NATURAL RESOURCES LAW AND POLICY

SECOND EDITION

by

JAMES RASBAND

Dean and Hugh W. Colton Professor of Law
J. Reuben Clark Law School
Brigham Young University

JAMES SALZMAN

Samuel F. Mordecai Professor of Law &
Nicholas Institute Professor of Environmental Policy
Duke University

MARK SQUILLACE

Professor of Law and Director of Natural Resources Law Center
University of Colorado

FOUNDATION PRESS
2009

THOMSON REUTERS™

© 2004 FOUNDATION PRESS
© 2009 By THOMSON REUTERS/FOUNDATION PRESS
      195 Broadway, 9th Floor
      New York, NY 10007
      Phone Toll Free 1–877–888–1330
      Fax (212) 367–6799
      foundation–press.com
Printed in the United States of America

ISBN 978–1–59941–344–0

To Mary
J.R.R.

To Andy and David
J.S.

To Sam, Tom, and Cooper
M.S.

*

INTRODUCTION

As the long-running debates over oil drilling in the Arctic National Wildlife Refuge, fire policy in our national forests, and salmon protection in the Pacific Northwest show, high-profile conflicts over natural resource management continue to capture the public's imagination. This is evident not only in newspaper headlines but in law school offerings, as well, with most law schools offering courses in natural resources law.

In writing a second edition of this book, we continue to strive to provide teachers and students with a resource that is (1) user-friendly, (2) comprehensive, and (3) as fascinating as the field itself. Likewise, we retain our goal of imbuing the text with the experience that the three of us share from industry, government, and environmental groups and with our varied perspectives on the proper role and scope of natural resource management. Perhaps as a consequence of this approach, we do not purport to promote a "right way" to manage resources. Rather we seek to set out relevant materials so that students can meaningfully assess the sources of resource conflicts and reach their own informed conclusions.

The second edition of this casebook arrives at a time when the Obama Administration is too new (we were tempted to say "too green") to have left its mark on the field of natural resources law and policy. But the winds of change have begun to blow and we try to signal the advent of new policies that are sure to influence the future of the field. For example, the Obama Administration has already pushed back against the limits on consultation under the Endangered Species Act announced towards the end of the Bush Administration, and the roller coaster ride that has characterized the debate over the protection of Forest Service roadless areas seems destined to swing back toward preservation. Furthermore, while prognosticators have been wrong time and again in predicting the demise of the 1872 Mining Law, reform of that law is a hot topic once again. Finally, though national climate change legislation is still gestating, few doubt that climate change and climate policy will take on growing importance for natural resources, and we try to anticipate the influence that possible changes to our natural world and to our legal regime will have on the field of natural resources law.

Traditionally, natural resource teaching materials have focused largely on the management of the Western public lands. These vast resources surely are a concern to all Americans but so, too, are fisheries, marine mammals, eastern forests, endangered species and biodiversity on private lands, state water law regimes, transboundary river regimes, etc. In seeking to give the casebook greater coverage, we have addressed both national and international resource management issues.

The best classes, we have found, are those where students grapple with real life legal and policy challenges. To that end, we have included a variety of problem exercises and case studies. The problems require students to apply the analytical tools and legal doctrines they have learned in the text to factual scenarios based on current or classic natural resource dilemmas. In our teaching of natural resource law, we have also found that students engage better with complex legal issues if they first know and feel the rich texture of history, geography, community, and ecology that underlie natural resources law and give it meaning. We provide some of this context for each resource before tackling the law for that resource. We also have tried to incorporate excerpts from Abbey, Leopold, Reisner, Wilkinson, Sax, and others whose writing so powerfully describes and gives voice to the intricate tapestry on which natural resources law has been written. Our hope is that by the end of the course the students will not only know something about the law but feel some of the passion we each do for our land, its resources, and this field of the law.

The study of natural resources law and policy is, initially, the study of management challenges that are found in virtually all resource conflicts. Thus Part I of the casebook (Chapters 1, 2 and 3) provides the "tools of the trade." Chapter 1 presents a conceptual overview introducing the field of natural resource law. It is designed to confront and force consideration of basic questions such as what "natural resources" are and why we might choose to protect or use those resources. It also introduces the various arguments for and against resource preservation, consumption, and extraction, ranging from ethical to utilitarian justifications. It then turns to the basic drivers that shape virtually any natural resource conflict, focusing on the deceptively simple question "why are natural resources so difficult to manage?" These drivers include the tragedy of the commons, problems with political and biophysical scale, clashes of values, scientific uncertainty, and institutional problems related to public choice theory. Armed with that foundation, students will better understand why these problems recur again and again across the range of natural resources as well as be able to assess the relative merits of the legal and management regimes set forth in the remainder of the casebook. The last part of the chapter addresses policy instruments to overcome these challenges—such as prescriptive regulation, market mechanisms, information, etc.

Our view is that it is also next to impossible to understand fully most natural resource disputes without a basic understanding of the history of how resources have been managed in the country, the resulting public/private geography of the national landscape, and the constitutional provisions applicable to resource problems. Chapter 2 thus describes the historical geography of natural resource management in the United States, explaining how we have arrived at a situation where one-third of the nation's lands are publicly owned and the consequences of that distribution for natural resource management. It then sets out the key constitutional doctrines that shape government actions, such as takings and federalism questions. Chapter 3 turns to federal natural resource agencies, the basic actors in resource management, highlighting their different missions and organic acts. This is followed by a brief introduction to administrative law and the special role of citizen suits. The chapter concludes with a section on resource planning processes, with a special focus on the National Environmental Policy Act (NEPA) and the Federal Land Policy Management Act (FLPMA). The planning process section is transitional. It serves the foundational purpose of providing a window into agency action and plays an important role in many of the natural resource management regimes addressed in Part II.

Part II of the casebook focuses on specific natural resource issues. Separate chapters address biodiversity and living marine resource conservation, protected lands, water, rangelands, minerals, and forests, applying the broad themes and tools developed in Part I to each resource. By way of example, the chapter on grazing uses historical narrative, edited cases, problem exercises and case studies to illustrate the various challenges of rangeland management and the limits of potential remedies—the tragic outcome of open access grazing on the public lands which led to the adoption of the Taylor Grazing Act; the capture of the Bureau of Land Management by cattlemen; the limits of range science to predict the impact of cattle on range ecosystems; the appropriate balance between preservation-induced limits on grazing and expectation interests of ranchers and rural communities in the West; and whether market mechanisms such as privatizing grazing permits or allowing conservation use of existing federal allotments are preferable on either a moral or utilitarian basis to stricter regulation of grazing.

By integrating the book's foundational themes into each section in this fashion, we seek to drive home the point that problems affecting management of a particular resource share similar theoretical and practical origins. This insight allows for a wiser assessment of alternative management regimes. From a teacher's perspective, the integration of the various resources into a broader scheme will also allow a course to be tailored to those resources that are of most interest to the teacher and students without sacrificing coherence in the course's thematic content. This is a particular benefit given that few teachers are likely to cover the entire gamut of resources during the typical three-credit-hour natural resource law class. Indeed, we do not anticipate that the casebook will be taught cover-to-cover. Rather, we encourage you to teach Chapter 1 and then pick and choose from the remaining chapters as best suits your interests.

To make the casebook more user-friendly, we have prepared a casebook website, described on the following page, and a Teacher's Manual. For access to the online Teacher's Manual, professors should e-mail Jim Rasband at rasbandj@law.byu.edu.

Such an undertaking would not have been possible without the assistance of many people. We thank our research assistants, Dave Newman, Kelly Yasaitis, Erin Morrow, Daniel Bower, Marie Bradshaw Durrant, Joshua Ellis, Megan Jill Falor, Garrett, Iantha Haight, Melinda Hill, Kent Ohlsen, Paul Shakespear, Ed Spear, Jay Wahlquist, Jenny Riegle, Shelby Cully, Jon Hanna, Jay Perry, Alison Flint, and Joshua Neely. We express gratitude to our libraries for their support, particularly Steve Averett,

David Armond, Molly Brownfield, Shawn Nevers, Nick Newton, Spencer Kellis, and Bruce Kennedy. We are also grateful for the support of our secretaries, Marcene Mason, Julie Hunt, and Peggye Cummings. We also thank experts in the field who have graciously reviewed drafts and provided comments—Josh Eagle, Will Irwin, Constance Lundberg, Richard Lazarus, and Chris Zeman. Any remaining errors, however, are ours alone. We are grateful to the Foundation for Research on Economics and the Environment for providing the gathering where the idea for this book originated. Generous research support was provided by the Rocky Mountain Mineral Law Foundation, Dean Claudio Grossman, Dean Kevin Worthen, Dean Phillip Closius, and Dean David Getches. A special thanks is due to those scholars, teachers, and colleagues who have so strongly influenced our perspectives on natural resources law and policy. If we have succeeded in opening up some new routes to study this field, it is because they blazed the first trails. Most of all, though, we are grateful for the support and patience of our wives: Mary, Lisa, and Maureen.

We welcome comments on the casebook, on both its strengths and areas for improvement. They may be sent to Jim Rasband at rasbandj@ law.byu.edu.

JIM RASBAND
JIM SALZMAN
MARK SQUILLACE

FOREWORD

Gus Speth*

This casebook is the first to address natural resources law from the broad and encompassing perspective it deserves. *Natural Resources Law and Policy* does not see the natural world only as a source of raw materials for the economy. Rather, it furthers recognition in the law of "existence" and recreational values in such resources as biological diversity and pristine areas. Temporally, it sees that the rights of future generations must be considered along with present-day claimants. Geographically, it breaks the mold of focusing predominantly on the American West and takes up national and even global dimensions. In moving in these directions, *Natural Resources Law and Policy* makes an important contribution to legal education.

The "production function" of today's neo-classical economists sees economic output as a function of inputs of labor, capital, and natural resources, all influenced by available technology. This formula is more profound than many imagine, with some tinkering. Instead of annual economic output measured in GDP, think of the annual capacity to satisfy the full range of human needs and aspirations. Instead of labor inputs, think of us, all six billion of us. Instead of capital, think of the entire built environment, from microchips to megacities. Instead of natural resources, think of the natural world with all its biological, mineral and scenic wealth. And instead of technology, think of the entire corpus of human knowledge and culture acquired over the centuries. In the beginning, it was just us and the rest of the natural world. Over the eons we applied our growing knowledge to transforming the gifts of nature into a world of things. As human beings, this is really all we have–ourselves, our knowledge and our natural and built environments–to apply to our quest to achieve human fulfillment.

If we look at this broader production function, focusing on the capacity to meet human needs and aspirations, an important conclusion emerges. Despite some twists, turns and setbacks, the overall trajectory of three of the factors is upward, but the trend line in the quality of our natural world is downward. There are certainly more and more of us. Meanwhile, the accumulation of things we have built and manufactured has grown much faster than our populations. And our knowledge and technological prowess is expanding even faster. But the capacity of the natural world and its resources to meet human needs is in decline, and has been for a long time.

---

* Gus Speth has been at the center of environmental law and policy for four decades. Following law school he co-founded the Natural Resources Defense Council and served as Chair of the Council on Environmental Quality under President Carter. He co-founded and served as President of the World Resources Institute prior to heading the United Nations Development Program. He served as Dean of the Yale School of Forestry & Environmental Studies from 1999 to 2009.

In some areas, increasing resource scarcities could drive up prices and have serious economic and social repercussions. In other areas, substitution of labor, capital and technology for declining resources could postpone adverse economic consequences, especially given the way GDP is measured. But whatever the economic consequences, nature's capacity to meet the non-economic and non-market needs and aspirations of human societies will be severely undermined if current trends in resource degradation continue.

Consider the following environmental trends. Scientists estimate we have entered the sixth wave of mass extinction, approaching rates of species extinctions not seen in the fossil record since 65 million years ago. We continue to increase the concentrations of atmospheric greenhouse gases with the likely result, if the consensus estimate of over 2,000 of the world's scientists proves accurate, of significantly increased global average temperatures and sea level rise over the coming decades. Seventy percent of the world's fisheries are overfished or fully exploited. This list could go on, but the message is clear. We need to re-think our management strategies and the non-market value of natural resources.

Natural resources law can help resolve conflicting claims among private parties, whether those claims are economic or environmental. But there should always be three other seats at the table: one for the public interest (which may or may not be represented by governments), one for future generations, and one for nature itself. This is just another way of saying that our deliberations cannot be entirely egocentric or contempocentric or anthropocentric.

Natural resources law and its practitioners should strive to ensure that all these voices are heard and their messages considered. In this pathbreaking volume, James Rasband, James Salzman and Mark Squillace have taken a major step in this direction. This casebook should help us act on the wisdom in Antoine de Saint Exupery's *The Little Prince*:

> The fox said to the little prince: Men have forgotten this truth, but you must not forget it. You remain responsible, forever, for what you have tamed.

As lords and masters of all we survey, we now have that responsibility for the natural world, its resources, and its beauty.

JAMES GUSTAVE SPETH

New Haven, Connecticut

NOTE ON THE CASEBOOK WEB SITE

In writing this book, we found the internet to be a rich resource for materials on natural resources law and policy. Our casebook website provides both students and teachers easy access to these materials and to additional teaching materials such as PowerPoint slides, maps, diagrams, and excerpted cases and articles that we were unable to include in the book because of space constraints. The website has links for each chapter which contain additional information students may want to access for proposed rules, guidance documents, opinions, photographs, maps, etc. There are also links to relevant statutes and the natural resource agencies. The casebook website also provides access (password protected) to the Teacher's Manual. The address for the website is:

http://www.naturalresources.byu.edu

*

SUMMARY OF CONTENTS

INTRODUCTION v
FOREWORD ix
NOTE ON CASEBOOK WEBPAGE xi
TABLE OF CASES xxxi
ACKNOWLEDGEMENTS xlv

CHAPTER ONE. Thinking About Natural Resources 1

    I. What Is a Natural Resource? 2
        A. The Nature of "Natural" 2
        B. Why Should We Protect or Use Natural Resources? 11
   II. Why Are Natural Resources Difficult to Manage? 36
        A. Scarcity 36
        B. Clash of Values Among Competing Interests 38
        C. Problems of the Commons 39
        D. Market Forces and Market Failures 41
        E. Scientific Uncertainty 43
        F. Scale 51
        G. Institutional Adequacy 60
  III. Tools for Managing Natural Resources—"The Five P's" 69
        A. Property Rights 70
        B. Prescriptive Regulation 71
        C. Financial Penalties 73
        D. Financial Payments 73
        E. Public Disclosure and Persuasion 74

CHAPTER TWO. The Historical and Constitutional Geography of Natural Resources Law 80

    I. Introduction 81
   II. Acquisition of the Public Lands 82
        A. Acquisition of Lands from the States with Western Land Claims 83
        B. Acquisition of Public Lands from European Powers 84
        C. Acquisition of Public Lands from Indian Tribes 87
  III. Allocating the Nation's Lands and Natural Resources 94
        A. The Equal Footing Doctrine 96
        B. The Public Trust Doctrine 104
        C. Federal Disposition of the Nation's Resources 115
        D. Federal Retention of Public Lands and Resources 129
  IV. Federal Power Over Natural Resource Management 146
        A. Federal Power Derived from Federal Land Ownership: The Property Clause 148
        B. Federal Power Over Natural Resources: Other Constitutional Sources 162

C. The Takings Limitation on Federal and State Power Over Natural Resources -- 184

D. Free Exercise and Establishment Clause Limitations on Federal and State Power Over Natural Resources ----------- 201

CHAPTER THREE. The Role of Agencies in Natural Resources Management -- 208

I. The Federal Natural Resource Agencies ----------------------------- 210
   A. The Rise of Federal Natural Resource Agencies ---------------- 210
   B. The Constitutional Challenge to Agency Action ---------------- 212
   C. The Basic Missions and Organization of the Federal Natural Resource Agencies -- 214
   D. Public Choice Challenges for Agency Management of Natural Resources -- 219
II. Improving Agency Decision–Making ----------------------------------- 223
   A. The Administrative Procedure Act ---------------------------------- 223
   B. The Role of Nongovernmental Organizations (NGOs) --------- 236
III. Improving Agencies' Environmental Decision–Making ------------- 258
   A. The National Environmental Policy Act -------------------------- 258
   B. Resource Planning on Public Lands ------------------------------- 292

CHAPTER FOUR. Wildlife and Biodiversity --------------------------- 320

I. Life on Earth --- 320
   A. What is Biodiversity? -- 321
   B. Biodiversity Over Time --- 323
   C. Is There an Extinction Crisis? ------------------------------------- 326
   D. Why Preserve Biodiversity? -- 330
II. Managing the Wildlife Commons ------------------------------------- 338
   A. Who Owns Wildlife? -- 338
   B. Policy Instruments -- 342
III. The Endangered Species Act -- 348
   A. Listing -- 349
   B. Designation of Critical Habitat ------------------------------------ 362
   C. Conservation --- 366
   D. Consultation, Jeopardy, and Adverse Modification of Critical Habitat -- 369
   E. Prohibition Against Takes -- 384
   F. Creating Incentives for Species Protection --------------------- 417
   G. Does It Work? -- 424

CHAPTER FIVE. Living Marine Resources -------------------------- 441

I. Fisheries -- 442
   A. Introduction --- 442
   B. Drivers of Fishery Collapse -- 449
   C. A Primer on Fisheries Science ------------------------------------- 457
   D. Fishery Management Tools -- 466
   E. Fishery Law --- 478

  II. Marine Mammals 528
    A. Whales 529
    B. Marine Mammal–Fishery Conflicts 549

CHAPTER SIX. Protected Lands 577

  I. Introduction 578
  II. The Case for Preservation 582
    A. The Economic Case for Preservation 582
    B. Preservation as Historical and Cultural Documentation 586
    C. The Ecological Case for Preservation 586
    D. The Moral Case for Preservation 588
    E. The Darker Side of Preservation 591
  III. National Parks 599
    A. The Park Service Organic Act 601
  IV. National Monuments 619
    A. The Antiquities Act 620
    B. The Clinton Monuments 625
  V. Wilderness 636
    A. The Evolution of the Wilderness Idea 636
    B. The Wilderness Act 637
  VI. National Wildlife Refuges, Wild and Scenic Rivers, and The
    Land and Water Conservation Fund 662
    A. National Wildlife Refuges 662
    B. Wild and Scenic Rivers 665
    C. The Land and Water Conservation Fund and Federal Reac-
     quisition of Land and Resources 667
  VII. Preservation on Multiple Use Lands 673
    A. Protecting Land in a Multiple Use Regime 673
    B. FLPMA Withdrawal Authority 687
  VIII. The Impact of Access on Preservation 696
    A. Access Across Federal Lands to Private and State Property 699
    B. R.S. 2477 707
  IX. Alternatives to Public Lands Preservation 727

CHAPTER SEVEN. Water 739

  I. Introduction 740
  II. Understanding the Water Resource 741
    A. The World's Water 741
    B. The United States' Water 744
    C. Water Uses and Water Users 748
    D. Valuing Water 751
    E. Dams 755
  III. The Law of Water Allocation 758
    A. Riparian Rights 760
    B. Eastern Permit Systems 767
    C. Prior Appropriation 777
    D. The Law of Groundwater 810

IV. Water Federalism -- 825
    A. Who Owns and Regulates Water? ------------------------------------ 825
    B. Indian and Federal Reserved Water Rights ---------------------- 830
    C. Intersecting Federal Statutes ------------------------------------ 851
    D. Allocating Water Between the States ---------------------------- 881
V. International Water Law -- 900
    A. Customary Law of Transboundary Watercourses -------------- 901
    B. The 1997 Convention on Non–Navigational Uses of International Watercourses -- 904

CHAPTER EIGHT. Rangelands -------------------------------------- 913

  I. Introduction -- 914
 II. Home on the Range -- 914
    A. What Are Rangelands? -- 914
    B. Rangeland Goods and Services ------------------------------------ 915
    C. Impacts of Grazing on Rangelands -------------------------------- 917
    D. The Passions Stirred By Public Lands Grazing ------------------ 925
III. Carving Up The Commons: A Brief History of Ranchers' Efforts to Control Western Rangelands ------------------------------------ 934
    A. The Rise of Ranching on the Public Commons ------------------ 934
    B. Fence Law -- 937
    C. Initial Federal Limitations on Open Access Grazing ------------ 939
    D. Ending Open Access to the Public Rangelands ------------------ 941
IV. Environmental Law Comes to the Range ... Slowly -------------- 949
    A. The Taylor Grazing Act as Environmental Law ---------------- 949
    B. Early Range Planning Efforts ------------------------------------ 950
    C. FLPMA: The BLM Gets an Organic Act ------------------------ 952
    D. PRIA: Environmental Mandate or More Congressional Ambivalence? -- 954
    E. Can the Grazing Statutes Be Made to Work for the Environment? -- 972
V. Rangeland Reform -- 975
    A. Grazing Fees and Subsidies -------------------------------------- 975
    B. Privatizing Grazing Permits ------------------------------------ 977
    C. Buying Back the Range -- 978
    D. Collaboration, Consensus, and Local Control ------------------ 978
    E. Grazing Reform Administrative Style ------------------------ 983
VI. Intersecting Laws and Their Impact on Range Management ------ 1011
    A. The Clean Water Act -- 1011
    B. The Wild and Scenic Rivers Act -------------------------------- 1012
    C. The Endangered Species Act ------------------------------------ 1013
VII. Grazing on State Lands -- 1015

CHAPTER NINE. Minerals -- 1021

  I. An Introduction to Mining -- 1022
    A. A Brief History of Mining -------------------------------------- 1024
    B. Mining and the Environment ------------------------------------ 1030
    C. Mining and Worker Safety -------------------------------------- 1031
    D. Mineral Economics -- 1033
    E. Methods for Developing Minerals -------------------------------- 1036
    F. Mineral Development Outside the United States ---------------- 1041

II. Mineral Property -- 1043
    A. Who Owns the Minerals? Acquisition and Loss of Mineral
        Rights--- 1043
    B. Defining the Mineral Resources------------------------ 1059
III. Mining on the Public Lands--------------------------------- 1077
    A. An Introduction to the General Mining Law of 1872----------- 1077
    B. Public Lands Open to Location----------------------- 1084
    C. Types of Mining Claims------------------------------ 1087
    D. Staking a Mining Claim------------------------------ 1097
    E. Pedis Possessio ----------------------------------- 1119
    F. Discovery of Valuable Minerals-------------------- 1122
    G. Challenges to the Validity of Mining Claims ----------- 1135
    H. Mining Claim Patents ----------------------------- 1139
    I. The Mechanics of Mining Claim Transactions---------- 1145
IV. Mineral Sales and Leases on Public Lands------------------ 1146
    A. The Common Varieties Act------------------------- 1147
    B. The Surface Resources Act-------------------------- 1150
    C. The Mineral Leasing Act --------------------------- 1153
    D. Multiple Mineral Development --------------------- 1168
V. Environmental Regulation of Mining--------------------- 1170
    A. Environmental Regulation of Hard Rock Mining--------- 1170
    B. Environmental Regulation of Coal Mining ----------- 1186

CHAPTER TEN. Forests--------------------------------- 1194

I. Forests and the American Mind ------------------------- 1195
II. The Forest Resource ----------------------------------- 1196
    A. Global Forest Resources --------------------------- 1196
    B. The Forest Resources of the United States----------- 1198
    C. Forest Ecosystem Services ------------------------- 1206
III. The Timber Industry---------------------------------- 1211
    A. Logging Methods----------------------------------- 1211
    B. Environmental Impacts of Logging ----------------- 1214
    C. Customs, Cultures, and Local Timber Economies------- 1216
IV. Forestry Law-- 1227
    A. National Forests---------------------------------- 1228
    B. Private Forests ----------------------------------- 1300

Common Acronyms-------------------------------------- 1319
Index -- 1323

*

TABLE OF CONTENTS

INTRODUCTION v
FOREWORD ix
NOTE ON CASEBOOK WEBPAGE xi
TABLE OF CASES xxxi
ACKNOWLEDGEMENTS xlv

CHAPTER ONE. Thinking About Natural Resources 1

I. What Is a Natural Resource? 2
   A. The Nature of "Natural" 2
      Questions and Discussion 8
   B. Why Should We Protect or Use Natural Resources? 11
      1. Biocentrism 12
         a. Deep Ecology 12
         b. The Land Ethic 13
      2. Anthropocentrism 16
         a. Utilitarianism 16
         b. Ecosystem Services, Use and Non–Use Values 18
      3. Intergenerational Equity 20
      4. Why Values Matter in Natural Resources Law 21
         Questions and Discussion 22
         Case Study: The Nature of Wilderness 28
         Questions and Discussion 33
II. Why Are Natural Resources Difficult to Manage? 36
   A. Scarcity 36
   B. Clash of Values Among Competing Interests 38
   C. Problems of the Commons 39
   D. Market Forces and Market Failures 41
   E. Scientific Uncertainty 43
      Questions and Discussion 45
   F. Scale 51
      1. Biophysical Scale 51
      2. Political Scale 52
         a. Getting Political Scale Right 54
         b. The Relationship Between Property and Jurisdiction 56
      3. Temporal Scale 57
         Case Study: The Quincy Library Group 58
   G. Institutional Adequacy 60
      Questions and Discussion 62
      Case Study: The Arctic National Wildlife Refuge 67
      Questions and Discussion 69
III. Tools for Managing Natural Resources—"The Five P's" 69
   A. Property Rights 70
   B. Prescriptive Regulation 71
      1. Tradable Permits 72
   C. Financial Penalties 73
   D. Financial Payments 73

E. Public Disclosure and Persuasion ----------------------------- 74
   Questions and Discussion ------------------------------- 74
   Case Study: Privatizing Parks ------------------------- 77

CHAPTER TWO. The Historical and Constitutional Geography of Natural Resources Law ----------------------------- 80

  I. Introduction --- 81
 II. Acquisition of the Public Lands --------------------------- 82
    A. Acquisition of Lands from the States with Western Land Claims --- 83
    B. Acquisition of Public Lands from European Powers ----------- 84
    C. Acquisition of Public Lands from Indian Tribes ------------- 87
     Questions and Discussion ------------------------------- 91
III. Allocating the Nation's Lands and Natural Resources ------------- 94
    A. The Equal Footing Doctrine ------------------------------ 96
     Questions and Discussion ------------------------------- 101
    B. The Public Trust Doctrine ------------------------------- 104
     Questions and Discussion ------------------------------- 108
     Problem Exercise: Indian Treaty Rights in Washington's Tidelands --- 111
    C. Federal Disposition of the Nation's Resources ------------- 115
     1. The Jeffersonian Survey System ----------------------- 116
     2. Land Grants to States ------------------------------- 118
     3. Land Grants to Settlers ----------------------------- 119
     4. Land Grants to Railroads ---------------------------- 125
     Questions and Discussion ------------------------------- 128
    D. Federal Retention of Public Lands and Resources ---------- 129
     1. Early Federal Retention and National Parks ----------- 129
     2. National Forests ------------------------------------ 131
     3. National Wildlife Refuges and Executive Withdrawals ----- 133
     Questions and Discussion ------------------------------- 137
     4. The Decision to Retain the Public Domain Lands --------- 139
     5. The Geographic Legacy of Federal Public Lands Policy --- 141
     Questions and Discussion ------------------------------- 142
 IV. Federal Power Over Natural Resource Management ----------------- 146
    A. Federal Power Derived from Federal Land Ownership: The Property Clause --- 148
     Questions and Discussion ------------------------------- 154
     Problem Exercise: The Sagebrush Rebellion ------------- 156
     Questions and Discussion ------------------------------- 161
    B. Federal Power Over Natural Resources: Other Constitutional Sources --- 162
     Questions and Discussion ------------------------------- 166
     Questions and Discussion ------------------------------- 171
     Questions and Discussion ------------------------------- 182
    C. The Takings Limitation on Federal and State Power Over Natural Resources --- 184
     Questions and Discussion ------------------------------- 194
     Problem Exercise: Applying the Law of Takings --------- 200
    D. Free Exercise and Establishment Clause Limitations on Federal and State Power Over Natural Resources ---------- 201
     Questions and Discussion ------------------------------- 206

CHAPTER THREE. The Role of Agencies in Natural Resources Management ... 208

I. The Federal Natural Resource Agencies ... 210
   A. The Rise of Federal Natural Resource Agencies ... 210
   B. The Constitutional Challenge to Agency Action ... 212
   C. The Basic Missions and Organization of the Federal Natural Resource Agencies ... 214
   D. Public Choice Challenges for Agency Management of Natural Resources ... 219
      Questions and Discussion ... 220
II. Improving Agency Decision–Making ... 223
   A. The Administrative Procedure Act ... 223
      1. Rulemaking ... 224
      2. Adjudication ... 225
      3. Judicial Review of Agency Actions ... 226
         Questions and Discussion ... 233
   B. The Role of Nongovernmental Organizations (NGOs) ... 236
      1. Lobbying for Legislative and Administrative Action ... 237
         Questions and Discussion ... 239
      2. Citizen Suits and Litigation ... 239
      3. Standing ... 241
         Questions and Discussion ... 253
      4. Ripeness, Exhaustion, and the Timing of Judicial Review ... 256
         Problem Exercise: Standing to Challenge a Draft EIS ... 257
III. Improving Agencies' Environmental Decision–Making ... 258
   A. The National Environmental Policy Act ... 258
      1. NEPA's Evolution ... 261
      2. When Must an Agency Prepare an EIS? ... 262
         a. Timing ... 264
         b. The Scale of a Proposed Action and Tiering ... 265
         c. The Scope of Agency Action ... 266
            Questions and Discussion ... 272
            Problem Exercise: Winter Park Ski Resort ... 277
      3. The Essential Elements of an EIS ... 277
         a. Alternatives Analysis ... 278
            Questions and Discussion ... 284
         b. The Adequacy of the Analysis ... 285
            Problem Exercise: Natural Disaster and Scientific Uncertainty in Environmental Analysis ... 286
         c. Supplemental EISs ... 288
            Problem Exercise: Supplementation of Environmental Analyses ... 289
      4. Does It Work? ... 290
         Problem Exercise: Thinking Beyond NEPA ... 291
   B. Resource Planning on Public Lands ... 292
      1. A Brief History of Public Land Planning ... 294
      2. Planning Under NFMA and FLPMA ... 297
         Questions and Discussion ... 303
         Questions and Discussion ... 313
         Problem Exercise: Land Use Planning on the Public Lands ... 317

CHAPTER FOUR. Wildlife and Biodiversity 320

I. Life on Earth 320
  A. What is Biodiversity? 321
  B. Biodiversity Over Time 323
  C. Is There an Extinction Crisis? 326
    Questions and Discussion 328
  D. Why Preserve Biodiversity? 330
    Questions and Discussion 334
II. Managing the Wildlife Commons 338
  A. Who Owns Wildlife? 338
    Questions and Discussion 339
  B. Policy Instruments 342
    1. Restricting Access and Take 343
    2. Landscape Management and Captive Breeding 344
    3. Market Instruments 344
    4. Restricting the Market for Sale 344
    Questions and Discussion 345
III. The Endangered Species Act 348
  A. Listing 349
    Questions and Discussion 351
    Case Study: Should the Prairie Dog Be Listed? 353
    Case Study: Should Hatchery Salmon Be Listed? 354
    Questions and Discussion 360
  B. Designation of Critical Habitat 362
    Questions and Discussion 366
  C. Conservation 366
  D. Consultation, Jeopardy, and Adverse Modification of Critical Habitat 369
    Questions and Discussion 371
    Questions and Discussion 379
    Problem Exercise: Critical Habitat for the Grizzly 380
    Problem Exercise: What to Do About Climate Change? 381
  E. Prohibition Against Takes 384
    1. Direct Takes 386
    2. Indirect Takes 386
    Questions And Discussion 398
    Problem Exercise: Grizzlies and Corn on the Tracks 404
    Problem Exercise: Pygmy Owls on the Double R Ranch 404
    Case Study: Reintroduction of Wolves 405
    Questions and Discussion 407
    3. Vicarious Takes 409
    Questions and Discussion 414
  F. Creating Incentives for Species Protection 417
    Questions and Discussion 422
  G. Does It Work? 424
    Case Study: The Delhi Sands Flower–Loving Fly 426

CHAPTER FIVE. Living Marine Resources 441

I. Fisheries 442
   A. Introduction 442
      Questions and Discussion 444
   B. Drivers of Fishery Collapse 449
      1. Overfishing and Overcapitalization 450
      2. Subsidies 450
      3. Bycatch 451
      4. Habitat Loss and Degradation 452
      Questions and Discussion 453
   C. A Primer on Fisheries Science 457
      Questions and Discussion 461
   D. Fishery Management Tools 466
      1. Restrictions 466
      2. Capacity Reduction 468
      3. Limited Access Privilege Programs 469
      Questions and Discussion 472
      4. Aquaculture 476
   E. Fishery Law 478
      1. UNCLOS and EEZs 478
      Questions and Discussion 479
      2. Magnuson–Stevens Fishery Conservation and Management Act 482
         a. Regional Fishery Management Councils (RFMCs) 486
         b. Fishery Management Plans (FMPs) 488
         Questions and Discussion 489
         c. Consistency With National Standards 494
         Questions and Discussion 496
         Questions and Discussion 502
         Questions and Discussion 510
         Problem Exercise: Stock Rebuilding 511
         d. Ecosystem Management 513
         Questions and Discussion 516
         Case Study: The Red Snapper Fishery 518
II. Marine Mammals 528
   A. Whales 529
      1. History of Whaling 529
      2. International Convention on the Regulation of Whaling 531
         a. The Moratorium and Responses 533
         b. Breaking the Stalemate 537
         Questions and Discussion 539
         Case Study: Aboriginal Subsistence Whaling 543
         Questions and Discussion 547
   B. Marine Mammal–Fishery Conflicts 549
      1. Overview of the Marine Mammal Protection Act of 1972 549
      Questions and Discussion 552

B. Marine Mammal–Fishery Conflicts—Continued

    2. Pinnipeds and the Salmon Fishery ------------------------------- 557
       Questions and Discussion-------------------------------------- 563
    3. Dolphin Mortality in the Tuna Fishery ----------------------- 565
       a. U.S. Legislative Response ------------------------------- 566
       b. International Response to U.S. Sanctions --------------- 568
       Questions and Discussion ------------------------------------- 572

CHAPTER SIX. Protected Lands ------------------------------------- 577

  I. Introduction-- 578
  II. The Case for Preservation ----------------------------------- 582
    A. The Economic Case for Preservation ------------------------- 582
    B. Preservation as Historical and Cultural Documentation------- 586
    C. The Ecological Case for Preservation------------------------ 586
    D. The Moral Case for Preservation ---------------------------- 588
    E. The Darker Side of Preservation---------------------------- 591
    Questions and Discussion ------------------------------------- 596
  III. National Parks -- 599
    A. The Park Service Organic Act ------------------------------- 601
    Questions and Discussion ------------------------------------- 602
    Questions and Discussion ------------------------------------- 612
    Problem Exercise: Snowmobiles in Yellowstone National
    Park --- 617
  IV. National Monuments--- 619
    A. The Antiquities Act -- 620
    B. The Clinton Monuments------------------------------------- 625
    Questions and Discussion ------------------------------------- 632
  V. Wilderness -- 636
    A. The Evolution of the Wilderness Idea----------------------- 636
    B. The Wilderness Act--- 637
      1. Designating Wilderness --------------------------------- 639
       a. Wilderness in the National Forests ----------------- 640
       b. Wilderness on BLM Lands --------------------------- 642
       Questions and Discussion ----------------------------- 644
      2. Managing Designated Wilderness ----------------------- 649
      Questions and Discussion------------------------------------ 656
      Case Study: Roading the Izembek National Wildlife Ref-
      uge -- 661
  VI. National Wildlife Refuges, Wild and Scenic Rivers, and The
    Land and Water Conservation Fund ------------------------ 662
    A. National Wildlife Refuges --------------------------------- 662
    B. Wild and Scenic Rivers------------------------------------ 665
    C. The Land and Water Conservation Fund and Federal Reac-
    quisition of Land and Resources -------------------------- 667
    Questions and Discussion ------------------------------------- 670

VII. Preservation on Multiple Use Lands ------------------------------- 673
    A. Protecting Land in a Multiple Use Regime ----------------- 673
        Questions and Discussion -------------------------------- 684
        Problem Exercise: Wilderness Reinventory and the Utah
           Settlement Agreement ------------------------------- 684
    B. FLPMA Withdrawal Authority ------------------------------ 687
        Questions and Discussion -------------------------------- 689
        Questions and Discussion -------------------------------- 695
VIII. The Impact of Access on Preservation------------------------------ 696
    A. Access Across Federal Lands to Private and State Property 699
        Questions and Discussion -------------------------------- 706
    B. R.S. 2477--- 707
        Questions and Discussion -------------------------------- 720
        Problem Exercise: Obtaining Access to an Inholding --------- 724
IX. Alternatives to Public Lands Preservation ------------------------- 727
    Questions and Discussion------------------------------------- 733

CHAPTER SEVEN. Water -- 739

  I. Introduction-- 740
  II. Understanding the Water Resource ------------------------------ 741
    A. The World's Water --------------------------------------- 741
    B. The United States' Water -------------------------------- 744
    C. Water Uses and Water Users------------------------------- 748
    D. Valuing Water-- 751
    E. Dams-- 755
  III. The Law of Water Allocation --------------------------------- 758
    A. Riparian Rights--- 760
        Questions and Discussion -------------------------------- 764
    B. Eastern Permit Systems --------------------------------- 767
        Questions and Discussion -------------------------------- 775
    C. Prior Appropriation ------------------------------------- 777
        1. Overview --- 779
            Questions and Discussion----------------------------- 782
        2. Beneficial Use and Waste------------------------------ 784
            Questions and Discussion----------------------------- 788
        3. Permit Systems and the Public Interest Requirement ----- 790
            Questions and Discussion----------------------------- 792
        4. Instream Flow Appropriations ------------------------ 793
            Questions and Discussion----------------------------- 796
            Problem Exercise: Forming a Water Trust----------------- 797
        5. Los Angeles, Water, and the Public Trust Doctrine -------- 797
            Questions and Discussion----------------------------- 807
    D. The Law of Groundwater--------------------------------- 810
        1. The Groundwater Resource----------------------------- 810
        2. Legal Regimes for Allocating Groundwater----------------- 815
            Questions and Discussion----------------------------- 821
            Problem Exercise: Allocating a Simple Groundwater
              Aquifer-- 825

IV. Water Federalism --- 825
   A. Who Owns and Regulates Water? ---------------------------------- 825
   B. Indian and Federal Reserved Water Rights --------------------- 830
      Questions and Discussion -------------------------------------- 833
      Questions and Discussion -------------------------------------- 839
      Questions and Discussion -------------------------------------- 846
      Problem Exercise: Reserved Water Rights for Wilderness in
        Idaho -- 848
   C. Intersecting Federal Statutes ----------------------------------- 851
      1. The Clean Water Act and Wetlands ----------------------- 851
        Questions and Discussion --------------------------------- 865
        Case Study: The Navigation Servitude ------------------ 868
        Questions and Discussion --------------------------------- 869
      2. The Endangered Species Act ---------------------------- 870
        Questions and Discussion --------------------------------- 878
   D. Allocating Water Between the States -------------------------- 881
      1. Judicial Allocation -------------------------------------- 882
      2. Allocation By Compact --------------------------------- 884
      3. Congressional Allocation ------------------------------- 887
        Questions and Discussion --------------------------------- 888
        Case Study: The Law of the Colorado River ------------ 890
        Questions and Discussion --------------------------------- 899
V. International Water Law -- 900
   A. Customary Law of Transboundary Watercourses ------------- 901
      Questions and Discussion -------------------------------------- 904
   B. The 1997 Convention on Non–Navigational Uses of Interna-
      tional Watercourses -- 904
      Questions and Discussion -------------------------------------- 908
      Problem Exercise: Allocating the Waters of the Nile River ---- 908

CHAPTER EIGHT. Rangelands ------------------------------------ 913

  I. Introduction --- 914
 II. Home on the Range -- 914
   A. What Are Rangelands? --- 914
   B. Rangeland Goods and Services ------------------------------------ 915
   C. Impacts of Grazing on Rangelands ------------------------------- 917
      Questions and Discussion -------------------------------------- 922
   D. The Passions Stirred By Public Lands Grazing --------------- 925
      Questions and Discussion -------------------------------------- 930
III. Carving Up The Commons: A Brief History of Ranchers' Efforts
    to Control Western Rangelands --------------------------------------- 934
   A. The Rise of Ranching on the Public Commons --------------- 934
   B. Fence Law --- 937
   C. Initial Federal Limitations on Open Access Grazing ---------- 939
   D. Ending Open Access to the Public Rangelands ---------------- 941
      Questions and Discussion -------------------------------------- 945
IV. Environmental Law Comes to the Range ... Slowly --------------- 949
   A. The Taylor Grazing Act as Environmental Law -------------- 949
   B. Early Range Planning Efforts ------------------------------------- 950
   C. FLPMA: The BLM Gets an Organic Act ----------------------- 952

D. PRIA: Environmental Mandate or More Congressional Ambivalence? 954
  Questions and Discussion 959
  Questions and Discussion 966
  Questions and Discussion 971
E. Can the Grazing Statutes Be Made to Work for the Environment? 972
  Questions and Discussion 974
  Problem Exercise: Determining Whether Public Lands Are Chiefly Valuable for Grazing 974
V. Rangeland Reform 975
  A. Grazing Fees and Subsidies 975
  B. Privatizing Grazing Permits 977
  C. Buying Back the Range 978
  D. Collaboration, Consensus, and Local Control 978
    Questions and Discussion 980
  E. Grazing Reform Administrative Style 983
    Questions and Discussion 987
    Questions and Discussion 995
    Questions and Discussion 1004
    Problem Exercise: The Grand Canyon Trust Retires Grazing Permits 1005
    Questions and Discussion 1008
VI. Intersecting Laws and Their Impact on Range Management 1011
  A. The Clean Water Act 1011
  B. The Wild and Scenic Rivers Act 1012
  C. The Endangered Species Act 1013
    Questions and Discussion 1014
VII. Grazing on State Lands 1015
  Questions and Discussion 1018

CHAPTER NINE. Minerals 1021

I. An Introduction to Mining 1022
  A. A Brief History of Mining 1024
    Questions and Discussion 1026
  B. Mining and the Environment 1030
  C. Mining and Worker Safety 1031
    Questions and Discussion 1032
  D. Mineral Economics 1033
    Questions and Discussion 1035
    Problem Exercise: Exploring the Volatility of Minerals Markets 1036
  E. Methods for Developing Minerals 1036
    Questions and Discussion 1039
  F. Mineral Development Outside the United States 1041
II. Mineral Property 1043
  A. Who Owns the Minerals? Acquisition and Loss of Mineral Rights 1043
    Questions and Discussion 1045

A. Who Owns the Minerals? Acquisition and Loss of Mineral Rights—Continued
  1. The Broad Form Deed 1046
    Questions and Discussion 1052
    Problem Exercise: Legal Limits on the Terms of a Lease 1054
  2. Split Estates 1055
    Questions and Discussion 1059
B. Defining the Mineral Resources 1059
  Questions and Discussion 1062
  Questions and Discussion 1065
  1. Coal Bed Methane 1067
    Questions and Discussion 1074
    Mineral Conveyance Drafting Exercise 1076
III. Mining on the Public Lands 1077
A. An Introduction to the General Mining Law of 1872 1077
  Questions and Discussion 1082
B. Public Lands Open to Location 1084
  Questions and Discussion 1086
C. Types of Mining Claims 1087
  1. Lode and Placer Claims 1087
    Questions and Discussion 1089
  2. Mill Sites 1094
    Questions and Discussion 1095
    Problem Exercise: Mining and Mill Sites 1097
D. Staking a Mining Claim 1097
  1. Federal and State Standards 1097
    Questions and Discussion 1098
    Problem Exercise: Location and Recording Requirements 1100
    Questions and Discussion 1101
  2. Amendment and Relocation 1102
    Questions and Discussion 1102
  3. Assessment Work 1103
    Questions and Discussion 1106
  4. Recording Requirements Under FLPMA 1111
    Questions and Discussion 1117
E. Pedis Possessio 1119
  Questions and Discussion 1120
  Problem Exercise: Pedis Possessio Rights 1121
F. Discovery of Valuable Minerals 1122
  Questions and Discussion 1123
  Questions and Discussion 1126
  Questions and Discussion 1127
  Questions and Discussion 1134
G. Challenges to the Validity of Mining Claims 1135
  Questions and Discussion 1136
H. Mining Claim Patents 1139
  Questions and Discussion 1141
I. The Mechanics of Mining Claim Transactions 1145
  Mining Claim Purchase Review Process 1145
IV. Mineral Sales and Leases on Public Lands 1146
A. The Common Varieties Act 1147
  Questions and Discussion 1149
B. The Surface Resources Act 1150
  Questions and Discussion 1151
  Problem Exercise. Discovery Problems and the Surface Resources Act 1153

C. The Mineral Leasing Act ----- 1153
1. Onshore Oil and Gas Leasing ----- 1154
Questions and Discussion ----- 1157
2. Coal Leasing ----- 1160
Questions and Discussion ----- 1164
3. Leasing of Minerals Other Than Coal ----- 1167
D. Multiple Mineral Development ----- 1168
Questions and Discussion ----- 1169
V. Environmental Regulation of Mining ----- 1170
A. Environmental Regulation of Hard Rock Mining ----- 1170
1. Federal Regulation of Mining to Protect the Environment ----- 1170
2. State Regulation of Mining to Protect the Environment -- 1174
Questions and Discussion ----- 1180
Problem Exercise: Environmental Restrictions That Preclude Mining ----- 1183
Problem Exercise: The Glamis Imperial Mine ----- 1183
Questions and Discussion ----- 1185
B. Environmental Regulation of Coal Mining ----- 1186
Questions and Discussion ----- 1189

CHAPTER TEN. Forests ----- 1194

I. Forests and the American Mind ----- 1195
II. The Forest Resource ----- 1196
A. Global Forest Resources ----- 1196
B. The Forest Resources of the United States ----- 1198
Questions and Discussion ----- 1201
Problem Exercise: Tree Spiking ----- 1206
C. Forest Ecosystem Services ----- 1206
Questions and Discussion ----- 1209
III. The Timber Industry ----- 1211
A. Logging Methods ----- 1211
B. Environmental Impacts of Logging ----- 1214
1. Soil Erosion and Compaction ----- 1214
2. Water ----- 1215
3. Wildlife Habitat ----- 1215
Questions and Discussion ----- 1216
C. Customs, Cultures, and Local Timber Economies ----- 1216
Questions and Discussion ----- 1224
IV. Forestry Law ----- 1227
A. National Forests ----- 1228
1. The History of Federal Forestry Law ----- 1228
Questions and Discussion ----- 1238
2. Modern Management Law, Policies, and Practices ----- 1240
a. National Forest Land and Resource Management Planning ----- 1241
b. NFMA and Clearcutting ----- 1246
Questions and Discussion ----- 1251
c. Biodiversity Conservation and National Forests ----- 1254
QUESTIONS AND DISCUSSION ----- 1259
Questions and Discussion ----- 1270
d. Roads and National Forests ----- 1272
Questions and Discussion ----- 1279

A. National Forests—Continued
    e. The Role of Fire in Forest Management........................ 1281
        Questions and Discussion 1289
        Problem Exercise: Forests and Fire............................ 1292
    3. The Economics of Logging on National Forests 1293
        Questions and Discussion.................................... 1298
B. Private Forests 1300
    1. Acquisition of Private Timber Rights............................ 1300
        Questions and Discussion.................................... 1304
    2. Federal and State Regulation of Private Logging Activities 1308
        Questions and Discussion.................................... 1316

Common Acronyms.. 1319
Index 1323

TABLE OF CASES

Principal cases are in bold type. Non-principal cases are in roman type. References are to Pages.

Abbott Laboratories v. Gardner, 387 U.S. 136, 87 S.Ct. 1507, 18 L.Ed.2d 681 (1967), 257

Access Fund v. United States Dept. of Agriculture, 499 F.3d 1036 (9th Cir.2007), 207

Ace Lobster Co., Inc. v. Evans, 165 F.Supp.2d 148 (D.R.I.2001), 504

Adair, United States v., 723 F.2d 1394 (9th Cir.1983), 835

Adams v. Lang, 553 So.2d 89 (Ala.1989), 816

Agins v. City of Tiburon, 447 U.S. 255, 100 S.Ct. 2138, 65 L.Ed.2d 106 (1980), 198

Akers v. Baldwin, 736 S.W.2d 294 (Ky.1987), 1052

Alaska v. United States, 545 U.S. 75, 125 S.Ct. 2137, 162 L.Ed.2d 57 (2005), 104

Alaska, United States v., 521 U.S. 1, 117 S.Ct. 1888, 138 L.Ed.2d 231 (1997), 103

Alaska Airlines, Inc. v. Brock, 480 U.S. 678, 107 S.Ct. 1476, 94 L.Ed.2d 661 (1987), 691

Alaska Factory Trawler Ass'n v. Baldridge, 831 F.2d 1456 (9th Cir.1987), 495

Alaska Pacific Fisheries Co. v. United States, 248 U.S. 78, 39 S.Ct. 40, 63 L.Ed. 138 (1918), 103

Albuquerque, City of v. Reynolds, 71 N.M. 428, 379 P.2d 73 (N.M.1962), 823

Alden v. Maine, 527 U.S. 706, 119 S.Ct. 2240, 144 L.Ed.2d 636 (1999), 240

Alford, United States v., 274 U.S. 264, 47 S.Ct. 597, 71 L.Ed. 1040 (1927), 162

Algonquin Coal Co. v. Northern Coal & Iron Co., 162 Pa. 114, 29 A. 402 (Pa. 1894), **1044**

Allegretti & Co. v. County of Imperial, 42 Cal.Rptr.3d 122 (Cal.App. 4 Dist.2006), 880

Alliance Against IFQs v. Brown, 84 F.3d 343 (9th Cir.1996), 470, 504

Alsea Valley Alliance v. Evans, 161 F.Supp.2d 1154 (D.Or.2001), **356**

American Bald Eagle v. Bhatti, 9 F.3d 163 (1st Cir.1993), 402

American Falls Reservoir Dist. No. 2 v. Idaho Dept. of Water Resources, 143 Idaho 862, 154 P.3d 433 (Idaho 2007), 822

Amoco Production Co. v. Guild Trust, 636 F.2d 261 (10th Cir.1980), 1066

Amoco Production Co. v. Southern Ute Indian Tribe, 526 U.S. 865, 119 S.Ct. 1719, 144 L.Ed.2d 22 (1999), **1169**

Anderson v. Evans, 371 F.3d 475 (9th Cir. 2004), 545

Andrus v. Charlestone Stone Products Co., Inc., 436 U.S. 604, 98 S.Ct. 2002, 56 L.Ed.2d 570 (1978), **1063**

Andrus v. Shell Oil Co., 446 U.S. 657, 100 S.Ct. 1932, 64 L.Ed.2d 593 (1980), 1129

Andrus v. Sierra Club, 442 U.S. 347, 99 S.Ct. 2335, 60 L.Ed.2d 943 (1979), 260

Andrus v. Utah, 446 U.S. 500, 100 S.Ct. 1803, 64 L.Ed.2d 458 (1980), 128

Animal Protection Institute, Center for Biological Diversity v. Holsten, 541 F.Supp.2d 1073 (D.Minn.2008), 415

Appalachian Elec. Power Co., United States v., 311 U.S. 377, 61 S.Ct. 291, 85 L.Ed. 243 (1940), 868

Appleby v. City of New York, 271 U.S. 364, 46 S.Ct. 569, 70 L.Ed. 992 (1926), 109

Arbogast v. Pilot Rock Lumber Co., 215 Or. 579, 336 P.2d 329 (Or.1959), **1301**

Arizona Cattle Growers' Ass'n, v. United States Fish and Wildlife Service, 63 F.Supp.2d 1034 (D.Ariz.1998), 1014

Arizona Center For Law In Public Interest v. Hassell, 172 Ariz. 356, 837 P.2d 158 (Ariz. App. Div. 1 1991), 109

Arizona, State of v. State of California, 373 U.S. 546, 83 S.Ct. 1468, 10 L.Ed.2d 542 (1963), 834, 835, 896, 897

Arizona, State of v. State of California, 298 U.S. 558, 56 S.Ct. 848, 80 L.Ed. 1331 (1936), 895

Arizona, State of v. State of California, 292 U.S. 341, 54 S.Ct. 735, 78 L.Ed. 1298 (1934), 895

Arizona, State of v. State of California, 283 U.S. 423, 51 S.Ct. 522, 75 L.Ed. 1154 (1931), 895

Arizona, State of, United States v., 295 U.S. 174, 55 S.Ct. 666, 79 L.Ed. 1371 (1935), 895

Arkla Exploration Co. v. Texas Oil & Gas Corp., 734 F.2d 347 (8th Cir.1984), 1155

Ashwander v. Tennessee Valley Authority, 297 U.S. 288, 56 S.Ct. 466, 80 L.Ed. 688 (1936), 184

Atherley v. Bullion Monarch Uranium Co., 8 Utah 2d 362, 335 P.2d 71 (Utah 1959), 1099

Aurora Lode v. Bulger Hill & Nugget Gulch Placer, 23 L.D. 95 (1896), 1093

A.V. Toolson, 66 I.D. 48 (1959), 1168

Babbitt v. Sweet Home Chapter of Communities for a Great Oregon, 515 U.S. 687, 115 S.Ct. 2407, 132 L.Ed.2d 597 (1995), 230, **389**, 1013, 1014

Baca Land & Cattle Co. v. Savage, 440 F.2d 867 (10th Cir.1971), 1304

Baker v. Carr, 369 U.S. 186, 82 S.Ct. 691, 7 L.Ed.2d 663 (1962), 930

Baker v. Ore–Ida Foods, Inc., 95 Idaho 575, 513 P.2d 627 (Idaho 1973), 818

Ball v. James, 451 U.S. 355, 101 S.Ct. 1811, 68 L.Ed.2d 150 (1981), 750

Baltimore Gas and Elec. Co. v. Natural Resources Defense Council, Inc., 462 U.S. 87, 103 S.Ct. 2246, 76 L.Ed.2d 437 (1983), 262

Barrick Goldstrike Mines, Inc. v. Babbitt, 1995 WL 408667 (D.Nev.1994), 1143

Barshop v. Medina County Underground Water Conservation Dist., 925 S.W.2d 618 (Tex.1996), 816

Barton v. Morton, 498 F.2d 288 (9th Cir. 1974), 1126

Beanal v. Freeport–McMoran, Inc., 197 F.3d 161 (5th Cir.1999), 1042

Bear Lodge Multiple Use Ass'n v. Babbitt, 175 F.3d 814 (10th Cir.1999), 206

Bear Lodge Multiple Use Ass'n v. Babbitt, 2 F.Supp.2d 1448 (D.Wyo.1998), **203,** 207

Beartooth Alliance v. Crown Butte Mines, 904 F.Supp. 1168 (D.Mont.1995), 1182

BedRoc Ltd., LLC v. United States, 541 U.S. 176, 124 S.Ct. 1587, 158 L.Ed.2d 338 (2004), 1066

Belk v. Meagher, 104 U.S. 279, 14 Otto 279, 26 L.Ed. 735 (1881), 1110

Bellingham Bay Boom Co., United States v., 176 U.S. 211, 20 S.Ct. 343, 44 L.Ed. 437 (1900), 827

Bennett v. Spear, 520 U.S. 154, 117 S.Ct. 1154, 137 L.Ed.2d 281 (1997), 242, 243, 254

Bergquist v. West Virginia–Wyoming Copper Co., 18 Wyo. 234, 106 P. 673 (Wyo.1910), 1103

Best v. Humboldt Placer Min. Co., 371 U.S. 334, 83 S.Ct. 379, 9 L.Ed.2d 350 (1963), 1137

Bicycle Trails Council of Marin v. Babbitt, 82 F.3d 1445 (9th Cir.1996), 612

Biggs, United States v., 211 U.S. 507, 29 S.Ct. 181, 53 L.Ed. 305 (1909), 124, 1229

Billie, United States v., 667 F.Supp. 1485 (S.D.Fla.1987), 201

Block v. Community Nutrition Institute, 467 U.S. 340, 104 S.Ct. 2450, 81 L.Ed.2d 270 (1984), 1144

Blue Water Fisherman's Ass'n v. Mineta, 122 F.Supp.2d 150 (D.D.C.2000), 490

Bob Marshall Alliance v. Hodel, 852 F.2d 1223 (9th Cir.1988), 287, 695

Boerne, City of v. Flores, 521 U.S. 507, 117 S.Ct. 2157, 138 L.Ed.2d 624 (1997), 202, 1185

Boesche v. Udall, 373 U.S. 472, 83 S.Ct. 1373, 10 L.Ed.2d 491 (1963), 1159

Book v. Justice Mining Co., 58 F. 106 (C.C.D.Nev.1893), 1123

Border Power Plant Working Group v. Department of Energy, 260 F.Supp.2d 997 (S.D.Cal.2003), 288

Botton v. State, 69 Wash.2d 751, 420 P.2d 352 (Wash.1966), 766

Branson School Dist. RE–82 v. Romer, 161 F.3d 619 (10th Cir.1998), 129, 1018

Brower v. Daley, 93 F.Supp.2d 1071 (N.D.Cal. 2000), 575

Bruce W. Crawford, 92 I.D. 208 (1985), 1152

Buckeye Power, Inc. v. E.P.A., 481 F.2d 162 (6th Cir.1973), 273

Buford v. Houtz, 133 U.S. 320, 10 S.Ct. 305, 33 L.Ed. 618 (1890), 938

Bundy v. Myers, 372 Pa. 583, 94 A.2d 724 (Pa.1953), 1066

California v. Block, 690 F.2d 753 (9th Cir. 1982), 260, 278, 287, 642

California v. United States, 438 U.S. 645, 98 S.Ct. 2985, 57 L.Ed.2d 1018 (1978), 829

California Coastal Com'n v. Granite Rock Co., 480 U.S. 572, 107 S.Ct. 1419, 94 L.Ed.2d 577 (1987), 1135, 1175

California ex rel. Lockyer v. United States Dept. of Agriculture, 459 F.Supp.2d 874 (N.D.Cal.2006), 1279

California Oregon Power Co. v. Beaver Portland Cement Co., 295 U.S. 142, 55 S.Ct. 725, 79 L.Ed. 1356 (1935), 829

Calvert Cliffs' Coordinating Committee, Inc. v. United States Atomic Energy Commission, 449 F.2d 1109, 146 U.S.App.D.C. 33 (D.C.Cir.1971), 261

Cameron v. United States, 252 U.S. 450, 40 S.Ct. 410, 64 L.Ed. 659 (1920), 622, 1139

Camfield v. United States, 167 U.S. 518, 17 S.Ct. 864, 42 L.Ed. 260 (1897), 155, 937

Caminiti v. Boyle, 107 Wash.2d 662, 732 P.2d 989 (Wash.1987), 108

Campbell v. McIntyre, 295 F. 45 (9th Cir. 1924), 1121

Cape Hatteras Access Preservation Alliance v. United States Dept. of Interior, 344 F.Supp.2d 108 (D.D.C.2004), 365

Cappaert v. United States, 426 U.S. 128, 96 S.Ct. 2062, 48 L.Ed.2d 523 (1976), **835**

Carlisle, United States v., 67 I.D. 417 (1960), 1142

Carson–Truckee Water Conservancy Dist. v. Clark, 741 F.2d 257 (9th Cir.1984), 367

Casitas Mun. Water Dist. v. United States, 2007 WL 968154 (Fed.Cl.2007), 879

Cataract Mining Co., 43 L.D. 248 (1948), 1130

Catron County Bd. of Com'rs, New Mexico v. United States Fish & Wildlife Service, 75 F.3d 1429 (10th Cir.1996), 366

Center for Biological Diversity v. Bureau of Land Management, 422 F.Supp.2d 1115 (N.D.Cal.2006), 1260

Center for Biological Diversity v. Bureau of Land Management, 2001 WL 777088 (N.D.Cal.2001), 1014

Center for Biological Diversity v. Kempthorne, 466 F.3d 1098 (9th Cir.2006), 350

Chambers v. Harrington, 111 U.S. 350, 4 S.Ct. 428, 28 L.Ed. 452 (1884), 1110

Chandler–Dunbar Water Power Co., United States v., 229 U.S. 53, 33 S.Ct. 667, 57 L.Ed. 1063 (1913), 869

Chemical Waste Management, Inc. v. Hunt, 504 U.S. 334, 112 S.Ct. 2009, 119 L.Ed.2d 121 (1992), 166

Chevron U.S.A., Inc. v. Natural Resources Defense Council, Inc., 467 U.S. 837, 104 S.Ct. 2778, 81 L.Ed.2d 694 (1984), 228, 865, 1074, 1165, 1189

Chicago, B. & Q.R. Co. v. City of Chicago, 166 U.S. 226, 17 S.Ct. 581, 41 L.Ed. 979 (1897), 184

Chicago, M., St. P. & P. R. Co., United States v., 312 U.S. 592, 313 U.S. 543, 61 S.Ct. 772, 85 L.Ed. 1064 (1941), 868

Choctaw Nation v. Oklahoma, 397 U.S. 620, 90 S.Ct. 1328, 25 L.Ed.2d 615 (1970), 103

Cholla Ready Mix, Inc. v. Civish, 382 F.3d 969 (9th Cir.2004), 207

Chournos v. United States, 193 F.2d 321 (10th Cir.1951), 946

Chrisman v. Miller, 197 U.S. 313, 25 S.Ct. 468, 49 L.Ed. 770 (1905), 1130

Citizens Against Burlington, Inc. v. Busey, 938 F.2d 190, 290 U.S.App.D.C. 371 (D.C.Cir.1991), **279**

Citizens Coal Council v. Norton, 330 F.3d 478, 356 U.S.App.D.C. 214 (D.C.Cir.2003), 1189

Citizens for Better Forestry v. United States Dept. of Agriculture, 481 F.Supp.2d 1059 (N.D.Cal.2007), 298, 1244

Citizens to End Animal Suffering and Exploitation, Inc. v. New England Aquarium, 836 F.Supp. 45 (D.Mass.1993), 403

Citizens to Preserve Overton Park, Inc. v. Volpe, 401 U.S. 402, 91 S.Ct. 814, 28 L.Ed.2d 136 (1971), 227

City and County of (see name of city)

City of (see name of city)

Cleary v. Skiffich, 28 Colo. 362, 65 P. 59 (Colo.1901), 1096

Cliffs Synfuel Corp. v. Norton, 291 F.3d 1250 (10th Cir.2002), 1107

Clipper Min. Co. v. Eli Min. & Land Co., 29 Colo. 377, 68 P. 286 (Colo.1902), 1121

Clouser v. Espy, 42 F.3d 1522 (9th Cir. 1994), **701,** 721

Coffin v. Left Hand Ditch Co., 6 Colo. 443 (Colo.1882), 759, 829

Coho Salmon v. Pacific Lumber Co., 30 F.Supp.2d 1231 (N.D.Cal.1998), 403

Cole v. Ralph, 252 U.S. 286, 40 S.Ct. 321, 64 L.Ed. 567 (1920), 1088

Coleman v. Curtis, 12 Mont. 301, 30 P. 266 (Mont.1892), 1110

Coleman, United States v., 390 U.S. 599, 88 S.Ct. 1327, 20 L.Ed.2d 170 (1968), **1123**

Colorado v. New Mexico, 459 U.S. 176, 103 S.Ct. 539, 74 L.Ed.2d 348 (1982), 883

Colorado River Water Conservation Dist. v. United States, 424 U.S. 800, 96 S.Ct. 1236, 47 L.Ed.2d 483 (1976), 848

Colorado, State of v. State of Kan., 320 U.S. 383, 64 S.Ct. 176, 88 L.Ed. 116 (1943), 884

Colorado Wild, Heartwood v. United States Forest Service, 435 F.3d 1204 (10th Cir. 2006), 275

Committee for Humane Legislation, Inc. v. Richardson, 540 F.2d 1141, 176 U.S.App. D.C. 362 (D.C.Cir.1976), 551

Conner v. Burford, 848 F.2d 1441 (9th Cir. 1988), 265

Conner v. Burford, 836 F.2d 1521 (9th Cir. 1988), 1159

Connor v. Andrus, 453 F.Supp. 1037 (W.D.Tex.1978), 367

Conoco, Inc. v. Hodel, 626 F.Supp. 287 (D.Del.1986), 1165

Consejo de Desarrollo Economico de Mexicali, A.C. v. United States, 482 F.3d 1157 (9th Cir.2007), 374

Conservancy Holdings, Ltd. v. Perma–Treat Corp., 126 A.D.2d 114, 513 N.Y.S.2d 266 (N.Y.A.D. 3 Dept.1987), 1307

Conservation Law Foundation v. Evans, 209 F.Supp.2d 1 (D.D.C.2001), 501

Continental Oil Co. v. Natrona Service, Inc., 588 F.2d 792 (10th Cir.1978), 1121

Converse v. Udall, 399 F.2d 616 (9th Cir. 1968), 1151

Copper Glance Lode, 29 L.D. 542 (1900), 1140

Copper Valley Mach. Works, Inc. v. Andrus, 653 F.2d 595, 209 U.S.App.D.C. 340 (D.C.Cir.1981), 1157

Cox, United States v., 190 F.2d 293 (10th Cir.1951), 945

Coyle v. Smith, 221 U.S. 559, 31 S.Ct. 688, 55 L.Ed. 853 (1911), 98, 101

Creede & C. C. Min. & Mill. Co. v. Uinta Tunnel Min. & Transp. Co., 196 U.S. 337, 25 S.Ct. 266, 49 L.Ed. 501 (1905), 1101

Cruthers, United States v., 523 F.2d 1306 (9th Cir.1975), 1153

Current Creek Irr. Co. v. Andrews, 9 Utah 2d 324, 344 P.2d 528 (Utah 1959), 818

Curtis–Nevada Mines, Inc., United States v., 611 F.2d 1277 (9th Cir.1980), 1151

Cushing v. Maine, 434 A.2d 486 (Me.1981), 1306

Darby v. Cisneros, 509 U.S. 137, 113 S.Ct. 2539, 125 L.Ed.2d 113 (1993), 257

Daubert v. Merrell Dow Pharmaceuticals, Inc., 509 U.S. 579, 113 S.Ct. 2786, 125 L.Ed.2d 469 (1993), 1270

Davis v. United States, 495 U.S. 472, 110 S.Ct. 2014, 109 L.Ed.2d 457 (1990), 996

Dean, United States v., 14 I.B.L.A. 107, GFS(MIN) 8 (1974), 1096

Defenders of Wildlife v. Andrus, 627 F.2d 1238, 201 U.S.App.D.C. 252 (D.C.Cir. 1980), 267

Defenders of Wildlife v. Andrus, 455 F.Supp. 446 (D.D.C.1978), 664

Defenders of Wildlife v. Andrus, 428 F.Supp. 167 (D.D.C.1977), 367

Defenders of Wildlife v. Kimbell, 07–CV–194–RLJ (D.D.C), 1245

Denison, Estate of, United States v., 76 I.D. 233 (1969), 1128

Denver, By and Through Bd. of Water Com'rs, City and County of v. Bergland, 695 F.2d 465 (10th Cir.1982), 724

Devereux v. Hunter, 11 L.D. 214 (1890), 1136

Dimitrov v. Norton, 479 F.Supp.2d 1141 (D.Mont.2007), 1104

Dolan v. City of Tigard, 512 U.S. 374, 114 S.Ct. 2309, 129 L.Ed.2d 304 (1994), 198

Douglas v. Seacoast Products, Inc., 431 U.S. 265, 97 S.Ct. 1740, 52 L.Ed.2d 304 (1977), 339

Douglas County v. Babbitt, 48 F.3d 1495 (9th Cir.1995), 366

Dred Scott v. Sandford, 60 U.S. 393, 19 How. 393, 15 L.Ed. 691 (1856), 154

Dugan v. Rank, 372 U.S. 609, 83 S.Ct. 999, 10 L.Ed.2d 15 (1963), 848

Duke Power Co. v. Carolina Environmental Study Group, Inc., 438 U.S. 59, 98 S.Ct. 2620, 57 L.Ed.2d 595 (1978), 243

Duncan v. Eagle Rock Gold Min. & Reduction Co., 48 Colo. 569, 111 P. 588 (Colo.1910), 1109

Duncan Miller, 79 I.D. 416 (1972), 1157

Earl R. Wilson, 21 I.B.L.A. 392, GFS (O & G) 99 (1975), 1157

Earth Island Institute v. Mosbacher, 746 F.Supp. 964 (N.D.Cal.1990), 568

Earth Island Institute v. Pengilly, 376 F.Supp.2d 994 (E.D.Cal.2005), 1292

Earth Island Institute v. Ruthenbeck, 490 F.3d 687 (9th Cir.2007), 306, 1292

Earth Island Institute v. United States Forest Service, 442 F.3d 1147 (9th Cir.2006), 676

Edmonds Institute v. Babbitt, 93 F.Supp.2d 63 (D.D.C.2000), 615

Ellis v. Gallatin Steel Co., 390 F.3d 461 (6th Cir.2004), 241

Employment Div., Dept. of Human Resources of Oregon v. Smith, 494 U.S. 872, 110 S.Ct. 1595, 108 L.Ed.2d 876 (1990), 201, 549, 1185

Energy Development Corp. v. Moss, 214 W.Va. 577, 591 S.E.2d 135 (W.Va.2003), 1075

Eno, United States v., 171 IBLA 69, GFS(MIN) 4 (2007), 1086

Enterprise Min. Co. v. Rico–Aspen Consol. Min. Co., 167 U.S. 108, 17 S.Ct. 762, 42 L.Ed. 96 (1897), 1094

Environmental Defense Center v. Babbitt, 73 F.3d 867 (9th Cir.1995), 351

Environmental Defense Fund, Inc. v. Andrus, 596 F.2d 848 (9th Cir.1979), 287

Environmental Defense Fund, Inc. v. Hardin, 428 F.2d 1093, 138 U.S.App.D.C. 391 (D.C.Cir.1970), 257

Environmental Defense Fund, Inc. v. Massey, 986 F.2d 528, 300 U.S.App.D.C. 65 (D.C.Cir.1993), 276

Environmental Protection Information Center v. Blackwell, 389 F.Supp.2d 1174 (N.D.Cal.2004), 1260

Equal Employnent Opportunity Commission v. Arabian American Oil Co., 499 U.S. 244, 111 S.Ct. 1227, 113 L.Ed.2d 274 (1991), 276

Erhardt v. Boaro, 113 U.S. 527, 5 S.Ct. 560, 28 L.Ed. 1113 (1885), 1091

Estate of (see name of party)

Eureka Consol. Mining Co. v. Richmond Mining Co., 8 F.Cas. 819 (C.C.D.Nev. 1877), **1088**

Eveleigh v. Darneille, 276 Cal.App.2d 638, 81 Cal.Rptr. 301 (Cal.App. 3 Dist.1969), 1109, 1110

Exxon Mobil Corp. v. Norton, 346 F.3d 1244 (10th Cir.2003), 1107

Federal Election Com'n v. Akins, 524 U.S. 11, 118 S.Ct. 1777, 141 L.Ed.2d 10 (1998), 254

Federal Power Commission v. State of Or., 349 U.S. 435, 75 S.Ct. 832, 99 L.Ed. 1215 (1955), 835

Feldsite Corp. of America, 88 I.D. 643 (1981), 1118

Ferdinand Marcos, Human Rights Litigation, In re Estate of, 25 F.3d 1467 (9th Cir. 1994), 1042

Filartiga v. Pena–Irala, 630 F.2d 876 (2nd Cir.1980), 1042

First English Evangelical Lutheran Church of Glendale v. Los Angeles County, Cal., 482 U.S. 304, 107 S.Ct. 2378, 96 L.Ed.2d 250 (1987), 195, 197

Fleming Foundation v. Texaco, Inc., 337 S.W.2d 846 (Tex.Civ.App.-Amarillo 1960), 1067

Forest Guardians v. Johanns, 450 F.3d 455 (9th Cir.2006), 1013

Forest Guardians v. Powell, 130 N.M. 368, 24 P.3d 803 (N.M.App.2001), 1019

Forest Guardians v. Wells, 201 Ariz. 255, 34 P.3d 364 (Ariz.2001), 1019

Foster v. Seaton, 271 F.2d 836, 106 U.S.App.D.C. 253 (D.C.Cir.1959), **1126**

Franco–American Charolaise, Ltd. v. Oklahoma Water Resources Bd., 855 P.2d 568 (Okla.1990), **769**

Fredricks v. Klauser, 52 Or. 110, 96 P. 679 (Or.1908), 1109

Freese v. United States, 226 Ct.Cl. 252, 639 F.2d 754 (Ct.Cl.1981), 1141

Friends of Earth, Inc. v. Mosbacher, 488 F.Supp.2d 889 (N.D.Cal.2007), 288

Friends of Santa Fe County v. LAC Minerals, Inc., 892 F.Supp. 1333 (D.N.M.1995), 1182

Friends of the Bow v. Thompson, 124 F.3d 1210 (10th Cir.1997), 290, 1253, 1254

Friends of the Earth v. Hintz, 800 F.2d 822 (9th Cir.1986), 285

Friends of the Earth, Inc. v. Laidlaw Environmental Services (TOC), Inc., 528 U.S. 167, 120 S.Ct. 693, 145 L.Ed.2d 610 (2000), 243

Friends of Yosemite v. Frizzell, 420 F.Supp. 390 (N.D.Cal.1976), 616

Friendswood Development Co. v. Smith–Southwest Industries, Inc., 576 S.W.2d 21 (Tex.1978), 816

Fuller, United States v., 409 U.S. 488, 93 S.Ct. 801, 35 L.Ed.2d 16 (1973), **943**

Garcia v. San Antonio Metropolitan Transit Authority, 469 U.S. 528, 105 S.Ct. 1005, 83 L.Ed.2d 1016 (1985), 173

Gardner, United States v., 107 F.3d 1314 (9th Cir.1997), 101, 158

Garfield County, United States v., 122 F.Supp.2d 1201 (D.Utah 2000), 722

Geer v. State of Conn., 161 U.S. 519, 16 S.Ct. 600, 40 L.Ed. 793 (1896), 53, **163,** 339, 825

General Adjudication of All Rights to Use Water in Gila River System and Source, In re, 195 Ariz. 411, 989 P.2d 739 (Ariz. 1999), 839

General Adjudication of All Rights to Use Water in the Big Horn River System, In re, 753 P.2d 76 (Wyo.1988), 839

Geomet Exploration, Ltd. v. Lucky Mc Uranium Corp., 124 Ariz. 55, 601 P.2d 1339 (Ariz.1979), 1120

Gerlach Live Stock Co., United States v., 339 U.S. 725, 70 S.Ct. 955, 94 L.Ed. 1231 (1950), 184

Gettysburg Electric R. Co., United States v., 160 U.S. 668, 16 S.Ct. 427, 40 L.Ed. 576 (1896), 102

Gibbs v. Babbitt, 214 F.3d 483 (4th Cir. 2000), **174**

Gibson v. United States, 166 U.S. 269, 17 S.Ct. 578, 41 L.Ed. 996 (1897), 868

Glenn–Colusa Irr. Dist., United States v., 788 F.Supp. 1126 (E.D.Cal.1992), 871

Globe Min. Co. v. Anderson, 78 Wyo. 17, 318 P.2d 373 (Wyo.1957), 1091

Goldblatt v. Town of Hempstead, N. Y., 369 U.S. 590, 82 S.Ct. 987, 8 L.Ed.2d 130 (1962), 307

Gold Leaf Enterprises, 105 IBLA 282 (1988), 1071

Gonzales v. Raich, 545 U.S. 1, 125 S.Ct. 2195, 162 L.Ed.2d 1 (2005), 174, 182

Gratiot, United States v., 39 U.S. 526, 14 Pet. 526, 10 L.Ed. 573 (1840), 96, 99, 130

Gray v. Handy, 349 Mass. 438, 208 N.E.2d 829 (Mass.1965), 1045

Great Eastern Mines, Inc. v. Metals Corp. of America, 86 N.M. 717, 527 P.2d 112 (N.M. 1974), 1109

Greater Yellowstone Coalition v. Babbitt, 952 F.Supp. 1435 (D.Mont.1996), 613

Greenpeace Foundation v. Mineta, 122 F.Supp.2d 1123 (D.Hawai'i 2000), 401

Grimaud, United States v., 220 U.S. 506, 31 S.Ct. 480, 55 L.Ed. 563 (1911), 213

Guam v. Guerrero, 290 F.3d 1210 (9th Cir. 2002), 1185

Gustin v. Nevada–Pacific Development Corp, 125 F.Supp. 811 (D.Nev.1954), 1100

Guzzman, United States v., 81 I.D. 685 (1974), 1088

Gwillim v. Donnellan, 115 U.S. 45, 5 S.Ct. 1110, 29 L.Ed. 348 (1885), 1141

Hadaja, Inc. v. Evans, 263 F.Supp.2d 346 (D.R.I.2003), 496

Hage v. United States, 2002 WL 122918 (Fed. Cl.2002), 947

Hage, Estate of v. United States, 2008 WL 2358593 (Fed.Cl.2008), 947

Hall v. Evans, 165 F.Supp.2d 114 (D.R.I. 2001), 496, 503

Hall v. McKinnon, 193 F. 572 (9th Cir.1911), 1092

Hamilton v. Ertl, 146 Colo. 80, 360 P.2d 660 (Colo.1961), 1109

Harris v. Brooks, 225 Ark. 436, 283 S.W.2d 129 (Ark.1955), **760**

Hawaiian Crow ('Alala) v. Lujan, 906 F.Supp. 549 (D.Hawai'i 1991), 403

Hawksbill Sea Turtle v. Federal Emergency Management Agency, 11 F.Supp.2d 529 (D.Virgin Islands 1998), 401

Hayashi, United States v., 22 F.3d 859 (9th Cir.1993), 557

Headwaters, Inc. v. Bureau of Land Management, Medford Dist., 914 F.2d 1174 (9th Cir.1990), 1240

Heart of Atlanta Motel, Inc. v. United States, 379 U.S. 241, 85 S.Ct. 348, 13 L.Ed.2d 258 (1964), 173

Heartwood, Inc. v. United States Forest Service, 73 F.Supp.2d 962 (S.D.Ill.1999), 274

Heinatz v. Allen, 147 Tex. 512, 217 S.W.2d 994 (Tex.1949), 1066

Hells Canyon Alliance v. United States Forest Service, 227 F.3d 1170 (9th Cir.2000), 667

Henault Min. Co. v. Tysk, 419 F.2d 766 (9th Cir.1969), 1123

Henderson, United States v., 68 I.D. 26 (1961), 1150

Henry Friedman, 49 IBLA 97, GFS(MIN) 178 (1980), 1118

Hickel v. Oil Shale Corp., 400 U.S. 48, 91 S.Ct. 196, 27 L.Ed.2d 193 (1970), **1104,** 1129

Hicks v. Dowd, 157 P.3d 914 (Wyo.2007), 735

High Country Citizens Alliance v. Clarke, 454 F.3d 1177 (10th Cir.2006), 1144

High Sierra Hikers Ass'n v. Moore, 561 F.Supp.2d 1107 (N.D.Cal.2008), 658

High Sierra Hikers Ass'n v. United States Forest Service, 436 F.Supp.2d 1117 (E.D.Cal.2006), 657

Hinderlider v. La Plata River & Cherry Creek Ditch Co., 304 U.S. 92, 58 S.Ct. 803, 82 L.Ed. 1202 (1938), 889

Hinsdale Livestock Co. v. United States, 501 F.Supp. 773 (D.Mont.1980), 971

Hodel v. Indiana, 452 U.S. 314, 101 S.Ct. 2376, 69 L.Ed.2d 40 (1981), 1189

Hodel v. Virginia Surface Min. and Reclamation Ass'n, Inc., 452 U.S. 264, 101 S.Ct. 2352, 69 L.Ed.2d 1 (1981), 1189

Hoglund v. Omak Wood Products, Inc., 81 Wash.App. 501, 914 P.2d 1197 (Wash.App. Div. 3 1996), 1304

Holmes v. Westvaco Corp., 289 S.C. 591, 347 S.E.2d 887 (S.C.App.1986), 1306

Holt State Bank, United States v., 270 U.S. 49, 46 S.Ct. 197, 70 L.Ed. 465 (1926), 103, 868

Huber v. Merkel, 117 Wis. 355, 94 N.W. 354 (Wis.1903), 815

Hughes v. Oklahoma, 441 U.S. 322, 99 S.Ct. 1727, 60 L.Ed.2d 250 (1979), 167, 339, 826

Humane Soc. of United States v. Lujan, 768 F.Supp. 360 (D.D.C.1991), 664

Hunt v. Washington State Apple Advertising Com'n, 432 U.S. 333, 97 S.Ct. 2434, 53 L.Ed.2d 383 (1977), 242

Idaho v. United States, 533 U.S. 262, 121 S.Ct. 2135, 150 L.Ed.2d 326 (2001), 103, 104

Idaho Dept. of Parks, State of v. Idaho Dept. of Water Administration, 96 Idaho 440, 530 P.2d 924 (Idaho 1974), 796

Idaho ex rel. Director, Idaho Dept. of Water Resources, United States v., 508 U.S. 1, 113 S.Ct. 1893, 123 L.Ed.2d 563 (1993), 847

Idaho Sporting Congress, Inc. v. Rittenhouse, 305 F.3d 957 (9th Cir.2002), **1254**

Idaho Watersheds Project v. State Bd. of Land Com'rs, 133 Idaho 64, 982 P.2d 367 (Idaho 1999), 129, **1016**

Illinois Cent. R. Co. v. State of Illinois, 146 U.S. 387, 13 S.Ct. 110, 36 L.Ed. 1018 (1892), **105,** 167

Immigration and Naturalization Service v. Chadha, 462 U.S. 919, 103 S.Ct. 2764, 77 L.Ed.2d 317 (1983), 690

Imperial Irrigation Dist. v. State Wat. Resources Control Bd., 225 Cal.App.3d 548, 275 Cal.Rptr. 250 (Cal.App. 4 Dist. 1990), **784**

Independence Min. Co., Inc. v. Babbitt, 105 F.3d 502 (9th Cir.1997), 1144

Ingemarson v. Coffey, 41 Colo. 407, 92 P. 908 (Colo.1907), 1099

Inland Empire Public Lands Council v. United States Forest Service, 88 F.3d 754 (9th Cir.1996), 1260

In re (see name of party)

International Snowmobile Mfrs. Ass'n v. Norton, 340 F.Supp.2d 1249 (D.Wyo.2004), 618

Inyo Marble Co. v. Loundagin, 120 Cal.App. 298, 7 P.2d 1067 (Cal.App. 4 Dist.1932), 1093

Iowa Coal Min. Co., Inc. v. Monroe County, 494 N.W.2d 664 (Iowa 1993), 307

Iron Silver Min. Co. v. Mike & Starr Gold & Silver Min. Co., 143 U.S. 394, 143 U.S. 430, 12 S.Ct. 543, 36 L.Ed. 201 (1892), 1091, 1093

Irwin v. Phillips, 5 Cal. 140 (Cal.1855), 828

Izaak Walton League of America, Inc. v. Kimbell, 516 F.Supp.2d 982 (D.Minn.2007), 659

James v. Krook, 42 Ariz. 322, 25 P.2d 1026 (Ariz.1933), 1109

James Stewart Co. v. Cattany, 134 Ariz. 484, 657 P.2d 897 (Ariz.App. Div. 2 1982), 1109

Japan Whaling Ass'n v. American Cetacean Soc., 478 U.S. 221, 106 S.Ct. 2860, 92 L.Ed.2d 166 (1986), 249

Jaramillo, United States v., 190 F.2d 300 (10th Cir.1951), 945

Johanson v. White, 160 F. 901 (9th Cir.1908), 1121

John C. Teller, 26 L.D. 484 (1898), 1102

Johnson v. M'Intosh, 21 U.S. 543, 5 L.Ed. 681 (1823), **88**

Jones v. Adams, 19 Nev. 78, 6 P. 442 (Nev. 1885), 830

Joseph E. McClory, 50 L.D. 623 (1924), 1168

J.W. Hampton, Jr., & Co. v. United States, 276 U.S. 394, 48 S.Ct. 348, 72 L.Ed. 624 (1928), 214, 314

Kaiser Aetna v. United States, 444 U.S. 164, 100 S.Ct. 383, 62 L.Ed.2d 332 (1979), 870

Kane County, Utah v. Kempthorne, 495 F.Supp.2d 1143 (D.Utah 2007), 723

Kane Land and Livestock, Inc. v. United States, 964 F.Supp. 1538 (D.Wyo.1997), 971

Kansas City Life Ins. Co., United States v., 339 U.S. 799, 70 S.Ct. 885, 94 L.Ed. 1277 (1950), 869

Kansas, State of v. State of Colo., 206 U.S. 46, 27 S.Ct. 655, 51 L.Ed. 956 (1907), 882, 884

Kentuckians for Commonwealth Inc. v. Rivenburgh, 317 F.3d 425 (4th Cir.2003), 1191

Kentuckians For the Commonwealth, Inc. v. Rivenburgh, 204 F.Supp.2d 927 (S.D.W.Va.2002), 1192

Klamath Irrigation Dist. v. United States, 2005 WL 2100579 (Fed.Cl.2005), 881

Kleppe v. New Mexico, 426 U.S. 529, 96 S.Ct. 2285, 49 L.Ed.2d 34 (1976), 99, **148,** 339, 721

Kleppe v. Sierra Club, 427 U.S. 390, 96 S.Ct. 2718, 49 L.Ed.2d 576 (1976), 265

Kootenai Tribe of Idaho v. Veneman, 313 F.3d 1094 (9th Cir.2002), **1273**

Kosanke Sand Corp., United States v., 80 I.D. 538 (1973), 1130, 1135, 1166

Kramer v. Taylor, 200 Or. 640, 266 P.2d 709 (Or.1954), 1109

Krichbaum v. Kelley, 844 F.Supp. 1107 (W.D.Va.1994), 1251, 1261

Lands Council v. Powell, 395 F.3d 1019 (9th Cir.2005), 1271

Langley, United States v., 587 F.Supp. 1258 (E.D.Cal.1984), 1152

Lassen v. Arizona ex rel. Arizona Highway Dept., 385 U.S. 458, 87 S.Ct. 584, 17 L.Ed.2d 515 (1967), 1018

Layman v. Ellis, 52 I.D. 714 (1929), 1088

Leary, United States v., 63 I.D. 341 (1956), 1135

LeFaivre v. Environmental Quality Council of Dept. of Environmental Quality, 735 P.2d 428 (Wyo.1987), 1181

Leo Sheep Co. v. United States, 440 U.S. 668, 99 S.Ct. 1403, 59 L.Ed.2d 677 (1979), 707

Light v. United States, 220 U.S. 523, 31 S.Ct. 485, 55 L.Ed. 570 (1911), 99, 939

Lingle v. Chevron U.S.A. Inc., 544 U.S. 528, 125 S.Ct. 2074, 161 L.Ed.2d 876 (2005), 198

L.N. Hagood, 65 I.D. 405 (1958), 1168

Locke, United States v., 471 U.S. 84, 105 S.Ct. 1785, 85 L.Ed.2d 64 (1985), 199, **1111,** 1142

Loggerhead Turtle v. County Council of Volusia County, Fla., 148 F.3d 1231 (11th Cir. 1998), 402, 414

Lopez, United States v., 514 U.S. 549, 115 S.Ct. 1624, 131 L.Ed.2d 626 (1995), 173

Loveladies Harbor, Inc. v. United States, 28 F.3d 1171 (Fed.Cir.1994), 200

Lucas v. South Carolina Coastal Council, 505 U.S. 1003, 112 S.Ct. 2886, 120 L.Ed.2d 798 (1992), 185, 879

Lujan v. Defenders of Wildlife, 504 U.S. 555, 112 S.Ct. 2130, 119 L.Ed.2d 351 (1992), 244

Lyng v. Northwest Indian Cemetery Protective Ass'n, 485 U.S. 439, 108 S.Ct. 1319, 99 L.Ed.2d 534 (1988), 201

MacGuire v. Sturgis, 347 F.Supp. 580 (D.Wyo.1971), 1120

Maddocks v. Giles, 728 A.2d 150 (Me.1999), 816

Maine v. Taylor, 477 U.S. 131, 106 S.Ct. 2440, 91 L.Ed.2d 110 (1986), 166

Maine, United States v., 420 U.S. 515, 95 S.Ct. 1155, 43 L.Ed.2d 363 (1975), 1158

Mammoth Oil Co. v. United States, 275 U.S. 13, 48 S.Ct. 1, 72 L.Ed. 137 (1927), 1159

Manuel v. Wulff, 152 U.S. 505, 14 S.Ct. 651, 38 L.Ed. 532 (1894), 1099

Marathon Oil Co. v. Lujan, 937 F.2d 498 (10th Cir.1991), 1144

Marbled Murrelet v. Babbitt, 83 F.3d 1060 (9th Cir.1996), 401, 672

Marbled Murrelet (Brachyramphus Marmoratus) v. Pacific Lumber Co., 880 F.Supp. 1343 (N.D.Cal.1995), 402

Marincovich v. Tarabochia, 114 Wash.2d 271, 787 P.2d 562 (Wash.1990), 474

Marks v. Whitney, 98 Cal.Rptr. 790, 491 P.2d 374 (Cal.1971), 108

Marsh v. Oregon Natural Resources Council, 490 U.S. 360, 109 S.Ct. 1851, 104 L.Ed.2d 377 (1989), 288

Martin v. Kentucky Oak Min. Co., 429 S.W.2d 395 (Ky.1968), **1048,** 1305

Martin v. Waddell's Lessee, 41 U.S. 367, 16 Pet. 367, 10 L.Ed. 997 (1842), 100

Massachusetts v. Environmental Protection Agency, 549 U.S. 497, 127 S.Ct. 1438, 167 L.Ed.2d 248 (2007), 255, 1144

Maurice Tanner, 141 I.B.L.A. 373 (1997), 1060

Mausolf v. Babbitt, 125 F.3d 661 (8th Cir. 1997), 613

McCall v. Andrus, 628 F.2d 1185 (9th Cir. 1980), 1092

McCarthy v. Speed, 11 S.D. 362, 77 N.W. 590 (S.D.1898), 1121

McClanahan v. Arizona State Tax Commission, 411 U.S. 164, 93 S.Ct. 1257, 36 L.Ed.2d 129 (1973), 114

McClarty v. Secretary of Interior, 408 F.2d 907 (9th Cir.1969), **1147**

McClarty, United States v., 81 I.D. 472 (1974), 1149

McCready v. State of Virginia, 94 U.S. 391, 4 Otto 391, 24 L.Ed. 248 (1876), 167

McCullagh, United States v., 221 F. 288 (D.Kan.1915), 168

McEvoy v. Hyman, 25 F. 596 (C.C.D.Colo. 1885), 1102

McKillop v. Crown Zellerbach, Inc., 46 Wash. App. 870, 733 P.2d 559 (Wash.App. Div. 3 1987), 1306

McKinley v. United States, 828 F.Supp. 888 (D.N.M.1993), **968**

McKinley Creek Mining Co v. Alaska United Mining Co, 183 U.S. 563, 22 S.Ct. 84, 46 L.Ed. 331 (1902), 1098

McKirahan v. Gold King Mining Co., 39 S.D. 535, 165 N.W. 542 (S.D.1917), 1109

McLennan v. Wilbur, 283 U.S. 414, 51 S.Ct. 502, 75 L.Ed. 1148 (1931), 1167

Mead Corp., United States v., 533 U.S. 218, 121 S.Ct. 2164, 150 L.Ed.2d 292 (2001), 229, 1189

Menzer v. Village of Elkhart Lake, 51 Wis.2d 70, 186 N.W.2d 290 (Wis.1971), 108

Merrell v. Thomas, 807 F.2d 776 (9th Cir. 1986), 273

Metcalf v. Daley, 214 F.3d 1135 (9th Cir. 2000), 545

Metropolitan Edison Co. v. People Against Nuclear Energy, 460 U.S. 766, 103 S.Ct. 1556, 75 L.Ed.2d 534 (1983), 275

Michels Pipeline Const., Inc., State v., 63 Wis.2d 278, 217 N.W.2d 339 (Wis.1974), 810

Midwest Oil Co., United States v., 236 U.S. 459, 35 S.Ct. 309, 59 L.Ed. 673 (1915), **133,** 621, 1153

Miehlich v. Tintic Standard Mining Co., 60 Utah 569, 211 P. 686 (Utah 1922), 1110

Milestone Petroleum, Inc. v. Phillips Oil Co., 85 I.B.L.A. 96 (1985), 1156

Miller Land & Mineral Co. v. State Highway Com'n of Wyoming, 757 P.2d 1001 (Wyo. 1988), 1066

Mineral Policy Center v. Norton, 292 F.Supp.2d 30 (D.D.C.2003), 1174, 1184

Minnesota v. Block, 660 F.2d 1240 (8th Cir.1981), **158**

Missouri v. Holland, 252 U.S. 416, 40 S.Ct. 382, 64 L.Ed. 641 (1920), **169**

Mitchell, United States v., 553 F.2d 996 (5th Cir.1977), 556

M. & I. Timber Co. v. Hope Silver–Lead Mines, Inc., 91 Idaho 638, 428 P.2d 955 (Idaho 1967), 1304

Monongahela Nav. Co. v. United States, 148 U.S. 312, 13 S.Ct. 622, 37 L.Ed. 463 (1893), 868

Montana v. United States, 450 U.S. 544, 101 S.Ct. 1245, 67 L.Ed.2d 493 (1981), 102, 833

Montana Cent. R. Co. v. Migeon, 68 F. 811 (C.C.D.Mont.1895), 1093

Montana Envtl. Info. Ctr v. Department of Envtl. Quality, No. CDV–92–486 (Montana First Judicial District Court), 1040

Montana Trout Unlimited v. Montana Dept. of Natural Resources and Conservation, 331 Mont. 483, 133 P.3d 224 (Mont.2006), 819

Montgomery v. Lomos Altos, Inc., 141 N.M. 21, 150 P.3d 971 (N.M.2006), 822

Morrison, United States v., 529 U.S. 598, 120 S.Ct. 1740, 146 L.Ed.2d 658 (2000), 174

Morros, State v., 104 Nev. 709, 766 P.2d 263 (Nev.1988), 846

Motor Vehicle Mfrs. Ass'n of United States, Inc. v. State Farm Mut. Auto. Ins. Co., 463 U.S. 29, 103 S.Ct. 2856, 77 L.Ed.2d 443 (1983), 227, 235, 997, 1004, 1270

Mountain States Legal Foundation v. Andrus, 499 F.Supp. 383 (D.Wyo.1980), 1157

Mountain States Legal Foundation v. Bush, 306 F.3d 1132, 353 U.S.App.D.C. 306 (D.C.Cir.2002), **628**

Mountain States Legal Foundation v. Hodel, 668 F.Supp. 1466 (D.Wyo.1987), **692,** 1160

Mulkern v. Hammitt, 326 F.2d 896 (9th Cir. 1964), 1128

Mullins v. Beatrice Pocahontas Co., 432 F.2d 314 (4th Cir.1970), 1054

Murray Hill Min. & Mill. Co. v. Havenor, 24 Utah 73, 66 P. 762 (Utah 1901), 1141

Mutchmor v. McCarty, 149 Cal. 603, 87 P. 85 (Cal.1906), 1093

National Audubon Society v. Superior Court, 189 Cal.Rptr. 346, 658 P.2d 709 (Cal. 1983), 108, 799

National Audubon Society v. United States Forest Service, 4 F.3d 832 (9th Cir.1993), 1262

National Fisheries Institute, Inc. v. Mosbacher, 732 F.Supp. 210 (D.D.C.1990), 496

National Organization for Reform of Marijuana Laws (NORML) v. United States Dept. of State, 452 F.Supp. 1226 (D.D.C.1978), 276

National Wildlife Federation v. Babbitt, 128 F.Supp.2d 1274 (E.D.Cal.2000), 4274

National Wildlife Federation et al. v. BLM, 140 I.B.L.A. 85 (1997), **962**

National Wildlife Federation v. Burford, 677 F.Supp. 1445 (D.Mont.1985), 1165

National Wildlife Federation v. Burlington Northern R.R., Inc., 23 F.3d 1508 (9th Cir.1994), 404

National Wildlife Federation v. Cosgriffe, 21 F.Supp.2d 1211 (D.Or.1998), 1012

National Wildlife Federation v. Hodel, 839 F.2d 694, 268 U.S.App.D.C. 15 (D.C.Cir. 1988), 1166

National Wildlife Federation v. National Park Service, 669 F.Supp. 384 (D.Wyo.1987), 616

National Wildlife Federation v. Watt, 571 F.Supp. 1145 (D.D.C.1983), 690

Natural Resources Defense Council v. United States Forest Service, 421 F.3d 797 (9th Cir.2005), 1281

Natural Resources Defense Council, Inc. v. Berklund, 609 F.2d 553, 197 U.S.App.D.C. 298 (D.C.Cir.1979), 1166

Natural Resources Defense Council, Inc. v. Daley, 209 F.3d 747, 341 U.S.App.D.C. 119 (D.C.Cir.2000), **508**

Natural Resources Defense Council, Inc. v. Daley, 62 F.Supp.2d 102 (D.D.C.1999), **505**

Natural Resources Defense Council, Inc. v. Evans, 279 F.Supp.2d 1129 (N.D.Cal. 2003), 552

Natural Resources Defense Council, Inc. v. Hodel, 624 F.Supp. 1045 (D.Nev.1985), **955**

Natural Resources Defense Council, Inc. v. Hodel, 618 F.Supp. 848 (E.D.Cal. 1985), **984**

Natural Resources Defense Council, Inc. v. Jamison, 815 F.Supp. 454 (D.D.C.1992), 1165

Natural Resources Defense Council, Inc. v. Morton, 388 F.Supp. 829 (D.D.C.1974), 260, 952

Natural Resources Defense Council, Inc. v. United States Dept. of Interior, 2001 WL 760519 (9th Cir.2001), 365

Natural Resources Defense Council, Inc. v. Winter, 518 F.3d 704 (9th Cir.2008), 554

Natural Resources Defense Council, Inc. v. Winter, 518 F.3d 658 (9th Cir.2008), 554

Natural Resources Defense Council, Inc. v. Winter, 2007 WL 2481037 (C.D.Cal.2007), 553

Navajo Nation v. United States Forest Service, 535 F.3d 1058 (9th Cir.2008), 292, 1185

Navajo Nation v. United States Forest Service, 479 F.3d 1024 (9th Cir.2007), 1185

Navajo Nation v. United States Forest Service, 408 F.Supp.2d 866 (D.Ariz.2006), 202

NCNB Texas Nat. Bank, N.A. v. West, 631 So.2d 212 (Ala.1993), 1075

Nebraska v. Wyoming, 325 U.S. 589, 65 S.Ct. 1332, 89 L.Ed. 1815 (1945), 883

New Jersey, State of v. State of New York, 283 U.S. 336, 51 S.Ct. 478, 75 L.Ed. 1104 (1931), 883

Newman v. RAG Wyoming Land Co., 53 P.3d 540 (Wyo.2002), 1075

New Mexico, State of, United States v., 536 F.2d 1324 (10th Cir.1976), 129

New Mexico, United States v., 438 U.S. 696, 98 S.Ct. 3012, 57 L.Ed.2d 1052 (1978), **840**

New York v. United States, 505 U.S. 144, Nuclear Reg. Rep. P 20553, 112 S.Ct. 2408, 120 L.Ed.2d 120 (1992), 173

9,947.71 Acres of Land, More or Less, in Clark County, State of Nev., United States v., 220 F.Supp. 328 (D.Nev.1963), 1110

Niobrara River Ranch, L.L.C. v. Huber, 277 F.Supp.2d 1020 (D.Neb.2003), 670

Noe v. Metropolitan Atlanta Rapid Transit Authority, 644 F.2d 434 (5th Cir.1981), 289

Nogueira, United States v., 403 F.2d 816 (9th Cir.1968), 1152

Nollan v. California Coastal Com'n, 483 U.S. 825, 107 S.Ct. 3141, 97 L.Ed.2d 677 (1987), 197

Norris v. United Mineral Products Co., 61 Wyo. 386, 158 P.2d 679 (Wyo.1945), 1109

North Carolina Fisheries Ass'n, Inc. v. Daley, 27 F.Supp.2d 650 (E.D.Va.1998), **499**

Northern Plains Resource Council v. Fidelity Exploration and Development Co., 325 F.3d 1155 (9th Cir.2003), 1182

Northern Spotted Owl (Strix Occidentalis Caurina) v. Hodel, 716 F.Supp. 479 (W.D.Wash.1988), **230**

Northwest Environmental Defense Center v. Brennen, 958 F.2d 930 (9th Cir.1992), 496

Norton v. Southern Utah Wilderness Alliance, 542 U.S. 55, 124 S.Ct. 2373, 159 L.Ed.2d 137 (2004), **307,** 1259, 1272

Noyes v. Mantle, 127 U.S. 348, 8 S.Ct. 1132, 32 L.Ed. 168 (1888), 1093

Nye County, Nev., United States v., 920 F.Supp. 1108 (D.Nev.1996), 158

Oberbillig v. Bradley Min. Co., 372 F.2d 181 (9th Cir.1967), 1046

Oceana, Inc. v. Evans, 2005 WL 555416 (D.D.C.2005), 498

Ohio Forestry Ass'n, Inc. v. Sierra Club, 523 U.S. 726, 118 S.Ct. 1665, 140 L.Ed.2d 921 (1998), 257, 314, 1251

Ohio Valley Environmental Coalition v. Bulen, 429 F.3d 493 (4th Cir.2005), 1192

Ohio Valley Environmental Coalition v. Bulen, 410 F.Supp.2d 450 (S.D.W.Va.2004), 1192

Olmsted Falls, OH, City of v. F.A.A., 292 F.3d 261, 352 U.S.App.D.C. 30 (D.C.Cir.2002), 254

Omaechevarria v. State of Idaho, 246 U.S. 343, 38 S.Ct. 323, 62 L.Ed. 763 (1918), 147, 155, 939

Oregon Natural Desert Ass'n v. Bureau of Land Management, 531 F.3d 1114 (9th Cir.2008), **675**

Oregon Natural Desert Ass'n v. Dombeck, 172 F.3d 1092 (9th Cir.1998), 1012

Oregon Natural Desert Ass'n v. Green, 953 F.Supp. 1133 (D.Or.1997), 667, 1012

Oregon Natural Desert Ass'n v. Singleton (Singleton II), 75 F.Supp.2d 1139 (D.Or. 1999), 666, 1012

Oregon Natural Desert Ass'n v. Singleton (Singleton I), 47 F.Supp.2d 1182 (D.Or. 1998), 1012

Oregon Natural Desert Ass'n v. Thomas, 940 F.Supp. 1534 (D.Or.1996), 1012

Oregon Natural Desert Ass'n v. United States Forest Service, 2008 WL 140657 (D.Or.2008), 1012

Oregon Natural Desert Ass'n v. United States Forest Service, 465 F.3d 977 (9th Cir.2006), 967

Oregon Trollers Ass'n v. Gutierrez, 2005 WL 2211084 (D.Or.2005), 361

Osborne v. United States, 145 F.2d 892 (9th Cir.1944), 945

Pacific Coast Federation of Fishermen's Ass'n, Inc. v. Secretary of Commerce, 494 F.Supp. 626 (N.D.Cal.1980), 495

Pacific Coast Molydenum Co., 90 I.D. 352 (1983), 1130

Pacific Coast Molybdenum Co., In re, 68 I.B.L.A. 325 (1983), 1136, 1141

Pacific Legal Foundation v. Watt, 529 F.Supp. 982 (D.Mont.1981), 660, 690

Pacific Marine Conservation Council, Inc. v. Evans, 200 F.Supp.2d 1194 (N.D.Cal. 2002), 502

Pacific Rivers Council v. Thomas, 30 F.3d 1050 (9th Cir.1994), 1014

Palazzolo v. Rhode Island, 533 U.S. 606, 121 S.Ct. 2448, 150 L.Ed.2d 592 (2001), 197, 879

Palila v. Hawaii Dept. of Land and Natural Resources, 852 F.2d 1106 (9th Cir. 1988), **387,** 1013, 1014

Palila v. Hawaii Dept. of Land and Natural Resources, 639 F.2d 495 (9th Cir.1981), 1013

Palila v. Hawaii Dept. of Land and Natural Resources (Palila I), 471 F.Supp. 985 (D.Hawai'i 1979), 386

Park County Resource Council, Inc. v. United States Dept. of Agriculture, 817 F.2d 609 (10th Cir.1987), 265, 1158

Parker v. United States, 309 F.Supp. 593 (D.Colo.1970), 641

Pascoe v. Richards, 201 Cal.App.2d 680, 20 Cal.Rptr. 416 (Cal.App. 5 Dist.1962), 1110

Peevyhouse v. Garland Coal & Min. Co., 382 P.2d 109 (Okla.1962), 1046

Penn Cent. Transp. Co. v. City of New York, 438 U.S. 104, 98 S.Ct. 2646, 57 L.Ed.2d 631 (1978), **185**

Pennsylvania Coal Co. v. Mahon, 260 U.S. 393, 43 S.Ct. 158, 67 L.Ed. 322 (1922), 185, 186

Pfizer & Co., United States v., 76 I.D. 331, 15 I.B.L.A. 43 (1969), 1150

Phillips Petroleum Co. v. Mississippi, 484 U.S. 469, 108 S.Ct. 791, 98 L.Ed.2d 877 (1988), 102, 109

Pittsburgh Pacific Co., United States v., 84 I.D. 282 (1977), **1083,** 1130, 1166

Pierce, United States v., 75 I.D. 270 (1968), 1126

Pit River Tribe v. United States Forest Service, 469 F.3d 768 (9th Cir.2006), 676

Pitkin Iron Corp., United States v., 170 IBLA 352, GFS(MIN) 30(2006), 1150

Platt v. Bagg, 77 Ariz. 214, 269 P.2d 715 (Ariz.1954), 1109

Plymouth, Mass., Town of, United States v., 6 F.Supp.2d 81 (D.Mass.1998), 416

Pollard v. Hagan, 44 U.S. 212, 3 How. 212, 11 L.Ed. 565 (1845), 97, 833

Portland Audubon Soc. v. Endangered Species Committee, 984 F.2d 1534 (9th Cir. 1993), 370

Port of Astoria, Or. v. Hodel, 595 F.2d 467 (9th Cir.1979), 267

Postema v. Pollution Control Hearings Bd., 142 Wash.2d 68, 11 P.3d 726 (Wash.2000), 822

Potlatch Corp. v. United States, 134 Idaho 916, 12 P.3d 1260 (Idaho 2000), 850

Pressentin, United States v., 71 I.D. 447 (1964), 1080

Printz v. United States, 521 U.S. 898, 117 S.Ct. 2365, 138 L.Ed.2d 914 (1997), 173

Protective Min. Co. v. Forest City Min. Co., 51 Wash. 643, 99 P. 1033 (Wash.1909), 1110

Public Lands Council v. Babbitt, 529 U.S. 728, 120 S.Ct. 1815, 146 L.Ed.2d 753 (2000), **989, 997**

Public Service Co. of Oklahoma v. Bleak, 134 Ariz. 311, 656 P.2d 600 (Ariz.1982), 1119

Public Utility Dist. No. 1 of Pend Oreille County v. State, Dept. of Ecology, 146 Wash.2d 778, 51 P.3d 744 (Wash.2002), 792

PUD No. 1 of Jefferson County v. Washington Dept. of Ecology, 511 U.S. 700, 114 S.Ct. 1900, 128 L.Ed.2d 716 (1994), 852

Rands, United States v., 389 U.S. 121, 88 S.Ct. 265, 19 L.Ed.2d 329 (1967), 869

Rapanos v. United States, 547 U.S. 715, 126 S.Ct. 2208, 165 L.Ed.2d 159 (2006), **854,** 1309

Rasmussen Drilling, Inc. v. Kerr–McGee Nuclear Corp., 571 F.2d 1144 (10th Cir. 1978), 1100, 1120

Red Canyon Sheep Co. v. Ickes, 98 F.2d 308 (D.C.Cir.1938), 946

Reid v. Covert, 354 U.S. 1, 77 S.Ct. 1222, 1 L.Ed.2d 1148 (1957), 171

Reynolds v. Sims, 377 U.S. 533, 84 S.Ct. 1362, 12 L.Ed.2d 506 (1964), 930

R. Gail Tibbetts, 43 I.B.L.A. 210, GFS(MIN) 92 (1979), 869

Rio Grande Dam & Irrigation Co., United States v., 174 U.S. 690, 19 S.Ct. 770, 43 L.Ed. 1136 (1899), 830

River Runners for Wilderness v. Martin, 2007 WL 4200677 (D.Ariz.2007), 613

Riverside Irr. Dist. v. Andrews, 758 F.2d 508 (10th Cir.1985), 871

Rizzinelli, United States v., 182 F. 675 (D.Idaho 1910), 1152

Roberts v. Morton, 549 F.2d 158 (10th Cir. 1976), 1126

Roberts v. Morton, 389 F.Supp. 87 (D.Colo. 1975), 1099

Robertson v. Methow Valley Citizens Council, 490 U.S. 332, 109 S.Ct. 1835, 104 L.Ed.2d 351 (1989), 249, 259, 261, 285, 286

Robertson v. Seattle Audubon Soc., 503 U.S. 429, 112 S.Ct. 1407, 118 L.Ed.2d 73 (1992), 1262

R.O. Corp. v. John H. Bell Iron Mountain Ranch Co., 781 P.2d 910 (Wyo.1989), 939

Rothrauff v. Sinking Spring Water Co., 339 Pa. 129, 14 A.2d 87 (Pa.1940), 816

Rummell v. Bailey, 7 Utah 2d 137, 320 P.2d 653 (Utah 1958), 1123

Sanders v. Noble, 22 Mont. 110, 55 P. 1037 (Mont.1899), 1091

San Juan County, Utah v. United States, 503 F.3d 1163 (10th Cir.2007), 723

Sarei v. Rio Tinto PLC., 221 F.Supp.2d 1116 (C.D.Cal.2002), 1042

Save the Yaak Committee v. Block, 840 F.2d 714 (9th Cir.1988), 260

Scientists' Institute for Public Information, Inc. v. Atomic Energy Commission, 481 F.2d 1079, 156 U.S.App.D.C. 395 (D.C.Cir. 1973), 254

S.D. Warren Co. v. Maine Bd. of Environmental Protection, 547 U.S. 370, 126 S.Ct. 1843, 164 L.Ed.2d 625 (2006), 1012

Seattle Audobon v. Sutherland, 2007 WL 130324 (W.D.Wash.2007), 414

Seattle Audubon Soc. v. Moseley, 798 F.Supp. 1484 (W.D.Wash.1992), 1262

Seven-Up Pete Venture v. Montana, No. BDV–2000–250 (Montana First Judicial District Court), 1041

Shauver, United States v., 214 F. 154 (E.D.Ark.1914), 168

Shiny Rock Min. Corp. v. United States, 629 F.Supp. 877 (D.Or.1986), 1086

Shokal v. Dunn, 109 Idaho 330, 707 P.2d 441 (Idaho 1985), 808

Shope v. Sims, 658 P.2d 1336 (Alaska 1983), 1099

Sierra Club v. Babbitt, 15 F.Supp.2d 1274 (S.D.Ala.1998), 424

Sierra Club v. Butz, 1972 WL 2683 (N.D.Cal. 1972), 641

Sierra Club v. Department of Interior, 376 F.Supp. 90 (N.D.Cal.1974), 615

Sierra Club v. Espy, 38 F.3d 792 (5th Cir. 1994), **1247**

Sierra Club v. Glickman, 156 F.3d 606 (5th Cir.1998), 367

Sierra Club v. Hardin, 325 F.Supp. 99 (D.Alaska 1971), 60, 220

Sierra Club v. Hodel, 848 F.2d 1068 (10th Cir.1988), **709**, 721

Sierra Club v. Lujan, 716 F.Supp. 1289 (D.Ariz.1989), 616

Sierra Club v. Lyng, 663 F.Supp. 556 (D.D.C. 1987), 658

Sierra Club v. Lyng, 662 F.Supp. 40 (D.D.C. 1987), 658

Sierra Club v. Mainella, 459 F.Supp.2d 76 (D.D.C.2006), 613

Sierra Club v. Marita, 46 F.3d 606 (7th Cir.1995), 286, 304, **1262**

Sierra Club v. Morton, 405 U.S. 727, 92 S.Ct. 1361, 31 L.Ed.2d 636 (1972), 27, 242, 253, 1144

Sierra Club v. Penfold, 857 F.2d 1307 (9th Cir.1988), 1092

Sierra Club v. Peterson, 717 F.2d 1409, 230 U.S.App.D.C. 352 (D.C.Cir.1983), 1158

Sierra Club v. Robertson, 845 F.Supp. 485 (S.D.Ohio 1994), 1251

Sierra Club v. Robertson, 810 F.Supp. 1021 (W.D.Ark.1992), 1261

Sierra Club v. State Bd. of Forestry, 32 Cal.Rptr.2d 19, 876 P.2d 505 (Cal.1994), **1310**

Sierra Club v. United States Army Corps of Engineers, 701 F.2d 1011 (2nd Cir.1983), 285, 288

Sierra Club v. United States Fish and Wildlife Service, 245 F.3d 434 (5th Cir.2001), 364, 365

Sierra Club v. United States Forest Service, 878 F.Supp. 1295 (D.S.D.1993), 1261

Sierra Club v. Watt, 608 F.Supp. 305 (E.D.Cal.1985), 643

Sierra Club v. Watt, 659 F.2d 203, 212 U.S.App.D.C. 157 (D.C.Cir.1981), 848

Sierra Club v. Yeutter, 926 F.2d 429 (5th Cir.1991), 416

Silver Chief Mining, United States v., 40 I.B.L.A. 244, GFS(MIN) 36 (1979), 1096

Simmons v. Muir, 75 Wyo. 44, 291 P.2d 810 (Wyo.1955), 1109

Sipriano v. Great Spring Waters of America, Inc., 1 S.W.3d 75 (Tex.1999), 816

Skidmore v. Swift & Co., 323 U.S. 134, 65 S.Ct. 161, 89 L.Ed. 124 (1944), 229, 1165

Skidmore, United States v., 10 I.B.L.A. 322, GFS(MIN) 53 (1973), 1096

Skokomish Indian Tribe v. France, 320 F.2d 205 (9th Cir.1963), 103

Slothower v. Hunter, 15 Wyo. 189, 88 P. 36 (Wyo.1906), 1099

Sleeper, In re Application of, Rio Arriba County, No. RA 84–53(C) (N.M. 1st Jud. Dist. April 16, 1985), **792**

Smith v. Maryland, 59 U.S. 71, 18 How. 71, 15 L.Ed. 269 (1855), 167

Smith v. Pittston Co., 203 Va. 711, 127 S.E.2d 79 (Va.1962), 1054

Snow Flake Fraction Placer, 37 L.D. 250 (1908), 1093

Soda Mountain Wilderness Council v. Norton, 424 F.Supp.2d 1241 (E.D.Cal.2006), 1260

Solid Waste Agency of Northern Cook County v. United States Army Corps of Engineers, 531 U.S. 159, 121 S.Ct. 675, 148 L.Ed.2d 576 (2001), 171, 1309

South Dakota, State of v. Andrus, 614 F.2d 1190 (8th Cir.1980), 1142

Southern Appalachian Biodiversity Project v. United States Fish and Wildlife Services, 181 F.Supp.2d 883 (E.D.Tenn.2001), 365

Southern Offshore Fishing Ass'n v. Daley, 995 F.Supp. 1411 (M.D.Fla.1998), 501

Southern Pac. Co., United States v., 259 U.S. 214, 42 S.Ct. 496, 66 L.Ed. 907 (1922), 1033

Southern Utah Wilderness Alliance v. Bureau of Land Management, 425 F.3d 735 (10th Cir.2005), 709, 721

Southern Utah Wilderness Alliance v. Bureau of Land Management, 147 F.Supp.2d 1130 (D.Utah 2001), 721

Southern Utah Wilderness Alliance v. National Park Service, 387 F.Supp.2d 1178 (D.Utah 2005), **604**

Southwest Center For Biological Diversity v. Bartel, 470 F.Supp.2d 1118 (S.D.Cal. 2006), 424

Southwest Center for Biological Diversity v. United States Bureau of Reclamation, 143 F.3d 515 (9th Cir.1998), **375**

Sparks v. Mount, 29 Wyo. 1, 207 P. 1099 (Wyo.1922), 1121

Speckert, United States v., 75 I.D. 367 (1968), 1103, 1105, 1151, 1153

Sporhase v. Nebraska, 458 U.S. 941, 102 S.Ct. 3456, 73 L.Ed.2d 1254 (1982), 166

Spur Industries, Inc. v. Del E. Webb Development Co., 108 Ariz. 178, 494 P.2d 700 (Ariz.1972), 923

Stanton v. Weber, 218 Or. 282, 341 P.2d 1078 (Or.1959), 1121

State v. _____ (see opposing party)

State Engineer v. City of Golden, 69 P.3d 1027 (Colo.2003), 796

State Engineer v. Eagle River Water and Sanitation Dist., 69 P.3d 1028 (Colo.2003), 796

State of (see name of state)

Steel Co. v. Citizens for a Better Environment, 523 U.S. 83, 118 S.Ct. 1003, 140 L.Ed.2d 210 (1998), 243

Stephenson Lumber Co. v. Hurst, 259 Ky. 747, 83 S.W.2d 48 (Ky.1934), 1307

Stewart v. Kempthorne, 593 F.Supp.2d 1240 (D.Utah 2008), 1009

St. Louis Smelting & Refining Co. v. Kemp, 104 U.S. 636, 14 Otto 636, 26 L.Ed. 875 (1881), 1103

Strahan v. Coxe, 127 F.3d 155 (1st Cir. 1997), **409**

Stratford, Connecticut, Town of v. FAA, 285 F.3d 84, 350 U.S.App.D.C. 432 (D.C.Cir. 2002), 255

Strong v. United States, 5 F.3d 905 (5th Cir.1993), 557

Strycker's Bay Neighborhood Council, Inc. v. Karlen, 444 U.S. 223, 100 S.Ct. 497, 62 L.Ed.2d 433 (1980), 261

Students Challenging Regulatory Agency Procedures (SCRAP), United States v., 412 U.S. 669, 93 S.Ct. 2405, 37 L.Ed.2d 254 (1973), 253

Summers v. Earth Island Institute, ___ U.S. ___, 129 S.Ct. 1142, 173 L.Ed.2d 1 (2009), 255, 1292

Sutton v. Providence St. Joseph Medical Center, 192 F.3d 826 (9th Cir.1999), 202

Swanson v. Babbitt, 3 F.3d 1348 (9th Cir. 1993), 1141

Sylvester v. United States Army Corps of Engineers, 884 F.2d 394 (9th Cir.1989), 267, 277

Tahoe–Sierra Preservation Council, Inc. v. Tahoe Regional Planning Agency, 535 U.S. 302, 122 S.Ct. 1465, 152 L.Ed.2d 517 (2002), 195, 879

Tasmania, Commonwealth v., 158 C.L.R. 1 (HCA 1983), 172

Taxpayers Watchdog, Inc. v. Stanley, 819 F.2d 294, 260 U.S.App.D.C. 334 (D.C.Cir. 1987), 266

Telecommunications Research and Action Center v. F.C.C., 750 F.2d 70, 242 U.S.App.D.C. 222 (D.C.Cir.1984), 1144

Teller v. United States, 113 F. 273 (8th Cir. 1901), 1152

Tennessee Valley Authority v. Hill, 437 U.S. 153, 98 S.Ct. 2279, 57 L.Ed.2d 117 (1978), 221, 369

Texaco, Inc. v. Short, 454 U.S. 516, 102 S.Ct. 781, 70 L.Ed.2d 738 (1982), **1055,** 1142

Texas v. New Mexico, 462 U.S. 554, 103 S.Ct. 2558, 77 L.Ed.2d 1 (1983), 886, 889

The Abby Dodge, 223 U.S. 166, 32 S.Ct. 310, 56 L.Ed. 390 (1912), 168

The Daniel Ball, 77 U.S. 557, 19 L.Ed. 999 (1870), 101

The Fund for Animals v. Norton, 294 F.Supp.2d 92 (D.D.C.2003), 618

The Propeller Genesee Chief v. Fitzhugh, 53 U.S. 443, 12 How. 443, 13 L.Ed. 1058 (1851), 827

The Wilderness Society v. United States Fish & Wildlife Service, 353 F.3d 1051 (9th Cir.2003), 649

Thomas v. Peterson, 753 F.2d 754 (9th Cir.1985), 260, **268,** 727

Thompson v. Spray, 72 Cal. 528, 14 P. 182 (Cal.1887), 1099

Toivo Pottala Logging, Inc. v. Boise Cascade Corp., 112 Idaho 489, 733 P.2d 710 (Idaho 1987), 1308

Topaz Beryllium Co. v. United States, 649 F.2d 775 (10th Cir.1981), 1118

Town of (see name of town)

Trout Unlimited v. Lohn, 2007 WL 1730090 (W.D.Wash.2007), 361

Tucker v. Masser, 113 U.S. 203, 5 S.Ct. 420, 28 L.Ed. 979 (1885), 1140

Tulare County v. Bush, 306 F.3d 1138, 353 U.S.App.D.C. 312 (D.C.Cir.2002), **629**

Tulare Lake Basin Water Storage Dist. v. United States, 59 Fed.Cl. 246 (Fed.Cl. 2003), 878

Tulare Lake Basin Water Storage Dist. v. United States, 49 Fed.Cl. 313 (Fed.Cl. 2001), **872**

Twin City Power Co., United States v., 350 U.S. 222, 76 S.Ct. 259, 100 L.Ed. 240 (1956), 869

Udall v. Tallman, 380 U.S. 1, 85 S.Ct. 792, 13 L.Ed.2d 616 (1965), 1160, 1167

Union Oil Co., 26 L.D. 245 (1958), 1141

Union Oil Co., 25 L.D. 351 (1897), 1092

Union Oil Co. of California v. Smith, 249 U.S. 337, 39 S.Ct. 308, 63 L.Ed. 635 (1919), 1119

Union Pac. R. Co., United States v., 226 U.S. 61, 33 S.Ct. 53, 57 L.Ed. 124 (1912), 1033

United Mining Corp., United States v., 142 I.B.L.A. 339, GFS(MIN) 38 (1998), 1129

United Plainsmen Ass'n v. North Dakota State Water Conservation Commission, 247 N.W.2d 457 (N.D.1976), 808

United States v. _____ (see opposing party)

United States ex rel. v. _____ (see opposing party and relator)

United States Borax Co., United States v., 58 I.D. 426 (1943), 1168

United States Pumice Corp., United States v., 37 I.B.L.A. 153, 159, GFS(MIN) 106 (1978), 1135

United States Steel Corp. v. Hoge, 503 Pa. 140, 468 A.2d 1380 (Pa.1983), 1075

Utah v. United States Dept. of Interior, 535 F.3d 1184 (10th Cir.2008), 686

Utah Div. of State Lands v. United States, 482 U.S. 193, 107 S.Ct. 2318, 96 L.Ed.2d 162 (1987), 101

Utah International, United States v., 45 I.B.L.A. 73, GFS(MIN) 25 (1980), 1096

Utah Standard Mining Co. v. Tintic Indian Chief Min. & Mill. Co., 73 Utah 456, 274 P. 950 (Utah 1929), 1109

Utah, State of v. Babbitt, 137 F.3d 1193 (10th Cir.1998), 685

Valley Forge Christian College v. Americans United for Separation of Church and State, Inc., 454 U.S. 464, 102 S.Ct. 752, 70 L.Ed.2d 700 (1982), 241

Ward v. Harding, 860 S.W.2d 280 (Ky.1993), 1053

Washington v. Washington State Commercial Passenger Fishing Vessel Ass'n, 443 U.S. 658, 99 S.Ct. 3055, 61 L.Ed.2d 823 (1979), 113

Washington Audubon Soc. v. Robertson, 1991 WL 180099 (W.D.Wash.1991), 1224

Washington, State of, United States v., 157 F.3d 630 (9th Cir.1998), 115

Washington, State of, United States v., 909 F.Supp. 787 (W.D.Wash.1995), 115

Washington, State of, United States v., 898 F.Supp. 1453 (W.D.Wash.1995), 115

Washington, State of, United States v., 873 F.Supp. 1422 (W.D.Wash.1994), 115

Washington, State of, United States v., 384 F.Supp. 312 (W.D.Wash.1974), 113

Waskey v. Hammer, 223 U.S. 85, 32 S.Ct. 187, 56 L.Ed. 359 (1912), 1140

Water Right Permits in the Sacramento–San Joaquin Delta Watershed (Term 80 Permits), In re, 1984 WL 19050, *14 (Cal. St. Water Res. Control Bd., Feb. 1, 1984), 809

Watt v. Alaska, 451 U.S. 259, 101 S.Ct. 1673, 68 L.Ed.2d 80 (1981), 996

Watt v. Western Nuclear, Inc., 462 U.S. 36, 103 S.Ct. 2218, 76 L.Ed.2d 400 (1983), 1065

Webb v. American Asphaltum Min. Co., 157 F. 203 (8th Cir.1907), 1092

Webb's Fabulous Pharmacies, Inc. v. Beckwith, 449 U.S. 155, 101 S.Ct. 446, 66 L.Ed.2d 358 (1980), 184

West Coast Forest Resources Ltd. Partnership, United States v., 2000 WL 298707 (D.Or.2000), 401

Western Aggregates, LLC, 169 IBLA 64, GFS(MIN) 18 (2006), 1137

Western Watersheds Project v. Bennett, 392 F.Supp.2d 1217 (D.Idaho 2005), 968

Western Watersheds Project v. Fish and Wildlife Service, 535 F.Supp.2d 1173 (D.Idaho 2007), 1014

Western Watersheds Project v. Kraayenbrink, 2007 WL 1667618 (D.Idaho 2007), **999**

West Virginia Division of Izaak Walton League of America v. Butz, 522 F.2d 945 (4th Cir.1975), 297, 1234

Wickard v. Filburn, 317 U.S. 111, 63 S.Ct. 82, 87 L.Ed. 122 (1942), 173, 827, 854

Wight v. Dubois, 21 F. 693 (C.C.D.Colo.1884), 1136

Wilbur, United States ex rel. McLennan v., 283 U.S. 414, 51 S.Ct. 502, 75 L.Ed. 1148 (1931), 1167

Wilderness Public Rights Fund v. Kleppe, 608 F.2d 1250 (9th Cir.1979), 616

Wilderness Society v. Kane County, Utah, 560 F.Supp.2d 1147 (D.Utah 2008), 723

Wilderness Society v. United States Fish and Wildlife Service, 316 F.3d 913 (9th Cir. 2003), 657, 670

Wilke Window & Door Co. v. Peabody Coal Co., 2007 WL 924463 (S.D.Ill.2007), 1190

Wilkins v. Secretary of Interior, 995 F.2d 850 (8th Cir.1993), 612

William Dunn, 157 I.B.L.A. 347 (2002), 1086

Willow River Power Co., United States v., 324 U.S. 499, 65 S.Ct. 761, 89 L.Ed. 1101 (1945), 869

Wiltsee v. King of Arizona Min. & Mill. Co., 7 Ariz. 95, 60 P. 896 (Ariz.Terr.1900), 1091

Winans, United States v., 198 U.S. 371, 25 S.Ct. 662, 49 L.Ed. 1089 (1905), 112, 834

Wind River Multiple–Use Advocates v. Espy, 835 F.Supp. 1362 (D.Wyo.1993), 1253

Winnebago Tribe of Nebraska v. Ray, 621 F.2d 269 (8th Cir.1980), 267

Winter v. Natural Resources Defense Council, Inc., ___ U.S. ___, 129 S.Ct. 365, 172 L.Ed.2d 249 (2008), 554

Winters v. Burkland, 123 Or. 137, 260 P. 231 (Or.1927), 1101

Winters v. United States, 207 U.S. 564, 28 S.Ct. 207, 52 L.Ed. 340 (1908), **831**

Wurts, United States v., 76 I.D. 6 (1969), 1126

Wyoming v. United States Dept. of Agriculture, 414 F.3d 1207 (10th Cir.2005), 1279

Wyoming v. United States Dept. of Agriculture, 277 F.Supp.2d 1197 (D.Wyo.2003), 1279

Wyoming v. United States Dept. of Agriculture, 570 F.Supp.2d 1309 (D.Wyo.2008), 1279

Wyoming Farm Bureau Federation v. Babbitt, 987 F.Supp. 1349 (D.Wyo.1997), 406

Wyoming Farm Bureau Federation v. Babbitt, 199 F.3d 1224 (10th Cir.2000), 407

Wyoming Outdoor Coordinating Council v. Butz, 484 F.2d 1244 (10th Cir.1973), 641

Wyoming, State of v. State of Colo., 259 U.S. 419, 42 S.Ct. 552, 66 L.Ed. 999 (1922), 883, 892

Zweifel, United States v., 508 F.2d 1150 (10th Cir.1975), 1137

ACKNOWLEDGEMENTS

The authors gratefully acknowledge the permissions granted to reproduce the following materials.

ATLAS OF THE NEW WEST: PORTRAIT OF A CHANGING REGION 58 (William E. Riebsame, ed., 1997). © 1997 by the Regents of the University of Colorado. Reprinted with permission.

Terry L. Anderson et al., *How and Why to Privatize Federal Lands*, POLICY ANALYSIS 2, 4, 6, 21 (No. 363, Dec. 9. 1999). Reprinted with permission of Cato Institute.

SARAH F. BATES ET AL., SEARCHING OUT THE HEADWATERS: CHANGE AND REDISCOVERY IN WESTERN WATER POLICY 8–9 (1993). © 1993 by Island Press. Reprinted with permission of Island Press, Washington, D.C.

WILLIAM BAXTER, PEOPLE OR PENGUINS: THE CASE FOR OPTIMAL POLLUTION 4–9, 12 (1974). © 1974. Reprinted with permission of Columbia University Press.

Michael C. Blumm, *Reversing the Winters Doctrine?: Denying Reserved Water Rights for Idaho Wilderness and Its Implications*, U. COLO. L. REV. 173, 186–89 (2002). Reprinted with permission of the University of Colorado Law Review.

Stephen Bodio, *Struck with Consequence, in* John A. Baden and Donald Snow, eds., THE NEXT WEST: PUBLIC LANDS, COMMUNITY, AND ECONOMY IN THE AMERICAN WEST 18, 20 (1997). © 1997 by Island Press. Reprinted with permission of Island Press, Washington, D.C.

Jutta Brunnee & Stephen J. Toope, *The Changing Nile Basin Regime: Does Law Matter?* 42 HARV. INT'L L.J. 105, 117–18, 120–29 (2002). © 2002 by the President and Fellows of Harvard College and the Harvard International Law Journal.

James M. Buchanan, *What Is Public Choice Theory?* 32 IMPRIMIS No. 3, at 3–5 (March 2003) (*Imprimis* is the national speech digest of Hillsdale College, *see* www.hillsdale.edu) Reprinted with permission.

David D. Caron, *The International Whaling Commission and the North Atlantic Marine Mammal Commission: The Institutional Risks of Coercion in Consensual Structures*, 89 AM. J. INT'L L. 154, 159–67 (1995). © 1995 The American Society of International Law. Reproduced with permission from 89 AM. J. INT'L L. 154, 159–67 (1995).

VERNON CARSTENSEN, THE PUBLIC LANDS: STUDIES IN THE HISTORY OF THE PUBLIC DOMAIN xxi–xxvi. © 1963. Reprinted with permission of the University of Wisconsin Press.

HARRY CAUDILL, NIGHT COMES TO THE CUMBERLANDS 72–75 (1962). Reprinted with permission of Marian Reiner on behalf of the Jesse Stuart Foundation.

ALSTON CHASE, PLAYING GOD IN YELLOWSTONE: THE DESTRUCTION OF AMERICA'S FIRST NATIONAL PARK 92–93, 95–97 (1987). Reprinted with permission.

Federico Cheever, *The United States Forest Service and National Park Service: Paradoxical Mandates, Powerful Founders, and the Rise and Fall of Agency Discretion*, 74 DENV. U. L. REV. 625, 629 (1997). Reprinted with permission.

Hoyt Childers, *The Essential Issue*, 81 NATIONAL FISHERMAN 36 (Nov. 2000). Reprinted with permission.

Craig Childs, *The Millworker and the Forest: Notes on Natural History, Human Industry and the Deepest Wilds of the Northwest*, HIGH COUNTRY NEWS, (Vol. 31 No. 18, Sept. 27, 1999). Reprinted with permission of author and High Country News.

ROBIN CLARKE, WATER: THE INTERNATIONAL CRISIS 91–92 (1993). Reprinted with permission.

Felix S. Cohen, *Original Indian Title*, 32 MINN. L. REV. 25, 34–36, 38 (1947). Reprinted with permission.

DANIEL H. COLE, POLLUTION & PROPERTY: COMPARING OWNERSHIP INSTITUTIONS FOR ENVIRONMENTAL PROTECTION 7–8, 13, 17–18 (2002). © 2002 Cambridge University Press. Reprinted with the permission of Cambridge University Press.

WILLIAM CRONON, UNCOMMON GROUND: TOWARD REINVENTING NATURE 34–52 (William Cronon ed., 1995). Copyright © 1995 by William Cronon. Reprinted with permission of W.W. Norton & Company, Inc.

Gretchen Daily, *Introduction: What Are Ecosystem Services?*, in NATURE'S SERVICES: SOCIETAL DEPENDENCE ON NATURAL ECOSYSTEMS 3–4 (Gretchen Daily ed., 1997). © 1997 by Island Press. Reprinted with permission of Island Press, Washington, D.C.

SAMUEL TRASK DANA & SALLY K. FAIRFAX, FOREST AND RANGE POLICY 21–24 (2d ed. 1980). Reprinted with permission.

Tony Davis, *Will Bulldozers Roll into Arizona's Eden?*, HIGH COUNTRY NEWS, Feb. 18, 2002. Reprinted with permission.

DEBRA L. DONAHUE, THE WESTERN RANGE REVISITED 5 (1999). Reprinted with permission.

Holly Doremus, *Restoring Endangered Species: The Importance of Being Wild*, 23 HARV. ENVTL. L. REV. 1, 61 (1999). Reprinted with permission.

Holly Doremus, *Patching the Ark: Improving Legal Protection of Biological Diversity*, 18 ECOLOGY L.Q. 265, 275–81 (1991). Reprinted with permission of the Regents of the University of California. © 1991 by the Regents of the University of California.

Holly Doremus, *Water, Population Growth, and Endangered Species in the West*, 72 U. COLO. L. REV. 361, 369–78 (2001). Reprinted with permission of the University of Colorado Law Review and with permission from Professor Doremus.

Josh Eagle & Barton H. Thompson Jr., *Answering Lord Perry's Question: Dissecting Regulatory Overfishing*, 46 OCEAN & COASTAL MANAGEMENT 649, 651–53 (2003). Reprinted with permission.

Tim Findley, *Making Monuments, Taking Towns*, RANGE (Summer 2001). Reprinted with permission.

Dave Foreman, *The Wildlands Project and the Rewilding of North America*, 76 DENV. U. L. REV. 535, 535–36, 545–46, 549, 551–52 (1999). Reprinted with permission.

Friends of Lake Powell (www.lakepowell.org), *Draining Lake Powell: Myths vs. Reality, available at* http://www.lakepowell.org/Page_two/ Information/Myths/myths.html. Reprinted with permission.

Toni Frohoff, *Scapegoating Seals and Sea Lions, available at* http://www. hsus.org/ace/11732. Reprinted with permission from the Humane Society of the United States. © 2004 by the Humane Society of the United States. Reprinted with permission.

PETER H. GLEICK, THE WORLD'S WATER 2000–2001: THE BIENNIAL REPORT ON FRESHWATER RESOURCES 20–22, 24 (2000). © 2000 by Island Press. Reprinted with permission of Island Press, Washington, D.C.

The Glen Canyon Institute, *Why the Colorado River Through Glen Canyon Should Be Restored, available at* http://www.glencanyon.org/why.htm. Reprinted with the permission of the Glen Canyon Institute.

Robert Jerome Glennon & Peter W. Culp, *The Last Green Lagoon: How and Why the Bush Administration Should Save the Colorado River Delta*, 28 ECOLOGY L.Q. 903, 933–35 (2002). Reprinted with permission of the Regents of the University of California. © 2002 by the Regents of the University of California.

Robert Glennon, *The Perils of Groundwater Pumping*, 19 ISSUES IN SCIENCE AND TECHNOLOGY 73, 73–77 (2002). Reprinted with permission.

George A. Gould, *A Westerner Looks at Eastern Water Law: Reconsideration of Prior Appropriation in the East*, 25 U. ARK. LITTLE ROCK L. REV. 89, 99–103 (2002). Reprinted with permission.

Douglas L. Grant, *Interstate Water Allocation Compacts: When the Virtue of Permanence Becomes the Vice of Inflexibility*, 74 U. COLO. L. REV. 105, 105–08 (2003). Reprinted with permission of the University of Colorado Law Review.

Douglas Grant, *The Complexities of Managing Hydrologically Connected Surface Water and Groundwater Under the Appropriate Doctrine*, 22 LAND & WATER L. REV. 63, 74, 80–81 (1987). Reprinted with permission.

Scott W. Hardt, *Federal Land–Use Planning and Its Impact on Resource Management Decisions*, 4–7 to 4–32, ROCKY MTN. MIN. L. FOUND., PUBLIC LAND LAW SPECIAL INSTITUTE (Nov. 1997). Reprinted with permission.

SAMUEL P. HAYS, CONSERVATION AND THE GOSPEL OF EFFICIENCY: THE PROGRESSIVE CONSERVATION MOVEMENT 1890–1920 2–3 (1959). © 1999 by University of Pittsburgh Press. Reprinted with permission of the University of Pittsburgh Press.

Geoffrey Heal et al., *Protecting Natural Capital Through Ecosystem Service Districts*, 20 STAN. ENVTL. L. J. 333, 353–56 (2001). Reprinted with permission.

Bill Hedden, *Grand Canyon Trust Grazing Retirement Program*, *available at* http://www.grandcanyontrust.org/arches/grazing.html. Reprinted with permission of Bill Hedden, Executive Director of the Grand Canyon Trust.

Oliver A. Houck, *On the Law of Biodiversity and Ecosystem Management*, 81 MINN. L. REV. 869, 945–48. Reprinted with permission.

Moana Jackson, *Indigenous Law and the Sea, in* FREEDOM FOR THE SEAS IN THE 21ST CENTURY 46 (JON M. VAN DYKE ET AL., EDS., 1993). © 1993 by Island Press. Reprinted with permission of Island Press, Washington, D.C.

Matt Jenkins, *U.S. Mills Fall Under Canadian Ax*, HIGH COUNTRY NEWS, March 26, 2001. Reprinted with permission.

Keith Johnson, *An Open Letter To The Public From The President Of The Makah Whaling Commission*, Aug. 6, 1998, *available at* http://www.cnie.org/NAE/docs/makaheditorial.html. Reprinted with permission.

Robert B. Keiter, *Preserving Nature in the National Parks: Law, Policy, and Science in a Dynamic Environment*, 74 DENV. U. L. REV. 649, 675–78 (1997). Reprinted with permission.

DANIEL KEMMIS, COMMUNITY AND THE POLITICS OF PLACE 126–28 (1990). Reprinted with permission.

Chester Kirby, *The English Game Law System*, 38 AM. HISTORICAL REV. 240, 240–50, 256 (1933). Reprinted with permission of the American Historical Review.

Christine A. Klein, *On Dams and Democracy,* 78 OREGON L. REV. 641, 647–51, 665–67, 671–72, 675–84, 695–96, 705–08 (1999). Reprinted with permission.

Sarah Krakoff, *Mountains without Handrails . . . Wilderness Without Cellphones*, 27 HARV. ENVTL. L. REV. 417, 450–53 (2003). © 2003 by The President and Fellows of Harvard College and The Harvard Environmental Law Review. Reprinted with permission.

Douglas J. Krieger. *Economic Value of Forest Ecosystem Services: A Review* iii–vii (The Wilderness Society, Washington, DC. 2001). Reprinted with permission of The Wilderness Society.

Paul Lagasse, *Mining, in* THE COLUMBIA ENCYCLOPEDIA (6th ed. 2000). © 2000 Columbia University Press. Reprinted with permission.

Erik Larson, *Unrest in the West*, TIME, Oct. 23, 1995, 7–9, 12. © 1995 TIME Inc. Reprinted with permission.

ALDO LEOPOLD, A SAND COUNTY ALMANAC AND SKETCHES HERE AND THERE 201–04, 210–12, 223–26, © 1949, 1977 by Oxford University Press, Inc. Reprinted with the permission of Oxford University Press, Inc.

JOHN LESHY, THE MINING LAW: A STUDY IN PERPETUAL MOTION, 79–80 (Res. for the Future, 1987). Reprinted with permission.

E. Michael Linscheid, Comment, *Living to Fish, Fishing to Live: The Fishery Conservation and Management Act and its Implications for Fishing–Dependent Communities*, 36 U.S.F. L. REV. 181, 190–92 (2001). Reprinted with permission.

Louise Liston, *Sustaining Traditional Community Values*, J. LAND RESOURCES & ENVT'L LAW 585, 585–86, 592 (2001). Reprinted with permission.

Nancy A. McLaughlin, *The Role of Land Trusts in Biodiversity Conservation on Private Lands,* 38 IDAHO L. REV. 453, 465–66 (2002). Reprinted with permission.

Andrew P. Morriss et al., *Between a Hard Rock and a Hard Place: Politics, Midnight Regulations and Mining*, 55 ADMIN. L. REV. 551, 592–94 (2003). © 2003 by the American Bar Association. Reprinted with permission.

Pete Morton, *The Economic Benefits of Wilderness: Theory and Practice*, 76 DENV. U. L. REV. 465 (1999). Reprinted with permission.

JOHN COPELAND NAGLE & J.B. RUHL, THE LAW OF BIODIVERSITY AND ECOSYSTEM MANAGEMENT 403–04 (2002). Reprinted with permission.

National Research Council, SUSTAINING MARINE FISHERIES 84–86 (1999). © 1999 by the National Academy of Sciences. Reprinted with permission from the National Academies Press, Washington, D.C.

National Resource Defense Council, *End of the Road The Adverse Ecological Impacts of Road and Logging: A Compilation of Independently Reviewed Research, available at* http://www.nrdc.org/land/forests/roads/eotrinx.asp. Reprinted with permission from the Natural Resources Defense Council.

Dale A. Oesterle, *Public Land: How Much Is Enough?,* 23 ECOLOGY L.Q. 521, 534–36 (1996). Reprinted with permission of the Regents of the University of California. © 1996 by the Regents of the University of California.

Randy Olson, *Shifting Baselines: Slow Motion Disaster in the Sea, available at* http://www.actionbioscience.org/environment/olson.html. Reprinted with permission.

TIM PALMER, THE SNAKE RIVER: WINDOW TO THE WEST 83–86 (1991), *in* SARAH F. BATES ET AL., SEARCHING OUT THE HEADWATERS: CHANGE AND REDISCOVERY IN WESTERN WATER POLICY 59–61 (1993). © 1991 by Island Press. Reprinted with permission of Island Press, Washington, D.C.

Wilson Parker, *Makah Culture and Tradition*, PAWS MAGAZINE, *available at* http://www.paws.org/about/mag/issues/issue39/culture.html. Reprinted with permission.

THOMAS MICHAEL POWER, LOST LANDSCAPES AND FAILED ECONOMIES: THE SEARCH FOR THE VALUE OF PLACE 134–46, 151–69 (1996). Reprinted with permission.

Jeffrey Rachlinski, *Noah by the Numbers: An Empirical Evaluation of the Endangered Species Act*, 82 CORNELL L. REV. 356, 369–83 (1997). Reprinted with permission.

James R. Rasband, *Priority, Probability and Proximate Cause: Lessons from Tort Law about Imposing ESA Responsibilities for Wildlife Harm on Water Users and Other Joint Habitat Modifiers*, 33 ENVTL. L. J. 595, 613–615 (2003). Reprinted with permission.

James R. Rasband, *The Rise of Urban Archipelagoes in the American West: A New Reservation Policy?*, 31 ENVTL. L. 1, 13–19, 28–33, 44–45, 49–52 (2001). Reprinted with permission.

Leigh Raymond & Sally K. Fairfax, *The "Shift to Privatization" in Land Conservation: A Cautionary Essay*, 42 NATURAL RES. J. 599, 625–30 (2002). Reprinted with permission.

MARC REISNER, CADILLAC DESERT: THE AMERICAN WEST AND ITS DISAPPEARING WATER, 3–5, 9–12, 120–22, 149–50, by Marc P. Reisner, copyright © 1986, 1993 by Marc P. Reisner. Reprinted with the permission of Viking Penguin, a division of Penguin Group (USA) Inc.

Carmen Revenga & Greg Mock, *Freshwater Biodiversity in Crisis*, World Resources Institute (2000), *available at* http://earthtrends.wri.org/features/view_feature.cfm?theme=2 & fid=9. Reprinted with permission.

Valerie Richardson, *Despite an Adequate Supply of Timber, Environmentalists Cost Hundreds Their Jobs in Logging*, WASH. TIMES, Nov. 25, 2001, at A1. Copyright © 2001 News World Communications, Inc. Reprinted with permission of The Washington Times.

Alison Rieser, *Prescriptions For The Commons: Environmental Scholarship And The Fishing Quotas Debate*, 23 HARV. ENVTL. L. REV. 393, 404–06 (1999). © 1999 by the President and Fellows of Harvard College and the Harvard Environmental Law Review. Reprinted with permission.

William Rodgers, *Defeating Environmental Law: The Geology of Legal Advantage*, 19 PACE ENVTL. L. REV. 687, 706–13 (2002). Reprinted with permission.

J.B. Ruhl, *A Manifesto for the Radical Middle*, 38 IDAHO L. REV. 385, 402–03 (2002). Reprinted with permission.

CARL SAFINA, SONG FOR THE BLUE OCEAN: ENCOUNTERS ALONG THE WORLD'S COASTS AND BENEATH THE SEAS. Reprinted with permission.

James Salzman et al., *Protecting Ecosystem Services: Science, Economics, and Law*, 20 STAN. ENVTL. L. J. 309, 310–12 (2001). Reprinted with permission.

Joseph L. Sax, *Do Communities Have Rights? The National Parks as a Laboratory of New Ideas*, 45 U. PITT. L. REV. 499, 504. 507–09 (1984). Reprinted with permission from the University of Pittsburgh Law Review.

JOSEPH SAX, MOUNTAINS WITHOUT HANDRAILS: REFLECTIONS ON THE NATIONAL PARKS 6–7, 11–15, 104 (1980). Reprinted with permission from the University of Michigan Press. © 1980 by the University of Michigan Press.

Joseph Sax, *Proceedings of the 2001 Symposium on Managing Hawaii's Public Trust Doctrine*, 24 HAWAII L. REV. 21, 24, 25–28, 33 (2001). Reprinted with permission.

Karin P. Sheldon, *Habitat Conservation Planning: Addressing the Achilles Heel of the Endangered Species Act*, N.Y.U. ENVT'L. L. J. 279, 286, 295–326 (1998). Reprinted with permission.

Vic Sher, *Breaking Out of the Box: Toxic Risk, Government Actions, and Constitutional Rights*, 13 J. ENVTL. L. & LITIG. 145, 146–50 (1998). Reprinted with permission.

Robert H. Smith, *Livestock Production: The Unsustainable Environmental and Economic Effects of An Industry Out of Control*, 4 BUFF. ENVTL. L. REV. 45, 48–73 (1996). Reprinted with permission.

Mark Squillace, *The Monumental Legacy of the Antiquities Act of 1906*, 37 GEORGIA L. REV. 473, 490–507 (2003). Reprinted with permission.

Dustin S. Stephenson, *The Tri–State Compact: Falling Waters and Fading Opportunities*, 16 J. LAND USE & ENVTL. L. 83, 97–100 (2000). © 2000 Journal of Land Use & Environmental Law. Reprinted with permission.

CASS SUNSTEIN, LAWS OF FEAR: BEYOND THE PRECAUTIONARY PRINCIPLE 26–29, 129–30 (2005). Reprinted with permission.

The Essential Issue, 81 NATIONAL FISHERMAN 36 (Jan. 2001). Reprinted with permission.

Barton H. Thompson, Jr., *Markets for Nature*, 25 WM. & MARY ENVTL. L. & POLICY REV. 261, 287–92, 271–78 (2000). Reprinted with permission.

Barton H. Thompson Jr., *Institutional Perspectives on Water Policy and Markets*, 81 CAL. L. REV. 671, 687–89 (1993). Reprinted with permission.

Randall Udall & Steve Andrews, *The Illusive Bonanza: Oil Shale in Colorado "Pulling the Sword from the Stone"*, available at, http://www.aspencore.org/images/pdf/OilShale.pdf. Reprinted with permission.

Edith Brown Weiss, *What Obligation Does Our Generation Owe To The Next? An Approach to Global Environmental Responsibility*, 84 AM. J. INT'L. L. 198, 199–202, (1990). © 1990 The American Society of International Law. Reprinted with permission from The American Society of International Law

We're Not Getting Through, 81 NATIONAL FISHERMAN 4 (Jan. 2001). Reprinted with permission.

Richard White, *"Are You An Environmentalist or Do You Work for a Living?" Work and Nature*, in UNCOMMON GROUND: TOWARD REINVENTING NATURE 171–75, 181–85 (William Cronon, ed., 1995). © 1995 by William Cronon. Used by permission of W.W. Norton & Company, Inc.

The Wilderness Society, *Economic Value of Forest Ecosystem Services: A Review*, pages iii-vii (2001). Reprinted with permission.

CHARLES F. WILKINSON, CROSSING THE NEXT MERIDIAN: LAND, WATER, AND THE FUTURE OF THE WEST 53–54, 57–58, 75–80, 85–86, 231–35 (1992). © 1992 by Island Press. Reprinted with permission of Island Press, Washington, D.C.

MICHAEL WILLIAMS, DEFORESTING THE EARTH: FROM PRE-HISTORY TO GLOBAL CRISIS 290, 446–47, 452, 457, 497–98 (2003). Reprinted with permission.

WORLD RESOURCES INSTITUTE ET AL., GLOBAL BIODIVERSITY STRATEGY 14–15 (1992). Reprinted with permission.

GEORGE WUERTHNER, SMOKEY THE BEAR'S LEGACY ON THE WEST, *in* WILDFIRE!: AN ENDANGERED ECOSYSTEM PROCESS, Vol. 1, Cascadia Fire Ecology Education Project, 1994, *available at* http://www.fire-ecology.org/research/smokey-bear-legacy.htm. Reprinted with permission.

NATURAL RESOURCES LAW AND POLICY

*

CHAPTER ONE

THINKING ABOUT NATURAL RESOURCES

I. **WHAT *IS* A NATURAL RESOURCE?**
   A. THE NATURE OF NATURAL
   B. WHY SHOULD WE PROTECT OR USE "NATURAL" RESOURCES?
      1. BIOCENTRISM
         a. Deep Ecology
         b. The Land Ethic
      2. ANTHROPOCENTRISM
         a. Utilitarianism
         b. Ecosystem Services, Use and Non–Use Values
      3. INTERGENERATIONAL EQUITY
      4. WHY VALUES MATTER IN NATURAL RESOURCES LAW
      CASE STUDY: THE NATURE OF WILDERNESS
II. **WHY ARE NATURAL RESOURCES DIFFICULT TO MANAGE?**
   A. SCARCITY
   B. CLASH OF VALUES AMONG COMPETING INTERESTS
   C. PROBLEMS OF THE COMMONS
   D. MARKET FORCES AND MARKET FAILURES
   E. SCIENTIFIC UNCERTAINTY
   F. SCALE
      1. BIOPHYSICAL SCALE
      2. POLITICAL SCALE
         a. Getting Political Scale Right
         b. The Relationship Between Property and Jurisdiction
      3. TEMPORAL SCALE
      CASE STUDY: THE QUINCY LIBRARY GROUP
   G. INSTITUTIONAL ADEQUACY
      CASE STUDY: THE ARCTIC NATIONAL WILDLIFE REFUGE
III. **TOOLS FOR MANAGING NATURAL RESOURCES—"THE FIVE P'S"**
   A. PROPERTY RIGHTS
   B. PRESCRIPTIVE REGULATION
      1. TRADABLE PERMITS
   C. FINANCIAL PENALTIES
   D. FINANCIAL PAYMENTS
   E. PUBLIC DISCLOSURE AND PERSUASION
      CASE STUDY: PRIVATIZING PARKS

Chapter One provides an introduction to the basic drivers and cross-cutting themes that shape virtually all natural resource problems, regardless of the specific resource at issue. We start by exploring the assumptions of what natural resources are as well as why we should protect or consume them. While discussing values may seem a "squishy" subject for a course on natural resource law and policy, our conceptions of natural resources and the source of their values are crucial to understanding resource conflicts. In creating management regimes for natural resources, we are making concrete our relationship with nature. While the chapters in Part II of this book explain *how* natural resource conflicts are fought over forests, fish or grasslands, this section explores *why* the conflicts are fought. We then explore why natural resources are difficult to manage, considering how basic problems posed by scarcity, uncertainty, market failures and other challenges make it unlikely there will be a single "correct" solution to any resource conflict. While water, a California condor, and Yosemite Valley may seem as different as resources could be, understanding their basic similarities is critical in resolving conflicts over their use and management. We end by examining the range of tools available to implement resource management goals. In many respects, this is a foundational chapter, for the issues we consider will come up again and again throughout the casebook.

I. WHAT IS A NATURAL RESOURCE?

A. THE NATURE OF "NATURAL"

Snakes, a coral reef, maple trees, oil, coal, water, copper, soil, a wetland, Pike's Peak, the Grand Canyon, Yellowstone, clean air, the ozone layer. It may seem too obvious to mention, but the key feature that distinguishes these resources from other types of resources is that they are all "natural resources." We're familiar enough with the meanings of the term, "resource," whether as human resources, financial resources, or legal resources. But what does the term, "natural," add?

We surely hear the term, "natural," all the time. You may shop at a "natural food store"; you may be a "natural athlete"; you may hike to spots of "natural beauty"; or nod in agreement with someone who says we should "get back to nature." Historically, nature was often used to describe something unrefined or useless. Jeremy Bentham, for example, referred to wilderness as offering "only a frightful solitude, impenetrable forests or sterile plains, stagnant waters and impure vapours; such is the earth when left to itself." By contrast, today almost all of its connotations are positive. The opposite term, "unnatural," has a formidably wide range of meanings and uses, as well, almost all of them negative. Think about environmental groups' criticism of development of a wilderness area or use of genetically modified organisms as "unnatural."

Before reading further, take a moment and think how you would define the word, "natural."

On its face, identifying something as natural seems easy. Most people, for example, would agree that Yellowstone National Park is natural and that New York City is not. Perhaps your definition of natural used "artificial," "synthetic," or "man-made" as helpful antonyms. Despite its apparently obvious meaning, it is surprisingly difficult to determine what natural means in a human-dominated landscape, and this has critically important implications for natural resource policy decisions. There's abundant evidence, for example, that the nature around us is not nearly as natural as it seems. In terms of pollution, there are precious few spots left on the globe (if any) with no traces of synthetic chemicals such as DDT. You might well think of the remote arctic areas north of the Hudson Bay as natural settings. Yet because of the prevailing air currents, the indigenous inhabitants there, the Inuit, have among the highest PCB levels in their blood of any community on earth.

Or take Yellowstone. Because humans long ago killed off the wolves in Yellowstone, there were no significant predators left to reduce the elk herds until wolves were recently "reintroduced" into the ecosystem. As a result, the elk population grew far beyond its pre-park designation numbers and extensive elk grazing changed the relative abundance of much of the park's vegetation. Some have argued that this altered the forage available for other species, driving down populations of other pre-park animals, most notably the grizzly bear. Absent significant predators, what should the park managers do? Try to mimic the "natural predation" the elk faced prior to Western settlement and cull the herd to a smaller size, or take a hands-off attitude and let "nature" run its course? What about the hunters and outfitters who have grown dependent on the large elk population to sustain their activities? The problem, of course, is that Yellowstone itself is profoundly unnatural—the park's protected areas are limited to the park borders, restricting the natural ranges of its larger mammals, and human hunting and development have effectively removed large predators, not to mention the roads, trails, and various concessions that are scattered throughout the park.

To take another example, until fairly recently the policy of the Forest Service was to put out fires when they started—known as "100% fire suppression." Not only was this unnatural—both in the sense of interfering with a fire caused by lightning strike and because fire is an important disturbance mechanism for many ecosystems—but it built up a large amount of fuel in the form of dead fallen wood. At a certain point, there was so much fuel available that the fires could not be easily controlled, leading to many of the large fires reported in the news in recent years. The current fire policy of the Forest Service is no longer one of control but, rather, to mimic "natural" burns. But mimicking nature has not been that easy. Some of the fires have burned out of control and caused tremendous property damage. But even where the fires are "successful," is the Forest Service really "mimicking" nature? What's more natural? Suppressing fire for 100 years and allowing the forest to grow undisturbed or a controlled burn that produces a forest more like those prior to European contact? Indeed, a number of scholars argue that the pre-Columbian forests were not "natural," either, since Native Americans dramatically influenced the flora and fauna of the American continent through controlled burning. As related in the following excerpt, this remains a controversial debate.

ALSTON CHASE, PLAYING GOD IN YELLOWSTONE: THE DESTRUCTION OF AMERICA'S FIRST NATIONAL PARK 92–93, 95–97 (1987)

"[I]t is often assumed," historian Stephen J. Pyne writes, "that the American Indian was incapable of greatly modifying his environment and that he would not have been much interested in doing so if he did have the capabilities. In fact, he possessed both the tool and the will to use it. That tool was fire.''

Fire improves nature in many ways. It changes the chemical composition of the soil, promoting more varied vegetation and supporting more diverse wildlife. It releases soluble mineral salts in plant tissue, and increases the nitrogen, calcium, potassium, and phosphorus in the soil that act as fertilizers. It decreases soil acidity, neutralizing the effects of acid rain, not only in the earth but in the streams and lakes as well.... Burning forests stimulates germination in some trees, such as lodgepole pine; it produces habitat for nesting birds, such as the mountain bluebird. But the most important result of burning is that it arrests or reverses the normally inexorable seral succession.

Left undisturbed, areas such as Yellowstone would progress from grasslands, to shrub, to deciduous stands or aspen, then to lodgepole pine, and finally to spruce and fir, a succession that takes around three hundred years. As succession progresses, the variety of plant life diminishes and thus the capacity of the land to support wildlife declines as well. Fire is the only way to interrupt seral succession, and human beings apparently learned that lesson long ago.
* * *

It has been documented that at least one hundred tribes of North America used fire for at least fifteen purposes, but nearly all these uses dramatically affected the landscape and ecosystem ... Recent research has established that the Indian practice of burning around Yellowstone was not only widespread, but had been practiced for millennia. * * *

This activity profoundly affected the environment around and on the Yellowstone plateau. Human burning kept large areas in open grassland, forests from reaching climax, sagebrush from spreading, and many edible plants prolific. The many open parks, the riparian thickets of willow, the aspen colonies, the lush patches of berries that early explorers wrote about, were helped along by the kinds of fires that [Native Americans regularly set].

The challenge for the Park Service, Forest Service and other resource managers, then, is how to manage natural resources in an unnatural setting. In the excerpt below (taken from the Introduction to a collection of essays), noted environmental historian, William Cronon, examines the different meanings of nature today. Cronon argues that the term, "nature," has *no* independent meaning but, rather, is necessarily a social construct. He identifies distinct (often opposing) ways in which we think of nature and usefully divides them into categories such as "nature as naive reality" and "nature as moral imperative." Cronon's thesis is that how we use the word "nature" says as much about ourselves as about the things we label with that word. It is precisely this battle between people's differing visions of nature that makes natural resource policy so contentious.

As a starting point, Cronon asks how we should think about the Rocky Mountain Arsenal. The Arsenal is located outside Denver and long served as a chemical weapons factory for highly toxic compounds, including chlordane, mustard gas, and napalm. Heavy contamination of the soil and water forced the Arsenal to be shut down and listed as a high priority Superfund site. Ironically, though, because the high levels of pollution precluded human activity for decades, the Arsenal served as an unwitting wildlife refuge within the rapid housing development along the Front Range and now hosts arguably the most diverse ecosystem in the central Rockies. Indeed the Arsenal is becoming better known for its "natural" wonders than for its "unnatural" contamination. Cronon queries whether the site should be cleaned up or left as is. Which action best protects nature?

WILLIAM CRONON, ED., UNCOMMON GROUND: TOWARD REINVENTING NATURE 34–52 (1995)

There is nothing natural, surely, about the arsenal's toxicity—and yet the toxicity is itself one of the most important things supporting the wild nature for which the place is now celebrated. The familiar categories of environmentalist thinking don't seem to work here, since we have no clear indication of what would be "natural" or "unnatural" to do in such a case.... The ability to blur the boundaries between "natural" and "unnatural" is precisely what makes the Rocky Mountain Arsenal ... so useful for encouraging us to question our assumptions about what nature means and how we should relate to it. * * *

Perhaps the most important lesson to remember ... is that none of these natures is natural: all are cultural constructions that reflect human judgments, human values, human choices. *We could* choose to think about nature different-ly, and it is surely worth pondering what would happen if we did.

To make this provocative claim is, of course, to fly in the face of what people commonly mean when they speak of "nature," because one of the most important implications of that word is that the thing it describes is *not* of our own making. This is the view of nature the essays in this book most explicitly seek to critique. We might call it *nature as naive reality*. It is in language: the sense that when we speak of the *nature* of something, whatever the usage may be, it is dangerous for what it tempts us to assume: the naturalness. When we refer to "the nature of X," we usually imply that there is no further need to analyze or worry about that nature. We need not ask where it came from or on what contingencies it depends, for it is simply the way X is. Its meaning is transparent and uncomplicated, so we can take it for granted as a given: that is its nature. * * *

I simply wish to argue that the burden of proof should be with those who assert the universal nature of nature, for the evidence against such a view is enormous. Ideas of nature never exist outside a cultural context, and the meanings we assign to nature cannot help reflecting that context. The main reason this gets us into trouble is that nature as essence, nature as naive reality, wants us to see nature as if it *has* no cultural context, as if it were everywhere and always the same.... If we wish to understand the values and motivations that shape our own actions toward the natural world, if we hope for an environmentalism capable of explaining why people use and abuse the earth as they do, then the nature we study must become less natural and more cultural.

The appeal to nature as naive reality is often linked to a second major cluster of ideas that surround this word: *nature as moral imperative*. One need not travel a very great distance in speaking of the "nature of X" to get from "this is the way X really is" to "this is way X ought to be." The great attraction of nature for those who wish to ground their moral vision in external reality is precisely its capacity to take disputed values and make them seem innate, essential, eternal, nonnegotiable. When we speak of the "natural way of doing things," we implicitly suggest that there can be no other way, and that all alternatives, being unnatural, should have no claim on our sympathies. Nature in such arguments becomes a kind of trump card against which there can be no defense, at least not as long as our opponents share our values—and how could they not, if those values are as natural as we claim. Only a fool or an incorrigible sinner could fail to respond to so compelling a moral imperative. This habit of appealing to nature for moral authority is in large measure a product of the European Enlightenment. By no means all people in history have sought to ground their beliefs in this particular way. Indeed, it would have been far more common in the past for people in Western traditions to cite God as the authority for their beliefs. The fact that so many now cite Nature instead (implicitly capitalizing it as they once might have capitalized God) suggests the extent to which Nature has become a secular deity in this post-romantic age.

Because the values that people attach to nature as moral imperative are so dependent on cultural context, it makes little sense to discuss this phenomenon in the abstract. Nature as moral imperative always implies a very particular vision of what ideal nature is supposed to be. For some modern Americans, ideal nature is clearly a pristine wilderness.... For others ... ideal nature is the pastoral countryside or the small town, while others still would celebrate the suburb or even the city as the natural home of humankind. It hardly needs saying that nothing in physical nature can help us adjudicate among these different visions, for in all cases nature merely serves as the mirror onto which societies project the ideal reflections they wish to see.

The Judeo–Christian tradition nonetheless has one core myth that is so deeply embedded in Western thought that it crops up almost anytime people speak of nature. It is so widespread in modern environmental thinking that it deserves to be labeled as a separate cluster of ideas in its right: *nature as Eden*.... [A] great many environmental controversies revolve around ... "Edenic narratives," in which an original pristine nature is lost through some culpable human act that results in environmental degradation and moral jeopardy. The tale may be one of paradise lost or paradise regained, but the role of the narrative is always to project onto actual physical nature one of the most powerful and value-laden fables in the Western intellectual tradition. The myth of Eden describes a perfect landscape, a place so benign and beautiful and good that the imperative to preserve or restore it could be questioned only by those who ally themselves with evil. Nature as Eden encourages us to celebrate a particular landscape as the ultimate garden of the world.... [T]he Amazon rain forest now plays this role for a great many people in the United States and Europe who have never actually seen that forest for themselves. * * *

Eden can point in another direction as well: *nature as artifice, nature as self-conscious cultural construction*. What is so striking about the southern California landscape is the extent to which it has been transformed into a vision of nature utterly different from the ecosystems that once characterized the region.... Once we believe we know what nature *ought* to look like—once our vision of its ideal form becomes a moral or cultural imperative—we can remake it so completely that we become altogether indifferent or even hostile toward its prior condition. Taken far enough, the result can be a landscape in which nature and artifice, despite their apparent symbolic opposition, become indistinguishable because they finally merge into one another. One might go so far as to say that the replacement of nature by self-conscious artifice is a key defining quality of the modern landscape. * * *

Sea World implicitly exemplifies one of the most powerful cultural constructions that shape modern American attitudes toward nature: *nature as commodity*, a thing capable of being bought and sold in the marketplace quite apart from any autonomous values that may inhere in it. Market exchange and commodified relations with nature have been transforming the landscape of America, indeed, of the entire planet, for centuries. Few cultural conceptions have had greater ecological impact. Whether one looks at the destruction of the great herds of bison or flocks of passenger pigeons in the nineteenth century, the extirpation from North America of whole ecosystems like the tallgrass prairie, or the increasing assaults on biodiversity worldwide, the immense power of a political economy based on culturally commodified nature is everywhere apparent, producing an alienation from the natural world—and from the effects human actions have thereon—that is all too characteristic of modernity. Looking at the environment in this way comes so easily to members of modern Western cultures that it is virtually second nature. It is present in the trading pits of the Chicago Board of Trade, where all manner of natural resources become commodities, and it is no less present in places like Sea World, where nature itself—or rather, a particular *idea* of nature—is bought and sold as a consumable experience. * * *

[A last vision of nature is the nightmare inversion of Eden]: *nature as demonic other, nature as avenging angel, nature as the return of the repressed.* It can range from something as trivial as those uncooperative snails in our Irvine garden, to natural disasters like earthquakes or floods, to the hypothetical horrors of global warming. At whatever scale we experience them, these things represent a nonhuman world that despite our best effort we never quite succeed in fully controlling. Often we come close enough that we congratulate ourselves prematurely for our own triumph—and then are surprised when the long-silent fault or the hundred-year flood suddenly reveals our hubris. * * *

[I]n April a young woman jogging near her home in the Sierra Nevada foothills was stalked and pulled from the trail by a female mountain lion and then quickly mauled to death. The lioness was hunted down and shot, lest she kill again. The woman left behind two small children; the lion, a seven-week-old cub. It undoubtedly says something about peoples' ideas of nature, perhaps even their ideas of human nature, that public appeals on behalf these young orphans soon yielded $9,000 for the two children ... and $21,000 for the cub.

What is interesting about such events is not that they occur. After all, what could be more natural than a mountain lion killing its prey or a great fault relieving its pent-up strain? What is really intriguing is the meaning we assign to them, for we have an inveterate habit of turning them into moral fables.... People are drawn to nature as an avenging angel for much the same reason they are drawn to nature as Eden. It should by now be clear that the two are in fact opposite sides of the same moral coin. The one represents our vision of paradise: the good that is so utterly compelling that we feel no hesitation in claiming nature as our authority for embracing it. The other is our vision of hell: the place where those who transgress against nature will finally endure the pain and retribution they so justly deserve. There is a wonderfully attractive clarity in this way of thinking about nature, for it turns the nonhuman world into a moral universe whose parables and teachings are strikingly similar to those of a religion. We need such teachings, for they give meaning and value to our lives. To the extent that environmentalism serves as a kind of secular religion for many people in the modern world, it is capable of doing great good if it can teach us the stories, as religions often try to do, that will help us to live better, more responsible lives.

And yet: we must never forget that these stories are *ours*, not nature's. The natural world does not organize itself into parables. Only people do that, because this is our peculiarly human method for making the world make sense. And because people differ in their beliefs, because their visions of the truth, the good, and the beautiful are not always the same, they inevitably differ as well in their understanding of what nature means and how it should be used—

because nature is so often the place where to go searching for the fulfillment of our desires. This points to one final vision of nature that recurs everywhere in this book: *nature as contested terrain.*

Over and over again in these essays, we encounter the central paradox of this complex cultural construct. On the one hand, people in Western cultures use the word "nature" to describe a universal reality, thereby implying that it is and must be common to all people. On the other hand, they also pour into that world all their most personal and culturally specific values: the essence of who they think they are, how and where they should live, what they believe to be good and beautiful, why people should act in certain ways. All these things are described as *natural*, even though everything we know about human history and culture flies in the face of that description. The result is a human world in which these many human visions of nature are always jostling against each other, each claiming to be universal and each soon making the unhappy discovery that even its nearest neighbors refuse to acknowledge that claim. The history of environmentalism is fraught with this paradox ... precisely because these groups do not agree on what counts as a nature worth protecting. * * *

Perhaps the most important message of this book is that such disagreement is inevitable—one might even be tempted to say natural—given the universalizing tendencies that lie at the very core of this human construct called nature. The question "whose nature?" again emerges as central. As soon as we project our values onto the world and begin to assert their primacy by calling them natural, we declare our unwillingness to consider alternative values that in all likelihood are no less compelling for the people who hold them dear. Nature becomes our dogma, the wall we build around our own vision to protect it from competing views. And like all dogmas, it is the death of dialogue and self-criticism. This is its seductive power. This is the trap it has set for us.

As we try to make sense of these many natures all claiming to be one, we would do well to stop hoping that any single one of them can ever finally triumph. Nature will *always* be contested terrain. We will never stop arguing about its meanings, because it is the very ground on which our debates must occur. This is *not* to say that all visions of nature are equally good, or that we can never persuade others that one of them is better, truer, fairer, more beautiful than another. It is simply to state that such persuasion will never occur if all we do is assert the naturalness of our own views. Tempting as it may be to play nature as a trump card in this way, it quickly becomes a self-defeating strategy: adversaries simply refuse to recognize each other's trump and then go off to play by themselves. This can often feel quite satisfying, since it reinforces our dogma and makes it that much easier to berate our enemies and celebrate our own moral superiority. But it is surely not a very promising path for trying to understand our differences. Without such understanding, the prospect for solving environmental problems, to say nothing of working toward a juster world for all the peoples and creatures of the earth, would seem very grim indeed.

―――――

QUESTIONS AND DISCUSSION

1.   Do you find Cronon's categories a useful way to break down the many meanings we attribute to nature? See if you can give specific examples of Cronon's categories. If you visit the websites of opponents to oil drilling in the Arctic National Wildlife Refuge, for example, you will find the Refuge described as a "truly pristine wild place," "America's Serengeti," and "one of the last areas of virgin wilderness in the United States"—all clear examples of "Nature as Eden" arguments. What other examples can you think of that describe:

- Nature as naive reality
- Nature as moral imperative
- Nature as Eden
- Nature as artifice
- Nature as demonic other
- Nature as commodity

Which categories do opponents of genetically modified organisms use? What about supporters of wheelchair-accessible trails in National Parks? How about supporters of logging in old-growth forests? What about supporters of breaching dams?

2. Does Cronon's excerpt help you appreciate why it is often so difficult to manage "natural" resources? Differing views about the nature of "natural" lead to very different management choices. Who should decide which view of nature prevails in a given context? Consider, for example, the problem of managing elk in Yellowstone National Park and the possibility of reintroducing wolves into that ecosystem. How would the differing views of nature, as described by Cronon, influence the management choice?

By all accounts, the reintroduction of the wolf into the Greater Yellowstone Ecosystem has been very successful in producing a stable wolf population. Does this mean that the natural balance has been restored? What continuing problems might you anticipate? This reintroduction is examined in a case study in Chapter 4 (page 405).

3. The challenge for the Department of Defense in managing the Arsenal—the "Nation's Most Ironic Nature Wildlife Refuge"—is considerable. If you were in charge and had been told to make the Rocky Mountain Arsenal a more natural site, what would you do? Would you continue to clean up the site and restore it to its pre-development "natural" condition (i.e., soil free of chemical and nuclear contamination), even though it will harm most of the now-resident flora and fauna, or would you favor "nature protection" over the interest of nearby communities concerned over health and real estate values? How would you justify your decision to the local Audubon Society and the local Chamber of Commerce?

4. Do you agree with the contention that a management strategy of "letting nature take its course" is meaningless in a human-dominated landscape so long as we disagree over which vision of nature should take precedence? The excerpt on Native American management of the land, for example, suggests that the habitat around Yellowstone was no less human-dominated before Europeans arrived than afterward. If this is the case, should the Forest Service have a restoration goal as its management strategy? If so, should it be to pre-Columbian habitat? Pre-human settlement? In either case, why should "pre-anything" restoration be a legitimate goal?

5. How does our understanding of nature and wilderness change as we live in an increasingly human-made landscape? Consider writer Bill McKibben's thoughts on this subject:

> If nature were about to end, we might muster endless energy to stave it off; but if nature has already ended, what are we fighting for? Before any redwoods had been cloned or genetically improved, one could understand clearly what the fight against such tinkering was about. It was about the idea that a redwood was somehow sacred, that its fundamental identity should remain beyond our control. But once that barrier has been broken, what is the fight about, then? . . . [H]ow can there be a mystique of the rain now that every drop—even the drops that fall as snow on the Arctic, even the drops that fall deep in the remaining forest primeval—bears the permanent stamp of man? Having lost its separateness, it loses its special power. Instead of being a category like God— something beyond our control—it is now a category like the defense budget or the minimum wage, a problem we must work out. This in itself changes its meaning completely, and changes our reaction to it.
>
> A few weeks ago, on the hill behind my house, I almost kicked the biggest rabbit I had ever seen. She had nearly finished turning white for the winter, and we stood there watching each other for a pleasant while, two creatures linked by curiosity. What will it mean to come across a rabbit in the woods once genetically engineered "rabbits" are widespread? Why would we have any more reverence or affection for such a rabbit than we would for a Coke bottle?

BILL MCKIBBEN, THE END OF NATURE 210–11 (1989).

In arguing that nature "has ended," what assumption is McKibben making about the prior state of the environment 20, 50, or 150 years ago? How would Cronon respond to McKibben's argument?

6. Our strong affinity for nature is certainly well understood by marketers. How else can one explain the message implicit in popular ads showing Sport Utility Vehicles improbably parked on mountain tops? Is it not the notion that you can "get back to nature" and "explore the great outdoors" behind the wheel, enjoying air conditioning, a V–8 engine, and stereophonic sound? A magazine ad for the Ford Explorer reads:

> Tom and Sally worked hard to get where they are. But now that they've arrived, all they want to do is get the heck out. So, last weekend, they traded business talk for a babbling brook and conference calls for conifer pines. They aimed their new Ford Explorer Sport toward the country, took turns driving, and sang out loud whenever they felt the urge: "Bye-bye blacktop."

As quoted in Sarah Krakoff, *Mountains Without Handrails . . . Wilderness Without Cellphones*, 27 HARV. ENVT'L. L. REV. 417, 438 (2003).

Or consider the market strategy of the aptly named "Nature Company." Here, in an upscale mall surrounded by trendy stores, the Nature Company offers:

> a calm woodsy space where shoppers can enjoy the pleasures of our national pastime—shopping—while still affirming their green values by purchasing recycled greeting cards, rustic bird feeders, ecologically educational toys, ambient environmental sound CDs, and hand-made crafts from the indigenous peoples of the rain forest. What the Nature Company sells is not so much nature as authenticity—or what passes for authenticity in a consumer culture. It reassures its customers that they can participate in consumerism with their values intact, go to the mall and still get back to nature.

Cronon, *op. cit.*, at 47. This is a prime example of nature as commodity and Cronon, even with his light touch, seems rather dismissive of such a "nature experience." But is this criticism justified? Indeed are any of the competing visions of nature identified by Cronon more or less legitimate than the others? If shopping at the Nature Company or driving an SUV to a campground is no less meaningful for most people than communing with nature by hiking in the back country of Yellowstone, is this commodity vision any less worthwhile? Isn't this really an example of elitism? Even if it is, is there anything wrong with that? We will return to this question in Chapter 6, when we consider the implications of Joe Sax's plea for mountains without handrails (page 589).

7. Is there a better phrase to describe natural resources than "natural resources" that provides different, and more accurate, connotations? What do you think of the terms, "natural heirlooms," or "environmental goods and services"?

———

B. WHY SHOULD WE PROTECT OR USE NATURAL RESOURCES?

Consider the following paragraph from a front page story in the *New York Times*. The writer is describing a group of young men on rafts paddling out to the coral reefs surrounding Sri Lanka.

> Carrying crowbars and hammers, the divers break up rocks and branches and smash coral formations that have taken thousands of years to grow. Like pearl divers, they hold their breath at length and work until their rafts are full. Once ashore, the coral is carried to kilns where it is pulverized and meets its destiny as cement. "This is what I live off," said a miner who had set up a makeshift kiln on a secluded cove behind his home. He had stacked coral rocks on top of a car tire, ready for burning.

Marlise Simons, *Indian Ocean Coral Reefs Are Ravaged by Mining*, N.Y. TIMES, Aug. 8, 1993, at 1.

While coral mining is illegal, roughly 10,000 tons of coral are collected in Sri Lanka every year for use as construction materials. Although such coral has been used as a building material for at least 400 years, recent explosions in tourism and construction created a huge market for slaked lime. Up to 80% of the country's reefs have been harmed. As a result, not only have fish stocks dropped but, without the breakwaters of the reef to dampen wave action, serious erosion is occurring along Sri Lanka's west coast. Such "coral strip mining" destroys the complex community of hundreds of marine plant, animal and fish species that live amidst the coral. Despite these harms, local mining continues as the livelihood for many islanders. When the government offered to give 41 families farming land as an alternative to coral mining, only 9 accepted.

———

What is your reaction to this story? Do you approve of the young men's actions and, if not, why is it that you object to their mining the reef? Is the disturbing part that their destruction of the reef seems economically wasteful and shortsighted? Have they violated some type of stewardship obligation for their descendants? Have they somehow violated their ethical obligations to the reef itself? You might ask yourself similar questions about drilling for oil in the Arctic National Wildlife Refuge, snowmobiling in Yellowstone, or clearcutting in national forests. Having a gut reaction to different types of resource management is easy; what's more difficult is providing a reasoned explanation for why you feel that way. While discussing values may seem tangential to studying natural resources law and policy, our conceptions of what natural resources are and why they're valuable underpin most resource conflicts.

While rarely at the surface, values drive both management strategies and, more important, conflicts over management strategies. The protection and use of natural resources are often in conflict. We cannot have wilderness and allow logging or mining on the same lands. On what philosophical foundation should we as a society make these tough choices?

A vast subject in itself, environmental ethics encompasses our relationship with the environment. The brief excerpts that follow set out a number of the dominant positions across the spectrum from biocentric (a nature-based ethical system) to anthropocentric (a human-based system). As you read the following sections, think about which passages resonate with your personal views and, building off the Cronon excerpt, the authors' visions of nature.

1.   BIOCENTRISM

Many scholars of indigenous communities have documented varied forms of pantheism, where the people are spiritually connected within rather than apart from their environment. In describing pre-Christian Greek religion, for example, Arnold Toynbee notes that "divinity was inherent in all natural phenomena.... Divinity was present in springs and rivers and the seal in trees . . .; in mountains; in earthquakes and lightning and thunder. The godhead was diffuse." Arnold Joseph Toynbee, *The Religious Background of the Environmental Crisis,* 3 INT'L J. ENVTL. STUD. 143 (1972). Toynbee goes on to argue that Christianity drained the divinity out of nature. *Id.* Likewise, many Native American tribes dance and pray to their prey following a hunt to thank them. As an anthropologist recounts, in one of these ceremonies the hunter declares:

> We know your life is as precious as ours. We know that we are both children of the same Great True Ones. We know that we are all one life on the same Mother Earth, beneath the same plains and sky. But we also know that one life must sometimes give way to another so that the one great life of all may continue unbroken. So we ask your permission, we obtain your consent to this killing.

See CHARLES ADAMS, ED., FRANK WATERS: A RETROSPECTIVE ANTHOLOGY 60 (1985).

a.   Deep Ecology

A recent environmental ethic, the philosophy of "deep ecology," builds off this foundation of kinship with nature. The term "deep ecology" was coined by Norwegian philosopher Arne Naess, and was founded on the twin principles of self-realization and biocentric equality. In the excerpt below, Bill Devall and George Sessions set out the need to develop a more profound relationship with nature and establish a new ecological connection. They believe that such a relationship will not only provide greater human fulfillment and quality of life, but that deep ecology is the only effective way to reestablish our natural connections to the environment and to protect it.

Bill Devall & George Sessions, Deep Ecology: Living as if Nature Mattered ix, 65–70 (1985)

The intuition of biocentric equality is that all things in the biosphere have an equal right to live and blossom and to reach their own individual forms of unfolding and self-realization within the larger Self-realization. The basic intuition is that all organisms and entities in the ecosphere, as parts of the interrelated whole, are equal in intrinsic worth. . . . Deep ecology goes beyond a limited piecemeal shallow approach to environmental problems and attempts to articulate a comprehensive religious and philosophical worldview. [Devall and Sessions then set out the core principles of deep ecology.] * * *

1. The well being and flourishing of human and nonhuman Life on Earth have value in themselves. These values are independent of the usefulness of the nonhuman world for human purposes.

2. Richness and diversity of life forms contribute to the realization of these values and are also values in themselves.

3. Humans have no right to reduce this richness and diversity except to satisfy *vital* needs.

4. The flourishing of human life and cultures is compatible with a substantial decrease of the human population. The flourishing of nonhuman life requires such a decrease.

5. Present human interference with the nonhuman world is excessive, and the situation is rapidly worsening.

6. Policies must therefore be changed. These policies affect basic economic, technological, and ideological structures. The resulting state of affairs will be deeply different from the present.

———

b. *The Land Ethic*

The following passage is probably the most influential statement of ethics in the American environmental movement. Its author, Aldo Leopold, was a pioneer in the field of resource management. In addition to his efforts in the U.S. Forest Service to preserve wild tracts of land, Leopold helped found the Wilderness Society in 1935. *A Sand County Almanac*, from which this excerpt is drawn, was published posthumously, after Leopold died of a heart attack fighting a forest fire. In the chapter entitled "The Land Ethic," Leopold traces the development of ethics, arguing that the time has come to enlarge its breadth. Consider whether Leopold's notion of rights is narrower or broader than that of deep ecology. Though written over sixty years ago, Leopold's observations have direct relevance to management debates today, particularly his criticisms of an economics-based view of resource management and the implications of ecological interdependence (that living resources are always "in use," even when left undisturbed).

ALDO LEOPOLD, A SAND COUNTY ALMANAC—AND SKETCHES HERE AND THERE 201–204, 210–212, 223–226 (1949)

When God-like Odysseus returned from the wars in Troy, he hanged all on one rope a dozen slave-girls of his household whom he suspected of misbehavior during his absence.

This hanging involved no question of propriety. The girls were property. The disposal of property was then, as now, a matter of expediency, not of right and wrong.

Concepts of right and wrong were not lacking from Odysseus' Greece: witness the fidelity of his wife through the long years before at last his black-prowed galleys clove the wine-dark seas for home. The ethical structure of that day covered wives, but had not yet been extended to human chattels. During the three thousand years which have since elapsed, ethical criteria have been extended to many fields of conduct, with corresponding shrinkages in those judged by expediency only. * * *

The first ethics dealt with the relation between individuals; the Mosaic Decalogue is an example. Later accretions dealt with the relation between the individual and society. The golden rule tries to integrate the individual to society; democracy to integrate social organization to the individual.

There is as yet no ethic dealing with man's relation to land and to the animals and plants which grow upon it. Land, like Odysseus' slave-girls, is still property. The land-relation is still strictly economic, entailing privileges but not obligations.

The extension of ethics to this third element in human environment is, if I read the evidence correctly, an evolutionary possibility and an ecological necessity. * * *

The Community Concept

All ethics so far evolved rest upon a single premise; that the individual is a member of a community of interdependent parts. His instincts prompt him to compete for his place in the community, but his ethics prompt him also to co-operate (perhaps in order that there may be a place to compete for).

The land ethic simply enlarges the boundaries of the community to include soils, waters, plants, and animals, or collectively: the land.

This sounds simple: do we not already sing our love for and obligation to the land of the free and the home of the brave? Yes, but just what and whom do we love? Certainly not the soil, which we are sending helter-skelter downriver. Certainly not the waters, which we assume have no function except to turn turbines, float barges, and carry off sewage. Certainly not the plants, of which we exterminate whole communities without batting an eye. Certainly not the animals, of which we have already extirpated many of the largest and most beautiful species. A land ethic of course cannot prevent the alteration, management, and use of the "resources," but it does affirm their right to continued existence, and, at least in spots, their continued existence in a natural state. In short, a land ethic changes the role of *Homo sapiens* from conqueror of the land-community to plain member and citizen of it. It implies respect for his fellow-members, and also respect for the community as such. * * *

One basic weakness in a conservation system based wholly on economic motives is that most members of the land community have no economic value. Wildflowers and songbirds are examples. Of the 22,000 higher plants and animals native to Wisconsin, it is doubtful whether more than 5 per cent can be sold, fed, eaten, or otherwise put to economic use. Yet these creatures are members of the biotic community, and if (as I believe) its stability depends on its integrity, they are entitled to continuance.

When one of these non-economic categories is threatened, and if we happen to love it, we invent subterfuges to give it economic importance. At the beginning of the century songbirds were supposed to be disappearing. Ornithologists jumped to the rescue with some distinctly shaky evidence to the effect that insects would eat us up if birds failed to control them. The evidence had to be economic to be valid.

It is painful to read these circumlocutions today. We have no land ethic yet, but we have at least drawn nearer to the point of admitting that birds should continue as a matter of biotic right, regardless of the presence or absence of economic advantage to us. * * *

To sum up: a system of conservation based solely on economic self-interest is hopelessly lopsided. It tends to ignore, and thus eventually to eliminate, many elements in the land community that lack commercial value, but that are (so far as we know) essential to its healthy functioning. It assumes, falsely, I think, that the economic parts of the biotic clock will function without the uneconomic parts. It tends to relegate to government many functions eventually too large, too complex, or too widely dispersed to be performed by government.

An ethical obligation on the part of the private owner is the only visible remedy for these situations.

The Land Pyramid

... Plants absorb energy from the sun. This energy flows through a circuit called the biota, which may be represented by a pyramid consisting of layers. The bottom layer is the soil. A plant layer rests on the soil, an insect layer on the plants, a bird and rodent layer on the insects, and so on up through various animal groups to the apex layer, which consists of the larger carnivores.

The species of a layer are alike not in where they came from, or in what they look like, but rather in what they eat. Each successive layer depends on those below it for food and often for other services, and each in turn furnishes food and services to those above. Proceeding upward, each successive layer decreases in numerical abundance. Thus, for every carnivore there are hundreds of his prey, thousands of their prey, millions of insects, uncountable plants. The pyramidal form of the system reflects this numerical progression from apex to base. Man shares an intermediate layer with the bears, raccoons, and squirrels which eat both meat and vegetables.... Land, then, is not merely soil; it is a fountain of energy flowing through a circuit of soils, plants, and animals. Food chains are the living channels which conduct energy upward; death and decay return it to the soil. * * *

The Outlook

It is inconceivable to me that an ethical relation to land can exist without love, respect, and admiration for land, and a high regard for its value. By value, I of course mean something far broader than mere economic value; I mean value in the philosophical sense.

Failures of the economic-based system

Perhaps the most serious obstacle impeding the evolution of a land ethic is the fact that our educational and economic system is headed away from, rather than toward, an intense consciousness of land. Your true modern is separated from the land by many middlemen, and by innumerable physical gadgets. He has no vital relation to it; to him it is the space between cities on which crops grow. Turn him loose for a day on the land, and if the spot does not happen to be a golf links or a "scenic" area, he is bored stiff. If crops could be raised by hydroponics instead of farming, it would suit him very well. Synthetic substitutes for wood, leather, wool, and other natural land products suit him better than the originals. In short, land is something he has "outgrown." * * *

The "key-log" which must be moved to release the evolutionary process for an ethic is simply this: quit thinking about decent land-use as solely an economic problem. Examine each question in terms of what is ethically and esthetically right, as well as what is economically expedient. A thing is right when it tends to preserve the integrity, stability, and beauty of the biotic community. It is wrong when it tends otherwise.

———

2.   ANTHROPOCENTRISM

In the Judeo–Christian tradition, our relations to the natural world have largely been anthropocentric (i.e., human-centered). In the well known text of Chapter 1, Verse 28, of Genesis, for example, God commands Adam (and by extension his descendents) to "Be fruitful and multiply and replenish the earth and subdue it: and have dominion over the fish of the sea, and over the fowl of the air and over every living thing that moveth upon the earth." As Note 6 in this section's *Questions and Discussion* points out, whether Genesis 1:28 commands aggressive development or careful stewardship has been interpreted differently over time. Nor does dominion necessarily portend destruction. George Perkins Marsh, the famous 19th Century ecologist, argued that, as the dominant species, humans have a responsibility to act as stewards of the Earth's resources. "Man has too long forgotten that the earth was given to him for usufruct alone, not for consumption, still less for profligate waste." GEORGE PERKINS MARSH, MAN AND NATURE; OR PHYSICAL GEOGRAPHY MODIFIED AS HUMAN ACTION 35 (1869).

Genesis 1:28 — what does "dominion" mean?

a.   *Utilitarianism*

Utilitarianism is perhaps the most widely accepted argument for anthropocentrism. As John Stuart Mill famously described, utilitarianism seeks to provide the greatest good to the greatest number of people. While some may find it odd to think of utilitarianism as an ethical viewpoint, it is a rights-based view of the world insofar as decisions ought to be made on the basis of social welfare (as measured for humans). Utilitarianism served as the basis for Gifford Pinchot's, the first head of the U.S. Forest Service, "wise use" management strategy (described in the case study that follows this section at page 28). In the classic excerpt below, the late Professor Bill Baxter provocatively defends utilitarianism as the proper guiding ethic for environmental policy. Do you agree with his assertion that, moral posturing aside, this is how most people really think? How would he respond to Leopold's critique of over-reliance on economics?

WILLIAM BAXTER, PEOPLE OR PENGUINS:
THE CASE FOR OPTIMAL POLLUTION 4–9, 12 (1974)

Recently scientists have informed us that use of DDT in food production is causing damage to the penguin population. For the present purpose let us accept that assertion as an indisputable scientific fact. The scientific fact is often asserted as if the correct implication—that we must stop agricultural use of DDT—followed from the mere statement of the fact of penguin damage. But plainly it does not follow if my criteria are employed.

My criteria are oriented to people, not penguins. Damage to penguins, or sugar pines, or geological marvels is, without more, simply irrelevant. One must go further, by my criteria, and say: Penguins are important because people enjoy seeing them walk about rocks; and furthermore, the well-being of people would be less impaired by halting use of DDT than by giving up penguins. In short, my observations about environmental problems will be people-oriented, as are my criteria. I have no interest in preserving penguins for their own sake.

It may be said by way of objection to the position, that it is very selfish of people to act as if each person represented one unit of importance and nothing else was of any importance. It is undeniably selfish. Nevertheless I think it is the only tenable starting place for analysis for several reasons. First, no other position corresponds to the way most people really think and act—i.e., corresponds to reality.... I do not know how we could administer any other system.... Penguins cannot vote now and are unlikely subjects for the franchise—pine trees more unlikely still. Again each individual is free to cast his or her vote so as to benefit sugar pines if that is his inclination. But many of the more extreme assertions one hears from some conservationists amounts to tacit assertions that they are specially appointed representatives of sugar pines, and hence that their preferences should be weighted more heavily than the preferences of other humans who do not enjoy equal rapport with "nature." * * *

[I]f polar bears or pine trees or penguins, like men, are to be regarded as ends rather than means, if they are to count in our calculus of social organization, someone must tell me how much each one counts, and someone must tell me how these life forms are to be permitted to express their preferences, for I do not know either answer. If the answer is that certain people are to hold their proxies, then I want to know how these proxyholders are to be selected: self-appointment does not seem workable to me. * * *

I reject the proposition that we *ought* to respect "the balance of nature" or to "preserve the environment" unless the reason for doing so, express or implied, is the benefit of man.

I reject the idea that there is a "right" or "morally correct" state of nature to which we should return. The word "nature" has no normative connotations. Was it "right" or "wrong" for the earth's crust to heave in contortion and create mountains and seas? Was it "right" for the first amphibian to crawl up out of the primordial ooze? ... No answers can be given to these questions because they are meaningless questions.

All this may seem obvious to the point of being tedious, but much of the present controversy over environment and pollution rests on tacit normative assumptions about just such nonnormative phenomena: that it is "wrong" to impair penguins with DDT, but not to slaughter cattle for prime rib roasts.... Every man is entitled to his own preferred definition of Walden Pond, but there is no definition that has any moral superiority over another, except by reference to the selfish needs of the human race. * * *

People enjoy watching penguins. They enjoy relatively clean air and smog-free vistas. Their health is improved by relatively clean water and air. Each of these benefits is a type of good or service. As a society we would be well advised to give up one washing machine if the resources that would have gone into that washing machine can yield greater human satisfaction when diverted into pollution control.... And so on, trade-off by trade-off, we should divert our productive capacities from the production of existing goods and services to the production of a cleaner, quieter, more pastoral nation up to—and no further than—the point at which we value more highly the next washing machine or hospital that we would have to do without than we value the next unit of environmental improvement that the diverted resources would create.

---

b.   *Ecosystem Services, Use and Non–Use Values*

Baxter is quick to note that a purely economic, anthropocentric view need not lead to environmental destruction. Quite the opposite, in fact, since people depend on natural systems and enjoy their amenities. Assume, for example, we're trying to determine the value of a wetland along the banks of the Potomac. Economists classify the valuable benefits of the wetland through separate categories. The most obvious category includes consumable ecosystem goods such as cranberries and crabs that are exchanged in markets and easily priced (direct market uses). Activities such as hiking and fishing are direct, non-market uses. Another source of value derives from the fact that even if we've never visited and used the wetland, we may benefit from knowing it exists ("existence value"), visiting it in the future ("option value"), or knowing that our children and their children will be able to enjoy the wetland ("bequest value"). Such non-market, non-use values are not exchanged in markets but, make no mistake, they are very real, as evidenced by the strong nationwide support for the Endangered Species Act.

[margin note: examples of non-market, non-use values]

A final category includes indirect non-market uses, such as pollination, water purification, maintenance of biodiversity, etc. These "ecosystem services" provide clear benefits to humans, but they are neither directly "consumed" nor exchanged in markets.

James Salzman et al., *Protecting Ecosystem Services: Science, Economics, and Law*, 20 STAN. ENVTL. L.J. 309, 310–312 (2001)

Largely taken for granted, healthy ecosystems provide a variety of critical services. Created by the interactions of living organisms with their environment, these "ecosystem services" provide both the conditions and processes that sustain human life—purifying air and water, detoxifying and decomposing waste, renewing soil fertility, regulating climate, mitigating droughts and floods, controlling pests, and pollinating plants. Although awareness of ecosystem services dates back to Plato, ecologists, economists, and lawyers have only recently begun systematically examining the extent and implications of these services' valuable contributions to social welfare. Not surprisingly, recent research has demonstrated the extremely high costs to replace many of these services if they were to fail, on the order of many billions of dollars in the United States for water purification alone. Such estimates are inherently uncertain, but the extraordinary costs required to substitute for many important services by artificial means are beyond dispute. * * *

Despite their obvious importance to our well being, ecosystem services have largely been ignored in environmental law and policy. Provision of services is only rarely considered in cost-benefit analyses, preparation of environmental impact statements, wetlands mitigation banking, Superfund remediations, and oil spill clean-ups. Nor have significant markets arisen that capitalize on the commercial value of these services. We have no shortage of markets for ecosystem goods (such as clean water and apples), but the services underpinning these goods (such as water purification and pollination) are free. The services themselves have no market value for the simple reason that no markets exist in which they can be exchanged. As a result, there are no direct price mechanisms to signal the scarcity or degradation of these public goods until they fail. Partly as a result, ecosystems are degraded.

An explicit ecosystem services perspective provides two obvious benefits. The first is political. Understanding the role of ecosystem services powerfully justifies why habitat preservation and biodiversity conservation are vital, though often overlooked, policy objectives. While a wetland surely provides existence and option values to some people, the benefits provided by the wetland's nutrient retention and flood protection services are both universal and undeniable. Tastes may differ over beauty, but they are in firm accord over the high costs of polluted water and flooded homes.

The second benefit is instrumental. Efforts to capture the value of ecosystem services may spur institutional designs and market mechanisms that effectively promote environmental protection at the local, regional, national, and international levels. To realize this potential, however, we must first create market mechanisms and institutions that can capture and maximize service values. If given the opportunity, natural systems can, in many cases, quite literally "pay their way." The key challenge is how to make this happen.

––––––––

In principle, then, a utilitarian ethic can dictate strong environmental protection if the values of the ecosystem are accurately captured. One can be sure that residents of New Orleans, harshly educated by Katrina, now understand the value of wetlands in buffering storm surge. Capturing ecosystems' value, however, in most circumstances is far easier said than done. Recall Baxter's challenge that if polar bears or penguins are "to count in our calculus of social organization, someone must tell me how much each one counts." An ecosystem services approach can indicate how much each one counts in biophysical terms—how much water is purified by the trees and vegetation in a watershed, how much a wetland slows flood waters, etc. But Baxter likely has something else in mind—monetary value. This can be done with ecosystem services in some instances through replacement cost methodology (i.e., how much it would cost to replace the service of water purification provided by a wetland, for example, by building a water treatment plant), but once one moves from such straightforward examples the going becomes less clear. After all, how can one possibly place a value on the benefit of saving penguins from DDT?

As described in more detail in Note 7 on page 24, cost-benefit analysis attempts to do just this by comparing the total social costs of a proposed action with the total benefits. In principle this seems unobjectionable. Making decisions that maximize societal benefit is surely a valid governmental goal. The key practical question, though, is the unit of measurement. Cost-benefit analysis generally monetizes costs and benefits, and that's where things get complicated. The benefits of development are relatively easy to calculate, whether as projected growth in jobs, additional tourists, timber board feet cut, etc. But the value of the benefits provided by natural systems (which will be lost or degraded by the development) are not exchanged in markets. Think about water purification, climate stability, pest control, and soil fertility. It would be foolish to argue that these have no value, but is there a legitimate way to convert their value into dollars and cents?

3.   INTERGENERATIONAL EQUITY

In legal philosopher John Rawls' famous "veil of ignorance" thought experiment, he asks you to decide what kind of society you would want to live in if you had no way of knowing beforehand who you would be in that society—rich or poor, male or female, young or old, black or white. Presumably, you would want a society with rules that ensured basic dignity and rights for all members of society, since you could just as likely be disadvantaged as powerful. Placing this in a temporal context, now ask what kind of society you would want if you were also ignorant of *when* you would be living? And, focusing the question, how you would want natural resources to be managed today if you were ignorant of when you would be living?

Acknowledging that we have an obligation to future generations, of course, still leaves unanswered the critical practical question of what that means for natural resource management decisions today. Just witness the unending debates over how we should implement the policy of sustainable development—development that meets the needs of the current generation without compromising the ability of future generations to meet their own needs. In the excerpt below, Edith Brown Weiss addresses this issue, arguing that holding the earth in trust for future generations requires that we pass the planet on in no worse condition than we received it and provide equitable access to its resources and benefits.

Edith Brown Weiss, *What Obligation Does Our Generation Owe to The Next? An Approach to Global Environmental Responsibility*, 84 AMERICAN J. INT'L. L. 198, 199–202 (1990)

To define intergenerational equity, it is useful to view the human community as a partnership among all generations. In describing a state as a partnership, Edmund Burke observed that "as the ends of such a partnership cannot be obtained in many generations, it becomes a partnership not only between those who are living but between those who are living, those who are dead, and those who are to be born." The purpose of human society must be to realize and protect the welfare and well-being of every generation. This requires sustaining the life-support systems of the planet, the ecological processes and the environmental conditions necessary for a healthy and decent human environment.

In this partnership, no generation knows beforehand when it will be the living generation, how many members it will have, or even how many generations there will ultimately be. It is useful, then, to take the perspective of a generation that is placed somewhere along the spectrum of time, but does not know in advance where it will be located. Such a generation would want to inherit the earth in at least as good condition as it has been in for any previous generation and to have as good access to it as previous generations. This requires each generation to pass the planet on in no worse condition than it received it in and to provide equitable access to its resources and benefits. Each generation is thus both a trustee for the planet with obligations to care for it and a beneficiary with rights to use it. * * *

I have proposed three basic principles of intergenerational equity. First, each generation should be required to conserve the diversity of the natural and cultural resource base, so that it does not unduly restrict the options available to future generations in solving their problems and satisfying their own values, and should also be entitled to diversity comparable to that enjoyed by previous generations. This principle is called "conservation of options." Second, each generation should be required to maintain the quality of the planet so that it is passed on in no worse condition than that in which it was received, and should also be entitled to planetary quality comparable to that enjoyed by previous generations. This is the principle of "conservation of quality." Third, each generation should provide its members with equitable rights of access to the legacy of past generations and should conserve this access for future generations. This is the principle of "conservation of access."

These proposed principles constrain the actions of the present generation in developing and using the planet, but within these constraints do not dictate how each generation should manage its resources. * * *

Intergenerational rights of necessity inhere in all generations, whether these be immediately successive generations or ones more distant. There is no theoretical basis for limiting such rights to immediately successive generations. If we were to do so, we would often provide little or no protection to more distant future generations. Nuclear and hazardous waste disposal, the loss of biological diversity and ozone depletion, for example, have significant effects on the natural heritage of more distant generations.

———

4. WHY VALUES MATTER IN NATURAL RESOURCES LAW

Clashes over environmental values have two important implications for natural resources law and policy. First is the nature of the laws themselves. In looking closely at resource laws, one finds an almost schizophrenic divide. Certain laws, such as the Endangered Species Act and the Marine Mammal Protection Act, may be described in some respects as biocentric, in the sense that individual endangered species and marine mammals are effectively given the legal right not to be taken or harmed. Other laws, such as the Magnuson–Stevens Fisheries Conservation and Management Act, by contrast, are hard-nosed commercial regulations, aimed at ensuring stocks of fish remain at commercially viable harvest levels. Understanding the values divide—biocentric versus anthropocentric—explains why these laws appear to be so different.

Realize, though, that this is a broad brush description. The political process requires a series of compromises among differing values and this is evident even in "biocentric laws" such as the Endangered Species Act. This rights-based law, for example, provides for permits that may be issued to legally kill endangered species. While the Wilderness Act designates lands where the hand of man is supposed to be substantially unnoticeable, the same act permits pre-existing grazing and mining rights to continue.

Second, understanding the values divide explains why so many natural resource conflicts seem intractable. Philosophers use the term, "categories," to explain the problem. One can say that the grass is green or that two plus two equals four. But the concepts in the two sentences exist in different, mutually exclusive, categories. It makes no sense to say that "the grass is four" or that "two plus two is green." Similarly, a number of schools of environmental ethics are irreconcilable and act as different categories. If someone is morally outraged over cutting old growth timber stands, for example, the economic trade-offs are irrelevant and unpersuasive. It's like telling someone that grass is four. To make the point in a different context, think of the abortion debate. If someone believes that abortion is murder, whether the abortion occurs in the first rather than second trimester is meaningless. Thus in the old growth timber and abortion examples, the conflicting parties are, quite literally, speaking past one another, making principled compromise difficult, if not impossible.

QUESTIONS AND DISCUSSION

1. For each school of environmental ethics described above (i.e., deep ecology, the land ethic, utilitarianism, etc.), in whom or in what do the rights inhere?

- In inanimate objects (e.g., rocks or a river)?

- In living things (e.g., a newt or whale)?

- In living communities (e.g., a particular forest)?

- In people living today in America?

- In future generations of people?

2. How would the major schools of thought described above analyze the decisions:

(1) To kill a few individuals of an endangered moth population to build a new hospital?

(2) To kill half the population of the endangered moth to build a new hospital?

(3) To kill the only known population of the endangered moth to build a new hospital?

Assume that the moth has been studied and has no clear commercial value. Assume the hospital will provide jobs and health care to an economically depressed community. Would the answers differ if the species were a cuddly panda instead of a moth? How about if it were an endangered bacteria?

3. The exercises in Questions 1 and 2 are useful in understanding an important distinction between deep ecology and the land ethic—the same distinction that plays out between animal rights groups and environmental groups today. It is also evident in the Endangered Species Act. Section 10 of the Endangered Species Act, for example, expressly provides for "incidental takes" of protected species so long as a permit has been issued. In simple terms, the permit allows people to kill or harm individual endangered species so long as the population remains viable. Most environmental groups have no ethical problem with this provision. Indeed, it's the basis for habitat conservation plans and is consistent with an overriding concern for the species' survival. Animal rights advocates, though, oppose killing individual animals for the simple reason that, in their worldview, rights inhere in individuals, not species or species populations. This distinction between individual and community rights has played an important role in frustrating closer alliances between environmental and animal rights groups.

4. What about ethical obligations to inanimate objects? To say we owe an ethical duty to a rock may seem a singularly stupid assertion. But not all commentators agree. The historian Lynn White has suggested that accepting such a duty is a crucial first step toward addressing our ecological problems:

> Do people have ethical obligations toward rocks? . . . To almost all Americans still saturated with ideas historically dominant in Christianity . . . the question makes no sense at all. If the time comes when to any considerable group of us the question is no longer ridiculous, we may be on the verge of a change of values that will make possible measures to cope with the growing ecological crisis. One hopes there is enough time left.

Lynn White Jr., *Continuing the Debate, in* WESTERN MAN AND ENVIRONMENTAL ETHICS 63 (Ian Barbour, ed. 1973). What is White talking about? Does he mean to say we have an ethical obligation toward any rock that we may kick along the street? Or is he referring perhaps to special rocks, like Devil's Tower in Wyoming, Half Dome in Yosemite National Park, or the Grand Canyon in Arizona? It makes no sense to say that Half Dome has a right to live. Can we say it has a right to exist undisturbed by humans?

Assume the government decided to flood the Grand Canyon (as the Bureau of Reclamation remarkably once proposed to do). Which school of thought described above do you think provides the strongest explanation for why most of us would be disturbed by this idea? Joe Sax has explored a similar notion in his provocatively titled book, PLAYING DARTS WITH A REMBRANDT (1999), where he queries whether the owner of a Rembrandt masterpiece should be legally barred from using it as a dartboard. Should it matter whether the Rembrandt is private or public property?

5. Interestingly, in his earlier writings, Leopold appears a more pragmatic balancer. Consider the following:

> What I am trying to make clear is that if in a city we had six vacant lots available to the youngsters of a certain neighborhood for playing ball, it might be "development" to build houses on the first, and the second, and the third, and the fourth, and even the fifth, but when we build houses on the last one,

we forget what houses are for. The sixth house would not be development at all, but rather it would be mere short-sighted stupidity.

ALDO LEOPOLD, ALDO LEOPOLD'S WILDERNESS 159 (Daniel E. Brown & Neil B. Carmony eds. 1990). Is this excerpt compatible with the earlier excerpt from *The Land Ethic*? Is Leopold's land ethic compatible with modern societies? In what cases would such societies justify loss to the "integrity, stability and beauty of the biotic community" for building the sixth house, additional roads, or extracting basic resources?

6. As the main text noted, in Genesis God commands Adam to "Be fruitful and multiply and replenish the earth and subdue it: and have dominion over the fish of the sea, and over the fowl of the air and over every living thing that moveth upon the earth." It has long been debated, however, whether Genesis 1:28 commands aggressive development or careful stewardship. Lewis Cass asserted in 1830 "There can be no doubt . . . the Creator intended the earth should be reclaimed from a state of nature and cultivated." *See* FRANCIS P. PRUCHA, AMERICAN INDIAN POLICY IN THE FORMATIVE YEARS 143 (1962).

This view of the meaning of Genesis 1:28 has more recently been challenged. As Michael Northcott has argued:

> Dominion has frequently been misinterpreted as meaning domination and possession. But the Hebrew root of the verb translated subdue or rule means vice-regent or steward and not ruler. God puts humans over nature not as owner or exploiter but as the steward who shares the creative care of the creator.

MICHAEL NORTHCOTT, THE ENVIRONMENT AND CHRISTIAN ETHICS 181 (1997). *See also* WESLEY GRANBERG-MICHAELSON, A WORLD SPIRITUALITY: THE CALL TO REDEEM LIFE ON EARTH 63 (1984) (asserting that "[o]ur call" is "to be stewards of [God's] creation").

7. As noted in the text, cost-benefit analysis relies on converting costs and benefits into a common unit of value (generally dollars). But how can the value of ecosystem services that are not exchanged in markets, such as climate stability, be converted to their value in dollars and cents?

Economists have devised a range of methodologies to do just that. These include contingent valuation (asking how much people would be willing to pay for various environmental goods and services), hedonic pricing (assessing how particular environmental amenities, such as proximity to a wetland, affect real estate prices), replacement cost (how much it would cost to replace the degraded ecosystem service), etc. All of these methodologies have shortcomings. In contingent valuation studies, for example, how the question is framed can significantly change the values given and, more fundamentally, when respondents are asked their willingness to accept a payment to degrade a resource instead of their willingness to pay to protect the resource, the value for willingness to accept is higher (this is known as the endowment effect—if you are given something, you have an increased interest in keeping it). Thus while all of these techniques provide numbers, there is considerable debate over whether the numbers are accurate or, indeed, whether many environmental values (like an unspoiled vista) can or should be valued at all.

Not surprisingly, there is a huge literature on cost benefit analysis. For an overview of the current debate, see David Driesen, *The Societal Cost of Environmental Regulation: Beyond Administrative Cost–Benefit Analysis,* 24 ECOLOGY L.Q. 545 (1997). For the public policy advantages provided by cost benefit analysis, see, for example, Robert Hahn and Cass Sunstein, *A New Executive Order for Improving Federal Regulation? Deeper and Wider Cost–Benefit Analysis,* 150 U. PA. L. REV. 1489 (2002); Sidney A. Shapiro and Christopher H. Schroeder *Beyond Cost–Benefit Analysis: A Pragmatic Reorientation,* 18 Harvard Environmental L. Rev. (2008).

8. Another challenge in cost-benefit analysis arises from the problem of benefits or costs in the future. What if an action taken today will have little effect in the present but will prove harmful and entail costs 50 or 100 years hence (such as emissions of ozone depleting chemicals over the last several decades)? Similarly, how does one compare the benefits of an action with clear costs today, such as not logging an old-growth forest, if the benefits will be accrued both today and into the future? These questions require assessing today the costs and benefits to future generations.

Economists use *discount rates* to address this dilemma. If you were offered $100 today or $110 a year from now, which would you accept? The answer would depend on what you would do with the money during the year. If you could place it in a bank account with 12% interest, presumably you would take the money now and invest it. In this manner, $100 today is the equivalent of $112 in a year. While this may seem an eminently reasonable way to take future costs and benefits into account, it poses serious problems over extended time periods. For instance, assume you want to grow a forest that will generate $1,000,000 in pleasure to recreationists in its 100th year. How much is that future $1,000,000 benefit worth today? If one uses the discount rate of 7% (which is the standard rate for these calculations used by the Office of Management and Budget), the answer is $1,152 (PV = $1,000,000/(1 + 0.07)^{100}$). In other words, it is a poor investment to allow a forest to grow if other uses will generate more than $1,153 today. Over long periods of time the choice of discount rates can significantly affect the interests we ascribe to future generations. An increasing number of scholars have called for low or no discount rates when valuing intergenerational costs and benefits.

Despite the many criticisms of cost-benefit analysis, it has become a standard exercise in many government decisions. Starting in a 1981 Executive Order by President Reagan and amended by President Clinton in Executive Order 12866 (Sept. 30, 1993), agencies must conduct cost-benefit analyses of major decisions (i.e., over $100 million impact on the economy). "Recognizing that some costs and benefits are difficult to quantify," the agency must "propose or adopt a regulation only upon a reasoned determination that the benefits of the intended regulation justify its costs." *See* 58 FED. REG. 51735.

For the problems posed by discounting (i.e., converting future benefits and harms into current dollars), see, for example, Lisa Heinzerling, *Regulatory Costs of Mythic Proportions,* 107 YALE L.J. 1981 (1998). For practical objections to the malleability of cost-benefit analysis, see, for example, Daniel Farber, *Revitalizing Regulation,* 91 MICH. L. REV. 1278 (1993). For normative objections to cost benefit analysis, see, for example, Steven Kelman, *Cost–Benefit Analysis: An Ethical Critique*, 5 REG. 33 (Jan–Feb 1981).

9. With its emphasis on the need for fundamental changes in the relations between the human and non-human world, deep ecology represents one of the more extreme perspectives on environmental ethics. James Lovelock has proposed an alternate theory which, like deep ecology, finds its foundation in a holistic or biocentric view of nature. Lovelock argues that we should consider the Earth or "Gaia" as a single, super organism. As he describes,

> The entire range of living matter on Earth from whales to viruses and from oaks to algae could be regarded as constituting a single living entity capable of maintaining the Earth's atmosphere to suit its overall needs and endowed with faculties and powers far beyond those of its constituent parts.... [Gaia can be defined] as a complex entity involving the Earth's biosphere, atmosphere, oceans, and soil; the totality constituting a feedback of cybernetic systems which seeks an optimal physical and chemical environment for life on this planet.

JAMES LOVELOCK, GAIA: A NEW LOOK AT LIFE ON EARTH 9 (1979).

To disrupt this dynamic system, Lovelock has argued, is "as foolish as it would be to consider our brains supreme and the cells of other organisms expendable." James E. Lovelock, *The Earth as a Living Organism*, reprinted in E.O. WILSON, BIODIVERSITY 488–89 (1988). Does Lovelock's position strike you as closer to deep ecology, the land ethic, or ecosystem services?

10. An early law review article by Chris Stone on environmental ethics and the law has remained very influential. Suggestively titled, *Should Trees Have Standing?*, Stone, echoing the point of Leopold in the text, argued that "Throughout legal history, each successive extension of rights to some new entity has been, theretofore, a bit unthinkable. We are inclined to suppose the rightlessness of rightless 'things' to be a decree of Nature, not a legal convention acting in support of some status quo." Christopher Stone, *Should Trees Have Standing?*, 45 S. CAL. L. REV. 450, 453 (1972). He goes on to recount the progressive granting of rights throughout the history of Anglo–American law. The Magna Carta extended authority from the king to barons. The Declaration of Independence extended rights to colonists (albeit white male colonists). Notwithstanding the Dred Scott decision, the Emancipation Proclamation extended legal rights to black Americans. And the Nineteenth Amendment extended suffrage to women. Continuing this evolution, Stone explains, "I am quite seriously proposing that we give legal rights to forests, oceans, rivers, and other so-called 'natural objects' in the environment—indeed to the natural environment as a whole."

Stone had been inspired to write the article by a Ninth Circuit decision denying standing to the Sierra Club's challenge of a Forest Service permit for Walt Disney to develop Mineral King Valley in the Sierra Nevadas into a ski resort. Stone rushed to finish the piece so that Justice William Douglas, who had agreed to write the preface for a special issue of the *U.S.C. Law Review*, would read the piece before voting on the case, then before the Supreme Court on appeal. Douglas not only read Stone's article but, in the very first paragraph of his dissent, bluntly called for a "federal rule that allowed environmental issues to be litigated before federal agencies or federal courts in the name of the inanimate object about to be despoiled, defaced, or invaded by roads and bulldozers and where injury is the subject of public outrage. Contemporary public concern for protecting nature's ecological equilibrium should lead to the conferral of standing upon environmental objects to sue for their own preservation." *Sierra Club v. Morton*, 405 U.S. 727, 741–742 (1972). In a whimsical reply to Justice Douglas' dissent, an attorney rhymed:

> If Justice Douglas has his way—
> O come not that dreadful day—
>
> We'll be sued by lakes and hills
> Seeking a redress of ills.
>
> Great mountain peaks of name prestigious
> Suddenly become litigious.
>
> Our brooks will babble in the courts,
> Seeking damages for torts.
>
> How can I rest beneath a tree
> If it may soon be suing me?
>
> Or enjoy the playful porpoise
> While it's seeking habeas corpus?
>
> Every beast within his paws
> Will clutch an order to show cause.
>
> The courts, besieged on every hand,
> Will crowd with suits by chunks of land.
>
> Ah! But vengeance will be sweet,
> Since this must be a two-way street.
>
> I'll promptly sue my neighbor's tree
> For shedding all its leaves on me.

Naff, *Reflections on the Dissent of Douglas, J., in Sierra Club v. Morton*, 58 A.B.A. J. 820, 820 (1972), as quoted in Christopher Stone, *Should Trees Have Standing? Revisited: How Far Will Law and Morals Reach? A Pluralist Perspective*, 59 S. Cal. L. Rev. 1, 3 (1985).

Bill Baxter ridicules the notion of legal guardians acting on behalf of environmental interests, arguing that forests and oceans cannot represent themselves in court much less make clear their desires (if they can even be said to have desires). It bears remembering, though, that corporations, while obviously not people, are legal persons and can defend their rights in court. Just as minors have guardians, corporations have court-recognized representatives. In a similar manner, Stone argues that the environment should be represented by a guardianship approach and Edith Brown Weiss argues for this in the context of future generations. How might such an arrangement work? Is it possible to discern the best interests of the environment as something separate from the interests of its putative guardian? What might William Cronon have to say about Chris Stone's proposal?

11. At first blush, Weiss' arguments seem unassailable. We clearly have a moral obligation to future generations. But is it so obvious what future generations would want us to do today? How do we decide who gets to make this decision, and how could it possibly be challenged? If you were asked to design a process that set forth concrete recommendations of how to manage resources for the benefit of future generations, what would the process look like?

————

CASE STUDY: THE NATURE OF WILDERNESS

Natural resources law and policy is shaped by its history. One cannot understand current conflicts over allocation and protection of our nation's natural resources—whether water, timber, wilderness, or rangelands—without some grasp of the changing perceptions of those resources over the course of our nation's history and of the ways in which policies to dispose or retain, to exploit or preserve, have responded to those changing norms. Thus many of the chapters will imbed their discussions in a broader historical context. As an initial overview of how we got to our present vantage, though, there is no better place to start than with wilderness and its amazing transformation in the public mind from daunting wasteland to sacred treasure.[1] As you read, note how society's dominant environmental ethics and, in turn, our constructions of nature have shifted over time.

————

Wilderness holds a special place in the American consciousness. The stillness of a remote forest lake, the imposing crags of a mountain peak, and the bewitching shades of color in a desert sunset etch themselves in our deep memories, providing a sense of connection both to a larger world and a sense of inner wonder. Wilderness is also big business. It primes our economy through eco-tourists paying top dollar for trips to Antarctica, backpackers buying high-tech gear for trekking in Alaska, and families enjoying Disneyworld's Jungle Cruise. Wilderness holds a strong grip in our collective imagination and the marketplace provides a dizzying number of ways for us to enjoy a range of "wilderness experiences."

Our love affair with things wild, however, is quite recent. To the Europeans who first came to America, eagerly seeking out the wilderness would have been incomprehensible. Indeed for most of the last two millennia, wilderness has more often been viewed with repugnance, as something dangerous and even an affront to civilization. The roots of this view go back to the Bible and earlier. After Adam and Eve taste the forbidden fruit, for example, their punishment is exile from the Garden of Eden into the wilderness. This is the same harsh, inhospitable region where Moses and the tribes of Israel must wander for forty years, where Christ is sorely tempted by the Devil for forty days. The Biblical wilderness is unforgiving, a wasteland of physical hardship and spiritual testing that forges iron faith.

---

1. The authors are grateful for the assistance of Professor Lewis Grossman in relating this history.

The later folk traditions in Europe reflected this harsh view. In many of the fairy tales of the Brothers Grimm, for example, when the protagonists leave the village bad things surely follow. For Hansel and Gretel, the forest is a place of monstrous beasts and creatures, surely no place for innocent children to wander. In the same manner, William Bradford, the first governor in Plymouth Plantation, described the surrounding wilderness as "hideous and desolate." To be fair, he had his reasons. The forests posed a very real threat to survival, hiding wild animals and potentially hostile (and heathen) tribes. Faced with this presumed absence of morality and civilization, the Puritans and their successors felt both a religious and practical compulsion to "civilize" the wilderness. As with the earlier Conquistadors, extending European conquest was rationalized in part by converting Indians to Christianity.

This is not to say that wilderness had no positive characteristics for early Americans. The goal of conquering the wilderness was usually not to convert it into cities but, rather, to a rural, pastoral state—a controlled, managed nature. Thus was wasteland converted to garden. One could have too much civilization as well as too little. The city—a pure civilized state— was equally viewed by many as immoral and disconnected from God. To the degree that the earliest Americans did admire the unspoiled American landscape, these were either areas that reminded them of cultivated landscapes in England, or particular aspects of the landscape—birds, flowers— that could be incorporated into a garden view.

During the age of Enlightenment in Europe, tamed wilderness began to take on positive overtones. The European landscape paintings that came into vogue, for example, were not pictures of wilderness but, instead, man-made rural landscapes (meadows, fields, farms, etc.) or wilderness scenes with people present or Greek temples in various states of decay—rarely nature alone.

To the early settlers, it seemed that much of Europe had gone too far toward the pole of civilization to achieve the ideal pastoral state. But it wasn't too late for America. Thus early American writers, such as Crevecoeur, despised wild areas but praised the improved, managed nature of the rural landscape. As he described, "I will revert into a state approaching nearer to that of nature, but at the same time sufficiently remote from the brutality of unconnected savage nature." Thomas Jefferson's ideal citizens were those yeoman farmers who labored on the earth (unlike city dwellers and industrial laborers). They were virtuous, close to God, and independent—the moral center of democratic society.

During the Westward expansion and development that long accompanied America's growth, the frontier mantra was largely one of taming the wilderness. Wilderness posed a barrier to progress and prosperity. It was an obstacle, something to be conquered. As Aldo Leopold later wrote in the 1930s, "A stump was our symbol of progress." But the era of frontier settlement coincided with the rise of the Age of Romanticism, and a broader appreciation for wilderness was developing. The Romantics (such as Byron, Wordsworth and Tennyson) associated God with wilderness. In their "sublime" view of nature, beauty was not only found in comfortable and well-ordered scenery but in the great outdoors, as well. To be fair, this view was mostly shared among people in the cities or comfortable farms who did not have to struggle with frontier living on a daily basis (indeed this split between urban and rural attitudes toward wilderness continues today). In art and literature, the presence of a grand and ancient wilderness in America assumed a role as a distinctive source of American identity and superiority. This embrace of wilderness was evident in the poetry of William Cullen Bryant, the novels of James Fenimore Cooper, the art of Thomas Cole, Asher Durand, Albert Bierstadt, and, most famously, in the writings of Henry David Thoreau.

The best known of the Transcendentalists, Thoreau's writings sprang from his belief in a connection between the higher realm of spiritual truth and the lower one of material objects. Thus God could be found in nature through intuitive contemplation. For Thoreau, modern industrial society, by cutting people off from nature, was cutting them off from God. The commercial spirit of civilization kept people from contemplation of the divine. Wilderness was a source of vigor, inspiration, and strength. It stripped life down to its essentials. As Thoreau simply stated, "In Wildness is the preservation of the world." Yet Thoreau's terrifying account of climbing Mount Katahdin in Maine leaves little doubt that he believed one could experience too much wilderness, as well as too little. In fact, Thoreau's ideal was really a middle landscape rather than pure wilderness, a life alternating between wilderness and civilization or residence in "partially cultivated country." This middle landscape is the essence of Walden, a subsistence farming existence near a town. Similarly, Ralph Waldo Emerson's famous essay, "Nature," was about a walk through Boston Common.

Neither Thoreau nor Emerson was particularly influential in their day, however, and the notion of preserving wilderness was not a serious option. Indeed, as described in Chapter 2, the opposite was true. Throughout most of the nineteenth century, federal policy was to settle the western wilderness with Jefferson's virtuous yeoman farmers. A series of preemption and donation acts followed by the Homestead Act and a variety of other statutes gave successive waves of settlers title to millions of acres of public lands. Often the statutes required some effort to cultivate the land before title would vest. To the extent there was federal supervision of the often chaotic process, it was to assure that wilderness was being tamed, not protected. And if wilderness could not necessarily be turned to farmland, particularly in the arid lands between the hundredth meridian and the Sierra Nevada and Cascade mountain ranges, its natural resources could at least be developed and exploited. Cattle were allowed freely to graze the public grasslands and miners were promised exclusive control of minerals they were able to discover on the public lands. Akin to the cultivation requirement, maintaining a mining claim necessitated diligently working the land. Leaving the land in its natural state meant losing the claim. At the same time public lands were being granted for agriculture, mining and other development, Congress was granting railroads millions of acres of alternating sections of public lands in an effort to speed the process along. The predominant public ethic was not to preserve wilderness but to subdue it or give it away as an incentive for further Westward expansion.

Nevertheless, while this mass transfer of land from public to private ownership was taking place, halting steps toward preserving wilderness began, albeit from very modest beginnings. George Catlin, a painter of Indians and prairie life, had proposed in 1832 the concept of preserving Indians, buffaloes, and their wilderness home in a park. And there was some early action. In 1832, Arkansas Hot Springs was set aside as a national reservation; in 1864, the federal government granted Yosemite Valley to California as a park "for public use, resort, recreation"; in 1872, President Grant signed an act creating Yellowstone "as a public park or pleasuring ground for the benefit and enjoyment of the people"; and, in 1885, New York State created a huge forest reserve in the Adirondacks. Indeed, Article 4 of the New York Constitution declares that "The lands of the state, now owned or hereafter acquired, constituting the forest preserve as now fixed by law, shall be forever kept as wild forest lands." Yet few of these acts were motivated solely by the aesthetic, spiritual, or cultural values of wilderness. The Adirondacks forest reserve was created in part to ensure clean water for New York City. Arkansas Hot Springs and Yellowstone were given protection primarily to prevent commercial exploitation of curiosities such as geysers. They were museums for oddities of nature.

As the nineteenth century drew to a close, though, public attitudes about wilderness preservation began to change. As Frederick Jackson Turner famously observed in 1893, "The frontier has gone, and with its going has closed the first period of American history." To Turner and many others, wilderness in American history had served as a fundamental source of democracy and rugged individualism. If the frontier was vanishing, preservation of the remaining wild areas had now become a matter of public concern. The success of the frontier movement had ironically raised the fear that wilderness, and the prized social values it had come to represent, might be lost, as well.

The dominant personality of the movement to preserve wilderness was a remarkable Scot named John Muir. Like Thoreau, Muir celebrated the presence of the divine in wilderness. It was not trite for him to proclaim that forests were temples on earth and mountains their steeples. He and other preservationists praised wilderness as a source of toughness and ethical values. Indeed he argued that many of the nation's difficulties could be attributed to too much civilization and effete, corrupt urban culture. Unlike the earlier transcendentalists, however, Muir had no ambivalence about pure wilderness. He was the first great public defender of wilderness for its own sake. When asked what rattlesnakes are good for, Muir famously was said to have replied, "They are good for themselves."

Muir was enough of a pragmatist, however, to realize that the public and politicians needed to be persuaded of the wisdom of preserving wilderness. He founded the Sierra Club in 1892 and, as its first president, through prolific writing and public speeches, argued for what became known as a "preservationist" approach to resource management—protecting the nation's special lands for all to experience through designation as parks and monuments.

Gifford Pinchot was an important early ally of Muir. The first American professionally trained as a forester in Europe, Pinchot became the consummate Washington insider. He was made the first Chief of the U.S. Forest Service by Teddy Roosevelt and later helped found the Yale School of Forestry, the first of its kind in America. Like Muir, Pinchot opposed the wholesale exploitation of public lands, but for very different reasons. In contrast to Muir's preservationist philosophy, Pinchot's views rested on a philosophy of "wise use," the view that expert management would ensure the optimal use of natural resources. The key words here are management and use. Pinchot recognized that there would always be competing demands for natural resources, and thus championed what came to be labeled as a "conservationist" approach to resource management. Its current equivalent is the strategy of multiple use.

In many conflicts the conservationists would agree with preservationists. But under the conservationist perspective, preservation was only one of several legitimate uses of national lands. To ensure the greatest good for the greatest number of people, the expert resource manager might dedicate different parts of the public lands for forestry, grazing, hunting, water power, or preservation. The most prominent policy manifestation of Pinchot's wise use strategy was his management of the National Forests for timber production (discussed in Chapter 10).

The great battle that catapulted the preservationist and conservationist movements into national prominence involved the Hetch Hetchy Valley in Yosemite National Park. From 1901 through 1913, there were repeated calls for damming the Tuolomne River in Hetch Hetchy Valley to increase San Francisco's water and electricity supply. Despite support of the dam by the President, Congress, and Pinchot, Muir led a more effective opposition campaign than anyone anticipated. Against the claims of dam supporters praising the beauty and potential recreational uses of the reservoir, Muir and grassroots opponents denounced as wasteful and sinful this "destruction" of a valley they claimed was more sublime than Yosemite. In response, the pro-dam San Francisco Chronicle ridiculed Muir's supporters as "hoggish and mushy esthetes" who favored a stroll in the woods over the needs of a city of 400,000.

In a fascinating reversal of the Adam and Eve story, Muir wrote that the dam supporters' arguments were "curiously like those of the devil, devised for the destruction of the first garden—so much of the very best Eden fruit going to waste." A century, or even a few decades earlier, the dominant argument would likely have been the reverse—a utilitarian claim that the dam improved the wasted flow through Hetch Hetchy Valley. Now this same development was portrayed as sacrilegious destruction.

The preservationists lost and Hetch Hetchy was dammed, but through the process of a sustained political campaign they gained many supporters and popularized the wilderness ethic.

Following World War II, the growth of America's middle class, and construction of the interstate highway system, America's public lands became both more familiar and cherished. While there had been only a handful of conservation groups at the time of the Hetch Hetchy dispute, by the early 1950s there were over 300. Thus when the dam battle was rejoined, the results were different. In 1954, a dam was proposed at Echo Park that would threaten Dinosaur National Monument on the Colorado–

Utah border. This time, the far larger preservation movement enjoyed greater support and created an unprecedented grassroots campaign against the dam. Mail to Congress was almost eighty-to-one against the dam. After five years, the dam proponents gave up.

The first great preservation victory behind them, environmental groups continued to organize and keep up their pressure on Congress. Perhaps their greatest successes came a decade later in a battle over a proposal to build two dams on the Colorado River that would have flooded a portion of the Grand Canyon. In addition to producing vast amounts of electricity, supporters claimed it would increase public access to the Grand Canyon. As absurd as this proposal seems today, at the time it was proposed it seemed unstoppable. It had the backing of Secretary of the Interior Stewart Udall, a person who had historically enjoyed strong support from the conservation community. But led by its iconoclastic leader, David Brower, the Sierra Club launched an unprecedented public relations blitz. Full page ads denouncing the proposal were placed in the *New York Times* and *Washington Post*. One such ad asked its readers, "Should we also flood the Sistine Chapel so tourists can get nearer its ceiling?" The public response was immediate and overwhelmingly negative. When the IRS sought to stifle the Sierra Club's voice by seeking to revoke its tax-exempt status because it was advocating legislation, the outcry against the proposal grew even worse. Eventually, Udall took his family on a raft trip down the Colorado River and concluded that his support for the dams was a mistake. In 1968, Congress passed legislation expressly prohibiting dams between the Glen Canyon and Hoover Dams, encompassing the entire length of the Grand Canyon.

The 1960s saw passage of landmark laws such as the Wilderness Act of 1964, the Land and Water Conservation Act of 1965, the National Historic Preservation Act of 1966, and the National Wild and Scenic Rivers System in 1968. Totally unlike earlier laws that had encouraged disposal of the public lands, this new wave of legislation took the opposite approach of retention and preservation. Recent conversion of public lands into national monuments is only the latest example of this counter-trend. Passage of these laws, of course, has not resolved the conflict between conservationists and preservationists. The decade-long debates over oil drilling in the Arctic National Wildlife Refuge and logging in public forests are proof of that.

Today our natural resource policies must ford the raging confluence of distinct historical perspectives—the view of wilderness as an obstacle to human welfare and a resource to be shaped and managed for society's benefit, in one stream, and the role of wilderness as sacred and essential to defining what we are as a people, in the other. As Wallace Stegner succinctly described, our position is unique. "No other nation on Earth so swiftly wasted its birthright; no other, in time, made such an effort to save what was left."

QUESTIONS AND DISCUSSION

1. Try to place the different cultural constructions of wilderness over time within Cronon's categories of nature (e.g., nature as commodity). Can you identify different schools of environmental ethics over time, as well? How are these related? How, for example, would you describe the settlers', Bradford's, and Crevecouer's views of nature? Were their ethics simply utilitarian, or was something else driving their attitudes to wilderness?

2. Is there a class divide over wilderness protection? Many critics of wilderness preservation argue that "locking up public lands" is elitist, favoring the interests of a few wealthy urban residents over poorer rural interests dependent on resource-based economies. As a columnist in *The Idaho Statesman* has argued, "Environmentalists tend to be elitist. They demonize opposition and shun contrarians. Snowmobilers, four-wheelers, ATVers [all terrain vehicle users], loggers and miners are regarded as lower life forms." Mark Tokarski, *It's Time to Move Beyond the Endless, Unproductive Bickering*, THE IDAHO STATESMAN, Jan. 25, 2000, at 9B. What if polls showed that preserving land as wilderness rather than for timber, motorized recreation, or coal mining was supported much more strongly by wealthy, urban white segments of the population than by rural and minority segments? Should that matter?

3. As mentioned earlier, the general notion of pre-Columbian wilderness as uninhabited and pristine is largely a fiction. As Bill Cronon has observed,

> The movement to set aside national parks and wilderness areas followed hard on the heels of the final Indian wars, in which the prior human inhabitants of these areas were rounded up and moved onto reservations. The myth of the wilderness as "virgin," uninhabited land had always been especially cruel when seen from the perspective of the Indians who had once called that land home. Now they were forced to move elsewhere, with the result that tourists could safely enjoy the illusion that they were seeing their nation in its pristine, original state, in the new morning of God's own creation.... The removal of Indians to create an "uninhabited wilderness"—uninhabited as never before in the human history of the place—reminds us just how invented, just how constructed, the American wilderness really is.

CRONON, *op. cit.*, 79.

4. Beyond his pivotal roles in the Hetch Hetchy dispute and the founding of the Sierra Club, John Muir led a remarkable life. Born in Scotland in 1838, Muir's family moved to Wisconsin when he was eleven. His upbringing was hard, with a strong disciplinarian father and most of his childhood spent at work on the farm. In 1867, while working in a carriage shop in Indianapolis, Muir was blinded when a file he was working with pierced his eye. Over the next few months, his sight gradually returned but the accident changed his life. Making good on his vow that if he ever regained his sight he'd see the world, Muir walked a thousand miles down to the Gulf of Mexico. Muir relates that when he finally landed in San Francisco and was looking for the nearest way out of town, he was asked where he wanted to go. In reply, he said, "To any place that is wild." That wild place ended up being the Yosemite Valley in the Sierra Nevada mountains.

While eventually settling near San Francisco, Muir regularly returned to the Sierras for the rest of his life. Indeed he would often take off for weeks at a time with nothing more than a small blanket and a loaf of bread. One of his more hair-raising exploits involved clinging to the top of a wildly swaying pine tree during a mountain storm. Known to the public through his prolific writings, primarily on the Sierras, Muir published over 300 articles and 10 books. His 1901 book, *Our National Parks*, caught the attention of President Theodore Roosevelt, who traveled in Yosemite with Muir and was influenced by his preservationist message. Muir died in 1914, but since his death his legacy has only grown. In 1976, the California Historical Society selected him as "The Greatest Californian." For a wide range of articles on Muir's life and his legacy, see <http://www.sierraclub. org/john_muir_exhibit/frameindex.html>.

5. For a better sense of Muir's arresting writing style and advocacy, below is an excerpt from a pamphlet Muir published during the Hetch Hetchy conflict. JOHN MUIR, THE HETCH-HETCHY VALLEY 2–6 (1908).

> Garden- and park-making goes on everywhere with civilization, for everybody needs beauty as well as bread, places to play in and pray in, where Nature may heal and cheer and give strength to body and soul. This natural beauty-hunger is displayed in poor folks' window-gardens made up of a few geranium slips in broken cups, as well as in the costly lily gardens of the rich, the thousands of spacious city parks and botanical gardens, and in our magnificent National Parks,—the Yellowlands, Yosemite, Sequoia, etc.,—Nature's own wonderlands, the admiration and joy of the world. Nevertheless, like everything else worth while, however sacred and precious and well-guarded, they have always been subject to attack, mostly by despoiling gain-seekers,—mischief-makers and robbers of every degree from Satan to senators, supervisors, lumbermen, cattlemen, farmers, etc., eagerly trying to make everything dollarable, often thinly disguised in smiling philanthropy, calling pocket-filling plunder "Utilization of beneficent natural resources, that man and beast may be fed and the dear Nation grow great." Thus long ago a lot of enterprising Jerusalem merchants made part of the temple into a place of business instead of a place of prayer, changing money, buying and selling cattle and sheep and doves. Ever since the establishment of the Yosemite National Park by act of Congress, October 8, 1890, constant strife has been going on around its borders, and I suppose will go on as part of the universal battle between right and wrong, however its boundaries may be shorn or its wild beauty destroyed.

6. For further background on wilderness in American history, you may want to read the following:

RODERICK NASH, WILDERNESS AND THE AMERICAN MIND (1982)

> The classic work on changing conceptions of nature

RODERICK NASH, THE RIGHTS OF NATURE: A HISTORY OF ENVIRONMENTAL ETHICS (1989)

> A comprehensive review of the foundations of environmental ethics

WILLIAM CRONON, ED., UNCOMMON GROUND: TOWARD REINVENTING NATURE (1995)

> Series of essays on our different conceptions of nature and their implications for environmental protection

WILLIAM CRONON, CHANGES IN THE LAND: INDIANS, COLONISTS, AND THE ECOLOGY OF NEW ENGLAND (1983)

> A seminal book on the relationships of the colonial inhabitants of New England with the natural landscape

JOHN MCPHEE, ENCOUNTERS WITH THE ARCHDRUID (1971)

> Wonderful sketch of David Brower, leader of the Sierra Club leader and founder of Friends of the Earth, and his encounters with three individuals—a mining proponent, a land developer, and a water developer

II.   WHY ARE NATURAL RESOURCES DIFFICULT TO MANAGE?

Recall the different natural resources listed at the beginning of the book, ranging from plants, animals, and oil to wilderness, the ozone layer, and water. At first glance, the main similarity among these resources seems to be that they are all so different. Yet despite the clear differences, conflicts over these resources tend to share the same aspects—themes we will see again and again throughout the course. These include the themes of scarcity, value clashes, commons problems, market failures, uncertainty, scale, and institutional failures. These common themes are so prevalent that it is hard to think of any resource conflict where they are not significant drivers. In the sections that follow, we briefly describe these themes. Such categorization is analytically helpful because determining the underlying management challenge determines which legal and policy approaches will prove most relevant.

A.   SCARCITY

Scarcity is perhaps the most basic feature of any natural resource conflict for the simple reason that if the resource were not scarce there would be no need for law, i.e., there would be plenty to go around. As soon as there is scarcity, competing interests arise over use of the resource, and the job of the natural resource policy-maker, and often the natural resource lawyer, will be to propose solutions that will likely make some groups happy and some unhappy when they can't have what they want. The types of scarcity depend, however, on the type of resource, as do the range of management challenges. Thus it is critical to understand specific challenges posed by specific types of natural resources.

The category of *extractive resources* includes those resources we take out of nature, modify and use. This is the traditional meaning of natural resources and would encompass plants, animals, fish, oil, coal, water, and mineral resources.

Within this broad category, *nonrenewable resources* exist in finite quantities. Use them and they're gone (over human time scales). It took tens of millions of years to form coal, but once it's burned it's gone. For these resources, management is a zero sum game. Extracting and using more now means less available in the future. In truth, though, some nonrenewable resources are not quite as scarce as may first appear because they are recyclable. Thus minerals such as gold or aluminum are not consumed when used. If they can be collected, they can be recycled and used again. And some nonrenewable resources can effectively increase over time because of improvements in technology (e.g., as more oil is discovered and extracted through improved exploration and drilling technologies).

Renewable resources exist in finite quantities at any point in time, but if properly managed can last indefinitely. These include plants, animals, soil, and some groundwater aquifers. Thus fisheries can provide food indefinitely so long as the population is maintained above replacement levels. Similarly, groundwater can provide water indefinitely so long as the rate of extraction does not exceed the rate of recharge (i.e., water percolating from the surface back into the underground aquifer).

The management concern for renewable resources, such as fisheries, lies in ensuring that the rate and type of consumption do not threaten the overall population viability. Hence we find rules for not taking juveniles (i.e., allowing fish to reach reproductive age) and take limits (making sure the total size of the population does not become too small). The key idea underlying management of renewable resources is sustainably using the resource, managing the optimum yield of the resource so that it remains productive over the longer term.

The main concern with nonrenewable resources, by contrast, is one of allocating a finite amount. "Sustainable use" makes little sense in this context because the resource will eventually be used up. The major problem is inefficient use as people race to get their share as quickly as possible. Hence management of nonrenewable resources generally concentrates not on rate of extraction but on ensuring equitable allocation of the depletable resource between competitors (for example, between and among those who would like to mine or drill for coal, petroleum or gold and those who would like the resource left in place to promote environmental values).

A second category of natural resources may be classified as *ecosystem services*, described *supra* at page 18. These are the streams of services provided by natural systems, including water purification, biodegradation, flood protection, pollination, climate stability, protection from ultraviolet radiation, and others. These services are not extracted or harvested. We rely on them every day and they are, quite literally, indispensable to human life and well-being. Because no markets exist to trade these services, they have no price and, in the commercial market, apparently no value. Ecosystem services may be thought of as renewable resources. The key to protecting these public goods, then, lies in creating market mechanisms and regulatory instruments that explicitly value and conserve services at sustainable levels.

A final category may be described as *spiritual or aesthetic resources.* These would include a particular mountain, scenic vista, national park, or a soaring bald eagle. We don't "use" these resources, in the sense that in appreciating them we don't extract or consume them, but they provide us a sense of well-being and connectedness nonetheless. The challenge in managing spiritual and aesthetic resources lies in maintaining their special status while allowing public access. In the case of national parks, for example, unrestricted public access can diminish everyone's enjoyment. There aren't a lot of happy faces sitting in traffic jams in the Yosemite Valley. With such "congestible goods," open access reduces the value of others' experience. At the same time, the special nature of the resource requires that we provide some level of access so that people can enjoy it. The proper level of access for national parks, lands that "belong to everyone," is as much a political as economic or scientific decision and, in this respect, mirrors the management goal of equitable allocation for extractive resources.

The chart below summarizes these categories in broad brush strokes. Note how many of the management challenges overlap. Consider, as well, how a single resource may fit into more than one category and how that multiplies the management challenges. A forest, for example, can be managed as a renewable extractive resource, an aesthetic resource and a source of ecosystem services.

RESOURCE CATEGORY		EXAMPLES	PRIMARY MANAGEMENT CHALLENGES
EXTRACTIVE	*Nonrenewable*	Coal, Oil, Copper	Provide incentives for further development; equitable allocation
	Renewable	Fish, Timber, Soil, Groundwater	Ensure sustainable yield; equitable allocation
ECOSYSTEM SERVICES		Pollination, Water purification, Flood control, Climate stability	Public goods – markets do not capture value of services; few explicit legal protections
SPIRITUAL / AESTHETIC		Scenic vistas, Mount Denali, Yellowstone	Congestible goods – ensure use of, and equitable access to, at levels that don't diminish value of experience

B.   CLASH OF VALUES AMONG COMPETING INTERESTS

As should be evident both by the earlier discussion of why we should protect natural resources and the example of Hetch Hetchy, competition over scarce natural resources inevitably causes a clash of competing interests. Resource managers must make the difficult decision over whose interest, whose competing right to the resource, prevails. Complicating matters, many of the protected interests in resource conflicts do not have a voice of their own or, for that matter, are not even human. But consideration of non-human interests poses its own challenges. To paraphrase the Lorax of Dr. Seuss, who should speak for the trees? And how should nonhuman interests be balanced against those of people? The spotted owl conflict in the Pacific Northwest has pitted environmentalists against logging communities, with loggers complaining that environmental groups care more about birds than people. While "win-win" compromises can sometimes be found, the different values of the interested parties, the different ways in which environmental problems impact people, and the scientific uncertainty that often surrounds key facts make many conflicts inevitable.

To someone new to natural resources law, it may seem odd that our wildlife conservation laws protect endangered species, such as the Stephens' Kangaroo rat, that many people would consider pests, at best. It may give one pause to realize that our natural resource management laws require protection of parks and refuges that few people will ever visit. The simplest explanation of these observations is that there is clearly something going on beyond the classic protection of human health and economic interests that drives the pollution laws. If you think back to the earlier section on environmental ethics, all of the perspectives were rights-based. The problem with a rights-based perspective, though, is that rights trump. If one group believes X is morally right and another that X is wrong, there's little room for compromise. The challenge to natural resource managers, then, is more than simply cutting up the natural resources pie in equal slices. They must determine *how* best to mediate among competing perspectives. As a result, and in significant contrast to pollution laws, much natural resource legislation is concerned primarily with rules for decision making.

C.   Problems of the Commons

Imagine you are a shepherd who grazes twenty sheep on a village common. Along with your pan pipe and bag lunch, you take your flock to the common every day. So long as the number of sheep on the common remains small, the grass in the common remains plentiful. Life is good. Assume, though, that shepherds from over the mountain have heard of the wonderful grass in the common and bring their flocks. Things are starting to get crowded. With each hour these sheep graze, less grass is available for future grazing. In fact, you realize, this increased level of grazing will soon nibble the grass down to the roots, resulting in not enough forage in the future for *anyone's* flock, including your own. Yet you and the other shepherds will likely continue to allow your sheep to graze, leading to an overgrazed common. Why?

The answer lies in economic incentives. The more the sheep graze, the more valuable they will be when they come to market. You could stop your flock's grazing, of course, to try to preserve the pasture for future grazing; but there is no guarantee your fellow shepherds will be similarly conscientious. As a result, you may well encourage your sheep to graze as much as possible, and your neighbors will do the same. "Might as well get the grass in my sheep's tummies before it disappears in others'," you think. The result is individually rational in the short term—if the resource will be depleted, you might as well ensure you get your fair share—but collectively disastrous in the long term. It would have been far better for each shepherd to restrain her flock's grazing but, when each seeks to maximize immediate economic gain, long term economic—and environmental—collapse is ensured.

This phenomenon, known as "the tragedy of the commons," is a fundamental, inherent challenge for many natural resources because they have similar open access qualities. Farmers will race to pump water from an underground aquifer, fishing boats with ever larger nets will chase fewer and fewer fish, and wildcat drillers will race to pump out oil as fast as they can. In each case, individually rational behavior is collectively deficient. Individuals' personal incentives work against the best long-term management solution.

So what can be done? Perhaps you could negotiate with all the shepherds and collectively agree to graze less. This may work when there are a handful of shepherds who all come from the same village. But it becomes increasingly difficult to agree as the number of shepherds increases (and more difficult still if they come from different places without shared cultural norms). This obstacle is known as a "collective action" problem and is due to the increased transaction costs in negotiating solutions as the number of parties increases. At a certain point, it's simply too difficult to reach consensus agreement. To see this in action, try to decide which movie to see with more than three friends.

Perhaps, as a last resort, in frustration at the inability to agree on a common solution, some of you decide to stop grazing your flock so that the grass on the common can grow back. Noble intent, no doubt, but there is a risk that other shepherds will take advantage of your generosity and keep their sheep on the common. More food for their flocks, they may smirk, while the common continues to be grazed. These shepherds benefiting from your sacrifice are known as "free riders." The similar phenomenon might occur even if all the shepherds agreed to graze less. Some new shepherd might come in and start grazing all the time, free-riding off of your agreement. Thus any solution to commons problems must overcome both the high transaction costs in reaching agreement among many parties (collective action) and counterproductive behavior by parties outside the agreement (free riders).

Given these management difficulties, one might well ask why we have natural resource commons at all. In some cases, commons cannot be avoided because of the physical nature of the resource. It cannot easily be subdivided into private property (think of underground aquifers or fisheries). In this regard, it's worth noting that physical commons can change over time because of technology. The invention of barbed wire allowed landholders in the West to fence off their land from grazing cattle. Before the cheap and easy-to-use barbed wire, there was no economical means to fence off huge properties. Similarly, fifty years ago, the television airwaves were a commons. Anyone could receive a signal and watch a TV station's program. With the development of scrambling technology, however, stations could send signals that could only be viewed through the use of a purchased box that unscrambled the signal.

In some cases, the resource may be so important that everyone must be able to use it. Imagine the effect on commerce if the public lacked general navigable rights on surface water. Similarly, the public interest in recreation or culture ensures that sea shores and national parks are generally managed for open access. Finally, we may want to keep a resource as a common because any other management regime would change its very nature. That is, for some resources, such as wildlife, what we appreciate about the resource is that it is common. If we privatized and collared animals, they would no longer be wild.

As with the different types of resources described above, to craft effective resource management strategies we need a clear sense of the types of problems commons present. The most obvious problem is scarcity—not enough resources for everyone to use—that leads to over-using the resource because each person does not take into account the impact of her appropriation and amount. This raises management challenges of allocation. Less obvious, but equally important, commons raise problems of provision because people are reluctant to invest in the resource out of concern that others will free-ride. In the case of fisheries, for example, individuals can under-invest in maintaining the stock. Individual fishers may be unwilling to pay to restock the fish (since others who are not paying will catch many of the released hatchery fish). They may not commit the resources to study the population structure (and therefore know how to regulate the harvest to ensure a maximum sustainable yield) or research diseases harming the fishery. Given these different types of problems, it should be clear that there is no single solution to the tragedy of the commons. We will explore the range of policy responses in more detail at page 69.

D. MARKET FORCES AND MARKET FAILURES

The market obviously has a huge impact on the management of natural resources. Why do industries extract copper from the ground or timber from forests? The simple answer is that there is demand for these resources, that supplies of these resources are limited, and that resource producers are often able to profit by selling them on the market.

But markets are not simply passive places of exchange. The prices of goods in markets send strong messages that direct people's behavior. As Adam Smith observed, this can promote the common good in many cases. But if, for example, the market prices of natural resources do not accurately reflect their full cost to society, then resource management can be directed in socially harmful ways.

In some cases, natural resource pricing causes problems because there is no market for the goods. Try to buy some clean air. Sure, you can buy real estate in the wilds of Alaska where the air is clean, but you own the land there, not the air. In fact, your neighbor can breathe it right after it blows through. Environmental amenities, such as clean air and water, are sometimes called "public goods." Their benefits can be shared by everyone, but owned by no one. No one owns the air. No one can sell it or prevent others from using it. So what is it worth? Perhaps surprisingly, in the eyes of the market it is not worth anything because it is free. There is no market to exchange public goods and, as a result, they have no price. This explains the riddle of why pollution does not become expensive as clean air is "used up." Because there's no market for clean air, there are no price signals to indicate its increasing scarcity or to drive the price up and discourage overconsumption.

Subsidies cause another kind of market problem. Suppose, for example, that the market price of gold equaled the cost of producing the gold. A mining company would have little incentive to develop the mine. But suppose that the government subsidized gold production by providing special tax incentives, waiving royalty payments, or directly subsidizing production costs. In this situation, a mine might be opened even if the market price of gold would not support it. As described earlier, subsidies have commonly been used to encourage natural resource development. Recall, for example, that in the nineteenth century Congress granted vast swathes of public lands to encourage agriculture, mining and other development. To encourage further Westward expansion, railroads were granted millions of acres of alternating sections of public lands. As note 7 at page 49 in the *Questions and Discussion* section below describes, federal subsidy of resource extraction continues today. This encourages more extraction of resources than the market, left alone, would support. We also give indirect subsidies. For example, the government in the past has granted flood relief to those who destroyed wetlands. The development of barrier islands has only been possible because of government-built roads. Development on these same barrier islands is encouraged by a government-subsidized "beach nourishment" program, dumping sand and sand bags to literally hold back the tide.

Perhaps most important, the market price may be too low because of externalities. Even when we do charge for natural resources, many values are left out. Assume, for example, you have moved on from the trampled and scraggly common and now own a mountain pasture above a populated valley. The main source of water for the valley's towns flows through your pasture. When you balance your financial books, you notice something odd. In figuring out your bottom line, you set off your income from wool sold against your costs to operate (such as labor, medicine for the sheep, pan pipes, and so on). But what about the reduction of fish downstream because of the silting of the river caused by your sheep eroding the stream bank? What about people who have had to miss work because they got sick drinking the water polluted by sheep droppings? Make no mistake, your grazing is causing real costs but, as described above, because clean water is a public good you do not have to pay for it. The stream acts as a sink for your grazing pollution at no cost. As a result, in seeking to maximize short-term economic gain, you "overuse" the stream and continue grazing your sheep alongside it. The costs from fewer fish, lost work days, and polluted water in the valley are very real, but they are external to the costs you currently pay to operate. These costs are borne by the public and known as "externalities."

If, on the other hand, you have to pay for the external harm your grazing causes, then you will likely change your behavior. This would incorporate the full costs into the market value of your resource and you might find it cheaper to fence off the stream to keep your sheep away from it. The process for forcing you to recognize the environmental and social costs caused by your activities is known as *internalizing externalities* and reflects a basic lesson of economics—when we have to pay more for something, we use less of it than if it is free. By internalizing externalities, we correct the market failure by charging for environmental harms and providing more accurate price signals to buyers.

Just as the grazing example demonstrated negative externalities (i.e., social costs that are not reflected in the market price), there are, of course, positive externalities, as well (where social benefits are not reflected in the market price). The market price of a wetland, for example, is its real estate price based on location and the potential for development. The price assuredly does not include the social benefits provided by the wetlands, such as flood control, water purification, and habitat for young fish. Our earlier discussion of ecosystem services described social benefits provided by public goods. All of these are positive externalities.

If all environmental externalities were internalized—both positive and negative—then more environmentally harmful products and processes would be relatively more costly and the market would reinforce environmental protection. One remaining problem, of course, is setting the right price for externalities. Even if we had the authority to charge shepherds for the damage their grazing caused, how much would that be? What is the monetary benefit provided by a specific wetland in terms of flood protection and water purification? As with clean air, there are no markets for environmental harms or goods, thus their costs must be estimated. Another stumbling block is the public's resistance to tax increases of any kind, much less "environmental taxes." One of the key goals of environmental law is to bring environmental externalities into the market and we discuss policy instruments to internalize externalities at page 69.

*[handwritten margin note: ** Market-based env'l protection]*

E. SCIENTIFIC UNCERTAINTY

Scientific uncertainty is an inescapable aspect of natural resource management. Most natural resource and environmental problems involve complex technical and economic issues. But lawmakers rarely have anything approximating perfect knowledge when asked to make specific decisions. Scientific certainty may come too late, if ever, to design optimal legal and policy responses.

In fact, uncertainties over the magnitude of environmental problems, their causes, and future impacts bedevil law and policy. What we would like to know as policy makers rarely approaches our actual knowledge. But if we do not understand well the current situation, then how can we predict the future impacts of our laws and policies?

In the context of climate change, for example, the detailed mechanisms of global warming are still only partly understood. Will increases in the earth's temperature lead to greater cloud formation, acting as a negative feedback to warming? Are measured temperature increases over the last century due to increased carbon in the atmosphere, the onset of an unrelated global warming trend, or a combination of the two? If atmospheric carbon dioxide concentrations continue to increase, what will the mean global temperature be in 20, 40 and 140 years, and what will this mean for sea levels?

All of these questions bear directly on our decisions today to regulate emissions of greenhouse gases or introduce carbon taxes. The Intergovernmental Panel on Climate Change has provided conclusions based on the judgment of over 2,000 scientists researching these issues from around the globe, but no one can claim with certainty that these conclusions are correct. They are simply the best consensus estimates we have.

Troubling levels of uncertainty are present when conserving natural resources, as well. Perhaps developers have proposed setting aside an acre beside a new mall to provide habitat for an endangered salamander population. Will an acre provide sufficient habitat for its survival? Is the main reason for the salamander population's collapse loss of habitat or, rather, predation by feral cats? We do not know enough about the salamander's life history or recent population declines to be certain. The same dilemma faces fishery management where, in setting fishing quotas, agency officials must find the "true" state of the population amidst conflicting claims of fishers who say their catches are going up and marine biologists whose modeling (based on less data than they'd like) predicts the stock is close to crashing.

Another source of uncertainty lies in the complex interrelations among causes of environmental harms. Environmental problems often have multiple causes and addressing one cause may have little effect or, even worse, exacerbate another problem. Rather than resulting from a single, identifiable action, many environmental harms are caused by cumulative, multiple actions. This makes disentangling causation a difficult undertaking. Take the example of endangered salmon in the Pacific Northwest. Why are so many stocks collapsing? One can point to overfishing, damming of rivers, logging practices that lead to erosion and silt in the rivers, pollution, and over-reliance on hatchery fish. Good luck figuring out how much relative harm each one contributes. To conserve and restore salmon populations, we must address most, if not all, of these causes, yet there is enormous debate over which particular action will be most effective. And solving one problem may simply cause it to reappear in another guise.

Consider, for example, Bob Adler's assessment of uncertainty in environmental restoration efforts:

> A large degree of real-world experimentation may be necessary to test which restoration strategies are effective, usually under variable conditions that can cloud experimental results with additional uncertainty, due to both natural and artificial changes. Did fish return to a particular stretch of river this year because of increased flows from the upstream dam (the restoration action), or was it because of an unusually large supply of food (environmental variability)? Did fish continue to decline because the restoration action (more water) was ill-conceived, or because of polluted runoff from a new construction project?

ROBERT W. ADLER, RESTORING COLORADO RIVER ECOSYSTEMS: A TROUBLED SENSE OF IMMENSITY 11 (2007)

Judgments over the "true" state of the resource drive policy and legal responses. In the climate change debate, global warming skeptics argue that scientific uncertainty counsels prudence. The "problem" of global warming has not been rigorously established and our limited knowledge of atmospheric physics severely restricts our ability to predict future temperatures or climates. And even if global warming is happening, there are enormous unknowns over how much warming will occur and at what rate. If the threat of global warming turns out to have been an exaggerated threat, then actions taken today to reduce fossil fuel consumption will have been an overreaction. Spending money to reduce fossil fuel use, they argue, will have caused more harm than good because of increased unemployment and diversion of resources away from other worthy causes. The best response is more research and development. After all, how can one craft an effective policy without understanding the problem we're trying to solve?

The obvious response to such an argument is that waiting for more scientific certainty, if it ever comes, imposes costs of its own. In the face of a credible and significant threat, the opposing argument goes, we must act today so as to avoid the present and future harms (which may well be greater) imposed by delay. To employ a nautical metaphor, we should be bailing water out of our sinking ship as fast a possible, not standing on the deck and studying the angle and rate of descent.

The same dynamic is at work in the example of the endangered salamander. Delay for further study of the salamander may lead to greater understanding, but of a now-extinct species. Yet, as the voices of caution warn, overreaction imposes its own real costs in the form of foregone development and public monies that would have been better spent elsewhere. In these and countless other examples, there are good reasons to wait and reduce the uncertainty, and good reasons to avoid potential future costs by acting now. Thus perhaps the first question of natural resource law and policy is how to act in the face of uncertainty.

There are two basic strategies to address this intractable problem. The first is to develop better information. Many natural resource statutes require generation of considerable information to provide a surer basis on which to create policy. A second strategy, known as the precautionary principle, effectively shifts the burden of proof from those who would challenge the offending activity to those who wish to continue the activity. This shift in burden could shorten the time period between when a threat to the environment is recognized and a legal response is developed.

In the climate change context, for example, the burden would fall on oil companies to establish that global warming is not a serious and credible threat. In the salamander example, the developer would shoulder the burden of proving that the loss of habitat will not threaten the salamander's survival. This shift in burden changes the tenor and nature of the debate over how well understood the problem must be before taking action. But it does not shed light on an equally important question—how serious the problem must be before taking action, much less the appropriate action to take. These are fundamentally political, not scientific, questions and they pose additional levels of uncertainty.

QUESTIONS AND DISCUSSION

1. Do you see how the tragedy of the commons can be explained as a problem of negative externalities? How would you explain overfishing to someone as an externality problem?

2. Drawing on the table of resource categories described at page 38, how would you categorize the following natural resources?

- Biodiversity
- The human genome
- Fossils
- The ozone layer

To what extent do these share the same management challenges?

3. *Revisiting the Commons:* The model of the tragedy of the commons described in Section C (most famously set out in an article by Garrett

Hardin in 1968) paints a bleak picture of the world. As Hardin bluntly asserted, economic incentives make overconsumption inevitable. "Therein is the tragedy. Each man is locked into a system that compels him to increase his herd without limit—in a world that is limited. Ruin is the destination toward which all men rush, each pursuing his own interest in a society that believes in the freedom of the commons." Garrett Hardin, *The Tragedy of the Commons*, 162 SCIENCE 1243, 1244 (1968). While tremendously influential, Hardin's conclusions have been subject to heavy criticism, as well. Are resource commons necessarily tragic?

In thinking about this important question, it's helpful to consider the unstated assumptions at play in the tragedy of the commons. The most important is that individuals are unable to reach agreement and impose constraints on their behavior. This occurs in part because it is assumed that (1) selfish behavior for short term-benefit is rational, in part because (2) absent government there are no effective constraints on behavior, and in part because (3) the resource is truly open access. Each of these assumptions is open to challenge, however.

Research by Elinor Ostrom and others has identified many examples of commons from around the world that have worked well and endured for centuries, from communal fishing grounds of the Maori in New Zealand and grazing in Switzerland to irrigation systems in Spain and the Philippines. Described as "common-pool resources," these self-governing commons are not open access. Unlike the grazing commons described above, in these cases, even without government intervention, there is decentralized enforcement and relatively clear assignment of property rights. The key factor in such common-pool resources is that informal operational rules are in place, accepted by the users and open to collective change over time. Critically (and again, without government intervention), use of the resource is monitored and those who violate the shared norms (broadly accepted rules) are subject to graduated sanctions.

In a well-studied example of such a common-pool resource, for example, the lobstermen on Monhegan Island, Maine, have well-understood, informal rules for who may place lobster traps where, when, and how many. If these rules are violated, low-level sanctions include moving traps and cutting buoys. The allocation of fishing locations reflects standing in the community, kinship, fishing skill, etc. Most assuredly, the lobster grounds are not open access resources and it is the ability of the community to keep out other fishers and police the resource that makes the common-pool resource sustainable.

Do these "comedy of the commons" examples share certain similarities? In what types of resource conflicts do you suspect these non-legal arrangements will fail to be effective?

See generally JAMES M. ACHESON, THE LOBSTER GANGS OF MAINE (1988); BONNIE J. MCCAY & JAMES M. ACHESON, EDS., THE QUESTION OF THE COMMONS: THE CULTURE AND ECOLOGY OF COMMUNAL RESOURCES (1987); ELINOR OSTROM, GOVERNING THE COMMONS (1990); Carol Rose, *The Comedy of the Commons: Custom, Commerce, and Inherently Public Property*, 53 U. CHI. L. REV. 711 (1986); ROBERT C. ELLICKSON, ORDER WITHOUT LAW: HOW NEIGHBORS SETTLE

DISPUTES (1991); JOHN BADEN AND DOUGLAS NOONAN, EDS. MANAGING THE COMMONS (1998).

4. Convincing users of a commons to reduce their use is almost always difficult. Those asked to cut back want a credible commitment that they— and not someone else—will reap the fruit of their sacrifice, that there will not be free riders. This explains why the examples in Note 3 above are so important. Elinor Ostrom and others have shown that users can be persuaded to restrict their use of the commons, but only if they are convinced that the governing institutions will be stable and effective.

As Brigham Daniels has pointed out, however, this necessary stability can also result in unintended negative consequences, and more often than we might think. Brigham Daniels, *Emerging Commons and Tragic Institutions*, 37 ENVTL. L. 515 (2007). This is most likely to occur when a commons potentially has multiple uses and can serve multiple values. In such cases, the stable governing institutions of a commons, intended to manage the resource for a particular use or value, may actively thwart those wishing to pursue alternate values. In this way, stability suddenly becomes rigidity.

Thus, for example, while the legislation governing the Alaska National Wildlife Reserve (ANWR) may effectively ensure its scenic, recreational, and wildlife values, it blocks oil exploration and other resource extraction. Changing this regime has proven extremely difficult because vested interests (in this case, conservation groups) are unwilling to shift the status quo. The roles were reversed in the example of forest management, where a single-minded focus on timber harvests squeezed out scenic, recreational, and wildlife values for decades until sufficient political pressure forced a change in governance.

Can you think of other instances where maximizing a particular value of a commons resource may interfere with and block other values the commons could provide?

5. In one of the most widely-cited law review articles of all time, University of Chicago economist Ronald Coase challenged the idea that pollution or other such harms caused by property uses were externalities problems. As Coase theorized, the real problem was one of transaction costs. "The question is commonly thought of as one in which A inflicts harm on B and what has to be decided is how should we restrain A? But this is wrong. We are dealing with a problem of reciprocal nature. To avoid the harm to B would inflict harm on A. The real question that has to be decided is: should A be allowed to harm B or should B be allowed to harm A?" R.H. Coase, *The Problem of Social Cost*, 3 J. LAW & ECON. 1, 2 (1960). Coase argued that no matter who was initially assigned the right to inflict harm, if "the pricing system is assumed to work smoothly (that is, costlessly)," the ultimate allocation of resources will be the same. *Id*. at 6. In other words, with perfect information about real costs and benefits of the competing property uses, the parties would be able to negotiate a socially optimal allocation without the need for a tax or regulation to mandate internalization of the externalities. Of course, said Coase, it was "a very unrealistic assumption" to assume there were no costs to a market transaction. *Id*. at 15.

> In order to carry out a market transaction it is necessary to discover who it is
> that one wishes to deal with, to inform people that one wishes to deal and on
> what terms, to conduct negotiations leading up to a bargain, to draw up the
> contract, to undertake the inspection needed to make sure that the terms of the
> contract are being observed, and so on. These operations are often extremely
> costly, sufficiently costly at any rate to prevent many transactions that would
> be carried out in a world in which the pricing system worked without cost.

Id. Thus, concluded Coase, the real market failure is not the failure to
internalize externalities but the inability to eliminate transaction costs. As
Coase saw it then, " 'externalities' are a joint product of 'polluter' and
'victim,' and ... a legal rule that arbitrarily assigns blame to one of the
parties only gives the right result if that party happens to be the one who
can avoid the problem at the lower cost." David Friedman, *How to Think
About Pollution or, Why Ronald Coase Deserved the Nobel Prize*, LIBERTY 5,
no. 3, 55–59 (1992).

6.   Will the market reflect important externalities? This debate has played
out publicly in response to concerns over scarcity. In 1980, in an unusual
dispute resolution process, academics Julian Simon and Paul Ehrlich made
a bet. In a $1,000 wager, Simon asked Ehrlich to choose any five commodi-
ties whose price would increase in real terms over the coming decade. If
their prices rose, Simon would pay $1,000. If they fell, Ehrlich would pay
$1,000. The bet seemed a fair test since basic supply and demand would
dictate that as resources become scarce their price will rise. Ehrlich and his
colleagues chose copper, chrome, nickel, tin, and tungsten. In 1990, Ehrlich
sent Simon a check in the mail. Three of the five metals had dropped in
price since 1980.

Simon trumpeted the results of this wager, arguing it proved the
correctness of "technology optimists" who contend that resource scarcity is
simply an artificial construct and that humans will always find more
efficient ways to extract resources and develop substitutes. They believe
that technology ultimately will solve our environmental problems. On the
other hand, technology pessimists such as Ehrlich point out the perils of
technology and the unintended environmental impacts whenever we try to
solve our problems solely through this strategy. What did the bet between
Ehrlich and Simon prove? Are the technology pessimists wrong? Was
choosing the relative market price of commodities over a time period an
accurate measure of resource depletion? What real costs would not be
captured in the market price for a commodity?

Simon attempted to follow up his wager with a bet for the 1990s,
challenging Ehrlich to choose any trend pertaining to material human
welfare that will get worse rather than improve by the year 2000. As
examples, Simon suggested life expectancy, the price of a natural resource,
some measure of air or water pollution, or the number of telephones per
person. In response, Ehrlich and his colleagues offered to wager that within
ten years ozone levels, global temperatures, the gap in wealth between the
richest and poorest 10% of humanity, and AIDS deaths will rise, while
human sperm counts, the amount of fertile cropland, rain forest acreage,
rice and wheat production and the fisheries harvest will fall. Simon rejected
these trends as too indirectly related to human welfare. Do you agree?

Mark Sagoff has argued that while resource scarcity may not be the problem we once thought it was, we still consume too much if consumption becomes an end in itself and severs our ties with the natural world. *See* Mark Sagoff, *Do We Consume Too Much?*, THE ATLANTIC MONTHLY, June 1997, at 80. In a reply to Sagoff, Paul Erhlich criticized Sagoff for his failure to consider the impact of consumption on ecosystem services. *See* Paul Ehrlich et al., *No Middle Way on the Environment*, THE ATLANTIC MONTHLY, Dec. 1997, at 98.

7. As the text indicates, one market-oriented approach for resource conservation or environmental protection is to curtail subsidies. There is no shortage of targets, from fisheries, water and hard rock mining to oil and gas extraction and timber. As an example, consider the Forest Service's timber sale program. The Forest Service has traditionally spent more each year to administer the program than it collected in revenues from timber sales on public lands. In 1997 the Forest Service stated it lost $88 million and in 1998 it lost $126 million. In addition, the Forest Service spent on the order of $50 million each year to build logging roads for the timber companies. It is estimated that the Forest Service has constructed more than 377,000 miles of logging roads, eight times longer than the national highway system. The General Accounting Office estimates that the timber subsidy from 1992–1997 approached $2 billion. *See* http://www.fs.fed.us/forestmanagement/reports/tspirs/index.shtml; MAJORITY STAFF REPORT OF THE HOUSE SUBCOMMITTEE ON OVERSIGHT AND INVESTIGATIONS OF THE COMM. ON NATURAL RESOURCES, 103rd Cong., 2d Sess., TAKING FROM THE TAXPAYER: PUBLIC SUBSIDIES FOR NATURAL RESOURCE DEVELOPMENT (1994).

8. In considering whether the precautionary principle can practically resolve instances of scientific uncertainty, ask yourself whether Sri Lankan policy-makers in the coral reef example discussed at page 11 should be more concerned about the impact of a conservation rule on the local community or on the coral reef? Is there any reason why caution might be more appropriate in one context than another? Does your answer depend in part on whether you think the ecological community is replaceable?

As another example, consider the practice of the State of Montana and the National Park Service of killing bison that leave the boundaries of Yellowstone National Park because they may carry a contagious bacterial disease known as brucellosis. Cattle ranchers are concerned that bison may transmit the disease to their livestock. Brucellosis causes cattle to abort their fetuses, thereby reducing their reproductive rates. Even more commercially important, many states and countries will not accept cattle from states where livestock may be infected with brucellosis, and states work very hard to be sure that their livestock are certified as "brucellosis-free." The ranchers and some others have also expressed concern that the brucellosis may then be transmitted to humans (and cause what is known as undulant fever). The view of most scientists is that the risk of transmission from bison to cattle is very low and the risk of transmission to humans even lower. Bison in captivity have transmitted brucellosis to cattle but there are not any documented cases of transmission in the wild. Which way does the precautionary principle cut in this case? *See generally* Peter

Morrisette, *Is There Room for Free–Roaming Bison in Greater Yellowstone?*, 27 ECOLOGY L.Q. 467 (2000).

Cass Sunstein has been quite critical of the Precautionary Principle. He argues that cost-benefit balancing holds significant advantages over the Precautionary Principle. The cost-benefit balancing he envisions is not a mere efficiency analysis but a broader analysis of trade-offs to identify the interests at stake. Do you agree with his assertions below?

> It is tempting to object that the Precautionary Principle is hopelessly vague. How much precaution is the right amount of precaution? By itself, the principle does not tell us. It is also tempting to object, as I have suggested, that the principle is cost-blind. Some precautions simply aren't worthwhile. But the most serious problem lies elsewhere. The real problem is that the principle offers no guidance—not that it is wrong, but that it forbids all courses of action, including regulation. It bans the very steps that it requires. . . .
>
> [C]onsider the case of genetic modification of food. Many people believe that a failure to allow genetic modification might well result in numerous deaths, and a small probability of many more. The reason is that genetic modification holds out the promise of producing food that is both cheaper and healthier—resulting, for example, in "golden rice," which might have large benefits in developing countries. My point is not that the benefits of genetic modifications will likely have those benefits, or that the benefits of genetic modification outweigh the risks. The claim is only that if the Precautionary Principle is taken literally, it is offended by regulation as well as by nonregulation.

CASS SUNSTEIN, LAWS OF FEAR: BEYOND THE PRECAUTIONARY PRINCIPLE 26–29 (2005).

9. Given the inherent uncertainty in managing complex natural systems, there have been strong calls for a more dynamic management approach that flexibly adjusts over time in response to new information and the results of past management efforts. Called "adaptive management," this management approach was developed by C.S. Holling in a 1970s book titled *Adaptive Environmental Assessment and Management* (1978). As Professor J.B. Ruhl describes,

> Holling and his fellow researchers found conventional environmental management methods at odds with the emerging model of ecosystem dynamics. They focused on four basic properties of ecological systems to provide the premises of a new management method. First, although the parts of ecological systems are connected, not all parts are strongly or intimately connected with all other parts. It cannot possibly be the case, for example, that every species in an ecosystem depends for its survival on the survival of every other species. The connections within ecosystems are themselves selective and variable, meaning what should be measured will depend on our understanding of the way the system as a whole works. Second, events are not uniform over space, meaning that impacts of development do not gradually dilute with distance from the development. In particular, induced effects of developments such as pipelines and water reservoirs may be of greatest magnitude at distant points. Third, ecological systems exhibit multi-equilibrium states between which the system may move for unpredictable reasons, in unpredictable manners, and at unpredictable times. Small variations in conditions such as temperature, nutrient content, or species composition can "flip" ecosystems into vastly different behavioral states, sometimes well after the event that started the reaction. The upshot is that the unexpected can happen, and it will be difficult to predict

when, where, and to what degree. Finally, Holling's group observed that because ecosystems are not static but in continual change, environmental quality is not achieved by eliminating change. Flood, fire, heat, cold, drought, and storm continually test ecosystems, enhancing resilience through system "self-correction." Efforts to suppress change are thus not only futile, but counter-productive.

Under this model of ecosystems, they concluded, management policy must put a premium on collecting information, establishing measurements of success, monitoring outcomes, using new information to adjust existing approaches, and a willingness to change. Whereas resourcists and preservationists have battled to "lock in" positions through fixed rules and standards and preserve every inch of incremental ground gained, an adaptive management framework is more experimentalist, relying on iterative cycles of goal determination, performance standard setting, outcome monitoring, and standard recalibration. This brand of adaptive management has evolved well beyond an idea, as FWS [U.S. Fish and Wildlife Service] and NMFS [National Marine Fisheries Service] have portrayed adaptive management as an important practical tool that "can assist the Services and the applicant in developing an adequate operating conservation program and improving its effectiveness." Indeed, there is broad consensus today among resource managers and academics that adaptive management is the only practical way to implement ecosystem management.

What practical constraints do you expect the National Park Service or Forest Service would face in applying adaptive management to their decision making? *See* J.B. Ruhl, *A Manifesto for the Radical Middle*, 38 IDAHO L. REV. 385, 402–403 (2002); *see also* Bradley C. Karkkainen, *Collaborative Ecosystem Governance: Scale, Complexity, and Dynamism*, VIRGINIA ENVTL. L.J. 189, 200–01 (2002).

F. SCALE

To this point, we have described natural resource management problems under the assumption that the resources are managed by a political jurisdiction whose authority matches the biophysical scale of the resource. This is a helpful simplification for teaching basic concepts such as the tragedy of the commons but, unfortunately, is usually not the case in real life. Problems of scale (or, more accurately, mismatching scales) are inescapable in natural resource management. They arise along three separate dimensions: biophysical, political, and temporal.

1. BIOPHYSICAL SCALE

Biophysical scale presents challenges of uncertainty and optimization. Consider the difficulty, for example, of determining the range of the endangered (and highly migratory) Southern bluefin tuna, delineating the boundaries of a groundwater aquifer, or establishing the minimum habitat necessary to support a population of an endangered wolf species. Any effective management regime will need these types of information to make intelligent decisions, but in practice they come with considerable uncertainties. Moreover, depending on the species, biophysical scales overlap. The range of a grizzly will encompass the ranges of many other mammals, birds, and insects. One cannot simultaneously manage at all these scales. If one manages primarily for a few species, this can have significant impacts (often negative) on species whose ranges fall within this area. In this context, think about the plea from many environmentalists to preserve old growth timber. If one manages a forest primarily for old growth, a likely consequence is that the habitat will not have a sustainable distribution of age classes. This can, ironically, reduce the area's biodiversity as a result.

2. POLITICAL SCALE

Natural boundaries rarely track political boundaries. A map of the western United States shows states and counties with straight lines and right angles. Map the region's watersheds, ecosystems, or forests, however, and nary a straight line will appear. Ecological concerns were, not surprisingly, far from the politicians' and surveyors' minds when these political jurisdictions were created, but the mismatch of natural and political scales poses challenges for natural resource management.

Consider a migratory goose whose flyway traverses Canada and the United States. Draining or filling prairie potholes in Kansas may benefit local farmers but imperil migratory birds along their entire flyway. As another illustration, the Colorado River flows through seven states, past various Indian reservations, and over an international border. Its watershed covers approximately 242,000 square miles in the United States and 3,000 square miles in Mexico. In this zero sum game, the more water used by one jurisdiction the less water available for others. Those downstream with greatest cause for concern do not live in the areas where their concerns could be most effectively expressed. The downstream jurisdictions rarely have political authority over the upstream users. As a result of these geographical "spillovers" across political jurisdictions, natural resource management presents problems of collective action (high transaction costs to bring differing parties together), equitable distribution (ensuring that the parties enjoying the benefits of resource use and protection also bear a share of the costs), and enforcement (monitoring compliance at a distance from the source of authority).

Mismatched political and natural boundaries also pose challenges of management authority. This is often expressed as a problem of federalism. A recurring issue in natural resource law is whether states or the federal government should be the primary manager of natural resources. Recall the basic postulates of our federal system. Following the American revolution the states and/or the people (itself a complex constitutional question) assumed all power held by both crown and parliament in England. They were independent sovereigns over all of the natural resources within their boundaries with full police power to regulate those resources. In the Constitution each state agreed to give up portions of that police power to the federal government.

The ink had barely dried on the Constitution before disputes arose between the states and federal government over the extent of their regulatory power over natural resources. As described in Chapter 2, over the course of the nation's legal history the resolution of these disputes exhibits a rather consistent trend toward increased federal jurisdictional power.

That trend, of course, is manifest across various areas of the law and is largely independent of natural resource management concerns, but it is important to understand why increasing federal jurisdictional control has had independent appeal in natural resource law.

To give one brief example, for the first century of the republic, wildlife regulation was primarily the province of the states. Indeed, at the close of the nineteenth century, in *Geer v. Connecticut*, 161 U.S. 519 (1896), the Supreme Court declared that the states owned the wildlife within their borders. Today, however, the Supreme Court's decision in *Geer* has been overruled and the federal government extensively regulates wildlife, most prominently under the Endangered Species Act (ESA). Why did this happen? Although it is possible to explain the change as just one more example of increasing federal power, it can also be explained by natural resource management concerns. Return for a moment to the migratory goose whose flyway traverses Canada and the United States. From an ecological standpoint, it makes little sense to have bird hunting or the preservation of its habitat decided independently by every state and province in the two countries through which it flies. Do you see how this would be a recipe for a tragedy of the commons? Why should a state set aside land or restrict hunting for migratory bird protection if other states will free ride, develop their land, and still allow hunting? Restricting state authority over wildlife helps prevent this market failure by conforming jurisdictional scale with biophysical scale.

In other instances, however, the broader trend toward federal jurisdictional control may not be so clearly consistent with sound natural resource management. Consider the wonderfully-named endangered insect, the Delhi Sands Flower–Loving Fly (discussed in a case study in Chapter 4). It lives in only one place, San Bernardino County, California, yet within at least three overlapping political jurisdictions. Who should regulate the fly? Is the fly's continued existence a matter of national interest, California's interest, or should it be an issue primarily for San Bernardino County's zoning officials to decide? In contrast to the migratory bird, the jurisdictional dilemma is not a function of the fly's movement but of a federalism that creates concentric circles of jurisdictional control.

Federalism, then, is not simply an abstract question for classroom discussion but a foundational question of proper natural resource management. Answering the legal question of who may regulate only begs the question of who should regulate, and what will be the consequences?

In this vein, consider the saga surrounding the Northern Spotted Owl. Its habitat is largely in timbered land in the states of Washington, Oregon, and California. Although the owl can range across state lines, most dwell within a single state. Some live on National Park and National Forest lands, others on state lands, and others on private timber farms, or even backyards. As a matter of natural resource management policy, what does the range of the owl suggest for the appropriate scale for management jurisdiction? Should the states or the federal government manage the owls? Should jurisdiction be purely a function of land ownership? Should the Northwest's rural timber communities, who may own no land but whose livelihood depends on how the forest is managed, have any say on whether and how to protect the owl? Perhaps the jurisdiction question should be resolved with reference solely to expertise and competence. But how do we figure out the answer to the competence question? Is it a question of management resources, experience with and proximity to the resource, scientific expertise, or something else? The key point, of course, is that who controls a resource can have a significant impact on how the resource is managed and allocated. And there are no simple answers.

States, and particularly local communities, are typically closer to the problem, often understand it better, and have to live with the consequences of the policy. Moreover, after generations of relying upon a natural resource for their economic and cultural sustenance, whether a forest, grass, or water supplies, locals may well feel a sense of entitlement to continue their use. A rancher's parents, grandparents and great-grandparents may have grazed their herds on the same public land that a far-away official in Washington now wants to fence off from cattle. Does that seem fair?

At the same time, locals are not the only ones with interests in the resource or its use. Harvesting timber, for example, can increase run-off and erosion, resulting in harm to salmon spawning habitat. The impact on the salmon is felt not just locally but by all those who might come into contact with the salmon during its life-cycle, whether tourist or fisher. Even where the harm is geographically localized, to the extent the harm occurs on or to public lands, it is visited upon more than the local community. If public lands are being degraded by over-use, the argument goes, then the federal government has no choice but to restrict use, regardless of local tradition or expectations. More broadly, if the public lands belong to the nation as a whole, shouldn't they be managed at the national level? This conflict has no clear solution and has led in the past to occasionally violent intimidation of federal officials and broad political movements such as "the sagebrush rebellion" in the 1970s and the "wise use" movement today.

Another commonly voiced concern about local control is that local jurisdictions may have an incentive to compete with one another by lowering environmental standards to attract industry. States without timber harvest limitations will attract more logging investment, the argument goes, than those that impose greater restrictions on logging; those that don't require reclamation bonding (financing to pay for restoration of a mining site) will attract more mining than those that do, and so on. Are nationwide standards necessary to halt such environmental "races-to-the-bottom"? Perhaps, though, it's worth considering whether it's just as likely that local jurisdictions will engage in an *upward* race, competing for industry by offering higher environmental quality. In this regard, think of all the communities across the nation advertising their proximity to wilderness and open space. In either case, the difficult question becomes when, if ever, should a state or local community be free to adopt its own natural resource preference? Should it depend whether that preference is upward or downward?

a. Getting Political Scale Right

Efforts to find an appropriate match between biophysical and political scale have been a source of ongoing debate and experimentation. As early as 1890, John Wesley Powell, the famous explorer of the Colorado River and first head of the U.S. Geological Survey, proposed that in the arid western part of the United States political jurisdictions should be organized around watersheds. As Powell saw it, within a watershed there was "a body of interdependent and unified interests and values" where the people have "common interests, common rights, and common duties and must necessarily work together for common purposes." *See* John Wesley Powell, *Institutions for the Arid Lands*, 40 CENTURY 111, 114 (1890); WALLACE STEGNER, ED., JOHN WESLEY POWELL, REPORT ON THE LANDS OF THE ARID REGIONS OF THE UNITED STATES (1962).

Powell's early plea was ignored but with the development of the science of ecology, the last couple of decades have seen a renewed push to look beyond traditional political boundaries in resolving natural resource management issues. In the water area, this renewed effort has followed Powell's insight that the water resource is best managed on a watershed basis. Yet, if there is broad agreement about the wisdom of managing a watershed as a unified whole, there is much less agreement about which jurisdictional entity should have the final say. In recent years an increasing number of watershed stakeholders have formed themselves into variously named watershed groups and councils. Such initiatives are relatively uncontroversial where they focus on voluntary cooperation, consultation, and grants for organizational and technological assistance. But when talk has turned to replacing state or federal control with local watershed group decisionmaking authority, many people's enthusiasm has waned.

At first glance, such opposition may seem contrary to the basic goal of matching political and biophysical scale, but opponents of local watershed control may be advocating management on a larger biophysical scale that would capture the positive and negative externalities generated by watershed use. Or, more concerned about politics, they may fear that decisionmakers have been "captured" by important local industries that generate many of the jobs and tax base of the community and, as a result, give scant protection to environmental interests (agency capture and public choice theory are discussed *infra*, page 62).

Outside the water resource context, the effort to re-match biophysical and management scale has traveled under the banner of "ecosystem management." Professor Bob Keiter explains:

> Whether the controversy involves spotted owls in the Pacific Northwest, visibility on the Colorado Plateau, or grizzly bears in Greater Yellowstone, the solution being espoused today is to manage the ecosystem as an entity. Indeed, each of the principal federal land management agencies—the Forest Service, Bureau of Land Management, National Park Service, and U.S. Fish & Wildlife Service—is openly touting ecosystem management as the panacea for today's natural resource controversies. Congress, tribal governments, state agencies, and private landowners, too, are beginning to explore the benefits of ecosystem-based management. Embedded in the concept of ecosystem management, however, are enormous complexities that natural resource managers are just beginning to confront. The scientific complexity of ecosystems is rivaled by the legal complexities involved in breaching jurisdictional boundaries and overcoming often outdated laws to facilitate management at an appropriate scale. The political obstacles to implementing such fundamental change on the public

domain are equally formidable. Nonetheless, with lawmakers and lawyers also beginning to speak in ecosystem terms, fundamental changes in federal natural resources law and policy are imminent.

The concept of ecosystem management, though still often misunderstood, has now been defined with sufficient precision to constitute a viable natural resource management policy. Drawing heavily upon ecological and biological sciences, particularly the field of conservation biology, ecosystem management views the land and resource base in its entirety, as a holistic or integrated entity. Management focuses on entire ecosystems, not just individual resources such as timber and forage. Recognizing that natural systems often cross jurisdictional boundaries, ecosystem management emphasizes the need for inter-jurisdictional coordination to ensure ecological integrity and sustainable resource systems.

Robert B. Keiter, *Beyond the Boundary Line: Constructing a Law of Ecosystem Management*, 65 U. COLO. L. REV. 293, 294–95 (1994). Although they remain rare, a number of initiatives have sought to better align political and biophysical scale in the manner described by Keiter. A commonly noted effort is the creation of the Chesapeake Bay Program by Virginia, Maryland and Pennsylvania to work on restoring the Bay's ecosystem. Several states have also matched political and natural boundaries, such as the New Jersey Pinelands Commission and the Adirondack Park Agency of New York. Regional habitat conservation plans developed under the Endangered Species Act can also be characterized as efforts to manage resources across political boundaries. Such cross-jurisdictional and collaborative approaches to resource management have been gaining momentum and will only increase in the coming years.

b.   The Relationship Between Property and Jurisdiction

The relationship between ownership and jurisdiction animates a number of natural resource law conflicts. In contrast to environmental law, whose roots are generally in tort and nuisance law, the roots of natural resource law are, in the main, in property law. Traditionally, the focus of natural resource law has been on allocation—who owned what rights in a resource. For example, with water the focus was on dividing a watercourse among various users rather than leaving the water in place for public recreation or endangered fisheries. Mining law focused on sorting out claims and rights between competing miners, not on the environmental harm caused by mining operations. In part because of this property focus, for years natural resource law was largely the province of state law. The exception was on federal land. Under the Constitution's Property Clause, Congress has the power to "make all needful rules and regulations respecting the territory or other property belonging to the United States." Art. IV, § 3. Thus, with United States' ownership came potential jurisdictional control over the natural resources on public lands. There are, of course, other sources of federal power, most prominently the Commerce Clause, but sorting out ownership questions has long been an important part of figuring out who has the power to protect, exploit and regulate natural resources on or near federal lands.

Determining the appropriate (and legal) scale on which to manage a natural resource thus also requires consideration of ownership. This, in turn, presents two complex issues which you will study later in this casebook: first, the confusing array of checker-boarded and overlapping ownership of natural resources; and second, the nature of property rights and whether certain resources can even be owned. The pattern of existing ownership will be studied largely in Chapter 2, where we study the history of the acquisition, disposition and retention of our nation's public lands. The result of that history is that the federal government owns land within states while states own some parcels wholly surrounded by federal land. In some instances, the federal government owns the subsurface mineral estate and a state or private party will own the surface right. In other cases, the opposite is true. Add to this the significant landholdings of Indian tribes and the result presents even greater obstacles to aligning management scale with biophysical scale.

Indeed, in some cases it is important to consider not just overlapping ownership but the very nature of property rights in natural resources. Whether natural resources are a different sort of property, or even capable of ownership at all, is an important consideration for defining the scope of management authority. This was part of the debate about our migratory goose and the *Geer* decision. To the extent the goose was viewed as "owned" by the states through which it flew, it made sense to give primacy to state regulation. But if the goose is viewed as a shared national, or even international, heritage, not subject to "ownership," the calculus of political scale necessarily changes.

3. TEMPORAL SCALE

Scale problems are not limited to those of biophysical and political scale. They also have a temporal dimension. The decision to dam a river today will have impacts 100 years from now. Tailings from long-abandoned mines continue to leak toxic substances into aquifers and creeks. Greenhouse gases we emit today will cause impacts over the next 50 years or longer. The same distributional asymmetry is at play here as with the examples of waterfowl and the Colorado River. The costs of refraining from an action fall on us today, while the benefits are enjoyed (perhaps by others) far later. Yet these future beneficiaries can't express their preferences in today's voting booth or court. Indeed, the temporal scale of many natural resource problems makes it difficult even to hold current elected officials accountable to voters today, since many of their actions will not cause harms until they are no longer in office. The impacts of overfishing today, for example, will only be seen several years later when the stock has collapsed.

Many advocates of "sustainable" resource management claim to be acting on behalf of the interests of future generations, but how can we know the preference of a future generation? Seemingly, they would prefer robust fish stocks and clean aquifers, but at what cost? Surely the interests of our future grandchildren and their children should be explicitly considered, but determining how much we should sacrifice today (and perhaps how much they should sacrifice in the future by way of foregone economic development) in order to obtain future benefits that may or may not be appreciated is no easy task.

As you study the different natural resources in this casebook, problems of scale will inevitably arise. In assessing the various management regimes, it is important to consider explicitly whether questions of political, temporal and biophysical scale have been adequately resolved. Have the resource and its scale been properly identified? Has the appropriate entity been given management authority over an adequate geographic area? Over what time period is the resource being managed? What are the likely costs and benefits associated with the scale of the particular management regime chosen?

CASE STUDY: THE QUINCY LIBRARY GROUP

A fascinating conflict over political scale has been playing out in a dispute over logging in Northern California. Frustrated over the contentious "timber wars" that had raged between environmentalists and logging companies through litigation over timber sales in national forests from the mid–1980s, in 1992 a Sierra Pacific Industries forester, a Plumas County supervisor, and a local environmental attorney began to discuss whether there was a way of putting in place a local compromise that provided for both logging and forest protection the parties could live with. These discussions grew to include other locals and took place in the Quincy Library. The Quincy Library Group, as this forum came to be known, grew to over 170 participants, with about 30 regulars on the steering committee. If they could convince the Forest Service to adopt their plan, the Group members felt, it could provide a win-win case for conservation and forestry while ending the seemingly endless cycle of litigation and ill will surrounding timber sales.

While the key protagonists in conflicts over resource management had been environmentalists and loggers, there was a wide range of potentially concerned parties. The area of concern covered three counties (Lassen, Plumas and Sierra Counties in northeastern California), most of which are within national forest. Home to 50,000 residents, the area also provides the headwaters for the Feather River, a key source of irrigation and drinking water for Southern California, and important habitat for the spotted owl and Chinook salmon. The region is an important provider of hydroelectric power and home to a number of Native American tribes.

Through a series of meetings, the Quincy Library Group formally developed a consensus plan that called for annual removal of dead and diseased trees from up to 60,000 acres to reduce fire risks, selective harvesting of timber from 9,000 acres per year to ensure multiple-age, multiple-species forests, riparian habitat protection, and other prescribed management steps. The plan made clear that all its measures must comply with all federal regulations, including endangered species protections. When the plan was proposed to the Forest Service for consideration as an amendment to the regional forest plan, however, it was rejected with the explanations of insufficient resources, staff, and national approval.

Going over the heads of the Forest Service, the Quincy Library Group contacted its Congressional representatives, and Representative Wally Herger introduced a bill *requiring* the Forest Service to implement the plan as a five-year demonstration project. Despite opposition from national environmental groups, the House of Representatives adopted the bill by a vote of 429–1, the Senate passed a similar bill, and President Clinton signed it into law. As a follow up, millions of dollars have been provided for implementation and study of the forest plan.

Many have hailed the Quincy Library Group as an important model for resolving other resource conflicts with multiple stakeholders. It's hard to argue against local consensus since, after all, the locals know the resource best and are most affected by management decisions. Timber companies have supported the model because it provides them with immediate certainty over what steps they can and can't take without fear of litigation delay. And local environmentalists have praised the initiative as a means to impose conservation measures they might otherwise not have been able to achieve. And adoption of the plan by Congress ensures it received the most democratic approval possible.

The Group is not without critics, however. Simply because locals participated in the process does not mean it was a true consensus. Ranchers, for example feel their concerns over water rights were not adequately considered. Group members respond that ranchers could have taken a more active role in the process but, the ranchers contend, they were told the Group would not be addressing grazing issues and many lived over two hours from Quincy, making meaningful participation impractical. Moreover, ranchers have raised the broader problem of not knowing in the future which stakeholder groups they should participate in, given their time constraints.

National environmental groups have opposed the model, arguing it was captive to special interests. The national forests belong to the nation, not locals. No matter how representative the 30 regular members of the Group were (and many critics contend that even local environmental interests were not adequately represented), they did not represent the interests of the three counties' 50,000 residents or, more important, the interests of the general public. As one environmentalist from a national group complained, "Here's a little group of people that can decide public policy." Moreover, allowing a local stakeholders group to bypass NEPA and the requirements of the National Forest Management Act for public participation and involvement frustrated the very purpose of these laws to ensure local interests do not capture the political process in developing the management plan.

Group supporters, however, counter that the opposition from national environmental groups stems from their fear that decision making over resources will shift from their power base in Washington to the grassroots, undercutting their political muscle and fundraising opportunities. Much more material, both positive and negative, is available on the Group's website at http://www.qlg.org/.

———

Stakeholder and consensus management of natural resources have become very popular in recent years as a means of ensuring the divergent interests affected by natural resource policies all have a seat at the table. The Quincy Library Group provides an example of this in practice.

- What is your view of the Quincy Library Group process as a model for resolving other resource conflicts?

- Given how contentious logging in national forests has become, if the locals have reached a consensus plan that is supported by local environmental groups, shouldn't the Forest Service presumptively favor that plan? Are you troubled that the Forest Service was forced to adopt the Group's plan despite development of its own plan over several years?

- How should management policies in national forests take account of local concerns? What is the proper level of authority for determining the management of national forests in northeastern California?

- How could collaborative decisionmaking be adapted to the scale of the resource?

- Does Congressional approval of the plan strike you as democratic or anti-democratic? Does it allow politicians to support the popular will or provide a politically expedient means to avoid responsibility and accountability for contentious decisions?

G.   INSTITUTIONAL ADEQUACY

As we will see in Chapter 3, our natural resource laws largely rely on "expert" agency management of resources, requiring agency personnel to take account of particular factors but giving them significant discretion in determining the optimal allocation or extraction level of resources. This is fine in principle so long as the agencies act in an expert, disinterested manner. The approach runs into serious problems, however, if it systematically favors certain interests over others. This phenomenon can take the form of "agency capture" and describes the tendency of agencies to align their goals with the interests of their regulated community rather than a more general public interest. Unfortunately, the natural resource field has often served as the poster child for agency capture examples, with the Bureau of Land Management historically favoring grazing interests and the Bureau of Reclamation favoring irrigation farmers. Indeed, the classic example of capture may be the Forest Service's management of the Tongass National Forest in the 1960s. Mandated by its "multiple use" mandate to determine how much of the forest should be dedicated to timber production, how much to recreation, wildlife, etc., the Forest Service decided that *100%* of the forest should be dedicated to timber production. Though challenged in court, the decision was upheld out of deference to agency expertise. *Sierra Club v. Hardin*, 325 F.Supp. 99 (D. Alaska 1971), *rev'd sub nom. Sierra Club v. Butz*, 3 ENVT'L L. REP. (ELI) 20,292 (9th Cir. 1973).

To some extent, agencies might identify their interests with those of the regulated community as the result of statutory mandate and history—i.e., promoting particular interests may have been the main reason the agencies were set up in the first place. In part, agency capture occurs because of revolving-door personnel, with agency personnel leaving for jobs in the regulated sector and people with regulated sector experience working in the agency. Agency officials' identification with regulated parties may be inevitable when they deal with them on a daily basis and are geographically dispersed. Nor is capture restricted to natural resource agencies. President Dwight Eisenhower warned of the dangers posed by the "military industrial complex" five decades ago.

The tendency toward agency capture is one of the insights of *public choice theory*, which suggests that governments and bureaucracies, just like markets, are susceptible to failures that a policy-maker must keep in mind. Another way in which public choice theory accounts for capture is through what is called the "rent-seeking" actions of concentrated special interests. Rent-seeking can take the form of lobbying Congress or an administrative agency to erect barriers to entry from competitors (such as limiting the number of liquor licenses in a community), distributing narrow subsidies (such as extending copyright to the Disney corporation or patent protections to drug manufacturers), or creating special protections (such as imposing tariffs or import restrictions on foreign steel). Hence rent seeking is sometimes also described as "policy investing." As Professor Bob Ellickson explains,

> Why do inefficient government programs persist in a democracy, where political aspirants might be expected to win election by campaigning to eliminate waste? According to public choice theory, the explanation lies in asymmetries in the ability of the gainers and losers from government programs to organize themselves for political action. An inefficient regulatory or spending program can be predicted to emerge and endure when its (relatively concentrated) beneficiaries have more influence than the (relatively diffuse) taxpayers and consumers whose interests are disserved by it.... This theory goes a long way toward explaining the persistence of many ... inefficient programs.... A subdivision regulation that imposes wasteful street-width standards is likely to be strongly defended by the contractors who build streets. A building code with excessive sprinkler specifications is warmly embraced by pipe manufacturers, plumbers' unions, and firefighters.

Robert C. Ellickson, *Taming Leviathan: Will the Centralizing Tide of the Twentieth Century Continue into the Twenty–First?*, 74 S. Cal. L. Rev. 101, 114 (2000).

Agency capture, public choice theory predicts, is an inevitable consequence of collective action. Because it's much more difficult to organize diffuse public interests that are only marginally affected than concentrated interests that are directly affected, we can expect concentrated interests to dominate the regulatory process. Parties that benefit from regulations will often form a more concentrated and effective opposition to reform than the diffuse public interest that suffers.

Agencies, public choice theory suggests, act similarly in protecting their own narrow self-interests. Because agencies need not pay the costs that their regulations impose and are only remotely accountable at the voting booth, they have little incentive to stick their necks out and oppose powerful special interests. As John Baden and Douglas Noonan, advocates of "free market environmentalism," argue,

> Rather than steward our resources "for the greatest good, for the largest number, for the long run," the [natural resource] agencies systematically advocate programs that (1) have environmental costs that exceed environmental benefits, (2) are financially wasteful, and (3) increase the command sector of the economy at the expense of voluntary exchange and coordination.... Bureaucracies tend to replace the goals that justified their creation with actions which protect their budgets. Bureaucracies are relentless. They pursue a budget-maximizing agenda with tenacity, single-mindedness, and even occasional creativity.... [O]ver the long run we should expect bureaucracies to be run for the benefit of those running them and the clientele upon whom they depend for authority and budget appropriations.

John Baden and Douglas Noonan, *The Federal Treasury as a Common–Pool Resource: The Predatory Bureaucracy as a Management Tool*, MANAGING THE COMMONS 205 (1998). Do you find this view of government unduly cynical? While the problems raised by Baden and Noonan undoubtedly occur, isn't it reasonable to think that many people choose a career in government service because of their commitment to serve the broad public interest? Does public choice theory suggest that individual commitment is less important than institutional interests?

To the extent that this problem is real, how can it best be addressed? "Free market environmentalists" call for private management and ownership of many resources now held by the government. Administrative law reformers call for more transparent decisionmaking processes to ensure hidden deals are opened to the public. Economists often call for mandatory cost-benefit analysis to smoke out inefficient subsidies and favors.

———

QUESTIONS AND DISCUSSION

1.   Consider the previous examples of the Delhi Sands Flower–Loving Fly and the Northern Spotted Owl (page 53). Planning decisions have to be made that could site a hospital directly beside the fly's habitat or would allow clearcut logging in the owl's habitat. Assuming there is no Endangered Species Act, what level of management authority do you think is appropriate to make these decisions—local, state or federal? How would you justify your decision in terms of fairness to local expectations and economic impacts, externalities and the ecological insight of interconnectedness, national concerns, and interests of future generations?

2.   Public choice theory provides a useful explanation of why agencies are sometimes captured or appear to make decisions that do not accord with the public interest. But does the theory explain most agency failings? Do people act the same as grocery store shoppers when politics is involved, or does acting as a citizen change our sense of values? In contemplating these questions, consider the following excerpt from James Buchanan, one of the founders of public choice theory.

James M. Buchanan, *What Is Public Choice Theory?*
32 Imprimis No. 3, at 3–5 (March 2003)

In essence, [public choice theory and its insight into "rent-seeking"] extends the idea of the profit motive from the economic sphere to the sphere of collective action. It presupposes that if there is value to be gained through politics, persons will invest resources in efforts to capture this value. * * *

[Much of the social science at the midpoint of the 20th Century was focused on a] research program called "theoretical welfare economics," which concentrated on identifying the failures of observed markets to meet idealized standards. In sum, this branch of inquiry offered theories of market failure. But failure in comparison with what? The implicit presumption was always that politicized corrections for market failures would work perfectly. In other words, market failures were set against an idealized politics.

Public choice then came along and provided analyses of the behavior of persons acting politically, whether voters, politicians or bureaucrats. These analyses exposed the essentially false comparisons that were then informing so much of both scientific and public opinion. In a very real sense, public choice became a set of theories of governmental failures, as an offset to the theories of market failures that had previously emerged from theoretical welfare economics. Or, as I put it in the title of a lecture in Vienna in 1978, public choice may be summarized by the three-word description, "politics without romance." * * *

[A] provocative criticism of public choice centers on the claim that it is immoral. The source of this charge lies in the application to politics of the assumption that individuals in the marketplace behave in a self-interested way.... The moral condemnation of public choice is centered on the presumed transference of this element of economic theory to political analysis. Critics argue that people acting politically—for example, as voters or as legislators—do not behave as they do in markets. Individuals are differently motivated when they are choosing "for the public" rather than for themselves in private choice capacities. Or so the criticism runs.

At base, this criticism stems from a misunderstanding that may have been fostered by the failure of economists to acknowledge the limits of their efforts. The economic model of behavior, even if restricted to market activity, should never be taken to provide the be-all and end-all of scientific explanation. Persons act from many motives, and the economic model concentrates attention only on one of the many possible forces behind actions. Economists do, of course, presume that the "goods" they employ in their models for predicting behavior are relatively important. And in fact, the hypothesis that promised shifts in net wealth modify political behavior in predictable ways has not been readily falsifiable empirically.

Public choice, as an inclusive research program, incorporates the presumption that persons do not readily become economic eunuchs as they shift from market to political participation. Those who respond predictably to ordinary incentives in the marketplace do not fail to respond at all when they act as citizens. The public choice theorist should, of course, acknowledge that the strength and predictive power of the strict economic model of behavior is somewhat mitigated as the shift is made from private market to collective choice. Persons in political roles may, indeed, act to a degree in terms of what they consider to be the general interest. Such acknowledgment does not, however, in any way imply that the basic explanatory model loses all of its predictive potential, or that ordinary incentives no longer matter. * * *

Armed with nothing more than the rudimentary insights from public choice, persons could understand why, once established, bureaucracies tend to grow apparently without limit and without connection to initially promised functions. They could understand why pork-barrel politics dominate the attention of legislators; why there seems to be a direct relationship between the overall size of government and the investment in efforts to secure special concessions from government (rent seeking); why the tax system is described by the increasing number of special credits, exemptions, and loopholes; why balanced budgets are so hard to secure; and why strategically placed industries secure tariff protection.

3. As the text noted, who controls a resource can have a significant impact on how the resource is managed and allocated. Can you come up with hypothetical examples for water, minerals, endangered species, or timber management and show how the different constituencies of federal, state, tribal, and local governments might lead to different natural resource management preferences and allocations?

4. In addition to overlapping political and geographic jurisdictions, there are often overlapping substantive jurisdictions. Thus, for example, at the federal level, water resource issues are overseen by thirteen different congressional committees and subcommittees, eight cabinet agencies, six independent regulatory agencies, and two White House offices. At the state level, water is typically managed by multiple state agencies and hundreds of local entities. Geoffrey Heal et al., *Protecting Natural Capital Through Ecosystem Service Districts*, 20 STAN. ENVTL. L.J. 333, 355 (2001). The competing missions and interests of these overlapping substantive jurisdictions can produce inconsistent and conflicting management approaches and at the very least increase the costs of collective action.

5. Despite its predictive power in explaining agency capture, public choice theory, ironically, cannot easily explain the fact that we have environmental laws in the first place. As Professor Richard Revesz explains in the context of air pollution legislation,

> given the standard public choice argument for federal environmental regulation, it is not clear why the problems observed at the state level would not be replicated at the federal level. The logic of collective action would suggest that the large number of citizen-breathers, each with a relatively small stake in the outcome of a particular standard-setting proceeding, will be overwhelmed in the political process by concentrated industrial interests with a large stake in the outcome. . . . In fact, the logic of collective action makes it difficult to explain why there is any federal regulation at all.

Richard L. Revesz, *The Race to the Bottom and Federal Environmental Regulation: A Response to Critics*, 82 MINN. L. REV. 535, 542 (1997).

If concentrated special interest groups will generally provide more effective political pressure than the general public, it is hard to see how general interest legislation can overcome special interest opposition. Yet that clearly seems to have occurred with pollution law, vindicating the diffuse general interest in clean air and water over the more concentrated interests of the regulated industries. Why might this have happened? For a law review issue dedicated to this problem, see the *Cummings Colloquium on Environmental Law and the Rents of Nature: Special Interests and the Puzzle of Environmental Legislation*, 9 DUKE ENVT'L L. & POL'Y F. 1 (1998).

6. One proposal for matching management scale to biophysical scale has been the creation of ecosystem service districts (ESDs). These would be governmental authorities dedicated to the management and protection of ecosystem services (described at page 18). The United States already has thousands of districts for soil conservation, resource conservation, flood control, and other local services. There are 2,935 soil conservation districts alone (encompassing 3,209 counties). While in many instances these districts have been provided with significant legal authority, including the powers of taxation, eminent domain, and zoning, as a rule they have not generally considered ecosystems as providers of services.

> As a matter of coordination, the larger the number of political entities required for a decision, the greater the costs of collective action and, therefore, the less likely action will be taken. All other things being equal, those ecosystem services requiring larger areas for their provision—and hence involving more political entities—will prove more difficult to administer. * * *

> ... [To be effective, ESDs will require a range of legal powers]. The least controversial power is the authority to *generate information*. For example, existing districts could be mandated by state legislatures to explicitly compare the cost of service provision through both natural and built means. ... This type of reflexive mandate would force at least minimal consideration of service provision by ecosystems. ...

> ESDs could also play a *coordinating function* across districts. Because district jurisdictions rarely track ecological or watershed boundaries, efforts in one district to enhance ecosystem services can be weakened or, in some cases, frustrated by activities in another district working at cross-purposes. One district's management for natural pollination, for example, can be nullified by a neighboring district's spraying of pesticides on crops and adjacent lands. Information exchange among ESDs could result in better-coordinated actions or, at a minimum, highlight counterproductive activities.

> More controversially, ESDs could be granted *zoning authority* or other land use powers (such as condemnation). The grant of such authority would, however, require transferring that power from its current source (unless the ESD acted concurrently with the zoning authority) and no doubt could threaten certain vested interests. Finally, the ESD might be granted *taxation authority*. Taxes could provide funds to pay for condemnation and, through charges and subsidies, facilitate the movement toward the optimal allocation of services through pricing.

> The various powers listed above may be found together in municipal governments but are rarely found together in districts. ... Thus from both environmental and economic efficiency perspectives, single coordinated districts aimed at the production of mixed services would be significantly outside the historical norm.

Geoffrey Heal et al., *Protecting Natural Capital Through Ecosystem Service Districts*, 20 Stan. Envtl. L.J. 333, 353–356 (2001).

ESDs are not merely thought experiments. In New Zealand, regional government councils have been established along the boundaries of major watershed catchments. Another interesting example can be found in the Australian city of Sydney. In 1998, the presence of the pathogens Cryptosporidium and Giardia in the Sydney water supply forced residents to boil their water for six weeks. A government commission, created during the public scare, later concluded that Sydney's water catchments had been seriously compromised by many sources of contamination and that the municipal supplier did not have sufficient regulatory control of the catchments to guarantee safe drinking water. In response, the New South Wales government created a new governmental body known as the Sydney Catchment Authority (SCA). The SCA's mandate is to manage and protect Sydney's water supply catchments, dams, raw water transfer pipelines and canals, and associated infrastructure. Its creators hope it will function as a kind of super-authority. It is well-funded, has solid public support, and significant but ill-defined regulatory powers to influence and, in some cases, determine land use decisions in the catchment area. The interesting part, of course, is currently playing out, as the SCA exercises its authority on behalf of the watershed.

Which range of powers listed above do you think are necessary to create an effective ESD? If you were the head of the SCA, what would your concerns be in modifying or overruling land management decisions by the existing authorities (i.e., local councils and planning boards)?

7. The EPA has been a strong proponent of managing watersheds at the proper biophysical scale, supporting a number of watershed initiatives. The EPA Watershed Initiative website is at http://www.epa.gov/owow/water shed/approach.html. A research project at the University of California, Davis, has examined many of these watershed partnerships, relying on social science techniques to understand better why people collaborate to address complex watershed problems. Its reports are on the web at www. wpp.ucdavis.edu/default.htm. The website for the Chesapeake Bay Program is at www.chesapeakebay.net; the New Jersey Pinelands Commission is at www.state.nj.us/pinelands/; and the Adirondack Park Agency is at http:// www.northnet.org/adirondackparkagency/.

8. *Sustainable Development:* Perhaps the greatest current challenge of management scale is taking place at the international level. Economic development has long been a defining goal of governments. Economic expansion has been considered fundamental to ending poverty in the developing world and raising standards of living worldwide. As global warming, loss of biodiversity, crashing fisheries, ozone depletion and other recent environmental crises make clear, however, the current pace and manner of global economic expansion may be incompatible with environmental protection. The development goal cannot, however, be abandoned. Poverty still must be reduced and standards of living raised throughout the developing world, as well as in the poorest sections of industrialized nations. Development cannot simply be subordinated to environmental protection. Instead, development and environmental protection must be integrated, and this process of integration lies at the core of the concept of "sustainable development."

The principle of sustainable development provided the core message for the 1992 Earth Summit (the largest international governmental meeting ever held). It was defined as "development that meets the needs of the present without compromising the ability of future generations to meet their own needs." Sustainable development provides an important overarching theme for three reasons. First, in historical terms, sustainable development tied together two disparate fields—development and environmental protection. Prior to the 1990s, those working in the development world saw their goal primarily as poverty alleviation and those in the environmental field as environmental protection, with little overlap between the two. As a result, development projects often had unnecessarily destructive environmental impacts and environmental protection efforts too often took little heed of economic impacts. Creating a park in a developing country might be viewed as a conservation success, for example, despite the potentially adverse economic consequences for the local community. Gandhi is said to have remarked that poverty is the greatest threat to the environment. By linking environmental protection and poverty alleviation to economic development, sustainable development forged the key insight that development and environmental protection efforts must be mutually reinforcing.

Second, sustainable development focuses both on intragenerational equity (allowing those of the present to meet their needs) and on intergenerational equity (meeting the needs of future generations). Thus sustainable development lengthens the geographic and time horizons of decisions, ensuring that both long and short-term interests are considered. What this means for foreign aid policies and nonrenewable resources remains contentious, as does the matter of deciding what future generations would want us to do, but these are important policy debates that might otherwise not have occurred. Third, sustainable development challenges the common assumption that growth is good. Importantly, "growth" is not the same thing as "development." In order to create a sustainable economy—one that provides goods and services to ensure a positive quality of life into the future—the model cannot be one of growth based on current practices for the simple reason that our natural systems cannot indefinitely continue to assimilate the impacts of growth. Thus, central to the concept of sustainable development is the importance of limits—that we must develop within the constraints of natural systems. Hence to many environmental policy experts, the greatest challenge posed by sustainable development is that of re-orienting our economies so they develop (providing greater value and standards of living) while not physically growing (in terms of resource consumption and pollution).

CASE STUDY: THE ARCTIC NATIONAL WILDLIFE REFUGE

The Arctic National Wildlife Refuge spans almost 20 million acres across the North Slope of Alaska, including parts of the rugged Brooks Range, barrier islands, coastal lagoons, and the vast tundra plains leading up to the sea. Three times the size of Vermont, it is the largest wildlife refuge in the country and boasts diverse flora and fauna, including 36 fish species, 36 land mammal species, 9 marine mammal species, and over 160 migratory and resident bird species. By executive action in 1960, President Eisenhower established the Refuge to protect its "unique wildlife, wilderness, and recreational values."

In 1968, North America's largest oil field was discovered at the adjacent Prudhoe Bay. In 1980, Congress passed the Alaska National

Interest Lands Conservation Act (ANILCA), doubling the size of the Refuge. Almost all of the Refuge was designated as a part of the National Wilderness Preservation System but, in a compromise acknowledging the potential oil fields, 1.5 million acres of the coastal plain (known as Section 1002) were set aside to study its potential for oil and gas production. The bill provided that Section 1002 would remain closed to oil and gas exploration until Congress legislated otherwise.

The battle over the Refuge was joined in 1987, when the Reagan Administration's Department of the Interior recommended leasing of Section 1002 for oil and gas exploration. Following the Gulf War in 1991, the Bush Administration's National Energy Policy again called for opening up Section 1002, but a Senate bill was defeated by a filibuster. Four years later, the Alaskan Congressional delegation attached a rider to the federal budget reconciliation bill mandating Arctic Refuge oil development. President Clinton vetoed the bill, naming the Refuge provision as the main reason. This veto caused the federal government to shut down. President George W. Bush's National Energy Plan called for opening the Refuge to drilling, as well. Despite the large increase in gas prices, at the time of this book's publication, political efforts to open the Refuge have continued to fail.

There is considerable debate over the likely reserves of recoverable oil beneath the Refuge. Nearby Prudhoe Bay is the largest working oil field in North America. The U.S. Geological Survey's estimates of the Refuge's recoverable oil range from 3.2 billion to 16 billion barrels of oil. Supporters of drilling point out that foreign imports comprise nearly 60% of U.S. oil consumption and claim that Refuge oil could provide the equivalent of 30 years of oil imports from Saudi Arabia. The Governor of Alaska claims that drilling would create up to 735,000 new jobs and generate billions of dollars in leases and tax revenue (much of it to Alaska, whose citizens receive a yearly check from the state—$1,654 per person in 2007). Not surprisingly, the opponents of drilling characterize the data as suggesting the Refuge's oil supply would make little difference to the nation's oil consumption over the medium or long term (providing less than 2% of the nation's oil consumption even at peak production), making far less impact on our dependence on foreign oil than simple efficiency measures would (such as increased vehicle fuel efficiency).

There is considerable debate, as well, over the environmental impacts of drilling for oil in the Refuge. Drilling opponents often cite the conclusions of studies by the U.S. Fish and Wildlife Service that drilling in the coastal plain, the Refuge's biologically most productive area, would cause major impacts to the caribou, musk oxen, polar bears and other Refuge wildlife. The plain is the main calving ground for the Porcupine River caribou herd, the end destination of the 129,000–strong herd's annual 700 mile migration from their winter range. Opponents also point out the heavy impacts of infrastructure to support drilling, ranging from roads, drill pads, and processing facilities to airports, power stations, and pipelines, not to mention the inevitable oil spills from operations and transport. These impacts could last for decades, given the slow rate of plant growth in the Arctic.

Drilling supporters tend to characterize the drilling as affecting less than one-tenth of one percent of the entire Refuge, emphasizing that there is plenty of habitat on the North Slope of Alaska for the Porcupine herd and other wildlife. Recent developments in drilling technology have shrunk the footprint of drilling infrastructure. They also note that only a few hundred people visit the Refuge each year.

It goes without saying that environmental groups have opposed drilling while oil companies and the state of Alaska have supported it. Indeed, it is not an exaggeration to state that the conflict over drilling in the Refuge has become a defining issue for both the environmental movement and the oil industry. Beyond the obvious interests, however, the conflict has drawn in many other parties. Both the International Brotherhood of Teamsters and the Seafarer's International Union have aggressively campaigned for drilling, seconding the claims that drilling would create over 735,000 jobs. The Inupiat Eskimos, who own 92,000 acres of land within the Coastal Plain, also support drilling, arguing it would provide valuable jobs, revenue and infrastructure to their poor community. The Inupiat largely depend on fishing and whaling for subsistence.

Another indigenous group, the Gwich'in Nation, just as strongly opposes drilling, fearful that it will drive off or harm the Porcupine caribou herd on which they depend for food, clothing, tools, and their cultural life. The Gwich'in argue that weakening the herd or changing its migration routes would threaten both their economic and spiritual survival.

QUESTIONS AND DISCUSSION

1.   What are the valuable natural resources in the Arctic National Wildlife Refuge?

2.   What are the major uncertainties in this decision? Do they counsel in favor of allowing drilling? How would the precautionary principle apply to this situation?

3.   Whose interests should be considered in deciding whether to allow drilling, and which should be given greatest weight?

4.   Leaving aside the statutory requirements for a moment, who do you think should make the final decision?

5.   Given the fact that only a tiny percentage of Americans will ever visit the Refuge, how do you explain the fact that drilling in the Refuge has become one of the dominant national environmental conflicts over the last two decades?

III.   TOOLS FOR MANAGING NATURAL RESOURCES—"THE FIVE P'S"

While values, market failures, scientific uncertainty and the other themes discussed in this chapter drive natural resource policies, policies still need to be implemented. The rubber meets the road in determining which type of instrument to use in the regulatory toolkit. To explore the possibilities, let's return to the classic natural resource problem—the tragedy of the commons. Recall that you have a herd of sheep that grazes on the public common. The common, though, is an open access resource (the defining problem for many natural resource issues). This means that anyone can graze as many sheep as she likes. So long as the resource is under little pressure (i.e., few sheep are grazing) there is no need for government intervention because there is no problem of scarcity. Once significant competing uses of a resource develop, however, then the need for state action arises. In the context of the commons, once more and more people graze more and more sheep, the commons is in danger of becoming overgrazed and denuded. So we need to do something, but how should we best head off the tragedy currently in the making? What is the appropriate mix of property and regulation? It is useful to think of the range of policy instruments as "The Five P's"—Property rights, Prescriptive regulation, financial Penalties, Payments, and Public disclosure and Persuasion.

A. PROPERTY RIGHTS

A classic solution to the tragedy of the commons is reliance on private property rights. Assume the state carves up the common into square parcels of land and grants fee simple title to the current shepherds using the common, including you. Are you still as eager to overgraze as before? All of a sudden, your previous incentive to use up the resource as fast as possible (before everyone else did) is no longer relevant. Instead, your interests are probably best served by carefully tending your part of the common so it remains fertile long into the future—so it is sustainably managed. In a variant of the privatization approach, assume the entire commons now belongs to you. What would you do? You may well charge other shepherds to use the commons, or even let them on for free, but you would only do so to the extent that the resource base remains intact and productive—i.e., so long as the commons are not overgrazed. The property rights approach is based on the common sense intuition that people take better care of their own property. In financial terms, people will safeguard their assets over the longer term to maximize long term profits.

Implicit in a property rights approach is the importance of technology. To enforce your rights, you need both to know whether someone is making unauthorized use of your resource (an issue of monitoring capacity) as well as to have the ability to exclude others' use. As described earlier in the chapter, it was only with the invention of barbed wire that settlers in the American west could effectively exclude cattle from grazing on their lands (i.e., could privatize the commons). Prior to this technology, there was no affordable way to keep cattle from grazing wherever they wanted. In a more modern context, decoders have allowed satellite television channels to privatize the airwave commons. Unless satellite channel providers could exclude other's use of their signal by scrambling it and then selling decoders, there would be no way for them to sell their product (since people would use it for free).

Reliance on property rights has proven effective in the case of trading systems, where rights to catch a ton of fish or emit a ton of pollution are allocated and traded on an open market. Indeed, some commentators have called for far greater reliance on property rights approaches to environmental protection. Sometimes called "free market environmentalism," this strategy would privatize as many environmental resources as possible, arguing that markets are better mechanisms for allocation of scarce goods than governmental regulators. We explore this in more detail in a problem exercise at the end of the chapter.

Despite the increasing interest and application of property rights approaches to environmental protection, there are some significant obstacles. The first is that many environmental resources are not easily amenable to commodification. Consider endangered species, for example. One might privatize their habitat, but what if the species is mobile? There may be normative concerns, as well, that are raised by proposals for privatization of national parks or other environmental amenities in the public domain. If the Disney Corporation owned Yellowstone, for example, would you would feel the same way about your visit even if the experience were identical in every other way to that of the current national park?

Practically, there are difficult allocation issues for the initial privatization of environmental resources. Using the commons as an example, assume that the government has decided to divide up the land into 50 separate parcels. Who should be given title? Should the land be auctioned to the highest bidder? This might ensure the most efficient use of the resource, but it would likely favor wealthier newcomers and corporate interests over traditional, small-scale users. Giving more deference to communities, perhaps the allocation should be based on historic use or current levels of consumption. This approach might seem more equitable, though realize that it freezes out newcomers who might use the land more efficiently or even set it aside for conservation. And if these lands belong to the nation, where's the fairness in effectively shutting out outsiders? Any allocation mechanism will tend to favor some groups at the expense of others.

Nor, finally, is it clear that privatization will lead to the most socially most beneficial use of the land. It is easy to imagine, for example, the problem of holding out. Perhaps the new owners of the commons wish to use it for mini-golf while the sheep starve. This may be economically efficient if it accurately reflects the land's most valuable use (as measured by willingness to pay). If the government wishes to ensure the important public goals of a secure food supply or supporting family farms, they will need to step in. Property rights advocates would approve of this course of action, so long as the government paid the property holders. But, one might ask, if the most valuable use, as demonstrated by the market, is for the commons to be used for mini-golf, why should government intervene at all? We will return to this in the *Questions and Discussion* section that follows.

B.   PRESCRIPTIVE REGULATION

In relying on prescriptive regulation, the government mandates how the resource may be used (regardless of whether it is publicly or privately held). This strategy explicitly directs behavior of regulated parties and is the most common policy approach in natural resource law. In the case of the commons, for example, the government might decide to limit access. The most obvious measure would be to restrict the number of sheep that may graze, perhaps allowing no more than 250 sheep per month. The government may further determine that certain commons areas must be set aside for re-vegetation and allow no grazing at all.

Such prescriptive regulation, also referred to as "command-and-control" regulation, can be very effective but there is considerable debate over its efficiency. The underlying assumption, of course, is that the natural resource management agency, staffed with experts, knows best. For the resource management agency to make wise decisions, though, it must have access to accurate information and not be subject to capture by special interest groups or to other public choice pressures. It needs monitoring capabilities to check for compliance and credible sanctioning authority to ensure rules will be followed. In practice, none of these preconditions are guaranteed. And even if they are, satisfying these requirements suggests that administrative costs could be significant.

1. TRADABLE PERMITS

As mentioned above, environmental markets have been growing in popularity and represent a hybrid of private property and regulation. To date, trading programs have reduced emissions of a wide range of pollutants, managed fisheries and lobster harvests, and channeled habitat development. The basis for trading environmental commodities is a regulatory proscription of behavior followed by regulatory permission of the behavior under controlled conditions. In establishing a market, the government first creates a new form of property—legal entitlements to emit pollutants, catch fish, develop habitat—then bans an activity absent these entitlements, and finally imposes a set of rules governing their exchange—i.e., creates a market. In the context of scarce natural resources, permits cap the bearer's right to take a specified amount of the resource and the total quantity of permits is equal to the aggregate extraction or harvest level set by policymakers. All trading programs therefore take place within carefully constructed markets. Absent legal restrictions on pollutant emissions, fish landings, or wetlands development, and the creation of alienable entitlements to these activities, few if any trades would take place.

To make this more concrete, imagine how a trading program would work with grazing on the commons. Government policy makers decide that the commons can sustain no more than 400 sheep grazing per year. It therefore creates 400 permits. Each permit entitles the holder to graze one sheep for the calendar year. Unless the shepherd has a separate permit for each sheep grazing on the commons, he is breaking the law. The government then allocates the permits in some fashion and lets trading commence. In theory, those for whom grazing is most valuable will buy the permits, ensuring that the commons are dedicated to the most valuable use.

One downside of trading is similar to that for private property rights approaches—the difficulty of initial allocation of permits in an equitable fashion. Moreover, constructing smoothly functioning markets is not simple. There must be a refined currency of trade, one that is fungible and reflects the desired environmental quality. There must also be a sufficient and well-defined marketplace and community of market participants. Thus, for example, it would be a stretch to consider allowing coastal developers in Florida to "trade" wetland values they eliminate for increasing endangered species habitat in Oregon. But where the environmental good (or bad, so to speak) can be captured in a measurable unit (whether that be kilos of fish or acres of wetland) and market service areas and participants are well-defined, trading programs have had demonstrable success in a variety of contexts, increasing the efficiency and flexibility of prescriptive instruments.

C. Financial Penalties

Another strategy of environmental protection relies explicitly on economic incentives and disincentives. Using the commons example again, these may take the form of an entrance fee to graze on the commons. One might levy a tax, perhaps on the number of sheep or time spent grazing. Such market instruments are attractive because they lead to self-regulation of use. If the fees and taxes are set correctly, this instrument quite literally internalizes externalities and provides a direct incentive to modify behavior, aligning environmental and economic interests. People will find cheaper ways to conserve those scarce resources and less of the resource will be used over time.

Setting the correct level of the tax, though, can be difficult. After all, what natural resource managers care about is the overall effect of many polluting sources or resource users. What level should the individual tax or fee be set at to reach the desired aggregate resource extraction level? More practically, there is strong public and political opposition to significant taxes. President Clinton's carbon tax proposal at the start of his presidency proved politically radioactive. In most cases, even when environmental taxes have been set, they've been intended more for revenue-raising than serious behavior modification.

D. Financial Payments

Another market approach with broad use in the field of natural resources is public subsidy. Rather than financially penalizing undesirable behavior, one rewards the desired behavior. If the government wants to reduce the loss of wetlands on farms, rather than banning farmers from draining and filling wetlands, it may subsidize those that set aside wetlands alongside their plowed fields. In contrast to such "environmental subsidies," however, many (in fact, most) subsidies promote degradation of environmental amenities. Suppose, for example, you graze your sheep on public lands. The government charges you less than the private lessee across the fence pays to graze his sheep. It sends you a check when you are unable to sell your lambs or their wool at a statutory target price. And it sells you water at a below-market price which you use to grow alfalfa to feed your sheep in the winter when the grazing land is covered with snow. If the subsidies are reduced, you may decide to stop grazing altogether, reduce the number of sheep you run, or perhaps find a more efficient way to graze, all of which will benefit an overgrazed range. Subjecting you to the discipline of the market can turn out to be good for the environment, but eliminating subsidies won't always produce environmental gains. Suppose that you stop grazing and the pasture is replaced with tract homes.

E.   PUBLIC DISCLOSURE AND PERSUASION

If the common law, prescriptive regulation, and market instruments represent "hard" regulatory approaches, then the softer approach may be found in laws requiring information production and dissemination. The theory behind such approaches is that forcing a regulated party or government agencies, themselves, to gather information and make it public, or at least to consider information, will change the party's behavior. In the context of the commons, the government might require shepherds to record and publish the number of sheep that graze or the amount of time they graze, subjecting them to peer pressure from the community. They may try to educate the shepherds with brochures or presentations on the causes and dangers of overgrazing. It may be more effective, though, to bypass the regulated party entirely and go directly to the consumer. As described at page 565, in the early 1990s, labeling cans of tuna "dolphin friendly" rapidly changed the fishing practices of tuna fleets in the Southern Pacific, from purse seine netting that killed tens of thousands of dolphins annually to much less harmful techniques. California passed a law requiring all 2009 model cars for sale to display a global warming score, on a scale of one to 10, based on how vehicles in the same model year compare to one another for emissions and fuel efficiency. New York has adopted a similar measure for 2010. California's data is posted on the web at the state's DriveClean website, <www.driveclean.ca.gov/index.php>.

Similar (often nongovernmental) eco-labeling initiatives certify and label sustainably harvested timber, coffee, etc. The theory behind such programs is to provide green consumers reliable information on which to base their purchases and favor environmentally friendlier products in the marketplace. Government can also support pilot programs or demonstration projects to show industries or farmers the benefits of alternative approaches to production or farming.

In general, information approaches are used when there is either inadequate political support to impose regulatory instruments or such instruments are ill-suited to the problem. In a number of cases, particularly in the case of pollution, requirements to collect and disseminate information on regulated parties' behavior have led to concrete changes even in the absence of overt prescriptive regulation. *See* Eric Orts, *Reflexive Environmental Law*, 89 Nw. U.L. Rev. 1227 (1995).

QUESTIONS AND DISCUSSION

1. All of the tools listed above have been used to manage fisheries. Assume you work for NOAA Fisheries and have been asked to analyze the potential application of the "Five P's" to the Red Snapper fishery (the subject of a case study in Chapter 5). This stock is currently being overfished by both commercial boats and recreational fishermen. For each type of instrument, describe examples of how it might work in practice and who the regulatory targets would be.

- Which instrument do you think will be most effective?
- Which most efficient?
- And which most equitable?

2. Given that public subsidies often result in environmentally-damaging resource allocation, a number of environmental groups have joined forces with taxpayers' groups and fiscal conservatives to lobby against particular congressional subsidies. The *Green Scissors Report*, for example, published annually by Friends of the Earth, the U.S. Public Interest Research Group, and Taxpayers for Common Sense, identifies environmentally wasteful programs. Operating for close to a decade, the Green Scissors Campaign claims to have "successfully cut or eliminated more than 20 environmentally wasteful programs, saving taxpayers more than $26 billion." Their most recent report can be found at http://www.greenscissors.com. This strategy, however, can act as a double-edged sword. Should the campaign be concerned over subsidies for renewable energy research and national park visitors? Is it possible, or fair, to pick and choose among subsidies or are subsidies simply the oil that makes the wheels of politics run? How do you think subsidies are viewed by free market environmentalists?

3. The Political Economy Research Center (better known as PERC), is one of the leading think tanks for free market environmentalism. Their approach to resource management is based on four tenets:

- Private property rights encourage stewardship of resources.
- Government subsidies often degrade the environment.
- Market incentives spur individuals to conserve resources and protect environmental quality.
- Polluters should be liable for the harm they cause others.

None of these contentions are exceptional, so why is PERC so controversial? Primarily because their policy prescriptions often call for much stronger reliance on markets, property rights and the common law than the current emphasis on prescriptive regulation. In advocating repeal of the Endangered Species Act, for example, PERC Executive Director Terry Anderson has argued that

> This Act creates perverse incentives by penalizing people who oversee resources. I'd start by scrapping the approach that's there and implementing new ones. First, by encouraging private environmental groups to contract with land owners, and second, by using financial resources (from user fees on public land, for example) to compensate land owners for preservation procedures.

http://www.perc.org/articles/article435.php. Does PERC's approach adequately account for the transaction costs incurred by those with diffuse interests? Consider for example, what it will take for multiple private environmental groups to marshal their resources to compete with a single landowner for the purchase of an old growth forest that provides critical habitat for an endangered species. While PERC's views have surely been controversial, it has succeeded in pushing the envelope of policy tools. PERC's website has a number of "success stories" it argues should serve as models for resource management. *See* http://www.perc.org/psolutions.php. For further reading on free market environmentalism, *see* TERRY L. ANDERSON & DONALD R. LEAL, FREE MARKET ENVIRONMENTALISM (2nd ed. 2001). For the views of the other influential free market environmentalist think tank, see the Foundation for Research on Economics and the Environment's website, at www.free-eco.org.

4.   Although regulation, property rights and market instruments can be categorized as separate approaches to the difficulties of managing an open access resource, it should be evident that there is significant overlap among them. Taxes and trading programs, for example, are obviously forms of regulation. At the same time, prescriptive regulation can also be understood as a public assertion of property rights in a resource. For example, a regulation prohibiting a timber company from logging within 100 feet of a riparian area so as to protect an endangered fish can equally be viewed as the assertion of a public property right in the riparian corridor. Professor Dan Cole explains this further in the excerpt below.

DANIEL H. COLE, POLLUTION & PROPERTY: COMPARING OWNERSHIP INSTITUTIONS FOR ENVIRONMENTAL PROTECTION 7–8, 13, 17–18 (2002)

Scholars have discussed and distinguished Hardin's two solutions to the tragedy of the commons, but almost all have failed to recognize that both are property-based: each involves the imposition of property rights on formerly open-access (or nonproperty) resources. This is obviously true of privatization, but it is also true of many forms of government regulation. A government can, of course, assert public rights by explicitly claiming the resource as public property. Most countries have done precisely this in establishing "national parks," "national forests," and other "public lands." * * *

Explicit claims of public ownership are not the only way, however, by which governments establish public property rights in resources. Governments frequently impose public rights through the regulation of private resource use. When the government regulates air pollution, for example, it imposes a system of public rights and private duties with respect to the atmosphere. Whether it chooses to regulate with command-and-control measures (such as technology-based standards), transferable pollution rights, or other "market-based" approaches, the state imposes on air polluters a legally enforceable duty to comply with all restrictions on use of (what amounts to) the public's atmosphere. What distinguishes this regulatory approach from "privatization" is not the existence or nonexistence of property rights but only the *type* of property regime imposed. Privatization converts nonproperty into private (individual or common) property. Government regulation typically (if tacitly) converts nonproperty into public/state property or some mixed form of public and private property. It may be objected that government regulation constitutes an exercise in *imperium* (*sovereign* authority) rather than *dominium* (ownership). However, this old Roman-law distinction marks little practical difference. Property and sovereignty are both forms of power—as Denman puts it, a "sanction and authority for decision-making"—over resources. Whether the state is purporting to act as sovereign or owner, the rights it asserts are in the nature of property. * * *

There is no such thing as a pure or unadulterated public or private property system. As Charles Geisler has noted, all existing property regimes are more or less admixtures, comprising various individual, group, and public rights. A property regime can only be *relatively* public or private.... So, when I refer to "private" property in this book, I do not mean allodial property, devoid of public rights, but property nominally owned by private individuals, subject to various group or public interests. * * *

Because all solutions to the tragedy of common access inevitably involve the imposition of property rights on previously owned environmental goods, the choice in environmental protection is not *whether* to adopt a property-based approach but *which* property-based approach(es) to adopt. To what extent should the state assert public rights (*res publicae*) as opposed to vesting (limited or unlimited) private property rights in individual users (*res individuales*) or groups of users (*res communes*)? An adequate theory of property rights in natural resources must consider the full range of possible property-based solutions to the tragedy of open access, recognizing that, in this second-best world, no single regime is likely to be the first-best solution for every resource in every institutional, technological, and ecological setting.

How does Professor Cole's view of property differ from the traditional view of Blackstone and others about the fee simple absolute of a property owner? What are the implications of his suggestion that "[t]here is no such thing as a pure or unadulterated public or private property system"? What might it mean for the law of takings, discussed in Chapter 2, page 184?

————

Case Study: Privatizing Parks

Terry L. Anderson et al., *How and Why to Privatize Federal Lands*, Policy Analysis 2, 4, 6, 21 (No. 363, Nov. 9, 1999)

Public land management ... does not always deliver what the citizens expect either for the treasury or for the environment. It is remarkable that the federal government actually loses money in the course of managing federal land assets estimated to be worth billions. Moreover, the federal government has a poor record of ecological stewardship. The argument that federal agents are better land managers than are private owners is not only suspect in theory; it is dubious in fact. * * *

[L]and-management agencies face conflicting policy goals, political pressures, perverse incentives, and poorly defined property rights. Managers are far removed from the actual costs and benefits associated with their actions, and the result is poor resource economics and stewardship. Instead of seeking profit, public managers seek larger budgets, more personnel, and expanded power. Instead of producing the goods that are most highly valued by users, managers produce the goods demanded by politically powerful special interests. Rather than face and charge market prices determined by supply and demand, managers face and set prices determined by politics, which usually equate to low or zero prices for those in political control. Not surprisingly, low receipts and high operating costs combine to create huge deficits for the federal land-management agencies.

... In 1995 the Forest Service managed 192 million acres worth $100 billion. The agency returned only $465 million to the treasury and spent $2.4 billion for a net loss of $1.9 billion. In the same year the BLM managed 220 million acres worth $25 billion. It returned $134 million to the treasury and incurred costs of over $1 billion for a net loss of $913 million. And the National Park Service netted a loss of $1.3 billion on an 87–million–acre asset worth $25

billion. Expenditures were $1.3 billion, and receipts were a paltry $1 million.
* * *

[T]he Yellowstone range is overpopulated by elk and bison resulting in starvation of thousands of elk, an overgrazed range, the destruction of plant communities, the elimination of critical habitat, and a serious decline in biodiversity. The starving elk and bison have repeatedly browsed willow communities and aspen stands on the northern range, causing a 95 percent decline in tall willows and aspens since the establishment of the park. * * *

[I]t is important to get beyond the visceral misidentification of government with the proper stewardship and husbanding of such resources. It is also important to realize that the public management of lands, which is subjected to a spectrum of conflicting political interests, creates common property-like incentives to overgraze grassland, overcut some forests (but undercut others), or overcrowd many parks. And where public land management encounters weakly organized political opposition, the budget-expanding incentives of government agencies tend to dominate policy determination. That is particularly evident in the 80–year history of large dam construction by the Bureau of Reclamation and the Army Corps of Engineers. No private power company, no consortium of such companies, and no industrial combine would have wasted its capital by flooding 186 miles of the Colorado River from Glen Canyon to Cataract Canyon then followed with a downstream proposal to flood Marble Canyon and Grand Canyon behind two great new dams.

[In his proposal for privatizing public lands, Anderson suggests a plan where action bids would not be made in money but in public land share certificates (analogous to no-par value stock certificates) which would be distributed equally to all Americans in advance of any auction and would be freely exchanged, assigned, or bequeathed during the auction period. Once all of the public lands were divested, the tract deed rights would be freely transferable.]

The above proposal would recognize each citizen's right to share in the wealth created by privatizing the public lands. Individuals without competence or interest in the productive use of any of the auctioned rights would be free to sell their initial assignment of share certificates in the open market. Oil companies, forest product companies, home builders, ranchers, farmers, outdoor recreation companies, private individuals, environmentalists, and environmental organizations would be free to purchase share certificates or receive them by donation or bequest. Environmental groups, such as the Sierra Club, Friends of the Earth, and the Audubon Society, instead of dissipating their resources in political action and lobbying for conservationist policies on public lands, could purchase certificates in the open market and actively campaign for the American people to donate their certificates to preservationist funds. Those certificates could be pooled and used to bid for the surface or other rights to any tracts the environmental groups chose. They could then manage those tracts as they saw fit.

———

- How would you argue against this proposal?
  - How would you argue *in favor* of this proposal?
- If the proposal were implemented as Anderson proposes, do you think the result would be more or less preservation?

- If less preservation would be the result, is that only because the government has currently over-valued the preservation resource?
- What types of lands are more or less likely to be preserved?
    - Would you be more willing to privatize some public lands than others? Why?
- Is bottom-line monetary profit or loss in managing public lands a useful measure of success or failure?

CHAPTER TWO

THE HISTORICAL AND CONSTITUTIONAL GEOGRAPHY OF NATURAL RESOURCES LAW

I. INTRODUCTION

II. ACQUISITION OF THE PUBLIC LANDS
   A. ACQUISITION OF LANDS FROM THE STATES WITH WESTERN LAND CLAIMS
   B. ACQUISITION OF PUBLIC LANDS FROM EUROPEAN POWERS
   C. ACQUISITION OF PUBLIC LANDS FROM INDIAN TRIBES

III. ALLOCATING THE NATION'S LAND AND NATURAL RESOURCES
   A. THE EQUAL FOOTING DOCTRINE
   B. THE PUBLIC TRUST DOCTRINE
      PROBLEM EXERCISE: INDIAN TREATY RIGHTS IN WASHINGTON'S TIDE-LANDS
   C. FEDERAL DISPOSITION OF THE NATION'S RESOURCES
      1. THE JEFFERSONIAN SURVEY SYSTEM
      2. LAND GRANTS TO STATES
      3. LAND GRANTS TO SETTLERS
      4. LAND GRANTS TO RAILROADS
   D. FEDERAL RETENTION OF PUBLIC LANDS AND RESOURCES
      1. EARLY FEDERAL RETENTION AND NATIONAL PARKS
      2. NATIONAL FORESTS
      3. NATIONAL WILDLIFE REFUGES AND EXECUTIVE WITHDRAWALS
      4. THE DECISION TO RETAIN THE PUBLIC LANDS
      5. THE GEOGRAPHIC LEGACY OF FEDERAL PUBLIC LANDS POLICY

IV. FEDERAL POWER OVER NATURAL RESOURCE MANAGEMENT
   A. FEDERAL POWER DERIVED FROM FEDERAL LAND OWNERSHIP: THE PROPERTY CLAUSE
      PROBLEM EXERCISE: THE SAGEBRUSH REBELLION
   B. FEDERAL POWER OVER NATURAL RESOURCES: OTHER CONSTITUTIONAL SOURCES
   C. THE TAKINGS LIMITATION ON FEDERAL AND STATE POWER OVER NATURAL RESOURCES
      PROBLEM EXERCISE: APPLYING THE LAW OF TAKINGS
   D. FREE EXERCISE AND ESTABLISHMENT CLAUSE LIMITATIONS ON FEDERAL AND STATE POWER OVER NATURAL RESOURCES

"[N]atural resource policy is dominated by the lords of yesterday, a battery of nineteenth-century laws, policies, and ideas that arose under wholly different social and economic conditions but that remain in effect due to inertia, powerful lobbying forces, and lack of public awareness."

CHARLES F. WILKINSON, CROSSING THE NEXT MERIDIAN: LAND, WATER, AND THE FUTURE OF THE WEST 17 (1992).

I. Introduction

Natural resources law is at once an old and new course. It is as old as property law itself. It is no coincidence that so many first-year students are introduced to property law by way of *Pierson v. Post*, an 1805 common law case about the ownership of a fox. Yet natural resources law is also decidedly "modern," as the various public and administrative law cases in this casebook attest. In tracking the course of the law from old to new, this chapter explores how the foundations of natural resources law have shaped the contours of our current legal edifice. The chapter does so by tracing the history of how the people of the United States have chosen to allocate ownership and regulatory authority over land and natural resources between themselves and different political institutions.

That history begins with the Revolution and the Declaration of Independence, when each of the colonies and their citizens gained sovereignty over the natural resources that had been possessed and controlled by Crown and Parliament. Once vested with that sovereignty, the people set about allocating ownership and regulatory power over their land and resources amongst themselves and the state and federal governments. The preeminent tool for that allocation was the United States Constitution. Precisely what the broad mandates of the Constitution meant for specific questions, however, remained for the courts to decide. As new questions arose about lands acquired from Indian tribes and European nations, about formation of new states, about continued federal ownership of land and resources within those new states, and about the authority of new federal agencies to manage that land, it fell to the courts to decide what distribution of ownership and authority had been intended, or was permissible, under the Constitution. This chapter can only skim the surface of this rich legal and natural resource history. By doing so, however, it provides a context for better understanding some of the foundational issues that lie at the heart of many current natural resource conflicts in the United States.

The law governing the allocation of natural resource ownership and regulatory authority among the federal government, states, and Indian tribes, along with the law respecting management of the lands and resources held by the federal government (the public lands), has traditionally been called "public land law." This appellation distinguished it from private land law or property law, which was essentially the law regarding land and other natural resources owned by private parties and regulated by states. This casebook looks at natural resources law through the lens of both private and federal lands. It does so for a number of reasons but primarily because regulation of natural resources has become less and less tied to *public land* ownership. The Endangered Species Act is perhaps the most prominent illustration of this development with federal authority following threatened and endangered species far beyond federal property.

Nevertheless, for a long period of time and still for many purposes today, land ownership largely determined regulatory control and thus partially the content of natural resources law. Because about thirty percent of our nation's lands are owned by the federal government, and because those lands contain a significant portion of our nation's biodiversity, understanding the legal history of our public lands is important to any understanding of natural resources law more generally. It is also critical because public land law established so much of the current distribution of entitlements, interests and expectations of individuals, communities, and the public which make resource management so complex. In addition to explaining why natural resource ownership and jurisdictional patterns look the way they do, the history of the public lands is a macro-level case study of policy approaches to an open access resource. As the United States heeded the call of manifest destiny and pushed westward throughout the nineteenth century, the lands that it acquired were essentially one great open access resource, with the exception of those lands and resources reserved for Indian tribes. Thus, the various public land laws that disposed of, reserved, and regulated these acquired lands were a century-long—indeed, a continuing—experiment in responses to the problems created by open access, the core concern of natural resource management.

The story of federal disposition of the public domain, and particularly that part of the story from the last half of the nineteenth century, referred to by historian Vernon Parrington as "The Great Barbecue," when land speculators, miners, railroads and timber companies took advantage of the laws to develop large holdings, is more than just backdrop. It is foundation. Many of the 3,500 public land laws adopted by Congress between 1785 and 1880 are still on the books. In Professor Charles Wilkinson's words at the beginning of this chapter, these laws are "the lords of yesterday" and continue to affect the way we manage natural resources, particularly in the public lands states of the West.

II. ACQUISITION OF THE PUBLIC LANDS

The seminal questions of public land law—whose public lands and who has sovereignty over those lands?—are ones that have bedeviled our country from the time that Great Britain, by means of generous charters and land grants to various proprietors, created the original thirteen colonies. Some of the grants were particularly large. Massachusetts, Connecticut, New York, Virginia, North and South Carolina, and Georgia were given the land between parallels of latitude extending "from sea to sea." PAUL W. GATES, HISTORY OF PUBLIC LAND LAW DEVELOPMENT 49 (1968).* For most of the seventeenth and well into the eighteenth century, Great Britain let the colonies develop their own policies for the management of these granted lands, and the primary policy was promoting their settlement and development. Although part of the incentive for that promotion was to raise revenue, it was also a reflection of political philosophy. The colonies' lands were the place where John Locke's ideas could be worked out in practice.

---

* With this first citation to Professor Gates' work it is important to acknowledge our debt to his landmark study on public land law. His careful and thorough research was performed on behalf of the Public Land Law Review Commission in 1968, the influential commission created as part of the 1964 Wilderness Act. *See* Pub. L. No. 88–606, §§ 1–3, 78 Stat. 982, 982 (1964).

Land ownership would be within the grasp of those willing to invest their labor. For some, such as Thomas Jefferson, the abundant lands would be the cradle of a citizenry of yeoman farmers, steadfastly clearing and breaking an inhospitable wilderness and virtuously cultivating the reclaimed lands. As Jefferson saw it, "Cultivators of the earth are the most valuable citizens. They are the most vigorous, the most independent, the most virtuous, and they are tied to their country, and wedded to its liberty and interests, by the most lasting bonds." Thomas Jefferson, *Notes on the State of Virginia*, Query XIX, at 157 (quoted in Daniel Kemmis, Community and the Politics of Place 20 (1990)).

This Jeffersonian vision of the public lands as a nursery of virtuous citizens was long to hold sway in public land policy and even today exerts significant influence. Great Britain's interference with this vision was one of the triggering events of the Revolution. In the Proclamation of 1763 and the Quebec Act of 1774, Great Britain insisted on a common land policy, prohibiting further settlement west of the Appalachians, halting grants by colonial governors and requiring that in the future land be surveyed and sold at public auction. Jefferson denounced this exercise of British authority over land title and two years later, in the Declaration of Independence, he raised the same grievance, accusing Great Britain of endeavoring "to prevent the population of these States" and "raising the conditions of new appropriations of lands."

Although the Declaration of Independence and the Revolution solved the problem of Great Britain imposing a common land policy on the colonies, it only ushered in a new set of perplexing questions. Would the colonies, now states, set their own land policies? How would the overlapping land claims of the new states be resolved? Would the newly-formed federal government assume ownership of any of these lands? Could additional states be created out of these western lands? Under what terms? And what about competing claims of other European sovereigns? How could those be resolved? Finally, what about the land claims of Indian tribes? The sections that follow sketch the nation's continuing efforts to answer these questions.

A. Acquisition of Lands from the States with Western Land Claims

After the Revolution, the Continental Congress had the monumental task of paying war debts and organizing the federal union. The greatest stumbling block in ratifying the Articles of Confederation was the issue of what to do about the western lands. As noted above, some of the original charters had granted the colonies land "from sea to sea." The states with such generous charters saw no reason to hand over their control. But led by Maryland, the states without western lands argued that those western territories had been "wrested from the common enemy by the blood and treasure of the thirteen states [and] should be considered as common property." 14 Journal of the Continental Congress 621 (May 1779); 17 Journal of the Continental Congress 806–08 (Sept., 1780) (1910). They threatened not to ratify the Articles of Confederation until the western territories were recognized as the property of the confederation and used to retire the heavy debt from the Revolutionary War. 11 JOURNAL OF THE CONTINENTAL CONGRESS 650 (June 1778).

Virginia responded that the complaints were the result of more cynical motives, noting that the legislatures of Maryland and New Jersey were both heavily influenced by prominent individuals who had invested in land companies and speculative land ventures in the west. *See* GATES, *supra*, at 50–51. Nevertheless, the Continental Congress, in dire need of money and in need of lands promised as bounties to Revolutionary War veterans, recommended to the legislatures of the landholding states that they cede their western territories. 17 JOURNAL OF THE CONTINENTAL CONGRESS 807 (Sept. 1780) (1910). It was only when Virginia and New York indicated that they would do so that Maryland acceded to the Articles of Confederation. GATES, *supra* at 51–52. As it turned out, it took until 1802 for all of the seven landholding states to make their cessions. *See* Figure 1 *below*.

B.   ACQUISITION OF PUBLIC LANDS FROM EUROPEAN POWERS

Federal acquisition of land from the landholding states is, of course, only a part of the acquisition story. Although some of the crown grants nominally extended from sea to sea, the reality was that they extended as far as British possession, which at the time of the Revolution was to the Mississippi River, with a couple of exceptions such as the Spanish claim to Florida, which stretched along the Gulf Coast to New Orleans. As reflected in the following map and in the discussion below, the next part of the acquisition story—the acquisition of land from European sovereigns—is spread out over almost 100 years, until the purchase of Alaska in 1867. (Although Hawaii was not annexed until 1898, the United States acquired very little public land when it annexed Hawaii.)

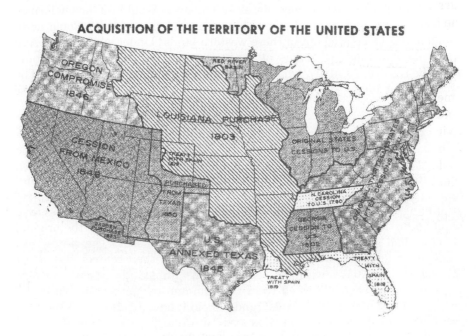

Figure 1 Acquisition of the Territory of the United States
(reproduced from GATES, *supra*, at 76.)

Early in our nation's history, the primary artery of commerce was rivers, and the primary artery beyond the Alleghenies was the Mississippi. Thus as settlers pushed westward, an area of immediate concern was Spain's control of New Orleans at the mouth of the Mississippi. When Napoleon and France secured Louisiana from Spain in 1800, the Mississippi problem became a French problem. President Jefferson sent representatives to France to negotiate the purchase of New Orleans at the mouth of the river and, he hoped, a part of Louisiana. Progress in the negotiations was slow until French military reverses prompted Napoleon to offer the entire Louisiana territory. Despite some concern about the constitutional authority for the purchase and objections from New Englanders disturbed about the growing political power of the new West, Jefferson quickly accepted the offer. The 1803 Louisiana Purchase roughly doubled the national area, adding more than 523 million acres at a cost of about 3 cents per acre. GATES, *supra*, at 75–78.

As Georgia's population increased and settlers pushed into the Mississippi territory, Spain's remaining territorial claims in Florida came under increasing pressure. The result was an 1819 treaty with Spain ceding all of Florida. In return, the United States surrendered a weak claim to Texas and agreed to pay $5 million of U.S. citizens' claims against Spain, the effective price for Florida. Just the year before, the United States had firmed up its northern border, at least as far as the Rocky Mountains, agreeing with Great Britain that the border separating the two countries would extend from the northwest point on the Lake of the Woods (in current Minnesota) down to the 49th parallel and from there westward to the Rockies. GATES, *supra*, at 78–79.

Some time elapsed before Texas became the next territorial addition, although not much time considering the amount of land the young nation needed to digest. Following its independence from Spain, Mexico welcomed American immigrants, offering land at favorable prices (2.5 cents to 5.6 cents per acre compared with the $1.25 per acre in the United States) and giving particularly large grants to boosters like Stephen Austin who agreed to bring a certain number of settlers. Mexico, however, was sowing the seeds of its own downfall. By 1830, there were 20,000 Americans in Mexico who were becoming increasingly disenchanted with Mexican rule. In 1835 this produced a revolution, famous for defeat at the Alamo and ultimately victory over Santa Anna at San Jacinto, leading to Mexico's recognition of Texas's independence in 1836. Concern about Texas altering the balance of power too much in favor of slave states, however, delayed Texas's admission to the Union until nine years later in 1845. From the public lands perspective, a chief outcome of this delay was that Texas, which during the interim period had been an independent sovereign managing its own public lands, was able to retain its public lands when it entered the Union. Texas in 1850 did sell just under 79 million acres along its western border to the United States but within Texas's remaining borders, the United States owns very little public land. Thus it is that most public land law books skip over Texas despite its abundant natural resource base. GATES, *supra* at 80–83.

Increasing contacts with Mexico in Texas and California prompted yet more expansion to the southwest. Professor Gates summarizes the story.

> President Polk and the expansionists were becoming anxious to acquire California from Mexico. Polk had tried to buy California and to pay Mexico a fair price for the disputed territory between the Rio Grande and the Nueces Rivers, but, having lost Texas, no official of Mexico dared to favor sale of any part of its territory. There were numerous issues between the two countries in addition to the boundary disputes that were exasperating both sides. They were sufficient, Polk thought, to justify the declaration of war for which he was preparing when Mexican troops crossed into the disputed territory, fired on American troops that were already there, and gave Polk a better pretext. War was promptly declared. Generals Scott and Taylor proceeded to defeat the Mexican armies, captured Mexico City, and were in a position to compel surrender of the country and make a peace acceptable to the Americans.

> All that Polk and the moderate expansionists wanted was gained in the [1848] Treaty of Guadalupe Hidalgo, though some politicians were disappointed that a larger part of Mexico was not gained. Mexico recognized the Rio Grande as the boundary separating Texas from Mexico, and agreed to sell for $15 million all of what is now California, Nevada, Utah, Arizona north of the Gila River, New Mexico west of the Rio Grande, and parts of southwestern Wyoming, and southwestern Colorado. Included in this great area containing 334,479,360 acres were the enormously rich mineral and agricultural regions of California, the Interior Basin that the Mormons were just beginning to develop, and some of the most spectacular scenery in the world, such as the Grand Canyon, and ... present day Bryce and Zion National Parks....

PAUL W. GATES, HISTORY OF PUBLIC LAND LAW DEVELOPMENT 83 (1968).

Along with Stephen Austin's move into Texas and Brigham Young and the Mormons' trek into the Great Basin, missionary settlers like Marcus Whitman, following the path of Lewis and Clark, were moving into the Oregon region, creating tension with its British occupants (primarily the Hudson's Bay Company). In 1846, the United States and Great Britain ended their joint occupation of the Oregon country, extending the border between the two nations along the 49th parallel from the Rocky Mountains to the Pacific Coast. This division of the Oregon country (present day Oregon, Washington, Idaho, and part of Montana) added another 180.6 million acres to public domain. GATES, *supra*, at 80–84.

With the Treaty of Guadalupe Hidalgo and the Treaty of 1846 with Great Britain, the borders of the contiguous United States were largely complete. The last piece of the puzzle was the 1853 purchase from Mexico of a tract of land south of the Gila River, the purpose of which was to facilitate construction of a railroad from New Orleans to San Diego. This $10 million Gadsden Purchase (named after James Gadsden, a South Carolina railroad promoter) added almost 19 million acres to the public domain in present-day Arizona and New Mexico. Although the Gadsden purchase marked the end of land acquisition in the contiguous United States, one significant addition remained—Alaska. Hoping in part to bracket British Columbia and make its annexation possible, Secretary of State Seward negotiated the purchase of Alaska from Russia in 1867. Although annexation of British Columbia was never to occur, at a relative bargain of $7.2 million (about 2 cents per acre), 325 million resource-rich acres were added to the public lands. Gates, *supra*, at 84–86.

C. Acquisition of Public Lands from Indian Tribes

Although describing the entire process of land acquisition from the original states and the European powers is a useful organizational approach, it should not be mistaken for telling the entire acquisition story. Throughout the same time period and continuing beyond it, another story was unfolding; namely the United States' acquisition of land and resources from the Indian tribes who had peopled the continent prior to European arrival. In essence, the agreements with European powers merely cleared the way for bilateral dealings with the tribes actually dwelling in the area. The history of the United States' dealings with Indian tribes is complex, tragic, and mostly beyond the scope of this casebook. Yet some understanding of that history is critical to natural resources law because it is entwined with a wide range of current natural resource disputes. Indian tribes have treaty rights to half the salmon runs in the states of Washington and Oregon and claims to potentially vast quantities of water throughout the western United States. The Clean Water Act gives tribes authority to regulate water quality, including off-reservation discharges. Indian reservations contain significant reserves of timber, coal, natural gas and critical biodiversity. To think about resource allocation and preservation without considering Native Americans is to exclude a critical stakeholder and to ignore an important example of the sort of political scale challenge discussed in Chapter 1 (pages 52–57) that makes natural resource management so complex. Our focus in this section is on acquisition. Other portions of the casebook address the role of Native Americans in the context of specific resources.

Recall that prior to the Proclamation of 1763, the colonies had largely set their own land policies within the extent of their generously interpreted charters. This meant that each colony decided upon its own approach for treating with Indian tribes. Most of the colonies prohibited individuals from purchasing land from Indian tribes without prior governmental permission, although in some instances individuals were allowed to negotiate on their own. At the beginning of the French and Indian war in 1754, however, Great Britain, mostly in an effort to win the tribes of the Ohio and Mississippi River basins to their side, took control of land policy from the individual colonies and prohibited further settlement west of the Appalachians. To the frustration of the colonies, this war-time policy was formalized in the Proclamation of 1763. Although a number of the colonists, including leading Founders, continued to purchase land from Indian tribes in the speculation that Crown policy would change, the policy itself remained a significant source of colonial angst and, as discussed above, was another significant grievance cited in the Declaration of Independence.

Following the Revolution, the question whether states or the federal government would have authority to treat with Indian tribes was bound up with the question of who would have ownership of the western lands. Just as the lands ultimately came to the federal government, so too did the power to treat with Indian tribes, although for a period of time under the Articles of Confederation, states retained the right to purchase Indian lands within their boundaries. Art. IX (4). Nevertheless, when the Constitution was ratified, Congress, under what has been termed the "Indian Commerce Clause," was authorized to "regulate Commerce with foreign Nations, and among the several States, and with the Indian Tribes." U.S. CONST. art. I, § 8, cl. 3. The practical import of this language has been to vest the federal government with complete control over Indian affairs. The following case addresses the residue of the shift from colonial and individual land purchases to federal control. More importantly, for purposes of public land and natural resources law, it describes the nature of the property interest that the United States received in the deeds of cession and then in subsequent agreements with European powers.

JOHNSON v. M'INTOSH,
21 U.S. (8 Wheat.) 543 (1823)

MR. CHIEF JUSTICE MARSHALL delivered the opinion of the Court.

[Johnson and the other plaintiffs claimed title to certain land under two grants made by chiefs of the Illinois and Piankeshaw Indian tribes in 1773 and in 1775. The defendant, M'Intosh, claimed title to the same land through an 1818 United States patent. The tribes had ceded the land to the United States in a 1795 treaty.]

The facts ... show the authority of the chiefs who executed this conveyance, so far as it could be given by their own people; and likewise show, that the particular tribes for whom these chiefs acted were in rightful possession of the land they sold. The inquiry, therefore, is, in a great measure, confined to the power of Indians to give, and of private individuals to receive, a title which can be sustained in the Courts of this country. * * *

On the discovery of this immense continent, the great nations of Europe were eager to appropriate to themselves so much of it as they could respectively acquire. Its vast extent offered an ample field to the ambition and enterprise of all; and the character and religion of its inhabitants afforded an apology for considering them as a people over whom the superior genius of Europe might claim an ascendancy. The potentates of the old world found no difficulty in convincing themselves that they made ample compensation to the inhabitants of the new, by bestowing on them civilization and Christianity, in exchange for unlimited independence. But, as they were all in pursuit of nearly the same object, it was necessary, in order to avoid conflicting settlements, and consequent war with each other, to establish a principle, which all should acknowledge as the law by which the right of acquisition, which they all asserted, should be regulated as between themselves. This principle was, that discovery gave title to the government by whose subjects, or by whose authority, it was made, against all other European governments, which title might be consummated by possession.

The exclusion of all other Europeans, necessarily gave to the nation making the discovery the sole right of acquiring the soil from the natives, and establishing settlements upon it. It was a right with which no Europeans could interfere. It was a right which all asserted for themselves, and to the assertion of which, by others, all assented. * * *

In the establishment of these relations, the rights of the original inhabitants were, in no instance, entirely disregarded; but were necessarily, to a considerable extent, impaired. They were admitted to be the rightful occupants of the soil, with a legal as well as just claim to retain possession of it, and to use it according to their own discretion; but their rights to complete sovereignty, as independent nations, were necessarily diminished, and their power to dispose of the soil at their own will, to whomsoever they pleased, was denied by the original fundamental principle, that discovery gave exclusive title to those who made it.

While the different nations of Europe respected the right of the natives, as occupants, they asserted the ultimate dominion to be in themselves; and claimed and exercised, as a consequence of this ultimate dominion, a power to grant the soil, while yet in possession of the natives. These grants have been understood by all, to convey a title to the grantees, subject only to the Indian right of occupancy.

The history of America, from its discovery to the present day, proves, we think, the universal recognition of these principles. * * *

Thus, all the nations of Europe, who have acquired territory on this continent, have asserted in themselves, and have recognised in others, the exclusive right of the discoverer to appropriate the lands occupied by the Indians. Have the American States rejected or adopted this principle?

By the treaty which concluded the war of our revolution, Great Britain relinquished all claim, not only to the government, but to the "propriety and territorial rights of the United States," whose boundaries were fixed in the second article. By this treaty, the powers of government, and the right to soil, which had previously been in Great Britain, passed definitively to these States. We had before taken possession of them, by declaring independence; but neither the declaration of independence, nor the treaty confirming it, could give us more than that which we before possessed, or to which Great Britain was before entitled. It has never been doubted, that either the United States, or the several States, had a clear title to all the lands within the boundary lines described in the treaty, subject only to the Indian right of occupancy, and that the exclusive power to extinguish that right, was vested in that government which might constitutionally exercise it. * * *

The States, having within their chartered limits different portions of territory covered by Indians, ceded that territory, generally, to the United States, on conditions expressed in their deeds of cession, which demonstrate the opinion, that they ceded the soil as well as jurisdiction, and that in doing so, they granted a productive fund to the government of the Union. * * *

The ceded territory was occupied by numerous and warlike tribes of Indians; but the exclusive right of the United States to extinguish their title, and to grant the soil, has never, we believe, been doubted. * * *

The United States, then, have unequivocally acceded to that great and broad rule by which its civilized inhabitants now hold this country. They hold, and assert in themselves, the title by which it was acquired. They maintain, as all others have maintained, that discovery gave an exclusive right to extinguish the Indian title of occupancy, either by purchase or by conquest; and gave also a right to such a degree of sovereignty, as the circumstances of the people would allow them to exercise. * * *

We will not enter into the controversy, whether agriculturists, merchants, and manufacturers, have a right, on abstract principles, to expel hunters from the territory they possess, or to contract their limits. Conquest gives a title which the Courts of the conqueror cannot deny, whatever the private and speculative opinions of individuals may be, respecting the original justice of the claim which has been successfully asserted. The British government, which was then our government, and whose rights have passed to the United States, asserted title to all the lands occupied by Indians, within the chartered limits of the British colonies. It asserted also a limited sovereignty over them, and the exclusive right of extinguishing the title which occupancy gave to them. These claims have been maintained and established as far west as the river Mississippi, by the sword. The title to a vast portion of the lands we now hold, originates in them. It is not for the Courts of this country to question the validity of this title, or to sustain one which is incompatible with it.

Although we do not mean to engage in the defence of those principles which Europeans have applied to Indian title, they may, we think, find some excuse, if not justification, in the character and habits of the people whose rights have been wrested from them.

The title by conquest is acquired and maintained by force. The conqueror prescribes its limits. Humanity, however, acting on public opinion, has established, as a general rule, that the conquered shall not be wantonly oppressed, and that their condition shall remain as eligible as is compatible with the objects of the conquest. Most usually, they are incorporated with the victorious nation, and become subjects or citizens of the government with which they are connected. The new and old members of the society mingle with each other; the distinction between them is gradually lost, and they make one people. Where this incorporation is practicable, humanity demands, and a wise policy requires, that the rights of the conquered to property should remain unimpaired; that the new subjects should be governed as equitably as the old, and that confidence in their security should gradually banish the painful sense of being separated from their ancient connexions, and united by force to strangers.
* * *

But the tribes of Indians inhabiting this country were fierce savages, whose occupation was war, and whose subsistence was drawn chiefly from the forest. To leave them in possession of their country, was to leave the country a wilderness; to govern them as a distinct people, was impossible, because they were as brave and as high spirited as they were fierce, and were ready to repel by arms every attempt on their independence.

What was the inevitable consequence of this state of things? The Europeans were under the necessity either of abandoning the country, and relinquishing their pompous claims to it, or of enforcing those claims by the sword, and by the adoption of principles adapted to the condition of a people with whom it was impossible to mix, and who could not be governed as a distinct society, or of remaining in their neighbourhood, and exposing themselves and their families to the perpetual hazard of being massacred.

Frequent and bloody wars, in which the whites were not always the aggressors, unavoidably ensued. European policy, numbers, and skill, prevailed. As the white population advanced, that of the Indians necessarily receded. The country in the immediate neighbourhood of agriculturists became unfit for them. The game fled into thicker and more unbroken forests, and the Indians followed. The soil, to which the crown originally claimed title, being no longer occupied by its ancient inhabitants, was parceled out according to the will of the sovereign power, and taken possession of by persons who claimed immediately from the crown, or mediately, through its grantees or deputies. * * *

However extravagant the pretension of converting the discovery of an inhabited country into conquest may appear; if the principle has been asserted in the first instance, and afterwards sustained; if a country has been acquired and held under it; if the property of the great mass of the community originates in it, it becomes the law of the land, and cannot be questioned. So, too, with respect to the concomitant principle, that the Indian inhabitants are to be considered merely as occupants, to be protected, indeed, while in peace, in the possession of their lands, but to be deemed incapable of transferring the absolute title to others. However this restriction may be opposed to natural right, and to the usages of civilized nations, yet, if it be indispensable to that system under which the country has been settled, and be adapted to the actual condition of the two people, it may, perhaps, be supported by reason, and certainly cannot be rejected by Courts of justice. * * *

Another view has been taken of this question, which deserves to be considered. The title of the crown, whatever it might be, could be acquired only by a conveyance from the crown. If an individual might extinguish the Indian title for his own benefit, or, in other words, might purchase it, still he could acquire only that title. Admitting their power to change their laws or usages, so far as to allow an individual to separate a portion of their lands from the common stock, and hold it in severalty, still it is a part of their territory, and is held under them, by a title dependent on their laws. The grant derives its efficacy from their will; and, if they choose to resume it, and make a different disposition of the land, the Courts of the United States cannot interpose for the protection of the title. The person who purchases lands from the Indians, within their territory, incorporates himself with them, so far as respects the property purchased; holds their title under their protection, and subject to their laws. If they annul the grant, we know of no tribunal which can revise and set aside the proceeding. We know of no principle which can distinguish this case from a grant made to a native Indian, authorizing him to hold a particular tract of land in severalty.

As such a grant could not separate the Indian from his nation, nor give a title which our Courts could distinguish from the title of his tribe, as it might still be conquered from, or ceded by his tribe, we can perceive no legal principle which will authorize a Court to say, that different consequences are attached to this purchase, because it was made by a stranger. By the [1795 Treaty of Greenville] concluded between the United States and the Indian nations, whose title the plaintiffs claim, the country comprehending the lands in controversy has been ceded to the United States, without any reservation of their title. These nations had been at war with the United States, and had an unquestionable right to annul any grant they had made to American citizens. Their cession of the country, without a reservation of this land, affords a fair presumption, that they considered it as of no validity. They ceded to the United States this very property, after having used it in common with other lands, as their own, from the date of their deeds to the time of cession; and the attempt now made, is to set up their title against that of the United States. * * *

After bestowing on this subject a degree of attention which was more required by the magnitude of the interest in litigation, and the able and elaborate arguments of the bar, than by its intrinsic difficulty, the Court is decidedly of opinion, that the plaintiffs do not exhibit a title which can be sustained in the Courts of the United States....

QUESTIONS AND DISCUSSION

1. Johnson was hardly unique in his purchase of western lands from Indian tribes. A number of the leading founding fathers—Washington,

Franklin, and Paine among them—had speculated in western lands hoping to turn a profit as the United States expanded westward. The importance of the case to such claimants is perhaps best illustrated by the fact that Daniel Webster represented Johnson in the litigation.

2. Based on *Johnson v. M'Intosh*, describe the probable chain of title to an initial homestead grant in Kansas or to a federal patent (essentially a federal quitclaim deed) in Indiana.

3. The Indians' right to use and occupy the land, subject to purchase or conquest by the "discovering" nation, is more generally described as aboriginal title, Indian title, or original Indian title. The United States' underlying fee simple title

> can be conveyed by the holder of the fee subject to the Indian right of occupancy. * * * The naked fee title in lands subject to original Indian title gives the holder, whether the state or private party, no present possessory interest in the land. Naked fee title merely constitutes a reversionary interest that becomes possessory only if Congress clearly and plainly extinguishes the Indian title. * * *
>
> Generally, the Supreme Court has held that the tribes are entitled to full use and enjoyment of the surface and mineral estate, and to the fruits of the land, such as timber resources.
>
> Although aboriginal title is similar to other forms of tribal title, there is one significant difference: aboriginal title may be extinguished by the United States without creating a constitutional obligation to pay compensation.
>
> In order to prove aboriginal possession, a tribe must prove actual, rather than constructive, possession of the land in question. The occupation shown must have been continuous and exclusive unless it was during a period of forcible, involuntary dispossession.

FELIX S. COHEN, HANDBOOK OF FEDERAL INDIAN LAW 489–92 (1982 ed.).

4. Under the Court's reasoning, were the Tribes' grants to Johnson wholly valueless? Could the Tribes have sold to Johnson their right of use and occupancy? If so, where was Johnson to seek a remedy? How eager do you suppose future settlers or speculators would have been to purchase a tribe's right to use and occupy? Whatever the eagerness of a potential purchaser, the power to purchase land from Indian tribes was essentially eliminated by the Trade and Non–Intercourse Act of 1790 which prohibited any conveyance of Indian lands without congressional approval. *See generally* FELIX S. COHEN, HANDBOOK OF FEDERAL INDIAN LAW 212, 489 (1982 ed.).

5. Consider the legitimacy of Chief Justice Marshall's decision to adopt the discovery doctrine as the foundation of United States' title. Do you see the decision as grounded in principles of natural law or positive law? Is there a natural law or positive law critique of the decision? What other approaches could Marshall have taken? What would have been the implication of those approaches?

6. The Court states that Indian title may be terminated by purchase or conquest. With respect to method, the United States chose a combination of purchase and conquest. Generally, the United States purchased Indian lands. In the absence of any legal impediment, however, the price was often negotiated under a threat to forcibly remove uncooperative tribes or at very least under the harsh light of the United States' vastly superior power. Professor Cohen describes this process below, although he takes a somewhat more positive view of the bargaining process.

Felix S. Cohen, *Original Indian Title*, 32 Minn. L. Rev. 25, 34–36, 38 (1947)

Every American schoolboy is taught to believe that the lands of the United States were acquired by purchase or treaty from Britain, Spain, France, Mexico, and Russia, and that for all the continental lands so purchased we paid about 50 million dollars out of the Federal Treasury. Most of us believe this story as unquestioningly as we believe in electricity or corporations. We have seen little maps of the United States in our history books and big maps in our geography books showing the vast area that Napoleon sold us in 1803 for 15 million dollars and the various other cessions that make up the story of our national expansion. As for the original Indian owners of the continent, the common impression is that we took the land from them by force and proceeded to lock them up in concentration camps called "reservations."

Notwithstanding this prevailing mythology, the historic fact is that practically all of the real estate acquired by the United States since 1776 was purchased not from Napoleon or any other emperor or czar but from its original Indian owners. What we acquired from Napoleon in the Louisiana Purchase was not real estate, for practically all of the ceded territory that was not privately owned by Spanish and French settlers was still owned by the Indians, and the property rights of all the inhabitants were safeguarded by the terms of the treaty of cession. What we did acquire from Napoleon was not the land, which was not his to sell, but simply the power to govern and to tax, the same sort of power that we gained with the acquisition of Puerto Rico or the Virgin Islands a century later.

It may help us to appreciate the distinction between a sale of land and the transfer of governmental power if we note that after paying Napoleon 15 million dollars for the cession of political authority over the Louisiana Territory we proceeded to pay the Indian tribes of the ceded territory more than twenty times this sum for such lands in their possession as they were willing to sell. And while Napoleon, when he took his 15 million dollars, was thoroughly and completely relieved of all connections with the territory, the Indian tribes were wise enough to reserve from their cessions sufficient land to bring them a current income that exceeds each year the amount of our payment to Napoleon. One of these reservations, that of the Osages, has thus far brought its Indian owners 280 million dollars in oil royalties. Some other Indian tribes, less warlike, or less lucky, than the Osages, fared badly in their real estate transactions with the Great White Father. But in its totality the account of our land transactions with the Indians is not small potatoes. While nobody has ever calculated the total sum paid by the United States to Indian tribes as consideration for more than two million square miles of land purchased from them, and any such calculation would have to take account of the conjectural value of a myriad of commodities, special services, and tax exemptions, which commonly took the place of cash, a conservative estimate would put the total price of Indian lands sold to the United States at a figure somewhat in excess of 800 million dollars. * * *

Granted that the Federal Government bought the country from the Indians, the question may still be raised whether the Indians received anything like a fair price for what they sold. The only fair answer to that question is that except in a very few cases where military duress was present the price paid for the land was one that satisfied the Indians. Whether the Indians should have been satisfied and what the land would be worth now if it had never been sold are questions that lead us to ethereal realms of speculation. The sale of Manhattan Island for $24 is commonly cited as a typical example of the white man's overreaching. But even if this were a typical example, which it is not, the matter of deciding whether a real estate deal was a fair bargain three hundred years after it took place is beset by many pitfalls. Hindsight is better than foresight, particularly in real estate deals. Whether the land the Dutch settlers bought would become a thriving metropolis or remain a wilderness, whether other Indian tribes or European powers would respect their title, and how long the land would remain in Dutch ownership were, in 1626, questions that were hid in the mists of the future. Many acres of land for which the United States later paid the Indians in the neighborhood of $1.25 an acre, less costs of surveying, still remain on the land books of the Federal Government, which has found no purchasers at that price and is now content to lease the lands for cattle grazing at a net return to the Federal Government of one or two cents per annum per acre.

7. For more detailed overviews of the history of federal Indian policy, see ROBERT N. CLINTON ET AL., AMERICAN INDIAN LAW 137–65 (3d ed. 1991); FRANCIS P. PRUCHA, THE GREAT FATHER (1984); FRANCIS P. PRUCHA, AMERICAN INDIAN POLICY IN THE FORMATIVE YEARS (1962); FRANCIS P. PRUCHA, AMERICAN INDIAN POLICY IN CRISIS: CHRISTIAN REFORMERS AND THE INDIANS, 1865–1890 (1964); RICHARD WHITE, IT'S YOUR MISFORTUNE AND NONE OF MY OWN: A HISTORY OF THE AMERICAN WEST 85–118 (1991).

8. In various cases and excerpts you will see two terms used to describe those lands that are the subject of public land law: the public domain and the public lands. Although there is considerable overlap in usage, "public lands" most often refers to all lands that are in federal ownership. National parks, national forests, wildlife refuges, and military installations are all part of the public lands. References to the "public domain" are typically to a subset of the public lands, namely those public lands that are unreserved for any specific purpose (in contrast to national forests and parks which are reserved for specific purposes) and were subject to disposition under the general land laws until the passage of the Federal Land Policy Management Act of 1976 and are now managed by the Bureau of Land Management. SAMUEL TRASK DANA & SALLY K. FAIRFAX, FOREST AND RANGE POLICY 8 (2d ed. 1980).

At the end of the Bush administration, Interior Secretary Dirk Kempthorne signed a secretarial order designating the 258 million acres of land managed by the BLM as the "National System of Public Lands." Ceasing to categorize these lands as part of the "public domain" does not formally change their status but identifying them as part of a system may increase their prominence in competition with the National Forest System, the National Park System, and the National Wildlife Refuge System.

III.   ALLOCATING THE NATION'S LANDS AND NATURAL RESOURCES

By virtue of the deeds of cession and negotiations with European powers and Indian tribes, the United States took ownership of vast lands and natural resources. Along with that ownership came a number of what Professor Gates identifies as "nagging" questions:

> Did the acts of cession of those early years and the later acquisitions of Florida, Louisiana, and California require that the lands be administered for the benefit of all the states, as the Original Thirteen States were inclined to maintain? Or should they be managed to assure speedy settlement of the newer communities into which they were being divided, without regard to the effects their rapid development would have on the older ones? Should the development of western states be promoted by generous grants of public land within their boundaries to aid educational institutions and finance internal improvements such as roads, canals, and railroads? Should the states in which the lands lay, and not the Federal government, be the major dispenser of land titles? Had the older communities no right to share in this largesse?

GATES, *supra*, at 3. This section of the chapter investigates these nagging questions along with a few others. It begins, however, with the question Professor Gates asks last: who would be the primary decision-maker with respect to the distribution of land and resources, the states within which the public lands lay or the federal government? Part A below takes up this issue. As with any question respecting the relationship between the states and the federal government, this is one of constitutional law. Stated in terms of the federal government's enumerated powers, the issue is federal power to create new states and to retain and own land within newly created states. As Part A discusses, over time the courts decided that the United States could dispose of or retain public lands as it chose, although a presumption in favor of state ownership would develop for land under navigable waters. The inquiry in Part A will introduce you to constitutional provisions with which you may have little familiarity, mostly from Article IV of the Constitution. Of greatest importance will be the Property Clause which gives to Congress the power to "dispose of and make all needful Rules and Regulations respecting the Territory or other Property belonging to the United States." U.S. CONST. art. IV, § 3, cl. 2.

Part B of this Section then looks at a companion question, namely state power to dispose of or retain the land and resources granted to it by the federal government (or, in the case of the original thirteen states, received at the time of the Revolution). As discussed in Part B, a state's power over its land and resources is plenary, except as preempted by federal action and except for those resources that the state is obligated to hold in trust for the whole people under the public trust doctrine, which focuses on the special case of land under navigable waters. Part B concludes with a problem exercise involving a dispute between the United States, the State of Washington, several Indian tribes, and private property owners that should allow you to apply the principles of Parts A and B as well as review the *Johnson v. M'Intosh* case.

Having reviewed the legal sources of federal power to grant or retain public lands as the government saw fit, Parts C and D look at the historical and practical application of that power. What did the United States actually do with the lands it had acquired from the original states, European powers, and Indian tribes? As Part C reveals, for most of the nineteenth and into the twentieth century, the primary goal of United States policy was to dispose of as much of the public lands and natural resources as possible. Reservation of public lands for the public would occur sporadically in the nineteenth century, as for example with the mineral leases discussed below in *United States v. Gratiot*, 39 U.S. (14 Pet.) 526, 538 (1840), and the creation of Yellowstone National Park in 1872. But it was not until 1891 and the creation of large forest reserves that later became our national forests that the federal government began more broadly and systematically to retain public lands under federal management. Part D recounts the creation of the national forests and the other moves toward federal retention of the public lands and resources over the course of the twentieth century.

A.   THE EQUAL FOOTING DOCTRINE

In the debate over whether Virginia should cede its western lands and, if ceded, what sort of states might be created from the western territories, Thomas Jefferson was one of the powerful voices. Jefferson understood that the western territories were more than a source of income. They were a key to the political balance of power in North America. The British and Spanish could entice away the loyalty of disgruntled occupants of the territory, shifting the balance of power in favor of old adversaries and jeopardizing the stability of the United States. Alternatively, subservient colonies might easily become disgruntled with a secondary political status given to them by the United States and seek their independence. Many in the East had serious doubts about the western settlers' loyalty to the United States. By offering fair and equitable terms of admission into the Union, the fledgling nation could better ensure the ongoing loyalty of the territories and the further expansion of the Union. Gordon T. Stewart, *The Northwest Ordinance and the Balance of Power in North America, in* THE NORTHWEST ORDINANCE: ESSAYS ON ITS FORMULATION, PROVISIONS AND LEGACY (Frederick D. Williams ed., 1988). Thus, in its instrument conveying its territories northwest of the Ohio River, Virginia stipulated that the states formed out of this ceded territory "shall be distinct republican states, and admitted members of the federal union; having the same rights of sovereignty, freedom and independence, as the other states." 26 JOURNALS OF THE CONTINENTAL CONGRESS 113, 114 (Mar. 1784) (1928) (Virginia's cession).

In the end, the land and sovereignty afforded new states would reflect the tension between the Jeffersonian concern about political equality and the original states' concern of sharing in the benefits of the West's resources. Reflecting the vision of Virginia's deed of cession, the Northwest Ordinance, which served as a constitutional document for the political structure of new states northwest of the Ohio River, decreed that new states would be admitted into the Union "on an equal footing with the original States, in all respects whatever...." 1 U.S.C. § 22. On the other hand, the new states' enabling acts (the legislation authorizing a new state to enter the Union) provided for federal retention of significant lands within each state. From the perspective of some of the original states this was only a good beginning. In 1826, for example, the Rhode Island legislature directed its congressional representatives to seek an act of Congress appropriating for Rhode Island "her proportion of the public lands" for "the establishment of an educational fund in this State." GATES, *supra*, at 7. Over the years other states floated similar proposals. Most did not bear fruit with the notable exception of the 1862 Morrill Act, which gave each state scrip for 30,000 acres of public land per representative and senator in Congress for purposes of funding state colleges of agricultural and mechanic arts. These "A & M" or "land grant" colleges have evolved into some of the leading institutions of higher learning in the nation, including, for example, Cornell University, the University of Illinois, the Massachusetts Institute of Technology, Michigan State University, Ohio State University, and the University of Wisconsin. Gates, *supra*, at 22–23. (The states received scrip rather than land in an effort to avoid the jurisdictional conflicts that could arise if one state owned land within another.)

From the perspective of many in the new states, the Morrill Act and like legislation appeared less like an equitable distribution of the benefits of the nation's resources and more like a "plunder scheme." Gates, *supra*, at 22. Although the new states' enabling acts had given them some land to support education and a small percentage of the proceeds from land sales to support internal improvements like roads and canals, from their perspective this was far too little. Between 1828 and 1833, state legislatures in Alabama, Indiana, Louisiana, Missouri, Illinois, and Indiana demanded cession of all federal lands. Indiana's memorial is typical: "This State, being a sovereign, free, and independent State, has the exclusive right to the soil and eminent domain of all the unappropriated lands ... which right was reserved for her by the State of Virginia, in the deed of cession...." Gates, *supra*, at 9. From Indiana's perspective, for new states to enter the Union on an equal footing with the original states, the federal government could not retain land within those new states. Indiana's position would subsequently be tested in *Pollard v. Hagan*, 44 U.S. (3 How.) 212 (1845), a classic public land law case, and one that wise use advocates still rely upon to argue that the federal government has no legal authority to retain ownership of the public lands.

Pollard involved a dispute about the United States' power to grant title to tidelands in Alabama's Mobile Bay. To those who have never heard of *Pollard*, it may seem odd that this particular dispute caused Justice Catron, in dissent, to proclaim that "this is deemed the most important controversy ever brought before this court, either as in respects the amount of property involved, or the principles on which the present judgment proceeds." 44 U.S. (3 How.) at 235. What Catron understood to be at stake in *Pollard* was not just whether the United States could grant Pollard the particular property at issue, but the entire question of federal power to retain and manage land and natural resources within the area to the west of the original thirteen states. Without that power, national parks like Yellowstone and Yosemite would not exist, nor would national forests or wilderness areas, or even federal grazing districts.

In reaching its conclusion that the United States' grant of the tidelands was invalid, the *Pollard* Court addressed three distinct issues. The Court first held that the Northwest Ordinance's command that new states enter the Union on an equal footing was not only a statutory requirement but was also a constitutional imperative. Congress, suggested the Court, did not have the power to admit states of lesser sovereignty than the original thirteen because Article IV, § 3, gave Congress only the power to "admit new states into this Union." 44 U.S. at 222–23. As the Supreme Court later explained in *Coyle v. Smith*, 221 U.S. 559 (1911):

> To maintain otherwise would be to say that the Union, through the power of Congress to admit new states, might come to be a union of states unequal in power, as including states whose powers were restricted only by the Constitution, with others whose powers had been further restricted by an act of Congress accepted as a condition of admission. Thus it would result, first, that the powers of Congress would not be defined by the Constitution alone, but in respect to new states, enlarged or restricted by the conditions imposed upon new states by its own legislation admitting them into the Union; and, second, that such new states might not exercise all of the powers which had not been delegated by the Constitution, but only such as had not been further bargained away as conditions of admission.

Id. at 567.

If all states were to be on an equal sovereign footing with the original thirteen, the obvious next issue is what it meant for a new state to be *equal*. Although *Pollard*'s answer to this question has not stood the test of time, the answer is one that is critical to understanding the evolution of public land law and to comprehending the foundation of many current natural resource policy debates. As the Court saw it, Georgia ceded the Alabama territory to the United States for the purpose of paying off the war debt. It was only when the United States sold the land into private ownership that Alabama would be a complete sovereign like the original thirteen states. Essentially, the Court viewed the federal government as an ordinary proprietor with respect to the public lands. The United States, the Court said over and over, had no "municipal sovereignty," which was another way of saying that the United States lacked police power over the public lands.

The Court recognized that in the Property Clause of the Constitution, Art. IV, § 3, Congress had been given the "power to dispose of and make all needful rules and regulations respecting the territory or other property of the United States." But this provision, said the Court, merely "authorized the passage of all laws necessary to secure the rights of the United States to the public lands, and to provide for their sale, and to protect them from taxation." 44 U.S. at 224. It was not intended to give the United States the authority to keep and regulate public lands. Instead, the Property Clause was something like temporary management authority pending the final sale and disposition of the public lands that would make Alabama a full sovereign.

According to *Pollard*, the Constitution provided only one way for the United States to obtain complete authority over public land and that way was the Enclave Clause. *Id.* at 223–24. The Enclave Clause gives Congress the power

> to exercise exclusive legislation in all cases whatsoever, over such district (not exceeding ten miles square) as may by cession of particular states, and the acceptance of Congress, become the seat of government of the United States, and to exercise like authority over all places purchased, by the consent of the

legislature of the state in which the same may be, for the erection of forts, magazines, arsenals, dock-yards, and other needful buildings.

U.S. Const., art. I, § 8, cl. 16. The need for the Enclave Clause with respect to the original thirteen states is relatively clear. Absent such a provision, the United States would not be able to obtain either the land or the exclusive jurisdiction necessary to perform various federal functions. What the Court was suggesting is that the United States should be under the same disability with respect to lands it acquired in the deeds of cession and then later from other European sovereigns and Indian tribes. Although it might hold such lands to fulfill any trust obligations imposed by the deeds or by treaties, it was like any other proprietor with respect to such lands. It did not have any particular regulatory authority except that which could be obtained through the Enclave Clause.

The import of the Court's reasoning is breathtaking in its scope. Imagine what our national landscape would have looked like if the Court's understanding of severely limited federal ownership and jurisdiction had been implemented. As we will explore further in Parts B and C below, the Court's view of severely limited federal power is long gone. Even before *Pollard*, the Supreme Court had confirmed federal power to issue short-term mineral leases for public land mining, remarking that "the words 'dispose of' [in the Property Clause], cannot receive the construction ... that they vest in Congress the power only to sell, and not to lease such lands. The disposal must be left to the discretion of Congress." *See United States v. Gratiot*, 39 U.S. (14 Pet.) 526, 538 (1840). Subsequent to *Pollard*, the Court on a number of occasions has made clear that the Property Clause power to "dispose of and make all needful rules and regulations respecting the territory and other property belonging to the United States," U.S. Const. art. IV, § 3, cl. 2, is plenary and presumes federal power to retain the public lands until it chooses to dispose of them. *See, e.g., Light v. United States*, 220 U.S. 523 (1911) ("The United States can prohibit absolutely or fix the terms on which its property may be used. As it can withhold or reserve the land, it can do so indefinitely."); *Kleppe v. New Mexico*, 426 U.S. 529 (1976).

One of the reasons why subsequent cases were so easily able to dismiss *Pollard*'s narrow view of federal power to retain and regulate land within the states is that it was dicta. Recall that *Pollard* held that the patent issued by the United States was invalid. In light of the Court's conclusion that the United States was obligated to sell its lands into private ownership to ensure Alabama's equal footing, this conclusion may seem strange. Why couldn't the United States grant the disputed patent if the Court's reasoning was controlling? The answer is that the Court applied a different rule to the particular land at issue because it was former tideland that had been overflowed by Mobile Bay prior to statehood.

At first glance, it would seem as though selling land formerly covered by Mobile Bay would be no different than any other non-overflowed land. Yet the Court held that unlike non-overflowed lands—which the United States was under a duty to sell—the United States lacked the power to convey the lands under Mobile Bay because those lands had to pass to Alabama when it entered the Union. As the Court saw it, navigable waters were even more closely bound up with state sovereignty than non-over-flowed lands and thus for Alabama to enter the Union on an equal sovereign footing, the United States needed to retain for Alabama all of its land under navigable waters. Whereas with respect to non-overflowed lands Alabama's equal sovereignty could be protected by a federal commitment to sell them to private owners, with respect to land under navigable water, Alabama's sovereignty could only be assured by holding those lands in trust for the future state.

In support of its conclusion that the United States could not convey away land under navigable water prior to statehood, the Court relied on *Martin v. Waddell*, 41 U.S. (16 Pet.) 367 (1842). *Martin* is one of the Supreme Court's earliest natural resource decisions. It involved a dispute over ownership of oyster lands in Raritan Bay in New Jersey. Martin claimed title to the oyster land by virtue of a lease issued by New Jersey. Waddell's lessee claimed title by a series of conveyances tracing back to the royal charter from Charles II. The Court sided with Martin. Although the Court never directly decided that Charles II was incapable of conveying these submerged lands, in dicta it suggested that he could not have done so because "[t]he dominion and property in navigable waters, and in the lands under them" were "held by the king as a public trust." 41 U.S. (16 Pet.) at 411. Land under navigable water was part and parcel of the crown's sovereign authority. The crown held title to all such submerged lands but was prohibited from conveying them into private ownership because it had an obligation to hold them in trust for public navigation, commerce, and fishery. Upon the Revolution, said the *Martin* Court, "the people of each state became themselves sovereign; and in that character hold the absolute right to all their navigable waters and the soils under them for their own common use, subject only to the rights since surrendered by the Constitution to the general government." *Id.* at 410–11. It is this last sentence that the *Pollard* court used as the basis for its conclusion that like Raritan Bay for New Jersey, Mobile Bay must have been part of Alabama's sovereign inheritance. And without its full inheritance, Alabama could not enter the Union on an equal footing.

Unlike the Court's dicta about the United States being obligated to dispose of non-overflowed lands, this core holding of *Pollard*—that the United States lacks power to grant away land under navigable water prior to statehood, or to retain it after statehood, because state ownership of such lands is critical to equal sovereign footing—has had real impact on the distribution of land and natural resources between the states and the federal government, although again the doctrine has changed over time. The Court now recognizes that land under navigable water is not part and parcel of state sovereignty and thus the United States may convey such lands prior to statehood, or retain them following statehood, without running afoul of the Constitution's equal footing mandate. However, in recognition of how critical navigable waters are to the public for navigation, commerce, and fishery, the Court requires that any prestatehood grant or retention be expressed in unmistakably clear language.

[A] court deciding a question of title to the bed of a navigable water must . . . begin with a strong presumption against conveyance by the United States, and must not infer such a conveyance unless the intention was definitely declared or otherwise made very plain, or was rendered in clear and especial words, or unless the claim confirmed in terms embraces the land under the waters of the stream.

Utah Div. of State Lands v. United States, 482 U.S. 193 (1987). The strong presumption in favor of state ownership of land under navigable water has left an interesting geographical legacy. In the midst of the vast swaths of federal land in the western United States are long ribbons of state-owned beds of navigable rivers and patches of state-owned bedlands under navigable lakes.

In the end, invocations of *Pollard* and the equal footing doctrine must be understood in context. Sometimes the reference is to the well-established rule that the United States will be presumed to have held land under navigable water in trust for the future state unless it very plainly indicates a contrary intent. In other cases, talk of *Pollard* and the "equal footing doctrine" refers to its constitutional holding that new states must enter the Union on an equal sovereign footing. This is still basic constitutional law, although as subsequent courts have clarified, equal footing "applies to political rights and sovereignty, not to economic or physical characteristics of the states." *United States v. Gardner*, 107 F.3d 1314, 1319 (9th Cir. 1997), *cert. denied*, 522 U.S. 907 (1997). *See also Coyle v. Smith*, 221 U.S. 559 (1911) (striking down as violating equal footing a provision in Oklahoma's enabling act requiring it to locate the state capitol in Guthrie). In still other cases, invocations of equal footing are an argument from *Pollard*'s dicta that the federal government should not be able to retain and regulate land within the states except under the Enclave Clause. It is this argument that forms the legal core of the Sagebrush Rebellion and wise use movement, a topic discussed more fully in Section IV.A of the casebook.

QUESTIONS AND DISCUSSION

1. The presumption of state ownership applies to land under *navigable* water. To the extent the water is non-navigable, the bed is owned by the landowner adjacent to the watercourse. In the case of a non-navigable stream with different land-owners on either side, for example, each owns the bed to the midpoint of the stream. *See generally* 1 WATERS AND WATER RIGHTS § 6.03(a)(3) (Robert E. Beck ed., 1991). The focus on navigability derives from England and the idea that it was the navigable waterways that the crown was obligated to hold in trust for the people because those waterways were particularly important for navigation, commerce (transportation was easiest along navigable waterways), and the fishery. The United States, however, departed from England in its definition of navigability. Whereas in England the term navigable waters had application almost exclusively to waters that ebbed and flowed with the tide, in the United States navigable waters has been expanded to include all water bodies that are navigable in fact, that is to say, capable of sustaining commerce. In *The Daniel Ball*, 77 U.S. (10 Wall.) 557, 563 (1871) the Court set forth the test:

> Those rivers must be regarded as public navigable rivers in law which are navigable in fact. And they are navigable in fact when they are used, or are susceptible of being used, in their ordinary condition, as highways for com-

merce, over which trade and travel are or may be conducted in the customary modes of trade and travel on water.

Thus, the equal footing presumption of state ownership applies to all waters navigable in fact. In keeping with its English tidewater heritage, however, the doctrine has also been held to apply to land under waters subject to the ebb and flow of the tide that are not navigable in fact. *See Phillips Petroleum Co. v. Mississippi*, 484 U.S. 469 (1988).

2. Suppose that *Pollard*'s dicta about the United States' obligation to sell all non-overflowed lands in Alabama had carried the day. How might you argue that the reasoning is less persuasive with respect to those public lands not acquired by virtue of deeds of cession?

3. Is there anything to the argument that federal ownership of land within a state limits state sovereignty? So long as Nevada has the same jurisdiction and police power as New York, does it matter that the federal government owns some 83% of Nevada and only 0.3% of New York? What should be the respective rights and obligations of the states within which resources lie and of the rest of the states in the Union? What might the national landscape look like if *Pollard*'s dicta had prevailed and what we now know as our public lands had been the subject of state and private ownership instead?

4. *Pollard*'s suggestion that the Enclave Clause was the only constitutional option for the United States to obtain ownership and jurisdiction over land within the states suffered a further blow when the United States passed the General Condemnation Act of 1888, authorizing the condemnation of land for public uses whenever it is "necessary or advantageous to the Government to do so." 40 U.S.C. § 257. *See also United States v. Gettysburg Elec. R.R. Co.*, 160 U.S. 668 (1896) (upholding United States' condemnation of land for inclusion in Gettysburg National Military Park). No provision of the Constitution explicitly gives the United States the power of eminent domain, but as the *Gettysburg* Court observed:

> It is, of course, not necessary that the power of condemnation for such purpose be expressly given by the Constitution. The right to condemn at all is not so given. It results from the powers that are given, and it is implied because of its necessity, or because it is appropriate in exercising those powers.

Id. at 681. Which of the "powers that are given" in the Constitution might the *Gettysburg* Court have had in mind when it suggested that condemnation was a necessary and proper extension of those powers? Does the Fifth Amendment's prohibition on taking property for public use without payment of just compensation support the United States' position?

If the federal government can condemn land within the original thirteen states and condemn or simply retain land within the new states, what purpose is left for the Enclave Clause? You might want to reconsider this question again after studying Section IV below, which explains the seemingly unlimited federal regulatory authority over any public lands under the Property Clause.

5. Probably the most controversial cases applying this presumption of state ownership are those involving disputes about pre-statehood reservations of land under navigable water on behalf of Indian tribes. *Montana v.*

United States, 450 U.S. 544 (1981), for example, involved a dispute between the Crow Indian tribe and Montana over the right to regulate hunting and fishing along the portion of the Big Horn River that flowed through the Crow Tribe's reservation. Key to the Tribe's claim of jurisdiction was whether the Tribe or Montana owned the river bed. The Court's decision in favor of Montana indicates the strength of the presumption in favor of state ownership of land under navigable water.

> In 1868, the Second Treaty of Fort Laramie established a Crow Reservation of roughly 8 million acres, including land through which the Big Horn River flows. By Article II of the treaty, the United States agreed that the reservation "shall be . . . set apart for the absolute and undisturbed use and occupation" of the Crow Tribe, and that no non-Indians except agents of the Government "shall ever be permitted to pass over, settle upon, or reside in" the reservation. * * *

> Whatever property rights the language of the 1868 treaty created, however, its language is not strong enough to overcome the presumption against the sovereign's conveyance of the riverbed. The treaty in no way expressly referred to the riverbed, nor was an intention to convey the riverbed expressed in "clear and especial words," *Martin* v. *Waddell*, 16 Pet., at 411, or "definitely declared or otherwise made very plain," *United States* v. *Holt State Bank*, 270 U.S., at 55. Rather, as in *Holt*, "[the] effect of what was done was to reserve in a general way for the continued occupation of the Indians what remained of their aboriginal territory." *Id.*, at 58. * * *

> The mere fact that the bed of a navigable water lies within the boundaries described in the treaty does not make the riverbed part of the conveyed land, especially when there is no express reference to the riverbed that might overcome the presumption against its conveyance.

Montana, 450 U.S. at 552–54. *Montana* is not alone in applying a very strong presumption against pre-statehood grants of land under navigable water. *See, e.g., United States v. Holt State Bank*, 270 U.S. 49, 55 (1926) (ruling that Minnesota owned the bed of Mud Lake within the Red Lake Indian Reservation); *Skokomish Indian Tribe v. France*, 320 F.2d 205 (9th Cir. 1963) (concluding that tidelands adjacent to Skokomish reservation passed to the State of Washington upon its entrance into the Union), *cert. denied*, 376 U.S. 943 (1964). In other instances, however, the Supreme Court has been willing to find reservations of sufficiently clear language to defeat the presumption favoring state title. *See, e.g., Idaho v. United States*, 533 U.S. 262 (2001) (holding that the United States had granted a portion of the bed of Lake Coeur d'Alene to the Coeur d'Alene Indian tribe prior to statehood); *Choctaw v. Oklahoma*, 397 U.S. 620, 635 (1970) (finding tribal title to bed of Arkansas River in part because the U.S. had promised that no part of the Tribe's land would ever become part of a state); *Alaska Pac. Fisheries v. United States*, 248 U.S. 78, 87–90 (1918) (holding that the United States had clearly granted the submerged land around the Annette Islands as part of the Metlakahtla Indian reservation).

6. In recent years, the Supreme Court has seemed to apply the presumption of state ownership less strongly. In *United States v. Alaska*, 521 U.S. 1 (1997), the Court considered Alaska's claim to the petroleum-rich submerged lands within the Arctic National Wildlife Refuge. The Court found that the United States had plainly expressed its intent to defeat Alaska's title to the submerged lands within the refuge and reserved the lands for itself. In *Idaho v. United States*, 533 U.S. 262 (2001), the Court decided that the executive order creating the Coeur d'Alene Indian Tribe's reservation had plainly expressed federal intent to retain a portion of the bed of Lake Coeur d'Alene in trust for the Tribe. Then, in *Alaska v. United States*, 545 U.S. 75 (2005), the Court held that the United States had clearly reserved for itself title to the submerged lands underlying the waters of Glacier Bay National Monument (now Glacier Bay National Park), primarily because the Monument had the stated purpose of protecting wildlife.

7. For a discussion of the origins and application of the equal footing doctrine, see James R. Rasband, *The Disregarded Common Parentage of the Equal Footing and Public Trust Doctrines*, 32 LAND & WATER L. REV. 1 (1997).

————

B. THE PUBLIC TRUST DOCTRINE

The prior section focused on whether the states or the federal government would be the primary holder and dispenser of land and resources in the United States. Despite *Pollard*'s dicta, that constitutional question was resolved in favor of the United States. The federal government was free to acquire, dispose, or retain lands and their accompanying natural resources as it saw fit. In fact, given the federal power of eminent domain, this is even true, as a theoretical matter, for lands, like those in the original thirteen states, that never passed through federal possession. Likewise, even for land under navigable water, although there is a strong presumption against federal disposition or retention, the federal government can defeat that presumption by using clear and unmistakable language.

If the federal government is the ultimate arbiter of natural resource ownership, that does not mean the states are irrelevant with respect to ownership of land and natural resources. As discussed below, the federal government granted states vast acreages of land in their enabling acts and in subsequent legislation, and states have significant regulatory authority. This section looks briefly at the power of states (the other main political entity within our federal system) with respect to the land and natural resources that ended up within their possession. Are states, like the federal government, free to dispose of or retain their lands? At first glance this may seem an easy question. Unlike the federal government, which is one of limited and enumerated powers, states have general police power to regulate in any way necessary to promote public health and welfare. In theory, that would mean that states could retain or dispose of their land and resources subject only to federal constitutional limits and preemption via the Supremacy Clause. In general that has been true. However, just as is the case with federal power prior to statehood, the power of the state after statehood is murkier with respect to land under navigable water. The following famous Supreme Court case addresses the question of state authority to dispose of land under navigable water. As the case reveals, state power to dispose of such lands may not be the equivalent of federal power prior to statehood.

ILLINOIS CENTRAL R.R. CO. V. ILLINOIS,
146 U.S. 387 (1892)

MR. JUSTICE FIELD delivered the opinion of the court.

[In 1869, the Illinois legislature passed, over the governor's veto, what was commonly known as the Lake Front Act, granting to the Illinois Central Railroad "all the right and title of the State of Illinois" to more than 1000 acres of submerged lands extending out from the City of Chicago under Lake Michigan. The alleged consideration for the grant was the Railroad's agreement to pay the State semi-annually, and in perpetuity, seven percent of its gross earnings derived from use of the submerged lands. In 1873, Illinois reconsidered its largesse, repealing the Lake Front Act and revoking the title of the Railroad to the submerged lands. Disputing the repeal, the Railroad continued to build piers and assert ownership of the harbor lands. Finally, in 1883, the State Attorney General filed suit in state court, seeking a declaration of the State's title to the disputed lands. Upon the Railroad's motion, the case was removed to federal circuit court.]

The question, therefore, to be considered, is whether the legislature was competent to thus deprive the state of its ownership of the submerged lands in the harbor of Chicago, and of the consequent control of its waters; or, in other words, whether the railroad corporation can hold the lands and control the waters by the grant, against any future exercise of power over them by the state.

That the state holds the title to the lands under the navigable waters of Lake Michigan, within its limits, in the same manner that the state holds title to soils under tide water, by the common law, we have already shown; and that title necessarily carries with it control over the waters above them, whenever the lands are subjected to use. But it is a title different in character from that which the state holds in lands intended for sale. It is different from the title which the United States hold in the public lands which are open to pre-emption and sale. It is a title held in trust for the people of the state, that they may enjoy the navigation of the waters, carry on commerce over them, and have liberty of fishing therein, freed from the obstruction or interference of private parties. The interest of the people in the navigation of the waters and in commerce over them may be improved in many instances by the erection of wharves, docks, and piers therein, for which purpose the state may grant parcels of the submerged lands; and, so long as their disposition is made for such purpose, no valid objections can be made to the grants. It is grants of parcels of lands under navigable waters that may afford foundation for wharves, piers, docks, and other structures in aid of commerce, and grants of parcels which, being occupied, do not substantially impair the public interest in the lands and waters remaining, that are chiefly considered and sustained in the adjudged cases as a valid exercise of legislative power consistently with the trust to the public upon which such lands are held by the state. But that is a very different doctrine from the one which would sanction the abdication of the general control of the state over lands under the navigable waters of an entire harbor or bay, or of a sea or lake. Such abdication is not consistent with the exercise of that trust which requires the government of the state to preserve such waters for the use of the public. The trust devolving upon the state for the public, and which can only be discharged by the management and control of property in which the public has an interest, cannot be relinquished by a transfer of the property. The control of the state for the purposes of the trust can never be lost, except as to such parcels as are used in promoting the interests of the public therein, or can be disposed of without any substantial impairment of the public interest in the lands and waters remaining. It is only by observing the distinction between a grant of such parcels for the improvement of the public interest, or which when occupied do not substantially impair the public interest in the lands and waters remaining, and a grant of the whole property in which the public is interested, that the language of the adjudged cases can be reconciled. General language sometimes found in opinions of the courts, expressive of absolute ownership and control by the state of lands under navigable waters, irrespective of any trust as to their use and disposition, must be read and construed with reference to the special facts of the particular cases. A grant of all the lands under the navigable waters of a state has never been adjudged to be within the legislative power; and any attempted grant of the kind would be held, if not absolutely void on its face, as subject to revocation. The state can no more abdicate its trust over property in which the whole people are interested, like navigable waters and soils under them, so as to leave them entirely under the use and control of private parties, except in the instance of parcels mentioned for the improvement of the navigation and use of the waters, or when parcels can be disposed of without impairment of the public interest in what remains, than it can abdicate its police powers in the administration of government and the preservation of the peace. In the administration of government the use of such powers may for a limited period be delegated to a municipality or other body, but there always remains with the state the right to revoke those powers and exercise them in a more direct manner, and one more conformable to its wishes. So with trusts connected with public property, or property of a special character, like lands under navigable waters; they cannot be placed entirely beyond the direction and control of the state.

The harbor of Chicago is of immense value to the people of the state of Illinois, in the facilities it affords to its vast and constantly increasing commerce; and the idea that its legislature can deprive the state of control over its bed and waters, and place the same in the hands of a private corporation, created for a different purpose,—one limited to transportation of passengers and freight between distant points and the city,—is a proposition that cannot be defended.

The area of the submerged lands proposed to be ceded by the act in question to the railroad company embraces something more than 1,000 acres, being, as stated by counsel, more than three times the area of the outer harbor, and not only including all of that harbor, but embracing adjoining submerged lands, which will, in all probability, be hereafter included in the harbor. It is as large as that embraced by all the merchandise docks along the Thames at London; is much larger than that included in the famous docks and basins at Liverpool; is twice that of the port of Marseilles, and nearly, if not quite, equal to the pier area along the water front of the city of New York. And the arrivals and clearings of vessels at the port exceed in number those of New York, and are equal to those of New York and Boston combined. * * * It is hardly conceivable that the legislature can divest the state of the control and management of this harbor, and vest it absolutely in a private corporation. Surely an act of the legislature transferring the title to its submerged lands and the power claimed by the railroad company to a foreign state or nation would be repudiated, without hesitation, as a gross perversion of the trust over the property under which it is held. So would a similar transfer to a corporation of another state. It would not be listened to that the control and management of the harbor of that great city—a subject of concern to the whole people of the state—should thus be placed elsewhere than in the state itself. * * *

Any grant of the kind is necessarily revocable, and the exercise of the trust by which the property was held by the state can be resumed at any time. Undoubtedly there may be expenses incurred in improvements made under such a grant, which the state ought to pay; but, be that as it may, the power to resume the trust whenever the state judges best is, we think, incontrovertible. The position advanced by the railroad company in support of its claim to the ownership of the submerged lands, and the right to the erection of wharves, piers, and docks at its pleasure, or for its business in the harbor of Chicago, would place every harbor in the country at the mercy of a majority of the legislature of the state in which the harbor is situated.

We cannot, it is true, cite any authority where a grant of this kind has been held invalid, for we believe that no instance exists where the harbor of a great city and its commerce have been allowed to pass into the control of any private corporation. But the decisions are numerous which declare that such property is held by the state, by virtue of its sovereignty, in trust for the public. The ownership of the navigable waters of the harbor, and of the lands under them, is a subject of public concern to the whole people of the state. The trust with which they are held, therefore, is governmental, and cannot be alienated, except in those instances mentioned, of parcels used in the improvement of the interest thus held, or when parcels can be disposed of without detriment to the public interest in the lands and waters remaining.

This follows necessarily from the public character of the property, being held by the whole people for purposes in which the whole people are interested. As said by Chief Justice Taney in *Martin v. Waddell*, 16 Pet. 367, 410: "When the Revolution took place the people of each state became themselves sovereign, and in that character hold the absolute right to all their navigable waters, and the soils under them, for their own common use, subject only to the rights since surrendered by the constitution to the general government." In *Arnold v. Mundy*, 6 N. J. Law, 1, which is cited by this court in *Martin v. Waddell*, 16 Pet. 418, and spoken of by Chief Justice Taney as entitled to great weight, and in which the decision was made "with great deliberation and research," the supreme court of New Jersey comments upon the rights of the state in the bed of navigable waters, and, after observing that the power exercised by the state over the lands and waters is nothing more than what is called the "jus regium," the right of regulating, improving, and securing them for the benefit of every individual citizen, adds: "The sovereign power itself, therefore, cannot, consistently with the principles of the law of nature and the constitution of a well-ordered society, make a direct and absolute grant of the waters of the state, divesting all the citizens of their common right. It would be a grievance which never could be long borne by a free people." * * *

In *Newton v. Commissioners*, 100 U.S. 548, it appeared that by an act passed by the legislature of Ohio in 1846 it was provided that upon the fulfillment of certain conditions by the proprietors or citizens of the town of Canfield the county seat should be permanently established in that town. Those conditions having been complied with, the county seat was established therein accordingly. In 1874 the legislature passed an act for the removal of the county seat to another town. Certain citizens of Canfield thereupon filed their bill setting forth the act of 1846, and claiming that the proceedings constituted an executed contract, and prayed for an injunction against the contemplated removal. But the court refused the injunction, holding that there could be no contract and no irrepealable law upon governmental subjects, observing that legislative acts concerning public interests are necessarily public laws; that every succeeding legislature possesses the same jurisdiction and power as its predecessor; that the latter have the same power of repeal and modification which the former had of enactment,—neither more nor less; that all occupy in this respect a footing of perfect equality; that this is necessarily so, in the nature of things; that it is vital to the public welfare that each one should be able at all times to do whatever the varying circumstances and present exigencies attending the subject may require; and that a different result would be fraught with evil.

As counsel observe, if this is true doctrine as to the location of a county seat, it is apparent that it must apply with greater force to the control of the soils and beds of navigable waters in the great public harbors held by the people in trust for their common use and of common right, as an incident to their sovereignty. The legislature could not give away nor sell the discretion of its successors in respect to matters, the government of which, from the very nature of things, must vary with varying circumstances.... Every legislature must, at the time of its existence, exercise the power of the state in the execution of the trust devolved upon it. We hold, therefore, that any attempted cession of the ownership and control of the state in and over the submerged lands in Lake Michigan, by the act of April 16, 1869, was inoperative to affect, modify, or in any respect to control the sovereignty and dominion of the state over the lands, or its ownership thereof, and that any such attempted operation of the act was annulled by the repealing act of April 15, 1873, which to that extent was valid and effective. There can be no irrepealable contract in a conveyance of property by a grantor in disregard of a public trust, under which he was bound to hold and manage it.

QUESTIONS AND DISCUSSION

1. In subsequent state court decisions, the public trust doctrine of *Illinois Central* has been expanded beyond its application to land under navigable water. It has been enlarged to include water rights obtained by prior appropriation. *See, e.g.*, *National Audubon Soc'y v. Superior Court of Alpine County*, 658 P.2d 709 (Cal. 1983), *cert. denied*, 464 U.S. 977 (1983) (holding that Los Angeles' water right to the tributaries of Mono Lake was revocable without payment of compensation). It has been enlarged to include non-navigable tributaries of navigable waters. *Id.* It has been expanded beyond the traditional purposes of navigation, commerce and fishery to include various forms of recreation. *See, e.g.*, *Marks v. Whitney*, 491 P.2d 374, 380 (Cal. 1971); *Caminiti v. Boyle*, 732 P.2d 989, 994 (Wash. 1987) (public trust includes the right of navigation "together with its incidental rights of fishing, boating, swimming, water skiing, and other related recreational purposes generally regarded as corollary to the right of navigation and the use of public waters"), *cert. denied*, 484 U.S. 1008 (1988); *Menzer v. Village of Elkhart Lake*, 186 N.W.2d 290, 296 (Wis. 1971) (public trust encompasses all public uses of water). *See generally* Scott Reed, *The Public Trust Doctrine: Is It Amphibious?* 1 ENVTL. L. & LIT. 107, 116–21 (1986) (collecting cases extending the public trust doctrine beyond its traditional scope).

Should the public trust doctrine of *Illinois Central* be expanded further? Should the government—whether state or federal—have a trust obligation to the public with respect to all of the natural resources it manages? Should it be any more able to abuse that trust with respect to precious land-based resources? If Illinois can't give away Chicago Harbor, should there be a limitation on the United States' power to give away Yosemite? But if there is to be a trust on behalf of the people, who should manage that trust? The executive branch? The legislature? The courts? For an exploration of whether the public trust doctrine can be applied to the public lands more generally, see Charles F. Wilkinson, *The Public Trust Doctrine in Public Land Law*, 14 U.C. Davis. L. Rev. 269 (1980). More broadly, in contemplating the policy and institutional consequences of the public trust doctrine, ask yourself how a society should make decisions about what to do with its natural resources. To whom would you allocate the power to make such decisions? Why? What sort of mechanism would you put in place to prevent or remedy bad decisions?

2. Does the Court's holding mean that a state may never grant away land under navigable water? How would you describe the public trust doctrine in property law terms? If you had a client seeking to purchase some sub-merged lands from the state, what would you advise?

3. In *Illinois Central*, it is the state legislature that uses the public trust doctrine to set aside a prior legislature's grant of land under navigable water. In subsequent cases, private plaintiffs have convinced courts to rely upon the public trust doctrine to invalidate legislative decisions. *See, e.g., Arizona Center for Law in the Public Interest v. Hassell*, 837 P.2d 158 (Ariz. Ct. App. 1991) (striking down as a violation of the public trust doctrine a 1987 Arizona statute quitclaiming to the record title riparian owners any interest held by the State of Arizona in lands under most of Arizona's navigable waters). Does one of the two approaches to the public trust doctrine seem more appropriate? In the latter case, where a court overturns the will of the legislature, what is the basis of its authority? One of the academic debates about the public trust doctrine is whether it is a product of state common law or state or federal constitutional law. Despite the *Illinois Central* Court's statement that a "State can no more abdicate its trust over property in which the whole people are interested . . . than it can abdicate its police powers," the Supreme Court later stated that the public trust doctrine is a common law doctrine that each state is free to adopt and adapt on its own. *See Phillips Petroleum Co. v. Mississippi*, 484 U.S. 469, 475 (1988) ("it has been long established that the individual States have the authority to define the limits of the lands held in public trust and to recognize private rights in such lands as they see fit."); *Appleby v. New York*, 271 U.S. 364, 395 (1926) ("the conclusion reached [in *Illinois Central*] was necessarily a statement of Illinois law"). Do you understand why the question still engages the academic community?

4. As you might imagine, the expansion of the public trust doctrine has proven controversial. What are the key concerns that exercise of the public trust doctrine raises in terms of separation of powers, good governance, governmental accountability, respect for property rights, and procedural fairness?

Illinois Central has spawned a multitude of law review articles. Most praise the decision and the public trust doctrine as a useful check on legislative improvidence and malfeasance with respect to critical natural resources. *See, e.g.,* Joseph L. Sax, *The Public Trust Doctrine in Natural*

Resource Law: Effective Judicial Intervention, 68 MICH. L. REV. 471 (1970); Charles F. Wilkinson, *The Headwaters of the Public Trust: Some Thoughts on the Source and Scope of the Traditional Doctrine*, 19 ENVTL. L. 425 (1989); Michael C. Blumm, *Public Property and the Democratization of Western Water Law: A Modern View of the Public Trust Doctrine*, 19 ENVTL. L. 573 (1989). Others are more critical of the doctrine, arguing that it is a common law principle improperly relied upon by courts to reverse legislative resource allocations without paying just compensation under the Fifth and Fourteenth Amendments. *See* James L. Huffman, *Trusting the Public Interest to Judges: A Comment on the Public Trust Writing of Professors Sax, Wilkinson, Dunning and Johnson*, 63 DEN. U. L. REV. 565 (1986); James R. Rasband, *Equitable Compensation for Public Trust Takings*, 69 U. COLO. L. REV. 331 (1998).

5.   Under the Court's holding in *Illinois Central*, how does state power to dispose of land under navigable water pursuant to the public trust doctrine differ from federal power to dispose of such lands under the equal footing doctrine? Is there any reason why the two should be different?

6.   Like the *Pollard* Court, the *Illinois Central* Court relies heavily on its prior decision in *Martin v. Waddell's Lessee*. Recall the discussion of *Martin*, page 100 *supra*. Does *Martin* support the proposition that a state has an obligation to hold land under navigable water in trust for its people? If so, how do you explain that although the Court rejected the claim of Waddell's lessee of an oyster lease from the crown, it upheld New Jersey's oyster lease? Should a state's trust obligation be the same as the crown's? In a passage in *Martin* not discussed in *Illinois Central*, the Court suggested that a grant made by the state's authority must "manifestly be tried and determined by different principles from those which apply to grants of the British crown, when the title is held by a single individual in trust for the whole nation." *Id.* at 411. Do you agree?

7.   For a detailed discussion of the history of the *Illinois Central* case, see Joseph D. Kearney and Thomas W. Merrill, *The Origins of the American Public Trust Doctrine: What Really Happened in Illinois Central*, 71 U. CHI. L. REV. 799 (2004). Professors Kearney and Merrill suggest that the standard narrative of the public trust doctrine being a check on legislative malfeasance is not supported by the actual historical setting for the case, which involved a long-term struggle among the City of Chicago, the State of Illinois, the United States, the railroad and other private interests, all of whom were competing for economic control of the Chicago waterfront and had very little concern about preservation of the lake itself. Those interested in the history of the public trust doctrine should read Professor Jim Huffman's article, *Speaking of Inconvenient Truths—A History of the Public Trust Doctrine*, 18 DUKE ENVTL. L. & POL'Y F. 1 (2007). Professor Huffman suggests that the history of the public trust doctrine as described by most courts and commentators is largely "mythological":

> In a nutshell, the generally accepted history is that from Justinian's Institutes through Magna Carta and Bracton, Hale and Blackstone reporting on English law and Chancellor Kent acknowledging the reception of English and Roman law in America, the public has deeply rooted rights in access to and use of resources important to the public welfare. *Arnold v. Mundy, Martin v. Waddell*

and *Illinois Central Railroad v. Illinois* are cited repeatedly as precedent for present day recognition of a doctrine that will limit the authority of the state to alienate resources while imposing constraints on governmental and private use of those resources. . . .

The only problem for these ambitions for the public trust doctrine is that they rely on a mythological history of the doctrine. There was nothing resembling the modern idea of public trust in Roman law and the claimed restraint on alienation of state-owned waters and lands is belied by a history of pervasive private ownership in both Rome and England. Magna Carta had little or nothing to do with such public rights, nor is there significant support in Bracton, Hale or Blackstone for the imagined doctrine. The one concept of English law on which the modern public trust doctrine relies—the prima facie rule pursuant to which title to submerged lands is presumed to be in the Crown absent a showing to the contrary—was a sixteenth century fabrication that did not take hold in England until late in the nineteenth century, well after American law had developed on its own. Ironically, the invented prima facie rule served to feather the nest of the Crown, not to protect the rights of the public. . . .

Id. at 1–2. If Professor Huffman is correct about the historical roots of the public trust doctrine, does it matter now that the doctrine has become so rooted in modern jurisprudence?

Another thoughtful analysis of the *Illinois Central* decision is offered by Professor Grant who has suggested that the case, "at its core, concerned the Contract Clause of the Federal Constitution and the reserved powers doctrine [under which a] 'legislature can later repudiate contracts purporting to bargain away or alienate essential sovereign powers without violating the Contract Clause.' " Douglas L. Grant, *Underpinnings of the Public Trust Doctrine*, 33 ARIZ. ST. L.J. 849, 856–57 (2001). The Court's discussion of *Newton v. Commissioners* lends support to this position, but doesn't it leave open the underlying question of whether public ownership of land under navigable water, or perhaps other natural resources, is essential to sovereign power?

———

PROBLEM EXERCISE: INDIAN TREATY RIGHTS IN WASHINGTON'S TIDELANDS

In thinking about the relationship between the three cases and doctrines discussed in the Chapter thus far—*Johnson* and the discovery doctrine, *Pollard* and the equal footing doctrine, *Illinois Central* and the public trust doctrine—consider the following problem exercise.

The area now comprising the present State of Washington was first claimed by the United States around the turn of the nineteenth century, and its present boundary was established by the Treaty of 1846 with Great Britain. But before the Americans or James Vancouver, the Hudson Bay company, and the British showed up, the area was occupied by a variety of coastal Indian tribes such as the Tulalip, Lummi, Makah, Muckleshoot and Puyallup. One common characteristic of these tribes was their dependence on fish and shellfish to sustain their way of life. Fish, and particularly salmon (an anadromous fish that hatches in fresh water, migrates to the ocean, and eventually returns to its stream of origin to spawn), were vital to their diet, played an important role in their religious life, and were a major element of their trade and economy.

In 1853, the Washington Territory was formed out of the Oregon Territory and Isaac Stevens, politically ambitious, and number one in his class at West Point, was appointed governor of the newly formed territory. He was also the *ex officio* Territorial Superintendent of Indian Affairs. In both roles, he was to negotiate treaties with the Indian tribes to open up the territory to settlement, which was already beginning under the auspices of the 1850 Oregon Donation Act that had promised free land to settlers who would come into the territory (320 acres to individuals and 640 acres to couples). Stevens negotiated five treaties. In Article I of each treaty, the tribes ceded and relinquished "to the United States all their right, title, and interest in and to the lands and country occupied by them," thereby accomplishing the United States' title-clearing objective. Although the tribes agreed to move onto reservations, they successfully demanded the right to continue their fishing way of life. Article III of the Medicine Creek Treaty is illustrative:

> The right of taking fish, at all usual and accustomed grounds and stations, is further secured to said Indians, in common with all citizens of the Territory, and of erecting temporary houses for the purpose of curing, together with the privilege of hunting, gathering roots and berries, and pasturing their horses on open and unclaimed lands; *Provided, however,* That they shall not take shell fish from any beds staked or cultivated by citizens. . . .

In the early years after the treaty, population was relatively low, the salmon seemed inexhaustible, and the Tribes had little problem continuing their fishing. However, as the area began to be settled, and as the commercial value of salmon grew with the advent of commercial canning, competition for the resource increased. With that competition came efforts to exclude the Indians from their fishery. Beginning in the 1905 case of *United States v. Winans,* 198 U.S. 371 (1905), which involved the Yakima Tribe's successful challenge to a state licensee's use of a fish wheel (a device capable of catching salmon by the ton), which was effectively taking an entire run of salmon just before it reached the tribe's traditional fishing spot, issues respecting the meaning of the Stevens treaties' fishing clause made their way to the Supreme Court six times prior to 1970.

Matters came to a head in the fall of 1970 when the United States, as trustee for the tribes, filed a complaint against Washington, alleging that Washington's general laws and regulations restricting the time, place, manner, and volume of fishing could not be applied to the tribes, except to the extent necessary to preserve a particular species of fish. From the tribes' perspective, they did not need permission from the state of Washington. They had a federally protected treaty right to take fish. In the lead-up to the case, Washington had been arresting tribal members who fished without a license, precipitating a variety of "fish-ins" and fishing rights protests from tribal members and sympathetic activists. Washington's position was that the treaty only gave the tribes a right to fish "in common" with other citizens and that this meant that tribal members, just like other citizens of the state, had to obtain fishing licenses and conform to state limits.

In a now famous decision, federal district judge George Boldt handed the tribes a resounding victory. He decided that the "in common" language in the fishing clause gave the tribes the right to 50% of the salmon and steelhead runs in the state of Washington. *United States v. Washington*, 384 F.Supp. 312 (W.D. Wash. 1974). This decision was affirmed by the Ninth Circuit, and the Supreme Court initially denied certiorari. Implementation of the decision caused an uproar in Washington, particularly among its commercial fishermen. When the State Department of Fisheries issued regulations to implement Boldt's order, the commercial fishers went to state court to challenge them. The state supreme court then ruled that the Department of Fisheries did not need to comply with the federal injunction because Boldt's treaty interpretation had been wrong. The Washington Game Department, on the basis of those orders, then also refused to comply with the federal injunction. In response, Judge Boldt issued a series of orders requiring the local United States Attorney and other federal law enforcement officers to supervise the state's fisheries and enforce its orders. Amidst the widespread defiance of the federal court's order, the United States Supreme Court granted certiorari on both the state and federal cases. Its decision largely upheld Judge Boldt's, agreeing that the tribes were entitled to up to one-half of the salmon runs, although no more than was necessary to secure the tribes a "moderate living." *See Washington v. Washington State Commercial Passenger Fishing Vessel Ass'n*, 443 U.S. 658, 686 (1979).

Ten years after the Supreme Court's decision, the tribes returned to court to ask for a determination of their rights to take shellfish. The tribes argued that just as they were entitled to 50% of the salmon, they were entitled to 50% of the shellfish. A number of factors made the case interesting. The fishing clause had a special Shellfish Proviso that prohibited tribal taking from "any beds staked or cultivated by citizens." Moreover, a good portion of the shellfish in Washington dwell on privately-owned tidelands. Unlike most states in the Union, Washington had sold off some 80% of its tidelands to private owners. The shellfish attached to those tidelands, particularly clams and oysters, had been treated as private property just as if they were trees. Adding an additional layer of complexity, the indigenous littleneck clam and Olympia oyster had largely been replaced since treaty time by the exotic Manila clam and Pacific oyster from Japan, and many choice oyster and clam beds had been filled or developed since treaty time for cities, ports, U.S. naval bases, and the like. Almost all of Washington's tidelands still contain some shellfish, although density varies by location.

Because of Washington's decision to privatize its tidelands, the litigation implicated a range of stakeholders. The state owned tidelands of its own, some of which were set aside as state parks where the public could gather clams and oysters. In some cases, the state had leased its tidelands to private shellfish farmers. The state likewise regulated the shellfish industry. Some of the tidelands adjoined naval bases of the United States, which joined the tribes in the litigation. Private property owners who owned shoreline property and adjacent tidelands wanted to protect their property interest and opportunity for recreational harvest and personal use. Finally, Washington had a longstanding and successful shellfish industry.

Unlike the industry in other states, however, because the tidelands could be privately owned, Washington's clam and oyster industry had developed as something more akin to farming than fishing. The farming occurred by a variety of methods. In some cases, shellfish farmers would spread hatchery-raised clam and oyster seed on tidelands largely barren of shellfish, or even spread the seed on productive tidelands in order to raise their yield. In other cases, they would spread cultch (mostly broken oyster shells) on their tidelands in order to capture the floating oyster larvae released from natural oyster beds. In some bays, farmers had built dikes around their tidelands to create the ideal water level and conditions for oyster growth. Sometimes, the farming consisted of netting the tidelands to keep predators, such as crabs, from eating the clams. Such predator control could increase yields from five clams per square foot to ninety clams per square foot. While the farmers worked to improve yields it was also the case that they had purchased many of the tidelands that were naturally the most productive for clams and oysters. Thus, their harvests often consisted of a mix of shellfish produced by nature and shellfish produced by their effort. Whatever the mix or method, the shellfish farmers were out on their tidelands year-round during low tide (because of the shallow depth in the lower part of Washington's Puget Sound, a farmer's entire crop is often exposed at low tide) and had invested their life and labor in the tidelands. In fact, for a number of the farmers, their tidelands had been in the family for five, six, or seven generations. The Olympia Oyster Company, for example, was incorporated in 1878, and its farm included tidelands granted by the territorial legislature in 1864.

The dispute between the shellfish farmers and the tribes centered on the meaning of the Fishing Clause's Shellfish Proviso. The farmers contended that their beds were staked (many had staked out their beds prior to the litigation; others relied on recording as the modern equivalent of staking) and cultivated and thus off-limits to tribal harvest. The tribes' argument was more complex. They argued that at the time the treaties were negotiated, states on the East Coast did not allow private ownership of oyster beds because the beds were part of the public fishery. The tribes contended that at treaty time, the only staked or cultivated beds were tidelands otherwise barren of oysters where oystermen were allowed to store oysters taken from public beds for fattening or to lay out cultch to catch the natural larvae. The tribes also emphasized that to the extent the Shellfish Proviso was ambiguous, the basic rule of construction for Indian treaties is that "[d]oubtful expressions are to be resolved in favor" of the Indian tribes. *See, e.g., McClanahan v. Arizona State Tax Comm'n,* 411 U.S. 164, 174 (1973). The shellfish farmers countered that the East Coast oyster laws were not uniform and that in some cases the law allowed private ownership of oyster beds, particularly in Isaac Stevens' home state of Rhode Island. More broadly, the farmers made the point that whatever the specific laws, the law in the East was uniform on one point: each state was able to decide for itself whether to privatize its shellfish beds.

In light of these facts, consider the following questions:

- How would the equal footing doctrine or the public trust doctrine support or undermine the arguments of the various parties? If you represented the State of Washington, how vigorously would you defend the rights of the private tideland owners? What approach might you take?

- In the *Winans* case, the Supreme Court said that the treaty was not a grant of rights to the Indians, but a grant of rights from them—a reservation of those not granted. 198 U.S. at 381. Considering this language, can you see why the tribes might assert that the equal footing doctrine does not apply to their reservation of a right to take shellfish from Washington's tidelands? Would the United States necessarily concur in this particular argument? Think back to *Johnson v. M'Intosh.*

- From the language in the Fishing Clause and the facts summarized above, what other sorts of arguments do you think the various parties to the litigation might have made? Where the abbreviated factual summary provides insufficient information, what other sorts of evidence would you want to develop to help you resolve the treaty meaning?

- If the conclusion is that the tribes should receive an equal share of shellfish, what sort of remedy might you impose to accomplish that objective? Remember that a court sitting in equity has broad discretion in fashioning equitable relief, although probably not so broad as to deny the tribes their treaty right.

- From the facts related, can you discern a potential settlement outline? What obstacles do you think the parties faced to negotiating a settlement? What do you see as a fair and ethical allocation of the shellfish resource?

If you want to look at how the courts resolved some of these questions and ignored others, see *United States v. Washington*, 873 F.Supp. 1422 (W.D. Wash. 1994); 898 F.Supp. 1453 (W.D. Wash. 1995) (implementation order); 909 F.Supp. 787 (W.D. Wash. 1995) (amended implementation order); 157 F.3d 630 (9th Cir. 1998) (substantially affirming district court orders), *cert. denied*, 526 U.S. 1060 (1999).

———

C. FEDERAL DISPOSITION OF THE NATION'S RESOURCES

As discussed above, *supra* Part III.A, the United States had essentially plenary authority to dispose of or retain the lands it acquired from the original thirteen states, European powers, and the Indian tribes. This part and Part D that follows address what the United States actually did with the lands it acquired. Professors Dana and Fairfax have suggested that

public land policy can be divided into three periods: disposition, reservation and management. A period of disposition in which Congress disposed of the public domain lasted from about 1776 until 1891. It was followed by a brief period in which lands were reserved or withheld from disposition and lasted until 1905. The period of management dating from 1905 marks the beginning of government programs to manage actively rather than simply retain the public domain. These periods are useful analytic concepts because they characterize many statutes, conflicts, and policies into a generally accurate structure. However, the periods overlap considerably.

SAMUEL TRASK DANA & SALLY K. FAIRFAX, FOREST AND RANGE POLICY 10 (2d ed. 1980). The discussion that follows largely tracks Dana and Fairfax's convenient demarcation, although, as they note, it is not a fully accurate portrayal. All three activities were carried on to some extent during each period. The periods of disposition and reservation (often also called retention) are discussed in this Part C and the following Part D. The period of federal "management" is wrapped into Section IV's discussion of federal regulatory authority.

1.   THE JEFFERSONIAN SURVEY SYSTEM

To comprehend how the public lands were disposed of (whether to states, private individuals, or corporations), it is important to have some understanding of the way in which the United States was mapped and surveyed. Recall that prior to the Revolution, each colony largely formed its own land policies. The policy of the New England states was generally to grant to a group of proprietors a township of approximately six square miles on which to establish an entire community. Lots within each township were surveyed in advance of settlement with in-lots for residences and out-lots for cultivation and pasture. Because the groups typically had a common religion and background, lots were also reserved for the minister, the church, and for schools. The New England system contrasted with that of the middle and southern colonies which employed a more laissez-faire approach with individuals striking out westward and choosing land they desired. When it came time for the federal government to dispose of its lands, elements of both approaches were incorporated in a system devised in part by Thomas Jefferson and adopted by the Continental Congress as the Land Ordinance of 1785. Under this "rectangular survey system," the land was to be surveyed from a single point or meridian into 36-square-mile townships. Each township would be divided for sale into lots/sections one mile square containing 640 acres. While the selling of individual lots credited the approach of the middle and southern states, the Ordinance did not contain any preemption rights (a squatter's right to obtain title by settling and improving land rather than purchasing it at auction). As discussed below, whether to allow settlers such preemption rights would be a source of constant tension in federal land policy. Although there was no reservation for religion as had been the practice in New England, section 16 in every township was reserved for the maintenance of the schools within the township. GATES, *supra*, at 33–74. This reservation of school lands was to continue as a fixture of public lands policy. Figure 2 below is a diagram of a basic township with its 36 one-mile square sections.

6	5	4	3	2	1
7	8	9	10	11	12
18	17	16	15	14	13
19	20	21	22	23	24
30	29	28	27	26	25
31	32	33	34	35	36

Figure 2: Sample Township

The job of surveying—which was as difficult and hazardous as that of early settlers, fur traders and miners—originally fell to surveyors appointed by Congress and then in 1812 to the General Land Office, which was within the Department of Treasury until the Office was shifted to the Department of the Interior in 1846. While this survey material may seem somewhat esoteric, this basic township diagram provides critical context for many public land and natural resources law references that will otherwise remain opaque—references to checkerboarded ownership, to homestead grants of 160 acres or a quarter section, etc. How might this be relevant to the problem of mismatched scales, discussed in Chapter 1 at page 51? As Dana and Fairfax point out,

> The decision to divide the nation into a checkerboard ... has had a tremendous but frequently unnoticed effect on the way we think about and use land. For example, the grid system for land disposition led to a similar pattern of straight lines in field borders and furrows. Farmers simply plowed along the boundary lines of their property. Following the dust storms of the 1930s, we turned away from the grid pattern of plowing in favor of contour plowing, which adapts to the contours of the land. Moreover, political organization followed the same grid as the survey and plowing. The effort to manage irregularly shaped watersheds proposed by reformers in the 1880s floundered on county, township, and state boundaries, which were based on rectangular surveys. Thus, the first sales policy—the decision to divide the land into little blocks and sell it—had a critical influence on everything that followed.

Dana & Fairfax, *supra*, at 13. Most land outside the original thirteen colonies was originally described under the rectangular survey system. In urban and suburban areas, the rectangular survey has generally given way to a system of plat maps specific to the particular area, but the rectangular survey remains in use throughout much of rural America. For those who wish to explore further detail, including how the rectangular survey system explains the descriptions of property boundaries that occur in most deeds with which a property lawyer works, you may wish to visit the following website: http://nationalatlas.gov/articles/boundaries/a_plss.html. The arduous work of surveying, and in some cases resurveying, the United States is mostly completed but some areas, particularly in Alaska, remain unsurveyed. *See* U.S. Dep't of the Interior, Bureau of Land Management, *Cadastral History, available at* http://www.blm.gov/wo/st/en/prog/more/cadastralsurvey/cadastral_history.html.

2. LAND GRANTS TO STATES

The next step in understanding the geography of our nation's land and resources is reviewing how the federal government chose to dispose of the public lands to states. Federal grants to states fall within two broad categories: lands given to states at the time of their admission to the Union and lands granted to existing states by way of legislation enacted after statehood. Recall that before a state could be formed from a territory, Congress needed to authorize its admission by means of an "enabling act." This process sparked contention within Congress and between Congress and the people of the territory. Because admitting a new state with its two senators had the potential to alter the political balance of power, it usually resulted in a power struggle between the major political parties in Congress. Nowhere was this more evident than with the contentious debates about slavery and whether new states would be slave or free. For land and resource purposes, however, the more important negotiation was between Congress and the people of the territory about how much public land they would receive. The early enabling acts set a basic pattern that continued to be followed, although the federal government grew more generous over time. As the first state to be created out of the Northwest Territory, Ohio's 1803 enabling act was a key precedent. Under the terms of the Northwest Ordinance, Congress had provided that the legislatures of the new states "shall never interfere with the primary disposal of the soil by the United States . . . nor with any regulations Congress may find necessary for securing title in such soil to *bona fide* purchasers. No tax shall be imposed on lands the property of the United States." Relying on this language, Ohio's enabling act required Ohio to disclaim any right, title or interest in the public lands within its boundaries. In partial consideration for that disclaimer and also because it would not obtain tax revenue from the federal lands until they were sold to private owners, Ohio was granted one section (Section 16) in every township to generate income for the support of its common schools, given additional public lands for other purposes such as supporting a seminary, and promised five percent of the net proceeds from federal land sales for road building to and within the state.

Subsequent enabling acts took a similar approach, although they were increasingly generous in their funding of education. Beginning with Illinois, most of the proceeds clauses required that the five percent of federal land sales proceeds be devoted to education. With the admission of California in 1850, new states received two sections within each township for supporting their public schools. Then in 1894, when Utah was admitted to the Union, Congress set aside four sections for the support of the schools. Over time, the amount of land granted by enabling acts for other purposes also grew.

In addition to its four sections for school grants, Arizona, for example, received another 240,000 acres to support a University, 300,000 acres for an A & M College, 200,000 acres for Normal Schools, 200,000 acres for an Insane Asylum, 200,000 acres for a Penitentiary, 200,000 acres for a Deaf, Dumb & Blind Asylum, 100,000 acres for a Miner's Hospital, 200,000 acres for a School of Mines, and 200,000 acres for Military Institutes. Arizona ended up with some 14% of its area under the terms of its enabling act, whereas Illinois received only about 4% of its area. GATES, *supra*, at 291–316.

As soon as states received lands in the enabling acts, they were back to the bargaining table asking for more. As Professor Gates describes,

> They soon urged the Federal government to give them additional lands to help finance the building of specified canals and wagon roads and the improvement of waterways. Later they wanted land grants for railroads and for the endowment of agricultural colleges. They demanded also that the swamplands, that is, all the overflowed, wet, swampy or poorly drained land, be turned over to the states to be reclaimed by them and made into cultivable farmlands. Far more land went to the states under the many general and special laws granting land for various purposes than was transferred to them under the provisions of the various state enabling acts.

GATES, *supra*, at 319. Although in most of these cases of post-statehood land grants the federal government defined the amount of land to be granted, it departed from this practice by enacting a series of Swamp Land Acts allowing states to select "swamp and overflowed lands unfit for cultivation." In light of current federal efforts to protect wetlands from filling and development, this largesse may seem odd, but, at the time, wetlands/swamplands were considered a nuisance to be conquered by draining and filling rather than a provider of important ecosystem services. The federal government estimated that some 20 million acres might pass out of the public domain, but the states had a more generous interpretation of the Acts. By trading on the ambiguity of the "unfit for cultivation" language, by carefully timing their inspections for the wet season, and by promising selection agents a proportion of any land to which they could secure a patent, the states selected some 80 million acres of land, many of which bore little resemblance to a swamp. The selections taxed the resources of the General Land Office and resulted in frequent litigation. In fact, almost 200 swampland cases reached the Supreme Court by 1888. In the end, about 63 million acres (an area roughly the size of the state of Oregon) were patented under the Acts. GATES, *supra*, at 319–34.

3. LAND GRANTS TO SETTLERS

The driving purposes of early federal land policy were to open western lands for settlement and development and to produce revenue for the federal treasury. Ideally, both would occur by orderly survey and careful disposition of surveyed lands through the General Land Office. Reality, however, was a bit different. From the beginning, revenues were disappointing. Few settlers could afford the $640 necessary to purchase an entire section at the $1 per acre price set in the 1785 ordinance. And even those who could were more likely to take up state lands offered at more favorable prices or to simply squat on lands without payment or legal title. In an effort to promote more sales, in 1796, 1800, and 1804, Congress passed acts allowing settlers to pay for land on an installment basis. Although this increased sales, many settlers failed to pay their debt. In theory the government could have evicted these settlers, but there was little public support for such action, particularly in the areas where settlement was occurring. In 1820, Congress abandoned credit sales and returned to cash sales but reduced the minimum purchase from 640 acres to 80 acres. In 1832, the minimum was further reduced to 40 acres (a quarter quarter-section). Lands were to be sold at auction to the highest bidder but for no less than $1.25 per acre, and there was no limit on the number of acres any person could purchase.

If the federal land sales program was to generate revenue, it meant that something had to be done about "squatting" on the public lands. If persons could simply head west and claim land, there would be no incentive to buy the land at auction. The federal government made a variety of efforts to prosecute squatters, from imposing fines for trespass, to authorizing the army to eject the squatters from their lands. Almost all of these efforts proved useless. Not only was the burden of administering such a vast landscape overwhelming, but particularly in the western lands where squatters were regarded as hardy yeomanry fulfilling the Jeffersonian ideal, public opinion ran strongly against limiting access to the public domain and prosecuting squatters.

One manifestation of this opinion was the lack of interference with "claims associations" formed by the settlers who had preceded government survey and/or auction. The purpose of a claims association was to protect the settlers from subsequent survey and sale. Professor Gates relates a couple of accounts about their methods:

> There was little competitive bidding as "the settlers," or "squatters" as they are called by speculators, have arranged matters among themselves to their general satisfaction. If, upon comparing numbers, it appears that two are after the same tract of land, one asks the other what he will take not to bid against him. If neither will consent to be bought off, then they retire, and cast lots, and the lucky one enters the tract at Congress price—$1.25 per acre—and the other enters the "second choice on his list." If a speculator "showed a disposition to take a settler's claim from him, he sees the white of a score of eyes snapping at him, and at the first opportunity he craw-fishes out of the crowd." * * *

> [Claims associations] were designed to meet pressing emergencies which existing political institutions did not, or were not able to handle. Settlers on a new frontier ... soon made sufficient improvements that called for protection by the community. Squatters felt that their "right" to their claims should include protection against invaders or claim jumpers, the right to sell their claims, and the right to buy the land for its value before their improvements had been made at the usual government minimum of $1.25 an acre. * * *

> In northern Illinois in 1835 the squatters on unoffered land arrived at an "understanding" equivalent "to a law of the land," that they would "sustain each other against the speculator, no settler should bid on another's land. If a speculator should bid on a settler's farm, he was knocked down & dragged out of the office, & and if the striker was prosecuted and fined, the settlers paid the expense by common consent among themselves. But before a fine could be

assessed, the case must come before a jury" which would find the accused not guilty on grounds of self-defense.

GATES, *supra*, at 152, 154. As western states came into the Union and the composition of Congress changed, the squatter's view of his rights gained traction in Congress. The result was the passage of a series of "preemption acts." Although Congress had earlier allowed limited preemption, 1830 marked the first general preemption act. It provided a one-year window for every settler or occupant who could prove that he had settled and cultivated land to purchase up to 160 acres at the minimum price of $1.25 per acre. In the 1841 Preemption Act, Congress abandoned the view that settlement should occur only on land which had been auctioned (so-called "offered" land) and opened up all unoffered land to preemption claims. Although the 1841 Act only allowed preemption of *surveyed* land, by 1862 that limitation had also been removed and settlers were free to make preemption claims on public domain lands that were both unsurveyed and unoffered. Unfortunately, yeoman settlers were not the only ones to take advantage of the new Act. False swearing from family members or employees about occupation and cultivation allowed separate 160–acre claims to be collected. Other persons would file declarations of their intent to improve and preempt land, which allowed them to hold the land for one year prior to improvement, and then merely strip the land of timber and move on.

Although preemption avoided the problems, largely resolved by claims associations anyway, of claim jumpers and speculators coming along at a government auction and gaining title to land already occupied by a settler, it did not address the demand for free land. That demand was to be satisfied with the Homestead Act. Professors Dana and Fairfax tell the story.

SAMUEL TRASK DANA & SALLY K. FAIRFAX, FOREST AND RANGE POLICY 21–24 (2d ed. 1980)

Efforts to obtain public lands free of charge date from 1797, when settlers along the Ohio River asked for a grant of 400 acres per family in return for an agreement to remain on the land for three years before receiving title. From then on, petitions for donations reached Congress regularly. In 1828, the Public Lands Committee of the House, in the same report in which it urged legalizations of preemption, recommended the grant of 80 acres "to the heads of such families as will cultivate, improve, and reside on the same for five years." Four special "donation" acts, passed between 1842 and 1854, resulted in the granting of about 3.1 million acres to frontier settlers in Florida, Oregon, Washington, and New Mexico, with certain residence and cultivation restrictions.

Free land was always favored in the West, but at first it was generally opposed in the East, particularly in the South. As the population of the public land states increased, the pressure on Congress for free land also increased so that, during the twenty years preceding the outbreak of the Civil War, it was one of the hottest political issues of the day. The West received strong support from the Northeast, where increased federal receipts from the tariff and an increased labor supply had largely removed the region's former objections to cheap or free land. Rapid development of the West became a desirable objective as a means of expanding the market for eastern manufactures. The South, on the other hand, remained opposed because of the conviction that the plantation system, which depended on slave labor, could not compete with small farms operated by their owners. Conflict over the extension of slavery was a critical aspect of the debate. * * *

In 1862, in the absence of most of its members from the Southern states, Congress overwhelmingly passed the Homestead Act of May 20, 1862. The act provided that any family head or anyone over twenty-one years of age who was a citizen of the United States or had declared an intention to become a citizen could enter up to 160 acres of land for cultivation. Free patent to the land could be secured by settlers when they paid certain fees and proved that they had resided upon and cultivated the land for five years. Thus began one of the most durable and destructive myths in American folklore.

It is widely believed that the West was opened and settled by homesteaders who gained valuable free land by their honest toil. Reverence for this bucolic myth stalled for decades the reform of disastrous land disposition statutes. There is, to be sure, nobility and inspiration in the lives of homesteaders chronicled by such great American authors as Willa Cather (*My Antonia, O Pioneer!*), O. E. Rölvaag (*Giants in the Earth*), and Mari Sandoz (*Old Jules*). These stunning tales of human endurance are harshly at variance with the land-of-milk-and-honey versions of early American abundance. They speak tragically of the waste in human and physical resources begotten by land policies made in disregard for the productive capacity of the land. Most of the lush American land was occupied well before 1862, and successful homesteading took place primarily in the upper Midwest. The incredible toil of the Great Basin homesteader was frequently rewarded by drought, blizzard, dust storm and financial and physical ruin. * * *

Unfortunately, the act was based on experience in the humid parts of the East and was not suited to the semiarid conditions in the prairie states and Far West, where 160 acres was inadequate to support a family. Congress tardily tried to remedy this defect in two acts passed in 1909 and 1916. The Enlarged Homestead Act of 1909 enabled acquisition of homesteads of 320 acres anywhere in the nine Western states and territories of Arizona, Colorado, Montana, Nevada, New Mexico, Oregon, Utah, Washington, and Wyoming, but forbade commutation. The lands entered had to be nonmineral and nonirrigable and could not contain merchantable timber. The provisions of the act were later extended to Idaho, Kansas, North Dakota, South Dakota, and California. The 1916 Stockraising Homestead Act provided for 640–acre homesteads on nonirrigable land. [The Act also provided for the federal government to retain the mineral estate, resulting in 32 million acres of split estate land in the West (DANA & FAIRFAX, *supra*, at 103), an area about the size of North Carolina. The surface is privately owned but the subsurface mineral rights are retained by the federal government.] * * *

The economically inadequate homesteads virtually required land abuse, and the results are now familiar. It is frequently overlooked, moreover, that the Homestead Act was also the focus of fraudulent land operations. One of the most abused features of the Homestead Act was the commutation provision which permitted entrymen to purchase title to their claim for $1.25 per acre at any time after six months rather than occupying the land for the designated period. This provision was commonly used, particularly after 1880, by large stock operators or lumber companies in consolidating enormous landholdings. Phony entry men would enter the land, remain there for six months, purchase the land for $1.25 an acre with cash provided by unscrupulous operators, and then turn the land over to them. Cowhands were frequently required to ''homestead'' in this way as a condition of employment. * * *

Actual fraud took many forms. The "twelve-by-fourteen" house required to prove occupancy might be a dry-goods box, with the dimensions measured in inches instead of feet. A "shingle roof" might consist of two shingles. A house that from a distance looked habitable might lack a floor or have a wooden chimney. "Dummy" entrymen were hired to stake false claims on land and transfer title to speculators, who were thus able to block up large holdings. There is no way of knowing how many of the 285 million acres patented under the Homestead Act were acquired fraudulently, but the figure must be sizable. Land office officials were too few and far between for effective enforcement of the laws, and public opinion commonly tolerated or even supported the illegal practices.

—————

The opportunity to enter and take up land was not limited to the Homestead and Preemption Acts. A wide variety of additional disposal laws were also enacted. A few of the more prominent acts are mentioned below but they certainly do not cover the whole subject. In 1873, Congress passed the Timber Culture Act which allowed settlers to claim an additional 160 acre quarter-section if they planted and watered 40 acres of trees (this was later reduced to 10 acres). The purpose of the Act was to provide a source of fuel wood, fencing, and building materials for the future. And, reflecting the optimistic science of the times, it was hoped that planting trees would change the weather and bring more rainfall. More realistically, it would help hold the soil, thereby extending water flows and preventing erosion. Although there were entries on 43.5 million acres under the Timber Culture Act, only about 10.8 million acres actually went to patent, which was still about the equivalent of granting Vermont and New Hampshire. In truth, given the difficulty of successful forest planting on the Great Plains, the 10.8 million acres patented probably best illustrates that the strict terms of the Act were widely violated.

Because so much of the arid and semiarid land west of the 100th Meridian was unattractive for homesteading and preemption, Congress decided to encourage irrigation by promising a full 640 acre section at $1.25 an acre to anyone willing to irrigate the land within three years of filing. The plan was enacted as the Desert Land Act of 1877 and resulted in another 10 million acres leaving the public domain. The problem was that if the land were truly irrigated, 640 acres was well more than needed by an individual settler. The primary reason to go after the 640 acres was for grazing. The result again was a number of dubious entries. Often ditches were plowed, irrigation affidavits sworn out, but water was never applied. Indeed, in his 1883 annual message, the governor of Wyoming encouraged men to enter the cattle industry by suggesting that they could acquire 1,120 acres under the Preemption, Homestead, Timber Culture and Desert Land Acts. GATES, *supra*, at 640–41. In the end, the Desert Land Act promoted little irrigation. Nor did the Carey Act of 1894, which disposed of another million acres to Western states who promised to develop irrigation projects that mostly never materialized. 43 U.S.C. §§ 641–48. As discussed in Chapter 7, the federal government's efforts to promote irrigation took a much more direct form with the passage of the 1902 Reclamation Act which was to lead to federal water projects and dams throughout the West.

attempts to encourage irrigation failed

One additional piece of disposal legislation was passed the year after the Desert Land Act. In 1878, Congress, in an apparent effort to obtain a bit more revenue from timber lands, which were so frequently being taken up in violation of existing laws anyway, enacted the Timber and Stone Act. The Act authorized purchase for $2.50 per acre of 160–acre quarter-sections, chiefly valuable for timber or stone and unfit for cultivation. Buyers had to attest that they were purchasing the land for their own exclusive use and benefit. However, aided by the Supreme Court's decision that persons intending immediate sale were still entering for their own exclusive use and benefit, *see United States v. Biggs*, 211 U.S. 507 (1909), the timber companies were able to use the Act to increase their holdings. Almost 14 million acres of land ended up leaving the public domain under the Act.

A final area of federal disposal policy merits brief mention, although it will be considered more thoroughly in Chapter 9—namely disposition of the nation's mineral-bearing lands. For most of the first half of the nineteenth century, mineral lands were open for sale and preemption just like other lands, although in a few instances, the United States reserved or leased specified mineral lands. With the discovery of gold in 1848 at Sutter's Mill on the American River in California, the issue of what to do with public lands containing mineral resources became harder to ignore, although Congress still waited another 18 years to pass mining legislation. In the absence of federal law, the miners themselves were quick to develop local associations and to adopt rules governing their claims. Unsurprisingly, the miners recognized possessory rights in discovered minerals without regard to federal ownership of the land.

When Congress acted in 1866, it largely confirmed the miner's position, providing that the public domain, whether surveyed or unsurveyed, was "free and open to exploration by all citizens of the United States, and those declaring their intention to become citizens." 14 Stat. 251 (1866). Patents to lode claims (those that followed a vein of ore embedded in rock) could be had for $5 per acre as long as the claimant complied with local customs and rules for establishing his claim and as long as he could show that he had made a minimal investment in labor and improvements. In the Placer Act of 1870, Congress extended the offer to so-called placer claims which included "all forms of deposit, excepting veins of quartz, or other rock in place," 16 Stat. 217 (1870), the classic example of a "placer" being gold-bearing gravel in the bed of a stream or former river valley. Placer claims were available for $2.50 per acre.

In 1872, Congress amended the 1866 and 1870 acts, passing what is known as the General Mining Law. It provided that anyone who found a valuable mineral deposit on the public lands, staked it out and complied with local notice and recording rules, was free to mine without paying the government a dime. Although a miner could take a claim to patent and obtain fee title to the surface, in which case he would pay the $5 per acre for lode claims and $2.50 per acre for placer claims, he did not need to do so. As long as the miner fulfilled the customary obligation to actually work the claim, he had a protectible property interest in his unpatented mining claim. The 1872 Mining Law is still the primary legislation governing hardrock mining on the public lands. The most prominent recent patent was one issued in 1994 to Barrick Goldstrike Mines for a gold mine in Nevada. For just under $10,000, Barrick received title to about 2000 acres of the public domain, containing an estimated $11.5 billion of gold. Margaret Kriz, *Mine Games*, 26 NAT'L J. 1669 (1994). In addition to lands taken to patent under the Mining Law, there remain thousands of unpatented mining claims on public lands in the West. Chapter 9 will consider the 1872 Mining Act in further detail, along with the laws relating to other mineral resources, such as fuel minerals like coal and petroleum, that are not freely available to the discovering miner but are federally retained and then leased under the Mineral Leasing Act.

4. LAND GRANTS TO RAILROADS

Another aspect of federal land policy that had significant impact on the national geography is the federal land grants in aid of railroad construction. Early on, Congress granted railroads a free right-of-way through public lands, but the right-of-way alone proved insufficient to stimulate entrepreneurs to undertake the great task of extending railroads across the nation. The builders pushed for a stronger incentive, and Congress complied. In 1850, Congress decided to subsidize the construction of the Illinois Central Railroad from Chicago to Mobile by granting Alabama, Mississippi and Illinois a 200–feet–wide right-of-way and every even-numbered section of land for six sections on either side of the right-of-way, which the states could sell to subsidize Illinois Central. Congress saw this approach as more than a simple subsidy. As Congress envisioned it, the checkerboard grant assured that the railroads would not hold a monopoly along the lands near the primary transportation route and the presence of the railroad would allow the federal government to sell its own alternate sections at a premium, effectively paying for the subsidy to the railroad. Although the finances did not work out in practice, the approach continued.

[handwritten margin note: Checkerboard grants to states]

Many probably recall the story of the building of the first transcontinental railroad and the race between the Union Pacific and the Central Pacific to lay track, ending in the pounding of the Golden Spike at Promontory Point in the Utah Territory. While the railroad was undoubtedly a heroic achievement, the competition between the two railroad companies was about much more than pride. In 1862, Congress had promised that the railroads would receive alternate sections of the public land for a distance of 10 miles, and then later 20 miles, on either side of the railroad. In 1864, the Northern Pacific Railroad (to be built from Duluth to Tacoma and then Portland) was given the largest grant of all, alternate sections out to 40 miles on each side of the railroad within territories and to 20 miles within states, which amounted to approximately 45 million acres, an area slightly larger than the state of Missouri. A variety of other railroad grants followed. Although a number of the grants provided for the granted sections to be subject to settlement and preemption if not sold or otherwise disposed of within three years, courts upheld the railroads' argument that they had disposed of their lands by placing a blanket mortgage on them. By the time Congress reconsidered and ended railroad grants in 1871, railroad corporations had received more than 94 million acres of land (a million acres more than the entire acreage of Montana) and another 37 million acres had been given to states for the specific benefit of railroads. *See* DANA & FAIRFAX, *supra*, at 20; GATES, *supra*, at 356–86.

The natural resource legacy of these grants is significant. In conjunction with the grants to states of specific numbered sections of school lands, the alternate grants to railroads created an even more dramatic checkerboard pattern of ownership, exacerbating the difficulties of land and natural resource management. Another legacy of the railroad grants is their contribution to the large private timber holdings in the Pacific Northwest. Frederick Weyerhaeuser, who had already purchased vast timber lands in the Great Lakes region, purchased about 1.5 million acres of timber land from the Northern Pacific, much of it at $6 per acre. And much of the timbered land not sold by the Northern Pacific is now held by Plum Creek Timber Company, one of its corporate successors. *See* Roy E. Appleman, *Timber Empire from the Public Domain*, 26 MISSISSIPPI VALLEY HISTORICAL REVIEW, No. 2 (1939), *reprinted in* PUBLIC LAND POLICIES: MANAGEMENT AND DISPOSAL 203–08 (Paul W. Gates, ed.).

Certain lands in Oregon face a further complication. In the late 1860s Congress granted about four million acres of federal land in Oregon to the Oregon and California Railroad Company for construction of a rail line from Washington to the California border. The grant was contingent upon the sale of the granted lands in 40 acre parcels to actual settlers for no more than $2.50/acre. The rail line was built but the railroad failed to meet its obligation to sell the land to settlers. As a result, in 1916, Congress revoked its grant, making this one of the rare instances in which the terms of a railroad land grant were strictly enforced. In 1937, Congress adopted the O & C Act, which requires the Interior Department to manage these lands for a sustained yield of timber. Most of the substantial income that is derived from these lands is provided to the local counties under the terms of the O & C Act.

Throughout northwest timber country, therefore, federal lands are interspersed with state and private lands, presenting a host of issues to which we will return regarding access, forest management, and protection of endangered species, whose behavioral patterns ignore property boundaries. For a glimpse of what this problem looks like on the ground, you may want to look at the pictures of checkerboard timber clear-cuts and the ownership diagrams included on the casebook website.

————

Historian Vernon Carstensen offers the following conclusion on the entire federal land disposal saga:

THE PUBLIC LANDS: STUDIES IN THE HISTORY OF THE PUBLIC DOMAIN xxi–xxvi (Vernon Carstensen ed., 1968)

The disposal of the public domain was a matter of large importance throughout the first century of the Republic. Individuals, groups, associations, state, county, and city officials, all sent to Congress a stream of petitions, entreaties, protests, on the disposal of the public lands. The territorial and state legislatures larded the pages of their journals and sessions laws with their petitions, declarations, and directives on how the public lands should be distributed, and they argued endlessly on how land grants to the states should be used. In 1880 the Public Land Commission, in compiling the laws relating to the public lands, reported that about 3,500 laws dealing with public lands had been adopted by Congress between 1785 and 1880. They might have added that, for every law passed, a number of others had died somewhere along the line toward final passage. * * *

It took time for the bureaucracy to learn how to function effectively.... It was an enormous task, one which the Public Land Commission of 1880 thought was on the whole well done despite the numerous cries of incompetence and fraud. Leonard White in *The Jeffersonians*, a study of federal administration, describes the land operation as an immense task that would have been difficult even with the administrative resources of a later age. "That it was accomplished literally by hand, with the compass and chain, quill pen and ink, illuminated by candlelight in rough-hewn prairie offices, was in itself a Herculean performance, even though too slow to keep up with the westward migration."

Perhaps no one had a right to expect the task to be done well: the remarkable thing was that it was done at all, that the whole machinery did not collapse.

Historians, to a large extent, have not taken the tolerant view and have properly insisted upon using exacting standards in judging land policies and their execution. Hence they have been quick to see the wide gap that often existed between high intentions and low performance. The history of the public lands has been full of words such as *speculators, land monopolists, rings, corrupt officials, hush money, fraudulent entry, bogus entrymen, land lawyers, land sharks*. No doubt each new community in the public land states, at one time, had its tales of the "innocent deceits" employed to obtain land. The literal-minded eastern lawyer might regard the land-claim association as a conspiracy to prevent open bidding at the land sale, but westerners were inclined to view such associations as a necessary accommodation to inept federal legislation. Few people in the lead country were disturbed by the story of blindfolding a witness and leading him across land. He could then testify at the land office that he had been on the land and had seen no sign of mineral deposits. A boy might stand on the number 21 and answer truthfully, when asked by the land office official that he was indeed over 21, and an eight- or ten-year-old girl might serve as a wife of record and so give a man right to claim a double portion of land under the Oregon donation law. A bucket of water poured out in a recently ploughed furrow or a shack measured in inches not feet might be used in testimony as evidence of irrigation or habitation. A group of lumbermen in the Puget Sound area was called into court charged with timber theft. They were fined and also sentenced to one day in jail. Their story, told again and again at the annual meetings of the lumbermen's association, was that they paid their fines and then sent the sheriff out for "segars" and potables. When he returned, lumbermen, sheriff, and judge all retired to the jail, the key was turned in the lock, and all hands remained incarcerated for the day. Thus were the demands of the law satisfied. * * *

The land grabs, the water grabs, the mineral grabs, the timber grabs, all excite great interest and bring forth lamentations. This represents a melancholy part of the story, but it is not the whole story. The alienation of the public land exhibits much human cunning and avarice, but in many instances what was called fraud represented local accommodation to the rigidities and irrelevance of the laws. The part of the story that involves the vast number of land-seekers who got their land without violating either the spirit or the letter of the law is in one way the least exciting part, but this is the part of the story that provided a lure so strong that it drew millions of people across the Atlantic to the United States in the hope of obtaining land. It was about this aspect that Eugene Davenport, then Dean of the College of Agriculture of Illinois, might have been thinking when in 1915 he discussed briefly the distribution and use of the public domain. Waste and abuse there had been in abundance, "but we have these farms, these cities, these railroads, and this civilization to show for it, and they are worth what they cost."

———

QUESTIONS AND DISCUSSION

1. Recall Professor Charles Wilkinson's words in the introduction to this chapter:

> Westwide, natural resource policy is dominated by the lords of yesterday, a battery of nineteenth-century laws, policies, and ideas that arose under wholly different social and economic conditions but that remain in effect due to inertia, powerful lobbying forces, and lack of public awareness.

CHARLES F. WILKINSON, CROSSING THE NEXT MERIDIAN: LAND, WATER, AND THE FUTURE OF THE WEST 17 (1992). Can you think about ways in which resource policy continues to be dominated by nineteenth century law and policy? With respect to why those laws remain in effect, should Professor Wilkinson have added to his list the fact that many of those laws established property rights? How does that fact relate to the "inertia" and "powerful lobbying forces" identified by Professor Wilkinson? The laws relating to disposition of the federal lands are only one facet of the lords of yesterday. As we will discuss when we move into the different natural resources—whether minerals, water, timber, or grass—other nineteenth century laws also continue to have significant impact on our resource management.

2. Although this casebook cannot devote significant space to them, a few complications that arose as a result of the federal grants to states are worthy of note. Before a state could know the location of its specific numbered sections of school land within each township granted in its enabling act, a survey was necessary. Prior to survey the United States was free to dispose of or reserve its public lands for any purpose otherwise consistent with federal law. Settlers, for example, often arrived ahead of the surveyors and received federal lands (by purchase or for free) that later turned out to be on sections promised to the state in its enabling act. In such situations, the federal government promised the states that they could make other "indemnity" selections "in lieu" of the sections they had been promised. Over the years, this sparked significant litigation about what sort of in lieu selections states could make. Could they select more valuable land, such as federal land containing mineral resources, as long as it was equal acreage, or were they obligated to select in lieu lands of roughly equal value? *See Andrus v. Utah*, 446 U.S. 500 (1980) (upholding Interior Secretary's requirement that indemnity selections not involve grossly disparate values).

3. Although states have sold much of the land they were granted, the farther west the grants lay, the less likely they were to be sold. Beyond the 100th Meridian, which bisects the country from North Dakota down to Texas, and up to the Sierra Nevada and Cascade mountain ranges, where rainfall is less than the twenty inches per year necessary for agriculture without irrigation, many of the lands (both state and federal) went begging for a buyer. This has meant that federal lands are interspersed with numerous parcels of state school sections. These state "inholdings" create a variety of access issues. What happens, for example, when a state wants to issue an oil and gas lease on its lands that sit in the middle of a federal wilderness area? This problem has prompted efforts to exchange state inheld lands for federal lands elsewhere in the state. What basic rules do you think should govern such exchanges? How should equivalency of exchange be ensured? Should the exchanges require equal acreage, commercial real estate value, ecosystem service provision? Or should these exchanges be process-based, with acceptable trades approved by a board of representative stakeholders, state and federal officials, or some other process? Access issues are discussed in more detail in Chapter 6.

4. Another set of issues that arose out of the various enabling act grants concerns the extent of the trust obligation imposed upon states with respect to the lands they received from the federal government. Could New Mexico, for example, close down its miner's hospital and use the funds generated by the federal miner's hospital grant to support other state hospitals at which the miners would be eligible to receive care? *United States v. New Mexico*, 536 F.2d 1324 (10th Cir. 1976) (no). Could Idaho lease its school lands to grazers without opening the lands to bid by conservation organizations who might be willing to pay more to the school fund? *Idaho Watersheds Project v. State Bd. of Land Comm'rs*, 982 P.2d 367 (Idaho 1999) (no). Could Colorado set aside portions of its school trust lands in a stewardship trust for conservation purposes or must it open them up to economic development for the benefit of its schoolchildren? *Branson School Dist. RE–82 v. Romer*, 161 F.3d 619 (10th Cir. 1998) (affirming the trust against a facial challenge), *cert. denied*, 526 U.S. 1068 (1999). Do these decisions make sense? Given the clear public purpose for which these lands were granted, what's wrong with redirecting the funds to other activities that further the same goal? As state school trust land managers attempt to respond to changing public land use preferences, these issues are likely to continue to arise.

D. FEDERAL RETENTION OF PUBLIC LANDS AND RESOURCES

1. EARLY FEDERAL RETENTION AND NATIONAL PARKS

Although most of the nineteenth century was devoted to disposal, with the early stirring of the conservation movement, *see* Chapter 1, *supra*, federal policy began to incorporate the idea that some lands should be retained by the public. The idea that the federal government might retain some of the public lands was not a novel one. In 1817 the federal government had reserved for naval construction public lands containing live oak and red cedar and in 1832 had reserved Hot Springs, Arkansas because of its perceived medicinal value. The Supreme Court in *United States v. Gratiot*, 39 U.S. (14 Pet.) 526 (1840), had also upheld federal leasing of lead mines. But the first significant instance of retention for conservation purposes was Congress' 1864 decision to cede Yosemite Valley and Mariposa Big Tree Grove to California for public recreation. Act of June 30, 1864, 13 Stat. 325 (California later re-ceded the land to the federal government). Eight years later, Congress reserved two million acres of public land in the Wyoming Territory to create Yellowstone National Park as a "pleasuring ground for the benefit of the people." Act of March 1, 1872, ch. 24, 17 Stat. 32. Congress, however, appropriated no money for its management, and the Interior Department relied on the Army to do what little it could to manage the Park. Although the national park idea is one of the United States' unique contributions to world conservation, Yellowstone can only be described as a tentative first step. Nevertheless, it was a significant step because it symbolized not only that some public lands may be best left in government hands but that they should be left undeveloped. Wallace Stegner once described national parks as "the best idea we ever had. Absolutely American, absolutely democratic, they reflect us at our best rather than our worst...." Wallace Stegner, *The Best Idea We Ever Had*, *in* MARKING THE SPARROW'S FALL: THE MAKING OF THE AMERICAN WEST 137 (Page Stegner ed., 1998).

In the next 18 years, only one other park was created—Mackinac Island National Park in Michigan. But in 1890, Congress created Yosemite (a federal donut of land surrounding the land previously ceded to the state), Sequoia, and General Grant (later to become part of Sequoia). Other parks followed: Mount Rainier in 1899, Crater Lake in 1902, Mesa Verde in 1906, Grand Canyon in 1908, Zion and Olympic in 1909, Glacier in 1910, and Rocky Mountain in 1915. The number of parks was augmented by passage in 1906 of the Antiquities Act, which gave the president authority to declare national monuments. Using this Act, Theodore Roosevelt set aside 18 monuments, including the Petrified Forest and what became Grand Canyon. *See generally* Mark Squillace, *The Monumental Legacy of the Antiquities Act of 1906*, 37 GA. L. REV. 473 (2003). By 1916, the Interior Department was responsible for 14 national parks and 21 national monuments but had neither an organization nor policy guidance from Congress as to how it was to manage them. In 1916, Congress gave it both, passing the Park Service Organic Act, which created the National Park Service within the Department of the Interior and gave it the mission "to conserve the scenery and the natural and historic objects and the wildlife therein, and to provide for the enjoyment of the same in such manner and by such means as will leave them unimpaired for the enjoyment of future generations." 16 U.S.C. §§ 1–18f. *See* DYAN ZASLOWSKY & T. H. WATKINS, THESE AMERICAN LANDS: PARKS, WILDERNESS AND THE PUBLIC LANDS 11–27 (1994). The National Parks now comprise 391 areas and about 84 million acres of land. *See* National Park Service Website, *available at* http://www.nps.gov. The law relating to national parks, national monuments, and other public lands reserved for preservation purposes will be discussed in Chapter 6.

[handwritten margin notes: Pres'l auth. to declare Ntnl. monuments ✱ T. Roosevelt ✱]*

2. NATIONAL FORESTS

The 1870s saw not only the reservation of Yellowstone, but also the beginnings of a movement for forest protection. New York, in 1872, established a commission to consider the creation of a state forest preserve in the Adirondacks. Their initial recommendation was ignored, but in 1885 the state legislature designated as a "forest preserve" all of the lands in fourteen counties in the Adirondacks and Catskills. Although the purpose of the preserve was partly for aesthetic and recreational purposes, its primary purpose was watershed protection. During the same time frame, the American Forestry Association was formed, forestry classes sprang up at several universities, and John Muir had begun traipsing the Sierra Nevadas and extolling the virtues of California's magnificent forests. The stage was set for some federal action on forests. The vehicle came along in 1891, when Congress passed what it termed the General Revision Act. The primary purpose of the Act was to revise public land laws in light of a report that had been issued by the Public Lands Commission in 1879. Among its many revisions was the repeal of the Timber Culture Act and the Preemption Act. But what the Act became known for was a provision, added in conference committee, that gave the president authority to "set apart and reserve . . . public lands wholly or in part covered with timber or undergrowth, whether of commercial value or not, as public reservations . . . ." 26 Stat. 1095.

→ more pres'l auth. → public reservations

President Benjamin Harrison quickly took up Congress' offer, establishing one reserve the next month. Before he left office two years later, he had established 14 more forest reserves covering more than 13 million acres of public land. In his first year in office, President Cleveland added two more reserves with a combined area of about 4.5 million acres but then stopped because Congress had not provided any guidance for the forests' protection or management. A forest commission was appointed to make legislative recommendations, which it did as well as recommending the creation of another 13 forest reserves. Its legislative recommendations came too late for Congress to act prior to the conclusion of Cleveland's presidency but Cleveland at the close of his term (February 22, 1897) went ahead with the 13 forest reserves, concluding that his action would likely hurry along legislation. Cleveland was right. The 21 million acres he reserved created a firestorm in the West. On June 4, 1897, Congress passed the Forest Management Act. The Act suspended Cleveland's last-minute reserves and reopened them to settlement for one year until they could be redrawn. The Act gave the Department of the Interior authority to make rules and regulations regarding "the occupancy and use" of the forests. 30 Stat. 34. It also authorized the continuing creation of forest reserves "to improve and protect the forest . . . or for the purpose of securing favorable conditions of water flows, and to furnish a continuous supply of timber for the use and necessities of the citizens of the United States." 16 U.S.C. § 475.

Forests —
＊Harrison
＊Cleveland

Forest Mgmt. Act → DoI rules/regs.

Although the 1897 Forest Management Act placed the forest reserves under the management of the Interior Department, Congress had eleven years earlier tasked the Department of Agriculture with studying forestry and timber production. Soon after the Act's passage, Gifford Pinchot became the head of the Agriculture Department's Bureau of Forestry. Pinchot, who had studied forestry in France and Germany, was among the first professionally trained foresters in the United States, but more than that he proved to be one of the most capable public servants the country has seen. Soon after the Act's passage, Pinchot had been hired by Interior as a "Special Forest Agent" to propose a structure for a forest bureau at Interior. But he quickly became disenchanted with Interior officials, concluding that "the Interior Department, with its tradition of political toad-eating and executive incompetence, was incapable of employing the powers the act gave it." GIFFORD PINCHOT, BREAKING NEW GROUND, 116 (1947). At Pinchot's urging, Congress passed the Transfer Act of 1905 which transferred jurisdiction over the national forests to the Bureau of Forestry at the Department of Agriculture. Several months later, the Bureau of Forestry was renamed the United States Forest Service, and Pinchot was installed as its first Chief.

Together, Pinchot and President Theodore Roosevelt forged the program of conservation that was to become one of the hallmarks of the Roosevelt administration. The important role played by Roosevelt in the designation of our first national monuments, many of which are now national parks, is noted briefly above. On the forestry side, Roosevelt was just as aggressive, more than quadrupling the number of acres devoted to national forests. Western hostility to the forest reserves peaked in 1907. In an appropriations act for the Department of Agriculture, Congress forbade the further creation of forest reserves (which the Act renamed "National Forests") in Washington, Oregon, Idaho, Montana, Wyoming, and Colorado. Roosevelt was unwilling to veto the appropriations act and so Pinchot and his staff worked night and day to prepare a list of 32 last-minute forest proclamations, which Roosevelt made in the last two days before signing the bill. Senator Patterson of Colorado remarked that Congress had succeeded in shutting the barn door but only after the horse had been stolen. GATES, *supra* at 582. At the end of the McKinley presidency, there were 41 forest reserves with about 46 million acres. By the end of Roosevelt's presidency, there were approximately 172.5 million acres of national forest, mostly in the western part of the United States, which is just a bit less than the total combined acreage of California and Arizona. Today the Forest Service manages 193 million acres of land in 155 national forests and 20 national grasslands. *See* U.S.D.A. Forest Service, *About Us*, *available at* http://www.fs.fed.us/aboutus/meetfs.shtml. Maps depicting the location of the national forests are available at http://www.fs.fed.us/maps/.

In acreage terms, the reservation of national forests was certainly the most significant move by the federal government to assert permanent control over a portion of the public lands. That is why the reservations drew such ire in the West. Recognize, however, that federal retention of public lands is not the equivalent of federal preservation of those lands. Although the national forests can appropriately be described as part of Roosevelt's conservation legacy, they were not nature preserves. They remained open to entry under the mining law, and timber production remained one of the primary uses. Over the years, Congress has expanded the purposes served by national forests to encompass a wide range of uses including outdoor recreation, range, timber, watershed, minerals, and wildlife and fish purposes, but the sustained yield of the forest resources has remained an overarching goal. Management of the national forests is now governed by the Multiple-Use, Sustained-Yield Act of 1960, 16 U.S.C. §§ 528–31, and the National Forest Management Act of 1976, 16 U.S.C. §§ 1601 et seq. The forest resource is considered in detail in Chapter 10.

3. NATIONAL WILDLIFE REFUGES AND EXECUTIVE WITHDRAWALS

Another part of Roosevelt's conservation legacy—and another early example of federal retention of the public lands—was his effort to create bird and wildlife refuges. In 1903, Roosevelt asked an advisor, "Is there anything in the law that will prevent me from declaring Pelican Island [off the Florida coast] a Federal Bird Reservation? When told there was not, he replied, 'Very well, then I so declare it.'" Although Congress had not delegated any authority to do so, by the time Roosevelt left office in 1909, he had created 51 bird reservations, forming the foundation of the current national wildlife refuge system. *See generally* ZASLOWSKY & WATKINS, *supra*, at 151–93. The National Wildlife Refuge System is now managed by the U.S. Fish & Wildlife Service within the Department of the Interior and consists of 520 units encompassing over 93 million acres. *See* U.S.F.W.S., History of the National Wildlife Refuge System, *at* http://refuges.fws.gov/history/index.html.

President Roosevelt's designation of bird refuges without any express congressional delegation of authority highlights a significant issue that continues to be a source of dispute in public land management—namely, how does the Constitution divide authority between the executive and Congress over the public lands? As described above, retention of the public lands occurred in three primary ways. In some instances, most prominently the national parks, Congress passed legislation on its own to set aside and reserve portions of the public lands. In other cases, Congress delegated to the executive branch authority to reserve portions of the public lands. The proclamation of national forests under the General Revision Act of 1891 and the proclamation of national monuments under the Antiquities Act of 1906 are two prominent examples. The third approach to reservation is that employed by President Roosevelt with the bird refuges. The following case addresses the constitutionality of such executive reservations made in the absence of express congressional delegation.

UNITED STATES v. MIDWEST OIL CO., 236 U.S. 459 (1915)

MR. JUSTICE LAMAR delivered the opinion of the court.

All public lands containing petroleum or other mineral oils and chiefly valuable therefor, have been declared by Congress to be "free and open to occupation, exploration and purchase by citizens of the United States ... under regulations prescribed by law." [Oil Placer] Act of February 11, 1897.

As these regulations permitted exploration and location without the payment of any sum, and as title could be obtained for a merely nominal amount, many persons availed themselves of the provisions of the statute....

The result was that oil was so rapidly extracted that on September 17, 1909, the Director of the Geological Survey made a report to the Secretary of the Interior which, with enclosures, called attention to the fact that, while there was a limited supply of coal on the Pacific coast and the value of oil as a fuel had been fully demonstrated, yet at the rate at which oil lands in California were being patented by private parties it would "be impossible for the people of the United States to continue ownership of oil lands for more than a few months. After that the Government will be obliged to repurchase the very oil that it has practically given away...." "In view of the increasing use of fuel by the American Navy there would appear to be an immediate necessity for assuring the conservation of a proper supply of petroleum for the Government's own use ..." and "pending the enactment of adequate legislation on this subject, the filing of claims to oil lands in the State of California should be suspended."

This recommendation was approved by the Secretary of the Interior. Shortly afterwards he brought the matter to the attention of the President who, on September 27, 1909, issued the following Proclamation: "Temporary Petroleum Withdrawal No. 5." "In aid of proposed legislation affecting the use and disposition of the petroleum deposits on the public domain, all public lands in the accompanying lists are hereby temporarily withdrawn from all forms of location, settlement, selection, filing, entry, or disposal under the mineral or nonmineral public-land laws. All locations or claims existing and valid on this date may proceed to entry in the usual manner after field investigation and examination." The list attached described an area aggregating 3,041,000 acres in California and Wyoming....

On March 27, 1910, six months after the publication of the Proclamation, William T. Henshaw and others entered upon a quarter section of this public land in Wyoming so withdrawn. They made explorations, bored a well, discovered oil and thereafter assigned their interest to [Midwest Oil], who took possession and extracted large quantities of oil....

As the explorations by the original claimants, and the subsequent operation of the well, were both long after the date of the President's Proclamation, the Government filed, in the District Court of the United States for the District of Wyoming, a Bill in Equity against the Midwest Oil Company ..., seeking to recover the land and to obtain an accounting for 50,000 barrels of oil alleged to have been illegally extracted....

... On the part of the Government it is urged that the President, as Commander-in-Chief of the Army and Navy, had power to make the order for the purpose of retaining and preserving a source of supply of fuel for the Navy, instead of allowing the oil land to be taken up for a nominal sum, the Government being then obliged to purchase at a great cost what it had previously owned. It is argued that the President, charged with the care of the public domain, could, by virtue of the executive power vested in him by the Constitution (Art. 2, § 1), and also in conformity with the tacit consent of Congress, withdraw, in the public interest, any public land from entry or location by private parties.

The Appellees, on the other hand, insist that there is no dispensing power in the Executive and that he could not suspend a statute or withdraw from entry or location any land which Congress had affirmatively declared should be free and open to acquisition by citizens of the United States. They further insist that the withdrawal order is absolutely void since it appears on its face to be a mere attempt to suspend a statute—supposed to be unwise,—in order to allow

Congress to pass another more in accordance with what the Executive thought to be in the public interest.

We need not consider whether, as an original question, the President could have withdrawn from private acquisition what Congress had made free and open to occupation and purchase. The case can be determined on other grounds and in the light of the legal consequences flowing from a long continued practice to make orders like the one here involved. For the President's proclamation of September 27, 1909, is by no means the first instance in which the Executive, by a special order, has withdrawn land which Congress, by general statute, had thrown open to acquisition by citizens. And while it is not known when the first of these orders was made, it is certain that "the practice dates from an early period in the history of the government." Scores and hundreds of these orders have been made; and treating them as they must be, as the act of the President, an examination of official publications will show that (excluding those made by virtue of special congressional action) he has during the past 80 years, without express statutory authority—but under the claim of power so to do—made a multitude of Executive Orders which operated to withdraw public land that would otherwise have been open to private acquisition.... The number of such instances cannot, of course, be accurately given, but the extent of the practice can best be appreciated by a consideration of what is believed to be a correct enumeration of such Executive Orders mentioned in public documents. They show that prior to the year 1910 there had been issued:

Executive Orders establishing or enlarging Indian Reservations	99
Executive Orders establishing or enlarging Military Reservations and setting apart land for water, timber, fuel, hay, signal stations, target ranges and rights of way for use in connection with Military Reservations	109
Executive Orders establishing Bird Reserves	44

In the sense that these lands may have been intended for public use, they were reserved for a public purpose. But they were not reserved in pursuance of law or by virtue of any general or special statutory authority. For, it is to be specially noted that there was no act of Congress providing for Bird Reserves or for these Indian Reservations. There was no law for the establishment of these Military Reservations or defining their size or location. There was no statute empowering the President to withdraw any of these lands from settlement or to reserve them for any of the purposes indicated.

But when it appeared that the public interest would be served by withdrawing or reserving parts of the public domain, nothing was more natural than to retain what the Government already owned. And in making such orders, which were thus useful to the public, no private interest was injured. For prior to the initiation of some right given by law the citizen had no enforceable interest in the public statute and no private right in land which was the property of the people. The President was in a position to know when the public interest required particular portions of the people's lands to be withdrawn from entry or location; his action inflicted no wrong upon any private citizen, and being subject to disaffirmance by Congress, could occasion no harm to the interest of the public at large. Congress did not repudiate the power claimed or the withdrawal orders made. On the contrary it uniformly and repeatedly acquiesced in the practice and, as shown by these records, there had been, prior to 1910, at least 252 Executive Orders making reservation for useful, though non-statutory purposes. * * *

It may be argued that while these facts and rulings prove a usage they do not establish its validity. But government is a practical affair intended for practical men. Both officers, law-makers and citizens naturally adjust themselves to any long-continued action of the Executive Department—on the presumption that unauthorized acts would not have been allowed to be so often repeated as to crystallize into a regular practice. That presumption is not reasoning in a circle but the basis of a wise and quieting rule that in determining the meaning of a statute or the existence of a power, weight shall be given to the usage itself—even when the validity of the practice is the subject of investigation.

posibivism

These decisions do not, of course, mean that ... the Executive can by his course of action create a power. But they do clearly indicate that the long-continued practice, known to and acquiesced in by Congress, would raise a presumption that the withdrawals had been made in pursuance of its consent or of a recognized administrative power of the Executive in the management of the public lands. This is particularly true in view of the fact that the land is property of the United States and that the land laws are not of a legislative character in the highest sense of the term (Art. 4, § 3) "but savor somewhat of mere rules prescribed by an owner of property for its disposal." *Butte City Water Co. v. Baker*, 196 U.S. 126.

These rules or laws for the disposal of public land are necessarily general in their nature. Emergencies may occur, or conditions may so change as to require that the agent in charge should, in the public interest, withhold the land from sale; and while no such express authority has been granted, there is nothing in the nature of the power exercised which prevents Congress from granting it by implication just as could be done by any other owner of property under similar conditions. The power of the Executive, as agent in charge, to retain that property from sale need not necessarily be expressed in writing....

For it must be borne in mind that Congress not only has a legislative power over the public domain, but it also exercises the powers of the proprietor therein. Congress "may deal with such lands precisely as a private individual may deal with his farming property. It may sell or withhold them from sale." Like any other owner it may provide when, how and to whom its land can be sold. It can permit it to be withdrawn from sale....

The Executive, as agent, was in charge of the public domain; by a multitude of orders extending over a long period of time and affecting vast bodies of land, in many States and Territories, he withdrew large areas in the public interest. These orders were known to Congress, as principal, and in not a single instance was the act of the agent disapproved. Its acquiescence all the more readily operated as an implied grant of power in view of the fact that its exercise was not only useful to the public but did not interfere with any vested right of the citizen. * * *

The case is therefore remanded to the District Court with directions that the decree dismissing the Bill be *Reversed*.

MR. JUSTICE DAY with whom concurred MR. JUSTICE MCKENNA and MR. JUSTICE VAN DEVANTER, dissenting.

DISSENT

* * * The Constitution of the United States in Article IV, § 3, provides: "The Congress shall have power to dispose of and make all needful rules and regulations respecting the territory or other property belonging to the United States." In this section the power to dispose of lands belonging to the United

States is broadly conferred upon Congress, and it is under the power therein given that the system of land laws for the disposition of the public domain has been enacted. * * *

It is thus explicitly recognized, as was already apparent from the terms of the Constitution itself, that the sole authority to dispose of the public lands was vested in the Congress and in no other branch of the Federal Government. The right of the Executive to withdraw lands which Congress has declared shall be open and free to settlement upon terms which Congress has itself prescribed, is said to arise from the tacit consent of Congress in long acquiescence in such executive action resulting in an implied authority from Congress to make such withdrawals in the public interest as the Executive deems proper and necessary. There is nothing in the Constitution suggesting or authorizing such augmentation of executive authority or justifying him in thus acting in aid of a power which the framers of the Constitution saw fit to vest exclusively in the legislative branch of the Government.

It is true that many withdrawals have been made by the President and some of them have been sustained by this court, so that it may be fairly said that, within limitations to be hereinafter stated, executive withdrawals have the sanction of judicial approval, but, as we read the cases, in no instance has this court sustained a withdrawal of public lands for which Congress has provided a system of disposition, except such withdrawal was—(a) in pursuance of a policy already declared by Congress as one for which the public lands might be used, as military and Indian reservations for which purposes Congress has authorized the use of the public lands from an early day, or (b) in cases where grants of Congress are in such conflict that the purpose of Congress cannot be known and therefore the Secretary of the Interior has been sustained in withdrawing the lands from entry until Congress had opportunity to relieve the ambiguity of its laws by specifically declaring its policy.

It is undoubtedly true that withdrawals have been made without specific authority of an act of Congress, but those which have been sustained by this court, it is believed, will be found to be in one or the other of the categories above stated. On the other hand, when the executive authority has been exceeded this court has not hesitated to so declare, and to sustain the superior and exclusive authority of Congress to deal with the public lands. * * *

In our opinion, the action of the Executive Department in this case, originating in the expressed view of a subordinate official of the Interior Department as to the desirability of a different system of public land disposal than that contained in the lawful enactments of Congress, did not justify the President in withdrawing this large body of land from the operation of the law and virtually suspending, as he necessarily did, the operation of that law, at least until a different view expressed by him could be considered by the Congress. This conclusion is reinforced in this particular instance by the refusal of Congress to ratify the action of the President, and the enactment of a new statute authorizing the disposition of the public lands by a method essentially different from that proposed by the Executive.

———

QUESTIONS AND DISCUSSION

1. The chapter has thus far discussed federal retention of the public lands mainly in terms of "reservations." However, the chapter has also occasionally used the word "withdrawal," which is the term employed by the Court

"reservation"
vs.
"withdrawal"

in *Midwest Oil*. Although these terms overlap in their definition, they are terms of art in public land law. Reservations occur when the government decides to retain public lands for a specified purpose. Although other, theoretically nonconflicting, uses such as mining are sometimes allowed to continue on reserved lands such as national forests, the idea of a reservation is that the public land is set aside for a specific objective. A "withdrawal" by contrast refers to a federal decision to remove land from the applicability of a particular disposition statute. Federal land, for example, might be withdrawn from entry for oil exploration, as it was in this case, or from homestead entry. A withdrawal does not decide the purpose for which the federal land will be used. It simply eliminates one potential use. The broader the withdrawal, the more like a reservation the withdrawal will look. *See generally* DANA & FAIRFAX, *supra* at 29–30. Withdrawals are discussed at greater length in Chapter 6.

2. Although the Court declines to address whether the president has withdrawal authority as part of his executive powers, what do you think the United States' argument would have been in that regard?

3. Why does the Court suggest that Taft's withdrawal caused no injury to a private interest?

4. Is the Court correct when it says that its decision does not "mean that the Executive can by his course of action create a power"? Do you agree with the Court's conclusion that because an executive order is "subject to disaffirmance by Congress," it "could occasion no harm to the interest of the public at large"? In thinking about this question, consider the various procedural obstacles to passage of legislation such as committees, Senate rules of filibuster and cloture, and the presidential veto. Consider also whether the president or the Congress best represents the public interest. Is one or the other more likely to be a better steward of the public lands? Why? Some might argue that this debate is merely academic in light of the Property Clause. Why?

5. In the Oil Placer Act at issue in *Midwest Oil*, Congress directed that public lands containing petroleum were to be "free and open to occupation, exploration and purchase by citizens of the United States ... under regulations prescribed by law." Yet the Court confirmed executive power to close some of those lands to exploration. In the Alaska National Interest Lands Conservation Act (ANILCA), Congress directed that no oil and gas development of the Arctic National Wildlife Refuge (ANWR) was to occur without congressional approval. *See* Alaska National Interest Lands Conservation Act of 1980, 16 U.S.C. § 3143. Suppose the president were to issue an executive order opening up ANWR to drilling, in direct violation of the statute. Suppose further that for the next 15 years senators who were proponents of development were able to filibuster every attempt to renew protection for ANWR. If litigation were filed at the end of that time period, and the president defended his actions with reference to *Midwest Oil* and congressional acquiescence, what result? How might you distinguish a presidential decision to open ANWR from President Taft's action in the *Midwest Oil* case?

6. The principle that congressional acquiescence can operate as an implied grant of power from Congress also has application to those instances in which Congress has delegated withdrawal authority to the president, but the president arguably goes beyond the scope of his delegated authority. In this regard, consider the 1906 Antiquities Act. The Act authorizes the president to reserve "historic landmarks, historic and prehistoric structures, and other objects of historic or scientific interest that are situated upon the [public lands]...." 16 U.S.C. § 431 (2000). According to many commentators, the original purpose of the Antiquities Act was to allow the president to make small withdrawals of public lands in order to protect prehistoric ruins and Indian artifacts. Yet within two years of its enactment, President Theodore Roosevelt had proclaimed 11 national monuments, including 800,000 acres as the Grand Canyon National Monument. Since its enactment in 1906, presidents have used the Act over 100 times to withdraw lands from the public domain as national monuments. Assuming that the 1906 Congress intended the Act to have a narrower application—and this is the subject of some debate, *see* Mark Squillace, *The Monumental Legacy of the Antiquities Act of 1906*, 37 Ga. L. Rev. 473 (2003)—should courts consider the acquiescence of subsequent Congresses in determining the Act's meaning, or should they be limited to the text of the Act? The Antiquities Act will be considered in detail in Chapter 6.

7. The president's implied withdrawal authority was expressly repealed, along with 29 other statutory provisions granting withdrawal authority to the executive branch, by Congress in the 1976 Federal Land Policy Management Act (FLPMA). *See* Pub. L. No. 94–579, § 704(a), 90 Stat. 2744, 2792 (1976). The only significant withdrawal power that was not repealed was the Antiquities Act. Does this legislation provide a simple answer to the question in Note 5? Could congressional acquiescence in a new executive withdrawal reinvigorate the president's implied withdrawal powers? Does it matter that FLPMA set forth specific terms and conditions under which the executive could withdraw public lands? *See* 43 U.S.C. § 1714 (1994). The withdrawal provisions of FLPMA (pronounced "flip-ma") are considered in more detail in Chapter 6.

8. For an overview of executive withdrawal authority, see David H. Getches, *Managing the Public Lands: The Authority of the Executive to Withdraw Lands*, 22 Nat. Resources. J. 279 (1982) and Charles F. Wheatley, Jr., *Withdrawals Under the Federal Land Policy Management Act of 1976*, 21 Ariz. L. Rev. 311 (1979).

———

4.   THE DECISION TO RETAIN THE PUBLIC DOMAIN LANDS

The move toward reservation of public lands for national parks, forests, monuments, wildlife refuges, naval petroleum reserves, and the like, was a substantial change in public lands policy. Nevertheless, these reservations can still be understood as exceptions to the still-prevailing idea that the public lands were largely intended for disposition to private owners. The rest of the public domain remained open for entry under the Homestead Act and the General Land Office remained open for business. Remember that even the national forests remained open for entry under the mining laws and that in the same year (1916) Congress created the

still didn't presume retention of public lands...

National Park Service, it passed the Stock Raising Homestead Act under which 23 million acres of public lands were patented. The change to a presumption of federal retention of *all* the public lands, under which we operate today, was yet to come.

Before the Homestead Act and after, the primary use of that portion of the public domain that had not been taken up by settlers was grazing. Congress placed no restrictions on grazing the public domain. Although as discussed in Chapter 8, which contains a full account of grazing law, ranchers did manage in some instances to effectively exclude others from portions of the range, the public's grass was free to all comers. One of the reasons that national forests were initially so unpopular was that Gifford Pinchot began regulating grazing in the national forests and charging a small fee to graze. But, outside of national forests, grazing on the rest of the public domain required neither permit nor fee. The result of treating the public domain as a grazing commons had just the effect Garrett Hardin described. Ranchers overgrazed the land and range conditions deteriorated.

Overgrazing was not the only problem. During the teens and 1920s, with prices high and rainfall plentiful, more and more farmers had been willing to try dry farming farther and farther West. But all the sod-busting for dry land farms, along with profligate grazing, had left little vegetation to hold the soil in place. When the weather turned dry in 1934, disaster struck in the form of massive dust storms in the Plains states that continued through the spring and summer. The dust storms helped concentrate Congress' attention on the long-brewing problem of overgrazing, resulting in the passage that summer of the Taylor Grazing Act, which ended free grazing on the public domain. The Act authorized the Secretary of the Interior to create grazing districts from 80 million acres of the public domain "chiefly valuable for grazing and raising forage crops," to withdraw those acres from entry or settlement, and to then issue ranchers permits for grazing. 43 U.S.C. § 315. Because the 80 million acres was less than half of the remaining public domain, and because President Franklin D. Roosevelt was convinced that all of the public domain needed more orderly administration, he issued two executive orders that withdrew the rest of the public domain from settlement. Congress responded by adding 62 million acres of the land withdrawn by Roosevelt to the grazing districts. To administer the Taylor Act, the Interior Department established a Grazing Division, which was renamed the U.S. Grazing Service in 1941. In 1946, the Interior Department merged the Grazing Service and the General Land Office to create the Bureau of Land Management (BLM).

By setting aside almost all of the remaining public domain for grazing purposes, the Taylor Act, helped along by Roosevelt's executive orders, effectively ended disposition of the public domain, at least outside Alaska. Nevertheless, because the Taylor Act also stated that the land was only being placed in grazing districts "pending its final disposal," some still held out hope that the grazing districts would one day be reopened to entry and settlement. This hope was finally dashed in 1976 with the passage of the Federal Land Policy Management Act (FLPMA) in which Congress declared its intention that the "public lands be retained in Federal ownership, unless as a result of the land use planning procedure provided for in this Act, it is determined that disposal of a particular parcel will serve the national interest[.]'' 43 U.S.C. § 1701(a). FLPMA repealed scores of old public lands laws and also served as an organic act for the BLM, directing that the grazing and other lands managed by the BLM, like the national forests, should be managed for a range of uses including extraction, recreation, and preservation, a philosophy commonly called ''multiple use and sustained yield'' that had originally been championed by Gifford Pinchot. The BLM now administers about 258 million acres of land, including about 83 million acres in Alaska. *See* Bureau of Land Management, Public Land Statistics, *available at* http://www.blm.gov/wo/st/en/res/ Direct_Links_to_Publications/ann_rpt_and_pls.html. For a map depicting the lands managed by the BLM, visit http://www.blm.gov/nhp/facts/maps/ landsmap_m.html.

FLPMA changed the presumption officially [handwritten margin note]

5.   THE GEOGRAPHIC LEGACY OF FEDERAL PUBLIC LANDS POLICY

The passage of FLPMA confirmed what had been effectively true under the Taylor Grazing Act: disposition of the public domain had largely ended. Other than mining entries under the Mining Law, the configuration of the public lands is now basically set. After two centuries of disposal and retention decisions, about 69% of our nation's lands are owned by states or private persons. About 31% of it is owned by the federal government. The map below depicts the percentage of land within each state that is owned by the federal government.

Public West, Private East

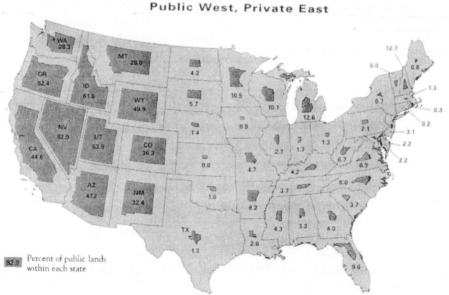

Percent of public lands within each state

Source: ATLAS OF THE NEW WEST: PORTRAIT OF A CHANGING REGION 58 (William E. Riebsame ed., 1997)

QUESTIONS AND DISCUSSION

1. Consider the map above showing that most of the public lands are located in the western part of the United States. What are the implications for natural resource policy and lawmaking?

2. It is fairly easy to find flaws in nineteenth century public lands policy, but if we could take a mulligan or "do-over" on the public lands, what should we have done? Given the different approaches to management of a common pool resource discussed in Chapter 1, what options should have been considered? More disposition to private parties? Disposal of about the same acreage but with a different distribution? Should the federal government have retained more? How practical is your solution? Would it have been politically feasible given the nation's other priorities? If you would have taken a different approach to the public lands, consider why that might be the case. Is it just that we know more about ecological impacts? Is it only that our utilitarian calculus about the value of the resources has changed? Or have our values changed? In this regard, think back to the case study in Chapter 1 on the "Changing Conception of Wilderness."

3. How might public choice theory help explain federal public land disposal and retention policies? How might natural resource economics and principles of scarcity help explain what happened?

4. Consider again the railroad grants and specifically the significant acreage granted to the Northern Pacific Railroad now held by timber companies. Returning such lands to federal ownership would do much to rationalize forest management in the Northwest and potentially to enhance protection of biodiversity. If the federal government decided to do so, how could it work to reacquire the checkerboarded lands? Is using the public trust doctrine a possibility, or would the government need to rely on purchase, exchange, or condemnation? More broadly, think about the many improvident or even fraudulent grants of federal land and resources. Short of buying back the West, is there any way for the public to reacquire some of these resources? To return to the question above, is reacquisition even a good idea from a perspective of natural resource management policy?

5. Supporters of federal retention raised three primary arguments in its favor. One was moral, an "appeal to social democratic ideals of equality and commonwealth" that argued for retaining these last remnants of a great heritage of land. Another was economic, embracing the premise that public ownership could better "insure the greatest return to the greatest number of people" (the classic Pinchot criterion). A third held that the "private entrepreneur simply could not be trusted to look out for the longer term ecological health of the range resource." DEBRA L. DONAHUE, THE WESTERN RANGE REVISITED 16 (1999), *quoting* DONALD WORSTER, NATURE'S ECONOMY: A HISTORY OF ECOLOGICAL IDEAS 267–68 (1977). Which of the three would you say is the dominant strain in today's thinking about the public lands?

6. The western states' frequent opposition to federal retention of land is not just about sovereignty and jurisdiction. It is also about revenue. Because federal land is exempt from state taxation, those states and counties with significant federal lands have a reduced base for property taxation. The school land grants were one effort to ameliorate this difficulty. Over time, a variety of other federal laws have been enacted to compensate states and counties. Perhaps the most prominent of these acts is the so-called Payment-in-Lieu-of-Taxes (PILT) Act which sends federal dollars to counties based on a formula of acreage and population. 31 U.S.C. § 6903 (1994). A variety of other acts pay counties based on federal revenues from commodity and extractive uses of the public lands. *See, e.g.,* 16 U.S.C. § 500 (promising counties 25% of the receipts from timber harvests in national forests); Mineral Leasing Act, 30 U.S.C. § 191 (providing for the state of origin to receive 50% of revenues from oil and gas leasing and for Alaska to receive 90%). Are these payment programs a good idea? What impact might such laws have on the way counties view resource development within their boundaries? If there is concern that it creates too strong an incentive to promote resource extraction and development, what is the alternative?

7. As mentioned in section III.C.2 above, many state enabling acts contained "proceeds clauses" under which the United States promised to pay the state five percent of the net proceeds from federal land sales to be used for a permanent fund for the support of the common schools within the state. As it turned out, of course, the federal government decided to retain a significant amount of public land in the western states. In 2007, a number of western representatives introduced H.R. 3614 to "authorize Western States to make selections of public land within their borders in lieu of receiving 5 percent of the proceeds of the sale of public land lying within said States as provided by their respective enabling Acts." The bill recites the following findings:

> (11) Despite the fact that Western States tax at a comparable rate and allocate as much of their budgets to public education as other States, Western States have lower real growth in per pupil expenditures and have higher pupil-per-teacher ratios.

> (12) The Federal Government is the source and potential solver of the problem because of the enormous amount of untaxed land the Federal Government owns in Western States.

> (13) All States east of an imaginary vertical line from Montana to New Mexico have, on average, 4.1 percent of their land federally owned, while the Western States on average have 51.9 percent of their land federally owned.

> (14) The plain language of these enabling Acts proclaims that the public land shall be sold by the United States subsequent to the admission of the States into the Union.

> (15) The United States honored those Acts by selling public land within the Western States until the passage of the Federal Land Policy and Management Act of 1976, wherein Congress declared that the policy of the United States was to retain public land in Federal ownership and management.

> (16) The United States has broken its solemn compact with the Western States and breached its fiduciary duty to the school children who are designated beneficiaries of the sale of Federal land under the terms of the respective enabling Acts of the Western States.

> (17) The current shortfall in funding public education in the Western States requires immediate Congressional action to remedy the above-described discriminatory Federal land policy and prevent the further disadvantaging of the school children of the Western States.

(18) The most efficient and cost effective remedy now available to the United States is to grant to the Western States 5 percent of the remaining Federal land located within each State, authorizing each State to select such land from the unappropriated public land within the boundaries of the State to satisfy the grant.

How likely do you think this legislation is to achieve passage? Are the federal transfer payments discussed in Note 6 a sufficient response to the concerns expressed in this legislation? Does the original promise to pay the states five percent of the proceeds include a promise to sell all of the public lands?

8. The existence of so much checkerboarded and split-estate land, along with more mundane issues such as urban growth abutting public lands in places like Las Vegas, has led Congress to give the federal land management agencies power to exchange federal lands for private lands. Exchanges are governed primarily by FLPMA, which requires that exchanges be of equal value and in the public interest. *See* 43 U.S.C. § 1716. In recent years, the BLM's exchange program has come under heavy criticism from those who allege that the agency is not getting equal value, failing to employ standard appraisal procedures, and not acting in the public interest. The equal value determination is not as straightforward as one might think. Suppose, for example, that a section of school trust lands within a national park contains a magnificent arch formation. On the one hand, the Park Service and many others may assert that the arch is priceless or, at very least, has great value to the public. The exchange regulations, however, provide that the school section is to be appraised at its fair *market* value. Its primary market value is for grazing. The state may be willing to negotiate an exchange but it wants the lands it receives to reflect the market and nonmarket value of the arch. What makes sense? How might the value of such a parcel be calculated? Think back to the discussion in Chapter 1 on resource valuation.

One approach to the problem is to have Congress pass legislation approving an exchange. Although the state-federal negotiation of value is still difficult, Congress is not bound by the equal value appraisal obligations of FLPMA. One example of such an exchange was the Utah School Lands Exchange Act of 1998. Pub. L. 105–35, 112 Stat. 3139 (Oct. 31, 1998). The catalyst for the exchange was President Clinton's proclamation of the Grand Staircase–Escalante National Monument, which contained within it about 180,000 acres of school trust lands, and his promise to work toward an exchange. In the end, Utah gave up all of its inholdings in the monument and in Utah's national parks, as well as most of its inheld school lands in Utah's national forests and Indian reservations. In total, Utah gave up over 376,000 acres of land and about 66,000 acres of mineral rights for about 139,000 acres of federal land plus $50 million. *See generally* Symposium, Robert B. Keiter, *Biodiversity Conservation and the Intermixed Ownership Problem: From Nature Reserves to Collaborative Processes*, 38 IDAHO L. REV. 301 (2002).

The problems and limitations of the exchange process led Congress to look at alternative ways to accomplish the same objective. In 1998, for example, Congress passed the Southern Nevada Public Land Management

Act of 1998. Pub. L. 106–263. Under this law, the BLM is permitted to sell certain public lands around the City of Las Vegas. The BLM uses the proceeds from the sale of these lands to purchase other environmentally sensitive lands around the State. As of 2006, auctions of nearly 13,000 acres had generated over $2.7 billion in revenue and another approximately 28,500 acres are slated to be sold. *See* Bureau of Land Management, *SNPLMA Quick Facts: Land Sale Statistics as of Oct. 31, 2006, available at* http://www.nv.blm.gov/snplma/quick_facts/land_sales.htm.

The success of this Nevada model persuaded Congress to enact general legislation in 2000. Under the Federal Land Transaction Facilitation Act, Pub. L. 106–248 (Title II), the BLM is authorized to sell lands and deposit the proceeds from such sales into a Federal Lands Disposal Account. Money from this account may be used by any of the federal land management agencies to purchase other lands. The law requires, however, that at least 80% of the money (less expenses and administrative costs) must be used in the state where it is generated.

9. A part of the public lands and natural resources story that this casebook will largely skip, but one that could justify an entire law school course on its own, is that of Alaska. Just a bit larger than California, Texas and Montana combined, Alaska and its 365 million acres rich in natural resources entered the Union in 1958. Obtaining a much better deal than any other state, Alaska's enabling act promised the state that it could select 103 million acres of land for itself. Alaska had selected about one-fourth of its lands when the Secretary of the Interior, pressed by land claims of native Alaskans and the discovery of oil on Alaska's North Slope, suspended Alaska's selection pending congressional action. Congress responded in 1971 by enacting the Alaska Native Claim Settlement Act (ANCSA). The Act assured the Alaska natives $462 million in grants, $500 million in mineral lease revenues, and 40 million acres of land. Although the Act allowed the state to resume selection, § d(2) of ANCSA also authorized the Secretary to withdraw 80 million acres of land from state or native entry that might merit status as national parks, forests, or wildlife refuges. Congress was to decide upon the Secretary's recommendations by December 1978. Congress, however, was not able to act by the deadline. To allow Congress more time to consider legislation, Secretary of the Interior Cecil Andrus, using his emergency withdrawal authority under FLPMA, withdrew almost 111 million acres of land and President Carter, using the Antiquities Act, placed 56 million of those acres in national monument status. With more time to act, Congress in 1980 passed the Alaska National Interest Lands Conservation Act (ANILCA). ANILCA superseded the national monuments and Andrus' withdrawals but in their place designated 53.7 million acres of wildlife refuges, 43.6 million acres of national parks, and 56 million acres of wilderness primarily within the refuges and parks. *See* G. FRANK WILLISS, DO THINGS RIGHT THE FIRST TIME: THE NATIONAL PARK SERVICE AND THE ALASKA NATIONAL INTEREST LANDS CONSERVATION ACT OF 1980 (1985), *available at* http://www.cr.nps.gov/history/online_books/williss/adhi. htm; DANA & FAIRFAX, *supra*, at 303–06. In looking at total acreage figures for wildlife refuges, national parks, and wilderness areas cited in this chapter and elsewhere in the casebook, it is wise to keep in mind the vast increases in those systems brought about by one piece of legislation in one state.

10.   Coming full circle back to acquisition, the federal government has now begun purchasing some lands for conservation and preservation purposes. Acquisition is carried out under a variety of federal statutes and programs, the most prominent of which is probably the Land and Water Conservation Fund, which is funded with revenues from oil and gas leasing on the outer continental shelf. *See* Land and Water Conservation Fund Act of 1965, 16 U.S.C. § 4601–4 to 4601–11. Since 1964, the public land base outside Alaska has increased approximately 19.8 million acres, an area equivalent to the size of the state of Maine. *See* James R. Rasband & Megan E. Garrett, *A New Era in Public Land Policy? The Shift Toward Reacquisition of Land and Natural Resources*, 53 ROCKY MTN. MIN. L. INST. 11–1. Two prominent examples of federal purchase are the Headwaters Forest to protect an ancient redwood grove in northern California and the New World Mine to protect Yellowstone's watershed. *See generally* Murray D. Feldman, *The New Public Land Exchanges: Trading Development Rights in One Area for Public Resources in Another*, 43 ROCKY MTN. MIN. L. INST. 2–1 (1997).

11.   For further reading about the acquisition, disposition and retention of the public lands, you may wish to read in the following books: SAMUEL TRASK DANA & SALLY K. FAIRFAX, FOREST AND RANGE POLICY (2d ed. 1980); PAUL W. GATES, HISTORY OF PUBLIC LAND LAW DEVELOPMENT (1968); PUBLIC LAND POLICIES: MANAGEMENT AND DISPOSAL (Paul Wallace Gates ed., 1979); THE PUBLIC LANDS: STUDIES IN THE HISTORY OF THE PUBLIC DOMAIN (Vernon Carstensen ed., 1962); CHARLES F. WILKINSON, CROSSING THE NEXT MERIDIAN: LAND, WATER, AND THE FUTURE OF THE WEST 1992.

IV.   FEDERAL POWER OVER NATURAL RESOURCE MANAGEMENT

Having reviewed the basic allocation of the nation's land and other resources, and the geographic jigsaw puzzle of checkerboarded and split-estate lands, Indian reservations, federal, state, and private lands, it is time to consider the question of regulatory power over the nation's land and natural resources. Put another way, Section III's main purpose was to set forth how the nation's resource geography took shape; this section's purpose will be to consider who gets to make the rules governing that geography. It is important to remember, however, that determining federal power to own and retain public lands depends in part on federal power to regulate. The opposite is also true. The power to regulate is enhanced by ownership. Despite the overlap, Sections III and IV separate out the federal vs. state ownership question from the federal vs. state regulatory authority question. They do so to emphasize the separate strands that you will often be required to pick from the more tangled web in cases and statutes you will encounter.

Recall that following the American Revolution, all power to regulate natural resources fell to the people and their fledgling states. The study of federal power over natural resources is thus an inquiry into how much of that power the people, or the states, gave up to the federal government in the Constitution. From one perspective, the answer that Congress and the courts gave for most of the nineteenth century was that the states had given up very little. From another perspective, however, the inquiry remained largely unanswered during that period because there was little need for the federal government to test the limits of its power. Natural resources were abundant and there was broad agreement that development of those resources was in the national and local interest. Whichever perspective is accurate, for most of the nineteenth century, natural resources were just another form of property and property was a matter of state, not federal, law. This was true even for the public lands, where state law applied in the absence of federal regulation. *See Omaechevarria v. Idaho*, 246 U.S. 343, 346–47 (1918) (holding that the "police power of the State extends over the federal public domain, at least when there is no legislation by Congress on the subject").

Although for the better part of the nineteenth century the federal government was largely content to allow state law to govern natural resource issues, when it did decide to assert its regulatory jurisdiction, it needed to point to some source of authority in the Constitution. This section of the chapter investigates the constitutional provisions upon which the federal government has relied as it has exercised increasing regulatory authority over natural resources. Part A of this section focuses on federal power over natural resources that flows from the Constitution's Property Clause, which gives to Congress the power to "dispose of and make all needful Rules and Regulations respecting the Territory or other Property belonging to the United States." U.S. CONST. art. IV, § 3, cl. 2. More specifically, to the extent the United States owns land within a state, what is the federal government's power to regulate not only its land but also activities on state or private land that may affect the federal land and resources?

While Part A focuses on the Property Clause and federal power derived from land and resources owned by the federal government, remember that federal power over land and natural resources is not solely, or even primarily, a function of federal land ownership. The federal government's power to regulate may be enhanced by a connection to federal lands, but it is not dependent on such a tie. Part B thus looks at the historical allocation of state and federal power over natural resources without regard to a public lands nexus. The constitutional provisions in this section will be more familiar to those who have taken a basic course in constitutional law. Whereas the Property Clause is commonly cited as a source of federal authority on public lands, or sometimes even when public lands are just nearby, in other locales (think particularly about the original thirteen states and most states east of the Mississippi which have little public land), the source of authority is more likely to be the Commerce Clause, or perhaps the treaty power, spending power, or even the war power. Although the casebook separates the study of federal power over land and resources into these two parts, recognize again that the inquiries typically overlap and support one another. Congress, for example, often cites multiple sources of constitutional authority for any particular statute. Finally,

Part C considers constitutional limits on both federal and state power, using, as primary examples, the Fifth Amendment's prohibition on taking private property for public use without just compensation and the First Amendment's prohibition on the establishment of religion.

A.   FEDERAL POWER DERIVED FROM FEDERAL LAND OWNERSHIP: THE PROPERTY CLAUSE

As discussed in Part III.A above, federal authority to retain the public lands rather than disposing of them to the states and people flows largely out of the Property Clause. The following two cases consider the related question of the extent of federal regulatory authority over land and natural resources derived from the Property Clause.

KLEPPE v. NEW MEXICO,
426 U.S. 529 (1976)

MR. JUSTICE MARSHALL delivered the opinion of the Court.

At issue in this case is whether Congress exceeded its powers under the Constitution in enacting the Wild Free-roaming Horses and Burros Act.

I

The Wild Free-roaming Horses and Burros Act, 16 U.S.C. §§ 1331–1340 (1970 ed., Supp. IV), was enacted in 1971 to protect "all unbranded and unclaimed horses and burros on public lands of the United States," § 2 (b) of the Act, 16 U.S.C. § 1332 (b) (1970 ed., Supp. IV), from "capture, branding, harassment, or death." § 1, 16 U.S.C. § 1331 (1970 ed., Supp. IV). [The wild horses and burros on the public lands are descendants of the horses which Spanish explorers introduced to North America starting in the late fifteenth century and which were then spread throughout the Great Plains and the West by Indian tribes. Later, horses were released onto the public lands by U.S. Cavalry, farmers, ranchers and miners.] The Act provides that all such horses and burros on the public lands administered by the Secretary of the Interior through the Bureau of Land Management (BLM) or by the Secretary of Agriculture through the Forest Service are committed to the jurisdiction of the respective Secretaries, who are "directed to protect and manage [the animals] as components of the public lands . . . in a manner that is designed to achieve and maintain a thriving natural ecological balance on the public lands." § 3 (a), 16 U.S.C. § 1333 (a) (1970 ed., Supp. IV). If protected horses or burros "stray from public lands onto privately owned land, the owners of such land may inform the nearest federal marshal or agent of the Secretary, who shall arrange to have the animals removed." § 4, 16 U.S.C. § 1334 (1970 ed., Supp. IV).

Section 6 authorizes the Secretaries to promulgate regulations and to enter into cooperative agreements with other landowners and with state and local governmental agencies in furtherance of the Act's purposes. On August 7, 1973, the Secretaries executed such an agreement with the New Mexico Livestock Board, the agency charged with enforcing the New Mexico Estray Law, N.M. Stat. Ann. § 47–14–1 et seq. (1966).[2] The agreement acknowledged the authori-

---

2. Under the New Mexico law, an estray is defined as: "Any bovine ani-   mal, horse, mule or ass, found running at large upon public or private lands,

ty of the Secretaries to manage and protect the wild free-roaming horses and burros on the public lands of the United States within the State and established a procedure for evaluating the claims of private parties to ownership of such animals.

The Livestock Board terminated the agreement three months later. Asserting that the Federal Government lacked power to control wild horses and burros on the public lands of the United States unless the animals were moving in interstate commerce or damaging the public lands and that neither of these bases of regulation was available here, the Board notified the Secretaries of its intent

> to exercise all regulatory, impoundment and sale powers which it derives from the New Mexico Estray Law, over all estray horses, mules or asses found running at large upon public or private lands within New Mexico.... This includes the right to go upon Federal or State lands to take possession of said horses or burros, should the Livestock Board so desire.

The differences between the Livestock Board and the Secretaries came to a head in February 1974. On February 1, 1974, a New Mexico rancher, Kelley Stephenson, was informed by the BLM that several unbranded burros had been seen near Taylor Well, where Stephenson watered his cattle. Taylor Well is on federal property, and Stephenson had access to it and some 8,000 surrounding acres only through a grazing permit issued pursuant to § 3 of the Taylor Grazing Act. After the BLM made it clear to Stephenson that it would not remove the burros and after he personally inspected the Taylor Well area, Stephenson complained to the Livestock Board that the burros were interfering with his livestock operation by molesting his cattle and eating their feed.

Thereupon the Board rounded up and removed 19 unbranded and unclaimed burros pursuant to the New Mexico Estray Law. Each burro was seized on the public lands of the United States and, as the director of the Board conceded, each burro fit the definition of a wild free-roaming burro under § 2(b) of the Act. On February 18, 1974, the Livestock Board, pursuant to its usual practice, sold the burros at a public auction. After the sale, the BLM asserted jurisdiction under the Act and demanded that the Board recover the animals and return them to the public lands.

On March 4, 1974, appellees filed a complaint in the United States District Court for the District of New Mexico seeking a declaratory judgment that the Wild Free-roaming Horses and Burros Act is unconstitutional and an injunction against its enforcement. * * *

Following an evidentiary hearing, the District Court held the Act unconstitutional and permanently enjoined the Secretary of the Interior (Secretary) from enforcing its provisions. The court found that the Act "conflicts with . . . the traditional doctrines concerning wild animals," *New Mexico v. Morton,* 406 F.Supp. 1237, 1238 (1975), and is in excess of Congress' power under the Property Clause of the Constitution, Art. IV, § 3, cl. 2. That Clause, the court found, enables Congress to regulate wild animals found on the public land only

either fenced or unfenced, in the state of New Mexico, whose owner is unknown in the section where found, or which shall be fifty (50) miles or more from the limits of its usual range or pasture, or that is branded with a brand which is not on record in the office of the cattle sanitary board of New Mexico. . . ." N.M. Stat. Ann. § 47–14–1 (1966). It is not disputed that the animals regulated by the Wild Free-roaming Horses and Burros Act are estrays within the meaning of this law.

for the "protection of the public lands from damage of some kind." 406 F.Supp., at 1239. Accordingly, this power was exceeded in this case because "[t]he statute is aimed at protecting the wild horses and burros, not at protecting the land they live on." *Ibid.*[6] We noted probable jurisdiction, 423 U.S. 818 (1975), and we now reverse.

II

The Property Clause of the Constitution provides that "Congress shall have Power to dispose of and make all needful Rules and Regulations respecting the Territory or other Property belonging to the United States." U.S. Const., Art. IV, § 3, cl. 2. In passing the Wild Free-roaming Horses and Burros Act, Congress deemed the regulated animals "an integral part of the natural system of the public lands" of the United States, § 1, 16 U.S.C. § 1331 (1970 ed., Supp. IV), and found that their management was necessary "for achievement of an ecological balance on the public lands." H.R. Conf. Rep. No. 92–681, p. 5 (1971). According to Congress, these animals, if preserved in their native habitats, "contribute to the diversity of life forms within the Nation and enrich the lives of the American people." § 1, 16 U.S.C. § 1331 (1970 ed., Supp. IV). Indeed, Congress concluded, the wild free-roaming horses and burros "are living symbols of the historic and pioneer spirit of the West." § 1, 16 U.S.C. § 1331 (1970 ed., Supp. IV). Despite their importance, the Senate committee found:

> "[These animals] have been cruelly captured and slain and their carcasses used in the production of pet food and fertilizer. They have been used for target practice and harassed for 'sport' and profit. In spite of public outrage, this bloody traffic continues unabated, and it is the firm belief of the committee that this senseless slaughter must be brought to an end." S. Rep. No. 92–242, pp. 1–2 (1971).

For these reasons, Congress determined to preserve and protect the wild free-roaming horses and burros on the public lands of the United States. The question under the Property Clause is whether this determination can be sustained as a "needful" regulation "respecting" the public lands. . . .

Appellees argue that the Act cannot be supported by the Property Clause. They contend that the Clause grants Congress essentially two kinds of power: (1) the power to dispose of and make incidental rules regarding the use of federal property; and (2) the power to protect federal property. According to appellees, the first power is not broad enough to support legislation protecting wild animals that live on federal property; and the second power is not implicated since the Act is designed to protect the animals, which are not themselves federal property, and not the public lands. As an initial matter, it is far from clear that the Act was not passed in part to protect the public lands of the United States[7] or that Congress cannot assert a property interest in the

---

6. The court also held that the Act could not be sustained under the Commerce Clause because "all the evidence establishes that the wild burros in question here do not migrate across state lines" and "Congress made no findings to indicate that it was in any way relying on the Commerce Clause in enacting this statute." 406 F.Supp., at 1239. While the Secretary argues in this Court that the Act is sustainable under the Commerce Clause, we have no occa-

sion to address this contention since we find the Act, as applied, to be a permissible exercise of congressional power under the Property Clause.

7. Congress expressly ordered that the animals were to be managed and protected in order "to achieve and maintain a thriving natural ecological balance on the public lands." § 3 (a), 16 U.S.C. § 1333 (a) (1970 ed., Supp. IV). Cf. *Hunt v. United States*, 278 U.S. 96 (1928).

regulated horses and burros superior to that of the State. But we need not consider whether the Act can be upheld on either of these grounds, for we reject appellees' narrow reading of the Property Clause.

Appellees ground their argument on a number of cases that, upon analysis, provide no support for their position. Like the District Court, appellees cite *Hunt v. United States*, 278 U.S. 96 (1928), for the proposition that the Property Clause gives Congress only the limited power to regulate wild animals in order to protect the public lands from damage. But *Hunt*, which upheld the Government's right to kill deer that were damaging foliage in the national forests, only holds that damage to the land is a sufficient basis for regulation; it contains no suggestion that it is a necessary one. * * *

Camfield v. United States, 167 U.S. 518 (1897), is of even less help to appellees. Appellees rely upon the following language from *Camfield*:

> "While we do not undertake to say that Congress has the unlimited power to legislate against nuisances within a State, which it would have within a Territory, we do not think the admission of a Territory as a State deprives it of the power of legislating for the protection of the public lands, though it may thereby involve the exercise of what is ordinarily known as the police power, so long as such power is directed solely to its own protection." *Id.*, at 525–526 (emphasis added).

Appellees mistakenly read this language to limit Congress' power to regulate activity on the public lands; in fact, the quoted passage refers to the scope of congressional power to regulate conduct on private land that affects the public lands. And *Camfield* holds that the Property Clause is broad enough to permit federal regulation of fences built on private land adjoining public land when the regulation is for the protection of the federal property. *Camfield* contains no suggestion of any limitation on Congress' power over conduct on its own property; its sole message is that the power granted by the Property Clause is broad enough to reach beyond territorial limits.

Lastly, appellees point to dicta in two cases to the effect that, unless the State has agreed to the exercise of federal jurisdiction, Congress' rights in its land are "only the rights of an ordinary proprietor...." *Fort Leavenworth R. Co. v. Lowe*, 114 U.S. 525, 527 (1885). *See also Paul v. United States*, 371 U.S. 245, 264 (1963). In neither case was the power of Congress under the Property Clause at issue or considered and, as we shall see, these dicta fail to account for the raft of cases in which the Clause has been given a broader construction.

In brief, beyond the *Fort Leavenworth* and *Paul* dicta, appellees have presented no support for their position that the Clause grants Congress only the power to dispose of, to make incidental rules regarding the use of, and to protect federal property. This failure is hardly surprising, for the Clause, in broad terms, gives Congress the power to determine what are "needful" rules "respecting" the public lands. And while the furthest reaches of the power granted by the Property Clause have not yet been definitively resolved, we have repeatedly observed that "[the] power over the public land thus entrusted to Congress is without limitations." *United States v. San Francisco*, 310 U.S. 16, 29 (1940).

The decided cases have supported this expansive reading. It is the Property Clause, for instance, that provides the basis for governing the Territories of the United States. And even over public land within the States, "[t]he general

Government doubtless has a power over its own property analogous to the police power of the several States, and the extent to which it may go in the exercise of such power is measured by the exigencies of the particular case." ... In short, Congress exercises the powers both of a proprietor and of a legislature over the public domain. Although the Property Clause does not authorize "an exercise of a general control over public policy in a State," it does permit "an exercise of the complete power which Congress has over particular public property entrusted to it." *United States v. San Francisco, supra,* at 30 (footnote omitted). In our view, the "complete power" that Congress has over public lands necessarily includes the power to regulate and protect the wildlife living there.

III

Appellees argue that if we approve the Wild Free-roaming Horses and Burros Act as a valid exercise of Congress' power under the Property Clause, then we have sanctioned an impermissible intrusion on the sovereignty, legislative authority, and police power of the State and have wrongly infringed upon the State's traditional trustee powers over wild animals. The argument appears to be that Congress could obtain exclusive legislative jurisdiction over the public lands in the State only by state consent, and that in the absence of such consent Congress lacks the power to act contrary to state law. This argument is without merit.

Appellees' claim confuses Congress' derivative legislative powers, which are not involved in this case, with its powers under the Property Clause. Congress may acquire derivative legislative power from a State pursuant to Art. I, § 8, cl. 17, of the Constitution by consensual acquisition of land, or by nonconsensual acquisition followed by the State's subsequent cession of legislative authority over the land. *Paul v. United States,* 371 U.S., at 264; *Fort Leavenworth R. Co. v. Lowe,* 114 U.S., at 541–542.[11] In either case, the legislative jurisdiction acquired may range from exclusive federal jurisdiction with no residual state police power, *e.g., Pacific Coast Dairy v. Dept. of Agriculture of Cal.,* 318 U.S. 285 (1943), to concurrent, or partial, federal legislative jurisdiction, which may allow the State to exercise certain authority. *E.g., Paul v. United States, supra,* at 265; *Collins v. Yosemite Park Co.,* 304 U.S. 518, 528–530 (1938); *James v. Dravo Contracting Co.,* 302 U.S. 134, 147–149 (1937).

But while Congress can acquire exclusive or partial jurisdiction over lands within a State by the State's consent or cession, the presence or absence of such jurisdiction has nothing to do with Congress' powers under the Property Clause. Absent consent or cession a State undoubtedly retains jurisdiction over federal lands within its territory, but Congress equally surely retains the power to enact legislation respecting those lands pursuant to the Property Clause. And when Congress so acts, the federal legislation necessarily overrides conflicting state laws under the Supremacy Clause. As we said in *Camfield v.*

---

11. Article I, § 8, cl. 17, of the Constitution provides that Congress shall have the power:

"To exercise exclusive Legislation in all Cases whatsoever, over such District (not exceeding ten Miles square) as may, by Cession of Particular States, and the Acceptance of Congress, become the Seat of the Government of the United States, and to exercise like Authority over all Places purchased by the Consent of the Legislature of the State in which the Same shall be, for the Erection of Forts, Magazines, Arsenals, Dock–Yards, and other needful Buildings...."

The Clause has been broadly construed, and the acquisition by consent or cession of exclusive or partial jurisdiction over properties for any legitimate governmental purpose beyond those itemized is permissible.

United States, 167 U.S., at 526, in response to a somewhat different claim: "A different rule would place the public domain of the United States completely at the mercy of state legislation."

Thus, appellees' assertion that "[a]bsent state consent by complete cession of jurisdiction of lands to the United States, exclusive jurisdiction does not accrue to the federal landowner with regard to federal lands within the borders of the State," is completely beside the point; and appellees' fear that the Secretary's position is that "the Property Clause totally exempts federal lands within state borders from state legislative powers, state police powers, and all rights and powers of local sovereignty and jurisdiction of the states," is totally unfounded. The Federal Government does not assert exclusive jurisdiction over the public lands in New Mexico, and the State is free to enforce its criminal and civil laws on those lands. But where those state laws conflict with the Wild Free-roaming Horses and Burros Act, or with other legislation passed pursuant to the Property Clause, the law is clear: The state laws must recede. * * *

The Act does not establish exclusive federal jurisdiction over the public lands in New Mexico; it merely overrides the New Mexico Estray Law insofar as it attempts to regulate federally protected animals. And that is but the necessary consequence of valid legislation under the Property Clause.

Appellees' contention that the Act violates traditional state power over wild animals stands on no different footing. Unquestionably the States have broad trustee and police powers over wild animals within their jurisdictions. *Toomer v. Witsell*, 334 U.S. 385, 402 (1948); *Geer v. Connecticut*, 161 U.S. 519, 528 (1896). But, as *Geer v. Connecticut* cautions, those powers exist only "in so far as [their] exercise may be not incompatible with, or restrained by, the rights conveyed to the Federal government by the Constitution." *Ibid.* "No doubt it is true that as between a State and its inhabitants the State may regulate the killing and sale of [wildlife], but it does not follow that its authority is exclusive of paramount powers." *Missouri v. Holland*, 252 U.S. 416, 434 (1920).... We hold today that the Property Clause ... gives Congress the power to protect wildlife on the public lands, state law notwithstanding.

IV

In this case, the New Mexico Livestock Board entered upon the public lands of the United States and removed wild burros. These actions were contrary to the provisions of the Wild Free-roaming Horses and Burros Act. We find that, as applied to this case, the Act is a constitutional exercise of congressional power under the Property Clause. We need not, and do not, decide whether the Property Clause would sustain the Act in all of its conceivable applications.

Appellees are concerned that the Act's extension of protection to wild free-roaming horses and burros that stray from public land onto private land, § 4, 16 U.S.C. § 1334 (1970 ed., Supp. IV), will be read to provide federal jurisdiction over every wild horse or burro that at any time sets foot upon federal land. While it is clear that regulations under the Property Clause may have some effect on private lands not otherwise under federal control, *Camfield v. United States*, 167 U.S. 518 (1897), we do not think it appropriate in this declaratory judgment proceeding to determine the extent, if any, to which the Property Clause empowers Congress to protect animals on private lands or the extent to which such regulation is attempted by the Act....

For the reasons stated, the judgment of the District Court is reversed, and the case is remanded for further proceedings consistent with this opinion.

QUESTIONS AND DISCUSSION

1. Recall the discussion about the meaning of nature in Chapter 1. Are wild horses and burros part of the "natural" environment? Are they part of Leopold's notion of "land" in his essay, *The Land Ethic*? Do either of these questions matter in terms of how these animals are managed or to the question whether federal power under the Property Clause extends to wild horses and burros?

2. Justice Marshall remarks that "appellees' fear that the Secretary's position is that 'the Property Clause totally exempts federal lands within state borders from state legislative powers, state police powers, and all rights and powers of local sovereignty and jurisdiction of the states,' is totally unfounded." Why might New Mexico have made that argument? Why would Justice Marshall have discounted the concern? Does the difference in their perspective depend upon a focus on latent vs. exercised power?

3. If Congress' power over its own property is "analogous to the police power of the . . . States" as the Court suggests, can you conceive of any limits on that power? Are there limits inherent in the language of the Property Clause itself? Does the language that Congress may make "needful" rules "respecting" public lands suggest any limit? What about limits on federal power that are external to the Property Clause? Could the United States exclude members of a certain religious group from a national park?

4. What does Justice Marshall mean when he says that "Appellees' claim confuses Congress' derivative legislative powers, which are not involved in this case, with its powers under the Property Clause"? Are appellees really confused? What point are they trying to make about the difference between Congress' power under the Enclave Clause and the Property Clause? If Congress' Property Clause power over the public lands is "without limitation" as the Court suggests, what purpose is left for the Enclave Clause?

5. Over the years, various commentators have advocated for broad and narrow readings of Congress' power under the Property Clause. *Compare* Eugene R. Gaetke, *Refuting the "Classic" Property Clause Theory*, 63 N.C. L. REV. 617 (1985) and Dale D. Goble, *The Myth of the Classic Property Clause Doctrine*, 63 DENV. U. L. REV. 495 (1986), *with* David E. Engdahl, *State and Federal Power over Federal Property*, 18 ARIZ. L. REV. 283 (1976). In a recent article advocating a broad view of Congress' power, Professor Peter Appel points out that proponents of a narrow view have ignored that perhaps the strongest precedent for a narrow interpretation of the Property Clause is the Court's infamous *Dred Scott* decision. *Dred Scott v. Sandford*, 60 U.S. (19 How.) 393 (1856). *Dred Scott* is today primarily known for its holding that the Court lacked diversity jurisdiction because Scott, as a black man, was not a citizen of any state and thus could not establish diversity jurisdiction. But in addressing the merits, the Court held that the Missouri Compromise (which prohibited slavery in the territory "north of thirty-six degrees and thirty minutes north latitude") was unconstitutional because its enactment was beyond Congress' Property Clause powers. Justice Taney opined that the word "territory" in the Property Clause applied only to the Northwest territory ceded to the United States in the

Articles of Confederation. *See* Peter A. Appel, *The Power of Congress "Without Limitation": The Property Clause and Federal Regulation of Private Property*, 86 MINN. L. REV. 1, 37–56 (2001).

6. Suppose the WFRHBA had never been enacted. Would anything prevent New Mexico from passing its Estray Law with respect to wild horses and burros on federal land? In *Omaechevarria v. Idaho*, 246 U.S. 343 (1918), the Supreme Court held that the "police power of the State extends over the federal public domain, at least when there is no legislation by Congress on the subject." *Id.* at 346–47. Might there be circumstances (as yet unexplored by courts) when the Property Clause has a dormant aspect similar to the dormant commerce clause that would preempt state regulation of activities on federal lands even in the absence of federal legislation?

7. The Court relies heavily on its prior decision in *Camfield v. United States*, 167 U.S. 518 (1897). *Camfield* addressed federal power to prosecute a Colorado rancher under an 1885 statute known as the Unlawful Inclosures Act, 23 Stat. 321, 43 U.S.C. §§ 1061–66, which Congress had passed in an effort to stop ranchers from stringing barbed wire around portions of the public domain and calling it their own. Camfield had managed to fence in 20,000 acres of public domain without placing any fence on public lands. He did so by acquiring title to the odd-numbered sections of a former railroad grant and then erecting his fence along the *top* edge of one odd-numbered section, leaving a six-inch gap, and then continuing the fence along the *bottom* edge of the diagonally-situated odd-numbered section. The diagram below from United States Reporter shows how it was done.

Camfield argued that the Unlawful Inclosures Act could not apply to his fence because it was entirely on private property and Congress' power under the Property Clause only extended to public lands. The Court rejected the argument, making the points quoted by Justice Marshall above. In light of *Camfield* is the holding in *Kleppe* particularly surprising? How might New Mexico have attempted to distinguish *Camfield* and make it fit its theory of the case?

8. The Bureau of Land Management Wild Horse and Burro Program website provides further information on the history of wild horses and burros, the WFRHB Act, and its current implementation by the Depart-

ment of the Interior. *See* http://www.blm.gov/wo/st/en/prog/wild_horse_and_
burro.html.

PROBLEM EXERCISE: THE SAGEBRUSH REBELLION

1976, the year *Kleppe v. New Mexico* was decided, was a tough year for
advocates of greater state and private control of the public lands. In June,
Kleppe emphasized that the Congress' power under the Property Clause
was without known limitations and gave the federal government "power
over its own property analogous to the police power of the several States."
426 U.S. at 540. Then, four months later, in October, Congress passed the
Federal Land Policy Management Act (FLPMA) which declared federal
policy that the "public lands be retained in federal ownership." 43 U.S.C.
§ 1701(a) (1976). Although western frustration with federal land ownership
and management has ebbed and flowed throughout our nation's history,
Kleppe and FLPMA precipitated an outspoken anti-Washington movement
among those in the West's rural communities whose livelihood depended
upon the public lands and among many state and federal politicians. The
movement, which became known as the Sagebrush Rebellion and Wise Use
Movement, had been percolating since the 1964 passage of the Wilderness
Act and its prohibition on most resource development within wilderness
areas. Further heightening their sensitivity, FLPMA had tasked BLM with
inventorying all of BLM's lands for areas suitable for wilderness designation.

The Sagebrush Rebellion had both a political and legal component. On
the political side, the next few years saw several western states pass related
legislation. Leading the way, Nevada's legislators appropriated $250,000 for
the state attorney general to pursue legal action to force a transfer of BLM
lands to the state and created a state board to supervise the sale of the
lands it hoped to receive. Utah, Arizona, New Mexico, and Wyoming
followed with similar bills, although Wyoming added a claim to the national
forests as well as BLM lands. In Washington, the legislature passed a
sagebrush bill, only to see it overturned by popular referendum. In California and Colorado, bills passed but were defeated by governors' vetoes. At
the federal level, in 1979, Utah's Senator Orrin Hatch, along with a
number of cosponsors from the interior West, introduced a sagebrush
rebellion bill that proposed transferring BLM lands to the states. S. 1680,
Congressional Record 26 (1979), S. 11657. Then, shortly after his election
in 1980, President Ronald Reagan pledged his support to "all my fellow
sagebrush rebels" and promised "to work toward a sagebrush solution."
With President Reagan's appointment of James Watt, an avowed sagebrush
rebel and former head of the Mountain States Legal Foundation (a public
interest law firm dedicated to protecting private property rights and to
promoting private access to and use of the public lands), to be his Secretary
of the Interior, it looked as though the Sagebrush Rebellion might produce
some real changes in the makeup of the public lands. In the end, between
Secretary Watt's caustic personality and the efforts of preservation groups,
the momentum of the Sagebrush Rebellion began to wane and the bills

introduced in Congress quietly expired. When Secretary Watt was forced to resign in 1983, the rebellion was effectively over. *See* WILLIAM L. GRAF, WILDERNESS PRESERVATION AND THE SAGEBRUSH REBELLIONS 226–31, 257 (1990).

The Sagebrush Rebellion, however, did not die. Hibernation would probably be a better description. The frustrations and anxieties that drove the wise use movement have continued to persist and, if anything, have increased as the West's demographics continue to change. As more and more people have flocked to the West's urban and suburban areas, the constituency for preservation and recreational use of the public lands instead of "wise use" (i.e., resource extraction and development under state governance) has only increased since the late 1970s and early 1980s. Thus, it was not surprising that in the 1990s the rebellion took shape again, this time under the banner of the "County Supremacy Movement." In 1995, Nevada rancher Dick Carver appeared on the cover of *Time* magazine under the title "Don't Tread on Me: An Inside Look at the West's Growing Rebellion." The following excerpt is from the cover story.

Erik Larson, *Unrest in the West,* TIME, Oct. 23, 1995, at 7–9, 12

SITTING ON A BALE OF BARLEY destined for his cattle, Dick Carver gets a little misty eyed as he recalls the moment that propelled him to leadership of a new rebellion now sweeping the West. Usually mild mannered and affable, the Nevada rancher and Nye County Commissioner reached a point last year when he had had enough. To him, federal intrusion into the daily life of his county had simply grown too great, so on July 4, 1994—Independence Day—he took the law into his own hands. His weapon of choice: a rusting, yellow D–7 Caterpillar bulldozer.

Carver sat astride the 22–ton machine, his dust caked face streaked with paths of recent tears. He remembers being frightened and tense as he guided the Cat towards an armed U.S. Forest Service agent holding a hand lettered sign ordering Carver to stop. The agent stumbled and wound up briefly crawling on hands and knees. But Carver kept coming. He pulled out a pocket sized copy of the U.S. Constitution, which he keeps with him always, and waved it defiantly at the agent as a crowd of about 200 people, a quarter of them armed, cheered him forward. "I was damned scared," says Carver. He was afraid someone—maybe the agent, maybe an overzealous spectator—would draw a gun and trigger a cascade of violence. "I told myself, 'Dick, you've got to keep going. Because if you stop, the people are going to do something and someone's going to get hurt.'"

Carver climbed aboard the Caterpillar to bulldoze open a weather-damaged road across a national forest. The hitch was, he wanted to do it without federal permission. Although plainly illegal, in Carver's mind it was an act of civil disobedience—a frontier Boston Tea Party—warranted by the tyranny he and his fellow citizens in Nye had long endured. But in this case, the purported tyrant was the U.S. government.

———

Carver's bulldozer made him a leading voice in the county-supremacy movement of the 1990s. In addition to Carver's Nye County, 35 more counties, primarily in Arizona, New Mexico, Nevada, and California, declared their control of federal lands within their boundaries. The movement sparked violence in some rural communities. "Pipe bombs have been found in the Gila wilderness in New Mexico. An unknown assailant fired shots at a Forest Service biologist in California.... And in Carson City, Nevada ... a bomb destroyed the family van of a forest ranger while it was parked in his driveway." Erik Larson, *Unrest in the West*, TIME, Oct. 23, 1995, at 12.

As long as there is a federal presence in the West and multiple claimants to the scarce natural resources on the public lands, the Sagebrush Rebellion and its progeny are likely to persist in some form. But are they ever likely to prevail? The story describes how Dick Carver waved his pocket-copy of the Constitution, but is there anything in the Constitution to support his arguments? If you were hired to represent Dick Carver or Nye County, what are the strongest legal and policy arguments you could make in support of your position? If you were a lawyer at the Department of Justice, how would you respond? How would you decide the case if you were a judge?

As you prepare to respond to these questions, you may want to review the discussion of *Pollard v. Hagan, supra* at pages 97–101, and reference the following materials: *United States v. Gardner*, 107 F.3d 1314 (9th Cir. 1997) (rejecting challenge to United States' title to lands with Nevada), *cert. denied*, 522 U.S. 907 (1997); *United States v. Nye County*, 920 F.Supp. 1108 (D. Nev. 1996) (same); John Leshy, *Unraveling the Sagebrush Rebellion: Law, Politics and Federal Lands*, 14 U.C.D. L. REV. 317 (1980); Ray Ring, *Rebels with a Lost Cause*, HIGH COUNTRY NEWS 10 (Dec. 10, 2007); Peter D. Coppelman, *The Federal Government's Response to the County Supremacy Movement*, 12 NAT. RESOURCES & ENV'T 30 (1997); Michael C. Blumm, *The Case Against Transferring BLM Lands to the States*, 7 FORDHAM ENVTL. L.J. 387 (1996); WILLIAM L. GRAF, WILDERNESS PRESERVATION AND THE SAGEBRUSH REBELLIONS (1990).

Review Note 7 at page 143. Do you see how the proceeds clause legislation discussed in the Note is another manifestation of the Sagebrush Rebellion?

———

Whereas *Kleppe* focused on the extent of Congress' Property Clause power over activities on federal lands, the next case explores the extent of Congress' Property Clause power off of federal land.

MINNESOTA v. BLOCK,
660 F.2d 1240 (8th Cir. 1981),
cert. denied, 455 U.S. 1007 (1982)

BRIGHT, CIRCUIT JUDGE.

These appeals arise from three consolidated cases involving multiple challenges to provisions of the Boundary Waters Canoe Area Wilderness Act of 1978, Pub.L.No. 95–495, 92 Stat. 1649 (BWCAW Act or the Act).... [A]ppellants allege that Congress unconstitutionally applied federal controls on the use of motorboats and snowmobiles to land and waters not owned by the United States. * * *

The State of Minnesota, joined by the National Association of Property Owners (NAPO) and numerous individuals, businesses, and organizations, brought suit against the United States, challenging the constitutionality of the BWCAW Act as applied to lands and waters that the federal government does not own. A group of organizations concerned with the environmental and wilderness aspects of the boundary waters intervened in support of the United States.

The challenged portion of the statute, section 4, prohibits the use of motorboats in the BWCAW in all but a small number of lakes. The Act also limits snowmobiles to two routes. The United States owns ninety percent of the land within the borders of the BWCAW area. The State of Minnesota, in addition to owning most of the remaining ten percent of the land, owns the beds of all the lakes and rivers within the BWCAW.

Appellants assert that Congress had no power to enact the motor vehicle restriction as applied to nonfederal lands and waters. We reject this contention and conclude that Congress, in passing this legislation, acted within its authority under the property clause of the United States Constitution.... Accordingly, we affirm.

I. Background.

The Boundary Waters Canoe Area Wilderness (BWCAW), a part of the Superior National Forest, consists of approximately 1,075,000 acres of land and waterways along the Minnesota–Canadian border. A sponsor of this legislation described the area in introducing the BWCAW Act on the House floor:

> The Boundary Waters Canoe Area is the largest wilderness area east of the Rocky Mountains and the second largest in our wilderness system. It is our Nation's only lakeland canoe wilderness a network of more than 1,000 lakes linked by hundreds of miles of streams and short portages which served as the highway of fur traders who followed water routes pioneered by Sioux and Chippewa Indians. Despite extensive logging, the BWCA still contains 540,000 acres of virgin forests, by far the largest such area in the eastern United States.
>
> This last remnant of the old "north-woods" is remarkable not only for its lakes and virgin forests, but also for its wildlife. * * *
>
> The BWCA is complemented on the Canadian side of our border by the Quetico Provincial Park of Ontario where commercial logging and nearly all motorized recreational activity are prohibited. Together, these areas encompass an area the size of Yellowstone National Park and constitute one of the finest wilderness areas on our continent. Not surprisingly, the BWCA is the most heavily used unit in the national wilderness system, drawing people from throughout the country who seek the solitude of a wilderness experience. (123 Cong.Rec. H621–22 (daily ed. Jan. 31, 1977), reprinted in Legislative History of the Boundary Waters Act of 1978, at 1–2.)

* * * At issue here are portions of section 4 of the Act, the provision barring the use of motorized craft in all but designated portions of the wilderness. Section 4(c) limits motorboat use to designated lakes and rivers, allowing a maximum of either ten or twenty-five horsepower motors on these waters. Section 4(e) permits certain limited mechanized portages. Section 4(e) restricts the use of snowmobiles to two designated trails. With these exceptions, the Act as construed by the federal government and by the district court,

prohibits all other motorized transportation on land and water falling within the external boundaries of the wilderness area.

The boundaries of the BWCAW circumscribe a total surface area of approximately 1,080,300 acres—920,000 acres of land and 160,000 of water. The United States owns approximately 792,000 acres of land surface, while the State of Minnesota owns approximately 121,000 acres of land,[12] in addition to the beds under the 160,000 acres of navigable water. Congress recognized that Minnesota would retain jurisdiction over the waters, but provided that the State could not regulate in a manner less stringent than that mandated by the Act.

Minnesota brought this action against the United States on December 27, 1979, challenging the application of section 4 to land and waterways under state jurisdiction that fall within the boundaries of the BWCAW. * * *

On appeal, Minnesota and the intervening plaintiffs renew their assertions . . . that Congress acted in excess of its authority under the property clause by curtailing the use of motor-powered boats and other motorized vehicles on lands and waters not owned by the United States. . . .

II.   Property Clause.

The property clause provides: "The Congress shall have Power to dispose of and make all needful Rules and Regulations respecting the Territory or other Property belonging to the United States * * *." U.S. CONST. art. IV, § 3, cl. 2. In a recent unanimous decision, the Supreme Court upheld an expansive reading of Congress' power under the property clause. *See Kleppe v. New Mexico*, 426 U.S. 529 (1976). The Court concluded that

> the Clause, in broad terms, gives Congress the power to determine what are "needful" rules "respecting" the public lands. * * * And while the furthest reaches of the power granted by the Property Clause have not yet been definitively resolved, we have repeatedly observed that "(t)he power over the public lands thus entrusted to Congress is without limitations." (Id. at 539.)

With this guidance, we must decide the question left open in *Kleppe*: the scope of Congress' property clause power as applied to activity occurring off federal land. Without defining the limits of the power, the Court in *Kleppe*, relying on its decision in *Camfield v. United States*, 167 U.S. 518 (1897), acknowledged that "it is clear the regulations under the Property Clause may have some effect on private lands not otherwise under federal control." 426 U.S. at 546. In *Camfield*, the Court concluded that Congress possessed the power to control conduct occurring off federal property through its "power of legislating for the protection of the public lands, though it may thereby involve the exercise of what is ordinarily known as the police power, so long as such power is directed solely to (the public lands') own protection." *Camfield v. United States, supra*, 167 U.S. at 526.

Under this authority to protect public land, Congress' power must extend to regulation of conduct on or off the public land that would threaten the designated purpose of federal lands. Congress clearly has the power to dedicate federal land for particular purposes. As a necessary incident of that power, Congress must have the ability to insure that these lands be protected against interference with their intended purposes. As the Supreme Court has stated, under the property clause "(Congress) may sanction some uses and prohibit

---

12. Private parties own approximately 7,300 acres of land.

others, and may forbid interference with such as are sanctioned." *McKelvey v. United States*, 260 U.S. 353, 359 (1922) (emphasis added).

This court has previously held that Congress, under the property clause, could prohibit hunting on waters within the boundaries of the Voyagers National Park in Minnesota, even though the waters were subject to state jurisdiction. *United States v. Brown*, 552 F.2d 817, 821 (8th Cir.), *cert. denied*, 431 U.S. 949 (1977). In *Brown*, the purpose of the challenged regulations extended beyond the mere protection of the federal land from physical harm. This court, in effect, affirmed the district court's approval of the regulations as necessary because "hunting on the waters in the park could 'significantly interfere with the use of the park and the purposes for which it was established.'" *Id.* at 822 (emphasis added).

[handwritten margin note: when regulating uses on private land is OK]

Having established that Congress may regulate conduct off federal land that interferes with the designated purpose of that land, we must determine whether Congress acted within this power in restricting the use of motorboats and other motor vehicles in the BWCAW. In reviewing the appropriateness of particular regulations, "we must remain mindful that, while courts must eventually pass upon them, determinations under the Property Clause are entrusted primarily to the judgment of Congress." *Kleppe v. New Mexico, supra*, 426 U.S. at 536. *Accord, United States v. San Francisco*, 310 U.S. 16, 29–30 (1940); *United States v. Brown, supra*, 552 F.2d at 822. Thus, if Congress enacted the motorized use restrictions to protect the fundamental purpose for which the BWCAW had been reserved, and if the restrictions in section 4 reasonably relate to that end, we must conclude that Congress acted within its constitutional prerogative. * * *

Hearings and other evidence provided ample support for Congress' finding that use of motorboats and snowmobiles must be limited in order to preserve the area as a wilderness. Testimony established that the sight, smell, and sound of motorized vehicles seriously marred the wilderness experience of canoeists, hikers, and skiers and threatened to destroy the integrity of the wilderness.

As a result of considerable testimony and debate and a series of compromises, Congress enacted section 4 in an attempt to accommodate all interests, determining the extent of motorized use the area might tolerate without serious threat to its wilderness values.

The motor use restrictions form only a small part of an elaborate system of regulation considered necessary to preserve the BWCAW as a wilderness. The United States owns close to ninety percent of the land surrounding the waters at issue. Congress concluded that motorized vehicles significantly interfere with the use of the wilderness by canoeists, hikers, and skiers and that restricted motorized use would enhance and preserve the wilderness values of the area. From the evidence presented, Congress could rationally reach these conclusions. We hold, therefore, that Congress acted within its power under the Constitution to pass needful regulations respecting public lands. * * *

QUESTIONS AND DISCUSSION

1. The court notes that Minnesota owns approximately 121,000 acres of land within the boundaries of the wilderness area, as well as title to the beds of about 160,000 acres of navigable water. How did Minnesota obtain title to its lands within the Boundary Waters Canoe Area Wilderness?

2. If Congress' power under the Property Clause extends beyond federal land, how far does it extend? Can Congress rely on the Property Clause to enact any natural resource or environmental legislation it chooses? Does the court propose any limits on Congress' power? How searching will a court be when it reviews a congressional determination about the need to regulate conduct off federal land? As you contemplate these questions, consider the following hypotheticals proposed by Professor Appel:

> First, suppose that Congress decides that it wants to relieve the tax burden on all citizens and that it will enter the casino gaming business to raise revenue. Congress decides to open casinos in five national forests under a hypothetical statute called the Forest Gaming Act, and coincidentally the states wherein those forests lie forbid all forms of gambling. Second, suppose that Congress enacts a law like the Gun Free School Zones Act held unconstitutional in *United States v. Lopez*, but that applies only to people who carry a firearm or explosives within 1000 feet of a federal building. For ease of reference, this hypothetical statute will be called the Gun Free Federal Building Zones Act. Suppose finally that Congress enacts a broad statute regulating the emission of sulfur dioxide (SO_2) and oxides of nitrogen (NOx) because these emissions are precursors to acid rain, which harms national parks. Instead of relying on the provisions of the federal Clean Air Act . . . Congress seeks to regulate sources of specified pollution both within and outside of the state in which federal lands lie. . . . For ease of reference, this hypothetical statute will be called the National Parks Clean Air Act.

Appel, *supra*, at 80–81. Would Congress have authority under the Property Clause to enact these hypothetical statutes?

3. How do you think Minnesota tried to distinguish the United States' regulation of the rancher's fence in *Camfield v. United States*, discussed *supra* at page 155, from regulation of snowmobiles and motorboats in the BWCAW? *Camfield* was not the only Supreme Court decision to have previously extended the Property Clause off federal land. In *United States v. Alford*, 274 U.S. 264 (1927), the Supreme Court had affirmed federal regulation of fires "in or near" national forests.

4. As you consider the cases in the following section addressing other constitutional sources of federal authority over natural resources, ask yourself whether the Property Clause would have been a viable alternative source of jurisdiction.

B.   FEDERAL POWER OVER NATURAL RESOURCES: OTHER CONSTITUTIONAL SOURCES

As discussed at the beginning of this section of the chapter, prior to the twentieth century, state law largely controlled the use of natural resources. The Property Clause is one vehicle through which the federal government began to assert its authority. But despite references in *Kleppe* and prior cases that Congress' power under the Property Clause is "without limitations," Congress' use of the Property Clause has been limited to regulation of the public lands themselves, with occasional forays onto adjacent private lands, as in *Minnesota v. Block*, or to closely connected natural resources, as in *Kleppe*. As far as regulating natural resources more generally, the question for Congress was whether it had such authority in another provision of the Constitution. Given Congress' Commerce Clause authority to regulate commerce "among the several states," one might think that Congress would early on have sought to regulate natural resources that transcended state boundaries, such as water or wildlife, but even there federal involvement was minimal. States were allowed to claim ownership of all the water within their boundaries and then to allocate property rights in that water as they saw fit (through a system of riparian rights or prior appropriation). *See* Chapter 7. Even federal regulation of navigation of interstate streams, a power at the core of the Commerce Clause, was limited. States merrily authorized obstructions to navigable waters until congressional authorization was finally required in 1899. *See* Rivers and Harbors Appropriation Act of 1899, ch. 425, § 10, 30 Stat. 1121, 1151. Just as states claimed ownership of the water within their boundaries, they also claimed ownership of wildlife, asserting that state ownership meant that wildlife was subject to exclusive state regulation.

This view of limited federal authority over natural resources which are not tied to federal lands began to change in the twentieth century. Over the last century, federal authority has waxed and state authority has correspondingly waned. In the last decade, the Supreme Court appears to have throttled back on this trend, although only on the margins. In part, this increase of federal natural resource regulation is another manifestation of the growth in federal jurisdiction that began with the New Deal. But as you read the cases that follow, consider why the growth of federal authority over natural resources law cannot simply be characterized as an appendage to the expansion of the modern welfare state but should also be understood as a considered response to the difficulties that plague natural resource management: scarcity, problems of commons, market failure, scientific uncertainty, problems of scale, and institutional adequacy.

The cases that follow consider the growth of federal power over natural resources largely in the context of wildlife law. We adopt this focus because the mobility of wildlife beyond state boundaries presented perhaps the best early justification for federal natural resource regulation. By studying wildlife law cases, we are able to consider the whole time line of growing federal jurisdiction. Moreover, as wildlife regulation has become more and more a function of protecting biodiversity and habitat, questions about authority over wildlife have largely merged with, or at least taken the same form as, questions about authority over other natural resources such as minerals, timber, and water. We begin with a case that has actually been overruled. Its purpose is to illustrate the regulatory baseline at the end of the nineteenth century, which was that state power over natural resources was practically complete.

Geer v. Connecticut,
161 U.S. 519 (1896)

[Mr. Justice White delivered the opinion of the Court]

[Geer killed a game bird during the state's hunting season but was convicted of selling the bird to someone outside the state in violation of Connecticut law.] The sole issue which the case presents is, was it lawful, under the constitution of the United States (section 8, art. 1), for the state of Connecticut ... to regulate the killing of game within her borders so as to confine its use to the limits of the state, and forbid its transmission outside of the state? * * *

The solution of the question involves a consideration of the nature of the property in game and the authority which the state had a right lawfully to exercise in relation thereto.

From the earliest traditions, the right to reduce animals *ferae naturae* [i.e., animals not yet reduced to possession] to possession has been subject to the control of the law-giving power. * * *

No restriction, it would hence seem, was placed by the Roman law upon the power of the individual to reduce game, of which he was the owner in common with other citizens, to possession, although the Institutes of Justinian recognized the right of an owner of land to forbid another from killing game on his property....

This inhibition was, however, rather a recognition of the right of ownership in land than an exercise by the state of its undoubted authority to control the taking and use of that which belonged to no one in particular, but was common to all. In the feudal as well as the ancient law of the continent of Europe, in all countries, the right to acquire animals *ferae naturae* by possession was recognized as being subject to the governmental authority and under its power, not only as a matter of regulation, but also of absolute control. * * *

The common law of England also based property in game upon the principle of common ownership, and therefore treated it as subject to governmental authority. * * *

[Blackstone] says:

... by the law of nature, every man, from the prince to the peasant, has an equal of pursuing and taking to his own use all such creatures as are ferae naturae, and therefore the property of nobody, but liable to be seized by the first occupant, and so it was held by the imperial law as late as Justinian's time. * * * But it follows from the very end and constitution of society that this natural right, as well as many others belonging to man as an individual, may be restrained by positive laws enacted for reasons of state or for the supposed benefit of the community. 2 Bl. Comm. 410.

The practice of the government of England from the earliest time to the present has put into execution the authority to control and regulate the taking of game.

Undoubtedly, this attribute of government to control the taking of animals *ferae naturae*, which was thus recognized and enforced by the common law of England, was vested in the colonial governments, where not denied by their charters, or in conflict with grants of the royal prerogative. It is also certain that the power which the colonies thus possessed passed to the states with the separation from the mother country, and remains in them at the present day, in so far as its exercise may be not incompatible with, or restrained by, the rights conveyed to the federal government by the constitution. * * *

While the fundamental principles upon which the common property in game rest have undergone no change, the development of free institutions had led to the recognition of the fact that the power or control lodged in the state, resulting from this common ownership, is to be exercised, like all other powers of government, as a trust for the benefit of the people, and not as a prerogative for the advantage of the government as distinct from the people, or for the benefit of private individuals as distinguished from the public good. Therefore, for the purpose of exercising this power, the state, as held by this court in *Martin v. Waddell*, 16 Pet. 410, represents its people, and the ownership is that of the people in their united sovereignty. The common ownership, and its resulting responsibility in the state, is thus stated in a well-considered opinion of the supreme court of California:

> "the wild game within a state belongs to the people in their collective sovereign capacity. It is not the subject of private ownership, except in so far as the people may elect to make it so; and they may, if they see fit, absolutely prohibit the taking of it, or traffic and commerce in it, if it is deemed necessary for the protection or preservation of the public good." *Ex parte Maier, ubi supra.* * * *

The foregoing analysis of the principles upon which alone rests the right of an individual to acquire a qualified ownership in game, and the power of the state, deduced therefrom, to control such ownership for the common benefit, clearly demonstrates the validity of the statute of the state of Connecticut here in controversy. The sole consequence of the provision forbidding the transportation of game killed within the state, beyond the state, is to confine the use of such game to those who own it,—the people of that state. The proposition that the state may not forbid carrying it beyond her limits involves, therefore, the contention that a state cannot allow its own people the enjoyment of the benefits of the property belonging to them in common, without at the same time permitting the citizens of other states to participate in that which they do not own. It was said in the discussion at bar, although it be conceded that the state has an absolute right to control and regulate the killing of game as its judgment deems best in the interest of its people, inasmuch as the state has here chosen to allow the people within her borders to take game, to dispose of it, and thus cause it to become an object of state commerce, as a resulting necessity such property has become the subject of interstate commerce; hence controlled by the provisions of article 1, § 8, of the constitution of the United States. But the errors which this argument involves are manifest. It presupposes that, where the killing of game and its sale within the state are allowed, it thereby becomes "commerce" in the legal meaning of that word. In view of the authority of the state to affix conditions to the killing and sale of game, predicated, as is this power, on the peculiar nature of such property and its common ownership by all the citizens of the state, it may well be doubted whether commerce is created by an authority given by a state to reduce game within its borders to possession, provided such game be not taken, when killed, without the jurisdiction of the state. The common ownership imports the right to keep the property, if the sovereign so chooses, always within its jurisdiction for every purpose. * * *

The fact that internal commerce may be distinct from interstate commerce destroys the whole theory upon which the argument of the plaintiff in error proceeds. The power of the state to control the killing of and ownership in game being admitted, the commerce in game which the state law permitted was necessarily only internal commerce, since the restriction that it should not become the subject of external commerce went along with the grant, and was a part of it. All ownership in game killed within the state came under this condition, which the state had the lawful authority to impose; and no contracts made in relation to such property were exempt from the law of the state consenting that such contracts be made, provided only they were confined to internal, and did not extend to external, commerce. * * *

QUESTIONS AND DISCUSSION

1.   The Commerce Clause (U.S. CONST., art. I, § 8) grants Congress authority to regulate interstate commerce. In its "negative" or "dormant" aspect, it limits the power of states to regulate in a way that discriminates against interstate commerce, even though Congress has not yet exercised its power to regulate. Thus, the question in *Geer* is whether the Connecticut statute barring the interstate sale of the game bird runs afoul of this dormant aspect of the Commerce Clause, or what is often just called the "dormant commerce clause."

2.   State regulation of natural resources is commonplace and, as a result, dormant commerce clause cases arise relatively frequently in the context of natural resource issues. The Supreme Court has set out a two-pronged analysis for such cases. First, the court asks whether the state law discriminates against interstate commerce. If a state law does not discriminate and its burden on commerce is only incidental, then the law will be upheld so long as the state can demonstrate that the burdens it imposes are not clearly excessive in relation to the local benefits. Generally, courts uphold state laws in this first category. If, however, the statute discriminates, then the state bears the much heavier burden of showing that the statute serves a legitimate local purpose that cannot be served just as well by less discriminatory means. *See Sporhase v. Nebraska*, 458 U.S. 941, 954 (1982). So, for example, in *Sporhase*, the Court struck down a Nebraska statute that restricted the export of water out of the state. While the court acknowledged that the state had a legitimate interest in protecting its water resources, it was not able to show that such protection required discrimination against out-of-state users. Likewise, in *Chemical Waste Management, Inc. v. Hunt*, 504 U.S. 334 (1992), the Court struck down an Alabama statute that imposed a hazardous waste disposal fee on waste generated outside Alabama but did not impose a fee on waste generated within the State. As in *Sporhase*, the Court acknowledged the State's legitimate concern with regulating hazardous waste and reducing the overall traffic in waste within the State. Nonetheless, the statute was rejected because less discriminatory means were available to achieve the desired purpose. How might the state have controlled and even limited hazardous waste disposal in Alabama without discriminating against out-of-state waste?

Maine v. Taylor, 477 U.S. 131 (1986) is one of the rare cases where the Supreme Court upheld a discriminatory state law. In *Maine*, the state had adopted a law banning the import of bait fish. Although economic protectionism was likely one of the reasons—perhaps the primary reason—for the law, Maine defended its statute on the grounds that imported bait fish could introduce parasites into Maine's waters, thereby threatening Maine's wild fish populations. Because Maine had no adequate way to test bait fish for these parasites, Maine's legitimate purpose in protecting its native fish could not be accomplished by less discriminatory means. As a result, the Maine statute was upheld.

3.   According to the Court, as of 1896, who owned the wildlife in Connecticut? In the Arizona Territory? On federal property in Minnesota?

4. What was the nature of individual and public rights to wildlife in Roman law and in English common law while the wildlife was *ferae naturae* (not yet reduced to possession)? What does the Court mean by its statement that the state owns the wildlife within its boundaries "as a trust for the benefit of the people, and not as a prerogative for the advantage of the government as distinct from the people, or for the benefit of private individuals as distinguished from the public good." Is the trust doctrine referenced in *Geer* the same public trust doctrine of *Illinois Central Railroad v. Illinois*, 146 U.S. 387 (1892), discussed *supra*? If so, why does the Court quote *Ex parte Maier* for the proposition that wildlife "is not the subject of private ownership, except in so far as the people may elect to make it so"? What sort of trust obligation does the Court have in mind? Could Connecticut give one hunting club the right to take all the birds of a certain species or give a riparian owner a private fishery along a stretch of navigable river? Suppose a bird watcher was upset by the state's management of birds to maximize hunting opportunities; could she sue on a claim that the state was violating its trust obligations?

5. As you read *Geer* and its recitation of some of the history of wildlife law, does it appear that state ownership of wildlife grew out of the sovereign's power to regulate or that the power to regulate was a function of state ownership? If it is the former, is "state ownership" just another way of saying "state police power"? Could the United States have condemned the state's ownership interest in wildlife?

6. Even if wildlife *ferae naturae* was owned by the state, why does the Court conclude that after a bird is reduced to possession, Connecticut may still prohibit its interstate sale without violating the dormant commerce clause?

7. As illustrated in further detail below, over the next 83 years a series of cases slowly eroded the state ownership doctrine until *Geer* was finally expressly overruled in *Hughes v. Oklahoma*, 441 U.S. 322 (1979) (holding that an Oklahoma statute prohibiting minnows procured within Oklahoma from being transported or sold for sale outside Oklahoma violated the dormant commerce clause).

  Geer represented the culmination of a line of Supreme Court cases giving the states the ownership of wildlife within their borders and effective regulatory control over resident species. *See also McCready v. Virginia*, 94 U.S. 391 (1876) (affirming Virginia's ownership of its fishery, even in navigable waters); *Smith v. Maryland*, 59 U.S. (18 How.) 71 (1855) (affirming Maryland's seizure of plaintiff's ship for dredging oysters in violation of state law despite fact that the ship was licensed under federal law). At the same time that the state ownership doctrine was reaching its zenith in *Geer*, the nation was starting to develop an ethos that favored conservation of natural resources. The national parks and national forests had just been given their start and President Theodore Roosevelt was to declare the first bird refuge at Pelican Island in 1903.

Roosevelt's withdrawal of lands for bird refuges was motivated by more than a general desire to promote conservation. Around the turn of the century, migratory bird populations were plummeting, primarily as a result of market hunting and the introduction of non-native species. The decimation of the passenger pigeon and the decline of other various grouse species and the prairie chicken were well known. Against this backdrop, in 1900, Congress made its first move into wildlife regulation with the passage of the Lacey Act. Reflecting Congress' tentative view of its jurisdiction in the face of the state ownership doctrine, the Lacey Act's key provision prohibited the interstate transportation of "any wild animals or birds" killed in violation of state law. Ch. 553, § 3, 31 Stat. 188 (1900) (current version at 16 U.S.C. § 3372(a)). The Act thus made no attempt to preempt state wildlife regulation, providing only an interstate commerce backstop to assist states in enforcing their own game laws. *See generally* Robert S. Anderson, *The Lacey Act: America's Premier Weapon in the Fight Against Unlawful Wildlife Trafficking*, 16 PUB. LAND L. REV. 27 (1995).

A less cautious Congress may have been more willing to assert its Commerce Clause power to act affirmatively to regulate wildlife, arguing that *Geer* was merely a dormant commerce clause case that considered whether Congress, if faced with the question, would have chosen to preempt Connecticut's protective legislation. But Congress' caution in the Lacey Act turned out to have been well taken because in 1912, the Supreme Court decided that the federal government did not have power under the Commerce Clause to affirmatively regulate wildlife within a state. *See The Abby Dodge v. U.S.*, 223 U.S. 166 (1912) (holding that a federal statute regulating the taking of sponges from the Gulf of Mexico and the Straits of Florida could not apply to sponges within Florida's waters).

Despite the decision in *The Abby Dodge*, Congress decided to test the constitutional waters the very next year. Claiming authority under the Commerce Clause, Congress enacted the Migratory Bird Act of 1913, which prohibited the hunting of migratory birds except pursuant to federal regulation. Two federal district courts, however, quickly struck down the Act. Relying on *Geer*, they concluded that the Act exceeded Congress' Commerce Clause authority. *See United States v. Shauver*, 214 F. 154 (E.D. Ark. 1914); *United States v. McCullagh*, 221 F. 288 (D. Kan. 1915). The *Shauver* case was appealed to the Supreme Court. While its appeal was pending, the Department of Agriculture encouraged the State Department to negotiate a treaty with Great Britain (for Canada) to protect migratory birds. The Department of Agriculture's theory was that if a treaty were negotiated, Congress could rely on the Constitution's treaty power to pass implementing legislation and simply bypass the question of its authority under the Commerce Clause. The Migratory Bird Treaty was signed by President Woodrow Wilson in 1916 and in 1918 Congress passed the Migratory Bird Treaty Act to implement the treaty. Ch. 128, 40 Stat. 755 (1918) (current version at 16 U.S.C. §§ 703–11). The Supreme Court then dismissed the government's appeal in *Shauver*. The states, however, were soon back in court, arguing that the federal government still lacked any authority to regulate wildlife. The fate of the states' argument is the subject of the following case.

Missouri v. Holland,
252 U.S. 416 (1920)

Mr. Justice Holmes delivered the opinion of the Court.

This is a bill in equity brought by the State of Missouri to prevent a game warden of the United States from attempting to enforce the Migratory Bird Treaty Act of July 3, 1918, c. 128, 40 Stat. 755, and the regulations made by the Secretary of Agriculture in pursuance of the same. The ground of the bill is that the statute is an unconstitutional interference with the rights reserved to the States by the Tenth Amendment, and that the acts of the defendant done and threatened under that authority invade the sovereign right of the State and contravene its will manifested in statutes. . . .

On December 8, 1916, a treaty between the United States and Great Britain was proclaimed by the President. It recited that many species of birds in their annual migrations traversed many parts of the United States and of Canada, that they were of great value as a source of food and in destroying insects injurious to vegetation, but were in danger of extermination through lack of adequate protection. It therefore provided for specified closed seasons and protection in other forms, and agreed that the two powers would take or propose to their lawmaking bodies the necessary measures for carrying the treaty out. 39 Stat. 1702. The above mentioned act of July 3, 1918, entitled an act to give effect to the convention, prohibited the killing, capturing or selling any of the migratory birds included in the terms of the treaty except as permitted by regulations compatible with those terms, to be made by the Secretary of Agriculture. Regulations were proclaimed on July 31, and October 25, 1918. It is unnecessary to go into any details, because, as we have said, the question raised is the general one whether the treaty and statute are void as an interference with the rights reserved to the States.

To answer this question it is not enough to refer to the Tenth Amendment, reserving the powers not delegated to the United States, because by Article 2, Section 2, the power to make treaties is delegated expressly, and by Article 6 treaties made under the authority of the United States, along with the Constitution and laws of the United States made in pursuance thereof, are declared the supreme law of the land. If the treaty is valid there can be no dispute about the validity of the statute under Article 1, Section 8, as a necessary and proper means to execute the powers of the Government. The language of the Constitution as to the supremacy of treaties being general, the question before us is narrowed to an inquiry into the ground upon which the present supposed exception is placed.

It is said that a treaty cannot be valid if it infringes the Constitution, that there are limits, therefore, to the treaty-making power, and that one such limit is that what an act of Congress could not do unaided, in derogation of the powers reserved to the States, a treaty cannot do. An earlier act of Congress that attempted by itself and not in pursuance of a treaty to regulate the killing of migratory birds within the States had been held bad in the District Court. *United States v. Shauver*, 214 Fed. 154. *United States v. McCullagh*, 221 Fed. 288. Those decisions were supported by arguments that migratory birds were owned by the States in their sovereign capacity for the benefit of their people, and that under cases like *Geer v. Connecticut*, 161 U.S. 519, this control was one that Congress had no power to displace. The same argument is supposed to apply now with equal force.

Whether the two cases cited were decided rightly or not they cannot be accepted as a test of the treaty power. Acts of Congress are the supreme law of the land only when made in pursuance of the Constitution, while treaties are declared to be so when made under the authority of the United States. It is open to question whether the authority of the United States means more than the formal acts prescribed to make the convention. We do not mean to imply that there are no qualifications to the treaty-making power; but they must be ascertained in a different way. It is obvious that there may be matters of the sharpest exigency for the national well being that an act of Congress could not deal with but that a treaty followed by such an act could, and it is not lightly to be assumed that, in matters requiring national action, "a power which must belong to and somewhere reside in every civilized government" is not to be found. *Andrews v. Andrews*, 188 U.S. 14. What was said in that case with regard to the powers of the States applies with equal force to the powers of the nation in cases where the States individually are incompetent to act. We are not yet discussing the particular case before us but only are considering the validity of the test proposed. With regard to that we may add that when we are dealing with words that also are a constituent act, like the Constitution of the United States, we must realize that they have called into life a being the development of which could not have been foreseen completely by the most gifted of its begetters. It was enough for them to realize or to hope that they had created an organism; it has taken a century and has cost their successors much sweat and blood to prove that they created a nation. The case before us must be considered in the light of our whole experience and not merely in that of what was said a hundred years ago. The treaty in question does not contravene any prohibitory words to be found in the Constitution. The only question is whether it is forbidden by some invisible radiation from the general terms of the Tenth Amendment. We must consider what this country has become in deciding what that amendment has reserved.

The State as we have intimated founds its claim of exclusive authority upon an assertion of title to migratory birds, an assertion that is embodied in statute. No doubt it is true that as between a State and its inhabitants the State may regulate the killing and sale of such birds, but it does not follow that its authority is exclusive of paramount powers. To put the claim of the State upon title is to lean upon a slender reed. Wild birds are not in the possession of anyone; and possession is the beginning of ownership. The whole foundation of the State's rights is the presence within their jurisdiction of birds that yesterday had not arrived, tomorrow may be in another State and in a week a thousand miles away. If we are to be accurate we cannot put the case of the State upon higher ground than that the treaty deals with creatures that for the moment are within the state borders, that it must be carried out by officers of the United States within the same territory, and that but for the treaty the State would be free to regulate this subject itself.

As most of the laws of the United States are carried out within the States and as many of them deal with matters which in the silence of such laws the State might regulate, such general grounds are not enough to support Missouri's claim. Valid treaties of course "are as binding within the territorial limits of the States as they are elsewhere throughout the dominion of the United States." No doubt the great body of private relations usually fall within the control of the State, but a treaty may override its power. * * *

Here a national interest of very nearly the first magnitude is involved. It can be protected only by national action in concert with that of another power. The subject matter is only transitorily within the State and has no permanent habitat therein. But for the treaty and the statute there soon might be no birds for any powers to deal with. We see nothing in the Constitution that compels the Government to sit by while a food supply is cut off and the protectors of our forests and our crops are destroyed. It is not sufficient to rely upon the States. The reliance is vain, and were it otherwise, the question is whether the United States is forbidden to act. We are of opinion that the treaty and statute must be upheld.

QUESTIONS AND DISCUSSION

1. What are the implications of the Court's reasoning in *Missouri v. Holland* for the state-ownership doctrine of *Geer*?

2. What are the implications of the Court's interpretation of the treaty power? Does the decision effectively give the federal government police power over any subject on which it negotiates a treaty? The Supreme Court has intimated that whether Congress has authority under the Commerce Clause to regulate isolated wetlands (wetlands not adjacent to navigable waters) presents "significant constitutional and federalism questions." *See Solid Waste Agency of Northern Cook County v. U.S. Army Corps of Engineers*, 531 U.S. 159, 161 (2001). To avoid these questions, could the United States find a friendly nation, negotiate a treaty in which both countries agree to protect their isolated wetlands, and then pass legislation for that purpose? Would the legislation be constitutional even if the wetlands have no effect on interstate commerce? Can you conceive of possible legal or practical limitations on this sort of use of the treaty power? *See generally* George Cameron Coggins & William H. Hensley, *Constitutional Limits on Federal Power to Protect and Manage Wildlife: Is the Endangered Species Act Endangered?*, 61 IOWA L. REV. 1099 (1976).

3. If the president's power to negotiate treaties is contained in Article II, Section 2, how can the enactment of a treaty create additional enumerated powers for Congress? Perhaps the answer lies in Article I, Section 8's Necessary and Proper Clause which gives Congress power to enact all laws "necessary and proper for carrying into execution ... all other powers vested by this constitution in the government of the United States, or in any department or officer thereof." *Missouri v. Holland* remains good law. In his plurality opinion in *Reid v. Covert*, 354 U.S. 1 (1957), Justice Black did say that a treaty may not contravene specific provisions of the Constitution. *Id.* at 16 ("[N]o agreement with a foreign nation can confer power on the Congress ... which is free from the restraints of the Constitution."). *Reid* addressed the question of whether the Bill of Rights applied to an overseas military trial despite an agreement between Britain and the United States to the contrary. Justice Black distinguished *Missouri v. Holland* on the ground that the MBTA did not interfere with the Tenth Amendment. *Id.* at 18. Black's focus on the Tenth Amendment suggests that he may not have viewed the lack of enumerated power as one of the "restraints of the Constitution." Does that distinction make sense?

4. Expansion of federal law-making under the Commerce Clause has left the treaty power largely unused. Perhaps the best illustration of its potential importance is from Australia. Like the United States, Australia has a federal system in which police power is vested in the states and the federal government is one of enumerated powers. The Australian Constitution confers no direct power over environmental matters and the courts have not given a broad definition to federal power over commerce. The result is that the states are the primary creators and enforcers of environmental law. The Australian Constitution does, however, give the federal government power over "external affairs." Echoing the reasoning of *Missouri v. Holland*, the Australian Supreme Court has upheld federal legislation premised on the external affairs power. *See, e.g., Commonwealth v. State of Tasmania*, 158 C.L.R. 1 (1983) (confirming federal power to overrule State of Tasmania's approval of a dam pursuant to the World Heritage Properties Conservation Act, which was enacted to implement the terms of the World Heritage Convention). Can you see why this would make Australians particularly interested in the content of international environmental and natural resources law?

Australia has imposed some limits on federal use of the external affairs power to justify legislation. For a period of time, the courts suggested that the issue had to be one of "international concern" for the external affairs power to apply. This standard now appears to have been discarded on the reasoning that the very existence of a treaty negotiated between two nations makes its subject matter one of "international concern." If this limitation applied to the treaty power, how would you go about establishing that natural resource issues included within a treaty were ones of "international concern"? Subsequently, the Australian courts have suggested two other limitations on the external affairs power: the legislation must be adapted to achieve an objective of the treaty; and the treaty must be bona fide and not just a way to increase the power of federal parliament beyond its constitutional scope. *See generally* Brian R. Opeskin & Donald R. Rothwell, *The Impact of Treaties on Australian Federalism*, 27 CASE W. RES. J. INT'L L. 1 (1995).

5. How can the Migratory Bird Treaty be viewed as a response to the tragedy of the commons? Why wasn't the state ownership doctrine a sufficient response to the open access resource problem presented by migratory birds? Isn't one response to overexploitation of an open access resource to assign property rights in the resource in order to give the owner (in this case the states) an incentive to conserve and care for the resource? Were there other potential responses to the overhunting of migratory birds? How well would different approaches work?

6. In this case and elsewhere we have seen arguments against the exercise of federal power lodged in the Tenth Amendment. The Tenth Amendment states: "The powers not delegated to the United States by the Constitution, nor prohibited by it to the States, are reserved to the States respectively, or to the people." In what sense is Missouri claiming that the MBTA violates the Tenth Amendment? Does the Tenth Amendment limit the exercise of federal powers otherwise enumerated in the Constitution? Alternatively, is the Tenth Amendment more like a rule of construction that should inform and narrow judicial interpretation of federal enumerated powers, perhaps as something like a counterweight to the Necessary and Proper Clause? Or is the Tenth Amendment just a truism that powers not otherwise enumerated are reserved to the states and the people? The Supreme Court has been wrestling with these questions. In most cases, the Tenth Amendment does not provide an independent limit on federal power. *See Garcia v. San Antonio Metro. Transit Auth.*, 469 U.S. 528 (1985). It has, however, been held to prohibit federal actions that commandeer the state legislative or executive branches to achieve federal purposes. *See New York v. United States*, 505 U.S. 144 (1992) (striking down a requirement that the states take title to radioactive waste generated within their borders); *Printz v. United States*, 521 U.S. 898 (1997) (holding unconstitutional that portion of Brady Handgun Violence Protection Act that obligated state law enforcement officers to perform background checks on handgun purchasers).

7. For an overview of federal wildlife law and the litigation and legislation leading up to *Missouri v. Holland*, see MICHAEL J. BEAN & MELANIE J. ROWLAND, THE EVOLUTION OF NATIONAL WILDLIFE LAW (1997).

———

In the years following *Missouri v. Holland*, the Supreme Court responded to pressure from President Franklin Roosevelt and his New Deal by adopting a much more generous view of Congress' powers under the Commerce Clause. As a result, congressional reliance on the Treaty Power fell into disuse. The preeminent example of the Court's expansive view of the Commerce Clause was the decision in *Wickard v. Filburn*, 317 U.S. 111 (1942), where the Court upheld a federal statute that imposed quotas on home-grown wheat. The Court held that growing wheat solely for personal consumption was subject to Commerce Clause regulation because aggregated together the acts of home wheat growers (about 20% of wheat grown in the United States) had a "substantial effect on interstate commerce." *Id.* at 125. Support for an expansive view of the Commerce Clause was further bolstered during the civil rights era when the Court again confirmed Congress' broad regulatory authority. *See, e.g., Heart of Atlanta Motel v. United States*, 379 U.S. 241 (1964) (upholding Title II of Civil Rights Act prohibiting discrimination in places of public accommodation).

Although *Wickard* and its progeny gave Congress broad authority, Congress still chose mostly to defer to state regulation of natural resources and the environment. That began to change in the late 1960s and early 1970s with the advent of the modern environmental movement. Relying on the broad view of its Commerce Clause powers evidenced in the Supreme Court's New Deal and civil rights cases, Congress enacted NEPA on New Years Day in 1970, 42 U.S.C. §§ 4321–61, the Clean Air Act later that same year, 42 U.S.C. §§ 7401–7642, the Clean Water Act in 1972, 33 U.S.C. §§ 1251–70, and the Endangered Species Act in 1973. 16 U.S.C. §§ 1531–43. Other natural resource legislation followed. Congress' power to enact this legislation seemed quite clear and by 1985, when the Court said in *Garcia* that the only real limits on federal commerce power were the "built-in restraints" of the "political process," *Garcia v. San Antonio Metro. Transit Auth.*, 469 U.S. 528, 556 (1985), the idea of any judicially imposed restrictions on Congress' commerce power seemed dead. In recent years, however, a narrower view of the Commerce Clause has been making a comeback. In 1995, in *United States v. Lopez*, 514 U.S. 549 (1995), the Court for the first time since early in the New Deal era struck down a federal statute regulating private conduct (possessing a gun within 500 feet of a school) as beyond Congress' power to regulate interstate commerce. Then, in 2000, in *United States v. Morrison*, 529 U.S. 598 (2000), the Court held that Congress lacked the power to enact the Violence Against Women Act of 1994, which created a federal civil remedy for victims of gender-motivated violence. In both cases, a closely-divided Court suggested that because the regulated activities were not "economic" in nature, the commerce power did not apply. *Lopez*, 514 U.S. at 567; *Morrison*, 529 U.S. at 613.

The pendulum may now be swinging back in the other direction. In *Gonzales v. Raich*, 545 U.S. 1 (2005), the Supreme Court recognized Congress' authority to enact the Controlled Substances Act, which prohibited the local cultivation and use of marijuana, thereby preempting a California law that allowed cultivation and use for medical purposes. The Court expressly reaffirmed the expansive view of Congress' Commerce Clause authority announced in *Wickard v. Filburn*, concluding that just as "when viewed in the aggregate, leaving home-consumed wheat outside the regulatory scheme would have a substantial influence on price and market conditions" and therefore a substantial effect on interstate commerce, so too did Congress have "a rational basis for concluding that leaving home-consumed marijuana outside federal control would similarly affect price and market conditions." *Id.* at 18–19.

Although *Raich* may indicate that *Lopez* and *Morrison* do not signal a new era in Commerce Clause jurisprudence, *Lopez* and *Morrison* triggered renewed questions about federal authority over natural resources. The following case was one of the first to address the implications of *Lopez* and *Morrison* for natural resource regulation, in particular the Endangered Species Act.

GIBBS V. BABBITT,
214 F.3d 483 (4th Cir. 2000),
***cert. denied*, 531 U.S. 1145 (2001)**

WILKINSON, CHIEF JUDGE:

The red wolf, *Canis rufus*, is an endangered species whose protection is at issue in this case. * * *

Activities such as wetlands drainage, dam construction, and hunting reduced the red wolf to such meager numbers that it was listed as endangered in 1976. Because of the paucity of animals left in the wild, their poor physical condition, and the threats posed by inbreeding, the FWS decided to trap the remaining red wolves in the mid–1970s and place them in a captive breeding program. The breeding program anticipated the eventual reintroduction of some red wolves into the wild.

In 1986, the FWS issued a final rule outlining a reintroduction plan for red wolves in the 120,000–acre Alligator River National Wildlife Refuge in eastern North Carolina. This area was judged the ideal habitat within the red wolf's historic range. Between 1987 and 1992, a total of 42 wolves were released in the Refuge.... Since reintroduction, some red wolves have wandered from federal refuges onto private property. From available data, as of February 1998 it was estimated that about 41 of the approximately 75 wolves in the wild may now reside on private land.

This case raises a challenge to 50 C.F.R. § 17.84(c), a regulation governing the experimental populations of red wolves reintroduced into North Carolina and Tennessee. [The regulation prohibits landowners from taking (harming, hunting, shooting, wounding, killing, trapping, etc.) wolves on private land, except to protect their own or other's lives or to protect their livestock or pets where the wolves are caught in the act of predation.] * * *

We consider this case under the framework articulated by the Supreme Court in *United States v. Lopez*, 514 U.S. 549 (1995), and *United States v. Morrison*, 529 U.S. 598 (2000), *aff'g Brzonkala v. Virginia Polytechnic Institute and State University*, 169 F.3d 820 (4th Cir.1999). While Congress's power to pass laws under the Commerce Clause has been interpreted broadly, both *Lopez* and *Morrison* reestablish that the commerce power contains "judicially enforceable outer limits." *See Lopez*, 514 U.S. at 566; *Morrison*, 120 S.Ct. at 1748–49. It is essential to our system of government that the commerce power not extend to effects on interstate commerce that are so remote that we "would effectually obliterate the distinction between what is national and what is local." *National Labor Relations Board v. Jones & Laughlin Steel Corp.*, 301 U.S. 1, 37 (1937). Indeed, the judiciary has the duty to ensure that federal statutes and regulations are promulgated under one of the enumerated grants of constitutional authority. It is our further duty to independently evaluate whether "a rational basis exist[s] for concluding that a regulated activity sufficiently affect[s] interstate commerce." *Lopez*, 514 U.S. at 557.

While this is rational basis review with teeth, the courts may not simply tear through the considered judgments of Congress. Judicial restraint is a long and honored tradition and this restraint applies to Commerce Clause adjudications. * * *

The *Lopez* Court recognized three broad categories of activity that Congress may regulate under its commerce power. "First, Congress may regulate the use of the channels of interstate commerce. Second, Congress is empowered to regulate and protect the instrumentalities of interstate commerce, or persons or things in interstate commerce, even though the threat may come only from intrastate activities. Finally, Congress' commerce authority includes the power to regulate those activities having a substantial relation to interstate commerce, i.e., those activities that substantially affect interstate commerce." 514 U.S. at 558–59 (citations omitted).

Section 17.84(c) is "not a regulation of the use of the channels of interstate commerce, nor is it an attempt to prohibit the interstate transportation of a commodity through the channels of commerce." *Lopez*, 514 U.S. at 559. The term "channel of interstate commerce" refers to, inter alia, "navigable rivers, lakes, and canals of the United States; the interstate railroad track system; the interstate highway system; . . . interstate telephone and telegraph lines; air traffic routes; television and radio broadcast frequencies." *United States v. Miles*, 122 F.3d 235, 245 (5th Cir. 1997). This regulation of red wolf takings on private land does not target the movement of wolves or wolf products in the channels of interstate commerce.

This case also does not implicate *Lopez's* second prong, which protects things in interstate commerce. Although the Service has transported the red wolves interstate for the purposes of study and the reintroduction programs, this is not sufficient to make the red wolf a "thing" in interstate commerce. . . . Therefore, if 50 C.F.R. § 17.84(c) is within the commerce power, it must be sustained under the third prong of Lopez. * * *

Under the third *Lopez* test, regulations have been upheld when the regulated activities "arise out of or are connected with a commercial transaction, which viewed in the aggregate, substantially affects interstate commerce." *Lopez*, 514 U.S. at 561. * * *

Although the connection to economic or commercial activity plays a central role in whether a regulation will be upheld under the Commerce Clause, economic activity must be understood in broad terms. Indeed, a cramped view of commerce would cripple a foremost federal power and in so doing would eviscerate national authority. The *Lopez* Court's characterization of the regulation of homegrown wheat in *Wickard v. Filburn*, 317 U.S. 111 (1942), as a case involving economic activity makes clear the breadth of this concept. * * *

To fall within Congress's commerce power, this regulation must have a "substantial relation to interstate commerce"—it must "substantially affect interstate commerce." *Lopez*, 514 U.S. at 559. The Supreme Court recently emphasized that "in those cases where we have sustained federal regulation of intrastate activity based upon the activity's substantial effects on interstate commerce, the activity in question has been some sort of economic endeavor." *Morrison*, 120 S.Ct. at 1750–51.... We therefore must consider whether the taking of red wolves on private land is "in any sense of the phrase, economic activity." *Morrison*, 120 S.Ct. at 1751–52. * * *

The relationship between red wolf takings and interstate commerce is quite direct—with no red wolves, there will be no red wolf related tourism, no scientific research, and no commercial trade in pelts. We need not "pile inference upon inference," *Lopez*, 514 U.S. at 567, to reach this conclusion. While a beleaguered species may not presently have the economic impact of a large commercial enterprise, its eradication nonetheless would have a substantial effect on interstate commerce. And through preservation the impact of an endangered species on commerce will only increase.

Because the taking of red wolves can be seen as economic activity in the sense considered by *Lopez* and *Morrison*, the individual takings may be aggregated for the purpose of Commerce Clause analysis. While the taking of one red wolf on private land may not be "substantial," the takings of red wolves in the aggregate have a sufficient impact on interstate commerce to uphold this regulation. This is especially so where, as here, the regulation is but one part of the broader scheme of endangered species legislation.

Further, § 17.84(c) is closely connected to a variety of interstate economic activities. Whether the impact of red wolf takings on any one of these activities qualifies as a substantial effect on interstate commerce is something we need not address. We have no doubt that the effect of the takings on these varied activities in combination qualifies as a substantial one. The first nexus between the challenged regulation and interstate commerce is tourism. The red wolves are part of a $29.2 billion national wildlife-related recreational industry that involves tourism and interstate travel. Many tourists travel to North Carolina from throughout the country for "howling events"—evenings of listening to wolf howls accompanied by educational programs. * * *

Appellants argue that the tourism rationale relates only to howling events on national park land or wildlife refuges because people do not travel to private land. They reason that without tourism on private land the regulated activity does not substantially affect interstate commerce. Yet this argument misses the mark. Since reintroduction, red wolves have strayed from federal lands onto private lands. Indeed, wolves are known to be "great wanderers." In 1998, it was estimated that 41 of the 75 wolves in the wild now live on private land. Because so many members of this threatened species wander on private land, the regulation of takings on private land is essential to the entire program of reintroduction and eventual restoration of the species. Such regulation is necessary to conserve enough red wolves to sustain tourism. * * *

Tourism, however, is not the only interstate commercial activity affected by the taking of red wolves. The regulation of red wolf takings is also closely connected to a second interstate market—scientific research. Scientific research generates jobs.... The red wolf reintroduction program has already generated numerous scientific studies.... By studying the effects of red wolves on the ecosystem, scientists learn about the interdependence of plants and animals, as well as how other threatened species may be reintroduced in the future. Scientific research can also reveal other uses for animals—for instance, approximately 50 percent of all modern medicines are derived from wild plants or animals.... Protection of the red wolves on private land thus encourages further research that may have inestimable future value, both for scientific knowledge as well as for commercial development of the red wolf.

The anti-taking regulation is also connected to a third market—the possibility of a renewed trade in fur pelts. Wolves have historically been hunted for their pelts. Congress had the renewal of trade in mind when it enacted the ESA. The Senate Report noted that the protection of an endangered species "may permit the regeneration of that species to a level where controlled exploitation of that species can be resumed. In such a case businessmen may profit from the trading and marketing of that species for an indefinite number of years, where otherwise it would have been completely eliminated from commercial channels." S. Rep. No. 91–526, at 3 (1969), *reprinted in* 1969 U.S.C.C.A.N. 1413, 1415. * * *

Finally, the taking of red wolves is connected to interstate markets for agricultural products and livestock. For instance, appellant landowners find red wolves a menace because they threaten livestock and other animals of economic and commercial value. By restricting the taking of red wolves, § 17.84(c) is said to impede economic development and commercial activities such as ranching and farming. This effect on commerce, however, still qualifies as a legitimate subject for regulation. It is well-settled under Commerce Clause cases that a regulation can involve the promotion or the restriction of commercial enterprises and development. Indeed, "[t]he motive and purpose of a regulation of interstate commerce are matters for the legislative judgment." *United States v. Darby*, 312 U.S. 100, 115 (1941).... The regulation here targets takings that are economically motivated—farmers take wolves to protect valuable livestock and crops. It is for Congress, not the courts, to balance economic effects— namely whether the negative effects on interstate commerce from red wolf predation are outweighed by the benefits to commerce from a restoration of this species. To say that courts are ill-suited for this act of empirical and political judgment is an understatement.

It is anything but clear, for example, that red wolves harm farming enterprises. They may in fact help them, and in so doing confer additional benefits on commerce. For instance, red wolves prey on animals like raccoons, deer, and rabbits—helping farmers by killing the animals that destroy their crops. *See* Robert J. Esher & Theodore R. Simons, *Red Wolf Propagation on Horn Island, Miss.: Red Wolf Ecological Studies* 13–16 (Sept. 1993) (unpublished, Joint Appendix at 890). On Horn Island, for instance, researchers found evidence of increased shore bird nesting, likely due to the reduction in raccoon predation. *See id.* at 15. * * *

The protection of the red wolf on both federal and private land substantially affects interstate commerce through tourism, trade, scientific research, and other potential economic activities. To overturn this regulation would start courts down the road to second-guessing all kinds of legislative judgments. There is a "rational basis" as defined by *Lopez* for sustaining this regulation. We therefore hold that the anti-taking provision at issue here involves regulable economic and commercial activity as understood by current Commerce Clause jurisprudence. * * *

This regulation is also sustainable as "an essential part of a larger regulation of economic activity, in which the regulatory scheme could be undercut unless the intrastate activity were regulated." The Supreme Court in *Hodel v. Indiana* stated: "A complex regulatory program ... can survive a Commerce Clause challenge without a showing that every single facet of the program is independently and directly related to a valid congressional goal. It is enough that the challenged provisions are an integral part of the regulatory program and that the regulatory scheme when considered as a whole satisfies this test." 452 U.S. 314, 329 n.17 (1981). * * *

Appellants repeatedly argue that individual takings of red wolves have only an insubstantial effect on interstate commerce and therefore that the application of the regulation to private landowners is invalid. But we emphasize that the effect on commerce must be viewed not from the taking of one wolf, but from the potential commercial differential between an extinct and a recovered species. A single red wolf taking may be insubstantial by some measures, but that does not invalidate a regulation that is part of the ESA and that seeks conservation not only of any single animal, but also recovery of the species as a whole. The Supreme Court in *Lopez* was emphatic on this point: " 'where *a general regulatory statute bears a substantial relation to commerce*, the *de minimis* character of individual instances arising under that statute is of no consequence.' " 514 U.S. at 558 (emphasis in original; [citations omitted]).

.... Section 17.84(c) must thus be evaluated against the overall congressional goal of restoring red wolves and endangered species generally. It would be perverse indeed if a species nearing extinction were found to be beyond Congress's power to protect while abundant species were subject to full federal regulatory power. Yet under appellants' theory, the more endangered the species, the less authority Congress has to regulate the taking of it. According to this view, endangered species would lie beyond congressional protection because there are too few animals left to make a commercial difference. Such reasoning would eviscerate the comprehensive federal scheme for conserving endangered species and turn congressional judgment on its head. * * *

Finally, we offer a brief response to the views of our dissenting brother. * * *

There should be no doubt about the implications of the dissenting opinion. Our dissenting colleague would rework the relationship between the judiciary and its coordinate branches. It is apparent that the dissent regards § 17.84(c) as ill-advised. That is fair enough, but a judge's view of the wisdom of enacted policies affords no warrant for declaring them unconstitutional. In recognition of the fact that the wisdom of legislation is different from its constitutionality, courts have always started with a presumption in favor of an enactment's constitutionality. *Lopez* and *Morrison* have not shifted this presumption. In fact, they have carefully maintained it. Our dissenting brother proceeds on the quite contrary premise that the burden now rests with those who wish to uphold legislation. We know of no other way to interpret the dissent's view that the empirical underpinnings of this regulation are inadequate.

Reversing the presumption in favor of constitutionality plunges our dissenting brother into the thick of political controversy. As the arguments and briefs in this case attest, the matter in question involves a rather traditional struggle between property owners on the one hand and environmentalists on the other. Both sides in this political stand-off have their legitimate points to make. Property owners understandably seek more freedom to take wolves on their property. Those opposing them seek to impress the fact that even private property has historically been imbued with public responsibilities. Why the judicial branch should place its thumb on either side of this old political scale is simply beyond our comprehension. Both concern for property rights and concern for the environment play important roles in shaping political decisions. But neither can automatically be allowed to grind the nation's commerce power to a constitutional halt. An indiscriminate willingness to constitutionalize recurrent political controversies will weaken democratic authority and spell no end of trouble for the courts. * * *

Finally, the dissenting opinion works a rent in the fabric of Our Federalism. Striking down this regulation will turn federalism on its head. *Lopez* and *Morrison* rightly emphasized the fact that the federal involvement with local school zones and the creation of civil causes of action to prevent gender-motivated violence encroached on what are traditional state functions. By contrast, the preservation of endangered species is historically a federal function. *Lopez* and *Morrison* recognized the importance of judicial review under the Commerce Clause. But, unlike the dissent, those cases set boundaries to that review and did not transform the reviewing function from a shield protecting state activities into a sword dismembering a long recognized federal one. It is as threatening to federalism for courts to erode the historic national role over scarce resource conservation as it is for Congress to usurp traditional state prerogatives in such areas as education and domestic relations. Courts seeking to enforce the structural constraints of federalism must respect the balance on both sides. * * *

LUTTIG, CIRCUIT JUDGE, dissenting:

* * * If one holds the views expressed by the Supreme Court majority in *Lopez* and *Morrison* ... a belabored discussion of the implications of those decisions for the regulation at issue before us today is not necessary.

Here, the Fish and Wildlife Service has promulgated a regulation that prohibits private landowners from shooting, wounding, killing, trapping, or otherwise harming the *canis rufus*, or the red wolf, even when the wolves are on the private landowners' property and threatening their crops and livestock. However, in what the majority characterizes as an act of beneficence by the government to benefit the landowners, the government does allow a property owner—even on his own property—to kill a wolf if the wolf is about to kill the property owner himself or his family. The question presented to us for decision is not "whether the national government can act to conserve scarce natural resources of value to our entire country," whether we should "hold as a basic maxim of judicial restraint that Congress may constitutionally address the problem of protecting endangered species," or whether our decision today will "work[] a rent in the fabric of Our Federalism," "turn federalism on its head," or "open the door to standardless judicial rejection of democratic initiatives of all sorts." Rather, the simple (and frankly, considerably less incitant) question of law for us to decide is whether, assuming its validity under statute, this one particular Fish and Wildlife regulation exceeds Congress' power under the Commerce Clause.

As the majority recites, there are an estimated 41 red wolves resident on private property and 75 red wolves total, in eastern North Carolina. The majority sustains the Fish and Wildlife's regulation unhesitatingly on the ground that the taking of the 41 red wolves that might occur as property owners attempt to protect themselves and their families, their property, their crops, and their livestock from these wolves, will have a "substantial effect" on interstate commerce. This substantial effect on interstate commerce comprises, according to the majority, four separate effects on such commerce, each of which the majority views as "substantial."

First, the majority concludes, in exclusive reliance upon a Cornell University professor's unpublished study entitled "Red Wolf Recovery in Northeastern North Carolina and the Great Smoky Mountains National Park," that "[m]any tourists travel to North Carolina from throughout the country for 'howling events'—evenings of listening to wolf howls accompanied by educational programs," and thus that the taking of these wolves will have a substantial effect on the interstate commercial industry of tourism.

Second, the majority concludes, largely in reliance, not upon their substantive conclusions, but rather upon the fact of the generation of two articles—"The Red Wolf as a Model for Carnivore Reintroductions," which was published in the Symposium of the Zoological Society of London, and the 1994 unpublished study "Alligator River National Wildlife Refuge Red Wolf (*Canis Rufus*) Scat Analysis"—that the taking of these red wolves will have a substantial effect on the "interstate market" of "scientific research."

Third, the majority concludes, largely on the strength of an article that appears in the University of Pennsylvania Journal of International Economic Law, that the taking of these wolves will have a substantial effect on the majority-anticipated resurrection of an interstate trade in fur pelts. In reliance upon an article that appeared two years ago in the *Calgary Herald* entitled "Hunters on Snowmobiles Cut Down Wolf Count in N.W.T.," the majority observes that "[f]or example, in the Northwestern Territories of Canada where wolves are plentiful, a hunter can command about $300 per pelt." The majority frankly acknowledges that there has not been a trade in wolf pelts since the 1800s, but, to the majority, "this temporal difference is beside the point."

Finally, in reliance upon yet another unpublished study by Robert Esher and Theodore Simons entitled "Red Wolf Propagation on Horn Island, Mississippi: Red Wolf Ecological Studies," and by analogy to the finding therein of "increased shore bird nesting, likely due to the reduction in raccoon predation," the majority concludes that the red wolves which the farmers and landowners have heretofore thought threatened their families, their crops, and their livestock, actually help the farmers, by killing the animals that destroy the farmers' crops, and thereby substantially affect interstate commerce.

That these conclusions are not even arguably sustainable under *Lopez* [and] *Morrison* ..., much less for the reasons cobbled together by the majority, is evident from the mere recitation of the conclusions. The killing of even all 41 of the estimated red wolves that live on private property in North Carolina would not constitute an economic activity of the kind held by the Court in *Lopez* and in *Morrison* to be of central concern to the Commerce Clause, if it could be said to constitute an economic activity at all. It is for this reason that the majority's attempted aggregation is impermissible: "While we need not adopt a categorical rule against aggregating the effects of any noneconomic activity in order to decide these cases, thus far in our Nation's history our cases have upheld Commerce Clause regulation of intrastate activity only where that activity is economic in nature." *Morrison*, 120 S.Ct. at 1751 (citations omitted). But even assuming that such is an economic activity, it certainly is not an activity that has a substantial effect on interstate commerce. The number of inferences (not even to mention the amount of speculation) necessary to discern in this activity a substantial effect on interstate commerce is exponentially greater than the number necessary in *Lopez* to show a substantial effect on interstate commerce from the sale of guns near schools or in *Morrison* to show a substantial effect on interstate commerce from domestic assault. * * *

In a word, the expansive view of the Commerce power expressed by the majority today is closely akin to that separately expressed by Justice Breyer in his dissent in *Lopez* and Justice Souter in his dissent in *Morrison*, and certainly more closely akin to those dissenting Justices' views than it is to the view of the *Lopez* majority in *Lopez* and *Morrison*. * * *

I would invalidate this particular agency regulation ... without any fear whatsoever that such "would place in peril the entire federal regulatory scheme for wildlife and natural resource conservation," as the majority over-rhetorically predicts would result from the invalidation of this lone regulation. * * *

While it could be lost in a reading of the majority opinion, we do not address here Congress' power over either the channels or instrumentalities of interstate commerce. We do not address activity that is interstate in character. We do not address in this case a statute or a regulation with an express interstate commerce jurisdictional requirement, which would all but ensure constitutional validity. We do not have before us an activity that has obvious economic character and impact, such as is typically the case with non-wildlife natural resources, and even with other wildlife resources. We are not even presented with an activity as to which a plausible case of future economic character and impact can be made.

To the contrary, we are confronted here with an administrative agency regulation of an activity that implicates but a handful of animals, if even that, in one small region of one state. An activity that not only has no current economic character, but one that concededly has had no economic character for well over a century now. An activity that has no foreseeable economic character at all, except upon the baldest (though admittedly most humorous) of speculation that the red wolf pelt trade will once again emerge as a centerpiece of our Nation's economy. And, importantly, an activity that Congress could plainly regulate under its spending power and under its power over federal lands, regardless.

Judge Wilkinson, for his part, has written that he regards *Lopez*, ... and presumably now *Morrison*, as examples in a "spate of decisions" of "contemporary judicial activism[.]" *Brzonkala*, 169 F.3d 820, 892–93 (Wilkinson, J., concurring).... The dissenting Justices in both *Lopez* and *Morrison* similarly regard these decisions. But I do not regard these decisions as such, and I certainly do not understand the majority of the Supreme Court to so regard these decisions. * * *

The majority of the Supreme Court in *Lopez* and *Morrison* has left no doubt ... that the interpretation of this clause of the Constitution, no less so than any other, must ultimately rest not with the political branches, but with the judiciary. *See Lopez*, 514 U.S. 549, 557 n.2 ("[W]hether particular operations affect interstate commerce sufficiently to come under the constitutional power of Congress to regulate them is ultimately a judicial rather than a legislative question, and can be settled finally only by this Court.")

Accordingly, I would faithfully apply in this case the Supreme Court's landmark decisions in *Lopez* and *Morrison*, as I would in any other case. The affirmative reach and the negative limits of the Commerce Clause do not wax and wane depending upon the subject matter of the particular legislation under challenge.

QUESTIONS AND DISCUSSION

1. What is the relevant activity for purposes of determining substantial effect on interstate commerce? Is it the protection of wolves? The farming activities with which the no-take rule might interfere? As a related question, what may be aggregated for purposes of showing a substantial effect on commerce? One wolf? The wolves on public land? All the wolves? The fully recovered wolf population to which the ESA aspires? All listed species under the ESA? Which view is more likely to lead to the conclusion that the challenged regulation is "economic" in character? In considering the answer to this question, remember that a key component of the *Lopez* decision was that a test which allows Congress to regulate anything under the Commerce Clause is incompatible with the principle that the powers of Congress are enumerated. *Lopez*, 514 U.S. at 564. Remember also, however, the Supreme Court's recent decision in *Gonzales v. Raich*, 545 U.S. 1 (2005), and the Court's reasoning that, just like the home-grown wheat in *Wickard*, marijuana grown at home for medical purposes should be aggregated for determining affect on interstate commerce.

2. How might Aldo Leopold's "land ethic" and principles of ecology aid the government in its efforts to establish that regulating wolves falls within the commerce power?

3. Will an endangered species that is not charismatic ever have a substantial economic effect on interstate commerce? The endangered Delhi Sands Flower–Loving Fly is one inch long and lives for only two weeks after it emerges from the ground. The fly's habitat is now limited to about a dozen patches of habitat in Riverside and San Bernardino counties in southern California. San Bernardino County wants to build a hospital on a portion of the fly's habitat. In light of *Gibbs*, does Congress' commerce power extend to the fly? What about a different species such as the Peck's Cave Ampiphod which lives in a zone of permanent darkness in one underground aquifer in Texas? Or the Cowhead Lake Tui Chub, which is a three-inch fish that lives in a three-mile stretch of river in an agricultural part of northern California? Is there any portion of the court's opinion that would allow Congress to reach these species? As Professor Nagle explains, the Commerce Clause issue in these three cases is about more than flies, ampiphods, and chubs:

> The Commerce Clause dilemma is whether Congress has the power to protect something that is very rare, very valuable, and seemingly entirely uninvolved with commerce between the states. It is a dilemma that transcends the preservation of endangered species and implicates federal efforts to protect historic buildings, scenic landscapes, works of art, and other valuable resources.

John Copeland Nagle, *The Commerce Clause Meets the Delhi Sands Flower–Loving Fly*, 97 MICH. L. REV. 174, 179 (1998).

4. Judge Wilkinson suggests that "the preservation of endangered species is historically a federal function." Is he right? Would he be right if he was talking about wildlife law more generally? What is the relevance of this issue to the Commerce Clause analysis?

5. If Judge Luttig's view of the commerce power is correct, does that mean there is no way for the federal government to protect the wolf? What does Luttig suggest?

6. Dismayed at the Supreme Court's decision in *Lopez* and writing on the eve of its decision in *Morrison*, one commentator asserted:

> If the Supreme Court strikes down the Violence Against Women Act, it will call into question scores of other federal laws and embolden states-rights judges on lower courts to declare war on Congress. The Endangered Species Act, for example, regulates violence against animals, many of whom don't engage in interstate travel. Will it soon be unconstitutional for Congress to prohibit shooting a puma for sport in a national park?

Jeffrey Rosen, *Hyperactive*, NEW REPUBLIC, Jan. 31, 2000, at 20. The Fourth Circuit's decision in *Gibbs* should alleviate some of his concerns. Suppose, however, that Judge Luttig's view of the Commerce Clause prevailed. Is there still reason to fear for Professor Rosen's puma?

7. One year after its decision in *Morrison*, the Supreme Court returned, albeit tangentially, to the Commerce Clause. In *Solid Waste Agency of Northern Cook County v. U.S. Army Corps of Engineers*, 531 U.S. 159 (2001), the Court addressed a challenge to the Corps of Engineers' "migratory bird" rule under which the Corps claimed the authority to apply its § 404 permit requirements to isolated wetlands (those wetlands not adjacent to navigable waters). The Court struck down the rule on the grounds that Congress did not intend to assert federal authority over isolated wetlands under the Clean Water Act. The Court declined to decide whether Congress could have extended federal authority over isolated wetlands had it chosen to do so. The Court's interpretation of the Clean Water Act has been subjected to heavy criticism. *See, e.g.*, William Funk, *The Court, the Clean Water Act, and the Constitution: SWANCC and Beyond*, 31 ENVTL. L. REP. (Envtl. L. Inst.) 10,741 (2001). Given this criticism, why might the Court have chosen to resolve the case as a matter of statutory interpretation rather than as one of constitutional law? The Court suggested that it was merely applying a prudential rule that statutes and regulations should be interpreted to "avoid the significant constitutional and federalism questions." *Id.* at 684. Does the fact that the justices were divided 5–4 suggest any other potential explanation? How would the case have been decided under the Commerce Clause? Could the migratory bird rule be sustained under another federal power?

8. *Gibbs* involves classical questions about both federalism and separation of powers. How far should a court go in overturning a decision of the legislative branch? Should courts, as suggested by Judge Wilkinson, generally leave the allocation of power between states and the federal government to the political process? Is there any more reason for a court to defer to Congress on the scope of its commerce power than on the scope of the Equal Protection Clause or the First Amendment?

9. Most of the foregoing questions ask you to analyze the Commerce Clause from a legal/formal perspective. But step back a bit further and ask yourself what is driving the Commerce Clause debate. Why is it that the environmental community is generally committed to a broad view of the Commerce Clause that maintains federal power over resource management? Are states more likely to favor resource exploitation over conservation? Will greater federal control lead to better resource management? Does it depend on the nature of the resource?

10. The text has focused on three sources of federal power over natural resources: the Commerce Clause, the treaty power, and the Property Clause. This is not an exclusive list. The Supreme Court has also held that Congress has authority to regulate natural resources under its spending power and its war power. *See United States v. Gerlach Live Stock Co.*, 339 U.S. 725 (1950) (holding that Congress' power to promote the "general welfare" of the United States gave it power to build large-scale, federal water projects); *Ashwander v. TVA*, 297 U.S. 288 (1936) (upholding federal power to construct a dam for purposes of producing electricity in the event of war; also concluding that water power generated by the dam was property of the United States and thus amenable to Property Clause regulation).

11. For detailed discussions of the Supreme Court's Commerce Clause jurisprudence and its potential implications for regulation of natural resources and the environment, see Bradford C. Mank, *After Gonzales v. Raich: Is The Endangered Species Act Constitutional Under the Commerce Clause?*, 78 U. COLO. L. REV. 375 (2007); Christine A. Klein, *The Environmental Commerce Clause*, 27 HARV. ENVTL L. REV. 1 (2003); John Copeland Nagle, *The Commerce Clause Meets the Delhi Sands Flower–Loving Fly*, 97 MICH. L. REV. 174 (1998).

C.   THE TAKINGS LIMITATION ON FEDERAL AND STATE POWER OVER NATURAL RESOURCES

Because most natural resources, including many resources on public lands, have long been regarded as private property, federal and state action with respect to those resources has the potential to implicate the Takings Clauses of the Fifth and Fourteenth Amendments. As you may recall from your property law class, the Fifth Amendment provides, in relevant part: "nor shall private property be taken for public use, without just compensation." This prohibition against the federal government has then been applied to the states via the Fourteenth Amendment's Due Process Clause. *See Chicago, Burlington and Quincy R.R. v. Chicago*, 166 U.S. 226, 234, 239, 241 (1897); *Webb's Fabulous Pharmacies, Inc. v. Beckwith*, 449 U.S. 155, 160 (1980). The core of the Takings Clause is the requirement that when the government physically expropriates property (e.g., to build a highway), it must pay just compensation. Such physical expropriations are relatively easy to identify and, although sometimes still controversial, have not occasioned anywhere near the commentary of so-called regulatory takings, which raise critical questions for regulation of natural resources and the environment. There is little question, for example, that if the state decides to take a farmer's land and convert it into a public park or to take his timber and use it to build homes, the state must pay the farmer compensation. But what happens if the government passes a regulation protecting wetlands which effectively prohibits the farmer from farming his land? What happens when the government enacts a law prohibiting harm to endangered species and the farmer's timber stand happens to be the last remaining nesting habitat for an endangered bird? Although it may not have been pointed out when you studied takings law in your property course, the majority of the Supreme Court's important regulatory takings decisions are at their core environmental and natural resources law cases. In subsequent chapters, you will often need to analyze whether a particular natural resource regulation amounts to a taking of that resource. This section is intended to give you the basic background on takings law necessary to perform that analysis.

As Justice Holmes first explained in *Pennsylvania Coal Co. v. Mahon*, 260 U.S. 393 (1922), a case involving mineral rights, "[g]overnment hardly could go on if to some extent values incident to property could not be diminished without paying for every such change in the general law. As long recognized, some values are enjoyed under an implied limitation and must yield to the police power." *Id.* at 413. On the other hand, if regulation of private property could never occasion compensation, the "natural tendency of human nature" would be to extend regulation further and further until private ownership essentially disappeared. *Id.* at 415. Holmes summarized with the familiar maxim that "while property may be regulated to a certain extent, if regulation goes too far it will be recognized as a taking." *Id.* Although Holmes' conclusion seems like common sense, in practical terms it is not easy to discern exactly when a regulation "goes too far" and merits compensation.

The key precedent on regulatory takings is the Supreme Court's decision in *Penn Central Transp. Co. v. New York City*, 438 U.S. 104 (1978). In *Penn Central*, the Court held that in deciding whether a regulation went "too far" so as to merit compensation, lower courts should focus on the economic impact of the regulation and the extent of its interference with distinct investment-backed expectations, as well as the character and purpose of the governmental regulation. *Id.* at 123–24. In practice, this *Penn Central* balancing test has led to very few regulations actually triggering a just compensation obligation. As the twentieth century drew to a close, however, the Supreme Court took a small step away from the *ad hoc* balancing approach of *Penn Central*. In an effort to give clearer guideposts to government and the regulated community, the Court carved out certain regulations that would amount to "categorical" or "per se" takings. The next case is a product of that effort. As you read the decision, contemplate whether it makes takings law any clearer or just produces another set of ambiguities and questions about when natural resource regulation rises to the level of a taking.

[handwritten margin note: Penn Central standard (balancing)]

Lucas v. South Carolina Coastal Council, 505 U.S. 1003 (1992)

Justice Scalia delivered the opinion of the Court.

In 1986, petitioner David H. Lucas paid $975,000 for two residential lots on the Isle of Palms in Charleston County, South Carolina, on which he intended to build single family homes. In 1988, however, the South Carolina Legislature enacted the Beachfront Management Act, S.C. Code § 48–39–250 *et seq.* (Supp. 1990) (Act), which had the direct effect of barring petitioner from erecting any permanent habitable structures on his two parcels. A state trial court found that this prohibition rendered Lucas's parcels "valueless." This case requires us to decide whether the Act's dramatic effect on the economic value of Lucas's lots accomplished a taking of private property under the Fifth and Fourteenth Amendments requiring the payment of "just compensation."

South Carolina's expressed interest in intensively managing development activities in the so-called "coastal zone" dates from 1977 when, in the aftermath of Congress's passage of the federal Coastal Zone Management Act of 1972, . . . the legislature enacted a Coastal Zone Management Act of its own. *See* S.C. Code § 48–39–10 *et seq.* (1987). In its original form, the South Carolina Act required owners of coastal zone land that qualified as a "critical area" (defined in the legislation to include beaches and immediately adjacent sand dunes) to obtain a permit from the newly created South Carolina Coastal Council (respondent here) prior to committing the land to a "use other than the use the critical area was devoted to on [September 28, 1977]." § 48–39–130(A).

In the late 1970s, Lucas and others began extensive residential development of the Isle of Palms, a barrier island situated eastward of the City of Charleston. Toward the close of the development cycle for one residential subdivision known as "Beachwood East," Lucas in 1986 purchased the two lots at issue in this litigation for his own account. No portion of the lots, which were located approximately 300 feet from the beach, qualified as a "critical area" under the 1977 Act; accordingly, at the time Lucas acquired these parcels, he was not legally obliged to obtain a permit from the Council in advance of any development activity. His intention with respect to the lots was to do what the owners of the immediately adjacent parcels had already done: erect single-family residences. . . .

The Beachfront Management Act brought Lucas's plans to an abrupt end. Under that 1988 legislation, the Council was directed to establish a "baseline" connecting the landward-most "point[s] of erosion . . . during the past forty years" in the region of the Isle of Palms that includes Lucas's lots. § 48–39–280(A)(2) (Supp. 1988). In action not challenged here, the Council fixed this baseline landward of Lucas's parcels. That was significant, for under the Act construction of occupiable improvements was flatly prohibited seaward of a line drawn 20 feet landward of, and parallel to, the baseline, § 48–39–290(A) (Supp. 1988). The Act provided no exceptions.

Lucas promptly filed suit in the South Carolina Court of Common Pleas, contending that the Beachfront Management Act's construction bar effected a taking of his property without just compensation. Lucas did not take issue with the validity of the Act as a lawful exercise of South Carolina's police power, but contended that the Act's complete extinguishment of his property's value entitled him to compensation regardless of whether the legislature had acted in furtherance of legitimate police power objectives. Following a bench trial, the court agreed. Among its factual determinations was the finding that "at the time Lucas purchased the two lots, both were zoned for single-family residential construction and . . . there were no restrictions imposed upon such use of the property by either the State of South Carolina, the County of Charleston, or the Town of the Isle of Palms." * * *

[Our decision in *Pennsylvania Coal Co. v. Mahon,* 260 U.S. 393 (1922)] * * * offered little insight into when, and under what circumstances, a given regulation would be seen as going "too far" for purposes of the Fifth Amendment. In 70–odd years of succeeding "regulatory takings" jurisprudence, we have generally eschewed any "set formula" for determining how far is too far, preferring to "engag[e] in ... essentially ad hoc, factual inquiries," *Penn Central Transportation Co. v. New York City,* 438 U.S. 104, 124 (1978) (quoting *Goldblatt v. Hempstead,* 369 U.S. 590, 594 (1962)). We have, however, described at least two discrete categories of regulatory action as compensable without case-specific inquiry into the public interest advanced in support of the restraint. The first encompasses regulations that compel the property owner to suffer a physical "invasion" of his property. In general (at least with regard to permanent invasions), no matter how minute the intrusion, and no matter how weighty the public purpose behind it, we have required compensation. For example, in *Loretto v. Teleprompter Manhattan CATV Corp.,* 458 U.S. 419 (1982), we determined that New York's law requiring landlords to allow television cable companies to emplace cable facilities in their apartment buildings constituted a taking even though the facilities occupied at most only 1½ cubic feet of the landlords' property, *see id.* at 438 n.16. *See also United States v. Causby,* 328 U.S. 256, 265, and n.10 (1946) (physical invasions of airspace).

The second situation in which we have found categorical treatment appropriate is where regulation denies all economically beneficial or productive use of land. *See Agins v. Tiburon,* 447 U.S. 255, 260; *see also Nollan v. California Coastal Comm'n,* 483 U.S. 825, 834 (1987); *Keystone Bituminous Coal Assn. v. DeBenedictis,* 480 U.S. 470, 495 (1987). As we have said on numerous occasions, the Fifth Amendment is violated when land-use regulation "does not substantially advance legitimate state interests *or denies an owner economically viable use of his land.*" *Agins, supra,* at 260 (citations omitted) (emphasis added).[7]

We have never set forth the justification for this rule. Perhaps it is simply, as Justice Brennan suggested, that total deprivation of beneficial use is, from the landowner's point of view, the equivalent of a physical appropriation. *See San Diego Gas & Electric Co. v. San Diego,* 450 U.S., at 652 (Brennan, J., dissenting). "[F]or what is the land but the profits thereof[?]" 1 E. Coke, Institutes § 1 (1st Am. ed. 1812). Surely, at least, in the extraordinary

---

7. Regrettably, the rhetorical force of our "deprivation of all economically feasible use" rule is greater than its precision, since the rule does not make clear the "property interest" against which the loss of value is to be measured. When, for example, a regulation requires a developer to leave 90% of a rural tract in its natural state, it is unclear whether we would analyze the situation as one in which the owner has been deprived of all economically beneficial use of the burdened portion of the tract, or as one in which the owner has suffered a mere diminution in value of the tract as a whole. (For an extreme—and, we think, unsupportable—view of the relevant calculus, *see Penn Central Transportation Co. v. New York City,* 366 N.E.2d 1271, 1276–77 (N.Y.1977), *aff'd,* 438 U.S. 104 (1978), where the state court examined the diminution in a particular parcel's value produced by a municipal ordinance in light of total value of the tak-

ing claimant's other holdings in the vicinity.) Unsurprisingly, this uncertainty regarding the composition of the denominator in our "deprivation" fraction has produced inconsistent pronouncements by the Court. The answer to this difficult question may lie in how the owner's reasonable expectations have been shaped by the State's law of property—*i.e.*, whether and to what degree the State's law has accorded legal recognition and protection to the particular interest in land with respect to which the takings claimant alleges a diminution in (or elimination of) value. In any event, we avoid this difficulty in the present case, since the "interest in land" that Lucas has pleaded (a fee simple interest) is an estate with a rich tradition of protection at common law, and since the South Carolina Court of Common Pleas found that the Beachfront Management Act left each of Lucas's beachfront lots without economic value.

circumstance when no productive or economically beneficial use of land is permitted, it is less realistic to indulge our usual assumption that the legislature is simply "adjusting the benefits and burdens of economic life," *Penn Central Transportation Co.*, 438 U.S. at 124, in a manner that secures an "average reciprocity of advantage" to everyone concerned. *Pennsylvania Coal Co. v. Mahon*, 260 U.S. at 415. And the functional basis for permitting the government, by regulation, to affect property values without compensation—that "Government hardly could go on if to some extent values incident to property could not be diminished without paying for every such change in the general law," *Id.* at 413—does not apply to the relatively rare situations where the government has deprived a landowner of all economically beneficial uses.

On the other side of the balance, affirmatively supporting a compensation requirement, is the fact that regulations that leave the owner of land without economically beneficial or productive options for its use—typically, as here, by requiring land to be left substantially in its natural state—carry with them a heightened risk that private property is being pressed into some form of public service under the guise of mitigating serious public harm. As Justice Brennan explained: "From the government's point of view, the benefits flowing to the public from preservation of open space through regulation may be equally great as from creating a wildlife refuge through formal condemnation or increasing electricity production through a dam project that floods private property." *San Diego Gas & Elec. Co.* 450 U.S. at 652 (Brennan, J., dissenting). The many statutes on the books, both state and federal, that provide for the use of eminent domain to impose servitudes on private scenic lands preventing developmental uses, or to acquire such lands altogether, suggest the practical equivalence in this setting of negative regulation and appropriation.

We think, in short, that there are good reasons for our frequently expressed belief that when the owner of real property has been called upon to sacrifice all economically beneficial uses in the name of the common good, that is, to leave his property economically idle, he has suffered a taking.

The trial court found Lucas's two beachfront lots to have been rendered valueless by respondent's enforcement of the coastal-zone construction ban. Under Lucas's theory of the case, which rested upon our "no economically viable use" statements, that finding entitled him to compensation. Lucas believed it unnecessary to take issue with either the purposes behind the Beachfront Management Act, or the means chosen by the South Carolina Legislature to effectuate those purposes. The South Carolina Supreme Court, however, thought otherwise. In its view, the Beachfront Management Act was no ordinary enactment, but involved an exercise of South Carolina's "police powers" to mitigate the harm to the public interest that petitioner's use of his land might occasion. 404 S.E.2d at 899. By neglecting to dispute the findings enumerated in the Act or otherwise to challenge the legislature's purposes, petitioner "concede[d] that the beach/dune area of South Carolina's shores is an extremely valuable public resource; that the erection of new construction, *inter alia*, contributes to the erosion and destruction of this public resource; and that discouraging new construction in close proximity to the beach/dune area is necessary to prevent a great public harm." *Id.* at 898. In the court's view, these concessions brought petitioner's challenge within a long line of this Court's cases sustaining against Due Process and Takings Clause challenges the State's use of its "police powers" to enjoin a property owner from activities akin to public nuisances. *See Mugler v. Kansas*, 123 U.S. 623 (1887) (law prohibiting manufacture of alcoholic beverages); *Hadacheck v. Sebastian*, 239 U.S. 394 (1915) (law barring operation of brick mill in residential area); *Miller v. Schoene*, 276 U.S. 272 (1928) (order to destroy diseased cedar trees to prevent infection of nearby orchards); *Goldblatt v. Hempstead*, 369 U.S. 590 (1962) (law effectively preventing continued operation of quarry in residential area).

It is correct that many of our prior opinions have suggested that "harmful or noxious uses" of property may be proscribed by government regulation without the requirement of compensation. For a number of reasons, however, we think the South Carolina Supreme Court was too quick to conclude that that principle decides the present case. The "harmful or noxious uses" principle was the Court's early attempt to describe in theoretical terms why government may, consistent with the Takings Clause, affect property values by regulation without incurring an obligation to compensate—a reality we nowadays acknowledge explicitly with respect to the full scope of the State's police power. * * *

The transition from our early focus on control of "noxious" uses to our contemporary understanding of the broad realm within which government may regulate without compensation was an easy one, since the distinction between "harm-preventing" and "benefit-conferring" regulation is often in the eye of the beholder. It is quite possible, for example, to describe in either fashion the ecological, economic, and aesthetic concerns that inspired the South Carolina legislature in the present case. One could say that imposing a servitude on Lucas's land is necessary in order to prevent his use of it from "harming" South Carolina's ecological resources; or, instead, in order to achieve the "benefits" of an ecological preserve.... A given restraint will be seen as mitigating "harm" to the adjacent parcels or securing a "benefit" for them, depending upon the observer's evaluation of the relative importance of the use that the restraint favors. Whether Lucas's construction of single-family residences on his parcels should be described as bringing "harm" to South Carolina's adjacent ecological resources thus depends principally upon whether the describer believes that the State's use interest in nurturing those resources is so important that any competing adjacent use must yield.

When it is understood that "prevention of harmful use" was merely our early formulation of the police power justification necessary to sustain (without compensation) any regulatory diminution in value; and that the distinction between regulation that "prevents harmful use" and that which "confers benefits" is difficult, if not impossible, to discern on an objective, value-free basis; it becomes self-evident that noxious-use logic cannot serve as a touchstone to distinguish regulatory "takings"—which require compensation—from regulatory deprivations that do not require compensation. A *fortiori* the legislature's recitation of a noxious-use justification cannot be the basis for departing from our categorical rule that total regulatory takings must be compensated. If it were, departure would virtually always be allowed. The South Carolina Supreme Court's approach would essentially nullify *Mahon*'s affirmation of limits to the noncompensable exercise of the police power. Our cases provide no support for this: None of them that employed the logic of "harmful use" prevention to sustain a regulation involved an allegation that the regulation wholly eliminated the value of the claimant's land.

Where the State seeks to sustain regulation that deprives land of all economically beneficial use, we think it may resist compensation only if the logically antecedent inquiry into the nature of the owner's estate shows that the proscribed use interests were not part of his title to begin with. This accords, we think, with our "takings" jurisprudence, which has traditionally been guided by the understandings of our citizens regarding the content of, and the State's power over, the "bundle of rights" that they acquire when they obtain title to property. It seems to us that the property owner necessarily expects the uses of his property to be restricted, from time to time, by various measures newly enacted by the State in legitimate exercise of its police powers; "[a]s long recognized, some values are enjoyed under an implied limitation and must yield to the police power." *Pennsylvania Coal Co. v. Mahon,* 260 U.S. at 413. And in the case of personal property, by reason of the State's traditionally high degree of control over commercial dealings, he ought to be aware of the possibility that new regulation might even render his property economically worthless (at least if the property's only economically productive use is sale or manufacture for sale), *see Andrus v. Allard,* 444 U.S. 51, 66–67 (1979) (prohibition on sale of eagle feathers). In the case of land, however, we think the notion pressed by the Council that title is somehow held subject to the "implied limitation" that the State may subsequently eliminate all economically valuable use is inconsistent with the historical compact recorded in the Takings Clause that has become part of our constitutional culture.

Where "permanent physical occupation" of land is concerned, we have refused to allow the government to decree it anew (without compensation), no matter how weighty the asserted "public interests" involved, *Loretto v. Teleprompter Manhattan CATV Corp.,* 458 U.S. at 426—though we assuredly *would* permit the government to assert a permanent easement that was a pre-existing limitation upon the landowner's title. We believe similar treatment must be accorded confiscatory regulations, *i.e.,* regulations that prohibit all economically beneficial use of land. Any limitation so severe cannot be newly legislated or decreed (without compensation), but must inhere in the title itself, in the restrictions that background principles of the State's law of property and nuisance already place upon land ownership. A law or decree with such an effect must, in other words, do no more than duplicate the result that could have been achieved in the courts—by adjacent landowners (or other uniquely affected persons) under the State's law of private nuisance, or by the State under its complementary power to abate nuisances that affect the public generally, or otherwise.

On this analysis, the owner of a lake bed, for example, would not be entitled to compensation when he is denied the requisite permit to engage in a landfilling operation that would have the effect of flooding others' land. Nor the corporate owner of a nuclear generating plant, when it is directed to remove all improvements from its land upon discovery that the plant sits astride an earthquake fault. Such regulatory action may well have the effect of eliminating the land's only economically productive use, but it does not proscribe a productive use that was previously permissible under relevant property and nuisance principles. The use of these properties for what are now expressly prohibited purposes was always unlawful, and (subject to other constitutional limitations) it was open to the State at any point to make the implication of those background principles of nuisance and property law explicit.... [T]hat the Takings Clause does not require compensation when an owner is barred from putting land to a use that is proscribed by those "existing rules or understandings" is surely unexceptional. When, however, a regulation that declares "off-limits" all economically productive or beneficial uses of land goes beyond what the relevant background principles would dictate, compensation must be paid to sustain it. * * *

It seems unlikely that common-law principles would have prevented the erection of any habitable or productive improvements on petitioner's land; they rarely support prohibition of the "essential use" of land, *Curtin v. Benson,* 222 U.S. 78, 86 (1911). The question, however, is one of state law to be dealt with on remand. We emphasize that to win its case South Carolina must do more than proffer the legislature's declaration that the uses Lucas desires are inconsistent with the public interest, or the conclusory assertion that they violate a common-law maxim such as *sic utere tuo ut alienum non laedas*. As we have said, a "State, by *ipse dixit*, may not transform private property into public property without compensation...." *Webb's Fabulous Pharmacies, Inc. v. Beckwith,* 449 U.S. 155, 164 (1980). Instead, as it would be required to do if it sought to restrain Lucas in a common-law action for public nuisance, South Carolina must identify background principles of nuisance and property law that prohibit the uses he now intends in the circumstances in which the property is presently found. Only on this showing can the State fairly claim that, in proscribing all such beneficial uses, the Beachfront Management Act is taking nothing.[18] * * *

The judgment is reversed and the cause remanded for proceedings not inconsistent with this opinion. * * *

Justice Blackmun, dissenting. * * *   DISSENT

Today the Court launches a missile to kill a mouse.

The State of South Carolina prohibited petitioner Lucas from building a permanent structure on his property from 1988 to 1990. Relying on an unreviewed (and implausible) state trial court finding that this restriction left Lucas' property valueless, this Court granted review to determine whether compensation must be paid in cases where the State prohibits all economic use of real estate. According to the Court, such an occasion never has arisen in any of our prior cases, and the Court imagines that it will arise "relatively rarely" or only in "extraordinary circumstances." Almost certainly it did not happen in this case.

Nonetheless, the Court presses on to decide the issue, and as it does, it ... creates simultaneously a new categorical rule and an exception (neither of which is rooted in our prior case law, common law, or common sense). I protest not only the Court's decision, but each step taken to reach it. More fundamentally, I question the Court's wisdom in issuing sweeping new rules to decide such a narrow case. * * *

In 1972 Congress passed the Coastal Zone Management Act. The Act was designed to provide States with money and incentives to carry out Congress' goal of protecting the public from shoreline erosion and coastal hazards. In the 1980 amendments to the Act, Congress directed States to enhance their coastal programs by "preventing or significantly reducing threats to life and the destruction of property by eliminating development and redevelopment in high-hazard areas."[1] 16 U.S.C. § 1456b(a)(2) (1988 ed., Supp. II).

---

18. Justice Blackmun decries our reliance on background nuisance principles at least in part because he believes those principles to be as manipulable as we find the "harm prevention"/"benefit conferral" dichotomy. There is no doubt some leeway in a court's interpretation of what existing state law permits—but not remotely as much, we think, as in a legislative crafting of the reasons for its confiscatory regulation. We stress that an affirmative decree eliminating all economically beneficial uses may be defended only if an objectively reasonable application of relevant precedents would exclude those beneficial uses in the circumstances in which the land is presently found.

1. The country has come to recognize that uncontrolled beachfront development can cause serious damage to life and property.... Hurricane Hugo's September 1989 attack upon South Carolina's coastline, for example, caused 29 deaths and approximately $6 billion in property damage, much of it the result of uncontrolled beachfront development.... The beachfront buildings are not only themselves destroyed in such a

Petitioner Lucas is a contractor, manager, and part owner of the Wild Dune development on the Isle of Palms. He has lived there since 1978. In December 1986, he purchased two of the last four pieces of vacant property in the development. The area is notoriously unstable. In roughly half of the last 40 years, all or part of petitioner's property was part of the beach or flooded twice daily by the ebb and flow of the tide. Between 1957 and 1963, petitioner's property was under water. Between 1963 and 1973 the shoreline was 100 to 150 feet onto petitioner's property. In 1973 the first line of stable vegetation was about halfway through the property. Between 1981 and 1983, the Isle of Palms issued 12 emergency orders for sandbagging to protect property in the Wild Dune development. Determining that local habitable structures were in imminent danger of collapse, the Council issued permits for two rock revetments to protect condominium developments near petitioner's property from erosion; one of the revetments extends more than halfway onto one of his lots. * * *

I first question the Court's rationale in creating a category that obviates a "case-specific inquiry into the public interest advanced," if all economic value has been lost. * * * This Court repeatedly has recognized the ability of government, in certain circumstances, to regulate property without compensation no matter how adverse the financial effect on the owner may be. More than a century ago, the Court explicitly upheld the right of States to prohibit uses of property injurious to public health, safety, or welfare without paying compensation: "A prohibition simply upon the use of property for purposes that are declared, by valid legislation, to be injurious to the health, morals, or safety of the community, cannot, in any just sense, be deemed a taking or an appropriation of property." *Mugler v. Kansas,* 123 U.S. 623, 668–69 (1887). On this basis, the Court upheld an ordinance effectively prohibiting operation of a previously lawful brewery, although the "establishments will become of no value as property." *Id.* at 664.

Mugler was only the beginning in a long line of cases. In *Powell v. Pennsylvania,* 127 U.S. 678 (1888), the Court upheld legislation prohibiting the manufacture of oleomargarine, despite the owner's allegation that "if prevented from continuing it, the value of his property employed therein would be entirely lost and he be deprived of the means of livelihood." *Id.* at 682. In *Hadacheck v. Sebastian,* 239 U.S. 394 (1915), the Court upheld an ordinance prohibiting a brickyard, although the owner had made excavations on the land that prevented it from being utilized for any purpose but a brickyard. *Id.* at 405. In *Miller v. Schoene,* 276 U.S. 272 (1928), the Court held that the Fifth Amendment did not require Virginia to pay compensation to the owner of cedar trees ordered destroyed to prevent a disease from spreading to nearby apple orchards. * * * And in *Keystone Bituminous Coal,* the Court summarized over 100 years of precedent: "the Court has repeatedly upheld regulations that destroy or adversely affect real property interests." 480 U.S. at 489, n.18.

The Court recognizes that "our prior opinions have suggested that 'harmful or noxious uses' of property may be proscribed by government regulation without the requirement of compensation," but seeks to reconcile them with its categorical rule by claiming that the Court never has upheld a regulation when the owner alleged the loss of all economic value. Even if the Court's factual premise were correct, its understanding of the Court's cases is distorted. In none of the cases did the Court suggest that the right of a State to prohibit certain activities without paying compensation turned on the availability of

storm, "but they are often driven, like battering rams, into adjacent inland homes." Moreover, the development of-

ten destroys the natural sand dune barriers that provide storm breaks.

some residual valuable use. Instead, the cases depended on whether the government interest was sufficient to prohibit the activity, given the significant private cost.

These cases rest on the principle that the State has full power to prohibit an owner's use of property if it is harmful to the public. "[S]ince no individual has a right to use his property so as to create a nuisance or otherwise harm others, the State has not 'taken' anything when it asserts its power to enjoin the nuisance-like activity." *Keystone Bituminous Coal,* 480 U.S. at 491, n.20. It would make no sense under this theory to suggest that an owner has a constitutionally protected right to harm others, if only he makes the proper showing of economic loss. * * *

Ultimately even the Court cannot embrace the full implications of its *per se* rule: it eventually agrees that there cannot be a categorical rule for a taking based on economic value that wholly disregards the public need asserted. Instead, the Court decides that it will permit a State to regulate all economic value only if the State prohibits uses that would not be permitted under "background principles of nuisance and property law." *Ante,* at 19.

Until today, the Court explicitly had rejected the contention that the government's power to act without paying compensation turns on whether the prohibited activity is a common-law nuisance. The brewery closed in *Mugler* itself was not a common-law nuisance, and the Court specifically stated that it was the role of the legislature to determine what measures would be appropriate for the protection of public health and safety. *See* 123 U.S. at 661. In upholding the state action in *Miller,* the Court found it unnecessary to "weigh with nicety the question whether the infected cedars constitute a nuisance according to common law; or whether they may be so declared by statute." Instead the Court has relied in the past, as the South Carolina Court has done here, on legislative judgments of what constitutes a harm. * * *

The threshold inquiry for imposition of the Court's new rule, "deprivation of all economically valuable use," itself cannot be determined objectively. As the Court admits, whether the owner has been deprived of all economic value of his property will depend on how "property" is defined. The "composition of the denominator in our 'deprivation' fraction," is the dispositive inquiry. Yet there is no "objective" way to define what that denominator should be. "We have long understood that any land-use regulation can be characterized as the 'total' deprivation of an aptly defined entitlement.... Alternatively, the same regulation can always be characterized as a mere 'partial' withdrawal from full, unencumbered ownership of the landholding affected by the regulation...." Michelman, *Takings, 1987,* 88 Colum. L. Rev. 1600, 1614 (1988).

The Court's decision in *Keystone Bituminous Coal* illustrates this principle perfectly. In *Keystone,* the Court determined that the "support estate" was "merely a part of the entire bundle of rights possessed by the owner." 480 U.S. at 501. Thus, the Court concluded that the support estate's destruction merely eliminated one segment of the total property. *Ibid.* The dissent, however, characterized the support estate as a distinct property interest that was wholly destroyed. *Id.* at 519. The Court could agree on no "value-free basis" to resolve this dispute.

Even more perplexing, however, is the Court's reliance on common-law principles of nuisance in its quest for a value-free taking jurisprudence. In determining what is a nuisance at common law, state courts make exactly the decision that the Court finds so troubling when made by the South Carolina General Assembly today: they determine whether the use is harmful. Common-law public and private nuisance law is simply a determination whether a particular use causes harm. There is nothing magical in the reasoning of judges long dead. They determined a harm in the same way as state judges and legislatures do today. If judges in the 18th and 19th centuries can distinguish a harm from a benefit, why not judges in the 20th century, and if judges can, why not legislators? There simply is no reason to believe that new interpretations of the hoary common law nuisance doctrine will be particularly "objective" or "value-free." Once one abandons the level of generality of *sic utere tuo ut alienum non laedas*, one searches in vain, I think, for anything resembling a principle in the common law of nuisance. * * *

I dissent.

QUESTIONS AND DISCUSSION

1. In light of the Court's opinion in *Lucas*, how would you describe the law of takings? Did Justice Scalia's decision significantly alter the balancing framework of *Penn Central*? How often will a regulation deny property of all economically beneficial use? What should a property owner have to show to demonstrate that her property has no remaining economic use?

2. Whether a regulation denies an owner all economically beneficial use of his property depends upon a critical question that Justice Scalia explores in footnote 7 but ultimately leaves unanswered: what precisely is the property interest against which the loss of value is to be measured? In *Penn Central*, the Court had said that a takings analysis "does not divide a single parcel into discrete segments and attempt to determine whether rights in a particular segment have been entirely abrogated"; rather it focuses "both on the character of the action and on the nature and extent of the interference with rights in the parcel as a whole." 438 U.S. at 130–31. But discerning what property interest is a "discrete segment" and what is the "parcel as a whole" is also uncertain. This "segmentation" or "denominator" question has perplexed the courts in the aftermath of *Lucas*. Suppose, for example, that application of the Endangered Species Act (ESA) precludes a landowner from harvesting any timber on 90% of his land. If the landowner sells the harvestable 10% to another company, can she then make a categorical takings claim on the remaining parcel (the original 90%) under *Lucas*? As a second illustration, suppose that application of the ESA prohibits a farmer from taking water from a stream, destroying his irrigated crops and requiring him to turn to dry-land farming. What is the relevant property interest? Is it his interest in diverting the water or is it the farmland? Does it matter if the right to withdraw water is a riparian right appurtenant to the land or an appropriative (usufructory) right to withdraw the water and put it to use wherever it is beneficial?

3. Suppose that application of the Endangered Species Act to prevent a timber harvest on 90% of a landowner's property does not rise to the level of a *per se* taking, does that mean that the 90% figure is irrelevant? How will it factor into the analysis of whether the regulation "goes too far"?

4. Once a court determines that a particular regulation denies the property owner of all economically beneficial use of his property, is compensation automatically warranted? What additional analysis must a court perform?

5. How might the recognition of the ecosystem services value of Lucas' sand dunes or of another landowner's wetland effect the Court's takings jurisprudence? Following the Court's decision, Professor Lazarus, who represented the South Carolina Coastal Council in *Lucas*, argued:

> The majority's current zeal to repel the perceived environmentalist assault on private property rests on serious misperceptions regarding the nature of land. The Court does not appreciate the now-settled ecological notion that land "is not merely soil; it is a fountain of energy flowing though a circuit of soils, plants, and animals." [ALDO LEOPOLD, A SAND COUNTY ALMANAC.] Land is not a discrete, severable resource that respects the surveyor's binary-based boundaries. It is part of a complex, interdependent ecological system. Nor does the Court appreciate that over the past century our relationship to the land has fundamentally changed. Land is now a highly regulated commodity, and its ownership is no longer the touchstone of human autonomy or the source of individual freedom.

Richard J. Lazarus, *Putting the Correct "Spin" on* Lucas, 45 STAN. L. REV. 1411, 1421 (1993). Is Professor Lazarus offering a description, making a normative argument, or both? If Professor Lazarus is right, how does Leopold's ecological insight fit into a *Lucas* or *Penn Central* analysis? Does it effect the analysis of the economically beneficial uses of the land? Is there any place in takings law for measuring the nonmarket value of land? Might an ecological understanding of the ecosystem services provided by land impact what land uses constitute a nuisance? Would it fit within Justice Scalia's view of the background principles of common law that inhere in the title of property? Professor Lazarus also argues that ownership of land and natural resources "is no longer . . . the source of individual freedom." What does he mean? How was the Takings Clause designed to protect individual freedom and what has changed?

6. On remand in *Lucas*, South Carolina decided that no common law principle justified the prohibition on Lucas' use of his land and thus the 1988 Beachfront Management Act had worked a taking of Lucas' property. 424 S.E.2d 484 (S.C. 1992). The court ordered that Lucas' damages be calculated from the time of the Act's passage to the time of its order. The court awarded this "temporary taking" remedy because in 1990, the South Carolina Legislature had amended the Beachfront Act to allow the issuance of "special permits" for the construction of habitable structures seaward of the baseline. Lucas, said the court, could seek compensation for a permanent taking if the permit was denied. In allowing compensation for a temporary taking, South Carolina was adhering to the United States Supreme Court's decision in *First English Evangelical Lutheran Church of Glendale v. County of Los Angeles*, 482 U.S. 304 (1987). There, the Court had held that "where the government's activities have already worked a taking of all use of property, no subsequent action by the government can relieve it of the duty to provide compensation for the period during which the taking was effective." *Id*. at 321.

7. Suppose that rather than prohibiting Lucas from developing his parcels, the Beachfront Management Act had instead imposed a three-year moratorium on any and all coastal zone development pending the adoption of a dunes management plan. Would the moratorium still have been a temporary taking of Lucas' property? In *Tahoe–Sierra Preservation Coun-*

cil, Inc. v. Tahoe Regional Planning Agency, 535 U.S. 302 (2002), the Court held that a 32–month moratorium on development around Lake Tahoe did not constitute a categorical taking. The Court explained:

> The categorical rule that we applied in *Lucas* states that compensation is required when a regulation deprives an owner of "all economically beneficial uses" of his land. *Id.*, at 1019. Under that rule, a statute that "wholly eliminated the value" of Lucas' fee simple title clearly qualified as a taking. But our holding was limited to "the extraordinary circumstance when no productive or economically beneficial use of land is permitted." *Id.*, at 1017.... Anything less than a "complete elimination of value," or a "total loss," the Court acknowledged, would require the kind of analysis applied in *Penn Central*. *Lucas*, 505 U.S., at 1019–1020, n. 8.

> * * * Petitioners seek to bring this case under the rule announced in *Lucas* by arguing that we can effectively sever a 32–month segment from the remainder of each landowner's fee simple estate, and then ask whether that segment has been taken in its entirety by the moratoria. Of course, defining the property interest taken in terms of the very regulation being challenged is circular. With property so divided, every delay would become a total ban; the moratorium and the normal permit process alike would constitute categorical takings. Petitioners' "conceptual severance" argument is unavailing because it ignores *Penn Central*'s admonition that in regulatory takings cases we must focus on "the parcel as a whole." 438 U.S., at 130–131. * * *

> An interest in real property is defined by the metes and bounds that describe its geographic dimensions and the term of years that describes the temporal aspect of the owner's interest. Both dimensions must be considered if the interest is to be viewed in its entirety. Hence, a permanent deprivation of the owner's use of the entire area is a taking of "the parcel as a whole," whereas a temporary restriction that merely causes a diminution in value is not. Logically, a fee simple estate cannot be rendered valueless by a temporary prohibition on economic use, because the property will recover value as soon as the prohibition is lifted. * * *

> [T]he duration of the restriction is one of the important factors that a court must consider in the appraisal of a regulatory takings claim, but with respect to that factor as with respect to other factors, the "temptation to adopt what amount to per se rules in either direction must be resisted." *Palazzolo*, 533 U.S., at 636 (O'Connor, J., concurring).... We conclude, therefore, that the interest in "fairness and justice" will be best served by relying on the familiar *Penn Central* approach when deciding cases like this, rather than by attempting to craft a new categorical rule.

535 U.S. at 330–32, 342. What is the "familiar *Penn Central* approach" to which the Court refers? In addition to including the temporal aspect of the owner's interest in valuing the property, the Court suggested that the focus of *Lucas* was on whether the moratorium or regulation at issue completely eliminates the property's value rather than whether it eliminates all economically beneficial use. In fact, although the Tahoe moratorium prohibited all development, the Forest Service purchased restricted lots while the moratorium was in effect. *Id.* at 317 n.12.

In dissent, Chief Justice Rehnquist criticized the majority's reading of *Lucas*, arguing that "the Court's position that value is the *sine qua non* of the *Lucas* rule proves too much. Surely, the land at issue in *Lucas* retained some market value based on the contingency, which soon came to fruition, that the development ban would be amended." *Id.* at 350 (Rehnquist, C.J., dissenting). Rehnquist also contended that the Court's previous "opinion in *First English Evangelical Lutheran Church of Glendale v. County of Los Angeles*, 482 U.S. 304 (1987), rejects any distinction between temporary and permanent takings when a landowner is deprived of all economically beneficial use of his land." 535 U.S. at 347 (Rehnquist, C.J., dissenting). But as the majority saw it, *First English* addressed only the remedy issue and not whether a temporary taking had occurred. *Id.* at 328 ("In *First English*, ... the Court's statement of its holding was ... unambiguous: 'We merely hold that where the government's activities have already worked a taking of all use of property, no subsequent action by the government can relieve it of the duty to provide compensation for the period during which the taking was effective.' ").

How much of the *Lucas* decision is left after *Tahoe–Sierra*? If regulations that deny an owner all economically beneficial use of land were infrequent before *Tahoe–Sierra*, why are they likely to be even less frequent now? How is the Court's focus on property value instead of economic use likely to impact takings law and *Lucas*? How is the Court's focus on the temporal component of property likely to impact the denominator analysis?

Suppose that in a drought year, there is not enough water in a stream to satisfy the uses of irrigation farmers and an endangered fish which needs a certain instream flow to survive. Suppose also that the United States Fish and Wildlife Service stops several farmers from exercising any portion of their water rights until the drought abates. Does Fish and Wildlife's order constitute a taking?

8. Suppose that Lucas had purchased his lots after passage of the Beachfront Management Act, paying a price that was discounted by the cost of filing a takings claim and the possibility that a takings claim would be unsuccessful. Would the Beachfront Management Act then inhere in his title, necessarily defeating any claim of a categorical taking? The Supreme Court addressed that issue in *Palazzolo v. Rhode Island*, 533 U.S. 606 (2001), although in a *Penn Central*-type context where the regulated property retained some economically beneficial use. The Court held that the fact that a property owner purchased property after passage of the regulation prompting the takings claim is not alone sufficient to avoid a takings claim. The timing of acquisition is simply one factor to be considered as part of the *Penn Central* analysis of the property owner's reasonable investment-backed expectations. *Id.* at 626–30. Could a post-regulation purchaser ever claim denial of all economically beneficial use or would his purchase alone defeat the claim? How likely are such cases to arise?

9. Another type of regulatory takings case are so-called exaction cases where the government conditions development of property upon the landowner giving up some interest in the land or paying a fee. To survive a takings challenge, the proposed exaction or condition must [1] have a reasonable nexus to a legitimate state interest and [2] be roughly proportional to the impact of the development. Thus, in *Nollan v. California Coastal Comm'n*, 483 U.S. 825 (1987), the State of California conditioned the permit for remodeling an oceanfront bungalow on the landowner's giving the public an easement across a portion of the beach between his house and the ocean. California asserted that, when viewed from the non-ocean side, the increased height of the remodeled bungalow would impair the public's visual access to the beach and thereby create a psychological barrier for passersby that could be remedied in part by giving the public increased access across the beach on the ocean side of the bungalow. Although the Supreme Court found the State's interest legitimate, it held that the condition was a taking because there was not a sufficiently close fit between the permit condition (an easement between the house and the ocean that would only help those already walking on the beach) and the justification for that condition (impairment of the public's visual and psychological access from the other side of the remodeled bungalow). In *Dolan v. City of Tigard*, 512 U.S. 374 (1994), the city conditioned plaintiff's permit to expand her hardware store and to pave thirty-nine parking places on her dedication of one part of her property for a public greenway to help with storm drainage and another part for a bicycle/pedestrian pathway. Although the Court found that the conditions bore a reasonable relationship to the development, it concluded that they were not roughly proportional to the impacts of the proposed development.

10. In *Agins v. City of Tiburon*, 447 U.S. 255, 260 (1980), the Supreme Court stated that a regulation could result in a taking if it failed to "substantially advance" a legitimate state interest. Whether this due process inquiry should provide a separate method for proving a Fifth Amendment taking has long troubled commentators. In 2005, in *Lingle v. Chevron*, 544 U.S. 528 (2005), the Supreme Court clarified this confused area of takings law. In *Lingle*, the lower courts had struck down a Hawaii statute limiting the rent oil companies could charge to dealers who leased service stations owned by the companies. The lower courts, relying on *Agins*, had said that the rent cap effected a taking because it did not substantially advance a legitimate state interest. In reversing, the Supreme Court made clear that regulatory takings law is targeted at regulations that are the functional equivalent of an appropriation of, or ouster from, private property. Whether a regulation substantially advances a legitimate state interest, said the Court, is not "an appropriate test for determining whether a regulation effects a Fifth Amendment taking." *Id.* at 532. Although *Lingle*'s repudiation of the *Agins* "substantially advances" due process inquiry substantially clarified takings law, it did raise a question whether the third prong of the traditional *Penn Central* balancing test—which considers the character of the governmental action—is still relevant. If takings law is to focus on severity of the burden imposed by the regulation as opposed to the legitimacy of the regulation, perhaps courts will limit themselves to consideration of *Penn Central*'s first two prongs, namely the magnitude of a regulation's economic impact and the degree to which it interferes with legitimate expectation interests of the owner.

11. Stepping back from positivist arguments about the meaning of the Fifth Amendment and the Supreme Court's precedents, consider how you might structure takings law if writing on a clean slate. Does your desired structure depend in part upon where you come down on the tension between the insights of public choice theory and the potential for administrative agency capture versus the progressive notion of expert administrative agencies working in a more disinterested fashion to achieve the public interest? Does your view depend upon how you perceive the distributional consequences of regulation and just compensation to property owners? What other premises underlie your reaction to the law of takings?

12. Does the fact that the property right allegedly taken has a close nexus to federal property make a difference in the takings analysis? In *United States v. Locke*, 471 U.S. 84 (1985), the Court, in deciding whether a provision of the Federal Land Policy Management Act that interfered with an unpatented mining claim (a property right to minerals contained in federal lands to which the United States retains underlying fee title) amounted to a taking, said,

> This power to qualify existing property rights is particularly broad with respect to the "character" of the property rights at issue here. . . . The United States, as owner of the underlying fee title to the public domain, maintains broad powers over the terms and conditions upon which the public lands can be used, leased, and acquired. . . . Claimants thus take their mineral interests with the knowledge that the Government retains substantial regulatory power over those interests.

Id. at 104–05. How might underlying federal fee title impact application of the *Penn Central* factor of the owner's investment-backed expectations? Where the United States owns the fee, how might that impact the denominator question raised by *Lucas*? Might it be easier to make out a takings claim where the regulation limits or eliminates an unpatented mining claim, a water right, a federal coal lease, or an Indian tribe's treaty right to hunt or fish?

13. Even when not obligated by the Constitution, Congress and state legislatures may award compensation to property owners whose land is devalued by government regulation. Congress, for example, has chosen to give compensation to those impacted by a federal assertion of its navigation servitude even though the federal government's exercise of its underlying servitude is not a taking. *See* 4 WATERS AND WATER RIGHTS § 35.02(c)(1) (Robert E. Beck ed., 1996). In recent years, Congress has considered but rejected a number of bills proposing that landowners be compensated when regulation devalues their property by a certain percentage. Are these compensation proposals wise public policy? Isn't part of the value of property created by the reciprocal benefits of land use regulation? Do we want regulators to think twice about the costs of regulation, or will it cause them to forego regulation that redounds to the public benefit? If the Endangered Species Act cuts in half the amount of timber a company can harvest or the amount of water a farmer can divert, should the public pay?

Since 1991, all fifty states have considered some kind of takings or compensation bill. Many states have enacted statutes requiring some form of takings impact analysis, which obligates state agencies, and sometimes local governments, to consider the possibility that the regulation will be ruled a taking and what the potential compensation obligation could be. Less frequently, states have imposed statutory limits on the percent reduction in property value that a regulation can impose without triggering a compensation requirement. "Mississippi places the compensation threshold at a 40% reduction of fair market value, Texas at 25%, Louisiana at 20%, and Oregon at any diminution in the fair market value of the private property." *See* Hannah Jacobs, *Searching for Balance in the Aftermath of the 2006 Takings Initiatives*, 116 Yale L. J. 1518, 1528–29 (2007).

14. For a thorough analysis of the Supreme Court's *Lucas* decision, you may want to review a symposium published at 45 STAN. L. REV. 1369 (1993) containing articles by Richard Epstein, William Fisher, Richard Lazarus, and Joseph Sax.

PROBLEM EXERCISE: APPLYING THE LAW OF TAKINGS

Consider the following facts from *Loveladies Harbor, Inc. v. United States*, 28 F.3d 1171 (Fed. Cir. 1994):

> The property at issue in this dispute is a 12.5 acre parcel (the parcel) consisting of 11.5 acres of wetlands and one acre of filled land, located on Long Beach Island, Ocean County, New Jersey. . . . The 12.5 acres is part of a 51 acre parcel owned by Loveladies, which in turn is part of an original 250 acre tract which Loveladies had acquired in 1958. The balance of the 250 acres—199 acres—had been developed before 1972 and the enactment of § 404 of the Clean Water Act.

> In order to develop the remaining 51 acre parcel for residential use, Loveladies needed to fill 50 acres, the one acre having been previously filled, and that in turn required Loveladies to obtain permission from both the New Jersey Department of Environmental Protection (NJDEP) and the [Army Corps of Engineers]. That process proved to be lengthy and contentious, marked by several years of negotiation (with Loveladies submitting progressively less ambitious and less environmentally objectionable proposals), a 1977 permit denial, appeal of that denial to the Commissioner of NJDEP, and judicial review in state court.

> During the course of the proceedings, NJDEP offered, as a compromise, permission for Loveladies to develop 12.5 of the 51 acres. Loveladies initially declined that offer. Eventually Loveladies acquiesced to the 12.5 acre limitation, the dispute was resolved, and the permit, on September 9, 1981, issued. The permit granted permission to fill and develop 11.5 acres in addition to the one acre which had been filled previously—this is the 12.5 acre parcel at issue—and to construct 35 single family homes thereon.

> Loveladies then sought the requisite federal [§ 404] permit for the development project. As required, the Corps sought the views of the counterpart state agency, the NJDEP. NJDEP in its response acknowledged that they had issued Loveladies the permit as they were obligated to do under the terms of the settlement, but denied that the permit approval was in compliance with the state's requirements. The response went on to explain that the 12.5 acre development would be "anachronistic," a "throwback to the 1950's–1960's style of shore development," and closed by noting, "[a] denial of the federal permit appears appropriate under this Division's understanding of the pertinent federal law."

> The Corps rejected Loveladies' § 404 permit application on May 5, 1982.

In light of *Lucas*, *Penn Central*, and *Tahoe–Sierra*, how do you think the Supreme Court would resolve a takings claim against the Corps? If you represented the plaintiff, what arguments would you make? If you worked at the Department of Justice, what arguments would you make on behalf of the United States?

———

D.   Free Exercise and Establishment Clause Limitations on Federal and State Power Over Natural Resources

Although the Takings Clause may be the most prominent limit on state and enumerated federal power over natural resources, it is not the only one. As described previously, the dormant commerce clause limits state power even in the absence of federal regulation. Federal and state authority over natural resources is also potentially limited by other provisions of the Bill of Rights and subsequent constitutional amendments. The primary controversies in this regard have revolved around whether certain federal natural resource policies violate the First Amendment's Free Exercise and Establishment Clauses. *See* U.S. Const. Amend. I ("Congress shall make no law respecting an establishment of religion, or prohibiting the free exercise thereof. . . ."). For example, in *United States v. Billie*, 667 F.Supp. 1485 (S.D. Fla. 1987), James Billie, a member and chairman of the Seminole Indian tribe, was charged with violating the Endangered Species Act for shooting an endangered Florida panther on the Seminole Indian reservation. In defense, Billie argued that prohibiting taking the panther violated his treaty right to hunt and his free exercise of religion because the panther played a role in Seminole religious and cultural practices. The court, however, rejected both arguments, noting that Congress could expressly abrogate treaty rights and had done so in the ESA and that the government's interest in protecting the panther outweighed Billie's religious interest. *Id.*

The Supreme Court's primary pronouncement on the issue of natural resource policy versus free exercise of religion came in *Lyng v. Northwest Indian Cemetery Protective Ass'n*, 485 U.S. 439 (1988). In *Lyng*, the plaintiffs challenged a Forest Service decision to build a logging road and permit timber harvesting in an area of the Six Rivers National Forest considered sacred by the Yurok, Tarok, and Tolowa Tribes. Plaintiffs, who used the area for religious rituals in which they would seek guidance and personal power by communing in solitude with pristine nature, asserted that the road and timber cut would hinder the free exercise of their religion. Asserting that plaintiffs' claim could give them "*de facto* beneficial ownership of some rather spacious tracts of public property" and would amount to a "subsidy of the Indian religion," the Court concluded that plaintiffs' free exercise rights could "not divest the Government of its right to use what is, after all, *its* land." *Id.* at 43 (emphasis in original). As the Court later clarified in *Employment Div. v. Smith*, 494 U.S. 872 (1990), neutral government policies of general application that impose burdens on religious action do not violate the Free Exercise Clause. Government is only prohibited from coercing or directly targeting religious beliefs or conduct.

In response to the Supreme Court's decision in *Smith*, Congress in 1993 passed the Religious Freedom Restoration Act (RFRA). 42 U.S.C. §§ 2000bb to 2000bb–4. RFRA statutorily reinstated the compelling government interest test rejected in *Smith*. Specifically, it provided that government action may not substantially burden an individual's free exercise of religion unless it furthers a compelling government interest and is the least restrictive means of furthering that interest. The Supreme Court declared RFRA unconstitutional as applied to the states in *City of Boerne v. Flores*, 521 U.S. 507 (1997), but did not address whether the Act was constitutional as applied to the federal government. Subsequent federal courts have upheld RFRA as applied to the federal government. *See, e.g., Sutton v. Providence St. Joseph Medical Center*, 192 F.3d 826, 832 (9th Cir. 1999).

How RFRA might impact a case like *Lyng* where the federal government has a proprietary interest in the public land associated with a free exercise claim is a difficult question. In *Navajo Nation v. U.S. Forest Service*, Native Americans from thirteen different Indian tribes protested a proposal to allow a ski resort in the San Francisco Peaks area of northern Arizona to use treated sewage effluent for snowmaking at the resort. The tribes consider the Peaks sacred, believing "that water, soil, plants, and animals from the Peaks have spiritual and medicinal properties; that the Peaks and everything on them form an indivisible living entity; that the Peaks are home to deities and other spirit beings; that tribal members can communicate with higher powers through prayers and songs focused on the Peaks; and that the tribes have a duty to protect the Peaks." 408 F. Supp. 2d 866 (D. Ariz. 2006). A Ninth Circuit panel reversed, finding that the Forest Service's action violated RFRA and observing that for Christians the equivalent harm would be requiring baptism of children with reclaimed effluent. 479 F.3d 1024, 1048 (9th Cir. 2007). The court distinguished *Lyng* on the grounds that it was a pre-RFRA, Free Exercise Clause case and that the *Lyng* plaintiffs demanded complete exclusion of non-Indians from the contested area. The Ninth Circuit, however, reheard the case en banc and subsequently rejected the panel's reasoning. 535 F.3d 1058 (9th Cir. 2008). The court assumed, without deciding, that RFRA applied to the government's use and management of its land. 535 F.3d at 1067 n.9. It then reasoned that RFRA should be interpreted in conformity with *Lyng* and other cases decided prior to *Employment Div. v. Smith*. *Id*. at 1074. Relying primarily upon *Lyng*, the en banc court concluded that using the effluent would not "substantially burden" the Tribes' free exercise of religion within the meaning of the RFRA.

Whatever the protection of Native Americans' religious and cultural interests in natural resources offered by RFRA, Congress has enacted a variety of other laws that are designed to give tribal interests some protection. The Archeological Resources Protection Act (ARPA), 16 U.S.C. § 470aa–470*ll* (1994), prohibits the unauthorized excavation, removal, damage or defacing of archaeological resources on public or Indian lands. *Id*. § 470ee. The Native American Graves Protection and Repatriation Act (NAGPRA), 25 U.S.C. § 3001–3013 (1994), gives Indian tribes ownership of human remains and funerary and other sacred objects and cultural items. *Id*. at § 3002. And the National Historic Preservation Act (NHPA), 16 U.S.C. § 470, 470a–470m, 470w (1994), requires federal agencies to consider the effect of federal action on sites included on the National Register, which includes "properties of traditional religious and cultural importance." *Id.* at §§ 470f & 470a(d)(6). In addition, Executive Order 13,007 on Sacred Sites directs agencies to accommodate "access to and ceremonial use of Indian sacred sites" and "avoid actions adversely affecting the physical integrity of such sacred sites." Exec. Order No. 13,007, 61 Fed. Reg. 26,771 (May 24, 1996). *See generally* Sandra B. Zellmer, *Sustaining Geographies of Hope: Cultural Resources on Public Lands*, 73 U. Colo. L. Rev. 413 (2002) (discussing protection of tribal cultural resources). These efforts to manage federal lands to protect religious and cultural resources have prompted another constitutional issue, namely potential violation of the First Amendment's prohibition on the establishment of religion. The following case addresses the potential tension between federal land management and the Establishment Clause.

Bear Lodge Multiple Use Association v. Babbitt, 2 F.Supp.2d 1448 (D. Wyo. 1998)

Downes, District Judge.

The United States Department of the Interior, National Park Service ("NPS") issued a Final Climbing Management Plan ("FCMP") . . . for Devils Tower National Monument[1] in February of 1995. The FCMP "sets a new direction for managing climbing activity at the tower for the next three to five years"; its stated purpose being, "to protect the natural and cultural resources of Devils Tower and to provide for visitor enjoyment and appreciation of this unique feature." To protect against any new physical impacts to the tower, the FCMP provides that no new bolts or fixed pitons will be permitted on the tower, and new face routes requiring new bolt installation will not be permitted. The FCMP does allow individuals to replace already existing bolts and fixed pitons. In addition, the plan calls for access trails to be rehabilitated and maintained, and requires camouflaged climbing equipment, and climbing routes to be closed seasonally to protect raptor nests. The FCMP further provides that "[i]n respect for the reverence many American Indians hold for Devils Tower as a *sacred* site, rock climbers will be asked to *voluntarily* refrain from climbing on Devils Tower during the culturally significant month of June." * * *

1. The Devils Tower National Monument is located in northeast Wyoming. The FCMP reports that the Tower is a "sacred site" to several American Indian peoples of the northern plains who are increasingly traveling to the monument to perform "traditional cultural activities." Devils Tower is also eligible for inclusion to the national Register of Historic Places as a traditional cultural property. The FCMP further reports:

Recreational climbing at Devils Tower has increased dramatically from 312 climbers in 1973 to over 6,000 annually. New route development in the last ten years resulted [in] accelerated route development and bolt placement. Today the tower has about 220 named routes. Approxi-

mately 600 metal bolts are currently embedded in the rock along with several hundred metal pitons. Devils Tower is world famous for its crack climbing, which depends primarily on removable protection placed by climbers in cracks.

Activities performed by the numerous climbers on the tower during the spring through fall climbing season have affected nesting raptors, soil, vegetation, the integrity of the rock, the area's natural quiet, and the rock's physical appearance. Some American Indians have complained that the presence of climbers on the sacred butte and the placement of bolts in the rock has adversely impacted their traditional activities and seriously impaired the spiritual quality of the site.

The NPS represents that it will not enforce the voluntary closure, but will instead rely on climbers' self-regulation and a new "cross-cultural educational program" "to motivate climbers and other park visitors to comply." The NPS has also placed a sign at the base of the Tower in order to encourage visitors to stay on the trail surrounding the Tower.... The NPS, however, states that the voluntary closure will be "fully successful" only "when every climber personally chooses not to climb at Devils Tower during June out of respect for American Indian cultural values." * * *

In this case Plaintiffs ... allege that the NPS's plan wrongfully promotes religion in violation of the Establishment Clause of the First Amendment.

The Establishment Clause of the First Amendment states that "Congress shall make no law respecting an establishment of religion...." (U.S. Const. amend. I) The Courts of this country have long struggled with the type and extent of limitations on government action which these ten words impose. At its most fundamental level, the United States Supreme Court has concluded that this provision prohibits laws "which aid one religion, aid all religions, or prefer one religion over another." *Everson v. Board of Ed. of Ewing,* 330 U.S. 1, 15 (1947). Defining this prohibition on a case by case basis has proven a difficult endeavor, but the Court has developed a number of useful frameworks for conducting the analysis. In *Lemon v. Kurtzman,* 403 U.S. 602 (1971), the court established a three part test for delineating between proper and improper government actions. According to this test a governmental action does not offend the Establishment Clause if it (1) has a secular purpose, (2) does not have the principal or primary effect of advancing or inhibiting religion, and (3) does not foster an excessive entanglement with religion. *Lemon,* 403 U.S. at 612–13. In a concurring opinion in the case of *Lynch v. Donnelly,* 465 U.S. 668 (1984), Justice O'Connor sought to clarify the *Lemon* analysis by focusing on whether the government action endorsed religion. "Applying Justice O'Connor's refined analysis, the government impermissibly endorses religion if its conduct has either (1) the purpose or (2) the effect of conveying a message that religion or a particular religious belief is favored or preferred." *Bauchman v. West High School,* 132 F.3d 542, 551 (10th Cir.1997). Noting the current disarray surrounding the analysis of Establishment Clause challenges, the Tenth Circuit has adopted the approach that an action must satisfy both prongs of Justice O'Connor's "endorsement" and *Lemon's* excessive entanglement test in order to be proper. *Id.* at 552. * * *

Purpose

The ability to accommodate religious practices is an important consideration in determining what constitutes a proper purpose under the *Lemon* test and Justice O'Connor's endorsement test. The Plaintiffs can succeed on this prong only if they show that the action has no clear secular purpose or that despite a secular purpose the actual purpose is to endorse religion. *Bauchman,* 132 F.3d at 554. The Supreme Court has noted that requiring a government action to serve a secular legislative purpose, "does not mean that the [policy's] purpose must be unrelated to religion." *Corporation of the Presiding Bishop of the Church of Jesus Christ of Latter–Day Saints v. Amos,* 483 U.S. 327, 335 (1987). In cases of accommodation the Court has stated that "it is a permissible ... purpose to alleviate significant governmental interference with the ability of religious organizations to define and carry out their religious missions." *Id.* 483 U.S. at 336.

In this case the Defendants contend that the climbing plan was designed, in part, to eliminate barriers to American Indian's free practice of religion.

They argue that this type of accommodation is particularly appropriate in situations like this where impediments to worship arise because a group's sacred place of worship is found on property of the United States. Defendants assert that their actions are also aimed at fostering the preservation of the historical, social and cultural practices of Native Americans which are necessarily intertwined with their religious practices. While the purposes behind the voluntary climbing ban are directly related to Native American religious practices, that is not the end of the analysis. The purposes underlying the ban are really to remove barriers to religious worship occasioned by public ownership of the Tower. This is in the nature of accommodation, not promotion, and consequently is a legitimate secular purpose.

accommodation vs. promotion

Effect

Accommodation also plays a role in considering whether the principal effect of a policy is to advance religion. The Supreme Court has said; "[a] law is not unconstitutional simply because it *allows* churches to advance religion, which is their very purpose. For a law to have forbidden 'effects' under *Lemon,* it must be fair to say that the government itself has advanced religion through its own activities or influence." *Id.* 483 U.S. at 337. "[O]n occasion some advancement of religion will result from governmental action." *Lynch,* 465 U.S. at 683. This is particularly true in cases of accommodation. Appropriate accommodation does not have a principal effect of advancing religion. Appropriate accommodation, however, is a matter of degree. *See Amos,* 483 U.S. at 334–35. Actions step beyond the bounds of reasonable accommodation when they force people to support a given religion. * * *

In the context of the Free Exercise Clause, the Tenth Circuit drew a line demarcating impermissible accommodation in the area of public lands, ruling that the "[e]xercise of First Amendment freedoms may not be asserted to deprive the public of its normal use of an area." *Badoni v. Higginson,* 638 F.2d 172, 179 (1980). The record clearly reveals that climbing at the Devils Tower National Monument is a "legitimate recreational and historic" use of Park Service lands. If the NPS is, in effect, depriving individuals of their legitimate use of the monument in order to enforce the tribes' rights to worship, it has stepped beyond permissible accommodation and into the realm of promoting religion. The gravamen of the issue then becomes whether climbers are allowed meaningful access to the monument. Stated another way, is the climbing ban voluntary or is it actually an improper exercise of government coercion?

Plaintiffs argue that the "voluntary" ban is voluntary in name only. In support of their argument Plaintiffs note that the NPS has established a goal of having every climber personally choose not to climb at the Tower during June. Plaintiffs also cite to possible modifications to the FCMP if the NPS deems the voluntary ban unsuccessful. Specifically, they draw the Court's attention to the fact that if the plan does not result in a significant reduction of climbers on Devils Tower each June, then the NPS may convert the closure to a mandatory closure.

Neither of these factors is sufficient to transform the voluntary ban into a coerced ban. The Park Service's stated goals are not the measure of coercion, rather the implementation of those goals is. The goal of reducing the number of climbers to zero may or may not be a desirable one, but coercion only manifests itself in the NPS's actions, not in its aspirations. The Park Service's stated goals would not be advanced at all by mandating that climbers not scale the Tower. Instead, it has stated that the "voluntary closure will be fully successful when every climber *personally chooses* not to climb at Devils Tower during

June." (FCMP at 23.) (emphasis added). Ordering climbers not to climb or deterring climbing through intimidation undermines this goal and robs individuals of the personal choice necessary to accomplish it. Yet, the Park Service's hopes that climbers will adhere to the voluntary climbing ban cannot be viewed as coercive.

The other purported indicia of coercion also fails to establish that the voluntary climbing ban is, in fact, mandatory. Although the NPS has stated that an unsuccessful voluntary ban may lead it to make the ban mandatory, that is far from an inevitable result. To the contrary, the conversion to a mandatory ban is only one of eight options which the NPS may consider in the event of a failed voluntary ban. While a more direct threat of a mandatory ban in the wake of a failed voluntary ban could evidence coercion, the remote and speculative possibility of a mandatory ban found in this case is insufficient to transform the Government's action into a coercive measure.

Excessive Entanglement

The Court concludes that the voluntary climbing ban also passes muster when measured against the excessive entanglement test. To determine whether a given policy constitutes an excessive entanglement the Court must look at "the character and purposes of the institutions that are benefited, the nature of the aid that the State provides, and the resulting relationship between the government and religious authority." *Lemon,* 403 U.S. at 615. In making this analysis the Court must be mindful that "[e]ntanglement is a question of kind and degree." *Lynch,* 465 U.S. at 668. The organizations benefited by the voluntary climbing ban, namely Native American tribes, are not solely religious organizations, but also represent a common heritage and culture. As a result, there is much less danger that the Government's actions will inordinately advance solely religious activities. The very limited nature of government involvement in this case also tends to undermine any argument of excessive entanglement. The government is merely enabling Native Americans to worship in a more peaceful setting. In doing so, the Park Service has no involvement in the manner of worship that takes place, but only provides an atmosphere more conducive to worship. This type of custodial function does not implicate the dangerously close relationship between state and religion which offends the excessive entanglement prong of the *Lemon* test. *See Westside Community Bd. of Educ. v. Mergens,* 496 U.S. 226, 253 (1990). * * *

The . . . voluntary climbing ban is a policy that has been carefully crafted to balance the competing needs of individuals using Devils Tower National Monument while, at the same time, obeying the edicts of the Constitution. As such, the plan constitutes a legitimate exercise of the Secretary of the Interior's discretion in managing the Monument.

QUESTIONS AND DISCUSSION

1. The district court's decision was affirmed on the ground that the plaintiffs lacked standing. *Bear Lodge Multiple Use Ass'n v. Babbitt,* 175 F.3d 814 (10th Cir. 1999), *cert. denied,* 529 U.S. 1037 (2000). It turned out that the named plaintiffs had actually climbed during the voluntary closure and thus could prove no injury in fact.

2. Suppose the voluntary climbing ban proves ineffective and the Park Service adopts a mandatory ban. What result under the Establishment Clause? In an earlier decision in the Devils Tower case, the district judge had issued a preliminary injunction against the Park Service's initial plan to impose a mandatory climbing ban, holding that "affirmative action by the NPS to exclude a legitimate public use of the tower for the sole purpose of aiding or advancing some American Indians' religious practices violates the First Amendment's establishment clause." *Bear Lodge Multiple Use Association v. Babbitt*, 2 F.Supp.2d 1448 (D. Wyo. 1998). Do you agree with the decision to grant the preliminary injunction?

In *Access Fund v. U.S. Dep't of Agriculture*, 499 F.3d 1036 (9th Cir. 2007), the Ninth Circuit upheld against an Establishment Clause challenge a Forest Service ban on rock climbing at Cave Rock, a site sacred to the Washoe Tribe and of archeological and historical significance. The court held that the climbing ban was directed primarily at preserving the cultural, historical and archeological features of Cave Rock and could not be understood as an endorsement of the Washoe religion because it allowed other activities (e.g., hiking and picnicking) incompatible with Washoe beliefs. The fact that the site's cultural and historical significance derived partly from its sacredness to the tribe was not enough to make the Forest Service's management decision unconstitutional. The court distinguished the *Bear Lodge* case on the grounds that the climbing ban in *Bear Lodge* advanced solely sacred goals. *See also Cholla Ready Mix, Inc. v. Civish*, 382 F.3d 969 (9th Cir. 2004), *cert. denied*, 544 U.S. 974 (2005) (holding that the Arizona Department of Transportation's refusal to purchase road construction materials from companies that mined its materials in a way that impacted a site sacred to the Hopi Tribe, Zuni Pueblo, and Navajo Nation did not violate the Establishment Clause because even though the state was motivated partly by a religious purpose, its broader purpose was secular).

3. As the court in the excerpted decision remarks, the FCMP required "climbing routes to be closed seasonally to protect raptor nests." Does it make sense that Devils Tower can be closed to protect raptor nests but that a mandatory closure of Devils Tower to protect the spiritual and cultural interests of Native Americans is suspect?

4. Suppose another tribe or climber asserted the ban interfered with their free exercise rights because part of their religious beliefs included a yearly climb of Devils Tower in search of spiritual solitude. What result under the Free Exercise Clause or the Religious Freedom Restoration Act (RFRA)? Think back to the discussion of *Employment Div. v. Smith* and RFRA in the text, *supra*.

5. Set aside the detailed legal arguments about Establishment and Free Exercise Clause doctrine (which, in any event, are beyond the scope of this natural resources law casebook) and contemplate your reaction to the facts in *Billie*, *Lyng*, and *Bear Lodge*. Should treaty rights and free exercise give way before federal land management and wildlife protection objectives? Should the competing values be balanced and, if so, what factors should be weighed in that balance?

CHAPTER THREE

THE ROLE OF AGENCIES IN NATURAL RESOURCES MANAGEMENT

I.   THE FEDERAL NATURAL RESOURCE AGENCIES
     A. THE RISE OF FEDERAL NATURAL RESOURCE AGENCIES
     B. THE CONSTITUTIONAL CHALLENGE TO AGENCY ACTION
     C. THE BASIC MISSIONS AND ORGANIZATION OF THE FEDERAL NATURAL
         RESOURCE AGENCIES
     D. PUBLIC CHOICE CHALLENGES FOR AGENCY MANAGEMENT OF NATURAL
         RESOURCES
II. IMPROVING AGENCY DECISION-MAKING
     A. THE ADMINISTRATIVE PROCEDURE ACT
         1. RULEMAKING
         2. ADJUDICATION
         3. JUDICIAL REVIEW OF AGENCY ACTIONS
     B. THE ROLE OF NONGOVERNMENTAL ORGANIZATIONS
         1. LOBBYING FOR LEGISLATIVE AND ADMINISTRATIVE ACTION
         2. CITIZEN SUITS AND LITIGATION
         3. STANDING
         4. RIPENESS, EXHAUSTION, AND THE TIMING OF JUDICIAL REVIEW
         PROBLEM EXERCISE: STANDING TO CHALLENGE A DRAFT EIS
III. IMPROVING AGENCIES' ENVIRONMENTAL DECISION-MAKING
     A. THE NATIONAL ENVIRONMENTAL POLICY ACT
         1. NEPA'S EVOLUTION
         2. WHEN MUST AN AGENCY PREPARE AN EIS?
             a. TIMING
             b. THE SCALE OF A PROPOSED ACTION AND TIERING
             c. THE SCOPE OF AGENCY ACTION
         PROBLEM EXERCISE: WINTER PARK SKI RESORT
         3. THE ESSENTIAL ELEMENTS OF AN EIS
             a. ALTERNATIVES ANALYSIS
             b. THE ADEQUACY OF THE ANALYSIS
         PROBLEM EXERCISE: NATURAL DISASTER AND SCIENTIFIC UNCERTAINTY IN
         ENVIRONMENTAL ANALYSIS
             c. SUPPLEMENTAL EISs
         PROBLEM EXERCISE: SUPPLEMENTATION OF ENVIRONMENTAL ANALYSES
         4. DOES IT WORK?
         PROBLEM EXERCISE: THINKING BEYOND NEPA
     B. RESOURCE PLANNING ON THE PUBLIC LANDS
         1. A BRIEF HISTORY OF PUBLIC LAND PLANNING
         2. PLANNING UNDER NFMA AND FLPMA
         PROBLEM EXERCISE: LAND USE PLANNING ON THE PUBLIC LANDS

"The procedure of administrative rulemaking is in my opinion one of the greatest inventions of modern government."

Kenneth Culp Davis

"I think the emphasis on the redemptive quality of procedural reform is about nine parts myth and one part coconut oil."

Joseph Sax

Understanding agencies is crucial to understanding natural resource law and policy because agencies manage virtually every natural resources issue. Grazing on public rangelands? The Department of the Interior (through the Bureau of Land Management). Wetlands? The Department of Defense (through the U.S. Army Corps of Engineers). National forests? The Department of Agriculture (through the U.S. Forest Service). Endangered species? The Department of the Interior (through the U.S. Fish & Wildlife Service). Marine fisheries? The Department of Commerce (through NOAA–Fisheries). The list goes on and on. And this doesn't begin to include the many state agencies that also manage resources, such as state fish and game agencies and departments of environmental quality. Resource management and environmental protection happen through agency action.

This chapter begins by introducing you to the key federal natural resource management agencies that have evolved over the last century as Congress has addressed various natural resource management challenges— whether disposing of the public lands, managing newly established national forests and parks, or managing grazing districts. The purpose of this chapter is not, however, to examine in detail the substantive responsibilities of each agency; that will come later as you study individual resources. Rather, it provides an overview of the administrative structure that overlays resource management, the processes that frame management activities, and the rules that encourage intelligent management choices. The first section of this chapter thus introduces the agencies and their organic acts (the legislation setting forth an agency's basic mission and duties). The second section moves to the study of the law that is common to all of the various natural resource agencies. That law, known as administrative law, is the set of rules—primarily procedural in nature—that control and limit the powers of all government agencies. Knowledge of administrative law is critical to understanding natural resources law because so many challenges to the actions of resource agencies are premised, in whole or in part, on administrative law principles. The section also addresses the critical role of nongovernmental actors in agency decision-making—how they help shape natural resources law through vehicles such as citizen suits against agencies and participation in the agency rulemaking process.

If administrative law can be described as an effort to control and improve agency decision-making generally, the third section of the Chapter focuses on the more specific issue of how to improve agencies' *environmental* decision-making. Section III of the chapter thus examines the National Environmental Policy Act (NEPA) and the effect of its mandate that agencies consider the environmental impacts of their proposed actions on both private and public lands. Section III also discusses the related natural resource management concept of planning. Decisions affecting resource development and protection do not occur in a vacuum. Typically, they evolve from both short and long-term planning processes. Understanding the planning process is therefore essential to understanding and influencing natural resource decisions.

I. THE FEDERAL NATURAL RESOURCE AGENCIES

A. THE RISE OF FEDERAL NATURAL RESOURCE AGENCIES

Chapter 2 told the story of the gradual increase in federal control over natural resource management that occurred over roughly the last half century. With that increase in federal control came an increasing number of federal agencies. Recall that the first federal involvement with natural resource issues concerned the public lands and consisted primarily of survey and disposal. Initially, Congress itself appointed surveyors and instructed the Department of the Treasury to supervise the sales and the War Department to handle military land warrants. But, in 1812, when it became apparent that this piecemeal approach could not handle the rapidly expanding public land business, Congress established a separate General Land Office (GLO) within the Department of Treasury and gave it the responsibility to "superintend, execute, and perform all such acts and things touching or respecting the public lands." Act of April 25, 1812, 2 Stat. 716. For quite a long time thereafter, the GLO was the primary federal natural resource agency. In 1849, Congress added to the three original executive agencies (Treasury, War, and State) by establishing a new agency—the Department of the Interior—to take charge of the nation's internal affairs. The Interior Department assumed responsibility for a wide range of domestic matters, including Indian affairs, regulation of the territorial governments, management of public parks, and further exploration of the West. It also took charge of the GLO. Interior, which at one time included the Bureau of Labor and the Interstate Commerce Commission, only later became the land- and resource-focused institution we know today. If 1849 represented an organizational change, it did not work much of a change in the way natural resources were managed. For the next few decades, the Interior Department continued dutifully disposing of the public lands without much thought for the natural resources on them.

The first stirrings of change can be traced to John Wesley Powell's 1878 *Report on the Lands of the Arid Region*, in which he suggested that federal policy in the West ought to take account of the landscape. He proposed that political jurisdictions be organized around watersheds and that the size of homestead grants should vary depending on whether the land could be irrigated (in which case 80 acres was enough to support a livelihood) or whether it was suitable only for livestock grazing (in which case he proposed 2,560 acre grants—four square miles of land). Congress wasn't prepared to adopt Powell's suggestions but, in 1879, at the urging of Powell and Interior Secretary Carl Schurz, Congress authorized a commission to study the public lands. The commission's 1880 Report demonstrated Powell's influence. The Report recommended that, for the first time, the public lands be inventoried and then classified according to their best use—whether for timber, mining, or pasturage—and that after classification, management policies should be designed for each type of land.

Both Powell and Schurz were great believers in scientific management of land and resources. They thought science could divine the wisest use of natural resources. If they and others could develop the data, Congress could act in light of that information to establish broad policy objectives that could then be turned into practical, on-the-ground policies by expert scientists and managers working for federal agencies. Congress, however, was not yet ready to move in that direction, and the Report's recommendations were largely ignored. Nevertheless, the efforts of Powell and Schurz laid the groundwork for the move toward expert agency management of natural resources. That move would begin in earnest during the conservation ferment of the 1890s and the Progressive Era policies of Theodore Roosevelt and Gifford Pinchot that followed. As described in more detail in Chapter 2, this period saw a boom in the designation of national parks, monuments, and wildlife refuges, and the creation of the national forests. Part of the reason for this increased focus on retaining land in public ownership was the preservationist movement promoted by John Muir and others. But a much more important reason was the belief that public ownership and scientific management of important natural resources would best insure their conservation. Samuel Hays describes this conservation ethic in the excerpt below.

SAMUEL P. HAYS, CONSERVATION AND THE GOSPEL OF EFFICIENCY: THE PROGRESSIVE CONSERVATION MOVEMENT, 1890–1920 at 2–3 (1959)

Conservation, above all, was a scientific movement, and its role in history arises from the implications of science and technology in modern society. Conservation leaders sprang from such fields as hydrology, forestry, agrostology, geology, and anthropology. Vigorously active in professional circles in the national capital, these leaders brought the ideals and practices of their crafts into federal resource policy. Loyalty to these professional ideals, not close association with the grass-roots public, set the tone of the Theodore Roosevelt conservation movement. Its essence was rational planning to promote efficient development and use of all natural resources. The idea of efficiency drew these federal scientists from one resource task to another, from specific programs to comprehensive concepts. It moulded [sic] the policies which they proposed, their administrative techniques, and their relations with Congress and the public. It is from the vantage point of applied science, rather than of democratic protest, that one must understand the historic role of the conservation movement.

The new realms of science and technology, appearing to open up unlimited opportunities for human achievement, filled conservation leaders with intense optimism. They emphasized expansion, not retrenchment; possibilities, not limitations. . . . The popular view that in a fit of pessimism they withdrew vast areas of the public lands from present use for future development does not stand examination. In fact, they bitterly opposed those who sought to withdraw resources from commercial development. They displayed that deep sense of hope which pervaded all those at the turn of the century for whom science and technology were revealing visions of an abundant future.

The political implications of conservation, it is particularly important to observe, grew out of the political implications of applied science rather than from conflict over the distribution of wealth. Who should decide the course of resource development? Who should determine the goals and methods of federal resource programs? The correct answer to these questions lay at the heart of the conservation idea. Since resource matters were basically technical in nature, conservationists argued, technicians, rather than legislators, should deal with them, Foresters should determine the desirable annual timber cut; hydraulic engineers should establish the feasible extent of multiple-purpose river development and the specific location of reservoirs; agronomists should decide which forage areas could remain open for grazing without undue damage to water supplies. Conflicts between competing resource users, especially, should not be dealt with through the normal processes of politics. Pressure group action, logrolling in Congress, or partisan debate could not guarantee rational and scientific decisions. Amid such jockeying for advantage with the resulting compromise, concern for efficiency would disappear. Conservationists envisaged, even though they did not realize their aims, a political system guided by the ideal of efficiency and dominated by the technicians who could best determine how to achieve it.

The conservation movement and the Progressive Era's penchant for expert agency management, led to the establishment of the U.S. Forest Service, an agency in the Department of Agriculture. (A predecessor agency, the Bureau of Forestry, within the Interior Department was transferred to the Department of Agriculture in 1905 at the request of Gifford Pinchot.) Similarly, along with national parks and monuments came the National Park Service in 1916, an agency within the Interior Department. In 1902, Congress passed the Reclamation Act to bring water to the West, *see infra* Chapter 7, and, along with the dams and canals, came the Reclamation Service, later renamed the Bureau of Reclamation, also located within the Interior Department. Management of the nation's grasslands began with the passage of the Taylor Grazing Act in 1934, *infra* Chapter 8, and the creation of the Interior Department's Grazing Service. The Grazing Service later merged with the General Land Office to form the Bureau of Land Management (BLM).

The conservationists' hope was that by turning the resources over to these agencies, the agencies could manage their assigned resources without fear or favor in a way that was both efficient and promoted the public interest. As it turned out, that hope has proved rather elusive. Some of the reasons why are discussed in Part D below.

B.   THE CONSTITUTIONAL CHALLENGE TO AGENCY ACTION

Federal agencies assume a rather uneasy position within the three branches of government. Agencies can issue rules, conduct inspections, issue permits, adjudicate disputes, demand information, hold hearings, and give and take money, just to name a few activities. Although agencies are located in the executive branch, they tread on the turf of all three branches of government—making rules (a legislative task), issuing permits, investigating compliance, punishing violations (executive tasks), and hearing appeals (a judicial task). This has created some tension with the Constitution's commitment to separation of powers. If the Constitution commits lawmaking authority to Congress in Article I and judicial authority to courts in Article III, then it might be argued that an executive agency acts without constitutional authority when it makes rules and adjudicates disputes. The standard response is that Congress is still in charge of lawmaking because agency authority to make rules is limited and delegated by Congress; the judiciary likewise is not cut out because judicial review of agency decisions and adjudications is available.

Few today would question Congress' authority to delegate rulemaking and adjudicatory authority to agencies, but that has not always been the case. Recall that for many decades, the GLO was the main federal "resource agency" and busied itself primarily with disposing of the nation's land and resources. As long as it focused on the ministerial task of selling land, there was little reason to challenge its authority. But when Congress began creating more agencies around the turn of the century and delegating to those agencies authority to actually *regulate* the use of the public lands, as it did in the Forest Service Organic Act, many in the West cried foul. Among the first were the ranchers who had been freely grazing their cattle within the national forests. When the Forest Service decided to adopt a small grazing fee that had not been specifically prescribed by Congress, ranchers in the Sierra Forest Reserve refused to pay and were then indicted for trespass. They defended by claiming that Congress had no business delegating to the Secretary of Agriculture the authority to make rules and regulations and to establish penalties for their violation. In *United States v. Grimaud*, 220 U.S. 506 (1911), the Court rejected the ranchers' argument:

> In the nature of things it was impracticable for Congress to provide general regulations for these various and varying details of management. Each reservation had its peculiar and special features; and in authorizing the Secretary of Agriculture to meet these local conditions Congress was merely conferring administrative functions upon an agent, and not delegating to him legislative power. * * *

> From the beginning of the Government various acts have been passed conferring upon executive officers power to make rules and regulations—not for the government or their departments, but for administering the laws which did govern. None of these statutes could confer legislative power. But when Congress had legislated and indicated its will, it could give to those who were to act under such general provisions "power to fill up the details" by the establishment of administrative rules and regulations, the violation of which could be punished by fine or imprisonment fixed by Congress, or by penalties fixed by Congress or measured by the injury done. * * *

> It is true that there is no act of Congress which, in express terms, declares that it shall be unlawful to graze sheep on a forest reserve. But the statutes, from which we have quoted, declare, that the privilege of using reserves for "all proper and lawful purposes" is subject to the proviso that the person so using them shall comply "with the rules and regulations covering such forest reservation." * * *

> The Secretary of Agriculture could not make rules and regulations for any and every purpose. As to those here involved, they all relate to matters clearly indicated and authorized by Congress. The subjects as to which the Secretary can regulate are defined. The lands are set apart as a forest reserve. He is required to make provision to protect them from depredations and from harmful uses. He is authorized "to regulate the occupancy and use and to preserve the forests from destruction." A violation of reasonable rules regulat-

ing the use and occupancy of the property is made a crime, not by the Secretary, but by Congress. The statute, not the Secretary, fixes the penalty.

Id. at 516–17, 521–22. As *Grimaud* suggests, Congress could hardly operate if it could not delegate some of the burden of managing resources to administrative agencies. That does not mean that agencies can make up any rule they want. The rule must, as the Court says, "relate to matters clearly indicated and authorized by Congress." *Id.* at 522. This limit is most frequently articulated as a requirement that the statutory language provide an "intelligible principle" to guide the agency's rulemaking discretion. *J.W. Hampton, Jr., & Co. v. United States*, 276 U.S. 394, 409 (1928). Although arguments that Congress improperly delegated legislative authority are infrequent (and have never been particularly successful, with only a few Supreme Court decisions from the New Deal era holding that Congress violated the so-called non-delegation doctrine), that does not mean that agency rules spark no controversy. On the contrary, vigorous argument and litigation continues over whether particular agency rules and actions are consistent with the congressional delegation. That issue is explored in Part II.A.3 below.

C.   THE BASIC MISSIONS AND ORGANIZATION OF THE FEDERAL NATURAL RESOURCE AGENCIES

If Congress must provide natural resource agencies with intelligible principles to guide their management of our natural resources, one important source of those principles is the agency's organic act, the basic statutory blueprint describing the agency's goals, policies, functions, and purpose. This section provides an overview of the missions of the important federal natural resource agencies. Although this section concentrates on federal agencies, the role of state agencies in resource management should not be forgotten. For example, the federal government owns only about 35% of forest land in the United States. Eleven million owners privately own about 60% of forests, and the states have primary regulatory authority over those forests. *See* Natural Resource Aspects of Sustainable Development in the United States of America, *at* http://www.un.org/esa/agenda21/natlinfo/countr/usa/natur.htm.

The following overview of federal natural resource agencies begins with the four primary federal land management agencies—the Forest Service, the Bureau of Land Management, the National Park Service, and the Fish and Wildlife Service. Its description of these four agencies will be cursory because their creation has already been partly described in Chapter 2 (pages 129–146) and because each agency will be discussed in greater detail in the specific chapters that address the resources over which the agencies have stewardship. The introduction to the four major land management agencies is followed by an even shorter summary of the other federal agencies with responsibility for natural resource issues.

The **United States Forest Service** (USFS) manages 155 national forests, 20 national grasslands, and a variety of other smaller units such as research and experimental areas. In total the Forest Service manages 193 million acres of land, an area almost as large as California and Montana combined. Although the national forests are concentrated in the West, both the East (12.1 million acres) and the South (13.3 million acres) contain significant national forests thanks largely to the 1911 Weeks Act, 36 Stat. 961, which authorized additions to the national forest system through the purchase of private lands. The Forest Service is divided into nine administrative regions headed by regional foresters who report to the Deputy Chief for the national forest system who, along with other deputies, reports to the Chief of the Forest Service.

As described in Chapters 2 and 10, the Forest Service is housed within the Department of Agriculture and for years managed the forests according to Congress' direction in the 1897 Forest Service Organic Act, 30 Stat. 11—

> to improve and protect the forest within the reservation, or for the purpose of securing favorable conditions of water flows, and to furnish a continuous supply of timber for the use and necessities of the citizens of the United States.

16 U.S.C. § 475. In 1960, the Forest Service's management goals were updated by the Multiple–Use, Sustained–Yield Act of 1960, which, as its name implies, required the Forest Service to manage the forests for multiple uses that best meet the needs of the American people, including "outdoor recreation, range, timber, watershed, and wildlife and fish purposes." 16 U.S.C. § 528. In 1976, Congress went further and replaced the 1897 Organic Act with a new organic act known as National Forest Management Act (NFMA), 16 U.S.C. §§ 1600–14. NFMA maintained the multiple use mandate but added to it detailed planning requirements and management criteria, which are discussed further in the planning section that ends this chapter. For further information about the Forest Service, see http://www.fs.fed.us and Betsy A. Cody, et al., *Major Federal Land Management Agencies: Management of Our Nation's Lands and Resources*, Congressional Research Report, 95–599 ENR (May 15, 1999).

The **Bureau of Land Management** (BLM), housed within the Department of the Interior, is, like the Forest Service, charged with managing the lands under its jurisdiction for multiple use and sustained yield. As described in Chapter 2, the BLM was formed in 1946 from a merger of two agencies within the Department of the Interior—the General Land Office and the United States Grazing Service, which had been created as part of the 1934 Taylor Grazing Act. For its first 30 years of existence, the BLM operated without any organic act. Congress remedied that in 1976 by passing the Federal Land Policy and Management Act (FLPMA), 43 U.S.C. §§ 1701–1785, which confirmed the agency's multiple use mandate. The BLM manages about 258 million acres, 83.5 million of which are in Alaska. The agency is headed by a Director, who is a political appointee and who reports to the Secretary of the Interior through the Assistant Secretary of Land and Minerals Management.

As discussed at greater length in Chapter 9, the BLM manages the onshore federal estate subject to mineral development under the auspices of such statutes as the General Mining Law of 1872, the Mineral Leasing Act of 1920, and the Materials Disposal Act of 1947. The BLM's administration of the federal mineral estate includes the lands managed by other agencies such as the Forest Service. In fact, 700 million acres of federal land are subject to mineral development. Although the BLM previously had responsibility for mineral leasing on the outer continental shelf (OCS), that responsibility has now been assigned to the Minerals Management Service, which is also within the Department of the Interior. As discussed in Chapter 8 on Rangelands, the BLM also manages grazing on approximately 160 million acres of public land. Finally, as discussed in Chapter 6, the BLM is the home to a relatively new program known as the National Landscape Conservation System (NLCS), which has responsibility for national monuments, wilderness areas, wilderness study areas, national conservation areas, wild and scenic rivers, and national scenic and historic trails within the BLM's jurisdiction. For further information about the Bureau of Land Management, see http://www.blm.gov and Betsy A. Cody, et al., *Major Federal Land Management Agencies: Management of Our Nation's Lands and Resources*, Congressional Research Report, 95–599 ENR (May 15, 1999).

Congress created the **National Park Service** (NPS) in 1916 to manage the national parks. Unlike the multiple use mandate of the Forest Service and the BLM, the Park Service Organic Act commands NPS "to conserve the scenery and the natural and historic objects and the wildlife therein, and to provide for the enjoyment of the same in such manner and by such means as will leave them unimpaired for the enjoyment of future generations." 16 U.S.C. § 1. The difficulties presented by this command to manage for public enjoyment of the parks while leaving them unimpaired for future generations are discussed in Chapter 6. In addition to 58 national parks, NPS administers many national monuments, national recreation areas, national seashores, national lakeshores, national historic sites, and national battlefields. In total, it manages 391 areas on about 84 million acres of land. *See* National Park Service Website, *available at* http://www.nps.gov.

The **United States Fish and Wildlife Service** (FWS), housed within the Department of the Interior, manages 520 wildlife refuges in 50 states totaling 93 million acres. As discussed in greater detail in Chapter 6, *infra* at pages 662–665, the organic act for management of wildlife refuges is the 1997 National Wildlife Refuge System Improvement Act, 16 U.S.C. §§ 668dd–668ee. The Act provides that the purpose of the Refuge System is to establish "a national network of lands and waters for the conservation, management, and where appropriate, restoration of . . . fish, wildlife, and plant resources and their habitats." 16 U.S.C. § 668dd(a)(2). In addition to the wildlife refuges, FWS administers more than 36,000 waterfowl production areas (WPAs), averaging about 90 acres in size. The National Wildlife Refuge Administration Act included WPAs in the National Wildlife Refuge System in 1966. 16 U.S.C. § 668dd(a)(1). Of the 95.3 million acres of land managed by FWS, more than 76 million are in Alaska.

In addition to its role as one of the four major federal land management agencies, FWS carries most of the burden of administering the Endangered Species Act, manages more than 800 species of migratory birds under the Migratory Bird Treaty Act, and maintains 69 federal fish hatcheries. It also administers the various federal statutes, such as the Pittman–Robertson Act, that provide for federal excise taxes on hunting and fishing equipment to be funneled to state fish and wildlife agencies.

For further information about the National Wildlife Refuge System and the Fish & Wildlife Service, see http://www.fws.gov.

The origins of the U.S. Fish and Wildlife Service trace back to 1871 when Congress established the U.S. Fish Commission to study the decrease in the nation's food fish and recommend ways to reverse the decline. The Commission was renamed the Bureau of Fisheries in 1903 and placed in the Department of Commerce. In 1885, Congress created the Office of Economic Ornithology in the Department of Agriculture to study the food habits and migratory patterns of birds, especially those that had an effect on agriculture. This Office was renamed the Bureau of Biological Survey in 1905, and Teddy Roosevelt's wildlife refuges were placed under its jurisdiction. The Bureau of Fisheries and the Bureau of Biological Survey were combined and renamed the U.S. Fish and Wildlife Service in 1939 and placed under the jurisdiction of the Interior Department.

Although these four major public land agencies receive the most attention in natural resources law, a variety of other federal agencies play an important regulatory role.

The **National Marine Fisheries Service (NOAA Fisheries Service)** within the Department of Commerce is the lead agency with respect to fisheries extending 200 miles offshore. It regulates the commercial fishery within those waters, primarily under the auspices of the Magnuson–Stevens Fishery Conservation and Management Act of 1976. It also administers the Marine Mammal Protection Act, which prohibits the taking of most marine mammals and handles the Endangered Species Act for the species within its jurisdiction, including anadromous fish, such as salmon, that spawn in freshwater but spend most of their life in the ocean. *See* NOAA Fisheries, *at* http://www.nmfs.noaa.gov.

The **U.S. Army Corps of Engineers** is one of two major federal water resource development agencies. Traditionally, the Corps focused on improving commercial navigation and flood control, including the nation's deep draft harbors as well as an extensive series of canals, locks, and dams. To maintain this system, the Corps dredges some 300 million cubic yards of material every year. To regulate private activities that may impact navigation, the Corps issues permits under the Rivers and Harbors Act. The Corps also operates 383 dams and reservoirs for flood control, which produce one-fourth of the country's hydropower, and it manages or leases to local authorities over 4300 recreation areas at those reservoirs and other lakes. In addition to these responsibilities, Section 404 of the Clean Water Act authorizes the Corps to issue permits for the disposal of dredged or fill material into the "waters of the United States." Such waters include many wetlands. Each year the Corps issues about 8,000 permits and approves some 80,000 activities by way of national and regional permits. *See* U.S. Army Corps of Engineers, *at* http://www.usace.army.mil/.

The primary responsibilities of the **Environmental Protection Agency** are in the area of pollution control, but EPA plays a role in resource management as well because it has veto power over the Army Corps' decision to issue permits under Section 404 of the Clean Water Act. EPA also has general authority to reviews all draft and final environmental impact statements prepared by all federal agencies. *See* http://www.epa.gov/

compliance/nepa/index.html. While EPA does not have the power to require agencies to make changes to their NEPA documents, it can refer disputes to the **Council on Environmental Quality**, which administers NEPA under the auspices of the Office of the President.

The **Bureau of Reclamation** within the Department of the Interior was established under the 1902 Reclamation Act. It has responsibility for federal water projects in 17 western states. In all, the Bureau has built more than 600 dams including such famous structures as the Hoover and Glen Canyon dams on the Colorado River and the Grand Coulee on the Columbia. It is the largest wholesaler of water in the country, supplying irrigation water to 20% of western farmers. It is also the second largest producer of hydropower in the West. More and more, the Bureau is focusing on balancing environmental and recreational considerations with its traditional development focus. *See* Bureau of Reclamation, *at* http://www.usbr.gov/.

The **U.S. Geological Survey** is the sole science agency for the Interior Department. It was first established in 1879 to conduct an "examination of the geological structure, mineral resources, and products of the national domain." 20 Stat. 394 (1879). In 1996, Interior Secretary Babbitt, interested in expanding the Survey's vision beyond minerals and other "products," created the Biological Resources Division of the Survey and charged it with researching biological information relating to fish and wildlife issues. *See* United States Geological Survey, *at* http://www.usgs.gov.

The **Minerals Management Service (MMS)** and the **Office of Surface Mining Regulation and Enforcement (OSM)** are both located within the Department of the Interior. MMS manages the country's oil, natural gas, and other mineral resources on the outer continental shelf. OSM operates under the Surface Mining Control and Reclamation Act, and regulates the environmental impacts of all coal mining in the United States. *See* http://www.mms.gov/ and http://www.osmre.gov/.

The **Bureau of Indian Affairs (BIA)** in the Interior Department manages about 56 million acres, including about 43.5 million acres of tribally owned land and 10 million acres that are owned by individual American Indians. The Interior Department as a whole is charged with ensuring that American Indian and Alaska Native lands and resources are properly managed, conserved, and protected. Thus, in addition to the BIA's activities, the BLM offers mineral management programs for tribes, OSM makes grants to tribes for the reclamation of abandoned mines and restoration of water quality affected by acid mine drainage and the Bureau of Reclamation offers financial and technical assistance to tribes on the planning, design, construction, and operation of water projects on reservations. The FWS also works with tribes to restore and manage fishery and wildlife resources. *See* http://www.doiu.nbc.gov/bureau-indian-affairs.html.

The **Natural Resources Conservation Service**, formerly the Soil Conservation Service, within the Department of Agriculture is tasked with providing technical assistance to private landowners to help conserve their soil, water, and other natural resources. It funds a variety of programs and local conservation districts with an eye toward protecting wildlife habitat on farms and ranches. *See* Natural Resources Conservation Service, *at* http://www.nrcs.usda.gov/about.

This cursory overview of the key federal natural resource agencies offers some indication of the vast reach and importance of agencies in natural resources law. Trying to understand or practice natural resources law without an understanding of agencies and how they work would be a fruitless exercise. In truth, it would be fruitless in most areas of the law. It may be hard to believe, but the Code of Federal Regulations' Alphabetical List of Agencies now runs over nine pages of fine print.

Having introduced the natural resource agencies and explored their basic constitutional validity, most of the remainder of this chapter is devoted to studying how agencies work or, in the view of some, don't work, and how the law circumscribes the duties of agencies and citizens as they interact with one another.

D. PUBLIC CHOICE CHALLENGES FOR AGENCY MANAGEMENT OF NATURAL RESOURCES

Remember the discussion above about the rise of federal natural resource agencies during the conservation boom of the 1890s and the Progressive Era that followed. The premise of much of that agency-creating energy was that agencies would produce rational scientific decisions free of the sort of log-rolling and lobbying pressure that affected legislative decisions. Under this *scientific expertise* model of administrative agencies, technocrats in white jackets faithfully implement congressional mandates by relying on their best professional judgment. Unfortunately, the history of both natural resource and other agencies indicates that this aspiration is not always fulfilled in practice. Indeed, some would say the aspiration of disinterested, technocratic decisions made in the public interest is seldom fulfilled. These skeptical views form the basis for a competing model of administrative agencies that might be called *interest group representation*. In this model, agencies act as mini-legislatures. Just as with Congress, special interests battle it out to influence the implementation of law. This is not necessarily a bad thing, but it can exacerbate some of the public choice concerns that are present with any government decision. *See generally* Richard Stewart, *The Reformation of American Administrative Law*, 88 HARV. L. REV. 1669 (1975).

As discussed in Chapter 1, public choice theory predicts that the efforts of concentrated interests (such as timber companies) will exercise greater influence in the political process than more diffuse, though larger, interests (such as supporters of wilderness). Because agencies work in a narrower field than the national legislature, the concentration, and thus the influence, of special interests can be greater. In some cases, this can lead to what is known as *agency capture*. Interested parties, who are willing to focus their time and energy on the regulatory process, are sometimes able to wield significant influence over an agency. Over time, the agency may so closely align itself with a particular interest group that it can be described as "captured." Thus, for a number of years the Bureau of Land Management (BLM) was known pejoratively as the Bureau of Livestock and Mining because it seemed, to many, to manage its lands solely for the benefit of ranchers and miners. In the past, the Forest Service has likewise been accused of being captured by the timber industry. A frequently cited example of that capture was the Forest Service's management of the Tongass National Forest. Despite a statutory mandate that the forest be managed for "multiple use," the Forest Service originally decided to dedicate almost all of the forested land to logging and to ignore the competing interests of recreation, wildlife protection, and preservation. As the Court explained in *Sierra Club v. Hardin*, 325 F.Supp. 99, 122 (D. Alaska 1971), *rev'd sub nom. Sierra Club v. Butz*, 3 Envtl. L. Rep. (ELI) 20,292 (9th Cir. 1973), of the approximately 4.5 million acres of commercial forest on the Tongass (out of more than 16 million total acres), only 0.6% was off limits to logging in 1958.

Another public choice concern is that of agency self-interest. To increase its power and perpetuate itself, the argument goes, agencies may act more out of bureaucratic self-interest than in the public interest. Historically, this charge was often leveled against the Army Corps of Engineers and the Bureau of Reclamation, which for years engaged in a contest for congressional funding of competing water projects. More and bigger projects meant more money, prestige, and job security, and thus it behooved both agencies to lobby for more dams rather than question whether construction of the dams was in the public interest. *See* MARC REISNER, CADILLAC DESERT (1986).

As these and other flaws predicted by public choice theory turned up again and again in agency actions, it led over the years to a variety of efforts to reform and improve agency decision-making. The remainder of this chapter considers three such reforms. The first reform was one directed at all federal agencies. It came in the form of the Administrative Procedure Act (APA), 5 U.S.C. §§ 551–559, passed by Congress in 1946. As originally created, federal agencies were mostly free to make management decisions without fear of public scrutiny or judicial review. Yet if agency officials were not really disinterested experts—but instead more like a legislature—it seemed to many that the public ought to have more knowledge about the decisions, that there ought to be additional opportunities for public input, and that there ought to be some vehicle for judicial review of agency decisions. The APA was Congress' effort to respond to those concerns. The other two reforms considered in Section III focus more explicitly on improving agencies' environmental, as opposed to their overall, decision-making. One is Congress' effort in the National Environmental Policy Act (NEPA) to get all federal agencies to consider the environmental impact of their proposed actions and to consider less harmful alternatives. The other is Congress' mandate, through a variety of statutes, that federal agencies with stewardship over natural resources engage in planning.

QUESTIONS AND DISCUSSION

1. As happens whenever two organizations have potentially overlapping authority, resource agencies often battle one another for natural resource management turf and disagree about management decisions. There is arguably even more interagency conflict in the resource area than in other regulated fields because agency mandates not only occasionally overlap (as with the competition between the Bureau of Reclamation and the Corps of Engineers to build dams) but often conflict, as well. Think of the agencies located within the Department of the Interior. Do you see why the Fish & Wildlife Service might oppose actions by the Bureau of Reclamation or the Park Service? Can you think of instances when the Bureau of Indian Affairs might oppose actions by the Fish & Wildlife Service?

How should interagency disputes be resolved? If there are policy disagreements, presumably the senior agency administrators should decide. But what if one agency believes another agency's actions violate the law? Assume that Fish & Wildlife Service biologists, for example, have written an opinion concluding that construction of a Forest Service road will jeopardize the existence of an endangered salamander. The Forest Service biologists disagree. Can the FWS sue the Forest Service?

Very few agencies (and none in the Interior Department) have independent litigating authority. As a result, decisions to sue are made by the Department of Justice, which, in theory, represents the agencies just as lawyers represent clients. An important difference, however, is that the Department of Justice sometimes decides not to file a case despite the wish of its client agencies to do so. In essence, the Attorney General, acting on behalf of the president, resolves the dispute.

While you might think that the president—as the chief executive—should be able to resolve all such interagency disputes, Congress has chartered some independent regulatory agencies, such as the Federal Communications Commission and the Federal Trade Commission, which are headed by a collegial body (a commission), and which have substantial executive power but operate largely independent of the president. (The constitutionality of such agencies raises an interesting question that has never been squarely addressed by the Supreme Court.)

One of the most famous cases involving an interagency dispute was *Tennessee Valley Authority v. Hill*, 437 U.S. 153 (1978). *TVA v. Hill*, which is discussed in Chapter 4, *infra*, involved an endangered species—the snail darter—listed by the Fish and Wildlife Service that threatened to block a nearly completed dam built by the TVA on the Little Tennessee River. When the case went to the Supreme Court, the Attorney General, Griffin Bell, chose to represent the TVA, but at the request of both the White House and Interior Secretary, Cecil Andrus, he included in his brief an appendix that argued for protecting the fish.

2. Agency capture is commonly criticized as preventing the agency from acting in the broader "public interest." Is that the appropriate critique of agency capture, or is the greater concern that the agency is departing from its statutory mandate? Is there a difference? Consider the comments of Professor Huffman:

> In the traditional democratic political system the public interest is determined by fifty percent plus one or more of those voting. In theory, and occasionally in practice, the vote of one person can be determinative of the public interest, a fact which underscores the idea that the public interest is an aggregation of individual interests, not something which exists independent

[handwritten margin note: interagency dispute → TVA v. Hill (snail darter)]

from individual interests. Different political institutions and processes do not alter this basic characteristic of public interest determinations. They only affect which individual interests will be aggregated and how much weight they will have relative to one another.

Meanwhile, the concepts of the body politic and the public interest have been consistently exploited by those who seek the attention and influence of governments. It is the rare advocate of government action, even in nondemocratic societies, who does not appeal to the public good to justify a favored policy or program.

James L. Huffman, *The Inevitability of Private Rights in Public Lands*, U. COLO. L. REV. 241, 264 (1994). Do you agree with Professor Huffman that the "public interest" has no independent existence but is only a function of the results churned out by any particular political process? Can a political decision be contrary to the public interest? How can you know?

When Congress charges a natural resource agency with acting in the public interest, how should the agency determine the public interest? Take the example of whether to allow snowmobiles in a national park. Should the number of visitors who might use snowmobiles in the park determine the public interest? The number of visitors who would approve such a change? The number of people across the nation who would approve such a change? Whether such a change would harm the interests of future park visitors? Or should the Secretary of the Interior who, after all, is the representative of the president—the official elected by the people—simply decide the public interest in this case? How should the interests of future generations be accounted for in determining the public interest?

Would a mandate to manage a national park "in the public interest" offer a sufficiently "intelligible principle" to satisfy the non-delegation doctrine?

3. It may surprise you that in addition to its many other duties, the Forest Service is authorized to issue permits for ski resorts within the national forests. Some 165 ski areas—including such famous areas as Aspen, Mammoth, Crested Butte, Heavenly Valley, Jackson Hole, Loon, Mt. Bachelor, Park City, Steamboat, Snowbird, Snowmass, Taos, Telluride, Wachusett, Waterville Valley, and Vail—are at least partly within national forests. Historically, the Forest Service issued 30–80 year permits for the base lodge, related buildings, lift equipment and the like, and it issued annual permits for the various runs. Under the National Forest Ski Area Permit Act of 1986, all permits are now for 40 years. 16 U.S.C. § 497b. Given the capital-intensive nature of ski resorts, such long-term permits are probably critical to a resort's viability. But does this accord with multiple use management principles? Is it contrary to the public interest to establish a single use for such a long period? Does it make sense to have ski resorts on national forest land? Considering the location of national forests, is there a viable alternative? Those who believe ski resorts are not a particularly wise use of public land will be encouraged to know that after a burst of one resort a year from 1960 to 1975, very few new ski resorts have been permitted in the last twenty years. *See generally* C. Wayne McKinzie,

Ski Area Development After the National Forest Ski Area Permit Act of 1986: Still an Uphill Battle, 12 VA. ENVTL. L.J. 299 (1993).

II.   IMPROVING AGENCY DECISION-MAKING

A.   THE ADMINISTRATIVE PROCEDURE ACT

Passed in 1946, the Administrative Procedure Act (APA), 5 U.S.C. §§ 551–559, and the "administrative law" it spawned are renowned as one of the great inventions of the American experience. Administrative law makes government activity more open, accountable, and responsive to the public than in any other country. Administrative law concerns *how agencies operate*—the processes and procedures they use to perform their functions—and the *separation of powers*—the competitive relationship and respective powers between the legislative and executive branches of government and the role of courts in refereeing this constant battle. In some ways, administrative law represents the flip side of corporate law. Just as corporate law regulates the conduct of private organizations, administrative law serves as the law of public organizations. The APA sets out procedures agencies must follow when promulgating rules and adjudicating conflicts. It also establishes the standard of judicial review (which varies depending on the type of action) when agency actions are challenged in court.

The APA breaks most agency actions into two broad categories—rules and orders. *See* 5 U.S.C. § 551(4), (6). Rules typically describe agency decisions that affect general classes of people. They establish standards of general or particular applicability and future effect and are designed to implement law or policy decisions. Orders, by contrast, are agency decisions relating to specific facts. The APA defines "rulemaking" as the agency process that produces rules. *Id.* § 551(5). The term "adjudication" describes the process for producing orders. *Id.* § 551(7). An agency decision, for example, to list an endangered species or a decision to adopt environmental protection measures for mining is a rule. If a particular mining company challenged the rule's applicability to its operations, the agency decision regarding that challenge would be an order. Likewise, the agency decision to approve or disapprove the mining company's application for a permit to mine is an order. Enforcement actions for violations of a rule or policy are also orders. In general, differentiating between rules and orders is straightforward, but it's an important distinction because the process set out in the APA for these two types of agency action are significantly different. As discussed in detail below, rules must be published and often require an agency to proceed through a notice and comment process, whereas orders are usually the product of an adjudicative process. Understanding these two common types of agency action is also important because the lines of attack against agency action are just as often procedural (e.g., the agency failed to comply with the APA's notice requirements for rulemaking) as they are substantive (e.g., the Fisheries Conservation Management Act forbids this agency action).

1. RULEMAKING

Where do agency rules come from? Usually they come from statutory mandates. In most environmental and natural resource laws, Congress simply passes broad framework legislation, leaving it up to the agency to fill in the (often extensive) details. The Clean Water Act, for example, requires the Army Corps of Engineers to issue permits for the discharge of dredged and fill material into the "waters of the United States." 33 U.S.C. §§ 1344; 1362(7). Federal jurisdiction under the Clean Water Act extends over all "waters of the United States", which presumably include at least some wetlands. But the Corps must define what a wetland is for purposes of the statute: does it include lands that are only wet a few months a year, or must there be standing water? The Corps decides what Congress intended or, more often, what definition would be consistent with the overall import of the statute. *See* 33 C.F.R. § 328. As another example, the Federal Land Policy and Management Act requires the Bureau of Land Management to regulate activities on the public lands that cause "unnecessary and undue degradation." *See* 43 U.S.C. § 1732(b). Before it can enforce the statute, the agency must determine what types of damage this includes. These are technical decisions with immense practical impact. Filling in the details can be especially contentious in those cases where Congress paints with a broad brush, requiring the agency, for example, to manage resources as necessary to "protect the public health." Clean Air Act, § 109(b)(1); 42 U.S.C. § 7409(b)(1). In these cases, the agency must decide how best to accomplish this broad goal and politics loom large.

Sometimes agencies are stymied either by political or resource limits, and they fail to address certain problems at all. In this case, the APA affords interested members of the public an opportunity to petition an agency to adopt a rule. 5 U.S.C. § 553(e).

The APA describes and establishes procedures for two types of rulemaking. Formal rulemaking requires a trial process with a hearing, testimony, and cross-examination of witnesses. It is rarely done today. Most rulemaking—and essentially all of it in the natural resources context—is *informal rulemaking* (sometimes called *notice and comment* rulemaking). The term *informal*, though, can be misleading. Notice and comment rulemaking is still a rigorous procedure and has become increasingly complex over the years as Congress and various presidents have imposed myriad requirements such as preparing environmental assessments, cost-benefit analyses, and assessments of the impact of the rule on small businesses and state and local governments.

Unless it meets one of the exceptions noted below, section 553 of the APA requires agencies to publish notice of a proposed rule in the *Federal Register* (the federal government's daily newspaper of announcements, notices, and rules), including the agency's source of authority to issue the rule, a description of the proposed rule, notice to interested persons of the location and time of public hearings, as well as opportunity to submit comments. The agency also must publish the final rule in the *Federal Register*, including a "concise general statement of [its] basis and purpose." 5 U.S.C. § 553(c). This statement generally includes responses to the categories of submitted comments, thereby justifying the rule's final form.

This is a far more rigorous process for agency action than in any other country in the world and seeks to ensure that agency rules are well crafted and consider the views of affected parties. Informal rulemaking creates a large record of information. This includes not only the *Federal Register* notices but also the often voluminous public comments that may be submitted on the proposed rule (and which may be viewed by the public in agencies' docket rooms, or increasingly on the internet). Final rules that follow the notice and comment process are compiled and published annually in the *Code of Federal Regulations* (C.F.R.). The C.F.R. has 50 titles that roughly correspond with the titles from the U.S. Code.

As noted above, the APA defines "rule" broadly and encompasses essentially any agency pronouncement of "general or particular applicability and future effect designed to implement, or prescribe policy." But the APA recognizes certain categories of rules, such as "interpretative rules" and "general statements of policy," for which notice and comment are not required. 5 U.S.C. § 553(b)(A). Notice and comment requirements are also waived "when the agency for good cause finds (and incorporates the finding and a brief statement of the reasons therefore in the rules issued) that notice and public procedure are impracticable, unnecessary, or contrary to the public interest." *Id.* at § 553(b)(B). Agencies can issue policy statements in the form of various guidance documents or legal opinions, and these documents can often make important statements about how a law should be interpreted or applied. As an example, the Bureau of Land Management publishes manuals for virtually every activity it regulates, from dam maintenance procedures and concession contracts to policies for making reasonable accommodations for persons with disabilities, prescribed fire management, and land exchange procedures. The BLM also issues a steady stream of Instruction Memoranda and Information Bulletins. *See* http://www.blm.gov/nhp/efoia/wo/woerr.html. Some of these documents must still be published in the *Federal Register* (see 5 U.S.C. § 552(a)(1)) and all of them must generally be made available for public inspection and copying—a task that has become much easier in the age of the internet. *Id.* at § 552(a)(2). While this provides some notice, it is much less than the practice of notice and comment rulemaking (and much less resource intensive). Still, the line between those types of rules that require notice and comment and those that don't has become blurred, and courts and agencies alike have struggled with where to draw the line. This problem has become more acute in recent years as agencies facing myriad new requirements for notice and comment rulemaking seek ways to minimize their burden.

2. ADJUDICATION

While rulemaking concerns prospective decisions affecting a class of people, the adjudication process, which produces an order, generally addresses present problems and issues such as permit issuance and enforcement actions. (The APA expressly defines an "order" to include licensing and sets some special procedures for these actions. See 5 U.S.C. §§ 551(6); 558.) Adjudicative actions might include, for example, issuing a permit to allow the disposal of dredged and fill material into a wetland, granting or

[handwritten margin notes: "RULES def." and "guidance – no N&C necessary"]

denying a right-of-way across federal land, or issuing or renewing a particular mineral lease. As with rulemaking, challenges to agency orders are often procedural, asking whether the proper process was followed.

Like rulemaking, the APA divides agency adjudications into formal and informal categories. Formal adjudication, which requires a formal, trial-type hearing, is generally reserved for those types of actions that involve property rights or other rights protected by the due process clause of the Constitution. In the extreme, for example, an order to close a mining operation because of health and safety concerns would clearly involve significant property rights subject to due process requirements. A more modest example might involve a decision to issue a fine for violating pollution standards established under a federal permit for a logging operation. The APA requires formal adjudication only where the relevant statute calls for it (*see* 5 U.S.C. § 554(a)). However, where due process rights are implicated, the Constitution requires some form of hearing anyway, and the APA procedures offer a safe option for most situations.

Informal adjudications are very common in the natural resources context. They might include, for example, agency decisions to open public lands to off-road vehicle use or to offer public lands for logging or leasing. The APA does not establish any particular procedures for such actions. Nonetheless, section 555 establishes general procedures that apply to all types of agency actions—including both rulemaking and adjudication, whether formal or informal—and have effectively become the minimal standards for informal adjudications. These requirements include the right to counsel, the right to appear before the agency in a proceeding, the right to receive a decision within a reasonable time, and, where a request made to an agency has been denied, a "brief statement of the grounds for denial." 5 U.S.C. § 555(e). This last requirement is especially important because it assures that a record is available upon which a court can review the agency's decision.

Agencies often establish additional procedures for both their formal and informal adjudications. These are generally published in the C.F.R. For example, the Department of the Interior has established a quasi-independent Office of Hearings and Appeals (OHA) to adjudicate a host of claims that might arise as a result of decisions by various Interior agencies. OHA has a pool of administrative law judges (ALJs) located in the Western states where most of the Interior's work occurs. These ALJs handle Interior's formal hearings. Challenges to decisions that do not require an ALJ are often handled initially within an agency and subsequently by one of several boards that are given the power to review Interior Department decisions. For example, decisions made by state directors of the various Bureau of Land Management offices are generally subject to review by the Interior Board of Land Appeals—a board that operates under OHA. 43 C.F.R. § 4.410 (2003). OHA has promulgated rules that establish the procedures that it will follow when cases are assigned to ALJs or one of the various boards. *See* 43 C.F.R. part 4 (2003).

3.   JUDICIAL REVIEW OF AGENCY ACTIONS

The Standard of Review. When final rules are challenged (as many in the natural resources field are), the key question for the courts is what the standard of review should be. The APA provides that courts reviewing *informal* agency actions, which are the most common actions taken by natural resource agencies, shall:

(1) compel agency action unlawfully withheld or unreasonably delayed; and

(2) hold unlawful and set aside agency action, findings, and conclusions found to be—

(A) arbitrary, capricious, an abuse of discretion or otherwise not in accordance with law;

(B) contrary to constitutional right, power privilege or immunity;

(C) in excess of statutory jurisdiction . . .

(D) without observance of procedure required by law. . . .

5 U.S.C. § 706.

Section 706(2)(A)–(D) is often referred to by the shorthand phrase, "the arbitrary and capricious standard," although as you can see, it is really much more than that. By contrast, Section 706(2)(E) provides for judicial review of *formal* agency actions under a "substantial evidence" standard. Although this standard was originally thought to be less deferential to agencies, in practice, it has been applied in similar fashion to the arbitrary and capricious standard. In rare cases, usually where the statute requires it, the APA allows courts to hold a *de novo* hearing, 5 U.S.C. § 706(2)(F), where the court reviews the administrative decision anew without any deference to the agency. Courts, for example, will hold a *de novo* hearing on an agency's failure to comply with a Freedom of Information Act request. 5 U.S.C. § 552(a)(4)(B).

In *Motor Vehicle Mfrs. Ass'n v. State Farm Mut. Auto. Ins. Co.*, 463 U.S. 29, 43–44 (1983), the Supreme Court offered one of its most useful explanations of the arbitrary and capricious standard:

> The scope of review under the "arbitrary and capricious" standard is narrow and a court is not to substitute its judgment for that of the agency. Nevertheless, the agency must examine the relevant data and articulate a satisfactory explanation for its action including a "rational connection between the facts found and the choice made." In reviewing that explanation, we must "consider whether the decision was based on a consideration of the relevant factors and whether there has been a clear error of judgment." *Normally, an agency rule would be arbitrary and capricious if the agency has relied on factors which Congress has not intended it to consider, entirely failed to consider an important aspect of the problem, offered an explanation for its decision that runs counter to the evidence before the agency, or is so implausible that it could not be ascribed to a difference in view or the product of agency expertise.* The reviewing court should not attempt itself to make up for such deficiencies; we may not supply a reasoned basis for the agency's action that the agency itself has not given. We will, however, "uphold a decision of less than ideal clarity if the agency's path may reasonably be discerned." (Emphasis added.)

Although the arbitrary and capricious standard of review sounds deferential to agencies, in the 1970s federal courts used it to take a "hard look" at agency actions. A prominent early case, *Citizens to Preserve Overton Park v. Volpe*, 401 U.S. 402 (1971), involved a statute that prohibited the approval of a federally funded highway through a public park unless there was no "feasible and prudent alternative." Despite this limitation, the Secretary of Transportation approved the construction of an interstate highway through Overton Park in Memphis, Tennessee, without indicating whether any feasible and prudent alternative existed. The Court rejected the Secretary's claim that the decision was unreviewable because it was committed to agency discretion by law. See 5 U.S.C. § 701(a)(2). According to the Court, this exception to judicial review applied only in the rare situation where the Court had no law to apply. The Court found sufficient "law to apply" in the "feasible and prudent" standard set forth in the statute. Nonetheless, the Court remanded the case because the agency had failed to provide the Court with the whole record upon which the decision had been made. Without the whole record, the Court was unable to determine whether the Secretary had acted arbitrarily or capriciously. *Overton Park* and similar decisions forced agencies to create more thorough records of decision in anticipation of judicial review.

Judicial review on the whole record before the agency at the time it made its decision has become a fundamental tenet of administrative law. It provides a powerful incentive for both the agency and interested parties to introduce key issues and evidence during the public processes provided by the agency. If the agency has failed to provide an adequate opportunity for the public to have their views considered, courts will usually remand the case to the agency for development of an adequate record. One of the consequences of "record review" is that the reviewing court rarely holds trial-type hearings when reviewing agency decisions. These cases usually look more like appellate review even when they are heard by district courts. The parties often file briefs, usually in support of, or in opposition to, motions for summary judgment, and they appear in court only for oral argument.

Chevron and *Skidmore* Deference. In the classic administrative law case of *Chevron U.S.A., Inc. v. Natural Resources Defense Council*, the United States Supreme Court clarified the role of courts in reviewing agency interpretations of statutory language. 467 U.S. 837 (1984). *Chevron* concerned the EPA's interpretation of the term "stationary source" as used in the Clean Air Act. The term "stationary source" was not defined in the statute, and the EPA promulgated an informal rule that allowed states to treat a whole plant, rather than the individual smokestacks in the plant, as a "stationary source." The issue before the Supreme Court was whether this was a lawful interpretation of the Clean Air Act. More broadly, the issue was how much deference should be given to an agency's interpretation of a statute where Congress has given little guidance over the meaning of a statutory term. The APA provides that "the reviewing court shall decide all relevant questions of law, [and] interpret constitutional and statutory provisions...." 5 U.S.C. § 706. But it does not clearly preclude the court from relying on agency expertise in deciding such questions.

The approach to statutory interpretation that the Court adopted in *Chevron* is sometimes called the "*Chevron* two-step." Step one asks whether Congress has spoken directly to the precise question at issue. If the statutory language is clear or congressional intent is otherwise clear, then the issue is simple. The court gives no deference to the agency but instead simply enforces the statute. If, though, as is far more often the case,

Congress has not directly addressed the specific question or has left a gap for the agency to fill, step two kicks in. In this instance, the court must decide only whether the agency's interpretation is based on a "permissible" construction of the statute. The agency's interpretation need not be the best or the one the court might have reached on its own; it simply must be reasonable.

In recent years, the Court has made clear that *Chevron* deference does not apply to every agency interpretation of a statute. It plainly applies to notice and comment rulemaking decisions, and to decisions reached after a formal adjudicatory hearing. However, it does not apply to agency decisions that are reached without adequate public involvement or sufficient agency process, unless perhaps Congress has expressly or implicitly indicated its intention that the agency should fill a regulatory gap. In *United States v. Mead Corporation*, 533 U.S. 218, 226–27 (2001), for example, the Court denied *Chevron* deference to a Customs "ruling letter" that treated Mead's three-ring binder "day-planners" as "diaries" subject to certain tariffs. By regulation, a Customs ruling letter "represents the official position of the Customs Service with respect to the particular transaction or issue described therein and is binding on all Customs Service personnel...." 19 C.F.R. § 177.9(a). As such, a ruling letter is essentially an informal adjudication of the application of tariff rules to a particular product. Although the regulations suggest that notice and comment may be available for ruling letters that have the "effect of changing a practice," notice and comment was not provided for the letter issued to Mead. The Court held that the ruling letter "fails to qualify" under *Chevron*. *Id.* at 226–27. Nonetheless, the Court held that the decision was entitled to a lesser form of deference, sometimes called *Skidmore* deference. This reference comes from the Court's decision in *Skidmore v. Swift and Co.*, 323 U.S. 134 (1944). In that case, the Court held that an agency's

> rulings, interpretations and opinions ... while not controlling upon the courts by reason of their authority, do constitute a body of experience and informed judgment to which courts and litigants may properly resort for guidance. The weight of such a judgment in a particular case will depend upon the thoroughness evident in its consideration, the validity of its reasoning, its consistency with earlier and later pronouncements, and all those factors which give it power to persuade, if lacking power to control.

Id. at 140.

There are, of course, many reasons why Congress might leave issues open by using vague statutory language. It might consciously desire the agency to make a policy choice; it may not have considered the specific issue (as was the case in *Chevron*); or it may have been unable to reach a compromise, so it passed over the issue. Deference to agency decisions is consistent with the argument that unelected judges should back off and let agencies do what they do best (i.e., apply their expertise), so long as the procedures are followed. In practice, however, even where the more deferential standard of *Chevron* applies, courts still overturn agency rules, usually relying on step one (that Congressional intent was clear and the agency got it wrong) rather than the more deferential step two. Perhaps one reason that courts carefully scrutinize agency decisions is their concern—rarely stated—about agency capture and influence of public choice theory. Plainly, agencies can and do make decisions contrary to the facts or statute. Courts afford the first, and sometimes only, line of protection against this. We will see these arguments play out in Chapter 4's discussion of *Babbitt v. Sweet Home Chapter of Communities for a Great Oregon*, upholding the Department of Interior's interpretation of "harm" in its regulations implementing the Endangered Species Act. 515 U.S. 687 (1995).

In the 1980s and 1990s, a political battle raged over the logging of old-growth stands in the forests of the Pacific Northwest. The listing of the Northern Spotted Owl under the Endangered Species Act ultimately proved a critical impetus for a regional management plan that addressed logging and environmental concerns. The well-known case excerpted below addresses the government's initial refusal to list the owl as an endangered species and raises many of the administrative law issues we have just reviewed.

NORTHERN SPOTTED OWL v. HODEL, 716 F. Supp. 479 (W.D. Wash. 1988)

ZILLY, DISTRICT JUDGE

A number of environmental organizations bring this action against the United States Fish & Wildlife Service ("Service") and others, alleging that the Service's decision not to list the northern spotted owl as endangered or threatened under the Endangered Species Act of 1973 ("ESA" or "the Act") was arbitrary and capricious or contrary to law.

Since the 1970s the northern spotted owl has received much scientific attention, beginning with comprehensive studies of its natural history by Dr. Eric Forsman, whose most significant discovery was the close association between spotted owls and old-growth forests. This discovery raised concerns because the majority of remaining old-growth owl habitat is on public land available for harvest.

In January 1987, plaintiff Greenworld, pursuant to Sec. 4(b)(3) of the ESA petitioned the Service to list the northern spotted owl as endangered. In August 1987, 29 conservation organizations filed a second petition to list the owl as endangered both in the Olympic Peninsula in Washington and in the Oregon Coast Range, and as threatened throughout the rest of its range.

The ESA directs the Secretary of the Interior to determine whether any species have become endangered or threatened due to habitat destruction, overutilization, disease or predation, or other natural or manmade factors.[1] The

---

1. Section 4(a)(1), codified at 16 U.S.C. § 1533(a)(1), provides that:

The Secretary [of Interior in the case of terrestrial species] shall ... determine whether any species is an endangered species or a threatened species because of any of the following factors:

(A) the present or threatened destruction, modification, or curtailment of its habitat or range;

(B) overutilization for commercial, recreational, scientific, or educational purposes;

(C) disease or predation;

Act was amended in 1982 to ensure that the decision whether to list a species as endangered or threatened was based solely on an evaluation of the biological risks faced by the species, to the exclusion of all other factors.

The Service's role in deciding whether to list the northern spotted owl as endangered or threatened is to assess the technical and scientific data in the administrative record against the relevant listing criteria in section 4(a)(1) and then to exercise its own expert discretion in reaching its decision.

In July 1987, the Service announced that it would initiate a status review of the spotted owl and requested public comment. The Service assembled a group of Service biologists, including Dr. Mark Shaffer, its staff expert on population viability, to conduct the review. The Service charged Dr. Shaffer with analyzing current scientific information on the owl. Dr. Shaffer concluded that:

> the most reasonable interpretation of current data and knowledge indicate continued old growth harvesting is likely to lead to the extinction of the subspecies in the foreseeable future which argues strongly for listing the subspecies as threatened or endangered at this time.

M. Shaffer, letter of November 11, 1987, to Jay Gore, U.S. Fish and Wildlife Service, Region 1, Endangered Species, attached to *Final Assessment of Population Viability Projections for the Northern Spotted Owl*.

The Service invited a peer review of Dr. Shaffer's analysis by a number of U.S. experts on population viability, all of whom agreed with Dr. Shaffer's prognosis for the owl, although each had some criticisms of his work.

The Service's decision is contained in its 1987 Status Review of the Owl ("Status Review") and summarized in its Finding on Greenworld's petition. The Status Review was completed on December 14, 1987, and on December 17 the Service announced that listing the owl as endangered under the Act was not warranted at that time.[2] This suit followed. Both sides now move for summary judgment on the administrative record before the Court. * * *

This Court reviews the Service's action under the "arbitrary and capricious" standard of the Administrative Procedure Act ("APA"), 5 U.S.C. § 706(2)(A). This standard is narrow and presumes the agency action is valid, but it does not shield agency action from a "thorough, probing, in-depth review," *Citizens to Preserve Overton Park v. Volpe,* 401 U.S. 402, 415 (1971). Courts must not "rubber-stamp the agency decision as correct." *Ethyl Corp. v. EPA,* 541 F.2d 1 (1976).

> Rather, the reviewing court must assure itself that the agency decision was "based on a consideration of the relevant factors...." Moreover, it must engage in a "substantial inquiry" into the facts, one that is "searching and careful." This is particularly true in highly technical cases....

(D) the inadequacy of existing regulatory mechanisms; or

(E) other natural or manmade factors affecting its continued existence.

2. The Service's Finding provides as follows:

A finding is made that a proposed listing of the northern spotted owl is not warranted at this time. Due to the need for population trend information and other biological data, priority given by the Service to this species for further research and monitoring will continue to be high. Interagency agreements and Service initiatives support continued conservation efforts. This finding will be published in the *Federal Register* and the petitioner will be notified.

Id. at 34–35. Agency action is arbitrary and capricious where the agency has failed to "articulate a satisfactory explanation for its action including a 'rational connection between the facts found and the choice made.'" *Motor Vehicle Mfrs. Ass'n v. State Farm Mut. Auto Ins.*, 463 U.S. 29, 43 (1983).

The Status Review and the Finding to the listing petition offer little insight into how the Service found that the owl currently has a viable population. Although the Status Review cites extensive empirical data and lists various conclusions, it fails to provide any analysis. The Service asserts that it is entitled to make its own decision, yet it provides no explanation for its findings. An agency must set forth clearly the grounds on which it acted. Judicial deference to agency expertise is proper, but the Court will not do so blindly. The Court finds that the Service has not set forth the grounds for its decision against listing the owl.

The Service's documents also lack any expert analysis supporting its conclusion. Rather, the expert opinion is entirely to the contrary. The only reference in the Status Review to an actual opinion that the owl does not face a significant likelihood of extinction is a mischaracterization of a conclusion of Dr. Mark Boyce:

> Boyce (1987) in his analysis of the draft preferred alternative concluded that there is a low probability that the spotted owls will go extinct. He does point out that population fragmentation appears to impose the greatest risks to extinction.

Dr. Boyce responded to the Service:

> I did not conclude that the Spotted Owl enjoys a low probability of extinction, and I would be very disappointed if efforts to preserve the Spotted Owl were in any way thwarted by a misinterpretation of something I wrote.

M. Boyce, letter of February 18, 1988, to Rolf Wallenstrom, U.S. Fish and Wildlife Service, Region 1, exhibit 7 to Complaint.

Numerous other experts on population viability contributed to or reviewed drafts of the Status Review, or otherwise assessed spotted owl viability. Some were employed by the Service; others were independent. None concluded that the northern spotted owl is not at risk of extinction. For example, as noted above, Dr. Shaffer evaluated the current data and knowledge and determined that continued logging of old growth likely would lead to the extinction of the owl in the foreseeable future. This risk, he concluded, argued strongly for immediate listing of the subspecies as threatened or endangered. M. Shaffer, *Final Assessment of Population Viability Projections for the Northern Spotted Owl*, Memorandum to Jay Gore, U.S. Fish and Wildlife Service, Region 1, Endangered Species (November 11, 1987). The Service invited a peer review of Dr. Shaffer's analysis. Drs. Michael Soule, Bruce Wilcox, and Daniel Goodman, three leading U.S. experts on population viability, reviewed and agreed completely with Dr. Shaffer's prognosis for the owl. * * *

The Court will reject conclusory assertions of agency "expertise" where the agency spurns unrebutted expert opinions without itself offering a credible alternative explanation. Here, the Service disregarded all the expert opinion on population viability, including that of its own expert, that the owl is facing extinction, and instead merely asserted its expertise in support of its conclusions.

The Service has failed to provide its own or other expert analysis supporting its conclusions. Such analysis is necessary to establish a rational connection between the evidence presented and the Service's decision. Accordingly, the

United States Fish and Wildlife Service's decision not to list at this time the northern spotted owl as endangered or threatened under the Endangered Species Act was arbitrary and capricious and contrary to law.

The Court further finds that it is not possible from the record to determine that the Service considered the related issue of whether the northern spotted owl is a threatened species. This failure of the Service to review and make an express finding on the issue of threatened status is also arbitrary and capricious and contrary to law.

In deference to the Service's expertise and its role under the Endangered Species Act, the Court remands this matter to the Service, which has 90 days from the date of this order to provide an analysis for its decision that listing the northern spotted owl as threatened or endangered is not currently warranted. Further, the Service is ordered to supplement its Status Review and Petition Finding consistent with this Court's ruling.

QUESTIONS AND DISCUSSION

1. As you probably noticed, the lead plaintiff in the foregoing case was the northern spotted owl (identified in the official opinion as *Strix Occidentalis Caurina*). Why would the plaintiffs make the lead plaintiff a bird? Why do you think the Service's lawyers didn't challenge this seemingly odd litigation tactic? Note that the plaintiffs also included the Seattle Audubon Society, the Pilchuck Audubon Society, The Washington Environmental Council, the Yakima Valley Audubon Society, the Washington Wilderness Coalition, the Natural Resources Defense Council, The Wilderness Society, and 15 other NGOs. For further discussion of the role of NGO's and their standing to sue, see pages 236–258.

2. What is the agency action challenged by the plaintiffs? Is it a rule or an order? How does the government attempt to claim deference for its decision not to list the owl? Why is it unsuccessful?

3. Despite Judge Zilly's almost contemptuous dismissal of the government's arguments, he remands the case back to the Fish and Wildlife Service for 90 days. It is extremely unlikely, though, that any serious field research could be undertaken in such a short time period. Why didn't he simply order the Service to list the owl under the ESA?

4. Does Judge Zilly say the agency made a mistake in not listing the owl? Under an APA claim, to what extent can he examine the actual merits of the agency's scientific conclusions?

5. Consider the candid comments below of Vic Sher on the difficulties of challenging agency actions in the environmental field. Sher, former president of the Sierra Club Legal Defense Fund, was the plaintiffs' lawyer in the *Spotted Owl* case.

In most instances, Congress passes laws with general goals, then vests executive agencies with discretion to carry them out. "Discretion" here means that Congress allows the agencies to decide which of a wide range of options they will adopt to accomplish the general goals established by the legislation. This is especially true in cases involving complex scientific or technical issues; Congress leaves it to the agencies to exercise their expertise in implementing the laws.

*courts'
role in
jud'l rvw.
of agency
action*

The role of the courts in this context is only to determine whether the agencies have exceeded the permissible bounds of the discretion granted to them by Congress. Thus, the question is never whether an agency's decision is "right" or "best," but only whether it is legal. The APA makes this clear by limiting a court's inquiry in two crucial, fundamental ways. First, the APA limits the court to determining only whether the agency's action was "arbitrary, capricious, an abuse of discretion, or otherwise not in accordance with law, or was taken without observance of procedures required by law." Second, the APA limits the court's inquiry to the appropriateness of the agency's decision in light of the record before the agency.

You can see that this is an extremely limited inquiry. That is why the APA standard of review is known as an extremely "deferential" standard. It is not the court's role to substitute its judgment for the expertise of the agency, but only to ensure that the agency has not acted in such an irrational ("arbitrary and capricious") manner as to constitute an abuse of discretion.

I cannot overstate the implications of this institutional framework for environmental litigation against the government. For example, the APA requires that conflicts among experts always be resolved in favor of the government. Always means that, even if you have one hundred experts holding an opinion in your favor while only one expert supports the government, you still lose.

Of course, the government still manages to lose cases. For example, the government may incorrectly assert that the court must defer to its expertise, even when all the experts disagree with the government. This happened in the first spotted owl listing case, *Northern Spotted Owl v. Hodel*. In that case, the United States Fish & Wildlife Service (FWS) decided not to list the spotted owl under the Endangered Species Act. Although experts in population dynamics agreed overwhelmingly that the owl faced potential extinction from continued loss of habitat to logging, FWS in its decision notice referred to a population dynamics expert as agreeing that the owl faced little risk. Subsequently, the Sierra Club Legal Defense Fund learned that the expert disagreed with this mischaracterization of his work. As we said in our briefs, it turned out that the agency's assertion of "expertise" was all "-tise" and no "expert." . . . We won the case, and the spotted owl ultimately received protection under the Endangered Species Act. * * *

The truth is that litigation victories against the government are more often a function of the government's arrogance, incompetence, or outright efforts to evade the law, than anything else. I wish this statement were hyperbole, but it is not. . . . The good news, if it may be called that, is that such boneheaded moves by the government are not that uncommon. As long as that circumstance persists, citizens will win lawsuits against the government—even under the APA—to enforce the laws as Congress intended them to be enforced.

Vic Sher, *Breaking Out of the Box: Toxic Risk, Government Actions, and Constitutional Rights*, 13 J. ENVTL. L. & LITIG. 145, 146–150 (1998).

6. Assume that the Bureau of Land Management issues an informal rule establishing an auction system for grazing allotments. Three years later, the agency announces that the auction approach has not performed well and rescinds the rule. Is this decision also subject to notice-and-comment rulemaking? *See* 5 U.S.C. § 551(5). Should it matter whether the reason for rescinding the rule is primarily factual—for example, because new data indicate a better approach, the rule has not worked well in practice, etc.— or political—the new administration is opposed to market mechanisms, effective lobbying by ranching interests, etc.? If challenged in court, how deferential do you think the judge should be in reviewing an agency's decision to change course?

Motor Vehicle Mfrs. Ass'n v. State Farm Mut. Auto. Ins. Co., 463 U.S. 29 (1983), involved a decision by the Department of Transportation to rescind a rule that would have required passive restraint systems on all automobiles produced after September, 1982. While the Court made clear that a decision to rescind a rule is subject to the same arbitrary and capricious standard that applies to promulgation of a new rule, it acknowledged that

> revocation of an extant regulation is substantially different than a failure to act. Revocation constitutes a reversal of the agency's former views as to the proper course. . . . Accordingly, an agency changing its course by rescinding a rule is obligated to supply a reasoned analysis for the change beyond that which may be required when an agency does not act in the first instance.

Id. at 41–42.

7. In addition to the procedural requirements of the APA, agencies must also comply with other statutory requirements. The National Environmental Policy Act (NEPA), 42 U.S.C. §§ 4321–4370, for example, requires agencies to prepare environmental impact statements on major federal actions that significantly affect the quality of the human environment. "Actions" are expressly defined to encompass "new or revised agency rules, regulations, plans, policies, or procedures. . . ." 40 C.F.R. § 1508.18 (2002). The Regulatory Flexibility Act, 5 U.S.C.A. §§ 601–612, requires agencies to prepare a regulatory flexibility analysis for any rule that may have important economic impact on a significant number of small businesses. Similarly, the Paperwork Reduction Act, 44 U.S.C. §§ 3501–3520, requires agencies to assess the impacts of their reporting and recordkeeping requirements, and the Unfunded Mandates Reform Act, 2 U.S.C. §§ 1501–1504, requires analysis of budgetary impacts if agency rules impose financial obligations on states or local government over $100 million.

NEPA

Presidents have also imposed analysis requirements on agencies through executive orders. President Reagan's E.O. 12291 required cost-benefit analysis for major rules (defined as a rule that has an annual economic impact of $100 million or more). Although Reagan's Order was superseded by President Clinton's E.O. 12886, the new order retains the basic requirement for cost-benefit analysis and further asks agencies to "select those approaches that maximize net benefits." President Clinton's E.O. 12988 requires agencies to review their laws and regulations to ensure they minimize litigation; and E.O. 12898 requires agencies to make achieving environmental justice part of their mission and, in particular, "to the greatest extent practicable and permitted by law," identify and address disproportionately high and adverse human health or environmental effects on minority and low-income populations.

Exec. orders

Cost-ben. analysis

While the stated goal of all these initiatives has been to ensure agencies fully consider the many possible impacts of their rules, the net effect has led to what some call "ossification"—the increasing costs and rigidity of the rulemaking process caused by extensive requirements for analysis and justification of individual rules. One result, whether intended or not, has been to make rulemaking an expensive and resource-intensive process. As a result, there has been a significant shift to greater reliance on non-legislative rules. *See, e.g.,* Thomas O. McGarity, *Some Thoughts on "Deossifying" the Rulemaking Process,* 41 DUKE L.J. 1315 (1992); Mark Seidenfeld, *Demystifying Deossification: Rethinking Recent Proposals to Modify Judicial Review of Notice and Comment Rulemaking,* 75 TEXAS L. REV. 483 (1997).

8. Complex agency rules are sometimes portrayed as the bane of industry, effectively giving foreign business a competitive edge in the increasingly global market. In *The Miasma of Regulation,* former Secretary of Labor Robert Reich suggests that clever industry lawyers are at least as culpable as government bureaucrats for our complex regulatory world. He uses a funny but compelling story about Henry, the inventor of a "turbo-charged, automatic vacuum cleaner," and his lawyer, Seymour. Henry's vacuum cleaner is quite popular but has one flaw—"[i]t emits a roar something like a jet engine at full throttle, but louder." The Environmental Protection Agency promulgates a simple rule to address the problem of excessive noise from consumer products, but the rule is no match for Seymour's legal prowess. He argues, for example, that the vacuum cleaner is not a consumer product, but an industrial product, and that indeed it is not a product at all but rather a service, because the machines are not sold but rather leased. The EPA responds with ever more complex standards to overcome Seymour's arguments, but Seymour finds ways to parry every EPA thrust. And even as the object of the EPA rules successfully avoids regulation, the manufacturers of other consumer products become burdened by the rules and complain bitterly about over-zealous government regulation. *See* Robert B. Reich, *The Miasma of Regulation, in* TALES OF A NEW AMERICA (1987); *see also* J.B. Ruhl & James Salzman, *Mozart and the Red Queen: The Problem of Regulatory Accretion in the Administrative State,* 91 GEO. L.J. 757 (2003). What are the lessons from Reich's story? What does it tell you about how litigation and the threat of litigation impacts regulatory policy. Can anything be done to overcome the gridlock and under-regulation that sometimes results?

B. THE ROLE OF NONGOVERNMENTAL ORGANIZATIONS (NGOS)*

The United States has long had the most dynamic and forceful environmental movement in the world. Environmental groups have been active in America since soon after Henry David Thoreau moved to Walden Pond. When the Audubon Society (a predecessor to today's National Audubon Society) was formed in 1886, almost 40,000 people joined. Within the next fifty years, conservationists formed such important national organizations as the Sierra Club, the Izaak Walton League, the National Wildlife Federation, and the Wilderness Society. By 1960, over 300,000 Americans belonged to the major conservation organizations. These organizations helped

* This section is adapted from JAMES SALZMAN & BARTON THOMPSON, JR., CONCEPTS AND INSIGHTS IN ENVIRONMENTAL LAW AND POLICY 68– 75 (2003). The authors are grateful for the contributions of Buzz Thompson.

to expand the vast system of national parks, forests, and wilderness areas that grace the United States today and to pass early environmental legislation.

The first Earth Day in 1970 saw a major change and expansion in the American environmental movement. The number of environmental organizations increased geometrically. The focus of the environmental movement, moreover, broadened to include pollution and toxic substances. Borrowing from the Civil Rights movement, environmental groups also adopted a more activist stance, filing litigation and aggressively lobbying Congress and administrative agencies. A number of the new environmental organizations specifically emphasized legal change. Among the most prominent were the Environmental Defense Fund, which was formed in 1967 in the wake of Rachel Carson's book, *Silent Spring*; the Natural Resources Defense Council, formed in 1969; and the Sierra Club Legal Defense Fund, founded in 1971 and now known as Earthjustice.

While environmental and conservation organizations have played an important role in the evolution of natural resources law, development interests have been well represented in the debate. In addition to the work of individual companies, trade organizations such as the National Mining Association and the National Cattlemen's Association, promote mining and grazing interests, respectively. Nonprofit groups representing development and property rights interests have also formed in recent years in an attempt to counterbalance the impact of environmental groups.

1. LOBBYING FOR LEGISLATIVE AND ADMINISTRATIVE ACTION

Based on public choice theory (discussed in Chapter 1, *supra* at pages 61–62), few political scientists would have predicted that the federal government would pass such strong environmental laws. Typically, industrial opponents of environmental laws are well organized and can afford to invest substantial resources to defeat or weaken legislation. Few members of the general public, by contrast, have a sufficient interest in any particular piece of environmental legislation to devote equivalent resources to ensuring the legislation's passage. When asked to participate in a collective lobbying effort, moreover, many members of the public may be tempted to decline, presuming that they can "free ride" on the efforts of other members of the public.

The major environmental organizations in the United States have found effective means of overcoming these "collective action" obstacles. Environmental groups have raised substantial money from the public both by framing environmental and natural resource issues in moral terms and by perfecting mass-mailing campaigns. Although many people still free ride on others' donations, environmental groups have used their limited resources efficiently. Unlike industry lobbyists, environmental organizations have been able to focus their resources solely on environmental issues. Through coordinated lobbying campaigns, the organizations have provided Congress and state legislatures with valuable scientific and legal expertise. Through member communications and skilled use of the media, they also have mobilized voters. As a result, the imprint of environmental organizations can be found throughout environmental law. The Natural Resources

Defense Council, for example, helped pass the Clean Water Act. The Environmental Defense Fund helped devise the Safe Harbor provisions of the Endangered Species Act. Moreover, depending on the administration, a revolving door operates between leaders of environmental groups and high-level government officials. Gus Speth, one of the cofounders of NRDC, for example, was appointed Chair of the Commission on Environmental Quality in the Carter administration. Don Barry, the Assistant Secretary for Fish, Wildlife, and Parks in the Clinton administration, now has a senior post in The Wilderness Society. This is equally true for groups that promote resource extraction interests. James Watt, the controversial Secretary of the Interior in the Reagan administration, previously directed the industry-friendly Mountain States Legal Foundation.

In broad terms, environmental NGOs fulfill three different roles. The first is advocacy. This is the most public face of NGOs, and would include most of the large membership organizations, such as the National Audubon Society and the Sierra Club, and hundreds of smaller groups, most of which operate at a local level. Many of these organizations have the resources and technical expertise to work on a full range of environmental issues. Their staffs often include lawyers, scientists, and economists in an effort to bring an interdisciplinary approach to environmental issues. Advocacy may, of course, be achieved through litigation, but lobbying, grassroots pressure, and public education can be equally, if not more, effective. Some of the most effective groups are local and issue-specific.

The second role is that of think tank and expert analysis. These organizations include the Environmental Law Institute, Resources for the Future, and the World Resources Institute. These groups seek to influence the policy process through their reports and studies on a range of issues. While not advocates in the sense of courtroom lawyers or congressional lobbyists, these groups have firm policy perspectives, ranging from greater reliance on economic instruments to the need for more effective environmental law.

The third role is that of market actor. Groups such as The Nature Conservancy and Conservation International dominate this sector, conserving and managing lands around the world. The Nature Conservancy is the world's richest environmental group, with assets of $3.3 billion and 3,200 employees. In order to ensure their support across the political spectrum, these groups intentionally do not take positions on environmental issues and explicitly do not regard themselves as advocacy organizations. This does not mean they lack critics, however. A series of investigative articles in the *Washington Post* accused the Nature Conservancy of drilling for oil on one of its holdings, lending employees money at below-market rates, selling undeveloped land to its trustees as home sites, etc. *See* David B. Ottaway and Joe Stephens, *Nonprofit Land Bank Amasses Billions; Charity Builds Assets on Corporate Partnerships*, WASH. POST, May 4, 2003, at A1. On the other hand, they have protected more than 100 million acres of land and more than 5,000 miles of rivers worldwide.

A hybrid category bears mentioning, as well: organizations that operate as parts of global networks. Most notable among these are the International Union for the Conservation of Nature (IUCN) (actually a network comprised of NGOs and government agencies concerned with nature conservation), Friends of the Earth–International (a network of 70 national member groups), Greenpeace International (present in 40 countries with more than 2.8 million members), and the World Wide Fund for Nature (a federation of national organizations boasting almost 5 million members). The Environmental Law Alliance Worldwide (ELAW) is a particularly interesting example of an international network of affiliated organizations. Comprised of over 300 public interest scientists and lawyers from 60 countries, ELAW is essentially the first global, virtual law firm dedicated to public interest environmental law. Advocates from over fifty countries access the ELAW network each year. Most of these NGOs have their own website, easily found on the internet.

Indeed, the environmental movement has "gone global." Virtually every country now has at least one environmental NGO, many of which are actively seeking partnerships and cooperative activities with their colleagues from other countries. In 2006, there were 7,432 intergovernmental organizations and 52,763 NGOs around the world. YEARBOOK OF INTERNATIONAL ORGANIZATIONS, 2006/2007.

QUESTIONS AND DISCUSSION

1. Politics makes strange bedfellows, and natural resource politics are no exception. One unlikely alliance, for example, has seen the hunting organization, Ducks Unlimited, working closely in alliance with wildlife groups to protect wetlands. Both groups' constituencies want to conserve ducks, though the former wish to shoot ducks with guns while the latter just shoot with their cameras. Economist Bruce Yandle has argued that, in some cases, environmental groups can provide political and public relations cover for quite different interests. He calls such alliances "Baptists and Bootleggers," referring to the unlikely partnership during the early 1900s when Baptists, who supported Prohibition and Sunday closing laws for alcohol sales, were supported by bootleggers, whose sales rose when their competitors were closed one day a week (and whose sales would rise even higher if their legal competitors were put out of business entirely). *See* Bruce Yandle, *The Golden Age of Risk,* THE INDEPENDENT INSTITUTE, Dec. 1998, *available at* http://www.independent.org/tii/news/981200Yandle.html.

---

2.   CITIZEN SUITS AND LITIGATION

NGOs have been very successful using litigation to influence environmental and natural resources law. As described above, the APA authorizes interested parties to seek judicial review of agency action that is arbitrary and capricious or that fails to conform to procedural standards. Indeed, the threat of litigation—backed up with a compelling legal argument—probably has a greater impact on agency action than the most compelling policy argument.

Beyond APA litigation, NGOs often file "citizen suits." Every major federal pollution law passed since 1970 contains a citizen suit provision (with the exception of the Federal Insecticide, Fungicide, and Rodenticide Act). By contrast, most of the important natural resource laws, including, for example, NEPA, NFMA, and FLPMA, lack citizen suit provisions. Two important exceptions are the Endangered Species Act and the Surface Mining Control and Reclamation Act. The absence of a citizen suit provision does not mean that citizens cannot sue. But it does mean that citizens must rely on the APA to obtain review. This generally limits actions to suits against government agencies alleging arbitrary and capricious action.

Citizen suits offer several advantages to plaintiffs over the APA. First, in addition to suits against agencies, citizen suit provisions allow actions to be brought directly against a person or company alleged to be in violation of the law, effectively empowering private attorneys general. Environmental groups have used this device frequently both to supplement the government's limited enforcement resources and to pursue violations that the government is ignoring. When governmental enforcement efforts declined at the beginning of the Reagan administration in the early 1980s, organizations such as the Natural Resources Defense Council organized an enforcement campaign to take up the slack. Second, they can sue the agency officials who fail to carry out a non-discretionary statutory duty. For example, the Endangered Species Act (ESA) requires the Secretary of the Interior to designate critical habitat for listed species within one year from listing the species. 16 U.S.C. § 1533(b)(6)(C). Failure to meet this deadline may lead to a citizen suit against the Secretary under the ESA's citizen suit provision. 16 U.S.C. § 1540(g)(1)(C). Third, citizen suit provisions generally allow prevailing plaintiffs to recover their legal costs, including their attorneys' fees. This can offer an attractive incentive for private lawyers to assist environmental groups in pursuing litigation. It should be noted, however, that even where a citizen suit provision is not available, Congress has authorized certain prevailing plaintiffs—generally those plaintiffs with limited assets—to recover their litigation costs, including "reasonable" attorney fees, when they prevail against a federal agency defendant and the agency's position is "substantially unjustified." *See* Equal Access to Justice Act, 28 U.S.C. § 2412; 5 U.S.C. § 504.

In keeping with the notion that citizen suit provisions are intended to encourage citizens to act essentially as attorneys for the state and not on their own behalf, the provisions generally authorize only injunctive relief. Several statutes authorize courts to impose monetary penalties in citizen suits, but the penalties are payable to the United States, not the private prosecutor. In practice, however, plaintiffs sometimes settle their citizen suits on terms that include not only the cessation of violations, but also agreements to engage in projects that benefit the environment.

Citizen suit provisions do not permit private plaintiffs to prosecute every violation of an environmental law. First, for largely political reasons, Congress purposefully has excluded some violations from the purview of citizen suits. Second, state sovereign immunity under the Eleventh Amendment precludes plaintiffs from pursuing citizen suits against non-consenting states for monetary damages—although purely injunctive actions (which have been far more important) are still permissible. *See Alden v. Maine*, 527 U.S. 706 (1999).

In authorizing citizen suits, Congress wanted to supplement, not duplicate, government enforcement efforts. As a result, citizen suit provisions prevent private plaintiffs from filing a lawsuit if the federal or state government has commenced and is "diligently prosecuting" a civil or criminal action or, under some statutes, has initiated at least some form of administrative enforcement proceeding. *See, e.g.,* ESA, 16 U.S.C. § 1640(g)(2). Furthermore, plaintiffs must generally provide the federal government and the alleged violator with 60 days prior notice of their intent to sue before commencing an action. This affords the government an opportunity to commence its own action first and the violator a chance to correct the problem that is identified. Courts are split on what happens if the government does not initiate an enforcement action before a citizen suit is filed, but subsequently enters into a consent decree—a court order based upon an agreement between the parties—with the defendant while the citizen suit is pending. Most courts have concluded that the consent decree bars the citizen suit if the decree reasonably ensures that the violation will not recur. *See, e.g., Ellis v. Gallatin Steel Co.,* 390 F.3d 461 (6th Cir. 2004) (holding that a consent decree regarding fugitive dust claims under the Clean Air Act bars all preexisting citizen claims).

———

3. STANDING

Not just anyone can file a case in court challenging an agency action. Indeed, whenever an NGO or individual seeks judicial review or files a citizen suit, one of the first questions that the court will ask is whether the plaintiff has "standing" to sue. This "standing" requirement comes from Article III of the Constitution, which limits the jurisdiction of federal courts to "cases or controversies." The Supreme Court has explained that a "case or controversy" exists when the parties before the court have an actual, as opposed to hypothetical, stake in the outcome. To the extent the parties have a stake in the outcome, the "legal questions presented will be resolved, not in the rarefied atmosphere of a debating society, but in a concrete factual context conducive to a realistic appreciation of the consequences of judicial action." *Valley Forge Christian College v. Americans United for Separation of Church and State, Inc.,* 454 U.S. 464, 472 (1982). The Supreme Court has held that an individual generally must demonstrate three facts to establish standing. First, the plaintiff must demonstrate that the challenged action has or will cause the plaintiff "injury in fact." Second, the plaintiff must show "causation"—that this injury can be traced to the challenged action. Third, the plaintiff must show "redressability"—that the court can afford relief that will redress the injury. An additional "prudential" requirement for standing must be met if the plaintiff is relying on the APA to support its action. This requirement stems from the provision in the APA that authorizes suits against the government whenever a person suffers an injury "within the meaning of a relevant statute." 5 U.S.C. § 702. Under this provision, plaintiffs must show that their injury is within the "zone of interests" sought to be protected by the statute. Since this requirement comes from the APA, it does not apply where a plaintiff can rely, for example, on a citizen suit provision. *See Bennett v. Spear*, 520 U.S. 154 (1997).

In addition, where an organization sues on behalf of one of its members, the organization must show that—(1) one or more of its members satisfy the basic standing requirements; (2) the relief being sought is "germane to the organization's purposes"; and (3) neither the claim asserted nor the relief requested requires the participation of individual members (as for example, where damages are sought for economic injuries to the particular member). *Hunt v. Washington State Apple Advertising Committee*, 432 U.S. 333, 343 (1977). Under this test, for example, the Minnesota Elk Breeder's Association would probably have problems satisfying the second part of the *Hunt* test if they were to sue the National Marine Fisheries Service for failing to list a tuna species as endangered.

Notwithstanding arguments that current standing rules are more burdensome than required by the "case or controversy" standard, a majority of the current Supreme Court appears committed to maintaining standing rules for several reasons. First, standing requirements such as "injury in fact" perform an important gate-keeping function to ensure that courts do not become embroiled in what otherwise might be largely academic questions. If no one has been hurt, judicial intervention is unnecessary. Second, the standing requirements ensure that the plaintiff has sufficient interest in the matter to provide adequate representation of the public interest. Finally, standing is a means of ensuring the separation of powers; absent injury in fact and the other standing findings, courts would be interfering unnecessarily in the activities of the other branches. Whether you agree with these arguments, and each has been challenged, they have led federal courts to throw a number of citizen suits and other cases out of court before any consideration of the merits of the actions. Indeed, environmentalists at times have worried that the courts have been trying to use standing as a roadblock to environmental change.

Injury in Fact. Most standing disputes focus on the first requirement of injury in fact. The Supreme Court helped to promote environmental litigation in the early 1970s by adopting a broad view of what constitutes an injury in the environmental field. In *Sierra Club v. Morton*, 405 U.S. 727 (1972), the Sierra Club challenged the Forest Service's approval of Walt Disney Enterprises' plan to develop a ski resort in the Sequoia National Forest. The Supreme Court held that the Sierra Club had not established standing to sue because it had not alleged that any of its members actually used the area of the proposed development and thus would be affected by Disney's plan. But the Court emphasized that standing did not require a showing of *economic* injury. For standing purposes, injuries can "reflect 'aesthetic, conservational, and recreational' as well as economic values" and can be widely shared among the population. *Id.* at 738. All the Sierra Club needed to do therefore was to allege that its members would suffer aesthetic or recreational injury as a result of the proposed development, and that's exactly what the Sierra Club did on remand. In a famous dissent, Justice William O. Douglas would have gone further and allowed lawsuits to be filed "in the name of the inanimate object about to be despoiled, defaced, or invaded by roads and bulldozers and where injury is the subject of public outrage." *Id.* at 741.

Traceability and Redressability. Tracing the plaintiff's injuries to the defendant's conduct (essentially showing causation) and demonstrating that the court can order relief that will redress the plaintiff's injuries are often related and can pose obstacles for plaintiffs. For example, in *Duke Power Co. v. Carolina Environmental Study Group,* 438 U.S. 59 (1978), the plaintiffs challenged the Price Anderson Act, which limits the liability of nuclear power plant licensees in the event of an accident at a nuclear power plant. The plaintiffs were hoping that if the Price Anderson Act were declared unconstitutional, the companies proposing to build two new nuclear power plants would withdraw their applications. The defendants argued that the plaintiffs lacked standing because they could not show that the power plants would not be built even without the Price Anderson Act and thus that their alleged injury would be redressed. Nonetheless, the Court found standing because there was a substantial likelihood that a favorable decision for the plaintiffs would cause the companies to withdraw their application.

Another example of redressability problems involves standing to bring a citizen suit for violations that have occurred entirely in the past. The Supreme Court has denied standing where neither of the remedies potentially available to the plaintiff (an injunction or a civil penalty payable to the government) could remedy any injury that the plaintiff suffered as a result of the past violation. *Steel Co. v. Citizens for a Better Environment*, 523 U.S. 83 (1998). In a subsequent decision, however, the Court held that an environmental organization has standing to seek civil penalties in the face of violations continuing at the time the suit was filed—even though any penalties awarded go to the government—because the penalties redress plaintiffs' injury by deterring future violations. *Friends of the Earth v. Laidlaw Environmental Services*, 528 U.S. 167 (2000).

Zone of Interests. The "zone of interests" requirement frequently becomes an issue when an industry group seeks to use environmental laws to thwart governmental actions protecting the environment. In a number of lawsuits, for example, industry groups have tried to block the government from reforming grazing, timber, water, or other resource policies on the ground that the government had not prepared an environmental impact statement under the National Envirnmental Policy Act (NEPA). Lower federal courts have generally rejected these lawsuits on the ground that NEPA's purpose is to protect the environment, not the economic interest of industry. In other cases, however, courts have concluded that Congress intended to provide standing to industry organizations.

In *Bennett v. Spear*, 520 U.S. 154 (1997), for example, ranchers and irrigation districts, upset by the Interior Department's decision to reduce their water deliveries because of endangered species concerns, filed a citizen suit under the Endangered Species Act (ESA) claiming that the department had failed to perform nondiscretionary duties—using the "best scientific data available" and considering the economic impact of designating a particular area as "critical habitat" for a species. Borrowing the logic of the NEPA cases, the lower court held that the ranchers and districts did not have standing because the purpose of the ESA was to protect the environment. The Supreme Court, however, reversed. Noting that the citizen suit provision granted a right to file a citizen suit to "any person," the Court concluded that Congress had not meant to restrict who could bring a citizen suit but had contemplated that industry groups might use the provision to avoid "over-enforcement" of the law.

Despite a broad trend over the last three decades to loosen standing requirements, more recent decisions appear to be narrowing the jurisdiction of the courts over resource issues in cases brought by third parties not directly involved in agency action. The case below is one of the most prominent examples of this development.

LUJAN v. DEFENDERS OF WILDLIFE
504 U.S. 555 (1992)

JUSTICE SCALIA delivered the opinion of the Court with respect to Parts I, II, III–A, and IV, and an opinion with respect to Part III–B, in which THE CHIEF JUSTICE, Justice WHITE, and Justice THOMAS join

This case involves a challenge to a rule promulgated by the Secretary of the Interior interpreting § 7 of the Endangered Species Act of 1973 (ESA), in such fashion as to render it applicable only to actions within the United States or on the high seas. The preliminary issue, and the only one we reach, is whether respondents here, plaintiffs below, have standing to seek judicial review of the rule. * * *

I

In 1978, the Fish and Wildlife Service (FWS) and the National Marine Fisheries Service (NMFS), on behalf of the Secretary of the Interior and the Secretary of Commerce respectively, promulgated a joint regulation stating that the obligations imposed by § 7(a)(2) extend to actions taken in foreign nations. [Section 7(a)(2) forbids the federal government from taking actions that will jeopardize or adversely modify the critical habitat of an endangered species.] The next year, however, the Interior Department began to reexamine its position. A revised joint regulation, reinterpreting § 7(a)(2) to require consultation only for actions taken in the United States or on the high seas, was proposed in 1983 and promulgated in 1986.

Shortly thereafter, respondents, organizations dedicated to wildlife conservation and other environmental causes, filed this action against the Secretary of the Interior, seeking a declaratory judgment that the new regulation is in error as to the geographic scope of § 7(a)(2) and an injunction requiring the Secretary to promulgate a new regulation restoring the initial interpretation. * * *

II

While the Constitution of the United States divides all power conferred upon the Federal Government into "legislative Powers," Art. I, § 1, "[t]he executive Power," Art. II, § 1, and "[t]he judicial Power," Art. III, § 1, it does not attempt to define those terms. To be sure, it limits the jurisdiction of federal courts to "Cases" and "Controversies," but an executive inquiry can bear the name "case" (the Hoffa case) and a legislative dispute can bear the name "controversy" (the Smoot–Hawley controversy). Obviously, then, the Constitution's central mechanism of separation of powers depends largely upon common understanding of what activities are appropriate to legislatures, to executives, and to courts. In The Federalist No. 48, Madison expressed the view that "[i]t is not infrequently a question of real nicety in legislative bodies whether the operation of a particular measure will, or will not, extend beyond the legislative sphere," whereas "the executive power [is] restrained within a narrower compass and ... more simple in its nature," and "the judiciary [is] described by landmarks still less uncertain." One of those landmarks, setting apart the "Cases" and "Controversies" that are of the justiciable sort referred to in Article III—"serv[ing] to identify those disputes which are appropriately resolved through the judicial process," is the doctrine of standing. Though some of its elements express merely prudential considerations that are part of judicial self-government, the core component of standing is an essential and unchanging part of the case-or-controversy requirement of Article III.

Over the years, our cases have established that the irreducible constitutional minimum of standing contains three elements. First, the plaintiff must have suffered an "injury in fact"—an invasion of a legally protected interest which is (a) concrete and particularized, and (b) "actual or imminent, not 'conjectural' or 'hypothetical.'" Second, there must be a causal connection between the injury and the conduct complained of—the injury has to be "fairly ... trace[able] to the challenged action of the defendant, and not ... th[e] result [of] the independent action of some third party not before the court." Third, it must be "likely," as opposed to merely "speculative," that the injury will be "redressed by a favorable decision."

The party invoking federal jurisdiction bears the burden of establishing these elements. Since they are not mere pleading requirements but rather an indispensable part of the plaintiff's case, each element must be supported in the same way as any other matter on which the plaintiff bears the burden of proof, i.e., with the manner and degree of evidence required at the successive stages of the litigation. At the pleading stage, general factual allegations of injury resulting from the defendant's conduct may suffice, for on a motion to dismiss we "presum[e] that general allegations embrace those specific facts that are necessary to support the claim." In response to a summary judgment motion, however, the plaintiff can no longer rest on such "mere allegations," but must "set forth" by affidavit or other evidence "specific facts," Fed. R. Civ. P. 56(e), which for purposes of the summary judgment motion will be taken to be true. And at the final stage, those facts (if controverted) must be "supported adequately by the evidence adduced at trial."

When the suit is one challenging the legality of government action or inaction, the nature and extent of facts that must be averred (at the summary judgment stage) or proved (at the trial stage) in order to establish standing depends considerably upon whether the plaintiff is himself an object of the action (or forgone action) at issue. If he is, there is ordinarily little question that the action or inaction has caused him injury, and that a judgment preventing or requiring the action will redress it. When, however, as in this case, a plaintiff's asserted injury arises from the government's allegedly unlawful regulation (or lack of regulation) of someone else, much more is needed. In that circumstance, causation and redressability ordinarily hinge on the response of the regulated (or regulable) third party to the government action or inaction—and perhaps on the response of others as well. The existence of one or more of the essential elements of standing "depends on the unfettered choices made by independent actors not before the courts and whose exercise of broad and legitimate discretion the courts cannot presume either to control or to predict"; and it becomes the burden of the plaintiff to adduce facts showing that those choices have been or will be made in such manner as to produce causation and permit redressability of injury. Thus, when the plaintiff is not himself the object of the government action or inaction he challenges, standing is not precluded, but it is ordinarily "substantially more difficult" to establish.

III

We think the Court of Appeals failed to apply the foregoing principles in denying the Secretary's motion for summary judgment. Respondents had not made the requisite demonstration of (at least) injury and redressability.

A

Respondents' claim to injury is that the lack of consultation with respect to certain funded activities abroad "increas[es] the rate of extinction of endangered and threatened species." Of course, the desire to use or observe an animal species, even for purely esthetic purposes, is undeniably a cognizable interest for purpose of standing. "But the 'injury in fact' test requires more than an injury to a cognizable interest. It requires that the party seeking review be himself among the injured." *Sierra Club v. Morton*, 405 U.S. 727, 734 (1972). To survive the Secretary's summary judgment motion, respondents had to submit affidavits or other evidence showing, through specific facts, not only that listed species were in fact being threatened by funded activities abroad, but also that one or more of respondents' members would thereby be "directly" affected apart from their " 'special interest' in th[e] subject." *Id.* at 735, 739.

With respect to this aspect of the case, the Court of Appeals focused on the affidavits of two Defenders' members—Joyce Kelly and Amy Skilbred. Ms. Kelly stated that she traveled to Egypt in 1986 and "observed the traditional habitat of the endangered Nile crocodile there and intend[s] to do so again, and hope[s] to observe the crocodile directly," and that she "will suffer harm in fact as the result of [the] American ... role ... in overseeing the rehabilitation of the Aswan High Dam on the Nile ... and [in] develop[ing] ... Egypt's ... Master Water Plan." App. 101. Ms. Skilbred averred that she traveled to Sri Lanka in 1981 and "observed th[e] habitat" of "endangered species such as the Asian elephant and the leopard" at what is now the site of the Mahaweli project funded by the Agency for International Development (AID), although she "was unable to see any of the endangered species"; "this development project," she continued, "will seriously reduce endangered, threatened, and endemic species habitat including areas that I visited ...[, which] may severely shorten the future of these species"; that threat, she concluded, harmed her because she "intend[s] to return to Sri Lanka in the future and hope[s] to be more fortunate in spotting at least the endangered elephant and leopard." When Ms. Skilbred was asked at a subsequent deposition if and when she had any plans to return to Sri Lanka, she reiterated that "I intend to go back to Sri Lanka," but confessed that she had no current plans: "I don't know [when]. There is a civil war going on right now. I don't know. Not next year, I will say. In the future."

We shall assume for the sake of argument that these affidavits contain facts showing that certain agency-funded projects threaten listed species— though that is questionable. They plainly contain no facts, however, showing how damage to the species will produce "imminent" injury to Mses. Kelly and Skilbred. That the women "had visited" the areas of the projects before the projects commenced proves nothing. As we have said in a related context, " 'Past exposure to illegal conduct does not in itself show a present case or controversy regarding injunctive relief ... if unaccompanied by any continuing, present adverse effects.' " *Los Angeles v. Lyons*, 401 U.S. 95, 102. And the affiants' profession of an "inten[t]" to return to the places they had visited before—where they will presumably, this time, be deprived of the opportunity to observe animals of the endangered species—is simply not enough. Such "some day" intentions—without any description of concrete plans, or indeed even any specification of when the some day will be—do not support a finding of the "actual or imminent" injury that our cases require.

B

Besides relying upon the Kelly and Skilbred affidavits, respondents propose a series of novel standing theories. The first, inelegantly styled "ecosystem nexus," proposes that any person who uses any part of a "contiguous ecosystem" adversely affected by a funded activity has standing even if the activity is located a great distance away. This approach, as the Court of Appeals correctly observed, is inconsistent with our opinion in *National Wildlife Federation*, which held that a plaintiff claiming injury from environmental damage must use the area affected by the challenged activity and not an area roughly "in the vicinity" of it. *Lujan v. National Wildlife*, 497 U.S. 871, 887–89. It makes no difference that the general-purpose section of the ESA states that the Act was intended in part "to provide a means whereby the ecosystems upon which endangered species and threatened species depend may be conserved," 16 U.S.C. § 1531(b). To say that the Act protects ecosystems is not to say that the Act creates (if it were possible) rights of action in persons who have not been injured in fact, that is, persons who use portions of an ecosystem not perceptibly affected by the unlawful action in question.

Respondents' other theories are called, alas, the "animal nexus" approach, whereby anyone who has an interest in studying or seeing the endangered animals anywhere on the globe has standing; and the "vocational nexus" approach, under which anyone with a professional interest in such animals can sue. Under these theories, anyone who goes to see Asian elephants in the Bronx Zoo, and anyone who is a keeper of Asian elephants in the Bronx Zoo, has standing to sue because the Director of the Agency for International Development (AID) did not consult with the Secretary regarding the AID-funded project in Sri Lanka. This is beyond all reason. Standing is not "an ingenious academic exercise in the conceivable," but as we have said requires, at the summary judgment stage, a factual showing of perceptible harm. It is clear that the person who observes or works with a particular animal threatened by a federal decision is facing perceptible harm, since the very subject of his interest will no longer exist. It is even plausible—though it goes to the outermost limit of plausibility—to think that a person who observes or works with animals of a particular species in the very area of the world where that species is threatened by a federal decision is facing such harm, since some animals that might have been the subject of his interest will no longer exist. It goes beyond the limit, however, and into pure speculation and fantasy, to say that anyone who observes or works with an endangered species, anywhere in the world, is appreciably harmed by a single project affecting some portion of that species with which he has no more specific connection. * * *

Besides failing to show injury, respondents failed to demonstrate redressability. Instead of attacking the separate decisions to fund particular projects allegedly causing them harm, the respondents chose to challenge a more generalized level of government action (rules regarding consultation), the invalidation of which would affect all overseas projects. This programmatic approach has obvious practical advantages, but also obvious difficulties insofar as proof of causation or redressability is concerned. As we have said in another context, "suits challenging, not specifically identifiable Government violations of law, but the particular programs agencies establish to carry out their legal obligations ... [are], even when premised on allegations of several instances of violations of law, ... rarely if ever appropriate for federal-court adjudication." *Allen,* 468 U.S. at 759–60.

The most obvious problem in the present case is redressability. Since the agencies funding the projects were not parties to the case, the District Court could accord relief only against the Secretary: He could be ordered to revise his regulation to require consultation for foreign projects. But this would not remedy respondents' alleged injury unless the funding agencies were bound by the Secretary's regulation, which is very much an open question.... When the Secretary promulgated the regulation at issue here, he thought it was binding on the agencies, *see* 51 Fed. Reg. at 19928 (1986). The Solicitor General, however, has repudiated that position here, and the agencies themselves apparently deny the Secretary's authority. * * *

A further impediment to redressability is the fact that the agencies generally supply only a fraction of the funding for a foreign project. AID, for example, has provided less than 10% of the funding for the Mahaweli Project. Respondents have produced nothing to indicate that the projects they have named will either be suspended, or do less harm to listed species, if that fraction is eliminated.... [I]t is entirely conjectural whether the nonagency activity that affects respondents will be altered or affected by the agency activity they seek to achieve. There is no standing.

IV

The Court of Appeals found that respondents had standing for an additional reason: because they had suffered a "procedural injury." The so-called "citizen-suit" provision of the ESA provides, in pertinent part, that "any person may commence a civil suit on his own behalf (A) to enjoin any person, including the United States and any other governmental instrumentality or agency ... who is alleged to be in violation of any provision of this chapter." The court held that, because § 7(a)(2) requires interagency consultation, the citizen-suit provision creates a "procedural right" to consultation in all "persons"—so that *anyone* can file suit in federal court to challenge the Secretary's (or presumably any other official's) failure to follow the assertedly correct consultative procedure, notwithstanding his or her inability to allege any discrete injury flowing from that failure. To understand the remarkable nature of this holding one must be clear about what it does *not* rest upon: This is not a case where plaintiffs are seeking to enforce a procedural requirement the disregard of which could impair a separate concrete interest of theirs (*e. g.,* the procedural requirement for a hearing prior to denial of their license application, or the procedural requirement for an environmental impact statement before a federal facility is constructed next door to them).[7] Nor is it simply a case where

---

7. There is this much truth to the assertion that "procedural rights" are special: The person who has been accorded a procedural right to protect his concrete interests can assert that right without meeting all the normal standards for redressability and immediacy. Thus, under our case law, one living adjacent to the site for proposed construction of a federally licensed dam has standing to challenge the licensing agency's failure to prepare an environmental impact statement, even though he cannot establish with any certainty that the statement will cause the license to be withheld or altered, and even though the dam will not be completed for many years. (That is why we do not rely, in the present case, upon the Government's argument that, *even if* the other agencies were obliged to consult with the Secretary, they might not have followed his advice.) What respondents' "procedural rights" argument seeks, however, is quite different from this: standing for persons who have no concrete interests affected—persons who

concrete injury has been suffered by many persons, as in mass fraud or mass tort situations. Nor, finally, is it the unusual case in which Congress has created a concrete private interest in the outcome of a suit against a private party for the Government's benefit, by providing a cash bounty for the victorious plaintiff. Rather, the court held that the injury-in-fact requirement had been satisfied by congressional conferral upon *all* persons of an abstract, self-contained, noninstrumental "right" to have the Executive observe the procedures required by law. We reject this view.[8] We have consistently held that a plaintiff raising only a generally available grievance about government— claiming only harm to his and every citizen's interest in proper application of the Constitution and laws, and seeking relief that no more directly and tangibly benefits him than it does the public at large—does not state an Article III case or controversy. For example, in *Fairchild* v. *Hughes*, 258 U.S. 126 (1922), we dismissed a suit challenging the propriety of the process by which the Nineteenth Amendment was ratified. Justice Brandeis wrote for the Court:

> [This is] not a case within the meaning of ... Article III.... Plaintiff has [asserted] only the right, possessed by every citizen, to require that the Government be administered according to law and that the public moneys be not wasted. Obviously this general right does not entitle a private citizen to institute in the federal courts a suit....

* * * To be sure, our generalized-grievance cases have typically involved Government violation of procedures assertedly ordained by the Constitution rather than the Congress. But there is absolutely no basis for making the Article III inquiry turn on the source of the asserted right. Whether the courts were to act on their own, or at the invitation of Congress, in ignoring the concrete injury requirement described in our cases, they would be discarding a principle fundamental to the separate and distinct constitutional role of the Third Branch—one of the essential elements that identifies those "Cases" and "Controversies" that are the business of the courts rather than of the political branches. "The province of the court," as Chief Justice Marshall said in *Marbury* v. *Madison*, 5 U.S. 137, 1 Cranch 137, 170, 2 L.Ed. 60 (1803), "is,

live (and propose to live) at the other end of the country from the dam.

8. The dissent's discussion of this aspect of the case distorts our opinion. We do *not* hold that an individual cannot enforce procedural rights; he assuredly can, so long as the procedures in question are designed to protect some threatened concrete interest of his that is the ultimate basis of his standing. The dissent, however, asserts that there exist "classes of procedural duties ... so enmeshed with the prevention of a substantive, concrete harm that an individual plaintiff may be able to demonstrate a sufficient likelihood of injury just through the breach of that procedural duty." If we understand this correctly, it means that the Government's violation of a certain (undescribed) class of procedural duty satisfies the concrete-injury requirement by itself, without any showing that the procedural violation endangers a concrete interest of the plaintiff (apart from his interest in having the procedure observed). We cannot agree. The dissent is unable to cite a single case in which we actually found standing solely on the basis of a "procedural right" unconnected to the plaintiff's own concrete harm. Its suggestion that we did so in *Japan Whaling Assn.* v. *American Cetacean Soc.*, 478 U.S. 221 (1986), and *Robertson* v. *Methow Valley Citizens Council*, 490 U.S. 332 (1989) is not supported by the facts. In the former case, we found that the environmental organizations had standing because the "whale watching and studying of their members w[ould] be adversely affected by continued whale harvesting," and in the latter we did not so much as mention standing, for the very good reason that the plaintiff was a citizens' council for the area in which the challenged construction was to occur, so that its members would obviously be concretely affected.

solely, to decide on the rights of individuals." Vindicating the *public* interest (including the public interest in Government observance of the Constitution and laws) is the function of Congress and the Chief Executive. The question presented here is whether the public interest in proper administration of the laws (specifically, in agencies' observance of a particular, statutorily prescribed procedure) can be converted into an individual right by a statute that denominates it as such, and that permits all citizens (or, for that matter, a subclass of citizens who suffer no distinctive concrete harm) to sue. If the concrete injury requirement has the separation-of-powers significance we have always said, the answer must be obvious: To permit Congress to convert the undifferentiated public interest in executive officers' compliance with the law into an "individual right" vindicable in the courts is to permit Congress to transfer from the President to the courts the Chief Executive's most important constitutional duty, to "take Care that the Laws be faithfully executed," Art. II, § 3. It would enable the courts, with the permission of Congress, "to assume a position of authority over the governmental acts of another and co-equal department," *Massachusetts* v. *Mellon*, 262 U.S. at 489, and to become " 'virtually continuing monitors of the wisdom and soundness of Executive action.' " *Allen, supra*, at 760 (quoting *Laird v. Tatum*, 408 U.S. 1, 15 (1972)). We have always rejected that vision of our role.

We hold that respondents lack standing to bring this action and that the Court of Appeals erred in denying the summary judgment motion filed by the United States. The opinion of the Court of Appeals is hereby reversed, and the cause is remanded for proceedings consistent with this opinion.

It is so ordered. * * *

Justice Kennedy, with whom Justice Souter joins, concurring in part and concurring in the judgment.

Although I agree with the essential parts of the Court's analysis, I write separately to make several observations.

I agree with the Court's conclusion in Part III–A that, on the record before us, respondents have failed to demonstrate that they themselves are "among the injured." *Sierra Club v. Morton,* 405 U.S. 727, 735 (1972). This component of the standing inquiry is not satisfied unless "[p]laintiffs . . . demonstrate a 'personal stake in the outcome.' . . . Abstract injury is not enough." * * *

While it may seem trivial to require that Mses. Kelly and Skilbred acquire airline tickets to the project sites or announce a date certain upon which they will return, this is not a case where it is reasonable to assume that the affiants will be using the sites on a regular basis, *see Sierra Club v. Morton, supra,* 405 U.S. at 735, n.8, nor do the affiants claim to have visited the sites since the projects commenced. With respect to the Court's discussion of respondents' "ecosystem nexus," "animal nexus," and "vocational nexus" theories, I agree that on this record respondents' showing is insufficient to establish standing on any of these bases. I am not willing to foreclose the possibility, however, that in different circumstances a nexus theory similar to those proffered here might support a claim to standing. *See Japan Whaling Assn. v. American Cetacean Soc., 478 U.S. 221, 231, n.4 (1986)* ("respondents . . . undoubtedly have alleged a sufficient 'injury in fact' in that the whale watching and studying of their members will be adversely affected by continued whale harvesting").

In light of the conclusion that respondents have not demonstrated a concrete injury here sufficient to support standing under our precedents, I would not reach the issue of redressability that is discussed by the plurality in Part III–B.

I also join Part IV of the Court's opinion with the following observations. As government programs and policies become more complex and far-reaching, we must be sensitive to the articulation of new rights of action that do not have clear analogs in our common-law tradition.... In my view, Congress has the power to define injuries and articulate chains of causation that will give rise to a case or controversy where none existed before, and I do not read the Court's opinion to suggest a contrary view. *See Warth v. Seldin,* 422 U.S. 490, 500 (1975). In exercising this power, however, Congress must at the very least identify the injury it seeks to vindicate and relate the injury to the class of persons entitled to bring suit. The citizen-suit provision of the Endangered Species Act does not meet these minimal requirements, because while the statute purports to confer a right on "any person ... to enjoin ... the United States and any other governmental instrumentality or agency ... who is alleged to be in violation of any provision of this chapter," it does not of its own force establish that there is an injury in "any person" by virtue of any "violation." 16 U.S.C. § 1540(g)(1)(A).

The Court's holding that there is an outer limit to the power of Congress to confer rights of action is a direct and necessary consequence of the case and controversy limitations found in Article III. I agree that it would exceed those limitations if, at the behest of Congress and in the absence of any showing of concrete injury, we were to entertain citizen suits to vindicate the public's nonconcrete interest in the proper administration of the laws. While it does not matter how many persons have been injured by the challenged action, the party bringing suit must show that the action injures him in a concrete and personal way. This requirement is not just an empty formality. It preserves the vitality of the adversarial process by assuring both that the parties before the court have an actual, as opposed to professed, stake in the outcome, and that "the legal questions presented will be resolved, not in the rarefied atmosphere of a debating society, but in a concrete factual context conducive to a realistic appreciation of the consequences of judicial action." *Valley Forge Christian College v. Americans United for Separation of Church and State, Inc.,* 454 U.S. 464, 472 (1982). In addition, the requirement of concrete injury confines the Judicial Branch to its proper, limited role in the constitutional framework of government. * * *

Justice Blackmun, with whom Justice O'Connor joins, dissenting.

Were the Court to apply the proper standard for summary judgment, I believe it would conclude that the sworn affidavits and deposition testimony of Joyce Kelly and Amy Skilbred advance sufficient facts to create a genuine issue for trial concerning whether one or both would be imminently harmed by the Aswan and Mahaweli projects. In the first instance, as the Court itself concedes, the affidavits contained facts making it at least "questionable" (and therefore within the province of the factfinder) that certain agency-funded projects threaten listed species. The only remaining issue, then, is whether Kelly and Skilbred have shown that they personally would suffer imminent harm.

I think a reasonable finder of fact could conclude from the information in the affidavits and deposition testimony that either Kelly or Skilbred will soon return to the project sites, thereby satisfying the "actual or imminent" injury standard. The Court dismisses Kelly's and Skilbred's general statements that they intended to revisit the project sites as "simply not enough." But those statements did not stand alone. A reasonable finder of fact could conclude, based not only upon their statements of intent to return, but upon their past visits to the project sites, as well as their professional backgrounds, that it was likely that Kelly and Skilbred would make a return trip to the project areas. Contrary to the Court's contention that Kelly's and Skilbred's past visits "prov[e] nothing," the fact of their past visits could demonstrate to a reasonable factfinder that Kelly and Skilbred have the requisite resources and personal interest in the preservation of the species endangered by the Aswan and Mahaweli projects to make good on their intention to return again. Similarly, Kelly's and Skilbred's professional backgrounds in wildlife preservation, also make it likely—at least far more likely than for the average citizen—that they would choose to visit these areas of the world where species are vanishing.

By requiring a "description of concrete plans" or "specification of when the some day [for a return visit] will be," the Court, in my view, demands what is likely an empty formality. No substantial barriers prevent Kelly or Skilbred from simply purchasing plane tickets to return to the Aswan and Mahaweli projects.

The Court also concludes that injury is lacking, because respondents' allegations of "ecosystem nexus" failed to demonstrate sufficient proximity to the site of the environmental harm. To support that conclusion, the Court mischaracterizes our decision in *Lujan v. National Wildlife Federation*, 497 U.S. 871 (1990), as establishing a general rule that "a plaintiff claiming injury from environmental damage must use the area affected by the challenged activity." In *National Wildlife Federation*, the Court required specific geographical proximity because of the particular type of harm alleged in that case: harm to the plaintiff's visual enjoyment of nature from mining activities. One cannot suffer from the sight of a ruined landscape without being close enough to see the sites actually being mined. Many environmental injuries, however, cause harm distant from the area immediately affected by the challenged action. Environmental destruction may affect animals traveling over vast geographical ranges, *see, e.g., Japan Whaling Assn. v. American Cetacean Society*, 478 U.S. 221 (1986) (harm to American whale watchers from Japanese whaling activities), or rivers running long geographical courses, *see, e.g., Arkansas v. Oklahoma*, 503 U.S. 91 (1992) (harm to Oklahoma residents from wastewater treatment plant 39 miles from border). It cannot seriously be contended that a litigant's failure to use the precise or exact site where animals are slaughtered or where toxic waste is dumped into a river means he or she cannot show injury.

The Court also rejects respondents' claim of vocational or professional injury. The Court says that it is "beyond all reason" that a zoo "keeper" of Asian elephants would have standing to contest his Government's participation in the eradication of all the Asian elephants in another part of the world. I am unable to see how the distant location of the destruction necessarily (for purposes of ruling at summary judgment) mitigates the harm to the elephant keeper. If there is no more access to a future supply of the animal that sustains a keeper's livelihood, surely there is harm.

I have difficulty imagining this Court applying its rigid principles of geographic formalism anywhere outside the context of environmental claims. As I understand it, environmental plaintiffs are under no special constitutional standing disabilities. Like other plaintiffs, they need show only that the action they challenge has injured them, without necessarily showing they happened to be physically near the location of the alleged wrong. The Court's decision today should not be interpreted "to foreclose the possibility ... that in different circumstances a nexus theory similar to those proffered here might support a claim to standing." Ante, at 2146 (KENNEDY, J., concurring in part and concurring in judgment).

QUESTIONS AND DISCUSSION

1. The plaintiffs produced two affidavits of members who had traveled to Egypt and Sri Lanka to observe endangered species and their habitats. Both members averred an intent to return to those countries in the future for the same purpose. Why were these affidavits inadequate to demonstrate injury? Does *Defenders* change the plaintiff's burden for demonstrating injury? If the plaintiff can refile or amend the complaint with the necessary allegations, does the Court's decision create a logical restriction or merely a formalistic barrier to standing, as suggested by Justice Blackmun's dissent?

2. What are the constitutional requisites of standing as described by Justice Scalia in *Defenders of Wildlife*? How do they limit Congress' authority to invest citizens with "private attorney general" status? Following the decision in *Defenders*, Professor Sunstein proposed that Congress enact bounties for citizens who file lawsuits to enforce statutes against the executive branch or private defendants. Cass Sunstein, *What's Standing After* Lujan? *Of Citizen Suits, "Injuries," and Article III,* 91 MICH. L. REV. 163 (1992). Alternatively, he proposed having Congress create a new property right—"a tenancy in common"—in an environmental asset such as clean air or the continued existence of endangered species. *Id.* at 234. If Congress were to adopt either of these ideas, do you think that the Court would grant such plaintiffs standing?

3. Justice Scalia's plurality opinion was joined by three other members of the Court (White, Rehnquist, and Thomas). Three other Justices (Stevens, Blackmun, and O'Connor) would have granted the plaintiffs standing. Two Justices (Souter and Kennedy) agreed that standing should be denied on the facts of the case, but were inclined to recognize Congress' authority to afford greater access to the courts. Given this split, what is the majority position of the *Defenders* court with respect to legal principles such as procedural standing and the various "nexus" theories. Justice Scalia's approach to standing as set forth in *Defenders* has been widely analyzed and criticized. *See, e.g.,* Karin Sheldon, Lujan v. Defenders of Wildlife: *The Supreme Court's Slash and Burn Approach to Environmental Standing,* 23 ENVTL. L. REP. (Envtl. L. Inst.) 10031 (1993); Cass Sunstein, *What's Standing After* Lujan? *Of Citizen Suits, "Injuries," and Article III,* 91 MICH. L. REV. 163 (1992).

4. Note the Court's statement in *Defenders* that "we have consistently held that a plaintiff raising only a generally available grievance about government ... does not state an Article III case or controversy." Notwithstanding this claim, the Court has been far from consistent. In *Sierra Club v. Morton,* 405 U.S. 727 (1972), for example, the Court held that "the fact that particular environmental interests are shared by the many rather than the few does not make them less deserving of legal protection...." And in *United States v. Students Challenging Regulatory Agency Procedures (SCRAP),* 412 U.S. 669 (1973), the Court noted that "standing is not to be denied simply because many people suffer the same injury." *Id.* at 687–88.

In one post-*Defenders* case, the Supreme Court again found standing where the plaintiffs' injury was "sufficiently concrete and specific," even though it was "widely shared." *Federal Election Commission v. Akins,* 524 U.S. 11, 25 (1998) (citizens can challenge agency action requiring recordkeeping of political action committees). It should come as no surprise that Justice Scalia (along with Justices Thomas and O'Connor) dissented from this decision essentially on the grounds that the plaintiffs' alleged injury was "plainly undifferentiated and common to all members of the public." *Id.* at 34.

5. In *Defenders,* Justice Scalia suggests that the alleged injury to the plaintiff may not have been redressable since two of the federal agencies involved in the projects (with the support of the Solicitor General) had denied the applicability of relevant U.S. Fish and Wildlife Service regulations to their actions. Compare Justice Scalia's analysis of this issue with his subsequent decision in *Bennett v. Spear,* 520 U.S. 154 (1997). In *Bennett,* Justice Scalia, writing for a unanimous Court, granted standing to ranchers to challenge an opinion of the Fish & Wildlife Service finding that a water project of the Bureau of Reclamation would illegally jeopardize the continued existence of endangered fish. The ranchers claimed that they would suffer economic harm if the Bureau reduced water deliveries to avoid jeopardy to the fish. The Court found the ranchers' imminent injury to be both fairly traceable to the Fish & Wildlife Service opinion as well as redressable by that agency despite the fact that the Bureau retained ultimate responsibility for determining how the water project should be administered. The Court found that although the Fish & Wildlife Service opinion serves only an advisory function, "in reality it has a powerful coercive effect on the action agency." *Id.* at 169. Is this holding consistent with *Defenders*?

6. The plurality, in footnote seven, recognizes the denial of procedural rights as the basis for standing and dismisses the requirement that a plaintiff show redressability when alleging a procedural injury. Without this concession, NEPA might have been rendered unenforceable, since the statute grants primarily procedural rights. Suppose, for example, that a citizens' group challenged an agency decision not to prepare an EIS on a proposed coal lease. But for Justice Scalia's concession, the group would be required to make the impossible showing that preparation of the EIS would result in a decision by the agency not to lease the coal.

7. Perhaps the most common kind of procedural injury occurs when an agency denies people information that they are entitled to receive by law. The concept of "informational standing" originated with a footnote in an early but important NEPA case. *Scientists' Institute for Public Information v. Atomic Energy Commission,* 481 F.2d 1079, 1087 n.29 (D.C. Cir. 1973). How should the language in footnote seven of the *Defenders* case be applied in the context of an informational standing claim under NEPA? In *City of Olmsted Falls v. Federal Aviation Administration,* 292 F.3d 261, 267 (D.C. Cir. 2002), the Court of Appeals for the District of Columbia Circuit held that "a NEPA claim may not be raised by a party with no claimed or apparent environmental interest. It cannot be used as a handy stick by a party with no interest in protecting against an environmental injury to attack a defendant." *Citing Town of Stratford v. FAA*, 285 F.3d 84, 88 (D.C. Cir. 2002). "Geographic proximity," the Court noted, "might be necessary to show such an injury, but it is not sufficient." *Id.* Is *City of Olmstead Falls* consistent with the *Akins* decision discussed in note 4?

8. In *Massachusetts v. EPA*, 549 U.S. 97 (2007), a sharply divided Supreme Court found that Massachusetts had standing to challenge the EPA's failure to regulate carbon dioxide emissions from motor vehicles under a provision in the Clean Air Act that required EPA to establish motor vehicle emission standards for new motor vehicles that in EPA's judgment "cause, or contribute to air pollution . . . reasonably . . . anticipated to endanger public health or welfare." 42 U.S.C. § 7521(a)(1). In so doing, the majority reaffirmed some of the Court's more expansive standing rules. For example, it emphasized that because the plaintiffs had invoked a *procedural* right under the Clean Air Act to challenge agency action unlawfully withheld, they did not need to meet the normal standards of immediacy and redressability. This was important because the alleged injuries to State resources from climate change that could be traced directly to EPA's failure to regulate vehicle emissions were somewhat speculative and remote. The Court also confirmed its holding in *Akins* (*see* note 4 above), that an injury that is "widely shared" does not diminish the State's claim of injury. *Id.* at 1456. Finally, the Court held that when a State acts on behalf of its citizens as *parens patriae* to protect its quasi-sovereign interests, it was "entitled to special solicitude in our standing analysis." In this case, a majority of the Court found that Massachusetts had standing because its coastal areas were impacted by sea level rise (injury in fact), the EPA's failure to regulate greenhouse gases were contributing to the rise (causation), and reductions in greenhouse gas emissions would slow the rise (redressability). *Id.* at 1455–58.

Chief Justice Roberts, joined by Justices Scalia, Thomas and Alito, dissented. Roberts was particularly critical of the majority's claim that States are entitled to "special solicitude" in deciding whether a claim is justiciable. He also questioned the State's showing of injury, causation, and redressability. "The very concept of global warming seems inconsistent with the requirement to show a particularized injury. . . . [T]he redress that petitioners seek is focused no more on them than on the public generally—it is literally to change the atmosphere of the world." *Id.* at 1467. Are you satisfied that Massachusetts made a credible claim of a "global warming" injury caused by motor vehicle emissions that can be effectively redressed by the regulation of such emissions? If not, can a plaintiff ever challenge an individual action that increases the prospects for global climate change? Has Massachusetts raised a "case" or "controversy" sufficient to warrant the intervention of the courts? Does this case suggest a need for broader reform of the standing doctrine?

9. In *Summers v. Earth Island Institute*, 129 S.Ct. 1142 (2009), the Supreme Court made it harder for plaintiffs to claim standing for a facial challenge to an agency regulation. *Summers* involved a challenge to the Forest Service's failure to provide notice, an opportunity to comment, and a right of appeal to the Burnt Ridge salvage timber sale as they claimed was required under the Forest Service rules implementing the ARA, which authorized the Forest Service to ignore the procedural requirements of the ARA for actions that were categorically excluded under NEPA, were unlawful. While the district court case was pending the parties settled their dispute over the Burnt Ridge sale, but the plaintiffs nonetheless went forward with their facial challenge to the rules. In a 5–4 decision, Justice Scalia, writing for the majority, held that the plaintiffs' could not challenge the rules because they failed to show concrete injury. The Court also denied the plaintiffs' procedural injury claim because they had not shown a concrete interest that might be affected by the denial of the procedural right.

A nagging question not answered by the Court is how it would handle a standing claim under a statute that specifically requires parties to file a lawsuit challenging an agency rule within 60 days after the rule was promulgated. *See e.g.*, Clean Air Act, 42 U.S.C. § 7606(b); The Surface Mining Control and Reclamation Act, 30 U.S.C. § 1276(a)(1). The failure to meet the filing deadline is jurisdictional but typically it is not long enough for the rule to have even been used. Is it possible that the courts lack standing to hear challenges to agency rules under these two major statutes unless plaintiffs suffer a concrete injury within 60 days after the rules are promulgated? Could the Court have avoided this problem by focusing on ripeness rather than standing? The ripeness doctrine is discussed briefly in the next section of the materials. Note that the *Summers* majority did not reach the ripeness claim because it resolved the case on standing grounds.

10. Read the citizen suit provision in the Endangered Species Act, 16 U.S.C. § 1640(g), reprinted on the casebook website. http://www.natural resources.byu.edu/. What types of actions can a plaintiff challenge? What steps must be taken before the case can proceed to trial? When can the government take over the case? Is there any assurance the government will pursue the case as diligently as the NGOs would have?

11. Why do you think Congress has made citizen suit provisions the rule for pollution laws but the exception for natural resources laws? Could this be a reflection of the fact that natural resources law is more management and value-based, so we want to leave value decisions to the political and administrative process and not to courts? Or is something else at work?

12. For a useful review of citizen suits and other mechanisms for enlisting the private sector in the enforcement of environmental laws, *see* Barton H. Thompson, Jr., *The Continuing Innovation of Citizen Enforcement*, 2000 U. ILL. L. REV. 185 (2000).

---

4.   RIPENESS, EXHAUSTION, AND THE TIMING OF JUDICIAL REVIEW

Related to the doctrine of standing are several other administrative law issues that concern the timing of judicial review. These issues often arise in resource cases. For example, the APA generally authorizes review only of "final agency action," 5 U.S.C. § 704, but it also makes clear that "action" can include the "failure to act." 5 U.S.C. § 551(13). So, for example, when the Environmental Protection Agency failed to finalize a decision on a request to cancel registration of the pesticide DDT, the court held that the lack of action was tantamount to a denial of the request and found that review was available. *Environmental Defense Fund v. Hardin*, 428 F.2d 1093 (D.C. Cir. 1970).

Closely related to both standing and finality principles is the doctrine that precludes judicial review of actions that are not "ripe" for review. The Supreme Court established a two-part test for ripeness in *Abbott Laboratories v. Gardner*, 387 U.S. 136 (1967). The first part asks whether the issues are fit for judicial resolution. The fitness prong assures that only final decisions with present impacts are subject to challenge. Once a court determines that the issues are fit for review, the second part of the ripeness inquiry requires a court to determine that withholding review will cause a hardship to the plaintiff.

Ohio Forestry Association v. Sierra Club, 523 U.S. 726 (1998), illustrates how the second prong of the ripeness test might arise in a resource context. In *Ohio Forestry*, the Sierra Club challenged the land and resource management plan approved by the Forest Service for the Wayne National Forest. The Club particularly objected to the fact that the plan zoned for logging as much as 126,000 acres of forest land. The plan itself did not approve any particular logging projects, and the Forest Service was not authorized to allow any logging until it prepared a new analysis and reached a separate decision on a particular logging tract. The Court found that the challenge to the land use plan was not ripe because the plaintiffs would suffer no hardship if they were simply forced to wait for any subsequent logging decision, at which point the factual record would be further developed. The *Ohio Forestry* case is noted below on page 314.

The doctrine of exhaustion of administrative remedies requires that prospective plaintiffs avail themselves of available administrative remedies before resorting to the courts. Moreover, parties who fail to raise issues in administrative proceedings may be barred from later raising those issues in court. So, for example, if an agency establishes an administrative procedure to review an enforcement action, a party against whom such action is taken must seek administrative review and raise all possible defenses to the action before seeking judicial review. There are a few exceptions to the exhaustion requirement, such as where the administrative process is inadequate or where exhaustion would be futile. Moreover, the Supreme Court has made clear that agencies may not compel litigants to seek administrative appeals from an adverse decision unless the agency stays the operation of its decision pending such review. *Darby v. Cisneros,* 509 U.S. 137 (1993); *see also* 5 U.S.C. § 704.

PROBLEM EXERCISE: STANDING TO CHALLENGE A DRAFT EIS

You are enrolled in a class on environmental activism at Oberlin College in Oberlin, Ohio. A portion of your grade will be based upon your participation in an action that has been proposed by a federal agency. You have chosen to write comments on a draft environmental impact statement prepared by the National Park Service that proposes to allow certain parts of Yellowstone National Park to remain open to snowmobile use. You have never been to Yellowstone National Park and have no present intention to go there, but you feel passionately that snowmobiles should not be allowed in Yellowstone.

In anticipation of your work on this project you have sent an e-mail message to the appropriate Park Service official requesting copies of the draft environmental impact statement and all other documents relevant to the agency's decision. The Park Service sent the draft EIS but has refused to send copies of an economic analysis that purportedly addressed the economic impacts associated with the elimination of snowmobiles from the Park. In a letter denying access to this document, the Park Service indicated that it had decided not to use the analysis and that it was accordingly not part of the administrative record. You believe that the economic analysis shows that elimination of snowmobiles will have only a minor impact on the economy and that the Park Service chose not to release the study because it did not support their proposed decision to allow snowmobiles to remain in the Park. Suppose that you sue the Park Service in an effort to obtain the economic analysis. What are your chances of surviving the government's expected motion to dismiss on the grounds that you lack standing?

[Note: Before considering this problem, you may want to review the introductory materials on NEPA, which appear below.]

III. IMPROVING AGENCIES' ENVIRONMENTAL DECISION-MAKING

A. THE NATIONAL ENVIRONMENTAL POLICY ACT

Passed in 1969, the National Environmental Policy Act (NEPA) was the first major statute of the modern era of environmental law. 42 U.S.C. §§ 4331–4370. A trailblazer, NEPA does not seek to ensure environmental protection through technology-forcing standards, market instruments, or prescriptive regulation, nor does it focus on conservation of endangered species or forests. Rather, NEPA relies on information, forcing agencies to consider the environmental impacts of their proposed actions and the comparative impacts associated with reasonable alternatives. This approach partly reflects a New Deal faith in agency management—a belief that government will do the right thing if it has all of the relevant information before it. It also relies on the insight about public disclosure discussed in Chapter 1. When an agency is required to disclose environmental impact information to the public, it allows the public to exert pressure on the agency to protect the environment. Without question, NEPA's influence has been far-reaching, with its progeny in the statute books of 15 states, the District of Columbia, and over 130 nations throughout the world.

The chief tool for implementing NEPA is the environmental impact statement or EIS. NEPA requires that all federal agencies prepare an EIS on every "recommendation or report on proposals for legislation and other major Federal actions significantly affecting the quality of the human environment." 42 U.S.C. § 4332(2)(C). NEPA requires agencies to use a "systematic, interdisciplinary approach."42 U.S.C. § 4332(2)(A) The EIS must contain a "detailed statement by the responsible [agency] official" on

(i) the environmental impact of the proposed action,

(ii) any adverse environmental effects which cannot be avoided should the proposal be implemented,

(iii) alternatives to the proposed action,

(iv) the relationship between local short-term uses of man's environment and the maintenance and enhancement of long-term productivity, and

(v) any irreversible and irretrievable commitments of resources which would be involved in the proposed action should it be implemented.

42 U.S.C. § 4332(2)(C).

[margin note: rqmts. w/in EIS]

Preparing an EIS is a considerable undertaking. Often the size of a metropolitan phone book, an EIS analyzes the environmental impacts across a range of proposed actions. The analysis considers both unavoidable adverse impacts and mitigation alternatives. For example, concerns about the amount of traffic in Yosemite Valley led the National Park Service to propose and implement a decision to close parking lots in the Valley and create a shuttle bus service. Before undertaking this action, the Park Service prepared an EIS that considered the environmental impacts of both the shuttle bus proposal and of doing nothing, as well as the impacts that would result from a range of other alternatives. The alternatives considered included, for example, consolidating parking in different areas of the Valley or adding bicycle and pedestrian paths along some of the Valley's roads. More creative alternatives, but perhaps less practical, might have included charging tolls for using the road or adding a light rail system. The agency's "record of decision" made on December 29, 2000, is available at http://www.nps.gov/yose/planning/yvp/rod.html. An EIS will sometimes indicate a preferred alternative, but often it simply lays out the various options for the decision-maker.

The regulations implementing NEPA define federal actions broadly to encompass wholly private actions that require a federal permit, or some other form of federal approval, before the action can proceed. 40 C.F.R. § 1508.18(b)(4). Development or use of natural resources frequently requires a federal permit, even when that development occurs wholly on private land. For example, a proposed mining operation on private lands that will damage or destroy wetlands may require a permit from the U.S. Army Corps of Engineers under Section 404 of the Clean Water Act. Likewise, a proposed power plant built on private lands that requires construction of new power lines across national forest lands will require a federal right of way from the Forest Service. A hydroelectric power project requires a license from the Federal Energy Regulatory Commission under the Federal Power Act, and a nuclear power plant requires a license from the Nuclear Regulatory Commission under the Atomic Energy Act.

[margin note: ✱ reach of NEPA is broad]

NEPA also created the Council on Environmental Quality (CEQ) to oversee the NEPA process and its implementation. 42 U.S.C. § 4321. The CEQ has promulgated detailed regulations to implement NEPA that are binding on all federal agencies, *Robertson v. Methow Valley Citizens Council*, 490 U.S. 332 (1989), and entitled to substantial deference by the courts.

[margin note: CEQ oversees NEPA]

Andrus v. Sierra Club, 442 U.S. 347 (1979); 40 C.F.R. part 1500. The CEQ rules are supplemented by individual agency rules. The CEQ does not have, and NEPA does not provide for, enforcement authority. However, under Section 309 of the Clean Air Act, the Environmental Protection Agency (EPA) provides oversight of all agency compliance with NEPA. 42 U.S.C. § 7609. That section requires EPA to review and comment publicly on all EISs. In addition, EPA must refer any EIS decision to the CEQ that it believes is not satisfactory from an environmental point of view. The CEQ rules establish procedures for resolving issues raised by such referrals. 40 C.F.R. part 1504. Finally, EPA is responsible for the administrative task of maintaining the national EIS filing system. *See* http://www.epa.gov/compli ance/resources/policies/nepa/fileguide.html.

In practice, NEPA enforcement has come primarily through legal actions filed under the Administrative Procedure Act. Two questions frequently arise in NEPA cases. First is the question of whether the agency should have prepared an environmental impact statement. Where an EIS has been prepared, the question is usually whether it was adequate. The general remedy for a NEPA violation is a remand to the agency and a stay of the proposed action until it prepares and considers a satisfactory EIS.

Given NEPA's limited purpose, it may seem surprising that interested parties have filed thousands of NEPA lawsuits. Indeed, NEPA's seemingly innocuous EIS requirement has led to more lawsuits than any other environmental statute. What purposes does this requirement serve and why are litigants so eager to enforce it? As described above, the fundamental goal of NEPA is to *educate* agency decision-makers, ideally by sensitizing them to environmental issues and helping the agencies find easy, inexpensive means of mitigating environmental impacts. From a *political* perspective, the EIS can be used to educate the public and provide information that can be used to fight the decision through the legislature, the voting booth, or the courts. Moreover, because the EIS was generated within the agency proposing the action, its information cannot easily be dismissed.

In addition to affording a basis for objections to an agency's NEPA compliance, the EIS might also provide information that can help litigants show that an agency action is "arbitrary and capricious, an abuse of discretion or otherwise not in accordance with the law." Under the Administrative Procedure Act, such a finding would require the court to "hold unlawful and set aside [the] agency action...." 5 U.S.C. § 706(2). Finally, NEPA litigation can *delay* a project (particularly if the EIS must be done again), allowing time to organize opposition and, in some cases, make the project so costly that it expires on its own. In sum, NEPA has provided plaintiffs with a powerful tool to stall or block agency action. In the context of natural resources management, for example, NEPA provided the essential legal basis for blocking the release of potential wilderness areas, *California v. Block,* 690 F.2d 753 (9th Cir. 1982), for ensuring consideration of the environmental impacts of grazing at the local level, *Natural Resources Defense Council v. Morton,* 388 F.Supp. 829 (D.D.C. 1974), *aff'd. mem.,* 527 F.2d 1386 (D.C. Cir. 1976), *cert. denied,* 427 U.S. 913 (1976), and for overturning numerous site-specific actions such as timber sales, *Save the Yaak Committee v. Block,* 840 F.2d 714 (9th Cir. 1988); *Thomas v.*

Peterson, 753 F.2d 754 (9th Cir. 1985). Such decisions clearly have important implications for resource management.

Before examining NEPA in more detail, you should note that even where federal approval may not be needed, state or local government approvals are often required, and many states have NEPA-like statutes that impose similar planning obligations on such agencies. Thus, resource development often cannot proceed without some form of environmental analysis. The following section focuses on federal NEPA law, first discussing whether NEPA's focus is procedural or substantive, then turning to when an EIS must be prepared, and finally looking at issues involving the adequacy of an EIS. Many of the same principles in NEPA case law apply to similar state laws.

1. NEPA'S EVOLUTION

Calvert Cliffs Coordinating Committee v. U.S. Atomic Energy Commission, 449 F.2d 1109 (D.C. Cir. 1971), was the first significant decision that interpreted NEPA, and it provides a useful insight into agencies' lack of environmental concern at the time of NEPA's passage. In arguing it had complied with NEPA for a nuclear plant licensing, the Atomic Energy Commission fully acknowledged that NEPA requires a "detailed statement" prepared by the responsible agency to "accompany" the licensing application for a nuclear plant. But in an astounding display of form over substance, *the agency claimed that the EIS need not be considered by the licensing board*. The EIS simply went along for the ride. In his opinion, Judge Skelly Wright decried the Commission's "crabbed interpretation of NEPA," finding that it made a "mockery of the Act." To survive judicial review, he said, agencies must prove that they have fully considered the detailed environmental statement "at every important stage in the decision making process." *Id.* at 1118.

The implications of *Calvert Cliffs* are significant. NEPA requires reviewing courts to examine the agency decision-making process and determine whether environmental concerns were adequately considered. Moreover, because adequate consideration of environmental concerns is best demonstrated by agency action, *Calvert Cliffs* seems to support the use of NEPA as a vehicle for reviewing the substance of agencies' environmental decision-making. In decisions that followed, however, particularly *Strycker's Bay Neighborhood Council, Inc. v. Karlen*, 444 U.S. 223 (1980), and *Robertson v. Methow Valley Citizen Council*, 490 U.S. 332 (1989), the Supreme Court made clear that NEPA is essentially a procedural statute. It does not require a particular substantive result. In *Robertson*, for example, the Forest Service prepared an EIS that addressed, among other things, the impacts of a planned ski resort on the area's mule deer population. The plaintiffs had argued that the agency's mitigation plan was inadequate. In rejecting this argument, the Court stated:

> If the adverse environmental effects of the proposed action are adequately identified and evaluated, the agency is not constrained by NEPA from deciding that other values outweigh the environmental costs. In this case, for example, it would not have violated NEPA if the Forest Service, after complying with the Act's procedural prerequisites, had decided that the benefits to be derived from

*Calvert Cliffs →
agencies must
also consider the
EIS findings*

*Limiting
Calvert Cliffs :
S.C. has said
NEPA is
procedural*

*agency doesn't
have to choose
the most
"env. friendly"
option*

downhill skiing at Sandy Butte justified the issuance of a special use permit, notwithstanding the loss of 15 percent, 50 percent, or even 100 percent of the mule deer herd. Other statutes may impose substantive environmental obligations on federal agencies, but NEPA merely prohibits uninformed—rather than unwise—agency action.

Id. at 350–51.

Thus, so long as the agency has complied with the NEPA process and fully considered the EIS, NEPA does not require the agency to choose the environmentally preferable option. Of course, other statutes, such as the Endangered Species Act, might provide a basis for reviewing the substance of an agency's decision, and the NEPA document might provide the prospective litigant with information needed to make that point. Moreover, as the legal realists suggested over 70 years ago, the line between procedural and substantive review is a grey one. Despite the Supreme Court's emphasis on NEPA being a procedural statute, when courts take a hard look at whether the agency complied with NEPA's procedural requirements (i.e., whether the agency fully considered the relevant factors), they often still do so by assessing the agency's final decision (a substantive analysis) under the arbitrary and capricious standard of the Administrative Procedure Act. For example, in *Baltimore Gas & Electric Co. v. Natural Resources Defense Council*, the Supreme Court held that in deciding to approve a nuclear power plant license, the Nuclear Regulatory Commission's "zero-release" assumption—that permanent storage of certain nuclear wastes would have no significant environmental impact because of complete repository integrity—was not arbitrary or capricious under the APA. 462 U.S. 87 (1983). To reach this holding, the Court had to decide not only that the NEPA analysis of the zero-release assumption was adequate, but also that the decision to use the assumption was "within the bounds of reasoned decisionmaking required by the APA," despite acknowledged uncertainties about it. *Id.* at 104.

2.   WHEN MUST AN AGENCY PREPARE AN EIS?

The logic behind the EIS requirement is straightforward: a better informed agency will make better decisions. Yet it is easy to see why some agencies prefer not to prepare an EIS. Preparing an EIS consumes considerable time and resources and it can increase conflict by exposing the environmental problems associated with government action. Recall that NEPA requires an EIS for any "recommendation or report on proposals for legislation and other major Federal actions significantly affecting" the human environment. 42 U.S.C. § 4332(2)(C). The EIS requirement for legislative proposals, however, has not proved especially important because it is difficult to enforce. *See, e.g.*, Joseph Mendelson III & Andrew Kimbrell, *The Legislative Environmental Impact Statement*, 23 ENV. L. REP. (Envtl. L. Inst.) 10653 (1993). Once Congress passes legislation proposed by an agency a court is unlikely to set that legislation aside simply because the agency failed to prepare an EIS. After all, Congress can act with or without an agency's recommendation.

The difficulty with enforcing the legislative EIS requirement has not carried over to the major federal action EIS. The CEQ has defined federal actions broadly to include a wide range of activities—such as approval of specific projects (e.g., construction of a road in a national park); approval of rules, regulations, and other official policies (e.g., adopting a new set of regulations for concessionaires in national parks); adoption of formal plans or programs to guide agency decisions (e.g., a land use plan, or a plan to permit local rangers greater discretion over their parks); and permitting or funding of private projects (e.g., approval of a river crossing for a power line). 40 C.F.R. § 1508.18. Federal actions can even include an agency's failure to act, where such failure is reviewable under the APA. *Id.; see also* 5 U.S.C. §§ 551(13); 706(1).

In addition to the broad EIS requirement for major federal actions, the CEQ regulations impose a range of requirements for EISs that can prove burdensome. *See* 40 C.F.R. subpart 1502. Moreover, agencies that fail to follow those requirements offer an easy target for future litigants. To help make EIS preparation manageable, the CEQ rules provide a mechanism to help agencies limit EIS preparation to those proposals that are truly significant. 30 C.F.R. § 1501.4. Under these rules, the agency first considers whether the proposal is one that either normally does or does not require an EIS. At this stage, an agency can decide against EIS preparation only if the action has been "categorically excluded." "Categorical exclusions" refer to those actions that have been found by rule not to individually or cumulatively have a significant effect on the environment. 40 C.F.R. § 1508.4.

Most often, the agency will not have enough information at this initial stage to decide that an EIS is needed and so the CEQ rules provide that the agency may prepare an "environmental assessment" (EA). An EA, which is intended to be a "concise public document," performs two important and distinct functions under NEPA. 40 C.F.R. § 1508.9. First, it provides the agency with sufficient information to decide whether a full EIS is warranted. In addition, it allows the agency to analyze possible alternatives to the proposed action even where an EIS is not needed. NEPA requires an alternatives analysis whenever a proposal involves "unresolved conflicts concerning alternative uses of available resources." 42 U.S.C. § 4332(2)(E).

For a variety of reasons, agencies rarely conclude that a full EIS is needed. Indeed, agencies prepare EAs about 100 times more often than they do EISs. *See The National Environmental Policy Act: A Study of Its Effectiveness After Twenty–Five Years*, at 19, (CEQ, 1997), *available at,* http://www.nepa.gov/nepa/nepa25fn.pdf. Because agencies are reluctant to prepare EISs if they can get by with an EA, EAs are often quite substantial documents, rivaling in size some EISs. From the agency's perspective, however, they have the advantage of not having to comply with the CEQ's specific requirements for EISs.

Agencies frequently provide interested persons with an opportunity to comment on EAs. If the EA ultimately concludes that an EIS is unnecessary, sometimes because the agency commits to mitigating the significant adverse impacts, the agency will issue a FONSI (Finding of No Significant Impact). Whether or not an EIS is prepared, resource agencies usually issue a "record of decision" (ROD) that memorializes the final decision reached by the agency, including any mitigation measures that the agency commits

ROD ~
finality (think
APA - ripe for
review)

to take. The <u>ROD, including any decision not to prepare an EIS, can then</u>
<u>be challenged in court.</u>

When an agency prepares an EIS, a draft EIS is first distributed and
made available for public comment for at least 45 days. Often agencies
provide a longer public comment period. The agency then prepares a final
EIS and responds to categories of public comments. Once the EIS and ROD
have been issued, there is a 30–day moratorium on agency action to afford
opponents of the decision an opportunity to file legal challenges. The
following diagram depicts the NEPA decision-making process in the form of
a flow chart.

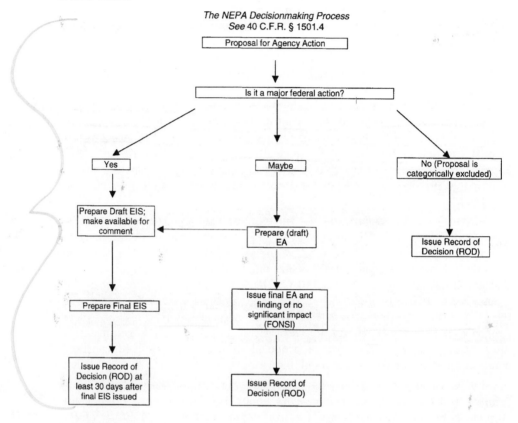

The NEPA Decisionmaking Process
See 40 C.F.R. § 1501.4

a. Timing

To prove useful, an EIS must be considered before the agency decides
on a course of action, and early enough that the EIS can meaningfully
contribute to the decision-making process. Otherwise it simply serves as a
post hoc rationalization for a decision already taken. Equally, the agency
must have something fairly concrete in mind, otherwise the scope of
potential EISs might be too broad to be meaningful. The CEQ regulations
address these concerns by requiring preparation of an EIS "as close as
possible to the time the agency is developing a proposal...." 40 C.F.R.
§ 1502.5. They further require that the EIS be prepared "early enough so
that it can serve practically as an important contribution to the decision-
making process...." *Id.*

Challenging the timing of an EIS can be difficult for outside parties lacking insiders' knowledge of the status of various initiatives under consideration. Indeed, in an iterative process within the agency with memoranda and suggestions circulating back and forth, it may not even be clear to those *inside* the agency when a recommendation has crystallized into a proposal. Nonetheless, numerous judicial opinions have made clear that agencies may not make an "irreversible and irretrievable commitment" of federal resources before complying with NEPA. One of the better known cases is *Conner v. Burford,* 848 F.2d 1441 (9th Cir. 1988), *cert. denied,* 489 U.S. 1012 (1989). *Conner* involved numerous federal oil and gas leases in a national forest in Montana. The government had prepared an EA describing the negligible effects of the paper transaction involved in issuing the lease, but had failed to analyze the impacts of possible oil and gas development should it occur on the leased land. For some of the leases the government had included "no surface occupancy" (NSO) stipulations, which precluded use of the surface unless and until the government lifted the stipulation. On other leases, however, no such stipulations were imposed. On these leases, the government had the right to impose reasonable regulations on mineral development, but could not wholly preclude a lessee from surface use. The court held that "the sale of non-NSO leases entailed an irrevocable commitment of land to significant surface disturbing activities, including drilling and road building, and that such a commitment could not be made under NEPA without an EIS." *Id.* at 1449. *But see Park County Resource Council v. Department of Agriculture,* 817 F.2d 609 (10th Cir. 1987) (reaching a different conclusion on similar facts).

b. The Scale of a Proposed Action and Tiering

Another way timing plays out is in the context of scale. In *Kleppe v. Sierra Club,* 427 U.S. 390 (1976), for example, the plaintiffs claimed that the government should prepare an EIS on its coal development plans for federal lands in the Northern Great Plains area. In the mid–1970s, it was clear to most observers that the Ford administration planned to lease major portions of the Northern Great Plains region to coal mining interests, but there was no official plan or announcement. The Department of the Interior prepared an EIS for its national coal leasing program as well as for individual leases. Against this backdrop, the Sierra Club sued the Secretary of the Interior seeking an EIS on the Department's regional development plans. The Club argued that the national EIS was too general, that the project-specific EISs were too narrow, and that the impacts were greatest at the regional level, where alternative approaches should be considered. From Interior's perspective, there were many levels of decision-making at which one could reasonably prepare an EIS, and it was unreasonable to demand an EIS at every level.

The Supreme Court sided with Interior, stating that an EIS is required only where there is an actual report or recommendation on a proposal for major federal action; "mere 'contemplation' of certain action is not sufficient to require an impact statement." *Id.* at 404. A comprehensive EIS is appropriate, the Court declared, where related proposals have significant cumulative or synergistic environmental effects, *id.* at 410, but it is left to the discretion of the agency to determine when this is the case. In other words, the Court deferred to agency discretion over the proper scale of analysis so as not to interfere with the agency decision-making process. *Id.* at 406. In practice, agencies have addressed this issue through the practice of "tiering," preparing successive EISs from broad scale to smaller. Thus an agency often prepares a "programmatic EIS" on the overall program, considering cumulative effects and overall alternatives, and then prepares site-specific supplemental EISs on specific projects as they become appropriate. By tiering, an agency does not have to consider general effects each time it prepares an individual EIS, and does not need to be comprehensive in its programmatic EIS. The CEQ rules encourage agencies "to tier their environmental impact statements to eliminate repetitive discussions of the same issues and to focus on the actual issues ripe for decision at each level of environmental review." 40 C.F.R. § 1502.20; *see also* 40 C.F.R. § 1508.28.

c.   The Scope of Agency Action

Deciding whether an agency is proposing a "major federal action that significantly affects the quality of the human environment" is not quite as simple as it may seem. The CEQ rules state that the word "major" "reinforces but does not have a meaning independent of significantly." 40 C.F.R. § 1508.18. Thus, a proposal that might otherwise seem major—for example, a proposal to consolidate the Forest Service and the Bureau of Land Management into a single agency—likely would not require an EIS because it would not significantly affect the environment. On the other hand, a project that at first blush might appear to be relatively minor may in fact require an EIS because its "scope" really encompasses much more than initially meets the eye. As described more fully in the *Thomas* case set forth below, the CEQ's rules define the "scope" of an agency action to encompass "connected actions" (actions that are automatically triggered by an agency action that otherwise might appear minor) and "cumulative actions" (actions that may be individually minor but when taken together would have cumulatively significant impacts). 40 C.F.R. § 1508.25.

The CEQ's broad definition of scope is intended in part to address instances in which agencies might try to avoid NEPA by dividing up or "segmenting" projects. At the extreme, for example, consider how the Forest Service might try to avoid preparing an EIS for its decision to build a 20-mile road in a National Forest. This 20-mile road would seem to be a major federal action significantly affecting the environment. But what if, instead, the Forest Service transformed the project into twenty separate projects to build one-mile roads? By segmenting, the agency can transform major projects into seemingly innocuous minor ones. In isolation, none of these one-mile roads will likely trigger the requirements for an EIS. Therefore, in scrutinizing examples like this, courts have asked whether the separate segments have independent utility or whether they are "connected." If the road segment along mile 16 makes no sense without miles 17 and 15, then the segments must be considered together. *See, e.g., Taxpayers Watchdog, Inc. v. Stanley,* 819 F.2d 294 (D.C. Cir. 1987) (upholding an agency EIS that addressed only a small segment of a much larger proposed subway system for Los Angeles because the segment was found to have sufficient independent utility to stand on its own, and did not irretrievably commit the agency to any particular future course of action).

A related question arises when an action may cause significant environmental impacts but the federal connection to the project may be too tenuous to warrant full NEPA compliance. Consider, for example, an application for a federal right-of-way to authorize a private power line to cross a navigable waterway. The crossing of the waterway will, by itself, have little environmental impact. But construction of the 67–mile power line will have significant impacts, and cannot be built unless it crosses the waterway. *Winnebago Tribe of Nebraska v. Ray*, 621 F.2d 269 (8th Cir. 1980). Minor federal actions associated with major private actions that might cause significant environmental consequences, are sometimes called the "small federal handle" problem. Do such cases require an EIS? The CEQ rules seem to say yes. "Cumulative impact" is defined to encompass "the incremental impact of past, present, and reasonably foreseeable future action *regardless of what agency (Federal or non-Federal) or person undertakes such other actions.*" 40 C.F.R. § 1508.7 (emphasis added). Nonetheless, small federal handle cases go both ways, with some courts focusing on the impacts of the entire project made possible by federal activity (EIS required) and others just focusing on the federal activity (no EIS). *Compare Sylvester v. U.S. Army Corps of Engineers*, 884 F.2d 394 (9th Cir. 1989) (an EA prepared for a dredge and fill permit for a golf course did not need to consider the impacts of a private resort complex, of which the golf course was a part, even though the golf course did not have independent utility), *with Port of Astoria v. Hodel*, 595 F.2d 467 (9th Cir. 1979) (EIS must address impacts from private magnesium plant in deciding whether to permit federal power source).

Another perplexing question in determining whether the scope of federal action is major and significantly affects the environment is in cases where an agency fails or refuses to act. Does an agency's omission constitute action? The CEQ rules state that major federal "[a]ctions include the circumstance where the responsible officials fail to act and that failure to act is reviewable by courts" under the APA. 40 C.F.R. § 1508.18. The APA further defines "agency action" to include "failure to act," and authorizes legal action for agency action "unlawfully withheld or unreasonably delayed." 5 U.S.C. §§ 551(13); 706(1). Still, courts have not been kind to citizens challenging an agency's failure to comply with NEPA when the challenge is based on the agency's failure to act. For example, in *Defenders of Wildlife v. Andrus*, 627 F.2d 1238 (D.C. Cir. 1980), the court rejected a claim that the Interior Department should have prepared an EIS before standing aside and allowing the State of Alaska to carry out a wolf hunt on federal lands. FLPMA plainly authorized the Department of Interior to take action, but FLPMA did not require any action. Although the court never cited the relevant APA provisions or the relevant CEQ rules, it held that when "the agency decides not to act, and thus not to present a proposal to act, the agency never reaches a point at which it needs to prepare an impact statement." *Id.* at 1244.

In deciding whether an action "significantly" affects the human environment, the CEQ's rules also require agencies to consider the "context" and "intensity" of the proposed action. 40 C.F.R. § 1508.27. Put another way, the significance of the impact may depend on the setting. An action in a pristine or environmentally sensitive or valued area would be more likely to trigger EIS preparation than the same action in a heavily developed area. Likewise, actions that are controversial, that involve uncertain effects, that have long-term, as opposed to short-term effects, or that impact endangered species are more likely to require an EIS. Yet even when relevant factors for determining significance can be identified, no bright-line rules apply, and agencies will necessarily have to use their judgment.

The following case wrestles with this basic problem of deciding when a federal action is sufficiently "major" and "significant" to require preparation of an EIS. Its particular focus is on the meaning of connected and cumulative actions.

THOMAS V. PETERSON,
753 F.2d 754 (9th Cir. 1985)

SNEED, CIRCUIT JUDGE:

Plaintiffs sought to enjoin construction of a timber road in a former National Forest roadless area. The District Court granted summary judgment in favor of defendant R. Max Peterson, Chief of the Forest Service, and plaintiffs appealed. We affirm in part, reverse in part, and remand for further proceedings consistent with this opinion.

I. STATEMENT OF THE CASE

This is another environmental case pitting groups concerned with preserving a specific undeveloped area against an agency of the United States attempting to obey the commands given it by a Congress which is mindful of both environmentalists and those who seek to develop the nation's resources. Our task is to discern as best we can what Congress intended to be done under the facts before us.

Plaintiffs—landowners, ranchers, outfitters, miners, hunters, fishermen, recreational users, and conservation and recreation organizations—challenge actions of the United States Forest Service in planning and approving a timber road in the Jersey Jack area of the Nez Perce National Forest in Idaho. The area is adjacent to the Salmon River, a congressionally-designated Wild and Scenic River, and is bounded on the west by the designated Gospel Hump Wilderness and on the east by the River of No Return Wilderness. The area lies in a "recovery corridor" identified by the U.S. Fish & Wildlife Service for the Rocky Mountain Gray Wolf, an endangered species.

The Jersey Jack area was originally part of the larger Gospel Hump roadless area, but when Congress created the Gospel Hump Wilderness in 1978 it did not include the Jersey Jack area. The Forest Service's Roadless Area Review and Evaluation in 1979 recommended that the Jersey Jack area be managed as non-wilderness. In 1980, Congress passed the Central Idaho Wilderness Act, Pub. L. 96–312, 94 Stat. 948, which created the River of No Return Wilderness to the east of the Jersey Jack area, but left the Jersey Jack area as non-wilderness. The Act stated as one of its purposes to assure that "adjacent lands better suited for multiple uses other than wilderness will be managed by the Forest Service under existing and applicable land management plans." 94 Stat. 948.

After the passage of the Central Idaho Wilderness Act, the Forest Service, in keeping with its earlier expressed intention, proceeded to plan timber development in the Jersey Jack area. In November, 1980, the Forest Service solicited public comments and held a public hearing on a proposed gravel road that would provide access to timber to be sold. The Forest Service prepared an environmental assessment (EA), see 40 C.F.R. § 1508.9 (1984), to determine whether an EIS would be required for the road. Based on the EA, the Forest Service concluded that no EIS was required, and issued a Finding of No Significant Impact (FONSI), see 40 C.F.R. § 1508.13. The FONSI and the notice of the Forest Supervisor's decision to go ahead with the road were issued in a single document on February 9, 1981. The decision notice stated that "no known threatened or endangered plant or animal species have been found" within the area, but the EA contained no discussion of endangered species.

The EA for the road discussed only the environmental impacts of the road itself; it did not consider the impacts of the timber sales that the road was designed to facilitate. Subsequently, on November 23, 1981, and on June 30, 1982, the Forest Service issued EAs for, and approved, two of the timber sales. An EA for a third timber sale was also issued prior to the commencement of this action in district court. Each EA covered only the effects of a single timber sale; none discussed cumulative impacts of the sales or of the sales and the road. Each EA resulted in a FONSI, and therefore no environmental impact statements were prepared.

[handwritten margin note: single timber sale EA's — no cum. impacts discussed]

The plaintiffs appealed the Forest Supervisor's decision on the road to the Regional Forester, who affirmed the decision on May 26, 1981. The Regional Forester's decision was then appealed to the Chief of the Forest Service, who affirmed the decision on November 24, 1981. The plaintiffs filed this action, challenging the Chief's decision, on June 30, 1992. * * *

After briefing and oral argument, the district court granted summary judgment for the Forest Service on all claims.

II.   THE NEPA CLAIM

The central question that plaintiffs' NEPA claim presents is whether the road and the timber sales are sufficiently related so as to require combined treatment in a single EIS that covers the cumulative effects of the road and the sales. If so, the Forest Service has proceeded improperly. An EIS must be prepared and considered by the Forest Service before the road can be approved. If not, the Forest Service may go ahead with the road, and later consider the environmental impacts of the timber sales.

[handwritten margin note: issue]

Section 102(2)(C) of NEPA requires an EIS for "major Federal actions significantly affecting the quality of the human environment." While it is true that administrative agencies must be given considerable discretion in defining the scope of environmental impact statements, see Kleppe v. Sierra Club, 427 U.S. 390, 412–15 (1976), there are situations in which an agency is required to consider several related actions in a single EIS, see id. at 409–10. Not to require this would permit dividing a project into multiple "actions," each of which individually has an insignificant environmental impact, but which collectively have a substantial impact. See Alpine Lakes Protection Society v. Schlapfer, 518 F.2d 1089, 1090 (9th Cir.1975).

Since the Supreme Court decided the Kleppe case, the Council on Environmental Quality (CEQ) has issued regulations that define the circumstances under which multiple related actions must be covered by a single EIS. The regulations are made binding on federal administrative agencies by Executive Order. *See* Exec. Order No. 11991. The CEQ regulations and this court's precedents both require the Forest Service to prepare an EIS analyzing the combined environmental impacts of the road and the timber sales.

A.   *CEQ Regulations*

1.   *Connected actions*

The CEQ regulations require "connected actions" to be considered together in a single EIS. *See* 40 C.F.R. § 1508.25(a)(1) (1984). "Connected actions" are defined, in a somewhat redundant fashion, as actions that

"(i) Automatically trigger other action which may require environmental impact statements.

"(ii) Cannot or will not proceed unless other actions are taken previously or simultaneously.

"(iii) Are interdependent parts of a larger action and depend on the larger action for their justification." *Id.*

The construction of the road and the sale of the timber in the Jersey Jack area meet the second and third, as well as perhaps the first, of these criteria. It is clear that the timber sales cannot proceed without the road, and the road would not be built but for the contemplated timber sales. This much is revealed by the Forest Service's characterization of the road as a "logging road," and by the first page of the environmental assessment for the road, which states that "[t]he need for a transportation route in the assessment area is to access the timber lands to be developed over the next twenty years." Moreover, the environmental assessment for the road rejected a "no action" alternative because that alternative would not provide the needed timber access. The Forest Service's cost-benefit analysis of the road considered the timber to be the benefit of the road, and while the Service has stated that the road will yield other benefits, it does not claim that such other benefits would justify the road in the absence of the timber sales. Finally, the close interdependence of the road and the timber sales is indicated by an August 1981 letter in the record from the Regional Forester to the Forest Supervisor. It states, "We understand that sales in the immediate future will be dependent on the early completion of portions of the Jersey Jack Road. It would be advisable to divide the road into segments and establish separate completion dates for those portions to be used for those sales."

We conclude, therefore, that the road construction and the contemplated timber sales are inextricably intertwined, and that they are "connected actions" within the meaning of the CEQ regulations.

2.   *Cumulative Actions*

The CEQ regulations also require that "cumulative actions" be considered together in a single EIS. 40 C.F.R. § 1508.25(a)(2). "Cumulative actions" are defined as actions "which when viewed with other proposed actions have cumulatively significant impacts." *Id.* The record in this case contains considerable evidence to suggest that the road and the timber sales will have cumulatively significant impacts. The U.S. Fish & Wildlife Service, the Environmental Protection Agency, and the Idaho Department of Fish & Game have asserted that the road and the timber sales will have significant cumulative effects that should be considered in an EIS. The primary cumulative effects, according to these agencies, are the deposit of sediments in the Salmon River to the detriment of that river's population of salmon and steelhead trout and the destruction of critical habitat for the endangered Rocky Mountain Gray Wolf.

These agencies have criticized the Forest Service for not producing an EIS that considers the cumulative impacts of the Jersey Jack road and the timber sales. For example, the Fish & Wildlife Service has written, "Separate documentation of related and cumulative potential impacts may be leading to aquatic habitat degradation unaccounted for in individual EAs (*i.e.,* undocumented cumulative effects).... Lack of an overall effort to document cumulative impacts could be having present and future detrimental effects on wolf recovery potential." These comments are sufficient to raise "substantial questions" as to whether the road and the timber sales will have significant cumulative environmental effects. Therefore, on this basis also, the Forest Service is required to prepare an EIS analyzing such effects.

B. *Ninth Circuit Precedents*

The Conclusion That Nepa Requires A Single Eis That Considers Both Road And Sales Is Supported By Our Precedents. In *Trout Unlimited v. Morton,* 509 F.2d 1276 (9th Cir. 1974), We Addressed The Issue Of When Subsequent Phases Of Development Must Be Covered In An Environmental Impact Statement On The First Phase. We Stated That An Eis Must Cover Subsequent Stages When "[T]he Dependency Is Such That It Would Be Irrational, Or At Least Unwise, To Undertake The First Phase If Subsequent Phases Were Not Also Undertaken." *Id*. At 1285. The Dependency Of The Road On The Timber Sales Meets This Standard; It Would Be Irrational To Build The Road And Then Not Sell The Timber To Which The Road Was Built To Provide access.

The same principle is embodied in standards that we have established for determining when a highway may be segmented for purposes of NEPA. In *Daly v. Volpe,* 514 F.2d 1106 (9th Cir. 1975), we held that the environmental impacts of a single highway segment may be evaluated separately from those of the rest of the highway only if the segment has "independent utility." 514 F.2d at 1110. In the light of *Trout Unlimited,* the phrase "independent utility" means utility such that the agency might reasonably consider constructing only the segment in question. The Forest Service has not alleged that the Jersey Jack road has sufficient utility independent from the timber sales to justify its construction. Severance of the road from the timber sales for purposes of NEPA, therefore, is not permissible.

C. *Timing of the EIS*

The Forest Service argues that the cumulative environmental effects of the road and the timber sales will be adequately analyzed and considered in the EAs and/or EISs that it will prepare on the individual timber sales. The EA or EIS on each action, it contends, will document the cumulative impacts of that action and all previous actions.

We believe that consideration of cumulative impacts after the road has already been approved is insufficient to fulfill the mandate of NEPA. A central purpose of an EIS is to force the consideration of environmental impacts in the decisionmaking process. That purpose requires that the NEPA process be integrated with agency planning "at the earliest possible time," 40 C.F.R. § 1501.2, and the purpose cannot be fully served if consideration of the cumulative effects of successive, interdependent steps is delayed until the first step has already been taken.

The location, the timing, or other aspects of the timber sales, or even the decision whether to sell any timber at all affects the location, routing, construction techniques, and other aspects of the road, or even the need for its construction. But the consideration of cumulative impacts will serve little purpose if the road has already been built. Building the road swings the balance decidedly in favor of timber sales even if such sales would have been disfavored had road and sales been considered together before the road was built. Only by selling timber can the bulk of the expense of building the road be recovered. Not to sell timber after building the road constitutes the "irrational" result that *Trout Unlimited*'s standard is intended to avoid. Therefore, the cumulative environmental impacts of the road and the timber sales must be assessed before the road is approved.

The Forest Service argues that the sales are too uncertain and too far in the future for their impacts to be analyzed along with that of the road. This comes close to saying that building the road now is itself irrational. We decline to accept that conclusion. Rather, we believe that if the sales are sufficiently certain to justify construction of the road, then they are sufficiently certain for their environmental impacts to be analyzed along with those of the road. *Cf. City of Davis v. Coleman,* 521 F.2d 661, 667–76 (9th Cir. 1975) (EIS for a road must analyze the impacts of industrial development that the road is designed to accommodate). Where agency actions are sufficiently related so as to be "connected" within the meaning of the CEQ regulations, the agency may not escape compliance with the regulations by proceeding with one action while characterizing the others as remote or speculative.

Moreover, the record contains substantial evidence that the timber sales were in fact at an advanced stage of planning by the time that the decision to build the road was made. The Forest Service issued EAs for, and approved, two of the timber sales nine and sixteen months after it issued the road EA, and it had issued an EA for a third sale by the time that this action was filed. In fact, one of the Forest Service's own affidavits shows that the Service was preparing the EA on at least one of the sales at the same time that it was preparing the EA on the road. The record plainly establishes that the Forest Service, in accordance with good administrative practices, was planning contemporaneously the timber sales and the building of the road. Either without the other was impractical. The Forest Service knew this and cannot insist otherwise to avoid compliance with NEPA.

We therefore reverse the district court on the NEPA issue and hold that, before deciding whether to approve the proposed road, the Forest Service is required to prepare and consider an environmental impact statement that analyzes the combined impacts of the road and the timber sales that the road is designed to facilitate.

QUESTIONS AND DISCUSSION

1. The *Thomas* court recognized the importance of considering, in the aggregate, the cumulative effects of otherwise insignificant impacts. The difficulty, of course, is determining when impacts are closely enough related to be considered cumulatively and when the idea of cumulative effects—which can easily be abused under the logic that everything is connected to everything else—is taken too far as a litigation technique. Recall that the CEQ rules define cumulative impact as "the impact on the environment which results from the incremental impact of the action when added to other past, present, and reasonably foreseeable future actions ... result[ing] from individually minor but collectively significant actions taking place over a period of time." 40 C.F.R. § 1508.7. The impact may include both direct and indirect ecological, aesthetic, historic, cultural, economic, social, or health effects. 40 C.F.R. § 1508.8. Based on this definition, how would you draw lines to limit the impacts that must be considered cumulatively? For example, must an agency consider the cumulative impacts of a project that affects an endangered species in one geographic region with other projects that affect the same species in entirely different geographic regions?

2. NEPA takes an informational approach to changing behavior. Information, however, comes at a cost. Agency resources (both cost and time) spent preparing an EIS are unavailable to spend on other pressing needs. How would one go about assessing the cost-effectiveness of NEPA? In 1997, the CEQ released a study that attempted to assess NEPA's achievements. *See The National Environmental Policy Act: A Study of Its Effectiveness After Twenty–Five Years*, (CEQ, 1997), *available at* http://www.nepa.gov/nepa/nepa25fn.pdf. The study makes some useful observations about the ways in which NEPA has changed agency behavior, and the public's ability to participate in government decision-making. It also makes recommendations for improving NEPA's utility. Unfortunately, the study does not offer empirical evidence that might help evaluate the extent of NEPA's success.

3. What standard of review does the *Thomas* court employ in reviewing the Forest Service's decision not to prepare an EIS? Does it give sufficient deference to the agency? Or is this one of those relatively rare cases identified by Vic Sher (*supra* at pages 233–234) where the plaintiffs' victory is "a function of the government's arrogance, incompetence, or outright efforts to evade the law"? Vic Sher, *Breaking Out of the Box: Toxic Risk, Government Actions, and Constitutional Rights*, 13 J. Envtl. L. & Litig. 145, 150 (1998). If *Thomas* is a relatively easy case because the road and the timber sales are so directly connected to one another, consider, instead, where two or more projects have cumulative impacts that are wholly unrelated. Suppose, for example, that the Bureau of Reclamation has proposed to change the management of certain federal dams in a way that will impact whooping crane habitat along the North Platte River in Nebraska and that the U.S. Minerals Management Service has simultaneously proposed to issue federal oil and gas leases for lands off the coast of the Arkansas National Wildlife Refuge in Texas, where the same cranes spend most of the winter. Should such projects be addressed in a single EIS? What if one or more of the projects is proposed by private parties on private lands? How can the federal agency obtain sufficient relevant information about both actions to analyze their cumulative impacts?

4. Not all federal actions trigger NEPA. Some statutes, such as the Clean Air Act and parts of the Clean Water Act, exempt the EPA from NEPA's EIS requirement on the theory that the underlying purpose of EPA's actions are environmental protection, and that an EIS would therefore be redundant. *See, e.g., Buckeye Power, Inc. v. EPA*, 481 F.2d 162 (6th Cir. 1973). Some courts have also found that certain activities that require other forms of environmental review and public participation are the "functional equivalent" of NEPA compliance. *See, e.g., Merrell v. Thomas*, 807 F.2d 776 (9th Cir. 1986), *cert. denied*, 484 U.S. 848 (1987) (no EIS required for EPA registration of pesticides). Given your understanding of NEPA's purposes, do these exceptions to NEPA compliance make sense? Wouldn't it be a good idea, for example, for the EPA to consider reasonable alternatives to proposed actions, such as a proposal to issue a Clean Air Act permit for a new coal-fired power plant in an area with marginal air quality? Why do you think the National Park Service has not been granted the same "functional equivalent exemption" as EPA?

5.   Recall that agencies can avoid preparing an EIS or EA if the action is "categorically excluded" from NEPA compliance. The CEQ rules define a "categorical exclusion" (CE) as "a category of actions which do not individually or cumulatively have a significant impact on the environment and which have been found to have no such effect in procedures adopted by the agency...." 40 C.F.R. § 1508.4.

One of the more controversial examples of a categorical exclusion was the Forest Service exclusion for

> Timber harvest which removes 250,000 board feet or less of merchantable wood products or salvage which removes 1,000,000 board feet or less of merchantable wood products; which requires one mile or less of low standard road construction, and assures regeneration of harvested or salvaged areas, where required.

57 Fed. Reg. 43209 (1992). In *Heartwood, Inc. v. United States Forest Service*, 73 F.Supp.2d 962 (S.D. Ill. 1999), *aff'd on other grounds*, 230 F.3d 947 (7th Cir. 2000), a federal district court struck down the timber sale categorical exclusion because the Forest Service had failed to explain its decision:

> The Court finds that the FS [Forest Service] did not provide any rationale for why this magnitude of timber sales would not have a significant effect on the environment. The Court cannot find and the defendants do not direct the Court to any evidence in the record to support the huge increase in the board feet limit from the prior 100,000 limit, except to refer to the FS' expertise and prior experience with timber sales having "these characteristics." 56 FED. REG. 19719. That is not sufficient. The FS does not identify nor detail the characteristics to which it refers (road construction length, size of salvage or live tree harvests, etc.) and provides absolutely no other rationale to the Court to explain how and why the agency arrived at these figures. In addition, the FS does not provide any documentation nor evidence regarding the details of these prior harvests nor the FS' analysis of their environmental effects upon which they based their opinion....
>
>   ... [T]he Court may not rely merely on the agency's expertise. To uphold the agency's decision, the Court must be convinced that the record contains adequate evidence supporting the agency's expert opinions and decisions, as well as evidence upon which the agency states it relied in making those decisions. When discussing an agency's fulfillment of its NEPA obligations, CEQ regulations state clearly that the record must contain the relevant environmental documents supporting the agency's decision. See 40 C.F.R. § 1505.1. That is what is missing from this record. What the record does contain is documentation from the agency's own Timber Salvage Task Force's Report and Recommendation, dated March 31, 1992, that runs counter the FS' decision. That report recommended two alternative options that would have either (1) kept the 100,000 board feet limit for both live tree and salvage sales but eliminate the acreage criteria; or (2) expanded the volume to 200,000 to 300,000 board feet for salvage only, keeping the live tree harvest limit at 100,000. The report noted that the draft FSH [Forest Service Handbook] published in the Federal Register in April, 1991, increased the volume require-

ment to one million board feet, but that public comments were strongly opposed to this harvest level for a categorical exclusion.

73 F. Supp.2d at 975–76. Notwithstanding its defeat in the *Heartwood* case, the Forest Service has moved aggressively to expand the number and type of activities categorically excluded from NEPA compliance. As of 2008, the Forest Service had promulgated new rules establishing numerous categorical exclusions. Among those likely to be controversial are the following:

- Short-term (1 year or less) mineral, energy, or geophysical investigations and their incidental support activities that may require cross-country travel by vehicles and equipment, construction of less than 1 mile of low standard road, or use and minor repair of existing roads.

- Hazardous fuels reduction activities using prescribed fire, not to exceed 4,500 acres; and mechanical methods for crushing, piling, thinning, pruning, cutting, chipping, mulching, and mowing, not to exceed 1,000 acres.

- Post-fire rehabilitation activities, not to exceed 4,200 acres ... to repair or improve lands unlikely to recover to a management approved condition from wildland fire damage, or to repair or replace minor facilities damaged by fire.

- Harvest of live trees not to exceed 70 acres, requiring no more than ½ mile of temporary road construction.

- Salvage of dead and/or dying trees not to exceed 250 acres, requiring no more than ½ mile of temporary road construction.

- Commercial and non-commercial sanitation harvest of trees to control insects or disease not to exceed 250 acres, requiring no more than ½ mile of temporary road construction.

- Land management plans, plan amendments, and plan revisions developed in accordance with 36 CFR 219 et seq. that provide broad guidance and information for project and activity decisionmaking in a NFS unit.

- Approval of a Surface Use Plan of Operations for oil and natural gas exploration and initial development activities, associated with or adjacent to a new oil and/or gas field or area.

71 Fed. Reg. 75481 (2006); Forest Service Handbook, 1909.15.30, *available at,* http://www.fs.fed.us/im/directives/. Typically, timber harvests average between 2000 and 3,500 board feet per acre. Thus, a timber harvest of 70 acres of live trees would likely yield at least 140,000 board feet and perhaps as much as 245,000 board feet. Are the new CEs consistent with the court's decision in *Heartwood*? Note that the Court of Appeals for the 10th Circuit upheld the CE for salvage logging on less than 250 acres. *Colorado Wild, Heartwood v. U.S. Forest Service,* 435 F.3d 1204 (10th Cir. 2006). Litigation over the land management plan CE is discussed in greater detail in the planning section of this chapter.

6. To trigger an EIS, the impact on the "human environment" must primarily be physical rather than social or economic. In *Metropolitan Edison Co. v. People Against Nuclear Energy,* 460 U.S. 766 (1983), for example, the Court reviewed a decision to allow an energy company to restart a companion reactor at Three Mile Island after the other reactor suffered a serious accident. The Nuclear Regulatory Commission performed an EIS that considered the effects of fog from cooling towers, the possibility of low-level radiation, or of another accident. Plaintiffs demanded, however, that the EIS also consider the psychological trauma to the community from restarting the reactor. The court rejected this claim, stating that even if psychological injuries are genuine, the risk of such injuries from restarting the reactor were too remote from the challenged action to be cognizable under NEPA. As Justice Brennan made clear in his concurring opinion, psychological injuries that arise from a "direct sensory impact of a change in the physical environment" remain cognizable under NEPA. But those psychological injuries that arise solely from a perception of risk associated with the agency's decision " 'lengthens the causal chain beyond' the reach of the statute." *Id.* at 775.

7. NEPA applies to international actions when the impacts occur in the United States. In perhaps the most creative of all NEPA challenges, the National Organization for the Reform of Marijuana Laws (NORML) alleged that a U.S.-supported narcotics program in Mexico that sprayed herbicide on marijuana and poppy plants would have significant health effects (by Americans smoking the herbicide-laden weed) in the United States and that an EIS must be prepared. The government agreed to prepare an EIS. *National Organization for the Reform of Marijuana Laws v. U.S. Dep't of State,* 452 F.Supp. 1226 (D.D.C. 1978). An EIS may not be required, however, when environmental impacts occur *exclusively* in a foreign jurisdiction because of a general presumption against the extraterritorial application of statutes. *Equal Employment Opportunity Commission v. Arabian American Oil Co.,* 499 U.S. 244 (1991). The case law regarding environmental impacts in the global commons such as the high seas or Antarctica, though, is less clear. In *Environmental Defense Fund v. Massey,* 986 F.2d 528 (D.C. Cir. 1993), the court held that NEPA applied to a proposal to build an incinerator on the global commons in Antarctica. The court reached this conclusion notwithstanding President Carter's 1979 Executive Order 12114, which requires analysis of environmental impacts abroad from major federal actions, including impacts in the global commons, but disclaims NEPA's application to such actions. The distinction between NEPA compliance and compliance with an Executive Order is important because, as with all Executive Orders, a violation does not create a cause of action and noncompliance cannot be challenged in courts. The Executive Order also exempts actions taken by the president or when national security is involved. President Clinton required environmental reviews for major trade agreements. *See* James Salzman, *Executive Order 13,141 and The Environmental Review of Trade Agreements,* 95 AM. J. OF INT'L L. 366 (2001).

8. At what point is the federal aspect of a proposed action that overall will have significant environmental impacts too small to warrant a federal EIS? Consider that question as you read the following problem.

PROBLEM EXERCISE: WINTER PARK SKI RESORT

A private resort developer has proposed to build a multimillion dollar, year-round resort near Winter Park, Colorado. The resort will be built entirely on private land. Among the projects planned for the resort are a major new ski area, a hotel, condominium, and retail complex, as well as a new, 18-hole championship golf course. Construction of the golf course will require the developer to fill 20 acres of wetlands adjacent to a navigable stream that will run through the course. Accordingly, the developer is required to obtain a permit from the U.S. Army Corps of Engineers in accordance with Section 404 of the Clean Water Act. The Corps is soliciting comments on the proper scope of the environmental analysis that it plans to prepare for the permit? How should you respond?

In answering this question, consider the CEQ regulations described in *Thomas* as well as the following rules adopted by the Corps.

   b. *Scope of Analysis.*

(1) In some situations, a permit applicant may propose to conduct a specific activity requiring a Department of the Army (DA) permit (*e.g.*, construction of a pier in a navigable water of the United States) which is merely one component of a larger project (*e.g.*, construction of an oil refinery on an upland area). The district engineer should establish the scope of the NEPA document (*e.g.*, the EA or EIS) to address the impacts of the specific activity requiring a DA permit and those portions of the entire project over which the district engineer has sufficient control and responsibility to warrant Federal review.

(2) The district engineer is considered to have control and responsibility for portions of the project beyond the limits of Corps jurisdiction where the Federal involvement is sufficient to turn an essentially private action into a Federal action. These are cases where the environmental consequences of the larger project are essentially products of the Corps permit action.

Typical factors to be considered in determining whether sufficient "control and responsibility" exists include:

(i) Whether or not the regulated activity comprises "merely a link" in a corridor type project (*e.g.*, a transportation or utility transmission project).

(ii) Whether there are aspects of the upland facility in the immediate vicinity of the regulated activity which affect the location and configuration of the regulated activity.

(iii) The extent to which the entire project will be within Corps jurisdiction.

(iv) The extent of cumulative Federal control and responsibility.

[The section elaborates further on how the agency might determine whether it has sufficient control, and then offers several examples to illustrate how these rules should be applied.]

33 C.F.R. part 325, App. B, § 7.b. *See Sylvester v. U.S. Army Corps of Engineers*, 884 F.2d 394 (9th Cir. 1989).

———

3. THE ESSENTIAL ELEMENTS OF AN EIS

Whether an EIS should be prepared formed the basis for much of the early NEPA litigation. But a good amount of NEPA litigation also focuses on the question whether the EIS, once prepared, is adequate. The CEQ rules establish a standard format for all EISs that "should be followed unless the agency determines there is a compelling need to do otherwise." 40 C.F.R. § 1502.10. An EIS should include, among other things, a statement of the purpose and need for action, a full description and analysis of the proposed action and reasonable alternative actions, a description of the affected environment, and an assessment of the environmental consequences of the various alternatives, including the means to mitigate the adverse impacts. In taking a hard look at an EIS, courts have focused on questions involving the range of alternatives to the proposed action, the adequacy of the analysis, the extent of uncertainty and the agency's good faith in addressing that uncertainty, and the problem of new information that becomes available after the final EIS is released.

a.   Alternatives Analysis

NEPA requires that the EIS contain a detailed statement on alternatives—what the CEQ has called the "heart" of the EIS. "[I]t should present the environmental impacts of the proposal and the alternatives in comparative form, thus sharply defining the issues and providing a clear basis for choice among options by the decision-maker and the public." 40 C.F.R. § 1502.14. Obviously, though, there are an endless number of potential alternatives an agency could consider. Note how the CEQ rules address this and other issues concerning the scope of the alternatives analysis.

[A]gencies shall:

(a) Rigorously explore and objectively evaluate all reasonable alternatives, and for alternatives which were eliminated from detailed study, briefly discuss the reasons for their having been eliminated.

(b) Devote substantial treatment to each alternative considered in detail including the proposed action so that reviewers may evaluate their comparative merits.

(c) Include reasonable alternatives not within the jurisdiction of the lead agency.

(d) Include the alternative of no action.

(e) Identify the agency's preferred alternative or alternatives, if one or more exists, in the draft statement and identify such alternative in the final statement unless another law prohibits the expression of such a preference.

(f) Include appropriate mitigation measures not already included in the proposed action or alternatives.

40 C.F.R. § 1502.14.

In implementing these requirements, courts have similarly required that agencies consider an array of actions that fairly represent the *range* of alternatives. In *California v. Block,* 690 F.2d 753 (9th Cir. 1982), for example, plaintiffs challenged the EIS informing the U.S. Forest Service's decision over which portions of a 62 million-acre national forest should remain roadless and designated wilderness. There was no lack of interest on the part of the public, and the Service's draft EIS drew 264,000 public comments. In its final EIS, the Service considered 11 alternatives, ranging from the extremes of all wilderness to no wilderness. In between, however, none of the alternatives considered allocating more than 33% of the roadless area to wilderness. In holding that this was inadequate, the Ninth Circuit emphasized that an agency need not consider every alternative or alternatives that are unlikely to be implemented for legitimate reasons, but equally, it must not ignore important alternatives or bias its evaluation by arbitrarily narrowing the range of options considered. While NEPA remains a procedural statute, this type of analysis suggests the overlapping relationship between NEPA challenges and arbitrary and capricious analyses under the APA.

Despite the importance of the alternatives analysis to NEPA compliance, agencies often struggle with this requirement because it can force them to consider options they may not prefer and that may even be outside of their jurisdiction to implement. The following case illustrates the problems that agencies sometimes face in addressing a proposal for a specific action that is proposed by someone from outside the agency. (It also provides a nice example of how local groups can use NEPA to try and preserve a local park.)

CITIZENS AGAINST BURLINGTON v. BUSEY
938 F.2d 190 (D.C. Cir. 1991), *cert. denied,* 502 U.S. 994 (1991)

CLARENCE THOMAS, CIRCUIT JUDGE:

The city of Toledo decided to expand one of its airports, and the Federal Aviation Administration decided to approve the city's plan. In this petition for review of the FAA's order, an alliance of people who live near the airport contends that the FAA has violated several environmental statutes and regulations. We hold that the FAA has complied with all of the statutes and all but one of the regulations.

I.

The Toledo Express Airport, object of the controversy in this case, lies about twenty-five miles to the west of downtown Toledo. Half a mile to the southwest of the airport, surrounded by four highways and intersected by three more, lies the Oak Openings Preserve Metropark, used by joggers, skiers, and birders, and site of one of the world's twelve communities of oak savannas. Within Oak Openings lies the Springbrook Group Camp, site of a primitive (tents only) campground, and used by hikers and campers, including Richard Van Landingham III, one of the petitioners in this lawsuit. Near the airport live Daniel Kasch, Carol Vaughan, and Professor William Reuter, three of the other petitioners. The Toledo–Lucas County Port Authority, one of the intervenors, wants to make the city of Toledo a cargo hub. Burlington Air Express, Inc., the other intervenor, wants to move its operations to Toledo. Kasch, Vaughan, Reuter, Van Landingham, and others have formed Citizens Against Burlington, Inc. to stop them.

Citizens Against Burlington first materialized about a year after the Port Authority first commissioned an "Airport Noise Compatibility Planning" study and began to consider the possibility of the airport's expansion. The Port Authority soon heard from Burlington Air Express, which had been flying its planes out of an old World War II hangar at Baer Field, an Air National Guard airport in Fort Wayne. After looking at seventeen sites in four midwestern states, Burlington chose the Toledo Express Airport. Among Burlington's reasons were the quality of Toledo's work force and the airport's prior operating record, zoning advantages, and location (near major highways and close to Detroit and Chicago). For its part, the Port Authority expects the new hub to create one thousand new jobs in Metropolitan Toledo and to contribute almost $68 million per year to the local economy after three years of the hub's operation. The Port Authority plans to pay for the new hub with both private and public funds. Much of the money, however, will come from user fees and lease agreements, and more than half will come from local bonds issued to private investors. Grants from the city of Toledo and the state of Ohio will make up another, much smaller portion of the costs. The Port Authority has applied for some federal funds as well, but the FAA has reacted coolly to the Port Authority's feelers. * * *

On May 11, 1990, the FAA published a final environmental impact statement. The first chapter of the statement explained that the Port Authority needed the FAA's approval for its plan to expand the Toledo Express Airport and described the role in that process that Congress meant for the agency to play. The second chapter of the EIS reviewed the particulars of the Port Authority's plan, listed the fourteen separate federal statutes and regulations that applied to the Port Authority's proposal, briefly described some alternatives to acting on the Port Authority's plan, and explained why the agency had decided not to discuss those possibilities more fully. The FAA then concluded that it had to consider in depth the environmental impacts of only two alternatives: the approval of the Port Authority's plan to expand the airport, and no action. The third chapter of the EIS described the environment affected by the proposal, and the fourth chapter detailed the environmental consequences of the two alternatives. After summarizing the environmental impacts in the fifth chapter, the agency listed in the sixth chapter the statement's preparers. Appendices to the statement collected scientific data and relevant inter-agency correspondence. In the second volume of the statement, the FAA compiled copies of the hundreds of letters concerning the draft EIS, a transcript of the public hearing, and written comments submitted after the hearing had ended.

* * * The problem for agencies is that "the term 'alternatives' is not self-defining." *Vermont Yankee Nuclear Power Corp. v. Natural Resources Defense Council, Inc.*, 435 U.S. 519, 551 (1978). Suppose, for example, that a utility applies for permission to build a nuclear reactor in Vernon, Vermont. Free-floating "alternatives" to the proposal for federal action might conceivably include everything from licensing a reactor in Pecos, Texas, to promoting imports of hydropower from Quebec. If the Nuclear Regulatory Commission had to discuss these and other imaginable courses of action, its statement would wither into "frivolous boilerplate," *id.*, if indeed the agency were to prepare an EIS at all and not instead just deny the utility a permit. If, therefore, the consideration of alternatives is to inform both the public and the agency decisionmaker, the discussion must be moored to "some notion of feasibility." *Vermont Yankee*, 435 U.S. at 551; *see id.* ("Common sense also teaches us that the 'detailed statement of alternatives' cannot be found wanting simply because the agency failed to include every device and thought conceivable by the mind of man.").

Recognizing the harm that an unbounded understanding of alternatives might cause, CEQ regulations oblige agencies to discuss only alternatives that are feasible, or (much the same thing) reasonable. 40 C.F.R. §§ 1502.14(a)–(c), 1508.25(b)(2); *see* Forty Most Asked Questions Concerning CEQ's NEPA Regulations, 46 FED. REG. 18,026, 18,026 (1981) [hereinafter Forty Questions]. But the adjective "reasonable" is no more self-defining than the noun that it modifies. Consider two possible alternatives to our nuclear reactor in Vernon. Funding research in cold fusion might be an unreasonable alternative by virtue of the theory's scientific implausibility. But licensing a reactor in Lake Placid, New York might also be unreasonable, even though it passes some objective test of scientific worth. In either case, the proposed alternative is reasonable only if it will bring about the ends of the federal action—only if it will do what the licensing of the reactor in Vernon is meant to do. If licensing the Vernon reactor is meant to help supply energy to New England, licensing a reactor in northern New York might make equal sense. If licensing the Vernon reactor is meant as well to stimulate the Vernon job market, licensing a reactor in Lake Placid would be far less effective. The goals of an action delimit the universe of the action's reasonable alternatives. * * *

We realize, as we stated before, that the word "reasonable" is not self-defining. Deference, however, does not mean dormancy, and the rule of reason does not give agencies license to fulfill their own prophecies, whatever the parochial impulses that drive them. Environmental impact statements take time and cost money. Yet an agency may not define the objectives of its action in terms so unreasonably narrow that only one alternative from among the environmentally benign ones in the agency's power would accomplish the goals of the agency's action, and the EIS would become a foreordained formality. Nor may an agency frame its goals in terms so unreasonably broad that an infinite number of alternatives would accomplish those goals and the project would collapse under the weight of the possibilities. * * *

In the second chapter of the environmental impact statement, the FAA begins by stating:

> The scope of alternatives considered by the sponsoring Federal agency, where the Federal government acts as a proprietor, is wide ranging and comprehensive. Where the Federal government acts, not as a proprietor, but to approve and support a project being sponsored by a local government or private applicant, the Federal agency is necessarily more limited. In the latter instance, the Federal government's consideration of alternatives may accord substantial weight to the preferences of the applicant and/or sponsor in the siting and design of the project. * * *

The FAA's reasoning fully supports its decision to evaluate only the preferred and do-nothing alternatives. The agency first examined Congress's views on how this country is to build its civilian airports. As the agency explained, Congress has told the FAA to nurture aspiring cargo hubs. At the same time, however, Congress has also said that the free market, not an ersatz Gosplan for aviation, should determine the sitting of the nation's airports. Congress has expressed its intent by statute, and the FAA took both of Congress's messages seriously.

The FAA also took into account the Port Authority's reasons for wanting a cargo hub in Toledo. In recent years, more than fifty major companies have left the Toledo metropolitan area, and with them, over seven thousand jobs. The Port Authority expects the cargo hub at Toledo Express to create immediately more than two hundred permanent and six hundred part-time jobs with a total payroll value of more than $10 million.... All of those factors, the Port Authority hopes, will lead to a renaissance in the Toledo metropolitan region.

Having thought hard about these appropriate factors, the FAA defined the goal for its action as helping to launch a new cargo hub in Toledo and thereby helping to fuel the Toledo economy. The agency then eliminated from detailed discussion the alternatives that would not accomplish this goal. Each of the different geometric configurations would mean technological problems and extravagant costs. So would plans to route traffic differently at Toledo Express, or to build a hub at one of the other airports in the city of Toledo. None of the airports outside of the Toledo area would serve the purpose of the agency's action. The FAA thus evaluated the environmental impacts of the only proposal that might reasonably accomplish that goal—approving the construction and operation of a cargo hub at Toledo Express. It did so with the thoroughness required by law. *See* 40 C.F.R. § 1502.16.

We conclude that the FAA acted reasonably in defining the purpose of its action, in eliminating alternatives that would not achieve it, and in discussing (with the required do-nothing option) the proposal that would. The agency has therefore complied with NEPA.

Citizens agree that the FAA need only discuss reasonable, not all, alternatives to Toledo Express. Relying on *Van Abbema v. Fornell,* 807 F.2d 633 (7th Cir. 1986), however, Citizens argues that "the evaluation of 'alternatives' mandated by NEPA is to be an evaluation of alternative means to accomplish the general goal of an action; it is not an evaluation of the alternative means by which a particular applicant can reach his goals." *Id.* at 638. According to Citizens, the "general goal" of the Port Authority's proposal is to build a permanent cargo hub for Burlington. Since, in Citizens' view, Fort Wayne (and perhaps Peoria) will accomplish this general goal just as well as Toledo, if not better, Baer Field is a reasonable alternative to Toledo Express, and the FAA should have discussed it in depth. Since it did not, this court should force the FAA to prepare a new (or supplemental) environmental impact statement.

We see two critical flaws in *Van Abbema,* and therefore in Citizens' argument. The first is that the *Van Abbema* court misconstrued the language of NEPA. *Van Abbema* involved a private businessman who had applied to the Army Corps of Engineers for permission to build a place to "transload" coal from trucks to barges. *See* 807 F.2d at 635. The panel decided that the Corps had to survey "feasible alternatives . . . to the applicant's proposal," or alternative ways of accomplishing "the general goal [of] deliver[ing] coal from mine to utility." *Id.* at 638. In commanding agencies to discuss "alternatives to the proposed action," however, NEPA plainly refers to alternatives to the "major *Federal* actions significantly affecting the quality of the human environment," and not to alternatives to the applicant's proposal. NEPA § 102(2)(C), 42 U.S.C. § 4332(2)(C) (emphasis added). An agency cannot redefine the goals of the proposal that arouses the call for action; it must evaluate alternative ways of achieving its goals, shaped by the application at issue and by the function that the agency plays in the decisional process. Congress did expect agencies to consider an applicant's wants when the agency formulates the goals of its own proposed action. Congress did not expect agencies to determine for the applicant what the goals of the applicant's proposal should be.

The second problem with *Van Abbema* lies in the court's assertion that an agency must evaluate "alternative means to accomplish the general goal of an action," 807 F.2d at 638—a statement that troubles us even if we assume that the panel was alluding to the general goals of the federal action instead of to the goals of the private proposal. Left unanswered in *Van Abbema* and Citizens' brief (and at oral argument) is why and how to distinguish general goals from specific ones and just who does the distinguishing. Someone has to define the purpose of the agency action. Implicit in *Van Abbema* is that the body responsible is the reviewing court. As we explained, however, NEPA and binding case law provide otherwise.

In chiding this court for having overreached in construing NEPA, a unanimous Supreme Court once wrote that Congress enacted NEPA "to ensure a fully informed and well-considered decision, not necessarily a decision the judges of the Court of Appeals or of this Court would have reached had they been members of the decisionmaking unit of the agency." *Vermont Yankee,* 435 U.S. at 558. We are forbidden from taking sides in the debate over the merits of developing the Toledo Express Airport; we are required instead only to confirm that the FAA has fulfilled its statutory obligations. Events may someday vindicate Citizens' belief that the FAA's judgment was unwise. All that this court decides today is that the judgment was not uninformed. * * *

BUCKLEY, CIRCUIT JUDGE, dissenting in part:

Burlington Air Express and the Federal Aviation Administration might be right: On substantial economic and environmental balance, Toledo Express Airport may well be the only suitable site for Burlington's air cargo hub. The public cannot know for certain, however, and neither can the FAA. By refusing to inquire into the feasibility of sites rejected by Burlington, the agency sidestepped its obligation to prepare "a detailed statement . . . on . . . alternatives to the proposed action." 42 U.S.C. § 4332(2)(C) (1988). The majority endorses this evasion. I cannot, and therefore I dissent from part II(A) of the majority opinion. While "the concept of 'alternatives' is an evolving one," *Vermont Yankee Nuclear Power Corp. v. NRDC,* 435 U.S. 519, 552 (1978), judicial evolution may not reduce it to a vermiform appendix. * * *

The majority would limit the consideration of alternatives to those available to the Toledo–Lucas County Port Authority. As the majority sees it, the FAA "defined the goal for its action as helping to launch a new cargo hub in Toledo and thereby helping to fuel the Toledo economy." As a consequence, airports outside the Toledo area were not to be considered because "[n]one . . . would serve the purpose of the agency's action." I read the EIS differently. Recognizing that Burlington is an essential party to the Port Authority's application, the FAA understands that the EIS must consider any reasonable alternative to Toledo Express Airport that might be available to Burlington, whether it lies within the Toledo area or outside it. * * *

I cannot fault the FAA for the attention given Burlington and its preferences. While both Toledo and Burlington are indispensable to the enterprise, Burlington is plainly the dominant partner; its requirements and desires shaped the project from the start. * * *

I do fault the agency for failing to attend to its own business, which is to examine all alternatives "that are practical or feasible from the technical and economic standpoint . . . rather than simply desirable from the standpoint of the applicant." Forty Most Asked Questions Concerning CEQ's National Environmental Policy Act Regulations ("Forty Questions"), 46 FED. REG. 18,026, 18,027 (1981). As far as I can tell, the FAA never questioned Burlington's assertions that of the ones considered, Toledo Express is the only airport suitable to its purposes. Instead, the agency simply accepted Burlington's "Toledo-or-bust" position. Thus, the EIS notes that Burlington hired consultants to help it choose a new hub site, and that the consultants prepared a confidential report. The impact statement fails to summarize the report; indeed, it does not say whether Burlington made the document available to the FAA. The EIS reports that a letter from the consultants demonstrates that Burlington's Toledo decision rests on "legitimate business interests." Of Burlington's decision to leave Fort Wayne, the FAA's Record of Decision similarly declares: "This is a business decision on the part of Burlington, in which the FAA has not been involved." The FAA thus accepts at face value Burlington's assertion that it had no second choice. * * *

I do not suggest that Burlington is untrustworthy, only that the FAA had the duty under NEPA to exercise a degree of skepticism in dealing with self-serving statements from a prime beneficiary of the project. It may well be that none of the sixteen other alternatives examined by Burlington and its consultants could be converted into a viable air cargo hub at acceptable cost. That, however, was something that the FAA should have determined for itself instead of accepting as a given. * * *

Even if the FAA had correctly concluded that the only reasonable alternative was "No Action," its EIS would still be flawed. By viewing the no-action alternative exclusively through Toledo's eyes, it failed to appreciate that that city's gains must necessarily be Fort Wayne's losses. Thus the EIS informs us that whereas the proposed project would produce 750 new jobs and $17 million for the Toledo economy during the first full year of operation, "the no-action alternative would mean foregoing . . . [these] economic benefits."

This analysis suggests that the jobs and dollars will arise spontaneously from the Toledo soil. In reality, Toledo's gains will come at Fort Wayne's expense. * * *

QUESTIONS AND DISCUSSION

1.   Judge (now Justice) Thomas distinguishes cases where a federal agency acts as a proprietor, itself engaging in a land-disturbing action, from cases, such as *Citizens Against Burlington,* where a federal agency's role is simply to approve or disapprove a project of a private applicant. What is the policy justification for such a distinction? If there are situations where it is important to distinguish the role of an agency as proprietor from its role as regulator, does it follow that the basis for NEPA compliance should change as well? For an argument that the dual standard for private and public projects is an incorrect interpretation of NEPA, see DANIEL R. MANDELKER, NEPA LAW AND LITIGATION § 9.05[7] (2d ed. 1992).

2.   The court notes that Burlington chose Toledo "[a]fter looking at seventeen sites in four Midwestern states." How likely is it that Burlington considered environmental impacts in choosing a site? Is it appropriate for a federal agency to influence a business decision by preparing an analysis that prefers a site already rejected by the applicant? Should such an analysis be used to demand additional mitigation at a site with greater impacts?

3.   How do you think the plaintiffs satisfied standing requirements? What type of agency action is being challenged, an adjudication or a rulemaking? To prevail, what did the plaintiffs need to establish?

4.   Review the language from the CEQ rules on alternatives analysis reproduced just before the *Busey* case. Is *Busey* consistent with these rules?

5.   Since many federal actions subject to NEPA involve the issuance of permits, what does the *Busey* decision suggest for NEPA's potential to improve agency decision-making?

6.   The CEQ rules define mitigation to include avoiding, minimizing, rectifying, reducing, or eliminating environmental impacts, or compensating for them by providing replacement or substitute resources. 40 C.F.R. § 1508.20. Mitigation is supposed to figure prominently in an environmental analysis. For example, the CEQ rules require agencies to describe appropriate mitigation measures for the proposed action and alternatives, and for the environmental consequences that are expected from agency actions. 40 C.F.R. § 1502.16(e)–(h). What mitigation actions should the FAA's EIS have considered?

7. NEPA does not require that agencies actually mitigate environmental harm, even if that mitigation can be accomplished at little or no additional cost. *Robertson v. Methow Valley Citizens Council,* 490 U.S. 332 (1989). By contrast, Canada has adopted an environmental assessment law that specifically mandates that government agencies implement appropriate mitigation measures when they approve actions that may adversely impact the environment. Canadian Environmental Assessment Act, ch. 37, § 37(2) (1992). Is there any downside to mandating that agencies take reasonable mitigation measures that are identified through the NEPA process?

8. Even though NEPA does not mandate mitigation, agency action can almost always be challenged on the grounds that it is arbitrary and capricious and an agency that fails to take reasonable actions to mitigate environmental harm may be vulnerable on those grounds. Still, such questions are rarely black and white, and an agency that refuses to mitigate environmental harm may be able to justify its decision on the grounds of cost or inconvenience. Suppose that agency comments to mitigate certain adverse impacts to justify its decision but then fails to take (or require a private applicant to take) the mitigation measure that were promised. On what basis might someone challenge such a decision?

9. The CEQ Forty Questions guidance, noted in the *Busey* case, is often cited to show the CEQ's intent in adopting particular rules. *See* 46 Fed. Reg. 18,026 (1981), *amended by* 51 Fed. Reg. 15,618 (1986); http://ceq.eh. doe.gov/nepa/regs/40/40p3.htm.? Is it binding on federal agencies? On courts? Can the court's support of the FAA's decision to evaluate only preferred and "do-nothing" alternatives be reconciled with NEPA's alternatives analysis requirement. *See also Friends of the Earth v. Hintz,* 800 F.2d 822, 837 n.15 (9th Cir. 1986).

---

b.   The Adequacy of the Analysis

While NEPA is primarily a procedural statute, courts are required to do some substantive review of the adequacy of the EIS analysis. This sometimes leads to a decision remanding the EIS to the agency. For example, in *Sierra Club v. U.S. Army Corps of Engineers,* 701 F.2d 1011 (2d Cir. 1983), the Corps prepared an EIS for filling part of the Hudson River to build a highway. The EIS described the area to be filled as a "biological wasteland," despite objections by EPA and the Fish & Wildlife Service. In requiring the Corps to prepare a supplemental EIS, the Second Circuit concluded that by ignoring the views of other expert agencies, and by not adequately compiling relevant data and analyzing it reasonably, the Corps had reached a "baseless and erroneous factual conclusion" that "cannot be accepted as a 'reasoned' decision." *Id.* at 1035. In most cases though, wary of appearing to engage in substantive review, courts are reluctant to reverse agencies on this ground. Thus, in *Sierra Club v. Marita*, 46 F.3d 606 (7th Cir. 1995), plaintiffs sued the Forest Service, claiming that NEPA and the National Forest Management Act required the agency to apply principles of conservation biology in developing a forest plan. Despite the testimony of thirteen distinguished scientists, the court rejected the plaintiffs' argument. According to the Seventh Circuit, agencies must use "high quality" science and ensure the "scientific integrity" of their analysis, but they don't have to use any particular methodology. *Id.* at 616, 620. *See also* 40 C.F.R. § 1502.24 (providing that agencies "shall insure the professional integrity, including scientific integrity, of the discussions and analyses in environmental impact statements").

As described in Chapter 1, scientific uncertainty is an unavoidable aspect of environmental decision-making. This arises in the context of NEPA when agencies must predict the impacts of particular options in the face of insufficient information. In particular, when do agencies have to conduct more research? The CEQ regulations state that if information essential to a reasoned choice among alternatives is not available, and the cost of obtaining the information is not exorbitant, the agency must include the information in its analysis before making a decision. 40 C.F.R. § 1502.22(a). If, however, obtaining the relevant information is too difficult, expensive, or time-consuming, the agency is obliged to include in the EIS, among other things, "a summary of existing credible scientific information" that is relevant to evaluating the "reasonably foreseeable significant adverse impacts" of the proposed action, and the agency's evaluation of such impacts "based upon theoretical approaches and research methods generally accepted in the scientific community." 40 C.F.R. § 1502.22(b). CEQ's rules provide that in deciding whether an impact is "reasonably foreseeable," agencies must include "impacts which have catastrophic consequences, even if their probability of occurrence is low...." *Id.* at 1502.22(b)(1). The Supreme Court has made clear, however, that agencies are not required to prepare a "worst case analysis" based upon a remote and hypothetical chance that an environmental problem might occur. *Robertson v. Methow Valley Citizens Council*, 490 U.S. 332 (1989).

PROBLEM EXERCISE: NATURAL DISASTER AND SCIENTIFIC UNCERTAINTY IN ENVIRONMENTAL ANALYSIS

In the aftermath of Hurricanes Katrina and Rita, New Orleans faced a state of emergency. Levees needed to be rebuilt and reinforced and the infrastructure needed to maintain the levees had to be reestablished. Given the potential for new storms, time was short. Yet all of the many proposed actions raised serious environmental issues. Full NEPA compliance seemed both impractical and impossible. The CEQ rules provide for emergency circumstances as follows:

> Where emergency circumstances make it necessary to take an action with significant environmental impact without observing the provisions of these regulations, the Federal agency taking the action should consult with the

Council about alternative arrangements. . . . [for] actions necessary to control the immediate impacts of the emergency.

40 C.F.R. § 1506.11.

On March 13, 2007, the Army Corps of Engineers announced that it had reached agreement with the CEQ to implement alternative arrangements that include preparation of a series of individual environmental reports (IERs) in place of an EIS. 72 Fed. Reg. 11337 (2007). These arrangements allowed the Corps to proceed quickly with projects focused on the 100–year level of storm protection by producing cursory IERs for groups of similar projects under circumstances where "risk to life, health, property, or severe economic loss is imminent." Projects such as levee reconstruction have proceeded under such analysis, despite the Corps' acknowledgment of unavoidable wetland impacts.

Ironically, coastal wetland degradation is a major aggravator in hurricane impact. For every 2.7 miles of wetlands between the Gulf and solid land, hurricane surges are lowered by one foot. Over the past century, taming of the rivers and maintenance of navigable channels have disrupted natural sediment deposition processes, which, augmented by the forces of the ocean and sea level rise, have resulted in wetland erosion at a current rate of around 60 feet per year. Hurricanes Katrina and Rita alone transformed 100 square miles into open water.

Although the Corps tends to focus on structural measures to hurricane protection, such as levees, pump stations, and floodgates, it has, along with other groups, proposed wetland restoration measures of varying degrees. The Corps is currently working on its Category 5 South Louisiana Coastal Protection and Restoration Report (LACPR) to "identify, describe and propose a full range of flood control, coastal restoration, and hurricane protection measures for south Louisiana." Considering that structural measures are necessary to maintain the Mississippi River Delta as a navigable waterway, and that some of the hurricane protection strategies are partly responsible for wetlands degradation and increased storm surges, how should the Corps strike the appropriate balance between structural and non-structural measures? *See* http://www.lacpr.usace.army.mil/default. aspx?p=Home.

According to the CEQ rule regarding emergency alternative arrangements, must the Corps prepare an IER or an EIS for the LACPR? Does it make sense to require such a document given the delay that this would likely cause for restoration efforts? In answering these questions, consider that an EIS is required before a federal agency makes an "irreversible and irretrievable commitment of the availability of resources." *Environmental Defense Fund, Inc. v. Andrus*, 596 F.2d 848, 852 (9th Cir. 1979); *see also Bob Marshall Alliance v. Hodel*, 852 F.2d 1223, 1225 (9th Cir. 1988); *California v. Block*, 690 F.2d 753, 761 (9th Cir. 1982). If the Corps commits substantial amounts of money to structural measures before it completes a comprehensive environmental analysis, would it undermine its ability to implement non-structural alternatives?

Complicating things further is the fact that climate change may be contributing to more frequent and more intense hurricanes, as well as to

sea level rise. *See e.g., Hurricanes and Climate Change, available at* http://
www.usgcrp.gov/usgcrp/links/hurricanes.htm. How should the scientific uncertainty surrounding the specific effects of global warming be addressed in
environmental analyses? Must the Corps address the impacts associated
with climate change? How should it inform the balance between structural
and non-structural hurricane protection measures? Consider CEQ rule 40
C.F.R. § 1502.22, discussed above. *See also Friends of the Earth v. Mosbacher*, 488 F.Supp.2d 889 (N.D.Cal. 2007); *Border Power Plan Working
Group v. Department of Energy*, 260 F.Supp.2d 997 (S.D.Cal. 2003).

---

c. Supplemental EISs

Related to the question whether an EIS is adequate is whether an
agency must prepare a supplemental EIS when new information becomes
available, perhaps significantly changing the range of impacts considered.
Imagine, for example, that the area to be filled in the Hudson River really
was a "biological wasteland," as suggested by the court in *Sierra Club v.
U.S. Army Corps of Engineers*, 701 F.2d 1011 (2d Cir. 1983), discussed
above. Soon after the filling of the river, though, a local fisherman caught
an endangered species and it now appears that a population of the fish lives
nearby. Must the Corps stop construction and prepare a supplemental EIS?
The CEQ regulations address this problem by requiring supplementation of
the EIS in two circumstances: (1) where the agency makes substantial
changes in the proposed action that are relevant to environmental concerns, or (2) where there are significant new circumstances or information
relevant to environmental concerns and bearing on the proposed action or
its impacts. 40 C.F.R. § 1502.9(c)(1). In *Marsh v. Oregon Natural Resources Council*, 490 U.S. 360 (1989), the Supreme Court rejected a claim
that the Army Corps of Engineers had violated NEPA when it failed to
prepare a second supplemental EIS on a proposal to build a dam in
southwest Oregon. In so doing, however, the Court made clear that agencies must consider new information even after a decision has already been
made. As Justice Stevens noted,

> It would be incongruous with ... the Act's manifest concern with preventing
> uninformed action, for the blinders to adverse environmental effects, once
> unequivocally removed, to be restored prior to completion of agency action
> simply because the relevant proposal has received initial approval.

Id. at 371. Of course, a "post-decision" supplemental EIS is not necessary
every time new information comes to light. Rather, an agency must look to
the significance of the new information, its value to the decision making
process, and whether the remaining governmental action is environmentally significant. *Id.*

And what if the predictions of the EIS, upon completion, turn out to be
inaccurate or ignored? Consider the plight of Ms. Noe. She owned a
bookshop that apparently was rattled to the core by the nearby construction of Atlanta's metro system, MARTA. She sued for a temporary injunction, among other remedies, asserting "that the failure of MARTA and its
builders to stay within the noise levels predicted by the environmental

impact statement constituted a violation of that section of NEPA that requires the filing of such statements prior to beginning construction." *Noe v. Metropolitan Atlanta Rapid Transit Authority*, 644 F.2d 434, 435 (1981), *cert. denied*, 454 U.S. 1126 (1981). Both the district and circuit courts, however, refused to imply a private right of action for Noe to sue. As the circuit court explained,

> NEPA contains no ... protections or prohibitions against conduct directed at private individuals. NEPA does not even require the protection of the environment. NEPA requires only that, prior to beginning construction of a project likely to affect the environment, an environmental impact statement be produced so that the individuals responsible for making the decision to go ahead with or stop the project do so on a well-informed basis. In that sense, NEPA provides procedural rather than substantive protection.

Id. at 438.

Problem Exercise: Supplementation of Environmental Analyses

Following preparation of an environmental assessment, the Forest Supervisor for the Medicine Bow National Forest approved the Banner Timber Sale. As approved, the sale would have allowed logging of five million board feet of timber. This was the highest volume of timber that was available from among the alternatives that the agency considered in the EA. The Supervisor justified his decision to approve the sale by citing, in particular, three "key" reasons:

(1) that the chosen alternative would do the most to help timber dependent communities;

(2) that the decision was consistent with the Forest Plan; and

(3) that the chosen alternative had the highest "benefit-cost" ratio of any of the alternatives considered.

After the timber sale was approved, the Forest Service revised its estimate of the amount of timber that was available from the sale downward to three million board feet, or 60% of the amount previously estimated. As a result of this revision, the economics of the sale changed so that the approved sale no longer had the highest "benefit-cost ratio" of the alternatives that had been considered in the EA prepared for the sale. Furthermore, the new data suggested—contrary to the findings in the EA—that the sale would cost more than it would generate in revenue, so the government would actually lose money if it went forward with the sale.

Friends of the Bow filed a lawsuit alleging that the decision was arbitrary and capricious on the basis of the revised economic analysis. The group further alleged that the Forest Service had failed to consider the relevance of a Forest Service study that indicated that the annual sustainable yield of the forest was about 6.4 million board feet/year rather than the 28.4 million board feet/year that had been presumed in the approved Forest Plan.[4]

---

4. Other timber sales that had been approved or were proposed for approval dur-   ing that year would have resulted in total sales that would have significantly exceeded

How should the Court analyze the agency's decision? What arguments can be made for or against the proposition that the decision approving the sale was arbitrary and capricious? *See Friends of the Bow v. Thompson,* 124 F.3d 1210 (10th Cir. 1997).

---

4.   DOES IT WORK?

Determining the effectiveness of NEPA is hard to do. Unlike the Clean Air Act or Clean Water Act, where one can measure air quality or water pollution over time, measuring the influence of environmental information on agency decision-making is no easy matter. At one extreme, the EIS could simply serve as a *post hoc* rationalization for decisions already taken— simply going through the bureaucratic motions. And there certainly is reason to fear that this may happen in some instances. After all, conflicts of interest run to the very core of NEPA. Some have commented that placing agencies in charge of conducting an EIS that may challenge their proposed actions is like placing the fox as guard of the henhouse. As Joe Sax noted at the beginning of this chapter, "I think the emphasis on the redemptive quality of procedural reform is about nine parts myth and one part coconut oil." Joseph Sax, *The (Unhappy) Truth About NEPA,* 26 OKLA. L. REV. 239 (1973). Given the concrete statutory mission of an agency with dedicated budgets, organized lobbies and congressional pressure, on the one hand, and the requirements of NEPA to consider environmental impacts of a range of actions, on the other, one might reasonably be skeptical of NEPA's influence. After all, there have traditionally been few political rewards for forests not cut or rangelands not grazed. Thus there are legitimate concerns over whether the benefit of generating information on impact analysis generally outweighs the cost and delays of producing such information.

EISs are usually several hundred pages long, not including sometimes lengthy appendices. The statutory requirement for an interdisciplinary analysis often leads to reports on a host of resources that may be impacted by a proposed action, including surface and groundwater, air quality, water quality, recreation, soils, plant and animal life, and cultural resources. As a result, preparing an EIS is an extremely expensive and time-consuming process. According to the Office of the Federal Environmental Executive, the average EIS costs over $150,000 and takes over 18 months to complete, while the average EA costs between $20,000 and $80,000 and takes over 6 months to complete. *See* http://www.ofee.gov/ems/training/hhs04/NEPA. ppt#285,10,Environmental.

Despite these concerns, NEPA has achieved a great deal. Talk to NGO litigators about NEPA, and many say it is critical in providing data on agency actions they could not otherwise obtain or use. In addition to

the 6.4 million board feet/year figure. The government had been working on this study for more than three years but abruptly abandoned the study within six weeks of its completion when the preliminary results of the study—noted above—became available. Although the study was abandoned, the government acknowledged that the study contained the best available information regarding sustained timber yield on the forest.

providing the public with the agency's environmental analysis, NEPA serves an important additional purpose as a kind of clearinghouse for information required by other relevant laws. Accordingly, the CEQ rules require that

> To the fullest extent possible, agencies shall prepare draft environmental impact statements concurrently with and integrated with environmental impact analyses and related surveys and studies required by the Fish and Wildlife Coordination Act (16 U.S.C. 661 et seq.), the National Historic Preservation Act of 1966 (16 U.S.C. 470 et seq.), the Endangered Species Act of 1973 (16 U.S.C. 1531 et seq.), and other environmental review laws and executive orders.

40 C.F.R. § 1502.25(a). One important result of this requirement is that the public participation procedures established under the CEQ regulations facilitate the public's ability to participate in the processes established under these other laws.

NEPA has played an important role in opening agency decision-making to the public. It also places constant pressure on agencies to broaden their missions to consider and adopt environmental values, and it has spurred agencies to modify proposals and mitigate adverse impacts. The circumstances described in *Calvert Cliffs*, where the Atomic Energy Commission prepared an EIS but refused even to read it, simply could not happen today. Indeed the numbers bear this out. Courts issued 202 NEPA injunctions in 1977, yet by 1997, only 102 NEPA cases were even filed and only two of those cases led to injunctions. (Perhaps not surprisingly, of those 102 cases, 59 were brought against the two major federal land management Departments—Interior and Agriculture.) Environmental impact analysis has become a standard part of federal decision-making.

————

Problem Exercise: Thinking Beyond NEPA

The Forest Service prepared an EIS and approved a proposal to expand the Snowbowl ski area, located on National Forest land in the San Francisco Peaks in northern Arizona. Part of the proposed expansion includes the use of recycled sewage effluent—"reclaimed water"—to make artificial snow, thereby greatly increasing the number of skiable days at Snowbowl. Water reclamation is an important strategy in assuring adequate supplies of drinking water in the rapidly developing southwest. Still, Snowbowl will be the only ski resort in the country to make its artificial snow exclusively out of treated sewage effluent. The EIS acknowledged that the treated effluent would contain "many unidentified and unregulated residual organic contaminants."

The San Francisco Peaks are also sacred ground for a variety of American Southwest Indian tribes, including the Hopi, the Navajo, the Hualapai, and the Havasupai. The Tribes' religious practices center around a spiritual connection with the mountain, which they believe is a pure, living being, and many of their ceremonies require harvesting water and other natural resources from the mountain. The Tribes sued the Forest Service, claiming that the use of sewage effluent on the Peaks would contaminate these resources and thereby substantially burden their exercise of religion under the Religious Freedom Restoration Act (RFRA). RFRA provides that:

(a) *In general.* Government shall not substantially burden a person's exercise of religion even if the burden results from a rule of general applicability, except as provided in subsection (b) of this section

(b) *Exception.* Government may substantially burden a person's exercise of religion only if it demonstrates that application of the burden to the person—

(1) is in furtherance of a compelling governmental interest; and

(2) is the least restrictive means of furthering that compelling governmental interest.

42 U.S.C. § 2000bb–1.

How should the court rule? Assuming it complied with NEPA, should the Forest Service's approval of the proposed expansion be overturned? In tackling this question, you may want to return to Chapter 2 and its discussion of potential tensions between certain federal natural resource policies and the First Amendment's Free Exercise and Establishment Clauses. More generally, how does NEPA compliance bring conflicts originating under other laws into play? *See* 40 C.F.R. § 1502.25(a). *See Navajo Nation v. U.S. Forest Service*, 535 F.3d 1058 (en banc) (9th Cir. 2008).

B.   RESOURCE PLANNING ON PUBLIC LANDS

When you travel, it's a good idea to bring along a map. Meetings usually work better when there is an agenda. Before you buy a car, it's generally wise to figure out how much money you have in your bank account and whether you'll still be able to afford the other items in your budget. Natural resource planning operates on the same commonsense principles. To manage a resource wisely it helps to have some idea of the quantity and nature of the resource (Is it scarce or plentiful? Is it renewable or non-renewable?); some knowledge of the competing uses of the resource (Does the resource have recreation, aesthetic, cultural, and/or commodity values? Is a particular use in the public interest?); and some sense of the impacts of using the resource (Will it cause environmental harm? Is it compatible with other uses? Does it limit future options?).

Given this simple intuition, it should not be surprising that planning mandates are pervasive in natural resource law and most natural resource decisions must reflect some type of broader resource management plan. Indeed, NEPA, while not usually described as a planning statute, requires agencies to follow basic planning principles. To grasp the pervasive role of planning in natural resources management, consider the planning provisions of the following important statutes:

• The Magnuson–Stevens Fishery Conservation and Management Act establishes Regional Fishery Management Councils to develop fishery management plans that are to provide the "measures necessary and appropriate for the conservation and management of the fishery to prevent overfishing and rebuild overfished stocks, and to protect, restore, and promote the long-term health and stability of the fishery [in a manner] consistent with the national standards." 16 U.S.C. 1853(a).

- The Endangered Species Act (ESA) requires the federal wildlife agencies to prepare "recovery plans" for the conservation of endangered species. 16 U.S.C. § 1533(f)(1). It also authorizes the agencies to issue "incidental take permits" (a sort of waiver for private activities that may incidentally harm—or "take"—a listed species) to private parties who prepare an acceptable "habitat conservation plan." 16 U.S.C. § 1539.

- The Coastal Zone Management Act presses states to develop coastal zone management plans. 16 U.S.C. § 1452(3).

- The National Forest Management Act (NFMA) requires the Secretary of Agriculture to "develop, maintain, and, as appropriate, revise land and resource management plans" for all of the national forests. 16 U.S.C. § 1604(a).

- The Federal Land Policy and Management Act (FLPMA) likewise requires the Secretary of the Interior to do land-use planning for the public lands by tract or area. 43 U.S.C. § 1712.

- The National Wildlife Refuge Improvement Act of 1997 guides the overall management of the Refuge System. It requires the Secretary of the Interior to maintain the biologic integrity, diversity and environmental health of the Refuge System, and to prepare comprehensive conservation plans. 16 U.S.C. § 668dd.

Planning statutes respond to several of the challenges that make natural resource management difficult. They address the problem of *scientific uncertainty* by imposing data collection requirements. FLPMA, for example, obligates the Interior Department to "prepare and maintain on a continuing basis an inventory of all public lands and their resource and other values." 43 U.S.C. § 1711. As a precursor to fishery planning, the Magnuson Act requires an assessment of "the present and probable future condition of, and the maximum sustainable yield and optimum yield from, the fishery," as well as the identification of "essential fish habitat." 16 U.S.C. § 1853(a). Planning provisions also represent an effort to respond to the *clash of values* problem. Because planning requirements are typically associated with multiple use management regimes, and because the planning process assures the public the opportunity to comment upon and participate in the formulation of a plan, all values are aired and usually, at least to some extent or in some location, accommodated under the final plan. *See, e.g.*, FLPMA, 43 U.S.C. § 1712(f).

The effort to respond to this clash of values is even more direct in those instances where the planning authority is delegated to a diverse group of stakeholders, as is the case with the Magnuson Act, which provides that the Regional Fishery Management Councils shall include the lead state fisheries official, the regional director of NOAA Fisheries, and commercial, recreational, and other fishing interests. 16 U.S.C. 1852(b)(2)(A). Including federal, state, and local officials in planning decisions is also a response to the challenge of *mismatched biophysical and political scale*, as are provisions, like that found in FLPMA, that require the Secretary to develop plans that are "consistent with State and local plans to the maximum extent consistent with Federal law and the purposes of this Act." 43 U.S.C. § 1712(c)(9). Finally, because most planning statutes bind federal officials to manage in accordance with the plan, plans provide an opportunity to influence resource management decisions and promote government accountability by creating a *handle for litigation* in those instances where federal resource managers ignore the plan.

In broad terms, federal planning statutes attempt to improve agencies' environmental decision-making much like NEPA. The focus is on process, although planning decisions are themselves substantive, and both are designed to make agencies pause and take a hard look at the environmental implications of their actions. Indeed, while this casebook treats NEPA and natural resource planning in two sections, recognize how closely intertwined they are. NEPA itself is essentially a planning statute. Moreover, because the development of a land use plan, a forest plan, a habitat conservation plan, or a fishery plan is a major federal action, the EIS process usually proceeds hand in hand with the development of such plans.

If planning promises to respond to so many natural resource management challenges, one might wonder why it took so long for planning to develop and why federal planning processes have so many critics. In an effort to consider those questions, the sections that follow trace the rise of two of the many federal planning regimes, namely those employed by the Forest Service on national forest lands and the BLM on public domain lands.

1. A BRIEF HISTORY OF PUBLIC LAND PLANNING

As described at the beginning of this chapter, the first century of our country's history saw very little land use planning, at least not the type we would recognize today. Certainly, the rectangular survey system imposed a rudimentary land use plan with its division of the public domain into 36–square–mile townships and one-square-mile sections. But the survey treated each lot as fungible, whether it contained gold, redwoods, a lake, sagebrush, or prairie. Other than the occasional consideration given to mineral-bearing lands, until well into the nineteenth century little thought was given to managing land with reference to the resources on that land. Although the 1872 creation of Yellowstone was arguably a planning decision, a better point from which to trace the birth of resource planning might be the 1879 Public Land Commission, described in the introduction to this chapter. It was in that report that John Wesley Powell and Interior Secretary Carl Schurz articulated their developing views that public land policy must, at some level, reflect the nature of land. The public lands, the report suggested, should be inventoried and then classified according to the resources they contained. Different laws and management regimes should then be developed for different resources.

Although today this does not seem like a particularly controversial proposition, it was at the time, and Congress initially rejected most of the report's recommendations. However, during the Progressive Era around the turn of the century, the ideas of Powell and Schurz bore fruit with the creation of the various federal agencies to manage portions of the public lands with reference to their resource characteristics. Yet, as explored above, for a variety of reasons expert agency management did not meet all of the expectations of its conservation era proponents. In the case of the two largest federal land management agencies—the Forest Service and the BLM—this was particularly true. As many saw it, the Forest Service was captured by the timber industry and, particularly after World War II, was managing the national forests almost exclusively for timber production. Professor Houck relates:

> To the American military, wood and wood products were "the most vital material" for winning [World War II], and the annual cut rose from an historic average of one billion board feet to 3.3 billion by 1944. When the war was over, the demand rose even higher, fueled by the promise of cheap housing and pulp and paper products. The nation's private timber lands had already been driven down to minimal production. Big timber would look to the public reserves. The most efficient harvest method available was clearcutting—the removal of every tree. The annual cut rose to eight billion board feet in 1959, and to twelve billion in 1966—a 600–percent increase in twenty-six years. The timber sales were increasingly subsidized by the American taxpayer. The Forest Service calculated its sale price not by the private market but, in the manner of electric power regulation, by a price that would guarantee the profit, usually fifteen percent, to each timber company. Excluded from the price were the costs of access roads, replanting, trimming, fencing, insect control, and administration of the sale program itself. Half the forest regions of the country were (and are) selling timber at a loss. The Tongass Forest of Alaska was selling at less than ten cents on the dollar of public expenditure, for trees exported to Japan; timber companies were paying from $2 to $20 for trees with an export value of $1,700 to $3,000. The Service promoted new sales even in times of plummeting demand, further undercutting the private market. It had every incentive to do so: Not only did it maintain the political support of its western constituents, it was authorized to keep a percentage of its timber sale receipts. The more trees it cut, the more the agency grew....

Oliver A. Houck, *The Water, the Trees, and the Land: Three Nearly Forgotten Cases That Changed the American Landscape*, 70 TUL. L. REV. 2279, 2294–95 (1996). The Forest Service's capture by the timber industry was exacerbated by the 1930 Knutsen–Vandenberg Act, which returns receipts from timber sales to the Forest Service to fund reforestation. 16 U.S.C. § 576b (2000). "K–V funds" give the Forest Service a perverse incentive to manage national forests for timber sales because excess funds go into the Service's reserve account. *See* Chapter 10, p. 1239 for further discussion of the K–V Act. Like the Forest Service, the BLM was also captured, many argued, by the livestock and mining industries and thus devoted the public domain and its natural resources almost wholly to commodity use.

As President Eisenhower's interstate highway system opened up more and more of the national forests and BLM lands to a public increasingly interested in outdoor recreation (visitor days in the National Forests climbed from 27.4 million in 1950 to 172.3 million in 1970) and with the rise of the environmental movement in the 1960s and 1970s, the management practices of the Forest Service and the BLM came under increasing scrutiny. *See generally* CHARLES I. ZINSER, OUTDOOR RECREATION: UNITED STATES NATIONAL PARKS, FORESTS, & PUBLIC LANDS 301 (1995). Because agency decision-making seemed so frequently captured by special interests, so often directed at commodity use of public natural resources, and so infrequently dictated by careful science and expert decisions, Congress eventually decided that change was needed. Part of the legal response was renewed emphasis on planning.

Planning statutes should thus be understood partly as a response to the failures of Progressive Era hopes for scientific management. Yet, because planning statutes also reflect a renewed effort to have agencies do a better, more expert, job of management, they also should be understood partly as products of a continuing Progressive Era impulse.

As part of its emphasis on increased resource planning, Congress began refocusing public land management on what it termed *multiple use* and *sustained yield*, passing the Multiple–Use, Sustained–Yield Act for the Forest Service in 1960. 16 U.S.C. §§ 528–531. FLPMA provides for the same standards to govern BLM management. 43 U.S.C. § 1712(c)(1). The Multiple–Use, Sustained–Yield Act defines the two key terms as follows:

(a) "Multiple use" means: The management of all the various renewable surface resources of the national forests so that they are utilized in the combination that will best meet the needs of the American people....

(b) "Sustained yield of the several products and services" means the achievement and maintenance in perpetuity of a high-level annual or regular periodic output of the various renewable resources of the national forests without impairment of the productivity of the land.

16 U.S.C. § 531. Planning was to be the method of implementing these concepts of multiple use and sustained yield and the way of mediating between the various public land interests.

During the 1960s, the Forest Service and the BLM began their initial efforts at public land use planning. One challenge that faced both agencies, and an issue with which federal land use planners have continued to struggle, was the scale at which to do planning. Local managers have a better understanding of local impacts and opportunities but have a hard time calibrating those impacts on a regional or national scale and a harder time resisting local political pressure to take actions contrary to the broader national interest. National planners, by contrast, are more likely to target the national interest in the public lands, but their broad policy pronouncements often do not fit particularly well with local circumstances. BLM's early planning efforts struggled to negotiate these competing concerns. Initially, BLM proposed that local officials would evaluate the costs and benefits of every land use. Where possible, they would rely on prices in private markets to value the resources involved, but in the case of resource values not priced in a market, they were to use a number administratively determined in Washington. This did not satisfy either BLM's Washington leadership, who felt that social and environmental values were receiving inadequate consideration in the local offices, or the field officers, who believed that the values assigned by Washington were arbitrary and bore little relationship to what was happening on the ground. In response to the criticism, BLM turned to a system in which various output categories, such as board feet cut and acres of rangeland improved, would be established at the national level. Field officers would then make a local evaluation of the potential outputs of any particular project and send their data to Washington where decisions would be made about which projects to fund. This system drew even stronger opposition from the field offices and was ultimately rejected by BLM's leadership. By 1969 BLM turned to a third approach, more closely related to urban land use planning, under which district managers prepared "management framework plans" (MFPs) designed to inventory existing and potential benefits from seven resources—lands, energy and minerals, livestock forage, timber, watershed, wildlife habitat, and recreation—and then decide on a priority among those uses in any particular area. Robert H. Nelson, Public Lands and Private Rights: The Failure of Scientific Management 133–36 (1995). Unfortunately, in 1970, soon after BLM hit upon this approach, the Classification and Multiple Use Act expired, leaving BLM planning largely in limbo until the passage of FLPMA in 1976, which served as an organic act for the BLM and set forth the planning obligations that guide the agency today.

The Forest Service was quicker to begin the planning process. Like the BLM, it borrowed from the discipline of urban planning and thought about planning in terms of zoning. Just as with municipal zoning that divides a community into areas of residential and industrial use and high and low density uses, ranger districts, for example, were divided into various zones, such as water influence zones, travel zones, and special zones for wilderness, scenic, and geologic areas. Each zone would then have a particular set of management priorities and requirements. This initial planning in the 1960s did not produce the result that many had hoped for because forest management continued to be tilted toward logging. Accordingly, criticism of the Forest Service's timber-driven management program continued into the 1970s, ultimately resulting in the famous *Monongahela* decision, *West Virginia Div. of Izaak Walton League v. Butz*, 522 F.2d 945 (4th Cir. 1975), in which the court interpreted the Forest Service's Organic Act to preclude clearcutting and to require marking each tree separately for cutting. The court's interpretation of the Act severely limited the Service's ability to engage in what had been its preferred harvest method. But as the court saw it, the Service had evolved from a "custodian to a production agency," and although the court's interpretation had "serious and far reaching consequences," those consequences were for Congress to fix. *Id.* at 955. It was in the aftermath of *Monongahela* that Congress passed the National Forest Management Act of 1976 (NFMA), Act of October 22, 1976, Pub.L. No. 94–588, 90 Stat. 2949, which continues to be the primary statute governing national forest planning. Its requirements are summarized in the next section, which describes the current agency planning processes.

2. PLANNING UNDER NFMA AND FLPMA

The planning requirements of NFMA and FLPMA are similar in many ways, which is not particularly surprising given that both statutes were enacted in 1976. The following excerpt describes the Forest Service process under NFMA, but it applies just as well to BLM planning under FLPMA:

> Public land and resource planning is basically a three-stage process. First, the foundation is set by gathering data in order to establish an inventory of commodity and noncommodity resources. The second stage is the creation of an integrated plan, which must be developed with the participation of the public and of professionals in the appropriate disciplines. The plan assesses the inventoried resources, reconciles competing demands for resources allocation, and proposes appropriate actions. Land classification, which prohibits or favors specified uses, is a crucial aspect of this stage. The third stage is the implementation of the plan on a site-specific basis, through such agency activities as

contracting for development, providing for construction of roads and other facilities, monitoring performance, and enforcing against infractions. The plan must also include procedures for revision as conditions change.

Charles F. Wilkinson & H. Michael Anderson, *Land and Resource Planning in the National Forests*, 64 OR. L. REV. 1, 10 (1985). Despite their similar approaches and challenges, there are important differences between the two planning regimes. To the extent these differences can be generally characterized, forest plans are more detailed and give the agency less discretion.

The following excerpt lays out the basics of Forest Service and BLM planning. Keep in mind, however, that the planning process is very much in flux, in large part due to the Supreme Court's decision in *Norton v. Southern Utah Wilderness Alliance*, excerpted below. That decision has called into question the very relevance of land use planning to project-level decisions. Under the George W. Bush Administration, the Forest Service was most aggressive in trying to exploit this decision. In 2005, it adopted new planning rules that were described as strategic rather than decisional. As a result, the Forest Service refused to prepare an EIS or even an EA on the proposed rules, claiming the right to categorically exclude them from NEPA compliance. Furthermore, in conjunction with the promulgation of planning rules the Forest Service proposed changes to its Handbook that allow forest planners to categorically exclude individual forest plans and amendments from NEPA. 70 Fed. Reg. 1023, 1032 (2005). Those handbook revisions were finalized in 2006. Forest Service Handbook, 1909.15, § 31.2(16), 71 Fed. Reg. 75481 (2006). Subsequently, the 2005 planning rules were struck down by a federal district court on various procedural grounds, including the agency's failure to comply with NEPA in preparing its programmatic planning rules. *See Citizens for Better Forestry v. U.S. Dept. of Agriculture*, 481 F. Supp.2d 1059, 1087–89 (N.D.Cal. 2007). In 2008, following preparation of an EIS, the Forest Service again adopted planning rules that allow the Forest Service to categorically exclude forest plans and amendments from NEPA. 73 Fed. Reg. 21468, 21473 (2008). Further litigation is expected over these rules, focusing in particular on the decision to categorically exclude forest plans from the NEPA process. Consider the language of NFMA. It requires the agency to—"insure that land management plans are prepared in accordance with NEPA....," 16 U.S.C. § 1604(g)(1). The Forest Service claims that it complied with this requirement by using the NEPA to categorically exclude plans. Note, however, that categorical exclusions under NEPA did not exist before the 1978 CEQ rules, two years after NFMA was enacted. How would you expect the court to rule?

Scott W. Hardt, *Federal Land–Use Planning and Its Impact on Resource Management Decisions*, 4–7 to 4–32, ROCKY MTN. MIN. L. FOUND., PUBLIC LAND LAW SPECIAL INSTITUTE (Nov. 1997)

* * *

IV. A.   THE GEOGRAPHIC SCOPE OF RMPs AND LRMPs

BLM RMPs [Resource Management Plans] are generally prepared by each BLM Area Manager and cover multiple-use management issues in the individual Resource Management Areas. District Managers are directed to assist in the planning effort, and all RMPs must be approved by the State Director....

... [A]t the national level, the Forest Service must prepare a Renewable Resources Assessment and Program. The Renewable Resource Assessment evaluates current and foreseeable demands for and supplies of renewable national forest resources, and opportunities available for improving the yield of goods and services provided by these resources. The Renewable Resources Program evaluates alternative national goals and objectives for renewable resource outputs and selects tentative resource objectives for each forest planning area. * * *

[Additionally], each Forest Supervisor must develop an LRMP. A separate LRMP is generally prepared for each national forest or grassland; however, where a single Forest Supervisor has responsibility for more than one such unit, a single LRMP may be prepared to cover those units. LRMPs must be approved by the appropriate Regional Forester.

In short, the geographic scope of RMPs and LRMPs are defined largely by administrative, and not ecological, boundaries....

B.   The Multiple-Use Mandate

* * * The courts have generally concluded that the Forest Service's and BLM's multiple-use mandates only require the agencies to consider the various multiple uses before committing land to a particular use. The agencies have broad discretion to decide the proper uses within any area under their management. The courts will not engage in a substantive evaluation of whether the agencies have chosen an appropriate balance of uses on any particular parcel. This is true even where the agencies have dedicated the majority of a forest to a single use, such as timber harvesting. It is clear that the multiple use doctrine does not require that every piece of land be put to every possible use, and that certain areas may be subject to limited or dominant uses in an overall multiple-use matrix. * * *

C.   What Do LRMPs and RMPs Decide?

1.   Plans Make Only Zoning/Suitability Decisions

Neither LRMPs nor RMPs authorize actual on-the-ground projects or activities. Instead, much like local zoning regulations, these plans merely articulate what types of activities may be allowed within the planning area, and under what conditions. LRMPs and RMPs essentially divide the planning area into different management areas and establish what future uses may be allowed in each area.

A plan prescription providing that certain activities may occur in a particular management area does not mean that such activities will subsequently be allowed, but only that they may be allowed consistent with the plan. In short, these plans limit the range of future options that federal land managers would otherwise have authority to implement....

Actual on-the-ground projects may be approved only after the Forest Service or BLM conducts further site-specific analyses to ensure compliance with the National Environmental Policy Act, the Endangered Species Act, and other applicable laws. The agencies should be able to tier their site-specific analysis to the plan-level environmental analyses and avoid readdressing all potential environmental issues when specific projects or activities are considered for approval.

2.   CONSISTENCY REQUIREMENTS

Once an LRMP or RMP is in place, all subsequent management decisions must be consistent with the plan. Consequently, while an RMP or LRMP does not approve on-the-ground activities, they are important documents for establishing what subsequent activities may be approved, and under what conditions. If approval of a proposed project or other management action would be inconsistent with the terms of an approved plan, the approval must be denied, unless the plan is amended. If such an amendment is deemed to be significant, it must be made in accordance with the public notice and comment procedures . . . for preparation and revision of plans, and can delay project-level permitting decisions. * * *

Because RMPs and LRMPs do not make actual land use decisions, the BLM or Forest Service must conduct additional environmental reviews when considering specific projects. During these project-specific reviews, the agencies frequently determine that additional mitigation measures or other land-use restrictions, above and beyond what is set forth in the RMP or LRMP are appropriate. Consequently, in effect, LRMPs and RMPs merely establish the minimum environmental restrictions that the agencies may impose, and do not set any ceiling on such restrictions. * * *

D.   SUBSTANTIVE REQUIREMENTS FOR NATIONAL FOREST SYSTEM PLANS

1.   GENERAL REQUIREMENTS * * *

NFMA . . . requires that the Forest Service regulations ensure that the management prescriptions in the LRMP "will not produce substantial and permanent impairment of the productivity of the land." In formulating these regulations, Congress directed the Forest Service to form and seek the advice of an independent committee of scientists to ensure that an effective interdisciplinary approach is utilized. This committee, which was composed of seven forestry and wildlife biology experts issued recommended regulations in 1979 that largely resemble the Forest Service's current planning regulations.

The Forest Service planning regulations provide that LRMPs "shall provide for multiple use and sustained yield of goods and services from the National Forest System in a way that maximizes long term net public benefits in an environmentally sound manner." The regulations then set forth 14 basic principles to guide forest planning in achieving that objective. Most of these principles promote the theme that planning should be interdisciplinary, and should provide for appropriate levels of environmental protection. For example, the guidelines require the Forest Service to recognize that the national forests are ecosystems and that their management requires consideration of the interrelationships between plants, animals, soil, water, air, and other environmental factors. Only one of these basic principles specifically addresses the need to consider economic interests.

In terms of their format, . . . LRMPs [generally divide the forest] into various management areas, which will have different management priorities, such as protection of habitat for certain species, or production of certain commodity resources. Different management prescriptions will then be established for each management area. It is these prescriptions and standards against which future land management activities and decisions will be measured to determine consistency with the LRMP. Finally, the LRMP will contain monitoring requirements for periodically evaluating the effects of management practices under the LRMP to determine whether plan objectives are being met.

The Forest Service has received recent criticism for failing to effectively monitor the implementation of its LRMPs.

All management prescriptions contained in an LRMP are required to meet certain minimum requirements for resource protection, which are identified in the Forest Service regulations. For example, all prescriptions must "[c]onserve soil and water resources and not allow significant or permanent impairment of the productivity of the land." Moreover, all prescriptions must be consistent with overall multiple-use objectives, provide for and maintain diversity of plant and animal communities, and provide for viable populations of existing vertebrate species. The Forest Service is also directed to give special attention to riparian areas, and no activities that would cause detrimental changes in water temperature or chemical composition, blockages of water courses, or sedimentation may be allowed in these areas if they would "seriously and adversely affect water conditions or fish habitat." * * *

2. Timber Harvesting Guidelines and Restrictions

In developing LRMPs, the Forest Service is required to identify, based upon economic, physical, and other factors, those lands that are not suitable for timber production. That suitability determination is to be reviewed by the Forest Service at least every 10 years. The courts have held that, at the LRMP stage, the Forest Service may identify categories of lands that are suitable and unsuitable, and need not specifically allocate each acre of land in the planning area. The Forest Service regulations provide that lands will be identified as unsuitable for timber production where technologies are not available to ensure that soil and watershed conditions will not be irreversibly damaged, or where there is not a reasonable assurance that the lands can be adequately restocked within five years after harvest. Moreover, NFMA requires that appropriate mitigation will be undertaken where the harvest is likely to seriously and adversely affect water conditions or fish habitat.

In addition, pursuant to NFMA's mandate, the Forest Service has adopted specific limitations on when clearcutting, seed tree cutting, and other even-aged management techniques may be used. These even-aged harvesting techniques may be used only where they can be carried out consistent with protection of other resource values, and clearcutting may be used only where it is determined to be the optimum method for achieving LRMP objectives. Although discouraged, LRMPs favoring these even-aged harvesting techniques will be upheld where these standards are satisfied.

Ultimately, LRMPs establish an allowable timber sale quantity from the planning area over the planning period, based upon the long-term sustained yield capacity of the forest. The allowable sale quantity sets only the upper limit on what may be cut and not the volume that actually will be cut. While the allowable sale quantity may never be realized due to restrictions adopted during site-specific analyses, the allowable sale quantity must be a realistic number that could plausibly be achieved. * * *

E. Substantive Requirements for Bureau of Land Management Plans

Distinct from the Forest Service's planning framework, FLPMA and the BLM's planning regulations provide only very general standards and guidelines for the content of BLM RMPs. FLPMA itself provides little guidance as to the contents of RMPs, other than to direct that the BLM "use and observe the principles of multiple use and sustained yield" and to require that RMPs "provide for compliance with applicable pollution control laws." BLM regulations governing preparation of RMPs also contain few substantive directives. Although they are not mandated requirements, the BLM regulations state that

RMPs should generally establish (i) land areas that will have limited, restricted or exclusive use; (ii) resource uses that will be allowed and levels of production or use that will be maintained; and (iii) resource condition goals and objectives to be attained. These regulatory guidelines are followed inconsistently.

FLPMA does direct the BLM, as part of the planning process, to "give priority to the designation and protection of areas of critical environmental concern" ("ACECs"). To qualify as an ACEC, the area must possess substantial resource values in need of protection. Significant fish and wildlife resources, scenic values or "natural systems" are among these values. The BLM uses ACECs to highlight areas needing special management attention and to impose additional management prescriptions. RMPs frequently designate ACECs based on the presence of important wildlife habitat or sensitive species, and impose specific mitigation measures for resource-development activities in these areas.

RMPs may contain decisions directly affecting future resource use activities. For example, with respect to mineral-development activities, RMPs may determine which lands will be open to mineral leasing, what types of stipulations will be attached to federal mineral leases, which areas will be open to motorized activities, and what mitigation measures may be required for development of leasable, salable and locatable minerals. . . .

In addition to RMPs, the BLM prepares a variety of activity-level plans, which provide more specific direction for certain management activities. Among these are habitat-management plans, which identify the wildlife-habitat management activities or conservation measures the BLM will implement to achieve RMP objectives. Habitat-management plans are to apply principles of ecosystem management to establish specific prescriptions for managing wildlife habitat, such as direct habitat-improvement measures and mitigation measures for resource-development activities. The BLM is also required to prepare site-specific plans for coal, oil shale and tar sand resources before selling leases for such resources, and may prepare allotment management plans for grazing permits and leases. * * *

V. * * * B. THE PUBLIC PROCESS

1. BLM LANDS * * *

BLM typically initiates the public process by publishing notice in the *Federal Register* of its intent to prepare or revise an RMP. This notice generally also serves as the scoping notice for purposes of NEPA. The public notice describes the geographic area covered by the plan, the key issues to be addressed in the plan, and a listing and schedule of opportunities for public participation. The notice should request public comments on issues or concerns to be addressed in the NEPA and planning documents. Parties having an interest in particular areas can request the BLM to place them on a list of interested parties, which will receive individual notices of all public participation opportunities associated with the plan preparation or revision. Second, the public will be given an opportunity to comment on the planning criteria that the BLM proposes to use in developing a proposed and alternative plans. Third, the BLM is required to publish a draft plan, along with the draft EIS, and accept public comments thereon for a minimum of 90 days. Finally, the BLM publishes the final proposed plan and EIS, and provides a minimum of 30 days for the public to review before it is finally approved by the State Director. * * *

Pursuant to NEPA and the BLM planning regulations, the BLM must evaluate the physical, biological, economic, and social effects of reasonable alternative plans. Based upon this comparison of reasonable alternatives, the

BLM selects a preferred alternative, which will be the basis for the draft RMP that is released for public comment.

After reviewing public comments on the draft plan, the District Manager recommends to the State Director a proposed RMP, which, after State Director review and initial approval, is published and notice of its availability is provided in the Federal Register. The State Director may not give final approval until the termination of 30 days following the date of publication of the final proposed plan or the resolution of any protests that may be filed during that period.

2. NATIONAL FOREST SYSTEM LANDS * * *

Like FLPMA, NFMA requires the Forest Service to provide for public participation in the development and revision of LRMPs. However, NFMA's guidance is limited, and it requires only that proposed plans or revisions be made available to the public for three months before final adoption and that the Forest Service hold public meetings or comparable processes to foster public participation in the planning process. The Forest Service regulations suggest more extensive opportunities for public involvement, and emphasize that early and frequent public participation shall be provided for when preparing LRMPs. Still, the specific mechanics for providing notice and opportunities for public hearings are left largely to the discretion of each Forest Supervisor who is to make such determinations based upon local circumstances.

NFMA requires that the Forest Service planning regulations insure that LRMPs are prepared in accordance with NEPA requirements, and that they specify when an EIS will be required. The Forest Service has determined that an EIS must be prepared for the preparation, revision, or significant amendment of an LRMP.* As with BLM RMPs, the opportunities provided by the Forest Service for public participation in preparing LRMPs are generally synonymous with those required by NEPA for preparing an EIS.

Initially, the Forest Service will provide public notice of its intent to prepare or revise an LRMP and will request comments on issues of concern that the Forest Service should address. The Forest Supervisor will then prepare a draft EIS identifying a preferred alternative LRMP and, after Regional Forester approval, make it available for public comment for at least three months. The Forest Supervisor then evaluates and addresses any public comments received, prepares a proposed plan and final EIS, and submits those documents to the Regional Forester for approval of the plan. Upon approval, the plan will not become effective until 30 days after public notice of the availability of the final EIS, to allow opportunities for appeal.

———

QUESTIONS AND DISCUSSION

1. Although the land use planning mandates of the BLM and the Forest Service are similar in many ways, the fact that the two agencies developed with such different histories and agency cultures may have had a greater impact on their approach to land management than the laws themselves. Although the Forest Service has at times strayed from its emphasis on

* Editor's note: As discussed in the introduction to this excerpt, the Forest Service's position as of 2008 was that forest plans and amendments could be categorically excluded under NEPA. *See* Forest Service Handbook, 1909.15, 31.2(16), available at, http://www.fs.fed.us/im/directives/. That decision will likely be challenged in court.

expert decision-making, Gifford Pinchot's initial commitment to science-based decision-making has given the Forest Service a reputation for professionalism that has largely endured throughout its history. This reputation has remained intact in part because of the ongoing tradition of appointing forest officers, including the chief, on the basis of merit, and invariably from the agency's own ranks. Indeed in the long history of the Forest Service there has never been a chief appointed from outside the agency. The BLM, by contrast, has a far more political management structure than the Forest Service. By statute, the BLM Director is appointed by the president with the advice and consent of the Senate. 43 U.S.C. § 1731(a)(1). Each state with substantial public domain lands has a "state director" who serves at the pleasure of the director. The BLM state office, which is generally located in the state's capital, oversees various District Offices. Each district may include several area offices. In contrast to the forest-based structure of the Forest Service, the state-based organization of the BLM further helps to promote the BLM's more political image.

Perhaps because of its reputation for professionalism, and perhaps also because national forests have been perceived as having greater aesthetic and economic value, congressional budget officials have been more generous to the Forest Service than to the BLM. Although the Forest Service manages about 25% fewer acres of land than the Bureau of Land Management, it has three times the number of employees, three times the appropriations, and four times as many offices located throughout the country. *See* UNITED STATES GENERAL ACCOUNTING OFFICE, LAND MANAGEMENT: THE FOREST SERVICE'S AND BLM'S ORGANIZATIONAL STRUCTURE AND RESPONSIBILITIES, 7 (GAO/RCED–99–227, July 29, 1999), *available at* http://www.fs.fed.us/servicefirst/gao_99_227.pdf. The Forest Service also generates more than three times the amount of revenue generated by the BLM. *Id.*

2. Public land use planning involves more than simply making choices among competing interests. It also requires agencies to consider the relevance of new scientific theories about the impacts of those choices on the ecological health of a management area. The Court of Appeals for the Seventh Circuit has made clear that agencies are not required to use any particular methodology in developing their plans. *Sierra Club v. Marita*, 46 F.3d 606 (7th Cir. 1995). But both the Forest Service and the BLM profess to focus on the ecological health of the lands they manage. The Forest Service rules, for example, provide that "[t]he first priority for planning to guide management of the National Forest System is to maintain or restore ecological sustainability of national forests and grasslands...." 36 C.F.R. § 219.2(a) (2003). Likewise, the BLM land use planning handbook provides that "the public lands must be managed in a manner that protects the quality of scientific, scenic, historical, ecological, environmental, air and atmospheric, water resource, and archaeological values...." BLM LAND USE PLANNING HANDBOOK, H–1601–1 (Rel. 1–1667, 11/22/00), *available at* http://www.blm.gov/nhp/200/wo210/landuse_hb.pdf.

These developments are, at least in part, a response to emerging theories about managing natural resources, such as landscape ecology and conservation biology. "Landscape Ecology is the study of structure, function and change in a heterogeneous land area composed of interacting ecosystems. "Structure" refers to the spatial patterns of landscape elements and ecological objects (such as animals, biomass and mineral nutrients). "Function" describes the flows of objects between landscape elements, and "change" reflects alterations in the mosaic through time." R.T.T. FORMAN AND MICHEL GODRON, LANDSCAPE ECOLOGY (1986). "[C]onservation biology represents an intersection of ecology, genetics, biogeography, and many traditional applied disciplines such as wildlife management and forestry. Its major concern is providing a valid scientific basis for actions that will slow or stop the accelerating loss of biological diversity world wide." Peter F. Brussard, *The Role of Ecology in Biological Conservation*, 1 ECOL. APPLIC. 6 (1991). The Society for Conservation Biology is a professional society that was formed to promote "the scientific study of the phenomena that affect the maintenance, loss, and restoration of biological diversity." *See* http://www.conbio.org. Do you see any parallels between these two emerging disciplines? How are they likely to influence the management of natural resources?

3. Professor George Coggins has summarized the planning responsibilities for each of the four principal types of federal lands—National Parks, National Wildlife Refuges, BLM public lands, and National Forests. *See* George Cameron Coggins, *The Developing Law of Land Use Planning on the Federal Lands*, 61 U. COLO. L. REV. 307 (1990). *See also* Charles F. Wilkinson & H. Michael Anderson, *Land and Resource Planning in the National Forests*, 64 OR. L. REV. 1 (1985).

4. Both the BLM and the Forest Service have promulgated rules to govern land use planning. The Forest Service rules are found at 36 C.F.R. part 219 (2008). The BLM rules are at 43 C.F.R. part 1600 (2006). In addition, and perhaps more importantly, both agencies have adopted detailed internal procedures for carrying out their land use planning responsibilities. Many of these procedures are contained in the complex agency manuals that agency personnel use to perform their assigned tasks. The Forest Service Manual contains detailed provisions for specific resource-related planning, although it does not address land use planning directly. http://www.fs.fed. us/im/directives/dughtml/serv_fsm.html. The Forest Service Handbook supplements these Manual provisions. The BLM's directives address land use planning very specifically. The BLM Manual procedures are fairly general, http://www.blm.gov/nhp/efoia/wo/manual/1601.pdf, but the BLM has promulgated a detailed Land Use Planning Handbook whose purpose is to "provide[] guidance for preparing and amending land use plan decisions through the planning process, and for maintaining both Resource Management Plans (RMPs) and Management Framework Plans (MFPs)." BLM Handbook H–1–1601–1 (Release 1–1667, 22 Nov 2000). http://www.blm.gov/ nhp/efoia/wo/handbook/h1601–1.pdf.

5. The Forest Service and the BLM have each established processes for administrative review of their decisions, but they take very different paths. The BLM appeals process is handled by a quasi-independent agency within Interior called the *Office of Hearings and Appeals (OHA)*. That Office supports administrative law judges, who handle formal hearings involving factual disputes like mining claim contest proceedings. It also has several appellate boards that hear legal challenges to agency decisions. These appellate boards may hear appeals from administrative law judge decisions, or directly from decisions made by the agency. The key board that hears appeals from BLM decisions is the *Interior Board of Land Appeals (IBLA)*. Most BLM decisions do not involve factual disputes because they are made on an administrative record that the parties must accept as the whole record for purposes of review. (An appellant may still argue, of course, that the record is not adequate to sustain the decision.) These decisions, usually made by the BLM State Directors, may be heard directly by the IBLA. *See e.g.,* 43 C.F.R. § 4.410 (2007).

By contrast, appeals from Forest Service decisions are heard, not by a quasi-independent board, but by the next highest official in the Forest Service line of authority. Thus, the decision of a District Ranger may be appealed to a Forest Supervisor. A Forest Supervisor's decision may be appealed to the Regional Forester, and decisions of the Regional Forester may be heard by the Chief. *See* 36 C.F.R. § 215.8 (2008). In 1992, the Forest Service proposed rules that would have excluded from notice, comment and appeal certain projects that the Forest Service deemed to be environmentally insignificant. The proposed rules were controversial, and led to the passage of the 1992 Appeals Reform Act (ARA). 16 U.S.C. § 1612 note (Pub. L. 102–381, § 322, 106 Stat. 1419). That law limits appeals in several significant ways. First, only persons who have been involved in the public comment process of a project or plan have a right to appeal. *Id.* at § 322(c). Second, the Forest Service must dispose of all appeals within 45 days, and may implement appealed projects 15 days later. *Id.* at § 322(d)(3). Finally, the Chief of the Forest Service may authorize projects to go forward despite pending appeals by declaring "that an emergency situation exists." *Id.* at § 322(e). On the other hand, the ARA does provide that the Forest Service—

> . . . *shall* establish a notice and comment process for proposed actions of the Forest Service concerning projects and activities implementing land an resource management plans . . ., and *shall* modify the procedure for appeals for decisions concerning such projects.

Id. at § 322(a) (emphasis added). Notwithstanding this language, the Forest Service promulgated new rules in 2003 that preclude both notice and comment and the right of appeal for decisions that are categorically excluded under NEPA, as provided in Forest Service rules. *See* 68 Fed. Reg. 33,582 (2003), *codified at,* 36 C.F.R. § 215.12(f) (2006). *Earth Island Institute v. Ruthenbeck,* 490 F.3d 687 (9th Cir. 2007) involved a claim by the plaintiffs that the new rules violated the ARA. The court agreed, finding the statute clear under a step one *Chevron* analysis, but noting that it would have found against the agency, even under the deferential step two test. The Supreme Court reversed on the grounds that the plaintiffs lacked standing. *Summers v. Earth Island Institute,* 129 S.Ct. 1142 (2009).

Additional information about the BLM and Forest Service appeals processes is available at the Red Lodge Clearinghouse website. *See* http://rlch.org/content/view/650/27/.

6. Most state and local planning is not directed at resources, but it certainly can impact resource development. Zoning laws, for example, may limit the kinds of uses that can be made of particular lands, and these uses will generally not accommodate activities such as mineral development. Mining companies have sometimes challenged these laws on the grounds that they cause a taking of private property rights in violation of the Fifth Amendment, but courts have not generally been sympathetic to these claims. *See, e.g., Goldblatt v. Hempstead,* 369 U.S. 590 (1962) (local ordinance prohibiting continuation of gravel mining operation does not violate takings clause); *Iowa Coal Mining Co., Inc. v. Monroe County,* 494 N.W.2d 664 (Iowa 1993) (local rules that preclude coal mining do not effect a taking.).

As you read the following case, consider how it will likely impact government planners and the public in their thinking about land use planning on public lands.

―――――

NORTON v. SOUTHERN UTAH WILDERNESS ALLIANCE
542 U.S. 55 (2004)

JUSTICE SCALIA delivered the opinion of the Court....

In this case, we must decide whether the authority of a federal court under the Administrative Procedure Act (APA) to "compel agency action unlawfully withheld or unreasonably delayed," 5 U.S.C. § 706(1), extends to the review of the United States Bureau of Land Management's stewardship of public lands under certain statutory provisions and its own planning documents.

I

Almost half the State of Utah, about 23 million acres, is federal land administered by the Bureau of Land Management (BLM), an agency within the Department of Interior. For nearly 30 years, BLM's management of public lands has been governed by the Federal Land Policy and Management Act of 1976 (FLPMA), 43 U.S.C. § 1701 *et seq.,* which "established a policy in favor of retaining public lands for multiple use management." *Lujan v. National Wildlife Federation*, 497 U.S. 871, 887 (1990). "Multiple use management" is a deceptively simple term that describes the enormously complicated task of striking a balance among the many competing uses to which land can be put, "including, but not limited to, recreation, range, timber, minerals, watershed, wildlife and fish, and [uses serving] natural scenic, scientific and historical values." 43 U.S.C. § 1702(c). A second management goal, "sustained yield," requires BLM to control depleting uses over time, so as to ensure a high level of valuable uses in the future. § 1702(h). To these ends, FLPMA establishes a dual regime of inventory and planning. Sections 1711 and 1712, respectively, provide for a comprehensive, ongoing inventory of federal lands, and for a land use planning process that "project[s]" "present and future use," § 1701(a)(2), given the lands' inventoried characteristics.

Of course not all uses are compatible. Congress made the judgment that some lands should be set aside as wilderness at the expense of commercial and recreational uses. A pre-FLPMA enactment, the Wilderness Act of 1964, 78 Stat. 890, provides that designated wilderness areas, subject to certain exceptions, "shall [have] no commercial enterprise and no permanent road," no motorized vehicles, and no manmade structures. 16 U.S.C. § 1133(c). The designation of a wilderness area can be made only by Act of Congress, *see* 43 U.S.C. § 1782(b).

Pursuant to § 1782 [of FLPMA], the Secretary of the Interior (Secretary) has identified so-called "wilderness study areas" (WSAs), roadless lands of 5,000 acres or more that possess "wilderness characteristics," as determined in the Secretary's land inventory. § 1782(a); *see* 16 U.S.C. § 1131(c). As the name suggests, WSAs (as well as certain wild lands identified prior to the passage of FLPMA) have been subjected to further examination and public comment in order to evaluate their suitability for designation as wilderness. In 1991, out of 3.3 million acres in Utah that had been identified for study, 2 million were recommended as suitable for wilderness designation. This recommendation was forwarded to Congress, which has not yet acted upon it. Until Congress acts one way or the other, FLPMA provides that "the Secretary shall continue to manage such lands ... in a manner so as not to impair the suitability of such areas for preservation as wilderness." 43 U.S.C. § 1782(c). This nonimpairment mandate applies to all WSAs identified under § 1782, including lands considered unsuitable by the Secretary. *See* §§ 1782(a), (b).

Aside from identification of WSAs, the main tool that BLM employs to balance wilderness protection against other uses is a land use plan—what BLM regulations call a "resource management plan." 43 CFR § 1601.0–5(k) (2003). Land use plans, adopted after notice and comment, are "designed to guide and control future management actions," § 1601.0–2. *See* 43 U.S.C. § 1712; 43 CFR § 1610.2 (2003). Generally, a land use plan describes, for a particular area, allowable uses, goals for future condition of the land, and specific next steps. § 1601.0–5(k). Under FLPMA, "[t]he Secretary shall manage the public lands under principles of multiple use and sustained yield, in accordance with the land use plans ... when they are available." 43 U.S.C. § 1732(a).

Protection of wilderness has come into increasing conflict with another element of multiple use, recreational use of so-called off-road vehicles (ORVs), which include vehicles primarily designed for off-road use, such as lightweight, four-wheel "all-terrain vehicles," and vehicles capable of such use, such as sport utility vehicles. *See* 43 CFR § 8340.0–5(a) (2003). According to the United States Forest Service's most recent estimates, some 42 million Americans participate in off-road travel each year, more than double the number two decades ago. United States sales of all-terrain vehicles alone have roughly doubled in the past five years, reaching almost 900,000 in 2003. The use of ORVs on federal land has negative environmental consequences, including soil disruption and compaction, harassment of animals, and annoyance of wilderness lovers. Thus, BLM faces a classic land use dilemma of sharply inconsistent uses, in a context of scarce resources and congressional silence with respect to wilderness designation.

In 1999, respondents Southern Utah Wilderness Alliance and other organizations (collectively SUWA) filed this action in the United States District Court for Utah against petitioners BLM, its Director, and the Secretary. In its second amended complaint, SUWA sought declaratory and injunctive relief for BLM's failure to act to protect public lands in Utah from damage caused by ORV use. SUWA made three claims that are relevant here: (1) that BLM had violated its nonimpairment obligation under § 1782(c) by allowing degradation in certain WSAs; (2) that BLM had failed to implement provisions in its land use plans relating to ORV use; and (3) that BLM had failed to take a "hard look" at whether, pursuant to the National Environmental Policy Act of 1969 (NEPA), 42 U.S.C. § 4321 *et seq.*, it should undertake supplemental environmental analyses for areas in which ORV use had increased. SUWA contended that it could sue to remedy these three failures to act pursuant to the APA's provision of a cause of action to "compel agency action unlawfully withheld or unreasonably delayed." 5 U.S.C. § 706(1).

The District Court entered a dismissal with respect to the three claims. A divided panel of the Tenth Circuit reversed. 301 F.3d 1217 (2002). The majority acknowledged that under § 706(1), "federal courts may order agencies to act only where the agency fails to carry out a mandatory, nondiscretionary duty." *Id.* at 1226. It concluded, however, that BLM's nonimpairment obligation was just such a duty, and therefore BLM could be compelled to comply. Under similar reasoning, it reversed the dismissal with respect to the land use plan claim; and likewise reversed dismissal of the NEPA claim. We granted certiorari. 540 U.S. 980 (2003).

II

All three claims at issue here involve assertions that BLM failed to take action with respect to ORV use that it was required to take. Failures to act are sometimes remediable under the APA, but not always. We begin by considering what limits the APA places upon judicial review of agency inaction.

The APA authorizes suit by "[a] person suffering legal wrong because of agency action, or adversely affected or aggrieved by agency action within the meaning of a relevant statute." 5 U.S.C. § 702. Where no other statute provides a private right of action, the "agency action" complained of must be "*final* agency action." § 704 (emphasis added). "[A]gency action" is defined in § 551(13) to include "the whole or a part of an agency rule, order, license, sanction, relief, or the equivalent or denial thereof, *or failure to act*." (Emphasis added.) The APA provides relief for a failure to act in § 706(1): "The reviewing court shall ... compel agency action unlawfully withheld or unreasonably delayed." * * *

The final term in the definition, "failure to act," is in our view properly understood as a failure to take an agency action—that is, a failure to take one of the agency actions (including their equivalents) earlier defined in § 551(13).... A "failure to act" is not the same thing as a "denial." The latter is the agency's act of saying no to a request; the former is simply the omission of an action without formally rejecting a request—for example, the failure to promulgate a rule or take some decision by a statutory deadline. The important point is that a "failure to act" is properly understood to be limited, as are the other items in § 551(13), to a *discrete* action.

A second point central to the analysis of the present case is that the only agency action that can be compelled under the APA is action legally *required*. This limitation appears in § 706(1)'s authorization for courts to "compel agency action *unlawfully* withheld." (Emphasis added.) In this regard the APA carried forward the traditional practice prior to its passage, when judicial review was achieved through use of the so-called prerogative writs—principally writs of mandamus under the All Writs Act, now codified at 28 U.S.C. § 1651(a). The mandamus remedy was normally limited to enforcement of "a specific, unequivocal command," *ICC v. New York, N.H. & H.R. Co.*, 287 U.S. 178, 204 (1932), the ordering of a " 'precise, definite act ... about which [an official] had no discretion whatever,' " *United States ex rel. Dunlap v. Black*, 128 U.S. 40, 46 (1888) (*quoting Kendall v. United States ex rel. Stokes*, 12 Pet. 524, 613 (1838)). * * *

Thus, a claim under § 706(1) can proceed only where a plaintiff asserts that an agency failed to take a *discrete* agency action that it is *required to take.* * * *

The limitation to *required* agency action rules out judicial direction of even discrete agency action that is not demanded by law (which includes, of course, agency regulations that have the force of law). Thus, when an agency is compelled by law to act within a certain time period, but the manner of its action is left to the agency's discretion, a court can compel the agency to act, but has no power to specify what the action must be. For example, 47 U.S.C. § 251(d)(1), which required the Federal Communications Commission "to establish regulations to implement" interconnection requirements "[w]ithin 6 months" of the date of enactment of the Telecommunications Act of 1996, would have supported a judicial decree under the APA requiring the prompt issuance of regulations, but not a judicial decree setting forth the content of those regulations.

III

A

With these principles in mind, we turn to SUWA's first claim, that by permitting ORV use in certain WSAs, BLM violated its mandate to "continue to manage [WSAs] ... in a manner so as not to impair the suitability of such areas for preservation as wilderness," 43 U.S.C. § 1782(c). SUWA relies not only upon § 1782(c) but also upon a provision of BLM's Interim Management Policy for Lands Under Wilderness Review, which interprets the nonimpairment mandate to require BLM to manage WSAs so as to prevent them from being "degraded so far, compared with the area's values for other purposes, as to significantly constrain the Congress's prerogative to either designate [it] as wilderness or release it for other uses."

Section 1782(c) is mandatory as to the object to be achieved, but it leaves BLM a great deal of discretion in deciding how to achieve it. It assuredly does not mandate, with the clarity necessary to support judicial action under § 706(1), the total exclusion of ORV use.

SUWA argues that § 1782 *does* contain a categorical imperative, namely, the command to comply with the nonimpairment mandate. It contends that a federal court could simply enter a general order compelling compliance with that mandate, without suggesting any particular manner of compliance. It relies upon the language from the Attorney General's Manual quoted earlier, that a court can "take action upon a matter, without directing how [the agency] shall act," and upon language in a case cited by the Manual noting that "mandamus will lie ... even though the act required involves the exercise of judgment and discretion," *Safeway Stores, Inc. v. Brown*, 138 F.2d 278, 280 (Emerg.Ct.App.1943). The action referred to in these excerpts, however, is *discrete* agency action, as we have discussed above. General deficiencies in compliance, unlike the failure to issue a ruling that was discussed in *Safeway Stores* lack the specificity requisite for agency action.

The principal purpose of the APA limitations we have discussed—and of the traditional limitations upon mandamus from which they were derived—is to protect agencies from undue judicial interference with their lawful discretion, and to avoid judicial entanglement in abstract policy disagreements which courts lack both expertise and information to resolve. If courts were empowered to enter general orders compelling compliance with broad statutory mandates, they would necessarily be empowered, as well, to determine whether compliance was achieved—which would mean that it would ultimately become the task of the supervising court, rather than the agency, to work out compliance with the broad statutory mandate, injecting the judge into day-to-day agency management. The prospect of pervasive oversight by federal courts over the manner and pace of agency compliance with such congressional directives is not contemplated by the APA.

B

SUWA's second claim is that BLM failed to comply with certain provisions in its land use plans, thus contravening the requirement that "[t]he Secretary shall manage the public lands ... in accordance with the land use plans ... when they are available." 43 U.S.C. § 1732(a); *see also* 43 CFR § 1610.5–3(a) (2003) ("All future resource management authorizations and actions ... and subsequent more detailed or specific planning, shall conform to the approved plan"). The relevant count in SUWA's second amended complaint alleged that BLM had violated a variety of commitments in its land use plans, but over the course of the litigation these have been reduced to two, one relating to the 1991 resource management plan for the San Rafael area, and the other to various aspects of the 1990 ORV implementation plan for the Henry Mountains area.

The actions contemplated by the first of these alleged commitments (completion of a route designation plan in the San Rafael area), and by one aspect of the second (creation of "use supervision files" for designated areas in the Henry Mountains area) have already been completed, and these claims are therefore moot. There remains the claim, with respect to the Henry Mountains plan, that "in light of damage from ORVs in the Factory Butte area," a sub-area of Henry Mountains open to ORV use, "the [plan] obligated BLM to conduct an intensive ORV monitoring program." This claim is based upon the plan's statement that the Factory Butte area "will be monitored and closed if warranted." SUWA does not contest BLM's assertion in the court below that informal monitoring has taken place for some years, but it demands continuing implementation of a monitoring *program*. By this it apparently means to insist upon adherence to the plan's general discussion of "Use Supervision and Monitoring" in designated areas, which (in addition to calling for the use supervision files that have already been created) provides that "[r]esource damage will be documented and recommendations made for corrective action," "[m]onitoring in open areas will focus on determining damage which may necessitate a change in designation," and "emphasis on use supervision will be placed on [limited and closed areas]." SUWA acknowledges that a monitoring program has recently been *commenced*. In light, however, of the continuing action that existence of a "program" contemplates, and in light of BLM's contention that the program cannot be compelled under § 706(1), this claim cannot be considered moot.

The statutory directive that BLM manage "in accordance with" land use plans, and the regulatory requirement that authorizations and actions "conform to" those plans, prevent BLM from taking actions inconsistent with the provisions of a land use plan. Unless and until the plan is amended, such actions can be set aside as contrary to law pursuant to 5 U.S.C. § 706(2). The claim presently under discussion, however, would have us go further, and conclude that a statement in a plan that BLM "will" take this, that, or the other action, is a binding commitment that can be compelled under § 706(1). In our view it is not—at least absent clear indication of binding commitment in the terms of the plan.

FLPMA describes land use plans as tools by which "present and future use is *projected*." 43 U.S.C. § 1701(a)(2) (emphasis added). The implementing regulations make clear that land use plans are a preliminary step in the overall process of managing public lands—"designed to guide and control future management actions and the development of subsequent, more detailed and limited scope plans for resources and uses." 43 CFR § 1601.0–2 (2003). The statute and regulations confirm that a land use plan is not ordinarily the medium for affirmative decisions that implement the agency's "project[ions]." Title 43 U.S.C. § 1712(e) provides that "[t]he Secretary may issue management decisions to implement land use plans"—the decisions, that is, are distinct from the plan itself. Picking up the same theme, the regulation defining a land use plan declares that a plan "is not a final implementation decision on actions which require further specific plans, process steps, or decisions under specific provisions of law and regulations." 43 CFR § 1601.0–5(k) (2003). The BLM's Land Use Planning Handbook specifies that land use plans are normally not used to make site-specific implementation decisions. * * *

Quite unlike a specific statutory command requiring an agency to promulgate regulations by a certain date, a land use plan is generally a statement of priorities; it guides and constrains actions, but does not (at least in the usual case) prescribe them. It would be unreasonable to think that either Congress or the agency intended otherwise, since land use plans nationwide would commit the agency to actions far in the future, for which funds have not yet been appropriated. Some plans make explicit that implementation of their programmatic content is subject to budgetary constraints. While the Henry Mountains plan does not contain such a specification, we think it must reasonably be implied. A statement by BLM about what it plans to do, at some point, provided it has the funds and there are not more pressing priorities, cannot be plucked out of context and made a basis for suit under § 706(1).

Of course, an action called for in a plan may be compelled when the plan merely reiterates duties the agency is already obligated to perform, or perhaps when language in the plan itself creates a commitment binding on the agency. But allowing general enforcement of plan terms would lead to pervasive interference with BLM's own ordering of priorities. For example, a judicial decree compelling immediate preparation of all of the detailed plans called for in the San Rafael plan would divert BLM's energies from other projects throughout the country that are in fact more pressing. And while such a decree might please the environmental plaintiffs in the present case, it would ultimately operate to the detriment of sound environmental management. Its predictable consequence would be much vaguer plans from BLM in the future-making coordination with other agencies more difficult, and depriving the public of important information concerning the agency's long-range intentions.

We therefore hold that the Henry Mountains plan's statements to the effect that BLM will conduct "Use Supervision and Monitoring" in designated areas—like other "will do" projections of agency action set forth in land use plans—are not a legally binding commitment enforceable under § 706(1). That being so, we find it unnecessary to consider whether the action envisioned by the statements is sufficiently discrete to be amenable to compulsion under the APA.

IV

Finally, we turn to SUWA's contention that BLM failed to fulfill certain obligations under NEPA. Before addressing whether a NEPA-required duty is actionable under the APA, we must decide whether NEPA creates an obligation in the first place. NEPA requires a federal agency to prepare an environmental impact statement (EIS) as part of any "proposals for legislation and other major Federal actions significantly affecting the quality of the human environment." 42 U.S.C. § 4332(2)(C). Often an initial EIS is sufficient, but in certain circumstances an EIS must be supplemented. See *Marsh v. Oregon Natural Resources Council*, 490 U.S. 360, 370–74 (1989). A regulation of the Council on Environmental Quality requires supplementation where "[t]here are significant new circumstances or information relevant to environmental concerns and bearing on the proposed action or its impacts." 40 CFR § 1502.9(c)(1)(ii) (2003). In *Marsh*, we interpreted § 4332 in light of this regulation to require an agency to take a "hard look" at the new information to assess whether supplementation might be necessary. 490 U.S. at 385, *see id.* at 378–85.

SUWA argues that evidence of increased ORV use is "significant new circumstances or information" that requires a "hard look." We disagree. As we noted in *Marsh*, supplementation is necessary only if "there remains 'major Federal actio[n]' to occur," as that term is used in § 4332(2)(C). *Id.* at 374. In *Marsh*, that condition was met: the dam construction project that gave rise to environmental review was not yet completed. Here, by contrast, although the "*[a]pproval* of a [land use plan]" is a "major Federal action" requiring an EIS, 43 CFR § 1601.0–6 (2003) (emphasis added), that action is completed when the plan is approved. The land use plan is the "proposed action" contemplated by the regulation. There is no ongoing "major Federal action" that could require supplementation (though BLM *is* required to perform additional NEPA analyses if a plan is amended or revised, *see* §§ 1610.5–5, 5–6).

* * *

The judgment of the Court of Appeals is reversed, and the case is remanded for further proceedings consistent with this opinion.

QUESTIONS AND DISCUSSION

1.   The *SUWA* decision has potentially far-reaching ramifications. Of particular importance, the Court holds that a claim to compel agency action under the APA can only be brought "where a plaintiff asserts that an agency failed to take a action that it is *required to take*." 542 U.S. at 64 (emphasis in original). Because FLPMA's nonimpairment mandate did not *specifically* require the BLM to completely exclude ORV use from the WSAs, the Court found the BLM's *general* deficiency in compliance insufficient to warrant judicial action under the APA. *Id.* at 66. The Court claims it was necessary to reach this result "to protect agencies from undue judicial interference with their lawful discretion, and to avoid judicial entanglement in abstract policy disagreements which courts lack both expertise and information to resolve." *Id.* Do you agree? If the Court had ordered the BLM to comply with FLPMA's nonimpairment standard would it have been necessary to specify the particular manner of compliance? Was the issue here an "abstract policy disagreement"?

2.   The *SUWA* case involves a claim for relief under 5 U.S.C. § 706(1), which authorizes courts to "compel agency action unlawfully withheld or unreasonably delayed." This standard is wholly separate from the more commonly invoked provisions at 5 U.S.C. § 706(2), which authorizes courts to set aside agency actions found to be "arbitrary, capricious, an abuse of discretion, or otherwise not in accordance with law." Does this suggest to you a possible way around the *SUWA* decision? Did SUWA make a mistake in failing not to seek relief in the alternative under 5 U.S.C. § 706(2)?

3.   The Court concedes that FLPMA's requirement that BLM manage "in accordance with" land use plans, and the BLM's own regulatory requirement that agency actions "conform to" those plans "prevent BLM from taking action inconsistent with the provisions of a land use plan." 542 U.S.

at 68. Nonetheless, the Court finds that a statement by the BLM in a land use plan that it "will" monitor and "if warranted" close an area to ORV use was not a "binding commitment that can be compelled under § 706(1)." *Id.* Why not? How does the Court reconcile these two conclusions?

4. The Court finds that evidence of increased ORV use in an area specifically targeted for monitoring in a land use plan was not significant new information requiring a supplemental NEPA analysis. Indeed, the Court appears to suggest that additional NEPA compliance is never required for land use plans (absent an agency proposal to amend a plan) because "the action is completed when the plan is approved." *Id.* How would the Court address this issue if it was discovered after approval of the land use plan that the area was home to a large community of desert tortoises—a species listed as threatened under the Endangered Species Act—and that ORV use would likely decimate the local tortoise population? Should this information trigger a new NEPA analysis? *See* 40 C.F.R. § 1502.7(c).

5. Consider the implications of the *SUWA* decision in the context of the following problems:

    a. A county government decides to build a road through a wilderness study area ("WSA") located within the county. Recall that FLPMA requires WSAs to be managed for non-impairment of their wilderness characteristics. The BLM refuses to take action, despite the fact that construction of the road is plainly illegal and will destroy the area's wilderness character. A private right of action against the county is not available under FLPMA, which does not have a citizen suit provision. Can a private party bring an action to compel the BLM to enforce the law? Is it arbitrary and capricious for the BLM to fail to take action against the county?

    b. A BLM land use plan designates an area off-limits to grazing because of a claimed need to protect the biological resources of the area. A rancher nonetheless brings cattle into the area and the BLM refuses to take any action to remove the cattle. Can a private citizen bring an action to compel the BLM to stop the grazing? Would it matter if the area was closed to grazing to protect an endangered species?

6. Justice Scalia suggests that when a matter is left to an agency's discretion a court "has no power to specify what the action must be." Keep in mind, however, that our Constitution does not generally authorize the Congress to delegate to agencies unfettered discretionary power. *J.W. Hampton, Jr., & Co. v. U.S.*, 276 U.S. 394, 409 (1928) (requiring Congress to "lay down by legislative act an intelligible principle" to guide the exercise of agency discretion.) Doesn't the existence of a standard make it possible to challenge the agency's decision on the grounds that it was arbitrary and capricious, an abuse of discretion, or otherwise inconsistent with the law?

7. In *Ohio Forestry Association v. Sierra Club*, 523 U.S. 726 (1998), the Supreme Court rejected a challenge to the legality of the Forest Service's management plan for Ohio's Wayne National Forest. The Sierra Club claimed that the plan unlawfully favored clearcutting in violation of NFMA. *Id.* at 732. The Court, however, found the case was not ripe for review because further agency action would be necessary before any logging could take place. *Id.* How does the *Ohio Forestry* decision limit review of agency land use plans? When, if ever, are land use decisions ripe for review? After *Ohio Forestry* and *SUWA*, what is left of judicial review of agency land use plans?

8. Consider that when viewed individually a decision to allow clearcutting may not be arbitrary and capricious, but what if the agency has repeatedly authorized such activities across an entire forest? This phenomenon is sometimes called the tyranny of small decisions. Alfred Kahn once described the problem with the following example. Suppose that in the nineteenth century some being had appeared from outer space and proposed an amazing "means of transportation that could . . . permit you to travel about, alone or in small groups, at 60 to 80 miles an hour" but that the cumulative toll would be the loss of 40,000 lives per year. As Kahn saw it, the cost might have made the proposal seem intolerable but that reaching "the same result gradually, unwittingly, by a series of individual purchases could represent a product of the tyranny of small decisions." Alfred E. Kahn, *The Tyranny of Small Decisions: Market Failures, Imperfections, and the Limits of Economics*, 19 Kyklos: Int'l Rev. Soc. Sci. 23, 29–30 (1966). Does Justice Breyer's suggestion—that "one initial site-specific victory (if based on the Plan's unlawfulness)" might "through preclusion principles, effectively carry the day"—solve this problem?

9. Why do you suppose that public land management plans often provide relatively little detail on specific resource use and protection? Professor Coggins and Glicksman suggest part of the reason:

> Agencies jealously guard their flexibility, which means, in essence, that they seek to retain the discretion to decide as they wish on any resource allocation question. Formal planning can destroy or curtail administrative flexibility if subsequent individual management decisions must conform to the plan. * * *

> It is not realistic to expect or require that plans be so specific that they eliminate managerial discretion—just as drafters of statutes can never anticipate all conceivable problems. For many public natural resources litigants, the greater danger is that the agency will promulgate plans so general as to be meaningless as limitations on or guidelines for subsequent management decisions. Some evidence indicates that agencies may prefer to write motherhood generalities rather than blueprints for future resource allocation and protection.

George C. Coggins & Robert L. Glicksman, Public Natural Resources Law, 2d ed. § 16:1 (2009). What are the implications of the *SUWA* decision for this common practice of providing relatively little detail? Although they are not sanguine about the quality of land use plans, Coggins and Glicksman argue that plans still serve an important purpose:

> Despite the typically vague, general and platitudinous language used by planners, lawyers should not discount the importance of plans, even when management decisions are not legally controlled or guided by plan provisions. Much federal land use planning is decentralized so that the planning official often is also the manager who will decide individual resource allocation questions. It is unlikely that he or she will not be influenced by his or her own handiwork—the purpose of which, of course, is to give direction and guidance to managers.

Id. Do you agree with this assessment? Are agency officials likely to follow established land use plans even if not required to do so?

10.   Robert Nelson argues that:

> Like earlier public land laws, while failing to realize the declared purposes, the FLPMA and NFMA mandates for land use planning also had other unintended (or at least unstated) consequences. Land use planning did not create a rational decision process but it did serve to redistribute political power. Environmental and recreation groups were able to manipulate the legal and procedural handles created by planning to obtain greater influence over public land decisions. The planning requirements of FLPMA and NFMA in this respect had practical consequences similar to NEPA.

ROBERT H. NELSON, PUBLIC LANDS AND PRIVATE RIGHTS: THE FAILURE OF SCIENTIFIC MANAGEMENT 123 (1995). Do you agree with Nelson that increasing the power of the recreation and environmental community was an "unintended" consequence of the planning regimes? Do you think that cases like *SUWA* are what Congress had in mind when it imposed a planning requirement on the BLM and the Forest Service?

11.   In March 2000, a Senate Subcommittee on Forests and Public Land Management held an oversight hearing on National Forest planning. At the hearing, Arthur Cooper, the head of the Society of American Foresters, testified that the planning process has "to put it charitably, fallen into disfavor and has not met the expectations for it that existed when it was created." *Oversight Hearing on National Forest Planning Regulations: Hearing Before the Subcomm. on Forests and Public Land Management of the Senate Comm. on Energy and Natural Res.*, 106th Cong. (Mar. 2, 2000). As he and others who testified saw it, the Committee of Scientists (of which Cooper had been an original member) who had developed the Forest Service's regulations had produced rules that made logical sense, but were so over-layered with documentation and process that they actually impeded wise forest planning and hindered the Forest Service from managing the forests in conformance with their other legal obligations. Robert Nelson offers a similar criticism of planning:

> Many strong proponents of planning have favored it not because they had a clear idea of how planning would make for better decisions, but because they have believed in planning as a virtuous undertaking. Seeing the big mistakes, the wastefulness, the confusion, the parochialism, and the many other liabilities of existing government, they have believed that there must be a better way. For them, planning grounded in the scientific method has stood for the possibilities of a rational world serving the interests of all the people.

The members of the legal profession have been particularly prone to think in this fashion. For them, planning also fills a critical niche in an abstract lawyer's argument. As legal thinking goes, government has large powers; these powers are subject to many potential abuses; there must therefore be strong guarantees that government will act fairly and responsibly; and the best way to ensure this result is to require that government actions follow an objective scientific plan prepared by professional experts. After the plan is prepared the judiciary must then be prepared to require that agencies act in accordance with the plan. It all makes for a precise legal logic and a well-defined set of procedures to follow, if it seldom has much correspondence with the real world.

Robert H. Nelson, Public Lands and Private Rights: The Failure of Scientific Management 143–44 (1995). Although the agencies' planning practices are easy targets for criticism, what is the alternative? Skip planning? Eliminate public process? Provide more funding for planning? Or is the frustration with planning simply a function of continuing disagreement about the best use of our public lands? Do you agree with the commentator who suggested that "[u]nless the conflicts between environmental protection, forest management statutes, and public values are resolved, it is unlikely that any form of forest management or planning will ever be made to work—with or without sound science"? Congress must establish a clearer framework for public lands policy. Without basic value assumptions to guide decision making, scientists cannot by themselves bring about a successful policy-making process." Brian Scott Pasko, Comment, *The Great Experiment that Failed? Evaluating the Role of a "Committee of Scientists" As a Tool for Managing and Protecting Our Public Lands*, 32 Envtl. L. 509 (2002).

––––––

Problem Exercise: Land Use Planning on the Public Lands

Perhaps the best way to understand land use planning on the public lands is to review an actual plan. Federal agencies are increasingly making their land use plans available online, and because land use plans must be revised periodically, several plans are in the process of being developed at any given time, with myriad opportunities for the public to participate. This helps insure a robust public debate over the many issues that arise in planning. Unfortunately, planning documents are long, and the issues that they raise are often complex. Furthermore, while federal planning agencies have made efforts to make their plans more accessible to the public, reviewing and understanding a land use plan remains a daunting task. Fortunately, it is not necessary to understand the complexities of an actual plan to understand planning. This case study describes a simple, hypothetical plan as a means for explaining how planning works.

The Fallen Pines National Forest in the State of Amarillo consists of one entire 36–square–mile township. The land use map from the current forest plan is set forth below with overlays that suggest some of the current issues. The current use zones with general "management prescriptions" for each of these planning areas are as follows:

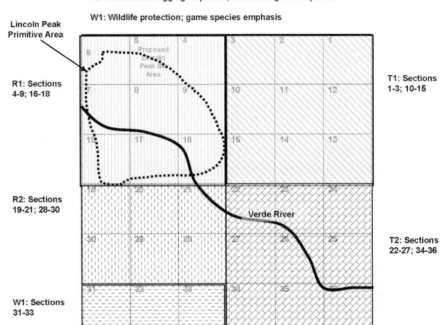

R1: Primitive, non-mechanized recreation

R2: Developed, motorized recreation

T1: Selective commercial tree harvesting with emphasis on watershed protection and wildlife protection and enhancement.

T2: Commercial logging emphasis; clearcutting is acceptable

W1: Wildlife protection; game species emphasis

Lincoln Peak Primitive Area

R1: Sections 4-9; 16-18

R2: Sections 19-21; 28-30

W1: Sections 31-33

T1: Sections 1-3; 10-15

T2: Sections 22-27; 34-36

Verde River

Three months ago, the United States Forest Service published in the *Federal Register* a notice of intent to prepare an environmental impact statement in conjunction with development of a new land and resource management plan (LRMP) for the forest. The notice also described the public scoping process (*see* 40 C.F.R. § 1501.7), whereby interested members of the public could express their opinions about issues and concerns that should be addressed in the development of a new plan. Through the scoping process, the Forest Service has identified the following key issues:

1. Whether to permit a new ski area near Lincoln Peak in Section 5. An economic study prepared by a private consulting firm on behalf of local investors has identified the Lincoln Peak area as the only area in the forest for which a ski area would be economically viable.

2. Whether to increase the annual sale quantity (ASQ) of timber as a means of minimizing fire risks and tree diseases, as well as to attract a new timber company to the area. (The ASQ is the maximum amount of timber (expressed in board feet) that the Service will sell in any given year, averaged over a 10–year planning cycle. The Service is free to sell less timber than authorized in the ASQ, but it may not sell more without amending the plan.) Logging is currently allowed everywhere other than the Lincoln Peak Primitive Area. Raising the ASQ would likely require removing some or all of the current protections in the Primitive Area.

3.   Whether to recommend that congress designate the Lincoln Peak Primitive Area as wilderness in accordance with the Wilderness Act.

4.   Whether to recommend that Congress designate some portion of the Verde River as it flows through the Forest as a wild, scenic or recreational river in accordance with the Wild and Scenic Rivers Act.

5.   Whether to curtail cattle and/or sheep grazing on any portion of the forest. (Grazing is currently allowed everywhere on the forest.)

6.   How the Forest can best meet its affirmative duty under the Endangered Species Act, to manage the Forest to recover the Amarillo toad, a species listed as threatened under the ESA. *See* 16 U.S.C. § 1536(a)(1). One of two known populations of the toad was recently found in a wetland area in Section 35.

7.   What species should the Forest Service identify as "management indicator species"? These are species that the Forest Service uses as surrogates to more generally assess forest health. Commentators have suggested the northern goshawk, the pine marten, and the lynx as indicator species. Historical data indicates that all of these species were found throughout the forest, but that their numbers have been declining over the past 50 years.

Imagine that you are the Supervisor for the Fallen Pines National Forest. You expect active interest and participation by logging, mining, grazing, recreation, and preservation interests.

- How do you go about involving the public in the planning process in a meaningful way? Should you invite representatives of the various interests groups to meet with you (either individually or together), or should you wait for them to contact you? Should you hold one or more public town-hall style meetings, or should you limit participation to private meetings and written comments?

- Note that congressional action, and action by other government agencies can significantly impact your discretion. For example, the designation of the Amarillo toad as an endangered species by the Fish and Wildlife Service may mean the toad's habitat will not be available for consumptive purposes. Likewise, if Congress chooses to designate lands in the forest as wilderness, or rivers in the forest as wild, scenic, or recreational, your planning options will be hampered. To what extent should a land manager welcome such intervention? When does it become officious meddling? From a land manager's perspective, how might a decision to list an endangered species be qualitatively different from a decision to designate an area as wilderness?

- Suppose that instead of working for the Forest Service you represent an organization that supports preservation of the maximum possible amount of forest land. How do you think your perspective would differ if you were representing a local organization rather than a regional or national organization? To what extent should federal land managers focus on local as opposed to national concerns?

In the chapters that follow we will study issues such as land preservation and endangered species in more detail, so don't be concerned if you lack a full understanding of the legal and policy implications of your ideas. Allow your experience and common sense to guide your analysis.

CHAPTER FOUR

WILDLIFE AND BIODIVERSITY

I. **LIFE ON EARTH**
    A. WHAT IS BIODIVERSITY?
    B. BIODIVERSITY OVER TIME
    C. IS THERE AN EXTINCTION CRISIS?
    D. WHY PRESERVE BIODIVERSITY?
II. **MANAGING THE WILDLIFE COMMONS**
    A. WHO OWNS WILDLIFE?
    B. POLICY INSTRUMENTS
        1. RESTRICTING ACCESS AND TAKE
        2. LANDSCAPE MANAGEMENT AND CAPTIVE BREEDING
        3. MARKET INSTRUMENTS
        4. RESTRICTING THE MARKET FOR SALE
III. **THE ENDANGERED SPECIES ACT**
    A. LISTING
    CASE STUDY: SHOULD THE PRAIRIE DOG BE LISTED?
    CASE STUDY: SHOULD HATCHERY SALMON BE LISTED?
    B. DESIGNATION OF CRITICAL HABITAT
    C. CONSERVATION
    D. CONSULTATION, JEOPARDY, AND ADVERSE MODIFICATION OF CRITICAL HABITAT
    PROBLEM EXERCISE: CRITICAL HABITAT FOR THE GRIZZLY
    PROBLEM EXERCISE: WHAT TO DO ABOUT CLIMATE CHANGE?
    E. PROHIBITION AGAINST TAKES
        1. DIRECT TAKES
        2. INDIRECT TAKES
    PROBLEM EXERCISE: GRIZZLIES AND CORN ON THE TRACKS
    PROBLEM EXERCISE: PYGMY OWLS ON THE DOUBLE R RANCH
    CASE STUDY: REINTRODUCTION OF WOLVES
        3. VICARIOUS TAKES
    F. CREATING INCENTIVES FOR SPECIES PROTECTION
    G. DOES IT WORK?
    CASE STUDY: THE DELHI SANDS FLOWER-LOVING FLY

Every country can be said to have three forms of wealth: material, cultural and biological. The first two we understand very well, because they are the substance of our everyday lives. Biological wealth is taken much less seriously. This is a serious strategic error, one that will be increasingly regretted as time passes.

E.O. WILSON, THE DIVERSITY OF LIFE (1992)

I. LIFE ON EARTH

Scientists estimate that anywhere from 3.5 to 3.9 billion years ago, in a process that may never be fully understood, life first appeared on earth in

320

the form of simple, single-celled organisms. It's hard to think of a more inhospitable place, with active volcanos, meteor bombardments, and a poisonous atmosphere. Some of these organisms, known as cyanobacteria, produced oxygen as a byproduct of their metabolism. Over a period of about 2 billion years, as mounds of these bacteria pumped out oxygen, the composition of the earth's atmosphere gradually changed from a poisonous mix to the oxygen-rich air we breathe today. Much later, some 540 million years ago, evidence of the first sea animals appears in the fossil record. About 350 million years ago, plants moved on to the land, followed 250 million years ago by the age of dinosaurs. Scientists and anthropologists then estimate that primate species appeared about 50 million years ago, evolved to walking upright and using tools around 3 million years ago and that *Homo sapiens*, our species, only came onto the scene roughly 300,000 years ago. To put this evolution in perspective, if we think of life on earth as a clock with the origin of life at the tick after midnight, the first fish and shells only appeared late the next evening, just before 10:00 p.m.; the age of the dinosaurs started around 10:30 p.m.; *Homo sapiens* burst onto the scene only 6 seconds ago, and human civilizations began developing in the last quarter second, faster than you've spent reading this line! We truly are newcomers to life on earth.

During this remarkable parade of life, many species have arisen and gone extinct, and some have evolved to the present day. Over time, life has become increasingly diverse. To get a sense of the remarkable complexity of living systems, consider that a single pinch of dirt contains roughly 30,000 protozoa, 50,000 algae, 400,000 fungi, and billions of bacteria, all interdependent through complex food webs, not to mention the nematodes, insects, plants, and animals the soil supports. GRETCHEN DAILY, NATURE'S SERVICES 4 (1997).

What is our relation to this diversity of life? What is our responsibility to preserve it? What are the trade-offs in protecting some species but not others, and how can we best manage these choices in the face of occasionally competing demands for development, food, and recreation? It is these questions, and none has an easy answer, that this chapter considers.

Section I provides background, drawing from a range of disciplines to examine why we should care about biodiversity and whether we are facing an extinction crisis that warrants a legal response. Section II examines who owns (and therefore controls) wildlife at the international, national and state level. It then reviews the range of policy instruments one might use to conserve biodiversity, many of which have been used for centuries. Section III briefly reviews the key U.S. wildlife laws before focusing on the Endangered Species Act, the most far-reaching and controversial of natural resource laws. The chapter ends with an in-depth case study of a conflict involving the expansion of a hospital in the habitat of the endangered Delhi Sands flower-loving fly.

A.   WHAT IS BIODIVERSITY?

Traditionally, conservation efforts have focused on protecting "wildlife." Hence one can find laws going back centuries to protect deer, partridge, and geese, or treaties at the turn of the twentieth century protecting migratory birds and whales. In recent decades, many biologists have argued that such a narrow focus on charismatic or tasty mammals and birds misses the more basic issue—the loss in the overall richness of life on the planet. To them, biological diversity (popularly known as "biodiversity") is a more appropriate object of conservation because it covers all forms of life. While there are many definitions of biodiversity, the Biodiversity Convention's definition captures well its breadth.

> [Biodiversity is] the variability among living organisms from all sources including, *inter alia*, terrestrial, marine and other aquatic ecosystems and the ecological complexes of which they are part; this includes diversity within species, between species and of ecosystems.

Convention on Biological Diversity, Jun. 5, 1992, 1760 U.N.T.S. 79, art. 2.

As this definition notes, biodiversity can be described usefully across at least four levels—ecosystem, species, population, and genetic. *Ecosystem diversity* describes the different combinations of geology, soil, climate, and other factors in an area that gives rise to specific types of plant and animal communities. A tropical savannah in Africa, arctic tundra in Canada, and mangrove swamp in the Everglades provide three obvious examples. Ecosystems can vary greatly, of course, in size—from a stream or pond to a mountain meadow. *Species diversity* refers to the number of species (e.g., the Black Rhinoceros, the White Rhinoceros and the Great White Shark) and their relative abundance. This is the most popular meaning of biodiversity and, while a useful measure, masks the enormous variety found within a single species. Just think, for example, of all the different types of dogs found within the species, *Canis familiaris*, ranging from Miniature Schnauzers and Chihuahuas to Dobermans and Great Danes. *Population diversity* refers to the variability among separate populations of a species. Living in distinct habitats, separate populations of the same species may become geographically isolated. Subject to differing pressures from natural selection, over time they will develop distinct traits that are passed on to their offspring. Thus, for example, some populations of the common fescue grass are tolerant of heavy metals and can grow on mine tailings while others cannot. *Genetic diversity* refers to the variability within members of the same population—the diversity of information contained in the genes of individual plants, animals, and microorganisms. Each organism holds an immense amount of genetic information, from 1,000 genes in some bacteria to more than 400,000 genes in many flowering plants.

One might think that species diversity is the most important measure of biodiversity, hence the occasional calls for a "Noah's Ark" approach to biodiversity conservation according to which the remedy for threats of extinction is keeping breeding groups of endangered species in zoos or reserves. Yet this misses the fact that preserving different populations and the genetic variability within populations are far more important than simply preserving species, for it is *the variation below the species level* that ensures the capacity of species to survive over time.

To use our own species as an example, consider what happened when Europe was exposed to the Black Death in the middle of the fourteenth century. While the death toll across Europe from bubonic plague was immense, killing up to one-third of the populace, there was sufficient genetic variability among populations and individuals that some groups and people had natural immunity to the disease and survived. Now imagine that all endangered species were preserved in zoos or preserves. Faced with a similarly lethal disease, would a captive breeding stock have the genetic variability to ensure enough individuals survived? Even if the zoo population survived, was eventually released to the wild, and expanded in number over its original range, much of the biodiversity would have been lost because of the low level of diversity within the breeding population (the so-called bottleneck effect). Because there would be much less genetic diversity in the zoo population than in the original wild population, the survivors would face greater susceptibility to disease and other negative effects of inbreeding depression.

Put simply, while a Noah's Ark approach to conservation would ensure species diversity was unchanged (at least for the short term), both population and genetic diversity would be greatly reduced. To preserve biodiversity, we must therefore be concerned not only with the existence of species in the wild but their location and relative abundance as well.

B. BIODIVERSITY OVER TIME

Roughly 1.5 million species have been described by taxonomists, though studies by conservation biologists suggest there are between ten and fifteen million species on earth. Well over half of the described species are insects. Vertebrates (i.e., species with backbones such as fish, birds, and mammals), while the best known taxonomic group, actually make up a very small percentage of species diversity, certainly less than 5%. Over long periods of time, the forces of natural selection ensure that new species are created while others go extinct. This is the way of the world and has been so since life first evolved billions of years ago. So why does the current level of biodiversity give cause for concern? After all, some ten to fifteen million species sounds like quite an impressive number.

Through studying the fossil record, evolutionary biologists estimate that the current rate of extinction is from 100 to 1,000 times the background rate, with most estimates around 1,000 times or greater. Put another way, if one compares today's extinction rates with extinctions over geologic periods of time (i.e., over many millions of years), we appear to be on the verge of the sixth great wave of extinction in geologic history. Mammals provide a depressingly illustrative example. Out of almost 4,400 mammal species, about 11 percent are already "endangered" or "critically endangered," with another 14 percent vulnerable to extinction (including nearly half of all primate species). One of every eight plant species are threatened or endangered; and studies of fish populations suggest that they may be the worst off—one-third of the world's fish species are already threatened with extinction. As habitat continues to be degraded in the tropics, these rates should be expected to increase. IUCN, IUCN RED LIST 2007, TABLE 1.

PERCENT OF THREATENED SPECIES BY MAJOR GROUPS OF ORGANISMS EVALUATED IN 2007

Status	Birds	Mammals	Reptiles/ Amphibians	Fish	Insects	Crustaceans	Plants
Threatened	12%	22%	30%	70%	50%	83%	70%
Not Threatened	88%	78%	70%	5%	50%	17%	30%

The last great extinction was caused by a meteor striking the earth and likely led to the end of dinosaurs. The current causes of extinctions, though, lie in our control. Regardless of the precise numbers of endangered species, and there is considerable debate over these numbers, the main drivers of extinction are clear, and we are behind the wheel.

WORLD RESOURCES INSTITUTE ET AL. GLOBAL BIODIVERSITY STRATEGY 14–15 (1992)

Habitat Loss and Fragmentation

Relatively undisturbed ecosystems have shrunk dramatically in area over past decades as the human population and resource consumption have grown. Ninety-eight percent of the tropical dry forest along Central America's Pacific coast has disappeared. Thailand lost 22 percent of its mangroves between 1961 and 1985, and virtually none of the remainder is undisturbed. In freshwater ecosystems, dams have destroyed large sections of river and stream habitat. In marine ecosystems, coastal development has wiped out reef and near-shore communities. In tropical forests, a major cause of forest loss is the expansion of marginal agriculture, though in specific regions commercial timber harvest may pose an even greater problem.

Introduced species

Introduced species are responsible for many recorded species extinctions, especially on islands. In these isolated ecosystems, a new predator, competitor, or pathogen can rapidly imperil species that did not co-evolve with the newcomer. In Hawaii, some 86 introduced plant species seriously threaten native biodiversity; one introduced tree species has now displaced more than 30,000 acres of native forest. [There are estimated to be over 4,500 introduced species in the United States.]

Over-exploitation of plant and animal species

Numerous forest, fisheries, and wildlife resources have been over-exploited, sometimes to the point of extinction. Historically, both the great auk and the passenger pigeon succumbed to such pressure, and the Lebanon cedar that once blanketed 500,000 hectares now is found in only a few scattered remnants of forest. Over-exploitation of the Peruvian anchovy between 1958 and 1970 dramatically reduced the population size and the catch. Today, the Sumatran and Javan rhinos have been hunted to the verge of extinction, along with numerous other vertebrates. Many extinctions attend the human harvest of food, but the search for precious commodities—notably, ivory—and for pets, curiosities, and collector's items has also impinged on some populations and obliterated others.

Pollution of soil, water, and atmosphere

Pollutants strain ecosystems and may reduce or eliminate populations of sensitive species. Contamination may reverberate along the food chain: barn owl populations in the United Kingdom have fallen by 10 percent since new rodenticides were introduced, and illegal pesticides used to control crayfish along the boundaries of Spain's Cora Donana National Park in 1985 killed

30,000 birds. Some 43 species have been lost in Poland's Ojcow National Park, due in part to severe air pollution. Soil microbes have also suffered from pollution as industry sheds heavy metals and irrigated agriculture brings on salinization. Acid rain has made thousands of Scandinavian and North American lakes and pools virtually lifeless, and, in combination with other kinds of air pollution, has damaged forests throughout Europe. Marine pollution, particularly from non-point sources, has defiled the Mediterranean and many estuaries and coastal seas throughout the world.

Global climate change

In coming decades, a massive "side-effect" of air pollution—global warming—could play havoc with the world's living organisms. Human-caused increases in "greenhouse gases" in the atmosphere are likely to commit the planet to a global temperature rise of some 1 to 3 degrees Celsius (2 to 5 degrees F) during the next century, with an associated rise in sea level of 1 to 2 meters. Each 1 degree Celsius rise in temperature will displace the limits of tolerance of land species some 125 km towards the poles, or 150 m vertically on the mountains. Many species will not be able to redistribute themselves fast enough to keep up with the projected changes, and considerable alterations in ecosystem structure and function are likely.... And protected areas themselves will be placed under stress as environmental conditions deteriorate and suitable habitat for their species cannot be found in the disturbed land surrounding them.

Industrial Agriculture and Forestry

Until this century, farmers and pastoralists bred and maintained a tremendous diversity of crop and livestock varieties around the world. But on-farm biodiversity is shrinking fast thanks to modern plant-breeding programs and the resulting productivity gains achieved by planting comparatively fewer varieties of crops that respond better to water, fertilizers, and pesticides. Similar trends are transforming diverse forest ecosystems into high-yielding monocultural tree plantations—some of which now resemble a field of maize as much as a natural forest—and even fewer tree genes than crop genes have been preserved off-site as an insurance policy against disease and pests.

———

These extinction forces can often reinforce one another. As a species population becomes smaller, for example, if the species has commercial value its price is driven up by the dynamic of supply and demand and hunting pressure increases. Reduced habitat area makes it easier for predators (often cats, snakes, and rats) to find and corner prey. And, over the longer term, smaller populations become less resilient overall. The tendency of small populations to become significantly more vulnerable than larger populations to environmental variability, loss of genetic variability, and external pressure such as hunting and loss of habitat is known as an *"extinction vortex"*—just as with a tornado, the closer one gets to the center, the smaller the population becomes, the faster it moves toward extinction.

Consider the global decline of frogs. When was the last time you saw a frog? Frogs, toads, and salamanders, which once were abundant, have all but disappeared from many areas. Since 1990, scientists have documented a worldwide decline in amphibians, with unrelated populations subject to different pressures around the globe experiencing significant decreases in numbers. There is no single reason for the decline of frogs and other amphibians. Dependent on both aquatic and terrestrial environments, amphibians are doubly vulnerable to development. Destruction of wetlands has resulted in a loss of breeding pools and other essential riparian habitats. The number of farm ponds in Britain, for example, has declined by 70% in the last century. Roads and habitat fragmentation disrupt migration and introduce threats from cars and pets. Chemical contamination threatens both amphibians and the aquatic ecosystems on which they depend, with slight changes in pH having dramatic effects on eggs and tadpoles. Hunting for consumption (frog legs) and sale in pet shops also takes its toll, as has the introduction of exotic species such as brook trout in mountain lakes. To make matters more complicated, populations in undisturbed, isolated areas have been declining, as well, possibly from the combined effects of climate change, ozone depletion, and acid rain. Other possible drivers include pesticides and herbicides, introduced species, and "cryptic kills." Halting this decline will not be easy, requiring actions to combat multiple threats. As Emily Yoffe has written, "Frogs are living environmental assayers, moving over their life cycles from water to land, from plant-eater to insect-eater, covered only by a permeable skin that offers little shield from the outside world." Emily Yoffe, *Silence of the Frogs*, in N.Y. TIMES MAGAZINE, Dec. 13, 1992, at 36; Andrew Blaustein and Joseph Kiesecker, *Complexity in conservation: lessons from the global decline of amphibian populations*, 5 ECOLOGY LETTERS 597 (2002).

C. IS THERE AN EXTINCTION CRISIS?

We are all familiar with the stories of the extinction of the Dodo and the Passenger pigeon, but how many other species have gone (and are going) extinct that we do not know about? The accuracy of the numbers in the biodiversity debate—how many species there are, how many are going extinct—is central to deciding whether there is a crisis justifying significant legal action. Not surprisingly, given the conflicting interests involved in the biodiversity debate at the national and international level (with developers, environmental groups, scientists, and governments among the obvious interested parties), there is significant debate over how accurate the biodiversity and extinctions estimates are. The paragraphs below briefly explain how these figures are calculated.

No one knows exactly how many species go extinct every year for the simple reasons that we neither know how many species there are (particularly invertebrates), nor do we track their populations. One of this casebook's authors had the opportunity to stay at a field station in a Costa Rican rainforest and, one afternoon, looked over an ecologist's shoulder as he identified insects he had collected that day. While stunned to learn that almost one-quarter of the insects had no names because they had not yet been formally identified, he was even more surprised when the ecologist just shrugged and said, "That's typical. Sometimes half are new."

In estimating biodiversity over large areas of habitat, scientists have relied on extrapolation from random sampling. In an early and well known example of this technique, two decades ago Terry Erwin fumigated the canopy of 19 specimens of a single species of evergreen tree in a Panamanian rainforest. Placing tarps under the trees, he collected all the dead insects as they fell to earth. To the amazement of the scientific community, he identified 1,143 different species of just beetles, most of which had never been collected or described. Based on the results of earlier research, he calculated that 162 species were host-specific (i.e., only lived on this particular species of tree). Assuming that similar numbers of beetle species live exclusively in canopies of other tree species, he multiplied 162 by the number of tree species in tropical rainforests (50,000 species) and came up with the estimate of 8.15 million specialist beetle species. Since beetles represent about 40% of all canopy arthropods, this provides a total of about 20 million arthropod species, which Erwin increased by 50% since there are generally double the number of canopy arthropod species as on the ground. His final figure came to 30 million tropical forest arthropods! These calculations are based, of course, on a series of assumptions (particularly the typical assemblage of insect species on tropical trees and their host-specificity). ANDREW BEATTIE, BIODIVERSITY: AUSTRALIA'S LIVING WEALTH 98–99 (1995).

While one can examine fossil records to see if species from the past have gone extinct, estimating extinctions over the last century is far more difficult, even if we can confidently estimate the number of species in a given habitat. On its face, this poses a real policy challenge because the direct evidence argues against a dire situation. As a number of biodiversity critics have been quick to point out, there are not enough dead bodies to warrant claims that we are in an extinction crisis. Based on Harvard entomologist E.O. Wilson's estimate that we are losing 50,000 species a year worldwide, journalist Gregg Easterbrook argues that:

> some 66,000 species should have been hounded out of existence in the United States alone since 1973, when the Endangered Species Act was passed in its current form.... [Yet] of the first group of species listed in 1973 under the Endangered Species Act, today 44 are stable or improving, 20 are in decline, and only seven, including the ivory-billed woodpecker and dusky seaside sparrow, are gone. This adds up to seven species lost over 20 years from the very group considered most sharply imperiled.... There is a rather amazing gap between a projected 66,000 and a confirmed seven. And the United States is the most carefully studied biosphere in the world, making U.S. extinctions likely to be detected.

GREGG EASTERBROOK, A MOMENT ON EARTH 558–59 (1995).

There have been roughly 726 documented extinctions since 1600 (primarily of flowering plants). RICHARD PRIMACK, ESSENTIALS OF CONSERVATION BIOLOGY 166 (2002). Cause for concern, surely, but seemingly not enough extinctions to warrant credible comparisons with the asteroid that struck the earth some 65 million years ago. Why such low numbers?

One reason for the low number of recorded extinctions is that invertebrates are not included. Another reason is that the accepted convention for declaring a species extinct is very conservative. To qualify as officially extinct, a species both has to be known to science (often not the case) and directly observed going extinct (unusual in the wild). Absent direct observation of the last individual dying, the species must not have been seen in nature for fifty years. Think about Terry Erwin's fumigation experiment and the estimate of 30 million tropical forest arthropods. While it is possible to estimate the number of arthropods that might be lost when a certain acreage of forest is cleared, it is hard to identify the individual species, particularly when so many are unknown to begin with. High extinction estimates, like that of E.O. Wilson's, include estimates about such invertebate loss. Lower estimates, like that of Easterbrook, do not consider such estimates. As Paul and Anne Ehrlich have argued, though, focusing on precise numbers of species loss risks missing the forest for the trees. As they note, this line of logic suggests equally that "no one can tell whether a beach is eroding away unless every grain of sand, seashell, piece of driftwood, and strand of seaweed has been counted, measured, and classified and a record kept of the ones that have disappeared." ANNE AND PAUL EHRLICH, BETRAYAL OF SCIENCE AND REASON 113 (1996). Focusing on dead bodies also implicitly suggests that undocumented extinctions are not significant. But how can one estimate extinctions without the bodies? As a police detective might explain, "we need to solve a victimless crime."

QUESTIONS AND DISCUSSION

1. Even relying on the same theories, respected scientists have provided widely ranging estimates of current extinction rates, anywhere from 100 to 1,500 times the background rate over geological time periods. But does it really matter what the precise number of extinctions is so long as we continue to reduce and fragment species-rich habitats? Or, if we are going to forgo development and its potential economic benefits, does prudence require more accurate and robust estimates?

2. Biodiversity is not spread evenly across the globe, with species richness increasing as one travels from the poles toward the tropics. As noted above, most documented extinctions over the last century have occurred on a relatively small number of islands and research suggests that current extinctions are also concentrated in particular areas. First proposed by Norman Myers, these "biodiversity hotspots" contain not only great species richness but many rare species that are found nowhere else (known as "endemic species"). Just think of the 162 beetle species found on a single species of tree by Terry Erwin. The policy implication of biodiversity hotspots is significant, for it suggests that much of the earth's biodiversity can be conserved by protecting a relatively small area. As E.O. Wilson has described,

> From the coastal sage of California to the rainforests of West Africa, the hottest of the terrestrial hotspots occupy only 1.4% of the world's land surface yet are the exclusive home of more than a third of the terrestrial plants and vertebrate species. Similarly, from the streams of Appalachia to the Philippine coral reefs, aquatic hotspots occupy a tiny fraction of the shallow water surface.

E.O. Wilson, *Vanishing Before Our Eyes,* TIME, Spring 2000, at 34. *See generally* John Charles Kunich, *Preserving the Womb of the Unknown Species with Hotspots Legislation,* 52 HASTINGS L.J. 1149 (2001).

It also suggests, of course, that any legal response must necessarily have a strong international component. Even if the United States were to conserve all of its biodiversity, global biodiversity would still continue its current decline if conservation were not strengthened in African, South American, and Asian hotspots. If our primary concern is loss of global biodiversity, would we be better served by taking the significant resources we dedicate to species conservation in the United States and spending them, instead, in foreign hot spots? This would surely provide more "biodiversity bang for the buck." Should the nationality of hot spots matter to us?

3. Natural selection does not cease once species are taken into captivity. A population's adaptation to captivity presents an important obstacle to reliance on zoos and refuges for maintenance of biodiversity. For populations that are maintained in captivity over several generations, natural selection will often favor traits that would be *selected against* in the wild, such as docility and tameness, for example. Thanks to cages and vets, populations are largely protected against disease and predators. Breeding success depends more on individuals' behavior in enclosed areas than competition among males. Carnivores are not required to hunt. After several generations, assuming the population can be released back into its habitat, it will likely be less fit to survive in the wild. There are numerous examples of such deleterious adaptations under captivity, ranging from fish and mammals to fruit flies, plants, and bacteria. *See* R. FRANKHAM ET AL., INTRODUCTION TO CONSERVATION GENETICS 453 (2002).

4. Do you see why scientists might prefer the concept of biodiversity conservation over, for example, wildlife conservation? Biodiversity offers a vehicle for discussing the importance of conserving all forms of life. Biodiversity also includes the concept of variability as an economic resource. As we shall discuss in the next section, the variation among and within species has great value in agriculture, medicine, and biotechnology. By focusing attention on the economic value of the variability of life, conservationists hoped they would be able to build broader support for overall conservation efforts—in addition to the broad support for conserving the last few rhinos or tigers. But there is a loss in terms of rhetoric. Do you think the general public is more concerned over threats to biodiversity or threats to wildlife?

5. As discussed in the Terry Erwin example, many of the numbers in the extinction debate are calculated indirectly through models—mathematical approximations of real life. Two models that have been particularly influential bear mentioning. The first determines species richness from a theory knows as the "species-area relationship." This theory, which has strong empirical support from many decades of field experiments, predicts that the number of species is directly related to the habitat area (with a coefficient based on the habitat in question). In mathematical notation,

[handwritten margin note: Models for species diversity & extinction]

$$S = cA^z$$

[handwritten note: ① species—area rel.]

where S is the number of species, c is the number of species per unit area, A is the area, and z is a coefficient reflecting the habitat's capacity to support biodiversity (e.g., a tropical rainforest has a higher z than the Sahara Desert). Not surprisingly, all else being equal, the larger the area, the more species it can support. This counsels against fragmenting productive habitats.

To estimate extinction rates, scientists rely on the theory of "island biogeography." Developed by Richard Macarthur and E.O. Wilson, this theory is, in some respects, the inverse of the species-area relationship. It starts from the observation that more species are found on larger islands and on closer islands than on smaller and more distant islands. Macarthur and Wilson explained this by proposing a dynamic equilibrium between the forces of immigration and extinction. The number of species on any island will depend upon both the rate of immigration of new species and the rate of extinction of existing species (it is assumed the time scale is too short for new species to evolve). As the island becomes smaller and more isolated, however, the species become more prone to extinction as a result of the extinction vortex described earlier. Thus, assuming no migration of new species, a 50% reduction in habitat area is predicted to result in a loss of 10% of biodiversity and a 90% reduction in habitat will result in extinction of 50% of the species present.

While the theory is based on species on islands (where most of the recent documented extinctions have taken place), Macarthur and Wilson argued that much the same process could be operating on "habitat islands"—that is, terrestrial habitat that is being fragmented. If, for example, a forest is broken into discrete fragments by clearing and roads for development, unless the species can safely move from one fragment to another (and are likely to do so), for all intents they could just as easily be on an island in the middle of the ocean. As the fragments grow smaller and more isolated, extinctions increase accordingly (though there may well be a lag time between fragmentation and extinction). Similar to the species-area relationship, there is strong empirical evidence supporting the theory of island biogeography's predictions in terrestrial environments. *See, e.g.,* RICHARD PRIMACK, ESSENTIALS OF CONSERVATION BIOLOGY 181 (2002); MATTHEW H. NITELKI, EXTINCTIONS (1984).

———

D.   WHY PRESERVE BIODIVERSITY?

Preserving biodiversity can often impose economic costs, whether in restoring habitat or modifying land uses. To be sure, it can provide benefits as well. But how much biodiversity we choose to preserve, and the related issue of how much we are willing to pay for this preservation, is ultimately determined by the basic questions, "why do we care about preserving biodiversity?" and, of particular relevance to our study, "do we care enough that we should use the law to preserve biodiversity?" In Chapter 1's section on environmental ethics (Section I.B), we explored the different ways of thinking about our relationship to nature, ranging from biocentric (a nature-based ethical system) to anthropocentric (a human-based system). The paragraphs below explore environmental ethics in a concrete setting, laying out the major arguments for biodiversity conservation. *See generally* ANDREW BEATTIE & PAUL EHRLICH, WILD SOLUTIONS: HOW BIODIVERSITY IS MONEY IN THE BANK (2001).

* We should preserve biodiversity because of its market values

Agriculture and food security. Although 30,000 species of plants are edible, only about 5,000 are consumed by humans and, of those, a mere 20 species provide 90% of the world's food. Wheat, maize, and rice together provide more than half. The genetic diversity of wild relatives and the numerous traditional varieties of these food crops act as a critical reservoir for adaptation to different conditions (such as disease, drought, or soil salinity) and for increasing the productivity of domestic strains. U.S. agricultural output is increased by an estimated $1 billion a year due to plant breeding programs that depend heavily on wild strains, but industrialized agriculture relies on ever bigger fields of fewer varieties of crops. The lack of diversity in such large "monocultures" not only displaces traditional varieties but makes crops highly susceptible to insects and diseases. For example, in 1970–71, the United States lost 15 percent of its corn crop due to corn blight. *See* John Kunich, *Preserving the Womb of the Unknown Species with Hotspots Legislation*, 52 HASTINGS L.J. 1149, 1166 (2001); NATURE'S SERVICES: SOCIETAL DEPENDENCE ON NATURAL ECOSYSTEMS 258 (Gretchen Daily ed., 1997).

Drugs and medicines. The development of pharmaceutical drugs and medicines strongly relies on derivatives from wild species of plants, microorganisms, fungi, and even animals. As of 1997, 118 of the top 150 prescription drugs used in the United States were based on natural sources: 74% of those on plants, 18% on fungi, 5% on bacteria, and 3% on one snake species. Nine of the top ten drugs in this list are based on natural plant products. Globally, approximately 80% of the human population relies on traditional medical systems, and about 85% of traditional medicine involves the use of plant extracts. Extracts from the rosy periwinkle, a plant found in Madagascar, have proven effective for many sufferers of Hodgkin's disease and acute lymphocytic leukemia, two deadly cancers. Taxol, a derivative from the bark of the pacific yew tree, is now used as a treatment for ovarian cancer. Even the lowly and slimy leech produces an anticoagulant called himdin, which now is used to treat rheumatism, hemorrhoids, and other conditions. Future discoveries of similar derivatives are considered quite likely as so few known species of plants have been examined for medicinal properties. F. GRIFO & J. ROSENTHAL EDS., BIODIVERSITY AND HUMAN HEALTH (1997); Farnsworth et al., *Medicinal Plants in Therapy*, 63 BULLETIN OF THE WORLD HEALTH ORGANIZATION, 965–81 (1985); P. Principe, *The Economic Significance of Plants and Their Constituents as Drugs, in* 3 H. WAGNER ET AL., ECONOMIC AND MEDICINAL PLANT RESEARCH 1–17 (1989).

Traditional uses. Wildlife as pets, ornaments, and tourist attractions (whether on safaris or birdwatching) is very big business. A conservative estimate places international trade in wildlife at over $10 billion a year. Up to one-third of the trade is likely illegal.

* We should preserve biodiversity because of its non-market values

Ecosystem services. To many analysts, the most important underlying cause of the loss of biodiversity is the failure to recognize the non-market benefits that wildlife and biodiversity provide or, to put it another way, the costs or loss of benefits that result from the loss of biodiversity. The most significant of these are ecosystem services (discussed at page 18). Created by the interactions of living organisms with their environment, ecosystem services provide both the conditions and processes that sustain human life. These include purifying air and water, detoxifying and decomposing waste, renewing soil fertility, regulating climate, mitigating droughts and floods, controlling pests, and pollinating plants. While none of these services are exchanged in markets, they clearly are of great value. Just think of the role natural pollinators play in producing fruit crops. Another example, is the role of ''keystone species.'' In some ecosystems, removing a particular species can dramatically alter the species composition of the ecosystem and, in some instances, its service provision. Beyond providing the foundation for the provision of ecosystem services, biodiversity can also be thought of as a service itself (i.e., as insurance for species resilience against disease and environmental change).

Option values. As a result of natural selection, every species alive today has had to solve threats to its existence—from defenses against microbes and predators to survival in sub-freezing temperatures or hot steam vents—and encode these solutions in its genome. Their unique solutions to challenges provide an enormous potential database for challenges we face. Yet beyond their physical appearance, we know remarkably little about the species we have named to date, much less the many more we have not. As biologist E.O. Wilson has written, this counsels prudence. ''We should judge every scrap of biodiversity as priceless while we learn to use it and come to understand what it means to humanity. We should not knowingly allow any species or race to go extinct.'' E.O. WILSON, THE DIVERSITY OF LIFE 34 (1992). If one is concerned with preserving options, species extinction must be avoided because, unlike many other environmental harms, it is final and irreversible.

* We should preserve biodiversity because of its aesthetic and spiritual values

Existence values. Tastes differ, but few would dispute that the existence of wildlife adds to the richness of our own life experiences. The flight of the Bald eagle in the wild has real meaning to many Americans. The same is true for koalas and platypus to Australians and lions to Kenyans. While such ''existence'' values may be impossible to quantify precisely, they surely are real. Even if we never see these animals in the wild, knowing that they exist is special to us. How else can one explain the overwhelming public support for whale conservation?

* We should preserve biodiversity because it is the right thing to do

Intrinsic values. To some, speaking of the economic value of wildlife misses the most important reasons for protecting them—they are living organisms that have a right to inhabit, evolve, and shape the planet. Animal rights activists argue forcefully that humans should be stewards of wildlife for ethical and moral reasons, that wildlife has an intrinsic value independent of its economic value for humanity. Some theologians argue that we must act as stewards for God's creations. Others contend that it is simply wrong to knowingly extirpate species that have evolved over millions of years.

While persuasive, each of these arguments also has shortcomings as a sole justification for biodiversity conservation.

Holly Doremus, *Patching the Ark* 18 ECOLOGY L.Q. 265, 275–281 (1991)

Although the utilitarian argument may be the easiest to sell to the public, it does not, by itself, provide a basis for preservation of the full spectrum of biological diversity. One common utilitarian argument is that, since most species have not been investigated with an eye to their exploitability, it would be foolhardy to allow them to become extinct before such an investigation has been made. This argument provides a solid basis for preservation of tropical systems, where little or nothing is known about a vast number of species, but is less applicable to developed countries like the United States, where, although large gaps in our knowledge remain, much of the flora and fauna has been at least cursorily investigated. Many species may have little or no utilitarian value, either individually or as components of an ecosystem. If utilitarian reasons are the only basis for preservation, we need not preserve these species. Similarly, there may be ecosystems which do not contribute noticeably to global stability, and which contain no useful species. A strict utilitarian would allow the elimination of these ecosystems, unless she defined human well-being as including exposure to the widest possible variety of other organisms. Such a definition would make the utilitarian argument tautological.

A strict utilitarian view would also justify extermination of a species or an ecosystem to serve a human purpose, even a fairly limited purpose.... The scope of an appeal for preservation based on utilitarian motives is also limited by the speculative and long-term nature of many of the expected benefits of biological diversity. Although true utilitarianism may require consideration of the needs of future generations, utilitarianism has come to signify the search for "whatever is of the greatest immediate benefit to the greatest number of people at the lowest cost." Because of this societal bias, where a development project provides short term, readily apparent benefits, a utilitarian argument for preservation of the biological resources which will be lost to the development may well fail. * * *

The esthetic argument, like the utilitarian one, is essentially anthropocentric: diversity is valued because it appeals to human tastes. This argument could allow the extermination of species and ecosystems which most people do not find appealing. For example, although many biologists would disagree, most people find swamps esthetically distasteful. Unless a scientific elite is made the arbiter of esthetic value, swamps might properly be turned into esthetically preferable meadows.

Similarly, if the purpose of preservation is primarily esthetic, people may demand that their esthetic experience be given first priority even when it conflicts with the health of the species or ecosystem. Such conflicts currently occur, for example, with respect to whale watching off the California coast. Because tourists demand the best possible view of the sounding whales, tour boats endeavor to get as close as possible. Some marine scientists believe that these intrusions have caused the whales to alter their migratory path significantly.... In the end, the esthetic argument may be indistinguishable from the utilitarian one: "enjoyment" of nature may simply be another use mankind makes of the natural world.... Like utilitarianism, esthetic arguments can provide a basis for the preservation of some biological resources, but not for the long-term preservation of the biota as a whole.

By contrast, non-anthropocentric moral arguments provide a basis for preservation of the entire range of biological diversity, at least if the ethical obligation runs primarily to species or natural systems rather than to individual creatures. An ethical obligation directed at individual organisms might lead indirectly to the protection of genetic diversity, but would not, in principle, allow one to distinguish between individuals of rare and abundant species. For example, under a view that primarily values individual creatures, it would be difficult to justify removal of feral goats or sheep from an island where they are eating the last examples of a rare plant.

Other factors also limit the reach of an ethical obligation running to individual organisms. Many (probably most) of the current threats to nonhuman species come from indirect causes, such as elimination of habitat, rather than from direct exploitation. Human activities causing these indirect threats are morally ambiguous compared to actions such as the clubbing of baby seals, as they often do not result in immediately apparent harm to individual animals.

QUESTIONS AND DISCUSSION

1. Which of the biodiversity conservation arguments resonate with you? Do you think preserving biodiversity is closer to protecting the Mona Lisa, safeguarding the Oxford English Dictionary, or buying a lottery ticket?

2. The different types of biodiversity can seriously complicate the justifications for conservation. Try to provide defensible answers to the following questions:

- Does the duty to preserve biodiversity run to individuals, populations, species, or ecosystems?

- Do you feel it is equally important to save the Coho salmon species and the stream and river systems in which they migrate?

- Do you think saving a unique population of slime mold with medicinal benefits is just as important as saving the Coho salmon?

- Does it make any sense to talk of a duty to preserve a genome?

In one of Aldo Leopold's most cited passages from *A Sand County Almanac*, he writes,

> If the biota, in the course of aeons, has built something we like but we do not understand, then who but a fool would discard seemingly useless parts? To keep every cog and wheel is the first precaution of intelligent tinkering.

Does this provide any guidance in answering the questions above?

3. What does the precautionary principle suggest about policy responses to extinction rates? Put another way, there will always be uncertainty over the rate and magnitude of current extinctions. Nor will we likely know with certainty the value of any particular endangered species to ecosystem function or future applications (such as pharmaceuticals). Given these inevitable uncertainties, does the precautionary principle serve a useful purpose in guiding policy? If you think it does, how would you respond to the criticism that "Saying we should conserve biodiversity in the face of its uncertain values begs the fundamental policy questions of 'how much biodiversity?' and 'at what cost?' Those are the real policy questions. Not whether conserving biodiversity is important or not."

4.   One of the classic justifications for biodiversity conservation is captured in Paul and Anne Ehrlich's famous metaphor of an airplane wing.

> As you walk from the terminal toward your airliner, you notice a man on a ladder busily prying rivets out of its wing. Somewhat concerned, you saunter over to the rivet popper and ask him just what the hell he's doing.
>
> "I work for the airline Growthmania Intercontinental," the man informs you, "and the airline has discovered that it can sell these rivets for two dollars apiece."
>
> "But how do you know you won't fatally weaken the wing doing that?" you inquire.
>
> "Don't worry," he assures you. "I'm certain the manufacturer made this plane much stronger than it needs to be, so no harm's done. Besides, I've taken lots of rivets from this wing and it hasn't fallen off yet. Growthmania Airlines needs the money; if we didn't pop the rivets, Growthmania wouldn't be able to continue expanding. And I need the commission they pay me—fifty cents a rivet!"
>
> "You must be out of your mind!"
>
> "I told you not to worry; I know what I'm doing. As a matter of fact, I'm going to fly on this flight also, so you can see there's absolutely nothing to be concerned about."
>
> Any sane person would, of course, go back into the terminal, report the gibbering idiot and Growthmania Airlines to the FAA, and make reservations on another carrier. You never have to fly on an airliner. But unfortunately all of us are passengers on a very large spacecraft—one on which we have no option but to fly. And, frighteningly, it is swarming with rivet poppers behaving in ways analogous to that just described.

PAUL & ANNE EHRLICH, EXTINCTION: THE CAUSES AND CONSEQUENCES OF THE DISAPPEARANCE OF SPECIES xi (1981)

To be sure, not every rivet is needed for the plane's safety. The plane was engineered with redundancy in mind. Equally clearly, though, at a certain point the wings will fall off, even if we do not know exactly the minimum number of rivets needed to hold the wing in place. What do the rivets in this tale symbolize? Who do the Ehrlichs think the rivet poppers are? What are the policy implications of this story and what are its limitations?

Extending the metaphor, what practical choices do we have? The Ehrlichs say we have no choice but to fly, and some might respond that popping rivets is an inevitable result of flying. But how we fly matters. The number of passengers we carry matters. And the type of plane we fly matters. What trade-offs are necessary to make these changes?

5.   Assume you challenge the rivet popper in the preceding note to stop and he says, "OK. No problem. Just tell me which rivets you need me to keep." You respond that you don't know the exact number, and, shrugging his shoulders, he keeps on popping away. A thought experiment created by John Holdren might change this response by framing the problem in a positive light. As ecologist Gretchen Daily explains:

One way to appreciate the nature and value of ecosystem services is to imagine trying to set up a happy, day-to-day life on the moon. Assume for the sake of argument that the moon miraculously already had some of the basic conditions for supporting human life, such as an atmosphere and climate similar to those on earth. After inviting your best friends and packing your prized possessions, a BBQ grill, some do-it-yourself books, the big question would be, Which of the earth's millions of species do you need to take with you?

Tackling the problem systematically, you could first choose from among all the species exploited directly for food, drink, spice, fiber and timber, pharmaceuticals, industrial products (such as waxes, rubber, and oils), and so on. Even being selective, this list could amount to hundreds or even several thousand species. The space ship would be filling up before you'd even begun adding the species crucial to *supporting* those at the top of your list. Which are these unsung heroes? No one knows which—nor even approximately how many—species are required to sustain human life. This means that rather than listing species directly, you would have to list instead the life-support functions required by your lunar colony; then you could guess at the types and numbers of species required to perform each. At a bare minimum, the spaceship would have to carry species capable of supplying a whole suite of ecosystem services that earthlings take for granted. These services include:

- purification of air and water
- mitigation of floods and droughts
- detoxification and decomposition of wastes
- generation and renewal of soil and soil fertility
- pollination of crops and natural vegetation
- control of the vast majority of potential agricultural pests
- dispersal of seeds and translocation of nutrients
- maintenance of biodiversity, from which humanity has derived key elements of its agricultural, medicinal, and industrial enterprise
- protection from the sun's harmful ultraviolet rays
- partial stabilization of climate
- moderation of temperature extremes and the force of winds and waves
- support of diverse human cultures
- providing of aesthetic beauty and intellectual stimulation that lift the human spirit

Armed with this preliminary list of services, you could begin to determine which types and numbers of species are required to perform each. This is no simple task! Let's take the soil fertility case as an example. Soil organisms play important and often unique roles in the circulation of matter in every ecosystem on earth; they are crucial to the chemical conversion and physical transfer of essential nutrients to higher plants, and all larger organisms, including humans, depend on them. The abundance of soil organisms is absolutely staggering: under a square yard of pasture in Denmark, for instance, the soil was found to be inhabited by roughly 50,000 small earthworms and their relatives, 50,000 insects and mites, and nearly 12 million roundworms. And that is not all. A single gram (a pinch) of soil has yielded an estimated 30,000 protozoa, 50,000 algae, 400,000 fungi, and billions of individual bacteria. Which to bring to the moon? Most of these species have never been subjected to even cursory inspection. Yet the sobering fact of the matter is, as Ed Wilson put it: they don't need us, but we need them.

Gretchen Daily, *Introduction: What Are Ecosystem Services?, in* NATURE'S SERVICES: SOCIETAL DEPENDENCE ON NATURAL ECOSYSTEMS 3–4 (Gretchen Daily ed., 1997).

There is some debate over the potential of an ecosystem services approach to biodiversity conservation. Does the fact that we cannot fully value wildlife and biodiversity suggest that we should not try to value it at all? Do environmentalists gain or lose by trying to engage in discussions of benefits and costs?

6. At the end of the day, does it really matter that no single argument fully justifies conserving biodiversity? Simply proving they are valuable, for example, does not mean that they must also be preserved. Isn't the question ultimately not *whether to preserve*, but *how much to preserve*? In other words, when we get down to practical decisions, isn't the real question what we are willing to pay? Or, to put it in less economic terms, what we are willing to give up for species preservation? And do the different justifications really help us answer these difficult questions?

7. In her excerpt, Holly Doremus notes that "Many species may have little or no utilitarian value, either individually or as components of an ecosystem." She is referring in part to the factor of system redundancy— the fact that some species can be removed from an ecosystem and its productivity will be unchanged (or may, in fact, increase). There has been a great deal of research in recent years examining the relationship between biodiversity and ecosystem function. Do greater assemblages of species lead to more productive systems? Does more biodiversity in a system lead to greater resilience in the face of environmental change? Despite concerted research efforts, the current answer to both these questions is, "sometimes." The complexity of soil biodiversity defies general conclusions. *See generally* M. LOREAU ET AL., BIODIVERSITY AND ECOSYSTEM FUNCTIONING (2002).

8. In the early 1990s, there was great optimism that the pharmaceutical benefits of plants would provide a strong economic incentive for drug companies to pay for rainforest conservation in exchange for local knowledge and access to the plants. Nature has produced a vast array of mostly undiscovered novel molecules, it was argued, some of which will become increasingly important as drug resistance develops globally and new diseases emerge. Thus there was a proliferation of smaller drug companies dedicated to natural product discovery, some of them using newer exploratory techniques involving knowledge of ecology, evolutionary biology, and natural history to target particular arrays of species (as opposed to screening everything).

Whether companies should pay for "biodiversity prospecting," as the search for medicinal compounds in the wild was called, how much, and to whom, were key stumbling blocks in negotiations over the Biodiversity Convention at the Earth Summit in 1992. The huge pharmaceutical company Merck, for example, signed a contract with a nonprofit Costa Rican scientific group, INBio, in 1991. INBio agreed to provide Merck with plants, insects, and microorganisms from Costa Rican forests and Merck, in turn, would have the right to develop the samples into drugs. If the drugs went to market, INBio would receive up to 10 percent of royalties, half of which would then go to the Costa Rican Ministry of Natural Resources (in addition to 10 percent of Merck's prospecting fee. The potential sums were staggering. An INBio employee claimed that a "two percent royalty on 20 products could yield more money than the Costa Rican Government now gets from exports.") In addition to money, the agreement also strengthened capacity, with Merck training Costa Rican scientists and field collectors in their identification and collection activities. *See* Merck–INBio Plant Agreement Case Study, at <http://www.american.edu/ted/merck.htm>.

Despite these heady beginnings, bioprospecting has not lived up to its potential as a major force for biodiversity conservation. Since the late 1990s, most drug companies have reduced or eliminated their investments in bioprospecting in favor of combinatorial chemistry and various drug designing techniques. It is unclear how much of this is due to the shortcomings of bioprospecting and how much to the size of the investment by drug companies in combinatorial chemistry and high throughput. With over a decade's experience of bioprospecting, the verdict remains mixed. It is clear from the behavior of the major drug companies that simply asserting that biodiversity is a vast, untapped cornucopia of immense commercial value has been unpersuasive. While there is continuing evidence that individual species can turn out to be of major commercial value, the costs of finding them and developing the products from them is also large and is being factored into more sober assessments. *See generally* ANDREW BEATTIE & PAUL EHRLICH, WILD SOLUTIONS: HOW BIODIVERSITY IS MONEY IN THE BANK (2001).

II.   MANAGING THE WILDLIFE COMMONS

A.   WHO OWNS WILDLIFE?

As any law student who has covered the venerable case of *Pierson v. Post* in the first property class can quickly assert, the traditional common-law view of wildlife going back at least to Roman times was that wild animals (known as animals *ferae naturae*) were the property of no one until reduced to possession. Thus, in the contest between two people, one who chased a fox and the other who killed it, the killer was the owner. Until you reduced the wildlife to possession, it was not your property. Even if the wildlife was roaming on your private land, it was not your property until you captured it (though property ownership would give the owner an exclusive right to kill or capture the wildlife while on his property). But when a wild animal had not yet been captured, when it was roaming in the fields, to whom did it belong?

As recounted in Chapter 2 (page 163), through the nineteenth century the law recognized that the state had authority to regulate wildlife within its boundaries on behalf of the people of the state, indeed even migratory wildlife that was just passing through the state. This authority to regulate, known as the "state ownership doctrine," was strongly supported by the

Supreme Court in 1896 in the case of *Geer v. Connecticut*, 161 U.S. 519 (1896), where the Court held that state laws restricting interstate trade were valid because the state "owned" the birds while they were within state boundaries. Following *Geer*, however, the state ownership doctrine went into a long, slow decline as the federal government continued to assert regulatory authority over wildlife and as the courts began to uphold federal efforts. Over the next 80 years, a series of Supreme Court cases eroded the state ownership doctrine, affirming the right of the government to regulate wildlife under its Property Clause power, *Kleppe v. New Mexico*, 426 U.S. 529 (1976), and Commerce Clause power, *Douglas v. Seacoast Products*, 431 U.S. 265 (1977). In 1979, the state ownership doctrine finally became extinct, with the Court expressly overruling *Geer* in *Hughes v. Oklahoma*, 441 U.S. 322 (1979).

Despite the demise of the state ownership doctrine, it is important to remember that most wildlife regulation still occurs at the state level, albeit those regulations are always susceptible to preemption by a conflicting federal law. State fish and game agencies retain broad authority over non-endangered fish and wildlife within state boundaries. Historically, they have tended to use that authority to focus on maintaining populations of wildlife for grazing, hunting, and fishing interests rather than on biodiversity conservation. Thus, state fish and game agencies are most widely known for deciding how many bear, elk, or deer permits should be issued and for determining how many thousands of hatchery trout should be released into any particular stream or lake within a state. In recent decades, however, states have become more and more involved with biodiversity concerns, and their regulations sometimes offer more protection for wildlife than do those of the federal government. Equally, in some cases they can conflict with endangered species conservation. As we shall see in discussing the Endangered Species Act, for example, the important *Palila* case was fought over whether the state of Hawaii's maintenance of mouflon sheep in a state park for hunting constituted a take of the endangered honeycreeper bird (page 386). While this chapter focuses on federal law, recognize that for any number of wildlife issues, state law may provide the solution (or the problem).

QUESTIONS AND DISCUSSION

1. The dispute between the federal government and states over the regulation and ownership of wildlife, and indeed between private property owners and either sovereign, reappears in the international context. Here, the conflict centers around whether biodiversity and other natural resources are "owned" by the nation within which they occur, by the nation that captures or reduces the biodiversity to possession, or by the larger global community. The use and protection of wildlife historically has been considered a matter of domestic law, reflecting every nation's claim to permanent sovereignty over its natural resources, including living natural resources.

The need for international wildlife law is obvious in the case of migratory species, which "belong" to several countries, as well as the case of the "global commons"—those areas beyond the limits of national jurisdiction such as the high seas, the sea-bed, and Antarctica. For many global commons resources, most notably the high seas fisheries, the general rule has been the right of capture—i.e., whoever captures a fish or other resource has the right to it. Concern that this right of capture penalizes under-developed and land-locked states, participants in the Law of the Sea Convention and other negotiations in the 1970s perceived a need for a new conceptual framework to address resources in the global commons. This doctrine became known as the "common heritage of mankind." As reflected in the 1982 UN Law of the Sea Convention, this doctrine instituted a common management regime for resources in the deep sea bed, providing that the benefits from the use and exploitation of common heritage natural resources must be shared among all countries. This was strongly opposed by the United States and, in fact, led to the U.S. decision not to ratify the treaty at the time.

Generally, developing countries have been the major supporters of the common heritage principle. They did not have the resources to mine the deep seabed, but this would allow them to share in the benefits. Their support changed, however, as the focus shifted from the global commons to resources within a nation's territory. As we have seen, national sovereignty must be restricted to some extent in the case of migratory wildlife to prevent harm to the interests of other countries where the wildlife resides or visits. But what about local wildlife? The biodiversity in the Amazon rainforest, for example, is staggering, and certainly is a concern of people outside of the Amazon. Should the common heritage of mankind principle apply to biodiversity, as well?

2. The debate over whether biodiversity should be treated as a common concern or common heritage of mankind shares important similarities with debates over application of the Endangered Species Act on private lands in the United States. The fundamental premise of the common heritage argument is that some resources are of such vital concern to the global community that their benefits should be shared. In the case of biodiversity, even if the species are located in a sovereign country, the global community has a legitimate interest in how the species are managed and, at a minimum, that they do not go extinct. In a strikingly similar way, the Endangered Species Act can restrict actions taken by private property owners that harm species on their property (such as adversely modifying the habitat or disrupting essential breeding or feeding behavior). At one extreme, property owners might argue that their property is their sovereign possession in a Blackstonian sense. Yet the Endangered Species Act makes clear that there exists an overriding public interest in species on their property, whether migratory or not.

3. The common heritage of humankind concept has not been widely accepted when it comes to resources or activities located within countries. Developing countries rich in biodiversity, such as Brazil and Colombia, viewed the common heritage principle as a threat and resisted the potential loss of sovereign control over development decisions and possibly profitable genetic resources. At the same time, a growing consensus has emerged that the planet is ecologically interdependent and that humanity may have a collective interest (based on environmental concerns) in certain activities that take place within or resources that are located wholly within national boundaries.

In the negotiations leading up to the Convention on Biological Diversity in 1992 (known as the Biodiversity Convention), the common heritage principle was specifically considered and rejected. Developing countries rejected application of the common heritage principle as "eco-imperialism," subjecting their natural resources to too much international control and the implication that benefits would have to be shared from these resources.

The compromise reached with respect to the Biodiversity Convention (and for the Climate Change Convention, where the same issue arose) was that these address common "concerns" of humankind. Thus, for example, the Biodiversity Convention's preamble affirmed that "the conservation of biological diversity is a common concern of humankind," even though most biodiversity is found within individual nations. *See* Convention on Biological Diversity, Preamble, June 5, 1992, 31 I.L.M. 818 (1992). Common concern was accepted in part because it did not carry with it any preconceived notions of benefit sharing or of joint management.

4. In a provocative analogy, Joe Sax has asked whether the law should prevent someone who owns a Rembrandt from throwing darts at the canvas. How would you describe this situation in terms of common heritage of mankind and common concern of mankind?

5. The most controversial aspect of the Convention on Biological Diversity has not been "who owns wildlife?" but "who owns the genome and products of wildlife?" The United States did not sign the Biodiversity Convention at the time of its adoption in 1992 because of concerns over the treaty's treatment of intellectual property rights. At the same time, biodiversity-rich developing countries were concerned that multinational corporations would continue to unfairly profit from local wildlife or knowledge. Imagine, for example, that a drug company researcher travels deep into the rainforest and learns from a local shaman which plants have powerful medicinal properties. Taking back samples to America or Europe, chemists at the drug company isolate the active ingredients, allowing the company to produce a successful patented medication. If the biodiversity belongs to the host country, shouldn't the host country be compensated for its vital contribution to this successful product? Or should they have no claim on the product which, after all, would never have been developed into a drug without the technical expertise of the drug company? Article 15 of the Convention addresses these situations. Do you see how the competing interests each got something in the final negotiated text excerpted below?

1. Recognizing the sovereign rights of States over their natural resources, the authority to determine access to genetic resources rests with the national governments and is subject to national legislation.

2. Each Contracting Party shall endeavour to create conditions to facilitate access to genetic resources for environmentally sound uses by other Contracting Parties and not to impose restrictions that run counter to the objectives of this Convention. * * *

4. Access, where granted, shall be on mutually agreed terms and subject to the provisions of this Article.

5. Access to genetic resources shall be subject to prior informed consent of the Contracting Party providing such resources, unless otherwise determined by that Party.

As Note 8 at page 337 explained, bioprospecting this has not turned into the large revenue source that parties had hoped. Nonetheless, it provides an important precedent for sharing the benefits of biodiversity. The issues surrounding bioprospecting in Yellowstone Park are discussed in Chapter 6, page 614.

––––––––––

B.   POLICY INSTRUMENTS

Regardless of whether an international body, the federal government, or a state government exercises primary legal authority over wildlife, one must still decide *how* to exercise this authority. Put simply, what is the range of policy instruments available to protect wildlife? While the difficulty of conserving wildlife may have increased over time, wildlife managers throughout history have faced similar challenges. Indeed it turns out that the small set of tools available hasn't changed much. This is clearly demonstrated in the following review of historic game laws in England. While the excerpt focuses on game laws from the fourteenth century through the eighteenth century, consider how many of the policy instruments in use at that time are still in use today, albeit in a more modern form.

Chester Kirby, *The English Game Law System*
38 AMERICAN HISTORICAL REV. 240, 240–250, 256 (1933)

The game laws, which defined and protected their sporting rights, had evolved by a long process out of the Norman forest laws. The ancient forests having been privileged places for royal sport, the barons when they increased in power or when they gained the favor of the sovereign, secured special franchises for themselves.... The first clear statute of this type was written into the statute book in 1390, when all persons were forbidden to keep hunting dogs or kill "Deer, Hares, nor Conies, nor other Gentlemen's Game" unless they had real estate worth forty shilling a year, or in the case of clergy and annual income of ten pounds. This meant in effect that sport was restricted to the governing classes. * * *

[The act of 1671] authorized every lord of a manor to appoint a gamekeeper who should have the power to confiscate all paraphernalia of sport, such as guns, dogs, or nets, found in the possession of unqualified persons. For this purpose he was to search the houses of suspected persons and thus he acted somewhat as a government official.... An act of 1691 gave almost unlimited authority to keepers of deer parks to resist poachers and by a heavy fine of twenty pounds for trespass in parks ensured that most trespassers would have to suffer a year's imprisonment and an hour in the pillory for non-payment of the penalty. * * *

The sale of game having been declared illegal early in the seventeenth century, Parliament in Queen Anne's reign declared a penalty of five pounds for every head of game found in possession of any "Higlar Chapman Carrier Innkeeper Victualler or Alehouse Keeper." The twenty shilling penalty of the act of 1692 on the possession of poaching dogs or instruments was increased to five pounds. This consequently meant three or four months' imprisonment for non-payment. The killing of game at night was absolutely prohibited, qualification or no qualification. * * *

The specter of scarcity constantly threatened sport. To dispel it the country gentlemen resorted to artificial methods of preservation. Every forest and franchise had been a game preserve. Now every squire, greatly aided, no doubt, by the rapid increase of enclosures in the eighteenth century, set about raising game by artificial means.... The Duke of Richmond for a time imported more than a thousand eggs annually from France to be hatched on his estates in Sussex. Hares took care of themselves, and, when they were not killed too rapidly, sometimes accumulated in fabulous numbers. The gamekeepers made it their business to encourage in every possible way the natural multiplication of game. Vermin they killed off as thoroughly as possible. They watched the nests of the birds and often took out the eggs to be hatched more safely under common hens.

Gang poaching and professional poaching depended upon the fact that game as a commodity commanded a ready sale.... To deal with this problem the sale of game under any circumstances had been altogether prohibited since the reign of James I.... [I]n any case game was in such universal demand and was so easy to dispose of that the traffic went on growing every year, *pari passu* with the increasing quantity of game in the preserves. It became a thriving business, in which poachers, wagoners, coachmen and town poulterers linked themselves together in a vast network. It had become a regular trade in London before 1750. * * *

Still another device for enforcement the ruling class found in taxation. When William Pitt in 1784 introduced his measure for the levying of a stamp tax on gamekeepers' deputations and the right to kill game he probably had in mind only the production of revenue for the government. He was taxing everything he could think of and the game privilege seemed convenient. But most sportsmen looked upon the new duty as a new game qualification, a game law pure and simple.... From that date forward, therefore, there existed in addition to the qualifications established during the last three decades of the seventeenth century a new qualification in the form of a game tax. It meant that the government became more interested than ever before in the game system. The poacher had now in the stamp office another enemy. And the financial success of the measure led to further taxes, while defects were ironed out to insure efficiency in the collection. The cost of the certificate was increased in 1791 to three guineas. Similarly a tax on dogs was established in 1796, and by 1812 it had risen to substantial rates which could not but serve as a restriction on sport.

———

As the excerpt described, there are four basic policy approaches to wildlife conservation that have been relied on for centuries.

1.   RESTRICTING ACCESS AND TAKE

The first strategy is to *restrict access to the habitat*. While the right to pursue animals was held in common until an animal was reduced to possession, this did not allow trespass on private property. Thus many of the great royal parks in Britain owe their origin to their role as exclusive

game parks. Today, we can exclude access through public land management—designation of habitat as parks or refuges—and private land management—preservation of habitat by The Nature Conservancy and other
land trusts through outright ownership or conservation easements. These
are discussed in detail in Chapter 6. One can also limit access through
hunting seasons and permits. While income and real estate served as the
limiting factor in England, modern practices can take additional forms such
as licenses or lotteries. A related approach is to *restrict the number of game.*
This can be done directly through setting a bag limit (which for an
endangered species is often zero without a permit) or indirectly through
gear restrictions (hence the gamekeepers' confiscation of "paraphernalia of
sport . . . found in the possession of unqualified persons").

2. LANDSCAPE MANAGEMENT AND CAPTIVE BREEDING

A second popular approach focuses not on reducing hunting but,
rather, increasing game. Thus habitat may be specially managed for the
benefit of particular species. We see this in wildlife refuges and parks that
actively remove invasive species (plant and animal) that compete with
native species or that actively remove predators (such as foxes on the
Aleutian Islands). This can also take a restrictive form, when we limit
certain types of development on private land that adversely modify habitat
or disrupt essential behavioral patterns.

Much as the Duke of Richmond imported eggs from France to hatch on
his estates, fish hatcheries remain a critical management tool for many
fisheries and captive breeding is relied on for severely endangered species
such as the California Condor and the Black Rhino. Later in this chapter
we will examine a case study of reintroducing wolves into the Greater
Yellowstone ecosystem.

3. MARKET INSTRUMENTS

A third approach relies on market instruments. The game tax limited
the number of people who could legally hunt. Hunting licenses do the same
today. A more sophisticated approach can be found in tradable permits.
Access and take are restricted by law, but the rights to hunt are alienable
and can be sold in the market. This can be seen in Individual Transferable
Quotas found in fisheries throughout the world (described in detail at page
469).

4. RESTRICTING THE MARKET FOR SALE

Restricting access to habitat and taking steps to increase the number
of game are both critical to wildlife conservation, but these efforts will
continually be frustrated if there is a strong market for the wildlife. As the
excerpt makes clear, despite all the wildlife protection instruments in place
in England, there was a thriving market in poached game, and this is no
less true today. The demand for game on the dinner table has been
replaced in importance by the demands of collectors of game trophies, rare
plants and birds, traditional medicinal practices, tropical aquariums, etc.
Between 1981 and 1989, elephant populations were reduced by half mainly

due to the trade in ivory. Trade is responsible for an estimated 40% of vertebrate species facing extinction. Ironically, market forces exacerbate the threats from illegal trade for, as species become rarer, their value on the market increases to reflect this scarcity, increasing the incentive for further poaching.

This threat is addressed through *restricting the market for sale*. In New Zealand, for example, for over 100 years it has been illegal to sell fishing rights for trout, to sell trout flesh, or to farm trout. The Lacey Act, the first federal wildlife law, outlaws interstate transport of any animal killed in violation of a state law (e.g., the sale across state lines of a protected species).

International cooperation has proven necessary, as well, to respond to the growing international trade in wildlife and plants. The Convention on International Trade and Endangered Species (CITES) was adopted in 1973, and has evolved into a detailed and complex regulatory regime covering thousands of plant and animal species. CITES enjoys a broad membership of over 150 parties. In simple terms, CITES acts as a border guard, restricting the flow of rare species and parts of species across national borders. The three levels of trade restriction (depending on whether a species is listed in Appendix I, II, or III) varies from strict (no trade for Appendix I species unless both the exporting and importing countries issue permits) to more lenient (no trade unless the exporting country issues a permit) depending on the level of the threat of extinction it faces. In all, CITES protections extend to some 34,000 plant and animal species. Only when an endangered species enters the stream of international commerce do CITES restrictions become legally applicable.

QUESTIONS AND DISCUSSION

1. As described in the text, historically state fish and game agencies have worked hard to manage the environment for the benefit of hunting, fishing, and grazing interests. These efforts to promote certain populations have significantly changed the environment. From the nineteenth century until recently, for example, state agencies sponsored predator eradication efforts on behalf of ranchers who worried about their livestock, poisoning and shooting wolves and coyotes. One can argue about how significant a threat coyotes and wolves ever posed to livestock, but it's clear that removing the top predators in the ecosystem changed the nature of the system itself, allowing their prey to thrive.

David Klein's classic study of the reindeer on St. Matthew Island illustrates well how deer populations respond to an environment without predators. In 1944, 29 reindeers were moved to St. Matthew Island. The island contained no predators and there was no hunting. In just 19 years, the population exploded to 6,000 and then, within just 3 years, crashed to a total of 41 females and one male, all in poor condition. Overgrazed by the massive deer population, the island had effectively been denuded of lichen and shrubs. *See* D.R. Klein, *The Introduction, Increase and Crash of Reindeer on St. Matthew Island*, 32 J. WILDLIFE MANAGEMENT 350 (1968).

2. Fish and game agencies must not only manage the size of populations but interest conflicts, as well. Their focus has shifted to encompass not only hunting concerns but also biodiversity conservation and animal rights. Big game hunters often oppose the reintroduction of endangered predators. They spent lots of time and effort to get big game sheep back into the wild, they argue, and now must face the introduction of animals who will kill them. Or consider deer populations. Absent predators, deer herds grow until they have overgrazed the habitat, and then suffer mass starvation. One could thin the herds by allowing hunting, but animal rights groups oppose this. At the National Elk Refuge outside Jackson Hole, for example, over 10,000 elk periodically face starvation every winter and are maintained by rangers who feed them.

3. As noted in the text, New Zealand's trout fishery was established over 140 years ago for recreational fishing, and it has long been illegal to sell fishing rights for trout, to sell trout flesh, or to farm trout. Trout management has always been paid for by anglers' license fees. There are surely far fewer anglers than there are New Zealand consumers who would prefer to buy trout at the market or at a restaurant. Why do you think efforts to end the New Zealand ban on the sale of trout have failed? Does public choice theory provide an explanation (*see* page 62).

4. CITES relies on trade restrictions to shut down the trade in wildlife, but it intentionally does not address species *unless* they are in commerce. Trade measures are also used, and quite effectively, to influence how countries manage endangered species. As described in Chapter 5, for example (page 565), in the 1980s Congress amended the Marine Mammal Protection Act to ban the import of tuna unless it could be demonstrated that the tuna had been caught using "dolphin-friendly" fishing gear. The tuna fishery in the Eastern Tropical Pacific had been killing over 100,000 dolphins annually, and animal rights advocates sought to use access to the U.S. market as a lever to force change. In response, Mexico challenged the U.S. trade restriction before the General Agreement on Tariffs and Trade (GATT). The dispute panel held for Mexico, stating that a country cannot base trade restrictions on processes and production methods (known as PPMs) in violation of Articles I and III of GATT. Trade restrictions must be product-specific. If tuna that had been caught by dolphin-friendly gear was indistinguishable from tuna caught by gear with high dolphin mortality, then trade restrictions were impermissible.

A similar issue was addressed several years later, when another U.S. trade sanction was challenged before the World Trade Organization. Seeking to protect sea turtle populations, which are endangered worldwide, Congress had banned the import of shrimp unless it could be shown that the shrimp had been caught using a turtle-excluder device, an attachment to a trawl that allows turtles to escape. This law was held to violate the GATT as well, not because it was based on a PPM but, rather, because the U.S. had not adequately consulted with its trading partners before imposing the ban. This decision focused on the unilateral nature of the ban.

Given the diplomatic rows caused by such trade sanctions, why do you think Congress and large parts of the environmental community continue to promote them?

5. Despite the efforts under CITES to control international wildlife trade and numerous other treaties aimed at migratory species conservation, wildlife populations are still plummeting in many regions, sometimes from commercial exploitation but just as often from habitat destruction and other causes. Efforts to identify and protect the most important wildlife habitats, particularly for migratory species, have led to some protection through the Convention on Migratory Species, the Ramsar Convention on Wetlands of International Importance, and the UNESCO World Cultural and Natural Heritage Convention. Through increased international interest and attention, these treaties help to provide resources and build political will for the conservation of particularly important habitats. *See generally,* DAVID HUNTER ET AL., INTERNATIONAL ENVIRONMENTAL LAW AND POLICY 1002 (3rd ed., 2007).

6. While most wildlife law is found at the state level, as described in Chapter 2, the federal government has played a central role in wildlife management for over a century. Its efforts have relied on the policy instruments described above—restricting access and take, landscape management and captive breeding, market instruments, and trade restrictions. The next section focuses in detail on the Endangered Species Act, but you should be aware that a broad variety of other federal laws address wildlife protection and management. To give you a flavor of their breadth, a sample of the more important statutes are briefly described below.

The Lacey Act, 18 U.S.C. §§ 41–47, is the oldest federal wildlife law addressed to the problem of extinction. Passed in response to the extermination of the carrier pigeon and rapid population declines of other bird species, the Lacey Act strengthened state laws protecting game and birds by prohibiting the transportation of wild animals or birds killed in violation of state or territorial law. All shipments of fish and wildlife moving in interstate or foreign commerce must accurately label their contents. The prohibitions of the Act apply broadly, including all wild animals (dead or alive) as well as any part, product, egg, or offspring.

The *Migratory Bird Treaty Act of 1918*, 16 U.S.C. §§ 703–711, is one of the oldest federal wildlife laws. It covers all migratory birds protected by international conventions with Canada, Mexico, Japan, and Russia and makes it unlawful to kill, capture, collect, possess, buy, sell, ship, import, or export listed species including their parts, nests, or eggs without a permit. This law is significant because of its potential reach. Migratory birds are far more widespread than endangered species listed under the Endangered Species Act and, therefore, the Act can prevent actions that would harm species that may be threatened or endangered but not listed under the ESA. See 50 CFR 10.13.

Passed in 1940, the *Bald Eagle Protection Act*, 16 U.S.C. §§ 668–668d, imposes criminal and civil penalties on anyone who takes, possesses, sells, purchases, barters a bald or golden eagle, or any part, nest or egg of a bald or golden eagle. "Take" is defined to include acts that pursue, shoot, shoot at, poison, wound, kill, capture, trap, collect, molest, or disturb eagles. Sanctions include civil fines or criminal penalties if the violator acted knowingly or with wanton disregard of the consequences. In an interesting provision, half of the fine (not exceeding $2,500) must be paid to whoever provided information leading to conviction. The Secretary of the Interior may issue permits authorizing the taking, possession and transportation of eagles for scientific or exhibition purposes, for religious purposes of Indian tribes, or for the protection of wildlife, agricultural, or other interests. If requested by a state governor, the Secretary must also authorize the taking of golden eagles to protect domesticated flocks and herds in the state.

Described in detail in Chapter 5 (page 549), the *Marine Mammal Protection Act*, 16 U.S.C. §§ 1361–1421h, establishes a moratorium on the taking, possession, transportation, and importation of marine mammals and marine mammal products. The Secretary of Commerce may issue a permit for takes under limited circumstances. These include scientific research, public display, photography for educational or commercial use, and enhancing the survival or recovery of a species. Most of the law's application has focused on incidental takes of marine mammals in commercial fishing operations. Incidental take permits may be issued by the Secretary, so long as they are consistent with the statute's goal of reducing takes from commercial fishing to insignificant levels approaching a zero mortality.

III.   THE ENDANGERED SPECIES ACT

The most powerful federal wildlife law, and perhaps the most powerful law in the whole field of natural resource management, is the 1973 Endangered Species Act (ESA). 16 U.S.C. §§ 1531–1544. The ESA embodies America's commitment to protect wildlife by mandating the dedication of resources and the tempering of development. The ESA intersects with (and trumps) many other natural resource management regimes. Its impacts are felt literally across the country—whether through red cockaded woodpeckers in Southeastern pine forests, salmon in Pacific Northwest rivers, desert tortoises in Southwest land developments, or gray wolves in the Intermountain West.

The ESA has been called ''the pit bull'' of environmental law and it is controversial for the simple reason that it has real teeth that can bite hard, though how hard the law actually bites in practice is strongly contested. Unlike many other natural resource laws that allow environmental benefits to be balanced against social and economic costs, the basic thrust of the ESA is that species should be protected, whatever the cost. This approach raises fundamentally difficult issues. Who should bear the burden of biodiversity conservation? Which endangered species should the law protect? Does the law's very effectiveness create perverse incentives that may undermine species conservation?

The predecessors to the ESA, the Endangered Species Preservation Act of 1966 and the Endangered Species Conservation Act of 1969, had afforded wildlife some protection, but neither of these laws prohibited the taking of endangered species nor mandated that all federal agencies act to preserve endangered species. Only species threatened with worldwide extinction qualified as endangered and, nationally, only a patchwork of protections existed. Indeed, it was legal in some states to kill animals listed as endangered. Dissatisfaction with this ineffective protection, coupled with growing recognition of the role of humans in extinctions, catalyzed statutory reform.

In 1973, Congress enacted the most comprehensive species protection program ever. Given the controversy the ESA has generated, it is ironic not only that it enjoyed near-unanimous support when adopted (passing unanimously in the Senate and with only four dissenting votes in the House) but that its supporters had no inkling of the conflicts it would generate. The goals of the bill were laudable and the rhetoric lofty. The House Committee Report of the ESA of 1973 stated that the loss of species threatened our genetic heritage, concluding, "the value of this genetic heritage is, quite literally, incalculable."

In broad brush, the ESA has a fairly simple structure. The ESA first provides a mechanism for identifying and "listing" threatened and endangered species that can benefit from the Act's protections. Once listed, federal agencies have a duty to conserve listed species and ensure their recovery. Federal agencies must also ensure that their actions neither jeopardize the continued existence of a species nor adversely modify its critical habitat. Agencies are to carry out this duty in consultation with the two federal wildlife agencies—the U.S. Fish & Wildlife Service (FWS) and NOAA Fisheries—who have been given primary responsibility for implementing the ESA.[1] All actors, including federal and state governments and private parties, are prohibited from killing, harming, or otherwise "taking" listed species. To soften the impact of the ESA and provide for flexible implementation, under certain circumstances an incidental take permit can be issued that will allow the taking of listed species.

The following sections of the chapter consider each of these basic parts of the ESA, starting where the ESA starts—with listing.

A. LISTING

There are many species in the United States and abroad facing the threat of extinction. Thus, given limited resources, a threshold question for any species conservation legislation is which species get protected and which do not. Should protection only be extended to species that people "really care about," such as whales, bald eagles and other charismatic megafauna? Or should protection avoid being "species-ist," providing equal levels of protection to all creatures great and small, from elephants to slime mold? There is no objectively "correct" answer to such questions but the resource implications are significant.

Under the ESA, only species that are "listed" are subject to the Act's protection, so getting formally listed is critically important. Section 4 sets

---

1. Specifically, the ESA charges the Secretary of the Interior with primary implementation responsibility. The Secretary, in turn, has delegated much of that authority to the FWS, an agency within the Department of Interior. Marine species are under the authority of the Department of Commerce, which has delegated ESA authority to NOAA Fisheries.

out the process and provides coverage only to species that are "endangered" or "threatened." A species is endangered if it is "in danger of extinction throughout all or a significant portion of its range" and threatened if it is "likely to become an endangered species in the foreseeable future." 16 U.S.C. §§ 1532(6) & (20). The ESA defines species to include subspecies and, for vertebrates, distinct population segments that interbreed. 16 U.S.C. § 1532(15). Distinct population segments are groups of the same species that occupy geographically discrete areas (such as grizzly bears in Alaska and in Yellowstone). Subspecies may occupy the same area but be distinct because of genetics, behavior, appearance, or other factors. The earlier discussion of different types of biodiversity, page 322, explains why listing authority below the species level is important but, given that the ESA does not define the terms "subspecies" or "distinct population segments," this can make listing decisions complicated.

The listing process may be initiated by anyone who files a petition (e.g., John Doe's proposal that the magenta-bellied warbler be listed). The contentious spotted owl litigation in the Pacific Northwest, for example, first started when the owl was proposed for listing by a tiny environmental group, called "Green World," that apparently operated out of a phone booth in Massachusetts. The agency has 90 days to decide whether the petition is warranted. If so, it then has up to a year to determine whether to list the species. Importantly, the agency may not consider economic costs or benefits in its listing decision. Only scientific data relating to the species status as endangered or threatened may enter into the decision. In the *Northern Spotted Owl v. Hodel* case excerpted in Chapter 3 (page 230), for example, despite strong scientific evidence in favor of listing the spotted owl, with little explanation the FWS decided not to list the owl. The court remanded the decision as arbitrary and capricious.

While the listing procedure is simple to describe, getting a species listed is no easy matter. Some petitions are rejected at the outset. But many are pushed off. In recent years, courts have upheld the requirements that the agency determine whether a petition is warranted within ninety days and whether listing is warranted within twelve months. FWS often exceeds these statutory deadlines, but usually loses when sued and the agency is then placed on a timeline by the court. Even when listing is warranted, however, the agency often concludes that it is "warranted but precluded" and placed effectively on hold. Thus, in 2008 there was a backlog of 283 species. The current numbers for listed and candidate species may be found at http://ecos.fws.gov/tess_public/.

Challenges to this practice have usually proven unsuccessful, with courts stating agencies' decisions how to operate within resource constraints are a substantive matters meriting discretion. *See, e.g., Center for Biological Diversity v. Kempthorne*, 466 F.3d 1098 (9th Cir. 2006) (describing the requirements for making a "warranted but precluded" finding for the Sierra Nevada Mountain Yellow–Legged Frog).

Following several extremely contentious battles in the late 1980s and early 1990s such as the listing of the Northern Spotted Owl and the designation of critical habitat in the Pacific Northwest, political opposition to the ESA increased. In April of 1995, this reached a head when the 104th

Congress established a moratorium on species listing, prohibiting the expenditure of any funds on listing or critical habitat designation (there was one exception to this zero-budgeting: funds could be spent to *downlist* a species from endangered to threatened). The Ninth Circuit rejected a challenge to this moratorium, holding that refusing funds for the Secretary of the Interior to carry out his duty under the ESA was a valid exercise of congressional authority. "The use of any government resources—whether salaries, employees, paper or buildings—to accomplish a final listing would entail government expenditure. The government cannot make expenditures, and therefore cannot act, other than by appropriation." *Environmental Defense Center v. Babbitt*, 73 F.3d 867, 871–872 (9th Cir. 1995). During the moratorium, the Listing Program operated on a series of continuing resolutions while approximately 100 Service biologists had to be reassigned. When President Clinton used executive authority to waive the moratorium in 1996, a large listing backlog had accrued.

Despite President Clinton's waiver of the moratorium, Congress continued to restrict listing activities through a smaller budget appropriation than before the moratorium. With fewer funds, the Listing Program not only had to address new petitions but also deal with the growing backlog mentioned above. Since then, FWS has issued periodic Listing Priority Guidance reports that detail how species listing activities should be prioritized. These have all taken a three- or four-tiered approach to prioritizing listing actions, ranging from emergency listing actions and processing final decisions on proposed listings (Tiers 1 and 2) to new proposed listings, petition findings, and critical habitat designations (Tier 4).

QUESTIONS AND DISCUSSION

1. How can the impasse between decision making by litigation and decision making by under-funding be resolved? Environmental groups argue that the answer is simple—fund the program properly. It is worth noting, for example, that at the time the 2001 moratorium went into effect, only $6.3 million of the $1.3 billion FWS budget was dedicated to listing activities. FWS says it needs $120 million to clear a backlog of requested endangered species listings. The president and Congress, environmental groups contend, should provide what is needed to carry out the law. Clearly, though, there has been little if any political price to pay for under-resourcing the listing process. Is this consistent with the strong public opposition that confronts congressional attempts to weaken the ESA through legislative amendment?

2. A March 2008 story in the *Washington Post* reported that the George W. Bush administration had made it substantially more difficult to list species. In the first seven years of his administration, the paper reported, 59 domestic species had been listed—roughly the same number listed *annually* during the first Bush administration in 1992 and the Clinton administration. Critics charged that this dramatic reduction was due to the creation of bureaucratic obstacles, including:

- considering only where candidate species live now rather than where they used to exist,

- rating threats to species based on international populations rather than their U.S. populations (thus, for example, deciding that the wolverine and jaguar should not be listed because there are populations in Canada and Mexico),

- refusing to consider citizen petitions if the agency had already identified the species as a listing candidate (this policy was overturned in a 2003 case),

- and a policy that FWS "files on proposed listings should include only evidence from the petitions and any information in agency records that could undercut, rather than support, a decision to list a species" (in other words, FWS information can be used to undercut but not support listing proposals)

Juliet Eilperin, *Since '01, Guarding Species Is Harder: Endangered Listings Drop Under Bush,* WASHINGTON POST, March 23, 2008 at A1.

In addition, the Department of Interior carried out an internal investigation in 2007 over allegations that Julie MacDonald, Deputy Assistant Secretary for Fish, Wildlife, and Parks at the Department of the Interior, had "bullied, insulted, and harassed the professional staff of the U.S. Fish and Wildlife Service (FWS) to change documents and alter biological reporting regarding the Endangered Species Program." The investigation found that MacDonald, who had no formal training in science, had "been heavily involved with editing, commenting on, and reshaping the Endangered Species Program's scientific reports from the field." The investigation did not suggest MacDonald had committed illegal acts and reached no conclusions whether her behavior was inappropriate. The report cited a number of cases where MacDonald had demanded that reports be altered or include scientific information she had independently collected. *See generally,* DEPARTMENT OF THE INTERIOR, OFFICE OF INSPECTOR GENERAL, REPORT OF INVESTIGATION OF JULIE MACDONALD (2007).

In response to the *Washington Post* article, FWS officials admit that over 280 species are warranted but precluded, but charge that they have been hamstrung by lawsuits against the agency. There certainly was more litigation against FWS than in past administrations—369 listing suits against the Bush FWS compared to 184 suits against the Clinton administration.

Politics seems unavoidable in listing decisions, whether in terms of which scientific data to use or the simple policies for how listing decisions are made within the agency. Is there a way to control politically motivated decisions in the listing process? Would greater transparency help in this regard? Do you think property rights advocates would have been just as critical of listing decisions during the Clinton administration as environmental groups were of the Bush administration?

3. Decisions not to list a species or that listing is "warranted but precluded" are subject to judicial review under the "arbitrary and capricious" standard of the Administrative Procedure Act. We saw an example of this in the Spotted Owl case in Chapter 3 (page 230), where the court remanded the agency's decision not to list. Do you think that *positive* decisions to list a species should be eligible for court challenge?

4. Do you think insects that harm crops or other "pests" that are endangered should be eligible for listing under the ESA? How do you think the ESA treats this class of insects?

CASE STUDY: SHOULD THE PRAIRIE DOG BE LISTED?

A longstanding listing decision that continues to generate controversy concerns the prairie dog. While there are five species of prairie dog, the Utah prairie dog is the only one listed under the ESA. The Black-tailed prairie dog has the widest distribution and occurs from Alberta to Mexico in the short grass and mid-grass prairies east of the continental Divide. Prairie dogs were the focus of a federally-sponsored eradication campaign early in the twentieth century to reduce suspected competition for forage between prairie dogs and domestic livestock. Prairie dogs are also susceptible to an exotic disease introduced from Asia, sylvatic plague, which is fatal to infected prairie dogs. As a result of hunting and disease, Black-tailed prairie dogs have been reduced to 1–2% of their original distribution and occur in isolated small populations throughout their former range (they have been fully eradicated only in Arizona).

This population decline has spurred efforts to list Black-tailed prairie dogs under the ESA. In response to a petition to list the prairie dog by the National Wildlife Foundation and a later petition by the Biodiversity Legal Foundation and the Predator Conservation Alliance, however, the FWS announced in February 4, 2000, that such a listing as threatened was warranted but precluded due to other listing priorities.

Supporters for listing contend that prairie dogs are keystone species of grass and shrub habitats, creating the conditions necessary for the survival of many other species including, most notably, the Black-footed ferret. Indeed, Black-footed ferrets are entirely dependent on large prairie dog colonies and because there are so few remaining colonies, ferrets have nearly become extinct. Prairie dog burrows provide valuable habitat for many other species such as burrowing owls and Mountain Plovers. They also are prey for important species such as coyotes, bobcats, eagles, hawks, badgers, and weasels.

Strong opposition to the protection of prairie dogs under the ESA has come from ranchers and other large landowners who contend that prairie dog holes reduce grazing for their livestock. Studies, though, indicate that the actual competition is much less than generally perceived and that in many cases cattle preferentially graze on prairie dog colonies. Most ranchers remain unconvinced by these studies and continue to argue that cattle or horses can break their legs by stepping in prairie dog burrows (an assertion environmental groups say has never been documented). Listing is also widely opposed by individuals and organizations involved in prairie dog (or "varmint") shooting. Prior to the listing petition, most states had little or no regulations restricting such shooting and prairie dogs were not subject to regulation by state fish and game departments. Instead, prairie dogs were managed as "pest species" by state agricultural agencies.

Following the positive (warranted but precluded) finding for listing prairie dogs, an eleven-state Prairie Dog Conservation Team was formed with the support of the Fish and Wildlife Foundation, and the Western Association of Fish and Wildlife Agencies. Seeking to avoid a listing by improving their management of prairie dogs, the states developed a conservation strategy that included recommended acreage of prairie dog habitat for each state and various standardized management and inventory practices. Under this multi-state umbrella, many of the participating states developed, for the first time, management plans for Black-tailed prairie dogs. The Fish and Wildlife Service has assisted these efforts by promoting Candidate Conservation Agreements with Assurances, which would allow states meeting certain standards in Black-tailed prairie dog conservation to be immunized from the effects of a listing decision. Most states, however, have not been interested in such agreements. The FWS has also worked hard to develop programs under the farm bill that would permit landowners to receive subsidies for maintaining prairie dogs on their lands.

Since the listing petition was filed, about half of the states have adopted management plans that will improve the status of prairie dogs. Under pressures from their state legislatures and fish and game commissions, other states such as Nebraska and Wyoming have been prohibited from developing management plans. All states have completed surveys that indicate the existence of more prairie dogs than were previously known. Based on this, the multi-state prairie dog conservation team has asked the FWS to remove Black-tailed prairie dogs from their list of candidate species. This request remains under review by the FWS. The Union of Concerned Scientists has charged that determinations by agency scientists to list prairie dog species have been overruled by political appointees. *See Systematic Interference with Science at Interior Department Exposed: Emails and Edited Documents Show Evidence of manipulation* <http://www.ucsusa.org/scientific_integrity/interference/endangered-species-act-interference.html>.

Although the prairie dog population is now at 1–2% of historical levels, there are still well over a million individual prairie dogs. Why do you think environmental groups are pushing to protect a species when there are over a million individuals in multiple habitats? If biodiversity conservation were the broader goal of these groups, how would listing prairie dogs under the ESA help achieve this? Is using individual listings to achieve landscape habitat management an appropriate use of the ESA?

––––––––

CASE STUDY: SHOULD HATCHERY SALMON BE LISTED?

Pacific salmon are among the most fascinating fish on earth. Originally found in almost every river between Monterey, California, and Alaska's Bering Peninsula, salmon are anadromous fish. They are born in freshwater, migrate to the ocean as tiny smolt—2 to 6 inches in length—where they live out their lives, only to return as they near death back to their freshwater birthplace to spawn. What is perhaps most remarkable is the Salmons' tenacity to fight back up the rivers to their place of their birth. Salmon born in Idaho's Sawtooth Mountains, for example, must traverse over 900 miles of river, winding their way from creeks and streams down the Snake River and finally into the mighty Columbia as they make their way to and from the ocean. On their way back the salmon relentlessly fight their way over obstacle after obstacle, in some cases leaping waterfalls. Describing a salmon run at Willamette Falls in 1841, Captain Charles Wilkes wrote:

The salmon leap the fall; and it would be inconceivable, if not actually witnessed, how they can force themselves up, and after a leap of from ten to twelve feet retain strength enough to stem the force of the water above. About one in ten of those who jumped, would succeed in getting by. They are seen to dart out of the foam beneath and reach about two-thirds of the height, at a single bound: those that thus passed the apex of the running water, succeed; but all that fell short, were thrown back again into the foam.

CHARLES F. WILKINSON, CROSSING THE NEXT MERIDIAN: LAND, WATER, AND THE FUTURE OF THE WEST 180–84 (1992) (quoting Wilkes and telling the story of the salmon's homeward journey). *See generally id.* at 175–218 (discussing history of salmon in the Northwest, particularly in relation to the Indian tribes' cultural and economic reliance on the salmon fishery). These magnificent salmon were once abundant. Professor Wilkinson relates:

> The size of the historical run was nothing short of fabulous. When the Lewis and Clark expedition crossed the Divide, moving down the Clearwater to the Snake and the Columbia, they were astonished by what they saw. Among many other comments in his journal, William Clark wrote that the river "was crouded with salmon." As one chronicler of the expedition commented, "[t]hey had never witnessed such a piscatorial spectacle before and would never again." John Muir, during his travels in the Alaska panhandle, observed, "The stream was so filled with them there seemed to be more fish than water in it, and we appeared to be sailing in boiling, seething silver light marvelously relieved in the jet darkness."
>
> A common metaphor in the early reports is that salmon were so thick that a person could cross a stream by walking across their backs.

Id. at 184. With the arrival of European–Americans, however, the fabulous salmon runs of the Columbia and Snake Rivers began a long, slow decline. The first great hit to salmon populations was the commercial salmon fishery and the advent of canning, which allowed as many salmon as could be harvested to be shipped eastward for sale. Later, it was the great dams along the Columbia and Snake Rivers. In some cases, as with Grand Coulee, the dams simply closed off all upstream salmon runs. Other dams included fish ladders, but even those dams were fish killers. Among other problems, salmon smolt are killed in turbines and they are subject to increased predation in the slackwater reservoirs that form behind dams in place of the free-flowing river. In addition to the dams and the commercial fishery, salmon are impacted by agriculture and logging which can cause increased siltation of the gravel beds that need to be clean for salmon to successfully spawn. Today, according to the American Fisheries Society, "[o]f 192 Columbia River stocks, 35 percent are extinct, 19 percent are at high risk for extinction, 7 percent are at moderate for extinction, 13 percent are of special concern, and only 26 percent are considered to be secure." Defenders of Wildlife, *Salmon Dam Dilemmas, quoting from* JIM LICHATOWICH, SALMON WITHOUT RIVERS: A HISTORY OF THE PACIFIC SALMON CRISIS (1999).

Because the dams bring water for irrigation and hydropower for cheap electricity, and because fishing, forestry, and farming are important component of the traditional economy in the Northwest, salmon have tended to take a backseat to river development. Despite a variety of proposals to tear down some of the dams on the Snake River and to spill more water so that smolt will be able to move through predator-infested reservoirs more quickly, the traditional solution to salmon issues, in use for over a century, has been salmon hatcheries. Each year, more than a billion salmon are raised in hatcheries and then placed in the river systems. In fact, because the juvenile salmon continue to struggle to make it downstream, each year many are recaught at dams, placed in barges or trucks, and shipped downriver beyond the last dam, at which point they are dumped back into the Columbia.

Despite the massive hatchery program, and some would argue in part because of the program, natural salmon stocks continue to decline, resulting in a number of salmon species being listed under the ESA. As discussed earlier in the text, the ESA defines species to include subspecies and distinct population segments that interbreed, 16 U.S.C. § 1532(15), but the lack of a definition for subspecies and distinct populations segments has spawned a good deal of controversy. One of the more prominent examples of that controversy relates to a listing of the coho salmon. In 1995, the National Marine Fisheries Service (NMFS) proposed listing the "Oregon Coast Evolutionary Significant Unit coho salmon" as threatened but did not include in its listing consideration coho raised in hatcheries. NMFS' decision was challenged in the case that follows.

ALSEA VALLEY ALLIANCE v. EVANS,
161 F. Supp. 2d 1154 (D. Or. 2001)

HOGAN, DISTRICT JUDGE.

On August 10, 1998, the National Marine Fisheries Services ("NMFS") published its final rule listing the Oregon Coast Evolutionary Significant Unit ("ESU") coho salmon as "threatened" pursuant to the Endangered Species Act ("ESA"), 16 U.S.C. §§ 1531, *et seq.* Plaintiffs bring this action challenging the validity of the listing decision....

I. *Background* * * *

Section 4(a) of the ESA commits to the Secretary of Commerce ("Secretary") the responsibility of determining whether certain species are "endangered" or "threatened." The Secretary has delegated this authority to the NMFS. * * *

When determining whether a species is "endangered" or "threatened," the NMFS must consider five statutorily prescribed factors: 1) "the present or threatened destruction ... of its habitat"; 2) the "overutilization" of the species by humans; 3) disease or predation pressures; 4) "the inadequacy of existing regulatory mechanisms"; and 5) "other natural or manmade factors affecting" the continued existence of the species. 16 U.S.C. § 1533(a). This determination is to be made "solely on the basis of the best scientific and commercial data available to [the Secretary]." 16 U.S.C. § 1533(b)(1)(A).

The ESA defines "species" to include "any subspecies of fish or wildlife or plants, and any *distinct population segment* of any species of vertebrate fish or wildlife which interbreeds when mature." 16 U.S.C. § 1532(16) (emphasis added). Congress did not define the term "distinct population segment" ("DPS") and the ESA does not set forth any restrictive criteria for defining a DPS.

Beginning in 1991, NMFS issued various policies that interpreted the ESA and its DPS provision, relevant to the Pacific salmon. NMFS eventually applied these policies to the coho salmon in its August 10, 1998, listing decision.

On November 20, 1991, NMFS issued its "Policy on Applying the Definition of Species Under the Endangered Species Act to Pacific Salmon" (hereinafter the "ESU Policy"). 56 Fed.Reg. 58,612 (1991). In the ESU Policy, NMFS introduced the term "evolutionary significant unit" ("ESU") to interpret the ESA's meaning of "distinct population segment." 56 Fed.Reg. at 58,613 (Nov. 20, 1991). NMFS explained:

> a stock of Pacific salmon will be considered a distinct population, and hence a "species" under the ESA, if it represents an Evolutionary significant unit (ESU) of the biological species. A stock must satisfy two criteria to be considered an ESU:
>
> > (1) It must be substantially reproductively isolated from other conspecific population units; and
> >
> > (2) It must represent an important component in the evolutionary legacy of the species.

56 Fed.Reg. at 58,618.

NMFS states that the first criterion can be measured "by movements of tagged fish, recolonization rates of other populations, measurements of genetic differences between populations, and evaluations of the efficacy of natural barriers." *Id.*

The second criterion is concerned with the "ecological/genetic diversity" of the species as a whole. *Id.* NMFS states that the following questions are relevant in determining whether this criterion is met 1) is the population genetically distinct from other conspecific populations, 2) does the population occupy unusual or distinctive habitat, 3) does the population show evidence of unusual or distinctive adaptation to its environment. *Id.*

On April 5, 1993, the NMFS published its policy entitled "Interim Policy on Artificial Propagation of Pacific Salmon Under the Endangered Species Act" (the "Hatchery Policy"). 58 Fed.Reg. 17,573 (1993). The Hatchery Policy describes how the NMFS considers hatchery populations when making listing decisions about the Pacific salmon. The Hatchery Policy interprets the ESA as requiring NMFS to focus its recovery efforts on "natural populations." The Hatchery Policy builds upon this cornerstone interpretation with the position that "artificial propagation *may* represent a potential method to conserve listed salmon species when the artificially propagated fish are determined similar to the listed natural population in genetic, phenotypic, and life-history traits, and in habitat use characteristics." 58 Fed.Reg. at 17,573–74 (April 5, 1993) (emphasis added). Although hatchery populations may be included as part of a listed species, NMFS policy is that it should be done sparingly because artificial propagation could pose risks to natural populations.[2] *Id.* at 17,575. Thus, the Hatchery Policy states:

> [I]f available information indicates that existing hatchery fish can be considered part of the biological ESU, a decision must be made whether to include them as part of the listed species. *In general, such fish will not be*

---

2. The Hatchery Policy defines "risks" to natural populations in terms of genetics, such as the loss of genetic diversity that could lead to greater in- stances of disease and/or the inability of natural populations to survive relative to hatchery populations. 58 Fed.Reg. 17,574.

included as part of the listed species. An exception may be made for existing hatchery fish if they are considered to be essential for recovery.

Id. at 17,575 (emphasis added).

NMFS excludes hatchery populations from its listing decision unless the hatchery population can be considered part of the ESU and the NMFS considers the hatchery population "essential to recovery." *Id.* at 17,575. Although the phrase "essential to recovery" is not specifically defined, NMFS gives the examples of a natural population facing a "high, short-term risk of extinction, or if the hatchery population is believed to contain a substantial proportion of the genetic diversity remaining in the species." *Id.*

...[On] August 10, 1998, NMFS issued a final rule listing the Oregon Coast coho ESU as threatened. 63 Fed.Reg. 42,587 (Aug. 10, 1998). However, within this ESU, NMFS only listed all "naturally spawned" coho inhabiting streams between Cape Blanco and the Columbia River. *Id.* In reaching this listing decision, NMFS applied its April 5, 1993 Hatchery Policy to the coho salmon. 63 Fed.Reg. 42,589. NMFS concluded that nine Oregon hatchery populations were part of the same Oregon Coast ESU as the natural populations. However, the hatchery populations were not included in the listing decision because the hatchery populations were not "deemed 'essential' to recovery." *Id.* Although excluded from the listing decision, NMFS stated that it might consider using these hatchery populations for future recovery but that "in this context, an 'essential' hatchery population is one that is vital for full incorporation into recovery efforts." *Id.*

Plaintiffs seek to invalidate the August 10, 1998 listing decision. Plaintiff's central argument is that NMFS' distinction between "naturally spawned" and "hatchery spawned" coho salmon is arbitrary and capricious and thus unlawful under the Administrative Procedures Act ("APA") 5 U.S.C. § 706. * * *

III. *Discussion*

...Plaintiffs argue that the distinction between hatchery spawned and naturally spawned coho is untenable under the ESA because the ESA does not allow the Secretary to make listing distinctions below that of species, subspecies or a distinct population segment of a species. Essentially, plaintiffs argue that the Secretary, in this instance, must include or exclude all members of a distinct population segment, as opposed to only some members of a distinct population segment. Defendants argue that the distinction between hatchery coho and natural coho is valid because the NMFS interpretation of the ESA, and in particular its interpretation of a "distinct population segment," should be afforded great deference by this court.

After reviewing the administrative record and the relevant statutes and legislative history, the court finds that the NMFS August 10, 1998 listing decision is arbitrary and capricious and therefore invalid because it relied on factors upon which Congress did not intend the NMFS to rely. The NMFS decision defines the ESU and thus DPS, but then takes an additional step, beyond its definition of an ESU, to eliminate hatchery coho from its listing decision.

NMFS defined a "distinct population segment" by making it the equivalent of a term (it created) called an "evolutionary significant unit" ("ESU"). A species is considered an ESU, and hence a DPS, if it is "substantially reproductively isolated from other conspecific population units" and "represent[s] an important component in the evolutionary legacy of the species." 56 Fed.Reg. at 58,618.

The NMFS interpretation of what constitutes a "distinct population segment" is a permissible agency construction of the ESA. *See PanAmSat Corp. v. Federal Communications Comm'n,* 198 F.3d 890, 894 (D.C. Cir. 1999) (citing *Chevron U.S.A., Inc. v. NRDC,* 467 U.S. 837, 842–43 (1984) (court must defer to a permissible agency construction of a statute)). Specifically, the NMFS creation of an ESU and the factors used to define it, geography and genetics, are within permissible limits under the ESA.

The central problem with the NMFS listing decision of August 10, 1998, is that it makes improper distinctions, below that of a DPS, by excluding hatchery coho populations from listing protection even though they are determined to be part of the same DPS as natural coho populations.

The ESA "specifically states in the definition of 'species' that a 'species' may include any subspecies. . . . and any distinct population segment (DPS) of any species . . . which interbreeds when mature." 16 U.S.C. § 1532(16); *Southwest Center for Biological Diversity v. Babbitt,* 980 F.Supp. 1080, 1085 (D.Ariz. 1997). Listing distinctions below that of subspecies or a DPS of a species are not allowed under the ESA. *Southwest Center,* 980 F.Supp. at 1085. Yet, this is precisely what the NMFS did in its final listing decision of August 10, 1998. NMFS concluded that nine hatchery stocks were part of the same Oregon Coast ESU/DPS as the "natural" populations but none of the hatchery stocks were included in the listing decision because NMFS did not consider them "essential for recovery." 63 Fed.Reg. 42,589.

The distinction between members of the same ESU/DPS is arbitrary and capricious because NMFS may consider listing only an *entire* species, subspecies or distinct population segment ("DPS") of any species. 16 U.S.C. § 1532(16). Once NMFS determined that hatchery spawned coho and naturally spawned coho were part of the same DPS/ESU, the listing decision should have been made without further distinctions between members of the same DPS/ESU.

The NMFS listing decision could arguably be proper under the ESA if the NMFS had defined "hatchery spawned" coho as a separate DPS, but it does not appear that this is possible. To classify hatchery spawned coho as a DPS under NMFS's own standard, hatchery spawned coho would have to be 1) "substantially reproductively isolated from other conspecific population units," and 2) "represent an important component in the evolutionary legacy of the species." 56 Fed.Reg. at 58,618. Here, hatchery spawned coho are likely not "substantially reproductively isolated" from naturally spawned coho because, once released from the hatchery, it is undisputed that "hatchery spawned" coho and "naturally spawned" coho within the Oregon Coast ESU share the same rivers, habitat and seasonal runs. It is undisputed that "hatchery spawned" coho may account for as much as 87% of the naturally spawning coho in the Oregon coast ESU. In addition, hatchery spawned and natural coho are the same species, and interbreed when mature. Finally, the NMFS considers progeny of hatchery fish that are born in the wild as "naturally spawned" coho that deserve listing protection.

Despite these facts, NMFS decided that hatchery coho, that are part of the same DPS/ESU as natural coho, should not be listed because they were not "essential" to recovery. Thus, the NMFS listing decision creates the unusual circumstance of two genetically identical coho salmon swimming side-by-side in the same stream, but only one receives ESA protection while the other does not. The distinction is arbitrary.

Finally, NMFS argues that its listing decision does not contradict the terms of the ESA because the listing decision, and relevant polices, are in accordance with ESA goals that prioritize "natural" salmon populations and "genetic diversity" within those populations. Although I agree with the general concept that "genetic diversity" is one factor in the long term success of a threatened species, and thus is one of many underlying goals of the ESA, genetics cannot, by itself, justify a listing distinction that runs contrary to the definition of a DPS.

The term "distinct population segment" was amended in the ESA in 1978 so that it "would exclude taxonomic [biological] categories below subspecies [smaller taxa] from the definition." H.R. CONF. REP. NO. 95–1804, at 17 (1978), *reprinted in* 1978 U.S.C.C.A.N. 9485, 14855.

Congress adopted the DPS language stating:

The committee agrees that there may be instances in which [the Fish and Wildlife Service] should provide for different levels of protection for populations of the same species. For instance, the U.S. population of an animal should not necessarily be permitted to become extinct simply because the animal is more abundant elsewhere in the world. Similarly, listing populations may be necessary when the preponderance of evidence indicates that a species faces a widespread threat, but conclusive data is available with regard to only certain populations.

S. Rep. No. 96–151.

Thus, Congress expressly limited the Secretary's ability to make listing distinctions among species below that of subspecies or a DPS of a species. Here, the NMFS listing decision was based on distinctions below that of subspecies or distinct population segment of a species.

Therefore, the NMFS's listing decision is arbitrary and capricious, because the Oregon Coast ESU includes both "hatchery spawned" and "naturally spawned" coho salmon, but the agency's listing decision arbitrarily excludes "hatchery spawned" coho. Consequently, the listing decision is unlawful. 5 U.S.C. § 706(2)(A).

IV. *Conclusion*

For the foregoing reasons, plaintiffs' motion for summary judgment is granted. Defendants' cross-motion for summary judgment is denied. The August 10, 1998 NMFS listing decision, contained at 63 Fed.Reg. 42,587, is declared unlawful and set aside as arbitrary and capricious. The matter is remanded to the NMFS for further consideration consistent with this opinion. The agency is further directed to consider the best available scientific information, including the most recent data, in any further listing decision concerning the Oregon coast coho salmon.

QUESTIONS AND DISCUSSION

1. Plaintiff, the Alsea Valley Alliance, is a property rights group opposed to listing the salmon. Why would it have brought this lawsuit seeking to include hatchery fish within the coho listing? What part did this litigation play in its overall strategy to oppose the listing?

2. Why do you think NMFS' hatchery policy provided that hatchery fish would generally not be included as part of a listed species unless "essential for recovery"? Is consideration of whether their inclusion is "essential for recovery" a legitimate listing criteria under the ESA?

3. Could NMFS have based its decision on population size not on the number of fish leaving the river but, rather, the number *returning* to spawn from the ocean? This approach would make no distinction between the fish origins. The focus would instead be on the ability of a fish stock to survive naturally in the wild and return to spawn. *See, Oregon Trollers Ass'n v. Gutierrez,* 2005 WL 2211084 (D. Or. 2005), for a similar analysis in a Magnuson–Stevens Fishery Conservation and Management Act case.

4. What were the potential implications of this decision for salmon in the Northwest? A commentator on this case later dramatically wrote that the decision "has put nearly all other Pacific salmon and steelhead listings . . . in doubt." Brian J. Perron, *Just Another Goldfish Down The Toilet? The Fate of Pacific Salmon After Alsea Valley and the De Facto Rescission of The 4(D) Rule,* 33 ENVTL. L. 547 (2003). Why did he fear the case could have such significant impact?

In the aftermath of the case, the Bush administration's Commerce Department declined to appeal the decision and instead decided to review the listing of 23 other salmon species to determine whether listing is still warranted. *Id.* at 549. In 2004, NMFS circulated a draft revision of the Hatchery Listing Policy (HLP). This generated a great deal of public interest, and NMFS held fourteen public hearings across the Pacific Northwest and California as well as soliciting technical review of its policy from over 50 independent experts from a variety of sectors. In all, there were over 27,000 comments submitted. The final HLP directed that so long as the fish were sufficiently genetically similar, hatchery fish and naturally spawning would be considered the same species for listing purposes. As a result, NMFS downlisted a steelhead population that inhabits the Upper Columbia River from endangered to threatened.

This was challenged in the case, *Trout Unlimited v. Lohn,* 2007 WL 1730090 (W.D. Wash. 2007). In its decision, the district court disagreed with the earlier *Alsea* decision, arguing that it neglected the importance of maintaining natural populations.

> [T]he record demonstrates that a healthy hatchery population is not necessarily an indication of a healthy natural population, and that in actuality, a healthy hatchery population can negatively affect the viability of a natural population. The scientific consensus is that artificial propagation has the potential to have either beneficial or deleterious effects on natural populations. Moreover, the possible negative effects of hatchery stocks on wild populations are scientifically well-established [citing studies that hatchery salmon have adverse impacts on wild stocks through interbreeding, ecological interactions in fresh water and mixed-stock fisheries.] . . . Thus, measuring the health of a salmon population by reference to the combined hatchery and natural populations does not necessarily provide an appropriate assessment of whether the natural population is on its way to becoming self-sustaining without human interference, and indeed, a healthy hatchery population may mask or obscure the decline of a natural population. Furthermore, the best available scientific evidence indicates that long-term reliance on hatcheries is at best an unproven strategy for the long-term conservation of a species or population, and may make its prospects for becoming self-sustaining more difficult with the passage of time. * * *
>
> Though it scarcely seems open to debate, the Court concludes that in evaluating any policy or listing determination under the ESA, its polestar must be the

viability of naturally self-sustaining populations in their naturally-occurring habitat. That the purpose of the ESA is to promote populations that are self-sustaining without human interference can be deduced from the statute's emphasis on the protection and preservation of the habitats of endangered and threatened species. The protection of the ecosystems upon which endangered and threatened species depend is explicitly recited as the statute's purpose... The Court concludes that the central purpose of the ESA, and the organizing principle upon which ESA listing determinations must be made, is the protection and promotion of endangered and threatened species to the point of being naturally self-sustaining... [As a result], the HLP is fatally deficient because it shifts status determinations away from the benchmark of naturally self-sustaining populations that is required under the ESA.

The Court held that the HLP and Upper Columbia River steelhead listing violated the ESA, requiring NMFS to follow the earlier Interim Hatchery Policy (which regarded the Upper Columbia River steelhead ESU as endangered) until a new HLP was developed. As this casebook was going to the printer, the Ninth Circuit had not resolved this district court split. Which decision, *Alsea* or *Trout Unlimited,* do you think the Court should favor? Recent developments can be tracked on the NMFS website at <http://www.nwr.noaa.gov/ESA–Salmon–Listings/Salmon–Populations/Al sea-Response/>.

5. If hatcheries can produce coho salmon that look and taste the same as natural salmon, is there any legitimate reason to prefer the natural salmon? Why might it be important to distinguish between natural and hatchery coho salmon in order to maintain genetic diversity? To answer this question you may wish to review the discussion of biodiversity at page 321.

B. DESIGNATION OF CRITICAL HABITAT

The ESA's focus on single-species conservation was not novel. Its attempts to protect both the species *and* its habitat, however, was an important innovation. During the ESA hearings, speaker after speaker emphasized the importance of habitat in efforts to protect and restore species. Section 5 of the Act responded to these concerns by providing for government purchase of habitat. However, Section 5 did not entirely address the habitat protection issues raised during the hearings. As a Department of Agriculture representative argued at the time: "Fundamental to the survival of any species, habitat describes the food and shelter requirements which enable species to reproduce and sustain viable populations; frequently these requirements are quite specific." 1973 House ESA Hearings on H.R. 37 and H.R. 1461 Before the Subcomm. on Merchant Marine and Fisheries, 93d Cong., 1st Sess. 236 (1973) (statement of Ray Housley, Associate Deputy Chief, U.S. Forest Service). The ESA embodied the belief that a discrete habitat, a "critical habitat," could be identified and protected for each listed species. Importantly, this added a spatial dimension to species protection, allowing a map to be developed of critically important areas. You can see such maps in the Code of Federal Regulations at 50 C.F.R. § 17.84 (2007).

Once a species has been listed, the agency is required to designate the species' critical habitat within one year. As with the listing decision, critical habitat designation originally was confined solely to scientific considerations. As we shall see in the next section, however, the *TVA v. Hill* decision caused a huge uproar, and one of its results was that the 1978 amendments to the ESA required the agency explicitly to consider economic factors when designating critical habitat. This stands in dramatic contrast with listing decisions, which, as described above, as purely scientific decisions explicitly may *not* consider economic factors.

In addition, the agency may decline to designate critical habitat if it is "not prudent" to do so or if the habitat is "not determinable." Both because of resource constraints and the controversy aroused by designation, the agency has not been eager to designate critical habitat. Thus it's not surprising that in 2008, critical habitat had been designated for roughly one in four domestic listed species. Citing concerns that maps revealing the locations of species would raise threats of vandalism, taking, collectors, and tourism, FWS has typically concluded that designation would not be "prudent." In some instances, a critical habitat map may well provide the equivalent of a treasure map for a collector or vandal (especially in the case of plants such as cacti) though it seems unlikely to the case for most species.

With critical habitat as a lowest-tier priority, in the late 1990s the Department of Interior declined as a matter of policy to designate critical habitat for species. It argued that designation of critical habitat provided no additional benefit beyond the protections available through Section 7's prohibitions on agency actions that "jeopardize" listed species. Section 7, which is discussed in section D below, requires federal agencies to "insure" that their actions are "not likely to jeopardize the continued existence" of a species or "result in the destruction or adverse modification of [the critical] habitat of such species." 16 U.S.C. § 1536(a)(2). In Interior's view, there would be very few, if any, examples of adverse modification of critical habitat that did not cause jeopardy. And even if there were any such instances, the cost of designating critical habitat consumed too much of the Department's ESA resources with little evident benefit. Consider, for example, that critical habitat designation can cost up to $500,000 per species out of a listing budget of a few million dollars.

A review of Section 7 cases suggested that the Secretary's position had some merit.

> [T]his synthesis of critical habitat and jeopardy is found throughout section 7 case law, for there appear to be no successful section 7 cases finding adverse modification of critical habitat without also finding jeopardy. The two section 7 protections have collapsed into a unified prohibition primarily because the two standards are redundant. Michael J. Bean, Chairman of the Wildlife Program at the Environmental Defense Fund, argues that "the adverse modification of any area that is in fact essential to the conservation of a listed species (whether it has been designated critical habitat or not) will also necessarily jeopardize the continued existence of that species." In fact, the regulatory definitions of these two standards both prohibit actions that appreciably diminish or reduce the likelihood of the survival and recovery of a listed species. Of the two prohibi-

tions, jeopardy encompasses more than critical habitat, for it follows the species wherever it moves.

James Salzman, *The Evolution and Application of Critical Habitat Under the Endangered Species Act,* 14 HARV. ENVTL. L. REV. 311, 326 (1990). But other species advocates have argued that critical habitat designation can provide important practical benefits. They contend, for example, that critical habitat has evolved into an important catalyst, a judicial red flag, to jeopardy violations. Critical habitat makes endangered species protection *spatial* and easier to understand. In practice, once an action occurs in a critical habitat it is subject to closer scrutiny. Moreover, proving adverse modification of critical habitat is much easier as an evidentiary matter.

> As Donald Carr, former Acting Assistant Attorney General in the Justice Department's Land and Natural Resources Division states: "Critical habitat does have advocacy value. It helps the prosecutor by getting rid of the necessity of showing the steps to jeopardy." The term "critical habitat" also has great rhetorical value for environmental groups outside of the courtroom. Michael Bean of the Environmental Defense Fund remarks: "It's easier for The Nature Conservancy to raise money if they can say, 'we're not just purchasing ordinary habitat, we're purchasing critical habitat.'"

Id. at 330.

However sensible from a budget allocation perspective, failure to designate habitat made FWS and NMFS an easy target for litigation, with environmental groups regularly winning in the courtroom. *See, e.g., Sierra Club v. United States Fish & Wildlife Service,* 245 F.3d 434 (5th Cir. 2001) (rejecting NMFS's argument that designation of critical habitat for the Gulf Sturgeon Services would provide no additional benefit to the sturgeon beyond the protections available through jeopardy consultation). Such "decision making by litigation," however, has created its own set of problems, placing the agency in the untenable position of complying with court orders while trying to chart its own course. The excerpt below from the 2000 Listing Priority Guidance makes this conflict clear.

> The numerous statutory responsibilities we bear under the Act do not come with an unlimited budget. We are sometimes required to make difficult choices about how to prioritize carrying out those statutory responsibilities in order to make the best use of our limited resources. Under these circumstances, technical compliance with the various sections of the Act with respect to one species can mean failure to comply with the other technical requirements of the Act for the same or another species. This guidance is part of a continuing effort to strive to achieve compliance with the Act in the manner that best fulfills the spirit of the Act, using our best scientific expertise. Individuals or organizations occasionally bring suit against us for failing to carry out specific actions with regard to specific species. Many of these suits question our judgment and priorities, and seek compliance with the Act in circumstances that do not, in our judgment, lead to the best use of our resources to provide the maximum conservation benefit to all species. In many of the outstanding Section 4 matters currently in litigation, the effect of what the plaintiff seeks is to require us to postpone or sacrifice conservation actions that we believe would have major conservation benefits in favor of actions that we believe would have lesser conservation benefits. In no case will we adjust our biological priorities to reflect the threat of litigation. We have sought and will continue to seek from

the courts recognition of our need to allocate our limited listing budget so as to best fulfill the spirit of the Act. We will, of course, comply with all court orders.

2000 Listing Priority Guidance, 64 Fed. Reg. 57, 114 (Oct. 22, 1999).

Not surprisingly, budgetary and litigation conflicts have continued, as Secretary of the Interior Gail Norton wrote in 2001:

> The United States Fish and Wildlife Service is currently engaged in 45 separate lawsuits relating to listing endangered species, and we have received notice of an additional 42 lawsuits on the way. Last fall, Secretary Bruce Babbitt announced that the Interior Department could not list any new species in the current fiscal year because a backlog of court orders ate up all the financing. President Bush has asked Congress for a 33 percent increase in the listing budget. The Interior Department remains committed to working with state and local governments, conservation groups, tribes, private landowners and others to focus on recovering endangered species and conserving their habitat—not just listing and litigation.

Gale A. Norton, *Letter to the Editor, A New Way to Save Species and Habitat*, N.Y. Times, Aug. 23, 2001.

In November 2001, FWS declared another moratorium on listing, claiming that it could not continue listing activities while most of its limited resources were spent dealing with lawsuits from environmental groups demanding habitat designation. *See, e.g., Southern Appalachian Biodiversity Project v. United States Fish and Wildlife Service*, 181 F. Supp. 2d 883 (E.D. Tenn. 2001); *Sierra Club v. United States Fish & Wildlife Service*, 245 F.3d 434 (5th Cir. 2001); *Natural Res. Defense Council v. United States Dept. of Interior*, 13 Fed. Appx. 612 (9th Cir. 2001). This decision halted listing consideration for 275 species. As a stopgap measure, Interior sought periodic ceasefires with litigating environmental groups. On August 29, 2001, for example, Interior announced an agreement with several groups (notably the Center for Biological Diversity and Defenders of Wildlife) where FWS committed to issue final listing decisions for 14 species and propose eight more for listing. In exchange, the organizations consented to extending deadlines for eight critical habitat designations. The Interior Department hailed it as a breakthrough because money that was going to litigation could now be used for protection of endangered species; critics charged that this simply allowed FWS to shift already inadequate funds from one important activity (critical habitat designation) to another (listing).

The tension between habitat designation and listing activities continued throughout the Bush administration. Indeed, the Center for Biological Diversity asserted in 2003 that "the Bush administration is the only administration in the history of the Endangered Species Act never to have listed an endangered species except in response to a court order or petition. It is the only administration never to have designated a critical habitat except in response to a lawsuit." *See* http://www.biologicaldiversity.org/swcbd/press/fox10-17-03.htm. A number of the decisions to designate critical habitat have been challenged, turning into a substantive battle over the methodology used to determine the critical habitat as well as its exact dimensions and location. *See, e.g., Cape Hatteras Access Pres. Alliance v. United States DOI*, 344 F. Supp. 2d 108 (D.D.C. 2004) (holding that the

FWS failed adequately to evaluate the economic impact of designating critical habitat for the piping plover).

QUESTIONS AND DISCUSSION

1. Should critical habitat designation decisions be subject to NEPA? Designating critical habitat seems environmentally benign; and we normally think of NEPA as applying to actions that are environmentally harmful. Courts, though, have split on this issue. In *Douglas County v. Babbitt,* 48 F.3d 1495 (9th Cir. 1995), *cert. denied,* 516 U.S. 1042 (1996), the Ninth Circuit held that NEPA did not apply to the listing and designation of critical habitat for the spotted owl. In *Catron County v. U.S. Fish and Wildlife Service,* 75 F.3d 1429 (10th Cir. 1996), the Tenth Circuit, by contrast, held that FWS should comply with NEPA in designating critical habitat when it is the equivalent of a major federal action significantly affecting the human environment. Whether or not NEPA applies, the ESA listing process requires notice and comment.

2. Is it appropriate or good policy for environmental groups such as the Center for Biological Diversity or Defenders of Wildlife to negotiate with Interior over which species should be listed and which critical habitat deadlines extended? Does such "policy by litigation" usurp fundamental policymaking authority from Interior? Does it squeeze out the voices of other environmental groups that do not litigate?

3. What is your view of the approach taken by the Clinton and Bush administrations to designation of critical habitat? After you read section D below on Section 7, you may want to return to this section and ask how much additional protection designation of critical habitat provides beyond the prohibition on jeopardy. Is the additional protection worth the cost?

C.   CONSERVATION

Once a species has been listed, the primary goal is to prevent it going extinct. Over the longer term, however, the basic challenge remains—how to restore populations. Remember that the goal of the ESA is not so much to list endangered species *but to get the species off the list.* Thus Section 7(a)(1) requires that federal agencies "carry ... out programs for the conservation of endangered species and threatened species." The conservation of protected species requires an agency to "use ... all methods and procedures which are necessary to bring any endangered species or threatened species to the point at which the measures provided pursuant to this chapter are no longer necessary." 16 U.S.C. § 1532(3). Such methods and measures cover a wide range of activities, including scientific research, census taking, "law enforcement, habitat acquisition and maintenance, propagation, live trapping, and transplantation, and, in the extraordinary case where population pressures within a given ecosystem cannot be otherwise relieved, may include regulated taking." *Id.* Taken together, these affirmative duties suggest Congress intended federal actors to do more than simply avoid causing harm on their own.

Several cases support the notion that agencies have an affirmative duty to conserve listed species, although the contours of that duty have not been fully developed. As Professor J.B. Ruhl has noted, Section 7(a)(1) can be used by the agency as a shield to defend its conservation activities and by agency critics as a sword to compel an agency to take further action to protect species. J.B. Ruhl, *Section 7(a)(1) of the "New" Endangered Species Act: Rediscovering and Redefining the Untapped Power of Federal Agencies' Duty to Conserve Species*, 25 Envtl. L. 1107, 1129–35 (1995). As a shield, for example, the Department of the Interior successfully defended its refusal to sell federal water resources to Nevada cities on the grounds that the water was needed downstream to protect stream flows for listed fish species. *Carson–Truckee Water Conservancy Dist. v. Clark*, 741 F.2d 257, 261 (9th Cir. 1984), *cert. denied*, 470 U.S. 1083 (1985). But in *Connor v. Andrus*, 453 F.Supp. 1037 (W.D. Tex. 1978), the court rejected the Fish and Wildlife Service's effort to use § 7(a)(1) as a shield to justify hunting closures in three southwestern states. The court found that the administrative record failed to support the agency's concerns about a threat to the endangered species and that, accordingly, the agency had failed to establish a rational connection between the closures and the recovery of listed species.

The most prominent cases are those that have successfully used § 7(a)(1) as a sword to challenge an agency's alleged failure to conserve species. For example, in *Defenders of Wildlife v. Andrus*, 428 F.Supp. 167 (D.D.C. 1977), a federal district court held that the Fish and Wildlife Service regulations allowing hunting of certain migratory birds from up to one half-hour before sunrise until sunset were arbitrary and violated the agency's duty to conserve. The court reached this conclusion because of the agency's failure to consider the likelihood that endangered birds might be mistaken for game birds during periods of low light. In *Sierra Club v. Glickman*, 156 F.3d 606 (5th Cir. 1998), the Fifth Circuit relied on § 7(a)(1) to require the Department of Agriculture to develop a program for conserving listed species threatened by certain agricultural and water management practices above Texas' Edwards Aquifer, and to consult with the Fish and Wildlife Service on that program. In strong language, the court rejected the conventional view of the conservation duty:

> At first blush, this section appears to suggest that federal agencies have only a generalized duty to confer and develop programs for the benefit of endangered and threatened species—*i.e.*, not with respect to any particular species.... When read in the context of the ESA as a whole, however, we find that the agencies' duties under § 7(a)(1) are much more specific and particular.

Id. at 615.

Despite these cases, however, § 7(a)(1) has not had nearly the influence NGO litigators had hoped for.

> To the chagrin of many environmental organizations, the affirmative conservation mandates of section 7(a)(1) have historically exerted little influence over the actions of federal agencies. FWS and NMFS have never issued regulations interpreting or implementing these requirements, save for a provision in their joint consultation regulations which authorizes these agencies to include a separate section in biological opinions that provides federal action agencies with "conservation recommendations." However, this regulatory provision explicitly

emphasizes that such recommendations "are advisory and are not intended to carry any binding legal force."

Daniel J. Rohlf, *Jeopardy Under the Endangered Species Act: Playing a Game Protected Species Can't Win*, 41 WASHBURN L.J. 114, 117 (2001) (*quoting* 50 C.F.R. § 402.14(j) (2002)). *See also* Federico Cheever, *Recovery Planning, the Courts and the Endangered Species Act*, 16 NAT. RESOURCES & ENV'T 106 (2001) (making the same point about the relatively small impact of § 7(a)(1)).

In addition to the federal conservation duty under § 7(a)(1), section 4(f) requires FWS and NMFS to develop recovery plans "for the conservation and survival of endangered species and threatened species," with priority given to those species "most likely to benefit" from a recovery plan, "particularly those species that are, or may be, in conflict with construction or other development projects or other forms of economic activity." 16 U.S.C. § 1533(f)(1). The ESA does not establish any deadlines for the preparation of a recovery plan and FWS does not need to prepare a recovery plan for a species if it will not promote recovery. In simple terms, the plan provides a road map of how the species will recover, setting out necessary steps such as identification of important habitat and management of the habitat to ensure recovery. As of 2008, FWS had prepared recovery plans for almost 1,200, or approximately two-thirds, of listed U.S. species. *See* http://ecos.fws.gov/tess_public/pub/speciesRecovery.jsp?sort=.

Despite the number of plans, their impact has been limited. This is due in large part to resources. The funding has been heavily skewed toward well-known species. From 1989 through 1991, for example, ten species, virtually all of which were charismatic birds or megafauna, received half of all government funding for endangered species. *See generally* JK Miller et al., *The Endangered Species Act: Dollars and Sense?*, 52 BIOSCIENCE 163 (2002). Nor has there been a great deal of funding. In 1993, the National Wilderness Institute estimated that implementing all the recovery plans would cost almost $1 billion. Congress has never provided anything approaching such funding for plans (in 2006, $69 million was provided) and every year hundreds of species receive no funding for their plans, at all. FWS has argued that focusing on the level of funding, however, misses the point. As the Frequently Asked Questions section of the FWS recovery website relates,

> The recovery plan is best thought of as a menu. To have a healthy meal at a restaurant, one would not total an entire menu to arrive at the cost of one dinner. Not all the tasks in a recovery plan need to be implemented to reach the recovery goal. For example, the recovery plan for the Ozark big-eared bat estimated spending for recovery at $2.6 million. This species is now considered stable; actual expenditures have totaled about $861,000.

STANFORD ENVIRONMENTAL LAW SOCIETY, THE ENDANGERED SPECIES ACT 71–72 (2001).

Professor Jeff Rachlinski, in a study of how listed species have fared, found promising results, as well.

> Species recovery plans did further species recovery. Although the existence of a recovery plan was closely associated with the length of time species were listed, recovery plans clearly benefited species, even when the length of time that

species were protected was controlled. In fact, recovery plans appeared to be the primary mechanism that set species on the road to recovery. Virtually all improving species had recovery plans. Listing and designating critical habitat stabilized species populations, and recovery plans facilitated improvement.

Jeffrey Rachlinski, *Noah by the Numbers: An Empirical Evaluation of the Endangered Species Act,* 82 CORNELL L. REV. 356, 384 (1997).

D.   CONSULTATION, JEOPARDY, AND ADVERSE MODIFICATION OF CRITICAL HABITAT

Section 7(a)(2) of the ESA requires federal agencies to "insure" that any action they authorize, fund, or carry out "is not likely to *jeopardize* the continued existence" of a species or "result in the destruction or *adverse modification* of [the critical] habitat of such species." 16 U.S.C. § 1536(a)(2) (emphasis added). In order to accomplish this objective, Section 7 requires the federal agency authorizing, funding, or carrying out an activity (the so-called "action agency") to consult with FWS or NOAA Fisheries on how to avoid jeopardy or adverse modification of critical habitat. *Id.* Hindsight reveals the potential power over federal projects of Section 7's jeopardy and adverse modification provisions, but Congress was oblivious to this consideration when passing the ESA in 1973. The committee reports of the ESA lacked any explanation of how Section 7 was to be interpreted and no industry representatives testified on this subject at the committee hearings.

The power of Section 7 became blindingly clear just a few years later, though, in one of the most famous cases in natural resources law, *Tennessee Valley Authority v. Hill,* 437 U.S. 153 (1978). Despite local opposition, the Tennessee Valley Authority (TVA) had long been seeking to dam the last free-flowing stretch of the Little Tennessee River, flooding a beautiful valley. The TVA's cost-benefit analysis suggested the dam would provide important benefits in hydroelectricity and tourism, but the estimates seemed overstated at best, given the sparse population in the area. Funding had first been approved in 1966 for damming the river to convert the valley into a 30–mile reservoir. By 1968, the concrete had been set at a cost of about $5 million. Following passage of NEPA, construction was halted in 1970 until an environmental impact statement could be drafted.

The TVA filed an appropriate EIS in 1973 and, the same year, an endangered perch, known as a snail darter, was found in the river by an ichthyologist. The fish was proposed for listing in 1974 and formally listed as an endangered species in 1975. There are 130 known snail darter species. The subspecies above the Tellico Dam was listed because it was "genetically distinct and reproductively isolated from other fishes." At the time of listing, the river was designated as critical habitat. This might have been the end of the story but for an enterprising University of Tennessee law student named Hiram Hill who, with the assistance of Professor Zyg Plater, filed an ESA challenge to completion of the dam. Hill argued that damming the river would result in the total destruction of the snail darter's critical habitat and constituted a clear violation of Section 7. In response, TVA proposed moving the fish to another river. In its court defense, TVA did not challenge the facts, arguing instead that almost $80 million had already been spent on the dam and that continued congressional funding clearly authorized an exception to the ESA.

In a 7–2 decision that sent shock waves around the country, the Supreme Court emphatically disagreed. As Chief Justice Burger wrote, "one might dispute this case by saying that the burden on the public through the loss of millions of unrecoverable dollars would greatly outweigh the loss of the snail darter. But neither the Endangered Species Act nor Article III of the Constitution provides federal courts with the authority to make such fine utilitarian calculations." 437 U.S. at 187. Underlining the absolute nature of Section 7, the opinion noted that that the 1966 ESA had contained a provision requiring preservation only "insofar as is practicable and consistent with the agency's primary purposes" but this language had specifically been dropped from the 1973 Act. *Id.* at 175.

This decision halted construction on the dam, led to sensational media coverage of the decision with editorial cartoons showing a dam being swallowed by a tiny fish, and triggered hearings on Capitol Hill. No one had opposed the ESA during the 1973 hearings. However, fear of halting federal projects in order to protect obscure organisms with strange names polarized the 1978 ESA amendment hearings that followed *TVA v. Hill*. The "incalculable genetic heritage" placed beyond valuation just four years earlier was now up for auction in the Merchant Marine and Fisheries Committee of the House.

As mentioned above, the amendments mandated cost-benefit analysis when designating critical habitat. They also created the Endangered Species Committee, consisting of the Secretaries of Agriculture, the Army, and Interior, the Administrators of EPA and the National Oceanic and Atmospheric Administration, the Chairman of the Council of Economic Advisors, and a state representative appointed by the president. Known colloquially as "The God Squad," the committee may vote to exempt an action from Section 7's authority and potentially drive a species to extinction if it decides (1) there are no "reasonable and prudent alternatives," (2) the benefits of the action "clearly outweigh" the environmental costs, and (3) the action is of "regional or national significance."

Interestingly, the first case the committee considered was the Tellico Dam. The God Squad unanimously denied an exemption, concluding that the project was pork barrel of the worst kind that deserved to be killed on its own merits. As Secretary of the Interior Cecil Andrus memorably said at the time, it was a pity "to see the snail darter get the credit for stopping a project that was ill-conceived and uneconomical in the first place." *As quoted in* CHARLES C. MANN & MARK L. PLUMMER, NOAH'S CHOICE: THE FUTURE OF ENDANGERED SPECIES 171 (1995). In practice, the God Squad has not been particularly important and has only exempted two projects (and one of these exemptions was later reversed, *Portland Audubon Society v. Endangered Species Committee*, 984 F.2d 1534 (9th Cir. 1993)). Despite the uproar following *TVA v. Hill*, the case was a defining moment for the ESA, both because it established the sheer power of Section 7 and because public support of the decision and the ESA prevented Congress from gutting the Act through later amendment.

TVA v. Hill made clear that Section 7's substantive prohibitions had teeth. Agency action could not jeopardize a species' existence or adversely modify its critical habitat, no matter the cost. And this went well beyond simply building a dam. All agency actions "authorized, funded, or carried out"—ranging from grants to permits for otherwise entirely private actions—that could jeopardize a species or adversely modify its critical habitat were covered.

Section 7's procedural obligations—specifically the obligation of federal "action" agencies to consult with the relevant federal wildlife agency about the potential impacts of its activities—are potentially just as important. To comply with Section 7's so-called consultation requirements, an agency proposing an action must first "inquire" of either FWS or NOAA Fisheries (the wildlife agencies) whether an endangered species may be present in the area affected (note that this is made much easier if critical habitat has been designated). If so, the action agency must prepare a Biological Assessment (BA) to determine whether the species is likely to be affected by the action. If, through this process known as "informal consultation," it is determined that a listed species is likely to be affected by the proposed action, the action agency must then formally consult with the relevant wildlife agency. This "formal consultation" results in preparation of a Biological Opinion (BO). The Biological Opinion must decide whether the action will jeopardize the continued existence of the species or result in the adverse modification of its critical habitat. If it will, the Secretary must suggest "reasonable and prudent alternatives" (RPA) that could be taken to avoid jeopardy or adverse modification. As we shall see later in the chapter, if the agency decides that the proposed action, or the action as mitigated by an RPA, would not cause jeopardy *but would result* in a "taking" of an endangered species, the agency can issue an incidental take statement along with its Biological Opinion.

While this may sound like a difficult gauntlet for the action agency to overcome, consultation has become routinized and rarely halts an agency action. Much more often, nothing happens or, at worst, the agency modifies or mitigates its proposed activity. A study by Professor Ollie Houck, for example, examined 186,000 federal projects from 1987–1995 that had been reviewed by FWS and NOAA Fisheries. Houck found that consultations delayed or modified less than 3% of the projects and halted less than 0.05%. Oliver Houck, *The Endangered Species Act and Its Implementation by the U.S. Departments of Interior and Commerce,* 64 U. Colo. L. Rev. 277 (1993). It's worth noting that, as a matter of law, neither FWS nor NOAA Fisheries can formally halt an agency project despite their issuance of an unfavorable Biological Opinion. In practice, however, for the action agency to ignore an unfavorable biological opinion makes it highly likely that its decision will appear arbitrary and capricious if challenged in a citizen suit.

QUESTIONS AND DISCUSSION

1. In *National Association of Home Builders v. Defenders of Wildlife*, the Supreme Court considered whether the Section 7 consultation duty of federal agencies applies to non-discretionary agency actions. The specific issue concerned whether EPA's decision to approve the transfer of Clean Water Act permitting authority to the state of Arizona needed to be reviewed by FWS and NMFS. The Clean Water Act provides that the EPA "shall" transfer such permitting authority to the requesting state unless the EPA determines that the state fails to meet one of the nine criteria provided in the statute. Defenders of Wildlife argued that EPA also needed to consider whether the transfer of permitting authority could result in a jeopardy or adverse modification violation under ESA Section 7(a)(2).

Justice Alito, writing for a 5–4 majority, held that Section 7(a)(2) applies solely to *discretionary* agency actions. If a statute states that the EPA "shall" do something (in this case, delegate Clean Water Act permitting authority), then the agency cannot be required to consider other criteria that have not been specified in the Act. The decision stated:

> Applying *Chevron*, we defer to the agency's reasonable interpretation of ESA § 7(a)(2) as applying only to "actions in which there is discretionary Federal involvement or control" [an interpretation of 50 C.F.R. § 402.03, stating that "Section 7 and the requirements of this part apply to all actions in which there is discretionary Federal involvement or control."] Since the transfer of NPDES permitting authority is not discretionary, but rather is mandated once a State has met the criteria set forth in § 402(b) of the CWA, it follows that a transfer of [CWA] permitting authority does not trigger § 7(a)(2)'s consultation and no-jeopardy requirements. Accordingly, the judgment of the Court of Appeals for the Ninth Circuit is reversed, and these cases are remanded for further proceedings consistent with this opinion.

In his dissent, Justice Stevens characterized the case as presenting "a problem of conflicting 'shalls.'"

> These cases present a problem of conflicting "shalls." On the one hand, § 402(b) of the Clean Water Act (CWA) provides that the Environmental Protection Agency "shall" approve a State's application to administer a National Pollution Discharge Elimination System (NPDES) permitting program unless it determines that nine criteria are not satisfied. On the other hand, shortly after the passage of the CWA, Congress enacted of the Endangered Species Act of 1973 (ESA), which commands that federal agencies "shall" insure that their actions do not jeopardize endangered species.
>
> When faced with competing statutory mandates, it is our duty to give full effect to both if at all possible. See, *e.g.*, *Morton* v. *Mancari*, 417 U.S. 535, 551 (1974) ("When two statutes are capable of co-existence, it is the duty of the courts, absent a clearly expressed congressional intention to the contrary, to regard each as effective"). The Court fails at this task. Its opinion unsuccessfully tries to reconcile the CWA and ESA by relying on a federal regulation, 50 CFR § 402.03 (2006), which it reads as limiting the reach of § 7(a)(2) to *only* discretionary federal actions. Not only is this reading inconsistent with the text and history of § 402.03, but it is fundamentally inconsistent with the ESA itself.
>
> In the celebrated "snail darter" case, *Tennessee Valley Auth.* v. *Hill*, 437 U.S. 153 (1978), we held that the ESA "reveals a conscious decision by Congress to give endangered species priority over the 'primary missions' of federal agencies." Consistent with that intent, Chief Justice Burger's exceptionally thorough and admirable opinion explained that § 7 "admits of no exception." Creating precisely such an exception by exempting nondiscretionary federal actions from the ESA's coverage, the Court whittles away at Congress'

comprehensive effort to protect endangered species from the risk of extinction and fails to give the Act its intended effect.

551 U.S. 644 (2007). Does this decision de-fang the "pit bull" of environmental law? Does it create an incentive for agencies to interpret their duties as nondiscretionary in order to limit the reach of the ESA over their activities? How could you use NEPA case law to argue that this actually is not a significant decision?

2.   In August, 2008, the Bush Administration proposed regulations that would allow agencies to bypass review of projects by FWS and NMFS. Instead, as described by the *Washington Post,* "Under the proposed new rules, dam and highway construction and other federal projects could proceed without delay if the agency in charge decides they would not harm vulnerable species." Juliet Eilperin, *Endangered Species Act Changes Give Agencies More Say,* WASH. POST, August 12, 2008 at A1. Secretary of the Interior, Dirk Kempthorne, described the proposed rule as a "narrow regulatory change ... [that] will provide clarity and certainty to the consultation process under the Endangered Species Act." Section 7(a) is excerpted below. Was the proposed change legal?

(a) Federal agency actions and consultations.

(1) The Secretary shall review other programs administered by him and utilize such programs in furtherance of the purposes of this Act. All other Federal agencies shall, in consultation with and with the assistance of the Secretary, utilize their authorities in furtherance of the purposes of this Act by carrying out programs for the conservation of endangered species and threatened species listed pursuant to section 4 of this Act.

[handwritten margin note: affirmative duty (not elaborated on by FWS)]

(2) Each Federal agency shall, in consultation with and with the assistance of the Secretary, insure that any action authorized, funded, or carried out by such agency (hereinafter in this section referred to as an "agency action") is not likely to jeopardize the continued existence of any endangered species or threatened species or result in the destruction or adverse modification of habitat of such species which is determined by the Secretary, after consultation as appropriate with affected States, to be critical, unless such agency has been granted an exemption for such action by the Committee pursuant to subsection (h) of this section. In fulfilling the requirements of this paragraph each agency shall use the best scientific and commercial data available.

[handwritten margin note: "negative" duty – do no harm]

(3) Subject to such guidelines as the Secretary may establish, a Federal agency shall consult with the Secretary on any prospective agency action at the request of, and in cooperation with, the prospective permit or license applicant if the applicant has reason to believe that an endangered species or a threatened species may be present in the area affected by his project and that implementation of such action will likely affect such species.

(4) Each Federal agency shall confer with the Secretary on any agency action which is likely to jeopardize the continued existence of any species proposed to be listed under section 4 or result in the destruction or adverse modification of critical habitat proposed to be designated for such species. This paragraph does not require a limitation on the commitment of resources as described in subsection (d).

3.   There are striking similarities between the ESA's consultation requirements and NEPA. Both require informal and formal assessments (NEPA for significant environmental impacts of major federal actions and the ESA for jeopardy and adverse modification). Just as most federal actions with environmental impacts do not require preparation of an EIS, the vast majority of actions that could affect endangered species never require a biological opinion. Moreover, even where there are potential adverse impacts, those impacts are mitigated up front as part of the EA (environmental assessment) or BA (biological assessment) process. What are the important differences between the ESA and NEPA? What would NEPA look like if it adopted its own Section 7(a)(2)?

4.   The Endangered Species Committee's decision not to grant an exemption seemed to be the end of the Tellico Dam story, but there was a plot-twisting chapter yet to come. In 1979, Senator Howard Baker from Tennessee slipped a rider onto an appropriations bill. Read in 42 seconds to a nearly empty chamber, the amendment repealed all protective laws applied to the Tellico dam. The appropriations bill passed and TVA flooded the valley in November, 1979. The reservoir never achieved any of the economic development that had been used as a justification for its construction. There was an epilogue, however. Relict populations of snail darters were later discovered in the main stretch of the Tennessee River and a number of its tributaries. In 1984, the FWS upgraded the snail darter's status from endangered to threatened. For a complete history of *TVA v. Hill* and its aftermath, see Zygmunt J.B. Plater, *In the Wake of the Snail Darter: An Environmental Law Paradigm and its Consequences,* 19 U. MICH. J. L. REFORM 805 (1986).

5.   Section 4 of the ESA allows FWS to list species if they are not found in the United States, but it remains an open question whether Section 7 applies to overseas federal actions. Prior to 1986, the FWS had applied Section 7(a)(2) to domestic and foreign federal actions. In 1986, the FWS revised its regulation, requiring agencies to consult only for domestic actions or for actions on the high seas. In *Lujan v. Defenders of Wildlife*, excerpted above with reference to the issue of standing (p. 244), environmental groups challenged the regulation and the court did not reach the merits of the case. In a concurring opinion, Justice Stevens suggested the ESA does not have extraterritorial application, arguing that there is a presumption against legislation applying to overseas actions unless Congress specifically provides otherwise. The only geographical reference in Section 7, he noted, is to critical habitat in "affected states," while other sections of the ESA, such as Section 8's implementation of the CITES Convention, do explicitly address international issues. Current FWS regulations only require consultation for federal actions either in the United States or on the high seas (i.e., beyond 200 miles from a nation's coast). 50 C.F.R. 402.01. It is also unsettled whether Section 7(a)(2) applies to federal agency actions taken within the United States that affect species abroad, such as federal water projects in the Southwest that reduce the flow to areas in Mexico with high biodiversity. *See Consejo de Desarrollo Economico de Mexicali v. U.S.A.,* 482 F.3d 1157 (9th Cir. 2007) (challenging federal water projects on the Colorado River in the United States that reduce the flow to the Colorado River Delta in Mexico, but dismissed for jurisdictional reasons and sovereign immunity).

The case below demonstrates how the consultation process can result in reasonable and prudent alternatives to mitigate actions that otherwise would clearly violate Section 7. As you read the case, consider what incentives Section 7 creates for the Bureau of Reclamation the next time an endangered bird starts building a nest on exposed lake bank.

Southwest Center for Biological Diversity v. U.S. Bureau of Reclamation
143 F.3d 515 (9th Cir. 1998)

Goodwin, Circuit Judge:

* * * In dry years, the Lake Mead delta ("the delta") which is exposed by low water impounded by Hoover Dam on the Lower Colorado River has provided a popular nesting ground for the Southwestern Willow Flycatcher ("the Flycatcher"), a migratory songbird which nests and breeds during spring and summer in dense cottonwood-willow riparian habitat. The bird has been "listed" by the Fish and Wildlife Service ("the FWS") as an endangered species under the ESA. Although periodically submerged by rising water during Reclamation's normal operations of the Hoover Dam and the Lower Colorado River, the delta experiences natural drying periods when upstream rain and snow conditions drop below normal.

In the late 1980s and early 1990s dry weather caused the water level to drop and encouraged expansion of the riparian growth of willow trees. This willow tree growth has gradually expanded to cover approximately 1,148 acres and now forms the second largest continuous patch of native willow habitat known to exist in the Southwest. More recently, however, the return of normal rainfall and runoff on the Colorado has caused the water impounded at Lake Mead to rise back to its normal levels, inundating the root crowns of the willows in the delta. Although the willows have shown resiliency to inundation for periods of over 13 months, the extended inundation of the delta has caused a loss of willows and cottonwoods. Continued inundation will result in the destruction of both the willows and cottonwoods. As the willow-cottonwood habitat is destroyed, Flycatcher nests and young have been, and will likely continue to be, lost.

In 1995, Reclamation began the process of consulting with the Fish and Wildlife Service ("FWS") pursuant to [Section 7 of] the ESA over the effects of its activities on the Lower Colorado River as they related to the Flycatcher and several other endangered species.... Following informal consultation, in August of 1996, Reclamation issued its biological assessment of the effects its operations were having on threatened and endangered species on the Lower Colorado River. See 50 C.F.R. § 402.12 (1998). Reclamation reported that its actions were affecting listed species, including the Flycatcher. In fact, direct take of Flycatchers due to water management had occurred at the Lake Mead delta in June of 1996 when willows subjected to prolonged inundation of root crowns lost the structural support of their root systems and fell into Lake Mead.

Approximately five months later, in January of 1997, the FWS, as the Secretary's special designee, issued a Biological Opinion ("BO") which concluded that Reclamation's continued operations on the Lower Colorado River for the next five years would jeopardize the continued existence and survival of the Flycatcher. In this BO, which was sent to Reclamation for comments, the FWS noted that, in light of the Flycatcher's status and riparian habitat on the Lower

Colorado River, the expected loss of habitat from Reclamation's continued activities at Lake Mead would prove catastrophic, both in the amount of Flycatcher habitat involved and the potential rate of loss. The FWS elaborated that there was an urgent need to protect breeding flycatchers and their habitat at Lake Mead.

The FWS then proposed a reasonable and prudent alternative ("RPA") which would permit Reclamation to continue its operations on the Lower Colorado River while still avoiding jeopardy to the Flycatcher. The proposed RPA was comprised of many short and long-term components. The first short-term provision of the RPA required Reclamation to use the full scope of its authority and discretion to immediately protect and maintain the 1,148 acres of riparian habitat at the delta. Reclamation was further required to provide the FWS with a detailed account of the type and extent of discretion available to it in the management of Lake Mead. If Reclamation was unable to implement this provision throughout the five-year consultation period, Reclamation was required to defer use of conservation space above elevation 2136 at Roosevelt Lake, Arizona, in order, in the short-term, to maintain Flycatcher habitat there until suitable flycatcher habitat could be developed elsewhere. The FWS issued a briefing statement on January 21, 1997, discussing the draft RPA. The FWS acknowledged that the proposed RPA actions for the Flycatcher were burdensome, but insisted that the actions were, at the time, considered the absolute minimum necessary to alleviate jeopardy.

After receiving the draft BO, the Regional Director of Reclamation sent a memorandum advising the Secretary that it should not be compelled to preserve any of the Lake Mead Flycatcher habitat because it lacked discretion to reduce the level of Lake Mead except for purposes of river regulation, improvement of navigation, flood control, irrigation, domestic uses, and power generation.

On April 30, 1997, the FWS issued its Final BO in which it confirmed that Reclamation's operation of Hoover Dam and Lake Mead over the next five years would place the Flycatcher in jeopardy. The FWS stated that the expected loss remained catastrophic and that there existed a critical need to protect breeding Flycatchers and their habitat at Lake Mead. The FWS admitted that extinction of the Flycatcher was foreseeable. The FWS nevertheless proposed a new RPA which no longer required Reclamation to take action to protect the habitat at the Lake Mead delta, because of its alleged lack of discretionary power to do so. This RPA further did not require Reclamation to defer use of conservation space above elevation 2136 at Roosevelt Lake, Arizona, in order, in the short-term, to maintain Flycatcher habitat there until suitable Flycatcher habitat could be developed elsewhere.

Instead, this RPA announced such short term mitigation measures as immediately initiating a program to procure and protect alternative compensation habitat. Specifically, the RPA required Reclamation to procure and protect approximately 1,400 acres of currently unprotected riparian habitat that is currently used by the Flycatcher, preferably on the Lower Colorado River. However, if insufficient occupied habitat could be identified, the RPA permitted Reclamation to instead procure and protect high potential, unoccupied habitat. All the required protections for at least 500 acres had to be put in place by January 1, 1999, including initiation (not completion) of any necessary ecological restoration or reforestation. All the required protection for the remaining acres had to be put in place by January 1, 2001.

The FWS did not identify specific areas available and suitable for acquisition and restoration, and did not mandate that the replacement habitat be established at a date certain before the destruction of the Lake Mead Habitat. The FWS, in adopting the RPA, did, however, expect the short-term mitigation measures, including habitat replacement, to be complemented by long-term mitigation measures, such as (1) an additional program of on and off-site compensation for historical Flycatcher habitat that represents the amount of historical Flycatcher habitat lost or precluded from developing because of the continuing effects of Reclamation's facilities, and (2) the continued development of the Multi–Species Conservation Program ("MSCP"). In fact, the FWS concluded that jeopardy to the Flycatcher could be avoided only if the long-term provisions were carried out. The RPA and Final BO were accompanied by an incidental take statement, in which the Secretary permitted an "unquantifiable" take of the Flycatcher at the Lake Mead Delta.

Sometime before this Final BO was issued, when it became clear to Southwest that no steps were being taken to preserve the Lake Mead habitat, Southwest initiated this lawsuit against Reclamation. As originally filed, the complaint charged that Reclamation was violating (1) 16 U.S.C. § 1536(d) by allowing continued inundation of the Lake Mead Delta before the completion of formal consultation; (2) 16 U.S.C. § 1536(a)(2) by allowing its operations to jeopardize the Flycatcher, and (3) 16 U.S.C. §§ 1538(a)(1)(B) and 1539(a) by "taking" Flycatchers in the Lake Mead delta without a valid incidental take statement.

Southwest also sought injunctive relief, asking the court to issue an order forcing Reclamation to lower Lake Mead to approximately 1178 feet above sea level in order to preserve the Lake Mead delta habitat. Reclamation responded by filing a motion to dismiss the complaint, arguing that Southwest failed to provide the requisite pre-suit notice necessary to invoke the court's jurisdiction over Reclamation under the citizen suit provision of the ESA.

Arizona Power Authority, the Metropolitan Water District of Southern California, the Salt River Project, and the Southern Nevada Water Authority filed motions to intervene as defendants. They argued that a reduction in the water level of Lake Mead to save the willow trees would ultimately require the release of 3.5 million to 5 million acre feet of water, and would harm the persons and entities who rely on Lake Mead water for domestic, power, and irrigation purposes. The district court granted the motions for intervention.

After the final BO was issued, and three days prior to the hearing on the motion for preliminary injunction and the motion to dismiss, Southwest amended its complaint to add a claim against the Secretary under the Administrative Procedure Act ("APA"), challenging the adopted RPA as arbitrary, capricious, and contrary to the ESA. Southwest also deleted its claim against Reclamation that it was violating the ESA by allowing continued inundation of the Lake Mead Delta before the completion of formal consultation. Nevertheless, Southwest continued its claims against Reclamation that it was violating the ESA by jeopardizing the continued existence of the Flycatcher and by unlawfully taking Flycatchers at Lake Mead in the absence of a valid RPA and incidental take statement. * * *

C.   Summary Judgment in favor of the Secretary.

The issuance of the BO, RPA, and Incidental Take Statement by the Secretary, through the FWS, constituted final agency action pursuant to 16 U.S.C. § 1536. Such administrative actions are, when final, subject to judicial review. However, because the ESA makes no specific provision for judicial review of final agency actions, the scope of review was governed by the APA, 5 U.S.C. § 701 et seq. The district court had to determine whether the Secretary's decision to adopt the BO, RPA and Incidental Take Statement in this case was "arbitrary, capricious, an abuse of discretion, or otherwise not in accordance with law." 5 U.S.C. § 706(2)(A).

The district court found that the Secretary's decision was not arbitrary, capricious, an abuse of discretion, or otherwise inconsistent with the law. Accordingly, the district court granted summary judgment in favor of the Secretary. Again, we review as a question of law the district court's grant of summary judgment in favor of the Secretary.

Southwest argues on appeal that the Secretary improperly rejected the draft RPA in favor of the final RPA, which does not preserve the Lake Mead habitat, based on Reclamation's alleged lack of discretion to lower the level of Lake Mead. Southwest complains that the Secretary never independently reviewed Reclamation's representation that it lacked such discretion. Southwest goes on to argue that the district court erred in holding that Reclamation's alleged lack of discretion was immaterial to its review of the Secretary's conduct under the APA.

We find Southwest's arguments problematic in several respects. First of all, under the ESA, the Secretary was not required to pick the first reasonable alternative the FWS came up with in formulating the RPA. The Secretary was not even required to pick the best alternative or the one that would most effectively protect the Flycatcher from jeopardy. The Secretary need only have adopted a final RPA which complied with the jeopardy standard and which could be implemented by the agency.

Secondly, under the ESA, the Secretary was not required to explain why he chose one RPA over another, or to justify his decision based solely on apolitical factors.[3] Accordingly, the district court had no reason to address the possible factors that might have motivated the Secretary in rejecting the draft RPA or to address the merits of Southwest's argument that the Secretary improperly rejected the draft RPA based on Reclamation's bare assertion that it lacked the discretion to lower the water level at Lake Mead.

The district court correctly held that the only relevant question before it for review was whether the Secretary acted arbitrarily and capriciously or abused his discretion in adopting the final RPA. In answering this question, the court had only to determine if the final RPA met the standards and requirements of the ESA. The court was not in a position to determine if the draft RPA should have been adopted or if it would have afforded the Flycatcher better protection.

Upon careful review of the evidence, we cannot say the district court erred in finding that the final RPA met the standards and requirements of the ESA. The district court determined that the FWS considered the relevant factors and reasonably found that the Flycatcher could survive the loss of habitat at Lake Mead for eighteen months until 500 acres could be protected, then survive an additional two years until an additional 500 acres could be protected, and finally survive through the MSCP process until compensation could be made for the historical habitat lost on the Lower Colorado River and until an extensive ecological restoration could be undertaken. Southwest failed to present any convincing evidence to contradict the FWS' findings. Southwest merely relied

3. The Secretary must rely on "the best scientific and commercial data available" in formulating an RPA, 16 U.S.C. § 1536(a)(2). However, the ESA does not explicitly limit the Secretary's analysis to apolitical considerations. If two proposed RPAs would avoid jeopardy to the Flycatcher, the Secretary must be permitted to choose the one that best suits all of its interests, including political or business interests.

upon the discarded draft RPA which had indicated that preservation of the Lake Mead habitat was necessary to the survival of the Flycatcher. However, upon further consideration of the matter, the FWS was entitled to, and did, in fact, change its mind. The FWS concluded in the final BO that the proposed short-term and long-term provisions of the final RPA would avoid jeopardy to the Flycatcher, notwithstanding the failure to modify Reclamation's operation of Hoover Dam at Lake Mead. Because there was a rational connection between the facts found in the BO and the choice made to adopt the final RPA, and because we must defer to the special expertise of the FWS in drafting RPAs that will sufficiently protect endangered species, we cannot conclude that the Secretary violated the APA.

Southwest's reliance on this court's decision in *Sierra Club v. Marsh*, 816 F.2d 1376 (9th Cir.1987), is misplaced. In *Marsh*, the FWS concluded that the Corps of Engineers' (COE) project to build a highway and flood control mechanism would jeopardize the continued existence of several bird species by destroying high-quality habitat. An RPA was consequently adopted to avoid jeopardy to the birds. One important provision of the RPA required the COE to acquire and preserve 188 acres of nearby wetlands as replacement habitat. When the transfer of the land failed to occur as anticipated, the COE refused to reinitiate consultation with the FWS, as requested, allegedly because it believed that it would eventually obtain the land through litigation with the current land owners. The COE further refused to halt construction, arguing that the Sierra Club had failed to show that the COE was not likely to acquire these mitigation lands.

This court ruled in favor of the Sierra Club, holding that COE violated the ESA by failing to ensure that its project did not jeopardize the continued existence of the endangered birds before allowing the adverse impact of its project to accumulate. Specifically, this court held that "if an agency plans to mitigate its project's adverse effects on an endangered species by acquiring habitat and creating a refuge, it must insure the creation of that refuge before it permits destruction or adverse modification of other habitat." By relying only on the outcome of uncertain litigation to provide replacement habitat, the COE had not done enough to make sure that the proposed mitigation measures would occur in time to avoid the jeopardy its actions posed to the endangered birds.

In this case, by contrast, there has been no violation of any of the terms of the RPA. There has also been no indication that Reclamation cannot acquire and restore the needed replacement habitat as specified in the final RPA by the required deadlines. Moreover, the FWS, which found the RPA insufficient in Marsh, fully supports the RPA at issue in this case, and has concluded that the RPA, as written, will avoid jeopardy to the Flycatcher. Thus, quite apart from the *Marsh* case, the RPA in this case insures the creation of replacement habitat, and the survival of the Flycatcher species, before it permits the destruction or adverse modification of the Lake Mead habitat.

We conclude that the district court did not err in holding that the Secretary did not act arbitrarily or capriciously in adopting the final RPA.

QUESTIONS AND DISCUSSION

1. How does the court take into account the interests of people who rely on Lake Mead's water for domestic use, power, and irrigation? How should their interests be considered? Do you think the RPA will likely work, or is it simply window dressing to allow the dam to operate?

2.   What should the baseline be? The flycatcher habitat did not exist when the dam operated at regular capacity. Nor did it exist before the construction of Hoover Dam. Willow trees only appeared during the drought period and would have been inundated when the dam returned to "normal" operating conditions. Recall our discussion in the first chapter of what should be considered natural. Should conditions that only occur during drought years in a constructed lake become the new, mandatory baseline once endangered species make use of the habitat? What's the natural condition of the human-made Lake Mead, or should that even matter to the court?

3.   What incentive does the court's decision create for dam operators and other resource professionals to manage habitat that attracts endangered species? What do you think the Bureau will do the next time willow trees start to establish along Lake Mead's banks?

4.   Assume that a population of an indigenous Colorado River fish—the Razorback Sucker—lives below the dam and has been listed under the ESA. In order to maintain habitat, the recovery plan for the fish calls for Hoover Dam to release a large burst of water every March, recreating the historically large Spring flow from the thawing snowpack that scours out riverbanks and creates favorable conditions for the fish. In order to create this large flow, however, Lake Mead levels need to be kept high. How should the court balance the needs of the endangered fish with the needs of the endangered flycatcher?

5.   Why didn't the Southwest Center for Biological Diversity bring a cause of action under Section 7(a)(1)? How would they argue that the Secretary violated his duty to conserve the flycatcher?

6.   As discussed earlier, one of the Department of Interior's arguments against designating critical habitat during the Clinton administration was that designation added no extra protection to Section 7's companion prohibition of jeopardy. Do you think it would have made a difference to the outcome of the *Southwest Center for Biological Diversity* case if the willows along the Lake Mead delta had been designated as critical habitat?

7.   Assume that the Bureau of Reclamation had no discretion to lower the level of Lake Mead. Would that matter under the ESA?

————

PROBLEM EXERCISE: CRITICAL HABITAT FOR THE GRIZZLY

There is a proposal to put a Forest Service road into an area in Montana to access an oil and gas wellsite for drilling. The government has never designated critical habitat for the grizzly bear because it was listed before designation provisions were mandatory. You are legal counsel for the group, Defenders of the Grizzly. Your staff biologist tells you that last month backpackers reported seeing a grizzly bear with two cubs just five miles from where the road would be built. Grizzlies are known to avoid roads and disturbances. What actions can your group take to help protect the grizzly? Would designation of critical habitat make the case easier to prove? Would you advise bringing a claim against the Fish & Wildlife Service for failure to designate the bear's critical habitat?

————

PROBLEM EXERCISE: WHAT TO DO ABOUT CLIMATE CHANGE?

J.B. Ruhl, *Climate Change and the Endangered Species Act: Building Bridges to the No–Analog Future* 88 BOSTON UNIV. L. REV. 1, 2–25 (2008)

The pika is toast. More specifically, the American pika (Ochotona princeps) is running out of places to live, and global climate change appears to be the primary cause of its decline. This tiny rabbit-like species has the unfortunate trait of being remarkably well-adapted to the cold, high-altitude, montane habitat of the Sierra Nevada and Rocky Mountain ranges in the North American Great Basin... The pika's problem is that as global climate change causes surface temperatures to rise, the altitude above which pikas can find suitable conditions for survival also is rising. In Yosemite National Park, for example, researchers have determined that the minimum average altitude for pika populations has risen from 7800 feet to 9500 feet in the past 90 years. Of course, if you think of a mountainous topography, you can quickly appreciate the pika's problem—most remaining pika populations are now stranded on scattered high mountain peaks in ranges separated by low-lying deserts, meaning they are stuck on mountaintop islands and the water is rising, so to speak. Seven of the twenty-five historically described pika populations in the Great Basin have gone extinct, and those remaining are in decline. * * *

Given the threat climate change poses to the pika and potentially many other species—one preeminent ecologist describes climate change as "a major threat to the survival of species and integrity of ecosystems world-wide"—it seems an appropriate target for the ESA. Indeed, although clearly not enthusiastic about the prospect, the FWS appears ready to carry the ESA into the climate change era, having recently proposed to extend ESA protection to the polar bear because of the diminishing ice habitat that the species depends upon for survival. The agency is getting strong nudges from the outside as well, as members of Congress have urged the agency to evaluate the effects of climate change on species generally, environmental advocacy groups have petitioned the agency to promulgate rules to address climate change, and one court has admonished the agency for failing to take climate change into account in its regulatory programs.

Practically speaking, however, what can the ESA do for the pika or the polar bear? The ESA takes a species-specific approach that has proven effective when employed to address discrete human-induced threats that have straight-forward causal connections to a species, such as clearing of occupied habitat for development or damming of a river. That is not the pika's or the polar bear's situation. Rather, all anthropogenic sources of greenhouse gases throughout the planet, from a small farm to a sprawling refinery, are contributing to the demise of the pika and polar bear, and the species' decline in both cases is gradual and largely invisible to human perception. The causal chain is less direct than, say, a salmon that finds a dam in its way. Pikas and polar bears will not drop dead because of exposure to greenhouse gas emissions—the species will just fade away as their habitats transform below their feet. The

ESA has proven to be unwieldy when applied on large working landscape levels, so is there reason to believe it will be any more effective when applied on global levels to this kind of creeping oblivion? * * *

Indeed, after *Massachusetts v. EPA* [holding that EPA must consider whether carbon dioxide is a pollutant under the Clean Air Act], one can argue it is incumbent on all federal regulatory agencies to assess how global climate change is to be integrated into their respective regulatory programs. There is no dodging the bullet—each agency must place the current knowledge of climate change and its reasonably anticipated trajectory next to its regulatory statute and ask how its knowledge and the statute fit together. * * *

The pika presents a relatively straightforward scenario of climate-induced species decline—the ecological conditions it needs for survival do not exist below a particular temperature regime. Of course, it is possible that as climate change takes hold, suitable conditions for the pika will materialize somewhere else in the world, but that will do the pikas of the Great Basin little good. They do not have the option of relocating once the temperature regime lifts above the peaks which they now call home. Rather, the pika and other species with specific ecological needs and limited migration capacity are likely to face significant threats from this kind of first order change in ecological conditions. Threats in this category will come in several forms:

Stranding. Some species will not be able to withstand the degradation or complete loss of essential habitat conditions beyond tolerable thresholds and will have no adaptive capacity to migrate and seek suitable conditions elsewhere.

Life–Stage Habitat Loss. Some species will find ecological conditions for essential life-stage junctures, such as migratory pathways or refuge habitat during juvenile stages, disrupted beyond tolerable thresholds, making the continued availability of suitable ecological conditions for other life-stages irrelevant.

Altered Biological Events. Some species will respond to climate change, particularly warming of surface and water temperatures, through phenologic changes such as shifts in the timing of budding, spawning, or migration. If, as is likely, all ecologically linked species do not shift in synch, some species may face significant threats.

Not all species will find it necessary and possible to depart their current ecosystems in order to withstand the direct effects of climate change, but many will. Others will stay to fight it out. While humans might cheer these species on, the aggregate effects of ecological disruption and species reshuffling are likely to lead to several secondary threats.

Increased Stress. Some species will not experience primary ecological changes beyond tolerable thresholds, but will experience increased stress as those thresholds are approached and will become more susceptible to disease, parasitism, predation, and other forms of mortality.

Successful Adaptive Migration. As some species adapt to climate change by successfully migrating to and establishing in areas that present suitable conditions, their introduction may disrupt predator-prey or other ecological conditions to the detriment of other species. One species' successful adaptive migration, in other words, can be another's demise.

Opportunistic Invasion. Rather than increased stress effects, some species will find an erosion of barriers, such as temperature limits or water availability, which formerly prevented them from successfully establishing in a particular area, notwithstanding a history of natural or human-induced introduction opportunities. Climate change will close down on some species, but open doors for others.

Just as the primary threats to species before climate change centered around human-induced ecological change, it is likely that human adaptation to climate change will play a leading role in threatening species...

Direct Habitat Conversion. Many human communities are likely to find it necessary and possible to migrate to avoid rising sea levels along coastal areas, to relocate agricultural land uses, and to obtain secure water supplies. These migrations will necessarily involve some conversion of land uses in areas that presently provide suitable ecological conditions for particular species, in some cases at scales sufficient to pose a threat to the species.

Degraded Ecological Conditions. Relocated human communities will likely introduce ecological degradations from new or amplified pollution, noise, water diversions, and other stresses. Many human communities, relocated or not, also will implement climate change mitigation and adaptation measures designed primarily to protect human health and welfare, such as coastal flood barriers, which in some cases could threaten ecological conditions for other species. Even planting of forests to sequester carbon could degrade conditions for some species.

Induced Invasions. Human adaptation to climate change is likely to involve spatial relocations, as well as increased flow of goods to new settlement areas, which, as in the past, are likely to introduce non-native species to local ecosystems, some of which will establish successfully. * * *

The "pit-bull" has met its match, but sometimes old dogs can learn new tricks... [T]he statute is neither designed to regulate something so ubiquitous as greenhouse gas emissions nor so sacrosanct as to survive the political battle attempting to do so would ignite. Support for the ESA, therefore, must be tempered by practical and political reality if the ESA itself is to survive climate change.

———

In a memo to the Secretary of the Interior, assess the different policy options listed below for how to treat the pika and future species threatened by climate change. Address both the requirements of the ESA and the political consequences of particular strategies.

Regulating Greenhouse Gas Emissions

- Should FWS assess specific activities that contribute to climate change that, in turn, threaten the pika?

- Should it consider whether federal actions that cause, fund, or authorize greenhouse gas emissions violate Section 7?

- Should it consider whether any person emitting or contributing to emissions of greenhouse gases constitutes a Section 9 take?

- What would FWS need to demonstrate in order to satisfy the evidentiary burden that specific, discrete activities emitting greenhouse gases jeopardize the pika, adversely modify its critical habitat, or constitute a take?

Designating Critical Habitat

- How should FWS designate critical habitat at a time of shifting climatic zones?

- Does it make sense to designate "potentially critical habitat"? In other words, can FWS designate habitat that is not currently necessary for the species' survival but which, if climate predictions prove accurate, will be necessary in a matter of decades (such as high peaks for the pika)?

Creating Recovery Plans

- Should FWS consider relocating the Pika on low peaks to habitat on higher peaks?

- Should it, as some have suggested, FWS consider creating large styrofoam "icebergs" for polar bears in the Arctic Ocean?

- At what point is a species doomed, either because of lost habitat or climatic shifts, such that resources spent in recovery attempts is effectively wasted money?

- How should FWS prioritize among species threatened by climate change?

E.   PROHIBITION AGAINST TAKES

The loss of habitat from human development activities is far and away the greatest cause of the decline and disappearance of wildlife and plant species. This loss is the principal basis for the endangerment of more than eighty percent of the species currently listed or proposed for listing under the Endangered Species Act. Federal lands alone cannot provide adequate endangered species habitat. Many protected species are migratory or have very large home ranges and cannot be confined to federally owned parks, wildlife refuges, or wilderness areas. More than fifty percent of all the species subject to the ESA have at least eighty-one percent of their habitat on privately owned lands. Between a third and a half of protected species do not live on federal land at all. Furthermore, the distribution of endangered and threatened species in the United States does not match the distribution of public land. Some states with high numbers of listed species have relatively little federal land within their borders. For example, the greatest numbers of endangered and threatened species in the United States occur in Hawaii, southern California, the southeastern coastal states, and southern Appalachia. The number of species in these areas exceeds the availability of federally owned habitat. Hawaii is home to 225 listed species, but only sixteen percent of its lands are managed by the federal government. Texas has seventy listed species within its borders, while only one percent of its land is federal. Florida has ninety-three listed species, and nine percent federal land. By contrast, some states have considerable federal lands, but few listed species. Alaska, for example, is more than sixty-eight percent federal land, but has only five listed species. * * *

Unfortunately, this conservation is not happening. Information compiled by the FWS and the General Accounting Office shows that endangered species on private lands are in much worse condition than those on federal land. Of the listed plants and animals found entirely on federal land, approximately eighteen percent are judged to be improving; and the ratio of declining species to improving species is approximately 1.5 to 1. In contrast, of the species found entirely on private lands (excluding property owned by conservation groups like the Nature Conservancy) only three percent are improving, and the ratio of declining species to improving species is 9 to 1. These figures fail to paint the complete picture, however, because the FWS does not know the status of over half of the species found exclusively on private land.

Karin P. Sheldon, *Habitat Conservation Planning: Addressing the Achilles Heel of the Endangered Species Act,* 6 N.Y.U. Envtl. L.J. 279, 286 (1998).

Clearly, any effective endangered species legislation must address private land, controversial though this may be. Section 5 of the Act allows the Secretary to purchase land or water rights for the purpose of conserving threatened or endangered species. Such purchases are not particularly controversial, but they can only address a small portion of what Professor Sheldon identifies as a much larger problem. A much more charged question has been whether, and to what extent, protecting habitat on private land is covered by Section 9's prohibition on take.

Section 9(a)(1) of the ESA states that it is unlawful for any "person"—including federal, state or local governments, corporations, or private parties—to *take* an endangered species of fish or wildlife. 16 U.S.C. § 1538(a)(1)(B). "Take" is defined as "to harass, harm, pursue, hunt, shoot, wound, kill, trap, capture, or collect, or to attempt to engage in any such conduct." 16 U.S.C. 1532(19). Section 9(a)(2) provides lesser protection for endangered plants, banning the removal, digging up, or destruction of plants on federal land, in knowing violation of a state law or regulation, or in violation of a state criminal trespass law. Section 9 does not extend these protections to *threatened* species. However, under § 4(d) of the ESA, the Secretary of the Interior "may by regulation prohibit with respect to any threatened species" those acts which are prohibited with respect to endangered species in § 9. 16 U.S.C. § 1533(d). Using this authority, the Secretary has decided that the take prohibition of § 9 will apply to all threatened species except in those instances where the Secretary develops a special 4(d) rule for a particular species. *See* 50 C.F.R. § 17.31(a). Most recently, this approach was taken in the Bush administration for the listing of the Polar Bear. The Department of Interior used a Section 4(d) rule to ensure that if an activity is permissible under the Marine Mammal Protection Act, it will also be permissible under the Endangered Species Act with respect to the polar bear. This rule effectively exempted activities that contribute to global warming (and presumably are linked to loss of Arctic sea ice) from consideration as potential violations of ESA Sections 7 or 9. *See* http://www.doi.gov/news/08_News_Releases/080514a.html.

Enforcement of section 9 against private parties has proven controversial. While Section 9 speaks of actions, as we shall see in the section on indirect takes, its application has often been directed toward land use. Section 9's strongest critics thus claim that the constitutional takings prohibition has been effectively hijacked by environmental groups and the ESA employed as federal land use regulation.

1. DIRECT TAKES

Reading the text of Section 9, the take prohibition seems straightforward. Take has a long-established definition at common law—reducing wildlife to possession by capturing or killing it. Thus, if a poacher kills a Florida panther or traps one for sale, she is guilty of a direct take. If a frustrated golfer starts hitting golf balls at an endangered plover and kills it, that could be a take. 16 U.S.C. § 1538(a)(1). If an overeager gardener putting in bulbs digs up endangered snails, that could be a take. *Id.* § 1538(a)(2). Specific intent is not required, nor is knowledge of the law a prerequisite for civil or criminal liability. The sanctions for such violations are heavy, and can include criminal penalties for "knowing violations." *See* 16 U.S.C. § 1540.

2. INDIRECT TAKES

Section 3(19) of the ESA, however, defines "take" more broadly than simply capture or killing.

> The term 'take' means to harass, harm, pursue, hunt, shoot, wound, kill, trap, capture, or collect, or to attempt to engage in any such conduct.

16 U.S.C. § 1532(19). What if the state government maintains a flock of sheep whose grazing prevents the regeneration of habitat for an endangered bird? What if a private landowner cuts down trees that may serve as habitat for an endangered woodpecker or paves over a sand dune that could serve as the habitat of the endangered Delhi Sands flower-loving fly? What if a farmer withdraws water from a river where endangered steelhead spawn? In none of these instances does the party directly kill or injure an endangered species. Although these may not be classic, common law takes, do any of these actions rise to the level of a take under Section 9 given the ESA's more expansive definition of the term?

In 1978, the Sierra Club and other environmental groups brought an action against Hawaii's Department of Land & Natural Resources. The Department had introduced and maintained a herd of feral goats and sheep in the Mauna Kea game management area for sport hunting. It was undisputed that the herd's grazing consumed the shoots and seedlings of mamane trees, which take 25 years to grow into mature trees. Thus the grazing prevented regeneration of the forest. This, in turn, plaintiffs argued, impaired the designated critical habitat for the palila, an endangered bird in the honeycreeper family, because the palila only nests in mature mamane trees. The net result, they contended, was a take under Section 9.

This was a bold claim. In previous cases, Section 9 had been applied to direct actions against listed species. Here, by contrast, no direct harm was being inflicted on a particular bird. The harm would be felt by future palila (or, more accurately, not felt because after a few generations there would be no trees for future palilas to nest in). Nonetheless, in *Palila v. Hawaii Dept. of Land & Natural Resources* ("*Palila I*"), 471 F.Supp. 985 (D. Haw. 1979), *aff'd*, 639 F.2d 495 (9th Cir. 1981), the court agreed with the Sierra Club. The court stated that "The mamane-naio forest is essential for the Palila's survival. The bird has evolved in the mamane-naio ecosystem over the centuries and is uniquely adapted to feeding upon the mamane. The mamane trees provide food, shelter and nest sites for the Palila." *Id.* at 995. Pointing to FWS regulations defining a "take" as "significant environmental modification or degradation," the court ordered the Department to adopt a program to eradicate the feral sheep and goats from the palila's habitat and enjoined the Department from taking any action with the effect of increasing or maintaining the existing population of feral sheep and goats. *Id.* at 995, 999.

In response to the *Palila I* decision, FWS promulgated new regulations defining the word "harm" in the definition of "take" as:

> an act which *actually* kills or injures wildlife. Such act may include significant habitat modification or degradation where it *actually* kills or injures wildlife by significantly impairing essential behavioral patterns, including breeding, feeding or sheltering. 50 C.F.R. § 17.3 (emphasis added).

[handwritten: post-Padila I def of "harm" in "take"]

This new regulation came into play soon after, in another iteration of the *Palila* litigation, this time involving mouflon sheep, which Hawaii had also introduced into the palila's habitat and which, like the feral sheep and goats in the earlier litigation, fed on mamane trees. The case, known as *Palila II*, is excerpted below.

PALILA (LOXIOIDES BAILLEUI, FORMERLY PSITTIROSTRA BAILLEUI) V. HAWAII DEPARTMENT OF LAND AND NATURAL RESOURCES
852 F.2d 1106 (9th Cir. 1988)

[handwritten: Padila II]

The Department [the Hawaii Department of Land and Natural Resources] argues that the district court construed the definition of "harm" in 50 C.F.R. § 17.3 too broadly. The scope of the definition of harm is important because it in part sets the limit on what acts or omissions violate the Act's prohibition against "taking" an endangered species. * * *

In making this argument, the Department suggests a dichotomy between "actual" and "potential" harm. The Department believes that actual harm only includes those acts which result in the immediate destruction of the Palila's food sources; all other acts are "potential" harm no matter how clear the causal link and beyond the reach of the Act. Thus, the Department challenges the district court's finding that habitat destruction which could drive the Palila to extinction constitutes "harm." * * *

While promulgating a revised definition of harm, the Secretary noted that harm includes not only direct physical injury, but also injury caused by impairment of essential behavior patterns via habitat modification that can have significant and permanent effects on a listed species. Moreover, in that same promulgation notice, the Secretary let stand the district court's construction of harm in *Palila I*. In *Palila I*, the district court construed harm to include habitat destruction that could result in the extinction of the Palila— exactly the same type of injury at issue here. We conclude that the district court's inclusion within the definition of "harm" of habitat destruction that could drive the Palila to extinction falls within the Secretary's interpretation. *(H)*

The Secretary's inclusion of habitat destruction that could result in extinction follows the plain language of the statute because it serves the overall purpose of the Act, which is "to provide a means whereby the ecosystems upon which endangered species and threatened species depend may be conserved...." 16 U.S.C. § 1531(b). The definition serves the overall purpose of the Act since it conserves the Palila's threatened ecosystem (the mamane-naio woodland).

The Secretary's construction of harm is also consistent with the policy of Congress evidenced by the legislative history. For example, in the Senate Report on the Act: " 'Take' is defined in ... the broadest possible manner to include every conceivable way in which a person can 'take' or attempt to 'take' any fish or wildlife." The House Report said that the "harassment" form of taking would "allow, for example, the Secretary to regulate or prohibit the activities of birdwatchers where the effect of those activities might disturb the birds and make it difficult for them to hatch or raise their young." If the "harassment" form of taking includes activities so remote from actual injury to the bird as birdwatching, then the "harm" form of taking should include more direct activities, such as the mouflon sheep preventing any mamane from growing to maturity.[3]

The decisions in the *Palila* cases—that the definition of take included habitat modification that could cause future harm to an endangered population—were a cause for significant concern among property owners and the regulated community. The courts' reasoning suggested that traditional land use activities like home building, farming, logging, grazing, and irrigation could violate Section 9.

The concerns of property owners and the regulated community came to a head in the early 1990s when the listing of the Northern Spotted Owl, Red–Cockaded Woodpecker and Marbled Murrelet brought § 9 to timber country and FWS began threatening timber harvesters with fines and criminal prosecution. In the case of the spotted owl, FWS issued Guidelines prohibiting logging within protective "owl circles", where the logging would reduce the standing timber below the percentage which FWS's biologists had determined was necessary for an owl's feeding and sheltering. Depending on the location, owl circles could have a radius between 1.2 and 2.2 miles. In one case, for example, FWS initiated a criminal prosecution against three Department of Defense employees for "taking Red–Cockaded Woodpeckers by conspiring to permit the harvest of Red–Cockaded Woodpecker habitat.... [T]he sole 'harm' alleged was permitting cavity trees where woodpeckers *might* nest to be harvested, thereby leaving

3. In addition, the Secretary's interpretation is consistent with the presumption that Congress is "aware of an administrative or judicial interpretation of a statute and [adopts] that interpretation when it reenacts a statute without change."

In June 1981, in reaction to *Palila I*, the Secretary promulgated a definition of harm which apparently left no room for any form of habitat destruction. However, the Secretary withdrew this new definition as the result of a large number of negative comments.

Instead, in November 1981, the Secretary introduced the present definition. In 1982, after the *Palila I* decision and the Secretary's redefinition of harm, Congress amended the Endangered Species Act. Endangered Species Act Amendments of 1982. So, Congress presumably was aware of the current interpretation of harm when it amended the Act in 1982. But Congress did not modify the taking prohibition in any matter. Thus, Congress' failure to act indicates satisfaction with the current definition of harm and its interpretation by the Secretary and the judiciary.

woodpecker colonies in the vicinity without sufficient habitat in which to forage." Albert Gidari, *The Endangered Species Act: Impact of Section 9 on Private Landowners*, 24 ENVTL. L. 419, 422 n.7 (1994).

In this enforcement action and others, harm was equated with habitat modification that either increased risk for identified animals or for animals that biological models predicted would likely use the habitat. From the timber community's perspective, this focus was wrong. As they saw it, take should never have been extended beyond its historical meaning and if habitat modification had to be the standard, FWS should have to prove that the modification had actually killed or injured some identifiable animal. *See* James R. Rasband, *Priority, Probability and Proximate Cause: Lessons from Tort Law about Imposing ESA Responsibilities for Wildlife Harm on Water Users and Other Joint Habitat Modifers*, 33 ENVTL. L. 595, 604 (2003).

Timber operators and timber communities had two primary reasons for concern. Old growth timber in the Northwest is worth a lot of money. One owl circle on Washington state's Olympic Peninsula could prohibit timber harvest of up to 3,960 acres. At 1994 market values, timber prices ranged from $10,000–$40,000 per acre depending on the wood species. Doing the math, a single owl circle could cost property owners from approximately $40 to $160 million, Gidari, *supra*, at 427; and there were lots of owl circles. Perhaps of even greater concern for timber company executives was the threat of criminal prosecution if they were found to have proceeded with a timber cut that was later determined to be a take. The following excerpt, for example, is from a typical letter sent by FWS to a city in California that had proposed to zone for development certain property that encompassed the habitat of an endangered species.

> Section 9 of the Endangered Species Act of 1973 ... makes it unlawful for any person to take an endangered species without a permit.... Section 11 of the Act prescribes civil penalties of up to $10,000, or imprisonment for up to one year, or both, for knowingly violating any provision of the Endangered Species Act.... [W]e must advise you, unless you first secure a section 10(a) permit authorizing the incidental take ..., the approval and implementation of the proposed action may subject ... city officials to investigation by our law enforcement branch regarding potential violations of the Endangered Species Act.

Id. at 422 n.6.

Such financial and personal concerns eventually prompted a challenge to the entire harm regulation. Led by the forest products industry, a group of property owners styled as the Sweet Home Chapter of Communities for a Greater Oregon argued that FWS had exceeded its statutory authority in promulgating the broad definition of harm. Take, the plaintiffs contended, was limited to direct applications of force and did not include habitat modification that might indirectly kill or injure wildlife. Their challenge made its way to the Supreme Court in 1995, resulting in the following decision.

BABBITT V. SWEET HOME CHAPTER OF COMMUNITIES FOR A GREAT OREGON
515 U.S. 687 (1995)

JUSTICE STEVENS delivered the opinion of the Court.

The Endangered Species Act of 1973 (ESA or Act) contains a variety of protections designed to save from extinction species that the Secretary of the

Interior designates as endangered or threatened. Section 9 of the Act makes it unlawful for any person to "take" any endangered or threatened species. The Secretary has promulgated a regulation that defines the statute's prohibition on takings to include "significant habitat modification or degradation where it actually kills or injures wildlife." This case presents the question whether the Secretary exceeded his authority under the Act by promulgating that regulation.

I

Section 9(a)(1) of the Act provides the following protection for endangered species: * * *

Except as provided in sections 1535(g)(2) and 1539 of this title, with respect to any endangered species of fish or wildlife listed pursuant to section 1533 of this title it is unlawful for any person subject to the jurisdiction of the United States to— . . .

(B) take any such species within the United States or the territorial sea of the United States.

Section 3(19) of the Act defines the statutory term "take":

stat. The term "take" means to harass, harm, pursue, hunt, shoot, wound, kill, trap, capture, or collect, or to attempt to engage in any such conduct.

The Act does not further define the terms it uses to define "take." The Interior Department regulations that implement the statute, however, define the statutory term "harm":

reg. Harm in the definition of 'take' in the Act means an act which actually kills or injures wildlife. Such act may include significant habitat modification or degradation where it actually kills or injures wildlife by significantly impairing essential behavioral patterns, including breeding, feeding, or sheltering. 50 CFR § 17.3 (1994).

This regulation has been in place since 1975. * * *

Respondents in this action are small landowners, logging companies, and families dependent on the forest products industries in the Pacific Northwest and in the Southeast, and organizations that represent their interests. They brought this declaratory judgment action against petitioners, the Secretary of the Interior and the Director of the Fish and Wildlife Service, in the United States District Court for the District of Columbia to challenge the statutory validity of the Secretary's regulation defining "harm," particularly the inclusion of habitat modification and degradation in the definition. Respondents *facial challenge* challenged the regulation on its face. Their complaint alleged that application of the "harm" regulation to the red-cockaded woodpecker, an endangered species, and the northern spotted owl, a threatened species, had injured them economically. * * *

Respondents advanced three arguments to support their submission that Congress did not intend the word "take" in § 9 to include habitat modification, as the Secretary's "harm" regulation provides. First, they correctly noted that *arguments* language in the Senate's original version of the ESA would have defined "take" to include "destruction, modification, or curtailment of [the] habitat or range" of fish or wildlife, but the Senate deleted that language from the bill before enacting it. Second, respondents argued that Congress intended the Act's express authorization for the Federal Government to buy private land in order to prevent habitat degradation in § 5 to be the exclusive check against habitat modification on private property. Third, because the Senate added the term "harm" to the definition of "take" in a floor amendment without debate, respondents argued that the court should not interpret the term so expansively as to include habitat modification. * * *

II

Because this case was decided on motions for summary judgment, we may appropriately make certain factual assumptions in order to frame the legal issue. First, we assume respondents have no desire to harm either the red-cockaded woodpecker or the spotted owl; they merely wish to continue logging activities that would be entirely proper if not prohibited by the ESA. On the other hand, we must assume, arguendo, that those activities will have the effect, even though unintended, of detrimentally changing the natural habitat of both listed species and that, as a consequence, members of those species will be killed or injured. Under respondents' view of the law, the Secretary's only means of forestalling that grave result—even when the actor knows it is certain to occur[9]—is to use his § 5 authority to purchase the lands on which the survival of the species depends. The Secretary, on the other hand, submits that the § 9 prohibition on takings, which Congress defined to include "harm," places on respondents a duty to avoid harm that habitat alteration will cause the birds unless respondents first obtain a[n incidental take] permit pursuant to § 10.

The text of the Act provides three reasons for concluding that the Secretary's interpretation is reasonable. First, an ordinary understanding of the word "harm" supports it. The dictionary definition of the verb form of "harm" is "to cause hurt or damage to: injure." *Webster's Third New International Dictionary* 1034 (1966). In the context of the ESA, that definition naturally encompasses habitat modification that results in actual injury or death to members of an endangered or threatened species.

Respondents argue that the Secretary should have limited the purview of "harm" to direct applications of force against protected species, but the dictionary definition does not include the word "directly" or suggest in any way that only direct or willful action that leads to injury constitutes "harm."[10]

9. As discussed above, the Secretary's definition of "harm" is limited to "act[s] which actually kil[l] or injur[e] wildlife." 50 CFR § 17.3 (1994). In addition, in order to be subject to the Act's criminal penalties or the more severe of its civil penalties, one must "knowingly violat[e]" the Act or its implementing regulations. 16 U.S.C. §§ 1540(a)(1), (b)(1). Congress added "knowingly" in place of "willfully" in 1978 to make "criminal violations of the act a general rather than a specific intent crime." * * *

10. Respondents and the dissent emphasize what they portray as the "established meaning" of "take" in the sense of a "wildlife take," a meaning respondents argue extends only to "the effort to exercise dominion over some creature, and the concrete effect of [sic] that creature." ... This limitation ill serves the statutory text, which forbids not taking "some creature" but "tak[ing] any [endangered] species"—a formidable task for even the most rapacious feudal lord. More importantly, Congress explicitly defined the operative term "take" in the ESA, no matter how much the dissent wishes otherwise, thereby obviating the need for us to probe its meaning as we must probe the meaning of the undefined subsidiary term "harm." Finally, Congress' definition of "take" includes several words—most obviously "harass," "pursue," and "wound," in addition to "harm" itself—that fit respondents' and the dissent's

Moreover, unless the statutory term "harm" encompasses indirect as well as direct injuries, the word has no meaning that does not duplicate the meaning of other words that § 3 uses to define "take." A reluctance to treat statutory terms as surplusage supports the reasonableness of the Secretary's interpretation.[11]

Second, the broad purpose of the ESA supports the Secretary's decision to extend protection against activities that cause the precise harms Congress enacted the statute to avoid. In *TVA v. Hill*, 437 U.S. 153 (1978), we described the Act as "the most comprehensive legislation for the preservation of endangered species ever enacted by any nation." *Id*. at 180. * * *

Respondents advance strong arguments that activities that cause minimal or unforeseeable harm will not violate the Act as construed in the "harm" regulation. Respondents, however, present a facial challenge to the regulation. Thus, they ask us to invalidate the Secretary's understanding of "harm" in every circumstance, even when an actor knows that an activity, such as draining a pond, would actually result in the extinction of a listed species by destroying its habitat. Given Congress' clear expression of the ESA's broad purpose to protect endangered and threatened wildlife, the Secretary's definition of "harm" is reasonable.[13]

Third, the fact that Congress in 1982 authorized the Secretary to issue permits for takings that § 9(a)(1)(B) would otherwise prohibit, "if such taking is incidental to, and not the purpose of, the carrying out of an otherwise lawful activity," 16 U.S.C. § 1539(a)(1)(B), strongly suggests that Congress understood § 9(a)(1)(B) to prohibit indirect as well as deliberate takings. The permit process requires the applicant to prepare a "conservation plan" that specifies how he intends to "minimize and mitigate" the "impact" of his activity on endangered and threatened species, 16 U.S.C. § 1539(a)(2)(A), making clear that Congress had in mind foreseeable rather than merely accidental effects on listed species. No one could seriously request an "incidental" take permit to

definition of "take" no better than does "significant habitat modification or degradation."

11. In contrast, if the statutory term "harm" encompasses such indirect means of killing and injuring wildlife as habitat modification, the other terms listed in § 3—"harass," "pursue," "hunt," "shoot," "wound," "kill," "trap," "capture," and "collect"—generally retain independent meanings. Most of those terms refer to deliberate actions more frequently than does "harm," and they therefore do not duplicate the sense of indirect causation that "harm" adds to the statute. In addition, most of the other words in the definition describe either actions from which habitat modification does not usually result (e.g., "pursue," "harass") or effects to which activities that modify habitat do not usually lead (e.g., "trap," "collect").

13. The dissent incorrectly asserts that the Secretary's regulation (1) "dispenses with the foreseeability of harm" and (2) "fail[s] to require injury to particular animals." As to the first assertion, the regulation merely implements the statute, and it is therefore subject to the statute's "knowingly violates" language, see 16 U.S.C. § 1540(a)(1), (b)(1), and ordinary requirements of proximate causation and foreseeability. [*See* note 9, *supra*.] Nothing in the regulation purports to weaken those requirements. To the contrary, the word "actually" in the regulation should be construed to limit the liability about which the dissent appears most concerned, liability under the statute's "otherwise violates" provision. The Secretary did not need to include "actually" to connote "but for" causation, which the other words in the definition obviously require. As to the dissent's second assertion, every term in the regulation's definition of "harm" is subservient to the phrase "an act which actually kills or injures wildlife."

avert § 9 liability for direct, deliberate action against a member of an endangered or threatened species, but respondents would read "harm" so narrowly that the permit procedure would have little more than that absurd purpose. "When Congress acts to amend a statute, we presume it intends its amendment to have real and substantial effect." Congress' addition of the § 10 permit provision supports the Secretary's conclusion that activities not intended to harm an endangered species, such as habitat modification, may constitute unlawful takings under the ESA unless the Secretary permits them.

The Court of Appeals made three errors in asserting that "harm" must refer to a direct application of force because the words around it do.[15] First, the court's premise was flawed. Several of the words that accompany "harm" in the § 3 definition of "take," especially "harass," "pursue," "wound," and "kill," refer to actions or effects that do not require direct applications of force. Second, to the extent the court read a requirement of intent or purpose into the words used to define "take," it ignored § 11's express provision that a "knowing" action is enough to violate the Act. Third, the court employed *noscitur a sociis* to give "harm" essentially the same function as other words in the definition, thereby denying it independent meaning. The canon, to the contrary, counsels that a word "gathers meaning from the words around it." The statutory context of "harm" suggests that Congress meant that term to serve a particular function in the ESA, consistent with, but distinct from, the functions of the other verbs used to define "take." The Secretary's interpretation of "harm" to include indirectly injuring endangered animals through habitat modification permissibly interprets "harm" to have "a character of its own not to be submerged by its association." * * *

Nor does the Act's inclusion of the § 5 land acquisition authority and the § 7 directive to federal agencies to avoid destruction or adverse modification of critical habitat alter our conclusion. Respondents' argument that the Government lacks any incentive to purchase land under § 5 when it can simply prohibit takings under § 9 ignores the practical considerations that attend enforcement of the ESA. Purchasing habitat lands may well cost the Government less in many circumstances than pursuing civil or criminal penalties. In addition, the § 5 procedure allows for protection of habitat before the seller's activity has harmed any endangered animal, whereas the Government cannot enforce the § 9 prohibition until an animal has actually been killed or injured. The Secretary may also find the § 5 authority useful for preventing modification of land that is not yet but may in the future become habitat for an endangered or threatened species. The § 7 directive applies only to the Federal Government, whereas the § 9 prohibition applies to "any person." Section 7 imposes a broad, affirmative duty to avoid adverse habitat modifications that

---

15. The dissent makes no effort to defend the Court of Appeals' reading of the statutory definition as requiring a direct application of force. Instead, it tries to impose on § 9 a limitation of liability to "affirmative conduct intentionally directed against a particular animal or animals." Under the dissent's interpretation of the Act, a developer could drain a pond, knowing that the act would extinguish an endangered species of turtles, without even proposing a conservation plan or applying for a permit under § 10(a)(1)(B); unless the developer was motivated by a desire "to get at a turtle," no statutory taking could occur. Because such conduct would not constitute a taking at common law, the dissent would shield it from § 9 liability, even though the words "kill" and "harm" in the statutory definition could apply to such deliberate conduct. We cannot accept that limitation. In any event, our reasons for rejecting the Court of Appeals' interpretation apply as well to the dissent's novel construction.

§ 9 does not replicate, and § 7 does not limit its admonition to habitat modification that "actually kills or injures wildlife." Conversely, § 7 contains limitations that § 9 does not, applying only to actions "likely to jeopardize the continued existence of any endangered species or threatened species," 16 U.S.C. § 1536(a)(2), and to modifications of habitat that has been designated "critical" pursuant to § 4, 16 U.S.C. § 1533(b)(2). Any overlap that § 5 or § 7 may have with § 9 in particular cases is unexceptional, and simply reflects the broad purpose of the Act set out in § 2 and acknowledged in *TVA v. Hill*. * * *

We need not decide whether the statutory definition of "take" compels the Secretary's interpretation of "harm," because our conclusions that Congress did not unambiguously manifest its intent to adopt respondents' view and that the Secretary's interpretation is reasonable suffice to decide this case. *See generally Chevron U.S.A. Inc. v. Natural Resources Defense Council, Inc.*, 467 U.S. 837 (1984). The latitude the ESA gives the Secretary in enforcing the statute, together with the degree of regulatory expertise necessary to its enforcement, establishes that we owe some degree of deference to the Secretary's reasonable interpretation. * * *

III

Our conclusion that the Secretary's definition of "harm" rests on a permissible construction of the ESA gains further support from the legislative history of the statute. The Committee Reports accompanying the bills that became the ESA do not specifically discuss the meaning of "harm," but they make clear that Congress intended "take" to apply broadly to cover indirect as well as purposeful actions. The Senate Report stressed that " '[t]ake' is defined . . . in the broadest possible manner to include every conceivable way in which a person can 'take' or attempt to 'take' any fish or wildlife." . . . The House Report stated that "the broadest possible terms" were used to define restrictions on takings. . . . The House Report underscored the breadth of the "take" definition by noting that it included "harassment, whether intentional or not." The Report explained that the definition "would allow, for example, the Secretary to regulate or prohibit the activities of birdwatchers where the effect of those activities might disturb the birds and make it difficult for them to hatch or raise their young." These comments, ignored in the dissent's welcome but selective foray into legislative history, support the Secretary's interpretation that the term "take" in § 9 reached far more than the deliberate actions of hunters and trappers.

Two endangered species bills, S. 1592 and S. 1983, were introduced in the Senate and referred to the Commerce Committee. Neither bill included the word "harm" in its definition of "take," although the definitions otherwise closely resembled the one that appeared in the bill as ultimately enacted. . . . Senator Tunney, the floor manager of the bill in the Senate, subsequently introduced a floor amendment that added "harm" to the definition, noting that this and accompanying amendments would "help to achieve the purposes of the bill." Respondents argue that the lack of debate about the amendment that added "harm" counsels in favor of a narrow interpretation. We disagree. An obviously broad word that the Senate went out of its way to add to an important statutory definition is precisely the sort of provision that deserves a respectful reading.

The definition of "take" that originally appeared in S. 1983 differed from the definition as ultimately enacted in one other significant respect: It included "the destruction, modification, or curtailment of [the] habitat or range" of fish and wildlife. Hearings, at 27. Respondents make much of the fact that the

Commerce Committee removed this phrase from the "take" definition before S. 1983 went to the floor. *See* 119 CONG. REC. 25663 (1973). We do not find that fact especially significant. The legislative materials contain no indication why the habitat protection provision was deleted. That provision differed greatly from the regulation at issue today. Most notably, the habitat protection provision in S. 1983 would have applied far more broadly than the regulation does because it made adverse habitat modification a categorical violation of the "take" prohibition, unbounded by the regulation's limitation to habitat modifications that actually kill or injure wildlife. The S. 1983 language also failed to qualify "modification" with the regulation's limiting adjective "significant." We do not believe the Senate's unelaborated disavowal of the provision in S. 1983 undermines the reasonableness of the more moderate habitat protection in the Secretary's "harm" regulation. * * *

The history of the 1982 amendment that gave the Secretary authority to grant permits for "incidental" takings provides further support for his reading of the Act. The House Report expressly states that "[b]y use of the word 'incidental' the Committee intends to cover situations in which it is known that a taking will occur if the other activity is engaged in but such taking is incidental to, and not the purpose of, the activity." This reference to the foreseeability of incidental takings undermines respondents' argument that the 1982 amendment covered only accidental killings of endangered and threatened animals that might occur in the course of hunting or trapping other animals. Indeed, Congress had habitat modification directly in mind: Both the Senate Report and the House Conference Report identified as the model for the permit process a cooperative state-federal response to a case in California where a development project threatened incidental harm to a species of endangered butterfly by modification of its habitat. Thus, Congress in 1982 focused squarely on the aspect of the "harm" regulation at issue in this litigation. Congress' implementation of a permit program is consistent with the Secretary's interpretation of the term "harm."

IV

When it enacted the ESA, Congress delegated broad administrative and interpretive power to the Secretary. *See* 16 U.S.C. § 1533, 1540(f). The task of defining and listing endangered and threatened species requires an expertise and attention to detail that exceeds the normal province of Congress. Fashioning appropriate standards for issuing permits under § 10 for takings that would otherwise violate § 9 necessarily requires the exercise of broad discretion. The proper interpretation of a term such as "harm" involves a complex policy choice. When Congress has entrusted the Secretary with broad discretion, we are especially reluctant to substitute our views of wise policy for his. In this case, that reluctance accords with our conclusion, based on the text, structure, and legislative history of the ESA, that the Secretary reasonably construed the intent of Congress when he defined "harm" to include "significant habitat modification or degradation that actually kills or injures wildlife."

In the elaboration and enforcement of the ESA, the Secretary and all persons who must comply with the law will confront difficult questions of proximity and degree; for, as all recognize, the Act encompasses a vast range of economic and social enterprises and endeavors. These questions must be addressed in the usual course of the law, through case-by-case resolution and adjudication.

The judgment of the Court of Appeals is reversed.

It is so ordered.

JUSTICE O'CONNOR, concurring.

My agreement with the Court is founded on two understandings. First, the challenged regulation is limited to significant habitat modification that causes actual, as opposed to hypothetical or speculative, death or injury to identifiable protected animals. Second, even setting aside difficult questions of scienter, the regulation's application is limited by ordinary principles of proximate causation, which introduce notions of foreseeability. These limitations, in my view, call into question *Palila v. Hawaii Dept. of Land and Natural Resources*, 852 F.2d 1106 (CA9 1988) (*Palila II*), and with it, many of the applications derided by the dissent. Because there is no need to strike a regulation on a facial challenge out of concern that it is susceptible of erroneous application, however, and because there are many habitat-related circumstances in which the regulation might validly apply, I join the opinion of the Court.

In my view, the regulation is limited by its terms to actions that actually kill or injure individual animals. Justice Scalia disagrees, arguing that the harm regulation "encompasses injury inflicted, not only upon individual animals, but upon populations of the protected species." At one level, I could not reasonably quarrel with this observation; death to an individual animal always reduces the size of the population in which it lives, and in that sense, "injures" that population. But by its insight, the dissent means something else. Building upon the regulation's use of the word "breeding," Justice Scalia suggests that the regulation facially bars significant habitat modification that actually kills or injures hypothetical animals (or, perhaps more aptly, causes potential additions to the population not to come into being). Because "[i]mpairment of breeding does not 'injure' living creatures," Justice Scalia reasons, the regulation must contemplate application to "a population of animals which would otherwise have maintained or increased its numbers."

I disagree. As an initial matter, I do not find it as easy as Justice Scalia does to dismiss the notion that significant impairment of breeding injures living creatures. To raze the last remaining ground on which the piping plover currently breeds, thereby making it impossible for any piping plovers to reproduce, would obviously injure the population (causing the species' extinction in a generation). But by completely preventing breeding, it would also injure the individual living bird, in the same way that sterilizing the creature injures the individual living bird. To "injure" is, among other things, "to impair." *Webster's Ninth New Collegiate Dictionary* 623 (1983). One need not subscribe to theories of "psychic harm," to recognize that to make it impossible for an animal to reproduce is to impair its most essential physical functions and to render that animal, and its genetic material, biologically obsolete. This, in my view, is actual injury.

In any event, even if impairing an animal's ability to breed were not, in and of itself, an injury to that animal, interference with breeding can cause an animal to suffer other, perhaps more obvious, kinds of injury. The regulation has clear application, for example, to significant habitat modification that kills or physically injures animals which, because they are in a vulnerable breeding state, do not or cannot flee or defend themselves, or to environmental pollutants that cause an animal to suffer physical complications during gestation. Breeding, feeding, and sheltering are what animals do. If significant habitat modification, by interfering with these essential behaviors, actually kills or injures an animal protected by the Act, it causes "harm" within the meaning of the regulation. In contrast to Justice Scalia, I do not read the regulation's "breeding" reference to vitiate or somehow to qualify the clear actual death or injury requirement, or to suggest that the regulation contemplates extension to nonexistent animals.

There is no inconsistency, I should add, between this interpretation and the commentary that accompanied the amendment of the regulation to include the actual death or injury requirement. *See* 46 Fed.Reg. 54748 (1981). Quite the contrary. It is true, as Justice Scalia observes, that the Fish and Wildlife Service states at one point that "harm" is not limited to "direct physical injury to an individual member of the wildlife species," *see* 46 Fed.Reg. 54748 (1981). But one could just as easily emphasize the word "direct" in this sentence as the word "individual."* Elsewhere in the commentary, the Service makes clear that "section 9's threshold does focus on individual members of a protected species." *Id.* at 54749. Moreover, the Service says that the regulation has no application to speculative harm, explaining that its insertion of the word "actually" was intended "to bulwark the need for proven injury to a species due to a party's actions." *Ibid.; see also ibid.* (approving language that "[h]arm covers actions ... which actually (as opposed to potentially), cause injury"). That a protected animal could have eaten the leaves of a fallen tree or could, perhaps, have fruitfully multiplied in its branches is not sufficient under the regulation. Instead, as the commentary reflects, the regulation requires demonstrable effect (i.e., actual injury or death) on actual, individual members of the protected species.

By the dissent's reckoning, the regulation at issue here, in conjunction with 16 U.S.C. § 1540(a)(1), imposes liability for any habitat-modifying conduct that ultimately results in the death of a protected animal, "regardless of whether that result is intended or even foreseeable, and no matter how long the chain of causality between modification and injury." *Post,* at 2421. Even if § 1540(a)(1) does create a strict liability regime (a question we need not decide at this juncture), I see no indication that Congress, in enacting that section, intended to dispense with ordinary principles of proximate causation. Strict liability means liability without regard to fault; it does not normally mean liability for every consequence, however remote, of one's conduct. I would not lightly assume that Congress, in enacting a strict liability statute that is silent on the causation question, has dispensed with this well-entrenched principle. In the absence of congressional abrogation of traditional principles of causation, then, private parties should be held liable under § 1540(a)(1) only if their habitat-modifying actions proximately cause death or injury to protected animals. The regulation, of course, does not contradict the presumption or notion that ordinary principles of causation apply here. Indeed, by use of the word "actually," the regulation clearly rejects speculative or conjectural effects, and thus itself invokes principles of proximate causation.

Proximate causation is not a concept susceptible of precise definition. It is easy enough, of course, to identify the extremes. The farmer whose fertilizer is lifted by a tornado from tilled fields and deposited miles away in a wildlife refuge cannot, by any stretch of the term, be considered the proximate cause of death or injury to protected species occasioned thereby. At the same time, the landowner who drains a pond on his property, killing endangered fish in the process, would likely satisfy any formulation of the principle.... Proximate causation depends to a great extent on considerations of the fairness of imposing liability for remote consequences. The task of determining whether

---

* Justice Scalia suggests that, if the word "direct" merits emphasis in this sentence, then the sentence should be read as an effort to negate principles of proximate causation. As this case itself demonstrates, however, the word "direct" is susceptible of many meanings. * * *

proximate causation exists in the limitless fact patterns sure to arise is best left to lower courts. But I note, at the least, that proximate cause principles inject a foreseeability element into the statute, and hence, the regulation, that would appear to alleviate some of the problems noted by the dissent. *See, e.g., post,* at 2423 (describing "a farmer who tills his field and causes erosion that makes silt run into a nearby river which depletes oxygen and thereby [injures] protected fish").

In my view, then, the "harm" regulation applies where significant habitat modification, by impairing essential behaviors, proximately (foreseeably) causes actual death or injury to identifiable animals that are protected under the Endangered Species Act. Pursuant to my interpretation, *Palila II*—under which the Court of Appeals held that a state agency committed a "taking" by permitting mouflon sheep to eat mamane-naio seedlings that, when full grown, might have fed and sheltered endangered palila—was wrongly decided according to the regulation's own terms. Destruction of the seedlings did not proximately cause actual death or injury to identifiable birds; it merely prevented the regeneration of forest land not currently sustaining actual birds.

This case, of course, comes to us as a facial challenge. We are charged with deciding whether the regulation on its face exceeds the agency's statutory mandate. I have identified at least one application of the regulation (*Palila II*) that is, in my view, inconsistent with the regulation's own limitations. That misapplication does not, however, call into question the validity of the regulation itself. One can doubtless imagine questionable applications of the regulation that test the limits of the agency's authority. However, it seems to me clear that the regulation does not on its terms exceed the agency's mandate, and that the regulation has innumerable valid habitat-related applications. Congress may, of course, see fit to revisit this issue. And nothing the Court says today prevents the agency itself from narrowing the scope of its regulation at a later date.

With this understanding, I join the Court's opinion.

[Justice Scalia's dissent, which the Chief Justice and Justice Thomas joined, is omitted]

QUESTIONS AND DISCUSSION

1. Both the Stevens and O'Connor opinions emphasize that this is a facial challenge and thus if *any* factual scenario in which habitat modification can constitute harm can be found, the regulation should be affirmed. As the majority opinion notes,

> Respondents, however, present a facial challenge to the regulation. Thus, they ask us to invalidate the Secretary's understanding of "harm" in every circumstance, even when an actor knows that an activity, such as draining a pond, would actually result in the extinction of a listed species by destroying its habitat.

Id. at 612. Given this low threshold for the government to win its case, why do you think the litigants decided to make a facial challenge to the guidelines? Wouldn't they have been better off waiting for a case with more favorable facts for a test case?

2. Does *Palila* survive *Sweet Home*? Justice O'Connor clearly would limit the application of the harm regulation to situations where significant habitat modification, by impairing essential behaviors, *proximately (foresee-*

ably) causes actual death or injury to *identifiable* animals. On this basis, Justice O'Connor questions the Ninth Circuit's interpretation of harm. Where do you think the *Sweet Home* majority would come out on this question?

3. How would Justice Stevens and Justice O'Connor respond to the criticisms of Justice Scalia's dissent excerpted below?

> Justice O'Connor supposes that an "impairment of breeding" intrinsically injures an animal because "to make it impossible for an animal to reproduce is to impair its most essential physical functions and to render that animal, and its genetic material, biologically obsolete." This imaginative construction does achieve the result of extending "impairment of breeding" to individual animals; but only at the expense of also expanding "injury" to include elements beyond physical harm to individual animals. For surely the only harm to the individual animal from impairment of that "essential function" is not the failure of issue (which harms only the issue), but the psychic harm of perceiving that it will leave this world with no issue (assuming, of course, that the animal in question, perhaps an endangered species of slug, is capable of such painful sentiments). If it includes that psychic harm, then why not the psychic harm of not being able to frolic about—so that the draining of a pond used for an endangered animal's recreation, but in no way essential to its survival, would be prohibited by the Act? That the concurrence is driven to such a dubious redoubt is an argument for, not against, the proposition that "injury" in the regulation includes injury to populations of animals. Even more so with the concurrence's alternative explanation: that "impairment of breeding" refers to nothing more than concrete injuries inflicted by the habitat modification on the animal who does the breeding, such as "physical complications [suffered] during gestation," *ibid.* Quite obviously, if "impairment of breeding" meant such physical harm to an individual animal, it would not have had to be mentioned.

4. Do you agree with Justice O'Connor's analysis of the hypothetical taking for razing the last remaining breeding habitat for the piping plover, making reproduction impossible? Suppose, for example, that a developer clears a large beach area along Lake Michigan for a commercial development. The beach was known to contain nesting habitat for the piping plover, a small shore bird species listed as endangered in the Great Lakes region and as threatened in other parts of the country. The developer takes care to clear the land during the winter months when the plover is not known to use the area. How might different interpretations of "harm" affect your answer? Would it matter if the area had been designated critical habitat for the plover? This issue is addressed more fully at note 6 below.

5. In the broadest sense, of course, *Sweet Home* is a loss for the plaintiffs because the Court clearly held that habitat modification could constitute a take. In a narrower sense, however, how could you argue that the decision has the potential to be something of a victory? Does the Court's explanation of why the regulation is valid effectively narrow its scope?

6. What proximate cause test will be applied after *Sweet Home*? Does the measure of impact focus on individuals or populations? And what constitutes "proof" of death or injury from an incidental take? Do you have to produce a dead body or is statistical evidence (such as a species viability model) sufficient? Is it now potentially *harder* to show a take? For a property owner contemplating whether to engage in a particular activity or

[handwritten margin note: prox. cause]

risk liability or even imprisonment, how much guidance is offered by a proximate cause test?

7. One of the perplexing questions left after *Sweet Home* is how to evaluate the issues of proximate cause and individual injury in light of background risks to a threatened or endangered species.

Consider a river system that is degraded by diversions, point and nonpoint source pollution, and hydroelectric projects. The population of an endangered fish in the river system has been declining over time as these various river uses have increased. The best biological evidence indicates that any individual endangered fish has a five percent chance of surviving to maturity in the river. Before any human uses of the river, fifty percent of the fish reached maturity. Plaintiff wants to enjoin a new diversion on the river and its experts are prepared to testify that the diversion will impair the spawning and feeding of the fish and reduce its chances of survival from five percent to three percent. If the focus is on individual fish, plaintiff has a causation problem. Plaintiff will not be able to prove that the project will harm any particular fish. Think about finding a dead fish after the new diversion. If there is no rusty hook, no cuts from turbines or the like, plaintiff would not be able to prove that the fish died because of the human-induced problems in the river. Given that fifty percent of the fish did not reach maturity in a state of nature, plaintiff cannot show on a more probable than not basis that the fish was killed by the collective impact of the various habitat modifications. The proof is even more difficult if the question is the new diversion. With respect to any particular fish, the chances of the diversion harming that fish are only two percent.

If the focus is on population, however, the entire analysis changes. A biologist may not know which fish will die but she can have a relatively high degree of confidence (enough to satisfy the more probable than not standard) that two out of every hundred fish will die if the new diversion occurs. Although the plaintiff can only prove harm at the population level, the fact remains that two fish suffer individual, if untraceable, deaths. How this case comes out after *Sweet Home* is a difficult question. With respect to any particular fish, the diversion merely impairs its chance at survival. The diversion does not make its survival impossible. This suggests that Justice O'Connor may not see harm in such a case. On the other hand, the fact that two individual, if unidentified, fish will die may satisfy the majority's requirement of "injury to particular animals," provided that the diversion is regarded as a significant impairment.

In the river hypothetical where the new diversion affects the entire habitat of the endangered fish population, it is relatively easy to conclude that the diversion will lead to two additional deaths. But it will not always be so easy to use population data to prove individual harm. Take one more example. Assume that in a forest untrammeled by man, or indeed in a forest where habitat modification has occurred but was regarded as reasonable when completed, there is a ten percent likelihood that any spotted owl will be killed by a predator. Then assume that a particular timber cut would increase to fifteen percent the likelihood that a pair of spotted owls will be subject to predation because the pair will then spend more time flying without canopy protection. If one of these owls ends up killed by a hawk, it cannot be proved, on a more probable than not basis, that the timber cut caused the take. More probably than not, the take would have happened even without the timber harvest.

Even with a population focus, causation is difficult. Unlike the river hypothetical where we assumed the particular diversion impacted the entire population, in the owl case, the particular timber cut potentially impacts only two owls. If a population biologist could review 100 timber harvests associated with fifteen acts of predation, theoretically she could be confident that five of those deaths were the result of timber harvests. What she could not do would be to associate any one bird kill with any particular timber harvest. To enjoin the timber harvest would be to make the single property owner responsible for a population-level risk.

James R. Rasband, *Priority, Probability and Proximate Cause: Lessons from Tort Law about Imposing ESA Responsibilities for Wildlife Harm on Water Users and Other Joint Habitat Modifers*, 33 ENVTL. L. 595, 613–15 (2003).

How do you think the *Sweet Home* majority or Justice O'Connor would resolve these hypotheticals? How should background risk to a species be taken into account in determining causation issues? What if, in contrast to the two hypotheticals, a proposed activity will more than double the background risk—say from 4% risk of mortality to 10% risk of mortality. Should the actor be responsible for every endangered animal that turns up dead in the project area?

In assessing causation, what should FWS even use as the baseline? If a river is severely degraded by other activities, or a forest significantly cut over by other harvesters, should the last diverter or the last harvester be identified as the cause of harm? If so, what incentives does that create for property owners?

8. In *Palila II*, the Ninth Circuit upheld the lower court's ruling that habitat degradation that could result in extinction is a Section 9 taking, but declined to "reach the issue of whether harm includes habitat degradation that merely retards recovery." 852 F.2d at 1110. Does *Sweet Home* provide an answer? What land management actions might modify habitat but still not constitute a take?

9. In the aftermath of *Sweet Home*, the courts continue to struggle with what sorts of activities will be considered the proximate cause of harm to a threatened or endangered species. Soon after *Sweet Home* was decided, the Ninth Circuit confirmed that *Palila II* was still good law and enjoined a timber harvest on a showing, that although no nests had been found, there had been one hundred detections of Marbled Murrelets in the proposed harvest area, and experts believed that the harvest would likely harm the birds "by impairing their breeding and increasing the likelihood of attack by predators." *Marbled Murrelet v. Babbitt*, 83 F.3d 1060, 1067–68 (9th Cir. 1996), *cert. denied*, 519 U.S. 1108 (1997). Other decisions, in both the Ninth Circuit and elsewhere, however, have seemed to take a narrower view of causation more in line with Justice O'Connor's concurrence. *See, e.g., Greenpeace Foundation v. Mineta*, 122 F. Supp. 2d 1123, 1134 (D. Haw. 2000) (holding that whether NMFS' operation of a lobster fishery caused a take of the endangered monk seal, which fed on lobsters, depended upon whether the "lobster plays such an essential role in the monk seal diet that a reduction of lobster prey dooms the monk seal to extinction"); *Hawksbill Sea Turtle v. FEMA*, 11 F. Supp. 2d 529 (D. V.I. 1998) (refusing to enjoin project which would cause runoff into Vessup Bay and kill the sponges and sea grasses which were a primary source of food for endangered turtles because there was no evidence that the sponges and grasses were the only food source for the turtles); *United States v. West Coast Forest Resources*

Ltd., No. CIV. 96–1575–HO, 2000 WL 298707 (D. Or. 2000) (refusing to enjoin a timber harvest without a showing that the area to be harvested was "essential to the owl's survival").

10. As a result of the *Sweet Home* and *Palila* decisions, has Section 9 implicitly incorporated Section 7's prohibition against adverse modification of critical habitat? Consider, for example, why it should matter to the *Palila I* and *II* courts that the mamane forest had been designated as critical habitat for the bird.

> The Mauna Kea area had been designated critical habitat for the palila, but this designation was legally irrelevant [for section 9 analysis] because of the absence of federal lands, funds, or participation. Even though section 7 could not be implicated, the court consistently referred to the "critical habitat" of the Palila. Finding a violation of the ESA through the takings restrictions in section 9, the court concluded that "defendants are violating the Endangered Species Act by maintaining feral sheep and goats in the palila's critical habitat." As with the dicta in *Froehlke*, the court emphasized the adverse modification of critical habitat, although it was not legally relevant.... The court justified its broad interpretation of section 9 by citing the discussion of habitat destruction in the ESA's legislative history. As it was with jeopardy under section 7, adverse modification seems redundant with the takings regulations. Indeed, the district court cited USFWS regulations defining "harm" under section 9 as "significant environmental modification or degradation."

James Salzman, *The Evolution and Application of Critical Habitat Under the Endangered Species Act*, 14 HARV. ENVTL. L. REV. 311, 327 (1990). If *Sweet Home* and *Palila* allow proof of harm by showing risks to the survival of the population, has Section 9 implicitly incorporated Section 7's jeopardy standard?

11. *Nature in the Dock.* Section 11 of the ESA allows "any person" to file suit to enjoin violations under the statute. In the first paragraph of *Palila II*, the judge notes that "The Palila (which has earned the right to be capitalized since it is a party to this proceeding) is represented by attorneys for the Sierra Club, Audubon Society, and other environmental parties...." 852 F.2d at 1107. Nor is this the only example of animal plaintiffs suing (successfully) under the ESA and other environmental statutes.

On its face, naming a bird as the lead plaintiff seems odd, to say the least. The Administrative Procedure Act entitles any person suffering legal wrong because of agency action to judicial review, and defines "person" as an "individual, partnership, corporation, association, or public or private organization other than an agency." 5 U.S.C. § 551(2). Federal Rule of Civil Procedure 17 speaks only of individuals, infants and incompetent persons, and the ESA grants a "person" the right to sue, not "winged creatures." There are, however, quite a few cases on record with non-human plaintiffs, including a Loggerhead turtle, a Bald eagle, a polluted river (the Byram River), a marsh (No Bottom), a brook (the Brown), a beach (Makena), a national monument (Death Valley), and a town commons (Billerica). *See, e.g., Loggerhead Turtle v. County of Volusia*, 148 F.3d 1231 (11th Cir. 1998), *cert. denied*, 526 U.S. 1081 (1999); *Marbled Murrelet v. Pacific Lumber Co.*, 880 F.Supp. 1343 (N.D. Cal. 1995), *aff'd*, 83 F.3d 1060 (9th Cir. 1996); *American Bald Eagle v. Bhatti*, 9 F.3d 163, 164 (1st

Cir. 1993). *See generally* Christopher Stone, Earth and Other Ethics 6–7 (1987).

Why do plaintiffs' attorneys do this? One obvious reason is the rhetorical benefit of having an endangered species as a party to the case—"Not only do I speak on behalf of the spotted owl, your Honor, but it was so incensed that it's become a party to the lawsuit!" From the perspective of the plaintiff groups, naming an object or species also has the advantage of avoiding turf wars. If several NGOs are participating in a lawsuit, there is sometimes disagreement over who will get to be the "named" plaintiff, i.e., the first plaintiff on the complaint. By naming an object or species as the lead plaintiff, that issue can be avoided entirely.

Perhaps the more important question, then, is why do defendants allow this? So long as the other named plaintiffs have standing, the Justice Department frequently chooses not to raise the issue of standing for non-humans since the case would go forward with the other plaintiffs, anyway.

The best insight on these issues comes from the description by Professor Denise Antolini, an attorney for the Sierra Club Legal Defense Fund (SCLDF, now Earthjustice) prior to becoming a law professor, of her involvement in *Hawaiian Crow v. Lujan*, 906 F.Supp. 549, 552 (D. Haw. 1991). SCLDF named the endangered crow, known locally as the 'Alala, as the lead plaintiff in a suit for implementation of the bird's recovery plan. As Professor Antolini relates,

> My experience litigating cases with SCLDF in Hawaii (1990–96) was that the federal government attorneys never used to care if we named critters as plaintiffs (and, of course, it makes no practical difference if you have the backup human or organizational plaintiff). Naming critters as plaintiffs in environmental cases is a time-honored tradition. But in our controversial 'Alala ESA case, the humorless private landowner intervenor decided that having the critically endangered crow as the lead plaintiff was just too much (the ranch did not like the adverse publicity, of course, and public image/message was our main reason for having the critter in the lead). The private defendant moved to dismiss the crow. I had a heck of a time writing the opposition brief given that the plain language of the ESA citizen suit provision says "any person may commence a civil suit...." We argued "time honored tradition" and "no prejudice to defendant," but in the end, the statute's plain language killed us. Judge Ezra dismissed the crow. (The ranch moved for Rule 11 sanctions too, which the judge graciously brushed aside.) No harm done, of course, because we had Audubon on the pleadings already, and the litigation moved forward without much of a hiccup.

E-mail from Denise Antolini, Feb. 1, 2004 (with reprint permission kindly granted by Denise).

Private defendants have successfully objected in other cases as well. The lawsuit, *Citizens to End Animal Suffering & Exploitation, Inc. v. The New England Aquarium*, 836 F.Supp. 45 (D. Mass. 1993), for example was originally brought in the name of Kama, a dolphin. The court concluded that Kama did not have standing. *See also Coho Salmon v. Pacific Lumber Co.*, 30 F. Supp. 2d 1231, 1239 n.2 (N.D. Cal. 1998) (observing that, "[w]ithout delving into the vagaries of the term 'entity,' the court notes that, to swim its way into federal court in this action, the coho salmon would have to battle a strong current and leap barriers greater than a waterfall or the occasional fallen tree'').

12. The majority decision in *Sweet Home* relies, in part, on the language from *T.V.A. v. Hill* that stresses the purpose of the law to recover species whatever the cost. What accounts for the consistent, expansive support by the Court of the ESA's goals, in contrast to the much more limited interpretation of NEPA's mandates? As a matter of statutory interpretation, how much weight should be given to an Act's broad purposes in determining the meaning of specific statutory language?

———

PROBLEM EXERCISE: GRIZZLIES AND CORN ON THE TRACKS

Three trains carrying corn derailed in northwestern Montana, spilling much of the corn. The corn spill attracted grizzlies to the site who, while feeding, were put at risk of being hit by passing trains. Grizzly bears are listed as threatened under the ESA. In just under two years, five more bears were killed in the immediate vicinity of the spill site. The train company spent $9.6 million to fix the track and $500,000 to clean up the site. An environmental group charges that the train company has been taking the grizzly bears by virtue of its train collisions. It files suit for an injunction requiring the railroad to take action to avoid future takes by reducing train speed near the spill site and studying the deployment of air bags on the front of trains. The injunction would also require that the train company obtain an incidental take permit. What should the court decide? Can the train company be prosecuted for a civil or criminal penalty? *See National Wildlife Fed'n v. Burlington Northern Railroad,* 23 F.3d 1508 (9th Cir. 1994).

———

PROBLEM EXERCISE: PYGMY OWLS ON THE DOUBLE R RANCH

The Pygmy owl is listed as an endangered species. Pygmy owls frequently nest in cavities in saguaro cactus trees. The Double R ranch, a 2,560–acre river ranch spread in the Sonoran desert of southern Arizona, contains some of the last remaining high quality saguaro habitat in areas surrounded by overgrazed BLM lands. Double R has been operating as a dude ranch. It recently was purchased to operate as a commercial ranch. The local group, Friends of the Pygmy Owl, is concerned because cattle grazing has been shown to trample young saguaro cactus, severely reducing cactus populations. Records from the last 50 years indicate that Pygmy owls have historically nested on the ranch, though none are known to be nesting at the moment (the ranch owners have not allowed Friends of the Pygmy Owl access to their property). A well-respected University of Arizona biologist has recently published a study showing that Pygmy owls are declining in the region because of a variety of factors, including development, feral cats, and grazing. Friends of the Pygmy Owl files a suit against the Double R ranch, which now has 10 head of cattle grazing, to enjoin it from increasing its herd to commercial levels (about 100 cattle).

(a) You have been hired by the Double R ranch to oppose a motion for summary judgment. What are your strongest arguments?

(b) Does it matter if the Double R lands have been designated as critical habitat?

(c) Does it matter whether any Pygmy owl nesting sites have been found on the property or is it sufficient that birds have historically been observed on the property?

(d) Suppose the rancher needs a permit to drill a water well on adjacent federal lands, and for a right-of-way for a pipeline to bring the water to the ranch. What litigation opportunities would now be available to Friends?

————

Case Study: Reintroduction of Wolves

In 1982, partially in response to the *Palila* decision, Congress amended the ESA by adding Section 10(j), allowing the Secretary of the Interior to limit the application of Sections 7 and 9 where the secretary issues a permit for the reintroduction and restoration of threatened or endangered species. 16 U.S.C. § 1539(j). Reintroductions are sometimes provided for in species recovery plans and have produced some successes, though often at a high price in both dollars and public relations. Reintroduction of the California condor, the black-footed ferret, and the Rocky Mountain gray wolf have cost more than $50 million, for example, and caused significant controversy.

Having studied the prohibitions of Sections 7 and 9, you can quickly see why reintroduction under the ESA would prove controversial. How will landowners react when they think that they may no longer be able to manage their land a certain way or may have to suffer livestock predation because the government is reintroducing an endangered species near them? This can be perceived as quite a different matter than proscribing behavior because an endangered species is already there.

Under Section 10(j), populations of endangered or threatened species that are reintroduced within their historic range, but outside of the areas they currently inhabit, are designated "experimental populations" that are either "essential" or "nonessential." 16 U.S.C. § 1539(j)(2)(B). An essential designation is issued if the population's loss "would be likely to appreciably reduce the likelihood of the survival of the species in the wild," and provides the reintroduced species with the full protection of Sections 7 and 9. This designation, not surprisingly, would be quite controversial. For this reason, Interior has never reintroduced a species under "essential" experimental status, so the "nonessential" designation is more relevant. This provides full ESA protections but only within the boundaries of national parks and national wildlife refuges. Outside federal lands, FWS has great discretion to prescribe the rules for introduced species, allowing takes in limited circumstances. This limited protective status has proven important in blunting much of the opposition from private landowners because they are not subject to full ESA restrictions from newly reintroduced endangered species on their land. At the same time, of course, this lack of full protection for the reintroduced species may make harder the ultimate goal of reintroducing species under the ESA—to reestablish truly wild populations.

GREATER YELLOWSTONE WOLF REINTRODUCTION

Gray wolves (*canis lupis*) are the largest wild members of Canidae, or dog family, with adult males weighing up to 100 pounds or more. They prey on large animals including deer, moose, elk, caribou, and mountain goats. They are social animals that live in packs of 2–10 members that occupy ranges of 20–200 square miles or more. Although gray wolves historically ranged across most of North America, they have been driven from 95% of their original range through eradication programs and loss of habitat. By the early 1970s, the few hundred estimated wolves remaining were isolated in Northern Minnesota and Michigan.

In 1978, the FWS listed the gray wolf as endangered throughout the lower 48 states outside of Minnesota, where the wolf was listed as threatened. In 1987, the FWS issued the Northern Rocky Mountain Wolf Recovery Plan, which concluded that approximately 300 wolves would need to be reintroduced for the species to recover in the Western United States. In conjunction with the National Park Service, FWS issued a final plan to release between 90–150 wolves from Canada into the Yellowstone and central Idaho areas over a three- to five-year period beginning in 1995. The final rules designated the wolves as part of a non-essential experimental population. 59 Fed. Reg. 60252 (Nov. 22, 1994).

Beginning in the winter of 1995, gray wolves captured in the Canadian Rockies were released into the greater Yellowstone ecosystem. The reintroduced wolves have thrived. In 2000, the FWS recorded that the goal of at least 30 breeding pairs in Wyoming, Montana, and Idaho had been met. Indeed, the Gray wolf in the northern Rockies was recently downlisted from endangered to threatened.

Not surprisingly, ranchers opposed the wolves' introduction. The FWS addressed this concern by expressly allowing private landowners to take any wolf caught killing, wounding, or biting livestock on their land. This exemption was complicated, however, by the fact that wolves from Northern Montana (which still received full ESA protection) occasionally wandered into the reintroduction areas. In *Wyoming Farm Bureau v. Babbitt*, 987 F.Supp. 1349 (D. Wyo. 1997), ranchers and other opponents to the wolf reintroduction program made two claims. The first was that the overlap between reintroduced wolves and those naturally occurring in the region created irreconcilable obstacles to enforcement. Ranchers would be unable to distinguish between naturally occurring individuals (afforded full endangered species protections) who wandered into an area where reintroduced experimental populations (with lesser ESA protections) had been released. The second claim was that the ESA does not allow reintroduction if there is already an existing population. If naturally occurring wolves occasionally wandered into the reintroduction area, plaintiffs argued, then they constituted an existing population. Indeed, some of the plaintiffs believed that the wolves in Wyoming were not strays that had wandered down from Montana, at all, but were wolves descended from a subspecies that had been there all along. This desire to protect the gene pool of the supposedly native wolves motivated some environmentalists to support the suit. The district court ordered the reintroduced wolves removed, but stayed that order pending appeal.

In reaching its conclusion, the district court relied substantially on the House Report on the 1982 legislation, which provides in relevant part as follows:

> The Committee carefully considered how to treat introduced populations that overlap, in whole or in part, [with] natural populations of the same species. To protect natural populations and to avoid potentially complicated problems of law enforcement, the definition [of "experimental population"] is limited to those introduced populations that are wholly separate geographically from nonexperimental populations of the same species. Thus, for example, in the case of the introduction of individuals of a listed fish species into a portion of a stream where the same species already occurs, the introduced specimens would not be treated as an "experimental population" separate from the non-introduced specimens. . . .

H. Rep. No. 97–567, 97th Cong., 2d Sess. § 5 (Merchant Marine and Fisheries Committee) (1982) U.S. Code Cong. & Admin. News 1982, p. 2833.

The decision for removal was reversed by the Tenth Circuit. *Wyoming Farm Bureau v. Babbitt*, 199 F.3d 1224 (10th Cir. 2000). The court held that determination of whether a reintroduced species is "wholly separate geographically from non-experimental populations" is left up to the discretion of the FWS. *Id.* at 1233. The court resolved the problem of distinguishing between reintroduced and naturally occurring wolves and their differing levels of protection by deferring to the Department's reliance on a special rule it adopted for the reintroduction, called "geographic separation." Under this rule, the level of protection afforded an individual wolf depended on where it was found, not whether it was part of the reintroduced population or a naturally occurring wolf who wandered into the reintroduction zone. *Id.* at 1235–36. Is the Tenth Circuit opinion consistent with congressional intent as set forth in the House Report? The Northern Rocky Mountain Gray wolves were delisted in February 2008, promptly followed by a lawsuit challenging the decision that forced their relisting. *See generally* <http://www.yellowstone-natl-park.com/wolfnews.htm>.

QUESTIONS AND DISCUSSION

1. Ranchers' concerns over livestock loss are deeply felt and, to ensure acceptance of the reintroduction program on the ground, needed to be addressed. Advocates of wolf reintroduction did just this through an innovative payment scheme. In 1987, Defenders of Wildlife established the Bailey Wildlife Foundation Wolf Compensation Trust to compensate ranchers whose livestock has been killed by wolves. The program effectively shifts the economic burden of wolf reintroduction from ranchers and other landowners to those who support reestablishing wild populations of wolves. Financed by private donors, the trust compensates people in both the greater Yellowstone region and throughout the Southwest, where the Mexican red wolf has been reintroduced. Since its inception, the program has paid out over $1,047,000 to a total of 738 ranchers, compensating for the loss of 1084 cattle and 2079 sheep killed by wolves.

The program has been hailed as an effective means to satisfy and neutralize opponents of predator reintroductions. What might be the down-sides to such an approach? Interestingly enough, a number of ranchers are program opponents. Why do you think they would oppose a program that promises them financial compensation for their losses?

2. Has reintroduction of wolves had the desired effect of recreating the natural environment? Consider the comments of Holly Doremus on how reintroduced wolves are managed.

> The agency frequently promises to capture and remove animals that stray from a restoration site.... [T]he agency has done everything short of fencing restoration zones to achieve that containment. It routinely installs monitoring devices such as radio-equipped collars on reintroduced animals, monitoring the population to ensure that it stays within a designated area. The most extreme example comes from the red wolf reintroduction in North Carolina. In order to fulfill its promise to capture and control strays in terrain that made live trapping impractical, Interior agreed to fit the wolves with "capture collars" designed to deliver a sedative dose in response to a radio signal. Other slightly less extreme examples abound. Many of the Yellowstone wolves have been captured and relocated at least once, and some many times, since their reintroduction. The unsuccessful sea otter relocation program included, at congressional direction, a commitment to contain otters within the transloca-tion area, maintaining an "otter free" zone between that area and the natural population that supplied the translocated otters. * * *

> Its nearly ubiquitous containment efforts also bring costs Interior does not appear to have considered, or even to have recognized. Both attachment of monitoring devices and repeated translocation can have biological effects, altering the animals' behavior in subtle, perhaps unrecognized respects. Al-though Interior's biologists should be sensitive to the possibility of such effects, the agency does not discuss them in the preambles to its special rules. The lay public is left to guess at whether these effects have been considered. Constant government monitoring and relocation of reintroduced animals also has impor-tant symbolic and aesthetic consequences. These direct control measures erect a virtual cage around the animals, converting them from wild creatures into semidomesticated ones, visibly under the control of wildlife agents. Collared wolves simply do not fulfill the same role as truly wild ones.

Holly Doremus, *Restoring Endangered Species: The Importance of Being Wild*, 23 HARV. ENVTL. L. REV. 1, 61 (1999). Are reintroduced wolves wild or simply "semidomesticated"? Does reintroduction under such controlled conditions simply create an outdoor zoo? Should collars be put on the the the next generation of wolves born in the wild?

3. Does it strike you as odd that the *Wyoming Farm Bureau* decision allows the FWS to *weaken* the protections for lone Gray wolves that wander into the reintroduction area? What does this suggest about the ESA's focus on species protection rather than individual animal protection? Do you think animal rights groups would support the wolf reintroduction program?

4. In March 2008, FWS delisted the entire Northern Rocky Mountain (NRM) Gray wolf population. Responsibility for management of the wolves now falls to state governments. According to FWS,

Montana, Idaho, and Wyoming have each committed to manage at least 15 breeding pairs and at least 150 wolves in mid-winter to provide a buffer to ensure that the NRM wolf population never falls below the mandated minimum level of 30 breeding pairs and 300 wolves (10 breeding pairs and 100 wolves per state). If the wolf population ever dropped below that level, the Service could take actions to protect wolves through the Service's emergency listing authority under the Endangered Species Act. Wyoming has committed to manage for at least 7 breeding pairs outside the national parks in Wyoming, regardless of how many wolves are in the national parks.

<http://www.fws.gov/mountain-prairie/species/mammals/wolf/delist_02202008/Qand A.pdf>

Wolves outside of the Northern Rocky Mountain region remain protected under the ESA (unless they make it to the Western Great Lakes, whose population was delisted in 2007).

————

3. VICARIOUS TAKES

We have seen how directly harming an endangered species or harming its habitat can lead to Section 9 takes, but what about when the government permits or allows these types of actions to occur but *does not itself* perform the offending activity. Consider, for example, the following situations:

- The Forest Service issues permits for private timber harvesting within a National Forest; the harvesting harms the endangered Red-cockaded Woodpecker;

- A state issues permits to set lobster traps; the lobstermen's pots and gear tangle endangered Right whales;

- A county has authority to regulate beachfront lighting from private homes but does not do so. The strong lighting disorients hatching turtles, who head inland toward the homes rather than toward the ocean and its reflected moonlight.

There are likely Section 9 causes of action against the loggers, lobstermen, and beachfront home owners, but should the government be liable for Section 9 takes, as well? In these examples and others, environmental groups have pushed the envelope of Section 9, arguing that states and municipalities that indirectly cause takes to be permitted are vicariously liable.

STRAHAN v. COXE
127 F.3d 155 (1st Cir. 1997), *cert. denied*, 525 U.S. 978 (1998)

TORRUELLA, CHIEF JUDGE.

In April 1995, Richard Strahan ("Strahan") filed suit against Trudy Coxe, Secretary of the Massachusetts Executive Office of Environmental Affairs, John Phillips, Commissioner of the Massachusetts Department of Fisheries, Wildlife, and Environmental Law Enforcement, and Philip Coates, Director of the Massachusetts Division of Marine Fisheries (together "defendants"), claiming that these Massachusetts state officers were violating the federal Endangered Species Act ("ESA"), 16 U.S.C. § 1531 et seq., and the Marine Mammals

Protection Act ("MMPA"), 16 U.S.C. § 1361 et seq. Strahan sought a preliminary injunction ordering the Commonwealth to revoke licenses and permits it had issued authorizing gillnet and lobster pot fishing and barring the Commonwealth from issuing such licenses and permits in the future unless it received "incidental take" and "small take" permits from the National Marine Fisheries Service ("NMFS") under the ESA and MMPA. Defendants moved to dismiss Strahan's complaint and, in the alternative, for summary judgment.

On September 24, 1996, the district court: (1) denied defendants' motion for summary judgment on Strahan's ESA claims; (2) dismissed Strahan's MMPA claims; and (3) granted summary judgment on Strahan's ESA claims in Count IV of Strahan's amended complaint. *Strahan v. Coxe*, 939 F.Supp. 963 (D. Mass. 1996). In this ruling, the district court declined to grant the preliminary injunctive measures sought by Strahan. Instead, the court issued a preliminary injunction ordering defendants to: (1) "apply for an incidental take permit [under the ESA] from NMFS ... for Northern Right whales"; (2) "apply for a permit under the [MMPA] for Northern Right whales"; (3) "develop and prepare a proposal ... to restrict, modify or eliminate the use of fixed-fishing gear in coastal waters of Massachusetts listed as critical habitat for Northern Right whales in order to minimize the likelihood additional whales will actually be harmed by such gear"; and (4) "convene an Endangered Whale Working Group and to engage in substantive discussions with the Plaintiff [Strahan], or his representative, as well as with other interested parties, regarding modifications of fixed-fishing gear and other measures to minimize harm to the Northern Right whales." * * *

BACKGROUND

I. Status of the Northern Right whale

Strahan is an officer of GreenWorld, Inc., an organization dedicated to the preservation and recovery of endangered species. Strahan brought suit on behalf of the Northern Right whale, listed as an endangered species by the federal government. Northern Right whales are the most endangered of the large whales, presently numbering around 300. Entanglement with commercial fishing gear has been recognized as a major source of human-caused injury or death to the Northern Right whale. * * *

The majority of Northern Right whales are present in Massachusetts waters only during spring feeding. The district court found, based on statements made by defendants as well as on affidavits from three scientists, that Northern Right whales have been entangled in fixed fishing gear in Massachusetts coastal waters at least nine times. * * *

II. Massachusetts' regulatory authority scheme

The Massachusetts Division of Marine Fisheries ("DMF") is vested with broad authority to regulate fishing in Massachusetts's coastal waters, which extend three nautical miles from the shoreline. Nearly all commercial fishing vessels must receive a permit from DMF in order to take fish, including shellfish, from Massachusetts coastal waters.... The DMF has limited the use of gillnets and lobster pot fishing gear in certain areas. * * *

In addition, the DMF has established a 500–yard "buffer zone" around Northern Right whales in Massachusetts coastal waters. Defendant Coates admitted that he had "issued a limited number of scientific research permits to some whale watch vessels exempting them from the 500 yard buffer zone surrounding right whales for scientific research purposes upon application."

STANDARD OF REVIEW

In ruling on a motion for preliminary injunction, a district court is charged with considering:

(1) the likelihood of success on the merits; (2) the potential for irreparable harm if the injunction is denied; (3) the balance of relevant impositions, i.e., the hardship to the nonmovant if enjoined as contrasted with the hardship to the movant if no injunction issues; and (4) the effect (if any) of the court's ruling on the public interest.

Under the ESA, however, the balancing and public interest prongs have been answered by Congress' determination that the "balance of hardships and the public interest tips heavily in favor of protected species." Our review of the district court's ruling on a motion for preliminary injunction is deferential and, "unless the appellant can show that the lower court misapprehended the law or committed a palpable abuse of discretion, the court of appeals will not intervene." * * *

B. Legal challenges

The district court's reasoning, in finding that Massachusetts' commercial fishing regulatory scheme likely exacted a taking in violation of the ESA, was founded on two provisions of the ESA read in conjunction. The first relates to the definition of the prohibited activity of a "taking," *see* 1538(a)(1)(B),* and the second relates to the solicitation or causation by a third party of a prohibited activity, such as a taking, *see* 1538(g).** The district court viewed these provisions, when read together, to apply to acts by third parties that allow or authorize acts that exact a taking and that, but for the permitting process, could not take place. Indeed, the district court cited several opinions that have also so held. *See*, e.g., *Sierra Club v. Yeutter*, 926 F.2d 429, 438–39 (5th Cir. 1991) (finding Forest Service's management of timber stands was a taking of the red-cockaded woodpecker in violation of the ESA); *Defenders of Wildlife v. EPA*, 882 F.2d 1294, 1301 (8th Cir. 1989) (holding that the EPA's registration of pesticides containing strychnine violated the ESA, both because endangered species had died from ingesting strychnine bait and because that strychnine could only be distributed pursuant to the EPA's registration scheme); *Palila v. Hawaii Dep't of Land and Nat. Resources*, 639 F.2d 495, 497–98 (9th Cir. 1981) (holding state's practice of maintaining feral goats and sheep in palila's habitat constituted a taking and ordering state to remove goats and sheep); *Loggerhead Turtle v. County Council of Volusia County*, 896 F.Supp. 1170, 1180–81 (M.D. Fla. 1995) (holding that county's authorization of vehicular beach access during turtle mating season exacted a taking of the turtles in violation of the ESA). The statute not only prohibits the acts of those parties that directly exact the taking, but also bans those acts of a third party that bring about the acts exacting a taking. We believe that, contrary to the defendants' argument on appeal, the district court properly found that a governmental third party pursuant to whose authority an actor directly exacts a taking of an endangered species may be deemed to have violated the provisions of the ESA.

The defendants argue that the statute was not intended to prohibit state licensure activity because such activity cannot be a "proximate cause" of the taking. The defendants direct our attention to long-standing principles of

---

* [This is the general take prohibition of Section 9.]

** ["It is unlawful for any person subject to the jurisdiction of the United States to attempt to commit, solicit another to commit, or cause to be committed, any offense defined in this section."]

common law tort in arguing that the district court improperly found that its regulatory scheme "indirectly causes" these takings. Specifically, the defendants contend that to construe the proper meaning of "cause" under the ESA, this court should look to common law principles of causation and further contend that proximate cause is lacking here. The defendants are correct that when interpreting a term in a statute which is, like "cause" here, well-known to the common law, the court is to presume that Congress intended the meaning to be interpreted as in the common law. We do not believe, however, that an interpretation of "cause" that includes the "indirect causation" of a taking by the Commonwealth through its licensing scheme falls without the normal boundaries.

The defendants protest this interpretation. Their first argument is that the Commonwealth's licensure of a generally permitted activity does not cause the taking any more than its licensure of automobiles and drivers solicits or causes federal crimes, even though automobiles it licenses are surely used to violate federal drug laws, rob federally insured banks, or cross state lines for the purpose of violating state and federal laws. The answer to this argument is that, whereas it is possible for a person licensed by Massachusetts to use a car in a manner that does not risk the violations of federal law suggested by the defendants, it is not possible for a licensed commercial fishing operation to use its gillnets or lobster pots in the manner permitted by the Commonwealth without risk of violating the ESA by exacting a taking. Thus, the state's licensure of gillnet and lobster pot fishing does not involve the intervening independent actor that is a necessary component of the other licensure schemes which it argues are comparable. Where the state has licensed an automobile driver to use that automobile and her license in a manner consistent with both state and federal law, the violation of federal law is caused only by the actor's conscious and independent decision to disregard or go beyond the licensed purposes of her automobile use and instead to violate federal, and possibly state, law. The situation is simply not the same here. In this instance, the state has licensed commercial fishing operations to use gillnets and lobster pots in specifically the manner that is likely to result in a violation of federal law. The causation here, while indirect, is not so removed that it extends outside the realm of causation as it is understood in the common law. * * *

The defendants' next argument need only detain us momentarily. They contend that the statutory structure of the ESA does not envision utilizing the regulatory structures of the states in order to implement its provisions, but that it instead leaves that implementing authority to NMFS. The point that the defendants miss is that the district court's ruling does not impose positive obligations on the Commonwealth by converting its regulation of commercial fishing operations into a tool of the federal ESA regulatory scheme. The Commonwealth is not being compelled to enforce the provisions of the ESA. Instead, the district court's ruling seeks to end the Commonwealth's continuing violation of the Act. * * *

Defendants also contend that the district court's ruling is erroneous because it fails to give deference to the position of NMFS, the federal agency charged with enforcing the ESA. The defendants' position is flawed for two reasons. First, the ESA gives NMFS, through the Secretary, discretion in authorizing takings incidental to certain commercial activity; the Act does not give a federal court, having determined that a taking has occurred, the same discretion in determining whether to grant injunctive relief. Second, the fact that NMFS has expressly declined to ban gillnet or lobster pot fishing in Cape Cod Bay does not reflect a policy determination by NMFS that such a ban is

III. The Endangered Species Act

unnecessary. For these two reasons, we find the defendants' deference arguments without merit.

C. Factual challenges

We review the district court's findings of fact for clear error. The district court found that entanglement with fishing gear in Massachusetts waters caused injury or death to Northern Right whales. Indeed, the district court cited several of the Commonwealth's documents in support of this finding, including its statement that "[f]ive right whales have been found entangled in fixed fishing gear in Massachusetts waters; three in gillnets and two in lobster lines." The court further cited to affidavits of three scientists that suggested that entanglement of Northern Right whales had harmed, injured, or killed those whales. The court cited eleven occasions on which Northern Right whales had been found entangled in fishing gear in Massachusetts waters between 1978 and 1995. The court also indicated that at least fifty-seven percent of all Northern right whales have scars indicating prior entanglement with fishing gear and noted that, even where the whale survives, the entanglement still wounds the whale. Although these findings indicate only that entanglements have occurred in Massachusetts waters, the district court determined that three whales had been found entangled in gear deployed in Massachusetts waters.
* * *

The defendants next contend that the district court ignored evidence of the significant efforts made by the Commonwealth to "minimize Northern Right Whale entanglements in fishing gear," and evidence of other causes of takings of Northern Right whales. With respect to the determination of whether a taking has occurred, the district court quite rightly disregarded such evidence. Given that there was evidence that any entanglement with fishing gear injures a Northern Right whale and given that a single injury to one whale is a taking under the ESA, efforts to minimize such entanglements are irrelevant. For the same reasons, the existence of other means by which takings of Northern Right whales occur is irrelevant to the determination of whether the Commonwealth has engaged in a taking.

Finding neither any error of law nor any clear error with respect to the factual findings, we believe that the district court properly applied the ESA to the facts presented and was correct in enjoining the Commonwealth so as to prevent the taking of Northern Right whales in violation of the ESA.

III. Scope of injunctive relief

Defendants claim that the injunctive relief granted by the district court goes beyond the scope of remedies available in an action against state officials. Specifically, defendants claim that, although the district court could have ordered an injunction barring all Commonwealth licensing activity, it could not require the Commonwealth to implement measures designed to accord Northern Right whales greater regulatory protection. Defendants argue that the statutory scheme, the Eleventh Amendment, and the Tenth Amendment all bar the measures ordered by the district court. [The Court rejected the Eleventh Amendment claim, holding it "does not place limits on the scope of the equitable relief that may be granted once appropriate jurisdiction is found."]
* * *

Strahan contends that the district court committed reversible error by refusing to grant the injunctive relief he sought. He contends that the Court in *TVA* ruled that injunctive relief is mandatory upon a finding of a violation of the ESA. In fact, the *TVA* Court specifically rejected this proposition, stating "[i]t is correct, of course, that a federal judge sitting as a chancellor is not mechanically obligated to grant an injunction for every violation of law." *TVA*, 437 U.S. at 193 (1976). The Court recognized, however, that in the instance presented, in which the activity at issue would have caused eradication of an entire endangered species if not enjoined, the only remedy that could prevent that outcome was a permanent injunction halting the activity. *Id.* at 194–95.

The district court, having determined that the Commonwealth's probable violation of the ESA could be curtailed without such extreme measures, declined to impose the injunction Strahan sought. The district court was not required to go any farther than ensuring that any violation would end.... We are satisfied that the district court was aware of the need to curtail any violation and bring about the Commonwealth's compliance with the ESA and that its order adequately achieves those ends. * * *

———

A year later, the Eleventh Circuit enlarged the scope of vicarious takes. In *Loggerhead Turtle v. County Council of Volusia City*, 148 F.3d 1231 (11th Cir. 1998), *cert. denied*, 526 U.S. 1081 (1999), artificial beachfront lighting from private homes evidently was confusing newly hatched logger-head turtles, who mistook the bright lights for moonlight over the ocean and, instead of heading for the sea (where their chance of survival might be approximately 1 in 100), headed for the inland lights (where their chance of survival was zero). Responding to a standing challenge to plaintiff's Section 9 taking claim, the court held that Volusia County's "harmfully inadequate regulation of artificial beachfront lighting in the non-party municipalities" in the county was sufficient to establish injury in fact for purposes of standing. *Id.* at 1249. The court stated that Volusia County was "vested with broad authority to regulate" artificial beachfront lighting. *Id.* at 1252. Although the County had developed standards to minimize artificial light on the beaches, the court found these standards insufficient. *See also, Seattle Audubon Soc'y v. Sutherland*, 2007 WL 130324 (W.D. Wash. 2007) (allowing suit to continue against state defendants where its authorization of acts by loggers was "fairly traceable" to ESA taking).

QUESTIONS AND DISCUSSION

1. As a matter of proximate causation, it might seem odd to argue that regulation can *cause* a take. Do activities that harm endangered species occur because the state allows it or because of private, intervening actions? The *Strahan* court addresses this concern by distinguishing between the issuance of a driver's license to a bank robber and a lobster permit to a lobsterman, stating that:

> whereas it is possible for a person licensed by Massachusetts to use a car in a manner that does not risk the violations of federal law suggested by the defendants, it is not possible for a licensed commercial fishing operation to use its gillnets or lobster pots in the manner permitted by the Commonwealth without risk of violating the ESA by exacting a taking. Thus, the state's licensure of gillnet and lobster pot fishing does not involve the intervening independent actor that is a necessary component of the other licensure schemes which it argues are comparable.

Strahan, supra, at 164. If you were preparing a brief for certiorari to the Supreme Court on behalf of Massachusetts, how would you rebut this part of the court's argument?

2. In terms of litigation strategy, why do think *Strahan* sued the state agency instead of the lobstermen in a class action? After all, if there were a bank robbery the prosecutor would bring the full force of the law against the driver, not the bureau of motor vehicles official who gave the driver his license.

3. *Problem Exercise.* Suppose a farmer intends to disc her land (i.e., turn over her topsoil) in preparation for planting. Worried about dust from the discing by its farmers, a county passes an ordinance requiring farmers to obtain discing permits. The only way to get a discing permit is to show that the discing machine has a dust-catching device. Suppose, upon obtaining the permit, the farmer discs the last remaining habitat of an endangered field mouse. Does the county's permit requirement "cause" a take in violation of Section 9 even though it makes discing less likely than before the permit requirement was instituted? Is this hypothetical any different than the facts in *Strahan*? In deciding whether the county ordinance and the state regulation cause takes, does it matter whether one conceives of activities like fishing and farming as authorized by the state in the first instance? If fishers, farmers, and others, in the initial position, are free to act without state permission, does the state's decision to prevent some harmful impacts of an activity *cause* other harmful impacts not restricted? What conception of property rights underlies the decisions in *Strahan* and *Volusia County*?

4. *Problem Exercise.*[4] The Minnesota Department of Natural Resources (DNR) supervises the licensing and regulation of trapping in Minnesota. Hunters set a range of traps, foothold or leghold traps with a spring loaded jaw that clamp down and hold the animal by the leg or foot, snare traps that use a loop or wire to catch the animal by the foot or neck, and others. The traps hold the animal in place until the hunter can check the traps, usually done every few days. DNR regulations include restrictions on trap type, jaw opening, size of loop, etc.

The Canada Lynx is listed as threatened under the ESA and its habitat range extends into Minnesota. In fact, the U.S. Fish and Wildlife Service published a pamphlet in 2003, "How to Avoid Incidental Take of Lynx, While Trapping or Hunting Bobcats and other Furbearers" and sent it to approximately 1,520 Minnesota trappers. The DNR also includes a warning in its Hunting and Trapping Handbook stating that the Canada Lynx had been listed and that any taking is a violation of federal law.

From 2002 through 2005, there have been thirteen reported takings of lynx by traps. Allegedly ten of the takings involved traps that were legally set. Friends of the Lynx have sued DNR for a section 9 taking under the ESA. How can DNR distinguish this situation from *Strahan*?

5. Supporters of such vicarious take decisions argue that they drive responsibility to conserve endangered species from the federal government

---

4. This is adapted from *Animal Protection Institute, Center for Biological Diversity v. Holsten,* 541 F.Supp.2d 1073 (D.Minn. 2008).

down to where it is really needed—at the level of local land use decisions. But is vicarious liability for takes consistent with the practice of federalism? Under the Clean Water Act, for example, state authorities issue NPDES permits to private parties, but the states don't assume responsibility for any contamination that results from the authorized activity. Can you draw a persuasive distinction between permitting under the Clean Air Act or Clean Water Act and under the ESA?

Does *Strahan* mean that, effectively, state and local governments have a greater obligation under Section 9 than the federal government has under Section 7 to protect listed species? Does it make sense, for example, that Massachusetts must regulate the lobster fishery so as to prevent take but that NMFS (NOAA Fisheries) can choose not to do so? Do you think Congress had this in mind when passing the ESA?

6. In *Strahan,* how does the court modify its standard test for an injunction? Why should requests for preliminary injunctions under the ESA be held to a different standard than all other settings? Was an injunction even necessary? Can Massachusetts comply with this decision short of refusing to issue lobster permits? Could Massachusetts avoid responsibility for take if it chose not to regulate at all? Is that a wise incentive to create?

7. Return to the three examples of vicarious takes at the introduction to this section at page 409. The first was based on *Sierra Club v. Yuetter*, 926 F.2d 429 (5th Cir. 1991), and the latter two on the *Strahan* and *Volusia County* you just read about. Is there any way to distinguish between the application of vicarious liability in these three cases? Is the case for vicarious liability stronger or weaker for any of the three?

In the same year as *Volusia County,* a federal district court in Massachusetts held that the town of Plymouth had violated Section 9 by failing to regulate adequately off-road vehicles on beaches. Finding that the vehicles driving on beaches harmed the threatened piping plover, the court granted a preliminary injunction. *United States v. Town of Plymouth*, 6 F. Supp. 2d 81, 90–91 (D. Mass. 1998). Is this closer to *Volusia County* or *Sierra Club v. Yuetter*? For a general consideration of the different kinds of vicarious liability cases, see J.B. Ruhl, *State and Local Government Vicarious Liability under the ESA*, 16 NAT. RESOURCES & ENV'T 70 (2001).

8. If *Strahan* is correctly decided, what does that mean for western state issuance of water permits? Are western states responsible for any harm to endangered species in western rivers? Suppose, for example, that a small creek in Arizona contains an endangered species of fish. The stream is fully appropriated by irrigators and in a particular drought year they dewater the stream despite the fact that the fish needs flow to survive. Could you sue the state? On what theory? Is a permit to appropriate water distinguishable from the fishing license in *Strahan*? For a discussion of this issue, see James R. Rasband, *Priority, Probability and Proximate Cause: Lessons from Tort Law about Imposing ESA Responsibilities for Wildlife Harm on Water Users and Other Joint Habitat Modifers*, 33 ENVTL. L. 595, 628–30 (2003).

9. In *Volusia County,* the plaintiffs also claimed that "takings" occurred when nesting female turtles aborted nesting attempts in brightly lit areas.

Is the court's decision on both the disoriented hatchling and nesting female turtles consistent with *Sweet Home*? With Justice O'Connor's concurring opinion in *Sweet Home*?

F. CREATING INCENTIVES FOR SPECIES PROTECTION

There is no more controversial aspect of the Endangered Species Act (ESA) than its application to development activities on privately owned lands. Newspapers carry tales of federal zealots seizing farm equipment from unwitting farmers,[2] homeowners barred from saving their property from wildfire because of brush clearing restrictions, and businesses losing decades of investment—all because of endangered species. A typical news article attacking the ESA begins: "Would you spend $2.6 million on a cockroach? The federal government does." This opening salvo is followed by a scathing review of the "tremendous economic damage" being done to citizens on behalf of a rat, mouse, mole, tortoise, or other lowly and contemptible creature whose earthly purpose cannot be fathomed, especially when measured against economic progress and individual freedom. Even United States Supreme Court Justices chime in. Justice Scalia accused the majority of the Court in *Babbitt v. Sweet Home Chapter of Communities for a Greater Oregon* of interpreting the ESA so as to "impose unfairness to the point of financial ruin . . . upon the simplest farmer who finds his land conscripted to national zoological use."

Karin P. Sheldon, *Habitat Conservation Planning: Addressing the Achilles Heel of the Endangered Species Act*, 6 N.Y.U. ENVTL. L.J. 279, 279–280 (1998).

As Karin Sheldon's description makes clear, Section 9 has generated even more opposition to the ESA than Section 7. As we shall see in the case study that follows this section, many think that halting expansion of a hospital to protect the habitat of the Delhi Sands Flower–Loving Fly would be laughable if there were not so much money involved.

We have already discussed how the ESA can impose burdens on agencies and private actors to further the conservation of endangered species. Section 9, though, raises other concerns, as well. To many critics, it's simply unfair to allocate all the costs of endangered species conservation to a small number of innocent landowners. If the benefits of biodiversity are shared nationally, the argument goes, so too should be the costs. It does seem inequitable, for example, that one property owner is prevented from plowing her fields or cutting her trees while another just down the road has free use of her land, all because of the random chance that some endangered species chose to live in one place and not another. To make

2. In February 1994, some twenty-five federal and state wildlife officials seized the tractor of an immigrant farmer and charged him with disturbing the habitat of the Tipton kangaroo rat and other endangered species. Although the farmer had received warnings that protected species were on his land, his case became a rallying cry for property rights activists, who pointed to the incident as an example of the excesses of the ESA. The case was publicized by conservative radio commentators G. Gordon Liddy and Rush Limbaugh and discussed on the editorial page of the *Wall Street Journal*. *See* Gideon Kanner, *Rule of Law: California Rat Killer Gets Off*, WALL ST. J., May 24, 1995, at A15; Todd Woody, *Taking on the Endangered Species: The Rat, the Farmer, and the Feds*, LEGAL TIMES, July 24, 1995, at 8.

matters worse, the main reason the species may be endangered is because the unaffected landowners *did develop their land*, destroying potential species habitat. To avoid problems of potential takes, some landowners may actively manage their land to make it *inhospitable* to endangered species—harming or destroying potential habitat before endangered species can establish populations. There is no prohibition against adversely modifying habitat prior to listing of a species or against habitat modification that does not satisfy the *Sweet Home* causation requirement. Given that roughly half of the species listed under the ESA have about 80% of their habitat on private lands, this problem of perverse incentives is a serious issue. Even worse, landowners may surreptitiously kill endangered species before their presence becomes known. This is popularly known as the "shoot, shovel, and shut up" approach. It is, of course, very difficult to know the extent to which such actions occur, but the signals provided by Section 9 certainly make such counterproductive activities more likely.

Taken together, these criticisms have fueled initiatives to amend the ESA. To address some of these concerns (and those raised by the *Palila* decisions,) in 1982 Congress amended Section 10(a) of the ESA and expanded authority for the issuance of *incidental take permits* beyond the earlier exceptions of research purposes, cases of emergency, or hardship. The excerpt below explains how implementation of Section 10(a) and two other important policies that have followed—the No Surprises and Safe Harbors policies—have fundamentally changed the practice of endangered species conservation.

Karin P. Sheldon, *Habitat Conservation Planning: Addressing The Achilles Heel of the Endangered Species Act* 6 N.Y.U. ENVTL. L.J. 279, 295–326 (1998)

The 1982 amendments to the ESA offer an exception for private landowners from the prohibition against the taking of endangered and threatened species. The exception was added "to give the Secretary [of the Interior] more flexibility in regulating the incidental taking of endangered and threatened species," and "to address the concerns of private landowners who are faced with having otherwise lawful actions not requiring federal permits prevented by Section 9 prohibitions against taking."

Section 10(a) of the ESA authorizes the Secretary of the Interior to allow a private property owner to engage in development or land use activities that may result in a taking of some members of a threatened or endangered species, so long as the taking is "incidental to, and not the purpose of, the carrying out of an otherwise lawful activity." The Secretary's approval is set forth in an "incidental take permit."

In order to qualify for this exception, a private landowner must submit a "conservation plan" designed to "minimize and mitigate" the impact of development activities on protected species. Such a plan has come to be known as a Habitat Conservation Plan (HCP). In addition to identifying the steps the landowner will take to "minimize and mitigate" the impacts of the development activities, an HCP must include a discussion of the potential impact of the taking, alternatives to the taking the landowner considered and the reasons for not choosing them, and other measures the Secretary may require.

The Secretary may issue an incidental taking permit, after public review and comment, if he finds that: (1) "the taking will be incidental;" (2) "the applicant will, to the maximum extent practicable, minimize and mitigate the impacts of such taking;" (3) the applicant will ensure that "adequate funding" will be provided for the plan; and (4) other required measures will be met.

Section 10(a) also directs the Secretary to determine that the proposed incidental take "will not appreciably reduce the likelihood of the survival and recovery of the species in the wild." This standard is a restatement of the regulatory definition of the "jeopardize the continued existence" standard of Section 7(a)(2).

Congress intended HCPs to be broad in scope. They are to include unlisted, as well as listed species, along with "assurances" to landowners that the terms of the plan will be adhered to and that further mitigation requirements will only be imposed in accordance with the terms of the plan. In the event an unlisted species addressed in an approved HCP is subsequently listed, no further mitigation requirements will be imposed, provided that the HCP addressed the conservation of that species. Congress did recognize that "unforeseen circumstances" might require changes in an HCP. Accordingly, each plan must include a procedure by which the parties will respond to such circumstances.

Although Congress enthusiastically endorsed HCPs in 1982, . . . the first ten years of experience with HCPs have been characterized as a "decade of disappointment." The numbers bear out this assessment: a total of fourteen HCPs were approved between 1982 and 1992; by the end of 1994, only thirty-nine HCPs had been approved.

The first generation of HCPs covered small areas. Only five of the fourteen HCPs approved between 1982 and 1992 encompassed more than a thousand acres; thirty-one of the thirty-nine HCPs approved by the end of 1994 involved less than a thousand acres. The resulting HCPs were parcel-specific and tailored to the needs of species at particular sites. Plans were developed in isolation with inconsistent mitigation and no evaluation of the cumulative effects of habitat fragmentation. The habitat was cut into smaller and smaller pieces incapable of supporting species. As one writer commented, the areas protected by many HCPs "amount to little more than small habitat 'postage stamps,' eventually surrounded by urban development and intense human activities."

On August 11, 1994, the Secretary of the Interior announced the *"No Surprises" policy.* "No Surprises" is perhaps the most significant of the policy changes in the HCP process. Under the "No Surprises" policy, landowners who enter into an HCP for the listed species on their property will not be required to pay more or provide additional land for mitigation, regardless of whether the needs of the species change over time. Except under "extraordinary circumstances," compliance with the terms and conditions of an HCP guarantees a property owner that development or land use activities can proceed, even if unlisted species covered by the plan are subsequently listed as threatened or endangered. * * *

The "No Surprises" policy provides certainty for private landowners in ESA Habitat Conservation Planning through the following assurances:

> In negotiating "unforeseen circumstances" provisions for HCPs, the Fish and Wildlife Service and National Marine Fisheries Service shall not require the commitment of additional land or financial compensation beyond the level of mitigation which was otherwise adequately provided for

a species under the terms of a properly functioning HCP. Moreover, FWS and NMFS shall not seek any other form of additional mitigation from an HCP permittee except under extraordinary circumstances.

As the Secretary put it, the "No Surprises" policy promises that "a deal is a deal." "The key issue for non-federal landowners is certainty. They want to know that if they make a good faith effort to plan ahead for species conservation, and do so in cooperation with the relevant agencies, then their plan won't be ripped out from under them many years down the road." * * *

The "No Surprises" policy applies to unlisted, as well as listed species. . . . The inclusion of unlisted species in an HCP is a voluntary decision of the landowner. The primary reasons to address unlisted species are greater planning certainty for the landowner and increased biological value of the HCP through comprehensive multi-species or ecosystem planning.

If an unlisted species not addressed in an HCP is subsequently listed, the landowner is subject to the take prohibitions of Section 9 or 4(d) of the ESA, regardless of the fact that an incidental take permit is held for other listed species. The landowner must either avoid a take of the newly listed species or revise the existing HCP and obtain a permit amendment. * * *

Under the "No Surprises" policy, if the condition of a species addressed in an HCP worsens, and additional mitigation measures are deemed necessary, the primary obligation for implementing such measures will be borne by the government, private conservation organizations, or private landowners who have not yet developed HCPs. Once an incidental take permit is issued and an HCP is being implemented, the permittee "may remain secure regarding the agreed upon cost of mitigation, because no additional mitigation land, funding, or land use restrictions will be requested by the Services." The "No Surprises" policy also "protects" a permittee from other forms of additional mitigation, except in "extraordinary circumstances."

In the event the FWS concludes that "extraordinary circumstances" warrant additional mitigation from an HCP permittee, the mitigation measures must be consistent with the original terms of the HCP, to the maximum extent possible. Unless the landowner consents, changes must be limited to modifications within areas designated for habitat protection or other conservation uses in the plan or to the plan's conservation programs for the affected species. The landowner will not be expected to pay the cost of these additional measures or to apply them on parcels of land committed to development under the original terms of the HCP.

The FWS has the burden of demonstrating that extraordinary circumstances do, in fact, exist, based upon "the best scientific and commercial data available." Its findings must be clearly documented and reflect reliable technical information regarding the status and habitat requirements of the affected species. The focus of the inquiry is the "level of biological peril" to the species in question, and the degree to which the welfare of the species is tied to the particular HCP. * * *

The *"Safe Harbors"* concept was created by the Environmental Defense Fund, which has argued for some time that landowners need incentives, not regulatory hammers, to protect wildlife. It was adopted by the FWS "to reduce the disincentives (*e.g.*, fear of regulatory restrictions) that often cause landowners to avoid or prevent land use practices that would otherwise benefit endangered species." . . . "Safe Harbors" offers assurances to private landowners that their development and land-use activities will not be restricted if they undertake voluntary, proactive conservation efforts. In other words, landowners who improve habitat conditions for threatened and endangered species can return to baseline conditions without penalty. * * *

Michael Bean has stated, "[t]he Achilles heel of the Endangered Species Act is the private landowner problem." He points out that Section 7 of the Act provides the government with tools to ensure that active management takes place on federal lands, but there are no comparable tools in Section 9 or elsewhere in the statute for non-federal land management. "In nearly a quarter century, there hasn't yet been a single example of Section 9 compelling a non-federal landowner to restore fire or manage to mimic its effects. In the same period, there has been only one example, the palila, of a species for which Section 9 has been employed to force a non-federal landowner to remove a non-indigenous species threatening it." For Bean, "The power of the safe harbor idea is that it not only provides habitat where otherwise there would be none, but it makes landowners willing partners in the endangered species conservation effort."

FWS bases the "Safe Harbors" policy on Section 10(a)(1)(A) of the ESA, which states: the "Secretary may permit . . . any act otherwise prohibited by section 1538 . . . to enhance the propagation or survival of the affected species." The permits to be issued under the "Safe Harbors" policy are called "enhancement of survival permits."

FWS's interp./ application of Safe Harbors approach

The goal of the "Safe Harbors" policy is to encourage private property owners to "restore, enhance, or maintain" habitats for listed species by undertaking a variety of proactive species conservation efforts on their lands. Examples of such beneficial management include prescribed burning to mimic natural fire regimes, removal of invasive, non-indigenous species, or restoration of hydrologic conditions. Priority for Safe Harbors will be given to "Agreements that provide the greatest contribution to the recovery of multiple listed species."

To qualify for a Safe Harbor Agreement a private property owner must be willing to undertake or forego land-use activities in order to provide a "net conservation benefit" to listed species present on her property. Net conservation benefits may include reduction of habitat fragmentation, the maintenance, restoration, or enhancement of habitat, the establishment of buffer zones for protected areas, and the reduction of the effects of catastrophic events. FWS must make a written finding that all protected species subject to the Safe Harbor Agreement will receive the net conservation benefit. Although a Safe Harbor does not have to offer permanent protection to covered species, it must be of "sufficient design and duration" to give net conservation benefits to all covered species. These "benefits must contribute to the recovery of the covered species."

Safe Harbor— qualify: need to provide "NET CONSV. BENEFIT"

In exchange for a commitment to carry out beneficial management of their lands, property owners are given assurances that additional land-use or resource-use restrictions will not be imposed. If a property owner meets all the conditions of a Safe Harbor Agreement, FWS will authorize the incidental take of covered species to enable the property owner to return the enrolled property to its "baseline conditions" in the future. * * *

Safe Harbor Agreements run with the land. The rights and obligations of the Agreement transfer with property ownership. A property owner must notify FWS of a proposed transfer so that the agency may explain the Agreement and determine whether the new owner wishes to continue the old Agreement or enter into a new one.

From humble beginnings, HCPs have become a key tool of ESA managers. When faced with endangered species or habitat on their property, developers, local governments, and other large landowners are increasingly turning to HCPs. As of May 2008, the FWS had approved more than 544 HCPs and issued accompanying incidental take permits, covering tens of millions of acres and hundreds of listed species. While most of these permits were issued to individual property owners, a number of communities and large developers entered into regional HCPs with multiple property owners and species. In one of the largest examples of this approach, in 1997, FWS, NMFS, and the Washington State Department of Natural Resources developed an HCP for 1.6 million acres of state-managed forest lands. The plan sought to protect more than 285 species of fish and wildlife. The Safe Harbor program has proven popular, as well. In South Carolina, for example, almost 100,000 acres of land have been enrolled to protect the red-cockaded woodpecker. As of May 2008, FWS had entered into 61 safe harbor agreements covering over three million acres of land.

Regulatory innovations such as incidental take permits, No Surprises, and Safe Harbors have served as critically important "political steam valves." In the 1990s, the ESA was under serious political attack in Congress. These innovations have taken the pressure off of crippling amendments, while at the same time demonstrating that the ESA can "work" without shutting down economic development.

QUESTIONS AND DISCUSSION

1. In assessing the success of Section 10(a) and the No Surprises and Safe Harbors policies, one must first ask, "compared to what?" There's no question that it would be far better for landowners to *want* endangered species on their property rather than dreading their appearance, but it has been hard to assess whether the "shoot, shovel and shut up" problem truly is widespread or more anecdote and legend than reality.

Economists Dean Lueck and Jeffrey Michael carried out a fascinating study to address this question empirically, examining how the presence of the red-cockaded woodpecker affected timber harvest rates and age of harvest in North Carolina pine plantations. Because these endangered birds prefer old-growth Southern pine trees for nesting, Lueck and Michael hypothesized that landowners could keep the woodpeckers from breeding on their property by harvesting their timber before it grew old enough to be attractive as nesting habitat for the birds. Using data from over 1,000 individual forest plots from the U.S. Forest Service's Forest Inventory and Analysis, a survey of over 400 landowners, and econometric analysis, they found statistically significant evidence that the closer woodpeckers were to a plot, the more likely it was both that the trees would be harvested and that the trees would be harvested at an earlier age. Dean Lueck & Jeffrey Michael, *Preemptive Habitat Destruction Under the Endangered Species Act*, 46 J. of Law and Economics 27 (2003). Their results were reinforced by a later study on the same species, which concluded that "a landowner is 25% more likely to cut forests when he or she knows or perceives that a red-cockaded woodpecker cluster is within a mile of the land than otherwise."

Daowei Zhang, *Endangered Species and Timber Harvesting: The Case of Red–Cockaded Woodpeckers*, 42 Economic Inquiry 150 (2004).

See also, Amara Brook et al., *Landowners' Responses to an Endangered Species Act Listing and Implications for Encouraging Conservation*, 17 Conservation Biology 1638 (2003) (finding that land designated as critical habitat for the Pygmy owl in Arizona was developed one year earlier than similar parcels not designated); Andrew P. Morriss & Richard L. Stroup, *Quartering Species: The "Living Constitution," the Third Amendment, and the Endangered Species Act*, 30 Envtl. L. 769, 796 (2000) (reporting similar anecdotal evidence of habitat destruction in Texas following listing of the Black-capped vireo and the Golden-cheeked warbler); Jonathan H. Adler, *Money or Nothing: The Adverse Environmental Consequences of Uncompensated Regulatory Takings*, 49 Boston College Law Review 301 (2008).

2. It is undeniable that the HCP, No Surprises, and Safe Harbors policies have dramatically reshaped ESA practice. Yet only Section 10(a) was passed by Congress. All the other initiatives have come from agency rulemaking and policy guidance. This has led a number of groups to question whether Interior should be making such sweeping changes on its own. *See, e.g.,* J.B. Ruhl, *Who Needs Congress? An Agenda for Administrative Reform of the Endangered Species Act*, 6 N.Y.U. Envtl. L.J. 367 (1998).

3. Given the flexible nature of HCPs and the contract-like obligations of the No Surprises policy, many environmental groups have voiced concerns over this approach to ESA implementation, arguing that it is inconsistent with adaptive management. In particular, they fear that the agency's knowledge of the listed species is too limited to ensure that the HCPs will provide adequate protection as more information is gained over time. Realize, as well, that HCPs can be in place for a long time. The first HCP, developed for San Bruno Mountain in 1983, expired after 30 years and today it is not unusual to have HCPs valid for up to 100 years (as is the case for an 11 acre HCP in Florida, which is also renewable!). Moreover, some argue that HCPs virtually ensure that there will be *less* habitat for listed species than before the HCP. Do you see why? If you were in the Solicitor's Office at Interior and speaking to a law school's environmental law society, how would you reply to these concerns?

[handwritten margin note: inadequate knowledge for current HCP practice? less habitat as a result of HCPs?]

4. Nor are there many safeguards in the process. Despite the broad public interest in HCPs, they remain a fairly closed process. FWS must publish notice of a proposed HCP in the *Federal Register* and provide at least 30 days for public comment on the documents (in practice, FWS gives up to 60 days for comments, and up to 90 days for large or complex HCPs). The environmental group, Defenders of Wildlife, studied the HCP permitting process of over twenty HCPs. Their conclusions were highly critical.

[handwritten margin note: not enough public participation in considering HCPs?]

> Citizens from various stakeholder groups have no formal role in the HCP process except through the public comment period and, for some plans, through the National Environmental Policy Act or requirements of state or local law. Often, by the time public meetings occur or official drafts are released for comment, however, both the regulated interests and the services have invested so much money and time in plan development that they are unlikely to change course.... Citizens (including those representing the environmental community) generally have not had a seat at the negotiating table in many major recent

negotiations despite the fact that conservationists (in addition to FWS) represent the public's interest in protecting endangered species. . . .

For the vast majority of plans . . . public participation was not adequate, given the plans' large effects on public resources. The most glaring examples are large-scale, single-landowner plans that significantly affect public resources . . . . While those plans did have public meetings and/or formal comment periods, the conservation strategies resulted from private negotiations with largely token attempts at listening to the public's concerns. In addition, numerous small-scale HCPs reviewed here involved exclusive negotiations between the landowner and FWS. . . . This lack of public participation has resulted from an absence of formal requirements to involve the public and the limited leverage of citizens who do not have a direct financial stake in negotiations.

DEFENDERS OF WILDLIFE, FRAYED SAFETY NETS 43–44 (1998).

While public participation avenues to influence HCPs have proven hard going, litigation has proven no easier. Until 1998, no court had overturned a Section 10(a) permit, deferring to expert agency judgment. There have been only a handful of successful challenges since. *See, e.g., Sierra Club v. Babbitt*, 15 F. Supp. 2d 1274 (D. Ala. 1998) (rejecting incidental take permits for two high density housing developments in the habitat of the endangered Alabama Beach Mouse because the FWS had failed to show that the off-site mitigation funding proposed in the HCPs would reduce the impact on the mouse to the "maximum extent practicable"); *NWF v. Babbitt*, 128 F. Supp. 2d 1274 (E.D. Cal. 2000) (remanding a 53,000 acre HCP because of unreasonable assumptions and failure to prepare an EIS), *Southwest Ctr. for Biological Diversity v. Bartel*, 470 F. Supp. 2d 1118 (S.D. Cal. 2006) (enjoining an incidental take permit governing 85 species because the conservation measures provided inadequate protection). For a more recent study critical of HCPs, See Alejandro Camacho, Can Regulation Evolve? Lessons from a Study in Maladaptive Management, 55 UCLA L. Rev. 293 (2007).

What are the downsides to mandating greater opportunity for public participation in HCPs? Realize, as well, that developers already believe the HCP process is unduly cumbersome and lengthy. What form could the participation take that would be meaningful but not bog down what is already a complicated negotiation? Do you feel differently about the discretionary power in HCPs and the No Surprises policy depending on which administration is in the White House?

––––––––

G.   DOES IT WORK?

By many measures, the ESA can be viewed as a success. Empirical evidence clearly demonstrates that after being listed, many species stabilize and some improve to the point of being taken off the list. As of 2008, 48 species had been delisted. The Peregrine falcon and Bald eagle are perhaps two of the best-known success stories. *See* http://ecos.fws.gov/tess_public/DelistingReport.do. Equally, though, at least 15 listed species have gone extinct. Despite the number of plans, their impact has been limited. A careful empirical study by Professor Jeff Rachlinski in 1999 provides a useful snapshot of failures and successes.

In its 1994 report, the FWS concluded that the length of time that a species has remained under the Act's protection correlates positively with species status. Specifically, the FWS observed that 58% of those species listed for twenty years or more have stable or improving populations, as opposed to 44% of those species listed for four to twenty years, and 22% of those species listed for less than four years. The FWS reported similar statistics in 1990. * * *

Since 1973, seven species have been removed from the lists due to extinction. Another eight species that are probably extinct remain listed, awaiting final confirmation of their fate. Thus, a total of fifteen extinctions may be said to have occurred among listed species. At least six are believed to have been extinct before the Act was passed, and the rest were probably already in serious decline. Nevertheless, the conclusion is unmistakable—extinctions have occurred in spite of the Act. By contrast, the FWS has declared eight species recovered to the point that protection is no longer needed. Although some of these successes may not have resulted from the Act's influence, the existence of some recoveries of listed species suggests that the Act can be successful. * * *

Listing appears to have turned the fortunes of about half of the species it protects. Although nearly half of all listed species remain in decline, virtually all species are in decline when originally listed. Most remain in decline for the first year after listing, but as time passes, species populations stabilize and even improve. Each year of protection under the Act improves the prospects for listed species. A year of listing turns the fortunes of three out of every 200 listed species. In addition to demonstrating the benefits of the Act to biodiversity, this study shows that analyzing the distribution of species status at a single point in time undervalues the Act. Because the FWS continuously adds species that are in decline, summary statistics will tend to understate the Act's positive impact. The trends over time indicate that although many species remain at risk of extinction, the biodiversity glass is half full, not half empty.

Despite the fact that the Act requires critical habitat and recovery plans to be created for all species, and despite the fact that both protections benefit species, 598 of the 835 species (71.6%) have recovery plans, 110 species (13.2%) have critical habitat, and only 99 species (11.9%) have both. Clearly, the lack of resources prevents the Act from being all that it can be. The failure to designate habitat and to adopt recovery plans jeopardizes species. As noted above, if the FWS designated both critical habitat and recovery plans for all threatened species, the number of species in decline would drop to less than one-third. * * *

The data clearly demonstrate that endangered and threatened species are better off with the Act than they would be without it. They undermine the conclusions that the Act's mandates stretch resources in a manner harmful to biodiversity and that it creates perverse incentives that overwhelm its benefits. Each aspect of the Act's protection—listing, designating critical habitat, and adopting a species recovery plan—benefits listed species. In short, the Act works.

Jeffrey Rachlinski, *Noah by the Numbers: An Empirical Evaluation of the Endangered Species Act,* 82 CORNELL L. REV. 356, 369–83 (1997).

Concluding that the ESA works, however, is not the same as concluding that it works well or could not be significantly improved. Listing, habitat designation, and enforcement of the Act remain highly contentious. While the benefits of biodiversity conservation are enjoyed by many, the costs are still borne by few. As a result, while perverse incentives for landowners to shoot, shovel, and shut up have been muted by the use of HCPs and Safe Harbors, they still exist. Perhaps most problematic, though, is the fact that the number of candidates for listing continues to grow. If an ounce of prevention is worth a pound of cure, perhaps it is well worth considering what types of legal responses would be effective *upstream* of the ESA, addressing populations that are in decline but not yet endangered.

CASE STUDY: THE DELHI SANDS FLOWER–LOVING FLY*

Introduction

By mid-October, the sun has retreated from its summer-long assault on Colton, California, an "Inland Empire" town about halfway between Los Angeles and the Mojave Desert. The temperature is only about 80, but it feels *hot* as you kick dust around at the construction site of the new San Bernardino County Medical Center ("Hospital"). It could be the arid appearance of the sand dunes and the scrub vegetation on the land in front of you. More likely, though, it's the growing sense of frustration you are feeling in your discussions with representatives of San Bernardino County ("County"). You are an attorney with the regional counsel's office of the U.S. Department of the Interior ("Interior"). The County wants to renegotiate an agreement that it made with your client, the U.S. Fish and Wildlife Service ("Service"), less than two years ago.

You first became involved in May of 1993, after the County had contacted the Service with a potential problem. The 73–acre site ("Site") where the County was planning to build the Hospital contained one and a half acres of the kind of sand dunes that were home to the Delhi Sands flower-loving fly ("Fly"). *See* Figure 1. The County had learned that the Fly had been proposed for listing under the Endangered Species Act of 1973 ("the Act") and wanted to know how it could build the Hospital without violating the law.

* This case was prepared by Josh Eagle, under the editorial guidance of Barton H. ("Buzz") Thompson, Jr., Robert E. Paradise Professor of Natural Resource Law, Stanford Law School, as a basis for classroom discussion rather than to illustrate either effective or ineffective handling of an environmental matter. Some or all of the characters or events may have been fictionalized for pedagogical purposes. Copyright © 1998 by the Board of Trustees of the Leland Stanford Jr. University. The casebook authors are grateful for permission from Stanford's Environment and Natural Resources Law Program to reproduce this abridged case study.

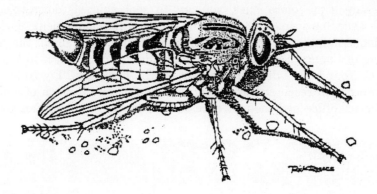

Figure 1. The Delhi Sands flower-loving fly *(Rhaphiomidas terminatus abdominalis)*.

The end result of those discussions was an agreement under which construction could proceed on most of the Site. To avoid an illegal "take" of the Fly, the County had agreed not to pave 8.35 acres in the southeast corner of the Site.

Under the terms of this written agreement, the County would create a "habitat enhancement area" ("Preserve") on the 8.35 acres. In addition, the County would fence off and maintain one 100–foot wide "corridor" of land running west from the Preserve to Pepper Avenue along the southern edge of the Site. The County would also maintain a 30–foot wide corridor running north along the eastern side of Pepper Avenue. The Service's theory was that this pair of corridors would allow Flies to travel to the northwestern corner of the Site. Once in the northwestern corner, Flies could potentially mix with another population of Flies off the site, if they could successfully fly across Pepper Avenue. This potential link, felt the Service, was crucial to the survival of the Fly population on the Site. *See* Figures 2 and 3.

As you stand there staring out at the dunes, County officials are telling you that they need to widen Valley Boulevard to accommodate the increased traffic into and out of the Hospital. Emergency vehicles must not be impeded by traffic congestion, they tell you. This is truly a matter of life and death.

The Valley Boulevard project would narrow the western half of the southern corridor from 100 to 18 feet, diminishing any potential for connectivity with nearby populations. The County's consultant, Tom Olsen, tells you that there is no biological evidence that the species uses corridors. "It's preposterous," he says. Following the terms of the agreement, his firm has conducted two biological surveys of the Site for the County. The entomologists he hired have not seen one Fly using the corridors.

Your own biologists and independent entomologists have told you that in order for the Fly population on the Site to persist, it will need access to at least one other Fly population. The experts are not sure, however, how wide an effective Fly corridor needs to be. They opine only that 18 feet is not wide enough.

Kicking some more dust, you try to cool yourself down. You had worked very hard in 1993 to craft the original agreement, feeling a tremendous amount of pressure from the County, the public, the media, members of Congress and especially from your Interior bosses in Washington, D.C. Your bosses did not want to see the headline: "Fly Kills Hospital." In order to reach an agreement, you had given up much of what the local Service office had thought necessary to protect the Fly. Can you give up more now?

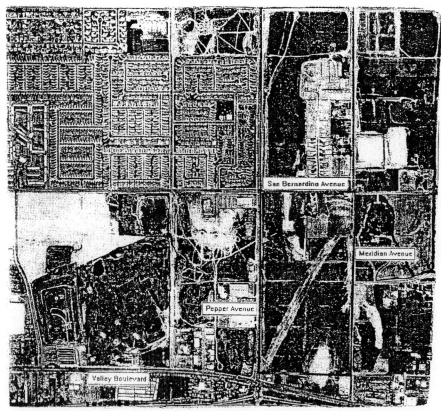

Figure 2. Site prior to construction.

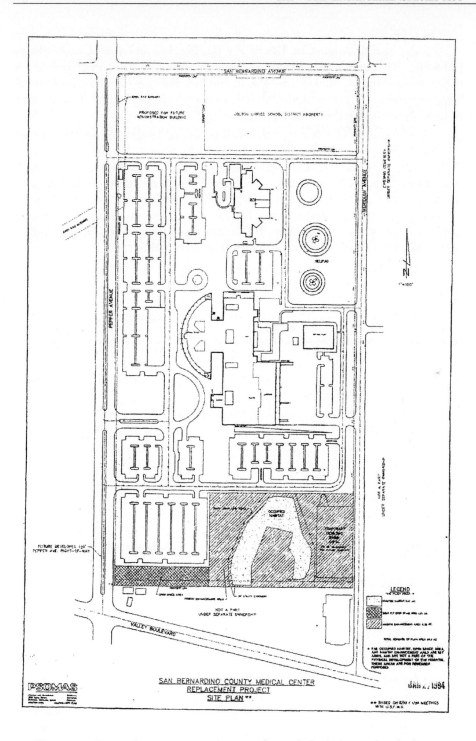

Figure 3. Hospital site, surrounding roads, and fly habitat (hatched area at bottom and bottom left).

Listing the Fly

It was during August of 1989—Fly mating season—that University of California Riverside Professor Greg Ballmer first saw Flies near Colton. A fellow entomologist, Rick Rogers, had alerted Ballmer to the presence of *Rhaphiomidas* in some undeveloped areas close to Interstate 10, and Ballmer went to see them for himself.

Rhaphiomidas is a North American genus of 19 species and 5 subspecies that inhabit arid regions of the southwestern United States and northwestern Mexico. Historically, there were two *Rhaphiomidas* subspecies in Southern California. By 1989 one of these, *Rhaphiomidas terminatus terminatus*, or the El Segundo flower-loving fly, was presumed to be extinct. This fly had resided in the coastal dunes of southwestern Los Angeles County and had apparently succumbed to loss of habitat due in part to the construction of Los Angeles International Airport.

Ballmer had taken an interest in the other member of the species, *Rhaphiomidas terminatus abdominalis:* the Fly. The Fly takes the first part of its common name from the fact that it is known to occur only on fine, sandy soil in wholly or partially consolidated dunes. Like all terrestrial features, dunes exist in continually changing form and location. The process whereby a dune is remade and relocated, primarily by wind, is known as consolidation. In Southern California, the soil types where wholly or partially consolidated dunes exist are generally classified as the Delhi (DELL-high) series of soils.

The Fly is called "flower-loving" because as an adult it uses its long proboscis to suck nectar from flowers while hovering like a hummingbird. In the course of feeding, the Fly pollinates at least one plant species, the common buckwheat *(Eriogonumfasiculatum).*

Other than what is captured in its name, precious little is known about the Fly. Making an entomologist's life difficult, Flies appear above ground only during a two-week-long adult life span. *See* Exhibit A, Declaration of Christopher D. Nagano. [All the exhibits are located on the Stanford case study website, which is described at the end of this case study.]

When he visited Colton in August of 1989, Ballmer managed to spot a few male Flies flying about in open spaces between vegetation. (Females tend not to move very much and are thus difficult to see.) Though excited by his find, Ballmer soon became concerned about the future of the Fly and several other rare insect species that had evolved to live in the harsh Delhi Sands. In addition to the Fly and four rare plant species, Delhi Sands habitat supports a number of animals of limited distribution including the legless lizard (*Anniellapulchra*), San Diego horned lizard (*Phrynosoma coronatum blainvillii*), Delhi Sands metalmark butterfly (*Apodemia mormo* new subspecies), Delhi Sands Jerusalem cricket (*Stenopelmatus* new species), convergent apiocerid fly (*Apiocera convergens*), and the Delhi Sands sandroach (*Arenivaga* new species).

Ballmer did not want the Fly, nor these other species, to end up like the El Segundo fly, victims of lost habitat. Over the years, Delhi Sands habitat had been degraded or eliminated as the result of various human activities. Some areas had been converted to vineyards, which had eventually failed due to shifting sand and the soil's inability to hold water. Other areas had served as dumping grounds for manure from dairy farms. The untreated manure created perfect conditions for an invasion of exotic plant species that were able to out-compete native species.

In the late 1980s, the threats were different, but the results were the same. Owing to the proximity of several major highways, land was being developed for industrial uses such as warehouses and factories. Growing population in the County led to an increase in residential development.

According to Ballmer, "the habitat was pretty much gone, and what was left was going fast."

More than 97 percent of the Fly's original habitat had been rendered unsuitable for the Fly. Of the historic 40 square miles of Delhi Sands, about one square mile of fragmented dunes remained. There were less than ten remaining sites, all within an eight-mile radius, where the Fly could be found. Each of these sites was smaller than ten acres. Given that Fly density is estimated to be about 10 per acre, there were at most about 1000 Flies remaining in 1989.

In the fall of 1989, Ballmer began assembling the information required for a petition to list the Fly as an endangered species under both the federal and California Endangered Species Acts. He gathered as much documentation as he could find about the Fly, its habitat, and the land uses that were threatening to render the Fly extinct. He felt that the Fly was "a very impressive insect and part of California's natural heritage." He was further motivated by his belief that extinction was a far greater tragedy than death: extinction meant an end to an evolutionary trajectory and an end to possibility.

Ballmer filed his petitions with the Service and the California Department of Fish and Game in October of 1989. Fearing that California would refuse to list the Fly for political and economic reasons, Ballmer soon withdrew his petition to the state.

In December of 1990, the Service issued notice pursuant to Section 4 of the Act, 16 U.S.C. § 1533(b)(3)(A), that sufficient information had been presented to indicate that listing the Fly as endangered might be warranted.

In November of 1992, pursuant to 16 U.S.C. § 1533(b)(5), the Service proposed to list the Fly.

On September 23, 1993, the Service added the Fly to its list of endangered species, where it joined about 850 other species in the United States, including 15 other species in the County. The "final rule" issued by the Service relied primarily on the fact that "extensive habitat loss and degradation" had reduced the range of the Fly "by over 97 percent." *See* Exhibit B, Final Rule.

In a 1998 interview, Tom Olsen said that while there "really wasn't much information available about the Fly or its habitat needs, since no one had ever really cared about the Fly," the logic used by the Service was sound. The Service's view was that since Fly habitat had declined by 97 percent, Fly population had probably declined by 97 percent. "Only five populations of [the Fly] exist," said the final rule. "All [are] threatened by urban development activities." Ballmer obviously agreed with the Service's conclusion as well, although he disagreed with Olsen's assessment that no one cared about the Fly.

"There were obviously people such as myself who cared," he said in 1998. "But no one had yet undertaken the laborious chore of studying its biology."

The Hospital and the County

Located about 25 miles east of Los Angeles (*see* Figure 4), San Bernardino County and the surrounding "Inland Empire" make up one of the fastest growing areas in California and the United States. According to John Husing, an economic analyst who has conducted in-depth studies of the region's economy, "the Inland Empire has become Southern California's metaphor for growth." Federal forecasts show that the area will add 928,000 people between 1993 and 2005—more than any other U.S. metropolitan area. A press release issued by SANBAG (San Bernardino Associated Governments) claims that the region has added "more than 80,000 jobs [between 1990 and 1998], four times that of second place San Diego."

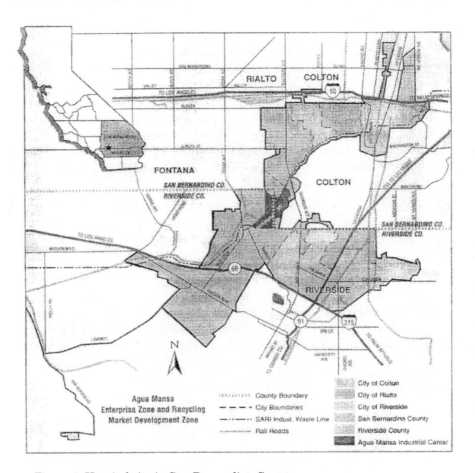

Figure 4. Hospital site in San Bernardino County.

Along with new residents and businesses comes a need for infrastructure, including roads and services. In the early 1980s, the County government had begun developing plans to construct a new medical center. The existing facility, located in the City of San Bernardino, was approaching fifty years of age, and there were concerns about its "seismic integrity." The County wanted to build a state-of-the-art facility that would resist earthquakes up to 8.0 in magnitude.

During the mid–1980's, the project was put on the back burner due to a sluggish local economy. When the economy and the County population began to grow, plans for the new medical center were revived.

In July of 1990, the County Board of Supervisors ("the Board") began the process of selecting a site for the Hospital. As part of this process, the Board selected a firm to perform an Environmental Impact Report ("EIR"), as required under the California Environmental Quality Act ("CEQA"), for several potential sites.

One of the sites to be covered by the EIR was the so-called "Arden" site in the City of San Bernardino. The Board selected this site as its "preferred" site for several reasons. It was close to several major roadways. It had good soil conditions and no geological hazards. It was of sufficient size to allow for future expansion. The City of San Bernardino supported the choice of the Arden site due to the economic benefits it would bring: construction jobs, hospital jobs, and new, hospital-related businesses.

At the public hearings on the EIR for the Arden site, significant neighborhood opposition was voiced. According to Randy Scott, Planning Manager for the County, this was a typical case of the NIMBY (Not in My Backyard) phenomenon. Neighborhood residents were concerned the Hospital would attract "the homeless, the indigent, and the criminal element that would be treated at the Hospital." As the County's public health facility, the Hospital would provide treatment to those who could not afford to pay for it. The neighborhood succeeded in killing the Arden site.

Anxious to keep the Hospital, the City offered another site. This site, though, had multiple constraints, including a lack of road infrastructure and soil with "potential liquefaction" characteristics. For these reasons, it was rejected.

It was at that point that the Colton Site became a contender. It was close to Interstate 10 ("I–10") and had good geological characteristics. It was centrally located in the County. The City of Colton, seeing the potential economic benefits, began lobbying for the Hospital.

In early 1991, the County held a public hearing on the EIR for the Site. Scott recalled that "the EIR" included a biological assessment and there was nothing in it about Flies. According to Scott, neither the Service nor any conservation group gave testimony or submitted comments about the potential biological impact of constructing the Hospital at the Site.

In August of 1991, the Board certified the EIR and designated a site in Colton as the location for the Hospital. In October of 1991, the Board approved the purchase of the majority of the Colton site. In July of 1992, the Board authorized acquisition of the final site parcels for the Hospital.

Between July of 1992 and September of 1993, the Board approved bids for quality control services, an inspector of record, seismic and geo-technical materials testing, insurance, management information systems, and site preparation package bids.

The estimated $487 million cost of the Hospital was to be paid for with a combination of County, state and federal funds. The County would raise part of the necessary money by issuing bonds. Interest payments on the debt incurred by the County would be reduced through a state program that provided about a 50/50 mix of state and federal aid to help finance the construction of new public hospitals. The (Riverside) Press–Enterprise reported that the County would receive more than $831 million through this program during the 30–year financing period.

The Hospital Site

The Site purchased by the County for the Hospital is located at the corner of Pepper Avenue and Valley Boulevard. *See* Figures 2 and 3, *supra*. Access to the Hospital from I–10 is *via* the Pepper Avenue exit. The Site is bounded on the north by San Bernardino Avenue, on the east by Meridian Avenue, on the south by Valley Boulevard, and on the west by Pepper Avenue.

At the time of the listing, prior to construction of the Hospital, the Site consisted of what most people would consider a "waste area," according to Ballmer. In an affidavit prepared for later litigation, Robert H. Gerdeman, County Project Manager for the Hospital, said that at the time of the listing, "homeless people were living on that portion of the Hospital site where the Fly was supposedly located. Trash and debris were everywhere. Also, the site was a popular place for riding all-terrain vehicles. . . . I observed teenagers riding through the dunes right up until the time of the Fly's listing."

The majority of the Site consisted of long-abandoned vineyards. Most of the area was covered by relatively dense vegetation; a small amount, where sand had been mined during the construction of I–10, contained so-called Riversidian Sage Scrub—less densely vegetated land containing "blowout" areas of wholly or partially consolidated dunes.

The County Learns About the Fly

A few months prior to publishing the proposed rule in November of 1992, the Service informed County officials of the impending listing of the Fly. According to Scott, County officials had "never heard a damn thing about the Fly" before this time.

Realizing that the listing of the Fly would probably impede construction of the Hospital, the County submitted comments to the Service opposing the listing. These comments did not attack the science behind the listing, but instead focused on the economic impacts that the listing would have. In addition, the County contacted the Service to begin discussions on how the potential conflict at the Hospital site might be resolved.

The Service and the County Attempt to Address the Conflict

In May of 1993, representatives of the Service and San Bernardino County held the first of several meetings aimed at resolving the situation. Present at some or all of these meetings were:

- Randy Scott, County Planning Manager
- John Giblin, Deputy County Administrative Officer
- Robert Gerdeman, County Project Manager for the Hospital
- Jeff Newman, the Service Branch Chief for Conservation Planning for San Bernardino, Riverside, Orange and Los Angeles Counties
- Linda Dawes, the Service biologist, Carlsbad, California
- Chris Nagano, the Service biologist, Carlsbad, California
- Tom Olsen, Consulting ecologist for the County
- J.B. Ruhl, Attorney/Consultant for the County
- Paul Mordy, Deputy County Counsel

The first meeting, according to many of those present, was characterized by a strong disagreement on the extent to which the Site actually contained Fly habitat. Some of the participants recalled that the disagreement quickly evolved into hostility coupled with the exchange of threats. In an interview, John Giblin recalled that "right off the bat this woman from Fish [the Service] started telling us that we're screwed, they had us over a barrel, and that we had to do everything they said or else." Robert Gerdeman stated in his affidavit that Service employees "were not concerned with causing additional cost or delay to the Hospital project." Giblin said that County representatives at this meeting responded to the Service's appearance of intransigence by "threaten[ing] to declare war in the newspapers."*

The initial Service position was that disturbing any part of the Site would likely result in a direct or indirect "take" of the Fly pursuant to 16 U.S.C. §§ 1538(a)(1) and 1532(18). The County's position was that only one and a half acres of the Site was "potential" habitat and that construction of the hospital would not result in a take. The County called it "potential" habitat because although it was Delhi Sands soil-type, there was no evidence that Flies existed there.

The next few months saw little progress in the negotiations, in part because of a lack of communication between the parties. In responding to a request from the County that it speed up the process of evaluating one of the County's proposals, the Acting Field Supervisor of the Service's Carls-

---

* An interesting side-note is the matter of the "I–10 slowdown." Giblin and Gerdeman (in a sworn affidavit) asserted that the Service employee Linda Dawes threatened at the May meeting to have traffic on I–10 slowed to 15 miles per hour during the Fly mating period. On the other hand, the Service employees present at the meeting insisted that no one had made such a statement. Whether it was made or not, the statement was attributed to Dawes in many newspaper articles about the controversy, and especially in opinion pieces attacking the Act. After hovering, the alleged quote finally landed in the dissenting opinion in a case eventually filed by the County against the United States. *See National Association of Home Builders, et al. v. Babbitt*, 130 F.3d 1041, 1060 (D.C. Cir. 1997) [, *cert. denied*, 524 U.S. 937 (1998)].

bad office replied that the Service was "reviewing [the County's] proposal as quickly as possible.... In view of the urgency of your need," he continued, "it is unfortunate that the County repeatedly cancelled meetings, and finally refused to schedule meetings with [the Service], despite numerous warnings that the occupied habitat on this site could present a problem if planning did not occur."

The County was feeling some urgency because, as Scott said, delays "would effectively terminate the project because conditions for financing the Hospital required that the monies be spent in a specified timeframe." Further, "[i]f the project was terminated, [it] would cause a public health crisis because the County's existing healthcare facilities [were] outdated and inadequate."

In August of 1993, the County hired two University of California Riverside entomologists to survey the Site for Flies. After scouring the entire Site for seven days between August 1 and September 4, the entomologists reported eight sightings within the one and a half-acre Delhi Sands area. It was unclear whether these were eight different Flies, because the Flies could not be marked for identification.

On October 18, 1993, the County submitted a written proposal to end the standoff. In this proposal, entitled the "Habitat Preservation, Habitat Enhancement, and Impact Avoidance Plan for the Delhi Sands Flower–Loving Fly at the San Bernardino County Hospital Replacement Site," the County offered to, among other things, "move" the Hospital location at the site 250 feet north and create the Preserve.

In a letter dated October 19,1993, the Service dismissed the proposal as insufficient to satisfy the Act, and noted the difficulty in trying to create a small preserve for the Fly. *See* Exhibit C, Correspondence re: Habitat Preservation, Habitat Enhancement, and Impact Avoidance Plan. The problem was this: the Fly needs wholly or partially consolidated dunes, habitat conditions created by wind-blown sand. Fly habitat in a small preserve would not last for very long, because sand in the preserve at the outset would soon be blown by the prevailing northerly winds out the south end. The construction of the Hospital and parking lots north of the Preserve would eliminate the replacement source of sand.

The County recognized the problem of creating a fixed preserve of shifting sand, and suggested that the problem could be solved by stabilizing the dunes. Stabilization could be achieved by planting native vegetation and by erecting wind barriers. These acts, said the Service, were unacceptable, as they would "constitute ... an artificial modification of habitat which may adversely impact" the Fly.

In the next few months, according to Scott, there was a tremendous amount of public and political pressure put on the Service to resolve the problem. The County spoke with California congressmen and Senator Alan Cranston. Scott recalled that County representatives "probably" went to Washington to meet with members of Congress and high-level Department of Interior staff.

As promised, the County declared war on the Service and the Act in the newspapers. This was apparently an appetizing case for the media because of the kind of species being protected and the type of growth and development being tempered. Articles and editorials appeared in many national newspapers. NBC Nightly News broadcast a segment on the controversy in its "Fleecing of America" series.

Most of the reporting focused on the issue of whether the Act had "gone too far." The editorials attacked the Act for "putting flies before people," calling The Fly, "Superfly: With the Power to Stop Bulldozers," "A Fly in the Ointment" of county plans, and other painful puns. *See* Exhibit D, Newspaper Articles.

In December of 1993, the Service accepted a County proposal that was nearly identical to the earlier one. *See* Exhibit E, Habitat Preservation, Habitat Enhancement, and Impact Avoidance Plan. The differences between the plan rejected in September and the plan accepted in December were that, under the latter plan, the County agreed to (1) set aside an additional amount of land to serve as a Fly "corridor," (2) engage in certain enhancement efforts in the preserve (the dune stabilization efforts which the Service had earlier called detrimental to the Fly), and (3) conduct certain studies, monitoring and educational programs regarding the Fly at the Site. The County also agreed to plant a 30–foot wide strip in natural vegetation up the western edge of the Site.

The 100–foot wide corridor would extend from the 8.35–acre preserve along the entire southern edge of the project site. The Service insisted that the corridor was essential because it could provide a link, in conjunction with the 30–foot wide strip along Pepper Avenue, to another stable Fly colony. (The location of this second Fly population can be seen in Figure 2: the sandy area west of Pepper Avenue and just south of San Bernardino Avenue.)

The plan approved by the Service was not a Habitat Conservation Plan ("HCP") under Section 10 of the Act. Such plans are required before the Service will issue an Incidental Take Permit, which allows the take of a species incidental to undertaking an otherwise lawful activity. *See* 16 U.S.C. § 1539. The plan submitted by the County and approved by the Service was a plan to avoid a take; because the Service determined that there would be no take under the plan, no permit was necessary.

Although it agreed to create and maintain the corridor as part of the agreement, the County believed the Service's demand for a corridor was not based on any sound scientific evidence. In an interview, Olsen said that there is no biology indicating that the species utilizes corridors and that the literature indicates that Flies are "wind dispersed." Giblin pointed out that Flies from the Hospital Site would have to fly northwest against prevailing winds to link with the second population.

After concluding the 1993 agreement with the Service, the County implemented the agreement, fencing off and maintaining the preserve, conducting some restoration work, and funding a five-year study of the Fly at the site.

It was uncertain to those outside the Service whether these activities would contribute in a meaningful way to the continued existence of the Fly as a species. According to Olsen, there were two views within the ecology community. There were those who believed that every little bit would help. There were others who believed that unless Fly conservation was addressed on a larger geographic scale, the County's actions would be futile.

The County estimated its cost in adjusting to the listing of the Fly as somewhere between three and four million dollars. *See* Exhibit F, Affidavit of Chief County Engineer Kenneth A. Taylor. These costs included modifying plans for the Hospital, setting up the Preserve and conducting the studies. "This insect that spends most of its life underground living as a fat, clumsy maggot cost the county more than a half million dollars per fly," said Joe Baca, a member of the California Assembly. Baca was the author of a bill passed by the California Assembly directing the Service to remove the Fly from the endangered list. The bill was eventually defeated in the California Senate.

Local environmental groups, who in interviews with the media supported the actions taken by the Service, felt differently about whether protecting the Fly was worth the monetary cost: "People think of flies as things that buzz around your home and lay eggs in your meat and give you maggots. That may be true of the housefly, but there are hundreds of fly species doing a lot of useful things out there that allow the ecosystem to operate properly," said John Hopkins, director of Sierra Club's California Biodiversity Program.

Round 2: The Interchange Impinges on the Corridor

In October of 1995, the County informed the Service of its plans to redesign the Valley Boulevard/Pepper Avenue intersection near the Hospital.

According to Selby Douglas Graybeal, an administrative analyst for the County, the County evaluated between 35 and 40 different plans designed to improve traffic flow and to allow for ease of access to the Hospital. "Each feasible alternative," he said in a 1996 affidavit, "underwent a cost analysis, an engineering analysis, and a traffic analysis." In the end, a plan called Alternative D was selected as "the most cost effective and best option for improving this section of road." In 1996, Anthony Gray, chief of transportation design for the County, wrote that Alternative D was "by far the least expensive" option. Alternative D involved moving Valley Boulevard northward 95 meters. *See* Exhibit G, County Interoffice Memorandum re: Valley Boulevard/Pepper Avenue.

While Alternative D was acceptable to the County, the California Transportation Department, and the City of Colton, it was unacceptable to the Service because it would reduce the potential effectiveness of the Fly corridor. *See* Figure 5 [redrawn from original, eds.].

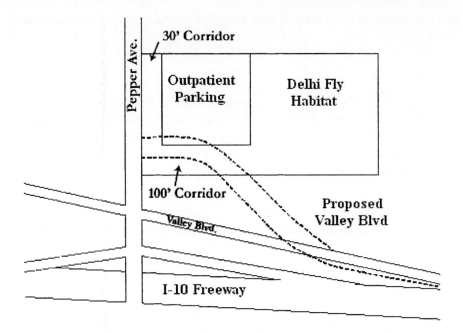

Figure 5. Proposed road construction across Fly habitat.

According to Newman, modifying the corridor by reducing its width would "eliminate . . . a critical part of the County's efforts to avoid a take of the [Fly]." The Service suggested that the County maintain the width of the corridor, but relocate it north of its original location, in an area that the County had designated for parking spaces.

The County rejected this proposal. Olsen told the Service that the relocation of the corridor would "seriously encroach into the hospital parking area and [would] have disastrous effects on parking that is critical to hospital operations" by eliminating 178 spaces. "At the current time," he wrote in November of 1995, "the hospital is approximately 700 parking spaces short of what is optimally needed for patrons and employees."

In the same letter, Olsen told the Service that "[t]he County is committed to preservation of the species and to financially supporting the ongoing research on behalf of the Fly in accordance with their original agreement." He suggested that "in addition to the standard twelve foot roadway maintenance strip, a six foot corridor be set aside and revegetated as per existing agreements." *See* Exhibit I, Correspondence re: Valley Boulevard/Pepper Avenue.

Jerry Eaves, an elected County Supervisor, wrote a second letter to the Service in January of 1996 stating that although the County had originally agreed to the creation of the corridor, "we felt that [it] was of dubious merit. . . . In two years of monitoring activity on the fly's behavior . . . no observations of [the Fly] have been made within the 'corridor'."

Ballmer's view was that the corridor would play an important part in the recovery of the Fly. "Ultimately," he wrote in 1993, "preservation of the Fly colony at the Hospital site will require linkage to at least one other stable colony."

———

Assume that you have a meeting tomorrow with County officials to discuss the situation. What are the major questions or issues that you believe that you must address in deciding how to approach this matter? In particular:

- What are your goals?
- Can the County go forward with its current plan without violating the ESA?
- Does Section 7 apply in this situation?
- Could the FWS give the County an incidental take permit? Should it develop an HCP?
- If you fight the County, is there any way of avoiding bad publicity and political consequences?
- How will the County likely respond?

In preparing your answers, you should first read the primary documents that form part of the record of decision.

To read the exhibits for this case study, please go to the website:

http://www.law.stanford.edu/casestudies/, and follow the prompts to register.

Once you have received a password, log in to the site, go to the Case Studies Subject Index, scroll down to the case, The Endangered Delhi Sands Flower–Loving Fly, Part–I, in the Endangered Species Act section, and click on the link, "Exhibits."

CHAPTER FIVE

LIVING MARINE RESOURCES

I. FISHERIES
    A. INTRODUCTION
    B. DRIVERS OF FISHERY COLLAPSE
        1. OVERFISHING AND OVERCAPITALIZATION
        2. SUBSIDIES
        3. BYCATCH
        4. HABITAT LOSS AND DEGRADATION
    C. A PRIMER ON FISHERIES SCIENCE
    D. FISHERY MANAGEMENT TOOLS
        1. RESTRICTIONS
        2. CAPACITY REDUCTION
        3. LIMITED ACCESS PRIVILEGE PROGRAMS
        4. AQUACULTURE
    E. FISHERY LAW
        1. UNCLOS AND EEZS
        2. MAGNUSON–STEVENS FISHERY CONSERVATION AND MANAGEMENT ACT
            a. REGIONAL FISHERY MANAGEMENT COUNCILS
            b. FISHERY MANAGEMENT PLANS (FMPS)
            c. CONSISTENCY WITH NATIONAL STANDARDS
                i.   NATIONAL STANDARD ONE
                ii.   NATIONAL STANDARD TWO
                iii. NATIONAL STANDARD EIGHT
                iv.   NATIONAL STANDARD NINE
                v.   CONFLICTING STANDARDS
            PROBLEM EXERCISE: STOCK REBUILDING
            d. ECOSYSTEM MANAGEMENT
        CASE STUDY: RED SNAPPER FISHERY
II. MARINE MAMMALS
    A. WHALES
        1. HISTORY OF WHALING
        2. INTERNATIONAL CONVENTION ON THE REGULATION OF WHALING
            a. THE MORATORIUM AND RESPONSES
            b. BREAKING THE STALEMATE
        CASE STUDY: ABORIGINAL SUBSISTENCE WHALING
    B. MARINE MAMMAL–FISHERY CONFLICTS
        1. OVERVIEW OF THE MARINE MAMMAL PROTECTION ACT OF 1972
        2. PINNIPEDS AND THE SALMON FISHERY
        3. DOLPHIN MORTALITY IN THE TUNA FISHERY
            a. U.S. LEGISLATIVE RESPONSE
            b. INTERNATIONAL RESPONSE TO U.S. SANCTIONS

No one can tell what a spot of time is until suddenly the whole world is a fish and the fish is gone.

NORMAN MACLEAN, A RIVER RUNS THROUGH IT (1976)

I. FISHERIES

A. INTRODUCTION

Covering 78% of the Earth's surface, the importance of the world's oceans cannot be overestimated. Life began in the oceans and it remains our link to life through its control of climate, provision of food and minerals, sequestration of carbon, assimilation of wastes, and other irreplaceable services. The seas have always been a source of goods and a dumping ground for wastes, but modern technology has tremendously increased both the resource extraction from the sea and the amount of discharges into the sea. To be sure, the seas have enormous capacity to assimilate wastes and support productive ecosystems, yet the oceans' ecosystems are under unprecedented stress. In earlier times, the bounty of the seas were thought limitless. But there are limits, and many have been reached or exceeded.

This section focuses on the fishery resources of the oceans. Commercial fishing is the last form of commercial hunting allowed in the United States. Mismanagement of marine fisheries has been spectacular and, in terms of direct human impact, overfishing remains arguably one of the greatest global threats. Since World War II, global catch has increased almost fivefold. The UN Food and Agriculture Organization (FAO) has estimated that about 10% of the world's major fisheries are significantly depleted, 18% are overexploited, and 47% are fully exploited, leaving just one-quarter of the world's marine fish populations at sustainable levels. Atlantic cod populations off Canada's Newfoundland coast—once the most abundant fish in the Northwest Atlantic—were long regarded by scientists as a limitless resource and supported a fishery for well over 500 years. MARK KURLANSKY, COD: A BIOGRAPHY OF THE FISH THAT CHANGED THE WORLD, 28 (1997). Technological advances, however, allowed fishermen from 1960 to 1975 to catch the same amount of cod estimated to have been caught between 1500 and 1750. MICHAEL HARRIS, LAMENT FOR AN OCEAN: THE COLLAPSE OF THE ATLANTIC COD FISHERY: A TRUE CRIME STORY, 62 (1998). In the years preceding the total collapse, overfishing was so great that from 1990 to 1993, the cod population fell nearly one hundred-fold. By 1994, the commercial cod fishery no longer existed. Such collapses, unthinkable in the past, have now become a terrible prospect in many countries. FAO, THE STATE OF THE WORLD'S FISHERIES AND AQUACULTURE 2000 (2000). The graph below shows the world's fish catch from 1950–2002 (note the increasing importance of aquaculture in China). FAO, THE STATE OF WORLD FISHERIES AND AQUACULTURE 2004, at 4.

World capture and aquaculture production

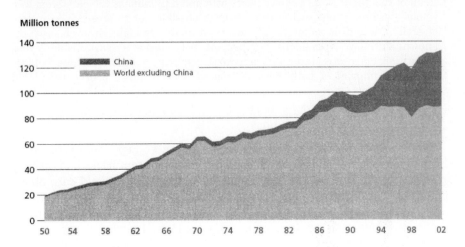

Million tonnes

Nor are such collapses isolated occurrences. As Oliver Houck describes below, U.S. fishery management has a sorry record. Of the 191 domestic fish stocks that have been studied, 82% are utilized or fully utilized.

Beyond public forests and rangelands, beyond the reach of piers and offshore oil platforms, lies one of the world's oldest economies: commercial fisheries. Since 1976, the United States has exercised an extended fisheries jurisdiction stretching 200 miles from the shoreline. This jurisdiction covers more than 100,000 miles of U.S. coastline, and more than 2.2 million nautical square miles of ocean—an area roughly doubling the size of the United States and encompassing nearly 20% of the world's maritime fisheries. As a matter of simple geography, the management responsibility is awesome. Only this decade have statistics revealed how poorly the United States has exercised this responsibility. Much of the New England fishing fleet, once the pride of the region, now sits grounded in port; the federal government is now trying to buy out the boats. Salmon fishing has been banned off the coast of Washington, and severely restricted down the western seaboard. Chesapeake Bay oysters are at 1% of historical levels; swordfish are landing at 60 pounds instead of 1000 pounds and more; bluefin tuna are down 90% since 1975; haddock are down 94% since 1960; and harvestable cod and yellowtail flounder are at their lowest levels on record. Between 1990 and 1992, the chief groundfish species of New England dropped 30% from historic averages. The biomass of bottomfish in the Gulf of Mexico has dropped 85% since 1973, largely due to shrimp trawling.... The collapse of the New England fishing industry alone cost 14,000 jobs and $350 million in annual revenues. Something went very wrong.

Fisheries management will never be a simple business. Managers often lack basic information on fish populations, and even healthy stocks fluctuate widely in nature, often undermined by natural or human events over which managers have no control. Managers also face the balkanization of law enforcement jurisdictions, with state, federal, and international authorities often exercising control over the same stocks and species. Add to this palette the growing conflicts among fisheries users and fishery-dependent communities: recreational fishers versus commercial, seiners versus longliners, large boats versus small, wild culture versus mariculture, and the ultimate enigma of whether the objective of management is to increase production, or biomass, or dollar value, or to lower consumer prices, or to preserve coastal traditions and ways of life. In all of this tug of war, we have never attempted to manage the ecosystem as a whole—assuming that such a thing is even possible—or to preserve ecosystem diversity. More disappointing, we have been unable to maintain even the best-known and most commercially-important fish stocks at sustainable levels, despite an elaborate statutory framework requiring just that. These failures reveal the imprint of both consensus-based politics and a poorly articulated standard of law.

Oliver A. Houck, *On the Law of Biodiversity and Ecosystem Management,* 81 Minn. L. Rev. 869, 945–48 (1997).

The facts of crashing stocks should be reason enough for concern over fisheries management, but it is worth taking a step back and asking ourselves why environmentalists and the general public should care about declining fisheries. American consumers eat over 15 pounds of seafood every year. Is concern over declining fisheries driven by individual economic interests—higher fish prices in the supermarket? Is it primarily a socio-economic concern—depleted fisheries lead to unemployment and related social problems? Perhaps the concern is more properly directed at cultural loss—crashing fisheries threaten traditional ways of life and fishing communities? Or are we driven more by moral concerns—an ethical obligation to protect ocean ecosystems and their populations?

Why are you concerned over crashing fisheries? Do you view fisheries management as primarily an economic, cultural, or moral challenge? As described in Chapter 1, the values issue—the reason we *ought* to conserve certain natural resources—drives management policies—*how* and *how much* we should conserve them. Whether our primary concern is preservation of an economic resource or respect for a sea ethic has a huge influence over what our policies look like and, as we shall see, nowhere is this clearer than in the contrast between the resource management policies for fish and for marine mammals.

QUESTIONS AND DISCUSSION

1. As Chapter 8 on rangelands describes, grazing policy has been driven in part by cultural respect for the "cowboy heritage" of cattle ranching. How important a driver of fisheries policy should concerns over the impact on local communities be? In this regard, consider the heartfelt congressional testimony of Pat Percy from the Maine Fishing Industry Development Center.

> Fishing in Maine has over a three hundred year history. Fishing was the foundation upon which communities up and down our 7,200 mile coast were built. Fishing families have carried on in the fishing traditions of their communities. Fishermen are committed to preserving the health and vitality of the fishery to ensure that generations to come can support themselves as fishermen and maintain their fishing and community traditions. They are core values that are very important to our rural fishermen. In many ways fishing defines our "way of life." While some of these coastal communities have developed into larger towns and cities, their character and primary occupation has changed little.

Certainly, the goal of promoting fishing related businesses has always been important to a state such as Maine and particularly so to the communities strung along Maine's vast coast line whose economic and social fabric is intertwined with fishing and dependent upon fishing related activities. For hundreds of years and through many generations, our perceptions of ourselves, of our families and of our community has been framed by fishing. * * *

In most of Maine's 144 communities, fishing and related businesses provide the main source of income for a significant part of the community. Property taxes on fishermen's houses support schools, mortgages on fishermen's boats and homes provide income for banks. Fuel and ice companies are all dependent on an active commercial fishery and provide jobs for fishing families ... Our fishermen are our selectmen and our school board members, our volunteer firemen and ambulance people, our basketball coaches, as well as soccer and baseball coaches, and yes even our Sunday school teachers ... We are the very fiber of America.

Testimony of Pat Percy, Maine Fishing Industry Development Center, House Committee on Resources, Subcommittee on Fisheries, Wildlife and Oceans (Aug. 1, 1996).

Assume you are the fishery manager for Maine's waters. The marine scientists argue that catch data indicate flounder are overfished and, therefore, the total catch level must be reduced. The local fishing community opposes reductions, arguing that (1) they are out there every day and know the stock better than anyone else and (2) it's obviously in their self-interest to preserve the fishery, and if the stock were truly threatened they would be the first to support reductions. How should you best respect community concerns? Perhaps the tragedy of the commons is at work here. Should you accede to locals and maintain the current catch levels? Isn't reducing the quota necessarily paternalistic—i.e., "I have you fishers' best interests in mind and you'd agree with me if you weren't so focused on short-term economic needs"? Think back to the discussion of scale at page 51. If determining the sustainable level of catch is a scientific question, why should the local fishermen have any influence on this process at all?

2.   There is no shortage of groups and individuals willing to donate time and money to help conserve pandas, elephants, and other endangered terrestrial species. Nor are marine mammals short of genuine concern. Just think of "Save the Whales" bumper stickers and efforts to protect dolphins and seals. Protecting fish, though, doesn't have the same ring to it. Is it that our native sympathies are not aroused by the plight of cold-blooded species that we are used to seeing on our dinner plates?

Not everyone, of course, views fish as hors d'oeuvres. What do you make of the argument of Carl Safina, below? How does it differ from the land ethic of Aldo Leopold discussed at page 13?

Today many typical people who do not particularly think of themselves as active conservationists or environmentalists apply the notion of "live and let live" to most species. Even if human use of species is deemed desirable, extermination is generally held unacceptable. Thus many people implicitly include nonhuman life in an unstated sense of extended community. They would not question a hawk's place in the sky, nor ask what good is a gazelle, nor wonder whether the world really needs wild orchids. Without stating it, they intuitively acknowledge other species' uncontested right to struggle for existence in life's harsh fabric.

Yet when told of the plight of, say, sharks, many of these same people still think it quite reasonable to inquire, "What good are they? Why do we need them?" * * *

What good, then, are sharks? Let's put all question of uses, products, and ecological significance aside for a moment. Perhaps we *most* need sharks and sea weeds, sea stars, sea slugs, squid, salmon, swordfish, seabirds, and singing cetaceans to test our ability *to* differentiate between right and wrong. If this answer seems silly, if refusing to answer the question of the value of sea creatures from an immediately utilitarian perspective just one time rings hollow, compare it to our unquestioning acceptance of the rightness of song-birds or elephants. The difference arises not because wet animals have lesser attributes than dry ones. Rather it is because we have yet to extend our sense of community below the high tide line. Many still view the ocean as the blank space between continents.

We now need a "sea ethic."

CARL SAFINA, SONG FOR THE BLUE OCEAN: ENCOUNTERS ALONG THE WORLD'S COASTS AND BENEATH THE SEAS 439 (1998).

3. While fish conservation may not evoke the same heartfelt response as opposition to whaling does, there is no love lost between many fishers and environmental groups. As an example, consider this editorial from the trade magazine, *National Fisherman*.

There is a gap in this country, in which sustainable fishing is the law of the land, between what our industry does and how it is perceived. White-tablecloth restaurants make a living presenting seafood dishes to diners who scarcely bat an eye paying $20 or more for an entrée. Nutritionists preach the gospel of heart-healthy fish. Supermarkets are chock-a-block full of economical frozen fish packages, and some fish products are so affordable, not to mention healthful, that they are a staple of school lunch and other programs. Yet to listen to our critics, you'd think fishermen produced nuclear weapons and sold them in the Middle East.

Fishing is a tough racket. It is arduous and sometimes dangerous work, and fisherman, like farmers, often deliver products to market at prices that preclude profitability. Comparisons between fishing and agriculture need not end there. Most fishermen, like most farmers, are family-orientated small businessmen at the mercy of the weather. Beyond the horizon—be it amber waves of grain or blue waves of ocean—are forces that ensure that life becomes more complex and paperwork-strewn every day. And like the farmer, the fisherman's capital needs often seem out of proportion to the potential profit.

Yet the small, family farmer remains an icon in this country, while the independent fisherman, once portrayed as the guileless weaver of nets, is today in everybody's bull's-eye. Environmental absolutists rail about highly mecha-nized fleets and industrial fishing. In truth, there are few, if any, more primitive occupations on earth. The twenty-first century fisherman chases albacore across the Pacific with a handful of fishhooks, throws spears at bluefin tuna who move like jaguars, and sets nets for Pollock where someone else caught them last year.

Politicians may not be aiming at this industry, but they'll fire in its direction. As a result, a lawmaker from landlocked Colorado becomes sponsor of a bill to ban bottom trawling. Another opposes a tribal hunt for gray whales, a species for which sustainability is not an issue. Yet another argues for sword-fish preserves in the mid-Atlantic to placate his sport-fishing constituents.

We're Not Getting Through, 81 NATIONAL FISHERMAN 4 (Jan. 2001). Do you think the comparison to farmers is fair? If so, why have farmers been so much more successful in staving off tough environmental regulation than fishers?

4. Whether strong legal responses are needed to conserve living marine resources depends on their current state. When someone asks, "how is the marine ecosystem doing?", a thoughtful answer implicitly first considers the question, "compared to what?" In the excerpt below, Randy Olson draws attention to this implicit question, raising issues we considered at the very beginning of the book—whether a "natural" state is desirable, achievable, or even knowable in a human-dominated environment.

Among environmentalists, a baseline is an important reference point for measuring the health of ecosystems. It provides information against which to evaluate change. It's how things used to be. It is the tall grass prairies filled with buffalo, the swamps of Florida teeming with bird life and the rivers of the Northwest packed with salmon. In an ideal world, the baseline for any given habitat would be what was there before humans had much impact. If we know the baseline for a degraded ecosystem, we can work to restore it. But if the baseline shifted before we really had a chance to chart it, then we can end up accepting a degraded state as normal—or even as an improvement.

The number of salmon in the Pacific Northwest's Columbia River today is twice what it was in the 1930s. That sounds great—if the 1930s are your baseline. But salmon in the Columbia River in the 1930s were only 10% of what they were in the 1800s. The 1930s numbers reflect a baseline that had already shifted. * * *

One of scientists' biggest concerns is that the baselines have shifted for many ocean ecosystems. What this means is that people are now visiting degraded coastal environments and calling them beautiful, unaware of how they used to look.

People go diving today in California kelp beds that are devoid of the large black sea bass, broomtailed groupers and sheephead that used to fill them. And they surface with big smiles on their faces because it is still a visually stunning experience to dive in a kelp bed. But all the veterans can think is, "You should have seen it in the old days."

Without the old-timers' knowledge, it's easy for each new generation to accept baselines that have shifted and make peace with empty kelp beds and coral reefs. Which is why it's so important to document how things are—and how they used to be.

For the oceans, there is disagreement on what the future holds. Some marine biologists argue that, as the desirable species are stripped out, we will be left with the hardiest, most undesirable species—most likely jellyfish and bacteria, in effect the rats and roaches of the sea. They point to the world's most degraded coastal ecosystems—places like the Black Sea, the Caspian Sea, even parts of the Chesapeake Bay. That's about all you find: jellyfish and bacteria. We have already become comfortable with a new term, "jellyfish blooms," which is used to describe sudden upticks in the number of jellyfish in an area.

Randy Olson, *Shifting Baselines: Slow Motion Disaster in the Sea, available at* www.actionbioscience.org/environment/olson.html. The effort to determine an environmental baseline is further complicated by the wide fluctuation in natural conditions:

> Not all ecological change is anthropogenic, however. Natural conditions in the oceans fluctuate greatly and sometimes suddenly on time scales that extend for decades to millennia. Thus, the filter of individual experience has two components. Changes caused by humans are the signal and natural variability constitutes the noise that obscures the human footprint. An important example of the potential magnitude of natural change comes from annually layered sediments of the Santa Barbara Basin. Abundances of fish scales of anchovies and sardines preserved in these sediments fluctuate more than an order of magnitude and exhibit nine major collapses and subsequent recoveries over 1700 years. These data and shorter records of fish catches suggest population cycles of 50 to 70 years associated with alteration of warm and cold physical regimes. These cycles exceed the longest instrumental temperature records for the region and greatly complicate management of fisheries. How can one determine a sustainable catch against a background of such extreme natural variation?

Jeremy B.C. Jackson, *What Was Natural in the Coastal Oceans?* 98 PNAS, Vol. 98, No. 10 (May 8, 2001), *available at* www.pnas.org/cgi/doi/10.1073/pnas.091092898.

An informative website dedicated to the issue of shifting baselines has been developed at www.shiftingbaselines.org/. For their excellent narrated slide show on shifting baselines, check out www.shiftingbaselines.org/slide show/pristine_hi.html or the Casebook website.

5. Another complication for fisheries policy and management is the relative lack of information about our oceans.

> Neotropical forests are greatly threatened by human activities and may disappear entirely within this century. The facts about tropical forests are widely known and much discussed by governments, international agencies, and the general public. By comparison, neotropical coral reefs are already effectively "deforested" throughout their entire range, but this fact received almost no comparable attention until the 1990s. Moreover, human activities leading to the destruction of coral and oyster reefs, seagrass beds, or kelp forests began early in the 19th century or earlier, long before comprehensive scientific study began. In general, we are more aware of the mass extinction of large vertebrates at the end of the Pleistocene than what happened in coastal seas only a century ago!

Jeremy B.C. Jackson, *What Was Natural in the Coastal Oceans?* 98 PNAS, Vol. 98, No. 10 (May 8, 2001), *available at* www.pnas.org/cgi/doi/10.1073/pnas.091092898.

6. While not addressed in this chapter, the state of living freshwater resources raises no less cause for concern than that of the marine environment.

> Freshwater ecosystems have lost a greater proportion of their species and habitat than ecosystems on land or in the oceans, and they face increasing threats from dams, overextraction, pollution, and overfishing.... Freshwater systems occupy only 0.8 percent of Earth's surface, but they are rich in species and vital as habitat. An estimated 12 percent of all animal species live in fresh water. Many others, including humans, depend on fresh water for their surviv-

al. In Europe, for example, 25 percent of birds and 11 percent of mammals use freshwater wetlands as their main breeding and feeding areas. Due to their limited area, freshwater ecosystems only contain about 2.4 percent of all Earth's plant and animal species. On a hectare-for-hectare basis, however, they are richer in species than the more extensive terrestrial and marine ecosystems. * * *

Threats to species in freshwater ecosystems are widespread. Habitat degradation, physical alteration from dams and canals, water withdrawals, overharvesting of fish and shellfish, pollution, and the introduction of nonnative species have all increased in scale and impact in the last century. As a consequence, the capacity of freshwater ecosystems to support biodiversity—the natural variety, abundance, and distribution of species across the aquatic environment—is highly degraded at a global level.... [W]hile many factors can simultaneously contribute to extinctions, habitat alteration and the introduction of nonnative species [are] the major causes driving the extinction of fish species. Building dams and water diversions, channelizing riverbeds, and draining wetlands are typical habitat alterations. * * *

Globally, scientists estimate that more than 20 percent of the world's 10,000 recorded freshwater fish species have become extinct, threatened, or endangered in recent decades. This number, however, may well be an underestimate. According to the 1996 IUCN Red List of Threatened Animals, 734 species of fish are classified as threatened, of which 84 percent are freshwater species.... In the United States, which has comparatively detailed data on freshwater species, 37 percent of freshwater fish species, 67 percent of mussels, 51 percent of crayfish, and 40 percent of amphibians are threatened or have become extinct. Indeed, studies indicate that freshwater species are being lost at an "ever-accelerating rate." * * *

World Resources Institute, Earthtrends: The Environmental Information Portal (2000), *available at* http://earthtrends.wri.org.

B.   Drivers of Fishery Collapse

As with all natural resources, so long as the levels of extraction and use remain below natural disturbance levels and within population fluctuations, there is no need for legal restrictions. There truly is enough for everyone to share. Thus the confident prediction in the nineteenth century of famed biologist Thomas Huxley: "I believe that the cod fishery ... and probably all the great sea fisheries are inexhaustible; that is to say, nothing we can do seriously affects the numbers of fish." Robert Kunzig, *Twilight of the Cod*, Discover, April 1995, at 52. Over time, however, our treatment of fisheries has belied this vision of infinite bounty. While Garrett Hardin's famous article on the tragedy of the commons relied on the example of grazing, this economic phenomenon had first been identified over a decade earlier in the context of fisheries. H. Scott Gordon, *The Economic Theory of a Common–Property Resource: The Fishery*, 62 J. Pol. Econ. 124, 135 (1954). While it is in the common interest of all to conserve fisheries, each fishing vessel's immediate interests are best served by catching as many fish as possible. This section sets out the main drivers behind the collapse of fisheries and, therefore, the challenges that any management regime must address.

1. OVERFISHING AND OVERCAPITALIZATION

At a certain level, the problem of fishery collapse boils down to the simple equation of too many boats chasing too few fish (and often at the wrong time and place). Over the last decade, the total marine fish catch has remained roughly constant. But because fishing fleet capacity has doubled since 1970, the global catch as measured by catch per unit of effort has markedly decreased. This suggests that harvested fish have become smaller, harder to locate and catch, or both.

Overfishing is tightly linked to the problem of overcapacity. The Nova Scotia trawler industry, for example, has roughly four times more capacity than necessary to catch its yearly cod quota. In the United States, in 1990 the East Coast surf clam fishery had over 100 boats, while 13 boats would have been sufficient to harvest the quota. FAO fisheries analyst Chris Newton observes that "We could go back to the 1970 fleet size and we would be no worse off—we'd catch the same number of fish." Peter Weber, *Net Loss: Fish, Jobs and the Marine Environment,* Worldwatch Paper No. 120, 1994, at 28.

This traditional view of overcapitalization is one of too many boats in the fishery, but it masks the crucial role of technology. Overcapitalization also occurs when the same number of boats, or even fewer, switch to newer and more effective gear or instruments. Advances in technology since the 1970s have transformed fishing from a skill to a science, from a challenge to near certainty. The introduction of nylon nets, outboard motors, sophisticated sonar, tracking buoys, and satellite data now allow astonishingly effective harvesting, enabling boats to locate schools of fish hundreds of meters under water, track their movements, and catch them. Modern factory trawlers can operate year-round, far offshore even in gale force winds. Advertisements in the trade magazines are not exaggerating when they boast: *"Now, fish have nowhere to hide!"*

At the same time, the growth of factory ships with flash-freezers that preserve fresh flavors and texture has greatly increased the amount of fish a ship can store. Fish used to be a perishable commodity, preserved only as dried and salted filets or, in the twentieth century, in cans. Coupled with changes in cold storage technology, dramatic drops in air-freight shipping costs over the last three decades have changed this reality by creating new global markets. Diners in a restaurant do not even give a second thought to ordering "fresh" fish that was caught halfway around the world.

2. SUBSIDIES

Subsidies contribute to declining fisheries by driving overcapacity. Make no mistake, fishing is big business, and big politics. The FAO estimated in 2003 that government subsidies account for more than 25% of the $56 billion global fish market. These occur through a dizzying range of programs, including grants for the purchase of boats and tackle, below-market rate loans and loan guarantees for buying new vessels, price supports for fish and fishers' wages, fuel tax credits, "disaster relief" payments when stocks crash or prices decline, etc. In the United States, the Capital Construction Fund creates tax-free accounts to repair or construct fishing vessels, while the Fishing Vessel Obligation Guarantee Program ensures long-term credit for fishing boats and facilities. U.S. COMMISSION ON OCEAN POLICY, AN OCEAN BLUEPRINT FOR THE 21ST CENTURY 290 (2004).

Opponents of fisheries subsidies argue that such aid reduces fishing costs, which leads to overexploitation and places a downward pressure on the price of fish. For a period of time, the government is able to maintain the economic well-being of the fishing industry, but overfishing continues to add to the decline in fish stocks. As Chris Stone has described, "the disease feeds on itself: the more subsidies, the more capacity; the more capacity, the fewer fish per unit effort; the lower the fishers' returns, the more intense the pressure for government relief." Christopher D. Stone, *The Maladies in Global Fisheries: Are Trade Laws Part of the Treatment?*, U.S.C. Law School Working Paper Series, No. 97–12, at 35. This helps explain why, despite the broad range of fishery subsidies, the industry lost $54 billion in 1994. Indeed fleets spent approximately 56% of their revenue paying back capital investment in their subsidized boats. *See* www.plank tos.com/eco-assets.htm.

In calculating total social costs of subsidies, consider, as well, the payments that follow failed fisheries. The Marine Fish Conservation Network reported in 2000 that American taxpayers had spent more than $160 million since 1994 to "mitigate the economic and ecological impacts of fishery management failures in New England, Alaska and along the West Coast." Cat Lazaroff, *New Law Could Save Millions Spent on Facilities Mismanagement*, ENVT'L NEWS SERVICE, Mar. 10, 2000.

3. BYCATCH

Most fishing is not like hunting, where a particular individual is selected and taken. Trawl nets and baited lines are indiscriminate, catching whatever becomes ensnared in their mesh or bites on their hooks. Because some fish are of little value in the marketplace (economic discards), regulations prohibit fishermen from landing high quantities, and boats have limited holds, a surprising amount of fish catch is wasted as fishers seek to maximize the value per pound of the fish they bring back to the dock. As a result, the common practices of "bycatch" (discarding of non target species, such as dolphins in the tuna fishery) and "high-grading" (discarding of small or otherwise unfit target species) have significantly exacerbated pressures on the ocean's living marine resources. Ironically, as fishing restrictions are tightened to prevent overfishing, bycatch and high-grading often increase as the fishing boats seek to maximize the value of the limited catch they can bring to shore by using non-selective fishing gear.

> FAO estimates that for every three tons of fish landed at the dock, another ton of unwanted creatures is thrown overboard dead or dying. That works out to 27 million tons of so-called bycatch killed each year. The annual death toll includes eighty thousand albatross drowned after taking bait on floating hooks trailed on miles of line behind "longliner" fishing vessels; one hundred thousand sea turtles ensnared in shrimp trawls; hundreds of thousands of seabirds ensnared in enormous open ocean driftnets; so many thousands of dolphins and porpoises drowned in traps and gill nets as to decimate seven stocks and threaten forty-

six others; untold billions of juvenile cod, redfish, pollock, and other valuable fish; and countless sharks, squids, crab, starfish, sponges, anemones, and other creatures ... Some fisheries are more damaging than others. Because their nets must be fine enough to catch tiny prey, shrimp trawls have enormous bycatch. Eight to nine pounds of unwanted creatures die for every pound of shrimp harvested in the Gulf of Mexico [not to mention the damage to the sea floor communities as shrimp trawls drag along the bottom]

COLIN WOODARD, OCEAN'S END 43–44 (2000).

4. HABITAT LOSS AND DEGRADATION

Most commercial and game fish reproduce and spend their juvenile life in coastal marshes and estuaries. Thus coastal development and pollution can cause significant indirect impact on fish health and habitat.

Environmental degradation has a major impact on fisheries resources. Industrial and agricultural effluents and municipal sewage may pollute waters to the point where they cannot support fish populations or they may simply contaminate the fish so that these are not suitable for consumption. Major rivers, which have historically served as transportation routes and therefore the focus of human settlement and industrial development, have been especially vulnerable to this kind of damage.

Land use also has an effect on fish habitat; for example, habitat may be lost to urban development. Deforestation causes increased run-off and loss of water quality because of siltation and alteration of water temperature. Anadromous fish such as salmon are particularly sensitive to these effects since damming rivers for hydro-electric power, irrigation or flood control impedes the movement of species that return to fresh water to spawn, effectively causing a loss of habitat. Wetlands, which often provide important spawning grounds or nursery areas for juvenile fish, may be taken out of production by being drained to provide land for agricultural use or urban development.

Fishing methods too are responsible for environmental damage. Heavy trawl nets have caused significant alteration to the sea bed by leveling out the bottom, cutting off coral heads in some areas, and turning over sediments, thereby disturbing and often killing the bottom-living fauna. The vast majority of shallow continental shelves have already been scarred by fishing; in the North Sea, most of the seabed is dragged by bottom trawlers at least once each year.

The detrimental impact of other fishing methods practiced in some areas of the world is even more drastic. For example, explosives or cyanide are used to stun fish in the coral reefs of some regions. This practice, which wreaks havoc on the whole ecosystem by killing smaller fish and vertebrates, has been fueled by the demand for live fish in some oriental restaurants.

ALAN NIXON, WORLD FISHERIES: THE CURRENT CRISIS (Canadian Parliament Research Branch Pub. BP434E, 1997).

Land-based marine pollution (LBMP) is the single most important source of pollution to the marine environment, contributing over 70% of total contaminants. LBMP is, however, exceedingly difficult to regulate and at its broadest includes any substance or energy from a land-based activity that pollutes the seas. In practice, this covers most activities in modern industrialized society and encompasses a vast range of substances and sources. These include garbage and sewage from municipalities, water effluent and air emissions from factories, pulp and paper mills, refineries and chemical plants, fertilizer and pesticides from farms, hot water from power stations, stormwater run-off, soil eroded from farms and logging, and atmospheric emissions from vehicles, utilities, and incinerators. Some of these pollutants are piped directly into the sea, while others enter through run-off into rivers or are washed out of the atmosphere by rain or dry deposition.

Given current demographic trends, LBMP will likely worsen in the future. In the United States, more than 50% of the people live within 50 miles of the ocean or the Great Lakes. Don Walsh, *America's Marine Sanctuaries*, 126 U.S. NAVAL INST. PROC. 89, June 1, 2000. Even the inland population contributes significantly to LBMP through drainage systems and rivers. In fact roughly 40% of the continental U.S. drains into the Gulf of Mexico through the Mississippi River. The combined run-off of fertilizer, sewage, and other nutrients into the sea has provided ideal conditions for explosive growth of algae. As the dead algae are decomposed by bacteria, the bacteria consume so much oxygen that other sea life that cannot swim away literally suffocates. Needless to say, this dramatically reduces the biological productivity of an area. This condition, known as "hypoxia," is the reason for the seven thousand square mile "dead zone" that regularly appears in the Gulf of Mexico. This dead zone is likely the result of urban and agricultural runoff from states along the Mississippi. The amount of pollution is considerable since, for example, industrialized hog farms in Missouri produce more waste than is produced by the city of St. Louis. *Hog Waste: A Dirty Job for the EPA*, ST. LOUIS POST-DISPATCH, Oct. 17, 1997, at 6B.

QUESTIONS AND DISCUSSION

1. Given the range of threats to fisheries, it should be clear that no single legal instrument or policy will "solve" the problem of fisheries decline. Efforts to address bycatch will likely have no effect on measures addressing land-based marine pollution. Indeed they will likely concern two entirely different constituencies, frustrating possible coalition-building. Do you see why? Moreover, as we saw in the description of bycatch, some efforts may be counterproductive.

2. Increasing attention has been focused on the threats posed by invasive aquatic species. The EPA estimates that over 21 billion gallons of ballast water are discharged in U.S. waters every year. As Colin Woodard describes,

> San Francisco Bay, a busy shipping port, is home to at least 212 exotic species. The fish population is now a bizarre mix of Mississippi catfish, East Asian gobies, Japanese carp, and aquarium goldfish. The bottom is controlled by Chinese mitten crabs (which can harbor human parasites and whose burrowing causes levees to collapse) and Asian clams (which filter out virtually all plankton, starving out native fish). A new species takes hold in the Bay every twelve weeks on average. Exotic invaders tend to wreak the most havoc in ecosystems already damaged by other stresses. A North American bristle worm now dominates the bottom of Poland's highly polluted Vistula lagoon. Mnemiopsis leidyi snuffed out most other life in the Black Sea after massive algae blooms, overfishing, and pollution weakened native communities.

COLIN WOODARD, OCEAN'S END 49 (2000).

The introduction of invasive species can disrupt local marine populations through predation, increased competition for food and habitat, habitat degradation, and spread of diseases. When engineering costs are included (e.g., clogged pipes), invasive species have been estimated to cost $137 billion annually in the United States. PEW OCEANS COMMISSION, AMERICA'S LIVING OCEANS: CHARTING A COURSE FOR SEA CHANGE 67 (2003).

Ships' ballast water are the primary means of transport for marine invasive species. Required for stability of a ship, ballast water is literally transported all over the globe. A team from the Smithsonian Environmental Research Center examined 15 ships coming into the Chesapeake Bay and found that 830 million bacteria and 7,400 million viruses could be found in the average liter of ballast water tested. The tests revealed *vibrio cholerae*, a bacteria that causes cholera, in the ballast water of all 15 ships. David Derbyshire, *Ship Water Spreading Disease,* DAILY TELEGRAPH, Nov. 2. 2000. The home aquarium industry provides another significant means of transport for invasive species. Residents around Washington, D.C., for example, were fixated by the catching of a Snakehead fish in 2004 in the Potomac River. Native to China and Korea, the Snakehead (described as a fish with the head of a snake and teeth of a shark) is a voracious freshwater predator. As Mike Slattery, assistant secretary of the Maryland Department of Natural Resources, described, finding the Snakehead is "the first act of the nightmare." Snakeheads are able to live for days out of water and wriggle to other water bodies. Snakeheads are imported as an aquarium fish and likely escape into the wild when aquaria are emptied. While states such as Florida and Virginia have outlawed the possession of a Snakehead without a permit, no federal laws prohibited the importation or interstate transportation of the fish. David Fahrenthold, *Snakeheads May be Making Home in Potomac,* WASH. POST, June 30, 2004, at B1.

Indeed, despite growing recognition of the threats posed by invasive species, domestic legislation protecting against the spread of invasive species remains weak.

> There is little law focusing on other vectors of invasive species. For example, there is no uniform regime in place to track live imports either entering or traveling around the country. There is no systematic process for determining which management approach is best when a species is found, no central source of information for researching species, and no dedicated source of funding to control invasive species....
>
> Currently, agencies at different levels of government report commodities using a different nomenclature and verification system. With such inconsistency, neighboring states could simultaneously be working to promote and eradicate the same species, and one agency's food list could be another agency's most wanted list of invaders.

PEW OCEANS COMMISSION, AMERICA'S LIVING OCEANS: CHARTING A COURSE FOR SEA CHANGE 69 (2003).

3.   The impacts of climate change on fisheries are still unclear but could be significant. Increasing ocean temperature will influence the ranges of marine organisms, likely reducing the habitat for species sensitive to warm temperatures at the ocean surface layers (the area where most marine life lives). As an example of possible impacts from changes in ocean temperature, Colin Woodard describes below the effect of recent warming in the Pacific (which may or may not be due to climate change).

> In the northwestern Pacific, the enormous swath of ocean bordering California and southern Alaska, average surface temperatures jumped by two degrees F in 1977 and have remained at these levels ever since. John McGowan of the Scripps Institution of Oceanography found that over the period there has been a 70 percent decline in zooplankton, the tiny animals that, directly or indirectly, feed virtually all higher life.... A once-common seabird, the sooty shearwater, declined by 90 percent. Most fish populations have fallen by 5 percent per year since 1986, and near shore species like kelp, urchins, and abalone have collapsed while warmer water species have moved in. The short-beaked dolphin, a species that prefers warm water, has undergone a twenty-five-fold increase in the waters off California, while Alaska's cold-water fur seals and sea lions have been dwindling.

Colin Woodard, Ocean's End 51 (2000).

Moreover, coral bleaching around the globe has been linked to rising sea-surface temperatures. Sea-level rise poses a threat to coral, as well, reducing light reaching coral. It is likely that coastal erosion caused by rising sea levels will increase turbidity and sedimentation, further stressing coral reefs. While shocking, it is perhaps not surprising that peer-reviewed scientific papers are predicting global destruction of coral reef ecosystems if mean sea-surface temperatures rise just 2 degrees Fahrenheit. Pew Oceans Commission, America's Living Oceans: Charting a Course for Sea Change 83–84 (2003).

4. LBMP has become a serious enough concern that many states now issue fish advisory warnings. Consider the press release below by the Maine Department of Human Services.

> "Because of emerging information on the toxicity of mercury, we are revising our warnings on eating freshwater fish in Maine," announced Dr. Dora Anne Mills, the Director of the Bureau of Health in the Department of Human Services. "These new advisories are:

> - Pregnant and nursing women, women who may get pregnant, and children under age 8 SHOULD NOT EAT freshwater fish, EXCEPT for 1 meal per month of either brook trout or landlocked salmon.

> - All other adults and older children CAN SAFELY EAT up to 2 meals per month of freshwater fish; but up to 1 meal per week of brook trout and landlocked salmon."

> * * * For the first time, the Department of Human Services is also providing warnings on eating ocean fish such as swordfish, shark and canned tuna. In doing so, Maine becomes the sixth state to extend mercury-related warnings to include commercially sold fish—the other states are Minnesota, Michigan, New Jersey, Vermont, and Connecticut. The U.S. Food and Drug Administration (FDA) already has warnings on eating swordfish and shark.

> "We are recommending that pregnant and nursing women, women who may get pregnant, and children under age 8 should not eat swordfish and shark," added Dr. Mills. "We are also recommending that they eat no more than 1 or 2 cans per week of canned tuna." * * *

> "We estimate that only about 40% of Maine women of childbearing age who eat freshwater fish are aware of the State's warnings on eating fish due to

mercury pollution. We hope to greatly increase this awareness with a new risk communication initiative starting this fall," added Dr. Mills. "Since fish is also one of the best sources of polyunsaturated fatty acids that are needed for the developing nervous system, our goal is to provide pregnant women and families the information they need to make safe choices about which fish to include in their diet."

How effective do you think such warnings are in changing consumption patterns? Do you think a requirement to post these warnings at fish counters in supermarkets, as is done on racks of cigarettes, would be more effective? What are the downsides to such an approach?

5. A frightening consequence of LBMP that still is not well understood concerns damage to the immune system of mammals. In particular, the persistence of toxic chemicals in body tissues leads to increasingly greater concentrations in organisms as they move up the food chain, reaching their highest concentrations in top predators like seals and dolphins. In graphic demonstration of this "bio-accumulation," a number of dead whales washed ashore have been disposed of as hazardous waste because of the concentrations of contaminants in their bodies. Indeed beluga whales from the St. Lawrence River in Canada have been called the most polluted animals on earth. In one case, autopsies of beluga whales revealed high concentrations of a pesticide called Mirex. This was difficult to explain, though, because no Mirex was used in the vicinity of the whales' habitat. How did it get in their bodies? Careful research showed that Mirex had accumulated in the tissues of migrating eels from Lake Ontario, more than 600 miles away. When the whales fed on the eels, the Mirex bio-accumulated in the whale's tissue. Polly Ghazi et al., *Our Plundered Seas,* OBSERVER, Apr. 2, 1995. Such contaminants in living marine resources are all the more worrying when one realizes that humans stand atop the food chain and many indigenous communities, such as the Inuit and the inhabitants of the Faroe Islands, depend almost entirely on marine mammals as a protein and fat source.

6. Surpassing the levels of sustainable fisheries has grave potential consequences, particularly for developing countries. It is estimated that developing countries take in a fishery trade surplus of $16.8 billion a year, exceeding income from coffee, tea, and rubber. Twenty percent of the world's population obtains its protein consumption from fish. In Asia, as much as 50% of the population's primary protein source is from fish. All but four of the 30 countries most dependent on fish as a primary source of protein are developing countries. Moreover, over a hundred million of the globe's poorest people depend on fisheries for jobs. While such figures are inexact, the importance of fisheries to the economy of developing countries and to the diet and employment of its inhabitants can scarcely be overestimated. THE STATE OF WORLD FISHERIES AND AQUACULTURE 2000, *available at* http://www.fao.org/fi/default.asp; Polly Ghazi et al., *Our Plundered Seas,* THE OBSERVER, Apr. 2, 1995.

This situation has been exacerbated by a common practice of developed country fishing fleets known as "pulse fishing." As a fishery is depleted, vessels simply move on to another foreign or high seas fishery until it has been overfished, repeating the pattern again and again. Though the official

European Union position has been to decommission 40 percent of its fishing capacity, it has actively provided "exit grants" so companies could relocate their boats outside European waters. Where are these boats "relocated" to? Often to developing countries, who are increasingly selling permits to foreign vessels to fish their waters. Senegal, for example, has been paid to allow intensive fishing of its waters by EU fleets. Dick Russell, *Vacuuming the Seas: Where Countries Collide,* E MAGAZINE, July 1996, at 28.

7.   Fishery issues are increasingly arising at the World Trade Organization (WTO). Peru, Australia, Iceland, New Zealand, the Philippines, Norway, and the United States have called for a WTO agreement to reduce fishery subsidies. Ideally, this would both reduce barriers to trade and protect the environment. As described above, reducing overcapacity would arguably lead to higher seafood prices and less pressure on already stressed fisheries. In one of the rare instances of free trade arguments clearly supporting environmental protection, a Communication from the United States to the WTO Committee on Trade and Environment argued that "subsidies in fisheries tend to promote harvesting operations and capitalization by reducing fixed and variable costs and supporting prices and incomes. Only rarely do they directly promote exports. Further it seems that cost reducing subsidies far outweigh subsidies that support incomes and prices, so their aggregate trade effect is usually to suppress prices." World Trade Organization, Committee on Trade Environment, WT/CTE/W/154, July 4, 2000, at 2. Proposals to reduce (and potentially remove) subsidies have received strong support during the Doha Round of trade negotiations and, assuming agreement is ever reached over agriculture, will likely be adopted in the package of trade agreements.

C.   A PRIMER ON FISHERIES SCIENCE

Fishing alters the age, size, and size structure of fish populations. In practice, there are two kinds of overfishing. *Recruitment overfishing* describes the problem of catching fish before they can spawn enough to replenish the stock. In other words, so many reproductive age fish are caught that not enough eggs can be produced to replace them. The net result is decline in population size. *Growth overfishing* describes the problem of harvesting fish before they have grown to their adult size. As a result, there are very few fully-grown fish in the population. Hence this is not an issue of crashing stocks but of changing the size distribution within the stock. The net result is decline in population biomass. The Red Snapper case study at the end of Part I of this chapter provides a good example of this effect. As a result of growth overfishing, from the 1980s through the 1990s, the mean size of Red Snappers caught in Florida decreased by fully one-fourth, from 24 inches down to 18 inches, as few fish escaped the baited hooks to reach full adult size.

Seeking to avoid the problems of recruitment and growth overfishing, fisheries management is based on the concepts of *carrying capacity* and *surplus production*. Any particular area of habitat should, all else being constant, support a maximum population of any particular species. This makes intuitive sense, since the sea's capacity to produce fish is ultimately limited by the amount of phytoplankton it produces. Assuming this and other key environmental factors remain stable, over time some fish die and others are born, but the overall biomass level (the total mass of the species) should, in theory, remain fairly constant at the habitat's carrying capacity.

In an area that is not subject to any fishing, a particular population will have relatively more large adult fish than in a fished area. Since the habitat can only support a set amount of biomass, the presence of the larger fish will make it difficult for young fish to reach reproductive age (if only because there is greater competition for food). As a result, the unfished area can be expected to be a low productivity system with an extremely competitive environment for fish trying to reach adulthood. As fishing commences, however, the larger fish will be among the first caught. This reduces the species biomass below the carrying capacity and enhances the likelihood of survival for younger fish that grow faster. There's now less competition for food. As a result, whereas before only 1 in 10,000 fish eggs laid might have reached spawning age, now perhaps double or triple the number do. Fishing, then, can result in a more dynamic population with a higher percentage of juvenile and young adult fish than in an unfished population. In this regard, fishing boats' nets and baited lines represent just one more source of fish mortality, no different in effect than predation or disease. The key challenge for fisheries managers is to determine the level of fishing (the maximum catch) that, in combination with natural sources of mortality, results in a maximally sustainable fishery and industry.

To make this clearer, consider the graph on the next page, a standard in fisheries management texts. The Y-axis shows yield. This is the amount of fish (by weight) caught. The X-axis shows population size, where 1.0 is the carrying capacity, 0.5 is half of the carrying capacity population, etc. The goal of the fishery manager is to determine the greatest annual catch that ensures a sustainable population, i.e., so that the same level of harvest can be caught every year. The trick is to catch enough fish so that, ironically, even more young fish can reach spawning age. This level is known as the "maximum sustainable yield" (MSY). In the example below, "X" marks the level of the MSY, which would be set at 0.5—half of the maximum population size. This is the highest level of catch that can be taken while maintaining a sustainable population size. Catching more than the MSY (say, 0.75 of the carrying capacity) is overfishing—the biomass level will fall below the maximum since the population's growth and reproduction will not be able to make up for the loss. Catching less than the MSY (say, 0.25 of the carrying capacity) is inefficient—you could have caught more fish and not risked lowering the MSY since the population's growth and reproduction can easily make up the loss.

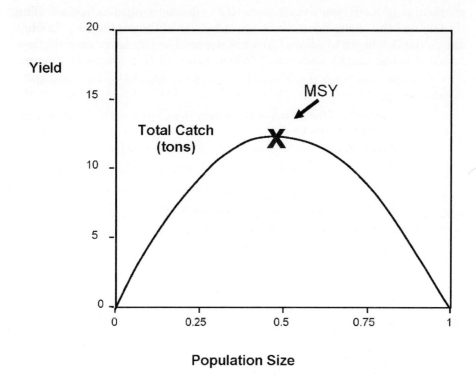

You can also think of this through the example of banking. Assume your account cannot hold more than $100. This represents the carrying capacity. Assume roughly a 6% rate of interest. The maximum continuous flow of interest will be $6 per year. This represents the MSY. Taking more than $6 per year will reduce the principal, thus reducing the annual interest you receive in the future. Taking less than $6 per year, though, doesn't help because your account cannot grow beyond $100 in principal. Taking less than $6 per year, less than the MSY, only makes sense when the principal is less than $100 and you need to grow it back up to its maximum level.

These descriptions have assumed that the habitat's carrying capacity remains constant, all else being equal. In reality, though, all else is far from equal. Environmental conditions may change from season to season, influencing salinity, water temperature, and other natural factors that can raise or lower carrying capacity as happens periodically in the Pacific Ocean with El Nino. Habitat loss and pollution, as described above, can drive down carrying capacity, as well. As a result, fish populations can fluctuate by orders of magnitude within a period of years. Thus determining the carrying capacity at any point in time is difficult, but even if this can be done, setting the appropriate catch level still remains challenging.

To see why, assume you are a marine biologist. You have been asked to set the annual quota for Red Snapper. What kind of information do you need to determine the "correct" MSY? We've already discussed the importance of knowing the carrying capacity. To guard against recruitment overfishing, though, you need a far better understanding of both the fishing activity and the stock. What is the age structure of the population? At what age do the fish begin to spawn? At what age are the fish being caught? How much is being caught each year? Which types of fish are being caught?

A full assessment would include some of the following information about the fishery.

1. The kinds of fishermen in the fishery (longliners, rod and reel, netters, recreational anglers, etc.).

2. Pounds of fish caught by each kind of fisherman over many years.

3. Fishing effort expended by each kind of fisherman over many years.

4. The age structure of the fish caught by each group of fishermen.

5. The ratio of males to females in the catch.

6. How the fish are marketed (preferred size, etc.).

7. The value of fish to the different groups of fishermen.

8. The time and geographical area of best catches.

The biological information would include:

1. The age structure of the stock.

2. The age at first spawning.

3. Fecundity (average number of eggs each age fish can produce).

4. Ratio of males to females in stock.

5. Natural mortality (the rate at which fish die of natural causes).

6. Fishing mortality (the rate at which fish die of being harvested).

7. Growth rate of the fish.

8. Spawning behavior (time and place).

9. Habitats of recently hatched fish (larvae), of juveniles and of adults.

10. Migratory habits.

11. Food habits for all ages of fish in the stock.

12. Estimate of the total number of weight of fish in the stock.

RICHARD WALLACE & KRISTEN FLETCHER, UNDERSTANDING FISHERIES MANAGEMENT 6–7 (1998).

Needless to say, full sets of the data described above have been provided for few, if any, fisheries. Much more often, fishery scientists must extrapolate from incomplete data (over two-thirds of U.S. commercial fish species remain unassessed). Assume you're a newly minted fisheries scientist, having been told by your boss that all the information listed above is relevant, and you should now find it. But where to go? The most obvious source is fishers themselves. Landings data might be useful. By visiting the docks, you can estimate the amount of fish being caught and the age and size distributions within the catch (assuming you can also account for the bycatch and high-grading that goes on before reaching port). Declining landings over time may be an obvious sign that the stock is overfished. But what if fewer boats are fishing than before? Landings data are hard to interpret without knowing how much time and effort went into catching the fish. This is reflected in the measure of "catch per unit effort" (CPUE).

This might be expressed, for example, as number of vessel days per pounds of fish. If the CPUE is declining, as boats find it harder and harder to catch the same amount of fish, the stock is likely overfished or at risk of becoming so. Even these relatively simple effort data, though, are often hard to come across. Worse still, by the time clear trends become evident, it may be too late to rebuild the stock easily. And finally, if the fishers are focused on short-term interests of keeping the fishery quotas high, they will have strong incentives to provide biased data suggesting a sustainable fishery.

Except for fish such as salmon or eels that migrate in rivers, it is not feasible to count individuals. As a result, scientists must rely on sampling methods, usually through federal and state annual trawl surveys. This is "fishery independent" data but still has inherent biases. Nets and other gear will catch certain size fish with particular behavioral characteristics (e.g., swimming in schools) more than others. One marine biologist described these kind of data (only half jokingly) as the equivalent of flying over the Serengeti at night in a helicopter, dropping a net, and using the snared zebra and wildebeest to estimate the population. In this regard, consider the observations of a National Academy of Science study of managing marine ecosystems.

> Central to the problem of uncertainty in fishery science and management is our difficulty in confronting it. Conventional fishery management relies on science, particularly our ability to determine appropriate target catches and to estimate actual fishing mortality or stock size as a basis for recommending effort or catch controls to meet these targets.... Experience and simulation analyses have shown that stock assessment methods sometimes are prone to errors exceeding 50%, even when costly monitoring programs are in place. Worse, errors tend to be correlated from year to year, compounding their effects over time. Retrospective analysis often reveal biases, with stock size initially overestimated or underestimated for several consecutive years. When scientists and managers depend on catch data from the fishery itself, levels of bycatch and discards at sea often are unknown, and these sources of fishing mortality may not be included properly in assessments. Fundamental parameters, such as the rate of natural mortality, can be specified only in a rather broad range, based on life-history correlates. Indices of abundance derived from research surveys are valuable, but they too can be imprecise or, in many fisheries, simply unavailable.

NATIONAL ACADEMY OF SCIENCES, MARINE PROTECTED AREAS: TOOLS FOR SUSTAINING OCEAN ECOSYSTEMS 40–41 (2000).

As we will discuss later in the chapter, fishery management tools are driven by data. Because uncertainties over stock size and population data structure are unavoidable, though, the process by which fisheries management decisions are made becomes critically important.

QUESTIONS AND DISCUSSION

1. While an important theoretical basis for fisheries management, the sustainable yield graph implies an unrealistic consequence. Assume, for example, an unexploited fishery is carefully studied by scientists. They determine that the current catch is below the MSY. Initially, therefore, managers may well open the fishery to unrestricted access and gear (if, indeed, it is managed at all) because the current fleet does not have sufficient capacity to harvest the MSY. Access to this bountiful resource will encourage investment and a great deal of fishing in the early years of the fishery (as the catch approaches the MSY). Once the fleet's capacity exceeds the MSY level, though, the story changes. The implication of the sustainable yield graph is that fishing quotas should be capped at the MSY for the foreseeable future. This is the most "interest" the fishery can yield. The fishery industry, though, is now overcapitalized. Loans need to be paid off, and fishers don't want to lose their jobs. As a result, there will be strong economic pressures to establish higher catch levels, even if this reduces the level of the MSY.

Standing up to such demands from fishing interests and their political supporters is difficult for fisheries managers and scientists, particularly when they have to acknowledge the high levels of uncertainty in their data and models. In such a context, it is easy to see why those in a fishery might hope for the best and systematically select the top range of uncertainty assessments in deciding management strategies. As the National Academy of Science study concluded, "Many scientists believe that a primary cause of fishery management failures is the inherent uncertainty in stock assessments. This uncertainty contributes to ineffective or untimely management actions and the reluctance of fishers to accept the economic costs of reducing effort even when stocks are in decline or their status is uncertain." *Id.* at 40. *See also*, Josh Eagle & Barton H. Thompson Jr., Answering Lord Perry's Question: Dissecting Regulatory Overfishing, OCEAN & COASTAL MANAGEMENT 649, 651–653 (2003).

2. One of the difficulties in setting the MSY is the time lag between fishery decline and when a decline in fish stocks shows up in the catch. Recall from the preceding note that a new fishery generally witnesses a rapid increase in capitalization. Boats quickly become better at catching the target fish. Because of this, as the graphs below demonstrate, while the fish stock is declining the catch can actually *increase*. Do you see why?

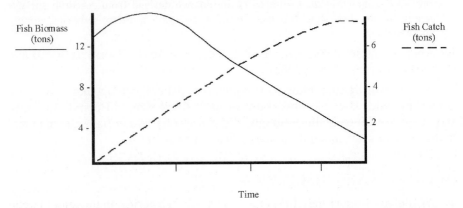

3. Read over the list above (on page 460) of the twelve types of data needed for a full stock assessment. How would the various categories of information provide useful insights into how to manage the fishery?

4. As Josh Eagle and Buzz Thompson have observed, the causes of overfishing are far more complex than simply too many boats catching too few fish.

> *Scientific error* occurs when scientists erroneously overestimate or underestimate the optimum annual level of fishing. A wide variety of factors, including poor data or inadequate population models, potentially can lead to scientific error.... *Decision overfishing* occurs ... when managers deliberately choose to disregard scientific advice and set a quota that allows more ... fishing to occur in a given year.

> *Implementation overfishing* ... is the result of managers failing to ensure that the quotas are enforced even though the fishing industry is accurately reporting its catch. There are three main sources of implementation overfishing in fisheries managed through numerical quotas. First, many quota management systems do not account for bycatch (regulatory or economic discards) of the target species. Most systems only require that fish actually landed at a port be counted toward the annual quota. Second, reporting systems for landed fish may have flaws that result in delayed reporting or inaccurate estimates of total landings. Delayed reporting or inaccurate estimates may result in managers' failure to close a fishery once a quota has been reached. Finally, managers may decline to close a fishery even when they know that the quota has actually been caught. * * *

> Finally, *illegal overfishing* occurs where fishers make illegal or unreported catches that result in fishing over the quota established by the fishery managers.... Although some amount of illegal overfishing is probably inevitable, managers have significant control over the total amount of illegal overfishing through the design and funding of enforcement. Because managers can control enforcement, illegal overfishing is another type of regulatory overfishing. While the other forms of regulatory overfishing are entirely within the control of the regulatory apparatus, however, illegal overfishing is determined by the joint interaction of the managers' efforts at enforcement and the fishers' efforts at evasion.

> In practice, regulatory overfishing may result from multiple sources simultaneously. Indeed, as discussed below, policymakers interested in eliminating overfishing must recognize the cumulative effects from and interactions among the various sources of regulatory overfishing. To the degree that one form of regulatory overfishing such as illegal overfishing is difficult or expensive to eliminate, for example, managers may need to compensate by setting lower quotas.

Josh Eagle & Barton H. Thompson Jr., *Answering Lord Perry's Question: Dissecting Regulatory Overfishing*, OCEAN & COASTAL MANAGEMENT 649, 651–653 (2003).

Which specific policy instruments are best suited to scientific overfishing, decision overfishing, implementation overfishing, and illegal overfishing?

5. Focusing solely on the decline of a fish stock may miss broader ecological effects, for selectively removing part of a marine food web can have important consequences for predator/prey relations and other feeding interactions. As more valuable fish stocks are depleted, for example, many fleets switch their efforts to less valuable species which are often lower down the food chain. Ironically, in many cases this slows the recovery of the more valuable species by reducing its food supply. This practice has now reached its logical conclusion with the advent of "biomass fishing," where "huge trawls with extremely fine mesh gather anything larger than an American quarter. Most of the net's contents are ground into meal and fed to farmed shrimp, fish, and poultry or simply spread on fields. The ecological effects can only be guessed at." COLIN WOODARD, OCEAN'S END 43–44 (2000).

A classic example of food web interdependencies was demonstrated in an experiment by marine ecologist John Paine. In 1960, Paine removed all the individuals of the sea star *Pisaster* from tide pools off the Washington coast in order to determine the effect of that removal on the surrounding ecosystem. He was astounded by the results. The tide pools are characterized by densely packed beds of mussels, barnacles, and seaweed, all attached to the rocky ocean floor, or to each other. *Pisaster* was the most important predator of one species of mussel, *Mytilus*. Once this predator was removed, the *Mytilus* population expanded unchecked, crowding out many other species. As a result, the entire nature of the ecosystem changed and seven of fifteen species disappeared. The system lost nearly half of its biodiversity because of the removal of a single species.

This same experiment has been repeated time and again, unintentionally, by non-scientists. During the nineteenth and early twentieth centuries, sea otters were heavily exploited all along the Pacific Coast of North America, both by indigenous hunters and by commercial operators. As a result of over hunting, sea otter populations eventually collapsed, with an unexpected result. Before the otters were over-hunted, the waters off the Pacific coast had been filled with thick forests of kelp, a type of blue-green algae that can grow as much as a hundred feet high. The kelp provided food and habitat for a rich variety of fish and invertebrate species. One of these species, the herbivorous sea urchin, feeds on kelp. Otters, in turn, feed on sea urchins. When the otters were removed from coastal ecosystems, the number of sea urchins increased dramatically. Uncontrolled, the sea urchins overgrazed the kelp, destroying the habitat it had provided for other species. As a result, once rich kelp beds were turned into vast "urchin barrens," inhospitable to most species. Fortunately, hunting of the sea otters ceased before the species was extinct. As sea otter populations have recovered, the kelp beds—and the ecosystems they support—have begun to return.

Focusing on multiple species (even at the same level of the food chain), however, is no easy task. Because most fishing gear is relatively indiscriminate, managing solely for one species often has harmful consequences. This becomes particularly problematic when, for example, different types of bottom-dwelling fish species are commercially caught. As a National Academy of Sciences report concluded:

> The problem of mixed-stock or mixed-species fisheries is that some species and stocks (populations) are more productive or less susceptible to fishing (catchable) than others, so if fishing pressure is low enough to protect the least productive or most catchable population, others are "underharvested" and there is great pressure to allow an increase in catch rate. When the catch rate increases, the less-productive populations ... or more catchable populations ... are depleted. This problem can be quite serious; it appears to have contributed or led to the loss of species from some environments and might even cause the

local extinction of a species.... But the precise nature and timing of the interactions related to multispecies fisheries are very hard to predict.

NATIONAL ACADEMY OF SCIENCES, SUSTAINING MARINE FISHERIES 69–70 (1998).

6.   How can the data underlying fisheries management be improved? The National Fisheries Institute (NFI), a trade association, has suggested that the fisheries agencies use independent peer reviews to assess data, reduce conflicts of interest, and improve confidence in the system. Cooperative research programs could also help increase the quantity and quality of research, while minimizing the financial burdens on the federal government. The NFI further supports the use of anecdotal information as an added source of data.

> The FCMA [Fisheries Conservation and Management Act] requires FMPs [fisheries management plans] ... to be based on the "best scientific information available." This requirement has resulted in the implementation of FMPs based on weak, poor, insufficient, and non-peer reviewed scientific information because it is the only information "available," even when such information is contradictory to the experiences and information from commercial fishermen and processors. Our proposal would add a more stringent definition of "best scientific information available" that would require such information to be peer-reviewed and to allow the consideration of anecdotal information gathered from the harvesting and processing of fish.

http://www.nfi.org/issues/management4.php

It stands to reason that fishers have the most direct knowledge about the state of fish stocks, but there are obvious disincentives to accurate reporting. The first is that reports of stock decline may lead to imposition of fishing restrictions. The second is that the agency may rely on reported data to prosecute overfishing violations. In pollution control law, limited immunity is sometimes granted to companies that uncover violations, report them immediately to the authorities, and take steps to correct them. Should there be the equivalent of self-audit immunity in fisheries, i.e., protection from prosecution for immediate reporting of discovered violations?

7.   Fisheries management has been advocated as an area for application of the precautionary principle. But how should it be applied? Does it provide useful guidance in determining *how much* we should lower catch rates or set aside marine reserves? Does it mean we should reduce the MSY by a factor of two to take into account uncertainties? By a factor of four? How would you respond to the argument excerpted below?

> Fisheries assessment is an inexact science, in which uncertainty is pervasive. At a certain level [there is] uncertainty, or, lack of predictability, and fisheries management has to learn to live with that.... [T]he existing statement of the Precautionary Principle (where there are threats of serious or irreversible damage, lack of full scientific information shall not be used as a reason for postponing cost-effective measures to prevent environmental degradation) is fine, albeit lacking in specifics ... But the Principle as stated offers no operational definition and the choice of language is poor. In science we can only disprove, not prove, so that there is never "full scientific certainty." These deficiencies have allowed free reign in interpreting the Principle. My chief argument is with those who cite the Precautionary Principle as the justification

to defend a "worst-case scenario" based management approach. But if we are honest with ourselves, that is simply not a practical approach to life.

Dr. Doug Butterworth of the University of Cape Town, South Africa, *as quoted* in the Congressional Testimony of Justin LeBlanc, National Fisheries Institute, House Committee on Resources, Subcommittee on Oceans, Fisheries, and Wildlife Conservation (Apr. 4, 2001).

———

D.   FISHERY MANAGEMENT TOOLS

The traditional approach to overfishing has been to restrict the activities of fishers, whether through the size of catch, length of season, areas that may be fished, or gear used. Eager to catch as many fish as possible, however, fishers' responses to these restrictions often create serious problems of their own. More recent management approaches have relied on targeted subsidies and trading programs known as individual transferable quotas (ITQs). All of these approaches have drawbacks and can prove painful to fishers and their communities. But as Frank Mirarchi, a fisherman from Massachusetts with over 35 years experience sadly observes, declining fisheries make all choices hard ones. Gone are the days where a day at sea brought 3,000–4,000 pounds of flounder to the dock. Today he's lucky to catch 500 pounds, barely enough to pay overhead. "I don't want to spend the rest of my life turning over costs, which is what I've been doing since about 1990. I hate to see people going out of business, but there aren't enough fish to support all the fishermen." Clarke Canfield, *New England's Groundfish Stocks Aren't Recovering Fast Enough. Neither Are Its Fisherman,* NATIONAL FISHERMAN, Mar. 1997, at 32.

1.   RESTRICTIONS

Often the first action of fishery managers to address overfishing is the imposition of *catch restrictions*. In principle, limiting the total allowable catch (known as the TAC) will allow the fish population to rise to levels that can produce the MSY. Setting the TAC at the correct level, of course, assumes accurate information on population size and structure and the current catch dynamics. For catch restrictions to work, the TAC must either be broken down into quotas for each fishing vessel that is allowed into the area or there must be adequate monitoring to determine when the fleet has reached the TAC so the fishery can be shut down. Fishery managers can avoid some of these monitoring difficulties by creating *seasonal restrictions*. These limit the times that fishers may harvest certain species. *Entry restrictions* limit the number of vessels that can fish in an area, but if the current fleet is already overcapitalized this only keeps the problem from getting worse.

While appealing at a first glance, these restrictions have serious shortcomings. If the TAC applies to the fleet rather than individual boats, or if the season is relatively short, fishers engage in what is known as *derby fishing*, where boats race to the grounds and catch as much as possible before the quota is exceeded or the season closes. This derby mentality encourages unsafe practices with serious loss of vessels and life. In less dire circumstances, the results would be laughable. Trawlers in British Columbia, for example, fished their annual quota of 847 tons of roe herring *after eight minutes*. Polly Ghazi et al., *Our Plundered Seas*, THE OBSERVER, April 2, 1995. Once the season starts, boats need to be out on the grounds, bad weather or not. Two days after the North Pacific halibut fishery commenced in 1994, the Coast Guard reported the death of one fisher and the rescue of fifteen others after their vessels sank or foundered. Moreover, such concentrated fishing effort lowers the profitability of fishing because the glut of fish on the market lowers their price. Catch restrictions also encourage investment and overcapitalization as boats race to become more efficient in order to catch the most fish before the quota ends. A seasonal restriction approach encourages bycatch, since a fish caught out of season must be thrown back and will likely die.

Another common management approach relies on *area restrictions*. The idea here is to allow fish populations in certain grounds to recover while other areas are fished. For obvious reasons, area restrictions often operate in combination with other catch or seasonal restrictions. Recent research on a type of area restriction known as marine protected areas (MPAs) has demonstrated a range of benefits. As a study by the National Research Council described,

> A primary purpose of such "no take" zones has been to protect target species from exploitation and to allow their populations to recover. Such protection has been shown to result quickly in increases in the number or size of individuals and many target species. MPAs can also protect critical habitats (like spawning grounds or nursery beds), provide some protection from pollution, protect the marine landscape from degradation caused by destructive fishing practices, provide an important opportunity to learn about marine ecosystems and species dynamics, and protect all components of a marine community. Protection against management uncertainty is another critical function of MPAs; the populations inside such areas can serve as a "bank" against fluctuations in outside populations caused by fishery management difficulties or miscalculations. Finally, and perhaps most important, MPAs represent an opportunity to protect ecosystems.

> Even small MPAs can result in rapid changes in local populations of fished species. Density and average size of populations often increase after protection. Even unexploited species can increase because of habitat protection. Larger individuals tend to have much increased reproductive output, suggesting that overall reproduction of a particular species may increase significantly after establishment of protected areas.

> Despite the overall success of MPAs that have been established and studied to date, there are important limitations to their effectiveness and huge gaps in our knowledge about how they function within broader marine ecosystems. Protected areas do not always result in higher density of target species or in higher biodiversity.... In many cases it is difficult to demonstrate the effectiveness of protected areas because of a lack of baseline data ... A critical area of ignorance is how a protected area functions within the broader marine ecosystem of which it is a part and if protected areas export biomass or eggs and larvae in the surrounding communities. The export problem is acute because the value of marine reserves as spawning banks depends on the movement of eggs, larvae or juveniles out of the protected area.

NATIONAL RESEARCH COUNCIL, SUSTAINING MARINE FISHERIES 84–86 (1999)

Equipment restrictions rely on the principles that if managers can restrict the efficiency of gear sufficiently, fewer fish will be caught and stocks should be able to recover. One might therefore limit the size of nets, increase the net's mesh size (thus allowing smaller fish to escape), cap the number of hooks per boat, etc. The problem here is that the contest between fishers and fisheries managers now resembles a Red Queen race, where each runs as fast as possible just to keep up. Recall that the derby fishing dynamic encourages fishers to invest in new and more effective fishing technology to be the first to the fishing ground, the most efficient boat hauling in the best catch ahead of the others. As other fishers improve their vessels and gear, a new investment cycle is launched for even faster and more efficient vessels and gear. With gear restrictions, fishery managers step into this arms race and force the fishers to be less efficient. There are now completely opposite races—fishers competing to increase efficiency and managers imposing restrictions to make fishing inefficient. Not surprisingly, fishers have been very adept at finding ways around gear restrictions. In Bristol Bay, Alaska, for example, salmon boats were restricted to 32 feet in length. With no restrictions on their beam, fishers built much wider boats so the cargo space would not diminish. In other cases fishers will simply increase their use of gear that has not yet been regulated.

2. CAPACITY REDUCTION

Acknowledging that fishing restrictions alone cannot fully address the problem of overfishing, state and federal governments have stepped in with a range of financial schemes to take vessels and gear out of the fishery. In some cases, capacity reduction is deemed necessary to prevent the collapse of a fishery; in others, the goal is to ensure greater profits for vessels that stay in the fishery. In *vessel buyback schemes,* fishers provide bids to the government for how much they are willing to sell their boats. The government then selects among these offers based on lowest price, length, tonnage, engine size, or a variety of other factors. The purchased vessels are then either destroyed, sold for non-commercial fishing purposes, or sold to another fishery (though this may simply exacerbate the problem of overcapacity somewhere else). Similarly, the government may pay for *fishing license retirement* in either a reverse auction or fixed payments. Finally, fleet overcapacity can be reduced by the government paying for *gear retirement.* Thus gear with a particularly high bycatch rate, for example, can be the target of government cash offers.

While such economic aid instruments soften the blow to fishers, they are an expensive approach to fishery management and, perhaps more important, have had limited effect on reducing capacity because the first fishers to accept buyback offers for vessels, licenses or gear are generally the least efficient and most out of date in the fleet. *See generally* Andrew Read and Eugene Buck, *Commercial Fishing: Economic Aid and Capacity Reduction,* CRS REPORT FOR CONGRESS 97–441 (April 14, 1997). In the late 1990s, NMFS sponsored a pilot program to buy back and destroy eleven New England fishing boats. In the tender process, 164 boat owners submitted bids totaling $58.2 million to remove their boats from the fishery. Some have criticized the project as a waste of taxpayer dollars, since a number of owners simply bought boats from other fishers and continued fishing; others have denounced it as too narrow, since no money goes to the crew members and deckhands who depended on the boat for their livelihoods.

3. LIMITED ACCESS PRIVILEGE PROGRAMS

Recall the classic approaches to resolving the tragedy of the commons—prescriptive regulation, penalties, payments, or property rights. Relying on a property rights approach, fisheries managers have recently made increasing use of a range of policies that grant the privilege to catch a fixed portion of the total catch to specific parties. This approach takes its simplest form in individual fishing quotas (IFQs). Fishers holding an IFQ have the right to catch a specific percentage of the total allowable catch over the fishing season. When these quotas are alienable, they are called Individual Transferable Quotas (ITQs). In principle, the ability to sell ITQs means that those fishers that finally end up holding fishing rights value them the most and are likely the most efficient operators.

In theory, limited access privileges offer significant advantages over current approaches. It eliminates the fishing derby problem because there is no race to catch fish before the TAC is reached or the season ends. All rights holders are assured that "their" fish will be available for them throughout the season, which can now extend over a much longer period. There should also less pressure on bycatch because fishers are not under pressure to meet their quota as quickly as possible. In turn, profits should be increased because there will no longer be a glut of fish on the market caused by derby fishing. Consumers are more likely to have fresh fish available throughout the year. Moreover, because the access privileges are explicitly not property rights, taking claims are precluded if the access privileges are later reduced or eliminated.

ITQs form a major part of fishery management in New Zealand and Iceland, and their experiences are encouraging. Starting with 29 commercial fisheries in 1986, New Zealand now relies on ITQs for fisheries worth nearly $1.4 billion. Not only has derby fishing stopped but quota holders are also cooperating to invest in research and enhancing fish stocks. In Iceland, the fishery productivity has increased, as well, with herring catch double the amount in 1980 and productivity five times greater. In Canada, the introduction of ITQs extended the season for halibut from six days to nine months. ITQs are also employed in specific fisheries in Australia, Italy, the Netherlands, and South Africa.

The United States has ITQs for the surf clam, ocean quahog, Alaskan halibut, and wreckfish fisheries and has had similar positive experiences. The Alaskan halibut season went from 3 days to 245 days once ITQs were introduced. The lack of a fishing derby glut on the market raised surf clam prices from an average of $8 per bushel to $12–$14. The fishery became safer as the Coast Guard reported a significant decrease in search and rescue missions. And fish losses through abandoned gear went down almost four-fold following introduction of the ITQ. *See* TERRY ANDERSON AND DONALD LEAL, FREE MARKET ENVIRONMENTALISM 113–114 (2001).

Given these results and seemingly clear benefits when compared to alternative management strategies, one might ask why ITQs haven't been adopted in more fisheries. A major concern has been the effect of ITQs on local communities. In virtually every fishery that has adopted an ITQ approach, the number of vessels has dropped dramatically. In the surf clam fishery, for example, the fleet dropped in three years from 128 to 59 vessels. In Iceland's fisheries, introduction of ITQs dropped fleet numbers in fifteen years from over 200 vessels to under 30. Economists might argue that this rationalization of the fishery is a good thing, clearly reducing overcapitalization and ensuring that only the most efficient operators remain in the fishery. For those holders of ITQs that can make more money through another activity, let them sell their quotas and everyone is better off from the exchange. To the fishing communities, though, fewer fishing jobs makes a difference that reverberates throughout the local economy. Moreover, there is a concern that in practice ITQs will end up being held by corporate interests as individual fishers are priced out of the market. Indeed, in the surf clam and ocean quahog ITQ program, the food company, Borden, held 40% of the quahog shares and 25–30% of the surf clam shares in 1990. The dominant holders later became National Westminster Bank and the accounting firm, KPMG. It should be noted, however, that overcapacity will eventually lead to a reduction in vessels anyhow, and at least an ITQ program ensures that some of the fishers are paid as they exit. *See generally* Eugene Buck, *Individual Transferable Quotas in Fishery Management,* CRS REPORT FOR CONGRESS 95–849 ENR (September 25, 1995); *Alliance Against IFQs v. Brown*, 84 F.3d 343 (9th Cir. 1996) *cert. denied*, 520 U.S. 1185 (1997). Finally, regardless of how well the ITQ program operates, unless the total allowable catch is set properly (i.e., at or below the MSY) the program will simply provide a more efficient means to overfish.

Just who is paid depends on how the ITQs are initially allocated. Allowing an open auction might make sense since, after all, these are public resources. But that will favor outside corporate interests over traditional fishers. One might allocate shares based on catches over the last year or two, but that awards the derby winners who overcapitalized or who over-reported their catches with future ITQ allocation in mind. One might allocate ITQs based on years in the fishery, though this works against outsiders and locals who recently entered. Should the ITQs be allocated only to the owners of fishing vessels or to the captains and crew of such vessels, as well? A number of programs have imposed restrictions on how quotas may be transferred. Some have placed limits on the total percentage of shares that any entity can own. Others have placed limits on foreign ownership or on ownership by non-resident owners. Do you see whose interests each of these restrictions would benefit?

Out of concerns such as those expressed above, dedicated access privileges have also been developed for larger interests. Cooperatives, for example, allocate all or part of the quota amongst fishing and processing parties through contractual agreement. The Pacific whiting, Bering Sea Pollock, and Chignik salmon fisheries in the U.S. all operate as cooperatives.

Community development quotas (CDQs) reserve a portion of the total allowable catch (TAC) for the purpose of stimulating economic growth in coastal fishing communities while also eliminating overfishing. CDQs come into play after the TAC is set by regional management councils. Communities come together and form non-profit CDQ groups to apply for a share of the TAC. The North Pacific Fishery Management Council has implemented a CDQ program as an amendment to its fishery management plan. According to its implementing regulations, the CDQ program allocates quotas "to eligible Western Alaska communities to provide the means for starting or supporting commercial fisheries business activities that will result in an ongoing, regionally based, fisheries-related economy." 50 C.F.R. 679.1.

At the time of the program's implementation in 1992, unemployment in Alaskan fishing communities was as high as 31%, the largest local employer was the government, and almost none of the fishery's value was captured by Native Alaskans. Kacy A. Collons, *ITQs as Collateral Rightly Understood: Preserving Commerce and Conserving Fisheries*, 14 UCLA J. ENVTL. L. & POL'Y 285, 308 (1995–1996). More recently, six CDQ groups representing 55 communities held a combined quota of 7.5% of the total Pollock catch. These Native coastal communities now had access to parts of the fishing industry that they previously lacked the resources to break into.

In many respects, the program has been a success. The *Alaska Journal* reported that the CDQ groups raised $128.8 million dollars between 1999–2000. Some of these proceeds were then used to invest in the fishing industry. One CDQ—the Norton Sound Economic Development Corporation—now "owns 50 percent of Seattle-based Glacier Fish Co., and ... 20 percent of American Seafoods, a major offshore vessel operator." *CDQ Groups Grow into Economic Force Worth $150 Million*, ALASKA JOURNAL, Dec. 24, 2001. Besides investing in fishing interests, the CDQ groups also invest in regional development projects. The Norton Sound CDQ, for example, donated $500,000 to improve the small boat harbor. In Savoonga, Alaska, the local CDQ group helped develop a Halibut fishery that employs 50 fishermen. This Halibut fishing quota alone yielded $150,000 in added income to the previously welfare-dependent community. *Id.* The groups have also used proceeds to upgrade boats, improve gear, and buy salmon at the highest price from local fishermen. One supporter has described the result as the "alaskanization of the offshore fishing industry" resulting in the construction of "docks, ports, seafood plants and other infrastructure." *Id.*

Despite these results, CDQs have faced challenges, as well. A 1999 review by the National Research Council concluded that:

> Perhaps the greatest weakness of the CDQ program as implemented is lack of open, consistent, communication between the CDQ groups and the communities they represent, particularly a lack of mechanisms for substantial input from the communities into the government structure.... Some controversy has surrounded the uncertainty about the intended beneficiaries of the program—essentially, whether the program is intended primarily for the Native Alaskan residents of the participating communities, and, if not, how to ensure that non-native participation is possible. Similarly, there has been dissatisfaction among segments of the fishing industry that are not involved either directly or as partners of CDQ groups, that the program unfairly targets a particular popula-

tion for benefits; this conflict is inevitable, given that the CDQ program is designed to provide opportunities for economic and social growth specifically to rural western Alaska. This policy choice specifically defines those to be included and cannot help but exclude others.

NATIONAL RESEARCH COUNCIL, THE COMMUNITY DEVELOPMENT QUOTA PROGRAM IN ALASKA 137 (1999).

Some fishing interests not included in the program have denounced it "as an unfair allocation of fish to a particular restricted group with no historic participation in the large scale fisheries." David Fluharty, *Magnuson Fishery Management and Conservation Act Reauthorization and Fishery Management Needs in the North Pacific Region*, 9 TULANE ENVT'L L. J. 301 (Summer 1996).

QUESTIONS AND DISCUSSION

1. If reports are to be believed, CDQs have created important social benefits and would seem clearly preferable to welfare payments and the related dependency and self-esteem problems they can generate. Are CDQs simply a better, more effective form of welfare? In some respects, perhaps yes, but there is an important difference to keep in mind. The costs of welfare payments are evenly distributed—they are borne by taxpayers across the state and country. In the case of CDQs, however, the losers are a discrete and easily identifiable group—those fishers who have smaller quotas than they otherwise would because of the CDQ allocation. Should the current fishers who are not eligible for CDQ quotas be paid, as well, to compensate them for their losses?

2. As a result of concerns over ITQs, Congress imposed a moratorium on ITQ programs in 1996, requesting a study from the National Research Council (the research arm of the National Academy of Sciences). In 1998, the NRC report concluded that ITQ programs were a valuable tool for fishery management and recommended lifting the moratorium. NATIONAL RESEARCH COUNCIL, SHARING THE FISH: TOWARD A NATIONAL POLICY ON INDIVIDUAL FISHING QUOTAS (1998). Congress did not act, although the moratorium expired on its own in October, 2002.

> Now that the moratorium is no longer in place, ITQs are under serious consideration in many fisheries and have been adopted in Alaska for halibut and king crab. Prior to adoption of the ITQ, these were classic derby fisheries. Indeed, the king crab fishery was so dangerous it had its own tv show, *The Deadliest Catch*. Following the adoption of ITQs, however, the fishing season for halibut extends over eight months, search-and-rescue missions have declined by over 70%, and deaths are down by 15%. *A Rising Tide*, THE ECONOMIST (Sept. 18, 2008).

Creation of ITQs, however, remains intensely political. For an excellent site showing the state of debate and development of a specific ITQs under consideration by the Pacific Fishery Management Council, visit http://www.pcouncil.org/groundfish/gfifq.html.

3. Who should be the beneficiaries of CDQs? According to the regulations, eligible communities must be (1) located within the proper geographic boundaries, (2) "[c]ertified by the Secretary of the Interior pursuant to the

Alaska Native Claims Settlement Act to be Native villages," (3) "consist of residents who conduct more than one-half of their current commercial or subsistence fishing effort in the waters of the Bering Sea or waters surrounding the Aleutian Islands," and (4) "[n]ot have previously developed harvesting or processing capability sufficient to support substantial participation in the groundfish fisheries in the Bering Sea. . . ." *See* http:// www.cdqdb.org/program/structure/eligibility.htm. But if poverty and lack of capital to invest in the fishery are endemic in coastal fishing communities, affecting both Native Americans and other ethnic groups, why should only Native villages be eligible?

4. In the excerpt below, Professor Alison Rieser points out the threats in private ownership of ITQs.

> Catching a species of fish for sale realizes one value of a rich and diverse marine ecosystem. If the right to engage in this activity is held exclusively by a group of individuals in the form of an ITQ, and these are traded actively in a market, there is a serious risk that all other valuable components of the ecosystem, which have no direct market value and whose contribution to the ecosystem's productivity is not understood, will be ignored. The value of the ecosystem itself is likely to be discounted by managers when setting regulations such as the total catch limit from which the annual, individual harvesting rights will be calculated. * * *

> Carol M. Rose has observed that environmentalists use the image of a particular resource as part of a larger ecosystem to argue against rights-based regulatory tools like ITQs. The effect of such measures, environmentalists fear, will be to elevate the significance of the propertized component and, in effect, over-value them. This overvaluation may lead people to ignore that their entitlements overlap the entitlements of others interested in the same resource or ecosystem. It may even cause the disintegration of the "larger and intricately interrelated ecosystem," as holders of one entitlement overstate what they "own" and block other management actions aimed at protecting other components of the same ecosystem.

> However, the need for management sensitive to the broader ecosystem may suggest, that, if property rights approaches are to be used to prevent resource depletion and spillover effects, these rights should take a particular form. These approaches should emphasize less the individual nature of the property right and more the community nature of the right. In fisheries management, for example, property rights could be allocated to a community, rather than an individual. Communities are more likely to embody a broader range of values and will therefore balance harvesting decisions against broader spatial and temporal views of the ecosystem. Communities can also enforce limits on individual appropriators through informal norms and sanctions.

Alison Rieser, *Prescriptions for the Commons: Environmental Scholarship and the Fishing Quotas Debate*, 23 HARV. ENVTL. L. REV. 393, 404–406 (1999).

Do you agree that community ownership offers significant benefits over an ITQ system? Given the terrible history of fishery management in the United States, is there any reason to think that "propertizing" fish would make things worse instead of provide for potential improvement?

5. Free market environmentalists hold out fisheries as a prime candidate for stronger property rights management strategies. Oyster beds, for example, have long been available for private management. A study comparing oyster fisheries in the southern United States from 1945–1970 found that privately leased beds in Louisiana were almost four times more profitable than open-access beds in Mississippi. In the first half of the Twentieth century, shrimp fishers along the Gulf Coast relied on informal arrangements and sanctions among unions and trade associations to limit access and conserve the fishery. These arrangements, however, ran afoul of antitrust laws. *See Marincovich v. Tarabochia*, 787 P.2d 562 (Wash. 1990).

Terry Anderson and Donald Leal have argued that, in a twist on marine protected areas, the government should establish "private fishery areas." A company called Ocean Farming, for example, fertilizes the ocean to increase phytoplankton growth and, in turn, fish biomass. They have signed a contract with the Marshall Islands for exclusive fishing rights in up to 800,000 square miles of ocean. Ocean Farming agrees to pay the government either $3.75 for each square mile of ocean they option or seven percent of the catch's value, whichever is greater. Ocean Farming also has the right to charge other fishers to use the optioned waters. TERRY ANDERSON & DONALD LEAL, FREE MARKET ENVIRONMENTALISM 119 (2001). Arguing to extend this practice, Anderson and Leal contend,

> Suppose the National Marine Fisheries Service allowed people to "homestead" sections of the ocean within the 200–mile limit and harvest bottom fish from their homestead. One company, Artificial Reefs, Inc., recently completed a multifaceted artificial reef structure off the waters of northwestern Florida to enhance recreational fishing and provide an area for skin diving ... Experiments with sinking oil drilling platforms have demonstrated the success of this approach in improving fish stocks, so it is but a small step to encourage such investment through property rights.... There is sufficient evidence that the costs in defining and enforcing property rights for non-migratory fish are low enough that we should lower the institutional barriers to such homesteading. In the Gulf waters off Alabama and Florida.... these two states allow private entities to create reefs out of certain permanent structures in parts of their territorial waters. The reefs are considered public property as soon as they hit the water, but the sense of ownership that comes from knowing the exact location of a reef has been enough to encourage private initiative. Unfortunately, the tenuous nature of reef ownership limits the potential for more privately created reefs.

Id. at 119–20.

Do you think there are strong parallels between "homesteading the oceans" and homesteading the West? What are the primary legal, technological, and social barriers to granting limited private property rights to sections of the ocean? Which do you think would be the most difficult to overcome?

Perhaps surprisingly, despite the potential benefits from establishing MPAs, "less than one-quarter of a percent of the sea is in areas termed marine parks, marine preserves, or no-fishing zones." *Id.* at 87. Why do you think a much higher percentage of land has been set aside for parks and private conservation than for ocean parks and conservation?

6. An indirect management strategy that has gained strength over the past decade is the use of consumer information to influence market choices. As described in the section on marine mammals and fish conflicts (page

565), the high mortality of dolphin bycatch in the tuna fishery was largely stopped by the decision of major canners to label their tuna cans with "dolphin friendly" logos. Consumer purchasing preferences eventually drove "unfriendly" tuna off the shelf.

The environmental group, SeaWeb, has taken a different approach in seeking to influence the food choices of chefs. Based on the idea that chefs are opinion leaders, SeaWeb has joined up with over 17 organizations (ranging from Greenpeace and the Monterey Bay Aquarium to the Chefs Collaborative and The Aquaculture Clearinghouse) to form the Seafood Choices Alliance. As its website describes:

> The Seafood Choices Alliance seeks to bring ocean conservation to the table by providing the seafood sector—fishermen, chefs and other purveyors—with the information they need to make sound choices about seafood and provide the best options to their customers. By working collaboratively with partners from conservation organizations, we connect professionals from the seafood and conservation community.... While better management and stronger regulations are a critical step, consumers can also make a difference by making better choices about what they eat and serve their families. Caught in the middle are chefs, retailers and the rest of the seafood industry who want to meet consumer demand for information while continuing to offer dishes seafood lovers enjoy. New opportunities are making environmentally responsible seafood a winning proposition for everyone.... These efforts are helping people make the connection between what's in the ocean and what's on their plates.

http://www.seafoodchoices.com/whoweare/index.html.

The campaign seeks to influence the purchasing decisions of "chefs, grocers, fishermen, distributors, restaurateurs, caterers, dieticians, hoteliers" and others who sell seafood. Subscription is free and includes information in a quarterly newsletter (*Afishianado*), networking opportunities, and answers to many questions on its website. In the earlier "Give Swordfish a Break" campaign, 27 high-profile East Coast chefs and dozens of others from around the country stopped serving swordfish. Royal Cruise lines agreed to stop serving swordfish on all of its ships and *Bon Appetit* magazine pledged not to publish swordfish recipes.

Such campaigns have been criticized by some as overly simplistic. As Thor Laass, president of Ocean Trust, has commented, "You don't ask the fisherman to cook up the dinner. Why are you asking the chef to manage the fishery?" More to the point, he notes that only the Atlantic population of swordfish was overfished, yet the campaign attacked all swordfish consumption.

In order to gain supporters, do such campaigns inevitably have to oversimplify issues such as not identifying which particular swordfish stocks are overfished? Do you think these campaigns are worthwhile or do they just provide a feel-good balm that really doesn't address the basic drivers of overfishing? Is the Seafood Choices campaign akin to someone feeling they've contributed to fighting climate change by buying one instead of two SUVs?

Perhaps the most influential information campaign has been directed by the Marine Stewardship Council (MSC). Jointly created in 1997 by Unilever, the world's largest buyer of seafood, and the World Wildlife Fund,

MSC has operated independently since 1999 as a certification organization. Seafood products that comply with MSC's environmental standard for sustainable and well-managed fisheries may use the MSC's eco-label, hopefully increasing their market share among environmentally-conscious consumers. MSC's informative website is at www.msc.org.

———

4. AQUACULTURE

One of the key questions for fisheries management is whether technology can give back—in the form of aquaculture or hatcheries—what it has taken away through overfishing. Aquaculture—the "farming" of captive fish in tanks on land or pens in the water—has become one of the world's fastest-growing food industries and, some argue, provides potential relief from overfishing pressures. Consider that roughly one-third of the seafood in global markets is farm-raised and the United States, ranked 11th in overall production, farms about one billion pounds of aquatic species annually. PEW OCEANS COMMISSION, AMERICA'S LIVING OCEANS: CHARTING A COURSE FOR SEA CHANGE 73 (2003).

According to the FAO, fish, crustaceans and mollusks grown in aquaculture grew from 3.9% of total seafood production by weight in 1970 to 29.9% in 2002. This represents more rapid growth than any other animal food producing sector, an average compounded rate of 8.9% per year since 1970, compared with only 1.2% for capture fisheries and 2.8% for terrestrial farmed meat production systems. Aquaculture continues to grow, with a 6.1% increase in production from 2000 to 2002 alone (with China accounting for over 70% of the production). Over this period, China has transformed into the world's largest producer and consumer of fish, with per capita consumption of 4.4 kilograms in 1972 to a remarkable 25.6 kilograms in 2002. FAO, THE STATE OF WORLD FISHERIES AND AQUACULTURE 2004 at 3, 6, 14, 18, 39. While over half of the world's aquaculture is carp raised in China for local consumption, salmon and shrimp farms have become multibillion dollar businesses providing important export earnings for countries such as Thailand and Ecuador. The World Bank reports that by 2010 aquaculture could provide 40% of the global fish consumed and over 50% of the commercial fish value. The chart below shows the growth trends of different aquaculture markets. *Id.* at 15.

Trends in world aquaculture production: major species groups

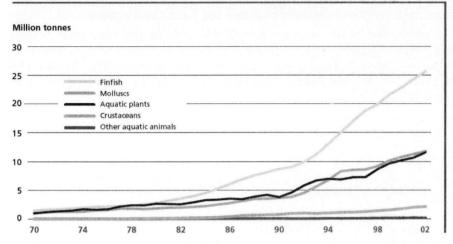

Million tonnes

Finfish
Molluscs
Aquatic plants
Crustaceans
Other aquatic animals

Aquaculture raises environmental concerns of its own, however, and has the potential to increase pressure on wild stocks for four reasons. The first is that carnivorous farmed fish take more out of the oceans than is kept in by their farmed production because their processed feed is largely made from ground-up wild fish taken from the oceans. Economist Rosamond Naylor estimates that almost two pounds of wild fish are needed for every pound of farmed fish. Second, disease and nutrient pollution can spread from fish pens (really, enclosed offshore cages) and harm water quality, wild fish populations and coastal marine life. In 2002, the Maine Department of Marine Resources ordered the destruction of 1.5 million farm-raised salmon in Cobscook Bay in order to prevent the spread of Infectious salmon anemia. PEW OCEANS COMMISSION, AMERICA'S LIVING OCEANS: CHARTING A COURSE FOR SEA CHANGE 4 (2003). The third is the destruction of mangrove wetlands, the nurseries for many species, to create ponds for shrimp aquaculture. Some environmentalists have called this practice as destructive as "slash-and-burn" deforestation.

Finally, crossbreeding between wild stocks and escaped domestic strains of fish could weaken the genetic robustness of wild populations as well as reducing genetic diversity over the longer term. While fish are kept in pens, breakouts are common. Since 1985, roughly one million Atlantic salmon have escaped in the Pacific Northwest and established breeding populations. A single storm in Maine in December, 2000, led to the escape of 100,000 salmon. PEW OCEANS COMMISSION, AMERICA'S LIVING OCEANS: CHARTING A COURSE FOR SEA CHANGE 76 (2003). The ecological risks posed by these non-native fish are considerable. If the Atlantic salmon were to return to streams ahead of wild Pacific salmon, they would gain a major competitive advantage in terms of habitat and spawning grounds. This could become an even greater issue of concern if genetically modified fish are allowed to be farmed in ocean pens (as one producer has requested a license to do). The biotech firm A/F Protein, Inc. has successfully introduced genes from the flounder into Atlantic salmon, creating a salmon that produces growth hormones year round and grows four to six times faster than normal.

Scientists are worried over competition with native fish if these GMO fish escaped and established wild populations. Only Maine and Washington state have banned genetically modified fish from their waters.

Regulation of aquaculture occurs primarily at the state level because the pens are located within three miles of the coast, and many states have little regulation beyond water pollution requirements. The Aquaculture Network Information Center, at http://aquanic.org/, provides links to a wide range of information on the web.

E.   FISHERY LAW

1.   UNCLOS AND EEZs

Management of a natural resource is always easier if one authority gets to make the rules for the entire resource. Because many fisheries are located in international waters, however, management for offshore fisheries has been a good deal more complex. Historically, a nation's fisheries authority extended 3 miles off its coast (known as "the cannon shot rule" because three miles was the limit of shore-based cannons' firing range). Beyond that, the oceans were an open-access commons. As a result, fisheries law has closely resembled property law. Living marine resources within a nation's territory belonged exclusively to the nation just as did its timber and coal. Fisheries beyond national jurisdiction—in the high seas— were common resources subject to the law of capture. Resources belonged to whomever took the property into possession first. Thus in an international arbitration between the United States and Great Britain in 1898, British ships were held to be exercising a legitimate freedom of the sea when they caught fur seals more than three miles off the U.S. coast. *Bering Sea Fur Seals Arbitration* (Gr. Brit. v. U.S.), *reprinted in* J. MOORE, INTERNATIONAL ARBITRATIONS 755 (1983).

This was an adequate management regime so long as there was low pressure on the resource. As technology improved, though, foreign fleets began fishing in other countries' traditional areas. This came to a head in the 1970s. Iceland, for example, unilaterally declared it was extending its exclusive fishing zone from 12 miles to 200 miles. British vessels, which had traditionally fished well within the 200–mile zone, refused to recognize Iceland's claim. A series of violent "cod wars" took place in the North Atlantic, with Iceland's coast guard chasing British fishing trawlers and, in turn, being rammed by British warships. In 1976 alone there were over four dozen rammings. Similarly, in 1974 New England fishermen were harvesting only 12% of the fish caught in their waters. Most were caught by boats from the Soviet Union, Poland, and elsewhere.

Thus when negotiations commenced at the United Nations to revise the international law on ocean fisheries (the Law of the Sea treaties), there was significant international pressure to revisit fisheries law and determine more clearly the scope of national fisheries management authority. The UN Third Conference on the Law of the Sea began in 1973 and concluded in 1982. Over almost a decade, nations cajoled, bickered, and negotiated a remarkably comprehensive document. The complexity of the negotiations is hard to imagine. Consensus was sought on virtually every issue governing humans' relationship with the sea, from fisheries, pollution, and conservation to mining, laying of sea cables, navigation, and jurisdictional authority. The final result was the United Nations Convention on the Law of the Sea (UNCLOS).

For our purposes, the most important part of UNCLOS is its treatment of jurisdictional zones. In striking a balance between the interests of coastal States, land-locked States and maritime powers, UNCLOS established a series of zones, varying in degrees of national control. From the baseline (usually the coast and harbor walls) to 12 nautical miles offshore is the *territorial sea* (a nautical mile is 1.15 miles). The coastal State exercises almost complete authority in the territorial sea. From the boundary of the territorial sea out to 200 nautical miles is the *exclusive economic zone* (EEZ). Beyond the EEZ, more than 200 nautical miles off the coast, lie the *high seas*, an area beyond national jurisdictions and part of the global commons.

Within the EEZ, coastal States have the sovereign right to explore, exploit, conserve and manage the natural resources, both mineral and living. Together, national EEZs cover over 30% of the world's seas, approximately 90% of the commercial fisheries, and almost all the presently exploitable mineral resources. Thus the creation of a 200–mile EEZ greatly increased coastal states' ability to manage fisheries. With the increased right to exploit resources, however, UNCLOS also imposed environmental responsibilities. A coastal state exercises authority to protect and preserve the marine environment in its EEZ and *"shall"* ensure the conservation and utilization of its living marine resources. UNCLOS Article 61. Coastal nations are also required to enter into agreements with other states to fish within the coastal state's EEZ (pursuant to conservation and compensation terms established by the coastal state), if the coastal nation lacks capacity to harvest the optimum yield, giving preference to landlocked and geographically disadvantaged states. UNCLOS Article 62.

It was thought at the time that bringing such an important part of the ocean's resources under national jurisdiction would encourage strict governmental oversight to ensure sound management and conservation of domestic fish stocks. After all, allocating property rights to common resources provides a classic resolution to the tragedy of the commons. Yet exactly the opposite has occurred. As described earlier in the section on subsidies, nations eager to exploit their new sovereign resources encouraged development of large fishing fleets. Between 1970 and 1990, the global fishing fleet doubled from 585,000 to 1.2 million commercial boats, in addition to millions of small fishing boats. In the United States, just the Arctic Alaska Fisheries Corporation received roughly $100 million in federal loan guarantees.

QUESTIONS AND DISCUSSION

1. UNCLOS Article 62 requires a coastal State to allow other nations to fish in its EEZ if it cannot harvest an optimum yield (similar in principle to a maximum sustainable yield), but the practice is more complicated. If a country does not want to open its EEZ to other nations' ships, it can either (a) play with its stock assessments to show a low optimum yield that is used, or (b) adjust its optimum yield down for "economic or environmental" reasons (Article 61(3)). Not surprisingly, developed countries have had no problem creating capacity to take their optimum yield. Many developing countries, on the other hand, employ "joint ventures" to sell access to their EEZs to distant water fishing nations such as Japan, Korea, Taiwan and Spain. A recurring problem with this practice, however, has been corruption and poor management. Agreements have been criticized for allowing access for too little money and for not reflecting scientific management practices. This practice, particularly in Africa, has depleted fisheries that support coastal, artisanal fishing communities.

2. The worldview reflected in UNCLOS' zones of jurisdictional authority is not universally shared. Indeed many indigenous cultures have long viewed the ocean as a common heritage. The law of the sea of the Maori (indigenous peoples of New Zealand) is described below.

> For the Maori people, *te tikanga o te moana*, or the law of the sea, is predicated on four basic concepts deeply rooted in Maori cultural values. First, the sea is part of a global environment in which all parts are interlinked. Second, the sea, as one of the *taonga*, or treasures of Mother Earth, must be nurtured and protected. Third, the protected sea is a *koha*, or gift, which humans may use. Fourth, that use is to be controlled in a way that will sustain its bounty.

> From this cultural and divinely ordained matrix the actual *tikanga*, or law, is developed. Thus, for example, *te tikanga o nga kaitaki* aims to stop pollution of coastal water not by seeking more effective methods of waste disposal, as is often advocated today, but by ensuring that any activity produces as little waste as possible at its source. Such laws were rigidly enforced by various sanctions and through *korero tunhonohono*, or agreements among the various tribal nations that make up the Maori people.

> It is impossible to detail here all of the various laws of *te tai ao*, the environment. It is submitted, however, that within the values and norms that shaped those laws are the seeds of understanding that could transform current international thinking on protection of the global marine environment.

> Two of the many claims laid by Iwi Maori before the Waitangi Tribunal give an indication of the interrelated view of the environment encapsulated within indigenous Maori law. In the Kaituna claim, the people of Te Arawa objected to the discharge of sewage into the Kaituna River. For the Maori, the river was part of an interconnected water system involving Lake Rotorua, Lake Rotoiti, and the Maketsu Estuary. Each body of water is important to the people of Te Arawa as a source of food, as the site of important historical events, and as the base of spiritual sustenance. To discharge sewage into such waterways not only would be a *hara*, or wrongful act that breached the laws protecting tangible food sources, but would also breach the laws protecting the intangible spiritual sources of the Iwi's well-being. *Nga tikanga o te tai ao*—the laws of the environment—sought to protect both the tangible and intangible, since together they strengthen *te korowai a Papatuanukau*—the cloak of Mother Earth.

Moana Jackson, *Indigenous Law and the Sea*, in JON VAN DYKE ET AL. EDS., FREEDOM FOR THE SEAS IN THE 21ST CENTURY 46 (1993).

Assume that *te tikanga o te moana* rather than UNCLOS formed the basis for the modern law of the sea. How might the law of the sea's treatment of jurisdictional zones and allocation of rights and obligations be different? The Maori's *te tikanga o te moana* is a common property regime which depended for its effectiveness upon a shared set of norms. Are there any similar norms shared by the global community? In the absence of shared norms, can a common property regime successfully manage a natural resource?

3. Ignorant of national jurisdictions, a number of fish stocks move freely in and out of EEZs and the high seas. Indeed, it would be a remarkable coincidence if ecosystems and habitats fit easily into jurisdictional lines determined by political negotiation. The habitats of some fish populations, such as halibut and pollock, overlap national and international waters and are known as "straddling stocks." Other "highly migratory" fish species, such as salmon, migrate from national into international waters and then back again to lay eggs and die. As a consequence of UNCLOS, such species fall in and out of domestic control. Thus the problem posed by conservation of straddling stocks and highly migratory fish is one of free riders. A coastal state can impose all types of fishing restrictions to build up depleted stocks, but once the fish swim beyond 200 miles, they can be caught freely by foreign boats, frustrating national conservation efforts. In the case of halibut in the George's Bank off of Canada, this conflict led to the Canadian navy boarding a Spanish fishing trawler 212 miles out to sea and towing it back to port. The "Donut Hole" in the Bering Sea is an area of high seas completely surrounded by the EEZ of the United States and Russia. Although the United States and Russia control most of the area where straddling stocks are found, other nations heavily fish in the Donut Hole, frustrating national conservation efforts.

In seeking to address the management challenges posed by straddling stocks and highly migratory species, UNCLOS Article 63 calls on coastal and other relevant fishing states to seek, either directly or through appropriate regional organizations, measures to conserve straddling stocks. Hence there are a number of regional organizations and conventions where fishing nations have established fishing rules for themselves beyond the EEZs. These include the North Atlantic Fisheries Organization (NAFO), the International Convention for the Conservation of Atlantic Tunas, the Convention for the Prohibition of Fishing with Long Driftnets in the South Pacific, the Convention Concerning Fishing in the Black Sea, and others.

In practice, these organizations' influence has been limited by a lack of consensus among its members on management measures and allocation levels. Gathering reliable fishing statistics has also proven difficult because not all nations provide catch data and the activities of non-contracting parties go unreported. The most significant practical constraint on effective conservation, however, has been the inability to allocate and enforce allowable catches once an organization has determined the maximum sustainable yield of fish stocks. Thus, for example, in the case of NAFO, the Organization had the authority to establish fishing quotas for each member nation, but the quotas were not binding. Once quotas had been allocated, if a member state disagreed with the decision it could use the Objection

Procedure within 60 days and declare its own quota. In 1986, for example, NAFO set a quota for flounder of 700 tons. The European Union formally objected to this quota and set itself one of 21,161 tons.

As one can easily imagine, this lack of real authority led to poor conservation and, in the case of NAFO, to the seizure of the Spanish fishing trawler by Canada as a means to highlight the toothless organization. In response to these problems, negotiations resulted in adoption of a binding treaty in 1995, known as "Straddling Stocks Convention" or "Fish Stocks Treaty." U.N. Doc. A/CONF.164/37 (1995). A significant achievement, the treaty directly limits the high seas freedom of fishing, subjecting it to the conservation mandates of regional organizations, as well as dramatically enhancing states' investigation and enforcement authorities on the high seas. Perhaps most important, if states refuse to comply with the organizations' rules or to become members, they are barred access to the fishery. This fundamentally shifts the traditional freedom of the high seas, effectively limiting for the first time open access to high sea fisheries.

4. In another interesting development, over 170 member States of the UN Food and Agriculture Organization (FAO) adopted the Code of Conduct for Responsible Fisheries in 1995. The Code is voluntary and contains a set of principles, goals and elements for action. Countries and regional organizations have since developed a number of International Plans of Action that set out concrete steps for complying with the Code of Conduct, including plans for seabirds, sharks, and illegal fishing. The Code is on the web at http://www.fao.org/fi/agreem/codecond/ficonde.asp#PRE and makes good reading as an example of "soft" international law (i.e., prescriptions or recommendations without the threat of sanction). The Plans of Action are available through http://www.fao.org/fi/ipa/ipae.asp.

5. Disagreements over the management regime governing deep seabed mining prevented the United States from ratifying UNCLOS after signing the treaty. Apart from the mining provisions, however, the United States has taken the formal position that UNCLOS is binding customary law. Despite periodic attempts in Congress to ratify UNCLOS, at the time this casebook went to press the United States still was not a party to the treaty.

———

2.   MAGNUSON–STEVENS FISHERY CONSERVATION AND MANAGEMENT ACT

The politics of national fishery management are more complicated than for most other natural resources. Fisheries disputes are rarely a two-player conflict between environmentalists and industry representatives. Fishing interests, in particular, are anything but monolithic. Commercial fishers are obviously a key player. In 2001, there were over 75,000 commercial vessels in U.S. fisheries with a direct contribution to gross domestic product of $28.1 billion. But the interests of commercial fishers differ substantially depending on their scale of operation (small boats versus factory ships), type of gear (shrimp trawls versus longlines versus nets), fishing area (inshore versus offshore), and end market (subsistence and indigenous consumption versus commercial sale). The recreational fishing industry (including charter boats, fly fishing, surf casting, etc.) has substantial clout, as well, with some 9 million saltwater anglers supporting 300,000 jobs and contributing over $20 billion of economic activity. Yet its catch is only 2% of the commercial fishery. Thus, as we will see in the Red Snapper case study at the end of this section, fishing vessels that catch groundfish may oppose the interests of shrimp trawlers, while both are opposed by recreational fishers, and all this *before* environmental groups get involved! Daniel Waldeck, Eugene Buck, The Magnuson–Stevens Fishery Conservation and Management Act: Reauthorization Issues for the 107th Congress 2–3 (Congressional Research Service 2001); U.S. Commission on Ocean Policy, An Ocean Blueprint for the 21st Century 275 (2004).

To get a sense of how strong these conflicts are, consider the homepage message of the Recreational Fishing Alliance website in 2002.

> For years, you and other recreational fishermen have done your part to conserve America's fisheries and fish stocks. You've released more fish, accepted shorter seasons, restricted bag limits and more. But it hasn't been enough to save fish.
>
> That's because, while you've tried to conserve, industrial fishing interests have embarked on a wholesale "search and destroy" mission to maintain their catch levels at a time when fish stocks are declining.
>
> Trawlers are dumping more "bycatch," dead and dying unwanted fish, back in the ocean. Commercial draggers are targeting wintering grounds and keeping smaller fish. They're using more advanced technologies to target more and more species—especially those which have traditionally been reserved for recreational anglers like you. And in Congress, the federal bureaucracy and coastal state legislatures, the industrial fishing lobby is demanding even more privileges, more restrictions on recreational anglers, and more opportunities to strip the ocean bare.
>
> The only way to stop them—to save the fish, and save your sport—is for fishermen like you to get involved in the political process and fight back. Now you can, through your membership in the Recreational Fishing Alliance!

http://www.savefish.com/index2.html

Both recreational and commercial fishing interests often oppose Native Americans with tribal fishing rights, some of whom fish for subsistence, others commercially. Fish processors and canneries represent the end market for most fishers and, thus, often have opposing interests. Hatchery and aquaculture interests can differ from fishery-dependent communities. Fisheries managers on the state and national level do not share identical interests, either, nor necessarily do scientists and environmental groups. Yet all play key roles in shaping fishery policies and deciding whether the overarching management goal should be to increase commercial harvests, maximize recreational harvests, preserve coastal fishing communities, reduce the consumer price of fish, or ensure a healthy marine ecosystem.

The Magnuson Fishery Conservation and Management Act (also known as the Magnuson Act or the FCMA; in 1996 its name was changed to Magnuson–Stevens) was passed in 1976 to create a process that mediated among all these contesting interests while also ensuring viable stocks. 16 U.S.C. 1801 et seq. It has been amended every ten years. Adopted during the UNCLOS negotiations, the FCMA is the primary domestic legislation governing fisheries and fishing activities in federal waters. As we shall see, as originally drafted, the FCMA was driven far more by domestic fishing interests than by environmental concerns. In the 1970s, massive "factory boats" from other countries had been catching fish within 200 miles of the U.S. coastline far more rapidly than U.S. boats. In 1974, for example, it was estimated that American boats caught $2.5 billion of fish in U.S. waters while foreign vessels took in $9 billion. When Congress stated in the FCMA's preamble that a "national program for the conservation and management of the fishery resources of the United States is necessary to prevent overfishing, to rebuild overfished stocks, to insure conservation, and to realize the full potential of the Nation's fishery resources," implicit in these ambitious goals was the sense that keeping out foreign boats was half the battle. 16 U.S.C. § 1801 (a)(6). Indeed it's worth noting that the law's main two sponsors, Senators Magnuson and Stevens, were from Washington and Alaska respectively, two states that suffered most from foreign fleets. Thus the FCMA extended the federal government's authority over fisheries from three to two-hundred miles offshore, giving it the largest EEZ in the world (note that, as a result of the Submerged Lands Act, coastal state governments control waters out to three nautical miles, nine nautical miles for Texas, Florida's Gulf coast and Puerto Rico).

The foundation for fisheries policy in the United States was laid out in the 1969 Stratton Commission's comprehensive review of ocean policy, *Our Nation and the Sea*. The Commission's recommendations led to creation of NOAA and passage of the Coastal Zone Management Act. Its assessment of marine fisheries, essentially unregulated at the time, was rosy.

> [F]ishery harvests around the world were increasing in the 1960s, and many people believed they would continue to increase indefinitely. The Stratton Commission predicted that enhanced technology and intensified exploitation of new species could eventually increase worldwide landings from 60 million metric tons in 1966 to 440–550 million tons. That Commission saw fisheries as an area of immense opportunity, and called for the expansion of U.S. fishing capability.

U.S. COMMISSION ON OCEAN POLICY, AN OCEAN BLUEPRINT FOR THE 21ST CENTURY 274–275 (2004).

The Magnuson Act provided a classic resolution to the tragedy of the commons—carving up the commons and setting rules for entry and use. As with other natural resources we study in this book, at the heart of fisheries management is a planning process. Congress charged the Department of Commerce with the ultimate authority to implement the Act. In practice, that has meant that the National Oceanographic and Atmospheric Administration (NOAA), located within Commerce, regulates fisheries management (Note that NOAA Fisheries agency was previously known as NMFS, the National Marine Fisheries Service, and the cases excerpted below and many practitioners continue to refer to the agency as NMFS). Freshwater fish are generally regulated by the Fish & Wildlife Service within the Department of the Interior. NOAA Fisheries' responsibility is, in turn, largely delegated to eight Regional Fishery Management Councils (FMCs). The Councils are responsible for initially preparing Fisheries Management Plans (FMPs) for those fisheries in need of conservation and management because of overfishing. These determine how each fishery within their geographic region will be managed—assessing the status of the fishery and proposing management restrictions (such as gear types, seasons, and quotas) to ensure conservation. All Management Plans and proposed regulations must be consistent with required provisions of the Act and the ten national standards set out in the Act. In principle, following these standards will ensure sustainable yields.

In terms of developing the U.S. fishing industry and driving foreign boats out of the EEZ, the Magnuson Act has been a great success. The percentage of fish harvested by foreign nationals in U.S. waters declined from 71% of the total annual catch in 1977 to near zero fifteen years later. From 1977 through 1997, commercial landings more than doubled. The Act's success in the conservation and restoration of U.S. fisheries, though, has been mixed. It has become apparent, for example, that overfishing poses greater risks than the initial legislation had contemplated. Despite (or perhaps because) foreign fleets no longer fished the EEZ, the domestic industry continued to build larger and more efficient fishing vessels and gear, increasing pressures on the fisheries. With loans to pay off and sunk costs, there were strong incentives for representatives of the fishing industry to hope for the best in the always uncertain estimates of stock size and push for increased catches, despite years of scientific recommendations to curb fishing effort, and to claim that the level of uncertainty in estimates of stock size was too great to jeopardize the short-term economic viability of the fishing industry. Dominated by commercial fishing interests, the regional Councils would often maintain unsustainable catch levels. In the worst cases, they would actually increase allowed catch levels. Indeed soon after its enactment, critics began to call into question whether the FCMA had introduced a new form of fisheries management or simply legalized the status quo.

In response to major fishery collapses in New England and the Gulf of Mexico, in 1996, the Sustainable Fisheries Act (SFA) reauthorized and amended the Magnuson Act, marking a significant shift in U.S. fisheries policy. P.L. 104–297. The amendments, among other things, required greater consideration of ecological factors in assessing catch levels and more attention to restoration and protection of habitat. Along with changes to the required provisions of FMPs, three new national standards were added, mandating Councils to accurately account for and reduce bycatch, to minimize adverse fishing impacts on Essential Fish Habitats, to consider the impact of FMPs on fishing communities, and to promote safety of human life at sea. These changes reflect a tension that has always existed in the FCMA—whether the law is a means to ensure a profitable fishing industry and allocate quotas among competing fishing groups or a law designed to ensure healthy fish populations and marine habitat. The 2006 amendments further strengthened the Act's conservation requirements, creating a stronger role for scientific advice in management decisions, increasing disclosure of conflicts of interest, requiring plans to end overfishing immediately, and encouraging greater use of market-based management tools.

Given all the conflicting interests described above, it should come as no surprise that fisheries policy remains highly contentious. The graph below charts the rise in litigation throughout the 1990s, with over 110 lawsuits pending against NOAA by the beginning of 2002. U.S. COMMISSION ON OCEAN POLICY, AN OCEAN BLUEPRINT FOR THE 21ST CENTURY 276 (2004).

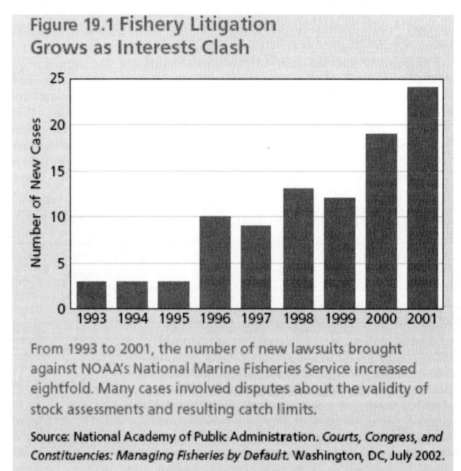

Figure 19.1 Fishery Litigation Grows as Interests Clash

From 1993 to 2001, the number of new lawsuits brought against NOAA's National Marine Fisheries Service increased eightfold. Many cases involved disputes about the validity of stock assessments and resulting catch limits.

Source: National Academy of Public Administration. *Courts, Congress, and Constituencies: Managing Fisheries by Default.* Washington, DC, July 2002.

a. Regional Fishery Management Councils (RFMCs)

The FCMA created eight Regional Fishery Management Councils charged with developing fishery management plans. 16 U.S.C. § 1852(a). As shown below, the Council regions include the Caribbean, Gulf, Mid–Atlantic, New England, North Pacific, Pacific, South Atlantic, and the Western Pacific. The number of voting members on each Council varies from seven on the Caribbean Council to twenty-one on the Mid–Atlantic Council, with each member serving a three-year term (maximum of three consecutive terms possible). U.S. OCEANS COMMISSION, AN OCEAN BLUEPRINT FOR THE 21ST CENTURY 283 (2004). The Council's voting members are set by statute and must include the principal state official that oversees each state's fisheries management and the regional director of NOAA Fisheries for the geographic area concerned. After that, the Secretary of Commerce appoints "individuals who, by reason of their occupational or other experience, scientific expertise, or training, are knowledgeable regarding the conservation and management, or the commercial or recreational harvest, of the fishery resources of the geographical area concerned." 16 U.S.C. § 1852(b)(2)(A). Potential appointees are nominated by the coastal state governors in the Fishery Management Council's region.

In selecting among qualified candidates, the Secretary:

> shall, to the extent practicable, ensure a fair and balanced apportionment, on a rotating or other basis, of the active participants (or their representatives) in the commercial and recreational fisheries under the jurisdiction of the Council.

Id. at § 1852(b)(2)(A). Non-voting members include a regional U.S. Fish and Wildlife representative, the Commander of the local Coast Guard, the executive director of the Marine Fisheries Commission for the geographical area concerned, and a representative of the State Department.

As with the International Convention for the Regulation of Whaling (page 529), the FCMA was originally designed to manage and support the fishery for the benefit of the fishing industry. Thus the statute makes no clear provision for the participation of conservation interests. True, the Councils must have a U.S. Fish and Wildlife representative, but only in a non-voting capacity. And note that the "fair and balanced apportionment" requirement for voting members quoted above is meant to ensure adequate representation from commercial, recreational, and other fishing interests. Traditionally, governors have selected representatives from the fishing industry and, over the past two decades, industry representatives have occupied roughly 80% of the Council seats. JOSH EAGLE, TAKING STOCK OF THE REGIONAL FISHERY MANAGEMENT COUNCILS 24 (2003).

Scientists and environmentalists may make their views known either through public comments on plans or, more directly, through serving on advisory panels, scientific committees, or stock assessment panels (to determine catch levels). At the end of the day, though, they have no vote in the Council. As a result, many have charged that the Councils' decisions systematically favor fishing interests and under-protect fish stocks. As Oliver Houck notes,

> The second unique feature of the FCMA is that the commercial fishing fleet of New Bedford and the agency promoting commercial fisheries in the State of Massachusetts are lead players in determining the harvest. The conflicts here have become obvious even to the popular press. A report of the American Fisheries Society asked: "Can people who clearly represent specific economic interests perform adequately as trustees of the public resources they use? On balance the answer is no...." Every reasoned critique of the FCMA has identified this conflict as a source of the catastrophe in the Northeast, and the ones elsewhere to come.... [I]t becomes clear that few public resource users, no matter what might come tomorrow, are going to conserve out of instinct, intelligence, or the goodness of their hearts. It is the classic prisoner's dilemma, and turning resource decisions over to the prisoners is not likely to achieve high levels of either self-restraint or resource protection.

Oliver Houck, *On the Law of Biodiversity and Ecosystem Management,* 81 MINN. L. REV. 869, 951–52 (1997). An editorial in the *Bangor Daily News* (Maine) makes a similar point.

The problem, at its core, is that an 18–member council responsible for the care of a public resource—the ocean and the fish within—is too dominated by offshore commercial fishing interests and by state agency officials with industry backgrounds. Science and the public interest are under-represented, as are fishermen who work inshore, such as lobstermen, whose livelihoods depend upon a healthy ecosystem. Calls to restructure the council to better reflect the varied interests with a stake in the ocean have long been ignored.

Fish Council Flounders, BANGOR DAILY NEWS, Jan. 5, 2002, at A6. Thus, it is not particularly surprising that fisheries management has produced decisions like that of the New England Fishery Management Council, which declared in 1983, just one decade before acknowledging the crash of the nation's oldest productive fishery, that its policy of fisheries management would involve "a minimum of regulatory intervention." *As quoted in* Clarke Canfield, *New England's Groundfish Stocks Aren't Recovering Fast Enough. Neither Are Its Fisherman*, NATIONAL FISHERMAN, March 1997, at 32.

b. *Fishery Management Plans (FMPs)*

Fishery Management Plans (FMPs) are the heart of the FCMA and the primary "on the water" management tool for the 4.5 million square miles of public domain that make up the U.S. Exclusive Economic Zone. FMPs are intended to reduce and ultimately halt overfishing, to control wasteful fishing gears that discard significant amounts of marine life, and to protect sensitive sea floor habitats from fishing and non-fishing human activities. Furthermore, as FMPs must comply with "any other applicable law" (16 U.S.C. § . 1853(a)(1)(C)), they must comply with other federal environmental laws, such as the National Environmental Policy Act and the Endangered Species Act.

Developing an FMP is an extensive undertaking and will often attempt to address species assemblages in similar habitat rather than a single fish stock. The current 45 FMPs address over seven hundred distinct populations, accounting for 99% of commercially-caught fish that are landed each year at U.S. ports.

The FCMA sets out fifteen required provisions of a FMP. Some of the most significant are set out below: The FMP "shall":

- [Contain measures] necessary and appropriate for the conservation and management of the fishery to prevent overfishing and rebuild overfished stocks, and to protect, restore, and promote the long-term health and stability of the fishery [in a manner] ... consistent with the national standards;

- Assess and specify the present and probable future condition of, and the maximum sustainable yield and optimum yield from, the fishery ...;

- Describe and identify essential fish habitat for the fishery ... [and] minimize to the extent practicable adverse effects on such habitat caused by fishing ... ;

- Include a fishery impact statement for the plan or amendment ... which shall assess, specify, and analyze the likely effects, if any, including the cumulative conservation and management measures on, and possible mitigation measures for—participants in the fisheries and fishing communities affected by the plan or amendment . . . ;

- Specify objective and measurable criteria for identifying when the fishery to which the plan applies is overfished . . . and, in the case of a fishery which the Council or the Secretary has determined is approaching an overfished condition or is overfished, contain conservation and management measures to prevent overfishing or end overfishing and rebuild the fishery;

- Establish a standardized reporting methodology to assess the amount and type of bycatch occurring in the fishery, and include conservation and management measures that to the extent practicable . . . minimize bycatch;

- allocate, taking into consideration the economic impact of the harvest restrictions or recovery benefits on the fishery participants in each sector, any harvest restrictions or recovery benefits fairly and equitably among the commercial, recreational, and charter fishing sectors in the fishery and;

- establish a mechanism for specifying annual catch limits in the plan (including a multiyear plan), implementing regulations, or annual specifications, at a level such that overfishing does not occur in the fishery, including measures to ensure accountability.

16 U.S.C. § 1853(a). In order to ensure the goals of the FMP are met, Section 303(b) grants the Council discretionary authority to require permits for vessels or operators, limit catch (based on area, species, size, number, weight, sex, bycatch, total biomass, or other factors), restrict gear, limit access entry, and use observers to facilitate information collecting.

FMPs are drafted by the Regional Councils, released for a 45–day public comment period, reviewed in light of the comments, and then forwarded to the Department of Commerce. NOAA Fisheries reviews the FMP to determine if it complies with the FCMA and other applicable law (including the FCMA's ten national standards, described in the section below). The FMP is published in the *Federal Register*, followed by a 60–day public comment period. The Secretary of Commerce may then approve, disapprove, or partially approve the FMP. 16 U.S.C. § 1854. Once approved, NOAA Fisheries is charged with issuing regulations to implement the FMP. These implementing regulations are subject to Administrative Procedure Act notice and comment rule-making procedures. 18 U.S.C. § 1854. Overall, this process may be quite lengthy if NOAA Fisheries rejects or partially rejects revisions to the FMP. Many FMPs are subsequently amended to take into account stock conditions and new data. Indeed one plan has been amended more than seventy-two times. While rarely exercised, the Secretary has the authority to draft his own management measures if the Council has developed no plan after a reasonable period of time or if, after rejecting a Regional Council's plan, the Council doesn't come up with another one. *Id.* § 1854(c)(1). In addition, the Secretary is authorized to implement emergency interim regulations to reduce overfishing "without regard to whether a fishery management plan exists for such fishery." *Id.* § 1855(c)(1).

QUESTIONS AND DISCUSSION

1. Consider again § 1852(b)(2)(A)'s requirement of a "fair and balanced apportionment" of voting members from the commercial and recreational fisheries under the Council's jurisdiction. Are there valid justifications for the required composition of the Councils, or is it simply public choice theory in action—concentrated fishing interests win out over diffuse public interests (recall that the FCMA's sponsors were senators from Washington and Alaska, two states with major fishing industries)? Put another way, why should conservation interests be made voting members on Councils? The reason for mandating adequate representation from commercial, recreational and other fishing interests on the Councils is obvious—their jobs and communities are at stake. Both the NMFS regional director and the principal state fisheries officials are voting members, as well, and their job is to ensure sustainable fish stocks. Thus they should be able to counterbalance any demands from fishing interests for overfishing. Given that the focus of the FCMA is not ecological (i.e., on behalf of the fish as fish), the key question seems to be how to ensure optimum commercial yields. In that setting, what would someone from Greenpeace have to offer?

It may be instructive to compare the Regional Councils under the Magnuson Act with the original Grazing Advisory Boards created under the Taylor Grazing Act. *See* Chapter 8. Like the Magnuson Act, the focus of the Taylor Act was on benefiting resource users rather than the environment per se. Just as with the fishery, open access to the range resource (grass) had resulted in over-exploitation of that resource to the detriment of all users. Because the Taylor Act, like the Magnuson Act, was focused on resource use, it is not particularly surprising that the Grazing Advisory Boards were to "offer advice or make recommendations concerning rules and regulations for the administration of" the Taylor Act and to advise on "the seasons of use and carrying capacity of the range." *See* 43 U.S.C. § 315o–1(b). As a result of rule-making during the Clinton Administration, the Grazing Advisory Boards were replaced by Range Advisory Councils whose membership includes a broader array of stakeholders, including ranchers, high and low-impact recreators, preservationists, states, Indian tribes, and local government officials. *See* 43 C.F.R. § 1784 (2000) (describing RACs). Has the time come for a similar change in the management approach to the fisheries resource? On what might the ability to effect such a change depend?

2.   Because FMPs are promulgated under informal rulemaking, they are subject to judicial review under the "arbitrary and capricious" standard set forth in the Administrative Procedure Act (for background on this standard of review, *see* page 226, or *Blue Water Fisherman's Assoc. v. Mineta*, 122 F. Supp. 2d 150, 158–59 (D.D.C. 2000)). A court does not review the plan directly but, instead, reviews the Secretary's determination that a plan is "consistent" with the Act's requirements (and, in particular, with the national standards). A reviewing court may not enjoin implementation of challenged regulations; it may declare them invalid if they are found to be arbitrary and capricious and remand for further development.

Declaring a plan invalid, however, can be counterproductive. Indeed, the myriad delays in developing and implementing FMPs pose significant problems. As the U.S. Oceans Commission explains,

> The difficult process of establishing allowable biological catch, and then determining allocations based on that figure, can result in lengthy delays in

developing or revising fishery management plans. The Magnuson–Stevens Act does not require RFMCs to submit a new or revised plan to NOAA on any specific schedule. As a result, Council delays can lead to a fishery having no management measures in place or relying on outdated, inadequate plans.

When that happens, the RFMCs are not penalized; instead, the adverse consequences are all borne by the fishery resource. There are two possible sources of delay: SSC [Scientific and Statistical Committee] difficulties in reaching agreement on allowable biological catch, and RFMC delays in submitting management plans to NOAA for approval. * * *

Delays in formulating management plans within the RFMC can be more intractable than reaching scientific consensus. Under the current system, RFMCs can simply avoid difficult decisions by postponing development of plans. While the Councils cannot be sued for their slowness, NMFS can be. In fact, an increasing number of lawsuits are prompted by delays in management actions, particularly for plans to end overfishing.

The very possibility of extended delays puts pressure on NMFS to recommend approval of inadequate management plans. Based on a recommendation from NMFS, the Secretary of Commerce may approve, partly reject, or fully reject a plan, but may not amend it. As part of its recommendation, NMFS is aware that rejection of a plan could result in no conservation measures being in place until the RFMC agrees on a revised plan—a process that could take many months.

Although the Secretary of Commerce can legally choose to develop a fishery management plan within the agency instead of waiting for a RFMC to do so, this is almost always impractical. Since Congress clearly desired the Councils to have the lead in fishery management, the Secretary can either enter into a protracted, contentious, and politicized process to develop a departmental plan, or continue to wait for the RFMC to act. Under either scenario, the resource may remain unprotected for an extended period of time.

U.S. OCEANS COMMISSION, AN OCEAN BLUEPRINT FOR THE 21ST CENTURY 279–280 (2004). Nor has NMFS strictly reviewed plans. A twenty-year study of NMFS reviews found that the agency had disapproved only 1 out of every 10,000 council management measures. JOSH EAGLE, TAKING STOCK OF THE REGIONAL FISHERY MANAGEMENT COUNCILS 43 (2003). With a likelihood of rejection of just 0.01%, what is the disincentive for FMCs proposing lax conservation measures?

3. To understand why the FCMA has been cited as an example of public choice theory in practice, consider that so long as Council members file financial disclosure forms, they are exempted from

> [the] section of the criminal code generally prohibiting official acts that advance a personal financial interest. . . . Notwithstanding loud complaints, three members of the North Pacific Fishery Management Council (responsible for Alaskan fisheries) recently voted with a 9–2 majority that reserved increased amounts of groundfish to shore-based Alaskan processors and the smaller inshore vessels that service them, even though two of the three owned such boats and the third soon became a paid lobbyist for the processors.

Robert McManus, *America's Saltwater Fisheries: So Few Fish, So Many Fishermen*, 9 NAT. RESOURCES AND ENVT. 13, 16 (Spring 1995). To be sure, there are opportunities for conflicts of interest in many natural resource planning bodies, but few are as brazen in admitting it.

The 2006 amendments to the FCMA added Section 302(j)(9) requiring the Secretary of Commerce annually to:

> submit a report to the Senate Committee on Commerce, Science, and Transportation and the House of Representatives Committee on Resources on action taken by the Secretary and the Councils to implement the disclosure of financial interest and recusal requirements of this subsection, including identification of any conflict of interest problems with respect to the Councils and scientific and statistical committees and recommendations for addressing any such problems.

What do you think will be the impacts of this disclosure requirement?

4. Ensuring meaningful public input on proposed FMPs is easier said than done. As a public comment letter from a fisherman to the Mid–Atlantic Council on a proposed fishery management plan amendment stated,

> Have you considered the time required to read 3 amendments of over 200 pages each? Working people don't have time for this. Overfishing definitions are indecipherable. They should be explained so a fisherman or even a member of Congress could understand them. It sounds like "We don't know this; so we're going to guess at it," written in gobbly gook.

5. In the United States, the federal government has primary jurisdiction over the EEZ, but there is no automatic preemption of state regulatory authority over fishing up to three miles off the coast. According to NOAA, in 1998 coastal states managed 74 "nationally significant fish and shellfish species and stock groups," and the federal government managed 201. The federal government may preempt the state's authority when the Secretary of Commerce, after notice and an opportunity for a full adversarial hearing, determines that: (1) the fishery is covered by a Fishery Management Plan predominantly within the EEZ and beyond, and (2) a state has taken or omitted to take action, with adverse effect on carrying out a fishery management plan. U.S.C. § 1856(b)(1). When state laws conflict with federal regulations under the FCMA, the Secretary must preempt state laws.

6. Despite criticism of the FCMA and the high-profile collapses of the cod and other fisheries, it is important to note that there have been some success stories in U.S. fishery management, as well. In response to the collapse of striped bass populations along the East Coast in the 1970s, Congress passed the Striped Bass Conservation Act which provided states the authority to restrict or ban fishing. As a result of stringent catch restrictions imposed by states (including moratoria by Maryland and Virginia), the striped bass population had fully recovered by 1996. Strong controls have helped restore the king mackerel and Spanish mackerel, as well. NATIONAL RESEARCH COUNCIL, SUSTAINING MARINE FISHERIES 80 (1999). The Department of Commerce report to Congress on the state of fisheries in 2000 stated that, of the 287 major fish stocks in the EEZ, 56 stocks were overfished and 47 stocks were experiencing overfishing. Rebuilding plans were in place or approved for 75 stocks. NMFS, REPORT TO CONGRESS: STATUS OF FISHERIES OF THE UNITED STATES 4–5 (2001).

7. In an effort to chart a new course in oceans policy, two high-level commissions issued reports in 2003 and 2004. The U.S. Commission on

Ocean Policy was created by Congress. Its report is entitled, *An Ocean Blueprint for the 21st Century*, and supporting documents are available on the web at http://oceancommission.gov/. The Pew Oceans Commission was a broad-based private effort composed of leaders in conservation, government, marine sciences, and fisheries. Their reports are available at http://www.pewtrusts.org/our_work.aspx?category=130. Commissioners from these two initiatives have joined efforts to promote ocean governance reform in a group known as the Joint Ocean Commission. http://www.joint oceancommission.org/. Their joint recommendations are presented in a 2007 report, *An Agenda for Action: Moving Regional Ocean Governance from Theory to Practice*. All three of these organizations offer superb online resources for further research.

8. One of the U.S. Oceans Commission's recommendations was to divide decision making authority between the scientists and RFMC officials. In particular,

> Because of their knowledge of the fisheries and communities in their region, RFMC members are best suited to make decisions about allocation of the available harvest and other issues related to the operations of regional fisheries. However, scientific decisions are more appropriately made by the SSCs [Scientific and Statistical Committees] created to support the RFMCs. Scientific decisions include stock assessments and determinations of allowable biological catch—the maximum amount of fish that can be harvested without adversely affecting recruitment or other key biological components of the fish population.... The role of scientific information should be as strong as possible in fishery management and subject to the least possible political influence. For this reason, many fishery managers and analysts have recommended separating scientific assessment decisions from the more political allocation decisions. While not required by law, some RFMCs have already taken this step. For example, the North Pacific council has a history of setting harvest levels at or below the level recommended by its SSC. Many policy makers believe this practice is largely responsible for the successful management of the fisheries in that region.

U.S. OCEANS COMMISSION, AN OCEAN BLUEPRINT FOR THE 21ST CENTURY 277–278 (2004). The Pew Commission made a similar recommendation. What are the strongest arguments *against* this division of responsibilities?

The 2006 amendments to the FCMA added Section 302(h)(6), which provides that each FMC "shall ... develop annual catch limits for each of its managed fisheries that may not exceed the fishing level recommendations of its scientific and statistical committee or the peer review process established under subsection (g)." Does this fully respond to the concerns raised by the commissions?

9. The lack of adequate staffing for the Councils is a major concern. America's EEZ is 23% larger than the land mass of the United States. In contrast to the tens of thousands of local, county, state and federal land use managers, however, there are approximately 200 staffers on the Council in charge of developing plans to manage this vast area.

c. Consistency With National Standards

Any FMP, or regulation implementing a FMP, must be consistent with ten national standards set out in section 301 of the Act (the FCMA had established seven national standards; the Sustainable Fisheries Act of 1996 added three more, numbers 8–10 below). All FMPs "shall be consistent" with the following conservation and management measures.

(1) Conservation and management measures shall prevent overfishing while achieving, on a continuing basis, the optimum yield from each fishery for the United States fishing industry.

(2) Conservation and management measures shall be based upon the best scientific information available.

(3) To the extent practicable, an individual stock of fish shall be managed as a unit throughout its range, and interrelated stocks of fish shall be managed as a unit or in close coordination.

(4) Conservation and management measures shall not discriminate between residents of different States. If it becomes necessary to allocate or assign fishing privileges among various United States fishermen, such allocation shall be (A) fair and equitable to all such fishermen; (B) reasonably calculated to promote conservation; and (C) carried out in such manner that no particular individual, corporation, or other entity acquires an excessive share of such privileges.

(5) Conservation and management measures shall, where practicable, consider efficiency in the utilization of fishery resources; except that no such measure shall have economic allocation as its sole purpose.

(6) Conservation and management measures shall take into account and allow for variations among, and contingencies in, fisheries, fishery resources, and catches.

(7) Conservation and management measures shall, where practicable, minimize costs and avoid unnecessary duplication.

(8) Conservation and management measures shall, consistent with the conservation requirements of this act (including the prevention of overfishing and rebuilding of overfished stocks), take into account the importance of fishery resources to fishing communities by utilizing economic and social data that meet the requirements of paragraph (2), in order to (A) provide for the sustained participation of such communities, and (B) to the extent practicable, minimize adverse economic impacts on such communities.

(9) Conservation and management measures shall, to the extent practicable, (A) minimize bycatch and (B) to the extent bycatch cannot be avoided, minimize the mortality of such bycatch.

(10) Conservation and management measures shall, to the extent practicable, promote the safety of human life at sea.

It is not surprising that, in such a broad list of objectives, national standards are in potential conflict. In particular, the requirements of Standards 5, 7 and 8 to consider efficiency, minimize costs and protect fishing communities can run counter to the various conservation Standards. When FMPs and amendments are challenged in court, plaintiffs generally allege violation of several Standards. The sections below briefly describe the Standards most often relied on by litigants.

i. National Standard One: Prevent Overfishing and Achieve the "Optimum Yield"

While seemingly obvious, National Standard One's dual mandates to prevent overfishing and achieve the optimum yield have proven complicated in practice. Overfishing is defined as "a rate or level of fishing mortality that jeopardizes the capacity of a fishery to produce the maximum sustainable yield on a continuing basis." 16 U.S.C. § 1802(29). We have already described the concept of a maximum sustainable yield (MSY). It is "the largest average annual catch" that can be taken from a stock "over a significant period of time" under average environmental conditions. 50 C.F.R. § 602.11(d)(1). In simple terms, it's the greatest harvest that can be consistently caught year after year. We have also explained why setting the MSY is so difficult. Absent perfect knowledge, Stock Assessment Panels must rely on past catches, computer models, and observer data in estimating the size and structure of the fish population. As the implementing regulations make clear,

> Because MSY is a theoretical concept, its estimation in practice is conditional on the choice of an MSY control rule. In choosing an MSY control rule [i.e., calculation method], councils should be guided by the characteristics of the fishery, the FMP's objectives, and the best scientific information available.

50 C.F.R. § 600.310(C)(2)(i).

Once calculated, the MSY serves as a ceiling on the allowable catch. It is then adjusted *down* to determine the optimum yield (OY) for the fishery. The OY is defined as the harvest rate for a fishery or a particular species that will "provide the greatest overall benefit to the Nation." 16 U.S.C. § 1802(28)(A). The OY need not be set at a level that will return the stock to MSY levels within a year. Rather, it should return the stock to levels that can support the MSY over the longer term. Importantly, the Council's determination of the OY is explicitly *not* a scientific measure. The OY starts at the MSY for the fishery, and is then "reduced by any relevant social, economic, or ecological factor." 16 U.S.C. § 1802(28). Implementing regulations make clear that, in determining the greatest benefit to the nation, the values to be considered range from food production, recreational opportunities, and protection afforded to marine ecosystems to a viable fishing industry and ecotourism, among many others. While these values must be weighed and compared, courts have held this does not require a formal cost/benefit analysis. *See, e.g., Alaska Factory Trawler Ass'n v. Baldridge*, 831 F.2d 1456, 1460 (9th Cir. 1987); *Pacific Coast Fed'n of Fishermen's Ass'n v. Secretary of Commerce*, 494 F.Supp. 626, 631 (N.D.Cal. 1980).

The key point to understand is that determining the OY is a political rather than scientific process. While calculating the MSY in the face of data gaps maintains at least a *presumption* of scientific credibility, calculating the OY is explicitly a social and economic decision. Given that, it's not surprising that OY determinations are extremely contentious, with fishing interests generally pushing for an OY close to the MSY ceiling while conservation groups push for lower catch levels.

ii. National Standard Two: Base Conservation Measures on the Best Scientific Information

National Standard Two requires Councils and the Secretary of Commerce to base FMPs on the "best available scientific information." Since perfect information will never be available, this really is a measure of whether the "second best information" is adequate. In general, courts have shown deference to agencies in this regard. In *National Fisheries Institute v. Mosbacher*, for example, plaintiffs challenged the FMP for blue marlin and other billfish.

> The parties agree that these billfish migrate over such great distances and are so widely distributed—both inside and outside the EEZ—throughout the Atlantic Ocean, the Gulf of Mexico, and the Caribbean Sea that commercial and recreational fishermen rarely encounter billfish. Consequently, specific biological and quantitative data regarding the billfish resource are relatively scarce compared with information available for most other species of fish regulated under the Magnuson Act. * * *

> The plaintiffs criticize the quality of this evidence, arguing that it is inconclusive and not sufficient to justify the FMP. The record reveals that the Secretary and the Councils were aware of the limitations on their billfish stock data due to the inherent difficulty of obtaining absolutely precise information about these highly migratory, widely dispersed species of fish. However, the Magnuson Act does not force the Secretary and Councils to sit idly by, powerless to conserve and manage a fishery resource, simply because they are somewhat uncertain about the accuracy of relevant information. Instead, one of the Act's national standards requires that "conservation and management measures shall be based upon the best scientific information *available*." 16 U.S.C. § 1851(a)(2) (emphasis added); *see also* 50 C.F.R. § 602.12(b) (1987) (emphasis added) ("The fact that scientific information concerning a fishery is incomplete *does not* prevent the preparation and implementation of an FMP."). Consequently, the Court will not construe the Magnuson Act to tie the Secretary's hands and prevent him from conserving a given species of fish whenever its very nature prevents the collection of complete scientific information. The record before the Court sufficiently supports the Councils' and the Secretary's conclusion, based on the best scientific information available to them, that the billfish resource was overfished and in need of conservation.

732 F.Supp. 210, 212, 220 (D.D.C. 1990); *see also Northwest Environmental Defense Center v. Brennen*, 958 F.2d 930 (9th Cir. 1992) (rejecting a challenge to the Secretary's consideration of socioeconomic as well as biological factors). Despite the strong language of the court and similar holdings in other cases, a number of contrary holdings have ensured that Standard 2 remains a frequent basis of challenge to FMPs. *See, e.g., Hall v. Evans*, 165 F. Supp. 2d 114 (D.R.I. 2001) (court carefully examined the Council's "copious evidence" and determined it did not justify the gear restrictions); *Hadaja v. Evans*, 263 F.Supp.2d 346 (D.R.I. 2003) (court states that "hallway compromise" over permit eligibility not justified by scientific information collected after compromise had been reached).

QUESTIONS AND DISCUSSION

1. In practice, the desirability of basing catch levels on the MSY remains questionable. Consider the dueling poems below.

Here lies the concept MSY.
It advocated yields too high,
And didn't spell out how to slice the pie.
We bury it with best of wishes.
Especially on behalf of fishes.
We don't know yet what will take its
place.
But hope it's as good for the human
race.

Peter Larkin (1977)

Up springs MSY.
No, it didn't die.
It just metamorphosed.
Ahead of his time was Larkin,
To him we would always harken.
But MSY has a cause,
It's the focus of many laws.
Now MSY has found a new niche,
And all that's needed is to make the
pitch.

Pamela Maces (1999)

2. The regulations for calculating the OY instruct the Councils to deter-mine catch limits of greatest benefit to the nation by considering the values of food production, recreational opportunities, and protection afforded to marine ecosystems.

(i) The benefits of food production are derived from providing seafood to consumers, maintaining an economically viable fishery together with its attend-ant contributions to the national, regional, and local economies, and utilizing the capacity of the Nation's fishery resources to meet nutritional needs.

(ii) The benefits of recreational opportunities reflect the quality of both the recreational fishing experience and non-consumptive fishery uses such as ecotourism, fish watching, and recreational diving, and the contribution of recreational fishing to the national, regional, and local economies and food supplies.

(iii) The benefits of protection afforded to marine ecosystems are those result-ing from maintaining viable populations (including those of unexploited spe-cies), maintaining evolutionary and ecological processes (e.g., disturbance re-gimes, hydrological processes, nutrient cycles), maintaining the evolutionary potential of species and ecosystems, and accommodating human use.

50 C.F.R. § 600.310(f)(2). Which of these benefits potentially conflict with one another? What are the likely consequences of giving such a laundry list of goals to a fisheries manager? What are the consequences of giving it to a decisionmaking body dominated by fishing interests?

3. If one agrees that economic and social factors should be considered when setting quotas, then it seems unavoidable that determining the OY will require considerable discretion in balancing competing goals. Consider Oliver Houck's criticism of this discretion in the excerpt below.

The opaque quality of this standard should be readily apparent. The legislative history of the FCMA explains the use of OY by noting that condi-tions may necessitate driving a stock below sustainability, if only temporarily, for the benefit of other stocks or the ecosystem as a whole. Fair enough—thus far, the bottom line remains reasonably objective. The House Report continues, however, by explaining that OY also compels fishery managers to consider "the economic well-being of the commercial fishermen, the interests of recreational fishermen, and the welfare of the nation and its consumers." OY "will be a carefully defined deviation from MSY" in order to accommodate these interests. Exactly how one might arrive at a "carefully defined" departure from the consideration of such broad and open-ended interests is not explained; nor can it be. Pitted against the relentless pressure toward overuse that affects all public resources, from grass to timber to fisheries to water, OY provides no effective brake. * * *

A second and corollary lesson is that, no matter who makes decisions this difficult, they will not be made in favor of conservation without a firm, fact-based standard: law to apply. The only reason that restraints on fishing finally came to New England—despite a level of resource devastation patent even to the most casual observer and long clear to the NMFS and the New England Regional Fisheries Management Council—is that the Conservation Law Foundation of New England brought a lawsuit to require them. Even on the waffling standards of the FCMA, the Foundation was so likely to prevail that the process blinked.

Stepping back from these lessons, one can see an unsettling parallel between fisheries management and the emerging trend towards terrestrial ecosystem management. It rests in the relationship between the people-are-part-of-ecosystems approach of the new ecosystem guidelines, and the people-are-part-of-acceptable-yield tenet of OY. Biological diversity and ecosystem protection are, like fisheries, basically about yield. Once people's wants and desires become the standard for the harvest—whether the subject is timber, grass, watersheds or tuna—there is no standard at all. There is only a process that will continue to lead back to derelict timber towns in the Northern Rockies and the moribund docks of New Bedford, Massachusetts.

Oliver Houck, *On the Law of Biodiversity and Ecosystem Management,* 81 MINN. L. REV. 869, 950, 952–3 (1997). Houck's implication is that discretion in setting the OY will ensure it is very close to the MSY. Do you think economic and ecological concerns should *not* be considered in lowering the MSY? Is Houck being unrealistic to think the political process could produce a firm, fact-based standard? How could one set a politically acceptable standard that was "reasonably objective"?

4. Recall Standard One's requirement that "conservation and management measures shall prevent overfishing while achieving, on a continuing basis, the optimum yield from each fishery." Does the "shall" mandate mean that the FMC must immediately end overfishing of depleted stocks or can it adopt a plan to end overfishing gradually over a period of time? In *Oceana v. Evans,* 2005 WL 555416 (D.D.C. 2005), the court upheld the FMC's decision to phase in stricter fishing limits over time, stating that it "enable[ed] more fishermen to remain in business while stocks rebuild." Is it appropriate for the FMC (and the reviewing court) to consider the short-term economic impact of restrictions on the fishing industry? Is it inevitable? As Josh Eagle has observed,

> Such holdings are, in part, a product of the hybrid nature of the statute. Despite its clear emphasis on conservation, the post–1996 Magnuson–Stevens Act includes a substantial amount of language expressing Congress' desire to protect the fishing industry from unnecessary economic shocks.... While the language of particular provisions is clear, the statute as a whole delivers a mixed message.
>
> Court-crafted compromises probably also reflect the fact that the 1996 amendments represented a dramatic departure from the prior law in terms of conservation. Twenty-five years of lax regulation meant that, by 1996, many fisheries were severely overfished and that probably even more were overcapitalized. The combination of the strict restrictions necessary for rebuilding and the thin profit margins characteristic of over-capitalized fisheries is not a recipe for painless transition. Their decisions seem to indicate that courts recognize the existence of this situation.

Josh Eagle, *Domestic Fishery Management, in* OCEAN AND COASTAL LAW DESK BOOK (DON BAUR ET AL., EDS., 2008).

iii.   National Standard Eight: Consider the Impacts on Fishing Communities

National Standard 8 (NS–8) was added during the 1996 amendments. It requires the Secretary to "take into account the importance of fishery resources to fishing communities in order to provide for the sustained participation of such communities and . . . to the extent practicable, minimize adverse economic impacts on such communities." 16 U.S.C. § 1851 (a)(8).

> The Code of Federal Regulations provides a framework for analyzing how fishing communities are to be protected under NS–8. First, the FMP must examine the social and economic importance of the fishery to the communities affected by the FMP using both qualitative and quantitative information. Second, the FMP is to analyze the sustained participation of these communities within a particular fishery by analyzing the history, extent, and type of participation within a specific fishery. The third step in the FMP analysis is to "assess the likely positive and negative social and economic impacts of the alternative management measures, over both the short and long term, on fishing communities." This third step takes into consideration the consumptive and non-consumptive uses of the fishery resources. NS–8 is the most important of the national standards for protecting fishing communities that face restrictions as a result of necessary conservation measures.

E. Michael Linscheid, Comment, *Living to Fish, Fishing to Live: The Fishery Conservation and Management Act and Its Implications for Fishing–Dependent Communities*, 36 U.S.F. L. REV. 181, 190–192 (2001).

National Standard 8's mandate to take fishing communities into account is not absolute. It must also be "consistent with the conservation requirements of this Act (including the prevention of overfishing and rebuilding of overfishing stocks)." Nonetheless, a number of courts have relied on the standard to reject FMPs. The following case is an example. In 1993, NMFS (the prior name of NOAA Fisheries) began imposing flounder quotas to address a serious decline in stocks that had started in the 1980s. North Carolina fishing interests, which land the most flounder of any Atlantic state, had challenged NMFS every step of the way, arguing that millions of dollars in seafood revenue and hundreds of jobs were threatened. In *North Carolina Fisheries Association v. Daley*, plaintiffs successfully challenged the summer flounder fishery quotas issued by the Secretary of Commerce, which had been justified in part by the agency's economic analysis of the quota's impacts. The court's harsh critique of the Secretary's analysis provides an example of the potential power of National Standard 8.

NORTH CAROLINA FISHERIES ASSOCIATION V. DALEY,
27 F. Supp. 2d 650 (E.D. Va. 1998)

. . . The Secretary has undertaken an Economic Analysis and concludes that the agency has complied with National Standard 8. . . . [T]he Secretary used the number of North Carolina fishing vessels identified by principal port, home port or residence as the sole basis for determining adverse effects on North Carolina's fishing communities. Moreover, he considered the entire state of North Carolina as one fishing community. Under the initial 1997 quota, the

Economic Analysis found that the North Carolina quota suffered a 50% reduction. Whether by home port or by principal port, even the Economic Analysis stated that 55% of the North Carolina vessels were impacted by 5% or more. Moreover, even the Economic Analysis projected that 43% of the North Carolina vessels would experience revenue reductions of more than 25%.

Against the weight of this empirical information, the Economic Analysis nevertheless maintained that the 1997 quota regulations posed no threat to the sustained participation of North Carolina's fishing communities. The Economic Analysis surmised that North Carolina's fishing vessels are broadly disseminated. From that supposition, the Economic Analysis inferred that adverse impacts are widely dispersed among fishing communities. Therefore, even though vessels' revenue reductions are between 5% and 60%, the Economic Analysis surmised that there is no economic threat posed by the quota regulations. * * *

After reviewing the Secretary's Analysis, this Court finds that the Secretary has completely abdicated his responsibilities under the Magnuson Act. In the report, the Secretary's narrow methodology ignores every relevant fact except where North Carolina's fishing vessels are located. It gives no consideration to the population size of communities, the significance of the fishing industry on local economies, or to what even constitutes a fishing community. * * *

First of all, the Secretary's examination failed to take into account the population size of particular fishing communities.... On top of this, the Secretary failed to take into account supporting empirical information tending to show the importance of the fishing industry to the local economies of selected communities. In his report, ... the independent expert selected by the Secretary, agrees that the seafood industry must be considered in assessing the economic impacts on affected communities.... [T]he Analysis should have examined potential effects on processors, wholesalers, distributors, boat yards, gear shops, ice houses and other fishery-dependent industries. * * *

In light of the Magnuson Act's own definition, an analysis of impacts on fishing communities should have been grounded in a geographical context. In [the expert's] view, fishing communities are better defined on a county-by-county basis in order to capture "the economic impacts of the quota changes at the 'community' level." * * *

In his own defense, the Secretary argues that requiring the agency to collect and analyze detailed information of the kind requested would place an "undue burden" on agency resources. According to the Secretary, the agency cannot consider every hamlet situated along the eastern seaboard. Nonetheless, the Court must deem the Secretary's contentions to be unacceptable because they are simply untrue. With the advent of the Internet, the burden on administrative agencies to collect data of this kind is considerably lessened. If the Secretary's designees wished to collect population figures, for instance, a simple search on the Internet would have provided that information through the website of the United States Census Bureau. Certainly, the Secretary need not consider every fishing community remotely affected by his quota regulations. Yet where an examination is warranted, the Court has no authority to waive the Secretary's obligations under the Act.

The Secretary's responsibilities include undertaking a reasonable examination of his own empirical findings. The Secretary may not turn a blind eye to the mounting statistical evidence his own agency has compiled. Under the initial 1997 quota, the Secretary's Economic Analysis showed that over half of North Carolina vessels are impacted by 5% or more. The Analysis found that 43% of the vessels suffer revenue reductions of more than 25%. Under the July

1997 Quota Adjustment, the percentages are more alarming. The Analysis determined that at least one-third of North Carolina vessels are projected to suffer a loss of revenue of 50% or more. * * *

[T]he Secretary is mistaken in the belief that his own regulatory requirements override the statutory provisions under National Standard 8. Legal constraints on the Secretary's decision making emanate from the statute, not from the agency's own regulations. As a rejoinder, the Secretary maintains that his regulations conform to the goals of the Magnuson Act "to rebuild overfished fisheries, and to achieve the optimum yield from each fishery." Even so, the purposes of National Standard 8 do not concern fishery conservation in isolation. To the contrary, the express terms of National Standard 8 provide for a balancing of conservation interests against the economic rights of commercial fishermen and fishing communities.

* * * The so-called Economic Analysis ... entirely failed to consider the effect on fishing communities or small entities. It failed to consider the economics as it may have affected actual fishermen. It never considered profitability or costs of any kind. It merely discussed gross revenues on a state-wide basis.

[The Court found that the Secretary acted arbitrarily and capriciously in failing to provide any meaningful consideration to the economic effects on fishing communities. *See also Southern Offshore Fishing Ass'n v. Daley,* 995 F.Supp. 1411 (M.D. Fla. 1998) (holding that that the NMFS conducted an inadequate economic analysis under National Standard 8).]

---

iv. National Standard Nine: Minimize Bycatch and Minimize Bycatch Mortality

As discussed earlier in this chapter, it is nearly impossible to fish commercially without catching "non-target" species. In some fisheries, this bycatch is significant, creating concerns not only about wasting the fishery resource but also for the bycatch species themselves. The classic examples of the latter are efforts of animal rights and conservation groups to protect dolphin killed as by-catch in purse seine nets employed in the tuna fishery and endangered turtles killed by shrimp trawls. As discussed at page 565, *infra,* in the 1980s Congress responded to these concerns by effectively banning the use of purse seine nets in the tuna fishery and mandating the use of turtle excluder devices by shrimp trawls. These moves provoked opposition not only nationally but internationally because the restrictions hindered other nations from exporting shrimp and tuna into the lucrative United States market. Bycatch also frustrates establishment of the MSY and OY because it increases the uncertainty of fishing-related mortality.

With passage of the Sustainable Fisheries Act in 1996, Congress addressed the bycatch problem more broadly by adding National Standard 9 to the Magnuson Act and Required Provision 11 (mandating the creation of a standard bycatch reporting methodology). Beyond calling for minimization of bycatch and bycatch mortality to the extent practicable, Standard 9 does not call for a specific reduction rate or target. As such, it leaves a great deal of discretion to the Councils to determine what methods of bycatch reduction to mandate. Nonetheless, the standard can have teeth. In *Conservation Law Foundation, et al. v. Evans,* 209 F. Supp. 2d 1 (D.D.C., 2001), for example, environmental groups alleged that NMFS had failed to prevent overfishing and minimize bycatch along the New England coast. Following passage of the Sustainable Fisheries Act (SFA), the New England Fishery Management Council had continued to rely on fishermen logbooks and minimal at-sea federal observer coverage as its "standardized bycatch reporting methodology"—even though it was well known that over 90% of all fishermen failed to report their discards on their logbooks. NMFS argued that this satisfied its requirements under Standard 9. The Court disagreed.

> In short, the record shows that, after the SFA was enacted, defendants adopted no new measures to minimize bycatch and bycatch mortality in the groundfish fishery. Such an approach both ignores and frustrates the will of Congress. When it enacted the SFA, Congress made clear that it sought to "bring to a stop this inexcusable amount of waste." Had Congress been content with the status quo, it would not have included the bycatch provisions in the SFA. Defendants' failure to minimize bycatch and bycatch mortality is arbitrary, capricious, and contrary to law, and in violation of the SFA and APA. * * *

Id. at 15. *See also Pacific Marine Conservation Council v. Evans,* 200 F.Supp. 2d 1194 (N.D. Cal. 2002) (holding that the council failed to fully consider the practicability of comprehensive bycatch observer programs).

QUESTIONS AND DISCUSSION

1. Are you persuaded by the court's assertion in *North Carolina Fisheries Association v. Daley* that collecting and analyzing data on the impact on communities won't be overwhelming? The court notes that reliance on the internet and census bureau data will considerably lessen the burden, nor must every community be examined. Maybe so, but recall the court's direction that the economic analysis "should have examined potential effects on processors, wholesalers, distributors, boat yards, gear shops, ice houses and other fishery-dependent industries" in at least some of the affected communities. Is surfing the web likely to provide much help in gathering these data? Try, as a small test, to gather some of this information for the fishing community of Buxton, North Carolina. Do you think this raises the danger of blocking new management actions from "paralysis through analysis?"

2. When considering catch reductions to address overfishing, why should the short-term impact on the local community matter? This may sound like a harsh question, but if the size of the total catch must be reduced in the short term or risk the long-term decline in landings or even collapse of the commercial fishery, shouldn't that be the overwhelming factor? After all, as hard as the economic impact will be with reduced fishing quotas, surely it will be even harder in the future if the stocks continue to fall.

3. In addition to adding National Standard 8, the 1996 Sustainable Fisheries Act also mandated greater diversity by adding one Indian tribe representative to the Pacific Council. Native Americans are key players in fishery management, particularly in the Pacific Northwest and Alaska because of treaties granting traditional fishing rights. Fifty percent of the Klamath River's Chinook salmon, for example, are allocated to tribes. If the quotas for a fish stock have to be reduced to prevent overfishing, how should the reductions be allocated? Should they be reduced across the board as an equal percentage or should some groups, such as Indian tribes, be given special preference either because of their treaty rights, historic injustices, or dependence on the harvest for subsistence diet?

4. National Standard 5 states that "[c]onservation and management measures shall, where practicable, consider efficiency in the utilization of fishery resources; except that no such measure shall have economic allocation as its sole purpose." 16 U.S.C. § 1851(a)(5). The 1996 SFA changed this standard from requiring that the Secretary and Councils "promote" efficiency to instead requiring that they "consider" efficiency in developing FMPs. Section 50 C.F.R. § 600.330(e) elaborates on the meaning of an "economic allocation":

> (e) Economic allocation. This standard prohibits only those measures that distribute fishery resources among fishermen on the basis of economic factors alone, and that have economic allocation as their only purpose. Where conservation and management measures are recommended that would change the economic structure of the industry or the economic conditions under which the industry operates, the need for such measures must be justified in light of the biological, ecological, and social objectives of the FMP, as well as the economic objectives.

Whom does Standard 5 favor, small fishing boats or factory ships?

In *Hall v. Evans*, 165 F. Supp. 2d 114 (D.R.I. 2001), the plaintiffs argued that a gear differential provision of the monkfish FMP violated national Standard 5. The FMP provision differentiated between vessels that used trawl gear and those that did not—allowing trawlers to land up to 1,500 pounds tail weight of monkfish a day and non-trawlers to land only 300 pounds. The court wrote that:

> The parties disagree about whether or not economic allocation was the sole justification for the gear differential regulations. . . . [V]ery little in the Record supports the argument that anything other than economics prompted the gear differential. As already noted, defendants have not directed this court to a single piece of biological or ecological evidence supporting the gear differential. There was some discussion at oral argument by defense counsel that the day at sea trip limits for different gear types represent an equitable, pro rata reduction based on the level of participation of each gear type in the monkfish market. If this is the case, that would constitute a rationale for the regulations based in something other than economics alone: namely, fairness. But there is no evidence in the Record documenting the calculation of such an equitable, proportional reduction—we have only the bald-faced, unsupported assertions of defense counsel to stack against the standard posed by National Standard Five. As it stands now, therefore, the regulations do not comply with National Standard Five.

Id. at 142–43.

Assuming the MSY is being caught and the stock is not overfished, why shouldn't the Councils be prevented from using economic efficiency as the basis for quota allocations?

5. National Standard 4 provides that:

> Conservation measures shall not discriminate between residents of different states. If it becomes necessary to allocate or assign fishing privileges among the various United States fishermen, such allocation shall be (A) fair and equitable to all such fishermen; (B) reasonably calculated to promote conservation; and (C) carried out in such a manner that no particular individual, corporation, or other entity acquires an excessive share of such privileges.

In the case, *Ace Lobster v. Evans*, 165 F. Supp. 2d 148 (D.R.I. 2001), lobster fishers and business owners challenged lobster regulations that significantly limited the numbers of traps that could be set. In arguing that the regulations violated National Standard 4, plaintiffs alleged in their brief that:

> the initial reduction of traps in the offshore industry will affect only 20 trap vessels. The problem with this is the fact that 18 of these 20 are located in Rhode Island. This impact evidences the fact that the regulation adopted by NMFS discriminates between residents of different states.... The effect of the flat trap cap is not fair and equitable to all fishermen because there are certain fishermen who fish below the caps proposed that would not be impacted at all by the regulation. Clearly, this is not a fair and equitable distribution of fishing privileges.

While acknowledging this disparate impact, the court held that disparate impacts on state residents are permissible if they are rationally connected to achievement of the OY or FMP, and if the hardship imposed on one group is outweighed by the total benefits received by others. 165 F. Supp. 2d at 181 (*reversed* on separate grounds, 311 F.3d 109 (1st Cir. 2002)).

———

v. Conflicting Standards

As noted above, many of the National Standards conflict with one another. As the Ninth Circuit has observed, "There is a necessary tension, perhaps inconsistency, among these objectives [set out in the national standards]. The tension, for example, between fairness among fishermen, preventing overfishing, promoting efficiency, and avoiding unnecessary duplication, necessarily requires that each goal be sacrificed to some extent to meeting the others." *Alliance Against IFQs v. Brown*, 84 F.3d 343, 348–349 (9th Cir. 1996), *cert. denied*, 520 U.S. 1125 (1997). How, though, should courts decide which standards to favor over others?

As noted in the text, if the Council determines that the fishery is "overfished," the FMP must ensure the stock is restored to levels able to support the MSY "on a continuing basis." One might think, therefore, that if the stock is below the level able to support the MSY, serious catch restrictions must be introduced. Often, though, this is not the case. Imagine, for example, that the stock must have a population level at least 50% of the estimated carrying capacity to support the MSY and that stock levels are currently well below that (say, at 25% of carrying capacity). The Council may not determine this to be an "overfished" fishery if the FMP provides for a fishing regime that, in theory, will bring the stock over time back to 50% of the carrying capacity (and therefore the capacity to sustain a harvest level at the MSY). Even if it may take as many as 15 years or more to build the stock back up, the fishery is not technically "overfished."

This issue plays out in the following two cases (a district court decision and its appeal), which also provide a nice illustration of how courts treat fishery agency discretion and the tension between preserving economic opportunity and protecting the resource. As mentioned earlier, summer flounder quotas have been the source of serious controversy for close to a decade. In North Carolina, flounder is an important commercial fish. The fishing industry has long complained that restrictions are not justified by the data and harm the local economy. At the same time, environmental groups have blamed the government for not taking strong enough conservation measures. As you read the cases, pay attention to how different the proposed catch limits (called the TAL quota) of the scientific Monitoring Body, the Council, and NMFS are. What would explain the differences?

NATURAL RESOURCES DEFENSE COUNCIL v. WILLIAM M. DALEY, 62 F. Supp. 2d 102 (D.D.C. 1999)

JUDGE JUNE L. GREEN:

This controversy arises from a rule issued by Defendants on December 31, 1998, that sets the 1999 summer flounder fishing quota, limiting the total amount of fish by weight that can be landed (brought to shore). The ruling was intended to comply with implementing regulations for the summer flounder Fishery Management Plan ("FMP") which requires Defendant National Marine Fisheries Service ("NMFS") to establish certain fishing conservation measures for the upcoming year.

The summer flounder fishery of the Atlantic coast, managed jointly by the Atlantic States Marine Fisheries Commission and the Mid–Atlantic Fishery Management Council, developed a summer flounder FMP (approved by the NMFS) in consultation with the New England and South Atlantic Fisheries Management Councils. Pursuant to 50 C.F.R. § 648.100 and in response to amendments to the FMP adopted as a result of continued population declines, NMFS is required to implement measures for the fishing year to ensure that the target fishing mortality (F), as specified in the FMP, is not exceeded.

The target fishing mortality rate (F) is a statistic that expresses the depletion of the stock of fish attributable to fishermen (reduced by commercial and recreational harvesting), whether by capture or by discard of fatally wounded fish or otherwise, in a given year. Its calculation is designed to maximize the harvest under prevailing ecological conditions on a sustainable basis. Therefore, F serves as a threshold index or biological reference point; a failure to achieve (exceeding) the target fishing mortality rate results in overfishing and will detract from the FMP's mission to rebuild the stocks. The 1999 target fishing mortality rate (F) for summer flounder was calculated to be 0.24 and thus required that any catch quota for 1999 be set at a level that would ensure that the actual F does not exceed 0.24. [In other words, if the mortality rate from fishing (F) is greater than 0.24, too little of the stock population will remain to ensure the population can grow to a size that sustains the OY harvest level.]

In accordance with 50 C.F.R. § 648.100(c), NMFS is required to implement the fishing mortality rate (F) through annual quotas, which are specified in terms of the amount of summer flounder by weight that fishermen can bring to shore, also known as total allowable landings ("TAL"). The TAL quota must necessarily "assure that the applicable specified F will not be exceeded." 50

C.F.R. 648.100(c). After proper notice and comment, NMFS finalized a rule that established the 1999 TAL quota for summer flounder to be 18.52 million pounds. This TAL quota was calculated to have an 18 percent chance of achieving (not exceeding) the specified target mortality rate (F) of 0.24.

The final rule also included a measure recommending the states implement an incidental catch allocation plan intended to "improve the probability of achieving the target [mortality rate of 0.24]" and to "further reduce the overall mortality." There is no evidence in the record that suggests the incidental catch provision influenced or was a factor in the calculation of the 18 percent probability of achieving the target (F). The measure specified that the states allocate a portion of the commercial quota to incidental catch resources so that a coastwide incidental catch allocation of 32.7 percent of the total commercial TAL of 18.52 million pounds can be achieved. Although initially proposed as mandatory, NMFS has corrected the measure to be only voluntary by the states. In addition, NMFS recognizes that the extent to which a voluntary incidental catch allocation plan would enhance the probability of achieving the target (F) is unknown. * * *

Plaintiffs claim that the Defendants, in determining the 1999 TAL fishing quota for summer flounder, violated the express mandate of the FCMA, or more specifically, National Standard 1. The Court concludes, however, that as a matter of law, Defendants' decision was reasonable in light of the competing interests of the National Standards, and therefore, finds that Defendants are not in violation of FCMA's mandates, FMP, or NMFS regulations. * * *

Plaintiffs assert that Defendants violated National Standard 1 which states that "[c]onservation and management measures shall prevent overfishing while achieving, on a continuing basis, the optimum yield from each fishery for the United States fishing industry." Id. § 1851(a)(1) (emphasis added). In 1996, however, section 1851 was amended to include, inter alia, National Standard 8 which states:

> Conservation and management measures shall, consistent with the conservation requirements of this chapter (including the prevention of overfishing and rebuilding of overfished stocks), take into account the importance of fishery resources to fishing communities in order to (A) provide for the sustained participation of such communities, and (B) to the extent practicable, *minimize adverse economic impacts* on such communities.

16 U.S.C. § 1851(a)(8) (Supp.1999) (emphasis added). It is evident that the policies of National Standards 1 and 8 are in competition. Yet, the FCMA mandates that NMFS fishery management measures be "consistent with" both National Standards 1 and 8 (in addition to the other National Standards). Therefore, a balance must be made so that both National Standards can be reconciled when provisions such as a TAL quota are implemented.

Applying the first prong of the *Chevron* analysis reveals that Congress provides no insight as to how National Standards 1 and 8 are to be reconciled when determining TAL fishing quotas. Nor is there any set formula or formal procedure expressed in the statute with which to calculate the factors of National Standards 1 and 8 in the regulations or fishery management plan. Finally, the FCMA does not mandate any particular level of certainty that must be attained for the TAL quota to be "consistent" with National Standard 1. Insofar as the statute is silent on this balancing issue, this Court must move to the second prong of the *Chevron* analysis to determine whether NMFS' decision is based on a permissible construction of the statute.

In deciding whether NMFS has permissibly construed the FCMA in making its 1999 TAL quota ruling, the analysis focuses on whether Defendants' interpretation of the statutory scheme was reasonable, based on the facts included in the administrative record. In this case, NMFS was required to consider both National Standard 1 and 8 in determining the 1999 TAL quota. Plaintiffs argue that the 18 percent probability of achieving the target fishing mortality rate (F) indicates that the TAL quota is virtually certain to cause overfishing and that the figure is "not in accordance with" FCMA National Standard 1.

Plaintiffs' argument is not persuasive. NMFS chose to compromise between the recommendation made by the Summer Flounder Monitoring Committee, which proposed a 14.97 million pounds TAL (having 50 percent probability of preventing overfishing) and the recommendation made by the Mid–Atlantic Fishery Management Council, which proposed a 20.20 million pounds TAL (having 3 percent chance of preventing overfishing). Pursuant to regulations, NMFS considered the recommendations, as well as public comments, and reasonably selected a TAL quota with a greater likelihood of preventing overfishing compared to that recommended by the Mid–Atlantic Fishery Management Council. NMFS also calculated a percent allocation (32.7 percent) of the total commercial TAL to be set aside for incidental catch of summer flounder. The purpose of the incidental catch allocation plan was to "improve the probability of achieving the target" and "reduce the overall mortality." 63 FED.REG. at 72204. In effect, the voluntary incidental catch allocation plan in conjunction with NMFS' rejection of a TAL quota having a 3 percent chance of achieving (F) was an effort to allow the TAL quota to be consistent with the mandate of National Standard 1.

Although facially it may appear to Plaintiffs that the TAL quota constitutes an unreasonably low probability of meeting National Standard 1, the Court recognizes the responsibility of NMFS in giving due consideration to National Standard 8 [impacts on fishing communities] and the fact that neither the statute nor Congress explicitly quantifies the precise probability by which the TAL quota (or even a range of probabilities) should be deemed consistent with National Standard 1. Just as the Supreme Court was convinced in *Chevron,* this Court, too, is convinced that when an agency primarily responsible for administering legislation interprets the authorizing Congressional statute, the interpretation is not conducted in a "sterile textual vacuum, but in the context of implementing policy decisions in a technical and complex arena."

Congress has specifically delegated policy-making responsibilities to the executive departments to formulate political decisions that the courts are less qualified to make. Therefore, deference should be accorded to agencies whose task it is to resolve competing interests "which Congress itself inadvertently did not resolve, or intentionally left to the resolved by the agency charged with the administration of the statute in light of everyday realities."

In conclusion, Defendants fairly conceptualized the construction of the FCMA given the multitude of variables and interests.... Defendants' action did not violate the FMP or NMFS' own regulations. Therefore, this Court denies Plaintiffs' Motion for Summary Judgment and grants Defendants' Motion for Summary Judgment on this issue. * * *

———

NATURAL RESOURCES DEFENSE COUNCIL v. WILLIAM M. DALEY,
209 F.3d 747 (D.C. Cir. 2000)

HARRY T. EDWARDS, CHIEF JUDGE:

* * * As an initial matter, we reject the District Court's suggestion that there is a conflict between the Fishery Act's expressed commitments to conservation and to mitigating adverse economic impacts. *Compare* 16 U.S.C. § 1851(a)(1) (directing agency to "prevent overfishing" and ensure "the optimum yield from each fishery"); with *id.* § 1851(a)(8) (directing agency to "minimize adverse economic impacts" on fishing communities). The Government concedes, and we agree, that, under the Fishery Act, the Service must give priority to conservation measures. It is only when two different plans achieve similar conservation measures that the Service takes into consideration adverse economic consequences. This is confirmed both by the statute's plain language and the regulations issued pursuant to the statute. *See id.* § 1851(a)(8) (requiring fishery management plans, "consistent with the conservation requirements of this chapter," to take into account the effect of management plans on fishing communities) (emphasis added); 50 C.F.R. § 600.345(b)(1) (1999) ("[W]here two alternatives achieve similar conservation goals, the alternative that ... minimizes the adverse impacts on [fishing] communities would be the preferred alternative.") (emphasis added).

The real issue in this case is whether the 1999 TAL satisfied the conservation goals of the Fishery Act, the management plan, and the Service's regulations. In considering this question, it is important to recall that the Service operates under constraints from three different sources. First, the statute requires the Service to act both to "prevent overfishing" and to attain "optimum yield." [The other constraints are that the quota must be consistent with the FMP and that the quota must be necessary to ensure the specified overfishing level (F, explained below) will not be exceeded.] * * *

All of these constraints, then, collapse into an inquiry as to whether the Service's quota was "consistent with" and at the level "necessary to assure" the achievement of an F of 0.24, and whether it reasonably could be expected to "prevent" an F greater than 0.24. In other words, the question is whether the quota, as approved, sufficiently ensured that it would achieve an F of 0.24. Appellants argue that the quota violates applicable standards under both *Chevron* Step One and *Chevron* Step Two. * * *

Nonetheless, we still view this case as governed by *Chevron* Step Two. The statute does not prescribe a precise quota figure, so there is no plain meaning on this point. Rather, we must look to see whether the agency's disputed action reflects a reasonable and permissible construction of the statute. In light of what the statute does require, short of a specific quota figure, it is clear here that the Service's position fails the test of *Chevron* Step Two.

The 1999 quota is unreasonable, plain and simple. Government counsel conceded at oral argument that, to meet its statutory and regulatory mandate, the Service must have a "fairly high level of confidence that the quota it recommends will not result in an F greater than [the target F]." We agree. We also hold that, at the very least, this means that "to assure" the achievement of the target F, to "prevent overfishing," and to "be consistent with" the fishery management plan, the TAL must have had at least a 50% chance of attaining an F of 0.24. This is not a surprising result, because in related contexts, the Service has articulated precisely this standard. *See* National Marine Fisheries Service, Final Fishery Management Plan for Atlantic Tunas, Swordfish and Sharks, Vol. I, at 288 (April 1999) (concluding that the Service should choose management measures that have "*at least* a 50–percent confidence in target reference points," and when choosing between two alternatives with a greater than 50% probability, should choose the higher "unless there are strong reasons to do otherwise").

The disputed 1999 TAL had at most an 18% likelihood of achieving the target F. Viewed differently, it had at least an 82% chance of resulting in an F greater than the target F. Only in Superman Comics' Bizarro world, where reality is turned upside down, could the Service reasonably conclude that a measure that is at least four times as likely to fail as to succeed offers a "fairly high level of confidence."

Rather than argue that the quota alone provided enough assurance, the Service contends instead that two additional measures were adopted to increase the likelihood of achieving the target F. These measures were: (1) the provision relating to minimum mesh size; and (2) the recommendation that states voluntarily allocate a certain portion of the directed commercial fishery toward incidental catch. There is nothing in this record, however, to indicate that the proposals on mesh size and voluntary state action would improve the level of confidence so as to assure a reasonable likelihood of achieving the target F.

The Service's reliance on its provision regarding minimum mesh size for fishing nets is rather perplexing. We do not question the Service's rational conclusion that it is important to reduce the number of undersized flounder being captured, given recent observations, in a species with a potential 20 year life span, that very few adult fish survive past three years of age. At the time the 1999 TAL was proposed, however, the Service acknowledged that the mesh size provision's "benefits have not yet been analyzed." In fact, the Service apparently placed little stock in MAFMC's [Mid–Atlantic Marine Fisheries Council's] prediction that the minimum mesh size of 5.5 inches would reduce the number of undersized fish caught. In the final rule, the Service stated only that the minimum mesh size provision was "intended to address" discarding due to undersized catch; the Service acknowledged, however, that the mesh provision had "not been in operation long enough to determine if an adjustment to the mesh size is warranted." In short, there are no meaningful data (or even well-founded predictions) to support the assertion that a larger mesh size would reduce the number of undersized fish caught. And the Service conducted no analysis whatsoever to determine the likely effect of this measure on the probability of meeting the target F. There is certainly nothing in the record to indicate that the larger mesh size would make it likely that the TAL had at least a 50% chance of achieving the target F.

The Service's second recommendation, that states set aside a certain percentage of the commercial fishing quota for incidental catch instead of directed commercial catch, also fails to ameliorate the deficient 18% figure. First, in concluding that the TAL had an 18% likelihood of achieving the target F, the Service assumed that at least 10% of the commercial fishing quota would be allocated to incidental catch. When defending its proposal to allocate 32.7% of the commercial quota to incidental catch against a comment that instead suggested a 10% figure, the Service observed that "[a] 10–percent incidental catch allocation in combination with the 18.52–million [pound] ... TAL would result in a *less than 18–percent* probability of achieving the target F." Therefore, at least some of the incidental catch proposal's assumed positive effects were already accounted for in the 18% starting probability. The agency's "double-counting" here indicates that the Service *overstated* the positive effects that might come from the incidental catch recommendation.

The second, and more serious, flaw in the Service's reliance on its incidental catch proposal is that the proposal is merely a recommendation to the states, not a mandatory requirement. The Service initially assumed that the incidental catch proposal would be mandatory. When it was revised from a mandatory to voluntary proposal, however, the Service never assessed the impact of the change. Indeed, the record is conspicuously silent on this point, almost as if the change never occurred. At oral argument before this court, counsel for the Government asserted that the Service could reasonably conclude that the states would comply with the recommendation on incidental catch. But counsel conceded that there is absolutely no demonstrated history in the relations between the federal and state agencies to support such an assumption, and there are no present assurances from the states that they will comply with the Service's recommendation. Indeed, there is evidence in the record to suggest resistance from some states to the Service's incidental catch proposal (reflecting comments from Connecticut, Massachusetts, New Jersey, New York, North Carolina, and Virginia stating, in sum, that the incidental catch allocation was too high, unenforceable, and beyond the Service's power). We are left only with the Service's unsupported conclusion that the incidental catch provision "increases the probability of meeting the target F." This is manifestly insufficient.

As we noted at the outset of this opinion, the Service's quota for the 1999 summer flounder harvest so completely "diverges from any realistic meaning" of the Fishery Act that it cannot survive scrutiny under *Chevron* Step Two. The Service resists this result by suggesting that we owe deference to the agency's "scientific" judgments. While this may be so, we do not hear cases merely to rubber stamp agency actions. To play that role would be "tantamount to abdicating the judiciary's responsibility under the Administrative Procedure Act." *A.L. Pharma, Inc. v. Shalala*, 62 F.3d 1484, 1491 (D.C. Cir. 1995). The Service cannot rely on "reminders that its scientific determinations are entitled to deference" in the absence of reasoned analysis "to 'cogently explain'" why its additional recommended measures satisfied the Fishery Act's requirements. *Id.* at 1492 (quoting *Motor Vehicle Mfrs. Ass'n, Inc. v. State Farm Mut. Auto. Ins. Co.*, 463 U.S. 29, 48 (1983)). Indeed, we can divine no scientific judgment upon which the Service concluded that its measures would satisfy its statutory mandate.

Here, the adopted quota guaranteed only an 18% probability of achieving the principal conservation goal of the summer flounder fishery management plan. The Service offered neither analysis nor data to support its claim that the two additional measures aside from the quota would increase that assurance beyond the at–least–50% likelihood required by statute and regulation. * * * [W]e reverse the District Court's judgment and remand the case to the Service for further proceedings consistent with this opinion.

―――――――

QUESTIONS AND DISCUSSION

1. What do you make of the fact that none of the proposed quotas offered even close to a 50% chance of restoring the stocks to the MSY? While the NMFS figure only offered an 18% chance of success, that is still six times greater than the Council's quota, which offered a 3% chance of success. Put another way, the multi-stakeholder management body that is supposed to manage the Mid–Atlantic fishery for sustainable stocks approved a quota with a 97% chance of failure. Given the high level of controversy surrounding the flounder quotas over the years, the Council must surely have known their quota would be challenged. Assuming they were not living in "Bizarro world," how do you think the Council selected and justified its quota?

2. Judge Edwards dismisses out of hand the lower court's decision that National Standards One and Eight must be balanced. Why is this such a crazy idea? Recall the statement of the court in *North Carolina Fisheries Association v. Daley* that "the express terms of National Standard 8 provide for a balancing of conservation interests against the economic rights of commercial fishermen and fishing communities." Presumably the whole point of the Standards is that they often conflict and that balancing must occur.

3. Does the FCMA incorporate the precautionary principle? If so, which opinion excerpted above suggests this? Who has the burden of proof? How can a group of fishers ever get sufficient data to overcome the presumption against overfishing? Since NMFS has greater access to data and fisheries expertise, is it not more appropriate to place the burden on them to justify restrictions?

4. Given the unavoidable uncertainty in stock estimates and predictions over whether particular management measures will prove effective, do you think the court should grant a large degree of deference to the agency? If so, is there any way to articulate a meaningful standard over how much the court should defer to agency expert judgments, or is it necessarily a case-by-case determination?

Problem Exercise: Stock Rebuilding[1]

You are the law clerk for a federal appellate judge on the Ninth Circuit. On a Friday afternoon, you find the following half-written opinion and research questions left on your desk, with instructions to get the completed draft opinion back to the judge by Monday morning and the hand-written message, "Enjoy your weekend!"

> Congress enacted the Magnuson Act to "conserve and manage the fishery resources found off the coasts of the United States." 16 U.S.C. § 1801(b)(1). The Agency is charged with developing and implementing rebuilding plans for overfished fish species. § 1854. In 1996, Congress amended the Act by passing the Sustainable Fisheries Act ("SFA"). The SFA added new requirements to the Act to accelerate the rebuilding of overfished species.
>
> The Act, as amended by the SFA, contains a provision the proper interpretation of which is the main subject of this case. Section 1854 of the Act provides in part that when any species is found to be overfished, the Agency must approve a rebuilding plan that:
>
> (A) specifies a time period for rebuilding the fishery that shall—

1. This exercise is based on a 2005 case in the 9th circuit.

(i) be as short as possible, taking into account the status and biology of any over-fished stock of fish, the needs of fishing communities, ... and the interaction of the overfished stock of fish within the marine ecosystem; and

(ii) not exceed 10 years, except in cases where the biology of the stock of fish, [or] other environmental conditions ... dictate otherwise.

§ 1854(e)(4).

The Act also sets forth a series of "national standards" with which any rebuilding plans must be "consistent," and provides for the establishment of National Standards Guidelines ("NSGs") that must be "based on the national standards" for use in "assisting in the development of fishery management plans." §§ 1851(a), (b). The Act provides that NSGs "shall not have the force and effect of law." *Id.*

There is some ambiguity to § 1854(e)(4). Section 1854(e)(4)(A)(i) specifies that the rebuilding time period be as "short as possible," but also directs that the Agency "take into account the status and biology of [the] ... overfished stock" and "the needs of fishing communities." Section 1854(e)(4)(A)(ii) in turn plainly mandates that the rebuilding plan be no longer than 10 years, so long as biologically or environmentally possible. However, if it is not possible to rebuild within 10 years, the Act is not clear as to the exact limits on the length of the rebuilding period.

Seeking to clarify the proper interpretation of § 1854(e)(4), the Agency in 1997 sought "comment on whether or not it is correct in its interpretation that the duration of rebuilding programs should not be unspecified and, if so, what factors should be considered in determining that duration." *See* 62 Fed. Reg. 67,610 (Dec. 29, 1997). The Agency propounded two alternate interpretations for public comment: that whenever it would take longer than 10 years to rebuild an overfished species, either (1) all fishing of that species would be banned until the rebuilding was complete or (2) the Agency would set a ceiling on the rebuilding duration that would be reached by adding the shortest possible time to rebuild plus "one mean generation time ... based on the species' life-history characteristics." A "mean generation time" is a scientific term, not mentioned in the Act itself, measuring how long it will take for an average mature fish to be replaced by its offspring. After notice and comment, the Agency adopted the second interpretation in a NSG ("the 1998 NSG"). The Agency reasoned that:

> for stocks that will take more than 10 years to rebuild, the guidelines [adopted] impose an outside limit that is objective, measurable, and linked to the biology of the particular species.... The guidelines strike a balance between the Congressional directive to rebuild stocks as quickly as possible, and the desire ... to minimize adverse economic effects on fishing communities. For stocks that cannot be rebuilt within 10 years, the guideline allows flexibility in setting the rebuilding schedule beyond the no-fishing mortality period, but places a reasonable, species-specific cap on that flexibility by limiting the extension to one mean generation time.

63 Fed. Reg. 24,217 (May 1, 1998).

The 2008 and 2009 Limits for Darkblotched Rockfish

The Pacific Coast Groundfish Fishery is one of the fisheries the Agency oversees, covering the bottom-feeding fish species dwelling in the waters off the coasts of California, Oregon and Washington. In 2007, the Agency assessed the status of one species of Pacific groundfish within the fishery—darkblotched rockfish. It found that the species was at 22% of its unfished population level (its predicted level absent any fishing), and therefore concluded that the species was "overfished" within the meaning of the Act. The Agency further concluded that the species could be rebuilt in 10 years or less, triggering § 1854(e)(4)(A)(ii)'s mandatory requirement that the rebuilding take place within 10 years. The Agency then set a 130 metric ton "fishing harvest level," or quota, i.e., a set limit of dark-blotched rockfish that could be fished in 2008.

In 2008, the Agency updated its assessment of dark-blotched rockfish and concluded that it had significantly over-estimated the health of the species. The Agency now estimated that the species was almost twice as depleted as previously thought—it was at only 12% of its unfished population level. In the Agency's calculations, rebuilding therefore could not be accomplished within 10 years; the minimum period for rebuilding was now 14 years.

This increased rebuilding time meant, by necessity, that the rebuilding plan was no longer limited by § 1854(e)(4)(A)(ii)'s mandatory 10–year cap; instead, the only applicable statutory time limit was § 1854(e)(4)(A)(i)'s command that the rebuilding period be "as short as possible." Further, according to the interpretation of the Act set forth in the 1998 NSG, the revised minimum rebuilding period triggered a new ceiling that was the 14–year period *plus* "one mean generation time," which in the case of the long-lived dark-blotched rockfish was 33 years. The Agency, in short, switched from operating under the statutory constraint of 10 years rebuilding time to a new constraint, dictated by the 1998 NSG, of 47 years. The Agency then set a "target" rebuilding time of 34 years, and in accordance with this target, raised the fishing level harvest for 2009 from the previous year's 130 metric tons to 168 metric tons.

NRDC brought suit alleging that the new quota violated the Act and the Administrative Procedure Act. The district court concluded that the quota violated none of these statutes and granted summary judgment for the Agency. We now review this case on appeal. * * *

- Under *Chevron* analysis, how should the court treat the 1998 NSG?
  - How can the issue be settled at Step 1 of *Chevron* analysis, which indicates that when congressional intent is clear, no deference to the agency is necessary?
  - If settled at Step 2 of *Chevron* analysis, where is the statute ambiguous and is the 1998 NSG a reasonable agency interpretation?
- How is the holding of *NRDC v. Daley* relevant to this decision?
- Which of the two proposed National Standard Guidelines best reflect the text of § 1854(e)(4) and the FCMA?
- Should the court uphold or reverse the district court's decision that the quota does not violate the FCMA or APA? If you recommend reversal, what is the basis for this decision?

---

d. *Ecosystem Management*

Despite the FCMA's requirement in National Standard 3 to manage interrelated stocks of fish "as a unit or in close coordination," fisheries management has traditionally been quite narrow, focusing on the population dynamics of a specific, commercially fished stock. Those FMPs that do focus on species assemblages, moreover, tend to focus on those species that are commercially significant or that are taken by particular gear. This approach risks ignoring species that, despite being commercially unimportant, remain quite important to the overall marine ecosystem.

Once a fishery has been depleted, fishers quickly begin targeting "new fisheries" and begin to overfish them. Indeed, in New England, fishery managers encouraged fishermen to shift to new fisheries after traditional cod, haddock and flounder species were overfished. Just a few years later, these "new fisheries" had also become overfished due to unregulated fishing. Most recently, New England fishery managers are encouraging fishermen to target herring. This serial overfishing is part of a phenomenon known as "fishing down the food web." The problems with such an approach are obvious. Depleting one population also often affects other populations because of predator-prey relationships. Marine biologists have suggested, for example, that overfishing and removal of oyster beds led to the explosion of comb jellies in the Chesapeake Bay. Fishing gear for some stocks can degrade habitat and drive down other stocks. The use of bottom trawls and clam dredges has been particularly controversial in this regard. An open-mouthed net is dragged along the bottom of the seabed. Held down by heavy steel weights, the trawls have large wheels (commonly called "roller" or "rockhopper" gear) to ride over boulders and coral and avoid snagging the net. Trawls are dragged for miles across the bottom, filling up with thousands of pounds of marine life, rocks, and mud. Environmental groups have denounced the use of trawls, calling it "ocean floor clear-cutting." As the Earth Island Institute describes below, focusing simply on the tonnage of groundfish catch misses almost completely the other effects of trawling.

> With the possible exception of agriculture, we doubt that any other human activity physically disturbs the biosphere to this degree. An activity that severely disturbs an area of seabed each year as large as Brazil, the Congo, and India combined must affect benthic ecosystems on both local and global scales. Like clear-cutting, use of mobile fishing gear converts ecosystems to domination by disturbance-tolerant opportunistic species. In general, trawling undermines fisheries for species that benefit from complex benthic structure. For fishes that do not need benthic structure, some trawling is likely to increase their populations by encouraging opportunistic prey species or reducing disturbance-intolerant competitors. A terrestrial equivalent is the change in animal species when virgin forest is converted for grazing. Trawling could prevent recovery of some diminished fish stocks, such as Georges Bank and Grand Banks Atlantic cod, but it can benefit fisheries for some other species. The sea's equivalents of ancient forests are becoming cattle pastures.

Elliot Norse & Les Watling, *Clearcutting the Ocean Floor*, 14 EARTH ISLAND JOURNAL (Summer 1999). For a remarkable video on the impact of trawls, *see* the Chapter 5 section on the casebook website.

What a range of commentators have called for, then, is a shift from single-species management to greater focus on habitat, species assemblages, and ecosystems. A great deal has been written on ecosystem-based fisheries management, with the many definitions and concepts coalescing around the need to consider complex interactions and interdependencies in a fishery. The Sustainable Fisheries Act required the creation of an Ecosystem Principles Advisory Panel to advise Congress on how best to apply ecosystem principles in fishery management. The Panel concluded that an ecosystem-based approach should

> require managers to consider all interactions that a target fish stock has with predators, competitors, and prey species; the effects of weather and climate on fisheries biology and ecology; the complex interactions between fishes and their habitat; and the effects of fishing on fish stocks and their habitat.

Ecosystem Principles Advisory Panel, *Ecosystem–Based Fishery Management: A Report to Congress,* Nov. 1998, *available at* http://www.nmfs.noaa.gov/sfa/EPAPrpt.pdf, at 1.

The Sustainable Fisheries Act's amendments to the FCMA required Fishery Management Plans to include "readily available information regarding the significance of habitat to the fishery and assessment as to the effects which changes to that habitat may have upon the fishery." 16 U.S.C. § 1853(a)(7) (1986). The amendments further required Councils to "describe and identify *essential fish habitat* for the fishery"—defined as those waters and substrate necessary to fish for spawning, breeding, feeding, or growth to maturity. In drafting FMPs, managers must assess the adverse effects that fishing activities may have on essential fish habitat (EFH) and ensure that steps are taken to "prevent, mitigate, or minimize any adverse effects from fishing, to the extent practicable" including "individual, cumulative, or synergistic consequences of actions." 50 C.F.R. 600.815. If a Council determines that a fishing activity may have a harmful effect on the EFH, it can "adopt any new measures that are necessary and practicable, . . . [taking into account] the nature and extent of the adverse effect on EFH and the long and short-term costs and benefits of potential management measures to EFH, associated fisheries, and the nation, consistent with national standard 7."

With little data to identify truly essential fish habitat, RFMCs have instead used a broad brush to identify EFH. As the U.S. Ocean Commission concluded,

> For example, in the case of Atlantic halibut, the New England RFMC designated the entire Gulf of Maine and almost all of Georges Bank as essential. The North Pacific council designated almost the entire EEZ below the Arctic Circle as essential for one species or another. But when everything is special, nothing is. The current methods have resulted in the designation of so much habitat that the original purpose of identifying areas that deserve focused attention has been lost.

> Perhaps in recognition of this, NMFS designated a subset of EFH called "habitat areas of particular concern." These areas were defined in 2002 NMFS regulations as "discrete areas within essential fish habitat that either play especially important ecological roles in the life cycles of federally managed fish species or are especially vulnerable to degradation from fishing or other human activities." Less than one percent of the area initially designated as EFH has been further characterized as habitat areas of particular concern.

U.S. OCEANS COMMISSION, AN OCEAN BLUEPRINT FOR THE 21ST CENTURY 297 (2004)

QUESTIONS AND DISCUSSION

1. The EFH provisions require all federal agencies to "consult with the Secretary with respect to any action authorized, funded, or undertaken, or proposed to be authorized, funded, or undertaken, by any agency that may adversely affect any essential fish habitat under this Act." 16 U.S.C. 1855(b)(2). The requirement for consultation is strikingly similar to Section 7 of the Endangered Species Act (ESA, page 369). While the ESA further requires that each agency insures that its actions do not jeopardize the continued existence of the endangered species or adversely modify its habitat, the FCMA is merely hortatory. If the Secretary finds that an action would adversely affect the essential fish habitat, "the Secretary shall recommend ... measures that *can be taken* by such an agency to conserve such habitat." 16 U.S.C. 1855(b)(4)(A) (emphasis added). There is no requirement that the agency follow these recommendations and hence little opportunity for citizen suits to enforce the law's requirements beyond ensuring the procedural steps were followed. In this respect, despite the similarity in language with the ESA, the essential fish habitat consultation provisions more closely resemble the procedural analysis of the National Environmental Policy Act (NEPA) and its obligation that agencies consider the environmental impacts of their activities. Why didn't the EFH drafters completely follow Section 7 of the ESA?

2. R. Edward Grumbine has conducted a thorough survey of the ecosystem management approach and concluded after "thousands of hours of discussion, and significant first attempts at implementation" that the term ecosystem management was "still being 'perceived by many as a buzzword'—a new and slippery concept that contending interests in resource exploitation and management (and also scholars in natural science, public policy, and law) were busy trying to capture on their own various terms." Harry N. Scheiber, *From Science to Law to Politics: An Historical View of the Ecosystem Idea and its Effect on Resource Management,* 24 ECOLOGY L. Q. 631, 633 (1997).

In creating an EFH, the FMC must gather a range of data for each managed species, including:

- the geographic range and habitat requirements by life stage, the distribution and characteristics of those habitats, and current and historic stock size as it affects occurrence in available habitats ...

- patterns of temporal and spatial variation in the distribution of each major life stage ...

- environmental and habitat variables that control or limit distribution, abundance, reproduction, growth, survival, and productivity of the managed species ...

50 C.F.R 600.815. Do you think the data-intensive requirements of the EFH provisions will give meaning to what Scheiber argues has otherwise

been a largely empty and politicized term, or are the information gathering requirements so unrealistic that little action will be taken?

3. Designation of EFH and other area restrictions have been extremely contentious. Consider, for example, the article below from the trade magazine, *National Fisherman.*

> This summer, for instance, even as George Clooney was riding the Andrea Gail's outriggers across the silver screen like Slim Pickens riding an A-bomb [in the movie, A Perfect Storm], a federal judge in Seattle was writing an order banning trawling in huge areas of the Bering Sea and the Gulf of Alaska. The court's objective? Protect the diet of Steller sea lions.

> U.S. District Court Judge Thomas Zilly's July order affected Pollock, cod and shallow-water flatfish grounds; and if it stands, dollar losses could run into the hundreds of millions for the industry and communities dependent on it. Zilly's order won't stop Alaska fishermen from working. But it does mean many of them will have to venture further offshore to steer clear of Steller rookeries and haulouts.

> "We're coming into the fall ... the bad weather," says Kodiak fisherman Doug Hoedel. "People are going to be venturing farther offshore to find these fish. You get offshore in a 50–foot vessel, you're just praying you can get back home." Hoedel says gale and storm warnings are "the norm" in fall and winter off Alaska. "A 60–foot boat being forced to fish 20 miles offshore is like going on a suicide mission," Laine Welch, a columnist for the *Kodiak Daily Mirror*, wrote in a July 24 column in response to Zilly's ruling.

> The ruling designates more than 100 sea lion rookeries and haulouts in the Bering Sea and the Gulf of Alaska—as well as waters within 20 miles of them—off limits to trawling. The closed areas are vast and sometimes overlapping. "It's a disaster," Hoedel says. "I don't know how to sum it all up. It's come to the point where they are taking an animal over a human being." Hodel believes the Steller sea lion issue gave the industry's opponents a place to hang their hats. "That was just a crutch, or an excuse to put fishing out of business," he says. "They're not happy until everybody's out of business."

> The Alaska groundfish closure is a formidable example of a heightened focus on habitat protection. However, it is by no means the only one; and as fishing effort comes under control, habitat issues are supplanting abundance concerns as the No. 1 challenge to the industry. From the Gulf of Maine to the Gulf of Mexico to the middle of the Pacific Ocean, parks, protected areas, sanctuaries and essential fish habitat considerations are poised to change the way fisherman operate, regardless of the health of their targeted species. * * *

> Bob Jones, executive director of the Southeastern Fisheries Association, contends that recreational fishing groups are using marine protected areas and other habitat issues to try to destroy the commercial fishing business. "I think it's an ongoing, articulated program," he says. "There are efforts to finish the cultural genocide that's already begun." Two groups in particular stand out, Jones says. "The Recreational Fishing Alliance would be No. 1. The CCA would be No. 2," he says, referring to the Coastal Conservation Association. "they've spread like a cancer from Texas all the way to Maine." The alliance has blamed "government-sanctioned, 'search-and-destroy'" commercial fishing for nationwide "overexploited and nearly collapsed" fisheries.

The Essential Issue, 81 NATIONAL FISHERMAN 36 (Nov. 2000).

CASE STUDY: THE RED SNAPPER FISHERY*

INTRODUCTION

It's January 1998, and you are the regional administrator for the southeast regional office of NMFS, the Department of Commerce agency responsible for regulating marine fishing. Your job is far from pleasant. Last year, you had to close the overfished red snapper fishery in the Gulf of Mexico to commercial fishers after only 73 days, the second, shortest commercial fishing season ever for red snappers. Moreover, for the first time ever, you had to close the fishery to recreational fishers before the end of the year. These actions were far from popular in a region where reef fish constitute the third most valuable fishery ($40 million annually in revenue, surpassed only by crab/oyster and shrimp fisheries), where recreational saltwater fishing contributes $7 billion annually to the local economy, and where December is one of the busiest recreational seasons. Yet you have no doubt that these actions were necessary if the red snapper fishery is to be restored.

In the Gulf coast fishery, red snapper has historically been the most valuable species. But its contribution to the value of the commercial Gulf fishery declined from 93 percent in 1970 to 36 percent in 1995. Scientists link the decline of the fishery to overfishing, loss of juvenile red snapper as shrimp trawler bycatch, and illegal fishing and fish sales. Despite these problems, red snapper remains a very popular sport fish for both private recreational anglers and charter boats and headboats.

The Gulf of Mexico Fishery Management Council ("Gulf Council"), the agency responsible under federal law for developing management plans for Gulf coast fisheries, has tried a variety of approaches to managing the red snapper fishery since the early '80s, in an attempt to develop a sustainable fishery with optimum annual yields. But past and existing management approaches appear to be inadequate. Annual commercial red snapper landings declined from over 10 million pounds in the 1960's to less than 6 million pounds in the 1980's. Since 1990, the Gulf Council has capped annual commercial red snapper landings at 2.04 to 4.65 million pounds, in an effort to allow the fishery to replenish itself. Scientific advisors to the Gulf Council currently estimate that under the existing fishery management plan, however, the red snapper fishery will not reach a sustainable level until 2019, *if then*.

You are faced with the question of what to do next. Although scientists believe that the total catch must be further reduced to save the fishery, the Gulf Council recently voted to use the same quota as last year. And you are

---

* This case was prepared by Mary Decker, under the editorial guidance of Barton H. ('Buzz') Thompson, Jr., Robert E. Paradise Professor of Natural Resource Law, Stanford Law School, as a basis for classroom discussion rather than to illustrate either effective or ineffective handling of an environmental matter. Some or all of the characters or events may have been fictionalized for peda-

gogical purposes. Copyright © 1998 by the Board of Trustees of the Leland Stanford Jr. University. The casebook authors are grateful for permission from Stanford's Environment and Natural Resources Law Program to reproduce this abridged case study. To access the background exhibits, please visit the case study website at http://www.law.stanford.edu/casestudies.

far from convinced that the Council is willing to adopt the tough measures needed to reduce fishing.

The Gulf Council is responsible under § 1851(a) of the Act for drawing up FMPs for fisheries in the Gulf of Mexico. *See* Figure 1. To date, the Gulf Council has developed FMPs for a number of Gulf fisheries including coastal pelagics (such as King mackerel & Spanish mackerel), reef fish (such as Red snapper, Vermillion snapper, and Red grouper), other varied fish (such as Red drum and Gulf butterfish), shrimp, and Spiny lobster. Exhibit C contains an overview of the Gulf of Mexico fishery that is excerpted from a recent report prepared by the Natural Resources Defense Council.

FIG. 1 COMMERCIAL AND RECREATIONAL RED SNAPPER FISHING GROUNDS

A BRIEF OVERVIEW OF THE RED SNAPPER FISHERY

Red snapper (*Lutjanus campechanus,* shown below) are sedentary reef fish that can live more than 50 years. The snapper gets its name from its habit of rising to the surface and snapping at bare hooks or whatever is offered. Fishermen catch red snapper in coastal reef areas, usually 15 to 20 miles offshore. Recreational charter boat and headboat expeditions usually last at least 12 hours, and are often overnight excursions. Much of the time on the charter boats and headboats is spent getting to and from the reef fishing areas, which can be as much as 50 miles off the coast. To catch red snapper, fishermen use baited hooks and lines on electric and hydraulic reels. Each line may hold two to forty hooks. Some commercial fishermen claim that in a good fishing spot, snapper will bite on all the exposed hooks within seconds.

In 1984, the Gulf Council determined that the red snapper fishery was "slightly overfished" and imposed a minimum size limit on catch and restrictions on gear. The Council expected that these initial regulatory measures would lead to noticeable stock improvements within a year. After assessing the fishing stock again, however, the Gulf Council concluded in 1988 that the red snapper fishery was "significantly overfished" and that current harvest levels could not be sustained.

Scientists all agree that the red snapper fishery remains overfished. According to a 1995 study by one scientist at the National Marine Fisheries

Southeast Fisheries Science Center, the red snapper fishery suffers from both recruitment overfishing and growth overfishing. The former results when fishing so reduces adult stocks and egg production that the fish population may not be able to reproduce itself; growth overfishing results when so many small fish are caught that the population shifts toward smaller fish. Except in 1989, recruitment (measured by the number of postlarval fish survivors) has been poor since 1981. The mean size of red snappers landed in Florida has decreased approximately a third from about 24 inches to less than 18 inches.

For regulatory purposes, the health of a fishery often is measured by its "spawning potential ratio" or SPR, the ratio of the number of eggs that can be produced by an average female over its lifetime under current fishing conditions to the number that could be produced by an average female if there were no fishing allowed. The target SPR for the red snapper fishery is 20%. By contrast, the NMFS in 1997 estimated that the red snapper fishery currently has a SPR of only 3 percent, and some scientists believe that the SPR is as low as 0.4%. According to NMFS predictions, current regulatory policies will return the fishery to a 20% SPR by the year 2019.

Most commercial and recreational fishers, as well as many members of the Gulf Council, do not share the pessimism of these numbers. Many fishers report encountering more and larger red snappers than in prior years. These fishers question the accuracy of the scientific models. Recent scientific studies also shows an improvement in recruitment, lending a degree of credibility to the fishers' perceptions. The "recruitment index" (which measures the number of age 1 fish entering the fishery each year) has risen from 2.96 in 1991 to 7.56 in 1996. And a recent stock assessment that attempted to calculate the total weight of all red snapper in the Gulf suggested that "red snapper biomass" might be six to ten times higher than it stood in 1990.

RED SNAPPER QUOTAS AND LANDINGS

In the 1990's, the Gulf Council began establishing an annual total allowable catch ("TAC") that represents the amount of fish that can be caught by all fishermen in the red snapper fishery. Based on historical data from 1979 (when recreational fishing survey data was first collected) through 1987, the Gulf Council allocated 51% of the TAC to the commercial sector and 49% to the recreational sector. Using historical landing data and real-time data, the NMFS projects the date on which the commercial fishing quota will be met and closes the commercial red snapper season on that date. As shown in Figure 2, the commercial fishing season since 1991 has lasted from a minimum of 52 days (in 1995) to a maximum of 236 days (in 1992). Prior to 1997, the Gulf Council did not try to enforce the recreational quota by limiting the recreational season; the recreational red snapper fishing season was permitted to operate year-round. In 1997, however, the NMFS closed the recreational red snapper fishing season on November 27 when the NMFS projected that the annual recreational quota had been met.

FIG. 2 COMMERCIAL RED SNAPPER HARVEST (IN MILLIONS OF POUNDS)

YEAR	Commercial Quota	Commercial Harvest	Days Open (# + # = split season)
1990	3.1	2.66	365
1991	2.04	2.23	236
1992	2.04	3.14	52 + 42
1993	3.06	3.45	104
1994	3.06	3.12	78
1995	3.06	2.95	50 + 2
1996	4.65	4.40	64 + 13
1997	4.65	4.68	53 + 20

As shown in Figure 3 below, the recreational fishermen have often dramatically exceeded their annual allocations; while doing a better job of compliance, the commercial fishermen also have often exceeded their quotas, with the net results shown in Figure 4. Pre–1990 harvest data is set forth in attached Exhibit B. Recreational red snapper harvest data is an estimate, based in part on the number of individual licenses issued, records of fish caught based on headboat log books, and dockside surveys of charter boat passengers and operators. (Headboats may carry 30–40 individuals out to the reef fishing areas; each passenger pays an individual fee. Charter boats are smaller; they usually carry six to ten individuals and charge a flat fee.) In comparison to recreational harvest data, commercial data is based on licensed fish dealer records.

FIG. 3 RECREATIONAL RED SNAPPER HARVEST (IN MILLIONS OF POUNDS)

YEAR	Recreational Allocation	Recreational Harvest
1990	No specified allocation	1.28
1991	1.96	1.28
1992	1.96	3.71
1993	2.94	5.91
1994	2.94	5.24
1995	2.94	4.18
1996	4.47	4.21
1997	4.47	5.73 (close date: 11/27/97)

FIG. 4 OVERALL RED SNAPPER HARVEST (IN MILLIONS OF POUNDS)

YEAR	TAC	Total Directed Harvest
1990	no specified TAC	3.94
1991	4.0	4.31
1992	4.0, plus emergency season	6.95
1993	6.0	9.36
1994	6.0	8.36
1995	6.0	7.13
1996	9.12	8.61
1997	9.12	10.41

The landing records, however, may not tell the whole story. Many experts believe that significant unreported red snapper fishing takes place, and that current surveillance by state agency enforcement officials, the U.S. Coast Guard, and the NMFS is inadequate to detect and stop illegal fishing by American and foreign fishing boats. Though red snapper dealers are required to be licensed and to keep records of their purchases from permitted reef fishing vessels, due to lack of enforcement personnel, no structured dealer enforcement program currently exists. While enforcement officials respond to tips and complaints regarding dealers that may be operating illegally, resulting in an occasional sting operation, most enforcement takes place through spot checks of vessels at sea for compliance with regulations. No on-boat observers are used. Identifying and verifying violations is challenging. In most of the Gulf states, recreational red snapper fishing is allowed year-round in state waters zero to three miles from shore. Enforcement authorities may find it difficult to prove that red snapper was caught illegally in federal waters unless the fishermen are literally caught "in the act." Commercial fishermen may also start fishing for red snapper a few hours (or days) before the federal season opens. The first day of the season historically has the most recorded landings, and some boats return to port with full loads just a short time after the season opens at noon.

Despite the enforcement difficulties, some successful enforcement actions have been taken. In June 1998, a federal district court in Texas sentenced a Louisiana seafood company owner to 18 months in federal prison, after the owner pled guilty to trafficking in out-of-season red snapper during 1995. The owner had purchased 9,000 pounds of red snapper for resale. When the government auctioned off the illegal snapper, the fish brought more than $27,000.

THE SHRIMP BYCATCH PROBLEM

Shrimp trawlers capture a significant amount of red snapper as bycatch. Some scientists predict that the shrimp bycatch will adversely impact the long term recovery of the red snapper fishery more than overfishing by commercial or recreational fishermen. The NMFS estimates that the current ratio of finfish bycatch to harvested shrimp is 4:1 by weight. The Gulf coast shrimp bycatch includes an estimated 34 million red snappers annually, most of them juveniles, or about 2.2 million pounds. Most shrimpers throw their bycatch back into the water, and therefore the bycatch does not appear on landing reports. An estimated ninety percent of the red snapper caught by shrimp trawlers as bycatch is dead or will die.

Many recreational and commercial red snapper fishermen object to red snapper fishing restrictions and early closures of their fishing seasons, while shrimp trawlers continue to pose a significant threat to the red snapper fishery's recovery. To address this problem, the Gulf Council has considered and rejected various fishery management techniques including seasonal shrimping closures and restriction of shrimping in specified areas. Biologists have concluded that these approaches would not significantly reduce bycatch. Shrimpers have also strongly resisted any attempt to limit shrimper licenses.

A BRIEF HISTORY OF RED SNAPPER FISHERY MANAGEMENT

The Gulf Council began to regulate the red snapper fishery in the Gulf of Mexico in 1984 with its adoption of the "Fishery Management Plan for the Reef Fish Resources of the Gulf of Mexico." Figure 5 on page 525 summarizes the major fishery management approaches adopted to regulate the commercial red snapper fishery in the Gulf of Mexico (source: *Managing the Gulf of Mexico Commercial Red Snapper Fishery* by P. Baker, F. Cox, and P. Emerson, January 27,1998 (GMFMC 1997)).

THE COMMERCIAL DERBY SYSTEM: ON YOUR MARK . . . GET SET . . . GO!

Commercial fishers of red snapper have faced the greatest regulatory restrictions. Since 1984, the Gulf Council has set minimum size limits (initially 12 inches and now 15 inches). In 1990, the Gulf Council set the first annual commercial fishing quota of 3.1 million pounds. Fishing was so bad that year, however, that commercial fishermen landed only 2.66 million pounds. Even so, with the imposition of a commercial fishing quota, commercial fishermen raced to the reefs to catch as much fish as possible as soon as the season opened.

The Gulf Council also required in 1990 that each commercial reef fishing vessel obtain a reef fish permit in order to fish for red snappers. To get a reef permit, a vessel owner or operator must prove that at least 50% of their earned income is derived from commercial reef fishing. The Council placed a moratorium on new reef permits in 1992, lasting until the year 2000.

Though red snapper fish prices had been rising steadily since the mid–1960s, during 1990 to 1994 prices fell from over \$2.00 per pound to under \$1.50, a drop attributed at least in part to this derby system in which fishermen landed massive quantities of red snapper during a short open season. Prior to the derby, red snapper fishing had been relatively uniform throughout the year. But by 1995, commercial fishermen were harvesting their annual quota in just 52 days. Some fishermen bought faster boats to increase their hauls during the short-lived derbies.

THE ENDORSEMENT PROGRAM

In 1993, the Gulf Council began issuing "endorsements," a special license issued to commercial fishermen that had a reef permit *and* a record of at least 5,000 pounds of red snapper landings in two of the three years between 1990 and 1992. Vessel owners and operators with endorsements could harvest up to 2,000 pounds of red snapper per trip. Fishermen that had reef permits but no endorsements could harvest up to 200 pounds per trip. The endorsements could be transferred only to another vessel owned by the endorsement holder, or if the endorsement holder died or became disabled. By 1996, the Gulf Council had issued endorsements to 129 red snapper fishermen, and had issued reef permits, but no endorsements, to another 302 vessels. Although the endorsement system limited how many pounds of red snapper any vessel could catch in a trip, it did not eliminate the derby mentality.

The 1995 Proposed ITQ Program

To replace the unsatisfactory derby system, the Gulf Council began putting together a proposed Individual Transferable Quota system for managing the commercial red snapper fishery. Several other regional fishery councils had already successfully implemented quota systems for other commercially valuable species. Under the Gulf Coast's proposed ITQ program, the commercial red snapper quota would be divided into individual shares and distributed to fishermen based on their historical participation in the red snapper fishery. The Gulf Council proposed to allocate ITQs to vessel owners or operators with red snapper landings between 1990 and 1992 *and* a reef permit as of August 29, 1995. The Council would issue shares of the commercial quota based on the average of the highest two years' landings in the three-year base period of 1990–1992. The minimum allocation would be equivalent to 100 pounds of red snapper. Individuals could adjust their harvest by buying or selling shares, the ITQs. The proposed ITQ program was to last for four years, after which it would be modified, extended, or terminated. The shares would be freely transferable to U.S. citizens and resident aliens.

Controversy Erupts

The ITQ proposal proved extremely controversial. Environmental organizations were largely opposed to it, with some notable exceptions such as the Environmental Defense Fund ("EDF"). EDF supported ITQs as the most cost-effective way to develop a sustainable fishery. Many other environmental groups opposed ITQs, fearing the approach would force small fishermen out of business and concentrate commercial fishing in the hands of a few large companies. (Experts estimate that four or five large commercial fishing vessels could catch the entire annual commercial quota. And, even under an ITQ system with a year-round fishing season, many experts agree that the red snapper commercial fishery in the Gulf can support only about 40 boats.)

Some small commercial fishermen who own and operate their own boats supported ITQs, because they felt they would benefit under the proposed baseline period and allocation formula. Other small commercial fishermen feared they would be pushed out of the industry by an ITQ system and that their share of the fishery would be absorbed by the recreational fishing sector, which was eagerly pursuing opportunities to enlarge its own red snapper allocation.

Larger commercial fishing operations and fish processing companies, who had perhaps reaped the greatest benefit from the derby system, opposed the ITQ program vehemently. These vessel operators, owners, and fish processors feared that using a pre-endorsement ITQ baseline period of 1990–1992, as proposed in 1995, would reduce their allowable catch. The processors, who rely on lower cost Mexican red snapper imports during the off-season, believed ITQs would drive up red snapper prices.

Congress in its 1996 amendments to the Act prohibited until October 1, 2000 the implementation of an individual transferable quota ("ITQ") program for the commercial red snapper fishery in the Gulf of Mexico. Any commercial red snapper ITQ program implemented after the moratorium expires must be approved by a special referendum described in the statute. Only commercial fishermen and vessel operators who held reef vessel permits and red snapper endorsements during the dates specified in the statute may participate in the referendum vote. The referendum must pass by a majority of the votes cast in order for the Gulf Council to adopt any future ITQ program. Implementation of the Gulf Council's proposed 1995 commercial red snapper ITQ program remains codified at 50 CFR § 622.16 (attached in Exhibit A), but implementation of the regulation had been stayed indefinitely as a result of the 1996 statutory amendment.

When the Gulf Council's proposed ITQ system did not come to fruition, the Council extended the endorsement system through 1997. The Gulf Council also established mini-derbies for 1997. Under the mini-derbies, the Gulf Council made two-thirds of the commercial quota available for catch beginning February 1. This quota was exhausted, and the fishery closed, after 53 days. The final one-third of the commercial quota became available at two week intervals beginning in September. The Gulf Council also restricted sale of red snapper to federally licensed buyers only.

The Recreational Fishery

Until 1997, recreational fishers could fish year-round, but they were subject to a variety of restrictions designed to minimize total catch and help preserve the red snapper fishery First, to avoid commercial fishers getting around their limits by claiming to be recreational fishers, the Gulf Council prohibited the sale of recreationally caught red snapper. Second, recreational fishers were required to comply with the same minimum size limits as commercial fishers. Third, "bag limits" were imposed on recreational fishers beginning in 1990. These "bag limits" originally prohibited any recreational fisher from catching more than seven fish on any trip; the bag limits were reduced to five fish in 1995.

In 1997, as noted earlier, the NMFS for the first time shut down the recreational fishery because data indicated that its quota had already been exhausted. The Gulf Council did not propose to include recreational red snapper fishers in its proposed ITQ program, though some argued that charter boat and headboat operators could easily be included in the initial ITQ allocation.

FIG. 5 SUMMARY OF RED SNAPPER COMMERCIAL FISHERY MANAGEMENT

DATE	MANAGEMENT ACTION
1984	**Reef Fish Fishery Management Plan implemented:** Minimum size limit set at 12 inches. Prohibitions set on using certain gear types in inshore stressed areas.
1988	**First red snapper stock assessment conducted:** Red snapper found to be "significantly" overfished.
1990	**Total Allowable Catch ("TAC") established:** Commercial quota set at 3.1 million pounds (but only 2.66 million pounds landed). **Reef fish vessel permits required for commercial fishing:** Sale of recreationally caught red snapper prohibited. Minimum size limit increased to 13 inches. Stock recovery target date set for the year 2000.
1991	**Commercial quota reduced to 2.04 million pounds.** Stock recovery target date moved to 2007.
1992	**Derby fishery begins.** **Moratorium imposed on new reef fish vessel permits.** Commercial quota set at 2.04 million pounds (but 3.14 million pounds landed).
1993	**Red snapper endorsement program implemented:** 2000 pound trip limit for endorsement holders; 200 pound limit for those with reef fish vessel permits but no endorsements. Commercial quota raised to 3.06 million pounds. Stock recovery target date moved to 2009.

1994	**Commercial quota remains at 3.06 million pounds.** Minimum size limit increased to 14 inches.
1995	**Individual Transferable Quota ("ITQ") program approved by NMFS.** Commercial quota remains at 3.06 million pounds. Minimum size limit increased to 15 inches. Stock recovery target date moved to 2019.
1996	**ITQ moratorium established by Congress until October I, 2000.** Reef fish vessel permit moratorium extended through 2000. Endorsement program extended through 1997. Commercial quota increased to 4.65 million pounds.
1997	**Mini-derbies established.** Commercial quota remains at 4.65 million pounds.

THE 1998 RED SNAPPER FISHING SEASON

As regional administrator for NMFS, you are faced with a number of decisions about the coming fishing season and about long-term management options. Although the Gulf Council prepares fishery management plans and amendments, NMFS must evaluate them to determine whether they are consistent with the national standards and other provisions of the Act. If the plans or amendments are not consistent with the Act, the Secretary must disapprove them.

The NMFS, however, must tread carefully, particularly in challenging the views of the Gulf Council. As an official at the Center for Marine Conservation has recently noted, "Anytime you're talking about a fishery issue in the Gulf, it's a highly politicized environment. The power of the Gulf congressional delegation always strikes fear into the hearts of NMFS."

---

1. **What, if any, steps should be taken to reduce the red snapper bycatch from shrimp trawling?**

Red snapper fishermen have lobbied strongly for new regulations requiring that shrimpers install equipment on their trawlers that would allow juvenile red snapper to escape unharmed. In 1996, the Gulf Council voted to require shrimp trawlers to use certified Bycatch Reduction Devices ("BRDs") to help reduce red snapper losses. BRDs provide small holes in the top of shrimp trawls so that red snapper and other finfish can escape. NMFS experts estimate that BRDs could reduce shrimp bycatch losses by as much as 77%, particularly once shrimpers have gained several years of experience using them, but also admit that the reduction in bycatch could be as low as 15 percent. Bycatch reduction will be only 0% if shrimpers launch a successful judicial challenge to any rule, as they threaten to do.

Shrimpers question whether BRDs will be very effective and suggest that any snappers that are released are likely to be eaten by pelicans and other sea birds waiting near the water. Shrimpers, moreover, complain that "fisheye" BRDs, which are the only BRD design currently approved, will permit shrimp to escape. Shrimpers claim that fisheye BRDs will result in a 10–30 percent decrease in their shrimp catches, cutting income and endangering jobs. Congressman Ron Paul (R–Surfside, TX) has threatened to introduce a bill voiding any rule mandating current use of BRDs on shrimp trawls.

Last summer, the NMFS expressed tentative approval of the Gulf Council's BRD requirement, but has not taken final action. One issue, therefore, is whether to issue a final rule mandating BRD use or to look for some other approach. Do any of the Magnuson Act national standards have a direct bearing on this decision?

2. What total allowable catch should be set for the red snapper fishery for 1998?

NMFS scientists have recommended an allowable biological catch ("ABC") of between 3–6 million pounds. The ABC represents the scientists' estimate of the amount of fish that can be taken without decreasing the population, assuming existing environmental conditions remain the same. Fishers, however, have lobbied to maintain the same total allowable catch ("TAC") as applied during the last two years' 9.12 million pounds.

Earlier this month, the Gulf Council voted 15–2 to permit the larger TAC. (You were one of the two dissenting votes.) The Gulf Council majority justified maintaining the larger TAC in part on the new requirement that shrimp trawlers use BRDs, which the Council majority argued will make more fish available to be caught by commercial and recreational fishers. As noted above, however, how well BRDs will reduce bycatch is open to considerable debate. The NMFS plans to conduct a four-month, intensive research program beginning May 1, in which 2000 observers will be placed on shrimp trawlers to try to measure the effectiveness of the BRDs. But preliminary data from this observation program will not be available until late summer or early fall at best.

3. How should the TAC be divided between commercial and recreational fishers?

The Gulf Council voted to divide the TAC by the same percentages as in all prior years, 51% to commercial fishers and 49% to recreational fishers.

4. How should commercial fishing be regulated?

The Gulf Council has recommended that the commercial-fishery's management rules remain largely the same as last year. You would like to eliminate the derby mentality created by the current regulatory system. You also would like to eliminate the many inefficiencies inherent in the current system, which seems to push all fishing into a few weeks of the year and to reward a small group of longterm fishers. But how? The Council believes that the commercial fishing year again should be divided into two seasons. The first season would begin in early February and run until two-thirds of the commercial quota is exhausted. The second season would begin in September and run two weeks on, two weeks off, until the remainder of the commercial quota is exhausted.

5. How should recreational fishing be regulated?

Recreational fishers clearly are a major source of the overfishing problem, but it's hard to see how best to regulate them. Last year, as noted earlier, NMFS had to close down the recreational fishery on November 27.

Because December is one of the most popular tourist months, the recreational fishery industry was irate over the shutdown. You would like to avoid another early shutdown this year, but under current management rules, recreational fishers are likely to exhaust their quota even earlier this year, particularly if they are awarded a smaller quota than last year.

> **6. Are there other changes that should be made in the current regulatory scheme? Are there more effective approaches to managing the red snapper fishery?**

You can't help but believe that there are better alternatives out there. The ITQ approach looked very attractive, but Congress appears to have limited that option, at least for the moment.[2]

————

In preparing your answers, you should first read the primary documents that form part of the record of decision.

* *To read the exhibits for this case study, please go to the website: http://www.law.stanford.edu/casestudies/ and follow the prompts to register.*

* *Once you have received a password, log in to the site, go to the Case Studies Subject Index, scroll down to the Red Snapper Fishery, Part 1 case in the Fisheries section, and click on the link, "Exhibits."*

————

II. MARINE MAMMALS

Historically, the law has treated marine mammals little different than fish. They have been commercially hunted for their fur, oil, and ivory, and were subject to the law of capture. At the turn of the twentieth century, rapidly declining marine mammal populations led countries to create management regimes, resulting in some of the very first international environmental treaties. The Fur Seal Treaty of 1911, for example, was signed by the United States, Russia, Japan, and Great Britain. The parties agreed to prohibit taking of fur seals and sea otters on the high seas and to manage populations of fur seals within territorial waters. This treaty, however, was firmly based on a fisheries model, concerned with ensuring marine mammal populations that could support a sustainable commercial harvest. Over the last few decades, however, the legal treatment of marine mammals has departed dramatically from the model of fisheries management. As you read the stories in this section about whales, pinnipeds (seals and sea lions), and dolphins, consider whether the overarching management goal is commercial (as we saw with fisheries in Section I), ecological, or rights-based. What are the practical legal implications of these differing goals? As the sections on whales and dolphins demonstrate, marine mammals also

————

2. As described at page 472, you should note that the ITQ moratorium expired in 2002 and Regional Councils now have the authority to institute ITQs. Assume for this exercise, however, that ITQs are not available.

provide a fascinating interplay between domestic and international law, with serious foreign policy implications.

A. WHALES

Suddenly bubbles seemed bursting beneath my closed eyes; like vices my hands grasped the shrouds; some invisible, gracious agency preserved me; with a shock I came back to life. And lo! close under our lee, not forty fathoms off, a gigantic Sperm Whale lay rolling in the water like the capsized hull of a frigate, his broad, glossy back, of an Ethiopian hue, glistening in the sun's rays like a mirror. But lazily undulating in the trough of the sea, and ever and anon tranquilly spouting his vapory jet, the whale looked like a portly burgher smoking his pipe of a warm afternoon. But that pipe, poor whale, was thy last. As if struck by some enchanter's wand, the sleepy ship and every sleeper in it all at once started into wakefulness; and more than a score of voices from all parts of the vessel, simultaneously with the three notes from aloft, shouted forth the accustomed cry, as the great fish slowly and regularly spouted the sparkling brine into the air.

HERMAN MELVILLE, MOBY DICK (1851).

1. HISTORY OF WHALING

Approximately 100 million years ago, the mammalian ancestors of today's whales left the dry land and returned to the sea. The descendants of this intrepid sea-dweller evolved into cetaceans, an order of marine mammals comprising 78 species and divided into two families. Toothed whales, including dolphins, porpoises, and killer whales, are the more ancient and varied of the two families. With the exception of the sperm whale, which grows up to 60 feet long, toothed whales are relatively small. The other family of cetaceans, baleen whales, comprise only eleven species. Over 18 million years ago, these whales' teeth developed into a series of plates hanging from the mouth that function as sieves to capture small organisms strained through sea water taken in the mouth. Baleen whales include some of the largest animals that have ever lived, such as Grey, Sei, Right, and Humpback whales. The enormous Blue Whale grows to a leviathan 115 feet and can weigh 200 tons. No one disputes that whales are intelligent. Though we cannot understand their communication, whales speak with one another through complicated clicking noises and long complex songs that travel great distances. As the table from the International Whaling Commission below shows, most baleen whales were at the brink of extinction several decades ago but only a few species still face the immediate threat of extinction.

Population	Year(s) to which estimate applies	Approximate point estimate	Approximate 95% confidence limits
MINKE WHALES			
Southern Hemisphere	1982–89	761,000 Under revision	510,000–1,140,000 The Commission is unable to provide reliable estimates at the present time. A major review is underway by the Scientific Committee.

North Atlantic	1987–95	Approx. 149,000	120,000–182,000
North West Pacific and Okhotsk Sea	1989–90	25,000	12,800–48,600
BLUE WHALES			
Southern Hemisphere	1980–2000	400–1,400	
FIN WHALES			
North Atlantic	1969–89	47,300	27,700–82,000
GRAY WHALES			
Eastern North Pacific	1997/98	26,300	21,900–32,400
BOWHEAD WHALES			
Bering–Chukchi–Beaufort Seas stock	1993	8,000	6,900–9,200
HUMPBACK WHALES			
Western North Atlantic	1992/93	11,570	
Southern Hemisphere	1988	10,000	5,900–16,800
PILOT WHALES			
Central & Eastern North Atlantic	1989	780,000	440,000–1,370,000

http://www.iwcoffice.org/conservation/estimate.htm#table.

Whales have been hunted through much of human history as a source of food, oil, building and artistic materials. Whale meat was said to be popular in medieval Europe because it was exempted from the church's ban on eating meat on Fridays. A strong whaling industry was present throughout much of the eighteenth and nineteenth centuries, but the threats to whale populations increased by an order of magnitude as technology improved through the development of steam ships and the invention of the harpoon gun by a Norwegian, Sven Foyn, in 1868. Under the doctrine of freedom of the seas there was no regulation of whaling. As with fisheries, when stocks of one species became depleted, whalers turned to others. Five species of large whales were hunted, four to the brink of extinction. Only when a glut in the market for whale oil developed due to overproduction at the turn of the twentieth century did the major whaling companies enter into inter-company agreements to regulate whaling. These agreements were based on the Blue Whale Unit (bwu), which allocated unit values to the three major whales taken: blue, humpback and sei. Under the formula, two-and-a-half humpbacks or six sei whales were equivalent to one blue whale. This early approach to managing the whale fishery largely failed as whale populations continued to decrease, and in 1902 governments became involved, creating the International Council for the Exploration of the Sea (ICES). Patricia Birnie, *International Legal Issues in the Management and Protection of the Whale: A Review of Four Decades of Experience*, 29 NAT. RESOURCES J. 903, 905–06 (1989).

ICES established a central bureau to collect statistics from the whaling industry in an attempt to establish a scientific basis for management. It also sought, with little success, to establish uniformity in the application of national laws. Even so, most whaling took place on the high seas beyond national jurisdictions. In 1931, the League of Nations adopted the Convention for the Regulation of Whaling to strengthen the ICES efforts. In an important advance in international environmental law, the convention's provisions were universal, applying to "all the waters of the world." State parties agreed to license their vessels and take appropriate measures to protect whales in their national jurisdictions. The Convention's protections, however, were quite limited, extending only to calves, immature whales, female whales accompanied by calves, and all right whales. It did not prohibit the taking of any other whale species or provide for any enforcement measures. Anthony D'Amato & Sudhir K. Chopra, *Whales: Their Emerging Right to Life,* 85 AM. J. INT'L L. 21, 30 (1991). The convention did improve the collection of statistical information which, over time, illustrated clearly the need for increased protection. Subsequent ad hoc protocols to the convention introduced new protection measures, but the protocols were signed by different parties and many never came into force.

Under this weak system, whale populations continued to decline and it became evident to whaling States that, to avoid the increasingly likely collapse of the fishery, an effective international system must be created with both the means to collect data and the authority to enforce whaling controls. This need was met in 1946 with passage of the International Convention on the Regulation of Whaling (ICRW), 161 U.N.T.S. 72.

2. INTERNATIONAL CONVENTION ON THE REGULATION OF WHALING

The ICRW has been, and remains, the dominant international agreement regulating whaling. Its influence has been dramatic. In just 35 years, its mandate transformed from regulation of the whaling fishery to a ban. How did such a remarkable reversal occur?

To regard the story of whaling as simply management of a specific resource misses the real story. The conflict over management of whales has been one of whaling versus whale conservation, of concerns over fishery management versus concerns over animal rights. Some indigenous communities, such as the Inuit and Makah, view whaling as an important part of their culture. Since the 1970s, though, increasing numbers of people from all walks of life have expressed strong ethical beliefs that whales should not be hunted at all, regardless of their population numbers. Indeed income from whale-watching now far exceeds the income from whaling. The dispute between traditional fisheries management and rights-based conservation has led to bitter conflict among traditional environmental allies. Readers familiar with the "sustainable development" paradigm may want to consider why it does not fit easily in the context of whaling.

As with the 1931 League of Nations Convention, the ICRW applies to all waters in which whaling occurs, thus protecting whales throughout their migration. At the time of its creation in 1946, the ICRW was intended to ensure the viability of commercial whaling—relying on scientific expertise in order to manage whale fishery stocks at a sustainable level for commercial fishing. Indeed if parties to the ICRW had intended to protect individual whales based on their inherent right to exist, they would have created a very different legal regime. While scholars generally agree that conservation of whales for ethical reasons was not the intention of the ICRW's drafters, the language of the Preamble has given rise to much debate over the purpose of the Convention. In particular, the Preamble seems to swing between the potentially contradictory goals of biodiversity conservation and fishery management.

RECOGNIZING the interest of the nations of the world in safeguarding for future generations the great natural resources represented by the whale stocks;

CONSIDERING that the history of whaling has seen over-fishing of one area after another and of one species of whale after another to such a degree that it is essential to protect all species of whales from further over-fishing;

RECOGNIZING that the whale stocks are susceptible of natural increases if whaling is properly regulated, and that increases in the size of whale stocks will permit increases in the number of whales which may be captured without endangering these natural resources; * * *

HAVING decided to conclude a convention to provide for the proper conservation of whale stocks and thus make possible the orderly development of the whaling industry;

HAVE agreed as follows . . .

The ICRW has broad coverage, applying not only to ships and land stations under the jurisdiction of the Contracting Governments but "to all waters in which whaling is prosecuted by such factory ships." The ICRW's most important innovation was the creation of a new institution known as the International Whaling Commission (IWC). The IWC is composed of one member from each Contracting Government. Each member has one vote. The Commission may encourage, recommend or organize studies and investigations of whale populations and whaling, as well as disseminate information concerning methods of maintaining and increasing the populations of whale stocks. All whales taken must be reported to the IWC, which uses the data to determine whether populations of species are threatened and require special protections from whaling.

Importantly, the IWC has no enforcement authority. Prosecution for infractions or contraventions of the ICRW are explicitly the responsibility of relevant national authorities in member States of vessels flying their flag. A reporting requirement mandates each Contracting Government to transmit to the IWC full details of each infraction of the Convention, measures taken for dealing with the infraction, and penalties imposed. It took 18 years after Norway's first proposal in 1972, however, to adopt an international observer program to ensure accurate reporting. In addition, there is no provision for dispute settlement.

The ICRW also created a "Schedule" of regulations. The Schedule lists the particular species covered by the ICRW and whaling controls, including open and closed seasons, designation of sanctuary areas, quotas, and gear restrictions. Decisionmaking under the Commission structure takes place through amendments to the Schedule and resolutions. Amendments to the Schedule are binding and require a three-fourths majority vote. Resolutions, while easier to pass in that they require only a simple majority, are non-binding. To date, the Schedule has only included large cetaceans because the countries supporting protection of dolphins and smaller cetaceans have never attained the requisite three-quarters majority necessary for amendment.

The Schedule amendments (called "regulations") have been the battleground for the conservation versus fisheries management debates. In fact, Article V, covering the Schedule amendment process and the objection procedures for newly passed regulations, has been the single most controversial provision of the ICRW. It provides that any regulations:

(a) shall be such as are necessary to carry out the objectives and purposes of this Convention and to provide for the conservation, development, and optimum utilization of the whale resources;

(b) shall be based on scientific findings;

(c) shall not involve restrictions on the number or nationality of factory ships or land stations, nor allocate specific quotas to any factory ship or land station or to any group of factory ships or land stations; and

(d) shall take into consideration the interests of the consumers of whale products and the whaling industry.

Pro-whaling States, as will be discussed below, have contended that these requirements have been ignored by the pro-conservation States. If a Contracting Government formally objects to a regulation within 90 days of notification, the regulation is not binding with regard to that Government and does not become binding until and unless the objection is withdrawn.

Article VIII establishes a Scientific Permit exception to the IWC. Any Contracting Government may grant to any of its nationals a special permit authorizing the killing of whales for purposes of scientific research subject to restrictions that the Contracting Government thinks fit. The exception allows contracting governments to issue whaling permits for the purposes of scientific research, notwithstanding stock status and any IWC quotas that may be in place. Following the imposition of a moratorium on whaling in the early 1980s, Japan, in particular, has been accused of misusing this exception to continue commercial whaling. As a consequence, subsequent regulations have granted the IWC Scientific Committee some influence over the issuance of such permits.

a. The Moratorium and Responses

The most significant amendment to the ICRW Schedule has been the moratorium on commercial whaling adopted in 1982 (in force from 1986). The seeds for this action had been sown ten years earlier at the Stockholm Conference on the Human Environment, which called for a 10–year moratorium on the catching of whales for commercial purposes. Declaration of Principles on the Human Environment, Report of the United Nations Conference on the Human Environment at 3, U.N. Doc. A/CONF. 48/14/ rev.2 (June 5–16, 1972). The IWC did not ban whaling but, rather, approved a "cessation" of all commercial whaling for an interim period. This moratorium would be kept under review based upon the best scientific advice and, by 1990 at the latest, the IWC would undertake a comprehensive assessment of the effects of this decision on whale stocks and consider modification of this provision and the establishment of other catch limits. The moratorium passed by a 25–to–7 vote with 5 abstentions. Four States (Japan, Norway, Peru, USSR) lodged formal objections to the moratorium; Peru later withdrew its objection. While the moratorium's provision for regular scientific review left open the possibility for resumption of whaling once whale populations recovered, the moratorium was extended following review in 1990. This decision reflected the success of NGOs (particularly Greenpeace and EarthTrust) to shift the debate from sustainable use to species conservation. This decision was controversial both inside and outside the IWC. The head of the Scientific Committee resigned, for example, accusing "the IWC of treating the committee's unanimous recommendations with contempt." Caron, *infra.* at 162.

In 1994, the IWC adopted the Revised Management Procedure (RMP), developed by its Scientific Committee over an eight year period. This procedure is based on a catch limit algorithm that calculates allowable catches based on population data and uncertainties. Described by the IWC as "the most rigorously tested management procedure for a natural resource yet developed," the RMP's catch limits would be set for five years. Despite the RMP's adoption, however, the moratorium has remained in place. As the IWC website explains, the RMP's "actual implementation in whale management (at least for those stocks for which it has been tested), is of course a political decision. The Commission will not set catch limits for commercial whaling until it has agreed and adopted a complete Revised Management Scheme (RMS). Any RMS will not only include the scientific aspects such as the RMP, but a number of non-scientific issues, including inspection and enforcement, perhaps to humaneness of killing techniques." http://www.iwcoffice.org/RMP.htm. In 1992, for example, the RMP suggested a catch could be authorized for Minke whales but the IWC extended the moratorium, stating that more work was needed "to agree on minimum standards for data, to prepare guidelines on the conduct of population surveys, and to devise and approve a system of measures for monitoring and inspection." Jeremy Cherfas, *Whalers Win The Numbers Game*, NEW SCIENTIST, July 11, 1992, at 12. Perhaps not surprisingly, the RMS, which still has not been established, has been condemned by pro-whaling nations a delaying tactic to keep the moratorium in place.

Following the IWC's extension of the moratorium, Iceland officially withdrew from the IWC in 1992. At the same time Japan and Norway threatened to leave the Commission, and Norway announced that it would resume commercial whaling in 1993. Norway's actions did not violate the ICRW because it had formally objected to the moratorium. Norway's role as an anti-conservationist pariah is strange because it was a founding member of the IWC and has been in the vanguard of whale conservation efforts throughout much of the IWC's history. Nonetheless, Norway, Japan and Iceland believe that the objectives and requirements of the ICRW have been flagrantly disregarded. The IWC is supposed to be an instrument for the sound management of whale stocks, they contend, not an instrument for a complete ban on whaling. Indeed, since the adoption of the moratorium most non-whaling States have shifted their stance in favor of outlawing whaling altogether.

This conflict has played out most clearly in the case of the minke whale. The IWC Scientific Committee estimates over 900,000 minke whales worldwide. Iceland, Japan and Norway argue that small numbers of minke whales can now be taken without risk to the population's viability. Yet the IWC continues to ban *all* commercial whaling, despite the opinion of the IWC Scientific Committee that minke whale stocks may be caught without threatening the population. In a fascinating response to the IWC's refusal to permit limited harvesting of minke whales, Norway, Iceland, Greenland and the Faeroe Islands have challenged the very legitimacy of the IWC, creating a new international whaling institution, the North Atlantic Marine

Mammal Commission (NAMMCO). Agreement on Cooperation in Research, Conservation and Management of Marine Mammals in the North Atlantic, April 9, 1992. The following excerpt describes the debate and origins of NAMMCO in more detail.

David D. Caron, *The International Whaling Commission and the North Atlantic Marine Mammal Commission: The Institutional Risks of Coercion in Consensual Structures* 89 AM. J. INT'L L. 154, 159–67 (1995)

Under its constitutive document, the IWC is given the task of adopting regulations "to provide for the conservation, development, and optimum utilization of the whale resources" with the condition that such regulations "shall be based on scientific findings." [Article V(2)] The perception of legitimacy of such an organization rests (1) on the integrity and accuracy of its science, and (2) on the political integrity and managerial accuracy of decisions taken on the basis of that science. Both of these aspects of institutional legitimacy have been suspect throughout the history of the IWC. For years prowhaling and antiwhaling states have debated what the scientific data indicate about the viability of whale stocks. During the first twenty-five years of the IWC's existence, the organization oversaw the continued overexploitation and depletion of whale stocks. The recommendations of the IWC Scientific Committee at that time, environmentalists allege, were distorted and ignored by the whaling states, a powerful allegation calling into question the integrity of the organization. Today the situation is reversed; the prowhaling nations, particularly Japan, Norway and Iceland, charge that the IWC is ignoring scientific findings in setting its policies. These nations allege that the IWC prohibits all whaling, even though the scientific community has concluded that some hunting of minke whales would be sustainable. The whaling states claim that the views of the Scientific Committee are distorted or ignored by nonwhaling states in order to prevent all whaling. They argue that the issue is not the conservation of whales. All parties involved have stated their acceptance of the importance of "conservation" and "sustainability." They contend instead that, under the guise of conservation, the IWC is attempting to grant whales an entitlement to life, absolute protection from further utilization. * * *

Within hours of the end of the 1993 [IWC] meeting in Tokyo, Norwegian Foreign Minister Johan Joergen Holst announced his country's intention to set commercial whaling quotas and dates for the 1993 season. Norway would take 296 minke whales: of those, 136 were intended for scientific research, and 160 were to be taken commercially. Norwegian Fisheries Minister Ian Olsen said that the numbers were "based on scientific evidence provided by the Scientific Committee of the International Whaling Commission." According to Foreign Minister Holst, the Norwegian quota was lower than it would have been under the IWC regulations. "We do this because we wish to indicate that our goal is regular IWC quotas." Philip Hammond, who had recently resigned as chairman of the Scientific Committee, supported Norway's plan, stating that the country was within its legal rights. Hammond believed that Norway's adoption of the procedure advocated by the Scientific Committee would protect minke stocks "not just for a year or two but . . . for a hundred years or more."

Shortly before Norway took its first whale in 1993 for commercial purposes, its Ambassador to the United States, Kjeld Vibe, said the IWC should be "analyzed anew," and that Norway's actions should serve as "a warning to the anti-all-whaling majority" that the IWC is supposed to be "an instrument for the sound management of whale stocks," not an "instrument for a complete ban on all whaling, regardless of whether we are talking about a threatened or endangered species." This "warning" to the IWC in 1993 leads us to consider the related challenge implicit in the 1992 creation of the North Atlantic Marine Mammal Commission.

Beginning in 1988, meetings sponsored by Norway, Iceland and others were held that brought "together countries which wish to emphasize a rational approach to marine mammal management, in contrast, for example, to the approach taken in recent years with respect to whales in the International Whaling Commission." At the fifth such conference, held in Nuuk, Greenland, on April 9, 1992, representatives of the Faroe Islands, Greenland, Iceland and Norway signed the Agreement on Cooperation in Research, Conservation and Management of Marine Mammals in the North Atlantic. The Agreement established a regional organization, NAMMCO, for the scientific study, conservation and management of marine mammals in the North Atlantic region. The document clearly responded to what the drafters regarded as inappropriate whale protectionist tendencies of the IWC. As Gudmundur Eiriksson of Iceland stated at NAMMCO's inaugural meeting in 1992, the organization was born out of dissatisfaction with the IWC's zero-catch quota, lack of IWC competence to deal with small cetaceans, and the need for an organization to deal with other marine mammals such as seals. * * *

The decision-making process within NAMMCO is highly protective of the interests of individual members. Since the management committees may only "propose" measures to members, the legal authority of NAMMCO over its members is merely recommendatory. Decisions of the Council and the management committees are to be made "by the unanimous vote of those members present and casting an affirmative vote." The Agreement does not provide mechanisms for implementing proposals, monitoring compliance with proposals, or obtaining definitive interpretation of the terms of either the Agreement or proposed conservation measures recommended thereunder. * * *

NAMMCO poses an interesting challenge to the IWC even though, strictly speaking, the organization does not conflict with the IWC. Indeed, the actions of NAMMCO's members need not necessarily conflict with their obligations under the IWC. Norway, for example, is a member of the IWC and, because of its earlier objection, is not legally bound by the moratorium. Yet, although NAMMCO and Norway have not yet acted in a manner legally in conflict with the IWC, the very existence of NAMMCO and the actions of Norway challenge the legitimacy of some of the IWC's decisions. In relying on the RMP of the IWC Scientific Committee in a way that appears appropriate but that the IWC itself has not yet done, NAMMCO and Norway are challenging the integrity of the political process of the IWC. In developing its own data base of marine mammal populations in the North Atlantic, NAMMCO will challenge the legitimacy of the IWC's decision making by contradicting the science and expertise that is the foundation of such legitimacy.

Norway has increased its minke whale quota since commercial hunting began, from 226 whales in 1993, to 674 in 2002 and 796 in 2005. Despite the mandates of the Pelly and Packwood–Magnuson Amendments (described in the *Questions and Discussion* section that follows), the United States has not certified or imposed sanctions on Norway for its whaling activities. Instead, the U.S. Commerce Department has officially expressed "regret" that Norway has resumed whaling.

Japan has taken a different approach to continue whaling, relying on the Scientific Permit exception. Throughout the 1990s, Japan authorized the taking of minke whales (965 minke whales, for example, in 1996). This whaling has been managed by the Institute of Cetaceous Research, which in 1996 received over $35 million for the sale of whale meat. Meat sales apparently account for 60% of its annual budget. Nick Smith, *University DNA testing exposes whale of a lie,* THE SUNDAY NEWS (AUCKLAND), August 24, 1997, at 11. The excerpt below sets out the Japanese Whaling Association's justification for this activity. http://www.jp-whaling-assn.com/index_eng. htm.

> The Japanese whale research program has obtained valuable information on whales by using non-lethal and lethal research. It has also enabled us to calculate the amount of fish consumed by whales—which is approximately between 280 million tonnes and 500 million tonnes per year. In contrast, humans harvest around 90 million tonnes of fish each year ... A large range of information is needed for the management and conservation of whales, such as population, age structure, growth rates, age of maturity, reproductive rates, feeding, nutrition and levels of contaminants. This type of important information cannot be obtained through small DNA samples or analysis of organochlorine, but only through lethal research.

> In the research program, the vessels are run on a predesigned track formulated by scientists, and conduct surveys and collects specimens such as earplug and ovaries. After scientific examination and removal of tissue and organ samples, the remains of the whales are frozen and marketed in compliance with the provisions of the Convention, which forbid any part of the carcass to be wasted. However, as the cost of research is expensive, the proceeds from sales of whale meat and parts alone cannot cover the costs. The Government of Japan pays the remainder of the costs.

In what has become a ritual, every IWC meeting adopts a resolution condemning this practice, but it has continued unabated. In 2005, for example, following its failure to gain IWC approval to lift the moratorium, Japan announced its research program in the North Pacific would continue to take annually 150 minke whales, 50 Bryde's whales, 50 fin whales and 10 Sperm whales. Japan's research program in the Antarctic announced it would take 850 minke whales, 50 humpback whales, and 50 fin whales. CHAIR'S SUMMARY REPORT FOR THE 57TH ANNUAL MEETING (2005).

b. Breaking the Stalemate

At the annual meeting of the IWC in 2000, its Secretary over the last 24 years, Dr. Ray Gambell, retired. In leaving the organization he had overseen both before and after the moratorium, Gambell issued a stark warning:

> Whaling is going on at a commercial level. It's outside IWC control. I would think it much better that it was brought within international regulations and oversight. I think the commission will need to move forward on measures which would allow controlled whaling, otherwise it will lose credibility. If the commission cannot set its house in order, people will start to ask: "Why do we need it at all?"

Whaling Ban Set to End (June 11, 2000) at http://news.bbc.co.uk.

Iceland's departure from the IWC, Norway's reservation to the moratorium, Japan's vigorous use of the scientific whaling exception, and NAMMCO's creation all call into question the effectiveness, indeed the relevance, of the IWC. The current situation clearly leaves much to be desired, but do the antagonists' fundamentally different visions of the problem—animal rights versus fisheries management—leave space for meaningful compromise? In 1997, Ireland and Australia called for establishment of a global whale sanctuary and, if this could not be achieved, a 50–year moratorium on commercial whaling. Realizing these proposals had little chance of success, and acknowledging the gap between the extremes of zero whaling and full scale commercial whaling, Ireland later proposed the following compromise at the 1997 IWC meeting:

1) The Revised Management Scheme should be completed and adopted. The scheme must be conservative and provide in particular for inspection and observation procedures that will engender public confidence.

2) Where quotas are justified under the RMS, these should be restricted to coastal areas only and to nations who are now whaling. This would result in a de facto sanctuary over the oceans of the world.

3) Quotas should be issued for local consumption only. This would avoid the pressure on whaling which would arise from international trade.

4) Lethal scientific whaling should be phased out over a period.

5) Regulations for whale-watching should be prepared to minimize the impacts of disturbance on whale populations.

Opening Statement of the Government of Ireland, International Whaling Commission, 1997 (IWC/49/OS Ireland).

In 1998, a revised proposal would have allowed countries the right to hunt whales in their own coastal waters up to 200 miles offshore but ban it elsewhere, turning the high seas in effect into a giant whale sanctuary. Neither of these proposals has been adopted, but countries have continued to search for compromises that will resolve the whaling stalemate. At the 2005 IWC meeting, Japan's motion to lift the moratorium attracted 23 votes in favor, 29 against, and five abstentions. This fell far short of the three-fourths majority required.

Despite the continuing bitter accusations of bad faith between parties to the ICRW, it should be remembered that the IWC has achieved a great deal since its founding. While the Humpback whale and, in particular, Blue whale populations remain at very low numbers, most large whales are still not commercially hunted. In addition to the basic conflict over hunting Minke, Bryde's and Sperm whales, the issues that will confront the ICRW in the next few years include: how to address the creation of a rival international institution based on its own legal procedures, the protection of small cetaceans, regulation of whale-watching and non-consumptive uses, and the treatment of aboriginal "small-type" or other local whaling. Patricia Birnie, *International Legal Issues in the Management and Protection of the Whale: A Review of Four Decades of Experience*, 29 NAT. RESOURCES J. 903, 933–34 (1989).

QUESTIONS AND DISCUSSION

1. Recalling the ICRW's Preamble—"HAVING decided to conclude a convention to provide for the proper conservation of whale stocks and thus make possible the orderly development of the whaling industry"—is the seemingly permanent moratorium on whaling contrary to the ICRW's objectives? Do you agree with Norway's argument that the IWC has been subverted from its original purpose of managing a commercial fishery to protection of animal rights by simply banning all whaling? If not, how do you justify the IWC's decision to ban hunting of Minke whales despite the contrary advice of the Scientific Committee (note that the ICRW leaves the decision on quotas in the hands of the IWC, not its Scientific Committee)? Conversely, is there any reason the ICRW's purpose cannot change over time? More specifically, can the meaning of "conservation of whale stocks" change over time?

2. Despite Japanese and Norwegian charges that the anti-whaling environmental groups are driven by concern over animal rights rather than science, Greenpeace justifies the moratorium on a scientific basis. It argues that whaling cannot be managed as a fishery because the whale's rate of reproduction is so slow. Instead of releasing enormous numbers of eggs into the water for fertilization by the male, as fish do, whales are mammals and give live birth to a single calf no more than once every year or two. Moreover, the calf needs a year of maternal care before it can survive on its own and many years before it reaches sexual maturity.

Greenpeace also criticizes the science underpinning IWC management, contending that neither the actual whale populations nor their growth rates are known well. Population estimates are extrapolated from sightings of a small fraction of the population. Read again the IWC chart on whale populations at the beginning of this section. The "95% confidence limits" column means that 95% of the time the actual population number will fall within the range between the two numbers. Put simply, there is a 95% probability that the actual population of blue whales lies between 210 and 1,000 individuals. Greenpeace argues that this supposed confidence is unfounded. As a powerful example, it points to evidence of illegal whaling that has brought into question the accuracy of the Scientific Committee's projections.

In 1994 it was revealed by a former Soviet Fisheries Ministry official that the Soviet Union had deliberately and egregiously misled the IWC over the number of whales it was killing. From 1948 to 1973, the Soviet Union officially reported killing 2,710 Humpback whales while, in fact, it killed over 48,000. This new information throws in doubt the extrapolations of recovery rates made by scientists over the last forty years. The IWC now admits that its estimates of whale harvests could be in error by two orders of magnitude. The sheer size of this deception, Greenpeace and others contend, clearly demonstrates the inability to estimate accurately whale populations and, as a consequence, allowable harvest quotas.

How should the precautionary principle apply to whaling? For which species does it suggest a total ban on whaling or quotas?

3. At the Convention on International Trade in Endangered Species conference of the parties in 1997, Japan and Norway proposed transferring Bryde's, Gray and Minke whales from Appendix I to II, thus permitting renewed commercial trade in those species. While Norway did not gain the two-thirds majority necessary for adoption, it did receive strong international support with 57 countries voting in favor and 51 against. This marked the first time there had ever been a CITES vote in favor of this issue. Japan's proposal that CITES establish its own policies on whaling in place of the IWC was defeated 51 to 27. In a suggestive example of deal-making among parties to international environmental agreements, it was reported that Norway would support southern African countries' proposal to renew trade in elephant ivory if they supported transferring the whales from Appendix I to Appendix II. Japan has made similar proposals at each subsequent CITES conference of the parties; and each has failed (with a majority opposed).

Charges of vote-buying have also surfaced at the IWC. Following a vote that fell six short of establishing a South Pacific whaling sanctuary, Patrick Ramage, of the International Fund for Animal Welfare, charged,

> This wasn't a vote, it was an auction, and Japan was the winning bidder. Japan has for several years pursued an international vote consolidation strategy, using development assistance and economic leverage to secure the votes of small developing countries in the IWC and other international conventions. In recent years, the Caribbean countries have been key targets of this effort. Each of the six Caribbean nation delegations to the Adelaide meeting today— Antigua, Dominica, Grenada, St. Kitts, St. Lucia, and St. Vincent—vocally supported the Japanese effort to sink the sanctuary proposal.

Andrew Darby, *South Pacific Whale Sanctuary Voted Down* (July 4, 2000), http://ens.lycos.com. Resorting to the same alleged tactics, a number of NGOs have been actively encouraging Pacific island nations to join the IWC and form a stronger anti-whaling bloc. As of the 2006 IWC meeting, the number of pro and anti-whaling nations were roughly equal, as evident from the vote on Japan's request for an exemption to the moratorium on commercial whaling for Minke and Bryde's whales—30 in favor, 31 against, and 4 abstentions.

Another unsuccessful motion by Japan at the 2006 IWC meeting was a proposal for secret ballots (33 votes against, 30 in favor). Do you think secret ballots would favor the interests of pro-whaling nations or anti-whaling nations?

4. The effectiveness of the IWC has been due in great measure to the threat of unilateral sanctions by the United States against countries that frustrate the IWC's efforts. The Pelly Amendment to the Fishermen's Protective Act of 1967 grants authority to the executive branch to impose sanctions on nations that violate the policies and objectives of the ICRW's conservation program. The Packwood–Magnuson Amendment allows the President to impose sanctions under the Pelly Amendment when foreign fisheries diminish the effectiveness of U.S. environmental laws. If a country is certified as acting contrary to the aims of the ICRW, the United States may put in place trade sanctions against any products from the certified country.

While foreign countries have been certified a number of times under these laws for diminishing the effectiveness of the ICRW, until the Japanese hunting of sperm and bryde's whales in 2000 no Pelly Amendment sanctions had ever been imposed and only a few Packwood–Magnuson sanctions had ever been imposed. Nonetheless, the threat of trade sanctions and loss of fishery access are serious and a number of countries, most notably Peru, have modified their behavior to comply with the IWC as a result. In December 1996, Canada was certified under the Pelly Amendment for conducting whaling activities that diminish the effectiveness of a conservation program of the IWC but no sanctions followed. Public Papers of the President, Message to the Congress on Canadian Whaling Activities, February 10, 1997.

Japan has been certified by the Pelly Amendment three times for conducting fishing operations that diminish the effectiveness of an international fishery conservation program. The most recent certification was the result of an expansion of Japan's North Pacific Program, which requested scientific permission to take 10 Sperm whales and 50 Bryde's whales, and which the Secretary said had "dubious scientific validity." Japan was also certified under the Packwood–Magnuson Amendment for its activities, which could potentially deprive it of future opportunities to fish in the U.S. exclusive economic zone.

In addition to the Pelly and Packwood–Magnuson Amendments, the U.S. Marine Mammal Protection Act and the Australian Whale Protection Act provide more direct species-specific protections. The U.S. law, for example, prohibits nationals from taking marine mammals from U.S. waters *or* the high seas. The New Zealand Marine Mammal Protection Act goes even farther, prohibiting its nationals from taking marine mammals within waters subject to the jurisdiction of another State. *See* Patricia Birnie, *International Legal Issues in the Management and Protection of the Whale: A Review of Four Decades of Experience*, 29 NAT. RESOURCES J. 903, 929 (1989).

These laws are reinforced by UNCLOS Article 65, which provides that other UNCLOS provisions shall not restrict the right of a coastal State or international organization to prohibit, limit or regulate the exploitation of marine mammals more strictly than provided for in UNCLOS. Moreover, parties must cooperate in conserving marine mammals and "in the case of cetaceans shall in particular work through appropriate international organizations for their conservation, management and study." The IWC, as an international organization, clearly is covered by this provision.

5. Article 5 of the ICRW provides for establishment of whale sanctuaries. At the 44th meeting of the IWC in 1992, France proposed a Southern Ocean Whaling Sanctuary. This proposal coincided with international efforts to establish a ban on mining and commercial operations in the Antarctic. In 1994 the IWC approved the creation of a sanctuary around Antarctica, banning commercial whalers from the Antarctic Ocean south of 40 degrees south latitude and in some areas below the 60th parallel. Japan strongly opposed creation of the Sanctuary, claiming there was no scientific basis for its creation. Since the Sanctuary's creation, Japan has taken minke whales there through its scientific whaling program. *Japan to*

Increase Minke Whale Catch Over Wider Area, JAPAN ECONOMIC NEWSWIRE, May 20, 1995.

6. The Convention on International Trade in Endangered Species (CITES) lists in Appendix I the species protected by the IWC moratorium, prohibiting trade in whale products. It is important to recognize that addressing the *trade* in whale products is not, technically, within the IWC's mandate. The IWC Infractions Subcommittee has, nonetheless, addressed the issue in order to increase public attention and national embarrassment. At the 1994 IWC meeting, for example, it was reported that a shipment of 232 tons of Bryde's whale meat had been discovered in Vladivostock, Russia. The meat had been transported from Taiwan by a Honduran-flagged ship for eventual sale in Japan. Discovering such illegal shipments, however, is rare. *See* PETER STOETT, THE INTERNATIONAL POLITICS OF WHALING 140–41 (1997).

DNA testing provides an enforcement mechanism to combat illegal whaling. Over a three-year period, researchers from the University of Auckland, in New Zealand, collected samples of whale meat sold in fish markets in Japan. Of thirty samples tested using DNA analysis, six samples were found to be from Whale species protected by the IWC—one came from Killer whale, one from Humpback whale, and four from Finback whale. An official at the Japanese Fisheries Agency claimed that these were likely from whale meat imported legally prior to 1991 and subsequently frozen for later sale. Natalie Angier, *DNA Tests Find Meat of Endangered Whales for Sale in Japan*, N.Y. TIMES, Sept. 13, 1994, at C4.

Perhaps they should test for more than DNA. In early 2001, five Japanese consumer groups opposed any trade of whale meat with Norway on health grounds. The groups cited a 1999 study showing that over half of the whale meat on the market in Japan exceeded national or international standards for at least one toxic chemical. As a wire service reported,

> The study of samples collected from Japanese shops and restaurants revealed that the blubber from 58% of North Pacific minke whales contained levels of at least one contaminant in excess of national or international standards. In a subsequent study, 80% of samples of Antarctic minke whale bacon or blubber and 100% of North Pacific minke whale bacon or blubber tested exceeded advisory limits set in Japan for ingestion of the dioxin group of chemicals. * * *

> Japanese law prohibits the sale and import of food that contains toxic substances or is suspected to contain toxic substances. However, the Japanese government remained cautious about the issue, saying that the country has yet to discuss possible whale meat imports with Norway.

Japanese Citizens Groups Oppose Imports of "Contaminated" Whalemeat, AGENCE FRANCE PRESSE ENGLISH, Jan. 19, 2001.

7. NAMMCO has developed into an active international organization strikingly similar to the IWC and has developed a real expertise on the conservation of marine mammals. Its members include the original signatories of Iceland, Norway, Greenland and the Faroe Islands, while officials from Russia, Canada, Denmark, St. Lucia and Japan often attend as observers. At annual meetings, NAMMCO's Scientific Committee presents its research findings on the population status of minke whales, fin whales, harp seals, hooded seals, etc. in the North Atlantic.

NAMMCO has proven effective in a number of cases. After an assessment of beluga and narwhal stocks off Greenland, the Scientific Committee concluded that the stocks were significantly depleted and recommended a reduction in harvests. Greenland, in response, adopted for the first time a set of quotas for belugas and narwhals. At its 16th Council meeting in 2006, NAMMCO issued a press release stating that:

> NAMMCO has previously expressed grave concern on the apparent decline of stocks of narwhal and belugas in west Greenland, and while commending Greenland for the recent introduction of quotas and the reduction in the harvest, there is still serious concern that present takes of narwhals and belugas in west Greenland, according to the advice of both the Scientific Committee and the JCNB (Canada Greenland Joint Commission on Narwhal and Beluga) Scientific Working Group are not sustainable and will lead to further depletion of the stocks.

Despite the expectations of some, pro-whaling nations in the Pacific have not formed their own regional management body based on NAMMCO. Why do you think NAMMCO has not developed into a threat to the legitimacy or jurisdiction of the IWC?

––––––

CASE STUDY: ABORIGINAL SUBSISTENCE WHALING

A number of indigenous cultures traditionally depended on the hunting of whales for physical, cultural and spiritual sustenance. Thus an aboriginal exception has existed as far back as the 1931 League of Nations convention for specific stocks such as Alaskan Bowhead whales (more commonly referred to as the Right whale because it is a slow swimmer and easy to hunt, making it the "right" whale for hunting). While the ICRW does not explicitly address the issue of indigenous whaling, the IWC has long provided for an aboriginal subsistence whaling exception. A three-quarters majority of IWC members must approve an aboriginal quota. The Schedule in 2002, for example, provided for six separate aboriginal subsistence whaling exceptions (e.g., up to 19 West Greenland Fin whales could be taken annually by Greenlanders from 2003–2006). The aboriginal exception has proven controversial both in determining which communities should qualify for the exception and, at the domestic level, in allowing whaling at all.

The ICRW Schedule does not define the terms, "aboriginal subsistence whaling," and the IWC still has not defined the term despite the establishment of a working group. This issue is significant because a number of pro-whaling States support limited exceptions for coastal communities that depend on whaling for their livelihood. Japan, for example, has consistently sought to apply the aboriginal exception to its small, coastal villages with whaling traditions because of their "shared characteristics" with aboriginal subsistence communities. To date the IWC has rejected this argument because of the commercial aspects of such whaling, i.e., the fact that it is not entirely for local consumption.

The United States has played an uncomfortable dual role—as an openly anti-whaling nation and staunch defender of the rights of its aboriginal communities for subsistence whaling. In 1977, for example, the United States was embarrassed by the Alaskan Eskimos' defiance of the IWC Scientific Committee's advice that a moratorium be implemented for bowhead whales. In response, the IWC removed the aboriginal exception on bowheads, placing the United States in a conflict between upholding the Eskimos' cultural rights while promoting the IWC. The United States challenged the legality of the IWC action, arguing that the moratorium only applied to commercial whaling. As the substantive articles of the ICRW make no reference to aboriginal exceptions and therefore do not guarantee them, a compromise was reached and the United States undertook research of the bowhead population. As a result of the lobbying efforts of the Eskimos at subsequent IWC meetings, a small quota has been regularly allowed for the Eskimos. Patricia Birnie, *International Legal Issues in the Management and Protection of the Whale: A Review of Four Decades of Experience*, 29 NAT. RESOURCES J. 903, 929–30 (1989).

More recently, much greater conflict has arisen (and continues) over the whale hunt conducted by the Makah tribe, which consists of about 1,800 Native Americans living at the tip of the Olympic Peninsula in northwest Washington state. The tribe has high unemployment (reportedly approaching 50%) and drug and alcohol concerns. There is debate over how long the Makah have been whaling and harvesting seals and sea otters, but written references date back to the eighteenth century and the practice likely originated long before then, influencing the tribe's culture, art and religion. Indeed, the treaty ceding the Makah's lands to the United States, the 1855 Treaty of Neah Bay, provides that:

> The right of taking fish and of whaling or sealing at usual and accustomed grounds and stations is further secured to said Indians in common with all citizens of the United States.

The Makah thus became the only tribe to gain a treaty right to whaling.

With the drastic decline of Gray whale populations at the turn of the century, in 1926 the Makah stopped whaling. In recognition of the Gray whale's plight, it was listed under the Endangered Species Act in 1969. Due to the protections of the ESA and the IWC, Gray whale populations made a remarkable recovery, increasing to about 26,000 individuals and growing roughly 2.5% per year. The Gray whale was delisted from the ESA in 1994 and the Makah notified the federal government that they wished to exercise their treaty rights and commence whaling. With federal support, the Makah requested permission from the IWC and, effectively in a trade, the United States obtained the rights for 20 Gray whales intended for Russia's Chukotka peoples and the Russians obtained the right to take 20 Bowhead whales intended for the Alaskan Inupiats.

The Makah have argued that the hunt represents an important opportunity for community self-respect and rejuvenation. As the president of the Makah Whaling Commission wrote in an editorial to the *Seattle Times* on August 23, 1998:

> Whaling has been part of our tradition for over 2,000 years. Although we had to stop in the 1920s because of the scarcity of gray whales, their abundance now makes it possible to resume our ancient practice of whale hunting. Many of our Tribal members feel that our health problems result from the loss of our

traditional sea food and sea mammal diet. We would like to restore the meat of the whale to that diet. We also believe that the problems which are troubling our young people stem from lack of discipline and pride and we hope that the restoration of whaling will help to restore that discipline and pride. But we also want to fulfill the legacy of our forefathers and restore a part of our culture which was taken from us.

Granted permits to take up to 5 Gray whales per year by NMFS for 5 years and supported by a federal grant, the Makah created a whaling commission with representatives from 23 traditional whaling families. The hunt would be carried out in a 36–foot, sea-going canoe carved out of a tree trunk, manned by eight Makah who had specially trained for whaling by paddling practice and spiritual preparations. Upon approaching a migrating Gray whale, the crew would strike it with a ceremonial harpoon and then shoot it with a retrofitted, high-powered rifle designed by a veterinarian to kill the whale immediately. A crew member would then dive in and sew shut the whale's mouth so it would not sink. The canoe would be followed by support boats in case of emergency. The Makah pledged not to sell any of the whale meat or whale products but, rather, distribute it to members of the tribe. They also pledged not to take calves or mothers with calves.

From the outset, the proposed hunt generated intense opposition, including a well-organized NGO campaign led by the Sea Shepherd Conservation Society and a unanimous resolution from the U.S. House of Representatives Resource Committee condemning the hunt. The Makah first started hunting in the Fall of 1998 but, in a spectacle widely reported in the media and that must have been seen to be believed, opponents moved into Neah Bay with up to fifteen boats, planes, and a submarine trailing the Tribe's canoe. The sub broadcast the underwater sounds of killer whales while those on the boats sought to disrupt the hunt with shouts and thrown objects. Sea Shepherd offered a reward of $2,000 for information on the Makah tribe's planned hunts provided at least three hours prior to the launch of whaling boats. The Coast Guard finally needed to come in and enforce a 500–yard exclusion zone around the canoe.

The battle has played out in court, as well, with a successful NGO challenge in 2000 to an environmental assessment prepared after NMFS had already signed an agreement with the Makah to support their whaling proposal. *Metcalf v. Daley*, 214 F.3d 1135 (9th Cir. 2000). In 2004, the Ninth Circuit ruled that the Makah must request a waiver under the Marine Mammal Protection Act before taking any more Gray whales. *Anderson v. Evans*, 371 F.3d 475 (9th Cir. 2004). At the time this book went to press, NOAA Fisheries had just released a draft Environmental Impact Statement for the Makah's request. The agency made clear that it would take additional time before it reached a decision on the waiver request. Assuming the final EIS is challenged in court, it could take a great deal of time.

The hunt has received strong support within the Makah community, with a 2001 referendum of Makah households showing over 90% approval for whaling under treaty rights. Perhaps even more telling, wealthy outside individuals have offered to support development projects and land acquisition on behalf of the Makah if they stop whaling and the Makah have refused. The Makah took a ten-meter long Gray whale in 1999, held a ceremony following the hunt, and distributed the meat in a tribal feast.

Opposition arguments to the hunt have covered the spectrum. In terms of its effect on the IWC, opponents fear that Makah whaling will provide meaningful precedent for increased aboriginal subsistence whaling around the world, not to mention the possibility of Japanese or Norwegian coastal communities eventually coming under the exception. Critics have also contended that the hunt is a cover for commercial whaling to sell meat to Japan. The animal rights opposition is obvious—killing whales is wrong, they argue, whether by indigenous groups or commercial vessels.

The cultural arguments have been more indirect, taking four basic forms. The first is that the lapse in time between hunting whales, from 1926 to 1998, shows that whaling is no longer central to the Makah culture and religion. Indeed, no one in the tribe is alive who took part in the earlier whaling. The second is that the lapse in time demonstrates that the Makah do not need whales for subsistence purposes because they have survived over seventy years without whale meat, oil, or bones. The third is that the modern equipment the Makah use in the hunt—a high-powered rifle and speedboat support—show the Makah have assimilated and cannot credibly claim the whale hunt is central to their historical identity. If that were so, the argument goes, they would honor their past by hunting with traditional means. As one whale tour operator has bluntly charged,

> If they [the Makah] are so hell bent on going back to their roots, why ... do they insist on: driving cars, using internal combustion engines, fiberglass, aluminum, roads, shopping centers, all the other stuff that has improved their lives ....

http://www.cnie.org/NAE/cases/makah/me.html#28.

The fourth argument attacks cultural relativism—the argument that we should allow the hunt to go forward out of respect for the Makah culture.

> From media reports, one would be tempted to conclude that whaling was the only "glue" that held together the ancient proud Makah. To argue that a return to whaling is the only way for the Makah to regain their lost culture, one must have an accurate understanding of the culture that was lost. * * *
>
> Slavery—Prior to their 1855 treaty with territorial governor Isaac Stevens, the Makah practiced slavery. Slaves were traded among tribal members and performed the menial and demanding tasks relegated to slaves.
>
> Human sacrifice—Upon the death of a chief, it was often the practice to sacrifice a slave.
>
> Polygamy—... [T]he Makah practiced limited polygamy, with some men having two wives.
>
> Warfare—The ancient Makah conducted warfare with other tribes on the modern Olympic Peninsula. Among the war practices were cutting off the heads of enemies and impaling the heads on poles for display back in the Makah village.
>
> The Makah whaling practices of ancient times were also quite complicated and involved. According to Curtis [an anthropologist in the early 1900s], at times the Makah would make use of a human corpse during their whaling

rituals. "The body must be that of a male not more than four days dead, and it is said that sometimes a small boy was killed for the purpose. Occasionally the whaler flayed the body after removing the forearms and the lower legs, cutting the skin down the median line from the forehead and along the inside of the legs. After being dried in the sun with as little handling as possible, the skin was hung over the back-piece of the whaler's head dress." Curtis goes on to describe how the whaler would then tie the corpse—sans arms and legs—onto his back and wear it during the hunt. * * *

The ancient Makah were a proud, resourceful people who hunted whales for subsistence needs. To adequately honor the Makah past it is important to understand ancient Makah society in its entirety, especially when people perceive that they are proposing a whole-scale return to the traditions of that era.

Wilson Parker, *Makah Culture and Tradition,* PAWS MAGAZINE, www.paws. org/about/mag/issues/issue39/culture.html. Not surprisingly, the Makah have strongly objected to all of these arguments.

QUESTIONS AND DISCUSSION

1. What is your gut reaction to the Makah hunt? Speaking for yourself, how would you defend your view that it should be allowed or stopped?

2. Which of the anti-hunt positions described above do you find most persuasive? Do you find any of the anti-hunt positions troubling?

Given the treatment of Native Americans since European settlement, one can understand why the Makah bristle at the notion of "outsiders" criticizing the morality of their hunt. In this regard, consider the comments of Keith Johnson, President of the Makah Whaling Commission.

Recently the Progressive Animal Welfare Society (PAWS) distributed a brochure in which they implied we have lost our cultural need for whaling because we have adapted to modern life. They cite our "... lighted tennis courts ... Federal Express ... and other amenities ..." Well, excuse me! I want to tell PAWS that the two tennis courts on our high school grounds have no lights. How about the fact that Federal Express makes deliveries to our reservation? Does that mean that we have lost our culture?

These attacks on our culture and our status are foolish. No one can seriously question who we are; we are a small Native American Tribe who were the whalers of the American continent. We retain our whaling traditions today. It resonates through all of our people from the youngest to the oldest, and we don't take kindly to other people trying to tell us what our culture is or should be. * * *

Whales have captured the public's fascination. Whales are definitely "in." Does that mean that Indians are "out?" The world has had a similar fascination with us and our cultures, but whenever we had something you wanted or did something you didn't like, you tried to impose your values on us. The Federal government even tried to stamp out our potlatch tradition because they thought it was backward and impoverishing. Too often white society has demonstrated this kind of cultural arrogance. We don't take well to Sea Shepherd or PAWS telling us we should rise to a "higher" level of culture by not whaling. To us the implication that our culture is inferior if we believe in whaling is demeaning and racist.

We feel that the whaling issue has been exploited by extremists who have taken liberties with the facts in order to advance their agenda. We understand that there are many people who legitimately believe that it is wrong to kill a whale. But we feel that the zealousness and self-righteousness which emanates from the animal rights community has led to dishonesty and extremism. To them I would say that we may have deeper feelings for the whale than you or your forebears. We ask that you show some respect for Indian culture and that you stop the lies and distortions. The Makah people have been hurt by these attacks, but nevertheless we are committed to continuing in what we feel is the right path.

We Makahs hope that the general public will try to understand and respect our culture and ignore the attacks of extremists.

http://www.cnie.org/NAE/docs/makaheditorial.html.

3. The IWC presumably has failed to define "aboriginal subsistence whaling" because of the difficulty in doing so. If you were creating an objective test for the exception, what would it look like? How would you take into account the following factors and concerns:

- *Length of tradition.*

  How should you take into account lapses between whaling? What if the Makah had last practiced whaling 200 years ago?

- *Recognition in domestic legal treaty.*

  This may seem a clinching argument for the Makah hunt going forward, but would it be as persuasive if the Gray whale were still listed under the Endangered Species Act?

- *Importance to local culture.*

- *Importance to diet*

- *Use of low-technology means*

- *Local consumption versus sale of meat*

These last two factors may seem relevant but, if the other factors are satisfied, why should they matter at all? Do you see why, in establishing the aboriginal whaling exception, one must also determine *the purpose* of the exception?

4. How should we regard the Japanese claims for an aboriginal exception? Is there a legitimate distinction between small-scale coastal whaling in countries like Norway, supposed village whaling called for by Japan, and the Makah? Is framing the distinction around where the meat ultimately ends up (consumed within the community or sold outside) persuasive?

5. The Makah controversy also raises the broader issue of balancing natural resource conservation with the free exercise of religion and respect for the nation's many cultures and religions. Do you find the arguments over cultural respect persuasive? The PAWS excerpt suggests that the Makah whaling tradition (as well as its other traditions) were unworthy of respect, much less emulation. What if the U.S. had signed a treaty with the Makah allowing bigamy? Would we allow that, even if it were not against the law? How would you rebut this argument?

As a matter of constitutional law, any free exercise challenge would be difficult. Even sincere religious adherents are not entitled to exemptions from neutral laws of general applicability. *See Employment Division v. Smith*, 494 U.S. 872 (1990) (holding that the Oregon's denial of unemployment compensation to Native American fired for ceremonial ingestion of peyote did not violate the Free Exercise Clause). *See also* Chapter 2 (discussing the relationship between the Free Exercise Clause and natural resources regulation). Although the free exercise clause may not entitle religious conduct to an exemption, it does not necessarily bar such an exemption. Thus the question remains whether it makes sense to grant the Makah an exception because of the whale's ceremonial importance. On the other hand, does the Makah whale hunt infringe on the rights of others? If so, how?

6. Is the US position on the Makah consistent with its IWC position or is it, as critics contend, hypocritically undermining its moral authority on the subject?

7. On September 12, 2007, NOAA Fisheries reported that

> [s]everal Makah tribal members shot and killed a gray whale on Sept. 8, without any NOAA Fisheries Service authorization or permit, or any apparent formal tribal authorization. Fisheries Enforcement is investigating, and NOAA is assessing how to proceed with processing the tribe's MMPA waiver request.

Should this have any impact on the decision whether or not to grant the Makah's waiver request to resume whaling?

8. Interestingly, the nationally prominent environmental groups Sierra Club and Greenpeace have not taken a position on the Makah hunt. Greenpeace, in particular, made its name racing in zodiac rafts between whaling vessels and whales on the high seas. Why do you think they have refused to condemn the Makah hunt?

—————

B. MARINE MAMMAL–FISHERY CONFLICTS

1. OVERVIEW OF THE MARINE MAMMAL PROTECTION ACT OF 1972

While the Fur Seal Treaty of 1911 represented an early attempt to protect marine mammals, federal wildlife law did not move much beyond bird conservation. This started to change in the late 1960s, however, with calls for a federal law to protect marine mammals. Calls for federal actions came from three separate quarters. Commercial interests were worried that, without stronger management authority, marine mammal stocks could not support sustainable harvests. Scientists and environmental groups pointed out the important ecological role of marine mammals in ocean ecosystems. And, as discussed in the preceding section on whaling, animal rights interests argued that marine mammals are highly intelligent and deserve special legal protections. The resulting legislation, the Marine Mammal Protection Act of 1972 (MMPA), 16 U.S.C. §§ 1361–1407, represented the most comprehensive conservation program to date. Because compromise among the three interests was necessary to assure passage, "the Act articulated only broad, general policy goals and implemented with specific directions that were neither purely protectionist nor purely exploitive but almost always complex." MICHAEL BEAN AND MELANIE ROWLAND, THE EVOLUTION OF NATIONAL WILDLIFE LAW 110–111 (3rd ed., 1997).

Focusing on population viability rather than solely on individuals, the MMPA preempted state regulation of marine mammals, placing control in the hands of the National Marine Fisheries Service (now also known as NOAA Fisheries) for pinnipeds (seals and sea lions) and cetaceans (whales, dolphins and porpoises). The U.S. Fish and Wildlife Service is responsible for walruses, sea otters, polar bears, manatees and dugongs. The primary responsibility for both these agencies is to ensure populations of marine mammals remain at their "optimum sustainable population" (OSP), defined as "the number of animals which will result in the maximum productivity of the population or species, keeping in mind the optimum carrying capacity of the habitat and the health of the ecosystem of which they form a constituent element." 16 U.S.C. § 1362(8). If the populations fall below this level, they are designated as "depleted" and a conservation plan must be developed to restore the population.

While the definition of the optimum sustainable population sounds a lot like the maximum sustainable yield in the Fisheries Conservation Management Act, the MMPA fundamentally differs from this fisheries approach by imposing a moratorium on the taking of marine mammals in U.S. waters (and by U.S. citizens on the high seas) and on the import of marine mammals and marine mammal products into the United States. Taking was defined to include acts that "harass, hunt, capture, or kill, or attempt to harass, hunt, capture or kill any marine mammal." On its face, the moratorium appeared absolute. The MMPA text called for a "complete cessation" on taking and a "complete ban" on imports. 16 U.S.C. § 1362(7). In practice, though, the moratorium story has been one of exceptions.

A major concern during passage of the MMPA and its subsequent implementation has been the tension between protecting marine mammals and protecting the commercial fishing industry. While the MMPA imposed a moratorium on taking marine mammals, this conservation goal had to be pragmatically balanced with commercial fishing interests and the fact that marine mammals sometimes become tangled in fishing gear and drown. Thus the Act states, for example, that "it shall be the immediate goal that the incidental kill or incidental serious injury of marine mammals permitted in the course of commercial fishing operations be reduced to insignificant levels approaching a zero mortality and serious injury rate." 16 U.S.C. § 1371(a)(2). At the same time, it allows taking marine mammals incidental to fishing operations so long as the taking "will not be to the disadvantage" of the species. 16 U.S.C. § 1373(a). How can one provide for incidental kills and ever achieve zero mortality, much less immediately?

This quandary has bedeviled the MMPA and was particularly controversial in the use of purse seine nets by the tuna fishery in the eastern tropical Pacific Ocean. The use of purse seine nets for yellowfin tuna traps and drowns many porpoises. In the early 1970s, NMFS estimated porpoise mortality ranging from 100,000–300,000 deaths annually, hardly approaching the goal of zero mortality. The MMPA included a two year exemption following its passage for incidental takes in the tuna fishery. In 1976, though, the government was ordered by a court to set a ceiling on the number of dolphins that could be incidentally taken. *See Committee for Humane Legislation, Inc. v. Richardson,* 540 F.2d 1141 (D.C. Cir. 1976) (denying the issuance of general permit for purse-seine fishing for yellowfin tuna). Over the next eight years, the tuna fleet's incidental dolphin mortality quota was reduced, from 78,000 in 1976 to 20,500 by 1985. The conclusion to this story and the key role of international law is discussed in more detail at the end of the chapter.

The current law, dating from the 1994 amendments, requires NMFS to undertake "stock assessments" for marine mammal populations in order to determine the "potential biological removal level." This is similar in principle to the MSY—a measure of the maximum number of animals that can be removed from a stock without causing it to drop below its OSP. A "Take Reduction Plan" is then developed that sets a level of take below the potential biological removal level. In essence, then, the zero mortality goal has developed into an approach that combines a stock assessment with a best available technology approach as developed in the Take Reduction Plan.

As a result, today the moratorium is really only relevant to taking marine mammals for recreational purposes or for the use of marine mammal products. As one commentator has noted, to accommodate concerns of the fishing industry, the amendments to the MMPA have clearly departed from the Act's original "zero mortality" conservation goal for marine mammals.

> The [1994] changes demonstrated to many observers that the MMPA had moved away from the concept of protecting each marine mammal and was now satisfied with merely protecting the populations of the species at high enough levels to prevent extinction.... In May of 1995, one year after these amendments were passed, researchers estimated that approximately 3200 marine mammals were being killed annually in Atlantic fisheries, most notably harbor porpoises killed by fishing in the Gulf of Maine. An additional 4400 animals were being killed annually in the Pacific. The new zero-mortality rate is 10% of the PBR [potential biological removal level].

Susan C. Alker, The *Marine Mammal Protection Act: Refocusing the Approach to Conservation*, 44 UCLA L. REV. 527, 551, 553 (1996). Michael Bean and Melanie Rowland agree that the 1994 amendments represent a major departure from the principles stated in the MMPA in 1972, but are less critical of this change.

> The 1972 law imposed a blanket moratorium on taking marine mammals and a virtual bar against waiving the moratorium for depleted stocks. The 1994 amendments grew out of a recognition that these requirements could not be enforced and probably were unnecessary in any event to achieve the law's conservation objectives. Although somewhat ambiguous, the amendments reflect the ascendancy of the view that rather than seeking to eliminate incidental deaths of marine mammals, it is sufficient to keep mortality within acceptable limits.... Rather than evidence of drafting ineptitude, the MMPA's incidental taking goals reflect the sort of purposeful ambiguity by which

opposing interests often reconcile their differing objectives. Unable to reach agreement on all details, they embrace a verbal formulation that leaves each the freedom to argue that its interpretation is what Congress truly intended.

MICHAEL BEAN & MELANIE ROWLAND, THE EVOLUTION OF NATIONAL WILDLIFE LAW 110–11 (3d ed., 1997).

QUESTIONS AND DISCUSSION

1. According to some scientists and NGOs, increasing use of sonar may pose serious threats to marine mammal populations. The U.S. Navy has been developing the use of "low frequency active" (LFA) sonar to detect the new generation of quiet diesel submarines and conducting training exercises in the waters off southern California. In contrast to "passive" sonar, which listens for sub engine noises, active sonar emits powerful sound waves that opponents contend can damage marine mammal hearing and disrupt their communication, thus also affecting breeding, feeding and other social interactions, resulting in a take under the ESA and MMPA.

In 1999, the Navy sought a five-year take permit for impacts on marine mammals during testing of the LFA sonar over an area of roughly 14 million square miles in the northwestern Pacific. The Humane Society, NRDC, Cetacean Society International and other groups sued, charging violations of the MMPA, NEPA and Endangered Species Act. In response to the request for a preliminary injunction, the judge ordered the Navy and plaintiffs to meet and determine areas for sonar testing in waters where few marine mammals are found. In August, 2003, the judge issued a permanent injunction against the navy's use of high-powered sonar during training exercises in areas that are particularly rich in marine life, stating that it posed too great a risk to whales and other ocean creatures. The court provided an exception, however, allowing use of technology "in self defense, times of defense and in times of war, combat or heightened threat conditions." *Natural Resources Defense Council, Inc. v. Evans*, 279 F. Supp. 2d 1129 (N.D. Cal. 2003).

Arguing that such decisions weaken national security, the Department of Defense has sought legislative exemptions from the Endangered Species Act and the Marine Mammal Protection Act. In its "Range Readiness and Preservation Initiative," the Department of Defense argues that these wildlife protection provisions often impede military training and readiness. In the specific context of the MMPA, a *Frequently Asked Questions* fact sheet published by the Department of Defense (DoD) states:

> The Navy faces major threats from new, quiet diesel submarines that a number of possible adversaries now possess. Training and testing with existing and new systems is necessary to effectively counter this threat and protect our young men and women in uniform. A single undetected submarine could sink a carrier, with its crew of approximately 5,000 sailors and marines. Several aspects of the MMPA, as interpreted by regulators and the courts, are severely inhibiting appropriate tests and training activities.

A bill was proposed that would enact DoD's proposed changes. The last clause in Section 2015 of the proposed legislation stated:

(e) EXEMPTION OF ACTIONS NECESSARY FOR NATIONAL DEFENSE.—The Secretary of Defense, after conferring with the Secretary of Commerce, the Secretary of Interior, or both, as appropriate, may exempt any action or category of actions undertaken by the Department of Defense or its components from compliance with any requirement of the Marine Mammal Protection Act, 16 U.S.C. 1361 et seq., if he determines that it is necessary for national defense. Exemptions granted under this section shall be for a period of not more than two years. Additional exemptions for periods not to exceed two years each may be granted for the same action or category of actions upon the Secretary of Defense, after conferring with the Secretary of Commerce, the Secretary of Interior, or both as appropriate, making a new determination.

If you were the legislative counsel for an animal rights group and testifying before Congress, how would you characterize and rebut the Department of Defense initiative? If the military exemption is too broad, how would you narrow its application? More broadly, what do you think is the proper balance between marine mammal protection and military operations?

2. Congress passed a military exemption similar to that described above in Question 1 and, in January 2007, the Department of Defense granted the Navy a two-year exemption from the MMPA for training purposes. 16 U.S.C. 1371(f)(1). The exemption was conditioned on the following mitigation measures:

(1) training lookouts and officers to watch for marine mammals;

(2) requiring at least five lookouts with binoculars on each vessel to watch for anomalies on the water surface (including marine mammals);

(3) requiring aircraft and sonar operators to report detected marine mammals in the vicinity of the training exercises;

(4) requiring reduction of active sonar transmission levels by 6 dB if a marine mammal is detected within 1,000 yards of the bow of the vessel, or by 10 dB if detected within 500 yards;

(5) requiring complete shutdown of active sonar transmission if a marine mammal is detected within 200 yards of the vessel;

(6) requiring active sonar to be operated at the "lowest practicable level"; and

(7) adopting coordination and reporting procedures.

In *NRDC v. Winter*, five environmental groups requested a preliminary injunction to halt the Navy's use of mid-frequency active (MFA) sonar in fourteen large-scale training exercises in the Southern California Operating Area (SOCAL). 2007 WL 2481037 (C.D. Cal. 2007). The primary claim focused on the Navy's failure to prepare an Environmental Impact Statement. The Navy had prepared an Environmental Assessment, concluding that the impacts were insufficient to require development of an EIS. Under the threat of litigation, the Navy subsequently agreed to prepare an EIS, but the plaintiffs moved for a preliminary injunction, trying to halt use of sonar until the EIS was completed. The district court, agreed, finding that plaintiffs had demonstrated a probability of success on the merits and concluding that:

From the numerous scientific studies, declarations, reports, and other evidence before the Court, Plaintiffs have established to a near certainty that use of MFA sonar during the planned SOCAL exercises will cause irreparable harm to the environment and Plaintiffs' standing declarants. The Court is also satisfied that the balance of hardships tips in favor of granting an injunction, as the harm to the environment, Plaintiffs, and public interest outweighs the harm that Defendants would incur if prevented from using MFA sonar, absent the use of effective mitigation measures, during a subset of their regular activities in one part of one state for a limited period. Accordingly, the Court grants Plaintiffs' requested relief and enjoins Defendants' use of MFA sonar during the remaining SOCAL exercises.

Id. at *10. In January, 2008, the district court issued a preliminary injunction permitting the Navy to complete its remaining exercises so long as it employed measures to mitigate the harm to marine mammals from sonar use. In particular, the court modified the fifth mitigation measure, requiring the Navy to suspend its use of sonar if a marine mammal is detected within 2,200 yards of the sonar source (rather than 200 yards), and reducing the acoustic energy level of sonar by 6 decibels whenever significant surface ducting conditions were detected. On appeal, the Ninth Circuit stayed these mitigation measures where the sonar was being used "at a critical point in the exercise" but kept in place the court's preliminary injunction on future use of sonar in training exercises. *NRDC v. Winter*, 518 F.3d 704, 705–06 (9th Cir. 2008) (order accompanying panel opinion). *See also NRDC v. Winter*, 518 F.3d 658 (9th Cir. 2008) (panel opinion).

The case was heard by the U.S. Supreme Court. In a decision focusing on the proper standard for issuing a preliminary injunction, the Court held for the Navy, concluding that:

Plaintiffs contend that the Navy's use of MFA sonar will injure marine mammals or alter their behavioral patterns, impairing plaintiffs' ability to study and observe the animals. While we do not question the seriousness of these interests, we conclude that the balance of equities and consideration of the overall public interest in this case tip strongly in favor of the Navy. For the plaintiffs, the most serious possible injury would be harm to an unknown number of the marine mammals that they study and observe. In contrast, forcing the Navy to deploy an inadequately trained antisubmarine force jeopardizes the safety of the fleet. Active sonar is the only reliable technology for detecting and tracking enemy diesel-electric submarines, and the President—the Commander in Chief—has determined that training with active sonar is "essential to national security."

The public interest in conducting training exercises with active sonar under realistic conditions plainly outweighs the interests advanced by the plaintiffs. Of course, military interests do not always trump other considerations, and we have not held that they do. In this case, however, the proper determination of where the public interest lies does not strike us as a close question.

Winters v. Natural Resources Defense Council, 129 S.Ct. 365 (2008).

Justice Ginsburg's dissent argues that the fourteen training exercises will be completed by the time the EIS is drafted. How can the Court conclude that the balance of interests (including potential harm to the marine mammals) favors the Navy and therefore that the use of LFA sonar should continue until the EIS is prepared, without the information the EIS would provide? What do you think plaintiffs would need to have demonstrated in order to satisfy the Court?

The long history of the navy sonar litigation is explained in Robin Kundis Craig, *Litigating the Navy's Use of Active SONAR: A Quick and Dirty Critique of the Current Statutory Exemptions* (2008); *available at* <http://papers.ssrn.com/sol3/papers.cfm?abstract_id=1278065>.

3. The MMPA bans the take of marine mammals without a permit. The law states:

> The term "take" means to harass, hunt, capture, or kill, or attempt to harass, hunt, capture or kill any marine mammal.

16 U.S.C. 1362(13). Compare this with the definition of "take" under the Endangered Species Act (which was passed a year later).

> The term "take" means to harass, harm, pursue, hunt, shoot, wound, kill, trap, capture, or collect, or to attempt to engage in any such conduct.

16 U.S.C. 1532(19). How are they different? If you have read the *Palila* and *Sweet Home* decisions, do you think an NGO litigator might be able to craft a similar argument that expanded the scope of takes for marine mammals? What kind of fact pattern would be needed for the equivalent of a *Palila* or *Sweet Home* decision for marine mammals?

4. On its face, the MMPA's goal of zero mortality seems fundamentally different from the management approach of the Fisheries Conservation Management Act, which focuses on sustainable management of the fishery for commercial purposes. Given the 1994 amendments to the MMPA and its current reliance on take reduction plans and potential biological removal levels, do the two statutes' management strategies differ all that much?

5. One of the major innovations of the MMPA was its focus on the role of a species within its ecosystem. Thus, for example, the preamble of the Act ("Congressional Findings"), states that marine mammal "species and population stocks should not be permitted to diminish beyond the point at which they cease to be a significant functioning element in the ecosystem of which they are a part.... In particular, efforts should be made to protect essential habitats, including the rookeries, mating grounds, and areas of similar significance of each species of marine mammal from the effects of man's actions." 16 U.S.C. § 1361(2). It is worth noting that this preceded the essential fish habitat requirements in the FCMA by almost a quarter century. It is also worth noting, however, how little has been done to protect marine mammal habitat. As Susan Alker observes,

> [Despite passage of the MMPA in 1972, the] 1994 amendments provided the first meaningful recognition of the need for habitat conservation, yet they mention only "monitoring" and "studying" the health and stability of ecosystems, not "protecting" or "preserving." Studying the problem is a valuable first step. However, after twenty years of MMPA protection efforts, more direct activities to preserve habitats are needed at this time. Because studying is all that is being done, the results will of necessity be limited to data and reports, not proactive implementation of protective measures.

Id. at 554.

6. The Act's moratorium on taking does not apply to taking by any Indian, Aleut, or Eskimo who resides in Alaska and who dwells on the coast of the North Pacific Ocean or the Arctic Ocean if such taking is for subsistence purposes or for creating and selling authentic Native articles of handicrafts and clothing, and is not done in a wasteful manner. Do you think this is an example of environmental justice done the right way?

7. Jerry Mitchell, a U.S. citizen, was arrested for capturing dolphins in Bahamian waters (in accordance with Bahamian law) and transporting them to an aquarium in England. He was charged with the unauthorized taking of a marine mammal by any person subject to the jurisdiction of the United States. Mitchell challenged his conviction, arguing that the MMPA's authority did not extend to foreign waters. The district court convicted Mitchell, ruling that Congress intended to extend coverage of the Act to all takings of marine mammals by U.S. citizens under the MMPA wherever such offenses occur, and that this moratorium was an absolute prohibition without geographical limitation. On appeal, however, the Fifth Circuit reversed the conviction. The Court found that although the MMPA expressly prohibited the taking of dolphins within the *territorial limits* of the United States and on the *high seas*, neither the language of the MMPA nor its legislative history demonstrated a congressional intent to prohibit a citizen of the United States from taking a dolphin while *in the territory* of another sovereign. *United States v. Mitchell*, 553 F.2d 996, 1003 (5th Cir. 1977).

> It is no small matter when, in effect, this nation countermands a permit of another nation allowing the permittee to work in the territorial waters of the foreign country. We cannot say that the interests of the United States in preserving dolphins outweighs the interest of the Commonwealth of the Bahamas in preserving its character as a tourist attraction by the issuance of a limited number of permits for the capture of dolphins within its narrow band of territorial waters. If the moratorium was meant to extend the reach of the statute to the territorial waters of every country in the world, the sponsors of the amendment would certainly have recognized a duty to explain the need for such an extension on the floors of Congress and in the committee reports.
>
> In summary, then, the Act and its legislative history do not demonstrate the clear intent required ... to overcome the presumption against extraterritorial extension of American statutes. Congress did extend the force of the MMPA to the high seas, but any further extension to regulate the taking of marine mammals in the territory of other sovereign states is not justified by the Act. The legislative scheme requires the State Department to pursue international controls by the usual methods of negotiation, treaty, and convention. Without a clearer expression from Congress to the contrary, we must presume that United States jurisdiction under the Act ceases at the territorial waters and boundaries of other states.

Id. at 1004–05. In its opinion, the Court argued that restricting the MMPA in scope to U.S. territories and the high seas would neither greatly curtail its scope and usefulness nor frustrate its purpose. But presumably the goal of Congress in passing the MMPA was to conserve marine mammal populations by shutting down *entirely* the commercial taking and capturing of marine mammals by U.S. citizens and vessels. Should it make a difference if the United States demonstrated that the dolphin population in Bahamian waters also spent time in U.S. waters?

8. *Problem Exercise.* The MMPA's definition of take includes "harass." This has been expanded in regulations to include "the negligent or intentional operation of an aircraft or vessel, or the doing of any other negligent or intentional act which results in disturbing or molesting a marine mammal." 50 C.F.R. § 216.3. Assume a commercial tour boat takes passengers into the Gulf of Mexico to feed wild dolphins. How would you argue this qualifies as a take? *See Strong v. United States,* 5 F.3d 905 (5th Cir. 1993). What about the case where a commercial fisherman fires a rifle to scare off porpoises he believes are eating fish off his line? *See United States v. Hayashi,* 22 F.3d 859 (9th Cir. 1993).

---

2. PINNIPEDS AND THE SALMON FISHERY

Thanks to the MMPA and earlier hunting bans, most pinniped populations (i.e., seals, sea lions and walruses) along the West coast of the United States have recovered remarkably well. In the 1920s, for example, there were roughly 1,500 California sea lions along the California coast. NMFS reported in the 1990s that sea lion populations had grown to 188,000, an annual growth rate of 5–7% and triple their number in the 1970s. NOAA 99–R107 Press Release, 2/11/99. With the increase in pinniped populations, however, have come increased concerns over their impacts on fish stocks and fishing vessel gear. Nowhere has this been clearer than with the story of Hondo and the Ballard Locks.

The Ballard Ship Locks are located in Seattle, providing the gateway into Lake Washington and its tributary streams. Starting in the early 1980s, Hondo and a number of other California sea lions took up residence at the locks during the steelhead trout migration from the sea to freshwater spawning grounds, essentially helping themselves to a buffet lunch as the fish slowed down and bunched together to go up the fish ladders at the Locks. Estimates varied, but predation by Hondo and his buddies was said to consume up to 65% of the steelhead passing through the locks, threatening the run, itself. In the excerpt below, Professor Bill Rodgers recounts Hondo's saga.

William Rodgers, *Defeating Environmental Law: The Geology of Legal Advantage* PACE ENVTL. L. REV. 687, 706–713 (2002)

The California sea lions that brought attention to the steelhead at the Ballard Locks were excellent scapegoats. They had recently arrived in the Puget Sound area—a legal by-product, some said, of the pro-pinniped sentiments bound up in the Marine Mammal Protection Act of 1970. They were native to California, which counts for two strikes in Washington. They were all male, another debit that made most of them biologically superfluous. And they ate fish in plain view, which stripped them of the pretense of innocence enjoyed by other offenders who did their steelhead malefactions in the anonymity of the high seas. It was easy enough for public opinion to saddle these proven killers with rumors of wrongs unconfirmed. These sea lions, it was believed, preferred heads, not the fillets of the fish. These wanton connoisseurs were suspected of killing eight or ten instead of one fully consumed. * * *

These troublesome sea lions who gathered at the Ballard Locks were given a name—"Hershel" was the moniker. In the early days, "Hershel" was a generic name applied to several of the sea lions who enjoyed the steelhead diet available at the Locks. But one "Hershel" soon emerged as the leader of the Hershels. He secured his reputation in the winter of 1993–94 when observers blamed him for consuming 60% of the dwindling steelhead run. He was given a name—Hondo, No. 17 by a biologist and longtime Boston Celtics fan and admirer of a great player from an earlier era, John Havlicek. Like the Havlicek of old, sea lion No.17 overwhelmed the defense set before him. Stopping him became a personal thing.

Eventually, Hondo, No. 17, would take the blame for the decline in the Ballard Locks Winter Steelhead Run. He would be the 255th victim in the war against pinnipeds that is now being waged in the name of the salmon. But he would be given every legal chance. He would enjoy the finest due process environmental law has to offer. He would hear the best of science brought to bear on his case. He would be the beneficiary of an exacting exercise in adaptive management.

The National Environment Policy Act (NEPA) was one of the first laws brought to bear to Hondo's advantage. It required carefully assessing the effects and evaluating the alternatives before undertaking a major action such as sea lion removal.... The NMFS staffers and their partners systematically rolled through the options that would save the fish and keep the sea lions alive.... The managers attempted to deter the sea lions with "seal bombs." But the clever respondents learned to dive to depth when the missiles entered the water. All that resulted from the failed experiment was the sea lions returning to the surface and picking up the struggling fish "incidentally" stunned by the "seal bombs."

The managers then sought to isolate the fish mingling at the mouth of the Locks with variously designed "entanglement nets." These were brushed aside by various "over, under and through" strategies that required little exertion from these 500–800 pound marine acrobats. The managers also ran "test aversion" experiments with chemically contaminated steelhead. The sea lions quickly learned to reject the proffer of dead fish from people in yellow suits.

The managers introduced a ten-inch mesh "sea lion barrier" that would allow the steelhead to pass, but not the sea lions. Unfortunately the steelhead did not know about this advantage; no one could make them aware of it, so they shied away from the ten-inch mesh as they might from a one-inch mesh. They were trapped there by the sea lions as efficiently as they could have been against a fine brick wall.

Increases in the degrees of violence made no difference. The managers turned to sea lion "anesthetics," and killed a few. However, the managers soon learned that dose-response rates derived from bears do not apply to marine mammals on a weight-for-weight basis. They turned to trapping the sea lions, putting them in trucks, and removing them to the Pacific Coast, only to learn that the animals returned rapidly to the Ballard Locks. One of the returnees was Rapid Rudy, whose feats received immediate consideration for North American marine mammal speed records.

Next came a serious removal strategy. It was aimed, as all effective removals are, not at individually identifiable candidates but at those who could be found and captured. Six of the animals were trapped at the Locks, trucked to southern California in the face of objections under the Coastal Zone Management Act, and released some 2000 miles from the forbidden waters of Puget Sound. Even this sea lion version of the Oklahoma territory was not sufficiently distant. Three sea lions returned in a matter of months. Two disappeared. One compromised by taking up residence in the Columbia River.

The sea lions at the Locks were attacked with "Bear Stingers" shot from crossbows. The sea lions met this strategy with hasty dives that created wicked ricochets as missiles glanced off the surface of the water. Lawyers, with recurring nightmares of wounded schoolchildren "incidentally" caught in the crossfire at the Locks, called off the campaign.

Then came the 220 decibels of sound in the hearing range of the sea lions— truly painful to the ones not already deaf. But more painful yet to the managers was the sight of Hondo, returning to the scene. Although obviously distressed by the noise, he succeeded in defeating it by the simple tactic of staying in turbulent water.

In the spring of 1995, Hondo was physically captured and detained for two months in a facility near Tacoma. To avoid imprinting, he had no human contact, a deprivation he did not noticeably regret. He was fed by remote control. The NMFS took pictures of him with mouth agape, beneath the chute of herring being refueled like a great tanker. He gained 120 pounds during captivity, and grew into what staffers describe as the most awesome sea lion they had ever seen. The literature speaks of monster California sea lions, weighing in at 800 to 900 pounds. Hondo tipped the scales at a svelte 1100 pounds. * * *

The adaptive management options ran out for Hondo in the spring of 1996 with the steelhead at an all-time low and official patience nearly expired. The state got its permit to kill five of these "identifiable" pinnipeds. But nobody shot Hondo. This is the age of win-win compromise. Even vindictive judgments are cautiously executed. So Hondo was captured once again, together with Bob and Big Frank. He was placed aboard a Federal Express cargo jet for a new home at Sea World of Florida in Orlando. A Sea World manager said this was a lovely spot: "It has a large body of water and rock work the animals can haul out on and there is a wave generating machine." * * *

Within a year, Hondo was dead at Sea World, unsustained even by the wave machine. But he had the best of care. No scientist could say that he died for want of freedom. And he certainly did not die in vain. The fish managers already see signs of recovery in the Ballard steelhead run, although the reasons for improvement remain unknown. It might have been the underwater transmitters, or a fake plastic orca brought into the area, or the removals, but fish passage at the Locks is no longer exploited by opportunistic sea lions. Many see this as validation of the "bad actor" sea lion theory.

––––––––

In addition to extreme examples such as the Ballard Locks, a series of studies have found evidence of salmonid scarring from unsuccessful pinniped predation attempts. A 1995 study of migrating steelhead and chinook at the Bonneville Dam and hatcheries on the Columbia and Snake Rivers, for example, found that 24% of the steelhead had pinniped marks and 16% of the chinook. *See* NOAA–NWFSC TECH MEMO-28: IMPACT OF SEA LIONS AND SEALS ON PACIFIC COAST SALMONIDS. According to fishers, predation at fish ladders is just the tip of the iceberg. The comments below from salmon fisher Lee Cerrutti, who fishes out of Moss Landing in Northern California, express these concerns well.

"Most of the fleet is tied up," the 66–year–old fisherman notes, gesturing to a jig-pole jungle crowding the port. "When we were catching 100 fish apiece per day and sea lions stole half of them, we could still make a living. But later in the season, when fishing slowed to 50 hookups per day, they took an even higher percentage, leaving us with about 20 fish apiece. The fewer salmon around, I suppose, the hungrier and more competitive they get. In any case, when we should have been landing 50 chinooks apiece, we had to tie up. At 20 fish, we simply couldn't make it—especially since the sea lions take so many hooks, leaders and flashers, too." * * *

Similar tales issue from the region's sablefish, rock-cod and charter-boat salmon fleets: sea lions stealing fish at 40 fathoms; sport anglers landing three salmon out of 50 hookups; pods of 20 sea lions surrounding a boat, waiting for rockfish to be hauled to the surface, then eating half the catch before it can be brought aboard; mammals nearly leaping into the trolling cockpit of small commercial boats—so close, says one fisherman, he could smell their breath. * * *

"For years, we've been told the problem with salmon and steelhead runs is their habitat," says Jack Harrell, former chairman of the Monterey Bay Salmon and Trout Project, a volunteer fish restoration group. "So we've rehabilitated streams and developed hatcheries. But hatchery returns are one-tenth of what they should be. And since 50% of our returning fish are 'raked' with claw or teeth marks from harbour seals and sea lions, it's obvious that marine mammals are eating the rest."

Mick Kronman, *Self–Service: Swollen Sea Lion Herds Push Fishermen and Fish to the Brink,* NATIONAL FISHERMAN, May 1998.

While California sea lion and Pacific harbor seal populations have soared over the last three decades, salmonid populations have been crashing, with a number now listed under the Endangered Species Act. Pinnipeds are not the sole or even primary cause of these declines for pinnipeds and salmonids have co-evolved as predator and prey for millions of years. Indeed, salmonids only make up about 5–10% of the diet of most pinnipeds, who feed on them primarily during the spawning runs. Other factors such as dams, degraded stream habitat, and overfishing have played key roles. Nonetheless, in the context of significant efforts to stabilize and restore declining salmonid populations, fishery managers have determined they cannot ignore the impact of pinniped predation.

As alluded to in the Rodgers excerpt, the MMPA already provides for non-lethal removal of identifiable "nuisance" marine mammals by local, state or federal officials (Section 109(h)(1)(C)). As described in the preceding section, while there are provisions for incidental takes of marine mammals during fishing (usually from drowning in nets), the intentional lethal take of any marine mammal in the course of commercial fishing operations is prohibited unless necessary for self defense or if a person is in immediate danger (Section 118(a)(5)). Section 120(b), however, does allow take permits to be issued for *"individually identifiable* pinnipeds which are having a significant impact on the decline or recovery of salmonid fishery stocks" that are listed under the Endangered Species Act, approaching threatened or endangered status, "or migrate through the Ballard Locks at Seattle, Washington." 16 U.S.C. 1389(b)(1)(A). In order to grant permits for lethal or non-lethal removals, however, NMFS must comply with NEPA and carry out an environmental assessment. *See, e.g., Environmental*

Assessment on Preventing California Sea Lion Foraging and Predation on Salmonids at the Willamette Falls, Oregon, 63 FED. REG. 55 (1998). These provisions have been viewed as insufficient, however, and fishing interests have lobbied NMFS and Congress to loosen the protections of the MMPA. Thus, when the MMPA was amended in 1994, Congress requested NMFS and the relevant agencies in California, Washington and Oregon to examine the impacts of the rising pinniped populations along the West Coast on salmonid stocks and fishing vessels. NOAA's summary of the report's three main recommendations is excerpted below, followed by a response from the Humane Society of the United States.

NMFS, SUMMARY OF CONGRESSIONAL REPORT: IMPACTS OF CALIFORNIA SEA LIONS AND PACIFIC HARBOR SEALS ON SALMONIDS AND WEST COAST ECOSYSTEMS (Feb. 11, 1999)

1. IMPLEMENT SITE–SPECIFIC MANAGEMENT FOR CALIFORNIA SEA LIONS AND PACIFIC HARBOR SEALS.

Congress should consider a new framework that would allow state and Federal resource management agencies to immediately address conflicts involving California sea lions and Pacific harbor seals. This framework should provide a streamlined approach for federal and state resource management agencies to take necessary and appropriate action with pinnipeds, including lethal taking where necessary, that are involved in resource conflicts. Any lethal takings would have to be within the Potential Biological Removal levels established by NMFS for all human causes of mortality. The three components of the framework are:

(a) In situations where California sea lions or Pacific harbor seals are preying on salmonids that are listed or proposed or candidates for listing under the ESA, immediate use of lethal removal by state or federal resource agency officials would be authorized;

(b) in situations where California sea lions or Pacific harbor seals are preying on salmonid populations of concern or are impeding passage of these populations during migration as adults or smolts, lethal takes by state or federal resource agency officials would be authorized if (1) non-lethal deterrence methods are underway and are not fully effective, or (2) non-lethal methods are not feasible in the particular situation or have proven ineffective in the past; and,

(c) in situations where California sea lions or Pacific harbor seals conflict with human activities, such as at fishery sites and marinas, lethal removal by state or federal resource agency officials would be authorized after non-lethal deterrence has been ineffective.

2. DEVELOP SAFE, EFFECTIVE NON–LETHAL DETERRENTS.

In order to provide an array of options broader than lethal removal to resolve West Coast pinniped problems, there is a pressing need for research on the development and evaluation of deterrent devices and further exploration of other non-lethal removal measures. * * *

3. SELECTIVELY REINSTATE AUTHORITY FOR THE INTENTIONAL LETHAL TAKING OF CALIFORNIA SEA LIONS AND PACIFIC HARBOR SEALS BY COMMERCIAL FISHERS TO PROTECT GEAR AND CATCH.

Prior to the 1994 Amendments to the MMPA, commercial fishers were allowed to kill certain pinnipeds as a last resort in order to protect their gear or catch. Although the 1992 NMFS legislative proposal contained provisions to continue such authority, it was not included in the 1994 Amendments to the MMPA. Congress should reconsider providing a limited authorization, based on demonstrated need, to certain commercial fishermen at specified sites to use lethal means, as a last resort, to protect their gear and catch from depredation by California sea lions and Pacific harbor seals until such time that effective non-lethal methods are developed for their specific situation.

Toni Frohoff, *Scapegoating Seals and Sea Lions,* http://www.hsus.org/ace/11732

Appalled by shrinking fish stocks, some U.S. fishermen—both commercial and recreational—have been casting about for something or someone to blame. Among their favorite scapegoats are seals and sea lions, who they say are eating more than their fair share of fish. Their claim has been taken seriously by the National Marine Fisheries Service (NMFS), the federal agency charged with protecting the nation's marine resources. In 1999 NFMS recommended the legalized killing of seals and sea lions in its report to Congress, *Impacts of California Sea lions and the Pacific Harbor Seals on Salmonids and West Coast Ecosystems*. Congress has yet to act on the recommendation, which means that no state agency can act on it either, but NMFS has held to all but the most extreme elements of its position.

The 1999 recommendation includes giving state and federal resource managers the ability to kill seals and sea lions without attempting reasonable nonlethal alternatives and without determining if the animals are actually impacting fish stocks. The Humane Society of the United States opposes the recommendation and is concerned that it represents a dangerous step toward further mismanagement of both marine mammal and fish populations.

The recommendation for lethal removal of seals and sea lions is ecologically, ethically, and scientifically indefensible and irresponsible. There are no data to support the contention that seals and sea lions are responsible for the decline of fisheries, and none to indicate that the recommendation will achieve the stated goal of enhancing depleted fish populations.

In fact, since the recommendation was issued, NMFS's own research and that of the states of Washington and Oregon have shown that seal and sea lion predation is occurring at a much lower rate than NMFS had suspected, and is not a significant factor in fish declines. Papers presented at the previous Society for Marine Mammalogy's biennial conference pointed out the same thing: Sea lions and seals are neither the proximal cause of the decline nor a significant contributor to it.

Even if seals and sea lions were responsible, it is NMFS's responsibility to examine promising and feasible nonlethal options for deterring their predation—something it has dropped the ball on repeatedly.

The recommendation that NMFS made to Congress also failed to mention that federal law already includes provisions for lethal removal of pinnipeds who threaten public safety. Ironically, the recommendation itself could threaten public safety by allowing certain commercial fishers to shoot pinnipeds from their boats to protect their gear and catch. Given the shooting skills of the average commercial fisherman, who undoubtedly spends little time on a shooting range, the possibility that a stray bullet could accidentally hit a pleasure-boat passenger or an endangered steller sea lion is very real.

NMFS also did not mention that the Marine Mammal Protection Act already provides for lethal removal of individually identifiable seals and sea lions who are having a significant adverse impact on the decline or recovery of salmonid stocks. NMFS's 1999 recommendation only serves to expand these provisions to allow for the indiscriminate and inhumane killing of these animals without addressing the real sources of fish declines, such as hatchery fish competition, habitat degradation, open ocean driftnet fishing, and fish passage problems caused by poor construction of fishways and dams. * * *

NMFS has selected an easy target to divert attention from the actual causes of fish declines, and in the process has misled the public about the valuable role of marine mammals in the ecosystem. The HSUS agrees with Hilda Diaz–Soltero, formerly of NMFS, who stated in a letter to the president of the California Fish and Game Commission on May 5, 1995, "I believe that sea lion predation on salmonids is currently serving as a scapegoat for the harm that has been rendered to anadromous fish habitat."

QUESTIONS AND DISCUSSION

1. Sea lion predation of salmon remains a hot topic. In 2006, the states of Oregon, Washington and Idaho formally requested under Section 120 of the MMPA that NOAA Fisheries authorize the killing of particular California sea lions below Bonneville Dam. The states claimed that the sea lions were eating at-risk federally protected salmon and steelhead. The U.S. Army Corps of Engineers monitoring data for pinniped predation of salmon near the Bonneville Dam are shown below. How do you think they gathered this data? How accurate do you think it is?

	2002	2003	2004	2005	2006	2007
Total Salmonid Run	284,733	217,185	186,804	82,006	105,063	88,474
Total Estimated Salmonid Take by Pinnipeds	1,010	2,329	3,533	2,920	3,023	3,859
% of Salmonid Run Taken by Pinnipeds	0.4%	1.1%	1.9%	3.4%	2.8%	4.2%

http://www.nwr.noaa.gov/Marine-Mammals/Seals-and-Sea-Lions/upload/HR_1769_hearing_Q_A.pdf.

NOAA Fisheries assembled an 18–member task force to examine the issues and all but one of the members recommended that NOAA Fisheries approve the request to "lethally remove" specific sea lions in the vicinity of the Bonneville Dam. FINAL REPORT AND RECOMMENDATIONS OF THE MARINE MAMMAL PROTECTION ACT, SECTION 120 PINNIPED-FISHERY INTERACTION TASK FORCE: COLUMBIA RIVER (November 5, 2007). In March, 2008, NOAA Fisheries granted the states' request to remove California sea lions that feed on ESA-listed salmon in the Columbia River Basin. It also issued a Finding of No Significant Impact, concluding an EIS was unnecessary. Relevant documents are posted on the web at http://www.nwr.noaa.gov/Marine-Mammals/Seals-and-Sea-Lions/States-MMPA-Request.cfm.

In March 2007, Congressional representatives from the states of Oregon, Washington, and Idaho introduced bill H.R. 1769, the *Endangered Salmon Predation Prevention Act*. As summarized by the Congressional Research Service, this law would amend the MMPA to authorize the Secretary of Commerce to issue one-year permits for the lethal taking of California sea lions if the Secretary determines that alternative measures to reduce sea lion predation on threatened or endangered salmonid stocks in the Columbia River do not adequately protect the salmonid stocks from such predation. Limits the cumulative annual taking of California sea lions to one percent of the annual potential biological removal level of such sea lions. Requires the Secretary to determine whether alternative measures to reduce sea lion predation on salmonid stocks will adequately protect such stocks.

Expresses the sense of Congress that: (1) nonlethal means of preventing sea lion predation of salmonid stocks in the Columbia River is preferable to lethal means; (2) permit holders exercising lethal removal authority should be trained in wildlife management; and (3) the federal government should continue to fund, research, and support effective nonlethal alternative measures for preventing such predation.

If you were writing a memo for the Administrator of NOAA Fisheries, how would you analyze the decision to issue lethal take permits for the Bonneville Dam? How would you assess the benefits and problems raised by supporting passage of H.R. 1769?

2. As a fisheries manager, how would you respond to the excerpted claims of Lee Cerruti, the Moss Landing salmon fisherman? NMFS research has shown evidence of pinniped scarring on salmonids, so clearly some predation is occurring outside of locks. If the fishers' claims are accurate, then pinnipeds pose a significant threat to the viability of fishing fleets along the central California coast. At the same time, however, surely it is easier for fishers to blame pinnipeds for declining catches than their own overfishing.

3. Are the proposed NMFS amendments for lethal takes by commercial fishers to protect their gear and catch too sweeping? Allowing lethal takes is unlikely, one would think, to threaten sea lion and seal populations growing at over 5% per year. In answering this question, do you see why you have to go back to the rationale for the MMPA itself and determine whether the driving paradigm should be fisheries management or rights-based protection?

4. The requirement that nuisance pinnipeds be "individually identifiable" before they may be taken seems consistent with the rights-based view of the MMPA, but does it make sense? Consider the critique of Bill Rodgers.

This bad-actor or deviancy theory may have some credence for humans trapped in unpromising environments. But who could imagine that a predation strategy that worked for sea lion A would not be immediately exploited by sea lion B if the opportunity arose? Who could presume that the cornering of steelhead was a specialized knowledge of a sea lion underworld? Only staffers and members of Congress who know nothing of Darwin, but who prefer to believe that pinniped extirpation is but a selective removal operation akin to taking a few criminals off the streets.

William Rodgers, *Defeating Environmental Law: The Geology of Legal Advantage*, 19 PACE ENVTL. L. REV. 687, 706–07 (2002).

5. Apparently a number of frustrated fishers have taken matters into their own hands. While shooting pinnipeds is a federal offense with penalties up to $20,000 and a year's jail term, 10% of the animals treated at the Marine Mammal Center in Sausalito, California, in 1997 had gunshot wounds. Enforcement in such cases is very difficult because there are no official observers on board, crews don't inform on each other, and, as a NMFS officer has observed, "dead sea lions don't talk." Mick Kronman, *Self–Service, Swollen Sea Lion Herds Push Fishermen and Fish to the Brink*, National Fisherman, May 1998. There have been occasional prosecutions for shooting sea lions. In June, 2007, for example, federal prosecutors filed charges against James Housley for allegedly shooting a sea lion twice in the head after the sea lion took a salmon off a companion's fishing line. *Feds Accuse Fisherman of Shooting Sea Lion,* http://blog.oregonlive.com/breakingnews/about.html The Oregonian, June 1, 2007. Under the MMPA, this would be a misdemeanor with a prison sentence of up to one year and up to $100,000 in fines.

6. Pinniped recovery under the MMPA has been mixed. While California sea lion, Harbor seal and Elephant seal populations have grown, establishing new colonies along the West coast, Steller sea lions and Hawaiian monk seals remain endangered. It is thought that a main cause for the failure of the Steller sea lion to recover has been the crash of certain fish stocks in Alaska, suggesting that fisheries management can be as important to pinniped conservation as protection from takes.

---

3.   DOLPHIN MORTALITY IN THE TUNA FISHERY

The legal protection of dolphins in the eastern tropical Pacific Ocean (ETP) provides a fascinating example of the intersection of international fisheries management, animal rights, and trade law. The history of the tuna/dolphin conflict provides the clearest possible example of how fish and marine mammals are treated differently under the law. In reading the story below, consider the legal/policy interplay between national action and international reaction. In the end, the U.S. actions proved effective, but at what cost?

No one knows exactly why, but yellowfin tuna tend to swim beneath certain species of dolphin in the ETP. Fisherman are well aware of this association and since the 1950s have taken advantage of it to catch large yellowfin tuna by surrounding schools of dolphin with purse seine nets. Purse seine nets can be up to a mile long and 600–800 feet deep. Once a school of dolphins is spotted, motorboats commence a high speed chase to herd the dolphins into a small enough circle so they can be surrounded by the purse seine net. Most chases last about 20 minutes, though they can take up to an hour. Once the dolphins are surrounded by the net the bottom is pulled together by cables (like a drawstring purse) to prevent escape beneath the net. Because dolphins must breathe at the surface, dolphins tangled in the net drown. Traditional purse seine net hauls have killed hundreds of dolphins at a time. Since the dolphins have no commercial value, they are simply discarded overboard as bycatch. Betsy Carpenter, *What Price Dolphin? Scientists Are Reckoning the True Cost of Sparing an Endearing Mammal*, U.S. News & World Rep., June 13, 1994.

The National Marine Fisheries Service estimated in 1992 that more than six million dolphins had been killed in the course of purse seine fishing operations by the United States and foreign fleets in the ETP since 1959. During the 1960s and early 1970s, the U.S. fleet dominated the tuna fishery in the ETP and was responsible for more than 80% of dolphin deaths. This was a period of expansion for the ETP tuna fishery to satisfy the growing popularity of tuna in the United States, which accounted for more than one-quarter of all fish Americans consumed in 1974. Roughly 30% of the world's yellowfin tuna comes from the ETP. The U.S. tuna fleet reached its peak in the ETP in 1979, with 140 purse seine boats actively fishing. The main target of purse seiners were spotted dolphins, accounting for about 88% of dolphin encirclements. While their numbers have sharply declined as a result of the tuna fishery in the ETP, spotted dolphins have not been listed as threatened or endangered by the U.S. Endangered Species Act, though they are listed as "depleted" under the Marine Mammal Protection Act. 57 FED. REG. 27010 (1992); MARINE MAMMAL COMMISSION, 1995 ANNUAL REPORT TO CONGRESS 99 (1996); EUGENE BUCK, DOLPHIN PROTECTION AND TUNA SEINING, CONG. RES. SERV. ISSUE BRIEF (1997).

a. U.S. Legislative Response

The incidental take of dolphin in the ETP purse seine tuna fishery was one of the factors leading to passage of the Marine Mammal Protection Act (MMPA) in the United States in 1972. The MMPA states that marine mammal species should be "protected and encouraged to develop to the greatest extent feasible commensurate with sound policies of resource management." 16 U.S.C. § 1361(6) (1995). As discussed earlier, the MMPA's restrictions on fishing established as a legislative goal that "the incidental kill or incidental serious injury of marine mammals permitted in the course of commercial fishing operations be reduced to insignificant levels approaching a zero mortality and serious injury rate." 16 U.S.C. § 1371(a)(2). Implementation took the form of a "general permit," which set limits for the taking of dolphins. In the years following enactment of the MMPA, tuna vessels continued to reach, and often exceed, the take limits set under the general permit. In 1976, dolphin mortality reached 108,000 animals, exceeding the incidental take limit of 78,000. That same year, the National Marine Fisheries Service issued a three-year general permit with annual limits set on a sliding scale, decreasing from 51,945 in 1978 to 31,150 in 1980. In addition, new restrictions on fishing gear and methods were implemented that would better ensure live release of dolphins from the net. To ensure compliance, National Marine Fisheries Service observers were placed on fishing vessels to oversee accurate reporting.

Largely due to the institution of these new requirements, by 1980 dolphin mortality had reached a new low of 15,305. While a significant improvement over past levels, it still was far distant from the zero mortality goal mandated by the MMPA. Congress amended the MMPA in 1981 in an attempt to address this issue, by defining zero mortality as a best available technology standard rather than a concrete goal. The relevant MMPA amendment stated that the goal of approaching zero mortality "shall be satisfied in the case of the incidental taking of marine mammals in the course of purse seine fishing for yellowfin tuna by a continuation of the application of the best marine mammal safety techniques and equipment that are ecologically and technologically practicable." 16 U.S.C. § 1371(a)(2).

As the decade passed, however, dolphin mortality from the U.S. fleet actually increased slightly, to 18,400 animals in 1988. During this same period, while the U.S. fleet in the ETP fishery declined, the number of foreign vessels participating in the fishery grew. In 1960, the tuna catch by U.S. vessels had comprised 90% of the ETP tuna fishery. But by 1991, this percentage had dropped to 11%. Over the same period, the catch by Latin American vessels had increased from 10% in 1960 to 57% in 1991. This shift in fleet composition was due in part to the growth of cannery industries in Asia and to re-flagging by U.S. vessels to foreign registries. As a result, the contribution of foreign tuna vessels began to weigh heavily on dolphin mortality in the ETP, killing roughly 100,000 dolphins in 1986. Seeking a level playing field in the ETP, U.S. fishermen requested as a matter of equity that Congress take steps to limit dolphin mortality caused by foreign vessels. H.R. Rep. No. 758, 98th Cong., 2d Sess. 6 (1984). This request for extraterritorial application of U.S. law, coupled with growing public concern over the protection of dolphins, led to congressional amendment of the MMPA in 1984 and 1988.

To address the issue of dolphin mortality in the ETP from foreign vessels, the 1984 MMPA amendments imposed trade restrictions banning the import of tuna into the United States unless each nation exporting tuna adopted a dolphin protection program comparable to that of the United States and attained an average rate of incidental take by its fleet that was comparable to that of the U.S. fleet. Pub. L. No. 98–364, 98 Stat. 440 (July 17, 1984). The 1988 MMPA amendments detailed the necessary documentation to certify comparability of programs. 16 U.S.C. § 1371(a)(2). In addition, the 1988 amendments imposed trade restrictions on *intermediary* nations exporting tuna to the United States, requiring them to provide proof that their shipments did not contain tuna from those nations prohibited from exporting tuna directly to the United States. In practice, these requirements effectively forbade the use of purse seine nets.

Despite this legislation, environmental groups kept the issue in the public's eye and consumers continued to pressure for further action to save dolphins. In 1990, Congress responded to public outcry by proposing the Dolphin Protection Consumer Information Act of 1990 (DPCIA). 16 U.S.C. § 1385. The DPCIA required that for any tuna caught in the ETP to receive a "dolphin safe" label, the tuna (1) must have been caught by a vessel too small to deploy its nets on dolphins, or (2) must be accompanied by a certification from a qualified observer that no dolphin purse seine sets were made for the entire trip on which the tuna was caught, or (3) cannot have been harvested using a large-scale driftnet. Regulations were implemented in 1991 establishing a tracking and verification system enabling the government to track tuna labeled "dolphin safe" back to the harvesting vessel in order to verify whether the product was properly labeled. Absent that certification, tuna imported into the U.S. could not be marketed as dolphin-safe on U.S. supermarket shelves. In practice, this measure was more effective and less interventionist than the MMPA ban because canners simply would not buy tuna that was not "dolphin-safe."

Anticipating the labeling requirement proposed by the DPCIA and faced with threatened consumer boycotts, the major American tuna canning companies took steps to preempt any adverse market impacts of the legislation. Starkist Seafood Company, a division of H.J. Heinz Company, was the first to announce that it would no longer purchase any tuna caught in association with dolphins and began labeling cans of Starkist tuna with "dolphin safe" symbols bearing the message: "No Harm to Dolphins." Within hours of Starkist's announcement, the other major canning companies announced that they would adopt the same purchasing practice and begin labeling their tuna as "dolphin safe." 56 FED. REG. 47,418, 47,419 (1991). In a matter of months 84% of tuna sold in the United States was labeled "dolphin safe."

As a consequence of these actions, most of the remaining U.S. purse seine fleet shifted to overseas operations in the western tropical Pacific where tuna and dolphins do not associate together as they do in the ETP.

b. International Response to U.S. Sanctions

By the end of the 1980s, environmental groups realized that, with the exodus of U.S. vessels from the ETP fishery, the practices of foreign boats were increasingly important. Yet the Department of Commerce had not imposed *any* of the trade bans required by the MMPA, presumably to avoid international disputes. As a result, environmental groups filed lawsuits in U.S. courts, the result of which was that the United States was ordered to impose embargoes against tuna-harvesting nations that did not have dolphin protection programs comparable to the U.S. or had average dolphin mortality rates that were in excess of those prescribed under the MMPA. *Earth Island Institute v. Mosbacher*, 746 F.Supp. 964 (N.D. Cal. 1990).

In October, 1990, because its domestic standard for regulating tuna harvesting techniques did not satisfy the MMPA's requirements, a number of countries' tuna exports, including Mexico's, were prohibited from import into the United States. In response, Mexico initiated a challenge under the GATT [General Agreement on Tariffs and Trade] dispute resolution process against the embargo provisions of the MMPA amendments and the tuna labeling provisions of the DPCIA. In its decision in *Tuna/Dolphin I*, the GATT Dispute Panel found that the MMPA import ban constituted both a quantitative restriction (i.e., an unlawful ban on imports from a GATT member country) and illegitimately regulated the method by which the tuna was caught (i.e., focusing on the process and production method rather than the product itself). *General Agreement on Tariffs and Trade: Dispute Settlement Panel Report on United States Restrictions on Imports of Tuna*, 30 I.L.M. 1594 (1991). The labeling provisions were upheld, however, because they applied equally to all nations fishing for tuna and did not restrict the sale of tuna products. A separate GATT challenge to the embargoes associated with intermediary nations was filed in July, 1992, by the European Union and the Netherlands, claiming that the secondary embargo on intermediary markets constituted an unfair trade practice. In February 1993, a different GATT Dispute Panel held that the MMPA's secondary embargo provisions also violated the GATT. *General Agreement on Tariffs and Trade: Dispute Settlement Panel Report on United States Restrictions on Imports of Tuna,* 33 I.L.M. 839 (1994). Deeply involved in negotiating the North American Free Trade Agreement with the United States, Mexico did not submit the dispute panel report for adoption by the Contracting Parties to the GATT nor did the European Union or the Netherlands. Thus neither dispute panel decision has been adopted by the GATT Parties. As a result, there was no congressional action to amend the MMPA.

The Inter–American Tropical Tuna Commission (IATTC) is the international body charged with oversight of the tuna fishery in the ETP. Established as a bilateral organization with Costa Rica in 1949, the original charge of the IATTC was to study tuna and other species affected by tuna vessels in the region and to recommend management measures designed to maintain fish stocks at levels capable of producing maximum sustainable yields. Convention for the Establishment of an Inter–American Tropical Tuna Commission, May 31, 1949, US–Costa Rica, 1 U.S.T. 230. The IATTC's membership includes the United States, Mexico, France, Japan, Venezuela, Panama, Costa Rica and Vanuatu. Mexico is not a member but attends IATTC meetings as an observer. In an early response to the tuna/dolphin issue in 1976, IATTC members resolved that the Commission should strive (1) to maintain a high level of tuna production, (2) to maintain dolphin stocks at or above levels that assure their survival in perpetuity, and (3) to make every reasonable effort to avoid needless or careless killing of porpoises. In 1979 the IATTC began its international observer program, placing observers on both foreign and domestic vessels. This observer program was perhaps the most significant conservation action because dolphin mortality was significantly higher on vessels not carrying observers than on vessels where observers were present. LouAnna Perkins, *International Dolphin Conservation Under U.S. Law: Does Might Make Right?,* 1 OCEAN & COASTAL L.J. 213, 233 (1995); 55 FED. REG. 42,235 (1990).

In response to U.S. legislation, the tuna embargo, and the GATT dispute panel's decision in *Tuna/Dolphin I,* in June 1992 the IATTC adopted the La Jolla Agreement—a non-binding multilateral program designed to reduce dolphin mortalities in the ETP over a seven-year period to "levels approaching zero," while maintaining the present maximum tuna yield. *Agreement to Reduce Dolphin Mortality in the Eastern Tropical Pacific Fishery,* 33 I.L.M. 936 (1992). The Agreement was ratified by IATTC member nations and four non-member nations that fish in the ETP (Mexico, Colombia, Ecuador and Spain); two member nations did not ratify the agreement (France and Japan). Under the Agreement, dolphin mortality limits for the ETP tuna fishery were set according to a schedule providing for 19,500 mortalities in 1993, reduced to under 5,000 annual mortalities by 1999. A system known as Dolphin Mortality Limit (DML) was used to allocate incidental takings to vessels and any vessel that reached its DML was required to cease further fishing associated with dolphins in the ETP for that season. The La Jolla Agreement also established an international research program and scientific advisory board to coordinate, facilitate, and guide research directed at reducing dolphin mortalities. It required that observers accompany all purse seine vessels with a carrying capacity of 400 short tons or more and established an international review panel to monitor compliance by the international fleet with the conservation program and DML.

The international dolphin conservation program established under the La Jolla Agreement and implemented by the IATTC proved extremely effective. In the first year of the program, dolphin mortality in the fishery was reduced to 3,601 animals, almost 12,000 less than the 1992 mortality level, and well below the 1999 target of 5,000 dolphins. MARINE MAMMAL COMMISSION, 1994 ANNUAL REPORT TO CONGRESS 117 (1995). By 1996, dolphin mortality in the fishery had been reduced further to an estimated 2,700 animals. And this was due entirely to foreign vessels. The five remaining U.S. tuna seiners operating in the ETP did not make any sets on dolphins during 1995.

The La Jolla Agreement was voluntary, however, and not legally binding. It had been created as a direct response to U.S. legislative demands and when the American embargo remained in place, despite significantly reduced dolphin mortality in the ETP, a number of nations threatened to reject the La Jolla agreement or even file additional WTO challenges against the MMPA. The political durability of the voluntary La Jolla Agreement weakened as major foreign fishing nations questioned why, with no reward for their good faith efforts in meeting the annual goals of the program, they should continue to comply. Indeed U.S. law provided that the encirclement of even one dolphin by a nation's fleet fishing in the ETP was grounds for an embargo, preventing the importation of technically "dolphin-safe" tuna into the U.S. market.

At the same time, a shift in the tuna market was taking place. While in the mid–1970s the United States had consumed 85% of the yellowfin tuna caught in the ETP, by the end of 1992, that percentage had declined to less than 10%. Most of the ETP tuna was now sold to Europe and Latin America, with Mexico increasing its tuna consumption five-fold between 1975 and 1992. Because markets were developing outside the United States that did not have the same harvesting restrictions, access to the U.S. markets no longer provided the same incentive it once had for these nations to achieve further dolphin mortality reductions.

Making this threat explicit, in July 1995 at the Intergovernmental Meeting of the La Jolla Agreement, the governments of Colombia, Costa Rica, Ecuador, Mexico, Panama and Venezuela signed the San Jose Declaration. The Declaration stated that these nations wished to

> reiterate their concern that the stability of the La Jolla Agreement is endangered if the United States fails during this session of the U.S. Congress to resolve these U.S. policy inconsistencies by implementing the following three indivisible acts: lifting the primary and secondary embargoes; codifying the La Jolla Agreement; and redefining dolphin safe to include all tuna and tuna products harvested in accord with the regulatory measures embodied within the framework of the La Jolla Agreement.

Declaration of San Jose, July 14, 1995. In addition, many of these countries were considering other international management bodies and mechanisms such as *Organizacion Latinamericana de Desarrolla Pesquero* to replace the

La Jolla Agreement. This action bears considerable similarity to the creation of NAMMCO by whaling nations as a legitimate institutional alternative to the International Whaling Commission (discussed *supra*).

To salvage the achievement of the La Jolla Agreement, five American environmental groups met with Mexican officials to explore a multilateral agreement that would strengthen dolphin conservation measures while lifting the U.S. tuna embargo. The result was signed by 12 nations in October 1995—The Declaration of Panama. In order to secure a binding international agreement, the Declaration required the United States to amend the MMPA's existing comparability standards that had served as the basis for the tuna embargo as well as amend the labeling standards for defining "dolphin safe." The Declaration was, at its core, a *quid pro quo* agreement. Foreign tuna fleets would maintain their dolphin conservation measures if the United States lifted its trade restrictions.

After nearly two years of failed attempts to pass the necessary legislation in Congress, the International Dolphin Conservation Program Act (IDCPA) was passed and signed in the summer of 1997. 16 U.S.C. § 1385(g). These 1997 amendments to the MMPA condition trade restrictions on compliance with the international dolphin conservation program outlined in the Panama Declaration, thus basing the embargo on multilateral rather than unilateral standards (a fundamental concern of the GATT Dispute Panels). The amendments improve the tracking and verification procedures by requiring periodic audits, spot checks, and an observer program. They also modify the "dolphin-safe" label by focusing on whether dolphins are killed rather than encircled in catching tuna. Hence the label is based on a "no mortality or serious injury" standard rather than a "no encirclement" standard. The end result allows the use of purse seine nets so long as no dolphins were killed or seriously injured during the set. It is a performance standard rather than an equipment standard. By conditioning the label on dolphin mortality rather than use of a particular fishing method and ensuring compliance with observers, supporters of the legislation have argued, there is more flexibility to achieve a zero mortality goal.

The IDCPA did not enter into effect until (1) the Secretary of Commerce certified a research program determining whether intentional encirclement of dolphins with purse seine nets was having a significant adverse impact on any depleted dolphin stock in the ETP and (2) the Secretary of State certified that an effective treaty was in place. By March 1999, the United States, Panama, Ecuador and Mexico had signed a treaty implementing the International Dolphin Conservation Program and the National Marine Fisheries Service had issued a report concluding that purse seine encirclement was not having a significant impact on depleted dolphin stocks. The treaty has since been ratified by El Salvador, Venezuela, Nicaragua and, significantly, the European Union.

The dolphin story could serve as a model for future international fisheries management agreements. The binding requirements of the International Dolphin Conservation Program have made the ETP the most heavily regulated international fishery in the world. This is no small accomplishment for a fishery that is conducted primarily on the high seas, beyond national jurisdictions. Stock-specific mortality had been capped at a

0.2% level of the total population and at or below the 0.1% level by 2001. While the permissible annual mortality level had been limited to 5,000 per year, in 1998 mortality was less than 2,000 dolphins. These mortality levels are more than four times lower than those recommended by the U.S. National Research Council and should permit the recovery of dolphin stocks in the fishery to their former abundance. Recent developments under the International Dolphin Conservation Program are tracked by NMFS at their website, http://www.nmfs.noaa.gov/ia/intlagree/aidcp.htm.

QUESTIONS AND DISCUSSION

1. What are the lessons of the Tuna/Dolphin story? Is this an example of international cooperation in dealing with a complex conservation issue or a case of a powerful nation exercising unilateral economic coercion to dictate other countries' actions? Looking only at the final result one conclusion seems obvious—unilateral trade restrictions *work*. Closure of the U.S. market forced foreign countries to regulate their fisheries and reduce dolphin mortality. Tuna boats in the ETP now have observers on board, are using better dolphin-safety equipment, and employing other dolphin-friendly procedures. One might argue that this has all happened because the United States used a trade ban.

But if the trade sanctions worked, what was the cost? Beyond trade issues, what are the consequences of forcing other countries to improve their environmental performance? Could the same results have been achieved through sole reliance on the labeling requirements? If American consumers want to buy only dolphin-friendly tuna, one might argue, that is their right and the market will respond accordingly. Labeling measures, as former GATT Secretary General Arthur Dunkel noted at the time, would have avoided entirely the GATT problems and unpopular threats of the MMPA ban. Would the labeling requirement alone have caused the same level of international discord?

2. While using purse seine nets to catch tuna clearly harms dolphins, the alternative fishing methods have serious drawbacks, as well. The two most common alternative fishing techniques are casting nets around free-swimming tuna and casting nets around floating logs (which tuna tend to congregate under). Purse seine nets catch far fewer immature tuna than the alternative methods, potentially weakening the population's viability over the longer term. Of greater concern to environmentalists is the bycatch problem. One thousand tons of tuna caught using purse seine nets around dolphins produces an average bycatch of 2 sharks, 29 dolphins, 5 billfish and less than 1 sea turtle. The bycatch from setting nets around logs, however, produces a staggeringly different average bycatch—2,950 sharks, 102 billfish, less than 1 dolphin and 8 sea turtles. All of these species reproduce slowly, making their deaths particularly significant to overall population stability. Carpenter, *What Price Dolphin? Scientists Are Reckoning the True Cost of Sparing an Endearing Mammal*, U.S. NEWS & WORLD REP., June 13, 1994.

As with so many environmental problems the cure may be, in some respects, worse than the problem. Unfortunately, efforts by scientists to develop ecologically and commercially viable alternatives to existing fishing methods, in particular to purse-seine setting on dolphin, have been unsuccessful. Fishing for yellowfin by encircling dolphins remains the "cleanest" fishing method to avoid bycatch.

An equally significant problem in finding less harmful fishing alternatives are the costs of failure. Government-sponsored research is necessary but can only do so much. The real test of alternative fishing gear is its performance in a commercial fishery. Yet in the early 1990s, vessels using alternative gear to reduce dolphin mortality reported losing up to $100,000 per trip because their gear was more effective at catching small skipjack and yellowfin tuna rather than the commercially valuable large yellowfin tuna. Few skippers are willing to risk the vessel's loan payments and crew's wages on unproven new fishing gear, regardless of the potential reduction in bycatch mortality. What role can government play in addressing this concern?

3. Debate over repeal of the MMPA trade ban deeply split the American NGO community. In simple terms, the division was between animal rights activists and traditional environmental groups. This debate centered on the question of whether the chase and encirclement method produces such levels of stress in dolphins that the recovery of their populations will be inhibited. The National Academy of Sciences concluded in 1993 that no direct evidence of harm had been associated with chase and encirclement, though the subject had not been extensively studied, and implications of any stress on individual animal and dolphin populations had not been determined. Others have claimed, however, that the chase and encirclement of dolphins causes stress of a duration and magnitude that severely impedes dolphin reproduction or even results in dolphin deaths, referred to as "cryptic kill."

During the 1995 and later congressional hearings, Earth Island Institute, Defenders of Wildlife, the Humane Society of the United States, and 13 other environmental and animal rights organizations argued against relaxing the trade ban on dolphin encirclement methods both because it was contrary to achieving the MMPA's mandated goal of zero mortality and because the harassment and stress of encircling dolphin populations would threaten the population's stability. These groups also attacked the objectivity of the IATTC and questioned the organization's science. Concerned that the IATTC was captive to tuna fishery interests, they alleged that IATTC observers were influenced to under-report dolphin mortalities. Indeed, public access to IATTC data is restricted, impeding independent verification of IATTC conclusions. These groups requested Congress to order a General Accounting Office investigation of the IATTC before accepting the IATTC data on the tuna fishery's impacts on dolphins.

Opposing these groups and arguing in favor of amending the MMPA, the World Wildlife Fund, the National Audubon Society, the National Wildlife Federation, Greenpeace, and three other environmental groups sought to eliminate the tuna embargo and adopt the Panama Declaration's conditions, contending that a multilateral international approach was preferable to unilateral action and that stress from encirclement was not a threat to dolphin survival. A number of these groups had been instrumental in the Panama Declaration negotiations and, with support from the Clinton administration, were successful in lobbying for passage of the International Dolphin Conservation Program Act. It is no exaggeration to say that the efforts of environmental groups were essential to resolving the tuna/dolphin dispute in a manner acceptable to all the countries involved.

4.   The IATTC's ability to enforce the fishery restrictions remains an issue of concern. Under the La Jolla Agreement, 53 major violations (such as non-cooperation with an observer) and several hundred minor violations were reported, but few penalties were imposed. Since the IATTC has no enforcement powers, it must rely on each vessel's flag State to punish violations under domestic law. This system of enforcement is, with some exceptions, similar to that provided by the U.N. Convention on the Law of the Sea. In reviewing 17 infractions of non-cooperation with the observer, the IATTC points out that two resulted in suspended licenses, one in a warning, three in sanctions still to be decided, three in decisions of no sanctions, and eight were still in judicial review. Eugene H. Buck, *Dolphin Protection and Tuna Seining*, CONG. RES. SERV. ISSUE BRIEF, updated June 11, 1997.

The monitoring and enforcement provisions of the International Dolphin Conservation Program may change this poor record, though, providing an important model for other fisheries agreements. The Program requires observers on board all large tuna purse seine boats in the ETP. As the Department of Commerce describes in its Frequently Asked Questions brochure, once the tuna are caught and the observer has verified it was a "dolphin safe" set:

> Dolphin-safe tuna will be stored in different storage wells on-board tuna fishing vessels from those in which non-dolphin-safe tuna will be stored. An Inter–American Tropical Tuna Commission (IATTC) observer will keep track of which storage wells contain dolphin-safe tuna and which do not. At the end of the fishing trip the observer and the vessel captain will sign and date the observer's report and the National Marine Fisheries Service will receive a copy of the observer's report for all U.S. vessels' fishing trips. When the tuna is delivered to U.S. canners, the dolphin-safe tuna will continue to be kept separated from the non-dolphin-safe tuna until it is canned. U.S. canners will be required to inform the NMFS as to where and how their frozen tuna supplies are stored, and NMFS will inspect U.S. canneries to verify the information NMFS is receiving. Non-dolphin-safe tuna can labels will not carry the official U.S. government dolphin-safe mark or any other dolphin-safe mark. From time to time, NMFS representatives will purchase cans of dolphin-safe tuna from food markets, and using can-codes stamped on all tuna cans, the contents of the cans will be checked back to their origin to verify that they are "dolphin-safe."

While this reads well, do you think this system will work? What practical problems might it encounter?

5.   The Tuna/Dolphin saga continues. The Department of Commerce has lifted the tuna embargo for Mexico and Ecuador. The major tuna processors (StarKist, Chicken of the Sea, and BumbleBee), however, have stated that they intend to retain their current dolphin-safe labels (i.e., meaning no encirclement) regardless of whether the IDCPA allows them to use a no mortality standard or not. Thus Mexican and Venezuelan tuna may be sold in the United States, but likely not by the major processors that account for roughly 90% of the market.

In April, 1999, the Secretary of Commerce issued a finding that chase and encirclement of dolphin by purse seine fishermen did not have a significant adverse impact on depleted populations. Under the International Dolphin Conservation Program Act, this finding was necessary for the new meaning of "dolphin safe" tuna to go into effect (i.e., purse seine nets allowed so long as no dolphins killed or injured). The Earth Island Institute, Defenders of Wildlife, and Humane Society filed a lawsuit in federal district court challenging this finding as an abuse of discretion under the Administrative Procedure Act. Reflecting the split among environmental groups, a lawyer for the Justice Department and lawyers for Greenpeace and World Wildlife Fund argued in favor of the finding. In a decision in April, 2000, the court granted plaintiffs summary judgment, ruling that the agency had not adequately taken into account preliminary results from the stress studies on dolphins in the ETP. *Brower v. Daley*, 93 F. Supp. 2d 1071 (N.D. Cal. 2000), *aff'd*, 257 F.3d 1058 (9th Cir. 2001).

The Earth Island Institute has also released a report it claims was written by NMFS scientists examining data on dolphin mortality from 1997 to 2002. According to Earth Island Institute, the report concludes that:

> Despite low reported dolphin kills from the tuna fleets, dolphin populations remain seriously depleted. Eastern Spinner dolphins remain at only 35% of their former numbers; Northeastern Offshore Spotted dolphins are at only 20% of their former numbers. More importantly, the research shows that dolphins are NOT recovering as expected. By some calculations, the populations may still be declining.

http://www.earthisland.org/news/new_news.cfm?newsID=292. Earth Island alleges that "the Bush Administration is hiding this damning report because it undermines its attempt to falsely label dolphin-deadly tuna as 'Dolphin Safe.'" *Id*. It has posted the report on the web at www.earth island.org/immp/secret_report.pdf and the report will surely play a role in future litigation.

6. Does public choice theory predict the MMPA amendments banning the use of purse seine nets? If you had been representing the U.S. tuna fleet as a lobbyist in the early 1980s, would you have supported the 1984 amendments?

7. The Earth Island Institute claims that about 100 boats (roughly 5% of the world's tuna fleet) still use purse seine nets. Given the domestic and international discord this conflict has engendered, would it not be more efficient simply to pay off these boats and put an end to the dispute?

8. While it was expected that populations would recover following the restrictions described above, the results have been disappointing. Below is a 2008 assessment by NOAA Fisheries.

> Since the early 1990s, reported dolphin mortality has been low enough that the dolphin populations should have started to recover. As of 2002, however, neither dolphin population was recovering at expected rates. Hypotheses to explain the lack of recovery have included underreporting of kill by observers, cryptic effects of the fishery not detectable by observers, such as stress, induced abortion or separation of mothers and calves, long-term ecosystem changes, and

a lag in recovery due to interactions with other species. In years with a high number of dolphin sets, there are fewer calves in the spotted dolphin population. Reproduction in both dolphin populations declined between 1993 and 2003, which is at least one reason why recovery has been at a lower-than-expected rate. On the other hand, perhaps pelagic dolphins inherently have low reproductive rates, and our expectation for rate of recovery needs to be revised. Research is continuing, but until there are clear recoveries of the affected dolphin stocks, the tuna-dolphin issue is likely to remain highly controversial.

NOAA SOUTHWEST FISHERIES SCIENCE CENTER, PROTECTED RESOURCES DIVISION, THE TUNA DOLPHIN ISSUE.

CHAPTER SIX

PROTECTED LANDS

I. INTRODUCTION
II. THE CASE FOR PRESERVATION
    A. THE ECONOMIC CASE FOR PRESERVATION
    B. PRESERVATION AS HISTORICAL AND CULTURAL DOCUMENTATION
    C. THE ECOLOGICAL CASE FOR PRESERVATION
    D. THE MORAL CASE FOR PRESERVATION
    E. THE DARKER SIDE OF PRESERVATION
III. NATIONAL PARKS
    A. THE PARK SERVICE ORGANIC ACT
    PROBLEM EXERCISE: SNOWMOBILES IN YELLOWSTONE NATIONAL PARK
IV. NATIONAL MONUMENTS
    A. THE ANTIQUITIES ACT
    B. THE CLINTON MONUMENTS
V. WILDERNESS
    A. THE EVOLUTION OF THE WILDERNESS IDEA
    B. THE WILDERNESS ACT
        1. DESIGNATING WILDERNESS
            a. WILDERNESS IN THE NATIONAL FORESTS
            b. WILDERNESS ON BLM LANDS
        2. MANAGING DESIGNATED WILDERNESS
        CASE STUDY: ROADING THE IZEMBEK NATIONAL WILDLIFE REFUGE
VI. NATIONAL WILDLIFE REFUGES, WILD AND SCENIC RIVERS, AND THE LAND
    AND WATER CONSERVATION FUND
    A. NATIONAL WILDLIFE REFUGES
    B. WILD AND SCENIC RIVERS
    C. THE LAND AND WATER CONSERVATION FUND
VII. PRESERVATION ON MULTIPLE USE LANDS
    A. PROTECTING LAND IN A MULTIPLE USE REGIME
    PROBLEM EXERCISE: WILDERNESS REINVENTORY AND THE UTAH SETTLEMENT
    AGREEMENT
    B. FLPMA WITHDRAWAL AUTHORITY
VIII. THE IMPACT OF ACCESS ON PRESERVATION
    A. ACCESS ACROSS FEDERAL LANDS TO PRIVATE AND STATE PROPERTY
    B. R.S. 2477
    PROBLEM EXERCISE: OBTAINING ACCESS TO AN INHOLDING
IX. ALTERNATIVES TO PUBLIC LANDS PRESERVATION

[M]ost conflict over national park policy does not really turn on whether we ought to have nature reserves (for that is widely agreed), but on the uses that people will make of those places—which is neither the subject of general agreement nor capable of resolution by reference to ecological principles. The preservationists are really moralists at heart, and people are very much at the center of their concerns. They encourage people to immerse themselves in natural settings and to behave there in certain ways, because they believe such behavior is redeeming.

JOSEPH L. SAX, MOUNTAINS WITHOUT HANDRAILS:
REFLECTIONS ON THE NATIONAL PARKS 103 (1980).

I.   INTRODUCTION

Chapter 2 described the history of our public lands and how, over time, the country moved from a policy of disposal to one of retention and management. As described there and in Chapter 3, which introduced federal agencies, the public lands can be roughly divided with reference to the federal agency tasked with managing a particular geographical area and the law that guides the agency's management decisions. Another way of understanding the division of the public lands, however, is with reference to the amount of protection afforded the land, or the number of uses of the land that are prohibited by any particular designation. If the amount or degree of protection is viewed along a spectrum, those federal lands designated as available for multiple use, which includes most, but not all, of the land managed by the Forest Service and the BLM, are on the less protective side of the spectrum with more uses permitted. Lands set apart as national parks, monuments, and wildlife refuges, by contrast, are toward the more protective part of the spectrum. And areas designated as wilderness, which can occur within any of the other areas, are still more protective, although even wilderness does not offer complete protection. The focus of this chapter is on federal efforts to protect, or, as it is more often described in natural resources law, "preserve," specific areas. Because they fall on the more protective side of the spectrum, wilderness, national parks, and monuments are the focus of the chapter, but the chapter also looks briefly at national wildlife refuges, wild and scenic rivers, and preservation as a component of multiple use management.

The law of "preservation" is concerned with the rules governing how much and what sort of use can be made within a designated area of the public lands. For example, does the designation of land as a national monument, national park, or wilderness area preclude mining, grazing, timber harvest, or motorized vehicles? Does it do so even where such uses predate the preservation designation? Because other chapters address the law governing the use of minerals, water, wildlife, grass, and timber, both on public and private lands, this chapter devotes little space to the limits imposed on these traditional resource activities by preservation designations. The chapter devotes more attention to another use of the public lands that is in tension with preservation, namely recreation. Although historically preservation and outdoor recreation were often partners in disputes against traditional commodity and extractive interests, that partnership began to fray as interest in motorized recreation grew. While the relationship between preservation advocates and low-impact recreation, such as hiking and bird-watching, retains quite a bit of vitality, preservationists are more and more finding themselves at odds with high-intensity recreators, such as off-road vehicle and personal watercraft users. The recreation versus preservation debate is now every bit as vociferous as the traditional debate between extractive resource users and preservationists.

Before turning to the law governing parks, monuments, refuges and wilderness, it is important to think a bit more broadly about preservation. Hark back to the case study in Chapter 1 (page 28) about how conceptions of wilderness or wild nature have changed over time. For most of the last two millennia, wilderness has mostly been viewed with repugnance, as something dangerous and even an affront to civilization. This same view held sway for most of our nation's first century of existence. The frontier mantra that animated natural resources policy was largely one of taming the wilderness. Wilderness posed a barrier to progress and prosperity. It was an obstacle, something to be conquered. As Aldo Leopold later wrote in the 1930s, "A stump was our symbol of progress."

The first hints of change in social attitudes were evidenced in the literature of Romantics such as Byron, Wordsworth, and Tennyson, who began to associate God with wild nature. This view had particular appeal in America where the country's vast wilderness was embraced as a distinctive source of American identity and superiority. This new appreciation of wilderness was evident in the poetry of William Cullen Bryant, the novels of James Fenimore Cooper, the art of Thomas Cole, Asher Durand, and Albert Bierstadt, and, most famously, in the writings of transcendentalist Henry David Thoreau. As Thoreau saw it, modern industrial society, by cutting people off from nature, was cutting them off from God. The commercial spirit of civilization kept people from contemplation of the divine. Wilderness was a source of vigor, inspiration, and strength. It stripped life down to its essentials. As Thoreau simply stated, "In wildness is the preservation of the world."

Although Thoreau praised "wildness," his vision of wilderness was actually more of a middle landscape, a life alternating between wilderness and civilization or residence in "partially cultivated country." This middle landscape is the essence of Walden, a subsistence farming existence near the village of Concord, Massachusetts. Similarly, fellow transcendentalist Ralph Waldo Emerson's famous essay, "Nature," was about a walk through Boston Common. If Thoreau's equation of Walden Pond with "wilderness" and Emerson's description of Boston Common as "nature" seem a bit odd, they well illustrate how variable individual conceptions of wilderness can be. Ask 100 Americans today whether they support "more wilderness" and a high percentage are likely to respond in the affirmative. Then ask them what wilderness means and you're likely to hear a variety of answers—everything from the public park down the street, to their favorite national park, to an isolated rainforest. One person's "wilderness" yearnings may be satisfied by a walk through Central Park, another's by a drive through Yosemite Valley, a third only by a weeklong backpacking trip through a roadless area. This wide array of interpretations of "wilderness" is of more than semantic interest. As the chapter relates, natural resources law has responded to these different perceptions and preferences with a range of federal land management designations and a variety of laws governing the use and protection of those areas.

As explored in prior chapters, the changing view of wilderness presaged by the Romantics and Transcendentalists began to take root in the second half of the nineteenth century with the 1864 federal grant of Yosemite Valley to California as a park "for public use, resort, and recreation" and the 1872 inauguration of the national park system with the creation of Yellowstone "as a public park or pleasuring ground for the benefit and enjoyment of the people." Like Thoreau's description of wilderness, these early protective designations also foreshadow another theme with which this chapter is concerned, namely the tension between preserving an area and managing it for public use and enjoyment. If parks, and other public lands, are to be enjoyed and used, it is hard to preserve them in a state of nature. Yet the Park Service's organic act charges it to regulate the use of national parks "to conserve the scenery and the natural and historic objects and the wild life therein and to provide for the enjoyment of the same in such manner and by such means as will leave them unimpaired for the enjoyment of future generations." 16 U.S.C. § 1. In truth, at the time of these designations, few people perceived any tension between building roads, campgrounds, lookouts, and lodges and preserving a park's wild and natural qualities. But as our conception of what really counts as wild or natural has changed, so, too, has our view of what sort of enjoyment and use is compatible with preservation for future generations. How the law can or should respond to such changes is a focus of this chapter.

The person most often described as the founder of the preservation movement was the remarkable Scot, John Muir. Unlike the earlier transcendentalists, Muir had no ambivalence about pure wilderness. He was the first great public defender of wilderness for its own sake. When asked what rattlesnakes are good for, Muir famously replied, "They are good for themselves." Muir's view that wilderness be preserved for its own sake was, however, a decidedly minority position, and probably remains so today. As highlighted in Bill Baxter's *People or Penguins* piece in Chapter 1, page 17, most people want to know what rattlesnakes and wilderness are good for or, in other words, what benefits they have for people. This utilitarian view almost inevitably leads to some weighing of costs and benefits and to compromises about appropriate uses that are the bread and butter of the law of preservation.

The utilitarian view was the one championed by Muir's philosophical counterpoint, Gifford Pinchot. Although Pinchot was an important early ally of Muir because he, too, opposed the wholesale exploitation of public lands, in contrast to Muir's preservationist philosophy, Pinchot emphasized "conservation" of natural resources for "wise use." His "conservationist" philosophy was that resources should be managed to produce the greatest good for the greatest number. The current equivalent of the conservationist approach is multiple use management. Because of Pinchot's own view that timber production was compatible with protection of the national forests, and because multiple use management has historically allowed extractive and commodity use of the public lands, the conservationist approach has tended to be regarded as different than the preservationist approach. But as you consider the cases and questions in this chapter, ask yourself whether the two are really that different in practice. Does Pinchot's utilitarian emphasis on using the public lands to benefit the public mean that a timber cut or a copper mine will always win out over a roadless area? Does the preservationist philosophy of Muir really mean no use at all? Muir may have worked to stop San Francisco from damming the Tuolomne River in Hetch Hetchy Valley, but he never advocated keeping people out of the Yosemite Valley. In truth, although labeling a particular law or land designation as intended for "preservation" or "multiple use" likely tells us something about the emphasis on use or protection, it will always be necessary to ask additional questions such as what uses are allowed, under what conditions, and in what location?

Although the concept of preservation took root with John Muir at the turn of the century, and even though many of our most treasured national parks were created in that period, it was not until after World War II that the preservationist philosophy truly captured the public's imagination. The period following the war saw the creation of a vast middle class with disposable income, automobiles, and leisure time. It also saw the creation of the interstate highway system that made America's public lands easily accessible to the average traveler. Recreation on the public lands began to grow and has hardly stopped.

Consider some numbers. Recreation in the national forests climbed from 27.4 million visitor days in 1950 to 204.8 million in 2004. Recreation visits to the national park system grew from 33 million visits in 1950 to over 275 million in 2007. Total visitor days on BLM lands climbed from just over 31 million in 1972 to over 66 million in 2004. Between 1960 and 1995, the percentage of Americans who camped nearly tripled, the percentage of cyclists more than tripled, and the percentage of canoers and kayakers more than quadrupled. In 2005, it was estimated that 161 million people, participated at least once in an outdoor activity—17.7 million campers, 51.7 million car campers, 76.7 million hikers, and 20.8 million canoers. Another important area of recreation is wildlife-associated recreation, which includes hunting, fishing and wildlife watching. In 2001, there were 13 million hunters, 34.1 million fishers, and 66.1 million wildlife watchers. James R. Rasband & Megan E. Garrett, *A New Era in Public Land Policy? The Shift Toward Reacquisition of Land and Natural Resources*, 53 ROCKY MTN. MIN. L. INST. 11–1, 11–13 to 11–15 (2007); *see National Park System Attendance Rises in 2007*, http://home.nps.gov/applications/release/Detail.cfm?ID=785.

As one might expect, the increasing demand for recreation use and additional protection of the public lands prompted, and continues to prompt, changes in the law. Thus the 1960s and 1970s saw passage of landmark laws such as the Wilderness Act of 1964, the Land and Water Conservation Act of 1965, the National Historic Preservation Act of 1966, the National Wild and Scenic Rivers Act of 1968, and the Alaska National Interest Lands Conservation Act of 1980. In addition to setting aside additional areas of the public lands primarily for preservation purposes, there has been a gradual alteration of the balance of uses on the public lands. A manifestation of this rebalancing is Congress' direction to the Forest Service in the 1976 National Forest Management Act (NFMA) and to the Bureau of Land Management (BLM) that same year in the Federal Land Policy Management Act (FLPMA) that both agencies consider recreation and preservation as part of their management objectives. FLPMA also required the BLM to look for lands within its jurisdiction that could be designated as wilderness. Nor is rebalancing relegated to multiple use lands. As discussed later in the chapter, the National Park Service has been rethinking some of its management of the parks, asking whether so many roads, lodges, and concessions are compatible with maintaining the parks unimpaired for future generations. Although the law has moved slower than some would like, but faster than others would prefer, over the second half of the twentieth century and now into the twenty-first, it has supplied more and more of the environmental good desired by the public—places for aesthetic and recreational enjoyment. Another goal of this chapter is to have you consider whether we have yet achieved the right balance.

Finally, as you study the law of preservation, it is important to consider not only how much land should be protected and what rules should govern the protection of that land but also who should answer those questions. Should Congress be the primary decisionmaker or should it be the president and executive agencies? And what role should the judiciary play? Even more broadly, are preservation decisions best made at a federal level or should some preservation choices be made at a state, local, or even private level? These are difficult questions on which there has always been vigorous debate. The important point is that there are a variety of ways to protect land and each will produce different benefits and raise separate concerns.

II.   THE CASE FOR PRESERVATION

Although Congress and the agencies have moved toward additional preservation, the public doesn't yet seem satisfied. Forest Service researchers, for example, found in a 2000–2001 poll that when asked about protecting more wilderness in their own state, 69.8% of the respondents were in favor and only 12.4% of the respondents were opposed. *See* Campaign for America's Wilderness, *A Mandate to Protect America's Wilderness* (2003), at 16, *available at* http://www.leaveitwild.org/docs/report_polling_report.pdf. In a 2003 Zogby poll, 64% of the respondents opined that Congress had not yet designated enough wilderness. *See* http://www.leaveitwild.org/docs/report_zogby_poll_01-03.pdf. What is it that underlies this polling data? The discussion above about increasing visitation to the public lands might be read as suggesting that public support for preservation derives from the increasing public preference for outdoor recreation. But does that motive offer a complete explanation? What other factors animate the public's support for additional preservation? This section briefly explores that question.

A.   THE ECONOMIC CASE FOR PRESERVATION

Traditionally, the largest opposition to setting aside public land as parks, monuments, and wilderness has come from the industries and communities dependent upon extractive and commodity uses of the public lands. Such economic arguments carried weight with Congress and other public officials because promoting job loss and economic hardship has never been the easiest way to get elected. If anything is surprising it is that so much preservation *was* accomplished in the face of these economic concerns that were largely accepted by both those in favor of preservation and those opposed to it. To the former, the economic sacrifice was worth it; to the latter, it was not. As it has turned out, however, preservation is not so clearly an economic burden; indeed, it may often prove an economic benefit.

Much of the recreation on the public lands discussed above produces huge economic benefits. In 2006, wildlife-associated recreation generated $122.3 billion dollars or 1% of the National GDP. Equipment sales and rentals totaled $64.1 billion and $37.4 billion went to trip expenses. In fact, according to the Heritage Forests Campaign, 85% of the total economic benefits generated by the national forests come from recreation. Ironically, playing on the public lands may pay more than working on them. *See* U.S. Fish and Wildlife Service, *2006 National Survey of Fishing, Hunting, and Wildlife-Associated Recreation* 4–5 (2007), http://www.census.gov/prod/2008 pubs/fhw06-errata.pdf; Outdoor Industry Ass'n., *State of the Industry Report* 2 (2006), http://www.outdoorindustry.org/images/researchfiles/SOI.pdf? 29; Heritage Forests Campaign, *Fact Sheet*, http://www.ourforests.org/fact/ access.html (noting that the revenue generated from recreation is more than five times the amount generated by logging).

The economic benefits of preservation extend far beyond the amount spent on recreation. Consider the array of benefits identified in the following excerpt.

Pete Morton, *The Economic Benefits of Wilderness:Theory and Practice,* 76 U. Denv. L. Rev. 465 (1999)

"I am afraid that I don't see much hope for a civilization so stupid that it demands a quantitative estimate of the value of its own umbilical cord." * * *

How can we put a dollar value on the wild experience of being high atop a mountain peak, alone with nature, miles from the sounds and stresses of modern civilization? Why is it necessary to quantify the benefits from the exhilarating auditory experience of bugling elk on a cool autumn eve? And, why is it necessary to estimate the economic value of the ecological processes necessary to sustain earth's life support system? Aren't some of life's necessities, pleasures and experiences invaluable—beyond quantification by "dismal scientists?" While many folks may find it unethical to place a dollar value on wilderness and wildness, it is important to at least recognize qualitatively the economic value of the ecological, personal and societal benefits of wilderness. The main justification for discussing and perhaps quantifying wildland economic benefits is to level the playing field with the more easily quantifiable benefits associated with marketable commodities (e.g., timber). While steadfastly acknowledging that the economic benefits of wilderness will never be fully quantified, without at least qualitatively describing and understanding these benefits, politicians and public land managers will continue to make policy decisions that shortchange wilderness in public land management decisions. * * *

To facilitate informed investment decisions about publicly owned wildlands, economic analysis must take into consideration both market and non-market goods and services. * * *

Wildland recreation results in a variety of individual and social benefits, which include personal development (spiritual growth, improved physical fitness, self-esteem, self-confidence, and leadership abilities), social bonding (greater family cohesiveness and higher quality of family life), therapeutic and healing benefits (stress reduction helping to increase worker productivity and reduce illness and absenteeism at work), and other social benefits (decreased social deviance, increased national pride). These are the perceived benefits of users, but rejecting them because they cannot be assigned a monetary value would be counterintuitive. Given the considerable amount of time, effort, and other personal resources people commit to outdoor recreation, they "either gain sizeable benefits or are quite foolish." * * *

Wildlands can also provide commercial benefits for private industry. For example, while most salmon harvesting occurs outside wilderness, salmon require the fresh water located in upper pristine reaches of wild river systems for spawning and rearing habitat. Hunting and fishing outfitters gain commercial benefits from wildlands by providing a primitive environment for their clients to experience. Wildlands are also a source of genetic material for propagators collecting seeds and tissue. Harvesting nontimber forest products from public wildlands has become a big business on national forests. Nationwide, nontimber forest products support a $130 million industry that employs over 10,000 people. * * *

At one end of the community economic development spectrum are communities where subsistence harvest of wildland products is an important component. Sustaining wildlands may be especially important for sustaining these communities. In Alaska, subsistence use of wild resources for food, clothing, and shelter is a customary and traditional use of the wildland resource. * * *

At the other end of the community economic development spectrum, wildland recreation directly generates thousands of jobs in local communities. Although many retail and service jobs associated with wildland recreation are low-paying and seasonal, they do provide local residents with employment opportunities in less skilled jobs for supplementing household income, helping to alleviate rural poverty.... And sometimes, these jobs simply allow folks to live in a place they love. Recreation jobs also support additional jobs, as the economic impact from visitor spending "multiplies" through a community. A perhaps more important role is the indirect role wildlands play in diversifying the economies of rural communities.

There is a growing body of literature suggesting that future diversification of rural economies is dependent on the ecological and amenity services provided by public wildlands. According to Whitelaw and Niemi, "the economic-development process is increasingly characterized, not by jobs-first-then-migration, but by the reverse." In other words, a rural development strategy can capitalize on the qualitative features of the wild landscape to attract a high quality work force and new businesses to an area. The extraction of publicly owned market resources should not degrade the long-term production of nonmarket goods and ecological services by wildlands on the public estate. It is the wildland-generated goods and services such as scenic landscapes and wildlife habitat that improve quality of life for local residents and drive the amenity-based development currently occurring throughout the nation.

The environmental, recreational, and scenic amenity resources generated on public wildlands improve quality of life for local residents and indirectly benefit rural communities by attracting and retaining businesses. Advances in telecommunications have allowed light manufacturers and "knowledge-based" business firms (e.g., computer programmers, engineers, and stockbrokers) to locate in relatively remote locations with desirable lifestyles. For many of these "footloose" businesses, information is the commodity exported (as opposed to a region's natural resources) and proximity to markets is a less important factor than in the past. Results from surveys on business location criteria indicate that scenic amenities, quality of life, and access to recreation are some of the most important reasons, relative to other more traditional economic criteria, for businesses to locate and stay in a rural region. Amenity factors have been deemed particularly important in the location decisions of four types of companies: corporate headquarters, high-technology, research and development, and services. * * *

The allure of the amenity and recreation resources available on public wildlands is illustrated by rural migration patterns. During the 1970s and 1980s, rural areas experiencing rapid population growth were highly concentrated in areas adjacent to large tracts of public lands that offered recreational and scenic amenities. Many of the migrants are amenity-seeking retirees who may have first visited public lands as recreationists or tourists. In general, retirement communities evolve from areas with recreation and tourism. The typical amenity-seeking retiree is married, well educated, newly retired, in good health, has ample financial resources, and more frequently lives in counties with public land. The economic contribution of migrating retirees to rural economies is significant. Retirees moving to rural communities buy or build houses, require medical assistance, and may need local banking services (e.g., mortgages) and investment advice. These needs translate into employment opportunities in construction, services (especially health services), retail, finance, insurance, and real estate. In addition, amenity-seeking retirees tend to increase county revenues while keeping costs low. For example, retirees increase the tax base for public schools and police services but they do not attend or send children to school, and they generally do not commit crimes. Retirement income is also less sensitive to the business cycle, which can stabilize the economic base and improve a community's ability to adjust to changing economic conditions. * * *

Scientific benefits are often cited as one justification for a network of wildlands. As Stankey stated: "[T]here remains the persuasive argument that science and scientific inquiry offer an important way of justifying the significant investment that society has made in the wilderness system." * * *

Biological diversity, or biodiversity, includes the full array of species, the genetic information they contain, the communities they form, and the landscapes they inhabit. Although biodiversity conservation obviously provides society with significant economic benefits, it is difficult to assign measurable values when evaluating wilderness proposals. * * *

Wildlands play an essential role in sustaining natural capital and ecological services that comprise our global life support system. The functioning of the earth's biosphere and hence the maintenance and enhancement of human life depend on a complex series of ecological processes or services. These ecological services can be global cycles (e.g., water, carbon, nitrogen, and oxygen), as well as more localized processes such as soil formation, pollination of crops, watershed protection, storage and cycling of nutrients, absorption and breakdown of pollutants, and maintenance of stream flows. Ecological services consist of flows of materials, energy, and information from natural capital stocks that combine with manufactured and human capital services to generate human welfare. The many nonmarket benefits provided by ecological services are not priced, are only partially understood, and their value is just starting to be recognized. The economic benefits to human welfare of sustaining natural capital and ecological services in the aggregate are significant. * * *

So do we really need economists to tell us how much our wildland life support system is worth? Is not that value infinitely obvious? In the past, many public investments were made without completing an economic analysis. Public assets that we take for granted, wilderness areas, national parks, wildlife refugees, Central Park, etc., would not be here today if we relied solely on markets and advice from market economists. Economics provides necessary information useful for policy discussions, but economics alone is not sufficient to promulgate policies. Economic efficiency is only one consideration when allocating multiple public resources.

————

B.   PRESERVATION AS HISTORICAL AND CULTURAL DOCUMENTATION

A non-economic, although still decidedly anthropocentric argument, for preservation of wild lands is their importance as historical "documents" that tell us something about our past. Roderick Nash writes:

> As historical document wilderness has meaning to any nation, but Americans claimed an especially intimate relationship to the wild. Following Frederick Jackson Turner and Theodore Roosevelt, philosophers of wilderness have contended that American culture bore the imprint of close and prolonged association with wilderness. * * *
>
> The lengthening distance from frontier conditions produced new and more eloquent articulations. One of the best was made ... by the novelist and historian Wallace Stegner. . . . To lose contact with wilderness, in Stegner's view, was to risk losing what was characteristically American. "Something will have gone out of us as a people," he continued, "if we ever let the remaining wilderness be destroyed." That "something" was the promise of a new start in a new world which, for Stegner, was the essence of the "American dream." . . . He urged ... keeping the remaining American Wilderness as "a sort of wilderness bank" in which a collective experience—pioneering on a frontier— could be safeguarded. Stegner knew that museums, roadside pioneer villages, and frontierlands were sorry substitutes for the opportunity of knowing wilderness first hand. * * *
>
> A related line of thinking about the historical value of wilderness stressed its special relationship to human freedom. Stegner expressed the relationship when he described wild country as "a part of the geography of hope." The Puritans understood this when they found in the wild New World a sanctuary in which to worship as they pleased. When Roger Williams dissented from the Puritan oligarchy, he too headed for the wilderness of Naragansett Bay, later Rhode Island. In the 1840s the Mormons also found freedom in wilderness, and so did some of the countercultural communities in the 1960s.

RODERICK NASH, WILDERNESS IN THE AMERICAN MIND 260–62 (1967).

C.   THE ECOLOGICAL CASE FOR PRESERVATION

Whether in lieu of, or as a supplement to, economic analysis, a number of preservation advocates have argued that the strongest case for preservation of public lands is on ecological grounds. Building on Aldo Leopold's land ethic that an activity is "right when it tends to preserve the integrity, stability, and beauty of the biotic community" and "wrong when it tends otherwise," and on biologists' advances in understanding about the ways in which natural systems function, many now call on public land agencies to practice ecosystem management and to protect biodiversity. The basic idea, which is discussed more fully in Chapter 1, is that preservation is an ecological necessity because if the natural system is interconnected, our health and welfare depend upon the adequate functioning of that system.

A passionate advocate of the ecological case for preservation is Dave Foreman, the chairman of the Wildlands Project, which promotes the creation of nature reserves made up of large wilderness areas surrounded by buffer zones and linked by habitat corridors. Among the Project's proposals is what is known as the Yellowstone to Yukon (Y2Y) project, which proposes an 1800–mile habitat corridor stretching from the northern Rocky Mountains, across the Canadian Rockies and into the Yukon Territory and which can be used by large carnivores like wolf and grizzly. Consider Foreman's thoughts in the following excerpt.

Dave Foreman, *The Wildlands Project and the Rewilding of North America,* 76 Denv. U. L. Rev. 535, 535–36, 545–46, 549, 551–52 (1999)

Ecological concerns, including the preservation of habitat for rare and imperiled species and the protection of representative examples of all ecosystems, have always been at least minor goals in wilderness area and national park advocacy in the United States. * * *

Some of this country's greatest conservationists have been scientists, too. One of the many hats John Muir wore was that of a scientist. Aldo Leopold was a pioneer in ecology and wildlife management and argued for wilderness areas as ecological baselines. Bob Marshall had a Ph.D. in plant physiology and explored the unmapped Brooks Range in Alaska not just for adventure, but also to study tree growth in that extreme climate. Olaus Murie, long-time President of The Wilderness Society, was an early wildlife ecologist and one of the first to defend the wolf.

Aesthetic, recreational, and utilitarian (e.g., watershed protection) arguments have traditionally dominated advocacy for national parks and wilderness areas and these values have had more influence on what areas were protected than have ecological arguments. In the last decade, however, ecological arguments have risen to the top of the conservation movement. Scientists, particularly from the new discipline of conservation biology, have become more prominent in conservation groups. * * *

This ecological renaissance in conservation has come about because of new research and theory in several branches of biology. Looking back over our shoulders, we see that five interrelated lines of scientific inquiry have led to the sort of wilderness networks now being proposed by the Wildlands Project and other conservation groups. These are extinction dynamics, island biogeography, metapopulation theory, large carnivore ecology, and natural disturbance ecology. * * *

As we have seen, wilderness areas and national parks are generally islands of wild habitat in a sea of human-altered landscapes. By fragmenting wildlife habitat, we imperil species from grizzlies to ovenbirds who need large, intact ecosystems. Because they have been chosen largely for their scenic and recreational values, and to minimize resource conflicts with extractive industries, wilderness areas and national parks are often "rock and ice"—high elevation, arid, or rough areas which are beautiful and are popular for backpacking, but which also are relatively unproductive habitats. For the most part, the richer deep forests, rolling grasslands, and fertile river valleys on which a disproportionate number of rare and endangered species depend have passed into private ownership or, if public, have been "released" for development and resource exploitation. * * *

To protect biological diversity, we must build on current national park, wildlife refuge, and wilderness area systems. The ecological model for nature reserves of large wilderness cores, buffer zones, and biological linkages is widely accepted by scientists and is the basis for proposals by the Wildlands Project. Core wilderness areas would be strictly managed to protect and, where necessary, to restore native biological diversity and natural processes. Traditional wilderness recreation is entirely compatible with preservation, so long as ecological considerations come first. Biological linkages (corridors) would provide secure routes between core reserves for the dispersal of wide-ranging species, for genetic exchange between populations, for the flow of ecological processes, and for migration of plants and animals in response to climate change. Surrounding the core reserves, stewardship zones (buffers) would allow increasing levels of compatible human activity away from the cores. Active intervention or protective management, depending on the area, would aid in the restoration of extirpated species and natural conditions. * * *

Existing wilderness areas and national parks and roadless or lightly roaded areas on the public lands are the building blocks for an expanded ecological nature reserve network. Far from tossing aside existing protected areas and the National Wilderness Preservation System and National Park System, conservation biologists and the Wildlands Project want to expand such areas and connect them. * * *

Let me be clear: Explanations for why national parks and wilderness areas have not fully protected nature in the United States and elsewhere are meant to help conservationists add areas to protected status, not to denigrate the considerable achievements of conservationists in the past. Ecological values for nature reserves are not meant to replace those values based on beauty, recreation, inspiration, or existence value, but to add to them.

D.   THE MORAL CASE FOR PRESERVATION

The ecological argument for preservation is at its core a moral argument. Its moral foundation is illustrated by Leopold's description of a land *ethic*: an activity is "right when it tends to preserve the integrity, stability, and beauty of the biotic community" and "*wrong* when it tends otherwise." However, it makes sense to separate out the ecological and moral cases for preservation because the reliance on ecology or science as a justification for preservation typically uses language of biological necessity rather than behavioral morality. There is a moral case to be made for preservation separate and apart from preserving the integrity of a biotic community. That moral argument can grow out of concerns about intergenerational equity, deep ecology beliefs in biocentric equity and ethical treatment of nature, or a religious sense of duty toward and stewardship over God's creation, all of which have already been elaborated upon in Chapter 1. Professor Sax offers another moral argument for preservation in the excerpt below.

Joseph Sax, Mountains Without Handrails 11–15, 104 (1980)

The preservationist constituency is disturbed not only—and not even most importantly—by the physical deterioration of the parks, but by a sense that the style of modern tourism is depriving the parks of their central symbolism, their message about the relationship between man and nature, and man and industrial society.

When the tourist of an earlier time came to the parks, he inevitably left the city far behind him. He may not have been a backpacker or a mountain climber, but he was genuinely immersed in a natural setting. He may only have strolled around the area near his hotel, but he was in a place where the sound of birds ruled rather than the sound of motors, where the urban crowds gave way to rural densities, and where planned entertainments disappeared in favor of a place with nothing to do but what the visitor discovered for himself.

Tourism in the parks today, by contrast, is often little more than an extension of the city and its life-style transposed onto a scenic background. At its extreme, in Yosemite Valley or at the South Rim of Grand Canyon, for example, one finds all the artifacts of urban life: traffic jams, long lines waiting in restaurants, supermarkets, taverns, fashionable shops, night life, prepared entertainments, and the unending drone of motors. The recreational vehicle user comes incased in a rolling version of this home, complete with television to amuse himself when the scenery ceases to engage him. The snowmobiler brings speed and power. Detroit transplanted, imposing the city's pace in the remotest backcountry.

The modern concessioner, more and more a national recreation conglomerate corporation, has often displaced the local innkeeper who adapted to a limited and seasonal business. There are modernized units identical to conventional motels, air conditioning, packaged foods, business conventions, and efforts to bring year-round commercial tourism to places where previously silent languid winters began with the first snowfall.

All these changes have made the preservationist, to whom the park is essentially a symbol of nature and *its* pace and power, an adversary of the conventional tourist. The clearest evidence that the preservationist and the tourist are not simply fighting over the destruction of resources or the allocation of a limited resource that each wishes to use in different, and conflicting ways, but are rather at odds over the symbolism of the parks, is revealed by the battles that they fight. One such recent controversy has arisen over the use of motors on concessioner-run boat trips down the Colorado River in Grand Canyon. In fact, motorized boats don't measurably affect the Canyon ecosystem, nor do they significantly intrude upon those who want to go down the river in oar-powered boats. Reduced to essentials, the preservationist claim is simply that motors don't belong in this remote and wild place; that they betray the idea of man immersed in nature and bring industrialization to a place whose meaning inheres in its isolation from, and contrast to, life in society.

Much the same observation may be made about the intense controversy over highly developed places like Yosemite Valley. Many of those who are most opposed to the claimed over-development of the valley do not themselves use it much. Wilderness lovers go into the wilderness, and Yosemite, like most national parks, has an abundance of undeveloped wilderness. What offends is not the unavailability of the valley as wild country, but the meaning national parks come to have when they are represented by places like Yosemite City, as the valley has been unkindly called.

What's wrong with the parks, says Edward Abbey—one of the most prominent contemporary spokesmen for the preservationist position—is that they have been too much given over to the clientele of "industrial tourism," people who visit from their cars and whose three standard questions are: "Where's the john? How long's it take to see this place? And where's the Coke machine?" * * *

The preservationist is not an elitist who wants to exclude others, notwithstanding popular opinion to the contrary; he is a moralist who wants to convert them. He is concerned about what other people do in the parks not because he is unaware of the diversity of taste in the society, but because he views certain kinds of activity as calculated to undermine the attitudes he believes the parks can, and should, encourage. He sees mountain climbing as promoting self-reliance, for example, whereas "climbing" in an electrified tramway is perceived as a passive and dependent activity. He finds a park full of planned entertainments and standardized activities a deterrent to independence, whereas an undeveloped park leaves the visitor to set his own agenda and learn how to amuse himself. He associates the motorcyclist roaring across the desert with aspirations to power and domination, while the fly-fisherman is engaged in reducing his technological advantage in order to immerse himself in the natural system and reach out for what lessons it has to offer him. The validity of these distinctions is not self-evident.... They are, however, what lies at the heart of the preservationist position.

The preservationist does not condemn the activities he would like to exclude from the park. He considers them perfectly legitimate and appropriate—if not admirable—and believes that opportunities for conventional tourism are amply provided elsewhere; at resorts and amusement parks, on private lands, and on a very considerable portion of the public domain too. He only urges a recognition that the parks have a distinctive function to perform that is separate from the service of conventional tourism, and they should be managed explicitly to present that function to the public as their principal goal, separate from whatever conventional tourist services they may also have to provide.

In urging that the national parks be devoted to affirming the symbolic meaning he attaches to them, the preservationist makes a very important assumption, routinely indulged but hardly ever explicit. The assumption is that the values he imputes to the parks (independence, self-reliance, self-restraint) are extremely widely shared by the American public. Though he knows that he is a member of a minority, he believes he speaks for values that are majoritarian. He is, in fact, a prophet for a kind of secular religion. You would like to emulate the pioneer explorers, he says to the public; you would like independently to raft down the wild Colorado as John Wesley Powell did a century ago. You would like to go it alone in the mountain wilderness as John Muir did. Indeed that is why you are stirred by the images of the great national parks and why you support the establishment of public wilderness. But you are vulnerable; you allow entrepreneurs to coddle you and manage you. And you are fearful; you are afraid to get out of your recreational vehicle or your car and plunge into the woods on your own. Moreover you want to deceive yourself; you would like to believe that you are striking out into the wilderness, but you insist that the wilderness be tamed before you enter it. So, says the secular prophet, follow me and I will show you how to become the sort of person you really want to be. Put aside for a while the plastic alligators of the amusement park, and I will show you that nature, taken on its own terms, has something to say that you will be glad to hear. This is the essence of the preservationist message. * * *

This is not to say that what they preach cannot be rejected as merely a matter of taste, of elitist sentiment or as yet another reworking of pastoral sentimentalism. It is, however, to admit that their desire to dominate a public policy for public parks cannot prevail if their message is taken in so limited a compass. If they cannot persuade a majority that the country needs national parks of the kind they propose, much as it needs public schools and libraries, then the role they have long sought to play in the governmental process cannot be sustained. The claim is bold, and it has often been concealed in a pastiche of argument for scientific protection of nature, minority rights, and sentimental rhetoric. I have tried to isolate and make explicit the political claim, as it relates to the fashioning of public policy, and leave it to sail or sink on that basis.

E. THE DARKER SIDE OF PRESERVATION

Despite the strong and growing public sentiment favoring preservation, many residents of rural, public land communities take a more negative view of the creation of monuments, parks, and wilderness areas. They view such designations as "locking up" the public lands upon which their communities have relied for economic sustenance over a number of generations. In such communities, the sentiment is often expressed that the increased tourism that accompanies a protective designation "is its own environmental disaster here in the West, the cause of strip development, clogged roads and towns, burger-flipper jobs and population increases." Sandra Dallas, *Tourism Takes Its Lumps in "Discovered Country,"* DENVER POST, Nov. 20, 1994, at E12. Although these sort of pejorative references to the service economy are legion, there is evidence that the transition to a service economy does more than produce low-paying positions in fast-foods, hotels, and retail. The service economy produces not only more lower-paying jobs but also more higher-paying jobs than the goods-production sector, although "a worker shifting from goods-production to services would have to move into a higher-skilled service job to make the same money." THOMAS MICHAEL POWER, LOST LANDSCAPES AND FAILED ECONOMIES: THE SEARCH FOR A VALUE OF PLACE 69 (1996).

Residents of public lands communities do not rely solely on economic arguments. Increased public lands tourism can take a toll on the culture of a rural community. Hal Rothman argued,

> As places acquire the cachet of desirability, they draw people and money; the redistribution of wealth, power, and status follows, complicating local arrangements. When tourism creates sufficient wealth, it becomes too important to be left to the locals. Power moves away from local decisionmakers, even those who physically and socially invest in the new system that tourism creates, and toward outside capital and its local representatives. . . . The new shape disenfranchises most locals even as it makes some natives and most neonatives—those who are attracted to the places that have become tourist towns because of the traits of these transformed places—economically better off and creates a place that becomes a mirror image of itself as its identity is marketed. * * *
>
> Tourism is the most colonial of colonial economies, not because of the sheer physical difficulty or the pain or humiliation intrinsic in its labor but because of its psychic and social impact on the people and their places. Tourism and the social structure it provides transform locals into people who look like them-

selves but who act and believe differently as they learn to market their place and its, and their, identity.

HAL ROTHMAN, DEVIL'S BARGAIN: TOURISM IN THE TWENTIETH-CENTURY AMERICAN WEST 11–12 (1998). Consider the case of Moab, Utah, a community just outside of Arches National Park:

> Originally founded by Mormon farmers and ranchers, Moab remained a quiet settlement until the twentieth century when intermittent discoveries of valuable mineral deposits, primarily uranium, vanadium and potash, led to a series of mini-booms and busts. Concerned about its fluctuating economic fortunes, Moab for years sought ways to attract industry and tourism to even out the economy. But it was not until the 1980s that tourism took off. Spurred by large visitation increases at Arches and Canyonlands National Parks and by the remarkable growth in the popularity of mountain biking, Moab has experienced exponential growth in the last 15 years. Long-time residents now barely recognize their town. Bill Hedden, vice-chairman of the county council, laments: "Our community leaders went fishing for a little tourism to revive and diversify our economy and they hooked a great white shark. This monster has swamped the boat and eaten the crew. At stake is not merely the community we used to be but also some of the best and most fragile country anywhere." [Describing the conversion of a local diner into a Burger King, the publisher of a local alternative newspaper suggested, "What happened to the Star Diner is a real metaphor for what's happening to Moab, and that story is being repeated all over the West. . . . Moab is no longer a community. It has lost its soul." Sam Allis, *Moab's Mutation*, CHICAGO TRIB., Jan. 16, 2000, at 24.]

> For many, Moab has become symbolic of growth gone awry. Rural residents voice the fear of their town becoming "another Moab" and talk about the "Moabization" of rural communities as if it were a plague. Whereas such sentiments had previously been reserved for ski-tourist communities like Aspen, Jackson, and Park City, Moab holds out the possibility that the undeveloped West alone holds sufficient attraction to be swamped by tourism and in-migration. Although this view of life before the bike in Moab is perhaps somewhat romanticized, it illustrates a genuine concern on the part of rural westerners about the economic and cultural dislocations that are a by-product of the shift to preservation and recreation as the new dominant uses of the public lands. * * *

James R. Rasband, *The Rise of Urban Archipelagoes in the American West: A New Reservation Policy?*, 31 ENVTL. L. 1, 44–45 (2001). If designation of parks, monuments, and wilderness, and the accompanying limitation of traditional uses of the public lands has this impact on rural communities, what does that mean for federal land policy? Is there some obligation to protect the traditional lifestyle of such rural communities? Is the lifestyle of rural communities dependent upon public land ranching, mining, logging, and the like really so unique that it merits special consideration? Consider further the questions raised by Professor Sax in this excerpt.

Joseph L. Sax, *Do Communities Have Rights? The National Parks As A Laboratory of New Ideas*, 45 U. PITT. L. REV. 499, 504, 507–09 (1984)

[A] number of newer units of the national park system are being established in places that already have existing human settlements, rather than, as was traditionally the case, on vast areas of public domain that were more or less uninhabited wilderness. Since parks are created to preserve natural resources, and to encourage public recreation, the question inevitably arises: How should the Park Service deal with the existing communities whose presence within these new enclaves advances neither of those goals. * * *

In 1972, Congress established, as a unit of the national park system, the Buffalo National River in Arkansas (hereafter 'the River'). Though there were several viable villages within the boundaries of the unit, no special attention was paid to them in the legislation, which provided only that the River was established 'for the purpose of conserving and interpreting an area containing unique scenic and scientific features, and preserving ... an important segment of ... the River.' * * *

Within the River is a tiny agricultural village known as Boxley Valley. It originally consisted of approximately twenty dwellings, with attached small farms, a little church, school and community building and a store. Boxley is not a very prepossessing place, but it presents a highly attractive example of a traditional Ozark Valley farming community. Some of its buildings, houses and barns are considered fine examples of vernacular country architecture.

Park Service policy for the Boxley Valley has gone through several stages. At first, the policy seems to have been to acquire all the properties and gradually move the residents out, with the notion that the land would revert to its natural condition and be available for River recreation. The store was acquired, as were a number of homes and farms. Some owners took their compensation and moved out; others took use and occupancy agreements for various terms of years. As of late 1983, the half-dozen homes and former stores owned in fee by the government are boarded up and stand empty. Eventually, the historical value of the Valley came to the fore, both as a traditional landscape, and as a setting for several architecturally significant structures, residences and barns. The Park Service, therefore, partially modified its policy and permitted some owners to remain as proprietors permanently. The Park Service negotiated for scenic easements designed to control development and to assure that the Boxley scene retained its rural, 1920's character. Plans for visitor use were largely abandoned.

Presently, the Park Service is in the process of developing a new plan for the future of the Boxley Valley. It seems to have decided that the village should not be returned to its natural, pre-settlement condition. Indeed, the Park Service is leaning in the opposite direction. It proposes to have the entire valley listed on the national register of historic properties so that the small farms, with their aesthetically pleasing fence lines, will be preserved and worked. The historically valuable houses and barns are to be occupied, maintained and, where necessary, restored.

While the inclination now is to save Boxley, rather than destroy it, such a plan raises problems of its own. If the place is to be preserved for its historic and aesthetic values, rigorous controls would seem to be called for. The sort of problems that arise seem small, but they are revealing. Should an owner be allowed to tear down a traditional style barn, and replace it with a cheaper, and more useful aluminum structure? What if the residents want to install the sort of obtrusive 'saucers' necessary to bring television to remote areas? Shall mobile homes be allowed in the Valley? May new houses—in what might be untraditional styles—be allowed to be built? Can fences be taken down to create bigger agricultural fields?

The Park Service realizes that it is faced with some unusual problems for which there are no conventional answers. By refraining from destroying the village and turning it into a picnic ground out of sensitivity to the interests of the residents, the Park Service has thrust itself into an almost equally uncomfortable opposite posture. Are the residents to be compelled to live as if they were the denizens of a museum, unable to grow and change simply because they happen to inhabit a quaint, historic town that others find interesting? But, are no controls permissible? Should farm practices be permitted that would impair the quality of the Buffalo River, and thus the recreational experience of those for whom Congress established the area? Should developers be allowed to come in to this charming valley and make it a weekend retreat for jaded urban residents, totally changing its character? Are controls here any different from those in the historic district of a large city, or the public interest in them any less? Ought the Park Service to withdraw entirely, selling back the properties to private owners, in order to let local autonomy prevail?

————

Although not really an argument against preservation, a number of writers have urged some caution about romanticizing preservation as selfless biocentrism. Designation of parks, monuments, and wilderness, they suggest, is mostly a manifestation of preferences for a different sort of use and a different type of impact, albeit usually a smaller one. Consider the following excerpt:

James R. Rasband, *The Rise of Urban Archipelagoes in the American West: A New Reservation Policy?*, 31 ENVTL. L. 1, 28–33 (2001)

[A]n increasing amount of research indicates that recreation has significant, negative impacts on biodiversity. This impact comes not just from intensive recreation activities like off-road vehicle use, but also from those activities that have long been touted as benign and non-consumptive—camping, hiking, angling, nature-viewing, and the like. Although a single backpacker, angler, or bird-watcher may not have much impact, the cumulative effect of repeated visitation does. Thus, in wilderness areas where the "imprint of man's work" is supposed to be "substantially unnoticeable," frequently used camping locations, such as areas adjacent to alpine lakes, have turned into permanent campsites. At such sites, ground vegetation has been worn away, tree roots exposed, and trash left behind, resulting in reduced numbers of ground and understory bird species in the area. An increased number of backpackers has also led to an increase in the number of streams polluted with giardia. Rock climbers in wilderness areas have left climbs littered with fixed anchors, prompting the Forest Service to prohibit the use of fixed anchors in all Forest Service wilderness areas. Climbing can also harm wildlife. Rock climbers typically choose routes that follow cracks and ledges, which are precisely the areas used by wildlife for breeding, foraging, and roosting. The problem is exacerbated by the fact that "the most popular time to climb mountains and cliffs coincides with the peak of the breeding season for many wildlife species." With such impacts, it is not surprising that in a recent survey of land managers, the most commonly cited problem with wilderness management was recreation overuse.

Research on recreation impacts outside of wilderness areas shows similar and even more extensive impacts result from camping, climbing, and other recreation activities. One study in Germany, for example, found that "[i]ntensive angling reduced the number of waterfowl nests by 80%, and the remaining nests were found only in areas inaccessible to anglers." In addition, hiking near nests has been found to increase predation of bird eggs or young birds.

Unfortunately, nature viewing is not benign. Indeed, one review of 166 articles containing data on the effects of "non-consumptive" outdoor recreation on wildlife found that 81% of the articles identified negative consequences.

Recreational impact can be particularly harmful in the fragile desert environments that abound in the Southwest.... A crucial component of the desert ecosystem is the cryptobiotic crust made up of mosses, fungi, and lichens. This crust grows on top of the sand, holds moisture, and stores carbon and nitrogen, in which larger plants can eventually take root. As hikers, bikers, and campers have ... dispersed themselves over the fragile cryptobiotic crust, formerly stable systems have given way to wind-blown sands. As Barbara Sharrow, BLM's lead recreational planner for the Grand Staircase–Escalante Monument, put it: "There's no doubt about it, recreation may have the same sorts of impacts that grazing did in the '20s and '30s and mining in the late 1800s."

———

Is any form of recreation or enjoyment of natural resources wholly compatible with preservation? Think about Professor Krakoff's comments on the phenomenon of ecotourism.

Alongside the plethora of adventure travel opportunities, the last two decades have witnessed the growth of a more environmentally and socially conscious method of travel dubbed "ecotourism." Ecotourism is defined as low impact nature tourism that aims to preserve species as well as local cultures. Ecotourism proponents and experts assert that it satisfies multiple conservation and development objectives, including: generation of financial support for the protection and management of natural areas; economic benefits for local residents; support for conservation among local residents; and, for the ecotourists, immersion in and appreciation of local nature and culture. * * *

This sounds good; is it too good to be true? ... One has reason to be skeptical, and in reality most such claims are sorely under-evaluated. There are, however, some spectacularly documented failures. In Thailand, sea-kayaking into limestone caves has gone from eco-friendly to eco-threatening. An American, John Gray, started a commercial venture with all of the motivations of the best eco-businessman: "Blend local people, uncompromising standards and sound management, and you'll not only have a business that's sustainable for nature, but for making money as well." Today, he characterizes his expectations as "fantasy land." When Gray started his business, he limited the daily visitors he took to the spectacular interior lagoons to fifty, hired an all-local staff, provided excellent training and compensation, and lectured the paying clients on proper cave etiquette. Then, the competition got in on it. Nineteen additional sea-kayaking tours now cater to eager foreigners. The result is that as many as 1,000 kayakers enter the delicate caves daily, and their behavior cannot be controlled. They break off stalactites, and their noise level scares away local wildlife. Gray concludes: "Eco-tourism rolls off the tongue quite easily. But quite honestly, there's very little around.... Looking back on it, I don't know if we did the right thing by commercializing caves." Despite ecotourism's promise, Gray's experience indicates that the buying and selling of nature can rarely avoid the material consequences of consumption; in other words, there is no non-consumptive consumption.

Sarah Krakoff, *Mountains Without Handrails ... Wilderness Without Cellphones*, 27 HARV. ENVTL. L. REV. 417, 450–53 (2003).

QUESTIONS AND DISCUSSION

1. Is "ecotourism" an oxymoron? Is Hal Rothman right that "[w]e are all industrial tourists. Physically we take only pictures and leave only footprints. Psychically, socially, culturally, and environmentally, we inexorably change all that we touch"? HAL ROTHMAN, DEVIL'S BARGAIN: TOURISM IN THE TWENTIETH-CENTURY AMERICAN WEST 377 (1998). If recreation is a consumptive use of natural resources, what is the relevance of that insight to resource managers? Does it mean that high-intensity recreation is no different than low-intensity recreation and that all recreation is no different than traditional natural resource uses like grazing, mining, logging, and hydropower dams?

2. While it is possible to articulate economic, ecological, and moral arguments for preservation, are those ideas what drives the public preference for preservation? Would you describe the public preference as anthropocentric, biocentric, or a mixture of the two? A 1993 survey sponsored by Defenders of Wildlife found that seventy-three percent of adults were unfamiliar with the issue of loss of biodiversity. MICHAEL E. KRAFT, ENVIRONMENTAL POLICY AND POLITICS: TOWARD THE TWENTY-FIRST CENTURY 78 (1996). Is this result surprising?

3. In the quote at the beginning of this chapter, Professor Sax argues that preservationists "are really moralists at heart." Do you think that is a fair characterization of most preservation advocates or would it be more accurate to say that they are really ecologists at heart?

4. The increased interest in recreation and preservation is not limited to the United States. It is a worldwide phenomenon. "Since the 1970s, more protected areas have been established worldwide than during all preceding periods." MARTHA HONEY, ECOTOURISM AND SUSTAINABLE DEVELOPMENT 11 (1999). By 2007 there were 107,034 nationally designated protected sites, which covered over 19.5 million square kilometers of land, territorial waters and marine and coastal areas (7.5 million square miles). Tourism worldwide is on the increase. In 2009, the World Travel and Tourism Council estimated that personal travel and tourism would generate $ 2.9 trillion of economic activity. Domestically, the U.S. travel and tourism industry was expected to generate $814.9 billion in personal travel and tourism expenditures in 2009. Additionally, the travel and tourism industry in the United States in 2009 employed 13.8 million people or 1 out of every 10 jobs in the country. *See* UNEP World Conservation Monitoring Centre, *World Database on Protected Resources, Statistics,* http://www.unep-wcmc. org/wdpa/; WORLD TRAVEL AND TOURISM COUNCIL, TRAVEL AND TOURISM ECONOMIC IMPACT, UNITED STATES 2009, http://www.wttc.org/bin/pdf/original_pdf_file/unitedstates.pdf; MARK HOY, TIA'S CENTRAL ROLE IN TOURISM RECOVERY STRATEGIES FOR THE UNITED STATES 1 (2003).

5. Are we loving our parks to death? Consider the following description of Yosemite National Park.

> Towering falls, ancient sequoias, and the world's most famous sheer rock outcroppings attract millions of visitors to Yosemite National Park. Unfortunately, when visitors arrive they encounter traffic gridlock, pine scent smothered by exhaust, sold-out campgrounds, and long lines to buy food, catch a

shuttle ride, or ride a horse. On peak summer weekends in Yosemite Valley, the park's scenic heart, it is common to see rangers directing traffic and rows of tour buses idling at top attractions. It is also common to see cars endlessly circling jammed parking lots, shuttles filled to standing room only, and highways littered with cars lined bumper-to-bumper. These conditions leave many visitors feeling disappointed. The pristine, peaceful park they hoped to visit is no different from the noise and pollution they had hoped to escape.

Richard J. Ansson, *Funding for Our National Parks in the 21st Century: Will We Be Able to Preserve and Protect Our Embattled National Parks?*, 11 FORDHAM ENVTL. L.J. 1, 1 (1999). Yosemite is not alone. A number of other popular national parks experience similar congestion problems. What is the appropriate response to this problem of uncontrolled access? Yosemite began offering visitors the option of free shuttle buses to move them around the park. Acadia National Park took the same approach. Zion National Park went further and banned cars from the park. Visitors park their cars at the entrance and then ride propane-powered shuttles into the park with stops at popular trailheads and features. A light rail system has been proposed for the Grand Canyon, and legislation has been unsuccessfully introduced that would have spent $540 million to increase mass transit in national parks. *See* Transit in Parks Act, § 1032, 108th Cong., 1st Sess. (May 8, 2003). What is your reaction to these solutions? Can you think of a better one?

6. Another problem caused by the dramatic increase in use of our public lands is that the land management agencies have developed a tremendous maintenance backlog. They haven't had the funds or the personnel to keep up with public impacts. One of Congress' responses was to pass what it called the Recreational Fee Demonstration Program, which authorized the National Park Service, the Fish and Wildlife Service, the Bureau of Land Management, and the Forest Service to charge fees to visitors. By 2003, fee demonstration projects were in place at 637 sites. Originally authorized for three years, the program was extended four times and replaced in 2004 by the Federal Lands Recreation Enhancement Act, which will sunset in 2014. By 2006, the four agencies had collected over $1.5 billion in fees. Eighty percent of the fees received may be used by the particular park, monument, refuge, or forest where the money was collected. What incentives does the fee demonstration program create for land managers? What might be the advantages and disadvantages of requiring users to pay a fee? Although most visitors are happy to pay a fee where the money will be used to improve the area they visit, the fees have been opposed by some. What arguments against the program would you expect to see? Shouldn't public land visitors be obligated at least to pay a fee sufficient to internalize their externalities? Is there any reason to treat a park visitor differently than a mining company? *See* U.S. Dep't of the Interior & U.S. Dep't. of Agric., *Recreational Fee Demonstration Program, Progress Report to Congress, Fiscal Year 2003* (May 2004), http://www.nps.gov/feedemo/reports/FinalFY 03FeeDemoAnnualReport.pdf; U.S. Dep't of the Interior & U.S. Dep't. of Agric., *Federal Lands Recreation Enhancement Act, First Triennial Report to Congress, Fiscal Year 2006* (May 2006), http://www.nps.gov/feedemo/ reports/FinalTriennial2006Report.pdf. For a review of the program, see Holly Lippke Fretwell & Michael J. Podolsky, *A Strategy for Restoring*

America's National Parks, 13 DUKE ENVTL. L. & POL'Y FORUM 143 (2003); U.S. GEN. ACCOUNTING OFFICE, RECREATION FEES: INFORMATION ON FOREST SERVICE MANAGEMENT OF REVENUE FROM THE FEE DEMONSTRATION PROGRAM (GAO–03–470, Apr. 2003).

7.   Since 2000, visits to National Park Service lands have remained relatively flat—visitation in 2007 was essentially the same as visitation in 1997. *See National Park System Attendance Rises in 2007*, http://home.nps.gov/applications/release/Detail.cfm?ID=785. Exactly why park visitation seems to have leveled off is not fully understood. Some have suggested that aging baby-boomers prefer softer king-size beds to tents, others have noted kids' preference for video games over the outdoors. Still others have suggested some correlation with the increase in fees under the fee demonstration program described in note 6. What other reasons might explain this leveling off of visitation? Is it likely to be a long- or short-term trend? If the trend continues or visitation declines, what are the implications for public land policy?

8.   Think back on the excerpt discussing the presence of Boxley Valley within the Buffalo National River unit of the park system. How would you respond to Professor Sax's question about whether an owner should be allowed to tear down a traditional style barn and replace it with a cheaper, and more useful aluminum structure? What land use controls are permissible or appropriate? These same questions arise frequently with historic buildings in cities. Do you see any difference between preserving nature and preserving culture? Is there a stronger justification for one of the two?

9.   As the excerpt from Pete Morton above indicates, many preservation advocates are uncomfortable with economic or utilitarian arguments for preservation. Sometimes, as is the case with Pete Morton, their view is that economic arguments are second-best or incomplete. For some others, however, economic arguments are dangerous or even immoral; preservation is both an ecological and moral imperative without respect to costs or benefits. As Ed Abbey once remarked: "The idea of wilderness needs no defense. It only needs more defenders." EDWARD ABBEY, THE JOURNEY HOME 223 (1977). Consider the response to such concerns from two free market environmentalists:

> Economists understand that whatever people claim, environmental quality is only one of several competing values they seek. They must trade-off more of some values for less of another. Scarcity—the fact that virtually no resources are abundant enough to satisfy all human demands at zero cost—dictates that choices must be made among competing values or goods. Just as people on fixed budgets must choose between buying a new television or a new sofa, societies must choose among competing goods (e.g., more health care, safer roads, or more environmental protection). Open space and wildlife habitat provided by parks, ranches, and wilderness are among the goods involved in the trade-offs. It is intellectually and ethically impossible to pretend away the necessity of such choices.

John A. Baden & Pete Geddes, *Environmental Entrepreneurs: Keys to Achieving Wilderness Conservation Goals?*, 76 DENV. U. L. REV. 519, 527 (1999). Is Abbey correct that "wilderness needs no defense," or are you more persuaded by the views of Baden and Geddes? Is it possible to think about preservation without weighing its value against other uses of natural resources? Does that weighing of values need to be monetized, or can cost-benefit analysis have a broader conception?

III. NATIONAL PARKS

Wallace Stegner once described national parks as "the best idea we ever had. Absolutely American, absolutely democratic, they reflect us at our best rather than our worst...." Wallace Stegner, *The Best Idea We Ever Had*, *in* MARKING THE SPARROW'S FALL: THE MAKING OF THE AMERICAN WEST 137 (Page Stegner ed., 1998). The casebook has already introduced the national parks and the Park Service in Chapters 2 and 3. As discussed there, the national park idea was inaugurated with the creation of Yellowstone National Park in 1872. During the conservation era that spanned the turn of the century, a number of new parks were created by Congress, including Yosemite in 1890, Mount Rainier in 1899, Crater Lake in 1902, Mesa Verde in 1906, Grand Canyon in 1908, Zion and Olympic in 1909, Glacier in 1910 and Rocky Mountain in 1915. By 1916, the Interior Department was responsible for 14 national parks but had neither an organization nor policy guidance from Congress for managing those parks. In 1916, Congress gave it both, passing the Park Service Organic Act, which created the National Park Service within the Department of the Interior. Act of August 25, 1916; ch. 408, 39 Stat. 535. 16 U.S.C. §§ 1–4. Over time the National Park System expanded to include units with nineteen different types of designations, including national parks, national monuments, national recreation areas, national seashores, national lakeshores, national historic sites, and national battlefields. The National Park System now comprises 391 areas, 58 of which are national parks, and 84 million acres. *See* National Park Service, *Frequently Asked Questions*, http://www.nps.gov/faqs.htm; National Park Service, *National Park System*, http://www.nps.gov/pub_aff/refdesk/classlst.pdf; DYAN ZASLOWSKY & T.H. WATKINS, THESE AMERICAN LANDS: PARKS, WILDERNESS AND THE PUBLIC LANDS 11–27 (1994).

Truth be told, national parks have been one of the less contentious areas of natural resources law. Partly because park designations usually include lands for which there is widespread agreement about their outstanding scenic qualities and even more because Congress itself creates parks, the designation process has produced precious little litigation or case law. Even the most committed sagebrush rebels and wise use advocates have been careful not to concentrate their antifederal fire on national park designations, preferring instead to focus on national forest and BLM lands. The facet of national parks that has triggered more disputes, particularly in recent years, is their management and thus that is where this section of the chapter will focus. To grasp why management of the parks more often triggers litigation, consider the following excerpt in which Professor Sax gives a brief overview of federal national park policy:

JOSEPH SAX, MOUNTAINS WITHOUT HANDRAILS 6–7 (1980)

If the government had a plan for the parks it was establishing, it was certainly casual about it. No bureau existed to manage these places until 1916, forty-four years after the Yellowstone reservation. Yellowstone, in fact, was run by the United States Cavalry, and the others were pretty much left to themselves and to a few hardy innkeepers and adventurous tourists. The modern desire to view the parks as the product of a prophetic public ecological conscience has little history to support it. The early parks were reserved for their scenery and their curiosities, and they reflect a fascination with monumentalism as well as biological ignorance or indifference. * * *

For a good many years, this fragile ideological coalition held together with only modest conflict. The preservationists (as they are now called), who always comprised the most active and interested constituency in favor of national parks, had little to complain about. The parks were there, but they were so little used and so little developed—Congress was always grudging with appropriations: "Not one cent for scenery" was its long-standing motto—that those who wanted to maintain the parks as they were, both for their own use and as a symbol of man's appropriate relationship to nature, had what they wanted.

The professional park managers, organized as the National Park Service in 1916, also found circumstances generally to their liking. Like all bureaucrats they had certain imperial ambitions. But the park system was steadily growing, and that was satisfying. Some of their gains were made at the expense of the national forests, housed in another federal department, and while inter-bureau infighting was at times intense, the general public was indifferent to such matters. Moreover, in its early years, and particularly before the full blossoming of the automobile era, the Park Service was able to take an actively promotional posture, encouraging increasing tourism, road building, and hotel development without losing the support of its preservationist constituency. It was then in everyone's interest to create greater public support for the parks. If more people came to the national parks, more people would approve the establishment of new parks and would approve funding for management needed to protect and preserve them. Even the most ardent wilderness advocate complained little about the Park Service as a promotional agency. The adverse effects tourism might have were long viewed as trivial.

The tourists who came to the parks in the early days were in general not much different from those who come today. They arrived in carriages, slept in hotels, and spent a good deal of their time sitting on verandas. But of course they came in much smaller numbers, their impact on the resources was much less, and, despite the comforts they provided themselves, the setting in which they lived in the parks was fairly primitive and marked a sharp contrast with life at home. A visit to a national park was still an adventure, quite unlike any ordinary vacation. The alliance of preservationists (whose interest in parks was essentially symbolic and spiritual) and vacationers (to whom the parks were a commodity for recreational use) was not threatened by the low intensity use the parks received for many decades. The contradiction Congress had enacted into law in the 1916 general management act, ordering the National Park Service at once to promote use and to conserve the resources so as to leave them unimpaired, was actually a workable mandate.

The recreation explosion of recent years has unraveled that alliance and brought to the fore questions we have not previously had to answer: For whom and for what are the parks most important? Which of the faithful national park constituencies will have to be disappointed so that the parks can serve their "true" purpose?

A. THE PARK SERVICE ORGANIC ACT

In the preceding excerpt Professor Sax concludes by asking "[w]hich of the faithful national park constituencies will have to be disappointed so that the parks can serve their 'true' purpose?" His placement of quotation marks around the word "true" suggests that park purposes are and inevitably will remain contested terrain. In a broad sense, this is certainly true. Park management is always subject to Congress' will. A closer question is whether the parks have a "true" purpose under current law? Is there a correct balance between recreation and preservation, between protection and use? Or is park management purely a matter of Park Service discretion under which the agency effectively decides park purposes? The first place to look for an answer to that question is the Park Service Organic Act, which gave the Park Service the mission "to conserve the scenery and the natural and historic objects and the wildlife therein, and to provide for the enjoyment of the same in such manner and by such means as will leave them unimpaired for the enjoyment of future generations." 16 U.S.C. §§ 1–18f. In addition to the Organic Act, separate missions for individual parks are spelled out in their individual authorizing legislation and then additional management criteria are developed in planning documents prepared for each park. Disputes about park use and management tend, however, to come back to the terms of the Organic Act and its mandate to provide for enjoyment of the parks while leaving them unimpaired for future generations. Professor Sax and many others have suggested that this language creates a contradiction and he questions whether it provides a workable mandate. Is he right? Professor Keiter takes a somewhat different view in the following excerpt explaining the basics of the Organic Act and park management:

Robert B. Keiter, *Preserving Nature in the National Parks: Law, Policy, and Science in a Dynamic Environment*, 74 DENV. U. L. REV. 649, 675–78 (1997)

Under the Organic Act, the Park Service is obligated to administer national parks to conserve scenery, wildlife, natural and historic objects, and to provide for public enjoyment, while ensuring that parks are left "unimpaired for the enjoyment of future generations." Although the Act speaks in terms of both preservation and public use, the statutory "nonimpairment" standard indicates that resource preservation responsibilities should take precedence over public use in the event of conflict. The 1978 amendments to the Organic Act, which provide that national parks shall be protected and managed "in light of the high public value and integrity" of the system, reaffirms and strengthens Congress' commitment to the basic Organic Act preservation tenets. Indeed, several courts have concluded that the amended statute clearly gives primacy to resource preservation over competing uses or interests. This construction of the Organic Act, with its emphasis on preserving nature, supports the basic nonintervention and ecological restoration premises of the Park Service's preservation policy.

Under the Organic Act, the Secretary of the Interior is vested with broad regulatory authority over the national parks. This provision provides the Secretary with adequate legal authority to implement nonintervention and restoration preservation policies. The courts have consistently sustained Park Service regulations and policies designed to protect park resources, including limitations on hunting, fishing, rafting, mountain biking, and vehicle use within the parks. Where the Park Service has sought to limit visitor activities in deference to protecting the ecological health or appearance of park resources, the courts have deferred to the agency's judgments.... Nevertheless, despite its considerable authority, the Park Service generally has not translated its resource management policies into governing regulations, choosing instead to define its preservation policies through general policy statements.

The Park Service has implemented its preservation policy through the park planning process. Under the Organic Act, the Park Service is obligated to develop general management plans "for the preservation and use of each unit of the National Park system." General management plans are required to address park resource preservation measures, visitor facilities plans, visitor carrying capacities, and boundary modifications. Most national parks ... have prepared management plans that contain general wildlife and fire management principles as well as policies governing individual species and ecological processes. These general management plans are sometimes supplemented by more specific management plans, such as Yellowstone's rather detailed bison and fire management plans. Given the environmental consequences attached to both types of plans, they ordinarily should be subject to NEPA compliance requirements. This would provide the public an opportunity to participate in formulating and implementing preservation policy, and subject underlying ecological assumptions to some degree of scrutiny. However, it is unclear whether preservation policies established in general management plans would be subject to judicial review at this planning stage.

The Organic Act and individual park enabling statutes also contain specific exceptions to the notion that national parks are inviolate natural sanctuaries. Under the Organic Act, the Secretary of the Interior may cut timber to protect park resources and scenery against insects or disease, and destroy animals or plants "as may be detrimental to the use of ... parks." These provisions evidently allow the Secretary to elevate other park resource considerations above preservation, so long as intervention can be reconciled with these statutory responsibilities. Individual park enabling acts also may require or authorize management approaches inconsistent with general preservation policy. For example, elk hunting is statutorily sanctioned in Grand Teton National Park, and Yellowstone National Park is authorized to "sell or otherwise dispose of" its surplus bison. Although neither provision precludes Park Service officials from pursuing a nonintervention preservation policy, they nonetheless indicate that other specified considerations may take precedence.

QUESTIONS AND DISCUSSION

1. Has Congress given the Park Service an impossible task? Is it possible to simultaneously provide for enjoyment of a resource without in any way impairing the resource for future generations? What about a road? A lodge? A trail? Do they impair the Park's resources for future generations? How can the Park Service avoid impairing park resources while accommodating a projected 275 million visitors a year? For a thorough consideration of the Organic Act's legislative history leading to the conclusion that the Organic Act "is not, in fact, contradictory and that Congress did not regard it as contradictory," see Robin W. Winks, *The National Park Service Act of 1916: "A Contradictory Mandate"?*, 74 DENV. U. L. REV. 575, 622 (1997).

2. The Park Service Organic Act is not the only place where Congress has charged an agency with mediating between positions in apparent conflict. Multiple use management creates the same tensions. Under FLPMA, for example, multiple use is defined as management of the public lands

> in the combination that will best meet the *present and future* needs of the American people; ... that takes into account the long-term needs of future generations for renewable and nonrenewable resources, including but not limited to, recreation, range, timber, minerals, watershed, wildlife and fish, and natural scenic, scientific and historical values; and harmonious and coordinated management of various resources without permanent impairment of the productivity of the land and the quality of the environment. . . .

43 U.S.C. § 1702 (emphasis added). Why might Congress issue such conflicting mandates to an agency? Does the existence of tension between different management mandates argue for more or less deference to agency decisionmaking? Think about Professor Cheever's comments on such paradoxical mandates:

> At present, the paradoxical mandates of the two agencies [NPS and USFS] facilitate the generation of perceptions of agency purpose at odds with actual agency conduct. They allow those of us who are interested in public land management to project our vision and values onto the language Congress used to instruct these agencies. This almost insures that some significant part of the interested public will believe that the agencies conduct is not only wrong but illegal.

> Federal officials are fond of saying that when they anger both sides in a dispute, they are probably doing their jobs. In fact, operating in a manner that defies the expectations of interested outside groups has a corrosive quality. It corrodes working relationships between the agency and its potential partners in the community in which it operates, and it corrodes judicial deference to agency action. When a Winnebago tourist, who believes the national parks exist for his enjoyment, hears that the Park Service is planning to ban cars from Zion National Park, he feels betrayed. When a wilderness enthusiast, who believes the national parks exist to preserve natural wonders, finds the equivalent of a shopping mall in Yosemite Valley, she feels betrayed. . . .

> So how did these agencies get stuck with such counter-productive mandates, and why did it take the better part of the twentieth century for the mandates to create such problems? I suggest that these paradoxical mandates once served to enhance agency prestige and esprit de corps by giving the powerful men who influenced the agencies' early years language onto which they could project their vision and that, in a world in which Congress and the Cabinet provided the only arenas for disputes about the public land, their opacity did little or no harm. Times have changed; ambiguity which once provided agencies necessary latitude before Congress and the Cabinet now inspire sophisticated western interest groups to challenge agency policy. Mandates which once contributed to the rise of agency discretion now contribute to its decline.

Federico Cheever, *The United States Forest Service and National Park Service: Paradoxical Mandates, Powerful Founders, and the Rise and Fall of Agency Discretion*, 74 DENV. U. L. REV. 625, 629 (1997).

———

To place the Organic Act mandate within a specific context, consider the following decision addressing the use of four-wheel drive vehicles within an environmentally sensitive area of Canyonlands National Park. The case describes 2001 Management Policies adopted by the Park Service that affirm the primacy of the nonimpairment mandate in line with the reasoning of Professor Keiter in the excerpt above. As you read the opinion, consider whether the Management Policies remove the management tensions faced by the Park Service.

SOUTHERN UTAH WILDERNESS ALLIANCE V. NATIONAL PARK SERVICE, 387 F. Supp. 2d 1178 (D. Utah 2005)

KIMBALL, DISTRICT JUDGE.

This matter is before the court on Defendant–Intervenors Utah Shared Access Alliance, Blue Ribbon Coalition, High Desert Multiple Use Coalition, United Four Wheel Drive Associations of U.S. and Canada, and Historic Access Recovery Project's (collectively "USA–ALL") Administrative Appeal of the National Park Service's ("NPS") Final Rule. The Final Rule, which is codified at 36 C.F.R. § 7.44, amends the NPS's regulations for Canyonlands National Park by prohibiting motor vehicles in Salt Creek Canyon above the Peekaboo campsite. * * *

Salt Creek Canyon

Salt Creek Canyon, which is located within the Needles District of Canyonlands, supports the most extensive riparian ecosystem in Canyonlands, other than the Colorado and Green Rivers.... The Salt Creek Road is an unpaved and ungraded jeep trail that runs in and out of Salt Creek. In various places, the road is the creek bed. NPS maintenance of the road is limited to occasional grading or filling of sections that have become impassable due to flooding or erosion from vehicle travel. To navigate this road safely, a high clearance four-wheel drive vehicle and some experience in four-wheeling, or the participation in a commercially guided tour, is necessary. Because of the condition of the road, vehicles using the road periodically break down or become stuck, requiring NPS assistance for removal. There have been instances where vehicles have lost transmission, engine, or crankcase fluids in Salt Creek's water. There is no practical way to reroute the road to avoid the watercourse.

A tributary canyon to Salt Creek contains a well-known landmark, Angel Arch. Angel Arch is a popular destination among four-wheel drivers. The Salt Creek Road is the only means of vehicular access to Angel Arch.

Backcountry Management Plan

Between 1984 and 1992, the number of annual visitors to Canyonlands quadrupled. The increase in visitation directly resulted in an increase of adverse impacts to Canyonlands' resources and diminishment in the quality of visitor experience. In response, the NPS began developing a new Backcountry Management Plan ("BMP"). The purpose of the BMP was to "develop backcountry management strategies to protect park resources, provide for high quality visitor experiences, and be flexible to deal with changing conditions."

On December 18, 1993, the NPS released a draft management plan and environmental assessment ("EA") that addressed, among other things, the impacts of the use of Salt Creek Road by four-wheel drive vehicles. The EA assessed various alternatives, including closing the entire road to vehicle use, closing a portion of the road to vehicle use, and a no-action alternative allowing continued unrestricted use of the road. The EA identified the NPS's preferred alternative as closing the road to vehicles beyond Peekaboo campsite, leaving the approximately ten miles to Angel Arch to be traversed by foot....

On January 6, 1995, the NPS released the final BMP. The final BMP did not completely close the ten-mile portion of Salt Creek Road to motor vehicles. Instead, because of the popularity of four-wheel drive travel on Salt Creek Road, the NPS decided to close a one-half mile segment of the road and leave the remainder of the road open to vehicles on a limited permit system. Specifically, the BMP provided that day-use permits for Salt Creek Canyon would be limited to ten permits for private motor vehicles and two permits for commercial motor vehicle tours per day.

District Court Decision

On June 22, 1995, SUWA filed the above-captioned action challenging the NPS's implementation of the BMP. USA–ALL, a combination of groups supporting four-wheel drive vehicle recreation, intervened as defendants. The parties subsequently filed cross-motions for summary judgment. Among other things, SUWA alleged in its motion that continued vehicular use of Salt Creek Road would cause impairment of unique park resources and thus would violate the Organic Act and Enabling Act.

As to Salt Creek Canyon, the court granted summary judgment in favor of SUWA. The court determined that the Organic Act unambiguously prohibits activities in national parks that would permanently impair unique park resources. The court then further concluded that the motorized vehicle use of Salt Creek Road from Peekaboo Spring to Angel Arch would cause significant, permanent impairment to unique park resources in violation of the Organic Act. *See Southern Utah Wilderness Alliance v. Dabney*, 7 F. Supp.2d 1205 (D.Utah 1998). The court consequently entered a final judgment on September 23, 1998, enjoining the NPS from permitting motorized vehicle travel in Salt Creek Canyon above the Peekaboo campsite.

Tenth Circuit Decision

USA–ALL appealed this court's June 1998 decision to the United States Court of Appeals for the Tenth Circuit. On August 15, 2000, the Court of Appeals reversed the district court decision and remanded it for further consideration. The Court of Appeals determined that the Organic Act's phrase "unimpaired for the enjoyment of future generations" is inherently ambiguous. Accordingly, the Court of Appeals found that the district court erred in finding that step one of *Chevron U.S.A., Inc. v. Natural Res. Def. Council*, 467 U.S. 837, 842–43 (1984), was determinative with respect to the issue of vehicle access on the ten-mile segment of Salt Creek Road. The Court of Appeals held that the analysis must instead proceed under step two of *Chevron*. * * *

2001 Management Policies

While this case was pending before the Court of Appeals, the NPS commenced a revision of its Management Policies.... Section 1.4 of the 2001 Management Policies defines the "impairment" prohibited by the Organic Act as "an impact that, in the professional judgment of the responsible NPS manager, would harm the integrity of the park resources or values, including the opportunities that otherwise would be present for the enjoyment of those resources or values." § 1.4.5, 2001 Management Policies (hereinafter referred to as the "Impairment Definition" or "Section 1.4"). Whether an impact meets this definition "depends on the particular resources and values that would be affected; the severity, duration, and timing of the impact; the direct and indirect effects of the impact; and the cumulative effects of the impact in question and other impacts." *Id.* The Management Policies then set forth a definition of what constitutes park resources and values. *Id.* § 1.4.6.

2002 Environmental Assessment

This court's September 22, 1998 Order, which prohibited motor vehicle use, was the beginning of the first period of significant length—since the inception of Canyonlands—that vehicles had not traveled on the Salt Creek Road between the Peekaboo campsite and Angel Arch. This extended prohibition on vehicular use made it possible for the NPS, as well as independent researchers, to monitor Salt Creek's riparian conditions when not subject to motor vehicle use. In light of the new scientific information gathered during this period, and in light of the NPS's new Management Policies, the NPS decided to conduct a new Environmental Assessment for Salt Creek Canyon. * * *

This court stayed its proceedings on remand until completion of the Environmental Assessment. This June 2002 Environmental Assessment, Middle Salt Creek Canyon Access Plan ("Salt Creek EA") analyzed in detail four alternatives. "Alternative A" allowed year-round vehicle travel subject to the permit system set forth in the BMP, "Alternative B" allowed part-year vehicle travel subject to the permit system set forth in the BMP, "Alternative C" realigned portions of the road to avoid the streambed and riparian area where feasible and allowed year-round vehicle travel subject to the permit system set forth in the BMP, and "Alternative D" prohibited year-round all motor vehicle travel above Peekaboo campsite but continued to allow hiking and pack/saddle stock travel. The NPS determined that Alternative D was the environmentally preferred alternative. * * *

Final Rule

. . . On June 14, 2004, the NPS issued a Final Rule amending the NPS's regulations for Canyonlands by [adopting Alternative D and] prohibiting motor vehicles on Salt Creek Road above the Peekaboo campsite. 69 Fed.Reg. 32,871 (June 14, 2004) (codified at 36 C.F.R. § 7.44). * * *

DISCUSSION

USA–ALL claims that the NPS's Final Rule . . . violates the 1916 National Park Service Organic Act (the "Organic Act"), as amended by the 1978 "Redwoods Amendments." The relevant provision of the Organic Act provides that the NPS is to "regulate the use" of national parks by means that conform to their "fundamental purpose," namely:

> to conserve the scenery and natural historic objects and the wildlife therein and to provide for the enjoyment of the same in such manner and by such means as will leave them unimpaired for the enjoyment of future generations.

16 U.S.C. § 1 (the "no-impairment mandate"). A provision added in 1978 prohibits the authorization of activities that derogate park values:

> The authorization of activities shall be construed and the protection, management, and administration of these areas shall be conducted in light of the high public value and integrity of the National Park System and shall not be exercised in derogation of the values and purposes for which these various areas have been established, except as may have been or shall be directly and specifically provided by Congress.

16 U.S.C. § 1a–1. The Enabling Act, which created Canyonlands, identifies that park's unique values and purposes. That legislation provides:

In order to preserve an area in the State of Utah possessing superlative scenic, scientific, and archaeologic features for the inspiration, benefit, and use of the public, there is hereby established the Canyonlands National Park. . . .

16 U.S.C. § 271. . . .

USA–ALL asserts that the Organic Act and its amendments authorize a balancing between competing mandates of resource conservation and visitor enjoyment and that the Final Rule violates the Organic Act and the Enabling Act because it deprives the public of its ability to use and enjoy significant portions of Canyonlands.

The NPS, on the other hand, asserts that its primary responsibility pursuant to the Organic Act is to prevent the impairment of park resources and values. The NPS claims that because motor vehicle use in Salt Creek will impair park resources key to the natural integrity of the park, the Final Rule prohibiting such use is a permissible interpretation of the Organic Act and should be accorded deference.

Accordingly, because the issue before the court involves the NPS's interpretation of a statute it administers, the precise question before the court is whether the Final Rule, which prohibits motor vehicle use in Salt Creek Canyon above Peekaboo campsite, is inconsistent with a clear intent of Congress expressed in the Organic Act and the Enabling Act. *See Southern Utah Wilderness Alliance v. Dabney,* 222 F.3d 819, 826 (10th Cir. 2000). Because of the ambiguity inherent in the Organic Act's "no-impairment" mandate, the court cannot resolve this question under step one of *Chevron* and instead must look to step two. *See Dabney,* 222 F.3d at 828. The question for the court under step two of *Chevron* is "whether the agency's answer is based on a permissible construction of the statute." *Chevron,* 467 U.S. at 843. * * *

I. NPS'S 2001 MANAGEMENT POLICIES

The Management Policies, specifically Section 1.4 of the Management Policies, constitute the NPS's interpretation of the Organic Act's "no-impairment mandate." As stated previously, the "no-impairment" mandate is inherently ambiguous. Before addressing "whether the agency's answer is based on a permissible construction of the statute," *Chevron,* 467 U.S. at 843, the court must determine whether the Management Policies "have been expressed in a binding format through the agency's congressionally delegated power." *Dabney,* 222 F.3d 819, 829 (finding that agency policy statements do not usually warrant deference under step two of *Chevron*).

A. *The 2001 Management Policies Are the Type of Agency Decision Intended to Carry the Force of Law.*

USA–ALL asserts that the 2001 Management Policies are not entitled to *Chevron* deference because they were not finalized and adopted pursuant to formal rulemaking procedures. * * *

[T]he Supreme Court has made clear that an agency interpretation reached through means less formal than notice-and-comment rulemaking can be entitled to *Chevron* deference. In *United States v. Mead Corp.,* 533 U.S. 218 (2001), the Court held that *Chevron* deference is warranted when Congress has delegated to the agency authority "generally to make rules carrying the force of law, and . . . the agency interpretation claiming deference was promulgated in the exercise of that authority." *Mead,* 533 U.S. at 226–27. * * *

The fact that the 2001 Management Policies were not implemented pursuant to formal rulemaking procedures . . . does not automatically foreclose the application of *Chevron* deference. In light of *Mead,* the court must assess whether the 2001 Management Policies are the type of agency decision that Congress intended to "carry the force of law." *Mead,* 533 U.S. at 221.

* * * The court finds . . . that the procedural and substantive nature of the 2001 Management Policies are so closely analogous to that of a formal regulation, Congress would expect the 2001 Management Policies to carry the force of law.

For example, unlike typical informal agency policy manuals, the 2001 Management Policies were implemented after undergoing an almost-complete, formal notice-and-comment process. The NPS published notice of the availability of the draft Management Policies in the Federal Register and invited comments from the public for a 60–day period. The NPS subsequently reviewed [and responded to] all of the public comments received. * * *

The procedures used by the NPS in implementing the 2001 Management Policies do not technically conform to all of the rulemaking requirements set forth in the APA. *See* 5 U.S.C. § 553. Most obviously, a concise general statement of basis and purpose was not incorporated into the Management Policies, and the Management Policies were not themselves published in the Federal Register. *See* 5 U.S.C. §§ 553(c),(d). The procedures followed by the NPS in implementing the Management Policies, however, satisfy the purpose behind formal rulemaking procedures, which is to "assure fairness and mature consideration of rules. . . ." *N.L.R.B. v. Wyman–Gordon Co.,* 394 U.S. 759, 764 (1969).

In addition, although the Management Policies are not technically formal regulations, they are procedurally and substantively much closer to a legislative rule than they are to an opinion letter or policy manual. The Management Policies were implemented pursuant to a "relatively formal administrative procedure tending to foster . . . fairness and deliberation," *Mead,* 533 U.S. at 230, and they have the characteristics of a substantive rule. Given the importance of the "no-impairment" standard to the NPS's administration of the statute, the expertise of the NPS in managing national parks, and Congress' express intent that the NPS have the force of law to issue substantive rules pursuant to notice-and-comment rulemaking procedures, the Court finds that the 2001 Management Policies are the type of agency decision Congress intended to "carry the force of law," and therefore eligible for *Chevron* deference.

B. The Management Policies' Interpretation of the Organic Act's "No–Impairment" Clause Is Permissible.

Pursuant to *Chevron,* the next "question for the court is whether the agency's answer is based on a permissible construction of the statute." *Chevron,* 467 U.S. at 843. In making this determination, the court need not conclude that the NPS's interpretation of the Organic Act's "no-impairment" clause is the only permissible interpretation, or even the best interpretation. *Id.* at 843 n. 1. The court must determine only that the interpretation is reasonable and not contrary to congressional intent. *Id.* at 844–45.

"The Organic Act mandates that the NPS provide for the conservation and enjoyment of the scenery and natural historic objects and the wildlife therein 'in such manner and by such means as will leave them unimpaired for the enjoyment of future generations.'" *Dabney,* 222 F.3d at 826; *see* 16 U.S.C. § 1. The Organic Act, however, does not define the word "unimpaired" or the phrase "unimpaired for the enjoyment of future generations." Thus, while the Act clearly directs the NPS to regulate parks pursuant to broad objectives, the agency is left with the task of further defining and applying this standard. As explained previously, Congress has granted the NPS express authority to manage national parks, including the authority to issue regulations which it "deems necessary or proper for the use and management of the [national] parks. . . ." 16 U.S.C. §§ 1,3. Further defining and applying the "no-impairment" standard is therefore within the NPS's delegation of authority. * * *

The Management Policies . . . define "impairment" as:

> an impact that, in the professional judgment of the responsible NPS manager, would harm the integrity of park resources or values, including the opportunities that otherwise would be present for the enjoyment of those resources or values. Whether an impact meets this definition depends on the particular resources and values that would be affected; the severity, duration, and timing of the impact; the direct and indirect effects of the impact; and the cumulative effects of the impact in question and other impacts.

Id. at § 1.4.5.

Although any impact to a park resource or value may constitute an impairment, it is more likely to constitute an impairment if it affects a resource or value whose conservation is "[n]ecessary to fulfill specific purposes identified in the establishing legislation . . . of the park; [k]ey to the natural or cultural integrity of the park . . . [or] [i]dentified as a goal in the park's general management plan or other relevant NPS documents." *Id.* . . .

USA–ALL contends that Section 1.4 of the NPS's 2001 Management Policies defines "impairment" so broadly that the NPS will manage national parks so as to avoid any impairment, with use and enjoyment being a secondary consideration. USA–ALL argues that the Organic Act mandates that the NPS balance preservation with public access when making management decisions. According to USA–ALL, by placing "no-impairment" above "use," the NPS exceeds its statutory authority. . . .

The express language of the Organic Act does not, as USA–ALL suggests, mandate that the NPS equally balance preservation with public use in making its management decision. In fact, the Organic Act specifically mandates that the NPS provide for the conservation and enjoyment of the scenery and natural historic objects and the wildlife therein "in such manner and by such means as will leave them unimpaired for the enjoyment of future generations." 16 U.S.C. § 1. The court finds that the 2001 Management Policies' interpretation of the Organic Act, is not manifestly contrary to the express language of the Organic Act.

In addition, the legislative history of the Organic Act suggests that the "overriding purpose of the bill was to preserve 'nature as it exists.' " *Nat'l Rifle Assoc. of Am. v. Potter,* 628 F. Supp. 903 (D.D.C.1986) (citing H. Rep. No. 700, 64th Cong., 1st Sess. 31 (1916)). Moreover, the court finds that the no-impairment interpretation set forth in the Management Policies is not inconsistent with the interpretation given the Organic Act by those officials initially charged with implementing the Organic Act. The NPS's first management policies, issued by Secretary Franklin K. Lane to Director Stephen T. Mather on May 13, 1918, established "that the national parks must be maintained in absolutely unimpaired form for the use of future generations as well as those of our own time." *See* Secretary Lane's Letter on National Park Management (May 13, 1918), *America's National Park System: The Critical Documents,* 48 (Lary M. Dilsaver, ed., 1994). * * *

In addition, the majority of courts that have interpreted the "no-impairment" mandate have interpreted it as placing an "overarching concern on preservation of resources." *Dabney,* 222 F.3d at 826; *see also Bicycle Trails Council v. Babbitt,* 82 F.3d 1445, 1453 (9th Cir. 1996) (recognizing that "resource protection [is] the overarching concern" of the Organic Act); *Conservation Law Found. v. Clark,* 590 F. Supp. 1467, 1479 (D. Mass. 1984) (characterizing the Organic Act as having an "overriding preservation mandate"). The Management Policies' interpretation therefore is consistent with over twenty years of federal court decisions confirming that conservation is the predominant facet of the Organic Act.

Next, USA–ALL argues that the interpretation set forth in the Management Policies should be entitled to no deference because it reverses the NPS's longstanding interpretation of the Organic Act without providing a reasoned analysis for such a change. *See Motor Vehicle Mfrs. Assn. v. State Farm,* 463 U.S. 29, 57 (1983) ("An agency's view of what is in the public's interest may change, either with or without a change in circumstances . . . [b]ut an agency changing its course must supply a reasoned analysis . . .").

The court finds that the NPS, however, has provided a reasoned analysis for its change in position. As part of the NPS's review of its 1988 Management Policies, a question arose as to whether the 1988 Management Policies provided adequate guidance to managers as to the no-impairment clause of the Organic Act. The NPS notes that several developments indicated that the policy needed further clarification. First, some NPS Managers interpreted the clause to authorize a balancing that would allow them to impair park resources if necessary to create opportunities for public use and enjoyment. Conversely, the NPS recognized that a number of courts had determined that although the Organic Act provides a balance between resource protection and public use, Congress intended resource protection to be the "overarching concern." *Id.*

As a result of the diverse and conflicting interpretations given to the "no-impairment" standard, the NPS decided to reevaluate its position. In doing so, the NPS requested public input, circulated service-wide two draft revisions of the policies, and published for review and comment a third draft. The NPS determined that because preventing the impairment of resources is its primary responsibility under the Organic Act, Congress intended conservation be the predominant consideration in making management decisions where there is a conflict between conserving resources and providing for the enjoyment of them. *Id.* at 13; 2001 Management Policies § 1.4.4. The court finds that this well-considered position, which resolves conflicting interpretations of the Organic Act in favor of the interpretation given it by a majority of courts, is reasonable.

In sum, . . . the court is satisfied that the interpretation of the "no-impairment" mandate of the Organic Act set forth in section 1.4 of the 2001 Management Policies is permissible. The interpretation is entitled to deference under *Chevron.*[5] Accordingly, the court finds no merit to USA–ALL's contention that the NPS's interpretation of the "no-impairment" mandate is in violation of the Organic Act.

---

5. The Court finds that in light of the validity of the Management Policies' reasoning and the thoroughness evident in their consideration, they should be given controlling weight regardless of whether they are entitled to *Chevron* deference. *Martinez v. A.M. Flowers,* 164 F.3d 1257 (10th Cir. 1998) (citing *Skidmore v. Swift & Co.,* 323 U.S. 134, 140 (1944) (informal agency interpretations of statutes are entitled to respect if they are "well reasoned" and have the "power to persuade")).

II. NPS's FINAL RULE DOES NOT VIOLATE THE ORGANIC ACT OR ENABLING ACT.

Having found Section 1.4 of the 2001 Management Policies to be a permissible interpretation of the Organic Act, the court next addresses whether the Final Rule, which closes portions of Salt Creek Road to motor vehicle use, is "based on a permissible construction of the [Organic Act and Enabling Act]." *Chevron*, 467 U.S. at 843....

As explained previously, the Organic Act mandates that the NPS provide for the conservation and enjoyment of the scenery and natural historic objects and wildlife therein "in such manner and by such means as will leave them unimpaired for the enjoyment of future generations." 16 U.S.C. § 1. While the Organic Act directs the NPS to regulate the parks pursuant to these broad objectives, it is silent as to the specifics of park management. The Organic Act instead explicitly delegates to the NPS the authority to determine which avenues best achieve the Organic Act's mandate. 16 U.S.C. § 3 (granting the NPS authority to make such rules as is deems "necessary or proper for the use and management of the parks"); *see also Isle Royale Boaters Ass'n v. Norton*, 330 F.3d 777, 782–83 (6th Cir. 2003); *Bicycle Trails*, 82 F.3d at 1454. Legislative regulations formulated pursuant to this delegation of authority "are given controlling weight unless they are arbitrary, capricious, or manifestly contrary to the statute." *Chevron*, 467 U.S. at 844.

Section 1.4 of the Management Policies, to which this court gives deference, provides that the primary responsibility of the NPS under the Organic Act is to ensure that park resources and values remain unimpaired. The NPS, having determined that closing Salt Creek Road above Peekaboo campsite to vehicular use is necessary to prevent the impairment of a park resource, *i.e.*, the Salt Creek riparian/wetland ecosystem, implemented the Final Rule. The court finds that this decision falls well within the NPS's broad grant of discretion and constitutes a permissible interpretation of the Organic Act and the Enabling Act (sometimes referred to as the "Acts"). * * *

USA–ALL next claims that the Final Rule violates the Organic Act and Enabling Act because it deprives the public of its ability to use and enjoy significant portions of Canyonlands. The Final Rule was issued, however, pursuant to the Organic Act's mandate that park resources be managed "unimpaired for the enjoyment of future generations." 16 U.S.C. § 1.

As discussed above, the court gives deference to the NPS's interpretation of this phrase. Section 1.4 defines "impairment" as prohibiting "an impact that, in the professional judgment of the responsible NPS manager, would harm the integrity of park resources or values...." 2001 Management Policies § 1.4.5.... The NPS, relying on this interpretation of "impairment," determined that vehicular traffic in Salt Creek Canyon constitutes an impairment to the Salt Creek riparian/wetland ecosystem. The court finds that the evidence in the Administrative Record fully supports this determination.... The Salt Creek EA determined that vehicular traffic, even on a part-year permit system, would put Salt Creek Canyon at risk of a major erosion and degradation, rendering the flood area nonfunctional, from a flood of a magnitude which recurs regularly. Based on this evidence, the NPS determined that the potential major indirect adverse impacts that would result to this "key" resource constitute an "impairment." Thus, the court finds that the Final Rule ... is supported by sufficient evidence and is a permissible construction of the statute. * * *

B. The NPS Considered the Impact of Non–Motorized Use on Salt Creek.

USA–All argues that the Final Rule is arbitrary because the NPS failed to consider the potential impacts on park resources that might be caused if closure to vehicular traffic leads to an increase in hiking and backpacking. The Salt Creek EA, however, specifically addresses the potential for increased hiking and backpacking and concludes that the potential impacts from such increased use will not cause major direct, indirect or cumulative impacts or impair park resources or values.

The Salt Creek EA specifically noted that there is a potential for increased backpacking as a result of prohibiting motor vehicle use above Peekaboo campsite. The Salt Creek EA determined, however, that any potential impacts are mitigated by the BMP's existing restrictions on backpack camping. The Salt Creek EA also analyzed the potential impacts that any increased hiking may have on archeological cultural resources. The Salt Creek EA found that while there would be continued pedestrian ground trampling, it would not involve degradation of any archeological cultural resources. The Salt Creek EA also determined that because no coliform bacteria has been detected, even during the busiest months since the vehicle prohibition, increased hiking and back-packing would have no effect on water quality. In light of this evidence, the court concludes that the NPS did not fail to consider the impact of an increase in non-motorized use on park resources. * * *

CONCLUSION

For the foregoing reasons, IT IS HEREBY ORDERED that the relief requested in USA–ALL's administrative appeal is DENIED. The court finds that the 2001 Management Policies are a permissible construction of the Organic Act and that the Final Rule prohibiting motor vehicle use in Salt Creek Canyon above Peekaboo campsite is consistent with the Organic Act and the Enabling Act.

———

QUESTIONS AND DISCUSSION

1. What are the implications of the nonimpairment definition adopted in the 2001 Management Policies? USA–All argues that the definition of "impairment" is so broad "that the NPS will manage national parks so as to avoid any impairment, with use and enjoyment being a secondary consideration." Indeed, USA–All argued that the NPS's non-impairment policy will effectively ensure that parks are managed like wilderness. Do you agree with this characterization of the impairment standard in the 2001 Management Policies? How much does the "impairment" definition limit the discretion of a particular park manager?

2. Would the court's decision have been any different if the Park Service had decided to prohibit vehicle use in Salt Creek Canyon without reference to the 2001 Management Policies?

3. As it did in the excerpted *SUWA v. NPS* case, the Park Service has typically prevailed in cases where its management decisions are challenged. *See Wilkins v. Secretary of Interior*, 995 F.2d 850 (8th Cir. 1993) (upholding Secretary's decision to remove wild horses from the Ozark National Scenic Riverways), *cert. denied*, 510 U.S. 1091 (1994); *Bicycle Trails Council of Marin v. Babbitt*, 82 F.3d 1445, 1454 (9th Cir. 1996) (upholding prohibition on bicycle use in certain off-road areas); *Greater Yellowstone Coalition v. Babbitt*, 952 F. Supp. 1435 (D. Mont. 1996) (rejecting challenge to Yellowstone's bison management plan), *Mausolf v. Babbitt*, 125 F.3d 661 (8th Cir. 1997) (affirming Park Service decision to prohibit snowmobiling on frozen lakes in Voyageur National Park because of evidence that the snowmobiling disrupted eagles and wolves), *cert. denied*, 524 U.S. 951 (1998).

Although the 2001 Management Policies could help further insulate the Park Service from challenges to management decisions that are more protective than a particular plaintiff might prefer, might the "impairment" definition open up the Park Service to challenges that its management is not protective enough? In *Sierra Club v. Mainella*, 459 F. Supp. 2d 76 (D. D.C. 2006), this seems to have been the case. There, the court found that the Park Service's unexplained conclusion that directional drilling for oil and gas under the Big Thicket National Preserve in Texas would not cause impairment was a arbitrary and capricious under the Organic Act. However, observing that historically courts had shown deference to the Park Service's management decisions, the court remanded to give NPS an opportunity to explain and justify its no-impairment conclusion. *Id.* at 98–103.

In *River Runners for Wilderness v. Martin*, 2007 WL 4200677 (D. Az. 2007), however, the plaintiffs claimed that the Park Service's management plan for the Colorado River through the Grand Canyon violated the 2001 Management Policies because it allowed motorized rafts and allocated too many river days to commercial operations. Distinguishing *SUWA*, the court concluded that the 2001 Management Policies were not binding on the Park Service, reasoning:

> There is a difference ... between application of the *Chevron* doctrine in *SUWA* and the question to be decided in this case. The plaintiffs in *SUWA* argued that the 2001 Policies were not entitled to deference and that a decision based on them should be set aside. The District Court relied on the *Chevron* doctrine to conclude that the 2001 Policies provided a sound basis for deference to the Park Service—a shield for the agency's decision concerning the proper administration of Canyonlands National Park. Plaintiffs in this case seek an opposite result—to use the same 2001 Policies as a sword to set aside Park Service decisions concerning the proper administration of Grand Canyon National Park.

Id. at *8. Setting aside the fairly complex administrative law question about whether and when the definition of "impairment" in the 2001 Management Policies should have the force of law and be binding on the NPS, there remains the underlying question of what management obligations the Organic Act's "impairment" language creates for the Park Service. On that issue, the court concluded:

> Plaintiffs contend that the 2006 CRMP [Colorado River Management Plan] is arbitrary and capricious because it permits commercial boaters to use the river at levels that interfere with free access by the public, and because it concludes that motorized uses do not impair the natural soundscape of the Park.

> Plaintiffs argue that the allocation of river access between commercial and noncommercial users is inequitable and thus limits the free access of members of the public. As noted above, however, the Park Service has significantly increased the access of noncommercial users. The 2006 CRMP allocates 115,500

user days to commercial users and an estimated 113,486 user days to non-commercial users.... [T]he allocation of river time between commercial and non-commercial user days changed from 66.5% commercial and 33.5% non-commercial under the 1989 CRMP, to 50.4% commercial and 49.6% non-commercial under the 2006 CRMP. The 2006 CRMP also reduced the number of launches and passengers for commercial users while nearly doubling both categories for non-commercial users....

Plaintiffs argue that non-commercial users are required to wait for permits to run the river—sometimes for 10 or more years—while clients of commercial rafting companies usually can book a trip within one year. They also assert that the current allocation favors the wealthy who can afford commercial trips, and they criticize the Park Service for not conducting a demand study that would have revealed the most equitable allocation. The Court cannot conclude on this basis, however, that the CRMP is arbitrary and capricious. The 2006 CRMP significantly revised the system for private boaters to obtain permits by establishing a lottery system that is weighted to favor those who have not received a permit in previous years. Moreover, surveys show that 61% of private boaters have floated the Colorado River Corridor before, while only 20% of commercial boaters were on repeat trips. The existence of a waiting list therefore does not necessarily show that more private boaters than commercial customers are awaiting their first river trip. * * *

Plaintiffs make several arguments in support of their claim that the Park Service acted arbitrarily and capriciously when it concluded that motorized uses of the Corridor do not impair the natural soundscape of the Park within the meaning of the Organic Act. The Court finds these arguments unpersuasive. * * *

[I]f a cumulative analysis were to result in the elimination of all sounds that can be eliminated by the Park Service—in this case, all sounds other than aircraft overflights, which are not within the jurisdiction of the Park Service—then all human activity in the Park would be eliminated. And still the aircraft overflights would create substantial and adverse sound effects in the Park. Plaintiffs have articulated no principled basis upon which the Court can conclude that the Park Service should have eliminated motorized noises on the basis of such cumulative analysis, but not other human-caused noises such as hiking or non-motorized raft trips. The Court cannot conclude that the Park Service acted arbitrarily and capriciously when it concluded from a cumulative-effects analysis that motorized river traffic noise was not the source of serious sound problems in the Park and that elimination of such noise would not significantly improve the overall soundscape.

Id. at *16–18. Was the court right to defer to the Park Service? If it were to reject the CRMP, what remedy would it impose? How well equipped is a court to order a remedy in this case?

4. Another issue that has attracted the attention of park managers is whether bioprospecting is compatible with park management. In 1997, the Park Service entered into an agreement with Diversa Corporation, a biotechnology company, to allow Diversa to sample microorganisms from Yellowstone National Park's various hot springs. Diversa's hope is that the organisms that are able to survive in the harsh chemical conditions of Yellowstone's hot springs will contain enzymes capable of functioning in similarly difficult industrial situations. Under the agreement, Yellowstone receives some cash up front as well as the promise of future royalties should Diversa be able to develop any commercial products from the organisms it removes. Diversa's bioprospecting activities will have no noticeable physical impact on Yellowstone because only tiny samples will be removed. The revenues from the contract could help close the substantial gaps in the Yellowstone's budget. What is your reaction to Yellowstone's contract with Diversa?

Soon after the contract was announced, several environmental groups filed suit. *Edmonds Inst. v. Babbitt*, 93 F. Supp. 2d 63 (D. D.C. 2000). Can you think of any arguments against the contract under the Organic Act or under Yellowstone's own enabling legislation that directs the Secretary of the Interior to make such regulations as may be necessary for the management and care of the park and "for the protection of the property therein, especially for the preservation from injury or spoliation of all ... natural curiosities, or wonderful objects" within the park, and the maintenance of those resources "in their natural condition"? Act of Mar. 1, 1872, ch. 24, 1, 17 Stat. 32, 32. Setting aside the legal arguments, is the agreement good park policy? Consider the argument of Professor Doremus:

> From the inception of the national park system preservation, rather than economic use, of park resources has been its goal. Where exploitation is permitted, bioprospecting may represent a valuable sustainable form of exploitation. But exploitation, even sustainable exploitation, is not what the parks are about. Our willingness to hold nature above commercial exploitation in these few special places is a crucial aspect of their symbolic importance to the nation and the world, not to be lightly sacrificed.

Holly Doremus, *Nature, Knowledge and Profit: The Yellowstone Bioprospecting Controversy and the Core Purposes of America's National Parks*, 26 ECOLOGY L. Q. 401, 487 (1999). Do you agree that the Diversa agreement is a dangerous step down a slippery slope of commodifying park resources? What are the implications of Professor Doremus's argument about the symbolic importance of the parks for issues like park concessions and fire suppression policy?

5. In *Sierra Club v. Department of the Interior*, 376 F. Supp. 90 (N.D. Cal. 1974), the court found that the Park Service had a duty under the Organic Act and the Redwood National Park Act to protect Redwood National Park from logging outside park boundaries that was damaging the park resource. The court also observed that the Secretary of the Interior is "the guardian of the people of United States over the public lands" with "fiduciary obligations" and with a "trust responsibility" for the public lands. What is the source of the Secretary's trust responsibility? Can the Secretary have a trust obligation that results from something other than Congress' statutory commands? If so, what is the nature of that trust responsibility? Should the public trust doctrine of *Illinois Central* apply to the management of national parks? No other court has endorsed the *Sierra Club* court's rationale of an extra-statutory trust responsibility for the Park Service. Indeed, some courts have specifically rejected the notion. GEORGE CAMERON COGGINS & ROBERT L. GLICKSMAN, PUBLIC NATURAL RESOURCES LAW § 8:27 (2003). Why do you suppose they have rejected it?

6. Another issue for park policy is what to do about concessions within the parks. The Park Service has always been authorized to enter into contracts with concessionaires to provide for visitor accommodation. Concession contracts were first authorized in the Organic Act, 16 U.S.C. §§ 3 and 17b, and later by the Concessions Policy Act of 1965. *Id.* §§ 20–20g. In 1998, Congress passed the National Park Service Concessions Management Act, 16 U.S.C. §§ 5951–5983, which replaced the Concessions Policy Act except for the concessions agreements entered into prior to 1998, a sizeable number given the long-term nature of many concessions contracts. Although the new statute adds a number of provisions respecting such issues as competitive bidding, renewal of contracts, and the nature of a concessionaire's property interest, its basic guidance on concessions is largely the same as that in the 1965 Act. Concessions in a national park are to be

> limited to those accommodations, facilities, and services that—(1) are necessary and appropriate for public use and enjoyment of the unit of the National Park System in which they are located; and (2) are consistent to the highest practicable degree with the preservation and conservation of the resources and values of the unit.

16 U.S.C. § 5951. *Compare* Concessions Management Act, 16 U.S.C. § 20. As this language reveals, the concessions policy reflects the same dichotomy as other aspects of park management—concessions should promote public use and enjoyment but be as consistent as possible with preservation of park resources. Courts have consistently afforded the Park Service wide discretion in deciding what concessions to allow or exclude from the parks. *See, e.g., Wilderness Public Rights Fund v. Kleppe*, 608 F.2d 1250 (9th Cir. 1979) (upholding NPS allocation of most of the rafting rights on the Colorado River within Grand Canyon to commercial outfitters rather than individual rafters), *cert. denied*, 446 U.S. 982 (1980); *Friends of Yosemite v. Frizzell*, 420 F. Supp. 390, 393 (N.D. Cal. 1976) (refusing to limit advertising campaign that was allegedly causing overuse of Yosemite); *National Wildlife Fed'n v. NPS*, 669 F. Supp. 384 (D. Wyo. 1987) (refusing to close campground that was allegedly hindering grizzly bear recovery and emphasizing that the NPS's management discretion was "very broad"). In only a couple of situations have the courts found NPS's concession decisions to be arbitrary and capricious. *E.g., Sierra Club v. Lujan*, 716 F. Supp. 1289 (D. Ariz. 1989) (enjoining construction of hotel on north rim of Grand Canyon).

7. Although the Park Service has broad discretion in its concession management, there is significant debate about whether the Park Service is exercising that discretion wisely. On its website, the Park Service describes its concessions policy in the following terms:

> "Scenery is a hollow enjoyment to the tourist who sets out in the morning after an indigestible breakfast and a fitful night's sleep on an impossible bed." Stephen T. Mather, first Director of the National Park Service[,] * * * believed that only well-rested and well-fed visitors would be fully capable of appreciating the wonders of our national parks. The present day concession program is mindful of this legacy, ensuring that park visitors have access to high quality commercial visitor services at reasonable prices.

> The concession program of the National Park Service administers over 600 concession contracts that gross over $800 million annually. Our concessioners employ over 25,000 hospitality industry people during peak seasons, providing services ranging from food and lodging to white water rafting adventures. The National Park Service develops these contracts, and monitors the performance of concessioners.

Concessioners fill a vital role in helping the National Park Service carry out its mission. Private companies are drawn to the national parks to offer services to park visitors, which are not provided by National Park Service personnel. By welcoming the private sector as a partner in park operations, the National Park Service broadens the economic base of the region in general and the communities surrounding the parks in particular.

See http://concessions.nps.gov. Do you agree with the Park Service's vision of concessions? Professor Sax contends that traditionally the Park Service has tipped too far toward "the windshield tourist" and comfort for park visitors. He laments the way in which both park managers and private concessionaires strive to create illusory wilderness experiences that do not expose people to the real rigors and power of nature. He points to commercial rafting companies that play on our aspirations for independence and self-reliance by proposing to take us where John Wesley Powell once traveled, but promise to do so with all of the luxuries of a resort—fine meals, portable toilets, and river guide valets to carry our gear. The United States Forest Service Manual likewise explains the development of modern campsites to "satisfy the urbanite's need for compensating experiences and relative solitude" while ensuring that it will be "obvious to the user that he is in a secure situation where ample provision is made for his personal comfort and he will not be called upon to use undeveloped skills." JOSEPH SAX, MOUNTAINS WITHOUT HANDRAILS, *supra*, at 99–100. Is there anything wrong with national park policy focusing on the creation of these sorts of illusory experiences? How much risk or hardship should the public encounter as part of a national park experience? Who is to say that rafting down the Colorado with modern conveniences is any less meaningful than traveling rough?

As you studied in Chapter 3, when a court reviews an agency's management decision, it is usually obliged to show some deference to the agency as long as the agency is operating within the parameters set forth in its governing legislation and in the Constitution. But how much deference should a court give to Park Service management decisions?

PROBLEM EXERCISE: SNOWMOBILES IN YELLOWSTONE NATIONAL PARK

Yellowstone National Park is a snowmobile mecca. Since 1968, it has groomed some 185 miles of roads to facilitate snowmobiling. By 2001, winter days at Yellowstone found an average of 840 snowmobiles, and sometimes as many as 1650, roaring through the park visiting famous sites such as Old Faithful and the Grand Canyon of the Yellowstone. For some, the scenery is almost an afterthought. It's "for the thrill, ... the rush, ... the wind in your face...." Dennis McAuliffe Jr., *Snowmobilers Could Shift Into Park Again: U.S. May Ease Ban on Vehicles in Yellowstone*, WASH. POST, Feb. 15, 2002, at A3. For others, the snowmobiles are an efficient means of getting to the backcountry. Once there, the machines can be turned off and the beauty of the Yellowstone winter landscape and its abundant wildlife can be enjoyed. *Id*. For communities like West Yellowstone, that sit just outside the park, such snowmobile tourism is also an important source of revenue during the winter off-season.

Unfortunately, these various recreational benefits come at some cost. Snowmobiles generate a lot of air pollution. One thousand two-stroke snowmobiles during a day's worth of recreation can put out as much nitrous oxide and hydrocarbons as 1.7 million cars (four-stroke snowmobiles are less polluting but give less power because only every fourth stroke is a power stroke). Sometimes the pollution from snowmobiles lined up at the park entrance becomes so bad that park rangers wear gas masks to avoid feeling dizzy and ill. *See* Blaine Harden, *Snowmobilers Favoring Access to Yellowstone Have Found an Ally in Bush*, N.Y. TIMES, Mar. 6, 2002, at A16; Michael Satchell, *Parks in Peril*, U.S. NEWS & WORLD REPORT, July 21, 1997, at 22. Snowmobiles are also noisy. The sometimes ear-splitting roar of a snowmobile can disturb and drive away wildlife and change the visitor experience for other recreators, such as cross-country skiers and snowshoers, seeking a lower intensity experience.

In 1997, the Fund for Animals sued the Park Service, calling for an end to snow road grooming because of snowmobiling's various impacts on park wildlife. As a result of the lawsuit, NPS issued a Winter Use Plan that proposed a complete phase out of all snowmobiles in Yellowstone by the winter of 2003–2004, concluding that "[m]itigation of snowmobile use is not enough to reduce the adverse impacts to acceptable levels." *See* Record of Decision, 65 Fed. Reg. 80908, 80915 (Nov. 22, 2000). Upset about the proposed ban, the BlueRibbon Coalition (an interest group devoted to all forms of motorized recreation), and the Wyoming State Snowmobile Association sued, arguing that the Park Service's EIS was inadequate and hoping that the newly installed Bush Administration would take a different view on snowmobiles. Their hopes were rewarded when the NPS reached a settlement under which it agreed to prepare a Supplemental Environmental Impact Study (SEIS). Based on the SEIS, the NPS decided not to ban snowmobiles but instead limited the number of snowmobiles allowed in the park to 950 per day. More lawsuits resulted in yet more changes to snowmobiles in Yellowstone. *See The Fund for Animals v. Norton*, 294 F. Supp. 2d 92 (D. D.C. 2003) (throwing out the Bush Administration's SEIS and reinstating the Clinton plan); *International Snowmobile Manufacturer's Ass'n v. Norton*, 340 F. Supp. 2d 1249, 1266 (D. Wyo. 2004) (invalidating the Clinton snowmobile rules as "a product of a prejudged political decision"). The Park Service's most recent winter use plan allows 540 best available technology (BAT) snowmobiles and 83 snowcoaches per day, both of which must be commercially guided and stay on existing park roads. *See* 72 Fed. Reg. 70781 (Dec. 13, 2007).

The debate over how snowmobiles should be managed in Yellowstone is likely to continue. With reference to the Park Service's obligations under the Organic Act, how should it end? Was the NPS correct during the Clinton Administration, the Bush Administration, both, neither?

In 2006, the National Park Service issued new Management Policies that preserved the no-impairment standard articulated in the 2001 Management Policies described in the Salt Creek case excerpted at page 604. *See* National Park Service, *Management Policies 2006* (Aug. 31, 2006), http://www.nps.gov/policy/mp/policies.html#_Toc157232605. Section 1.4.6 lists the following park resources and values as being subject to the no-impairment standard:

- the park's scenery, natural and historic objects, and wildlife, and the processes and conditions that sustain them, including, to the extent present in the park: the ecological, biological, and physical processes that created the park and continue to act upon it; scenic features; natural visibility, both in daytime and at night; natural landscapes; natural soundscapes and smells; water and air resources; soils; geological resources; paleontological resources; archeological resources; cultural landscapes; ethnographic resources; historic and prehistoric sites, structures, and objects; museum collections; and native plants and animals;

- appropriate opportunities to experience enjoyment of the above resources, to the extent that can be done without impairing them;

- the park's role in contributing to the national dignity, the high public value and integrity, and the superlative environmental quality of the national park system, and the benefit and inspiration provided to the American people by the national park system; and

- additional attributes encompassed by the specific values and purposes for which the park was established.

park resources subject to "non-impairment" standard in 2006 Management Policies

Id. What are the implications of this list for the snowmobile dispute? Can the Park Service legitimately allow snowmobiles in Yellowstone? What about cars during the summer? Recalling other provisions of the NPS Management Policies and the *SUWA v. NPS* and *River Runners* cases discussed above, how might one argue that snowmobiles are an acceptable activity in Yellowstone?

IV.   NATIONAL MONUMENTS

Although national parks tend to have a higher profile in the American consciousness, national monuments have been and remain a critical component of the nation's preservation history. Between 1906 and 2001, thirteen presidents established 122 national monuments covering approximately 70 million acres in twenty-eight states, one territory, and the District of Columbia. In 2006, President George W. Bush designated two more national monuments—the African Burying Ground National Monument, on about one-third of an acre in New York City, and the Papahnaumokukea Marine National Monument, which covers 89.6 million acres of the Pacific Ocean, submerged lands, and coral reefs northwest of the Hawaiian Islands.

Many of our most treasured national parks—including Grand Canyon, Olympic, Zion, Bryce Canyon, Capitol Reef, Canyonlands, and Glacier Bay—began as national monuments. Like the national parks, national monuments have been managed primarily by the Park Service, although, as discussed below, President Clinton for the first time allowed the BLM and the Forest Service to share in those duties. If monuments are mostly managed by the Park Service, mostly managed like parks, and in fact the precursor to many national parks, they nevertheless remain distinct from the parks in one crucial way—they are the products of presidential action rather than congressional action. It is this critical fact that merits separate treatment. Whereas congressional creation of parks has engendered little conflict, presidential proclamation of monuments, albeit pursuant to authority delegated by Congress in the Antiquities Act of 1906, 16 U.S.C. § 431, has often generated public outcry. That outcry has generally been limited to directly affected communities and has been relatively short-lived, but it is worth study because it is a recurring feature of public lands debate that has significant implications for executive preservation efforts more generally. This section of the chapter focuses on the debate over the creation of national monuments and does not delve deeply into their management. Recognize, however, that just as parks must be managed in accordance with the Park Service Organic Act and the specific park creation acts, monuments must be managed under the mandates of the Antiquities Act and the specific proclamation creating any particular monument.

A.   The Antiquities Act

National monuments are a product of the Antiquities Act, which authorizes the President of the United States,

> in his discretion, to declare by public proclamation historic landmarks, historic and prehistoric structures, and other objects of historic and scientific interest that are situated upon lands owned or controlled by the Government of the United States to be national monuments, and may reserve as a part thereof parcels of land, the limits of which in all cases shall be confined to the smallest area compatible with the proper care and management of the objects to be protected.

16 U.S.C. § 431. The Antiquities Act has its origin in concerns about protecting noted archaeological sites such as Chaco Canyon and Mesa Verde, as well as dozens of lesser sites, from private collecting of artifacts by both professionals and amateurs which threatened to rob the public of its cultural heritage. By the turn of the century, a consensus had emerged among policy officials that this practice had to be stopped and that even surveys conducted by qualified researchers had to be carefully regulated. In light of this origin, most commentators who have considered the Antiquities Act and its legislative history have concluded that it was designed to protect only small tracts of land around archeological sites. The complex political history of the law, however, suggests that some of the Act's promoters intended a broader design.

In keeping with the general conservation ferment of the times, officials within the Department of the Interior consistently pushed to give the president more expansive preservation power than was needed to address the specific problem of harm to archeological sites. An early draft bill introduced by congressman Lacey and authored within the Interior Department, proposed to give the President authority to

> [s]et apart and reserve tracts of public land, which for their scenic beauty, natural wonders or curiosities, ancient ruins or relics, or other objects of scientific or historic interest, or springs of medicinal or other properties it is desirable to protect and utilize in the interest of the public; and the President shall, by public proclamation, declare the establishment of such reservations and the limits thereof.

H.R. 11021, 58th Cong. § 1 (1900). The bill met resistance because of its expansive language and during the next few years underwent a series of changes designed to resolve that objection. As ultimately enacted in 1906, the Antiquities Act did not authorize protection of lands for their "scenic beauty" or "natural wonders" and it limited reservations of land to the *"smallest area compatible* with the proper care and management of the objects to be protected." 16 U.S.C. § 431 (emphasis added). Nevertheless, the Act still included the language from Lacey's original bill authorizing the protection of "objects of historic or scientific interest." As discussed further below, this language was to prove key in future judicial decisions supporting an expansive interpretation of the Antiquities Act. *See generally* Mark Squillace, *The Monumental Legacy of the Antiquities Act of 1906*, 37 GA. L. REV. 473, 476–86 (2003) (describing background and legislative history of the Antiquities Act).

While the Act's language left room for debate about the scope of authority that Congress intended to give the president, Theodore Roosevelt quickly resolved upon an expansive interpretation of presidential authority under the Act. His resolve can at least partly be explained by the fact that when enacted in 1906, the Antiquities Act was unique in affording the president clear authority to set aside lands for preservation purposes. Congress had enacted the General Revision Act of 1891, which authorized the president to set aside forest reserves. But while forests were generally withdrawn from disposition and entry under the homestead and other laws, they were not protected from other forms of development, especially mining. As a result of Gifford Pinchot's utilitarian approach to forest management, the focus of the Forest Service was on the conservation and use of forest resources, and not on their preservation. Presidents, including Roosevelt in the case of bird refuges, had also asserted an implied power to reserve lands for conservation purposes, and this authority would later be upheld in *United States v. Midwest Oil Co.*, 236 U.S. 459 (1915), excerpted in Chapter 2. But at the time of the Antiquities Act, no legislative authority was available that provided for the preservation of public lands. *See generally* Mark Squillace, *The Monumental Legacy of the Antiquities Act of 1906*, 37 GA. L. REV. 473, 487–89 (2003).

Beginning with Roosevelt, the Antiquities Act has left a remarkable legacy of preservation. The story is told in the following excerpt.

Mark Squillace, *The Monumental Legacy of the Antiquities Act of 1906*, 37 GA. L. REV. 473, 490–507 (2003)

Soon after the Antiquities Act was passed, Roosevelt designated Devil's Tower in Wyoming as the nation's first monument. He followed that decision with seventeen more proclamations in less than three years, including, most importantly, the more than 800,000–acre Grand Canyon National Monument. The Grand Canyon National Monument was important not only because of its significance to our national heritage, but also because it spawned the lawsuit that seemed destined from the start to secure the expansive interpretation of the Antiquities Act that would make the Act's legacy possible.

If one were to choose a set of facts from which to promote a broad reading of the Antiquities Act, one might very well have chosen the Grand Canyon as the setting, and invented a character like Ralph Henry Cameron. Cameron, along with his brother Niles and a local prospector named Peter Berry, had located mining claims along the South Rim of the Grand Canyon and had successfully developed a copper mine in the canyon below Grandview Point. Cameron's real interests, however, were along the Bright Angel Trail where he was able to use the mining law to exploit tourists rather than minerals. Initially, Cameron charged a toll for access along the trail as authorized under an Arizona territorial law. When his toll rights expired in 1906, Cameron used numerous strategically-located, but probably invalid, mining claims along the trail as a pretense for continuing to charge an access fee. Unfortunately for Cameron, his interests conflicted with those of the Santa Fe Railroad Company, and the railroad challenged Cameron's claims in the courts and before the Department of the Interior.

In 1909, Secretary of the Interior James Garfield declared that Cameron's claims lacked sufficient mineral values to justify issuing a patent. Still, Cameron persisted in charging fees for access to public land that he did not own and for which he lacked any lawful claim, using his various political offices to keep the authorities at bay. Eventually, Cameron's case wound up in the United States Supreme Court [*Cameron v. United States*, 252 U.S. 450 (1920)]. Among other things, Cameron alleged that President Roosevelt lacked the authority to designate the Grand Canyon as a national monument. The Court quickly dismissed Cameron's Antiquities Act claim. Quoting from Roosevelt's proclamation, the Court found that the Grand Canyon "is an object of unusual scientific interest." The Court went on to note:

> [The Grand Canyon] is the greatest eroded canyon in the United States, if not in the world, is over a mile in depth, has attracted wide attention among explorers and scientists, affords an unexampled field for geologic study, is regarded as one of the great natural wonders, and annually draws to its borders thousands of visitors.

Nowhere does the court specifically address the language from the Antiquities Act that the monument must be "the smallest area compatible with the proper care and management of the objects to be protected," but the clear implication of the Court's decision was that the size of the monument was not disqualifying if the "protected object" was otherwise of "scientific interest."
* * *

Franklin Roosevelt created eleven new monuments including the Joshua Tree National Monument in California, Cedar Breaks in southwestern Utah, Capitol Reef in southern Utah, Channel Islands off the coast of southern California, the Badlands National Monument in western South Dakota, and the Jackson Hole National Monument in Wyoming. This last decision sparked the next major lawsuit under the Antiquities Act. * * *

In *Wyoming v. Franke*, the State challenged Roosevelt's proclamation on the grounds that the evidence failed to support the claim that the monument contained "historic landmarks, [and] historic or prehistoric structures or objects of historic or scientific interest." After hearing evidence on both sides, the court noted that it had limited authority to review the proclamation:

> If there be evidence in the case of a substantial character upon which the President may have acted in declaring that there were objects of historic or scientific interest included within the area, it is sufficient upon which he may have based a discretion. * * *

The controversy over the Jackson Hole National Monument also sparked what was perhaps the most successful congressional opposition to a monument proclamation. Lengthy hearings were held before the House Committee on Public Lands, and virtually every prominent Wyoming politician offered testimony opposing the monument. In 1944, Congress actually passed legislation that would have abolished the monument, but Roosevelt pocket vetoed the bill. In response, Congress refused to appropriate money for the management of the monument for seven years after it was proclaimed. Finally, in 1950, Congress negotiated a compromise with President Truman that provided for adding the monument lands to the Grand Teton National Park, but amending the Antiquities Act to prohibit the President from designating any further monuments in Wyoming. * * *

After Franklin Roosevelt and until Jimmy Carter, presidents continued to expand and otherwise modify existing monuments, but new monuments slowed to a trickle. There were, however, two important monuments established during this period. The first was the C & O Canal proclaimed by Dwight Eisenhower at the end of his administration in 1961. The canal, which stretches more than 180 miles between Washington and Cumberland, Maryland, operated from 1828–1924, primarily to haul coal from western Maryland. * * *

Some members of Congress held continuing disdain for these executive branch proclamations. In fact, Eisenhower's decision so piqued Congressman Wayne Aspinall of Colorado, the powerful chair of the House Committee on Interior and Insular Affairs, that Aspinall blocked funding for the C & O Canal National Monument for many years. Aspinall's action, like the action of an earlier Congress with respect to the Jackson Hole National Monument, served as a continuing warning to future presidents that national monument proclamations under the Antiquities Act carried risks. A President might be able to preserve the status quo on public lands through a monument proclamation, but he might be denied the money that was needed to protect the monument's resources. * * *

The other important monument proclaimed during this period was Marble Canyon, adjacent to the former Grand Canyon National Monument and now part of the Grand Canyon National Park. * * *

President Jimmy Carter did not make extensive use of the Antiquities Act, with one remarkable exception. On December 1, 1978, Carter proclaimed seventeen new or enlarged national monuments in Alaska, covering fifty-six million acres. [He did so because under the 1971 Alaska Native Claims Settlement Act about 80 million acres of land that had been set aside for study for protective designation was about to be reopened for entry and development.] For their sheer size, Carter's proclamations were unparalleled, and it is unlikely that land-based monuments will ever again approach their scale. The path that led to protecting these lands serves as a testament to the significant role that the Antiquities Act continues to play in land preservation in the United States. * * *

The Carter monuments sparked bitter opposition in Alaska, but the withdrawals effectively halted mineral development in Alaska and thereby provided the impetus for congressional action. On December 2, 1980, two years after these executive actions, Congress passed the Alaska National Interest Lands Conservation Act (ANILCA). ANILCA designated more than one-hundred million acres of land in new conservation units, including 43.6 million acres of new parklands, 53.7 million acres of new wildlife refuge land, twenty-five new wild and scenic rivers, and 56.4 million acres of wilderness. Many of the protected areas were carved out of the monuments that had been declared just two years earlier by President Carter. * * *

Despite the fact that the conservation units established under ANILCA ultimately supplanted the monuments proclaimed by Carter, it was the Antiquities Act decision that prompted two lawsuits, one brought by the State of Alaska and the other by the Anaconda Copper Company. In *Alaska v. Carter*, [462 F. Supp. 1155 (D. Alaska 1978),] the State claimed that the President's decision to designate a monument, and the Secretary of the Interior's recommendation to the President that he declare a monument, were subject to NEPA's environmental impact statement requirement. The court did not address the scope of the Antiquities Act directly, but did conclude that the President was not an agency subject to NEPA's impact statement requirement. Furthermore, the court found that since the Interior Department's recommendation was made at the President's request, the Interior Department could not be compelled to file an impact statement before making its recommendation. According to the court, to hold otherwise "would raise serious constitutional questions." * * *

As reflected in the litigation described above, national monuments have often proved controversial. It should be clear that the controversies were not simply abstract disagreements about whether particular lands were of sufficient "scientific or historic interest" to merit designation. Rather, two core concerns animated the disputes. The first was the sense of those rural public lands communities adjacent to the new monument that the monument would "lock up" the natural resources upon which the community depended for its economic livelihood, whether for ranching, mining, or logging. The second was a perception that the proclamations were an abuse of executive power. The reactions of Wyoming's congressional delegation to the creation of Jackson Hole National Monument are illustrative. As Wyoming Senator Joseph O'Mahoney saw it, the Jackson Hole proclamation was "not only an invasion of the rights of the sovereign State of Wyoming ... [and] an invasion of the sacred rights of people affected, it is also an invasion of the rights of Congress to legislate in connection with something definitely within the jurisdiction of the Congress alone." *A Bill to Abolish the Jackson Hole National Monument*, Hearings on H.R. 2241 Before the House Comm. on Public Lands, 78th Cong. 114 (1943). Wyoming Congressman Frank A. Barrett added: "The Park Service is just like every other bureau. They are exceedingly avaricious." *Id*. at 52. Similarly when President Johnson, in January 1969, just 90 minutes before he was to leave office, signed Antiquities Act proclamations adding some 264,000 acres to Arches and Capitol Reef National Monuments, Utah's Senator Wallace Bennett argued that the proclamations were a "last gasp attempt to embalm a little more land in the West," and protested that the actions were "arbitrary" and "unilateral ... with no notice whatsoever, without hearing any interested group, without prior consultation with Congress and without consultation or discussion with state officials." James R. Rasband, *Utah's Grand Staircase: The Right Path to Wilderness Preservation?* 70 U. Colo. L. Rev. 483, 490–91 (1999).

In the long run, even the most hotly disputed monuments have come to be valued by almost all constituents. Arches and Capitol Reef are now crown jewels of Utah's tourism industry and Wyoming Senator Alan

Simpson concluded years later: "All of us agree that Teton County would not look like it does today if they hadn't (established the monument and expanded the park). Instead of open space there would be gas stations, motels and other businesses on Antelope Flats north of Jackson where the view of the Tetons remains largely unobstructed by development. It was great in hindsight." Candy Moulton, *National Monuments? Not in Wyoming*, Casper Star Trib., Jan. 1, 2001, at A1. If most monuments look "great in hindsight," what explains the continuing opposition to monuments at the time they are created? Consider this question again at the conclusion of the following section describing the flurry of monument proclamations by President Clinton.

B. The Clinton Monuments

Following President Carter's Alaska monuments, the Antiquities Act went unused during the Reagan and Bush administrations, and it continued to lie idle for most of President Clinton's first term. President Clinton had come to office with ambitious environmental goals, but most of his efforts were rebuffed, particularly after the Republicans took over congress in 1994. Taking stock of its options, the President decided to turn where so many other presidents had and to use his authority under the Antiquities Act. The prime candidate for a monument was Utah's spectacular red rock country, which had for a number of years seen fierce disputes about the amount of land deserving of wilderness protection, a subject discussed further in the wilderness section below. Aware of previous controversies generated by the Act, the president first sought advice about the political repercussions of a proclamation. The answer given to President Clinton by both his advisors and prominent Democrats in the West was positive. As they saw it, the designation would have particular appeal in the urban areas of the West where the president had the best opportunity for capturing votes, and would only hurt him in staunchly Republican Utah and with rural constituencies who were unlikely to vote for him in any event. Convinced of its positive political repercussions, in September 1996, President Clinton proclaimed the creation of a new, 1.7 million acre national monument in southern Utah—The Grand Staircase–Escalante National Monument. *See generally* James R. Rasband, *Utah's Grand Staircase: The Right Path to Wilderness Preservation?*, 70 U. Colo. L. Rev. 483 (1999).

In complaints that had a familiar ring in Antiquities Act controversies, Utah's congressional delegation, which had only learned of the President's intentions in a *Washington Post* story some 11 days before the proclamation, described the President's actions as a shameful and arrogant act of political opportunism and cried foul over the administration's failure to consult them or to give any public notice of the proposal. Utah's Senator Hatch declared that "[i]n all my years in the U.S. Senate, I have never seen a clearer example of the arrogance of federal power. . . . Indeed, this is the mother of all land grabs." Laurie Sullivan Maddox, *Taking Swipes at Clinton, Utahns Vow to Fight Back*, Salt Lake Trib., Sept. 19, 1996, at A5. Politicians from other Western states joined in the chorus, with Senator Burns of Montana calling the proclamation the act of a "tyrant" and

Senator Craig of Idaho describing it as a "phenomenal misuse of power." *Id.* The view of the residents of Kane and Garfield counties, the southern Utah counties within which the Monument is located, was even less kind. President Clinton and Interior Secretary Babbitt were hung in effigy and were subjected to vituperative criticism. Four years after the Monument's creation, Louise Liston, chairman of the Garfield County Commission and a rancher from the community of Escalante adjacent to the Monument, offered the following criticisms:

Louise Liston, *Sustaining Traditional Community Values,*
J. LAND, RESOURCES & ENVTL. L. 585, 585–86, 592 (2001)

The creation of the Monument has literally changed the course of our lives. As a result of the Monument's designation, the people of my county have suffered a great loss. In addition to lost revenues, a lifestyle of values and work ethics is being replaced with a lifestyle encumbered by federal regulations, restrictions, and threats. A once proud and peace-loving people are being turned into a hostile, antagonistic, suspicious, and distrustful community. * * *

This change in attitude is a result of people's fear of how to proceed, what to expect, and how to preserve the lifestyle they love and have sacrificed over many years to preserve. Those of us called to work with the federal agencies are often perceived as traitors to those values and traditions these people hold dear. I have found through my involvement with county government at the national level, that congressmen and residents in eastern states, where federal ownership of land is meager, cannot begin to comprehend the impacts on local governments and local economies that rely upon the land for their survival.

It is very destructive when the fate of a region is determined by people who do not have to live with the direct results of their decisions, and that is what we are experiencing. We have shared the beauty of our deserts, high plateaus, and pine-scented mountains in Garfield County for decades. We have borne the monetary burden of caring for the millions of visitors that traverse the lands. We rescue them when they get lost, provide emergency services when they get hurt, take care of their garbage, keep the roads safe and passable, put out the fires they carelessly start, provide law enforcement, and a myriad of other services they demand. This care is provided on a very limited budget by volunteer workers who must miss work and leave their families to help. * * *

In conclusion, the economic, social and environmental concerns facing Garfield County and other counties throughout the West are real. The lives of people living in areas adjacent to public lands and special designations such as the Monument, are being directly impacted by land management decisions. Historically, the consideration of those impacts has not been sufficiently addressed in legislation, regulation, or implementation by the federal government. I am keenly aware of the unmatched beauty of the deserts, the high plateaus and the mountains, and of the limitless opportunities for solitude and rejuvenation to the soul. However, I am also keenly aware of the communities, schools, families, and friends who struggle and sacrifice to live in the shadow of that beauty and maintain a quality of life not found in modern urban societies. What most Americans do not realize at this point in time is that the most valuable renewable natural resource is the human resource, and this resource must be put back into the environmental equation or we will not survive.

————

Although the Grand Staircase–Escalante National Monument proved controversial in Utah, it was highly popular elsewhere around the country and, indeed, was quite popular in Utah's urban and suburban areas. Following his re-election in 1996, and acting on the recommendations of Secretary of the Interior Bruce Babbitt, Clinton embarked on what was arguably the most ambitious expansion of the national monument system ever, exceeding even the prodigious efforts of the Theodore Roosevelt administration nearly one hundred years earlier. By the end of his second term, Clinton had proclaimed twenty-two new or expanded national monuments, thereby adding approximately six million acres to the national monument system. The monuments were a diverse collection. They included four small historic sites, one new and one expanded monument in the Virgin Islands that consisted entirely of submerged lands, and the California Coastal National Monument, which included all unappropriated islands, rocks, pinnacles, and exposed reefs in the jurisdictional waters of the United States for the 841 miles of California coastline. Fourteen of the monuments, including the Grand Staircase, were assigned to the Bureau of Land Management's (BLM) management responsibility, marking the first time the BLM had been assigned such a preservation task. Another of the monuments—Giant Sequoia in California—was to be managed primarily by the United States Forest Service, and another—Hanford Reach, which protects the last free-flowing nontidal stretch of the Columbia River—was to be managed primarily by the United States Fish and Wildlife Service, in cooperation with the Department of Energy. *See generally* Mark Squillace, *The Monumental Legacy of the Antiquities Act of 1906*, 37 GA. L. REV. 473, 507–14 (2003).

In response to the criticism of the Grand Staircase–Escalante proclamation, and to defuse efforts by some in Congress to amend or repeal the Antiquities Act, Interior Secretary Babbitt, who was the architect of the president's monument proclamation policy, took a different approach with respect to these later monuments. Although not obligated to do so by the Antiquities Act, he committed to a three-part process—which he often described as a "no surprises" policy—before recommending any new national monuments to the president. First, he expressed a willingness to personally visit any area that his office was considering for monument status. Second, he agreed to meet personally with local officials and interested members of the public about different strategies for protecting the area under review. Finally, he agreed to afford local members of Congress and senators the opportunity to adopt appropriate legislation to protect the area under consideration for national monument status before making a recommendation to the president. This last concession resulted in legislation protecting several remarkable areas that would not likely have received congressional attention without indications from the Secretary that these areas were being considered for national monument status. *Id.* at 539–40.

Despite Secretary Babbitt's efforts, many of the new monuments proved just as locally unpopular as the Grand Staircase. The result was a variety of legal challenges to the proclamations. Two of those cases were decided on the same day by the D.C. Circuit. In the first, the court addressed the threshold question of the appropriate standard of review for a court hearing a challenge to a monument proclamation.

Mountain States Legal Foundation v. Bush,
306 F.3d 1132 (D.C. Cir. 2002), *cert. denied* 540 U.S. 812 (2003)

Presidential Proclamations designating national monuments have been challenged in only a handful of cases; in each the court has upheld the President's action. The Supreme Court has considered the Antiquities Act in three cases, each time confirming the broad power delegated to the President under the Act. *United States v. California,* 436 U.S. 32 (1978); *Cappaert v. United States,* 426 U.S. 128, 141–42 (1976); *Cameron v. United States,* 252 U.S. 450 (1920).

Although the Supreme Court has never expressly discussed the scope of judicial review under the Antiquities Act, the Court has directly addressed the nature of review of discretionary Presidential decisionmaking under other statutes. The Court has highlighted the separation of powers concerns that inhere in such circumstances and has cautioned that these concerns bar review for abuse of discretion altogether. *United States v. George S. Bush & Co.,* for example, involved § 336(c) of the Tariff Act of 1930, which provided that the President:

> shall by proclamation approve rates of duties and changes in classification and in basis of value specified in any report of the [Tariff] [C]ommission . . . if *in his judgment* such rates of duty and changes are shown by such investigation of the commission to be necessary to equalize such differences in costs of production.

310 U.S. 371, 376–77 (1940) (quoting 19 U.S.C. § 1336(a)) (emphasis added). The statute provided for judicial review only of legal questions. The Court held that "[t]he President's method of solving the problem [of foreign exchange value] was open to scrutiny neither by the Court of Customs and Patent Appeals nor by us." *Id.* at 379. Similarly, in *Dalton v. Specter,* the Court considered a statute—the Defense Base Closure and Realignment Act of 1990— that did "not at all limit the President's discretion. . . ." 511 U.S. 462, 476 (1994). Judicial review was unavailable under the Administrative Procedures Act ("APA") because the President is not an "agency" within the meaning of that statute. *Id.* at 469–70 (citing *Franklin v. Massachusetts,* 505 U.S. 788, 800– 01 (1992)). The Court then "assume[d] for the sake of argument that some claims that the President has violated a statutory mandate are judicially reviewable outside the framework of the APA," *id.* at 474 (citation omitted), but it reiterated that "such review is not available when the statute commits the decision to the discretion of the President." *Id.* The Court held, "[h]ow the President chooses to exercise the discretion Congress has granted him is not a matter for our review." *Id.* at 476.

A somewhat different case is presented, however, where the authorizing statute or another statute places discernible limits on the President's discretion. Judicial review in such instances does not implicate separation of powers concerns to the same degree as where the statute did "not at all limit" the discretion of the President. *Id.* at 476. As this court observed in *Chamber of Commerce v. Reich,* "*Dalton's* holding merely stands for the proposition that when a statute entrusts a discrete specific decision to the President and contains no limitations on the President's exercise of that authority, judicial review of an abuse of discretion claim is not available." 74 F.3d 1322, 1331 (D.C. Cir. 1996) (footnote omitted). "*Dalton* is inapposite," the court explained, "where the claim instead is that the presidential action . . . independently violates" another statute. *Id.* at 1332. The court rejected the government's position "that the Procurement Act grants the President such broad discretion ... that the case reduces only to a claim that the President abused his discretion—a claim that [the court is] not authorized to entertain." *Id.* at 1326. It would be "untenable," the court stated, "to conclude that there are no judicially enforceable limitations on presidential actions, besides actions that run afoul of the Constitution or which contravene direct statutory prohibitions, so long as the President *claims* that he is acting pursuant to" a statutory directive. *Id.* at 1332. Rather, the court emphasized that "'[t]he responsibility of determining the limits of statutory grants of authority ... is a judicial function entrusted to the courts by Congress. . . .'" *Id.* at 1327 (quoting *Stark v. Wickard,* 321 U.S. 288, 310 (1944)). The court then held that the President had exceeded his authority under the Procurement Act in issuing an Executive Order barring federal contractors from hiring replacement workers during an economic strike because the Order was preempted by an independent statute, the National Labor Relations Act. *Id.* at 1339.

Although the limits on Presidential authority at issue derive from the Antiquities Act itself rather than an independent statute, *Reich* is instructive, for the same policy considerations apply. Courts remain obligated to determine whether statutory restrictions have been violated. In reviewing challenges under the Antiquities Act, the Supreme Court has indicated generally that review is available to ensure that the Proclamations are consistent with constitutional principles and that the President has not exceeded his statutory authority. *United States v. California,* 436 U.S. at 35–36; *Cappaert,* 426 U.S. at 141–42; *Cameron,* 252 U.S. at 455–56. * * *

In its second Antiquities Act decision issued later that day, the court applied the *Mountain States* standard of review to a challenge to President Clinton's proclamation of the Giant Sequoia National Monument.

TULARE COUNTY v. GEORGE W. BUSH,
306 F.3d 1138 (D.C. Cir. 2002), *cert. denied,* **540 U.S. 813 (2003)**

ROGERS, CIRCUIT JUDGE:

In April 2000 President Clinton established by proclamation the Giant Sequoia National Monument pursuant to his authority under the Antiquities Act. Proclamation 7295, 65 Fed. Reg. 24,095 (Apr. 15, 2000). The Monument, which encompasses 327,769 acres of land in the Sequoia National Forest in south-central California, contains groves of giant sequoias, the world's largest trees, and their surrounding ecosystem. *Id.* at 24,095–97, 24,100.

Tulare County, which contains land near and within the Grand Sequoia National Monument ("Monument"), along with a number of other public and private entities that use the Monument area for business or recreational purposes (hereinafter "Tulare County"), filed a complaint seeking declaratory and injunctive relief. Tulare County alleged that the Proclamation violated various provisions of the Antiquities Act and the Property Clause of the Constitution, as well as the National Forest Management Act, the National Environmental Policy Act, and the parties' existing rights under a prior mediated settlement agreement. The district court, concluding that only facial review was appropriate, dismissed the complaint. *Tulare County v. Bush,* 185 F. Supp. 2d 18 (D. D.C.2001).

On appeal, Tulare County contends that in dismissing its complaint prior to discovery, the district court erred in failing to accept as true the facts alleged in the complaint and in limiting its review to the face of the Proclamation rather than reviewing the President's discretionary factual determinations. Tulare County does not contend that the President lacks authority under the Antiquities Act to proclaim national monuments like Giant Sequoia, as the Supreme Court has long upheld such authority. *Cappaert v. United States,* 426 U.S. 128, 142 (1976); *Cameron v. United States,* 252 U.S. 450, 455 (1920). Rather, in Counts 1–4 of the complaint, Tulare County alleged that the Proclamation violated the Antiquities Act because it: (1) failed to identify the objects of historic or scientific interest with reasonable specificity; (2) designated as the basis for the Monument objects that do not qualify under the Act; (3) did not confine the size of the Monument "to the smallest area compatible with proper care and management of the objects to be protected," 16 U.S.C. § 431; and (4) increased the likelihood of harm by fires to any objects of alleged historic or scientific interest within the Monument rather than protecting those objects. In Count 5, Tulare County argued that, absent judicial review of the President's action under the Antiquities Act, the statute constitutes an unconstitutional delegation of congressional authority....

The Antiquities Act provides, in relevant part, that the President, "in his discretion" may declare "historic landmarks ... and other objects of historic or scientific interest ... situated upon [federal] lands ... to be national monuments, and may reserve ... parcels of land ... confined to the smallest area compatible with the proper care and management of the objects to be protected...." 16 U.S.C. § 431.... [W]e review Tulare County's complaint to determine whether it contains factual allegations to support an *ultra vires* claim that would demonstrate the district court erred in declining to engage in a factual inquiry to ensure that the President complied with the statutory requirements.

Count 1 of Tulare County's complaint is premised on the assumption that the Antiquities Act requires the President to include a certain level of detail in the Proclamation. No such requirement exists. The Act authorizes the President, "in his discretion, to declare by public proclamation historic landmarks, historic and prehistoric structures, and other objects of historic or scientific interest." 16 U.S.C. § 431. The Presidential declaration at issue complies with that standard. The Proclamation lyrically describes "magnificent groves of towering giant sequoias," "bold granitic domes, spires, and plunging gorges," "an enormous number of habitats," "limestone caverns and ... unique paleontological resources documenting tens of thousands of years of ecosystem change," as well as "many archaeological sites recording Native American occupation ... and historic remnants of early Euroamerican settlement." Proclamation at 24,095. By identifying historic sites and objects of scientific interest located within the designated lands, the Proclamation adverts to the statutory standard. Hence, Count 1 fails as a matter of law.

Count 2 alleges that the President has designated nonqualifying objects for protection. The Antiquities Act provides that, in addition to historic landmarks and structures, "other objects of historic or scientific interest" may qualify, at the President's discretion, for protection as monuments. 16 U.S.C. § 431. Inclusion of such items as ecosystems and scenic vistas in the Proclamation did not contravene the terms of the statute by relying on nonqualifying features. In *Cappaert,* 426 U.S. at 141–42, the Supreme Court rejected a similar argument, holding that the President's Antiquities Act authority is not limited to protecting only archeological sites.

As relevant to Count 3 of the complaint, the Proclamation states that the Monument's 327,769–acre size "is the smallest area compatible with the proper care and management of the objects to be protected." Proclamation at 24,097. It also states that the sequoia groves are not contiguous but instead comprise part of a spectrum of interconnected ecosystems. *Id.* Tulare County alleges that no one in the Clinton Administration "made any meaningful investigation or determination of the smallest area necessary to protect any specifically identified objects of genuine historic or scientific interest." Compl. ¶ 149. Instead, it alleges, President Clinton "bowed to political pressure ... in designating a grossly oversized Monument unnecessary for the protection of any objects of genuine historic or scientific interest." Compl. ¶ 150. This allegation is a legal conclusion couched as a factual allegation. "Although in reviewing the dismissal of a complaint the court must take 'all factual allegations in the complaint as true,' the court is 'not bound to accept as true a legal conclusion couched as a factual allegation.'" *Mountain States,* 306 F.3d at 1137 (quoting *Papasan v. Allain,* 478 U.S. 265, 286 (1986)).

Contrary to the assumption underlying Count 3, the Antiquities Act does not impose upon the President an obligation to make any particular investigation. And to the extent that Tulare County alleges that the Proclamation designates land that should not be included within the Monument, the complaint fails to identify the improperly designated lands with sufficient particularity to state a claim. *Id.* Insofar as Tulare County alleges that the Monument includes too much land, i.e., that the President abused his discretion by designating more land than is necessary to protect the specific objects of interest, Tulare County does not make the factual allegations sufficient to support its claims. This is particularly so as its claim that the Proclamation covered too much land is dependent on the proposition that parts of the Monument lack scientific or historical value, an issue on which Tulare County made no factual allegations. *Cf. Dalton v. Specter,* 511 U.S. 462, 473–74 (1994); *United States v. George S. Bush & Co.,* 310 U.S. 371, 379 (1940).

Count 4 of the complaint alleges that the Monument designation actually increases the risk of harm from fires to many of the objects that the Proclamation aims to protect. However, the Proclamation expressly addresses the threat of wildfires and the need for forest restoration and protection. The Proclamation observes that forest renewal is needed because environmental change "has led to an unprecedented failure in sequoia reproduction," and that "a century of fire suppression and logging" has created "an increased hazard of wildfires of a severity that was rarely encountered in pre-Euroamerican times." Proclamation at 24,095. Count 4 contains no factual allegations, only conclusions, *see, e.g.,* Compl. ¶ 160, and it refers to current management rather than the designation under the Proclamation as the cause for likely increases in catastrophic fires, Compl. ¶ 159.

Count 5, alleging that if judicial review is not available under the Antiquities Act then the Act violates the Property Clause of the Constitution as an improper delegation of congressional authority to the President, fares no better. As the court held in *Mountain States,* "[n]o Constitutional Property Clause claim is before us, as the President exercised his delegated powers under the Antiquities Act, and that statute includes intelligible principles to guide the President's action." 306 F.3d at 1136–37 (citing *Whitman v. Am. Trucking Ass'ns, Inc.,* 531 U.S. 457, 474 (2000); *Dalton,* 511 U.S. at 473–74 & n. 6). * * *

Accordingly, because "[a]t no point has [Tulare County] presented factual allegations that would occasion ... *ultra vires* review of the Proclamation[,]" *Mountain States,* 306 F.3d at 1136–37, we affirm the dismissal of the complaint.

QUESTIONS AND DISCUSSION

1. Given the standard of judicial review adopted by the court, is a monument decision ever likely to be overturned provided that the president's proclamation is prepared by a competent draftsman? How much deference should be afforded presidential decisions about monument size and appropriate objects for protection?

2. The proclamation for the Sonoran Desert National Monument describes the area as "a magnificent example of untrammeled Sonoran desert landscape" and as encompassing "a functioning desert ecosystem." Proclamation No. 7397, 3 C.F.R. § 22 (2001). Although the proclamation also describes in detail the specific plant and animal communities and the historic and archaeological objects located within the monument, could the president have acted to protect only the desert "landscape" and "ecosystem"? Would the literature that has developed in recent years describing landscape ecology and ecosystem management be sufficient support for the assertion that a landscape or ecosystem is a legitimate object of scientific interest? If so, is it possible to conceive of land that could not be described as an object of "scientific interest"?

3. Did Congress intend for the president to exercise such broad discretion under the Antiquities Act? Does congressional intent over 100 years ago matter if the language of the Act is broad enough to encompass the creation of such large monuments? If looking beyond the statutory language to congressional intent is important, how should the determination of statutory meaning be affected by the fact that the Department of the Interior participated in drafting the early versions of the Act and plainly hoped for a broad delegation of preservation authority to the President?

4. Even if one assumes that the Antiquities Act as originally enacted had the narrow purpose of protecting Indian ruins and artifacts in the Southwest, is the *Tulare County* court unwise in affirming a broad interpretation of the Act? Should it matter to the court that Congress has seemingly acquiesced in prior broad interpretations of the Antiquities Act? Does it matter that when Congress enacted the Federal Land Policy Management Act (FLPMA) in 1976 it repealed 29 statutes giving the executive branch withdrawal authority, as well as the president's implied withdrawal authority under *Midwest Oil* (excerpted in Chapter 2, *supra*), *see* Pub. L. No. 94–579, § 704(a), 90 Stat. 2744, 2792 (1976), but left the Antiquities Act undisturbed?

5. Review the language of the Antiquities Act (page 620). Does the President have the authority to abolish a national monument, reduce its size, or refuse to protect a monument's designated objects of historic or scientific interest? By way of a new proclamation? By way of a monument management plan? By some other means? For a discussion of these issues, see Mark Squillace, *The Monumental Legacy of the Antiquities Act of 1906*, 37 GA. L. REV. 473, 554–68 (2003); James R. Rasband, *The Future of the Antiquities Act*, 21 J. LAND, RESOURCES & ENVTL. L. 619 (2001).

6. Following President Clinton's designation of the Grand Staircase–Escalante National Monument, a variety of bills were introduced proposing to amend the Antiquities Act so as to limit the president's power to designate national monuments. Among them were bills to repeal the Antiquities Act outright, bills that would require an act of Congress to establish any national monument over 50,000 acres, and bills requiring public notice prior to designation and compliance with all applicable federal land management and environmental statutes. *See generally* James R. Rasband, *Utah's Grand Staircase: The Right Path to Wilderness Preservation?*, 70 U. COLO. L. REV. 483, 531–32 (1999). Would any of these bills be wise? Should the Antiquities Act be repealed or amended? Why shouldn't Congress just take charge of all preservation decisions? Why do you think proponents and opponents of the Antiquities Act have not been able at least to agree on the value of giving affected states and communities notice prior to a monument designation?

7. Think on the excerpt from Louise Liston sharing her views of the impact of a monument designation on a local public land community. What, if any, implications do these views have for the Antiquities Act or for preservation policy more generally? Should rural public land communities be allowed to participate in decisions about national monument designation, boundaries, or management? If so, what form should their participation take? Should it go beyond an opportunity for notice and comment that is available to the entire public? Is there any reason they should be afforded special status over members of the general public who do not live in the immediate vicinity of the monument?

Would participation really make a difference in rural communities' acceptance of monument designations? Several commentators have argued that the basic assumptions underlying public participation—that public involvement will lead to wiser decisions and greater acceptance by the public—are "largely unfounded." Gail L. Achterman & Sally K. Fairfax, *Public Participation Requirements of the Federal Land Policy and Management Act*, 21 ARIZ. L. REV. 501, 507–08 (1979). *See also* George C. Coggins, *Abdication Can Be Fun, Join the Orgy Everyone: A Simpleton's Perspective on Abdication of Federal Land Management Responsibilities, in* CHALLENGING FEDERAL OWNERSHIP AND MANAGEMENT: PUBLIC LANDS AND PUBLIC BENEFITS, at 14 (Univ. of Colorado School of Law, Natural Resources Law Center, Conference Proceedings, Oct. 11–13, 1995) ("Sitting down and feeling good are merely phony substitutes for real conflict resolution.").

8. One approach to encouraging local participation while maintaining primary federal control would be to allow local communities to participate in the management of preservation lands through some sort of trust arrangement. The terms of the trust could specify certain preservation objectives but allow local inhabitants to implement those objectives in ways least harmful and most beneficial to their economic standing and cultural identity. For a discussion of how such a trust arrangement might work, see Terry L. Anderson & Holly Lippke Fretwell, *A Trust for the Grand Staircase–Escalante*, POLITICAL ECONOMY RESEARCH CENTER (PERC) POLICY SERIES (Issue No. PS–16, Sept. 1999). Anderson and Fretwell actually suggest that the trustees be nominated from various interest groups without regard to residency in the local community. Would this be a better idea?

9. The idea that the local community should participate in decisions that impact their living environment is at the core of the environmental justice movement and literature. *See, e.g.*, DANIEL FABER, INTRODUCTION TO THE STRUGGLE FOR ECOLOGICAL DEMOCRACY: ENVIRONMENTAL JUSTICE MOVEMENTS IN THE UNITED STATES 1 (Daniel Faber ed., 1998) (arguing that the "fundamental" claim of the environmental justice movement is that local communities "be afforded greater participation in the decisionmaking processes of capitalist industry and the state (at all levels), as well as the environmental movement itself"). How would you respond to the argument that it is no less unjust for well-off urban and suburban areas to off-load their waste and environmental problems onto poorer communities than it is for those same areas to set aside rural communities as their playgrounds?

10. Why is it that the public overwhelmingly supports national monuments and that even monument opponents usually come to appreciate the value of the designations? Does that support delegitimize the arguments of those who oppose unilateral executive action?

11. President Clinton's monument proclamations were dramatic not just in the amount of acreage they set aside but also in their provisions for management responsibility. At Secretary Babbitt's urging, President Clinton for the first time placed the Bureau of Land Management (BLM) in charge of managing fifteen monuments. Given the BLM's traditional multiple-use focus and what some have perceived as its capture by the livestock and mining industries, many within the environmental community were skeptical of the BLM's ability to manage according to a preservation mandate. Secretary Babbitt, however, sensed that at least some within the BLM were ready to assume the preservation mantle, and believed that the monument initiative was just the vehicle to steer the agency in this new direction. In a question and answer session following a speech at the University of Denver Law School, Secretary Babbitt put it this way:

> The traditional approach is, you see something nice, you get up a big movement to protect it, and you take it away from the Bureau of Land Management and give it to somebody else, namely typically the National Park Service [and] in some cases the National Wildlife Refuge System. And out of that has grown a kind of perception that the BLM is sort of the Bureau of Leftovers, livestock and mining—whatever you want to call it. But, it doesn't seem to me to be an adequate way of looking at the Western landscape, because the largest land manager ought to be induced to have a sense of pride rather than simply having a bunch of inventory out in the garage that is discovered and given to someone else. * * * And my hope is that out of this will emerge not two but three land management agencies in charge of administering live, vibrant, carefully protected conservation units—Fish and Wildlife Service, Park Service, [and the] Bureau of Land Management.

Bruce Babbitt, *From Grand Staircase to Grand Canyon Parashant: Is There a Monumental Future for the BLM? available at* http://www.doi.gov/news/archives/000222b.html.

12. To help promote BLM's change in focus, Secretary Babbitt also established a new subagency within the BLM known as the National Landscape Conservation System (NLCS). The NLCS was assigned responsibility not only for the monuments but also for the wilderness areas, wilderness study areas, national conservation areas, wild and scenic rivers, and national scenic and historic trails within the BLM's jurisdiction. Although this step did not create any new legal protections for the areas included within the NLCS, Secretary Babbitt hoped that the NLCS would give the Bureau a conservation mission distinct from the other land protection agencies such as the National Park Service. Does public choice theory suggest anything about whether these changes are likely to make BLM more preservation-minded? What are the potential benefits and risks of assigning the BLM to manage national monuments? For more information on the National Landscape Conservation System, including a map of the units in the system, see http://www.blm.gov/nlcs.

In March 2009, Congress passed legislation formally establishing the NLCS. *See* Omnibus Public Land Management Act of 2009, H.R. 146, 111th Cong., 1st Sess. (2009)

> The Secretary shall manage the system—(1) in accordance with any applicable law (including regulations) relating to any component of the system ... ; and (2) in a manner that protects the values for which the components of the system were designated.... Nothing in this subtitle enhances, diminishes, or modifies any law or proclamation (including regulations relating to the law or proclamation) under which the components of the system described in subsection (b) were established or are managed.... Nothing in this subtitle shall be construed as affecting the authority, jurisdiction, or responsibility of the several States to manage, control, or regulate fish and resident wildlife under State law or regulations, including the regulation of hunting, fishing, trapping and recreational shooting on public land managed by the Bureau of Land Management. Nothing in this subtitle shall be construed as limiting access for hunting, fishing, trapping, or recreational shooting.

Id. at § 2002. Despite the fact that the legislation does not alter the legal status of lands managed by the BLM and does little more than assign a collective label to those lands, there was significant opposition in the House, particularly from western representatives. What do you think may have been the source of the opponents' concern? How important is naming and labeling in natural resources law?

13. As recounted in the text, in 2006, President George W. Bush designated the Papahnaumokukea Marine National Monument covering 89.6 million acres of the Pacific Ocean, submerged lands, and coral reefs northwest of the Hawaiian Islands. Later that fall, at a conference celebrating the 100–year anniversary of the Antiquities Act, which was attended by two of the authors, former Interior Secretary Bruce Babbitt commented that during President Clinton's second-term flurry of monument-making, the administration had come close to designating a similar Hawaiian Islands monument, partly because that would have given President Clinton first place among presidents in terms of acreage proclaimed under the Antiquities Act, topping President Carter's 56 million acre Alaska proclamations. Babbitt lamented the irony of President Bush—no friend of preservation in Secretary Babbitt's view—now holding the acreage lead among all presidents. Former Secretary's Babbitt's usual candor and good humor aside, does toting up acreage tell a cautionary tale about broad executive withdrawal authority? Is acreage a good way to judge the real preservation impacts of any proclamation, withdrawal or designation?

V. WILDERNESS

National parks and national monuments are both federal efforts to preserve wild nature from man's use and exploitation. And in casual conversation one can often hear such areas described as "wilderness," generally meaning an area that has seen little or no human development. There is nothing particularly wrong with calling a national park or a national monument "wilderness" because the meaning of the word is so often in the eye of the beholder. But in natural resources law, the word "wilderness" has a more particular definition. It is a legal term of art referring to those areas designated as wilderness by Congress and thereafter managed pursuant to the Wilderness Act of 1964, Pub. L. No. 88–577, 78 Stat. 890, 16 U.S.C. § 1131, et seq. Thus, a national park or monument may contain wilderness within its boundaries, but the park itself is not wilderness. The same is true for the "wilderness areas" on lands managed by the Bureau of Land Management, the Fish and Wildlife Service, and the Forest Service. Wilderness areas are managed on more protective terms than other federal lands. The sections of the chapter that follow briefly recount the evolution of the wilderness idea, the history of the Wilderness Act of 1964, its primary provisions, and the current debate over expansion of the wilderness system.

A.   THE EVOLUTION OF THE WILDERNESS IDEA

From the perspective of preservationists such as John Muir, the creation of national parks, monuments and wildlife refuges was a triumph, but only an incomplete one. As roads, lookout points, developed campgrounds, lodges, and various concessions sprouted in the parks, monuments and refuges, and as the national forests were covered with logging roads and mining claims, preservationists began to argue that additional protective measures were necessary. Some land should be left in a wild state—roadless and undeveloped. In 1919, Arthur Carhart, a young Forest Service employee, was assigned to submit plans for a road and vacation homes beside Trappers Lake, Colorado, in the White River National Forest. Upon surveying the area, however, Carhart recommended that the best use of the lake was for wilderness recreation. Going further, he recommended that the Forest Service manage more areas of spectacular wild scenery as wilderness. The next year Trappers Lake became the first area purposely designated as roadless and off limits to development. About the same time, Aldo Leopold, who was then a Forest Service employee in New Mexico, was developing a more broad-ranging conception of wilderness. Writing in the *Journal of Forestry* in 1921, Leopold attempted to give content to the notion of "wilderness," defining it as a "continuous stretch of country preserved in its natural state, open to lawful hunting and fishing, big enough to absorb a two weeks' pack trip, and kept devoid of roads, artificial trails, cottages, or other works of man." RODERICK NASH, WILDERNESS IN THE AMERICAN MIND 186 (1967). Leopold's vision bore fruit in 1924 when the Forest Service designated 574,000 acres of the Gila National Forest as a "wilderness area" to be devoted primarily to wilderness recreation. In

1926, additional roadless areas were set aside in the Superior National Forest in Northern Minnesota and in 1929, the Forest Service issued regulations providing that certain areas within the national forests could be designated as "primitive areas," although the primitive areas still allowed some mining, grazing, and logging. Revised in 1939, the so-called U–Regulations prohibited roads, motorized vehicles, and timber cutting in these primitive areas and provided for the designation of additional wilderness areas like that in the Gila National Forest. *See* Michael McCloskey, *The Wilderness Act of 1964: Its Background and Meaning*, 45 OR. L. REV. 288, 296 (1966).

The U–Regulations were a product of a period of significant wilderness ferment. The Wilderness Society had been formed in 1935 and proved to be a persuasive advocate for the wilderness idea. The Society's founder, Robert Marshall, was a Ph.D. plant pathologist and an avid wilderness backpacker. (The stories of Marshall's backpacking prowess are legendary. In the early 1930s he spent thirteen months alone in Alaska's Brooks Range exploring and collecting data on tree growth, and, according to his brother, by 1937 had done more than 200 hikes of thirty miles in a day, fifty-one forty mile hikes, and several trips up to seventy miles.) The effectiveness of The Wilderness Society was in no small part due to Marshall's ability to direct his energy and passion for the outdoors to the wilderness project. Although the push for wilderness went through a relatively quiescent period during World War II, by the 1950s, The Wilderness Society, led then by Howard Zahniser, began again to push for stronger legislative protection for roadless areas on the public lands. Legislation was necessary, he and others believed, because there were questions about whether the Forest Service really had authority to prohibit mining and other development in administratively designated wilderness and primitive areas. Zahniser's argument caught the attention of Minnesota Senator Hubert Humphrey, who encouraged Zahniser to draft a bill. Zahniser, assisted by the Sierra Club, the National Parks Association, the National Wildlife Federation and others, prepared the first version of the Wilderness Act, which Senator Humphrey introduced in the Senate in 1956. RODERICK NASH, WILDERNESS IN THE AMERICAN MIND 200–26 (1967); Michael McCloskey, *The Wilderness Act of 1964: Its Background and Meaning*, 45 OR. L. REV. 288, 296–98 (1966). It took eight more years and sixty-five more versions of the bill but, in 1964, the Wilderness Act was enacted into law and the National Wilderness Preservation System was established. Pub. L. No. 88–577, 78 Stat. 890, 16 U.S.C. § 1131, et seq.

B. THE WILDERNESS ACT

The Wilderness Act stands as an important symbol of Americans' increasing preference for preservation of the public lands and, to some extent, of the idea that preservation is valuable for its own sake and not only for recreation, enjoyment, or other forms of use. The symbolic importance of the Act is evident in its declaration of congressional policy and its definition of wilderness.

16 U.S.C. § 1131. National Wilderness Preservation System

(a) In order to assure that an increasing population, accompanied by expanding settlement and growing mechanization, does not occupy and modify all areas within the United States and its possessions, leaving no lands designated for preservation and protection in their natural condition, it is hereby declared to be the policy of the Congress to secure for the American people of present and future generations the benefits of an enduring resource of wilderness. For this purpose there is hereby established a National Wilderness Preservation System to be composed of federally owned areas designated by Congress as "wilderness areas," and these shall be administered for the use and enjoyment of the American people in such manner as will leave them unimpaired for future use and enjoyment as wilderness, and so as to provide for the protection of these areas, the preservation of their wilderness character, and for the gathering and dissemination of information regarding their use and enjoyment as wilderness; and no Federal lands shall be designated as "wilderness areas" except as provided for in this chapter or by a subsequent Act. * * *

(c) A wilderness, in contrast with those areas where man and his own works dominate the landscape, is hereby recognized as an area where the earth and its community of life are untrammeled by man, where man himself is a visitor who does not remain. An area of wilderness is further defined to mean in this chapter an area of undeveloped Federal land retaining its primeval character and influence, without permanent improvements or human habitation, which is protected and managed so as to preserve its natural conditions and which (1) generally appears to have been affected primarily by the forces of nature, with the imprint of man's work substantially unnoticeable; (2) has outstanding opportunities for solitude or a primitive and unconfined type of recreation; (3) has at least five thousand acres of land or is of sufficient size as to make practicable its preservation and use in an unimpaired condition; and (4) may also contain ecological, geological, or other features of scientific, educational, scenic, or historical value.

Once designated, wilderness areas are managed by the federal agency that had jurisdiction over the land immediately prior to its inclusion in the system. 16 U.S.C. § 1131(b). Thus, the National Park Service, the Forest Service, the BLM, and the Fish and Wildlife Service all have management responsibility for wilderness. The Wilderness Act describes the basic management responsibility as follows:

16 U.S.C. § 1133. Use of Wilderness Areas

(b) Except as otherwise provided in this chapter, each agency administering any area designated as wilderness shall be responsible for preserving the wilderness character of the area and shall so administer such area for such other purposes for which it may have been established as also to preserve its wilderness character. Except as otherwise provided in this chapter, wilderness areas shall be devoted to the public purposes of recreational, scenic, scientific, educational, conservation, and historical use.

(c) Except as specifically provided for in this chapter, and subject to existing private rights, there shall be no commercial enterprise and no permanent road within any wilderness area designated by this chapter and, except as necessary to meet minimum requirements for the administration of the area for the purpose of this chapter (including measures required in emergencies involving the health and safety of persons within the area), there shall be no temporary road, no use of motor vehicles, motorized equipment or motorboats, no landing of aircraft, no other form of mechanical transport, and no structure or installation within any such area.

Having read these basic management responsibilities and the rather lyrical definition of wilderness above, one might assume that the Wilderness Act was a complete triumph for the preservation community. The truth is that in order to enact these provisions, wilderness proponents agreed to a number of compromises that increased the challenges for both designating and managing wilderness areas. Some of those compromises are detailed in the sections that follow, which divide consideration of the Wilderness Act and the wilderness debate into three basic issues: first, what public lands will be designated as part of the wilderness preservation system; second, how wilderness will be managed once it is designated; third, how areas with wilderness potential, but not yet officially designated as wilderness, should be managed.

1. DESIGNATING WILDERNESS

The Wilderness Act of 1964 designated as wilderness areas only the 9.1 million acres of land that had previously been set aside by the Forest Service as "wilderness," "wild," or "canoe" areas. 16 U.S.C. § 1132(a). In addition, however, the Act provided for a review, to be completed within ten years, of the wilderness potential of all the areas within the national forests that had previously been designated as "primitive areas," as well as a review of "every roadless area of five thousand contiguous acres or more in the national parks, monuments and other units of the national park system and every such area of, and every roadless island within, the national wildlife refuges and game ranges." 16 U.S.C. § 1132(c). BLM lands were not mentioned in the Wilderness Act and their review only began in 1976 with the passage of the Federal Land Policy Management Act (FLPMA) and its requirement of a wilderness review. 43 U.S.C. § 1782. Following the various reviews, the relevant Secretary was to report to the president and the president was to recommend to Congress which of the potential wilderness areas should actually be designated as wilderness. *Id.*

As a result of the various reviews, Congress began expanding the system in 1968, adding four more areas within national forests and one in a national wildlife refuge. Two years later, the first National Park wilderness areas were established. The greatest expansion of the system came as a result of the 1980 Alaska National Interest Lands Conservation Act (ANILCA) which created 35 new wilderness areas in Alaska totaling more than 56 million acres. Today, the National Wilderness Preservation System contains 703 areas totaling 107.4 million acres. *See The National Wilderness Preservation System*, at http://www.wilderness.net/index.cfm?fuse=NWPS &sec=fastFacts. For a clickable map identifying all of these wilderness areas including descriptions and photographs, see http://www.wilderness. net/index.cfm?fuse=NWPS.

This brief description of the designation process leading to the rather dramatic figure of 107.4 million acres of wilderness belies the complex and contentious process that actually produced those numbers. Although the process within national parks and wildlife refuges has not been particularly controversial because wilderness is not a dramatic departure from the existing preservation mandate for those land systems, within national forests and BLM lands, the process has been much more controversial because those lands would otherwise be available for multiple uses, which include logging, grazing, mining, and other extractive and commodity uses, as well as high intensity, motorized recreation. The controversies that have swirled around national forests and BLM lands are considered further below, but before doing so it is necessary to consider for a moment how the statutory definition of wilderness allows for such varying interpretations about what lands actually deserve the "wilderness" label.

The Wilderness Act's definition of wilderness is quite subjective. Wilderness is said to be an area "which (1) generally *appears* to have been affected *primarily* by the forces of nature, with the imprint of man's work *substantially* unnoticeable; (2) has outstanding opportunities for solitude or a primitive and unconfined type of recreation; ... (4) may also contain ecological, geological, or other features of scientific, educational, scenic, or historical value." 16 U.S.C. § 1132(c) (emphasis added). Even its most objective components—that a proposed wilderness area should be without permanent improvements or human habitation and should contain 5,000 roadless acres—have been subject to plenty of disagreement. The Act, for example, contains an explicit exception to the 5,000 acre requirement, allowing designation of areas that are "of sufficient size as to make practicable its preservation and use in an unimpaired condition." *Id.* And deciding what really constitutes a road or what counts as a permanent improvement has not been as straightforward as it may seem. The Forest Service, for example, has identified as wilderness, areas with fences, water troughs, small airstrips and abandoned mines; it has decided that the only roads that disqualify an area from wilderness consideration are those roads passable by standard, passenger-type vehicles; and in the eastern United States, the Forest Service, because there would otherwise be so few qualifying areas, has said that areas which contain no more than a half mile of improved road for each 1,000 acres have wilderness potential. *See* FOREST SERV., U.S. DEP'T OF AGRIC., FOREST SERVICE MANAGEMENT HANDBOOK § 71.12, ch. 70 (2007). In the end, Congress is free to designate an area as wilderness regardless of its physical characteristics, and Congress has occasionally been willing to designate areas which do not seem to fulfill the basic criteria enumerated in the Wilderness Act. Nevertheless, as a shorthand or working description, the requirements that an area be roadless, at least 5,000 acres, and without permanent improvements provide a fairly objective baseline for which areas may even be considered as wilderness. Once that baseline is established, the more subjective factors of opportunities for solitude and primitive recreation, and features of ecological, scenic or other value can be applied to the decision about wilderness quality.

a.   Wilderness in the National Forests

Recall that the Wilderness Act required the Secretary of Agriculture to, within ten years of the Act's passage, "review, as to its suitability or nonsuitability for preservation as wilderness, each area in the national forests classified on September 3, 1964 by the Secretary of Agriculture or the Chief of the Forest Service as 'primitive' and report his findings to the President." 16 U.S.C. § 1132. The Act also specified that "[n]othing herein contained shall limit the President in proposing, as part of his recommendations to Congress, the alteration of existing boundaries of primitive areas or recommending the addition of any contiguous area of national forest lands predominantly of wilderness value." *Id.* On its face, the Forest Service's review obligations were quite modest. The Forest Service, however, voluntarily undertook a wider-ranging review, inventorying not just primitive areas (as required by the Act) and areas contiguous to those primitive areas (as allowed by the Act) but also all roadless tracts over 5,000 acres. This process, known as the Roadless Area Review and Evaluation (RARE I) found some 56 million acres of land in the national forests that could qualify as wilderness.

Although the Forest Service found 56 million acres of potential wilderness, it did not believe that it was obligated to preserve the wilderness characteristics of that entire acreage pending the president's recommendation to Congress. After all, a good portion of the acreage had been identified voluntarily. The courts, however, saw things differently. While the RARE I process was ongoing, the Forest Service proposed to allow logging in an area contiguous to a primitive area. The Tenth Circuit, however, affirmed a district court's injunction against the timber harvest, reasoning that logging the area would prevent the president from proposing and Congress from designating the area as wilderness. *See Parker v. United States*, 309 F. Supp. 593 (D. Colo. 1970), *aff'd*, 448 F.2d 793 (10th Cir. 1971), *cert. denied*, 405 U.S. 989 (1972). The court reasoned that the Wilderness Act's provision that "[n]othing herein contained shall limit the president in proposing, as part of his recommendations to Congress, the alteration of existing boundaries of primitive areas or recommending the addition of any contiguous area of national forest lands predominantly of wilderness value," meant that the Forest Service could not do anything that would take away the president's discretion to designate such a contiguous area. The Forest Service primitive areas and contiguous areas were off-limits to logging until the president submitted his recommendation. With an eye on the "contiguous" language in the Act, the Forest Service had proposed a buffer area, where there would be no logging, between the primitive area and the area to be harvested. The court rejected this attempt to render the logging area noncontiguous, 448 F.2d at 796, thereby suggesting a broad interpretation of which lands were contiguous and had to be preserved pending the president's opportunity to recommend them as wilderness.

The obligation of the Forest Service to delay logging of potential wilderness was further strengthened in the next couple of years when the courts decided that any area identified as potential wilderness in the RARE I process could not be logged until the Forest Service first prepared an environmental impact statement that looked at the impact of logging on the area's potential for wilderness designation. *See Wyoming Outdoor Coordinating Council v. Butz*, 484 F.2d 1244 (10th Cir. 1973); *Sierra Club v. Butz*, 3 Envtl. L. Rep. 20071 (N.D. Cal. 1972). Logging the 56 million acres of potential wilderness identified in RARE I wasn't necessarily prohibited by these decisions, but it would certainly be more difficult. Partly in response to the problems with the RARE I process and partly because the Carter administration was committed to more wilderness, the Forest Service in 1977 embarked upon a second wilderness review of its lands. The resulting RARE II report and its accompanying EIS, which took a somewhat more generous view of what lands had wilderness potential, found about 62 million acres of potential wilderness. The report suggested that of those 62 million acres, 15 million be designated as wilderness, about 11 million be studied further, and that 36 million acres be made available for multiple use. Again, however, the Forest Service was blocked from allowing logging of any part of the 62 million acres. In what many in the Forest Service viewed as a case of no good deed going unpunished, in *California v. Block*, 690 F.2d 753 (9th Cir. 1982), the Ninth Circuit decided that the 36 million acres could not be released from wilderness management because the RARE II EIS had failed to adequately consider the implications of releasing the 36 million acres from wilderness consideration. The basic effect of the decision in *California v. Block* was that logging was enjoined on all 62 million acres of the RARE II inventory, an area that encompassed about one-third of the national forests. In response to the *Block* decision, the Forest Service, now operating under the Reagan administration, suggested in 1983 that it might simply drop RARE II and do a RARE III. Congress, however, intervened and in 1984 passed twenty statewide wilderness bills that designated wilderness and released unchosen RARE II lands from wilderness management for at least one forest planning cycle. With the passage of these statewide wilderness bills, and several more in subsequent years, the small wilderness beachhead within the national forests seemingly envisioned by the Wilderness Act has grown to more than 33 million acres. *See generally* George Cameron Coggins & Robert L. Glicksman, Public Natural Resources Law § 14B:9 (2003).

b.   *Wilderness on BLM Lands*

Hewing to the old adage that the public lands managed by the BLM were the lands no one wanted, the Wilderness Act completely ignored BLM lands. As preservation sentiments continued to mount, Congress decided to rectify that omission when it passed the Federal Land and Policy Management Act (FLPMA) in 1976. Section 603 of FLPMA provided that

> Within fifteen years after October 21, 1976, the Secretary shall review those roadless areas of five thousand acres or more and roadless islands of the public lands, identified during the inventory required by section 1711(a) of this title as having wilderness characteristics described in the Wilderness Act of September 3, 1964 (78 Stat. 890; 16 U.S.C. 1131 et seq.) and shall from time to time report to the President his recommendation as to the suitability or nonsuitability of each such area or island for preservation as wilderness. . . .

43 U.S.C. § 1782(a). Having received the recommendation from the Secretary of the Interior, the president was to make a separate recommendation to the Congress within two years with respect to what areas should be designated as wilderness. *Id.* at 1782(b). One of the linchpins of the current wilderness debate came in the next part of Section 603. There, Congress provided that the areas identified by the Secretary as potential wilderness (what are typically called "wilderness study areas" or "WSAs") were to be managed by the Secretary of the Interior, and therefore the BLM,

> . . . until Congress has determined otherwise, . . . in a manner so as not to impair the suitability of such areas for preservation as wilderness, subject, however, to the continuation of existing mining and grazing uses and mineral leasing in the manner and degree in which the same was being conducted on

October 21, 1976. Once an area has been designated for preservation as wilderness, the provisions of the Wilderness Act [16 U.S.C.A. § 1131 et seq.] which apply to national forest wilderness areas shall apply with respect to the administration and use of such designated area. . . .

Id. § 1782(c). In basic terms, wilderness study areas are to be managed for nonimpairment of their wilderness characteristics until Congress decides to designate the WSAs as part of the wilderness preservation system or release them for multiple use management.

Like the RARE process for the national forests that preceded it, the inventory of the BLM's lands for wilderness proceeded on a state-by-state basis. By the conclusion of the initial inventory in November 1980, out of almost 174 million acres surveyed, BLM had identified 919 WSAs covering some 24 million acres. 45 Fed. Reg. 77,574 (Nov. 14, 1980). Its conclusions proved quite controversial. The focus of that controversy were disputes about whether BLM was identifying enough areas and acreage with wilderness potential. From the environmental community's perspective, the BLM was far too stingy in its views of what lands had wilderness quality. Moreover, they claimed, BLM had conveniently excluded from WSAs roadless areas that had significant mineral potential. Most of these concerns played out in administrative litigation before the Interior Board of Land Appeals (IBLA) and the BLM's inventory decisions were largely, although not entirely, upheld. One prominent dispute that did reach federal court was over Interior Secretary Watt's order not to designate as wilderness study areas any split estate lands or any roadless areas of less than 5,000 acres. A court invalidated both components of the order in *Sierra Club v. Watt*, 608 F. Supp. 305, 335–38 (E.D. Cal. 1985). Even though preservation advocates were able to fend off Secretary Watt's order which would have eliminated 1.5 million acres of potential wilderness, the inventory resulted in far less acreage in WSAs than many preservation advocates believed existed. The gap between the two sides grew even greater when BLM recommended wilderness designation of only a percentage of the WSAs it had established. *See generally* Jim DiPeso & Tom Pelikan, *The Republican Divide on Wilderness Policy*, 33 GOLDEN GATE U. L. REV. 339 (2003) (recounting history of inventory process).

In the years following completion of the inventories, Congress added 6.7 million acres of BLM lands to the National Wilderness Preservation System, most prominently in the Arizona Desert Wilderness Act of 1990 (104 Stat. 4496), which designated 1.1 million acres, and the California Desert Protection Act of 1994 (108 Stat. 4471), which designated 3.5 million acres. However, since 1994, the wilderness situation on BLM lands has remained largely stalemated. In broad brush strokes, Western Republicans in whose states the wilderness study areas lie have proposed state-by-state wilderness bills that largely track the BLM's wilderness recommendations while congressional Democrats and like-minded Republicans have proposed wilderness bills that include not just the BLM's recommended wilderness, but also all WSAs and areas identified by preservation advocates as having wilderness potential that were rejected by the BLM in the inventory process. At first glance, the stalemate might seem odd—why not at least designate as wilderness those areas on which the two sides agree? One prominent source of the stalemate is disagreement about what is known as "release" language. So-called soft release language in wilderness legislation removes non-designated land from wilderness study area status but does not prohibit the area from being designated as wilderness in the future. The "hard release" language favored by some Western Republicans bars non-designated areas of the state from being considered for possible wilderness designation forever or for some fixed period of time. In essence, hard release language is designed to eliminate wilderness management from the range of multiple uses available to the BLM in its land use planning. For preservation advocates it makes little sense to compromise on release language when wilderness study areas must already be managed for non-impairment.

It was this congressional stalemate which in part prompted the Clinton administration to take the national monument route, discussed above, because the Antiquities Act allowed the President to circumvent Congress. The debate has left BLM lands with two pressing preservation issues: what are BLM's management obligations with respect to wilderness study areas; and what authority does BLM have outside of wilderness study areas to manage its lands so as to preserve their wilderness characteristics? Those issues are discussed below in section V.C.

QUESTIONS AND DISCUSSION

1. Why do you suppose that it took eight years and sixty-five bills to achieve passage of the Wilderness Act? In light of the management provisions ultimately included within the Act, what objections do you suspect may have been raised by the federal land management agencies? By public land resource users? Is the passage of the Wilderness Act compatible with public choice theory?

2. With reference to the definition of wilderness in 16 U.S.C. § 1131 quoted above, which of the following areas might be entitled to designation as wilderness:

- A remote 100,000 acre area of a national forest that was completely logged early in the twentieth century but that is now recovered with trees of roughly the same size?
- What if the same logged-over area of the National Forest had an abandoned logging road roughly bisecting it but the road was mostly overgrown with bushes and small trees?
- 4,000 roadless acres of spectacular alpine country in Glacier National Park?
- 65,000 acres of red rock desert country containing three small, abandoned uranium mines and several areas recently disturbed by zealous off-road vehicle users who abandoned the jeep trails that run adjacent to the 65,000 acre area?

3. Is "wilderness" real or is it simply a cultural construct? Recall the Cronon excerpt in Chapter 1. Cronon argues: "Far from being the one place on earth that stands apart from humanity, [wilderness] is quite profoundly a human creation—indeed, the creation of very particular human cultures at very particular moments in history." William Cronon, *The Trouble with*

Wilderness; or, Getting Back to the Wrong Nature, in UNCOMMON GROUND: TOWARD REINVENTING NATURE 69, 69 (William Cronon ed., 1995). As Cronon sees it, "elite urban tourists and wealthy sportsmen projected their leisure-time frontier fantasies onto the American landscape and so created wilderness in their own image." *Id.* at 471, 482. Do you agree? J. Baird Callicott has even more aggressively asserted that early wilderness thinkers imagined a fictitious pre-Columbian wilderness of a pristine, untouched nature. His view is that this concept of wilderness improperly ignores aboriginal peoples, separates all people from nature, and assumes that nature and ecosystems are static. J. Baird Callicott, *The Wilderness Idea Revisited, in* THE GREAT NEW WILDERNESS DEBATE 337 (J. Baird Callicott & Michael P. Nelson eds., 1998). Is this a fair critique of Leopold, Marshall, and others? As you read the language of the Wilderness Act does it give a warranty of pristineness?

4. An argument raised again and again by opponents of wilderness is that wilderness is elitist and caters to the young, healthy, and wealthy, and to those with enough leisure time to explore backcountry. One study found that "[b]lue-collar workers account for only 5 percent of all wilderness visits" and another found that "two-thirds of wilderness users were college graduates and one-fourth of them had done graduate work." JOSEPH L. SAX, MOUNTAINS WITHOUT HANDRAILS 48 (1980). This elitist argument is belied somewhat by the polling which suggests widespread public support for more wilderness, even among those who may not use it. Economists' estimates of the existence and bequest value of wilderness also indicate that wilderness matters even to those who cannot use it. Nevertheless, the public perception of elitism is an issue that preservation advocates are constantly battling. Part of their response is the moral argument suggested by Professor Sax, *supra*, page 577. Consider these thoughts of Dr. Richard White, an environmental and western historian and self-proclaimed environmentalist:

Richard White, *"Are You An Environmentalist or Do You Work for a Living?" Work and Nature, in* UNCOMMON GROUND: TOWARD REINVENTING NATURE 171–75, 181–85 (William Cronon ed., 1995)

In Forks, Washington, a logging town badly crippled by both over-cutting and the Spotted owl controversy, you can buy a bumper sticker that reads "Are You an Environmentalist or Do You Work for a Living?" It is an interesting insult, and one that poses some equally interesting questions. How is it that environmentalism seems opposed to work? And how is it that work has come to play such a small role in American environmentalism? * * *

Modern environmentalism lacks an adequate consideration of this work. Most environmentalists disdain and distrust those who most obviously work in nature. Environmentalists have come to associate work—particularly heavy bodily labor, blue-collar work—with environmental degradation. This is true whether the work is in the woods, on the sea, in a refinery, in a chemical plant, in a pulp mill, or in a farmer's field or a rancher's pasture. Environmentalists usually imagine that when people who make things finish their day's work, nature is the poorer for it. Nature seems safest when shielded from human labor.

This distrust of work, particularly of hard physical labor, contributes to a larger tendency to define humans as being outside of nature and to frame environmental issues so that the choice seems to be between humans and nature. * * *

My work, I suspect, is similar to that of most environmentalists. Because it seems so distant from nature, it escapes the condemnation that the work that takes place out there, in "nature," attracts. I regularly read the *High Country News*, and its articles just as regularly denounce mining, ranching, and logging for the very real harm they do. And since the paper's editors have some sympathy for rural people trying to live on the land, letters from readers denounce the paper for not condemning these activities enough. The intention of those who defend old growth or denounce overgrazing is not to denounce hard physical work, but that is, in effect, what the articles do. There are few articles or letters denouncing university professors or computer programmers or accountants or lawyers for sullying the environment, although it is my guess that a single lawyer or accountant could, on a good day, put the efforts of Paul Bunyan to shame.

Most humans must work, and our work—all our work—inevitably embeds us in nature, including what we consider wild and pristine places. Environmentalists have invited the kind of attack contained in the Forks bumper sticker by identifying nature with leisure, by masking the environmental consequences of their own work. To escape it, and perhaps even to find allies among people unnecessarily made into enemies, there has to be some attempt to come to terms with work. Work does not prevent harm to the natural world—Forks itself is evidence of that—but if work is not perverted into a means of turning place into property, it can teach us how deeply our work and nature's work are intertwined.

And if we do not come to terms with work, if we fail to pursue the implications of our labor and our bodies in the natural world, then we will return to patrolling the borders. We will turn public lands into a public playground; we will equate wild lands with rugged play; we will imagine nature as an escape, a place where we are born again. It will be a paradise where we leave work behind. Nature may turn out to look a lot like an organic Disneyland, except it will be harder to park.

There is, too, an inescapable corollary to this particular piece of self-deception. We will condemn ourselves to spending most of our lives outside of nature, for there can be no permanent place for us inside. Having demonized those whose very lives recognize the tangled complexity of a planet in which we kill, destroy and alter as a condition of living and working, we can claim an innocence that in the end is merely irresponsibility.

If, on the other hand, environmentalism could focus on our work rather than on our leisure, then a whole series of fruitful new angles on the world might be possible. It links us to each other, and it links us to nature. It unites issues as diverse as workplace safety and grazing on public lands. It unites toxic sites and wilderness areas. In taking responsibility for our own lives and work, in unmasking the connections of our labor and nature's labor, in giving up our hopeless fixation on purity, we may ultimately find a way to break the borders that imprison nature as much as ourselves. Work, then, is where we should begin.

———

5.   Does public support for wilderness amount to a vote for preservation for preservation's sake? Consider the following:

> [P]olling that goes beyond the simple question of whether a person supports wilderness consistently indicates that most citizens have very little understanding of the highly protective nature of a wilderness designation. For example, in an opinion survey of Colorado voters who were highly supportive of wilderness, 42.1% of those surveyed thought that snowmobiling could take place in wilderness areas and 31.1% believed that energy production by wind and hydro facilities could occur, despite the fact that motorized vehicles as well as structures and installations are generally prohibited in wilderness areas. Of the respondents, 46.8% believed that Rocky Mountain National Park was a wilderness area. Apparently, voters were not supporting wilderness because it was the designation most likely to protect biodiversity. Instead, their support seemed to be a function of a more generalized preference for parks and open space. In fact, when actually asked to compare parks and open space to wilderness, their clear preference was for the former.
>
> In other surveys analyzing attitudes toward wilderness in Utah similar results appear. A number of respondents indicated that they had used recreational vehicles within designated wilderness and wilderness study areas, and only one in five Utahns understood that bicycles were prohibited in wilderness areas. Another interesting study in British Columbia of urban and rural attitudes toward wilderness found that when shown photographs of natural areas with varying levels of activity or human impact, urbanites "often regarded depicted areas as wilderness notwithstanding evidence of logging activity, ranging, grazing, villages, roads, and hydroelectric dams," whereas rural respondents "generally considered areas with any such activities as nonwilderness." * * *

James R. Rasband, *The Rise of Urban Archipelagoes in the American West: A New Reservation Policy?*, 31 ENVTL. L. 1, 31–32 (2001). If the public does not have a solid understanding of the legal status of wilderness, what is the message for Congress? Is it an argument for leaving all of the public lands in multiple use status? How much should polling data matter to Congress anyway?

6.   A number of commentators have asked whether it makes sense to have wilderness managed by four different agencies and, more broadly, whether it makes sense to have the Forest Service and the BLM be tasked with multiple use management that necessarily pulls those agencies in different directions. Professors Coggins and Glicksman have proposed the following solution:

> At the risk of oversimplification, one can view federal lands as the source of two kinds of "goods"—commodities and personal pleasure. One obvious course of reform then, is to condense the four existing agencies into two; the National Park and Wildlife Service (NPWS) which would take charge of the lands devoted primarily to noncommodity uses, and the National Forest and Range Service (NFRS), which would control the lands set aside principally for resource extraction. The new NPWS would assume jurisdiction over all current units of the national park and wildlife refuge systems plus all adjacent or (more-or-less) freestanding wilderness areas.... The new NFRS would then be responsible for the remaining lands, which would remain open to extractive activities under the multiple use, sustained yield laws.

Robert L. Glicksman & George Cameron Coggins, *Wilderness in Context*, 76 DENV. U. L. REV. 383, 394 (1999). What is your reaction to their proposal?

How likely is it that this idea, or any other reconfiguration of the federal natural resources agencies, will be enacted? What makes such changes so difficult? Do you think that Secretary Babbitt's creation of the National Landscape Conservation System within the BLM (*supra* at 634)—which includes BLM wilderness and wilderness study areas, along with 15 national monuments—is likely to facilitate a reconfiguration of agency responsibilities or make it less likely?

7. Who has the authority to designate wilderness? The answer to this question may appear relatively straightforward because the Wilderness Act provides that the Wilderness Preservation System shall be composed "of federally owned areas designated by *Congress*" and that "no Federal lands shall be designated as 'wilderness areas' except as provided for in this chapter or by subsequent Act." 16 U.S.C. § 1131 (emphasis added). Fixing the meaning of this language is not, however, as simple as it might first appear. Does it mean that the agencies may not "manage" or "administer" land within their jurisdiction as wilderness even if it is not designated as part of the Wilderness Preservation System? Elsewhere the Act provides that "[n]othing contained herein shall, by implication or otherwise, be construed to lessen the present statutory authority of the Secretary of the Interior with respect to the maintenance of roadless areas within the national park system." 16 U.S.C. § 1132(c). The Act also states that "[n]othing in this Act shall be deemed to be in interference with the purpose for which national forests are established as set forth in the Act of June 4, 1897," 16 U.S.C. § 1133(a), and it was under that authority that the Forest Service set aside the wilderness and primitive areas that became the foundation of the Wilderness Preservation System. Moreover, multiple use management of the national forests and the BLM lands allows for management for "watershed, wildlife and fish, and natural scenic, scientific and historical values," 43 U.S.C. § 1702(c) (FLPMA), all of which are compatible with wilderness-type management.

8. In a 1969 essay, Garrett Hardin proposed a stratified system of wilderness areas and parks based on a people/acre ratio. For the wildest areas, where use would be restricted to one person per 1000 aces, Hardin suggested that admission could be reserved to those who were sufficiently skilled and strong to withstand the difficulties and danger of the area. These areas, Hardin recognized, were ones for which he himself would fail the test of admission because he was a victim of childhood polio. Garrett Hardin, *The Economics of Wilderness*, 78 NAT. HISTORY 20, 20–27 (1969). What do you think of Hardin's proposal for a greater range of wilderness classifications? Do we already have such variations? What of his proposal to allocate entrance by physical merit? Recognize that federal land management agencies already limit access to a variety of national parks and wilderness areas. Persons who want to backpack in Yellowstone, for example, must apply for backcountry permits months in advance. Upon their arrival they must watch a video on grizzly bear encounters and while backpacking must stay in designated backcountry campsites. Other parks and wilderness areas have similar sorts of queuing systems because of the large numbers of people seeking a backcountry experience. Is allocation by queuing more or less fair than allocation by physical merit? If neither approach is appealing, how should entrance be allocated? by the market? by lottery?

9. Roderick Nash describes how some have suggested that "the need for wilderness is transitory, frontier-related enthusiasm that Americans will outgrow just as have, to a large extent, the Italians and the Chinese." NASH, *supra*, at 387. Do you agree with this view or do you think that there is something more at work in the desire to preserve wilderness?

———

2. MANAGING DESIGNATED WILDERNESS

As introduced in the prior section, once designated, wilderness areas are to be managed by the federal agency that had jurisdiction over the land immediately prior to its inclusion in the system. 16 U.S.C. § 1131(b). The agency administering the wilderness is "responsible for preserving the wilderness character of the area." *Id.* Subject to valid existing rights, "there shall be no commercial enterprise and no permanent road within any wilderness area ... [and] there shall be no temporary road, no use of motor vehicles, motorized equipment or motorboats, no landing of aircraft, no other form of mechanical transport, and no structure or installation within any such area." *Id.* at § 1133(c). These limitations on activities within wilderness can be quite strict, as the next case reveals.

THE WILDERNESS SOCIETY v. UNITED STATES FISH AND WILDLIFE SERVICE, 353 F.3d 1051, *en banc* (9th Cir. 2003)

GOULD, CIRCUIT JUDGE.

We consider an action brought by the Wilderness Society and the Alaska Center for the Environment ("Plaintiffs") challenging a decision by the United States Fish and Wildlife Service ("USFWS"), to grant a permit for a sockeye salmon enhancement project ("Enhancement Project") that annually intro- duces about six million hatchery-reared salmon fry into Tustumena Lake, the largest freshwater lake in the Kenai National Wildlife Refuge ("Kenai Refuge") and the Kenai Wilderness. Plaintiffs assert that the USFWS permit for the Enhancement Project violated the Wilderness Act by offending its mandate to preserve the "natural conditions" that are a part of the "wilderness character" of the Kenai Wilderness, 16 U.S.C. §§ 1131, 1133, and by sanctioning an impermissible "commercial enterprise" within a designated wilderness area. *Id.* § 1133(c).... The district court denied Plaintiffs' motion for summary judg- ment and sua sponte entered summary judgment in favor of the USFWS.... We conclude that the district court erred in finding that the Enhancement Project is not a "commercial enterprise" that Congress prohibited within the designated wilderness. We reverse and remand so that the final decision of the USFWS may be set aside, the Enhancement Project enjoined, and judgment entered for Plaintiffs. * * *

In 1941, President Franklin D. Roosevelt issued an Executive Order designating about two million acres of land on Alaska's Kenai Peninsula, including Tustumena Lake, as the Kenai National Moose Range for the purpose of "protecting the natural breeding and feeding range of the giant Kenai moose." Exec. Order No. 8979, 6 Fed.Reg. 6471 (Dec. 16, 1941). * * *

In 1980, Congress enacted the Alaska National Interest Lands Conserva- tion Act ("ANILCA"), Pub.L. No. 96–487, Title III, § 702(7), 94 Stat. 2371

(1980), to control the management of Alaska refuge lands. ANILCA expanded the Kenai National Moose Range by nearly a quarter-million acres, renamed it the Kenai National Wildlife Refuge, ANILCA § 303(4); 16 U.S.C. § 668dd notes, and further set aside 1.35 million acres of the Refuge, including Tustumena Lake, as the Kenai Wilderness, a designated wilderness pursuant to Congress's authority to protect lands under § 1132(c) of the Wilderness Act. ANILCA § 702(7); 16 U.S.C. § 1132(c) & notes. * * *

Tustumena Lake lies near the western edge of the Kenai [National Wildlife] Refuge and within the Kenai Wilderness. Tustumena Lake is the largest freshwater lake located within the Kenai Refuge and is the fifth largest freshwater lake in the State of Alaska. The lake's outlet is the Kasilof River, which drains into the Cook Inlet, a tidal estuary that flows into the Gulf of Alaska and the Pacific Ocean.

As a result of its remote location, the ecosystem around and within Tustumena Lake is in a natural state. This ecosystem supports several species of anadromous fish, including sockeye salmon, which spawn within the Kasilof River watershed. A commercial fishing fleet, operating outside the boundaries of the Kenai Refuge, intercepts and harvests these sockeye salmon during their annual run from the Gulf of Alaska back to the Kasilof River, Tustumena Lake, and other spawning streams.

The antecedents of the present Enhancement Project date back to 1974, when the Alaska Department of Fish and Game ("ADF & G") first conducted a sockeye salmon egg collection at Tustumena Lake as part of a research project designed to test the ability of the ecosystem to produce fish. The eggs were incubated at the Crooked Creek Hatchery, outside of the Kenai Refuge, and the resulting fry were stocked outside of the Kenai Refuge in the spring of 1975. In 1976, fry were first released into Tustumena Lake, and since have been released into Tustumena Lake in all but two subsequent years. The number of fry stocked yearly in Tustumena Lake has ranged from a low of 400,000 in 1978 to a high of 17,050,000 in 1984. Since 1987, the number of fry released annually into the lake has been slightly greater than 6 million.

Before 1980, ADF & G operated the Enhancement Project without a special use permit, and ADF & G did not seek permits for the operation of the project. In 1980, following passage of ANILCA, the USFWS's Refuge Manager for the Kenai Refuge notified ADF & G that special use permits would be required for all ongoing projects within the Refuge. In 1985, the USFWS and ADF & G entered into a Memorandum of Understanding that allowed ADF & G annually to obtain a special use permit for the Enhancement Project to study the effect of stocking on native lake fish and on the incidence of disease within the fish population.

In 1989, the USFWS and ADF & G reached a joint agreement that by 1993 a decision should be made either to discontinue the research project at Tustumena Lake or to elevate it to enhance commercial fishing operations for the benefit of the Cook Inlet fishing industry. In a 1992 report, ADF & G requested that the project become an operational enhancement project. This report cited two reasons for conversion of the project. First, ADF & G concluded that the risk of adverse impacts on the Tustumena Lake ecosystem appeared to be lowered at a stocking rate of about 6 million fry per year. Second, ADF & G noted that, beginning in fiscal year 1992, a reduced state budget would require curtailing project evaluation. In 1993, ADF & G entered into a contract with the Cook Inlet Aquaculture Association ("CIAA") to staff and run the Crooked Creek Hatchery and its hatchery programs.

The CIAA is a private, non-profit corporation "comprised of associations representative of commercial fishermen in the region" as well as "other user groups interested in fisheries within the region." Alaska Stat. § 16.10.380(a) (2003). According to the USFWS's final Environmental Assessment of the Enhancement Project, the CIAA is "organized for the purpose of engaging in salmon enhancement work throughout the Cook Inlet Region." * * *

[T]he USFWS on August 8, 1997, issued a Special Use Permit to the CIAA for the Enhancement Project. Under the terms of this permit, each summer the CIAA establishes a temporary camp within the Kenai Wilderness at the mouth of Bear Creek, which flows into Tustumena Lake, and catches about 10,000 returning sockeye salmon, which yield about 10 million eggs. These eggs are transported to a hatchery outside the Kenai Wilderness. The following spring about six million salmon fry produced by the eggs are stocked and returned to the wilderness in Bear Creek. * * *

II

* * * In *Chevron,* [467 U.S. 837 (1984)], the Supreme Court set forth a two-step test for judicial review of administrative agency interpretations of federal law. Under the first step: "If the intent of Congress is clear, that is the end of the matter; for the court, as well as the agency, must give effect to the unambiguously expressed intent of Congress." *Chevron,* 467 U.S. at 842–43. . . . Conversely, at step two of *Chevron,* when applicable, we recognize that if a statute is silent or ambiguous with respect to the issue at hand, then the reviewing court must defer to the agency so long as "the agency's answer is based on a permissible construction of the statute." 467 U.S. at 843. In such a case an agency's interpretation of a statute will be permissible, unless "arbitrary, capricious, or manifestly contrary to the statute." *Id.* at 844. * * *

Addressing the first step in the *Chevron* analysis, we ask "whether Congress has directly spoken to the precise question at issue." 467 U.S. at 842. "If a court, employing traditional tools of statutory construction, ascertains that Congress had an intention on the precise question at issue, that intention is the law and must be given effect." *Id.* at 843 n. 9. * * *

With these principles in mind, we assess Plaintiffs' contention that the Enhancement Project offends the Wilderness Act. Most pertinent to our analysis is the Wilderness Act's prohibition of commercial enterprise within designated wilderness. Section 4(c) of the Wilderness Act states that, subject to exceptions not relevant here, "there shall be no commercial enterprise . . . within any wilderness area." 16 U.S.C. § 1133(c). The Wilderness Act does not define the terms "commercial enterprise" or "within." The district court considered these terms ambiguous and concluded that they do not bar the Enhancement Project.

Because no statutory or regulatory provision expressly defines the meaning of the term "commercial enterprise" as used in the Wilderness Act, we first consider the common sense meaning of the statute's words to determine whether it is ambiguous. *See Iverson,* 162 F.3d at 1022. Webster's defines "enterprise" to mean "a project or undertaking." Webster's Ninth New Collegiate Dictionary 415 (1985). Webster's defines "commercial" as "occupied with or engaged in commerce or work intended for commerce; of or relating to commerce." *Id* at 264–65. The American Heritage Dictionary of the English Language provides a strikingly similar definition, viewing "commercial" as meaning "1.a. of or relating to commerce, b. engaged in commerce, c. involved in work that is intended for the mass market." American Heritage Dictionary of the English Language 371 (4th ed. 2000).... These definitions suggest that a commercial enterprise is a project or undertaking of or relating to commerce.

We also consider the purposes of the Wilderness Act. The Act's declaration of policy states as a goal the "preservation and protection" of wilderness lands "in their natural condition," so as to "leave them unimpaired for future use and enjoyment as wilderness and so as to provide for the protection of these areas, [and] the preservation of their wilderness character." 16 U.S.C. § 1131(a). The Wilderness Act further defines "wilderness," in part, as "an area where the earth and its community of life are untrammeled by man." *Id.* § 1131(c). These statutory declarations show a mandate of preservation for wilderness and the essential need to keep commerce out of it. Whatever else may be said about the positive aims of the Enhancement Project, it was not designed to advance the purposes of the Wilderness Act. The Enhancement Project to a degree places the goals and activities of commercial enterprise in the protected wilderness. The Enhancement Project is literally a project relating to commerce.

The structure of the relevant provisions of the Wilderness Act may also be considered. The Wilderness Act's opening section first sets forth the Act's broad mandate to protect the forests, waters and creatures of the wilderness in their natural, untrammeled state. 16 U.S.C. § 1131. Section 1133, devoted to the use of wilderness areas, contains a subsection entitled "[p]rohibition provisions." *Id.* § 1133(c). Among these provisions is a broad prohibition on the operation of all commercial enterprise within a designated wilderness, except as "specifically provided for in this Act." *Id.* The following subsection of the Act enumerates "special provisions," including exceptions to this prohibition. *Id.* § 1133(d). This statutory structure, with prohibitions including an express bar on commercial enterprise within wilderness, limited by specific and express exceptions, shows a clear congressional intent generally to enforce the prohibition against "commercial enterprise" when the specified exceptions are not present. There is no exception given for commercial enterprise in wilderness when it has benign purpose and minimally intrusive impact.

The language, purpose and structure of the Wilderness Act support the conclusion that Congress spoke clearly to preclude commercial enterprise in the designated wilderness, regardless of the form of commercial activity, and regardless of whether it is aimed at assisting the economy with minimal intrusion on wilderness values.

C

Because the aim of Congress in the Wilderness Act to prohibit commercial enterprise within designated wilderness is clear, we do not owe deference to the USFWS's determination regarding the permissibility of the Enhancement Project if it is a commercial enterprise. *Chevron,* 467 U.S. at 842–43.

The district court grounded its decision in part on an assessment that the impact on wilderness of millions of fry unseen beneath the waters of Bear Creek and Tustumena Lake was not terribly intrusive on wilderness values and that the project would hardly be noticed by those visiting the wilderness. The district court also was impressed that the CIAA was a nonprofit entity, that the State of Alaska heavily regulated the Enhancement Project, and that commercial effects of the project generally occurred years after the collection of salmon eggs and later release of the fry and were realized by commercial fishermen who sought their catch outside the wilderness bounds.

We thus deal with an activity with a benign aim to enhance the catch of fishermen, with little visible detriment to wilderness, under the cooperative banner of a non-profit trade association and state regulators. Surely this fish-stocking program, whose antecedents were a state-run research project, is nothing like building a McDonald's restaurant or a Wal–Mart store on the shores of Tustumena Lake. Nor is it like conducting a commercial fishing operation within designated wilderness, which we have previously proscribed. *See Alaska Wildlife Alliance v. Jensen,* 108 F.3d 1065, 1069 (9th Cir. 1997). Nor is the project like cutting timber, extracting minerals, or otherwise exploiting wilderness resources in a way that is plainly destructive of their preservation.

Conversely, the challenged activities do not appear to be aimed at furthering the goals of the Wilderness Act. The project is not aimed at preserving a threatened salmon run. Looked at most favorably, for the proponents of the fish-stocking project, it might be concluded that the project only negligibly alters the wild character of Tustumena Lake and is not incompatible with refuge values, though those issues are disputed. And it might also be considered that, to the extent the project is a servant of commerce, it may pose a threat to the wild, even if it operates under the eye of state and federal regulators.

Before further addressing the reasoning of the district court, we acknowledge that none of our precedent, and no explicit guidance from the United States Supreme Court, has addressed how to assess "commercial enterprise" when faced with activities involving mixed purposes and effects. The lack of explicit guidance on this issue in part led the district court to defer to the agency action. Yet we have determined that Congress absolutely proscribed commercial enterprise in the wilderness, and it is a traditional judicial function to apply that prohibition to the precise facts here, to determine if the challenged project may continue consistent with the will of Congress.

In light of Congress's language and manifest intent, we conclude that the most sensible rule of decision to resolve whether an activity within designated wilderness bounds should be characterized as a "commercial enterprise" turns on an assessment of the purpose and effect of the activity. *See Sierra Club v. Lyng,* 662 F. Supp. 40, 42–43 (D. D.C. 1987). *Lyng,* though it involves a different issue under the Wilderness Act, is instructive on the issue of whether the Enhancement Project should be considered a commercial enterprise. In *Lyng,* plaintiffs challenged the legality of a United States Forest Service program to control pine beetle infestations in designated wilderness areas by an extensive tree-cutting and chemical-spraying campaign. Defendant urged that the eradication program was permissible, without justification, under section 4(d)(1) of the Wilderness Act, 16 U.S.C. § 1133(d)(1), under which the Secretary of Agriculture may take "such measures ... as may be necessary in the control of fire, insects, and diseases," within the designated wilderness. Rejecting this contention, the district court stressed that the "purpose and effect of the program [was] solely to protect commercial timber interests and private property," and imposed an affirmative burden on the Secretary of Agriculture to justify the eradication program in light of wilderness values. *Lyng,* 662 F. Supp. at 42–43.

The consideration of purpose and effect of challenged actions not infrequently assists in determining whether a prohibition is to be applied to complex conduct. For example, the United States Supreme Court has long looked to the purpose and effect of state action to determine whether it violates the Establishment Clause. *E.g., Agostini v. Felton,* 521 U.S. 203, 218 (1997); *Lemon v. Kurtzman,* 403 U.S. 602, 612–13 (1971). It is also commonplace to assess purpose and effect to determine whether a trade restraint is unreasonable. *E.g., Chicago Bd. of Trade v. United States,* 246 U.S. 231, 238 (1918). Similarly, the Supreme Court has directed us to rely on considerations of purpose and effect in determining whether there is a conflict between state and federal law that leads to preemption of the state law. *E.g. Gade v. Nat'l Solid Wastes Mgmt. Ass'n,* 505 U.S. 88, 106–07 (1992). The Supreme Court has also focused our review on purpose and effect in evaluating whether a statute is properly characterized as civil or criminal. *E.g., Hudson v. United States,* 522 U.S. 92, 99 (1997). * * *

For all these reasons, we conclude that as a general rule both the purpose and the effect of challenged activities must be carefully assessed in deciding whether a project is a "commercial enterprise" within the wilderness that is prohibited by the Wilderness Act.... This familiar test looking to "purpose and effect" is persuasive here because it gets to the heart of what has occurred in the wilderness.

The primary purpose of the Enhancement Project is to advance commercial interests of Cook Inlet fishermen by swelling the salmon runs from which they will eventually make their catch. The Enhancement Project is operated by an organization primarily funded by a voluntary self-imposed tax instituted by the Cook Inlet fishing industry on the value of its salmon catch. In the words of the Kenai Refuge Manager, in a memorandum to the Department of Interior's Regional Solicitor:

> The *primary purpose of the enhancement activity is to supplement sockeye catches* for East Side Cook Inlet set-net commercial fishermen, and for lower Cook Inlet enhancement projects.
>
> A secondary purpose is use of the excess eggs taken from Tustumena in a CIAA cost recovery project to help finance the Tustumena lake and lower Cook Inlet sockeye salmon enhancement projects.
>
> *The activity is no longer experimental in nature, nor is restoration of fish stocks an objective. It is strictly an enhancement effort to increase the number of sockeye salmon available to the commercial fishery.*

Memorandum from Kenai Refuge Manager to Regional Solicitor 2–3 (undated), ER 224–26 (emphasis added). The Fishery Management Plan for the Kenai Refuge characterizes the purpose of the Enhancement Project as "commercial enhancement of sockeye salmon populations in ... Tustumena lake[ ]." This primary purpose is not contradicted by evidence that the Enhancement Project serves other secondary noncommercial purposes, including providing a general benefit to the fishery commonly used by commercial and recreational fishermen alike. Incidental purposes do not contradict that the Enhancement Project's principal aim is stock enhancement for the commercial fishing industry.

The primary effect of the Enhancement Project is to aid commercial enterprise of fishermen. More than eighty percent of the salmon produced by the Enhancement Project are caught by commercial fishermen, who realize over $1.5 million in additional annual revenue from project-produced fish. USFWS documents highlight the primary effect of the Enhancement Project to aid commercial enterprise. For example, the July 1997 EA states that "[i]t is apparent because commercial fishing economics is emphasized ... the main reason for continuing the project is economic[ ] in nature." Similarly a USFWS "Briefing Statement" concludes that "[w]e should consider [CIAA's cost-recovery harvest] to be a commercial fishing operation." The 1997 Compatibility Determination concludes that the Enhancement Project "primarily benefits Eastside Cook Inlet set-net commercial fishermen." In light of this primary effect, any incidental benefit to sport fishermen or others is not controlling. The incidental benefit that the program may provide to recreational and sport fishermen is subordinate to the primary benefit conferred on the commercial fishing industry.

In light of the unmistakable primary purpose and effect of the Enhancement Project, we reject arguments advanced by the USFWS that were credited by the district court. The district court reasoned in part that the CIAA is itself a nonprofit organization. But the non-profit status of the CIAA cannot be controlling because its non-profit activities are funded by the fishing industry and are aimed at providing benefits to that industry. The CIAA's continued funding and operation is dependent upon the revenues of commercial fishermen, and we have previously recognized that even non-profit entities may engage in commercial activity. *Dedication and Everlasting Love to Animals v. Humane Soc.,* 50 F.3d 710, 713 (9th Cir. 1995). * * *

Furthermore, the essential nature of the Enhancement Project is not changed merely because the commercial benefit derived from the Enhancement Project is conferred when fishermen make their salmon catch outside the bounds of the Kenai Wilderness. It is correct that what the Wilderness Act bars is the operation of a "commercial enterprise ... *within* any wilderness area." 16 U.S.C. § 1133(c) (emphasis added). But it is not disputed that substantial and essential parts of the Enhancement Project's operation, the collection of eggs taken to a hatchery and the stocking of six million fry returned to Bear Creek, occur within the Kenai Wilderness.[13]

Implicit in the justifications urged for the project is the premise that we may recognize that the benign purposes of the project should be permitted to continue because the Wilderness Act resulted from a "compromise" of the legislature. But regardless of any tradeoffs considered by Congress in enacting the Wilderness Act, we interpret and apply the language chosen by Congress, for that language was chosen in order to incorporate and effectuate those tradeoffs. The plain language of the Wilderness Act states that there shall be "*no* commercial enterprise" within designated wilderness. 16 U.S.C. § 1133(c) (emphasis added). This mandatory language does not provide exception to the prohibition on commercial enterprise within wilderness if aimed at achieving a benign goal for commerce with modest impact on wilderness. That compromises may have been made in the legislative process does not alter an analysis of Congress's words of proscription based on traditional canons of statutory construction.

We must abide by Congress's prohibition of commercial enterprise in wilderness and may not defer to the contrary interpretation argued by the USFWS. In light of the clear statutory mandate, the Wilderness Act requires that the lands and waters duly designated as wilderness must be left untouched, untrammeled, and unaltered by commerce. By contrast, the Enhancement Project is a commercial enterprise within the boundaries of a designated wilderness and violates the Wilderness Act. * * *[18]

13. If we were to accept the argument that the Enhancement Project, despite its commercial aims, is exempt from the Wilderness Act because the project's commercial benefit is conferred outside the wilderness, we would likely soon face arguments that other commercial operations, more intrusive on the wilderness, might be sustained under the Wilderness Act, if transactions constituting commerce occur outside of the wilderness area's bounds. The weakness in this line of argument is obvious if we consider that a logging operation within the wilderness could not sensibly be urged to be permissible, even though the trees harvested were sold outside of the wilderness area.

18. Plaintiffs also assert that the Enhancement Project violates the Wilderness Act's requirement that any action taken within a federally-designated

REVERSED and REMANDED for further proceedings not inconsistent with this opinion. * * *

QUESTIONS AND DISCUSSION

1. As the court remarks in footnote 18, it did not reach plaintiffs' additional argument that the Enhancement Project also violated the Wilderness Act's requirement that the agency preserve the "natural conditions" and "wilderness character" of the area. 16 U.S.C. §§ 1131, 1133. Had it reached that issue, what should the court have decided? The Ninth Circuit's en banc decision vacated a decision of a three-judge panel upholding the decision of the Fish and Wildlife Service to permit the enhancement project. The panel majority had reasoned:

> [I]t is not obvious how an agency must protect and manage an area "so as to preserve its natural conditions." In general, the term "natural" means wild, formed by nature, and not artificially made. *See* Black's Law Dictionary 1026 (6th ed. 1990). However, there are two plausible inferences to be drawn from the quoted phrase in this context. On the one hand, to preserve the "natural conditions" of the Refuge could mean protecting against the introduction of artificial propagation programs, like the Project, that alter the natural ecological processes within the Refuge. On the other hand, to preserve the "natural conditions" of the Refuge could mean preserving the natural ecological processes as they *would* exist in their wild state, in the absence of artificial disturbance from outside the wilderness area. * * *

> The difference between those two interpretations is profound. If, for example, hunting *outside* the wilderness area threatens a particular animal with extinction, and that animal used to be plentiful in the wilderness area, under the former interpretation no project to reintroduce the animal into the wilderness area can occur if it involves any artificial process (e.g., trapping and artificial insemination). By contrast, under the latter interpretation interventions can occur if they restore the "natural" balance of the wilderness area as it *would* exist without the external human forces that have altered it. Both interpretations are plausible and permissible.

> Indeed, the [Wilderness Act's] use of the phrase "protected and managed" highlights this ambiguity. "Management" suggests affirmative steps taken to maintain wilderness character, while "protection" suggests a more hands-off approach. If "natural conditions" may be preserved only through a program of strict nonintervention, what is the purpose of the word "managed" in the definition? If strict nonintervention was Congress' intent, the word "protect" would have sufficed.

> A reasonable interpretation of this ambiguity is that a "wilderness" does not exist in a vacuum. Human activities outside the wilderness continue, with effects that most certainly are felt within the wilderness area. While the

wilderness area preserve the "natural conditions" that are a part of the "wilderness character" of such an area, 16 U.S.C. §§ 1131, 1133, and also that the project violates the Refuge Act's mandate that special use permits be issued only after a determination that "such uses are compatible with the major purposes for which such areas were es-

tablished." 16 U.S.C. § 668dd(d)(1)(A). Because we have determined that the district court erred in granting summary judgment to the USFWS because the Enhancement Project is a prohibited commercial enterprise, we need not and do not consider these additional claims.

wilderness must be "protected" so that its natural processes dominate, it also must be "managed" so that human activities from outside the area do not interfere unduly. * * *

The Project reasonably can be seen as a legitimate measure taken to restore fish runs to their "natural conditions," that is, to make the runs as plentiful as they would be in the absence of interference from outside the Refuge. The statute is reasonably susceptible to the agency's interpretation, which is all that we require.

Wilderness Society v. United States Fish and Wildlife Service, 316 F.3d 913, 923–25 (9th Cir. 2003). Is this reasoning persuasive? Is the term "wilderness management" an oxymoron? How would you factor into the obligation to preserve the Lake's "natural conditions" the fact that the stocking of Tustumena Lake with salmon fry was occurring before the designation of the area as wilderness? Should the predesignation stocking have made a difference to the en banc court's interpretation of the "commercial enterprise" language?

2. By way of review of administrative law, Chapter 3 *supra*, was there sufficient ambiguity in the "no commercial enterprise" language that the court should have proceeded to the second step of the *Chevron* analysis? Assuming the court had reached step two of *Chevron*, did the Fish and Wildlife Service offer a permissible interpretation of the "no commercial enterprise" language? In light of the fact that the Service's interpretation of the language was the product of a permit decision and not notice-and-comment rulemaking, is it possible that *Chevron* deference would not have been appropriate in any event? What alternative level of deference may have been available?

With respect to the question of appropriate deference consider the district court decision in *High Sierra Hikers Ass'n v. U.S. Forest Service*, 436 F. Supp. 2d 1117 (E.D. Cal. 2006). There, the court enjoined the Forest Service from repairing and maintaining eleven dams within the Emigrant Wilderness in the High Sierras, although the dams had been within the wilderness at the time it was designated. Following the reasoning of the en banc panel in *Wilderness Society*, the court concluded that under step one of *Chevron*, the operation and maintenance of the dams violated the Wilderness Act's plain prohibition against "structures."

[T]here is no logical necessity in maintaining, repairing, or operating the dams in order to administer the area for purposes of the Wilderness Act. The area manifested its wilderness characteristics before the dams were in place and would lose nothing in the way of wilderness values were the dams not present. What would be lost is some enhancement of a particular use of the area (fishing), but that use, while perhaps popular, is not an integral part of the wilderness nature of that area.

In sum, Defendants' basic argument with regard to the Wilderness Act centers around the level of deference owed to Forest Service with regard to its findings and conclusions. The flaw in Defendants' argument is that, regardless of how carefully and thoroughly Forest Service considered the various action plans, the plans considered and the plan finally chosen are predicated on the legal contention that maintenance, repair and operation of the dams is "necessary to meet minimum requirements for the administration of the area for purposes of this chapter"—a contention that is without legal or logical support. While

> Forest Service's factual findings are due considerable deference under *Skidmore*, the legal foundations of Forest Service's actions are due no deference because the proposed actions are contrary to the express purposes of the Wilderness Act.

Id. at 1137. Thinking about the basic precepts of administrative law, does it make sense for courts to defer to the Service with respect to wilderness management decisions?

3.   Do you agree with the en banc panel that the fact that the Wilderness Act is a product of compromise is not particularly important to its interpretation of the phrase "no commercial enterprise"? Elsewhere in the Wilderness Act, Congress was explicit that it was not willing to let the ideal of wilderness as pristine, *terra incognita*—if that ideal even exists—stand in the way of a historic move toward greater preservation. The Wilderness Act contains a series of what it termed "special provisions" explicitly allowing activities seemingly incompatible with the Act's definition of wilderness. 16 U.S.C. § 1133(d). One such special provision allows agencies to take the measures "necessary in the control of fire, insects, and diseases." 16 U.S.C. § 1133(d)(1). This provision, which the court briefly discusses, has been a source of some tension in wilderness management. In one series of cases involving Forest Service efforts to deal with a Southern Pine Beetle infestation, the courts held that the Forest Service may cut corridors through wilderness areas in order to contain the spread of the beetle, as long as it does so to protect the wilderness and not "for the benefit of outsiders." *Sierra Club v. Lyng*, 662 F. Supp. 40, 43 (D. D.C. 1987). The Secretary, said the court, had the burden of justifying that the cuts are necessary. *Id. See also Sierra Club v. Lyng*, 663 F. Supp. 556 (D. D.C. 1987) (finding that the Forest Service had met its burden as defined in the prior case). Why would Congress have allowed the Forest Service to protect wilderness from a *natural* pine beetle infestation? Is "protecting wilderness" really the purpose of the exception or did Congress have something else in mind? What about fighting fires? Should there be any limits on firefighting in wilderness?

4.   Among the "special provisions" in the Wilderness Act is also one that allows commercial services to be performed within wilderness area "to the extent necessary for activities which are proper for realizing the recreational or other wilderness purposes of the areas" 16 U.S.C. § 1133(d)(5). This provision was tested in *High Sierra Hikers Ass'n v. Moore*, 561 F. Supp. 2d 1107 (N.D. Cal. 2008), where the plaintiffs claimed that the Forest Service's issuance of special use permits for commercial packstock operators in the Ansel Adams and John Muir wilderness areas was degrading the wilderness. Evaluating the extent to which the packstock operations were necessary, the court entered a detailed order which included a stock-to-person ratio of 1:1.5 and a limit on overnight pack trips to 95% of the historical average. Plaintiffs had sought a 30% reduction in trips and the Forest Service had argued that no reduction was necessary. Are commercial pack trips "necessary" to realize the purpose of wilderness areas? How much deference is it appropriate for a court to show the agency about this sort of determination?

5. In *Izaak Walton League of America, Inc. v. Kimbell*, 516 F. Supp. 2d
982 (D. Minn. 2007), the plaintiffs challenged the Forest Service's proposal
to construct a snowmobile trail in the Superior National Forest, which is
adjacent to, but not within, the Boundary Waters Canoe Area Wilderness,
because of concerns about the noise impact of the snowmobiles. The
plaintiffs relied on section 4(b) of the Wilderness Act, which provides:

> Except as otherwise provided in this chapter, each agency administering any
> area designated as wilderness *shall be responsible for preserving the wilderness
> character of the area* and shall so administer such area for such other purposes
> for which it may have been established as also to preserve its wilderness
> character.

16 U.S.C. § 1133(b) (emphasis added). The Forest Service countered that
this language did not create an obligation with respect to activities outside
of wilderness areas, reasoning that such an interpretation "would have no
limiting principle" and "would create a judicial 'buffer zone' around any
wilderness area, effectively expanding the wilderness beyond the areas
designated by Congress." *Id.* at 987–88. The court disagreed and concluded
that the "agency's duty to preserve the wilderness [in § 4(b)] is wholly
independent of the source or location of that activity." *Id.* at 988. Before
deciding whether the snowmobile trail within the adjacent national forest
would violate the Wilderness Act, the court ordered the Forest Service to
prepare an EIS considering the noise impacts. How far can this holding be
extended? Is the court suggesting a duty to regulate activities on *private*
property outside wilderness areas?

6. Another of the "special provisions" of the Wilderness Act provides that
within wilderness areas in national forests "the grazing of livestock, where
established prior to September 3, 1964, shall be permitted to continue
subject to such reasonable regulations as are deemed necessary by the
Secretary of Agriculture." 16 U.S.C. § 1133(d)(4). Does this provision mean
that the Forest Service lost its previous authority to cancel grazing permits
in these parts of the national forests? Does it seem likely that Congress in
the Wilderness Act intended to create a permanent right to graze where
one did not previously exist? In the Colorado Wilderness Act of 1980,
Congress provided that grazing in wilderness would be governed by the
guidelines articulated in the House Report accompanying the Act, 94 Stat.
3271, § 108 (1980), insofar as consistent with the terms of the Wilderness
Act. Those guidelines provided, in part:

> There shall be no curtailments of grazing in wilderness simply because an area
> is, or has been designated as wilderness, nor should wilderness designations be
> used as an excuse by administrators to slowly 'phase out' grazing. Any
> adjustments in the numbers of livestock permitted to graze in wilderness areas
> should be made as a result of revisions in the normal grazing and land
> management planning and policy setting process, giving consideration to legal
> mandates, range condition, and the protection of the range resources from
> deterioration. It is anticipated that the numbers of livestock permitted to graze
> in wilderness would remain at the approximate levels existing at the time an
> area enters the wilderness system.

H.R. REP. No. 617, 96th Cong., 1st Sess. 11 (1979). Although the Colorado
Wilderness Act indicates that Congress did not intend to create a right to
graze, it does raise difficult questions about how far the Forest Service may

go in regulating grazing so as to protect the wilderness qualities of an area. Suppose, for example, that grazing along a particular stream within a wilderness is raising the fecal coliform level of the water and interfering with backpackers' wilderness experience. Could the Forest Service require the rancher to remove the cattle? What if grazing is causing the condition of a wilderness riparian area to deteriorate? On the issue of grazing in wilderness, see Mitchel P. McClaran, *Livestock in Wilderness: A Review and Forecast*, 20 Envtl. L. 857 (1990).

7. The "special provision" which made perhaps the greatest compromise with the notion of pristine wilderness was the exception for mining. The Wilderness Act provided that

> Notwithstanding any other provisions of this chapter, until midnight December 31, 1983, the United States mining laws and all laws pertaining to mineral leasing shall, to the same extent as applicable prior to September 3, 1964, extend to those national forest lands designated by this chapter as "wilderness areas"; subject, however, to such reasonable regulations governing ingress and egress as may be prescribed by the Secretary of Agriculture.... Mineral leases, permits, and licenses covering lands within national forest wilderness areas designated by this chapter shall contain such reasonable stipulations as may be prescribed by the Secretary of Agriculture for the protection of the wilderness character of the land consistent with the use of the land for the purposes for which they are leased, permitted, or licensed. Subject to valid rights then existing, effective January 1, 1984, the minerals in lands designated by this chapter as wilderness areas are withdrawn from all forms of appropriation under the mining laws and from disposition under all laws pertaining to mineral leasing and all amendments thereto.

16 U.S.C. § 1133(d)(3). Under this exception, miners and prospective lessees were given 20 years to locate mining claims and pursue leases. It seemed like a potentially gaping hole in the statute's protective cover. As it turned out, however, few hard rock claims were located and a succession of Interior Department secretaries declined to issue leases within wilderness, as was within their discretion under the Mineral Leasing Act. *See* Chapter 9, *infra*. When Secretary Watt took over the Department in 1981, he decided to change the policy and proposed to issue leases in three Montana wilderness areas. Pursuant to the withdrawal provisions of FLPMA, the House Interior Committee directed Secretary Watt to make an emergency withdrawal of the lands from mineral leasing. As discussed further below, *infra* at 687–91, the provision of FLPMA allowing a single House committee to direct a withdrawal was challenged as a violation of the Constitution's bicameralism and presentment requirements but the lawsuit failed. *See Pacific Legal Foundation v. Watt*, 529 F. Supp. 982 (D. Mont. 1981), *supplemented by* 539 F. Supp. 1194 (D. Mont. 1982). The lawsuit did have one effect—it precipitated a series of congressional and executive withdrawals of all wilderness areas from mineral leasing up through December 31, 1983, the time when leasing was to stop under the terms of the Wilderness Act.

Although the time for locating hard rock claims or applying for leases ended in 1984, mining within wilderness continues to pose management difficulties, particularly with respect to access to pre–1984 mining claims within wilderness. The issue of access to mining and other inholdings is discussed further below in a section devoted entirely to that issue.

————

CASE STUDY: ROADING THE IZEMBEK NATIONAL WILDLIFE REFUGE

Izembek National Wildlife Refuge is a 315,000 acre refuge on the Alaska Peninsula near the beginning of Aleutian Island chain. It contains world-class wetlands and was the first place in the United States designated under the Convention on Wetlands of International Importance Especially as Waterfowl Habitat (known as Ramsar). In 1980, the Alaska National Interest Lands Conservation Act (ANILCA) set aside 95% of the refuge as wilderness. Each fall, Izembek hosts the world's entire population of Pacific black brant (approximately 150,000 birds) as they migrate along the Pacific Flyway. The entire population of emperor geese use the refuge during their annual spring and fall migrations and the threatened Stellar's Eider uses the refuge during the winter. In 1998 Congress considered the Department of the Interior and Related Agencies Appropriations Act of 1999 (S. 2237, 105th Cong.). The Act contained § 126, a rider otherwise known as the King Cove Health and Safety Act of 1998 (S. 1092, 105th Cong.), which proposed to create an easement through Izembek in order to create an unpaved, one-lane road connecting the communities of King Cove and Cold Bay. The road would have traversed seven miles of wilderness and would have been the first time Congress had authorized a road to be built through an existing wilderness area.

King Cove, an Aleut village of approximately 800 permanent residents and between 400–600 seasonal workers, has no hospital and is accessible only by boat or plane. The airport in King Cove has a small, dirt runway with mountains and steep valleys on all sides. During harsh weather conditions, which occur frequently, travel from this airport is dangerous. The airport at Cold Bay is the third largest airport in Alaska and not only functions in all weather conditions 24 hours a day but also serves as an alternative to the Anchorage airport in emergencies. The citizens of King Cove believed that the road was necessary to help them secure adequate medical attention when travel by air or sea was not possible. Traffic, they argued, would be minimal because there are only about 250 vehicles in the two cities combined. Opponents of the road, which included the Department of the Interior, the Fish and Wildlife Service, and an array of sportsmen's and environmental organizations, argued that the road would damage pristine habitat and harm the various species which rely on the refuge for their survival. They also argued that any road would be contrary to the Wilderness Act and to the Alaska National Interest Lands Conservation Act (ANILCA). Finally, they asserted that it was not necessary to run the road through the wilderness because alternatives, including ferry and helicopter service as well as telemedicine, were available.

In the end, Congress did not approve the road through the wilderness but instead appropriated $37.5 million to improve the medical facility in King Cove and to build a transportation system between the two communities that constructed some road outside the wilderness and relied primarily on a hovercraft to provide ferry service between King Cove and Cold Bay. *See* Pub. L. No. 105–277 § 353, 112 Stat. 2681 (1998). Do you think the 1998 Congress made a wise decision in requiring a combined boat and road route? Suppose the Fish and Wildlife Service had approved the road on its own. Could it have done so?

In 2008, Alaska's delegation proposed the road again, although this time with the sweeteners of an exchange of state and King Cove Native Corporation lands. Then, in 2009, as part of a massive piece of omnibus legislation, Congress authorized an exchange of 56,400 acres of state land and 13,300 acres of King Cove land for about 1,800 acres of federal land to allow construction of a single-lane gravel road between King Cove and Cold Bay. The road must be used primarily for health and safety purposes and may not be used for commercial purposes. The building plan also requires various mitigation measure to protect wetlands. Omnibus Public Land Management Act of 2009, H.R. 146, 111th Cong., 1st Sess., §§ 6401–6406. Did Congress finally reach the right result or should it have held firm to its prior opposition?

————

VI.   NATIONAL WILDLIFE REFUGES, WILD AND SCENIC RIVERS, AND THE LAND AND WATER CONSERVATION FUND

National parks, monuments, and wilderness areas do not, of course, describe the full range of federally protected landscapes. While detailed consideration of other protective land designations is beyond the scope of this casebook, this section briefly introduces you to two additional federal preservation efforts—the National Wildlife Refuges and Wild and Scenic River designations. It also introduces the Land and Water Conservation Fund, which provides money for the acquisition of lands to support outdoor recreation.

A.   NATIONAL WILDLIFE REFUGES

Of the major federal land designations, the National Wildlife Refuge System is the only one devoted primarily to the preservation of wildlife. Administered primarily by the Fish and Wildlife Service, the purpose of the Refuge System is to provide "a national network of lands and waters for the conservation, management, and where appropriate, restoration of . . . fish, wildlife, and plant resources and their habitats." 16 U.S.C. § 668dd(a)(2). As described briefly in Chapter 2, the first wildlife refuge was established by executive order by President Theodore Roosevelt at Pelican Island, Florida, in 1903. The System's subsequent growth is described in the following excerpt.

Carol Hardy Vincent et al., *Federal Land Management Agencies: Background on Land and Resource Management,* **Congressional Research Report, RL 32393, 43–48 (Aug. 2, 2004)**

By September 30, 2002, there were 540 refuges totaling 92.1 million acres in 50 states, the Pacific Territories, Puerto Rico, and the Virgin Islands. The largest increase in acreage by far occurred with the addition of 53 million acres of refuge land under the Alaska National Interest Lands Conservation Act of 1980. Alaska now has 76.8 million acres of refuge lands—80.5% of the system. Within 63 of the refuges are 78 designated wilderness areas, ranging from 2 acres at Green Bay National Wildlife Refuge (NWR) in Wisconsin to 8.0 million acres at Arctic NWR in Alaska.

The NWRS [National Wildlife Refuge System] includes two other categories of land besides refuges: (1) the 203 Waterfowl Production Area (WPA) districts, private lands managed in accordance with agreements between the farmers and ranchers who own the land and the FWS; and (2) 50 Wildlife Coordination Areas (WCAs), owned primarily by FWS, but also by other parties, including some federal agencies; they generally are managed by state agencies under agreements with the FWS. These bring the NWRS to 793 units. These two additional categories bring the total land in the NWRS (counting refuges, WPAs, and WCAs) to 95.4 million acres. In approximately 1.7 million acres of the NWRS, FWS has secondary jurisdiction: the FWS has some influence over activities on these lands, but the lands are owned or managed principally by some other agency, subject to the mandates of that agency. * * *

WPAs are managed primarily to provide breeding habitat for migratory waterfowl. As of September 30, 2002, these areas totaled 2.9 million acres, of which 0.7 million acres were federally owned and 2.2 million acres were managed by the private landowners under leases, easements, or agreements with FWS. These areas are found mainly in the potholes and interior wetlands of the North Central states, a region sometimes called "North America's Duck Factory." In these areas, there is considerably less conflicting resource use, in part because the areas managed under lease are not subject to the federal mining and mineral leasing laws, and because the size of individual tracts is relatively small. However, the leased lands may be less secure as wildlife habitat because they may be converted later to agricultural use by the private owners. The WCAs (0.3 million acres) are owned primarily by FWS, but also by other parties, including some federal agencies; they are managed by state wildlife agencies under cooperative agreements with FWS. * * *

Growth of the NWRS may come about in a number of ways. Certain laws provide general authority to expand the NWRS, including primarily the Migratory Bird Treaty Act (MBTA) of 1929, but also the Fish and Wildlife Coordination Act, the Fish and Wildlife Act of 1956, and the Endangered Species Act. These general authorities allow the FWS to add lands to the Refuge System without specific congressional action.

Some units have been created by specific acts of Congress (e.g., Protection Island NWR, WA; Bayou Sauvage NWR, LA; or John Heinz NWR, PA).71 Other units have been created by executive order. Also, FLPMA authorizes the Secretary of the Interior to withdraw lands from the public domain for additions to the NWRS, although all withdrawals exceeding 5,000 acres are subject to congressional approval procedures (43 U.S.C. § 1714(c)).

... The primary FWS land acquisition authority has been the MBTA [Migratory Bird Conservation Act of 1929, 16 U.S.C. § 715 et seq.] This Act authorizes the Secretary to recommend areas "necessary for the conservation of migratory birds" to the Migratory Bird Conservation Commission, after consulting with the relevant governor (or state agency) and appropriate local government officials (16 U.S.C. § 715c). The Secretary may then purchase or rent areas approved by the Commission (§ 715d(1)), and "acquire, by gift or devise, any area or interest therein. . . ." (§ 715d(2)). * * *

The purchase of refuge lands is financed primarily through two funding sources: the Migratory Bird Conservation Fund (MBCF) and the Land and Water Conservation Fund (LWCF). . . . MBCF acquisitions have emphasized wetlands essential for migratory waterfowl, while LWCF acquisitions have encompassed the gamut of NWRS purposes. MBCF is supported from three sources (amounts in parentheses are FY2000 receipts deposited into the MBCF):

- the sale of "hunting and conservation stamps" (better known as "duck stamps") purchased by hunters and certain visitors to refuges ($25.1 million);

- import duties on arms and ammunition ($18.5 million); and

- 70% of certain refuge entrance fees ($0.15 million). * * *

The predictability of MBCF funding makes it assume special importance in the FWS budget. This contrasts with LWCF funding, which has fluctuated significantly from year to year. * * *

Until the 1960s, federal wildlife refuges were not governed by any single law. Each unit was administered under the standards of the legislation or executive order under which it was created. Then, in 1962, Congress enacted the Refuge Recreation Act, 16 U.S.C. § 460k, which provided that the Secretary could administer Refuges for "public recreation when in his judgment public recreation can be an appropriate incidental or secondary use: Provided, That such public recreation use shall be permitted only to the extent that is practicable and not inconsistent with . . . the primary objectives for which each particular area is established." *Id.* In 1966, Congress confirmed that the Secretary had authority to allow not only recreation consistent with refuge objectives but other activities as well. In the National Wildlife Refuge System Administration Act, 16 U.S.C. § 668dd & 668ee, Congress authorized the Secretary of the Interior to "permit the use of any area within the System for any purpose, including but not limited to hunting, fishing, public recreation and accommodations, and access whenever he determines that such uses are *compatible* with the major purposes for which such areas were established." 16 U.S.C. § 668dd(d)(1)(a) (emphasis added).

The compatibility standard of the Refuge System Administration Act became the touchstone for wildlife refuge management. It also produced a good number of disputes. The result has been a few cases indicating that the compatibility standard created judicially enforceable limits on the discretion of FWS to allow secondary uses, *see, e.g., Defenders of Wildlife v. Andrus*, 455 F. Supp. 446, 449 (D. D.C. 1978) (finding that regulations permitting motorboats with unlimited horsepower on the Ruby Lake National Wildlife Refuge violated the consistency requirements of the Refuge Recreation Act), and a number of other cases upholding FWS's decision to allow secondary uses within wildlife refuges. *See, e.g., Humane Society of the United States v. Lujan*, 768 F. Supp. 360 (D. D.C. 1991) (rejecting challenge to FWS's decision to allow deer hunting within the Mason Neck

National Wildlife Refuge). Over the years, one of the great concerns of wildlife conservationists was that FWS was merely paying lip service to the compatibility standard. This concern was somewhat alleviated in 1993, when, as a result of a lawsuit filed by the National Audubon Society, the Clinton administration reached a settlement agreement under which it agreed to make a written compatibility determination for any new secondary use of a wildlife refuge. In 1996, President Clinton went further and issued an executive order that established a hierarchy of purposes for the Refuge System with preservation as the dominant goal. Exec. Order 12,996, 61 Fed. Reg. 13,647 (Mar. 25, 1996).

The 1993 settlement, along with the Executive Order and a 1989 GAO Report that had been highly critical of refuge management, paved the way for passage of the 1997 National Wildlife Refuge System Improvement Act, 16 U.S.C. § 668dd & 668ee, which now functions as the basic organic act for the Wildlife Refuges just as FLPMA serves as the organic act for the public lands managed by the BLM. Although the Improvement Act modified and changed the 1966 Refuge Administration Act, it did not repeal it. Indeed, it left intact the basic policy of the 1966 Act that activities unrelated to the purpose for which a wildlife refuge was created may be permitted if they are wildlife-compatible. 16 U.S.C. § 668dd(d)(1). On the other hand, the Improvement Act places greater emphasis on maintaining the "biological integrity, diversity, and environmental health" of the refuges, *id.* § 668dd(a)(4)(B), and, following the approach taken in President Clinton's executive order, it establishes a hierarchy of management purposes. The primary purpose remains management for the conservation and restoration of "the fish, wildlife, and plant resources and their habitats" and management in accordance with the directives of the legislation or executive order creating the particular refuge. *Id.* § 668dd(a)(2)–(3). But to the extent management for secondary and compatible purposes is allowed, the Improvement Act gives express priority to compatible *wildlife-dependent* "recreational uses involving hunting, fishing, wildlife observation and photography, and environmental education," over uses that are potentially compatible (grazing, motorboating, etc.) but not wildlife-dependent. *Id.* § 668dd(a)(3)(C). Before allowing any secondary use, FWS must prepare a written compatibility determination and allow for public comment. *Id.* § 668dd(d)(3)(A). Finally, like the organic acts for the BLM and Forest Service, the Improvement Act requires the development of a comprehensive management plan for each refuge and then management in conformity with the plan. *Id.* § 668dd(e). *See generally* Michael J. Bean & Melanie J. Rowland, The Evolution of National Wildlife Law 283–305 (3d. ed. 1997); Robert L. Fischman, *The National Wildlife Refuge System and the Hallmarks of Modern Organic Legislation*, 29 Ecology L.Q. 457 (2002).

B. Wild and Scenic Rivers

The Wild and Scenic Rivers Act, 16 U.S.C. §§ 1271–1287, provides that certain selected rivers which "possess outstandingly remarkable scenic, recreational, geologic, fish and wildlife, historic, cultural, or other similar values, shall be preserved in free-flowing condition, and that they and their immediate environments shall be protected for the benefit and enjoyment of present and future generations." 16 U.S.C. § 1271.

> Rivers may come into the System either by congressional designation or state nomination to the Secretary of the Interior. Congress initially designated 789 miles in 8 rivers as part of the National Wild and Scenic Rivers System. Congress began expanding the System in 1972, and made substantial additions in 1976 and in 1978 (413 miles in 3 rivers, and 688 miles in 8 rivers, respectively). As with the National Wilderness Preservation System, the National Wild and Scenic Rivers System was more than doubled by designation of rivers in Alaska in ANILCA in 1980. In January 1981, Interior Secretary Cecil Andrus approved 5 rivers designated by the state of California, increasing the System mileage by another 20% (1,235 miles). The first additions under the Reagan Administration were enacted into law in 1984, with the addition of 5 rivers including more than 300 miles. The next large addition came in 1988, with the designation of more than 40 river segments in Oregon, adding 1,400 miles. In 1992, 14 Michigan river segments totaling 535 miles were added. The 106th and 107th Congresses added new designations to the system which now includes 163 river units with 11,302.9 miles in 38 states and Puerto Rico.

Carol Hardy Vincent et al., *Federal Land Management Agencies: Background on Land and Resource Management*, Congressional Research Report, RL32393, 43–48 (Aug. 2, 2004). Once a river has been designated as part of the Wild and Scenic Rivers System, it must

> be administered in such manner as to protect and enhance the values which caused it to be included in said system without, insofar as is consistent therewith, limiting other uses that do not substantially interfere with public use and enjoyment of these values.

16 U.S.C. § 1281. This duty to "protect and enhance" applies not just to management of the river itself but also to management of the watershed. Section 12 of the Act provides that

> The Secretary of the Interior, the Secretary of Agriculture, and the head of any other Federal department or agency having jurisdiction over any lands which include, border upon, or are adjacent to, any river included within the National Wild and Scenic Rivers System ... shall take such action respecting management policies, regulations, contracts, plans, affecting such lands, ... as may be necessary to protect such rivers in accordance with the purposes of this chapter.

Id. § 1283(a). Finally, as of 1986, the Act required that the federal agency charged with administering a component of the Wild and Scenic Rivers System must "prepare a comprehensive management plan for such river segment to provide for the protection of the river values." *Id.* § 1274(d). *See generally* Charlton H. Bonham, *The Wild and Scenic Rivers Act and the Oregon Trilogy*, 21 PUB. LAND & RESOURCES L. REV. 109, 117–26 (2000).

The focus of litigation under the WSRA has been on Section 10's command that river values be protected and enhanced "without, insofar as is consistent therewith, limiting other uses that do not substantially interfere with public use and enjoyment of these values." 16 U.S.C. § 1281. Although this standard, combined with an arbitrary and capricious standard of review, affords significant discretion to federal agencies in their management of river segments, in a few cases courts have found agencies in violation of Section 10's command. *See, e.g., Oregon Natural Desert*

Ass'n v. Singleton, 75 F. Supp. 2d 1139, 1152 (D. Or. 1999) (ordering BLM to exclude cattle from the Owyhee River corridor to comply with the WSRA); *Oregon Natural Desert Ass'n v. Green*, 953 F. Supp. 1133 (D. Or. 1997) (finding BLM's management plan for the Donner and Blitzen River in violation of the WSRA because it did not consider excluding cattle from the river area). *But see Hells Canyon Alliance v. United States Forest Service*, 227 F.3d 1170 (9th Cir. 2000) (rejecting challenge by nonmotorized boaters to management plan providing specified periods for motorized water craft use on wild section of the river and emphasizing that the WSRA did not prohibit any interference but "substantial" interference).

C.   THE LAND AND WATER CONSERVATION FUND AND FEDERAL REACQUISITION OF LAND AND RESOURCES

Historically, it has most often been the case that national parks, monuments, or refuges have been created by the reservation of public lands. Early on it was apparent that reservation of existing public lands would not be sufficient to accomplish certain preservation goals. In some cases, desirable private land might adjoin or be intermixed with a federal designation. A portion of the watershed of a national park might, for example, be privately owned. In other cases, private land might be critical habitat or have other qualities that the public would like to preserve. A variety of statutes allow the United States to purchase private land, or exchange federal for private land, to obtain these public benefits. Perhaps the most prominent of these statutes is the Land and Water Conservation Fund [LWCF], Act of Sept. 3, 1964, Pub. L. No. 88–578, 78 Stat. 897, which Congress passed in 1964 to provide money for the acquisition of land to support outdoor recreation. 16 U.S.C. 460*l*–4. According to a report from the Congressional Research Service, the LWCF

> * * * has been the principal federal source of monies to acquire new recreation lands. Four federal agencies—the Park Service, Bureau of Land Management, Fish and Wildlife Service, and Forest Service—receive a portion of these funds. The remainder is a matching grants program to assist states (and localities) in acquiring and developing recreation sites and facilities. The fund accumulates $900 million annually from designated sources. Congress allocates these funds through appropriations each year. * * *

> These four [federal] agencies have used LWCF funds to acquire approximately 4.5 million acres, an area slightly smaller than New Jersey. (Viewed in a different way, 4.5 million acres is less than 1% of the almost 672 million acres owned by the federal government.) Another portion of the LWCF, administered by the NPS, provides matching grants to states for recreation planning, land acquisition, and facility development. These grants have funded about 38,000 state and local projects. Recipients have acquired approximately 2.3 million acres and have developed recreation facilities at about 27,000 of these projects. Acquisitions funded through LWCF grants must remain in recreation use in perpetuity. * * *

> The LWCF is a "trust fund" that accumulates revenues from federal outdoor recreation user fees, the federal motorboat fuel tax and surplus property sales. To supplement these sources to reach the authorized level of $900 million, it accumulates revenues from oil and gas leases on the Outer Continental Shelf (OCS). During the past decade, the OCS revenues have

accounted for more than 90% of the deposits each year (and almost 100% in most recent years).

The LWCF is not a true trust fund in the way "trust fund" is generally understood in the private sector. The fund is credited with revenues totaling to $900 million annually, but Congress must appropriate funds; unappropriated funds remain in the U.S. Treasury and can be spent for other federal activities. Interest is not accrued on the accumulated unauthorized balance that has been credited to the LWCF account. In addition, the LWCF is subject to earmarks and other directions from Congress during the annual appropriations process. From FY1965 through FY2005, $28.1 billion has been credited to the LWCF. However, only about half that amount—$14.3 billion—has been appropriated.

* * *

Jeffrey Zinn, *Land and Water Conservation Fund: Current Status and Issues*, Congressional Research Report, RS21503 (Feb. 14, 2005).

Although the LWCF may be the most prominent federal acquisition program, there are a number of additional sources of federal funding and authority that support federal acquisition of private lands.

James R. Rasband & Megan E. Garrett, *A New Era in Public Land Policy? The Shift Toward Reacquisition of Land and Natural Resources*, 53 ROCKY MTN. MIN. L. INST. 11–1, 11–21 to 11–26 (2007).

In the 2004 Appropriations Act for Interior and Related Agencies, the House Report directed the Secretaries of Interior and Agriculture to develop "a long-term national plan outlining the acreage goals and conservation objectives for Federal land acquisition." In response the agencies published in February 2005 a National Land Acquisition Plan. [T]he Plan identifies three goals that motivate its reacquisition program: protecting the "[n]ation's natural, cultural and heritage resources;" providing recreation opportunities for America; and improving the quality of life for the communities served by the agencies. To achieve these goals, the agencies emphasize that they will employ "a suite of tools that include cooperative conservation and land acquisition." In addition to the LWCF . . . , that suite of tools includes several other programs. . . .

North American Wetland Conservation Act (NAWCA). NAWCA was enacted in 1989, and provides funding to FWS for acquisition of wetland habitat, with a particular focus on protecting and restoring migratory bird habitat. The program works by providing matching grants, both internationally and domestically, for projects that accomplish this goal. In the United States, about 5.8 million acres have been enrolled in this program, providing long-term protection of the wetlands. Another portion of the program, the "small grants" program, has protected another 117,818 acres of land.

Migratory Bird Conservation Fund (MBCF). The MBCF, which is funded primarily by the sale of duck stamps and by import duties on arms and ammunition, is a fairly significant source of funding for the Fish and Wildlife Service. MBCF funding is generally in the neighborhood of $40–$50 million per year and can be used to fund the acquisition of land within wildlife refuges. Since its inception, over 4 million acres have been acquired by FWS by fee purchase, easement, or lease with revenue from the MBCF.

Forest Legacy Program. The Forest Service's Forest Legacy Program, which was created as part of the 1990 Farm bill and is now funded as part of the LWCF, works in partnership with states to protect environmentally sensitive forests, either through fee simple purchase or the use of conservation easements. As of February 2006, the program had protected over 1.4 million acres of land.

Forest Stewardship Program. Recognizing that almost half of the nation's forests (45%, or 354 million acres) are owned by non-industrial private owners, the Forest Stewardship Program provides technical assistance to private landowners for preparation of forest management plans, which can include conservation easements. Under the program, plans have been developed for more than 25 million acres of private forest land.

Farm and Ranch Lands Protection Program. The Farm and Ranch Lands Protection Program "provides matching funds to State, Tribal, or local governments and non-governmental organizations with existing farm and ranch land protection programs to purchase conservation easements." In order to be eligible for grants under this program, the land must meet various requirements, inter alia, have a conservation plan, be under private ownership, and "[c]ontain prime, unique, or other productive soil or historical or archaeological resources." As of 2003, this Program had protected more than 300,000 acres in 42 states.

Cooperative Endangered Species Conservation Fund. In section 6 of the Endangered Species Act, Congress created the Cooperative Endangered Species Conservation Fund. The fund provides financial assistance to states and territories to implement conservation projects, to develop habitat conservation plans, to obtain land associated with approved habitat conservation plans and to acquire habitat in support of approved species recovery plans. In FY 2006, approximately $77 million in funding was available for these purposes and $60 million of that amount was spent on acquisition.

Private Stewardship Grants Program. FWS also administers a Private Stewardship Program that awards grants on a competitive basis to private individuals "and groups engaged in . . . voluntary conservation efforts that benefit . . . listed, proposed or candidate species." Since the Program's initiation in 2002, FWS awarded approximately $7 million per year to landowners willing to initiate projects to benefit imperiled species.

Wetlands Reserve Program. The Wetlands Reserve Program is administered by the Natural Resources Conservation Service and aims to "protect, restore and enhance wetlands" on private property. It pays for conservation easements and restoration costs associated with retiring marginal farmlands and protecting and restoring those farmlands as wetlands. As of April 2007, approximately 1.9 million acres were enrolled in the program, close to the 2,275,000 acre limit allowed by the Farm Bill.

Farmable Wetlands Program. The Farmable Wetlands Program is managed by the Farm Service Agency within the Department of Agriculture. Similar to the Wetlands Reserve Program, it is directed at restoring and protecting "farmed and prior converted wetlands." The program is voluntary and limited to restoration of one million acres of farmable wetlands and up to 100,000 acres in any state. As of the beginning of 2005, the Farmable Wetlands Program had enrolled 122,800 acres of land.

Partners for Fish and Wildlife Program. The Partners for Fish and Wildlife Program provides "technical assistance and cost-share incentives" to private landowners and Indian tribes "to restore fish and wildlife habitats." Between its inception in 1987 and 2006, the program had established agreements with more than 41,000 private landowners and had restored or enhanced two million acres of uplands, 800,000 acres of wetlands, and 6,500 miles of stream habitat.

QUESTIONS AND DISCUSSION

1. Suppose that at a particular wildlife refuge the Fish and Wildlife Service determines that cattle grazing is compatible with the primary purpose of managing the refuge to promote conservation but that the grazing is driving the resident bison herd into a part of the refuge less accessible to visitors who enjoy photographing and watching the bison. May FWS continue to allow the grazing?

2. There has been little litigation interpreting the 1997 National Wildlife Refuge System Improvement Act. In one case a district court rejected a challenge to FWS's decision not to issue a license for a commercial canoe enterprise to operate within the Niobrara NWR. *See Niobrara River Ranch, L.L.C. v. Huber*, 277 F. Supp. 2d 1020 (D. Neb. 2003). Probably the most important interpretation to date has been the panel's decision in *Wilderness Society v. United States Fish & Wildlife Service*, 316 F.3d 913 (9th Cir. 2003) which was vacated by the Ninth Circuit's *en banc* decision in the same case that is excerpted in the wilderness section of this chapter (page 649). 353 F.3d 1051 (9th Cir. 2003) (en banc). Because the en banc court found that FWS's proposed salmon enhancement project violated the Wilderness Act, it never reached the question, addressed by the panel, of whether the project was compatible with the primary purposes of the Kenai National Wildlife Refuge. The panel had found that the project was a compatible use of the refuge and offered the following rationale.

> The Refuge Act tells the Service to permit only those uses within the Refuge that "are compatible with the major purposes" for which the area was established. 16 U.S.C. § 668dd(d)(1)(A). Congress has clearly delegated to the Secretary the authority to determine whether a use is "compatible" with those purposes. *Id.* ("The Secretary is authorized, under such regulations as he may prescribe, to ... permit the use of any area within the System for any purpose ... *whenever he determines* that such uses are compatible with the major purposes for which such areas were established." (emphasis added)). The definition of "compatible use" similarly confers broad discretion: " 'compatible use' means a wildlife-dependent recreational use or any other use of a refuge that, *in the sound professional judgment of the Director,* will not materially interfere with or detract from the ... purposes of the refuge." 16 U.S.C. § 668ee(1) (emphasis added).

> Plaintiffs argue that the Project is incompatible with the first stated purpose of the Refuge: to "conserve fish and wildlife populations and habitats in their natural diversity." ANILCA § 303(4)(B)(i). The Service defines "natural diversity" to mean the "number and relative abundance of native species which would occur without human interference." Final Plan at 174.

> Again, the ambiguity in the text is apparent. Is the purpose of the Refuge to conserve the number and relative abundance of native species within the Refuge as they would be without human interference from *outside* the Refuge? If so, then a restoration program may be "compatible." Or, is the purpose of the Refuge to leave the Refuge wholly untouched so that, whatever a species'

"natural diversity" is or becomes, no human interference may occur? Also, does "diversity" refer to the number of species within a Refuge, or to genetic diversity within a single species?

Perhaps more important to our analysis is the fact that the statute refers not to a *single* purpose, but instead refers in the plural to "the major purposes" for which the refuge is established. 16 U.S.C. § 668dd(d)(1)(A). When the *entire* Refuge Act is considered, it becomes apparent that one of the *other* major purposes may be to maintain the size of a population of fish even if that result requires artificial aquaculture activities in a refuge. * * *

The Service's decision that the Project is "compatible" with the purposes of the Refuge is entitled to deference. Considering the ambiguities within the list of statutory purposes and within the underlying definition of "natural diversity," the Service's conclusion that the Project could continue is permissible. Further, a use need not *support* Refuge purposes in order to be compatible, as the definition clearly provides. In order to be "compatible," a use simply must not "materially interfere" with stated Refuge purposes. The Service concluded that this use did not so interfere. Because that is a reasonable conclusion, we must affirm the decision of the Service.

316 F.3d at 925–27. Do you agree with the panel's reasoning? If you think the panel was correct to defer to the FWS, do you agree with FWS's interpretation of compatibility? Is the project compatible with the primary purpose of wildlife refuges to conserve and, if necessary, restore fish, wildlife, and plant resources and their habitats? Does the project conserve the "natural diversity" of the Kenai refuge as required by ANILCA, the Refuge's enabling legislation?

3. How might the source of funds used to acquire Wildlife Refuges impact refuge management? Does public choice theory provide any insight?

4. The most prominent debate over the management of national wildlife refuges has been over whether to allow exploration and drilling for oil in the 19 million acre Arctic National Wildlife Refuge (ANWR). You may want to return to the ANWR case study in Chapter 1 (page 67) at this point.

5. There has been quite a bit of opposition in some quarters of the West to additional funding for the Land and Water Conservation Fund. In fact, one rallying cry in the West has been that there should be "no net gain" of federal land ownership. What do you think is the basis for this opposition? Does the concern have any justification?

6. Why is it that most of Congress supports the LWCF in concept but has so rarely appropriated all of the available funds? The fact that the LWCF requires Congress to annually appropriate funds from the $900 million credited to the LWCF has been one of its most criticized features. LWCF supporters have long advocated altering the LWCF to make it a true trust fund under which the money allocated to the LWCF cannot be used for other purposes. In 2000, Congress looked set to take a significant step in this direction. The Conservation and Reinvestment Act (CARA), H.R. 701, 106th Cong. (2000) proposed to guarantee $3 billion per year for 15 years to a number of different conservation programs. The money was to come from Outer Continental Shelf Lands Act royalties. Although CARA passed the House by a wide margin (315 to 103), it died before it reached the floor of the Senate, partly because of appropriation committee concerns about ceding power and partly because of the concerns of property rights advocates who feared additional public ownership in the West. It also died because House and Senate appropriators put forward a substitute bill dubbed "CARA-lite" which Congress ultimately passed. CARA-lite authorized additional spending of approximately $1.6 billion per year for six years for various conservation programs under the aegis of the LWCF. Pub. L. No. 106–291 (Oct. 11, 2000). CARA-lite, however, remained largely dependent upon federal budget issues and the decisions of the House and Senate appropriations committees. As it has turned out, the appropriations committees have failed to fully fund CARA-lite as well. *See* Jeffrey Zinn, *Land and Water Conservation Fund: Current Status and Issues*, Congressional Research Report, RS21503 (Feb. 14, 2005), at CRS–3 (table reflecting total LWCF appropriations).

7.   Two prominent uses of the LWCF were the Clinton administration's negotiation of purchase and exchange agreements for the New World Mine near Yellowstone National Park and the Headwaters ancient redwood grove in California. The New World Mine exchange arose out of a plan by Noranda, a Canadian mining company, to extract an estimated $800 million in gold, silver, and copper from Forest Service lands upstream from Yellowstone National Park, the Wild and Scenic Clarks Fork of the Yellowstone River, and the Absaroka–Beartooth Wilderness. Responding to significant opposition to the potential environmental hazards posed by the mine, Noranda and its subsidiary, Crowne Butte, agreed with the Department of the Interior to trade all of its claims in the New World Mine District, covenant not to pursue future mining in the area, and to establish a $22.5 million escrow account to be applied towards cleanup of existing pollution in the area in return for an anticipated $65 million worth of federal lands and the settlement of pending and future litigation related to the mine. Congress appropriated the money from the Land and Water Conservation Fund, and the President signed the deal into law on November 20, 1997. *See* Pub. L. No. 105–83, § 502, 111 Stat. 1543, 1614–15 (1997). *See also Clinton Signs Money Bill; Vetoes New World Mine Transfer*, PUBLIC LANDS NEWS, Nov. 27, 1997, at 1; Bob Ekey, *The New World Agreement: A Call For Reform of The 1872 Mining Law*, 18 PUB. LAND & RESOURCES L. REV. 151, 152 (1997); Murray D. Feldman, *The New Public Land Exchanges: Trading Development Rights in One Area for Public Resources in Another*, 43 ROCKY MTN. MIN. L. INST. 2–1, 2–16 to 2–18 (1997) (discussing the deal and other administration efforts to use land exchanges to protect sensitive areas).

The Headwaters grove exchange grew out of concerns over the logging of what was the largest old-growth stand of coastal redwoods in private hands. In 1996, Pacific Lumber, which had previously been enjoined from harvesting parts of the forest that were critical habitat for the endangered Marbled Murrelet, *see Marbled Murrelet v. Babbitt*, 83 F.3d 1060 (9th Cir. 1996), *cert. denied*, 519 U.S. 1108 (1997), began threatening to "salvage log" the trees in the Headwaters forest and also initiated a takings claim, arguing that the government had effectively turned the company's forest into a wildlife preserve. In response to public outcry over the threatened logging and the fear that Pacific Lumber's takings claim might succeed, the Interior Department and the State of California negotiated an agreement to buy the Headwaters and other forest tracts for $380 million. In the same legislation as the New World mine deal, Congress appropriated $250 million from the Land and Water Conservation Fund toward acquisition of the Headwaters forest. *See* Pub. L. No. 105–83, § 501, 111 Stat. 1543, 1610–11 (1997); *Clinton Signs Money Bill; Vetoes New World Mine Transfer*, PUBLIC LANDS NEWS, Nov. 27, 1997, at 1–2; William Booth, *Calif., U.S. to Pay $495 Million For Ancient Redwood Grove*, WASH. POST, Sept. 2, 1998, at A3; Feldman, *supra*, at 2–24 to 2–25.

Using the LWCF for the Headwaters and New World Mine deals drew opposition in some quarters. Some believed that the developers were effectively shaking down the government in circumstances where the government could have simply regulated the development to protect the resources. *See* Ryan Lizza, *Gold Diggers: How Developers Mine the Government*, THE NEW REPUBLIC, May 1998, at 17. Do you think these two cases were appropriate uses of the LWCF? Is regulation and litigation a better answer? What principles should guide use of the LWCF?

8. Between 1964, which was the year in which both the LWCF and the Wilderness Act were enacted, and 2006, the total acreage managed by the BLM, FS, NPS, and FWS in the lower 48 states "increased from 371 million acres ... to 390.8 million acres ..., a gain of approximately 19.8 million acres, which is about the size of the state of Maine, and about nine and one-half times the size of Yellowstone National Park." James R. Rasband & Megan E. Garrett, *A New Era in Public Land Policy? The Shift Toward Reacquisition of Land and Natural Resources*, 53 ROCKY MTN. MIN. L. INST. 11–1, 11–28 (2007). This increase is a function of the LWCF and the various other programs described in the text above as well as federal land exchanges and other purchases. What do you think accounts for this increase in federal ownership? Is the trend likely to continue? What are its implications for natural resource policy?

VII. PRESERVATION ON MULTIPLE USE LANDS

A. PROTECTING LAND IN A MULTIPLE USE REGIME

Although the last century saw millions of acres set aside as parks, monuments, refuges, and wilderness areas, a still greater amount of public land, managed by the BLM and the Forest Service, continues to be managed for "multiple use and sustained yield." *See* FLPMA, 43 U.S.C. § 1732(a) (directing the Secretary of the Interior to employ multiple use management principles); Multiple–Use, Sustained–Yield Act of 1960, 16 U.S.C. § 529 (similar direction for Secretary of Agriculture). "Multiple use" and "sustained yield" are defined in FLPMA as follows:

> (c) The term "multiple use" means the management of the public lands and their various resource values so that they are utilized in the combination that will best meet the present and future needs of the American people; making the most judicious use of the land for some or all of these resources or related services over areas large enough to provide sufficient latitude for periodic adjustments in use to conform to changing needs and conditions; the use of some land for less than all of the resources; a combination of balanced and diverse resource uses that takes into account the long-term needs of future

generations for renewable and nonrenewable resources, including, but not limited to, recreation, range, timber, minerals, watershed, wildlife and fish, and natural scenic, scientific and historical values; and harmonious and coordinated management of the various resources without permanent impairment of the productivity of the land and the quality of the environment with consideration being given to the relative values of the resources and not necessarily to the combination of uses that will give the greatest economic return or the greatest unit output. * * *

(h) The term "sustained yield" means the achievement and maintenance in perpetuity of a high-level annual or regular periodic output of the various renewable resources of the public lands consistent with multiple use.

43 U.S.C. § 1702. *See also* Multiple–Use, Sustained–Yield Act of 1960, 16 U.S.C. § 531 (giving similar definitions with respect to national forest management). As revealed in the definition, multiple use management gives the agencies wide latitude in choosing how the public lands will be used. The agencies are to decide upon some "combination of balanced and diverse resource uses" that includes not only traditional commodity and extractive uses like range, timber, and minerals but also more preservation-minded uses like "watershed, wildlife and fish, and natural scenic, scientific and historical values." 43 U.S.C. § 1702.

Because the multiple use standard gives such wide discretion to the BLM and the Forest Service, the lands managed by those agencies have triggered perhaps the most frequent and bitter disputes about public land management as different interests have worked to encourage the agencies to exercise their discretion in favor of particular resource uses and values. Thus, commodity and extractive interests have urged the agencies in one direction, preservation interests have pushed in another, and recreation and other interests have tugged in still more directions. The same push and pull has occurred within the agencies themselves as different administrations have emphasized different multiple use values.

Although different administrations have been more or less amenable to the preservation side of multiple use management, as a general matter it is fair to say that the focus of the BLM and the Forest Service has remained on extractive and commodity uses of the land they manage. In light of that focus, in most conversations about the public lands, "multiple use management" is understood to mean extractive and commodity use management, although that is not what FLPMA says. While it is perhaps a stretch to say that the "multiple use" vocabulary has been captured by industry, it does often seem to be the case that BLM field officers feel an obligation to allow drilling, exploration, or other extractive activities on any lands open to "multiple use." Indeed, to many ears, the title of this section—Protecting Land in a Multiple Use Regime—may seem incongruous. Nevertheless, any account of preservation on the public lands must include multiple use lands because even though they are not designated specifically for protective purposes and have not generally been managed that way, as a matter of administrative discretion, they can be managed to accomplish preservation objectives.

The exercise of multiple use discretion to accomplish preservation can occur in a wide variety of ways, most of which are discussed in separate chapters. Chapter 3, for example, discussed the foundational multiple use decisions made in the land use planning process under which the public lands are effectively zoned for different resource values, including preservation. FLPMA specifically provides that the management decisions taken under a land use plan can include the "exclusions . . . of one or more of the principal or major uses." 43 U.S.C. § 1712(e)(1). The Act also directs the BLM "[i]n the development and revision of land use plans" to "give priority to the designation and protection of areas of critical environmental concern [ACECs]." 43 U.S.C. § 1712(c)(3). These ACECs are defined as

> areas within the public lands where special management attention is required (when such areas are developed or used or where no development is required) to protect and prevent irreparable damage to important historic, cultural, or scenic values, fish and wildlife resources or other natural systems or processes, or to protect life and safety from natural hazards.

43 U.S.C. § 1702(a). Although they fall under the broad multiple use umbrella, management of ACECs can be quite similar, if not functionally equivalent, to management of parks, monuments, and wilderness more traditionally associated with preservation. Even where a land use plan "zones" an area for extractive or commodity use, agencies have discretion to manage in ways more or less compatible with preservation. As discussed in Chapter 8, an area might be designated for grazing, but one administration may be more aggressive about limiting harmful grazing practices than another. With respect to mining on the public lands, for example, administrations have differed on whether to make certain lands available for leasing, *see infra* page 692, and in their interpretation of FLPMA's mandate that in allowing multiple uses of the public lands, the BLM prevent "unnecessary or undue degradation of the lands." 43 U.S.C. § 1732(b). *See generally* Chapter 9 (discussing these aspects of the mining law).

The following case illustrates how multiple use management can include management to protect the wilderness qualities of BLM lands even if those lands are not congressionally designated wilderness or wilderness study areas (WSAs), which under FLPMA are to be managed for nonimpairment of their wilderness characteristics pending a congressional decision on their status. 43 U.S.C. § 1782(c).

OREGON NATURAL DESERT ASS'N V. BUREAU OF LAND MANAGEMENT, 531 F.3d 1114 (9th Cir. 2008)

BERZON, CIRCUIT JUDGE:

The Bureau of Land Management (the "BLM" or the "Bureau") is charged with managing "the public lands and their various resource values so that they are utilized in the combination that will best meet the present and future needs of the American people." 43 U.S.C. § 1702(c); *see also id.* § 1712(a), (c). That task, which the Supreme Court has characterized as "enormously complicated," *Norton v. Southern Utah Wilderness Alliance* ("*SUWA*"), 542 U.S. 55, 58 (2004), requires careful planning.

The issue in this case is whether the BLM complied with the requirements of the National Environmental Policy Act of 1969 ("NEPA"), 42 U.S.C. §§ 4321 *et seq.,* when it developed a land use plan covering a large portion of Oregon. The Oregon Natural Desert Association, Committee for the High Desert, and

Western Watersheds Project (collectively "ONDA") contend that the BLM has not done so because it has failed . . . properly to analyze the effects of the plan on lands under its control possessing "wilderness characteristics." . . . The district court granted summary judgment for the BLM. We reverse and remand to the district court with instructions to remand to the Bureau.

The BLM-managed land at issue (which we will sometimes refer to as the "planning area") spreads over roughly four and a half million acres of rugged, remote land in southeastern Oregon's Malheur, Grant, and Harney Counties. These lands lie in the rain shadow of the Cascade and Coastal ranges, and so are sunny and semi-arid. The sagebrush plains that characterize the region are varied by high mountains, rising to over 8,000 feet, and by the valleys of the Malheur and Owyhee rivers. * * *

Federally owned land makes up a large portion of the region, giving the BLM an important role. Its land use planning choices influence both the unique and irreplaceable natural resources of the planning area and the local economy, which is strongly tied to the outdoors. * * *

In August 1995, the BLM, in accordance with its regulations, published a public notice that it would prepare a resource management plan for the region. The Southeastern 8566 Oregon Management Plan (the "Southeast Oregon Plan" or the "Plan") is intended to guide management of the area for the next twenty years.

["Approval of a resource management plan is considered a major Federal action significantly affecting the quality of the human environment." 43 C.F.R. § 1601.0–6. For that reason, the land use planning process implicates . . . NEPA, which requires the preparation of an environmental impact statement ("EIS") for such actions. *See* 42 U.S.C. § 4332(C). * * * To fulfill its purpose, an EIS must "provide full and fair discussion of significant environmental impacts and shall inform decisionmakers and the public of the reasonable alternatives which would avoid or minimize adverse impacts or enhance the quality of the human environment." 40 C.F.R. § 1502.1. To fulfill this mandate, agencies must "consider every significant aspect of the environmental impact of a proposed action" in an EIS. *Pit River Tribe v. U.S. Forest Serv.*, 469 F.3d 768, 781 (9th Cir. 2006) (quoting *Earth Island Inst. v. U.S. Forest Serv.*, 442 F.3d 1147, 1153–54 (9th Cir. 2006)).]

Some three years after initiating the planning process, the BLM announced that the draft Plan and an accompanying EIS were available for public comment. * * * After receiving ONDA's comments on the draft EIS and Plan suggesting the need to give more attention to lands with wilderness characteristics, the Bureau wrote in the final EIS that:

> A global reinventory by BLM to address wilderness values within the planning area is outside the scope of this plan. In accordance with FLPMA, with substantial public input and review, BLM has completed its required evaluation and assessment of wilderness values on public lands with earlier planning efforts. The agency's wilderness recommendations in Oregon derived from those planning efforts have been submitted and are presently awaiting consideration by Congress.

FEIS, Vol. III at 105. . . . The EIS therefore did not consider the effects of the Plan on areas with wilderness characteristics not already designated as WSAs, nor analyze management options for the wilderness values in such areas. * * *

The BLM did consider granting some degree of additional protection from development and other disruptive uses to several hundred thousand acres of land in "areas of critical environmental concern." FEIS, Vol. I at 276–368; *see also* 43 U.S.C. § 1712(c)(3) (requiring the BLM to give priority to area of critical environmental concern in land use planning). These critical areas are broadly defined as "areas within the public lands where special management attention is required ... to protect and prevent irreparable damage to important historic, cultural, or scenic values, fish and wildlife resources, or other natural systems or processes, or to protect life and safety from natural hazards." 43 C.F.R. § 1601.0–5(a). Designation as a critical area does not, of itself, "change or prevent change of the management or use of public lands." *Id.* The Plan, however, contemplated various limitations on ORV use, mineral leasing, and plant collection, among other protections, for such areas.

The critical areas protected by the Southeast Oregon Plan are limited, however. Also, the overlap between the critical area criteria and the statutory definition of wilderness values is only partial. *Compare* 43 C.F.R. § 1601.0–5(a) (defining areas of critical environmental concern) *with* 16 U.S.C. § 1131(c)(1)–(4) (describing wilderness characteristics). As a consequence, the BLM does not structure its critical area decisions to protect wilderness characteristics, nor does designation as a critical area necessarily imply the presence of wilderness characteristics. In fact, several of the areas of critical environmental concern contain roads or other signs of human use that would be incompatible with wilderness values. * * *

In December 2001, ONDA filed a protest with the BLM of the Plan and final EIS.... ONDA ... charged that the BLM had failed to analyze wilderness values in the EIS and Plan.... This failure to provide information on wilderness values, ONDA argued, violated NEPA's requirement that the Bureau engage in fully-informed decisionmaking. ONDA further argued that the BLM's response to ONDA's comments on the draft EIS, in which the Bureau had maintained that its wilderness obligations were at an end with the completion of the 1991 wilderness report, was mistaken. It contended that the BLM had a continuing duty to inventory wilderness values on its lands under 43 U.S.C. § 1711 and that it could protect lands with such values using the broad multiple use authority provided by 43 U.S.C. § 1712. * * *

The BLM denied the protest in September 2002. * * *

2. ONDA's Survey

Because the BLM had not responded to its wilderness concerns, ONDA decided to undertake a survey of land with wilderness characteristics outside of the WSAs, documenting changes that had occurred since November 1980, when the BLM completed the inventory supporting its 1991 preservation recommendations. In doing so, ONDA relied upon wilderness inventory procedures described in the BLM's guidance documents. The wilderness characteristics ONDA reviewed were those described in the Wilderness Act and incorporated into the FLPMA. In February 2004, ONDA submitted the results of its survey to the BLM. * * *

ONDA explained that there had been significant changes since the BLM's last inventory. Lands the BLM had previously determined lacked wilderness characteristics had reverted to a more natural state and, ONDA maintained, now did have such characteristics. Many of these changes occurred, ONDA reported, because little-used roads had deteriorated since November 1980. * * *

In all, the ONDA study concluded that there are now more than 1.3 million acres of land in the planning area outside the WSAs that display wilderness characteristics. The BLM did not, however, alter the Plan or otherwise take action on ONDA's new information.

D. The Litigation

Continuing to pursue the issues raised in its comments and protest, ONDA contended in its complaint that the BLM had violated NEPA by ... "fail[ing] to take a 'hard look' at the environmental consequences of the proposed action, because the Plan and FEIS do not present adequate baseline information and discussion on critical environmental resources and/or resource issues, including ... current conditions of ... non-WSA roadless areas." * * *

[T]he district court ... held that the BLM was not "legally required to perform a wilderness inventory," and so could not be faulted for failing in the EIS to analyze non-WSA land that might now have wilderness characteristics, or to discuss management options for such lands. . . .

ONDA timely appealed.

II. Analysis

A. Standard of Review

... Judicial review of the BLM's compliance with NEPA is governed by the Administrative Procedure Act of 1946 ("APA"), 5 U.S.C. § 551 *et seq. Pit River Tribe,* 469 F.3d at 778. Under the APA, we must "hold unlawful and set aside agency action, findings, and conclusions" if, among other things, they are "arbitrary, capricious, an abuse of discretion, or otherwise not in accordance with law." 5 U.S.C. § 706(2)(A); *see also, e.g., Pit River Tribe,* 469 F.3d at 778 (reviewing an EIS under § 706(2)(A)).

B. Land with Wilderness Characteristics

The BLM did not explicitly consider wilderness values in its EIS, despite ONDA's repeated requests that it discuss and analyze wilderness characteristics on its lands in southeastern Oregon. To determine whether it violated NEPA by failing to do so, we consider the nature of the BLM's authority and obligations with regard to wilderness characteristics and the BLM's rationale for not considering lands with wilderness values. * * *

Here, the BLM is charged with "manag[ing] the public lands under principles of multiple use and sustained yield," 43 U.S.C. § 1732(a), and with developing a resource management plan which would allow it do so, *id.* § 1712(c). . . . Among the BLM's "primary goal[s]" was to "develop management practices that ensure the long-term sustainability of healthy and productive land, consistent with principles of ecosystem management." To fulfill this purpose, then, the EIS supporting the Plan had to consider the land resources and values relevant to its long-term management strategy.

In ONDA's view, the remaining analysis is straightforward: The BLM did not consider wilderness values, despite comments urging it do so. ONDA observes that the Plan itself identifies wilderness as "part of the spectrum of resource values considered in the land use planning process," Plan ROD at 104, and argues that the FLPMA places management of wilderness values squarely within the BLM's land use planning authority. ONDA also observes that the Plan could affect such values on lands outside of the WSAs. So, in light of the Plan's purpose of providing a "comprehensive framework for managing public land," NEPA requires analysis of these issues in the EIS. Because the EIS offers no discussion of non-WSA lands with wilderness values other than a disclaimer of any obligation to consider them, it did not provide a "full and fair discussion" of the impacts of the Plan and the alternatives before the BLM, and so violated NEPA.

The BLM sees the question very differently. In its view, "wilderness characteristics" matter for one, and only one, purpose: They provide criteria to be used in the 43 U.S.C. § 1782 survey of lands to recommend for permanent preservation, which, the Bureau argues, was a "one-time" duty. No other provision of the FLPMA, the Bureau maintains, "requires BLM to conduct inventories of, or otherwise specially consider, 'wilderness characteristics' in land use planning, and BLM completed the [§ 1782] wilderness review in 1991." * * *

The BLM ... acknowledges that it *could* manage its lands to promote such characteristics, just as it could manage its land to promote many other goals, it does not acknowledge wilderness characteristics as a value of the public lands specifically identified by the FLPMA, and so sees no reason to address "wilderness characteristics" as a discrete resource category in its EIS. Following this line of argument, the BLM points out that it has considerable methodological discretion as to how it complies with NEPA and argues that its consideration of the Plan's effects need not embrace "ONDA's notion of the 'wilderness resource,'" as long as it otherwise provides a full and fair discussion of the Plan....

Our question, then, is whether ONDA is right, and wilderness characteristics are among the values the FLPMA specifically assigns to the BLM to manage in land use plans, or whether the BLM is right, and wilderness characteristics have no independent vitality apart from their use in the § 1782 process....

This question is placed in sharper focus because, after the EIS was completed, the BLM entered into a settlement regarding the reach of the BLM's management authority concerning wilderness. In an April 2003 settlement with the state of Utah, the BLM agreed to an interpretation of 43 U.S.C. § 1782 limiting the BLM to a one-time review of areas with wilderness characteristics, for the purpose of recommending such areas for permanent congressional preservation, with the review power expiring "fifteen years after October 21, 1976," *see* 43 U.S.C. § 1782(a). The BLM therefore agreed (1) that it would cease recommending lands for permanent preservation as wilderness; (2) that it would not, going forward, "establish, manage or otherwise treat public lands ... as WSAs or as wilderness ... absent congressional authorization"; and (3) that it would withdraw the 2001 Handbook, which contained guidelines for further wilderness recommendations. *See Utah v. Norton,* 396 F.3d 1281, 1284–85 (10th Cir. 2005) (describing the history of the litigation leading to the settlement); *see generally Utah v. Norton,* 2006 WL 2711798 (D. Utah 2006) (describing the settlement). The settlement, then, tracks—but, as we shall see, only in part—the BLM's position in this case regarding its one-time obligation to consider wilderness characteristics on BLM land.

The Attorney General lacks the power "to agree to settlement terms that would violate the civil laws governing the agency," *United States v. Carpenter,* 526 F.3d 1237, 1242 (9th Cir. 2008) (quoting *Executive Bus. Media, Inc. v. U.S. Dep't of Def.,* 3 F.3d 759, 761 (4th Cir. 1993)), so the Utah settlement is only valid if it comports with the FLPMA, NEPA, and other relevant law. The parties maintain, nonetheless, that we need not directly consider the legality of the 2003 Utah settlement agreement in this case.[12]

---

12. The matter is presently before the Tenth Circuit, *see Utah v. Kempthorne,* No. 06–4240 (10th Cir.). [Eds. On August 4, 2008, the Tenth Circuit decided that it lacked subject matter jurisdiction to hear the case because appellants' claims were not ripe. *Utah v. U.S. Dep't of Interior,* 535 F.3d 1184 (10th Cir. 2008).]

We agree. Wilderness values are among the resources which the BLM can manage under 43 U.S.C. §§ 1712 and 1732. Wilderness characteristics are not simply a checklist to be used in completing the § 1782 survey.... As a result, the BLM's response to ONDA's concerns in the EIS—that, because it had completed the § 1782 survey wilderness characteristics were "outside the scope" of the EIS for the land use plan—was incorrect and, standing alone, does not satisfy NEPA's requirements. * * *

1. Statutory and Regulatory Authority

Read carefully and in context, the FLPMA makes clear that wilderness characteristics are among the values which the BLM can address in its land use plans, and hence, needs to address in the NEPA analysis for a land use plan governing areas which may have wilderness values.

As we have explained, wilderness characteristics are enumerated by the Wilderness Act, in 16 U.S.C. § 1131(c)(1)–(4). They are incorporated into the FLPMA in several ways. In addition to the language of 43 U.S.C. § 1782, 43 U.S.C. § 1702(i) provides that "[t]he term 'wilderness' as used in section 1782 of this title shall have the same meaning as it does in section 1131(c) of Title 16"—which is the Wilderness Act definition. The BLM similarly records in its current land use planning handbook that wilderness characteristics are "naturalness, outstanding opportunities for solitude, and outstanding opportunities for primitive and unconfined recreation," a paraphrase which closely tracks 16 U.S.C. § 1131(1)–(3). BUREAU OF LAND MGMT., U.S. DEP'T OF THE INTERIOR, LAND USE PLANNING HANDBOOK, H–1601–1 ("2005 Handbook") Appx. C 12 (2005)....

As noted earlier, the FLPMA's provision directing the BLM to conduct an initial wilderness review provides that "those roadless areas of five thousand acres or more and roadless islands of the public lands ... having wilderness characteristics described in the Wilderness Act" are to be "identified during the inventory required by section 1711(a)." 43 U.S.C. § 1782(a). Notably, the statute does not direct that areas with wilderness characteristics be identified only as part of recommending such areas for "preservation as wilderness." *Id.* Instead, it contemplates a *"review"* of areas *already* so "identified," *id.* (emphasis added), in the course of the general BLM "inventory of all public lands and their resource and other values," an inventory process which is to be "kept current so as to reflect changes in conditions and to identify new and emerging resource and other values." *Id.* § 1711(a). In other words, reading §§ 1711(a) and 1782(a) together, the statute specifically contemplates that the § 1711(a) inventory process includes identification of wilderness characteristics—including those that are "new and emerging" or which arise from "changes in conditions"—and that it will do so continuously, with no time limit.

As to the BLM's authority to include such identified lands in its management planning, the multiple use management and planning mandates of 43 U.S.C. §§ 1712 and 1732 pertain to the "management of the public lands and their various resource values." *Id.* § 1702(c). Section 1711(a), again, provides for "an inventory of all public lands and their resource and other values." Because wilderness characteristics are to be identified by that inventory, they are, as we earlier explained, necessarily among those "resource and other values." And, as wilderness characteristics are among the "resource and other values" recognized under the FLPMA, they are to be managed as part of the complex task of managing "the various resources without permanent impairment of the productivity of the land and the quality of the environment." *Id.*

§ 1702(c); *see also id.* § 1732(a) ("The Secretary shall manage the public lands under principles of multiple use...."). This management is to be done "in accordance with land use plans developed ... under section 1712 ... when they are available." *Id.* § 1732(a). Land use plans, in turn, must "use and observe the principles of multiple use." *Id.* § 1712(c)(1), whether or not the § 1711 inventory "is available," *id.* § 1712(c)(4).

Once the statute is so understood, it becomes evident that permanent preservation of wilderness using the 43 U.S.C. § 1782 process is just one aspect of the BLM's broader management authority for lands with wilderness characteristics.... At the same time, the BLM's wide authority to "manage the public lands under principles of multiple use and sustained yield," 43 U.S.C. § 1732(a), allows it ample discretion for management of lands with wilderness values. * * *

[T]he BLM could place many lands with wilderness characteristics in special management categories that, while not as protective as the non-impairment standard, still afford considerable protection. Designating some such regions as areas of critical environmental concern is one obvious option. *See* 43 C.F.R. § 1610.7–2. The BLM might also designate such lands "that have ecological or other natural history values of scientific interest" as research natural areas to protect them for research and education. *See id.* §§ 8200.0–1 to 8223.1.

The BLM could also—according to its own representations to the Tenth Circuit in the Utah settlement litigation—adopt for some non-WSA lands with wilderness characteristics a temporary "modified non-impairment" policy, quite different from the permanent non-impairment policy imposed on WSAs by § 1782(c). As the BLM put it in its brief to the Tenth Circuit:

> [The BLM] has the authority under [43 U.S.C. § 1712] to manage lands in a manner that is similar to the non-impairment standard that applies to wilderness study areas under [§ 1782], by emphasizing the protection of wilderness-associated characteristics as a priority over other potential uses.... [U]nder [§ 1712] the agency retains the discretion to change its designation and management of public lands through the land use planning process, whereas [§ 1782(c)] requires BLM to manage lands pursuant to the non-impairment standard 'until Congress has determined otherwise.'

Brief of the Federal Appellees at 41, *Utah v. Kempthorne,* No. 06–4240 (filed Feb. 2007) (footnote omitted, quoting 43 U.S.C. § 1782(c)). Under this standard, the BLM could later—within the time period covered by a particular land use plan, if the plan so provides, or afterwards—reconsider the restrictions on use of the area under the Bureau's multiple use mandate and, perhaps, determine that the non-impairment standard for that particular land with wilderness characteristics should be abandoned. Because such an approach entails alterable rather than permanent protection of land as wilderness, it is not at all equivalent to § 1782(c) protection.

Finally, the BLM could, with adequate consideration during the planning process, decide not to manage some lands with wilderness characteristics so as to preserve those characteristics, but instead manage them for uses which would be inconsistent with long-term wilderness preservation.

Our point, simply put, is that various options for the management of lands with wilderness characteristics remain even if permanent congressional preservation of non-WSA land is no longer an option. As a result, wilderness characteristics retain vitality as a resource category covered by the BLM's multiple-use land use planning mandate. The BLM was therefore incorrect when it asserted, in its responses to ONDA and this court, that it had no duty to inventory or analyze wilderness characteristics because it had years ago completed a § 1782 review. Even assuming its § 1782 obligation was a "one-time" duty, the BLM's authority to manage this statutorily-defined resource nevertheless continues in other ways. * * *

3. Case Law

Our view of the BLM's powers and obligations under NEPA and the FLPMA is further supported by our own cases considering the related question of whether agencies need consider in NEPA documents the roadless character of lands under their management. As we have earlier explained, *see supra* Part I(C)(II), roadlessness is critical to fulfilling the "natural conditions" wilderness characteristic, *see* 16 U.S.C. § 1131(c). And, as roadlessness alone may require NEPA consideration in some circumstances, even though it chiefly relates to only one of several wilderness characteristics, wilderness characteristics themselves must also require NEPA consideration when they are implicated by land use planning efforts.

We analyzed roadlessness in the related context of the United States Forest Service's land management and NEPA responsibilities. In *Smith v. United States Forest Service,* we made clear that "an area's roadless character has . . . environmental significance," and required NEPA analysis. 33 F.3d at 1078. The Forest Service, not unlike the BLM in this case, argued that "the sole significance of [roadlessness] is that the [roadless] parcel is potentially eligible for wilderness designation." *Id.* at 1077. Because the Forest Service was not required to consider permanent protection for the areas at issue, *see id.* at 1074 (citing the Washington State Wilderness Act, Pub.L. No. 98–339, 98 Stat. 299 (1984)), the Forest Service maintained that "the fact that a parcel of . . . land is roadless is, in itself, immaterial and need not be addressed in NEPA documents." *Id.* at 1078. We rejected that argument, observing that roadlessness has environmental significance apart from permanent wilderness preservation and, as a result, "[t]hat the land has been released by Congress for nonwilderness use does not excuse the agency from complying with its NEPA obligations when implementing a land-use program." *Id.* * * *

Because "[r]oadless areas . . . also help conserve some of the last unspoiled wilderness in our country," *Kootenai Tribe of Idaho v. Veneman,* 313 F.3d 1094, 1121 (9th Cir. 2002), there is no reason to suppose that such characteristics, when they appear on BLM land, rather than on Forest Service land, do not implicate the planning process. They therefore also implicate NEPA. And it would be very strange if roadlessness, a key factor in determining one of the wilderness characteristics, was alone worthy of NEPA consideration, while other statutorily-enumerated wilderness characteristics were not. Our roadlessness cases, then, are consistent with our holding that a landscape's wilderness characteristics generally must be considered in NEPA documents prepared for land use plans concerning that landscape, regardless of whether permanent wilderness preservation is an option.

4. The BLM's Response * * *

[T]he BLM provides a laundry list of other resource values that it *did* consider, ranging from animal habitat quality to visual resources. Although it does not argue that its analysis of these other resources was identical to an analysis of wilderness characteristics, it contends that the analysis had the "incidental benefit of capturing the [Southeast Oregon Plan's] effects on many 'wilderness characteristics.'" The BLM supposes, apparently, that members of the public and government decisionmakers might be able to piece together a wilderness characteristics analysis from what the Bureau did say. The BLM is wrong in several regards. * * *

[T]he premises of the argument are wrong. Although the BLM suggests that "wilderness characteristics" is a nebulous term, capable of being addressed simply by generally examining resources having to do with nature, that is not so. As we have discussed at length, "wilderness characteristics" is a carefully-defined statutory concept, originating in the Wilderness Act, incorporated into the BLM's mandate by the FLPMA, and used by the BLM in its own Handbook and by the IBLA in reviewing the BLM's actions. In *Smith,* the Forest Service similarly argued that roadlessness was "merely a synonym" for other resources that it *had* considered. 33 F.3d at 1078. We expressed some sympathy for the idea that it might be possible to address roadlessness by considering other factors, but explained that the Forest Service's analysis had never comprehensively analyzed the land at issue in that case and held that it had to "at the very least, ... acknowledge the existence of the 5,000 acre roadless area" at issue in that case. *See id.* at 1078–79.

So here it is. Even had the BLM professed in the EIS to use such a consideration-by-proxy approach, it is far from clear that it would have provided adequate disclosure of any wilderness values potentially in the planning area. And, in any event, the BLM never purported to have developed such a proxy methodology, by which consideration of other resource types could be melded together to produce an analysis of wilderness characteristics. Instead, it firmly maintained that, because of its § 1782 survey, it need not address the fate of non-WSA lands with wilderness characteristics at all. * * *

5. Conclusion on Wilderness Issues

In sum, the BLM misunderstood the role of wilderness characteristics in its land use planning decisions. Contrary to the understanding it expressed, wilderness characteristics are a value which, under the FLPMA, the Bureau has the continuing authority to manage, even after it has fulfilled its 43 U.S.C. § 1782 duties to recommend some lands with wilderness characteristics for permanent congressional protection. As a result, the BLM's completion of its permanent preservation recommendations for the planning area does not mean that the Bureau may entirely decline to consider wilderness characteristics presently existing in the area.

ONDA drew the BLM's attention to the fact that, in some regions of the planning area not designated as WSAs when the BLM conducted its § 1782 survey prior to November 1980, wilderness characteristics may now be present. In view of the broad management purposes of the Southeast Oregon Plan, and the possibility that the Plan could affect wilderness values, ONDA requested that the BLM give some attention to the matter in its EIS. The BLM's management of any lands with wilderness characteristics is likely to be vigorously debated. It is fairly debatable issues of this kind that NEPA was designed to bring out in the open, for analysis and discussion in the service of sound decisionmaking. The BLM's response to ONDA's concern—that it had completed the § 1782 survey and that it had no further duty to inventory or analyze wilderness characteristics as such—was wrong. It did not provide the "full and fair discussion" of the issue required by NEPA, and also did not properly respond to ONDA's comments. *See* 40 C.F.R. §§ 1502.1, 1503.4.

We therefore vacate the ROD approving the EIS and Plan. *See* 5 U.S.C. § 706(2). We remand to the district court with instructions to remand to the BLM for it to address in some manner in its revised EIS whether, and to what extent, wilderness values are now present in the planning area outside of existing WSAs and, if so, how the Plan should treat land with such values. We prescribe no particular methodology for that consideration. The BLM must, however, do more than simply assert that it need not consider wilderness values because of the completion of the § 1782 process, as it did in the present EIS. * * *

QUESTIONS AND DISCUSSION

1. What are the implications of this decision for BLM's land use planning? If BLM must consider wilderness values outside WSAs, must it manage to protect those values? If not, is the decision likely to produce greater protection of BLM lands with wilderness quality? Why?

2. Resource inventories of resource planning areas can be quite time-consuming and expensive. Does this decision mean that a new land use plan cannot be prepared without preparing a new inventory? Is that what congress intended in Section 201 of FLPMA, 43 U.S.C. § 1711, when it directed the Secretary to "prepare and maintain on a continuing basis an inventory of all public lands and their resource and other values"?

3. Does this decision help explain why the title of this section of the chapter—"Protecting Land in a Multiple Use Regime"—may not be such an oxymoron? Or, does the BLM's litigation position suggest the contrary?

PROBLEM EXERCISE: WILDERNESS REINVENTORY AND THE UTAH SETTLEMENT AGREEMENT

The court in *ONDA v. BLM* mentions the Utah Settlement Agreement with the Department of the Interior. That agreement arose out of a similar dispute in Utah where the Department of the Interior, while Bruce Babbitt was secretary, had actually conducted an additional wilderness inventory of BLM lands. The inventory was described as a "reinventory" because the BLM relied upon its continuous inventorying and land use planning authority under sections 201 and 202 of FLPMA, respectively, rather than on its authority under section 603 to designate wilderness study areas (WSAs). The reinventory found that in addition to the 3.2 million acres originally identified as wilderness study areas in Utah, another roughly 2.6 million acres of BLM lands in Utah had wilderness quality. To distinguish the areas inventoried pursuant to its § 201 authority from those areas originally inventoried and designated WSAs during the 15-year window provided in § 603, the Department of the Interior called the new areas "Wilderness Inventory Areas" or "WIAs."

Utah didn't like the reinventory and the friction only increased when in April 1999, the Department of the Interior Solicitor issued a directive that the BLM should use NEPA to give "careful attention" to any proposal for development within a WIA, including consideration of a "no action" alternative to preserve the area's wilderness characteristics. Later, on January 10, 2001, BLM adopted a new Wilderness Inventory and Study Procedures Handbook which provided that the § 201 WIAs could be designated as WSAs through § 202's land use planning process (at which point they would become § 202 WSAs), after which they would be managed for nonimpairment just as if they were § 603 WSAs. Based on these documents, on August 20, 2001, the Utah BLM State Director instructed all Utah field office managers to manage WIAs so as to prevent any change that might prevent their designation as wilderness. Even before this document, and certainly after, BLM field office managers in Utah declined mineral leases within WIAs despite the fact that almost all such areas were open to leasing under the current land use plans.

At that point, Utah proposed to amend a complaint it had originally filed in a lawsuit to stop the reinventory, in which it had been denied standing on the theory that the reinventory would only label lands as potential wilderness but wouldn't decide how the lands were to be managed. *Utah v. Babbitt*, 137 F.3d 1193 (10th Cir. 1998). The proposed amended complaint alleged that the BLM had improperly adopted a de facto wilderness management standard for WIAs without having amended the relevant land use plans as required by sections 202 and 302 of FLPMA. 43 U.S.C. §§ 1712, 1732(a). In April 2003, the Department of the Interior announced that it had settled the case with Utah. The settlement document provided:

3. The authority of Defendants to conduct wilderness reviews, including the establishment of new WSA's, expired no later than October 21, 1993, with submission of the wilderness suitability recommendations to Congress pursuant to Section 603. As a result, Defendants are without authority to establish post–603 WSAs, recognizing that nothing herein shall be construed to diminish the Secretary's authority under FLPMA to: * * *

   b. utilize the criteria in Section 202(c) to develop and revise land use plans, including giving priority to the designation and protection of areas of critical environmental concern (Section 202(c)(3)). * * *

7. Defendants will not establish, manage or otherwise treat public lands, other than Section 603 WSAs and Congressionally designated wilderness, as WSAs or as wilderness pursuant to the Section 202 process absent congressional authorization.... However, nothing herein is intended to diminish BLM's authority under FLPMA to prepare and maintain on a continuing basis an inventory of all public lands and their resources and other values, as described in FLPMA Section 201. These resources and other values may include, but are not limited to, characteristics that are associated with the concept of wilderness.

The settlement agreement frustrated preservation advocates, particularly when the Interior Department announced that the policy reflected in the settlement applied not only to Utah but also to other public land states where the Interior Department had conducted wilderness reinventories similar to that accomplished in Utah. As mentioned in *ONDA v. BLM*, a lawsuit was filed challenging the settlement agreement. The Tenth Circuit ultimately concluded that it lacked subject matter jurisdiction to resolve the dispute because "the question of whether the settlement violates FLPMA and other statutes turns primarily on the settlement's meaning," which, said the court, was not ripe for consideration in the absence of "a record illustrating how BLM applies the settlement in the context of specific land management decisions." *See Utah v. Department of Interior*, 535 F.3d 1184 (10th Cir. 2008). The court reasoned:

> SUWA [the Southern Utah Wilderness Alliance] develops a detailed argument that wilderness management is just one form of multiple-use management, and that by forbidding [non-impairment management in] areas other than § 603 WSAs, the settlement illegally curtails BLM's § 202 powers. In response, BLM contends that although the settlement forbids designating lands as "WSAs" under § 202, it does nothing to limit BLM's authority to manage lands, including applying policies similar to [the non-impairment standard, if not the non-impairment standard itself] to areas other than § 603 WSAs. In order to reach the merits of this claim, we would have to decide which side has the better reading of the settlement. Specifically, is this "really just a disagreement over nomenclature" as BLM would have us accept, or does the settlement require BLM to rule out certain management options in developing land use plans? BLM's application of the settlement in context may well help answer this question. * * *
>
> In addition, SUWA charges that the settlement violates NEPA by limiting BLM's options during the land use planning process.... By removing the option of WSA designation for three pending land use plan revisions in Utah, SUWA reasons that the settlement "commit[s] BLM to ignoring possible WSA designation in the NEPA analyses...." BLM offers two retorts. First, it argues that because FLPMA precludes the agency from creating any WSAs after § 603's 1993 deadline, such a designation is not within BLM's "reasonable alternatives" when considering land use plans. Second, BLM contends that it may still consider all reasonable options under § 202, including land use plans that "would protect wilderness-associated characteristics to an extent equivalent to the non-impairment standard." Utah apparently disagrees with this view, maintaining in their briefs and at oral argument that, after the settlement, BLM may not manage lands exclusively for wilderness values under § 202. As with SUWA's other arguments, this issue turns on the meaning and force of the settlement, which is unclear at this juncture.

Id. at 1193–94.

Why do you suppose the Department of the Interior settled the case with Utah? What do you think of the practice of making policy via settlement agreement? In this regard consider again the discussion, *supra* page 665, where the Clinton administration agreed to make a written compatibility determination for any new secondary use of a wildlife refuge. Ought such decisions to be made by more formal rulemaking with notice and comment?

If the Interior Department had not settled the case and gone forward to trial on its management of the WIAs, what would have likely been the result? As you consider this question, compare the management directives of the Interior Solicitor's office with the management actions of the Utah BLM prior to the settlement. Which would have been more likely to withstand legal challenge? What does the comparison tell you about the way agencies operate?

What are the BLM's options for implementing the terms of the settlement agreement in its land use planning process? How might *ONDA v. BLM* impact its process? What if, in preparing an EIS for a revised land use plan, the BLM stated that designating § 202 WSAs was not a legitimate alternative but that it was willing to consider the alternative of designating all former wilderness inventory areas (WIAs) as Areas of Critical Environmental Concern (ACECs) and of managing them for nonimpairment of their wilderness characteristics? Might SUWA still sue? Would the *ONDA v. BLM* court find this permissible? Why would SUWA care about the label under which the BLM managed for nonimpairment? Alternatively, might Utah view managing ACECs for nonimpairment as a breach of the settlement agreement? Would it violate the settlement's provisions described above?

———

B. FLPMA Withdrawal Authority

While the BLM and the Forest Service have the ability to achieve preservation objectives through planning and land management, an even more direct source of authority to protect public lands is their authority under FLPMA to make specific withdrawals. *See* 43 U.S.C. § 1714. Recall that historically the term "withdrawal" has referred to the removal of land from the applicability of a particular disposition statute. Federal land, for example, might be withdrawn from entry for mineral exploration. A withdrawal does not decide the purpose for which the federal land will be used. It simply eliminates one potential use. Withdrawals were distinguished from "reservations" which occurred when the government decided to retain public lands for a specified purpose, such as a national park. In practice distinguishing withdrawals from reservations has not always been easy. The broader the withdrawal, the more like a reservation the withdrawal looks. *See generally* Dana & Fairfax, *supra*, at 29–30. Recognizing the difficulty of drawing the distinction, FLPMA's definition of "withdrawal" encompasses the traditional understanding of both withdrawals and reservations, empowering the Secretary of the Interior to withhold an area "from settlement, sale, location, or entry" or to "reserve[e] the area for a particular public purpose." 43 U.S.C. § 1702(j).

Before elaborating upon the nature of the agencies' FLPMA withdrawal authority, it is necessary to hark back to Chapter 2 and the Supreme Court's decision in *Midwest Oil* that the president had authority to withdraw lands from entry under the Oil Placer Act and set them aside as a naval petroleum reserve. *See supra* page 133. As the Court saw it, congressional acquiescence in the president's withdrawal amounted to an implied delegation of withdrawal authority from Congress. The Court's decision in *Midwest Oil* confirmed the validity of a range of prior executive withdrawals including 99 Indian reservations and 44 bird refuges. Together with the president's authority under the Antiquities Act to proclaim national monuments, discussed *supra*, the implied withdrawal authority under *Midwest Oil* gave the president significant authority to designate public lands for preservation without waiting for congressional action. This authority was further enhanced by congressional enactment of the 1910 Pickett Act which gave the president authority to withdraw public lands from all uses except mineral entry for "public purposes to be specified in the orders of withdrawals." Act of June 25, 1910, ch. 421, § 1, 36 Stat. 847 (1910), 43 U.S.C. §§ 141–42 (repealed 1976). Over the years, presidents, and by delegation the Secretary of the Interior, withdrew millions of acres of public lands from various forms of entry. In fact, prior to land use planning, executive withdrawals were the primary method by which federal agencies zoned the public lands. *See generally* David Getches, *Managing the Public Lands: The Authority of the Executive to Withdraw Lands*, 22 Nat. Resources J. 279 (1982); George Cameron Coggins & Robert L. Glicksman, Public Natural Resources Law §§ 10D9–10D12 (2003).

The broad withdrawal authority exercised by the executive branch generated significant tension over the years. Those whose interests were negatively impacted by such withdrawals argued that it was Congress, and not the executive, that should be the primary arbiter of what uses were allowed on the public lands. After all, they said, the Property Clause gives *Congress* the power to "dispose of and make all needful Rules and Regulations respecting the Territory or other Property belonging to the United States." U.S. Const. art. IV, § 3, cl. 2. Proponents of executive authority, on the other hand, argued that the executive and its land management agencies were better situated to act quickly to preserve the public interest in the public lands and that Congress could always reverse executive withdrawals if it chose to do so. When Congress passed FLPMA in 1976, it attempted to deal with this conflict. It did so by repealing the Pickett Act and 29 other statutes granting executive withdrawal authority, as well as by specifically rejecting the president's implied withdrawal authority under *Midwest Oil*. *See* Pub. L. No. 94–579, § 704(a), 90 Stat. 2744, 2792 (1976). Congress, however, left untouched the president's authority to create national monuments under the Antiquities Act. It also enacted elaborate procedures under which the Secretary of the Interior could withdraw public lands.

FLPMA's withdrawal procedure, set forth in Section 204, provide for three categories of withdrawals—withdrawals of less than 5000 acres, which can be made for "such period of time" as the Secretary "deems desirable for a resource use"; withdrawals of more than 5000 acres, which are limited to twenty years; and emergency withdrawals, which are limited to three years. 43 U.S.C. § 1714. The following provisions of Section 204 further describe the requirements for the latter two categories of withdrawal, including provisions allowing for congressional veto of the Secretary's withdrawal decisions.

(c) Congressional approval procedures applicable to withdrawals aggregating five thousand acres or more

(1) On and after October 21, 1976, a withdrawal aggregating five thousand acres or more may be made (or such a withdrawal or any other withdrawal involving in the aggregate five thousand acres or more which terminates after such date of approval may be extended) only for a period of not more than twenty years by the Secretary on his own motion or upon request by a department or agency head. The Secretary shall notify both Houses of Congress of such a withdrawal no later than its effective date and the withdrawal shall terminate and become ineffective at the end of ninety days (not counting days on which the Senate or the House of Representatives has adjourned for more than three consecutive days) beginning on the day notice of such withdrawal has been submitted to the Senate and the House of Representatives, if the Congress has adopted a concurrent resolution stating that such House does not

approve the withdrawal. If the committee to which a resolution has been referred during the said ninety day period, has not reported it at the end of thirty calendar days after its referral, it shall be in order to either discharge the committee from further consideration of such resolution or to discharge the committee from consideration of any other resolution with respect to the Presidential recommendation. A motion to discharge may be made only by an individual favoring the resolution, shall be highly privileged (except that it may not be made after the committee has reported such a resolution), and debate thereon shall be limited to not more than one hour, to be divided equally between those favoring and those opposing the resolution. An amendment to the motion shall not be in order, and it shall not be in order to move to reconsider the vote by which the motion was agreed to or disagreed to. If the motion to discharge is agreed to or disagreed to, the motion may not be made with respect to any other resolution with respect to the same Presidential recommendation. When the committee has reprinted, or has been discharged from further consideration of a resolution, it shall at any time thereafter be in order (even though a previous motion to the same effect has been disagreed to) to move to proceed to the consideration of the resolution. The motion shall be highly privileged and shall not be debatable. An amendment to the motion shall not be in order, and it shall not be in order to move to reconsider the vote by which the motion was agreed to or disagreed to. * * *

(e) Emergency withdrawals; procedure applicable; duration

When the Secretary determines, or when the Committee on Natural Resources of the House of Representatives or the Committee on Energy and Natural Resources of the Senate notifies the Secretary, that an emergency situation exists and that extraordinary measures must be taken to preserve values that would otherwise be lost, the Secretary notwithstanding the provisions of subsections (c)(1) and (d) of this section, shall immediately make a withdrawal and file notice of such emergency withdrawal with both of those Committees. Such emergency withdrawal shall be effective when made but shall last only for a period not to exceed three years and may not be extended except under the provisions of subsection (c)(1) or (d), whichever is applicable, and (b)(1) of this section. The information required in subsection (c)(2) of this subsection shall be furnished the committees within three months after filing such notice. * * *

In addition to the legislative veto, FLPMA's withdrawal procedure further limits the Secretary's flexibility by requiring a public hearing prior to any non-emergency withdrawal. For withdrawals over 5000 acres, the Secretary is also required to file an elaborate report giving Congress a variety of information, including its proposed use, an inventory of the site's natural resource values, impacts on present users of the land to be withdrawn, an investigation of suitable alternative sites, and a report on the existence of mineral deposits. 43 U.S.C. § 1714(c)(2).

QUESTIONS AND DISCUSSION

1. Recall the discussion of the Antiquities Act and presidential declaration of national monuments. Why isn't the FLPMA withdrawal process an adequate substitute for Antiquities Act withdrawals? What benefits does it offer? What costs might it impose?

2. FLPMA's withdrawal procedure has remained relatively unused. The most prominent exception is Interior Secretary Andrus' use of FLPMA's emergency withdrawal procedures to set aside 111 million acres of land in Alaska in conjunction with President Carter's national monument proclamations under the Antiquities Act, both of which were done pending negotiation of the Alaska National Interest Lands Conservation Act (ANILCA). *See supra* page 623. One reason for this reticence may be the comparative ease of using the Antiquities Act. Another may be the reluctance of the Secretary to subject the withdrawal to legislative veto. There are, however, significant questions about whether the legislative veto provisions are constitutional. In *Immigration and Naturalization Service v. Chadha*, 462 U.S. 919 (1983), the Supreme Court addressed a similar provision of the Immigration and Nationality Act which authorized either house of Congress, by resolution, to invalidate the decision of the Executive Branch to allow an otherwise deportable alien to remain in the United States. The Court held that allowing such a one-house veto of executive action violated the Constitution's bicameralism and presentment requirements, *see* U.S. CONST. Art. I, § 7, cl. 2 (requiring that all bills "shall have passed" both the House and the Senate and "be presented to the President" for signature or veto). Reviewing the language of Section 204 of FLPMA, 43 U.S.C. § 1714, are there any arguments that would distinguish FLPMA's withdrawal procedures from the one-house veto in *Chadha*? Most commentators don't think so. As a matter of constitutional law, what concerns might the Founders have had in mind when they included a bicameralism and presentment requirement in the Constitution? Are those concerns still valid for a complex administrative state? What was Congress trying to accomplish in the way it crafted the FLPMA withdrawal procedures?

3. The primary judicial comment on FLPMA's withdrawal procedures came in two federal district court decisions in the 1980s. In *Pacific Legal Foundation v. Watt*, 529 F. Supp. 982 (D. Mont. 1981), the House Interior Committee, concerned about Interior Secretary Watt's announced plan to open certain wilderness areas to oil and gas leasing, used its authority under § 1714(e) of FLPMA to direct the Secretary to make an emergency withdrawal of wilderness areas from mineral leasing. When the Secretary reluctantly made the withdrawals, the Pacific Legal Foundation sued. The court held that although allowing a single committee to direct the action of the executive branch seemed constitutionally dubious, any problem was cured by the Secretary's discretion to establish the duration of the withdrawal and to revoke it after a reasonable time. *Id.* at 1002–04. Soon thereafter, the House Interior Committee directed Secretary Watt to withdraw coal-bearing lands in the Upper Great Plains which he had proposed to lease. This time the Secretary refused and environmental groups sued. In *National Wildlife Federation v. Watt*, 571 F. Supp. 1145 (D. D.C. 1983), the court enjoined the Secretary from issuing any coal leases. The court reasoned that it did not need to decide upon the constitutionality of § 1714(e) because the Interior Department had adopted regulations implementing § 1714(e), *see* 43 C.F.R. § 2310.5(a), and the Secretary was obligated to follow those regulations until they had been rescinded by notice and comment. With respect to the constitutional issue, the court offered:

> It may well be that when this Court, the Court of Appeals, or the Supreme Court has had comprehensive briefs and an adequate opportunity to consider all the relevant historical evidence about the drafting and context of Article IV, Section 3, as well as its application over the years, they will reach a conclusion contrary to the opinions relied upon by the defendant here. The Supreme Court has stated that Congress' proprietary interest in public lands gives it constitutional prerogatives which transcend those which it enjoys in its purely legislative role in respect of immigration. *See, e.g., United States v. California*, 332 U.S. 19, 27 (1947). Moreover, it is common historical knowledge that in the years before the Constitution was adopted (and for many years thereafter) Congress was in session for only brief periods and in recess for many months at a time. Public lands were matters of even greater public and political interest than they are now. It is not inconceivable that courts will decide from the text and context of Article IV, Section 3, that its Framers contemplated that Congress' proprietary power to "dispose of" public lands included the power to delegate power to dispose of public land to the Executive as a trustee. The Framers may well have contemplated that such an Article IV delegation might be subject to an express and narrow condition that a specified Committee of Congress could, during or in anticipation of a congressional recess, temporarily suspend that delegation in the manner now provided for in section 204(e) of the 1976 Act. Such a condition would be analogous to limitations traditionally imposed by settlors under familiar principles of trust law.

571 F. Supp. at 1156–57. Are you persuaded by the district court's analysis? Are FLPMA's withdrawal provisions constitutional? Does the questionable constitutionality of the legislative veto provisions provide a third reason why Interior Secretaries have apparently been reluctant to use FLPMA's withdrawal procedures? If the legislative veto were struck down as unconstitutional, a question would arise about whether the withdrawal procedures were severable from the veto provisions. *See Alaska Airlines, Inc. v. Brock*, 480 U.S. 678, 685 (1987) ("The . . . relevant inquiry in evaluating severability is whether the statute will function in a manner consistent with the intent of Congress."). Given this test for severability, if § 1714's veto provisions were struck down, would the Secretary's withdrawal authority survive? If the withdrawal provisions were found to be severable, might that cause Congress to consider legislation less favorable to executive action?

4. On June 25, 2008, responding to a flurry of uranium mining claims in the West, the House Natural Resources Committee invoked its rarely used FLPMA withdrawal authority and approved a resolution ordering the Interior Department to make an emergency withdrawal of just over one million acres of land near Grand Canyon National Park from any uranium mining during the next three years. Committee Republicans walked out of the meeting. Said Utah representative Rob Bishop: "We will not be part of this resolution. It's the wrong thing to do. It's the wrong process. It is the wrong subject. It is not an emergency. It's clearly an unconstitutional action." *House Panel Orders Mining Withdrawal Near Grand Canyon*, PUBLIC LANDS NEWS, June 27, 2008, at 5. Interior Secretary Dirk Kempthorne refused to make the withdrawal, arguing that Congress must make the request. This was apparently expected by Arizona representative Raul

Gijalva, who reportedly stated, "This will be good for three to six months.... Even if it's challenged and we lose, I think the focus on the Grand Canyon is good." *Resolution Saves Canyon From Mining—For A While*, ARIZONA DAILY STAR, June 27, 2008.

On September 29, 2008 various conservation groups sued Secretary Kempthorne, seeking an injunction ordering him to comply with the withdrawal order of the House Natural Resources Committee. Two weeks later, Secretary Kempthorne initiated a rulemaking to rescind the regulation implementing the Natural Resources Committee withdrawal provision of FLPMA. The rule became effective on January 5, 2009. *See* 43 C.F.R. § 2310.5. Harking back to the preceding note, why did Secretary Kempthorne take this step? What do you expect the outcome of the litigation to be?

5. FLPMA's withdrawal procedures apply not only to BLM lands but also to lands administered by the Forest Service and other agencies. With respect to lands administered by other agencies, FLPMA provides that "the Secretary shall make, modify, and revoke withdrawals only with the consent of the head of the department or agency concerned, except [for emergency withdrawals]." 43 U.S.C. § 1714(i). As a practical matter, the way this works is that another agency, such as the Forest Service, will propose to the Secretary of the Interior that a withdrawal be made of land the Forest Service manages.

Those who have suggested that the executive branch should follow FLPMA's withdrawal procedure, with its various procedural protections, rather than use the Antiquities Act to preserve public land, often raise a related concern. They argue that the Secretary's decisions, pursuant to his or her multiple use management authority, not to issue mineral leases in certain areas are really the equivalent of a withdrawal triggering the various procedural safeguards in Section 204 of FLPMA. The following case addresses that issue.

MOUNTAIN STATES LEGAL FOUNDATION v. HODEL, 668 F. Supp. 1466 (D. Wyo. 1987)

KERR, DISTRICT JUDGE.

* * * [P]laintiff Mountain States Legal Foundation (Foundation) filed suit against the Secretaries of the Department of Interior and the Department of Agriculture to challenge the suspension of mineral leasing by the Forest Service and Bureau of Land Management. The Foundation alleges that this suspension of mineral leasing and the delays in acting upon leases in the Shoshone, Targhee, and Bridger–Teton National Forests violates the ... the Federal Land Policy and Management Act, 43 U.S.C. § 1701 et seq. * * *

FACTS

At the time this action was filed on January 15, 1986, there were at least 72 lease offers, some as old as twelve years, pending for lands located in the

Shoshone National Forest. There were also 94 tracts of land in the Shoshone National Forest available for mineral leasing under the simultaneous oil and gas leasing program.

As of February 19, 1987, in the Bridger–Teton National Forest, there were six over-the-counter lease applications and over 100 SIMO lease offers affecting more than one million acres of forest land which were subject to oil and gas leases which have now expired, terminated, or been relinquished. . . .

On May 29, 1985, the Regional Forester for Region IV in a letter to the Wyoming State Director of the Bureau of Land Management, suspended mineral leasing in the Bridger–Teton National Forest, requesting the Bureau of Land Management to delay further processing of oil and gas leases in this area. The Regional Forester based this request on the land's environmental sensitivity and the pending completion of further environmental documentation including a final Environmental Impact Statement and/or a Forest Plan pursuant to the Forest and Rangeland Resources Planning Act, 16 U.S.C. § 1604, as amended by the National Forest Management Act of 1976, 16 U.S.C. § 1604. . . . The Bureau of Land Management has since honored the Forest Service request to suspend such mineral leasing in the Bridger–Teton Forest. * * *

Pursuant to the Mineral Leasing Act, the Secretary of the Interior has authority to issue mineral leases on federal lands, 30 U.S.C. § 226. That authority in turn has been delegated to the Bureau of Land Management, 43 U.S.C. § 1731. The Bureau of Land Management has entered into an inter-agency agreement with the Forest Service, whereby the Forest Service makes recommendations to the Bureau of Land Management as to whether a lease application or offer should be issued and under what terms and conditions a lease should be issued in order to protect the surface resources. * * *

Based upon the requests and recommendations of the Forest Service through the Regional Forester, the Bureau of Land Management has ceased to act upon or issue leases. * * *

WITHDRAWAL OF LANDS UNDER THE FEDERAL LAND POLICY AND MANAGEMENT ACT 43 U.S.C. § 1714

The Foundation asserts that the defendants' suspension of mineral leasing in the Bridger–Teton National Forest and their failure to act upon pending lease applications and offers in the National Forests is an unlawful withdrawal of lands in violation of the Federal Land Policy Management Act, 43 U.S.C. § 1714. The defendant Secretaries claim, however, that a withdrawal of lands can only occur when affirmative action is taken and an order of withdrawal entered. Furthermore, the Secretaries contend that mineral leasing does not come within the purview of the withdrawal statutes.

Defendants' arguments ignore the reality of the present situation in light of the federal laws and have previously been rejected by the courts in the cases of *Mountain States Legal Foundation v. Andrus,* 499 F. Supp. 383 and *Pacific Legal Foundation v. Watt,* 529 F. Supp. 982 (D. Mt. 1981). In *Mountain States Legal Foundation v. Andrus,* Judge Brimmer held that the moratorium placed on mineral leasing in wilderness study areas under the RARE II program and the failure to act upon leases was a withdrawal within the meaning of 43 U.S.C. § 1702(j) and could, therefore, only be implemented by proper compliance with procedural requirements of the Federal Land Policy and Management Act. In the *Pacific Legal Foundation* case, the court found that the term "withdrawal" as used in the Federal Land Policy and Management Act includes a withdrawal of public lands from mineral exploration and leasing.

The definition of withdrawal under the Federal Land Policy and Management Act states that:

> ['w]ithdrawal' means *withholding an area of* Federal land from settlement, sale, location, or *entry, under some or all of the general land laws,* for the purpose of *limiting activities* under those laws in order to *maintain other public values* in the area or reserving the area for a particular public purpose or program; . . .

43 U.S.C. § 1702(j).

Clearly, the acts of suspension of mineral leasing and the unreasonable delay in mineral leasing in the Shoshone, Targhee, and Bridger–Teton National Forests fall squarely within the definition of withdrawal for purposes of the Federal Land Policy and Management Act. The Forest Service is seeking to protect and elevate the use of environmentally sensitive lands above other statutorily mandated uses by stopping mineral leasing until an Environmental Impact Statement or Forest Plan is completed. The action of the Secretaries is more than mere delay in the leasing process; rather, it involves affirmative action to withhold these forest lands from mineral leasing, thereby limiting leasing activities in order to maintain basic environmental values for an indefinite period of time.

In contrast to arguments asserted by the defendants here, the Montana District Court in the case of *Pacific Legal Foundation v. Watt,* 529 F. Supp. at 995–997, concluded that mineral leasing is included in the definition of a withdrawal based on several factors. First, the term "mineral leasing" appears in several subsections of 43 U.S.C. § 1714. Second, the legislative history's reference to retaining the "traditional meaning" of a withdrawal does not support the conclusion that Congress intended to exclude mineral leasing from the procedural provisions regarding withdrawals of federal land. Third, . . . the district court noted that other Secretaries have withdrawn land from mineral leasing under the authority in 43 U.S.C. § 1714 of the Federal Land Policy and Management Act. For all of these reasons, the district court held that the definition of a withdrawal includes mineral activities under the Mineral Leasing Act.

This Court is persuaded by the sound reasoning and analysis made by Judge Jameson in *Pacific Legal Foundation* and concludes that mineral leasing activities pursuant to the Mineral Leasing Act are included within the purview of the Federal Land Policy and Management Act's withdrawal provisions.

Further, this Court concludes that the fact that the Secretary of Interior has discretionary authority in leasing government lands under oil and gas leases, pursuant to the Mineral Leasing Act of 1920, *McDonald v. Clark,* 771 F.2d at 463, does not extend to permit the Secretary of the Interior, acting together with the Secretary of Agriculture, to deprive lease applicants or offerors of the right to have their leases fairly considered under the proper statutory requirements. *Schraier v. Hickel,* 419 F.2d at 667. The Secretaries' suspension and delay in mineral lease processing under the present circumstances has deprived plaintiff and its members of just that right. Therefore, the Secretaries' actions are clearly an abuse of discretion and not in accordance with the law and must be set aside as unlawful. Administrative Procedure Act, 5 U.S.C. § 706(2)(A).

Moreover, the Secretary of Interior's mineral leasing discretion is not so broad as to allow the Secretary to refuse to act upon lease applications and offers in large areas of land, thereby effectively removing the lands from the operation of the Mineral Leasing Act without following the proper procedural requirements of the withdrawal provisions, § 204 of the Federal Land Policy and Management Act, 43 U.S.C. § 1714; *Mountain States Legal Foundation v. Andrus,* 499 F. Supp. at 391–392; 1 American Law of Mining § 20.02[3] at 20–12 (Rocky Mtn. Min. L. Inst. 2d ed. 1986).

In *Mountain States Legal Foundation v. Andrus,* 499 F. Supp. at 392, 395, the district court considered and rejected the government's argument that the definition of a withdrawal does not apply to mineral leasing because it is a discretionary decision, finding that there are limits to the Secretary's exercise of that discretion. The court there also suggested that applicability of the Secretary's discretion as pertaining to a specific lease must be differentiated from general applicability of that discretion. *Id.* citing *Edras K. Hartley,* 23 IBLA 102 (1975).

Under the provisions of the Federal Land Policy and Management Act, 43 U.S.C. § 1714, certain procedures must be followed by the Secretary to properly effectuate a withdrawal. These procedures include such matters as a hearing (§ 1714(h)), publication of notice in the Federal Register (§ 1714(b)), and a report to Congress (§ 1714(c)). The Secretary of Interior has admittedly failed to follow the withdrawal procedures of 43 U.S.C. § 1714 under the Federal Land Policy Management Act.

Based on all the foregoing, this Court, therefore, concludes the actions taken by the Secretaries in delaying and suspending mineral leasing in the aforementioned forests is an impermissible withdrawal of land by failure to comply with the requirements of 43 U.S.C. § 1714, and that such action is unlawful as an abuse of discretion and not in accordance with the law. 5 U.S.C. § 706(2)(A). * * *

NOW, THEREFORE, IT IS ORDERED that plaintiff's motion for summary judgment be, and the same is, hereby granted to the extent set forth herein; it is

FURTHER ORDERED that the suspension of mineral leasing in the National Forests as initiated by the Forest Service and followed by the Bureau of Land Management as it now exists, be, and the same is, hereby set aside as unlawful; it is

FURTHER ORDERED that the Secretary of Interior shall report the withdrawal of the affected lands in the National Forests to Congress within thirty (30) days from the date of this Order pursuant to 43 U.S.C. § 1714(c), or cease withholding said lands from oil and gas leasing exploration and development for the purpose of elevating environmental concerns pending the completion of the Forest Plan. . . .

QUESTIONS AND DISCUSSION

1. In *Bob Marshall Alliance v. Hodel,* 852 F.2d 1223 (9th Cir. 1988), *cert. denied,* 489 U.S. 1066 (1989), the Ninth Circuit opined that the denial of mineral leases was not a withdrawal triggering the FLPMA withdrawal provisions. Responding to the lessee's (Kohlman) argument that denying or deferring action on several mineral leases within the Deep Creek area of the Lewis and Clark National Forest would have obligated the agency to comply with FLPMA's withdrawal procedures, the Court said:

We reject this argument. "Withdrawal" of public lands requires a formal procedure which, for parcels exceeding 5000 acres, includes congressional approval; the land is effectively segregated from the operation of public land laws for a period of up to 20 years. Federal Land Policy and Management Act, 43 U.S.C. § 1714 (1982). We fail to see how a decision not to issue oil and gas leases on Deep Creek would be equivalent to a formal withdrawal. Kohlman cites only one case, *Mountain States Legal Foundation v. Andrus*, 499 F. Supp. 383 (D. Wyo. 1980), as authority for the proposition that deferring action on oil and gas lease applications can constitute an unlawful administrative withdrawal. *Mountain States* is not binding on us and we do not find its reasoning persuasive. In that case, the court concluded that the Interior and Agriculture Departments had illegally withdrawn over a million acres of land because they had failed to act on oil and gas lease applications and had thereby removed the land from the operation of the Mineral Leasing Act of 1920. Yet as the court acknowledged, the Mineral Leasing Act gives the Interior Secretary discretion to determine which lands are to be leased under the statute. 30 U.S.C. § 226(a) (1982); *see Mountain States*, 499 F. Supp. at 391–92. We have held that the Mineral Leasing Act "allows the Secretary to lease such lands, but does not require him to do so.... [T]he Secretary has discretion to refuse to issue any lease at all on a given tract." *Burglin v. Morton*, 527 F.2d 486, 488 (9th Cir. 1975) (*citing Udall v. Tallman*, 380 U.S. 1, 4 (1965)), *cert. denied*, 425 U.S. 973 (1976). Thus refusing to issue the Deep Creek leases, far from removing Deep Creek from the operation of the mineral leasing law, would constitute a legitimate exercise of the discretion granted to the Interior Secretary under that statute.

Id. at 1229–30. Which court is correct? Does the BLM make a "withdrawal" within the meaning of FLPMA every time it exercises its discretion not to issue a mineral lease? Can the Forest Service prepare a land use plan which prevents mineral leasing within an entire national forest without complying with FLPMA's withdrawal procedures? What did Congress intend under FLPMA?

2. *Problem Exercise.* Suppose you are a counselor to the Secretary of the Interior. The new Secretary is committed to dedicating more of the public lands to preservation purposes. She has asked you to prepare a basic users guide that informs her of the various options available for protecting lands and what constraints apply to those options. Thinking back over the entire chapter, what options are available to the Secretary?

————

VIII. THE IMPACT OF ACCESS ON PRESERVATION

Recall the discussion in Chapter 2 about the checkerboard status of land ownership in much of the West. As a result of federal grants, such as the 94 million acres of alternate sections of land given to railroads along their rights of way and the enabling act grants to states of one, two, and later four sections of land within each township for purposes of financing schools, most federal land is interspersed with state and private land. As further discussed in the chapter on mining law, the public lands are also shot through with literally hundreds of thousands of unpatented mining claims and mineral leases. Accordingly, whenever Congress sets aside a portion of the public lands as a park, monument, wilderness area, refuge, recreation area, or the like, the area designated is likely to include within its boundaries state and private parcels or mining claims. Federal designations of preservation lands typically provide that the owners of these parcels, claims, and leases will be protected in their valid existing rights. *See, e.g.*, Wilderness Act, 16 U.S.C. § 1133(c) ("subject to existing private rights there shall be no commercial enterprise and no permanent road within any wilderness area"). *See generally* James N. Barkeley & Lawrence V. Albert, *A Survey of Case Law Interpreting "Valid Existing Rights"— Implications for Unpatented Mining Claims*, 34 ROCKY MTN. MIN. L. INST. 9-1, 9-6 n.7 (1988) (noting that over 100 statutes in the United States Code employ the term "valid existing rights"). But what exactly does the protection of valid existing rights entail? Prior to the designation, the property rights in these inheld parcels, mining claims, and mineral leases were subject to the authority of the federal government to regulate with reference to changing public needs and interests, subject only to the limitations of the Constitution's takings clause. Does the protection of valid existing rights offer any additional protection beyond that already afforded by the takings clause—by promising, for example, to regulate as if the protective designation never happened—or is the promise to "protect" valid existing rights really just a statement by the federal government that it does not intend the designation itself to be a taking?

The nature of valid existing rights in inheld parcels and mining claims has critical implications for federal preservation efforts. Consider a situation where Congress declares a wilderness area or the president proclaims a national monument. If a state remains free to issue a mineral lease to its land within the wilderness or monument, the characteristics of the area that triggered its proclamation can be defeated by the roads and other development attendant to the mineral lease. On the other hand, if the designation of surrounding federal lands effectively precludes any development of a state or private inholding or mining claim, is that fair to the property owner? This section of the chapter takes up the conflict between federal preservation efforts and the property rights of states and private persons in lands that are interspersed with or surrounded by federal lands. It does so by focusing on one particular conflict—the interest of states and private persons in obtaining access across federal lands.

From a preservation perspective there are few issues more important than access. The type and scope of access can have a dramatic impact on the uses to which property can be put. The more limited the access the less likely property is to be used and developed. But access is even more important for another reason. Access usually means roads; and roads have tremendous implications for preservation. As an initial matter, the existence of a road usually precludes an area from being assigned the highest level of federal protection as wilderness, which by definition is to be "roadless." Roads, however, do more to limit preservation than simply curtail the opportunity for an area to be designated as wilderness. Consider the following excerpt from the Natural Resources Defense Council's compilation of research on the ecological impact of roads.

> Roads displace species sensitive to disturbance or dependent on forest interior habitat. For example, species like grizzly bears, wolves, and elk avoid otherwise suitable habitat near roads. They may modify their home range, and they have been shown to select areas with lower road densities than the

average on the landscape. As a result, high-quality habitat becomes effectively unavailable to them.

Roads also create barriers to the movement of many species. In particular, small animals such as salamanders, frogs, and mice will rarely cross roads or are killed by vehicles when crossing. As barriers to dispersal, roads isolate populations on one side of the road from those on the other. Biologists fear a likely consequence of this isolation and the resultant loss of gene flow between populations is, over the long-term, increased vulnerability of some species to inbreeding or environmental catastrophes. Larger species such as moose, white-tailed deer, and mule deer also have high rates of mortality due to roadkill. * * *

Roads facilitate the spread of invasive non-native (exotic) plants, animals, and insects. For example, vehicles can transport the seeds of exotic plants to new areas.... Over time, some exotic species spread from roadsides into adjacent, undisturbed areas. * * *

Logging and road construction compact soils, disturb or destroy organic layers, and cause high rates of soil erosion. Soil compaction, which can last for several decades, is typically measured by changes in soil bulk density or porosity. Trees' access to nutrients and water is reduced because of restricted root growth in compacted soils, reduced water infiltration rates, and decreased oxygen and water available to root systems. * * *

Compacted soils are also more susceptible to surface erosion. The frequency of mass erosion events, such as debris slides, also increases in landscapes that have been roaded or logged, thus increasing total soil loss. In forests where overland (surface) water flow is unlikely, roads have been documented to intercept water at road cuts, converting subsurface flow to surface flow. This greatly increases runoff-related erosion.

This loss of soil due to erosion not only reduces the productivity of the local site by removing top, nutrient-rich layers of soil, but the sediment that is generated often runs into streams, where it has a range of detrimental impacts on aquatic ecosystems. * * *

Roads and logging can significantly degrade stream ecosystems by introducing high volumes of sediment into streams, changing natural streamflow patterns, and altering stream channel morphology. The frequency of landslides in steep terrain is higher in roaded areas and in forests that have been clearcut. Much of the resultant eroded soil ends up in streams. Fine sediment from road surfaces runs into streams during storm events....

Streamflow patterns can change in watersheds that are roaded and/or have been logged. Roads, ditches, and new gullies form new, large networks of flow paths across the landscape; this changes the rate at which water reaches streams. As a result, peak discharge volumes in some watersheds are higher and after large storms begin earlier than they would in undisturbed watersheds.

These changes in stream habitat affect the health of aquatic organisms. The survival rates of many salmonid species, for instance, decrease as fine sediment levels increase. Deposition of fine sediment on the stream bed degrades spawning areas, reduces pool refuge habitat, decreases winter refuge areas for juveniles, and impedes feeding visibility. * * *

See Natural Resources Defense Council, *End of the Road: The Adverse Ecological Impacts of Roads and Logging: A Compilation of Independently Reviewed Research, available at* http://www.nrdc.org/land/forests/roads/

eotrinx.asp. One of the reasons that roads have had such impacts is that we have so many of them. In 1999, the "national forest road system include[d] 380,000 miles of road, enough road to circle the globe more than 15 times." National Forest System Roadless Areas, 64 Fed. Reg. at 56,306 (Oct. 19, 1999). BLM lands currently contain 75,959 miles of roads; and wildlife refuges and national parks contain 12,145 and 8,500 miles of roads respectively. *See* DOI Quick Facts, *available at* http://mits.doi.gov/quickfacts/facts 2.cfm.

If roads cause harm to the environment, they also bring benefits. As George Bernard Shaw once remarked, "What Englishman will give his mind to politics as long as he can afford to run a motorcar." *See* MARK NICHOLSON & MARK WHEATLEY, MARKET DRIVERS: ENDING ROAD RATIONING AND REFINING THE TRANSPORT MARKET 13 (2003). Most of us benefit from the country's vast transportation infrastructure. Roads create opportunities for economic development. They open up access to recreation opportunities that would otherwise be unavailable to all but a few. And for rural communities surrounded by a sea of public lands, roads are seen as an economic lifeline, providing access to markets, grazing allotments, and recreational sites, as well as routes for off-road vehicle use. To an individual owner of an inheld parcel, of course, all of these arguments are often secondary to the owner's deeply held conviction that her basic constitutional right to use and enjoy her property necessarily includes access to that property.

With this basic background about roads in mind, this section of the chapter now turns to two issues. It first addresses the law regarding access to inheld parcels and mining claims. The section then turns to the related but distinct issue of claims by state and local governments to ownership of roads and rights of way across federal land that were granted as part of the 1866 mining law under a statutory provision known as R.S. 2477. *See* § 8 of the Act of July 26, 1866, 14 Stat. 253 ("That the right of way for the construction of highways over public lands, not reserved for public uses, is hereby granted.").

A.   ACCESS ACROSS FEDERAL LANDS TO PRIVATE AND STATE PROPERTY

Although a full discussion of the laws governing access to inholdings, unpatented mining claims, and mineral leases is beyond the scope of this casebook, it is possible to consider the basic issues that underlie most access disputes. The first access question for inholders and mining claimants is whether they have an actual property right to access. The answer depends on the nature of their interest in the land or minerals they are trying to reach. With respect to inheld school trust lands, inheld private parcels, or unpatented mining claims, there is an implied property right of access over federal lands. There is, however, no implied right of access with respect to mineral leases issued under the Mineral Leasing Act. Although the former group has a property right to access and mineral lessees do not, this distinction may not be as significant as it first appears. Although mineral lessees have no property right to access, FLPMA still authorizes them to apply to the Secretary for a right-of-way permit. 43 U.S.C.

§§ 1761–65. And even though unpatented mining claimants and inholders have a property right to access, that right, like all property, is subject to reasonable regulation. The terms and conditions imposed on the exercise of a property right to access imposed as part of an agency's regulatory authority—and often imposed as part of a permitting process—can closely resemble the terms and conditions imposed on a discretionary right-of-way permit under FLPMA. While the relevant agency surely feels more free to deny, or impose conditions on, a FLPMA permit where the access seeker has no claim of right and therefore cannot make a takings claim, that does not mean that persons with a property right to access can expect easy approval for their access plans. *See generally* Daniel A. Jensen, *How Do I Get There? Access to and Across Mining Claims and Mineral Leases*, 45 ROCKY MTN. MIN. L. INST. 20–1 (1999).

In those instances, like mineral leases, where there is no property right to access, the course of action is quite clear. The person seeking a right of way must apply to the Secretary of the Interior or the Secretary of the Agriculture for a permit under the process outlined in Subchapter V of FLPMA. 43 U.S.C. §§ 1761–65. The Secretaries are authorized, in their discretion, to issue permits for roads, canals, ditches, pipelines, utility corridors, and the like, but each right of way must contain:

> such terms and conditions as the Secretary concerned deems necessary to (i) protect Federal property and economic interests; (ii) manage efficiently the lands which are subject to the right-of-way or adjacent thereto and protect the other lawful users of the lands adjacent to or traversed by such right-of-way; (iii) protect lives and property; (iv) protect the interests of individuals living in the general area traversed by the right-of-way who rely on the fish, wildlife, and other biotic resources of the area for subsistence purposes; (v) require location of the right-of-way along a route that will cause least damage to the environment, taking into consideration feasibility and other relevant factors; and (vi) otherwise protect the public interest in the lands traversed by the right-of-way or adjacent thereto.

43 U.S.C. § 1765.

Where the access seeker has an implied property right to access, a variety of statutory and regulatory provisions can apply depending on the designation of the federal lands within which access is sought and on the type of activity for which the access is desired. Thus, for example, with respect to the national forests, Congress has provided that

> Notwithstanding any other provision of law, and subject to such terms and conditions as the Secretary of Agriculture may prescribe, the Secretary shall provide such access to nonfederally owned land within the boundaries of the National Forest System as the Secretary deems adequate to secure to the owner the reasonable use and enjoyment thereof: Provided, That such owner comply with rules and regulations applicable to ingress and egress to or from the National Forest System.

16 U.S.C. § 3210. (Oddly enough, this particular provision giving direction for all national forests is contained within the Alaska National Interest Lands Conservation Act (ANILCA).) The obvious question left by such statutory provisions is exactly what counts as "adequate" access? Is it enough to provide helicopter access to a company seeking to log its checkerboarded land within a national forest? How should the agency

balance the right of access against the need to maintain the character of the surrounding lands? The following case wrestles with these issues with respect to a mining claim within a wilderness area.

CLOUSER V. ESPY,
42 F.3d 1522 (9th Cir. 1994), *cert. denied,* **515 U.S. 1141 (1995)**

THELTON E. HENDERSON, DISTRICT JUDGE:

This case is a lawsuit by holders of certain mining claims located on federal land within National Forests. The claim holders challenge rulings by the U.S. Forest Service that, among other things, refused under certain circumstances to permit them to use motor vehicles to access their claims, requiring them instead to use pack animals. On the parties' cross motions for summary judgment, the district court granted summary judgment for defendants and plaintiffs appealed. For the reasons set forth below, we affirm.

I.   BACKGROUND

A.   OVERVIEW

This lawsuit is brought by three different sets of plaintiffs, all of whom have asserted rights to mine in areas located wholly within federal national forest lands. Two of the claims are located in regions designated "wilderness areas" pursuant to the Wilderness Act of 1964, 16 U.S.C. §§ 1131–1136, and the third is located on national forest land that is part of the National Wild and Scenic Rivers System, 16 U.S.C. § 1271. In each case, the national forest land in which the mining claims are located was at one time open to the public for exploration, prospecting, and the extraction of minerals; however, the land was subsequently withdrawn from mineral entry under the Wilderness Act or the Wild and Scenic Rivers Act, so that only persons establishing that they discovered a valuable mineral deposit prior to the withdrawal possess a valid right to mine claims there (a "valid claim"). All three sets of claims at issue are unpatented.[2] * * *

The challenged Forest Service decisions are . . . [the] Forest Service rulings that . . . access to claims located within federal national forest lands should be limited to non-motorized means where the Forest Service considers such means adequate to carry out the proposed mining operations (the "Robert E." and "Thunderbolt" claims). . . .

B.   DESCRIPTION OF THE THREE GROUPS OF MINING CLAIMS AT ISSUE AND THE ADMINISTRATIVE PROCEEDINGS PRECEDING THIS LITIGATION * * *

2.   THE THUNDERBOLT MINING CLAIMS

The Thunderbolt claims, owned by plaintiffs Carl, Judith, and Anthony Setera, are located in the Umatilla National Forest in Oregon. The lands on which the claims are located were included in the Blue Mountain Forest Reserve on March 15, 1906; these lands were withdrawn from mineral entry and became part of the North Fork John Day Wilderness Area on June 26,

---

2. An "unpatented" claim is a possessory interest in a particular area solely for the purpose of mining; it may be contested by the government or a private party. By contrast, if a claim is patented, the claimant gets a fee simple interest from the United States and no contest can be brought against the claim. *See Northern Alaska Envtl. Ctr. v. Lujan,* 872 F.2d 901, 904 n.2 (9th Cir. 1989).

1984. There are six claims; five were located in 1980 and the sixth in 1982. For purposes of this case only, the government has agreed to assume that Thunderbolt claim #2, the only claim involved in this case, is valid.

In August 1988, the plaintiffs filed a notice of intent and plan of operations proposing the use of a "suction dredge" and other equipment to test Thunderbolt claim #2. They proposed motorized access over two Forest Service trails covering a distance of approximately four miles in the wilderness. This proposed route had been gated and blocked from traffic in 1984 after the land was included in the North Fork John Day Wilderness Area. In November 1988, the Forest Supervisor issued a decision restricting plaintiffs to using pack animals or other non-motorized means of access, on the ground that motorized access was not essential due to the limited nature of the proposed operation.

In May 1989, plaintiffs proposed another plan of operations, which they revised in July 1989. The revised plan proposed use of a five-inch suction dredge and motorized access over the same two Forest Service roads. In August 1989, the Forest Supervisor determined, based on an environmental assessment that had been conducted in 1988, that the plan could not be approved as submitted because motorized access was not necessary given the low level of proposed operations and because of the Forest Service's statutory mandate to preserve the wilderness characteristics of the lands in question. The Forest Supervisor directed the plaintiffs to amend the operating plan and to provide for access by horses or other non-motorized means.

Plaintiffs appealed, and in February 1990 the Deputy Regional Forester affirmed the Forest Supervisor's decision limiting access to non-motorized means. The plaintiffs filed a petition for discretionary review of this decision with the Chief of the Forest Service, but it was denied. * * *

C.   THIS LAWSUIT

Plaintiffs filed suit jointly against the Secretary of Agriculture and various Forest Service and Interior officials, seeking only declaratory and injunctive relief requiring the defendants to grant plaintiffs motorized access to their mining claims and permit them to conduct mining operations. The district court referred the case to a magistrate judge. On the parties' cross-motions for summary judgment, the magistrate judge recommended granting the government's summary judgment motion and denying plaintiffs' summary judgment motion. The district court, after reviewing plaintiffs' objections to the magistrate's report, adopted most of the findings of the magistrate and proceeded to grant defendants' summary judgment motion and deny plaintiffs'. This appeal followed. * * *

III.   THE FOREST SERVICE'S AUTHORITY TO REGULATE INGRESS TO AND EGRESS FROM MINING CLAIMS LOCATED IN NATIONAL FOREST LANDS * * *

A.   PLAINTIFFS' ARGUMENT

Plaintiffs assert—no doubt correctly—that the means of access permitted materially affects the commercial viability of mining claims. Under the legal standard applied by the Department of the Interior to determine whether a putative claim is "valid," validity depends in part on commercial viability.[6] On

---

6. "A mining claimant has the right to possession of a claim only if he has made a mineral discovery on the claim." *Lara v. Secretary of Interior,* 820 F.2d 1535, 1537 (9th Cir. 1987). A "discovery" is defined as having occurred in circumstances "[w]here minerals have been found and the evidence

this basis, plaintiffs argue that adjudication of questions concerning access materially affects claim validity. They therefore contend that adjudication of such issues is committed to the exclusive jurisdiction of the Department of the Interior since, the parties agree, Interior is the agency authorized to adjudicate the validity of mining claims.

Although all three of the claims at issue in this suit are located within national forests, only two of them—the Robert E. and Thunderbolt claims—are located within areas that have been designated "wilderness areas" pursuant to the Wilderness Act. Because the Forest Service has special statutory authority to regulate activities in wilderness areas, we shall address separately the question of Forest Service regulation of access to claims located in wilderness areas and non-wilderness areas.

B. CLAIMS ON NATIONAL FOREST LANDS THAT ARE DESIGNATED AS "WILDERNESS AREAS": THE ROBERT E. AND THUNDERBOLT CLAIMS

As to these two claims located in wilderness areas, there can be no doubt whatsoever that the Forest Service enjoys the authority to regulate means of access, for the Department of Agriculture has expressly been granted statutory authority to do so. 16 U.S.C. § 1134(b) provides that

> In any case where valid mining claims or other valid occupancies are wholly within a designated national forest wilderness area, the Secretary of Agriculture shall by reasonable regulations consistent with the preservation of the area as wilderness, permit ingress and egress to such surrounded areas by means which have been or are being customarily enjoyed with respect to other such areas similarly situated.

This provision's unambiguous instruction to the Secretary of Agriculture to permit ingress and egress to such areas "by means which have been or are being customarily enjoyed with respect to other such areas similarly situated" clearly implies an authority and duty to determine what means are being or have been "customarily enjoyed" in like areas. Indeed, the provision expressly empowers the Secretary to promulgate "reasonable regulations" implementing the statutory mandate. Although Forest Service decisions regarding access may indeed affect whether a claim is found to be "valid," that fact in no way alters 16 U.S.C. § 1134(b)'s unequivocal delegation of authority to the Secretary of Agriculture. While Congress has assigned to Interior authority to adjudicate claim validity, it is free to allocate regulatory authority as it chooses and in 16 U.S.C. § 1134(b) it has empowered Agriculture to make decisions regarding a particular issue that happens to have collateral consequences for claim validity.

C. CLAIMS ON NATIONAL FOREST LANDS THAT ARE *NOT* DESIGNATED "WILDERNESS AREAS": THE WILSON CLAIM

National forest lands that are not designated as wilderness areas are not covered by 16 U.S.C. § 1134(b). However, the government maintains that other grants of statutory authority empower the Department of Agriculture to regulate the means that may be used to access mining claims that are located in

---

is of such a character that a person of ordinary prudence would be justified in the further expenditure of his labor and means, with a reasonable prospect of success, in developing a valuable mine. . . ." *Chrisman v. Miller,* 197 U.S. 313, 322 (1905), *quoted in Lara,* 820 F.2d at 1541. The Supreme Court subsequently refined this prudent person

test, holding that "profitability is an important consideration in applying the prudent-[person] test." *United States v. Coleman,* 390 U.S. 599, 602 (1968), *quoted in Lara,* 820 F.2d at 1541. Thus, the profitability of a putative claim can affect whether the claim is found to be valid.

nonwilderness area national forest lands. The government relies on two provisions of the Organic Administration Act of 1897, which established the national forest system. That statute authorizes the Secretary of Agriculture to promulgate rules and regulations to protect the national forest lands from destruction and depredation. 16 U.S.C. § 551. Further, it specifies that persons entering the national forests for the purpose of exploiting mineral resources "must comply with the rules and regulations covering such national forests." 16 U.S.C. § 478.

Interpreting the scope of the Forest Service's grant of regulatory authority, this circuit has held that

> The Forest Service may properly regulate the surface use of forest lands. While the regulation of mining per se is not within Forest Service jurisdiction, where mining activity disturbs national forest lands, Forest Service regulation is proper. *See United States v. Weiss,* 642 F.2d 296, 298 (9th Cir. 1981) (Secretary of Agriculture has "power to adopt reasonable rules and regulations regarding mining operations within the national forests"); *United States v. Richardson,* 599 F.2d 290 (9th Cir. 1979), *cert. denied,* 444 U.S. 1014 (1980) (recognizing the conflict between mining and forest land policies and holding that the district court may properly enjoin unreasonable destruction of surface resources).

United States v. Goldfield Deep Mines Co., 644 F.2d 1307, 1309 (9th Cir. 1981), *cert. denied,* 455 U.S. 907 (1982). * * *

In light of the broad language of § 551's grant of authority, § 478's clarification that activities of miners on national forest lands are subject to regulation under the statute, and this substantial body of case law, there can be no doubt that the Department of Agriculture possesses statutory authority to regulate activities related to mining—even in non-wilderness areas—in order to preserve the national forests. 16 U.S.C. § 551.

As noted above, plaintiffs argue that because the permissibility of motor-vehicle access may affect whether a claim is deemed to be "valid," the issue of access is different from other matters that the Forest Service may permissibly regulate. Plaintiffs contend that means of access go to the validity of the claim and, as such, are committed to the jurisdiction of Interior. Rejecting this argument, the district court wrote:

> I find that it is the nature of the issue presented (i.e. mode of access), not the *effect* of the determination which determines the appropriate agency forum. Thus, the fact that the Forest Service's rejection of a particular method of access may have a "material impact" on the mining claim activity does not *transform* the determination from one within the province of the Forest Service to one within the exclusive province of the Interior Department.

ER at 218 (emphasis in original). We concur in this conclusion. Virtually all forms of Forest Service regulation of mining claims—for instance, limiting the permissible methods of mining and prospecting in order to reduce incidental environmental damage—will result in increased operating costs, and thereby will affect claim validity, for the reasons explained above. However, the above case law makes clear that such matters may be regulated by the Forest Service, and plaintiffs have offered no compelling reason for distinguishing means of access issues from other such forms of regulation. * * *

For the above reasons, we affirm the district court's ruling that the Forest Service enjoys authority to regulate access to mining claims located within national forest lands, and hold that that authority extends both to national forest lands that have been designated wilderness areas and those that have not. * * *

V. SUBSTANTIVE VALIDITY OF THE FOREST SERVICE'S DECISIONS UNDER THE APA

In addition to challenging the Forest Service's authority to regulate access to mining claims, plaintiffs challenge the Service's particular rulings and actions on the merits, charging that they are otherwise illegal. The district court rejected all of these arguments, and plaintiffs challenge those rulings on appeal. * * *

B. THE THUNDERBOLT CLAIM: FOREST SERVICE RULING DENYING MOTORIZED ACCESS

1. BACKGROUND: THE FOREST SERVICE ACCESS REGULATIONS

As noted above, Forest Service regulations provide that miners should be permitted access to claims that are surrounded by national forest wilderness lands "by means consistent with the preservation of National Forest Wilderness which have been or are being *customarily used* with respect to other such claims," 36 C.F.R. § 228.15(c) (emphasis added), and that "the use of mechanized transport . . . or motorized equipment" need not be permitted unless *"essential"* to mining activities. 36 C.F.R. § 228.15(b) (emphasis added). As these regulations draw their operative language nearly verbatim from the statute, there can be no question that the regulations are a valid exercise of the agency's delegated rulemaking authority. However, plaintiffs challenge on other grounds the validity of the Forest Service's application of these regulations in the case of the Thunderbolt claim.

2. FOREST SERVICE RULINGS

In its 1989 ruling on plaintiffs' appeal of its denial of permission for motorized access to the Thunderbolt claim, the Forest Service found (1) that the trails that plaintiffs proposed to use for motorized access to the claim had not been used by motor vehicles since the area was designated a wilderness area in 1984; and (2) that the scope of the proposed operation was relatively small, and that consequently the volume of material and equipment that would need to be transported to the claim was not great. On the basis of these findings, the Service concluded that motorized access was not "essential" for the operation of the claim under 36 C.F.R. § 228.15(b), and therefore reaffirmed its earlier denial. In the second 1990 appeal of the same ruling, the Forest Service further found that the scope of the proposed operation was relatively small, and that the equipment that plaintiffs proposed using—a five-inch suction dredge—was sufficiently small in size that it could be transported using pack horses. (A five-inch dredge had been carried in by pack horse when the claim was examined by the Forest Service to assess its validity.) On the basis of this finding, the Service concluded that motorized access was not being "customarily used with respect to other such claims," and that therefore motorized access need not be granted under 36 C.F.R. § 228.15. * * *

3. ANALYSIS OF GROUNDS ON WHICH PLAINTIFFS CHALLENGE FOREST SERVICE RULINGS

Plaintiffs challenge the above rulings on various grounds. First, they challenge the fact-finding on the basis of which the Service concluded that motorized access was neither "essential" to the operation of the claim under 36 C.F.R. § 228.15(b), nor "customarily used with respect to other such claims" under 36 C.F.R. § 228.15(c). However, federal court review of agency fact-finding—other than fact-finding made in the course of formal adjudications which the instant proceedings are not—is conducted under the deferential "arbitrary and capricious" standard, pursuant to 706(2)(A) of the APA. *Mt. Graham Red Squirrel v. Espy,* 986 F.2d 1568, 1571 (9th Cir. 1993); II Davis & Pierce, *Administrative Law Treatise* § 11.4 (3d ed. 1994).... As explained above, the Forest Service concluded, based on the fact that the Service's own examiner had carried in a five-inch dredge by pack horse when evaluating the claim, and the fact that the operation proposed was a small one for which plaintiffs also planned to use a five-inch dredge, that motorized access was not "essential" to the mining operation under 36 C.F.R. § 228.15(b). Regarding the "customarily used" standard of 36 C.F.R. § 228.15(c), the record also shows that the access trails plaintiffs proposed using have been blocked by a gate and closed to traffic since 1984. Since that date the trails have not been maintained by the Forest Service, and consequently they are returning to a natural condition.

Moreover, plaintiffs have pointed to no evidence in the administrative record that would tend to show motorized access is, in fact, "essential" to the operation of this claim or is "customarily used with respect to other such claims." In the absence of such record evidence, there can be no question but that the challenged agency ruling holding that motorized access is not required under 36 C.F.R. § 228.15 is not arbitrary and capricious in violation of § 706(2)(A) of the APA. * * *

QUESTIONS AND DISCUSSION

1. How is the court defining access that is "essential" for a mining operation? If the economic viability of a particular mining claim depends on motorized access, does that make motorized access "essential"?

2. Plaintiffs in *Clouser* also argued that the Forest Service's denial of motorized access to their claims was a taking of their property without just compensation in violation of the Fifth Amendment. The court dismissed their claim because subject matter jurisdiction over the takings claim would lie in the U.S. Court of Federal Claims which, under the Tucker Act, is to hear claims against the United States for money damages in excess of $10,000. 28 U.S.C. §§ 1346, 1491. If plaintiffs had subsequently filed suit in the Court of Federal Claims, would they have prevailed on their takings claim?

3. The *Clouser* case addresses the issue of access to a mining claim which is governed by § 1134(b) of the Wilderness Act. The Wilderness Act in § 1134(a) similarly provides for access to state or privately owned land surrounded by wilderness.

> In any case where State-owned or privately owned land is completely surrounded by national forest lands within areas designated by this chapter as wilderness, such State or private owner shall be given such rights as may be necessary to assure adequate access to such State-owned or privately owned land by such State or private owner and their successors in interest, or the State-owned land or privately owned land shall be exchanged for federally owned land in the same State of approximately equal value under authorities available to the Secretary of Agriculture....

16 U.S.C. § 1134(a). Suppose that Clouser had owned a 160–acre inholding within the North Fork John Day Wilderness Area and had sought access for the purpose of opening a fishing lodge on his property. What result? As

quoted above, § 1134(a) provides that in lieu of access, state-owned land or privately-owned land may "be exchanged for federally owned land in the same State or approximately equal value." 16 U.S.C. § 1134(a). When might an exchange be a wiser approach to an access problem?

Would it matter if Clouser's inholding was within a wilderness area managed by the BLM? FLPMA provides that when BLM lands are designated as wilderness, the access provisions of the Wilderness Act which apply to national forest wilderness areas will also apply to the BLM wilderness. 43 U.S.C. § 1782.

4. Is the effort to regulate access and roads properly described as an attempt to make the access user internalize her negative externalities or as an effort to protect existing positive externalities? Does the distinction matter?

5. The converse of the problem of private access over federal land is federal access over private land. Whether the federal government has an implied right of access over state or private lands was addressed by the Supreme Court in *Leo Sheep Co. v. United States*, 440 U.S. 668 (1979). There, the plaintiff, Leo Sheep Company, who was a successor in interest to the checkerboard blocks of land granted to the Union Pacific Railroad under the Union Pacific Act of 1862 (discussed *supra* at page 125), challenged the United States' decision to build a road across the company's odd-numbered parcels to provide public recreational access to a reservoir. The Supreme Court held that the United States did not have an easement across private land, reasoning first that the Union Pacific Act contained no reservation of such a right and, second, that no access right could be implied because "whatever right of passage a private landowner might have, it is not at all clear that it would include the right to construct a road for public access to a recreational area" and "the easement is not actually a matter of necessity in this case because the Government has the power of eminent domain." *Id.* at 679–80.

———

B. R.S. 2477

Although today the roads that crisscross our public lands are a source of environmental concern for many, that has not always been the case. During the nineteenth century, and even for much of the twentieth, roads were viewed as an almost unqualified good. During the period when the United States was focused on disposing of the public lands and exploiting their natural resources (*see* Chapter 2), roads could hardly be created fast enough. Early state enabling acts promised money for building roads and Congress in a variety of statutes promised rights of way to settlers, miners, and other public land users who needed to construct roads, ditches, or canals across the public lands. Perhaps the most famous of these promises came in the 1866 Mining Law where Congress, in a provision known as R.S. 2477, stated: "*And be it further enacted,* That the right of way for the construction of highways over public lands, not reserved for public uses, is hereby granted." *See* § 8 of the Act of July 26, 1866, 14 Stat. 253. In basic terms, R.S. 2477 allowed state and local governments to acquire a right of way over the public lands by the simple expedient of constructing a road. No application was required; constructing the road created the right of way. This generous grant was repealed by FLPMA in 1976, 43 U.S.C. § 706(a), Pub. L. No. 94–579, 90 Stat. 2793, but FLPMA also promised to protect R.S. 2477 rights-of-way in existence on the date of its passage. *See* FLPMA 43 U.S.C. §§ 509(a), 701(a), and 701(h), codified respectively at 43 U.S.C. §§ 1769(a) and 1701(a), (h) (protecting valid existing rights).

At first glance, R.S. 2477 may not seem particularly significant but, depending on what actually counts as the "construction" of a "highway[,]" it may have created thousands of rights of way across public lands prior to its 1976 repeal. Consider this criticism of R.S. 2477 by two preservation advocates:

> [I]t is hard to imagine a policy that could have more of an impact for the nation's public lands treasures. For example, the state of Utah claims that hiking trails in virtually every park in Utah's scenic treasures, like Arches, Zion, Bryce, and Canyonlands National Parks as well as the Grand Staircase–Escalante National Monument, are actually immune from federal protection and management. Additionally, the State of Utah and a number of rural counties have asserted at least 10,000 and as many as 20,000 R.S. 2477 claims throughout national parks, wilderness areas, proposed wilderness areas, and critical wildlife habitat. Most of these are abandoned mining trails, dry stream bottoms, off-road vehicle routes, and some are not even visible on the ground.
> * * *
> The R.S. 2477 movement has spread beyond Utah. In California, for example, San Bernardino County has begun the process of compiling its R.S. 2477 claims. With its review eighty percent complete, the county has thus far claimed 4,986 miles of "highways," 2,567 of which are in the Mojave National Preserve, protected by the California Desert Protection Act of 1994. In Colorado, Moffatt County officials have claimed a spiderweb of trails in Dinosaur National Monument. In Alaska, the state has claimed that nearly 900,000 miles of section lines (used for survey purposes) with no apparent surface manifestation, are R.S. 2477 highways.
> These claims all have one characteristic in common: they are used as ammunition in the battle against wilderness designation, land preservation and against attempts to regulate the proliferation of off-road vehicles on the public lands.

Stephen H.M. Bloch & Heidi J. McIntosh, *A View from the Front Lines: The Fate of Utah's Redrock Wilderness Under the George W. Bush Administration*, 33 GOLDEN GATE U. L. REV. 473, 489–90 (2003). In light of these stakes, it should not be surprising that FLPMA's repeal of R.S. 2477 triggered a long-running debate about precisely what counted as "construction" of a "highway" triggering an R.S. 2477 right of way.

Most of that debate has taken place at an administrative level. In 1980, the Carter Interior Department's Solicitor office issued a letter concluding that "whether a particular highway has been legally established under R.S. 2477 remains a question of federal law," and that as a matter of federal law, the word "construction" meant that "for a valid right-of-way to come into existence, there must have been the actual building of a highway; i.e., the grant could not be perfected without some actual construction.... 'Mere use' was not sufficient." *See* Letter from Frederick N. Ferguson,

Deputy Solicitor, to James W. Moorman, Assistant Attorney General (Apr. 28, 1980). The Reagan Interior Department, however, looked to state law interpreting R.S. 2477 rights of way and took the position that a road could be constructed by "[r]emoving high vegetation, moving large rocks out the way, or filling low spots" and that the "passage of vehicles by users over time may equal actual construction." Memorandum re: Departmental Policy on Section 8 of the Act of July 26, 1866, Revised Statute 2477 (Repealed), Grants of Right-of-Way for Public Highways (RS–2477), approved Dec. 7, 1988. Then, in 1994, the Clinton administration proposed regulations that would have established an administrative procedure for determining the validity of R.S. 2477 claims under an actual construction standard similar to that in the Ferguson letter. The proposed rules, however, were not finalized because Congress imposed first a temporary and then a permanent moratorium on further Interior Department R.S. 2477 regulations. *See* National Highway System Designation Act of 1995, Pub. L. No. 104–59, § 349(a), 109 Stat. 568, 617–18 (1995); Omnibus Consolidated Appropriations Act, 1997, Pub. L. No. 104–208, 110 Stat. 3009 (1996).

While this administrative tug-of-war was going on, little was happening in the courts. In 1988, in *Sierra Club v. Hodel*, 848 F.2d 1068 (10th Cir. 1988), the Tenth Circuit held that the *scope* of an R.S. 2477 right of way was a question of state law, but the rules for determining the actual existence of an R.S. 2477 right of way remained judicially unresolved.

As discussed earlier in this chapter, on September 24, 1996, President Clinton used his authority under the Antiquities Act to proclaim the Grand Staircase–Escalante National Monument. About two weeks later, three southern Utah counties, including the two in which the Monument had been created, sent out their road crews to blade (i.e., to use a road grader to move earth with a snowplow-like blade) claimed R.S. 2477 rights-of-way within the Monument and elsewhere, including within wilderness study areas and land proposed as wilderness in legislation supported by the environmental community. Kane County Commissioner Joe Judd described the decision this way.

> "What we said was, if they are having trouble judging if it's a road, we are going to brighten those roads up," said Judd. "We went out and reestablished our roads. We smoothed them out. Then they can't say it wasn't graded or it wasn't maintained. It was to help them with their judgment."

> How extensive was that effort in Kane County? Work crews "brightened up" some 500 to 600 miles of back-country roads, Judd said.

Tom Kenworthy, *Blazing Utah Trails to Block a Washington Monument*, WASH. POST, Nov. 30, 1996, at A1. Joe Judd's question about what counted as a road is precisely the one that had been a source of dispute since FLPMA's repeal of R.S. 2477 in 1976. The following case grapples with that question, as well as the subsidiary issues of what law governs the question and who gets to make the decision in the first instance.

SOUTHERN UTAH WILDERNESS ALLIANCE V. BUREAU OF LAND MANAGEMENT,
425 F.3d 735 (10th Cir. 2005)

McCONNELL, CIRCUIT JUDGE.

This case involves one of the more contentious land use issues in the West: the legal status of claims by local governments to rights of way for the construction of highways across federal lands managed by the Bureau of Land Management (BLM). In 1866, Congress passed an open-ended grant of "the right of way for the construction of highways over public lands, not reserved for public uses." Act of July 26, 1866, ch. 262, § 8, 14 Stat. 251, 253, *codified at* 43 U.S.C. § 932, *repealed by* Federal Land Policy Management Act of 1976 (FLPMA), Pub.L. No. 94–579 § 706(a), 90 Stat. 2743. This statute, commonly called "R.S. 2477," remained in effect for 110 years, and most of the transportation routes of the West were established under its authority. During that time congressional policy promoted the development of the unreserved public lands and their passage into private productive hands; R.S. 2477 rights of way were an integral part of the congressional pro-development lands policy.

In 1976, however, Congress abandoned its prior approach to public lands and instituted a preference for retention of the lands in federal ownership, with an increased emphasis on conservation and preservation. *See* FLPMA, 43 U.S.C. § 1701 *et seq.* As part of that statutory sea change, Congress repealed R.S. 2477. There could be no new R.S. 2477 rights of way after 1976. But even as Congress repealed R.S. 2477, it specified that any "valid" R.S. 2477 rights of way "existing on the date of approval of this Act" (October 21, 1976) would continue in effect. Pub.L. No. 94–579 § 701(a), 90 Stat. 2743, 2786 (1976). The statute thus had the effect of "freezing" R.S. 2477 rights as they were in 1976.

The difficulty is in knowing what that means. Unlike any other federal land statute of which we are aware, the establishment of R.S. 2477 rights of way required no administrative formalities: no entry, no application, no license, no patent, and no deed on the federal side; no formal act of public acceptance on the part of the states or localities in whom the right was vested.…

To make matters more difficult, parties rarely had an incentive to raise or resolve potential R.S. 2477 issues while the statute was in effect, unless the underlying land had been patented to a private party. If someone wished to traverse unappropriated public land, he could do so, with or without an R.S. 2477 right of way, and given the federal government's pre–1976 policy of opening and developing the public lands, federal land managers generally had no reason to question use of the land for travel. Roads were deemed a good thing.… Thus, all pre–1976 litigated cases involving contested R.S. 2477 claims (and there are dozens) were between private landowners who had obtained title to previously-public land and would-be road users who defended the right to cross private land on what they alleged to be R.S. 2477 rights of way.

Now that federal land policy has shifted to retention and conservation, public roads and rights of way in remote areas appear in a different light.… Conservationists and federal land managers worry that vehicle use in inappropriate locations can permanently scar the land, destroy solitude, impair wilderness, endanger archeological and natural features, and generally make it difficult or impossible for land managers to carry out their statutory duties to protect the lands from "unnecessary or undue degradation." FLPMA § 302(b), 43 U.S.C. § 1732(b). They argue that too loose an interpretation of R.S. 2477 will conjure into existence rights of way where none existed before, turning every path, vehicle track, or dry wash ... into a potential route for cars, jeeps, or off-road vehicles. For their part, the Counties assert that R.S. 2477 rights of way are "major components of the transportation systems of western states," and express the fear that federal land managers and conservationists are attempting to redefine those rights out of existence, with serious "financial and other impacts" on the people of Utah. Thus, the definition of R.S. 2477 rights of way across federal land, which used to be a non-issue, has become a flash point, and litigants are driven to the historical archives for documentation of matters no one had reason to document at the time.

I. FACTUAL AND PROCEDURAL BACKGROUND

In September and October of 1996, road crews employed by San Juan, Kane, and Garfield Counties entered public lands managed by the BLM and graded sixteen roads (or "primitive trails," as the BLM calls them) located in southern Utah. The Counties did not notify the BLM in advance, or obtain permission to conduct their road grading activities. With a few possible exceptions, none of these roads had previously been graded by the Counties, though some of them showed signs of previous construction or maintenance activity. The roads are claimed by the Counties as rights of way under R.S. 2477. Six of the routes lie within wilderness study areas. Nine are within the Grand Staircase–Escalante National Monument. Six others traverse a mesa overlooking the entrance corridor to the Needles District of Canyonlands National Park. According to the Complaint filed by a consortium of environmental organizations including the Southern Utah Wilderness Alliance (hereinafter collectively referred to as "SUWA"), the areas affected by the Counties' road grading activities "contain stunning red-rock canyon formations, pristine wilderness areas, important cultural and archeological [sites], undisturbed wildlife habitat, and significant opportunities for hiking, backpacking and nature study in an area largely undisturbed by road or human ... development."

SUWA protested to the BLM, but these initial protests resulted in no apparent action against the road grading actions of the Counties. In October of 1996, SUWA filed suit against the BLM, San Juan County, and later Kane and Garfield Counties, alleging that the Counties had engaged in unlawful road construction activities and that the BLM had violated its duties under FLPMA, the Antiquities Act, and the National Environmental Policy Act by not taking action. The complaint sought declaratory and injunctive relief requiring the BLM to halt the Counties' construction activities and enjoining the Counties from further road construction or maintenance without the BLM's permission. The BLM filed cross-claims against the Counties, alleging that their road construction activities constituted trespass and degradation of federal property in violation of FLPMA. . . .

The Counties defended on the ground that their road improvement activities were lawful because the activities took place within valid R.S. 2477 rights of way. The district court acknowledged that "the validity and scope of the claimed rights-of-way [were the] key to resolving the trespass claims," but it also concluded that binding Tenth Circuit precedent required that "the initial determination of whether activity falls within an established right-of-way ... be made by the BLM and not the court." It therefore stayed the litigation and referred the issue of the validity and scope of the claimed rights of way to the BLM. * * *

In January of 2000, [the BLM] issued final administrative determinations, concluding that the Counties lacked a valid right of way for fifteen of the sixteen claims. * * *

The district court affirmed the BLM's determinations in their entirety, concluding that the BLM's factual determinations were supported by substantial evidence in the record and that its interpretation of R.S. 2477 was persuasive under *Skidmore v. Swift & Co.*, 323 U.S. 134, 140 (1944). * * *

IV.   PRIMARY JURISDICTION OVER R.S. 2477 RIGHTS OF WAY

We turn now to the district court's holding that none of the fifteen contested routes falls within a valid R.S. 2477 right of way. We address first the question of whether the district court should have treated this dispute as an appeal of an informal, but legally binding, administrative adjudication, or instead should have treated it as a de novo legal proceeding. We then turn to questions of substantive law.

[O]n May 11, 1999, the district court stayed the litigation in order to allow the BLM to make an initial determination regarding the validity and scope of the Counties' claimed rights of way. The BLM ruled against the Counties, and SUWA filed a motion seeking to enforce that decision in the district court. The district court treated SUWA's motion as an appeal of informal agency action and therefore limited its review to the administrative record and employed the arbitrary and capricious standard of review under the Administrative Proce- dure Act, 5 U.S.C. § 706(2)(A). In effect, it treated the initial stay as a binding primary jurisdiction referral. The Counties argue that the district court should have treated the BLM's decision not as a binding primary jurisdiction referral but as an internal, non-binding administrative determination. * * *

Primary jurisdiction is a prudential doctrine designed to allocate authority between courts and administrative agencies. An issue of primary jurisdiction arises when a litigant asks a court to resolve "[an] issue[] which, under a regulatory scheme, ha[s] been placed within the special competence of an administrative body." *United States v. Western Pac. R.R. Co.,* 352 U.S. 59, 64 (1956). If the issue is one "that Congress has assigned to a specific agency," *Williams Pipe Line Co. v. Empire Gas Corp.,* 76 F.3d 1491, 1496 (10th Cir. 1996), the doctrine of primary jurisdiction allows the court to stay the judicial proceedings and direct the parties to seek a decision before the appropriate administrative agency. *Western Pac.,* 352 U.S. at 64. The agency is then said to have "primary jurisdiction." * * *

[W]e . . . must determine whether Congress has granted the BLM authori- ty to determine validity of R.S. 2477 rights of way in the first place.

R.S. 2477 is silent on this question. It makes no mention of what body— courts or agencies—should resolve disputes over R.S. 2477 rights of way.

The BLM argues that we should interpret this silence against the backdrop of general statutory provisions that give the BLM authority to execute the laws regulating the acquisition of rights in the public lands. According to the BLM, there is a presumption that when Congress makes a grant of land and does not specify which agency, if any, is to administer the grant, the general statutory provisions giving the BLM authority over the public lands also give it authority over the grant. The Counties counter that we should interpret the statutory silence against the backdrop of over one hundred years of practice under R.S. 2477. They maintain that both the BLM and the courts have always operated under the assumption that courts are the final arbiters of R.S. 2477 rights of way, and that this practice should inform our interpretation of the statute.

The BLM's argument, we believe, confuses a land agency's responsibility for carrying out the executive function of administering congressionally deter- mined procedures for disposition of federal lands with the authority to adjudi- cate legal title to real property once those procedures have been completed. The latter is a judicial, not an executive, function. It is one thing for an agency to make determinations regarding conditions precedent to the passage of title, and quite another for the agency to assert a continuing authority to resolve by informal adjudication disputes between itself and private parties who claim that they acquired legal title to real property interests at some point in the past. . . .

Perhaps more to the point, for over a century, in every Land Department or BLM decision in which parties sought a ruling on the validity of an R.S. 2477 claim, the agency maintained that this was a matter to be resolved by the courts. And in prior cases in this Circuit, the BLM has appeared as a litigant, without ever suggesting that its administrative determinations are entitled to legally enforceable status as a matter of primary jurisdiction. This case is the first occasion the government has ever purported to exercise the authority to resolve the validity of R.S. 2477 claims in an informal adjudication before the agency. * * *

According to the BLM, the same general statutory provisions giving [it] authority to rule on the validity of unpatented mining claims should give the BLM authority to rule on the validity of R.S. 2477 rights of way. However, this argument ignores a fundamental difference between mining claims and R.S. 2477 rights of way: title to a mining claim passes by means of a patent, which is issued by the agency in accordance with specified procedures and subject to specified substantive prerequisites. Title to an R.S. 2477 right of way, by contrast, passes without any procedural formalities and without any agency involvement. * * * All that is required . . . are acts on the part of the grantee sufficient to manifest an intent to accept the congressional offer. In fact, because there were no notice or filing requirements of any kind, R.S. 2477 rights of way may have been established—and legal title may have passed— without the BLM ever being aware of it. Thus, R.S. 2477 creates no executive role for the BLM to play. * * *

In sum, nothing in the terms of R.S 2477 gives the BLM authority to make binding determinations on the validity of the rights of way granted thereunder, and we decline to infer such authority from silence when the statute creates no executive role for the BLM. This decision is reinforced by the long history of practice under the statute, during which the BLM has consistently disclaimed authority to make binding decisions on R.S. 2477 rights of way. Indeed, there have been 139 years of practice under the statute—110 years while the statute was in force, and 29 years since its repeal—and the BLM has not pointed to a single case in which a court has deferred to a binding determination by the BLM on an R.S. 2477 right of way. We conclude that the BLM lacks primary jurisdiction and that the district court abused its discretion by deferring to the BLM.

This does not mean that the BLM is forbidden from determining the validity of R.S. 2477 rights of way for its own purposes. The BLM has always had this authority. It exercises this authority in what it calls "administrative determinations." . . . These procedures "are not intended to be binding, or a final agency action." *1993 D.O.I. Report to Congress,* at 25. Rather, "they are recognitions of 'claims' and are useful only for limited purposes," namely, for the agency's internal "land-use planning purposes." *Id.* at 25–26. Nonetheless, they may reflect the agency's expertise and fact-finding capability, and as such will be of use to the court. * * *

V.   LEGAL ISSUES ON REMAND

Because the BLM lacks primary jurisdiction over R.S. 2477 rights of way, a remand is required to permit the district court to conduct a plenary review and resolution of the R.S. 2477 claims in this case. . . .

Bearing in mind the burden this places on the district court, and the importance of these issues to resolution of potentially thousands of R.S. 2477 claims in the State of Utah and elsewhere, this Court will proceed now to address some of the significant legal issues that have been briefed by the parties on appeal and ruled on by the court below. . . .

A. State or Federal Law

The central question in this case is how a valid R.S. 2477 right of way is acquired. As framed by the parties, the answer to this question turns on whether federal or state law governs the acquisition of rights of way under R.S. 2477. For reasons discussed below, we are more doubtful than the parties that the choice between federal and state law is outcome determinative. The principal difference between the federal and state standards, according to the parties, is whether acceptance of an R.S. 2477 right of way is dependent on actual "construction," meaning that "[s]ome form of mechanical construction must have occurred to construct or improve the highway," (the supposed "federal" standard adopted by the BLM), or whether it can be established by the "passage of vehicles by users over time" (the supposed "state" standard advocated by the Counties). [I]t . . . is far from clear that any of the R.S. 2477 claims under adjudication would pass the "usage" test and flunk the "construction" test, or vice versa. . . .

We nonetheless begin with this question: which law applies? * * *

R.S. 2477 was originally enacted as Section 8 of An Act Granting the Right of Way to Ditch and Canal Owners over the Public Lands, and for other Purposes, commonly called the Mining Act of 1866. Act of July 26, 1866, ch. 262, § 8, 14 Stat. 251, 253. The language is short, sweet, and enigmatic: "And be it further enacted, that the right of way for the construction of highways over public lands, not reserved for public uses, is hereby granted." There is little legislative history. Interestingly, Sections 1, 2, 4, 5, and 9 of the Act make explicit reference either to state law or to the "local customs or rules of miners" in the district. For example, Section 2 gives persons who discover certain minerals on public land, "having previously occupied and improved the same according to the local custom or rules of miners in the district where the same is situated," the right to apply for and obtain a patent for the tract. Section 5 provides that "in the absence of necessary legislation by Congress, the local legislature of any State or Territory may provide rules for working mines involving easements, drainage, and other necessary means to their complete development." This shows that when Congress intended application of state laws it did so explicitly. On the other hand, Sections 7, 10, and 11 make explicit reference to other federal laws. Section 7 refers to laws authorizing the President to appoint certain officers, Section 10 preserves the prior claims of homesteaders under the Homestead Act, and Section 11 authorizes the Secretary of the Interior to designate portions of the mineral lands that are "clearly agricultural lands" as such, making them subject to "all the laws and regulations applicable to the same." Section 8 refers to neither state law nor federal law. . . .

The real question, we think, is not whether state law applies or federal law applies, but whether federal law looks to state law to flesh out details of interpretation. R.S. 2477 is a federal statute and it governs the disposition of rights to federal property, a power constitutionally vested in Congress. U.S. Const. art. IV, § 3, cl. 2. As the Supreme Court has stated, "The laws of the United States alone control the disposition of title to its lands. The states are powerless to place any limitation or restriction on that control." *United States v. Oregon*, 295 U.S. 1, 27–28 (1935). "The construction of grants by the United States is a federal not a state question." *Id.* at 28.

Even where an issue is ultimately governed by federal law, however, it is not uncommon for courts to "borrow" state law to aid in interpretation of the federal statute. . . . In the specific context of federal land grant statutes, the Court has explained that courts may incorporate state law "only in so far as it may be determined as a matter of federal law that the United States has impliedly adopted and assented to a state rule of construction." *Oregon*, 295 U.S. at 28.

In determining when to borrow state law in the interpretation of a federal statute, the Supreme Court has instructed courts to consider: whether there is a "need for a nationally uniform body of law," whether state law would "frustrate federal policy or functions," and what "impact a federal rule might have on existing relationships under state law." *See Wilson v. Omaha Indian Tribe*, 442 U.S. 653, 672 (1979). . . . It follows that to the extent state law is "borrowed" in the course of interpreting R.S. 2477, it must be in service of "federal policy or functions," and cannot derogate from the evident purposes of the federal statute. . . .

To modern eyes, R.S. 2477 may seem to stand on its own terms, without need for reference to any outside body of law. At the time of its enactment, however, the creation and legal incidence of "highways" was an important field within the common law, with well-developed legal principles reflected in numerous legal treatises and decisions. When Congress legislates against a backdrop of common law, without any indication of intention to depart from or change common law rules, the statutory terms must be read as embodying their common law meaning. *Nationwide Mut. Ins. Co. v. Darden*, 503 U.S. 318, 322 (1992). It is reasonable to assume that when Congress granted rights of way for the construction of highways across the unreserved lands of the West in 1866, it was aware of and incorporated the common law pertaining to the nature of public highways and how they are established.

In the decades following enactment of R.S. 2477, when disputes arose, courts uniformly interpreted the statute in light of this well-developed body of legal principles, most of which were embodied in state court decisions. . . . The *Hodel* court cited some fifteen decisions in which state law definitions of "acceptance" of a public highway were employed to resolve R.S. 2477 disputes, 848 F.2d at 1082 n.13, and we have located many more. . . . In contrast to . . . the many . . . decisions employing state law standards to resolve R.S. 2477 disputes, the parties have not cited, and we have not found, any cases before its repeal in which R.S. 2477 controversies were resolved by anything other than state law. This unanimity of interpretation over a great many years is entitled to weight. *See Sierra Club v. Hodel*, 848 F.2d 1068, 1080 (10th Cir. 1988) (practice under a statute is relevant evidence of how that statute should be interpreted) (quoting *United States v. Midwest Oil Co.*, 236 U.S. 459, 473 (1915)).

It was the consistent policy of the BLM, as well as the courts, to look to common law and state law as setting the terms of acceptance of R.S. 2477 grants. * * * In its first regulation addressing R.S. 2477 claims, issued in 1939, the BLM stated that "[t]he grant [under R.S. 2477] becomes effective upon the construction or establishing of highways, *in accordance with the State laws,* over public lands not reserved for public uses." 43 C.F.R. § 244.55 (1939) (emphasis added). BLM regulations continued to incorporate state law as the standard for recognizing R.S. 2477 rights of way until the repeal of R.S. 2477 in 1976. * * *

This did not mean, and never meant, that state law could override federal requirements or undermine federal land policy. For example, in an early decision, the BLM determined that a state law purporting to accept rights of way along all section lines within the county was beyond the intentions of Congress in enacting R.S. 2477. *Douglas County, Washington,* 26 Pub. Lands Dec. 446 (1898). The Department described this state law as "the manifestation of a marked and novel liberality on the part of the county authorities in dealing with the public land," and stated that R.S. 2477 "was not intended to grant a right of way over public lands in advance of an apparent necessity therefor, or on the mere suggestion that at some future time such roads may be needed." *Id.* at 447.... In none of the cases applying state law was there any suggestion of a conflict between the state law and any federal principles or interests. Rather, state law was employed as a convenient and well-developed set of rules for resolving such issues as the length of time of public use necessary to establish a right of way, abandonment of a right of way, and priorities between competing private claims.

We do not believe application of state law in this fashion offends the criteria set forth in *Wilson* for appropriate borrowing of state law in the interpretation of federal statutes. The first question is whether there is a "need for a uniform national rule" regarding what steps are required to perfect an R.S. 2477 right of way. 442 U.S. at 672. We think not. Although the substantive content of state law could in some cases conflict with the purposes of federal law (the second *Wilson* criterion), we do not think uniformity for uniformity's sake is necessary in this area of the law. Indeed, there is some force to the view that interpretation of R.S. 2477 should be sensitive to the differences in geographic, climatic, demographic, and economic circumstances among the various states, differences which can have an effect on the establishment and use of routes of travel. * * * Moreover, for over 130 years disputes over R.S. 2477 claims were litigated by reference to non-uniform state standards, a fact that casts serious doubt on any claims of a need for uniformity today.

The second *Wilson* criterion is whether "application of state law would frustrate federal policy or functions." *Id.* As we discuss specific state law standards, we will advert to congressional intention and other indications of federal policy. To the extent adoption of a state law definition would frustrate federal policy under R.S. 2477, it will not be adopted.

The third *Wilson* criterion, the "impact a federal rule might have on existing relationships under state law," *id.,* points in favor of continued application of state law. Both right-of-way holders and public and private landowners faced with potential R.S. 2477 claims have an interest in preservation of the status quo ante. That is best accomplished by not changing legal standards. In *Hodel,* this Court observed that "R.S. 2477 rightholders, on the one hand, and private landowners and BLM as custodian of the public lands, on the other, have developed property relationships around each particular state's definition of the scope of an R.S. 2477 road." 848 F.2d at 1082–83. The same can be said of the *existence* of an R.S. 2477 road.

We therefore conclude that federal law governs the interpretation of R.S. 2477, but that in determining what is required for acceptance of a right of way under the statute, federal law "borrows" from long-established principles of state law, to the extent that state law provides convenient and appropriate principles for effectuating congressional intent. The applicable state law in this case is that of the State of Utah, supplemented where appropriate by precedent from other states with similar principles of law.

B. Specific Legal Issues

We turn now to the criteria governing recognition of a valid R.S. 2477 right of way. First we address burden of proof, and then we turn to substantive standards. For reasons explained in the previous section, we begin with the common law standard as developed in the law of the State of Utah, a standard which is based on continuous public use. We will then address arguments by the BLM and SUWA that, instead of the public use standard, we should adopt a "mechanical construction" standard, as set forth in the BLM administrative determinations, and that valid R.S. 2477 claims should further be limited by the BLM's proposed definition of "highway" * * *

1. Burden of proof

The district court correctly ruled that the burden of proof lies on those parties "seeking to enforce rights-of-way against the federal government." 147 F. Supp. 2d at 1136.... Because evidence in these cases is over a quarter of a century old, the burden of proof could be decisive in some cases.... On remand, therefore, the Counties, as the parties claiming R.S. 2477 rights, bear the burden of proof.

2. The public use standard

Under the common law, the establishment of a public right of way required two steps: the landowner's objectively manifested intent to dedicate property to the public use as a right of way, and acceptance by the public. Isaac Grant Thompson, *A Practical Treatise on the Law of Highways* 48–52 (1868) (dedication); *id.* at 54–57 (acceptance). Dedication by the landowner could be manifested by express statement or presumed from conduct, usually by allowing the public "the uninterrupted use and enjoyment of their privilege" over a specified period of time. *Thompson on Highways, supra,* at 48–49. In the years after its enactment, R.S. 2477 was uniformly interpreted by the courts as an express dedication of the right of way by the landowner, the United States Congress. The difficult question was whether any particular disputed route had been "accepted" by the public before the land had been transferred to private ownership or otherwise reserved. * * *

The rules for "acceptance" of a right of way by the public (whether under R.S. 2477 or otherwise) varied somewhat from state to state. Some states required official action by the local body of government before a public highway could be deemed "accepted." *E.g., Tucson Consol. Copper Co. v. Reese,* 100 P. 777, 778 (Ariz. Terr. 1909). In such states, the appropriation of public funds for repair was generally deemed sufficient to manifest acceptance by the public body. In most of the western states, where R.S. 2477 was most significant, acceptance required no governmental act, but could be manifested by continuous public use over a specified period of time. This was the common law rule. "The common law mode of indicating an acceptance by the public of a dedication is by a user of sufficient length to evince such acceptance...." *Thompson on Highways, supra,* at 54. In some states, the required period was the same as that for easements by prescription, in some states it was some other specified period, often five to ten years, and in some states it was simply a period long enough to indicate intention to accept.

In the leading Utah decision interpreting R.S. 2477, the state Supreme Court explained:

> It has been held by numerous courts that the grant may be accepted by public use without formal action by public authorities, and that continued use of the road by the public for such length of time and under such circumstances as to clearly indicate an intention on the part of the public to accept the grant is sufficient. Other decisions are to the effect that an acceptance is shown by evidence of user for such a length of time and under such conditions as would establish a road by prescription, if the land

over which it passed had been the subject of private ownership[,] or of public user for such time as is prescribed in state statutes upon which highways are deemed public highways.

Lindsay Land & Live Stock Co. v. Churnos, 285 P. 646, 648 (Utah 1929). Looking to the Utah statutes in force at the time the right of way was claimed to have been accepted, the Court held that the period of user necessary for acceptance of an R.S. 2477 right of way was ten years. *Id.,* citing Laws of Utah 1886, ch. 12, § 2 ("A highway shall be deemed and taken as dedicated and abandoned to the use of the Public when it has been continuously and uninterruptedly used as a Public thoroughfare for a period of ten years.").

Acceptance of an R.S. 2477 right of way in Utah thus requires continuous public use for a period of ten years. The question then becomes how continuous and intensive the public use must be. The decisions make clear that occasional or desultory use is not sufficient. In the decision just quoted, the Utah Supreme Court stated: "While it is difficult to fix a standard by which to measure what is a public use or a public thoroughfare, it can be said here that the road was used by many and different persons for a variety of purposes; that it was open to all who desired to use it; that the use made of it was as general and extensive as the situation and surroundings would permit, had the road been formally laid out as a public highway by public authority." *Lindsay Land & Live Stock,* 285 P. at 648.

[To aid the district court on remand, the court set forth in great detail the factual circumstances of state court decisions in Utah and other jurisdictions recognizing and rejecting R.S. 2477 claims.]

3.   *The "mechanical construction" standard*

The BLM and SUWA argue that mere public use cannot suffice to establish an R.S. 2477 right of way. Instead, ... they contend that R.S. 2477 requires that "[s]ome form of mechanical construction must have occurred to construct or improve the highway." "A highway right-of-way cannot be established by haphazard, unintentional, or incomplete actions. For example, the mere passage of vehicles across the land, in the absence of any other evidence, is not sufficient to meet the construction criteria of R.S. 2477 and to establish that a highway right-of-way was granted." ...

The BLM and SUWA cite no pre–1976 authority for this interpretation of R.S. 2477, and we are aware of none. No judicial or administrative interpretation of the statute, prior to its repeal, ever treated "mechanical construction" as a pre-requisite to acceptance of the grant of an R.S. 2477 right of way. The standard has no support in the common law, which, as we have noted, formed the statutory backdrop for R.S. 2477. In no state was mechanical construction of a highway deemed necessary for acceptance of a public right of way. * * *

Consistent with our conclusion that acceptance of the grant of R.S. 2477 rights of way is governed by long-standing principles of state law and common law, we cannot accept the argument that mechanical construction is necessary to an R.S. 2477 claim. Adoption of the "mechanical construction" criterion would alter over a century of judicial and administrative interpretation. This is not to say that evidence of construction is irrelevant. Construction or repair at public expense has sometimes been treated as a substitute for public use, as shortening the period of public use necessary for establishing acceptance, or as evidence of public use or lack thereof. Thus, ... we hold that evidence of actual construction (appropriate to the historical period in question), or lack thereof, can be taken into consideration as evidence of the required extent of public use, though it is not a necessary or sufficient element.

The BLM and SUWA defend their proposed "mechanical construction" standard primarily as dictated by the "plain meaning" of R.S. 2477, which grants the rights of way for the "construction" of highways. The BLM quotes the definition of "construction" from an 1860 edition of Webster's Dictionary as "[t]he act of building, or of devising and forming, fabrication." SUWA quotes a similar definition from an 1865 edition of Webster's as:

> 1. The act of construction; the act of building, or of devising and forming; fabrication; composition. 2. The manner of putting together the parts of any thing so as to give to the whole its peculiar form; structure; conformation.

SUWA Br. 21. That same dictionary supplies these synonyms: to "build; erect; form; make; originate; invent; fabricate."

We are not persuaded. First, it would take more semantic chutzpah than we can muster to assert that a word used by Congress in 1866 has a "plain meaning" that went undiscerned by courts and executive officers for over 100 years. But even confining ourselves to the quoted dictionary definitions of "construction," we are left with a wide range of meanings, including "build," "form," and "make." If nineteenth-century pioneers made a road across the wilderness by repeated use—the so-called "beaten path"—this would fall squarely within the scope of the quoted definition. Such a road would be "formed" and "made" even if no mechanical means were employed. *See Cent. Pac. Ry. Co. v. Alameda County,* 284 U.S. 463, 467 (1932) (referring to R.S. 2477 roads originally "*formed* by the passage of wagons, etc., over the natural soil") (emphasis added). * * *

SUWA supplements its argument that "construction" must refer to "resource-intensive construction," by reference to the probable intention of Congress in granting rights of way for highways. According to SUWA, Congress enacted R.S. 2477 "to spur investment in and development of internal improvements" by "grant[ing] a permanent right-of-way in exchange for the 'construction' of highways." "Like other land-grant statutes, R.S. 2477 provided an incentive and reward for the expenditure required to construct a highway." The trouble with this theory is that those who made the investment in the road did not receive any rights to it; R.S. 2477 rights of way are owned by the public and not by the individuals who "constructed" the highways. A more probable intention of Congress was to ensure that widely used routes would remain open to the public even after homesteaders or other land claimants obtained title to the land over which the public traveled. That explanation of congressional intent is more consistent with the common law interpretation than with the Appellees' proposed substitute. * * *

[W]e are skeptical that there is much difference, in practice, between a "construction" standard (if applied in light of contemporary conditions) and the traditional legal standard of continuous public use. If a particular route sustained substantial use by the general public over the necessary period of time, one of two things must be true: either no mechanical construction was necessary, or any necessary construction must have taken place. It is hard to imagine how a road sufficient to meet the user standard could fail to satisfy a realistic standard of construction. * * *

Indeed, contrary to the apparent assumptions of the parties, it is quite possible for R.S. 2477 claims to pass the BLM's "mechanical construction" standard but to fail the common law test of continuous public use. *See Town of Rolling v. Emrich,* 99 N.W. 464, 464 (Wis. 1904) (rejecting R.S. 2477 claim despite evidence that two men "cut out a road ... through the 80 acres in question to haul logs upon"); *Roediger v. Cullen,* 175 P.2d 669, 674, 677 (Wash.

1946) (rejecting R.S. 2477 claim despite evidence of construction and repair by members of the community).... Large parts of southern Utah are crisscrossed by old mining and logging roads constructed for a particular purpose and used for a limited period of time, but not by the general public. Thus, we cannot agree with Appellees' argument that a "mechanical construction" standard is necessary to avoid recognition of "a multitude of property claims far beyond the scope of Congress's express grant in R.S. 2477." The common law standard of user, which takes evidence of construction into consideration along with other evidence of use by the general public, seems better calculated to distinguish between rights of way genuinely accepted through continual public use over a lengthy period of time, and routes which, though mechanically constructed (at least in part), served limited purposes for limited periods of time, and never formed part of the public transportation system.

We therefore see no persuasive reason not to follow the established common law and state law interpretation of the establishment of R.S. 2477 rights of way.

4. Definition of "highway"

R.S. 2477 grants "the right of way for the construction of highways over public lands, not reserved for public uses." At common law the term "highway" was a broad term encompassing all sorts of rights of way for public travel. In his magisterial *Commentaries on American Law,* Chancellor James Kent wrote that "Every thoroughfare which is used by the public, and is, in the language of the English books, 'common to all the king's subjects,' is a highway, whether it be a carriage-way, a horse-way, a foot-way, or a navigable river." James Kent, 3 *Commentaries on American Law* 572–73, *432 (10th ed. 1860). Under traditional interpretations, therefore, the term "highway" is congruent with and does not restrict the "continuous public use" standard: any route that satisfies the user requirement is, by definition, a "highway." * * *

The parties disagree ... over whether R.S. 2477 routes are limited to roads that lead to "identifiable destinations or places." Cases interpreting R.S. 2477, and analogous cases involving claims to public easements across private land under state law, occasionally refer to a lack of identifiable destinations as one factor bearing on the ultimate question of continuous public use.... It is far from clear that this factor has much practical significance.... It is hard to imagine a road satisfying the "continuous public use" requirement that did not "lead anywhere." We therefore hold that, on remand, the district court should consider evidence regarding identifiable destinations as part of its overall determination of whether a contested route satisfies the requirements under state law for recognition as a valid R.S. 2477 claim. * * *

VI. CONCLUSION

This case is REMANDED to the district court for a de novo proceeding, in accordance with this opinion.

QUESTIONS AND DISCUSSION

1. What are the implications of the court's interpretation of R.S. 2477? How much easier will it be to establish R.S. 2477 rights of way now that the mechanical construction standard has been rejected? Do you agree with the court that continuous public use will be just as hard, if not harder, to prove? How much is your answer to these questions affected by the court's rejection of the BLM's primary jurisdiction and its decision that state, rather than federal, law will apply? For a detailed argument in favor of the

BLM's primary jurisdiction, authored before this decision, see Bret C. Birdsong, *Road Rage and R.S. 2477: Judicial and Administrative Responsibilities for Resolving Road Claims on Public Lands*, 56 HASTINGS L.J. 523 (2005).

2. In his effort to interpret the meaning of R.S. 2477, Judge McConnell relies almost exclusively on pre–1976 case law and administrative rules and decisions. The district court, whose decision the panel overruled, had emphasized that the House Conference Report on FLPMA had provided that the validity of an R.S. 2477 claim " 'should be drawn from the intent of R.S. 2477 and FLPMA.' " *Southern Utah Wilderness Alliance v. Bureau of Land Management*, 147 F. Supp. 2d 1130, 1139 (D. Utah. 2001) (citing H.R. CONF. REP. NO. 102–5503 (1992); 138 Cong. Rec. H9306–01, at H9325). And because FLPMA's purpose was that the public lands be retained in federal ownership, the word "construction" should be interpreted to help achieve that goal. *Id.* at 1139–40. Which approach to interpreting R.S. 2477 is sounder?

3. Recall the court's conclusion that the party seeking to establish an R.S. 2477 right of way bears the burden of proof. Why might this burden be significant to the outcome of many R.S. 2477 cases?

4. Once an R.S. 2477 road is established, questions arise about the scope of the right of way and federal authority to regulate the use of the right of way to protect adjoining lands. In *Sierra Club v. Hodel*, 848 F.2d 1068 (10th Cir. 1988), the Tenth Circuit held that Garfield County had the right to widen an existing R.S. 2477 right of way—along a route known as the "Burr Trail"—as necessary to meet the exigencies of increased travel. The Burr Trail "winds for sixty-six miles through federally owned land in the rugged, dramatic terrain of southern Utah's Garfield County. Connecting the town of Boulder with Lake Powell's Bullfrog Basin Marina, the road at various points traverses across or next to unreserved federal lands, two wilderness study areas, the Capitol Reef National Park, and the Glen Canyon National Recreation Area." *Id.* at 1073.

What is the federal government's authority over Garfield County's actions on the Burr Trail? It comes from two sources. First, the federal government is a sovereign with the authority to regulate use of the right of way. Recall from Chapter 2 that it is well-established under the Property Clause that federal regulatory authority can extend beyond the public lands to adjacent private property. *See Kleppe v. New Mexico*, 426 U.S. 529, 539–44 (1976). *See also Clouser v. Espy*, 42 F.3d 1522, 1538 (9th Cir. 1994) (holding that "regardless whether the trails in question are public highways under R.S. 2477, they are nonetheless subject to the Forest Service regulations"). Second, the United States is the owner of the servient estate and, as such, entitled to common law protection of its interest in the lands through which an R.S. 2477 right of way runs. *See Hodel*, 848 F.2d at 1087 (holding that the county's plans for the Burr Trail could not "unreasonably interfere with (*i.e.,* unnecessarily or unduly degrade)" the BLM's "servient estate"); *see also SUWA v. BLM*, 425 F.3d 735, 745 (10th Cir. 2005) (requiring holders of an R.S. 2477 right of way, before undertaking any improvements in the road along its right of way beyond mere maintenance, to advise the federal land management agency of its plans). In light of both the regulatory and common law limits on an R.S. 2477 right of way, it should be clear that when a county "wins" on R.S. 2477, it does not mean the county will have the unfettered ability to control what happens within its right of way.

Thus, following the court's decision in *Hodel*, Garfield County paved the Burr Trail except for the ten-mile portion traversing Capitol Reef National Park. In February 1996, County road crews performed what they described as routine road improvement along the Burr Trail at the entrance to Capitol Reef National Park, bulldozing a portion of a hillside to improve sight lines for travelers. They did so without the approval of the Park Service. The United States sued and the federal district court held that the County had exceeded the scope of its right-of-way and trespassed on federal lands, awarding the United States $6840.00 in damages. *United States v. Garfield County*, 122 F. Supp. 2d 1201, 1265 (D. Utah 2000).

5. Part of the fascination with R.S. 2477 cases is the sorts of "roads" that are sometimes claimed as R.S. 2477 rights of way. For a view of some particularly dubious R.S. 2477 claims, see http://www.suwa.org/site/Photo AlbumUser?AlbumID=5171&view=UserAlbum. On the other hand, in the *Garfield County* case discussed in Note 4, the United States alleged that the county had "completely transformed the gateway to [Capitol Reef] National Park" by "removing half of the hillside that framed its entrance." This sounds fairly egregious but consider the before and after pictures of Garfield County's road work, *see* http://www.rs2477roads.com/2bora1.htm, and ask whether the United States is taking a similarly uncompromising view.

6. Suppose that the section of the Burr Trail through Capitol Reef National Park had been bull-dozed in 1973, prior to Congress' repeal of R.S. 2477 in FLPMA. What result? R.S. 2477 rights of way may be established only over lands that are "not reserved for public uses." Act of July 26, 1866, ch. 262, § 8, 14 Stat. 251, 253. In a part of Judge McConnell's opinion not included in the excerpt above, he rejected the BLM's argument that a 1910 coal withdrawal defeated the counties' R.S. 2477 claims:

> We must decide whether the coal withdrawal constitutes a "reserv[ation] for public use" under R.S. 2477. The text of the coal withdrawal states:
>
> > "[S]ubject to all of the provisions, limitations, exceptions, and conditions contained in [the Pickett Act and the Coal Lands Act], there is hereby withdrawn from settlement, location, sale or entry, and reserved for classification and appraisement with respect to coal values all of those certain lands of the United States ... described as follows: [describing over 5.8 million acres of land in Utah]."
>
> It is important to note ... that "withdrawal" and "reservation" are not synonymous terms. Although Congress and the Supreme Court have occasionally used the terms interchangeably, that does not eliminate their distinct meaning. A withdrawal makes land unavailable for certain kinds of private appropriation under the public land laws. It temporarily suspends the operation of some or all of the public land laws, preserving the status quo while Congress or the executive decides on the ultimate disposition of the subject lands.

> A reservation, on the other hand, goes a step further: it not only withdraws the land from the operation of the public land laws, but also dedicates the land to a particular public use.... Thus, a reservation necessarily includes a withdrawal; but it also goes a step further, effecting a dedication of the land "to specific public uses." ... The text of R.S. 2477 reinforces this point by requiring not merely that the land be "reserved," but that it be reserved "for public uses."

After a detailed historical analysis, Judge McConnell concluded that the coal withdrawal was not a reservation because it did not dedicate the land to a specific public purpose. *Id.* at 785.

7. In the wake of Judge McConnell's opinion in *SUWA v. BLM*, counties took a more aggressive posture in asserting R.S. 2477 claims. One southern Utah county passed an ordinance opening up to ORV use roads that had been closed by the BLM and the National Park Service, claiming that the roads were R.S. 2477 rights of way. In fact, the county removed federal agency road closure signs and posted in their place county road signs with ORV decals. In *Wilderness Society v. Kane County*, 560 F. Supp. 2d 1147 (D. Utah 2008), the court held that the county's actions violated the Constitution's Supremacy Clause and were preempted by various federal laws and regulations because the county had not yet established its ownership of the claimed R.S. 2477 rights of way. As a matter of sequencing, the county had to bring a quiet title action and prove its claims before it could assert such ownership interests. In *Kane County v. Kempthorne*, 495 F. Supp. 2d 1143 (D. Utah 2007), another district court rejected a similar argument that BLM could not regulate ORV use on any roads within the Grand Staircase–Escalante National Monument that the county claimed as R.S. 2477 rights of way. The BLM, it said, was free to regulate until the county met its burden of proving an R.S. 2477 right of way. By doing so, the BLM was not asserting primary jurisdiction and determining the rights of way. It was only making an administrative determination for its internal management purposes that was not binding on any future federal court addressing the existence of the right of way claims. *Id.* at 1154–55.

8. Notice in Note 7 that the plaintiff in the case where Kane County removed federal road closure signs was actually The Wilderness Society. Neither the U.S. Attorney nor the BLM was willing to take action against Kane County for putting up its own signs. Why do you suspect they were reticent? What happens when counties actually sue for quiet title under the Quiet Title Act, 28 U.S.C. § 2409a? Do environmental organizations have standing to intervene as defenders of the United States' title? In *San Juan County v. United States*, 503 F.3d 1163 (10th Cir. 2007), an en banc court for the Tenth Circuit addressed whether the Southern Utah Wilderness Alliance (SUWA) could intervene in a quiet title action brought by San Juan County to establish title to the Salt Creek Road, which was the subject of an earlier discussion in this chapter about national park management. *See supra* at page 604. The court held that SUWA could not intervene as of right because it had not established that its interests were not adequately represented by the federal government. *Id.* at 1167. Should third parties be allowed to intervene in title disputes? What are the relevant considerations?

9. R.S. 2477 was not the only instance in which rights-of-way across public land were granted by the federal government. In the same statute, Congress also granted the right-of-way for "the construction of ditches and canals" on federal lands, 43 U.S.C. 1769 (repealed, along with R.S. 2477, by FLPMA in 1976), a grant that was repeated in subsequent statutes. *See City & County of Denver v. Bergland*, 695 F.2d 465 (10th Cir. 1982) (discussing Denver's claim to a ditch right-of-way under various federal statutes, all of which were also repealed by FLPMA).

PROBLEM EXERCISE: OBTAINING ACCESS TO AN INHOLDING

Tony Davis, *Will Bulldozers Roll into Arizona's Eden?*
HIGH COUNTRY NEWS, Feb. 18, 2002

Alaskans Erik and Tina Barnes made their fortunes working as commercial fishermen, ski instructors, veterinarians and pilots. But they'd always wanted to run a ranch. In 1990, they found their opportunity: The Santa Maria Ranch, straddling a river of the same name just outside the Arrastra Mountain Wilderness Area in central Arizona, was not only stunningly beautiful, it also had an access road, an airstrip for their Cessna 180 and proximity to shopping in Wickenburg, about 45 miles south.

Intending to ranch part-time and continue the family fishing business, they paid $350,000 for 980 acres on the river and a 40–acre inholding along a wilderness canyon. * * *

But the Barneses' last decade on the ranch has been far from peaceful. Their plans to use heavy construction equipment to fix up old roads and livestock watering tanks in the wilderness have run up against one of the nation's top anti-grazing activists. * * *

"We have to remind ourselves not to stay angry," says Erik Barnes, 67. "My assumption 10 years ago was that they would take care of the inholding problem and the maintenance problems prior to declaring this wilderness. The problems are the result of Joe Feller. Every time the BLM has made a decision in favor of the rancher, he's found a way to stop it. It's unfair." * * *

Joe Feller, of course, sees things differently. The Arizona State University law professor and activist discovered the Arrastra Wilderness a year before Congress designated it in November of 1990. Feller was looking for a riverside grazing issue to sink his teeth into, he acknowledges. After learning from a top BLM official in Kingman that the bureau was doing a management plan for another grazing allotment next to the Barneses' Santa Maria Ranch, Feller dove in. Drawn to steep-walled Peeples Canyon in the heart of the Arrastra Mountains, enchanted by the area's curious blend of junipers, Joshua trees and saguaros, Feller, 48, soon took the first of approximately 50 hikes in the area.

Feller wasn't alone in his attraction to Peeples Canyon. In 1990, Arizona Highways described it "as one of the wonders of public land in Arizona." In 1994, Phoenix Magazine called it "Arizona's answer to Eden." BLM reports label the canyon "a unique desert oasis" that is "among the rarest and most productive wildlife habitat."

Feller learned that the Barneses wanted to bring bulldozers and backhoes into the canyon to improve one mile of a 7.5–mile stretch of dirt roads. The key stretch was 1,000 feet of a narrow, World War II-era access road that slices through hills covered with saguaro and prickly pear, and leads to the Barneses' 40–acre inholding. Erik and Tina Barnes and three other ranchers also wanted to rebuild and repair 15 abandoned and rotting livestock watering tanks. * * *

Feller discovered that the jeep road to the inholding had been closed shortly after the Arrastra became a wilderness, and that it hadn't been used since 1980. In a series of legal briefs Feller helped research for the National Wildlife Federation, the group contended that the road-grading would violate a Wilderness Act ban on new roads in wilderness areas. They said the bulldozing would create long-lasting scars, and that the ensuing cattle grazing would devastate sensitive springs. * * *

The BLM's environmental assessment, completed in 1996, acknowledged that the road "would look maintained and appear to casual observers as a road receiving regular and continuous use." Increased noise could drive raptors such as peregrine falcons and zone-tailed hawks off their nests, and possibly lead them to abandon the canyon.

But the agency also said that denying the proposal might make forage in the area unavailable to livestock and force the owners to abandon their water rights to the canyon, thus reducing the value of the inholding and the ranch. Other development, such as rental cabins or other eco-tourism services, could replace ranching there, the Bureau warned.

John R. Christensen, field manager of BLM's Kingman office, says Congress gave the Bureau a "difficult set of cards to play with," with a law to manage this as wilderness while still allowing grazing: "It's hard to make those two mesh, but they wanted to allow that to happen. We're trying to have a minimum effect, yet still allow livestock grazing to continue." * * *

But despite protests of Feller and environmental groups, in 1996 the BLM approved the Arrastra Wilderness projects. In November 2000, though, the outgoing Clinton administration's Interior Department put the ruling on hold before rescinding it two months later.

Then, last fall, the Bush administration's Interior Department again authorized the road and water tank construction. But Barnes still can't start his engines. In December, with both sides pressing lawsuits, a federal judge ordered that an existing stay precluding ground disturbance would continue until the court makes a final decision. * * *

Erik Barnes says that even if he gains access to his inholding, it won't make up for the lost decade. He says that he has not made a cent at the ranch, because his cattle numbers are one-fourth what they could be with road and water improvements. According to BLM's environmental assessment, though, Barnes likely would earn only $5,000 a year, even if allowed to make his improvements.

Barnes also chafes at the regulations the BLM will impose limiting motor vehicle access to the inholding to 80 to 150 days the first year and even shorter amounts of time in the future.

"The assumption that most Americans have is that if there's a road to your property, you can drive to it," he says.

Feller agrees with Barnes that the federal government has been slow to make decisions, but insists that delays don't mean environmentalists should give up their right to challenge decisions they believe are wrong. Walking down a rutted dirt road through the wilderness toward Barnes' inholding, Feller beams when he spots palo verde and mesquite trees and yellow grasses growing on the now-unused road:

"I try to imagine a bulldozer here and that is not right," he says. "To me, this is wilderness."

But Barnes threatens to build a resort in his inholding if the case keeps dragging. The BLM offered him $200,000 for the 40 acres a few years ago. He sought $1.2 million and today contends his inholding is worth $7 million as Arrastra's "crown jewel." He envisions customers riding horseback into Peeples Canyon, just as they ride mules into the Grand Canyon.

––––––

When the Arizona State Director of the BLM completed the office's environmental assessment of the Barnes' proposal, the Director concluded that in light of the various limitations imposed on the access by the BLM, the project would not have a significant impact. Both the Barnes and the National Wildlife Federation appealed the Director's decision to the Interior Board of Land Appeals (IBLA), the Barnes challenging the limitations and NWF the finding of no significant impact. *See Erik and Tina Barnes,* 151 IBLA 128 (Nov. 30, 1999); *National Wildlife Federation, et al.,* 151 IBLA 104 (Nov. 24, 1999). In response to the Barnes' appeal, the IBLA provided the following additional facts:

Access to the inholding parcel is by a partially overgrown and eroded jeep trail which crosses 2.4 miles of the wilderness between the wilderness border and the private property. This trail was closed to motorized traffic at the time of designation of the wilderness. The WIAEA [Wilderness Inholding Access Arrastra Mountain Wilderness Environmental Assessment] states that the jeep trail access was built by the Santa Maria Ranch more than 50 years ago across state land to access the private land, private water rights, Tina High Spring and the Upper and Lower Red Tank livestock watering facilities. BLM acquired these lands and associated access routes from the state by means of two land exchanges in the 1980's. At one time, about 1940, a road was bulldozed to the bottom of Peeples Canyon to haul in supplies necessary to maintain the water pump and pipeline. The road was not maintained and was impassible to the rim of Peeples Canyon and the boundary of the private land before 1980.

Public lands in the eastern part of the Arrastra Mountain Wilderness are managed under the Lower Gila North Management Framework Plan (March 1983), which recommended that the Peeples Canyon Wilderness Study Area be designated as a wilderness. It also recommended that the 40–acre private parcel, later acquired by the Barnes, be acquired through purchase or land exchange. The BLM explored various options with the Barnes but made no formal land exchange, sale or lease offers until May 1995. At that time, BLM offered to acquire the Barnes' 40 acre parcel for an "exchange value of approximately $200,000." The Barnes rejected BLM's offer.

The access specifications of BLM's chosen Alternative are narrated beginning at page 4 of the WIAEA. In summary, bulldozer, truck and/or backhoe access is allowed to "complete initial repairs" to about 1,000 feet of the 2.4 mile route, as staked by BLM. The remainder of the route would not be maintained or bladed. Pickup truck, all terrain vehicle and trailer access is permitted for "initial pump and pipeline installation" and maintenance on the Barnes' parcel. The WIAEA emphasizes that only such traffic by motorized vehicles is permitted as is necessary to active grazing operations, estimated at 120 days annually, and preparatory activities on this portion of the allotment. Further, bulldozer or backhoe access would be authorized in writing on a case-by-case basis "for repair of damage to the access route and for reestablishing authorized access," and only if route damage is so extensive as to preclude repair with hand tools. The anticipated frequency of need for such access is "on the average of once every three to 5 years." The WIAEA lists a number of mitigation actions/stipulations which include the prohibition of mechanized access from April 1 through July 31 "if the peregrine falcon aerie is in use."

Erik and Tina Barnes, 151 IBLA at 130–31.

———

With reference to the facts described above, consider the following questions:

- Do the Barnes have an implied right of access to their 40–acre inholding? Can they really bulldoze a road in a wilderness area?

- What legal arguments do you suppose the Barnes made in their effort to defeat the limitations imposed upon their access by the BLM? Would those arguments be likely to succeed? In responding to this question it will be helpful to review note 3 at page 706, which describes the law regarding access to wilderness inholdings.

- What sorts of arguments might the National Wildlife Federation have made in contesting the finding of no significant impact? In responding to this question, you may want to review the holding in *Thomas v. Peterson*, 753 F.2d 754 (9th Cir. 1985), excerpted in Chapter 3 (page 268, *supra*).

- If the Barnes were to go ahead with their idea of a resort, could the BLM or the environmental groups stop it? How?

- Can you think of a compromise solution that will satisfy all the parties? In the absence of a compromise, what would be the best solution to impose?

- How do you explain the difference in values assigned to the 40–acre parcel by BLM and the Barnes? How would you calculate the value of a wilderness inholding?

IX. ALTERNATIVES TO PUBLIC LANDS PRESERVATION

To this point, this chapter has focused on federal efforts to preserve portions of the public lands under various designations and management regimes. The truth is that protecting federal public lands is only part of the preservation picture. There are more than 5,842 state park areas that offer some measure of protection to more than 13 million acres of land. California, for example, has 1.5 million acres of state parks and New York has 178 state parks totaling about 300,000 acres. New York's primary preservation commitment, Adirondacks State Park, which is discussed in Chapter 2 (page 131), is not even included in these figures. Adirondacks alone encompasses 5.8 million acres, about 2.5 million of which are state-owned.

In fact, despite the large visitation increases at national parks, in 2001, the various state parks received more than double the visitation of the national parks *See* The National Association of State Parks Directors, *State Park Facts*, http://www.naspd.org/; California State Park Quick Facts, http://www.parks.ca.gov/pages/23509/files/natural%20resources%20of %20california%20state%20parks.pdf; National Park Service Public Use Statistics Office, *Annual Summary Report for: 2001*, http://www.nature.nps. gov/stats/viewReport.cfm?selectedReport=SystemSummaryReport.cfm.

Another critical component of the public preservation landscape, and one that is the most widely used but often ignored, is our system of urban and suburban parks, trails, and open space. Although almost all of these parks lack the dramatic or sublime characteristics of wilderness or the national parks, as Frederick Law Olmsted, the designer of New York's Central Park and the founder of American landscape architecture, saw it, urban parks fulfill a similar purpose by serving as an antidote to the stress and artificiality of urban life. Even more important to Olmsted, and in this sense better than the national parks, parks located in urban settings would be available to the masses. Professor Sax describes Olmsted's philosophy:

> It is unquestionably true, but it is not inevitable, [Olmsted] said, "that excessive devotion to sordid interests," to the constant and degrading work upon which most people are engaged, dulls the aesthetic and contemplative faculties. It is precisely to give the ordinary citizen an opportunity to exercise and educate the contemplative faculty that establishment of nature parks as public places is "justified and enforced as a political duty."

> No one, he thought, was more relentlessly tied to unreflective activity than the ordinary working citizen. The worker spends his life in almost constant labor, and he has done so traditionally because the ruling classes of the Old World had nothing but contempt for him. They thought "the large mass of all human communities should spend their lives in almost constant labor and that the power of enjoying beauty either of nature or art in any degree, require[d] a cultivation of certain faculties which [are] impossible to these humble toilers." Olmsted rejects this belief categorically. Behind his rather archaic vocabulary, and pseudoscientific proofs, lies a prescription for parks as an important institution in a society unwilling to write off the ordinary citizen as an automaton. * * *

> [T]he new, close-to-home parks provide an opportunity to show the urban-ite what it means to be without what Olmstead called distractions. Though Olmstead's Central Park was not a natural wilderness (indeed it was extensive-ly and cunningly landscaped), it was to be a place without amusements and hawkers to amuse the masses. Olmsted's goal at Central Park—lamentably later betrayed in many instances—was to put the New Yorker into a setting designed to stimulate his imagination, and then leave him alone so that his own inclinations and thoughts could take over.

JOSEPH SAX, MOUNTAINS WITHOUT HANDRAILS: REFLECTIONS ON THE NATIONAL PARKS 21, 85 (1980). A 2003 study by The Trust for Public Land reports:

> The total area covered by urban parkland in the United States has never been counted, but it certainly exceeds one million acres. The 50 largest cities (not including their suburbs) alone contain more than 600,000 acres. . . .

> The exact number of annual visitors has not been calculated either, but it is known that the most popular major parks, such as Lincoln Park in Chicago

and Griffith Park in Los Angeles, receive upwards of 12 million users each year, while as many as 25 million visits are made to New York's Central Park annually—which is more than the total number of tourists coming to Washington, D.C.

Peter Harnik, *The Excellent City Park System*, at 9, THE TRUST FOR PUBLIC LAND (2003), *available at* http://www.tpl.org/content_documents/excellent_city_parks.pdf.

The state laws and local ordinances that govern the management of the various state and local parks are beyond the scope of this chapter but the importance of these parks, as well as trails and open space, to the preservation landscape should not be forgotten. Another part of the protected lands picture that should not be ignored are what might be called private preservation efforts. The remainder of this section of the chapter is designed to give you a brief introduction to that topic.

As discussed elsewhere in this casebook, the last few decades have seen an increasing understanding that natural resources are best managed on a landscape or ecosystem level. Because national parks and other federal designations only infrequently encompass an entire ecosystem, watershed, or habitat, it has become increasingly clear that protecting natural resources requires a mix of public and private land. Moreover, aside from this ecological motivation, it can also be said that the public's increasing demand for recreational, scenic, and other amenities provided by preservation has simply not been satisfied by the existing supply of public land protective designations.

Protecting the necessary or desired mix of public and private lands can occur any number of ways. In theory, the public, acting through the federal government, could acquire the necessary property by eminent domain or by purchase through the Land and Water Conservation Fund (*supra* p. 667). Alternatively, it could regulate the land to achieve preservation objectives. In this regard, think about Section 9 of the Endangered Species Act, which prohibits private property owners from engaging in harmful habitat modification, and Section 404 of the Clean Water Act, which prohibits filling of wetlands. However, neither the broad use of eminent domain nor comprehensive regulation (and aggressive enforcement) has garnered particularly broad political support. Another approach to bridging the gap between existing public land preservation and ecosystem preservation needs—or more broadly the gap between the supply of protected lands and the demand for more such lands—is private preservation efforts. As elaborated below, the preservation of private land, whether through land trusts, conservation easements or other mechanisms, is a significant and growing part of the protected lands picture.

Private preservation and conservation easements are not particularly novel. Private forests and game preserves have been with us since the Middle Ages, and the Fish & Wildlife Service began purchasing conservation easements to preserve bird habitat in the upper Midwest during the 1930s. Nevertheless, private preservation efforts truly took off in 1976 when Congress approved tax deductions for land and conservation easements given to environmental charities for conservation purposes. *See* 26

U.S.C. § 170(f)(3)(B) (1976). Since 1976, there has been a rather spectacular boom in land trusts.

> In 1950, there were 53 land trusts. By 1976, on the eve of the enactment of Section 170(h), there were approximately 300. As of 2005, the number of land trusts had increased to 1,667. Along with the boom in the number of land trusts has come a dramatic increase in the acres protected. According to the Land Trust Alliance (LTA), since 1985, state and local land trusts have protected 11.9 million acres of land via purchase and conservation easement. The national land trusts—organizations like The Nature Conservancy, Ducks Unlimited and the Trust for Public Land—have protected another approximately 25 million acres of land. In total, land trusts have protected 37 million acres of land, which is an area 16½ times the sizes of Yellowstone National Park and approximately the same size as the state of Georgia.

James R. Rasband & Megan E. Garrett, *A New Era in Public Land Policy? The Shift Toward Reacquisition of Land and Natural Resources*, 53 ROCKY MTN. MIN. L. INST. 11–1, 11–33 to 11–34 (2007). As this data makes clear, land trusts are a significant player in preservation policy.

As described in the following excerpt, land trusts accomplish their work in three basic ways:

Leigh Raymond & Sally K. Fairfax, *The "Shift to Privatization" in Land Conservation: A Cautionary Essay*, 42 NATURAL RES. J. 599, 625–30 (2002)

A.   Flip or Assisted Transactions

In flip transactions, the land trust acquires land and transfers title to the government at a later date. LTA data ... shows that between one-third and one-half of the land "protected" by land trusts actually winds up being paid for and managed by the government. Land trusts act as procurers for the government for many reasons: landowners may not want to deal with government bureaucrats, government acquisition procedures may be too clunky and rule-bound to meet the family and estate planning needs of potential sellers, or land trusts may be able to move faster in a competitive market. * * *

B.   Conservation Easements

Like the term "land trust," a "conservation easement" has no specific content. It is a contract negotiated by two parties that separates some of the rights of ownership from the underlying fee title. The landowner retains ownership of the land but transfers some use or development options to the trust. The land trust also accepts responsibility for monitoring and enforcing the contract. The transaction is registered as a part of the deed to the property and constrains all future owners. Because the easement typically lowers the value of the parcel, the landowner may be entitled to lower property or estate taxes and may, if the easement was donated, receive income tax benefits as well.

Land trusts and easements can be criticized for just this reason: almost uniformly, easement deals are constructed to meet the specific financial and real estate needs of the donor or seller. Conserved land thus comes under protection because it is available to a land trust, not necessarily because it is an appropriate parcel to conserve. The landowner, rather than the trust, drives the process. Moreover, during negotiations private landowners can reserve rights, exclude portions of the property in order to allow construction of homes for children and grandchildren, and generally define the nature of the protection on the land to suit their own priorities. * * *

C.   Private Reserves

Not infrequently, a land trust makes a fee acquisition with the intention of holding and managing the property on a continuing basis. This is the strongest example of a private alternative to public land use incentives and regulation. Private reserves, rather than conservation easements, would appear as the archetypal private, voluntary, compensated conservation transaction. For example, imagine that a group of private individuals wants a tract of land protected. They join together to buy it from the owner and protect it. No appropriated funds are involved and no government resources are committed to long-term management. While only a small percentage of land trust transactions are of this type, surely one might conclude that they at least represent a truly "private" alternative.

Typically, however, even these deals depend upon public money. Some acquisitions involve corporate sponsors seeking public relations benefits. Individual and corporate contributions to preserve acquisitions are also typically viewed as charitable donations by the Internal Revenue Service. So, while the seller of the land enters the deal voluntarily and is undeniably compensated, even this type of transaction is not appropriately considered wholly private. The transaction almost inevitably will include tax benefits for the seller, hence an infusion of government funds.

Although the land trust movement has accomplished significant preservation, it is not without its abuses. In 2003, the *Washington Post* published a series of articles highly critical of the conservation easement and land trust practices of The Nature Conservancy. According to the *Post*, the Conservancy "had repeatedly bought scenic properties, added development restrictions, then resold the land at reduced prices to Conservancy trustees and supporters. The buyers, some of whom retained the right to build houses on the land, in turn gave the Conservancy cash donations that supplied them with hefty tax write-offs." Joe Stephens & David B. Ottaway, *Developers Find Payoff in Preservation*, WASH. POST, Dec. 21, 2003, at A1. The Conservancy reacted to the articles by prohibiting such sales, but the series may have broader repercussions. Media and scholars are beginning to look with a more critical eye on the land trust movement. One issue that has been raised is whether the tax deductions taken by donors are fair. In theory, a tax deduction is allowed because a conservation easement will decrease the value of the property, but in some cases the easements actually increase property values by reducing the density of a neighborhood and making it more scenic. A 2003 news story related:

> In the Great Smoky Mountains near Asheville, N.C., investors two years ago bought 4,400 acres, placed an easement on 3,000 acres and then began developing 350 home sites and an 18–hole golf course on the remaining property. A master plan for the development, ... shows that the easement area is broken up by the fairways and home sites, which spot the land like mushrooms on a pizza.
>
> Investors paid about $10 million for the land and shared in a tax write-off "in the $20 million range," said James A. Anthony, a partner in the South

Carolina development firm of Chaffin/Light Associates. The deduction was based, in part, on an appraiser's assessment of how much the land would have been worth had they filled the acreage with 1,400 homes, Anthony said.

Far from a liability, the easement has become a marketing tool. Sales literature describes the subdivision as "a community within a park" and the undeveloped portions as maintained "for the quiet enjoyment of members."

Joe Stephens & David B. Ottaway, *Developers Find Payoff in Preservation*, WASH. POST, Dec. 21, 2003, at A1. The same story discussed a 1978 easement that chemical heiress Wilhelmina duPont Ross gave to The Nature Conservancy with respect to her 27,000–acre family estate in the Adirondack Mountains. According to the story, the easement restricted commercial development and required that the estate

remain forever a "natural and scenic area." Backed by an appraisal, she claimed that the restrictions slashed the property's market value by 44 percent. That qualified her for a federal income tax break of more than $1 million—$2.5 million in today's dollars.

Two decades later, during a local property tax dispute, a panel of state judges pointed out that Ross had retained the right to build 10 additional homes, mine gravel pits, drill for oil, cut trees, subdivide the land and expel the public. They pointed out that local governments already heavily regulated development of the estate, meaning that Ross actually had "parted with very little" when she donated her easement. * * *

Another criticism of land trusts has been that they do not do an adequate job of monitoring and enforcing the terms of the conservation easements they negotiate. Stephens and Ottaway noted a 1999 survey of conservation easements in the San Francisco area that found that "only half of the preserved tracts in the region were regularly monitored by the nonprofit or government agency holding the easement" and that of those monitored, 14 percent were violating the terms of the easement. *Id.* On the other hand, a study by the Land Trust Alliance found that 93% of the easements they studied were complying with the terms of their agreements. *Id.*

Although land trusts are the most prominent manifestation, private preservation can be understood to include a much wider array of practices. In broad relief, private preservation encompasses any effort to use positive incentives rather than prohibitory regulation to influence individuals to preserve nature. In the words of two free-market environmentalists, the goal is to create "environmental entrepreneurs" who "specialize in identifying conservation opportunities, mobilizing resources, and building a constituency for conservation. A key to their success is the recognition that solutions will be more acceptable and successful if locals are both the beneficiaries of and participants in conservation efforts." John A. Baden & Pete Geddes, *Environmental Entrepreneurs: Keys to Achieving Wilderness Conservation Goals*, 76 DENV. U. L. REV. 519, 521 (1999). One example of this sort of entrepreneurial activity is the "wolf insurance program" of the Defenders of Wildlife discussed in Chapter 4 (page 407). By compensating ranchers for wolf predation of their livestock, Defenders was able to recalibrate private incentives and at least ease opposition to wolf reintroduction. As another illustration, California has adopted a "conservation bank" program, based on wetlands mitigation banking, that allowed parties, who agreed permanently to manage their land to protect specific endangered species, to sell a fixed number of mitigation credits to developers to offset adverse effects on a species elsewhere. Minnesota exempts from property tax undisturbed wetlands and ungrazed native prairie upon certification by the state department of natural resources. Minn. Stat. §§ 272.02(10), (11) (1993). The Oregon Water Trust, discussed in Chapter 7 (page 797), which purchases water rights and converts them to instream flow, is yet another example of environmental entrepreneurial activity. Without multiplying illustrations further, it can fairly be said that private preservation—or what some might call incentive-based public preservation policy—is playing an increasingly important role in protecting valuable landscapes and biodiversity.

QUESTIONS AND DISCUSSION

1. Reading the discussion of private preservation might give one the impression that there is a clear distinction between private preservation efforts on the one hand and public preservation on the other. Is that distinction real? Which of the various arrangements discussed above are truly "private" preservation and which might be more accurately characterized as simply a different manifestation of public preservation policy?

2. Publication of the Stephens and Ottaway *Washington Post* story discussed in the text drew a quick rebuke from the land trust community, including the following letter from the president of the Land Trust Alliance.

> By focusing on the worst abuses of conservation easements, Joe Stephens and David B. Ottaway did not clearly distinguish con artists from the land trusts doing legitimate conservation work. Most landowners who donate conservation easements are not wealthy developers or golf course owners. They are farmers, ranchers and other ordinary Americans who love their land and want to preserve it forever, forgoing the profits of development.
>
> The article suggests that most landowners initiate the easement process to get big tax breaks when, in fact, it is usually the land trust that approaches the landowner to encourage a donation. It is an indication of the magnitude of property value lost through a conservation easement that so many landowners cannot afford to make that sacrifice.
>
> The article quoted an academic who said that regulations are superior to easements for accomplishing conservation goals. Land-use regulations are a powerful tool, but they can be overturned, while easements last forever. Also, many regions lack even minimum land-use regulations.
>
> Conservation easements are a relatively new legal tool, and the article identifies several areas in which they have been abused. Since most of the abuses involve exaggerated appraisals, we need legislation to stop the abuse of the tax code by those whose motive is private gain instead of conservation. Also, to protect the reputation of legitimate land trusts, the Land Trust Alliance is revising its ethical standards and practices and developing an accreditation program.
>
> RAND WENTWORTH
>
> President
> Land Trust Alliance
> Washington

Letters to the Editor, WASH. POST, Jan. 3, 2004, at A20. If you were hired by the Land Trust Alliance to prepare a set of ethical standards and practices for land trusts, what would you include?

3.   From a basic tax law course you may be familiar with the idea of a "tax expenditure"—the insight that there is no economic or legal difference between the government's direct subsidy of an activity and the government's decision to grant an equivalent tax break for that activity. If this insight holds for land trusts, would the public be better off if the federal government eliminated the tax break for conservation easements and simply spent the money, perhaps through the Land and Water Conservation Fund, to purchase land or easements for the public?

Would a program of government purchase accomplish the same amount of preservation? Would it be accomplished in the same place? Consider the thoughts of Professor McLaughlin:

> It is arguable that the public funds expended on the conservation easements acquired by land trusts, at least those easements that have habitat protection as their conservation purpose, would be better spent in programs that more effectively plan for biodiversity protection by targeting land with the highest conservation value and in most critical need of protection. However, as discussed by Holly Doremus, it is becoming increasingly apparent that a biodiversity conservation approach that focuses only on the protection of reserves or "hot spots" likely will not be successful over the long term because such an approach ignores and, in some respects, exacerbates the growing disconnect in our society between humans and nature. Recognizing that "the more completely we isolate our daily lives from nature, the more tenuous our commitment to protecting nature is likely to become," Doremus argues for finding ways to "focus the law, and the public, on protecting ordinary nature."

> Land trusts, and the conservation easements they acquire, provide a means through which individuals, families, and communities can participate in the protection of ordinary nature—the working farms, the family homesteads, the public trails and parks, the urban gardens. The variety of missions pursued by individual land trusts and the broad conservation purposes for which deductible easements may be granted under section 170(h) allows land trusts to cast a much wider net of land protection than is found in more targeted land conservation programs—ones that take into account and, indeed rely on, the accumulated wisdom of the local inhabitants and their personal connections to the land. Individual landowners, families, and communities are able to take an active role in and responsibility for the protection of the lands they cherish through the sale or donation of conservation easements and through involvement in the founding and ongoing operations of land trusts as board members, staff members, volunteers, and donors.

Nancy A. McLaughlin, *The Role of Land Trusts in Biodiversity Conservation on Private Lands*, 38 IDAHO L. REV. 453, 465–66 (2002).

4.   In the preceding excerpt, Professor McLaughlin identifies as a benefit of conservation easements their ability to involve individuals and communities in the task of preservation. In what other ways might private preservation through the land trust movement differ from traditional public preservation methods? Which of the two is likely to better protect entire ecosystems? Which will have better monitoring and enforcement to assure that preservation objectives are being accomplished? Which is likely to include public participation and accountability? Which is more likely to result in an equitable distribution of public goods and services? Which is more likely to be politically popular?

5. In theory, conservation easements are supposed to be perpetual but what happens when circumstances change? Wyoming has seen an interesting dispute in this regard. In the early 1990s, the Lowham family put a conservation easement on their 1000 acre ranch in Johnson County. The easement required that the ranch continue to be used for agriculture and never be subdivided for residential development. In 1999, the Lowhams sold their ranch to Fred and Linda Dowd who understood the restrictions. Two years later, an energy company with mineral interests underlying the ranch showed up and began exploring for coal bed methane. The Dowds, in turn, went to the County Commissioners and asked them to terminate the conservation easement. They claimed that the coal bed methane development was unpreventable, unanticipated, and inconsistent with the terms of the conservation easement. The commissioners unanimously agreed and rescinded the easement. Rob Hicks, the owner of the local newspaper, the *Buffalo Bulletin*, was furious, particularly when the mineral development didn't go forward on the ranch and the Dowds put part of the ranch up for sale as new home sites. He sued, but the Wyoming Supreme Court ruled that Hicks lacked standing to enforce the terms of the easement. *Hicks v. Dowd*, 157 P.3d 914 (Wyo. 2007). The court observed, however, that the state attorney general was free to sue. *Id.* On July 8, 2008, the state attorney general did so, arguing that rescinding the agreement breached the commissioner's fiduciary obligations as trustee and violated the Wyoming Constitution's prohibition against using public funds for private purposes. WYO. CONST. art. 16 § 6.

What are the implications of this litigation for conservation easements? If the county commissioners' action is upheld, will it reduce charitable organizations' incentives to pay for conservation easements? Or does there need to be some flexibility in managing properties with conservation easements? For an article addressing these and other issues, see Nancy A. McLaughlin, *Conservation Easements: Perpetuity and Beyond*, 34 ECOLOGY L.Q. 673 (2007) (suggesting that perpetual land protection is not appropriate in all instances and that courts and state legislature should look to the common law *cy pres* doctrine, which allows adjustments when the charitable purpose to which the property has been devoted becomes obsolete or inappropriate due to changed circumstances).

6. The basic idea of land trusts, conservation easements, and other private incentive schemes is to *augment* public preservation efforts with private ones. An alternative vision of private preservation is that it should *replace* public preservation. Recall the discussion in Chapter 1 (page 77) about the proposal from the Political Economy Research Center (PERC) for privatizing and auctioning off the public lands. *See* Terry L. Anderson et al., *How and Why to Privatize Federal Lands*, POLICY ANALYSIS (No. 363, Nov. 9, 1999). How likely is it that privatization would produce environmental benefits? If privatization produced less preservation, would that be because the government has currently over-valued the preservation resource, or would it be the result of market failures? Even if one assumed that privatization would bring environmental benefits, would you be willing to privatize all of the public lands?

7. Debt-for-nature swaps remain one of the more innovative and successful efforts to develop alternative financing for environmental protection in developing countries. The following excerpt explains how these swaps work:

> A typical debt-for-nature swap transaction involves a purchase of [a debtor country's] commercial bank debt by a foreign nonprofit organization or a foreign government agency acting in conjunction with a local private conservation or environmental organization.... After purchasing the debt, the investor presents it to the debtor country's central bank in exchange for ecological bonds or local currency at the prevailing exchange rate or at near face value. The investor then uses the converted funds for the management and the preservation of the environment, usually with the support of the host country government and local environmental group. The debtor country's rules govern the redemption of external debt claims. These rules may be foreign investment laws, exchange control laws, or special regulations promulgated to govern such transactions. * * *

> Bolivia was the first country to implement a debt-for-nature swap program. The transaction was concluded in 1987 and covered some 4 million acres of forest and grassland in the Beni River Region. Under the arrangement Conservation International (a U.S conservation organization) purchased $650,000 of substantially discounted Bolivian debt for about $100,000 and swapped it for the shares of a new company set up to help preserve some 1.6 million hectares of forests and grasslands. The debts used in this transaction were owed to private lenders. Citicorp Investment Bank (a subsidiary of Citibank) brokered the transaction and arranged the debt purchase from undisclosed foreign debt creditors. * * *

> The transaction sought to protect land adjoining the Beni Biosphere Reserve. This reserve was created in 1982 as a model for the preservation of flora and fauna, water resources, and the native peoples. Under the agreement, the Bolivian Government undertook to pass legislation to protect the parcels of the land adjoining the 334,000 acre reserve. Part of the area covered by the agreement will be designated exclusively for research while the other part will be open to the nomadic Himane Indians and to agriculture and forestry development. To ensure effective management of the project, an endowment fund of approximately $250,000 in local currency, was created.

Derek Asiedu-Akrofi, *Debt-for-Nature Swaps: Extending the Frontiers of Innovative Financing in Support of the Global Environment*, 25 THE INT'L LAWYER 557, 564–65 (Fall 1991). Debt-for-nature swaps have been used effectively in Ecuador, Costa Rica, the Philippines, Madagascar, and Poland, among others. Although innovative and important in certain specific instances, debt-for-nature swaps will never meet a significant part of the overall demand for sustainable development financing.

To facilitate transactions, the Tropical Forest Conservation Act of 1998, Pub. L. No. 105–214 (TFCA), provides for the alleviation of debt in countries with tropical forests. The TFCA authorizes the President to reduce certain bilateral government debt owed to the United States under the Foreign Assistance Act of 1981 or Title 1 of the Agricultural Trade

Development and Assistance Act of 1954. In exchange, the eligible developing country agrees to place local currencies in a tropical forest fund, which are then used to fund local conservation efforts designed to preserve, restore, or maintain its tropical forests. The TFCA also allows some developing countries to restructure their debt at an amount that is lower than the asset or face value of the debt. Federal appropriations are then used to compensate the Treasury for reductions in the anticipated revenue stream following the debt reduction. The law allows private organizations to contribute their funds to help facilitate a debt swap.

8. For additional discussion of the use of incentives to encourage private preservation, see Christopher S. Elmendorf, *Ideas, Incentives, Gifts and Governance: Toward Conservation Stewardship of Private Land, in Cultural and Psychological Perspective*, 2003 U. ILL. L. REV. 423; Dana Clark & David Downes, *What Price Biodiversity? Economic Incentives and Biodiversity Conversion in the United States*, 11 J. ENVTL. L. & LITIG. 9 (1996).

9. As mentioned in the text, consideration of the law with respect to urban and suburban parklands is beyond the scope of this chapter and casebook. A number of interesting things are happening in the area. The heyday of the urban park was between about 1890 to 1940 as various major cities developed city park systems, but following World War II, as Americans moved to suburbia, parks went into a period of decline where there was relatively little investment in open space. Of late that has been changing as cities have been devoting more resources to revitalizing their parks. *See* Peter Harnik, *The Excellent City Park System*, at 11–13, THE TRUST FOR PUBLIC LAND (2003), *available at* http://www.tpl.org/content_docu ments/excellent_city_parks.pdf. The environmental justice movement is also taking an increased interest in urban parks and landscapes, recognizing that parks "provide outlets for physical activity, recreation, and relaxation," but worrying that historically urban park development has not focused on low-income neighborhoods. Michel Gelobter, *The Meaning of Urban Environmental Justice*, 21 FORDHAM URB. L.J. 841, 853 (1994) (noting that between 1930 and 1939, Robert Moses, the famed New York City Parks Commissioner, built 255 parks, but only two of those were in African–American neighborhoods). What are the implications of this environmental justice insight for park policy more generally—whether national, state, or local?

10. As mentioned above (note 1), the land trust movement and the use of economic incentives to encourage private preservation can be seen as either an alternative to public preservation or as a separate means of accomplishing public preservation objectives. Under this latter view, this section of the chapter can be understood as one that focuses on mechanisms for preservation that go beyond the traditional model of reserving an area of the public lands and turning its management over to a federal agency. In that regard consider two experiments in preservation management that attempted to overcome opposition to preservation by another means—allowing private and local participation in public land management decisions.

The Valles Caldera National Preserve. One of the more interesting experiments in public land management involves the Baca Ranch in New Mexico. The National Park Service had eyed the ranch for many years as a possible extension of the nearby Bandelier National Monument because of its scenic and ecological values. But the high cost of the 89,000–acre ranch and New Mexico Senator Domenici's reluctance to see the property managed solely by the Forest Service put off any action. Finally, on July 25, 2000, President Clinton signed the Valles Caldera Preservation Act which provided for the purchase of the Baca Ranch and its redesignation as the Valles Caldera National Preserve. 16 U.S.C. § 698v *et seq.* (2000). The Preserve, which takes its name from a large, resurgent lava dome with the potential for geothermal activity, operates under a unique management scheme. The Act establishes the Valles Caldera Trust as a wholly-owned government corporation. The Trust is managed by a nine-member Board of Trustees that includes the Superintendent of the Bandelier National Monument, the Supervisor of the Santa Fe National Forest, and seven members appointed by the President to represent the following areas of experience and expertise: (1) livestock management; (2) game and nongame wildlife; (3) sustainable forestry; (4) nonprofit conservation organizations; (5) financial management; (6) cultural and natural history; and (7) state and local governments. 16 U.S.C. § 698v–5 (2000).

As might be surmised from the diverse group of trustees, the Preserve is not managed as wilderness or anything like it. Rather it is intended to be run as a "working ranch" to "protect and preserve the scientific, scenic, geologic, watershed, fish, wildlife, historic, cultural, and recreational values of the Preserve, and to provide for multiple use and sustained yield of renewable resources within the Preserve...." 16 U.S.C. § 698v(b)(2) (2000). How difficult do you think it will be to accommodate the diverse interests represented on the Board of Trustees? Perhaps as unique as the management scheme, is the provision in the law that requires the Trustees to develop a plan that will make the Preserve "self-sustaining" within 15 years. 16 U.S.C. § 698v–9 (2000). How might this requirement help the diverse interests to find common ground? Further information about the Preserve is available at its website. *See* http://www.vallescaldera.gov/.

The Pinelands National Reserve. Another unique management approach is represented in the Pine Barrens of New Jersey, an area popularized in a 1978 John McPhee book. JOHN MCPHEE, THE PINE BARRENS (1978). In that same year, the federal government established the Pinelands National Reserve and called upon the State of New Jersey to adopt a plan to protect the area. One year later, the State of New Jersey enacted the Pinelands Protection Act, which established the Pinelands Commission to help manage this unique resource. The Commission includes 15 members. Seven are appointed by the New Jersey Governor; one by each of the seven counties encompassed by the Reserve, and one by the Secretary of the Interior. The 1.1 million acres of farms, forests, and wetlands that comprise the Pinelands contains 56 communities and more than 700,000 permanent residents. It includes the largest body of open space on the Mid–Atlantic seaboard between Richmond and Boston, and is underlain by aquifers containing 17 trillion gallons of some of the purest water in the world. In 1983, the Pinelands was designated a Biosphere Reserve by the U.S. Man and the Biosphere (MAB) Program and the United Nations Educational, Scientific and Cultural Organization (UNESCO), recognizing the Pinelands as an example of the world's major ecosystem types. Further information about the Pinelands National Reserve can be found at http://www.nps.gov/pine, and http://www.state.nj.us/pinelands.

CHAPTER SEVEN

WATER

I.   INTRODUCTION
II. UNDERSTANDING THE WATER RESOURCE
    A. THE WORLD'S WATER
    B. THE UNITED STATES' WATER
    C. WATER USES AND WATER USERS
    D. VALUING WATER
    E. DAMS
III. THE LAW OF WATER ALLOCATION
    A. RIPARIAN RIGHTS
    B. EASTERN PERMIT SYSTEMS
    C. PRIOR APPROPRIATION
        1. OVERVIEW
        2. BENEFICIAL USE AND WASTE
        3. PERMIT SYSTEMS AND THE PUBLIC INTEREST REQUIREMENT
        4. INSTREAM FLOW APPROPRIATIONS
        PROBLEM EXERCISE: FORMING A WATER TRUST
        5. LOS ANGELES, WATER, AND THE PUBLIC TRUST DOCTRINE
    D. THE LAW OF GROUNDWATER
        1. THE GROUNDWATER RESOURCE
        2. LEGAL REGIMES FOR ALLOCATING GROUNDWATER
    PROBLEM EXERCISE: ALLOCATING A SIMPLE GROUNDWATER AQUIFER
IV. WATER FEDERALISM
    A. WHO OWNS AND REGULATES WATER?
    B. INDIAN AND FEDERAL RESERVED WATER RIGHTS
    PROBLEM EXERCISE: RESERVED WATER RIGHTS FOR WILDERNESS IN IDAHO
    C. INTERSECTING FEDERAL STATUTES
        1. THE CLEAN WATER ACT AND WETLANDS
    CASE STUDY: THE NAVIGATION SERVITUDE
        2. THE ENDANGERED SPECIES ACT
    D. ALLOCATING WATER BETWEEN THE STATES
        1. JUDICIAL ALLOCATION
        2. ALLOCATION BY COMPACT
        3. CONGRESSIONAL ALLOCATION
    CASE STUDY: THE LAW OF THE COLORADO RIVER
V.   INTERNATIONAL WATER LAW
    A. CUSTOMARY LAW OF TRANSBOUNDARY WATERCOURSES
    B. THE 1997 CONVENTION ON NON-NAVIGATIONAL USES OF INTERNATIONAL
        WATERCOURSES
    PROBLEM EXERCISE: ALLOCATING THE WATERS OF THE NILE RIVER

Fresh water is the blood of our land, the nourishment of our forests and crops, the blue and shining beauty at the heart of our landscape. Religions bathe their children and their saved with water. Greek philosophers described water as one of the four elements that made up the earth. To the Kogi Indians of Columbia the three things at the beginning of life are mother, night, and water. The Koyukon Indians of Alaska define cardinal directions not as north or south but as upstream or down. Where there is no water, there is no life. A healthy human being can live for a month without food, but will die in less than a week without fresh water. We live by the grace of water.

Michael Parfit, *Water*, 184 NATIONAL GEOGRAPHIC 7–12 (1993).

Whiskey is for drinkin' and water is for fightin'.

Attributed to Mark Twain.

I. INTRODUCTION

A central theme of this casebook is that similar policy concerns and prescriptions drive most natural resource problems. That is no less true of water. Yet water does present an opportunity to think about natural resources and law a bit differently. As Professor Sax explains:

> Water is unique among resources and it's not unique simply because it sustains us, though, of course, it does that. Unlike other resources, unlike land, oil, or timber, which are also essential to our modern lives, water, whether we find it beneath the earth or in surface streams, is a moving and cyclical resource. Its supply is uncertain and changeable from season to season and from year to year. By its very nature, it is a shared common property. We cannot command it as a fixed object as we do with land or with other minerals. The water we use today is not the same water we'll use tomorrow, and the water we use is routinely used again and again by someone else downstream or downgradient, and ultimately water returns to the sea. It is a continuum. Surface water and underground water are parts of a single integrated system. For these reasons, the legal regime applied to water is unlike any other, and this has been true in every state and in every nation and at all times. Water is never owned in the usual sense. We acquire only use rights in it, or what lawyers call a "usufruct." Because water is inherently a common resource, it is subject to common servitudes, such as the right of public navigation. We find these concepts in various forms in all legal systems, not only those familiar remnants of the ancient Roman law ... but also, for example, in Spanish law, some elements of which are still operative in the American Southwest.
>
> * * * All these diverse laws from widely separated places on the globe emphasize one idea: Water is first and foremost a community resource whose fate tracks the community's needs as time goes on.

Joseph Sax, *Proceedings of the 2001 Symposium on Managing Hawai'i's Public Trust Doctrine*, 24 U. HAW. L. REV. 21, 24 (2001). Do you agree with Professor Sax? Is water "unique among resources"? The fact that water is a "moving and cyclical resource" may distinguish it from timber or minerals, but what about fish, wildlife, and marine mammals? And what about groundwater? In some cases groundwater aquifers have a significant annual recharge just like a river. In others, groundwater is little different than oil. It has collected over millions of years, has little recharge, and is essentially nonrenewable. Water is a classic renewable resource, replacing itself every year, albeit subject to weather. But timber and fish are also renewable resources. Water is a resource that flows across boundaries. The same molecules of water can flow past multiple riparians, through several counties, states, and even nations. But migratory birds and whales do the same thing and wetlands and oil deposits often stretch across jurisdictional boundaries. So, should water be managed like wildlife, like trees, like oil, a combination of the three, or as something unique?

What of Professor Sax's broader theme—that water is "never owned in the usual sense" and is "inherently a common resource"? What is Professor Sax getting at when he distinguishes water from resources "owned in the usual sense"? Does this mean that water rights are, or should be, inherently less secure? Should the community, or the state, have greater power to regulate private water use than other extractive or consumptive natural resource activities because of water's physical qualities? And if so, as some have suggested, should public rights in water serve as a model for public rights in other natural resources? Alternatively, as free market environmentalists have suggested, should we be making greater efforts to treat water more like other property owned "in the usual sense" and subject to price signals and market discipline? These are just a few of the many questions that you should consider as you study the water law materials in this chapter.

The chapter begins with a brief overview of the physical qualities of water. It considers the basic hydrologic cycle and the physical distribution of the water resource on earth and in the United States. It then sets forth the basic consumptive and nonconsumptive uses of water and introduces the basic stakeholders in most water allocation debates. The section follows with a brief discussion of some of the difficulties of valuing water and concludes with a consideration of one more basic physical characteristic of water use—its historic relationship to dams. The chapter then moves to a consideration of the basic state laws governing the allocation of water, beginning first with the riparian rights scheme that largely controls in the eastern United States and then turning to the system of prior appropriation that predominates in the West. The consideration of state water law also investigates the basic rules governing groundwater allocation. The next section of the chapter studies the federal role in water law. It considers historic federal deference to state management of the water resource and the exceptions to that deference, such as the doctrine of federal and Indian reserved water rights, the navigation servitude, congressional allocation of interstate rivers, and the increasing instances in which intersecting federal laws, such as the Endangered Species Act and Clean Water Act, are limiting the exercise of state-created water rights. The chapter concludes with a consideration of international water law, investigating the basic principles that have animated nation-state disputes over allocation of transboundary watercourses.

II. UNDERSTANDING THE WATER RESOURCE

A. THE WORLD'S WATER

Look at any picture of the earth from space. What is the most dominant physical characteristic? It is water. Given its abundance, one might think there would be little reason for law. After all, the catalyst for all natural resources law is scarcity. Why does the need for water law arise? The answer begins with an understanding of water's physical characteristics. The following diagram illustrates the hydrologic cycle.

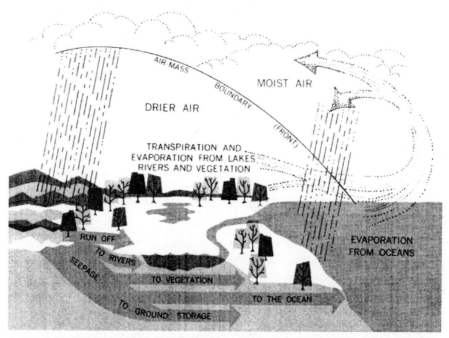

MOIST AIR

DRIER AIR

AIR MASS BOUNDARY (FRONT)

TRANSPIRATION AND EVAPORATION FROM LAKES RIVERS AND VEGETATION

RUN OFF

TO RIVERS

SEEPAGE

TO VEGETATION

TO THE OCEAN

TO GROUND STORAGE

EVAPORATION FROM OCEANS

Source: United States Water Resources Council, The Nation's Water Resources 1–3 (1968)

With the diagram in mind, consider this description of the hydrologic cycle and the world's water by Peter Gleick.

Peter H. Gleick, The World's Water 2000–2001: The Biennial Report on Freshwater Resources 20–22, 24 (2000)

Water is found in many places and forms, and it is in continuous and rapid transformation from one form and stock to another. Fresh water is a renewable resource made available on an ongoing basis by the flow of solar energy reaching the earth from the sun. This energy evaporates fresh water into the atmosphere from the oceans and land surfaces and redistributes it around the world in what is known as the hydrologic cycle—the stocks, flows, and interactions of water as ice, liquid, and vapor. The quantity of water in the atmosphere is reduced by precipitation and replenished by evaporation. Less water falls on the oceans as precipitation than leaves through evaporation; thus there is a continuous transfer of water to the land, which runs off in rivers and streams or is stored in lakes, soils, and groundwater aquifers.

Because of the heterogeneous nature of our atmosphere, land surfaces, and energy fluxes, the distribution of fresh water around the world is also heterogeneous in both space and time. This uneven distribution of water determines the nature of many of the problems related to freshwater management and use. Some places receive enormous quantities of water regularly; others are extremely dry and arid. Seasonal cycles of rainfall and evaporation are the rule, not the exception, and variability from one period to another can be large.

The total volume of water on earth is approximately 1.4 billion cubic kilometers (km^3) and only 2.5 percent of it . . . is fresh water. The vast majority of fresh water is in the form of permanent ice or snow, locked up in Antarctica and Greenland, or in deep groundwater aquifers. The principal sources of water for human use are lakes, rivers, soil moisture, and relatively shallow groundwater basins. The usable portion of these sources is estimated to be . . . less than 1 percent of all fresh water on earth and only one one-hundredth of a percent (0.01%) of all water on the planet. And much of this water is located far from human populations. * * *

The major source of fresh water is evaporation off the surface of the oceans. Approximately 505,000 km³ a year, or a layer 1,400 mm thick, evaporates from the oceans. Another 72,000 km³ evaporates from land surfaces annually. Approximately 80 percent of all precipitation, or about 458,000 km³, falls on the oceans; the remaining 119,000 km³ of precipitation falls over land. The difference between precipitation onto land surfaces and evaporation from those surfaces (119,000 km³ annually minus 72,000 km³ annually) is runoff and groundwater recharge—approximately 47,000 km³ per year.

These global averages hide considerable variation in both the spatial and the temporal distribution of water. Precipitation and evaporation vary on every time scale, ranging from interannual variations to sharp differences in the intensity of storm events. Nearly 80 percent of all runoff in Asia occurs between May and October; three-quarters of runoff in Africa occurs between January and June; in Australia as much as 30 percent of runoff may occur in the single month of March. Another way to think about these variations over time is to realize that nearly 7,000 km³ more water is stored on land in snow, soil moisture, and lakes in March than in September, and that 600 km³ more water is stored in the atmosphere in September than in March. A few spots on earth receive essentially no regular rainfall for long periods, while others are deluged, receiving as much as 10 meters in the span of a few months.

The total volume of stocks and flows provides only a single measure of water availability. From a human perspective, *relative* or *specific* . . . water availability per person (per capita) or per unit area can be more enlightening and useful for public policy. . . . Total volumes of water availability are greatest in Asia. Using per capita measures, however, Asia has the lowest per capita water availability because of its large population. Australia and Oceania have the lowest total volume of water of these continental regions, but by far the greatest per capita availability.

Gleick's description of the world's water is a useful reminder about the nature of resource scarcity. Scarcity is not simply a function of the absolute amount of a resource. It is also related to costs associated with making the resource usable. If rainfall comes at the wrong time, it can't be used unless it can be captured and stored, most often in dams but increasingly by injecting the water into depleted groundwater aquifers. But dams and aquifer recharge cost money and cost the environment. If water is not located where it is needed, it must be moved. Historically, this has meant systems of canals, ditches, pumps, and pipelines. More recently, water has been shipped in tankers, and aspiring entrepreneurs have proposed lassoing icebergs and towing them to thirsty cities or shipping water in football-field-size plastic bags. But moving water also costs money and creates undesired externalities. Another way to make water usable is to desalinate it. But again, although desalination technology has been improving and the price of desalinating water has been coming down, for most nations the costs are simply too high. Water scarcity is thus less a function of absolute amounts than a result of location, timing, and cost. Water law ends up mediating these constraints.

Another contributor to water scarcity is water quality. Access to safe drinking water is probably the number one health problem in the world. All the water in the world won't help if it is too polluted to drink. A recent United Nations report paints a grim picture.

WATER FOR PEOPLE, WATER FOR LIFE: THE UNITED NATIONS WORLD WATER DEVELOPMENT REPORT 9–12 (Executive Summary 2002)

Freshwater resources are further reduced by pollution. Some 2 million tons of waste per day are disposed of within receiving waters, including industrial wastes and chemicals, human waste and agricultural wastes (fertilizers, pesticides and pesticide residues).... As ever, the poor are the worst affected, with 50 percent of the population of developing countries exposed to polluted water sources. * * *

Water-related diseases are among the most common causes of illness and death, affecting mainly the poor in developing countries. Water-borne diseases causing gastro-intestinal illness (including diarrhea) are caused by drinking contaminated water; vector-borne diseases (e.g. malaria, schistosomiasis) are passed on by the insects and snails that breed in aquatic ecosystems; water-washed diseases (e.g. scabies, trachoma) are caused by bacteria or parasites that take hold when there is insufficient water for basic hygiene (washing, bathing, etc.). In 2000, the estimated mortality rate due to water sanitation hygiene-associated diarrheas and some other water/sanitation-associated diseases (schistosomiasis, trachoma, intestinal helminth infections) was 2,213,000.... Worldwide, over 2 billion people were infected with schistosomes and soil-transmitted helminthes, of whom 300 million suffered serious illness. The majority of those affected by water-related mortality and morbidity are children under five. The tragedy is that this disease burden is largely preventable. * * *

Presently, 1.1 billion people lack access to improved water supply and 2.4 billion to improved sanitation. In the vicious poverty/ill-health cycle, inadequate water supply and sanitation are both underlying cause and outcome: invariably, those who lack adequate and affordable water supplies are the poorest in society. If improved water supply and basic sanitation were extended to the present-day 'unserved', it is estimated that the burden of infectious diarrheas would be reduced by some 17 percent annually; if universal piped, well-regulated water supply and full sanitation were achieved, this would reduce the burden by some 70 percent annually.

Water quality and water quantity are related in another way as well. Because water dilutes waste products, more water generally means healthier water. Although laws relating to water quality are left to your environmental law course and not covered in this natural resources law casebook which focuses on allocation, make no mistake—water quantity and water quality are integrally related.

B.   THE UNITED STATES' WATER

Scarcity, as noted above, is a function of place. Some places have water and others don't. The spatial and temporal variation of water is a defining physical characteristic of water in the United States. As reflected in the diagram below, water is unevenly distributed across the country.

100th Meridian

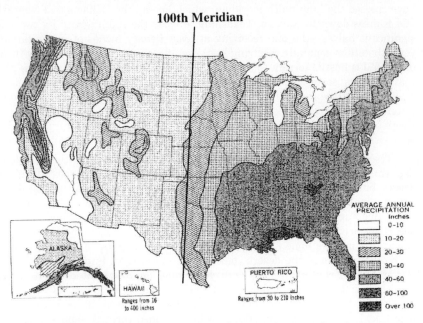

Source: United States Water Resources Council, The Nation's Water Resources 3–2–2 (1968) (100th Meridian added)

To the east of the 100th Meridian, water is relatively plentiful. Most areas receive at least 20 inches of rainfall per year, which is the minimum amount of water necessary to farm in reliance on rainfall rather than irrigation. To the west of the 100th Meridian up to the coastal mountain ranges, precipitation is generally less than 20 inches per year and even where it exceeds that amount, the rainfall occurs only during certain months of the year and water flow fluctuates dramatically, coming in torrents during the spring snow melt in April, May, and June and then dropping to a trickle in late summer and early fall. To make land productive in the West generally requires irrigation—taking water out of streams, rivers, lakes, and aquifers and applying it to the soil. And because the flow in the West is so variable, successful irrigation often necessitates building dams to store water for the dry season. As discussed below, the variation in the scarcity and distribution of water between East and West has led to different legal approaches to allocation of the water resource and distinct cultural outlooks on water. The following excerpt gives some insight into the two different cultures of water use.

Marc Reisner, Cadillac Desert: The American West and Its Disappearing Water 3–5, 9–12 (1993)

If you begin at the Pacific rim and move inland, you will find large cities, many towns, and prosperous-looking farms until you cross the Sierra Nevada and the Cascades, which block the seasonal weather fronts moving in from the Pacific and wring out their moisture in snows and drenching rains. On the east side of the Sierra–Cascade crest, moisture drops immediately—from as much as 150 inches of precipitation on the western slope to as little as four inches on the eastern—and it doesn't increase much, except at higher elevations, until you have crossed the hundredth meridian, which bisects the Dakotas and Nebraska and Kansas down to Abilene, Texas, and divides the country into its two most significant halves—the one receiving at least twenty inches of precipitation a year, the other generally receiving less. Any place with less than twenty inches of rainfall is hostile terrain to a farmer depending solely on the sky, and a place that receives seven inches or less—as Phoenix, El Paso, and Reno do—is arguably no place to inhabit at all. Everything depends on the manipulation of water—on capturing it behind dams, storing it, and rerouting it in concrete rivers over distances of hundreds of miles. Were it not for a century and a half of messianic effort toward that end, the West as we know it would not exist.

The word "messianic" is not used casually. Confronted by the desert, the first thing Americans want to do is change it. People say that they "love" the desert, but few of them love it enough to live there. I mean in the real desert, not in a make-believe city like Phoenix with exotic palms and golf-course lawns and a five-hundred-foot fountain and an artificial surf. Most people "love" the desert by driving through it in air-conditioned cars, "experiencing" its grandeur. That may be some kind of experience, but it is living in a fool's paradise. To *really* experience the desert you have to march right into its white bowl of sky and shape-contorting heat with your mind on your canteen as if it were your last gallon of gas and you were being chased by a carload of escaped murderers. You have to imagine what it would be like to drink blood from a lizard or, in the grip of dementia, claw bare-handed through sand and rock for the vestigial moisture beneath a dry wash.

Trees, because of their moisture requirements, are our physiological counterparts in the kingdom of plants. Throughout most of the West they begin to appear high up on mountainsides, usually at five or six thousand feet, or else they huddle like cows along occasional streambeds. Higher up the rain falls, but the soil is miserable, the weather is extreme, and human efforts are under siege. Lower down, in the valleys and on the plains, the weather, the soil, and the terrain are more welcoming, but it is almost invariably too dry. A drought lasting three weeks can terrorize an eastern farmer; a drought of five months is, to a California farmer, a normal state of affairs. (The lettuce farmers of the Imperial Valley don't even *like* rain; it is so hot in the summer it wilts the leaves.) The Napa Valley of California receives as much Godwater—a term for rain in the arid West—as Illinois, but almost all of it falls from November to March; a weather front between May and September rates as much press attention as a meteor shower. In Nevada you see rainclouds, formed by orographic updrafts over the mountains, almost every day. But rainclouds in the desert seldom mean rain, because the heat reflected off the earth and the ravenous dryness can vaporize a shower in midair, leaving the blackest-looking cumulonimbus trailing a few pathetic ribbons of moisture that disappear before reaching the ground. And if rain does manage to fall to earth, there is nothing to hold it, so it races off in evanescent brown torrents, evaporating, running to nowhere.

One does not really conquer a place like this. One inhabits it like an occupying army and makes, at best, an uneasy truce with it. New England was completely forested in 1620 and nearly deforested 150 years later; Arkansas saw nine million acres of marsh and swamp forest converted to farms. Through such Promethean effort, the eastern half of the continent was radically made over, for better or worse. The West never can be. The only way to make the region over is to irrigate it. But there is too little water to begin with, and water in rivers is phenomenally expensive to move. And even if you succeeded in moving every drop, it wouldn't make much of a difference. John Wesley Powell, the first person who clearly understood this, figured that if you evenly distributed all the surface water flowing between the Columbia River and the Gulf of Mexico, you would *still* have a desert almost indistinguishable from the one that is there today. Powell failed to appreciate the vast amount of water sitting in underground aquifers, a legacy of the Ice Ages and their glacial melt, but even this water, which has turned the western plains and large portions of California and Arizona green, will be mostly gone within a hundred years—a resource squandered as quickly as oil. * * *

As is the case with most western states, California's very existence is premised on epic liberties taken with water—mostly water that fell as rain on the north and was diverted to the south, thus precipitating the state's longest-running political wars. With the exception of a few of the rivers draining the remote North Coast, virtually every drop of water in the state is put to some economic use before being allowed to return to the sea. Very little of this water is used by people, however. Most of it is used for irrigation—80 percent of it, to be exact. That is a low percentage, by western standards. In Arizona, 87 percent of the water consumed goes to irrigation; in Colorado and New Mexico, the figure is almost as high. In Kansas, Nevada, Nebraska, North Dakota, South Dakota, and Idaho—in all of those states, irrigation accounts for nearly all of the water that is consumptively used.

By the late 1970s, there were 1,251 major reservoirs in California, and every significant river—save one—had been dammed at least once. The Stanislaus River is dammed fourteen times on its short run to the sea. California has some of the biggest reservoirs in the country; its rivers, seasonally swollen by the huge Sierra snowpack, carry ten times the runoff of Colorado's. And yet all of those rivers and reservoirs satisfy only 60 percent of the demand. The rest of the water comes from under the ground. The rivers are infinitely renewable, at least until the reservoirs silt up or the climate changes. But a lot of the water being pumped out of the ground is as nonrenewable as oil. * * *

During the first and only term of his presidency, Jimmy Carter decided that the age of water projects had come to a deserved end. As a result, he drafted a "hit list" on which were a couple of dozen big dams and irrigation projects, east and west, which he vowed not to fund. Carter was merely stunned by the reaction from the East; he was blown over backward by the reaction from the West. Of about two hundred western members of Congress, there weren't more than a dozen who dared to support him. One of the projects would return five cents in economic benefits for every tax payer dollar invested; one offered irrigation farmers subsidies worth more than $1 million each; another, a huge dam on a middling California river, would cost more than Hoover, Shasta, Glen Canyon, Bonneville, and Grand Coulee combined. But Carter's hit list had as much to do with his one-term presidency as Iran.

Like millions of easterners who wonder why such projects get built, Jimmy Carter had never spent much time in the West. He had never driven across the country and watched the landscape turn from green to brown at the hundredth meridian, the threshold of what was once called the Great American Desert—but which is still wet compared to the vast ultramontane basins beyond. In southern Louisiana, water is the central fact of existence, and a whole culture and set of values have grown up around it. In the West, lack of water is the central fact of existence, and a whole culture and set of values have grown up around it. In the East, to "waste" water is to consume it needlessly or excessively. In the West, to waste water is *not* to consume it—to let it flow unimpeded and undiverted down rivers. Use of water is, by definition, "beneficial" use—the term is right in the law—even if it goes to Fountain Hills, Arizona, and is shot five hundred feet into 115–degree skies; even if it is sold, at vastly subsidized rates, to farmers irrigating crops in the desert which their counterparts in Mississippi or Arkansas are, at that very moment, being paid not to grow. To easterners, "conservation" of water usually means protecting rivers from development; in the West, it means building dams. * * *

In the West, it is said, water flows uphill toward money. And it literally does, as it leaps three thousand feet across the Tehachapi Mountains in gigantic siphons to slake the thirst of Los Angeles, as it is shoved a thousand feet out of Colorado River canyons to water Phoenix and Palm Springs and the irrigated lands around them. It goes 444 miles (the distance from Boston to Washington) by aqueduct from the Feather River to south of L.A. It goes in man-made rivers, in siphons, in tunnels. In a hundred years, actually less, God's riverine handiwork in the West has been stood on its head. A number of rivers have been nearly dried up. One now flows backward. Some flow through mountains into other rivers' beds. There are huge reservoirs where there was once desert; there is desert, or cropland, where there were once huge shallow swamps and lakes.

C.   WATER USES AND WATER USERS

To understand the task of water law and policy, it is necessary to have some conception of the uses to which water can be put as well as the people and organizations who use it. Those uses and users define the competing interests that struggle over how the water resource should be allocated. Initially, it is instructive to think about water use by differentiating between instream and out-of-stream uses or what might also be called on-site and off-site uses. Instream or on-site uses include fish and wildlife uses, recreation uses, and ecosystem service provision, for example the nursery and water purification services provided by wetlands. They also include navigation, hydroelectric power, and waste dilution. Out-of-stream or off-site uses include using water for irrigated agriculture and domestic or industrial purposes.

Another axis along which to divide water use is between consumptive and nonconsumptive uses. Water withdrawn is not necessarily water consumed. Water can often be reused several times, although not always in the same location as the first withdrawal. Typically, for example, 50% of the water used for flood irrigation makes its way back to the stream from which the water was diverted. With respect to instream or on-site uses, one might initially suppose that all such uses are nonconsumptive. In one sense, that is true. They don't make the water in a stream disappear. But in other ways they can be just as consumptive. To the extent stream flow is used for waste dilution, its diluting qualities are consumed by each additional quantum of waste. More broadly, any time one particular use of water precludes another (for example, a minimum instream flow to protect a fishery), that use can be said to "consume" the water.

To describe the various uses of water is in large measure to describe various water users. Nevertheless, it is worth pausing to consider those interested in any decision about water allocation. Who exactly are the stakeholders in water use decisions? Should decisions be made by those who hold some sort of property interest in the water (riparians and permit holders in the East and prior appropriators in the West)? Or should they include a broader range of users and interests without respect to formal property rights? If you wanted to hold a public meeting about what to do with a local river, whom would you invite? In contemplating the breadth of interests impacted by a single river, consider the following excerpt.

SARAH F. BATES ET AL., SEARCHING OUT THE HEADWATERS: CHANGE AND REDISCOVERY IN WESTERN WATER POLICY 8–9 (1993)

In modern water policy decisions it is important to recognize the breadth of communities of interest. The demands of the Seattle and Portland metropolitan areas for low-cost power from hydroelectric dams affect commercial fishers and their customers from Alaska to British Columbia to Northern California; Indian tribes with treaty-guaranteed fishing rights on nearly every river system in the Pacific Northwest; sportsfishers ... from the coast of Alaska to the interior of Idaho; irrigators and electric rate-payers in Oregon, Washington, Idaho, Montana, and Canada; and people the world over who visit, or plan to visit, the wondrous rivers of the Northwest.

The same is true in other metropolitan areas. Because Denver's reach extends far beyond its political boundaries, the city's desire for water for urban growth affects competitors for water development from Nebraska to Southern California to the state of Sonora in Mexico. Also affected are citizens of the United States and the world who treasure the in-river values from the Rocky Mountain snowmelt that carves and enlivens the deep redrock canyons of Colorado, Utah, and Arizona, all of which are impacted by Denver's water use....

Just as the geographic reach of communities of interest has broadened, so too the membership within water communities has expanded far beyond the small number of interest groups that structured western water policy in the last century.... Today's community of interest is likely to include—in place of the old miner-farmer-rancher-industrial coalition that made western water policy—citizens determined to reduce government expenses; Indian tribes; residents opposed to continued rapid growth in their geographic communities; environmentalists; citizens who want western rivers, lakes, and aquifers managed to guarantee sustainability for their children and grandchildren; recreationists of all stripes; businesspeople whose livelihoods depend on the West's emerging recreation economy; and those who simply believe, fervently, that western rivers should be allowed to retain the incomparable, eternal qualities that provide so much inspiration, reflection, and fulfillment.

All of these and other identifiable interests need to be represented in modern water policy, and in most watersheds nearly all of them are already clamoring for recognition. They will be heard, one way or another.

If water communities of interest are moving beyond "the old miner-farmer-rancher-industrial coalition," of the past, should the broader community do anything to recognize or protect the "old-timers" longstanding water uses? And if so, what?

The preceding excerpt used the term "water communities" to describe communities of interest. Understand, however, that reference to "water communities" also has a much more literal application. More than with any other resource, water users have tended to group themselves into self-governing units for purposes of using the resource. The irrigation districts, flood control districts, conservancy districts, drainage districts, mutual water companies, groundwater districts, and canal companies that dot the water law landscape are cooperative efforts to control, capture, store, and transport water. In studying water law and policy, it is important to remember the existence of these water institutions. Whether a particular water user has an entitlement to water, or can transfer water, can often depend not so much on water law per se, but on the by-laws of the particular organization of which she is a member and on the basic law applicable to business associations. Indeed, water institutions present an array of issues that transcend water law. Certain water districts, for example, have been given powers akin to those held by local government, such as the power to tax land. Their quasi-governmental status has generated significant controversy. In *Ball v. James*, 451 U.S. 355 (1981), for example, the Supreme Court, in a departure from its one-person, one-vote jurisprudence, upheld a rule that limited voting in water district elections to landowners. Professor Thompson outlines the current state of water institutions.

Barton H. Thompson Jr., *Institutional Perspectives on Water Policy and Markets*, 81 CAL. L. REV. 671, 687–89 (1993)

Water institutions form a complex, multilayered industry. Consumers receive water from various "retailing" institutions, which in turn often obtain their supplies from various "wholesaling" institutions. Some institutions serve both roles, supplying water simultaneously to ultimate consumers and to other institutions. The institutional layers are also often nested; retailing institutions are commonly members of wholesaling institutions. [T]he principal agricultural retailers are mutual water companies ("mutuals") and irrigation and other governmental water districts ("water districts"). Of these two, the older are the mutuals—private nonprofit associations (typically corporations) whose customers are also their shareholders. Slightly eclipsing mutuals in importance today, however, are the water districts, which are governed by elected boards much like other local governments. Both types of institutions engage in a broad set of activities, including obtaining and storing necessary water supplies, transporting the water to their service areas, and distributing it to their members.

Governmental institutions are even more prominent suppliers of domestic water, furnishing about eighty-five percent of the water that domestic users receive from institutions. In some cases, cities and counties themselves furnish water to their residents; in other cases, municipal or other water districts supply the water. Privately-owned utilities furnish most of the remaining fifteen percent, although mutuals also serve some domestic consumers.

Although many retailing institutions hold their own appropriative water rights, many obtain at least some of their supply from a diverse assortment of "wholesaling" institutions, including local umbrella agencies, state agencies, and the federal Bureau of Reclamation. The Bureau, the most important wholesaler, supplies water to over twenty percent of all irrigated acreage in the West, as well as to twenty million domestic users—almost entirely through water districts and other retailing governmental agencies.

Although the rise of our urban and suburban culture has moved most water users, both in the East and in the West, toward reliance on institutional water providers, historically cooperative efforts occurred first in the arid West, because the cost of building water storage and then moving the water through systems of canals and ditches was more than most individual farmers could handle. As it turned out, the cost of such major water projects was also more than most private cooperative associations could manage, although there were notable exceptions such as the early Spanish and Mormon settlements. In 1902, Congress responded to these many private and cooperative failures by passing the Reclamation Act, 43 U.S.C. §§ 371–431, which proposed to construct water projects to promote the agricultural settlement of the western United States. The Reclamation Service (later renamed the Bureau of Reclamation) proceeded to build the dams, canals, and water projects that have become such a fixture of the western landscape. Although federal participation in water projects may now seem commonplace, recognize that, in 1902, the Reclamation Act constituted a dramatic departure from the basic nineteenth century ethos that if water development was to occur, dams and ditches should be built by private initiative and with private money. Indeed, in theory, even the Reclamation Act would only provide a loan to individual irrigators who would pay back the government the cost of building the project, albeit interest free and over a long period of time. In practice, however, most irrigators were unable to meet even these generous terms and the Bureau and Congress consistently extended the repayment period.

D. VALUING WATER

For years, students in introductory economics courses have been asked the seemingly simple question, "which is more valuable, water or diamonds?" A cup of water has almost no value to someone drinking a glass of freshly-squeezed juice while shopping for an engagement ring. But if you were dying of thirst in the desert, would you pay more for an engagement ring or water? The fact that we can survive without diamonds but not without water suggests that water is more valuable, yet we pay far more for diamonds than water. Why is that? The answer, and the point of the question, is that one cannot determine value in the abstract. Asking whether diamonds or water is more valuable also asks a hidden question—valuable to whom? An economist might describe this question as one of marginal utility. The real issue is the value of more water or more diamonds. Because water is usually plentiful and diamonds are scarce, an additional cup of water is almost always less valuable than an additional diamond pendant. To the shopper the next drink matters little—but not so in the blazing heat of the desert.

Recall the discussion in Chapter 1 about the difficulties associated with economic valuation of natural resources. Water has not only economic value but also aesthetic, recreational, and cultural values that are much more difficult to price. As long as there is a limited supply of water, valuing water will depend upon understanding the alternative uses to which water could be put. Water is also difficult to value because it is difficult to define what constitutes water "use." As explained above, some uses, like relaxing alongside a lake or stream, have almost no impact. Others, like navigation, fishing, and recreation, leave the water in place but usually a bit more polluted. By contrast, municipal, industrial, and agricultural use tend to consume the water, although even those uses typically are not entirely consumptive. Thus, understanding the cost of a particular water use requires understanding not just the quantity of water used but also the impact of that use upon water quality and upon the timing and location of other potential uses of those same water molecules.

In considering the value of water, we must consider not only the opportunity costs of alternative uses, but also remember that the real cost of water is a function of the infrastructure costs necessary to move the water from the river to the sprinkler. It may surprise some to learn that a farmer diverting water from a public stream often pays nothing for the water, except perhaps a nominal fee to the permitting agency for the original permit. The real cost of the water to the farmer is a function of the cost of whatever works are necessary to divert, store and deliver the water to her crops. Much the same is true for all water users: the cost of water is an amalgam of the water itself and the service performed by the entity, such as a water district, that diverts, stores, cleans, and delivers that water.

An additional challenge of valuing water or, more precisely, allocating water according to its most valuable use, is that of subsidies. Because the public often subsidizes the infrastructure costs, particularly on behalf of irrigation farmers in the form of dam building, canal building and the like, the individual user does not pay the real costs of the water use. The following excerpt gives some indication of the extent of subsidies for water users provided by the Bureau of Reclamation.

MAJORITY STAFF REPORT OF THE HOUSE SUBCOMMITTEE ON OVERSIGHT AND INVESTIGATIONS OF THE COMMITTEE ON NATURAL RESOURCES, 103RD CONG., 2D SESS., TAKING FROM THE TAXPAYER: PUBLIC SUBSIDIES FOR NATURAL RESOURCE DEVELOPMENT 41, 43–44, 50, 52, 56–57 (Comm. Print 1994)

Perhaps the single area in which federal policies provide the greatest number of overlapping programs and the deepest array of supports to resource users is irrigation. The federal government provides Bureau of Reclamation (BuRec) water to farmers and urban consumers in the seventeen Reclamation states. This report focuses largely on BuRec's irrigation water deliveries, because water for urban uses is not intentionally subsidized, and in fact receives far less subsidy.

BuRec constructs major projects throughout the West, then sells the water to farms, or to local water and irrigation districts that in turn supply the water to individual farms. For example, the largest project, the Central Valley Project in California, has thus far involved a capital investment of $4 billion to construct several dams and related distribution systems traveling hundreds of miles to supply irrigation water to more than 2.5 million acres of land on almost 20,000 farms. The terms of sale for BuRec water provide a substantial discount to the irrigators compared to the cost of developing and operating the projects themselves. * * *

The basic subsidy incorporated into the Reclamation program is the interest-free repayment of the construction costs of irrigation projects, including dams, distribution systems and sometimes drainage systems. Under Reclamation law, the cost of constructing these projects is repaid to the federal government over a 40 to 50–year period. Irrigators are required to repay the portion of the construction costs allocated to irrigation; that is, that portion of the costs that BuRec determines is the share of the project that supports irrigation. [Portions of the project allocated, either during construction or during operation, to hydropower or recreation use are not repaid by irrigators. Thus, allocation or reallocation of project costs can reduce the repayment obligation of the irrigators.] The irrigators, however, pay no interest on the unpaid irrigation construction costs. Thus, Reclamation construction repayment is like receiving an interest-free loan for 40 or 50 years. * * *

Another large subsidy for the users of many irrigation projects derives from the Secretary of the Interior's determination of the irrigators' "ability to pay" for water. The Reclamation Project Act of 1939 allows the Secretary of the Interior to reduce water charges to irrigators, based on a calculation of whether the interest-free project repayment cost would exceed their ability to pay for the water. This unpaid portion of the project repayment is then reallocated to the share of the project repaid through sales of federal hydropower. * * *

Although it is nearly impossible to determine the total benefit, ... some 1991 BuRec data provides insight into the overall benefits derived from the program. The following table compares the actual prices being paid for each acre-foot of irrigation water [an acre-foot or "af" is the amount of water necessary to cover one acre of land with one foot of water, which is the equivalent of 325,851 gallons—eds.] on various projects with the "full cost" price for irrigation water. "Full cost" is calculated as the cost for irrigation water if full repayment of the irrigation portion of the project, included any deferred O & M [operation and maintenance expenses], is amortized with interest from the date of construction expenditures. * * *

Project District	$/af Contract Price	$/af Full Cost
CVP* Westlands	8.00	45.79
CVP* Broadview	3.50	30.62
CVP* Glenn–Colusa	2.00	9.77
CAP Central Arizona	2.00	209.49
CAP New Magma	2.00	248.52
Pick–Sloan Riverton Valley	0.75	8.18
Pick–Sloan Torrington	2.80	7.27 * * *

* By contrast, irrigators receiving water from the California State Water Project may pay $100–$200 per acre-foot.

Most of the farmers who purchase subsidized irrigation water also receive support of one kind or another from various agencies of the Department of Agriculture (USDA). These benefits result from the entire array of USDA programs, except for a few programs specific to crops that are not irrigated or not grown in the western states. The following summary of these benefits includes price support (surplus crop) programs, income support programs, disaster assistance programs, conservation programs, loan programs, and pest control programs. Other more indirect benefits derive from agricultural research programs and extension services. * * *

Certain large agribusinesses have historically abused the restrictions on the size of farms that may receive BuRec irrigation water. Because it was originally intended to assist family farmers, the law limits the number of acres of each farm receiving Reclamation water. Originally, the acreage limit was set at 160 acres, but BuRec often interpreted the limit in a loose fashion, permitting a husband and wife to own 320 acres and allowing an unlimited amount of leased land to be added to the 160–acre farm ownership receiving cheap water.

In 1982, Congress attempted to remedy these abuses by passing the Reclamation Reform Act of 1982. The Reform Act acknowledged the existence of the larger farms and expanded the qualified farm to 960 acres, but tightened up the definition of a single farm. All lands operated as a single farming unit were to be counted into the 960–acre limit by 1987. Congress adopted further refinements to close potential loopholes in the acreage limit in 1987.

Unfortunately, BuRec's enforcement of the Reform Act was often selective. Further, large agribusinesses receiving Reclamation water again found loopholes in BuRec's loose interpretation of the Reform Act. Huge farms were reorganized into interconnected farm corporations and trusts, operated together but having a single owner. In some cases, these paper reorganizations existed only for Reclamation purposes; on loan applications and USDA forms, they still operated as a single farm. * * *

———

Undoubtedly, federal water projects involve significant subsidies, and those subsidies are often directed at large agribusinesses. But federal efforts also helped establish a large number of farming communities, and their survival is considered by some as a nonmarket, cultural value that must be included in the water valuation calculus. The following excerpt gives a glimpse into the life of an irrigation farmer. While the farmer described in the excerpt, Ken Mulberry, is like many multigenerational farmers who rely on a steady source of water to keep alive their farms and communities, he provides an interesting counter-example to the irrigation farmers nurtured by the Bureau of Reclamation because he receives his water from one of the few successful large, private irrigation projects in the West.

TIM PALMER, THE SNAKE RIVER: WINDOW TO THE WEST (1991), *reproduced in* SARAH F. BATES ET AL., SEARCHING OUT THE HEADWATERS: CHANGE AND REDISCOVERY IN WESTERN WATER POLICY 59–61 (1993)

His grandfather raised potatoes, his father raised potatoes, and now Ken Mulberry raises potatoes. And other crops. "We have 400 acres here and 330 down the river. About half are in grains—red wheat for milling, barley, and other cow feed. Then there's the feedlot with 2,000 head of cattle, and the potato packing plant. We ship out a million bags a year to eastern markets." Each bag weighs 100 pounds.

Mulberry stood about six feet tall, strong in build, fair-haired under his baseball cap, friendly and ready to share information. His farm lay just above the rim of the Snake River canyon near Twin Falls. Jenny Mulberry tended to five children, all blonde. "Another on the way," she said as she poured a row of orange juices. "Would you like a glass?" * * *

"Let me show you the farm. I have some time now. I got some sleep last night." He slept nine hours for the last three nights, altogether. "We'll stay busy the rest of the season."

We left the wood-sided ranch house, crossed the dirt yard where landscaping was in process, stepped into the pickup, and rode down a lane to a ditch.

"This is out of the Twin Falls Main Canal. Our water rights were established when the canal system was built in 1910. On a dry year, if anyone has to cut back, they cut out the users with the junior water rights. Down here, you hardly ever have to worry about managing your water. I watch it real close anyway, but you don't have to." * * *

We stopped at an overhead sprinkler—a pipe mounted on wheels powered by a motor. Water sprays downward as the pipe progresses slowly across the field. Evaporation consumes less water than in the old lines that sprayed the water upward. "By going to sprinklers and larger fields, we use one-third the water we used in furrow irrigation." * * *

Ken drove to the top of a furrowed field. "There are new things coming out of the research center at Kimberly, like this gated pipe." At the top of the field, perpendicular to the rows of crops, I didn't see a leaking, open, muddy ditch, but a large plastic pipe. At regular intervals, holes had been cut one-inch square. A roped device traveled down the inside of the pipe and opened and closed the holes—miniheadgates—to allow a precise amount of water to leave the pipe and flow down the furrow. "It saves soil, saves water, saves labor, and makes the field look nice. It's efficient." Wastewater that might flow to the bottom corner of the field was pumped back to the top. "That also carries the suspended soil back to the top, right where it ought to be."

"These guys have enough water rights to irrigate constantly, but that doesn't make sense. If you save water, you save oil and have efficient production." Ken looked at me and shrugged his shoulders, as if his statement was obvious to everyone. * * *

"I used to say, 'Damn the conservationists,' but now I see the need to compromise. If we're going to have an organized society, we need some power plants and some irrigation, but some land should never have been put into production. Now they have this CRP program [Conservation Reserve Program]. I call it CPR [cardiopulmonary resuscitation]. It's giving farmers who are going out of business a chance to start something else."

"Isn't that just another subsidy?"

"Yes. I'd like to see an end to the subsidies; let the most efficient farmers win." Ken drove back toward the house.

E. DAMS

To understand the legal and policy context of water, it is finally necessary to understand a bit about dams. Dams have been around for thousands of years, providing a steady, reliable supply of water for livestock, for drinking, for irrigating fields, for water wheels. The last century has seen the development of large dams—Aswan, Grand Coulee, Hoover, Three Gorges—that tame major rivers. The *Report of the World Commission on Dams* observes that nearly half of the world's rivers have at least one large dam, defined by the Commission as a dam over four stories high. More than 45,000 large dams have been constructed around the world. DAMS AND DEVELOPMENT: A NEW FRAMEWORK FOR DECISION-MAKING, THE REPORT OF THE WORLD COMMISSION ON DAMS xxix, 6 (2000). The United States has been a major participant in this worldwide effort.

The United States has joined this world dam-building frenzy, constructing some 5500 large and 100,000 small dams. Although about ninety-five percent of those dams are privately owned, federal dams overshadow them in size, importance, and storage capacity. Together, this country's dams can store approximately one billion acre-feet of water, a volume sufficient to submerge the entire state of Texas beneath six feet of water. Most of the major waterways in the continental United States have been reduced to "staircases of reservoirs," with only the Yellowstone River remaining in the lower forty-eight states as a major, wild river. These dams have inundated an area the size of New Hampshire and Vermont combined.

Christine A. Klein, *On Dams and Democracy*, 78 Or. L. Rev. 641, 646 (1999).

Dams, like most natural resource development, generate significant social benefits. As reported by the World Commission on Dams, "one-third of the countries in the world rely on hydropower for more than half their electricity supply, and large dams generate 19% of electricity overall. Half the world's large dams were built exclusively or primarily for irrigation, and some 30–40% of the 271 million hectares irrigated worldwide rely on dams." Dams and Development: A New Framework for Decision-Making, The Report of the World Commission on Dams 6 (2000). If dams produce social benefits, they also impose significant costs.

Christine A. Klein, *On Dams and Democracy*, 78 Or. L. Rev. 641, 647–49 (1999)

Undoubtedly, dams have brought many critical benefits to society. They have made the desert bloom, providing irrigation water to the most arid portions of the nation. They have tamed mighty rivers, shielding communities from rushing floodwaters and storing spring torrents to provide a dependable year-round supply of water. They have generated inexpensive electricity, bringing warmth and light to impoverished, rural areas. Additionally, they have created great watery playgrounds for activities such as water-skiing and power-boating. * * *

But, these benefits have come at great, and often ignored, environmental, social, and economic costs. * * *

From an environmental perspective, dams create an utter transformation of the downstream ecosystem, affecting the temperature, flow rate, and sediment load of streams. Reservoirs change flowing rivers into deep pools with wide thermal variations, from sun-warmed surface to bone-chilling depths. Seasonal flow rhythms of spring floods and winter trickles are now computer-regulated to match peak power demands and irrigation needs. In addition, dams trap stream sediment, releasing clear powerful waters capable of scouring downstream riverbed and shoreline habitats. As a result of these riverine changes, native fauna has experienced severe and often lethal stresses. One study has identified dams as the predominant factor contributing to the decline of aquatic fauna, finding that sixty-seven percent of freshwater mussels, sixty-four percent of crayfish, thirty-six percent of fish, and twenty percent of dragonfly species are either "extinct, imperiled, or vulnerable" due in large part to dams.

As Professor Klein notes, about 95% of the dams in the United States are the product of private construction. But the biggest dams, the ones with the greatest storage capacity on the largest rivers and the ones that are part of our nation's lore, are federal dams built primarily by the Bureau of Reclamation, the Army Corps of Engineers and the Tennessee Valley Authority. Although federal involvement in navigation projects dates back to the early part of the nineteenth century, its involvement in dam-building and major irrigation projects did not come until the turn of the century with passage of the 1902 Reclamation Act, 43 U.S.C. §§ 371–431. As discussed in Section II.C, *supra*, the purpose of the Act was to construct water projects to promote the agricultural settlement of the western United States.

As citizens have come to value more and more free-flowing rivers for their recreational, aesthetic, and ecological benefits, the legacy of the Bureau, the Corps, and the TVA appears more mixed. Certainly the dams were great engineering achievements that have provided and continue to provide significant economic, recreational, and even some environmental benefits. Judged by the standard of a different era, the agencies delivered what people wanted. Today, however, the agencies preside over a product— dams—whose value more and more people are questioning. The increasing public preference for recreation and preservation has, not surprisingly, slowly been changing the way we think about dams.

Christine A. Klein, *On Dams and Democracy*, 78 Or. L. Rev. 641, 705–08 (1999)

Like all great empires of history, the glory years of the federal dam-building agencies have come to an end. The movement from construction toward demolition began quietly, but has continued to build a relentless momentum. As early as 1931, the Sunbeam Dam was removed from Idaho's Salmon River. Since that time, over 100 of the nation's 100,000 dams have been demolished. In most instances, the removals were relatively noncontroversial, involving important public safety considerations or small, obsolete dams that no longer fulfilled their original purpose. The organization American Rivers observes:

> Thousands of dams in the US were built generations ago, powering mills that fueled this country's leap into the industrial age. Although these dams served an important purpose in their day, today many of them have outlived that purpose. The mills have gone, but the dams remain as a memory of an age gone by. These dams often become abandoned by the original owner, requiring the state to take over the obligation of safety repairs and other maintenance, and putting large economic burdens on taxpayers.

In virtually all cases, deconstruction has occurred with the voluntary cooperation of the dam owner, albeit the threat of federal regulation was a catalyst for action on several occasions. On Butte Creek in California, for example, the threat that the federal government would list as endangered spring-run chinook salmon prompted the 1988 removal of four dams at a cost of $9.13 million. Likewise, an owner in Vermont agreed to the 1996 removal of a dam on the Clyde River when the Federal Energy Regulatory Commission indicated its preliminary preference for dam removal during a relicensing proceeding. Similarly, major electric utility PacifiCorp announced in September 1999 that it would remove the Condit Dam on the White Salmon River in Washington State at an estimated cost of fourteen million dollars in order to avoid thirty million dollars worth of fish ladders and environmental improvements that FERC would have imposed as a condition of relicensing.

The movement continues, with more than one hundred active campaigns seeking the demolition of additional dams. One particular focus of the deconstruction lobby is the Pacific Northwest, where fourteen dams obstruct the Columbia River and its largest tributary, the Snake, is impeded by twelve additional dams. Despite a predictable opposition from some sectors of the population, a surprisingly broad coalition of interests have joined together in the name of river restoration.

With respect to the Lower Snake River, for example, over two hundred entities, including Indian tribes, environmental organizations, scientists, and business and taxpayer groups, have argued for the partial removal of Ice Harbor, Lower Monumental, Little Goose, and Lower Granite dams. Those four structures, operated by the Corps, currently obstruct the migration of endangered salmon populations in Washington. *The Idaho Statesman*, regarded generally as a conservative publication, has come out in support of the proposal, arguing that breaching the dams would produce an annual net benefit to taxpayers of approximately $183 million. * * *

A similar campaign has been mounted to restore Washington salmon and steelhead populations in the Elwha River by removing two private hydropower dams. A group of tribal, environmental, and congressional interests have united to urge the FERC to deny the relicensing applications for the Elwha and the Glines Canyon Dams. Through the Elwha River Ecosystem and Fisheries Restoration Act of 1992, Congress approved the purchase of those dams at a cost of up to $29.5 million, provided that the Secretary of the Interior determines that "removal of the ... dams is necessary for the full restoration of the Elwha River ecosystem and native anadromous fisheries and that funds for that purpose will be available for such removal within two years after acquisition."

III. THE LAW OF WATER ALLOCATION

Two major legal regimes govern water allocation in the United States. Eastern states have employed various forms of riparian rights derived from English common law. Under riparian theory, the right to use water derives from ownership of the land that borders on a watercourse. Western states, by contrast, have adopted a system of prior appropriation more suited to their arid condition under which water rights are determined not by streamside property ownership but by being the first in time to take water out of a stream and put it to use. While this division of water laws into two distinct camps is a useful simplification, certain western states employ a hybrid approach that incorporates riparian rights within a broader appropriation framework. Likewise, many eastern states have begun to condition water use on administrative permit schemes that delink riparian ownership and water use and begin to look more like the permit systems in the West. Within each broader scheme, the states have developed a number of variations. This section of the chapter introduces a few of these variations but it leaves most of them for full-semester courses in water law and instead paints with a broader brush to introduce the major legal and policy questions that animate state water allocation regimes. Before we discuss the basics of riparian theory and prior appropriation, it is worth contemplating the question of why two systems evolved and why water law has changed over time. In that regard consider the following excerpt.

Joseph Sax, *Proceedings of the 2001 Symposium on Managing Hawai'i's Public Trust Doctrine*, 24 U. Haw. L. Rev. 21, 25–28, 33 (2001)

There's one other feature of water law that reveals its essential status as a common resource.... Because water is so central to the life of a community of which it is a part, water law has shown itself to be remarkably adaptable to the evolving needs of the community. Some of these transformations are well known. In pre-industrial England and America, ... the natural flow doctrine prevailed. Rivers were left to flow as they did in the state of nature, which suited agricultural and pastoral landscapes prior to the nineteenth century. As industrialization got under way, most prominently with the mills that powered the early industries of New England, natural flow doctrine yielded to a more industry-friendly doctrine known as "reasonable use." The law changed to permit the diversions to produce hydropower, and natural flow doctrine gave way, though versions of it are making a strong comeback in the context of environmental restoration. * * *

As population moved west past the hundredth meridian, the line dividing the so-called humid and arid regions of North America, another and even more dramatic change occurred. Riparianism, the very essence of water law in Anglo–American tradition, was simply not recognized in most of the West. Instead, western states fashioned the prior appropriation system which, among other things, abolished watershed of origin restrictions, and permitted water to be moved out of the basin where it was needed, first for mining, later for irrigation, and finally to support municipal development in cities like Los Angeles, Denver, Albuquerque, and San Francisco. Riparian landowners object-ed that no such change could be achieved as against their traditional riparian rights to the water and that such rights were implicit in their land titles. Of course, as we now know, those claims too were overwhelmingly swept aside by the same reasoning that had led to the modification of the natural flow doctrine and to the redefinition of navigability. The courts found that water was a community resource and that rights in water were always contingent on the fundamental needs of the community at the time, reflecting natural conditions, such as aridity, or the evolution of social goals.

In a famous opinion in 1882, the Colorado Supreme Court said "we conclude that the common law doctrine is inapplicable here. Imperative necessi-ty, unknown to the countries which gave it birth, compels the recognition of another doctrine in conflict with the old." [*Coffin v. The Left Hand Ditch Co.*, 6 Colo. 443, 447 (1882)]. The evolutionary character of water law has continued in a variety of contexts. The principle of the *Coffin* case that I just quoted, and the commitment to beneficial use which, at that time, meant economically productive use as the source and limit of water rights, gave rise to another Colorado case some twenty-five years later in which it was determined that leaving water instream could not qualify as a beneficial use and no one could acquire a right to leave water instream. Why? Because by the standards and the goals of that day, water was considered too precious to be left in the river. Indeed, it was standard law that the only way to perfect the beneficial right of use was physically to take the water out of the river and to apply it to some economic purpose. When more contemporary values to protect fish and riparian services, as well as recreation, came to the fore, it was argued, as it had been when the appropriation doctrine first displaced the riparian doctrine, that to treat instream flows as beneficial and to allow an individual or a state agency to appropriate water instream for environmental protection was to take away the established property rights of others to appropriate the water. But the courts rejected this claim just as they had rejected the previous traditional claims, and today instream uses are everywhere considered beneficial, even essential, uses of water.

So once more, history's wheel turned. I noted ... that Colorado eliminated riparian rights from the very beginning of settlement. Many other western states, the Dakotas, Oregon, and California, retained some of these riparian rights at least for a while. Then in various ways, with the one exception of Oklahoma, they either eliminated or restricted the acquisition of future riparian rights, although loss by nonuse was absolutely antithetical to traditional riparian doctrine. In each such instance, it was asserted that the abolition of unused riparian rights was a violation of vested property rights. Those claims too have failed. * * *

I could extend this list almost endlessly. To your relief, I will not, but I hope the central point I'm trying to make is by now obvious. The rules governing the use of water have always been in a dynamic relationship with the evolving values of the community.

———

As you study the following sections on riparian rights and prior appropriation consider Professor Sax's point that the "rules governing the use of water have always been in a dynamic relationship with the evolving values of the community." Is that true for all natural resources and property? If so, what does that suggest about the nature of property rights? If not, why is water different?

A.   RIPARIAN RIGHTS

As described by Professor Sax in the excerpt above, the United States inherited from England the property law concept that one of the sticks in the bundle possessed by property owners whose land was adjacent (riparian) to a watercourse was the right to make use of the water (a riparian right). The dominant understanding of a riparian right was that each riparian property owner was entitled to have any stream flowing through his land remain in its natural condition without diminishing its quality or quantity. When this doctrine began to interfere with productive uses of the stream, jurisdictions gravitated to what became known as the reasonable use rule. The following case discusses this change and begins an explanation of how the reasonable use rule works in practice.

HARRIS v. BROOKS,
225 Ark. 436, 283 S.W.2d 129 (1955)

The issues presented by this appeal relate to the relative rights of riparian landowners to the use of a privately owned non-navigable lake and the water therein.

Appellant, Theo Mashburn, lessee of riparian landowners, conducts a commercial boating and fishing enterprise. In this business he rents cabins, sells fishing bait and equipment, and rents boats to members of the general public who desire to use the lake for fishing and other recreational purposes. He and his lessors filed a complaint ... to enjoin appellees from pumping water from the lake to irrigate a rice crop, alleging that, as of that date, appellees had reduced the water level of the lake to such an extent as to make the lake unsuitable 'for fishing, recreation, or other lawful purposes.' After a lengthy hearing, the chancellor denied injunctive relief, and this appeal is prosecuted to reverse the chancellor's decision.

Factual Background. Horseshoe Lake, located about 3 miles south of Augusta, is approximately 3 miles long and 300 feet wide, and, as the name implies, resembles a horseshoe in shape. Appellees, John Brooks and John Brooks, Jr., are lessees of Ector Johnson who owns a large tract of land adjacent to the lake, including three-fourths of the lake bed.

For a number of years appellees have intermittently raised rice on Johnson's land and have each year, including 1954, irrigated the rice with water pumped from the lake. They pumped no more water in 1954 than they did in 1951 and 1952, no rice being raised in 1953. Approximately 190 acres were cultivated in rice in 1954.

... Mashburn began operating his business about the first of April, 1954, and fishing and boat rentals were satisfactory from that time until about July 1st or 4th when, he says, the fish quit biting and his income from that source and boat rentals was reduced to practically nothing.

Appellees began pumping water with an 8 inch intake on May 25, 1954 and continued pumping until this suit was filed on July 10, and then until about August 20th. They quit pumping at this time because it was discovered fish life was being endangered. * * *

The Testimony.... The burden of appellants' testimony, given by residents who had observed the lake over a period of years and by those familiar with fish life and sea level calculations, was directed at establishing the *normal* or *medium* water level of the lake. The years 1952, 1953 and 1954 were unusually dry and the water levels in similar lakes in the same general area were unusually low in August and September of 1954. During August 1954 Horseshoe Lake was below "normal", but it is not entirely clear from the testimony that this was true on July 10 when the suit was filed. It also appears that during the stated period the water had receded from the bank where Mashburn's boats were usually docked, making it impossible for him to rent them to the public. There is strong testimony, disputed by appellees, that the *normal* level of the lake is 189.67 feet above sea level and that the water was below this level on July 10. Unquestionably the water was below normal when this suit was tried the latter part of September, 1954.

On the part of appellees it was attempted to show that: they had used the water for irrigation several years dating back to 1931 and Mashburn knew this when he rented the camp site; although they had been pumping regularly since May 25, 1954 the water did not begin to fall in the lake until July 1st or 4th; an agent of the Arkansas Game and Fish Commission examined the lake and the water about July 2nd and found no condition endangering fish life, and similar examinations after suit was filed showed the same condition, and; they stopped pumping about August 20th when they first learned that fish life was being endangered.

Issues Clarified. In refusing to issue the injunction the chancellor made no finding of facts, and did not state the ground upon which his decision rested. Appellants strongly insist that the chancellor was forced by the testimony to conclude first that the normal level of the lake was 189.67 feet above sea level and second that the water in the lake was at or below this level when the suit was filed on July 10th. This being true, appellants say, it was error for the chancellor to refuse to enjoin appellees from pumping water out of the lake. If it be conceded that the testimony does show and the chancellor should have found that the water in Horseshoe Lake was at or below the normal level when this suit was filed on July 10th, then appellants would have been entitled to an injunction provided this case was decided strictly under the uniform flow theory mentioned hereafter. However as explained later we are not bound by this theory in this state. * * *

In view of the above situation it is urged by appellees that the case should therefore be affirmed, but we have concluded that the best interest of the parties hereto and the public in general will be served by concluding this case in the light of the announcements hereafter made and the conclusions hereafter reached. Before attempting such conclusion it appears proper to make some general observations relative to the law regulating the use of water in lakes and streams. * * *

Riparian Doctrine. This doctrine, long in force in this and many other states, is based on the old common law which gave to the owners of land bordering on streams the right to use the water therefrom for certain purposes, and this right was considered an incident to the ownership of land. Originally it apparently accorded the landowner the right to have the water maintained at its normal level, subject to use for strictly domestic purposes. Later it became evident that this strict limitation placed on the use of water was unreasonable and unutilitarian. Consequently it was not long before the demand for a greater use of water caused a relaxation of the strict limitations placed on its use and this doctrine came to be divided into (a) the natural flow theory and (b) the reasonable use theory.

(a) *Natural Flow Theory.* Generally speaking again, under the natural flow theory, a riparian owner can take water for domestic purposes only, such as water for the family, live stock, and gardening, and he is entitled to have the water in the stream or lake upon which he borders kept at the normal level.

(b) *Reasonable Use Theory.* This theory appears to be based on the necessity and desirability of deriving greater benefits from the use of our abundant supply of water. It recognizes that there is no sound reason for maintaining our lakes and streams at a normal level when the water can be beneficially used without causing unreasonable damage to other riparian owners. The progress of civilization, particularly in regard to manufacturing, irrigation, and recreation, has forced the realization that a strict adherence to the uninterrupted flow doctrine placed an unwarranted limitation on the use of water, and consequently the court developed what we now call the reasonable use theory. This theory is of course subject to different interpretations and limitations. In 56 Am.Jur., page 728, it is stated that 'The rights of riparian proprietors on both navigable and unnavigable streams are to a great extent mutual, common, or correlative. The use of the stream or water by each proprietor is therefore limited to what is reasonable, having due regard for the rights of others above, below, or on the opposite shore. In general, the special rights of a riparian owner are such as are necessary for the use and enjoyment of his abutting property and the business lawfully conducted thereon, qualified only by the correlative rights of other riparian owners, and by certain rights of the public, and they are to be so exercised as not to injure others in the enjoyment of their rights.' It has been stated that each riparian owner has an equal right to make a reasonable use of waters subject to the equal rights of other owners to make the reasonable use. The purpose of the law is to secure to each riparian owner equality in the use of water as near as may be by requiring each to exercise his right reasonably and with due regard to the rights of others similarly situated.

This court has to some extent recognized the reasonable use theory, but we have also said in the City of Conway case that the uniform flow theory and the reasonable use theory are inconsistent and further that we had not yet made a choice between them.... The nucleus of this opinion is, therefore, a definite acceptance of the reasonable use theory. We do not understand that the two theories will necessarily clash in every case, but where there is an inconsistency, and where vested rights may not prevent, it is our conclusion that the reasonable use theory should control. * * *

The result of our examination of the decisions of this court and other authorities ... justifies the enunciation of the following general rules and principles:

(a) The right to use water for strictly domestic purposes—such as for household use—is superior to any other uses of water—such as for fishing, recreation and irrigation.

(b) Other than the use mentioned above, all other lawful uses of water are equal. Some of the lawful uses of water recognized by this state are: fishing, swimming, recreation, and irrigation.

(c) When one lawful use of water is destroyed by another lawful use the latter must yield, or it may be enjoined.

(d) When one lawful use of water interferes with or detracts from another lawful use, then a question arises as to whether, under all the facts and circumstances of that particular case, the interfering use shall be declared unreasonable and as such enjoined, or whether a reasonable and equitable adjustment should be made, having due regard to the reasonable rights of each. * * *

We do not minimize the difficulties attendant upon an application of the reasonable use rule to any given set of facts and circumstances and particularly those present in this instance. It is obvious that there are no definite guide posts provided and that necessarily much must be left to judgment and discretion. The breadth and boundaries of this area of discretion are well stated in Restatement of the Law, Torts, § 852c in these words: 'The determination in a particular case of the unreasonableness of a particular use is not and should not be an unreasoned, intuitive conclusion on the part of the court or jury. It is rather an evaluating of the conflicting interests of each of the contestants before the court in accordance with the standards of society, and a weighing of those, one against the other. The law accords equal protection to the interests of all the riparian proprietors in the use of water, and seeks to promote the greatest beneficial use of the water, and seeks to promote the greatest beneficial use by each with a minimum of harm to others. But when one riparian proprietor's use of the water harmfully invades another's interest in its use, there is an incompatibility of interest between the two parties to a greater or lesser extent depending on the extent of the invasion, and there is immediately a question whether such a use is legally permissible. It is axiomatic in the law that individuals in society must put up with a reasonable amount of annoyance and inconvenience resulting from the otherwise lawful activities of their neighbors in the use of their land. Hence it is only when one riparian proprietor's use of the water is unreasonable that another who is harmed by it can complain, even though the harm is intentional. Substantial intentional harm to another cannot be justified as reasonable unless the legal merit or utility of the activity which produces it outweighs the legal seriousness or gravity of the harm.'

In all our consideration of the reasonable use theory as we have attempted to explain it we have accepted the view that the benefits accruing to society in general from a maximum utilization of our water resources should not be denied merely because of the difficulties that may arise in its application. In the absence of legislative directives, it appears that this rule or theory is the best that the courts can devise.

Our Conclusion. After careful consideration, an application of the rules above announced to the complicated fact situation set forth in this record leads us to conclude that the Chancellor should have issued an order enjoining appellees from pumping water out of Horseshoe Lake when the water level reaches 189.67 feet above sea level for as long as the material facts and circumstances are substantially the same as they appear in this record. We make it clear that this conclusion is not based on the fact that 189.67 is the normal level and that appellees would have no right to reduce such level. Our conclusion is based on the fact that we think the evidence shows this level happens to be the level below which appellants would be unreasonably interfered with. * * *

Reversed with direction to the trial court to enter a decree in conformity with this opinion.

QUESTIONS AND DISCUSSION

1. The court suggests that the "determination in a particular case of the unreasonableness of a particular use is not and should not be an unreasoned, intuitive conclusion on the part of the court or jury." Does the court heed its own advice in this case?

2. The *Restatement (Second) of Torts* § 850A sets forth a list of nine factors relevant to the consideration of the reasonableness of a particular use.

reasonable use factors

> The determination of the reasonableness of use of water depends upon a consideration of the interests of the riparian proprietor making the use, of any riparian proprietor harmed by it and of society as a whole. Factors that affect the determination include the following: (a) The purpose of the use, (b) the suitability of the use to the watercourse or lake, (c) the economic value of the use, (d) the social value of the use, (e) the extent and amount of the harm it causes, (f) the practicability of avoiding the harm by adjusting the use or method of use of one proprietor or the other, (g) the practicality of adjusting the quantity of water used by each proprietor, (h) the protection of existing values of water uses, land, investments and enterprises, and (i) the justice of requiring the user causing the harm to bear the loss.

Using these factors, what arguments would you expect Mashburn or Brooks to have made in advocating the relative reasonableness of their competing uses? Does it matter who began using the water first? Section 850A suggests that one of the reasonableness factors is "the extent and amount of harm [the use] causes." If riparian rights are correlative, what does this factor mean? Is Mashburn, Brooks, or both of them causing the harm in this case? Think back to Ronald Coase's article on *The Problem of Social Cost*, discussed in Chapter 1, page 47.

3. How would you critique riparian rights and the reasonable use doctrine as a matter of fairness and efficiency? Are riparian rights more or less likely to encourage investment in water-dependent activities than the prior appropriation doctrine?

4. Defining riparian land and the extent of riparian rights is not quite as simple as it might appear. Although property ownership has much to do with the nature of riparian rights, it is not as simple as saying that riparian rights include the full acreage of any tract of property bordering on a watercourse. Riparian rights do not extend to any portion of the tract outside the watershed. Moreover, to the extent an owner subdivides and sells riparian property, those tracts no longer adjacent to the watercourse typically lose their riparian rights. Whether a tract without riparian rights can obtain riparian rights when its ownership is later unified with a riparian parcel depends on the jurisdiction. Most apply what is called the "unity of title" rule, which extends riparian rights to all land within a riparian parcel held by a single owner regardless of whether some of the parcel was once not in riparian ownership. Other states, most frequently those in the West with hybrid riparian-appropriation systems, apply a "source of title" test under which riparian rights apply only to that portion of the land that has always had riparian rights. Hybrid states' preference for this approach is understandable because it leads to less and less riparian ownership and thus to a more unified system of appropriative rights. Although these rules generally define the riparian land to which riparian rights will attach, the owner of a riparian parcel may defeat these presumptions by making an express grant—which must be in writing to defeat the Statute of Frauds—of riparian rights to a nonriparian land owner, although in a majority of jurisdictions a grant of riparian rights to nonriparian land is only valid against the grantor and not against other riparians.

Traditionally, owners of land without riparian rights—e.g., land outside the watershed or simply nonriparian land—were not entitled to use a watercourse. Over time, a number of exceptions developed. Although some states allow any riparian to enjoin a nonriparian use regardless of harm, other states hold that a riparian must prove he has been harmed before the nonriparian use will be enjoined. The former approach may seem more protective of riparians, but it actually made it easier for nonriparians to acquire prescriptive rights to water. Do you see why? In addition to these two approaches, other jurisdictions follow the approach advocated in § 855 of the *Restatement (Second) of Torts*, which allows for nonriparian uses as long as the use is reasonable in comparison with all other uses, and as long as the user owns some riparian land, however small the parcel. Finally, recognize that with the adoption of permit statutes in so many states, discussed in section III.C.3 *infra*, all of these common-law limitations have become less of an impediment to nonriparian water use.

5. *Problem Exercise.* Imagine a river with an average flow of 40 cubic feet per second (cfs)* of water with three riparian water users. Annually since

---

* Cubic feet per second is a measurement of water flow. One cfs of water is a flow of 449 gallons per minute or 646,317 gallons per day. Water is also measured in "acre feet."

1950, Jones has been diverting 20 cfs to irrigate a wheat crop. Since 1970, Smith, pursuant to the terms of a contract, has piped 20 cfs to a local municipality, which is a nonriparian. Last year Computer Inc. began diverting 10 cfs to produce computer chips. Smith and Jones have sued to enjoin Computer Inc.'s diversion, arguing that it unreasonably interferes with their riparian rights. What result?

6. For landowners adjacent to water, the riparian stick in their bundle of property rights has always consisted of more than the right to divert water. Traditionally, riparian rights have also included the right to build docks, piers, and wharves, and the right to use the waters for fishing, boating, swimming, and other recreation. Although the state typically owns the beds of all navigable watercourses (remember the equal footing doctrine discussed in Chapter 2, *supra*), the adjacent riparians own the bed of non-navigable watercourses, usually to the midpoint of the watercourse. The extent of a riparian's right to make surface use of a non-navigable water-course differs by jurisdiction. In some jurisdictions, each riparian has a common right to make reasonable use of the entire surface. Other jurisdictions limit riparian surface use to that portion of the lake overlying the portion of the bed owned by the riparian (imagine wedges of pie formed by an extension of the property lines to the center of the lake). In the case of navigable waters, the riparian shares a right of surface access along with the public, although the riparian does enjoy the unique right of wharfing out, namely the right to build docks and bulkheads out into the water-course as long as they do not interfere with navigation. *See generally* Peter N. Davis, *Recreational Use of Watercourses*, 4 Mo. ENVTL. L. & POL'Y REV. 71 (1996).

7. As noted in the prior question, for *navigable* waters, the riparian shares a right of surface access with the public. But what happens when the state is the owner of riparian land along a *non-navigable* watercourse? Should public access be treated any differently? The Washington State Supreme Court addressed this question in *Botton v. State*, 69 Wash.2d 751, 420 P.2d 352 (1966). There, the state had purchased a small lot along a 63 acre lake and had developed the lot to provide public fishing access. Other waterfront property owners eventually sued the state on the ground that it was making unreasonable use of its riparian right of access. The other riparians' complaints about the public access included the following:

1. The fair market value of plaintiffs' property has been decreased.

2. Thievery on the lake has greatly increased, particularly the stealing of boats, oars, outdoor furniture, tools and miscellaneous items of personal property of all kinds. In many of the cases it was definitely ascertained that the thieves gained access to the lake from the public access area.

An acre foot of water is the amount of water necessary to cover one acre of land one foot deep. It amounts to 325,851 gallons of water. The use of "acre feet" rather than "gallons" becomes more understandable when one recognizes that Lake Mead, the reservoir created by Hoover Dam, has a capacity of 28.5 million acre feet. In gallons, that is 9,286,753,-500,000 (9.28 trillion), a rather more cumbersome figure. For those who prefer numbers in metric format, one acre foot is the equivalent of 1,233.5 cubic meters, and one cfs is equal to 28.317 liters per second of water flow.

3.   Persons relieving themselves in the lake as well as on the property and front yards of various of the plaintiffs, to the considerable embarrassment and annoyance of the plaintiffs, their families and guests.

4.   Beer cans, worm cans, sandwich bags, pop bottles, rafts, and other assorted trash has been deposited in the lake and on the plaintiffs' beaches in considerable quantity.

5.   Repeated and frequent trespasses on the plaintiffs' front yards, docks, beaches and property. . . .

6.   Numerous of the plaintiffs, their children and grandchildren, have severely and frequently been cut by broken beer bottles left on the beaches.

7.   Fishermen using plaintiffs' docks, and fishing immediately adjacent to their beaches and front yards, would refuse to leave when requested and would stare and make remarks when plaintiffs, their wives and daughters would try to use their beaches for sun bathing, swimming or the entertainment of guests. . . .

8.   Although hunting and shooting on the lake are illegal, hunters come in and hunt and shoot on the lake. Persons also come in and shoot at ducks with air rifles.

9.   Speed boating on the lake has greatly increased. In some cases it has increased to the extent that it has become a danger to the plaintiffs' children.

10.   The public use of the lake has interfered with the plaintiffs' use of the lake for boating, swimming, fishing and recreational purposes.

11.   The noise on the lake has substantially increased.

Id. at 353–54. The court decided to enjoin the state from allowing public access until it could present a plan to control and regulate its licensees so that the rights of other riparian owners would be adequately safeguarded.

A dissenting justice argued that the state had already provided such a plan through its general misdemeanor laws, which the other riparians had never sought to enforce. Moreover, argued the dissent, the state could not reasonably be expected to post a sheriff at the lake to assure proper behavior. The dissent's prediction proved accurate. When the Department of Game could not afford to place a deputy on site, the public access to Phantom Lake was closed. In 1993, it was finally reopened, although it has continued to suffer intermittent closings because of riparian complaints about harm caused by members of the recreating public. *See* Joseph L. Sax et al., Legal Control of Water Resources: Cases and Materials 527 (3d ed. 2000). Is this an appropriate outcome? Should the state be treated just like any other riparian owner where the lake is non-navigable?

―――――

B.   Eastern Permit Systems

During the last few decades, as concerns about environmental protection have increased, many eastern states have been moving away from a common law reasonable use approach and moving to a permit system that looks more like that of the western states, although the permits are not ranked based on temporal priority. By adopting permit systems, the states are better able to consider the public impact of water uses. As Professor Dellapenna explains, these eastern permit regimes were "not originally introduced as a radical revision of the water law of a particular state. Rather, in most states, it emerged gradually through a process of small legislative interventions that eventually cumulatively did fundamentally change the water law of the state. As a result, it is sometimes difficult to determine precisely when, in a particular state, the transition from riparian rights ... occurred." AMERICAN SOCIETY OF CIVIL ENGINEERS, THE REGULATED RIPARIAN MODEL WATER CODE, at v–viii (Joseph W. Dellapenna ed., 1997). As of 2006, seventeen states had enacted some sort of permit system for surface water resources. 1 WATER AND WATER RIGHTS, § 9.01 (Robert E. Beck ed., replacement vol. 2001, Cumm. Supp. 2006).

Although varied, the permit systems of eastern riparian states share several basic characteristics. Probably the most fundamental departure from common-law riparian rights is that a permit is necessary to withdraw water, except for certain categories of small withdrawals, see, e.g., GA. CODE ANN. § 12–5–31(a) (exempting withdrawals averaging less than 100,000 gallons per day); KY. REV. STAT. ANN. § 151.140 & 151.210(a) (exempting irrigation withdrawals and withdrawals for domestic use), and receipt of a permit does not depend upon ownership of riparian land. The relevant state agency issues the permit based upon an evaluation of whether the withdrawal would exceed the safe yield of the water source, whether the withdrawal is consistent with any applicable water allocation planning, and most significantly, whether the proposed use is reasonable. Reasonableness is a function of factors like those outlined in *Restatement (Second) of Torts* § 850A above, including whether the proposed withdrawal is consistent with the public interest. The public interest analysis is typically quite broad and can include such factors as the withdrawal's effect on ecology and aesthetics, domestic and municipal uses, aquifer recharge, wetlands, flood plains, and the water source's capacity to assimilate waste. To the extent the water source is insufficient to satisfy all prospective users, allocation is made not by temporal priority but by a preference system that ranks various uses, with first preference generally being given to domestic uses. The permits themselves are usually issued for a limited duration, typically 10–20 years, although public uses are generally authorized for a longer period such as 50 years. At the expiration of that period, the permit holder must apply to the state for a renewal, at which time the state reconsiders the permit based on the same criteria it applied initially, although the current permittee is usually afforded some preference over competing applicants to the extent either withdrawal would equally serve the public interest. To the extent a permit holder wants to modify their permit or transfer it to a person who plans on changing the type of use or the place of use or diversion, the permit holder must again obtain state approval based upon the same initial criteria. *See generally* MODEL WATER CODE, *supra*, at 201–11, 236–49, 272–76, 285–93.

One of the difficult questions that has faced eastern states moving to a permit system is how to deal with existing riparians. In general, the states have provided that riparians must obtain a permit to continue any existing withdrawals. The state will issue the permit for the full amount of the existing withdrawal as long as the existing use is reasonable. To the extent the withdrawals of existing riparians exceed the safe yield of the water source, the permits will be allocated between them based on reasonable use principles. The key factor in converting existing riparians over to a permit system is that the failure to apply for a permit constitutes an abandonment of any claim to make a future withdrawal based on riparian status. *See generally* MODEL WATER CODE, *supra*, at 212–15. It is that facet of the eastern permit systems that triggered the following case.

FRANCO-AMERICAN CHAROLAISE, LTD. V.
OKLAHOMA WATER RESOURCES BOARD,
855 P.2d 568 (Okla. 1990)

OPALA, JUSTICE.

[In August of 1980 the City of Ada made application for a permit to increase its existing appropriation of water. The Oklahoma Water Resources Board [OWRB] granted the permit subject to certain conditions. Various riparian owners and appropriators challenged the decision of the OWRB to issue the permit. Among other arguments, the plaintiffs claimed that the legislation authorizing the permit was unconstitutional.]

This appeal challenges the constitutionality of the 1963 amendments to Oklahoma's water law insofar as the amendments regulate riparian rights. . . . The questions of law tendered for our resolution are:

1.   What is the nature of the riparian right under Oklahoma common law?

2.   To what extent did the 1963 amendments abrogate the common-law riparian right?

3.   Are the 1963 amendments constitutional when measured by Art. 2, § 24 Okl. Const.? * * *

We hold that the Oklahoma riparian owner enjoys a vested common-law right to the reasonable use of the stream. This right is a valuable part of the property owner's "bundle of sticks" and may not be taken for public use without compensation. We further hold that, inasmuch as 60 O.S. 1981 § 60, as amended in 1963, limits the riparian owner to domestic use and declares that all other water in the stream becomes public water subject to appropriation without any provision for compensating the riparian owner, the statute violates Art. 2 § 24, Okl. Const. * * *

The Organic Act of 1890 extended England's common law over Indian Territory. The same year the Territorial Legislature adopted a statute declaring the nature of water rights in the Territory:

> The owner of land owns water standing thereon, or flowing over or under its surface, but not forming a definite stream. Water running in a definite stream, formed by nature over or under the surface may be used by him as long as it remains there; but he may not prevent the natural flow of the stream, or of the natural spring from which it commences its definite course, nor pursue nor pollute the same. Terr. Okla. Stat. § 4162 [1890].

This codification of the common-law riparian doctrine of water rights remained the law in Oklahoma until legislative adoption of the 1963 amendments.

In 1897 the legislature provided for the appropriation of the ordinary flow or underflow of stream water for the irrigation of arid sections of the State. The statute protected the riparian owner from the appropriation of the ordinary flow of the stream *without* the riparian owner's consent except by condemnation. In 1905 the provision protecting the riparian right was omitted. It was reinstated in 1909, then finally eliminated in 1910. In 1925 the legislature added a provision recognizing the priority of all beneficial uses of water initiated prior to statehood.

Since 1897 both the common law and the statutes have operated in Oklahoma to confer riparian and appropriative rights. Though these rights have coexisted in the State for almost 100 years, they are theoretically irreconcilable.[15] The common-law riparian right extends to the reasonable use of the stream *or* to its natural flow, depending on the jurisdiction; the appropriative right attaches to a fixed amount. The last riparian use asserted has as much priority as the first; the appropriator who takes first has the senior right. In 1963 the legislature attempted to reconcile the two doctrines. The amendments, shown in italics, are as follows:

> The owner of the land owns water standing thereon, or flowing over or under its surface but not forming a definite stream. . . . Water running in a definite stream, formed by nature over or under the surface, may be used by him *for domestic purposes as defined in Section 2(a) of this Act,* as long as it remains there, but he may not prevent the natural flow of the stream, or of the natural spring from which it commences its definite course, nor pursue nor pollute the same, *as such water then becomes public water and is subject to appropriation for the benefit and welfare of the people of the state, as provided by law* . . . .

Companion statutes limit riparian domestic use to household purposes, to the watering of domestic animals up to the land's normal grazing capacity, and to the irrigation of land not exceeding a total of three acres. . . . In addition, the 1963 amendments provided a validation mechanism as a method for protecting pre-existing beneficial uses, including those of the riparian owner and pre-existing appropriators. All subsequent rights to the use of stream water, except for riparian domestic uses, are to be acquired by appropriation. The stream's natural flow is considered public water and subject to appropriation. Riparian owners may not assert their common-law right to the use of stream water other than for the domestic uses.

Riparian rights arise from land ownership, attaching only to those lands which touch the stream. A riparian interest, though one in real property, is not absolute or exclusive; it is usufructuary in character and subject to the rights of other riparian owners. A riparian right is neither constant nor judicially quantifiable *in futuro.* * * *

The natural flow doctrine, which prevents any consumptive use, was early modified to allow for "natural" or domestic uses such as bathing, drinking, gardening, and stock watering. Because the natural flow doctrine when "pressed to the limits of its logic enabled one to play dog-in-the-manger" and fostered waste, the majority of American courts [including Oklahoma in 1933] have expressly adopted the reasonable use doctrine. * * * We said that the

---

15. This dual system of water rights is known nationally as the "California Doctrine" and at one time was the rule in all West Coast states and the tier of the Great Plains from North Dakota to Texas. Only California and Nebraska retain it. Most dual-system states have since adopted the appropriation doctrine as controlling all rights to stream water.

accepted rule allows a riparian owner the right to make any use of water beneficial to himself as long as he does not substantially or materially injure those riparian owners downstream who have a corresponding right.

Mindful of these decisions and of the co-existence of appropriative with riparian rights in this state since 1897, we hold that the modified common-law riparian right to the reasonable use of the stream is the controlling norm of law in Oklahoma. We further hold that, consistently with the California Doctrine, the statutory right to appropriate stream water coexists with, but does not preempt or abrogate, the riparian owner's common-law right. * * *

The issue here is whether the legislature can validly abrogate the riparian owner's right to initiate non-domestic reasonable uses in stream water without affording compensation. Art. 2, § 24, Okl. Const. provides in part:

> Private property shall not be taken or damaged for public use without just compensation. Such compensation, irrespective of any benefit from any improvements proposed shall be ascertained by a board of commissioners of not less than three freeholders, in such a matter as may be prescribed by law.

Private property protected by Art. 2, § 24 includes "easements, personal property, and every valuable interest which can be enjoyed and recognized as property." *Graham v. City of Duncan*, 354 P.2d 458, 461 (Okl. 1960). Further, in *Oklahoma Water Resources Board v. Central Oklahoma Master Conservancy District*, we held:

> A "vested right" is the power to *do certain actions* or possess certain things lawfully, and is substantially a property right. It may be created by common law, by statute or by contract. Once created, it becomes absolute, and is protected from legislative invasion.... 464 P.2d 748, 755 (Okl. 1969) (emphasis added).

Therefore, the common-law riparian right to use stream water, as long as that use is reasonable, has been long recognized in Oklahoma law as a private property right. * * *

[I]n *C.C. Julian Oil & Royalties Co. v. Capshaw*, 292 P. at 847, we declared that the legislature could regulate a landowner's use and enjoyment of natural resources to prevent waste and infringement on the rights of others. Thus, a statutory regulation of the methods to be used in extracting hydrocarbons was a constitutional exercise of police power where none of the hydrocarbons was taken for public use. Then, in *Frost v. Ponca City*, 541 P.2d 1321, 1324 (Okl. 1975), we held that in the interest of health and safety, the city could exercise its police power to restrict the plaintiff's right to capture hydrocarbons underlying his property, but the city could not remove the hydrocarbons and sell them without compensating the plaintiff.

We, therefore, hold that the 1963 water law amendments are fraught with a constitutional infirmity in that they abolish the right of riparian owners to assert their vested interest in the prospective reasonable use of the stream. Under the 1963 amendments, riparian owners stand on equal footing with appropriator; ownership of riparian land affords *no right* to the stream water except for limited domestic use.

This case must be remanded for the trial court to determine whether the appellee-riparian owners' claim to the use of the stream flow ... is reasonable.

The OWRB argues the 1963 amendments are a permissible exercise of the police power just as a zoning ordinance would be. That contention is inapposite when, as here, the use of stream water is *not just restricted but is taken for public use.*

Although the 1963 water law amendments provided a mechanism for a riparian owner to "perfect" all beneficial uses initiated prior to the legislation, that mechanism falls short of protecting the riparian owner's common-law appurtenant right. The mechanism is constitutionally inadequate first of all because the full sweep of the riparian right is much broader than the validation mechanism could ever shield. The heart of the riparian right is the right to assert a use at *any time* as long as it does not harm another riparian who has a corresponding right. Further, yesterday's reasonable use by one riparian owner may become unreasonable tomorrow when a fellow riparian owner asserts a new or expanded use. After the 1963 amendments, the riparian owner who wants to expand a use or assert a new use may do so *only as an appropriator.* His use is not judged by its reasonableness but only by its priority in time.

Furthermore, the validation mechanism attempted to forever set in stone the maximum amount of stream water the landowner, *as a riparian owner,* can use. Any use asserted by the landowner, *as an appropriator,* is either denied because no water is available or is given a lower priority than all other uses, including those of appropriators who are non-riparian to the stream. It matters not that the riparian owner's use is reasonable when compared with prior uses. This result is antithetical to the very nature of the common-law riparian right, which places no stock in the fact of past use, present use, or even non-use. * * *

Upon remand, should the trial court find that any or all of the riparian owners' asserted uses of the stream for their claimed purposes is unreasonable, such uses do not fall under the mantle of constitutionally protected property rights. On the other hand, should the trial court find that an asserted riparian use of the stream is reasonable, the right to a flow sufficient to supply the riparian owners' reasonable use must be preserved in the owners. * * *

LAVENDER, VICE CHIEF JUSTICE, concurring in part; dissenting in part:

I must respectfully dissent from that part of the majority opinion holding the 1963 legislative amendments to our State's stream water law unconstitutional under the guise the amendments effected a taking of property without just compensation in violation of OKLA. CONST. art. 2, § 24. In reaching this result the majority makes several errors.

Initially, it misperceives that future, unquantified use of stream water by a riparian is a vested property right that can only be limited or modified pursuant to judicially mandated common law factors that were generally used to decide piecemeal litigation between competing riparians in water use disputes. Secondly, it misinterprets the plain and unambiguous legislation at issue and it fails to recognize that even assuming a vested property right is at issue, such rights in natural resources like water, may be subject to reasonable limitations or even forfeiture for failure to put the resource to beneficial use. Thirdly, its analysis of the law as to what constitutes a taking of private property requiring just compensation is flawed. In my view the majority errs in such regard by failing to view the legislation as akin to zoning regulation, which although [it] may limit a riparian's open-ended common law right to make use of the water to benefit his land and thereby effect the value of his land, does not deprive him of all economic use of his land or absolutely deprive him of water. The lack of water to a riparian, if it occurs, is caused by his own neglect or inaction by years of failure either to put the water to beneficial use or failure to gain an appropriation permit from the Oklahoma Water Resources Board (OWRB) for uses being made prior to passage of the 1963 amendments or uses made or sought to be made between passage of the amendments and the City of Ada's appropriation at issue here. This mistake of the majority is particularly egregious because it wholly ignores the virtually admitted fact that neither riparians or appropriators *own* the water they are being allowed to use. All of the people in this State own the water and that ownership interest by the legislation before us is merely being channeled by the Legislature, for the benefit of those owners (i.e. the people), to those uses deemed wise.

The majority has failed to consider persuasive case law from the highest courts of other jurisdictions upholding analogous legislation over similar attacks and pronouncements of the United States Supreme Court which lead me to conclude the legislation *on its face* is constitutional. The majority finally seems to confuse *public* fundamental and preeminent rights in the streams of this State, protected through the public trust doctrine, as being the private property of landowners (riparians) owning land adjacent to the stream waters in Oklahoma.

In place of the statutory scheme drafted by the Legislature after years of study and debate the majority acts as a super-legislature by rewriting the water law of this State in accord with its views of prudent public policy, something neither this Court or any court has the power to do. The foundation of this judicial "legislation," relying as it does on the so-called California Doctrine, is illusory at best because the majority ignores pronouncements from the California Supreme Court which has itself recognized the common law doctrine of unquantified future riparian use of stream water is not a vested right, even in the face of a California constitutional provision specifically interpreted to protect it, when it may impair the promotion of reasonable and beneficial uses of state waters and, in effect, constitute waste of the resource.[2] * * *

In order to understand the erroneous nature of the majority opinion it is first necessary to understand the "property" right of riparians it purportedly protects and the central rationale given for holding the 1963 water law amendments unconstitutional. The "property" interest is supposedly the prospective or future reasonable use of stream water. The opinion posits that this unquantified *prospective or future use* is a vested right. Although the majority discusses preexisting water uses by riparians (i.e. uses initiated prior to passage of the 1963 amendments), as I read the opinion, it is the effect the legislation had on future use which is the basis for finding constitutional infirmity. In my view such future use was never a vested property interest inuring to the benefit of a riparian such that if it was changed or modified as accomplished by the 1963 stream water laws just compensation was due for a taking of property. Furthermore, even assuming future use could be considered a vested property interest under Oklahoma law prior to passage of the 1963 amendments, the Legislature had the authority, without providing a mechanism for compensation, to provide that the unexercised "right" to use water at some unspecified time in the future could be limited to domestic use because continuous nonuse

2. *In re Waters of Long Valley Creek Stream System,* 158 Cal.Rptr. 350, 355, n. 3, 599 P.2d 656, 661, n. 3 (1979). In said case the California Supreme Court said:

> [A]ppellant also asserts that these common law cases disclose his future right to an unquantified amount of water has become "vested." The assertion is without merit. As discussed *post,* riparian rights are limit-

ed by the concept of reasonable and beneficial use, and they may not be exercised in a manner that is inconsistent with the policy declaration of article X, section 2 of the [California] Constitution. Thus, to the extent that a future riparian right may impair the promotion of reasonable and beneficial uses of state waters, it is inapt to view it as vested. (emphasis added).

of water was determined by the Legislature to be wasteful and injurious to a comprehensive State plan regulating the beneficial use of such a valuable resource and, thus, subject to forfeiture or limited to those uses, in addition to domestic use, for which an appropriation was sought and granted by the OWRB. * * *

The majority also fails to understand the import of the reasonable use doctrine as it existed in Oklahoma prior to passage of the 1963 stream water law amendments and that the State for the benefit of all the people *owned* the waters at issue in this case and had plenary control over their disposition. In my view only preexisting uses (i.e. uses initiated prior to passage of the amendments and subject to validation thereunder) can be said to be property in any real or actual sense. *Such uses the majority admits were subject to validation under the 1963 amendments.* As to any common law claim to use an unquantified amount of water in the future such open-ended claim was lost or forfeited because it was determined to be wasteful by the Legislature and was properly limited to domestic use. Furthermore, riparians, just as other potential future water users, may obtain their future needs of water in addition to domestic use by applying for an appropriation under our water laws. If the water is not then available it is their own inaction or neglect which deprives them of water and not action of the State under the involved legislation. In effect, all the legislation at issue did was to put water users in this State on an equal footing (except for a statutory preference in favor of riparian domestic use) and provide a statewide *unitary* system for the acquisition of water rights. * * *

In the instant case the majority ... says riparians have a right to insist that things remain as they were under the common law in regard to future use. Other states have concluded differently.

The South Dakota Supreme Court in the case of *Belle Fourche Irrigation District v. Smiley*, 176 N.W.2d 239 (1970), *after remand* 204 N.W.2d 105 (1973), rejected a similar argument to that raised by Appellees here and approved of by the majority.... Another court upholding legislation of a similar nature was the Texas Supreme Court in *In re Adjudication of the Water Rights of the Upper Guadalupe Segment of the Guadalupe River Basin*, 642 S.W.2d 438 (Tex. 1982). * * *

The [Texas] court further relied on *Texaco, Inc. v. Short*, 454 U.S. 516 (1982), where the United States Supreme Court upheld the Indiana Dormant Mineral Act which provided that severed mineral interests not used for a period of twenty years automatically lapsed and reverted to the current surface owner, unless certain procedural steps were taken. In said case the Supreme Court stated:

> We have concluded that the State may treat a mineral interest that has not been used for twenty years and for which no statement of claim has been filed as abandoned; it follows that, after abandonment, the former owner retains no interest for which he may claim compensation. It is the owner's failure to make any use of the property—and not action of the State—that causes the lapse of the property right; there is no "taking" that requires compensation. The requirement that an owner of a property interest that has not been used for twenty years must come forward and file a current statement of claim is not itself a "taking." *Id.* at 530.

Thus, even if it be assumed the majority is correct that the riparian had a protectible property interest to some unquantified right to make use of the water at some unspecified time in the future, this common law right could be lost or forfeited by nonuse or, at least, limited to domestic use and appropriative uses granted by the OWRB as sought to be accomplished by the legislation under review. To rule otherwise simply places a common law doctrine as an impenetrable barrier to efficient management of a natural resource never deemed to be owned by private landowners. * * *

The United States Supreme Court has long recognized that land use regulations normally do not effect a taking of property as long as the regulations at issue substantially advance legitimate state interests and do not deny a landowner economically viable use of his land. No one argues here, including the majority, that the statutory scheme under review does not substantially advance legitimate state interests. The State interests advanced are numerous. Among them are direct promotion of the efficient management of our State's water resources by preventing waste. It provides a semblance of certainty in the area of water rights and distributes this valuable resource *which is owned by all the public* in response to demonstrated need. Therefore, the only real question in the taking context is whether the legislation has deprived riparians of the economically viable use of their land. I do not think it has nor from my review of the record herein do I read Appellees' submissions to assert otherwise. * * *

QUESTIONS AND DISCUSSION

1. The court decides that the 1963 amendments to Oklahoma's water law are unconstitutional because they effected a taking without payment of just compensation. The first step in any takings analysis is to define the nature of the property taken. How do the majority and dissenting opinions differ on that issue? If unexercised riparian rights are a protectible property interest, did the 1963 legislation cause a physical taking or a regulatory taking? How does the answer to this question affect the takings analysis? In contemplating these questions, consider whether an unused riparian right is akin to part of a farmer's land not yet put into cultivation, or is the elimination of an unused riparian right more like downzoning that reduces the number of uses to which property can be put? To the extent the 1963 amendments can be characterized as a regulatory takings issue, what is the relevant property interest or denominator?

2. Does the fact that the court was applying the Oklahoma Constitution make any difference in the takings analysis?

3. Recall Professor Sax's observation at the beginning of this chapter that the nature of water rights has always been responsive to community needs. In fact, the *Franco–American* court discusses how Oklahoma had proceeded from the natural flow doctrine to a reasonable use doctrine and then to a hybrid appropriative rights/riparian rights system before the 1963 amendments. If compensation was not required for these previous changes, should it be for this one? More broadly, should water rights be subject to changing community needs without any possibility of just compensation? If not, how is an appropriate line to be drawn?

4. Oklahoma's effort to depart from its hybrid system of water rights parallels that of most other hybrid states. As the court notes, unused riparian rights have been abolished in all dual system (California doctrine) states except California, Nebraska, and, in light of *Franco–American*, Oklahoma. And, as indicated in the dissenting opinion, California has severely curtailed riparian rights. Only Oklahoma's effort to eliminate riparian rights failed to pass judicial muster. Oklahoma's desire to adopt a unitary system is understandable. As Professor Allison explains:

> Given the substantive differences between the riparian and appropriation doctrines, dual rights systems contain three major irreconcilable contradictions:
>
>> (1) the reciprocal rights of riparian landowners to initiate or maintain reasonable water uses, regardless of when, if ever, they have used water, cannot be preserved without depriving senior appropriators the security afforded by the appropriation doctrine's "first-in-time, first-in-right" and "use it or lose it" principles;
>>
>> (2) the riparian reasonable use requirement, by which the merits of each riparian use are determined by a comparison of all riparian uses, cannot be upheld without subverting the appropriation doctrine's beneficial use requirement, which determines the merits of each appropriation use individually based on its economic, social, aesthetic, or environmental benefits; and,
>>
>> (3) appropriators not owning riparian lands may initiate a water use without seeking permission or a conveyance from riparian landowners only by destroying the core principle of riparianism, which confers rights to use water only on riparian landowners and generally requires such uses to be on riparian lands.
>
> Consequently, a dual rights system inevitably frustrates the chief advantages of one or both doctrines. The systems are also difficult to administer when there are conflicts between riparian landowners and appropriators. Accordingly, many dual rights states have converted their water law into unitary appropriation systems.

Gary D. Allison, *Franco–American Charolaise: The Never Ending Story*, 30 TULSA L.J. 1, 12 (1994). Do any Oklahoma water users have secure water rights after the court's decision in *Franco–American*? Is there anything to prevent a riparian from proposing the initiation of a large new water use on a fully appropriated stream?

5.   As described in the text, eastern permit systems like that proposed by Oklahoma generally limit the duration of permits, typically for a 10–20 year period, and require a public interest review prior to issuing a new permit. Are such limits wise water policy?

6.   Although this casebook uses the moniker "eastern permit systems," there is some disagreement about using that label to describe the combination of common law riparianism with statutory permitting schemes. Professor Dellapenna has argued that such regimes are better described as "regulated riparianism."

> [R]egulated riparianism appears to be about as succinctly descriptive as one can hope. Suggested alternative names have serious defects. "Eastern permit systems" or the like tell us nothing about the nature of the legal regime, and leave one more open to the charge that the new system has taken rather than regulated pre-existing property rights. "No-temporal priority permit systems" is more immediately descriptive than "regulated riparianism" but it is rather too much to expect people to say frequently and also leaves more room for the allegation that property was taken by the legislation. The name "regulated riparianism" both emphasizes that the administrative permit process proceeds

on essentially riparian principles, and that the new system is a regulation of rather than a taking of the older riparian rights. * * *

AMERICAN SOCIETY OF CIVIL ENGINEERS, THE REGULATED RIPARIAN MODEL WATER CODE, at v–vii (Joseph W. Dellapenna ed., 1997). Do you agree with Professor Dellapenna that "regulated riparianism" is the most appropriate description? How much of riparianism is left by a system that does not even require that permittees own riparian land?

C. PRIOR APPROPRIATION

Prior appropriation is the primary water law in the western United States. That is partly a function of history but also a function of geography. As Marc Reisner's earlier excerpt made clear, the defining geographic feature of the American West is its aridity. In arid country, allowing riparian property owners to control all of the water and to decide whether and how to use the water was simply not acceptable. Throughout the country in the nineteenth century and throughout most of the twentieth, the cultural imprimatur was growth and development. And in arid country, development requires water. Water was too precious to be left in the stream. Its use needed to be encouraged. And the best way to do that was to promise water to those willing to use it. This reasoning was not unique to the western United States. Variants of prior appropriation (most often permit systems where water is owned by the state and parceled out to users) are the law in a number of arid nations. *See* LUDWICK A. TECLAFF, WATER LAW IN INTERNATIONAL PERSPECTIVE 21–59 (1985).

Although prior appropriation is rooted in aridity and water scarcity, its birth in the West is also tied closely to mining and mining law, another legal regime for allocating a scarce and precious natural resource. Professor Wilkinson explains:

CHARLES F. WILKINSON, CROSSING THE NEXT MERIDIAN: LAND, WATER, AND THE FUTURE OF THE WEST 231–35 (1992)

Early western water law was symbiotic with hardrock mining law. This was natural, since from 1848 on water was the engine for the mining camps. The early-arriving miners used mining pans to work placer deposits, in which the gold was found in loose soil and gravel. The goldbearing ore was heavier than the sand and gravel in which it was found. A skillful miner could fill the pan with water and potential pay dirt, swirl the pan in a circular fashion, and slosh the water and gravel over the sloped sides of the pan. The heavier gold would remain in the bottom of the pan. The miner would then rework the discarded material, hoping to recover traces of gold.

The same principles were used for increasingly larger operations. Long Toms and other forms of sluices, some of them hundreds of feet long, were sloped wooden chutes with cleats in the bottom. Gravel was shoveled into the upper end and forced down the sluice by water. With luck, pieces of gold would be caught in the cleats and the dirt and sand would be washed out. By the late 1850s and the 1860s, the size and efficiency of the operations multiplied many times over as hydraulic mining moved into the gold country. A head of water pressure was built up and forced into large firefighting hoses. A stream of water from the hoses, which had enough power to kill a man, was then trained on a hillside. The process was so effective that in a matter of minutes, the force of the water could literally tear out tons of earth, which would then be worked through sluices. These were the same hydraulic mining operations that California finally banned in the 1880s because countless thousands of tons of rocks and soil had cascaded down into the rivers and laid waste to the salmon runs in the Sacramento River system. In the meantime, however, the big hoses served the mining industry's ends beautifully. As mining became ever more industrial, milling operations required large amounts of water.

Many mining camps were located in rugged country far from any watercourse. They all had need for water and required the elaborate, serpentine ditch systems that even today wind their way through the foothills and mountains of western states. These ingenious conduits wrapped around hillsides, moving from one watershed to another, often seeming to run uphill to serve high-elevation camps. In reality, of course, amateur engineers, predecessors to the professionals who would remake the West, played the law of gravity to a T.

The miners, just as they did with the mining laws, developed their own water laws before any state or federal court or legislature spoke. As might be expected, the rules for water looked a lot like the rules for minerals.

The miners used a simple, primitive rule of capture for water: "first in time, first in right." Some scholars believe that the idea was borrowed from Mexico, where many of the earlier miners had previously labored, but it is at least as likely that they used their own inventiveness and common sense—reinforced, no doubt, by the equity and inevitability in the cold-eyed glare of a bearded, pistoled miner who was already hard at work.

The rule of priority based on time amounted to a direct rejection of riparian water law, which applied in England and the eastern United States. Riparianism requires the sharing of a watercourse by all of the landowners bordering it, regardless of whether a water user had ever put water to work previously. That made no sense at all to these miners. If two men, or companies, came in and diverted a whole stream, so be it. If just one took the whole stream, so be it. They needed it; they depended on it; they had rights to it. In one sense: absolute anarchy. In another, one that made much better logic in those days: absolute order. In a mining society, how could a person operate without being able to rely on a stable possession of the claim and the water necessary to operate it.

The rules paralleled those for mining in other respects. The due diligence rule that required a miner actively to work a claim operated with equal force as to water; otherwise, the water right was abandoned. (This applied only to the seasons when the water right was actually diverted, so abandonment did not run, for example, during winter months, when mining, and water use, was impractical.) In the meantime, as with hardrock minerals, water users had the right—a vested property right, like title to land—to keep using the water. Of course, the water, like the minerals, was free for the taking. In real terms, to whom would payment be made in those frontier times? After the initial appropriation, however, the water right, like a mining claim, could be leased or sold. It was property—from the very moment it was first put to use. First in time, first in right. * * *

Later developments in the prior appropriation doctrine added other provisions that were inherent in, or consistent with, the intensely utilitarian objectives of the mining camps. To obtain a water right, an appropriator had to "divert" the water—physically take it out of a watercourse, which included running it through turbines to generate electrical power. In addition, water had to be put to a "beneficial use." Beneficial use, as defined first by courts and later by state legislatures, merely ratified the customary rules of western water users and was not nearly as broad as it might sound. To rise to the level of being beneficial, a use had to be consumptive, usually extractive. The list was limited to mining, agriculture, industrial, municipal, domestic, stock-raising, and hydropower. Among other things, these rules meant that in-stream uses could not qualify as appropriations. They were not diversions. Nor did using water—a stream, a lake, or a waterfall—to protect wildlife, to swim in or boat on, or to enjoy for its beauty make a beneficial use. In-stream uses were doubly disqualified.

Early on, the rubric of beneficial use also came to encompass the idea that water, once validly diverted and put to use, could not be wasted. But the language decrying waste was mostly theoretical. It was always difficult to police waste, and in some cases to define it, so the prohibition against waste, although an announced principle in the cases and statutes of every western state, has been enforced sporadically at best.

This was the classic prior appropriation doctrine, and it was adopted nearly wholesale in every western state. As late as the mid–1970s, water law and policy were essentially monolithic throughout the region. To be sure, there were variations. Following the lead of Elwood Mcad and Wyoming, ... states set up agencies to administer prior appropriation rights, except Colorado, which granted its water rights through the courts. As we shall see, however, these procedural changes did little to affect the traditional workings of prior appropriation. Beginning in 1915, Oregon had withdrawn from appropriation the streams above some of its scenic waterfalls. California, Washington, Oregon, and the states along the 100th meridian recognized some riparian rights along with appropriation rights before abolishing or sharply limiting these vestiges of riparianism. There were other differences. But in the larger scheme, such exceptions were wrinkles at best. The classic prior appropriation doctrine governed nearly all water usage in the West.

————

1. OVERVIEW

To make the foregoing description of the classic prior appropriation doctrine a bit more concrete, consider the following hypothetical which illustrates the basic structure of prior appropriation law. Suppose a river with an average flow of 40 cubic feet per second (cfs) of water on which there are four diverters as outlined in the diagram below. Jones diverts 10 cfs of water with a priority date of 1890, the date on which the water was first put to beneficial use on his land. Jones uses his 10 cfs to irrigate his wheat crop. Smith diverts 10 cfs of water with a priority date of 1970. She uses drip irrigation to grow a large crop of organic vegetables. Computer Inc. diverts 10 cfs with a priority date of 1990. It uses its water to produce computer chips. Williams diverts 10 cfs with a priority date of 1900. He uses his water to flood irrigate a field of alfalfa to provide winter feed for his cattle.

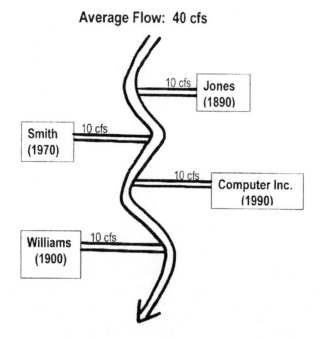

Average Flow: 40 cfs

With reference to this diagram, consider how the law of prior appropriation applies to several allocation questions. As you read the questions and answers below, understand that this is only a basic overview of the doctrine. Many of the concepts have been contested or modified over time. This hypothetical simply provides an introduction to the foundational principles of the law of prior appropriation.

• Suppose a drought year in which the river has only 20 cfs of flow, the basic case for which prior appropriation was designed. Who gets the water? In such a drought, Jones and Williams are each entitled to take their entire 10 cfs because they are the senior-most appropriators—their water rights are first in time. Smith and Computer Inc. are left high and dry.

• Suppose that, in a drought year, of the 10 cfs still in the stream following Jones' diversion, all but 1 cfs of it will have been lost to evaporation, seepage into the underlying aquifer, and transpiration from riparian vegetation by the time the water reaches Williams. Can Williams still demand that Smith and Computer Inc. not touch the water? The answer again is generally yes, unless their forbearance would not allow Williams to receive any water at all.

• Does it matter that Computer Inc. uses its water in a way that employs many people in the community and that Smith uses a more efficient drip irrigation system and grows more valuable crops than Williams, who flood irrigates to produce water for alfalfa? Historically, the answer has most often been no. Although the doctrine of prior appropriation conditions a water right on making "beneficial use" of the water, the fact that Williams is growing alfalfa using a common irrigation method has generally been sufficient to satisfy the standard, even if his methods for doing so are less efficient than some others along the watercourse.

• Does it matter that the diversions of Jones and Williams in a drought year, or of all diverters in an average flow year, will completely dewater the stream? Traditionally, this has not mattered at all. Many streams in the West are fully appropriated or even overappropriated. Until recently, conservation of water in the West meant not allowing a drop of it to get to the sea.

• Does it matter whether a diverter's property is adjacent to the stream? In other words, does it matter if she is not a riparian? No. Prior appropriation does not depend upon the location of the property. As long as the diverter puts the water to beneficial use, she can use it wherever she desires.

• If Computer Inc. wants to obtain a more senior water right that will protect it in times of drought, can't it simply purchase 10 cfs from Jones? It depends. Some jurisdictions limit transfers on the theory that the water right is appurtenant to the land. Most jurisdictions allow transfers but apply what is called the "no harm" rule, which prohibits any change in the location of use, type of use, time of use, point of diversion, or point of return flow that might harm a junior appropriator. If, for example, water from Jones' sprinklers percolates into the ground and makes its way back to the river (with typical irrigation methods about one-half of the water diverted returns to the stream), Smith might object to Computer Inc.'s attempt to purchase 10 cfs from Jones. If one-half of the amount used by Jones typically returned to the river, then even in a drought year of 20 cfs flow, Smith would have been able to divert 5 cfs. (Jones would take 10 cfs; Smith could divert the 5 cfs of return flow and still leave 10 cfs for Williams.) Thus, Computer, Inc. may also need to negotiate with Smith or Williams if it wants a more senior water right. Indeed, it may want to skip Jones and just negotiate with Williams because Williams is the last diverter along the hypothetical river.

• Suppose another farmer moved into the area and wanted to divert water for a trout farm. Could she? It depends. The existing appropriators have already claimed the full average flow of the stream. Some jurisdictions, worrying about the administrative burden of enforcing seniority, would not allow an additional appropriation. Other jurisdictions, however, allow streams to be overappropriated, assigning "paper water rights" that will only yield "wet water" in high flow years. In such situations, the junior appropriator sometimes builds storage (read dams) to capture the water from high-flow years for later use in low-flow years. Even if the jurisdiction allows our hypothetical river to be overappropriated, the trout farmer would need to show that her appropriation will not harm existing users and will be in the public interest. Suppose, for example, that the trout farm was upstream of Computer, Inc., which needs particularly clean water for its chip manufacturing process. If waste from the fish farm lowered the quality of the water too far, Computer Inc. could object to the new diversion.

• Suppose that Jones decides not to farm wheat anymore but to simply hold his water right as an investment, hoping perhaps that another computer manufacturer will relocate to the area and want to buy his water rights. Can he? Generally, no. A diverter who ceases to make beneficial use of his water right loses that water right. Speculation is not considered a beneficial use. In prior appropriation states, water has long been considered too valuable to sit idle in the stream.

- If water cannot sit idle in the stream, what are the environmental implications? Could a conservation organization like Trout Unlimited obtain a water right in our hypothetical river to assure a certain instream flow for protecting a fishery? Historically, water rights for instream flow were not available. Water had to be diverted out of the stream and put to use. Most western states have now passed legislation allowing state agencies, and in rare cases private organizations, to obtain water rights for instream flow purposes.

QUESTIONS AND DISCUSSION

1. The rule of prior appropriation has been criticized as economically inefficient:

> Under the "first in time, first in right doctrine," appropriators are senior and junior to one another along a scale from the first to the last. When water runs low, the juniors drop out first and lose everything before the next senior appropriator loses anything. In result, there is no pooling of risk whatever. The top senior has a 100 per cent firm supply; the last junior has a supply so uncertain it is unusable. Two basic economizing principles are denied. One is marginal productivity. The junior appropriator who loses all his water obviously loses marginal units of high productivity, while the senior retains marginal units of low productivity.

M. Mason Gaffney, *Economic Aspects of Water Resource Policy*, 28 AM. J. ECON. & SOC. 131, 140 (1969). Is there a response to this criticism? Does the fact that water may be transferred defeat the criticism? Is a system of riparian rights likely to achieve a more efficient result? What sort of system would?

2. The no-harm rule that prohibits changes in water rights harmful to junior users has been criticized as severely hampering any market in water rights. While it certainly makes transfers more difficult, they still occur.

George A. Gould, *A Westerner Looks at Eastern Water Law: Reconsideration of Prior Appropriation in the East*, 25 U. ARK. LITTLE ROCK L. REV. 89, 99–103 (2002)

> There is some truth to charges regarding water markets in the West. Few, if any, markets exist if one has in mind a setting in which water rights are transferred from anonymous buyers to anonymous sellers at prices set by the invisible hand of the market. A variety of factors impede the development of such markets for appropriation water rights, including the uniqueness of each right, the existence of externalities (third-party effects), the lack of facilities to transport large quantities of water, deficiencies in information, and institutional resistance to transfers. The term "water marketing," however, is seldom used in a strict sense in the West; instead it typically refers to any transfer of water rights from a willing seller to a willing buyer.

The development of additional supplies, the traditional western response to new needs, is frequently difficult or impossible because of lack of water to develop, high costs of development, environmental damage of large development projects, and social and political resistance. As a result, the West increasingly relies on reallocation to meet new needs, and some observers have dubbed the present "the Era of Reallocation." Reallocation in the West is achieved almost exclusively through voluntary transfers, i.e., through markets.

A few illustrations may be useful in demonstrating western efforts to implement water transfers. The California Water Bank, although not without its critics, is generally considered a success. In 1991 the bank transferred almost 400,000 acre-feet of water to meet critical water needs in a severe, multi-year drought. Most of the water was purchased from farmers, who fallowed ground or substituted groundwater for surface water, and was primarily sold to large urban entities. * * *

A study of transfers in six western states from 1975 to 1984 found that there were 3853 applications for changes in use in Utah, 1133 in New Mexico, and 858 in Colorado. At the other extreme, the study found only three applications in California during this period, but noted that this number understates transfer activity in California because a large number of water rights are not subject to the jurisdiction of the state water agency. The study also noted that the water supply in California is dominated by large supply agencies and that transfers within and between such agencies are often outside the jurisdiction of the water agency. Although many of these transfers involved small amounts of water, particularly in Utah, New Mexico, and Colorado, the level of activity illustrates that water transfers are a viable mechanism for reallocation in many western states.

Transfers from agricultural use in the Imperial Valley in southern California are a critical component in meeting the water needs of the great municipalities in the southern coastal area. Approximately 110,000 acre-feet of water annually is currently being transferred pursuant to a 1988 agreement between the Metropolitan Water District and the IID. Additionally, transfer[] of another 200,000 acre-feet annually from the Imperial Valley to the south coast, said to be the largest agriculture to urban transfer ever, is being implemented pursuant to a 1998 agreement between the IID and the San Diego County Water Authority. * * *

Interstate transfers of water have also begun to occur. Arizona and Nevada just completed a historic agreement which will permit 1.2 million acre-feet of Colorado River water to be transferred from Arizona to Nevada. Nevada's current diversions from the Colorado River slightly exceed its apportionment. Southern Nevada, unlike California, cannot meet new urban demands by intrastate transfers of water from agriculture because there are no significant agricultural uses of water in southern Nevada. Thus, the Arizona transfer is critical to continued growth of Las Vegas and other urban areas in southern Nevada.

Finally, transfers between users within irrigation districts and other water supply entities are very common and are accomplished with relative ease. Factors which contribute to the frequency and ease of such transfers include the homogeneous nature of the rights, the brokering role of the supply entity in matching potential buyers and sellers, the existence of distribution facilities to redirect water from sellers to buyers, and the fact that intra-institution transfers typically do not require approval by state water officials.

2. BENEFICIAL USE AND WASTE

Although the law of prior appropriation is significantly more complex than the simple scenarios above might indicate, we will leave most of those complexities for the casebooks and courses devoted entirely to the subject of water law. A couple of the key water law doctrines do, however, merit additional attention because of their currency and centrality to broader issues of water resources policy. As discussed above, the standard explanation of a water right is that a diverter has a property right in the amount of water diverted from a stream or lake and put to "beneficial use." Beneficial use means that the water is used for a purpose that is beneficial (e.g., agriculture, domestic, municipal, and industrial uses) and in a reasonable amount. Waste is not allowed. Thus it is often said that beneficial use is the basis, measure, and limit of a water right. As Professor Neuman notes,

> The requirement of "beneficial use without waste" sounds tight, as if water users must carefully husband the resource, using every drop of water completely and efficiently to avoid both forfeiture and waste. In actuality, the system is quite loose. Beneficial use is in fact a fairly elastic concept that freezes old customs, allows water users considerable flexibility in the amount and method of use, and leaves line drawing to the courts. The prohibitions against waste— even the threat of forfeiture for nonuse—are mostly hortatory concepts that rarely result in cutbacks in water use.

Janet C. Neuman, *Beneficial Use, Waste, and Forfeiture: The Inefficient Search for Efficiency in Western Water Use*, 28 ENVTL. L. 919, 922 (1998). Although courts have generally been slow to find waste in irrigation practices that have continued unchanged since the 1800s, the following case represents a departure from that norm. As you read the case, think about how the beneficial use doctrine makes water different than real property. If you buy a parcel of real property with the intention to build a home but then decide against building, you will still own the property, home or no. Absent allowing your property to become a nuisance, the state doesn't care whether you are "using" your property. Why is water different? Should it be treated any differently? Should real property rights be treated more like water rights?

IMPERIAL IRRIGATION DIST. v. STATE WATER RES. CONTROL BOARD, 225 Cal. App. 3d 548, 275 Cal. Rptr. 250 (1990), *cert. denied*, 502 U.S. 857 (1991)

This is an appeal from a judgment denying the petition for writ of mandate brought by Imperial Irrigation District (IID) to overturn a decision of the State Water Resources Control Board (Board).... In 1980 a private citizen requested the Department of Water Resources to investigate alleged misuse of water by IID which had resulted in a rise in the level of the Salton Sea, flooding the citizen's farmland. After an investigation, an initial conclusion of water waste, and unproductive communications with IID, the Department of Water Resources referred the matter to the Board for investigation and action.... On June 21, 1984, the Board issued its decision regarding misuse of water by IID, herein designated Decision 1600 (hereafter sometimes referred to as Board Decision) ... and an order requiring certain action to be taken by the IID.
* * *

As IID concedes in its brief, the essential facts of this case are not in dispute. The experts on any particular issue were never in complete agreement, but their differences were of degree, not kind. For instance, estimates of water lost through "canal spill" ranged from 53,000 to 135,000 acre feet per annum; and water lost through excessive "tailwater" ranged from 312,000 to 559,000 acre feet per annum. There was no dispute, however, that very large quantities of water in each case were being lost. The dispute is whether such loss (and this is but one example of such decisions made by the Board) was or was not reasonable. * * *

Water used by IID and its customers is diverted from the Colorado River. Diversion instrumentalities, including dams, power plants and the All–American Canal, which brings water from the river to the Imperial Valley, were authorized by the Boulder Canyon Project Act, enacted December 21, 1928. (43 U.S.C. § 617 et seq.).... Allocation of Colorado River water among users in Southern California was achieved through mutual agreement, however. The agreement, termed the "California Seven–Party Agreement," was executed on August 18, 1931, and remains in effect. Amount of entitlement and priority of distribution to IID are established in this agreement. * * *

Water rights within the state of California traditionally were derived from riparian rights or entitlement based upon prior appropriation. It is conceivable that IID's water rights, based as they are upon a unique blend of statutory and contractual origins, could be characterized as somehow more stable or securely vested than water rights from traditional sources. IID does not, however, make this claim. It simply contends that a right to use water, no matter how derived, once vested, becomes a property right which cannot be undermined without due compensation. * * *

As a preliminary matter we should note exactly what the Board did require of IID. The principal mandate contained in the Board Decision was an injunction that IID develop and present a water conservation plan. The trial court in its memorandum of decision noted that "except for requiring the District to repair defective tailwater structures, Decision 1600 itself requires no specific conservation measures, nor does it compel IID to sell, transfer, or otherwise convey water to the Metropolitan Water District or any other party. Decision 1600 simply requires the District to prepare plans to remedy its misuse of water, while retaining jurisdiction to review the adequacy of IID's plans."

We are unable, however, to agree that Decision 1600 did not substantially erode IID's otherwise virtually complete control over its water use. IID was required within a period of eight months to submit a plan for reservoir construction and to affirm its intent to construct one reservoir per year. Once a general plan of water conservation was achieved, IID was required to submit progress reports every six months "until the objectives have been achieved." The board reserved jurisdiction to monitor IID progress and to "take such other action" as might be required to assure compliance with an approved plan. There can be no doubt that the Board's intrusion into IID's previously untrammeled administration of the use of water in its district was substantial....

Our conclusion that the Board Decision substantially impacted the practical use and administration by IID of its water does not, however, result in our acceptance of IID's contention of unconstitutional interference with "vested" rights. Historic concepts of water "rights" in California were dramatically altered by the adoption in 1928 of [Article X, Section 2 of the California Constitution which prohibits "waste or unreasonable use or unreasonable method of use of water."]

The concept of the dimension of rights remaining to the water user after the constitutional amendment was fully developed in *Joslin v. Marin Mun. Water Dist.*, 67 Cal.2d 132, 429 P.2d 889 (1967). In that case a lower user attempted to enjoin upstream diversion by a municipal water company upon the contention that the downstream prior use for deposit of sand and gravel was a vested, protectible use. The Supreme Court held that simply because a use is beneficial it does not become "reasonable" under the Constitution. Denying the plaintiff's assertion of compensability for its loss of water, the court focused on the *nature* of water rights after 1928. "While plaintiffs correctly argue that a property right cannot be taken or damaged without just compensation, they ignore the necessity of first establishing the legal existence of a compensable property interest. Such an interest consists in their right to the *reasonable* use of the flow of water.... [While a] vested right *as now defined* may not be destroyed or infringed upon without due process of law or without just compensation ... [there is] no provision of law which authorizes an unreasonable use or endows such use with the quality of a legally protectible interest merely because it may be fortuitously beneficial to the lands involved." *Id.* at 143–44.

Put simply, IID does not have the vested rights which it alleges. It has only vested rights to the "reasonable" use of water. It has no right to waste or misuse water. The interference by the Board with IID's misuse (this finding of fact by the Board being accepted for purposes of the present issue) does not constitute a transgression on a vested right. * * *

IID contends that all of the water introduced into its district is used for "beneficial" purposes, including the excess water which finds its way to the Salton Sea. Such water prevents excessive salinization of the sea, protecting it as a fishery and wildlife sanctuary. It also finds beneficial use in the generation of electric power. There has never been, IID contends, an adjudication of constitutional misuse of water when the water is being beneficially used and there is no controversy between competing water users. Further, IID contends, both the Board and the attorney general have conceded that IID's use of water is "reasonable." Having made this concession, it is inconsistent and reversible error for the Board to reach a bottom-line conclusion of unreasonable use. IID's argument is bolstered, it contends, by the superior court's finding that "The Board did not find that IID's uses of water, in themselves, were unreasonable."

We believe IID has mischaracterized the Board's findings. The Board found (and IID does not dispute) that substantial losses of water resulted from canal spills, excess tailwater (the water running off the "tail" of a farm as the result of excess water being introduced at the "head" of the system), and other wasteful practices, such as canal seepage. Such runoff of water provided no alternative use for downstream users since IID's customers are at the end of the river, so to speak, the downstream being the Salton Sea. The totality of this waste of water was found by the Board to be "unreasonable and ... a misuse of water." Admitting that fresh flow into the Salton Sea might have some temporary fishery benefit, the Board found it to be an unpersuasive factor in that "prolonged delay in water conservation measures would not save the fishery for an appreciable length of time."

IID is also in error in contending that all "beneficial" uses are by definition "reasonable." The Constitution requires not only that water use be "reasonable" but that "the water resources of the State be put to beneficial use to the fullest extent of which they are capable." Obviously, this mandate requires a comparison of uses. As stated in *Tulare Dist. v. Lindsay–Strathmore Dist.* 3 Cal.2d 489, 567, 45 P.2d 972 (1935), "What is a beneficial use, of course, depends upon the facts and circumstances of each case. What may be a reasonable beneficial use, where water is present in excess of all needs, would not be a reasonable beneficial use in an area of great scarcity and great need. What is a beneficial use at one time may, because of changed conditions, become a waste of water at a later time."

In *Joslin v. Marin Municipal Water Dist., supra*, 67 Cal.2d at 141, the court noted the limited water resources available to the state, and that "conservation [must] be exercised 'in the interest of the people and for the public welfare.' " These cases, along with others which have been cited above, note the evolution of water rights from a concept of absolute right of use to one of comparative advantage of use. The fact that a diversion of water may be for a purpose "beneficial" in some respect (as for desalinization of lakes or generation of electric power) does not make such use "reasonable" when compared with demands, or even future demands, for more important uses. * * *

The tenor and taste of the appeal is that IID is being unfairly treated. It has occupied a position of strength, discretion and vested right in a geographical part of the country that is "far western," embracing a philosophy that is independent in every sense of the word. Recent trends in water-use philosophy and the administration of water law have severely undermined the positions of districts such as IID. IID's core complaint, if not completely valid, is at least understandable. It has been deprived of a great deal of the property rights which it thought were inherent in its allocation of Colorado River waters, made many years ago by federal and state statute and private contract. The loss of these rights undoubtedly will result in practical and monetary losses for IID and its customers. An obvious conclusion is that *Imperial I* and the rulings of the Board have eroded IID's bargaining position in terms of the sale of its water to other districts, such as the Metropolitan Water District. * * *

IID reviews its past record of activities designed to conserve water, reminding that in the last 20 years or so it has constructed four reservoirs, evaluated cost effectiveness, lined 732 miles of canals, constructed 6 additional units for power production, initiated conservation studies, and achieved water use efficiencies which are above average for comparable projects. IID itself has recognized the desirability of water conservation by adopting in January of 1984 a resolution calling for reduction of inflow to the Salton Sea by 100,000 acre feet annually. In light of this evidence of responsible water trusteeship, IID finds the Board's mandates (such as item 1.2 of the Board's order, that IID require its water users to repair defective tailwater structures by a certain date in 1985) to be excessive. * * *

All things must end, even in the field of water law. It is time to recognize that this law is in flux and that its evolution has passed beyond traditional concepts of vested and immutable rights. In his review of our Supreme Court's recent water rights decision in *In re Water of Hallett Creek Stream System*, 44 Cal.3d 448, 749 P.2d 324 (1988), Professor Freyfogle explains that California is engaged in an evolving process of governmental redefinition of water rights. He concludes that "California has regained for the public much of the power to prescribe water use practices, to limit waste, and to sanction water transfers." He asserts that the concept that "water use entitlements are clearly and permanently defined," and are "neutral [and] rule-driven," is a pretense to be discarded. It is a fundamental truth, he writes, that "everything is in the process of changing or becoming" in water law.

In affirming this specific instance of far-reaching change, imposed upon traditional uses by what some claim to be revolutionary exercise of adjudicatory power, we but recognize this evolutionary process, and urge reception and recognition of same upon those whose work in the practical administration of water distribution makes such change understandably difficult to accept.

QUESTIONS AND DISCUSSION

1. What are the implications of the court's acceptance of Professor Freyfogle's argument that "everything is in the process of changing or becoming" in water law? Is the court's suggestion that the "concept that 'water use entitlements are clearly and permanently defined' . . . is a pretense to be disregarded" descriptive, normative, or both? Is uncertainty about the nature of water rights wise water policy?

2. The Imperial Irrigation District's history is bound up with some of the most important stories in western water law. Located just north of Mexico at the southern end of California, the IID is essentially a desert. When Juan Bautista de Anza, a captain in the Spanish army, crossed the area in the eighteenth century he declared that he had made "*la jornada de los muertos*" [the journey of the dead]. And in a sense he was right. The District averages about 2.9 inches of rainfall a year, with average high temperatures of 105 degrees in July and 67 degrees in January. On the other hand, because the District sits in the archeological flood plain of the Colorado River, its soil is incredibly fertile—200 inches of sediment that poured out of the southwest over the centuries. The first to notice the possibility of irrigation was a geologist with the Southern Pacific railroad survey party. Crossing the area in 1853, he took barometric readings which showed that the entire desert lay below sea level and could be irrigated by a gravity-flow canal from the Colorado River. The story of the District's subsequent efforts to build a canal from the Colorado River and a dam to help corral the River is retold in the Colorado River case study later in this chapter. *Infra* p. 890. The end result was that IID became the largest irrigation district in the nation. Of the 7.5 million acre feet (MAF) of Colorado River water allocated to the lower basin states of California, Nevada, and Arizona, IID has a senior right to 2.6 MAF. With that 2.6 MAF, IID irrigates about 500,000 acres and produces about $1 billion worth of crops annually. *See* Imperial Irrigation District, 2005 Annual Water Report, *available at http://www.iid.com/Media/2005IIDWaterAnnualReport. pdf.*

3. One of IID's arguments in the case is that the water that escapes its system is still put to beneficial use because it ends up in the Salton Sea. The Salton Sea has a fascinating history. When Europeans first came to the IID area, the Salton Sea did not exist. Although there were signs of an ancient sea bed, there was no water in it.

> The Sea owes its current existence to a twentieth century engineering catastrophe. In the early 1900s, Anglo speculators dug a large diversion canal from the Colorado River (near Yuma), passing through Mexico to the newly-named town of Imperial, California. By 1904, Imperial Valley had 7,000 settlers who irrigated farmland with Colorado River water. Nevertheless, the poorly constructed main canal soon clogged with sediment. To bypass the clog, the Colorado Development Company cut a new canal in the river's banks, but failed to install a control gate. The next spring, heavy snowmelt from the Rocky Mountains produced severe flooding along the Gila and the Lower Colorado

Rivers, and the river broke through the primitive canal banks. By summer, the entire flow of the Colorado River had moved from its natural channel into the new canal and was flowing into the Imperial Valley, rapidly flooding more than a quarter of a million acres of farmland. A massive one and a half year effort eventually pushed the river back into its natural channel, but the gigantic inland sea created by the flood remained and continued to grow, fed by irrigation outflows from the Imperial, Coachella, and Mexicali valleys, and later by Mexican municipal wastewater flows from the New River.

The Sea has no outlet, and its size depends solely on the amount of wastewater inflow balanced against the rate of evaporation from the Sea's surface. Today, it is about 35 miles long, from 9 to 15 miles wide, and lies 227 feet below sea level. Due to years of high-salinity agricultural wastewater inflow and the concentrating effects of evaporation, the salinity of the Sea now exceeds that of the ocean; at the same time, nutrient loading from fertilizers has produced gigantic toxic algae blooms within the Sea. Nevertheless, the Salton Sea is a critical environmental refuge, serving as a stopping point for more than 380 species of birds on the Pacific Flyway. The Salton Sea is one of the few remaining refuges along the Pacific Flyway north of the Delta because most wetlands in California's Central Valley have been drained or filled. Unfortunately, due to avian cholera and botulism, the Sea produces enormous mortality among these birds. As the water quality of the Sea continues to deteriorate due to salt, pesticide, toxics, and nutrient concentration, it is likely that this bird mortality will increase.

Recent interest in the Sea as a refuge for migratory waterfowl has spawned efforts to save it. In the mid–1990s, the late Sonny Bono, a United States Representative from Southern California, took on the Salton Sea as his personal crusade. In his honor, Congress passed the Salton Sea Reclamation Act in 1998, which authorized the BOR [Bureau of Reclamation], U.S. Fish and Wildlife Service, and U.S. Environmental Protection Agency to undertake a feasibility study for restoring the Salton Sea. The Act renamed the refuge the Sonny Bono Salton Sea National Wildlife Refuge and provided $8 million for the feasibility study and for clean-up efforts along the New and Alamo rivers (which empty into the Sea). . . .

While the Act precluded any option that "relies on the importation of any new or additional water from the Colorado River," several environmental groups, including the Audubon Society, remain in favor of diverting additional Colorado River water into the Sea in order to dilute salinity. A number of other environmental groups oppose such a plan, preferring to reserve additional flows for restoration along the Lower Colorado River and Delta.

Regardless of the alternative selected, restoration of the Sea will be enormously expensive. According to *High Country News*, "[E]ven the cheapest proposed solution would require a congressional appropriation of more than $300 million." In addition, despite the elaborate engineering fixes designed to cope with salt loads in the Sea, none of the proposed solutions deals with the real problem facing the Sea: the growing demands on the water that feeds it. Regional water conservation and municipal wastewater reuse efforts are underway that will inevitably reduce flows of water to the Sea. The conservation/transfer agreements between southern California cities and the Imperial Irrigation District are one serious threat. Though laudable for their conservation goals, such efforts will only increase the environmental problems of the Sea by reducing the fresh water inflows.

Robert Jerome Glennon & Peter W. Culp, *The Last Green Lagoon: How and Why the Bush Administration Should Save the Colorado River Delta,*

28 ECOLOGY L.Q. 903, 933–35 (2002). Is the IID correct that preservation of the Salton Sea is a beneficial use, or should the area be allowed to return to its pre–1905 status? Would you characterize the Salton Sea as "natural" or "artificial"? Does that characterization help answer the policy conundrum of what to do about the Salton Sea? For useful websites about the history of the Salton Sea and the continuing debate about the best ways to restore it, see U.S. Bureau of Reclamation, Salton Sea Restoration Project, *at* http://www.usbr.gov/lc/region/saltnsea/index.html; Salton Sea Authority, *at* http://www.saltonsea.ca.gov.

4. The court notes that the California Water Resources Control Board's ruling had "eroded IID's bargaining position in terms of the sale of its water to other districts." This may have been true with respect to price but the decision helped catalyze IID to think creatively about its water. Prompted by the Board's decision, in 1989, IID negotiated an agreement with the Metropolitan Water District (MWD) under which MWD agreed to undertake a variety of improvements within IID, such as lining canals with cement, in exchange for 106,000 acre feet of water. In 2003, IID signed a similar agreement with the San Diego County Water Authority for 200,000 acre feet.

5. Professor Gould has argued that "the excesses and deficiencies attributed to the [prior appropriation] doctrine, most notably environmental degradation, reflect nineteenth century values, not inherent flaws in the doctrine. [I]f the doctrine is viewed as a tool, the alleged excess and deficiencies are not the result of a poor tool but merely of its improper use...." George A. Gould, *A Westerner Looks at Eastern Water Law: Reconsideration of Prior Appropriation in the East*, 25 U. ARK. LITTLE ROCK L. REV. 89, 98 (2002). What do you think he means? Do you agree? Are the doctrines of beneficial use and waste useful tools to correct environmental degradation? Do you see why most commentators consider them harmful to the environment? Is the decision in *IID* a "victory" for the environment?

6. For a thorough overview of the legislation and case law addressing the beneficial use doctrine, see Janet C. Neuman, *Beneficial Use, Waste, and Forfeiture: The Inefficient Search for Efficiency in Western Water Use*, 28 ENVTL. L. 919 (1998).

───────

3.   PERMIT SYSTEMS AND THE PUBLIC INTEREST REQUIREMENT

Although the roots of prior appropriation are in the common law, today the law of prior appropriation is mostly administered through comprehensive statutory and regulatory systems. In large measure the statutes and regulations replicate the common-law rules. Their purpose was not so much to supplant as to organize and make administrable the underlying common law allocation of water rights. To accomplish these tasks, states adopted permit systems under which prospective water users are obligated to apply for a permit from a state agency. The state generally provides a form for this purpose. *See, e.g.,* http://www1.wrd.state.or.us/pdfs/surfacewaterapp.pdf. Colorado is the only appropriation state that never adopted a statutory permit procedure, instead employing a system of seven water divisions with water judges who adjudicate the water rights within the division. In those states with permit systems, an application to appropriate water is typically filed the state engineer or other equivalent administrator and must describe the nature of the proposed use, the quantity of water to be appropriated, the name of the stream, the point of diversion on the stream, etc. Upon receipt of the application, the state engineer publishes notice of the application and usually contacts affected parties. Interested persons are given some period of time—e.g., 20 days—to file a protest. If a protest is filed, the agency holds a public hearing, relying heavily on the factual investigation of the state engineer who opines on whether the basic statutory criteria for an appropriation have been met. If the requirements of state law are satisfied, the state will issue a permit. The permit is not itself a water right, but will ripen into a water right, with a priority date as of the date of filing, provided that the applicant constructs the diversion works with due diligence and applies the water to a beneficial use. The agency will then issue a "certificate of appropriation" or similar document signifying that the water right has been perfected.

The primary focus of western permit systems remains on taking water out of the stream and putting it to use. Certain aspects of the permit systems do, however, have potential for protecting and conserving water for fish and wildlife habitat and recreation opportunities. One such component of most permit systems is the requirement that the state agency responsible for administering the state's water conduct a public interest analysis before issuing any permit. Almost all western states require some sort of public interest review prior to issuing a permit to appropriate water. *See generally* Douglas L. Grant, *Public Interest Review of Water Right Allocation and Transfer in the West: Recognition of Public Values*, 19 Ariz. St. L.J. 681, 683 & n.16 (1987). California's public interest provision is typical.

> In acting upon applications to appropriate water, the [state water resources control] board shall consider the relative benefit to be derived from (1) all beneficial uses of the water concerned including, but not limited to, use for domestic, irrigation, municipal, industrial, preservation and enhancement of fish and wildlife, recreational, mining and power purposes, and any uses specified to be protected in any relevant water quality control plan, and (2) the reuse or reclamation of the water sought to be appropriated, as proposed by the applicant. The board may subject such appropriations to such terms and conditions as in its judgment will best develop, conserve, and utilize in the public interest, the water sought to be appropriated.

Cal. Water Code § 1257. Although application of the public interest analysis prior to issuing a permit can be contentious, the more controversial application of the public interest rules has been in cases where one water user proposes to transfer her water right to another user. Many of the states requiring a public interest analysis to obtain a permit also require a public interest review prior to water transfers. In one much discussed case, a ski resort in northern New Mexico, hoping to construct an artificial lake for summer recreation, bought the property of two farmers and then sought to change their irrigation use and places of diversion. The New Mexico state engineer approved the transfer application and a group of local irrigators appealed, resulting in the following decision.

IN RE APPLICATION OF SLEEPER, RIO ARRIBA COUNTY,
No. RA 84–53(C) (N.M. 1st Jud. Dist. April 16, 1985)

ART ENCINAS, DISTRICT JUDGE:

[I]t is simply assumed by the Applicants that greater economic benefits are more desirable than the preservation of cultural identity. This is clearly not so. . . . This region of Northern New Mexico and its living culture are recognized . . . as possessing significant cultural value, not measurable in dollars and cents. The deep-felt and tradition bound ties of northern New Mexico families to the land and water are central to maintenance of that culture. * * *

I am persuaded that to transfer water rights, devoted for more than a century to agricultural purposes, in order to construct a playground for those who can pay is a poor trade, indeed. Indeed, I find that the proposed transfer of water rights is clearly contrary to the public interest.

QUESTIONS AND DISCUSSION

1. The court of appeals reversed Judge Encinas' decision on the grounds that New Mexico's public interest statute in force at the time of Judge Encinas' decision did not apply to transfers of previously appropriated water but only to applications for new appropriations. 107 N.M. 494, 760 P.2d 787 (N.M. Ct. App. 1988). Subsequent to the ski resort's transfer application, New Mexico had passed a statute providing for the consideration of the public interest prior to approving a transfer. *See* N.M.S.A. § 72–5–23 (providing that irrigation water transfers not be detrimental to the "public welfare").

What if a public interest test had applied to the ski resort's proposal to transfer the irrigation water right to a new recreational use. Is this the sort of analysis that judges and state engineers should conduct? As a matter of institutional competence, who is best situated to determine whether a water rights transfer conforms to the public interest? Does it matter how broadly the public interest is defined?

2. Is the case for performing a public interest analysis any different for new appropriations than for transfers? Why would you expect senior water rights holders to object to the idea that a transfer must satisfy public interest criteria? Are their objections at all justified? In *Public Utility Dist. No. 1 of Pend Oreille County v. State, Dept. of Ecology*, 146 Wash.2d 778, 51 P.3d 744 (2002), the Washington Supreme Court held that Washington's public interest statute did not apply to transfers. Although it focused on the statutory language and legislative intent, the court noted that "when an application for change . . . is made, the allocation of public waters has already occurred, and the right involved is a perfected water right." *Id.* at 796. Is this a persuasive reason to reject public interest analysis of changes? Arguing for its authority to conduct a public interest analysis, the Washington Department of Ecology expressed concern that "one could essentially avoid public interest review by applying for a permit to appropriate water, undergoing public interest review, obtaining a water right, and then seeking to change it without further public interest review." *Id.* at 797. Is this a valid concern? How might legislation address it? On public interest analysis generally, see Douglas L. Grant, *Public Interest Review of Water Right Allocation and Transfer in the West: Recognition of Public Values*, 19 ARIZ. ST. L.J. 681 (1987); Owen L. Anderson et al., *Reallocation, Transfers, and Changes*, *in* 2 WATER AND WATER RIGHTS, § 14.04(d) (Robert E. Beck ed., 1991).

————

4.   INSTREAM FLOW APPROPRIATIONS

At common law one of the basic requirements for perfecting a water right was that the water actually be diverted from the stream. Speculation in water was forbidden. No water right could be obtained for the purpose of leaving water in the stream. If a water right was not put to beneficial use— and instream uses were historically not considered beneficial—it would be lost. These basic common law doctrines were not particularly friendly to the riparian ecosystem or to recreation, both of which depend upon having a sufficient amount of water in the stream. Considering environmental and recreation impacts of appropriations as part of the public interest analysis is one approach to this problem. Another approach has been to give the relevant state agency authority to condition permits on maintaining certain instream flows or to simply instruct the agency not to issue permits that would diminish the flow below a certain level. A third strategy that most states in the West now employ is to allow water to be appropriated for the maintenance of stream flow. Typically, they authorize a specific public agency to appropriate instream flows. Some allow appropriation only of unappropriated water. *See, e.g.*, WYO. STAT. ANN. § 41–3–1001 & 41–3–1003. Others allow instream rights to be created only from existing rights. Utah, for example, allows its Division of Wildlife Resources or Division of Parks and Recreation to apply for permanent or temporary changes to provide water for instream flows for the propagation of fish, public recreation, or the reasonable preservation or enhancement of the natural stream environment.

Adhering to the traditional common-law requirement of diversion and the prohibition on speculation, most states do not allow private appropriation of instream flow. A few states do. In addition to the legislation in Montana, Oregon and California described below, Utah recently began allowing private "fishing groups" to file change applications on perfected, consumptive water rights for the purpose of providing water for instream flow. UTAH CODE ANN. § 73–3–30 (2008). In the excerpt below, Professor Thompson describes some of the reasons why private appropriation of instream flow is not commonly permitted and considers arguments for and against such a change in the common law.

Barton H. Thompson, Jr., *Markets for Nature*,
25 WM. & MARY ENVTL. L. & POL'Y REV. 261, 287–92, 271–78 (2000)

[O]nly a handful of states explicitly authorize private acquisitions. Montana authorizes private individuals and entities of any kind to lease water for up to ten years for instream purposes. Oregon permits "any person" to acquire an instream right by purchase, lease, or donation.... California permits anyone, including implicitly the private purchaser of a water right, to dedicate some or all of their water to "preserving or enhancing wetlands habitat, fish and wildlife resources, or recreation in, or on, the water." * * *

Why have only a limited number of states authorized the private acquisition of instream flow—and then only reluctantly? Some observers have suggested that legislatures may view instream flows as uniquely public in character, reflecting collective decisions about the commonweal. Although governments must be involved in the provision of instream flows, however, there is no reason why governments must monopolize the field. Instream flows are largely public goods: the benefits of instream flows are nonexclusive, and one person can enjoy the benefits without taking away from someone else's enjoyment of them. As a result, nonprofits and private organizations cannot be counted on to provide a level of instream flows that maximizes societal benefits . . . ; although some individuals will contribute toward instream flows, many others will free ride on the contributions of others. This is an argument for public provision of instream flow, but it does not justify banning those who wish even greater levels of instream flows from using the marketplace to achieve those levels— any more than the public character of education or welfare justifies banning their provision by nonprofits or other private entities. * * *

The government can provide a desired level of instream flow in a variety of fashions other than through acquisition, including regulation and condemnation. Why acquisition? Regulation avoids a drain on the public fisc and is more consistent with the traditional view that water is a public resource to which individuals should hold only limited, usufructuary rights and only when consistent with the overall public interest. If the government believes for policy or constitutional reasons that water users subject to reduced diversions should be compensated, condemnation of the needed water rights would provide adequate compensation. Market acquisitions run the risk that water users will hold out for prices greater than the "market value" of the water, raising the specter in some people's minds of unjust enrichment. Voluntary acquisition would seem the inferior approach.

Political feasibility explains much of the reason for the government's turn to voluntary acquisition. Existing water users have strongly and successfully opposed efforts to return significant amounts of water to western waterways. Legislatures and administrative agencies sometimes have mustered the political courage to reserve unappropriated water for instream purposes or to strip water users of unexercised paper rights. But legislatures and agencies have balked at stripping users of water they are currently using. Virtually all of the major regulatory reallocations of water to the environment have involved the judicial invocation of either the court-created public trust doctrine or the Endangered Species Act, which few, if any, members of the adopting Congress ever expected to interfere with longstanding water uses. Even in these limited contexts, administrative discretion and political opposition have combined to limit the law's potential value in restoring instream flow. . . . Legislative efforts to reduce historic diversions, moreover, raise constitutional takings questions. * * *

Any effort to reallocate water to instream flow, whether compulsory or voluntary, raises concerns within the water community. Downstream water users, for example, fear that reallocations will negatively affect the timing of flows that are crucial to their operations. In the dry season, farmers often depend on the return flow from earlier upstream irrigation; if an upstream irrigator transfers his water to instream flow, the delayed return flow upon which the downstream users rely will disappear. Agricultural communities also fear that irrigators who transfer their water to instream flow will fallow their lands, injuring the local economy. Water users also fear a slippery policy slope. The legislative adoption of an instream acquisition program endorses the importance of instream flows and undercuts the traditional preference in western water law for consumptive uses; instream acquisition programs thus undermine policy arguments against involuntary instream reallocations. Finally, water users who anticipate needing more water in the future may not want the added competition of the government bidding for instream flows; an instream acquisition program might bid up the cost of water available on the market. Where the government acquires water that otherwise might have gone unused, the acquisition might also take water away from junior appropriators. Under prior appropriation law, moreover, water that remains unused for a sufficient period of time is "abandoned" or "forfeited" and becomes permanently available to other appropriators. * * *

Some environmental advocates ... have questioned the political wisdom of using voluntary acquisition programs to increase instream flows. Budgetary outlays for voluntary acquisitions have historically been quite low, and political theory would suggest that legislative appropriations are unlikely to fully reflect public support for instream acquisitions. Because support for environmental amenities such as higher stream flow is relatively diffuse, demands from more concentrated constituencies are likely to dominate the appropriation process. Although some instream acquisition programs have gotten around the appropriation process by funding acquisitions through a fee on water use, water users are likely to oppose such fees as strongly and effectively as they have opposed mandated instream flows. Many water users, moreover, have refused to participate in instream acquisition programs either out of lingering suspicions that the programs are regulations in disguise or because of local community opposition to water transfers. For these reasons, voluntary acquisition programs may never provide levels of instream flow reflective of the actual public demand for stream restoration.

None of this would argue against voluntary acquisition programs if they did not reduce the chances of increasing instream flows through other means. Instream proponents could enjoy the limited fruit of voluntary acquisitions while pursuing other avenues of restoration. But by paying some water users for instream flows, the government may undercut the argument for direct regulation. Opponents of regulation are likely to point to the voluntary acquisition program as evidence that mandated reallocations are unfair and unnecessary. While mandatory reallocations may be a tough political sell, some environmentalists would prefer that fight over under-funded acquisition programs that give regulatory opponents yet another argument against mandatory reallocations.

Some environmental advocates, moreover, fear that, by paying for instream flow, the government also may undercut an ethos of conservation. Aldo Leopold believed that the only effective means to achieve sustainable resource use was by developing a new norm, a "land ethic," under which property owners would incorporate the needs of the ecosystem as a whole into their stewardship of land, water, and other resources. Several recent scholars, in turn, have suggested that legal regulations or standards may encourage the development of new norms consistent with those regulations or standards. Some have worried that government acquisition programs, by contrast, might undermine the fostering of a new land ethic by making environmental stewardship an issue of money rather than fundamental values.

QUESTIONS AND DISCUSSION

1. After reviewing Professor Thompson's comments, whose argument do you find more persuasive—the opponents or the proponents of private instream appropriations? In light of growing public preference for river protection and recreation, is speculation still a legitimate concern of water policy? If instream flow appropriations are a good idea, why do many states limit those appropriations to the amount of water necessary to protect fish and wildlife habitat?

2. Idaho's Constitution provides that the "right to divert and appropriate the unappropriated waters of any natural stream to beneficial uses, shall never be denied." IDAHO CONST. art. XV, § 3. Would a state statute directing the Idaho Department of Parks to appropriate instream flows violate this constitutional provision? What arguments would you envision on either side of this question? *See State of Idaho Department of Parks v. Idaho Department of Water Administration*, 96 Idaho 440, 530 P.2d 924 (1974) (addressing this issue).

3. Preserving minimum stream flows has typically been an easier task in states employing riparian rights. Not only do such states have more water to begin with, but also riparian doctrine generally prohibited unreasonable depletion of stream flows. Nevertheless, as eastern states have moved to permit systems, most have included statutory provisions obligating an agency to set or protect minimum stream flows. Florida, for example, obligates the relevant agency to establish a "[m]inimum flow for all surface watercourses in the area. The minimum flow for a given watercourse shall be the limit at which further withdrawals would be significantly harmful to the water resources or ecology of the area." FLA. STAT. § 373.042(1)(a). Likewise, before any permit is issued, a public interest analysis, which includes potential environmental impacts, is required. FLA. STAT. § 373.223(3).

4. Instream flow is not only about protecting fish and wildlife habitat. Increasingly it is about preserving recreational amenities. In 2003, Colorado awarded the communities of Golden, Vail, and Breckenridge instream flow rights sufficient to operate their whitewater kayaking courses. *See State Engineer v. City of Golden*, 69 P.3d 1027 (Colo. 2003) (affirming water court's recognition of water right by virtue of an equally divided Colorado Supreme Court); *State Engineer v. Eagle River Water & Sanitation Dist.*, 69 P.3d 1028 (Colo. 2003) (same). The Colorado Attorney General had contended that using the water for kayaking courses was not the sort of beneficial use allowed by Colorado law because the water was not physically removed from the stream or impounded behind a dam. Golden, which was awarded a water right to 1000 cfs, countered that during its first three years of existence, its Clear Creek Whitewater Park, which has spectator seating, had 45,000 users and injected $23 million into Golden's economy. Golden had also built seven boat chutes that it argued were effectively diversions. *See* Howard Pankratz, *Recreational Water Use Buoyed*, DENVER POST, May 20, 2003, at A1; *Concerning the Application for Water Rights of the City of Golden*, No. 98CW448, Dist. Ct. Water Div. No. 1 (Colo. Jan. 13, 2001). What do you suppose the reaction in Colorado was to the Court's decision? Is the granting of recreational water rights unmitigated good news for the environment?

5. On instream flow rights generally, see Jack Sterne, *Instream Rights and Invisible Hands: Prospects for Private Instream Water Rights in the Northwest*, 27 ENVTL. L. 203 (1997); Cynthia Covell, *A Survey of State Instream Flow Programs in the Western United States*, 1 U. DENV. WATER L. REV. 177 (1998).

———

PROBLEM EXERCISE: FORMING A WATER TRUST

The state in which you live has just passed legislation modeled on Oregon's allowing any person to purchase or lease existing water rights. The relevant provision states:

> (1) Any person may purchase or lease all or a portion of an existing water right or accept a gift of all or a portion of an existing water right for conversion to an in-stream water right. Any water right converted to an in-stream water right under this section shall retain the priority date of the water right purchased, leased or received as a gift.... A person who transfers a water right by purchase, lease or gift under this subsection shall comply with the requirements for the transfer of a water right [including the no harm rule.]

> (2) Any person who has an existing water right may lease all or a portion of the existing water right for use as an in-stream water right for a specified period without the loss of the original priority date. During the term of such lease, the use of the water right as an in-stream water right shall be considered a beneficial use. * * *

OR. REV. STAT. 537.348 (2002). An avid fisher and river enthusiast, you and several other attorneys decide to form a water trust. Although you have a few backers, your funds will be quite limited initially. How should you allocate those limited funds? On which watercourses would you focus? Would you direct your efforts at senior rights or junior rights? Purchase or lease? Would you focus on upstream or downstream water rights? Why? What sort of political and public relations obstacles might you face? How would your strategy take account of those obstacles? In considering these questions, you may wish to peruse Professor Neuman's account of her work to form the Oregon Water Trust, the first such trust in the nation. *See* Janet C. Neuman & Cheyenne Chapman, *Wading into the Water Market: The First Five Years of the Oregon Water Trust*, 14 J. ENVTL. L. & LITIG. 135 (1999). *See also* Janet C. Neuman, *Sometimes a Great Notion: Oregon's Instream Flow Experiments*, 36 ENVTL. L. 1125 (2006).

———

5. LOS ANGELES, WATER, AND THE PUBLIC TRUST DOCTRINE

Retold in fiction in Roman Polanski's movie *Chinatown* and in scholarly detail in William L. Kharl's *Water and Power*, the story of Los Angeles and its water is one of the classics of western water law. As an introduction to the most significant public trust doctrine decision since the Supreme

Court decided *Illinois Central, supra* Chapter 2, a brief retelling of that story is necessary.

During the nineteenth century Los Angeles took a decidedly back seat to San Francisco in the hierarchy of California prestige and power. As Marc Reisner described it, during most of the latter half of the nineteenth century,

> Los Angeles . . . remained a torpid, suppurating, stunted little slum. It was too far from the gold fields to receive many fortune seekers on their way in or to detach them from their fortunes on the way out. It sat forlornly in the middle of an arid coastal basin, lacking both a port and a railroad. During most of the year, its water source, the Los Angeles River, was a smallish creek in a large bed; during the winter weeks when it was not—when supersaturated tropical weather fronts crashed into the mountains ringing the basin—the bed could not begin to contain it, and the river floated neighborhoods out to sea. Had humans never settled in Los Angeles, evolution, left to its own devices, might have created in a million more years the ideal creature for the habitat: a camel with gills. * * *
>
> In this freakish climate—semitropical but dry, ocean-cooled but lavishly sunny—you could grow almost anything. Corn and cabbages sprouted next to oranges, avocados, artichokes and dates. The capitalists of San Francisco did not remain oblivious; the Southern Pacific ran a spur line to Los Angeles in 1867, finally linking it to the rest of the world. On this same line, huge San Bernardino Valencias found their way to the 1884 World's Fair in New Orleans, where they attracted crowds. No one could imagine *oranges* grown in the western United States. It was then and there, more or less, that the phenomenon of modern Los Angeles began.

MARC REISNER, CADILLAC DESERT: THE AMERICAN WEST AND ITS DISAPPEARING WATER 52–54 (1986). As Los Angeles grew it needed more water. Mostly it found that water in the artesian aquifers underlying the city. But around the turn of the century, when the city's population doubled in just four years and when artesian wells which had gushed eight feet high were reduced to gurgles, the city's water masters recognized that they were going to need more water to support the growth. The closest rivers of any note were the Colorado and the Kern, but to bring either to L.A. would have required lifting the water up over intervening mountain ranges, a task requiring a lot of energy which just wasn't available at the time. Instead, Los Angeles, led by former mayor Fred Eaton and the chief of the Department of Water and Power, William Mulholland, turned their gaze some 250 miles away, to the Owens River. The Owens River rises southeast of Yosemite and flows south along the eastern side of the Sierra Nevada mountains and into Owens Lake, or what used to be Owens Lake. Before Owens Lake, the river passes through a long mountain valley flanked by the Sierra Nevadas on one side and the White Mountains on the other. By 1899, this valley, the Owens Valley, had about 40,000 acres under cultivation, a patch of green in the midst of California's high desert. In fact, its cultivation was so promising that in 1903 the newly-minted U.S. Reclamation Service identified Owens Valley as one of the first places for an irrigation project.

But Los Angeles had other things in mind. Although the Owens River wasn't as big as the Colorado, it had one great advantage. The Owens

Valley sat at about 4000 feet above sea level. Los Angeles, just a few feet above sea level, could get the waters of the Owens River by gravity alone. No pumping would be required. Quietly, Eaton and Mulholland began buying up land and water rights in the Owens Valley. They also managed to hire J.B. Lippincott, who just happened to be the district engineer for the Reclamation Service, as a part-time consultant. Not surprisingly, Lippincott ended up recommending against a Reclamation Service irrigation project in the Valley. Between the negative recommendation and the fact that Los Angeles by then controlled some 40 miles of riverbank and most of the key water rights, the project never got off the ground. All that was left was for Los Angeles to build the aqueduct. No small feat at the time, the aqueduct included 53 miles of tunnels and traversed a total of 223 miles. After six years of labor, the Department of Water and Power turned on the spigots and water poured down the final sluice-way into Los Angeles' San Fernando Valley. Mulholland's 1913 ribbon-cutting speech was short. As the water cascaded down the man-made waterfall, still visible today from the freeway as one drives out of Los Angeles, he turned to the mayor and said: "There it is. Take it."

At first, life in the Owens Valley seemed relatively unaffected. But when the inevitable drought came ten years later, the impact of the city's diversion hit home. The Valley's farmers and ranchers didn't have enough water to make it. Things turned nasty. In May of 1924, a group of farmers dynamited a portion of the aqueduct; in November, after the aqueduct had been repaired, a group of citizens managed briefly to turn the river back into the now dry bed of Owens Lake. By liberally spending more money to buy yet more land and water rights, Los Angeles, with the help of a couple of injunctions, was able to pacify the protests. But the Owens Valley just got drier. Indeed, as Los Angeles grew and the Owens River wasn't enough, the city began pumping the Valley's groundwater as well. By the 1970s, what had been Owens Lake was a dust bowl and the single largest source of particle air pollution in the United States. In the last couple of decades, Los Angeles has negotiated agreements with Inyo County to rewater portions of the Owens River and revegetate portions of the Valley but the area today remains a shadow of what might have been. *See generally* REISNER, *supra*, at 52–103 (telling the Owens Valley story).

As it turned out, all of the water from the Owens Valley could not slake the thirst of Los Angeles' growing population. The Department of Water and Power would subsequently turn to the Colorado River, a story told later in this chapter, to northern California, and to another mountain lake on the east side of the Sierra Nevada mountains—Mono Lake. The following case tells that story and reintroduces you to the public trust doctrine of *Illinois Central* from Chapter 2.

NATIONAL AUDUBON SOCIETY V. SUPERIOR COURT OF ALPINE COUNTY, 33 Cal. 3d 419, 189 Cal. Rptr. 346, 658 P.2d 709 (1983), *cert. denied*, 464 U.S. 977 (1983)

BROUSSARD, JUSTICE.

Mono Lake, the second largest lake in California, sits at the base of the Sierra Nevada escarpment near the eastern entrance to Yosemite National

Park. The lake is saline; it contains no fish but supports a large population of brine shrimp which feed vast numbers of nesting and migratory birds. Islands in the lake protect a large breeding colony of California gulls, and the lake itself serves as a haven on the migration route for thousands of Northern Phalarope, Wilson's Phalarope, and Eared Grebe. Towers and spires of tufa on the north and south shores are matters of geological interest and a tourist attraction.

Although Mono Lake receives some water from rain and snow on the lake surface, historically most of its supply came from snowmelt in the Sierra Nevada. Five freshwater streams—Mill, Lee Vining, Walker, Parker and Rush Creeks—arise near the crest of the range and carry the annual runoff to the west shore of the lake. In 1940, however, the Division of Water Resources, the predecessor to the present California Water Resources Board, granted the Department of Water and Power of the City of Los Angeles (hereafter DWP) a permit to appropriate virtually the entire flow of four of the five streams flowing into the lake. DWP promptly constructed facilities to divert about half the flow of these streams into DWP's Owens Valley aqueduct. In 1970 DWP completed a second diversion tunnel, and since that time has taken virtually the entire flow of these streams.

As a result of these diversions, the level of the lake has dropped; the surface area has diminished by one-third; one of the two principal islands in the lake has become a peninsula, exposing the gull rookery there to coyotes and other predators and causing the gulls to abandon the former island. The ultimate effect of continued diversions is a matter of intense dispute, but there seems little doubt that both the scenic beauty and the ecological values of Mono Lake are imperiled. [Plaintiffs alleged that the declining lake level and correspondent increase in salinity would harm the Lake's brine shrimp population to the detriment of the migratory birds which relied upon the shrimp. Plaintiffs also alleged that as the lake receded it had exposed portions of the lake bed composed of very fine silt containing alkali and other minerals which, once dry, easily became airborne in winds resulting in toxic dust storms.]

Plaintiffs filed suit in superior court to enjoin the DWP diversions on the theory that the shores, bed and waters of Mono Lake are protected by a public trust. * * *

This case brings together for the first time two systems of legal thought: the appropriative water rights system which since the days of the gold rush has dominated California water law, and the public trust doctrine which, after evolving as a shield for the protection of tidelands, now extends its protective scope to navigable lakes. Ever since we first recognized that the public trust protects environmental and recreational values (*Marks v. Whitney*, 491 P.2d 374 (1971)), the two systems of legal thought have been on a collision course. They meet in a unique and dramatic setting which highlights the clash of values. Mono Lake is a scenic and ecological treasure of national significance, imperiled by continued diversions of water; yet, the need of Los Angeles for water is apparent, its reliance on rights granted by the board evident, the cost of curtailing diversions substantial.

Attempting to integrate the teachings and values of both the public trust and the appropriative water rights system, we have arrived at certain conclusions which we briefly summarize here. In our opinion, the core of the public trust doctrine is the state's authority as sovereign to exercise a continuous supervision and control over the navigable waters of the state and the lands underlying those waters. This authority applies to the waters tributary to Mono Lake and bars DWP or any other party from claiming a vested right to divert waters once it becomes clear that such diversions harm the interests protected by the public trust. The corollary rule which evolved in tideland and lakeshore cases barring conveyance of rights free of the trust except to serve trust purposes cannot, however, apply without modification to flowing waters. The prosperity and habitability of much of this state requires the diversion of great quantities of water from its streams for purposes unconnected to any navigation, commerce, fishing, recreation, or ecological use relating to the source stream. The state must have the power to grant nonvested usufructuary rights to appropriate water even if diversions harm public trust uses. Approval of such diversion without considering public trust values, however, may result in needless destruction of those values. Accordingly, we believe that before state courts and agencies approve water diversions they should consider the effect of such diversions upon interests protected by the public trust, and attempt, so far as feasible, to avoid or minimize any harm to those interests.

The water rights enjoyed by DWP were granted, the diversion was commenced, and has continued to the present without any consideration of the impact upon the public trust. An objective study and reconsideration of the water rights in the Mono Basin is long overdue. The water law of California—which we conceive to be an integration including both the public trust doctrine and the board-administered appropriative rights system—permits such a reconsideration; the values underlying that integration require it. * * *

1. *Background and history of the Mono Lake litigation.*

DWP supplies water to the City of Los Angeles. Early in this century, it became clear that the city's anticipated needs would exceed the water available from local sources, and so in 1913 the city constructed an aqueduct to carry water from the Owens River 233 miles over the Antelope–Mojave plateau into the coastal plain and thirsty city. * * *

The city's rapid expansion soon strained this new supply, too, and prompted a search for water from other regions. The Mono Basin was a predictable object of this extension, since it lay within 50 miles of the natural origin of Owens River, and thus could easily be integrated into the existing aqueduct system.

After purchasing the riparian rights incident to Lee Vining, Walker, Parker and Rush Creeks, as well as the riparian rights pertaining to Mono Lake, the city applied to the Water Board in 1940 for permits to appropriate the waters of the four tributaries. At hearings before the board, various interested individuals protested that the city's proposed appropriations would lower the surface level of Mono Lake and thereby impair its commercial, recreational and scenic uses.

The board's primary authority to reject that application lay in a 1921 amendment to the Water Commission Act of 1913, which authorized the board to reject an application "when in its judgment the proposed appropriation would not best conserve the public interest." (Stats. 1921, ch. 329, § 1, p. 443, now codified as Wat. Code, § 1255.) The 1921 enactment, however, also "declared to be the established policy of this state that the use of water for domestic purposes is the highest use of water" (id., now codified as Wat. Code, § 1254), and directed the Water Board to be guided by this declaration of policy. Since DWP sought water for domestic use, the board concluded that it had to grant the application notwithstanding the harm to public trust uses of Mono Lake.

The board's decision states that "[i]t is indeed unfortunate that the City's proposed development will result in decreasing the aesthetic advantages of Mono Basin but *there is apparently nothing that this office can do to prevent it.*

The use to which the City proposes to put the water under its Applications . . . is defined by the Water Commission Act as the highest to which water may be applied. . . . This office therefore has *no alternative but to dismiss all protests based upon the possible lowering of the water level in Mono Lake and the effect that the diversion of water from these streams may have upon the aesthetic and recreational value of the Basin.*" (Div. Wat. Resources Dec. 7053, 7055, 8042 & 8043 (Apr. 11, 1940), at p. 26, italics added.) * * *

Between 1940 and 1970, the city diverted an average of 57,067 acre-feet of water per year from the Mono Basin. The impact of these diversions on Mono Lake was clear and immediate: the lake's surface level receded at an average of 1.1 feet per year.

In June of 1970, the city completed a second aqueduct designed to increase the total flow into the aqueduct by 50 percent. Between 1970 and 1980, the city diverted an average of 99,580 acre-feet per year from the Mono Basin. By October of 1979, the lake had shrunk from its prediversion area of 85 square miles to an area of 60.3 square miles. Its surface level had dropped to 6,373 feet above sea level, 43 feet below the prediversion level. * * *

DWP expects that its future diversions of about 100,000 acre-feet per year will lower the lake's surface level another 43 feet and reduce its surface area by about 22 square miles over the next 80 to 100 years, at which point the lake will gradually approach environmental equilibrium (the point at which inflow from precipitation, groundwater and nondiverted tributaries equals outflow by evaporation and other means). * * *

To abate this destruction, plaintiffs filed suit for injunctive and declaratory relief in the Superior Court for Mono County on May 21, 1979.[11] * * *

2. *The Public Trust Doctrine in California.*

"By the law of nature these things are common to mankind—the air, running water, the sea and consequently the shores of the sea." (Institutes of Justinian 2.1.1.) From this origin in Roman law, the English common law evolved the concept of the public trust, under which the sovereign owns "all of its navigable waterways and the lands lying beneath them 'as trustee of a public trust for the benefit of the people.' " (*Colberg, Inc. v. State of California ex rel. Dept. Pub. Works* (1967) 67 Cal.2d 408, 416, 62 Cal.Rptr. 401, 432 P.2d 3.) The State of California acquired title as trustee to such lands and waterways upon its admission to the union (*City of Berkeley v. Superior Court* (1980) 26 Cal.3d 515, 521, 162 Cal.Rptr. 327, 606 P.2d 362 and cases there cited); from the earliest days its judicial decisions have recognized and enforced the trust obligation.

Three aspects of the public trust doctrine require consideration in this opinion: the purpose of the trust; the scope of the trust, particularly as it applies to the nonnavigable tributaries of a navigable lake; and the powers and duties of the state as trustee of the public trust. We discuss these questions in the order listed.

11. DWP contended that plaintiffs lack standing to sue to enjoin violations of the public trust. . . . *Marks v. Whitney, supra,* expressly held that any member of the general public has standing to raise a claim of harm to the public trust. (Pp. 261–262; *see also Environmental Defense Fund, Inc. v. East Bay Mun. Utility Dist.* (1980) 26 Cal.3d 183 [161 Cal.Rptr. 466, 605 P.2d 1], in which we permitted a public interest organization to sue to enjoin allegedly unreasonable uses of water.) We conclude that plaintiffs have standing to sue to protect the public trust.

(a) *The purpose of the public trust.*

The objective of the public trust has evolved in tandem with the changing public perception of the values and uses of waterways. As we observed in *Marks v. Whitney, supra,* 6 Cal.3d 251, 98 Cal.Rptr. 790, 491 P.2d 374, "[p]ublic trust easements [were] traditionally defined in terms of navigation, commerce and fisheries. They have been held to include the right to fish, hunt, bathe, swim, to use for boating and general recreation purposes the navigable waters of the state, and to use the bottom of the navigable waters for anchoring, standing, or other purposes." (P.259, 98 Cal.Rptr. 790, 491 P.2d 374.) We went on, however, to hold that the traditional triad of uses—navigation, commerce and fishing— did not limit the public interest in the trust res. In language of special importance to the present setting, we stated that "[t]he public uses to which tidelands are subject are sufficiently flexible to encompass changing public needs. In administering the trust the state is not burdened with an outmoded classification favoring one mode of utilization over another. There is a growing public recognition that one of the most important public uses of the tidelands— a use encompassed within the tidelands trust—is the preservation of those lands in their natural state, so that they may serve as ecological units for scientific study, as open space, and as environments which provide food and habitat for birds and marine life, and which favorably affect the scenery and climate of the area." (Pp. 259–260, 98 Cal.Rptr. 790, 491 P.2d 374.)

Mono Lake is a navigable waterway. It supports a small local industry which harvests brine shrimp for sale as fish food, which endeavor probably qualifies the lake as a "fishery" under the traditional public trust cases. The principal values plaintiffs seek to protect, however, are recreational and ecologi- cal—the scenic views of the lake and its shore, the purity of the air, and the use of the lake for nesting and feeding by birds. Under *Marks v. Whitney,* it is clear that protection of these values is among the purposes of the public trust.

(b) *The scope of the public trust.*

Early English decisions generally assumed the public trust was limited to tidal waters and the lands exposed and covered by the daily tides; many American decisions, including the leading California cases, also concern tide- lands. It is, however, well settled in the United States generally and in California that the public trust is not limited by the reach of the tides, but encompasses all navigable lakes and streams. *See Illinois Central Railroad Co. v. Illinois* 146 U.S. 387 (1892) (Lake Michigan).

Mono Lake is, as we have said, a navigable waterway. The beds, shores and waters of the lake are without question protected by the public trust. The streams diverted by DWP, however, are not themselves navigable. Accordingly, we must address in this case a question not discussed in any recent public trust case—whether the public trust limits conduct affecting nonnavigable tributar- ies to navigable waterways. * * *

We conclude that the public trust doctrine, as recognized and developed in California decisions, protects navigable waters from harm caused by diversion of nonnavigable tributaries.

(c) *Duties and powers of the state as trustee.*

In the following review of the authority and obligations of the state as administrator of the public trust, the dominant theme is the state's sovereign power and duty to exercise continued supervision over the trust. One conse- quence, of importance to this and many other cases, is that parties acquiring rights in trust property generally hold those rights subject to the trust, and can assert no vested right to use those rights in a manner harmful to the trust.

As we noted recently in *City of Berkeley v. Superior Court*, the decision of the United States Supreme Court in *Illinois Central Railroad Company v. Illinois, supra,* 146 U.S. 387, "remains the primary authority even today, almost nine decades after it was decided." 26 Cal.3d 521, 162 Cal.Rptr. 327, 606 P.2d 362. * * *

[I]n our recent decision in *City of Berkeley v. Superior Court, supra,* we considered whether deeds executed by the Board of Tidelands Commissioners pursuant to an 1870 act conferred title free of the trust. Applying the principles of earlier decisions, we held that the grantees' title was subject to the trust, both because the Legislature had not made clear its intention to authorize a conveyance free of the trust and because the 1870 act and the conveyances under it were not intended to further trust purposes.

Once again we rejected the claim that establishment of the public trust constituted a taking of property for which compensation was required: "We do not divest anyone of title to property; the consequence of our decision will be only that some landowners whose predecessors in interest acquired property under the 1870 act will, like the grantees in *California Fish,* hold it subject to the public trust." (P. 532, 162 Cal.Rptr. 327, 606 P.2d 362.)

In summary, the foregoing cases amply demonstrate the continuing power of the state as administrator of the public trust, a power which extends to the revocation of previously granted rights or to the enforcement of the trust against lands long thought free of the trust. Except for those rare instances in which a grantee may acquire a right to use former trust property free of trust restrictions, the grantee holds subject to the trust, and while he may assert a vested right to the servient estate (the right of use subject to the trust) and to any improvements he erects, he can claim no vested right to bar recognition of the trust or state action to carry out its purposes.

Since the public trust doctrine does not prevent the state from choosing between trust uses, the Attorney General of California, seeking to maximize state power under the trust, argues for a broad concept of trust uses. In his view, "trust uses" encompass all public uses, so that in practical effect the doctrine would impose no restrictions on the state's ability to allocate trust property. We know of no authority which supports this view of the public trust, except perhaps the dissenting opinion in *Illinois Central R. Co. v. Illinois, supra,* 146 U.S. 387. Most decisions and commentators assume that "trust uses" relate to uses and activities in the vicinity of the lake, stream, or tidal reach at issue. The tideland cases make this point clear; after *City of Berkeley v. Superior Court, supra,* 26 Cal.3d 515, 162 Cal.Rptr. 327, 606 P.2d 362, no one could contend that the state could grant tidelands free of the trust merely because the grant served some public purpose, such as increasing tax revenues, or because the grantee might put the property to a commercial use.

Thus, the public trust is more than an affirmation of state power to use public property for public purposes. It is an affirmation of the duty of the state to protect the people's common heritage of streams, lakes, marshlands and tidelands, surrendering that right of protection only in rare cases when the abandonment of that right is consistent with the purposes of the trust.

3. *The California Water Rights System.*

"It is laid down by our law writers, that the right of property in water is usufructuary, and consists not so much of the fluid itself as the advantage of its use." (*Eddy v. Simpson* (1853) 3 Cal. 249, 252.) Hence, the cases do not speak of the ownership of water, but only of the right to its use. Accordingly, Water Code section 102 provides that "[a]ll water within the State is the property of the people of the State, but the right to the use of water may be acquired by appropriation in the manner provided by law." * * *

4.   *The relationship between the Public Trust Doctrine and the California Water Rights System.*

As we have seen, the public trust doctrine and the appropriative water rights system administered by the Water Board developed independently of each other. Each developed comprehensive rules and principles which, if applied to the full extent of their scope, would occupy the field of allocation of stream waters to the exclusion of any competing system of legal thought. Plaintiffs, for example, argue that the public trust is antecedent to and thus limits all appropriative water rights, an argument which implies that most appropriative water rights in California were acquired and are presently being used unlawfully. Defendant DWP, on the other hand, argues that the public trust doctrine as to stream waters has been "subsumed" into the appropriative water rights system and, absorbed by that body of law, quietly disappeared; according to DWP, the recipient of a board license enjoys a vested right in perpetuity to take water without concern for the consequences to the trust.

We are unable to accept either position. In our opinion, both the public trust doctrine and the water rights system embody important precepts which make the law more responsive to the diverse needs and interests involved in the planning and allocation of water resources. To embrace one system of thought and reject the other would lead to an unbalanced structure, one which would either decry as a breach of trust appropriations essential to the economic development of this state, or deny any duty to protect or even consider the values promoted by the public trust. Therefore, seeking an accommodation which will make use of the pertinent principles of both the public trust doctrine and the appropriative water rights system, and drawing upon the history of the public trust and the water rights system, the body of judicial precedent, and the views of expert commentators, we reach the following conclusions:

a.   The state as sovereign retains continuing supervisory control over its navigable waters and the lands beneath those waters. This principle, fundamental to the concept of the public trust, applies to rights in flowing waters as well as to rights in tidelands and lakeshores; it prevents any party from acquiring a vested right to appropriate water in a manner harmful to the interests protected by the public trust.

b.   As a matter of current and historical necessity, the Legislature, acting directly or through an authorized agency such as the Water Board, has the power to grant usufructuary licenses that will permit an appropriator to take water from flowing streams and use that water in a distant part of the state, even though this taking does not promote, and may unavoidably harm, the trust uses at the source stream. The population and economy of this state depend upon the appropriation of vast quantities of water for uses unrelated to in-stream trust values. California's Constitution (see art. X, § 2), its statutes (see Wat. Code, §§ 100, 104), decisions, and commentators all emphasize the need to make efficient use of California's limited water resources: all recognize, at least implicitly, that efficient use requires diverting water from in-stream uses. Now that the economy and population centers of this state have developed in reliance upon appropriated water, it would be disingenuous to hold that such appropriations are and have always been improper to the extent that they harm public trust uses, and can be justified only upon theories of reliance or estoppel.

c.   The state has an affirmative duty to take the public trust into account in the planning and allocation of water resources, and to protect public trust uses whenever feasible. Just as the history of this state shows that appropriation may be necessary for efficient use of water despite unavoidable harm to public trust values, it demonstrates that an appropriative water rights system administered without consideration of the public trust may cause unnecessary and unjustified harm to trust interests. As a matter of practical necessity the state may have to approve appropriations despite foreseeable harm to public trust uses. In so doing, however, the state must bear in mind its duty as trustee to consider the effect of the taking on the public trust and to preserve, so far as consistent with the public interest, the uses protected by the trust.

Once the state has approved an appropriation, the public trust imposes a duty of continuing supervision over the taking and use of the appropriated water. In exercising its sovereign power to allocate water resources in the public interest, the state is not confined by past allocation decisions which may be incorrect in light of current knowledge or inconsistent with current needs.

The state accordingly has the power to reconsider allocation decisions even though those decisions were made after due consideration of their effect on the public trust.[28] The case for reconsidering a particular decision, however, is even stronger when that decision failed to weigh and consider public trust uses. In the case before us, the salient fact is that no responsible body has ever determined the impact of diverting the entire flow of the Mono Lake tributaries into the Los Angeles Aqueduct. This is not a case in which the Legislature, the Water Board, or any judicial body has determined that the needs of Los Angeles outweigh the needs of the Mono Basin, that the benefit gained is worth the price. Neither has any responsible body determined whether some lesser taking would better balance the diverse interests. Instead, DWP acquired rights to the entire flow in 1940 from a water board which believed it lacked both the power and the duty to protect the Mono Lake environment, and continues to exercise those rights in apparent disregard for the resulting damage to the scenery, ecology, and human uses of Mono Lake.

It is clear that some responsible body ought to reconsider the allocation of the waters of the Mono Basin. No vested rights bar such reconsideration. We recognize the substantial concerns voiced by Los Angeles—the city's need for water, its reliance upon the 1940 board decision, the cost both in terms of money and environmental impact of obtaining water elsewhere. Such concerns must enter into any allocation decision. We hold only that they do not preclude a reconsideration and reallocation which also takes into account the impact of water diversion on the Mono Lake environment. * * *

6. *Conclusion.*

This opinion is but one step in the eventual resolution of the Mono Lake controversy. We do not dictate any particular allocation of water. Our objective is to resolve a legal conundrum in which two competing systems of thought— the public trust doctrine and the appropriative water rights system—existed independently of each other, espousing principles which seemingly suggested

28. The state Attorney General asserts that the Water Board could also reconsider the DWP water rights under the doctrine of unreasonable use under article X, section 2 [of the California Constitution]. DWP maintains, however, that its use of the water for domestic consumption is prima facie reasonable. The dispute centers on the test of un- reasonable use—does it refer only to inordinate and wasteful use of water, as in *Peabody v. City of Vallejo, supra,* 2 Cal.2d 351, 40 P.2d 486, or to any use less than the optimum allocation of water? In view of our reliance on the public trust doctrine as a basis for reconsideration of DWP's usufructuary rights, we need not resolve that controversy.

opposite results. We hope by integrating these two doctrines to clear away the legal barriers which have so far prevented either the Water Board or the courts from taking a new and objective look at the water resources of the Mono Basin. The human and environmental uses of Mono Lake—uses protected by the public trust doctrine—deserve to be taken into account. Such uses should not be destroyed because the state mistakenly thought itself powerless to protect them.

Let a peremptory writ of mandate issue commanding the Superior Court of Alpine County to vacate its judgment in this action and to enter a new judgment consistent with the views stated in this opinion.

QUESTIONS AND DISCUSSION

1. How does the version of the public trust doctrine articulated by the California Supreme Court differ from the public trust doctrine of *Illinois Central*? As the court recites, prior to its decision, the public trust doctrine had been expanded well beyond its original application to land under navigable water. *See generally* Scott Reed, *The Public Trust Doctrine: Is It Amphibious?* 1 ENVTL. L. & LIT. 107, 116–21 (1986) (collecting cases extending the public trust doctrine beyond its traditional scope). In the *Mono Lake* case, however, the court went further and expanded the doctrine to include water rights obtained by prior appropriation. What are the justifications for this gradual expansion of the public trust doctrine? Why might some be skeptical about the expansion of the doctrine? With the rise of the modern regulatory state and environmental regulation is the public trust doctrine really necessary? In this case, for example, were there any other legal doctrines available to reduce Los Angeles' appropriations? Were there any other solutions to the ecological disaster at Mono Lake?

2. In *National Audubon*, the original plaintiff was the National Audubon Society. Should it matter whether the proponent of the public trust doctrine is the state (as it was in *Illinois Central*) or a private plaintiff? Unless the state is joined and then supports plaintiff's position, a court could end up revoking or altering a grant even though the state actually supports the grantee's current use of the trust resource, or at worst acquiesces in it. Is that an appropriate exercise of judicial power? Is that what happened in this case? Did the court actually deprive Los Angeles of its water rights? If so, in what sense? Who makes the ultimate decision about the content of Los Angeles' water right?

3. Although the California Supreme Court handed down the *National Audubon* decision in 1983, it was not until 1989 that an injunction was entered limiting Los Angeles' diversions. And it was 1994 before the state water board amended Los Angeles' water rights to establish a permanent plan for raising the level of Mono Lake to 20 feet higher than its historic low, although still 25 feet lower than the Lake was at the time Los Angeles began its diversions. The board estimated that the annual costs of replacement water and lost hydropower would be $36.3 million over the next 20 years and $23.5 million per year after the lake reached the designated level. To offset the impact, the State appropriated $36 million to contribute to a $55 million waste-water reinfiltration project of the Los Angeles Department of Water and Power which was designed to provide 35,000 acre-feet per year of treated wastewater to recharge an underground aquifer in the Los Angeles area. The Bureau of Reclamation agreed to contribute another $12.8 million. *See* CAL. WATER CODE § 12929.14 (1994) (appropriating money); Environmental Water Act of 1989, CAL. WATER CODE § 12929.20 (1989) (initially authorizing appropriation); Reclamation Projects Authorization and Adjustment Act of 1992, 102 Pub. L. 575 § 1613, 106 Stat. 4600, 4667–68 (1992) (authorizing expenditures on Los Angeles Area Water Reclamation and Reuse Project). *See generally* Cynthia L. Koehler, *Water Rights and the Public Trust Doctrine: Resolution of the Mono Lake Controversy*, 22 ECOLOGY L.Q. 541, 571–76 (1995) (discussing the aftermath of the Mono Lake litigation); Michael C. Blumm & Thea Schwartz, *Mono Lake and the Evolving Public Trust in Western Water*, 37 ARIZ. L. REV. 701, 719–20 (1995).

Once the Water Resources Control Board had reestablished Los Angeles' water right with reference to specific lake-level targets, does that mean that Los Angeles then has a vested right in its new allocation?

4. Although the public trust doctrine of *National Audubon* has great potential to remake water law in the West, the decision has had relatively little impact. A couple other states have suggested that the public trust doctrine requires some planning and consideration of the public interest before issuing a new permit to appropriate water, *see Shokal v. Dunn*, 707 P.2d 441 (Idaho 1985); *United Plainsmen Ass'n v. North Dakota State Water Conservation Comm'n*, 247 N.W.2d 457 (N.D. 1976), but no state has adopted the approach of *Mono Lake*. Even California has been slow to use the doctrine. As Professor Weber notes, "[w]e know the doctrine exists and might compel potentially massive water reallocations.... The doctrine's potential judicial articulation remains almost fully inchoate. In this virtually unbridled potential lies much of the doctrine's mystique and some of its power." Gregory S. Weber, *Articulating the Public Trust: Text, Near–Text and Context*, 27 ARIZ. ST. L.J. 1155, 1235 (1995). Why this hesitancy to extend the public trust doctrine?

5. In 1997, Idaho, responding to suggestions from its courts that water rights were held subject to the public trust, passed a statute declaring that the public trust doctrine "is solely a limitation on the power of the state to alienate or encumber the title to the beds of navigable waters" and prohibiting application of the doctrine to the "appropriation or use of water, or the granting, transfer, administration or adjudication of water or water rights." IDAHO CODE § 58–1203(2)(a)–(c). *See generally* Michael C. Blumm et al., *Renouncing the Public Trust Doctrine: An Assessment of the Validity of Idaho House Bill 794*, 24 ECOLOGY L.Q. 461 (1997). Suppose California were to adopt the same statute. Would it bind the California Supreme Court?

6. Section III.C.3 of this chapter discussed how most states now analyze the public interest of any water use before issuing a permit. Does that public interest analysis eliminate the need for the public trust doctrine? Is there a difference between the public interest and the public trust?

7. In an excised portion of the opinion, Los Angeles argued that any obligation to reduce diversions should be shared by all users of Mono Lake water and thus cross-complained against 117 other individuals and entities claiming water rights in the Mono Basin. 658 P.2d at 716. As discussed in note 3 above, the Water Resources Control Board ultimately imposed the trust obligation solely on Los Angeles. *See In re* Amendment of the City of Los Angeles' Water Right Licenses for Diversion of Water from Streams Tributary to Mono Lake (Water Right Licenses 10191 and 10192, Applications 8042 and 8043) City of Los Angeles, Licensee, Decision 1631, 1994 WL 758358, at *1–2 (Cal. St. Water Res. Control Bd., Sept. 28, 1994). In another decision, the Board made clear its assumption that public trust responsibility could be allocated to the party against whom the complaint was drawn. *See In re* Water Right Permits in the Sacramento–San Joaquin Delta Watershed (Term 80 Permits), 1984 WL 19050, *14 (Cal. St. Water Res. Control Bd., Feb. 1, 1984) ("Nothing in the Audubon decision requires the Board to initiate proceedings to exercise jurisdiction over every possible water right on public trust grounds."). What are the alternatives to this sort of joint and several liability approach to public trust responsibilities? Would it have made more sense to allocate responsibility by priority? Is there any reason why priority should not be the principle of allocation in all cases where there is insufficient water to satisfy all diverters, whether that insufficiency is a result of natural drought, regulation, or imposition of the public trust doctrine? What would have been the advantages and disadvantages of allocating by priority?

8. Partly in response to stories like that of Los Angeles and the Owens Valley and Mono Lake, California and a number of other states have enacted so-called area-of-origin statutes that impose some limits on out-of-basin transfers. With respect to the water rights held by the massive Central Valley and State Water Projects, California provided that "any permit hereafter issued pursuant to such an application, and any license issued pursuant to such a permit, shall provide, that the application, permit, or license shall not authorize the use of any water outside of the county of origin which is necessary for the development of the county." CAL. WATER CODE § 10505.5. *See, e.g.*, KAN. STAT. ANN. § 82a–1502 ("No water transfer shall be approved which would reduce the amount of water required to meet the present or any reasonably foreseeable future beneficial use of water by present or future users in the area from which the water is to be taken for transfer unless" the state concludes that benefits of export outweigh the benefits of not exporting the water); ALASKA STAT. § 46.15.035 (no out-of-basin transfer unless water is surplus).

Are these limitations wise policy? Should there be some protection for rural and late-growing communities from expanding urban areas? Do communities have some special interest in the water within their boundaries? How is the community of origin to be defined? Are there other instances in which local communities are treated as having a special connection to a resource? Should states, for example, be allowed to issue fewer hunting permits to out-of-state residents? On what grounds? Should nations or indigenous peoples have any particular rights in local biodiversity? Under the Biodiversity Convention, parties are enjoined to share benefits "arising from the commercial or other utilization of genetic resources" with the nation in which the biodiversity originates. Convention on Biological Diversity, U.N. Doc. DPI/130/7, June 2, 1992, *reprinted in* 31 I.L.M. 818 (1992), at Art. 15. Notice that all of these questions have at their foundation the basic issues discussed in Chapter 1 of who owns natural resources and who has the right to regulate their use.

9. After reading *National Audubon*, who would you say "owns" the water in California? Individual permit holders? The people? The courts? Is the ownership divided among them? Or is "ownership" even a useful way to describe the various interests?

10. By way of review, compare and contrast the following water law doctrines: reasonable use, beneficial use, no harm rule, public interest analysis, and the public trust doctrine. What is the source of each doctrine and to what situations do the doctrines apply?

————

D.   THE LAW OF GROUNDWATER

At common law, both in England, and for a long time in the United States, the law of groundwater was a rule of capture. A landowner had an absolute right to pump and consume as much water as he wanted. Water was part of the realty, which, in Blackstone's terms, extended from the center of the earth to the heavens. That groundwater pumping might cause a neighbor's well to go dry or a nearby river to have diminished flow was ignored. The basis for this rule of capture was the feeling that "the ways of underground water were too mysterious and unpredictable to allow the establishment of adequate and fair rules for regulation of competing rights to such water." *State v. Michels Pipeline Construction, Inc.*, 63 Wis.2d 278, 217 N.W.2d 339 (1974). As the use of groundwater has accelerated in the last fifty years, and as scarcity and competition for the resource have become more common, the need both to understand groundwater and to regulate its extraction has grown. The indulgence that groundwater was simply too complex to regulate has given way to a variety of approaches to groundwater management which are outlined in this section of the chapter. Before considering these varied approaches to groundwater law, we first consider the groundwater resource itself.

1.   THE GROUNDWATER RESOURCE

Hearing the word "groundwater," our first images may be more literary than factual. We may think of the underground rivers and subterranean lakes that dominate Greek and Roman mythology and appear in literature like *The Hobbit*. Although such lakes and rivers do exist, they don't describe the vast majority of groundwater, which is instead water that exists in the interstices of rock and soil. Picture a vase containing a layer of moist clay, a layer of sand, and a layer of pea-sized gravel. Pour some water into the vase. The water will seep into the sand and gravel but will probably not penetrate (at least very quickly) the moist clay. The water in the interstices of the sand and gravel is groundwater. The water in the clay is also groundwater, although it's not very usable. James Crosby explains groundwater hydrology in more detail.

James W. Crosby III, A Layman's Guide to Groundwater Hydrology 38–42, 45, 56–59, *in* Charles E. Corker, National Water Commission, Legal Study No. 6 (1971)

To understand the groundwater environment, one needs only to consider the void spaces, or *porosity*, of an accumulation of sand and gravel; or to view the fractures and crevices in the granites and limestones that form the walls of a road cut.... Picture then, the environment that would exist if these unconsolidated or consolidated rock masses were partially submerged beneath water.... The air occupying the different types of openings would be displaced by water which, in the natural setting, would be called groundwater. The upper surface of the water-saturated zone, or the air-water interface, would be called the water table.... Groundwater sometimes is confined under pressure between or under impermeable or semi-permeable rock in much the same manner that water is pressurized in a pipeline network. Water in wells penetrating through impermeable material into the underlying permeable materials may rise above the top of the aquifer or water-bearing formation. Such groundwater is said to be under artesian pressure. The pressure is from gravity, just as is the water pressure on a dam impounding water in a surface reservoir.

Depending upon the type of rock material saturated, the voids or empty spaces can be expected to range from about one percent to more than 30 percent. At saturation, in other words, such rocks can contain between one and 30 or more percent of their total volume as water. Much of this water might be contained in voids so small that, even given the opportunity, it could never drain out; it would be retained as though the rock were a blotter. Such water would not flow into wells, and hence it could not be extracted from the ground by any normal means.

The capacity of a rock to transmit water through its interconnected pore spaces is called its *permeability*. The capacity of porous material to store water need have no bearing on its capacity to transmit water. Thus, a clay usually has high porosity but low permeability. On the other hand, an unconsolidated gravel may have both high porosity and high permeability....

The relatively small size of rock openings and the tortuous nature of the tunnel-like interconnected pore spaces present tremendous frictional resistance to the movement of groundwater. This factor is dominant in establishing the permeability of a porous material. Frictional limitations to flow, coupled with the typically low gradients (or slopes), contribute to the very low flow velocities prevalent in the groundwater environment. Normal flow velocities range from five feet per day to five feet per year. However, velocities as high as 100 feet per day have been reported.

The saturated, permeable earth materials from which significant quantities of water can be produced are called *aquifers*. * * *

[M]oving water which is groundwater in one location, surface water in another location, and again groundwater is a very common phenomenon which complicates water "ownership." Nearly all groundwater originates from surface sources and is subject to just such a succession of metamorphoses. Depending upon the fluid circulation pattern the time sequence can be measured in minutes, days, years, or geologic periods. * * *

For all practical purposes, the origin of groundwater can be regarded as meteoric, meaning that it comes from the atmosphere.... Much of the precipitation falling on the earth's surface infiltrates the soil zone where it is utilized by plants.... Infiltrating precipitation in excess of these requirements tends to move downward through the zone of aeration under the influence of gravity until it reaches the water table. Some of the excess precipitation moves directly or indirectly by flow over the land surface to streams, from which it may, in part, move into a groundwater body. * * *

Surface streams are sometimes classified as gaining streams or losing streams.... That is, they acquire water from or lose water to the groundwater body, depending on whether the stream is incised below or elevated above the water table. * * *

Water may be imported to a drainage basin or existing basin waters may be allocated for the express purpose of storage underground.... Groundwater recharge may be induced or facilitated by spreading over areas of high infiltration capacity or by injection into deep wells under pressure.

The following excerpt goes beyond this basic description of the resource and discusses the connection between groundwater, people, and the environment.

Robert Glennon, *The Perils of Groundwater Pumping,* 19 ISSUES IN SCIENCE AND TECHNOLOGY 73, 73–77 (2002)

The next time you reach for a bottle of spring water, consider that it may have come from a well that is drying up a blue-ribbon trout stream. The next time you dine at McDonald's, note that the fries are all the same length. That's because the farmers who grow the potatoes irrigate their fields, perhaps with groundwater from wells adjacent to nearby rivers. The next time you purchase gold jewelry, consider that it may have come from a mine that has pumped so much groundwater to be able to work the gold-bearing rock that 60 to 100 years will pass before the water table recovers. The next time you water your suburban lawn, pause to reflect on what that is doing to the nearby wetland. And the next time you visit Las Vegas and flip on the light in your hotel room, consider that the electricity may have come from a coal-fired power plant supplied by a slurry pipeline that uses groundwater critical to springs sacred to the Hopi people.

These and countless other seemingly innocuous activities reflect our individual and societal dependence on groundwater. From Tucson to Tampa Bay, from California's Central Valley to Down East Maine, rivers and lakes have disappeared, and fresh water is becoming scarce. Groundwater pumping—for domestic consumption, irrigation, or mining—causes bodies of water and wetlands to dry up; the ground beneath us to collapse; and fish, wildlife, and trees to die. The excessive pumping of our aquifers has created an environmental catastrophe known to relatively few scientists and water management experts and to those who are unfortunate enough to have suffered the direct consequences. This phenomenon is occurring not just in the arid West with its tradition of battling over water rights, but even in places we think of as relatively wet. * * *

Groundwater pumping in the United States has increased dramatically in the past few decades. For domestic purposes alone, groundwater use jumped from 2.9 trillion gallons in 1965 to about 6.8 trillion gallons in 1995, or 24,000 gallons for every man, woman, and child. But domestic consumption is only a small fraction of the country's total groundwater use, which totaled almost 28 trillion gallons in 1995. Farmers used two-thirds of that to irrigate crops; the mining industry, especially for copper, coal, and gold production, pumped about 770 billion gallons. Groundwater constitutes more than 25 percent of the nation's water supply. In 1995, California alone pumped 14,500 billion gallons of groundwater per day. Groundwater withdrawals actually exceeded surface water diversions in Florida, Kansas, Nebraska, and Mississippi. In the United States, more than half of the population relies on groundwater for their drinking water supply. Groundwater pumping has become a global problem because 1.5 billion people (one-quarter of the world's population) depend on groundwater for drinking water.

Groundwater is an extraordinarily attractive source of water for farms, mines, cities, and homeowners because it is available throughout the year and it exists almost everywhere in the country. During the various ice ages, much of the country was covered with huge freshwater lakes. Water from these lakes percolated into the ground and collected in aquifers. Unlike rivers and streams, which are few and far between, especially in the West, aquifers exist below almost the entire country. * * *

Overdrafting or "mining" groundwater creates serious problems. Because water is heavy, about two pounds per quart, more energy is needed to lift water from lower levels. The costs of this energy may be substantial: In Arizona, the electric energy to run a commercial irrigation well may cost $2,000 per month. The drilling of new and deeper wells may be required, which is often a considerable expense. Pumping from lower levels may produce poorer quality water because naturally occurring elements, such as arsenic, fluoride, and radon, are more prevalent at deeper levels in the earth, and the earth's higher internal temperature at these levels dissolves more of these elements into solution. As the water deteriorates in quality, it may violate U.S. Environmental Protection Agency regulations, requiring either that the water be subject to expensive treatment processes or that the well be turned off, thus eliminating that source of water. Along coastal areas, overdrafting may cause the intrusion of saltwater into the aquifer, rendering the water no longer potable. This problem is quite serious in California, Florida, Texas, and South Carolina. Another consequence of overdrafting is the prospect of land subsidence, in which the land's surface actually cracks or drops, in some cases dramatically. In California's San Joaquin Valley, the land surface dropped between 25 and 30 feet between 1925 and 1977. Land subsidence has damaged homes and commercial structures and reduced property values. Pumping north of Tampa Bay in Pasco County has cracked the foundations, walls, and ceilings of local resident's homes, resulting in lawsuits, insurance claims, and considerable ill will.

A final consequence of groundwater pumping is its impact on surface water, including lakes, ponds, rivers, creeks, streams, springs, wetlands, and estuaries. These consequences range from minimal to catastrophic. An example of the latter is the Santa Cruz River in Tucson. Once a verdant riparian system with a lush canopy provided by cottonwood and willow trees, groundwater pumping has lowered the water table, drained the river of its flow, killed the cottonwood and willow trees, and driven away the local wildlife. The river has become an oxymoron—a dry river—a pathetic desiccated sandbox. * * *

Fueled by the energy of the sun and the force of gravity, water continually moves through a succession of different phases, called the hydrologic cycle ... When the water falls to earth, some of it immediately evaporates into the sky, another portion runs off the land to creeks, streams, and rivers, and some infiltrates the ground, in a process known as recharge. A portion of the groundwater near rivers and streams eventually emerges from the ground, in a process called discharge, to augment the surface flows of rivers or streams. Groundwater pumping essentially interrupts this cycle by removing water, directly or indirectly, that would otherwise discharge from aquifers to rivers, streams, and other surface water bodies.

Groundwater and surface water are not separate categories of water any more than liquid water and ice are truly separate. The designations groundwater and surface water merely describe the physical location of the water in the hydrologic cycle. Indeed, groundwater and surface water form a continuum. In some regions of the country, virtually all groundwater was once stream flow that seeped into the ground. The converse is also true but not obvious. Consider the following puzzle: Where does water in a river come from if it has not rained in a while? The water comes from groundwater that has seeped from the aquifer into the river, in what's known as base flow.

Whether water will flow from the river to the aquifer or vice versa depends on the level of the water table in the aquifer and on the elevation of the river. If the water table is above the elevation of the river, water will flow laterally toward the river and augment the flow in the river. In most regions of the country, this is the process that occurs. But as groundwater pumping lowers the water table, the direction of the flow of water changes. Once the water table is below the elevation of the river, water flows from the river toward the aquifer. * * *

In considering other examples of environmental problems caused by groundwater pumping, the first thing to note is that the impact of groundwater pumping on the environment is not confined to the arid West. Consider Florida. * * *

Florida's population jumped from 2.7 million people in 1950 to 16 million in 2000, making Florida the fourth most populous state. A region that is experiencing particularly explosive growth is Tampa Bay. In search of additional supplies during the 1970s, Tampa Bay Water (the local water utility) purchased large tracts of rural areas in adjoining counties and drilled a huge number of wells. By 1996, groundwater withdrawal had risen to approximately 255 million gallons per day, a 400 percent increase over 1960 levels. When lakes and ponds began to dry up—one study found that fewer than 10 of 153 lakes in the region were healthy—Tampa Bay Water knew it had a public relations disaster on its hands. Homeowners who had bought lakefront property only to watch it dry up were not amused. In response, Tampa Bay Water began to dump hundreds of thousands of gallons of water per day into the dry lakebeds. Where did Tampa Bay Water get this additional water? From groundwater pumping. Yet this additional groundwater would inevitably drain back into the ground in search of the water table. It was like trying to keep water in a colander.

Tampa Bay is not the only area where officials have tried to mask the consequences of groundwater pumping. In San Antonio, Texas, Paseo del Rio, or River Walk, has become the city's most popular tourist attraction. A 2.5–mile section of the San Antonio River that flows through the heart of downtown, River Walk anchors a $3.5 billion-per-year tourist industry. Most tourists would be surprised to learn that the river they enjoy is the creation of dams, floodgates, and groundwater pumped from the Edwards Aquifer and dumped into the San Antonio River above River Walk. The San Antonio River was once navigable through the River Walk stretch, but it dried up because of groundwater pumping. In short, the city of San Antonio pumps millions of gallons a day of groundwater into the river in order to create an economically useful fiction. As San Antonio has continued to expand, the San Antonio Water System began to search for new sources of water and to look for ways to reuse existing supplies. In 2000, the system began to dump treated municipal effluent into

River Walk as a substitute for groundwater. The water creating the illusion of a real river is still groundwater, but it has been used before.

Americans use groundwater to grow all kinds of things, even where there is no need to do so. Until rather recently, many U.S. farms were "dryland" farmed, meaning that the farmers had no irrigation system. However, Americans' love affair with processed foods caused some potato farmers to shift from dryland to irrigation farming. The problem with dryland potatoes is that their size, shape, and texture depend heavily on seasonal weather patterns. During the growing season, potatoes need constant moisture or they will have knobs and odd shapes. A misshapen or knobby potato is perfectly edible, but it is not an acceptable potato for the fast-food industry. In 1998, McDonald's began to offer consumers "super-sized" meals with larger portions of french fries served in rectangular boxes with flat bottoms. Only potatoes grown through irrigation produced a uniform length fry that would jut out of the super-size box just the right amount so that the consumer could grasp the potato between index finger and thumb and dip it in ketchup. The desire for the perfect fry is felt by the trout in north central Minnesota, where potato farms rely on groundwater that is very closely connected hydrologically to blue-ribbon trout streams. Increased pumping to support additional potato production threatens the survival of trout.

----

2.   LEGAL REGIMES FOR ALLOCATING GROUNDWATER

Like surface water, the task of allocating groundwater fell initially to the courts as part of their effort to articulate the common law of property. Unsurprisingly, with 50 states in different geographic circumstances with different groundwater resources, the courts developed a variety of approaches to groundwater allocation. Those approaches are generally divided into the five categories discussed below. Before delving into those categories, it is again important to recognize that the law of groundwater in any particular jurisdiction does not often neatly fall wholly within one of these categories. The truth is that the law in a particular state is more likely to resemble one category but partake of elements of the others. This is particularly true now that so many states have passed legislation and promulgated regulations that overlie and supplant the common law. Thus, the discussion below of the different common law approaches to groundwater should not be understood as a careful guide to the details of current groundwater law in any particular jurisdiction, which is a topic beyond this survey course, but as an introduction to the basic management options and allocation issues that drive groundwater law.

Rule of Capture. As mentioned in the introduction of this section, at common law in England, and throughout much of the United States for a good portion of the nineteenth and early twentieth centuries, the law of groundwater was a rule of capture. As the Wisconsin Supreme Court explained, it was the consensus of judicial opinion that "[i]f the waters simply percolate through the ground, without a definite channel," which is a description of most groundwater, those waters "belong to the realty in which they are found, and the owner of the soil may divert, consume or cut them off with impunity." *Huber v. Merkel*, 117 Wis. 355, 94 N.W. 354 (1903). Under this basic rule of capture, landowners could take as much water as they wanted, as fast as they wanted, for whatever purpose they wanted, and use the water wherever they wanted. The only limitation was that water could not be withdrawn maliciously, for the sole purpose of harming a neighboring landowner. Under the rule of capture, water wasn't much different from berries or minerals. The rule of capture, or absolute dominion, is no longer the law in most jurisdictions, but in 1999, the doctrine was reaffirmed in both Maine and Texas. *See Maddocks v. Giles*, 728 A.2d 150, 153 (1999); *Sipriano v. Great Spring Waters of America*, 1 S.W.3d 75 (Tex. 1999). In Texas, despite the reaffirmation, absolute dominion is not quite so absolute. Texas has also ruled that landowners can be held liable for pumping that negligently causes subsidence to another's land, *see Friendswood Dev. Co. v. Smith–Southwest Indus. Inc.*, 576 S.W.2d 21 (Tex. 1978), and that the state may appropriately regulate withdrawals from the Edwards Aquifer. *See Barshop v. Medina County Underground Water Conservation Dist.*, 925 S.W.2d 618 (Tex. 1996).

Reasonable Use (American Rule). One of the first modifications to the rule of capture was the inclusion of two basic limits on groundwater use—that the water be put to reasonable use and that the water be used only on the land overlying the aquifer from which the water was withdrawn, unless its use elsewhere caused no injury to overlying landowners. *See Adams v. Lang*, 553 So.2d 89 (Ala. 1989); *Rothrauff v. Sinking Spring Water Co.*, 339 Pa. 129, 134, 14 A.2d 87, 90 (1940). The first requirement was not a significant departure from the rule of capture because it did not entail evaluating the relative reasonableness of one use against another. However, the second requirement did impose a significant new limit on groundwater use. So many jurisdictions adopted this reasonable use (modified capture) rule that it became known as the ''American Rule'' of reasonable use. Its dominance has begun to decline in favor of the other rules to be discussed below, but it remains the basic common law in a number of jurisdictions.

Correlative Rights. Although the American Rule was seen as an advance over the traditional rule of capture, in the view of many it still partook too much of that traditional rule because it allowed unlimited reasonable use of groundwater without concern for any other overlying landowners. As many saw it, the reasonableness of groundwater pumping ought to be determined just like the reasonableness of diverting surface water in a system of riparian rights. Each overlying landowner (just like each riparian) ought to have correlative rights in the water; the reasonableness of their respective uses ought to be determined correlatively, with reference to one another. The result of this ferment was the adoption of the so-called rule of correlative rights. Under the doctrine of correlative rights, all overlying landowners have coequal or correlative rights to pump the groundwater and use it on their overlying land. The rule of correlative rights retained the American Rule's principle that water could only be used on overlying land unless there was a surplus. But in contrast to the common law reasonable use rule, overlying owners are not free to pump as much as they want for any beneficial use until the water is gone. Instead, they must share the water equitably. Because the correlative rights rule limits use in times of shortage to overlying land, the equitable share of competing users has often been determined not by the relative reasonableness of their use but by the proportion of overlying land they own, a more concrete and predictable basis for sharing. Although correlative rights can be distinguished from the American Rule, some courts purportedly applying the American Rule have required some form of sharing between overlying landowners, suggesting that they are really applying a rule of correlative rights. The foremost practitioner of correlative rights is California, although it has modified the doctrine to allow off-site users to acquire rights through a relatively short five-year period of adverse use. *See generally* Earl F. Murphy, *The Status of the Correlative Rights Doctrine in Groundwater Today, in* 3 WATERS AND WATER RIGHTS § 22.01, at 195–289 (Robert Beck ed., 2d ed. 1991).

Reasonable Use (Restatement). Although the correlative rights rule responded to the concern that the American Rule did not require sharing between beneficial users, it has been criticized for retaining the American Rule's limitation to overlying uses in the absence of a surplus. From critics' perspective, this limitation hindered efficient off-site uses of the water, particularly by municipalities that did not overlie an aquifer and needed to import groundwater. In response to these criticisms, § 858 of the *Restatement (Second) of Torts* proposed that landowners could pump water for any beneficial purpose, whether on overlying land or not, as long as their use did not cause unreasonable harm to other users. Moreover, because the reasonableness of the competing water uses would be determined by comparing overlying *and* off-site uses, the proportion of overlying acreage could not be the focus of equitable sharing. Instead, § 858 proposed that reasonableness would be determined by the reasonable use principles governing allocation of water between riparians. *See Restatement (Second) of Torts* §§ 850–57. The *Restatement*'s approach to reasonable use, which compares the relative reasonableness of all uses, has been making headway in groundwater law. As one commentator noted: "Further modifications of the American rule can be expected, just as modifications have overtaken the absolute dominion rule in the jurisdictions that adhere to it. Whether § 858 of the *Restatement (Second) of Torts* truly 'restated' the law in 1979 or, instead, 'redefined' it, the general broadening intent of that section has become more acceptable to courts and legislatures." Earl F. Murphy, *Reasonable Use Rule, in* 3 WATERS AND WATER RIGHTS § 23.03, at 365 (Robert Beck ed., 2d ed. 1991).

Prior Appropriation. As with surface water, most of the arid states in the West have adopted some form of prior appropriation for groundwater. Rather than viewing groundwater as part of the land from which it is pumped, those states have declared that groundwater, like surface water, belongs to all the people and is the property of the state, to be distributed to promote public ends. Except for small domestic wells, the water codes in these states require a permit to appropriate groundwater.

Although allocating groundwater by priority can result in shutting down junior wells, the issue is not always the absolute amount of water in the aquifer. Often it is about allocating pumping costs. In basic terms, the further water must be lifted from the ground, the more energy it requires and the costlier it becomes. Thus, the first appropriator of an aquifer typically sinks a relatively shallow and inexpensive well. Later, however, junior appropriators come along and sink deeper wells, the water table declines and reduces or eliminates the flow of water to the senior's well. There is still water in the aquifer, so the senior is unlikely to be able to enjoin the junior pumpers. But should the senior be required to pay for a deeper well, or is her means of diversion also a part of her original appropriative right? In most jurisdictions, for both surface and groundwater, a user is entitled to prevent interference with not only her proscribed amount of water but also with reasonable means of diversion (or reasonable pumping lift) to get at the water. *See, e.g., Current Creek Irrigation Co. v. Andrews*, 344 P.2d 528, 531 (Utah 1959) (articulating this "junior pays" rule); *but see Baker v. Ore–Ida Foods, Inc.*, 513 P.2d 627 (Idaho 1973) (holding that what constitutes "reasonable pumping levels can be modified to conform to changing circumstances"); *see generally* GEORGE A. GOULD & DOUGLAS L. GRANT, CASES AND MATERIALS ON WATER LAW 382–86 (6th ed. 2000).

Another perplexity prior appropriation jurisdictions face is that priority only matters where there is a limited supply and with groundwater the yearly "supply" is not as easily defined as with surface water. Suppose an aquifer containing 1000 acre feet (AF) of water that has an annual recharge of 1000 AF. This is basically like a surface stream. If there are ten appropriators each with a right to 100 AF, the state permitting agency is almost sure to deny a new permit to another appropriator seeking another 100 AF. There simply isn't any water available. But what if the aquifer contains 50,000 AF of water with an annual recharge of 1000 AF? Should the state agency grant a permit to the eleventh appropriator? If it does, the aquifer will slowly be *mined*. Yet, if the eleventh appropriator takes only 100 AF per year, the aquifer would still take 500 years to fully dewater. States have adopted different approaches to this mining dilemma. Some have limited withdrawals to the amount of average annual recharge, what some refer to as the aquifer's *safe yield*. Other states (or local groundwater districts to which the state has delegated management authority) allow withdrawals to exceed the safe yield. The key question in such cases is the period of time over which the water in the aquifer should be amortized. Talk of safe yield and amortization may sound much more scientific than is the case. Determining safe yield is not a simple process. It is difficult to map the precise contours of an aquifer. Local aquifer conditions—soil type, porosity, permeability, etc.—vary greatly. Computer groundwater modeling is improving but still lacks precision. Thus, whether the goal is to pump at safe yield or for a set period of years, the decision whether to give a prospective pumper a permit is ultimately a mix of the best available science, preference for precaution, and the jurisdiction's policy goals.

A third key issue that comes up most frequently in the arid, prior appropriation states but also in others is how to integrate rights to surface and ground water that are hydrologically connected. As mentioned above, for a long time, this connection was poorly understood and thus largely ignored. Most state permitting schemes now make some effort to integrate the two. In the West, the key issue has been how to integrate priorities to ground and surface water. Typically, the specific question is how much a groundwater withdrawal should be curtailed in favor of a surface right given that surface rights were usually the first ones developed. Professor Grant explains the difficulty:

When water is diverted from a surface stream, the flow is directly reduced, and the reduction is soon felt by downstream users unless the distances involved are great. When water is withdrawn from an aquifer, however, the impact elsewhere in the basin or on a hydrologically connected stream is typically much slower. If a well withdraws groundwater that is tributary to a surface stream, the stream will be depleted gradually, and the full impact might not be felt for weeks, months, years, or even decades. Conversely, if the well is closed after a period of operation, the stream depletion does not terminate immediately but may continue, gradually diminishing for weeks, months, years, or decades. Delayed impact complicates the administration of priorities. * * *

The priority principle is supplemented by rules that (1) a junior appropriator may divert excess water in the source of supply beyond that appropriated by holders of senior rights, and (2) a junior appropriator may also divert water to which senior rights would otherwise attach when the senior appropriators do not need the water. These rules originated long ago to regulate the rights of successive appropriators from surface streams, and in that setting they usually enabled greater productive use of water without prejudice to senior rights. If a junior appropriator took excess water or took water when a senior did not need it, and later the streamflow decreased or the senior needed water, the junior could be shut down. Typically, the supply to the senior would increase promptly.

With extension of the appropriation doctrine to groundwater, these rules must now operate in situations where delayed impact is common. * * *

When a junior well withdraws groundwater connected with a surface stream, the resulting depletion of the stream might be less than the consumptive use from the well. One cause of attenuated impact is an incomplete tributary connection between the groundwater and the streamflow. An aquifer might discharge water not only into a stream but through springs or into a connecting aquifer. It might also lose water by evapotranspiration if the water table is near enough to the surface. Consequently, part of the groundwater withdrawn by a well and consumed on the surface might never have reached the stream even if left in the aquifer. * * *

Douglas Grant, *The Complexities of Managing Hydrologically Connected Surface Water and Groundwater Under the Appropriation Doctrine*, 22 LAND & WATER L. REV. 63, 74, 80–81 (1987). The following case explores some of the issues raised by Professor Grant.

MONTANA TROUT UNLIMITED v. MONTANA DEPARTMENT OF NATURAL RESOURCES AND CONSERVATION, 331 Mont. 483, 133 P.3d 224 (Mont. 2006)

JUSTICE BRIAN MORRIS delivered the Opinion of the Court. * * *

[In 1993, Montana enacted a moratorium on new water right applications in certain over-appropriated basins.] The legislature included a basin closure for the Upper Missouri River basin, encompassing the drainage area of the Missouri River and its tributaries above Morony Dam. The Smith River is a tributary of the Upper Missouri River and subject to the Upper Missouri River basin moratorium (hereafter Basin Closure Law).

The Basin Closure Law provides that [the Montana Department of Natural Resources and Conservation] DNRC may not "process or grant an application for a permit to appropriate water ... within the upper Missouri River basin until the final decrees have been issued...." Section 85–2–343, MCA. The legislature provided for several exceptions to the general ban on processing or granting applications. New groundwater applications represent one of the exceptions. Section 85–2–343(2)(a), MCA. The legislature recognized, however, that some groundwater bears a close relationship with surface water and that allowing unrestricted appropriations of groundwater would defeat the purpose of the Basin Closure Law. Thus, the Basin Closure Law also forbids the processing of new applications for groundwater that is "immediately or directly connected" to the Upper Missouri River basin's surface water. Sections 85–2–342 and –343, MCA.

DNRC recognized the particularly intimate relationship between groundwater and surface water along the Smith River. DNRC prepared a Supplemental Environmental Assessment (Supplemental EA) for the Smith River Basin in February of 2003. Therein DNRC noted that the Smith River and its principal tributaries are hydrologically connected to groundwater. The Supplemental EA further noted two ways that groundwater pumping affects surface stream flows. First, pumping may intercept groundwater that otherwise would have entered the stream thereby causing a reduction in surface flows. This phenomenon is called the prestream capture of tributary groundwater. Second, groundwater pumping may pull surface water from the stream toward the well. The DNRC refers to this pulling as induced infiltration. DNRC's hydrogeologist reports that a stream takes longer to recover from prestream capture of its tributary groundwater than from depletion through induced infiltration.

New irrigation developers began turning to groundwater to supplement limited surface water supplies in closed basins. DNRC, as the agency charged with implementation of the Basin Closure law, reviews groundwater applications. DNRC must determine whether an application for groundwater includes groundwater that is "immediately or directly connected to surface water" for the application to qualify under the groundwater exception to the Basin Closure Law. The legislature did not define "immediately or directly connected to surface water" in the Basin Closure Law. DNRC interpreted the language to mean that a groundwater well could not pull surface water directly from a stream or other source of surface water. This interpretation makes no mention of the potential influence of the prestream capture of tributary groundwater on surface flow. DNRC processed new applications before making a threshold determination that the applications fell within an exception to the Basin Closure Law. It is against this backdrop that Trout Unlimited initiated its suit against DNRC.

Trout Unlimited . . . argued that DNRC had adopted an inappropriately narrow interpretation of the "immediately or directly connected to surface water" language in the Basin Closure Law by considering groundwater to have an immediate or direct connection to surface water only if it induced infiltration. * * *

Trout Unlimited sought a declaratory judgment that DNRC's interpretation of the Basin Closure Law conflicted with the clear statutory language of §§ 85–2–342 and –343, MCA. * * *

Trout Unlimited argues that DNRC abused its discretion by failing to interpret the statutory language in a manner consistent with the legislature's intent. Specifically, Trout Unlimited argues that by failing to recognize the direct effect of prestream capture of tributary groundwater DNRC fails to give meaning to each word in the Basin Closure Law. * * *

The legislature defined the groundwater exception in the conjunctive as "water that is beneath the land surface or beneath the bed of a stream, lake, reservoir, or other body of surface water and that is not immediately *or* directly connected to surface water." Section 85–2–342(2), MCA (emphasis added). The plain language of the statute demonstrates the legislature's intent to prohibit the processing or granting of applications for groundwater that either has an immediate connection to surface flows or has a direct connection to surface flows, or both. The legislature did not define "immediately or directly connected to surface water."

DNRC's [regulatory] interpretation of "immediately or directly" indicates that DNRC considers groundwater to have an immediate or direct connection to surface water if groundwater "pumped at the flow rate requested in the application and during the proposed period of diversion, induces surface water infiltration." Rule 36.12.101(33), ARM. . . . DNRC's interpretation of "immediately or directly connected" therefore fails to account for impacts to surface flow caused by the prestream capture of tributary groundwater.

DNRC's own hydrogeologist recognized the impact to surface flows caused by the prestream capture of tributary groundwater. Bill Uthman (Uthman) of DNRC's Water Management Bureau drafted a memo to the Water Resources Division outlining the hydrologic interactions that occur between groundwater and surface water and how groundwater development may impact surface water. Uthman explained therein that groundwater pumping produces two separate components that contribute to total streamflow depletion:

> The first component, groundwater capture, is interception of groundwater flow tributary to the stream, that ultimately reduces the hydraulic gradient near the stream and baseflow to the stream. *Streamflow depletion from groundwater capture usually continues after pumping ends and may require long periods of time to recover.* The second component, induced streambed infiltration, *usually has less impact on streamflow depletion,* and its effects dissipate soon after pumping ends. [Emphasis added.]

As evidenced by DNRC's own hydrogeologist, not only does the prestream capture of tributary groundwater have an impact on surface flows, it has a more significant and longer lasting impact than does induced infiltration. * * *

The legislature provided an exception to the Basin Closure Law for groundwater, provided it is not "immediately or directly connected to" the Upper Missouri River's surface flow. DNRC's interpretation of the Basin Closure Law conflicts with the statute, and does not provide sufficient protection to reasonably effectuate its purpose. DNRC's interpretation recognizes only immediate connections to surface flow caused by induced infiltration and ignores the less immediate, but no less direct, impact of the prestream capture of tributary groundwater. The Basin Closure Law serves to protect senior water rights holders and surface flows along the Smith River basin. It makes no difference to senior appropriators whether groundwater pumping reduces surface flows because of induced infiltration or from the prestream capture of tributary groundwater. The end result is the same: less surface flow in direct contravention of the legislature's intent.

We therefore reverse and remand for further proceedings consistent with this opinion.

QUESTIONS AND DISCUSSION

1. What does the court's decision mean for future groundwater permits in closed basins? Does it effectively prohibit the Montana DNRC from issuing a permit anytime a connection—whether large or small, currently or in the future—can be shown between a proposed groundwater withdrawal and some surface water in the basin? Is this likely what the Montana legislature intended? On the other hand, would the legislature have intended to ignore all prestream capture of groundwater?

2.   In response to the *Trout Unlimited* decision, Montana revised its law governing groundwater permits in closed basins. The legislation requires an applicant to conduct a hydrogeologic assessment to determine whether the proposed appropriation will result in a "net depletion" of surface water and whether that depletion will harm senior appropriators. MCA 85–2–360. The legislature was careful to emphasize, however, that "the prediction of a net depletion does not mean that an adverse effect on a prior appropriator will occur." Instead, the determination of adverse effect "must be made by the department based on the amount, location, and duration of the amount of net depletion that causes the adverse effect relative to the historical beneficial use of the appropriation right that may be adversely affected." MCA 85–2–360(5). What are the implications of this provision? How might it be interpreted by the Montana DNRC? The Idaho Department of Water Resources has issued a similar rule, deciding that a senior appropriator may only enforce priority against a groundwater pumper if the senior suffers a material injury *and* the senior is diverting and using the water efficiently without waste. *See American Falls Reservoir Dist. No. 2 v. Idaho Dep't of Water Resources*, 154 P.3d 433, 447 (Idaho 2007) (upholding the rule against challenge under the state constitution).

Even where the Montana DNRC determines that the groundwater withdrawal would harm a senior appropriator, the applicant can compensate by purchasing part of the senior right or establishing an aquifer recharge plan. MCA 85–2–362. What are the implications of this exception for developers, farmers, and other water users?

3.   Because the hydrologic connection between groundwater and surface water can be small and, as Professor Grant notes above, "delayed by weeks, months, years, or even decades," the determination of just how significant a hydrologic connection must be established before a proposed groundwater appropriation will be prohibited is one with which other states have struggled. In Colorado, the state engineer may not issue a permit for a new well if the well will "materially injure the vested rights of others." Colo. Rev. Stat. § 37–90–137(2)(b). In Washington, the standard is any "impair[ment]," *see* RCW 90.03.290, although the courts have made clear that proving hydraulic continuity is not sufficient to show impairment. *Postema v. Pollution Control Hearings Board*, 142 Wash.2d 68, 11 P.3d 726 (2000). *See also Montgomery v. Lomos Altos, Inc.*, 150 P.3d 971 (N.M. 2006) (suggesting that impairment requires a case-by-case inquiry). What should the standard be? If significance or material injury is the standard, is there a risk that senior surface water appropriators will suffer death by a thousand cuts? If any diminishment is prohibited, does that prevent some efficient uses of groundwater? How might the use of presumptions and allocation of the burden of proof be a part of any solution?

New Mexico's approach to the time-lag management problem has been to issue conditional permits to new groundwater pumpers. The city of Albuquerque, for example, sought a permit to pump groundwater hydrologically connected to the Rio Grande. Over a 75 year period, approximately one-half of the water pumped would be taken from Rio Grande surface flows and one-half from the aquifer. Rather than denying the permit, the state engineer issued a permit conditioned on Albuquerque adhering to a timetable for purchasing and retiring senior surface water rights as the impacts of the pumping progressed. *See City of Albuquerque v. Reynolds*, 379 P.2d 73 (N.M. 1962). What are the implications of this approach to managing hydrologically connected surface and groundwater?

4. Western states are not the only ones to have adopted groundwater permit regimes. Just like many eastern states have moved toward permit systems with respect to surface water, many have moved in that direction for groundwater. Some states have simply provided that groundwater and surface water will be treated the same way. *See, e.g.,* ALA. CODE § 9–10B–3(3), (19); N.J. STAT. ANN. § 58:1A–3(g). Others have adopted separate permitting regimes that leave in place various components of the existing common law. Although the legislation varies in many details, generally the regimes provide for a state agency to issue and record permits for a specific amount of groundwater that may be pumped, provided that water is available, that the use will be beneficial, and that the withdrawal will be consistent with the public interest. Many also provide for the creation of special groundwater management districts. Indiana's, for example, calls for the creation of "groundwater restricted areas" where the withdrawal "exceeds or threatens to exceed natural replenishment." IND. CODE ANN. §§ 14–25–3–4, 14–25–3–6 (2003). Within the groundwater restricted areas, withdrawals are limited to 100,000 gallons per day. However, the Department of Natural Resources may grant a permit to pump more based on consideration of several factors, including the effect of the withdrawal on future supply, the use to be made of the water, the impact on other users, and the "health and best interests of the public." IND. CODE ANN. 14–25–3–8 (2003). *See generally* Joseph W. Dellapenna, *The Law of Water Allocation in the Southeastern States at the Opening of the Twenty–First Century*, 25 U. ARK. LITTLE ROCK L. REV. 9, 45–47 (2002).

5. In most jurisdictions, small domestic wells (and domestic is often defined to include some amount of irrigation and stockwatering) are exempt from permit requirements. The primary reason for these exemptions is the view that the pumping will have only a de minimis impact on other water users and sources. Collectively, however, small groundwater withdrawals and exempt wells can have an impact.

> In discussing the federal budget and efforts to curb profligate spending on defense items, the late Senator Everett McKinley Dirksen once commented: "A million here and a million there, and pretty soon you're talking big money." The same is true with respect to exempt wells. * * * A closer look at the category of exempt wells indicates that they are hardly de minimis and, in certain areas, will have a dramatic impact on streams and rivers. According to the National Ground Water Association, there are approximately 800,000 boreholes drilled annually in the United States. Private household wells constitute the largest share of all water wells in the United States. Approximately 40,000,000 Americans are served from over 15,000,000 private water wells.

Robert Jerome Glennon & Thomas Maddock III, *The Concept of Capture: The Hydrology and Law of Stream/Aquifer Interactions*, 22 ROCKY MTN. MIN. L. INST. 22–1, 22–47 to 22–48 (1997).

6. Think back to the chart at page 38 describing various resource categories. How would you classify groundwater? Is it a renewable or nonrenewable resource? Does it provide any ecosystem services? Does it make an aesthetic contribution?

7. The text discussed how a number of states have limited groundwater pumping to the safe yield of particular aquifers. Given the uncertainty in determining safe yield with precision, how should jurisdictions perform that complex task? What is the role of the precautionary principle? What does public choice theory suggest about how safe yield is likely to be determined? More broadly, why worry about limiting pumping to safe yield? Does it ever make sense to amortize a groundwater resource over a period of years? Is there any reason that groundwater should be treated differently than petroleum? Imagine an oil field with a ten percent annual recharge. Would we limit pumping to the extent of the annual recharge? What sorts of factors might influence our decision?

8. As the discussion in the text indicates, the basic groundwater law inherited from England has changed significantly over the last century. What prompted those changes? Was it science? Scarcity? A change in values? If it was a combination of the three, which do you think predominated?

9. T. Boone Pickens, the famous Texas oil entrepreneur, has turned his attention to another resource—Texas' groundwater. Pickens' company, Mesa Water, Inc., has spent about $100 million purchasing 150,000 acres of land in West Texas overlying the Ogallala aquifer. His plan is to mine groundwater from the aquifer and then sell it to thirsty cities like Dallas. *See generally* Susan Berfield, *There Will Be Water*, BUSINESS WEEK (June 12, 2008). Pickens' plan has many in West Texas worried:

> C.E. Williams runs the Panhandle Groundwater Conservation District, which is responsible for managing the competing demands on the region's share of the Ogallala. He puts it this way: "As a district, we cannot pick and choose where the water goes. But personally I am concerned. I have a son who is an irrigated farmer, and I have grandkids, and I want to make sure that they can conduct commerce when they want to."

> Pickens has a way of dismissing the complexity of a situation, sometimes even the possibility of an opinion contrary to his own. In this case, any opposition to his plan from anyone who is not a Roberts County landowner, who is not essentially a shareholder in this venture, he deems irrelevant. Williams, he points out, doesn't himself have any property. "Water is a commodity," he says. "Heck, isn't it like oil? You have to come back to who owns the water. The groundwater is owned by the landowner. That's it." When it comes to potential buyers, Pickens cares about only one thing: how much they're willing to pay. "Do I care what Dallas does with the water? Hell no."

Id. As noted in the text, *supra*, Texas already allows local groundwater conservation districts to set terms on permits. What would you recommend the local groundwater districts in West Texas do? Would Pickens have any legal recourse if new groundwater rules diminished the value of his investment?

10. On groundwater generally, see ROBERT JEROME GLENNON, WATER FOLLIES: GROUNDWATER PUMPING AND THE FATE OF AMERICA'S FRESH WATERS (2002); 3

WATERS AND WATER RIGHTS 1–550 (Robert E. Beck ed., 1991); Joseph W. Dellapenna, *The Law of Water Allocation in the Southeastern States at the Opening of the Twenty–First Century*, 25 U. ARK. LITTLE ROCK L. REV. 9 (2002).

————

PROBLEM EXERCISE: ALLOCATING A SIMPLE GROUNDWATER AQUIFER

To test your understanding of the different common law regimes for allocating groundwater, consider a simplified hypothetical aquifer with a known amount of water and constant porosity and permeability throughout a known boundary. Assume the aquifer has 4000 acre feet (af) of water with an annual recharge of 100 af. Suppose that overlying the aquifer are three property owners: X, Y, and Z. X owns 100 acres, and Y and Z own 50 acres each. Suppose X has been diverting 200 af since 1970 to irrigate his alfalfa crop, 100 af of which seeps back into the aquifer as return flow. Last year, Y began pumping 100 af per year to run a trout farm. All of the water Y uses is consumed by evaporation. Z has just negotiated a 25–year contract with a nearby municipality to provide it 100 af of water per year. There will be no return flows into the aquifer from this use. X, Y, and Z's water demands cannot all be satisfied. As long as X was the only pumper, the aquifer remained at equilibrium. Although X diverted 200 af per year, the aquifer level remained steady because X's withdrawal was replaced by 100 af of return flow and the 100 af annual recharge. As soon as Y began pumping last year, however, the water level of the aquifer began to decline by 100 af per year. In 38 years, there will no longer be enough to satisfy both Y's demand and that of X (at the beginning of year 39, the aquifer will have only 200 af remaining, not enough for X and Y both to make their full withdrawals). If Z starts sending 100 af per year to the municipality, the aquifer will decline twice as fast. *See generally* JOSEPH L. SAX ET AL., LEGAL CONTROL OF WATER RESOURCES 362–64 (2000) (developing similar hypothetical).

How might this hypothetical groundwater aquifer be allocated under each of the five common law legal regimes described above? As you consider that question, think also about which of the rules are likely to produce a tragedy of the commons and which might avoid it.

IV. WATER FEDERALISM

A. WHO OWNS AND REGULATES WATER?

Recall the discussion in Chapter 1 about the overlap between ownership and regulation and the story in Chapter 2 about the demise of the state ownership doctrine in wildlife law. At the turn of the century, wildlife *ferae naturae* (wildlife not reduced to possession) was understood to be owned by the state until it was reduced to individual possession. *See Geer v. Connecticut*, 161 U.S. 519 (1896). The state's authority to regulate wildlife was said to flow out of that ownership interest. However, as the federal government stepped forward and began to regulate wildlife, first under its treaty power and then under its Property and Commerce Clause powers, it became more and more apparent that wildlife had not really been owned by the state. Instead, wildlife had simply been regulated by the states in the absence of any federal regulation to the contrary. *See Hughes v. Oklahoma*, 441 U.S. 322 (1979) (overruling *Geer* and rejecting state ownership doctrine). The tangled relationship of ownership and regulatory authority in water shares many of the same characteristics as wildlife, although it remains significantly more complex and uncertain. This section of the chapter describes some of the basic doctrines and cases creating that complex relationship.

To this point in the chapter, water, like the land to which it is appurtenant, has largely been treated as a subject of private ownership allocated according to state property law. Riparian rights attach to land ownership. Appropriative rights are usufructuary rights assigned by the state to private individuals. And the state's power to assign that usufructuary right has historically been understood to derive from the state's ownership of the water, an ownership interest asserted over and over in state constitutions in the West. *See, e.g.*, COLO. CONST. art. XVI, § 5 ("The water of every natural stream, not heretofore appropriated, within the state of Colorado, is hereby declared to be the property of the public. . . ."); WYO. CONST. art. VIII, § 1 ("The water of all natural streams, springs, lakes or other collections of still water, within the boundaries of the state, are hereby declared to be the property of the state."); N.M. CONST. art. XVI, § 2 (similar language); N.D. CONST. art. XI, § 3 (similar language); ALASKA CONST. art. VIII, § 3 (similar language). But if water is the property of the states or of private owners, what is the federal role in water ownership and regulation? Is the federal government merely an ordinary proprietor? Is its regulatory role limited to restricting interference with navigation? Alternatively, is state ownership of water an outmoded conception like state ownership of wildlife? Is it all just a matter of dividing regulatory authority over the resource between the states and the federal government?

Think back to Chapter 2 and the geographical development of the United States. When the original thirteen states formed the Union, what was their relationship to the water within their boundaries? As England's heir, they inherited the common law with its understanding of riparian rights. Those rights attached to riparian land, some of which was private and some of which was owned by the states themselves. From Parliament, the new states also inherited the police power and the power of eminent domain and with them the right to regulate and control resource use within their boundaries. Although the matter is one of historical debate, by the account of cases like *Illinois Central* and *National Audubon*, the states also inherited from the Crown an obligation to hold the land under navigable waters and the waters themselves in trust for the public to assure their use for navigation, commerce, and fishery. With that inheritance in place, the states, or the people collectively depending on one's constitutional perspective, then gave up certain powers to the United States. The key one where water was concerned was the power for Congress to regulate commerce between the states. Because most interstate commerce in the eighteenth and early nineteenth centuries was conducted on navigable waterways, the Commerce Clause turned out to be a particularly significant concession of federal power over water within the states. Although in the post-New Deal and *Wickard v. Filburn* era the Commerce Clause is recognized as a wide-ranging source of general federal regulatory power, its impact on regulation of the water resource has proven more significant. As discussed below, in the water arena, the federal commerce power has been the source of not only federal regulatory authority but also of federal ownership claims (with reserved water rights and the navigation servitude, both of which are discussed further below).

Although the states and the people gave the federal government power to regulate interstate commerce, that concession for a long time did not have much meaning with respect to state water law. Federal power over the water resource initially extended only to watercourses navigable in fact—in other words, those watercourses on which commerce could be conducted. *See The Propeller Genesee Chief v. Fitzhugh*, 53 U.S. (12 How.) 443 (1852) (rejecting the English rule that navigability was determined by whether waters ebbed and flowed with the tide and adopting navigability in fact as the standard for determining the extent of the admiralty jurisdiction committed to the federal courts by art. III, § 2 of the Constitution). Even with respect to navigable waters, for most of the nineteenth century, the federal government made little effort to exercise its authority. Water allocation was left up to state property law. And the regulation of activities that tended to obstruct navigation was left largely in the hands of the states.

The first significant federal foray into regulating even navigable waters came in the Rivers and Harbors Appropriation Act of 1890, when Congress passed general legislation prohibiting the creation of obstructions to navigable waters, unless the obstruction was "affirmatively authorized by law." Act of Sept. 19, 1890, ch. 907, § 10, 26 Stat. 454. But even in that Act, the reference to obstructions "authorized by law" was taken to include obstructions authorized by state law. *See United States v. Bellingham Bay Boom Co.*, 176 U.S. 211 (1900). It was not until the Rivers and Harbors Appropriation Act of 1899, Act of Mar. 3, 1899, ch. 425, 30 Stat. 1121, that Congress stated its intention to preempt state authority over obstructions and required *congressional* authorization to build an obstruction in navigable waters. *Id.* § 10. But even the Rivers and Harbors Act was not an effort to intervene in state *allocation* decisions. The Act retained a traditional Commerce Clause focus on navigable waters and on ensuring that those waters were not obstructed in a way that would hinder commerce. It would not be until the New Deal and the Supreme Court's adoption of the "affecting commerce" test in *Wickard v. Filburn*, 317 U.S. 111 (1942), *see* Chapter 2, page 173, that federal authority would be understood to extend—or, more precisely, to have the potential to extend—to non-navigable waters and to questions of water allocation. Thus for much of our nation's history, the states, and particularly those without much federal land, were largely left free to apply their own laws to water and to decide for themselves how water should be allocated.

Ownership and regulatory authority over water in the public land states in the West, however, present some additional complexities because in those states, the United States was not simply a regulator but was also a riparian owner. As discussed in Chapter 2, section III.D, the United States retained vast acreages of public lands in many states but particularly those west of the hundredth meridian. That made the United States the largest riparian owner in those states and created questions about the nature of any water rights in the federal government, in the private riparians who had taken up their land pursuant to a federal grant, and in those who, typically hoping for later preemption, had simply established themselves on federal land in the absence of any grant. As some viewed it, the matter was quite simple. The common-law system of riparian rights inherited from England and adopted in the East should define the water rights of the United States and its grantees. But miners, irrigators, and other settlers in the arid West had different ideas. They were convinced that water use should not be limited to riparian property but should be directed toward any location where it could be put to beneficial use. Prior use, not streamside ownership, would create water rights. But if using water created a prior right, what about the United States, who left so much of its land—and the water running through it—idle? Could the western states adopt prior appropriation and impose it on federal land and federal grantees without federal consent?

An early and incomplete answer to these questions came in the famous water law case of *Irwin v. Phillips*, 5 Cal. 140 (1855), a dispute between two miners in California's gold country, neither of whom had any federal title to the lands they occupied. Irwin had diverted water from a stream and brought it via ditch to his mining operations. Phillips arrived later, took up riparian land along the banks of the stream, and cut down Irwin's diversion dam, claiming that as a riparian he, rather than Irwin, was entitled to the water. Irwin sued, and the California Supreme Court ruled in his favor. The Court decided that at least as between two squatters on the public lands, the controlling law should not be the common-law doctrine of riparian rights but the customary law of the mining camps that had been tacitly approved by the California legislature. Said the court: "the policy of the State ... has ... conferred the right to divert the streams from their natural channels, and as these two rights [of Irwin and Phillips] stand upon an equal footing, when they conflict, they must be decided by the fact of priority, upon the maxim of equity, *qui prior est in tempore, potior est in jure.*" *Id.* at 147. Although a first step toward prior appropriation, the *Irwin v. Phillips* decision can hardly be described as securing a system of prior appropriation for all land, including federal land, in California. The decision did nothing to answer whether riparian rights would have existed had Phillips been a federal patentee rather than a squatter and, more broadly, whether the United States itself could claim riparian rights.

Given this uncertainty, western interests began encouraging the federal government to recognize appropriative rights in water on federal lands. Congress responded by adding language to the 1866 Mining Act confirming that rights to water acquired by prior appropriation were good against subsequent federal patentees if the rights "are recognized and acknowledged by the local customs, laws, and decisions of courts." Mining Act of 1866, § 9, 14 Stat. 251, 253. This provision addressed the concern about federal patentees having riparian rights that trumped the state water rights of appropriators but left open the question whether the United States could claim riparian rights for the public lands.

In the 1877 Desert Land Act, 19 Stat. 377, Congress seemed to sanction prior appropriation as the general rule for at least a portion of the public lands. As discussed in Chapter 2, the Desert Land Act increased the amount of land that a settler could acquire from 160 acres under the Homestead Act to 640 acres, as long as at least one-fourth of the acres were put under irrigation. The Act provided that a settler could "appropriate[]" the amount of water necessary to accomplish that irrigation and that "the surplus water over and above such actual appropriation and use, together with the water of all lakes, rivers, and other sources of water supply upon the public lands and not navigable, shall remain and be held free for the appropriation and use of the public for irrigation, mining and manufacturing subject to existing rights." 19 Stat. 377. The effect of this language, said the Supreme Court, was to sever the waters from the public domain and make those waters subject to whatever state law was applicable. *See California Oregon Power Co. v. Beaver Portland Cement Co.*, 295 U.S. 142, 158 (1935) (stating that "following the act of 1877, if not before, all non-navigable waters then a part of the public domain became *publici juris*, subject to plenary control of the designated states, ... with the right in each to determine for itself to what extent the rule of appropriation or the common-law rule in respect of riparian rights should obtain"). As a further confirmation of state control of water resources, under the 1902 Reclamation Act, Congress provided:

> [N]othing in this Act shall be construed as affecting or intended to affect or to in any way interfere with the laws of any States or Territory relating to the control, appropriation, use or distribution of water used in irrigation, or any vested rights acquired thereunder, and the Secretary of the Interior, in carrying out the provisions of this Act, shall proceed in conformity with such laws ...

43 U.S.C. § 383 (§ 8 of the Reclamation Act). *See also California v. United States*, 438 U.S. 645 (1978) (discussing the various federal efforts to assure the states control of the water resource).

By recognizing western states' authority over water allocation, the language of the 1866 Mining Act, the 1877 Desert Land Act, and the 1902 Reclamation Act only speeded along a process that was already well under way. As evidenced by the various state constitutions cited above, the western states early on claimed ownership of the water within their boundaries. In the view of many westerners, the various federal statutes were not giving anything to the West but only confirming what the states already had. With their ownership of the water, the states presumed, came the right to allocate and regulate the water. And the manner of allocation many chose was prior appropriation. Although dual riparian and appropriative rights systems were adopted in some western states, more states rejected riparian rights altogether. The claims of riparians that the adoption of prior appropriation unfairly denied their preexisting riparian rights were swept aside by state courts. In *Coffin v. Left Hand Ditch Co.*, 6 Colo. 443 (1882), for example, despite strong evidence that common-law riparian principles had prevailed before 1876, the Colorado Supreme Court held that

> the common law doctrine giving the riparian owner a right to the flow of water in its natural channel upon and over his lands, even though he makes no beneficial use thereof, is inapplicable to Colorado. Imperative necessity, unknown to the countries which gave it birth, compels the recognition of another doctrine in conflict therewith.

Id. at 447. Other state courts were just as direct in rejecting riparian rights. In Nevada, only thirteen years after affirming the natural flow rule of riparian rights, the Supreme Court overruled its decision and said that prior appropriation had long been the "universal custom" in the western states. *Jones v. Adams*, 19 Nev. 78, 6 P. 442, 445 (1885).

By the turn of the century, as a result of this conglomeration of state and local custom, state constitutional and statutory law and judicial decisions, and federal statutes, the western states assumed almost complete control of the water within their boundaries. It looked as though the federal government was largely out of the water business. It could regulate to prevent interference with navigation, but that was about it. Thus, as indicated by the first half of this chapter, states have largely made the rules with respect to the water resource. The rest of this section of the chapter, however, details how this understanding of state ownership and regulatory control over water has eroded over time.

B.   INDIAN AND FEDERAL RESERVED WATER RIGHTS

An early move away from complete state control of water diversions came in the Supreme Court's decision in *United States v. Rio Grande Dam & Irrig. Co.*, 174 U.S. 690 (1899), in which the Court upheld federal power to prohibit a dam from being built in a navigable portion of the Rio Grande, stating:

> Although this power of changing the common-law rule as to streams within its dominion undoubtedly belongs in each state, yet two limitations must be recognized: First, that, in the absence of specific authority from congress, a state cannot, by its legislation, destroy the right of the United States, as the owner of lands bordering on a stream, to the continued flow of its waters, so far, at least, as may be necessary for the beneficial uses of the government property; second, that it is limited by the superior power of the general government to secure the uninterrupted navigability of all navigable streams within the limits of the United States.

Id. at 703. Although the latter point was the one on which the decision turned and was not particularly controversial because of Congress' enumerated authority in the Commerce Clause to protect navigation, it was the former point that suggested state control over water may not be as secure as some imagined. By stating that when the United States is a riparian owner, it is entitled to make beneficial uses of the water and that state interference with federal riparian rights depends upon congressional consent, the court made clear that legislation like the 1866 Mining Act and the 1877 Desert Land Act was discretionary and that federal interest in water was not limited to regulation on behalf of navigation. The following case, which is the first to describe what has become known as the doctrine of Indian reserved water rights, represents another significant limitation on the notion of state ownership of water resources.

WINTERS V. UNITED STATES,
207 U.S. 564 (1908)

Statement by MR. JUSTICE MCKENNA:

This suit was brought by the United States to restrain appellants and others from constructing or maintaining dams or reservoirs on the Milk river in the state of Montana, or in any manner preventing the water of the river or its tributaries from flowing to the Fort Belknap Indian Reservation.

* * * [The] Milk river, designated as the northern boundary of the reservation, is a nonnavigable stream. . . . [It is alleged that] on the 5th of July, 1898, the Indians residing on the reservation diverted from the river for the purpose of irrigation a flow of 10,000 miners' inches of water to and upon divers and extensive tracts of land, aggregating in amount about 30,000 acres, and raised upon said lands crops of grain, grass, and vegetables. And ever since . . ., the . . . Indians have diverted and used the waters of the river in the manner and for the purposes mentioned. . . .

It is alleged that, 'notwithstanding the riparian and other rights' of the United States and the Indians to the uninterrupted flow of the waters of the river, the defendants, in the year 1900, wrongfully entered upon the river and its tributaries above the points of the diversion of the waters of the river by the United States and the Indians, built large and substantial dams and reservoirs, and, by means of canals and ditches and water ways, have diverted the waters of the river from its channel, and have deprived the United States and the Indians of the use thereof. . . .

The allegations of the answer, so far as material to the present controversy, are as follows: That the lands of the Fort Belknap Reservation were a part of a much larger area in the state of Montana, which, by an act of Congress, approved April 15, 1874 [18 Stat. at L. 28, chap. 96], was set apart and reserved for the occupation of the Gros Ventre, Piegan, Blood, Blackfeet, and River Crow Indians, but that the right of the Indians therein 'was the bare right of the use and occupation thereof at the will and sufferance of the government of the United States.' That the United States, for the purpose of opening for settlement a large portion of such area, entered into an agreement with the Indians composing said tribes, by which the Indians 'ceded, sold, transferred, and conveyed' to the United States all of the lands embraced in said area, except Fort Belknap Indian Reservation, described in the bill. This agreement was ratified by an act of Congress of May 1, 1888 [25 Stat. at L. 113, chap. 213], and thereby the lands to which the Indians' title was thus extinguished became a part of the public domain of the United States and subject to disposal under the various land laws, 'and it was the purpose and intention of the government that the said land should be thus thrown open to settlement, to the end that the same might be settled upon, inhabited, reclaimed, and cultivated, and communities of civilized persons be established thereon.' * * *

That the defendants, prior to the 5th day of July, 1898, before any appropriation, diversion, or use of the waters of the river or its tributaries was made by the . . . Indians on the Fort Belknap Reservation, . . . without having notice of any claim made by . . . the Indians that there was any reservation made of the waters of the river or its tributaries for use on said reservation, and believing that all the waters on the lands open for settlement as aforesaid were subject to appropriation under the laws of the United States and the laws, decisions, rulings, and customs of the state of Montana, in like manner as water on other portions of the public domain, entered upon the public lands in the vicinity of the river, made entry thereof at the United States land office, and thereafter settled upon, improved, reclaimed, and cultivated the same and performed all things required to acquire a title under the homestead and desert land laws, made due proof thereof, and received patents conveying to them, respectively, the lands in fee simple.

That all of said lands are situated within the watershed of the river, are riparian upon the river and its tributaries, but are arid and must be irrigated by artificial means to make them inhabitable and capable of growing crops.... The defendants and the stockholders of the defendant corporations have expended many thousands of dollars in constructing dams, ditches, and reservoirs, and in improving said lands, building fences and other structures, establishing schools, and constructing highways and other improvements usually had and enjoyed in a civilized community, and that the only supply of water to irrigate the lands is from Milk river. If defendants are deprived of the waters their lands cannot be successfully cultivated, and they will become useless and homes cannot be maintained thereon. * * *

MR. JUSTICE McKENNA delivered the opinion of the court:

* * * The case, as we view it, turns on the agreement of May, 1888, resulting in the creation of Fort Belknap Reservation. In the construction of this agreement there are certain elements to be considered that are prominent and significant. The reservation was a part of a very much larger tract which the Indians had the right to occupy and use, and which was adequate for the habits and wants of a nomadic and uncivilized people. It was the policy of the government, it was the desire of the Indians, to change those habits and to become a pastoral and civilized people. If they should become such, the original tract was too extensive; but a smaller tract would be inadequate without a change of conditions. The lands were arid, and, without irrigation, were practically valueless. And yet, it is contended, the means of irrigation were deliberately given up by the Indians and deliberately accepted by the government. The lands ceded were, it is true, also arid; and some argument may be urged, and is urged, that with their cession the 'civilized communities could not be established thereon.' And this, it is further contended, the Indians knew, and yet made no reservation of the waters. We realize that there is a conflict of implications, but that which makes for the retention of the waters is of greater force than that which makes for their cession. The Indians had command of the lands and the waters—command of all their beneficial use, whether kept for hunting, 'and grazing roving herds of stock,' or turned to agriculture and the arts of civilization. Did they give up all this? Did they reduce the area of their occupation and give up the waters which made it valuable or adequate? ... If it were possible to believe affirmative answers, we might also believe that the Indians were awed by the power of the government or deceived by its negotiators. Neither view is possible. The government is asserting the rights of the Indians. But extremes need not be taken into account. By a rule of interpretation of agreements and treaties with the Indians, ambiguities occurring will be resolved from the standpoint of the Indians. And the rule should certainly be applied to determine between two inferences, one of which would support the purpose of the agreement and the other impair or defeat it. On account of their relations to the government, it cannot be supposed that the Indians were alert to exclude by formal words every inference which might militate against or defeat the declared purpose of themselves and the government, even if it could be supposed that they had the intelligence to foresee the 'double sense' which might some time be urged against them.

Another contention of appellants is that if it be conceded that there was a reservation of the waters of Milk river by the agreement of 1888, yet the reservation was repealed by the admission of Montana into the Union, February 22, 1889, 'upon an equal footing with the original states.' The language of counsel is that 'any reservation in the agreement with the Indians, expressed or implied, whereby the waters of Milk river were not to be subject of appropriation by the citizens and inhabitants of said state, was repealed by the act of admission.' But to establish the repeal counsel rely substantially upon the same argument that they advance against the intention of the agreement to reserve the waters. The power of the government to reserve the waters and exempt them from appropriation under the state laws is not denied, and could not be. *United States v. Rio Grande Dam & Irrig. Co.*, 174 U.S. 702; *United States v. Winans*, 198 U.S. 371. That the government did reserve them we have decided, and for a use which would be necessarily continued through years. This was done May 1, 1888, and it would be extreme to believe that within a year Congress destroyed the reservation and took from the Indians the consideration of their grant, leaving them a barren waste,—took from them the means of continuing their old habits, yet did not leave them the power to change to new ones.

[Decree enjoining diversion of waters of the Milk River] affirmed.

QUESTIONS AND DISCUSSION

1. What constitutional text does the Supreme Court have in mind when it says that "the power of the government to reserve the waters and exempt them from appropriation under state laws is not denied, and could not be"? Is it the treaty power? The Property Clause? The Commerce Clause? Is it even necessary to identify a source of federal power to uphold the decision?

2. Do you see how the *Winters* doctrine of Indian reserved water rights can be understood as an exception to the 1877 Desert Land Act? If the Court is correct that the federal government had the power to reserve the waters, how does it know that the federal government intended to do so here when Congress had stated in the Desert Land Act that non-navigable waters "shall remain and be held free for the appropriation and use of the public for irrigation, mining and manufacturing subject to existing rights." 19 Stat. 377. Does the court's citation of the rule of construction that ambiguities in "treaties with the Indians ... will be resolved from the standpoint of the Indians" help answer this question?

3. What of Montana's argument that the equal footing doctrine should have given it the authority to dispose of the Milk River? What is it about the Milk River that makes that argument difficult? Suppose the Milk River were navigable and recall that, under the equal footing doctrine, courts are obligated to employ a strong presumption against any claim that the United States made a prestatehood grant of land under navigable water because those lands are so intimately associated with the state's sovereignty. *See Pollard v. Hagan*, 44 U.S. (3 How.) 212 (1845); *Montana v. United States*, 450 U.S. 544 (1981). Should the equal footing doctrine apply to water just as it does to the land under the water? Should the courts employ a strong presumption against any prestatehood grants? If the equal footing doctrine should not be expanded beyond submerged lands, what about the public trust doctrine? Should it similarly be limited to land under navigable water as it was in *Illinois Central*, or was its expansion in *National Audubon* to include water itself appropriate? For a discussion of the two doctrines, see James R. Rasband, *The Disregarded Common Parentage of the Equal Footing and Public Trust Doctrines*, 32 LAND & WATER L. REV. 1 (1997). If the equal footing doctrine of *Pollard* and *Montana* had been applied in *Winters*, what result?

Why might the tribes argue that the equal footing doctrine simply has no application in this case or, for that matter, in any case where a tribe reserves for itself certain of the natural resources whose use it enjoyed prior to any treaty with the United States? A partial answer to this question may come from the Supreme Court's citation of *United States v. Winans*, 198 U.S. 371 (1905), where the Court had stated the treaty at issue "was not a grant of rights to the Indians, but a grant of rights from them,—a reservation of those not granted." *Id.* at 381.

4. The *Winters* decision gave little content to Indian reserved water rights. It did not quantify the water right except to intimate that the treaty necessarily reserved an amount of water sufficient for the tribe to change from its nomadic ways and "old habits" to a more "pastoral" lifestyle dependent upon irrigation. Nor did the court explain how the Indians' right would fit within Montana's appropriation system. It was not until 1963 that the Court gave additional guidance. In *Arizona v. California*, 373 U.S. 546 (1963), the Court held that reserved water rights had a priority date as of the date of the treaty or executive order establishing the reservation. *Id.* at 600. The Court also held that the quantity of the water reserved for irrigation was to be calculated by reference to the number of practically irrigable acres (PIA) on the reservation. *Id.* With these two characteristics in mind, would you characterize Indian reserved water rights as riparian or appropriative in nature?

5. The potential quantity of Indian reserved water rights is quite large. As explained in one government report:

> [W]ater rights claims of the Missouri River basin tribes could total more than 19 million acre-feet, or approximately 40 percent of the total flow of the Missouri. As of 1995, there are more than 60 cases in courts involving the resolution of Indian water rights claims. The total amount of water potentially involved in these claims ranges from 45 million to over 65 million acre-feet.

WATER IN THE WEST: CHALLENGE FOR THE NEXT CENTURY 3–48 (1998) (final report of the Western Water Policy Review Advisory Commission). What are the implications of these numbers for water policy in the West? Despite the significant water rights of the tribes, the paper rights have amounted to relatively little wet water. This is in part because many of the tribes' water rights have not been adjudicated and quantified. It is also a result of the high cost of water development and the increasing public opposition to water development projects.

6. Although *Arizona v. California* resolved the quantification of Indian reserved rights for agricultural purposes, agriculture was not the sole purpose for which reservations were created, nor was it the sole object of Indian treaties. A number of treaties, particularly those negotiated with Indian tribes in the Northwest and upper Midwest, reserved hunting and fishing rights for certain Indian tribes. A right to fish isn't much good if there is so little water that the fish cannot survive. Does that mean that the treaties also reserved a sufficient amount of water to protect the fishery? In *United States v. Adair*, 723 F.2d 1394 (9th Cir. 1983), *cert. denied*, 467 U.S. 1252 (1984), the Ninth Circuit held that an 1864 treaty with the Klamath Indian tribe did indeed reserve instream flows sufficient to protect the fishery. With respect to the priority date of the reserved instream right, the court said that it dated not from the treaty but from the Indians' first use of the water for that purpose, or from time immemorial. On what basis do you suppose the court assigned a different priority date for water reserved for agriculture than for water reserved for the fishery? In practice, will it often matter which of the two priority dates is assigned?

7. For a historical examination of the *Winters* case, see Norris Hundley, *The Winters Decision and Indian Water Rights: A Mystery Reexamined*, 13 W. HIST. Q. 20 (1982).

For quite some time after the *Winters* decision, most commentators saw the case as a narrow Indian law exception to the severance doctrine of *Beaver Portland Cement*, which, as described above, held that the Desert Land Act severed water from the public domain and made it subject to state regulation. However, in 1955, in *FPC v. Oregon*, 349 U.S. 435, 448 (1955) (*Pelton Dam*), the Court, in rejecting Oregon's protest that the federal government lacked authority to license a hydropower project on federal property on a non-navigable river, announced that the Desert Land Act did not apply to federal lands reserved for a specific purpose, effectively reopening the question of water ownership and control within federal reservations. Then, in *Arizona v. California*, 373 U.S. 546, 601 (1963), the Court affirmed without any discussion its special master's decision that the United States could reserve water not only for Indian tribes but also for a national recreation area, two wildlife refuges, and a national forest. The next two cases describe the development of what has become known as the doctrine of federal reserved water rights.

CAPPAERT V. UNITED STATES, 426 U.S. 128 (1976)

MR. CHIEF JUSTICE BURGER delivered the opinion of the Court.

The question presented in this litigation is whether the reservation of Devil's Hole as a national monument reserved federal water rights in unappropriated water.

Devil's Hole is a deep limestone cavern in Nevada. Approximately 50 feet below the opening of the cavern is a pool 65 feet long, 10 feet wide, and at least 200 feet deep, although its actual depth is unknown. The pool is a remnant of the prehistoric Death Valley Lake System and is situated on land owned by the United States since the Treaty of Guadalupe Hidalgo in 1848, 9 Stat. 922. By the Proclamation of January 17, 1952, President Truman withdrew from the public domain a 40–acre tract of land surrounding Devil's Hole, making it a detached component of the Death Valley National Monument. The Proclamation was issued under the American Antiquities Preservation Act, 16 U.S.C. § 431, which authorizes the President to declare as national monuments "objects of historic or scientific interest that are situated upon the lands owned or controlled by the Government of the United States. . . ."

The 1952 Proclamation notes that Death Valley was set aside as a national monument "for the preservation of the unusual features of scenic, scientific, and educational interest therein contained." The Proclamation also notes that Devil's Hole is near Death Valley and contains a "remarkable underground pool." Additional preambulary statements in the Proclamation explain why Devil's Hole was being added to the Death Valley National Monument:

> WHEREAS the said pool is a unique subsurface remnant of the prehistoric chain of lakes which in Pleistocene times formed the Death Valley Lake System, and is unusual among caverns in that it is a solution area in distinctly striated limestone, while also owing its formation in part to fault action; and

> WHEREAS the geologic evidence that this subterranean pool is an integral part of the hydrographic history of the Death Valley region is further confirmed by the presence in this pool of a peculiar race of desert fish, and zoologists have demonstrated that this race of fish, which is found nowhere else in the world, evolved only after the gradual drying up of the Death Valley Lake System isolated this fish population from the original ancestral stock that in Pleistocene times was common to the entire region; and

> WHEREAS the said pool is of such outstanding scientific importance that it should be given special protection, and such protection can be best afforded by making the said forty-acre tract containing the pool a part of the said monument. * * *

The Cappaert petitioners own a 12,000–acre ranch near Devil's Hole, 4,000 acres of which are used for growing Bermuda grass, alfalfa, wheat, and barley; 1,700 to 1,800 head of cattle are grazed. The ranch represents an investment of more than $7 million; it employs more than 80 people with an annual payroll of more than $340,000.

In 1968 the Cappaerts began pumping groundwater on their ranch on land 2 1/2 miles from Devil's Hole; they were the first to appropriate groundwater. The groundwater comes from an underground basin or aquifer which is also the source of the water in Devil's Hole. After the Cappaerts began pumping from the wells near Devil's Hole, which they do from March to October, the summer water level of the pool in Devil's Hole began to decrease. Since 1962 the level of water in Devil's Hole has been measured with reference to a copper washer installed on one of the walls of the hole by the United States Geological Survey. Until 1968, the water level, with seasonable variations, had been stable at 1.2 feet below the copper marker. In 1969 the water level in Devil's Hole was 2.3 feet below the copper washer; in 1970, 3.17 feet; in 1971, 3.48 feet; and, in 1972, 3.93 feet.

When the water is at the lowest levels, a large portion of a rock shelf in Devil's Hole is above water. However, when the water level is at 3.0 feet below the marker or higher, most of the rock shelf is below water, enabling algae to grow on it. This in turn enables the desert fish (*Cyprinodon diabolis*, commonly known as Devil's Hole pupfish), referred to in President Truman's Proclamation, to spawn in the spring. As the rock shelf becomes exposed, the spawning area is decreased, reducing the ability of the fish to spawn in sufficient quantities to prevent extinction. * * *

In August 1971 the United States, invoking 28 U.S.C. § 1345, sought an injunction in the United States District Court for the District of Nevada to limit, except for domestic purposes, the Cappaerts' pumping from six specific wells and from specific locations near Devil's Hole. The complaint alleged that the United States, in establishing Devil's Hole as part of Death Valley National Monument, reserved the unappropriated waters appurtenant to the land to the extent necessary for the requirements and purposes of the reservation.... The United States asserted that pumping from certain of the Cappaerts' wells had lowered the water level in Devil's Hole, that the lower water level was threatening the survival of a unique species of fish, and that irreparable harm would follow if the pumping were not enjoined. * * *

On June 5, 1973, the District Court ... held that in establishing Devil's Hole as a national monument, the President reserved appurtenant, unappropriated waters necessary to the purpose of the reservation; the purpose included preservation of the pool and the pupfish in it. The District Court also held that the federal water rights antedated those of the Cappaerts ... and that the public interest required granting the injunction. On April 9, 1974, the District Court entered its findings of fact and conclusions of law substantially unchanged in a final decree permanently enjoining pumping that lowers the level of the water below the 3.0–foot level.

The Court of Appeals for the Ninth Circuit affirmed, 508 F.2d 313 (1974), ... holding that the implied-reservation-of-water doctrine applied to groundwater as well as to surface water. * * *

We granted certiorari to consider the scope of the implied-reservation-of-water-rights doctrine. We affirm.

I

Reserved–Water–Rights Doctrine

This Court has long held that when the Federal Government withdraws its land from the public domain and reserves it for a federal purpose, the Government, by implication, reserves appurtenant water then unappropriated to the extent needed to accomplish the purpose of the reservation. In so doing the United States acquires a reserved right in unappropriated water which vests on the date of the reservation and is superior to the rights of future appropriators. Reservation of water rights is empowered by the Commerce Clause, Art. I, § 8, which permits federal regulation of navigable streams, and the Property Clause, Art. IV, § 3, which permits federal regulation of federal lands. The doctrine applies to Indian reservations and other federal enclaves, encompassing water rights in navigable and nonnavigable streams. *Colorado River Water Cons. Dist. v. United States*, 424 U.S. 800, 805 (1976); *United States v. District Court for Eagle County*, 401 U.S. 520, 522–523 (1971); *Arizona v. California*, 373 U.S. 546, 601 (1963); *FPC v. Oregon*, 349 U.S. 435 (1955); *United States v. Powers*, 305 U.S. 527 (1939); *Winters v. United States*, 207 U.S. 564 (1908).

Nevada argues that the cases establishing the doctrine of federally reserved water rights articulate an equitable doctrine calling for a balancing of competing interests. However, an examination of those cases shows they do not analyze the doctrine in terms of a balancing test. For example, in *Winters v. United States, supra,* the Court did not mention the use made of the water by the upstream landowners in sustaining an injunction barring their diversions of the water. The "Statement of the Case" in *Winters* notes that the upstream users were homesteaders who had invested heavily in dams to divert the water to irrigate their land, not an unimportant interest. The Court held that when the Federal Government reserves land, by implication it reserves water rights sufficient to accomplish the purposes of the reservation.

In determining whether there is a federally reserved water right implicit in a federal reservation of public land, the issue is whether the Government intended to reserve unappropriated and thus available water. Intent is inferred if the previously unappropriated waters are necessary to accomplish the purposes for which the reservation was created. Both the District Court and the Court of Appeals held that the 1952 Proclamation expressed an intention to reserve unappropriated water, and we agree.[5] The Proclamation discussed the pool in Devil's Hole in four of the five preambles and recited that the "pool . . . should be given special protection." Since a pool is a body of water, the protection contemplated is meaningful only if the water remains; the water right reserved by the 1952 Proclamation was thus explicit, not implied. * * *

The implied-reservation-of-water-rights doctrine, however, reserves only that amount of water necessary to fulfill the purpose of the reservation, no more. Here the purpose of reserving Devil's Hole Monument is preservation of the pool. Devil's Hole was reserved "for the preservation of the unusual features of scenic, scientific, and educational interest." The Proclamation notes that the pool contains "a peculiar race of desert fish . . . which is found nowhere else in the world" and that the "pool is of . . . outstanding scientific importance. . . ." The pool need only be preserved, consistent with the intention expressed in the Proclamation, to the extent necessary to preserve its scientific interest. The fish are one of the features of scientific interest. The preamble noting the scientific interest of the pool follows the preamble describing the fish as unique; the Proclamation must be read in its entirety. Thus, as the District Court has correctly determined, the level of the pool may be permitted to drop to the extent that the drop does not impair the scientific value of the pool as the natural habitat of the species sought to be preserved. The District Court thus tailored its injunction, very appropriately, to minimal need, curtailing pumping only to the extent necessary to preserve an adequate water level at Devil's Hole, thus implementing the stated objectives of the Proclamation. * * *

II

Groundwater

No cases of this Court have applied the doctrine of implied reservation of water rights to groundwater. Nevada argues that the implied-reservation doctrine is limited to surface water. Here, however, the water in the pool is surface water. The federal water rights were being depleted because, as the evidence showed, the "(g)roundwater and surface water are physically interrelated as integral parts of the hydrologic cycle." C. CORKER, GROUNDWATER LAW, MANAGEMENT AND ADMINISTRATION, NATIONAL WATER COMMISSION LEGAL STUDY No. 6, p. xxiv (1971). Here the Cappaerts are causing the water level in Devil's Hole to drop by their heavy pumping. . . . Thus, since the implied-reservation-of-water-rights doctrine is based on the necessity of water for the purpose of the federal

5. The District Court and the Court of Appeals correctly held that neither the Cappaerts nor their predecessors in interest had acquired any water rights as of 1952 when the United States' water rights vested. Part of the land now comprising the Cappaerts' ranch was patented by the United States to the Cappaerts' predecessors as early as 1890. None of the patents conveyed water rights because the Desert Land Act of 1877, 19 Stat. 377, 43 U.S.C. § 321, provided that such patents pass title only to land, not water. Patentees acquire water rights by "bona fide prior appropriation," as determined by state law. *California Oregon Power Co. v. Beaver Portland Cement Co.*, 295 U.S. 142 (1935). * * *

reservation, we hold that the United States can protect its water from subsequent diversion, whether the diversion is of surface or groundwater. * * *

We hold, therefore, that as of 1952 when the United States reserved Devil's Hole, it acquired by reservation water rights in unappropriated appurtenant water sufficient to maintain the level of the pool to preserve its scientific value and thereby implement Proclamation No. 2961.

QUESTIONS AND DISCUSSION

1. By way of reviewing the basic legal reasoning in *Cappaert*, by what authority did the United States reserve Devil's Hole? What is the content of the United States' reserved water right? How much water? What is its priority date? Suppose the Cappaerts had begun pumping groundwater in 1950. Would that have made a difference?

2. Recall the *Winters* case, *supra*. Is the rationale for Indian reserved water rights the same as that for non-Indian federal reserved rights? Is there any reason to treat the two differently?

3. Does the court describe the federal reserved water right at Devil's Hole as a matter of ownership or of regulatory authority? How would you describe it? Does the distinction matter?

4. If the Court had denied the United States' claim, what would have been the result? Is the federal reserved rights doctrine sound water and natural resource policy? Would it make more sense to require the United States to apply for a groundwater permit like any other property owner in Nevada? What sort of concerns might arise with such an approach?

5. What if Nevada did not apply the law of prior appropriation to groundwater but instead adhered to a common law reasonable use approach? What result? Would the Commerce Clause and Property Clause give the United States the authority to curtail diversions otherwise allowed by the common law reasonable use doctrine? Would the exercise of such power trigger takings scrutiny?

6. *Cappaert* avoids expressly addressing the question of how the reserved rights doctrine applies to groundwater. Nevertheless, recognition of reserved rights in groundwater presents some interesting issues. In this case, for example, how much groundwater is included within the reserved right? What are the implications of allowing the United States to reserve the top part of the aquifer? The courts are divided on whether the reserved rights doctrine applies to groundwater. The Ninth Circuit in *Cappaert* concluded that it did. 508 F.2d 313, 317 (9th Cir. 1974). And in *In re the General Adjudication of All Rights to Use Water in the Gila River System and Source*, 989 P.2d 739 (Ariz. 1999), *cert. denied*, 530 U.S. 1250 (2000), the Arizona Supreme Court said that there could be a reserved right in groundwater where the surface water was inadequate to accomplish the purposes of the reservation. *Id.* at 746–47. The Wyoming Supreme Court, however, has concluded that there is not a reserved right to groundwater. *See In re the General Adjudication of All Rights to Use Water in the Big Horn River System*, 753 P.2d 76, 99 (Wyo. 1988), *aff'd by equally divided Court*, 492 U.S. 406 (1989).

7.   *Problem Exercise.* Consider a groundwater dispute between the Lummi Indian tribe in Washington and various non-Indian landowners. Under the 1855 Treaty of Point Elliot, 12 Stat. 927, a reservation bordering on the Puget Sound was set aside for the Tribe, and the Tribe reserved the right of taking fish. The Tribe claims a right to pump groundwater for a number of purposes, but most prominently for the supply of a salmon hatchery, designed in part to compensate for salmon runs depleted by dams, overfishing, and pollution. Although surface water is available, its quality is insufficient for purposes of operating the hatchery. The non-Indians, who also dwell within the boundaries of the Lummi reservation, claim groundwater rights under state law. The groundwater pumping of all parties has led to saltwater intrusion into the fresh groundwater. What sort of arguments do you expect would be raised by the opposing sides? Should it matter if the aquifer was discovered recently? Should it matter if the aquifer is found to extend beyond the exterior boundaries of the reservation?

UNITED STATES v. NEW MEXICO,
438 U.S. 696 (1978)

MR. JUSTICE REHNQUIST delivered the opinion of the Court.

The Rio Mimbres rises in the southwestern highlands of New Mexico and flows generally southward, finally disappearing in a desert sink just north of the Mexican border. The river originates in the upper reaches of the Gila National Forest, but during its course it winds more than 50 miles past privately owned lands and provides substantial water for both irrigation and mining. In 1970, a stream adjudication was begun by the State of New Mexico to determine the exact rights of each user to water from the Rio Mimbres. In this adjudication the United States claimed reserved water rights for use in the Gila National Forest. The State District Court held that the United States, in setting aside the Gila National Forest from other public lands, reserved the use of such water "as may be necessary for the purposes for which [the land was] withdrawn," but that these purposes did not include recreation, aesthetics, wildlife preservation, or cattle grazing. The United States appealed unsuccessfully to the Supreme Court of New Mexico. We granted certiorari to consider whether the Supreme Court of New Mexico had applied the correct principles of federal law in determining petitioner's reserved rights in the Mimbres. We now affirm.

I

The question posed in this case—what quantity of water, if any, the United States reserved out of the Rio Mimbres when it set aside the Gila National Forest in 1899—is a question of implied intent and not power. In *California v. United States*, 438 U.S. 645, at 653–663, we had occasion to discuss the respective authority of Federal and State Governments over waters in the Western States. The Court has previously concluded that whatever powers the States acquired over their waters as a result of congressional Acts and admission into the Union, however, Congress did not intend thereby to relinquish its authority to reserve unappropriated water in the future for use on appurtenant lands withdrawn from the public domain for specific federal purposes. *Winters v. United States*, 207 U.S. 564, 577 (1908); *Cappaert v. United States*, 426 U.S. 128, 143–146 (1976).

Recognition of Congress' power to reserve water for land which is itself set apart from the public domain, however, does not answer the question of the amount of water which has been reserved or the purposes for which the water may be used. Substantial portions of the public domain *have* been withdrawn and reserved by the United States for use as Indian reservations, forest reserves, national parks, and national monuments. And water is frequently necessary to achieve the purposes for which these reservations are made. But Congress has seldom expressly reserved water for use on these withdrawn lands. If water were abundant, Congress' silence would pose no problem. In the arid parts of the West, however, claims to water for use on federal reservations inescapably vie with other public and private claims for the limited quantities to be found in the rivers and streams. This competition is compounded by the sheer quantity of reserved lands in the Western States, which lands form brightly colored swaths across the maps of these States.[3]

The Court has previously concluded that Congress, in giving the President the power to reserve portions of the federal domain for specific federal purposes, *impliedly* authorized him to reserve "appurtenant water then unappropriated *to the extent needed to accomplish the purpose of the reservation.*" *Cappaert, supra*, at 138 (emphasis added). While many of the contours of what has come to be called the "implied-reservation-of-water doctrine" remain unspecified, the Court has repeatedly emphasized that Congress reserved "only that amount of water necessary to fulfill the purpose of the reservation, no more." *Cappaert, supra*, at 141. Each time this Court has applied the "implied-reservation-of-water doctrine," it has carefully examined both the asserted water right and the specific purposes for which the land was reserved, and concluded that without the water the purposes of the reservation would be entirely defeated.

This careful examination is required both because the reservation is implied, rather than expressed, and because of the history of congressional intent in the field of federal-state jurisdiction with respect to allocation of water. Where Congress has expressly addressed the question of whether federal entities must abide by state water law, it has almost invariably deferred to the state law. Where water is necessary to fulfill the very purposes for which a federal reservation was created, it is reasonable to conclude, even in the face of Congress' express deference to state water law in other areas, that the United States intended to reserve the necessary water. Where water is only valuable for a secondary use of the reservation, however, there arises the contrary inference that Congress intended, consistent with its other views, that the

---

3. The percentage of federally owned land (*excluding* Indian reservations and other trust properties) in the Western States ranges from 29.5% of the land in the State of Washington to 86.5% of the land in the State of Nevada, an average of about 46%. Of the land in the State of New Mexico, 33.6% is federally owned. Because federal reservations are normally found in the uplands of the Western States rather than the flat lands, the percentage of water flow originating in or flowing through the reservations is even more impressive. More than 60% of the average annual water yield in the 11 Western States is from federal reservations. The percentages of average annual water yield range from a low of 56% in the Columbia–North Pacific water resource region to a high of 96% in the Upper Colorado region. In the Rio Grande water resource region, where the Rio Mimbres lies, 77% of the average runoff originates on federal reservations.

United States would acquire water in the same manner as any other public or private appropriator.

Congress indeed has appropriated funds for the acquisition under state law of water to be used on federal reservations. Thus, in the National Park Service Act of Aug. 7, 1946, 60 Stat. 885, as amended, 16 U.S.C. § 17j–2 (1976 ed.), Congress authorized appropriations for the "[i]nvestigation and establishment of water rights *in accordance with local custom, laws, and decisions of courts,* including the acquisition of water rights or of lands or interests in lands or rights-of-way for use and protection of water rights necessary or beneficial in the administration and public use of the national parks and monuments." (Emphasis added.) The agencies responsible for administering the federal reservations have also recognized Congress' intent to acquire under state law any water not essential to the specific purposes of the reservation.[7] * * *

The United States contended that it was entitled to a minimum instream flow for "aesthetic, environmental, recreational and 'fish' purposes." 90 N.M., at 412, 564 P.2d, at 617. The Supreme Court of New Mexico concluded that, at least before the Multiple–Use Sustained–Yield Act of 1960, 74 Stat. 215, 16 U.S.C. § 528 et seq., national forests could only be created "to insure favorable conditions of water flow and to furnish a continuous supply of timber" and not for the purposes upon which the United States was now basing its asserted reserved rights in a minimum instream flow. 90 N.M., at 412–413, 564 P.2d, at 617–619. . . .

II

A

The quantification of reserved water rights for the national forests is of critical importance to the West, where, as noted earlier, water is scarce and where more than 50% of the available water either originates in or flows through national forests. When, as in the case of the Rio Mimbres, a river is fully appropriated, federal reserved water rights will frequently require a gallon-for-gallon reduction in the amount of water available for water-needy state and private appropriators. This reality has not escaped the attention of Congress and must be weighed in determining what, if any, water Congress reserved for use in the national forests.

The United States contends that Congress intended to reserve minimum instream flows for aesthetic, recreational, and fish-preservation purposes. An examination of the limited purposes for which Congress authorized the creation

---

7. Before this Court's decisions in *FPC v. Oregon,* 349 U.S. 435 (1955) and *Arizona v. California,* recognizing reserved rights outside of Indian reservations, the Forest Service apparently believed that all of its water had to be obtained under state law. "Rights to the use of water for National Forest purposes will be obtained in accordance with State law." Forest Service Manual (1936). While the Forest Service has apparently modified its policy since those decisions, their Service Manual still indicates a policy of deferring to state water law wherever possible. "The right of the States to appropriate and otherwise control the use of water is recognized, and the policy of the Forest Service is to abide by applicable State laws and regulations relating to water use. When water is needed by the Forest Service either for development of programs, improvements, or other uses, action will be taken promptly to acquire necessary water rights. . . ." Forest Service Handbook § 2514 (Feb. 1960). "The rights to use water for national forest purposes will be obtained in accordance with State law. This policy is based on the act of June 4, 1897 (16 U.S.C. [§] 481)." Forest Service Manual § 2514.1 (Jan. 1960).

of national forests, however, provides no support for this claim. [In the Organic Administration Act of June 4, 1897, 30 Stat. 34, 16 U.S.C. § 473 *et seq.* (1976 ed.), which governs the Forest Service,] Congress provided:

> *"No national forest shall be established, except to improve and protect the forest within the boundaries, or for the purpose of securing favorable conditions of water flows, and to furnish a continuous supply of timber for the use and necessities of citizens of the United States*; but it is not the purpose or intent of these provisions, or of [the Creative Act of 1891], to authorize the inclusion therein of lands more valuable for the mineral therein, or for agricultural purposes, than for forest purposes." 30 Stat. 35, as codified, 16 U.S.C. § 475 (1976 ed.) (emphasis added).

The legislative debates surrounding the Organic Administration Act of 1897 and its predecessor bills demonstrate that Congress intended national forests to be reserved for only two purposes—"[t]o conserve the water flows, and to furnish a continuous supply of timber for the people." 30 Cong.Rec. 967 (1897) (Cong. McRae). National forests were not to be reserved for aesthetic, environmental, recreational, or wildlife-preservation purposes.

> The objects for which the forest reservations should be made are the protection of the forest growth against destruction by fire and ax, and preservation of forest conditions upon which water conditions and water flow are dependent. The purpose, therefore, of this bill is to maintain favorable forest conditions, without excluding the use of these reservations for other purposes. They are not parks set aside for nonuse, but have been established for economic reasons. 30 Cong.Rec. 966 (1897) (Cong. McRae).
> * * *

Any doubt as to the relatively narrow purposes for which national forests were to be reserved is removed by comparing the broader language Congress used to authorize the establishment of national parks. In 1916, Congress created the National Park Service and provided that the

> "fundamental purpose of the said parks, monuments, and reservations ... is to conserve the scenery and the natural and historic objects and the wild life therein and to provide for the enjoyment of the same ... unimpaired for the enjoyment of future generations." National Park Service Act of 1916, 39 Stat. 535, § 1, as amended, 16 U.S.C. § 1 (1976 ed.).

When it was Congress' intent to maintain minimum instream flows within the confines of a national forest, it expressly so directed, as it did in the case of the Lake Superior National Forest:

> In order to preserve the shore lines, rapids, waterfalls, beaches and other natural features of the region in an unmodified state of nature, no further alteration of the natural water level of any lake or stream ... shall be authorized. 16 U.S.C. § 577b (1976 ed.). * * *

B

Not only is the Government's claim that Congress intended to reserve water for recreation and wildlife preservation inconsistent with Congress' failure to recognize these goals as purposes of the national forests, it would defeat the very purpose for which Congress did create the national forest system.

> [F]orests exert a most important regulating influence upon the flow of rivers, reducing floods and increasing the water supply in the low stages. The importance of their conservation on the mountainous watersheds

which collect the scanty supply for the arid regions of North America can hardly be overstated.... S. Doc. No. 105, 55th Cong., 1st Sess., 10 (1897).

The water that would be "insured" by preservation of the forest was to "be used for domestic, mining, milling, or irrigation purposes, under the laws of the State wherein such national forests are situated, or under the laws of the United States and the rules and regulations established thereunder." Organic Administration Act of 1897, 30 Stat. 36, 16 U.S.C. § 481 (1976 ed.). As this provision and its legislative history evidence, Congress authorized the national forest system principally as a means of enhancing the quantity of water that would be available to the settlers of the arid West. The Government, however, would have us now believe that Congress intended to partially defeat this goal by reserving significant amounts of water for purposes quite inconsistent with this goal.

C

In 1960, Congress passed the Multiple–Use Sustained–Yield Act of 1960, 74 Stat. 215, 16 U.S.C. § 528 *et seq.* (1976 ed.), which provides

> It is the policy of Congress that the national forests are established and shall be administered for outdoor recreation, range, timber, watershed, and wildlife and fish purposes. The purposes of sections 528 to 531 of this title are declared to be supplemental to, but not in derogation of, the purposes for which the national forests were established as set forth in the [Organic Administration Act of 1897.]

The Supreme Court of New Mexico concluded that this Act did not give rise to any reserved rights not previously authorized in the Organic Administration Act of 1897.... While we conclude that the Multiple–Use Sustained–Yield Act of 1960 was intended to broaden the purposes for which national forests had previously been administered, we agree that Congress did not intend to thereby expand the reserved rights of the United States.[21]

The Multiple–Use Sustained–Yield Act of 1960 establishes the purposes for which the national forests "*are* established and *shall* be administered." (Emphasis added.) The Act directs the Secretary of the Agriculture to administer all forests, including those previously established, on a multiple-use and sustained-yield basis. H.R. 10572, 86th Cong., 2d Sess., 1 (1960). In the administration of the national forests, therefore, Congress intended the Multiple–Use Sustained–Yield Act of 1960 to broaden the benefits accruing from all reserved national forests.

---

21. The United States does not argue that the Multiple–Use Sustained–Yield Act of 1960 reserved additional water for use on the national forests. Instead, the Government argues that the Act confirms that Congress *always* foresaw broad purposes for the national forests and authorized the Secretary of the Interior as early as 1897 to reserve water for recreational, aesthetic, and wildlife-preservation uses. As the legislative history of the 1960 Act demonstrates, however, Congress believed that the 1897 Organic Administration Act only authorized the creation of national forests for two purposes—timber preservation and enhancement of water supply—and intended, through the 1960 Act, to *expand* the purposes for which the national forests should be administered. *See, e.g.,* H.R. Rep. No. 1551, 86th Cong., 2d Sess., 4 (1960), U.S. Code Cong. & Admin. News 1960, p. 2377. Even if the 1960 Act expanded the reserved water rights of the United States, of course, the rights would be subordinate to any appropriation of water under state law dating to before 1960.

The House Report accompanying the 1960 legislation, however, indicates that recreation, range, and "fish" purposes are "to be supplemental to, but not in derogation of, the purposes for which the national forests were established" in the Organic Administration Act of 1897. H.R. Rep. No. 1551, 86th Cong., 2d Sess., 4 (1960), U.S. Code Cong. & Admin. News 1960, p. 2380. * * *

As discussed earlier, the "reserved rights doctrine" is a doctrine built on implication and is an exception to Congress' explicit deference to state water law in other areas. Without legislative history to the contrary, we are led to conclude that Congress did not intend in enacting the Multiple–Use Sustained–Yield Act of 1960 to reserve water for the *secondary* purposes there established. A reservation of additional water could mean a substantial loss in the amount of water available for irrigation and domestic use, thereby defeating Congress' principal purpose of securing favorable conditions of water flow. Congress intended the national forests to be administered for broader purposes after 1960 but there is no indication that it believed the new purposes to be so crucial as to require a reservation of additional water. By reaffirming the primacy of a favorable water flow, it indicated the opposite intent. * * *

IV

Congress intended that water would be reserved only where necessary to preserve the timber or to secure favorable water flows for private and public uses under state law. This intent is revealed in the purposes for which the national forest system was created and Congress' principled deference to state water law in the Organic Administration Act of 1897 and other legislation. The decision of the Supreme Court of New Mexico is faithful to this congressional intent and is therefore

Affirmed.

MR. JUSTICE POWELL, with whom MR. JUSTICE BRENNAN, MR. JUSTICE WHITE, and MR. JUSTICE MARSHALL join, dissenting in part.

I agree with the Court that the implied-reservation doctrine should be applied with sensitivity to its impact upon those who have obtained water rights under state law and to Congress' general policy of deference to state water law. . . .

I do not agree, however, that the forests which Congress intended to "improve and protect" are the still, silent, lifeless places envisioned by the Court. In my view, the forests consist of the birds, animals, and fish—the wildlife—that inhabit them, as well as the trees, flowers, shrubs, and grasses. I therefore would hold that the United States is entitled to so much water as is necessary to sustain the wildlife of the forests, as well as the plants. . . .

My analysis begins with the language of the statute. The Organic Administration Act of 1897, as amended, 16 U.S.C. § 475, provides (1976 ed.), in pertinent part:

No national forest shall be established, except to improve and protect the forest within the boundaries, or for the purpose of securing favorable conditions of water flows, and to furnish a continuous supply of timber for the use and necessities of citizens of the United States. . . .

Although the language of the statute is not artful, a natural reading would attribute to Congress an intent to authorize the establishment of national forests for three purposes, not the two discerned by the Court. The New Mexico Supreme Court gave the statute its natural reading in this case when it wrote:

The Act limits the purposes for which national forests are authorized to: 1) improving and protecting the forest, 2) securing favorable conditions of water flows, and 3) furnishing a continuous supply of timber. *Mimbres Valley Irrigation Co. v. Salopek*, 564 P.2d 615, 617 (1977).

Congress has given the statute the same reading, stating that under the Organic Administration Act of 1897 national forests may be established for "the purposes of improving and protecting the forest or for securing favorable conditions of water flows, and to furnish a continuous supply of timber...." H.R. Rep. No. 1551, 86th Cong., 2d Sess., 4 (1960), U.S. Code Cong. & Admin. News 1960, p. 2380. * * *

One may agree with the Court that Congress did not, by enactment of the Organic Administration Act of 1897, intend to authorize the creation of national forests simply to serve as wildlife preserves. But it does not follow from this that Congress did not consider wildlife to be part of the forest that it wished to "improve and protect" for future generations. It is inconceivable that Congress envisioned the forests it sought to preserve as including only inanimate components such as the timber and flora. Insofar as the Court holds otherwise, the 55th Congress is maligned and the Nation is the poorer, and I dissent.

QUESTIONS AND DISCUSSION

1. How does the Court's decision in *New Mexico* further refine and limit the reserved rights doctrine of *Cappaert*? What reasons does Justice Rehnquist give for narrowly construing the federal reserved rights doctrine? Are his reasons persuasive? What does Justice Rehnquist mean when he says that the "question posed in this case ... is a question of implied intent and not power"?

2. As indicated in the opinion, fully 60% of the water in the West originates in or flows through the national forests. How do you think that geophysical fact influenced the majority opinion?

3. Western water interests often ask: why imply water rights at all? Why not require the federal government to obtain state permits as it has done in numerous other instances? How would you respond to that argument? Does it matter that most of the states that issue permits for instream flow purposes assign that power to a state agency? *See supra* at 793. *But see State v. Morros*, 766 P.2d 263 (Nev. 1988) (affirming *in situ* water right granted to the BLM by the Nevada state engineer). If a state permit won't work, and if the purpose for which water is needed is secondary, is the federal government simply out of luck? Is there any way to obtain what has been awkwardly called a "non-reserved" federal water right other than under state law? Under the Supremacy Clause, the federal government can preempt state water laws that conflict with federal purposes and programs enacted within the scope of federal enumerated powers. But if Congress were to assert a water right by virtue of its regulatory authority, what would be the character of that right? Could Congress pass legislation asserting an out-of-priority right, or is it bound by the state priority system? If it did assert an out-of-priority right, would that be a taking? Consider a regulatory demand for water under the Clean Water Act or the Endangered Species Act. Are these non-reserved instream flow rights or just regulation? Does the distinction matter? A more difficult question is whether a federal natural resource agency, acting pursuant to its organic act, could assert a non-reserved water right for a secondary purpose, particularly when Congress in the Desert Land Act provided that non-navigable waters would be available for appropriation.

4. As is the case with Indian reserved water rights, many federal reserved rights remain unquantified because river basin adjudications are extremely complex. Professor Getches explains:

> Basin-wide adjudications can be massive in scope. In Idaho, the Snake River basin adjudication involves approximately 185,000 claims and has been in active litigation since 1987. The Gila River adjudication in Arizona began in 1974 and seeks to resolve the claims of 24,000 water users. In Oregon, the Department of Water Resources began an adjudication process in 1990, joining 25,000 claimants to determine federal and pre–1909 water rights in the Klamath Basin. Washington has been adjudicating rights in the Yakima River basin since 1977, with as many as 40,000 water users' interests at stake.

David H. Getches, *The Metamorphosis of Western Water Policy: Have Federal Laws and Local Decisions Eclipsed the States' Role*, 20 STAN. ENVTL. L.J, 3, 49 (2001). Adjudications are also time-consuming and costly. Professor Thorson notes:

> The commencement dates for most western adjudications suggest that the life of these proceedings is measured in decades. The commencement of the New Mexico adjudications extends from 1956 to 1984 and includes the Aamodt case, which is the oldest active case pending before a federal trial court in the entire country. In Utah, the adjudications have been ongoing in a serial fashion since the turn of the century and are likely to continue indefinitely. All the adjudications commenced in the 1970s, including those in Arizona, Montana, Washington, and Wyoming, are ongoing. Even in those states that are reasonably close to completion, Washington and Wyoming, judicial personnel estimate that at least five more years will be necessary. In the other large adjudications, such as Idaho, Montana, and Arizona, the cases can be expected to last another decade or two. * * *

> In addition to time, these adjudications take millions of dollars to complete. In proceedings that involve so many people and such an important resource, financial information is surprisingly fragmentary and incomplete, but even these figures are daunting. In Arizona, one attorney has estimated that state agency expenses and attorney's fees incurred by the major parties since 1974 total somewhere between $50 and $100 million. In Wyoming, the state agencies and court probably have spent between $30 and $40 million. In Idaho, the state has spent $20 million since 1985. In Montana, $22 million has been spent by the state agencies and water court since 1979. Texas' adjudication was completed at an estimated cost to the state of $20 million. Except for Arizona, these estimates do not include attorneys' fees and costs paid by private parties. None of these estimates includes the opportunity cost to the state as a result of its choice of expenditures.

See generally John E. Thorson, *State Watershed Adjudications: Approaches and Alternatives*, 42 ROCKY MTN. MIN. L. INST. 22–1, 22–43 (1996). *See also, United States v. Idaho*, 508 U.S. 1 (1993) (holding that United States consent to suit did not amount to a consent to pay the $10 million filing fees).

For the first half of the twentieth century, federal reserved rights (which at that time consisted of Indian reserved rights held in trust by the federal government) were also difficult to adjudicate because federal sovereign immunity precluded joining the United States in any litigation without its consent. In 1952, however, Senator McCarran of Nevada was able to attach a rider to a Department of Justice appropriations bill. The rider, which became known as the McCarran Amendment, gave consent "to join the United States as a defendant in any suit (1) for the adjudication of rights to the use of water of a river system or other source, or (2) for the administration of such rights, where it appears that the United States is the owner of ... water rights by appropriation under State law, by purchase, by exchange, or otherwise, and the United States is a necessary party to such suit." 43 U.S.C. § 666. Subsequent court decisions have elaborated on the McCarran Amendment. The waiver includes Indian reserved rights held in trust by the United States. *See Colorado River Water Conservation Dist. v. United States*, 424 U.S. 800 (1976). The waiver applies to suits in state or federal court, the result of which is that general adjudications usually occur in state court because federal courts typically abstain in favor of comprehensive state court adjudications of water rights. *Id.* The waiver applies only to *comprehensive* stream adjudications and not to private litigation. *See Dugan v. Rank*, 372 U.S. 609 (1963).

5.   National forests, of course, are only part of the federal landscape. Given what you know about other federal reservations (national parks and monuments, national recreation areas, wildlife refuges, wild and scenic rivers), do you think reserved water rights can be implied for them? On what would your analysis depend? The D.C. Circuit held that reserved rights do not attach to BLM lands because they are not dedicated to a particular purpose but are managed for multiple use. *Sierra Club v. Watt*, 659 F.2d 203 (D.C. Cir. 1981). The Wild & Scenic Rivers Act expressly reserves water rights, providing that "[d]esignation of any stream or portion thereof as a national wild, scenic or recreational river area shall not be construed as a reservation of the waters of such streams for purposes other than those specified in this chapter, or in quantities greater than necessary to accomplish these purposes." 16 U.S.C. § 1284(c). However, in the immediately preceding section of the statute, Congress stated: "Nothing in this chapter shall constitute an express or implied claim or denial on the part of the Federal government as to exemption from State water laws." *Id.* at 1284(b). Can these two sections be reconciled?

———

PROBLEM EXERCISE: RESERVED WATER RIGHTS FOR WILDERNESS IN IDAHO

The Snake River Basin Adjudication (SRBA) began in 1987 and now includes about 150,000 water rights claims, including 50,000 claims filed by the federal government for ten of its own agencies and four Indian tribes. Among the federal claims are claims to all unappropriated water in three wilderness areas: the Frank Church River of No Return Wilderness, the Gospel–Hump Wilderness, and the Selway–Bitterroot Wilderness. With reference to the following provisions of the Wilderness Act and the Central

Idaho Wilderness Act, analyze the United States' claim to a reserved right to all unappropriated water within Idaho's wilderness areas.

Wilderness Act of 1964, 16 U.S.C. § 1131(a). In order to assure that an increasing population, accompanied by expanding settlement and growing mechanization, does not occupy and modify all areas within the United States and its possessions, leaving no lands designated for preservation and protection in their natural condition, it is hereby declared to be the policy of the Congress to secure for the American people of present and future generations the benefits of an enduring resource of wilderness. For this purpose there is hereby established a National Wilderness Preservation System to be composed of federally owned areas designated by Congress as "wilderness areas," and these shall be administered for the use and enjoyment of the American people in such manner as will leave them unimpaired for future use and enjoyment as wilderness, and so as to provide for the protection of these areas, the preservation of their wilderness character, and for the gathering and dissemination of information regarding their use and enjoyment as wilderness; and no Federal lands shall be designated as "wilderness areas" except as provided for in this Act or by a subsequent Act.

§ 1131(c). A wilderness, in contrast with those areas where man and his own works dominate the landscape, is hereby recognized as an area where the earth and its community of life are untrammeled by man, where man himself is a visitor who does not remain. An area of wilderness is further defined to mean in this chapter an area of undeveloped federal land retaining its primeval character and influence, without permanent improvements or human habitation, which is protected and managed so as to preserve its natural conditions.

Wilderness Act of 1964, 16 U.S.C. § 1133(a). The purposes of this chapter are hereby declared to be within and supplemental to the purposes for which national forests and units of the national park and national wildlife refuge systems are established and administered. * * *

§ 1133(b). Except as otherwise provided in this chapter, each agency administering any area designated as wilderness shall be responsible for preserving the wilderness character of the area and shall so administer such area for such other purposes for which it may have been established as also to preserve its wilderness character. Except as otherwise provided in this chapter, wilderness areas shall be devoted to the public purposes of recreational, scenic, scientific, educational, conservation, and historical use. * * *

§ 1133(d)(4). Within wilderness areas in the national forests designated by this chapter, (1) the President may, within a specific area and in accordance with such regulations as he may deem desirable, authorize prospecting for water resources, the establishment and maintenance of reservoirs, water-conservation works, power projects, transmission lines, and other facilities needed in the public interest, including the road construction and maintenance essential to development and use thereof, upon his determination that such use or uses in the specific area will better serve the interests of the United States and the people thereof than will its denial....

§ 1133(d)(5). Nothing in this chapter shall constitute an express or implied claim or denial on the part of the Federal Government as to exemption from State water laws.

Central Idaho Wilderness Act of 1980, Pub. L. No. 96–312 § 2(a), 94 Stat. 948 (1980). The Congress finds that—,

(1) certain wildlands in central Idaho lying within the watershed of the Salmon River—the famous "River of No Return"—, constitute the largest block of

primitive and undeveloped land in the coterminous United States and are of immense national significance;

(2) these wildlands and a segment of the Salmon River should be incorporated within the National Wilderness Preservation System and the National Wild and Scenic Rivers System in order to provide statutory protection for the lands and waters and the wilderness-dependent wildlife and the resident and anadromous fish which thrive within this undisturbed ecosystem; and

(3) such protection can be provided without conflicting with established uses.

———

You may be curious to know the importance of this particular issue in Idaho. In October 1999, the Idaho Supreme Court, by a 3–2 decision, decided that the United States had impliedly reserved all unappropriated waters within the three wilderness areas. *See Potlatch Corp. v. United States*, No. 24546, 1999 WL 778325 (Idaho Oct. 1, 1999). The reaction was swift and negative. As Professor Blumm describes:

> Howls of protest in response to the court's wilderness reserved rights decision were registered by virtually every newspaper in the state. The largest, the Idaho Statesman, featured the decision across four columns on its front page and nearly a full page of the interior under the headline: "Court ruling could siphon Idahoans' water rights: If decision holds, thousands may lose water for homes, farming, business." Four days later, the paper's editorial page suggested that the result should cost Justice Silak [who was soon to sit for re-election] her Supreme Court seat.

> The virulent nature of the protest had to do with the fact that, unlike most wilderness areas, the Idaho wilderness areas are not at the headwaters of their watersheds. Instead, for example, the Salmon River flows through the towns of Stanley, Challis, and Salmon, as well as numerous private lands before entering the Frank Church River of No Return Wilderness downstream. * * *

> The court agreed to rehear the case in response to petitions from the state, several mining and irrigation companies, and upstream cities—and no doubt the public protest, which included sharp criticism from Idaho Governor Dirk Kempthorne. On February 12, 2001, Daniel Eismann, a district court judge and brother-in-law of then SRBA Presiding Judge Barry Wood, accepted the Idaho Statesman's challenge and decided to campaign against Justice Silak. Two days later, the Idaho Supreme Court reheard the case. In May 2000, ... Justice Silak was defeated for reelection by 32,000 votes, or eighteen percent....

> On October 27, 2000, five months after the election, and just over a year after its initial decision, the court reversed itself. [*Potlatch Corp. v. United States*, 12 P.3d 1260, 1264 (Idaho 2000)]. Just as in the initial decision, the decision on rehearing was by a 3–2 vote. This time, however, Chief Justice Trout—scheduled to face reelection [the following year]—switched her position and provided the necessary vote to deny the existence of federal wilderness water rights. Justice Silak, who remained on the court until her term expired at the end of 2000, wrote now in dissent instead of for the majority.

Michael C. Blumm, *Reversing the Winters Doctrine?: Denying Reserved Water Rights for Idaho Wilderness and Its Implications*, 73 U. COLO. L. REV. 173, 186–89 (2002). Professor Blumm describes the ultimate outcome of the case as a classic example of public choice theory. Why might he describe the result that way? Should the public reaction to the case have impacted the judges' interpretation of the law?

———

C. INTERSECTING FEDERAL STATUTES

As with the other resources studied in this casebook, until 1970, water law was primarily about allocation. Except for regulation, primarily under the Rivers and Harbors Act, of projects that had the potential to interfere with navigation, to the extent the federal government made inroads into water law, its focus was also largely on allocation. Although the doctrine of reserved rights, particularly reservations of instream flow, has significant environmental implications, that element of the doctrine was largely latent until the 1970s. Similarly, when the federal government passed the Reclamation Act and began its massive dam and irrigation projects, and when it involved itself in the allocation of interstate watercourses, a subject discussed later in this chapter, the federal focus was hardly environmental. Quite the contrary. Its actions had tremendous, often negative, impacts on the natural environment. With the rise of the environmental movement, this federal focus on water as a commodity began to change. And with that changing federal focus came the next challenge to the tradition of state control over water resources. In the sections that follow, we look briefly at two statutes that have had significant impact on state control of water resources and promise to have even greater impact in the future, namely the Clean Water Act and the Endangered Species Act.

1. THE CLEAN WATER ACT AND WETLANDS

Until 1972, states and local governments were the primary regulators of water quality. Historically, the primary form of "regulation" was common-law public and private nuisance claims. When state and local governments began to get involved and passed legislation or ordinances, their typical approach was to decide upon the use they wanted to make of a particular water body and then to set water quality standards to assure that the water was clean enough to support the identified use. Theoretically, if a particular pollutant exceeded the established water quality standard, the state would determine the respective contributions of the various polluters within the watershed and then "abate those discharges that cause[d] the criteria to be exceeded." Oliver A. Houck, *TMDLs: The Resurrection of Water Quality Standards–Based Regulation Under the Clean Water Act*, 27 ENVTL. L. RPTR. 10329, 10330 (1997). Unfortunately, assigning responsibility and enforcing compliance proved largely unworkable, and, by 1972, Congress decided that federal involvement was necessary. Congress' response came in the form of the 1972 Federal Water Pollution Control Act, denominated the Clean Water Act (CWA) in 1977 amendments. 33 U.S.C. §§ 1251–1387. The CWA took a different approach to water quality, largely eschewing water quality standards and instead adopting specific effluent limitations by reference to the best practical control technologies currently available. Compliance with those limitations would allow a polluter to obtain a National Pollutant Discharge Elimination System (NPDES) permit. 33 U.S.C. §§ 1342, 1311, 1362(14). Although the CWA removed significant control over the water resource from the states, the Act did require permit applicants to seek state certification of compliance with the CWA, which can include any appropriate requirement of state law. 33 U.S.C. § 1341(a). *See also PUD No. 1 v. Washington Dep't of Ecology*, 511 U.S. 700 (1994) (upholding Washington's imposition of minimum stream flow requirements to protect salmon and steelhead).

Although not without its critics, and even though it has not achieved its stated goal that "the discharge of pollutants into navigable waters be eliminated by 1985," 33 U.S.C. § 1251(a)(1), the CWA has been a significant success story. When the CWA was passed, it was estimated that 60–70% of the nation's lakes, rivers, and coastal waters were unsafe for fishing and swimming. The number has now been reduced to 39% for rivers, 45% for lakes, and 51% for estuaries, still high but certainly moving in a positive direction. *See* NANCY STONER, CLEAN WATER AT RISK (Natural Resources Defense Council 2002) (citing EPA statistics). Beyond this truncated description of the CWA's pollution control mechanisms, this casebook leaves that success story and the Act's details to survey courses on environmental law or to courses devoted entirely to the subject of water pollution control. This is not intended to ignore the real connections between water quality and water quantity (discussed at page 744) but simply to keep the focus on the policy and legal conundrums that animate natural resource use and preservation issues.

The aspect of the CWA that aligns itself most closely with natural resource policy drivers is the regulation of wetlands. Wetlands provide a range of ecosystem services, from trapping nutrients and sediments, to water purification and groundwater recharge, to support of bird, fish, and mammal populations. Wetlands also serve as natural sponges, soaking up water during times of peak runoff and then releasing the water slowly over time. A 1993 study in Illinois, for example, estimated that every 1% increase in wetlands along a stream corridor decreased peak stream flows by 3.7%. *See* James Salzman et al., *Protecting Ecosystem Services: Science, Economics and Law*, 20 STAN. ENVTL. L.J. 309, 319 (2001). While not sold in markets, all of these services have real value. Often, however, their value is only realized after the wetlands have been destroyed—when property owners survey their flooded homes or face a large tax increase to pay for a new plant to treat polluted drinking water. Opinions may differ over the value of a wetland's scenic vista, but they are in universal accord over the contributions of clean water and flood control to social welfare.

Since European settlement, the continental United States has lost roughly half of its wetlands through drainage, conversion, and erosion. The loss of wetlands slowed during the latter half of the twentieth century (from 458,000 acres per year from the mid 1950s to the mid 1970s, to 290,000 acres per year through the mid 1980s, to 58,500 acres per year between 1986 and 1997). U.S. Fish & Wildlife Service, *Status and Trends of Wetlands in the Coterminous United States 1998–2004, available at* http://www.fws.gov/nwi/PubsReports/trends_2005_report.pdf. The slowing of wetland destruction came as the public recognized the general importance of wetlands and administrations responded. During President George H.W.

Bush's campaign in 1988, he pledged to ensure there would be "no net loss" of wetlands. President Clinton reiterated this commitment in his own campaign four years later and then, on Earth Day 2004, President George W. Bush's administration called for a new commitment to attaining an overall increase in the quality and quantity of wetlands. Although wetland losses continue to occur in coastal areas and as a result of urban development, between 1998 and 2004, there was an estimated net gain of 32,000 acres per year and between 2004 and 2008 almost 1.2 million acres of wetlands were either restored or created. *See* http://www.whitehouse.gov/ceq/wetlands/2008/index.html. Whether the net gains have continued will await FWS publication of the next status and trends report, scheduled for 2010.

The CWA is the primary law conserving wetlands in the United States. Section 311 of the CWA broadly prohibits "the discharge of any pollutant by any person" into navigable waters and "pollutant" is defined broadly to include not only traditional contaminants but also solids such as "dredged spoil, . . . rock, sand, [and] cellar dirt." 33 U.S.C. § 1362(6). On its face, this would seem to prevent the filling of most wetlands. The CWA provides a limited exception to this prohibition in Section 404, which authorizes the Secretary of the Army to "issue permits, after notice and opportunity for public hearings, for the discharge of dredged or fill material into navigable waters at specified disposal sites." These permits, administered principally by the Army Corps of Engineers and known as "404 permits," "wetland permits," or "Corps permits," are the cornerstone of federal efforts to encourage protection of wetland resources. In granting 404 permits, the Corps' guidelines call for a "sequencing" approach which essentially lists wetland protection actions in the following order of desirability: (1) avoid filling wetland resources; (2) minimize adverse impacts to those wetlands that cannot reasonably be avoided; and (3) provide compensatory mitigation for those unavoidable adverse impacts that remain after all minimization measures have been exercised. *See Memorandum of Agreement Between Department of the Army and the Environmental Protection Agency Concerning the Clean Water Act Section 404(b)(1) Guidelines*, 55 Fed. Reg. 9210, 9211–12 (1990). Thus, when applying for a 404 permit, a developer must convince the Corps that no reasonable alternatives exist to the development of the wetlands, that the design of the development minimizes harm to the wetlands, and, if these two conditions have been satisfied, that other wetlands have been restored to compensate for the wetlands destroyed (known as "compensatory mitigation").

The 404 permit program has had a significant influence on development around the country, generating considerable opposition. Legal challenges to wetlands protections have attacked the definition of wetlands, the sequencing requirements, and the authority of the federal government. This last avenue has had some success, for if water quality and wetlands need to be regulated at a federal level, the question remains whether the federal government has the authority to do so, how far that authority extends, and just how much of that authority Congress intended to assert.

The following case touches on these questions, but before delving into the case, it is useful to recall the discussion at the beginning of this section on water federalism. Remember that federal authority over water was conceived initially as extending only to waters navigable in fact and that Congress did not even attempt general regulation of navigable waters until the Rivers and Harbors Acts in the 1890s. *Supra* at page 827. Given that history, when Congress in the Rivers and Harbors Act stated its intention to regulate "the navigable waters of the United States," Act of Mar. 3, 1899, ch. 425, 30 Stat. 1121, § 10, its meaning was relatively clear. It intended to extend its authority only to waters navigable in fact (i.e., those waters on which commerce could be conducted). But then came *Wickard v. Filburn*, 317 U.S. 111 (1942) which suggested that Congress had authority over any waters "affecting commerce" whether navigable or not. This change has wreaked some havoc in statutory interpretation. Although Congress could simply state its intention to regulate any waters affecting commerce, it has in certain statutes, including the Clean Water Act at issue in the following case, continued to state its intention to regulate only "navigable waters," "the waters of the United States," or similar phrases. Thus, discerning how much of its Commerce Clause authority Congress intended to assert is a more difficult interpretive task than it was with the Rivers and Harbors Act. The question is now whether Congress intended to regulate only waters navigable in fact, whether it meant to reach any activity on waters "affecting" interstate commerce, or whether it intended something in between those two.

RAPANOS v. UNITED STATES, 547 U.S. 715 (2006)

JUSTICE SCALIA announced the judgment of the Court, and delivered an opinion, in which THE CHIEF JUSTICE, JUSTICE THOMAS, and JUSTICE ALITO join.

In April 1989, petitioner John A. Rapanos backfilled wetlands on a parcel of land in Michigan that he owned and sought to develop. This parcel included 54 acres of land with sometimes-saturated soil conditions. The nearest body of navigable water was 11 to 20 miles away. Regulators had informed Mr. Rapanos that his saturated fields were "waters of the United States," 33 U.S.C. § 1362(7), that could not be filled without a permit. Twelve years of criminal and civil litigation ensued.

The burden of federal regulation on those who would deposit fill material in locations denominated "waters of the United States" is not trivial. In deciding whether to grant or deny a permit, the U.S. Army Corps of Engineers (Corps) exercises the discretion of an enlightened despot, relying on such factors as "economics," "aesthetics," "recreation," and "in general, the needs and welfare of the people," 33 CFR § 320.4(a) (2004). The average applicant for an individual permit spends 788 days and $271,596 in completing the process, and the average applicant for a nationwide permit spends 313 days and $28,915—not counting costs of mitigation or design changes. Sunding & Zilberman, The Economics of Environmental Regulation by Licensing: An Assessment of Recent Changes to the Wetland Permitting Process, 42 Natural Resources J. 59, 74–76 (2002). "[O]ver $1.7 billion is spent each year by the private and public sectors obtaining wetlands permits." *Id.,* at 81. These costs cannot be avoided, because the Clean Water Act "impose[s] criminal liability," as well as steep civil fines, "on a broad range of ordinary industrial and commercial activities." *Hanousek v. United States,* 528 U.S. 1102, 1103 (2000)

(THOMAS, J., dissenting from denial of certiorari). In this litigation, for example, for backfilling his own wet fields, Mr. Rapanos faced 63 months in prison and hundreds of thousands of dollars in criminal and civil fines. *See United States v. Rapanos,* 235 F.3d 256, 260 (C.A.6 2000). * * *

I

Congress passed the Clean Water Act (CWA or Act) in 1972. The Act's stated objective is "to restore and maintain the chemical, physical, and biological integrity of the Nation's waters." 86 Stat. 816, 33 U.S.C. § 1251(a). The Act also states that "[i]t is the policy of Congress to recognize, preserve, and protect the primary responsibilities and rights of States to prevent, reduce, and eliminate pollution, to plan the development and use (including restoration, preservation, and enhancement) of land and water resources, and to consult with the Administrator in the exercise of his authority under this chapter." § 1251(b).

One of the statute's principal provisions is 33 U.S.C. § 1311(a), which provides that "the discharge of any pollutant by any person shall be unlawful." "The discharge of a pollutant" is defined broadly to include "any addition of any pollutant to navigable waters from any point source," § 1362(12), and "pollutant" is defined broadly to include not only traditional contaminants but also solids such as "dredged spoil, . . . rock, sand, [and] cellar dirt," § 1362(6). And, most relevant here, the CWA defines "navigable waters" as "the waters of the United States, including the territorial seas." § 1362(7).

The Act also provides certain exceptions to its prohibition of "the discharge of any pollutant by any person." § 1311(a). Section 1342(a) authorizes the Administrator of the EPA to "issue a permit for the discharge of any pollutant, . . . notwithstanding section 1311(a) of this title." Section 1344 authorizes the Secretary of the Army, acting through the Corps, to "issue permits . . . for the discharge of dredged or fill material into the navigable waters at specified disposal sites." § 1344(a), (d). It is the discharge of "dredged or fill material"— which, unlike traditional water pollutants, are solids that do not readily wash downstream—that we consider today.

For a century prior to the CWA, we had interpreted the phrase "navigable waters of the United States" in the Act's predecessor statutes to refer to interstate waters that are "navigable in fact" or readily susceptible of being rendered so. *The Daniel Ball,* 10 Wall. 557, 563 (1871). After passage of the CWA, the Corps initially adopted this traditional judicial definition for the Act's term "navigable waters." *See* 39 Fed.Reg. 12119, codified at 33 CFR § 209.120(d)(1) (1974). After a District Court enjoined these regulations as too narrow, *Natural Resources Defense Council, Inc. v. Callaway,* 392 F. Supp. 685, 686 (DC 1975), the Corps adopted a far broader definition. *See* 40 Fed.Reg. 31324–31325 (1975); 42 Fed.Reg. 37144 (1977). The Corps' new regulations deliberately sought to extend the definition of "the waters of the United States" to the outer limits of Congress's commerce power. *See id.,* at 37144, n. 2.

The Corps' current regulations interpret "the waters of the United States" to include, in addition to traditional interstate navigable waters, 33 CFR § 328.3(a)(1) (2004), "[a]ll interstate waters including interstate wetlands," § 328.3(a)(2); "[a]ll other waters such as intrastate lakes, rivers, streams (including intermittent streams), mudflats, sandflats, wetlands, sloughs, prairie potholes, wet meadows, playa lakes, or natural ponds, the use, degradation or destruction of which could affect interstate or foreign commerce," § 328.3(a)(3); "[t]ributaries of [such] waters," § 328.3(a)(5); and "[w]etlands adjacent to [such] waters [and tributaries] (other than waters that are them-selves wetlands)," § 328.3(a)(7). The regulation defines "adjacent" wetlands as those "bordering, contiguous [to], or neighboring" waters of the United States. § 328.3(c). It specifically provides that "[w]etlands separated from other waters of the United States by man-made dikes or barriers, natural river berms, beach dunes and the like are 'adjacent wetlands.' " *Ibid.*

We first addressed the proper interpretation of 33 U.S.C. § 1362(7)'s phrase "the waters of the United States" in *United States v. Riverside Bayview Homes, Inc.,* 474 U.S. 121 (1985).... Noting that "the transition from water to solid ground is not necessarily or even typically an abrupt one," and that "the Corps must necessarily choose some point at which water ends and land begins," 474 U.S., at 132, we upheld the Corps' interpretation of "the waters of the United States" to include wetlands that "actually abut[ted] on" traditional navigable waters. *Id.,* at 135.

Following our decision in *Riverside Bayview,* the Corps adopted increasing-ly broad interpretations of its own regulations under the Act. For example, in 1986, to "clarify" the reach of its jurisdiction, the Corps announced the so-called "Migratory Bird Rule," which purported to extend its jurisdiction to any intrastate waters "[w]hich are or would be used as habitat" by migratory birds. 51 Fed.Reg. 41217. In addition, the Corps interpreted its own regulations to include "ephemeral streams" and "drainage ditches" as "tributaries" that are part of the "waters of the United States," *see* 33 CFR § 328.3(a)(5), provided that they have a perceptible "ordinary high water mark" as defined in § 328.3(e). 65 Fed.Reg. 12823 (2000). This interpretation extended "the waters of the United States" to virtually any land feature over which rainwater or drainage passes and leaves a visible mark—even if only "the presence of litter and debris." 33 CFR § 328.3(e)....

In *Solid Waste Agency of Northern Cook Cty. v. Army Corps of Engineers,* 531 U.S. 159 (2001) (*SWANCC*), we considered the application of the Corps' "Migratory Bird Rule" to "an abandoned sand and gravel pit in northern Illinois." 531 U.S., at 162. Observing that "[i]t was the *significant nexus* between the wetlands and 'navigable waters' that informed our reading of the CWA in *Riverside Bayview," id.,* at 167 (emphasis added), we held that *Riverside Bayview* did not establish "that the jurisdiction of the Corps extends to ponds that are not adjacent to open water." 531 U.S., at 168 (emphasis deleted). On the contrary, we held that "nonnavigable, isolated, intrastate waters," *id.,* at 171, which, unlike the wetlands at issue in *Riverside Bayview,* did not "actually abu[t] on a navigable waterway," 531 U.S., at 167, were not included as "waters of the United States."

Following our decision in *SWANCC,* the Corps did not significantly revise its theory of federal jurisdiction under § 1344(a). The Corps provided notice of a proposed rulemaking in light of *SWANCC,* 68 Fed.Reg.1991 (2003), but ultimately did not amend its published regulations. Because *SWANCC* did not directly address tributaries, the Corps notified its field staff that they "should continue to assert jurisdiction over traditional navigable waters ... and, generally speaking, their tributary systems (and adjacent wetlands)." 68 Fed. Reg.1998. In addition, because *SWANCC* did not overrule *Riverside Bayview,* the Corps continues to assert jurisdiction over waters " 'neighboring' " tradi-tional navigable waters and their tributaries. 68 Fed.Reg.1997 (quoting 33 CFR § 328.3(c) (2003)). * * *

II

In these consolidated cases, we consider whether four Michigan wetlands, which lie near ditches or man-made drains that eventually empty into traditional navigable waters, constitute "waters of the United States" within the meaning of the Act. The Rapanos and their affiliated businesses, deposited fill material without a permit into wetlands on three sites near Midland, Michigan: the "Salzburg site," the "Hines Road site," and the "Pine River site." The wetlands at the Salzburg site are connected to a man-made drain, which drains into Hoppler Creek, which flows into the Kawkawlin River, which empties into Saginaw Bay and Lake Huron. The wetlands at the Hines Road site are connected to something called the "Rose Drain," which has a surface connection to the Tittabawassee River. And the wetlands at the Pine River site have a surface connection to the Pine River, which flows into Lake Huron. It is not clear whether the connections between these wetlands and the nearby drains and ditches are continuous or intermittent, or whether the nearby drains and ditches contain continuous or merely occasional flows of water.

The United States brought civil enforcement proceedings against the Rapanos petitioners. The District Court found that the three described wetlands were "within federal jurisdiction" because they were "adjacent to other waters of the United States," and held petitioners liable for violations of the CWA at those sites. On appeal, the United States Court of Appeals for the Sixth Circuit affirmed, holding that there was federal jurisdiction over the wetlands at all three sites because "there were hydrological connections between all three sites and corresponding adjacent tributaries of navigable waters." 376 F.3d, at 643.

Petitioners in No. 04–1384, the Carabells, were denied a permit to deposit fill material in a wetland located on a triangular parcel of land about one mile from Lake St. Clair. A man-made drainage ditch runs along one side of the wetland, separated from it by a 4–foot–wide man-made berm. The berm is largely or entirely impermeable to water and blocks drainage from the wetland, though it may permit occasional overflow to the ditch. The ditch empties into another ditch or a drain, which connects to Auvase Creek, which empties into Lake St. Clair.

After exhausting administrative appeals, the Carabell petitioners filed suit in the District Court, challenging the exercise of federal regulatory jurisdiction over their site. The District Court ruled that there was federal jurisdiction because the wetland "is adjacent to neighboring tributaries of navigable waters and has a significant nexus to 'waters of the United States.' " Again the Sixth Circuit affirmed, holding that the Carabell wetland was "adjacent" to navigable waters. 391 F.3d 704, 708 (2004) *(Carabell)*.

We granted certiorari ... to decide whether these wetlands constitute "waters of the United States" under the Act, and if so, whether the Act is constitutional.

III

* * * We need not decide the precise extent to which the qualifiers "navigable" and "of the United States" restrict the coverage of the Act. Whatever the scope of these qualifiers, the CWA authorizes federal jurisdiction only over "waters." 33 U.S.C. § 1362(7). The only natural definition of the term "waters," our prior and subsequent judicial constructions of it, clear evidence from other provisions of the statute, and this Court's canons of construction all confirm that "the waters of the United States" in § 1362(7) cannot bear the expansive meaning that the Corps would give it.

The Corps' expansive approach might be arguable if the CSA defined "navigable waters" as "water of the United States." But "the waters of the United States" is something else. The use of the definite article ("the") and the plural number ("waters") show plainly that § 1362(7) does not refer to water in general. In this form, "the waters" refers more narrowly to water "[a]s found in streams and bodies forming geographical features such as oceans, rivers, [and] lakes," or "the flowing or moving masses, as of waves or floods, making up such streams or bodies." Webster's New International Dictionary 2882 (2d ed. 1954) (hereinafter Webster's Second). On this definition, "the waters of the United States" include only relatively permanent, standing or flowing bodies of water.[5] The definition refers to water as found in "streams," "oceans," "rivers," "lakes," and "bodies" of water "forming geographical features." *Ibid.* All of these terms connote continuously present, fixed bodies of water, as opposed to ordinarily dry channels through which water occasionally or intermittently flows. Even the least substantial of the definition's terms, namely "streams," connotes a continuous flow of water in a permanent channel—especially when used in company with other terms such as "rivers," "lakes," and "oceans." None of these terms encompasses transitory puddles or ephemeral flows of water.

The restriction of "the waters of the United States" to exclude channels containing merely intermittent or ephemeral flow also accords with the commonsense understanding of the term. In applying the definition to "ephemeral streams," "wet meadows," storm sewers and culverts, "directional sheet flow during storm events," drain tiles, man-made drainage ditches, and dry arroyos in the middle of the desert, the Corps has stretched the term "waters of the United States" beyond parody. The plain language of the statute simply does not authorize this "Land Is Waters" approach to federal jurisdiction. * * *

Our subsequent interpretation of the phrase "the waters of the United States" in the CWA likewise confirms this limitation of its scope. In *Riverside Bayview,* we stated that the phrase in the Act referred primarily to "rivers, streams, and other *hydrographic features more conventionally identifiable as 'waters' "* than the wetlands adjacent to such features. 474 U.S., at 131 (emphasis added). We thus echoed the dictionary definition of "waters" as referring to "streams and bodies *forming geographical features* such as oceans, rivers, [and] lakes." Webster's Second 2882 (emphasis added). Though we upheld in that case the inclusion of wetlands abutting such a "hydrographic featur[e]"—principally due to the difficulty of drawing any clear boundary between the two, *see* 474 U.S., at 132—nowhere did we suggest that "the waters of the United States" should be expanded to include, in their own right, entities other than "hydrographic features more conventionally identifiable as 'waters.' " * * *

Even if the phrase "the waters of the United States" were ambiguous as applied to intermittent flows, our own canons of construction would establish that the Corps' interpretation of the statute is impermissible. As we noted in *SWANCC,* the Government's expansive interpretation would "result in a significant impingement of the States' traditional and primary power over land and water use." 531 U.S., at 174. Regulation of land use, as through the issuance of the development permits sought by petitioners in both of these cases, is a quintessential state and local power. *See FERC v. Mississippi,* 456 U.S. 742,

---

5. By describing "waters" as "relatively permanent," we do not necessarily exclude streams, rivers, or lakes that might dry up in extraordinary circumstances, such as drought. We also do not necessarily exclude *seasonal* rivers, which contain continuous flow during some months of the year but no flow during dry months—such as the 290-day, continuously flowing stream postulated by Justice STEVENS' dissent (hereinafter the dissent). Common sense and common usage distinguish between a wash and seasonal river....

768, n. 30 (1982). The extensive federal jurisdiction urged by the Government would authorize the Corps to function as a *de facto* regulator of immense stretches of intrastate land—an authority the agency has shown its willingness to exercise with the scope of discretion that would befit a local zoning board. *See* 33 CFR § 320.4(a)(1) (2004). We ordinarily expect a "clear and manifest" statement from Congress to authorize an unprecedented intrusion into traditional state authority. *See BFP v. Resolution Trust Corporation,* 511 U.S. 531, 544 (1994). The phrase "the waters of the United States" hardly qualifies.

Likewise, just as we noted in *SWANCC,* the Corps' interpretation stretches the outer limits of Congress's commerce power and raises difficult questions about the ultimate scope of that power. *See* 531 U.S., at 173. (In developing the current regulations, the Corps consciously sought to extend its authority to the farthest reaches of the commerce power. *See* 42 Fed.Reg. 37127 (1977).) Even if the term "the waters of the United States" were ambiguous as applied to channels that sometimes host ephemeral flows of water (which it is not), we would expect a clearer statement from Congress to authorize an agency theory of jurisdiction that presses the envelope of constitutional validity. *See Edward J. DeBartolo Corp. v. Florida Gulf Coast Building & Constr. Trades Council,* 485 U.S. 568, 575 (1988).

In sum, on its only plausible interpretation, the phrase "the waters of the United States" includes only those relatively permanent, standing or continuously flowing bodies of water "forming geographic features" that are described in ordinary parlance as "streams[,] ... oceans, rivers, [and] lakes." *See* Webster's Second 2882. The phrase does not include channels through which water flows intermittently or ephemerally, or channels that periodically provide drainage for rainfall. The Corps' expansive interpretation of the "the waters of the United States" is thus not "based on a permissible construction of the statute." *Chevron U.S.A. Inc. v. Natural Resources Defense Council, Inc.,* 467 U.S. 837, 843 (1984).

IV

... [The Sixth Circuit] ... stated that, even if the ditches were not "waters of the United States," the wetlands were "adjacent" to *remote* traditional navigable waters in virtue of the wetlands' "hydrological connection" to them. *See id.,* at 639–640. This statement reflects the practice of the Corps' district offices, which may "assert jurisdiction over a wetland without regulating the ditch connecting it to a water of the United States." GAO Report 23. We therefore address in this Part whether a wetland may be considered "adjacent to" remote "waters of the United States," because of a mere hydrologic connection to them. * * *

When we characterized the holding of *Riverside Bayview* in *SWANCC,* we referred to the close connection between waters and the wetlands that they gradually blend into: "It was the *significant nexus* between the wetlands and 'navigable waters' that informed our reading of the CWA in *Riverside Bayview Homes.*" 531 U.S., at 167 (emphasis added). In particular, *SWANCC* rejected the notion that the ecological considerations upon which the Corps relied in *Riverside Bayview*—and upon which the dissent repeatedly relies today— provided an *independent* basis for including entities like "wetlands" (or "ephemeral streams") within the phrase "the waters of the United States." *SWANCC* found such ecological considerations irrelevant to the question whether physically isolated waters come within the Corps' jurisdiction. It thus confirmed that *Riverside Bayview* rested upon the inherent ambiguity in defining where water ends and abutting ("adjacent") wetlands begin, permitting the Corps' reliance on ecological considerations *only to resolve that ambiguity* in favor of treating all abutting wetlands as waters. Isolated ponds were not "waters of the United States" in their own right, *see* 531 U.S., at 167, and presented no boundary-drawing problem that would have justified the invocation of ecological factors to treat them as such.

Therefore, *only* those wetlands with a continuous surface connection to bodies that are "waters of the United States" in their own right, so that there is no clear demarcation between "waters" and wetlands, are "adjacent to" such waters and covered by the Act. Wetlands with only an intermittent, physically remote hydrologic connection to "waters of the United States" do not implicate the boundary-drawing problem of *Riverside Bayview,* and thus lack the necessary connection to covered waters that we described as a "significant nexus" in *SWANCC.* 531 U.S., at 167. Thus, establishing that wetlands such as those at the Rapanos and Carabell sites are covered by the Act requires two findings: First, that the adjacent channel contains a "wate[r] of the United States," (*i.e.,* a relatively permanent body of water connected to traditional interstate navigable waters); and second, that the wetland has a continuous surface connection with that water, making it difficult to determine where the "water" ends and the "wetland" begins.

V * * *

[R]espondents and many *amici* admonish that narrowing the definition of "the waters of the United States" will hamper federal efforts to preserve the Nation's wetlands. It is not clear that the state and local conservation efforts that the CWA explicitly calls for, *see* 33 U.S.C. § 1251(b), are in any way inadequate for the goal of preservation. In any event, a Comprehensive National Wetlands Protection Act is not before us, and the "wis[dom]" of such a statute (opinion of STEVENS, J.), is beyond our ken. What is clear, however, is that Congress did not enact one when it granted the Corps jurisdiction over only "the *waters* of the United States." * * *

VIII

Because the Sixth Circuit applied the wrong standard to determine if these wetlands are covered "waters of the United States," and because of the paucity of the record in both of these cases, the lower courts should determine, in the first instance, whether the ditches or drains near each wetland are "waters" in the ordinary sense of containing a relatively permanent flow; and (if they are) whether the wetlands in question are "adjacent" to these "waters" in the sense of possessing a continuous surface connection that creates the boundary-drawing problem we addressed in *Riverside Bayview.* * * *

We vacate the judgments of the Sixth Circuit in both No. 04–1034 and No. 04–1384, and remand both cases for further proceedings.

It is so ordered. * * *

JUSTICE KENNEDY, concurring in the judgment.

These consolidated cases require the Court to decide whether the term "navigable waters" in the Clean Water Act extends to wetlands that do not contain and are not adjacent to waters that are navigable in fact. In *Solid Waste Agency of Northern Cook Cty. v. Army Corps of Engineers,* 531 U.S. 159 (2001) *(SWANCC),* the Court held, under the circumstances presented there, that to constitute " 'navigable waters' " under the Act, a water or wetland must possess a "significant nexus" to waters that are or were navigable in fact or that could reasonably be so made. *Id.,* at 167, 172. In the instant cases neither the plurality opinion nor the dissent by Justice STEVENS chooses to apply this test; and though the Court of Appeals recognized the test's applicability, it did not consider all the factors necessary to determine whether the lands in question had, or did not have, the requisite nexus. In my view the cases ought to be remanded to the Court of Appeals for proper consideration of the nexus requirement. * * *

Twice before the Court has construed the term "navigable waters" in the Clean Water Act. In *United States v. Riverside Bayview Homes, Inc.,* 474 U.S. 121 (1985), the Court upheld the Corps' jurisdiction over wetlands adjacent to navigable-in-fact waterways. *Id.,* at 139. * * *

In *SWANCC,* the Court considered the validity of the Corps' jurisdiction over ponds and mudflats that were isolated in the sense of being unconnected to other waters covered by the Act. 531 U.S., at 171. The property at issue was an abandoned sand and gravel pit mining operation where "remnant excavation trenches" had "evolv[ed] into a scattering of permanent and seasonal ponds." *Id.,* at 163. Asserting jurisdiction pursuant to a regulation called the "Migratory Bird Rule," the Corps argued that these isolated ponds were "waters of the United States" (and thus "navigable waters" under the Act) because they were used as habitat by migratory birds. *Id.,* at 164–165. The Court rejected this theory. "It was the significant nexus between wetlands and 'navigable waters,'" the Court held, "that informed our reading of the [Act] in *Riverside Bayview Homes.*" *Id.,* at 167. Because such a nexus was lacking with respect to isolated ponds, the Court held that the plain text of the statute did not permit the Corps' action. *Id.,* at 172.

Riverside Bayview and *SWANCC* establish the framework for the inquiry in the cases now before the Court: Do the Corps' regulations, as applied to the wetlands in *Carabell* and the three wetlands parcels in *Rapanos,* constitute a reasonable interpretation of "navigable waters" as in *Riverside Bayview* or an invalid construction as in *SWANCC?* Taken together these cases establish that in some instances, as exemplified by *Riverside Bayview,* the connection between a nonnavigable water or wetland and a navigable water may be so close, or potentially so close, that the Corps may deem the water or wetland a "navigable water" under the Act. In other instances, as exemplified by *SWANCC,* there may be little or no connection. Absent a significant nexus, jurisdiction under the Act is lacking. Because neither the plurality nor the dissent addresses the nexus requirement, this separate opinion, in my respectful view, is necessary. * * *

Congress' choice of words creates difficulties, for the Act contemplates regulation of certain "navigable waters" that are not in fact navigable. Nevertheless, the word "navigable" in the Act must be given some effect. . . .

Consistent with *SWANCC* and *Riverside Bayview* and with the need to give the term "navigable" some meaning, the Corps' jurisdiction over wetlands depends upon the existence of a significant nexus between the wetlands in question and navigable waters in the traditional sense. The required nexus must be assessed in terms of the statute's goals and purposes. Congress enacted the law to "restore and maintain the chemical, physical, and biological integrity of the Nation's waters," 33 U.S.C. § 1251(a), and it pursued that objective by restricting dumping and filling in "navigable waters," §§ 1311(a), 1362(12). With respect to wetlands, the rationale for Clean Water Act regulation is, as the Corps has recognized, that wetlands can perform critical functions related to the integrity of other waters—functions such as pollutant trapping, flood control, and runoff storage. 33 CFR § 320.4(b)(2). Accordingly, wetlands possess the requisite nexus, and thus come within the statutory phrase "navigable waters," if the wetlands, either alone or in combination with similarly situated lands in the region, significantly affect the chemical, physical, and biological integrity of other covered waters more readily understood as "navigable." When, in contrast, wetlands' effects on water quality are speculative or insubstantial, they fall outside the zone fairly encompassed by the statutory term "navigable waters." * * *

As applied to wetlands adjacent to navigable-in-fact waters, the Corps' conclusive standard for jurisdiction rests upon a reasonable inference of ecologic interconnection, and the assertion of jurisdiction for those wetlands is sustainable under the Act by showing adjacency alone. . . .

The Corps' existing standard for tributaries, however, provides no such assurance. . . . [T]he breadth of this standard—which seems to leave wide room for regulation of drains, ditches, and streams remote from any navigable-in-fact water and carrying only minor water-volumes towards it—precludes its adoption as the determinative measure of whether adjacent wetlands are likely to play an important role in the integrity of an aquatic system comprising navigable waters as traditionally understood. Indeed, in many cases wetlands adjacent to tributaries covered by this standard might appear little more related to navigable-in-fact waters than were the isolated ponds held to fall beyond the Act's scope in *SWANCC*.

When the Corps seeks to regulate wetlands adjacent to navigable-in-fact waters, it may rely on adjacency to establish its jurisdiction. Absent more specific regulations, however, the Corps must establish a significant nexus on a case-by-case basis when it seeks to regulate wetlands based on adjacency to nonnavigable tributaries. Given the potential overbreadth of the Corps' regulations, this showing is necessary to avoid unreasonable applications of the statute. . . .

In both the consolidated cases before the Court the record contains evidence suggesting the possible existence of a significant nexus according to the principles outlined above. Thus the end result in these cases and many others to be considered by the Corps may be the same as that suggested by the dissent, namely, that the Corps' assertion of jurisdiction is valid. Given, however, that neither the agency nor the reviewing courts properly considered the issue, a remand is appropriate, in my view, for application of the controlling legal standard. * * *

JUSTICE STEVENS, with whom JUSTICE SOUTER, JUSTICE GINSBURG, and JUSTICE BREYER join, dissenting. * * *

In my view, the proper analysis is straightforward. The Army Corps has determined that wetlands adjacent to tributaries of traditionally navigable waters preserve the quality of our Nation's waters by, among other things, providing habitat for aquatic animals, keeping excessive sediment and toxic pollutants out of adjacent waters, and reducing downstream flooding by absorbing water at times of high flow. The Corps' resulting decision to treat these wetlands as encompassed within the term "waters of the United States" is a quintessential example of the Executive's reasonable interpretation of a statutory provision. *See Chevron U.S.A. Inc. v. Natural Resources Defense Council, Inc.,* 467 U.S. 837, 842–845 (1984). * * *

II

Our unanimous opinion in *Riverside Bayview* squarely controls these cases. * * *

Contrary to the plurality's revisionist reading today, *Riverside Bayview* nowhere implied that our approval of "adjacent" wetlands was contingent upon an understanding that "adjacent" means having a "continuous surface connection" between the wetland and its neighboring creek. Instead, we acknowledged that the Corps defined "adjacent" as including wetlands " 'that form the border of or are in reasonable proximity to other waters' " and found that the Corps reasonably concluded that adjacent wetlands are part of the waters of the United States. 474 U.S., at 134 (quoting 42 Fed.Reg. 37128 (1977)). Indeed, we explicitly acknowledged that the Corps' jurisdictional determination was reasonable even though

> not every adjacent wetland is of great importance to the environment of adjoining bodies of water. . . . If it is reasonable for the Corps to conclude that in the majority of cases, adjacent wetlands have significant effects on water quality and the ecosystem, its definition can stand. That the definition may include some wetlands that are not significantly intertwined with the ecosystem of adjacent waterways is of little moment, for where it appears that a wetland covered by the Corps' definition is in fact lacking in importance to the aquatic environment . . . the Corps may always allow development of the wetland for other uses simply by issuing a permit.

474 U.S., at 135 n.9. * * *

Disregarding the importance of *Riverside Bayview,* the plurality relies heavily on the Court's subsequent opinion in *Solid Waste Agency of Northern Cook Cty. v. Army Corps of Engineers,* 531 U.S. 159 (2001) *(SWANCC).* In stark contrast to *Riverside Bayview,* however, *SWANCC* had nothing to say about wetlands, let alone about wetlands adjacent to traditionally navigable waters or their tributaries. Instead, *SWANCC* dealt with a question specifically reserved by *Riverside Bayview,* namely, the Corps' jurisdiction over isolated waters— " 'waters that are *not* part of a tributary system to interstate waters or to navigable waters of the United States, the degradation or destruction of which could affect interstate commerce.' " 531 U.S., at 168–169 (quoting 33 CFR § 323.2(a)(5) (1978); emphasis added). . . .

Unlike *SWANCC* and like *Riverside Bayview,* the cases before us today concern wetlands that are adjacent to "navigable bodies of water [or] their tributaries," 474 U.S., at 123. Specifically, these wetlands abut tributaries of traditionally navigable waters. . . . Given that wetlands serve these important water quality roles and given the ambiguity inherent in the phrase "waters of the United States," the Corps has reasonably interpreted its jurisdiction to cover non-isolated wetlands. *See* 474 U.S., at 131–135.

This conclusion is further confirmed by Congress' deliberate acquiescence in the Corps' regulations in 1977. *Id.,* at 136. Both Chambers conducted extensive debates about the Corps' regulatory jurisdiction over wetlands, rejected efforts to limit this jurisdiction, and appropriated funds for a " 'National Wetlands Inventory' " to help the States " 'in the development and operation of programs under this Act.' " *Id.,* at 135–139 (quoting 33 U.S.C. § 1288(i)(2)). . . .

The Corps' exercise of jurisdiction is reasonable even though not every wetland adjacent to a traditionally navigable water or its tributary will perform all (or perhaps any) of the water quality functions generally associated with wetlands. *Riverside Bayview* made clear that jurisdiction does not depend on a wetland-by-wetland inquiry. 474 U.S., at 135, n. 9. Instead, it is enough that wetlands adjacent to tributaries generally have a significant nexus to the watershed's water quality. If a particular wetland is "not significantly intertwined with the ecosystem of adjacent waterways," then the Corps may allow its development "simply by issuing a permit." *Ibid.* * * *

In final analysis, however, concerns about the appropriateness of the Corps' 30–year implementation of the Clean Water Act should be addressed to Congress or the Corps rather than to the Judiciary. Whether the benefits of particular conservation measures outweigh their costs is a classic question of public policy that should not be answered by appointed judges. * * *

IV

While I generally agree with Parts I and II–A of Justice KENNEDY's opinion, I do not share his view that we should replace regulatory standards that have been in place for over 30 years with a judicially crafted rule distilled from the term "significant nexus" as used in *SWANCC.* * * *

V

I would affirm the judgments in both cases, and respectfully dissent from the decision of five Members of this Court to vacate and remand. I close, however, by noting an unusual feature of the Court's judgments in these cases. It has been our practice in a case coming to us from a lower federal court to enter a judgment commanding that court to conduct any further proceedings pursuant to a specific mandate. That prior practice has, on occasion, made it necessary for Justices to join a judgment that did not conform to their own views. In these cases, however, while both the plurality and Justice Kennedy agree that there must be a remand for further proceedings, their respective opinions define different tests to be applied on remand. Given that all four Justices who have joined this opinion would uphold the Corps' jurisdiction in both of these cases—and in all other cases in which either the plurality's or Justice Kennedy's test is satisfied—on remand each of the judgments should be reinstated if *either* of those tests is met.

JUSTICE BREYER, dissenting.

In my view, the authority of the Army Corps of Engineers under the Clean Water Act extends to the limits of congressional power to regulate interstate commerce. *See Solid Waste Agency of Northern Cook Cty. v. Army Corps of Engineers,* 531 U.S. 159, 181–182 (2001) (*SWANCC*) (STEVENS, J., dissenting). I therefore have no difficulty finding that the wetlands at issue in these cases are within the Corps' jurisdiction, and I join Justice STEVENS' dissenting opinion.

My view of the statute rests in part upon the nature of the problem. The statute seeks to "restore and maintain the chemical, physical, and biological integrity of the Nation's waters." 33 U.S.C. § 1251(a). Those waters are so various and so intricately interconnected that Congress might well have decided the only way to achieve this goal is to write a statute that defines "waters" broadly and to leave the enforcing agency with the task of restricting the scope of that definition, either wholesale through regulation or retail through development permissions. That is why I believe that Congress, in using the term "waters of the United States," § 1362(7), intended fully to exercise its relevant Commerce Clause powers.

I mention this because the Court, contrary to my view, has written a "nexus" requirement into the statute. But it has left the administrative powers of the Army Corps of Engineers untouched. That agency may write regulations defining the term—something that it has not yet done. And the courts must give those regulations appropriate deference. *Chevron U.S.A. Inc. v. Natural Resources Defense Council, Inc.,* 467 U.S. 837 (1984).

If one thing is clear, it is that Congress intended the Army Corps of Engineers to make the complex technical judgments that lie at the heart of the present cases (subject to deferential judicial review). In the absence of updated regulations, courts will have to make ad hoc determinations that run the risk of transforming scientific questions into matters of law. That is not the system Congress intended. Hence I believe that today's opinions, taken together, call for the Army Corps of Engineers to write new regulations, and speedily so.

QUESTIONS AND DISCUSSION

1. Which opinion controls? How helpful will *Rapanos* be to lower courts and the agency attempting to implement its guidance?

2. How does each opinion ultimately propose to define waters of the United States?

3. What range of regulatory options are open to the Corps of Engineers? How far can it go in redefining "waters of the United States"? What range of options are available to Congress?

4. How faithful is each opinion to the Supreme Court's holding in *Chevron U.S.A., Inc. v. Natural Resources Defense Council, Inc.,* 467 U.S. 837 (1984), discussed in Chapter 3 above, that in the absence of clear statutory language, the Court should defer to an agency's interpretation as long as it is a "permissible" construction of the statute?

5. The various opinions in the case focus on whether Congress intended the Corps to be able to regulate the type of wetlands at issue when it used the phrase "waters of the United States." But what of the constitutional issue? How would the justices have decided the case if Congress had specifically asserted authority to protect the wetlands at issue in this case or the isolated ponds in *SWANCC*?

6. Is it a sufficient answer to critics of the plurality and Justice Kennedy that Congress can simply legislate to make clear its intention to assert the widest possible jurisdiction under the Clean Water Act? If not, how much weight should be given to Congress' 1977 acquiescence in the Corps' regulation, which is discussed by Justice Stevens?

7. Do you see any similarities between the plurality opinion in *Rapanos* and Chief Justice Rehnquist's opinion in *New Mexico*? Do you see similarities between the primary purpose doctrine of *New Mexico* and the narrow construction of the Corps' jurisdiction over wetlands? What do these Justices seem to be saying to Congress?

8. Whatever the limitation on federal power over wetlands, can't states pass laws protecting wetlands? Is that a satisfactory answer to the decision's critics?

9. Think about the ecosystem services provided by wetlands. Is the interest in those services primarily local or national? Are the services best secured by state or federal regulation? In the absence of federal regulation of isolated wetlands, what is likely to happen to such wetlands?

10. Thinking broadly about the Clean Water Act and wetlands, what sorts of policy justifications are there for federal regulatory intervention? Is it enough to justify federal involvement that the states simply were not doing a very good job of cleaning up their water? Are there any scale concerns that justify federal involvement in this area? To the extent the Court takes a narrower view of the scope of regulation permitted by the Commerce Clause, as it hints in this case, how often will that limitation inhibit management of water resources according to the appropriate scale?

11. Notwithstanding its official status as the least-favored alternative in the agencies' sequence of preferences, compensatory mitigation quickly proved popular because it freed at least some highly valued wetlands for more comprehensive and flexible development. Building a shopping center around an avoided wetlands site on choice commercial development land could, for example, present costly design constraints. Compensatory mitigation allowed the developer to evaluate whether the compensatory land swap was superior to the avoidance strategy. Compensatory mitigation thus took some of the "sting" out of 404 permits and reduced the frequency of incidents when 404 permitting could be portrayed as unreasonably obstructive.

Nonetheless, the strict mitigation requirements remained unpopular with developers, who started exerting significant political pressure in the 1980s to loosen up the 404 permitting process. Of particular concern to developers was that, if closely followed, the Corps' guidelines provided few opportunities for market transactions to arise because the mitigation was supposed to take place onsite. Calls for reform of the 404 program came from environmentalists, as well. While attractive in theory and providing some political shelter, the project-by-project compensatory mitigation approach was widely regarded as having failed miserably in terms of environmental protection. Whether on-site or near-site, the piecemeal approach complicated the Corps' ability to articulate mitigation performance standards, monitor success, and enforce conditions. Many developers went through the motions of so-called landscape mitigation—planting what was required or regrading where required to meet the minimum letter of the permit—then moved on, leaving the "restored wetland" to revert back to its original habitat, usually a wetland in name only, if even that. A Florida state agency study found a meager 27 percent success rate of such projects. Lawrence R. Liebesman & David M. Plott, *The Emergence of Private Wetlands Mitigation Banking*, 13 NAT. RESOURCES & ENV'T 341 (1998).

In light of these problems, the Corps and EPA (supported by many scholars) started shifting compensatory activities from on-site to off-site mitigation, thus opening the door for greater use of market instruments, in particular, the wetlands mitigation banking (WMB) technique. This approach, its proponents argued, would prove advantageous both in terms of efficiency and ecological benefits, aggregating small wetlands threatened by development into larger restored wetlands in a different location. As the diagram below shows, in WMB, a "bank" of wetlands habitat is created, restored, or preserved and then made available to developers of wetlands habitat who must "buy" habitat mitigation as a condition of government approval for development. This mechanism has also provided a model for endangered species protection and is in the process of being extended to other settings including watershed protection.

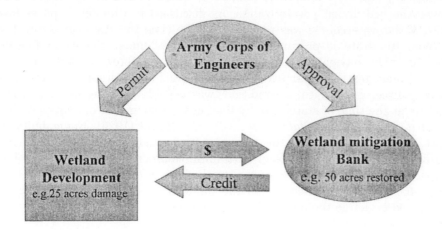

In commercial terms WMB has been a great success, with commercial wetlands banks being created all over the country. Politically, WMB has been effective, as well, muting calls for weakening of the 404 permit program. In terms of ecosystem service provision, however, the program has fared less well. For example, despite claims by the Maryland Department of the Environment that the state had gained 122 acres of wetlands between 1991 and 1996, a Chesapeake Bay Foundation study found that there had been a net *loss* of fifty-one acres of wetlands functions. In the most comprehensive study to date on this issue, in 2001 the National Academy of Sciences examined the practice of wetlands compensatory mitigation. The very first of the Committee's Principal Findings was that "the goal of no net loss of wetlands is not being met for wetland functions by the mitigation program."

One of the main reasons for this poor performance is that the currency used for trading is inadequate. Destroyed and restored wetlands are usually measured solely in terms of acreage rather than service provision. That is, developers are commonly required to mitigate two acres of wetland for every acre of filled wetland (or some other ratio). They are not required to mitigate based on how much flood control or water quality the filled wetland provided. Not surprisingly, most wetlands development takes place in densely populated areas, where the services are highly valued, and most wetland banks are located in rural, sparsely populated areas where land is cheap and services are likely redundant. For more on the WMB program and an explanation for its failure to ensure service provision, see James Salzman and J. B. Ruhl, *Currencies and the Commodification of Environmental Law*, 53 STAN. L. REV. 607 (2000).

How does this information about mitigation projects affect your view of the relatively encouraging report in the text (p. 853) that there has been a net gain in wetland acreage since 1998?

12. The meaning of navigability turns out to be important in a variety of contexts in water law. In addition to defining the scope of admiralty jurisdiction and indicating Congress' intent to assert some or all of its regulatory authority under the Commerce Clause, navigability decides who owns the bed under a watercourse. As discussed in Chapter 2, pages 96–104, if the watercourse was navigable at the time the state came into the Union, the state is presumed to own the bed under the equal footing doctrine. This navigability-for-title test is slightly different than the navigability-in-fact test. Navigability for title depends on whether the particular watercourse, in its natural condition, was capable of being used for commerce, at the time of statehood, by then customary modes of transport. *See United States v. Holt State Bank*, 270 U.S. 49, 56 (1926). Navigability in fact depends on whether the waterway previously, presently, or in the future was/is/will be capable of sustaining commerce with reasonable improvements. *See United States v. Appalachian Elec. Power Co.*, 311 U.S. 377, 407 (1940). As discussed in the following case study, navigability is also used to define the scope of what is known as the navigation servitude.

———

CASE STUDY: THE NAVIGATION SERVITUDE

Until the 1890s, federal power over navigation was infrequently asserted and understood as wholly regulatory in nature. The federal government could regulate what happened on navigable waters, but that regulatory authority did not create any ownership interest in those waters. As the Court stated in 1893:

> It cannot be doubted, in view of the long list of authorities,—for many more might be cited,—that Congress has the power in its discretion to compel the removal of this lock and dam as obstructions to the navigation of the river, or to condemn and take them for the purpose of promoting navigability. . . .

> But like the other powers granted to Congress by the Constitution, the power to regulate commerce is subject to all the limitations imposed by such instrument, and among them is that of the Fifth Amendment. . . .

Monongahela Navigation Co. v. United States, 148 U.S. 312, 336 (1893). In 1897, however, the Court changed its tune and held that federal power to protect navigation actually constituted federal immunity from compensation when submerged lands were taken to promote or protect navigation. *See Gibson v. United States*, 166 U.S. 269 (1897). A commonly-cited explanation for this immunity, which is known as the navigation servitude, was offered by the Supreme Court in *United States v. Chicago, M., St. P. & P.R.R.*, 312 U.S. 592 (1941):

> The dominant power of the federal government, as has been repeatedly held, extends to the entire bed of a stream, which includes the lands below ordinary high-water mark. The exercise of the power within these limits is not an invasion of any private property right in such lands for which the United States must make compensation. The damage sustained results not from a taking of the riparian owner's property in the stream bed, but from the lawful exercise of a power to which that property has always been subject.

Id. at 596–97 (citations omitted). The navigation servitude has thus some-times been conceived of as an easement that grows out of federal power to regulate navigation but that is different from, and narrower than, the power to regulate commerce. *See United States v. Kansas City Life Ins. Co.*, 339 U.S. 799, 808 (1950) ("It is not the broad constitutional power to regulate commerce, but rather the servitude derived from that power and narrower in scope, that frees the government from liability. . . ."). As the navigation servitude doctrine has developed, the United States need not pay compensation when it removes a riparian's access to a navigable waterway or impairs the flow of a navigable waterway. *United States v. Willow River Power Co.*, 324 U.S. 499 (1945); *United States v. Chandler–Dunbar Water Power Co.*, 229 U.S. 53, 74–76 (1913). And when the United States condemns land adjacent to a navigable watercourse, it need not compensate the owner of the land for the portion of its value attributable to the presence of the navigable waterway. *See, e.g., United States v. Rands*, 389 U.S. 121, 124–25 (1967); *United States v. Twin City Power Co.*, 350 U.S. 222, 225–26 (1956). Even though property next to a navigable stream may be valuable chiefly as a potential port site or hydroelectric site, that fact will not be part of the just compensation calculation. *Id.*

This general immunity from Fifth Amendment takings claims under the navigation servitude is much like the state's immunity from Fourteenth Amendment takings claims under the public trust doctrine. As suggested by *Illinois Central* and its progeny, because of the state's public trust obligation, it cannot convey fee title in land beneath navigable water. The most that a grantee can receive is title subject to an easement in favor of the state. And thus any subsequent exercise of the state's dominant servitude could not be a taking of private property. If the states had a trust obligation to protect navigation, commerce, and fishery, the United States can be said to have inherited from the states in the Constitution, via the Commerce Clause, the dominant servitude (and trust obligation) with respect to navigation. Thus, when the United States exercises its dominant servitude in favor of navigation, it likewise need not pay any compensation. As discussed previously, this conception of the sovereign's trust obligation is historically debatable, but it forms the core of the current understanding of both the public trust doctrine and the navigation servitude. The alterna-tive view, which has not carried the day, is that Congress and state legislatures, as the people's representatives, should have the authority, limited by the federal and state constitutions, to grant private rights in navigation, the fishery, and other trust resources, and when subsequent regulation of those private rights "goes too far," compensation should be awarded. *See* James R. Rasband, *Equitable Compensation for Public Trust Takings*, 69 U. COLO. L. REV. 331, 360–71 (1998).

QUESTIONS AND DISCUSSION

1. Just as the expansion of the public trust doctrine in cases like *National Audubon*, *supra* page 799, from *land* under navigable water to appropria-tive water rights has significant implications for allocation of the water resource, so too would expansion of the navigation servitude. What if, for example, the no compensation rule of the navigation servitude were extended to water rights themselves? Suppose, for example, the United States intended to build a hydropower dam on a navigable river and proposed to condemn the adjacent lands that would be flooded. Under the *Rands* decision, *supra*, the navigation servitude exempts the United States from paying for that portion of the land's value attributable to the presence of the navigable waterway. 389 U.S. at 124–25. Does that mean that if the adjacent land were irrigated farmland, the farm land would have to be valued as desert land for purposes of determining the United States' compensation obligation? Or to take it the next step, suppose the United States were to demand an irrigator's water to provide an endangered fish greater river flow, a goal plainly within Congress' Commerce Clause power although one not particularly related to navigation. Could the United States claim that the protection of the fish was within the scope of the United States' navigation servitude and thus taking the water was noncompensable? *See* Eva H. Morreale, *Federal Power in Western Waters: The Navigation Power and the Rule of No Compensation*, 3 Nat. Resources J. 1, 75 (1963) (concluding that on purely logical terms the navigation servitude could extend that far).

Despite the potential reach of the navigation servitude, its scope has been limited by subsequent events. In *Kaiser Aetna v. United States*, 444 U.S. 164 (1979), the Supreme Court rejected an argument that the servitude was coextensive with the test of navigability-in-fact and held that the servitude does not extend to waters rendered navigable in fact by improvement (in that case a marina in Hawaii for which an ocean outlet had been dredged). Also, in Section 111 of the Rivers and Harbors Flood Control Act of 1970, Congress waived its immunity from compensation and provided that where the United States takes real property "for the public use in connection with any improvement of rivers, harbors, canals, or waterways of the United States," compensation should be calculated based upon the property owner's access to or utilization of navigable waters. 33 U.S.C. § 595a.

2. In light of federal reserved water rights, Congress' power over water under the Commerce Clause, and the navigation servitude, do the states really "own" the water within their boundaries? What is the real content and meaning of a state constitutional provision like that of Colorado which declares that "[t]he water of every natural stream, not heretofore appropriated, within the state of Colorado, is hereby declared to be the property of the public"? *See* Colo. Const. art. XVI, § 5.

---

2.   THE ENDANGERED SPECIES ACT

The Endangered Species Act (ESA) is considered more fully in Chapter 4, *supra*, but it merits consideration in this chapter because it is probably the most significant current source of federal influence over water allocation. The number of water-related activities authorized, funded, or carried out by federal agencies and thus subject to section 7's no jeopardy rule and consultation obligations, 16 U.S.C. § 1536, is considerable and continues to grow. Most significant private and municipal dams are licensed by the

Federal Energy Regulatory Commission (FERC) and must be relicensed. In fact, by 2013, some 550 projects will need to be relicensed. *See generally* AMERICAN RIVERS, HYDROPOWER DAM REFORM, http://www.americanrivers.org/ site/PageServer?pagename=AMR_hydroabout; SIERRA CLUB, DOWN COME THE DAMS, *at* http://www.sierraclub.org/sierra/199805/lol.asp. There are also numerous federal water projects. "As found in one 1996 study, 184 species with habitat impacted by federal Reclamation projects and water service areas had either been listed or were proposed for listing under the ESA." Michael R. Moore et al., *Water Allocation in the American West: Endangered Fish Versus Irrigated Agriculture*, 36 NAT. RESOURCES J. 319, 320–21 (1996). Section 9's prohibition on taking any endangered species also has the potential to impose significant limits on water diversion. As of May 2009, 151 fish species and another 34 amphibian species had been listed as threatened or endangered. *See* U.S. Fish and Wildlife Service, *Threatened and Endangered Species System, Summary of Listed Species*, *at* http://ecos. fws.gov/tess_public/TESSBoxscore. To the extent a particular water use causes harm to any of these species, it can be enjoined as a violation of Section 9. 16 U.S.C. §§ 1538(a)(1)(B) (take prohibition); 16 U.S.C. § 1540(e)(6), (g) (authorizing injunctive relief).

The tension between the ESA and water is particularly acute in the western United States because the number of threatened and endangered species is greater in the West and the water which they need to survive is scarcer. One of the common refrains in ESA litigation has been that the federal government is improperly interfering in the state's management of its water resources. To make this claim, water users have emphasized the ESA's declaration that it is "the policy of Congress that Federal agencies shall cooperate with State and local agencies to resolve water resource issues in concert with conservation of endangered species," 16 U.S.C. § 1531(c)(2) (2000), and the Act's requirement that the Secretary, in implementing the ESA, "cooperate to the maximum extent practicable with the States." *Id.* § 1535(a). The courts, however, have dismissed such arguments, noting that the provisions do not require "that state water rights should prevail over the restrictions set forth in the Act. Such an interpretation would render the Act a nullity." *United States v. Glenn–Colusa Irrigation Dist.*, 788 F. Supp. 1126, 1134 (E.D. Cal. 1992).

This approach to the ESA is like that applied to similar language in the Clean Water Act. In the so-called Wallop Amendment to the Clean Water Act, Congress provided: "It is the policy of Congress that the authority of each State to allocate water within its jurisdiction shall not be superseded, abrogated or otherwise impaired by this Act. It is further the policy of Congress that nothing in this Act shall be construed to supersede or abrogate rights to quantities of water which have been established by any State." 33 U.S.C. § 1251(g). The Wallop Amendment, like its ESA counterpart, has packed little punch. In *Riverside Irrigation Dist. v. Andrews*, 758 F.2d 508 (10th Cir. 1985), the Corps of Engineers denied plaintiffs a nationwide dredge and fill permit on the grounds that their proposed dam and reservoir would harm the habitat of the endangered whooping crane. When the plaintiffs argued that the Corps could not deny the permit because doing so would impair the state's right to allocate water in violation of the Wallop Amendment, the court disagreed, noting that the

Amendment, "which is only a general policy statement, cannot nullify a clear and specific grant of jurisdiction, even if the particular grant seems inconsistent with the broadly stated purpose." *Id.* at 513. Although to encourage passage of the legislation Congress apparently perceives the need to include such policy language accommodating state water law, in practice the authority of the states over water has been superseded by the specific commands in the ESA and CWA.

Another issue that always lurks in the background whenever the application of Section 7 or Section 9 causes a water user to lose a portion of their water is whether the regulatory demand amounts to a taking of a water right. The following case addresses that issue. It is first decision to hold that a regulatory limitation on an appropriative water right can constitute a taking.

TULARE LAKE BASIN WATER STORAGE DIST. v. UNITED STATES, 49 Fed. Cl. 313 (2001)

WIESE, JUDGE.

Plaintiffs are California water users who claim that their contractually-conferred right to the use of water was taken from them when the federal government imposed water use restrictions under the Endangered Species Act. They now seek Fifth Amendment compensation for their alleged loss.... We now rule in favor of plaintiffs, and deny the government's cross-motion for summary judgment.

FACTS

This case concerns the delta smelt and the winter-run chinook salmon—two species of fish determined by the United States Fish and Wildlife Service ("USFWS") and the National Marine Fisheries Service ("NMFS") to be in jeopardy of extinction. The efforts by those agencies to protect the fish—specifically by restricting water out-flows in California's primary water distribution system—bring together, and arguably into conflict, the Endangered Species Act and California's century-old regime of private water rights. The intersection of those concerns, and the proper balance between them, lie at the heart of this litigation.

The development of California's water system has a long and detailed history well chronicled in case law. That system, in brief, involves the transport of water from the water-rich areas in northern California to the more arid parts of the state. Various water projects or aqueduct systems have been built to facilitate that goal; two—the Central Valley Project ("CVP") and the State Water Project ("SWP")—are the focus of the present litigation.

Although CVP is a federal project managed by the Bureau of Reclamation ("BOR") and SWP is a state project managed by the Department of Water Resources ("DWR"), the two projects share a coordinated pumping system that requires, as a practical matter, that the systems be operated in concert. That arrangement has been formalized both by statute and by subsequent agreement. In order to operate the two projects, water is diverted from the Feather and Sacramento Rivers, captured by pumping systems located at the southern edge of the Sacramento–San Joaquin Delta, and then distributed, through a series of canals, to end-users in southern California. Water that is not diverted from the Delta flows into the San Francisco Bay.

Both BOR and DWR are granted water permits by the State Water Resources Control Board ("SWRCB" or "the Board")—a state agency with the ultimate authority for controlling, appropriating, using and distributing state waters. BOR and DWR in turn contract with county water districts, conferring on them the right to withdraw or use prescribed quantities of water. [Tulare Lake Basin Water Storage District has a contract directly with the State Water Project for 118,500 acre feet per year.]

By law, the water projects are required to be financially self-sustaining, with the costs of construction and maintenance to be paid entirely by those who ultimately receive the water. The water contractors are thus obligated to pay to maintain the operation of the system regardless of the amount of water actually received. Because the amount of water available to water users in a particular year is largely a function of natural causes, however, the permits explicitly provide that the state will not be held liable for shortages due to drought or other causes beyond its control. * * *

In fulfillment of the duties assigned to it under the ESA, the National Marine Fisheries Service initiated discussions with the federal Bureau of Reclamation and state Department of Water Resources to determine the impact of the Central Valley Project and the State Water Project on the winter-run chinook salmon. As a result of those discussions, the NMFS issued a biological opinion on February 14, 1992, concluding that the proposed operation of SWP and CVP was likely to jeopardize the continued existence of the salmon population. Included in the agency's findings was a reasonable and prudent alternative ("RPA")[2] designed to protect the fish by restricting the time and manner of pumping water out of the Delta. As a result, water that would otherwise have been available for distribution by the water projects was made unavailable.

The process was repeated the following year, with the issuance of a second biological opinion by NMFS, again finding the winter-run chinook salmon to be in jeopardy. The U.S. Fish and Wildlife Service then issued its own biological opinion—this one identifying the delta smelt to be at risk. Following each of these later-issued opinions, RPAs were adopted that again restricted the time and manner in which water could be pumped from the Delta, thereby limiting the water otherwise available to the water distribution systems.

The RPAs were thus implemented in each of the years in question, giving rise to the present claims. According to plaintiffs, the restrictions imposed by the RPAs deprived Tulare Lake Basin WSD of at least 9,770 acre-feet of water in 1992; at least 26,000 acre-feet of water in 1993, and at least 23,050 acre-feet of water in 1994. . . .

DISCUSSION

The Fifth Amendment to the United States Constitution concludes with the phrase: "nor shall private property be taken for public use, without just compensation." The purpose of that clause—as the oft-quoted language from *Armstrong v. United States*, 364 U.S. 40, 49 (1960) explains—is "to bar Government from forcing some people alone to bear public burdens which, in all fairness and justice, should be borne by the public as a whole." At issue,

---

2. Where the activities of a federal agency are seen to jeopardize the continued existence of listed species or cause the destruction or adverse modification of critical habitats, the Endangered Species Act directs the Secretary to suggest "reasonable and prudent alternatives" to avoid such harms. 16 U.S.C. § 1536(b)(3)(A) (1994).

then, is not whether the federal government has the authority to protect the winter-run chinook salmon and delta smelt under the Endangered Species Act, but whether it may impose the costs of their protection solely on plaintiffs.

In arguing against the existence of a taking, the government ... argues that the criteria for a regulatory taking—specifically the existence of reasonable, investment-backed expectations and of a significant decrease in economic value—have not been met. Finally, defendant contends that the federal government cannot be held liable for a taking when it does no more than impose a limit on plaintiffs' title that the background principles of state law would otherwise require. We address these arguments in turn.

II.

Turning then to the merits of plaintiffs' claim, we begin by determining the nature of the taking alleged. Courts have traditionally divided their analysis of Fifth Amendment takings into two categories: physical takings and regulatory takings. A physical taking occurs when the government's action amounts to a physical occupation or invasion of the property, including the functional equivalent of a "practical ouster of [the owner's] possession." *Transportation Co. v. Chicago*, 99 U.S. 635, 642 (1878); *Loretto v. Teleprompter Manhattan CATV Corp.*, 458 U.S. 419 (1982). When an owner has suffered a physical invasion of his property, courts have noted that "no matter how minute the intrusion, and no matter how weighty the public purpose behind it, we have required compensation." *Lucas v. South Carolina Coastal Council*, 505 U.S. 1003, 1015 (1992).

A regulatory taking, in contrast, arises when the government's regulation restricts the use to which an owner may put his property. In assessing whether a regulatory taking has occurred, courts generally employ the balancing test set forth in *Penn Central*, weighing the character of the government action, the economic impact of that action and the reasonableness of the property owner's investment-backed expectations. *Penn Central Transp. Co. v. New York*, 438 U.S. 104, 124–125 (1978). Regulations that are found to be too restrictive, however—i.e., those that deprive property of its entire economically beneficial or productive use—are commonly identified as categorical takings and, like physical takings, require no such balancing. *Lucas*, 505 U.S. at 1015–1016.

Plaintiffs urge us to consider this action as a case involving a physical taking of property. Under that theory, plaintiffs possessed contract rights entitling them to the use of a specified quantity of water. By preventing them from using that water, plaintiffs argue, the government deprived them of the entire value of their contract right.

Defendant sees the case differently. In defendant's view, the court must examine the government's conduct under the three-part test that *Penn Central* prescribes for the evaluation of regulatory action that interferes with an owner's use of his property. Under that rubric, defendant contends, the claim must fail because plaintiffs' reasonable contract expectations were necessarily limited by regulatory concern over fish and wildlife; and because the economic loss asserted here—a fraction of the master contract's overall value—was de minimis.

Of the two positions, plaintiffs', we believe, is the correct one. Case law reveals that the distinction between a physical invasion and a governmental activity that merely impairs the use of that property turns on whether the intrusion is "so immediate and direct as to subtract from the owner's full enjoyment of the property and to limit his exploitation of it." *United States v. Causby*, 328 U.S. 256, 265 (1946). In *Causby*, for instance, the Court ruled that frequent flights immediately above a landowner's property constituted a taking, comparing such actions to a more traditional physical taking: "If, by reason of the frequency and altitude of the flights, respondents could not use this land for any purpose, their loss would be complete. It would be as complete as if the United States had entered upon the surface of the land and taken exclusive possession of it." *Id.* at 261 (footnote omitted).

While water rights present an admittedly unusual situation, we think the *Causby* example is an instructive one. In the context of water rights, a mere restriction on use—the hallmark of a regulatory action—completely eviscerates the right itself since plaintiffs' sole entitlement is to the use of the water. Unlike other species of property where use restrictions may limit some, but not all of the incidents of ownership, the denial of a right to the use of water accomplishes a complete extinction of all value. Thus, by limiting plaintiffs' ability to use an amount of water to which they would otherwise be entitled, the government has essentially substituted itself as the beneficiary of the contract rights with regard to that water and totally displaced the contract holder. That complete occupation of property—an exclusive possession of plaintiffs' water-use rights for preservation of the fish—mirrors the invasion present in *Causby*. To the extent, then, that the federal government, by preventing plaintiffs from using the water to which they would otherwise have been entitled, have rendered the usufructuary right to that water valueless, they have thus effected a physical taking. * * *

III.

Having concluded that a deprivation of water amounts to a physical taking, we turn now to the question of whether plaintiffs in fact owned the property for which they seek to be compensated. Defendant argues that both the terms of plaintiffs' contracts and the background principles of state law impose limits on plaintiffs' titles that render their loss of water non-compensable. That is the case in the first instance, defendant contends, because plaintiffs' contracts entitle them only to the water made available to the Department of Water Resources. As the water—through no fault of DWR—was not made available to DWR, plaintiffs have no claim to the foregone flow. Additionally, defendant argues that plaintiffs' contract rights are subject to the public trust doctrine, the doctrine of reasonable use, and common law principles of nuisance, all of which provide for the protection of fish and wildlife. To the extent that the reductions in the water supply that plaintiffs suffered are designed to advance those interests, defendant argues, the reductions merely reflect the limitations of title inherent in the background principles of state law. And, defendant adds, no right to compensation attends the assertion of such background principles.

i. Contract Language as a Limitation on Title

Under the terms of the water supply contracts, neither the state nor its agents may be held liable for "any damage, direct or indirect, arising from shortages in the amount of water to be made available for delivery to the Agency under this contract caused by drought, operation of area of origin statutes, or any other cause beyond its control." Para. 18(f). Defendant reads that language to mean that plaintiffs are entitled to receive water only to the extent that water is available to DWR. Because the imposition of federal use restrictions constitutes a cause beyond DWR's control, defendant argues, plaintiffs' contract rights are contingent on a condition that never occurred: the availability of water to DWR. Defendant's argument, in other words, amounts to the assertion that a litigant has a compensable property interest in a contract right only if he can press for its enforcement at law. Defendant cites *O'Neill v. United States*, 50 F.3d 677 (9th Cir. 1995) in support of this position.

Having considered *O'Neill*, however, we conclude that it has no application to the present case. In *O'Neill*, water contractors in the federally-owned Central Valley Project sued under a breach of contract theory when the enforcement of the Endangered Species Act deprived them of water under their contracts. The *O'Neill* Court concluded that the government was not liable based on a provision in the contract holding the government not responsible for "any damage, direct or indirect, arising from a shortage on account of errors in operation, drought, or any other causes." That broad exemption from liability was found to include shortages of water due to implementation of the ESA.

In the present case, the federal government enjoys no such contractual immunity from liability. The comparable term in the plaintiffs' contracts—Paragraph 18(f)—insulates *DWR* from liability for circumstances beyond its control; not the federal government. The inclusion of Paragraph 18(f) in the contract does not render plaintiffs' interest in the water contingent; it merely provides DWR with a defense against a breach of contract action in certain specified circumstances. With that exception, plaintiffs' contract rights are otherwise fully formed against DWR, and certainly against a third party seeking to infringe on those rights. *O'Neill* can provide the government no defense to a taking.

ii. The Public Trust Doctrine, the Doctrine of Reasonable Use and Nuisance Law

In addition to its contract-based argument, defendant offers a number of common law justifications for limiting the scope of plaintiffs' property right: specifically, that plaintiffs can have no vested right in a use or method of diverting water that is unreasonable or violates the public trust. In support of that position, defendant refers us to various SWRCB decisions, as well as to assorted background principles of state law for the proposition that plaintiffs' proposed use is unreasonable or in contravention of California water law. The difficulty with defendant's argument, however, is that the water allocation scheme in effect for the period 1992–1994, as set forth in D–1485, specifically allowed for the allocations of water defendant now seeks to deem unreasonable. We explain further.

There is, as an initial matter, no dispute that all California water rights are subject to the universal limitation that the use must be both reasonable and for a beneficial purpose. Cal. Const. art. XIV, § 3, amended by Cal. Const. art. X, § 2. Included in that definition of reasonable use is the preservation of fish and wildlife. Indeed, the California legislature has specifically declared that the protection of fish and wildlife is among the purposes of the state water projects. Cal. Water Code § 11900 (Deering 1977).

Whether a particular use or method of diversion is unreasonable or violative of the public trust is a question committed concurrently to the State Water Resources Control Board and to the California courts. See *National Audubon Soc'y v. Superior Court of Alpine County*, 33 Cal.3d 419, 451–452, 189 Cal.Rptr. 346, 658 P.2d 709 (1983). Thus, while we accept the proposition that plaintiffs have no right to use or divert water in an unreasonable manner, nor in a way that violates the public trust, the issue now before us is whether such a determination has in fact been made.

Plaintiffs argue that the State Water Resources Control Board's decision D–1485—a comprehensive water rights scheme balancing the needs of and allocating water rights among competing users—defines the full scope of their contract rights. In plaintiffs' view, D–1485 represents the state's determination of various water rights, thereby reflecting the amount of water, under state law, they reasonably can expect and to which they are reasonably entitled. Plaintiffs argue that unless and until D–1485 is modified by the State Water

Resources Control Board, or the terms of D–1485 are declared by that board or a California court to be unreasonable or violative of the public trust, DWR has a right recognized and protected under California law to divert water in accordance with D–1485.

In defendant's view, D–1485 fails to encapsulate the board's approach to the endangerment of the delta smelt and salmon, both because it was promulgated before the fish were found to be in jeopardy, and because the board enacted D–95–1—a 1995 decision whose provisions adopt measures found in the RPAs—to protect the fish. Additionally, defendant argues that D–1485 should be read as an evolving document, one informed by later developments in water needs and altered by subsequent state actions. . . .

We cannot accept defendant's position. As an initial matter, the responsibility for water allocation is vested in the State Water Resources Control Board. Cal. Water Code §§ 174, 179. Once an allocation has been made—as was done in D–1485—that determination defines the scope of plaintiffs' property rights, pronouncements of other agencies notwithstanding. While we accept the principle that California water policy may be ever-evolving, rights based on contracts with the state are not correspondingly self-adjusting. Rather, the promissory assurances they recite remain fixed until formally changed. In the absence of a reallocation by the State Water Resources Control Board, or a determination of illegality by the California courts, the allocation scheme imposed by D–1485 defines the scope of plaintiffs' contract rights. None of the doctrines to which defendant resorts—the doctrine of reasonable use, the public trust doctrine or state nuisance law—are therefore availing. * * *

Nor do we believe that the subsequent actions by the SWRCB were designed to supplant the findings of D–1485. Although the Board agreed to waive salinity requirements to enable compliance with the RPA, for instance, it did not revisit the water allocations set forth in D–1485 that were established after some eleven months of hearings. And while the administrative determinations issued by the SWRCB in 1995—the 1995 the Water Control Plan and the Water Right Decision 95–6—served to reallocate water allotments, they did so only after the period in dispute, and cannot therefore be construed as altering the scope of plaintiffs' contract rights for the 1992–1994 period. * * *

Defendant argues against this position, urging us to anticipate how the Board or the California courts would apply the doctrine of reasonable use if the issue were before them. * * *

Defendant [argues] that the state does not have to declare a use a nuisance or unreasonable before the federal government can, without effecting a taking, exercise its own regulatory powers to abate that use. Put differently, the issue, in defendant's view, is whether the use *could* have been prohibited under state water or nuisance law. If so, defendant argues, the federal government is free to operate within the regulatory space carved out by the state background principles, whether or not the state has preceded it. * * * As the *Lucas* Court explained in describing those interests that, on the basis of nuisance principles, are non-compensable: "The use of these properties for what are now expressly prohibited purposes was *always* unlawful, and (subject to other constitutional limitations) it was open to the State at any point to make the implication of those background principles of nuisance and property law explicit." *Lucas*, 505 U.S. at 1030.

That the use now being challenged was not always unlawful is evident from the fact that it was specifically authorized by the state in D–1485. Were we now to deem that use a nuisance, we would not be making explicit that which had always been implied under background principles of property law, but would

instead be replacing the state's judgment with our own. That we cannot do.
* * *

To the extent that water allocation in California is a policy judgment—one specifically committed to the SWRCB and the California courts—a finding of unreasonableness by this court would be tantamount to our *making* California law rather than merely applying it. This is especially true where, as here, the Board charged with such determinations has responded, and continues to respond, to the concerns about fish and wildlife that the government was seeking to address through the implementation of the ESA.

While we are often asked to interpret state or federal statutes or regulations to determine the scope of a property interest under a takings claim, those determinations do not extend to matters of discretion committed to the authority of the state. Accordingly, we conclude that plaintiffs' right to divert water in the manner specified by their contracts and in conformance with D–1485 continued until a determination to the contrary was made either by the SWRCB or by the California courts. As no such determination was made during the period 1992–1994, and subsequent amendments to policy cannot, for contract purposes, be made retroactive, plaintiffs were indeed entitled to the water use provided for in D–1485 and in their contracts.

CONCLUSION

There is, in the end, no dispute that DWR's permits, and in turn plaintiffs' contract rights, are subject to the doctrines of reasonable use and public trust and to the tenets of state nuisance law. Nor is there serious challenge to the premise that the SWRCB, under its reserved jurisdiction, could at any time modify the terms of those permits to reflect the changing need of the various water users. The crucial point, however, is that it had not.

D–1485 is a comprehensive balancing of interests that recognized that while the "full protection" of fish was perhaps possible, it was not ultimately in the public interest. The SWRCB chose not to revisit that in-depth balancing of water needs and uses even as it reviewed the salinity standards it had set in response to NMFS's biological opinion. We need not attempt to discern the state's response to the threat, then, because the state has in fact spoken.

Nor can we, as defendant urges, make that determination ourselves. It is the Board that must provide the necessary weighing of interests to determine the appropriate balance under California law between the cost and benefit of species preservation. The federal government is certainly free to preserve the fish; it must simply pay for the water it takes to do so.

For the reasons stated, plaintiffs' motion for summary judgment must therefore be granted and defendant's cross-motion for summary judgment denied.

QUESTIONS AND DISCUSSION

1. In a subsequent decision, the district judge determined that the federal government owed the water districts almost $14 million plus interest from the date of the taking. *Tulare Lake Basin Water Storage Dist. v. United States*, 59 Fed. Cl. 246 (2003).

2. The introduction to this chapter quoted Professor Sax's observation that

[b]ly its very nature, [water] is a shared common property. Water is never owned in the usual sense. We acquire only use rights in it, or what lawyers call a "usufruct." Because water is inherently a common resource, it is subject to common servitudes, such as the right of public navigation. We find these concepts in various forms in all legal systems. * * *

All these diverse laws from widely separated places on the globe emphasize one idea: Water is first and foremost a community resource whose fate tracks the community's needs as time goes on.

Joseph Sax, *Proceedings of the 2001 Symposium on Managing Hawai'i's Public Trust Doctrine*, 24 U. HAW. L. REV. 21, 24 (2001). How does the court's view of the nature of property rights in water differ from that of Professor Sax? Why is that distinction so important to the takings analysis?

3. Suppose that the water rights of the Bureau and the SWP, and therefore the contract right of the District, had a priority date of 1980, seven years later than the 1973 passage of the ESA. Would that impact the court's takings analysis? Should it? Recall that in *Lucas v. South Carolina Coastal Council*, 505 U.S. 1003 (1992), *supra* page 185, the Court held that where a regulation denied a property owner all economically viable use of her property it would be a *per se* taking unless the regulation was justified by background principles of common law that inhered in the property right to begin with. *Id.* at 1015–16. Although the *Tulare Lake* court does not seem to accept that regulatory limitations inhere in every water right, would it agree that ESA limitations inhere in a permit with a 1980 priority date? In *Palazzolo v. Rhode Island*, 533 U.S. 606 (2001), the Court held that the mere fact that a property owner purchased property after passage of the regulation prompting the takings claim is not alone sufficient to avoid a takings claim. *Id.* at 626–30 (also holding that the timing of acquisition could be considered as part of the *Penn–Central* balancing test which includes the property owner's reasonable investment-backed expectations). Does it make a difference that in *Palazzolo* the property owner acquired the property from another private owner rather than directly from the state in the form of a permit to appropriate water?

4. In the *Tulare Lake* case, the RPAs (reasonable and prudent alternatives) are each for different amounts of water and presumably were only temporary until enough water was available to remove any limitations. Should the temporary nature of the RPAs affect the takings analysis? In considering this question, review note 7 at page 195 discussing the Supreme Court's decision in *Tahoe–Sierra Preservation Council v. Tahoe Regional Planning Agency (Tahoe)*, 535 U.S. 302 (2002), where the Court held that a thirty-two-month moratorium on development was not a taking. Would the *Tulare Lake* case have come out the same way if it had been decided after *Tahoe–Sierra*? Can *Tahoe–Sierra* be distinguished?

5. In 2007, Judge Wiese, the same judge who decided *Tulare Lake*, concluded that *Tulare Lake* was not consistent with the Supreme Court's subsequent decision in *Tahoe–Sierra*. In *Casitas Mun. Water Dist. v. U.S.*, 76 Fed. Cl. 100 (2007), Judge Wiese faced another takings challenge for water lost due to application of the ESA.

[In *Tulare*] we concluded that where a nonpossessory right of use—such as a water right—is displaced or abridged by a governmental action, the property owner has been caused to suffer a loss—the imposition of a servitude—that is akin to the dislocation occasioned by a physical occupation. . . .

Admittedly, in *Tulare*, our focus was upon the finality of the plaintiffs' loss rather than upon the character of the government's action. * * *

In its motion for partial summary judgment, defendant asks us to reexamine this ruling. * * * [D]efendant refers us to a number of cases, among them *Tahoe–Sierra Preservation Council, Inc. v. Tahoe Regional Planning Agency*, 535 U.S. 302 (2002). In *Tahoe–Sierra*, the Supreme Court rejected the assertion that a moratorium on residential land development was analogous to a physical taking and thus constituted a categorical or per se taking. The Court explained its ruling as follows:

> This longstanding distinction between acquisitions of property for public use, on the one hand, and regulations prohibiting private uses, on the other, makes it inappropriate to treat cases involving physical takings as controlling precedents for the evaluation of a claim that there has been a "regulatory taking," and vice versa. For the same reason that we do not ask whether a physical appropriation advances a substantial government interest or whether it deprives the owner of all economically valuable use, we do not apply our precedent from the physical takings context to regulatory takings claims. . . . [P]hysical appropriations are relatively rare, easily identified, and usually represent a greater affront to individual property rights.

535 U.S. at 323–25 (footnotes omitted).

Defendant urges us to heed the caution expressed in *Tahoe–Sierra* and thus to recognize that restrictions on the use of property, short of those that deprive an owner of all economically beneficial use of the property, do not qualify as categorical takings but must be treated as regulatory takings subject to analysis under the Penn Central factors. * * *

Despite the seeming simplicity of the question before us, we do not find it an easy one to decide. . . . [T]he question becomes whether the restrictions on plaintiff's water diversion, like a permanent physical invasion, and the accompanying loss those restrictions engender, constitute "government action of such a unique character that it is a taking without regard to other factors a court might ordinarily examine." Loretto, 458 U.S. at 432.

Tempted though we may be to answer this question in the affirmative, *Tahoe–Sierra* counsels against our doing so. That case compels us to respect the distinction between a government takeover of property (either by physical invasion or by directing the property's use to its own needs) and government restraints on an owner's use of that property. Although from the property owner's standpoint there may be no practical difference between the two, *Tahoe–Sierra* admonishes that only the government's active hand in the redirection of a property's use may be treated as a per se taking.

Applying a *Penn–Central* analysis is typically fatal for a takings claim. Should that be any less likely in the context of water rights? Alternatively, should water claims be even less likely to succeed than cases where land is regulated?

6. *Tulare Lake* has not fared well with other courts who have faced similar issues. *See, e.g., Allegretti & Co. v. County of Imperial*, 138 Cal. App. 4th 1261, 42 Cal. Rptr. 3d 122 (Cal.App. 2006) ("*Tulare Lake*'s reasoning disregards the hallmarks of a categorical physical taking, namely, actual physical occupation or physical invasion of a property interest.");

Klamath Irrigation Dist. v. United States, 67 Fed. Cl. 504 (2005) (*"Tulare* appears to be wrong on some counts, incomplete in others and, distinguishable, at all events.").

7. When water is unavailable for diversion due to the application of a regulation, it is sometimes referred to as a "regulatory drought" or an "artificial drought" to distinguish it from a "natural drought" where there is insufficient water because of a lack of rain. Professor Brian Gray has criticized the metaphor of "regulatory drought" and its companion "artificial drought" and suggested the term "hybrid drought" is more accurate because the lack of water is usually a function of both natural and regulatory causes. How could Professor Gray's "hybrid drought" concept influence the physical taking analysis?

8. The Bureau and SWP likely hold some of the more senior water rights in the river system. How is it that they (more specifically the districts who contracted with them though the DWR) should bear the burden of providing additional water for the endangered salmon? Under basic prior appropriation principles, when there is insufficient water to satisfy all users' needs, it is the juniors who must stop their diversions and not the seniors. Does it make sense to disregard the priority principle when the lack of water is caused by a regulatory or hybrid drought rather than a purely natural drought? For a discussion of this issue, see James R. Rasband, *Priority, Probability, and Proximate Cause: Lessons from Tort Law About Imposing ESA Responsibility for Wildlife Harm on Water Users and Other Joint Habitat Modifiers* 33 ENVTL. L. 595 (2003). What concerns might the federal wildlife agencies have if they were obligated to pursue junior appropriators first to satisfy the water needs of threatened or endangered species?

9. Why must the Bureau of Reclamation seek a permit from the California Water Resources Control Board? Section 8 of the 1902 Reclamation Act provides that:

> [N]othing in this Act shall be construed as affecting or intended to affect or to in any way interfere with the laws of any State or Territory relating to the control, appropriation, use or distribution of water used in irrigation, or any vested rights acquired thereunder, and the Secretary of the Interior in carrying out the provisions of this Act, shall proceed in conformity with such laws....

43 U.S.C. § 383. Under the Reclamation Act, therefore, the Bureau must apply for a state permit from the relevant state agency and then turn around and enter into water delivery contracts of the sort described in this case with individuals, irrigation districts, and water districts. If you were a lawyer for the Bureau of Reclamation, what steps would you take in the future to avoid an outcome like that in this case?

D. ALLOCATING WATER BETWEEN THE STATES

Water does not neatly confine itself to jurisdictional boundaries; nor do watersheds. This fact triggers many of the natural resource management challenges that were identified in Chapter 1, including the challenge of managing a resource on the appropriate scale, the issue of externalities and transaction costs, and the difficulty of managing a common pool resource. This section considers a particular transboundary management problem, namely the law regarding allocation of interstate watercourses. Consideration of the problem occurs along two axes. First, there is the procedural and jurisdictional question of who should make the final determination of how interstate rivers are to be divided. Should it be the states themselves by compact under Article I, § 10 of the Constitution? The Supreme Court by means of its original and exclusive jurisdiction over disputes between states? U.S. CONST. art. III, § 2, cl. 2 (original jurisdiction); 28 U.S.C. § 1251(a) (exclusive jurisdiction). Or should it be Congress, justified by its regulatory role over interstate commerce or its Property Clause authority over waters relating to federal lands? It turns out that all three approaches have been tried and remain viable options for allocating an interstate watercourse.

The second axis along which the problem of interstate watercourse allocation must be considered is the substantive question of what rules should govern the apportionment of a transboundary watercourse. Should riparian-type principles apply between two states? Should the upstream or downstream location of the state matter? Should prior appropriation principles apply to the benefit of the state whose citizens are the first to use a watercourse? Should it be a matter of contract, left to the negotiation of the two states? Or should there be some sort of equitable division of the water resource? Although in the end some form of equitable division typically carries the day, equity is often defined with an eye on one or more of the alternative allocation approaches. The sections that follow consider these alternative allocation regimes in the context of the three basic procedural approaches to allocation, namely allocation by Supreme Court decision, by compact, and/or by Congress.

1.   JUDICIAL ALLOCATION

The Supreme Court was not asked to decide how an interstate watercourse should be apportioned between two states until 1908, when Kansas sued Colorado, arguing that Colorado farmers were taking too much of the Arkansas River and its subterranean flow and effectively precluding development along the river in Kansas. *Kansas v. Colorado*, 206 U.S. 46 (1907). The ensuing arguments of both states reflected a posture that has been repeated over and over again in water disputes between competing sovereigns. Colorado, the upstream state, claimed that it was sovereign over all resources within its boundaries and therefore had a right to use the entire flow of the river if it chose. Kansas, on the downstream side, asserted that it was entitled to its own territorial integrity which included a river undiminished in flow from its natural state. Putting the argument in terms of riparian rights, Kansas contended that Colorado had an obligation not to disrupt the natural flow of the river. The Supreme Court decided that a more equitable solution was in order.

> One cardinal rule, underlying all the relations of the states to each other, is that of equality of right. Each state stands on the same level, with all the rest. It can impose its own legislation on no one of the others, and is bound to yield

its own views to none. Yet, whenever ... the action of one state reaches through the agency of natural laws, into the territory of another state, the question of the extent and the limitations of the rights of the two states becomes a matter of justiciable dispute between them, and this court is called upon to settle that dispute in such a way as will recognize the equal rights of both and at the same time establish justice between them. In other words, through these successive disputes and decisions this court is practically building up what may not improperly be called interstate common law.

Id. at 97–98. Although the Court concluded that Kansas had not yet shown sufficient injury to entitle it to relief, it held that Kansas was entitled to "an equitable apportionment of benefits" and that if Colorado's diversions continued to increase, Kansas was entitled to return to the Court to seek relief. *Id.* at 118.

The rule of equitable apportionment adopted by the Court in *Kansas v. Colorado* has been the lodestar for all subsequent interstate allocation disputes. As Justice Holmes explained in another dispute between New Jersey and New York over the waters of the Delaware River and its tributaries, "different traditions and practices in different parts of the country may lead to varying results but the effort always is to secure an equitable apportionment without quibbling over formulas." *New Jersey v. New York*, 283 U.S. 336, 343 (1931). Holmes' reference to "different traditions" was directed primarily at explaining the import of the Court's decision nine years earlier, in *Wyoming v. Colorado*, 259 U.S. 419 (1922), where the Court had held that as between two states that adhered to the prior appropriation doctrine, it was "just and equitable" to use priority of appropriation as a rule of decision. *Id.* at 470. In *Nebraska v. Wyoming*, 325 U.S. 589 (1945), the Court emphasized that priority was just one factor in the equitable calculus, albeit a particularly important one in disputes between two prior appropriation states.

[I]f an allocation between appropriation States is to be just and equitable, strict adherence to the priority rule may not be possible. For example, the economy of a region may have been established on the basis of junior appropriations. So far as possible those established uses should be protected though strict application of the priority rule might jeopardize them. Apportionment calls for the exercise of an informed judgment on a consideration of many factors. Priority of appropriation is the guiding principle. But physical and climatic conditions, the consumptive use of water in the several sections of the river, the character and rate of return flows, the extent of established uses, the availability of storage water, the practical effect of wasteful uses on downstream areas, the damage to upstream areas as compared to the benefits to downstream areas if a limitation is imposed on the former—these are all relevant factors. They are merely an illustrative not an exhaustive catalogue.

Id. at 618.

In subsequent decisions the Court has continued to elaborate upon the details of equitable apportionment. In *Colorado v. New Mexico*, 459 U.S. 176 (1982), a dispute involving the Vermejo River, a small, non-navigable river that originates in southern Colorado and flows into New Mexico, the Court held:

Our cases establish that a state seeking to prevent or enjoin a diversion by another state bears the burden of proving that the diversion will cause it "real or substantial injury or damage." . . .

New Mexico must therefore bear the initial burden of showing that a diversion by Colorado will cause substantial injury to the interests of New Mexico. In this case New Mexico has met its burden since any diversion by Colorado, unless offset by New Mexico at its own expense, will necessarily reduce the amount of water available to New Mexico users.

The burden has therefore shifted to Colorado to establish that a diversion should nevertheless be permitted under the principle of equitable apportionment. Thus, with respect to whether reasonable conservation measures by New Mexico will offset the loss of water due to Colorado's diversion, or whether the benefit to Colorado from the diversion will substantially outweigh the possible harm to New Mexico, Colorado will bear the burden of proof. It must show, in effect, that without such a diversion New Mexico would be using "more than its equitable share of the benefits of a stream." Moreover, Colorado must establish not only that its claim is of a "serious magnitude," but also that its position is supported by "clear and convincing evidence."

Id. at 188 n.13.

Although the Court's decisions have moved in the direction of articulating a more formulaic list of factors and evidentiary burdens, the Court has remained reluctant to impose its will on disputes between states, issuing decrees in only three cases. As the Court explained in *Colorado v. Kansas*, 320 U.S. 383 (1943):

The reason for judicial caution in adjudicating the relative rights of states in such cases is that, while we have jurisdiction of such disputes, they involve the interests of quasi-sovereigns, present complicated and delicate questions, and, due to the possibility of future change of conditions, necessitate expert administration rather than judicial imposition of a hard and fast rule. Such controversies may appropriately be composed by negotiation and agreement, pursuant to the compact clause of the Federal constitution.

Id. at 392. Partly because the Supreme Court has viewed its role as primarily to establish guidelines rather than to allocate interstate rivers, and partly because the risk of litigation is significant, the states have often turned to negotiation as a way of resolving interstate water clashes.

2.   ALLOCATION BY COMPACT

In *Kansas v. Colorado*, 206 U.S. 46 (1907), the Court remarked that "[i]f the two States were absolutely independent nations," interstate water disputes "would be settled by treaty or by force" but "neither of these ways being practicable, it must be settled by decision of this court." *Id.* at 98. As rhetoric the statement is unobjectionable but it isn't entirely accurate. Resolving interstate water disputes by treaty is more than impracticable. It is unconstitutional. Article I, Section 10, Clause 1 provides that "No State shall enter into any Treaty, Alliance, or Confederation." In addition to overselling states' power to make treaties, the Court's rhetoric oversold its own obligation to settle the dispute. While the Constitution precludes treaties, it provides for states to negotiate compacts with the consent of Congress. Article I, Section 10 goes on to provide in Clause 3: "No State shall, without the Consent of Congress . . . enter into any Agreement or

Compact with another State." The following excerpt describes how this provision, known as the "Compact Clause," has provided states a practical, if still arduous, method of settling interstate water conflicts without calling on the Supreme Court for help.

Dustin S. Stephenson, *The Tri–State Compact: Falling Waters and Fading Opportunities*, 16 J. LAND USE & ENVTL. L. 83, 97–100 (2000)

The process of creating an interstate compact often begins with the states requesting congressional authorization to negotiate a resolution among themselves. Once Congress grants authorization (often mandating that a federal representative be present at the negotiations), the states may begin the negotiation process. When the states reach an agreement, they must then seek congressional approval of the terms of that agreement. Only after Congress has given final consent does the compact become federal law.

Beyond the approval process itself, no additional federal regulations govern interstate compacts. Since the agreement reached is based on negotiations between the states involved, Congress assumes the compact is suitable to the states involved. Thus, once the negotiations have yielded an agreement, Congress almost always ratifies it. In fact, Congress rarely restricts, or gets involved with, the mechanics of an interstate water compact. Therefore, interstate compacts can be set up in virtually any manner to solve any type of interstate water rights dispute.

... The first interstate compact resolving a water rights dispute was the Colorado River Compact of 1922 [discussed *infra*], which simply allocated the waters of the Colorado River between the states involved. Since that time, Congress has approved over thirty interstate water compacts, each with varying complexities stemming from various water resource disputes. The vast majority of these water compacts have taken place in the arid western states where the water supply is relatively scarce. In fact, every western state has participated in at least one interstate water compact.

A significant dynamic underlying these water compacts is that the states are negotiating their water allocations for future use. As such, the states must anticipate their future water needs as accurately as possible and negotiate an appropriation accordingly. However, even the best estimates are sometimes off the mark and as a result, the compact's enforcement mechanism becomes extremely important. A water compact can be enforced in two ways: through the compact itself or through an interstate commission. The compact itself acts as the enforcement mechanism by providing certain guidelines for state agencies to follow in allocating the water supply. This prescriptive scheme was used in the early water compacts. Today, this scheme is disfavored because ... any enforcement of the compact usually requires court intervention, at a significant cost to the litigants.

It is far more common today to use the second model, which incorporates a standing interstate commission or agency to plan, operate, monitor, and enforce the compact. These commissions all vary to some degree but most include one or more federal representatives for each state involved, usually appointed by the respective governors. Depending on how the compact arranged the commission, the federal representative(s) may or may not have full voting rights.

These permanent commissions are how interstate water compacts make their greatest contribution to water resource management. Through these commissions, compacts create the much-needed authoritative structure for true regional water-resource management. The permanent commission can constantly gather new information and can remain in continuous negotiation, allowing adaptation to new circumstances. Also, because the commission is one centralized body, the costs normally associated with information gathering and continuous negotiation may be drastically reduced.

––––––––––

Because Congress must consent to any compact, a ratified compact is more than a contract between two states; it is federal law and thus supreme to any inconsistent state laws and, presumably, any state efforts to withdraw from the compact in a way inconsistent with the terms of the compact. As long as a compact is constitutional, as legislation, it is also theoretically supreme to any potentially inconsistent Supreme Court allocation or remedy. What sort of remedies the Court can deploy that are not accounted for by the compact itself is a tricky question. It was most closely faced in *Texas v. New Mexico*, 462 U.S. 554 (1983). Texas and New Mexico had negotiated the Pecos River Compact, 63 Stat. 159, which created a three-member Pecos River Commission comprised of a voting member from each state and a nonvoting representative of the United States. Rather than establishing a specific division of the river between the two states, the compact had created a complex methodology for allocating the water. When the methodology led to a result that New Mexico viewed as mistaken, New Mexico refused to deliver the disputed amount. Unsurprisingly, the Pecos River Commission could not reach a resolution because New Mexico, as the upstream state, had no incentive to instruct its commissioner to vote with Texas. Texas sought relief in the Supreme Court, and the Special Master recommended that the Court order the United States representative, or some other third party, to vote decisively when the states could not agree. The Court rejected the recommendation, reasoning that it could not order relief inconsistent with the express terms of a compact that had been ratified by Congress and was otherwise constitutional. Although it declined to reconfigure the Commission contrary to the express terms of the compact, the Court refused New Mexico's suggestion that the entire case be dismissed:

> If it were clear that the Pecos River Commission was intended to be the exclusive forum for disputes between the States, then we would withdraw. But the express terms of the Pecos River Compact do not constitute the Commission as the sole arbiter of disputes between the States over New Mexico's ... obligations.... Texas' right to invoke the original jurisdiction of this Court was an important part of the context in which the Compact was framed; indeed, the threat of such litigation undoubtedly contributed to New Mexico's willingness to enter into a compact. It is difficult to conceive that Texas would trade away its right to seek an equitable apportionment of the river in return for a promise that New Mexico could, for all practical purposes, avoid at will. In the absence of an explicit provision or other clear indications that a bargain to that effect was made, we shall not construe a compact to preclude a State from seeking judicial relief when the compact does not provide an equivalent method of vindicating the State's rights.

Id. at 569–70.

Suppose that the Pecos River Compact had established a specific allocation that turned out to be a particularly bad deal for New Mexico or Texas. If the Supreme Court is prohibited from revising the allocation because of its status as federal law, would the harmed state have any options? Could Congress simply step in and override the compact by passing a new federal law that allocated the River? The answer is yes, but, as the next section explains, that does not mean Congress would be eager to do so.

3. CONGRESSIONAL ALLOCATION

As a function of its power over interstate commerce, U.S. CONST. art. I, § 8, Congress has the power to apportion the waters of interstate rivers. Congress, however, has done so only twice. The latest was in the Truckee–Carson–Pyramid Lake Water Rights Settlement Act of 1990. Pub. L. No. 101–618, § 204, 104 Stat. 3289, 3295–3304. The Settlement Act had the approval of both California and Nevada and largely tracked a compact negotiated in the 1950s and 1960s by the two states. Congress had previously been unwilling to ratify the compact because it did not adequately consider the water needs of the Pyramid Lake Paiute Tribe's traditional fishery in Pyramid Lake. The ultimate settlement passed by Congress addressed tribal demands, as well as issues raised by endangered species, Indian reserved water rights, and water needs for a federal reclamation project and a wildlife refuge. As Professor Grant has remarked, given the Act's complexity and its approval by both affected states, the Act "hardly serves as political precedent for Congress to apportion interstate waters routinely or to force an apportionment upon an unwilling state." Douglas L. Grant, *Interstate Water Allocation Compacts: When the Virtue of Permanence Becomes the Vice of Inflexibility*, 74 U. COLO. L. REV. 105, 173 (2003).

The only other instance of congressional apportionment is in the case of the lower Colorado River. In *Arizona v. California*, the Supreme Court, to the surprise of most commentators, ruled that Congress, in the Boulder Canyon Project Act, 43 U.S.C. § 617 *et seq.* (1928), had decided to apportion between California, Arizona, and Nevada the portion of the Colorado River allocated to those "Lower Basin States" under the Colorado River Compact. This story is told more fully in the Colorado River case study, *infra* page 890, but the Court's conclusion that Congress intended to require an apportionment of the Colorado River was certainly an aggressive interpretation of Congress' 1928 view of its own power.

The fact that these are the only two instances of congressional apportionment well illustrates Congress' reluctance to join the allocation fray. In part that reluctance is a function of a historical and continuing sense on the part of many in Congress that water allocation is a state matter. In part, it derives from the reluctance of representatives to impose natural resource decisions on colleagues from the states in which those resources are located, again a function of historical deference to state control of natural resources. And where colleagues agree, a compact is usually possible. Nevertheless, congressional apportionment looms over all compact negotiations and any judicial apportionment as the final trump card. As long as its apportionment is constitutional, Congress has the final say on allocation of interstate waters.

QUESTIONS AND DISCUSSION

1. Which method of apportionment—judicial, compact, or congressional— is wisest? What are the advantages and disadvantages of each? Do you see how all three are a response to a potential tragedy of the commons?

2. Professor Douglas Grant observes that when the Supreme Court first created the doctrine of equitable apportionment, "it assumed that Congress lacked the power to make an apportionment" and "[w]ater law experts assumed the same for decades thereafter." Douglas L. Grant, *Interstate Water Allocation Compacts: When the Virtue of Permanence Becomes the Vice of Inflexibility*, 74 U. COLO. L. REV. 105, 173 (2003). Why would they have made such an assumption? If Congress has the power to apportion interstate waters, is that power unlimited? Is there any allocation that could be invalidated by a court?

3. Professor Grant has argued that compacts should not necessarily bind the states that agreed to them.

> Western states negotiated most of their compacts between the 1920s and 1960s, an era when westerners widely viewed water as a commodity that should be used to promote economic development. Not surprisingly, the compacts of that era focused mainly on allocating water between states for present and future uses related to economic development, mainly irrigation but also industrial and municipal uses.

> Since states formed these compacts, the West has undergone some dramatic changes affecting water use. First, some cities have experienced once-unimagined population explosions that show few signs of slowing. Of course, growing populations need water. Second, although the doctrine of Indian reserved water rights predates the compacts, compact negotiators generally underestimated the magnitude of these rights and largely ignored them. Now Indian reserved water rights loom over water planning in much of the West. Third, public opinion has changed regarding desirable uses of water. Modern public sentiment supports maintaining instream flows to promote recreational and ecological values, and this has led to environmental legislation such as the federal Endangered Species Act and state minimum streamflow laws. In surveying the last thirty-five years of federal environmental programs, an expert on interstate water allocation recently said "many of the allocation compacts, most of which are at least forty years old, are so environmentally outdated in many respects that, in my opinion, it is unlikely that most of them should or would currently receive congressional consent."

> The expanding water demands for urban, Indian, recreational, and ecological uses create a major challenge for western water managers. They must find ways to meet these demands despite overallocation of water in many areas. They are responding to the challenge with various innovative measures that involve mainly water conservation and water marketing. Although these measures are important and desirable, they may prove inadequate to cope with increasingly outdated compact water allocations. Even if the measures fulfill demands for a time, they may fail after decades of further changes, some now foreseeable and others surely not. And even in the shorter term, the social, political, and economic costs of coping with outdated compact allocations may become inordinate from any perspective other than that of a state advantaged

by an old compact. Therefore, it is worth inquiring whether interstate allocations made long ago by compact can be modified to facilitate regionally desirable solutions to changing water needs.

Douglas L. Grant, *Interstate Water Allocation Compacts: When the Virtue of Permanence Becomes the Vice of Inflexibility*, 74 U. Colo. L. Rev. 105, 105–08 (2003). How would you answer Professor Grant's inquiry? What obstacles do you think a state would face in withdrawing from a compact? Would the Court invalidate such an effort?

4. What if Nevada had not consented to the Truckee–Carson–Pyramid Lake Water Rights Settlement Act of 1990? Pub. L. No. 101–618, § 204, 104 Stat. 3289, 3295–3304. What objections, both legal and political, might Nevada have raised? Is congressional apportionment likely to be as attractive to Nevada as it is to California?

5. In the Pecos River Compact litigation described in the text, the Court encouraged New Mexico and Texas to resolve their dispute by further negotiations. *Texas v. New Mexico*, 462 U.S. 554, 565, 568–69 (1983). When the states were not able to compromise, the Court adopted a modified methodology for calculating New Mexico's obligation, 467 U.S. 1238 (1984), and ultimately determined that New Mexico had taken more than its share of water from 1950 to 1983 and owed Texas 340,100 acre feet. 482 U.S. 124 (1987). The two states finally settled upon New Mexico making a payment of $14 million to Texas. In subsequent years New Mexico has spent about $50 million to purchase, lease, and retire water rights within the state in order to meet its recalculated obligation to Texas. Rather than paying for additional water, could the New Mexico legislature have simply declared that the water was unavailable and reduced the diversions of junior appropriators of the Pecos? In *Hinderlider v. La Plata River & Cherry Creek Ditch Co.*, 304 U.S. 92 (1938), the Court held that Colorado's decision to temporarily shut off diversions in order to comply with the La Plata River Compact did not take any vested rights of the complaining ditch company.

6. In some instances, the federal government does more than simply approve a compact between states and actually becomes a party to the compact. Two examples of such a federal-interstate compact are the Apalachicola–Chattahoochee–Flint River Basin Compact (among Florida, Georgia, and Alabama), Public L. No. 105–104, 111 Stat. 2219, 2223 (1997), and the Alabama–Coosa–Tallaposa River Basin Compact (between Georgia and Alabama), Public L. No. 105–105, 111 Stat. 2219, 2233 (1997). The compacts create a commission which is directed to allocate basin waters while protecting water quality, ecology, and biodiversity. The commission is made up of one voting member from each state and a nonvoting federal member who nevertheless retains the right to veto allocation formulas that do not comply with federal law. Given federal common law on interstate allocation, how much discretion does this arrangement leave with the federal member of the commission?

7. For a table listing all water compacts and their signatory states, see Douglas L. Grant, *Water Apportionment Compacts Between States* § 46.01, *in* 4 Waters and Water Rights (Robert E. Beck ed., replacement vol. 1996).

———

CASE STUDY: THE LAW OF THE COLORADO RIVER*

Among all the quirky, tragic and fascinating stories of water law, perhaps none is more compelling than that of the Colorado River. The tale of the Colorado River's allocation between its basin states and the creation of the "Law of the River" has been the life study of historians and water lawyers and is not yet anywhere near complete. The story begins with the river itself.

MARC REISNER, CADILLAC DESERT: THE AMERICAN WEST AND ITS DISAPPEARING WATER 120–22 (1993)

The Colorado is neither the biggest nor the longest river in the American West, nor, except for certain sections described in nineteenth-century journals as "awful" or "appalling," is it the most scenic. Its impressiveness and importance have to do with other things. It is one of the siltiest rivers in the world—the virgin Colorado could carry sediment loads close to those of the much larger Mississippi—and one of the wildest. Its drop of nearly thirteen thousand feet is unequaled in North America, and its constipation-relieving rapids, before dams tamed its flash floods, could have flipped a small freighter. The Colorado's modern notoriety, however, stems not from its wild rapids and plunging canyons but from the fact that it is the most legislated, most debated, and most litigated river in the entire world. It also has more people, more industry, and a more significant economy dependent on it than any comparable river in the world. If the Colorado River suddenly stopped flowing, you would have four years of carryover capacity in the reservoirs before you had to evacuate most of southern California and Arizona and a good portion of Colorado, New Mexico, Utah, and Wyoming. The river system provides over half the water of greater Los Angeles, San Diego, and Phoenix; it grows much of America's domestic production of fresh winter vegetables; it illuminates the neon city of Las Vegas, whose annual income is one-fourth the entire gross national product of Egypt—the only other place on earth where so many people are so helplessly dependent on one river's flow. The greater portion of the Nile, however, still manages despite many diversions, to reach its delta at the Mediterranean Sea. The Colorado is so used up on its way to the sea that only a burbling trickle reaches its dried-up delta at the head of the Gulf of California, and then only in wet years. . . .

The Colorado has a significance that goes beyond mere prominence. It was on this river that the first of the world's truly great dams [Hoover Dam] was built—a dam which gave engineers the confidence to dam the Columbia, the Volga, the Paraná, the Niger, the Nile, the Zambezi, and most of the world's great rivers. The dam rose up at the depths of the Depression and carried America's spirits with it. * * *

In terms of annual flow, the Colorado isn't a big river—in the United States it does not even rank among the top twenty-five—but, like a forty-pound wolverine that can drive a bear off its dinner, it is unrivaled for sheer orneriness. The virgin Colorado was tempestuous, willful, headstrong. Its flow

---

* The description of the history that follows relies heavily on the work of Norris Hundley, Jr., the preeminent historian on the Colorado River Compact and the Law of the River. Specifically, it uses *The West Against Itself: The Colorado River—An Institutional History, in* NEW COURSES FOR THE COLORADO RIVER 9 (Gary D. Weatherford & F. Lee Brown eds., 1986) and NORRIS HUNDLEY, JR., WATER AND THE WEST: THE COLORADO RIVER COMPACT AND THE POLITICS OF WATER IN THE AMERICAN WEST (1975). The description also relies upon MARC REISNER, CADILLAC DESERT 120–44, 255–305 (1993).

varied psychotically between a few thousand cubic feet per second and a couple of hundred thousand, sometimes within a few days. Draining a vast, barren watershed whose rains usually come in deluges, its sediment volume was phenomenal. If the river, running high, were diverted through an ocean liner with a cheesecloth strainer at one end, it would have filled the ship with mud in an afternoon. The silt would begin to settle about two hundred miles above the Gulf of California, below the last of the Grand Canyon's rapids, where the river's gradient finally moderated for good. There was so much silt that it raised the entire riverbed, foot by foot, year by year, until the Colorado slipped out of its loose confinement of low sandy bluffs and tore off in some other direction, instantly digging a new course. It developed an affection for several such channels, returning to them again and again—Bee River, New River, Alamo River, big braided washes that sat dry and expectant in the desert, waiting for the river to return. The New and Alamo channels drove into Mexico, then veered back north into the United States, a hundred-mile semi-loop, and ended at the foot of the Chocolate Mountains, where the delinquent river would form a huge evanescent body of water called the Salton Sea. After a while, the New and Alamo channels would themselves silt up and the Colorado would throw itself back into its old bed and return to the Gulf of California, much to the relief of the great schools of shrimp, the clouds of waterfowl, and the thousands of cougars, jaguars, and bobcats that prowled its delta. The Salton Sea would slowly evaporate and life would return to normal, for a while. The river went on such errant flings every few dozen years—a vanishing moment in geologic time, but long enough so that the first people who tried to tame it had no idea what they were in for.

––––––––

The legal development of the Law of the River, which touches upon all three methods of allocation—judicial, compact, and congressional—begins with those whom Reisner describes as "the first people who tried to tame it." They were farmers and speculators in California's Imperial Valley. As described in connection with the *Imperial Irrigation District* case, *supra* page 784, the Imperial Valley, located at the southern end of California just north of Mexico, is a desert with only 2.9 inches of rainfall a year. But it is a desert with 200 inches of the richest soil in the world, poured out of the entire Southwest over the ages by the Colorado River. The soil will grow anything. The first farmers who came to the Valley just had to find water. And water was there to be had. The Valley, which lies just below sea level, could be irrigated by a gravity-flow canal from the Colorado River. Unfortunately for those first farmers, because of a ridge of hills separating the Valley from the River, the easiest route for the water was through Mexico. Mexico agreed that the water could be diverted through its territory but demanded the right to take up to half of it. The farmers agreed to Mexico's terms and began diverting, putting 300,000 acres in production by 1901. What they really wanted, however, was a canal north of the border—an "All–American Canal." But such a canal would be expensive to build and even more expensive to maintain because of the annual flooding of the untamed Colorado; flooding, recall, which recreated the Salton Sea between 1905 and 1907. To make the canal work, the farmers would also need a dam.

In 1919, the farmers, by then organized as the Imperial Irrigation District, convinced Congressman William Kettner to introduce legislation authorizing construction of a canal. They were strongly supported by the Bureau of Reclamation. Eager to test its own development ideas, the Bureau thought the canal was a good idea and that a major dam was an even better one. The prospect of a major hydroelectric dam in turn attracted the interest of Los Angeles. While Los Angeles believed its Owens Valley project would provide it enough water, its rapid growth was creating increasing demand for electricity and a major dam on the mainstem of the Colorado seemed like a perfect opportunity to get it. (Only after a 1923 dry cycle would Los Angeles start thinking about the dam as a way of providing more water.) Early in 1922, Imperial Valley congressman Phil Swing and California Senator Hiram Johnson introduced revised bills that authorized not only an All–American Canal but also a hydropower dam at Boulder Canyon.

With the Bureau and both urban and agricultural interests in California lined up behind the legislation, it may have seemed that the way was clear. There was one big problem: the Colorado was an interstate river and the other states in the basin were opposed. Even then California's potential for growth was evident. If California were permitted to start using all of the waters of the Colorado, it might mean that the other states in the basin would never have their chance. This fear was only exacerbated by the Supreme Court's decision in *Wyoming v. Colorado*, 259 U.S. 419 (1922), that as between states that adhered to the prior appropriation doctrine, priority of appropriation would be the primary determinant of interstate allocation.

Prompted by the calls of Colorado water lawyer Delph Carpenter, who was a staunch advocate of using the Constitution's Compact Clause instead of relying on the vagaries of expensive apportionment litigation, the basin states had in 1921 sought and gained federal approval to negotiate a compact. Joined by Secretary of Commerce Herbert Hoover as the federal representative, the negotiations began in January of 1922. The early negotiations did not make much progress but the introduction of the Swing–Johnson bill and the decision in *Wyoming v. Colorado* later that year added a sense of urgency for the final round of talks scheduled for November, 1922 at Bishop's Lodge, a resort just outside Santa Fe. From the perspective of the basin states other than California, if the compact negotiations failed and the bill passed, California might just get all of the River, foiling Colorado's own nascent plans to divert water from the western slope of the Rockies to the growing cities on the Front Range and the even more inchoate plans of Arizona, Utah, and others some day to develop the River's waters for their citizens. On the other hand, California wanted the Swing–Johnson bill and understood that it was likely to remain bottled up in Congress until the other basin states had some security about their own share of the Colorado.

Eschewing the state-by-state allocation proposals on which early negotiations had foundered, Carpenter led off the November negotiation with a new proposal to divide the Colorado's waters equally between two basins rather than state-by-state. Lee's Ferry, an ancient river crossing in northern Arizona close to the Utah border, would be the dividing line between an Upper Basin (Colorado, Utah, Wyoming, and New Mexico, with a small slice of Arizona) and a lower basin (California, Nevada, and Arizona, with small slices of Utah and New Mexico). A map of the two basins is available at http://www.crwua.org/coloradoriver/index.cfm?action=rivermap. Most of the delegates agreed with the plan but Arizona was a holdout. It wanted to assure that the water from its tributaries—primarily the Gila which flowed into the Colorado near the end of the Colorado's journey—would not be included in the calculus of the water available for division. Without support, Arizona gradually gave ground and finally agreed to a plan under which the two basins would each receive 7.5 million acre feet (maf) per year and, in recognition of Arizona's tributary claim, the lower basin states could increase their diversions by 1 maf per year. More specifically, the Upper Basin assumed an obligation to deliver 75 maf to Lee's Ferry every ten years in recognition of the significant fluctuations in river flow from year to year. The parties also agreed that if the United States were to negotiate a water treaty with Mexico, any obligation to Mexico would be met with surplus water or shared equally by the two basins. Unfortunately, the states' understanding of how often the River would run a surplus was mistaken. The negotiators had worked on the assumption that the River's average flow was 16.4 maf. As it turns out, the average flow of the Colorado since the Compact was negotiated has been closer to 13.9 maf. The following are some of the key provisions of the Compact.

ARTICLE I

The major purposes of this compact are to provide for the equitable division and apportionment of the use of the waters of the Colorado River System; to establish the relative importance of different beneficial uses of water; to promote interstate comity; to remove causes of present and future controversies; and to secure the expeditious agricultural and industrial development of the Colorado River Basin, the storage of its waters, and the protection of life and property from floods. To these ends the Colorado River Basin is divided into two Basins, and an apportionment of the use of part of the water of the Colorado River System is made to each of them with the provision that further equitable apportionments may be made.

ARTICLE II

As used in this compact—

(a) The term "Colorado River System" means that portion of the Colorado River and its tributaries within the United States of America.

(b) The term "Colorado River Basin" means all of the drainage area of the Colorado River System and all other territory within the United States of America to which the waters of the Colorado River System shall be beneficially applied. * * *

(h) The term "domestic use" shall include the use of water for household, stock, municipal, mining, milling, industrial, and other like purposes, but shall exclude the generation of electrical power.

ARTICLE III

(a) There is hereby apportioned from the Colorado River System in perpetuity to the Upper Basin and to the Lower Basin, respectively, the exclusive beneficial consumptive use of 7,500,000 acre-feet of water per annum, which shall include all water necessary for the supply of any rights which may now exist.

(b) In addition to the apportionment in paragraph (a), the Lower Basin is hereby given the right to increase its beneficial consumptive use of such waters by one million acre-feet per annum.

(c) If, as a matter of international comity, the United States of America shall hereafter recognize in the United States of Mexico any right to the use of any waters of the Colorado River System, such waters shall be supplied first from the waters which are surplus over and above the aggregate of the quantities specified in paragraphs (a) and (b); and if such surplus shall prove insufficient for this purpose, then the burden of such deficiency shall be equally borne by the Upper Basin and the Lower Basin, and whenever necessary the States of the Upper Division shall deliver at Lee Ferry water to supply one-half of the deficiency so recognized in addition to that provided in paragraph (d).

(d) The States of the Upper Division will not cause the flow of the river at Lee Ferry to be depleted below an aggregate of 75,000,000 acre-feet for any period of ten consecutive years reckoned in continuing progressive series beginning with the first day of October next succeeding the ratification of this compact.

(e) The States of the Upper Division shall not withhold water, and the States of the Lower Division shall not require the delivery of water which cannot reasonably be applied to domestic and agricultural uses. * * *

ARTICLE VII

Nothing in this compact shall be construed as affecting the obligations of the United States of America to Indian tribes.

ARTICLE X

This compact may be terminated at any time by the unanimous agreement of the signatory States. In the event of such termination all rights established under it shall continue unimpaired.

———

Within five months, six states had ratified the Compact. Arizona was a different story. Whereas the Compact protected the Upper Basins states from California's water ambitions, it offered no such protection to Arizona. The principle of priority might still result in California taking the full share of the lower basin's water, particularly now that the Upper Basin states were ready to withdraw their opposition to the Swing–Johnson, Boulder Canyon legislation. Although Arizona's negotiator, William Norviel, had been convinced that the trajectory of California's growth would not limit Arizona's ambitions, Arizona's new governor disagreed and ultimately so did much of the state. The result was that Arizona refused to ratify the Compact and insisted that the deal be renegotiated. Without Arizona's ratification, the Upper Basin states wouldn't support the Swing–Johnson bill. Colorado's Carpenter again proved key to resolving the impasse. He proposed a six-state agreement that excluded Arizona. If California would agree to the division, the Upper Basin would be protected from California, whose development they most feared. The six-state compact wouldn't protect the Upper Basin from Arizona, particularly if California used up the full lower basin share and Arizona decided to look northward, but it was a reasonable second-best solution. California, however, was reluctant because it would more likely bear the full burden of whatever Arizona's share proved to be. Nevada, in which no one foresaw any significant development, remained an afterthought.

Finally, in 1928, Congress stepped in to resolve the impasse with a bill that authorized construction of the All–American Canal and Boulder Dam, but only if at least six states, including California, ratified the Compact. To further protect themselves, the Upper Basin insisted that California agree to limit itself to a specific share of the River and leave a significant amount of lower basin water for Arizona, in the hopes that Arizona would then not need to ever pursue the Upper Basin's water. Still eager for the canal and dam after all these years, California reluctantly agreed to limit itself to 4.4 maf of water plus one-half of any surplus. Finally, in a provision which was later to prove critical, Congress gave its advance approval to a proposed lower basin compact. The preapproved compact assigned 4.4 maf to California plus one-half of any surplus, 2.8 maf to Arizona, plus the other half of any surplus, and 0.3 maf to Nevada. It also assured that Arizona would receive the entire flow of the Gila. Arizona strenuously objected to the bill, but the Boulder Canyon Project Act, 43 U.S.C. § 617 *et seq.*, was approved by Congress in December and by the following June, after California's legislature had agreed to the limitations included in the Act, it became effective. By 1935, Hoover Dam had been completed (as it turned out, in Black Canyon rather than Boulder Canyon) and by 1941 Imperial Valley was receiving water through the All–American canal.

Arizona, however, was not about to give up. It embarked upon a series of fruitless lawsuits. In 1930, Arizona asked the Supreme Court to declare the Boulder Canyon Project Act unconstitutional on the ground that it authorized construction of a dam on Arizona's soil without Arizona's permission and that Congress' claim that it was acting to improve navigation was a sham. The Court refused. *Arizona v. California*, 283 U.S. 423 (1931). Four years later, in 1934, Arizona asked the Court for permission to perpetuate oral testimony on the meaning of the Compact but the Court again refused, concluding that Arizona had no business worrying about the interpretation of a Compact it had refused to ratify. *Arizona v. California*, 292 U.S. 341 (1934). In 1935, Arizona followed with a request for judicial apportionment of the Colorado River which the Court rejected because the United States refused to be party to the suit. *Arizona v. California*, 298 U.S. 558 (1936). Arizona at one point even dispatched its state national guard unit to Parker Dam in an effort to stop the Bureau from building what Arizona claimed was an unauthorized bridge to the Arizona shore. This time the Court agreed, *United States v. Arizona*, 295 U.S. 174, 192 (1935), but Congress quickly authorized the dam and Arizona's militia was withdrawn. At various times throughout this period, Arizona tried to reopen negotiations with California, but neither party was willing to give ground and incidents like those with the national guard made compromise even less likely.

Although California was growing faster, Arizona was growing too, and relying mostly on pumping groundwater. Without signing the compact, Arizona had little hope of getting its own federal water project, a project that was destined to be very expensive because it required pumping 1.2 maf of Colorado River water up nearly 2000 feet and then through a 335–mile–long series of aqueducts and canals to the growing cities of Phoenix and Tucson. That fact, along with a 1944 treaty with Mexico fixing Mexico's share of the River at 1.5 maf, led Arizona finally to ratify the Compact. If Arizona thought its troubles were over, it was mistaken. When its representatives introduced a bill authorizing the Central Arizona Project (CAP), California objected that Arizona was proposing to take more than its share of the Colorado. As California saw it, under the Compact, Arizona's tributaries were part of the river system, and thus when Arizona used its tributaries, it was using its share of the River. The tributaries, in other words, were excess to the water delivered at Lee's Ferry, and under the Boulder Canyon Project Act, one-half of any excess was available to California, which even then had contracts with the Bureau for the delivery of 5.3 maf, some 900,000 af more than its 4.4 maf share. This interpretation of the Compact, insisted California, necessarily followed from the Compact provision allowing the lower basin to use an additional 1 maf. Arizona countered that its tributaries were for its use alone. With Congress unwilling to authorize the CAP until Arizona and California resolved their differences, in 1952 Arizona sued California again.

The case was to last eleven years and to entail 22 hours of oral argument, but when it was over Arizona won an overwhelming victory. *Arizona v. California*, 373 U.S. 546 (1963). The Court decided that the key document was not the Compact but the Boulder Canyon Project Act. As the Court viewed it, the lower basin compact to which Congress had given its preapproval (4.4 maf to California, 2.8 maf to Arizona, 0.3 maf to Nevada, with Arizona receiving the entire flow of its tributaries) was not simply a proposal. Instead, "Congress in passing the Project Act intended to and did create its own comprehensive scheme for the apportionment among California, Arizona, and Nevada of the Lower Basin's share of the mainstream waters of the Colorado River." *Id.* at 564–65. Not only that, but by giving the Secretary of the Interior authority to enter into water delivery contracts, said the Court, Congress intended the Secretary to have discretion with respect to which states and which users would receive any excess or bear the burden of any shortage. *Id.* at 580–81. According to the Court, the Project Act was thus not only the first congressional apportionment but also made the Secretary of the Interior the permanent water master of the lower Colorado River.

In contrast to the fireworks in the Lower Basin, the Upper Basin remained relatively quiet. Only Colorado had significant immediate ambitions for the Colorado River, and in 1937 it managed to win congressional approval of the Colorado–Big Thompson project, which would bring water from the Colorado River basin on the west slope of the Rockies to the cities and farms on the plains to the east. With Arizona's ratification of the Compact, the resolution of Mexico's share, and the end of World War II, the Upper Basin states decided it was time to divide their share of the Colorado among themselves. In 1948, they entered into a separate compact assigning

Colorado 51.75% of the Upper Basin's share, Utah 23%, Wyoming 14%, New Mexico 11.25%, and Arizona 50,000 af per year. With this agreement in place, the states renewed their push for the Bureau to start construction of the Upper Basin water projects, whose feasibility had been studied as part of the Boulder Canyon Project Act. Most particularly, the Upper Basin desired a large storage reservoir that would allow it to meet its Compact obligation of delivering 75 maf at Lee's Ferry every ten years. That reservoir turned out to be Lake Powell. But the Glen Canyon dam was not the only project authorized by the 1956 Colorado River Storage Project Act. It also gave the go-ahead for major dams on three tributaries to the Colorado—Blue Mesa on the Gunnison, Navajo on the San Juan, and Flaming Gorge on the Green.

With its victory in *Arizona v. California*, 373 U.S. 546 (1963) in hand, Arizona hoped that now surely the Central Arizona Project could be authorized. But if it could not win in court, California was going to exercise its political muscle in Congress. The California delegation managed to hold off CAP authorization for five years and dropped its opposition only when Arizona agreed that California would have first priority to its 4.4 maf no matter how much water was available, a critical concession given that the average flow of the Colorado was so much less than the Compact's negotiators had originally anticipated.

Not to be denied an opportunity, the Upper Basin states conditioned their own approval of CAP on the authorization of five additional major projects for the Upper Basin. In the end, the bill authorized projects which the river's water supply had little chance of fulfilling. Unfazed, all of the basin states proposed that the Bureau of Reclamation study ways of moving water from other river systems into the Colorado River basin. Recognizing that the Columbia River was directly in their sights, representatives from the Northwest, led by Senator Scoop Jackson, won inclusion of a provision imposing a ten-year ban on any interbasin transfer studies.

Perhaps the most controversial aspect of the CAP bill, enacted as the Colorado River Basin Project Act, 43 U.S.C. §§ 1501–56, was its proposal to build dams at Marble Canyon, just east of the Grand Canyon, and Bridge Canyon, just to the west. Bridge Canyon's reservoir would have inundated portions of Grand Canyon National Park. The purpose of the dams was to generate the hydropower necessary to pay for the CAP and to provide the power to lift the water up and out of the Colorado and send it to central Arizona. In a fight reminiscent of the one waged over the proposed Echo Park dam, *see supra* at page 32, the environmental community managed to defeat the dams. Key to the campaign were the Sierra Club's full-page advertisements in major newspapers. One such ad, responding to the Bureau's argument that the reservoirs would actually give boaters a better view of the Grand Canyon, asked, "Should we also flood the Sistine Chapel so tourists can get nearer the ceiling?" Although the dams were defeated, in their place the bill authorized a coal-fired power plant at Page in northern Arizona, which today generates air pollution over the Grand Canyon and important jobs for members of the Navajo and Hopi tribes.

The CAP was finally completed in the 1990s (at a cost of $4.7 billion), but the water was mostly too expensive for the irrigators for whom it was intended. With municipal and industrial users not able to take up the slack, CAP water was underutilized. That, of course, was just fine with California, as long as the water was left in the Colorado. But in 1996, Arizona's legislature created the Arizona Water Bank to store Arizona's unused share of CAP water. The Bank pays for the delivery and then either stores the water in underground aquifers or allows irrigation districts to use the water in exchange for future ground water recovery rights. Arizona also claims the right to market its banked water to California and to Nevada, which in 2000 used its full 300,000 af allotment for the first time, largely because of Las Vegas' dramatic growth. In 1999, the Bureau issued a regulation to facilitate such voluntary transactions without taking a position on their legality under the Law of the River. 64 Fed. Reg. 58,986 (Nov. 1, 1999); 43 C.F.R. § 414.1 to § 414.6 (2003). In 2004, Nevada agreed to pay Arizona $330 million ($100 million in 2005 and then $23 million per year for ten years beginning in 2009) for banking 1.25 maf of water. *See* Southern Nevada Water Authority, *Arizona Water Bank, available at* http:// www.snwa.com/html/wr_colrvr_azbank.html; Arizona Water Banking Authority, *Annual Report 2007, available at* http://www.azwaterbank.gov/ awba/documents/Final2007AnnualReport.pdf. The idea is that in some future year Nevada could take, for example, an extra 50,000 af of water out of the Colorado River and Arizona would then take 50,000 less acre feet of its Colorado River share.

Each passing year seems to bring new management challenges for the Colorado River and new complexities to the Law of the River. In recent years there has been increasing attention to the plight of endangered species dependent on the Colorado River ecosystem. The Upper Basin states have been required to develop a recovery plan for several endangered native fish species. In the Lower Basin, a multi-species conservation plan has been developed to address 26 federal- and state-listed candidate and sensitive species. As part of the Glen Canyon Dam Adaptive Management Program, the Bureau has experimented with mimicking natural floods in the Grand Canyon by releasing greater flows from Glen Canyon Dam and an array of officials, scientists, and environmental organizations are also at work thinking about how to restore the Colorado River delta, whose wetlands have been reduced from 1.8 million acres rich in biodiversity to only 40,000 acres. *See* ROBERT W. ADLER, RESTORING COLORADO RIVER ECOSYS-TEMS: A TROUBLED SENSE OF IMMENSITY (2007); Robert Jerome Glennon & Peter W. Culp, *The Last Green Lagoon: How and Why the Bush Administration Should Save the Colorado River Delta*, 28 ECOLOGY L.Q. 903 (2002). The one thing in common with all of these efforts is that they require more water to be left in the River.

In response to these ever-increasing demands, and pressure from the other basin states, in 2003 the Secretary of the Interior finally exercised the discretion given the Secretary in *Arizona v. California* to limit California's water use to the 4.4 maf limit of the Boulder Canyon Project Act. California had for a long time been using about 5.2 maf. Under guidelines issued by the Secretary, California must reduce its consumption to 4.4 maf by 2016. Part of the way California has agreed to accomplish this is to transfer water from the agricultural use of the Imperial Irrigation District to municipal and industrial use of the San Diego County Water Authority.

See supra page 790. *See also* Quantification Settlement Agreement, *available at* http://www.crss.water.ca.gov/crqsa/index.cfm (agreement between California and four state water agencies on the water transfers and supply programs necessary to reduce California's consumption to 4.4 maf).

These topics cannot all be covered in this casebook. Nor can a host of others that influence management of the Colorado River, among them Indian tribes' reserved rights to significant quantities of the Colorado's water and the historical and continuing efforts of the United States to limit the increasing salinity of the water that is delivered to Mexico after being leached through so many saline soils on its way down river. But this case study should give you some idea of the sorts of challenges that can be faced in allocating an interstate river. Whereas the historic Colorado River once spread layer after layer of sediment, in its place the river now pours out a succession of statutes, regulations, judicial decisions, contracts, guidelines, and orders that are as meandering and complex as the River itself.

QUESTIONS AND DISCUSSION

1. Return to the question posed by Professor Grant: Can an individual state choose to withdraw from or to modify an interstate compact to which it is a party? Stepping back from the interests of the individual states, what sorts of modifications, if any, would you propose to the Compact? How might the various Colorado River basin states react to any effort to modify the Colorado River Compact?

2. As of 2005, the Upper Basin was using 3.6 maf of its 7.5 maf share. *See* Colorado River Water Use, at http://www.usbr.gov/lc/region/g4000/uses.html. Under the Compact, can an Upper Basin state sell its unused share to California or Nevada?

3. Suppose there were no Compact or Boulder Canyon Project Act and all of the Colorado River basin states were before the Supreme Court in an allocation dispute. If you were clerking for the Special Master assigned to make an allocation recommendation to the Court, what would you recommend? Why?

4. Why not simply shortcut the whole process of compacts and judicial apportionment and just have Congress pass legislation mandating that interstate waters will be divided by priority of appropriation? Given the mobility of the United States citizenry, does it make sense to allocate water with reference to state boundaries?

5. For further reading on the cultural and legal geography of the Colorado River see PHILLIP FRADKIN, A RIVER NO MORE: THE COLORADO RIVER AND THE WEST (1981).

6. For further background reading on water law and the history of water allocation, see the following: ROBERT JEROME GLENNON, WATER FOLLIES: GROUNDWATER PUMPING AND THE FATE OF AMERICA'S FRESH WATERS (2002); WILLIAM KAHRL, WATER AND POWER (1982); MARC REISNER, CADILLAC DESERT: THE AMERICAN WEST AND ITS DISAPPEARING WATER (1993); WALLACE STEGNER, BEYOND THE HUNDREDTH MERIDIAN: JOHN WESLEY POWELL AND THE SECOND OPENING OF

THE WEST (1954); WATERS AND WATER RIGHTS vols. 1–7 (Robert E. Beck ed., 1991).

V. INTERNATIONAL WATER LAW

Arizona may have sent its national guard to Parker Dam to challenge the Bureau of Reclamation and a lot of harsh words have been exchanged between riparian states, but in the end interstate water allocation disputes have been settled peacefully because the states have consented in the Constitution to federal jurisdiction over commerce and to Supreme Court resolution of disputes between states. The task of international water law is to resolve the same sort of disputes between nation-states without the benefit of an international legislature or preexisting consent to jurisdiction. Generally, that occurs by negotiation of agreements—in the form of treaties, conventions, and other instruments, both bilateral and multilateral—in the shadow of international legal norms, norms that are themselves developed partly by the growing corpus of treaties. This final section of the chapter briefly considers the treaties and international legal norms that bind or guide (depending on one's view of the meaning and force of international law) the allocation of transboundary watercourses between riparian nations. It turns out that the international law of water has much in common with the interstate allocation doctrines discussed in the prior section. Before turning to the doctrine, however, it will be useful to have some sense of the scope of the international challenge.

ROBIN CLARKE, WATER: THE INTERNATIONAL CRISIS 91–92 (1993)

The potential for conflict is enormous. Globally, 47 per cent of all land falls within international river basins, and nearly 50 countries on four continents have more than three-quarters of their total land in international river basins. Two hundred and fourteen basins are multinational, including 57 in Africa and 48 in Europe.

In human terms, this means that almost 40 per cent of the world's population lives in international river basins. These two billion people are dependent on the cooperation of all the countries sharing the basin for a guaranteed water supply of consistent quality, and for their environmental stability.

Thirteen river basins are shared by five or more countries. Ten are shared mostly by developing countries, and have few or no treaties to regulate water use; and a number are in areas where water is otherwise scarce. It is not surprising that many [shared rivers] have a history of international tension, particularly the Jordan and Euphrates in the Near and Middle East; the Ganges in Asia; the Nile in Africa; and the Colorado and Rio Grande in North America.

In developed countries, many international agreements have been drawn up to regulate shared basin areas and, as a result, use of shared water supplies is more rarely a source of international dispute. Europe, for instance, has four river basins shared by four or more countries, but these are regulated by no less than 175 treaties.

An absence of regulation on shared water resources is common in developing countries. Africa, in comparison to Europe, has a vast and complex system of river basins: 12 are shared by four or more nations, but only 34 treaties regulate their use. In Asia, only 31 treaties have been drawn up to regulate the five basins shared by four or more countries.

A. CUSTOMARY LAW OF TRANSBOUNDARY WATERCOURSES

Recall the first interstate water dispute that came before the United States Supreme Court. Colorado, the upstream state, claimed the right to use as much of the Arkansas River as it desired. Kansas, the downstream state, contended that Colorado had an obligation to forego diversions that would disrupt the natural flow of the river. In the end, the Court rejected both positions and adopted a rule of equitable apportionment. International disputes have traditionally evolved much the same way. The upstream nation makes a claim of absolute territorial sovereignty, asserting the right to use the natural resources within its territory as it sees fit. The downstream state argues for absolute integrity of the river. Historically, although watercourse states assert these irreconcilable claims to establish an initial bargaining position, most have then negotiated a compromise that provides for some form of equitable utilization and that may or may not include some mechanisms for common management of the watercourse. Out of this oft-repeated process of claim, counterclaim, and compromise apportionment, commentators have chosen to label four theories of transboundary water allocation: territorial sovereignty; territorial (or river) integrity; equitable utilization (sometimes called limited territorial sovereignty); and common management (sometimes called the community of interests theory).

Probably the most often cited example of the territorial sovereignty theory is the dispute between the United States and Mexico over allocation of the waters of the Rio Grande. In 1894, Mexico complained to the United States that the water supply of several Mexican cities was being jeopardized by the diversions of United States' irrigators. In response to a request from the Secretary of State, United States Attorney General Harmon issued an opinion.

Attorney General Opinion, 21 Op. Atty. Gen. 274, 280–83; 1895 WL 391 (U.S.A.G.)

The fundamental principle of international law is the absolute sovereignty of every nation, as against all others, within its own territory. Of the nature and scope of sovereignty with respect to judicial jurisdiction, which is one of its elements, Chief Justice Marshall said (*Schooner Exchange v. McFaddon*, 7 Cranch, p. 136):

> The jurisdiction of the nation within its own territory is necessarily exclusive and absolute. It is susceptible of no limitation not imposed by itself. Any restriction upon it, deriving validity from an external source, would imply a diminution of its sovereignty to the extent of the restriction and an investment of that sovereignty to the same extent in that power

which could impose such restriction. 'All exceptions' therefore, to the full and complete power of a nation within its own territories must be traced up to the consent of the nation itself. They can flow from no other legitimate source. * * *

The immediate as well as the possible consequences of the right asserted by Mexico show that its recognition is entirely inconsistent with the sovereignty of the United States over its national domain. * * *

It is not suggested that the injuries complained of are or have been in any measure due to wantonness or wastefulness in the use of water or to any design or intention to injure. The water is simply insufficient to supply the needs of the great stretch of arid country through which the river, never large in the dry season, flows, giving much and receiving little.

The case presented is a novel one. Whether the circumstances make it possible or proper to take any action from considerations of comity is a question which does not pertain to this Department; but that question should be decided as one of policy only, because in my opinion, the rules, principles, and precedents of international law impose no liability or obligation upon the United States.

———

Attorney General Harmon's opinion is a classic expression of the doctrine of absolute territorial sovereignty. Indeed, the doctrine of territorial sovereignty is often referred to as the "Harmon Doctrine." As even the last paragraph of the excerpt hints, the doctrine was never one to which the United States could reasonably adhere. Not only was there the matter of comity and policy mentioned by Harmon, but also there was the matter of geography. The Rio Grande is part of the southern border between the United States and Mexico and thus some United States' users were downstream of Mexican users. Moreover, to the north, the United States was a downstream user of waters that flowed out of Canada. It is thus not particularly surprising that even though the United States continued to assert that it did not have any legal obligation to Mexico, by 1906 it had negotiated the *Convention Between the United States of America and Mexico Concerning the Equitable Distribution of the Waters of the Rio Grande for Irrigation Purposes*. 34 Stat. 2953 (1906).

Although the Harmon Doctrine remains a useful negotiating tool for upstream riparians, its underlying premise that nation states have complete sovereignty over the resources within their country has been significantly undermined by a growing body of international legal norms. The most prominent of these norms is the basic standard articulated in the famous *Trail Smelter* case involving a United States protest of harm caused by sulphur dioxide pollution from a smelter across the border in Canada. The arbitral tribunal to whom the countries had agreed to submit the dispute ruled that "[n]o State has the right to use or permit the use of its territory in such a manner as to cause injury.... in or to the territory of another or the properties or persons therein, when the case is of serious consequence...." Trail Smelter Case (U.S. v. Canada), Arbitral Tribunal, 3 R. Int'l Arb. Awards 1905 (1941). This standard, familiar to those who have studied common law nuisance and the *sic utere* principle, has since become one of the bedrocks of the field of international environmental law and is enshrined in Principle 21 of the Stockholm Declaration and then repeated in Principle 2 of the Rio Declaration:

> States have, in accordance with the Charter of the United Nations and the principles of international law, the sovereign right to exploit their own resources pursuant to their own environmental policies, and the responsibility to ensure that activities within their own jurisdiction or control do not cause damage to the environment of other States or of areas beyond the limits of national jurisdiction.

Although the principle that one state should not exploit its resources in a way that damages another state might at first appear to give some impetus to the competing water allocation theory of absolute river integrity, that view ignores the principle of *Trail Smelter* that the injury must be of "serious consequence," which is another articulation of the common nuisance requirement that the harm be significant and unreasonable. One important articulation of this requirement came in the *Lac Lanoux Arbitration* between Spain and France. France sought to build a reservoir at Lake Lanoux that would reduce the natural flow of water from the Lake into the Carol River which flowed into Spain. France proposed to substitute from another river the equivalent amount of water into the Carol River before it reached Spain. Fearing that France's plan would give it the ability to stop water from reaching Spain should it choose to stop the substitution, Spain objected. When the parties were unable to reach a solution, they agreed to submit their dispute to arbitration. Before the tribunal, Spain argued that France should be enjoined unless it received Spain's approval, even though France's plan promised to substitute the same quantity and quality of water to Spain. By claiming a veto right even in the absence of harm, Spain was essentially arguing for absolute river integrity. The tribunal rejected Spain's demand of a right to veto as an unwarranted infringement on France's sovereignty. In doing so, it observed:

> [w]hile admittedly there is a rule prohibiting the upper riparian State from altering the waters of a river in circumstances calculated to do *serious injury to* the lower riparian State, such a principle has no application to the present case, since it was agreed by the Tribunal ... that the French project did not alter the waters of the Carol.

Lac Lanoux Arbitration (Spain v. France), Arbitral Tribunal, 12 R. Int'l Arb. Awards 281 (French; English trans. in 24 I.L.R. 101, 197 (1961)) (emphasis added). The tribunal further emphasized that while the upstream state was not obligated to give up its sovereignty, "the upper riparian State, under the rules of good faith, has an obligation to take into consideration the various interests concerned, to seek to give them every satisfaction compatible with the pursuit of its own interests and to show that it has ... a real desire to reconcile the interests of the other riparian with its own." *Id.* at 198. In the end, because France had already made significant changes to its plans in an effort to assure that Spain would receive an equal amount of water, the Tribunal found that France was entitled to go forward with the project.

As revealed in the Harmon Doctrine and the Lake Lanoux case, nations are inclined to begin from the extreme positions of territorial sovereignty or territorial integrity and then move toward some equitable arrangement. In that regard, international allocation shares much in common with interstate allocation. But there is a critical difference. In contrast to Colorado, which had agreed in Article III of the Constitution that Kansas could take its claim before the Supreme Court, nations are free to cling to their initial positions. Because so many nations have negotiated some equitable utilization of their shared waters, the refusal to do so likely "violates" customary international law (the law that is created by the customary practice of states where that practice is undertaken out of a sense of legal obligation). But that violation is not easy to remedy, and even when some negotiated allocation occurs it is more likely to reflect considerations of political economy and power than is the case with congressional, judicial, or compact allocation of interstate waters.

QUESTIONS AND DISCUSSION

1.   The text asserts that negotiated solutions on an international level are more likely to reflect considerations of political economy and power than congressional, judicial, or compact allocation of interstate waters. Do you agree? Does that mean that such considerations are absent in interstate allocation?

2.   For a more detailed look at the Harmon Doctrine, see Stephen McCaffrey, *The Harmon Doctrine One Hundred Years Later: Buried, Not Praised*, 36 NAT. RESOURCES J. 549 (1996).

B.   THE 1997 CONVENTION ON NON-NAVIGATIONAL USES OF INTERNATIONAL WATERCOURSES

The repeated rejection of arguments for absolute territorial or river integrity and the acceptance of some form of equitable utilization in arbitral decisions like *Lac Lanoux* and in a wide array of treaties and agreements gradually developed into customary international law. By 1966, it had come far enough for the International Law Association to draft its Helsinki Rules on the Uses of International Rivers, *reprinted in* 52 I.L.M. 484 (1967), which provided in Article IV that "Each basin State is entitled, within its territory, to a reasonable and equitable share in the beneficial uses of the waters of an international drainage basin." Then, in 1970, the Sixth Committee of the UN General Assembly asked the International Law Commission (a UN commission created to promote the development and codification of international law) to develop a convention to codify these understandings and practices. Draft articles were finally submitted in 1990, and after seven more years of comments from governments and revisions from another General Assembly working group, the following Convention was approved by the General Assembly and opened for signature.

UN Convention on the Law of the Non–Navigational Uses of International Watercourses, May 21, 1997, *reprinted in* 36 I.L.M. 700 (1997)

I. INTRODUCTION

Article 1

Scope of the present Convention

1. The present Convention applies to uses of international watercourses and of their waters for purposes other than navigation and to measures of protection, preservation and management related to the uses of those watercourses and their waters.

2. The uses of international watercourses for navigation is not within the scope of the present Convention except insofar as other uses affect navigation or are affected by navigation.

Article 2

Use of terms

For the purposes of the present Convention:

(a) "Watercourse" means a system of surface waters and groundwaters constituting by virtue of their physical relationship a unitary whole and normally flowing into a common terminus;

(b) "International watercourse" means a watercourse, parts of which are situated in different States; * * *

II. GENERAL PRINCIPLES

Article 5

Equitable and reasonable utilization and participation

1. Watercourse states shall in their respective territories utilize an international watercourse in an equitable and reasonable manner. In particular, an international watercourse shall be used and developed by watercourse States with a view to attaining optimal and sustainable utilization thereof and benefits therefrom, taking into account the interests of the watercourse States concerned, consistent with adequate protection of the watercourse.

2. Watercourse States shall participate in the use, development and protection of an international watercourse in an equitable and reasonable manner. Such participation includes both the right to utilize the watercourse and the duty to cooperate in the protection and development thereof, as provided in the present Convention.

Article 6

Factors relevant to equitable and reasonable utilization

1. Utilization of an international watercourse in an equitable and reasonable manner within the meaning of article 5 requires taking into account all relevant factors and circumstances, including;

(a) Geographic, hydrographic, hydrological, climatic, ecological and other factors of a natural character;

(b) The social and economic needs of the watercourse States concerned;

(c) The population dependent on the watercourse in each watercourse State;

(d) The effects of the use or uses of the watercourses in one watercourse State on other watercourse States;

(e) Existing and potential uses of the watercourse;

(f) Conservation, protection, development and economy of use of the water resources of the watercourse and the costs of measures taken to that effect.

(g) The availability of alternatives, of comparable value, to a particular planned or existing use.

2. In the application of article 5 or paragraph 1 of this article, watercourse States concerned shall, when the need arises, enter into consultations in a spirit of cooperation.

3. The weight to be given to each factor is to be determined by its importance in comparison with that of other relevant factors. In determining what is a reasonable and equitable use, all relevant factors are to be considered together and a conclusion reached on the basis of the whole.

Article 7

Obligation not to cause significant harm

1. Watercourse States shall, in utilizing an international watercourse in their territories, take all appropriate measures to prevent the causing of significant harm to other watercourse States.

2. Where significant harm nevertheless is caused to another watercourse State, the States whose use causes such harm shall, in the absence of agreement to such use, take all appropriate measures, having due regard for the provisions of articles 5 and 6, in consultation with the affected State, to eliminate or mitigate such harm and, where appropriate, to discuss the question of compensation.

Article 8

General obligation to cooperate

1. Watercourse States shall cooperate on the basis of sovereign equality, territorial integrity, mutual benefit and good faith in order to attain optimal utilization and adequate protection of an international watercourse.

2. In determining the manner of such cooperation, watercourse States may consider the establishment of joint mechanisms or commissions, as deemed necessary by them, to facilitate cooperation on relevant measures and procedures in the light of experience gained through cooperation in existing joint mechanisms and commissions in various regions.

Article 9

Regular exchange of data and information

1. Pursuant to article 8, watercourse States shall on a regular basis exchange readily available data and information on the condition of the watercourse, in particular that of a hydrological, meteorological, hydrogeological and ecological nature and related to the water quality as well as related forecasts.

2. If a watercourse State is requested by another watercourse State to provide data or information that is not readily available, it shall employ its best efforts to comply with the request but may condition its compliance upon payment by the requesting State of the reasonable costs of collecting and, where appropriate, processing such data or information.

3. Watercourse States shall employ their best efforts to collect and, where appropriate, to process data and information in a manner which facilitates its utilization by the other watercourse States to which it is communicated.

Article 10

Relationship between different kinds of uses

1. In the absence of agreement or custom to the contrary, no use of an international watercourse enjoys inherent priority over other uses.

2. In the event of a conflict between uses of an international watercourse, it shall be resolved with reference to articles 5 to 7, with special regard being given to the requirements of vital human needs.

III. PLANNED MEASURES

Article 11

Information concerning planned measures

Watercourse States shall exchange information and consult each other and, if necessary, negotiate on the possible effects of planned measures on the condition of an international watercourse. * * *

Article 20

Protection and preservation of ecosystems

Watercourse States shall, individually and where appropriate, jointly, protect and preserve the ecosystems of international watercourses. * * *

Article 22

Introduction of alien or new species

Watercourse States shall take all measures necessary to prevent the introduction of species, alien or new, into an international watercourse which may have effects detrimental to the ecosystem of the watercourse resulting in significant harm to other watercourse States. * * *

Article 24

Management

1. Watercourse States shall, at the request of any of them, enter into consultations concerning the management of an international watercourse, which may include the establishment of a joint management mechanism.

2. For the purposes of this article, "management" refers, in particular to:

   (a) Planning the sustainable development of an international watercourse and providing for the implementation of any plans adopted; and

   (b) Otherwise promoting the rational and optimal utilization, protection and control of the watercourse.

The Convention provides that it will enter into force after thirty-five nations have ratified the Convention. As of May 2009, only sixteen nations (the United States is not among them) had ratified the Convention, meaning that it has not yet entered into force. *See* United Nations Treaty Collection Website, *located at* http://treaties.un.org/Pages/Home.aspx?lang=en. Nevertheless, the Convention is a useful compilation of customary international law on transboundary water allocation and is thus likely to have significant influence on state negotiations. The following questions and case study provide an opportunity to consider the potential influence of the Convention on transboundary water disputes.

QUESTIONS AND DISCUSSION

1. What are the implications of the way in which the Convention defines a watercourse? Does it cover all transboundary water? Should it? Would a broader definition of a watercourse be more or less likely to attract signatories to the Convention? Is there any reason why the right to use a watercourse should be limited to riparian states?

2. Would you describe the Convention as focusing on the principle of equitable utilization or on the obligation not to cause significant harm?

3. Does the Convention suggest that concern for the environment should be a factor in allocating a transboundary watercourse? Which provisions address ecological concerns?

4. A number of commentators have suggested that access to safe and affordable water is a human right and thus states are obligated by international law to provide clean water to their citizens. *See, e.g.,* Stephen C. McCaffrey, *A Human Right to Water: Domestic and International Implications*, 5 Geo. Int'l L. Rev. 1, 22 (1992); Peter Gleick, *The Human Right to Water*, 1(5) Water Policy 487–503 (1999). Do you agree? What are the implications of making the availability of water, or other natural resources, a human right?

5. For an authoritative review of international water law, see Stephen C. McCaffrey, The Law of International Watercourses (2001). *See also* Patricia Birnie & Alan Boyle, International Law and the Environment 298–346 (2d ed. 2002); David Hunter et al., International Environmental Law and Policy 769–829 (2d ed. 2002).

6. Useful international water law websites include:

- *The International Water Law Project, at* http://internationalwater law.org.

- *Transboundary Freshwater Dispute Database, at* http://www.trans boundarywaters.orst.edu.

———

Problem Exercise: Allocating the Waters of the Nile River

In preparation for considering the questions that follow, review this excerpt about the history and geography of the Nile River basin.

Jutta Brunnée & Stephen J. Toope, *The Changing Nile Basin Regime: Does Law Matter?*, 43 Harv. Int'l L.J. 105, 117–18, 120–29 (2002)

The Nile is one of the world's great rivers, flowing for 6825 kilometers through much of Northeastern Africa, draining approximately 2.9 million square kilometers of territory, and nourishing the bodies and imaginations of roughly 280 million people in ten riparian (or water-supplying) states. The geographic and climatic setting of the basin is varied, ranging from tropical rain forest to mountains, plateaus, and deserts. Roughly 85% of the Nile's water originates in the highlands of Ethiopia, from which three rivers flow into the main body of the Nile: the Blue Nile (draining Lake Tana) and the Atbara and

Sobat Rivers (through Eritrea and Sudan, and Ethiopia and Sudan, respectively). The remainder of the water flows along the White Nile from Central and East Africa, originating in Lake Victoria (Kenya, Uganda, and Tanzania) and the mountains of Burundi, Rwanda, and the Democratic Republic of Congo. The White Nile flows through and feeds the great Sudanese swamps (The Sudd). The White Nile and Blue Nile meet at Khartoum, the former "clear and limpid" and the latter carrying "the fertilizing lime which in the past has been so helpful to Sudan and to Egypt." From Khartoum, the Nile is a single river, flowing through Egypt on its way to the Mediterranean Sea.

Although "flow" statistics for the Nile can be quite imprecise for a number of technical reasons, it is fair to conclude that annual flow of the Nile, measured at Aswan in Egypt, has diminished significantly over the last century. The river is also highly seasonal, with roughly 80% of its discharge occurring between August and October. Many scientists believe that with the completion of the Aswan High Dam, and the creation of the huge reservoir known as Lake Nasser, controlled discharge has saved Egypt both from major floods and from major droughts. However, as a result of the same project, only about 2% of the Nile's flow actually reaches the sea. Such low flow levels have contributed to ecological problems that have reached crisis proportions....

The Nile is essentially Egypt's sole source of water, sustaining a population of over sixty-eight million, estimated to be growing at a rate of one million every nine months. Over 95% of Egypt's population resides in the Nile Valley. Population growth is even faster in Ethiopia, where it is expected that by 2025, there will be more people to feed than in Egypt. A World Bank study has predicted that by 2025, the amount of water available to each person in North Africa will have dropped by roughly 80% in a single lifetime. Water planners describe a country as "water scarce" when annual renewable freshwater is less than 1000 cubic meters per person per year. By this measure, as of 1990, Burundi, Kenya, and Rwanda were already subject to water scarcity. Egypt and Ethiopia are expected to fall into that category by 2025, and Tanzania and Uganda will join the group by 2050. * * *

Water quality is especially important to Egypt because it is so dependent upon the Nile for agricultural production. Although Egypt has, over the last thirty years, substituted food imports (funded massively by the United States) for indigenous production, it remains true that without a secure and clean water supply from the Nile, poorer Egyptians would starve. This outcome is not currently likely for any other Nile riparian. Even in Ethiopia, with its fast-growing population, "food supply ... is not much affected by Nile flow." Of course, Ethiopia has not previously exploited the Nile to support food production, depending instead upon rain based agriculture....

The greatest use of water from the Nile, especially within Egypt, is irrigation for agricultural production. "The Nile Basin is water-scarce not because of too many people but because of too much agriculture relative to water supply. Agriculture here, as just about anywhere else in the world, accounts for upward of 80% of all water use." * * *

To a significant degree, the political context in the Nile Basin is conditioned by the region's colonial history and the strategic concerns of its colonial powers. Control over, and competition for, the waters of the Nile were central colonial preoccupations, pursued either through efforts to gain direct control over key areas, or through treaties designed to establish legal control over the Nile. The colonial patterns of competition and quest for control were subsequently replicated by the newly independent states in the region and the influence of a competitive legal environment continues to be felt. * * *

As colonial "protector," Britain undertook a series of initiatives to ensure the almost unimpeded flow of Nile waters into Egypt. Indeed, it was the British who imposed a basin-wide regime to the benefit of Egypt, a regime only now undergoing significant change. Although the hegemonic aspect of the regime is deeply problematic, it had the virtue of treating the entire Nile Basin as a unit, a feature that the modern "ecosystem approach" to water management seeks to recreate, albeit for fundamentally different reasons. Believing initially that the main supply of Nile water came from the East African tropical lakes, Britain's first initiatives were concentrated in Central and Eastern Africa, particularly Uganda. Concern over secure water supplies in Egypt in part explains the massive British colonial engagement in East Africa in the mid to late nineteenth century. Under British patronage, the Egyptian and Ugandan colonial governments reached a series of agreements allowing the damming of Lake Victoria so as to raise water flow rates to buttress Egyptian hydroelectric needs and to provide for year-round regulation of water flow. Egyptian engineers were stationed at Owens Falls to oversee implementation, and remain there to this day.

British efforts to protect the White Nile flow continued into the twentieth century with a 1906 British–Belgian agreement guaranteeing water flow from the Congo into the Nile Basin, and similar agreements with Italy and France regarding their colonial territories. The most far-reaching agreement was the 1929 Nile Waters Agreement, a colonial treaty involving Britain, as the governing power in Sudan, and Egypt. The Treaty specifically granted priority to Egyptian water needs and forbade any construction on the Nile in Sudan that would restrict Nile flow....

Finally understanding the central importance of flow from the Ethiopian highlands to overall Nile water flow, Britain concluded a treaty with the Italian colonialists in 1891 to preclude the building of any structures that would impede the flow of the Atbara River into the Nile. When the Ethiopians succeeded in expelling the Italians and claiming the eastern banks of the White Nile, the British and Egyptians again seized control of Sudan in 1898, putting down the Mahdist rebellion and at the same time ensuring their control over the river. Then, in 1902, King Edward VII sent an emissary to Addis Ababa to negotiate a treaty with Emperor Menelik II, recognizing Sudan's borders and governing the use of the Blue Nile. Article III of the 1902 Anglo–Ethiopian Treaty contained an undertaking by the Ethiopian Emperor "not to construct or allow to be constructed, any works across the Blue Nile, Lake Tana or the Sobat, which could arrest the flow of their waters into the Nile" without the prior consent of the British and the Government of Sudan. This concession facilitated British recognition of Ethiopian independence.

Ethiopia later repudiated the Anglo–Ethiopian agreement of 1902. In an Aide Memoire of September 1957, the Ethiopian Government asserted that it "has the right and obligation to exploit its water resources for the benefit of present and future generations of its citizens." ...

In 1959, Egypt and Sudan concluded a treaty to replace the 1929 Treaty, which Sudan had long found unpalatable. The 1959 version was not, however, markedly different from the 1929 Treaty, although it did implicitly repudiate the provision in the 1929 Treaty that granted Egypt complete control over the Nile.... Another problem with the 1959 Treaty, one that is the root of much regional tension, is that while it is purely bilateral, it seeks to apportion the entire flow of the Nile to Egypt and Sudan, excluding the interests of any other riparian, notably Ethiopia. Bilateral treaties can certainly consider the needs of third parties under the concepts of good faith and reasonableness. However, the

1959 Treaty fails to do so, implicitly supporting a "prior appropriation" approach to water apportionment favorable to downstream states. * * *

The more immediate threat to the hegemonic aspirations of Egypt over the Nile is posed by Ethiopia. Ethiopia has never recognized the validity of the 1959 Sudanese–Egyptian Apportionment Treaty. Ethiopian distrust of Egypt has been strong almost since the time of Ethiopian independence, so much so that rumors of Egyptian policies of destabilization toward Ethiopia circulate widely. In 1988, Ethiopia launched the first phase of an ambitious hydroelectric scheme called the Tana Beles Project. The goal was to double hydroelectric production in Ethiopia and to provide irrigation for new settlements with up to 200,000 farmers. Water was to be taken from Lake Tana to the Beles River, where five dams were to be built. Egypt was deeply concerned about the potential effect of the scheme on the flow of the Blue Nile and in 1990 it blocked a loan provision for the project that Ethiopia had requested from the African Development Bank. This action prompted anger among other riparian states and led to complaints that Egyptian hegemonic goals had replaced the nineteenth-century British hegemony, and led to a view of Egypt as an indigenous colonialist.

Despite the recurring problems of drought and poor water distribution that have made Ethiopian famines a source of world concern since the 1980s, massive hydroelectric and irrigation schemes appear to be out of favor with the Ethiopian government. Environmental and developmental concerns, combined with prohibitive costs, have made such projects less attractive. However, greater political stability and a modestly growing economy have allowed Ethiopia to plan two smaller hydroelectric projects and a series of micro-dam projects, largely for irrigation. The micro-dam projects could reduce the flow of the Blue Nile and the Atbara, both of which flow into the Nile proper within Sudan. Creating new agricultural land will be increasingly important for the Ethiopians, as traditional farming in the highlands is adversely affected by environmental destruction, especially soil erosion due largely to deforestation.

Meanwhile, Egypt has gone ahead with ambitious irrigation plans of its own. Work is said to be underway on the Salaam Canal, designed to carry 12.5 million cubic meters of water per day from Lake Nasser to the northern Sinai in support of a huge resettlement scheme, which will eventually bring some three million new inhabitants to the region. The parallel New Valley Project will pump 4.94 billion cubic meters of water a year from Lake Nasser to irrigate up to 250,000 hectares in new settlement areas in the Western Desert outside the Nile Valley, the traditional home to almost all of Egypt's population. In his address inaugurating construction of the project, which coincided with the thirty-seventh anniversary of the inauguration of the Aswan High Dam project, President Mubarak referred to the New Valley scheme as a "giant national project," part of a plan to open up Egypt "outside the boundaries of the Nile Valley."

There simply is not enough water in the Nile to complete the irrigation plans of both Ethiopia and Egypt, much less to satisfy the ambitions of all the Nile riparians. Waterbury and Whittington suggest that even with zero use by upstream riparians, the Egyptians would have to "find" roughly five billion cubic meters of water a year to meet the requirements of the New Valley Project. Egyptian planners suggest that this water can come from more efficient use of existing supplies, but such projections are naively optimistic. Moreover, Egyptian projections are based on the continuing availability of the portion of Nile flow accorded to Egypt under the 1959 Treaty with Sudan....

––––––––

By the summer of 2008, Ethiopia had moved ahead with the construction of the dams mentioned in the excerpt but they were not yet completed. *See generally* Terri Hathaway *What Cost Ethiopia's Dam Boom?* (2008), *available   at*   http://internationalrivers.org/files/EthioReport06Feb08.pdf. The dams will generate significant hydropower and also have the potential to store and divert water for irrigated agriculture. Assume that the 1997 Convention represents customary international law to which Egypt and Ethiopia should adhere even though they are not signatories to the Convention. What obligations do the two countries have to each other under the Convention? If Egypt seeks to thwart or limit irrigation diversions from the dams and the case is submitted to arbitration, who would prevail? With respect to this last question, pay particular attention to articles 5, 6, and 7 of the Convention. How, if at all, should the colonial-era agreements influence any allocation decision? What sort of practical approaches might Egypt or Ethiopia rely on to resolve their dispute?

CHAPTER EIGHT

Rangelands

I. Introduction
II. Home on the Range
    A. What Are Rangelands?
    B. Rangeland Goods and Services
    C. Impacts of Grazing on Rangelands
    D. The Passions Stirred By Public Lands Grazing
III. Carving up the Commons: A Brief History of Ranchers' Efforts to Control Western Rangelands
    A. The Rise of Ranching on the Public Commons
    B. Fence Law
    C. Initial Federal Limitations on Open Access Grazing
    D. Ending Open Access to the Public Rangelands
IV. Environmental Law Comes to the Range ... Slowly
    A. The Taylor Grazing Act as Environmental Law
    B. Early Range Planning Efforts
    C. FLPMA: The BLM Gets an Organic Act
    D. PRIA: Environmental Mandate or More Congressional Ambivalence?
    E. Can the Grazing Statutes Be Made to Work for the Environment?
    Problem Exercise: Determining Whether Public Lands Are Chiefly Valuable for Grazing
V. Rangeland Reform
    A. Grazing Fees and Subsidies
    B. Privatizing Grazing Permits
    C. Buying Back the Range
    D. Collaboration, Consensus, and Local Control
    E. Grazing Reform Administrative Style
    Case Study: The Grand Canyon Trust Retires Grazing Permits
VI. Intersecting Laws and Their Impact on Range Management
    A. The Clean Water Act
    B. The Wild and Scenic Rivers Act
    C. The Endangered Species Act
VII. Grazing on State Lands

> I have said that my father studied cattle with the same fascination with which I study books, but ... [w]hat interested him more, on both the intellectual and emotional level, was grass. To the extent that he had a religion, it was grass, a religion whose grandeur and complexity were worthy of him....
>
> The tragedy of my father's life effort, and that of many ranchers up and down the West, was that, despite skill and hard work (application, my father called it), they could never really get ahead....
>
> He wanted very much to make the cowboying life last, and by dint of shrewd planning and very hard work, he did just manage to make it last his lifetime. But tragedy was woven into the effort anyway....
>
> Larry McMurtry, *Death of the Cowboy*,
>
> New York Review of Books, Nov. 4, 1999, at 17–18.

I. INTRODUCTION

Few natural resources better illustrate the challenges for natural resources law and policy than our nation's public rangelands. It is no coincidence that grazing provided the archetype for Garrett Hardin's tragedy of the commons nor that it has served as the classic example of agency capture. The current debate over rangeland management also provides a fascinating instance of environmental aspirations butting heads with long-standing tradition, culture and reliance interests. The chapter tells the historical tale of grazing in more detail than other resource regimes, in part because the history is a case study of a long and ongoing experiment with the management of a common pool resource, and in part because it is impossible to understand the nature and intensity of the current debate over appropriate allocation of rangeland goods and services without a firm understanding of its historical antecedents. Each case in this chapter is laden with historical references and subtexts that inevitably impact the interpretation of relevant statutes and regulations.

The chapter begins with an overview of some of the basic facts about rangelands—the types and uses of the rangeland resource, the economics of grazing, and grazing's impacts on rangeland ecosystem health. It then moves to culture, opening a window into the passions that have animated disputes over rangeland management policy. From there, the chapter begins the exploration of ranchers' 150–year effort to gain control of an open access resource and the related federal management responses. As with other natural resources, the historical allocation decisions turned out to have significant environmental implications, which have then been slowly addressed and further complicated by the statutes governing the range resource—primarily the Taylor Grazing Act, the Federal Land Policy Management Act, and the Public Rangeland Improvement Act, but increasingly such intersecting laws as the Clean Water Act and the Endangered Species Act. Tying together the allocation and environmental questions, the chapter then investigates various rangeland reform proposals. The chapter concludes with a brief look at grazing on state school trust lands in an effort to encourage further consideration of the appropriate political scale for public management of the rangeland resource.

II. HOME ON THE RANGE

A. WHAT ARE RANGELANDS?

Range managers and scientists define rangeland as lands that are neither developed nor cultivated that can provide food for livestock (generally cattle and sheep) or wildlife. Typically, this food consists of edible grasses and forbs (flowers) that are *grazed* and edible leaves and twigs from trees and shrubs that are *browsed*. A variety of different rangeland types exist within the United States, depending on climate (precipitation being the single most important factor), soil type, and topography. Grasslands, as the name implies, have few shrubs or trees and are the most productive rangelands for purposes of producing forage. The Great Plains and the inland valleys of California and Oregon are examples. Desert shrublands, which have less grass and mostly smaller woody plants like sagebrush, dominate the Great Basin and Southwest. Woodlands and forests, which can produce a lot of forage when the trees are small or scattered as with savanna or areas thinned by fire or logging, dominate the mountain and coastal areas with higher precipitation. Although these rangeland types can be broadly identified with certain geographical regions, they also overlap one another within each region depending on local factors. Thus, a relatively wet riparian area in the midst of desert shrubland may have grassland characteristics and so forth.

Despite the productivity of grassland areas, they have not been the focus of the national grazing debate. Not only does their productivity make them less susceptible to ecological harm, but much of the land that can be described as grassland, like the Great Plains and coastal state valleys, is privately owned and governed primarily by state law. This is not to suggest that grazing in these areas does not raise significant concerns for resource policy. It does. Private land grazing implicates state land use laws, water quality, and even global warming because of the methane produced by cattle. The rangeland areas that have triggered the most vociferous national debate are our desert shrublands and forests, most of the grazing on which is managed by the Bureau of Land Management (BLM) and the Forest Service, respectively. The BLM manages grazing on about 170 million acres of public land (about the size of Texas) and the Forest Service on about 100 million acres of public land (about the size of California), both almost exclusively in the West.

Although public land grazing in the western United States will be the focus of this chapter, primarily because of the fascinating theoretical and policy questions it presents, rangeland issues are not limited to the West or the United States. The issues are worldwide. Rangeland is the dominant land type on all continents. 70% of the world's land area is uncultivated and capable of sustaining grazing, and some 50% of that area is actually grazed by domestic animals. Only 7% of the world's cattle and 1% of its sheep are found in the United States. Both India (16%) and Brazil (12%) have more cattle; and China (11%) and Australia (11%) have many more sheep. JERRY L. HOLECHEK ET AL., RANGE MANAGEMENT: PRINCIPLES AND PRACTICES 14–18 (5th ed. 2004).

B. RANGELAND GOODS AND SERVICES

Until relatively recently, a question asking what rangelands were "good for" might have seemed rhetorical to many. Although memorialized in song as the place "where the deer and the antelope play," rangelands were generally viewed as providing one real good—forage for cows and sheep. The public lands on which grazing occurred were the lands "no one wanted." DYAN ZASLOWSKY, THESE AMERICAN LANDS 113 (1986). When homesteaders had not taken them up by 1934, the Taylor Grazing Act set them aside primarily for grazing. 43 U.S.C. § 315. For a long time, other than perhaps miners and a few hardy preservationists, no one saw rangelands as providing much of value beyond grazing.

During the last three or four decades this has begun to change. Whereas talk about allocating or managing range resources once meant allocating forage between and among cattle and sheep ranchers (and occasionally hunters seeking deer and elk) and setting the timing, intensity, and frequency of grazing to promote maximum use of the resource; more and more range policy has begun to integrate other concerns. The talk of range management which for years dominated BLM field offices and the land grant universities that dot the West has in some places, although certainly not all, given way to talk of range ecology. Range management courses have become courses in range science or given way to courses in conservation biology. The focus has begun to change because of the growing recognition of the other ecosystem goods provided by rangelands—including opportunities for people to hike, camp, fish, picnic, hunt, and bike—as well as the ecosystem services provided by rangelands—including habitat for wide varieties of animals and bird species, and the improvement of water quality and quantity.

With the recognition that rangelands are valuable for other purposes beyond livestock forage and that grazing can have negative impacts has come more and more hard questions about just how valuable public rangelands actually are for grazing. Recent economic research on this question indicates that the answer is, not very valuable. Approximately 30,000 permittees run cattle on the public lands. This is about 2% of the nation's ranchers and only about 7% of the ranchers in the West. Public rangelands provide forage for only 3.76% of the nation's beef cattle herd. HOLECHEK, *supra*, at 46. Not only are public land ranchers a relatively small percentage of the nation's ranchers, but also they are a relatively small part of the economy in the western states. Thomas Power, an economist at the University of Montana, has been a persistent critic of what he calls the "folk economics" of the West that overemphasizes the value of various natural resource extractive industries to the western economy. In 1996, Power reported that cattle and sheep production in the eleven western states with significant public lands, excluding Alaska, amounts to only 0.31% of total income and 0.53% of total employment. Federal public lands grazing is even less valuable, accounting for 0.04% of total income and 0.06% of total employment. Put another way:

> Potential job and income loss associated with federal grazing reform can be expressed in terms of the time it would take for local western economies to replace jobs through the normal expansion of the economy. If state economic growth since 1980 is taken as the reference point, the loss of all federal grazing would cause income growth in the eleven western states to pause for six days. To make up for lost jobs, economic growth would pause for a week and a half. That is, in even the most extreme case where all grazing on federal land was eliminated, direct income and job losses would be made up in a matter of a few days by normal economic expansion. Obviously some communities would be harder hit than others given the uneven distribution of public grazing land across states. While the potential for local disruption should be analyzed and mitigated where necessary, it is still the case that economies of broad parts of the West would not significantly suffer from reduced grazing on public land.

Thomas Michael Power, Lost Landscapes and Failed Economies: The Search for a Value of Place 186 (1996).

In 2004, grazing fees imposed by all federal agencies generated about $21 million, which is less than one-sixth of the expenditures to manage grazing. In contrast, that same year, recreation receipts ($13.5 million) brought in more money than grazing fees ($10 million) for the first time in the history of the BLM, causing one wag to propose changing the BLM's derisive nickname from the Bureau of Livestock and Mining to the Bureau of Leisure and Motorhomes. These revenues, which are generated from recreation user fees that are collected only sporadically at volunteer pay stations, are a small part of the economic impact of recreation on public lands communities. A 2003 Forest Service report estimated that recreation visitors spent over $7.5 billion dollars in communities near national forests. *See* U.S. Gen. Accounting Office, *Livestock Grazing* (September 2005), http://www.gao.gov/new.items/d05869.pdf; Brett French, *Rec Fees Surpass Grazing for First Time in BLM History*, Billings Gazette, Oct. 7, 2004; National Forest Visitor Use Monitoring Program, http://www.fs.fed.us/recreation/programs/nvum/national_report_final_draft.pdf.

C. Impacts of Grazing on Rangelands

Range policy must address not only whether grazing is compatible with the various recreational uses, but whether either use is compatible with habitat preservation and water quality and, if so, under what conditions. Put another way, range management has been moving from allocating one ecosystem good (forage) among a limited set of users to a much more complex task of allocating multiple ecosystem goods (forage and various types of recreational uses) and services (watershed, habitat, etc.) among a much broader group of consumers. The job is made more difficult because the goods and services are not always compatible. Professor Wilkinson offers the following example of how grazing can disrupt other rangeland goods and services.

Charles F. Wilkinson, Crossing the Next Meridian: Land, Water, and the Future of the American West 75–80 (1992)

The waters of Camp Creek gather in the rounded, low-lying area around the Maury Mountains and Hampton Butte in central Oregon. The small stream flows northward through open rangeland for some 40 miles, mostly at an elevation between 5200 and 4000 feet, until it discharges into the Crooked River. This is the arid eastern two-thirds of Oregon, not really of the Pacific Northwest but of the high plains country found throughout the Rocky Mountains. Average annual precipitation in the Camp Creek drainage is just 12–14 inches.

Peter Skene Ogden, the intrepid British fur trapper for the Hudson's Bay Company, led a hunting party up the Crooked River in December 1825. In his journal, the first written account of the region, he observed that the banks were "well lined with willows" and rejoiced at the fine feed for his horses: "The Soil on this Fork [is] remarkably rich in some parts [and] the Grass seven feet high." Ogden believed the Crooked River system to be a potential bonanza for the beaver men, saying, "I doubt if we should find another equal to it in any part of this country." A half century later, in 1875, the deputy surveyor of

Oregon examined Camp Creek, describing the valley floor as a "meadow" and noting several marshes. The surveyor's notes also pointed out the abundance of bunchgrass on the uplands of the Camp Creek watershed.

Excessive grazing of cattle since the 1880s has worked over Camp Creek in almost incredible ways. There are few beaver, no willows to speak of, and no 7–foot–tall grasses at all. The creek itself runs not through a grassy meadow but on a hard-packed floor at the bottom of deep cut-banks. The timing of the runoff has been thrown off: water shoots out during the spring melt, and little is held for late summer and fall. * * *

If you stand on Camp Creek's rocky bed today, you ... will be standing between the sheared-off banks, 50 feet away on each side. The banks rise up 20 or 25 feet. You can imagine the former meadow surface at the tops of the cut-banks high above your head, at the roof level of many houses. If you fix on a point upstream, say, 100 yards away, you can begin to comprehend the volume of soil and rock driven downstream—the equivalent of several neighborhoods of houses full of material—just on that one short, 100–yard stretch of stream.

The erosion of Camp Creek continues. Topographical maps show "Severance Reservoir" on Camp Creek about 7 miles up from Crooked River. A rancher named Ned Severance built this impoundment by putting in a dam across the creek in 1952, creating a 40–acre reservoir. It was 65 feet deep in places and was considered a fine trout lake by locals.

There is no longer a Severance Reservoir. By 1977, just a quarter of a century after the dam had been built, it had become completely filled with sediment carried into it by the flow of Camp Creek. In other words, if you stand on top of the earthen dam and face downstream, the trickle of Camp Creek will slip over the dam and drop down 40 or 50 feet below you to the channel. If you turn around and face upstream, you will be standing about a foot above a flat meadow of 40 acres, the former lake surface. Camp Creek, which runs along the top of this new meadow, has stacked up a million tons of sediment behind the dam.

All of this is due to cattle and sheep or, much better put, to the poor management of cattle and sheep by human beings. In the 1880s and 1890s ranchers took over the public domain rangeland and introduced thousands of cows, and significant numbers of sheep, into the Camp Creek valley. Understandably, when cows see green and smell water, they head for it. After all, riparian zones—the "green strips" along streams and creeks—produce twenty-five times more vegetation per unit of ground than do upland sites. And stream bottoms are cool. If you let them, those cattle will pound down the banks, crush the beaver dams, root out every last stalk of forage, and then wallow in the mud that is left. Some of them will literally stay on all spring and summer, drinking what water is left and losing weight steadily as the hot sun bakes down. Some cows will move into the uplands to graze, or be driven there by ranchers who locate a spring or build a water tank. * * *

Camp Creek ... was an elaborate holding filtering system. The broad, marshy meadowlands trapped sediment. The vegetation also slowed and caught water in its matrix of meanders, soil, and plants. Cool water seeped into the groundwater table, the top of which blended with the root systems of the plants. The blue ribbon of Camp Creek was only the visible tip of a vast, interconnected aquifer.

A healthy riparian system, such as existed in the Camp Creek valley before the 1880s, produces a range of economic benefits. It cools and purifies water. It is a deep and efficient reservoir—much like a great sponge—that stores water without evaporative loss and feeds it back into the stream conveyance channel, ensuring a reliable supply of water to downstream users during summer and fall and in dry years. Further, if proper land management practice are followed, cattle can graze in these exceptionally nutritious areas.

A riparian zone can also be a festival of wildlife species, and Camp Creek once was exactly that. Canada geese, wigeon, and green-winged teal nested there. The great blue heron coasted in on its 7–foot wingspread to feed on insects and minnows. Native rainbow trout lived in the water all year, and salmon and steelhead pushed up several hundred miles from the ocean to spawn. Raccoons prowled the stream bottom, and deer and elk stole down from the uplands at the close of day to drink. Beaver, which Peter Skene Ogden found so plentiful, were exceedingly important to the integrity of the old Camp Creek system. Pools behind the beaver dams stored water and spread it out, expanding the reach of the riparian zone. * * *

Poor ranching practices destroyed all of this at Camp Creek. When cows beat down the stream banks and destroyed the vegetation in the riparian zone, the creek's flow scoured out soil and rocks. This activity was particularly rapid in the spring. Camp Creek has a languid flow most of the year, but it can be a raging torrent, fifty times larger, in March and April, when the snow melts off. Unimpeded by vegetation, the big spring flow gouged out the exposed stream bottom, and the process snowballed as rocks and boulders tore down the channel. In many stretches, the scouring effect continued until the stream bottom cut down to bedrock. With no spongy soil to hold the water, the groundwater table was not recharged. The top of the aquifer declined, dropping below the reach of streamside trees. Valuable willows, whose root systems helped stabilize the soil, died out. The flow pattern radically changed. The snowmelt, much of which was once stored by the riparian zone, flushed down the rocky chute in a rush, leaving little or no flows for the dry months of summer and fall. Hundreds of animal species were driven out.

The uplands, the other component in a rangeland system, were also integrally involved in the deterioration at Camp Creek. Ranchers simply turned their cattle loose on the open public range in the early spring and rounded them up in the fall. The cows overgrazed the bunchgrasses on the uplands and pounded down the native plants with their hoofs. None of this was necessary. New growth in these grasses occurs at the "growing point" near the base of the plant, where new cells develop. Light grazing can actually promote growth: removing as much as 40 percent of a plant's leaves and stems is much the same as pruning for these wild grasses. In addition, the sharp hoofs of cattle can chip up the turf, loosen it, and promote water storage and seed regeneration. But these beneficial effects accrue only if the animals are present in the right numbers and if they are kept moving.

With native grasses being driven out of Camp Creek's uplands, a low canopy of juniper, sagebrush, and rabbitbrush moved in. These invaders, with their broad, shallow root systems, hastened the departure of the bunchgrasses by successfully competing for scarce water. The protective ground cover on the uplands was now gone, and the transformation of the Camp Creek watershed was complete. Rainwater, instead of seeping into the soft ground, washed unprotected soils down to the creek. The trench was now crisscrossed with small gullies and arroyos. Uncountable tons of sediment from the once-green bottomlands. Uncountable tons from the uplands.

There are Camp Creeks all across the American West—thousands of them. To be sure, factors that determine the amount of erosion—soil types, vegetation, gradient, and volume and regularity of stream flow—will differ from locale to locale. Camp Creek, for instance, is unusual because of its native tallgrasses; the tallgrass prairies were found mostly near the 100th meridian in the heart of the country and in the Central Valley of California. Nor is the sediment load of the little drainage in central Oregon necessarily typical; the soils of Bear Creek, the watershed adjacent to Camp Creek on the west, are considerably more stable, so erosion in Bear Creek, though substantial, is less than in Camp Creek. General regional differences also can be drawn—the ravages of overgrazing tend to be somewhat less severe, for example, in Montana and somewhat more severe in New Mexico. Nonetheless, Camp Creek fairly represents the current state of the western range.

———

Although Professor Wilkinson suggests that Camp Creek "fairly represents the current state of the western range," there is significant debate over range conditions. One popular grazing management textbook, for example, paints a different picture.

> Scientific evidence and other information indicate that, although public rangelands are being degraded in localized areas, current livestock-grazing practices are not degrading rangelands on a large scale. * * *

> Much of this destructive grazing occurred prior to World War I before the importance of placing grazing lands under proper management became widely known.... Many long term studies are available that show controlled livestock grazing using sound range management principles will sustain and in many cases improve range resources. Domestic livestock grazing at conservative levels appears to be sustainable, even on sensitive western rangelands.

JOHN F. VALLENTINE, GRAZING MANAGEMENT 19–20 (2d ed. 2001). Government statistics offer some support for this position. They show that, as of 2001, 37% of BLM lands were in either excellent or good condition, another 34% were in fair condition, and only 12% were in poor condition, compared with 1936 figures of 15.8%, 47.9%, and 36.3% respectively. *See* BLM Annual Report (2003), http://www.blm.gov/nhp/info/stratplan/ARFY03.pdf; HOLECHEK, *supra* at 39. Other range scholars have countered that assertions such as those in the grazing management textbook are dubious and "fueled by misrepresentations or biased characterizations of range condition and other grazing-related issues." DEBRA L. DONAHUE, THE WESTERN RANGE REVISITED 8–9 (1999). A 1994 appraisal of public rangeland conditions prepared by the BLM and Forest Service found that

> [M]anagement changes since the 1930s have brought improvements. But there is still much progress to be made. Rangeland ecosystems are not functioning properly in many areas of the West. Riparian area are widely depleted and some upland areas produce far below their potential. Soils are becoming less fertile. * * * Once altered, upland vegetation communities change or improve only gradually. Native grasses revegetate slowly, annual grasses cannot be removed once established, and disturbed or eroded soils require a long time to rebuild. When management improves, upland communities that receive more than 12 inches of annual precipitation have shown improvement within 20 years. Drier areas generally have not improved. * * * The amount and quality of riparian communities have been severely reduced since the settlement period. Although uplands have improved since rangeland management began in the 1930s, riparian areas have continued to decline and are considered to be in their worst condition in history. * * * Once riparian areas become nonfunctioning they usually will not recover without major changes in management. But, because they have moisture, most riparian areas will respond relatively rapidly once

disturbance factors are removed. Many riparian areas have improved and begun to function properly within 5 years of management changes.

RANGELAND REFORM '94, DRAFT ENVIRONMENTAL IMPACT STATEMENT 5, 24–25.

Whatever the precise distribution of range conditions, there is undoubtedly a notable effect that can be caused by poor grazing practices. The following BLM photographs show variations in rangeland health in riparian areas.

RIPARIAN VEGETATION—GOOD CONDITION CLASS

Department of Interior Draft Environmental Impact Statement on Grazing Management in the Randolph Planning Unit, Rich Country, Utah (June 15, 1979) at 2–23.

RIPARIAN VEGETATION—FAIR CONDITION CLASS

Department of Interior Draft Environmental Impact Statement on Grazing Management in the Randolph Planning Unit, Rich Country, Utah (June 15, 1979) at 2–23.

RIPARIAN VEGETATION—POOR CONDITION CLASS

Department of Interior Draft Environmental Impact Statement on Grazing Management in the Randolph Planning Unit, Rich Country, Utah (June 15, 1979) at 2–34.

For additional pictures depicting rangeland types and results of different range management approaches, see the casebook web page for this chapter.

QUESTIONS AND DISCUSSION

1.   Consider the various types of rangeland (grassland, woodlands and forest, and desert shrublands), rangeland topography (e.g., steep slope, riparian area), and climate. What sorts of rangelands would you expect to sustain the most harm from grazing, and what types of harm would you expect?

2.   Why is there so much disagreement over the physical condition of the range? Why should what is essentially a question of science be so difficult? Is there any way to reconcile the different viewpoints on range condition? Does it matter whether one focuses on riparian areas? If so, is that a legitimate focus of rangeland policy? Riparian vegetation communities occupy only one percent of rangelands. RANGELAND REFORM '94, *supra*, at 920. Does part of the distinction between the various views of range conditions also depend in part on whether the focus is on past or current grazing practices?

3.   The debate about the condition of the public rangelands is only part of a broader environmental debate about the livestock industry. Far more livestock are raised on private lands than on public lands, often in the sort of large feedlots that animate nuisance discussions in first year law classes.

See, e.g., Spur Industries v. Del E. Webb Development Co., 494 P.2d 700 (Ariz. 1972). As Professor Ruhl explains: "Only 190,000 of the 640,000 farms in the United States that raise or keep livestock rely on pasture land to feed the livestock. The remaining farms use animal feeding operations (AFOs) known as confined feedlots—food is brought to animals kept in confined quarters." *See* J.B. Ruhl, *The Environmental Law of Farms: 30 Years of Making a Mole Hill Out of a Mountain*, 31 ENVTL. L. RPTR. 10203, 10217–18 (2001). Such Concentrated Animal Feeding Operations (CAFOs) are regulated as point source polluters under the Clean Water Act. *See* 33 U.S.C. § 1362(14). The following excerpt captures the wide range of the national and global environmental community's concerns with livestock production.

Robert H. Smith, *Livestock Production: The Unsustainable Environmental and Economic Effects of an Industry Out of Control*, 4 BUFF. ENVTL. L. REV. 45, 48–73 (1996)

Perhaps the most significant environmental problem related to livestock production is its main role in the consumption, pollution, and depletion of water reserves. * * *

More than half of the water consumed for all purposes in the United States goes to grow cattle feed and provide water for livestock animals. This overuse is made more clear when the comparison is made between gallons of water used to produce vegetables and grains as compared to meat. For instance, it takes up to 137 times more water to create a pound of edible beef compared to that of edible vegetation. * * *

Organic waste from livestock, along with pesticides, chemical fertilizers, and agricultural salts and sediments are the primary non-point sources of water pollution in the United States. "American livestock contribute five times more harmful organic waste to water pollution than do people, and twice that of industry." * * *

U.S. livestock produces 250,000 pounds of excrement per second. Overall, cattle produce nearly two billion tons of organic waste (manure) each year. Dr. Harold Bernard, an agricultural expert for the environmental protection agency, reported to Newsweek that U.S. feedlot runoff is "ten to several hundred times more concentrated than raw domestic sewage." * * *

Currently, almost 17 million hectares of rain forest throughout the world are destroyed annually by deforestation. The leading cause of rainforest destruction in Central America is cattle production, where since 1960, more than 25% of all Central American forests have been razed and destroyed to produce beef. * * *

The Meat Importers Council of America reports that ten percent of the beef consumed in the U.S. is imported, with 90% of those imports coming from Central and Latin America. A single quarter-pound hamburger imported from Latin America causes the clearing of six square yards of rain forest. * * *

Throughout the world, productive land is being turned into deserts as a direct result of the overgrazing of cattle and other livestock. The four leading causes of desertification are overgrazing of livestock, over-cultivation of land, waterlogging and salinization of irrigated lands, and deforestation along with the prevention of reforestation; all of which have cattle production as the primary contributing factor. Currently 29% of Earth's landmass is suffering from desertification. Each year 52 million acres of land, an area equivalent to the size of Kansas, are eroded so severely by desertification that they are rendered unproductive for virtually any use.

The two means by which cattle directly degrade the land are by stripping vegetation and compacting the earth. * * *

Several estimates reveal that more than 85% of the annual loss of topsoil in the U.S. is directly attributable to livestock and livestock feed production. The U.S. Soil Conservation Service reports that each year in the U.S., more than 4 million acres of cropland are being lost to erosion. This loss of topsoil is a tremendously serious problem since it takes 100 to 500 years for nature to form an inch of topsoil. * * *

In addition to contributing to the depletion or destruction of fossil fuel, water, grassland, and tropical rain forest, livestock production is also a significant factor in the emission of greenhouse gases. * * *

Methane gas poses a greater threat to global warming since one molecule of methane traps 25 times more solar heat than a molecule of CO_2. All in all, livestock are estimated to account for 20% of global methane emissions. * * *

The overwhelming majority of crops grown are used for livestock feed, particularly in the U.S. The livestock industry is therefore responsible for a proportional amount of petrochemical agriculture. In the United States, pesticide use in agriculture increased from less than one million pounds in 1950 to 815 million pounds in 1987. Pesticide use has increased 3,300% since 1945. * * *

––––––––

Many of Smith's estimates are subject to dispute, but even if the numbers are half the estimates, should the focus of grazing policy be directed more at CAFOs?

4. An often underestimated issue in resource policy is personal consumption habits. What is the relationship between consumption and range policy? World Bank ecologist Robert Goodland asserts:

Affluent people in OECD countries consume about 800 kg of grain indirectly, much of it inefficiently converted into animal flesh, with the balance as milk, cheese, eggs, ice cream and yogurt.... In contrast, in low-consuming countries, annual consumption of grains averages 200 kg per person, practically all of it directly, with little inefficiency in conversion.... The grain consumption ratio between rich and poor countries is about four to one.

ROBERT GOODLAND, ENVIRONMENTAL SUSTAINABILITY: EAT BETTER AND KILL LESS 5–7 (1996). What impact, for example, might marginal declines in beef consumption have upon the public lands grazing industry?

5. What are the implications for grazing policy of the budding sales in meat from nontraditional "livestock" like buffalo, elk, ostrich, and emu, which are a very small but growing part of the market? If these sales grow significantly, would you expect opposition to the grazing of such animals to be less, more, or about the same than opposition to cattle and sheep?

6. An important environmental concern related to grazing is desertification. Rather than the common misperception that desertification involves sand dunes or the "desert" actually spreading into agriculturally productive land, desertification refers to prolonged abuse of land that weakens its ability to support plant growth through loss of soil productivity, increased soil deterioration, and loss of biodiversity. Overgrazing, along with poor agricultural practices and deforestation, is one of the prime contributors to desertification. The United Nations Environment Programme (UNEP) estimates that desertification currently affects about 30% of the world's land surface area and 70% of the world's drylands. *See* http://www.unccd.int/knowledge/faq.php#answer0; http://www.uncce.int/ publicinfo/factssheets-eng.pdf. While these and other desertification estimates are disputed, the existence of the problem is not.

Desertification is most pronounced in Africa because almost 70% of its land is either desert or drylands. But the poor condition of public rangelands in many riparian and arid areas of the American West can also be understood as a manifestation of desertification. The international community has begun taking steps to address desertification, focusing primarily on the developing world. In 1994 the Convention to Combat Desertification in Those Countries Experiencing Serious Drought and/or Desertification, Particularly in Africa, was adopted, *see* 33 I.L.M. 1328 (1994), and 191 countries (including the United States) have ratified it. The Convention does not create specific rules but instead encourages the development of National Action Programs and emphasizes collaborative decision making processes involving foreign donors, the affected country, local communities, and nongovernmental organizations.

7. Recall the comparison of economic returns from public land grazing and recreation. What does this cost-benefit analysis suggest about the value of grazing? Is this a full cost-benefit analysis? If not, what else should it include and do you think these could be readily quantified in dollars?

———

D. THE PASSIONS STIRRED BY PUBLIC LANDS GRAZING

Given the relatively low economic returns of public lands grazing and its potential for ecological harm, a person unfamiliar with the history and cultural geography of the American West might expect significant agreement on curtailing or eliminating public lands grazing. Yet there is nothing approaching such a consensus. Indeed, quite the opposite is true. The cultural place of ranching and cowboys stirs great passion. Part of that passion derives from the romantic image of ranching in the West. Other than perhaps the idyllic Jeffersonian yeoman farmer, few images have had as much staying power as that of the rugged and independent cowboy of the American West. It is no coincidence that the marketing image of the Marlboro Man drove that brand to the top of the cigarette market. The ranching industry has always had a place in the national psyche beyond its economic impact. Even at its historic peak, the western public lands cattle industry was a relatively small portion of the national total. In 1880, near the apex of the cattle kingdom (historian Walter Prescott Webb's name for the area of the Great Plains and West that came to be dominated by cattle drives, cattlemen, and cowboys in the aftermath of the Civil War), the western states accounted for only 34% of the United States' cattle, only 15.4% if Texas and the Pacific states are excluded. Walter Prescott Webb asked: "If the West produced comparatively so few cattle, then why is it that we think of the West, of the Plains, as the center of the cattle industry? Why do we call it the cattle kingdom?" WALTER PRESCOTT WEBB, THE GREAT PLAINS 226 (1931). His answer provides both explanation and example of the power of ranching's romantic image:

> The answer is found in the method and not in the results. The thing that has identified the West in the popular mind with cattle is not the number raised, but the method of handling them. A thousand farms in the East will each have six or seven cows, with as many more calves and yearlings—ten thousand head. But they attract no attention. They are incidents of agriculture. In the West a ranch will cover the same area as the thousand farms, and will have perhaps ten thousand head, round-ups, rodeos, men on horseback, and all that goes with ranching. Hot days in the branding pen with bawling calves and the smell of burned hair and flesh in the wind! Men in boots and big hats, with the accompaniment of jingling spurs and frisky horses. Camp cook and horse wrangler! Profanity and huge appetites! The cattle industry in the East and that in the West were two worlds as different from each other as the East is different from the West. And the ninety-eighth meridian lies between. The East did a large business on a small scale; the West did a small business magnificently.

Id. at 226–27.

If the romantic image of the cowboy generates favorable feelings about public lands ranching beyond its economic significance, it also provokes a strongly negative reaction from those who view the image as a dangerous myth that prevents sounder ecological thinking. Part of their project has thus been to dismantle the myth. Ed Abbey's famous comments about cowboys are a caustic but fairly accurate view of how many critics view the Western ranching industry:

Edward Abbey, *Even the Bad Guys Wear White Hats: Cowboys, Ranchers, and Ruin of the West,* HARPERS 55 (Jan. 1986)

> The rancher (with a few honorable exceptions) is a man who strings barbed wire all over the range; drills wells and bulldozes stock ponds; drives off elk and antelope and bighorn sheep; poisons coyotes and prairie dogs; shoots eagles, bears, and cougars on sight; supplants the native grasses with tumbleweed, snakeweed, povertyweed, cowshit, anthills, mud, dust, and flies. And then leans back and grins at the TV cameras and talks about how much he loves the American West....

> Do cowboys work hard? Sometimes. But most ranchers don't work very hard. They have a lot of leisure time for politics and bellyaching. Anytime you go into a small Western town you'll find them at the nearest drugstore, sitting around all morning drinking coffee, talking about their tax breaks.

> Is a cowboy's work socially useful? No. As I've already pointed out, subsidized Western range beef is a trivial item in the national beef economy. If all of our 31,000 Western public land ranchers quit tomorrow, we'd never miss

them. Any public school teacher does harder work, more difficult work, more dangerous work, and far more valuable work than any cowboy or rancher. The same thing applies to registered nurses and nurses' aids, garbage collectors, and traffic cops. Harder work, tougher work, more necessary work. We need those people in our complicated society. We do not need cowboys or ranchers. We've carried them on our backs long enough.

———

While Abbey's biting language is hardly the norm in the grazing debate, it highlights the passions involved with public lands grazing and the conflict of cultures. That conflict and passion is not found simply in the literature of historians and nature writers. It is part of the on-the-ground reality in the West. Two vignettes—one about a rancher running cattle on a federal grazing permit within the Grand Staircase–Escalante National Monument and the other about a law professor in Wyoming—are illustrative.

As discussed in Chapter 6, when President Clinton designated the Grand Staircase–Escalante National Monument on the eve of the 1996 election, it provoked a great outcry in Utah and in the rural West more generally. Although the proclamation did not prohibit grazing within the monument, it did bring greater scrutiny to the grazing allotments within the monument's boundaries. The following excerpt from *Range* magazine describes, from a rancher's viewpoint, a subsequent dispute over grazing within the monument.

Tim Findley, *Making Monuments, Taking Towns*, Range (Summer 2001)

In a one-room log house the size of a pantry, Quinn Griffin manages his struggling real estate business. It isn't going well these dreary days in Escalante, Utah, and Griffin would sooner be out at his ranch anyway, doing the work learned over lifetimes of his own family.

Griffin's name can be found everywhere in the two blocks of Main Street falling into the deep flat from all the surrounding high fortresses of cliffs and mesas. In the supermarket his uncle owns, in the hair salon run by his sister-in-law. The little cafe, the gift shop, the town garage, all can find some link to Griffin. . . .

Quinn turned his head slowly from side to side, chin down, choking back the regret. "Last week," he says, "I sent a rifleman up there to finish off the last of them. He killed 27, and he was ill when he came back."

They were the last of the Griffin cattle still on summer range in the broad mesa top known as "The 50," and they had been spotted by the helicopter patrols of federal authorities from the Grand Staircase Escalante Monument. Only a steep narrow trail, difficult in summer, deadly in the deep winter of this February, leads down from The 50 to lower pasture. The monument authorities gave Griffin a choice: remove his cattle all the way into town at once or federal helicopters would pick them up one by one in slings at a charge to him of $585 per animal. Already, from the bitter pressures put upon him since last summer, Griffin stands to owe the federal government more than $50,000 for just such removals as well as trespass fines on his allotment.

"No choice," Griffin says, turning his head again. "No choice really."

"It's a major tragedy," says Kate Cannon, ... manager of the Grand Staircase Escalante National Monument....

"A tragedy," she says, but she means the cattle, not the place, nor its people. * * *

Six months after its designation, Kate Cannon had won the job of Escalante Monument manager from her position as a Park Service superintendent in South Dakota.... In her office at Kanab, Cannon still spins with enthusiasm for what she regards as "a new look" in "public lands management." She supersedes the authority of BLM officials still in place on lands overwhelmed by the monument and guides them in the direction of new policy toward what she calls "applied science," for which she admits there is so far "no rule book."

It was something like that which prompted her to use evidence from the drought last year to demand that Quinn Griffin and two other ranchers immediately bring their cattle down from high summer range. Cannon has the law and what she calls her "science" on her side. Griffin wisely kept a journal telling more of the story.

"It was public land before and it's public land now," says Cannon. "All I did was apply the rules that already existed. I know these are difficult allotments that require huge effort. It's a matter of who is up to it."

Quinn Griffin's agony leading to tragedy began in the piercing heat of last summer's drought when monument authorities declared that continued presence of cattle on the high ranges would be ecologically devastating. By August he was directed to reduce his numbers of cattle by half. The following are excerpts from Griffin's personal journal:

Aug. 6—Trailed cattle to Willow Tank.... A cow and heifer died because of the heat, distance and lack of water. We normally just gather and shove them off to the next lowest level, but BLM closed our winter permit, forcing us to take them to town. First time in 30 years we've had to do this.

Aug. 18—Received notification that all cattle had to be removed by Sept. 1. We protested, saying there was still the problem of heat and distance and subjecting cattle to this would be inhumane.... Denied.

Sept. 6—Broke u-joint on truck.

Sept. 7—Returned home that day to learn grandson hospitalized with [E. coli] infection. Criticized by BLM for not staying to gather cattle.

Sept. 15—Lost some leaders in dense trees. Country rough. Another two head died.

All through September and October he and his wranglers urged the cattle down the narrow trails, unable to rest them at bench stops closed by the feds.

Oct. 13—Received trespass notice, tried to respond to BLM and media.

Oct. 20–23—Rain and fog. Rained all night. Led Mary's calf back in cold black wetness. Supper at 10:30 p.m.

Oct. 24—Patch fog and occasional rain. Shot two head. One ol' cow had some age on her. Gentle, but too late in the evening to get her to the Lake corral ... so rather than the BLM finding her out there and having to pay $1,000 for her, I chose to put her down....

And so it went into winter, cattle dying from the stress of heat or the threat of fines or the bitterness of an unfair season, and all but the impossible-to-reach town corrals denied to Griffin's desperate effort to save what he could, until finally, his and other ranchers' cattle were snatched and virtually stolen in helicopter slings sent by the monument. Feed and forage on the winter range where the cattle would naturally have gone remained strong but denied to Griffin's use. He had the last of his cattle on "The 50" shot from a helicopter.

————

A different tale would surely be told by the federal land managers (*see* note five *infra* at page 932), but the anger and frustration reflected in the article are real nonetheless and give a glimpse into the view of many in the rural West about federal involvement on the range.

A second glimpse into the cultural conflict over grazing involves University of Wyoming Law School professor Debra Donahue. In 1999, Professor Donahue wrote a powerful book critiquing grazing in the West and arguing that grazing has no place at all on any arid or semiarid public lands, which she defined as lands with less than twelve inches of rainfall. Debra L. Donahue, The Western Range Revisited 8–9 (1999). Although her view of ranchers was less belligerent than Abbey's, it was equally critical of romantic notions about ranching's role in the American West as attested by this short excerpt.

> In this "romantic view," ranchers are "cowboys," who are seen as synonymous with the American West. Yet ranchers have never filled the boots of the mythical cowboy—the independent, freedom-loving, self-reliant figure of the open range. The public land ranchers of today are something of a paradox. Their numbers are few, but their political power is substantial. They act like they own the range when, in fact, their toehold on it is but a revocable "privilege." They pride themselves on their self-reliance and rail against government meddling in their affairs, while availing themselves of every government benefit and fighting to maintain a grazing fee that fails to recoup even the government's administrative costs. They replace their own cowboys with new-fangled balers and four-wheelers and snowmobiles and yet appeal to public sentiment and nostalgia to help preserve their traditional way of life. Arguing that the economy of their local community depends on their staying in business, they "moonlight" to make ends meet. The animals they raise on the range deplete the very capital upon which their, the animals', living depends. They call themselves the "original conservationists," but they have a rifle slung behind the seat of their pickups for picking off coyotes and other "varmints." They poison prairie dogs and willows and sagebrush and replace native meadows with water-guzzling alfalfa.
>
> The foregoing is not an accurate depiction of every western rancher, of course. . . . The western livestock industry is not monolithic, nor was it in the early West. * * *

Debra L. Donahue, The Western Range Revisited 5 (1999). Professor Donahue and her book were vilified in various editorials and a number of influential ranchers cut off their contributions to the University of Wyoming. The president of the Wyoming State Senate, Jim Twiford, told the Casper Star Tribune that "We've got some unlicensed, unbridled folks running over there that ought to be smarter than to be biting the hand that's feeding them" and then drafted a bill, which he later dropped, to close the University of Wyoming College of Law. *See* Katharine Collins, *A Prof Takes on the Sacred Cow*, High Country News, Feb. 28, 2000.

QUESTIONS AND DISCUSSION

1.   Although Senator Twiford threatened the University of Wyoming Law School's funding because of Professor Donahue's book, in the end, the legislature approved a 12% increase in funding for the University, citing the need to promote education and create jobs so that the state would not continue to lose its youth. What does this tell you about the political economy of grazing in the West and whose view is ultimately likely to prevail?

2.   It is commonly asserted that cattle ranchers have long held "disproportionate" political power far in excess of their numbers or value to the economy. *See, e.g.*, Stephanie Parent, *Ranching Without Reason*, 5 GREAT PLAINS NAT. RES. J. 153, 156 (2001); George Cameron Coggins et al., *The Law of Public Rangeland Management I: The Extent and Distribution of Federal Power*, 12 ENVTL. L. 535, 557 (1982). It is difficult to find clear empirical support for the proposition. In the 2005–2006 election cycle, livestock interests (the primary component of which is cattle ranching interests) donated $4,823,199 to federal candidates in the form of contributions from individuals and political action committees (PACs). 67% of that amount went to Republicans and 32% to Democrats. By contrast, environmental groups donated $2,907,458 with 89% going to Democrats and 9% going to Republicans. *See* Center for Responsive Politics, *available at* http://www.opensecrets.org/industries/indus.asp?cycle=2008&ind=A06;   http://www.opensecrets.org/industries/indus.asp?Ind=Q11. Given the insights of public choice theory, might the donations of the livestock and cattle industry produce more legislative influence than the similar donations of environmental groups? Would you expect the contributions of the cattle interests to be more focused?

Setting aside donor impact, it is undoubtedly true that the influence of western senators on public lands decisions is disproportionate in terms of population. And traditionally they have also played a greater role on congressional committees devoted to public lands issues. Nevertheless, one might ask why western senators would have an incentive to support grazing interests at the expense of the recreation and preservation interests that predominate in the more populous, and vote-rich, urban and suburban areas of their states. At the state level, the political power of rural ranching communities has been dissipating since *Baker v. Carr*, 369 U.S. 186 (1962) and *Reynolds v. Sims*, 377 U.S. 533 (1964) mandated that state legislatures be apportioned by population. What then explains ranchers' political power or at least the perception of that power? Again, do the insights of public choice theory shed any light on why organized and persistent ranching interests may have greater influence than the interests in recreation and preservation of larger urban and suburban majorities? Might ranchers' political influence result from the romantic view of ranchers that is not really a function of ranchers' propaganda but of the way legislators and their constituents construct their view of themselves? Or is it the case that in politics only money talks?

3.   Edward Abbey's caustic critique of cowboys is certainly aggressive, but ranching advocates can give as good as they get. Consider the following criticism of urbanites and suburbanites from Stephen Bodio:

Stephen Bodio, *Struck with Consequence, in* John A. Baden & Donald Snow, The Next West: Public Lands, Community, and Economy in the American West, 18, 20 (1997)

I've rarely met happier people than cowboys who have work, nor ones who hate "regular hours" more, which may point to one reason ranch folks are hard for outsiders to understand. Urbanites, yuppies, suburbanites, call them what you will: they are all "middle class," bourgeois; they have jobs and routines from which they escape to an increasingly intricate web of pleasures. Ranchers and cowboys, whether owners or workers, stand outside this twentieth-century structure. They control baronial amounts of land, but their customs and language seem working-class to intellectuals. They have the frugality and generosity, the clannishness, the sirs-and-ma'am manners of the plain people of the South, from whom their culture descends. They are emotional, contrary to the John Wayne image, and can be moved to tears. But they don't show their tears to strangers.

A Montana friend pointed out a real difference between "modern" and country people. She said that urbanites tend to see all people who work with the soil and nature—farmers and fishermen as well as ranchers and cowboys— as people who are losers in their professional race, people "too dumb to be yuppies," too unintellectual to have real jobs. Because of this, they can be pitied but hardly consulted on important issues. And ranchers and landowners who are in the employer class must be out to make money off the land, to rape it as long as they are allowed to—why else would anyone live voluntarily in W.H. Auden's "desert full of bigots?"

There are consequences here, all around. * * *

The old people, the old cultures, knew something about consequence that the new ones don't. The new ones, both born-again and politically correct (two faces of the same coin, or hydra, eerily similar in their self-righteousness) are, of course, sure they know, surer than the old ones ever are. Luigi Barzini, an Italian journalist, once wrote of such people that "they lack the humble skills of men who have to work with lackadaisical unpredictable nature, the skills so to speak of sailors, fishermen, farmers, horse-tamers, the people who must at all cost avoid deceiving themselves and must develop prudence, patience, skepticism, resignation, as well as great fortitude and perseverance." * * *

The new ones all want to evade death and deny it, legislate against it, transcend it. They run, bicycle, network, and pray. They stare into their computer screens and buy their vitamins. Here, they want the street drunks locked up, cigarettes banned, and drunken driving met with more severe penalties than is armed assault. They fear guns, cowboys, Moslems, pit bulls, whiskey, homosexuals, and freedom. Strong smells offend them.

In my town, the new people are disgusted by the *matanzas* of the old Spanish culture. Who but the Spanish and Mexicans would call a joyous fiesta celebrating pork a *matanza*, a killing? The new ones hate dangerous hard work. Who but a cretin would voluntarily work on horseback, rope cows, unroll miles of barbed wire? Or, for that matter, cut trees, stack bricks, fish out of sight of shore in winter, plow, balance on high steel? * * *

New people . . . think they are victims, but they are conquerors.

According to an article in *High Country News*, "an important regional representative from a national conservation organization said in a meeting in Aspen that 'the role of environmental groups is to save the Colorado Plateau from the people who live there.' "

4. An emerging source of cowboy folklore is the annual gathering of cowboy poets in Elko, Nevada. *See* Western Folklife Center, http://www. westernfolklife.org/site1/index.php. Is the poetry festival perpetuating a romantic mythology or cataloguing and describing a unique way of life?

5. How did you feel about BLM's treatment of Quinn Griffin and his cattle? Should the fact that Griffin's family has been grazing cattle in the area for generations make a difference? The controversy over the removal of Griffin's cattle from the Fifty Mile Mountain allotment had an interesting twist not covered in the *Range* magazine article. In October of 2000, BLM land managers removed by helicopter those cows of Griffin's they could find—six cows and two calves. They also removed an estimated 37 head of cattle run by local rancher Mary Bulloch. The following month, the day before some of the cattle were to be auctioned, Bulloch and about a dozen sympathetic ranchers seized the cattle from a federal impoundment yard. The local sheriff, who was himself a rancher and who had refused assistance from the U.S. Marshals, initially rebuffed the ranchers' demands, but when it became apparent that they intended to take the cattle and "did not care how they got them," he relented, explaining "I did not want a Waco situation." The ranchers returned Griffin's cattle to him in Escalante and he subsequently negotiated an arrangement with the U.S. Attorney under which he would care and feed for the cattle pending an administrative ruling on the legality of removing them from the allotment. The U.S. Attorney ultimately decided not to file a criminal prosecution and to let the administrative action take its course, warning that if the Bulloch and Griffin did not pay their fines for failing to timely remove their cattle, they could lose their grazing permits. In yet another upshot of the Quinn Griffin story, after the change in presidential administrations, Kate Cannon, the BLM's monument manager, was reassigned to a deputy superintendent job at the Grand Canyon, apparently because of local criticism. In June 2003, Griffin paid a reduced fine and BLM agreed to the gradual return of 350 cattle to the Fifty Mile Mountain allotment. *See* Brent Israelsen, *Cows Remain in Overgrazed Area of Monument*, Salt Lake Trib., Sept. 25, 2000, at B2; Joe Bauman, *Cattle Deal Is Reached*, Deseret News, Nov. 18, 2000, at B1; Stephen Speckman, *Rancher Kills 27 Cattle to Comply with BLM Rules*, Deseret News, Feb. 28, 2001, at B6; *Ranchers Won't Face Charges in Cattle Rift*, Deseret News, Feb. 27, 2001, at A14; Brent Israelsen, *Politics Played Role in Staircase Boss' Departure*, Salt Lake Trib., Dec. 17, 2001, at B2; Greenwire, June 18, 2002.

6. Some commentators have argued that the rural ranching communities of the American West have a distinctive culture that must be factored into the changing western landscape where preservation and recreation are gaining favor over commodity and extractive uses of the public lands. *See* A. Dan Tarlock, *Can Cowboys Become Indians? Protecting Western Communities as Endangered Cultural Remnants*, 31 Ariz. St. L.J. 539, 539, 561–62 (1999); James R. Rasband, *The Rise of Urban Archipelagoes in the American West: A New Reservation Policy*, 31 Envtl. L. 1, 49–52 (2001). The latter article poses the question whether the growing preference for moving public land ranchers off federal allotments has echoes of earlier efforts to move Indian tribes off the land.

Although those ... of us who have flocked to the West's urban archipelagoes have a different view about how the West's natural resources are best used, often many of us seem to share with our nineteenth century counterparts the view that those who were here before we arrived are an obstacle and hindrance to achieving our desired use of the West's resources. This time it is not Native Americans and their hunter-gatherer lifestyle that stand in the way of farming, ranching, and extraction, but rather rural Westerners and their cattle, sheep, mines, and roads that seem to stand in the way of recreation and preservation. Indeed, there are profound nineteenth century echoes in the goal of many of the West's new immigrants to wean rural Westerners of their dependence on the public lands and to train them in the arts of city-bound, service economies so that the public lands will be available for the new Westerners' preferred uses. This parallel goal is accompanied by parallel arguments about economic productivity and land use morality, with the law again serving as a useful ally for elevating the new majority's land use preferences.

In the nineteenth century, most were certain that leaving the West undeveloped and using its abundant resources for hunting, gathering, and occasional agriculture was economically irrational. Now a variety of persuasive economic studies show that traditional public land economies, dependent upon timber, grazing, and mining, are not efficient and that recreation and preservation are far more productive uses of the public lands. Such studies point out that the percentage of the national and Western economy represented by Western extractive industries is small and getting smaller, making it less and less rational to devote the public lands to extractive interests. Likewise, the prevailing political and moral sentiment in the nineteenth century was that the yeoman farmer who mixed his labor with the soil and established community roots was engaged in an activity superior to the transitory act of hunting and gathering. Extraction and consumption of resources to promote economic development were viewed as better than eking out a subsistence. Now, many of us tout ecosystem preservation—largely for recreation—as a morally superior land use, whether as a matter of intergenerational equity or ecological necessity.

Thoroughly confident in our political and moral sentiments and in our economic calculus, we have set out, both consciously and unconsciously, de jure and de facto, to move many of our rural communities away from their dependence on the public lands and to create a new West of urban archipelagoes surrounded by public lands preserved for our aesthetic and recreational enjoyment. As in the nineteenth century, the law does little to hinder our aspirations. Grazers have no property rights in the lands on which they have grazed their cattle for multiple generations, but only a privilege to use and occupy the public lands until the United States decides to the contrary. And where public land users have property rights—unpatented mining claims, federal mineral leases, state-created water rights, or rights-of-way—Fifth Amendment takings jurisprudence presents little hindrance to regulations that make the exercise of such property rights unattractive.

Although the analogy between current and nineteenth century public lands policies is not perfect, it is useful in considering the impact of public lands policy on the rural West because such a contrarian lens may cause those in urban areas for whom preservation is the chief goal to exhibit a little less certainty about the superiority of our public lands aspirations. If the history of the American West has been "[c]onquest by certitude" as Charles Wilkinson suggests in his powerful and evocative book, *Fire on the Plateau*, the perils of such certitude remain every bit as real. Can those of us in the urban West be so certain that our motives for changing the paradigm of public lands use are any less self-interested than those of our nineteenth century counterparts? Or are the motives much the same, different only in the particular public lands amenity that we seek?

Rasband, *supra*, at 5–7. The excerpt goes on to note a number of differences with federal Indian policy, *id.* at 52–61, but does the analogy have any merit? How do you think the two circumstances can be distinguished? It should not be surprising that many disagree with the distinctive culture argument and the analogy. *See, e.g.*, Debra Thunder, *Cowboys Ain't Indians; Buffalo Ain't Cows*, HIGH COUNTRY NEWS, May 31, 1993, at 16; DONAHUE, *supra*, at 90–98, 112–13 (reviewing the "[m]any commentators" who "have undertaken to explain—and to debunk—the cowboy myth"); Ed Quillen, *The Mountain West: A Republican Fabrication*, HIGH COUNTRY NEWS, Oct. 13, 1997, at 9 (deriding as mythical the notion of the West as "a land of small family farms, skillful artisans and wholesome little towns, all populated by descendants of courageous rugged-individualist pioneers who moved into a vast empty space without any help from that pernicious federal government in Washington"). Even if the ranching culture has distinctive qualities, should grazing policy reflect that concern? If so, how? Does it mean that recreation and preservation should not be the preferred uses of our public lands?

III. CARVING UP THE COMMONS: A BRIEF HISTORY OF RANCHERS' EFFORTS TO CONTROL WESTERN RANGELANDS

The complexity and source of the passions behind the range debate can only be understood by reviewing the history of ranching in the West and the evolution of federal range policy. Similar to other natural resource legal regimes, grazing law for a significant period of time was more a species of property law than environmental law. For the first century or so, range policy was not about ecology; it was about the efforts of ranchers, primarily but not exclusively, to acquire rights, privileges, and control of the rangeland resource. This section of the chapter focuses on that effort, tracing the range from its time as largely an open-access resource up to the allocation of grazing permits under the Taylor Grazing Act. It concludes with a look at the continuing dispute about the nature of the rights associated with those grazing permits, a dispute which has significant implications for addressing the rangeland environmental issues raised in subsequent sections.

A. THE RISE OF RANCHING ON THE PUBLIC COMMONS

Cattle and sheep are not native to North America. They were introduced to the Americas between 1515 and 1530 by Hernando Cortez, Spanish conqueror of the Aztec Indians, in what is present-day Mexico, and first made their way into the present United States when Francisco Vasquez de Coronado in 1540 went searching for the Seven Cities of Cibola and their purported treasures of gold and silver. Some of the cattle and sheep Coronado took with him escaped and began stocking the ranges of New Mexico, Arizona, Texas, and Colorado. Coronado was followed by the Spanish mission system, which established outposts along the rivers in the Southwest and the coast of California and which brought more cattle and sheep. But all of this amounted to relatively few livestock and insignificant pressure on the range. The story of what Walter Prescott Webb called "the cattle kingdom" really begins in Texas in the decades preceding the Civil War. Starting from the wild and hardy cattle of Spanish origin later known as Texas longhorns, the cattle business took root. Texas went from an estimated 100,000 head of cattle in 1830 to 330,000 head in 1850 to 3,535,768 head in 1860. WALTER PRESCOTT WEBB, THE GREAT PLAINS 212 (1931).

At the end of the Civil War, northern markets were paying $30 to $40 per head for the same cattle that could be bought in Texas for $3 and $4 per head. WEBB, *supra*, at 216. Thus began the long cattle drives of western lore as cowboys trailed thousands of Texas cattle northward to the new railheads in now-historical cattle towns like Abilene and Dodge City. From there, spurred by the growing markets and a sea of free grass covering the plains, the cattle kingdom spread out over the West. For some fifteen years, the plains were almost the pure commons of Garrett Hardin's theory. Indian tribes were being pushed westward and forced onto reservations. Homesteaders had not yet come so far West; and barbed wire, which made fencing economical, had not yet been invented. The range was wide open to livestock grazing and more and more grazers came.

As more cattlemen, and then sheep ranchers and settlers, arrived, the pressure on the open access, rangeland resource increased. The ranchers' response to the open access problem took several forms but can be broadly characterized as an effort to maintain private rights in the common resource, whether by legal recognition or on-the-ground fiat. From the beginning, ranchers hoped that their use of the public domain would ripen into private title as had been the case with settlers/squatters under the various preemption acts (*supra* Chapter 2) and miners under the 1866 and 1872 mining laws. *See* Chapter 9. If the ranchers could just get control of the range, legal recognition, they hoped, would follow. Ranchers' control efforts took many forms. Perhaps the most common was by controlling water. Testifying before the Public Land Commission in 1879, a Colorado rancher remarked:

> Wherever there is any water there is a ranch. On my own ranch (320) acres I have two miles of running water; that accounts for my ranch being where it is. The next water from me in one direction is twenty-three miles; now no man can have a ranch between these two places. I have control of the grass, the same as though I owned it.... Six miles east of me, there is another ranch, for there is water at that place.... Water accounts for nine-tenths of the population in the West on ranches.

Valerie Weeks Scott, *The Range Cattle Industry: Its Effect on Western Land Law*, 28 MONT. L. REV. 155, 162 (1967). As evidenced by the 320 acre ranch, ranchers used the land disposal laws to their advantage. By using homestead or preemption laws to take up a base ranch of 160 acres along fertile riparian areas (or multiples of that acreage if members of his family or his cowhands were willing to enter additional and sometimes fraudulent claims), a rancher could exclude other aspiring grazers and settlers from the surrounding range and assure himself of water for growing winter feed.

Where control of the water was not sufficient, many ranchers asserted a "range right" to the land within the relevant watershed. Other cattle ranchers, and the cattlemen's associations into which they organized themselves, recognized these customary range rights. But homesteaders and sheep ranchers were not so accommodating and constantly tested the ranchers' claims. Homesteaders did so by taking up land within ranchers' customary ranges, and adjacent to water if possible. Sheepherders, who were typically more nomadic, did so by ignoring range rights and trailing their sheep across ranchers' customary areas. Ranchers also claimed that sheep caused particular harm because sheep consume plants all the way down to the ground whereas cattle, ranchers asserted, leave more of the plant, allowing for quicker regeneration. As depicted by Hollywood in movies like *Shane* and *Tom Horn*, the ranchers' reaction to homesteaders and sheepherders was sometimes violent. This 1904 letter to the editor of the *Oregonian* from the secretary of the Crook County Sheep–Shooting Association gives a glimpse.

CHARLES F. WILKINSON, CROSSING THE NEXT MERIDIAN: LAND, WATER, AND THE FUTURE OF THE WEST 85–86 (1992) (*quoting from* PAUL H. ROBERTS, HOOF PRINTS ON FOREST RANGES: THE EARLY YEARS OF NATIONAL FOREST RANGE ADMINISTRATION 22–23 (1963))

I am authorized by the association (The Inland Sheep Shooters) to notify the *Oregonian* to desist from publishing matter derogatory to the reputation of sheep-shooters in Eastern Oregon. We claim to have the banner County of Oregon on the progressive lines of sheep shooting, and it is my pleasure to inform you that we have a little government of our own in Crook County, and we would thank the *Oregonian* and the Governor to attend strictly to their business and not meddle with the settlement of the range question in our province.

We are the direct and effective means of controlling the range in our jurisdiction. If we want more range we simply fence it in and live up to the maxim of the golden rule that possession represents nine points of the law.... When sheepmen fail to observe these peaceable obstructions we delegate a committee to notify offenders....

These mild and peaceful means are usually effective, but in cases where they are not, our executive committee takes the matter in hand, and being men of high ideals as well as good shots by moonlight, they promptly enforce the edicts of the association.... Our annual report shows that we have slaughtered between 8,000 and 10,000 head during the last shooting season and we expect to increase this respectable showing during the next season providing the sheep hold out and the Governor and the *Oregonian* observe the customary laws of neutrality.... In some instances the Woolgrowers of Eastern Oregon have been so unwise as to offer rewards for the arrest and conviction of sheepshooters and for assaults of herders. We have therefore warned them by publication of the danger of such action, as it might have to result in our organization having to proceed on the lines that dead men tell no tales. This is not to be considered as a threat to commit murder, as we do not justify such a thing except where the flock-owners resort to unjustifiable means of protecting their property.

————

Range wars tend to make good copy but less violent tactics, albeit of dubious legality, were more common. Cattlemen's associations also drove newcomers from the range by denying them participation in local round-ups, use of common corrals, and group protection from Indians and rustlers. Scott, *supra* at 166. A more common tactic, as indicated in the passage from the *Oregonian*, was taking advantage of the new barbed wire technology to fence in portions of the public domain. Fencing led to more violence between so-called fenced range men and free grass men, the latter typically consisting of small stockmen and itinerant sheepherders who were dependent on open range. It also led to legislation and then to lawsuits.

B.   Fence Law

If the ranchers saw open access to the range (or at least any more access) as an evil to be remedied, the initial federal response was to remove impediments to open access. In 1885, Congress passed the Unlawful Inclo-sures Act, forbidding construction and enclosures on public lands. 23 Stat. 321 (1885). By 1886, the General Land Office had 375 fencing cases involving over six million acres of public land. Scott, *supra* at 170. Among the most interesting prosecutions under the Act were those involving ranchers who managed to fence in federal land without ever erecting a fence on public property. As discussed in Chapter 2, federal railroad land grants and state school trust grants of alternate sections of land resulted in a checkerboard pattern of public and private ownership. A rancher who had acquired title to all of the odd-numbered sections in a certain area could enclose a vast amount of federal land by erecting a fence along the *top* edge of an odd-numbered section, leaving a six-inch gap, and then continuing the fence along the *bottom* edge of the diagonally-situated odd-numbered section. By repeating this process at top and bottom of a number of sections, the rancher could construct a fence entirely on his own property that would close off access to and effectively control a large number of sections of public domain. (A diagram of such a fence is reproduced at page 155.) Whether this ingenious practice could be prosecuted led to one of the significant public land law decisions of the nineteenth century in *Camfield v. United States*, 167 U.S. 518 (1897), involving a Colorado rancher who had managed to enclose some 20,000 acres of the public domain. Finding that the Act was intended to prohibit even fences situated solely upon private land, the Court rejected the rancher's challenge that Congress lacked the power to regulate private land use:

> The general Government doubtless has a power over its own property analo-gous to the police power of the several states, and the extent to which it may go in the exercise of such power is measured by the exigencies of the particular case.... While we do not undertake to say that Congress has the unlimited power to legislate against nuisances within a State, which it would have within a Territory, we do not think the admission of a Territory as a State deprives it of the power of legislating for the protection of the public lands, though it may

thereby involve the exercise of what is ordinarily known as the police power, so long as such power is directed solely to its own protection. A different rule would place the public domain of the United States completely at the mercy of state legislation.

Id. at 525–26.

If they could not fence others out of the public domain, ranchers sought to accomplish the same purpose by claiming trespass when another user, most often itinerant sheepherders, crossed the rancher's privately-owned, odd-numbered sections to get at even-numbered sections of the public domain. One such claim made it to the Supreme Court in *Buford v. Houtz*, 133 U.S. 320 (1890). Buford was a partner in the Promontory Stock–Ranch Company which had purchased from the Central Pacific Railroad 350,000 acres of alternate, odd-numbered sections in the Utah Territory. On those sections and the adjoining sections of the public domain, totaling some 921,000 acres, the company ran 20,000 head of cattle. Houtz was a sheep rancher. Buford sought to enjoin Houtz from trailing his sheep across Buford's land to the interspersed sections of public domain which, conveniently, would have made Buford the effective owner of all 921,000 acres. The Court refused to enjoin Houtz, remarking that the "equity of this proceeding is something which we are not able to perceive." It did, however, articulate a justification for all grazing on the public domain:

> We are of the opinion that there is an implied license, growing out of the custom of nearly a hundred years, that the public lands of the United States, especially those in which the native grasses are adapted to the growth and fattening of domestic animals, shall be free to the people who seek to use them, where they are left open and unclosed, and no act of government forbids this use. . . . The government of the United States in all its branches has known of this use, has never forbidden it, nor taken any steps to arrest it. No doubt it may be safely stated that this has been done with the consent of all branches of the government, and, as we shall attempt to show, with its direct encouragement.

Id. at 526–27. The Court's message was a mixed bag for ranchers. They could not exclude others from the public domain, but they themselves also had "an implied license, growing out of the custom of nearly a hundred years," to use the public lands for grazing. On the other hand, that implied license fell well short of the title to which they aspired. The license only lasted as long as "no act of government" forbade the use.

In enterprising fashion, the ranchers worked to turn this state of affairs to their advantage. If the federal government was reluctant to order the range in the ranchers' favor, states were less so. Using their powerful influence in the state legislatures around the West, ranchers achieved passage of a number of state laws designed to protect their interests. Theft of cattle was punished more severely than theft of similarly valued property. Idaho passed legislation making sheep ranchers liable for grazing their sheep within two miles of a house and later prohibited sheep from grazing on range previously occupied by cattle. The United States Supreme Court affirmed both laws, reasoning: "The police power of the State extends over the federal public domain, at least when there is no legislation by Congress on the subject. We cannot say that the measure adopted by the State is unreasonable or arbitrary ... [f]or experience shows that sheep do not require protection against encroachment by cattle, and that cattle rangers are not likely to encroach upon ranges previously occupied by sheep herders." *Omaechevarria v. Idaho*, 246 U.S. 343, 346–47 (1918). In the absence of federal law, ranchers were free to ply their influence in state legislatures, and they often did so to great effect. Fence laws were changed from the common-law approach of strict liability for damage done by trespassing livestock to the rule that owners of wandering animals would not be liable for harm caused to another's unenclosed land. *See, e.g., R.O. Corp. v. John H. Bell Iron Mountain Ranch*, 781 P.2d 910 (Wyo. 1989) ("It is firmly settled in Wyoming that no trespass or liability for damages exists when livestock running at large stray upon and depasture the unenclosed lands of a private owner."). Farmers countered by persuading many legislatures to pass "herd laws," which essentially allowed individual counties to decide whether their crops or the ranchers' cattle needed to be fenced. But as a general matter most counties in the interior West continue to have fence-out rules.

C. Initial Federal Limitations on Open Access Grazing

The Supreme Court in *Buford v. Houtz* had warned that ranchers' implied license to graze the public domain was subject to revision by federal law, but in the years that followed, grazing on public lands continued to mean free grass and federal indifference. The first real federal foray into restricting open access to public rangelands did not come until 1906, and it was a modest one. Fresh from his success at convincing President Theodore Roosevelt to transfer the national forests from the Department of Interior to the Department of Agriculture where he was serving as chief of the Division of Forestry, Gifford Pinchot embarked upon a program to regulate grazing in the approximately 100 million acres of national forests now under his jurisdiction. The regulation consisted primarily of requiring ranchers to obtain a grazing permit and pay a fee. The fee was $.05 per animal unit month (AUM). An AUM is the amount of forage one cow (more precisely one cow and calf), one horse, or five sheep or goats would be expected to consume in one month.

> Pinchot's 1906 program may have been modest by today's lights, but it was incendiary to the cattle industry. Several western legislatures passed memorials denouncing regulation of the federal range. "Pinchotism" was front-page news in western newspapers, and the chief of the Forest Service was labeled a dictator and a carpetbagger. Many forest rangers, who had thrived on the support of their local communities, suffered harassment.

Wilkinson, Crossing, *supra*, at 91. A challenge to Pinchot's program filed by a Colorado rancher and funded by stock associations and the Colorado legislature found its way to the United States Supreme Court in 1911 in the form of a challenge to federal power to retain the public lands and restrict access to them. In *Light v. United States*, 220 U.S. 523 (1911), the Court upheld the regulations and affirmed the United States' power of retention. Although Pinchot's grazing regulations survived legal challenge, it would be a stretch to say they made much difference in range conditions. By 1915, the number of AUMs available for grazing in national forests had actually increased by more than half. Donahue, *supra*, at 18. More significantly, grazing outside of national forests on the rest of the public domain required neither permit nor fee. Overgrazing and deterioration of range conditions thus continued, sometimes faster during periods of drought or high demand, like World War I, and sometimes slower when the opposite conditions pertained.

As the condition of much of the open range continued to deteriorate, many ranchers started to look more favorably on federal intervention. When President Roosevelt's Public Lands Commission surveyed stockmen in 1903, 78% favored federal control of public lands grazing and the Commission recommended that grazing be allowed only by ten year permits. DONAHUE, *supra*, at 15. Roosevelt and Pinchot also proposed a grazing lease program that was strongly supported by large cattle operators and livestock associations who were most concerned about their ability to control the incursions of smaller operators, sheep ranchers, and farmers onto their customary ranges. Their leasing proposal and others introduced up through a 1929 bill in Congress continued to be rejected, partly on the ground that the land should be left available for Jefferson's yeoman farmers and John Wesley Powell's irrigators, and partly for fear that the public's resources should not be controlled by a few "cattle barons."

In 1928, Congress did pass the Mizpah–Pumpkin Creek bill which provided for a grazing management experiment on just over 100,000 acres of land in Montana. The experiment called for the lands to be leased for ten years at just over three cents an acre and managed largely by designated ranchers. The result was considered a success. With the leases in place, the ranchers constructed fences and artificial reservoirs and by 1932, the forage value of the area had increased by 38%. PAUL W. GATES, HISTORY OF PUBLIC LAND LAW DEVELOPMENT 610 (1968). Meanwhile, between 1931 and 1933, livestock prices fell by 50%, causing grazers to rely even more heavily on public rangelands, exacerbating their already poor condition.

Overgrazing was not the only problem. During the teens and 1920s, with prices high and rainfall plentiful, more and more farmers had been willing to try dry farming further and further West. When the weather turned dry, disaster struck. All the sod-busting for dry land farms, along with profligate grazing, had left little vegetation to hold the soil in place.

> The first of the storms blew through South Dakota on Armistice Day, November 11, 1933. By nightfall, some farms lost nearly all their topsoil. "Nightfall" was a relative term, because at ten o'clock the next morning the sky was still pitch-black. People were vomiting dirt. Machinery, fences, roads, shrubs, sheds—everything was covered by great hanging drifts of silt. "Wives packed every windowsill, door frame, and keyhole, with oiled cloth and gummed paper," William Manchester wrote, "yet the fine silt found its way in and lay in beach-like ripples on their floors." As a gallon jug of desert floodwater, after settling, contain a quart and a half of solid mud, the sky seemed to be one part dust to three parts air. A naked human tethered outside would have been rendered skinless—such was the scouring power of the dirt-laden gales. Huge numbers of jackrabbits, unable to close their eyes, went blind. That was a blessing. It gave the human victims something to eat.

> The storms, dozens of them, continued through the spring and summer of 1934. An old physician in southwestern Nebraska wrote in his diary, "Wind forty miles an hour and hot as hell. Two Kansas farms go by every minute." With the temperature up to 105 degrees and the horizon lined with roiling clouds that

seemed to promise ten inches of rain but delivered three feet of dirt, the plains took on a phantasmagorical dreadfulness. The ravenous storms would blow for days at a time, eating the land in their path, lifting dust and dirt high enough to catch the jet stream, which carried it to Europe. In 1934, members of Congress took time out from debating the Taylor Grazing Bill—designed to control overgrazing on the public lands—to crowd the Capitol balcony and watch the sky darken at noon. . . .

MARC REISNER, CADILLAC DESERT: THE AMERICAN WEST AND ITS DISAPPEARING WATER 149–50 (1993).

D. ENDING OPEN ACCESS TO THE PUBLIC RANGELANDS

The dust storms helped catalyze what had long been brewing in the leasing proposals and the Mizpah–Pumpkin Creek experiment—a decision by the federal government to end open access grazing on the rest of the public domain. The result was the 1934 passage of the Taylor Grazing Act with the acquiescence, and in some cases blessing, of ranchers. The Act provided:

> In order to promote the highest use of the public lands pending its final disposal, the Secretary of the Interior is authorized, in his discretion, by order to establish grazing districts . . . of vacant, unappropriated, and unreserved lands from any part of the public domain of the United States . . . which in his opinion are chiefly valuable for grazing and raising forage crops. . . .

43 U.S.C. § 315. Although the Taylor Act's "pending final disposal" language appeared to contemplate eventual transfer of the public lands to private ownership, the Act's focus was on increased federal control of the range. The Secretary was charged with insuring "the objects of such grazing districts, namely, to regulate their occupancy and use, to preserve the land and its resources from destruction or unnecessary injury, [and] to provide for the orderly use, improvement, and development of the range. . . ." 43 U.S.C. § 315a. Within the grazing districts, the Secretary was to issue grazing permits "upon the payment annually of reasonable fees," and to give preference, in the issuance of those permits,

> to those within or near a district who are landowners engaged in the livestock business, bona fide occupants or settlers, or owners of water or water rights, as may be necessary to permit the proper use of lands, water or water rights owned, occupied, or leased by them.

43 U.S.C. § 315b. In other words, in deciding to whom the new permits would be issued, the Act enshrined a significant part of prior custom: ranchers who had homesteaded, say, a 160 or 320 acre section along a river or creek would be given preference to permits on adjoining or nearby public rangelands and itinerant grazers would be last in line. This preference was one of the reasons why the Taylor Act attracted the support of a significant number of ranchers. The grazing permits were to be issued

> for a period of not more than ten years, subject to the preference right of the permittees to renewal in the discretion of the Secretary of the Interior, who shall specify from time to time numbers of stock and seasons of use. . . . So far as consistent with the purposes and provisions of this subchapter, grazing privileges recognized and acknowledged shall be adequately safeguarded, but the creation of a grazing district or the issuance of a permit pursuant to the

provisions of this subchapter shall not create any right, title, interest, or estate in or to the lands.

43 U.S.C. § 315b. In addition to the grazing permits within grazing districts, the Act also gave the Secretary authority to lease for grazing purposes lands "so situated as not to justify their inclusion in any grazing district." 43 U.S.C. § 315m. In the issuance of these leases, the Secretary was again generally to give preference to "owners, homesteaders, lessees, or other lawful occupants of contiguous lands to the extent necessary to permit proper use of such contiguous lands...." *Id.* The grazing leases outside of grazing districts are often called "Section 15 lands" with reference to the relevant provision of the Taylor Act and distinguished from the "Section 3 lands" within grazing districts for which permits are issued.

The Taylor Act set forth a daunting task for the Department of the Interior. It had to ascertain the bounds of the range, establish grazing districts, determine their grazing capacity, and divide that capacity among the various applicants with sometimes conflicting claims of historic use. To administer the Taylor Act, the Interior Department established a Grazing Division (which was renamed the U.S. Grazing Service in 1941 and in 1946 merged with the General Land Office to become the BLM) and named Farrington Carpenter, a lawyer and rancher from Colorado, to run it. Having been charged with administering an area larger than France with only seventeen other employees, Carpenter turned to local ranchers for help, setting up advisory boards of stockmen. The advisory boards were given clearer legal status by a 1939 amendment to the Taylor Act that provided for five to twelve local stockmen, and one wildlife representative, to give the Secretary "the benefit of the fullest information and advice concerning physical, economic and other local conditions." 43 U.S.C. § 315o-1(a). The boards were also to "offer advice or make recommendations concerning rules and regulations for the administration of" the Taylor Act and to advise on "the seasons of use and carrying capacity of the range." *See* 43 U.S.C. § 315o-1(b).

By 1938, 50 grazing districts had been established covering some 142 million acres with 19,342 permittees. PAUL W. GATES, HISTORY OF PUBLIC LAND LAW DEVELOPMENT 614–15 (1968). Although the configuration of grazing districts has undergone some change, ranchers' grazing privileges remained remarkably stable after their initial allocation. Permits were renewed year after year to the same individuals, typically for the same number of AUMs. WESLEY CALEF, PRIVATE GRAZING AND PUBLIC LANDS 43 (1960); Joseph Feller, *What Is Wrong with the BLM's Management of Livestock Grazing on the Public Lands?* 30 IDAHO L. REV. 555, 570–81 (1994). In part because of this consistent renewal, and despite the language in Section 315b of the Taylor Act providing that the Act "shall not create any right, title, interest, or estate in or to the lands," a recurring legal issue has been whether ranchers' grazing permits constitute a property right whose taking requires compensation under the Fifth Amendment. The Supreme Court's first clear statement on this issue did not come until 1973 in the following case.

UNITED STATES v. FULLER,
409 U.S. 488 (1973)

MR. JUSTICE REHNQUIST delivered the opinion of the Court.

Respondents operated a large-scale "cow-calf" ranch near the confluence of the Big Sandy and Bill Williams Rivers in western Arizona. Their activities were conducted on lands consisting of 1,280 acres that they owned in fee simple (fee lands), 12,027 acres leased from the State of Arizona, and 31,461 acres of federal domain held under Taylor Grazing Act permits issued in accordance with § 3 of the Act. The Taylor Grazing Act authorizes the Secretary of the Interior to issue permits to livestock owners for grazing their stock on Federal Government lands. These permits are revocable by the Government. The Act provides, moreover, that its provisions "shall not create any right, title, interest, or estate in or to the lands."

The United States, petitioner here, condemned 920 acres of respondents' fee lands. At the trial in the District Court for the purpose of fixing just compensation for the lands taken, the parties disagreed as to whether the jury might consider value accruing to the fee lands as a result of their actual or potential use in combination with the Taylor Grazing Act "permit" lands. The Government contended that such element of incremental value to the fee lands could neither be taken into consideration by the appraisers who testified for the parties nor considered by the jury. Respondents conceded that their permit lands could not themselves be assigned any value in view of the quoted provisions of the Taylor Grazing Act. They contended, however, that if on the open market the value of their fee lands was enhanced because of their actual or potential use in conjunction with permit lands, that element of value of the fee lands could be testified to by appraisers and considered by the jury. * * *

The question presented by this case is whether there is an exception to th[e] general rule where the parcels to be aggregated with the land taken are themselves owned by the condemnor [United States] and used by the condemnee [Fuller] only under revocable permit from the condemnor.

To say that this element of value would be considered by a potential buyer on the open market, and is therefore a component of "fair market value," is not the end of the inquiry. In *United States v. Miller, supra,* this Court held that the increment of fair market value represented by knowledge of the Government's plan to construct the project for which the land was taken was not included within the constitutional definition of "just compensation." 317 U.S., at 374. * * *

United States v. Cors, 337 U.S. 325 (1949), held that the just compensation required to be paid to the owner of a tug requisitioned by the Government in October 1942, during the Second World War, could not include the appreciation in market value for tugs created by the Government's own increased wartime need for such vessels. The Court said: "That is a value which the government itself created and hence in fairness should not be required to pay." *Id.,* at 334. A long line of cases decided by this Court dealing with the Government's navigational servitude with respect to navigable waters evidences a continuing refusal to include, as an element of value in compensating for fast lands which are taken, any benefits conferred by access to such benefits as a potential portsite or a potential hydroelectric site. *United States v. Rands,* 389 U.S. 121 (1967); *United States v. Twin City Power Co.,* 350 U.S. 222 (1956); *United States v. Commodore* Park, Inc., 324 U.S. 386 (1945).

These cases go far toward establishing the general principle that the Government as condemnor may not be required to compensate a condemnee for elements of value that the Government has created, or that it might have destroyed under the exercise of governmental authority other than the power of eminent domain. If, as in *Rands*, the Government need not pay for value that it could have acquired by exercise of a servitude arising under the commerce power, it would seem *a fortiori* that it need not compensate for value which it could remove by revocation of a permit for the use of lands that it owned outright. * * *

"Courts have had to adopt working rules in order to do substantial justice in eminent domain proceedings." Seeking as best we may to extrapolate from these prior decisions such a "working rule," we believe that there is a significant difference between the value added to property by a completed public works project, for which the Government must pay, and the value added to fee lands by a revocable permit authorizing the use of neighboring lands that the Government owns. The Government may not demand that a jury be arbitrarily precluded from considering as an element of value the proximity of a parcel to a post office building, simply because the Government at one time built the post office. But here respondents rely on no mere proximity to a public building or to public lands dedicated to, and open to, the public at large. Their theory of valuation aggregates their parcel with land owned by the Government to form a privately controlled unit from which the public would be excluded. * * *

We hold that the Fifth Amendment does not require the Government to pay for that element of value based on the use of respondents' fee lands in combination with the Government's permit lands. * * *

Reversed.

MR. JUSTICE POWELL, with whom MR. JUSTICE DOUGLAS, MR. JUSTICE BRENNAN, and MR. JUSTICE MARSHALL join, dissenting.

I dissent from a decision which, in my view, dilutes the meaning of the just compensation required by the Fifth Amendment when property is condemned by the Government. * * *

Contrary to the implication in the Government's framing of the question in this case, the jury was not allowed to include "the value of revocable grazing permits." The instruction expressly stated that "such permits are mere licenses which may be revoked and are not compensable as such." The emphasis of the instruction was on the location of the fee land, with the resulting "availability and accessibility" of the adjacent public grazing land. I find the instruction to be an appropriate statement of the applicable principles of just compensation.

The opinion of the Court recognizes that the just compensation required by the Fifth Amendment when the Government exercises its power of eminent domain is ordinarily the market value of the property taken. It is commonplace, in determining market value—whether in condemnation or in private transactions—to consider such elements of value as derive from the *location* of the land. But today the Court enunciates an exception to these recognized principles where the value of the land to be condemned may be enhanced by its location in relation to Government-owned property. * * *

Neither of the lines of cases on which the Court relies seems apposite. The first includes *United States v. Miller, supra*, in which the Court held that the Government need not pay for an increase in value occasioned by the very project for which the land was condemned, and *United States v. Cors*, 337 U.S. 325 (1949), in which the Court held that in condemning tugboats during wartime the Government need not offer compensation for an increase in value attributable to its own extraordinary wartime demand for such craft. These cases support only the modest generalization that compensation need not be afforded for an increase in market value stemming from the very Government undertaking which led to the condemnation.

The other cases on which the Court relies, *United States v. Rands*, 389 U.S. 121 (1967), and *United States v. Twin City Power Co.*, 350 U.S. 222 (1956), deal with the condemnation of lands adjacent to navigable waters. In *Rands*, the condemnee owned land on the Columbia River which the United States condemned "in connection with the John Day Lock and Dam Project, authorized by Congress as part of a comprehensive plan for the development of the Columbia River." 389 U.S., at 122. Relying on the "unique position" of the Government "in connection with navigable waters," *ibid.*, the Court held that no special element of value could be accorded the land by virtue of its possible use as a port. In *Twin City*, the condemnee was holding land on the Savannah River as a potential hydroelectric powersite. The Government condemned the land as part of a major flood control, navigation, and hydroelectric project. By a bare majority vote, the Court held that the condemnee was not entitled to the "special water-rights value" of the land as a potential powersite, distinguishing other cases with the comment: "We have a different situation here, one where the United States displaces all competing interests and appropriates the entire flow of the river...." 350 U.S., at 225.

The water rights cases may be subject to varying interpretations, but it is important to remember when interpreting them that they cut sharply against the grain of the fundamental notion of just compensation, that a person from whom the Government takes land is entitled to the market value, including location value, of the land. They could well be confined to cases involving the Government's "unique position" with respect to "navigable waters." * * *

QUESTIONS AND DISCUSSION

1. Prior to this decision, two circuit courts had reached conflicting results on whether the value of attached grazing permits would be included in the value of a condemned base ranch. The Ninth Circuit had denied compensation for permit value in a case involving permits on national forest land. *See Osborne v. United States*, 145 F.2d 892, 896 (9th Cir. 1944). The Tenth Circuit, however, had held that compensation was required. *See United States v. Jaramillo*, 190 F.2d 300, 302 (10th Cir. 1951) (government liable for permit value where permits in effect). *But cf. United States v. Cox*, 190 F.2d 293 (10th Cir. 1951) (denying compensation where permits were withdrawn as part of the condemnation), *cert. denied*, 342 U.S. 867 (1951).

2. If the Taylor Act provided that permits "shall not create any right, title, interest, or estate in or to the lands," 43 U.S.C. § 315b, why have ranchers argued so tenaciously that their permits were vested property rights? Ranchers could point to a longstanding federal practice of renewing their permits as a matter of course. *See, e.g.*, WESLEY CALEF, PRIVATE GRAZING AND PUBLIC LANDS 43 (1960) ("Although the service has never abandoned the position that grazing 'privileges' can be revoked at its discretion, in actual practice permits are renewed year after year to the same individuals. Moreover, except in unusual circumstances they are renewed annually for the same number of a.u.m.'s."); Joseph Feller, *What Is Wrong with the BLM's Management of Livestock Grazing on the Public Lands?*, 30 IDAHO L. REV. 555, 570–81 (1994) (describing similar current BLM practices). Ranchers would also emphasize that banks have accepted their grazing permits as collateral and that permits are typically capitalized into the value of a ranch. Ranchers also pinned some hopes on a 1938 opinion in *Red Canyon Sheep Co. v. Ickes*, 98 F.2d 308 (D.C. Cir. 1938). In that case, the court enjoined a land exchange that would have transferred out of federal ownership land on which a rancher was grazing sheep under a newly minted Taylor Act permit. The court stated: "We recognize that the rights under the Taylor Grazing Act do not fall within the conventional category of vested rights in property. Yet, whether they be called rights, privileges, or bare licenses, or by whatever name, while they exist they are something of real value to the possessors and something which have their source in an enactment of the Congress." *Id.* at 315. The court went on to admit that grazing permits were "subject to restriction or withdrawal," *id.* at 316, but concluded that they were a "proper subject of equitable protection against an illegal act." *Id.* 316. That illegal act, said the court, was an exchange that did not meet the statutory requirements. Is *Red Canyon Sheep* that helpful to the ranchers' argument for a property right in their permit? Is the case simply an expansive interpretation of the actual injury requirement of traditional standing law? *See supra*, Chapter 3, page 242.

3. Does the *Fuller* Court's opinion leave any unanswered questions about whether a rancher maintains a property right in a grazing permit? In a 1996 law review article, two livestock industry lawyers argued that it did:

> Appellants and Respondents stipulated that the grazing permit could be taken without just compensation. Therefore, the question of the legal status of the underlying preference was not addressed. Second, because not all of Fuller's private land was condemned, he still owned an adjudicated preference which he could attach to his remaining base property. Therefore, had the Court allowed Fuller to be paid, he would have been compensated for something he still possessed.... Third, although the courts have not ruled on the scope of rights that existed before the Taylor Grazing Act and the Organic Administration Act, prior rights or uses in the federal lands have been recognized. *See* McNeil v. Seaton, 281 F.2d 931, 933 (D.C. Cir. 1960) (stating that once a preference right is granted, the permittee is entitled to rely on it); Chournos v. United States, 193 F.2d 321 (10th Cir. 1951) (holding that the purpose of the Taylor Grazing Act is to "stabilize the industry and permit the use of the public range according to the needs and the qualifications of the livestock operators with base holdings"); Red Canyon Sheep Co. v. Ickes, 98 F.2d 308, 314 (D.C. Cir. 1938) (rejecting a proposed BLM exchange because it interfered with a permittee's adjudicated preference).

Frank J. Falen & Karen Budd–Fallen, *The Right to Graze Livestock on the Federal Lands: The Historical Development of Western Grazing Rights*, 30 Idaho L. Rev. 505, 524 (1994). Are their efforts to distinguish the case persuasive? Does it help their argument that the IRS has ruled the grazing preference is taxable and that preference rights are taxed in some western states? *See id.* at 522–24.

4. The latest twist on the issue of whether there is a property right in a grazing permit comes from litigation filed in the Federal Court of Claims by rancher-activist Wayne Hage. Hage and his wife, Jean, both of whom have now passed away, argued that by canceling their grazing permit and then denying them access to the associated state water rights and federal ditch rights (created by the 1866 Ditch Rights-of-Way Act), the government had taken not only the water and ditch rights, but also an appurtenant right to have livestock graze within the ditch right-of-way. In a bifurcated proceeding, the court first concluded that the Hages did indeed have a property interest in various water and ditch rights, as well as forage rights within the ditch right-of-way. *See Hage v. United States*, 51 Fed. Cl. 570 (Fed. Cl. 2002). As the court saw it, "[t]he government cannot cancel a grazing permit and then prohibit the plaintiff from accessing the water to redirect it to another place of valid beneficial use. The plaintiffs have a right to go on land and divert the water." *Id.* at 584.

In the second proceeding, the court emphasized that "for [the Hages'] claim to succeed, they must establish a taking of their property that is not related to the cancellation of grazing permits," but concluded that, under *Penn Central*, the federal government had taken the Hages' state water rights and 1866 Act ditch rights and that they should be awarded compensation of $2,854,816.20. *See Estate of Hage v. U.S.*, 82 Fed. Cl. 202 (Fed. Cl. 2008). The court accepted the Hages' argument that the Forest Service's threats of trespass and its prohibition on maintaining their ditches with anything other than hand tools was a taking:

> policies promoted by the Forest Service, including permitting brush to overgrow the stream beds and allowing beavers to establish dams in the upper reaches of streams, prevented Plaintiffs from accessing and using the water.... Spreading [from the beaver dams] and evapotranspiration were also issues. Evapotranspiration represents the water used by plants, and can represent a significant loss of water when plants develop root structure into existing shallow aquifers or groundwater. Plaintiffs offered evidence at trial that the willow growth in the creeks had gotten so thick that it was difficult to walk across, or even to see in some places, the stream bed. Plaintiffs' expert witness estimated the average historical flow in the seven creeks reaching the Ranch to be 13,000 acre feet. The actual flow at the time of trial was close to 5,000 acre feet, reflecting an 8,000 acre feet diminishment.

Id. at 211. The Hages' inability to access and maintain their water rights, said the court, deprived them of the water they needed for irrigation for their base ranch and prevented them from selling the water to another irrigator. On the third issue left over from the prior litigation, the court declined to find a taking of the forage rights within the ditch right-of-way because it would have been "economically unfeasible to graze cattle on the 100 foot wide strips while being unable to graze on land beyond that mark." *Id.* at 213 n.11.

Given the decision in *Fuller*, would you have expected this result? Is the decision likely to stand up on appeal? What are the implications of this takings decision for federal range management?

5. Does the "general principle" articulated by the Court in *Fuller* that "the Government as condemnor may not be required to compensate a condemnee for elements of value that the Government has created, or that it might have destroyed under the exercise of governmental authority other than the power of eminent domain," have any limits? Does this distinguish the post office hypothetical mentioned by the majority? Is the majority's primary concern that the base ranch not be "aggregated" with the allotment lands? If so, why was it not sufficient to emphasize that the rancher had no property interest in the allotment?

6. Is the dissent's effort to distinguish *Rands* and *Twin City Power* persuasive? *Rands* and *Twin City Power* were both grounded in the federal navigation servitude, a property and regulatory interest of the United States that is most often said to derive from Congress's power over commerce, although its precise origins are murky. *See generally* Amy K. Kelley, *Constitutional Foundations of Federal Water Law, in* 4 WATER AND WATER RIGHTS § 35.02(c) (Robert E. Beck ed., 1991). Because of the servitude, there is no constitutional right to compensation for federal actions that interfere with the flow, affect the bed or banks, or eliminate access to navigable waters. *Id.* § 35.02(c)(1). Nor, as *Rands* held, is there a constitutional right to include in the value of fast lands (the lands above the high water mark) the "special value" which "arises from access to, and use of, navigable waters." 389 U.S. at 124–25. Interestingly enough, following the Supreme Court's decision in *Rands*, Congress enacted legislation providing that it would pay the fair market value of fast lands even where a portion of that value was created by access to or utilization of navigable waters. *See* Section 111 of the Rivers and Harbors Act of 1970, 33 U.S.C. § 595a. Would it be appropriate for Congress to pass similar legislation with respect to compensation for base ranches taken by eminent domain? How might the two situations be distinguished?

7. Now that you have read something about the history of the western range and the *Fuller* case which suggests that ranchers have no right, title, or interest in their grazing permits, consider again whether public land ranchers have any reliance interests worthy of recognition in grazing policy. What about ranchers like Quinn Griffin, *supra*? Does it matter that he and his family have been running cattle on "The Fifty" since the late 1800s? If you were a BLM field office manager, would you feel any special obligation to preserve the grazing opportunities of a sixth- or seventh-generation rancher?

Professor Oesterle rejects the argument that ranchers have a reliance interest in continued grazing on the public domain. He asserts: "Personal decisions based on an expectation of government action do not necessarily justify an assertion of ownership rights. * * * Acquisition of permanent property rights by accretion, when the public is represented by transitory and often ineffectual government officials, stretches any notion of public consent to property transfers beyond reasonable boundaries." Dale A. Oesterle, *Public Land: How Much Is Enough?*, 23 ECOLOGY L.Q. 521, 532–33 (1996). When, if ever, is it appropriate to preserve or subsidize a natural resource dependent culture? Is canceling a rancher's grazing permit any different than issuing a pink slip to a computer programmer of a company whose software is no longer in demand? If so, can communities dependent upon grazing be distinguished from those dependent on mining, logging, or the family farm?

8. Before the federal government began to involve itself in regulating grazing, ranchers formed range associations which respected informal range rights and which took a variety of measures to protect the interests of the group. Are there any implications of these collective efforts for the efficacy of common property regimes in the face of pressure from competing resource users? Are you comfortable with the ranchers' informal enforcement of group rights? Another example of informal enforcement is that of some New England lobstermen. Because it is so difficult for government regulators to detect cheating on take limits, lobstermen, who are on the water every day, have enforced limits on their own through such measures as cutting the floating buoys that are attached to the poacher's lobster traps, simply opening the traps, or even sinking the boats of the cheater. *See* James M. Acheson, The Lobster Gangs of Maine (1988).

9. Dividing a common resource among private users is one of the classic solutions to the tragedy of the commons. *See* Chapter 1, page 70. As you read the following section, consider whether the grazing permit approach has been an effective solution for either ranchers or the environment. Consider also why the division of the range into individual grazing allotments has not been completely effective and what sorts of common pool resource management approaches may have worked better.

IV. Environmental Law Comes to the Range ... Slowly

A. The Taylor Grazing Act as Environmental Law

The Taylor Act's preamble describes the Act's purpose as:

> To stop injury to the public grazing lands by preventing overgrazing and soil deterioration, to provide for their orderly use, improvement, and development, to stabilize the livestock industry dependent on the public range, and for other purposes.

Act of June 28, 1934, Pub. L. No. 482, ch. 865, 48 Stat. 1269. Section 2 of the Act then instructs the Secretary to

> make such rules and regulations ... to insure the objects of such grazing districts, namely, to regulate their occupancy and use, to preserve the land and its resources from destruction or unnecessary injury, to provide for the orderly use, improvement and development of the range. . . .

43 U.S.C. § 315a. "[S]top[ping] injury to the public grazing lands" and "preserv[ing] the land and its resource from destruction and unnecessary injury," certainly suggest ecological concerns, but it would be a mistake to confuse the Taylor Grazing Act and its implementing regulations (often referred to as "The Range Code") with modern environmental regulation. Although the Act reflected concerns with soil deterioration, flood control, and watershed protection, those concerns were more utilitarian than aesthetic or ecological and are best understood as another manifestation of Gifford Pinchot's conservationist approach: resources should be managed to produce the greatest good for the greatest number in the long run. *See supra* Chapter 6, page 580 (discussing the influence of Pinchot's "conservationist" philosophy on the Forest Service). The primary thrust of the Taylor Act was wiser grazing of public rangelands. This focus is apparent in the above provisions. Although they exhibit concern about rangeland health, they also refer to "the public *grazing* lands," express concern about "stabiliz[ing] the livestock industry dependent on the public range" and

command the Secretary "to provide for the orderly *use*, improvement, and *development* of the range." The Taylor Act's language can certainly be mined for language allowing different range use and management, and some of that effort will be discussed below. But as you consider the progress of grazing law and range management following the passage of the Taylor Act, it is important to keep in mind the Act's grazing focus. Because of that focus, it is not particularly surprising that in the years following the adoption of the Taylor Act, the range continued to be managed primarily for the benefit of the grazing permittees.

As reflected in the data described in Part II.C above, range conditions improved somewhat under the Taylor Act, although that improvement was measured primarily with respect to production of forage for livestock. Whether the range ecosystem improved is more controversial, particularly in riparian areas. As with management of any natural resource, defining success depends in significant part on which resource use the manager seeks to maximize. As interest in managing the range for other purposes— e.g., watershed, recreation, wildlife—grew over the latter half of the twentieth century, so too did interest in altering or adding to the Taylor Act's tools for managing public rangelands. On its own, the Taylor Act provides few legal footholds for challenging BLM's grazing management or for managing for these other purposes. In the first thirty years of the Act's existence, very few cases addressed allocation of the range resource and most such cases involved allocation disputes between grazing and mining interests. In fact, the Taylor Act prompted little litigation with ranchers, with less than a dozen administrative appeals even reaching the courts. *See* Hugh E. Kingery, *The Public Grazing Lands*, 43 DENV. U. L. REV. 329, 336, 339–44 (1966).

B. EARLY RANGE PLANNING EFFORTS

The first significant manifestation of environmental concern over rangeland resources came in the form of the Classification and Multiple Use Act. *See* 43 U.S.C. § 1411–18 (expired 1970), passed by Congress in 1964. The Act, which is discussed further in Chapter 3, was based on the Multiple–Use, Sustained–Yield Act of 1960 for the national forests. It directed BLM to classify the public lands under its jurisdiction and gave BLM the authority to manage for multiple use and sustained yield. In theory, the BLM already had that authority under the Taylor Act. Section 7 of the Act authorized the Secretary "in his discretion, to examine and classify any lands ... within a grazing district which are more valuable or suitable for the production of agricultural crops than for the production of native grasses and forage plants, *or more valuable or suitable for any other use* than for the use provided for under this subchapter...." 43 U.S.C. § 315f (emphasis added). But the Secretary had not used this discretion to classify much public land for non-grazing purposes. Moreover, the Classification and Multiple Use Act, although hardly a ringing endorsement of environmental values, was more explicit in its direction to administer BLM lands "for multiple use," which included not only grazing and extractive uses but also fish and wildlife, watershed, and wilderness preservation. *See* 78 Stat. 986, §§ 1(a) & 3 (Sept. 19, 1964). The BLM did not, however, seize the opportunity to change its management approach and when the Classification and Multiple Use Act expired in 1970, not much in the way of classification or inventorying had been accomplished. Nevertheless, the Act did prompt BLM to start a new planning process and it serves as a useful marker for identifying the beginning of what is a still-unfolding shift by BLM toward range planning that incorporates broader environmental and recreational concerns.

Environmental concerns over the range resource took a significant step forward with the explosion of environmental laws during the Nixon administration—NEPA on New Years Day in 1970, the Clean Air Act later that same year, the Clean Water Act in 1972, and the Endangered Species Act in 1973. Although grazing and range problems did not drive these laws, they had, and still have, significant relevance to range management issues. The initially tentative, but increasingly significant, application of these statutes to range issues is discussed in Section VI below. NEPA's application to range management, however, needs some elaboration at this point in the chapter because the application of NEPA in grazing case law is so closely interwoven with the application of statutes more explicitly concerned with grazing that leaving its discussion until later risks confusion. Moreover, NEPA provided the first impetus for bringing environmental concerns to range management.

As discussed in Chapter 3, NEPA requires federal agencies to consider the environmental impacts of their actions. In the immediate aftermath of NEPA's passage, and even today, it was not self-evident what constituted "*major* federal actions *significantly* affecting the quality of the human environment," 42 U.S.C. § 4332(2)(C) (emphasis added), particularly as it related to grazing management on millions of acres of federal land. Could BLM get away with a single environmental impact statement (EIS) for the management of all resources (e.g., coal, timber, and grass) within its jurisdiction? On the other end of the scale, did the issuance of individual permits require an EIS? What about their renewal? Or was it the management of a grazing district? BLM's first approach was to prepare nationwide EISs for individual resources. Thus, in 1973 it released a draft programmatic EIS reviewing its entire grazing permit program. BLM also announced that it would complete environmental assessment reports on individual allotment management plans (the name for the planning document that typically covers one grazing allotment, although it may cover more) as they were developed.

Beginning what has become a more common refrain, many in the ranching community thought BLM's Draft EIS (DEIS) was too negative about rangeland conditions and "biased against livestock grazing." Bureau of Land Management, *Livestock Grazing Management on National Resource Lands: Final Environmental Impact Statement* supplement no. 1, comment no. 45 (1975). Environmental groups focused on a different point. They believed the BLM's draft national-scale, programmatic EIS had very little value, whatever its language, because it failed to consider local impacts of grazing on wildlife, soils, water quality, and alternative uses. Led by the Natural Resources Defense Council, which had been formed by a few Yale Law School graduates in 1969 on the eve of NEPA's passage, several environmental organizations sued, demanding that more localized EISs be prepared. *See NRDC v. Morton*, 388 F. Supp. 829 (D. D.C. 1974), *aff'd per curiam*, 527 F.2d 1386 (D.C. Cir.), *cert. denied*, 427 U.S. 913 (1976). The case turned out to be one of the most significant NEPA decisions of the 1970s. Judge Flannery ruled that BLM's programmatic EIS was inadequate and then charged the parties with developing a schedule for preparing more site-specific impact statements. After four months of negotiation, the parties presented an agreed order to the court under which BLM would prepare 212 EISs (later reduced to 144) over the next thirteen years (later extended). The EISs would be correlated with the ongoing process of developing management framework plans (MFPs) that had been started under the Classification and Multiple Use Act.

Despite its importance, the *Morton* case did not bring dramatic changes in range management. NEPA did not prescribe substantive range management standards and BLM continued to operate much as it had before. Nevertheless, *Morton* was a start, and more changes were in store.

C. FLPMA: THE BLM GETS AN ORGANIC ACT

Although grazing was the predominant use of the public lands (at least in its geographic scope), concern about the limits of the Taylor Grazing Act was only one of many issues relating to management of the public domain. In 1964, as part of the compromises involved with passage of the Wilderness Act, the Public Land Law Review Commission was tasked with studying the nation's approach to the public domain and making recommendations for modernization of public land management. Act of Sept. 19, 1964, Pub. L. No. 88–606, 78 Stat. 982. The Commission published its study in June of 1970 and one of its key recommendations—that an organic act be passed to direct the BLM's management—was achieved with the passage of the Federal Land Policy and Management Act in 1976. *See* 43 U.S.C. § 1701–84. FLPMA's passage was a triumph for the BLM. As one former associate director at the BLM remarked: "Many of us oldtimers in the Bureau said that before we retired we wanted a basic organic act—and not all this crossword puzzle kind of stuff we'd had to work with for 30 years." JAMES MUHN & HANSON R. STUART, OPPORTUNITY AND CHALLENGE: THE STORY OF BLM 170 (1988). FLPMA covered much more than grazing. As discussed in other chapters, it altered mining law, limited executive withdrawal power, required broad land use planning, and revised the process for acquiring rights-of-way across public lands.

Although FLPMA did not repeal the Taylor Act, it impacted grazing policy in a number of ways. Whereas the Taylor Act established grazing districts on the public lands "pending its [*sic*] final disposal," 43 U.S.C. § 315, FLPMA declared the policy of the United States that "the public lands be retained in Federal ownership." 43 U.S.C. § 1701(a)(1). This important shift in federal policy dampened the hopes of some that the public lands would be assigned to the states or that grazing permits would be privatized. FLPMA also required the Secretary of the Interior to manage the public lands for "multiple use and sustained yield." 43 U.S.C. § 1732(a). FLPMA defines "multiple use" as the management of the public lands and their various resources so that they are utilized in the combination that will best meet the present and future needs of the American people; ... a combination of balanced and diverse resource uses that takes into account the long-term needs of future generations for renewable and non-renewable resources, including but not limited to, recreation, range, timber, minerals, watershed, wildlife and fish, and natural scenic, scientific and historical values; and harmonious and coordinated management of the various resources without permanent impairment of the productivity of the land and the quality of the environment with consideration being given to the relative values of the resources and not necessarily to the combination of uses that will give the greatest economic return or the greatest unit output.

43 U.S.C. § 1702(c). "Sustained yield" is defined as

the achievement and maintenance in perpetuity of a high-level annual or regular periodic output of the various renewable resources of the public lands consistent with multiple use.

43 U.S.C. § 1702(h). FLPMA also mandated that the Secretary "[i]n managing the public lands ... shall, by regulation or otherwise, take any action necessary to prevent unnecessary or undue degradation of the lands." 43 U.S.C. § 1732(b).

Although BLM claimed to have been operating the public lands under multiple use principles, FLPMA's specific mandate helped clarify that grazing was not to be the dominant use of public rangeland. Adding further credence to this point, FLPMA obligated the Secretary to prepare and maintain land use plans observing the principles of multiple use and sustained yield, *id.* § 1712(c)(1), to allow the public to participate in that process, *id.* § 1712(f), and then to manage the public lands in accordance with the land use plans. *Id.* § 1732(a).

In addition to its dominant multiple use message, FLPMA dealt specifically with several range management issues. It conformed grazing permit duration (ten years) and the process for canceling a permit for both the BLM and the Forest Service. *See* 43 U.S.C. § 1752. It emphasized that both the Secretary of the Interior and the Secretary of Agriculture may

cancel, suspend, or modify, a grazing permit or lease, in whole or in part, pursuant to the terms and conditions thereof, or to cancel or suspend a grazing permit or lease, in whole or in part, pursuant to the terms and conditions thereof, or to cancel or suspend a grazing permit or lease for any violation of a grazing regulation or of any term or condition of such grazing permit or lease.

Id. § 1752(a). FLPMA also amplified the Taylor Act's statement that the Secretary should "specify from time to time number of stock and seasons of use," 43 U.S.C. § 315b, by providing that the Secretary

shall incorporate in grazing permits and leases such terms and conditions as he deems appropriate for management of the permitted or leased lands pursuant to applicable law ... [and] shall also specify therein the number of animals to be grazed and the seasons of use and that he may reexamine the condition of the range at any time and, if he finds on re-examination that the condition of the range requires adjustment in the amount or other aspect of grazing use, that the permittee or lessee shall adjust his use to the extent the Secretary ... deems necessary.

43 U.S.C. § 1752(e). Finally, FLPMA reemphasized that grazing permits could be canceled for other purposes such as when the agency decides in its

land use planning process to devote land to a different public purpose. FLPMA did, however, assure ranchers of some protection in such instances.

> Whenever a permit or lease for grazing domestic livestock is canceled in whole or in part, in order to devote the lands covered by the permit or lease to another public purpose, including disposal, the permittee or lessee shall receive from the United States a reasonable compensation for the adjusted value, to be determined by the Secretary concerned, of his interest in the authorized permanent improvements placed or constructed by the permittee or lessee.... Except in cases of emergency, no permit or lease shall be canceled ... without two years' prior notification.

43 U.S.C. § 1752(g).

Congress' command in FLPMA that BLM manage for multiple use contained an implicit criticism of BLM's grazing focus that had dominated since the Taylor Act. Indeed, Congress expressly observed "that a substantial amount of the Federal range lands is deteriorating in quality." *Id.* § 1751(b)(1). After FLPMA's passage, the question was whether its various commands to manage for "multiple use," to avoid "permanent impairment of the productivity of the land," and "to prevent unnecessary or undue degradation of the lands," created a substantive obligation to depart from historical grazing management practices. Some commentators thought that it did, predicting that courts were likely to enforce these standards in the future. What made such predictions difficult is that FLPMA also exhibits congressional ambivalence toward the role of grazing on the public domain. Grazing is included as one of the many multiple uses that BLM has discretion to allow. *See* § 1702(c). And in the provision deploring federal range conditions, Congress directs a program of range improvements which could lead, says Congress, "to substantial betterment of forage conditions with resulting benefits to wildlife, watershed protection, and livestock production." *Id.* § 1751(b)(1).

D.   PRIA: ENVIRONMENTAL MANDATE OR MORE CONGRESSIONAL AMBIVALENCE?

Two years after FLPMA's passage, Congress passed the Public Rangelands Improvement Act (PRIA). 43 U.S.C. §§ 1901–08. Congress reiterated that "vast segments of the public rangelands are producing less than their potential for livestock, wildlife habitat, recreation, forage, and water and soil conservation benefits, and for that reason are in unsatisfactory condition." *Id.* § 1901(a)(1). It then provided that "the goal" of rangeland management "shall be to improve the range conditions of the public rangelands so that they become as productive as feasible in accordance with the rangeland management objectives established through the land use planning process, and consistent with the values and objectives listed in sections 1901(a) and (b)(2) of this title." *Id.* § 1903(b). This directive "to improve the range conditions" gave some observers hope that Congress was telling the BLM to manage grazing more restrictively. As with FLPMA, however, Congress muddied the water. The directive "to improve range conditions" is stated as a "goal" and the "values and objectives" with which management is supposed to be consistent include not only environmental and recreation values but also "expansion of the forage resource."

Id. § 1901(a)(3). PRIA, like FLPMA, left BLM range managers with significant discretion in allocation of the range resource between livestock forage and other rangeland goods and services and left observers wondering whether there was a substantive hook to make BLM exercise its discretion in a more environmentally-friendly manner.

Since PRIA's passage in 1978, Congress has not passed any significant grazing legislation. Thus, the courts have been left to sort out the meaning and content of FLPMA's multiple use requirement, PRIA's improvement mandate, and the impact of those two statutes on underlying Taylor Act provisions. The following cases begin an investigation of these questions and introduce the effort to make these three statutes work for environmental protection on the range.

NATURAL RESOURCES DEFENSE COUNCIL V. HODEL,
624 F. Supp. 1045 (D. Nev. 1985),
***aff'd* 819 F.2d 927 (9th Cir. 1987)**

JAMES M. BURNS, DISTRICT JUDGE, Sitting by Designation.

This is a complex case of first impression, brought by environmental organizations seeking to overturn certain decisions made by the Bureau of Land Management (BLM) relating to livestock grazing on public lands in the Reno, Nevada area. The plaintiffs challenge the BLM's land use plan as being in conflict with Congressional statutory mandates, and as being arbitrary and capricious as a matter of administrative law. They also raise a variety of challenges to BLM's environmental impact statement which purports to evaluate its proposed plan in comparison to other alternatives. * * *

BACKGROUND

The BLM manages some 171 million acres of federal lands in 11 western states. . . . The BLM lands are divided for grazing purposes into districts, and subdivided into planning areas, such as the "Reno Planning Area" which is the subject of this action. The Reno Planning Area encompasses an overall area of just over 5 million acres, about 700,000 of which are under BLM supervision. The planning areas are further divided into grazing allotments, for which the BLM issues grazing permits or licenses.

In 1974 the BLM prepared a single, programmatic Environmental Impact Statement (EIS) to cover its entire grazing program. That EIS was declared to be inadequate by the U.S. District Court for the District of Columbia in *Natural Resources Defense Council v. Morton*, 388 F. Supp. 829 (D. D.C. 1974), *affirmed* 527 F.2d 1386 (D.C. Cir. 1976). The court found that the program-wide EIS "does not provide the detailed analysis of local geographic conditions necessary for the decision-maker to determine what course of action is appropriate under the circumstances." *Id.*, 388 F. Supp. at 838–39.

Subsequent to the *NRDC v. Morton* decisions Congress enacted comprehensive legislation intended to guide the BLM's management of public lands, including those used for grazing. The Federal Land Policy and Management Act of 1976 (FLPMA), 43 U.S.C. §§ 1701–1782, gave the BLM organic authority and set out both general and specific policies and guidelines to be applied by the agency. The Public Rangeland Improvements Act (PRIA), 43 U.S.C. §§ 1901–1908, supplemented and refined FLPMA's range management provisions, and authorized funding for specific on-the-ground range improvements designed to reverse the widespread downward trend in range conditions.

Pursuant to the decision in *NRDC v. Morton* and the new statutes, the BLM undertook steps in the late 1970s to lay the groundwork for a comprehensive grazing management plan and EIS for the Reno area. The agency began gathering inventory data, listing the available resources in portions of the planning area. Agency specialists then began preparation of the Management Framework Plan (MFP). . . .

[The final land use plan placed each of the approximately 55 grazing allotments contained within the Reno planning area into one of the following three categories: (1) *Maintenance,* for allotments which are in adequate ecological condition, and for which present management policies are satisfactory; (2) *Improvement,* for allotments which are in fair to poor ecological condition but have potential for improvement, and for which present management practices are not adequate to meet long term objectives; and (3) *Custodial,* for allotments which are in stable ecological condition but with limited potential for improvement. The plan focuses BLM efforts on allotments in the Improvement ["I"] category, by initially allowing grazing to continue at existing levels, while attempting to effect improvement through range improvements, monitoring, and consultation with affected parties. The plan called for continued monitoring of the allotments so that adjustments in grazing levels could be made later as needed.]

[NRDC raised a variety of NEPA arguments. In a lengthy part of the opinion rejecting those arguments the court made the following points.] An EIS of the specificity sought by plaintiffs is also unreasonable on another ground. Basically, plaintiffs want the EIS to spell out stocking levels for each of the 55 or so allotments both in the near term, and in the long term, and under each of the four (and preferably more) alternatives. Plaintiffs are really seeking an EIS for each allotment. A document addressing the ecological and other impacts for each set of permutations of stocking levels would be a completely unmanageable undertaking. * * *

Plaintiffs finally argue, . . . that the BLM was under an obligation to at least consider an alternative that attempts to redress the overall poor quality of the rangeland in the planning area. They point out that under all alternatives [in the draft EIS] nearly half of the Reno area will remain in poor condition, and that "there will be continued overuse of unprotected riparian habitat by livestock and/or wild horses causing a decline in vegetation quality." * * *

The fact that lands may be in a state below that of their aboriginal pristine condition is content neutral for policy purposes. The important characteristic is whether the lands are producing at or near their capacity, under multiple-use/sustained yield principles, as required by FLPMA and PRIA. *See* 43 U.S.C. §§ 1712(c), 1903(b). This includes productivity for livestock uses, which inherently involves a retreat from the land's native condition or ecological climax state. Thus the arguments raised by plaintiffs in this regard, while factually correct, do not represent NEPA violations. * * *

Plaintiffs here argue that the BLM's internal policies, as well as CEQ regulations, required the BLM to include in the EIS an alternative analyzing the effects of a complete ban on livestock grazing within the Reno area. I find this argument lacks merit.

This argument must be evaluated against the historical background of the Reno planning area, and against the regulations and case authorities that discuss the scope of alternatives that must be included for an EIS to be valid. First, it is an indisputable fact that livestock grazing has been going on in the Reno planning area, on public lands, for more than a century. For better or worse, production of forage for livestock use is at least an important priority in the overall resource picture of this area. Second, the mandate of Congress in PRIA was that livestock use was to continue as an important use of public lands; they should be managed to maximize productivity for livestock and other specified uses. 43 U.S.C. § 1903. Third, NEPA does not require examination of alternatives that are so speculative, contrary to law, or economically catastrophic as to be beyond the realm of feasibility. *Kilroy v. Ruckelshaus*, 738 F.2d 1448, 1454 (9th Cir. 1985); *California v. Block*, 690 F.2d 753, 767 (9th Cir. 1982). The complete abandonment of grazing in the Reno planning area is practically unthinkable as a policy choice; it would involve monetary losses to the ranching community alone of nearly 4 million dollars and 290 jobs, not to mention unquantifiable social impacts. Of course, compared with the economy of the Reno area as a whole, ranching plays only a negligible role. Nevertheless, eliminating all grazing would have extreme impacts on this small community. A "no grazing" policy is simply not a "reasonable alternative" for this particular area. *Citizens For A Better Henderson v. Hodel*, 768 F.2d 1051, 1057 (9th Cir. 1985). * * *

It is true that the DEIS does not explicitly detail the BLM's underlying reasoning, or forthrightly explain at any one place why the proposed action is felt to be superior to the other alternatives. This is perhaps confusing to the casual reader, who might observe that the proposed action is possibly more expensive than the "resource protection" alternative, results in less livestock grazing in the long run, and less overall improvement in ecological condition. Nevertheless, after a thorough and painstaking review of the EIS the reader understands that there are so many different tradeoffs and permutations of tradeoffs involved that no single explanation could fully justify every aspect of the MFP. The reader is left only with the impression that the BLM took its best cut at addressing the areas that it felt were in the most immediate need. It is also clear that subjective factors came into play, including the BLM's obvious desire to maintain for ranchers, what it describes (romantically perhaps) as a "preferred lifestyle." I believe that the DEIS adequately conveys to anyone who reads it in depth the reasons for (and the tradeoffs behind) the proposed action.

II.   The MFP Allows Continued Resource Deterioration, Contrary To Statute

In this section of the case, plaintiffs argue that the BLM has violated a number of statutory and regulatory provisions in its management of the Reno area. They argue that substantive mandates require the BLM to curb overgrazing, and to take affirmative actions to remedy past degradation of public rangelands. They conclude that because the BLM has not taken strong enough action in these matters that this court should intervene, overturning the MFP and directing the agency to take steps more in line with plaintiffs' interpretations of the law. * * *

A.   BLM Has Failed To Curtail Overgrazing

Plaintiffs first correctly point to the legislative histories of the Taylor Grazing Act, FLPMA, and PRIA, to demonstrate Congress' general concern about overgrazing by livestock, and to indicate that reductions in livestock levels were one of the methods mentioned by Congress to prevent further deterioration of rangelands. Plaintiffs then cite portions of the record, including the DEIS, which indicate that there has been overuse of some portions of the Reno area by livestock. The conclusion plaintiffs say should then follow is that BLM has violated the law, and that the relatively modest improvements predicted from the MFP are insufficient to comply with the statutory mandates. * * *

[E]ven where overgrazing is found to exist, the remedy is not necessarily the immediate removal of livestock. I give due weight to the proposition put forth by defendants' experts that other methods, such as vegetation manipulation and seeding, fencing, water development, or other range improvements or grazing systems may serve to address problems of selective overgrazing without a mandatory reduction in livestock use. While reductions in AUMs for livestock may be one accepted method of addressing range deterioration, as recognized by Congress (*see* 43 U.S.C. § 1903(b)), it is not the only method. * * *

Plaintiffs claim that the BLM is allowing overgrazing to continue. In reality, however, their complaint is with the *methods* selected by the BLM to allocate the resources within its control. Rather than immediate reductions in livestock numbers, the BLM chose to install range improvements and grazing systems on the areas ("I" allotments) that the BLM says are in need of the greatest attention. Moreover, the MFP does call for a significant reduction in livestock numbers, although this is to take place over a longer period of time than plaintiffs insist on. Finally, the MFP is predicted to bring about an overall improvement in the rated quality of many of the allotments. In sum, it is not entirely certain that the BLM has allowed continued overgrazing or deterioration of resources, in violation of statutory mandates.

B. PRIA Claims: Rangeland Improvement

The converse argument is also put forward by plaintiffs in this section of their case, namely that the BLM is violating the affirmative mandates of PRIA by failing to assure the *improvement* of the public rangelands. As noted immediately above, however, the MFP does result in limited improvements in overall ecological and forage conditions in the Reno area. Plaintiffs characterize the BLM's management as "do nothing," but in reality it appears that the real argument is that the BLM does not do what plaintiffs want, namely redress range conditions through immediate reduction or elimination of livestock grazing. * * *

Plaintiffs argue that FLPMA and PRIA provide "standards" against which the court can determine whether the MFP is "arbitrary, capricious or contrary to law." The declarations of policy and goals in 43 U.S.C. §§ 1701(a), 1732, 1901, 1903 and ancillary provisions contain only broad expressions of concern and desire for improvement. They are general clauses and phrases which "can hardly be considered concrete limits upon agency discretion. Rather, it is language which 'breathes discretion at every pore.'" *Perkins v. Bergland*, 608 F.2d at 806, quoting *Strickland v. Morton*, 519 F.2d 467, 469 (9th Cir. 1975). Although I might privately agree with plaintiffs that a more aggressive approach to range improvement would be environmentally preferable, or might even be closer to what Congress had in mind, the Ninth Circuit has made it plain that "the courts are not at liberty to break the tie choosing one theory of range management as superior to another." *Perkins v. Bergland*, 608 F.2d at 807. The modest plans adopted by the BLM for dealing with range conditions in the Reno area are not "irrational" and thus cannot be disturbed by the court. * * *

CONCLUSION

... After considerable thought and deliberation, I have come to the conclusion that the role plaintiffs would have me play in this controversy is an unworkable one. Plaintiffs are understandably upset at what they view to be a lopsided and ecologically insensitive pattern of management of public lands at the hands of the BLM, a subject explored at length by many commentators. Congress attempted to remedy this situation through FLPMA, PRIA and other acts, but it has done so with only the broadest sorts of discretionary language, which does not provide helpful standards by which a court can readily adjudicate agency compliance.

Boiled down and stripped of legalese this is a case in which plaintiffs ask me to become—and defendants urge me not to become—the rangemaster for about 700,000 acres of federal lands in western Nevada. For some reason, over the past 15 years or so, I and many of my Article III colleagues have become or have been implored to become forestmasters, roadmasters, schoolmasters, fishmasters, prisonmasters, watermasters, and the like. This trend has not escaped the notice and criticism of academic commentators.

That criticism has been based upon observations which include lack of training and expertise, lack of time, lack of staff assistance, and similar conditions. At bottom, however, the primary reason for the large scale intrusion of the judiciary into the governance of our society has been an inability or unwillingness of the first two branches of our governments—both state and federal—to fashion solutions for significant societal, environmental, and economic problems in America. Frankly, I see little likelihood that the legislative and executive branches will take the statutory (and occasional constitutional) steps which would at least slow, if not reverse, this trend. Fortunately, for reasons set out in this opinion which (to me) are legally correct, I am able to resist the invitation to become western Nevada's rangemaster.

Plaintiffs' motion for summary judgment is denied in its entirety, and defendants' motion for summary judgment is granted. The action will be dismissed.

QUESTIONS AND DISCUSSION

1. Judge Burns' decision was affirmed by the Ninth Circuit, which agreed that it was not arbitrary and capricious for BLM to postpone grazing adjustments until more reliable data was available. 819 F.2d 927, 930 (9th Cir. 1987).

2. What are the implications of this decision for protests to land use plans less favorable to grazing produced by a BLM and Interior Department in a different administration?

3. Is Judge Burns' view of a narrow role for the federal judiciary honorably restrained or merely an abdication of judicial responsibility? Is he as restrained with respect to the factors he is willing to consider in reviewing the management framework plan [MFP]?

4. Prior to *NRDC v. Hodel*, Professor Coggins had observed: "The conventional wisdom holds that multiple use statutes are little more than slogans or platitudes. Many managers and a few theorists contend that multiple use authority is only an invitation to make wise, balanced decisions unfettered by legal rules and standards.... The conventional wisdom is at least shortsighted and probably wrong. FLPMA and the MUSY Act do contain standards that bind land managers, and courts are more likely than not to enforce these standards in the future." George Cameron Coggins, *The Law of Public Rangeland Management IV: FLPMA, PRIA, and the Multiple Use Mandate*, 14 Envtl. L. 1, 33–34 (1983). Judge Burns' opinion about two years later plainly adopts the "conventional wisdom" criticized by Professor Coggins. Whose reading of FLPMA and PRIA do you find more persuasive? Do FLPMA's land use planning process and multiple use mandate, and PRIA's improvement command appear to be useful vehicles for pushing agencies to improve range conditions? Did Judge Burns misread the statutes? Is it true that they bleed discretion at every pore?

5.   Given the marginal economic value of grazing and its real environmental costs, should it be "practically unthinkable," as Judge Burns suggests, to abandon livestock grazing in the Reno planning area, or to consider modest and even substantial reductions in current grazing lands? What role does historical practice play in his opinion?

6.   Judge Burns seemed to take a charitable view of "BLM's obvious desire to maintain for ranchers, what it describes (romantically perhaps) as a 'preferred lifestyle.'" Does FLPMA's multiple use mandate allow the BLM to act on such a desire? If permitted, is that a wise approach for BLM to take?

7.   Was Judge Burns correct that studying each allotment was a "completely unmanageable undertaking"? Did BLM have the resources to accomplish the task? Consider that at the time of NEPA's passage BLM had fewer than 3,000 full-time employees managing approximately 485 million acres of land (approximately 178 million outside of Alaska). Its total budget for rangeland management in 1973 was $24 million. *See* SAMUEL TRASK DANA & SALLY K. FAIRFAX, FOREST AND RANGE POLICY 313 (1980); ROBERT H. NELSON, PUBLIC LANDS AND PRIVATE RIGHTS: THE FAILURE OF SCIENTIFIC MANAGEMENT 161– 62 (1995). If FLPMA and PRIA require more, what is the role of a court when Congress passes legislation requiring agency action but then fails to fund the agency at a level necessary to accomplish the statutory mandate? Should underfunding affect statutory interpretation? Is it a functional amendment to legislation? If underfunding does not impact interpretation, should it affect the remedy?

8.   As the opinion describes, BLM's Reno planning area was covered by a management framework plan (MFP), despite the fact that FLPMA requires preparation of what is known as a resource management plan (RMP). Why this is so requires a brief return to BLM land use planning. As reviewed above, and in the section on planning in Chapter 3, BLM's development of MFPs began just prior to the expiration of its authority under the Classification and Multiple Use Act and continued after Congress passed NEPA. In the wake of the *NRDC v. Morton* litigation, BLM combined the MFP process with the preparation of EISs for those areas ordered by the court in *Morton*. Then, with the passage of FLPMA, Congress directed BLM on a different course, requiring it to inventory the public lands for their resource values, 43 U.S.C. § 1712(a), and then develop new RMPs in accordance with nine statutory planning criteria. *Id.* § 1712(c). The RMPs cover more than just grazing and are designed to zone BLM resource areas (i.e., administratively designated portions of BLM land) for certain uses, set resource condition goals, and establish program constraints and general management practices. *See* 43 C.F.R. § 1601.0–5(k). FLPMA did not set forth any timetable for completion of the RMPs and the Secretary provided by regulation that MFPs may be used until an RMP is prepared. 43 C.F.R. § 1610.8. In the case of the Reno planning area, at the time this case was decided an RMP had not yet been prepared. Planning, public participation, and consideration of alternatives is time-consuming and costly and RMPs have still not been completed for portions of the public lands. As of 1993, the BLM had completed just over half of its intended 144 RMPs and was projecting a final completion date of 2013, thirty-seven years after FLPMA's passage. *See* BUREAU OF LAND MANAGEMENT, U.S. DEP'T OF INTERIOR, SUMMARY OF RMP BACKGROUND INFORMATION AND CURRENT PLANNING STATUS (June 2, 1993). Thus, grazing on public rangelands is subject to both MFPs and RMPs, depending on the particular area, and the various plans differ markedly in their quality and comprehensiveness.

Once an RMP or MFP is in place, a BLM field officer can do more specific planning for grazing in an effort to satisfy the conditions of the broader land use planning document. This more site-specific planning is typically accomplished through what are known as allotment management plans (AMPs), which are essentially land use plans for a single allotment. *See* 43 U.S.C. § 1752(d)–(f); 43 C.F.R. § 4120.2. BLM is not obligated to complete an AMP for every grazing permit and AMPs have not been prepared for a number of allotments. For more thorough reviews of BLM land use planning, see George Cameron Coggins, *The Law of Public Rangeland Management IV: FLPMA, PRIA, and the Multiple Use Mandate*, 14 ENVTL. L. 1, 79–109 (1983); Veronica Larvie, *Federal Land Planning Issues: Ecosystem Analysis, Forests, Oceans, and Public Lands*, SF34 ALI–ABA 127 (Oct. 2000); Erik Schlenker–Goodrich, *Moving Beyond Public Lands Council v. Babbitt: Land Use Planning and the Range Resource*, 16 J. ENVTL. L. & LITIG. 139, 157 (2001); Kelly Nolen, *Residents at Risk: Wildlife and the Bureau of Land Management's Planning Process*, 26 ENVTL. L. 771 (1996).

9. In contemplating BLM management in both this and the following cases, it may be helpful to have in mind an image of the geographic division of responsibility over grazing with the BLM. The BLM is divided into twelve administrative jurisdictions, which are known as state offices despite the fact that some of the jurisdictions encompass more than one state, most notably the "Eastern States Office." A state office is then subdivided into a number of field offices. Personnel in the field office manage the various grazing allotments within their area. Maps delineating these boundaries and links to each field office are available at the BLM web site—http://www.blm.gov/wo/st/en.html. Until recently, each state office was divided into a number of district offices and further subdivided into resource areas. The reference to the "Reno Planning Area" in *NRDC v. Hodel, supra*, and to the "San Juan Resource Area" in *National Wildlife Federation v. BLM, infra*, reflects this prior administrative division within BLM.

For a lawyer working with any administrative agency, it is important to understand who makes the decisions and where to seek relief from adverse decisions. In the BLM, the initial point of contact is typically a BLM employee within the BLM Field Office, headed up by a Field Office Manager. The Field Office Manager typically supervises a number of grazing districts and reports to the State Director. The BLM State Directors report to the Director of the BLM, who reports to the Assistant Secretary for Land and Minerals Management who, in turn, reports to the Secretary of the Interior. The administrative process follows the management chain of command, but there is not complete overlap. Absent emergency circumstances, a BLM officer, typically a field office manager, who makes a decision about grazing on a particular allotment must serve the decision on any applicant, existing permittee or lessee, and any interested member of the public who has submitted a written request to be involved in the decision-making process for that allotment. They, in turn, have 15 days to protest the decision. Assuming no protest, or an unsuccessful protest, the officer's decision becomes final, and there are 30 days during which "any person whose interest is adversely affected by a final decision" may appeal the officer's decision to an administrative law judge in the Office of Hearings and Appeals. The appeal is actually filed with the local BLM officer who then forwards the appeal to the State BLM Director, who functions as the adverse party in the litigation. The proceedings before the administrative law judge are the primary place where the administrative record is developed. If either party is dissatisfied with the administrative law judge's determination, it may appeal to the Interior Board of Land Appeals (IBLA). The decision of the IBLA constitutes final agency action. Finally, although it is rare that they do so, the Secretary of the Interior (or the Director of the BLM if the Secretary directs) may take jurisdiction of any case before any employee of the Department or before any administrative law judge or the IBLA, and render the agency's final decision in that case. *See* 43 C.F.R. § 4160.1–4, §§ 4.403, 4.410, and 4.470.

Judge Burns' refusal in *NRDC v. Hodel* to require more from BLM in the Reno planning area was a setback for advocates of greater environmental protection of range resources, but they were persistent. A few years later Professor Joseph Feller, a staunch critic of BLM's grazing management, filed a grazing protest before the Interior Board of Land Appeals (IBLA). Rather than attacking an entire planning area, he focused on a single allotment in southern Utah's spectacular red rock country. Not only did he assert that FLPMA's multiple use mandate imposed some limits on land managers, but also he argued that NEPA applied to BLM's permit issuance decision. As you read the following IBLA decision, consider the implications of moving from *NRDC v. Morton*'s requirement of 144 grazing management EISs (discussed *supra*) to a potential obligation to prepare EISs on each of thousands of individual allotments. With respect to the administrative law judge's FLPMA analysis, consider whether it can be reconciled with *NRDC v. Hodel* and whether Professor Coggins' prediction that multiple use would have teeth is beginning to bear fruit.

NATIONAL WILDLIFE FEDERATION ET AL. v. BLM,
140 I.B.L.A. 85 (1997)

OPINION BY DEPUTY CHIEF ADMINISTRATIVE JUDGE HARRIS

The Comb Wash Allotment encompasses nearly 72,000 acres, of which approximately 63,000 acres are public lands, the remainder being state and private.... Within the allotment boundaries is the geographic feature from which the allotment derives its name, Comb Wash, a narrow valley that runs north-south just west of the Comb Ridge for about 20 miles. Draining into

Comb Wash from the west are five canyons.... The canyons encompass about 7,000 acres, or 10 percent of the allotment land. Each canyon contains a perennial or ephemeral stream, with an associated riparian area. The canyons provide recreational opportunities for camping, hiking, photography, sightseeing, and the viewing of archaeological sites, including many remnants of the ancient Anasazi culture. * * *

[In 1989, BLM issued a ten-year grazing permit for the Comb Wash Allotment. That permit was challenged by Professor Feller who claimed that BLM had not consulted with affected parties as required by its regulations. The appeal also alleged violations of NEPA and FLPMA. The ALJ, Judge Rampton, ruled that issuing a grazing permit was an "action" within the meaning of BLM's regulations and thus required a statement of reasons, notice to affected parties, and opportunity for protest. Accordingly, he set aside the ten-year permit and remanded the matter to BLM. He did not reach the NEPA and FLPMA issues. On March 6, 1991, BLM issued its Notice of Final Decision responding to Judge Rampton's remand order. It asserted that the RMP/EIS for the San Juan Resource Area satisfied BLM's duties under NEPA and FLPMA. It also stated its intention to prepare an allotment management plan (AMP) for the Comb Wash Allotment. While the AMP was being developed, it would continue to allow grazing but by means of annual authorizations. Once the AMP was developed, a new ten-year permit would be issued.*

The annual grazing authorizations, two of which were challenged in this case, were issued by the San Juan Resource Area Manager, Edward Scherick, who believed he had discretion under the RMP to determine whether grazing should take place in the canyons. However, in exercising that discretion, he relied exclusively on the recommendations provided to him by Paul Curtis, the San Juan Resource Area range conservationist. * * *]

Curtis stated that it had been decided in the RMP that the canyons were available for livestock use. He came to that conclusion because the RMP did not preclude grazing in the Comb Wash Allotment. * * *

Curtis testified that he "monitor[s] the grazing in the San Juan resource area, and presently that covers approximately two million acres. And I deal with the biggest percent of that two million acres, and approximately 66 different allotments and 66 different permittees, give or take a few." Given the scope of his duties, it is not surprising that Curtis stated that he did not have the time or personnel to conduct the necessary monitoring in the canyons. * * *

The [National Wildlife Federation (NWF)] timely appealed the District Manager's Decision, as well as the Area Manager's subsequent grazing authorizations for the allotment for the 1991–92 and 1992–93 grazing seasons.

III. Judge's Decision

Judge Rampton ... set aside the District Manager's March 1991 Final Decision, to the extent it permitted authorized grazing use to continue at established levels, and remanded the case to BLM for further action consistent with his directives. Judge Rampton based his holding on the following conclusions: (1) BLM failed to comply with NEPA; (2) BLM violated FLPMA by "failing to make a reasoned and informed decision that the benefits of grazing the canyons outweigh the costs; (3) BLM violated FLPMA by failing to make a

---

* For complete details on the procedural history, see Joseph M. Feller, *The Comb Wash Case: The Rule of Law* *Comes to the Public Rangelands*, 17 Pub. Land L. Rev. 25, 29–31 (1996).

reasoned and informed decision establishing stocking rates for the whole allotment; ... and (5) BLM failed to conform to the forage utilization limits of the RMP.''

IV. Discussion

A. NEPA Violation

The first issue we will consider is whether Judge Rampton properly concluded that BLM violated NEPA in this case. The record in this case establishes, without doubt, that BLM failed to comply with NEPA.

Judge Rampton made the following findings regarding BLM's assertion that the RMP/FEIS provided adequate NEPA documentation for its grazing authorizations in the Comb Wash Allotment:

The Proposed RMP/FEIS is simply devoid of any site-specific information or analysis regarding the impacts of grazing on the resource values of the particular allotment in question. At best, it contains some general information regarding the impacts of grazing on the entire San Juan Resource Area as a whole. The discussion focuses upon broad descriptions of the types of vegetative zones found in the Area and the general problems of grazing management. The "Affected Environment" and the "Preferred Alternative" of the document do not mention the Comb Wash allotment other than to list it in summary tables showing such data as the number of acres, number of authorized AUM's, and number of acres in various ecological conditions.

Numerous BLM witnesses confirmed the following facts about the Proposed RMP/FEIS:

(1) That it is not useful or does not provide the detailed information necessary to determine whether to graze the canyons;

(2) That it does not contain an analysis of the 1990 proposed grazing plan or grazing system being implemented by issuance of the annual grazing authorizations nor does it contain information regarding the available forage, condition of the vegetation, or condition of the riparian areas in the canyons; and

(3) That it lacks any discussion of the relative values of the resources in the canyons and no balancing of the harms and benefits of grazing the canyons.

We are in complete agreement with those findings. * * *

In fashioning the appropriate relief for the violation of NEPA, Judge Rampton stated:

... With respect to the canyons, the evidence shows that any level of grazing use may significantly effect [sic] the quality of the human environment, and therefore BLM is prohibited from allowing any grazing in the canyons until an adequate EIS is prepared and considered.

Thus, Judge Rampton precluded any grazing in the canyons pending preparation of an EIS. * * *

[H]e found, quite properly, that the Proposed RMP/FEIS did not support BLM's site-specific actions. * * *

B. FLPMA Violation

The next issue for resolution is whether Judge Rampton properly held that BLM violated FLPMA. After citing section 302(a) of FLPMA, 43 U.S.C.

§ 1732(a) (1994), which requires the Secretary to "manage the public lands under principles of multiple use and sustained yield," Judge Rampton ... cited a statement by the court in *Sierra Club v. Butz*, 3 ENVT'L L. REP. 20,292, 20,293 (9th Cir. 1973), that the multiple-use principle "requires that the values in question be informedly and rationally taken into balance." He concluded that an agency is required to engage in such a balancing test in order to determine whether a proposed activity is in the public interest.

However, in applying those standards to the facts in this case, Judge Rampton held that "BLM violated FLPMA by failing to make a reasoned and informed decision that the benefits of grazing the canyons outweigh the costs." It is with this highlighted language that all Appellants disagree, asserting that FLPMA does not require an economic cost/benefits analysis.

It is not clear that Judge Rampton intended that BLM engage in an economic cost/benefits analysis. A reading of his Decision discloses that the sentence quoted above is the only place in his Decision where he uses the word "costs," other than in the heading to the discussion. Later in his Decision when he is addressing the appropriate relief for the various violations, he describes the violation as the failure to make a reasoned and informed decision to graze the canyons in violation of FLPMA. He mentions neither costs nor benefits. He described the appropriate relief, as follows: "Because BLM may choose to prohibit grazing in the canyons in the future, BLM is not compelled to make a reasoned and informed decision that grazing the canyons is in the public interest. However, until a decision is made, BLM is prohibited from allowing grazing in the canyons." Again, no mention is made of benefits and costs.

Judge Rampton's analysis of the evidence relating to BLM's decision-making process is as follows:

> The Area Manager, Mr. Scherick, correctly believed that he had discretion under the RMP to allow or disallow grazing on the Comb Wash allotment. He testified that, in exercising this discretion, he had not considered the relative values of the resources in the canyons because consideration of those values would take place during the activity planning stage (formation of the new AMP). * * *

> Mr. Scherick also admitted that neither he nor any document, including the Proposed RMP/FEIS, weighs the benefits and harms of grazing the canyons. In authorizing grazing in the canyons, Mr. Scherick simply relied upon the information and recommendations provided to him by Mr. Curtis, the range conservationist responsible for the allotment.

> Contrary to the evidence and Mr. Scherick's belief, Mr. Curtis thought that the RMP had already considered the impacts of grazing on the allotment's resources and determined that the allotment should be grazed, regardless of the recognized conflict with recreational uses and the need for adjustment confirmed by monitoring. He therefore felt it was not his responsibility to consider those impacts. Mr. Scherick's reliance upon Mr. Curtis, who believed that the decision to graze had already been made and was still binding, does not constitute a rational basis for determining whether the canyons should be grazed. * * *

> In sum, BLM's decision to graze the canyons was not reasoned or informed, but rather based upon Mr. Curtis' misinterpretation of the RMP and a totally inadequate investigation and analysis of the condition of the canyons' varied resources and the impacts of grazing upon those resources. (Decision at 23–25.)

We agree with that analysis. Even NWF does not argue that FLPMA requires an economic cost/benefits analysis. The NWF states: "To the extent the Judge's choice of words may be ambiguous, NWF has no objection to this Board clarifying that FLPMA does not require an economic cost-benefit analysis, but rather that BLM must informedly and rationally balance competing values."

To the extent Judge Rampton's Decision may be construed as requiring an economic cost/benefit analysis, it is modified to make it clear that no such analysis is required. * * *

We agree with BLM that FLPMA does not require a "specific" public interest determination for grazing. However, FLPMA's multiple-use mandate requires that BLM balance competing resource values to ensure that public lands are managed in the manner "that will best meet the present and future needs of the American people." 43 U.S.C. § 1702(c) (1994). Indeed, all parties agree that BLM must conduct some form of balancing of competing resource values in order to comply with the statute. * * *

What is important in this case, and what we affirm, is Judge Rampton's finding that BLM violated FLPMA, because it failed to engage in any reasoned or informed decisionmaking process concerning grazing in the canyons in the allotment. That process must show that BLM has balanced competing resource values to ensure that the public lands in the canyons are managed in the manner that will best meet the present and future needs of the American people. * * *

Judge Rampton found that BLM had violated NEPA by not preparing a site-specific analysis of the impact of grazing on the canyons in the allotment. He also found, based on the evidence presented by NWF, which he characterized as "overwhelming," that grazing had significantly degraded the human environment in the canyons and that grazing might continue to do so. Based on those findings, Judge Rampton properly granted NWF the relief it sought—the preclusion of grazing in the canyons pending the preparation and consideration of an EIS. The BLM has raised no objection to Judge Rampton's imposition of that duty on it. * * *

Accordingly, pursuant to the authority delegated to the Board of Land Appeals by the Secretary of the Interior, 43 C.F.R. § 4.1, the Decision appealed from is affirmed as modified.

QUESTIONS AND DISCUSSION

1. One interesting facet of the *Comb Wash* case is that because BLM proposed to issue annual grazing authorizations while an allotment management plan was being prepared for the Comb Wash Allotment, the second appeal was actually of the annual grazing authorizations rather than the ten-year permit. (In most cases, the annual grazing authorization is essentially the bill, with attached contractual language, sent each year to the permittee. Although it can fluctuate, most often the annual authorization follows the terms of the existing ten-year permit.) Assume you are the head of the BLM. How should BLM respond to this decision? Must BLM conduct an annual, site-specific analysis whenever it issues an annual grazing authorization? Or, did Judge Rampton and the IBLA intend NEPA to apply only to permit issuance? In either case, can BLM adequately comply with NEPA on all allotments within the San Juan Resource Area?

On all allotments nationwide? Where does this decision leave the EIS framework established by *NRDC v. Morton*? From its beginning, management of public land grazing has been understaffed. After passage of the Taylor Act, the Interior Department's Grazing Division had only 17 employees. Later, when the Grazing Service merged with the General Land Office in 1946, BLM had a staff of 86 persons to supervise grazing on 150 million acres. The BLM estimates that it and the Forest Service spent collectively about $94 million on their grazing management in 1993, about $5.76 per AUM when AUMs were priced at $1.86. Donahue, *supra* at 65; Rangeland Reform '94, *supra*, at 3–10; U.S. Gen. Accounting Office, BLM Resource Allocation 13 (1992).

[handwritten margin note: BLM historically understaffed]

2. In the wake of the *Comb Wash* case, BLM began performing a NEPA analysis (mostly an EA) on individual allotments when permits come up for renewal (typically every ten years). In some cases, BLM grouped together a number of similarly situated allotments (e.g., sheep in the same geographic area grazing during the same season) for NEPA compliance purposes. Does this approach meet the concerns and objectives expressed by Judge Rampton?

When BLM struggled to complete the NEPA analysis and issue permits in a timely fashion, Congress responded with series of riders to Interior Department appropriations bills authorizing the permits to be renewed on the same terms pending NEPA compliance. At the time of this writing, Congress had enacted a rider, valid between fiscal 2004 and 2008, that continued the terms of all existing permits on both BLM and Forest Service land. Pub. L. No. 108–108, 117 Stat. 1307 (2003). In an effort to streamline the NEPA process, in 2007, BLM categorically excluded NEPA compliance for issuance of most livestock grazing permits/leases as long as the permit is renewed under the same terms, the permit meets rangeland health standards, and there are no extraordinary circumstances such as threatened or endangered species on the allotment. *See* BLM, *National Environmental Policy Act Handbook H–1790–1* (Jan. 30, 2008). According to the BLM, between 1999 and 2004, almost 80% of grazing permit EAs resulted in a finding of no significant impact and most of the other permits were issued based on already-existing EISs. At most 3% of the grazing permits issued indicated that the grazing might produce some significant impact, and in those cases, the BLM modified the terms of the permit to mitigate the potential impacts. *See* BLM, *Grazing Permit Categorical Exclusion Analysis Report* (Mar. 22, 2007), *available at* http://www.doi.gov/oepc/cx reports/Grazing_CX_Analysis_Additional_CX.pdf. What does this suggest about the impact of the *Comb Wash* case during the last ten years since it was decided? Is it likely that only 3% of grazing permits have a significant impact on the environment?

[handwritten margin note: findings of "no significant impact"]

3. Although Congress and the Secretary have taken a go-slow approach to NEPA in the context of grazing permits, the courts have been less reluctant. In *Oregon Natural Desert Ass'n v. U.S. Forest Service*, 465 F.3d 977 (9th Cir. 2006), the Ninth Circuit held that the Forest Service's issuance of annual operating instructions (AOIs)—the annual instructions to the permittee which typically repeat the longer term directives in the grazing permit and allotment management plan but which can be adjusted to account for drought, rainfall, etc.—constitutes final agency action for purposes of judicial review under the Administrative Procedure Act. In dissent, Judge Fernandez argued:

> In pragmatic terms, if every AOI for every permit in every allotment every year is to be open to litigation by ONDA, and others, it is a little difficult to see how the grazing program can continue, if the purpose of the program is to feed animals. They need to eat now rather than at the end of some lengthy court process.

Id. at 991–92. Is Judge Fernandez's pragmatic analysis accurate? On the other hand, would his approach allow the agency to put forward generic resource management plans and allotment management plans and then do its real managing via AOIs, which would not be subject to review? Is Judge Fernandez correct to say that the purpose of federal range policy is to "feed animals"?

In *Western Watersheds Project v. Bennett*, 392 F. Supp. 2d 1217 (D. Idaho 2005), the court enjoined grazing on 28 allotments in the Jarbridge Resource Area in Nevada because BLM failed to follow NEPA and FLPMA in renewing grazing permits. The court expressed particular concern about the impact of grazing on the sage grouse, which had been identified by the BLM as a sensitive species within the resource area. In a series of Environmental Analyses (EAs), the BLM had asserted that renewing the grazing permits would cause no significant harm despite an 85% decline in the number of sage grouse over the last 20–50 years and despite the fact that all of the allotments had failed to meet the ecological standards of the Fundamentals of Rangeland Health set forth in the BLM's grazing regulations. How might the BLM's adoption of the categorical exclusion for grazing permit renewals, discussed in Note 2, impact the outcome of permit renewals at issue in *Bennett*?

4. What would be the implications of Judge Harris' suggestion in *Comb Wash* that FLPMA multiple use analysis creates a duty to "informedly and rationally balance competing values" and to allocate the range resource in a way that will "best meet the present and future needs of the American people"? What is the substantive content of that duty? In light of *Chevron* and traditional deference to agency decision making, is it possible, or wise, for a court to discern whether agency action is in the public interest? Is PRIA's command "to improve the range conditions," 43 U.S.C. § 1903(b), a better handle for environmental advocates?

––––––––

With respect to the Comb Wash allotment, BLM was reluctant to consider a reduction in grazing, but in other instances federal officials have taken steps to reduce grazing. And when they have, ranchers have been the ones attacking the agency's exercise of its discretion. The following case, which involves the Forest Service rather than the BLM, is illustrative.

McKINLEY v. UNITED STATES,
828 F. Supp. 888 (D. N.M. 1993)

HANSEN, DISTRICT JUDGE.

This lawsuit seeks to set aside a decision by officials of the U.S. Forest Service which provided for a reduction in the number of cattle permitted to graze on the 28,719 acre Barranca allotment located in the Cibola National Forest in the Manzano Mountains of central New Mexico.

[In 1973] appellant Weldon McKinley was issued a Term Grazing Permit for 201 cattle on the Barranca allotment. Range evaluations indicated that a small portion of the allotment was in fair condition with an upward trend, but that the majority of the range was in unsatisfactory condition with a downward trend. Beginning in 1975, appellant elected to graze less than the number of cattle permitted. According to the Forest Service, average use between 1973 and 1988 was 50% of permitted numbers.

On July 7, 1988, McKinley was advised that a reduction in livestock numbers on the allotment had been recommended, based on Forest Service range studies. In August, 1988, and January, 1989, the Forest Service met with McKinley to discuss the allegedly unsatisfactory range conditions.

On July 21, 1989, defendant Cibola Forest Supervisor C. Phil Smith decided that grazing should be reduced to 100 cattle. On September 5, 1989, McKinley appealed that decision. On October 10, 1989, Smith modified his July 21 decision, based in part on the results of the Production/Utilization Study completed on September 28, 1989, and determined that the Barranca Allotment should be permitted 112 head of cattle.

McKinley appealed the decision and following oral argument the supervisor's decision was affirmed by the Deputy Regional Forester on May 14, 1990. The Office of the Chief of the Forest Service declined to review the decision on June 15, 1990 and the Deputy Regional Forester's decision therefore became the final agency action. McKinley filed this lawsuit on August 20, 1991.

The U.S. Forest Service is authorized to issue grazing permits on lands within the National Forests by the general language of 16 U.S.C. § 580*l* and by the Federal Land Policy and Management Act (FLPMA), 43 U.S.C. § 1701 et seq. which provides in part that:

> ... permits and leases for domestic livestock grazing ... with respect to lands within National Forests ... shall be for a term of ten years subject to such terms and conditions the Secretary concerned deems appropriate and consistent with the governing law, including, but not limited to, the authority of the Secretary concerned to cancel, suspend, or modify a grazing permit or lease, in whole or in part, pursuant to the terms and conditions thereof.... 43 U.S.C. § 1752(a).

FLPMA further provides that:

> In all cases where the Secretary concerned has not completed an allotment management plan ..., the Secretary concerned shall incorporate in grazing permits and leases such terms and conditions as he deems appropriate for management of the permitted or leased lands pursuant to applicable law. The Secretary concerned shall also specify therein the numbers of animals to be grazed and the seasons of use and that he may reexamine the condition of the range at any time and, if he finds on reexamination that the condition of the range requires adjustment in the amount or other aspect of grazing use, that the permittee or lessee shall adjust his use to the extent the Secretary concerned deems necessary....

The Secretary of Agriculture has also promulgated regulations which address the administration of grazing lands. 36 C.F.R. § 222.5(a) provides that:

The Chief, Forest Service, is authorized to cancel, modify, or suspend grazing and livestock use permits in whole or in part as follows: ... (8) Modify the seasons of use, numbers, kind, and class of livestock allowed on the allotment to be used under the permit, because of resource condition, or permittee request. One year's notice will be given of such modification, except in cases of emergency. * * *

The function of this Court on review is to determine whether the defendants acted in a manner that was arbitrary, capricious, an abuse of discretion or contrary to law. 5 U.S.C. § 706(2)(A). * * *

The scope of review of a Forest Service decision to reduce permitted grazing was addressed by the Ninth Circuit which concluded that "the district court should ascertain whether the agency's factual findings as to range conditions and carrying capacity are arbitrary and capricious. If not, the matter ends there." *Perkins v. Bergland*, 608 F.2d 803, 807 (9th Cir. 1979).

Appellant seeks judicial review of the decision of the Cibola Forest Supervisor to reduce the number of cattle permitted to graze on the Barranca allotment. He argues that the Forest Service can modify the seasons of use, numbers, kinds and class of livestock allowed only because of resources condition or at the request of the permittee. He contends that because he did not request a modification and because the Barranca allotment is in a stable or upward condition, the decision was not in accordance with the provisions of 36 C.F.R. § 222.4.

It is clear that the Forest Supervisor has the ability to reduce permitted numbers on the allotment. The dispute in this case concerns the accuracy of the Forest Service studies which found that the range condition in the allotment was poor or very poor, indicating a need for a reduced stocking level on the allotment.

Range analysis of the allotment was performed in 1973, 1977–78, 1988 and 1989. The techniques utilized in this case included Parker Three Step Clusters, paced transects, and ocular estimates.

Parker Three Step Cluster studies were conducted in 1973, 1977–78 and 1988. The purpose of these studies is to compare range conditions at the same spot over time. Permanent iron makers are placed in the ground and metal tape is strung between the markers. Vegetative and soil conditions are examined and photographs taken to evaluate the current trend and these are compared with past data collected from the same location.

A paced transect was conducted by the Forest Service in June 1989 at the request of appellant's expert, Ralph Rainwater, who participated in the study. It involves walking a randomly selected line of 100 data points with soil and vegetation examined at a predetermined (i.e., every other pace) spacing.

Ocular estimates are merely visual observations of range conditions by range conservationists. They are conducted on an annual basis. * * *

Appellant's expert argues that the studies actually shows that the range condition is improving. Further, he contends that the sample size does not conform to the generally accepted sample size used by range experts.

The Forest Service argues that the evaluation of range trend is merely one factor to consider in the overall evaluation of range resources. Its findings demonstrate that in 1988, despite appellant's voluntary reduction in the number of grazing cattle on the property, only 8% of the allotment was in fair condition with 92% in poor or very poor condition and that the trend on 50% of the allotment was static, indicating that conditions were not improving, and a reduced stocking level was necessary.

The appellant's permit states that it "may be modified at any time during the term to conform with needed changes brought about ... because of resource condition or other management needs." The Court agrees with the Forest Service that by the permit's own terms it is range condition, not trend, which is evaluated to determine grazing capacity.

Appellant argues that the Forest Service's failure to use a larger sample size renders the range studies inaccurate. This contention is disputed by the Forest Service experts who claim that the methodology used is scientifically based and widely accepted. Their data was gathered over many years by several different range conservationists who consistently agreed that intensified management and decreased grazing was appropriate. That the agency chose to follow the opinions of its own experts is not grounds for overturning the decision under the arbitrary and capricious standard, providing that the reasons for choosing to follow its own technical employees are not arbitrary and capricious. To prove that the agency employed irrational methods for calculating carrying capacity, a contesting party must show that there is virtually no evidence in the record to support the agency's methodology in gathering and evaluating the data. *Perkins v. Bergland, supra*. The Court "must refrain from entering that fray if it turns out that the appellant's position would require a choice between experts." *Id*. at 807. The burden of proof under the arbitrary and capricious standard is on the party challenging the decision, and appellant has not met that burden. * * *

IT IS THEREFORE ORDERED that the May 14, 1990 decision by the Deputy Regional Forester is affirmed.

QUESTIONS AND DISCUSSION

1. Why did McKinley protest the reduction in AUMs if he had been grazing only 50% of the permitted number for the prior fifteen years? Does the *United States v. Fuller* decision, *supra*, or the *Public Lands Council v. Babbitt* decision, *infra*, give any clues? Might the reduction in AUMs have been considered a breach of McKinley's loan agreement with a bank?

2. What conclusions about the precision of range management decisions can be drawn from the methodology employed by the Forest Service to determine range condition?

3. What are the implications of the court's standard of review for ranchers or preservationists who seek to challenge a permit action? *McKinley* and the case on which it primarily relies, *Perkins v. Bergland*, suggest a fairly limited review of agency grazing decisions. *See also Kane Land and Livestock, Inc. v. United States*, 964 F. Supp. 1538 (D. Wyo. 1997) (upholding as not arbitrary or capricious the Forest Service's decision to suspend portion of rancher's grazing permit because he moved his cattle onto the grazing allotment five days prior to the "on-date" in violation of the terms of his permit). But in *Hinsdale Livestock Co. v. United States*, 501 F. Supp. 773 (D. Mont. 1980), the court took a more aggressive approach. The BLM had ordered Hinsdale to remove his cattle from his allotment to prevent what it believed would be severe damage to the range resource during the prevailing drought conditions. Noting that the plaintiffs had been ranching the land their entire adult lives, the court accepted their testimony that the range would not be damaged by continued grazing and, in fact, that "drought conditions never create an emergency with respect to the range resource, contrary to the opinion of defendant Bureau of Land Management." *Id.* at 777. Finally, the court found that by removing the cattle BLM violated a contract with Hinsdale represented by the allotment management plan which did not call for removal of the cattle. Does the Secretary's obligation to manage in accordance with the land use plan, 43 U.S.C. § 1732(a), create a contractual obligation? Does it matter that AMPs recite the Secretary's authority to suspend, modify or revoke grazing privileges as necessary to respond to changing land use plans or resource conditions? *See* 43 C.F.R. § 4130.3–1. How can it be that drought conditions will never create an emergency, as suggested by the court?

4. Although this chapter has mostly focused on grazing on BLM lands, as the *McKinley* case evidences, the Forest Service is also an important regulator of grazing. As discussed above (pages 939–40), the Forest Service was the first federal agency to begin regulating grazing and charging a grazing fee. The Forest Service currently regulates grazing on approximately 100 million acres as compared with the 170 million acres managed by the BLM. Grazing within national forests is governed by a number of statutes, including FLPMA and the PRIA, as well as the Forest Service's Organic Administration Act and the National Forest Management Act. *See* BUREAU OF LAND MANAGEMENT, RANGELAND REFORM '94 FINAL ENVIRONMENTAL IMPACT STATEMENT 3–5 (1994). The Forest Service's grazing regulations are located at 36 C.F.R. parts 219 (planning) and 222 (range management).

E.   CAN THE GRAZING STATUTES BE MADE TO WORK FOR THE ENVIRONMENT?

Given the holdings of the preceding cases, whether the Taylor Act, FLPMA, and PRIA are sufficient to protect the range ecosystem and also equitably address the concerns of the ranching community is, to put it mildly, unsettled. A number of commentators, however, have contended that the existing statutory framework is sufficient to provide strong environmental protection. Perhaps the leading exponent of this view is Professor Donahue, who has argued that if BLM were to follow the law it would prohibit grazing on public lands that receive less than twelve inches of annual rainfall or, at the very least, recognize its authority to allocate rangelands to biodiversity conservation purposes. DEBRA L. DONAHUE, THE WESTERN RANGE REVISITED: REMOVING LIVESTOCK FROM THE PUBLIC LANDS TO CONSERVE BIODIVERSITY 193–228 (1999).

Her argument begins with the Taylor Grazing Act's directive to the Secretary of the Interior to establish grazing districts from lands "which in his opinion are *chiefly valuable for grazing* and raising forage crops . . . [i]n order to promote the highest use of the public lands pending its [sic] final disposal." *Id.* at 192 (quoting 43 U.S.C. § 315) (emphasis added). She also emphasizes the Act's grant of authority to the Secretary to "classify" the land within grazing districts "which are more valuable or suitable for the production of agricultural crops than for the production of native grasses and forage plants, or more valuable or suitable for any other use...." 43 U.S.C. § 315f. *See generally* Donahue, *supra*, at 193–203. She concludes that

> grazing was not intended to be the predominant use of public lands under the Taylor Act; in fact, grazing was at best a co-equal use of the public domain, where it was not actually subordinated to other uses.... [T]he statute's provisions for establishing grazing districts on "lands chiefly valuable for grazing" and for promoting "the highest use" of the lands must be construed to allow for review over time. Public lands that become "more valuable or suitable for any other use"—including biodiversity conservation—should be reclassified for that use. Furthermore, where lands may be irreparably damaged by continued grazing, the agency is obliged to terminate such abuse.

Id. at 203.

Turning to FLPMA, Professor Donahue emphasizes the substantive content of the multiple use command and argues that the supplementary obligation to "take any action necessary to prevent unnecessary or undue degradation of the lands," 43 U.S.C. § 1732(b), "must, at a minimum, mean that resource condition may not be allowed to decline to a point that would interfere with the sustained yield of that, or any other, resource or with realizing the land's values." Donahue, *supra*, at 205. The application of this standard, she suggests, should obligate the Secretary in many instances to terminate grazing on arid lands. Donahue also emphasizes FLPMA's requirement that "[i]n the development and revision of land use plans, the Secretary shall ... give priority to the designation and protection of areas of critical environmental concern." 43 U.S.C. § 1712(c)(3). These areas, generally known by their acronym ACECs, are defined as "areas within the public lands where special management attention is required ... to protect and prevent irreparable damage to important historic, cultural, or scenic values, fish and wildlife resources or other natural systems or processes...." *Id.* § 1702(a). Arid lands, suggests Professor Donahue, are just the sort of area that the Secretary is obligated to protect from the "irreparable damage" caused by grazing.

Finally, with respect to PRIA she asserts:

> PRIA does nothing to weaken my assessment of the legality or propriety, under FLPMA or the Taylor Grazing Act, of the proposed biodiversity conservation strategy. In fact, by clarifying that "improving range conditions" is "*the* goal" of range management, even where livestock grazing continues, and by expressly recognizing that grazing may have to be discontinued in certain circumstances, PRIA probably strengthens the case for a biodiversity conservation plan on arid lands unsuited to livestock grazing. * * *

> It would be illogical at best to infer that Congress intended, via PRIA, to perpetuate the "unsatisfactory conditions" extant on "vast segments of the public rangelands" by sanctioning continued, unsustainable grazing on lands unsuited to that purpose. PRIA thus confirms that conservation of biodiversity and/or prevention of irreversible, grazing-induced vegetative changes would be legitimate bases for a decision to terminate grazing on arid and semi-arid rangelands.

Donahue, *supra*, at 221–22.

QUESTIONS AND DISCUSSION

1. Professor Donahue's critique of grazing law is more nuanced than the outline above, but from the excerpt, is her position persuasive? Do you agree that the Taylor Act and FLPMA obligate, or at very least allow, BLM to curtail grazing on arid lands with less than twelve inches of rainfall? If you are persuaded by Professor Donahue's ecological concerns, do you agree that the best way to accomplish them is by using the current statutory framework? Even if statutory amendment is not necessary, would it be advisable?

2. The "chiefly valuable" language of the Taylor Act emphasized by Professor Donahue was first employed in the Stock Raising Homestead Act of 1916. 43 U.S.C. §§ 291–302 (repealed by FLPMA in 1976). The Act's purpose was to promote the development of small stock ranches on the public domain in places where smaller homesteads did not make sense because of a lack of irrigation opportunities. Recognizing that 160 acres was more than enough land to support a family where water was available but too little when arid conditions obtained, Congress authorized the Secretary "to designate as stock raising lands ... lands the surface of which is, in his opinion, chiefly valuable for grazing and raising forage crops, do not contain merchantable timber, are not susceptible of irrigation from any known source of water supply, and are of such character that six hundred and forty acres are reasonably required for the support of a family." 43 U.S.C. § 292. The Act, however, reserved for the United States "all the coal and other minerals in the lands" entered and patented under the Act. *Id.* § 299. This reservation created yet another anomaly in the patchwork quilt of public and private land ownership in the West. Not only is public land interspersed with checkerboarded sections of state school trust lands and private land derived from railroad land grants, *see supra* Chapter 2, but the approximately 32 million acres of land disposed of under the Stock–Raising Homestead Act is subject to federal ownership of the mineral estate.

3. During the concluding months of the Clinton administration, the Interior Department prepared a new Land Use Planning Handbook for the BLM. As part of a broader effort to change the culture of the Agency and its historic practice of regular renewal of grazing permits, the Handbook, for the first time, instructed BLM officers and employees to consider whether grazing should be curtailed or eliminated on each allotment as part of the land use planning process. *See* BUREAU OF LAND MANAGEMENT, LAND USE PLANNING HANDBOOK VI–3 to VI–4 (Rel. 1–1667, Nov. 22, 2000). Adding this set of instructions to the Handbook was a contentious issue within the agency. In light of PRIA, FLPMA, and the Taylor Act, should it have been? What does this say about the prospects for success of Professor Donahue's biodiversity conservation proposal?

PROBLEM EXERCISE: DETERMINING WHETHER PUBLIC LANDS ARE CHIEFLY VALUABLE FOR GRAZING

In 1998, the Oregon Natural Desert Association (ONDA) filed a petition with the Secretary of the Interior. ONDA requested that the Secretary initiate a rulemaking (1) to establish procedural and substantive standards governing the BLM's determination of those BLM lands "chiefly valuable for grazing and raising forage crops" and (2) to require BLM to make this determination each time it prepared or revised a land use plan under FLPMA. More specifically, they requested a rule requiring the Secretary to issue a written order and opinion in conjunction with each management plan finding that all lands within a grazing district are chiefly valuable for grazing and not for another use.

Assume you are an attorney in the Solicitor's Office within the Department of the Interior. The Solicitor has requested your help in responding to ONDA's petition. His inclination is to deny the petition but he is not sure whether he can. He is also curious whether Section 15 of the Taylor Act (relating to leasing outside of grazing districts), 43 U.S.C. § 315m (*supra* at page 942), and FLPMA's land use planning provision, 43 U.S.C. § 1712 (*supra* at page 953), have any implications for the meaning of the chiefly valuable language. Considering these and other provisions of the Taylor Act and FLPMA, prepare to brief the Solicitor on potential reasons for rejecting the petition and potential counter-arguments.

V. Rangeland Reform

Given the passionate debate about the place of ranching in the West, the divergent views on whether PRIA, FLPMA, and the Taylor Act require, allow, or discourage reallocation of the range resource away from grazing, and the difficult practical questions with management of the allotments in the Comb Wash and *McKinley* cases (which are merely two of thousands of allotments on the public lands), it should be readily apparent why many have continued to push for reforms in the way the grazing resource is allocated and managed. This section considers the most significant grazing reform proposals, illustrating the various natural resource management approaches discussed in Chapter 1.

A. Grazing Fees and Subsidies

Under the Taylor Grazing Act, the Secretary is authorized to issue grazing permits "upon the payment annually of reasonable fees." 43 U.S.C. § 315b. Establishing a "reasonable" grazing fee has long been a focus of grazing reformers. The issue is not simply whether the federal government is charging a below-market price for its grazing lands, nor is it whether the fee strictly covers the costs of public lands grazing administration. A larger concern among many grazing reformers has been whether the price charged reflects the environmental externalities and opportunity costs of devoting the federal range to grazing. Raising the fee is viewed as a way of reflecting some of these costs (forcing ranchers to pay their way), and ultimately of decreasing ranchers' ability to engage in activities that impose such costs.

At the time of the Taylor Act's passage, the view of Interior Secretary Harold Ickes was that the statute's term "reasonable" meant that the fee would be sufficient to cover the costs of administering the range. Farrington Carpenter, the first head of the Department's Grazing Division, took a more practical view. Meeting with ranchers after the passage of the Act, he argued:

> If we charge no fee it would amount to a government subsidy, and a government subsidy is always subject to scrutiny, criticism and investigation. You stockmen should set some fair fee, so that you can go before any committee from Boston, or Newport, or anywhere else, and show it is fair. Otherwise you are never going to be away from constant criticism in the east and middle west, who feel that the way to solve the question is to throw all the cattle and sheep off the public domain.... So, we will want fees for our own protection.

PHILIP O. FOSS, POLITICS AND GRASS 173 (1960). Carpenter's warning was prescient. Whether the fee set by the Interior Secretary amounts to a subsidy has been a constant source of dispute since the passage of the Act. There is no question that the fees charged for BLM grazing permits have historically been lower than those charged on national forest lands, state lands, or private lands. The first grazing fee established by the Department was only $0.05 per AUM for cattle (the rate on national forest land at that time was $0.16) and even this fee was disputed. GATES, *supra*, at 615.

Despite Carpenter's advice, every proposal for a fee increase has since been met with strong opposition from ranchers and their supporters in the House and Senate. As a result, the fee only increased to $0.12 in 1950, $0.19 in 1958, $0.22 in 1959, and $0.33 in 1968. GATES, *supra*, at 615; Todd M. Olinger, Comment, *Public Rangeland Reform: New Prospects for Collaboration and Local Control Using the Resource Advisory Councils*, 69 U. COLO. L. REV. 633, 636 (1998). These minimal increases came despite the fact that by 1941 it was clear that the fees were not covering the program's administrative costs. Appropriations to run the Grazing Service were some $5.2 million whereas only $0.9 million was collected in fees. FOSS, *supra*, at 179. Ranchers responded that the Service had grown too fast and that it should tighten its own belt.

With the passage of FLPMA in 1976, Congress declared a policy that "the United States should receive fair market value of the use of the public lands." 43 U.S.C. § 1701(a)(9). However, it also imposed a moratorium on any increase pending a joint study by the Forest Service and BLM to determine a fee that would be "equitable" to both the treasury and to those who held grazing permits. *Id.* § 1751(a). Then, when the agencies proposed to collect fair market value, Congress in 1978 in the PRIA legislated a formula by which grazing fees would be set for both BLM and Forest Service lands. 43 U.S.C. § 1905. The formula uses a base value of $1.23 per AUM and then adjusts the fee depending on current private grazing land lease rates, cattle prices, and the cost of livestock production. *Id. See also* 43 C.F.R. § 4130.8–1. The formula resulted in a fee of $1.86 per AUM in 1993, whereas the average fee for comparable private lands was $9.80 per AUM. *Id.*

Since PRIA established its fee formula, there have been several subsequent attempts in Congress to increase the grazing fee, all of which have failed. Soon after the Clinton administration took office, Interior Secretary Babbitt as part of his grazing reform efforts, proposed that the fee be increased from $1.86 to $3.96 per AUM over three years but the proposal met with loud criticism in the West. *See* Karl N. Arruda & Christopher Watson, *The Rise and Fall of Grazing Reform*, 32 LAND & WATER L. REV. 413, 431 (1997). Having touched the third-rail of grazing policy, Babbitt withdrew the proposal and went back to the drawing board. By 1996, the Department had actually *lowered* the fee to $1.35 per AUM, the lowest possible fee under the 1978 formula. Olinger, *supra* at 638. It has remained at $1.35 per AUM, with the exception of a one-year increase to $1.43 in 2002, well below the rate charged for private lands (between $8 and $23 per AUM in 2004) and state lands (between $1.23 and $80 in 2004). U.S. Government Accountability Office, *Livestock Grazing (September 2005)*, http://www.gao.gov/new.items/d05869.pdf.

Although the disparity with state and private grazing rates is significant, the overall subsidy for the costs of grazing permits is relatively small in comparison to the many other federal subsidies. Whereas in 1998 federal spending was $1.65 trillion, even a partisan estimate of the subsidy to grazing is only $150 million per year. *See* MAJORITY STAFF REPORT OF THE HOUSE SUBCOMMITTEE ON OVERSIGHT AND INVESTIGATIONS OF THE COMM. ON NATURAL RESOURCES, 103RD CONG., 2d Sess., TAKING FROM THE TAXPAYER: PUBLIC SUBSIDIES FOR NATURAL RESOURCE DEVELOPMENT 87 (1994). Subsidy critics are quick to point out, however, that grazers receive other subsidies in addition to the below-market grazing permits, including cheap water from Bureau of Reclamation projects, federal assistance with predator control, and agricultural price supports for beef and alfalfa. *See id.* at 87–91.

B. PRIVATIZING GRAZING PERMITS

The debate about grazing fees and federal subsidies is a theoretical cousin of an approach long championed by free-market environmentalists and others: privatizing grazing permits. The following offers a succinct overview of the argument in favor of markets.

> Grazing permits should be marketable to people other than ranchers and for uses other than raising livestock. To that end, all statutory requirements that restrict grazing allotments to domestic livestock production should be eliminated, and regulations that either constrain or penalize grazing nonuse should be abolished. All Americans should be eligible to acquire, hold, and trade grazing permits and to apply them to uses that include, but are not limited to, forage for cattle, sheep, and horses. Ranchers should be free to destock their public-land ranges, and environmentalists, sportspeople, and community groups should be free to buy grazing permits from willing stockmen for wilderness protection, wildlife refuges, and outdoor recreation. All permit holders should pay fees and assume management costs sufficient to make the range programs of the BLM and the Forest Service fiscally sound. * * *

> Rangeland has economic value for recreation, wildlife viewing, big-game habitat, riparian health, clean water, and fisheries. For those values to be conserved, stewarded, and protected, permit holders—ranchers and nonranchers alike—must be allowed to capture the full value of their leased public forage. They should be given the opportunity to use riparian areas for fee-supported fishing and bird watching and upland ranges for fee-supported hunting, wildlife viewing, and recreation. If they are allowed to do those things, market forces will yield a far wider spectrum of desirable land-use outcomes than does multiple-use planning.

Karl Hess Jr. & Jerry L. Holechek, *Beyond the Grazing Fee: An Agenda for Rangeland Reform*, POLICY ANALYSIS, No. 234, July 13, 1995.

C. BUYING BACK THE RANGE

In the fall of 2001, a number of environmental groups formed the National Public Lands Grazing Campaign. They proposed to introduce legislation under which federal land management agencies would, on a voluntary basis, buy out grazing permits at $175 per AUM, a price well over market. The campaign's director asserted: "This is attractive to environmentalists.... This is attractive to taxpayer groups. This should provide a great deal for ranchers. It's a win, win, win." *Environmentalists Want Bill to Buy Out Grazing Permits*, PUBLIC LANDS NEWS, Dec. 7, 2001, at 8. *See also National Public Lands Grazing Campaign*, http://www.public landsranching.org. The legislation was first introduced in September 2003 and again in 2005 but it has not yet made a serious bid for passage. *See* H.R. 3324, 108th Cong., 1st Sess. (2003); H.R. 3166, 109th Cong., 1st Sess. (2005).

An even more aggressive buyout proposal has been advocated by Professor Robert Nelson. Rather than voluntary buyouts, he proposed that the federal government simply treat grazing permits as if they were private property and essentially "condemn" the permits by paying ranchers a reasonable compensation. Nelson's point is that it would ultimately be a lot cheaper to buy out the ranchers than to continue to regulate and manage grazing on public rangelands.

> The government might institute a long-run program with the objective of purchasing much or all of the grazing rights in certain areas or geographic conditions. The price of a BLM grazing permit in the market has typically been around $50 to $100 per AUM. Given that BLM administers somewhat less than ten million AUMs, a simple calculation suggests that the total capital value of all livestock grazing permits on all BLM lands is no more than $500 million to $1 billion. By comparison the true BLM livestock grazing management costs are perhaps $100 million to $200 million per year. Hence, the present value of all future BLM administrative costs that can be largely attributable to the management of livestock grazing is probably around $2 billion—or even more, depending on the discount rate used, the method of allocation of overhead, and other considerations that affect the determination of true cost.

ROBERT H. NELSON, PUBLIC LANDS AND PRIVATE RIGHTS: THE FAILURE OF SCIENTIFIC MANAGEMENT 265 (1995).

D. COLLABORATION, CONSENSUS, AND LOCAL CONTROL

An approach advocated by some grazing reformers is to rely on local stakeholders to manage the range resource by collaboration and consensus. The bottom-up consensus building process is championed as more flexible and responsive than the more top-down approach of command and control regulation. But these abstractions mean different things to different people when placed in the range context. To some, it is an affirmation of the management by grazing advisory boards made up of stockmen which for so long held sway under the Taylor Act. For others, including most of its proponents, it refers to efforts to bring together all stakeholders, including ranchers, high and low-impact recreators, preservationists, states, Indian tribes, and local government officials. For example, the Range Advisory Councils created as a part of Interior Secretary Babbitt's reform of the grazing regulations are based in part on the latter approach, although the Advisory Councils are just that, advisory—they do not have real decision-making authority. *See* 43 C.F.R. § 1784 (2000) (describing RACs); Todd M. Olinger, Comment, *Public Rangeland Reform: New Prospects for Collaboration and Local Control Using the Resource Advisory Councils*, 69 U. COLO. L. REV. 633, 665–69 (1998).

One ardent proponent of local control over natural resource management, including not only grazing but timber, watershed, wildlife, and other resources, is Daniel Kemmis, the former mayor of Missoula, Montana. He contends that "no real public life is possible except among people who are engaged in the project of inhabiting a place." DANIEL KEMMIS, COMMUNITY AND THE POLITICS OF PLACE 79–80 (1990). It is the shared and repeated practices involved with inhabiting a place, he suggests, that create a set of shared values that allow for real collaboration satisfactory to all stakeholders. *Id.* at 79–80, 116–17, 126–27.

> The pattern of federal ownership and management of Western land affects both the politics and the economics of the region. The concept of a place-focused economy—of a "marketplace"—is profoundly undermined by these extensive federal holdings. What emerges is neither a sense of inhabited *place* nor of a free *market*. National forest management illustrates this point. Both industry and environmentalists routinely berate the Forest Service for its anti-market activities. The wood products industry bemoans regulations and legislation which keep it from harvesting good, marketable timber, while environmentalists charge that many Forest Service timber sales have the effect of subsidizing the industry, especially by using public funds to build logging roads which an open market would not justify. Analogous arguments are levied against the Bureau of Land Management for its grazing land management. As both sides charge the federal bureaucracy with being the servant of the opposition, a potentially substantial arena of common ground is consistently ignored. * * *

> It would be an insult to assume that they are incapable of reaching some accommodation among themselves about how to inhabit their own place. Such accommodation would never be easy, and it would probably always be open to some redefinition. But if they were allowed to solve their problems (and manage their resources) themselves, they would soon discover that no one wants local sawmills closed, and no one wants wildlife habitat annihilated. If encouraged to collaborate, they would learn to inhabit the place on the place's own terms better than any regulatory bureaucracy will ever accomplish. * * *

Id. at 126–28. Kemmis ends up concluding that the West "will be successful only if it is willing to carry decentralization even further than states' rights—back to the *polis* itself." *Id.* at 139. *See also* DANIEL KEMMIS, THIS SOVEREIGN LAND: A NEW VISION FOR GOVERNING THE WEST (2001). Other advocates of local participation in range management do not go quite so far. They recognize a whole range of levels of local involvement, often with federal oversight or law to assure consideration of broader national interests. In broad relief, however, the message is the same: the best way to tackle natural resource management issues on the range specifically, or on the public lands generally, is to cede some decision-making authority to local control. *See, e.g.*, ACROSS THE GREAT DIVIDE: EXPLORATIONS IN COLLABORA-

TIVE CONSERVATION IN THE AMERICAN WEST (Philip D. Brick et al. eds., 2001); JULIA M. WONDOLLECK & STEVEN L. YAFFEE, MAKING COLLABORATION WORK: LESSONS FROM INNOVATION IN NATURAL RESOURCE MANAGEMENT (2000); Sarah F. Bates, *Public Lands Communities: In Search of a Community of Values*, 14 PUB. LAND L. REV. 81 (1993).

QUESTIONS AND DISCUSSION

1. Which interest groups do you think would support the particular proposals of higher fees, privatization, buyback, or collaboration? If the proposals sound wise, are they workable? Do you think any of the proposals could receive sufficient support to create an effective political coalition?

2. Should grazing fees be increased? If so, what should be the purpose of any increase? To reflect market rates? To internalize externalities? To capture the costs of administration? Where should the collected fees go? In 2004, grazing on BLM and Forest Service lands cost the BLM and the Forest Service $132.5 million to manage. By contrast, the agencies recovered $17.5 million in grazing fees. In order for grazing fees to actually pay for grazing on public lands, the BLM would need to charge $7.64 per AUM and the Forest Service would need to charge $12.26 per AUM. *See* United States Government Accountability Office, *Livestock Grazing* (September 2005), http://www.gao.gov/new.items/d05869.pdf; *see also* http://www.sage brushsea.org/mn_grazing_fees.htm. With respect to where any fees collected should go, BLM returns a part of its grazing collections to the states and local counties in which the grazing occurs under various federal programs. In fiscal 2004, BLM returned $2.1 million to states. *See* Bureau of Land Management, *Public Rewards from Public Lands 2004–2005*, http://www. blm.gov/nhp/pubs/rewards/2005/PR05NATLtxt.pdf.

3. If pricing federal grazing permits at their fair market value is a key to improving range ecosystems, is it even possible to determine fair market value? Professor Oesterle offers the following observations:

> Can we solve our public land management problems, short of privatization, by pressuring the federal government to set so-called fair market fees or prices that approximate what a private owner would charge? This is the "marketization" approach to allocation of federal land use. Experience with federal land management does not give us much cause for optimism about a marketization approach.
>
> Suppose the federal government attempted to set its prices, at a minimum, to cover its costs of operation—the normal approach taken by private firms that want to stave off bankruptcy. In allocating grazing leases, if the government set its fees based on its costs of administration, the fees could be well in excess of fair market prices charged by private land owners. At present, there is no strong incentive for BLM officials to keep administrative expenses of grazing leases down because the BLM does not worry about bankruptcy. In fact, it has converse incentives: higher administrative costs mean a larger agency budget, which is the ultimate goal of many bureaucrats. When a bureaucrat can dress up an increased budget request in the mantle of the public interest, so much the better.
>
> If the federal government is unable to set grazing fees based on a recovery of its costs, can it rely on a system that mimics fees set by private landowners?

Probably not. Federal grazing land is ubiquitous in local grazing markets. Finding private grazing leases that are priced without an overriding influence from adjacent federal grazing leases may be impossible. Moreover, grazing fees ought to vary from region to region and parcel to parcel, and ought to change periodically to reflect changing market conditions. Yet prices set by federal officials are sticky to the point of immutability. Inevitably, we would get what we have: one grazing price per AUM and AUM figures for each parcel fixed over long periods of time.

Alternatively, could the government rely on competitive bidding to create a system of fees based on fair market prices? Again, our experience with attempts to develop a competitive bidding system for coal leasing suggests that an auction system would not work. * * *

Another problem is designing an auction system that encourages competition; a 1983 study found that "competition has been the exception rather than the rule" in coal leasing. In both coal and grazing leases, bidding competition for some tracts tends to be weak because the location of the land makes it of interest to only a single firm or rancher. For example, where federal land is encircled by a private ranch, only the ranch owner and possibly a few others will be interested in it.

Dale A. Oesterle, *Public Land: How Much Is Enough?*, 23 ECOLOGY L.Q. 521, 534–36 (1996).

4. Why do you suppose states have been able to charge a higher fee for grazing than the federal government? Would public choice theory predict such a result?

5. Many trees have been sacrificed on the subsidy issue. For a sampling, see TAKING FROM THE TAXPAYER, *supra*, at 85–91; Todd M. Olinger, Comment, *Public Rangeland Reform: New Prospects for Collaboration and Local Control Using the Resource Advisory Councils*, 69 U. COLO. L. REV. 633, 638–40 (1998) (discussing the subsidization of grazing and the counter-arguments of ranchers); WAYNE HAGE, STORM OVER RANGELANDS 22 (1989) (arguing that grazing fees actually exceed the real value of public rangelands because they do not include the private owner's infrastructure like water rights, roads, fences, and corrals).

6. If you favor a privatization and trading approach, how would you implement it? To whom should the right be allocated initially? Should it go to existing permittees? Should they be required to pay for that right and, if so, what price? Ranchers would likely contend that they have already paid for the right because it is capitalized in the cost of their base ranch. Instead of assigning the property right to existing permittees, should grazing permits simply be put up for auction to the highest bidder? Who is likely to have an advantage in such a bidding situation?

7. What should be the nature of the privatized right? Could it include deed restrictions limiting use to protect the environment? For a review of the gradual movement toward marketable grazing permits and of implementation approaches, see Robert H. Nelson, *How to Reform Grazing Policy: Creating Forage Rights on Federal Rangelands*, 8 FORDHAM ENVTL. L.J. 645 (1997). Who do you think would support or oppose privatization of grazing permits?

8. Privatization of grazing permits has been criticized on a number of grounds. One objection is the holdout problem—some ranchers will refuse to sell even if it would be economically rational to do so. *See* Joseph M. Feller, *'Til the Cows Come Home: The Fatal Flaw in the Clinton Administration's Public Lands Grazing Policy*, 25 ENVTL. L. 703, 714 (1995). Another criticism is distributional—if permits were privatized by allocating the grazing right to current permittees, it would generate a windfall not only for small rural ranchers but for absentee owners and large corporate livestock interests. Professor Donahue points out the following pattern of permittees:

> According to a National Wildlife Federation (NWF) survey, "10 percent of the BLM's permittees control almost 50% of the AUMs permitted"; "the top 20 BLM permittees (or 0.1 percent of the total number) control 9.3 percent of the available forage" and "14 percent, or 20.7 million acres of the BLM's rangelands." The "top 20" permittees include corporations such as Nevada First Corp., Agri–Beef Co., and Metropolitan Life Co. (some are companies with $1 billion in assets) and such wealthy individuals as J.R. Simplot, one of the 400 richest people in the country.

DEBRA L. DONAHUE, THE WESTERN RANGE REVISITED 273 (1999). How might a privatization advocate respond to these criticisms?

9. Some commentators have gone further than advocating privatization of grazing permits and have argued for privatization of the public lands generally. *See* Richard L. Stroup, *Privatizing Public Lands: Market Solutions to Economic and Environmental Problems*, 19 PUB. LAND & RES. L. REV. 79 (1998); Terry L. Anderson et al., *How and Why to Privatize Federal Lands*, 363 POLICY ANALYSIS, Nov. 9, 1999; RICHARD L. STROUP & JOHN A. BADEN, NATURAL RESOURCES: BUREAUCRATIC MYTHS AND ENVIRONMENTAL MANAGEMENT 123–27 (1983) (advocating sale of the national forests). When there have been legislative proposals to sell off public lands, however, they have been met with widespread opposition. Professor Oesterle contends:

> Too many powerful political interest groups are aligned to oppose any sale. They are strange bedfellows. Commodity-based interest groups (ranchers, loggers, and miners), conservation-based interest groups, and recreation-based interest groups, who usually despise and distrust each other, have joined hands to oppose the sale of any federal land. Rather than buy land at auction, the players prefer to struggle among themselves over access to government-owned land, and the struggle takes the form of a contest over the process of choosing a political decisionmaker or a decisionmaking forum. Each side urges the adoption of a political process that allocates land use in their favor. The commodity-based interest groups urge us to put the land under state administrative control, while conservation-based interest groups lobby for federal legislation enforced through the federal courts.
>
> The balance of power in this struggle is shifting because the demographics of the West are moving away from commodity-based groups, who have dominated allocation decisions for more than fifty years, to recreation-based groups. This shift will cause new tensions in old alliances; recreationists and conservationists, for example, will disagree with each other over land use decisions. There will also be divisions among the recreationists: backpackers will clash with off-road vehicle enthusiasts, and birdwatchers will object to mountain bikers.

Oesterle, *supra*, at 575.

10.   As discussed above, Professor Nelson and the National Public Lands Grazing Campaign propose retiring grazing permits by paying ranchers a price well above the permits' putative market value. Do you have any concerns about this proposal? Spokesmen for the livestock industry oppose the legislation. *Environmentalists Want Bill to Buy Out Grazing Permits*, PUBLIC LANDS NEWS, Dec. 7, 2001, at 8. Why would they? Would you expect all environmental groups to join in the proposal? Might some of them be concerned about an unfair windfall to ranchers or about spending public dollars to retire grazing permits that under existing law may be terminated without compensation?

11.   The collaboration and consensus-based approach to range management discussed in the text also has its critics. The most common argument is that local groups are not entitled to any preferred place in allocating and managing public lands that belong to all citizens. Critics also argue that collaborative processes tend to favor the status quo by diverting time, money, and other resources away from activities that might better bring change. Moreover, participation in such processes by those who benefit from the status quo is virtually assured because they often have a direct economic stake in the outcome. Concern about public goods, such as clean water and habitat, tend to be under-represented because the benefits are diffuse and tend to be discounted when compared with the immediate private interests of local economic concerns. The interests of future generations, critics assert, also tend to be discounted by collaborative approaches. For a sampling of some of the criticisms of collaborative approaches, see George C. Coggins, *Regulating Federal Natural Resources: A Summary Case Against Devolved Collaboration*, 25 ECOLOGY L.Q. 602, 603 (1999); Rena Steinzor, *The Corruption of Civic Environmentalism*, 30 ENVTL. L. RPTR. 10909 (2000) (raising a number of concerns with "civic environmentalism" and the idea of delegating environmental decisions to local groups and interested parties). How might collaboration advocates respond to these criticisms?

E.   GRAZING REFORM ADMINISTRATIVE STYLE

Proposing the sort of rangeland management and allocation theories raised in the prior section is decidedly easier than convincing Congress to implement them. It was not until 1934 that Congress decided to regulate grazing at all. It took over forty years for Congress to return to the subject in FLPMA in 1976 and PRIA in 1978, and since then it has been largely silent. This story is not unique to grazing. It is difficult to move any sort of comprehensive natural resources or public land legislation through Congress. Sometimes, judicial interpretation of statutory meaning can move the law and policy toward a particular management approach. But given the discretionary standards in most natural resources laws, it remains difficult to litigate one's way to an alternative resource allocation or management approach. An approach with greater potential for changing rangeland management is administrative reform. Like litigation, agency rulemaking is in theory designed merely to implement principles already decided upon by Congress. In practice, however, it has significant potential to alter the rules of resource allocation and governance, particularly where the applicable legislation invests the agency with as much management discretion as do the statutes governing grazing and rangeland management. The following cases illustrate competing administrative efforts to incorporate elements of the grazing reform ideas outlined above. As you read them consider not only the merits of the specific reforms but also the merits of administrative reform more generally.

NATURAL RESOURCES DEFENSE COUNCIL V. HODEL,
618 F. Supp. 848 (E.D. Cal. 1985)

RAMIREZ, DISTRICT JUDGE.

[Plaintiffs challenged Interior Secretary Watt's new rule establishing the Cooperative Management Agreement (CMA) program. The program authorized BLM to enter into special permit arrangements with selected ranchers who had demonstrated "exemplary rangeland management practices." 43 C.F.R. § 4120.1(a). "Exemplary practices" were not defined in the regulation; the selection of ranchers was within the discretion of BLM officials.]

The expressed purpose of the CMA program is to allow these ranchers the heretofore *verboten* opportunity to "manage livestock grazing on the allotment as they determine appropriate." 48 Fed.Reg. at 21823–24 (proposed 43 C.F.R. § 4120.1). The BLM is bound by the terms of a CMA for ten years.... The rule envisions periodic evaluations and provides for cancellation or modification only in the event of unauthorized transfers, violation of whatever terms and conditions the Secretary inserts in the CMA, or violation of regulations unrelated to overgrazing. * * *

A review of the CMAs which have been drafted and executed by defendants, confirms that the Secretary's expressed purposes for the CMA program (secure rancher tenure and self-management) have been implemented. Example agreements cited by *both* plaintiffs' and defendants' counsel indicate that CMAs need not contain specific performance standards such as numbers of animals or seasons of use.... These agreements list no terms or conditions whatsoever which prescribe the manner in or extent to which livestock grazing shall be managed on these allotments. The permits which accompany these agreements are brief documents containing no grazing specifications. The agreements do contain, however, the BLM's promise of non-interference and secure tenure as outlined in the [BLM] Handbook. * * *

Defense counsel's chief argument to uphold the CMA Program is premised on a clever interpretation of the Experimental Stewardship Program (ESP), contained in PRIA of 1978. 43 U.S.C. § 1908.[32] Congress by enacting ESP

---

32. Section 1908 provides in relevant part, as follows:

(a) *Scope of program*

The Secretar[y] of Interior ... [is] hereby authorized and directed to develop and implement, on an experimental basis on selected areas of the public rangelands which are representative of the broad spectrum of range conditions, trends, and forage values, a program which provides incentives to, or rewards for, the holders of grazing permits and leases whose stewardship results in an improvement of the range condition of lands under permit or lease. Such program shall explore innovative grazing management policies and systems which might provide incentives to improve range conditions.

directed the Secretary to select areas of the rangelands of representative conditions, trends, and forages and in concentrating on these areas to "explore innovative grazing management policies and systems which might provide incentives to improve range conditions." *Id.* The incentive projects were to be experimental and ready for Congressional review by December of 1985 when the Secretary was directed to report the "results" of the program. *Id.*

The government has maintained that even if the CMA program cannot be upheld under the Taylor Act and FLPMA, it is nevertheless fully justified by ESP. For the reasons stated herein, the Court finds this argument unsound.

This Court would ordinarily defer to the Secretary's judgment on matters such as the applicability of a particular program to a concededly generous delegation of experimental authority. However, it is blatantly obvious from the record that the Secretary did not in fact rely upon ESP when he promulgated the regulation authorizing the CMA program. Not only is there no record of the Secretary ever relying on ESP for such authority, evidence in the record establishes that BLM has already completed its experimental stewardship projects. In fact, a brochure describing the completed ESP was produced by the ranchers participating in the three official "Experimental Stewardship Groups" organized by the BLM. Given the manner in which BLM carefully identified the three regions subject to ESP experiments in the past, it would be strange indeed for it to establish a fourth experiment without so much as brief mention of section 1908 in any of the documents pertaining to the new program. The apparent truth is that the CMA program was never intended as a stewardship experiment. The Court must therefore view counsel's ESP argument as a *post hoc* rationalization for the CMA program and, as such, deserving of none of the customary deference accorded agency interpretations.

However, assuming for the moment that the CMA program is not a lawful method of permit issuance under the Taylor Act and FLPMA, this Court is of the view that ESP would not create any additional authority for it even if the Secretary *had* relied upon section 1908. ESP did not create an exception to the permit issuance requirements of FLPMA. To the contrary, Congress ordered the Secretary to continue managing the lands "in accordance with" both the Taylor Act and FLPMA when it enacted PRIA in 1978. 43 U.S.C. § 1903(b).

Moreover, the legislative history, as cited to this Court by counsel on both sides, reveals that ESP vested no authority in the Secretary that was not *already available to him under the Taylor Act and FLPMA.* The legislative history also amply establishes that "experimentation" with FLPMA permit procedures was *not* what Congress had in mind when it enacted section 1908.

It is also manifest from the language of section 1908 that the CMA program simply does not meet the description of the projects ESP was intended to encourage. The CMA program is *not* an experiment, but is a permanent system of permit issuance aimed at a group of favored permittees. Significantly, there is no indication whatsoever that the "results" of the CMA program can be the subject of a report to Congress by December of 1985. None of the CMAs

These may include, but need not be limited to—

(1) cooperative range management projects designed to foster a greater degree of cooperation and coordination between Federal and State agencies charged with the management of the rangelands and with local private range users, * * *

(3) such other incentives as he may deem appropriate.

(b) *Report to Congress*

No later than December 31, 1985, the Secretar[y] shall report to the Congress the results of such experimental program.

will even be ripe for review until several years after the Congressional reporting deadline. * * *

Plaintiffs' principal contention is that the CMA regulation, as finally promulgated and implemented by the Secretary and the BLM, is a naked violation of defendants' affirmative duties under the Taylor Grazing Act, FLPMA, and PRIA. The Court agrees. The CMA program disregards defendants' duty to prescribe the manner in and extent to which livestock practices will be conducted on public lands. The program also overlooks defendants' duty of expressly reserving, in all permits, sufficient authority to revise or cancel livestock grazing authorizations when necessary.

1. Duty to Prescribe Practices. The CMA program authorizes a permanent system of preferential permit issuance. Since 1934, defendants have been authorized to issue such permits but have also been required "from time to time" to "specify" the "numbers of livestock" permittees may graze on the lands and the "seasons of use" for such livestock grazing purposes. 43 U.S.C. § 315b. By enacting FLPMA in 1976, Congress clarified this duty by obligating defendants to conform to one of two prescribed methods of permit issuance. 43 U.S.C. § 1752(d)–(e). Defendants may, after cooperation and consultation with ranchers, tailor a specific grazing prescription to each allotment by incorporating an AMP [Allotment Management Plan] into each permit. *Id.,* at § 1752(d).* Defendants may, instead, choose to forego incorporation of an AMP, and, in such case, specify in the *permit itself* the prescription of numbers of livestock and seasons of use. *Id.,* at § 1752(d). While these choices provide defendants with an extraordinary degree of flexibility and discretion, there is no question that defendants' choices under FLPMA are limited to these two. Because a CMA agreement represents a third choice, and one which violates the spirit and letter of the grazing statutes, the program is unlawful.

The original purpose of the CMA program was to allow selected permittees the opportunity to "manage livestock grazing on [their] allotment[s] as *they* determine appropriate." 48 Fed.Reg. at 21823 (proposed 43 C.F.R. § 4120.1) (emphasis supplied). Thus, any defense of the program begins on the shakiest of legs since the dominant message and command of defendants' Congressional mandate is that *defendants* shall prescribe the extent to which livestock grazing shall be conducted on the public lands. The apparent goal and inevitable result of the CMA program is to allow ranchers, for a term of at least ten years, to rule the range as they see fit with little or no governmental interference. Many of these ranchers may be fully qualified to prescribe their own management practices. Many are undoubtedly familiar, after years of ranching on the public lands, with the Congressional mandate that public lands be managed "in a manner that will protect the quality of scientific, scenic, historical, ecological, environmental, air and atmospheric, water resource, and archaeological values." 43 U.S.C. § 1701(a)(8). Some or all of these knowledgeable permittees may even be *inclined* to limit their livestock grazing to levels which will guarantee the vitality of such values, even at the expense of their own private ranching interests. Had Congress left a gap in its regulatory scheme which allowed defendants to decide whether individual ranchers should be entrusted with such decisions, this Court would be in no position to second guess the

---

* [Section 1752(d) provides, in relevant part, "Allotment management plans shall be tailored to the specific range condition of the area to be covered by such plan, and shall be reviewed on a periodic basis to determine whether they have been effective in improving the range condition of the lands involved or whether such land can be better managed.... The Secretary concerned may revise or terminate such plans or develop new plans from time to time after such review and careful and considered consultation...."]

wisdom of the CMA program. However, Congress, in directing that the Secretary prescribe the extent of livestock practices on each allotment, precluded such entrustment, apparently because after years of rancher dominance of range decisions, it found substantial evidence of rangeland deterioration.

According to defendants' own Handbook Manual, CMAs *may* incorporate the objectives of an existing AMP, but *must* provide the permittee with special management flexibility. Thus, any AMP which might be in existence when the CMA is signed retains no independent significance. The CMA itself need not be specially tailored to the allotment, and need not prescribe the extent to which livestock practices are conducted on the allotment. Thus, a decision by defendants to enter into a CMA with a permittee is plainly a decision by the Secretary and the BLM that an AMP need *not* be incorporated into the permit. 43 U.S.C. § 1752(e). Defendants are entitled to make such a determination, but Congress has instructed them that *"in all cases"* where an AMP is not incorporated, they "shall" specify in the permit "the numbers of animals to be grazed and the seasons of use ..." *Id.* Defendants' assertion that the CMA regulation is valid because it requires specification of "performance standards" is without merit. The statute requires specification of numbers and seasons, not generalized standards or responsibilities. CMAs, by definition and in practice, fail to comply with this Congressional mandate. * * *

2. Duty to Reserve Revision and Cancellation Authority. Defendants are also required to incorporate into each permit an express revocation or suspension clause, 43 U.S.C. § 1732(c), and must retain constant authority to "cancel, suspend, or modify" each permit "in whole or in part" for violations of permit or regulatory requirements. 43 U.S.C. § 1752(a). In permits without AMPs, such as those incorporating CMAs, defendants are required to specify in each permit that they "may reexamine the condition of the range at *any time*" and order whatever adjustments they deem appropriate. 43 U.S.C. § 1752(e) (emphasis supplied). Even permits incorporating AMPs must reserve authority for defendants to "revise or terminate such plans or develop new plans from time to time" after consultation with ranchers. 43 U.S.C. § 1752(d). * * *

The CMA regulation and program fall short of the standard set by Congress in FLMPA. While the rule, as promulgated, contains vague references to the BLM's authority to periodically evaluate the range, 43 C.F.R. § 4120.1(c), and to cancel or modify agreements under certain circumstances, § 4120.1(d), § 4170.1–4, the details of defendants' authority are left to the BLM's determination, and the BLM has determined to abdicate its authority in favor of secure ranching tenure.

The Handbook, which defendants concede has implemented the true intent of the Secretary's rule, sets up a range review schedule so lenient and favorable to ranchers, that permittees are virtually guaranteed a minimum ten years of uninterrupted self-management on each CMA allotment. * * *

It is for Congress and not defendants to amend the grazing statutes. In the meantime, it is the public policy of the United States that the Secretary and the BLM, not the ranchers, shall retain final control and decisionmaking authority over livestock grazing practices on the public lands. * * *

QUESTIONS AND DISCUSSION

1. The regulatory amendments allowing for cooperative management agreements were initiated during the tenure of President Reagan's first Secretary of the Interior, James Watt. CMAs were not the only regulatory amendments at issue in the case. The court struck down another change under which a regulation providing that grazing permits "shall" be modified as required by land use plans had been changed to provide that permits "may" be modified. *NRDC v. Hodel*, 618 F. Supp. at 875–76. It also invalidated an amendment deleting from the regulations penalties for livestock operators who violated state or federal environmental laws. *Id.* at 876–77. Finally, the court declined to rule on an amendment that narrowed the definition of those with "affected interests" entitled to participate in grazing decisionmaking to those designated as such by BLM officers. *Id.* at 880–81. The court did so because there was no evidence that anyone had yet been denied the opportunity to participate. *Id.*

2. Why didn't Judge Ramirez show more deference to the Secretary? Was he obligated to show deference? Is there any way he could have upheld the cooperative management agreements?

3. Setting aside the question of statutory authority for the CMA program, was it a good idea to give ranchers more secure tenure in their grazing permits? Would the program likely have harmed the range or improved it? Isn't this a practical example of the collaborative reforms described in the previous section? Alternatively, can you conceive of useful experimental stewardship programs that conform to the relevant statutes?

4. Interior Secretary Watt was vilified by many in the environmental community for his approach to the range and a whole host of other public lands issues. *See, e.g.*, George C. Coggins & Doris K. Nagel, *"Nothing Beside Remains": The Legal Legacy of James G. Watt's Tenure As Secretary of the Interior on Federal Land Law and Policy*, 17 B.C. Envtl. Aff. L. Rev. 473 (1990) (criticizing Secretary Watt's various efforts at administrative change, including proposing to sell 4.4 million acres of BLM lands, attempting to lease minerals in wilderness and wilderness study areas, refusing to spend money appropriated for national parkland acquisition, and reclassifying with less protective designations about 161 million acres of public lands); *Marching Backwards: The Department of Interior Under James G. Watt*, Nat'n Wildlife Fed'n, Apr. 29, 1982, at 365; Deanne Kloepfer et al., *The Watt Record*, James Watt and the Bureau of Land Management Lands 26–34 (The Wilderness Soc'y 1983).

––––––––

When President Clinton took office in 1993, he appointed as his Secretary of the Interior Bruce Babbitt, former governor of Arizona and president of The League of Conservation Voters. Secretary Babbitt immediately embarked upon another effort to change grazing law. Although he supported an early legislative effort at grazing reform, his focus was on amending grazing regulations. In 1993, the Secretary issued a first notice of proposed rulemaking. It called for more than a doubling of the grazing fee over three years, created a new set of national standards for range management, and replaced Grazing Advisory Boards with what would become Resource Advisory Councils made up of equal representation from resource and commodity users, preservation and recreation advocates, and public officials. The Secretary's proposal met strong opposition from ranching communities as well as an ultimately unsuccessful legislative effort to impose a moratorium on the regulations. Although he weathered the attempted moratorium, Secretary Babbitt decided to engage in a more inclusive process and began to meet with ranchers, environmentalists, local officials, and others about grazing reform. When the final regulations were issued in February of 1995, they had been changed considerably, including elimination of the grazing fee increase and the national ecological standards. For further discussion of the Secretary's grazing reform efforts, see RANGELAND REFORM '94, UNITED STATES DEPARTMENT OF THE INTERIOR (August 1993); Joseph M. Feller, *'Til the Cows Come Home: The Fatal Flaw in the Clinton Administration's Public Lands Grazing Policy*, 25 ENVTL. L. 703 (1995); Karl N. Arruda & Christopher Watson, *The Rise and Fall of Grazing Reform*, 32 LAND & WATER L. REV. 413, 458–59 (1997); Bruce M. Pendery, *Reforming Livestock Grazing on the Public Domain: Ecosystem Management–Based Standards and Guidelines Blaze a New Path for Range Management*, 27 ENVTL. L. 513 (1997); Todd M. Olinger, Comment, *Public Rangeland Reform: New Prospects for Collaboration and Local Control Using the Resource Advisory Councils*, 69 U. COLO. L. REV. 633, 638–40 (1998).

Despite the changes, the Secretary's regulations continued to draw the ire of much of the ranching community, leading to this lawsuit by the Public Lands Council. As you read the opinion, consider what motivated both the ranchers and the Secretary to dispute seemingly small changes in the regulations.

PUBLIC LANDS COUNCIL V. BABBITT, 529 U.S. 728 (2000)

JUSTICE BREYER delivered the opinion of the Court.

This case requires us to interpret several provisions of the 1934 Taylor Grazing Act, 48 Stat. 1269, 43 U.S.C. § 315 *et seq.* The Petitioners claim that each of three grazing regulations, 43 CFR §§ 4100.0–5, 4110.1(a), and 4120.3–2 (1998), exceeds the authority that this statute grants the Secretary of the Interior. We disagree and hold that the three regulations do not violate the Act.
* * *

A

... The Taylor Act seeks to "promote the highest use of the public lands." 43 U.S.C. § 315. Its specific goals are to "stop injury" to the lands from "overgrazing and soil deterioration," to "provide for their use, improvement and development," and "to stabilize the livestock industry dependent on the public range." 48 Stat. 1269. The Act grants the Secretary of the Interior authority to divide the public range lands into grazing districts, to specify the amount of grazing permitted in each district, to issue leases or permits "to graze livestock," and to charge "reasonable fees" for use of the land. 43 U.S.C. §§ 315, 315a, 315b. It specifies that preference in respect to grazing permits "shall be given ... to those within or near" a grazing district "who are landowners engaged in the livestock business, bona fide occupants or settlers, or owners of water or water rights." § 315b. And, as particularly relevant here, it adds:

> So far as consistent with the purposes and provisions of this subchapter, grazing privileges recognized and acknowledged shall be adequately safe-guarded, but the creation of a grazing district or the issuance of a permit ... shall not create any right, title, interest, or estate in or to the lands. *Ibid.*

The Taylor Act delegated to the Interior Department an enormous administrative task. To administer the Act, the Department needed to determine the bounds of the public range, create grazing districts, determine their grazing capacity, and divide that capacity among applicants. It soon set bounds encompassing more than 140 million acres, and by 1936 the Department had created 37 grazing districts. The Secretary then created district advisory boards made up of local ranchers and called on them for further help. Limited department resources and the enormity of the administrative task made the boards "the effective governing and administrative body of each grazing district."

By 1937 the Department had set the basic rules for allocation of grazing privileges. Those rules recognized that many ranchers had long maintained herds on their own private lands during part of the year, while allowing their herds to graze farther afield on public land at other times. The rules consequently gave a first preference to owners of stock who also owned "base property," *i.e.*, private land (or water rights) sufficient to support their herds, *and* who had grazed the public range during the five years just prior to the Taylor Act's enactment. They gave a second preference to other owners of nearby "base" property lacking prior use. And they gave a third preference to stock owners without base property, like the nomadic sheep herder. Since lower preference categories divided capacity left over after satisfaction of all higher preference claims, this system, in effect, awarded grazing privileges to owners of land or water. * * *

The grazing regulations in effect from 1938 to the present day made clear that the Department retained the power to modify, fail to renew, or cancel a permit or lease for various reasons. First, the Secretary could cancel permits if, for example, the permit holder persistently overgrazed the public lands, lost control of the base property, failed to use the permit, or failed to comply with the Range Code. Second, the Secretary, consistent first with 43 U.S.C. § 315f, and later the land use planning mandated by 43 U.S.C. § 1712, was authorized to reclassify and withdraw land from grazing altogether and devote it to a more valuable or suitable use. Third, in the event of range depletion, the Secretary maintained a separate authority, not to take areas of land out of grazing use altogether as above, but to reduce the amount of grazing allowed on that land, by suspending AUMs of grazing privileges "in whole or in part," and "for such time as necessary."

Indeed, the Department so often reduced individual permit AUM allocations under this last authority that by 1964 the regulations had introduced the notion of "active AUMs," *i.e.*, the AUMs that a permit *initially* granted *minus* the AUMs that the department had "suspended" due to diminished range capacity. Thus, three ranchers who had initially received, say, 3,000, 2,000, and 1,000 AUMs respectively, might find that they could use only two-thirds of that number because a 33% reduction in the district's grazing capacity had led the Department to "suspend" one-third of each allocation. The "active/suspended" system assured each rancher, however, that any capacity-related reduction would take place proportionately among permit holders, see 43 CFR § 4111.4–2(a)(3) (1964), and that the Department would try to restore grazing privileges proportionately should the district's capacity later increase, see § 4111.4–1. * * *

This case arises out of a 1995 set of Interior Department amendments to the federal grazing regulations. 60 Fed.Reg. 9894 (1995) (Final Rule). * * *

Petitioners Public Lands Council and other nonprofit ranching-related organizations with members who hold grazing permits brought this lawsuit against the Secretary and other defendants in Federal District Court, challenging 10 of the new regulations. The court found 4 of 10 unlawful. 929 F. Supp. 1436, 1450–1451 (D. Wyo. 1996). The Court of Appeals reversed the District Court in part, upholding three of the four. 167 F.3d 1287, 1289 (C.A. 10 1999).

[The Court of Appeals did agree with the District Court that Secretary had exceeded his authority in the 1995 regulations by adding "conservation use" as a permissible use of a grazing permit. *See* 43 C.F.R. § 4100.0–5 (1995). "Conservation use" was a potentially significant change of the permit system because it provided for permits to be issued for uses other than livestock grazing. As the name implied, "conservation use" would allow conservation groups to hold grazing permits for preservation purposes. The Court of Appeals, however, reasoned that allowing permits to be issued for conservation use was contrary to the plain language of the Taylor Grazing Act which authorized the Secretary only "to issue or cause to be issued permits to graze livestock ... on grazing districts," 43 U.S.C. § 315b., and of FLPMA and PRIA, both of which define "grazing permit and lease" as "any document authorizing use of public lands ... *for the purpose of grazing domestic livestock.*" 43 U.S.C. §§ 1702(p), 1902(c) (emphasis added). The Court of Appeals thus struck down the conservation use rule and the Secretary did not appeal. Only the ranchers' challenge to the other three regulations came before the Court.]

Those three (which we shall describe further below) (1) change the definition of "grazing preference"; (2) permit those who are not "engaged in the livestock business" to qualify for grazing permits; and (3) grant the United States title to all future "permanent" range improvements. * * *

II

A

The ranchers attack the new "grazing preference" regulations first and foremost. Their attack relies upon the provision in the Taylor Act stating that "grazing privileges recognized and acknowledged shall be adequately safeguarded...." 43 U.S.C. § 315b. Before 1995 the regulations defined the term "grazing preference" in terms of the *AUM-denominated amount* of grazing privileges that a permit granted. The regulations then defined "grazing preference" as

> the total number of animal unit months of livestock grazing on public lands apportioned and attached to base property owned or controlled by a permittee or lessee. 43 CFR § 4100.0–5 (1994).

The 1995 regulations changed this definition, however, so that it now no longer refers to grazing privileges "apportioned," nor does it speak in terms of AUMs. The new definition defines "grazing preference" as

> a superior or priority position against others for the purpose of receiving a grazing permit or lease. This priority is attached to base property owned or controlled by the permittee or lessee. 43 CFR § 4100.0–5 (1995).

The new definition "omits reference to a specified quantity of forage." 60 Fed.Reg. 9921 (1995). It refers only to a priority, not to a specific number of AUMs attached to a base property. But at the same time the new regulations add a new term, "permitted use," which the Secretary defines as the forage allocated by, or under the guidance of, an applicable land use plan for livestock grazing in an allotment under a permit or lease and is expressed in AUMs. 43 CFR § 4100.0–5 (1995).

This new "permitted use," like the old "grazing preference," is defined in terms of allocated rights, and it refers to AUMs. But this new term as defined refers, not to a rancher's forage priority, but to forage "allocated by, or under the guidance of *an applicable land use plan.*" *Ibid.* (emphasis added). And therein lies the ranchers' concern.

The ranchers refer us to the administrative history of Taylor Act regulations, much of which we set forth in Part I. In the ranchers' view, history has created expectations in respect to the security of "grazing privileges"; they have relied upon those expectations; and the statute requires the Secretary to "safeguar[d]" that reliance. Supported by various farm credit associations, they argue that defining their privileges in relation to land use plans will undermine that security. They say that the content of land use plans is difficult to predict and easily changed. Fearing that the resulting uncertainty will discourage lenders from taking mortgages on ranches as security for their loans, they conclude that the new regulations threaten the stability, and possibly the economic viability, of their ranches, and thus fail to "safeguard" the "grazing privileges" that Department regulations previously "recognized and acknowledged."

We are not persuaded by the ranchers' argument for three basic reasons. First, the statute qualifies the duty to "safeguard" by referring directly to the Act's various goals and the Secretary's efforts to implement them. The full subsection says:

> "*So far as consistent with the purposes and provisions of this subchapter,* grazing privileges recognized and acknowledged shall be adequately safeguarded, *but* the creation of a grazing district or the issuance of a permit pursuant to the provisions of this subchapter shall *not* create any right, title, interest or estate in or to the lands." 43 U.S.C. § 315b (emphasis added).

The words "so far as consistent with the purposes . . . of this subchapter" and the warning that "issuance of a permit" creates no "right, title, interest or estate" make clear that the ranchers' interest in permit stability cannot be absolute; and that the Secretary is free reasonably to determine just how, and the extent to which, "grazing privileges" shall be safeguarded, in light of the Act's basic purposes. Of course, those purposes include "stabiliz[ing] the livestock industry," but they also include "stop[ping] injury to the public grazing lands by preventing overgrazing and soil deterioration," and "provid[ing] for th[e] orderly use, improvement, and development" of the public range. 48 Stat. 1269.

Moreover, Congress itself has directed development of land use plans, and their use in the allocation process, in order to preserve, improve, and develop the public rangelands. See 43 U.S.C. §§ 1701(a)(2), 1712. That being so, it is difficult to see how a definitional change that simply refers to the use of such plans could violate the Taylor Act by itself, without more. Given the broad discretionary powers that the Taylor Act grants the Secretary, we must read that Act as here granting the Secretary at least ordinary administrative leeway to assess "safeguard[ing]" in terms of the Act's other purposes and provisions. Cf. §§ 315, 315a (authorizing Secretary to establish grazing districts "*in his discretion*" (emphasis added), and to "make provision for protection, administration, regulation, and improvement of such grazing districts").

Second, the pre–1995 AUM system that the ranchers seek to "safeguard" did not offer them anything like absolute security—not even in respect to the proportionate shares of grazing land privileges that the "active/suspended" system suggested. As discussed above, the Secretary has long had the power to reduce an individual permit's AUMs or cancel the permit if the permit holder did not use the grazing privileges, did not use the base property, or violated the Range Code. See *supra,* at 1820 (collecting CFR citations 1938–1998). And the Secretary has always had the statutory authority under the Taylor Act and later FLMPA to reclassify and withdraw range land from grazing use, see 43 U.S.C. § 315f (authorizing Secretary, "in his discretion, to examine and classify any lands ... which are more valuable or suitable for the production of agricultural crops ... or any other use than [grazing]"); §§ 1712, 1752(c) (authorizing renewal of permits "so long as the lands ... remain available for domestic livestock grazing *in accordance with land use plans*" (emphasis added)). The Secretary has consistently reserved the authority to cancel or modify grazing permits accordingly. Given these well-established pre–1995 Secretarial powers to cancel, modify, or decline to review individual permits, *including the power to do so pursuant to the adoption of a land use plan,* the ranchers' diminishment-of-security point is at best a matter of degree.

Third, the new definitional regulations by themselves do not automatically bring about a self-executing change that would significantly diminish the security of granted grazing privileges. The Department has said that the new definitions do "not cancel preference," and that any change is "merely a clarification of terminology." 60 Fed.Reg. 9922 (1995). It now assures us through the Solicitor General that the definitional changes "preserve all elements of preference" and "merely clarify the regulations within the statutory framework."

The Secretary did consider making a more sweeping change by eliminating the concept of "suspended use"; a change that might have more reasonably prompted the ranchers' concerns. But after receiving comments, he changed his mind. *See* 59 Fed.Reg. 14323 (1994). The Department has instead said that "suspended" AUMs will continue to be recognized and have a priority for additional grazing use within the allotment. "Suspended use provides an important accounting of past grazing use for the ranching community and is an insignificant administrative workload to the agency." Bureau of Land Management, Rangeland Reform '94: Final Environmental Impact Statement 144 (1994).

Of course, the new definitions seem to tie grazing privileges to land-use plans more explicitly than did the old. But, as we have pointed out, the Secretary has since 1976 had the authority to use land use plans to determine the amount of permissible grazing, 43 U.S.C. § 1712. The Secretary also points out that since development of land use plans began nearly 20 years ago, "all BLM lands in the lower 48 states are covered by land use plans," and "all grazing permits in those States have now been issued or renewed in accordance with such plans, or must now conform to them." Yet the ranchers have not provided us with a single example in which interaction of plan and permit has jeopardized or might yet jeopardize permit security. An *amicus* brief filed by a group of Farm Credit Institutions says that the definitional change will "threate[n]" their "lending policies." But they do not explain *why* that is so, nor do they state that the new definitions will, in fact, lead them to stop lending to ranchers.

We recognize that a particular land use plan could change pre-existing grazing allocation in a particular district. And that change might arguably lead to a denial of grazing privileges that the pre–1995 regulations would have provided. But the affected permit holder remains free to challenge such an individual effect on grazing privileges, and the courts remain free to determine its lawfulness in context. We here consider only whether the changes in the definitions by themselves violate the Taylor Act's requirement that recognized grazing privileges be "adequately safeguarded." Given the leeway that the statute confers upon the Secretary, the less-than-absolute pre–1995 security that permit holders enjoyed, and the relatively small differences that the new definitions create, we conclude that the new definitions do not violate that law.

B

The ranchers' second challenge focuses upon a provision of the Taylor Act that limits issuance of permits to "settlers, residents, and other *stock owners....*" 43 U.S.C. § 315b (emphasis added). In 1936, the Secretary, following this requirement, issued a regulation that limited eligibility to those who "ow[n] livestock." But in 1942, the Secretary changed the regulation's wording to limit eligibility to those "engaged in the livestock business," and so it remained until 1994. The new regulation eliminates the words "engaged in the livestock business," thereby seeming to make eligible otherwise qualified applicants even if they do not engage in the livestock business. See 43 CFR § 4110.1(a) (1995).

The new change is not as radical as the text of the new regulation suggests. The new rule deletes the entire phrase "engaged in the livestock business" from § 4110.1, and seems to require only that an applicant "own or control land or water base property...." But the omission, standing alone, does not render the regulation facially invalid, for the regulation cannot change the statute, and a regulation promulgated to guide the Secretary's discretion in exercising his authority under the Act need not also restate all related statutory language. Ultimately it is *both* the Taylor Act and the regulations promulgated thereunder that constrain the Secretary's discretion in issuing permits. The statute continues to limit the Secretary's authorization to issue permits to "bona fide settlers, residents, and *other stock owners.*" 43 U.S.C. § 315b (emphasis added).

Nor will the change necessarily lead to widespread issuance of grazing permits to "stock owners" who are not in the livestock business. Those in the business continue to enjoy a preference in the issuance of grazing permits. The same section of the Taylor Act mandates that the Secretary accord a preference to "landowners engaged in the livestock business, bona fide occupants or settlers." * * *

The ranchers nonetheless contend that the deletion of the term "engaged in the livestock business" violates the statutory limitation to "stock owners" in § 315b. The words "stock owner," they say, meant "commercial stock owner" in 1934, and a commercial stock owner is not simply one who owns livestock, but one who engages in the business. Hence, they argue, the Secretary lacks the authority to allow those who are not engaged in the business to apply for permits.

The words "stock owner" and "stock owner engaged in the livestock business," however, are not obvious synonyms. And we have found no convincing indication that Congress intended that we treat them as such. Just two sentences after using the words "stock owner," Congress said that, among those eligible for permits (*i.e.,* stock owners), preference should be given to "landowners *engaged in the livestock business,* bona fide occupants or settlers, or owners of water or water rights." § 315b (emphasis added). Why would

Congress add the words "engaged in the livestock business" if (as the ranchers' argument implies) they add nothing? The legislative history to which the ranchers point shows that Congress expected that ordinarily permit holders would be ranchers, who do engage in the livestock business, but does not show any such absolute requirement. Nor does the statute's basic purpose require that the two sets of different words mean the same thing. Congress could reasonably have written the statute to mandate a preference in the granting of permits to those actively involved in the livestock business, while not absolutely excluding the possibility of granting permits to others. The Secretary has not exceeded his powers under the statute.

The ranchers' underlying concern is that the qualifications amendment is part of a scheme to end livestock grazing on the public lands. They say that "individuals or organizations owning small quantities of stock [will] acquire grazing permits, even though they intend not to graze at all or to graze only a nominal number of livestock—all the while excluding others from using the public range for grazing." The new regulations, they charge, will allow individuals to "acquire a few livestock, . . . obtain a permit for what amounts to a conservation purpose and then effectively mothball the permit."

But the regulations do not allow this. The regulations specify that regular grazing permits will be issued for livestock grazing, or suspended use. *See* 43 CFR §§ 4130.2(a), 4130.2(g) (1998). New regulations allowing issuance of permits for conservation use were held unlawful by the Court of Appeals, *see* 167 F.3d, at 1307–1308, and the Secretary did not seek review of that decision.

Neither livestock grazing use nor suspended use encompasses the situation that the ranchers describe. With regard to the former, the regulations state that permitted livestock grazing, "*shall be based* upon the amount of forage available for livestock grazing as established in the land use plan. . . ." 43 CFR § 4110.2–2(a) (1998) (emphasis added). Permitted livestock use is not simply a symbolic upper limit. Under the regulations, a permit holder is expected to make substantial use of the permitted use set forth in the grazing permit. For example, the regulations prohibit a permit holder from "[f]ailing to make substantial grazing use as authorized for 2 consecutive fee years." § 4140.1(a)(2). If a permit holder does fail to make substantial use as authorized in his permit for two consecutive years, the Secretary is authorized to cancel from the grazing permit that portion of permitted use that the permit holder has failed to use. *See* § 4170.1–2. On the basis of these regulations, the Secretary has represented to the Court that "[a] longstanding rule requires that a grazing permit be used for grazing." Suspended use, in turn, is generally imposed by the Secretary in response to changing range conditions. Permittees may also apply to place forage in "[t]emporary nonuse" for financial reasons, but the Secretary must approve such nonuse on an annual basis and may not grant it for more than three consecutive years. 43 CFR § 4130.2(g)(2) (1998). A successful temporary nonuse application, moreover, does not necessarily take the land out of grazing use—the Secretary may allocate to others the forage temporarily made available via non-renewable permit. *See* §§ 4130.2(h), 4130.6–2. In short, nothing in the change to § 4110.1(a) undermines the Taylor act's requirement that the Secretary grant permits "to graze livestock." 43 U.S.C. § 315b. * * *

The judgment of the Court of Appeals is *Affirmed.*

QUESTIONS AND DISCUSSION

1. As the Court discusses, prior to 1995, the regulations defined the term "grazing preference" with respect to the historical number of AUMs apportioned to a particular allotment. 43 C.F.R. § 4100.0–5 (1994). This historic number was then further subdivided into active use (the number of AUMs the rancher was currently allowed to graze) and suspended use (the preference minus the number of active AUMs). Secretary Babbitt's amended regulations changed the definition of "grazing preference" from one that focused on the original apportionment of AUMs to a definition that merely recognized priority for receiving a permit, without reference to a priority to any particular amount of AUMs. 43 C.F.R. § 4100.0–5 (1995). As the Court makes clear, even under the old regulation, the Secretary was not obligated to let a rancher graze the full preference/historical apportionment. The Secretary could always reduce the amount grazed under the Taylor Act or FLPMA. Indeed, that is why the entire concept of active use and suspended use had developed. Given the parties' seeming agreement on this issue, why the litigation? Why did ranchers and credit institutions view the new definition as an impairment of their collateral when the Secretary had always had authority to reduce the amount of forage attached to a particular permit? Did they perhaps believe the preference figure served to influence BLM field officers to come as close as possible to the "preference" marker when deciding upon an appropriate amount of active use even though the officer was not obligated to do so? Does eliminating a persuasive but unenforceable marker really impair the bank's collateral? Is that historical marker part of the grazing "privilege" that the Taylor Act requires to be "adequately safeguarded" because it is not inconsistent with the Act's other purposes?

2.   If the ranchers' vehement objections to elimination of an unenforceable preference seems odd, so too does the Solicitor General's concession that " 'suspended' AUMs will continue to be recognized and have a priority for additional grazing use within the allotment." On its face, this appears to be a concession that the historical preference figure will be retained because calculation of suspended use requires subtracting the active use from the historical apportionment/"preference." If that is the case, the Secretary's new regulation does not seem to change much. Perhaps that is why the ranchers contended that the Court's emphasis on the Secretary's suspended use clarification was a victory for them despite the 9–0 ruling. *See, e.g.,* Edward Walsh, *Court Backs U.S. on Land Use,* WASH. POST, May 16, 2000, at A19. If this regulatory arcana strikes you as worrying about how many angels can dance on the head of a pin—given that the Secretary is always free to reduce or eliminate grazing on any particular allotment—why do you suppose the ranchers and the Secretary went to so much trouble? Was the grazing preference a historical marker worth fighting over?

3.   Whatever the meaning of "preference" in the Taylor Act, was this decision particularly surprising as a matter of administrative law? Is there an argument that the Court should not have deferred to the Secretary's interpretation of the relevant statutes? Does it matter that a contrary definition of preference had been in place for a number of years? *See, e.g., Davis v. United States,* 495 U.S. 472, 484 (1990) ("[W]e give an agency's interpretations and practices considerable weight where they involve the contemporaneous construction of a statute and where they have been in long use."); *Watt v. Alaska,* 451 U.S. 259, 272–73 (1981) (agency's interpretation of an amendment that was contemporaneous with the amendment's passage was entitled to greater deference than an agency's current, inconsistent interpretation). When agencies depart from previous rules, they will be found to have acted arbitrarily and capriciously unless they "supply a reasoned analysis for the change." *Motor Vehicle Mfrs. Ass'n of United States, Inc. v. State Farm Mut. Automobile Ins. Co.*, 463 U.S. 29, 42 (1983). In what was perhaps a tactical error, the Public Lands Council did not raise such a *State Farm* argument before the Supreme Court. *See Public Lands Council v. Babbitt*, 529 U.S. 728 (2000) (O'Connor, J., concurring) (noting this omission). Had it done so, the Solicitor General may have been more reluctant to argue that the new regulations "preserve[d] all elements of preference," 529 U.S. at 743, and thus served little practical purpose.

4. Does it make sense to give deference to agency interpretations and reinterpretations of their governing statutes when rulemaking is capable of such shifts in the law? Are courts competent to exercise any more scrutiny?

5. Do the grazing reform approaches of Secretary Babbitt strike you as more legitimate or appropriate than those of Secretary Watt? Can they be meaningfully distinguished, or is it the case that one took the side of ranchers and the other took the side of environmentalists? As governor of Arizona, Secretary Babbitt was a critic of Secretary Watt's aggressive use of administrative power:

> If President Reagan and Secretary Watt are serious about efforts to establish a "good neighbor policy" between Washington and the West, they should work to strengthen, not weaken, mechanisms for joint decisionmaking on public lands. In particular, the states must be given a more meaningful role in planning development on federal lands within their borders.... What angers most westerners is not the fact of federal ownership, but the federal government's insistence that it is entitled to exercise power "without limitation." When this sovereign power is wielded by a continually changing parade of federal administrators, each with a different agenda, the situation becomes intolerable.

See Bruce Babbitt, *Federalism and the Environment: An Intergovernmental Perspective of the Sagebrush Rebellion*, 12 ENVTL. L. 847, 857 (1982). He argued that if there were a public lands issue of truly national interest, then Congress "ought to identify that interest explicitly through legislation, rather than leaving identification to agency administrators." *Id.* at 858. After serving six years as the Interior Secretary, Secretary Babbitt observed: "When I got to town, what I didn't know was that we didn't need more legislation.... We've switched the rules of the game. We're not trying to do anything legislatively." Carl M. Cannon, *The Old–Timers*, 1999 NAT'L J. 1386, 1391. Are his comments as Governor reconcilable with his approach as Secretary? If not, is Governor Babbitt or Secretary Babbitt correct about administrative reform of natural resource management?

6. A recent commentary on the *Public Lands Council* decision argued: "Taking a bird's eye view of the Court's legal reasoning, it is reasonable to conclude that the politics and history of the range, though still relevant, are appropriately receding to the rule of law." Erik Schlenker–Goodrich, *Moving Beyond* Public Lands Council v. Babbitt: *Land Use Planning and the Range Resource*, 16 J. ENVTL. L. & LITIG. 139, 157 (2001). Is the author's optimism well founded? Whether or not grazing is receding to the rule of law, it has been receding.

From the mid–1930s to the early–1940s, the number of AUMs increased with the number of grazing districts established under the new regulatory framework. BLM grazing remained constant from the 1940s until the late 1950s, but then began a long-run decline in the early 1960s that lasted through the 1990s. By 1996, grazing had dropped over 45% from its peak level in 1955. The general downward trend follows the net decline seen for grazing of all stock in the national forests. Overall, livestock in the West is down from 20 million head in 1900 to less than 2 million in 1998.

Jan G. Laitos & Thomas A. Carr, *The Transformation on Public Lands*, 26 ECOLOGY L.Q. 140, 155 (1999).

7. Justice Breyer notes that the Secretary created Grazing Advisory Boards made up of local ranchers and that the Boards made most grazing decisions within the grazing districts. Colorado Representative Taylor, the original sponsor of the Act bearing his name, had called these advisory boards "democracy on the range" and "home rule on the range." E. LOUISE PEFFER, THE CLOSING OF THE PUBLIC DOMAIN 221 (1972). Yet it is partly because of the role played by the Grazing Advisory Boards that the BLM has often been derisively called the "Bureau of Livestock & Mining" and a classic case of agency capture. Why might the Grazing Service have relied so heavily on the advisory boards? Is the creation of the boards consistent with public choice theory? The Forest Service was consistently less accommodating to ranching interests, treating grazing as secondary to forestry in its management. Can this also be explained by public choice theory? The Secretary's 1995 grazing reform eliminated Grazing Advisory Boards and replaced them with Resource Advisory Councils made up of equal representation from resource and commodity users, preservation and recreation advocates, and public officials. *See* 43 C.F.R. § 1784.6–1 (2000) (describing membership of Resource Advisory Councils). Why the switch to Resource Advisory Councils? How might this switch be explained by public choice theory? Does the switch reduce the likelihood that the BLM will be captured by one particular interest group?

8. The Public Lands Council also challenged a change in the regulations governing title to structural or removable range improvements made pursuant to cooperative agreements with the United States. Previously, title was shared according to the respective contributions of the United States and the rancher. Under the new regulations, title "shall be in the name of the United States." 43 CFR § 4120.3–2(b) (1995). The ranchers argued that this change violated 43 U.S.C. § 315c, which says that "No permit shall be issued which shall entitle the permittee to the use of such [range] improvements constructed *and owned* by a prior occupant until the applicant has paid to such prior occupant the reasonable value of such improvements. . . ." In their view, the word "owned" foresees ownership by a "prior occupant," a possibility they argued was denied by the new rule mandating Government ownership of permanent range improvements. The Secretary responded that, because section 315c gives him the power to *authorize* range improvements pursuant to a cooperative agreement, he necessarily has the lesser power to set the terms of title ownership to such improvements. "Under this reading, the subsequent statutory provision relating to 'ownership' simply provides for compensation by some future permit holder *in the event* that the Secretary decides to grant title." *Public*

Lands Council, 529 U.S. at 749–50. The Court agreed with the Secretary's position. Why did the Secretary depart from a long-standing practice and shift title to all new range improvements to the United States? The Secretary asserted that shifting the title of all new range improvements would unify BLM practice with that of the Forest Service, simplify negotiation with permittees over title to range improvements if lands were taken out of grazing, and eliminate the sometimes confusing distinction between structural and nonstructural range improvements discussed in the opinion. Are these reasons convincing?

As one might expect after reading about the regulatory tug-of-war from Secretary Watt to Secretary Babbitt, in 2006 the George W. Bush Administration issued a new rule, amending the grazing regulations once again and largely reversing course in favor of the approach used prior to the Clinton administration's 1995 rulemaking. *See* 43 C.F.R. Part 4100. The new rule was challenged and the result was the following opinion.

WESTERN WATERSHEDS PROJECT V. KRAAYENBRINK
2007 WL 1667618 (D. Idaho 2007)

B. LYNN WINMILL, Chief United States District Judge.

The parties seek a ruling on the legality of the BLM's revisions to nationwide grazing regulations. Past BLM regulations imposed restrictions on grazing and increased the opportunities for public input to reverse decades of grazing damage to public lands. Without any showing of improvement, the new BLM regulations loosen restrictions on grazing.

They limit public input from the non-ranching public, offer ranchers more rights on BLM land, restrict the BLM's monitoring of grazing damage, extend the deadlines for corrective action, and dilute the BLM's authority to sanction ranchers for grazing violations. * * *

After thoroughly reviewing the extensive Administrative Record in this case, ... the Court finds that ... BLM violated the National Environmental Policy Act (NEPA) by failing to take the required "hard look" at the environmental effects of the regulations. For many of same reasons, the Court also finds that the regulations violate the Federal Land Policy and Management Act (FLPMA).

Based on these violations, the Court will issue an injunction enjoining the revised regulations from taking effect until the BLM ... takes the requisite "hard look" at the environmental impacts under NEPA. * * *

2.   *2006 Regulatory Changes* * * *

The BLM asserts that the changes were necessary to "improv[e] the working relationship with permittees and licensees and increas[e] administrative efficiency and effectiveness, including resolution of legal issues." By July of 2002, the BLM had developed a list of proposed changes, and assembled an interdisciplinary team of experts to review and report on the planned changes. The team's report, dated November 29, 2002, predicted that the limitations on public input would "lead to poorer land management decisions" and to "greater environmental harm, without necessarily sustaining or improving economic conditions." Based on these findings, the team recommended that "the definition of *interested public* be changed to specifically allow for broader public participation...." AR at 67848 (emphasis in original).

[The BLM decided not to alter the proposed changes and instead assembled a second interdisciplinary team to review the proposed rules.... This team issued a report referred to as the Administrative Review Copy Draft EIS (ARC–DEIS). The ARC–DEIS was issued on November 17, 2003, just three weeks before the publication of the proposed changes on December 8, 2003. The BLM set November 28th—just 11 days after the ARC–DEIS was issued—as the deadline for internal comments. To review these comments and the ARC–DEIS "as rapidly as possible," the BLM assembled a small team. Before this team was done reviewing the ARC–DEIS, the BLM published the proposed regulations on December 8, 2003. That publication was not accompanied by a Draft EIS (DEIS), which would not be completed for another month.]

The revision team responsible for the DEIS substantially re-wrote the ARC–DEIS. For example, the DEIS deleted, without comment, the ARC–DEIS's conclusions that the proposed changes would have adverse impacts on wildlife, biological diversity, and riparian habitats. As another example, the ARC–DEIS's conclusion that ownership of water rights or range improvements will greatly diminish the BLM's ability to regulate grazing and have long-term impacts on wildlife was re-written to state that the changes in ownership would have little or no impact. * * *

[In an Addendum to the FEIS, the BLM explained] that the ARC–DEIS was revised "in an effort to produce a factually accurate, scientifically sound and reasoned DEIS." The changes were made, according to the BLM, "to correct erroneous interpretations of the proposed rule, correct misstatements of law, and improve its logic." * * *

About four months after the Addendum was issued, the BLM issued its Final Rule and Record of Decision (ROD), adopting the proposed changes on July 12, 2006.

3. *Changes to Public Participation*

The Final Rule makes two major changes to the public participation process. First, the BLM modified the definition of "interested publics." Under the old definition, an individual or group that submitted a written request to the BLM to be involved in the decision-making process as to a specific allotment would be put on a list of "interested publics" and receive notice of issues arising concerning that allotment—including notice of day-to-day management issues. Under the new rule, the group would be dropped from that list if it received notice but did not comment.

The second major change in public input comes from a narrowing of the BLM's duty to consult, cooperate, and coordinate (CCC) with the interested public. Under the old rules, the BLM's CCC duties ran to the interested public, the affected ranchers, and the state whenever the BLM issued, renewed, or modified a grazing permit for a certain allotment. The new rules no longer require the BLM to CCC with the interested public on the following decisions: (1) adjustments to allotment boundaries, (2) changes in active use, (3) emergency allotment closures, (4) issuance or renewal of individual permits or leases, and (5) issuance of temporary nonrenewable grazing permits and leases. For these matters, the interested public would be cut out of the discussions between the BLM and the ranchers at the formulation stage of decisions. * * *

5. *Changes to Range Improvement Ownership & Control*

The Final Rule amends 43 C.F.R. § 4120.3–2 to allow shared title of permanent range improvements constructed under cooperative range improvements agreements. Title would be shared in proportion to the permittee's and Government's contributions to the on-the-ground project development and construction costs.

The Final Rule also (1) removes the prior requirement that livestock water rights on BLM land be acquired and perfected in the name of the United States only, and not in the permittee's name, (2) redefines the definitions of "grazing preference" and "active use" to be an historic forage allocation (expressed in AUMs) attached to the base property; (3) allows permittees to extend both livestock numbers and periods of use so long as overall AUMs remain within the amount of "active use" authorized by permit; (4) limits the BLM's ability to withhold, suspend or cancel grazing permits for violations of laws by permittees committed on lands other than the allotment covered by the permittee's permit; and (5) added Tribal, state, local, and county-established grazing boards to those groups the BLM routinely cooperates with in administering laws related to grazing. * * *

[A. The NEPA Challenge]

... NEPA requires that the BLM take a hard look in the FEIS as to why public participation and CCC duties should be more limited than those in the 1995 regulations. One reason advanced by the BLM for this change involves the cost of maintaining a list of "interested publics" that must get "periodic mailings at taxpayer expense" but have not "participated ... in years." The BLM does not list the specific costs it incurs, beyond noting that it has incurred "substantial expenses" in supporting public participation generally and that "[s]ome of these resources have been devoted to tasks such as maintaining lists" of persons that have not participated in years. *Id.*

The BLM has advanced other reasons for the changes, including the following:

> BLM believes that in-depth involvement of the public in day-to-day management decisions is neither warranted nor administratively efficient and can in fact delay BLM remedial response actions necessitated by resource conditions. Day-to-day management decisions implement land use planning decisions in which the public has already had full opportunity to participate. Also, such in-depth public involvement can delay routine management responses, such as minor adjustments in livestock numbers or use periods to respond to dynamic on-the-ground conditions. Cooperation with permittees and lessees, on the other hand, usually results in more expeditious steps to address resource conditions and can help avoid lengthy administrative appeals.

See FEIS at pp. 5–24 to 5–25.

Public participation is, by nature, messy. To manage it, agencies must be "given ample latitude to adapt their rules and policies to changed circumstances." *Motor Vehicle Mfgs.*, 463 U.S. at 42. * * *

The FEIS makes no attempt to explain how things have changed since 1995 to justify curtailing public input. *See Motor Vehicle Manufacturers Assoc. v. State Farm*, 463 U.S. 29, 42 (1983). The required "reasoned analysis" for changing course on public input is entirely missing. There is no detailed discussion of either the volume or quality of comments the BLM receives on day-to-day issues. Has the volume become overwhelming? Are the comments mostly specious? What are the costs and employee resources involved? These questions are not addressed in the FEIS.

When "the information in the ... EIS [is] so incomplete ... that the ... public could not make an informed comparison of the alternatives, revision of the EIS may be necessary...." *Ecology Center, Inc. v. Austin*, 430 F.3d 1057, 1067 (9th Cir. 2005). In this case, the FEIS does not contain enough information to allow decision-makers and the public to make an informed evaluation of the BLM's claim that efficiency compels these changes. * * *

NEPA's "hard look" requires "a discussion of adverse impacts that does not improperly minimize negative side effects." *Earth Island*, 442 F.3d at 1159. The FEIS violates NEPA because it improperly minimizes the negative side effects of limiting public input.

[B. The FLPMA Challenge]

With regard to their FLPMA challenge, WWP must carry a "heavy" burden, as discussed above. WWP, in its facial challenge, "must establish that no set of circumstances exists under which the [regulations] would be valid." *Rust*, 500 U.S. at 183.

That standard requires the Court to examine first whether the BLM's regulatory revisions are authorized by Congress under FLPMA. The revised regulations delete the requirements to consult, cooperate and coordinate with the "interested public" on crucial decisions involving the issuance of grazing permits. The BLM's intent was to "[k]eep[] day-to-day stuff between the agency and permittee." Explaining this revision in similar terms, the FEIS stated that it "focuses the role of the interested public on planning decisions and reports that influence daily management, rather than on daily management decisions themselves."

Yet this revision is in direct conflict with the language of FLPMA and cannot be reconciled by some later interpretation. In FLPMA, Congress stated that the BLM, "by regulation *shall* establish procedures ... to give ... the public adequate notice and an opportunity to comment upon the formulation of standards and criteria for, and to participate in the preparation and execution of plans and programs for, and the management of, the public lands." See 43 U.S.C. § 1739(e) (emphasis added). * * *

The clear meaning of the statutory language quoted above is that public input is required on long-range issues ("preparation ... of plans and programs") as well as on day-to-day issues ("the management of" and "execution of" those long-range plans). *See National Wildlife Federation v. Burford*, 835 F.2d 305, 322 (9th Cir. 1987) (rejecting BLM's argument that FLPMA's public input provisions only apply to land use planning process as opposed to individual revocation decisions).

Grazing permit issues are the crucial "management" and "execution" tools of the BLM to carry out its long-range plans. In the management of BLM lands, this is where the rubber meets the road. It is the grazing permit (or TNR permit) that determines the amount and season of use, the grazing boundaries, and the myriad of details that directly affect the land.

Congress, in FLPMA, did not give the BLM any discretion to cut the public out of these management and execution issues. Yet the BLM seeks to grant itself that forbidden discretion in its regulatory revisions. Accordingly, under *Rush* and *Salerno*, WWP has met its "heavy" burden of proving that those revisions limiting public input constitute a facial violation of FLPMA.

3.   *Changes to FRH & Range Improvement Ownership*

WWP argues that the BLM's own experts concluded in the ARC–DEIS that the proposed regulatory changes concerning the FRH and ownership of range improvements and water rights would have adverse effects on wildlife and riparian conditions. WWP asserts that these expert opinions were suppressed by the BLM and never presented to the public.

Under NEPA "[a]gencies shall insure the professional integrity, including scientific integrity, of the discussions and analyses in environmental impact statements. They shall identify any methodologies used and shall make explicit reference by footnote to the scientific and other sources relied upon for conclusions in the statement." *Earth Island*, 442 F.3d at 1159–60. The BLM failed to comply with this standard. * * *

On closer review, the "hard look" is missing. The BLM's own experts found in the ARC–DEIS that the proposed regulatory changes would have "a slow long-term adverse effect on wildlife and biological diversity, including threatened and endangered and special status species," and would lead to a continual decline in upland and riparian habitats, and would cause "the numbers of special status species [to] continue to increase." These findings are supported by lengthy and detailed citations to scientific authorities. Yet there is no evidence that the BLM considered these substantial criticisms before publishing the proposed rules just 3 weeks after the ARC–DEIS was issued. * * *

It is true that the Addendum does address *some* of the ARC–DEIS analysis. But the FEIS had already been issued, raising a serious question whether the Addendum contains analysis or justification for a decision already made. Supporting the latter conclusion is the fact that the Addendum's discussion of the ARC–DEIS only identifies minor inaccuracies and is buried deep in the Addendum, almost as an aside. The public never got a chance to comment on what discussion there was in the Addendum.

Most importantly, however, the Addendum never refuted the more substantive criticisms of the ARC–DEIS. The BLM's failure to explain itself in the DEIS and FEIS deprived the public of its ability to comment on the BLM's reasoning process. *See Earth Island*, 442 F.3d at 1159 (holding that an FEIS meets the hard look requirement only if it "foster[s] both informed decision-making and informed public participation").

Certainly the BLM has broad discretion to resolve conflicts among its own experts. *Greenpeace Action v. Franklin*, 14 F.3d 1324, 1332 (9th Cir. 1992). However, a recitation of that conflict and its resolution must take place in the EIS. *State of California v. Block*, 690 F. 2d 753, 770–71 (9th Cir. 1982). Here, the conflict among experts was not revealed until the Addendum was filed after the public comment period was closed.

For all of these reasons, the Court finds that the FRH changes and the changes to ownership of range improvements and allowing entities other than the BLM to hold water rights violate NEPA.

6.   *Remedy*

The Court has found that the BLM's regulatory revisions violate NEPA [and] FLPMA. * * *

[T]he BLM must give a "hard look" at these revisions under NEPA, and the Court will accordingly enjoin the operation of these revisions until that "hard look" is completed. Finally, the injunction would also be supported by the FLPMA violations set forth above.

If the revisions are enjoined, an issue arises as to whether the prior regulations are revived. In *Citizens for Better Forestry v. United States*, 2007 WL 966985 (N.D. Ca. March 30, 2007), the court enjoined Forest Service regulations known as the "2005 Rule" and then stated "it would seem that the rule immediately preceding the 2005 Rule would control future agency action. Nevertheless this is a determination for the USDA to make in the first instance." *Id.* at *59.

The Court agrees with this analysis. While it would seem that the 1995 regulations would govern until new compliant regulations are passed, that determination is for the BLM to make in the first instance. * * *

QUESTIONS AND DISCUSSION

1. What vision of natural resources policy underlies the BLM's new rules?

2. Although the new regulations preserved the Range Advisory Councils rather than returning to Grazing Advisory Boards, they did add a requirement, as noted by the court, that the BLM cooperate with tribal, state, local and county-established grazing boards when reviewing allotment management plans. Is this a move in favor of public participation? Does public choice theory help explain the answer?

3. The court comments in the first paragraph of the opinion: "Without any showing of improvement, the new BLM regulations loosen restrictions on grazing." Later, the court cites *Motor Vehicle Manufacturers Ass'n v. State Farm*, 463 U.S. 29, 42 (1983), which is discussed in note 3 on page 997, and remarks: "The FEIS makes no attempt to explain how things have changed since 1995 to justify curtailing public input. The required 'reasoned analysis' for changing course is entirely missing." 2007 WL 1667618, at *10. How might the BLM have responded to this reasoning if given the chance?

4. Were the BLM's concerns about in-depth public involvement, discussed by the court on page 1002, well founded? Think back to the two models of administrative law discussed in Chapter 3—scientific expertise and interest group representation. Which model is the BLM espousing? Why not just let the experts at the agencies make the decisions? Is the political process a sufficient check on mismanagement?

5. The court concludes that FLPMA requires the Secretary to seek public input on day-to-day management issues. Is that what Congress likely intended in § 1739(e) quoted in the opinion above? Did the BLM propose to entirely cut out the public? Should the court have shown more deference to the BLM's interpretation and application of FLPMA? If you were given an assignment to draft an amended FLPMA, what sort of public participation requirements would you write into the law?

6. Recall the discussion of the Wayne Hage case at note 4 on page 946. Hage was awarded compensation on the theory that the Forest Service had precluded him from transferring the state water rights associated with his terminated grazing permits. As noted in the opinion, one of the rule changes proposed by the BLM was to remove the "requirement that livestock water rights on BLM land be acquired and perfected in the name of the United States only, and not in the permittee's name." Before 1995, ownership of water rights for livestock grazing varied, depending on whether the state allowed water rights to be acquired in the name of the permittee. What incentives and concerns are created by these two alternative versions of ownership of water rights?

7. Reflecting on the regulatory changes from Secretary Watt to Secretary Babbitt and then this latest attempt at regulatory change from the Bush Administration, what does it say about the nature of rulemaking and agency decisionmaking and about natural resource lawmaking more generally?

PROBLEM EXERCISE: THE GRAND CANYON TRUST RETIRES GRAZING PERMITS

The Grand Canyon Trust (GCT) is a conservation organization dedicated to protecting and restoring the red rock canyons of the Colorado Plateau. One of its protection and restoration efforts focused on negotiating with ranchers to retire their grazing permits in places like Canyonlands and Capitol Reef National Parks, Glen Canyon National Recreation Area, and the Grand Staircase–Escalante National Monument. The following is an excerpt from GCT's description of its efforts:

Bill Hedden, *Grand Canyon Trust Grazing Retirement Program, available at* http://www.grandcanyontrust.org/arches/grazing.html

The Trust negotiates directly with willing ranchers to structure agreements in which either the ranchers are compensated for relinquishing their grazing privileges to BLM, or the permits are sold directly to our non-profit grazing corporation. In the latter case, the grazing corporation offers to relinquish the permits to BLM if the agency concludes, through an appropriate public process (generally an Environmental Assessment), to amend its resource management plan to cancel grazing on the allotment. Any water rights associated with the grazing permits are transferred to the State Division of Wildlife Resources to be held perpetually for wildlife use.

The risk of this method is that the permanence of such actions is not ironclad. During reasonable times it is very unlikely that grazing would ever be successfully reinitiated in one of the high profile areas where we apply this technique. First, we only do this where the resource professionals within the agencies themselves consider grazing inappropriate, and second, any future applicant for reinstitution of grazing would have to go through a daunting NEPA process that would provide opportunities for us and others to defend the allotment closures. * * *

Our first application of this technique, in partnership with the Conservation Fund, resulted in retirement of grazing from 55,000 acres around the Horseshoe Canyon section of Canyonlands National Park. The springs and archaeological treasures of the canyon have been protected from cows since 1996. Next, we structured a deal to retire grazing from the Lost Spring Canyon area, which was added to Arches National Park in November 1998 through legislation crafted by the Trust. Immediately after the park expansion, the Trust bought out the rancher, permanently removing cows from the entire system of five canyons added to the park. Within the first year after cows were removed, NPS documented a 30% increase in native species diversity in the canyons.

Establishment of the new Grand Staircase/Escalante National Monument set the stage for one of the Trust's most significant grazing retirement projects thus far. With five ranching families, we negotiated agreements that completely removed grazing from the entire main canyon of the Escalante River and from more than a dozen of the most important side-canyons, as well.... The retirement encompasses 132 miles of some of the loveliest stream-filled canyons on earth, including more than 67 miles of the Escalante River. * * *

The Trust's recent grazing deals were the first transacted through the new non-profit Canyonlands Grazing Corporation. This corporation is qualified to hold federal grazing permits through base property consisting of leases on state lands and easements on private property. In early June, 2001 the corporation bought the 78,000 acre Drip Tanks pasture of the Headwaters allotment on the Kaiparowits Plateau, with its 906 AUMs, from rancher Franklin O'Driscoll. The allotment is held in non-use due to drought. In August, the corporation bought the 43,000 acre Moody allotment on the east side of the Escalante River, on the border of Capitol Reef National Park and Glen Canyon National Recreation Area. This area, too, is held in drought-induced non-use. Consideration of the future status of these allotments has been deferred to a monument-wide Grazing EIS which is in the early stages of preparation.

The final transaction in this series was made in late fall of 2001. Canyonlands Grazing Corporation purchased the federal and state permits for the Last Chance allotment in the Grand Staircase–Escalante National Monument. * * *

The Last Chance is the largest and most remote allotment in the entire monument. It includes great areas of wildlands and remote canyons where cattle do not belong, plus a smaller area that has been developed as rangeland. The developed area has fenced sections of State Land that serve as base property, windmills and areas seeded with crested wheatgrass. We negotiated a deal to retire grazing on the wild sections of the allotment and exchange grazing privileges on the developed area to retire yet another high priority allotment in the monument. Rancher Dell LeFevre, who held the permit for the 18,245 acre Big Bowns Bench allotment along Horse Canyon and the Escalante River, traded his permit and relocated to the developed portion of Last Chance.

Retiring Big Bowns Bench was a top priority [for] all the conservation groups working in the monument because the allotment's Horse Canyon is a critical riparian area that also allows cattle into the retired portions of the Escalante Canyon. Closing the allotment makes it possible for BLM to close an administrative road that cuts the Escalante Canyons Wilderness Study Area in half, and forecloses agency plans to construct a $400,000 cattle-watering system at the confluence of Horse Creek and the Escalante River. At the end of 2001, BLM began an Environmental Assessment of the Last Chance, Big Bowns Bench proposal. [eds. The Environmental Assessment was undertaken as part of the monument-wide Grazing EIS.]

At the same time, developments on the larger stage helped focus on this program the resentment of local people opposed to President Clinton's 1996 designation of the Grand Staircase–Escalante National Monument. Just as the three grazing EAs were publicly announced, the National Public Lands Grazing Campaign went public with its proposal to enact federal legislation creating a grazing buyout fund coupled with permanent retirement of allotments purchased with these public monies.... Suddenly, there was an audience for southern Utah wise-use activists who claimed that there is a conspiracy to eliminate all grazing in the West. The local chapter of People for the USA became the Canyon Country Rural Alliance, lobbying at every level of state and federal government to prevent our market-based transactions from succeeding.

Secretary Norton, who had written in support of the Last Chance deal as an excellent way of resolving resource conflicts, was caught between her fondness for the free market and her allegiance to old guard Bureau of Livestock and Mining staffers. Nonetheless, when BLM completed the EAs in the spring of 2002, it decided to close the allotments because managers and scientists had found that alternative would provide important benefits like: richer soils; more diverse and healthy vegetation; better wildlife diversity and abundance; cleaner, healthier streams; and better opportunities for recreation. * * *

Locals charge that the ranchers are being forced out of business by environmental groups, but Grand Canyon Trust has never filed an appeal, protest or lawsuit on any grazing issue anywhere. In fact, ranchers in the region have been nearly free of environmentalist interference because the conservation community has been giving this market-based approach a chance, to learn if it can work. That honeymoon is soon to end as lawsuits are now in preparation.

The decisions in the EAs were immediately protested by the counties, who claimed that the 30 month process, which generated nearly 4,000 public comments, was secretive and rushed. In fact, the EAs were some of the most comprehensive BLM has ever produced about grazing decisions, relying on the abundance of data and staff available to the agency's flagship national monument. * * *

DOI [the Department of the Interior] dithered for months until Chief Solicitor William Myers produced a new Opinion about grazing retirement in October 2002. He said that an amendment of the Resource Management Plan is the proper way to close a portion of the public lands to grazing, adding: "If the lands are within an established grazing district, BLM must analyze whether the lands are no longer 'chiefly valuable for grazing and raising forage crops' and express its rationale in a record of decision." If such a determination is made, Myers contends that the lands will then be removed from the Taylor Grazing District and closed to grazing. Absent such a finding, Myers says that the lands are subject to application for renewed grazing by a qualified permittee.

In January 2003, DOI finally issued decisions denying all points in the counties' protests; but refusing to make the Myers determination about whether the lands are chiefly valuable for grazing. The EAs laid a solid foundation for such a finding, but the agency had apparently reconsidered the larger implications of making such determinations. Instead, BLM offered to temporarily close the allotments, if we would relinquish the permits. The future status of the allotments would then be reconsidered in the Grazing EIS that is already underway. On the advice of our attorneys we refused to relinquish the permits with no assurance about their future, so we now hold the permits in non-use due to drought like so many of the other permittees in the region. When the restrictions are lifted, we will begin taking our three year period of voluntary non-use, evaluating our options based on what happens in the Grazing EIS. We may be forced to occasionally graze the allotments or sell them if BLM refuses the advice of its range scientists and insists on keeping the allotments open. Meanwhile, ranchers continue to ask whether we will buy their permits so they can get out of debt and save their private lands. Until the administration establishes a regular procedure for considering and implementing grazing closures, the answer is, "No."

QUESTIONS AND DISCUSSION

1. Could the BLM and GCT agree to retire grazing permits without amending the relevant land use plan or would an allotment need to remain available for grazing until the plan is amended? In a Solicitor's Opinion authored just prior to the end of the Clinton administration, Solicitor Leshy concluded that the Secretary could decide to retire grazing permits outside the FLPMA land use planning process. As authority, he cited Section 4 of PRIA which provides, in relevant part,

> Except where the land use planning process required pursuant to section 202 of [FLPMA] determines otherwise *or* the Secretary determines, and sets forth his reasons for this determination, that grazing uses should be discontinued (either temporarily or permanently) on certain lands, the goal of such management shall be to improve the range conditions of the public rangelands. . . .

43 U.S.C. § 1903(b) (emphasis added). He did, however, go on to say:

> As a general matter, even though PRIA contemplates that the Secretary may make decisions to retire public lands from grazing outside the FLPMA land use planning process, I believe it is preferable that the Secretary use the FLPMA process wherever possible, because of the opportunities it offers for public participation, consultation with affected governments and interests, and environmental assessment.

Authority for BLM to Act on Requests for Voluntary Retirement of Livestock Grazing Permits on BLM–Managed Public Lands, Interior Solicitor Op., Jan. 19, 2001, at 4. Solicitor Leshy's opinion was reversed by an opinion from Solicitor Myers during the Bush Administration. As the excerpt notes, Solicitor Myers opined that the BLM could only retire grazing permits if it amended the land use plan *and* determined that the lands within a grazing district were no longer "chiefly valuable for grazing and raising forage crops." 43 U.S.C. § 315. This "chiefly valuable" determination was not necessary, said Myers, for so-called Section 15 lands outside of grazing districts. *See Authority for the Bureau of Land Management to Consider Requests for Retiring Grazing Permits and Leases on Public Lands*, Interior Solicitor Op., Oct. 4, 2002.

Does it make sense that there must be a determination that land is *not* chiefly valuable for grazing before grazing is terminated even though the BLM never engaged in specific fact-finding that the lands within grazing districts were chiefly valuable for grazing purposes? If Solicitor Myer's proposal makes it harder to retire grazing permits, does it also make it harder to lease oil, gas or coal within a grazing district? Must the Secretary first determine that the lands are not "chiefly valuable" for grazing?

2. Why do you think the Department of the Interior decided not to make a determination that the allotments within the monument purchased by GCT were not "chiefly valuable" for grazing? Doesn't the existence of the buyouts themselves indicate that the land is not chiefly valuable for grazing purposes?

3. Without a determination that the allotments were not chiefly valuable for grazing, GCT's plan to relinquish the allotments to the BLM as part of a land use plan revision stalled. This did not mean that grazing immediately resumed on the GCT's allotments. As the excerpt indicates, GCT was not obligated to graze the allotments because they were in nonuse due to drought. What the excerpt did not address is what would happen if grazing were allowed to resume before the land use plan could be amended to eliminate grazing. As discussed in the *Public Lands Council* case, grazing permits must be used for grazing and may not be used for conservation purposes. Under BLM's grazing regulations, a permittee may elect not to place any livestock on an allotment (i.e., take "temporary nonuse") for a three year period, 43 C.F.R. § 4130.2(g)(2). Under the new regulations enjoined in *Kraayenbrink*, excerpted *supra*, the three year limit has been eliminated in favor of a year-to-year determination. *See* 43 C.F.R. § 4130.4. If the BLM decides against allowing a permittee to take nonuse, the permittee must use the approved number of AUMs or risk the BLM canceling the permit and making the AUMs available to another rancher. 43 C.F.R. §§ 4130.2(h), 4130.6–2.

In fact, as Bill Hedden feared, grazing was allowed to resume on two of three allotments purchased by GCT and GCT was faced with a choice—it could relinquish the grazing permits to BLM, which would allow other ranchers to graze the permits pending BLM's revision of a land use plan precluding grazing, or GCT could become a rancher and graze the allotments itself. As Hedden suggested GCT would, GCT, or more accurately, GCT's subsidiary—the nonprofit Canyonlands Grazing Corporation—chose the latter approach. The Canyonlands Grazing Corporation (CGC) retained the permits and started grazing two of the three allotments, but at much reduced levels approved by the BLM. Several local ranchers, including Dell LeFevre, applied to use the AUMs not used by the CGC. The BLM denied the applications on the ground that there was not any additional forage beyond what was already allocated to CGC.

After the rancher's appeal was denied by the Department of the Interior's Office of Hearings and Appeals, the ranchers filed suit in federal district court, arguing that CGC was not qualified to hold a grazing permit because (1) it was not a stock owner at the time it originally applied for a transfer of the grazing permits and (2) it did not have an intent to graze the allotments. The court rejected the arguments. *Stewart v. Kempthorne*, 593 F. Supp. 2d 1240 (D. Utah 2008). With respect to the first argument, the court observed that persons starting up a ranching operation should not be precluded from acquiring permits for the purpose of doing so. It then observed:

> [S]ubstantial evidence supports the ALJ's finding that CGC owned four head of cattle before BLM issued CGC the grazing permits for the allotments.... In addition to the four cattle that CGC owned in January 2003, CGC acquired more cattle so that by the time of the hearing in May 2005, CGC owned 20 head of cattle on the allotments. In fact, based on the substantial evidence submitted at the hearing regarding CGC's stock ownership, the ALJ found that CGC "has become a classic example of a grazing success story. What began as a few inherited cattle ... and then grew into a small herd of some 20 cattle at the time of BLM's Decisions on appeal herein, has subsequently grown into the

acquisition of the Kane and Two–Mile ranches on the so-called Arizona Strip. With these acquisitions, [CGC] has become one of the largest, active grazing permittees in the Southern–Utah, Northern–Arizona region.... With the acquisition of the Kane and Two–Mile ranches in 2005 for some $4.5 million, [CGC] has become a much bigger, active grazing permittee than any of the [Plaintiffs] in this case, thereby proving the wisdom of BLM in transferring permits to [CGC] when it was merely a start-up organization."

Id. at 1249–50. What motivated the ranchers to file this lawsuit? Why not allow CGC to use its grazing permits as it sees fit? A rural county commissioner suggested the following:

"If this process of buyout, relinquishment and permanent closure of the allotment to grazing—if that process can take hold, it'll sweep like wildfire through the grazing communities," he said.

Federal agencies will apply pressure on ranchers, driving them to sell to environmentalists, he worries.

"It's the path of least resistance to the ranchers," he said.

According to Habbeshaw, it's important to support the tradition of public land grazing, "rather than the closure of the allotment because somebody doesn't believe cows should be out there." ...

"I think ... it threatens the livestock industry in the west, which relies on public land grazing," he said.

Joe Bauman, *Grazing Permit a Threat?*, DESERET NEWS, Jan. 31, 2006. Are you persuaded by this argument? How does this argument fit with the assertion that ranchers retain a property right in their grazing permits?

4. Recall that FLPMA requires the BLM to manage the public lands "in accordance with the land use plans developed by [the Secretary]." 43 U.S.C. § 1732(a). If BLM amends its relevant land use plan to preclude grazing in an area covered by a grazing retirement agreement, could a rancher challenge the plan on the grounds that conforming a land use plan to satisfy a private, monetary transaction is a decision made outside the FLPMA land use planning process (43 U.S.C. § 1712(c))? Is such a claim likely to be successful or is a court likely to show deference to the Secretary's land use planning?

5. Do the previous notes help explain why the Grand Canyon Trust believes that the permanence of these retirement agreements is not "ironclad"? Why might this be the case even in those instances where the BLM amends its land use plans to prohibit grazing on an allotment relinquished by GCT? Do you agree with Bill Hedden's assessment that grazing is unlikely to be reinstated once a land use plan is amended? Do the statistics in Chapter 6 (page 581) on increasing use of the public lands for recreation and preservation suggest an additional answer to those offered by Hedden?

6. From the environmentalists' perspective, are there any downsides to these retirement agreements? Do the agreements allow federal land managers to abdicate their regulatory responsibilities to prevent grazing harm?

7. What do you suppose catalyzed the Escalante Canyons retirement agreement? Dell LeFevre, one of the ranchers participating in the deal, remarked that increased tourism in the area since President Clinton's declaration of the monument had made ranching more difficult: "People keep going through and leaving the gate open. Then my cows get into areas they're not supposed to be and that means trouble for me." Lisa Church, *Fun–Hogs to Replace Cows in Utah Monument*, High Country News, Feb. 1, 1999, at 4. What sort of trouble might LeFevre have been talking about?

8. Hedden concludes the excerpt by noting that buyouts cannot continue "[u]ntil the administration establishes a regular procedure for considering and implementing grazing closures." In fact, the GCT has not pursued buyouts after the Myer's opinion. Instead it has concentrated on buying base ranches (like those described in Note 3) and then running as few cattle on the adjoining federal lands as possible. What sort of regular procedure would make the most sense? Can there be such a procedure without an amendment of existing statutes and regulations?

9. What do these grazing retirement deals suggest about the desirability of privatizing grazing permits? Would such deals be more or less common if grazing permits were privatized? Whose approach to restricting grazing do you prefer, that of Professor Feller in the *Comb Wash* litigation or that of the Grand Canyon Trust? Are the two mutually exclusive or does the success of the Grand Canyon Trust depend in part on Professor Feller's success? Do you think the price per AUM paid by the Grand Canyon Trust is more or less than it would pay in an open market?

10. As noted above (page 978), several environmental groups have formed the National Public Lands Grazing Campaign with the intent of pushing legislation allowing for a federal buyout of grazing permits at $175 per AUM. Would a federal buyout have any advantages over private agreements like those negotiated by the Grand Canyon Trust? Any disadvantages?

VI. Intersecting Laws and Their Impact on Range Management

Given the limitations of FLPMA's multiple use management command, range reform activists have looked more and more to other environmental statutes, even though those statutes are not directed specifically at grazing, for leverage to change grazing management. The first instance of this approach was NRDC's use of NEPA discussed earlier in Section IV.B. Additional approaches include the Clean Water Act, the Wild and Scenic Rivers Act, and the Endangered Species Act.

A. The Clean Water Act

Another environmental group that has led in seeking environmental protection of range resources is the Oregon Natural Desert Association (ONDA), an environmental organization dedicated to restoring and protecting eastern Oregon's high deserts and ending grazing on the public lands. *See* http://www.onda.org (ONDA's web site). In 1996, ONDA led several other environmental groups and the Warm Springs Indian tribe in filing a lawsuit alleging that the Forest Service was violating § 401 of the Clean Water Act, 33 U.S.C. § 1341(a)(1), by issuing grazing permits without first obtaining a certification from the state that allowing grazing would not violate state water quality standards. *See Oregon Natural Desert Ass'n v. Thomas*, 940 F. Supp. 1534 (D. Or. 1996). Section 401 requires state certification for any person applying for a federal permit for any activity that may result in a discharge. 33 U.S.C. § 1341(a)(1). ONDA's argument was that the term "discharge" in the Act was not limited to "point sources" (defined in the act as "any discernible, confined and discrete conveyance ...," 33 U.S.C. § 1362(14)) but also includes nonpoint source pollution like livestock waste. When the district court accepted the argument, grazing activists had hope that future permittees would be required to ensure their grazing would not violate state water quality standards. The decision, however, was reversed on appeal. *See Oregon Natural Desert Ass'n v. Dombeck*, 172 F.3d 1092 (9th Cir. 1998), *cert. denied*, 528 U.S. 964 (1999). *See also Oregon Natural Desert Ass'n v. U.S. Forest Service*, 2008 WL 140657 (D. Or. 2008) (rejecting ONDA's argument that the decision in *Dombeck* should be revisited because of the Supreme Court's 2006 decision in *S.D. Warren Co. v. Maine Board of Environmental Protection*, 547 U.S. 370 (2006), which determined that release of water from hydroelectric dams constituted a discharge). For a brief in favor of applying section 401 in the grazing context, see Debra L. Donahue, *The Untapped Power of Clean Water Act Section 401*, 23 ECOLOGY L.Q. 201 (1996). *See also* Peter M. Lacy, *Addressing Water Pollution from Livestock Grazing After* ONDA v. Dombeck*: Legal Strategies Under the Clean Water Act*, 30 ENVTL. L. 617 (2000) (advocating use of other provisions of the Clean Water Act to address livestock pollution, including using the Act's total maximum daily load provisions).

B.   THE WILD AND SCENIC RIVERS ACT

Although it did not prevail under the Clean Water Act, ONDA has had more success attacking public lands grazing under the Wild and Scenic Rivers Act. 16 U.S.C. §§ 1271–84. In a series of lawsuits, ONDA convinced courts that BLM was required to manage grazing near wild and scenic designated rivers to "protect and enhance the values which caused [the river] to be included in said system," with primary emphasis given to "esthetic, scenic, historic, archaeologic, and scientific features" (16 U.S.C. § 1281(a)). *See Oregon Natural Desert Ass'n v. Green*, 953 F. Supp. 1133 (D. Or. 1997) (ordering BLM to work with ONDA to craft the terms of a permanent injunction that would protect and enhance the river's outstanding values); *National Wildlife Fed'n v. Cosgriffe*, 21 F. Supp. 2d 1211 (D. Or. 1998) (ordering BLM to prepare a plan protecting the river's values but refusing to enjoin grazing before preparation of a plan); *Oregon Natural Desert Ass'n v. Singleton (Singleton I)*, 47 F. Supp. 2d 1182 (D. Or. 1998) (ordering BLM to prepare an EIS and consider whether cattle grazing was consistent with the WSRA's objectives). ONDA's biggest success came in *Oregon Natural Desert Ass'n v. Singleton (Singleton II)*, 75 F. Supp. 2d 1139 (D. Or. 1999), where the court required BLM to remove cattle from portions of the Ohwyee River watershed. As in any case weighing injunctive relief, the court balanced the competing claims of injury and concluded that the degradation to the river trumped the loss of 26,976 AUM, which amounted to about 26% of the AUMs in the river corridor, particularly when the overall effect on the county's economy was negligible. *Id.* at 1152.

See generally Charlton H. Bonham, *The Wild and Scenic Rivers Act and the Oregon Trilogy*, 21 PUB. LAND & RESOURCES L. REV. 109 (2000).

C. THE ENDANGERED SPECIES ACT

While ONDA worked with the Clean Water Act and Wild and Scenic Rivers Act, others have focused their grazing reform efforts on the Endangered Species Act (ESA). The ESA's potential for affecting grazing practices was evidenced in two seminal cases involving the endangered Palila bird. *Palila v. Hawaii Dep't of Land & Natural Resources*, 639 F.2d 495 (9th Cir. 1981); *Palila v. Hawaii Dep't of Land & Natural Resources*, 852 F.2d 1106 (9th Cir. 1988). As described in Chapter 4 (pages 386–87), the Audubon Society filed suit on behalf of the Palila seeking an order requiring Hawaii to remove feral goats and sheep from the Palila's habitat on the slopes of Mauna Kea. It later added mouflon sheep to its complaint, triggering the second case. The Palila depends for its survival on mature mamane-naio woodlands, both for food and shelter and nesting sites. The sheep and goats were browsing on the seedlings of the mamane-naio tree, which severely limited the number of trees reaching maturity. The Ninth Circuit concluded that Hawaii, by not removing the feral sheep and goats and by introducing the mouflon sheep for the enjoyment of sport hunters, had violated Section 9 of the ESA which makes it unlawful to "take" any endangered species. 16 U.S.C. § 1538(a)(1). Despite the fact that the grazing did not cause any direct, immediate physical harm to the Palila, the Court ordered Hawaii to remove the offending animals. As discussed in Chapter 4, recall that the term "take" is defined to include conduct that causes "harm." *Id.* § 1532(19). And by regulation, the Secretary has defined harm to include "significant habitat modification or degradation where it actually kills or injures wildlife by significantly impairing essential behavioral patterns, including breeding, feeding, or sheltering." 50 C.F.R. § 17.3.

Palila's implications for grazing management are significant. If habitat modification can constitute a "take," then whenever there is a threatened or endangered species present on a grazing allotment, private grazers are at risk under Section 9's take prohibition and the BLM and Forest Service are obligated under Section 7 "to insure that any action authorized, funded, or carried out by such agency . . . is not likely to jeopardize the continued existence of any endangered species." 16 U.S.C. § 1536(a)(2). The potential breadth of the holding in *Palila* may be one reason why Justice O'Connor in her concurrence in *Babbitt v. Sweet Home Chapter of Communities for a Greater Oregon*, 515 U.S. 687 (1995), emphasized that the harm regulation was limited by "ordinary principles of proximate causation," which in her view "call into question" the *Palila* decision. *Id.* at 708–09.

Testing the application of the ESA to federal grazing management, environmental groups have had their greatest success in compelling relevant federal agencies to consult about grazing impacts on listed species under Section 7 of the ESA. 16 U.S.C. § 1536(a)(2). *See Forest Guardians v. Johanns*, 450 F.3d 455 (9th Cir. 2006) (requiring the Forest Service to reinitiate § 7 consultation on thirty grazing allotments because the inadequacy of its monitoring constituted a modification to the AMP not previously considered), *Pacific Rivers Council v. Thomas*, 30 F.3d 1050 (9th Cir. 1994), *cert. denied*, 514 U.S. 1082 (1995) (enjoining the Forest Service from conducting any range or logging activities affecting the threatened Snake River chinook salmon pending consultation on its existing land and resource management plans); *Center for Biological Diversity v. Bureau of Land Management*, 2001 WL 777088 (N.D. Cal. 2001) (approving consent decree under which cattle were removed from certain desert tortoise habitat pending BLM's completion of consultation). The impact of these suits has been more than procedural. As a result of a suit filed by the Center for Biological Diversity and Forest Guardians in 1997, the Forest Service agreed to remove or fence out some 15,000 cattle from 230 miles of streams on 75 federal grazing allotments in Arizona and New Mexico. *See* Tony Davis, *Healing the Gila*, HIGH COUNTRY NEWS, Oct. 22, 2001, at 1, 8–11.

It is not clear whether Section 9 will be as effective a tool against grazing. Along the lines of Justice O'Connor's *Sweet Home* concurrence, there remain questions about the difficulty of proving grazing as a cause of "take." In *Arizona Cattle Growers' Ass'n v. U.S. Fish & Wildlife Service*, 63 F. Supp. 2d 1034 (D. Ariz. 1998), *aff'd* 273 F.3d 1229 (9th Cir. 2001), the court found that BLM's issuance of an incidental take statement was arbitrary and capricious because the agency had not developed a sufficient factual record that grazing would result in the actual death or injury of the affected species. *Id.* at 1042. In fact, the Fish & Wildlife Service had not produced evidence that the listed species were even present on the particular allotments at issue. *Id.* The court concluded: "The ITS [incidental taking statements] identify only degradation to potential habitats, rather than actual injury or death to existing members of the listed species. Thus, Defendants are unable to demonstrate that cattle grazing will result in 'harm'...." *Id.* at 1045.

Before either Section 7 or Section 9 can have an impact, a species must be listed. A potentially significant decision in that regard was *Western Watersheds Project v. Fish and Wildlife Service*, 535 F. Supp. 2d 1173 (D. Idaho 2007). The court found that the Fish & Wildlife Service had acted arbitrarily and capriciously when it decided not to list the Greater Sage Grouse because it had failed to use the best science, particularly where a deputy assistant secretary with no background in biology had edited scientific findings and intimidated FWS staffers. *Id.* at 1176. The Sage Grouse's habitat and diet are defined by sagebrush, which is the primary habitat in which cattle graze in the western United States. If this decision results in listing, and a status review was underway when this book went to press, it could have significant potential implications for cattle grazing in the West.

QUESTIONS AND DISCUSSION

1. What proximate causation principles might Justice O'Connor have had in mind when she criticized *Palila v. Hawaii Dep't of Land & Natural Resources*, 852 F.2d 1106 (9th Cir. 1988) in her concurrence in *Babbitt v. Sweet Home Chapter of Communities for a Greater Oregon*, 515 U.S. 687, 708–09 (1995)? What sort of difficulties will proximate cause present in applying the Secretary's harm regulation to grazing? Does *Arizona Cattle Growers* suggest any answers to this question?

2. As mentioned in the text, in response to a suit filed by the Center for Biological Diversity and Forest Guardians, the Forest Service agreed to remove or fence out some 15,000 cattle from 230 miles of streams on 75 federal grazing allotments in Arizona and New Mexico. Reports suggested that grasses, sedges, willows, and other riparian vegetation have improved significantly but that there was not much improvement in the populations of the imperiled species on whose behalf the litigation was filed, although there have been rapid increases in the population of Chiricahua leopard frogs which had been proposed for listing. Unable to make a go of it under the terms of the agreement, several ranchers removed their cattle from their entire allotments: " 'It just broke me. This will break anyone,' says Glen McCarty, who pulled 175 cattle from the river northwest of Reserve. 'I'm having to sell cattle at one-fifth the normal price. How would you like to work at one-fifth of your income?' " Given the results, does it appear as if the litigation was successful? Would other approaches work better? *See* Tony Davis, *Healing the Gila*, HIGH COUNTRY NEWS, Oct. 22, 2001, at 1, 8–11.

VII. GRAZING ON STATE LANDS

Although public debate tends to focus on federal range policy, it is worth recalling that western states also operate significant grazing lease programs on the school trust lands given to the states upon their entry into the Union. *See supra* Chapter 2 (discussing how western states received two to four sections of land from each surveyed township, the income from which was to be used to support their public schools). The amount of land is substantial. About 78,000,000 acres were given in support of common schools. SENATE COMMITTEE ON INTERIOR AND INSULAR AFFAIRS, THE PUBLIC LANDS, 88TH CONG. 60 (Comm. Print 1963).

Although the state and federal permit programs have a number of similarities, there are significant differences. As discussed above (page 977, one difference is that states generally charge more per AUM than does the federal government. Another difference is that there has been more movement in the states toward allowing preservation groups to bid on grazing permits and, if successful, to dedicate the land to nongrazing use. This movement has come primarily as a result of litigation. Jon Marvel, an acerbic and controversial antigrazing activist, and his Western Watersheds Project (previously the Idaho Watersheds Project) have taken the lead in this effort. Idaho essentially prohibited grazing leases from being used for nongrazing purposes. *See* Idaho Code § 310B. Nevertheless, Marvel regularly bid against ranchers for permits to graze state school trust lands, with the intent of subleasing the lands for grazing, hopefully for less intensive use, and, if nothing else, driving up the ranchers' costs. At first, this tactic was unsuccessful because the State Land Board refused to award the permits to Marvel even where he outbid the rancher. Marvel then sued the State Land Board in the following case.

IDAHO WATERSHEDS PROJECT V. STATE BOARD OF LAND COMMISSIONERS, 133 Idaho 64, 982 P.2d 367 (1999)

In 1996, the Idaho Watersheds Project (IWP) submitted twenty-four conflict grazing lease applications (the applications) to the Idaho Department of Lands (the Department) for expiring state endowment land leases (the leases). The Department recommended to the [State Board of Land Commissioners] that IWP be deemed a "qualified applicant" for auction purposes pursuant to I.C. § 58–310B(4)* on only six of the applications. In addition, IWP filed one application for a lease that had been canceled in 1996 prior to its expiration. The Department recommended to the Board that this lease be awarded to IWP as the only applicant, but later recommended that IWP be rejected as a bidder because IWP was not a "qualified applicant." The Board decided IWP was a "qualified applicant" for three lease auctions. When these auctions were conducted, IWP was the highest bidder in two of them. The Department recommended that IWP be disqualified as the high bidder in those two auctions, and the Board approved this recommendation, citing land management considerations. Therefore, IWP received no lease awards out of its 1996 lease applications.

IWP filed suit against both the Board and the Department (collectively the State), seeking ... a declaratory judgment that I.C. § 58–310B is unconstitutional on its face and as applied.... The trial court ruled that I.C. § 58–310B is constitutional and upheld the actions of the State concerning the auctions and award of the leases. IWP appealed.

I.C. § 58–310B VIOLATES ARTICLE IX, § 8.

IWP asserts that I.C. § 58–310B violates Article IX, § 8 of the Idaho Constitution. We agree. * * *

Article IX, § 8 directs that the Board provide *"rental* of all the lands heretofore, or which may hereafter be granted to or acquired by the state by or from the general government, *under such regulations as may be prescribed by law,* ..."" (emphasis added). Therefore, we must determine whether I.C. § 58–310B is constitutional as a "regulation ... prescribed by law."

Article IX, § 8 provides that the objective of sales and leases of state endowment lands is to "secure the maximum long term financial return to the institution to which granted or to the state if not specifically granted." This is in keeping with the Idaho Admission Bill admitting Idaho into the union, which indicates that monies received from the sale or lease of school endowment lands

---

* [Eds.—Idaho Code § 58–310B provides, in relevant part,

(2) It is hereby declared that the purposes of this section are:

(a) To support the endowed institutions and the state by encouraging a healthy Idaho livestock industry so as to generate related business and employment opportunities on a state and local level, thus supporting additional sales, income and property taxes; * * *

(4) To be a qualified applicant and therefore entitled to participate at an auction for a lease under this section: * * *

(b) The applicant must be capable of and willing to fulfill all provisions of any existing written grazing management plan which meets department standards associated with the parcel;

(c) The conflict applicant's proposed use of the state land must be compatible with the purpose and terms of a written grazing management plan which meets department standards; * * *]

"shall be reserved for school purposes only." Idaho Admission Bill, 26 Stat. L. 215, ch. 656, § 5(a).

Prior to the enactment of I.C. § 58–310B, hearings in the Senate Resources and Environment Committee (the committee) disclosed that the Idaho livestock industry contributes somewhere between $1.2 and $3.8 billion to the economy of Idaho, as compared to only $78,000 earned from conflict bids for public grazing lands. Aside from the strict financial gain to the state, supporters of I.C. § 58–310B urged the committee to consider several other factors, all financially related, including the stability of the livestock industry, the effect on the overall economy of ranchers going out of business, jobs and additional tax funds generated by the livestock industry, and the effect on those who supply the livestock industry. As a result of those factors, the proponents argued that if the livestock industry were weakened, the monies to be obtained from bidding auctions would also be weakened since there would be fewer participants in the livestock industry to place bids in the first place.

During a December 1996 hearing before the Board, the Board indicated that it needed to consider sales, income, and property taxes from the businesses conducted on the leased lands in determining the "maximum long term financial return." The Board also stated that in the previous year, $22.4 million had been earned from rents on school endowment lands, which monies were funneled directly to the schools of Idaho, while an additional $800 million had been collected in various taxes that benefit the state as a whole. The factors considered by the Board in this case mirror the factors presented to the Senate and discussed prior to the enactment of I.C. § 58–310B.

Rather than seeking to provide income to the schools *and* the state in general, Article IX, § 8 requires that the State consider only the "maximum long term financial return" to the schools in the leasing of school endowment public grazing lands. Article IX, § 8 requires the Legislature to "provide by law that the general grants of land made by congress to the state shall be judiciously located and carefully preserved and held in trust, subject to disposal at public auction *for the use and benefit of the respective object for which said grants of land were made....*" (emphasis added). By attempting to promote funding for the schools *and* the state through the leasing of school endowment lands, I.C. § 58–310B violates the requirements of Article IX, § 8. By the Board's application of the considerations contained in I.C. § 58–310B, IWP was denied the opportunity to participate in auctions for the leases for which it had applied.

We acknowledge that "[t]he Board is granted broad discretion in determining what constitutes the maximum long term financial return for the schools." *Idaho Watersheds Project v. Board of Land Comm'rs*, 128 Idaho 761, 765, 918 P.2d 1206, 1210 (1996) (IWP I). Section 58–310B removes much of the Board's broad discretion, however, by impermissibly directing the Board to focus on the schools, the state, and the Idaho livestock industry in assessing lease applications, all to the detriment of other potential bidders like IWP, which might provide "maximum long term financial return" to the schools, but not to the state and the Idaho livestock industry.

Having declared I.C. § 58–310B to be unconstitutional, it necessarily follows that the 1996 leases the Board awarded for which IWP was an applicant but was not allowed to bid at an auction were improperly awarded and must be opened for applications again....

QUESTIONS AND DISCUSSION

1. Jon Marvel, who has derided ranchers as "welfare queens," "champion whiners," and members of "a violent subculture," has few friends in the Idaho ranching community. *See* Stephen Stuebner, *Jon Marvel vs. The Marlboro Man: Idaho Architect Gets Nasty in Hopes of Healing Public Lands*, HIGH COUNTRY NEWS, Aug. 2, 1999, at 1, 8. Despite, or perhaps because of, his confrontational tactics, he has now succeeded in acquiring a number of grazing leases. Their cost has actually been quite low. For one lease of 777 acres he outbid the rancher $1,500 to $1,200; on another lease of 1,236 acres he prevailed $750 to $500, and on a 3,986 acre parcel, his bid of $1,800 topped the rancher's bid of $1,600. *See* Western Watersheds Project, *Sample Press Coverage, 2000*, http://www.westernwatersheds.org/news_media/press/press_2000/1press00.html.

2. Are you persuaded by the Board's arguments about the financial benefits of the livestock industry? If you represented the Idaho Watersheds Project how might you answer this economic argument?

3. The Idaho Supreme Court's decision turned on its interpretation of the state constitution, but would the Court have reached a different result if the constitution specifically dedicated school trust lands to grazing purposes? In *Lassen v. Arizona ex rel. Arizona Highway Dep't*, 385 U.S. 458 (1967), the United States Supreme Court held that Arizona was obligated to obtain "full value" when it disposed of school trust lands granted in its state enabling act (the federal legislation authorizing a state constitutional convention). Idaho's constitutional obligation to receive the "maximum long term financial return" from its school lands thus may also be a federal obligation. Does this suggest that the Idaho decision can be exported to other states in the West?

If states have a federally created trust obligation to obtain the maximum economic returns for their school children, does it necessarily follow that the range will be managed in a more environmentally friendly manner? What if, for example, a bidder sought to use the land for an ORV track or a dude ranch?

Will managing school trust lands for preservation purposes typically satisfy *Lassen*'s standard of obtaining "full value" from trust lands? In *Branson School Dist. RE–82 v. Romer*, 161 F.3d 619, 633 (10th Cir. 1998), *cert. denied*, 526 U.S. 1068 (1999), the Tenth Circuit reviewed a 1996 amendment to the Colorado constitution which made a number of changes to management of school trust lands, including establishing a permanent 300,000 acre "stewardship trust" under which the acres were to be managed only for uses that would "enhance [their] beauty, natural values, open space, and wildlife habitat." *Id.* at 629. The court found that Colorado, by virtue of its enabling act, had a fiduciary obligation with respect to its school land grants but ruled that the 300,000 acre stewardship trust was not a facial violation of that fiduciary obligation because Colorado still had plenty of other school lands to sell and it was possible to conceive of income being derived from compatible uses on the 300,000 acres. *Id.* at 640.

4. Like Jon Marvel and the Idaho Watersheds Project, Forest Guardians has bid on state grazing leases in the Southwest and then filed litigation when unsuccessful. In *Forest Guardians v. Wells*, 34 P.3d 364 (Ariz. 2001), the Arizona Supreme Court held that the State Land Commissioner could not reject conservationists' bids on grazing permits simply because they did not intend to use the land for grazing. The bids, said the court, had to be reviewed with an eye toward whether they were "in the long term, best for the school trust lands and their beneficiaries." *Id.* at 373. Forest Guardians has successfully leased state trust lands for restoration purposes in New Mexico. *See New Mexico Environmentalists Lease State Lands*, HIGH COUNTRY NEWS, Nov. 25, 1996, http://www.hcn.org/servlets/hcn.Article?article_id=2924. However, a New Mexico court of appeals held that Forest Guardians lacked standing to make a facial challenge to State Land Office procedures inhibiting conservation groups from bidding successfully on grazing leases. *Forest Guardians v. Powell*, 24 P.3d 803 (2001), *cert. denied*, 26 P.3d 103 (N.M. 2001). For a review of nongrazing use of state trust lands, see Sally K. Fairfax & Andrea Issod, *Trust Principles as a Tool for Grazing Reform: Learning from Four State Cases*, 33 ENVTL. L. 341 (2003).

5. What does the experience of Idaho, and the other western states in note three, *supra*, suggest about the appropriate scale for managing public resources? Are grazing reform efforts more promising at the state level? Is that a function of anything other than the unique trust obligation with respect to school trust lands? What opportunities and concerns are presented by state management? What does the basic postulate of public choice theory—that small, well-organized groups will capture governmental decisionmaking and economic rents and pass the costs on to an unorganized and more numerous public—suggest about state grazing management?

6. At various times, there have been efforts to have the federal government transfer ownership of the public lands to the states in which those lands are situated. Commenting on this phenomenon, Professor Coggins asks:

> why on earth do the states want these lands? They were rejected as worthless by waves of settlers for nearly a century, and they remain in federal ownership for precisely that reason.... It is true that depletion of resources on private lands has enhanced the value of the public lands, and there is an oft-expressed dislike of federal 'oppression.' Nevertheless, transfer of ownership under present conditions seems to make little financial sense for states. The federal presence means payrolls, in lieu tax payments, highway subsidies, water subsidies, tourism, revenue sharing, subsidized grazing, and a spectrum of other direct and indirect dollar benefits to western states. Even acknowledging the imprecision of economic cost benefit balancing, one must still surmise that the West, if it won divestiture, could end up holding a pig in a poke.

George Cameron Coggins, *Some Disjointed Observations on Federal Public Land and Resources Law*, 11 ENVTL. L. 471, 495–96 (1981). *See also* Michael C. Blumm, *The Case Against Transferring BLM Lands to the States*, 7 FORDHAM ENVTL. L.J. 387 (1996). Do you agree with Professor Coggins? Regardless whether states want the lands, would transferring them be a good idea? Who would be benefited or hurt the most by transfer?

7. If you would like to do further reading on rangelands, the following websites may be helpful:

- http://www.rangebiome.org/ (assembling links to individuals and organizations devoted to improving rangeland condition and who generally oppose grazing)

- http://www.westernwatersheds.org/ (organization devoted to restoring western watersheds by the removal of livestock)

- http://rangelands.org/ (Society of Range Management website devoted to promoting sustainable rangeland management with tremendous number of useful links)

- http://www.beefusa.org/ (National Cattlemen's Beef Association)

The most comprehensive analysis of rangeland management is a series of five articles in which Professor George Coggins was the primary author. *See* George Cameron Coggins & Margaret Lindeberg–Johnson, *The Law of Public Rangeland Management V: Prescriptions for Reform*, 13 STAN. ENVTL. L.J. 497 (1984); George Cameron Coggins, *The Law of Public Rangeland Management IV: FLPMA, PRIA, and the Multiple Use Mandate*, 14 ENVTL. L. 1 (1983); George Cameron Coggins, *The Law of Public Rangeland Management III: A Survey of Creeping Regulation at the Periphery, 1934– 1982*, 13 ENVTL. L. 295 (1983); George Cameron Coggins & Margaret Lindeberg–Johnson, *The Law of Public Rangeland Management II: The Commons and The Taylor Act*, 13 ENVTL. L. 1 (1982); Coggins et al., *The Law of Public Rangeland Management I: The Extent and Distribution of Federal Power*, 12 ENVTL. L. 535 (1982).

CHAPTER NINE

MINERALS

I. AN INTRODUCTION TO MINING
  A. A BRIEF HISTORY OF MINING
  B. MINING AND THE ENVIRONMENT
  C. MINING AND WORKER SAFETY
  D. MINERAL ECONOMICS
  PROBLEM EXERCISE: EXPLORING THE VOLATILITY OF MINERALS MARKETS
  E. METHODS FOR DEVELOPING MINERALS
  F. MINERAL DEVELOPMENT OUTSIDE THE UNITED STATES
II. MINERAL PROPERTY
  A. WHO OWNS THE MINERALS? ACQUISITION AND LOSS OF MINERAL RIGHTS
    1. THE BROAD FORM DEED
    PROBLEM EXERCISE: LEGAL LIMITS ON THE TERMS OF A LEASE
    2. SPLIT ESTATES
  B. DEFINING THE MINERAL RESOURCE
    1. COAL BED METHANE
  MINERAL CONVEYANCE DRAFTING EXERCISE
III. MINING ON THE PUBLIC LANDS
  A. AN INTRODUCTION TO THE GENERAL MINING LAW OF 1872
  B. PUBLIC LANDS OPEN TO MINERAL LOCATION
  C. TYPES OF MINING CLAIMS
    1. LODE AND PLACER CLAIMS
    2. MILL SITES
    PROBLEM EXERCISE: MINING AND MILL SITES
  D. STAKING A MINING CLAIM
    1. FEDERAL AND STATE STANDARDS
    PROBLEM EXERCISE: LOCATION AND RECORDING REQUIREMENTS
    2. AMENDMENT AND RELOCATION
    3. ASSESSMENT WORK
    4. RECORDING REQUIREMENTS UNDER FLPMA
  E. PEDIS POSSESSIO
  PROBLEM EXERCISE: PEDIS POSSESSIO RIGHTS
  F. DISCOVERY OF VALUABLE MINERALS
  G. CHALLENGES TO THE VALIDITY OF MINING CLAIMS
  H. MINING CLAIM PATENTS
  I. THE MECHANICS OF MINING CLAIM TRANSACTIONS
  MINING CLAIM PURCHASE REVIEW PROCESS
IV. MINERAL SALES AND LEASES ON THE PUBLIC LANDS
  A. THE COMMON VARIETIES ACT
  B. THE SURFACE RESOURCES ACT
  PROBLEM EXERCISE: DISCOVERY PROBLEMS AND THE SURFACE RESOURCES ACT
  C. THE MINERAL LEASING ACT
    1. ONSHORE OIL AND GAS LEASING
    2. COAL LEASING
    3. LEASING OF MINERALS OTHER THAN COAL
  D. MULTIPLE MINERAL DEVELOPMENT

V. ENVIRONMENTAL REGULATION OF MINING
    A. ENVIRONMENTAL REGULATION OF HARD ROCK MINING
        1. FEDERAL REGULATION OF MINING TO PROTECT THE ENVIRONMENT
        2. STATE REGULATION OF MINING TO PROTECT THE ENVIRONMENT
    PROBLEM EXERCISE: ENVIRONMENTAL RESTRICTIONS THAT PRECLUDE MINING
    PROBLEM EXERCISE: THE GLAMIS IMPERIAL MINE
    B. ENVIRONMENTAL REGULATION OF COAL MINING

Minerals are where you find them. The quantities are finite. It's criminal to waste minerals when the standard of living of your people depends upon them. A mine cannot move. It is fixed by nature. So it has to take precedence over every other use. If there were a copper deposit in Yellowstone Park, I'd recommend mining it.

Geologist Charles Park, *quoted in* JOHN MCPHEE, ENCOUNTERS WITH THE ARCHDRUID 21 (1971)

I. AN INTRODUCTION TO MINING

Minerals are indisputably important in a civilized society. We use minerals such as oil, gas, and coal to heat our homes, to fuel our cars and other forms of transportation, and to generate electricity. We mix iron ore with other minerals such as manganese, silicon, and copper to make steel, which is used in products as diverse as cars and washing machines. (Stainless steel is an alloy of iron mixed with chromium, nickel and molybdenum.) Among the many uses for bauxite, which is the ore used to make aluminum, are soft drink cans and airplanes. Limestone is used to make cement. Gold is used not only for jewelry but also in electronic components due to its superior electrical conductivity and resistance to rust. Gold is also the most malleable metal. A single ounce of gold can be made into a length of wire five miles long! Like gold, silver has many uses beyond jewelry, including for photographic paper and film, and for electronics.

But unregulated mineral production invariably leads to serious environmental problems. Open pit mining, which is often used in mining metals such as copper, gold, and silver, requires the removal and disposal of massive quantities of earth or "spoil" material just to expose the ore. Even the mineral veins from which the metals are extracted contain very small percentages of metal. A valuable gold deposit, for example, may contain ore with only a tiny percentage of gold. Most gold mines process between 3 and 10 tons of ore to produce a single ounce of gold, but gold mining can be profitable with even lower grade ores. The Cripple Creek and Victor Gold Mine in Colorado, for example, processes as much as 100 tons of ore per ounce of gold. *See* Steve Raabe, *A Major Miner of Colorado Gold*, THE DENVER POST, Jan. 20, 2002. And the proposed Glamis Imperial Mine in California would process an incredible 422 tons of ore for every ounce of gold produced. *See* Regulation of Hardrock Mining, Interior Solicitor's Opinion, M–36999 (Dec. 27, 1999).

When mining is completed, often many years after it begins, a massive pit and enormous spoil piles are left behind. The spoil often includes acidic soils, and the spent ore frequently contains residual amounts of highly toxic heavy metals. With the help of the acid-forming soils, these metals can contaminate surface and ground water supplies. Given the problems associated with open pit mining, it is not surprising that many old mine sites are now listed on the National Priorities List under the Superfund law, as among the most toxic sites in the country. Indeed, Earthworks, a nonprofit group that supports mining law reform, claims that "[i]n 2001 alone, the hardrock mining industry released 2.8 billion pound of toxic waste, according to the EPA's Toxics Release Inventory." *See* http://www.earthworks action.org/EnvironmentalImpacts.cfm.

Modern reclamation laws generally address water quality problems but rarely require backfilling of the large mining pits, which will likely remain as a scar on the landscape for hundreds of years to come. Mining operations can also incur costs that may have been unexpected. For example, before closing in 2005 the Black Mesa coal mine, on the Navajo Reservation in northeastern Arizona, pumped one billion gallons of water a year from groundwater aquifers for a coal slurry line. Mixing the coal with water creates coal slurry which enables transportation of the material through a pipeline, but the long-term damage to groundwater supplies may prove to be devastating for an arid region dependent upon such resources. *See* http://ludb.clui.org/ex/i/AZ3134. The Black Mesa mine provided coal to the Mohave Generation Station in Laughlin, Nevada, which was closed on December 31, 2005. As a result, Peabody Energy, which operates the Black Mesa mine, had suspended mineral extraction activities at Black Mesa but it is actively negotiating to find new markets for the coal so that it can reopen the mine. http://www.blackmesais.org/latest_indfo.htm

Over time, state and federal governments have begun to take more seriously their responsibility to regulate mining activities. One result has been increased scrutiny of proposals to site mining operations in pristine areas with important biological and aesthetic resources. The notion expressed by Charles Park that "[m]inerals are where you find them," and that accordingly, mining should be allowed wherever minerals occur, may resonate within the mineral industry, but it does not seem to reflect public opinion. Indeed, political decisions to block mining activities are often quite popular, especially when they encompass sensitive federal lands. A good example was the proposed New World Mine, just outside of Yellowstone National Park. After years of litigation over the proposal, the federal government agreed to pay the mining company, Crown Butte Resources, $65 million to relinquish its mineral development rights in the area. *New World Gold Mine and Yellowstone National Park,* C.R.S. Report 96–669 ENR (1996). The Congressional Research Service estimated that the proposed mine would have yielded ore valued at $800 million over 10–15 years of operation. *Id.*

The law relating to mining and mineral development has two distinct parts. The first deals with the ownership and control of natural resources and the authority of the landowner to limit or preclude mining activities. This first part is the focus of this chapter. The second part concerns the environmental regulation of mining operations and the reclamation of mineral properties. With the exception of coal mining, which is subject to federal standards under the Surface Mining Control and Reclamation Act of 1977, 30 U.S.C. § 1201–1328 (2006), mining and reclamation operations are generally covered by state laws that vary widely. As a result, comprehensive treatment of this topic is not practical in a course that focuses generally on natural resources law. In the case of coal mining, the laws and regulations are quite complex and time and space allows these issues to be addressed in only summary fashion. Before we consider the law of mining, however, we first consider the basic facts and history of mining and minerals in order to give context to the discussion that follows.

A.   A BRIEF HISTORY OF MINING

Mining and mineral development have a long and fascinating history. Mining originated in Africa in the Stone Age, perhaps as early as 300,000 years ago. Early mining involved extraction and processing of flint and stone for use as tools and implements, and salt for preserving food. Clay was another important early mineral because it could be fashioned into vessels to store food and liquids. Potters' kilns, which were used to set the clay vessels, may have inspired the later development of smelters to extract metal from ore. Some of the earliest forms of trade involved minerals such as flint and salt.

The mining of metals began around 6,000 B.C. when miners in the Mediterranean region fashioned raw copper into crude tools and weapons. About 1,000 years later, miners discovered that the application of heat to ore made the metal in the ore malleable and easier to work. Smelting was born. Still later, miners discovered that metal alloys were stronger than a single metal alone. Copper and tin were made into bronze. Sometime later, copper and zinc were fashioned into brass. Advances in mining and metallurgy—the science of separating metal from its ore—made possible the Industrial Revolution of the eighteenth century.

As mining methods became more sophisticated and evolved to include underground extraction, mining institutions developed to accommodate the increasingly complex operations. Both the corporate form and trade unions can trace at least some aspects of their existence to early mining operations.

If mining played an important role in the early history of the world, it was also important to the history of the United States. An early Spanish explorer, Hernando DeSoto, used his position as Governor of Cuba to explore the southeastern United States for gold. Although unsuccessful in his pursuit of gold, he was the first European to find the Mississippi River, near present-day Memphis, Tennessee.

At the same time that DeSoto was exploring the southeastern United States, Francisco Coronado led an expedition into the southwestern United States in a futile search for the mythical Seven Golden Cities of Cibola. Coronado, like DeSoto, never found gold, but he was the first European to set his eyes on the Grand Canyon.

Long before gold discoveries in the West spurred a wave of Western migration, gold rushes occurred in several Eastern states. Gold was discovered in Georgia and North Carolina in the early part of the nineteenth century, and North Carolina was the leading gold-producing state. But there is surely no event in the history of American mining that better

captures the spirit of the times than James Marshall's discovery of gold at
John Sutter's mill on January 24, 1848. Within four years of Marshall's
discovery, California's population skyrocketed from about 14,000 in 1848 to
250,000 in 1852. Mining, it turned out, was as much a part of settling the
West as it was about producing precious metals.

The gold rush in California was repeated throughout the West—at the
Comstock silver lode in Nevada, at the gold deposits near Pike's Peak in
Colorado, and at numerous mining camps throughout the West. The
mining camps themselves became the most important governmental institution in many parts of the Western United States. Esther Hobart Morris,
who gained fame for persuading the legislature of the Wyoming territory to
give women the right to vote, the right to serve on juries, and the right to
own property, became the first female justice of the peace anywhere in the
world—in the mining camp at South Pass City, Wyoming.

If the mining camps were designed to impose order on mineral development and the mining communities, their legal system was often rudimentary and lawyers were not always welcome. Indeed, the regulations of the
Union District in Clear Creek County, Colorado, which were adopted on
December 10, 1860, provided that—"No lawyer shall be permitted to
practice law in any court in any district under a penalty of not more than
fifty nor less than twenty lashes and be forever banished from the district."
Clarence King, comp., *The United States Mining Laws and Regulations
Thereunder, quoted in* John Leshy, The Mining Law: A Study in Perpetual
Motion at 386 n. 18 (1987).

Even Mark Twain became "smitten with the silver fever" and spent
about six months in a mining camp along the Humboldt River in the
Nevada Territory in the early 1860s. Twain wrote one of the most memorable accounts of that era in his popular book, *Roughing It* (1872). Twain and
his partners staked the "Monarch of the Mountains" claims amid the
speculative frenzy that gripped the area. Twain's description of the mood in
the camp is palpable:

> We were stark mad with excitement—drunk with happiness—smothered
> under mountains of prospective wealth—arrogantly compassionate toward the
> plodding millions who knew not our marvelous canyon—but our credit was not
> good at the grocer's.
>
> It was the strangest phase of life one can imagine. It was a beggar's revel.
> There was nothing doing in the district—no mining—no milling—no productive
> effort—no income—and not enough money in the entire camp to buy a corner
> lot in an Eastern village, hardly; and yet a stranger would have supposed he
> was walking among bloated millionaires....

Id. at 166.

In the latter part of the nineteenth century smaller gold deposits were
also discovered in northern Michigan and Minnesota. The Little American
gold mine in northern Minnesota led to the settlement of several small
communities, including International Falls. More important than the gold
itself, however, was the impetus that it gave to finding other minerals.
Lead deposits were discovered in Illinois, Wisconsin, and Missouri and
significant copper deposits were found in Michigan, most notably on the
Keweenaw Peninsula. Between 1867 and 1884 the Calumet & Hecla Mining

Company, based in Calumet, Michigan, produced half the nation's copper. The main shaft at the mine was more than 8,000 feet deep—the deepest in the world at that time.

The most important mineral to the Midwestern economy was probably iron ore, which is used to make steel. Iron ore was first discovered in the Upper Peninsula of Michigan in 1844 by William Burt, a federal surveyor, and later in Minnesota, where mines were opened in the Mesabi, Cuyuna, and Vermilion iron ranges. Minnesota soon became the largest iron-producing state in the country, and held that position well into the twentieth century. A lower grade form of iron ore called taconite continues to be mined in large quantities in northern Minnesota.

While the metals industry played a critical role in industrial development, such development would not have been possible without the production of oil, gas, and coal to fuel the smelters and the electrical power plants. Demand for coal in particular helped to secure a prominent role for coal mining, first primarily in Appalachia, but eventually in the Midwest and Western United States as well.

QUESTIONS AND DISCUSSION

1.   Mining and mineral development are often in conflict with other land uses, but supporters of mining are quick to point out the essential benefits that mining brings to a civilized world. In *Encounters with the Archdruid,* Charles Park, a former Stanford University geology professor, engages the renowned conservationist, David Brower, in a discussion of mining during a hike through the Glacier Peak Wilderness Area in northwestern Washington. Glacier Peak is home to a copper deposit that Park thinks should be developed. Brower, not surprisingly, opposes the mine. At one point in their discussion, Park emphasizes the importance of minerals to everyday life, including the construction of Brower's own home:

> "Most people don't think about pigments in paint. Most white paint now is titanium. Red is hematite. Black is often magnetite. There's chrome yellow, molybdenum orange. Metallic paints are a little more permanent. * * *. Dave's electrical system is copper, probably from Bingham Canyon. He couldn't turn on a light or make ice without it. The nails that hold the place together come from the Mesabi Range. His downspouts are covered with zinc that was probably taken out of the ground in Canada. The tungsten in his light bulbs may have been mined in Bishop, California. The chrome of his refrigerator door probably came from Rhodesia or Turkey. His television set almost certainly contains cobalt from the Congo. He uses aluminum from Jamaica, maybe Suriname; silver from Mexico or Peru; tin—it's still in tin cans—from Bolivia, Malaya, Nigeria. People seldom stop to think about these things—planes in the air, cars on the road, Sierra Club cups—once, somewhere were rock.... Oh, gad! I haven't even mentioned manganese or sulphur. You won't make steel without them. You can't make paper without sulphur."

JOHN MCPHEE, ENCOUNTERS WITH THE ARCHDRUID 48–49 (1971). If, as Park suggests, our society has come to depend fundamentally on minerals, is it realistic to think we can avoid developing them where they are found in commercial quantities? Short of returning to a more primitive lifestyle, what alternatives, if any, exist?

2. Charles Park's argument that our society has become dependent on minerals and mining will likely be true for many years to come. But the advent of the "hydrogen economy" holds the prospect at least for radically changing our dependence on fossil fuel minerals such as coal, oil, and natural gas. Whether and when we actually make the transition to the hydrogen economy depends upon the development and refinement of fuel cell technology and at least for the near term, on the adoption of regulations or carbon taxes that would provide market demand for such technologies. Fuel cells produce electricity that can power our cars, heat our homes, and provide a clean and, because they use hydrogen—the most abundant element in the universe—as their fuel, a potentially limitless source of energy. Jeremy Rifkin describes how fuel cells work:

> Pure hydrogen gas is fed to the anode, one of two electrodes in each cell. The process strips the hydrogen atoms of their electrons, turning them into hydrogen ions, which then pass through an electrolyte (which, depending on the type of fuel cell, can be phosphoric acid, molten carbonate or another substance) to the second electrode, known as the cathode. This electron movement produces electric current, the intensity of which is decided by the size of the electrodes. At the cathode, the electrons are brought back together with their ions and combined with oxygen to produce one of the fuel cell's major byproducts, water. The other byproduct is heat, which can be captured and reused in a cogeneration process.

Jeremy Rifkin, *The Hydrogen Economy: After Oil, Clean Energy from a Fuel–Cell–Driven Global Hydrogen Web*, E–Magazine Vol. XIV, No. 1 (Jan./Feb. 2003). As Rifkin notes, fuel cells produce electricity, heat, and water. That's all.

The technology for producing fuel cells is well understood, but the cost of producing electricity from these cells remains high, largely because of the cost associated with producing and storing the highly flammable hydrogen gas. Still, fuel cells hold great promise, not only as a clean and abundant energy source, but also because of their potential to democratize the energy industry by allowing for the production of electricity on-site. Drawing on the work of Amory Lovins, for example, Rifkin notes that fuel cell powered cars are essentially 20–25 kilowatt power stations on wheels that could be plugged in to ports at the office and at home and become part of the electrical grid. Doesn't the prospect for "democratizing" the energy industry pose a threat to current energy producers? How would you expect them to respond to that threat? What response might public choice theory predict? What opportunities might be available to profit from the transition to a hydrogen economy?

3. Fossil Fuels and Climate Change. The most pressing threat to the fossil fuel industry is global climate change. Carbon dioxide in our atmosphere is part of a complex global carbon cycle. Produced naturally by the respiration of animals, carbon dioxide is, in turn, absorbed by plants, trees, and other vegetation through photosynthesis, and by our oceans. Burning fossil fuels releases additional carbon dioxide that disrupts the natural equilibrium of the carbon cycle. Carbon dioxide and other gases (such as methane) absorb energy in the atmosphere, increasing the energy of the world's climate systems. The net result (first theorized by Swedish chemist Svante Arrhenius in 1896) is the "greenhouse effect." The existence of the greenhouse effect is not disputed. It's why Venus is always covered in clouds and why we have a climate that supports life. What remains contentious, though, is the impact of carbon dioxide released by fossil fuels on the world's climate.

From analyzing bubbles trapped in ice cores, scientists have established that, prior to the commencement of the Industrial Revolution, atmospheric CO_2 concentrations stayed roughly between 265 parts per million (ppm) and 280 ppm. Anthropogenic contributions since then have led to a steady increase of atmospheric CO_2 concentration. By 2008 they had reached approximately 385 ppm and were growing at a rate of about 2 ppm per year. To put this in perspective, annual emissions of CO_2 grew by about 80% between 1970 and 2004 from 21 gigatons of CO_2 to 38 gigatons per year. Most of this comes from burning fossil fuels for energy, transportation, and industry. So long as fossil fuels continue to serve as the world's primary energy source, this trend is likely to continue. Emissions of CO_2 from energy use are projected to increase between 40% and 110% between 2000 and 2030. Atmospheric concentrations of methane and other greenhouse gases have also increased, in some cases, at even faster rates.

As greenhouse gas concentrations increased so did global average surface temperatures, by about 1.33F over the last century. Eleven of the twelve years between 1995 and 2006 were among the twelve warmest since instrumental records were first kept in 1850. The past century has also seen global average sea levels rise between 4 and 8 inches with contributions from thermal expansion, and the melting of glaciers, ice caps, and the polar ice sheets. Rising sea levels are consistent with warming.

We know all this as a result of data collected by the Intergovernmental Panel on Climate change (IPCC), established in 1988 by the United Nations Environment Programme (UNEP) and the World Meteorological Organization (WMO) to study the impact of anthropogenic sources of carbon and other chemicals on climate. *See* http://www.ipcc.ch. In 2007, the IPCC's Fourth Assessment Report concluded that "[m]ost of the observed increase in global average temperatures since the mid–20th century is very likely due to the observed increase in anthropogenic GHG (greenhouse gas) concentrations." IPCC, Fourth Assessment Report (2007). The report further projects a warming of about 0.2C for the next two decades, with subsequent warmly highly dependent on greenhouse gas emissions scenarios. Increases could range from 1.1C to 6.4C by 2100. Increases at the higher end would be unprecedented over the last ten thousand years.

The earth's climate system, of course, is dauntingly complex, and the models used to predict climatic changes are far from perfect. Still, the IPCC's assessment represents the best consensus estimates of over 2,000 scientists from around the world.

4. Climate Change Law. The international community has made strides toward addressing climate change on a global scale. The United Nations Framework Convention on Climate Change, adopted in 1992 (and ratified by the United States), committed its signatories to "the aim of returning individually or jointly to their 1990 levels of . . . emissions of carbon dioxide and other greenhouse gases." UNFCCC, Article 2(a). This goal has not been met, as global greenhouse gas emissions have continued to rise. An agreement establishing specific targets and timetables for reducing greenhouse gases was adopted at Kyoto, Japan in 1997. *See*, http://unfccc.int. It did not take effect, however, until February 15, 2005 when the necessary number of countries had ratified. The United States never ratified Kyoto and even countries that did have struggled to meet the goals established for the first commitment period which ends in 2012. Much of the debate now focuses on the negotiating the goals for the next commitment period.

Efforts to enact federal climate change legislation failed in 2008 as a result of a filibuster of the Lieberman–Warner bill that would have established a national "cap and trade" program. *See* Climate Security Act, S. 3036 (2008). Prospects for similar legislation in 2009 seem brighter due to strong support from the Obama Administration. Although the push for a "cap and trade" program seems inexorable, many economists question whether a greenhouse gas tax might offer a more efficient way to deal with multiple greenhouse gases from a wide variety of sources. *See* Dr. Robert Shapiro, *Addressing the Risks of Climate Change: The Environmental Effectiveness and Economic Efficiency of Emissions Caps and Tradable Permits, Compared to Carbon*, Feb. 2007, *available at* http://www.the americanconsumer.org/Shapiro.pdf.

The failure of the United States to adopt climate change legislation has prompted states to initiate their own efforts. The Regional Greenhouse Gas Initiative (RGGI) is a cooperative effort by Northeastern and Mid–Atlantic states to reduce carbon dioxide emissions through a "cap-and-trade" and emissions trading program. http://www.rggi.org/. In May 2007, several Western states embarked on a similar effort—the Western Regional Climate Action Initiative (WRCAI). http://www.westernclimateinitiative.org/. That effort now includes the Canadian Provinces of British Columbia and Manitoba). Another such agreement was reached in November 2007 among Midwestern states. The Midwestern Greenhouse Gas Reduction Accord (MGGRA) represents a significant step in state initiated efforts, as the Midwest's intensive manufacturing and agriculture sectors make it the most coal-dependent region in North America. http://www.midwestern accord.org/.

Given the major contribution of fossil fuels to climate change, individual states have been calling for regulation to cap carbon dioxide emissions and increase fuel efficiency of cars and trucks. In December 2007, President Bush signed into effect an energy plan that requires an increase in average fuel efficiency to 35 mpg by 2020 for cars and light trucks. Energy Independence and Security Act of 2007, § 102(b)(2)(A), Pub.L. 110–140, 110 Cong., 1st Sess. (2007). However, a proposal to impose a four percent increase every year from 2021 to 2030 was dropped. Instead, the Department of Transportation (DOT) is authorized to set the "maximum feasible" standard for yearly increases. *Id*. at § 102(b)(2)(B). Hybrid engine cars that run on both electricity and gasoline are increasingly popular, with U.S. sales jumping from under 10,000 annually in 2000 to more than 181,000 in 2007, before dipping to just over 158,000 in 2008 as a recession took hold. Even with the ever increasing sales numbers of hybrids, however, their total sales only represent around 3% of the total market. *See* http://www. hybridcars.com/market-dashboard.html.

How likely is it that these measures will be adequate? What more can be done to reduce greenhouse gases emissions? Why not go further upstream and regulate or tax the source of the fossil fuels themselves? How should the threat of climate change influence our regulation of mining? Should the law discourage development of fossil fuel resources altogether? Should the law favor fuels with lower global warming potential over other fuels (such as methane over coal)?

5.   Climate Change and Environmental Justice. While climate studies often look at global averages, climate change will plainly affect some disproportionately. The effects are more pronounced, for example, towards the north and south poles. Arctic temperatures have risen at almost twice the rate of the rest of the world, with temperatures in Alaska and western Canada rising between 3–4C in the last 50 years. *Impacts of a Warming Arctic: Supporting Evidence for Key Findings* 1 (Arctic Council & International Arctic Science Committee, 2004). The dramatic changes to the natural environment accompanying climate change in these regions may present especially difficult challenges for native communities that depend on their regions' natural resources. *See* Jonathan M. Hanna, *Native Communities and Climate Change: Protecting Tribal Resources as Part of National Climate Policy* (Natural Resources Law Center, 2007). Others facing disproportionate threats include small island nations and coastal areas due to rising sea levels, and subsistence farmers in desert environments who are likely to see further strains on their limited water supplies. How should these disparate impacts affect climate law and policy?

———

B.   MINING AND THE ENVIRONMENT

If mining, and the mining culture that figures so prominently in American history, has a romantic side, it also has a dark side. Mining and mineral development have often come at substantial cost—especially to the environment and worker health and safety. Environmental regulations are commonplace today, but regulation came too late to prevent the proliferation of old abandoned mine pits that still scar the countryside, leaving a legacy of land that is not only unproductive for other uses but that itself contributes to pollution. Streams and rivers around mine sites—some long ago abandoned—remain polluted. Acid mine drainage, which occurs when acid-forming materials in the overburden material extracted during mining became exposed to the elements, is itself toxic to stream life, and is made worse by its ability to leach toxic heavy metals from the soil. The Appalachian region has particular problems with coal mining sites that were abandoned before the Surface Coal Mining and Reclamation Act of 1977 went into effect. But the problem is not limited to coal mines. The Mineral Policy Center has estimated that there are more than half a million abandoned hard rock mining sites. Most of these are on public lands. *See* http://www.mineralpolicy.org/us/abandoned.php; Michael N. Greeley, *National Reclamation of Abandoned Mine Lands* (Mar. 1999), *available at* http://www.fs.fed.us/geology/amlpaper.htm.

Toxic pollution from mine sites continues many years after the mines are closed. Many former mine sites are now listed as "Superfund" sites under the Comprehensive Environmental Response and Comprehensive Liability Act, 42 U.S.C. § 9607 (2006). One of the most notorious sites is at Butte, Montana. *See* William Langewiesche, *The Profits of Doom,* The Atlantic Monthly, Apr. 2001 (describing the legacy of mining in Butte, Montana). Water pollution and runoff from mine sites is now generally covered by the permit program of section 402 of the Clean Water Act, but the law has proved only a partial palliative to the water pollution problems associated with mining.

Water pollution is not the only mining-related environmental problem. Air pollution from the dust that is created when surface vegetation is disturbed is a common problem. Mineral processing also adds to the air pollution problem. Underground mining frequently causes surface subsidence, damaging ground water supplies and surface uses. Blasting at mine sites causes flyrock (just what it sounds like) to leave the mine site, putting property and public safety at risk.

C. Mining and Worker Safety

Mining, and in particular underground mining, has long been the most dangerous occupation in the world. An average of 5,000 mine worker deaths throughout the world are reported each year, and the questionable reporting practices of some countries has led some to speculate that total deaths are at least twice that high. Most mine-related deaths are not the result of mining accidents but rather of poor air quality in underground mine tunnels. Black lung disease, or pneumoconiosis, is a particularly serious condition caused by inhaling coal dust, and afflicts as many as 5% of all coal miners, especially those who work underground. The Black Lung Benefits Act, 30 U.S.C. § 901–45 (2003), provides benefits to miners afflicted with the disease.

The dangers to mine workers, especially in underground coal mines, sparked violence between workers and mining companies, and spawned what was at one time at least the most radical union in the country—the United Mine Workers. John L. Lewis served as the UMW president for nearly 40 years beginning in 1920, and helped the union achieve much success, including a health and welfare fund assuring a pension of $100 per month to all miners over 62. But Lewis was controversial as, for example, when he ordered a mine workers strike in 1943 during World War II, leading to the government's seizure of the mines.

The Federal Mine Safety and Health Act, 30 U.S.C. § 801–962, provides comprehensive protection for mine workers under the auspices of the Mine Safety and Health Administration. Several high-profile accidents in recent years, however, have called into question the adequacy of that law. A methane explosion at the Sago Mine in West Virginia in January 2006 killed 12 miners. *See* http://www.msha.gov/Fatals/2006/Sago/ftl06C1-12.pdf. In May, 2006, a similar explosion killed three miners at the Darby Mine in Kentucky. *See* http://www.msha.gov/FATALS/2006/Darby/FTL06c2731.pdf. In August, 2007 six miners were killed when a wall collapsed at the Crandall Canyon Mine in central Utah, and three others were killed when a second wall collapsed during rescue efforts. *See* http://www.msha.gov/ Genwal/CrandallCanyonupdates.asp. Recent reforms have included the PROP (Preventive Roof/Rib Outreach Program) Safety Initiative, which lays out a series of "Best Practices" guidelines aimed at improving the stability and safety of underground mines. *See* http://www.msha.gov/S& HINFO/Prop/prophome.htm. Additionally, the Mine Improvement and New Emergency Response Act of 2006 (the MINER Act) has expanded the scope of all "accident response plans" for underground coal mine operators, Pub. L. No. 109–236, § 2, 120 Stat. 493, 493–503.

QUESTIONS AND DISCUSSION

1. As mentioned in the introduction, the law rarely requires backfilling of large mining pits. One exception is for coal mining operations. The history of coal mining was one of profound neglect for the environment. Comprehensive federal legislation that included the backfilling of the mine pit, was adopted against the backdrop of one of the worst mining tragedies in mining history, at Buffalo Creek, West Virginia in 1972. The Pittston Mining Company, one of the largest coal operators in the country, also had one of the industry's worst safety records. In 1971, Pittston had been cited for more than 5,000 safety violations at its various mines and had challenged every single one. As a result, it had paid only $275,000 of the $1.3 million in fines that had been assessed against it. *See* http://www.wv culture.org/history/buffcreek/frmngtn.html.

Pittston maintained a series of coal waste dams at the top of a hollow above the community of Buffalo Creek. Coal waste typically consists of fine particles that are notoriously unstable, especially when they become saturated with water. On the morning of February 26, 1972, following several days of continuous rain, the lowest dam broke, sending a 20 to 30 foot wall of coal waste sludge through the community destroying everything in its path. The thick sludge reportedly moved through the valley at speeds up to 30 miles per hour. Before it was over, 125 people were killed—buried by the sludge—and thousands of homes and vehicles were destroyed. A popular account of the Buffalo Creek disaster was written by the lawyer from Arnold & Porter who represented the plaintiffs in the ensuing civil lawsuit. *See* GERALD STERN, THE BUFFALO CREEK DISASTER (1977). A sociologist subsequently chronicled the devastating impact that the incident had on the community beyond the direct loss of life and property. KAI ERICKSON, EVERYTHING IN ITS PATH (1978).

The tragedy at Buffalo Creek was often cited to support efforts to enact a comprehensive national program to regulate the adverse environmental impacts of coal mining—a goal that was achieved five years later when President Jimmy Carter signed the Surface Mining Control and Reclamation Act of 1977, 30 U.S.C. § 1201–1328. Still, the legacy of past coal mining that went largely unregulated for so many years continues to cause adverse environmental and land use impacts, especially in the coal mining districts of Appalachia.

2. Consider the various levels and bodies of government that might have an interest in regulating mining operations, mine development, mine reclamation, mine worker safety, and public safety from mining activities. What are the federal interests in these activities; what are the states' interests? Are any of these issues so localized that they should not be addressed by federal and state authorities at all?

3. In addition to environmental and worker problems, mineral development offered unparalleled opportunities for monopolies to thrive. Before Teddy Roosevelt and his "trustbusters" broke it up, Standard Oil controlled as much as 90% of the oil produced in the United States. During the early part of the twentieth century, the railroad monopoly of Edward H. Harriman's Union Pacific Railroad Company, while not directly tied to the energy business, effectively controlled the means for getting coal and other goods to market. In 1912, the Supreme Court ordered Union Pacific to sell its interests in Southern Pacific. *United States v. Union Pacific R.R.Co.*, 226 U.S. 61 (1912). Ten years later the Court ordered Southern Pacific to divest itself of Central Pacific. *United States v. Southern Pacific Co.*, 259 U.S. 214 (1922).

———

D. MINERAL ECONOMICS

Minerals present the classic case of a scarce resource whose price is highly dependent on supply and demand. Most minerals are traded on national and international commodity markets. While these markets appear to work well over the long term for many minerals, distortions in these markets, almost exclusively on the supply side, are commonplace and can cause both local and international prices to fluctuate well beyond what supply and demand might dictate. Examples abound, of which the most obvious is the market for oil. Since 1960, the Organization of Petroleum Exporting Countries (OPEC) attempted to control the supply of oil, thereby controlling its price. Historically, OPEC was most effective in controlling prices on the high side because its members, and in particular Saudi Arabia, had enough excess production capacity to increase oil supplies thereby depressing the price. OPEC had more problems controlling prices on the low side because OPEC members account for only about 44% of world oil production and 16% of the world's natural gas. If the supply from other producers increases, or if demand decreases, thereby driving down prices, OPEC had to curtail its own production significantly to force prices back up. OPEC members, which include many developing countries like Venezuela and Mexico, have been reluctant to forego this important source of their national income, even if forbearance might inure to their long-term economic benefit. *See generally* http://www.opec.org/library/faqs/opec.htm

The surge in the price of oil and other commodities in 2007 and 2008 may portend a change of historic patterns. This increase was rapid and dramatic. For example the price of a barrel of oil increased from $25 in 2003 to over $140 in July of 2008 before collapsing to around $50 as the world faced a serious recession. *See* Energy Information Administration (EIA), http://www.eia.doe.gov, for the current price. Some argue that we are at or very near to "peak oil"—the point where oil supplies will be in a continual decline. *See e.g.* Robert Hirsch et al., Department of Energy,

Peaking of World Oil Production: Impacts, Mitigation & Risk Management (2005), *available at* http://www.netl.doe.gov/publications/others/pdf/Oil_Peaking_NETL.pdf. Notwithstanding the temporary decline in demand brought on by the recession, increasing fossil fuel use, especially from rapidly developing countries like China and India, can be expected to further exacerbate the ability of producers to meet what will likely be a long-term spike in demand. The EIA forecasts an increase of 74% in worldwide consumption of liquid fuels between 2005 and 2030. *Highlights—International Energy Outlook 2008,* Figure 7, *available at* http://www.eia.doe.gov/oiaf/ieo/pdf/highlights.pdf. Some have argued that speculation in commodity markets by large investors has also played a role, leading Congress to place limits on such investment. These unprecedented high prices and a growing international awareness of the dangers of climate change have also provided a strong impetus for a move away from traditional carbon based energy sources.

One of the reasons for the distortions in some mineral markets is that the price does not always reflect the cost of producing minerals. Saudi Arabia produces oil for far less than it receives for its product. It can easily make a handsome profit by selling oil for $10 a barrel or less. By withholding sufficient oil from the market to keep prices at a much higher level, OPEC essentially allows producers who could not compete in a truly free market to make a profit. Therein lies the difficult balancing act that OPEC must engineer. If it allows the price to rise too much, thousands of new producers are encouraged to enter the market. Once their wells are drilled and they begin producing, the market may be flooded with new supplies thereby keeping prices low.

Additionally, the recent price spikes have revealed another danger to OPEC members in high prices. High prices provide short term benefits to OPEC members but also provide a market incentive for the emergence of new energy technologies. A shift away from a petroleum based energy system would prove disastrous for the economies of OPEC nations. Thus, OPEC members such as Saudi Arabia have shrewdly promised to increase production in the hopes of bringing down prices and maintaining high demand.

Of course, quantities of oil and other minerals are finite. Once used these minerals may be difficult or impossible to recapture. Thus, even if mineral producers were not able to control the supply, government agencies might want to limit production to ensure that minerals are used conservatively. This might be done, for example, by taxing mineral consumption, as is done with gasoline. The uncertainties and disagreements about long-term supply and demand of minerals, however, make any such policy controversial and politically difficult to implement.

A more palatable government tool for increasing supply is recycling. While minerals themselves may be finite, consumer products that contain minerals can often be collected, remanufactured, and reused for the same or other purposes. In recent years, communities throughout the world have implemented programs to collect aluminum cans, glass, paper, and plastics for reuse in a host of other products. The Environmental Protection Agency (EPA) estimates that approximately 32% of all discarded materials in the

United States are recycled. *See Municipal Solid Waste Generation, Recycling, and Disposal in the United States: Facts and Figures for 2006,* *available at* http://www.epa.gov/garbage/pubs/msw06.pdf. Vast quantities of virgin materials have been saved by such efforts. Short-term mineral markets can also be distorted by third-party brokers who are sometimes in a position to control supplies especially in local markets. In the summer of 2000, California faced a crisis in the supply of electricity that now appears to have been at least partially orchestrated by third party brokers, including Enron and Dynergy. Harvey Wasserman, *Our Fake Energy Crisis: What Really Happened in California, available at,* http://www.local.org/wasser man.html.

The price of minerals can also be controlled on the demand side, but such controls are more difficult to contrive. To be sure, the free market works pretty well on the demand side. When energy prices rose dramatically in California during the summer of 2000, Californians conserved energy. As soon as energy prices came down, however, demand went back up. American Council for an Energy Efficient Economy, *Energy Efficiency Has Proven It Can Avert a Major Energy Supply Crisis* (2003), *available at* http://www.aceee.org/energy/calsnlrnd.pdf

QUESTIONS AND DISCUSSION

1. Less well-known, but almost certainly more effective than OPEC in controlling the market is the diamond cartel that is essentially the province of a single South African company—De Beers. Consider the following description from an Oxford University economist:

> Diamonds are . . . cheap to produce and would in fact be lower in price but for the global cartel operated by De Beers. Its aim is to maintain a strong monopoly position, an objective it has successfully achieved for several decades, notwithstanding the pundits' predictions to the contrary. In controlling the diamond market, De Beers has exploited a relatively simple idea: put an armlock on production and keep prices high. What makes De Beers so special is its execution of the idea. Over the past 60 years the cartel has done for diamonds something that has eluded the oil producers of OPEC and even the cocaine barons of the Medellin cartel. It had the muscle and the nerve to impose its own order on the market and it built a syndicate not for weeks or months but for decades.

Muireann A. Kelliher, *Diamonds Are Forever: An Econometric Investigation, available at* http://www.tcd.ie/Economics/SER/sql/download.php?key= 152. Why do you think De Beers has been so successful in maintaining its "armlock" on diamond production? Consider that diamonds are unlike many other minerals in that they vary considerably in quality. As a result, the diamond market is really a series of submarkets for different types of diamonds. De Beers maintains an enormous supply of all the various diamond types. How would you expect De Beers to react if a company tries to undercut De Beer's price for diamonds of a particular type or quality?

———

PROBLEM EXERCISE: EXPLORING THE VOLATILITY OF MINERALS MARKETS

The price of gold on international markets is among the most volatile of all minerals. Gold prices peaked in 1980 at a price of $850/ounce. By 1998 the price per ounce had fallen below $300. The surge in commodity prices in 2007 and 2008 caused gold to spike once again, surpassing even 1980 levels. While some gold is used for dentistry, electronics, and for other industrial purposes, the vast majority of gold—about 89% in 2000—is used to make jewelry. The Earth Protection Society is concerned about the increasing number of environmental problems at gold mines in the United States and other parts of the world. While the Society recognizes that gold has important industrial uses, it is also aware that the vast majority of gold is used for jewelry, a highly discretionary consumer product.

The Society believes that many gold mines operate on a sufficiently small margin that they would likely close if the price of gold were to drop by 20% or more. The Society is interested in designing a public campaign that would either increase the supply of recycled gold or decrease the demand for virgin gold such that the market price of gold would fall enough to discourage new mines from opening and to force the closure of marginal mines.

If you represented the Society, what particular mechanisms might you suggest to achieve the Society's goals? What problems, if any, might you anticipate with such a campaign? How would you propose to address those problems? If you represented the mining industry, how might you respond to such a campaign?

––––––––

E.   METHODS FOR DEVELOPING MINERALS

Mineral development takes many different forms. Liquid and gaseous deposits are typically developed through wells, which can be drilled thousands of feet underground. Because these oil and gas deposits migrate underground, their ownership can raise difficult legal issues. In the early development of oil and gas in the United States, a "rule of capture" prevailed that allowed the owner of an oil and gas property to drill a well and extract as much oil and gas as possible, even where the drill operator was draining the resources underneath neighboring properties. The ensuing race to develop resulted in anarchy in the oil fields. State governments eventually intervened to set well spacing and well number requirements that limited the amount of oil and gas that a single producer could take.

One of the earliest forms of equitable sharing of oil and gas resources was the pooling agreement whereby owners of land overlying a common oil and gas reservoir on which there was a single well site agreed to share equitably the costs and revenues from oil and gas production. Many states provide for compulsory pooling so that landowners demand an equitable share of the revenues and costs of a neighbor's well. *See, e.g.*, TEX. NAT. RES. CODE § 102.011. While pooling agreements can help avoid the most egregious problems with common oil and gas reservoirs, they do not adequately address concerns relating to efficient resource development because they are generally limited to a single well. *Unitization agreements* try to solve this problem by providing for common development of an entire oil field. Unitization promotes maximum recovery of oil and gas resources with the fewest possible wells, thereby reducing costs and surface disturbance. As with pooling, many states provide for compulsory unitization. Of the major oil-producing states, Texas is the only state that does not. William F. Carr, *Compulsory Fieldwide Unitization*, 49 Rocky Mtn. Min. L. Inst. 21–1 (2003). Oil and gas law generally, and the law of pooling and unitization in particular, are complex subjects that are usually addressed in separate courses. *See* John Lowe et. al., Cases and Materials on Oil and Gas 668–835 (4th ed. 2002); *see also* Bruce Kramer & Patrick Martin, The Law of Pooling and Unitization (1997). For that reason, these issues are addressed only briefly here and again later in this chapter in the context of mineral leasing on federal lands.

Solid minerals can sometimes be developed "in situ," which literally means developing the minerals "in place." In situ mining is common with uranium and some soluble minerals like salt. *See* http://www.world-nuclear. org/info/inf27.html for a description of uranium mining using this technique. Solid minerals are usually developed through extraction, although mining methods vary greatly, as described in the excerpt below.

The Columbia Encyclopedia, (6th Ed. 2001)
Available at http://www.bartleby.com/65/mi/mining.html

Surface Mining Methods

Strip mining, open-pit (or open-cut) mining, and quarrying are the most common mining methods that start from the earth's surface and maintain exposure to the surface throughout the extraction period. The excavation usually has stepped, or benched, side slopes and can reach depths as low as 1,500 ft. (460 m). In strip mining, the soft overburden, or waste soil, overlying the ore or coal is easily removed. In open-pit mining the barren rock material over the ore body normally requires drilling and blasting to break it up for removal. A typical mining cycle consists of drilling holes into the rock in a pattern, loading the holes with explosives, or blasting agents, and blasting the rock in order to break it into a size suitable for loading and hauling to the mill, concentrator, or treatment plant. There the metals or other desired substances are extracted from the rocks.

Underground Mining Methods

Under certain circumstances surface mining can become prohibitively expensive and underground mining may be considered. A major factor in the decision to operate by underground mining rather than surface mining is the strip ratio, or the number of units of waste material in a surface mine that must be removed in order to extract one unit of ore. Once this ratio becomes large, surface mining is no longer attractive. The objective of underground mining is to extract the ore below the surface of the earth safely, economically, and with as little waste as possible. The entry from the surface to an underground mine may be through an adit, or horizontal tunnel, a shaft or vertical tunnel, or a declined shaft. A typical underground mine has a number of roughly horizontal levels at various depths below the surface, and these spread out from the access to the surface. Ore is mined in stopes, or rooms. Material left in place to support the ceiling is called a pillar and can sometimes be recovered afterward. A vertical internal connection between two levels of a mine is called a winze if it was made by driving downward and a raise if it was made by driving upward.

A modern underground mine is a highly mechanized operation requiring little work with pick and shovel. Rubber-tired vehicles, rail haulage, and multiple drill units are commonplace. In order to protect miners and their equipment much attention is paid to mine safety. Mine ventilation provides fresh air underground and at the same time removes noxious gases as well as dangerous dusts that might cause lung disease, *e.g., silicosis*. Roof support is accomplished with timber, concrete, or steel supports or, most commonly, with roof bolts, which are long steel rods used to bind the exposed roof surface to the rock behind it.

Other Methods

Although surface and underground mining are the most common techniques, there are a number of other mining methods. In solution mining the valuable mineral is brought into a liquid solution by some chemical or bacteria. The resultant liquid is pumped to the surface, where the mineral or metal is taken out of solution by *precipitation* or by ion exchange (*e.g., the Frasch process*). In glory-hole mining a steep-sided, funnel-shaped surface excavation is connected to tunnels below it. Rocks blasted off the sides of the excavation fall into the tunnels, from which they are then removed. Gopher mining is an old-fashioned method still used in very small mines. Narrow, small holes are driven in order to extract the ore (*e.g.,* gold) as cheaply as possible. In placer mining no excavation is involved; instead, gravel, sand, or talus (rock debris) is removed from deposits by hand, hydraulic nozzles, or dredging. The ore is separated from the waste by panning or sluicing. * * *

Concentration of Ore

When an ore has a low percentage of the desired metal, a method of physical concentration must be used before the extraction process begins. In one such method, the ore is crushed and placed in a machine where, by shaking, the heavier particles containing the metal are separated from the lighter rock particles by gravity. Another method is the *flotation process*, used commonly for copper sulfide ores. In certain cases (as when gold, silver, or occasionally copper occur "free," *i.e.,* uncombined chemically in sand or rock), mechanical or ore dressing methods alone are sufficient to obtain relatively pure metal. Waste material is washed away or separated by screening and gravity; the concentrated ore is then treated by various chemical processes.

Separation of Metal

Processes for separating the metal from the impurities it is found with or the other elements with which it is combined depend upon the chemical nature of the *ore* to be treated and upon the properties of the *metal* to be extracted. Gold and silver are often removed from the impurities associated with them by treatment with mercury, in which they are soluble. Another method for the separation of gold and silver is the so-called *cyanide process*. The Parkes process, which is based on silver being soluble in molten zinc while lead is not, is used to free silver from lead ores. Since almost all the metals are found combined with other elements in nature, chemical reactions are required to set them free. These chemical processes are classified as pyrometallurgy, electrometallurgy, and hydrometallurgy.

Pyrometallurgy, or the use of heat for the treatment of an ore, includes smelting and roasting. If the ore is an oxide, it is heated with a reducing agent, such as carbon in the form of coke or coal; the oxygen of the ore combines with the carbon and is removed in carbon dioxide, a gas (see *oxidation and reduc-*

tion). The waste material in the ore is called gangue; it is removed by means of a substance called a flux which, when heated, combines with it to form a molten mass called slag. Being lighter than the metal, the slag floats on it and can be skimmed or drawn off. The flux used depends upon the chemical nature of the ore; limestone is usually employed with a siliceous gangue. A sulfide ore is commonly roasted, *i.e.,* heated in air. The metal of the ore combines with oxygen to form sulfur dioxide, which, being a gas, passes off. The metallic oxide is then treated with a reducing agent. When a carbonate ore is heated, the oxide of the metal is formed, and carbon dioxide is given off; the oxide is then reduced.

Electrometallurgy includes the preparation of certain active metals, such as aluminum, calcium, barium, magnesium, potassium, and sodium, by *electrolysis*: a fused compound of the metal, commonly the chloride, is subjected to an electric current, the metal collecting at the cathode.

Hydrometallurgy, sometimes called leaching, involves the selective dissolution of metals from their ores. For example, certain copper oxide and carbonate ores are treated with dilute sulfuric acid, forming water-soluble copper sulfate. The metal is recovered by electrolysis of the solution. If the metal obtained from the ore still contains impurities, special *refining* processes are required.

The cyanide process or *cyanidation*, is a method for extracting *gold* from its ore. The ore is first finely ground and may be concentrated by flotation; if it contains certain impurities, it may be roasted. It is then mixed with a dilute solution of sodium cyanide (or potassium or calcium cyanide) while air is bubbled through it. The gold is oxidized and forms the soluble aurocyanide complex ion, $Au(CN)_2$. (Silver, usually present as an impurity, forms a similar soluble ion.) The solution is separated from the ore by methods such as filtration, and the gold is precipitated by adding powdered zinc. The precipitate usually contains silver, which is also precipitated, and unreacted zinc. The precipitate is further refined, *e.g.,* by smelting to remove the zinc and by treating with nitric acid to dissolve the silver. The cyanide process was developed (1887) by J.S. MacArthur and others in Glasgow, Scotland. It is now the most important and widely used process for extracting gold from ores.

Flotation in mineral treatment and mining is a process for concentrating the metal-bearing mineral in an *ore*. Crude ore is ground to a fine powder and mixed with water, frothing reagents, and collecting reagents. When air is blown through the mixture, mineral particles cling to the bubbles, which rise to form a froth on the surface. The waste material (gangue) settles to the bottom. The froth is skimmed off, and the water and chemicals are distilled or otherwise removed, leaving a clean concentrate. The process, also called the froth-flotation process, is used for a number of minerals, especially silver.

QUESTIONS AND DISCUSSION

1. What environmental impacts would you expect to encounter with each of the mining methods described above? Should the law be designed to favor certain methods over others?

2. Different mineral development methods raise different legal and practical issues. Surface mining, for example, requires removal of the "overburden"—the rock layer above the mineral deposit-and-produces large quantities of waste material or "spoil." This spoil material must be deposited somewhere and can pose daunting economic and environmental problems. The problem is exacerbated by the fact that when overburden is removed it increases in volume, usually by about 25% or more. (This is called the "swell factor.") One of the most difficult issues posed by surface mining is whether to require backfilling of the mine pit. As noted previously, backfilling is required for surface coal mining, which occurs over a relatively short period of time. *See* 30 U.S.C. § 1265(b) (2006). It is generally not the law, however, for "hard rock" mining, which often occurs over a much longer period. The mine pit at the Bingham Canyon Copper Mine, for example— the largest open pit mine in the world—was first opened in 1906, and continues to produce copper and other minerals today. Kennecott Utah Copper, which operates the mine, runs public tours at the site, and proudly advertises that:

> The mine is 2–1/2 miles across at the top and 3/4 of a mile deep. You could stack two Sears Towers on top of each other and still not reach the top of the mine.
>
> The mine is so big, it can be seen by the space shuttle astronauts as they pass over the United States.

http://www.kennecott.com/?id=MjAwMDEzMQ==. It seems a virtual certainty that this "pit" will never be backfilled.

3. In June, 2002, a Montana state district court ruled that a state law that precludes backfilling a mine pit except as required to meet air and water quality laws violated a state constitutional provision requiring reclamation of all lands disturbed by the taking of natural resources. The court did not hold that backfilling is required in all cases but rather that the state must keep the requirement available as a possible reclamation tool to be used in appropriate cases. In the specific case the court ordered the Montana Department of Environmental Quality to "immediately implement" a backfill requirement. *Montana Envtl. Info. Ctr. v. Department of Envtl. Quality*, No. CDV–92–486 (Montana First Judicial District Court). To this date, the CEQ has not implemented the backfill requirement and the Montana Environmental Information Center recently filed a petition with the court seeking implementation of their order. *See generally* http://www.meic.org/mining/cyanide_mining/golden_sunlightMine/golden-sunlight-mine.

In 2003, California became the first state to enact legislation requiring certain mining operators to backfill the mine pit to premining contours for noncoal mining operations. S.B. 22 (2003). The law applies only to metal mines located within one mile from a Native American sacred site and other areas of special concern. By emergency regulation, however, the State has adopted rules that require open pits at certain metallic mines to be backfilled whether or not they impact sacred sites. These rules have been unpopular with the mining industry but after examination in 2006, the State Mining and Geology Board reaffirmed them stating that the "backfilling requirements were of significant environmental importance." REPORT ON BACKFILLING OF OPEN-PIT METALLIC MINES IN CALIFORNIA, at 28 (Jan. 2007), *available at* http://www.conservation.ca.gov/smgb/reports/Documents/SMGB%20IR%202007-02.pdf.

4. In recent years, cyanide heap-leach mining has become the preferred method for extracting precious metals from ore. Cyanide is sprayed or poured over piles of ore, dissolving the metal in the ore. Distilling the spent cyanide results in recovery of pure metals. This technique has become popular because it allows profitable mining operations on low-grade ore bodies. But cyanide is, of course, toxic. Just a teaspoonful of two-percent cyanide solution can kill a human adult, not to mention a bird or a fish. Thus, the emergence of this mining method has not occurred without controversy. In 1998, Montana voters approved an initiative that bans cyanide heap-leach mining in that State. A Montana state district court ruled that a standard provision included in state mineral leases requiring the lessee to comply with applicable state laws barred contract impairment and takings claims based on the cyanide ban. *Seven–Up Pete Venture v. Montana,* No. BDV–2000–250 (Montana First Judicial District Court), *affirmed, Seven Up Pete Venture v. State,* 114 P.3d 1009 (Mont. 2005). Montana Supreme Court also held that the restriction upon cyanide heap-leach mining is not a taking when the mining company had not already secured this express property right through contract and applicable permit.

5. Underground mining raises its own set of challenges. One of the more significant is the problem of surface subsidence. Longwall mining of coal, for example, which has become the preferred method of underground coal mining in recent years, results in the removal of the entire coal seam and thus all of the subjacent support for the land. Surface subsidence is inevitable—indeed, it is called "planned subsidence." Unfortunately, structures over a longwall operation are likely to suffer damage. Moreover, subsidence can cause breaks in the bed of material that confines any aquifer above the coal seam. The result may be drainage of the aquifer to a lower elevation, and the permanent loss of streams and water wells. Trees and other vegetation that rely on the water table may also die.

––––––

F.   MINERAL DEVELOPMENT OUTSIDE THE UNITED STATES

Even as the rules and requirements for domestic mining have become more complex, a strong trend has emerged toward increasing mineral development in foreign countries. Some in the domestic industry have argued that the trend toward foreign mineral development is a direct result of increased domestic regulation, but other factors likely contribute as well. First, geological information about domestic mineral supplies has been available and accessible to mineral operators for many years. As a result, significant new mineral deposits are less likely to be found in the United States than elsewhere. Conversely, information from other countries is becoming more accessible, thereby increasing interest in foreign deposits. Also, while foreign interests may have become aware of valuable mineral deposits, these foreign interests often lack the capital to successfully develop a major new mineral deposit. Finally, the increased ease with which information and ideas can be traded over vast distances has helped facilitate partnerships and agreements between American companies and companies based in other countries. American capital and expertise, including legal expertise, has helped open new opportunities for domestic firms even as the domestic industry itself seems to be waning. Companies that operate in the host country help provide the American firms with a better understanding of the local culture and of the institutional norms that will likely apply to the mineral development project.

The law relating to mineral development overseas is well beyond the scope of this chapter. Nonetheless, a few general observations can be made. First, government officials in foreign countries, especially developing countries, may have greater flexibility in setting operation and reclamation standards for mining operations than their U.S. counterparts. But mining companies face some risks if they fail to deal forthrightly with foreign officials, and if they fail to follow reasonable reclamation practices. For example, certain parties, such as domestic companies, who make payments to foreign officials for the purpose of "obtaining or retaining business for or with, or directing business to any person," may be violating the Foreign Corrupt Practices Act, 15 U.S.C. § 78dd–1 (2006). That law prohibits companies subject to regulation under the Securities Exchange Act to offer or give "anything of value ... to a foreign official for purposes of ... influencing any act or decision of such foreign official in his official capacity...." *Id.* Serious penalties attach to violations of the law including criminal fines of up to $2 million, and imprisonment for up to five years.

Moreover, companies whose mining operations cause significant but reasonably avoidable environmental harm may face risks under the Alien Torts Claims Act (ATCA), even if they are otherwise in compliance with their foreign permit. The ATCA, which was enacted as part of the Judiciary Act of 1789, 28 U.S.C. § 1350 (2003), gives federal district courts jurisdiction over "any civil action by an alien for a tort claim only, committed in violation of the law of nations or a treaty of the United States." *Id.* To be actionable under the ATCA, "violations of international law must be of a norm that is specific, universal, and obligatory." *In Re Estate of Ferdinand Marcos, Human Rights Litigation,* 25 F.3d 1467, 1475 (9th Cir. 1994), *cert. denied,* 513 U.S. 1126 (1995). While cases under the ATCA have historically focused on torture and human rights abuses, *see, e.g., Filartiga v. Pena–Irala,* 630 F.2d 876 (2d Cir. 1980), more recent cases have raised at least the possibility that mine operators might be liable for significant environmental harm. In *Sarei v. Rio Tinto PLC,* 221 F. Supp. 2d 1116 (C.D. Cal. 2002), a federal district court rejected a claim that environmental harm violated international law principles supporting a right to life and health, but upheld the plaintiff's right to claim environmental harm based upon an alleged violation of international principles of sustainable development. In *Beanal v. Freeport–McMoran, Inc.,* 197 F.3d 161 (5th Cir. 1999), however, the Court of Appeals for the Fifth Circuit rejected the plaintiffs' ATCA claims because they failed to provide specific information regarding the alleged ATCA violations, as necessary to put the defendants on notice of their claims.

Perhaps the most difficult problem facing mining companies operating in foreign countries, especially developing countries is knowing what standards to follow. A number of international organizations have made efforts to provide guidance to the industry. A particular focus in recent years has been on sustainable development practices. For example, the International Institute for Economic Development has sponsored the Mining, Minerals, and Sustainable Development Project (MMSD) to promote sustainable development practices by the mining industry. In recent years, the United Nations Environment Programme (UNEP) has sponsored a number of conferences and publications relating to sustainable mineral development, best environmental management practices for mining, and similar initiatives that provide guidance for mining companies operating in foreign countries. *See* http://www.unep.fr/scp/metals/publications/. Finally, the International Organization for Standardization (ISO) provides general guidance for companies interested in following accepted international standards. ISO 14000, for example, encompasses a series of environmental management standards, many of which are relevant to mining operations. *See* http://www.iso.ch. ISO claims that by 2001, their ISO 14001 environmental management systems (EMS) standard was being used as a model by nearly 37,000 organizations operating in 112 countries. *See* http://www.iso.org/iso/business_benefits_of_iso_14001.

II.   Mineral Property

A.   Who Owns the Minerals? Acquisition and Loss of Mineral Rights

Real property rights are generally described as estates in land. Minerals make up one part of a fee estate—one stick from the bundle of the fee owner's property rights—but these rights can and are frequently severed from the fee estate using a variety of either permanent or temporary forms of reservation or conveyance.

One of the most common forms of mineral right is the mineral *lease*. A lease is a possessory right to develop a mineral deposit, generally for a set term of years, but the term is usually extended indefinitely during mineral production. As a possessory right the lessee may exclude others from the leased land. The landowner receives compensation for the lease in the forms of bonus payments, royalties, and/or rentals, and retains ownership of the land, which will be unencumbered once the lease term expires or otherwise terminates by operation of law. In exchange, the mineral lessee receives the right to extract minerals along with any necessary incidental rights such as access and surface use. *See* 4 Am. L. of Mining § 131.02 (2d ed. 1995).

In addition to leases, interests in minerals may be held by license, a profit a prendre, a royalty interest, or by ownership of a full mineral estate. A mineral *license* creates a personal privilege in the licensee to remove minerals in accordance with the terms of the license. A license is revocable, and generally cannot be assigned or inherited. A *profit a prendre* is a nonpossessory, usufructuary, commercial right to remove minerals and is "presumptively assignable, inheritable, and exclusive." 3 Am. L. of Mining § 82.03[3]. Profits differ from leases because profits are not possessory estates and because they do not generally expire after a term of years. Thus, while the profit owner may remove minerals from the land, the landowner retains the right to use the land in a manner that is consistent with the profit owner's reasonable mineral development activities. *Royalty interests* are "non-expense bearing [commercial] interests in gross production...." *Id.* § 82.03[4]. They differ from leases, fee estates, and profits in that they exist independent of any rights to control development, or responsibility for development costs. *Mineral fee estates* usually arise from grants or reservations of minerals in place. Under the common law of most jurisdictions, mineral estates are the dominant estate and they thus assure the owner the right to develop the minerals even if such development may injure the surface owner. The following materials help to explain these various instruments of mineral acquisition.

Algonquin Coal Co. v. Northern Coal & Iron Co.,
162 Pa. 114, 29 A. 402 (1894)

Williams, J.

The plaintiff does not claim to own the surface of the land covered by the description filed in this case, but does claim to be the owner of the coal below the surface. This action is brought, therefore, to recover for an alleged invasion of the underlying estate, which the plaintiff says was severed from the surface in 1801, and has continued to belong to its grantors down to the time of the lease or conveyance to itself. The facts found by the learned trial judge show that prior to 1801 the surface and the subsurface were owned by Thomas Wright. In that year he sold the land to Henry Courtright, and made a conveyance therefor in the usual form, in which he incorporated the following clause: "The said Thomas reserves for himself, his heirs and assignees, a free toleration of getting coal for their own use, without hindrance or denial." The plaintiff contends that these words amount to a reservation of all the coal under the land conveyed, and, as the assignee or holder of Wright's title, claims an absolute and exclusive right to mine all the coal. The defendant claims under one Myers, who acquired Courtright's title by an adverse possession, and insists that, if any right to take coal from the land survives in Wright or his grantees, it is an incorporeal one, to be exercised concurrently with its own, and to no greater extent than may be necessary for "their own use." The first question, therefore, is over the proper construction of the reservation in the deed made by Wright to Courtright in 1801. At the outset of this inquiry, we should bear in mind the well-settled rule that words in a deed or other written instrument should be taken most strongly against him whose words they are. We should remember, also, that these words of reservation are found in a deed that in every other respect purports to convey, by formal and apt words, a fee simple title to the land described. Coming now to the words of the reservation, we notice (a) that they do not expressly embrace all the coal under the tract. The words are, "coal for their own use;" not the coal, or all the coal, or coal for the market, but so much, and no more, as the grantor, or his heirs or assignees, may need for his own personal use. We notice (b) that the right reserved is not, in terms, exclusive, but is capable of exercise concurrently with the exercise of mining rights on the part of the grantee. The words are, "reserves a free toleration of getting coal." This is equivalent to the words, "reserves the privilege" of getting coal. But for what? The words of the reservation make the reply, "for their own use." This does not exclude the idea that the coal passed, with the surface, to the grantee, but does reserve a right of entry upon the land conveyed, to get and carry away coal for the use of the grantor. But (c) the words do not necessarily or naturally imply more than is obviously expressed by them. "Toleration for getting coal for one's own use" does not necessarily or naturally mean getting coal for the market, or the exclusive right to get all the coal underlying the tract. On the other hand, the words are capable of being understood as a reservation of the privilege to the grantor, his heirs and assignees, of supplying their personal needs for fuel from the coal granted by the deed, into which the reservation is incorporated, to the buyer. This, if all artificial rules are left out of view, is the plain, natural meaning of the words employed, when read in connection with the deed in which they are found.

The land, with its minerals, passed to Courtright, subject only to the privilege reserved; and, his title being now held by the defendant, it follows that the title to the coal, as severed and separate estate, is not in the plaintiff, but was acquired, together with the surface by Myers, and passed from him to the coal company, defendant.

The judgment is affirmed.

QUESTIONS AND DISCUSSION

1.   What was the nature of the reservation in the deed made by Wright?

2.   The court notes the "well-settled rule" that ambiguous language in the deed should be construed against the party who drafted the language. What other general rules of property and contract law might help courts construe transactions such as these?

3.   Suppose that a developer is interested in exploring for minerals rather than acquiring mineral rights outright. What terms should be included in an exploration agreement to protect the interests of the landowner and the developer? The American Law of Mining treatise suggests the following:

> An exploration agreement should establish the exclusivity of the mineral developer's exploration rights, the period during which those rights may be exercised, and the duty, if any, of the mineral developer to actually explore the property. In addition, the agreement should contain an option allowing the mineral developer to acquire complete mining and development rights. An exploration agreement should also address whether or not exploration data must be supplied to the landowner, confidentiality of exploration results, any special requirements governing the conduct of exploration activities, surface protection, payment of damages, and assignability of the agreement.

4 AM. L. OF MINING § 130.05 (2d ed. 1995). Can you think of any other provisions that might be included in such an agreement?

4.   One of the more obscure types of property rights is the *profit a prendre*. The decision of the Supreme Court of Massachusetts in *Gray v. Handy,* 208 N.E.2d 829 (1965), illustrates the nature of such rights. The deeds involved in this case conveyed perpetual "privileges of taking sands from the land." The Court found that the deeds created a profit, which it described as follows:

> A profit [a prendre] is a right in one person to take from the land of another either a part of the soil, such as minerals of all kinds from mines, stone from quarries, sand and gravel; or part of its produce, such as grass, crops of any kind, trees, timber, fish from lakes or streams, game from the woods, seaweed and the like. * * * A profit [a prendre] is appurtenant when created for the benefit of the dominant estate. It is then in all respects, except the character of the user, of the same nature as an easement, passing with the dominant estate as an incident thereof whenever the estate passes by deed, devise, or inheritance....

> A conveyance of a profit a prendre is to be distinguished from a 'conveyance of an interest in real estate which will give complete ownership of a valuable part of the property. . . .'
>
> So also, a profit a prendre is to be distinguished from a mere license to enter upon the land and remove portions thereof . . . since a license, unlike a profit a prendre, creates no interest in the land, and is revocable not only at the will of the owner of the property on which it is exercised, but also by his death or by his alienation of demise [sic; should probably be 'devise'] of the land. . . .

Id. at 832. Is it clear to you how a profit a prendre differs from a license? From a lease?

5. Compare the property interests described in the previous notes with a royalty interest. A royalty interest guarantees the owner a percentage of the value of the minerals if and when they are produced and sold. Does a seller have any recourse against a buyer who refuses to develop the minerals and thereby deprives the royalty interest owner of any remuneration? In *Oberbillig v. Bradley Mining Co.*, 372 F.2d 181 (9th Cir. 1967), the court found that Bradley, the mineral developer, had an obligation to act in good faith, but he was not required, as the plaintiff claimed, to exercise diligence in developing the minerals unless required by the terms of the royalty contract. What is the difference between an obligation to exercise good faith and one to exercise diligence?

6. An obligation to diligently develop minerals is common in lease/royalty arrangements. Why would a person holding a royalty interest want to include such a requirement? What problems might such a clause pose for the mineral developer?

7. Diligent development is sometimes described as the obligation to exercise "due diligence," but this concept should not be confused with the more common meaning of that phrase in the context of mineral contracts. "Due diligence" usually describes the investigation performed by a buyer in the period between the execution of a purchase and sale agreement and the closing of a transaction. A due diligence inquiry typically examines, among other things, the property, all title matters, liens, geologic engineering data, financial records, equipment, inventory, and water rights. A satisfactory due diligence investigation confirms the representations and warranties of the seller and identifies undisclosed or unforeseen liabilities. It will also confirm the expectations of the buyer concerning the property. *See* Dean R. Massey, *Due Diligence in Modern Mining Deals: How to Protect Your Client from Buying a Pig in a Poke*, 33 ROCKY MTN. MIN. L. INST. § 2 (1988).

———

1.   THE BROAD FORM DEED

The history of mineral development is in part a history of exploitation of unsophisticated fee owners. *See, e.g., Peevyhouse v. Garland Coal & Min. Co.*, 382 P.2d 109 (Okla. 1962), *cert. denied*, 375 U.S. 906 (1963). Few examples, however, compare with the devastatingly methodical approach taken by the coal developers in the poorest parts of the coal-rich Appalachian Mountains at the turn of the twentieth century. In his prize-winning book, *Night Comes to the Cumberlands*, Harry Caudill describes the techniques of these developers:

Night Comes to the Cumberlands
Harry Caudill, 72–75 (1962)

In the summer of 1885, gentlemen arrived in the county seat towns for the purpose of buying tracts of minerals, leaving the surface of the land in the ownership of the mountaineers who resided on it. The Eastern and Northern capitalists selected for this mission were men of great guile and charm. They were courteous, pleasant, and wonderful storytellers. Their goal was to buy the minerals on a grand scale as cheaply as possible and on terms so favorable to the purchasers as to grant them every desirable exploitive privilege, while simultaneously leaving to the mountaineer the illusion of ownership and the continuing responsibility for practically all the taxes which might be thereafter levied on the land. * * *

With every convincing appearance of complete sincerity the coal buyer would spend hours admiring the mountaineer's horse and gazing over a worm-rail fence in rapt approbation of his razorback hogs while compliments were dropped on every phase of his host's accomplishments. * * *

When the highland couple sat down at the kitchen table to sign the deed their guest had brought to them they were at an astounding disadvantage. On the one side of the rude table sat an astute trader, more often than not a graduate of a fine college and a man experienced in the business world. He was thoroughly aware of the implications of the transactions and of the immense wealth he was in the process of acquiring. Across the table ... sat a man and woman out of a different age. Still remarkably close to the frontier of a century before, neither of them possessed more than the rudiments of an education. Hardly more than 25% of such mineral deeds were signed by grantors who could so much as scrawl their names. Most of them "touched the pen and made their mark," in the form of a spidery X, in the presence of witnesses whom the agent had thoughtfully brought along.... Unable to read the instrument or able to read it only with much uncertainty, the sellers relied upon the agent for an explanation of its contents—contents which were to prove deadly to the welfare of generations of the mountaineer's descendants. * * *

[T]he great majority of these deeds were the "broad-form" and, in addition to the minerals conveyed a great number of specific contractual privileges and immunities.

The broad-form deeds passed to the coal companies title to all the coal, oil and gas and all "mineral and metallic substances and all combinations of the same." They authorized the grantees to excavate for the minerals, to build roads and structures on the land and to use the surface for any purpose "convenient or necessary" to the company and its successors in title. Their wordy covenants passed to the coal men the right to utilize as mining prop the timber growing on the land, to divert and pollute the water and to cover the surface with toxic mining refuse. The landowner's estate was made perpetually "servient" to the superior or "dominant" rights of the owner of the minerals. And, for good measure, a final clause absolved the mining company for such damages as might be caused "directly or indirectly" by mining operations on his land.

Beneath the feet of the highlander lay quantities of minerals, the magnitude of which would have dumbfounded him. In practically every ridge a vein of coal was to be found near the top of the hill, sometimes with as little as forty feet of overburden on it. Other seams ran through the mountains at intervals all the way through the base of the hill. * * * The agents assured him that that the coal would not be mined for many years, and then only under circumstances harmless to him and his children. So, the deeds were signed and duly recorded in the clerk's offices of the county courts, and then the coal buyers, or most of them departed.

————

The following case addresses the legal implications of the broad form deeds discussed in the Caudill excerpt. As revealed in the Questions and Discussion section that follows the case, the decision has now been overruled by state constitutional amendment. Nevertheless, it provides a useful perspective on the history of mineral development and how mineral property rights work.

MARTIN V. KENTUCKY OAK MINING COMPANY
429 S.W.2d 395 (Ky. Ct. App. 1968)

CULLEN, COMMISSIONER

Under standard "broad form" mineral deeds of the character commonly employed in the Appalachian region in the early 1900's in the acquisition of mineral rights, the Kentucky River Coal Corporation owns the coal rights in a large acreage in eastern Kentucky. Coal mining operations on various of its lands are carried on, under leases, by Kentucky Oak Mining Company, Oak Branch Mining Company, Midland Mining Company and North Fork Coal Company.

LeRoy Martin and his wife own a 10–acre parcel of land in Knott County which in former ownership was part of a larger, 90–acre tract. Most of the parcel is hillside land but there is a small area of bottom land which is occupied by the Martins' dwelling house, outbuildings, and garden. In 1905 the mineral rights under the entire 90–acre tract were conveyed by the then owners to the predecessor in title of the Kentucky River Coal Corporation, under a "broad form" deed.

In September 1965 the Martins, alleging that the Kentucky River Coal Corporation and its lessee-operators were proposing the commencement of strip or auger mining operations on the Martins' land, brought the instant action seeking a declaration that under the mineral deed the owner of the minerals had no right to remove the coal by strip or auger mining. The coal companies answered asserting that they did have such right, and setting forth various other defenses. Ultimately, judgment was entered declaring that the mineral owner has the right to remove the coal by strip or auger mining but must pay damages to the surface owner for any destruction of the surface.

The Martins have appealed, maintaining that the judgment is erroneous in holding that the right to use strip or auger methods exists, and Kentucky River Coal Corporation, Kentucky Oak Mining Company and Oak Branch Mining Company have cross-appealed, contending that the judgment is in error in imposing upon the mineral owner the obligation to pay damages.

This is not a new problem. In *Buchanan v. Watson, Ky.*, 290 S.W.2d 40, this court held squarely that under the broad form deed coal may be removed by strip mining without any obligation to pay damages except for those caused by oppressive, arbitrary, wanton or malicious action. (Ten years before *Buchanan*, in *Treadway v. Wilson,* 301 Ky. 702, 192 S.W.2d 949, the court in effect held that strip mining can be done under the broad form deed so long as it is not done "oppressively".) . . . So the issue in the instant case is simply whether the court shall stay with *Buchanan v. Watson* and the subsequent cases based upon it. * * *

The court has been favored with briefs amicus curiae on behalf of the Kentucky Civil Liberties Union, the Commonwealth, The Appalachian Group to Save the Land and People, Inc., the Kentucky Members of the National Council of Coal Lessors, Inc., the Sierra Club, and the Big Sandy–Elkhorn Coal Operators Association. The briefs have been most helpful and have presented ably and forcefully (as have those of the parties) the arguments pro and con.

The court is fully aware of the great public concern with the conservation problems attendant upon strip and auger mining, and the urgent necessity to protect the soil and the water courses from destruction and pollution. However, counsel for the landowners, and for those amicus curiae who side with them in arguing that the broad form deed does not permit strip or auger mining, frankly concede that a decision of this court upholding their contention as to the construction of the deed will not stop strip or auger mining. They admit that in Pennsylvania and West Virginia, where the courts have held that the broad form deed does not authorize strip or auger mining, that type of mining is even more prevalent than in eastern Kentucky. And of course it is common knowledge that strip mining has been done on a large scale in western Kentucky where the broad form deed was not commonly used.

So conservation is not in issue. The issue is whether the owners of minerals, who clearly have the right to remove the coal by deep mining processes, must purchase from the landowner the right to use strip or auger processes.

The arguments by the landowners and their adherents are that (1) the parties to the mineral deeds could not reasonably have intended that the surface could be "destroyed" in the removal of the minerals, because there would have been no point in the landowners' retaining surface title if it could be rendered worthless by the mineral owner; (2) it is unfair, unjust and inequitable to construe the deeds to allow "destruction" of the surface; (3) the parties to the deeds did not contemplate the development of strip and auger mining; (4) the word "mining" in the deeds embraces only mining by underground workings; (5) the right to "use" the surface granted to the mineral owner does not include the right to "destroy"; (6) the mineral owners should be estopped from strip or auger mining any area upon which they have permitted the surface owner to make improvements.

We think the first five arguments can be refined into one basic argument, that the broad form deed does not mean, and could not reasonably have been intended to mean, when it grants to the mineral grantee the right to use the surface of the land "as may be necessary or convenient to the exercise and enjoyment of the property rights and privileges hereby . . . conveyed," that the use, regardless of old or new methods, could be such as to destroy the value of the surface for agricultural or residential purposes. Whether or not the parties actually contemplated or envisioned strip or auger mining is not important— the question is whether they intended that the mineral owner's rights to use the surface in removal of the minerals would be superior to any competing right of the surface owner.

Of course in endeavoring to find the intent of the parties we must consider the situation and circumstances existing when the deeds were made. Of significance, we think, are the following circumstances which relate particularly to the execution of the deed here in issue but which are typical of the circumstances attending the execution of a great many of the broad form deeds. In 1900 only 17 percent of the land in Knott County was improved agricultural land. A great percentage of the land (as was the case with the 90–acre tract of which the Martin parcel was a part) was hillside land of no productive value. The average value per acre of land in Knott County (in 1900) was only $2.90 per acre. The predecessors in title to the Martin land were paid $3.00 per acre in 1905 for the mineral rights only.

So the argument that no farmer reasonably would have intended that his fields be destroyed by mining operations must be weighed in the light of the fact that there were very few farmers and very few fields involved in the mineral deed transactions. It is of course true that in a number of instances (as in the case before us) there was some bottom land embraced in the deed, and it reasonably can be argued that the owner would not have intended that his bottom land be destroyed. But on the other hand it can just as reasonably be argued that in order to obtain the best price for the mineral rights in his hillside land the owner had to throw in the rights in the bottom land also, and he was willing to take the chance on future destruction of his bottom land to get the immediate money. Otherwise, why did not the landowners simply exclude their bottom land from the deeds? * * *

The argument that the landowners would not have undertaken to sever the mineral title from the surface title, and retain the latter, instead of simply deeding the whole title to the mineral buyers, if they had not contemplated that the surface would retain its value for agricultural and residential uses, is not fully persuasive. We think the fact that in many instances, as here, the landowner was being paid, for the mineral rights alone, practically the full value of his land, might well indicate that the landowner chose to retain the bare title simply for what little value, if any, it might have.

If, as appears well may have been the case, the landowners who executed the broad form mineral deeds at the turn of the century were paid prices which substantially or in large part equaled the full value of the land (at least of the hillside land) we see nothing unfair, unjust or inequitable in construing the deeds in favor of the grantees. Certainly the fact that the surface of the land is worth much more today than it was in 1905 is not a valid reason for saying that the landowners should be paid again.

As concerns the matter of estoppel, we find no basis for an estoppel in the fact that an owner of thousands of acres of mineral rights does not advise a surface owner who is commencing to make improvements that the latter's rights are subordinate by law to those of the mineral owner, and that some day the mineral owner may reach that land in his mining operations. If there were any estoppel in this case it would be against the Martins, in that they built their improvements after *Buchanan v. Watson* had been decided, advising the public that strip mining could be done under the broad form deed.

We do not mean to discredit the arguments on behalf of the landowners. They have elements of merit and a degree of persuasiveness. However, they do not have the overwhelming force necessary to prevail against the long entrenched rule of our previous cases in reliance upon which property rights have vested. *See Blue Diamond Coal Company v. Neace, Ky.*, 337 S.W.2d 725. * * *

There remains for consideration the cross-appeal attacking that portion of the judgment which requires the mineral owner to pay damages for destruction of the surface caused by legitimate strip or auger mining operations. The appellants, as cross-appellees, do not undertake with any enthusiasm to argue that this portion of the judgment is correct. It appears to us that if, as we in substance are holding, the mineral owner bought and paid for the right to destroy the surface in a good faith exercise of the right to remove the minerals, then there is no basis upon which there could rest an obligation to pay damages for exercising that right. Certainly it could not rest upon any tort principle, and the only other possible basis—a contractual one—does not exist in the terms of the deed. So in our opinion the judgment is erroneous in declaring the obligation to pay damages (except of course for arbitrary, wanton or malicious acts).

On the direct appeal the judgment is affirmed; on the cross-appeal the judgment is reversed with directions to enter judgment in conformity with this opinion.

Edward P. Hill, Judge (dissenting).

I dissent from the majority opinion.

This case presents a question of the interpretation of a deed executed December 29, 1905, known and designated as "broad form" or "northern" deeds. These deeds, including the one in question, give the owner of the coal the right to use the surface for any and all purposes "deemed necessary" by the grantee to remove the coal. In a number of counties uniform blank deeds were used so that only the description and the name of the grantor were required above the certificate of the acknowledging officer. In many instances deed books were ordered by the clerk at the request of the mineral purchasers. I mention the foregoing circumstances in connection with the so-called rule that a deed should be construed against the grantor.

The question here is whether the grantee may use mining methods (stripping) not known or contemplated by the parties at the time the deed was made to such an extent as to destroy the surface rights of the grantor.

By every rule of contract construction, including construction of deeds, the intention of the parties is the ultimate quest of the interpreter. 17A C.J.S. Contracts § 295. The authorities supporting this proposition are so legion I consider it unnecessary to cite further authority except to say that this jurisdiction has followed the universal rule announced in *Parrish v. Newbury,* Ky., 279 S.W.2d 229, 233, wherein this court said: "Notwithstanding these general rules, always, as a fundamental and supreme rule of construction of contracts, the intention of the parties governs."

What was the intention of the parties in 1905? This question provokes another question, What were the usual, known, and accepted mining methods at that time? Certainly strip mining was then unknown and unaccepted. I find a note in Kentucky Law Journal, volume 50, page 525, note 5, which states: "Strip mining was of no importance until 1914 but 'knob' or 'channel' coal was mined near Cumberland Lake, Kentucky about 1927. These early operations used picks, shovels, and slip-scrapers drawn by mules to remove the thin overburden." (Emphasis added.)

Strip mining was neither heard of nor dreamed of in 1905 in Knott County, the locality of the coal land in question. There was no railroad in Knott County until long thereafter. Neither was there a navigable stream in that county. About the only coal mined in those days was from the outcroppings in creek beds, where a small quantity was obtained by the use of a new-found tool—the coal pick.

I contend first that inasmuch as the parties to the "broad form" deeds never contemplated the use of the then unknown method of strip mining and never dreamed of the cataclysmic destruction of the surface, the grantee and his successor in title have no right to remove the coal by stripping methods. Secondly, I contend that if rules of construction are so modified and distorted as to authorize the grantee to use stripping methods, he should be answerable in damages to the surface owners for just compensation. * * *

Not only is the majority opinion contrary to the laws of sister coal states, such as West Virginia and Pennsylvania, as I shall point out later, but the majority opinion is inconsistent with other opinions of this court in similar situations. This court decided in *Wiser Oil Company v. Conley*, Ky., 346 S.W.2d 718 (1960), that the owner of oil and gas rights had no right to use the water-flooding method of recovering oil without the consent of the owner of the surface. This court said in *Wiser* at page 721: "Even though appellants assert that the water-flooding process was known prior to March 10, 1917, the date of execution of the lease, and was employed to some extent in other states before that time, *we conclude it was the intention* of the parties that oil should be produced by drilling in the customary manner *that prevailed when the lease was executed*. Any exemption from liability would therefore be limited to the damages which might be caused by this *contemplated* means of bringing oil to the top." (Emphasis added.) *Wiser* and *Buchanan* are as inconsistent as sin and salvation.

I am shocked and appalled that the court of last resort in the beautiful state of Kentucky would ignore the logic and reasoning of the great majority of other states and lend its approval and encouragement to the diabolical devastation and destruction of a large part of the surface of this fair state without compensation to the owners thereof. * * *

I cannot bring myself to the conclusion that it was the intention of the parties at the time the minerals were reserved to permit the owner of the minerals to completely destroy the surface of the farm which is now owned by the defendants.

I confess I think strip mining without proper reclamation procedures is a catastrophe. I consider it against public policy and detrimental to the general welfare of the state, and any contract pertaining thereto is illegal as being against public policy. Of course, where the land is not steep and proper reclamation practices are followed, strip mining may be justified.

The majority opinion attempts to justify the harsh rule applied in this case by comparing the value of the consideration paid for the mineral to the assessed value of the surface at the date of the deed. This is a poor comparison when it is universally recognized that in this state land values were assessed at 10 to 15 percent of their market value until recently.

I would affirm the judgment of the trial court and go further and hold that the grantee has no legal right to strip or auger mine coal under the deed in question.

QUESTIONS AND DISCUSSION

1. In 1984, the Kentucky Legislature enacted a law that created a presumption that coal deeds conveyed the right to mine "only by the method or methods of commercial coal extraction commonly known to be in use in Kentucky in the area affected at the time the instrument was executed." The presumption could be rebutted only by "clear and convincing evidence to the contrary." KY. REV. STAT. ANN. § 381.940 (1902). Nonetheless, in *Akers v. Baldwin*, 736 S.W.2d 294 (Ky. 1987), the Kentucky Supreme Court held the statute unconstitutional, essentially reaffirming the decision in

Martin. The Court did overturn that aspect of *Martin* that denied damages for injury to the surface, but then held that its decision would not apply to any deeds executed between 1956 (when it had first denied surface damages) and the date of the *Akers* decision, or to any future conveyance to the same mineral property. Did fairness to mining interests compel the Court to so limit its decision?

Kentucky finally amended its constitution in 1988 with language that tracked the 1984 statute. KY. CONST. 19(2) (amended 1988). In *Ward v. Harding*, 860 S.W.2d 280 (Ky. 1993), *cert. denied*, 510 U.S. 1177 (1994), the Kentucky Supreme Court upheld the amendment against challenges under the contracts and takings clauses of the federal constitution. *See* Dean Hill Rivkin, *Lawyering, Power and Reform: The Legal Campaign to Abolish the Broad Form Deed*, 66 TENN. L. REV. 467 (1999).

2. The broad form deed involved in the *Buchanan* decision, the case cited by the *Martin* court, provided in relevant part as follows:

> . . . [granting the] property, rights and privileges, in, of, to, on, under, concerning and appurtenant . . . all the coal, minerals and mineral products, . . . such of the standing timber as may be, or by the Grantee, his heirs or representatives, its successors, or assigns, be deemed necessary for mining purposes, . . . [to] use and operate the same and surface thereof, . . . in any and every manner that may be deemed necessary or convenient for mining, and there from removing, . . . and in the use of said land and surface thereof by the Grantee his heirs or representatives, successors and assigns, shall be free from and is, and are, hereby released from liability or claim of damage to the said Grantor, their representatives, heirs and assigns, ...

Does this broad form deed clearly grant the mineral owner the right to conduct strip mining operations? What arguments might you make to support a claim that it does not? Does the language give the coal company the right to maintain a nuisance? Are you persuaded by Judge Hill's dissent in *Martin*?

Harry Caudill, the author of NIGHT COMES TO THE CUMBERLANDS, which is excerpted above, represented the plaintiffs in the *Martin* case. In a more recent book, THEIRS BE THE POWER: THE MOGULS OF EASTERN KENTUCKY (1983), Caudill offers extensive background information about the *Martin* case.

3. Although strip mining of coal ravaged many parts of the country, especially in the coal fields of Appalachia, the mining and reclamation standards established under the Surface Mining Control and Reclamation Act of 1977 (SMCRA), 30 U.S.C. § 1201–1328, have fundamentally changed the way that strip mining is carried out in the United States. In addition to mandating strict permitting and performance standards, SMCRA generally requires restoration of mined lands to their "approximate original contour," and requires that the lands be restored to a condition capable of supporting their pre-mining uses or "higher and better uses." 30 U.S.C. § 1265(b)(2) (2006). Despite the strict standards established by SMCRA, many citizen groups, like Save Our Cumberland Mountains in Tennessee, initially supported an outright ban on strip mining because of their past experience with the poor mining practices of the industry. Despite this opposition, Congress chose to allow strip mining because it is safer and it generally has a distinct economic advantage over underground mining. SMCRA is addressed more fully at the end of this chapter.

4. Is the court right in suggesting that conservation is not an issue in construing broad form deeds? Suppose that the broad form deed were construed to limit the rights of the coal owner such that only those mining methods that existed at the time of the deed would be allowed, unless the coal owner received the surface owner's permission to use other methods. Assuming that the surface owner maintains a home on the surface of the land, as is often the case in Kentucky, is it likely that the surface owner's only concern will be securing additional money from the coal owner as a condition for allowing strip mining? What other considerations will likely affect the surface owner's willingness to grant permission to strip mine?

5. In *Mullins v. Beatrice Pocahontas Co.*, 432 F.2d 314 (4th Cir. 1970), the plaintiffs filed an action for damages and injunctive relief against a coal company that was allegedly creating a nuisance as a result of air pollution from its coal processing facilities. The relevant deeds contained broad language granting the coal company all rights incidental to mining. Some of the deeds even included language exonerating the coal company from "all claims ... for damages for incidental activities, including ... pollution of the air, or the emission of dust, smoke, fumes or noxious gases." Nonetheless, the court held that under Virginia law, a coal company had no right "to process coal by methods which unreasonably impair the use of the surface." How does *Pocahontas* limit the rights that can be granted by a lease or mineral estate?

Pocahontas reversed a district court decision in favor of the coal company. On remand, how should the court rule if air pollution adversely affects the health of local residents but the cost of available emission controls could force *Pocahontas* out of business?

6. Under the decision in *Pocahontas* can a coal operator maintain a nuisance if specifically allowed under the terms of the deed? Are there any limitations on that right? If the deed is sufficient to protect Pocahontas from an action by the surface owner, should it protect Pocahontas from an action by tenants of the surface owner? From people who work but do not live in the area? From an adjacent surface owner who is not subject to the deed under which the right to conduct incidental mining activities is claimed? *See Smith v. Pittston Co.*, 127 S.E.2d 79 (Va. 1962) (upholding the liability of a coal company for causing a private nuisance to adjacent land, regardless of the degree of care exercised by the company).

7. Even without explicit language, mineral estates are generally considered to be dominant estates as compared with the surface estate. ROCKY MOUNTAIN MINERAL FOUNDATION, 3 AM. L. OF MINING § 84.02(4)(a) (2d ed. 1997). Why? What rights does this secure for the mineral estate owner?

PROBLEM EXERCISE: LEGAL LIMITS ON THE TERMS OF A LEASE

Freda Farmer, who owns a large tract of farm land, negotiates a coal lease with the Carbon Coal Company (CCC) in 1995. The lease imposes no reclamation obligations on CCC and provides that CCC is not liable in any way in damages to Freda for destruction of the surface or for any pollution that mining may cause. In exchange Freda receives an 18% net royalty—about twice the standard royalty rate for coal leases in the area. The following year the state legislature enacts comprehensive mining and reclamation standards applicable to CCC's mining operation. As a result, CCC must now conduct its mining operations in a manner that avoids pollution and must fully reclaim the land after mining to its pre-mining condition. Suppose that the new law combined with the high royalty rate make it impossible for CCC to mine coal profitably. Does the law effect a "taking" of CCC's property? Is CCC entitled to renegotiate the royalty rate? If so, on what possible grounds?

---

2. SPLIT ESTATES

"Split estates," in which one person owns the surface and one owns the minerals, are often disfavored by state and local governments because they limit the economic development and use of the land surface. As noted previously, property law treats the mineral estate as the dominant estate, assuring a preference for mining when conflicts with the surface arise. Notwithstanding this preference, the state's interest in promoting economic development and the tendency of some mineral estate holders to sit on their rights for long periods of time may make the mineral estate a less secure estate, as the following case illustrates.

Texaco, Inc. v. Short,
454 U.S. 516 (1982)

Justice Stevens delivered the opinion of the Court.

In 1971 the Indiana Legislature enacted a statute providing that a severed mineral interest that is not used for a period of 20 years automatically lapses and reverts to the current surface owner of the property, unless the mineral owner files a statement of claim in the local county recorder's office. The Indiana Supreme Court rejected a challenge to the constitutionality of the statute. 406 N.E.2d 625 (Ind., 1980). We noted probable jurisdiction, 450 U.S. 993, and now affirm.

As the Indiana Supreme Court explained, the Mineral Lapse Act "puts an end to interests in coal, oil, gas or other minerals which have not been used for twenty years." The statute provides that the unused interest shall be "extinguished" and that its "ownership shall revert to the then owner of the interest out of which it was carved." The statute, which became effective on September 2, 1971, contained a 2–year grace period in which owners of mineral interests that were then unused and subject to lapse could preserve those interests by filing a claim in the recorder's office.

The "use" of a mineral interest that is sufficient to preclude its extinction includes the actual or attempted production of minerals, the payment of rents or royalties, and any payment of taxes; a mineral owner may also protect his interest by filing a statement of claim with the local recorder of deeds. The statute contains one exception to this general rule: if an owner of 10 or more interests in the same county files a statement of claim that inadvertently omits some of those interests, the omitted interests may be preserved by a supplemental filing made within 60 days of receiving actual notice of the lapse.

The statute does not require that any specific notice be given to a mineral owner prior to a statutory lapse of a mineral estate. The Act does set forth a procedure, however, by which a surface owner who has succeeded to the ownership of a mineral estate pursuant to the statute may give notice that the mineral interest has lapsed. * * *

In [the two cases consolidated before the Court] it is agreed that if the statute is valid, appellants' mineral interests have lapsed because of their failure to produce minerals, pay taxes, or file a statement of claim within the statutory period. In neither case does the agreed statement of facts indicate whether any of the appellants was aware of the enactment of the Mineral Lapse Act, or of its possible effect on his mineral interests, at any time after the enactment of the statute and before the appellees published notice of the lapse of the mineral estates. At all stages of the proceedings, appellants challenged the constitutionality of the Dormant Mineral Interests Act. Appellants claimed that the lack of prior notice of the lapse of their mineral rights deprived them of property without due process of law, that the statute effected a taking of private property for public use without just compensation, and that the exception contained in the Act for owners of 10 or more mineral interests denied them the equal protection of the law; appellants based these arguments on the Fourteenth Amendment of the United States Constitution. Appellants also contended that the statute constituted an impairment of contracts in violation of Art. 1, § 10, of the Constitution. The state trial court held that the statute deprived appellants of property without due process of law, and effected a taking of property without just compensation.

On appeal, the Indiana Supreme Court reversed. * * *

I

Appellants raise several specific challenges to the constitutionality of the Mineral Lapse Act. Before addressing these arguments, however, it is appropriate to consider whether the State has the power to provide that property rights of this character shall be extinguished if their owners do not take the affirmative action required by the State.

In *Board of Regents v. Roth*, 408 U.S. 564, 577, the Court stated: "Property interests, of course, are not created by the Constitution. Rather, they are created and their dimensions are defined by existing rules or understandings that stem from an independent source such as state law, rules or understandings that secure certain benefits and that support claims of entitlement to those benefits." The State of Indiana has defined a severed mineral estate as a "vested property interest," entitled to "the same protection as are fee simple titles." Through its Dormant Mineral Interests Act, however, the State has declared that this property interest is of less than absolute duration; retention is conditioned on the performance of at least one of the actions required by the Act. We have no doubt that, just as a State may create a property interest that is entitled to constitutional protection, the State has the power to condition the permanent retention of that property right on the performance of reasonable conditions that indicate a present intention to retain the interest. * * *

It is also clear that the State has not exercised this power in an arbitrary manner. The Indiana statute provides that a severed mineral interest shall not terminate if its owner takes any one of three steps to establish his continuing interest in the property. If the owner engages in actual production, or collects rents or royalties from another person who does or proposes to do so, his interest is protected. If the owner pays taxes, no matter how small, the interest is secure. If the owner files a written statement of claim in the county recorder's office, the interest remains viable. Only if none of these actions is taken for a period of 20 years does a mineral interest lapse and revert to the surface owner.

Each of the actions required by the State to avoid an abandonment of a mineral estate furthers a legitimate state goal. Certainly the State may encourage owners of mineral interests to develop the potential of those interests; similarly, the fiscal interest in collecting property taxes is manifest. The requirement that a mineral owner file a public statement of claim furthers both of these goals by facilitating the identification and location of mineral owners, from whom developers may acquire operating rights and from whom the county may collect taxes. The State surely has the power to condition the ownership of property on compliance with conditions that impose such a slight burden on the owner while providing such clear benefits to the State.

II

Two of appellants' arguments may be answered quickly. Appellants contend that the Mineral Lapse Act takes private property without just compensation in violation of the Fourteenth Amendment; they also argue that the statute constitutes an impermissible impairment of contracts in violation of the Contract Clause. The authorities already discussed mandate rejection of each of these arguments.

In ruling that private property may be deemed to be abandoned and to lapse upon the failure of its owner to take reasonable actions imposed by law, this Court has never required the State to compensate the owner for the consequences of his own neglect. We have concluded that the State may treat a mineral has not been used for 20 years and for which no statement of claim has been filed as abandoned; it follows that, after abandonment, the former owner retains no interest for which he may claim compensation. It is the owner's failure to make any use of the property—and not the action of the State—that causes the lapse of the property right; there is no "taking" that requires compensation. The requirement that an owner of a property interest that has not been used for 20 years must come forward and file a current statement of claim is not itself a "taking."

Nor does the Mineral Lapse Act unconstitutionally impair the obligation of contracts. In the specific cases under review, the mineral owners did not execute the coal and oil leases in question until after the statutory lapse of their mineral rights. The statute cannot be said to impair a contract that did not exist at the time of its enactment. Appellants' right to enter such an agreement of course has been impaired by the statute; this right, however, is a property right and not a contract right. In any event, a mineral owner may safeguard any contractual obligations or rights by filing a statement of claim in the county recorder's office. Such a minimal "burden" on contractual obligations is not beyond the scope of permissible state action.

III

Appellants' primary attack on the Dormant Mineral Interests Act is that it extinguished their property rights without adequate notice. In advancing this argument, appellants actually assert two quite different claims. First, appellants argue that the State of Indiana did not adequately notify them of the legal requirements of the new statute. Second, appellants argue that a mineral interest may not be extinguished unless the surface owner gives the mineral owner advance notice that the 20–year period of nonuse is about to expire. When these two arguments are considered separately, it is clear that neither has merit.

A

The first question raised is simply how a legislature must go about advising its citizens of actions that must be taken to avoid a valid rule of law that a mineral interest that has not been used for 20 years will be deemed to be abandoned. The answer to this question is no different from that posed for any legislative enactment affecting substantial rights. Generally, a legislature need do nothing more than enact and publish the law, and afford the citizenry a reasonable opportunity to familiarize itself with its terms and to comply. In this case, the 2–year grace period included in the Indiana statute forecloses any argument that the statute is invalid because mineral owners may not have had an opportunity to become familiar with its terms. It is well established that persons owning property within a State are charged with knowledge of relevant statutory provisions affecting the control or disposition of such property. * * *

B

We have concluded that appellants may be presumed to have had knowledge of the terms of the Dormant Mineral Interests Act. Specifically, they are presumed to have known that an unused mineral interest would lapse unless they filed a statement of claim. The question then presented is whether, given that knowledge, appellants had a constitutional right to be advised—presumably by the surface owner—that their 20–year period of nonuse was about to expire.

In answering this question, it is essential to recognize the difference between the self-executing feature of the statute and a subsequent judicial determination that a particular lapse did in fact occur. As noted by appellants, no specific notice need be given of an impending lapse. If there has been a statutory use of the interest during the preceding 20–year period, however, by definition there is no lapse—whether or not the surface owner, or any other party, is aware of that use. Thus, no mineral estate that has been protected by any of the means set forth in the statute may be lost through lack of notice. It is undisputed that, before judgment could be entered in a quiet title action that would determine conclusively that a mineral interest has reverted to the surface owner, the full procedural protections of the Due Process Clause—including notice reasonably calculated to reach all interested parties and a prior opportunity to be heard—must be provided. * * *

The judgment of the Supreme Court of Indiana is affirmed.

JUSTICE BRENNAN, with whom JUSTICE WHITE, JUSTICE MARSHALL, and JUSTICE POWELL join, dissenting.

There is no measurable dispute in these cases concerning Indiana's power to control, define, and limit interests in land within its boundaries. Nor is there any question that Indiana has a legitimate interest in encouraging the productive use of land by establishing a registration system to identify the owners of mineral rights. Nor indeed is there any question that extinguishment of a mineral owner's rights may be an appropriate sanction for a failure to register. The question presented here is simply whether the State of Indiana has deprived these appellants of due process of law by extinguishing their pre-existing property interests without regard to whether they knew, and without providing any meaningful mechanism by which they might have learned, of the imminent taking of their property or their obligations under the law. * * *

[T]he Due Process Clause of the Fourteenth Amendment was designed to guard owners of property from the wholly arbitrary actions of state governments. As applied retrospectively to extinguish the rights of mineral interest owners for their failure to have made use of their interests within a prior 20–year period, Indiana's statutory scheme would likely effect an unlawful taking of property absent the proviso that such mineral interest owners could preserve their rights by filing a notice of claim within the 2–year grace period. Given the nature of the scheme established, there is no discernible basis for failing to afford those owners such notice as would make the saving proviso meaningful. As applied to mineral interest owners who were without knowledge of their legal obligations, and who were not permitted to file a saving statement of claim within some period following the giving of statutory notice by the surface owner, the statute operates unconstitutionally. In my view, the provision of no process simply cannot be deemed due process of law. I respectfully dissent.

QUESTIONS AND DISCUSSION

1. The dissent argues that the state's interests are best served by requiring the surface owner to notify the mineral owner before title is extinguished. How would the majority respond?

2. What does the *Texaco* decision tell you about the nature of a mineral estate? Do you think that the Court would have reached the same result if the statute had provided for forfeiture of the full fee estate?

3. Why would Indiana adopt a statute that extinguished a mineral estate in favor of the surface estate owner? What problems do split estates pose for the state? Why do states allow mineral estates to be severed from the surface estate in the first place if split estates limit the productive use of the surface?

4. The Court notes that due process requires notice to the record owner of a mineral estate in a quiet title action to determine whether a mineral interest has reverted to a surface owner, but that such individualized notice is not required before a reversion takes place by operation of law. Why so? In answering this question, consider that the reversion occurs as a result of legislative action, whereas quiet title requires judicial action.

—————

B. DEFINING THE MINERAL RESOURCES

Does a mineral estate include everything below the surface of the land? Does it include the migrating fluids and gases, and just the plain dirt and other materials that support the surface? Put another way, when a deed or conveyancing instrument grants a mineral estate to a party, just exactly what does the party get? A simplistic approach might divide all matter into the classic three categories of animal, vegetable, and mineral, and allocate the mineral portion to the estate owner. Even this division, however, does not answer all of the legal questions, as the following case suggests.

MAURICE TANNER,
141 I.B.L.A. 373 (1997)

Opinion by Administrative JUDGE BURSKI

[Tanner traced his title to a patent under the Stock Raising Homestead Act (SHRA). Under the terms of this statute, the government reserved "all the coal and other minerals." (43 U.S.C. § 299 (2003)). Tanner had removed "humate" from the land but the government claimed that Tanner was trespassing because humate is part of the mineral estate owned by the federal government. Tanner challenged an adverse decision of the Bureau of Land Management to the Interior Board of Land of Appeals. Set forth below is an excerpt from the Board's decision.]

. . . Since 1979, extraction of humate has been unauthorized by the BLM. Although Tanner owns the surface estate and recognizes that the United States reserved to itself ownership of "all the coal and other minerals," he contends that "humate" is an organic substance which, like peat, should not be considered reserved as a mineral. Tanner has requested a hearing to present evidence on the organic nature of peat. The Bureau does not dispute that humate is organic in origin but considers it, nevertheless, to be a low grade of coal which is reserved to the United States.

Before giving further consideration to humate's legal status as a vegetative or mineral material, it is helpful to develop a general understanding of what humate is. One of the standard authorities states:

> Humate, derived from weathered coal and associated carbonaceous shales and claystones, has become an important nonfuel, mineral commodity in the State [of New Mexico]. Enormous reserves of the humic-acid rich material have been identified, and in 1990 there were two producing mines. * * * Humate is used chiefly as an additive in drilling muds and soil conditioners.

U.S. Department of the Interior, Bureau of Mines, 1990 Minerals Yearbook, Vol. 2, at 353.

A somewhat different definition, however, appeared in a later publication of the Bureau of Land Management:

> The New Mexican variety of humate can best be described as a carbonaceous mudstone or shale-like material made up of totally decomposed humus and salts of humic acids such as humic, ulmic, and fluvic acids. . . .
> Although not well understood in terms of agricultural effects, humate seems to aid plant uptake of nutrients via the acids. Humate also aids soil by increasing the water holding capacity, and acts as a buffer for alkaline soils. Microorganism growth also seems to be positively affected by the introduction of humate material.

B. Lloyd, Humates in Northwestern New Mexico (Snake Oil or Wonder Product), Energy and Minerals Newsline, October/November 1991, at 9–10.

Although the record does not contain an analysis or detailed description of the material recently excavated by Tanner in this trespass action, a Mineral Report dated September 20, 1985, was prepared for a coal and humate trespass from three pits, and pit #1 appears to be in the same location as the pit in the instant appeal. * * *

In support of his contention that material such as humate is not a reserved mineral and, indeed, not a mineral at all, Tanner relies on a discussion appearing in the leading decision construing the mineral reservation in the

SRHA, *Watt v. Western Nuclear, Inc.,* 462 U.S. 36, 53–54 (1983). In that case, the Supreme Court grappled with the question whether gravel was a mineral reserved under an SRHA patent:

> Given Congress' understanding that the surface of SRHA lands would be used for ranching and farming, we interpret the mineral reservation in the Act to include substances that are mineral in character (*i.e.,* that are *inorganic*), that can be removed from the soil, that can be used for commercial purposes, and that there is no reason to suppose were intended to be included in the surface estate.

(Emphasis added.) Elsewhere, the Court had declared that "[w]hile it may be necessary that a substance be inorganic to qualify as a mineral under the SRHA, it cannot be sufficient." *Id.* at 43. Appellant relies upon these statements and argues that humate is clearly "organic" in nature and, therefore, under the Supreme Court's analysis, not mineral in character. * * *

If the Supreme Court had utilized the term "inorganic" in its technical sense to exclude substances which contained carbon as a constituent element, it would have excluded diamonds, graphite, coal, petroleum, and asphalt from the definition of "mineral" under the laws of the United States. This the Court clearly did not intend. Not only are all of these substances considered to be mineral within the meaning of the mining and mineral leasing laws of the United States, * * * but all entries made and patents issued under the SRHA were expressly subject to "a reservation to the United States of all the coal and other minerals in the lands so entered and patented." 43 U.S.C. § 299 (1994). Yet, coal has, in fact, been defined as "an organic rock." *See* Encyclopedia Britannica, Macropaedia (1979), Vol. 4 at 790. * * *

Contextually, it is clear that the term "inorganic" was used by the Court to describe substances that were neither animal nor vegetable and not in the sense that substances which contain carbon as a constituent were necessarily excluded from classification as a mineral. * * *

Where, then, does humate figure in this equation? Humate is not a vegetative material that has undergone only slight modification. On the contrary, unlike peat moss which still retains its vegetative character, humate is "a carbonaceous mudstone or shale-like material." Unlike peat moss which dates from the present epoch (the Holocene), humate dates from the Upper Cretaceous period, *i.e.,* at least 65 million years ago, such that the forces of nature have, indeed, had ample opportunity to act upon it and alter its original nature. And, unlike peat moss which is primarily used as an additive for improving the physical character of the soil, it seems clear that the major incentive for humate use is an alteration in the chemical character of soil by improving plant uptake of nutrients via the humic and other acids present in the humate. . . . It seems clear from the foregoing that humate is far more akin to coal in being an "organic rock" than it is to peat moss which has retained its essential vegetable character. * * *

We conclude, therefore, that humates are a mineral reserved under patents issued pursuant to the SRHA and that the disposition of such mineral constitutes a trespass for which the United States is properly compensated. Therefore, pursuant to the authority delegated to the Board of Land Appeals by the Secretary of the Interior, 43 C.F.R. § 4.1, the decision appealed from is affirmed.

QUESTIONS AND DISCUSSION

1. What are the indicia for determining whether material is classified as vegetable or mineral? Why is peat recognized as vegetative material, whereas humates are classified as minerals? Are there any circumstances where peat might be classified as a mineral?

2. The Interior Board of Land Appeals (IBLA) is an administrative board within the Interior Department's Office of Hearings and Appeals (OHA). The IBLA hears appeals from a wide variety of both formal and informal BLM decisions, as well as from decisions by administrative law judges who rule on BLM matters. 43 C.F.R. § 4.410 (2008). IBLA decisions are considered as binding precedent on the Department unless overturned by the Director of OHA, the Secretary, or a later IBLA decision. 43 C.F.R. § 4.5 (2008). The decisions of administrative law judges, however, are not treated as precedent but as *ad hoc* resolutions of particular cases. Most mining claims challenges involve contest proceedings, which are first heard by an administrative law judge. 43 C.F.R. § 4.450–1(2008). IBLA decisions decided after 1993 are available on the web at http://www.ibiadecisions.com/Ibla/iblamainpage.html. Contest proceedings are described in greater detail at Part III.G of this chapter.

The federal government publishes all IBLA decisions and the Rocky Mountain Mineral Law Institute publishes most of these in Gower's Federal Service (GFS). Gower's contains exact reproductions of IBLA decisions and divides those decisions into three categories—mining (green binder), oil and gas (red binder), and miscellaneous (blue binder). In addition, selected cases are separately published in the federal government's annual volume of Interior Decisions (I.D.).

3. The Board of Land Appeals found that humates are minerals, but this finding in itself does not resolve the case. Why not? What else must be considered?

4. The Board finds that Tanner was an innocent trespasser. Accordingly, the measure of damages was the value of the material in place. Is it clear that Tanner was acting in good faith? What should the damages be where a party has acted in bad faith? Generally, it is the minerals' market value rather than their value in place. *See* 6 AM. L. OF MINING, § 203.01[2][b] (2d ed. 1987).

5. Until 2003, the BLM regulations provided that "[w]hatever is recognized as a mineral by the standard authorities, whether metallic or other substance, when found in public lands in quantity and quality sufficient to render the lands valuable on account thereof, is treated as coming within the purview of the mining laws." 43 C.F.R. § 3812.1 (2003). These rules were revised and reorganized in 2004 and now simply provide that minerals must be recognized as such "by the scientific community." 43 C.F.R. § 3830.12(a)(1) (2007). What does the "scientific community" have to say about "humates"? Is the decision in *Tanner* consistent with the BLM's definition of mineral?

6. What does the *Tanner* case teach you about drafting a mineral reservation clause or other conveyance instruments?

7. Under the Board's analysis in *Tanner*, is water a mineral? Is it reserved under the SRHA? Consider these questions as you read the following case.

Andrus v. Charlestone Stone Products Co.,
436 U.S. 604 (1978)

Mr. Justice Marshall delivered the opinion of the Court.

[*Andrus* involved various mining claims that had been located under the General Mining Law of 1872. As will be described later in this chapter, such claims are valid only where—at a minimum—they contain valuable deposits of minerals. The district court held that one of the mining company's claims was not valid, but that the government was nonetheless obliged to provide the claimant with access to the property to remove water resources that would be used to develop minerals on other valid claims. The Court of Appeals for the Ninth Circuit affirmed the lower court's decision, but on different grounds. The Ninth Circuit held that because water is a mineral and the claim contained valuable water supplies, the claim should be considered valid under the mining law. The court reached this surprising conclusion without the benefit of briefs or argument. Indeed, the mining claimant had never made such a claim. Supreme Court review followed.]

Under the basic federal mining statute, which derives from an 1872 law, "all valuable mineral deposits in lands belonging to the United States" are declared "free and open to exploration and purchase." 30 U.S.C. § 22. The question presented is whether water is a "valuable mineral" as those words are used in the mining law. * * *

II

We may assume for purposes of this decision that the Court of Appeals was correct in concluding that water is a "mineral," in the broadest sense of that word, and that it is "valuable." Both of these facts are necessary to a holding that a claimant has located a "valuable mineral deposit" under the 1872 law, 30 U.S.C. § 22, but they are hardly sufficient.

This Court long ago recognized that the word "mineral," when used in an Act of Congress, cannot be given its broadest definition. In construing an Act granting certain public lands, except "mineral lands," to a railroad, the Court wrote:

The word "mineral" is used in so many senses, dependent upon the context, that the ordinary definitions of the dictionary throw but little light upon its signification in a given case. Thus the scientific division of all matter into the animal, vegetable or mineral kingdom would be absurd as applied to a grant of lands, since all lands belong to the mineral kingdom.... Equally subversive of the grant would be the definition of minerals found in the Century Dictionary: as "any constituent of the earth's crust...." *Northern Pacific R. Co. v. Soderberg*, 188 U.S. 526, 530 (1903).

In the context of the 1872 mining law, similar conclusions must be drawn. As one court observed, if the term "mineral" in the statute were construed to encompass all substances that are conceivably mineral, "there would be justification for making mine locations on virtually every part of the earth's surface," since "a very high proportion of the substances of the earth are in that sense 'mineral.' " *Rummell v. Bailey,* 7 Utah 2d 137, 140, 320 P.2d 653, 655 (1958). *See also Robert L. Beery,* 25 I.B.L.A. 287, 294–296 (1976) (noting that "common dirt," while literally a mineral, cannot be considered locatable under the mining law); *Holman v. Utah,* 41 L.D. 314, 315 (1912); 1 American Law of Mining, *supra,* § 2.4, p. 168.

The fact that water may be valuable or marketable similarly is not enough to support a mining claim's validity based on the presence of water. Many substances present on the land may be of value, and indeed it seems likely that land itself—especially land located just 15 miles from downtown Las Vegas, *see* 553 F.2d, at 1211—has, in the Court of Appeals' words, "an intrinsic value," *id.* at 1216. Yet the federal mining law surely was not intended to be a general real estate law. * * *

Our opinions ... recognize that, although mining law and water law developed together in the West prior to 1866, with respect to federal lands Congress chose to subject only mining to comprehensive federal regulation. When it passed the 1866 and 1870 mining laws, Congress clearly intended to preserve "pre-existing [water] right[s]." *Broder v. Natoma Water & Mining Co.,* 101 U.S. 274, 276 (1879). Less than 15 years after passage of the 1872 law, the Secretary of the Interior in two decisions ruled that water is not a locatable mineral under the law and that private water rights on federal lands are instead "governed by local customs and laws," pursuant to the 1866 and 1870 provisions. *Charles Lennig,* 5 L.D. 190, 191 (1886); *see William A. Chessman,* 2 L.D. 774, 775 (1883). The Interior Department, which is charged with principal responsibility for "regulating the acquisition of rights in the public lands," *Cameron v. United States,* 252 U.S. 450, 460 (1920), has recently reaffirmed this interpretation. *Robert L. Beery,* 25 I.B.L.A. 287 (1976)....

IV

The conclusion that Congress did not intend water to be locatable under the federal mining law is reinforced by consideration of the practical consequences that could be expected to flow from a holding to the contrary.

A

Many problems would undoubtedly arise simply from the fact of having two overlapping systems for acquisition of private water rights. Under the appropriation doctrine prevailing in most of the Western States, the mere fact that a person controls land adjacent to a body of water means relatively little; instead, water rights belong to "[t]he first appropriator of water for a beneficial use," but only "to the extent of his actual use," *California Oregon Power Co. v. Beaver Portland Cement Co., supra,* 295 U.S. at 154, *see Jennison v. Kirk, supra,* 98 U.S. at 458. Failure to use the water to which one is entitled for a certain period of time generally causes one's rights in that water to be deemed abandoned. *See generally* 2 W. Hutchins, *Water Rights Laws in the Nineteen Western States* 256–328 (1974).

With regard to minerals located under federal law, an entirely different theory prevails. The holder of a federal mining claim, by investing $100 annually in the claim, becomes entitled to possession of the land and may make any use, or no use, of the minerals involved. *See* 30 U.S.C. § 28. Once fee title by patent is obtained, *see supra,* at 2006, even the $100 requirement is eliminated.

One can readily imagine the legal conflicts that might arise from these differing approaches if ordinary water were treated as a federally cognizable "mineral." A federal claimant could, for example, utilize all of the water extracted from a well like respondent's, without regard for the settled prior appropriation rights of another user of the same water. Or he might not use the water at all and yet prevent another from using it, thereby defeating the necessary Western policy in favor of "actual use" of scarce water resources. *California Oregon Power Co. v. Beaver Portland Cement Co.*, 295 U.S. at 154. As one respected commentator has written, allowing water to be the basis of a valid mining claim "could revive long abandoned common law rules of ground water ownership and capture, and ... could raise horrendous problems of priority and extra lateral rights." We decline to effect so major an alteration in established legal relationships based on nothing more than an overly literal reading of a statute, without any regard for its context or history....

V

It has long been established that, when grants to federal land are at issue, any doubts "are resolved for the Government, not against it." *United States v. Union Pacific R. Co.*, 353 U.S. 112, 116 (1957). A fortiori, the Government must prevail in a case such as this, when the relevant statutory provisions, their historical context, consistent administrative and judicial decisions, and the practical problems with a contrary holding all weigh in its favor. Accordingly, the judgment of the Court of Appeals is reversed.

QUESTIONS AND DISCUSSION

1. Following the Court of Appeals decision, the reversal by the Supreme Court was widely anticipated. Why? Was the appeals court decision consistent with the BLM regulations in effect at the time? (The pertinent language appears at note 5 on page 1060.)

2. The development of mining law generally pre-dated the development of water law in the Western United States. But the early mining camps that developed in the West around major mineral deposits recognized that miners needed water to process and develop their minerals. Not surprisingly, and as discussed in more detail in Chapter 7, they followed the same rules for water rights as they did for mineral rights—first in time, first in right. The agricultural settlers who largely followed the miners in settling the West realized that the rules developed for water allocation in the mining camps were far better suited to agricultural development than were the rules that had developed in the East under the riparian doctrine. The prior appropriation doctrine was thus born, and rather quickly became the law throughout the arid West. *See* WELLS A. HUTCHINS, WATER RIGHTS LAWS IN THE NINETEEN WESTERN STATES 254 (1971).

3. Somewhat surprisingly, the courts have struggled with the characterization of one of the most common of all minerals—gravel. *See* John S. Lowe, *What Substances Are Minerals?* 30 ROCKY MTN. MIN. L. INST. 2–1 (1983). Gravel is an important mineral because it is used in virtually all construction, and especially in road construction. In *Watt v. Western Nuclear, Inc.*, 462 U.S. 36 (1983), the U.S. Supreme Court held that gravel is a mineral for purposes of the general mineral reservation clause included in patents issued under the Stock Raising Homestead Act of 1916. You may recall that this was the statute described in the *Tanner* case as reserving to the United States "all the coal and other minerals." 43 U.S.C. § 299 (2003). In 2004, the Supreme Court had an opportunity to reconsider its opinion in *Watt v. Western Nuclear, Inc.*, when looking at the reservation of minerals to the United States in patents issued under the Pittman Act of 1919. The Pittman Act reserved only "valuable minerals" to the U.S., and the Court held that gravel was not a "valuable mineral" under the Act. *BedRoc Limited, LLC v. United States,* 541 U.S. 176 (2004). Thus, while gravel is considered a "mineral" it is not considered a "valuable mineral", which makes the exact language of the reservation clause important

Most state courts have held that gravel is not included in a general mineral reservation clause. For example, in *Miller Land & Mineral Co. v. State Highway Commission of Wyoming,* 757 P.2d 1001 (Wyo. 1988), the Wyoming Supreme Court held that a general reservation of all minerals did not reserve gravel. *Western Nuclear* was not deemed persuasive authority because it "relied heavily upon Congressional intent under the [Stock Raising Homestead Act]...." In narrowly construing the mineral reservation clause, the Court followed Texas' lead in using the "ordinary and natural meaning" test. This test, announced in *Heinatz v. Allen,* 147 Tex. 512, 217 S.W.2d 994, 997 (1949), holds that—

> ... [S]ubstances such as sand, gravel, and limestone are not minerals within the ordinary and natural meaning of the word unless they are rare or exceptional in character or possess a peculiar property giving them special value....

Why do you think the state courts have been so reluctant to treat gravel as a mineral? Does the Texas test adequately resolve the issue? How would you draft a deed to overcome the problems that arose in these cases? Does *Western Nuclear* reach the right result? How might the fact that public lands are involved affect the analysis?

4. In *Amoco Production Company v. Guild Trust,* 636 F.2d 261 (10th Cir. 1980), *cert. denied,* 452 U.S. 967 (1981), the Court of Appeals for the Tenth Circuit held that the reservation of "coal and other minerals" creates a rebuttable presumption that the reservation includes oil and gas. What evidence might be offered to rebut the presumption? Is it appropriate to consider extrinsic evidence such as past dealings between the parties, or the custom or practice in the industry? Should it matter that in the *Guild Trust* case the reservation was for "coal and other minerals," rather than simply "all minerals"?

5. Pennsylvania takes a view seemingly contrary to *Guild Trust.* In *Bundy v. Myers,* 372 Pa. 583, 94 A.2d 724 (1953), the Court held that a reservation or grant of "oil, coal, fire clay, and minerals of every kind and character" creates a rebuttable presumption that natural gas was not included. Can *Guild Trust* be distinguished? Which is the better rule? *See* 3 AM. L. OF MINING § 84.02[1][a] (2d ed. 1961). As you try to answer this question, consider the relevant public policy issues. One of these is surely to promote the development of valuable minerals. But the development of multiple minerals—such as coal and oil and gas—at the same site can create conflicts, especially when the ownership of these minerals is in different parties. Which result—common ownership or split ownership—will best assure maximizing recovery of the most valuable mineral resources?

6. Does a reservation of "oil, gas, and other minerals" include subsurface water? What arguments might you make for or against such a claim? As with the previous question, consider the public policy implications of the different outcomes. Mining and mineral development frequently intercept groundwater. The water is largely a nuisance to mineral operators, who must find a way to dispose of it in order to develop their minerals. Should it matter that the mineral operator will usually want to dispose of the water in the most efficient manner possible, even if that results in wasting water resources? In *Fleming Foundation v. Texaco, Inc.*, 337 S.W.2d 846 (Tex.Civ. App. 1960), the Texas Court of Civil Appeals held that a reservation of "oil, gas, and other minerals" did not include the water, and that the surface owner retained the groundwater rights. Assuming this holding is correct, should a mineral developer be liable to the surface owner for the loss of ground water resources or water pressure when water is released during mineral production?

————

1. COAL BED METHANE

One of the most important contemporary issues in mineral development involves coal bed methane or "CBM." Methane, more commonly known as "natural gas," has become the fuel of choice in many parts of the country because it burns more efficiently than coal or oil and causes fewer environmental problems. As a result, the demand for natural gas has soared in recent years, pushing up prices to record levels. The increased demand and higher prices have caused a boom in natural gas development, and growing interest in the potential for CBM.

According to the CBM Association of Alabama, 13% of the land in the lower 48 states is underlain with coal. *See* http://waterquality.montana.edu/ docs/methane/cbm101.shtml. Much of this coal, however, is too deep or too poor in quality to warrant development. But most deep coal contains methane, and thus, the potential importance of CBM is enormous. For many years, the methane gas that was trapped in the coal was viewed as a serious safety hazard, especially for underground miners, both because of its potentially toxic impact on the air quality in the mine, and because of the potential that methane might cause mine explosions. Before modern ventilation and testing equipment became available, the canary in the coal mine offered a relatively simple way to assess methane conditions underground.

Although underground coal mining continues in many parts of the world, mining companies today generally favor surface mining methods for both safety and economic reasons. In the early 1970s most coal mining was underground; today, however, less than one-half of U.S. production comes from underground mines. *See* Annual Coal Report, 2006, DOE/EIA–0584 (2006), *available at* http://www.eia.doe.gov/cneaf/coal/page/acr/acr.pdf.

As underground coal mining became less attractive in certain areas, mineral operators began to look at ways to exploit the coal resource without actually extracting the coal. In situ coal mining, which involves altering the coal itself for extraction through wells, has eventually given way to the more promising strategy of developing the embedded CBM gas itself from otherwise uneconomical coal deposits. Where mineral reservation clauses reserved only the coal, the question then arose as to who owned the CBM.

The case that follows offers important insights into both the legal and political importance of coal mining. As the Supreme Court notes, the Tenth Circuit had held that the owner of the coal estate—in this case, an Indian Tribe—owned the CBM. The legal issue involved was relatively simple, and there was no conflict in the federal courts on the issue. Does it surprise you then that the Supreme Court agreed to hear this case? Do you think the Court was influenced by the fact that billions of dollars were at stake? While the Southern Ute Tribe lost this particular case, the bigger loser may well have been the federal government, which owns the coals rights under vast stretches of Western lands.

The diagram below illustrates how coal bed methane is produced. The Supreme Court's decision follows.

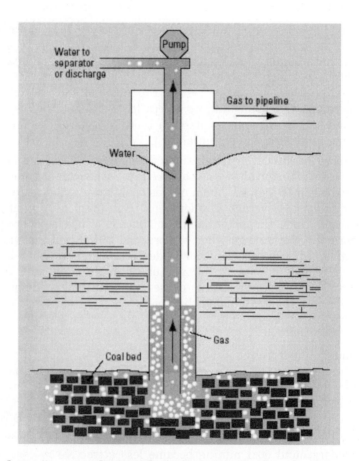

**http://serc.carleton.edu/images/research_education/
cretaceous/cbmrecovery.jpg**

AMOCO PRODUCTION CO. V. SOUTHERN UTE INDIAN TRIBE, 526 U.S. 865 (1999)

JUSTICE KENNEDY delivered the opinion of the Court

Land patents issued pursuant to the Coal Lands Acts of 1909 and 1910 conveyed to the patentee the land and everything in it, except the "coal," which was reserved to the United States. The United States Court of Appeals for the Tenth Circuit determined that the reservation of "coal" includes gas found within the coal formation, commonly referred to as coal bed methane gas (CBM gas). See 151 F.3d 1251, 1256 (1998) (en banc). We granted certiorari, 525 U.S. 1118 (1999), and now reverse.

I

During the second half of the nineteenth century, Congress sought to encourage the settlement of the West by providing land in fee simple absolute to homesteaders who entered and cultivated tracts of a designated size for a period of years. *See, e.g.*, 1862 Homestead Act, 12 Stat. 392; 1877 Desert Land Act, ch.107, 19 Stat. 377. Public lands classified as valuable for coal were exempted from entry under the general land-grant statutes and instead were made available for purchase under the 1864 Coal Lands Act, which set a maximum limit of 160 acres on individual entry and minimum prices of $10 to $20 an acre. Lands purchased under these early Coal Lands Acts—like lands patented under the Homestead Acts—were conveyed to the entryman in fee simple absolute, with no reservation of any part of the coal or mineral estate to the United States. The coal mined from the lands purchased under the Coal Lands Acts and from other reserves fueled the Industrial Revolution.

At the turn of the twentieth century, however, a coal famine struck the West. At the same time, evidence of widespread fraud in the administration of federal coal lands came to light. Lacking the resources to make an independent assessment of the coal content of each individual land tract, the Department of the Interior in classifying public lands had relied for the most part on the affidavits of entrymen. *Watt v. Western Nuclear, Inc.*, 462 U.S. 36, 48 (1983). Railroads and other coal interests had exploited the system to avoid paying for coal lands and to evade acreage restrictions by convincing individuals to falsify affidavits, acquire lands for homesteading, and then turn the land over to them. C. MAYER & G. RILEY, PUBLIC DOMAIN, PRIVATE DOMINION 117–118 (1985).

In 1906, President Theodore Roosevelt responded to the perceived crisis by withdrawing 64 million acres of public land thought to contain coal from disposition under the public land laws. As a result, even homesteaders who had entered and worked the land in good faith lost the opportunity to make it their own unless they could prove to the land office that the land was not valuable for coal.

President Roosevelt's order outraged homesteaders and western interests, and Congress struggled for the next three years to construct a compromise that would reconcile the competing interests of protecting settlers and managing federal coal lands for the public good. President Roosevelt and others urged Congress to begin issuing limited patents that would sever the surface and mineral estates and allow for separate disposal of each. Although various bills were introduced in Congress that would have severed the estates—some of which would have reserved "natural gas" as well as "coal" to the United States—none was enacted.

Finally, Congress passed the Coal Lands Act of 1909, which authorized the Federal Government, for the first time, to issue limited land patents. In contrast to the broad reservations of mineral rights proposed in the failed bills, however, the 1909 Act provided for only a narrow reservation. The Act authorized issuance of patents to individuals who had already made good-faith agricultural entries onto tracts later identified as coal lands, but the issuance was to be subject to "a reservation to the United States of all coal in said lands, and the right to prospect for, mine, and remove the same." 30 U.S.C. § 81. The Act also permitted the patentee to "mine coal for use on the land for domestic purposes prior to the disposal by the United States of the coal deposit." *Ibid.* A similar Act in 1910 opened the remaining coal lands to new entry under the homestead laws, subject to the same reservation of coal to the United States. 30 U.S.C. §§ 83–85.

Among the lands patented to settlers under the 1909 and 1910 Acts were former reservation lands of the Southern Ute Indian Tribe, which the Tribe had ceded to the United States in 1880 in return for certain allotted lands provided for their settlement. Act of June 15, 1880, ch. 223, 21 Stat. 199. In 1938, the United States restored to the Tribe, in trust, title to the ceded reservation lands still owned by the United States, including the reserved coal in lands patented under the 1909 and 1910 Acts. As a result, the Tribe now has equitable title to the coal in lands within its reservation settled by homesteaders under the 1909 and 1910 Acts.

We are advised that over 20 million acres of land were patented under the 1909 and 1910 Acts and that the lands—including those lands in which the Tribe owns the coal—contain large quantities of CBM gas. At the time the Acts were passed, CBM gas had long been considered a dangerous waste product of coal mining. By the 1970's, however, it was apparent that CBM gas could be a significant energy resource and, in the shadow of the Arab oil embargo, the Federal Government began to encourage the immediate production of CBM gas through grants and substantial tax credits.

Commercial development of CBM gas was hampered, however, by uncertainty over its ownership. "In order to expedite the development of this energy source," the Solicitor of the Department of the Interior issued a 1981 opinion concluding that the reservation of coal to the United States in the 1909 and 1910 Acts did not encompass CBM gas. *See Ownership of and Right to Extract Coal Bed Gas in Federal Coal Deposits,* 88 Interior Dec. 538, 539. In reliance on the Solicitor's 1981 opinion, oil and gas companies entered into leases to produce CBM gas with individual landowners holding title under 1909 and 1910 Act patents to some 200,000 acres in which the Tribe owns the coal.

In 1991, the Tribe brought suit in Federal District Court against petitioners, the royalty owners and producers under the oil and gas leases covering that land, and the federal agencies and officials responsible for the administration of lands held in trust for the Tribe. The Tribe sought, inter alia, a declaration that Congress' reservation of coal in the 1909 and1910 Acts extended to CBM gas, so that the Tribe—not the successors in interest of the land patentees—owned the CBM gas.

The District Court granted summary judgment for the defendants, holding that the plain meaning of "coal" is the "solid rock substance" used as fuel, which does not include CBM gas. 874 F. Supp. 1142, 1154 (Colo. 1995). On appeal, a panel of the Court of Appeals reversed. 119 F.3d 816, 819 (CA10 1997). The court then granted rehearing en banc on the question whether the term "coal" in the1909 and 1910 Acts "unambiguously excludes or includes CBM." 151 F.3d at 1256. Over a dissenting opinion by Judge Tacha, joined by two other judges, the en banc court agreed with the panel. *Ibid.* The court held that the term "coal" was ambiguous. *Ibid.* It invoked the interpretive canon that ambiguities in land grants should be resolved in favor of the sovereign and concluded that the coal reservation encompassed CBM gas. *Ibid.*

The United States did not petition for, or participate in, the rehearing en banc. Instead, it filed a supplemental brief explaining that the Solicitor of the Interior was reconsidering the 1981 Solicitor's opinion in light of the panel's decision. On the day the Government's response to petitioners' certiorari petition was due, see id. at 47, n. 37, the Solicitor of the Interior withdrew the 1981 opinion in a one-line order. The United States now supports the Tribe's position that CBM gas is coal reserved by the 1909 and 1910 Acts. * * *

III

* * * The question is not whether, given what scientists know today, it makes sense to regard CBM gas as a constituent of coal but whether Congress so regarded it in 1909 and 1910. In interpreting statutory mineral reservations like the one at issue here, we have emphasized that Congress "was dealing with a practical subject in a practical way" and that it intended the terms of the reservation to be understood in "their ordinary and popular sense." *Burke v. Southern Pacific R. Co.,* 234 U.S. 669, 679 (1914) (rejecting "scientific test" for determining whether a reservation of "mineral lands" included "petroleum lands"); see also *Perrin v. United States,* 444 U.S. 37, 42 (1979) ("Unless otherwise defined, words will be interpreted as taking their ordinary, contemporary, common meaning" at the time Congress enacted the statute). We are persuaded that the common conception of coal at the time Congress passed the1909 and 1910 Acts was the solid rock substance that was the country's primary energy resource.

A.

At the time the Acts were passed, most dictionaries defined coal as the solid fuel resource. For example, one contemporary dictionary defined coal as a "solid and more or less distinctly stratified mineral, varying in color from dark-brown to black, brittle, combustible, and used as fuel, not fusible without decomposition and very insoluble." 2 Century Dictionary and Cyclopedia 1067 (1906). *See also* American Dictionary of the English Language 244 (N. Webster 1889) (defining "coal" as a "black, or brownish black, solid, combustible substance, consisting, like charcoal, mainly of carbon, but more compact"); 2 New English Dictionary on Historical Principles 549 (J. Murray ed.1893) (defining coal as a "mineral, solid, hard, opaque, black, or blackish, found in seams or strata in the earth, and largely used as fuel"); Webster's New International Dictionary of the English Language 424 (W. Harris & F. Allen eds.1916) (defining coal as a "black, or brownish black, solid, combustible mineral substance").

In contrast, dictionaries of the day defined CBM gas—then called "marsh gas," "methane," or "fire-damp"—as a distinct substance, a gas "contained in" or "given off by" coal, but not as coal itself. *See, e.g.,* 3 Century Dictionary and Cyclopedia 2229 (1906) (defining "fire-damp" as "the gas contained in coal, often given off by it in large quantities, and exploding, on ignition, when mixed with atmospheric air"; noting that "fire-damp is a source of great danger to life in coal-mines").

As these dictionary definitions suggest, the common understanding of coal in 1909 and 1910 would not have encompassed CBM gas, both because it is a gas rather than a solid mineral and because it was understood as a distinct substance that escaped from coal as the coal was mined, rather than as a part of the coal itself.

B.

As a practical matter, moreover, it is clear that, by reserving coal in the 1909 and 1910 Act patents, Congress intended to reserve only the solid rock fuel that was mined, shipped throughout the country, and then burned to power the Nation's railroads, ships, and factories. In contrast to natural gas, which was not yet an important source of fuel at the turn of the century, coal was the primary energy for the Industrial Revolution.

As the history recounted in Part I, supra, establishes, Congress passed the 1909 and 1910 Acts to address concerns over the short supply, mismanagement, and fraudulent acquisition of this solid rock fuel resource. Rejecting broader proposals, Congress chose a narrow reservation of the resource that would address the exigencies of the crisis at hand without unduly burdening the rights of homesteaders or impeding the settlement of the West.

It is evident that Congress viewed CBM gas not as part of the solid fuel resource it was attempting to conserve and manage but as a dangerous waste product, which escaped from coal as the coal was mined. Congress was well aware by 1909 that the natural gas found in coal formations was released during coal mining and posed a serious threat to mine safety. Explosions in coal mines sparked by CBM gas occurred with distressing frequency in the late nineteenth and early twentieth centuries. Congress was also well aware that the CBM gas needed to be vented to the greatest extent possible. Almost 20 years prior to the passage of the 1909 and 1910 Acts, Congress had enacted the first federal coal-mine-safety law which, among other provisions, prescribed specific ventilation standards for coal mines of a certain depth "so as to dilute and render harmless ... the noxious or poisonous gases." 1891 Territorial Mine Inspection Act, § 6, 26 Stat. 1105. *See also* 3 CENTURY DICTIONARY AND CYCLOPEDIA, *supra*, at 2229 (explaining the dangers associated with fire-damp).

That CBM gas was considered a dangerous waste product which escaped from coal, rather than part of the valuable coal fuel itself, is also confirmed by the fact that coal companies venting the gas to prevent its accumulation in the mines made no attempt to capture or preserve it. The more gas that escaped from the coal once it was brought to the surface, the better it was for the mining companies because it decreased the risk of a dangerous gas buildup during transport and storage. *Cf.* E. MOORE, COAL: ITS PROPERTIES, ANALYSIS, CLASSIFICATION, GEOLOGY, EXTRACTION, USES AND DISTRIBUTION 308 (1922) (noting that the presence of gases such as methane in the coal increases the risk of spontaneous combustion of the coal during storage). * * *

The limited nature of the 1909 and 1910 Act reservations is confirmed by subsequent congressional enactments. When Congress wanted to reserve gas rights that might yield valuable fuel, it did so in explicit terms. In 1912, for example, Congress enacted a statute that reserved "oil and gas" in Utah lands. Act of Aug. 24, 1912, 37 Stat. 496. In addition, both the 1912 Act and a later Act passed in 1914 continued the tradition begun in the 1909 and 1910 Acts of reserving only those minerals enumerated in the statute. *See ibid.*; Act of July 17, 1914, 38 Stat. 509, *as amended*, 30 U.S.C. §§ 121–123 (providing that "lands withdrawn or classified as phosphate, nitrate, potash, oil, gas or asphaltic minerals, or which are valuable for those deposits" could be patented, subject to a reservation to the United States of "the deposits on account of which the lands so patented were withdrawn or classified or reported as valuable"). It was not until 1916 that Congress passed a public lands act containing a general reservation of valuable minerals in the lands. *See* Stock–Raising Homestead Act, ch. 9, 39 Stat. 862, *as amended*, 43 U.S.C. § 299 (reserving "all the coal and other minerals in the lands" in all lands patented under the Act). *See also Western Nuclear,* 462 U.S. at 49 ("Unlike the preceding statutes containing mineral reservations, the [1916 Stock–Raising Homestead Act] was not limited to lands classified as mineral in character, and it did not reserve only specifically identified minerals").

C.

Respondents contend that Congress did not reserve the solid coal but convey the CBM gas because the resulting split estate would be impractical and would make mining the coal difficult because the miners would have to capture and preserve the CBM gas that escaped during mining. We doubt Congress would have given much consideration to these problems, however, because—as noted above—it does not appear to have given consideration to the possibility that CBM gas would one day be a profitable energy source developed on a large scale.

It may be true, nonetheless, that the right to mine the coal implies the right to release gas incident to coal mining where it is necessary and reasonable to do so. The right to dissipate the CBM gas where reasonable and necessary to mine the coal does not, however, imply the ownership of the gas in the first instance. Rather, it simply reflects the established common-law right of the owner of one mineral estate to use, and even damage, a neighboring estate as necessary and reasonable to the extraction of his own minerals. *See, e.g., Williams v. Gibson,* 84 Ala. 228, 4 So. 350 (1888); ROCKY MOUNTAIN MINERAL FOUNDATION, 6 AMERICAN LAW OF MINING § 200.04 (2d ed. 1997). Given that split estates were already common at the time the 1909 and 1910 Acts were passed, see, e.g., *Chartiers Block Coal Co. v. Mellon,* 152 Pa. 286, 25 A. 597 (1893), and that the common law has proved adequate to the task of resolving the resulting conflicts between estates, there is no reason to think that the prospect of a split estate would have deterred Congress from reserving only the coal.

Were a case to arise in which there are two commercially valuable estates and one is to be damaged in the course of extracting the other, a dispute might result, but it could be resolved in the ordinary course of negotiation or adjudication. That is not the issue before us, however. The question is one of ownership, not of damage or injury. * * *

Because we conclude that the most natural interpretation of "coal" as used in the 1909 and 1910 Acts does not encompass CBM gas, we need not consider the applicability of the canon that ambiguities in land grants are construed in favor of the sovereign or the competing canons relied on by petitioners. * * *

JUSTICE GINSBURG, dissenting.

I would affirm the judgment below substantially for the reasons stated by the Court of Appeals and the federal respondents. *See* 151 F.3d 1251, 1256–1267 (CA10 1998) (en banc). As the Court recognizes, in 1909 and 1910 coal bed methane gas (CBM) was a liability. *See ante,* at 4, 9–10. Congress did not contemplate that the surface owner would be responsible for it. More likely, Congress would have assumed that the coal owner had dominion over, and attendant responsibility for, CBM. I do not find it clear that Congress understood dominion would shift if and when the liability became an asset. I would therefore apply the canon that ambiguities in land grants are construed in favor of the sovereign. *See Watt v. Western Nuclear, Inc.,* 462 U.S. 36, 59 (1983) (noting "established rule that land grants are construed favorably to the Government, that nothing passes except what is conveyed in clear language, and that if there are doubts they are resolved for the Government, not against it.")

QUESTIONS AND DISCUSSION

1. *Charlestone Stone Products*, as well as Justice Ginsburg's dissent in the *Southern Ute* case, note the cardinal rules of interpretation that "land grants are construed favorably to the Government, that nothing passes except what is conveyed in clear language, and that if there are doubts they are resolved for the Government, not against it." How does the Court avoid application of these rules in this case?

2. Is the issue as simple as understanding the normal meaning of the word "coal," as suggested in the opinion by Justice Kennedy? Consider that impurities are often found in minerals. Gold ore, for example, often includes other valuable metals, such as silver, platinum, and copper. Oil and coal often contain sulfur and other minerals that are generally considered undesirable. Suppose that the owner of an oil estate finds a way to remove and market the sulfur contained in the oil. Is the owner of the oil estate liable to the owner of the remaining mineral estate for the value of the sulfur?

3. Which party has the better argument regarding the "plain meaning" of the statute? What is the best result from a policy perspective? Why? How does the analysis differ where public lands rather than private lands are involved?

4. What are the implications of the *Southern Ute* decision for persons seeking to purchase or lease coal rights on federal coal lands reserved under the 1909 and 1910 laws? For persons seeking to purchase coal rights on other lands, whether private or public? What are the policy implications of the Court's decision?

5. If the government leases coal on lands patented under the Coal Lands Act, does the developer owe damages to the owner of the remaining estate for venting gas trapped in the coal? Conversely, if CBM is developed in a way that damages the coal resources, does the developer of the CBM owe damages to the United States for injury to the coal estate?

6. The three judge panel decision of the Court of Appeals for the Tenth Circuit had rejected a claim that an opinion of the Interior Department Solicitor, holding that CBM was not part of a federal coal reservation, was entitled to judicial deference under *Chevron USA, Inc. v. Natural Resources Defense Council, Inc.,* 467 U.S. 837 (1984). The court found that *Chevron* deference was limited to those circumstances where an agency interpretation of a statute was made following a rulemaking or adjudicative process. Suppose that the Secretary had chosen to promulgate rules finding that CBM was a part of the coal reservation. Would the Court have likely deferred to those rules? The issue of *Chevron* deference did not arise in the Supreme Court at least in part because the Solicitor withdrew his opinion after the Court had granted certiorari.

7. Recovery of CBM has skyrocketed in recent years with the refinement of new development techniques. CBM is attractive because it occurs at relatively shallow depths, thus making drilling costs quite modest. In the Powder River Basin of Wyoming, more than 20,000 CBM wells have already been drilled, and the Bureau of Land Management estimates an eventual total of between 81,000–139,000 CBM wells in Wyoming alone. Reasonable

Foreseeable Development Scenario for Oil and Gas Development in the Buffalo Field Office Area, Wyoming (BLM), *available at* http://www.blm. gov/pgdata/etc/medialib/blm/wy/information/NEPA/prb-deis.Par.9930.File. dat/02rfd.pdf. One of the potentially serious environmental consequences of massive CBM development involves the production of water resources.

CBM is generally held in the ground by groundwater. In order to release the gas, substantial quantities of groundwater must be pumped from the ground. In the early days of CBM development this water was simply released onto the ground and allowed to flow wherever the terrain would take it. More recently, operators have been able to reduce the amount of water produced from an average well from about 16,000 gallons per day, to approximately 6,700 gallons per day. Cynthia A. Rice et al., *Limits on Produced Water Management Resulting from the Composition of Coalbed Methane Produced Water: The Powder River Basin, available at* http://ipec.utulsa.edu/Conf2003/Abstracts/rice.html. They have also made efforts to ensure that produced groundwater is properly managed. Nonetheless, water damage to property has become fairly common. Moreover, long-term questions about the loss of substantial groundwater resources have yet to be answered. These issues continue to attract attention as CBM development increases in other parts of the country.

8. Compare the result in *Southern Ute* with *United States Steel v. Hoge,* 468 A.2d 1380 (Pa. 1983). In *Hoge,* the Pennsylvania Supreme Court found that a deed which conveyed "[a]ll the coal" and expressly reserved "the right to drill and operate through said coal for oil and gas, 'included the CBM so long as it remains within his property and subject to his exclusive dominion and control.' " The court further found it "inconceivable" that the grantor would have intended to reserve the CBM, which at the time of the deed was thought to be a "waste product with well-known dangerous properties." Can *Hoge* be distinguished from *Southern Ute* because it involved a conveyance rather than a reservation of coal? Which approach— granting the CBM to the coal owner or the gas owner—makes more sense from a legal perspective? From a policy perspective? Compare *Hoge* and *Southern Ute* with two more recent decisions. *Newman v. RAG Wyoming Land Company,* 53 P.3d 540 (Wyo. 2002) involved a deed that conveyed "all the coal and the minerals commingled with the coal that may be mined or extracted in association therewith. . . . " The Wyoming Supreme Court held that this language did not reflect an intent to convey the CBM associated with the coal since the CBM could not practically be developed in association with coal development. By contrast, in *Energy Development Corp. v. Moss,* 591 S.E.2d 135 (W.Va. 2003), the West Virginia Supreme Court held that an oil and gas lease did not include the right to develop the CBM from a coal seam within the boundaries of the lease. Should it matter that the Wyoming case involved a dispute between the coal lessee and the oil and gas lessee, whereas the West Virginia case involved a dispute between the oil and gas lessee and the surface owner and mineral estate owner? *See also NCNB Texas National Bank et al.* v. *Neva Watkins West et al.,* 631 So.2d 212 (Ala. 1993), where the Alabama Supreme Court held that the owners of the coal estate retained the right to the gas while it was still within the coal seams, but that the owners of the gas estate acquired the right to the gas once it migrates out of the seams. Is this a practical solution?

––––––––

MINERAL CONVEYANCE DRAFTING EXERCISE

The best way to understand the problems that may arise with mineral conveyancing instruments is to draft such an instrument yourself. Set forth below is a brief outline of the key elements of a mineral lease adapted from the sample leases included in 4 AM. L. OF MINING Title XII, App. 2, 4. After reviewing these materials, you will be asked to negotiate a lease or other mineral conveyance instrument based upon a fact pattern provided to you by your professor. As you negotiate please bear in mind possible ethical issues that may arise as you consider whether to reveal or withhold information that might best be kept confidential.

While the focus of this exercise is on mineral leases because they are the most common method for conveying mineral rights, you are free to consider other methods as well. The outline below will provide you with an appropriate checklist of items that should be addressed.

The Elements of a Mineral Lease

Granting clause: Describes the property and mineral rights to be leased, along with incidental rights (for example, access, surface disturbance, and surface use) that are intended to be conveyed with the lease. Describes any reservations or exceptions to the grant of mineral rights, including any limits on surface use, rights of access, and subjacent support. If the lease grants rights to less than all minerals, describes how conflicts with other mineral development will be resolved.

Habendum clause: Describes the term of the lease. If the lease has an initial term that can be extended either by renewal or by mineral production, describes the terms for extension.

Lessee's rights and obligations: Describes any diligence requirements and any payment obligations in lieu of diligence. Describes the lessee's obligation regarding removal of merchantable minerals. Describes the lessee's obligations regarding compliance with reclamation, environmental and waste disposal laws, and such other standards as may be established by the lessor. Describes the lessee's obligations to inform the lessor regarding mining plans and mining operations. Describes the lessee's right to assign the lease. Describe the lessee's obligations to pay taxes. Describes the lessor's rights to inspect the premises. Describes the lessee's right to remove improvements upon termination of the lease.

Rents and royalties: Describes rental and royalty obligations of the lessee. This may include a minimum annual rent (in lieu of diligence), and/or a minimum per unit royalty. The royalty may be based upon the market value of the mineral or on the price received for its sale. If a royalty is payed on the net profit, the lessor must rely on the efficiency of the operator thus suggesting the need to exercise caution in choosing a lessee, and authorizing assignment of the lease.

Insurance and performance bonds: Describes the lessee's obligation to obtain insurance and performance bonds.

Force majeure: Defines a force majeure and describes its effects on the terms of the lease.

Lessor's warranties: Describes the lessor's warranties as to ownership of the property in question, and any material facts about the property that may affect mining.

Default and forfeiture: Describes with specificity the bases upon which default or forfeiture of the lease may occur.

Other provisions: Describes the impact of condemnation of all or part of the property by the government. Describes how resolution of disputes will be handled, including for example, binding arbitration, or mediation. Describes any choice of law. Describes any terms whereby the lease may be terminated at the option of either the lessor or the lessee. Describes the obligation of the lessee or lessor to record the lease.

III.   MINING ON THE PUBLIC LANDS

A.   AN INTRODUCTION TO THE GENERAL MINING LAW OF 1872

As described in Chapter 2, the General Mining Law of 1872, 30 U.S.C. § 21–54, allows any citizen or domestic corporation to go on to public lands,* including most of the lands managed by the BLM and the Forest Service, for the purpose of prospecting for minerals. If valuable minerals are found, the prospector may stake a mining claim, and can eventually purchase the land from the federal government for either $2.50/acre or $5.00/acre, depending on the type of claim.

The Mining Law was passed at a time when the federal government was promoting Western migration, and it accomplished this goal, at least in part, by providing legal protection to those who followed its fairly simple requirements. But, in the eyes of most commentators, the Mining Law is an anachronism—a massive subsidy to the mining industry that no longer serves the public interest.

The following excerpt is from a 1977 Council on Environmental Quality (CEQ) report that advocated substantial changes to the General Mining Law of 1872. Despite the abuses documented by the CEQ, substantial mineral deposits have been and continue to be developed from mining claims on federal lands. These materials also introduce the reader to the substantial body of law governing such development.

---

* The General Mining Law applies only to the public domain, or those lands that the federal government has owned from the time they became part of the United States. A separate statute establishes a leasing process for lands that have been acquired by the federal government after they passed into private ownership. These "acquired lands" include most of the Eastern national forests. *See* Acquired Lands Act of 1947, 30 U.S.C. § 351–360.

HARDROCK MINING ON THE PUBLIC LANDS, COUNCIL ON ENVIRONMENTAL QUALITY (1977)

"The general mining laws extend an express invitation to enter [public lands] and explore and, upon discovery, to claim by location with the promise of full reward. This is the free enterprise system in action."

U.S. Forest Service, 1975

Roughly one-third of the land in the United States is owned by the public. Of these 743.2 million acres, about 68 percent is open to hard rock exploration (the modern term for prospecting) and mining. In fact, miners have free access to these public lands.

For purposes of public policy analysis, the key word here is "free." That is, the miner can go onto these lands and drill or dig for copper, zinc, gold, uranium, or any other hard rock mineral, and no permit, license, or fee is required of him by the owners' agent—the federal government. If the miner locates a "marketable" ore body which is unclaimed, he can stake a claim to it. The claim also gives him free use of the land above and adjoining the deposit. Then the miner is free to dig the ore and sell it. He pays no royalty to the owners. The miner can also use surface resources on the claim, such as timber and water, free of charge for mining purposes. On the land, the miner is free to build any structure, a mill, an office, a shed, or whatever, as long as it relates directly to the mining operation. No rent is paid the owners.

unpatented mining claims

To hold his claim from year to year, the miner need only do $100 worth of work upon it. Most mining claims are never mined. They are held for speculative purposes. Individuals or small companies hold onto their claims, perhaps for years, in the hope that a large mining company will come along, do a professional assessment of their claims' mineral potential, find something worth mining, and then buy them out. It is easy enough to stake a claim. At present, you need only file a simple location notice at the nearest county courthouse and post a copy of the notice at the site. [Ed. note: As a result of the Federal Policy and Land Management Act of 1976, miners must also file claims with the local Bureau of Land Management office.]

patented mining claims

Further, by applying for a patent from the Department of the Interior, the miner can seek outright ownership of his mining claim. If the patent is granted, the land is his, not the public's. The miner pays the public either $2.50 per acre (if it is a placer deposit) or $5 per acre (if it is a lode deposit) for the land, which is probably one of today's great real estate bargains. * * *

Most states require some kind of permit for mineral exploration on state-owned lands. Then, if a deposit is found, they lease the mineral rights, requiring a royalty payment on production. The notable exceptions to this approach are Alaska and Arizona, which operate both a location system and a leasing system, depending on the category of land involved, for state owned lands.

A VERY BRIEF HISTORY

During its first 83 years, the United States did not have an explicit and coherent mineral policy for the public lands. Officials such as Alexander Hamilton advocated the sale of mineralized lands on the public domain because of the money it would bring into the U.S. Treasury. But during the early days of the Republic, minerals such as iron and lead were leased more often than not, and the public retained ownership of the land or sold it later for farming. Administration of the public lands, however, was lax. It was not until 1845, for instance, that unauthorized mining on the public domain was established to be an actionable trespass (*United States v. Gear*).

As the country expanded, so did the belief that land was an unlimited asset and if public it should be disposed of as rapidly as possible in the interest of development and exploitation "in order that all might prosper." Increasingly, mineralized lands on the public domain were sold to private interests, often at extremely low prices. Such was the case with the extensive copper and iron ore deposits in Michigan and Wisconsin. And in the rush to dispose of public mineral resources, "gross fraud" was not uncommon.

With the California gold rush of 1848 and the western mining boom which followed, events moved too swiftly for the distant federal government to affect their course. (Needless to say, the environmental impacts of mining were not a consideration in those days. That does not mean, however, that they were insignificant. The abundant flora and fauna of San Francisco Bay were ravaged by polluted waters flushed out of gold mines and mills, for example, and they never recovered.)

By the time Congress finally acted, passing the Lode Law of 1866, in reality it could do little else than "legalize what would otherwise have been a trespass," which is what it did. The miners had already appropriated the mineral resources on the public land as well as the surface resources above them. Interestingly, even at this early date, mining on the public land was mostly done under the supervision of trained mining engineers and was financed by wealthy investors in this country and England. Except for the early California gold rush days, the individual miner—the mythologized prospector riding a burro—never profited greatly from the exploitation of minerals on the public lands. The Lode Law of 1866 was amended by the Placer Act of 1870, and the two were consolidated in the Mining Law of 1872. Although hardly a model of legislative draftsmanship (almost every term in it has been the subject of controversy and litigation), the Law's purpose is abundantly clear: *To promote the mining resources of the United States.*

And this is the sole purpose of the 1872 Mining Law. No mention is made in it of the nonmineral uses of the public lands, be they grazing, hunting, fishing, or whatever. The 1872 Mining Law is based on a single premise, one which dates back to Roman times: Mineral exploration and development should have preference over all uses of the land because they are the highest economic use of the land. * * *

[handwritten margin note: mining = highest economic use]

The policy of promoting mining has deep historical roots. Under Germanic law of the 13th century, at a time when agricultural workers were shackled by feudal serfdom, miners were a skilled and privileged class who enjoyed considerable freedom. To encourage mining, the overlords permitted miners to go upon "wastrel" lands and stake out claims. Upon discovery of a vein or other mineral deposit, the miner obtained a permanent concession to hold and work this property, subject only to continued payment of royalties to the overlord (usually one-tenth of production). The most important feature of this system was the overlord's relinquishing his right to select personally those who might mine the wastelands of his jurisdiction. The rights of the miner subsequently spread into other parts of Europe and eventually reached the western United States of the last century. * * *

Here, on a continent whose mineral resources were still to be discovered, a laissez-faire policy of "finders keepers" became the rule. More and more often during the second half of the nineteenth century, the "finders" of mineral deposits sold them to mining corporations, which possessed the wherewithal to mine and process the ore. These corporations became the "keepers" as they gained control over more and more hard rock mineral reserves—and thus were born the oligopolies in copper, aluminum, nickel, iron, molybdenum, and other minerals of the twentieth century.

THE EVOLUTION OF FEDERAL MINERAL POLICY FOR THE PUBLIC LANDS

Since 1872 Congress, the administrative agencies, and the courts have been chipping away at the policy of free access to minerals on the public's land. To be sure, the change has been glacial at times, but the direction is unmistakable. Along the way, three federal government systems of mineral disposal have evolved.

The claim-patent (location) system, established by the Mining Law of 1872, still applies for hard rock mineral deposits on public domain lands, i.e., those lands which the United States obtained from other countries—Great Britain, Spain, Russia, and so on.* The others include lease and sale systems.

Leasing

In 1920 Congress passed the Mineral Leasing Act. Under this system, the federal government retains ownership of the land and of certain minerals. The government has discretionary power to permit prospecting for development of these minerals under specified conditions in return for payment of certain fees—rentals, royalties, and, in competitive bidding situations, bonuses; limitations are placed on the number of acres any one company can lease in any given state. This kind of government control over mineral resources is the rule rather than the exception in most of the world. Minerals covered by the Leasing Act include: coal, oil, gas, and oil shale; phosphates or phosphate rock; chlorides, sulfates, carbonates, borates, and silicates or nitrates of potassium and of sodium; sulphur in Louisiana and New Mexico; and native asphalt, bitumen, and bituminous rock.

The legislative history of the Mineral Leasing Act shows that Congress intended to prevent development of monopolies, to discourage holding mineral rights without development for speculative purposes, and to provide a return to the U.S. Treasury for the exploitation of public resources.

It is important to note that according to the Department of the Interior, the leasing system does apply to hard rock minerals found on lands *acquired* by the federal government from private owners—some 56.3 million acres, or about 8 percent of the total area of the public's land. On these lands, hard rock mineral development is subject to prospecting permit and lease by the Secretary of Interior. For example, there exists an active program for leasing lead deposits on acquired lands in Missouri (with a production value of over $42 million in 1972). * * *

Sale

Under the Materials Disposal Act of 1947, the federal government can sell such materials as sand, gravel, stone, and clay which are on the public land, but the public retains ownership of the land. The Act was amended by the Multiple Surface Use Act of 1955, which removed certain common varieties of sand, stone, gravel, pumice, pumicite, and cinders from coverage under the Mining Law of 1872.

We have seen how the Congress has altered mineral policy for the public's land since 1872. So too have the courts, especially in regard to the difficult

---

* Ed.—Since 1994, however, Congress has imposed a moratorium on new patent applications for public domain lands.

matter of what constitutes the discovery of "a valuable mineral deposit," for it is this which determines whether or not a mining claim staked under the Mining Law of 1872 is valid. For many years, the courts used the "prudent man" rule requiring "evidence of such a character that a person of ordinary prudence would be justified in the further expenditure of his labor and means, with a valuable mine...." But in *United States v. Coleman* (1968), the Supreme Court introduced the "marketability rule" as a "logical complement to the prudent man rule." A patent applicant must prove that he has discovered a deposit of minerals which can be mined and marketed at a profit under the economic conditions at the time of application. * * *

Except in the area of granting mineral patents, [however] there is no evidence to suggest that the Law has become "an instrument of regulation." To the contrary, available evidence suggests that laissez-faire is still very much in force when it comes to staking mining claims on the public domain under the terms of the 1872 Mining Law.

For example, in an investigation of 240 randomly selected claims in mining districts in Arizona, California, Colorado, and Wyoming, the General Accounting Office (GAO) found that only one was actually being mined. There was evidence on only three claims that minerals had ever been extracted. Most mining claims appear to be held for speculative purposes and not for the development of mineral resources.

The vast majority of claims are never checked by federal administrative agencies to determine whether a "discovery of a valuable mineral" has been made. No one knows for sure how many mining claims have been staked on the public domain—though they certainly number in the millions. An administrative-legal process does exist for invalidating illegal claims, but it is very cumbersome and expensive and is usually instigated by the federal government only in cases of flagrant violation, e.g., someone builds a resort on his mining claims or uses the claimed land as a junkyard. (Neither of these instances is apocryphal; they happened.)

A continuing administrative headache for BLM and the Forest Service is the use of mining claims for nonmineral purposes. The system itself seems to invite abuse. It is so much easier to go out and stake a mining claim on the public's land and build, say, a home on it than it is to have to buy land from a private owner. These abuses are well documented.

The Congress has sought to remedy this situation through such measures as the Mining Claims Occupancy Act and the Surface Resources Act. Indeed, the Surface Resources Act of 1955 represents the first significant legislation in which Congress asserted its authority over the public land vis-a-vis the miner:

> Any mining claim hereafter located under the mining laws of the United States shall not be used, prior to issuance of patent ... for any purposes other than prospecting, mining or processing operations and uses reasonably incident therein.

Nevertheless, the abuses continue, although BLM and the Forest Service believe they are on the wane. But these agencies are responsible for vast expanses of land and due to their limited resources personnel and money—they have not been able to eliminate the problem. The Forest Service reported nearly 2,000 cases of "questionable occupancy on its land," and there may well be even more on BLM lands. It is difficult and expensive to dislodge these squatters, according to BLM and the Forest Service.

Discerning what exactly constitutes questionable occupancy is not always clear-cut, but in *Cynthia Balser*, 170 IBLA 269, GFS(MIN) 27 (2006), the IBLA held that surface occupancy rules extend to activities deemed "casual" use, thus reversing a cessation order by the BLM. Additionally, the Board held that seasonal work can satisfy the requirements for occupancy, as long as the work program is regularly recurring. This ruling helps identify what claims are subject to questionable occupancy.

To get some notion of the difficulties involved in regulating mining claims, consider the Department of the Interior's program to clear the titles to mining claims on oil shale lands in Colorado, Utah, and Wyoming. Between September 1968 and February 1974, Interior spent over 100 man-years and $1.9 million on this effort; yet approximately 50,000 claims identified as of February 1974 still have to be cleared.

The Federal Land Policy and Management Act of 1976 (the BLM Organic Act) for the first time requires that mining claims be filed with the federal government. (Persons with claims which predate the Act have 3 years to file their claims with the federal government.) This measure should make the administrative task of keeping track of mining claims on the public domain possible. The problem of determining whether a claim represents "the discovery of a valuable mineral deposit" will remain, however.

mining patents used for nonmineral purposes

It is perfectly legal, of course, for the holder of a mineral patent to do with the once public land what he will. Throughout the western United States, land acquired through mineral patents is used for all manner of nonmineral purposes—including trailer parks, housing developments, drive-in movies, shopping centers, and occasionally even a house of prostitution. * * *

QUESTIONS AND DISCUSSION

1. While the General Mining Law has evolved over its history so that it now excludes the "fuel and fertilizer" minerals that are subject to leasing, and the common variety minerals that are subject to direct sale, most commentators agree that the General Mining Law is still in need of a serious overhaul. The alleged problems with the current system include— (1) the failure to require mine operators to pay royalties for removing valuable mineral deposits from public lands; (2) the failure to impose adequate standards to ensure that mine operators exercise diligence in developing federal minerals; (3) the need to impose mine operation and reclamation standards to ensure protection of the environment and maximization of recovery of the mineral resource; (4) the need to reform the system of self-initiation to afford the federal government an opportunity to determine whether mining operations should be allowed on particular lands even where those lands have not otherwise been withdrawn from location under the law; and (5) the need to remove the option of patenting public lands that contain valuable mineral deposits. *See, e.g.,* Mark Squillace, *The Enduring Vitality of the General Mining Law of 1872*, 18 ENVTL. L. REP. (News and Analysis) 10261 (1988). Opponents of reform argue that the current system works reasonably well and that significant problems can be addressed through regulatory interpretations of the existing law.

During the Clinton administration, Secretary of the Interior Bruce Babbitt, and his Solicitor, John Leshy, appeared poised to push reform legislation through the Congress. On two occasions, conservation minded legislators combined with fiscal conservatives in the House of Representatives to pass reform legislation. *See, e.g.,* H.R. 322, 93d Cong. 1st Sess.

(1993). But each time the Senate balked and mining law reform remains an elusive goal.

The most recent effort is a bill put forward by Congressman Rahall of West Virginia, the Chairman of the House Committee on Natural Resources and a long-time advocate of reform. Rahall's bill, the *Hardrock Mining and Reclamation Act of 2009*, H.R. 639 (2009), would accomplish most of the objectives of reform advocates. It would:

- Put certain environmentally sensitive lands off limits to exploration and development
- Allow land managers to better balance mineral activities with other uses of public land
- Set comprehensive environmental protection standards for mining
- End mineral patenting
- Set an 8% gross royalty[†] on mineral production
- Require reclamation bonding
- Establish a fund to clean up abandoned mines on federal lands and assist impacted communities
- Establish a program of regular inspections and enforcement of violations at mines on federal lands
- Authorize citizen suits to enforce the law

See http://www.earthworksaction.org/2007MiningReformBill.cfm.

What the proposed reform legislation does not do is alter the General Mining Law's system of self-initiation. Some have argued that hardrock minerals should be subject to a leasing system much like all other public minerals. How are the two systems different? To what extent might a leasing system avoid the problems caused by the recent location of more than 1,000 new mining claims near the Grand Canyon? On June 25, 2008, in accordance with § 204(e) of FLPMA, the House Natural Resources Committee passed a binding resolution that requires the Department of the Interior to withdraw approximately one million acres adjacent to Grand Canyon National Park. 43 U.S.C. § 1714(e). *See New Mining Claims Banned in Region Around Grand Canyon National Park,* Las Vegas Sun, June 26, 2008. Would this withdrawal have been necessary if a leasing system was in place?

2. Speculation and the location of mining claims for unlawful purposes, such as recreation, has been hampered by a congressional requirement that most claimants pay a $100 annual fee for each mining claim they hold, in

---

† The two types of royalties being considered are "net proceeds" or "net profit", and "net smelter" or "gross" royalties. The distinction is critical. A net proceed/net profits royalty allows a mining company to deduct all expenses associated with mineral production including administrative and business operating expenses, which are difficult to monitor. A gross royalty is based on the revenue received from the sale of the minerals. The net smelter royalty allows deduction for mineral processing costs but not other costs. *See* http://www.earthworksaction.org/pubs/AHardrockRoyalty.pdf. Earthworks, a mining law reform advocacy group, claims that the two states that use a net profit royalty—Alaska and Nevada—receive less than 1% of the value of the minerals in royalties. This compares to 8–16.7% of the gross value for other federal minerals. *Id.*

lieu of performing "assessment work," which the law had previously required. Persons who hold fewer than ten claims, however, may continue to perform assessment work instead of paying the fee. 30 U.S.C. § 28f (2006).

3. The Congressional Research Service has prepared a more recent, though less engaging study, of the Mining Act. It does, however, include a discussion of several current issues that are addressed later in the text, including, for example, the mill site debate, the moratorium on patents, and claim maintenance issues. *See* Marc Humphries *Mining on Federal Lands, (2005) available at* http://www.aleec.org/nle/crsreports/05Feb/IB 89130.pdf

---

B.   PUBLIC LANDS OPEN TO LOCATION

Not all public lands are open to location under the mining law. First, the mining law only applies on "public domain" lands. These are lands that have been held by the federal government since they became part of the United States. Mining claims are not permitted on "acquired lands"—lands that were transferred to private ownership and then reacquired by the United States, although these lands may be available for leasing under the Acquired Lands Act of 1947. Virtually all of the Eastern National Forests are acquired lands.

Eastern National Forests = "acquired lands"

In addition, lands may be "withdrawn" from location under the mining laws. A recent study indicates that "of the approximately 700 million acres of federal subsurface minerals under the agency's jurisdiction in 2000, approximately 165 million acres have been withdrawn from mineral entry, leasing and sale, subject to valid existing rights." Marc Humphries, *Mining on Federal Lands, supra* at Ch. 9, III.A. note 3. Land use restrictions, including, for example, federally-mandated protections for wilderness study areas, may further limit the availability of lands for mining.

Withdrawing land from location under the General Mining Law (or from the operation of other public land laws) is no simple task. As a general rule, agencies that want to withdraw lands must do so in accordance with Section 204 of the Federal Land Policy and Management Act. 43 U.S.C. § 1714 (2000). For any tracts of significant size (over 5000 acres), the cumbersome process described in Chapter 6, *supra* at page 688, must be followed. Moreover, Section 204 withdrawals remain in effect for only 20 years and must be renewed thereafter. Congress can, of course, enact legislation withdrawing lands from various uses, and the President retains authority under the Antiquities Act to withdraw lands, but such authorities have historically been used sparingly.

To ascertain the effect of a particular withdrawal on the right to locate mining claims one must review the Executive Order or legislation which brought about the withdrawal. Nonetheless, certain generalizations can be made about categories of withdrawals as described below.

(a) ***National Parks and Monuments.*** National parks are all creatures of federal legislation and, with a few exceptions, are closed to mineral development. By contrast, national monuments are established by Presidential proclamation under the authority of the Antiquities Act of 1906. 16 U.S.C. § 431 (2006). (As noted in Chapter 6, *supra* at page 687, the withdrawal authority under the Antiquities Act was one of few such provisions that survived the passage of FLPMA.) As with the national parks, most but not all monuments are closed to mineral entry and location. In 1976, Congress passed the Mining in the Parks Act, 16 U.S.C. § 1902 (2006), which closed those parks and monuments that had previously been opened to location under the General Mining Law. In addition, it required the Secretary of the Interior to adopt regulations to control mining operations on valid existing claims.

(b) ***National Forests.*** Under the so-called Creative Act of 1891, 26 Stat. 1103, the President was authorized to set aside public domain forest lands as forest reserves, thereby withdrawing these lands from entry and location. The plethora of withdrawals that resulted soon thereafter prompted criticism from the Western states where all of the forest reserves had been created. In 1897, in response to this criticism, Congress enacted the National Forest Organic Administration Act, 16 U.S.C. § 473 (2006), which set guidelines for the establishment of new forests and opened all forests to mineral entry and location. Notwithstanding the provision opening forest lands to mineral entry, much national forest land has been closed to entry or location by subsequent executive or legislative action. Thus, even where national forest lands are not in a protected category such as wilderness, the land may not be open to location under the mining laws.

(c) ***Wilderness Areas.*** Under the Wilderness Act of 1964, 16 U.S.C. §§ 1131–36 (2006), national forest lands designated by Congress as wilderness were closed to mineral entry on December 31, 1983. Section 603 of FLPMA, 43 U.S.C. § 1782, provides for the designation of wilderness study areas and requires the Secretary of the Interior "to manage such land . . . in a manner so as not to impair the suitability of such areas for preservation as wilderness, subject, however to the continuation of existing mining and grazing uses and mineral leasing in the manner and degree in which the same was being conducted on the date of approval of this Act." *Id. See Edmund Key*, 117 I.B.L.A. 274, GFS (MIN) 7 (1991).

(d) ***Wild and Scenic Rivers.*** The Wild and Scenic Rivers Act of 1968, 16 U.S.C. § 1271, provides for designation of river segments as wild, scenic, or recreational, with varying degrees of protection afforded to each classification. Wild rivers are the most protected, and the public land within the boundaries of these components (up to one quarter of a mile from the banks of the river) is closed to mineral entry and location. 16 U.S.C. § 1279. Mineral entries are allowed on scenic and recreational rivers subject to strict regulation. 16 U.S.C. § 1280. Rivers under study for designation and the public lands within one quarter-mile from the banks of such rivers are closed to entry under the mining laws for a ten-year period beginning on the date that Congress designated the river for potential inclusion in the system.

(e) ***Fish and Wildlife Refuges.*** As the *Midwest Oil* opinion (*supra,* Chapter 2, page 133) notes, the president created numerous bird reserves by executive order. Since that time numerous additional units have been set aside for wildlife preserves, primarily under the authority of the Fish and Game Sanctuaries Act 1934, 16 U.S.C. § 694, and the National Wildlife Refuge System Administration Act of 1966, 16 U.S.C. § 668dd. With the exception of several such preserves in Alaska, these units are closed to location under the mining laws. The Secretary of the Interior does have discretion, however, to open these lands for mineral leasing subject to certain restrictions.

(f) ***Other.*** Numerous other public lands have been withdrawn from location under the mining laws, most notably those lands set aside for Indian reservations and military reservations. Mining at power site (land allocated for hydroelectric power development) and reclamation withdrawals is generally permitted but remains subject to the superior right of the government to use the lands for the purposes for which they were withdrawn. 30 U.S.C. §§ 621–625. The Mining Claims Rights Restoration Act of 1955, 30 U.S.C. §§ 621–625 (2000), opened power site withdrawals to mining claim entry. For a case upholding the right of a power site mining claim to develop the minerals over the objection of the Forest Services, *see United States v. Eno,* 171 IBLA 69, GFS(MIN) 4 (2007).

QUESTIONS AND DISCUSSION

1. *Master Title and Use Plats.* Each BLM State Office maintains a set of Master Title (MT) plats that depict the status of all lands within the state. These plats, which have been prepared for each township, show whether the federal government owns all or any part of the land (e.g., surface and/or mineral estate) and whether the land has been withdrawn from various uses. This information is extremely useful in ascertaining whether land is open for location under the mining laws. In addition, an *historical index* contains the chronological history of each tract of land until the time it passes into private ownership. Finally, *use plats* are maintained which contain much of the same information as the MT plats but which also contain information regarding temporary uses of the land, such as mineral leases. Master title plats for some states are now available on the internet. *See, e.g.,* http://www.blm.gov/az/cadastral/cadhome.htm.

The master title and use plats do not generally contain information about previously located mining claims unless those claims have been patented. The BLM maintains records on all mining claims and basic information about all claims, including the names of claims, claimants, and geographic location, is available in various reports that can be accessed at http://www.blm.gov/lr2000. Additional information about unpatented mining claims must generally be obtained from the property records of the local county courthouse in the county where the claim is located.

2. Under the "notation rule," a BLM record which indicates that lands are withdrawn is binding even if the withdrawal is later found to be void. *See Shiny Rock Mining Corp. v. United States,* 629 F. Supp. 877 (D. Or. 1986); *William Dunn,* 157 I.B.L.A. 347 (2002). Suppose the BLM fails to include a withdrawal on its records. Should those lands be deemed open to location under the "notation rule"?

———

Having introduced the history and structure of the General Mining Law, as well as some basic information about where mineral exploration can occur, the chapter now proceeds to consider particular components of the federal mining law. It first investigates the different types of mining claims—lode claims, placer claims, and mill site claims. It then discusses how a miner goes about staking and recording these claims, the rules for which are mostly a matter of state law. The chapter next looks at what miners must do to maintain their claims. Following this discussion of the formalities of locating and maintaining mining claims, the discussion shifts to consideration of the property rights acquired by mining claimants. After a brief discussion of the temporary right to explore, known as *pedis possessio* the chapter moves to the key question of whether the miner has discovered a valuable mineral deposit. If so, the miner is said to have an unpatented mining claim. Finally, this section of the chapter discusses the opportunity of the miner to turn an unpatented mining claim into a fee simple property interest by taking the claim to patent.

C.   TYPES OF MINING CLAIMS

1.   LODE AND PLACER CLAIMS

There are two basic types of mining claims—lode claims and placer claims. At a very basic level, lodes are vein-like deposits, picture a miner following a spidery vein of gold running along the ceiling of a mine. A placer (pronounced "plass-er") refers to unconsolidated mineral deposits; think of James Marshall panning for gold at Sutters Mill or a Forty–Niner shoveling gravel into a sluice (or "Long Tom"), in the hopes that heavier gold will fall through the screen as the gravel is washed down the box. Although this distinction may appear simple, it can actually be quite complex in practice, and there seems little reason to make the legality of a mining claim depend upon getting it right. And yet depend it does. Whatever the geological significance of the distinction between lode and placer deposits, the distinction made in the General Mining Law seems more an accident of history than a reasoned policy choice. Congress passed the first form of the mining law in the Lode Law of 1866. As its name implies, the law authorized the appropriation of lode or vein-like deposits on public lands. When Congress realized that the law did not encompass unconsolidated mineral deposits it passed a separate statute, the Placer Act of 1870, which authorized the location of deposits not found in vein form. When Congress enacted the General Mining Law of 1872, it combined the two earlier laws but retained the distinction between lode and placer deposits.

Under the General Mining Law, a placer is said to include "all forms of deposit, excepting veins of quartz, or other rock in place." 30 U.S.C. § 35. Thus, while placer deposits are most commonly described as deposits that have been removed from a lode by erosion and deposited in streambeds or other such bodies, they actually encompass all mineral deposits that fail to meet the somewhat ambiguous definition of a lode.

Whether a particular mineral deposit is a lode or placer matters. In *Cole v. Ralph*, 252 U.S. 286, 295 (1920), the Supreme Court held that "[a] placer discovery will not sustain a lode location, nor a lode discovery a placer location." And in *Layman v. Ellis*, 52 I.D. 714 (1929), the Department of the Interior declared invalid a valuable deposit of gravel which had been located as a lode, but which plainly did not occur as "rock in place." *See also United States v. Guzzman*, 81 I.D. 685 (1974).

As the decisions in *Cole* and *Layman* make clear, a miner who mistakenly locates a lode as a placer claim does not have a valid claim. Although the validity of the claim is plainly the most important reason to accurately identify a mineral deposit, it is not the only reason. The size and layout of lode and placer claims are different, the formalities for locating the claims are distinct, and patent fees ($5.00 per acre for lodes and $2.50 per acre for placers) are also different. And while the distinction between lodes and placers may seem uncomplicated in the abstract, the cases attest to the difficulty that miners and courts alike have had in identifying a deposit as a lode or placer. Consider the following decision.

EUREKA CONSOLIDATED MINING CO. v. RICHMOND, 8 F. Cas. 819 (1877), *aff'd* 103 U.S. 839 (1880)

FIELD, CIRCUIT JUSTICE. * * *

The definition of a "lode" given by geologists is, that of a fissure in the earth's crust filled with mineral matter, or more accurately, as aggregations of mineral matter containing ores in fissures.... But miners used the term before geologists attempted to give it a definition. One of the witnesses in this case, Dr. Raymond, who for many years was in the service of the general government as commissioner of mining statistics, and in that capacity had occasion to examine and report upon a large number of mines in the states of Nevada and California, and the territories of Utah and Colorado, says that he has been accustomed, as a mining engineer, to attach very little importance to those cases of classification of deposits which simply involve the referring of the subject back to verbal definitions in the books. The whole subject of the classification of mineral deposits he states to be one in which the interests of the miner have entirely overridden the reasonings of the chemists and geologists. "The miners," to use his language, "made the definition first." As used by miners, before being defined by any authority, the term "lode" simply meant that formation by which the miner could be led or guided. It is an alteration of the verb "lead", and whatever the miner could follow, expecting to find ore, was his lode. Some formation within which he could find ore, and out of which he could not expect to find ore, was his "lode." The term "lode-star," "guiding-star," or "north star," he adds, is of the same origin. Cinnabar is not found in any fissure of the earth's crust, or in any lode, as defined by geologists, yet the acts of congress speak, as already seen, of lodes of quartz, or rock in place, bearing cinnabar. Any definition of "lode," as there used, which did not embrace deposits of cinnabar, would be as defective as if it did not embrace deposits of gold or silver. The definition must apply to deposits of all the metals named, if it apply to a deposit of any one of them. Those acts were not drawn by geologists or for geologists; they were not framed in the interests of science, and consequently with scientific accuracy in the use of terms. They were framed for the protection of miners in the claims which they had located and developed, and should receive such a construction as will carry out this purpose. The use of the terms "vein" and "lode" in connection with each other in the act of 1866, and their use in connection with the term "ledge" in the act of 1872, would seem to indicate that it was the object of the legislator to avoid any limitation in the application of the acts, which a scientific definition of any one of these terms might impose.

It is difficult to give any definition of the term as understood and used in the acts of congress, which will not be subject to criticism. A fissure in the earth's crust, an opening in its rocks and strata made by some force of nature, in which the mineral is deposited, would seem to be essential to the definition of a lode, in the judgment of geologists. But to the practical miner, the fissure and its walls are only of importance as indicating the boundaries within which he may look for and reasonably expect to find the ore he seeks. A continuous body of mineralized rock lying within any other well-defined boundaries on the earth's surface and under it, would equally constitute, in his eyes, a lode. We are of opinion, therefore, that the term as used in the acts of congress is applicable to any zone or belt of mineralized rock lying within boundaries clearly separating it from the neighboring rock. It includes, to use the language cited by counsel, all deposits of mineral matter found through a mineralized zone or belt coming from the same source, impressed with the same forms, and appearing to have been created by the same processes.

QUESTIONS AND DISCUSSION

1.   The Court finds that the mining laws were "framed for the protection of miners in the claims which they had located and developed." Suppose that the customs of miners differ in different jurisdictions, such that in one jurisdiction a deposit would be located as a lode and yet in another the same deposit would be located as a placer. How should a court ascertain the custom of a particular area and to what extent should it rely on those customs?

2.   A lode claim has end lines that run roughly perpendicular to the vein and sidelines that run roughly parallel to the vein. Only the endlines of a claim must be straight and parallel. Figure 1 illustrates a typical lode claim.*

* The three drawings in these notes are   Claim Laws, (5th ed. 1996).
taken from Robert Pruitt, Digest of Mining

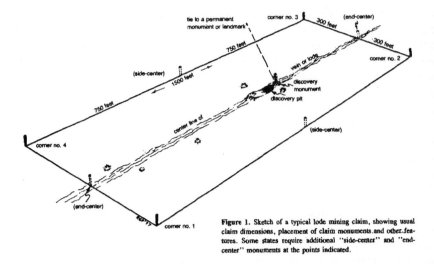

Figure 1. Sketch of a typical lode mining claim, showing usual claim dimensions, placement of claim monuments and other features. Some states require additional "side-center" and "end-center" monuments at the points indicated.

3. As *Eureka* suggests, lode claims are those where a zone or vein of mineralized rock occurs "in place." Placer claims include all other forms of mineralized deposits. 30 U.S.C. § 35. Under the terms of the statute, a lode claim may not exceed 1500 feet in length or 600 feet in width. *Id.* § 23. The width, however, is measured at a maximum of 300 feet from the center of the vein. A claimant is entitled to a full 600 feet only if he takes care to locate the center of the claim along the "strike" of the vein. The strike is the course or bearing of the vein along its length. A lode claimant must also take care to locate his claim along the "apex" of the vein. The apex is the uppermost portion of the vein. The claimant who has the apex may follow his lode along the "dip" or downward course of the vein, through the sidelines of his claim, even where a senior locator holds a claim that encompasses the dipping vein. *Id.* § 26. These "extralateral rights" are described by the figure below.

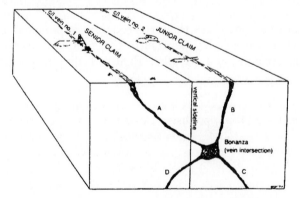

Note that the senior claimant can follow the lode through the side line of the junior's claim. Likewise, the junior can follow his vein through the sidelines of the senior's claim. The area where the two veins intersect—the bonanza—belongs to the senior claimant.

4. A claimant staking a lode claim may lack sufficient information to determine the direction, or "strike," of the vein. Most states afford claimants between 30 and 90 days to complete the formalities of locating a mining claim, including, for example, recording their claims in the local county recorder's office. These formalities are described in the section below. During this time, claimants are generally allowed to "swing" their claims, essentially using the point of discovery as a pivot. Some courts suggest that claims can be swung in a full circle. *See, e.g., Sanders v. Noble,* 22 Mont. 110, 55 P. 1037 (1899). Other courts appear to require claimants to indicate the general direction of the claim, and then allow the claimant to swing the claim 45 degrees in either direction. *Wiltsee v. King of Ariz. Mining & Milling Co.,* 7 Ariz. 95, 60 P. 896 (1900).

Some commentators have also suggested that claimants have the right to "float" their claims, or slide them up and down along the discovery point, as long as the discovery point remains somewhere within the 1,500 feet allowed for such claims. *See* 2 AM. L. OF MINING, § 33.04[4]; L. Mall, PUBLIC LAND AND MINING LAW 263 (3d ed. 1981). Floating claims, however, appears to conflict with the Supreme Court's decision in *Erhardt v. Boaro,* 113 U.S. 527 (1885). In *Erhardt,* the original claimants posted a notice on the discovery monument claiming "1,500 feet on this mineral-bearing lode, vein, deposit." Thirteen days later, subsequent claimants, Boaro and Hull, established a new monument at the same point as Erhardt and Caroll, but specifically claiming 600 feet northeast of the monument, and 900 feet to the southwest. The Court upheld the validity of the original claim but limited its scope to "750 feet on the course of the lode or vein in each direction from that point." If the claimants had been allowed to float their claims, then presumably they could have moved them a full 1500 feet in either direction.

5. Some deposits like uranium are inherently difficult to characterize. Uranium often occurs in a pancake shape, and while it has a pretty clear "hanging wall" and "footwall," (the nonmineral strata above and below the mineralized zone), it lacks an obvious dip or strike. In most jurisdictions, uranium is located as a lode, but because it does not dip, uranium claims, and other types of "blanket lode" claims are usually denied extralateral rights. *See, e.g., Globe Mining Co. v. Anderson,* 318 P.2d 373 (Wyo. 1957); *see also* 1 AM. L. OF MINING, § 32.03[3].

6. Where the controversy is between rival claimants, one claimant holding a lode claim and the other a placer claim for the same deposit, the cases seem to favor the senior claimant, regardless of claim type at least where a reasonable dispute exists as to the form of the deposit. *See, e.g., Iron Silver Mining Co. v. Mike & Starr Gold & Silver Mining Co.,* 143 U.S. 394 (1892). Does *Eureka* support this conclusion? Are there any good policy reasons for supporting such an outcome?

7. In its description of lode claims, the General Mining Law specifically mentions only metallic minerals—gold, silver, cinnabar, lead, tin, and copper. (Cinnabar is the mineral associated with mercury. At room temperature mercury exists as a liquid and is often called quicksilver.) Some had argued that the lode statute was thus intended to be limited to metals. This argument was rejected in *Webb v. American Asphaltum Mining Co.,* 157 F. 203, 204–07 (8th Cir. 1907) and has not been seriously contested since.

8.   Some commentators have urged that the distinction between lode and placer claims be abolished. *See, e.g.,* Mark Squillace, *The Enduring Vitality of the General Mining Law of 1872,* 18 ENVTL. L. REP. (News and Analysis), 10261 (1988); Clyde O. Martz, *Pick and Shovel Mining Laws in an Atomic Age: A Case for Reform,* 27 ROCKY MTN. L. REV. 375, 384 (1955). Can you think of any reasons for maintaining the distinction?

9.   In *Sierra Club v. Penfold,* 857 F.2d 1307, 1309 (9th Cir. 1988), the court described the procedures for removing the mineral from a gold placer deposit. "To extract the gold, a miner first removes the vegetation and surface soil. The gold-bearing soil (pay dirt) is then removed and put in a sluice box. A sluice box is a channel with intermittent dams. When water is run through the box, the lighter materials are flushed away while the gold remains. The lighter materials, sands, silts and clays, are discharged from the box. When the discharge is excessive, it can enter streams, killing fish, aquatic life and vegetation, and generally contaminate the wastewater in surrounding areas. The size of a placer mine can vary greatly—from very large mines using bulldozers, pumps and heavy equipment, to small one-person pick and shovel operations."

10.   The provisions governing placer claims have their own peculiar aspects. Individual placer claims may not exceed 20 acres, but the statute allows two or more persons to make joint entry and claim as much as 160 acres. 30 U.S.C. § 36. These "association placers" require that each member of the association hold a bona fide interest and no member may hold an interest in excess of 20 acres. Thus, a minimum of 8 people are needed for a 160 acre association placer claim. The figure below depicts typical types of placer claims.

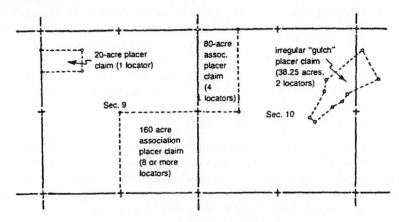

11.   An association placer is a single mining claim and thus a single discovery will support an entire 160 acre claim. *Hall v. McKinnon,* 193 F. 572 (9th Cir. 1911); *Union Oil Co,* 25 L.D. 351 (1897). But each ten acre tract must be "mineral in character, ensuring that unprofitable lands are not needlessly developed." *See McCall v. Andrus,* 628 F.2d 1185 (9th Cir. 1980) *cert. denied,* 450 U.S. 996 (1981).

12.   Under the statute, placer claims must conform "as near as practicable" to the public land surveys. 30 U.S.C. § 35. This means that the claims should, if possible, be laid out in rectangular shape along the boundaries of the legal subdivisions of a section. Irregular placer claims are allowed where, for example, the terrain makes conformity impracticable, but long, serpentine-shaped claims will not be sustained. The basic rule for irregular placer claims was adopted in *Snow Flake Fraction Placer,* 37 L.D. 250 (1908), and later codified at 43 C.F.R. § 3832.12(c) (2008). The rule currently provides that—

> If you are describing an association placer claim by metes and bounds, you must meet the following requirements, according to the number of persons in your association, as described in *Snow Flake Fraction Placer*, 37 Pub. Lands Dec. 250 (1908), in order to keep your claim in compact form and not split Federal lands into narrow, long or irregular shapes:
>
> (i) A location by 1 or 2 persons must fit within the exterior boundaries of a square 40–acre parcel;
>
> (ii) A location by 3 or 4 persons must fit within the exterior boundaries of 2 square contiguous 40–acre parcels;
>
> (iii) A location by 5 or 6 persons must fit within the exterior boundaries of 3 square contiguous 40–acre parcels; and
>
> (iv) A location by 7 or 8 persons must fit within the exterior boundaries of 4 square contiguous 40–acre parcels.

Id. § 3832.12(c)(3). Why do you think that the preference for conformity was limited to placer claims?

13.   As the statute indicates, a placer patentee acquires no rights to lodes that are known to exist at the time of the patent application. 30 U.S.C. § 37. Further, a placer claimant acquires no rights in a known lode until he makes a lode location. *Inyo Marble Co. v. Loundagin,* 7 P.2d 1067 (Cal. Ct. App. 1932). If a placer claimant applies for a patent, he cannot amend his application to include lodes or veins that were known prior to the time of the application. *Aurora Lode v. Bulger Hill & Nugget Gulch Placer,* 23 L.D. 95, 101–103 (1896).

14.   A strong presumption exists that lodes in placers were not known. *Montana Central Ry. v. Migeon,* 68 F. 811 (C.C. D.Mont. 1895), *aff'd,* 77 F. 249 (9th Cir. 1896); *Mutchmor v. McCarty,* 149 Cal. 603, 87 P. 85, 87 (1906). Further, mere indications of a lode do not make the lode known. *McCarthy v. Speed, supra.* But personal knowledge of the existence of the lode is not required, *Noyes v. Mantle,* 127 U.S. 348 (1888), and the applicant is chargeable with knowledge of what is generally known in the community, or what would be disclosed by a reasonable and fair inspection of the premises. *McCarty, supra; Iron Silver Mining Co. v. Mike & Starr Gold & Silver Mining Co.,* 143 U.S. 394, 403 (1892).

15.   As a precaution, some miners will double stake a claim, first as a placer then as a lode. This is because any attempt to stake a placer over a lode may be construed as abandonment of the lode. By contrast, since the law recognizes lodes *in* placers, 30 U.S.C. § 37, the earlier placer claim might not be deemed abandoned. *See* 1 Am. L. Of Mining, § 32.02[4][b]. Do you see any possible problems with this practice?

16. *Tunnel Sites.* The General Mining Law makes special provision for tunnels that are designed to locate mining claims. Tunnel sites are not themselves mining claims, but they can lead to the discovery of such claims. The statute provides at 30 U.S.C. § 27 that—

> When a tunnel is run for the development of a vein or lode, or the discovery of mines, the owners of such tunnels shall have the right of possession of all known veins or lodes within 3,000 feet from the face of such tunnel on the line thereof, not previously known to exist, to the same extent as if discovered on the surface ...; but failure to prosecute work on the tunnel for six months shall be considered as an abandonment of the right to all undiscovered veins....

This provision essentially gives the owner of a tunnel site who is diligently prosecuting work on the tunnel prior rights over claimants who discover valuable minerals on the surface, along a 3,000–foot line that runs from the tunnel face. Tunnel locators must record evidence of their tunnel rights with the county recorder, 43 C.F.R. § 3833.1 (2008), and file notice of their locations with the Bureau of Land Management. 30 U.S.C. § 1744.

Even where a third-party mining claimant obtains a patent for his claim while a tunnel is being diligently prosecuted by another miner, the Supreme Court has held that the patent is void and the tunnel locator who later discovers the same mineral deposit should prevail. *Enterprise Mining Co. v. Rico–Aspen Consol. Min. Co.,* 167 U.S. 108 (1897). This result seems at odds with the language of 30 U.S.C. § 29 which provides that—

> If no adverse claim shall have been filed ... at the expiration of sixty days of publication, it shall be assumed that the applicant is entitled to a patent ..., and that no adverse claim exists; and thereafter no objection from third parties to the issuance of a patent shall be heard....

Why did the Court nonetheless rule for the tunnel locator?

Because the time and money involved in digging a tunnel are substantial, the tunnel site provision encourages exploration that might not otherwise be undertaken. Nonetheless, modern drilling practices, which allow core samples to be removed from depth, generally make tunnels uneconomical, even given the substantial rights acquired by the tunnel owner.

----

2.   MILL SITES

In addition to lode and placer claims and the tunnel sites discussed in note 16 above, the General Mining Law provides for two types of mill sites. The most common—the dependent mill site—requires that it be associated with a valid mining claim. An independent mill site for a "quartz mill or reduction works," by contrast, does not require a valid mining claim. (A quartz mill crushes the ore; the reduction works processes the ore to recover the gold.) The statute provides in relevant part that:

> (a) Where nonmineral land not contiguous to the vein or lode is used or occupied by the proprietor of such vein or lode for mining or milling purposes, such nonadjacent surface ground may be embraced and included in an application for a patent for such vein or lode, and the same may be patented therewith, subject to the same preliminary requirements as to survey and notice as are applicable to veins or lodes, but no location made of such

nonadjacent surface land shall exceed five acres. . . . The owner of a quartz mill or reduction works, not owning a mine in connection therewith, may also receive a patent for his mill site, as provided in this section.

30 U.S.C. § 42 (2000).

Mill sites have commanded substantial attention in recent years because of a controversial legal opinion issued by former Interior Solicitor John Leshy in November 1997. That opinion found that mining claimants are entitled to receive only one dependent mill site of five acres or less for each valid mining claim. *Limitation on Patenting Millsites Under the Mining Law of 1872,* Solicitor's Opinion, M–36988, (Nov. 7, 1997). Multiple mill site claims were allowed so long as the total acreage for a single claim did not exceed five acres. The opinion purported to be based on the plain language of 30 U.S.C. § 42(a), but was contrary to the Department's recent practice of authorizing multiple mill sites for individual claims. The Leshy opinion noted that while operators can use public lands for mining purposes without a mill site by obtaining a special use permit or arranging an exchange of private for public lands, the government has no obligation to issue a special use permit or approve an exchange. If the use of additional public lands is necessary for a viable mining operation, the federal government would retain significant discretion over the development of a new mine—discretion that is largely denied the government under the General Mining Law itself.

When George W. Bush became President, the Interior Department rejected the Leshy Opinion as a departure from the Department's longstanding practice of allowing multiple mill sites for individual claims. It issued a second opinion finding that multiple mill sites for individual mining claims were allowed so long as the sites were used for "mining or milling purposes." *Mill Site Location and Patenting Under the 1872 Mining Law,* Solicitor's Opinion, M–37010. (Oct. 7, 2003). The new opinion cites provisions that were included in the BLM Manual for many years authorizing multiple mill sites for each mining claim with a total acreage in excess of 5 acres per claim. It also describes the BLM's recent practice of issuing patents for such mill sites. Earlier decisions that supported a five-acre per claim limit on mill sites were rejected as dicta. Several unequivocal statements from leading mining authorities over many years were also rejected on the grounds that they had relied on the dictum from these earlier opinions.

QUESTIONS AND DISCUSSION

1. Read 30 U.S.C. § 42(a) again. Do you think the language is clear? What was the purpose of limiting mill sites to five acres if a claimant could avoid that limit simply by locating multiple millsites? Should a policy or practice, however longstanding, be sufficient to overcome conclusions reached in agency decisions, even if those conclusions might be characterized as dicta? Why do you think that the Interior Department chose to adopt this policy— and then change it—through a legal opinion, rather than the more conventional process of informal rulemaking? Note that after the Leshy opinion was published, Interior proposed rules in 1999 that would have codified that opinion. The final rules were not published, however until shortly after the 2003 opinion was published. As a result, the final rules were modified to delete the one mill site per claim limitation that was originally proposed. *See* 68 Fed. Reg. 61045, 61055 (2003). How might the decision to proceed by legal opinion affect a judicial challenge to the policy? Will it matter that the issue was eventually addressed in the agency's rules? Given the controversy surrounding this issue, and the fact that numerous mines around the country are impacted by this policy, litigation over this issue seems likely.

2.   In *United States v. Silver Chief Mining*, 40 I.B.L.A. 244, GFS (MIN) 36 (1979), the mining company had proposed a mining and reclamation plan that required the use of certain mill sites for deposition of mine waste. The federal government argued, however, that the mill sites were not valid because they were not presently being used for mining or milling purposes. The Board held that only present mining or milling activities satisfy the requirement for a valid mill site patent notwithstanding Silver Chief's argument that the mill site claims were necessary to meet state reclamation standards. Suppose the state refused to approve Silver Chief's plan until title to the claims was established. This would seem like a reasonable requirement since the State would want to know that the mining company had a place where it could lawfully dispose of its mine waste. Can Silver Chief ever satisfy this requirement under the Board's test? Note that the Board has previously held that occupancy coupled with a good faith intent to use a site for mining and milling purposes satisfies the statute. *United States v. Dean*, 14 I.B.L.A. 107, GFS (MIN) 8 (1974); *United States v. Skidmore*, 10 I.B.L.A. 322, GFS (MIN) 53 (1973).

3.   What are the two kinds of mill sites authorized by the General Mining Law statute? What are the purposes of each? "Mining and milling purposes" have been broadly construed to encompass mill tailings storage, ore storage, housing or offices for miners, and equipment storage. *See* 4 AM. L. OF MINING § 110.03[3] (2d ed. 1984).

4.   In *Cleary v. Skiffich*, 28 Colo. 362, 65 P. 59 (1901), the Colorado Supreme Court held that the date for determining whether land is mineral in character is the date of location of the mill site or the date on which improvements are made on the site if such improvements do not follow shortly after location. *Id.*, at 62. In *United States v. Utah Int'l, Inc.*, 45 I.B.L.A. 73, 76, GFS (MIN) 25 (1980), the Board held that the date for determining the mineral character is the date that the patent would issue. Which is the better rule? Does the Board's ruling bind the states? Is this a question of federal or state law?

5.   Under the terms of the statute, a millsite dependent on a mining claim may not be contiguous to the vein or lode. 30 U.S.C. § 42. Early cases interpreted this language to prohibit mill sites contiguous to the claim, but in the *Yankee Mill Site* case the Interior Department held that the purpose of this provision was "to prevent appropriation ... of a further segment of the actual vein." 37 L.D. 674, 677 (1909). Thus, a mill site that is nonmineral in character and contiguous to the side lines of a lode claim is valid. *Id.*

PROBLEM EXERCISE: MINING AND MILL SITES

The Lucky Strike Mining Company owns 20 unpatented lode mining claims. The claims have been found to contain valuable gold deposits and Lucky Strike is planning to open a gold mining operation soon. The proposed mine is controversial because it is located in the Deep Creek Wilderness Study Area—an area that the BLM has recommended for inclusion in the National Wilderness Preservation System. Mining would likely preclude further consideration of the area as wilderness.

In order to begin mining, Lucky Strike must receive approval from the BLM for its "plan of operations." This is a plan that describes the company's proposed mining and reclamation operations. The claims are surrounded by federal land managed by the BLM. To facilitate mining the company has located 125 mill sites of 5 acres each. Lucky Strike claims that these 625 acres of land are necessary to support its mining operations, especially the placement of overburden and other waste rock. Lucky claims that this amount of land—almost a full square mile—is needed because of the low grade of ore that Lucky will be mining. Approximately 200 tons of ore must be mined for each ounce of gold that will be produced.

In addition to relevant provisions of the Mining Law, the Federal Land Policy and Management Act contains two provisions that are potentially relevant to this conflict. Section 302(b) provides in relevant part that—

> . . . In managing the public lands, the Secretary shall, by regulation or otherwise, take any action necessary to prevent unnecessary and undue degradation of the lands.

43 U.S.C. § 1732(b). Section 603(c) provides—

> During the period of review of [areas recommended for wilderness designation], and until Congress has determined otherwise, the Secretary shall continue to manage such lands according to his authority under this Act and other applicable law in a manner so as not to impair the suitability of such areas for preservation as wilderness, . . .

43 U.S.C. § 1782(c). Friends of the Deep Creek is a conservation group that is dedicated to promoting wilderness designation for the Deep Creek Wilderness Study Area. It opposes Lucky's proposed mining operation due to the irreparable damage that it will likely cause to the roadless character of the area. What legal arguments can you make to support Friends' claim that the BLM has the authority, and perhaps a legal obligation, to reject Lucky's mining operations in the Deep Creek Wilderness Study Area? If the BLM rejects the plan will it effect a "taking" of Lucky's mining claims in violation of the constitution?

D. STAKING A MINING CLAIM

1. FEDERAL AND STATE STANDARDS

You now have some familiarity with the basic requirements of the 1872 Mining Law. But suppose you actually want to stake a claim. What do you do? As described above, you will first want check the BLM's Master Title

Plats and local county records to be sure that the lands on which your claims will be located are open to location under the Mining Law. Then, keeping in mind the dimensional requirements for mining claims described previously, you will need to actually "stake" your claim. The statute requires that—(1) "[t]he location . . . be distinctly marked on the ground so that its boundaries can be readily traced"; (2) all records of mining claims contain the names of the locators, the date of the location, and a description of the claim; and (3) $100 worth of labor be performed or improvements made each year (assessment work). 30 U.S.C. § 28.*

In addition to these federal requirements, the mining law invites state and local authorities to establish rules that are not in conflict with the federal standards. 30 U.S.C. § 26. In response to this invitation, each public land state has adopted procedures for staking mining claims. While the specific procedures vary, all states adhere to the same basic requirements:

1. A discovery of valuable minerals subject to appropriation under the mining laws;

2. Notice of discovery made on a monument at or near the time and place of the discovery;

3. Boundary markers on the ground at sufficient points—usually each corner, and in some case, the center of the sidelines—to identify the boundaries of the claim; and

4. Recordation of a certificate of location and an affidavit of assessment work in the county recorder's office for the county in which the claim is situated.

Until fairly recently, most states also required *discovery work* on lode claims. Discovery work usually took the form of a shaft or hole, dug to a certain minimum depth that would expose the ore or vein. Today, only North Dakota and Colorado retain discovery work requirements. Even in these states the old requirements for digging a discovery shaft can generally be avoided by performing some alternative work on the claim.

The requirements for a *discovery* of valuable minerals are addressed in greater detail at section F., below. The remaining requirements are the subject of the cases in this section. Discovery monuments and boundary markers are most commonly made with 4 x 4 wooden posts. Metal tags are often tacked on to these posts with pertinent information about the claim.*

QUESTIONS AND DISCUSSION

1. The General Mining Law expressly states that mining claims may be located only "by citizens of the United States and those who have declared their intention to become such. . . ." 30 U.S.C. § 22. Nonetheless, in *McKinley Creek Mining Co. v. Alaska United Mining Co.*, 183 U.S. 563

---

* Since 1993, Congress has imposed a requirement that claimants pay a $100 fee in lieu of assessment work. 30 U.S.C. § 28f (2003). The only exception is for claimants who hold ten or fewer claims. *Id.* § 28f(d).

* Drawings of discovery monuments and mining claim are available in ROBERT PRUITT, DIGEST OF MINING CLAIM LAWS (6th ed. 1996). This Digest also contains a useful collection of the mining statutes for all of the public land states.

(1902), the Court held that aliens may locate mining claims and only the federal government may challenge such claims on the grounds that the owner is not a U.S. citizen. Furthermore, *Manuel v. Wulff*, 152 U.S. 505 (1894), makes clear that aliens can acquire mining claims by purchase.

2. Agents may locate claims so long as their principals are qualified locators. 43 C.F.R. § 3830.3 (2007). According to the California Supreme Court, minors can also locate mining claims so long as they are the actual party in interest and are otherwise qualified. *See Thompson v. Spray*, 72 Cal. 528, 14 P. 182 (1887). The BLM regulations at 43 C.F.R. § 3830.3 (2007) expressly recognize the right of minors who have reached the "age of discretion" to locate claims.

3. In *Roughing It,* Mark Twain recounts how he and his partners located a valuable claim only to lose it soon thereafter for failing to perform the required discovery work. The claim was sufficiently valuable that one of Twain's partners was offered (and refused) $250,000 for his one-third share of the claim. As Twain notes:

> By the laws of the district, the "locators" or claimants of a ledge [lode] were obliged to do a fair and reasonable amount of work on their new property within ten days after the date of the location, or the claim was forfeited, and anybody could go seize it that chose.

MARK TWAIN, ROUGHING IT 214 (1872). The partners had planned to go out the next day, but each of them was called away on other business, and thinking that the other would take care of the work did not check the claim before the ten days expired. Twain recounts that "[a]t midnight on the woeful tenth day the ledge would be relocatable, and by eleven o'clock the hill was black with men prepared to do the relocating." *Id.* at 219.

4. A claimant's failure to comply with state procedures may be grounds for cancellation of the claim by the federal government. *Roberts v. Morton*, 389 F. Supp. 87, 93 (D. Colo. 1975), *aff'd*, 549 F.2d 158, 161–62 (10th Cir. 1976), *cert. denied, sub nom., Roberts v. Andrus*, 434 U.S. 834 (1977); *U.S. v. Weber Oil Co.*, 89 I.D. 538, 548, GFS (MIN) 306 (1982). Furthermore, the statutory time period begins to run from the date posted on the discovery monument. Posting a notice of location is expressly required by federal rules. 43 C.F.R. § 3832.11(3) (2007). A claimant cannot change that date to allow additional time to complete the formalities. *Ingemarson v. Coffey*, 41 Colo. 407, 92 P. 908 (1907).

5. The failure to record a certificate of location within the period prescribed by statute does not render the claim void. An unrecorded claim, however, will not protect a claimant against intervening rights. Thus, if a claimant fails to comply with the requirements of the statute within the prescribed period, a subsequent claimant may acquire rights to that claim by making a new discovery. *Slothower v. Hunter*, 15 Wyo. 189, 88 P. 36 (1906). Suppose a subsequent claimant has actual knowledge of an unrecorded claim. Can he nonetheless make a valid location? *Compare Atherley v. Bullion Monarch Uranium Co.*, 8 Utah 2d 362, 335 P.2d 71 (1959) (protecting the earlier claimant where the later claimant had actual knowledge of an inadequately recorded prior claim), *with Shope v. Sims*, 658 P.2d 1336 (Alaska 1983) (holding that the exception that allows a prior claimant to prevail over a later claimant with actual knowledge does not apply where the prior claimant fails to record a certificate of location within 90 days as required by state law).

PROBLEM EXERCISE: LOCATION AND RECORDING REQUIREMENTS

(Based upon *Rasmussen Drilling, Inc. v. Kerr–McGee Nuclear Corp.*, 571 F.2d 1144 (10th Cir. 1978), *cert. denied*, 439 U.S. 862 (1978))

In late 1967 and early 1968, Kerr–McGee located numerous uranium lode claims on public lands in Wyoming. Subsequently, in the summer of 1968, Rasmussen staked over certain claims that had been located by Kerr–McGee in Section 17 of Township 35 North, Range 74 West, 6th Principal Meridian, but that, as a result of a clerical error, were mistakenly recorded in Section 19 of that same township. Because Kerr–McGee had other claims in Section 19, the county records showed a double filing in Section 19 and no filing in Section 17. The evidence regarding Rasmussen's knowledge of Kerr–McGee's claims was in dispute, but a jury found that Rasmussen was aware of Kerr–McGee's mistake at the time it staked its claims in Section 17.

The relevant Wyoming statutes describe the process for locating a lode mining claim as follows:

§ 30–1–101

(a) A discoverer of any mineral lead, lode, ledge or vein shall, within sixty (60) days from the date of discovery, cause the claim to be recorded in the office of the county clerk and ex officio register of deeds in the county within which the claim may exist, by a location certificate which shall contain the following facts:

1. The name of the lode claim;

2. The name of the locator or locators;

3. The date of location;

4. The length of the claim and the general course of the vein as far as it is known;

5. The amount of surface ground claimed;

6. A description of the claim by such designation of natural or fixed object, or if upon ground surveyed by the United States system of land survey, by reference to section or quarter section corners, as shall identify the claim beyond question.

§ 30–1–102:

Any certificate of the location of a lode claim which shall not fully contain all the requirements named in the preceding section [§ 30–1–101], together with such other description as shall identify the lode or claim with reasonable certainty, shall be void.

As between Kerr–McGee and Rasmussen, which party holds the valid claims? Does it matter whether Rasmussen knew about and deliberately took advantage of Kerr–McGee's clerical error? Suppose that Rasmussen knew of the double filing in Section 19. Did this information obligate him to ascertain whether one of those filings should have been in Section 17? *Compare* 2 AM. L. OF MINING § 33.09[7] *with Gustin v. Nevada–Pacific Dev.*

Corp., 125 F. Supp. 811 (D. Nev. 1954), *aff'd*, 226 F.2d 286, *cert. denied*, 351 U.S. 930 (1956); *Winters v. Burkland*, 123 Or. 137, 260 P. 231 (1927).

Suppose that Rasmussen had sold his interest to a third party, Dakota Minerals. Before purchasing the claims from Rasmussen, Dakota checked the dates on several of the Kerr–McGee discovery monuments in Section 17 and determined that Kerr–McGee had failed to record its locations in Section 17 within the statutory 60–day period. On this basis, Dakota decided that Rasmussen held good title to the claims. Assume from the original facts that that Kerr–McGee prevailed because Rasmussen was found to have acted in bad faith. Who should prevail as between Dakota and Kerr–McGee?

QUESTIONS AND DISCUSSION

1. Under Wyoming law as described in the problem above, a lode claimant has 60 days from the date of discovery to record a certificate of location and to perform the other formalities required by law. WYO. STAT. ANN. § 30–1–101 (1983). But often a claimant, in anticipation of a discovery, will perform the formalities first. This is not objectionable, but the claim does not become valid until the discovery is made. *Creede & Cripple Creek Mining & Milling Co. v. Uinta Tunnel Mining & Transp. Co.*, 196 U.S. 337 (1905); *see also* 30 U.S.C. § 23.

Like Wyoming, most states allow claimants a specified period of time (between 20–90 days) to complete the formalities of location after discovery. 2 AM. LAW OF MINING, § 33.04[3]. During this time, a claimant is protected against adverse claims, including those that may be located without actual notice of the initial claim.

2. State requirements for posting the notice of location vary. Some states require only the name of the locator, the name of the claim, and the date of location. Others require that a copy of the recorded notice be posted. Despite these requirements, the cases agree that any form that adequately provides notice to subsequent locators will be sustained. With the exception of the claimant's name, erroneous or omitted information is often excused. *See* 2 AM. L. OF MINING § 33.03[6].

3. As described in Chapter 2, the Stockraising Homestead Act of 1916 allows persons qualified to make an entry on public lands under the homestead laws to make a stockraising homestead entry for up to 640 acres of unappropriated and unreserved public domain land. 43 U.S.C. § 291, repealed by the Federal Land Policy and Management Act of 1976, 43 U.S.C. § 1701. Entrymen who complied with the requirements of the law were eligible for patents to these lands. The law expressly reserved to the United States, however, all minerals contained within these lands. 43 U.S.C. § 299. Furthermore, the Act authorized mineral entrymen to enter and prospect for minerals on such lands. The mineral locator, however, was required to pay damages to the agricultural entrymen for any injury or damage caused by the prospecting activities. In order to develop minerals on such lands, the mining claimant must either obtain the consent of the surface entryman or post a bond sufficient to cover the potential damage that may be caused by the mining operations.

————

2.   AMENDMENT AND RELOCATION

Once a claim is located changes may be necessary. As described previously, claimants generally have the right to hold off marking the boundaries of their claims until the statutory time period for completing the formalities of location has expired. Once those boundaries have been set, however, and the claimant has recorded the claim in the local county recorder's office, changes may only be made by amending the claim. The Mining Law does not itself provide for amending claims, but courts have generally allowed parties to amend their claim to correct minor defects, including clarifying the precise physical boundaries of a claim. *See, e.g., McEvoy v. Hyman,* 25 F. 596 (C.C.D. Colo. 1885). Furthermore, most state statutes expressly provide for amending mining claims. *See, e.g.,* NEV. REV. STAT. § 517–200.

An amendment is made "in furtherance of the original location and for the purposes of giving additional strength . . . thereto." *John C. Teller,* 26 L.D. 484 (1898). An amendment will not protect a claimant against intervening claims. In contrast to an amendment, a relocation is really just a new location made by the same claimant. It is adverse to an original location and "can only be made where the original location and all the rights thereunder have been lost by failure to make the necessary annual expenditures." *Id.* at 486.

A case that illustrates the distinction between amendment and relocation is *R. Gail Tibbetts,* 43 I.B.L.A. 210, GFS (MIN) 92 (1979). In *Tibbetts,* the claimant along with several other parties had filed numerous mining claims in southern Utah. In 1972, the lands on which the claims were located were withdrawn from the operation of the Mining Law when they were made part of the Glen Canyon National Recreation Area. Subsequently, Tibbetts filed new location certificates over some of these same lands. The certificates did not on their face purport to amend the pre-existing claims, but when the BLM contested the claims, Tibbetts claimed that he was the successor in interest to the prior claims and that the new certificates were amendments rather than relocations. The Board noted that if the amended certificates were relocations, then they were null and void *ab initio* because they were filed on lands that had been withdrawn. If they were amendments, however, as Tibbetts claimed, then they would relate back to the date of the original locations, which were made before the lands were withdrawn. The Board remanded the case to the administrative law judge for further fact-finding as to whether the new certificates should be treated as amendments or relocations.

QUESTIONS AND DISCUSSION

1. On remand in *Tibbetts,* who has the burden of proof? Should the government be required to show that Tibbetts had filed relocations and that the claims were thus void, or should Tibbetts be required to show that he had filed amendments to the original claims so that the claims were still valid? The Administrative Procedure Act provides that the "proponent of a rule or order has the burden of proof." 5 U.S.C. § 556(d). Who is the proponent in a government proceeding contesting the validity of a claim?

2. Sometimes a claimant is uncertain as to whether her claim remains valid. Questions may arise, for example, as to whether a valid senior claim existed at the time of a location, *see Bergquist v. West Virginia–Wyoming Copper Co.*, 18 Wyo. 234, 106 P. 673 (1910), or as to assessment work that was not carried out for several years prior to the mandatory filing requirements imposed by FLPMA. Should the claimant relocate and risk losing his rights to intervening claimants or to the federal government? Some operators use a "hybrid certificate," which purports to amend the certificate of location unless the claim should for some reason be deemed void, in which case the hybrid certificate is treated as a relocation. For a further discussion of the dilemma posed by the amendment/relocation distinction, see James Aronstein, *Simultaneous Amendment and Conditional Relocation*, 33 ROCKY MTN. MIN. L. INST. 10–1 (1987). *See also* George Reeves, *Amendment v. Relocation*, 14 ROCKY MTN. MIN. L. INST. 207 (1968).

———

3. ASSESSMENT WORK

In order to ensure that mining claimants were acting in good faith with the intention of developing a mine in a timely fashion, the General Mining Law imposed a requirement that claimants perform "not less than one hundred dollars' worth of labor ... or improvements ... each year." 30 U.S.C. § 28; *St. Louis Smelting & Refining Co. v. Kemp*, 104 U.S. 636 (1881). Like the use-it-or-lose-it aspect of the beneficial use doctrine in water law (Chapter 7, page 784), the assessment fee was designed to ensure that claimants who failed to diligently work their claims would forfeit their rights.

Assessment work requirements have been largely eliminated as a result of recent legislation enacted by Congress. In the Dep't of the Interior and Related Agencies Appropriations Act, Pub. L. No. 103–381, 106 Stat. 1378–79 (1993), Congress imposed a $100 claim maintenance fee for all mining claims, mill and tunnel sites in lieu of assessment work for the assessment year ending in 1994. This requirement was regularly extended in the various annual budget bills until the 2003 assessment year when it was finally codified. *See* 30 U.S.C. § 28f–k. This legislation also authorized the Secretary to adjust the fees, and the maintenance fee was raised to $125/claim in 2004. 43 C.F.R. § 3830.21 (2008). Payment must be made *before* the assessment year begins except in the case of newly located claims, in which case payment is required at the time the location notice is recorded with the BLM, which must be within 90 days of location. Failure to pay the fee as required by the law "shall conclusively constitute a forfeiture of the unpatented mining claim, mill or tunnel site ..."; 30 U.S.C. § 28i. The maintenance fee requirement may be waived, however, for claimants who certify in writing to the Secretary that the claimant and all related parties held no more than 10 mining claims, mill sites, or tunnel sites and have done assessment work on these claims as required by law. 30 U.S.C. § 28f(d).

While assessment work may largely be a relic of the past, the issue remains important for miners with no more than 10 claims, and in litigating title to mining claims established prior to the adoption of the claim maintenance procedure. If a "small miner certification" is filed without express language stating that the miner owns less than 10 claims, such defects are not fatal to the claim if the document "easily could and should have been construed" as such. See *Dimitrov v. Norton*, 479 F. Supp. 2d 1141 (D. Mont. 2007). Thus, the courts prefer to allow for defect cure. This prevents the BLM or Forest Service from abusing their discretion to forfeit claims due to filing of a defective waiver, if the intent of the claimant to retain their mineral rights is easily ascertained. The following case illustrates how historical assessment work can retain continuing importance. The case arises in the context of oil shale claims, which have proved to be a particularly thorny problem despite the fact that oil shale was removed from the operation of the mining law in 1920 and that oil shale development has not yet proved profitable.

HICKEL v. THE OIL SHALE CORP. (TOSCO), 400 U.S. 48 (1970)

MR. JUSTICE DOUGLAS delivered the opinion of the Court.

This case involves six groups of claims to oil shale located in Colorado and asserted under the General Mining Act of 1872, 17 Stat. 91, now 30 U.S.C. §§ 22, 26, 28, and 29. Section 28 provides that until a patent issued "not less than $100 worth of labor shall be performed or improvements made during each year." And § 29 provides that a patent to the claim could issue on a showing that the claimant had expended $500 worth of labor or improvements on the claim. These claims are not patented and were canceled in the early 1930's on the ground that the amount of labor or improvements specified in '28 had not been made "during each year."

Some of the claimants in this case applied for patents between 1955 and 1962. The General Land Office rejected the patent applications because the claims had been canceled. On appeal, the Secretary of the Interior, acting through the Solicitor, ruled that these cancellations were effective, later judicial determinations of the invalidity of the grounds for cancellation notwithstanding. *Union Oil Co.*, 71 I.D. 169. These claimants then sought an order to compel the Department to issue the patents. They argued that the Land Office was without authority to cancel the claims when it did and that the Secretary of the Interior had nullified all the contest proceedings in 1935. In the alternative, they sought judicial review of those contest rulings. Respondent Oil Shale Corp. commenced this action in the District Court, not to require the Secretary to issue a patent, but to expunge the rulings of the Secretary canceling the claims and to enjoin him from enforcing them. All the cases were consolidated for trial in the District Court. The District Court granted the relief, 261 F. Supp. 954, and the Court of Appeals affirmed, 406 F.2d 759, both holding that cancellations for lack of assessment work were void because the Department did not have jurisdiction over the subject matter. The case is here on petition for certiorari, which we granted to consider whether *Wilbur v. U.S. ex rel. Krushnic*, 280 U.S. 306 and *Ickes v. Virginia–Colorado Development Corp.*, 295 U.S.

639, had been correctly construed and applied to invalidate the Secretary's action in protection of the public domain.

Before we come to a consideration of the *Krushnic* and *Virginia–Colorado* cases it should be noted that in 1920, Congress by enacting § 21 of the Mineral Lands Leasing Act, 41 Stat. 445, 30 U.S.C. § 241(a), completely changed the national policy over the disposition of oil shale lands. Thereafter such lands were no longer open to location and acquisition of title but only to lease. But § 37 contained a Saving Clause which covered "valid claims existent on February 25, 1920, and thereafter maintained in compliance with the laws under which initiated, which claims may be perfected under such laws, including discovery." 30 U.S.C. § 193. Respondents contend that their claims fall within that exception.

Respondents assert that a like claim was recognized and approved in the *Krushnic* case. In that case, however, labor in the statutory amount had been performed, including the aggregate amount of $500. The only default was in the failure to perform labor for one year during the period. * * *

The Court further held that the claims were "maintained" within the Saving Clause of the Leasing Act by a resumption of the assessment work before a challenge of the claim by the United States had intervened.

Virginia–Colorado also involved claims on which labor had been expended except for one year. It was alleged, however, that the claimant had planned to resume the assessment work but for the Secretary's adverse action and that the claims had not been abandoned. The Court held that the claims had been "maintained" within the meaning of the Saving Clause of the Leasing Act of 1920.

Those two cases reflect a judicial attitude of fair treatment for claimants who have substantially completed the assessment work required by 30 U.S.C. § 28. There are, however, dicta both in *Virginia–Colorado* and in *Krushnic* that the failure to do assessment work gives the Government no ground for forfeiture but inures only to the benefit of relocators.

Indeed 30 U.S.C. § 28, which derives from the 1872 Act, as already noted, provides that upon the failure to do the assessment work, "the claim or mine upon which such failure occurred shall be open to relocation in the same manner as if no location of the same had ever been made," provided the assessment work has not been "resumed" upon the claim "after failure and before such location." It is therefore argued that so far as the 1872 Act is concerned the failure to do the assessment work concerns not the Government but only "rival or adverse claimants."

The problem in those two cases and the present one concerns the Saving Clause in the Leasing Act which, as noted, makes available for patent "valid claims existent on February 25, 1920, and thereafter maintained in compliance with the laws under which initiated." Concededly, failure to maintain a claim made it "subject to disposition only" by leasing by the United States. *See* § 37 of the 1920 Act, 30 U.S.C. § 193. Hence if we assume, arguendo, that failure to do assessment work as provided in the 1872 Act concerned at the time only the claimant and any subsequent relocator, the United States, speaking through the Secretary of the Interior, became a vitally interested party by reason of the 1920 Act. For it was by that Act that Congress reclaimed portions of the public domain so that land might be disposed of by a different procedure (leasing) to the same end (oil shale production) or devoted to wholly different purposes within the purview of public policy as determined by Congress.

It appears that shortly before 1920 oil shale claims were affected by a speculative fever. Then came a period of calm. By the late forties and continuing into the sixties speculators sought out the original locators or their heirs, obtained quitclaim deeds from them, and thereupon eliminated all other record titleholders by performing assessment work for one year. It appears that 94 of the 98 claims involved in the present litigation were of that character. There is nothing reprehensible in the practice, if the procedure is one which Congress has approved. But the command of the 1872 Act is that assessment work of $100 be done "during each year" and the Saving Clause of § 37 of the 1920 Act requires that for lands to escape the leasing requirement the claims must be "maintained in compliance with the laws under which initiated." * * *

If we were to hold to the contrary that enforcement of the assessment work of § 28 was solely at the private initiative of relocators, the "maintenance" provision of § 37 becomes largely illusory, because relocation of oil shale claims became impossible after the 1920 Act. So if enforcement of the assessment work requirement of § 28 were dependent solely on the activities and energies of oil shale relocators, there was no effective enforcement device. While the area covered by the claims might possibly be relocated for wholly different purposes, the likelihood was so remote that the Court of Appeals concluded that: "The old claims were thus sheltered by the (1920) Act." 406 F.2d at 763. That meant that a claim could remain immune from challenge by anyone with or without any assessment work, in complete defiance of the 1872 Act.

The Court concluded in *Virginia–Colorado* that the lapse in assessment work was no basis for a charge of abandonment. 295 U.S. at 645–646. We construe that statement to mean that on the facts of that case failure to do the assessment work was not sufficient to establish abandonment. But it was well established that the failure to do assessment work was evidence of abandonment. *Union Oil Co. v. Smith*, 249 U.S. 337, 349; *Donnelly v. United States*, 228 U.S. 243, 267. If, in fact, a claim had been abandoned, then the relocators were not the only ones interested. The United States had an interest in retrieving the lands. *See* G. WIDMAN, T. BRIGHTWELL, & J. HAGGARD, LEGAL STUDY OF OIL SHALE ON PUBLIC LANDS, 189–193 (1969). The policy of leasing oil shale lands under the 1920 Act gave the United States a keen interest in recapturing those which had not been "maintained" within the meaning of § 37 of that Act. We agree with the Court in *Krushnic* and *Virginia–Colorado* that every default in assessment work does not cause the claim to be lost. Defaults, however, might be the equivalent of abandonment; and we now hold that token assessment work, or assessment work that does not substantially satisfy the requirements of 30 U.S.C. § 28, is not adequate to "maintain" the claims within the meaning of '37 of the Leasing Act. To hold otherwise would help defeat the policy that made the United States, as the prospective recipient of royalties, a beneficiary of these oil shale claims. We cannot support *Krushnic* and *Virginia–Colorado* on so broad a ground. Rather, their dicta to the contrary, we conclude that they must be confined to situations where there had been substantial compliance with the assessment work requirements of the 1872 Act, so that the "possessory title" of the claimant, granted by 30 U.S.C. § 26, will not be disturbed on flimsy or insubstantial grounds. * * *

We conclude therefore that the judgments below must be reversed. * * *

QUESTIONS AND DISCUSSION

1. What test does the *TOSCO* (*The Oil Shale Corporation*) case adopt for determining whether a mining claim lapses for failing to perform annual assessment work? Is the decision limited to oil shale claims? *See* 43 C.F.R. § 3836.15 (2007). Does *TOSCO* require affirmative action on the part of the government to cancel a mining claim or is forfeiture automatic?

2. Suppose that a claimant failed to maintain a non-Mineral Leasing Act claim over a period of 50 years and that, in the intervening period, the government withdrew the land from location under the Mining Law. Does *TOSCO* suggest that the government cannot contest that claim for failing to perform assessment work?

3. In two recent cases before the Tenth Circuit, the court rejected various arguments that certain oil shale claims should be found valid notwithstanding the claimants' failure to comply substantially with the applicable assessment work requirements. In particular, the court determined that the claimants' failure to perform assessment work requirements over a period of many years could not be overcome either by performing at least $500 worth of assessment work—the amount required for obtaining a patent—or by resuming assessment work before the government contested the claim. *See Exxon Mobil Corp. v. Norton*, 346 F.3d 1244 (10th Cir. 2003), *cert. denied*, 541 U.S. 904, 124 S.Ct. 1606 (2004); *Cliffs Synfuel Corp. v. Norton*, 291 F.3d 1250 (10th Cir. 2002).

4. Oil shale development advocates received a boost with the passage of the Energy Policy Act of 2005. Section 369(d) of the Act required the Secretary of the Interior to prepare a programmatic environmental impact statement in accordance with the National Environmental Policy Act for commercial leasing program for oil shale and tar sands on public lands within 18 months after passage of the law. Within six months thereafter, the Secretary was directed to prepare final regulations establishing a commercial leasing program. The final EIS was released in September, 2008, but the Obama Administration has signaled that it intends to move more cautiously before embarking on a commercial leasing program. Nonetheless, it is easy to see the attraction of oil shale. In a press release issued with the final EIS, the BLM claimed that oil shale deposits in Colorado, Utah, and Wyoming "hold the equivalent of 800 billion barrels of oil—enough to meet U.S. demand for imported oil at current levels for 110 years." http://www.blm.gov/wo/st/en/info/newsroom/2008/september/ NR_09_04_2008.html. Yet critics argue that extracting the oil from the shale remains impractical. Consider, for example, this description of the "in situ" process currently being considered by Royal Dutch/Shell:

> Time will tell whether the company's "in-situ" process is madness or genius. The vision is breathtaking. The company proposes to electrically heat a 1,000 foot-thick section of the Green River Formation to 700 degrees Fahrenheit, then keep it that hot for three years. Beam me up, Scotty, but first share some details. Imagine a ten-acre production plot, 2,000 feet on a side. Inside that area, the company would drill up to 200 closely spaced wells. After those wells are lined with steel casing, 1,000 foot-long electric heaters would be inserted in preparation for the "bake." Before the fire comes the ice. Since it's impractical to heat the rock if it's in contact with groundwater, Shell has to dewater the production area first. To do that, it proposes to construct a "frost wall" to isolate the production zone from the surrounding area. (Frost walls are routinely used in skyscraper foundations, but of course few foundations are 2,000 feet deep.) To build the frost wall, the company will drill a narrowly

spaced line of wells, case them, then circulate a frigid coolant until the rock freezes solid. If the frost wall holds, the company will drill dewatering wells inside the production zone. Once the shale is dry, it will be heated, and if all goes well, three years later oil and natural gas will flow. The company hopes to recover up to one million barrels per acre—$60 million worth at today's prices. It's a high-stakes gamble, but if it works a six mile-by-six mile area could produce twenty billion barrels, roughly equal to remaining reserves in the Lower 48.

Although Shell's method avoids many of the negative impacts of mining oil shale, it requires a mind-boggling amount of electricity. To produce 100,000 barrels a day would require raising the temperature of 700,000,000,000 pounds of shale by 700 degrees F. How much power would be needed? A gigabunch—in rough numbers, about $500,000,000 per year. The least expensive source for electricity is a coal-fired power plant. How much coal, how many power plants? To produce 100,000 barrels per day, the RAND Corporation recently estimated that Shell will need to construct the largest power plant in Colorado history, large enough to serve a city of 500,000. This power plant, costing about $3 billion, would consume five million tons of coal each year, producing ten million tons of greenhouse gases, some of which would still be in the atmosphere a century from now. To double production, you'd need two power plants. One million barrels a day would require ten new power plants, five new coal mines.

Randall Udall & Steve Andrews, *The Illusive Bonanza: Oil Shale in Colorado "Pulling the Sword from the Stone"*, available at, http://www.aspencore.org/images/pdf/OilShale.pdf. Are you persuaded that oil shale development is "a fool's bargain"? What if the electricity needed for this enterprise came from nuclear power rather than coal? Would that adequately address the greenhouse gas issue? For a detailed assessment of the technical and policy issues surrounding oil shale development, *see* JAMES T. BARTIS ET AL., OIL SHALE DEVELOPMENT IN THE UNITED STATES (2005), *available at* http://www.rand.org/pubs/monographs/2005/RAND_MG414.pdf.

5. The Energy Policy Act of 1992 limited the patent right of oil shale claimants. Pub. L. No. 102–486, 106 Stat. 2776, 3109–11 (1992). Unless patent applicants had completed essentially all of their responsibilities for a patent application by October 24, 1992, applicants are limited to patenting the oil shale and associated minerals at a cost of $2.50/acre. Surface rights and other minerals are retained by the federal government. Furthermore, holders of unpatented oil shale claims may keep their claims only upon payment of a holding fee of $550/year. This payment is in lieu of assessment work and of the $100 maintenance fee imposed on most other mining claims.

6. Does the *TOSCO* decision provide an independent basis for rejecting the mining claims at issue in the *R. Gail Tibbetts* case described in the previous section? Who bears the burden of proving substantial compliance with assessment work requirements?

7 Suppose that a mining claimant has held a gold mining claim for 30 years. During the first ten years he diligently worked the claim and easily performed more than $100 of assessment work annually. During the following ten years, however, the market for gold declined and no work was performed. Subsequently, the gold market recovered and the claimant has performed his annual assessment work for the past ten years. May the government cancel his claim? Should it matter whether the ten-year period without assessment work occurred during the beginning or at the end of the twenty-year period? Should it matter if the land was withdrawn from location during the ten-year period in which the assessment work lapsed? During the period after assessment work had resumed?

8. Suppose that $500 worth of assessment work has been performed offsite for the benefit of eight claims. In this circumstance, the requirement for $100 of annual assessment work for *each* claim has plainly not been met. But are all eight of the claims subject to relocation? Courts have split on this issue. Some have held that the work must be apportioned equally such that all of the claims will be open to relocation. *Platt v. Bagg*, 77 Ariz. 214, 269 P.2d 715 (1954); *Duncan v. Eagle Rock Gold Mining & Reduction Co.*, 48 Colo. 569, 111 P. 588 (1910). Other courts have allowed the claim owner to choose the claims to which the work will apply. *Utah Standard Mining Co. v. Tintic Indian Chief Mining & Milling Co.*, 73 Utah 456, 274 P. 950 (1929); *McKirahan v. Gold King Mining Co.*, 39 S.D. 535, 165 N.W. 542 (1917). Which is the better rule? Why?

9. The cost of materials used on a claim may be included in the assessment work calculation, as may any equipment that is permanently attached to the property. However, tools and equipment which are merely used on the property qualify as assessment work only to the extent of the reasonable value for their use. Suppose a watchman is hired to guard a mining claim and ward off trespassers. Does the watchman's salary qualify as assessment work? *See James v. Krook*, 42 Ariz. 322, 25 P.2d 1026 (1933) *and Fredericks v. Klauser*, 52 Ore. 110, 96 P. 679 (1908) (both holding that cost of watchman did not qualify where there was no machinery or equipment on site that required the services of a watchman).

10. Following a 1958 amendment to the mining law, *on the ground* geological, geochemical and geophysical surveys are authorized as assessment work subject to certain filing and reporting requirements. 30 U.S.C. §§ 28–1, 28–2. Such surveys, however, may not be used for more than two consecutive years or five total years as assessment work. 30 U.S.C. § 28–1. *See also Great Eastern Mines, Inc. v. Metals Corp. of America*, 86 N.M. 717, 527 P.2d 112 (1974). To what extent should exploratory work qualify as assessment work? If the work is done in order to determine whether a valuable deposit of minerals exists, then the work plainly does not qualify as assessment work. (Why not?) If, however, a valuable discovery has been made and the exploratory work is undertaken to test or establish the extent of the deposit, the work qualifies as assessment work in most jurisdictions. *Eveleigh v. Darneille*, 276 Cal.App.2d 638, 81 Cal.Rptr. 301 (1969); *Hamilton v. Ertl*, 146 Colo. 80, 360 P.2d 660 (1961); *Simmons v. Muir*, 75 Wyo. 44, 291 P.2d 810 (1955). Oregon appears to be the only state adhering to a contrary view. *Kramer v. Taylor*, 200 Or. 640, 266 P.2d 709 (1954).

11. How should the requirement for $100 *worth* of labor be measured—by the value of the work performed or the price that is paid for the work? *See James B. Stewart Co. v. Cattany*, 134 Ariz. 484, 657 P.2d 897 (App. 1982); *Norris v. United Mineral Products Co.*, 61 Wyo. 386, 158 P.2d 679 (1945); *McKirahan v. Gold King Mining Co.*, 39 S.D. 535, 165 N.W. 542 (1917). Is the assessment work requirement satisfied even by work performed gratuitously or where payment for work performed is otherwise withheld? *See Eveleigh v. Darneille,* 276 Cal.App.2d 638, 81 Cal.Rptr. 301 (1969); *Pascoe v. Richards,* 20 Cal.Rptr. 416 (Cal. Ct. App. 1962); *Coleman v. Curtis,* 12 Mont. 301, 30 P. 266 (1892). Suppose a claimant, acting in good faith, pays for work that is not performed. Is such a claim subject to forfeiture? *See Protective Mining Co. v. Forest City Mining Co.,* 51 Wash. 643, 99 P. 1033 (1909).

12. The most common question about assessment work concerns the kind of work that qualifies. As a general rule, any work performed in good faith and tending to develop the claim and facilitate the extraction of minerals from it will qualify. For example, in *Chambers v. Harrington,* 111 U.S. 350 (1884), the claimant owned three adjacent claims and had dug a vertical shaft on one claim that was designed to support the development of the minerals on all of the claims. An intervening locator argued that the assessment work had to be performed on the claim itself to qualify. The Court disagreed. Quoting an earlier decision, the Court held that " '[w]ork done outside of the claim, or outside of any claim, if done for the purpose and as a means of prospecting or developing the claim ... is as available for holding the claim as if done within the boundaries of the claim itself.' " *Id.* at 354.

Chambers has been interpreted to support a three-part test for determining whether assessment work performed offsite to benefit a group of claims may be applied to an individual mining claim: (1) the work must benefit the claim for which the work is performed; (2) the claims must be held in common; and (3) the claims must be contiguous. These tests are often repeated by commentators. The key requirement, however, is the first, and so long as the offsite work tends to benefit or develop a claim to which the work will be applied, the requirements of the law are met. *See* 2 AM. L. OF MINING § 45.04[7][b][ii] ("[I]t would seem that the contiguity test is unrealistic, and that the true test should be whether the work tends to benefit the particular claim."). So, for example, an access road that allows the claimant to transport materials and ore to and from the site qualifies for the claim or claims that it serves even though the work is not done on any claim. *United States v. 9,947.71 Acres of Land,* 220 F. Supp. 328 (D. Nev. 1963). Likewise, as *Chambers* suggests, a *shaft* dug pursuant to a general plan or scheme to develop a group of claims will qualify as assessment work for each claim for which access will be obtained through the shaft. Suppose, however, that, pursuant to this general scheme, a *drift* is dug in a direction away from one or more of the claims. Should work on this drift qualify as assessment work for the claims located in a direction opposite the drift? *See Miehlich v. Tintic Standard Mining Co.,* 60 Utah 569, 211 P. 686 (1922) (upholding work on drift going away from a claim where it tended to promote development of the entire deposit); *see also* 2 AM. L. OF MINING § 45.04[7][b][iii] (2d ed. 1986).

13. Suppose Claimant A locates a mining claim. Before he is delinquent on his assessment work Claimant B stakes over the claim. After the original Claimant A is delinquent, Claimant C stakes over the same land. Who holds rights to the claims? *See Belk v. Meagher,* 104 U.S. 279 (1881); 2 AM. L. OF MINING § 45.09[2] (2d ed. 1984).

14. Even where assessment work has been performed, a mining claim will be "conclusively" deemed abandoned if the claimant fails to file an affidavit of assessment work as required by Section 314(c) of the Federal Land Policy and Management Act (FLPMA). This provision of FLPMA is discussed in greater detail in the following section.

———

4. RECORDING REQUIREMENTS UNDER FLPMA

Section 314 of the Federal Land Policy and Management Act, 43 U.S.C. § 1744, fundamentally altered the relationship between mining claimants and the federal government. Before FLPMA, the federal government had no easy way to keep track of the number, location, and ownership of mining claims. The only recording requirements were those imposed by state law. As described previously (page 1098), state laws typically require claimants to file their notice of location and annual affidavit of assessment work in the county recorder's office for the county where the claim is located. If the federal government wanted to know whether a particular tract of land was burdened with one or more claims, it had to go to the county office and check the records. But there are important reasons why the federal government needs to know about certain mining claims. If, for example, the federal government wants to authorize a reservoir on public lands, if it wants to sell a tract of land, if it wants to exchange public lands for private lands, or if it wants to allow any other use potentially incompatible with mining claims, it needs to know whether any mining claims will be impacted. If the claims are valid, the government may need to purchase them; if not, they must contest them.

Requiring mining claimants to record their notice of location and their annual proof of assessment work with the Bureau of Land Management, gives the federal government ready access to information about all valid mining claims. But it does much more. By making clear that mining claims that fail to comply with FLPMA's recording requirements are void, FLPMA cleared the public land of thousands of stale mining claims that had not been maintained. Contest proceedings against claimants that could often not even be found were no longer necessary. But as the following case illustrates, FLPMA's recording requirements can impose a harsh result.

UNITED STATES v. LOCKE,
471 U.S. 84 (1985)

JUSTICE MARSHALL delivered the opinion of the Court.

The primary question presented by this appeal is whether the Constitution prevents Congress from providing that holders of unpatented mining claims who fail to comply with the annual filing requirements of the Federal Land Policy and Management Act of 1976 (FLPMA), 43 U.S.C. § 1744, shall forfeit their claims.

I

From the enactment of the general mining laws in the nineteenth century until 1976, those who sought to make their living by locating and developing minerals on federal lands were virtually unconstrained by the fetters of federal control. The general mining laws, 30 U.S.C. § 22 *et seq.*, still in effect today, allow United States citizens to go onto unappropriated, unreserved public land to prospect for and develop certain minerals. "Discovery" of a mineral deposit, followed by the minimal procedures required to formally "locate" the deposit, gives an individual the right of exclusive possession of the land for mining purposes, 30 U.S.C. § 26; as long as $100 of assessment work is performed annually, the individual may continue to extract and sell minerals from the claim without paying any royalty to the United States, 30 U.S.C. § 28. For a nominal sum, and after certain statutory conditions are fulfilled, an individual may patent the claim, thereby purchasing from the federal government the land and minerals and obtaining ultimate title to them. Patenting, however, is not required, and an unpatented mining claim remains a fully recognized possessory interest. *Best v. Humboldt Placer Mining Co.*, 371 U.S. 334, 335 (1963).

By the 1960s, it had become clear that this nineteenth century laissez faire regime had created virtual chaos with respect to the public lands. In 1975, it was estimated that more than six million unpatented mining claims existed on public lands other than the national forests; in addition, more than half the land in the National Forest System was thought to be covered by such claims. S. Rep. No. 94–583, p. 65 (1975). Many of these claims had been dormant for decades, and many were invalid for other reasons, but in the absence of a federal recording system, no simple way existed for determining which public lands were subject to mining locations, and whether those locations were valid or invalid. As a result, federal land managers had to proceed slowly and cautiously in taking any action affecting federal land lest the federal property rights of claimants be unlawfully disturbed. Each time the Bureau of Land Management (BLM) proposed a sale or other conveyance of federal land, a title search in the county recorder's office was necessary; if an outstanding mining claim was found, no matter how stale or apparently abandoned, formal administrative adjudication was required to determine the validity of the claim.

After more than a decade of studying this problem in the context of a broader inquiry into the proper management of the public lands in the modern era, Congress in 1976 enacted the Federal Land Policy and Management Act, Pub. L. No. 94–579, 90 Stat. 2743. Section 314 of the Act establishes a federal recording system that is designed both to rid federal lands of stale mining claims and to provide federal land managers with up-to-date information that allows them to make informed land management decisions. For claims located before FLPMA's enactment, the federal recording system imposes two general requirements. First, the claims must initially be registered with the BLM by filing, within three years of FLPMA's enactment, a copy of the official record of the notice or certificate of location. 43 U.S.C. § 1744(b). Second, in the year of the initial recording, and "prior to December 31" of every year after that, the claimant must file with state officials and with BLM a notice of intention to hold the claim, an affidavit of assessment work performed on the claim, or a detailed reporting form. 43 U.S.C. § 1744(a). Section 314(c) of the Act provides that failure to comply with either of these requirements "shall be deemed conclusively to constitute an abandonment of the mining claim ... by the owner." 43 U.S.C. § 1744(c).

The second of these requirements—the annual filing obligation—has created the dispute underlying this appeal. Appellees, four individuals engaged "in the business of operating mining properties in Nevada,'' purchased in 1960 and 1966 ten unpatented mining claims on public lands near Ely, Nevada. These claims were major sources of gravel and building material: the claims are valued at several million dollars, and, in the 1979–1980 assessment year alone, appellees' gross income totalled more than one million dollars. Throughout the period during which they owned the claims, appellees complied with annual state law filing and assessment work requirements. In addition, appellees satisfied FLPMA's initial recording requirement by properly filing with BLM a notice of location, thereby putting their claims on record for purposes of FLPMA.

At the end of 1980, however, appellees failed to meet on time their first annual obligation to file with the Federal Government. After allegedly receiving misleading information from a BLM employee, appellees waited until December 31 to submit to BLM the annual notice of intent to hold or proof of assessment work performed required under section 314(a) of FLPMA, 43 U.S.C. § 1744(a). As noted above, that section requires these documents to be filed annually "prior to December 31.'' Had appellees checked, they further would have discovered that BLM regulations made quite clear that claimants were required to make the annual filings in the proper BLM office "on or before December 30 of each calendar year.'' 43 C.F.R. § 3833.2–1(a) (1980) [current version at 43 C.F.R. 3833.2–2(b) (1997)]. Thus, appellees' filing was one day too late.

This fact was brought painfully home to appellees when they received a letter from the BLM Nevada State Office informing them that their claims had been declared abandoned and void due to their tardy filing. In many cases, loss of a claim in this way would have minimal practical effect; the claimant could simply locate the same claim again and then rerecord it with BLM. In this case, however, relocation of appellees' claims, which were initially located by appellees' predecessors in 1952 and 1954, was prohibited by the Common Varieties Act of 1955, 30 U.S.C. § 611; that Act prospectively barred location of the sort of minerals yielded by appellees' claims. Appellees' mineral deposits thus escheated to the Government.

After losing an administrative appeal, appellees filed the present action in the United States District Court for the District of Nevada. Their complaint alleged, *inter alia*, that § 314(c) effected an unconstitutional taking of their property without just compensation and denied them due process. On summary judgment, the District Court held that § 314(c) did indeed deprive appellees of the process to which they were constitutionally due. The District Court reasoned that § 314(c) created an impermissible irrebuttable presumption that claimants who failed to make a timely filing intended to abandon their claims. Rather than relying on this presumption, the Government was obliged, in the District Court's view, to provide individualized notice to claimants that their claims were in danger of being lost, followed by a post-filing-deadline hearing at which the claimants could demonstrate that they had not, in fact, abandoned a claim. Alternatively, the District Court held that the one-day late filing "substantially complied'' with the Act and regulations.

Because a District Court had held an Act of Congress unconstitutional in a civil suit to which the United States was a party, we noted probable jurisdiction under 28 U.S.C. § 1252. We now reverse. . . .

III

Before the District Court, appellees asserted that the section 314(a) requirement of a filing "prior to December 31 of each year'' should be construed to require a filing "on or before December 31.'' Thus, appellees argued, their

December 31 filing had in fact complied with the statute, and the BLM had acted ultra vires in voiding their claims.

Although the District Court did not address this argument, the argument raises a question sufficiently legal in nature that we choose to address it even in the absence of lower court analysis.... While we will not allow a literal reading of a statute to produce a result "demonstrably at odds with the intentions of its drafters," *Griffin v. Oceanic Contractors, Inc.*, 458 U.S. 564, 571 (1982), with respect to filing deadlines a literal reading of Congress' words is generally the only proper reading of those words. * * *

Moreover, BLM regulations have made absolutely clear since the enactment of FLPMA that "prior to December 31" means what it says. * * *

Leading mining treatises similarly inform claimants that "[i]t is important to note that the filing of a notice of intention or evidence of assessment work must be done *prior* to December 31 of each year, *i.e.*, on or before December 30." 2 AMERICAN LAW OF MINING § 7.23D, p. 150.2 (Supp. 1983) (emphasis in original); *see also* 23 ROCKY MOUNTAIN MINERAL LAW INSTITUTE 25 (1977). If appellees, who were businessmen involved in the running of a major mining operation for more than 20 years, had any questions about whether a December 31 filing complied with the statute, it was incumbent upon them, as it is upon other businessmen, *see United States v. Boyle, supra,* to have checked the regulations or to have consulted an attorney for legal advice. Pursuit of either of these courses, rather than the submission of a last-minute filing, would surely have led appellees to the conclusion that December 30 was the last day on which they could file safely. * * *

"Section 314(c) states that failure to comply with the filing requirements of §§ 314(a) and 314(b) shall be deemed conclusively to constitute an abandonment of the mining claim." We must next consider whether this provision expresses a congressional intent to extinguish all claims for which filings have not been made, or only those claims for which filings have not been made and for which the claimants have a specific intent to abandon the claim. * * *

The District Court ... noted correctly that the common law of mining traditionally has drawn a distinction between "abandonment" of a claim, which occurs only upon a showing of the claimant's intent to relinquish the claim, and "forfeiture" of a claim, for which only noncompliance with the requirements of law must be shown. *See, e.g.*, 2 AMERICAN LAW OF MINING § 8.2, pp. 195–196 (1983) (relied upon by the District Court). Given that Congress had not expressly stated in the statute any intent to depart from the term-of-art meaning of "abandonment" at common law, the District Court concluded that § 314(c) was intended to incorporate the traditional common-law distinction between abandonment and forfeiture. Thus, reasoned the District Court, Congress did not intend to cause a forfeiture of claims for which the required filings had not been made, but rather to focus on the claimant's actual intent. As a corollary, the District Court understood the failure to file to have been intended to be merely one piece of evidence in a factual inquiry into whether a claimant had a specific intent to abandon his property.

This construction of the statutory scheme cannot withstand analysis.... Although § 314(c) is couched in terms of a conclusive presumption of "abandonment," there can be little doubt that Congress intended § 314(c) to cause a forfeiture of all claims for which the filing requirements of §§ 314(a) and 314(b) had not been met.

To begin with, the Senate version of § 314(c) provided that any claim not properly recorded "shall be conclusively presumed to be abandoned and shall be void." S. 507, 94th Cong., 1st Sess. § 311. The Committee Report accompanying S. 507 repeatedly indicated that failure to comply with the filing requirements would make a claim "void." *See* S. Rep. No. 94–583, p. 65, 66 (1975). The House legislation and reports merely repeat the statutory language without offering any explanation of it, but it is clear from the Conference Committee Report that the undisputed intent of the Senate—to make "void" those claims for which proper filings were not timely made—was the intent of both chambers. * * *

In addition, the District Court's construction fails to give effect to the "deemed conclusively" language of § 314(c). If the failure to file merely shifts the burden to the claimant to prove that he intends to keep the claim, nothing "conclusive" is achieved by § 314(c). * * *

For these reasons, we find that Congress intended in § 314(c) to extinguish those claims for which timely filings were not made. * * *

A final statutory question must be resolved before we turn to the constitutional holding of the District Court. Relying primarily on *Hickel v. Shale Oil Corp.*, 400 U.S. 48. (1970), the District Court held that, even if the statute required a filing on or before December 30, appellees had "substantially complied" by filing on December 31. We cannot accept this view of the statute.

The notion that a filing deadline can be complied with by filing sometime after the deadline falls due is, to say the least, a surprising notion, and it is a notion without limiting principle. If 1–day late filings are acceptable, 10–day late filings might be equally acceptable, and so on in a cascade of exceptions that would engulf the rule erected by the filing deadline; yet regardless of where the cutoff line is set, some individuals will always fall just on the other side of it. Filing deadlines, like statutes of limitations, necessarily operate harshly and arbitrarily with respect to individuals who fall just on the other side of them, but if the concept of a filing deadline is to have any content, the deadline must be enforced. "Any less rigid standard would risk encouraging a lax attitude toward filing dates," *United States v. Boyle*, 469 U.S., at 241. A filing deadline cannot be complied with, substantially or otherwise, by filing late—even by one day.

Hickel v. Shale Oil Co., supra, does not support a contrary conclusion. *Hickel* suggested, although it did not hold, that failure to meet the annual assessment work requirements of the general mining laws, 30 U.S.C. § 28, which require that "not less than $100 worth of labor shall be performed or improvements made during each year," would not render a claim automatically void. Instead, if an individual complied substantially but not fully with the requirement, he might under some circumstances be able to retain possession of his claim.

These suggestions in *Hickel* do not afford a safe haven to mine owners who fail to meet their filing obligations under any federal mining law. Failure to comply fully with the physical requirement that a certain amount of work be performed each year is significantly different from the complete failure to file on time documents that federal law commands be filed. In addition, the general mining laws at issue in *Hickel* do not clearly provide that a claim will be lost for failure to meet the assessment work requirements. Thus, it was open to the Court to conclude in *Hickel* that Congress had intended to make the assessment work requirement merely an indicia of a claimant's specific intent to retain a claim. Full compliance with the assessment work requirements would establish conclusively an intent to keep the claim, but less than full compliance would not by force of law operate to deprive the claimant of his claim. Instead, less than full compliance would subject the mine owner to a case-by-case determination of whether he nonetheless intended to keep his claim. *See Hickel, supra,* 400 U.S., at 56–57. * * *

IV

* * * There are suggestions in the District Court's opinion that, even understood as a forfeiture provision, § 314(c) might be unconstitutional. We therefore go on to consider whether automatic forfeiture of a claim for failure to make annual filings is constitutionally permissible. The framework for analysis of this question, in both its substantive and procedural dimensions, is set forth by our recent decision in *Texaco, Inc. v. Short,* 454 U.S. 516 (1982). There we upheld a state statute pursuant to which a severed mineral interest that had not been used for a period of 20 years automatically lapsed and reverted to the current surface owner of the property, unless the mineral owner filed a statement of claim in the county recorder's office within two years of the statute's passage.

Under *Texaco,* we must first address the question of affirmative legislative power: whether Congress is authorized to "provide that property rights of this character shall be extinguished if their owners do not take the affirmative action required by the" statute. *Id.* at 525. Even with respect to vested property rights, a legislature generally has the power to impose new regulatory constraints on the way in which those rights are used, or to condition their continued retention on performance of certain affirmative duties. As long as the constraint or duty imposed is a reasonable restriction designed to further legitimate legislative objectives, the legislature acts within its powers in imposing such new constraints or duties. *See, e.g., Village of Euclid v. Ambler Realty Co.,* 272 U.S. 365. (1926); "[L]egislation readjusting rights and burdens is not unlawful solely because it upsets otherwise settled expectations." *Usery v. Turner Elkhorn Mining Co.,* 428 U.S. 1, 16 (1976). * * *

This power to qualify existing property rights is particularly broad with respect to the "character" of the property rights at issue here. Although owners of unpatented mining claims hold fully recognized possessory interests in their claims, *see Best v. Humboldt Placer Mining Co.,* 371 U.S. 334, 335 (1963), we have recognized that these interests are a "unique form of property." *Id.,* 371 U.S. at 335. The United States, as owner of the underlying fee title to the public domain, maintains broad powers over the terms and conditions upon which the public lands can be used, leased, and acquired. *See, e.g., Kleppe v. New Mexico,* 426 U.S. 529, 539. * * *

Claimants thus must take their mineral interests with the knowledge that the Government retains substantial regulatory power over those interests. *Cf. Energy Reserves Group, Inc. v. Kansas Power & Light Co.,* 459 U.S. 400, 413 (1983). * * *

Against this background, there can be no doubt that Congress could condition initial receipt of an unpatented mining claim upon an agreement to perform annual assessment work and make annual filings. That this requirement was applied to claims already located by the time FLPMA was enacted and thus applies to vested claims does not alter the analysis, for any "retroactive application of (FLPMA) is supported by a legitimate legislative purpose furthered by rational means. . . ." *PBSC v. R.A. Gray & Co.,* 467 U.S. 717 (1984). The purposes of applying FLPMA's filing provisions to claims located before the Act was passed—to rid federal lands of stale mining claims and to provide for centralized collection by federal land managers of comprehensive and up-to-date information on the status of recorded but unpatented mining claims—are clearly legitimate. In addition, § 314(c) is a reasonable, if severe, means of furthering these goals; sanctioning with loss of their claims those claimants who fail to file provides a powerful motivation to comply with the filing requirements, while automatic invalidation for noncompliance enables federal land managers to know with certainty and ease whether a claim is currently valid. Finally, the restriction attached to the continued retention of a mining claim imposes the most minimal of burdens on claimants; they must simply file a paper once a year indicating that the required assessment work has been performed or that they intend to hold the claim. Indeed, appellees could have fully protected their interests against the effect of the statute by taking the minimal additional step of patenting the claims. * * *

We look next to the substantive effect of § 314(c) to determine whether Congress is nonetheless barred from enacting it because it works an impermissible intrusion on constitutionally protected rights. With respect to the regulation of private property, any such protection must come from the Fifth Amendment's proscription against the taking of private property without just compensation. On this point, however, *Texaco* is controlling: "this Court has never required (Congress) to compensate the owner for the consequences of his own neglect." 454 U.S. at 530. Appellees failed to inform themselves of the proper filing deadline and failed to file in timely fashion the documents required by federal law. Their property loss was one appellees could have avoided with minimal burden; it was their failure to file on time—not the action of Congress—that caused the property right to be extinguished. Regulation of property rights does not "take" private property when an individual's reasonable, investment-backed expectations can continue to be realized as long as he complies with reasonable regulatory restrictions the legislature has imposed. *See, e.g., Miller v. Schoene*, 276 U.S. 272, 279–280 (1928); *Terry v. Anderson*, 95 U.S. at 632–633. * * *

Finally, the Act provides appellees with all the process that is their constitutional due. In altering substantive rights through enactment of rules of general applicability, a legislature generally provides constitutionally adequate process simply by enacting the statute, publishing it, and, to the extent the statute regulates private conduct, affording those within the statute's reach a reasonable opportunity both to familiarize themselves with the general requirements imposed and to comply with those requirements. *Texaco*, 454 U.S., at 532. Here there can be no doubt that the Act's recording provisions meet these minimal requirements. Although FLPMA was enacted in 1976, owners of existing claims, such as appellees, were not required to make an initial recording until October 1979. This three-year period, during which individuals could become familiar with the requirements of the new law, surpasses the two-year grace period we upheld in the context of a similar regulation of mineral interests in *Texaco*. * * *

QUESTIONS AND DISCUSSION

1. What does the *Locke* decision indicate about the nature of the mining claimant's property right if a claim can be lost because an affidavit of assessment work was filed one day late? Can the government lawfully impose other restrictions on a claimant's rights *after* a claim has been located? Can the government take away the right to patent? Consider for example whether Congress could apply the Surface Resources Act, which requires all post–1955 claimants to provide surface access to persons with consistent uses, retroactively to all claims located before 1955. The Surface Resources Act is discussed *infra* at Section IV.B.

2. As the Court points out, FLPMA required the owners of all mining claims located before FLPMA's passage to make an initial filing with the BLM within three years of the law's enactment. 43 U.S.C. § 1744(a). For claims located after FLPMA was enacted in 1976, a claimant has 90 days within which to file a certificate of location with the BLM. 43 U.S.C. § 1744(b). Annual filings are required for all claims each year thereafter *prior to* December 31. *Id.* § 314(c) (emphasis added).

3. The Bureau of Land Management has promulgated regulations implementing § 314 of FLPMA which require a claimant to file general information about the claim beyond that specifically required by FLPMA. 43 C.F.R. § 3833.11 (2007). The failure to file this supplemental information in a timely fashion, however, does not automatically lead to forfeiture of the claim. Rather, the BLM treats the failure as a "curable defect." A claimant has sixty days within which to cure the defect and the failure to do so results in a forfeiture of the claim. 43 C.F.R. § 3830.94(d) (2008).

4. The BLM rules also provide that notice of actions affecting a mining claim need only be provided to those who have either filed their claim with the BLM, or filed notice that an interest in a claim has been transferred. These rules relieve the BLM of the burden of checking county records when taking action involving a claim. *See* 43 C.F.R. §§ 3833.92 (2008). The regulations respecting supplemental filings and notices of transfer were upheld against a legal challenge by several industry representatives in *Topaz Beryllium Co. v. United States*, 649 F.2d 775 (10th Cir. 1981).

5. In *Feldsite Corp. of America*, 88 I.D. 643 (1981), the IBLA held that a millsite was not abandoned upon failure to make an annual filing because a millsite is not a mining claim. Thus, millsites (and most likely tunnel sites) are subject only to the initial filing requirements set out at 43 U.S.C. § 1744(b). Nonetheless, they are subject to the annual rental fee requirements imposed by Congress in lieu of assessment work. 106 Stat. 1378–79 (1992).

6. In *Henry Friedman*, 49 IBLA 97, GFS (MIN) 178 (1980), Friedman located a mining claim in Alaska on October 12, 1979. He postmarked a copy of his certificate of location to the Alaska BLM office on January 6, 1980. Under § 314(b), the certificate was due to be filed by January 10, 1980, or 90 days after location. The record showed that there was daily service between the place where the certificate was posted and Anchorage where the BLM office was located, but that the certificate was not "received and date stamped" by the BLM until January 15, 1980—five days late. As a result, the BLM declared the claim abandoned and void. On appeal, how should the Board rule? Can *Locke* be distinguished?

7. The documents required by Section 314 of FLPMA must be filed in the *proper* BLM state office, usually the state office where the claim is located. (Some state offices encompass more than one state.) *See* 43 C.F.R. §§ 1822.12; 3833.11 (2007). Failure to file in the appropriate office may render a claim void. *Gold Leaf Enterprizes*, 105 IBLA 282 (1988).

The BLM's acceptance of filings under Section 314 of FLPMA does not render a claim valid. 43 C.F.R. § 3833.1(b) (2007). It does, however, provide federal land managers with an efficient means for determining what claims people are asserting on the public lands, and perhaps more importantly, for determining what claims are no longer valid. This helps to streamline a whole variety of federal land management activities.

8. As noted above, an initial filing of a notice of location must be received and date stamped by the BLM within the 90–day period established by FLPMA. For filing proof of assessment work, however, the BLM accepts as timely filed any document which is postmarked on or before December 30, of the relevant year, and received no later than January 19 of the following year. 43 C.F.R. §§ 3830.5; 3835.31 (2007).

9. FLPMA's filing requirements have not entirely eliminated the problem of a claimant's failure to meet the annual requirements. Consider, for example, the following sequential series of events, all occurring before FLPMA's annual filing requirements became applicable—(1) a claimant locates mining claims; (2) the claimant fails to perform assessment work; (3) a second claimant stakes claims over the original claims; (4) the second claimant fails to perform assessment work; (5) the original claimant resumes assessment work; and (6) a third claimant stakes over the original claims. As between the original claimant and the third claimant, who should prevail? In *Public Service Co. of Oklahoma v. Bleak*, 656 P.2d 600 (Ariz. 1982), the Arizona court found that once a claim has been abandoned and relocated by another party, it can never be revived. As a result, the court held for the third claimant. Is this a fair result? *See* 2 Am. L. of Mining § 45.09[5] (2d ed. 1984) ("While [the] rule which permits the revival of an old claim after its forfeiture and after the abandonment or loss of a later location has been criticized as being contrary to the wording of the federal statute, it accomplishes an equitable result as between the parties directly concerned.") The result in *Bleak* appears to have been codified in rules promulgated by the BLM. 43 C.F.R. § 3836.15 (2008). Do the BLM rules trump inconsistent state law? While FLPMA's annual filing requirement makes it impossible for new conflicts like this to develop, a thorough title search of pre-FLPMA claims may still reveal a past problem that could affect the validity of the claim.

E.   Pedis Possessio

Early on it became clear that in order to avoid a free-for-all on potentially valuable mineral lands, miners engaged in exploration needed some protection on the ground they were actually working. The doctrine of *pedis possessio* evolved to respond to this need. In *Union Oil Co. v. Smith*, 249 U.S. 337, 346–48 (1919), the Supreme Court described the doctrine as follows:

> Those who, being qualified, proceed in good faith to make such explorations and enter peaceably upon vacant lands of the United States for that purpose are not treated as mere trespassers, but as licensees or tenants at will. For since, as a practical matter, exploration must precede the discovery of minerals, and some occupation of the land ordinarily is necessary for adequate and systematic exploration, legal recognition of the *pedis possessio* of a bona fide and qualified prospector is universally regarded as a necessity. It is held that upon the public

domain a miner may hold the place in which he may be working against all others having no better right, and while he remains in possession, diligently working towards discovery, is entitled at least for a reasonable time to be protected against forcible, fraudulent, and clandestine intrusions upon his possession. * * *

Whatever the nature and extent of a possessory right before discovery, all authorities agree that *such possession may be maintained only by continued actual occupancy by a qualified locator or his representatives engaged in persistent and diligent prosecution of work looking to the discovery of mineral.* (Emphasis added.)

Consider the following questions and problems that arise in the context of the pedis possessio doctrine.

QUESTIONS AND DISCUSSION

1. Some mineral deposits such as uranium and limestone often occur over large areas and the pedis possessio doctrine can stymie the efforts of a single entity to acquire minerals rights over such an area as may be necessary to ensure the most economical mining operation. *Geomet Exploration, Ltd. v. Lucky McUranium Corp.,* 601 P.2d 1339 (Ariz. 1979) involved a dispute between the original prospector, Lucky, and a subsequent claimant, Geomet. Lucky had filed on 200 uranium claims encompassing 4,000 acres (more than 6 square miles) on the basis of positive radioactive readings, but it had not actually made a discovery on all of the claims and was not physically occupying all of the land. Subsequently, Geomet entered peaceably and filed its own claims staking over much of the land claimed by Lucky. Lucky claimed that while it was not in actual possession of all the land it had constructive possession because it was actually drilling on some of its claims and it had a comprehensive plan to develop the entire area. The Court rejected Lucky's claim. The Court noted that even assuming Lucky was found to be in constructive possession of the land, it was not diligently searching for minerals on every claim—a separate requirement under the pedis possessio doctrine. The Court further found that Geomet was not acting in bad faith merely because it was aware that Lucky was claiming the same land.

2. Suppose that Lucky forcibly restrained Geomet from entering the claims during the day? To avoid detection, Geomet entered at night. Would the result be the same? Compare *Geomet* with *Rasmussen Drilling, Inc. v. Kerr–McGee Nuclear Corp.,* 571 F.2d 1144 (10th Cir. 1978), *cert. denied,* 439 U.S. 862 (1978). In *Rasmussen,* Kerr–McGee had mistakenly filed claims with the wrong legal description. When he became aware of Kerr–McGee's mistake, Rasmussen subsequently filed claims on the lands that Kerr–McGee had intended to locate. The Court rejected Rasmussen's claims on the grounds that he did not act in good faith. Is *Geomet* consistent with *Rasmussen?*

3. The federal district court for the district of Wyoming reached a result contrary to Geomet in *MacGuire v. Sturgis,* 347 F. Supp. 580 (D. Wyo. 1971). In *MacGuire,* both parties had attempted to locate a substantial number of uranium claims covering an area of approximately 36,000 acres (about 56.25 square miles). Though neither party could claim actual occupancy of all claims, MacGuire had a systematic plan for developing them. The court sustained MacGuire's pedis possessio rights over the entire group of claims despite the lack of actual occupancy. The court based its decision on its finding that the following standards had been met: (a) the geology of the area was similar and the size of the area claimed was reasonable; (b) the discovery work required by Wyoming law had been completed; (c) an overall work program was in effect for the area claimed; (d) the work program was being diligently pursued; and (e) the nature of the mineral claimed and the cost of development would make it economically impracticable to develop the mineral if the locator was awarded only those claims on which he was actually present and currently working. *Id.* at 582.

4. The *MacGuire* test appears to have been accepted by the Court of Appeals for the Tenth Circuit. *Continental Oil Co. v. Natrona Service*, 588 F.2d 792 (10th Cir. 1978). Which case establishes the better rule— *MacGuire* or *Geomet*? Does *Continental Oil* bind the state courts located in the Tenth Circuit? *See also* Terry Fiske, *Pedis Possessio—Modern Use of an Old Concept*, 15 Rocky Mtn. Min. L. Inst. 181, 190–91 (1969). Is *MacGuire* consistent with the Supreme Court's decision in *Union Oil*, as described in *Geomet*?

5. Is the doctrine of pedis possessio a matter of state or federal law? To what extent does an individual state have the authority to alter its law of possession as it applies to mining claims?

6. In *Johanson v. White*, 160 F. 901 (9th Cir. 1908), the plaintiff staked a mining claim, and then left the site for about two weeks to get the supplies and equipment that would be necessary to expose the minerals. In the plaintiff's absence, the defendant staked over the claim. Upon the plaintiff's return, he entered the claim peaceably and proceeded to work alongside the defendant. The plaintiff was the first to locate valuable minerals, but the defendant claimed that he should prevail because he had pedis possessio rights that were superior to the plaintiff. Who wins? Should it matter whether the defendant protested plaintiff's entry upon his return from his trip for supplies and equipment? *See Sparks v. Mount*, 29 Wyo. 1, 207 P. 1099 (1922).

Problem Exercise: *Pedis Possessio* Rights

The Gemstone Mining Co. holds a valid, unpatented placer claim in northeastern Nevada. Jack Feldspar has been prospecting for unknown lode claims on the site of the placer. His activities have not interfered in any way with Gemstone's work on the placer claim. Nonetheless, Gemstone objects to Feldspar's presence and has repeatedly ordered him off the land. Feldspar seeks your advice. What rights does Feldspar have to prospect on Gemstone's claim? *See Clipper Mining Co. v. Eli Mining & Land Co.*, 29 Colo. 377, 68 P. 286 (1902), *aff'd*, 194 U.S. 220 (1904); *Campbell v. McIntyre*, 295 F. 45 (9th Cir. 1924).

Suppose that Gemstone consents to Feldspar's prospecting. *See Stanton v. Weber*, 218 Ore. 282, 341 P.2d 1078 (1959); *McCarthy v. Speed*, 11

S.D. 362, 77 N.W. 590 (1898). Suppose that Gemstone has patented the placer claim and that thereafter, Feldspar wants to prospect for unknown lode claims. *See* 30 U.S.C. § 37.

––––––

F. DISCOVERY OF VALUABLE MINERALS

Even if a mining claim is properly staked and recorded, and even if the claimant is in compliance with all assessment work and maintenance fee requirements, the claimant may still lack a valid mining claim. In order to have a valid "unpatented" mining claim, which gives a miner the right to develop the minerals, the miner must also have discovered a valuable mineral deposit. The following four cases describe different aspects of the law of discovery.

CASTLE v. WOMBLE,
19 L.D. 455 (1894)

[Martin Womble made an agricultural entry on unappropriated public lands in California. Such entries were permitted only on lands that are nonmineral in character. The following excerpt is from a decision by Secretary of the Interior Hoke Smith to the Commissioner of the General Land Office following a protest from a conflicting mining claimant Walter Castle. Castle prevailed in the earlier proceedings.] * * *

[On] April 15, 1892, Womble filed notice of intention to submit final proof June 13, 1892, and Walter Castle filed protest, alleging in substance that, March 15, 1890, he, with others, located the Empire Quartz mining claim, embracing a portion of lots 10 and 11, and the NW quarter of the SE quarter of said section thirty; that said mining claim contains a lode of quartz rock in place, carrying gold in paying quantities; that said land is more valuable for mineral, than for agricultural, grazing, or other purposes.

On this protest a hearing was had before the register and receiver, testimony taken, and a decision rendered by them, finding the land to contain gold sufficient to justify further development, and that Womble's declaratory statement having expired by limitation of law, and the Empire Quartz mining claim having attached to the land by location, Womble should be required to procure, at his own expense, a segregation of the Empire Quartz mining claim, before he be permitted to enter the remainder of the land embraced by his declaratory statement.

Womble appealed, and your office held that the part of the land embraced within the limits of the Empire Quartz mine contains sufficient mineral to justify the belief that it will develop into a paying mine, and affirmed the judgment of the local officers. Womble appealed to the Department.

The law is emphatic in declaring that "no location of a mining claim shall be made until the discovery of the vein or lode within the limits of the claim located." (Revised Statutes, 2320.) And this Department said in the *Cayuga Lode*, 5 L.D. 703—"This is a prerequisite to the location, and, of course, entry of any mining claim. Without compliance with this essential requirement of the law no location will be recognized, no entry allowed." Has such discovery been made in this case? * * *

In this case the presence of mineral is not based upon probabilities, belief and speculation alone, but upon facts, which, in the judgment of the register and receiver and your office, show that with further work, a paying and valuable mine, so far as human foresight can determine, will be developed.

After a careful consideration of the subject, it is my opinion that where minerals have been found and the evidence is of such a character that a person of ordinary prudence would be justified in the further expenditure of his labor and means, with a reasonable prospect of success, in developing a valuable mine, the requirements of the statute have been met. To hold otherwise would tend to make of little avail, if not entirely nugatory, that provision of the law whereby "all valuable mineral deposits in lands belonging to the United States.... are ... declared to be free and open to exploration and purchase." For, if as soon as minerals are shown to exist, and at any time during exploration, before the returns become remunerative, the lands are to be subject to other disposition, few would be found willing to risk time and capital in the attempt to bring to light and make available the mineral wealth, which lies concealed in the bowels of the earth, as Congress obviously must have intended the explorers should have proper opportunity to do.

Entertaining these views, your judgment is affirmed.

QUESTIONS AND DISCUSSION

1.   The "prudent person" test set forth in *Castle v. Womble* retains as much vigor today as it did when it was announced in 1894. Though it has been explained and refined in numerous decisions over the years, it remains the basic test against which a discovery of valuable minerals is measured.

2.   The prudent person test is an objective test. It does not matter that a reasonable locator may be *willing* to expend further resources to develop a mine. He must be *justified* in doing so. *Book v. Justice Mining Co.*, 58 F. 106 (C.C. D. Nev. 1893).

3.   A discovery of valuable minerals must be made on the claim itself. Geological inferences, made from data gathered outside the claim, however compelling, will not sustain a discovery on the claim. *Henault Mining v. Tysk*, 419 F.2d 766 (9th Cir. 1969), *cert. denied*, 398 U.S. 950 (1970); *Rummell v. Bailey*, 7 Utah 2d 137, 320 P.2d 653 (1958).

4.   What kinds of factors must be considered in determining whether a prudent person would be justified in the expenditure of his labor and means with a reasonable prospect for developing a valuable mine? While the quality and quantity of the ore are important factors, they are by no means the only factors. The following case offers a glimpse at the ever-evolving standards facing the miner seeking to prove a discovery.

————

UNITED STATES V. COLEMAN,
390 U.S. 599 (1968)

Mr. Justice Black delivered the opinion of the Court.

In 1956 respondent Coleman applied to the Department of the Interior for a patent to certain public lands based on his entry onto and exploration of these lands and his discovery there of a variety of stone called quartzite, one of the most common of all solid materials. It was, and still is, respondent Coleman's contention that the quartzite deposits qualify as "valuable mineral deposits" under 30 U.S.C. § 22 and make the land "chiefly valuable for building stone" under 30 U.S.C. § 161.[1] The Secretary of the Interior held that to qualify as "valuable mineral deposits" under 30 U.S.C. § 22 it must be shown that the mineral can be "extracted, removed and marketed at a profit"—the so-called "marketability test." Based on the largely undisputed evidence in the record, the Secretary concluded that the deposits claimed by respondent Coleman did not meet that criterion. As to the alternative "chiefly valuable for building stone" claim, the Secretary held that respondent Coleman's quartzite deposits were a "common variet[y]" of stone within the meaning of 30 U.S.C. § 611[2] and thus they could not serve as the basis for a valid mining claim under the mining laws. The Secretary denied the patent application, but respondent Coleman remained on the land, forcing the Government to bring this present action in ejectment in the District Court against respondent Coleman and his lessee, respondent McClennan. The respondents filed a counterclaim seeking to have the District Court direct the Secretary to issue a patent to them. The District Court, agreeing with the Secretary, rendered summary judgment for the Government. On appeal the Court of Appeals for the Ninth Circuit reversed, holding specifically that the test of profitable marketability was not a proper standard for determining whether a discovery of "valuable mineral deposits" under 30 U.S.C. § 22 had been made and that building stone could not be deemed a "common variet[y]" of stone under 30 U.S.C. § 611. We granted the Government's petition for certiorari because of the importance of the decision to the utilization of the public lands. 389 U.S. 970.

We cannot agree with the Court of Appeals and believe that the rulings of the Secretary of the Interior were proper. The Secretary's determination that the quartzite deposits did not qualify as valuable mineral deposits because the stone could not be marketed at a profit does no violence to the statute. Indeed, the marketability test is an admirable effort to identify with greater precision and objectivity the factors relevant to a determination that a mineral deposit is "valuable." It is a logical complement to the "prudent-man test" which the Secretary has been using to interpret the mining laws since 1894.... Under the mining laws Congress has made public lands available to people for the purpose of mining valuable mineral deposits and not for other purposes. The obvious intent was to reward and encourage the discovery of minerals that are valuable in an economic sense. Minerals which no prudent man will extract because there is no demand for them at a price higher than the costs of

---

1. The 1872 Act, *supra*, was supplemented in 1892 by the passage of the Act of August 4, 1892 ... which provides in pertinent part: "That any person authorized to enter lands under the mining laws of the United States may enter lands that are chiefly valuable for building stone under the provisions of the law in relation to placer mineral claims." [30 U.S.C. § 161].

2. Section 3 of the Act of July 23, 1955, 69 Stat. 368, 30 U.S.C. § 611, provides in pertinent part as follows: "A deposit if common varieties of sand, gravel, pumice, pumicite, or cinders shall not be deemed a valuable mineral deposit within the meaning of the mining laws of the United States so as to give effective validity to any mining claim hereafter located under such mining laws ... 'Common varieties' as used in this Act does not include deposits of such materials which are valuable because the deposit has some property giving it distinct and special value...."

extraction and transportation are hardly economically valuable. Thus, profitability is an important consideration in applying the prudent-man test, and the marketability test which the Secretary has used here merely recognizes this fact.

The marketability test also has the advantage of throwing light on a claimant's intention, a matter which is inextricably bound together with valuableness. For evidence that a mineral deposit is not of economic value and cannot in all likelihood be operated at a profit may well suggest that a claimant seeks the land for other purposes. Indeed, as the Government points out, the facts of this case—the thousands of dollars and hours spent building a home on 720 acres in a highly scenic national forest located two hours from Los Angeles, the lack of an economically feasible market for the stone, and the immense quantities of identical stone found in the area outside the claims—might well be thought to raise a substantial question as to respondent Coleman's real intention.

Finally, we think that the Court of Appeals' objection to the marketability test on the ground that it involves the imposition of a different and more onerous standard on claims for minerals of widespread occurrence than for rarer minerals which have generally been dealt with under the prudent-man test is unwarranted. As we have pointed out above, the prudent-man test and the marketability test are not distinct standards, but are complementary in that the latter is a refinement of the former. While it is true that the marketability test is usually the critical factor in cases involving nonmetallic minerals of widespread occurrence, this is accounted for by the perfectly natural reason that precious metals which are in small supply and for which there is a great demand, sell at a price so high as to leave little room for doubt that they can be extracted and marketed at a profit.

We believe that the Secretary of the Interior was also correct in ruling that "[i]n view of the immense quantities of identical stone found in the area outside the claims, the stone must be considered a 'common variety' and thus must fall within the exclusionary language of § 3 of the 1955 Act, 69 Stat. 368, 30 U.S.C. § 611, which declares that '[a] deposit of common varieties of . . . stone . . . shall [not] be deemed a valuable mineral deposit within the meaning of the mining laws. . . .' " Respondents rely on the earlier 1892 Act, 30 U.S.C. § 161, which makes the mining laws applicable to "lands that are chiefly valuable for building stone" and contend that the 1955 Act has no application to building stone, since, according to respondents, "[s]tone which is chiefly valuable as building stone is, by that very fact, not a common variety of stone." This was also the reasoning of the Court of Appeals. But this argument completely fails to take into account the reason why Congress felt compelled to pass the 1955 Act with its modification of the mining laws. The legislative history makes clear that this Act (30 U.S.C. § 611) was intended to remove common types of sand, gravel, and stone from the coverage of the mining laws, under which they served as a basis for claims to land patents, and to place the disposition of such materials under the Materials Act of 1947, 61 Stat. 681, 30 U.S.C. § 601 *et seq.*, which provides for the sale of such materials without disposing of the land on which they are found. For example, the Chairman of the House Committee on Interior and Insular Affairs explained the 1955 Act as follows: "The reason we have done that is because sand, stone, gravel . . . are really *building materials*, and are not the type of material contemplated to be handled under the mining laws, and that is precisely where we have had so much abuse of the mining laws. . . ." 101 Cong. Rec. 8743. (Emphasis added.)
* * *

Thus we read 30 U.S.C. § 611, passed in 1955, as removing from the coverage of the mining laws "common varieties" of building stone, but leaving 30 U.S.C. § 161, the 1892 Act, entirely effective as to building stone that has "some property giving it distinct and special value" (expressly excluded under § 611).

For these reasons we hold that the United States is entitled to eject respondents from the land and that respondents' counterclaim for a patent must fail. The case is reversed and remanded to the Court of Appeals for the Ninth Circuit for further proceedings to carry out this decision.

QUESTIONS AND DISCUSSION

1. Is a mineral deposit "marketable" within the meaning of the *Coleman* test merely because a market exists for that particular mineral? Because a particular deposit is of sufficient quality to satisfy standards for sale of that mineral? *See United States v. Wurts*, 76 I.D. 6, 13 (1969); *United States v. Pierce*, 75 I.D. 270, 278 (1968). What more must be shown? Can one pass the marketability test without having actually sold any minerals? *See* 2 Am. L. of Mining, § 35.14[2][f] (2d. ed. 1984).

2. Does the term "marketability" accurately describe the test established by *Coleman*? What better term might be used?

3. The Common Varieties Act, which is described in the *Coleman* opinion, will be addressed in greater detail in the next section of the chapter. Is the Court's analysis of the Common Varieties Act consistent with the Building Stone Act of 1892?

4. In *Barton v. Morton*, 498 F.2d 288 (9th Cir. 1974), Barton's applications for patents on two lode mining claims were denied even though he had discovered veins of gold, silver, and base metals, and had shown that further tunneling along the veins could yield a profitable discovery. The court found that the initial discovery of mineralization was too spotty and uneven to meet the test of actual discovery of a valuable mineral deposit for purposes of granting patents. It was not sufficient that a prudent person would be justified in expending labor and means on further exploration; to meet the prudent person test a miner must show that he or she would be justified in spending labor and means in developing the minerals.

5. In *Roberts v. Morton*, 549 F.2d 158 (10th Cir. 1976), *cert. denied*, 434 U.S. 834 (1977), an application for a patent was denied even though a market existed for alumina, the mineral discovered by the claimants. A profitable means of extracting the mineral from the particular formation was unavailable at that time. Accordingly, the discovery did not meet the marketability test.

FOSTER V. SEATON,
271 F.2d 836 (D.C. Cir. 1959)

Per Curiam

This case relates to appellants' claims under provisions of the mining laws which authorize "occupation and purchase" of Government lands containing "valuable mineral deposits." Rev. Stat. 2319, 2325, 2329 (1875), 30 U.S.C.A. 22, 29, 35. The Department of the Interior instituted proceedings contesting the claims on the ground that the allegedly "valuable mineral deposits" of sand and gravel, located thirteen miles from the center of Las Vegas, Nevada, were insufficient, *inter alia*, in quantity, quality and accessibility to a market to constitute a valid discovery. The hearing officer rendered a decision favorable to appellants, but it was reversed by the Director of the Bureau of Land Management upon an appeal by rival claimants who had intervened to assert an interest in the land under the Small Tract Act, 68 Stat. 239 (1954), 43 U.S.C.A. 682a *et seq.* The Secretary of the Interior sustained the Director's ruling. Appellants then instituted this suit in the District Court under the Administrative Procedure Act to review the Secretary's decision. On cross motions, the District Court granted a summary judgment in favor of appellee and this appeal followed. * * *

Appellants' principal assignment of error is that the Secretary misinterpreted the statute by requiring a demonstration of present value. They earnestly contend that their claim can also be sustained on the basis of prospective market value.

The statute says simply that the mineral deposit must be "valuable." Rev. Stat. 2319, 30 U.S.C.A. 22. Where the mineral in question is of limited occurrence, the Department, with judicial approval, has long adhered to the definition of value laid down [under the prudent person test] in *Castle v. Womble*, 19 I.D. 455, 457 (1894) * * *.

With respect to widespread nonmetallic minerals such as sand and gravel, however, the Department has stressed the additional requirement of present marketability in order to prevent the misappropriation of lands containing these materials by persons seeking to acquire such lands for purposes other than mining. Thus, such a "mineral locator or applicant, to justify his possession, must show that by reason of accessibility, *bona fides* in development, proximity to market, *existence of present demand*, and other factors, the deposit is of such value that it can be mined, removed and disposed of at a profit." *Layman v. Ellis*, 54 I.D. 294, 296 (1933), *emphasis supplied. See also Estate of Victor E. Hanny*, 63 I.D. 369, 370–72 (1956). Particularly in view of the circumstances of this case, we find no basis for disturbing the Secretary's ruling. The Government's expert witness testified that Las Vegas valley is almost entirely composed of sand and gravel of similar grade and quality. To allow such land to be removed from the public domain because unforeseeable developments might some day make the deposit commercially feasible can hardly implement the congressional purpose in encouraging mineral development.

Thus the case really comes down to a question whether the Secretary's finding was supported by substantial evidence on the record as a whole. We think it was. * * *

QUESTIONS AND DISCUSSION

1. *Foster* appears to represent the prevailing view, but statements to the contrary can be found in many cases and legal writings. One prominent example is found in the *American Law of Mining* treatise published by the Rocky Mountain Mineral Law Foundation. In the chapter on discovery, the authors state as follows:

> Inherent in the concept of reasonable *prospect* of success is the concept of *prospective* value, and it has been recognized that either a present or a prospective value will satisfy the prudent man rule.

2 AM. L. OF MINING § 35.11[6][c] (2d ed. 1984) (emphasis in original). Several mostly older Interior Department decisions are cited to support this proposition. The only recent case, *United States v. Pressentin*, 71 I.D. 447 (1964), does suggest that present *or prospective* value will suffice to sustain a discovery but in that case the Department found that no discovery had been made. Five pages after the above statement appears in the mining law treatise, the authors continue with the following:

> One of the distinguishing elements of the marketability rule is the requirement of a present market or demand for the minerals in question. . . .

> Speculation that there might be a market at some future date is not sufficient, nor is a "prospective market" or even a "likely future market" sufficient.

2 AM. L. OF MINING, § 35.12[4] (2d ed. 1984). Numerous cases, many of them of recent vintage, are cited to support this proposition. Most prominent among these is the Ninth Circuit's decision in *Mulkern v. Hammitt*, 326 F.2d 896, 898 (9th Cir. 1964). Can these two statements be reconciled by noting that the first addresses the prudent man test and the second the marketability test? That the first deals with "value" and the second with "marketability"? How do the two tests interrelate? Is it the value or market for the mineral, or is it the value of the claim that determines its validity?

2. The court states that "[w]ith respect to widespread, nonmetallic minerals . . . the Department has stressed the additional requirement of present marketability. . . ." Is *Foster* limited to nonmetallic minerals of widespread occurrence? Is there any rational basis for so limiting the decision? *See United States v. Estate of Denison*, 76 I.D. 233, 238–39 (1969).

3. On March 22, 1996, Interior Solicitor John Leshy issued Opinion M–36984, entitled "Excess Reserves Under the Mining Law." The Opinion concluded that the BLM may contest the validity of a discovery on a mining claim if the mineral deposits within the mining claim exceed the "reasonably foreseeable market demand" for the mineral, taking into account other resources in the mining area held by the claimant. This follows from the fact that the Mining Law requires mineral deposits to be "presently marketable." The Opinion generally applies to common variety minerals such as limestone, pumice, gypsum, perlite, cinders, sand, and gravel. To implement this policy, the BLM issued Instruction Memorandum 98–167 (September 28, 1998), which provides that minerals that cannot be marketed in the "reasonably foreseeable future" are "excess reserves" and not subject to location. The BLM defines "reasonably foreseeable future" as 40 years. This policy was reaffirmed by the Bush administration in Instruction Memorandum 2003–130 (April 2, 2003). Are materials that will not be sold for 40 years "presently marketable"? Should persons claiming "common variety" minerals be limited to that amount necessary to allow a reasonable return on investment? Since common variety minerals were removed from the operation of the Mining Law in 1955, why are any of these claims still valid under the current excess reserves policy?

4. Compare the result in *Foster* with the decision of the Supreme Court in *Andrus v. Shell Oil Co.*, 446 U.S. 657 (1980). *Shell Oil* involved oil shale claims. The Mineral Leasing Act of 1920 removed oil shale from minerals that could be located under the General Mining Law but many oil shale claims were located before the Mineral Leasing Act was passed. Oil shale development has never proved profitable, but oil shale claims are arguably valuable because a substantial increase in the price of oil could make oil shale development economically viable. During the energy crisis of the early 1970s, speculation over oil shale led to a resurgence of interest in old oil shale claims. While the Supreme Court's decision in *Hickel v. The Oil Shale Corp.*, 400 U.S. 48 (1970), *supra* at 1104, had required oil shale claimants to show substantial compliance with assessment work requirements, the district court's decision on remand, and the federal government's generous settlement of an appeal from that decision, revived many long dormant claims. Compliance with assessment work requirements, however, did not resolve the larger question of whether oil shale claimants could demonstrate a discovery given their inability to demonstrate that oil shale could be developed and marketed at a profit. In *Shell Oil*, the Court held that oil shale claims could be patented on the basis of their future marketability. In reaching this conclusion, the Court relied on the legislative history of the Mineral Leasing Act, as it related to oil shale, and on a "savings" clause in the Mineral Leasing Act that preserved "claims existent on February 25, 1920, and thereafter maintained in compliance with the laws under which initiated...." The Court also relied upon a long-standing but controversial policy of the Department of the Interior to sustain oil shale claims based upon their future value. The policy had been expressly disavowed by the Department in the *Shell Oil* case.

The *Shell Oil* decision seems to be limited to oil shale claims and perhaps to other pre–1920 claims for Mineral Leasing Act minerals. Nonetheless, if future marketability is good enough to show a discovery for some mining claims, it is hard to see why it is not good enough for all of them. In this sense, the *Shell Oil* decision casts some doubt over the present marketability test that seems to apply to all other minerals.

5. Is *Shell Oil* consistent with *Castle v. Womble*? With *Coleman*? As you consider these questions, note that the decision in *Shell Oil* purports to construe a "savings clause" in the Mineral Leasing Act. By definition, a savings clause does not create new rights; it merely preserves rights that existed before the new law was passed—in this case, the right to keep mining claims for Mineral Leasing Act minerals.

6. Does the Mining Law require a showing that the land on which claims are located is more valuable for mineral production than other purposes? The argument that it does arose in *United States v. United Mining Corp.*, 142 IBLA 339; GFS (MIN) 38 (1998), reversed following review by Secretary of the Interior Bruce Babbitt, (May 15, 2000). *See Mineral Law Newsletter*, Vol. XVII, No. 3 (2000). The case involved 14 placer claims in Idaho for large, water-sculpted basalt boulders, which were prized for landscaping and similar decorative uses. These boulders also had a high value—arguably a higher value—for scenic and recreational purposes if left in place. Because the boulders were a common variety mineral they were subject to location only if they were not "common variety" boulders. (The Common Varieties Act is discussed in greater detail in the next section of the chapter.) For purposes of this case, the government conceded that these boulders were uncommon. Nonetheless, the government argued that these claims were not valid because they were found on lands that were "chiefly valuable" for purposes other than mineral development. While the government argued that a comparative value test should be employed for all mining claims, this particular case arguably raised the question only in the narrower context of the Building Stone Act of 1892, which authorizes any person "to enter lands . . . that are *chiefly valuable* for building stone." 30 U.S.C. § 161 (emphasis added).

A majority of judges on the Board of Land Appeals, sitting *en banc*, held that the comparative value test was not applicable to claims located under either the General Mining Law or the Building Stone Act. 142 IBLA 339; GFS (MIN) 38 (1998). But in an unusual move, the Secretary assumed jurisdiction over the case and found that the "chiefly valuable" test of the Building Stone Act did in fact require a comparison of values between mining and other uses, and that the BLM had properly declared the claims invalid on that basis. Decision Upon Review of *United States v. United Mining Corp.* (May 15, 2000).

7.   The idea that the General Mining Law requires a "comparative value test" received support from Professor John Leshy in a book that he wrote well before he became the Interior Solicitor. JOHN LESHY, THE MINING LAW: A STUDY IN PERPETUAL MOTION 132, 140–48 (1987). In support of this claim, Professor Leshy cites *Chrisman v. Miller* 197 U.S. 313 (1905), which involved pre–1920 oil and gas claims. The statute under which those claims had been located, however, authorized their location only on lands "chiefly valuable therefore." Thus, the *Chrisman* decision does not seem to apply generally to all mining claims. Moreover, as Professor Leshy acknowledges, in *Cataract Mining Co.*, 43 L.D. 248 (1948), the First Assistant Secretary expressly rejected the comparative value test, and while it has occasionally been used by both the Department and the courts since that time, it was again specifically rejected by the IBLA in 1973. *U.S. v. Kosanke Sand Corp.*, 80 I.D. 538, 547, 553–54 (1973); *see also, Pacific Coast Molydenum Co.*, 90 I.D. 352, 361–63 (1983).

———

UNITED STATES V. PITTSBURGH PACIFIC CO., 84 I.D. 282 (1977)

Opinion by Administrative JUDGE GOSS

The United States appeals from so much of a decision of Administrative Law Judge John R. Rampton, Jr., as dismissed a contest proceeding against a mineral patent application filed by appellee Pittsburgh Pacific Company for twelve 20–acre lode mining claims located within the Black Hills National Forest, Lawrence County, South Dakota. The claims are contiguous and stretch in a north/south direction for somewhat over a mile. Upon request of the Forest Service, U.S. Department of Agriculture, the Bureau of Land Management filed a contest complaint against appellee's patent application contending there had been no discovery of valuable mineral deposits and asking that the claims be held invalid. By order, the Board granted petitions of State of South Dakota and American Mining Congress to file briefs as amici curiae.

The United States contends generally that Pittsburgh has not proved the discovery of valuable deposits, and supports its argument with allegations of error in the geological and economic analysis performed. Additionally, the State of South Dakota argues, *inter alia*, that adequate consideration has not been given to cost of compliance with environmental quality statutes and regulations.

Pittsburgh claims discovery of some 160 million tons of relatively low grade iron ore, including specular hematite and martite. Pittsburgh intends to mine 96 million tons under a plan of operation which includes the annual removal of 7,200,000 long tons of ore; the crushing of the best 4,900,000 long tons; the cobbing (preliminary separation) of that ore; the reduction roasting of the best 2,300,000 long tons until all of the iron is magnetized and more readily ground and separated; grinding and magnetic separation, with gangue rock washed away; and the compression, into hard pellets, of 1,000,000 long tons of ore. The process of reduction roasting followed by fine grinding and magnetic separation of iron has not been used except on an experimental basis in a laboratory or pilot project. Each year 10,000 rail cars of such pellets, containing 62.68 percent natural iron, would be loaded and shipped. Pittsburgh states that unless patents are issued, the necessary financing cannot be obtained. Assuming a 20–year payout on investment, and pellet prices as of Feb. 1975, the proposed operation would involve well over one-half billion dollars in gross revenue.

For reasons set forth hereafter, the decision of the Administrative Law Judge must be set aside and the case remanded. The decision, however, is well reasoned, and except as modified herein, the findings and conclusions are accepted.

Pittsburgh is entitled to a patent for a particular claim if a "valuable mineral deposit" has been discovered on that claim. 30 U.S.C. §§ 22, 29 (1970). The prudent person test for determining whether or not deposits are "valuable" was set forth in *Castle v. Womble*, 19 L.D. 455, 457 (1894) * * *.

While Pittsburgh has submitted considerable evidence which indicates that a discovery has been obtained, there remain factors—some of which may be beyond the control of Pittsburgh—which could stand in the way of a profitable mining operation. After evaluating the evidence, we conclude that substantial questions exist with respect to adequacy and cost of water supply, additional land, financing, labor costs, and expense of compliance with environmental protection laws.

Water Supply

No significant dispute exists over the amount of water needed for the mining and beneficiating process. It is agreed some 20,000 to 25,000 gallons per minute (gpm) of water will be used, with a recycle rate of approximately 95 percent, thus requiring 1,000 to 1,250 gpm of new water during operation. As possible sources, Pittsburgh has cited Box Elder Creek and nearby flooded abandoned mines, natural springs, and wells. It will be necessary for Pittsburgh to construct ponds of substantial acreage and depth for water storage, to supply water during relatively dry spells.

The United States argues that Pittsburgh has failed to prove that sufficient water would be available at the claims in South Dakota. Noting problems of obtaining ownership of water from private sources and permits for water from public sources, the Government characterizes Pittsburgh as "seem[ing] to have assumed that", with so much water around, additional land for storage and tailings reservoirs, possible pipeline easements, and pumping costs. *See United States v. Osborne* (Supp. on Judicial Remand), 28 I.B.L.A. 13 (1976) * * *. In *Osborne* at 35, the Board indicated that a prudent man would be assured that an element essential to his mining operation was available, before he would make further expenditures:

> Since water is essential, and its lack makes aggregate production "very costly," it would seem that prudence would demand that the claimants satisfy themselves as to its availability in sufficient quantity before they "[w]ould be justified in the further expenditure of their labor and means, with a reasonable prospect of developing a paying mine." * * *

The evidence adduced at the hearing does not fully establish that sufficient water is reasonably available. Pittsburgh stated its volume of water requirement, noted several possible sources for that much water, and argued that there would thus be sufficient water. There was, however, no detailed showing that the rights could be acquired, nor was there any specification of cost of such supply, beyond the general statement of construction costs. On remand, the parties will have the opportunity to show more clearly whether the requisite water supply can be obtained and delivered at a feasible cost.

Additional Land

Pittsburgh will require approximately 600 to 900 acres of land outside the mining claims upon which to construct its plants, tailings pond, and water storage reservoir. A small portion of this land may be available to appellants as millsites. 43 C.F.R. Subpart 3864. The Government alleges that Pittsburgh contends that there "is substantial land in private ownership adjacent to and in the near vicinity of the involved claims, ... [which] can be acquired in the normal course of business when the time comes." Additionally, Pittsburgh notes that it is possible to purchase lands in other areas and exchange them with the Forest Service for adjacent land within Black Hills National Forest.

* * * While there may be private tracts which are geographically and economically feasible, this is not clear from the record.

Apparently, the only other feasible land is in the National Forest, managed by the Forest Service. Since this contest was initiated at the request of the Forest Service, it is not clear whether the Service would be amenable to the necessary exchange.

A reasonably prudent man would take steps to assure that essential land is available to the project. *See Osborne, supra.* On remand, Pittsburgh will have an opportunity to show that it can acquire the requisite suitable acreage for the anticipated construction, in a feasible configuration and at a price harmonious with a profitable mining operation.

Financing

Pittsburgh estimated that as of October 1969, some $28,000,000 would be required to finance the project. The Government argues that Pittsburgh had shown no source of financing. Pittsburgh states that "normally financing is done or at least underwritten by the users of the product, the steel mills and companies desiring to insure a source of supply." * * *

The Department, of course, is most anxious that it not patent the land only to have the project fail for lack of financing. The upwards of $28,000,000 in financing is as essential to appellant's project as is the required water and land. If it could be shown by further evidence that a responsible financial source would probably furnish the funds needed, conditioned upon patents being issued by the United States, this would help to assuage Departmental questions as to the likelihood of full development of the deposit. The Board does not believe a prudent miner would continue making his own substantial investments until he has a reasonable expectation of success in developing a valuable mine and of the availability of additional funds, if necessary, at feasible interest cost. *See Osborne, supra.* On remand, the parties will have the opportunity to present evidence as to potential availability of financing and other matters as discussed herein.

Labor Costs

To determine the estimated cost of labor, the parties have introduced the cost experience of Pittsburgh and comparable companies. Pittsburgh's case re labor costs was made out by Pavel Zima, an engineer with the company, primarily by means of the economics section of the Mineral Evaluation Report, Exhibit M–4. This report shows operation-by-operation estimates of labor needs and costs, and labor expense is allocated to each processing step. Zima's labor estimates at each step are merely stated, however, and are not explained, describing the operation involved and detailing why the given number of men at a given wage cost is needed.

Government witness Dr. Alfred Petrick stated as his opinion that 252 persons, rather than 177, as estimated by Zima, would be necessary for the total operation, and that the increase in costs occasioned by the 75 extra persons would then be approximately $948,000 annually. A major factor in Petrick's analysis of Pittsburgh's total labor needs was a comparison of labor use experience in several other plants. * * *

We recognize that there can be differences in mining and engineering factors between various mines and plants producing the same iron pellets, and that these differences can have a substantial influence on labor costs, *e.g.*, the relative softness of the South Dakota ore compared with the ore of the Mesabi Range mines, or the possibility of higher percentage recovery of iron because of reduction roasting. Additional evidence is necessary to assess the accuracy of Pittsburgh's labor expense projections.

Cost of Compliance with Environmental Quality Statutes and Regulations

At the hearing, environmental costs were considered only to a limited degree. In Pittsburgh's testimony and in the economics section of Pittsburgh's Exhibit M–4, it was succinctly given that environmental protection costs were comprehended by the anticipated general construction costs listed in the report, plus 1 cent for miscellaneous environmental control for each ton shipped. Construction was to be undertaken as a matter of course in a manner which would assure environmental quality maintenance.

Neither did the government establish the environmental protection measures which would be required and the cost thereof. However, it is noted that considerable environmental legislation and regulations have been promulgated since the evidence herein was first formulated.

As amicus curiae, South Dakota has posed questions concerning water quality, air pollution, reclamation and other problems. The cost of compliance with governmental and other environmental requirements are of course significant in determining whether there has been a discovery. [*United States v. Kosanke Sand Corp.*, 12 I.B.L.A. 282, 298–99, 80 I.D. 538, 546–47.]

As stated, there would be a removal of some 7.2 million tons of material per year, ultimately affecting an area of about 240 acres now within a national forest. In addition, Pittsburgh would need to construct ponds and buildings over some 600 to 900 acres on other lands in the area. Some 4.9 million tons will annually move into the beneficiation process, and this may create the need for environmental controls as to dust and disposal of waste water and soil. All told, some 6.2 million tons of waste earth will have to be disposed of. Though Pittsburgh had proposed to use natural gas, the roasting of 2.3 million tons per year could create air pollution problems. A railroad spur will have to be constructed, presumably through the National Forest. Adjacent to the claims are two creeks which South Dakota states it has classified as cold water fisheries.

The State is therefore admitted as a party to the contest, in order that the State, together with the other parties, may offer new evidence as to environmental requirements, the cost of compliance, and other pertinent factors.

New Evidence

On remand, the Administrative Law Judge will have discretion to entertain any other issues which he deems proper, in order to formulate the required findings and conclusions.

Therefore, pursuant to the authority delegated to the Board of Land Appeals by the Secretary of the Interior, 43 C.F.R. § 4.1, the decision appealed from is set aside and the matter is remanded.

QUESTIONS AND DISCUSSION

1. As the *Pittsburgh Pacific* case suggests, proving discovery under the prudent person test may require an extended evidentiary hearing.

2. Can the BLM or the Forest Service lawfully stop a mining operation by refusing to give the mining company access to the land it needs? Would the government be liable for "taking" the claimant's property if the sole reason the mine cannot be developed is the lack of available land for mining purposes?

3. A mining claim contest is sometimes described as an action *in rem*, rather than *in personam*. Robert W. Mullen, *The Prudent Man Ain't What She Used to Be Many Long Years Ago,* 49 ROCKY MTN. MIN. L. INST. 10–1 (2003). This means that the focus of the proceedings is on the property and not the individual making the claim. Why then does the Board hold that Pittsburgh Pacific's ability to obtain financing for the project is a relevant consideration? Won't financing depend, to some extent at least, on the overall economic position of the particular company? If a company's ability to obtain financing must be considered, is it possible that a small company with limited assets might have a claim declared invalid, whereas a larger company, such as Exxon–Mobil, which might even be in a position to finance its own venture, could be awarded a patent to the very same claim?

4. The *Kosanke* case, cited by the Board in *Pittsburgh Pacific*, established the rule that the cost of compliance with environmental standards must be taken into account in determining whether the prudent person test has been satisfied. As stated by the Board:

To the extent federal, state, or local law requires that anti-pollution devices or other environmental safeguards be installed and maintained as part of the process of extraction and beneficiation of the minerals contained in the claims, the expenditures made necessary by such protective measures may properly be considered in connection with the issue of marketability, as part of the costs in determining whether appellant has a reasonable prospect of success in developing a valuable mind within the claims.

United States v. Kosanke Sand Corp., 80 I.D. 538, 546–47 (1971).

5. Suppose a state or local community wanted to limit the development of mining claims. Could it impose environmental standards that were so onerous that a claimant could never satisfy the prudent person test? *See California Coastal Comm'n v. Granite Rock Co.*, 480 U.S. 572 (1987), *infra* at 1175.

——

G. CHALLENGES TO THE VALIDITY OF MINING CLAIMS

An unpatented mining claim may be challenged at the agency level in either a *contest* or *protest* proceeding. Adverse proceedings following a patent application under 30 U.S.C. § 29 are addressed separately in the section on patents. The most common challenge is a *contest*, which may be filed either by a private individual or by a governmental agency. A private individual may initiate a contest if the challenging party claims an interest in public land that is adverse to another's interest in that land. 43 C.F.R. § 4.450–1 (2008); *see also United States v. U.S. Pumice Corp.*, 37 I.B.L.A. 153, 159, n.4; GFS (MIN) 106 (1978). Government contests may be initiated by the appropriate federal agency for any reason affecting the validity of a claim. 43 C.F.R. § 4.451–1 (2008). Contest proceedings are not limited to mining claims but they frequently involve such claims.

A contest is initiated by filing a complaint in the appropriate BLM state office. *Id.* § 4.450–3. The person against whom the complaint is filed (the contestee) has thirty days in which to file an answer to the complaint. An administrative law judge is appointed to hear the case and may hold a prehearing conference. *Id.* § 4.452–1. The regulations do not provide for discovery and in fact appear to discourage some aspects of it. *See id.* § 4.452–4 (empowering the administrative law judge to authorize depositions to be taken "but not for discovery"). Nonetheless, discovery may be an appropriate and useful tool in defining and narrowing the issues for the hearing. Thus, if the rules are not changed then at least they should be liberally construed to allow forms of discovery other than depositions. A formal adjudicatory hearing is then held before the administrative law judge in accordance with the Administrative Procedure Act. 5 U.S.C. § 554. *See United States v. Leary*, 63 I.D. 341 (1956) (holding that the APA applies to contest proceedings).

A decision by an administrative law judge is, of course, binding on the parties unless overturned on appeal. The administrative law judge, however, does not speak for the Secretary and thus such decisions have no precedential value. Either party may file an appeal from an ALJ decision with the Interior Board of Land Appeals. The Board serves an appellate review function for the Secretary. Its decisions are published and serve as precedent for later cases. The Secretary, however, as the Department head, may assume jurisdiction over a case either before or after it is decided by the Board. 43 C.F.R. § 4.5 (2008). The Secretary rarely asserts such authority.

Because the Board speaks for the Secretary (and because the Secretary ultimately can reverse any decision with which he disagrees), the Department of the Interior may not seek judicial review of a decision by the Board. Other federal agencies (such as the U.S. Forest Service) and other parties adversely affected by a Board decision in contest proceedings may file an appeal with the appropriate federal district court in accordance with the appropriate jurisdictional and venue provisions of the U.S. Code.

Protests are allowed for any objections "to any action proposed to be taken in any proceeding before the Bureau [of Land Management]" "where the elements of a contest are not present." 43 C.F.R. § 4.450–2. Thus, where a person objects to a proposed action by the Bureau, but has no claim or interest in the public lands that is adverse to the interests of another, his administrative remedy is to file a protest. *In re Pacific Coast Molybdenum Co.*, 68 I.B.L.A. 325, GFS (MIN) 329 (1982). The protest is much less attractive than a contest to a party challenging another's mining claim. First, protests are limited to objections to proposed actions "in any proceeding" before the Bureau. In the mining claim context the only proceedings likely to be of interest to a protestant are patent application proceedings and applications for approval of a plan of operations. *See* 43 C.F.R. § 3872.1(a) (2007) (describing the right to protest patent applications "upon any ground tending to show that the applicant has failed to comply with the law in any matter essential to a valid entry. . . ."), and 43 C.F.R. § 3809.411(d) (2007) (describing the approval of a plan of operations). Arguably then, so long as a claimant refuses to file a patent application or fails to develop his mining operation so as to require a plan of operations, a protest may not be filed. Furthermore, the Department has broad discretion as to how it handles a protest. It may, of course, hold a hearing on a protest. *Devereux v. Hunter*, 11 L.D. 214 (1890); *Alice Placer Mine*, 4 L.D. 314, 317 (1886). But the rules allow whatever action "is deemed appropriate under the circumstances." 43 C.F.R. § 4.450–2 (2007). This may be nothing more than a letter responding to the protest. An adverse decision from a protest may be appealed to the Board of Land Appeals. 43 C.F.R. § 4.410 (2007). But the protestant will have to demonstrate some personal interest that is or may be adversely affected by the government's action on the protest, in order to establish standing to seek administrative or judicial review. *See, e.g., Wight v. Dubois*, 21 F. 693 (C.C.D. Colo. 1884); *In re Pacific Coast Molybdenum Co., supra*, at 331–32.

QUESTIONS AND DISCUSSION

1. Contest proceedings are often commenced by federal agencies that want to free a certain tract of land for other, potentially incompatible uses. Sometimes the government cannot wait for the administrative process to run its course before it takes possession of the land. When this happens, the federal government might simply bring a quiet title action in federal court. But suppose that it initiates a court action to obtain possession and then seeks a stay of that action pending completion of contest proceedings.

Can the government have its cake and eat it too? In *Best v. Humboldt Placer Mining Co.,* 371 U.S. 334 (1963), the United States sued to obtain possession of lands that were set to be inundated as a result of construction of Trinity Dam in California. In its complaint, the government asked the court to confirm its right to occupy the land notwithstanding the existence of potentially valid mining claims, even while it sought to preserve its right to challenge the validity of those claims in administrative contest proceedings. By taking possession of the land, the government was effectively announcing its intention to condemn any claims that proved to be valid through eminent domain proceedings. After filing its lawsuit, the government did in fact initiate contest proceedings against Humbolt Placer Mining. Humbolt argued that once the government invoked the jurisdiction of the federal courts, all relevant issues, including the validity of Humbolt's mining claims, would have to be resolved in those judicial proceedings. The Supreme Court disagreed and upheld the government's strategy. The Court noted that while appropriate, it was not necessary for the government to file an action in court. It could simply have taken physical possession of the land and relied on private parties with property claims to bring inverse condemnation actions. Thus, the decision to file suit was not inconsistent with the administrative remedy for determining the validity of Humbolt's claims. Notwithstanding its right to proceed in this fashion, do you see any reason why this might be a risky strategy for the government to pursue?

2. In *Western Aggregates, LLC,* 169 IBLA 64, GFS(MIN) 18 (2006), the BLM did, in fact, take physical possession over lands, when it withdrew several lots near a river in 1899 and 1905. The claimant alleged that his modern claims were not invalid, despite the removal of these parcels from mineral exploration, because they were on land that had been newly formed by accretion of river sediment. The IBLA held that all federally owned riverbeds take on the same status as the neighboring lands, and that the claimant's claims were void regardless of how and when this new land was formed. Can you see any potential problems that this IBLA decision hopes to circumvent?

3. Compare *Best* with the subsequent Tenth Circuit decision in *United States v. Zweifel,* 508 F.2d 1150 (10th Cir. 1975), *cert. denied,* 423 U.S. 829 (1975). In that case, Merle I. Zweifel and his associates filed association placer mining claims over large tracts of public land in Wyoming. The claims covered lands known to be valuable for coal—a "leasable" mineral not subject to the General Mining Law. The claims were almost certainly designed to force a buy-out by coal interests rather than to promote development of any hard rock minerals. (As noted below, Zweifel was well known for such tactics.) The federal government sued Zweifel and others in federal court. The district court held that the claims were not located in good faith and that the defendants failed to demonstrate a discovery or compliance with the procedural requisites of federal and state law. On appeal, the defendants claimed that under the decision in *Best*, the federal government should have been required to bring administrative contest proceedings against the claims before resorting to the courts. The Tenth Circuit disagreed, holding that the federal government had the authority to clear title to federal lands under 28 U.S.C. § 1345, which authorizes actions by the federal government as a plaintiff. Is *Zweifel* consistent with *Best*? Is it fair that claimants must resort to administrative procedures, but that the federal government is exempt from that requirement?

4. Merle Zweifel was one of the more colorful and, some would say, unscrupulous characters to take advantage of the General Mining Law. In his wonderfully readable account of the abuses of the Mining Law, Professor and former Interior Solicitor, John Leshy, offers the following portrait of Zweifel:

> A seasoned observer of the uranium booms on the Colorado plateau has observed: "There are a lot of cases in which individuals have located claims over recently located claims of mining companies solely with the thought that the mining companies will buy them out rather than litigate the conflicts involved." The expectation of a buyout is often not unreasonable. A Forest Service publication has noted that "[s]ometimes the mining company's counsel mistakenly advise a payoff; each time this is done it only compounds future difficulties."

> The master of this gambit ... was Merle Zweifel. Until his flamboyance, greed, and disarming candor about the game he was playing attracted so much attention that he could no longer be tolerated, the "old prospector," as he styled himself, filed mining claims on millions of acres of federal land all over the West. (He himself put the figure at 30 million acres, which included an unspecified amount of land claimed on the outer continental shelf.) When Congress authorized the Central Arizona Project in 1968, part of which required construction of an aqueduct from the Colorado River to Phoenix and Tucson, the old prospector was there, filing claims on 600,000 acres along the aqueduct route. When interest in oil shale development began to revive on Colorado's west slope after 1960, Zweifel surfaced with 465,000 acres of mining claims in the Piceance Basin. Acknowledging that he would never actively explore the land (because that would damage the scenery, he said) he exploited the Law's offer of free access to the federal lands with a vengeance, though the character of his claims reflected the German meaning of his name—doubt. His "real goal in life," he was reported as saying, was to "discredit bureaucrats and their hypocritical ways," though he also admitted that fighting large companies "is an enjoyment I can't pass up," and that at last "I do have a lust for money."

> Zweifel is gone now, and most (if not all—it is difficult to tell) of his claims are gone too, as the state and federal bureaucracies eventually responded to the publicity generated by his shenanigans with unaccustomed vigor. Although in the long run authorities handed him a series of defeats, from all outward appearances Zweifel made a decent living by exploiting not minerals, but the Mining Law itself, dramatically demonstrating how the free-access policy could be converted into financial gain while at the same time mocking the policy's purpose—promotion of mineral development.

JOHN LESHY, THE MINING LAW: A STUDY IN PERPETUAL MOTION 79–80 (1987).

5. Merle Zweifel was certainly not the only person to take advantage of the generous invitation contained in the Mining Law. One of the earliest was Ralph Henry Cameron. Cameron, along with his brother Niles and a local prospector named Peter Berry, had located mining claims along the south rim of the Grand Canyon and had successfully developed a copper mine in the canyon below Grandview Point. But Cameron's real interests were along the Bright Angel Trail where he used the mining law to mine tourists rather than minerals. Initially, Cameron charged a toll for access along the trail as authorized under an Arizona territorial law. When his toll rights expired in 1906, Cameron used numerous, strategically located but probably invalid, mining claims along the trail, as a pretense for continuing to charge an access fee. Unfortunately for Cameron, his interests conflicted with those of the Santa Fe Railroad Company, and the railroad challenged Cameron's claims in the courts and before the Department of the Interior.

In 1909, Secretary of the Interior James Garfield, son of the former President James Garfield, declared that Cameron's claims lacked sufficient mineral values to justify issuing a patent. Still, Cameron persisted in charging fees for access to public land that he did not own, and for which he lacked any lawful claim, using his various political offices to keep the authorities at bay. Cameron was elected delegate from the Arizona Territory in 1908, a position he held until Arizona became a state in 1912. In 1914, he ran an unsuccessful campaign for governor, but in 1920 he became a U.S. Senator. Cameron was more than willing to exert his political influence to improve his personal position. Professor Sax has suggested that "[t]here has probably never been a more scandalous case of a member of Congress using his office to protect private interests." Joseph L. Sax, *Free Enterprise in the Woods,* 91 Nat. Hist., No. 6, at 14, 17 (June 1982). Eventually, Cameron's case wound up in the U.S. Supreme Court, which confirmed the government's authority to declare his claims invalid and oust him from the land. *Cameron v. United States,* 252 U.S. 450 (1920). When Cameron's antics finally came to the attention of the Attorney General, Harlan Stone, who later became chief justice of the Supreme Court, Stone appointed a special prosecutor who promptly ended Cameron's tenure on the Bright Angel Trail.

H. Mining Claim Patents

Any person who has made a valuable discovery of minerals on unappropriated public domain land, and has otherwise complied with the requirements of the state and federal mining laws, is entitled to purchase the land from the federal government for a nominal sum of money—five dollars per acre for a lode claim and two dollars and fifty cents per acre for a placer claim. 30 U.S.C. § 29. At these bargain prices, one might expect that the government would be flooded with patent applications. On the contrary, of nearly 1.5 million mining claims held by private parties in 1981, only 51 applications for patent were filed. *See* Terry Maley, The Handbook of Mineral Law 462–63 (5th ed. 1993). Growing talk of mining law reform increased the number of patent applications in the late 1980s and early 1990s but, as described below, Congress, by way of legislative moratoria, has effectively shut down new patent applications for now.

It is difficult to understand why patent applications were not more common. In many cases, claimants probably feared that trying to patent a claim would invite unwanted scrutiny as to the validity of the claim. To be sure, patent applicants face a stiff inquiry into the validity of their claims, whereas the government otherwise rarely investigates unpatented mining claims unless a conflict with land use arises. Moreover, unpatented mining claims are themselves property rights protected by the Fifth Amendment. Nonetheless, the advantages and certainties of ownership would seem to afford sufficient incentive for many claimants to seek a patent.

The first step in patenting a mining claim is to obtain a *mineral survey*. A survey is not required for placer claims that conform to the boundaries of a legal subdivision but must be obtained *prior to filing a patent application* on all other claims. 43 C.F.R. § 3861.1–1 (2007). The mineral survey is used to delineate the boundaries and set permanent monuments for the claim, to describe improvements made on the claim, and to resolve any conflicts with other claims to those lands.

A surveyor approved by the BLM must perform the mineral survey. A claimant can obtain a list of approved surveyors from the local BLM state office. The claimant may contact these surveyors directly and negotiate on the cost for the survey. However, when a mineral surveyor is performing a survey of a mining claim, he is acting as a federal government employee and not as an employee of the claimant. *Waskey v. Hammer*, 223 U.S. 85 (1912). Other than conducting the survey, he may not become involved in any way in the patent application process. 43 C.F.R. § 3861.3–1 (2006). The surveyor and any assistants he may hire must be disinterested parties without ties to the claim or the claimant. *Id.*

After a survey is completed, the surveyor must submit a copy of the plat or map, field notes, and a report on improvements to the Chief of Cadastral Surveys at the BLM state office. The claimant then receives a copy of those documents, which must be filed with his patent application. A copy of the plat must also be posted on the claim together with a notice indicating the claimant's intent to seek a patent. 43 C.F.R. § 3861.7–1 (2007). Notice must also be posted in the appropriate state BLM office and published in a local newspaper for at least 60 days.

In addition to the survey information, the patent applicant must submit an abstract or other evidence of title, proof of citizenship, payment of the purchase price, proof of the expenditure of $500 worth of labor, and a filing fee (currently $2520 for over 10 claims and $1260 for 10 or fewer claims included in a single application). *See* 43 C.F.R. §§ 3000.12 (2007); 2 AM. L. OF MINING § 51.01[2]. The requirement for an expenditure of at least $500 worth of labor on each claim is analogous to the assessment work requirement and the same rules generally apply. *Copper Glance Lode*, 29 L.D. 542 (1900). Patent applications may include multiple claims if those claims are contiguous. *Tucker v. Masser*, 113 U.S. 203 (1885). When a patent application is complete and no adverse claims have been filed, a BLM mineral examiner must review the claim to determine whether a valuable discovery of minerals has been made. The mineral report is then reviewed by a BLM minerals specialist and BLM managers who may ask for reconsideration of the recommendations or require that additional work be performed. If the final report supports the discovery and the applicant has paid all fees, including the purchase price, the BLM issues a "Mineral Entry Final Certificate." A patent is then signed by the Secretary or his designee. An unfavorable mineral report results in a government contest against the claim. Other details of the patent application process may be found in TERRY MALEY, THE HANDBOOK OF MINERAL LAW, *supra*, at 462–511.

Any person claiming an interest in a mining claim adverse to the patent applicant's interest must file an *adverse* claim with the appropriate BLM office before the end of the 60–day publication period. Failure to file within that period of time precludes any further challenge to the claim by a private party unless the notice was defective. 2 Am. L. of Mining, § 52.01. Once an adverse claim is filed, the adverse claimant has 30 days within which to commence an action in the appropriate state court to determine who has the right of possession. The adverse claimant has the burden of proving a superior right in a conflicting claim, *Gwillim v. Donnellan*, 115 U.S. 45 (1885), and he may not rely on the weakness of the title of the patent applicant. *Murray Hill Mining & Milling Co. v. Havenor*, 24 Utah 73, 66 P. 762 (1901). Once an adverse claim is filed, the patent application proceedings are stayed pending resolution of the court proceedings, including appeals. 43 C.F.R. § 3871.4 (2007).

Adverse claims may be filed only by competing mining claimants. *Union Oil Co.*, 65 I.D. 245, 248–49 (1958). Other persons with a conflicting interest may file an administrative contest or protest, or seek judicial relief. *See* 43 C.F.R. part 3870 (2006). Any person may file a protest under 43 C.F.R. § 4.450–2 (2007), but only those with an interest that may be adversely affected by the government's decision may appeal to the Board of Land Appeals. 43 C.F.R. § 4.410 (2007); *In re Pacific Coast Molybdenum Co.*, 68 I.B.L.A. 325 (1982).

In 1994, the Congress imposed a moratorium on processing new patent applications. Pub. L. No. 103–332, § 112, 108 Stat. 2519 (Sept. 30, 1994). Since 1994, Congress has extended the moratorium annually, and this policy seems likely to continue until mining law reform legislation is passed.

QUESTIONS AND DISCUSSION

1. The recent efforts to foreclose future patent applications raise questions about the nature of the right to patent. The issue arose well before the various moratoria on new applications as a result of the Sawtooth National Recreation Area Act (SNRA). 16 U.S.C. §§ 460aa *et seq.* The SNRA prohibited the issuance of patents on SNRA lands after that law was enacted. Rights of possession and enjoyment attached to valid claims under the SNRA, but the Act expressly denied the ability to obtain patents. In *Freese v. United States*, 639 F.2d 754, 226 Ct.Cl. 252, *cert. denied,* 454 U.S. 827 (1981), the court found that passage of the Act did not amount to a taking of a future option to patent because the claimant, Freese, had not filed a patent application before passage of the SNRA.

2. The issue that was not answered in *Freese* arose in *Swanson v. Babbitt,* 3 F.3d 1348 (9th Cir. 1993). Swanson claimed a right to patent claims in the Sawtooth National Recreation Area because he had filed a patent application for certain mill site claims in 1967, well before the SNRA was passed in 1972. The court rejected Swanson's claims because the government had filed contest proceedings challenging the validity of the claims. The court made clear, however, that the right to patent would have vested if all that remained to be done before granting patents were ministerial duties of the government.

The *Swanson* case arose because the government had found that Swanson's mill site claims occupied more land than was necessary for mining and milling purposes. Swanson had been offered the opportunity to amend the mill sites to conform to the government's requirements before the SNRA was enacted, but he had refused. By the time the government ordered their reduction, it was 1974. Suppose that Swanson had amended his application in accord with the government's recommendations before passage of the SNRA? How would the case have been decided?

3. Suppose you purchased an option to buy a piece of property at a specified price for one year. Shortly thereafter the state exercised its eminent domain authority to condemn the land for a public highway. Has the state deprived you of the option of a valuable property right for which compensation must be paid? Can this case be distinguished from *Swanson* and *Freese*?

4. When a patent application is rejected for lack of discovery, the claim itself is void and the Department will generally commence contest proceedings for a legal declaration to that effect. Rejection of the patent application, however, does not by itself invalidate the claim. *United States v. Carlisle*, 67 I.D. 417 (1960); *see also* 2 AM. L. OF MINING, § 51.02.

5. The Wilderness Act allows the issuance of mineral patents for mining claims located before the relevant wilderness area was withdrawn from location under the mining laws. Such patents convey title only to the mineral estate and must reserve to the United States title to the surface. 16 U.S.C. § 1133(d)(3).

6. The issue of when and how the right to patent vests will surely arise again if the right to patent is permanently denied in the context of mining law reform legislation. How would you expect the Supreme Court to view this issue in light of *United States v. Locke*, 471 U.S. 84 (1985), and *Texaco v. Short*, 454 U.S. 516 (1982), *supra*, at 1055 and 1111.

7. Is the government required to prepare an environmental impact statement in the course of processing a patent application? Recall that the National Environmental Policy Act requires preparation of an EIS for any "major federal action that significantly affects the quality of the human environment." In *South Dakota v. Andrus*, 614 F.2d 1190 (8th Cir. 1980), *cert. denied*, 449 U.S. 822 (1980), South Dakota claimed that NEPA required the Department to prepare an EIS on a patent application filed by the Pittsburgh Pacific Company. The Court of Appeals for the Eighth Circuit held that the issuance of a patent following receipt of an application is a ministerial act outside NEPA's scope. The court further noted that even if NEPA applied to ministerial acts, the decision to grant a patent on mining claims was not a "major" federal action because a person with a valid mining claim has the right to mine even without a patent.

Is the court's analysis in the *South Dakota* case sound? In answering this question, consider the import of the IBLA's decision in the *Pittsburgh Pacific* case, excerpted above, which involved the same claims as were involved in the *South Dakota* case. Suppose, for example, that the cost of conducting a proposed mining operation will be greatly affected by the environmental controls that are imposed by federal regulation, and that at some point those regulations, although reasonable in the abstract, could be so costly as to make the proposed mining operation unprofitable. Under *Pittsburgh Pacific*, "[t]he cost of compliance with governmental and environmental requirements are ... significant in determining whether there has been a discovery." 30 I.B.L.A. 388, 405, 84 I.D. 282 (1977). How can those costs be determined without preparing an EIS? Suppose, alternatively, that the availability of land, water, or financing necessary to carry out the mining operation is in doubt. Shouldn't the government prepare an EIS to resolve these issues? Do the decisions that result from this process seem "ministerial" to you? In responding to these questions consider the kind of information that is generally included in an EIS and how that information might be used to assist the agency in making a decision on a patent application. *See also* 40 C.F.R. Part 1500 (2007).

8. As noted previously, in 1994, Congress imposed a moratorium on accepting or processing new patent applications. *See* Department of the Interior and Related Agencies Appropriations Act, 1995, Pub. L. No. 103–332 § 112, 113, 108 Stat. 2499, 2519 (1994). Certain applications, however, were exempted from this provision:

> The [moratorium] provisions of section 112 shall not apply if the Secretary of the Interior determines that, for the claim concerned (1) a patent application was filed with the Secretary on or before the date of enactment of this Act, and (2) all requirements established under sections 2325 and 2326 of the Revised Statutes (30 U.S.C. 29 and 30) for vein or lode claims ... were fully complied with by the applicant by that date.

In 1996 the patent moratorium was extended until September 30, 1996; it has been extended every year since then. *See, e.g.,* Pub. L. No. 105–83, § 314, 111 Stat. 1543 (Nov. 14, 1997); Pub. L. No. 106–113 § 312, 113 Stat. 1501 (Nov. 29, 1999); Pub. L. No. 107–63 § 309, 115 Stat. 414 (Nov. 5, 2001); Pub. L. No. 108–7, § 307, 117 Stat. 11 (Feb. 20, 2003). Still, processing grandfathered patent applications has never been a high priority for the Department, and the process nearly ground to a halt during the Clinton administration as Secretary of the Interior Bruce Babbitt resisted what he perceived to be a give-away of public resources. Secretary Babbitt's "go slow" approach led to a lawsuit by Barrick Goldstrike Mines, a Canadian company which sought patents for 61 gold lode mining claims and 151 mill sites, in northern Nevada. The gross value of these claims was estimated to be 10 billion dollars. The Secretary refused to make a final decision on Barrick's patent applications until he was finally ordered to do so by the federal district court in Nevada. *Barrick Goldstrike Mines v. Babbitt*, 1995 WL 408667 (D. Nev. 1994). On May 16, 1994, Babbitt signed patents granting the lands to Barrick for $9,765 even as he denounced the transaction as "the biggest gold heist since the days of Butch Cassidy." WASH. POST, May 17, 1994, Section A.

From this single claim, the government would likely have realized tens of millions of dollars in royalties. Instead, all of the profits from this mine will go to a foreign company. Why do you think it has been so difficult to pass legislation that ensures that the federal government receives a reasonable return for the extraction of hard rock minerals from federal lands?

9. Despite the Department's foot-dragging in processing patent applications, litigation seeking to force the Department's hand has met with mixed results. In *Marathon Oil Co. v. Lujan,* 937 F.2d 498 (10th Cir. 1991), the court ordered the Department to reach a decision on certain oil shale patent applications within 15 days. The Department subsequently issued patents for those claims. But in *Independence Mining Co. v. Babbitt,* 105 F.3d 502 (9th Cir. 1997), the court refused to order the Department to make a decision on various patent applications that were pending for an existing mining operation. In denying the claimant's request, the court applied the six-factor test (TRAC factors) for determining whether the agency's delay was unreasonable, as set forth by the Court of Appeals for the District of Columbia Circuit in *Telecommunications Research and Action v. F.C.C.,* 750 F.2d 70, 79–80 (D.C. Cir. 1984).

10. *High Country Citizens Alliance v. Clarke,* 454 F.3d 1177 (10th Cir. 2006), *cert. denied,* 550 U.S. 929 (2007) explored the rights of private citizens and local government agencies to challenge patent decisions. An environmental group, along with two government entities—the Town of Crested Butte, Colorado, and Gunnison County, Colorado—alleged, among other things, that the patent applicant had failed to demonstrate a discovery of valuable minerals on mining claims located in the Gunnison National Forest, and that the issuance of patents thus violated the General Mining Law of 1872. The court held, however, that the General Mining Law allowed review of patent decisions only by parties with a competing interest in the lands. The court relied on a 1984 decision of the Supreme Court, *Block v. Community Nutrition Institute,* 467 U.S. 340, 349 (1984), which held that the general presumption of reviewability of agency action under the Administrative Procedure Act can be overcome by showing congressional intent in the statutory scheme to preclude review. The court found such an intent in 30 U.S.C. §§ 29 and 30. The language of § 30 expressly creates a right of action for adverse claimants, who were conceded to encompass only those with a property interest in the same land. The plaintiffs did not claim to have such an interest. Section 29, however, establishes a process for third parties who claim no ownership in the land to file protests with the BLM:

> [N]o objection from third parties to the issuance of a patent shall be heard, except it be shown that the applicant has failed to comply with the terms of [the General Mining Law].

Do you agree that General Mining Law evinces an intent to preclude review by persons without a property interest in land? Is there any doubt that such persons meet the test for standing under *Sierra Club v. Morton,* 405 U.S. 727 (1972). Should the participation of a city and county government make any difference to the court's assessment of the case? *Cf., Massachusetts v. EPA,* 549 U.S. 497 (2007). ("It is of considerable relevance that the party seeking review here is a sovereign State and not, as it was in *Lujan,* a private individual.")

I. The Mechanics of Mining Claim Transactions

Much of the legal work associated with the General Mining Law involves transactions for the sale and purchase of mining claims. Suppose, for example, that your client, the Lucky Strike Mining Co., wants to purchase a block of unpatented gold mining claims. The seller has had an active mining operation on the site for 20 years. As with other real estate contracts, a contract to purchase a mining claim generally occurs in three stages. First, the terms of the contract are negotiated by the parties. The buyer typically reserves in the contract the right to cancel the transaction if an investigation reveals any number of defects with the property or with the seller's authority to convey the property. During the second stage, the buyer conducts this investigation. The seller will normally require that the buyer exercise *due diligence* in carrying out this investigation. Finally, if the buyer is satisfied with the property, the deal is closed.

A lawyer representing a buyer in such a transaction must exercise extreme caution. Numerous complex issues can arise during an investigation of mineral properties. The lawyer must identify these issues and assure their resolution prior to closing or risk substantial costs for the client. The following outline briefly summarizes the scope of an investigation for a mining claim transaction. A more detailed discussion of this matter is found in Dean R. Massey, *Due Diligence in Modern Mining Deals: How to Protect Your Client from Buying a Pig in a Poke*, 33 Rocky Mtn. Min. L. Inst. 2–1 (1987).

MINING CLAIM PURCHASE REVIEW PROCESS

A. *Review the Property*. This should include a physical inspection as well as an inspection of all documents relevant to the seller's title. Among the questions that should be answered are the following:

1. *Title Search*. Does the seller hold legal title to all of the claims? Are there liens against the property? Does the transaction encompass other property rights such as easements or leases?

2. *Maintenance*. Has the seller regularly performed annual assessment work on all claims and made regular filings with the county and federal governments?

3. *Market Analysis*. What is the seller company's experience with mining and marketing minerals from the claim? If the claims are not patented will they meet the discovery test?

4. *Mineral Analysis*. What is the quality and quantity of the mineral reserves? Are there special costs associated with developing or processing the minerals?

5. *Water Rights*. Are water rights needed to use the property? If so, does the seller hold valid water rights in sufficient quantities to carry out the proposed mining activities? Will these rights be transferred with the claims?

6. *Property Rights*. What other property (equipment) and rights (e.g., power supply) are necessary to carry out the proposed mining activities? Are these matters addressed in the transaction? If equipment will be sold

with the mine, what is the condition of the equipment? How has it been maintained? What is its market value?

7.   *Personnel.* Does the transaction include any transfer of personnel? What general problems, if any, may exist with such a transfer (wages, benefits, etc.)? Will any individual transfers pose specific problems?

B.   *Review the Seller Company.* The buyer should know some basic information about the seller company. Among the questions to be considered:

1.   Does the seller have the authority to carry out the transaction? What further approval is needed?

2.   Is the corporation subject to any government investigation (e.g. SEC) which may interfere with the transaction?

3.   Will existing mineral supply contracts, if any, transfer to the buyer? Are they clearly assignable?

C.   *Conduct an Environmental Audit.* As environmental law becomes more complex, compliance can be difficult and expensive. Further, the seller company's liability may be transferred to the buyer. Consider the following questions.

1.   What federal, state, or local laws (including land use laws) apply to the conduct of the mining operation? Is the seller in compliance with those laws? Have all necessary permits been obtained? Is the seller in compliance with those permits? What are the annual operating costs?

2.   If the operation is not in compliance with state and federal laws, what measures are necessary to bring it into compliance? Who will pay for these compliance measures? What do they cost?

3.   What is the potential liability of the buyer for seller's violations of the law? (*See, e.g.,* David Tunderman, *Personal Liability for Corporate Directors, Officers, Employees and Controlling Shareholders Under State and Federal Environmental Laws*, 31 ROCKY MTN. MIN. L. INST. 2–1 (1985)).

D.   *Miscellaneous.* Other areas of inquiry may focus on pending litigation against the seller that may affect the transaction, the status of the seller's insurance, and whether buyer can obtain any necessary insurance in a timely manner to cover potential losses. *See also* Steven J. Christiansen, *Environmental Audits and Beyond*, 42 ROCKY MTN. MIN. L. INST. 7–1 (1996).

IV.   MINERAL SALES AND LEASES ON PUBLIC LANDS

As enacted in 1872, the General Mining Law applied to the broad category of "all valuable mineral deposits." That this definition extended to oil, gas, and oil shale was confirmed by Congress in the 1897 Oil Placer Act. This broad definition of minerals included within the General Mining Law began to prove problematic around the turn of the twentieth century when demand for oil, gas, and coal began to boom.

> The gasoline car came into vogue in the 1890s, and production of the Model T began in 1907. The United States became a world power with growing military obligations. Western coal production rose from 2 million tons in 1873, the year of the most recent federal coal law, to 58 million tons in 1912. Even more

dramatically, oil production in the public-land states jumped from 2 million barrels in 1897, when Congress confirmed oil and gas as being covered by the 1872 law, to 141 million barrels in 1912.

Charles F. Wilkinson, Crossing the Next Meridian: Land, Water, and the Future of the American West 50–51 (1992). With this explosion in oil and coal development, the federal government became concerned that it was going to give away the minerals it needed for its military and energy needs. In 1906, President Theodore Roosevelt responded by withdrawing from mineral entry 66 million acres of coal deposits. As discussed in the *Midwest Oil* case in Chapter 2 (page 133), President Taft followed by withdrawing three million acres of oil-producing lands as naval petroleum reserves. A key additional step for which many argued was to remove these valuable minerals from the operation of the General Mining Law. Although World War I delayed the reform, in 1920, Congress passed the Mineral Leasing Act, 30 U.S.C. §§ 181 *et seq.*, which removed the "fuel and fertilizer" minerals, including coal, oil and gas, and oil shale, from the operation of the Mining Law. Instead of a system of location and private patent, the Mineral Leasing Act adopted a new leasing regime which required federal permission to drill or mine in any particular location. The Mineral Leasing Act is discussed further below but first we consider two other statutes that limit the scope of the General Mining Law—the Common Varieties Act, 30 U.S.C. § 611, and the Surface Resources Act, 30 U.S.C. §§ 613–615.

A. The Common Varieties Act

In 1947 Congress passed the Material Sales Act, 30 U.S.C. §§ 601–604, which authorized the sale of such common materials as sand, stone, gravel, and pumice. But there was little reason for anyone to purchase such materials when they were available for free under the General Mining Law. Moreover, as described earlier in this chapter, mining claimants could get much more than the minerals; they could also obtain a patent to the lands by paying a nominal fee. But allowing people to obtain mining claims for common minerals like sand and gravel was an invitation to abuse. And abuse was rampant. Mining claims for common variety minerals were frequently located in scenic areas of national forests or along favorite fishing streams. *See* John Leshy, The Mining Law: A Study in Perpetual Motion at 55–67 (1987). The only real mining going on was of the nation's public land heritage. Finally, in 1955 Congress passed the Multiple Surface Use Act or, as it is more commonly known, the Common Varieties Act, which removed from the operation of the mining law common variety minerals, such as sand, stone, gravel, pumice, pumicite, cinders, and petrified wood. 30 U.S.C. § 611 (2000). As its popular name suggests, however, uncommon varieties of these minerals remain subject to location under the General Mining Law. Much of the litigation under the Common Varieties Act has focused on the distinction between common and uncommon varieties of minerals.

McClarty v. Secretary of Interior,
408 F.2d 907 (9th Cir. 1969)

THOMPSON, DISTRICT JUDGE

This is an appeal from a summary judgment entered May 27, 1966, by the District Court of the United States for the Eastern District of Washington, dismissing an action to review the decision of the Secretary of the Interior, *United States v. McClarty*, 71 I.D. 331 (1964), invalidating Appellant's mining claim located for building stone.

There have been significant developments in this area of the law since the processing of this case through the administrative appeals in the Interior Department and since the decision of the District Court. The Supreme Court has ruled (*United States v. Coleman*, 1968, 390 U.S. 599) that the Act of July 23, 1955, 30 U.S.C. 601–615, eliminating as minerals locatable under the mining laws a "deposit of common varieties of sand, stone, gravel, pumice, pumicite or cinders" applies to common varieties of building stone, but that the Act of August 4, 1892, 27 Stat. 348, 30 U.S.C. 161, authorizing mining locations of lands chiefly valuable for building stone remains viable and "effective as to building stone that has . . . some property giving it 'distinct and special value'." *United States v. Coleman, supra*, at 605.

And on April 30, 1968, the Secretary of the Interior, in *United States v. U.S. Minerals Development Corporation*, 75 I.D. 127, undertook to review and reconcile his many decisions with respect to building stone claims against the cogent charge that his rulings avoiding such claims had the effect of vitiating 30 U.S.C. 161 with the result that no building stone deposits are locatable under the mining laws. Among the decisions discussed was that in the instant case (*United States v. McClarty*, 71 I.D. 331). In the *U.S. Minerals Development Corporation* case, the Secretary, impelled by the *Coleman* decision to breathe some life into the building stone statute, has defined guidelines for distinguishing between common varieties and uncommon varieties of building stone. These guidelines, as we discern them, are (1) there must be a comparison of the mineral deposit in question with other deposits of such minerals generally; (2) the mineral deposit in question must have a unique property; (3) the unique property must give the deposit a distinct and special value; (4) if the special value is for uses to which ordinary varieties of the mineral are put, the deposit must have some distinct and special value for such use; and (5) the distinct and special value must be reflected by the higher price which the material commands in the market place. We accept this analysis as representing a genuine effort by the Secretary to implement the admonition of the *Coleman* case that certain kinds of building stone are still subject to location under the mining laws. The result in the *Minerals Development Corporation* case was a remand for further hearing to develop further evidence regarding the price commanded by the stone there in question as compared to other building stone on the market. The evidentiary record was deficient on this issue.

In the instant case, McClarty located a mining claim on a deposit of stone which was naturally fractured in regular shapes ready for use by the stonemason, with little, if any, cutting or shaping required. The deposit was unique in that seventy per cent or more of the stone had been shaped by nature into forms immediately useable in commercial and residential construction. This was determined by a comparison of this particular deposit with other deposits generally. The deposit had a unique and special property or characteristic for use as building stone, and it was used by the locator for that purpose in commercial and residential construction. It should be noted that the common varieties statute (30 U.S.C. 611) refers to a "deposit" which has "some property giving it distinct and special value" and not to the fabricated or marketed product of the deposit. Unquestionably, the evidence in the record requires a finding that this deposit of naturally fractured and regularly shaped stone was unique.

Thus, the only requirement elucidated in the *Minerals Development Corporation* case which remains to be considered is that of value. As to this requirement, the record is sketchy. If final decision must be predicated upon the present record, the claim of the locator should be sustained. The only evidence in the record is testimony that this building stone commanded $40 to $45 per ton on the market as compared with $6 to $7 per ton for common rock, and the testimony of a stonemason who had laid this and other building stone that the stone from this claim was easier to lay and required less time because of its shape and he hadn't seen any other stone as economical for laying as this. This testimony is undisputed and is the only testimony bearing on value; that is, value in terms of money. It, nevertheless, is evident that the hearing before the trial examiner did not focus on money value. The evidence of both the contestant and contestee aimed at the unique properties of the deposit, contestant asserting it to be an unlocatable common variety of building stone with which the contestee took issue. Accordingly, in this case, as in the *Minerals Development Corporation* case, the Department may conclude with propriety that the case should be remanded to the Hearing Examiner for further evidence on the issue of money value.

In the *Minerals Development Corporation* case, the claimed unique properties of the stone (color and cleavability) were thought to be characteristics that should be reflected in the price commanded for the stone on the market if these properties truly gave the stone a distinct and special value. In whatever way one may view that conclusion in that particular case, in the *McClarty* case, where the unique properties of the stone are the natural fracturing into regular shapes and forms suitable for laying without further fabrication, the distinct and special economic value of the stone may or may not be measurable by the retail market price in comparison with the price of other building stones. It is quite possible that the special economic value of the stone would be reflected by reduced costs or overhead so that the profit to the producer would be substantially more while the retail market price would remain competitive with other building stone. All we are attempting to indicate is that the guideline "the only practical factor for determining whether one deposit of material has a special and distinct value because of some property is to ascertain the price at which it is sold in comparison with the price for which the material in other deposits without such property is sold" (*United States v. U.S. Minerals Development Corporation*, 75 I.D. at 135) cannot be the exclusive way of proving that a deposit has a distinct and special economic value attributable to the unique property of the deposit.

The summary judgment entered by the District Court is reversed and this case is remanded to the District Court with instructions to enter a judgment remanding the case to the Secretary of the Interior * * *.

QUESTIONS AND DISCUSSION

1. On remand, the Board found that the stone deposit at issue, referred to by its trade name, "Heatherstone," possessed a unique property that permitted natural fracturing and flat surface cross-sectioning. This property reduced the cost of extracting and installing the stone. How should the Board rule? *See United States v. McClarty*, 81 I.D. 472 (1974).

2. Compare the result in *McClarty* with the Board's earlier decision in *United States v. Henderson*, 68 I.D. 26 (1961). In that case, Henderson argued that the sand and gravel on his claim occurred in a mixture that was nearly perfect for construction uses. This allowed Henderson to sell the material right out of the pit. Furthermore, the concrete made from this sand and gravel was unique in that it could be ground and polished to produce an attractive stone that looked like marble. Nonetheless, the Board held that "[t]he fact that these sand and gravel deposits may have characteristics superior to those of other sand and gravel deposits does not make them an uncommon variety of sand and gravel so long as they are used only for the same purposes as other deposits which are widely and readily available." *Id.* at 29–30. Can *Henderson* be reconciled with *McClarty*? Does *McClarty* effectively overturn *Henderson*?

3. In 2003, the BLM adopted rules that were designed to codify the *McClarty* test, and to further explain the distinction between common and uncommon varieties. 43 C.F.R. § 3830.12 (2008).

4. The definition of "common varieties" in the BLM regulations addresses limestone explicitly, stating that limestone suitable for certain uses (including cement production) is not a common variety. 43 C.F.R. § 3830.12(d) (2008). Suppose that a large deposit of limestone occurs over a 100–mile area and that most of this limestone is suitable for cement production. Clearly this deposit meets the BLM definition of an uncommon variety of limestone. Does it meet the statutory definition? Compare this with a recent IBLA decision, *United States v. Pitkin Iron Corp.*, 170 IBLA 352, GFS(MIN) 30(2006). Here, the board held that use of limestone as a soil additive was insufficient to qualify the limestone as an uncommon variety. The use of the limestone was deemed too common, and this specific stone could not be differentiated from other nearby deposits. Does this meet the BLM definition? The statutory definition? Should there be a difference? Regarding the locatability of limestone deposits *see United States v. Pfizer & Co.*, 76 I.D. 331, 15 I.B.L.A. 43 (1969), which provides detailed information about the extent and locatability of limestone deposits under the General Mining Law. Among other things, the Board found that limestone, which contains at least 95% calcium and magnesium carbonate, is a chemical or metallurgical grade limestone that is locatable under the law. *Id.* at 347.

5. The Mineral Sales Act of 1947 (*codified as amended at* 30 U.S.C. § 601–604 (1994)) allowed disposal of mineral materials, including common varieties, to the highest qualified bidder, *id.* § 602, so long as disposal was not detrimental to the public interest. Governmental units and subdivisions could remove materials free of charge for purposes other than commercial, industrial, or for resale. *Id.* § 601.

B. THE SURFACE RESOURCES ACT

Before 1955, mining claimants obtained "the exclusive right of possession and enjoyment of all the surface included within the lines of location." *See* 30 U.S.C. § 26. While this "exclusive right of possession" did not give the claimant the right to use his claim for purposes unrelated to mining, the government was slow to take action against people who used their mining claims even for a permanent residence.

In 1955, in the same legislation that removed common varieties from the operation of the Mining Law, Congress adopted several provisions designed to ensure that claimants who occupied public lands were focused on mining and not on other activities. Accordingly, § 4(a) of the Surface Resources Act reinforced the existing law by emphasizing that "[a]ny mining claim hereafter located ... shall not be used ... for any purpose other than prospecting, mining, or processing operations...." 30 U.S.C. § 612(a). Furthermore, for all claims located after 1955, the federal government reserved the right to manage and use the surface resources on such claims, so long as such uses did not interfere with mining operations. *Id.* § 4(b); 30 U.S.C. § 612(b). Finally, § 5 of the Act establishes a procedure whereby the federal agency with jurisdiction over lands on which mining claims have been located can seek a determination of surface rights on claims located *before* 1955. 30 U.S.C. § 613. Under this procedure, the Secretary publishes a notice in a local newspaper, and provides personal notice to identifiable claimants, that the agency is seeking a determination of surface rights. A claimant must then file a verified statement supporting the claimant's rights. Any claimant who fails to file such a statement (within 150 days from the date of the first newspaper publication) "shall be conclusively deemed" to have waived their surface rights to the same. If one or more verified statements are filed, a hearing is held solely to determine whether the claimant had a valid mining claim as of the date of the enactment of the Surface Mining Act. *See Converse v. Udall*, 399 F.2d 616 (9th Cir. 1968), *cert. denied*, 393 U.S. 1025 (1969). Significantly, however, § 5 proceedings do not result in a declaration that a claim is null and void, and the claimant may continue to engage in mining activities even though she no longer retains exclusive rights to the surface resources. *United States v. Speckert*, 75 I.D. 367, 371 (1968).

QUESTIONS AND DISCUSSION

1. In *United States v. Curtis–Nevada Mines, Inc.*, 611 F.2d 1277 (9th Cir. 1980), a claimant had staked 203 mining claims for "gold, platinum, copper, silver, tungsten, pitchblend, palladium, tridium, asmium, rhodium, ruthenium, scandium, vanadium, ytterbium, yttrium, europium, and 'all the rare earths,' " after passage of the Surface Resources Act. The claimant maintained that the minerals on the claims were worth "trillions," but little mining activity had occurred on the property. Nonetheless, the claimant had posted "No Trespassing" signs on the property, and barricaded roads that ran through the boundaries of his claims, thereby preventing access by recreational users to certain portions of the Toiyabe National Forest. Relying on the language from § 4(b), which authorizes surface access over mining claims by "the United States, its permittees or licensees," the district court held that the claimant could maintain the barricades so long as a guard was available to provide access to persons who possessed a valid written permit. On appeal, the Ninth Circuit reversed. The court held that the general public enjoys an implied license to use public lands and that the claimant could not deny access to anyone without a showing that they were interfering with mining operations.

2. Even after the Surface Resources Act was passed, many people used their mining claims for nonmining purposes, including their permanent residence. *Compare United States v. Nogueira*, 403 F.2d 816 (9th Cir. 1968) (reversing the district court's dismissal of government challenge to mining claim and remanding for the lower court to decide whether the claim used solely as a residence was entered in bad faith.), *with United States v. Langley*, 587 F. Supp. 1258 (E.D. Cal. 1984) (denying government's motion to eject mining claimant absent a showing of bad faith but granting motion to enjoin use of the claim as a residence without an approved plan of operations showing use for mining purposes). *See also United States v. Rizzinelli*, 182 F. 675 (D. Idaho 1910) (upholding decision enjoining claimant from operating a saloon on a mining claim as unrelated to mining purposes.); *Bruce W. Crawford*, 92 I.D. 208 (1985) (requiring the BLM to give notice and opportunity for a hearing before ordering removal of cabin and other structures unrelated to mining). Enforcement against these squatters was rare, and once they had become established federal land managers were reluctant to take any action that might force families from their homes. In 1962, Congress passed the Mining Claims Occupancy Act, which gave the Secretary of the Interior the power to convey small tracts of land not exceeding five acres that were actually being used as a permanent place of residence. 30 U.S.C. § 701.

3. A claimant's right to exclusive possession of the surface for a pre–1955 claim does not encompass the right to commit trespass or waste, or to use surface resources for nonmining purposes. *Teller v. United States*, 113 F. 273 (8th Cir. 1901), clearly demonstrates this principle. The claimant, Mullison, had located mining claims and on January 5, 1898 had filed a patent application for those claims. He had perfected his title to the claims by tendering the purchase price to the government on June 22, 1898. Between January 5 and June 22, however, Teller, who claimed a license from Mullison, had cut timber from the claim property. The court held that Mullison's title did not relate back to the date of his patent application and affirmed Teller's conviction for a criminal trespass.

4. The Surface Resources Act expressly addresses the problem of timber cutting on unpatented mining claims providing, in relevant part, as follows:

> Except to the extent required for the mining claimant's prospecting, mining or processing operations and uses reasonably incident thereto, or for the construction of buildings or structures in connection therewith, or to provide clearance for such operations or uses, or to the extent authorized by the United States, no claimant of any mining claim hereafter located under the mining laws of the United States shall, prior to issuance of patent therefor, sever, remove, or use any vegetative or other surface resources thereof which are subject to management or disposition by the United States under the preceding subsection (b). Any severance or removal of timber which is permitted under the exceptions of the preceding sentence, other than severance or removal to provide clearance, shall be in accordance with sound principles of forest management.

30 U.S.C. § 612(c). Subsection (b) noted in the above quotation allows a claimant to obtain timber in *addition* to that on his claim from the nearest source of mature federal timber available if such timber is necessary to

develop the claim. *See also United States v. Cruthers*, 523 F.2d 1306 (9th Cir. 1975).

5. Surface Resources Act procedures are described at 43 C.F.R. subpart 3712 (2008).

————

Problem Exercise. Discovery Problems and the Surface Resources Act

Adam Apple located a uranium mining claim in 1951 on public domain land in south central Wyoming. Mineral ore was extracted and sold from the claim at a profit between 1951 and 1965. In 1965, the market for uranium declined and for 5 years Apple was unable to market his ore profitably. He nonetheless faithfully maintained his claim. In 1970, Apple negotiated a long-term contract with a California utility company to supply uranium ore for two nuclear power plants. As a result of this contract Apple's mining operation has been turning a profit every year since 1970. In 1981, the Bureau of Land Management, which manages the land on which the claim is located, instituted proceedings under Section 5 of the Surface Resources Act to determine the surface rights to the claim. What is the likely outcome of these proceedings? *See United States v. Speckert*, 75 I.D. 367, 371–72 (1968). Suppose that a prior Section 5 hearing held in 1959 had sustained Apple's rights to the surface resources. No appeal was taken. Is the government barred by the doctrine of *res judicata* from instituting new proceedings in 1981?

————

C. The Mineral Leasing Act

As discussed above, widespread concern over private appropriation under the General Mining Law of vast quantities of federal oil and gas reserves, as described in *United States v. Midwest Oil*, 236 U.S. 459 (1915) (Chapter 2, *supra*, page 133), prompted Congress to pass the Mineral Leasing Act of 1920 (MLA). The purpose of this statute was to remove certain minerals from the operation of the General Mining Law and to make them available for leasing. The minerals to which the MLA applies are sometimes referred to as the "fuel and fertilizer" minerals and include coal, oil, gas, oil shale, phosphate, sodium, potassium and gilsonite, and sulfur in Louisiana and New Mexico. 30 U.S.C. §§ 181–287 (2001). Although a detailed discussion of the Mineral Leasing Act is beyond the scope of this casebook and is reserved for courses in Energy Law or Oil and Gas Law, the Act provides a useful contrast to the approach of the General Mining Law. Professor Wilkinson explains:

> The mineral leasing system, the major contrasting model for the self-initiation and patent approach taken in the 1872 act, has numerous special and technical provisions that apply to some leasable minerals and not others. But the following are the main features of leasing that distinguish it from the Hardrock Act:
>
> 1. There is no "right to mine." Permission must be obtained from the federal government to prospect or mine.

[handwritten margin note: differences between General Mining law of 1872 & Mineral Leasing Act of 1920]

2.   The United States receives an economic return in the form of royalties, rents, and bonus payments. Examples of royalties are 12.5 percent to 25 percent for oil and gas, depending on the amount of production; at least 12 percent for surface-mined coal; and 10 percent to 15 percent for geothermal steam. A bonus is also included in the bid, and leases are usually issued to the qualified bidder with the highest bonus bid, since the royalty is usually fixed by the BLM in advance.

3.   The United States has discretion to decide which, if any, competitive bidder may proceed.

4.   Each lease is for a fixed term—for example, five years for most oil and gas leases and twenty years for most coal leases. Usually, leases can be renewed if the miner is producing minerals in paying quantities.

5.   The United States can require reasonably prompt development of the resource through lease provisions providing for cancellation if a lessee does not proceed with due diligence.

6.   Provisions can be and are included in the lease to protect other, competing resources and the environment. Thus, federal officials often set construction standards and prescribe access routes for roads, a principal cause of erosion and disruption of wildlife habitat. In some instances, helicopter access has been required. Highly specialized conditions can be imposed, such as the "winter access only" provision in some Alaska leases to protect the delicate tundra environment during the summer months. Reclamation (restoration of the mined-over area to a natural-looking condition) is required of lessees when the operation is completed.

The leasing approach, then, was spawned by a crisis due to overextraction of public resources. It is premised on a fair monetary return to the United States and has evolved to include protections for the environment.

CHARLES F. WILKINSON, CROSSING THE NEXT MERIDIAN: LAND, WATER, AND THE FUTURE OF THE AMERICAN WEST 53–54 (1992). As described in the materials that follow, several different leasing systems have evolved for the different minerals encompassed by the Mineral Leasing Act (MLA).

1.   ONSHORE OIL AND GAS LEASING

Mineral leases on federal lands are similar in many respects to mineral leases on private lands. They are essentially contracts between the mineral developer (the lessee) and the federal government (the lessor) that provide for the development of federal minerals. Federal leases set the terms for mineral development. These include royalties and rental fees, as well as environmental and use restrictions.

Under the original terms of the Mineral Leasing Act, oil and gas leases could be issued on a competitive or noncompetitive basis. Leases were issued on a competitive basis only if they were located in a "known geologic structure" (KGS). The idea was that KGS lands were generally known to be valuable for oil and gas and thus should be leased competitively to assure the greatest dollar return to the government. Non–KGS lands were leased without competition to the first qualified offeror because the government assumed that it needed to provide incentives on these lands to encourage exploration and development. The KGS concept had no scientific significance but was incorporated into the 1920 law at the suggestion of Senator Kendrick of Wyoming. Interior rules defined a KGS as "the trap in which an accumulation of oil and gas has been discovered by drilling and determined to be productive, the limits of which include all acreage which is presumptively productive." 43 C.F.R. § 3100.0–5 (1987). Historically, this rule was construed narrowly so that many lands that were believed to be valuable for oil and gas were found not to be in a KGS and thus outside the competitive leasing process. This resulted in substantial losses to federal and state treasuries.

One of the most glaring examples of this problem occurred at the Fort Chaffee military reservation in Arkansas. The lands surrounding the reservation were known to be productive for oil and gas (and thus should have been leased competitively), but in 1979 the Interior Department leased 33,000 acres of land under the noncompetitive leasing provisions for the incredible price of $1 per acre. Just one year later, the Department changed its KGS determination and made an additional 24,000 acres in the area available for lease competitively. These lands were leased for approximately $1,705 per acre! *See Issues Surrounding Continuation of the Noncompetitive Oil and Gas Lottery System* 5 (GAO/RCED–85–88, 1985).

Following a lawsuit by a lease competitor, and pressure from Congress, the BLM decided to cancel the original leases because of a technical violation under their regulations. The Court of Appeals for the Eighth Circuit eventually ruled that the KGS procedure used to classify the land was arbitrary and capricious. *Arkla Exploration Co. v. Texas Oil and Gas Corp.*, 734 F.2d 347 (8th Cir. 1984), *cert. denied*, 469 U.S. 1158 (1985).

Problems like the Fort Chaffee leases led Secretary of the Interior Cecil Andrus to impose a moratorium on noncompetitive oil and gas leases in 1980. But the moratorium was lifted by Secretary Watt in 1981, and soon thereafter another controversy arose over the issuance of fourteen noncompetitive leases in the Amos Draw area of the Powder River Basin of Wyoming. Many of the lessees immediately sold their leases—in some cases for millions of dollars. *See* Laura Lindley, *Of Teapot Dome, Wind River, and Fort Chaffee: Federal Oil and Gas Resources, available at* http://www.land man.org/content/104.pdf.

Bureaucratic abuses were not the only problem with the old oil and gas leasing system. Under the BLM's regulations, noncompetitive leases were issued either over-the-counter to the first qualified applicant or under the simultaneous leasing system. 43 C.F.R. §§ 3111.1 & 3112 (1987). Under the simultaneous leasing system, state BLM offices announced bi-monthly which of the non-KGS tracts would be made available for lease. A lottery was then held to determine who would receive the first opportunity to lease the tract. An individual or corporation was allowed only one filing on each tract. This system gave rise to a proliferation of filing services. For a fee, these services would choose the tracts that were supposedly the most valuable and would then file applications on those tracts on behalf of each of its customers thereby greatly increasing the chances that one of these customers would win the lease. At least some of these filing services were run by unscrupulous operators who made false promises to customers while filing on virtually worthless tracts of land.

The combination of these problems led to bipartisan cries for reform and after several years of debate the Federal Onshore Oil and Gas Leasing

Reform Act of 1987 was enacted. Pub. L. No. 100–203 (1987). The 1987 law retains the competitive/noncompetitive leasing system but in a substantially modified form. All lands made available for leasing must first be offered on a competitive basis. The size of the tracts available for lease was increased from 640 acres to 2,560 acres and 5,760 acres in Alaska. 30 U.S.C. § 226(b)(1)(A). If such lands do not receive the minimum bid required by law they become available for noncompetitive leasing for two years. 30 U.S.C. § 226(b)(1)(A). Noncompetitive leases are issued to the first qualified applicant upon payment of a nonrefundable $75 fee. 30 U.S.C. § 226(c)(1). The distinction between KGS and non-KGS lands has thus been eliminated entirely.

Competitive lease sales are conducted by oral bidding. Leases are awarded to the "highest bid from a responsible bidder which is equal to or greater than the national minimum acceptable bid...." 30 U.S.C. § 226(b)(1)(A). The minimum acceptable bid for two years from the date that the law was enacted (December 22, 1987) was $2 per acre. After that time the Secretary of the Interior may establish a higher minimum bid by regulation. 30 U.S.C. § 226(b)(1)(B).

All leases are subject to royalties as well as a minimum rental payment of $1.50 per acre for the first five years and $2 per acre thereafter. The rental payment may be deducted from the royalty payments which remain at a minimum of 12.5% of the amount or value of production removed or sold. 30 U.S.C. § 226(b)(1)(A).

Lease terms were not changed by the 1987 law. Noncompetitive oil and gas leases are issued for a primary term of ten years. Competitive leases have a primary term of five years. All leases continue in effect, however, "so long after [their] primary term as oil and gas is produced in paying quantities." 30 U.S.C. § 226(e). In addition, any lease which is part of an approved cooperative or unit plan of development continues in force so long as "production is had in paying quantities under the plan prior to the expiration ... of such lease." 30 U.S.C. § 226(j). Unit plans of development or pooling operations are encouraged to help conserve the affected resources. Leases can also be extended for two years beyond their primary term where actual drilling operations are commenced before the end of the lease term, and where such drilling operations are being diligently prosecuted at the *end* of that primary term. *See Milestone Petroleum, Inc. v. Phillips Oil Co.,* 85 I.B.L.A. 96 (1985).

Onshore oil and gas development on public lands generally occurs in three phases. First the government makes lands available for lease and issues leases to the highest bidder, or in the case of a noncompetitive lease sale, to the first qualified bidder. Then, the lessee engages in exploration activities to determine whether commercial quantities of oil and gas may exist on the leased land. Finally, if exploration reveals commercial deposits, development of the field occurs. Drilling activities may be necessary at either the exploration or development stages, and a lessee who wants to drill on its lease must first file an application for a permit to drill (APD) and receive the approval of the appropriate BLM state office before drilling activities commence.

The 1987 law also requires that the surface managing agency regulate all surface disturbing activities. Permits to drill may not be approved until a plan of operations has been approved. 30 U.S.C. § 226(g). Furthermore, the Secretary must promulgate regulations to ensure that an adequate bond or other surety is posted, and that "complete and timely reclamation of the lease tract, and the restoration of any lands or surface waters adversely affected by lease operations...." 30 U.S.C. § 226(g). Any person who fails to meet these requirements is barred from receiving new leases.

Before the 1987 law was enacted, the Interior Department took the position that it was the final arbiter of a decision to lease federal lands even on National Forest lands under the management of the Department of Agriculture. *See Earl R. Wilson*, 21 I.B.L.A. 392, GFS (O & G) 99 (1975). Under the previous system, the Forest Service made recommendations to the BLM on oil and gas applications in National Forests, and those recommendations were usually accepted, although occasionally modified by the BLM. *Mountain States Legal Foundation v. Andrus*, 499 F. Supp. 383, 388 (D. Wyo. 1980). The Reform Act now makes clear, however, that the Interior Secretary may not lease forest lands over the objection of the Secretary of Agriculture. 30 U.S.C. § 226(b).

A final significant change brought on by the new law was a prohibition on oil and gas leasing in wilderness study areas. 30 U.S.C. § 226-3. Such leasing had become popular during the Reagan Administration but could have effectively destroyed the eligibility of these areas for wilderness designation.

QUESTIONS AND DISCUSSION

1. Any lease under the Mineral Leasing Act may also be suspended by the Secretary to "encourage the greatest ultimate recovery of [the resource]" and "in the interest of conservation of natural resources." 30 U.S.C. § 209. During the period that the lease is suspended, rental and royalty payments are also suspended. In addition, the term of the lease is extended by adding the suspension period to that term. *Id.* In *Copper Valley Mach. Works, Inc. v. Andrus*, 653 F.2d 595 (D.C. Cir. 1981), the Court of Appeals for the D.C. Circuit held that suspensions "in the interest of conservation" were not limited to conservation of the mineral resource. Suspensions should also be granted to protect against environmental harm. Thus, a condition in a drilling permit prohibiting summer drilling on the Alaska tundra was held to be a suspension under the Mineral Leasing Act which resulted in a commensurate extension of the lease term.

2. The Mineral Leasing Act of 1920 does not apply to most Eastern national forest lands and other public lands that have been acquired by the United States. 30 U.S.C. § 181. A separate statute, the Mineral Leasing Act for Acquired Lands, 30 U.S.C. § 351 *et seq.*, was enacted in 1947 to fill this gap. The Act generally applies the terms of the MLA to acquired lands, 30 U.S.C. § 352, but makes clear that the Secretary of the Interior may not lease mineral deposits on acquired lands without the consent of the head of the executive office or agency having jurisdiction over the land. *Duncan Miller*, 79 I.D. 416 (1972).

3. Offshore oil and gas leasing poses special international relations and environmental problems. In recognition of these problems Congress enacted the Outer Continental Shelf Lands Act, 43 U.S.C. §§ 1331–43. This legislation regulates oil and gas leasing on the outer continental shelf which generally includes all lands three miles beyond the coast. *United States v. Maine*, 420 U.S. 515 (1975). Coastal states were granted title to the lands three miles from the coast under the Submerged Lands Act of 1952. 43 U.S.C. §§ 1301–15. Comprehensive treatment of the Outer Continental Shelf Lands Act is beyond the scope of this book. The law is summarized at http://www.csc.noaa.gov/opis/html/summary/ocsla.htm.

4. One issue not resolved by the 1987 legislation is the extent to which NEPA applies to the decision to issue oil and gas leases. On the one hand, a decision to lease lands does not mean that oil and gas development will ever take place. It simply determines who will be allowed to develop the oil and gas during a certain period of time, if it is going to be developed at all. On the other hand, if the lessee chooses to develop the oil and gas, the government's ability to stop it may be severely limited.

Three circuit courts have considered this problem. The issue first arose in *Sierra Club v. Peterson,* 717 F.2d 1409 (D.C. Cir. 1983). In *Sierra Club,* the plaintiffs challenged oil and gas leases issued by the Forest Service in the Targhee and Bridger–Teton National Forests in Idaho and Wyoming. Prior to issuing the leases, the government prepared environmental assessments that addressed the impacts from the leasing action, but not from possible future oil and gas development. For lands designated by the Forest Service as "highly environmentally sensitive," the agency imposed a "No Surface Occupancy" (NSO) stipulation. This stipulation prevented the lessee from engaging in surface disturbing activities unless and until the Forest Service lifted the stipulation, presumably after further environmental analysis of the impact of such a decision. Even with these stipulations, the oil and gas on these properties might have been developed. (How?) Other leases were issued without NSO stipulations. The court held that the government was required to analyze the impacts of any possible oil and gas development before leases were issued without NSO stipulations:

> While it may be true that the majority of these leases will never reach the drilling stage, . . . NEPA requires that federal agencies determine at the outset whether their major actions can result in "significant" environmental impacts. . . .
>
> . . . [O]nce the land is leased the Department no longer has the authority to preclude surface disturbing activities, even if the environmental impact of such activity is significant. . . .
>
> . . . [T]he decision to allow surface disturbing activities has been made at the leasing stage and, under NEPA, this is the point at which the environmental impacts of such activities must be evaluated.

717 F.2d at 1409.

5. The Court of Appeals for the Tenth Circuit reached a seemingly different result in a case involving a 10,174–acre lease on national forest lands which were not included in any wilderness or wilderness study area. *Park County Resource Council v. U.S. Dep't of Agriculture*, 817 F.2d 609 (10th Cir. 1987). The Court was apparently persuaded that an EIS should not be required prior to leasing because the BLM had prepared an environmental assessment in excess of 100 pages prior to leasing, and because the prospect of actual drilling at the time of lease issuance was remote. Although both cases involved leases issued by the BLM in national forests in Wyoming, the Court never cited the *Sierra Club* decision. Can the *Sierra Club* and *Park County* cases be reconciled? How should the BLM resolve a conflict between the circuits when it issues new leases in national forests?

6. The Court of Appeals for the Ninth Circuit appears to agree with the D.C. Circuit's opinion in *Sierra Club*. *Conner v. Burford*, 836 F.2d 1521 (9th Cir. 1988), involved numerous leases over 1.3 million acres of land in national forests in Montana. Some of the lands were roadless areas eligible for wilderness designation; others were not. No EIS was prepared prior to lease issuance. The court held that these leases must be preceded by a comprehensive EIS, covering all possible lease development, unless the leases contained NSO stipulations covering the entire lease. *Id.* at 1527–28. In response to the government's claim that the court should at a minimum distinguish between roadless and roaded areas, the court replied that nothing in the record supported such a distinction. *Id.* at 1529 n.17.

In addition to addressing NEPA, the decision in *Conner* considers possible conflicts between oil and gas leasing and the Endangered Species Act (ESA). As described in Chapter 4, the ESA, like NEPA, imposes certain procedural obligations on agencies engaged in federal actions. Under § 7 of the ESA, an agency must ensure that any actions "authorized, funded, or carried out" by the agency are not likely to "jeopardize" the continued existence of any endangered or threatened species or result in the adverse modification of their critical habitat. In meeting this mandate the action agency must first determine whether an endangered or threatened species may be present in the action area. If so, the action agency must prepare a biological assessment to determine whether the species is likely to be adversely affected. If adverse effects are likely then the action agency must consult with the U.S. Fish and Wildlife Service to ensure that the species are not jeopardized by the action.

Contrary to its decision on NEPA, the Court of Appeals for the Ninth Circuit held that an incremental step approach to consultation under the ESA was not lawful, even where the agency had included stipulations in the lease specifically authorizing the government to deny use or occupancy, if later consultations revealed a conflict with the ESA. Can you see any basis for the court's seemingly different treatment of NEPA and the ESA?

7. What effect, if any, should the Federal Onshore Oil and Gas Leasing Reform Act have on the *Sierra Club*, *Park County*, and *Conner* cases?

8. As the above cases suggest, once a lease is issued, the Secretary's authority to deny a lessee the right to develop that lease is limited. Nonetheless, the Secretary can cancel a lease that was issued in violation of the law. In *Boesche v. Udall*, 373 U.S. 472 (1963), the plaintiff was issued a lease that violated the acreage requirements of the federal regulations. After discovering the error, the Secretary cancelled the lease. The Court held that the Secretary had inherent authority to cancel an oil and gas lease issued in violation of law. *Id.* at 476, 484. *See also Mammoth Oil Co. v. United States*, 275 U.S. 13 (1927). The *Mammoth Oil* case involved the famous Teapot Dome scandal, where Secretary of the Interior Albert Fall allegedly accepted a bribe in exchange for an oil and gas lease within a naval petroleum reserve that had been withdrawn from leasing by executive order. The Court held that the United States could cancel any lease issued fraudulently.

9.   In *Udall v. Tallman*, 380 U.S. 1 (1965), the Supreme Court held that "the Mineral Leasing Act of 1920 ... gave the Secretary of the Interior broad power to issue oil and gas leases on public lands.... Although the Act directed that if a lease was [*sic*] issued on such a tract, it had to be issued to the first qualified applicant, it left the Secretary discretion to refuse to issue any lease at all in a given tract." Subsequently, however, in *Mountain States Legal Foundation v. Hodel,* 668 F. Supp. 1466 (D. Wyo. 1987), a federal district court held that the failure to process certain oil and gas lease applications in certain national forests in Wyoming—some of which had been pending for 12 years—violated both the Energy Security Act of 1980, and the Federal Land Policy and Management Act of 1976. The Energy Security Act required the National Forest leases to be *processed* regardless of the status of any land use planning effort by the Forest Service, and there was evidence that the Forest Service had stopped processing oil and gas lease applications while it was awaiting completion of its forest plans. As for FLPMA, the court found that the failure to process leases effectively constituted a withdrawal of the land which could only be accomplished under the withdrawal provisions at § 204 of that law. Could the agency avoid the outcome in *Mountain States* by simply rejecting all applications until its Forest Plan was complete rather than refusing to process them?

———

2.   COAL LEASING

The federal government owns about half of all U.S. coal reserves, which comprise about 25% of world reserves. Much of that coal is found in the Western United States. Federal coal has been available for lease since the enactment of the Mineral Leasing Act of 1920, and by 1970 nearly 16 billion tons of coal had been leased and were available for development. But only a tiny portion of this coal was actually being developed. Much of the coal was being held for speculative purposes by coal brokers who could obtain the coal from the federal government for a nominal sum and then turn around and market the coal at a substantial profit. Myriad other problems beset the federal coal leasing program, and in 1973 Secretary of the Interior Rogers Morton imposed a moratorium on new leasing. The House Report on the legislation that would become the Federal Coal Leasing Amendments Act (FCLAA) describes these problems as follows:

> *1. Speculation*: Under existing law, any coal lease issued by the Secretary is effective virtually forever. Although Section 7 permits revision of leasing terms every 20 years and a lease can be terminated for lack of compliance with the terms of the Act through lengthy court proceedings, no Federal coal lease has ever been cancelled in this manner.

The current law also specifies that a coal lease shall be subject to the conditions of "diligent development" and "continued operation." ... Since these terms had never been defined, cancellation of a lease for lack of compliance with the law ... would have been very difficult. * * *

In addition to the lack of development of existing leases, the provision of the existing law which allows issuance of preference rights associated with coal prospecting permits (Section 2(b)) has contributed to speculative holding of leases by making it possible to gain control of public resources at virtually no cost. According to the study "Leased and Lost," 45 percent of all Federal leases have been issued on a preference right basis, with no competitive bidding involved. * * *

2. *Concentration of Holdings*: Approximately 66 percent of the Federal and Indian acreage under lease is held by 15 leaseholders, although there are a total of 144 lessees. This data reflects the trend of dominance in the energy field by a handful of major corporations which is evident in virtually every resource area.

This dominance is due in part to the system of cash bonus bidding which is used when leases are offered on a competitive bidding basis. Such a bidding system requires substantial "front end" capital (i.e. a larger initial investment in the bonus bid). Smaller companies do not have the financial resources to compete with the giants in the energy and mining industries. * * *

3. *Fair Return to the Public*: Several aspects of the current law have contributed to a situation in which the public is being paid a pittance for its coal resources. The first such provision is that which establishes a prospecting system for lands in which the resource is not known to the Department of the Interior. Such permits are issued for specific plots of land and carry with them the right of a "preference lease." That is, if a holder of a prospecting permit demonstrates the existence of coal in commercial quantities in the permit area, he is entitled to a preference right lease. No competitive sale is held and the lessee is subject only to the minimum royalty and rental provisions of Section 7 of the Mineral Leasing Act of 1920 or such other rates of royalty and rental as the Secretary may determine.

Additionally, although more than 50 percent of all leases have been offered for competitive bid, 72 percent of these "competitive" sales had less than two bidders, not really reflective of a competitive environment. Since the bid is related to the number of bidders, those tracts which attract only one bid are not likely to result in payment of a fair return to the public.

... [T]he minimum royalty and rental established in the law (royalty—5 cents/ton; rental—$.25/acre–1st yr., $.50/acre for the 2nd to 5th years and $1.00/acre thereafter) also contributes to the lack of fair return to the public. According to the Council on Economic Priorities, the Federal government has collected a total of $23,373,920 in royalty payments in the last 54 years, from a total production of 189,099,653 tons of coal. This total represents an average royalty of 12.5 cents per ton. The study points out that although royalty rates have increased 75 percent in the last half century, the price of a ton of coal has more than doubled. Thus, the actual royalty being paid is a smaller percentage of the value of the coal now than it was in 1920. * * *

4. *Environmental Protection, Planning, and Public Participation*: Heretofore, there has been very little control exercised by the Department of the Interior over the effects that a mining operation on the Federal lands has upon the environment. * * *

5. *Social and Economic Impacts*: The current restrictions on the manner in which monies return to the States from the sale of Federal leases within their

borders are onerous. When an area is newly opened to large scale mining, local governmental entities must assume the responsibility of providing public services needed for new communities, including schools, roads, hospitals, sewers, police protection, and other public facilities, as well as adequate local planning for the development of the community. Since Section 35 of the Mineral Leasing Act of 1920 currently provides that the monies returned to the states be available only for schools and roads, it is difficult for affected areas to meet the needs of their new inhabitants. * * *

6. *Need For Information*: In light of the projections for rapid growth in coal production, especially with respect to disposition of Federal coal in the West, and the fact that the overwhelming majority of domestic coal reserves are recoverable through deep mining only, it is necessary for Congress to obtain an independent assessment of the existing situation with respect to outstanding Federal coal leases and the feasibility of the use of deep mining technology in these areas. * * *

7. *Maximum Economy Recovery of the Resource*: A primary concern of any future coal leasing program on public lands should be the maximum economic recovery of the available coal resources. At present, easily reached surface deposits which yield the highest profits are often the only resources developed in an area that contains vast amounts of coal not so easily or profitably extracted. This results in the waste of valuable resources, and the creation of severe environmental impacts. * * *

H.R. REP. No. 94–681 (1975).

The Federal Coal Leasing Amendments Act of 1975 addressed each of these issues. Speculation is addressed by requiring the termination of leases that are not producing coal in commercial quantities within 10 years. Moreover, pre-existing but undeveloped federal coal lessees may not obtain new federal mineral leases of any kind until they surrender their coal leases. The law addresses concentration of holdings by setting state and national limits on leased acreage by a single company, and by requiring the government to offer at least half of all leased lands under a system of deferred bonus bidding, thereby minimizing up-front capital outlays.

The law assures a fair return to the public by promoting more competitive bidding and by increasing royalties to a minimum of 12.5% of the value of the coal. Environmental protection is promoted by prohibiting leasing until the affected lands are included in a comprehensive land use plan. In addition, a public hearing—separate from any hearing on the land use plan—must be held in the affected area. Social and economic impacts are addressed by increasing the state's share of royalties and bonus bids from 37.5% to 50%. The additional 12.5% is not earmarked for schools and roads, thus providing states with greater flexibility to spend money where it is most needed.

Gaps in information are addressed through a required study of existing leases, and by requiring a comprehensive exploration program to better ascertain the extent of federal reserves. Finally, the law encourages the maximum recovery of coal by allowing federal leases to be consolidated with other federal, state, tribal, and private leases to form a "logical mining unit."

The basic structure for the current federal coal leasing program was set out in regulations promulgated in 1979. 43 C.F.R. part 3400 (2008).

IV. MINERAL SALES AND LEASES ON PUBLIC LANDS

Under the current federal coal management program, coal leasing is supposed to be carried out in three phases: (1) land use planning; (2) regional sale activity planning; and (3) lease sale activities. 43 C.F.R. subpart 3420 (2008).

Land use planning is intended to ensure that coal leasing passes through four screening procedures. *Id.* at 3420.1–4(e) (2008). The first screen requires the agency to determine the development potential of the area. This analysis includes estimates of the quality and amount of economically recoverable federal coal reserves. Next, the agency considers whether lands may be unsuitable for mining. Lands deemed unsuitable are dropped from consideration for leasing. Multiple use trade-offs are then assessed to determine whether other important uses may be incompatible with mining. Potential conflicts may lead to further removing areas from consideration for leasing. Finally, the agency consults with surface owners to obtain the necessary consent for mining as required by the Surface Mining Control and Reclamation Act. *Id.*

Once planning is completed and a final land use plan (Resource Management Plan) is adopted, regional coal lease activity planning begins. This process is guided by the Regional Coal Team (RCT), which is a federal-state advisory group chartered under the provisions of the Federal Advisory Committee Act.* The RCT reviews the land use plan and a long-range market analysis in an attempt to determine whether to proceed with leasing. If the RCT decides to move forward with leasing, a panel of science advisors and an internal BLM review council are appointed to assist the RCT in tract delineation, site specific analysis, and EIS preparation. A call for expressions of interest in leasing is also published in the Federal Register. Responses may be used by the RCT in delineating potential coal lease tracts. The RCT then recommends a regional leasing level to the Secretary and identifies, ranks, analyzes, and selects tracts for study in the regional coal lease sale EIS. A regional lease sale decision is then published in the Federal Register. 43 C.F.R. §§ 3420.3–3420.5 (2008).

Finally, the lease sale is scheduled. Public comment is solicited on fair market value and appropriate mining methods to achieve the maximum economic recovery of the coal resource. A regional evaluation team then prepares its own estimate of the value of each lease tract. Following a 30–

---

* 5 U.S.C. Appendix I (Supp. III, 1973), *as amended*, 5 U.S.C. Appendix I (Supp. I, 1975). The RCT role, however, appears to go beyond providing the BLM with advice. The Charter of the Powder River Regional Coal Team, for example, provides that "[t]he team's recommendations on regional leasing levels, tracts to be offered, and sales scheduled, *shall be accepted*, except in the case of an overriding national interest, or in the case that the advice of the Governor(s) is accepted pursuant to 43 C.F.R. § 3420.4–3(c)." Charter, 6.b(ii) (emphasis added). The Charter also provides, however, that "[o]peration and administration of the team will be in accordance with the Federal Advisory Committee Act of 1972 (FACA). 5 U.S.C. Appendix (1982). . . . " Charter, 13.e. Likewise, BLM regulations provide that with certain exception, Regional Coal Team recommendations on leasing levels and on regional lease sales "shall be accepted" by the Secretary. 43 C.F.R. § 3400.4(d) (2006). The FACA states clearly that "the function of advisory committees should be *advisory only*, and that all matters under their consideration should be determined in accordance with law, by the official, agency, or officer involved" (emphasis added). It thus appears that the RCT Charter, as well as the BLM regulations, violate the FACA.

day period of public notice, the lease sale is offered by means of sealed bids. A post-sale analysis of the bids is then made recommending acceptance of the high bids. Only high bids representing fair market value may be accepted. A successful bidder must also endure an antitrust review by the Department of Justice. 43 C.F.R. subpart 3422 (2008).

There are no exceptions to the phase one land use planning, and phase three, lease sale activity requirements. These apply to all coal leases. Regional sale activity planning (phase two), however, need not be carried out in two situations. First, emergency leasing is allowed within designated federal coal production regions in accordance with the standards at 43 C.F.R. § 3425.1–4 (2007). Such leases are issued following an application and are intended for those limited circumstances where federal coal might be bypassed or where the coal is needed to maintain production levels in the near term. Second, regional sale activity planning need not be carried out for leases "outside coal production regions." 43 C.F.R. § 3425.1–5 (2008).

The term "coal production region" is not defined, but the federal government has acquiesced in the view that an area is not a coal production region unless there exists substantial interest in new leasing. On this basis, the Powder River RCT has decided that the Powder River Basin, the largest coal production region in the world, is *not* a coal production region. In recent years, more than 3 billion tons of federal coal have been leased in the Powder River Basin by the BLM on tracts designed by existing coal operators and without regional sale activity planning. In only rare cases has the BLM received more than one bid for the tract. In one case, for example, the existing lessee designed an extension tract that was big enough to elicit a competing bid. The existing coal lessee bid $124 million; the competing (and winning) bidder offered $158 million, resulting in an additional $34 million for state and federal treasuries. If all of the lease sales were designed by the BLM to maximize revenues, rather than by the existing lessees to avoid competition, the federal and state governments which share equally the bonus bids received for the sale of a coal lease, would almost certainly have realized substantial additional revenues. *See* Mark Squillace, *Bring Back the Market for Federal Coal Leases*, CASPER STAR TRIBUNE, Nov. 8, 1998, at E.1.

QUESTIONS AND DISCUSSION

1. FCLAA amended Section 2 of the Mineral Leasing Act. As amended, this section provides that—

> The Secretary shall not issue a lease or leases under the terms of this Act to any person, association, corporation, or any subsidiary, affiliate, or persons controlled by or under common control with such person, association, or corporation, where any such entity holds a lease or leases issued by the United States to coal deposits and has held such lease or leases issued for a period of ten years when such entity is not, except as provided for in section 7(b) of this Act, producing coal from the lease deposits in commercial quantities. In computing the ten-year period referred to in the preceding sentence, periods of time prior to the date of enactment shall not be counted.

30 U.S.C. § 201(a)(2)(A) (2003).

In *Conoco, Inc. v. Hodel*, 626 F. Supp. 287 (D. Del. 1986), Conoco held various pre-FCLAA coal leases through a subsidiary, Consolidated Coal. The leases were not producing any coal, but contained an estimated 1.3 billion tons of recoverable coal. Conoco sought a declaratory judgment that § 2 applied only to coal leases. The federal government had published guidelines finding that the provision applied to all leases. 50 Fed. Reg. 35125 (1985). Under Conoco's interpretation, it would be precluded from acquiring any further coal lease unless it either relinquished its existing lease or began producing coal in commercial quantities on these leases. It would not, however, be precluded from acquiring oil and gas, and other noncoal leases. This was critical for Conoco, which claimed to add about 10,000 oil and gas leases, totalling between 48,000 and 365,000 acres each year. How should the court rule?

2. In construing the language of a statute, courts typically employ the standard established by the Supreme Court in *Chevron USA v. Natural Resources Defense Council, Inc.*, 467 U.S. 837 (1984). The *Chevron* standard was previously discussed in Chapter 3, *supra*, at 228. The *Conoco* court never mentions *Chevron* or its counterpart, *Skidmore v. Swift Co.,* 323 U.S. 134 (1944). How should the issue have been analyzed under *Chevron* and *Skidmore*?

3. The restrictions imposed by Section 2 of the Mineral Leasing Act, 30 U.S.C. § 201(a)(2)(A), have been controversial since their adoption in 1976 because, as *Conoco* suggests, they constrain large energy companies from engaging in speculative investments in coal. Repeated efforts to repeal them have thus far failed, though the effective date of the provision was pushed back from August 4, 1986, to December 31, 1986. Pub. L. No. 99–190, § 101(d), 99 Stat. 1266.

[handwritten margin note: Controversial Section 2 of MLA]

4. Despite the extensive changes in the coal leasing program ushered in by the enactment of FCLAA in 1976, the leasing program remained controversial, and many years passed before federal coal leasing resumed. In 1982, Interior finally offered for lease several tracts of land in the Powder River Basin in Montana and Wyoming. Those leases were the subject of much controversy due to charges that the leases were sold well below market value. In *National Wildlife Federation v. Burford*, 677 F. Supp. 1445 (D. Mont. 1985), the court sustained the Secretary's decision to sell the leases despite substantial evidence that the government received much less than the property was worth. Indeed, the Linowes Commission, which was established by Secretary Watt to investigate this sale and the Department's coal leasing policy in general, actually supported the plaintiff's position in that case. *See Fair Market Value Policy for Federal Coal Leasing* (Linowes Comm'n, Dept. of the Interior, Feb. 1984). (Readers may recall that it was Secretary Watt's comments about the makeup of this commission that led to his resignation.) A challenge to significant revisions to the 1979 programmatic regulations adopted by the Department of the Interior in 1982 was brought by the Natural Resources Defense Council (NRDC) with mixed results. *Natural Resources Defense Council v. Jamison*, 815 F. Supp. 454 (D.D.C. 1992). As noted previously, the current rules are available at 30 C.F.R. part 3400 (2008).

5. As noted above, prior to FCLAA the federal government issued prospecting permits that allowed parties to explore federal lands for coal deposits that were not previously known. A party who found commercial quantities of coal was entitled to obtain a "preference right" coal lease. In *Natural Resources Defense Council v. Berklund*, 609 F.2d 553 (D.C. Cir. 1979) the Court of Appeals for the D.C. Circuit rejected NRDC's contention that the Interior Department had the authority under either its general discretionary powers or under the National Environmental Policy Act to deny a coal lease application which otherwise met the requirements of the law. To what extent might Interior reject a preference right lease application on the ground that applicable environmental requirements rendered the coal resource noncommercial? *See* 43 C.F.R. § 3430.1–2 (2008), which defines "commercial quantities" consistent with the prudent person/marketability tests developed under the General Mining Law. Recall that under the Mining Law, the cost of reclamation had to be considered in deciding whether a discovery had been made. *See United States v. Kosanke Sand Corp.*, 80 I.D. 538, 546 (1973); *United States v. Pittsburgh Pacific*, 84 I.D. 282, 295 (1977); JOHN LESHY, THE MINING LAW: A STUDY IN PERPETUAL MOTION 208–209 (1987).

6. Because of the Interior Department's concern that some tracts of land eligible for preference right leases may not be the most appropriate places to encourage mining activity, the Secretary adopted regulations providing for exchanges of land subject to preference right leases with other coal lands. 43 C.F.R. subpart 3435 (2008). An exchange proposal may be initiated by the Secretary, a person holding a valid coal lease, or a person with a valid preference right lease application. *Id.* at § 3435.2(a).

7. While Congress was debating the FCLAA, they were also considering legislation to regulate the environmental impacts of all coal mining operations—not just those taking place on federal lands. This legislation was eventually enacted as the Surface Mining Control and Reclamation of 1977 (SMCRA). 30 U.S.C. § 1201–1328. Similar legislation had been vetoed by President Ford in 1975, and this led some members of Congress to support inclusion of the substantive provisions of the environmental legislation in the FCLAA. Most members, however, were apparently satisfied that environmental legislation would eventually be enacted. As a result, FCLAA only requires that the coal lessees obtain an approved mining plan before commencing mining operations. This mining plan must include an "operation and reclamation plan," 30 U.S.C. § 207(c), but that plan, which the BLM describes as a "resource recovery and protection plan," is defined to exclude environmental protection requirements. *See* 43 C.F.R. § 3480.0–5(a)(34) (2008). This does not mean that coal mining on federal lands can be carried out without meeting environmental protection requirements. This is required by SMCRA. But because SMCRA allows states to approve such requirements on federal leased land pursuant to cooperative agreements, the federal government does not generally perform NEPA analyses or otherwise approve mining and reclamation standards on federal lands. *See National Wildlife Fed'n v. Hodel*, 839 F.2d 694, 766–67 (D.C. Cir. 1988).

8. As the House Report notes, one of FCLAA's key purposes was to ensure the maximum economic recovery of coal. This goal is achieved primarily through the provision for consolidating coal lands into logical mining units (LMU). The act defines a "logical mining unit" as

> an area of land in which the coal resources can be developed in an efficient, economical, and orderly manner as a unit with due regard to conservation of coal reserves and other resources. A logical mining unit may consist of one or more Federal leaseholds, and may include intervening or adjacent lands in which the United States does not own the coal resources, but all the lands in a logical mining unit must be under the effective control of a single operator, be able to be developed and operated as a single operation and be contiguous.

30 U.S.C. § 202(a)(1) (2003). Consolidation of leases into an LMU allows a coal operator to meet diligent development requirements on federal leases, even where only nonfederal coal within the LMU is being mined.

---

3. LEASING OF MINERALS OTHER THAN COAL

The Mineral Leasing Act of 1920, 30 U.S.C. § 181 *et seq.*, sets separate standards for leasing federal deposits of phosphates, oil shale, sodium, sulfur, and potash. The BLM has issued rules that establish a single system for all solid minerals other than coal and oil shale. 43 C.F.R. part 3500 (2008). Under these rules, minerals that are known to exist in commercial quantities are subject to a competitive leasing system. A competitive lease sale can be initiated by an interested party or by the BLM. 43 C.F.R. § 3508.12 (2008). The BLM, however, has no obligation to grant a request for a lease sale or to lease lands for development. *Cf. Udall v. Tallman*, 380 U.S. 1 (1965); *McLennan v. Wilbur*, 283 U.S. 414 (1931). For minerals not known to exist, the BLM may issue a prospecting permit to an applicant interested in exploring for minerals. 43 C.F.R. § 3505.10 (2008). Prospecting permits are issued for an initial term of two years and are subject to certain acreage limitations set out in the rules. 43 C.F.R. §§ 3505.15; 3505.60 (2008). If the applicant finds commercial quantities of these minerals, the applicant has a "preference right" to receive a lease for those minerals.

The Mineral Leasing Act allows the BLM to authorize the exploration, development, and use of oil shale resources on the public lands. 30 U.S.C. § 241(a). Despite periodic interest in oil shale leasing, especially during the energy crisis of the 1970's, the program languished until the passage of the Energy Policy Act of 2005 (EPAct). Section 369 of EPAct authorized the Secretary to make lands available for leasing, first for research and development purposes, and subsequently for commercial leasing. 42 U.S.C. § 15927. Five companies were awarded six research and development leases (five in Colorado and one in Utah) in July, 2007. On November 18, 2008, shortly after the election of Barack Obama, the Bush Administration issued final regulations establishing a commercial oil shale leasing program, 73 Fed. Reg. 69414 (2008), but the initial signals from the Obama Administration are that it intends to move more slowly with the commercial leasing program.

A separate law, the Mineral Leasing Act for Acquired Lands, 30 U.S.C. § 351–360. (2006), allows leasing of hard rock and other minerals on public lands that were acquired by the federal government and thus not part of the public domain. Neither the General Mining Law nor the Mineral Leasing Act applies directly to these lands, although the Acquired Lands Act incorporates the provisions of the Mineral Leasing Act by reference. *Id.* at § 352.

Leasing of geothermal resources on public lands is provided for under the Geothermal Steam Act of 1970, 30 U.S.C. §§ 1001–1028., and the regulations at 43 C.F.R. part 3200 (2008).

D.   MULTIPLE MINERAL DEVELOPMENT

Following passage of the Mineral Leasing Act in 1920, conflicts began to arise between mining claimants and mineral lessees on the same lands. Suppose for example, that a claimant wanted to obtain a patent for land with a pre-existing lease. What happens to the lease? The Department of the Interior initially resolved the conflict by treating the two systems of mineral acquisition on the public lands as mutually exclusive. Thus, once a mineral lease was issued the land was withdrawn from entry under the mining law. *Joseph E. McClory,* 50 L.D. 623 (1924). In *United States v. U.S. Borax Co.,* 58 I.D. 426 (1943), the Department held that no mining claim could be made where the conditions at the time of the location were such as to engender a reasonable belief that the lands contained leasing act minerals in such quantity and quality as would render their extraction profitable. *Id.* at 433. Similarly, once a valid mining claim was located, the land covered by the claim could not be leased. *A.V. Toolson,* 66 I.D. 48 (1959); *L.N. Hagood,* 65 I.D. 405 (1958).

In 1954, in an effort to minimize these conflicts, Congress passed the Multiple Mineral Development Act. 30 U.S.C. §§ 521–531. The Act has several key components. Foremost is the provision for coexistence of mining claims with mineral leases. 30 U.S.C. § 526. Under this provision, mining claims and mineral leases obtained after the passage of the Act (August 13, 1954) must be conducted "so far as reasonably practical" in a manner compatible with multiple development. *Id.* § 526(a). Furthermore, all claims located after August 13, 1954 (and certain claims located between July 31, 1939 and February 10, 1954, as described below) are subject to a reservation in the United States of all Mineral Leasing Act minerals within the bounds of the claim. *Id.* § 524. A patent for any such claim must reserve all leasable minerals to the United States if the lands are known to be valuable for such minerals or are covered by a lease for such minerals.

The Act also validates claims that were located between July 31, 1939 and February 10, 1954, which at the time of their location would otherwise have been invalid because they were located on lands that were subject to a pre-existing lease. Finally, the Act establishes a procedure whereby a mineral lessee can seek a determination of the rights of a mining claimant to Leasing Act minerals located within the boundaries of a claim located before the Act became effective. 30 U.S.C. § 527. These "Section 7 proceedings" as they are sometimes called, are quite similar to the Section 5 proceedings for determining surface rights under the Surface Resources

Act, described earlier in this chapter. The principal difference is that a lessee or lease applicant rather than a federal agency initiates Section 7 proceedings.

Under Section 7, the Secretary publishes a notice at the request of an applicant, permittee, offeror, or lessee, in a local newspaper. He must also serve actual notice on known claimants on the lands in question. Persons claiming rights under claims located prior to August 13, 1954 must file a verified statement or be deemed to have relinquished all rights to the leasing act minerals located within the claim boundaries. If one or more verified statements is filed, a hearing is held to ascertain whether the claimant held a valid mining claim at the time of the passage of the Act and continuously thereafter. For a critical look at Section 7 proceedings and suggestions for alternative means of protecting a lessee's interests, see William S. Livingston, *Oil and Gas Title Examinations: What to Do About Mining Claims*, 15 ROCKY MTN. MIN. L. INST. 263 (1969).

QUESTIONS AND DISCUSSION

1. Suppose that leasable and locatable minerals are so commingled that one cannot be extracted without extracting or disturbing the other. Should a prior mining claimant on a claim located after the enactment of the Multiple Mineral Development Act be entitled to extract the leasable minerals? *See* M–36764.4357, *Mining Claims—Rights to Leasable Minerals*, 75 I.D. 397, 403 (1968) (concluding that mining claims convey no rights to leasable minerals nor even to locatable minerals that cannot be minted without extracting or disturbing the leasable minerals). *See also* 30 U.S.C. §§ 541–541i.

2. A conflict can also arise between leasable minerals. Suppose for example that a coal deposit contains recoverable quantities of methane (natural gas). A federal coal lease does not appear to allow a coal lessee to recover the methane that is embedded in the coal, even though venting of methane at underground coal mines to protect mine workers is commonplace. See *Amoco Production Company v. Southern Ute Indian Tribe*, 526 U.S. 865 (1999) *supra* at 1069. Suppose the methane could be recovered economically rather than vented. In order to recover the methane, it would have to be leased through a competitive bidding process and a party other than the coal lessee might very well win the methane lease. What conflicts might you anticipate between the coal lessee and the methane gas lessee? Is there a better way to promote the economic recovery of both resources? Should congress amend the law to require it? In answering this question, consider that methane is a greenhouse gas that is about 21 times more potent than CO_2. How should this figure into your analysis. Consider also that a single coal mine in Colorado vents enough gas to heat at least 34,000 homes annually and has a value of $21 million per year. *See Passing Gas: Western States Struggle to Capture Methane Emissions from Coal Mines,* High Country News, (Nov. 10, 2008), *available at,* http://www.hcn.org/issues/40.20/passing-gas

V.   ENVIRONMENTAL REGULATION OF MINING

This section has two parts. The first addresses the tortured path toward environmental regulation of hard rock mining on public lands. The second part briefly reviews environmental regulation of coal mining under the Surface Mining Control and Reclamation Act of 1977 (SMCRA), 30 U.S.C. § 1201–1328 (2006). As described below, SMCRA reflects Congress' recognition that coal mining raises unique challenges for environmental protection.

A.   ENVIRONMENTAL REGULATION OF HARD ROCK MINING

1.   FEDERAL REGULATION OF MINING TO PROTECT THE ENVIRONMENT

Historically, "hard rock" mining, including operations that occurred on federal lands, was subject to very little in the way of environmental regulation. The General Mining Law, passed as it was in 1872, did not specifically concern itself with the environment, and the Forest Service and BLM were reluctant to interfere with what had been historically perceived as the miners' right to mine. What little regulation existed was a matter of state laws and regulations, which varied considerably in their content and implementation. Many states, for example, exempt small mining operations from regulation, despite the fact that these small operations often cause significant environmental problems. *See, e.g.,* WYO. STAT. § 35–11–401(e)(vi). Moreover, states often lacked the financial resources or the commitment for strong inspection and enforcement programs or significant reclamation bonding requirements. The result of this laissez-faire approach to mining has been significant environmental harm. Much of that harm has come from the thousands of abandoned mines that litter the Western states. The Mineral Policy Center now known as Earthworks, a mining reform advocacy group, estimates that there are more than half a million abandoned mines sites throughout the United States.

The rise of the environmental movement in the 1970s put increasing pressure on the principal federal land management agencies with responsibility for mining—the Bureau of Land Management and the United States Forest Service—to adopt federal standards to protect the environment. The following excerpt briefly recounts the story.

> As late as the 1960s and early 1970s, most hardrock mining went entirely unregulated. Forest Service authority arguably could be found in its 1897 Organic Act, which does not mention regulation of mining but gives the agency broad authority to "regulate ... occupancy and use" within the forests. In addition, the General Mining Law itself provides that mining must proceed "under regulations prescribed by law," although the potential authority had never been exercised. Any regulation of mining by the Forest Service, however, was clouded by the agency's location in the Department of Agriculture and by the statutory designation of the BLM, in the Department of the Interior, as the administering agency for mining laws on all public lands, including the national forests. This did not deter conservationists from pressing the Forest Service to

take action. More fundamentally, the nation's oldest federal land agency had come to view the unparalleled autonomy of hardrock miners as an impediment to orderly land management and was ready to act.

In 1970, the Forest Service began working on mining regulations. The draft proposal—which, with a bow to politics and the Interior Department's authority to regulate mining, was couched in terms of regulating "the surface of [the] National Forest System lands," not minerals—was released for public comment in December 1973. Predictably, industry came up in arms, but the final regulations, effective in September 1974, were largely unchanged from the initial proposal. In general, the regulations require a miner to give notice to the agency before beginning any mining operation that could disturb surface resources. If the disturbance is "significant," the miner must file a "plan of operations," which must receive agency approval; while approval is pending, work may continue under agency guidelines "to minimize adverse environmental impacts." Reclamation is required after mining is completed. There are no provisions for fines or shutdown of mines in noncompliance. [eds. The Forest Service's regulations are at 36 C.F.R. subpart 228 (2008).]

The Forest Service's action in this historically sensitive area, relatively modest though it may be, took institutional courage. Those regulations, however, apply only in the national forests, less than a third of the public lands open for mining. The Bureau of Land Management, which is responsible for mining on the more than 270 million acres under its jurisdiction, took seven years longer to act, expressing concern about its limited discretion under the Hardrock Act and about any provisions that might be unduly burdensome on small miners. The resulting BLM regulations, adopted in 1981, are even more lax than the Forest Service program. Most notably, mining operations disturbing fewer than 5 acres are effectively outside the regulations—operators need only give notice to the BLM that they are going ahead with mining. These "notice" mines comprise 80 percent of all mines on BLM lands, and many of them hardly qualify as small; with a bulldozer operation, you can rearrange a very large amount of earth on 5 acres. For mines larger than 5 acres, operators must file a plan of operations, but the requirements for posting of bonds and for reclamation of mined-over land are vague. As with the Forest Service regulations, there are no provisions for fines or penalties for shutdown of noncomplying operations.

Charles F. Wilkinson, Crossing the Next Meridian: Land, Water, and the Future of the American West 57–58 (1992).

One of the reasons that the BLM was slower to act was that, until FLPMA was passed in 1976, it lacked clear authority. The General Mining Law authorized the BLM to regulate mining locations but the agency was reluctant to construe the law to encompass the authority to regulate environmental problems associated with mining. FLPMA clearly gave the BLM a stronger hook. In particular, Section 302(b) of FLPMA provides that "[i]n managing the public lands the Secretary shall, by regulation or otherwise, take any action necessary to prevent unnecessary or undue degradation." 43 U.S.C. § 1732(b). The BLM relied on this "unnecessary and undue degradation" standard to issue its environmental regulations for mining. The regulations are found at 43 C.F.R. subpart 3809 (2008) and are commonly referred to as the "3809 rules."

The 3809 rules, as well as those of the Forest Service, were a significant move forward in environmental protection. Nonetheless, the environmental community criticized the rules from their inception on the grounds that they failed to establish sufficiently stringent environmental standards and because they required very little in the way of reclamation bonding. Although reclamation bonds have been authorized for many years, in many cases the BLM failed to require bonds, and in other cases required bonds that were woefully inadequate. *See Interior Should Insure Against Abuses From Hardrock Mining,* GAO Report to the Secretary of the Interior, March, 1986 (GAO/RCED—86–48).

Part of the BLM's response to the criticism that the original 3809 rules were not sufficiently rigorous was that its authority under FLPMA was limited; FLPMA, argued the BLM, allowed the agency to stop "unnecessary or undue degradation" but not degradation that is a necessary by-product of the mining process. When the Clinton administration came to office in 1993, one of the items high on its environmental agenda was mining law reform. When efforts at legislative reform proved unavailing, the administration turned to a regulatory approach, one facet of which was revision of the 3809 regulations. For an extended discussion of the background to the original and revised 3809 rules, see Patrick Garver and Mark Squillace, *Mining Law Reform, Administrative Style,* 45 ROCKY MTN. MIN. L. INST. 14–1 (1999).

In November 2000, on the last day regulations could be issued during the Clinton administration and still become effective before the President left office, the Clinton administration issued revised "3809 rules." Among other things, the new rules required a detailed plan of operations for all mining activities beyond "casual use," and tightened many of requirements for operation plans and for environmental performance at mining operations. 43 C.F.R. §§ 3809.401, 428 (2001). The new regulations also required the BLM to inspect at least four times each year operations that use cyanide or other leachates that pose a threat of acid mine drainage and authorized the BLM to issue noncompliance orders and administrative civil penalties. 43 C.F.R. §§ 3809.600, 601, 702 (2001). In addition, the rules strengthened bonding requirements, requiring that bonds cover the full cost of reclamation "if the BLM were to contract with a third party to reclaim" the mine site. 43 C.F.R. § 3809.552(a) (2003). *See generally* Andrew P. Morriss et al., *Between a Hard Rock and a Hard Place: Politics, Midnight Regulations and Mining,* 55 ADMIN. L. REV. 551 (2003).

Several provisions of the new regulations proved particularly controversial with the mining industry. Foremost among these was the new definition of "unnecessary and undue degradation" to include "conditions, activities, or practices that ... result in substantial irreparable harm to significant scientific, cultural, or environmental resource values of the public lands that cannot effectively be mitigated." 43 C.F.R. § 3809.5. This new definition for the first time allowed the BLM to prohibit a mining operation that was otherwise in compliance with the relevant environmental laws if the BLM concluded that the operation would harm cultural or environmental resources. The impact of this new standard is explored further below in the Glamis Imperial Mine Problem Exercise (*infra* page 1183). The new 3809 regulations also provided for joint and several liability on mining claimants and operators, and included a series of environmental performance standards, such as a requirement that the BLM evaluate—

[handwritten margin note: Clinton-era 3809 regs, replaced by Bush in 2001]

over and above state and federal water quality standards—whether an operator has taken appropriate action to minimize water quality impacts from the mining operation. The regulations also obligated mining operators to "conduct operations affecting ground water, such as dewatering, pumping and injecting, to minimize impacts on surface and other natural resources, such as wetlands, riparian areas, aquatic habitat, and other features that are dependent on ground water." 43 C.F.R. § 3809.420(b)(2)(C).

Shortly after the Bush administration took office, the Department of the Interior suspended the Clinton administration's new 3809 rules. 66 Fed. Reg. 16,162 (2001). In October 2001, Interior published new rules that pulled back substantially from the year 2000 rules. 66 Fed. Reg. 54,834 (2001). A critic of the Clinton-era rules summarized the reversal in the following excerpt:

Between a Hard Rock and a Hard Place: Politics, Midnight Regulations and Mining Andrew P. Morriss et al., 55 Admin. L. Rev. 551, 592–94 (2003)

Briefly, of the thirty-nine categories of rule changes considered significant enough to warrant inclusion in the BLM's summary of changes made by the 2001 regulations, eighteen substantially returned to the 1980 regulations' provisions, eighteen retained the midnight regulations' provisions, and three (UUD [unnecessary and undue degradation] definition, penalty provisions, and environmental performance standards) contained unique features or significant alterations.

In short, the 2001 regulations made five major changes to the midnight 3809 regulations:

- restoration of the 1980 regulations' definition of operator [Eds. The original rules defined "operator" to mean "any person conducting or proposing to conduct mining operations." The Clinton Administration revised these rules to define an operator to encompass "persons who manage or direct operations and corporate parents and affiliates who materially participate in the operations." The Bush Administration restored the old definition, citing concerns that the Clinton rule might "authorize the BLM to routinely breach the corporate veil that generally is established under state corporate laws to protect such entities." 66 Fed. Reg. at 54837.];

- revision of the definition of "unnecessary or undue degradation" by removing the "substantial irreparable harm" clause of the definition, which had been the subject of challenges in several of the lawsuits over the midnight 3809 regulations because it was not contained in the proposed rule that led to those regulations;

- revision of the liability provisions to remove joint and several liability for environmental damage and provide for liability only for obligations that accrue while a claimant or operator holds its interest, essentially returning the rule to the pre-midnight regulation practice;

- removal of many of the specific environmental and performance standards in the midnight 3809 regulations, retaining only the sections codifying "longstanding BLM policies on acid mine drainage and the use of cyanide" and the general standard, which "form[s] a foundation upon

which operators should base their plans of operations" and about which
BLM had not received "widespread concern;" and

- elimination of the administrative civil penalty provisions, for which BLM
  now argued the legal authority was unclear.

How do you think the changes made by the Bush administration will
impact mining regulation? What is the likelihood that they will impel states
to take a more active role in environmental regulation of mining?

The Mineral Policy Center challenged various aspects of the Bush
Administration rules including the removal of the "substantial irreparable
harm" clause from the "unnecessary and undue degradation standard." In
Mineral Policy Center v. Norton, 292 F. Supp. 2d 30 (D.D.C. 2003), the
federal district court for the District of Columbia expressly rejected a legal
opinion by Interior Solicitor William Myers that determined that the BLM
could *not* disapprove of an otherwise lawful mining operation because it
would cause "substantial irreparable harm" to public lands. The court
found that

> the Solicitor misconstrued the clear mandate of FLPMA [because] FLPMA
> vests the Secretary of the Interior with the authority—and indeed the obli-
> gation—to disapprove of an otherwise permissible mining operation because the
> operation, though necessary for mining, would unduly harm or degrade public
> land.

Id. at 34–35. The court nonetheless upheld the Bush Administration rules
on the basis of assurances by Interior that it would protect public lands
from unnecessary and undue degradation "by exercising case-by-case discretion." *Id.* at 42. How difficult do you think it will be to challenge an
Interior decision that allows mining to go forward notwithstanding significant harm to public lands? Do the states retain any authority to protect
public lands if the federal government fails to do so? Consider these
questions as you read the following materials.

―――――――

2. STATE REGULATION OF MINING TO PROTECT THE ENVIRONMENT

As described previously in this chapter, mining claimants must generally comply with all procedural requirements of state laws for locating and
maintaining mining claims to the extent they are not in conflict with
federal requirements. To what extent should this same principle extend to
environmental regulation, particularly now that the federal agencies have
set their own standards? Clearly, states cannot adopt requirements that are
inconsistent with federal law, including federal regulations. But the decision of the federal government to back off from a strict regulatory program
has left the door open for states. Moreover, the BLM rules specifically
provide for state administration of the BLM regulatory program. 43 C.F.R.
§§ 3809.200 (2008). But what if the state rules go beyond federal law even
to the point of possibly making a mining operation technically or economically infeasible? As the following case illustrates, opinions vary considerably
on this question.

CALIFORNIA COASTAL COMMISSION V. GRANITE ROCK COMPANY,
480 U.S. 572 (1987)

JUSTICE O'CONNOR delivered the opinion of the Court.

This case presents the question whether Forest Service regulations, federal land use statutes and regulations, or the Coastal Zone Management Act (CZMA), 16 U.S.C. § 1451 *et seq.*, pre-empt the California Coastal Commission's imposition of a permit requirement on operation of an unpatented mining claim in a national forest.

I

Granite Rock Company is a privately owned firm that mines chemical and pharmaceutical grade white limestone. Under the Mining Act of 1872, [30 U.S.C. § 22 *et seq.*], a private citizen may enter federal lands to explore for mineral deposits. If a person locates a valuable mineral deposit on federal land, and perfects the claim by properly staking it and complying with other statutory requirements, the claimant "shall have the exclusive right of possession and enjoyment of all the surface included within the lines of their locations," 30 U.S.C. § 26, although the United States retains title to the land. The holder of a perfected mining claim may secure a patent to the land by complying with the requirements of the Mining Act and regulations promulgated thereunder, *see* 43 C.F.R. § 3861.1 *et seq.* (1986), and, upon issuance of the patent, legal title to the land passes to the patent-holder. Granite Rock holds unpatented mining claims on federally owned lands on and around Mount Pico Blanco in the Big Sur region of Los Padres National Forest.

From 1959 to 1980, Granite Rock removed small samples of limestone from this area for mineral analysis. In 1980, in accordance with federal regulations, *see* 36 C.F.R. § 228.1 *et seq.* (1986), Granite Rock submitted to the Forest Service a 5–year plan of operations for the removal of substantial amounts of limestone. The plan discussed the location and appearance of the mining operation, including the size and shape of excavations, the location of all access roads and the storage of any overburden. The Forest Service prepared an Environmental Assessment of the plan. *Id.*, at 38–53. The Assessment recommended modifications of the plan, and the responsible Forest Service Acting District Ranger approved the plan with the recommended modifications in 1981 shortly after Forest Service approval of the modified plan of operations, Granite Rock began to mine.

Under the California Coastal Act (CCA), Cal. Pub. Res. Code Ann. § 30000 *et seq.*, any person undertaking any development, including mining, in the State's coastal zone must secure a permit from the California Coastal Commission. Sections 30106, 30600. According to the CCA, the Coastal Commission exercises the State's police power and constitutes the State's coastal zone management program for purposes of the federal CZMA. In 1983 the Coastal Commission instructed Granite Rock to apply for a coastal development permit for any mining undertaken after the date of the Commission's letter.

Granite Rock immediately filed an action in the United States District Court for the Northern District of California seeking to enjoin officials of the Coastal Commission from compelling Granite Rock to comply with the Coastal Commission permit requirement and for declaratory relief under 28 U.S.C. § 2201. Granite Rock alleged that the Coastal Commission permit requirement was pre-empted by Forest Service regulations, by the Mining Act of 1872, and by the CZMA. Both sides agreed that there were no material facts in dispute. The District Court dismissed Granite Rock's motion for summary judgment and dismissed the action. 590 F. Supp. 1361 (1984). The Court of Appeals for the Ninth Circuit reversed. 768 F.2d 1077 (1985). The Court of Appeals held that the Coastal Commission permit requirement was pre-empted by the Mining Act of 1872 and Forest Service regulations. * * *

III

Granite Rock does not argue that the Coastal Commission has placed any particular conditions on the issuance of a permit that conflict with federal statutes or regulations. Indeed, the record does not disclose what conditions the Coastal Commission will place on the issuance of a permit. Rather, Granite Rock argues, as it must, given the posture of the case, that there is no possible set of conditions the Coastal Commission could place on its permit that would not conflict with federal law—that any state permit requirement is *per se* pre-empted. The only issue in this case is this purely facial challenge to the Coastal Commission permit requirement.

The Property Clause provides that "Congress shall have Power to dispose of and make all needful Rules and Regulations respecting the Territory or other Property belonging to the United States." U.S. Const., Art. IV, § 3, cl. 2. This Court has "repeatedly observed" that " '[t]he power over the public land thus entrusted to Congress is without limitations.' " *Kleppe v. New Mexico,* 426 U.S. 529, 539 (1976), *quoting United States v. San Francisco,* 310 U.S. 16, 29 (1940). Granite Rock suggests that the Property Clause not only invests unlimited power in Congress over the use of federally owned lands, but also exempts federal lands from state regulation whether or not those regulations conflict with federal law. In *Kleppe, supra,* at 543, we considered "totally unfounded" the assertion that the Secretary of Interior had even proposed such an interpretation of the Property Clause. We made clear that "the State is free to enforce its criminal and civil laws" on federal land so long as those laws do not conflict with federal law. *Ibid.* The Property Clause itself does not automatically conflict with all state regulation of federal land. Rather, as we explained in *Kleppe,*

> absent consent or cession a State undoubtedly retains jurisdiction over federal lands within its territory, but Congress equally surely retains the power *to enact legislation* respecting those lands pursuant to the Property Clause. *And when congress so acts,* the federal legislation necessarily overrides conflicting state laws under the Supremacy Clause. *Ibid.* [citations omitted] (emphasis supplied).

We agree with Granite Rock that the Property Clause gives Congress plenary power to legislate the use of the federal land on which Granite Rock holds its unpatented mining claim. The question in this case, however, is whether Congress has enacted legislation respecting this federal land that would pre-empt any requirement that Granite Rock obtain a California Coastal Commission permit. To answer this question we follow the pre-emption analysis by which the Court has been guided on numerous occasions:

> [S]tate law can be pre-empted in either of two general ways. If Congress evidences an intent to occupy a given field, any state law falling within that field is pre-empted. If Congress has not entirely displaced state regulation over the matter in question, state law is still pre-empted to the extent it actually conflicts with federal law, that is, when it is impossible to comply with both state and federal law, or where the state law stands as an

obstacle to the accomplishment of the full purposes and objectives of Congress. [citations omitted]

A

Granite Rock and the Solicitor General as amicus have made basically three arguments in support of a finding that any possible state permit requirement would be pre-empted. First, Granite Rock alleges that the Federal Government's environmental regulation of unpatented mining claims in national forests demonstrates an intent to pre-empt any state regulation. Second, Granite Rock and the Solicitor General assert that indications that state land use planning over unpatented mining claims in national forests is pre-empted should lead to the conclusion that the Coastal Commission permit requirement is pre-empted. Finally, Granite Rock and the Solicitor General assert that the CZMA, by excluding federal lands from its definition of the coastal zone, declared a legislative intent that federal lands be excluded from all state coastal zone regulation. We conclude that these federal statutes and regulations do not, either independently or in combination, justify a facial challenge to the Coastal Commission permit requirement.

* * * Congress has delegated to the Secretary of Agriculture the authority to make "rules and regulations" to "regulate [the] occupancy and use" of national forests. 16 U.S.C. § 551. Through this delegation of authority, the Department of Agriculture's Forest Service has promulgated regulations so that "use of the surface of National Forest System lands" by those such as Granite Rock, who have unpatented mining claims authorized by the Mining Act of 1872, "shall be conducted so as to minimize adverse environmental impacts on National Forest System surface resources." 36 C.F.R. § 228.1, § 228.3(d) (1986). It was pursuant to these regulations that the Forest Service approved the Plan of Operations submitted by Granite Rock. If, as Granite Rock claims, it is the federal intent that Granite Rock conduct its mining unhindered by any state environmental regulation, one would expect to find the expression of this intent in these Forest Service regulations. * * *

Upon examination, however, the Forest Service regulations that Granite Rock alleges pre-empt any state permit requirement not only are devoid of any expression of intent to pre-empt state law, but rather appear to assume that those submitting plans of operations will comply with state laws. The regulations explicitly require all operators within the National Forests to comply with state air quality standards, 36 C.F.R. § 228.8(a) (1986), state water quality standards, § 228.8(b), and state standards for the disposal and treatment of solid wastes, § 225.8(c). The regulations also provide that, pending final approval of the plan of operations, the Forest Service officer with authority to approve plans of operation "will approve such operations as may be necessary for timely compliance with the requirements of Federal and *State laws....*" § 228.5(b) (emphasis added). Finally, the final subsection of § 228.8, "[r]equirements for environmental protection," provides:

> (h) Certification or other approval issued by *State agencies* or other Federal agencies of compliance with laws and regulations relating to mining operations will be accepted as compliance with similar or parallel requirements of these regulations; (emphasis supplied).

It is impossible to divine from these regulations, which expressly contemplate coincident compliance with state law as well as with federal law, an intention to pre-empt all state regulation of unpatented mining claims in national forests. Neither Granite Rock nor the Solicitor General contends that these Forest Service regulations are inconsistent with their authorizing statutes.

Given these Forest Service regulations, it is unsurprising that the Forest Service team that prepared the Environmental Assessment of Granite Rock's plan of operation, as well as the Forest Service officer that approved the plan of operation, expected compliance with state as well as federal law. The Los Padres National Forest Environmental Assessment of the Granite Rock plan stated that "Granite Rock is responsible for obtaining any necessary permits which may be required by the California Coastal Commission." The Decision Notice and Finding of No Significant Impact issued by the Acting District Ranger accepted Granite Rock's plan of operation with modifications, stating:

> The claimant, in exercising his rights granted by the Mining Law of 1872, shall comply with the regulations of the Departments of Agriculture and Interior. The claimant is further responsible for obtaining any necessary permits required by State and/or county laws, regulations and/or ordinance.

B

The second argument proposed by Granite Rock is that federal land management statutes demonstrate a legislative intent to limit States to a purely advisory role in federal land management decisions, and that the Coastal Commission permit requirement is therefore pre-empted as an impermissible state land use regulation.

In 1976 two pieces of legislation were passed that called for the development of federal land use management plans affecting unpatented mining claims in national forests. Under the Federal Land Policy and Management Act (FLPMA), 43 U.S.C. § 1701 *et seq.*, the Department of Interior's Bureau of Land Management is responsible for managing the mineral resources on federal forest lands; under the National Forest Management Act (NFMA), 16 U.S.C. §§ 1600–1614, the Forest Service under the Secretary of Agriculture is responsible for the management of the surface impacts of mining on federal forest lands. Granite Rock, as well as the Solicitor General, point to aspects of these statutes indicating a legislative intent to limit States to an advisory role in federal land management decisions. For example, the NFMA directs the Secretary of Agriculture to "develop, maintain, and, as appropriate, revise land and resource management plans for units of the National Forest System, coordinated with the land and resource management planning processes of State and local governments and other Federal agencies." 16 U.S.C. § 1604(a). The FLPMA directs that land use plans developed by the Secretary of the Interior "shall be consistent with State and local plans to the maximum extent [the Secretary] finds consistent with Federal law," and calls for the Secretary, "to the extent he finds practical," to keep apprised of state land use plans, and to "assist in resolving, to the extent practical, inconsistencies between Federal and non-Federal Government plans." 43 U.S.C. § 1712(c)(9).

For purposes of this discussion and without deciding this issue, we may assume that the combination of the NFMA and the FLPMA pre-empt the extension of state land use plans onto unpatented mining claims in national forest lands. The Coastal Commission asserts that it will use permit conditions to impose environmental regulation. *See* Cal. Pub. Res. Code Ann. § 30233 (quality of coastal waters); § 30253(2) (erosion); § 30253(3) (air pollution); § 30240(b) (impact on environmentally sensitive habitat areas).

While the CCA gives land use as well as environmental regulatory authority to the Coastal Commission, the state statute also gives the Coastal Commission the ability to limit the requirements it will place on the permit. The CCA declares that the Coastal Commission will "provide maximum state involvement in federal activities allowable under federal law or regulations...." Cal.

Pub. Res. Code Ann. § 30004. * * * In the present case, the Coastal Commission has consistently maintained that it does not seek to prohibit mining of the unpatented claim on national forest land. *See* 768 F.2d at 1080 (The Coastal Commission also argues that the Mining Act does not preempt state environmental regulation of federal land *"unless the regulation prohibits mining altogether . . ."*) (emphasis supplied). * * *

The line between environmental regulation and land use planning will not always be bright; for example, one may hypothesize a State environmental regulation so severe that a particular land use would become commercially impracticable. However, the core activity described by each phrase is undoubtedly different. Land use planning in essence chooses particular uses for the land; environmental regulation, at its core, does not mandate particular uses of the land but requires only that, however the land is used, damage to the environment is kept within prescribed limits. * * *

Granite Rock suggests that the Coastal Commission's true purpose in enforcing a permit requirement is to prohibit Granite Rock's mining entirely. By choosing to seek injunctive and declaratory relief against the permit requirement before discovering what conditions the Coastal Commission would have placed on the permit, Granite Rock has lost the possibility of making this argument in this litigation. Granite Rock's case must stand or fall on the question whether any possible set of conditions attached to the Coastal Commission's permit requirement would be pre-empted. * * * In the present posture of this litigation, the Coastal Commission's identification of a possible set of permit conditions not pre-empted by federal law is sufficient to rebuff Granite Rock's facial challenge to the permit requirement.

C

Granite Rock's final argument involves the CZMA, 16 U.S.C. § 1451 *et seq.*, through which financial assistance is provided to States for the development of coastal zone management programs. Section 304(a) of the CZMA, 16 U.S.C. § 1453(1), defines the coastal zone of a State, and specifically excludes from the coastal zone "lands the use of which is by law subject solely to the discretion of or which is held in trust by the Federal Government, its officers or agents." The Department of Commerce, which administers the CZMA, has interpreted § 1453(1) to exclude all federally-owned land from the CZMA definition of a state's coastal zone. 15 C.F.R. § 923.33(a) (1986).

Granite Rock argues that the exclusion of "lands the use of which is by law subject solely to the discretion of or which is held in trust by the Federal Government, its officers or agents" excludes all federally-owned land from the CZMA definition of a State's coastal zone, and demonstrates a congressional intent to pre-empt any possible Coastal Commission permit requirement as applied to the mining of Granite Rock's unpatented claim in the national forest land. * * *

Absent any other expression of congressional intent regarding the pre-emptive effect of the CZMA, we would be required to decide, first, whether unpatented mining claims in national forests were meant to be excluded from the § 1453(1) definition of a State's coastal zone, and second, whether this exclusion from the coastal zone definition was intended to pre-empt state regulations that were not pre-empted by any other federal statutes or regulations. Congress has provided several clear statements of its intent regarding the pre-emptive effect of the CZMA; those statements, which indicate that Congress clearly intended the CZMA *not* to be an independent cause of pre-emption except in cases of actual conflict, end our inquiry. * * *

Because Congress specifically disclaimed any intention to pre-empt pre-existing state authority in the CZMA, we conclude that even if all federal lands are excluded from the CZMA definition of "coastal zone," the CZMA does not automatically pre-empt all state regulation of activities on federal lands.

IV * * *

The judgment of the Court of Appeals is reversed and the case is remanded for further proceedings consistent with this opinion.

JUSTICE SCALIA, with whom JUSTICE WHITE joins, dissenting.

I agree with the Court that this case is live because of continuing dispute over California's ability to assert a reclamation claim. In my view, however, the merits of this case must be decided on simpler and narrower grounds than those addressed by the Court's opinion. It seems to me ultimately irrelevant whether state environmental regulation has been pre-empted with respect to federal lands, since the exercise of state power at issue here is not environmental regulation but land use control. The Court errs in entertaining the Coastal Commission's contention "that its permit requirement is an exercise of environmental regulation," and mischaracterizes the issue when it describes it to be whether "any state permit requirement, whatever its conditions, [is] per se pre-empted by federal law." We need not speculate as to what the nature of this permit requirement was. We are not dealing with permits in the abstract, but with a specific permit, purporting to require application of particular criteria, mandated by a numbered section of a known California law. That law is plainly a land use statute, and the permit that statute requires Granite Rock to obtain is a land use control device. Its character as such is not altered by the fact that the State may now be agreeable to issuing it so long as environmental concerns are satisfied. Since, as the Court's opinion quite correctly assumes state exercise of land use authority over federal lands is pre-empted by federal law, California's permit requirement must be invalid. * * *

[A]ny lingering doubt that exercise of Coastal Act authority over federal lands is an exercise of land use authority pre-empted by federal laws is removed by the fact that that is not only the view of the federal agencies in charge of administering those laws, but also was the original view of California, which until 1978 excluded from the Coastal Act, in language exactly mirroring that of the federal lands exclusion from the CZMA, 16 U.S.C. § 1453(1), "lands the use of which is by law subject solely to the discretion of or which is held in trust by the federal government, its officers or agents." [Citation omitted.]

Any competent lawyer, faced with a demand from the California Coastal Commission that Granite Rock obtain a § 30600 coastal development permit for its Pico Blanco operations, would have responded precisely as Granite Rock's lawyers essentially did: Our use of federal land has been approved by the Federal Government, thank you, and does not require the approval of the State. * * *

I would affirm the court below on the ground that the California Coastal Act permit requirement constitutes a regulation of the use of the federal land, and is therefore pre-empted by federal law.

QUESTIONS AND DISCUSSION

1. Suppose that the Forest Service were to amend its regulations to provide specifically that an approved plan of operations was all that a mining claimant needed to conduct mining operations and that all state and local requirements were preempted. Would these rules be effective in overturning the *Granite Rock* decision? In his dissenting opinion, Justice Scalia notes that the United States filed a brief in this case supporting Granite Rock's position that the federal land use laws preempted State regulation of mining claims. Why then did the U.S. Forest Service specifically advise Granite Rock that it was "responsible for obtaining any necessary permits from the California Coastal Commission"?

2. Justice Scalia points to language from the CZMA at 16 U.S.C. § 1453(1) to bolster his argument that state land use authority was preempted by federal law. Are mining claims "lands the use of which is by law subject solely to the discretion of or which is held in trust by the federal government...."?

3. Justice Scalia rejects the majority opinion because he believes the California Coastal Act is a land use statute which conflicts directly with federal land use authority. The pertinent language from the statute provides that "any person, ... wishing to perform or undertake any development in the coastal zone, ... shall obtain a coastal development permit." CAL. PUB. RES. CODE § 30600(a). Suppose that rather than imposing regulatory standards under a coastal resource law, California adopted similar regulatory standards but under the guise of a mine regulation statute. Would Justice Scalia approve such a law?

4. Justice Scalia argues that "any competent lawyer ... would have responded precisely as Granite Rock's lawyers essentially did...." Do you agree? With the benefit of hindsight, how might you have better handled this case if you represented Granite Rock?

5. Keep in mind that 30 U.S.C. §§ 22 and 26 specifically disclaim any intent to preempt local standards and rules, except to the extent they are inconsistent with federal rules. This, of course, does not preclude a finding of preemption under another law, such as the CZMA, but it does confirm a long tradition of allowing states to exercise substantial regulatory authority over mining claims on federal lands.

6. In *LeFaivre v. Environmental Quality Council,* 735 P.2d 428 (Wyo. 1987), the plaintiff, a mining claimant, challenged a decision of the Wyoming Environmental Quality Council denying a permit to mine because the area possessed unique archaeological and geological resources. No one argued that the mining claims were invalid. Does the State have the authority to deny the permit under *Granite Rock*? (In a footnote, the Wyoming Supreme Court found that the state had such authority. 735 P.2d 428, 434 n.3.) Mr. LeFaivre appeared *pro se,* both before the hearing examiner and the Wyoming Supreme Court. How do you think this affected his case? If you had represented him, how would you have presented his case differently?

7. In 2003, California became the first jurisdiction (state or federal) to require backfilling and grading at certain hard rock metallic mining operations. Backfilling and grading has been standard practice at coal mines since the passage of the Surface Mining Control and Reclamation Act in 1977. *See* 30 U.S.C. § 1265(b) (2003). Moving the vast quantities of dirt required to backfill a mining operation is costly and because of this cost, the mining industry has long claimed that such practices are not practical, especially for hard rock mines. To be sure, hard rock mining and coal mining are very different enterprises. As the problem exercise below notes, for example, the ratio of waste rock to mineral at the Glamis Imperial mine was 13.5 million to one, although a more common ratio for a cyanide heap leach gold mine might be a million to one. At a coal strip mine, by contrast, the ratio might be better than one to one, as it is, for example, for a few of the large coal seams in the Powder River Basin of Wyoming, but it is rarely more than 20 to one. Does the difference adequately explain the reluctance of the federal and state governments to impose backfilling requirements on the hard rock mining industry?

8. Section 402 of the Clean Water Act authorizes the EPA (or the state under an approved program) to issue a permit for the discharge of a pollutant from a point source into the navigable waters of the United States. In *Beartooth Alliance v. Crown Butte Mines,* 904 F. Supp. 1168 (D. Mt. 1995), several environmental groups sued Crown Butte alleging violations of the Clean Water Act (CWA) from a mining site just outside of Yellowstone National Park. Beartooth claimed that Crown Butte was required to obtain a permit for its point source discharges from the mine site under § 402 of the Clean Water Act. Crown Butte was in the process of developing the site for future mining; the alleged violations came from old mine workings at the mine site that were being redeveloped in conjunction with the larger mining plan. The court held that to prove a violation of the § 402 permit requirement, the plaintiffs must show the "discharge" of a "pollutant" to "navigable waters" from a "point source" without a permit. The court found that the plaintiffs had met their burden and that the operator was liable for the violation.

9. In *Northern Plains Resource Council v. Fidelity Exploration & Development Co.,* 325 F.3d 1155 (9th Cir. 2003), *cert. denied,* 540 U.S. 967 (2003), the court held that groundwater discharged from a coal bed methane well was a point source pollutant as defined by the Clean Water Act (CWA). The court found that the groundwater, which is produced as a by-product during the process of extracting methane, was an "industrial waste." Industrial wastes are expressly included under the definition of "pollutant" under the Clean Water Act. 33 U.S.C. § 1362(6). Further, the discharge constituted "pollution" under the CWA since it resulted from a "man-induced" alteration of the integrity of the river. 33 U.S.C. § 1362(19). Moreover, neither the EPA nor the state had the authority to exempt the discharge, which was otherwise subject to the § 402 permitting requirements of the CWA. 33 U.S.C. § 1342.

10. The Clean Water Act is just one of many federal environmental statutes that may apply to a mining operation. Air pollution generated from surface disturbance or processing facilities may be regulated under the Clean Air Act. Contaminated lands from past mining activities may be subject to cleanup under the Comprehensive Environmental Response, Compensation and Liability Act (CERCLA or "Superfund"). The Resource Conservation and Recovery Act (RCRA), which establishes a "cradle to grave" system for managing hazardous wastes, generally does not apply to wastes from the extraction and beneficiation of ores, *see generally Friends* *of Santa Fe County v. LAC Minerals*, 892 F. Supp. 1333, 1339–1340 (D. N.M. 1995) but it does apply to other wastes which may be generated in the operation and maintenance of equipment and facilities. 5 Am. L. of Mining § 170.02[4][a] (1961, 1997). In addition, many states have set standards for mine operations and reclamation of mined lands. Added to these are a host of safety requirements imposed primarily under the Mine Safety and Health Act of 1977, 30 U.S.C. §§ 801 *et seq.* In short, the lawyer's task in helping mining companies to comply with this myriad of laws is daunting.

11. One approach that more and more companies are using to ascertain problem areas and promote compliance is the environmental audit. Periodic, comprehensive, and objective audits of environmental and safety compliance can give corporate officers a picture of a company's performance in relation to legal requirements. Where problems are identified, corrective action can be taken, often before serious problems arise, or substantial penalties are imposed. As a result of new laws and policies at the state and national levels, audits are increasingly attractive since they may allow companies that perform audits to limit or reduce liability for violations that are reported to the relevant regulatory agency and addressed with dispatch. *See generally* Steven J. Christiansen & Clay W. Stucki, *Environmental Audits and Beyond: Developing an Effective Environmental Management System,* 42 Rocky Mtn. Min. L. Inst. 7–1 (1996) (recommending an "environmental management system" of which the audit is only one component).

12. State laws governing environmental controls on hard rock mining are summarized in James M. McElfish, Jr. et al, Hard Rock Mining: State Approaches To Environmental Protection (1996).

———

Problem Exercise: Environmental Restrictions That Preclude Mining

Suppose that the State of Deseret adopts regulations for all noncoal mining operations within the state. Under these regulations, a person cannot obtain a permit to conduct mining operations unless the applicant demonstrates that the land surface can be restored to its pre-mining condition within five years after mining is completed. Suppose further that no comparable requirement exists under the federal regulations. The owner of a mining claim on federal lands in Deseret cannot make the required showing because the land proposed for mining receives insufficient rainfall to restore the vegetative cover within five years. The rain that does fall usually falls during violent storms. Such storms hinder rather than help reclamation by washing away seeds and topsoil from the exposed land. Reclamation experts hired by the owner of the claim estimate that it will take a minimum of 15 years of intensive management to return the land to its pre-mining condition. As a result, the state rejects the claimant's permit application. The claimant sues challenging the state's authority to do so. What result?

Problem Exercise: The Glamis Imperial Mine

In 1994, Glamis Gold, Ltd., a Canadian corporation, submitted a proposed plan of operations to the BLM for the Glamis Imperial open-pit gold mine in California. The proposed cyanide heap-leach mining operation would encompass three open pits and approximately 1,650 acres of land, and would likely destroy 55 recorded tribal sites eligible for listing on the National Register of Historic Places. A review of the proposed mine by the Advisory Council on Historic Preservation concluded that even with the proposed mitigation measures, the mine would cause "serious and irreparable damage to historic sites" of the Quechen Indian Tribe and to its ability to practice its sacred traditions. In 2002, as a result of the proposed mine, the National Trust for Historic Preservation listed the Indian Pass area, which includes the proposed mine site, as one of the 11 Most Endangered Historic Places.

The cyanide heap-leach mining method makes it economical for mining companies to recover gold from very low grades of ore. The proposed Glamis Imperial mine, for example, would recover, on average, one ounce of gold for every 422 tons of material mined—a ratio of one to 13.5 million. On December 27, 1999, Interior Solicitor John Leshy issued a legal opinion entitled *Regulation of Hardrock Mining on Federal Lands.* M–36999 (1999). That Opinion was primarily concerned with the proposed Glamis Imperial mine and addressed, among other issues, the standard contained in § 302(b) of FLPMA, which provides in relevant part as follows:

> In managing the public lands, the Secretary shall, by regulation or otherwise, take any action necessary to prevent unnecessary or undue degradation of the lands.

43 U.S.C. § 1732(b). The Solicitor concluded on the basis of this and other provisions of law that the BLM had the authority to reject the proposed mining plan if it found that the proposed plan would cause undue impairment. In January, 2001, the BLM rejected the proposed plan.

Shortly after the Bush Administration took office, Solicitor William Myers issued a new opinion reversing the position taken in the previous opinion that the BLM had the authority to reject the proposed plan of operations. *Surface Management Provisions for Hardrock Mining*, M–37007 (2001). The new opinion found that the 1999 Solicitor's opinion had unlawfully impaired the rights of the mining claimant. The BLM then issued revised rules that followed the conclusions contained in the Solicitor's opinion, thereby clearing the way for final approval of the Glamis Mine. As noted previously, the federal district court for the District of Columbia rejected the second Solicitor's opinion because it failed to acknowledge the Secretary's obligation under FLPMA to disapprove an otherwise permissible mining operation if it would unduly harm or degrade public land. *Mineral Policy Center v. Norton*, 292 F. Supp. 2d 30, 35 (D.D.C. 2003). Nonetheless, the court upheld the Bush Administration's rules on the grounds that they gave Interior sufficient authority to prevent unnecessary and undue degradation. *Id.* at 42–44.

Meanwhile, the State of California adopted emergency legislation that precludes open pit mining activities within one mile of any Native American sacred site. Cal. Pub. Resources Code § 2773.3. The legislation applies generally but was plainly intended to stop the proposed Glamis Mine.

You represent Glamis Gold, Ltd. The CEO of the company has asked you to assess Glamis' prospects for prevailing in any appeal of the district court's decision, as well as the anticipated litigation over the new California legislation. What are the legal issues that are likely to be raised? How should you respond to the CEO's request?

QUESTIONS AND DISCUSSION

1. Another possible avenue for challenging mining operations on public lands arises under the Religious Freedom Restoration Act (RFRA). RFRA prohibits the federal government from "substantially burden[ing] a person's exercise of religion even if the burden results from a rule of general applicability. . . ." 42 U.S.C. § 2000bb–1(a). The only exception is for burdens where the government demonstrates "that application of the burden to the person—(1) is in furtherance of a compelling governmental interest; and (2) is the least restrictive means of furthering that compelling governmental interest." RFRA was enacted largely in response to the Supreme Court's 1990 decision in *Employment Division, Department of Human Resources of Oregon v. Smith*, 494 U.S. 872 (1990). In *Smith*, the Court upheld an Oregon statute denying unemployment benefits to drug users, including Indians who used peyote in religious ceremonies. *Id.* at 890. The Court held that the first amendment does not prohibit burdens on religious practices if they are imposed by laws of general applicability, such as the Oregon statute. Subsequently, in *City of Boerne v. Flores*, 521 U.S. 507 (1997), the Court found RFRA unconstitutional as applied to state and local governments, *id.* at 529, 534–35, but the Ninth Circuit has held that the law remains valid as applied to the federal government. *See Guam v. Guerrero*, 290 F.3d 1210, 1220–21 (9th Cir. 2002).

In *Navajo Nation v. U.S. Forest Service*, 535 F.3d 1058, *en banc* (9th Cir. 2008) six tribes and several other individuals and organizations filed an action alleging that the decision of the U.S. Forest Service to authorize the use of reclaimed sewage water for making snow at a ski resort in the San Francisco Peaks area outside of Flagstaff, Arizona violated RFRA and NEPA. The mountains and waters in the area were used by the tribes in religious ceremonies and the tribes alleged that the use of sewage water burdened their exercise of religion by contaminating the water and soils. A 3–judge panel agreed, finding that the decision authorizing the use of reclaimed sewage for making snow imposed a substantial burden on the tribes, and that the government had failed to show that the proposed action serves "serves a compelling governmental interest by the least restrictive means." 479 F.3d 1024, 1046 (9th Cir. 2007).

Following rehearing *en banc*, the full 9th Circuit reversed holding that the use of recycled waste water to make artificial snow for the ski area would not "substantially burden" the free exercise of religion by tribal members. 535 F.3d at 1070.

Notwithstanding the result in this case, consider how RFRA might implicate mineral development on public lands that have religious significance to Indians? Consider, for example, the facts described in the Glamis Imperial mine controversy described in the problem exercise above. How might RFRA be used to stop or limit mineral development?

———

B.   ENVIRONMENTAL REGULATION OF COAL MINING

Regulation of coal mining operations and reclamation activities falls under an entirely different program from all other types of mining. Whereas other forms of mining are subject to a mix of federal and state requirements on both private and public lands, coal mining is regulated under the Surface Mining Control And Reclamation Act, 30 U.S.C. §§ 1201–1328 (SMCRA)—a comprehensive federal law that applies on all lands throughout the United States.

As with most other federal environmental regulatory statutes, SMCRA establishes a system of *cooperative federalism*. States may assume responsibility for regulating surface coal mining operations within their boundaries if they obtain Secretarial approval of a program that is found to be consistent with the federal law and regulations. 30 U.S.C. § 1253. The federal government, however, retains an active oversight responsibility.

The Act applies to all "surface coal mining and reclamation operations." This term is broadly defined to encompass the surface impacts of underground mines, coal processing facilities operated "in connection with" a mine, and virtually all other mine-related activities. 30 U.S.C. § 1291(28). The Act establishes its own federal agency, the Office of Surface Mining Reclamation and Enforcement (OSM), within the Department of the Interior to administer its provisions.

All major coal-producing states have received approval to administer their own programs. Two states, Tennessee and Oklahoma, have had their approval withdrawn because of their failure to comply with the law, although Oklahoma has regained primacy. Federal programs are administered in states lacking approved programs. There are currently 24 state-approved programs and twelve federal programs. 30 CFR parts 900–955 (2002).

The regulatory scheme of the Act has four primary components: (1) *permitting*; (2) *bonding and bond release*; (3) *performance standards*; (4) *inspection and enforcement*.

Permitting. Before conducting a surface coal mining operation, an operator must obtain a permit. The permitting requirements of both the Act and regulations are detailed and highly technical. Among the more significant requirements are: (a) a cumulative hydrologic impact assessment (CHIA) of all anticipated mining in the area; (b) a determination of the probable hydrologic consequences of mining (PHC); and (c) a reclamation plan which meets the standards of the Act. 30 U.S.C. §§ 1257, 1258.

Bonding and Bond Release. The Act requires a bond to be posted "sufficient to assure completion of the reclamation work if work had to be performed by the regulatory authority." 30 U.S.C. § 1259. The performance bond may not be fully released until revegetation success has been demonstrated for five full years *after* augmented seeding, fertilizing, irrigation, etc. (Ten full years in areas with less than 26' annual rainfall.) Partial release of the bond is allowed after completion of various stages of reclamation work. 30 U.S.C. § 1269.

Performance Standards. As with permitting, the Act and regulations set forth detailed performance standards. Among the more significant are: (a) restoring the land to a condition capable of supporting pre-mining uses or higher and better uses, § 515(b)(2); (b) restoring the approximate original contour (AOC) and elimination of all highwalls, § 515(b)(3); (c) removing, segregating, storing, and restoring the topsoil or best available soil for revegetation, § 515(b)(5); (d) minimizing disturbance to hydrologic balance, § 507(b)(11); (e) using best technology currently available (BTCA) to control sedimentation, § 515(b)(10)(B); (f) carrying out blasting activities in conformance with detailed standards, including notice to local residents (pre-blast surveys of homes and other structures must be carried out if requested), § 515(b)(15); and (g) replacing water supplies damaged by mining operations, § 507(b)(13). *See* 30 U.S.C. §§ 1265, 1266.

Inspections. SMCRA contains inspection and enforcement provisions, which, in many ways, are more progressive than those found in any other major environmental statute. Section 517 of the Act authorizes *warrantless* inspections of mine sites and requires that each site be inspected 12 times annually. 30 U.S.C. 1267(b)(3), (c). Inspections must occur without prior notice to the permittee and the inspector must file an inspection report following each inspection. *Id.* Further, persons who inform the regulatory authority of potential violations have a right to accompany the inspector on the mine site (or alternatively, to remain anonymous). 30 U.S.C. § 1271(a)(1).

Enforcement. The Act establishes a system of *mandatory enforcement.* When an inspector discovers a violation, she is required to issue a "notice of violation" (NOV) to the operator. The NOV must provide for abatement of the violation within a reasonable time, but in no case may the time for abatement exceed 90 days. If the operator fails to abate the violation within the time set in the NOV then the inspector must issue a "cessation order" (CO), which requires the operator to cease that portion of his operations contributing to the violation. 30 U.S.C. § 1271(a)(3). Further, if the violation is one that causes an imminent danger to the health and safety of the public, or a significant, imminent threat of environmental harm, the inspector must immediately issue a CO. *Id.* at § 1271(a)(2).

Penalties. Civil penalties may be assessed for any notice of violation and must be assessed for any cessation order. The maximum penalty is $5,000 per violation, but each day that a violation continues may be treated as a separate violation for purposes of assessment. 30 U.S.C. § 1268(a). The amount of civil penalty is supposed to be determined after consideration of four factors: (1) the permittee's history of past violations; (2) the seriousness of the violation; (3) whether the permittee was negligent; and (4) whether the permittee exercised good faith in achieving rapid compliance once the violation was identified. Where an operator fails to abate an NOV within the time specified, and a CO is issued, the operator must be assessed a minimum penalty of $750/day. *Id.* § 1268(h). Criminal penalties may be assessed for knowing and willful violations of the law. In addition, individual civil penalties may be assessed against any director, officer or agent of a corporation who willfully and knowingly authorized a violation of the law. 30 U.S.C. § 1268(e), (f).

The Act contains an innovative method for collecting civil penalties. If an operator desires to contest a penalty assessment, he may do so in a formal adjudicatory proceeding, but only if he first places the amount of the proposed penalty in an escrow account within 30 days from the date of the notice of assessment. 30 U.S.C. § 1268. This helps to ensure prompt payment of the penalty in the event that the operator loses his appeal.

Other important components of the law are as follows:

Public Participation/Citizen Complaints. The law encourages public participation in all facets of administration of the Act. 30 U.S.C. § 1202(i). Among other things, a citizen may file a complaint alleging that a violation of the Act exists at a particular mine site. If there is any reasonable support for the complaint, the agency must conduct an inspection of the mine site and allow the citizen an opportunity to accompany the inspector on the inspection. 30 U.S.C. § 1271(a)(1).

Unsuitability Designations. The Act formally designates certain lands such as national parks as off limits to surface coal mining. In addition, it authorizes petitions for designating other lands unsuitable. After a hearing and a study, the agency must designate lands subject to a petition if it finds that the land cannot be reclaimed in accordance with the requirements of the Act. Lands *may* be designated unsuitable for mining if mining would be incompatible with state or local land use plans, affect historic or fragile lands, affect natural hazard lands or adversely affect renewable resource lands. The Secretary is required to review all federal lands to determine whether any such lands should be designated unsuitable. 30 U.S.C. § 1272.

Citizen Suits. The Act authorizes citizen suits to enforce the law where the state and federal agencies fail to do so. It further authorizes private causes of actions against operators to enforce violations of the law. Successful litigants may recover their legal fees and other expenses. 30 U.S.C. § 1270.

Steep Slopes/Prime Farmlands/Alluvial Valley Floors (AVFs). Special permitting and performance standards are established for each of these types of lands. Steep slope standards address the special problems of soil erosion and backfilling in steep slope areas. Complete backfilling with spoil material is required to completely cover the highwall and return the site to its original contour. No spoil material or waste mineral matter is to be placed on the downslope below the bench or mining cut. The reclaimed area must be stable with the toe of the lowest coal seam and associated overburden retained in place as barriers to slides and erosion. 30 U.S.C. § 1265(c). Prime farmland requirements are intended to ensure the restoration of 100% of the pre-mining productivity of the soil after mining. Initially, a soil survey is done to determine the location of prime farmlands. 30 U.S.C. § 1257(b)(16). The mining operator must then separate the A, B, and C soil horizons, protect them from wind and water erosion or chemical contamination, then return them following mining in such a way as to create a root zone of comparable depth and quality as that existing in the natural soil. 30 U.S.C. § 1265(b)(7). The AVF requirements are intended to ensure that mining does not materially damage the important water resources of the Western United States. No mining application is approved unless the operator can show mining would not interrupt farming on alluvial valley floors that are irrigated or naturally subirrigated, nor materially damage the quantity or quality of water in surface or underground water systems that supply these valley floors. 30 U.S.C. § 1260(b)(5).

Judicial Review of Regulations/State Programs. Judicial review of national rules must be heard in the federal district court for the District of Columbia. Judicial review of state programs must be filed in the federal district court for the district where the state capitol is located. All must be filed within 60 days from publication of the final rule or program. 30 U.S.C. § 1276.

Employee "Whistleblower" Protection. State and federal agencies administering the law may not fire or discriminate against an employee for notifying officials of violations of the law. 30 U.S.C. § 1293.

QUESTIONS AND DISCUSSION

1. In *Hodel v. Virginia Surface Mining and Reclamation Association,* 452 U.S. 264 (1981), the Supreme Court upheld SMCRA against a series of constitutional challenges. The plaintiffs alleged that the law violated the Commerce Clause, the Tenth Amendment, the Due Process Clause, and the Takings Clause, in the context of the steep slope mining areas in Appalachia. A unanimous Supreme Court reversed a lower court decision in favor of the plaintiffs and upheld the statute against all of these claims. In a companion case, *Hodel v. Indiana,* 452 U.S. 314 (1981), the Court rejected a similar argument in the context of the Act's prime farmland provisions.

2. The scope of SMCRA was at issue in *Citizens Coal Council v. Norton,* 330 F.3d 478 (D.C. Cir. 2003), *cert. denied,* 540 U.S. 1180 (2004). The case involved the prohibitions on surface coal mining operations in certain protected areas like national parks and forests, and near homes, schools, and public buildings. *See* 30 U.S.C. § 1272(e). The Interior Department had issued an interpretive rule without following the notice and comment process, finding that "surface coal mining operations" do not include surface subsidence caused by underground mining. The effect of this rule was to allow mining in these areas that would have otherwise been off-limits. The federal district court for the District of Columbia struck down the rules, but the Court of Appeals for the District of Columbia Circuit reversed. The court analyzed the case under the two-part test of *Chevron v. Natural Resources Defense Council,* 467 U.S. 837 (1984). Under this familiar test, the court first determines whether the statute is ambiguous. If not, the court enforces the statute. But if the statute is ambiguous, then the court defers to any reasonable agency interpretation. In this case, the court found that the statute was ambiguous and that while the Secretary's interpretation was not the most natural one, it was reasonable. Accordingly, the rule was sustained.

Interestingly, the court apparently failed to consider the impact of the Supreme Court's decision in *United States v. Mead Corp.,* 533 U.S. 218 (2001). In *Mead,* the Court held that certain tariff classification rulings by the U.S. Customs Service were not entitled to *Chevron* deference. In reaching this holding, the Court noted that "the overwhelming number of our cases applying *Chevron* deference have reviewed the fruits of notice-and-comment rulemaking or formal adjudication." *Id.* at 230. The Court also cited with approval a law review article noting that "interpretive rules may sometimes function as precedents and they enjoy no *Chevron* status as a class." *Id.* at 232. Given the closeness of the question, it is unclear whether the court of appeals would have reached a different result if it had applied a lesser form of deference to the agency interpretive rule.

3. In another ruling that absolved a mining company from surface subsidence liability, a federal district court held that the construction of a coal mine is an "improvement to real property" under the Illinois Construction Statute of Repose. *Wilke Window & Door Co. v. Peabody Coal Co.*, 2007 WL 924463 (S.D.Ill.). This statute limits liability for any act or omission after 10 years have elapsed. Accordingly, the plaintiff could not recover from subsidence damage that had occurred 40 years after the closure of Peabody's mine. Given the nature of subsidence occurring over an extended period of time, does this result seem fair to you? Would a different result unfairly burden mining companies for actions that occurred many years before the damage?

4. A long-standing source of controversy under SMCRA concerns the extent to which it allows "mountaintop removal" mining. This method, which is very popular in the Appalachian Mountains, essentially involves lopping off the entire top of a mountain to a point just below the coal seam. As you might expect, mountaintop removal mining generates an enormous amount of spoil material and leaves no hole where the spoil can be placed once mining is completed. A compromise included in the final legislation allows mountaintop removal mining by authorizing a limited waiver from the general requirement that mine operators must restore the "approximate original contour." In particular, operators must propose a specific, productive post-mining land use following such mining activities. 30 U.S.C. § 1265(c). Despite the expectation that mountaintop mining removal would occur only in exceptional circumstances, it has now become commonplace throughout Appalachia. A great deal of controversy has followed.

Mountaintop removal operations generate vast amounts of excess spoil material. Typically this material is placed in a fill at the top of a valley. These enormous valley, or "head-of-hollow," fills interrupt natural drainage patterns and must be carefully engineered and constructed to avoid risks from landslides and serious environmental harm. Because these fills require the disposal of dredged and fill materials into stream beds and their tributaries, the U.S. Army Corps of Engineers (Corps) requires mine operators to obtain a permit in accordance with Section 404 of the Clean Water Act. 33 U.S.C. § 1344.

Under Section 404(e), the Corps may issue "general" or "nationwide" permits—

> for any category of activities involving discharges of dredged or fill material if the Secretary determines that the activities in such category are similar in nature, will cause only minimal adverse environmental effects when performed separately, and will have only minimal cumulative adverse effect on the environment.

33 U.S.C. § 1344(e). Nationwide permits (NWPs) are essentially rules that establish requirements and standards that apply "to any activity authorized by such general permit." *Id.* In 2007, the Corps promulgated 50 NWPs, including NWP 21, which applies to surface coal mining operations. 72 Fed. Reg. 11092, 11184 (2007). Only three of the 50 NWPs, including NWP 21 require that parties seeking to invoke the permit obtain prior approval from the Corps. *Id.* The purpose of the approval process is to allow the Corps to determine whether the proposed valley fills meet the requirements of 33 U.S.C. § 1344(e). Unfortunately, NWP 21 offers no guidance to help the Corps make this determination. *Id.* at 11114. It sets no limit, for example, on the length of a stream that can be buried, nor does it limit the total acreage within a watershed that can be impacted. *Id.* Think about the impact of burying miles of headwater streams under waste rock and soil. How likely is it that a valley fill will "cause only minimum adverse impacts" to the environment?

Note that the Corps prepared an environmental assessment when it issued NWP 21, but does not prepare any additional environmental analyses when it approves NWP 21 permits. Is this consistent with NEPA? Consider that the decision to issue NWP 21 was a rule. By contrast, the Corps' decision to approve an NWP 21 permit is an order. *Compare* 5 U.S.C. § 551(a)(4) and (6). Isn't that order necessarily a separate agency action that requires NEPA compliance? *See* 5 U.S.C. § 551(13); 40 C.F.R. § 1508.18(b).

5.   The NWP 21 approval process also allows mining companies to avoid the requirements of the stream buffer zone rule. That rule states that "no land within 100 feet of a perennial or intermittent stream shall be disturbed by surface mining activities" unless specifically authorized by the regulating agency under strict conditions. 30 C.F.R. § 816.57(a) (2008). Valley fills seem like a per se violation of the stream buffer zone rule, but as noted above, the regulatory agency can issue a variance to the rule as long as the proposed mining project will not violate state and federal water quality standards. *Id.* As a practical matter, valley fill projects are routinely granted variances to the stream buffer zone rule if the project is authorized by the Corps under NWP 21.

If a valley fill cannot be permitted under NWP 21 because it causes more than minimal adverse effects on the environment then an individual permit is required under 33 U.S.C. § 1344(b)(1). Individual permits require full NEPA compliance as well as compliance with the Corps and EPA rules. *See* 40 C.F.R. part 230 (2008).

Most mountaintop removal operations occur in the central Appalachian region and the Court of Appeals for the Fourth Circuit, which includes the states in that region, has considered several challenges to the practice. Two cases are noteworthy. *Kentuckians for the Commonwealth, Inc. v. Rivenburgh*, 317 F.3d 425 (4th Cir. 2003), involved a challenge to the Corp's issuance of a Section 404 permit for a mining operation in West Virginia. The plaintiffs had argued that the Corps' decision was arbitrary and capricious, and violated NEPA as well as the Corps' own rules. The Corps had approved the permit under NWP 21, which allowed the coal company to create 27 valley fills and bury approximately 6.3 miles of streams at the heads of the valleys. Rather than addressing the narrow issue presented by the plaintiffs, the district court ruled that Section 404 authorized the issuance of Section 404 permits only for discharges with a beneficial primary purpose. Because the permit issued in this case was for waste disposal, the district court held it unlawful. *Kentuckians for the Commonwealth, Inc. v. Rivenburgh*, 204 F. Supp. 2d 927 (S.D. W.Va. 2002). The Fourth Circuit reversed, holding that the Clean Water Act did not clearly prohibit the issuance of permits for waste disposal, and that the Corps' rules allowing such permits were entitled to *Chevron* deference. Furthermore, the court held that the district court's injunction was overbroad because it prohibited future Section 404 permits for all valley fills in the district, while the plaintiff had only requested the denial of a single permit.

Subsequently, in *Ohio Valley Envtl. Coalition v. Bulen*, 429 F.3d 493, 496 (4th Cir. 2005). the Fourth Circuit reversed a district court finding that the Corps had exceeded its statutory authority in issuing NWP 21. The lower court had found that—

> [T]he statute unambiguously requires determination of minimal impact before, not after, the issuance of a nationwide permit. The issuance of a nationwide permit thus functions as a guarantee *ab initio* that every instance of the permitted activity will meet the minimal impact standard. Congress intended for a potential discharger whose project fits into one of those categories to begin discharging with no further involvement from the Corps, no uncertainty, and no red tape. In issuing NWP 21, however, the Corps did not define activities that will invariably have only minimal effects; rather, NWP 21 provides for a *post hoc,* case-by-case evaluation of environmental impact.

Ohio Valley Envtl. Coalition v. Bulen, 410 F. Supp. 2d 450, 465–66 (S.D.W. Va. 2004). The Fourth Circuit reversed, pointedly disagreeing with the lower court's conclusion that the general permit provisions were intended to be used only where minimal impacts were certain. To the contrary, the Fourth Circuit found that the Clean Water Act fully anticipated uncertainty following the issuance of a general permit because Section 404(e)(2) allows the Corps to revoke or modify a general permit after issued if it finds that "the activities authorized by such general permit have an adverse impact on the environment." 33 U.S.C. § 1344(e)(2). Moreover, the Court found it impossible that "the Corps' *ex ante* determinations of minimal impact [could] be anything more than reasoned predictions." 429 F.3d at 501.

Even assuming that the Fourth Circuit was correct in finding that some level of uncertainty must surround the issuance of a general permit, does it make sense to you that general permits require individualized approval? If the issuance of a general permit is not itself adequate to determine whether impacts will be minimal, is it lawful to cut off the public comment and hearing processes established under NEPA and the Clean Water Act for individualized permits? *See* 33 U.S.C. § 1344(a); 42 U.S.C. § 4332(2)(C).

An excellent book on the legal battles over mountaintop removal mining in West Virginia is MICHAEL SHNAYERSON, COAL RIVER (2008).

6. SMCRA establishes an Abandoned Mined Land Reclamation (AML) program that is funded by a tax on every ton of coal produced in the United

States. 30 U.S.C. §§ 1232. Money from the fund is distributed to the states to carry out reclamation of pre-SMCRA abandoned mined lands. Historically, States with approved SMCRA regulatory programs receive at least half of the money paid into the AML fund by mining companies operating in their states. The Surface Mining Control and Reclamation Act Amendments of 2006, which were encompassed in the Tax Relief and Health Care Act of 2006, Pub. L. 109–432, revised the program to reduce the fees paid into the fund by 10% for 5 years beginning in October, 2007, and by another 10% for the nine years thereafter.

CHAPTER TEN

FORESTS

I. FORESTS AND THE AMERICAN MIND
II. THE FOREST RESOURCE
   A. GLOBAL FOREST RESOURCES
   B. THE FOREST RESOURCES OF THE UNITED STATES
   PROBLEM EXERCISE: TREE SPIKING
   C. FOREST ECOSYSTEM SERVICES
III. THE TIMBER INDUSTRY
   A. LOGGING METHODS
   B. ENVIRONMENTAL IMPACTS OF LOGGING
      1. SOIL EROSION AND COMPACTION
      2. WATER
      3. WILDLIFE HABITAT
   C. CUSTOMS, CULTURES, AND LOCAL TIMBER ECONOMIES
IV. FORESTRY LAW
   A. NATIONAL FORESTS
      1. THE HISTORY OF FEDERAL FORESTRY LAW
      2. MODERN MANAGEMENT LAW, POLICIES, AND PRACTICES
         a. NATIONAL FOREST LAND AND RESOURCE MANAGEMENT PLANNING
         b. NFMA AND CLEARCUTTING
         c. BIODIVERSITY CONSERVATION AND NATIONAL FORESTS
         d. ROADS AND NATIONAL FORESTS
         e. THE ROLE OF FIRE IN FOREST MANAGEMENT
   PROBLEM EXERCISE: FORESTS AND FIRE
      3. THE ECONOMICS OF LOGGING ON NATIONAL FORESTS
   B. PRIVATE FORESTS
      1. ACQUISITION OF PRIVATE TIMBER RIGHTS
      2. FEDERAL AND STATE REGULATION OF PRIVATE LOGGING ACTIVITIES

Notwithstanding all the waste and use which have been going on unchecked for more than two centuries, it is not too late—though it is high time—for the Government to begin a rational administration of its forests.

    JOHN MUIR, OUR NATIONAL PARKS 359 (1901)

A tree is a tree. How many more do you have to look at?

    Ronald Reagan, opposing expansion of Redwood National Park as governor of California, SACRAMENTO BEE, Mar, 12 1966

I am the Lorax. I speak for the trees, which you seem to be chopping as fast as you please.

    DR. SEUSS, THE LORAX.

I.   FORESTS AND THE AMERICAN MIND

Forests are inseparable from the American identity. We stand in awe of the towering old redwoods and sequoias along the West coast. During the autumn months we gladly endure traffic that can rival the worst urban rush hour to gaze at the many shades of reds and yellows that adorn maples and beech in the New England forests or quaking aspen in the Rockies. We celebrate our forests and our trees in the Shenandoah Valley and the Blue Ridge and Smoky Mountains, in the northern woods of Minnesota, Wisconsin and Michigan, in the Rocky Mountains, and the Sierra Nevada.

Forests and trees have long played a prominent role in our culture and folklore. The "tree of life" is a familiar symbol in many cultures, with its branches reaching into the heavens and its roots into the earth's depths. Christmas trees are a familiar sight every December. We all know the stories of Johnny Appleseed (a.k.a., John Chapman), who cultivated apple trees throughout the American frontier, and of the apocryphal Paul Bunyan and his blue ox, Babe, who helped clear our forests to make way for settlers. Since 1872, trees have even had their own holiday—National Arbor Day—celebrated on the last Friday in April.

Trees give value to our homes, protect our water supplies, and provide endless recreational opportunities. We hike, camp, hunt, and fish in our forests, and climb and swing in our backyard trees. Who among us didn't once dream of building and living in a tree house; we marveled at the Swiss Family Robinson who did. We are shocked and saddened by the devastation and loss of trees from forest fires, and we thank a forest icon—Smokey the Bear—for helping us prevent these fires. But our attachment to trees has not always been positive. In Chapter 1 we noted that the original settlers viewed the wild forests with a sense of foreboding. Jefferson applauded the yeoman farmers who cleared the forests and cultivated the land to make it fit for settlement.

We have built a society and lifestyle that is heavily dependent on the consumption of trees for the wood and wood products they provide. And as our population has grown and our personal wealth increased, our demand for these products has grown with them. Our love affair with trees and the natural amenities they provide is tempered by the reality that we have become ever more reliant on their bounty.

Despite the overwhelming public affinity for forests, their major uses are often incompatible. One cannot clearcut a forest and expect it to provide a wilderness camping experience. Mediating such competing uses has made forest management a deeply contentious policy area, with long-running and bitter disputes between the timber industry and environmentalists. Mention the words "spotted owl" in the Pacific Northwest and it's hard to find someone without a deeply-held opinion. Similarly strong feelings are evident in decisions over timber sales and road-building in national forests, fire management operations, and salvage logging following burns. To some in the timber industry, setting aside forest lands with high timber values is a commercially wasteful use of natural resources that, at the extreme, favors trees and birds over the jobs that are the life blood of local logging communities.

This chapter is about forests and the resources and amenities they provide. It begins with an overview of forest resources in the United States and around the globe. It describes their ecological value and their value for timber production. It reviews the economics of the timber industry, and then introduces silvicultural practices, and the environmental impacts that are caused by logging. This leads to a discussion of forestry law, with a primary focus on the law relating to national forests, followed by a review of state and private forestry practices.

II.   THE FOREST RESOURCE

In order to place the law and policy of America's forests in a broader context, we first review global forest resources, identifying the critical importance of tropical forests and the dire challenges posed by deforestation. This is followed by an overview of American forests and the benefits forest ecosystem services provide.

A.   GLOBAL FOREST RESOURCES

Look at a satellite picture of the earth and the universality of forests is readily apparent. Except for the ice of the poles and the vast desert swaths across Saharan Africa and Mongolia, the green of trees is readily evident on every continent. From the boreal forest spanning Eurasia (known as the taiga) and the temperate rainforests of western North America to the verdant rainforest of the Congo basin and the massive eucalyptus stands in southwestern Australia, forests cover roughly one-quarter of the earth's ice-free land surface, hosting well over half of the world's plant and animal species.

The earth's trees also provide amazing witness to our planet's life history. The same types of fern trees that were munched by dinosaurs can still be found in New Zealand. The Wollomi Pine, discovered in a park near Sydney, Australia in 1997, is over 1,000 years old. The giant sequoia tree in Sequoia National Park, known as General Sherman, is almost 275 feet tall with a massive trunk over 100 feet in circumference at its base. It weighs in at around 1400 tons, similar to 15 adult blue whales or 10 train engines. An aspen stand in the Wasatch Mountains of Utah is currently considered the heaviest living thing on earth. Over 47,000 stems of aspen trees, weighing roughly 6,500 tons, have sprouted from the same gigantic root system.

Despite our vast forests, they cover only half of the forest area that once blanketed the earth. Intact forest ecosystems are under threat today as never before. The primary drivers of deforestation have been conversion to agriculture and logging. By far the most critical losses have occurred in the tropical rainforests—the earth's oldest and richest living ecosystems. The primary rainforests of India, Bangladesh, Sri Lanka, and Haiti are now gone. Less than 5% of the primary rainforests of Thailand and the Philippines that once covered more than 80% of those countries remain. To put this loss in more familiar terms, the UN Food and Agriculture Organization has estimated that from 1990–1995 the net global forest loss was the equivalent of 33 soccer fields per minute. The United Nations currently estimates that rainforests are being lost at an annual rate of 7.3 million hectares per year, an area roughly the size of Panama. FAO, STATE OF THE WORLD'S FORESTS, 135 (1999); FAO, GLOBAL FOREST RESOURCE ASSESSMENT 2005, 12 (2005).

While rainforests make up a small fraction of forest vegetation (about 6% of the Earth's land area), their biodiversity is stunning. A National Academy of Sciences report, for example, estimated that a typical four square miles of rainforest can contain as many as 1500 species of flowering plants, 750 species of trees, 125 different mammals, 400 types of birds, 100 species of reptiles, 60 types of amphibians, and 150 different species of butterflies. *See* http://www.savetherainforest.org/savetherainforest_007.htm. Recall the experiment by Terry Erwin recounted in Chapter 4 (pages 326–327). On a single species of evergreen tree in Panama he collected 1,143 species of beetles *alone*.

It should be no surprise that as our rainforests disappear, so too do the species on which they depend. As explained in Chapter 4, scientists estimate that the rate of species extinction may be as much as 1,000 times the natural rate. Since many of these species have never even been identified, the consequences of their loss will never be known. But the known products that come from rainforests, which include the genetic stocks of important foods and medicines, are significant. The National Cancer Institute, for example, estimates that 70% of medicines useful in cancer treatment come from plants found only in rainforests; yet less than 1% of tropical forest species have been thoroughly examined for their medicinal value.

Despite such richness of life, rainforests are fragile ecosystems. Perhaps surprisingly, rainforest soil is nutrient-poor. As is the case with coral reefs, the rainforest ecosystem is remarkably efficient at recycling scarce nutrients. When the vegetation is removed or destroyed by logging or burning, so too are the nutrients. With vegetation removed, the nutrient poor soils compact easily and cannot sustain agricultural activities for very long.

Deforestation, however, is not confined to tropical rainforests. In North America, the temperate rainforests that once extended from California to Alaska have been decimated by logging. Only the Tongass National Forest in Alaska—home to one-third of the world's remaining temperate rain forest—remains largely intact, but that too may soon change. The Bush Administration approved an amended forest plan that opens roadless areas of the Tongass to logging. *Bush Opens Roadless Tongass National Forest to Logging*, ENV. NEWS SERVICE, Jan. 25, 2008, http://www.ens-newswire.com/ens/jan2008/2008-01-25-095.asp. Despite numerous appeals to the plan, the Forest Service upheld the amended forest plan in August, 2008. *See* http://tongass-fpadjust.net/Documents/AppealDecision.pdf. *See also* KATHIE DURBIN, TONGASS: PULP POLITICS AND THE FIGHT FOR THE ALASKAN RAIN FOREST (2005).

B. THE FOREST RESOURCES OF THE UNITED STATES

In 1630—around the beginning of European settlement—about 45 percent of the land area of what is now the United States contained commercial quality forest.

> Approximately one-fifth of that forest cover was located west of the Great Plains in the Pacific coast states of Washington, Oregon, and California and those portions of the Rocky Mountain states not too arid to support trees, such as upland Colorado, Wyoming, and Idaho. Over four-fifths, the greatest bulk of the forest, lay east of the Great Plains. It stretched from eastern Texas through the South, to a lesser extent from the extreme eastern portions of Kansas and Nebraska through the center of the continent, and in great profusion and density from mid-Minnesota through the Lake States to the Atlantic Coast and New England. In fact, the land east of the Mississippi to the Atlantic Ocean was an almost unbroken expanse of forest. * * *

MICHAEL WILLIAMS, AMERICANS AND THEIR FORESTS: A HISTORICAL GEOGRAPHY 3–4 (1989) [Hereinafter WILLIAMS, AMERICANS]. As settlers spread across the country, this forested landscape underwent dramatic changes. From the earliest days of settlement, Europeans began utilizing the vast forest treasury of the New World, cutting trees for building and then heating their homes, for fencing their lands, and for constructing their ships and masts. While many trees were felled because they could be utilized, many more were removed because they impeded farming and other development.

Indeed, of all the early drivers of deforestation, agricultural clearing was far and away the greatest. From the time Jamestown's Captain John Smith learned from the Indians how to kill trees by girdling (cutting a ring around the trunk of a tree so that food could not be carried upward from the roots), settlers used this and other methods to clear land for the agriculture that Benjamin Franklin declared the "great business of the Continent" and that Thomas Jefferson was convinced would create a class of yeomanry who would serve as the foundation of the democracy. THOMAS R. COX ET AL., THIS WELL-WOODED LAND: AMERICANS AND THEIR FORESTS FROM COLONIAL TIMES TO THE PRESENT 9, 51 (1985).

> For the poor settler, seeking to support a family while clearing a farm in the timber, the presence of a towering forest was more than an impediment; it was a threat to survival. In a society short on both labor and capital, an abundance of trees was an asset that few could capitalize on. Farmland, by contrast, was something that could be turned to profit with a rudimentary knowledge of husbandry and an abundance of hard work. Small wonder that many pioneers looked upon clearing the forest as freeing them from an alien, hostile environment. One frontier resident wrote of the "everlasting sound of falling trees" that accompanied life in a region freshly opened to settlement "and was a relief to the dreary silence of these wilds." * * *

> Some settlers, although viewing the forests as impediments to progress, also recognized the majesty of what they were destroying. William Nowlin described the clearing of his family's farm in Michigan: "The grand old forest was melting away.... Beautiful workmanship of nature was displayed in that timber." Yet he welcomed the change. "Now finally I thought we had quite a clearing.... I could look to the east and there, joining ours was the clearing of Mr. Asa Blare.... Then it began to seem as if others were living in Michigan, for we could see them. The light of civilization began to dawn on us."

Id. at 55, 52.

Trees were also a vital source of firewood for the home and later for steam-powered riverboats and trains. In 1865 railroads were using 6.5 million cords of wood annually for fuel. Another forest use, and one with increasing impact, was the commercial timber industry. Wood and wood products were one of the primary exports of the American colonies during the early period of the United States. To satisfy the voracious domestic appetite for wood, logging moved systematically across the country. "From a mere 0.5 billion board feet [bbf] cut in 1801, the amount of lumber rose and accelerated with each successive decade to form a new, upwardly sloping curve that reached 20 bbf in 1880 and peaked at nearly 46 bbf in 1906, an amount never reached since." MICHAEL WILLIAMS, DEFORESTING THE EARTH: FROM PRE-HISTORY TO GLOBAL CRISIS 317 (2003) [Hereinafter WILLIAMS, DEFORESTING].

In the early years of the nation's existence, the timber industry took root in Maine with its massive stands of white pine, which is light, strong, and durable. Maine was also close to the growing urban areas of the East, and the state's many rivers flowing from the interior to the coast facilitated moving logs to market. By 1820, Maine was the leader of the nation's young timber industry. COX ET AL., *supra*, at 74. By 1839, New York had taken the leading role, accounting for 30 percent of total lumber production as opposed to Maine's 14 percent. By 1860, the focus of the timber industry had shifted to the Lake states. From around 1860 to 1890, there was a dramatic assault on the forests of Michigan, Wisconsin, and Minnesota, aided in part by improvements in technology that allowed timber to be sawed at increasingly faster rates. Production in the Lake states fluctuated dramatically through that period—from approximately 3.5 bbf in 1869 to almost 10 bbf in 1889, only to drop back down to 1.7 bbf by 1929. As production in the Lake states was declining the timber industry in the southern states was expanding. Between 1880 and 1920, the original forested area in the South declined by 40 percent. From the South, the industry moved to the Pacific Northwest and by 1920 production there was almost equal to that of the South. *See* WILLIAMS, AMERICANS, *supra*, at 161–67, 200, 223–24, 238, 289; James L. Huffman, *A History of Forest Policy in the United States*, 8 ENVTL. L. 239, 242 (1978).

As a result of this 150–year wave of logging that swept across the country, as well as the aggressive agricultural clearing and cutting of timber for domestic fuel, by 1920 the original commercial forest cover of the United States had been reduced by almost half, from approximately 850 million acres to about 470 million acres. WILLIAMS, AMERICANS, *supra* at 4. But as partly recounted in Chapter 2, it was during the period of growth for the Pacific Northwest timber industry that things began to change.

> [I]t was no coincidence that in this, the last lumber frontier, where the green westward horizon of trees gave way to the blue horizon of the Pacific Ocean, other considerations began to hold sway. This was the last of the public lands, the remaining untouched, unalienated stock of forest left in the country. There were many people who thought this sizable section should not fall into private hands to be exploited for individual gain but should be preserved and managed by federal authorities for the good of the nation as a whole, especially at a time when timber prices seemed high and available resources were becoming scarce.

Thus, the Pacific Northwest, California, and portions of adjacent states in the Rocky Mountain region were the scene of the first federal intervention in forest exploitation, in the form of the national forests created.

Not only was this the last of the public lands and the remnant of the West, it was in many ways the most spectacular of lands, a treasure house of natural wonders and scenic beauties that captured the imagination and concern of the increasingly environment-conscious society emerging in the United States at the end of the nineteenth century. That foremost among these wonders were the very trees of redwood and sequoia forests themselves only added to the concern felt by many that this unique forest should be preserved for its own sake and that other forests should be preserved as a part of the general setting for the scenic beauties of the region. Thus, although the Pacific Northwest became the epitome of big business and big-scale lumber organization after 1900 because it was the last of the major forested regions to undergo exploitation, equally it was the scene of numerous experiments in preservation, ownership, and management.

WILLIAMS, AMERICANS, *supra*, at 290.

Beginning around 1920, the rate of logging in the Pacific Northwest began to stabilize and logging elsewhere in the country declined. Indeed, by 1977 the amount of commercial forest acres in the coterminous United States had actually increased slightly since 1920, growing from approximately 470 million acres to 483 million acres. This figure doesn't include the 250 million acres of noncommercial forest, where trees are either too small or sparse for commercial logging. Taken together, forests currently occupy one-third of the country. WILLIAMS, AMERICANS, *supra*, at 4, 433, 467. The timber acreage in the United States has remained steady not just because of increasing concerns about preservation but also because per capita consumption of wood products declined dramatically over the course of the twentieth century, as Americans learned to use wood much more efficiently and found substitutes such as steel, aluminum, concrete, petroleum, and plastic. Per capita wood consumption in 1980 was only one-sixth of per capita consumption in 1900. WILLIAMS, AMERICANS, *supra*, at 487–88.

Nonetheless, the commercial forests of today are quite different than the forests of 1630. The Forest Service reports that after the "intensive logging in the late 19th century and early 20th century, 55 percent of the forests on the Nation's timber land is less than 50 years old. Six percent of the Nation's timber land is more than 175 years old." U.S. DEP'T OF AGRIC., U.S. FOREST FACTS AND HISTORICAL TRENDS, FS–696, April 2001, at 10. It is this last six percent of so-called "old growth" timber that has been a particular source of contention in recent decades, revealed most prominently by the battle between loggers and the environmental community over the protection of the northern spotted owl, which favors old growth habitat. *See* Chapter 3, page 230.

With respect to the forests remaining in the United States (including both commercial and non-commercial acreage), their ownership varies by region. Private forest land predominates in the East, with 318 million acres of forests (82.6%) in private hands and 67 million acres (17.4%) in public ownership. The West is almost the reverse, with 250 million acres (68.9%) in public ownership and 113 million acres (31.1%) in private hands. U.S. DEP'T OF AGRIC., U.S. FOREST FACTS AND HISTORICAL TRENDS, FS–696, April

2001, at 6–7. Forest ecosystems vary by region, as well. A good summary of the types of trees and forests found in different parts of the United States is found in W. Brad Smith et al., *Forest Resources of the United States* (1997), *available at,* http://ncrs.fs.fed.us/pubs/gtr/gtr_nc219.pdf.

––––––––

QUESTIONS AND DISCUSSION

1.   Section 3 of the Forest and Rangeland Renewable Resources Planning Act of 1974 requires the Forest Service to periodically prepare a *Renewable Resource Assessment* that describes U.S. forest resources. 16 U.S.C. § 1601(a) (2000). The initial Assessment was required by 1975, and was supposed to be updated in 1979 and every ten years thereafter. The Assessment serves as the basis for setting national resource goals and objectives and must include, among other things:

> (1) an analysis of present and anticipated uses, demand for, and supply of the renewable resources, with consideration of the international resource situation, and an emphasis of pertinent supply and demand and price relationship trends; [and]

> (2) an inventory, based on information developed by the Forest Service and other Federal agencies, of present and potential renewable resources, and an evaluation of opportunities for improving their yield of tangible and intangible goods and services. . . .

Id. The most recent version of the Assessment was prepared in 2000, although an interim update was completed in 2007 and the agency was in the process of preparing an Assessment for 2010 at the time of this writing. *See* http://www.fs.fed.us/research/rpa/. Among the technical reports supporting the Assessment is a report on forest resources. *See* http://ncrs.fs. fed.us/pubs/gtr/gtr_nc241.pdf. This report focuses on timber, as opposed to forest resources more generally. For example, after describing U.S. forest resources, the report includes extended discussions of timber volume, timber growth, and timber products. Yet the report contains no discussion of recreational, biological, or other resources. Does it strike you as odd that an assessment of *forest* resources would focus almost exclusively on timber? Is the Forest Service missing the forest for the trees? How would you expect a report such as this to influence the policy choices made by the agency? Is the timber focus what Congress likely intended when it required an assessment of the forests' renewable resources?

2.   Feelings over forest management run high. One of this book's authors worked in Seattle in the early 1990s. In driving through the logging towns of Forks and Hoquiam on the Olympic Peninsula west of Seattle, he observed house after house with signs posted, "This house paid for by timber dollars." Many cars had bumper stickers with fiery messages such as, "Save a Job, Kill an Owl." Some of the more radical environmental activists have responded by "spiking" trees. Tree spiking involves driving long metal or ceramic spikes into trees and then publicly announcing the action. Spikes can interfere with a chainsaw used to cut trees, but they pose an even bigger problem for a sawmill because of the risk of serious injury to mill workers as well as substantial damage to the band saws used at mills. Metal spikes can be detected with metal detectors and then removed, but the process is time-consuming and costly. Ceramic spikes can be almost impossible to detect. A number of people have been convicted for these actions, with jail sentences and fines imposed. *See, e.g., Two Plead Guilty To Spiking Trees To Stop Sales In Idaho,* PORTLAND OREGONIAN, Jun. 5, 1993, at B8; *U.S. Tree–Spiker Sentences "Surprisingly" Stiff,* VANCOUVER SUN (British Columbia), Aug. 17, 1993, at C1.

3. Although most of the public's attention has focused on conflicts in public forests, high-profile conflicts occur in private forests, as well, especially when private companies are proposing to log "old growth" trees that may be hundreds or even thousands of years old. One of the most celebrated fights was led by Julia "Butterfly" Hill. On December 10, 1997, the twenty-three year old Hill climbed high into a 180–foot ancient redwood in northern California located on the private property of the Pacific Lumber Company. Pacific Lumber had planned to log the tree, which Hill had named "Luna," and the forest around it. But for more than two years Hill refused to come down, living on a platform. Eventually, the lumber company agreed to save Luna and a small preserve around it in exchange for a donation by Hill's supporters to Humboldt State University for forestry research. JULIA BUTTERFLY HILL, THE LEGACY OF LUNA (2000). While Hill viewed her actions as justifiable civil disobedience, she was clearly an illegal trespasser. Why do you think the timber company did not use the police and courts to forcibly remove her?

4. While there are only a few basic causes of deforestation, the drivers are complex. Just as it did early in America's history, forested lands are still cleared to make land available for cultivation or grazing. Commercial logging also plays a significant role in deforestation. The roads needed for logging and the heavy machinery used on the land cause significant environmental damage beyond that caused by the logging itself. A major cause of deforestation in developing countries is the need for fuel wood. Thus poverty and energy policies must play a key, though indirect, role in halting deforestation.

5. As you learned in high school biology class, a plant takes in carbon dioxide and transpires oxygen through photosynthesis. This ensures we have air to breathe and also provides the ecosystem service of "carbon sequestration." Thus, plants (and forests, in particular) play a key role in regulating the planet's carbon cycle by serving as a carbon "sink." The Kyoto Protocol, which was negotiated as part of the Framework Convention on Climate Change, recognized this explicitly. Article 3 of the Kyoto Protocol states that "net changes in greenhouse gas emissions by sources and removals by sinks resulting from direct human-induced land-use change and forestry activities ... shall be used to meet the commitments under the Article." Article 12 goes on to create a clean development mechanism (CDM). The CDM provides a means for developed countries to gain carbon emission credits by ensuring increased carbon sequestration in forests through reforestation and afforestation (planting trees where none existed in the past). *See* http://unfccc.int/kyoto_protocol/mechanisms/clean_development_mechanism/items/2718.php.

When adopted, it was hoped that the CDM would provide a powerful economic incentive to slow deforestation in developing countries. While the Kyoto Treaty became effective on February 16, 2005, the CDM has not yet proved an effective means to address deforestation. As this book goes to press, only one of the 1445 registered CDM projects dealt with reforestation or afforestation. *See* http://cdm.unfccc.int/Statistics/Registration/Registered ProjByScopePieChart.html.

What problems might arise with implementing the CDM? Should credits be granted for conserving existing forests or only for reforestation and afforestation? Given the variability in the rate of carbon sequestration among tree species and over the life of a tree, how should credits be measured? The Kyoto Protocol expires in 2012. Should some different mechanism for protecting forest resources be considered in the negotiations over a new agreement?

At the 13th Conference of Parties on the Framework Convention on Climate Change, held in Bali, Indonesia, in 2007 the Parties adopted a policy on Reducing Emissions from Deforestation in Developing Countries (REDD), that encourages voluntary efforts to reduce emissions from deforestation and forest degradation. *See* http://unfcccbali.org/unfccc/article/ article-climate-change/reducing-emissions-from-deforestation-and-degrada tion-redd.html. This policy is designed as a first step toward the development of more formal mechanisms that may give credit to developing countries for reducing emission from deforestation. At the time of this writing, proposed legislation in the United States (at both the federal and subnational level) contained significant provisions on REDD and international forest carbon management. *See* William Boyd, *Deforestation and Emerging Greenhouse Gas Compliance Regimes: Current Status and Prospects, in* Deforestation and Climate Change: Reducing Carbon Emissions from Deforestation and Forest Degradation (V. Bosetti & R. Lubowski eds., Edward Elgar) (forthcoming 2010). Additionally, further steps regarding REDD are expected to be discussed during negotiations at the United Nations Climate Change Conference in Copenhagen, Denmark, in December 2009. *See* http://unfccc.int/resource/docs/2009/awglca6/eng/08.pdf; *see also* http://en.cop15.dk/news/view + news?newsid=1305.

6. Another obstacle to implementation has been definitional. In particular, defining the terms "forest," "afforestation," and "deforestation" has been a real challenge. As Michael Williams describes,

> Before change in the forest can be measured, its extent and area must be known; and even more basically, before either can be delineated a "forest" must be defined, something that has not been attempted until recent years. Intuitive experience suggests that a broad distinction can be made between closed and open forest, and in practice most writers make such a distinction. FAO [UN Food and Agriculture Organization] defines *closed forest* as "land where trees cover a high proportion of the ground and where grass does not form a continuous layer on the floor," and *open forest* (sometimes called woodland) as "mixed forest/grasslands with at least 10 percent tree cover and a continuous grass layer." * * *
>
> [The variability of forest cover estimates] depends on definitions of what is deforestation and what is conversion, the role of logging and shifting agriculture, the types of forest considered (closed or open), and whether there are

specific measurements by remote sensing or subjective judgments, or a combination of both. Some are extrapolations from sample areas, some are averages, some are actual and some potential. In addition, it does not take too much imagination to realize that there may be good reasons to either exaggerate or play down the rate of deforestation for national political or economic ends, and even for personal professional reasons in the race for funding and status.

Thus, we are left with the knowledge that the exact magnitude, pace, and the nature of one of the most important processes in the changing environment of large portions of the earth is largely unknown. In all this uncertainty we can be sure that the debate on the rate of deforestation is not over. * * *

MICHAEL WILLIAMS, DEFORESTING, *supra* 446–47, 452, 457, 497–98. Following adoption of the Kyoto Protocol, negotiations to settle on definitions of "forest," "afforestation," "reforestation," and "deforestation" extended over four years. Why do you think it took so long to define these terms? How would you define these terms for legal effect?

7. The Clean Development Mechanism Executive Board, which oversees the CDM program, defines afforestation as ". . . conversion of land that has not been forested for a period of at least 50 years to forested land . . . ," reforestation as ". . . conversion of non-forested land to forested land . . . on land that was forested but that has been converted to non-forested land," and forest as "a minimum area of land of .05–1.0 hectares with tree crown cover . . . of more than 10–30 percent with trees with the potential to reach a minimum height of 2–5 metres at maturity. . . ." CDM EXECUTIVE BOARD, GLOSSARY OF CDM TERMS (VERSION 03) (November 2007), *available at* http://cdm.unfccc.int/Reference/Guidclarif/glos_CDM_v03.pdf. Why do you think the CDM executive board didn't define "deforestation"?

8. As noted in the introduction, Johnny Appleseed was a real person. John Chapman was born on September 26, 1774, near Leominster, Massachusetts. Son of a Continental soldier, at the age of 25 Johnny began his journey west as a "practical nurseryman." Apples were an essential part of early settlers' diets. In Pennsylvania, new homesteaders were required to plant fifty apple trees within the first year. Purchasing seeds from scattered cider mills, Johnny began creating nurseries by planting apple seeds and seedlings in western portions of New York and Pennsylvania. After clearing small portions of land, Johnny would plant apple seeds in concise rows and build a surrounding brush fence to keep out animals. He also used his own lands in Ohio and Indiana to grow and harvest apple trees, establish orchards, and sell both apples and trees for pennies, used clothing, or promises to pay later.

As pioneers pushed westward, Johnny was among the first to venture into the new lands. When settlers arrived in Ohio, Michigan, Indiana, and Illinois, they often found Johnny's apple trees ready for sale. A methodical businessman and successful nurseryman, later commentators remarked that it was "uncanny how many towns have risen on or near his nursery sites." Often traveling barefoot, Johnny supposedly ate no meat and was a welcome guest at settlers' cabins and Indian settlements, alike. Following his death in 1845, it was said that, "[t]hus died one of the memorable men of pioneer times, who never inflicted pain or knew an enemy—a man of strange habits, in whom there dwelt a comprehensive love that reached with one hand downward to the lowest forms of life, and with the other upward to the very throne of God." W.D. Haley, *Johnny Appleseed, A Pioneer Hero*, XLIII HARPER'S NEW MONTHLY MAGAZINE 830 (1871).

9. Forests provide a fascinating vantage on history. The spread of the British Empire, for example, was accomplished through its powerful navy and merchant fleet. This, in turn, depended on a steady source of timber. A single ship could require timber from 2,000 trees (about 50 acres of forest). Thus Ireland, a wooded island for over 10,000 years, was deforested and converted within a matter of centuries into the grass-covered "Emerald Isle" we know today. Similarly, the navy's demand inspired the charm of Britain's colonies in North America, with their straight, tall trees so well suited for ships' masts.

10. The United Nations Food and Agricultural Organization (FAO) reports on the state, changes, and conditions of the world's forests. The most recent survey, known as the Global Forest Resources Assessment (FRA 2005), includes detailed maps showing global forest cover and forest canopy density. *See* ftp://ftp.fao.org/docrep/fao/008/A0400E/A0400E00.pdf.

There is considerable debate, however, over these estimates and the true levels of global deforestation. As discussed in Note 6, *supra*, part of this turns on the various definitions of what constitutes deforestation, but a large part of the uncertainty stems from inadequate monitoring. The Global Forest Watch (GFW) project of the World Resources Institute is one of the most ambitious projects addressing this data gap. *See* http://www.wri.org/gfw.

11. The Amazon Conservation Team (ACT) protects Amazon basin rain forests by working to preserve indigenous cultures. Under the direction of its charismatic leader, Mark Plotkin, ACT pioneered a strategy that he calls "biocultural conservation," which aims to protect biodiversity by strengthening traditional health systems, and helping preserving culture in a holistic and synergistic way. According to Plotkin, "the people who best know, use, and protect biodiversity are the indigenous people who live in these forests.... ACT helps the keepers of the forest keep the forest!" *See* http://news.mongabay.com/2006/1031-interview_plotkin.html. ACT empowers indigenous peoples by: (1) helping them map and obtain legal rights to their traditional lands; (2) setting up clinics to provide traditional medicinal services under the control of elder shamans; and (3) coordinating with other indigenous groups. For example, ACT helped indigenous groups in Colombia set up a school to teach traditional medicine and worked with them to create the Indi Wasi National Park, which protects almost 170,000 acres of rain forest. The Park is co-managed by local indigenous groups and the Colombian government. Overall, the indigenous groups working with ACT control over 40 million acres of land in the Amazon basin. *See* http://www.amazonteam.org/. What advantages, if any, does ACT's approach have over traditional conservation?

PROBLEM EXERCISE: TREE SPIKING

Set forth below is an actual anonymous press release describing tree-spiking in a native forest north of Vancouver, British Columbia.

Communique from the Lorax, Wednesday, Feb. 16, 2000

The Lorax today took responsibility for spiking hundreds of ancient trees in the Elaho Valley, in areas approved for clearcut logging this year. The purpose of the tree spiking is to protect grizzly bear habitat and to deter International Forest Products (InterFor) from clearcutting this ancient coastal rainforest, located on Native land northwest of Whistler, BC. Hundreds of black bears and a small number of grizzlies inhabit the rugged mountains and canyons near the Elaho River.

The upper Elaho Valley is also known as the Randy Stoltmann Wilderness, and it is home to the oldest living Douglas firs in North America, the Elaho Giants. No one is likely to be injured as a result of the spikes. If InterFor decides to carry out its clearcut plans, workers will have to find the spikes with metal detectors and remove them by hand. Most sawmills screen logs for foreign objects that may damage the saw.

The Lorax encourages wood buyers worldwide to boycott InterFor. The company is destroying a unique cedar, hemlock and Douglas fir forest that is thousands of years old, without regard for wildlife, water quality or Native land claims. The Elaho River area is the southernmost remnant of grizzly bear habitat on the west coast of North America. * * *

http://www.geocities.com/riot_bitch2000/Communique.html. Suppose that you were the government official responsible for selling the timber to International Forest Products as well as for managing forest resources generally. How would you respond to this "communiqué"? If you represented International Forest Products, how would you respond?

———

C.   FOREST ECOSYSTEM SERVICES

As described in the excerpt below, forests provide important and valuable ecosystem services, offering shelter and habitat for a vast array of plant and animal species, purifying water, sequestering carbon, and slowing rainfall to prevent flooding. Most of these services are "free," in the sense that they are not captured in markets. As a result, with no obvious economic value they have often been ignored in management decisions.

DOUGLAS J. KRIEGER, ECONOMIC VALUE OF FOREST ECOSYSTEM SERVICES: A REVIEW III–VII (2001)

The importance of ecosystems to human well-being cannot be overstated. Forests provide raw materials for food, fuel and shelter. In forests, ecosystem components such as micro-organisms, soils and vegetative cover interact to purify air and water, regulate the climate and recycle nutrients and wastes. Without these and many other ecosystem goods and services, life as we know it would not be possible.

When we make decisions to alter natural forest ecosystems, we often give little thought to the consequences that change may have on forest ecosystem services or to the ultimate cost of losing those services. This oversight stems from our incomplete knowledge about how changes in ecosystems affect the level of services that the systems provide and our inadequate understanding of the roles played by seemingly trivial ecosystem components.

Perhaps the most significant factor is that few ecosystem services have clearly established monetary values. And this can have a strong impact, considering that many decisions about resource use are made by comparing benefits and costs. The decision to log a forest tract, for example, should be based on a comparison of the expected monetary value of the timber and the costs associated with the ecosystem goods and services foregone as a result of logging. Any ecosystem goods and services that do not have monetary values are generally not accounted for in the decision calculus. Neither is the fact that the benefits of many resource use decisions are usually enjoyed by small, fairly cohesive groups of people or the current generation, while the costs of foregone ecosystem goods and services are borne by larger, more dispersed groups or future generations.

Resource economists have long recognized the market distortions caused by unpriced goods. They have developed techniques to estimate monetary values, and ecological economists have applied those methods to estimate values for ecosystem services. This paper reviews estimates of the economic value of forest ecosystem goods and services in the United States. * * *

Watershed Services

Forested watersheds capture and store water, thus contributing to the quantity of water available and the seasonal flow of water. Forests also help purify water by stabilizing soils and filtering contaminants. The quantity and quality of water flowing from forested watersheds are important to agriculture, the generation of electricity, municipal water supplies, recreation and habitat for fish and other wildlife species. Estimates of water quantity values focus primarily on streamflow and range from $0.26 per acre-foot for electricity generation to as much as $50 per acre-foot for irrigation and municipal use.... In general, recreational values are probably higher in arid regions such as the Southwest and in regions that experience substantial seasonal variation in streamflow. * * *

Water quality is particularly important for municipal uses. The U.S. Environmental Protection Agency estimates that as many as 3,400 public water systems serving 60 million people obtain their water from watersheds that contain national forests. The value of the water purification services of forested water sheds is reflected in the costs that some communities incur to protect their watersheds. New York City spent $1.4 billion to protect the quality of water from the 80,000–acre forested watershed that serves much of the city [described *infra* at page 1209]. To protect their watersheds, Portland, Oregon spends $920,000 and Portland, Maine $729,000 per year. * * *

Soil Stabilization and Erosion Control

Forest vegetation helps stabilize soils and reduce erosion and sedimentation. Estimated values associated with soil stabilization primarily reflect the costs associated with sedimentation. Values range from $1.94 per ton in Tennessee to $5.5 million annually in Oregon's Willamette Valley. In Tucson, Arizona, a half million mesquite trees are expected to reduce runoff that would otherwise require construction of detention ponds costing $90,000.

Air Quality

Trees trap airborne particulate matter and thus improve air quality and human health. This paper discusses only one study of the value of air quality services from trees. That study concluded that the 500,000 mesquite trees which Tucson, Arizona, intends to plant will, once they reach maturity, remove 6,500 tons of particulate matter annually. Tucson spends $1.5 million on an alternative dust control program. Therefore, the air quality value of each tree equals $4.16.

Climate Regulation and Carbon Sequestration

Trees help regulate climate by trapping moisture and cooling the earth's surface.... Studies in urban settings conclude that 100,000 properly planted, mature trees in U.S. cities may save as much as $2 billion in heating and cooling costs. Trees also capture atmospheric carbon dioxide, thereby reducing global warming. The U.S. Forest Service estimates that such carbon sequestration services yield benefits of $65 per ton, which totals to $3.4 billion annually for all U.S. forests.

Biological Diversity

Biological diversity is important for many reasons, including its role as a store house of genetic material that can be used to selectively breed plants and animals, its contribution to natural pest and disease control and its ability to provide valuable pharmaceutical products. Few studies have addressed the value of biological diversity in forest ecosystems, but it is estimated that the cost to U.S. agriculture of using chemical pesticides to replace the natural pest control services from all natural ecosystems would be about $54 billion annually. The U.S. Forest Service estimates that it would cost more than $7 per acre to replace the pest control services of birds in forests with chemical pesticides. In addition, the pollination services of natural ecosystems provide U.S. agriculture benefits of $4 billion to $7 billion annually.

Recreation and Tourism

Scenic beauty and recreational amenities associated with forests make them popular recreation destinations. The U.S. Forest Service estimated that recreational activities on national forests alone contribute $110 billion annually to this nation's Gross Domestic Product. Regionally, the economic impact of forest-based recreation depends to some extent on the proximity of population centers as well as on the unique characteristics of a region's forest resources. Estimates of the economic impact of forest-influenced recreation vary from $736 million annually in Montana to $6 billion annually in the Southern Appalachians region.

Wild, unroaded lands offer a unique form of outdoor recreation, and many studies have estimated the value of wilderness-related recreation. Based on an average value of $41.87 per visitor day, the economic value of recreation on the 42 million acres of roadless areas in the U.S. national forests is $600 million annually. Among residents of the Northeast, use values for eastern wilderness total $29 million annually. Visitors to wilderness areas in Colorado are willing to pay $14 and in Utah $12 per visit for wilderness recreation.

Forest ecosystems are also important destinations for hunters and anglers. In 1996, hunters spent 19.4 million days hunting on national forests and more than 18 million people fished in national forests. The economic impact of these activities is substantial—between $1.3 and $2.1 billion for hunting and $1.4 and $2.9 billion for fishing nationwide. In the Southern Appalachians region, hunting generated impacts of $594 million and fishing $407 million in 1996. Hunters on federal lands in the Columbian River Basin spend as much as $150 million annually. In the Pacific Northwest, commercial and recreational fishing generate more than $1 billion in income annually. In Montana, anglers were willing to pay $2.07 million to protect high-quality recreational fishing in just one roadless study area.

Non–Timber Commercial Forest Products

Forests produce many commercially valuable products other than timber, including mushrooms, floral greens, medicinal plants and edible plant and wildlife species. The total market value of these non-timber products harvested in the Pacific Northwest amounted to about $300 million in 1992. In New York, a single community generated $910,000 in sales for non-timber forest products. Non-timber forest products are also important in sources of subsistence foods in some regions. In southeastern Alaska, the average household consumes an average of 889 pounds of edible resources annually. This includes 295 pounds of salmon with a market value of $590 and 118 pounds of venison with a market value of $472.

Cultural Values

Cultural values associated with forests include what economists call passive use values for forest goods and services (including endangered species habitat), the aesthetic value of forest scenery and values associated with a region's cultural heritage. The scenic characteristics of forests attract tourists to forested regions, and the resulting economic impact can be substantial. Visitors to the scenic Blue Ridge Parkway in North Carolina and Virginia, for example, contribute $1.3 billion to local economies. Visitors to the Southern Appalachians region reported a willingness to pay $18 to $99 per household per year to maintain the scenic quality of the region's forests. Forest ecosystems also provide habitat for some endangered species. Values attached to Pacific Northwest old-growth forests for northern spotted owl habitat range from $35 to $95 per household per year.

Many people attach value to knowing that forests exist now and into the future. Estimates of such existence value for old-growth forests west of the Cascade Mountains extend from $48 to $144 per U.S. household per year. Residents of Wisconsin revealed a willingness to pay $7 million to protect wilderness areas in Utah that they are unlikely to visit. A study in Vermont found passive use values for wilderness protection range from $14 to $92 per household per year.

———

QUESTIONS AND DISCUSSION

1. The preceding excerpt on the ecosystem goods and services of forests provides a range of specific monetary values determined by nonmarket methodologies. Krieger describes a study in Tucson, Arizona, for example, that concluded that planting 500,000 mesquite trees would remove 6,500 tons of particulate matter annually. "Tucson spends $1.5 million on an alternative dust control program. Therefore, the air quality value of each tree equals $4.16." He cites similar types of studies (relying on replacement cost methodology) to calculate values for erosion control and water quality. What do you think of these numbers? How should they be used to guide policy decisions?

2. The City of New York offers the best known example of payments for forest ecosystem services. In the early 1990s, a combination of federal regulation and cost realities drove New York City to reconsider its water supply strategy. New York City's water system provides 1.4 billion gallons of drinking water to almost nine million New Yorkers every day. Ninety percent of the water is drawn from the Catskill and Delaware watersheds located 125 miles north and west of the city. Under amendments to the federal Safe Drinking Water Act, municipal and other water suppliers were required to filter their surface water supplies unless they could demonstrate that they had taken other steps, including watershed protection measures, to protect their customers from harmful water contamination.

Presented with a choice between provision of clean water through building a filtration plant or managing the watershed, New York City easily concluded that the latter was more cost effective. New York City estimated that a filtration plant would cost between $6 billion and $8 billion to build and another $300 million annually to operate. By contrast, watershed protection efforts, which would include not only the acquisition of critical watershed lands but also a variety of other programs designed to reduce contamination sources in the watershed, would cost only about $1.5 billion. Acting on behalf of New Yorkers—the beneficiaries of the Catskills' water purification services—New York City chose to invest in natural rather than built capital.

While the New York approach provides a natural alternative to the standard, costly treatment plant, it has its critics. To maintain the pristine source of its water, New York City has been aggressively trying to curb development in the Catskill and Delaware watersheds. The City has devoted $250 million towards acquiring land in the area, proving that such ecosystem services come with a hefty price tag and often hinder local economies by denying new building. As in the spotted owl controversy, these ecosystem plans tend to pit environmental concerns of the greater public against economic concerns of the local citizenry. However, local citizen groups have formed to ensure the rural citizens have a voice, and conservation easements giving locals the incentive not to develop have gone a great way towards assuaging the public's concerns. *See* http://www.fathom.com/course/10701045/session3.html.

Nor is New York City alone. According to the International Institute for Environment and Development, there are over 280 actual and proposed payment plans dealing with carbon sequestration, biodiversity conservation, and watershed protection. There are scores of examples of payments for forest ecosystems in developing countries, as well. The non-governmental group, Forest Trends, works specifically on creating market opportunities for forest ecosystem service payments. For a comprehensive website on service markets, *see* www.ecosystemmarketplace.com; *see also* NATASHA LANDELL MILLS & INA PORRES, SILVER BULLET OR FOOL'S GOLD: A GLOBAL REVIEW OF MARKETS FOR FOREST ENVIRONMENTAL SERVICES AND THEIR IMPACTS ON THE POOR (International Institute for Environment and Development, 2002).

Which types of forest services do you think are most amenable to payment schemes? What are the necessary precursors for successful schemes? Why might payment programs be harder or easier to establish in developed or developing countries?

3. Ecosystem services can also aid planning for major industrial projects in developing regions, as evident in the Yangtze watershed of China.

Researchers used spatial models for water flow in different types of forests and soils to determine the potential for hydroelectric power in the region. The study found that terrestrial ecosystems regulate and stabilize the amount of water entering the Yangtze, which, in turn, maximizes the amount of power the river can generate. The study concluded that the economic benefit realized indirectly from the region's forest is actually 2.2 times more than the annual income from direct products of the forest like lumber. Not only does this project demonstrate the tangible economic benefits of maintaining the ecosystem services, but it also exemplifies the importance of strong scientific data to guide and support ecosystem services planning. Without such a strong study, both the economic and environmental windfall of the forest ecosystem could have been lost, especially in developing countries rushing to grow. Zhongwei Guo, *An Assessment of Ecosystem Services: Water Flow Regulation and Hydroelectric Power Production,* ECOLOGICAL APPLICATIONS: VOL. 10, No. 3, 925–36 (JUNE 2000).

4. One of the problems associated with non-timber values of forests—whether they relate to recreational or tourist value, aesthetic value, or the value of ecosystems services—is that they are not easily captured by the forest owner. While leases for hunting and fishing on private lands have become increasingly common and can generate significant revenues, other non-timber values are more difficult for the landowner to recover. *See* John S. Baen, *The Growing Importance and Value Implications of Recreational Hunting Leases to Agricultural Land Investors in America,* 14 J. OF REAL ESTATE RESEARCH 399 (1997). As a result, a forest owner seeking to maximize revenues might be inclined to allow logging that reduces social welfare, given the other non-market values of the forest. The same can be true for a country. Economist Robert Repetto argues that Indonesia, for example, is becoming impoverished by its logging policy, losing four times the value of its timber exports once one takes into account the loss of ecosystem services. ROBERT REPETTO, FOREST FOR THE TREES (1988).

III. THE TIMBER INDUSTRY

The sections below briefly describe the major logging methods, the environmental impacts of logging, and the economic and social dynamics of logging communities. As with ranching and fishing, the timber industry has long had a strong influence on local economies and culture, making changes in management practices a difficult undertaking.

A. LOGGING METHODS

Silviculture is the science of forestry. It encompasses the study of logging methods, as well as the study of the impacts of logging on the environment. Logging has four basic aspects—getting to the trees, cutting them down, getting the logs out, and (in most cases) ensuring the right trees grow so they can be harvested in the future. Each step in this process offers choices. Should one build roads or use cables and helicopters for access and removal of trees? Should heavy machinery be used to take out a large area of trees at one time or more carefully select only mature, high value trees for removal?

Because of its higher economic efficiencies, the method of choice for logging companies is *clearcutting*. Clearcutting involves the removal of all or most of the trees from the site and is often described as "even-aged management" because it helps ensure regeneration of trees of the same species, with the same age and roughly the same size, thereby facilitating future harvests. This suits shade-intolerant and fast-growing species best, such as jack pine, lodgepole pine, and black spruce. Beyond being the simplest and least expensive logging system, clearcutting is also the safest harvesting method.

In some cases, clearcut sites are regenerated by distributing seeds or planting seedlings to stabilize soils and promote faster regrowth. In other cases, trees are allowed to regenerate naturally, though this usually takes longer. This produces an even-aged monoculture, with great value as timber stock but poor biodiversity value. There are, though, several clear-cutting variations. The *seed tree harvesting* method removes all of the trees from the site except for a few that are intended to provide seeds for natural regeneration. Seed tree harvesting causes many of the same environmental impacts as clearcutting. Furthermore, isolated seed trees are susceptible to "windthrow" or being toppled by wind.

As a new stand of trees establishes itself, it often produces many trees that compete for space and soil nutrients. To promote the growth of larger trees, stands are often selectively thinned. Generally, the growth rate of a new tree stand increases steadily until it reaches its peak, or culmination of mean annual growth. The rate then begins to decline. To maximize wood products production, trees are usually not harvested until their rate of growth has begun to decline.

Shelterwood harvesting is done in phases and, as with the seed tree method, is designed to promote natural regeneration. In the first phase, the larger trees with dense canopies are removed, leaving enough trees to provide both shelter and seed dispersal for new growth. Once regrowth has been firmly established, additional logging may be allowed to remove the shelterwood. Because trees remain on-site throughout all phases of shelter-wood harvesting, many of the environmental problems associated with other forms of clearcutting can be avoided. Ideally, the seed trees that are allowed to remain after the first cut will be among the straightest and most disease-free, so that they will regenerate new trees of high quality. As a practical matter, however, this is more complex and costly than other types of clearcutting and these seed trees are most likely the ones that will be prized by the logging company.

To give a better sense of a clearcut landscape, we show below an aerial shot of the Coon Creek timber sale in the Medicine Bow National Forest in southeastern Wyoming. The photo was taken by Jeff Kessler of the Biodiversity Conservation Alliance in April, 1996. The Coon Creek timber sale was a "water yield augmentation project." This means it was designed not primarily to produce timber, but rather to provide greater water flows in the watershed for use primarily by farmers. The sale resulted in 224 clearcuts averaging 3.9 acres (totaling 887 acres) and 17 overstory removal cuts averaging 4.3 acres (totaling 73 acres). To log these 960 acres of timber, 27.4 miles of new roads were constructed in the 4,000–acre Coon Creek watershed. *See generally* Charles A. Troendle, Marc S. Wilcox, Greg S. Bevenger, and Laurie S. Porth, *The Coon Creek Water Yield Augmentation Project*, 143 Forest Ecology and Mgt. 179 (2001).

While such pictures of clearcut areas send shivers down the spines of many people, proponents of clearcutting argue that it mimics natural disturbances such as fire, wind storms, or insect infestations. There are, however, important ecological differences to keep in mind. Most forest fires are low intensity, producing a random mosaic of gaps and remnant stands that provide important wildlife habitat. Fire also kills pathogens and breaks up rock, providing nutrients for the soil. In contrast, clearcutting requires the use of heavy machinery and roads, accelerating soil erosion that results in soil and nutrient loss and stream pollution. "Slash," the waste materials left after logging, also increases the risk of fire.

Moreover, slash does not include most of the important biomass left after a fire. Fire leaves the burnt structures of the trees to decay within the forest and replenish the soil. Burnt embers remain on the land, while most of the smoke particles fall elsewhere in the forest. Clearcutting, on the other hand, removes the bulk of the natural biomass a forest creates. Because clearcutting takes the lion's share of this valuable regenerative debris, the resulting forest differs considerably from the natural, fire-inspired product.

The main alternative to clearcutting is known as *selection harvesting* or "uneven aged management." The selection method identifies individual trees or small groups of trees to be harvested at regular intervals. This promotes maintenance of a variety of tree species of different sizes and age classes and ensures a steady supply of mature trees and a more regular income stream. Areas logged using the selection method are more aesthetically attractive than clearcut areas and minimize loss of biodiversity. This is, however, a more expensive and complex system than clearcutting, requiring skilled workers to manage the cuts and, in some settings, may require as many or more roads than clearcut areas.

The diagram below depicts the different logging methods.

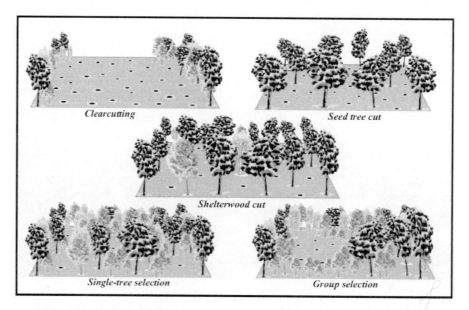

Clearcutting

Seed tree cut

Shelterwood cut

Single-tree selection

Group selection

From *A Landowners Guide To Sustainable Forestry in Indiana*, Purdue University Cooperative Extension Service at 9, FNR 182 (2002), *available at* http://www.ces.purdue.edu/extmedia/FNR/FNR–182.pdf. The Chapter 10 link on the casebook website contains additional information and photographs of logging machinery and methods.

B. ENVIRONMENTAL IMPACTS OF LOGGING

While clearcutting is the most efficient commercial logging method, it, and other methods, can cause a host of environmental problems. As described below, most of these problems relate to soils, water, and wildlife.

1. SOIL EROSION AND COMPACTION

Modern logging operations generally use large machinery to build roads into logging areas, to strip and remove trees from the ground, to skid trees along the ground so they can be brought to the landing where they are loaded for transportation, and to transport the logs to market. All of this heavy equipment disturbs the soil and vegetation, causing erosion and compacting the remaining soils. Soil compaction eliminates the air spaces in soil. This makes it more difficult for water to penetrate the soil, thereby inhibiting plant growth. Water runoff from compacted soils also increases erosion.

Compaction is a particular problem with wet or ''hydric'' soils, including wetlands, because of the important role that these areas play in the ecology of the forest. Modern practices like *cable logging,* in which logs are brought from the logging site to the landing where they will be loaded by an elevated cable, can help minimize compaction.

2. WATER

Logging impacts water resources in several ways. As noted above, road building and skidding disturb soils and lead to sedimentation of streams. Logging can also damage wetlands and disrupt their provision of water purification and flood control services. Logging can also increase water yields in streams by promoting run-off, and preventing the evapo-transpiration of water through the trees and into the atmosphere. In extreme cases this can cause flooding, though in the Western United States, where water resources are often scarce, increased water yields are often used to justify logging operations even where such operations might otherwise lose money.

3. WILDLIFE HABITAT

Forests provide important habitat for many species of wildlife. As the Spotted Owl saga described in Chapter 4 (page 388) made clear, logging can most directly affect habitat by destroying it. Logging also degrades habitat through *fragmentation*—the separation of large, unbroken habitats into isolated and small patches. Forest fragmentation is usually caused by logging or land clearing for agriculture. Forest roads also contribute to fragmentation. National forest lands in the United States host more than 430,000 miles of roads—enough to circle the globe more than 17 times. Most of these roads were built to promote logging and were heavily subsidized by taxpayers. Fragmentation alters the biodiversity of forests by disrupting migration patterns, reducing habitat area (usually older growth), and by increasing edge habitats and predation. As the theory of island biogeography would predict, (pages 1262–1272), all of these changes can wreak havoc on an ecosystem.

All of the environmental impacts described above have come together in the case of salmon populations in the Pacific Northwest. While dams and overfishing have been the primary causes of the decline of various salmon species, the timber industry has also been a significant contributor. Logging, and particularly the construction of logging roads, has resulted in increased sedimentation of salmon streams, covering gravel in which salmon have traditionally spawned and increasing the turbidity of streams, which can also disrupt salmon migration. Poorly designed road culverts have sometimes blocked salmon migration to spawning areas. Removal of trees, which create a shade canopy along stream banks, has increased stream temperatures and reduced the supply of large, woody debris that helps form fish habitat. This problem was particularly acute prior to the 1980s when timber companies actually removed woody debris from streams because biologists believed the removal would help salmon migrate upstream to spawn. *See generally* MICHAEL C. BLUMM, SACRIFICING THE SALMON: A LEGAL AND POLICY HISTORY OF THE DECLINE OF COLUMBIA BASIN SALMON (2002). Today, most state Forest Practice Acts (discussed later in this Chapter at pages 1308–1317), limit timber harvesting alongside riparian areas, with the width of the buffer zone depending upon a variety of habitat issues. To help alleviate the impact of these rules on small forest owners, the state of Washington created a Forest Riparian Easement Program that compensates qualifying landowners for a 50 year easement on streamside timber in return for the landowners' agreement not to harvest the timber. *See* WASH. ADMIN. CODE § 222–21 (2008).

QUESTIONS AND DISCUSSION

1. In addition to their importance for wood production and forest ecology, forest lands also serve important aesthetic and recreational functions. As we saw in Chapter 8 on Rangelands, competition for use of forest resources for non-consumptive purposes has been growing. *See also* Jan G. Laitos & Thomas A. Carr, *The Transformation on Public Lands*, 26 ECOL. L. Q. 140 (1999) ("In recent years ... America's public lands have undergone a fundamental change. They are now dominated by just two non-consumptive uses—recreation and preservation.") One economist has estimated, for example, that the six national forests that surround Yellowstone National Park produce $20 in recreational benefits for every dollar in timber benefits. Recreation also produces eight times as many jobs as timber in that region, not to mention the ecosystem services described in the preceding section. Randall O'Toole, *Reforming the Forest Service,* 13 COLUM. J. ENVTL. L. 299, 300 (1988).

2. If there are no endangered species in a forest or stand of trees, should the state or federal government have the power to deny a logging company the right to cut trees? What if, for example, the trees are truly ancient or extraordinary? Does it make sense to speak of legal rights for particular trees? If so, what types of specific rights do these entail? If the logging companies are restrained from harming extraordinary trees, should they be compensated by the government? Do the logging company's private property rights extend to logging as many trees as they desire so long as their activities do not cause tort harms? *See generally* Christopher Stone, *Should Trees Have Standing?*, 45 S. Cal. L. Rev. 450 (1972); JOSEPH SAX, PLAYING DARTS WITH A REMBRANDT: PUBLIC AND PRIVATE RIGHTS IN CULTURAL TREASURES (1999).

3. What is your reaction to the state of Washington's Forest Riparian Easement Program that compensates small forest owners for not harvesting timber adjacent to salmon streams? Is the state paying for something that it could accomplish less expensively with its police power? Why limit this program to small landowners?

——————

C.   CUSTOMS, CULTURES, AND LOCAL TIMBER ECONOMIES

Any discussion of the economics of forest resources inevitably conjures up images of logging camps and small towns built around a sawmill. That timber has long played an important role in the historical development of the United States, and in the economies and cultures of hundreds of small communities throughout the country, can hardly be denied. How, if at all, should the law respond to the relationship between communities and forests? In that regard consider the following three excerpts. The first two portray some of the anger and pathos generated by the closure of sawmills. The third, written by Tom Power, chair of the economics department at the University of Montana, refutes some of the most enduring myths surrounding timber communities.

Craig Childs, *The Millworker and the Forest: Notes on Natural History, Human Industry and the Deepest Wilds of the Northwest* HIGH COUNTRY NEWS, Sept. 27, 1999 at 1

There are two ways to see the interior of a thousand-year-old Douglas fir. One is to mill it, where it will smell of fresh, powder-burned wood and will be hot to the touch from the band saw. The cut will be straight, an artistry of mechanics, something a shadow will fall flat against. The other is to walk into the Olympic Mountains in Washington, where wind has chosen the largest fir and ruptured it near its base. It will have collapsed into a wreckage of slivers and knots.

It will leave splinters in your fingers. The heart of the tree will be red as salmon.

Jim Podlesny emerges from the fir, sawdust in his hair, blades of sunlight against his shirt. He tells me how it happened, the kinetic energy, the explosion, the force of one tree taking down another in the wind. He submits his arms to the sky when he talks. In his story is a driven rain, streams of water cascading from the canopy. His words carry the weight of the wind.

"Look up into the crowns," he says. "You can imagine the wrestling match they had, trees leveraging against each other as they fell."

This Douglas fir had stood with 3 tons of water in its bulk, so when it fell, it burst open. It is a sculpture of cataclysm. A four-door sedan would fit into the erupted remains of its trunk. The wood smells sweet where it has split, and is damp to the touch. * * *

Jim Podlesny, millworker, 41 years old. He was hired by Rayonier Inc. in Port Angeles, Washington, the year wood pulp hit its worldwide peak price.

Four years, one month and ten days later, he lost his job when the mill closed. There were cries of foul play against the company, against environmentalists, the spotted owl and anyone within earshot. Anguish was spray-painted on the inside of the mill like angry prayers.

He was among the last dozen to work at the mill after the first 350 were laid off. * * *

The pulp mill history of Port Angeles is a series of mergers, closings and receiverships dating to the early 1900s. Mills opened and closed, slowed by environmental regulations, sped by clear-cut programs.

Under one name or another, Rayonier had been a pillar of the town since 1927. The company supplied 10 percent of the town's revenue, dumped $60,000 into scholarships each year, and another $40 million into the general economy. Six hundred jobs, not actually on the company payroll, were directly related to the mill, a symbiosis as complex as nitrogen-fixing bacteria at the roots of a 200–foot cedar. The town and the mill had melted together.

Then the supply of wood abated. The price of pulp plummeted. Some locals said it had nothing to do with the spotted owl and the Endangered Species Act. There just weren't enough big trees anymore.

The shortage was no surprise. In the 1970s, the government made the unprecedented move of opening federal land to clear-cutting. It was a way of flushing fresh cash through the economy, booming the Northwest. The result was simple to predict: Once the forest is clear-cut, second-growth timber will not make near the profits. Rayonier Inc. knew this. Official predictions of it were published 10 years earlier.

When a Northwest coastal forest starts from leveled ground, the biomass of greenery hits a peak after 50 years. Wood, however, continues expansion for another 600 years. If you cut it before 600 years, you're only getting scraps. The thing to do was to move to Port Angeles, make as much money as possible off old-growth harvest, then brace for the inevitable crash. But a lot of children were born in that time, mortgages acquired, V–8 extra-cab trucks purchased, loans taken.

When forests thinned, when certain regions were closed to timber harvest due to declining spotted owl populations, the industry faltered. Rayonier went from using 242 million board-feet in 1985 to 13.6 million a decade later.

Podlesny kept careful notes, each comment and date and rumor that worked through the ranks. He witnessed every step of the process because it was not merely pulp and jobs and forest. It was history.

When he speaks of the pulp mill his words are steam and darkness and steel digesters with great welded rivets. People sweating, hauling, cursing; people with short, powerful nicknames, and sons of sons of sons who have always worked in the hiss and the groan of Rayonier.

There were, of course, those in the community who were ecstatic to witness the closure. The mill's effluent bore toxins of epic proportions. Sulfates and oil and a brew of nasties spilled into the Strait of Juan de Fuca. Sulfur dioxide and ammonia escaped into the atmosphere at regular intervals, altering the color of houses in certain parts of town.

The EPA has volumes of violations from Port Angeles alone, naming Rayonier as the heaviest single polluter in the state the year it closed. * * *

People who watched these forests become lunar landscapes and who protested the dumping of toxic mill waste tried to boycott Rayonier. But the product was not something you could isolate.

The mill produced raw cellulose, forced from wood chips in a 280 degrees Fahrenheit bath of sulfur and ammonia. The pulp comes out in the form of thick paper and is sold to unrelated companies; they dissolve and mold it into oil filters, toothbrush handles, rayon fabric, chewing gum, kitchen sponges, eyeglass frames, pudding thickeners, film and handy wipes.

To boycott Rayonier one would have to abandon most amenities of civilization, stripping naked to disappear into the wilderness. * * *

When I ask, [Podlesny] tells me that he does not need to reconcile wilderness and industry. They lead in and out of each other. Rayonier finally closed only 10 days ago and now he is in the forest. I ask him about toxins at Rayonier and about ethics, how he could live with these on his back.

"The paycheck," he says. "Too much is bad for the world, but a human has got to make a living." For Podlesny, the mill is history.... You can close your eyes to industry but your life is made of it. He tells me that it is the path society has chosen, living off cellulose pulp and steel.

Who is more part of it, the maker or the buyer? The man who works at the mill or the backpacker who wears the product? * * *

————

Valerie Richardson, *Despite an Adequate Supply of Timber, Environmentalists Cost Hundreds Their Jobs in Logging,* Wash. Times, Nov. 25, 2001, at A1

Look in any direction along this stretch of rural Idaho and the first thing you see are the trees. They're everywhere—thousands upon thousands of acres of lodgepole pine and Douglas fir, cascading down hills and blanketing mountains as far as the eye can see. For a century, the trees of the Boise, Payette, Nez Perce and Clearwater national forests provided the people here with shelter, work, recreation and a way of life.

No longer. As the poet Samuel Coleridge once observed about the ocean, that it has "Water, water everywhere/Nor any drop to drink," the national forests of Idaho are filled with millions of trees that cannot be touched.

For the past decade, timber communities throughout the Northwest have waged a legal and public-relations battle with environmental groups over how the trees should be used. By all accounts and on every front, the loggers are losing.

President Theodore Roosevelt's vision of maintaining the national forests as the nation's lumber supply was replaced during the Clinton administration by the idea that forests should be preserved in their natural state. The amount of timber that could be harvested was reduced drastically, both by the administration's moratorium on road-building and by the legal system, as environmentalists took to the courts to stop the logging.

That shift has come at a price. There are more trees and more old-growth, but also more disease and dead wood. There are fewer chainsaws in the forests, but also fewer mills, homes and families. And within the small, wooded hamlets whose denizens have cut and replanted the trees for generations, there is poverty, dislocation, anger—and a sense of disbelief that is slowly turning into resignation. * * *

Idaho and the rest of the Pacific Northwest have watched the timber economy plummet over the last decade, taking with it a dozen mills and at least 30,000 jobs. The reasons include automation and greater efficiency at timber mills and plants; falling lumber prices; and stiff competition from across the border in the form of cheaper Canadian lumber.

"The reason the mills closed is soft prices, imports from Canada, and the timber industry's willingness to move to other countries because of relaxed environmental standards under NAFTA," said Roger Singer, director of the Sierra Club's Idaho chapter. "The sudden downturn in the industry is due to market forces, not environmental challenges."

But those in the timber industry say they could have handled those fluctuations without closing the mills. What they couldn't handle was the political assault they faced from the environmental movement.

"All these mills have been around for almost a century. They've been through economic upturns and downturns. They went through the Depression," said Steve Bliss, a former millworker and union representative from Horseshoe Bend. "But you can't operate without raw materials."

"It has nothing to do with the economy and nothing to do with demand. It has everything to do with the environmental movement and political correctness," he said.

Starting in the mid–1980s, environmental groups began stepping up their opposition to timber sales in the national forests. * * *

Environmentalists have managed to bring the process to a grinding halt by filing legal challenges, or appeals, to most timber sales. The appeals are usually based on perceived problems with the sale, such as a failure to take into account endangered species or sensitive wildlife habitat.

Sometimes the appeals are successful, and a judge halts the sale. "The reason we're successful is because the Forest Service isn't playing by the rules," said John McCarthy, wildlife director of the Idaho Conservation League, which is responsible for many of the challenges.

"They can't account for old growth and how it affects endangered species. We can always find experts on the inside who will say, 'They're doing it wrong,' " he said.

Even when the appeals fail, the process can drag on for years. That's too much time for small logging outfits and mills, which can go out of business waiting for a challenge to move through the legal system. * * *

In February, Boise Cascade announced that it would shut down its mills in Cascade and Emmett, laying off 400 workers. While some critics blamed poor management, Chairman George J. Harad cited lack of raw materials.

The closures came as the end of an era for Boise Cascade, which has seen its mills in Idaho decline from five to none.

"Despite an adequate supply of timber, under the policies of the Clinton administration and pressure from environmental groups, the amount of timber offered for commercial harvest has declined more than 90 percent over the past five years," Mr. Harad said.

The ripple effect led to the closure of half-dozen other related businesses in Cascade, ranging from a rental equipment outlet to a flower shop. Soon the modest one-story homes in Cascade's neighborhoods were peppered with "For Sale" signs as families sought jobs elsewhere in the Northwest.

In Cascade, a town of a little more than a thousand, losing even one family leaves a void. After the mill closed, as many as 70 families moved, including some whose roots in the town went back three generations, said Mr. Vandenburg, the City Council member.

"I don't know what's worse, to leave town or to stay here and watch everyone else leave," he said.

Those fortunate enough to find jobs in Cascade were forced to take substantial pay cuts. Jobs at the Boise Cascade mill paid between $12 and $19 an hour with "the best benefits package in Idaho," said Ron Lundquist, a former millworker.

He now helps manage a trailer park, a job that pays well at $16 an hour but provides bare-bones benefits, not to mention less satisfaction.

"I enjoy this job," Mr. Lundquist said. "But I was raised in a resource family. There's something to be said for making something from a natural resource. It's rewarding because you're building something." * * *

Faced with double-digit unemployment and no second coming of the timber industry in sight, Idaho logging towns are trying to diversify their economies by luring other businesses, starting with tourism. Given the beauty of the forests, rivers and lakes, spotlighting the area's rafting, boating and hiking opportunities came as a natural move. * * *

Tourism offers its own set of problems. The work is seasonal—strong in the summer but virtually nonexistent in the winter—and the jobs don't pay as well as mill work. In Riggins, just north of Cascade, the town has a thriving river-rafting business, but the investment hasn't paid off as well as locals had hoped.

"They're relying on tourism for their funds, and frankly, there isn't any money in that," said Wayne Davis, superintendent of the local school district. "You get a few backpackers, a few rafters, but there's nothing to sustain jobs."

Tourism also tends to change the complexion of towns. Locals point to the example of McCall, about 30 miles north of Cascade, where the town managed to replace a closed mill with tourism, then watched as wealthy retirees moved in, drove up housing prices and began pushing out the middle class.

"McCall has gone from a working man's community to a rich man's playground," said Dave Rosen, a former co-worker of Mr. Lundquist. * * *

Perhaps the biggest untold story from the timber economy's decline is its impact on public schools. Most schools rely on property taxes for the bulk of their funding, but in the West, where most of the land is federally owned, there isn't enough of a tax base to maintain rural schools. As a result, the Forest Service sends 25 percent of its sale receipts back to the state. Of that, 70 percent goes toward state road projects and 30 percent goes to schools.

Consequently, as timber profits have fallen, so has money for education. Cascade has just begun to feel the pinch, but in communities whose mills shut down five or six years ago, school officials have been forced to fire teachers, eliminate elective classes, cut sports and music, even trim the school week down from five days to four. * * *

Millworkers seethed when Mr. McCarthy was quoted as saying they should all go work for Micron. "You notice that Micron's laying off people," Mr. Lundquist said. But state leaders are indeed looking for high-tech remedies for the ailing economy. Idaho recently became the first state to institute a tax credit for broadband companies that build in rural areas. * * *

"The pendulum is probably going to swing back, but for a lot of these towns, it's too late," said Mr. Bliss, the former millworker and union representative. "There's never going to be another sawmill in Horseshoe Bend or Cascade—it would cost $50 million in today's dollars to build it."

For anyone who lives in these woods, however, it doesn't take much to restore their faith in the forest's ability to provide for them.

"You drive out five minutes in any direction and you're in forest," Cascade School Principal Bill Leaf said. "My father logged the same lands that my grandfather was logging with a horse and teams. It's been here for generations and it's still beautiful land. It hasn't been pilfered."

————

THOMAS MICHAEL POWER, LOST LANDSCAPES AND FAILED ECONOMIES: THE SEARCH FOR THE VALUE OF PLACE 134–146 (1996)

The impact of timber harvest policies on local communities has long been recognized. Deforestation changes the possible mix of economic activities and has the potential to change watersheds and local climate. Clearly, communities can be and often are dependent on forests.

This social reality has colored discussions of American forest policy from at least the middle of the nineteenth century, when citizens of Maine and Pennsylvania began worrying about the future of their timber industries. Since then, forest policy has been entwined with concerns about social policy. Public dialogue on forestry practices has typically been couched in terms of "social forestry." The general idea that communities can depend on forest resources for their well-being, and that well-being is affected by forest management decisions, was converted into a vague concept of community stability that has been touted by almost every interest group concerned with public forest policy. * * *

Community stability obviously means a lot of different things to a lot of different people. It carries a lot of emotional and rhetorical weight, especially undefined, and dominates public discourse on forest policy while doing little to inform that discourse. For most of the last several decades the U.S. Forest Service has interpreted community stability to mean boosting the flow of raw materials from public lands to private lumber mills. * * *

Timber harvesting and processing are usually touted as one of the few high-paying and reliable sources of local employment and income. The argument is straightforward: the timber industry will significantly increase income-earning potential and employment opportunity in otherwise backwoods areas. The tax base from the mill and logging equipment will fund public infrastructure and services. Education, roads, parks, and law enforcement will improve, and with them the quality of life. Is this picture accurate, or just a deceptive lure? * * *

Solid-wood products (lumber and plywood mills) is one of the most volatile manufacturing industries in the American economy. Because a significant part of its output flows directly into the housing industry, the demand for wood products fluctuates with the volume of home building. Housing starts in the United States fluctuate widely, doubling in a matter of a year or so, then falling to half of their former level, depending on demographic changes, interest rates, and confidence in the national economy. The swings in income earned in wood products are two to four times as large as those in manufacturing as a whole. Real total income rarely declines by more than a few percentage points even in the worst recession, but real income from wood products can decline by as much as a third. During the 1970s, income from wood products boomed, expanding by 50 percent after adjusting for inflation, and then crashed, returning to the levels of ten years earlier. In the mid–1980s the industry recovered only to lose much of its gain in the late 1980s and early 1990s. When fluctuations in the national economy are compared to the ups and downs of the wood products roller coaster, the national economy looks like a smooth ride up.

Analysis of counties in timber states where wood products provide a large percentage of total income illustrates the destabilizing impact of this industry. For instance, in western Montana where the timber industry is considered dominant, the larger the industry is as a source of county income, the larger the declines in total county income over the last two decades. The relative importance of the wood products industry in any given county explains about 90 percent of the variation in income decline. A similar pattern of income decline tied to the predominance of the wood products industry can be found in the timber counties of Oregon. The more important the industry is to the local economy, the larger the periodic downward pressure on that economy is likely to be. * * *

One way to emotionally charge this normal and positive transformation of the economy is to raise the issue of disrupted ways of life. Several generations of families work in the timber industry, harvesting and processing trees. A community is established, complete with its own values and culture. Now with logging jobs threatened—even if they can be replaced by other jobs—a way of life, a part of American culture and history, will die. Who could be in favor of that? Loggers and mill workers have an aura that teachers, accountants, and computer consultants lack. There are no Paul Bunyan legends about service workers.

But is logging and lumber mill work a way of life, like farming and ranching, handed down from one generation to another? Or is it just another job that people move into and out of with considerable frequency? Data suggests the latter. In 1991 the median tenure of employment in lumber and wood products firms was 4.2 years, in sawmills 4.6 years, and in miscellaneous wood products 2.7 years. That is, over half of the employees in any given wood products firm worked there for only 3 to 5 years. And the median tenure as a worker in the industry was only 5.3 years. This is hardly what one would expect in an industry around which so much romanticized folklore has gathered. In fact, these job tenure statistics are lower than for the economy as a whole, where median job tenure is 4.5 years and median tenure in the industry is 6.5 years. People working in wood products hold those jobs for a shorter time than workers elsewhere in the economy. Notably, service workers, though they have about the same tenure with their current employers as wood products workers, about 4 years, have a much longer tenure in the industry, almost 7 years. The much-maligned service jobs that are increasing while wood products jobs disappear provide longer job tenure. If we are interested in promoting ways of life built around stable job tenure, maybe we should abandon the myth of the wood products industry.

What is actually being threatened by the downsizing of the wood products industry is not a time-honored profession passed down from generation to generation but rather high-paying jobs for relatively uneducated white males. High-school dropouts used to instantaneously enter the middle class by taking a wood products job. That particular route to a middle-class lifestyle is what is being closed. Following the alternative routes takes considerably more training and time. At any rate, white males are a politically powerful group and a potent symbol of middle America. It is not surprising that their way of life has attracted so much attention.

Another concern about job loss in wood products that has considerable emotional punch is forced outmigration. When longtime residents are forced to move away in search of work, the social fabric of a community is indeed damaged. But as mentioned above, the relationship between local economic conditions and outmigration is much more complicated than emotive rhetoric might suggest. Consider in- and out-migration over the last two decades in Oregon, the nation's most timber-dependent state. Outmigration actually rose during the boom years in the later 1970s (when inmigration was also rising). Then when the Oregon economy slipped into a depression in the early 1980s, the rate of outmigration actually declined. The same pattern appears on a smaller scale in Oregon's timber-dependent southwest counties. When the economy collapsed, outmigration was cut almost in half. This pattern is not unique to Oregon or to timber regions, as analysis of Great Plains counties from 1970 to 1990 shows. Hard economic times, then, are not what primarily drive outmigration. Good economic times can cause far more disruption in a community by boosting both immigration and outmigration. * * *

If wood products' jump-starting of local economies is of dubious value, there are other aspects of the industry that give more reason to pause. Forestry is one of the most dangerous occupations around. No other has a higher injury and mortality rate. The rate of disabling injuries in the lumber and wood products industry is 40 percent higher than in the construction industry and three times higher than in mining and manufacturing. In logging itself, in 1991, the average number of work days lost per worker due to injury was twice that in mining and construction and three times that in manufacturing.

The timber industry's record of investment in its workers is equally distressing. For instance, in 1990, 99 percent of the timber workers laid off in Oregon had no more than a high-school education, and 25 percent had not even completed high school. Local lumber mills have induced many young people to drop out of school, a decision that in an unstable industry can have serious negative consequences for them and for the community in the long run.

The timber industry does not represent a way of life that needs public subsidization. Rather, it is a mature primary industry that is in relative decline along with mining and agriculture as the U.S. economy continues to develop, shifting resources, including labor, from products that are less in demand to those that are more in demand. There is nothing special or central about the timber industry that should cause the government to give it privileged access to public resources.

QUESTIONS AND DISCUSSION

1. In 1991, a federal judge issued an order to protect the northern spotted owl. The order banned logging on 24 million acres in 17 national forests in Oregon, Washington, and Northern California. *Washington Audubon Society v. Robertson,* 1991 WL 180099 (W.D. Wash. 1991). Three economists who studied the impact of the logging ban supported Power's conclusion that the timber industry's importance to local economies of the Pacific Northwest has been waning even while forests resources remain important to the vitality of the region. The authors note:

> Although logging has been crucial to the development of the Pacific Northwest's economy over the past century, lumber and wood-products jobs represented only 1.9 percent of total employment in 1996. * * *
>
> The spotted-owl region, concentrated west of the Cascades, contains 38 counties and nine metropolitan areas. Several of these areas have experienced declines in employment since 1990, but only two counties (containing a small percentage of the region's overall employment) had fewer jobs in 1996 than in 1990, the year before Judge Dwyer's ruling. * * *
>
> In the past, regional economies grew largely because of their ability to exploit natural resources, yet in today's economy it is more important to have a productive workforce. Increasingly, the prosperity of the region and its communities depends on the ability to attract and retain skilled workers. Many firms choose the Pacific Northwest because of its good workforce, and many workers are here because they cherish the quality of life that healthy forests help provide. In addition, residents of the region have become increasingly aware of the high costs associated with the timber industry. These costs include subsidies and environmental repairs.

Ernie Niemi et al., *The Sky Did Not Fall: The Pacific Northwest's Response to Logging Reductions,* OREGON'S FUTURE 32–33 (Summer/Fall, 2000). How might Jim Podlesny or other timber community residents quoted in the preceding articles respond to this report?

2. Job losses in the timber industry of the Pacific Northwest as a result of the environmental restrictions on logging were far less than some had predicted. In 1989, the Northwest Forest Resource Council, an industry group, estimated that 65,700 jobs would be lost; government estimates were about 20,000 jobs. Actual job losses for the six year period between 1988 and 1994, however, were estimated at 16,695. Peter Sleeth, *NW Loses Fewer Timber Jobs Than Forecast,* THE OREGONIAN, May 21, 1995, at A01. Moreover, a substantial number of lost jobs were most likely the result of increasing automation in the timber industry and not environmental restrictions. Tom Gentle, *The Best and Worst of Times, in* A PORTRAIT OF POVERTY IN OREGON, (Oregon State Univ. Ext Service, 2000). Still, the impact of those job losses and ripple effects, especially in smaller communities, can be profound. Timber industry workers used to receiving good wages found that they lacked the skills to obtain jobs with similar pay. Many of the new jobs that were created by recreation and tourism were in the lower paying service industry. If government action knowingly causes these economic problems, what obligation should agencies have to soften the blow?

3. Forest products can produce significant revenues, but they do not comprise a substantial part of the U.S. economy. The federal Bureau of Economic Analysis, which publishes annual statistics on the gross domestic product, includes forestry in a category along with agricultural services and fishing. In 2005, this entire sector contributed 1% of the GDP and accounted for none of the growth in the national GDP that year. *See* http://www.bea.gov/scb/pdf/2006/12december/1206_indyaccts.pdf.

4. Consider the following story from the *High Country News.*

> It seemed an offer the Forest Service couldn't refuse: The government gets the best price for its timber, and the buyer never cuts down any trees. Yet on March 21, the agency rejected an environmental group's high bid of $28,875 for 275 acres of fire-damaged trees in the eastern Cascades of Washington near the Canadian border. Instead, it accepted the second-highest bid to ensure that the trees are cut.
>
> "Their decision makes terrible business sense," said Mitch Friedman of the Northwest Ecosystem Alliance. "We offered them more money and also said we would preserve the public's resource." But Sam Gehr, supervisor of the Okanogan National Forest, told the Seattle Times that he awarded the contract to a local logging company because the rules require the trees be cut. "The fact that they weren't going to fulfill the contract obligation was the key to our choice," he said. Gehr sold the estimated 750 trailer-loads of timber to Double A Logging for $28,000. The sale cost the agency $300,000 to prepare. Friedman said his group plans to appeal the decision.

Richard Hicks, *Forest Service Economics 101,* HIGH COUNTRY NEWS, Jan. 30, 2004. Why do you think the Forest Service was unwilling to sell the timber to a group that was not going to log? Why would the Forest Service spend $300,000 for a timber sale in the first place if that sale was only going to yield $28,000 from the sale of the timber? What similarities do you see between this decision and the attempts of environmental groups to purchase grazing permits, described in Chapter 8 at page 978?

5. United States forest policies impact not only U.S. forests but also forests elsewhere in the world. Consider the following excerpt:

> Gary Draper has worked in the timber industry for 25 years, and in that time he's lived through a string of mill closures.
>
> Now he's living through one again. Last month, Boise Cascade announced that both Draper's mill in Emmett, Idaho, and another in Cascade will close this June. About 375 people will lose their jobs in the two towns.
>
> The loss of the mills will cut deeply into these small rural communities where "everybody knows everybody else," Draper says. And it will add to an already remarkable number of mill closures in the state. Over the past decade, 33 sawmills have closed and 1,911 timber workers have lost their jobs, according to the Idaho Department of Commerce. Once the Boise Cascade mill in Emmett closes, only one large sawmill will remain in southern Idaho.
>
> The announcement has started an all-too-familiar blame game in Idaho. Boise Cascade points its finger at the environmental community for pushing the U.S. Forest Service to dramatically reduce the amount of federal timber made available to mills; environmentalists have responded by saying that Boise Cascade is finally paying the price for years of overcutting.
>
> But unlike past debates, this time everyone agrees on one point: The lumber market stinks. Industry analysts say a five-year-old trade agreement with Canada has allowed a flood of Canadian timber to depress lumber prices in the U.S. While no one claims that the agreement is the direct cause of the Emmett and Cascade closures, no one denies that it has had a dramatic impact on the U.S. timber industry. More than 100 U.S. mills have closed in the past six months.
>
> The loss of sawmills has attracted the concern of environmentalists, who recognize that less cutting in the U.S. means more cutting in Canada, where environmental regulations are looser. They have joined the timber industry in calling for a renegotiated agreement that will keep U.S. workers and Canadian forests whole. But time is running out. The trade agreement is due to expire on March 31, and it is unclear whether the Bush administration will renegotiate.

Matt Jenkins, *U.S. Mills Fall Under Canadian Ax*, HIGH COUNTRY NEWS, March 26, 2001, *available at* http://www.hcn.org/issues/199/10371.

The trade agreement to which the excerpt refers is the 1996 U.S.–Canada Softwood Lumber Agreement, which establishes a 14.7 billion board-feet limit on the quantity of lumber that Canada may ship duty-free to the United States. Although the Agreement was designed to help protect U.S. timber industry, the 14.7 bbf limit turned out to be far too high from the U.S. perspective. The original agreement expired in 2001 and subsequently, the U.S. imposed billions of dollars of tariffs on Canadian lumber. A new agreement was entered in 2006 whereby the U.S. agreed to refund 80% of the tariffs imposed between 2001 and 2006 and to allow the U.S. to impose export taxes on Canadian lumber if the price falls below $355/thousand board feet. Import restrictions may also be imposed if Canadian lumber captures more than 34% of U.S. market share. It was not long, however, before the U.S. alleged violation of these conditions in a complaint filed with the London Court of International Arbitration in accordance with the terms of the 2006 agreement. In early 2008, the Court entered a split decision that largely favored the Canadian position. *Canada Wins Split Decision in Softwood Ruling,* THE CANADIAN PRESS, March 4, 2008, *available at,*   http://www.ctv.ca/servlet/ArticleNews/story/CTVNews/20080304/soft wood_ruling_080304/20080304/.

Is there a way to negotiate a trade agreement that will protect U.S. workers and U.S. and Canadian forests? Would it make sense to restrict the import of Canadian timber and thereby provide additional market opportunities for U.S. harvesters? On the other hand, why not just allow free trade in forest products? Wouldn't that provide the greatest benefits to the American consumer? If Canada's comparative trade advantage is its lax environmental regulations, is that fair? What about a tariff that attempted to require Canada to internalize those externalities unaccounted for by Canadian regulation? The Bush administration later imposed tariffs of up to 40% on Canadian lumber. Was that approach wise? Should the United States environmental community care any more about protecting American forests than Canadian forests?

6. Sarah Bates has asked whether focusing solely on logging communities is mistaken. She suggests that geographic communities are not the only ones that matter and that we should instead be more willing to look to "communities of interest" for guidance on natural resource management questions. Sarah F. Bates, *Public Lands Communities: In Search of a Community of Values*, 14 PUB. LAND L. REV. 81, 90–92 (1993). Who would be included in the community of interest for forests? Is a community of interest entitled to the same voice and respect as a geographical community dependent upon a forest for its livelihood?

IV. FORESTRY LAW

If you have proceeded sequentially through this casebook you should already have learned a good deal about what might be labeled forestry law. In Chapter 2 you were introduced briefly to the creation of the national forests and to the vast timber holdings in the Northwest amassed by railroad corporations as a result of railroad land grants. In Chapter 3 you learned something about the Forest Service planning process as described in the *Ohio Forestry* case (page 257) and Forest Service NEPA compliance in *Thomas v. Peterson* (page 268), which addressed timber cuts and a logging road just outside the Jersey Jack wilderness in Idaho. Chapter 4's discussion of the Endangered Species Act (ESA) again drew attention to forests. Recall that the origin of the *Sweet Home* case (page 389) was the question whether habitat modification—cutting timber—could itself be a "take" of endangered or threatened species. Chapter 6 taught still more forest law, introducing you to wilderness designation on forest service lands and questions of access across forest service wilderness to mining claims in *Clouser v. Espy* (page 701). Chapter 7, although focused on water, considered still more forest law in *United States v. New Mexico* (page 840), which addressed the extent of federal reserved water rights in national forests. Finally, in Chapters 8 and 9 respectively, you learned something about the regulation of grazing permits and mining claims in national forests.

This brief review is intended not just as a reminder that you have already learned quite a bit about the law applicable to forests but also that natural resource laws often overlap and intersect. Although the focus of the materials below is on those laws directed exclusively at the forest resource, the ESA has arguably had a greater impact on forest management than many of the "forest" laws discussed in the section that follows. Until the northern spotted owl and the marbled murrelet came along, for example, "forest law" did little to stop the harvesting of old growth timber in the Pacific Northwest. Thus, as you study the materials that follow, keep in mind that a lawyer concerned with forest use, management, or protection must retain a broad perspective on the variety of legal hurdles and tools available.

The chapter's discussion of forestry law is organized into two parts. The first looks at national forests, and the second considers forests on state and private land. It will not be surprising that the part on national forests is focused on federal law and the part on state and private forests is focused on state law. However, it is important to keep in mind that dividing the chapter between national forests and private forests is not the same as dividing the chapter between federal and state law. Federal law can have a large impact on private forest practices. The ESA, for example, applies to both national and private forests. To the extent access across federal land is necessary to harvest timber on private land—a circumstance not at all rare given the checkerboard ownership problem described in Chapter 2—NEPA or federal access regulations are likely to be implicated. And state regulation may apply to activities within national forests. Witness the *Granite Rock* case excerpted in Chapter 9 (page 1175) where the Supreme Court upheld California's requirement that a miner secure a permit from the California Coastal Commission prior to undertaking mining operations within a national forest. The basic point to remember is that dividing the chapter by ownership is not the same as dividing the chapter by jurisdiction. Whatever the underlying land ownership, keep in mind that federal or state law may apply.

The national forests section will focus on those laws specifically governing the management of the national forests, namely the Forest Service's 1897 organic act, the Multiple–Use, Sustained–Yield Act of 1960 (MUSYA), the Forest and Rangeland Renewable Resources Planning Act of 1974 (RPA), and the National Forest Management Act of 1976 (NFMA). The focus of the part on state and private forests will be on state law relating specifically to forests, including basic common-law and contractual understandings of timber ownership and the state forest practice acts that regulate logging on state and private lands.

A.   NATIONAL FORESTS

1.   THE HISTORY OF FEDERAL FORESTRY LAW

The federal government's first foray into forest policy came quite soon in our nation's history. In 1799, as a result of growing pirate attacks on American merchant ships, Congress appropriated money to acquire a secure timber supply for building the navy's war ships. Act of Feb. 25,

1799, ch. 16, 1 Stat. 622. This money was used to purchase Grover's and Blackbeard's Islands off the Georgia coast, which contained some 2000 acres of prime timber land. After the War of 1812, Congress authorized the Secretary of the Navy to select, and the president to reserve from sale, vacant and unappropriated tracts of public land containing live oak and cedar to be used for shipbuilding by the Navy. Act of Mar. 1, 1817, ch. 22, 3 Stat. 347. *See* JOHN NAGLE & J.B. RUHL, THE LAW OF BIODIVERSITY AND ECOSYSTEM MANAGEMENT 402 (2002); SAMUEL TRASK DANA & SALLY K. FAIRFAX, FOREST AND RANGE POLICY 35 (2d. ed. 1980).

Despite these examples of federal reservations of timber, the overriding federal policy of the nineteenth century, as described in more detail in Chapter 2, was to dispose of land for purposes of settlement and development. The focus of most disposal legislation, however, was not to dispose of timber but to encourage agricultural settlement. Disposal legislation, such as the Homestead Act, thus typically required proof of cultivation efforts before the land could be patented. In many cases, however, persons and companies claimed to be homesteading just long enough to strip the land of timber before they moved along to another claim. Just as often, loggers didn't even bother with pretense and simply stole the timber from the public lands. Despite occasional federal efforts to discourage or restrict the rampant theft of timber, many forests, particularly those in the Great Lake states, were decimated by theft. *See* James L. Huffman, *A History of Forest Policy in the United States*, 8 ENVTL. L. 239, 243 (1978). In 1878, in an effort to obtain more revenue from public timber lands and curtail the abuse that was occurring under the existing laws, Congress enacted the Timber and Stone Act, which authorized purchase for $2.50 per acre of 160–acre, quarter-sections, chiefly valuable for timber or stone and unfit for cultivation. 20 Stat. 89 (1878). Buyers had to attest that they were purchasing the land for their own exclusive use and benefit but because the Supreme Court held that this standard could be satisfied by plans for immediate sale, *see United States v. Biggs*, 211 U.S. 507 (1909), most of the 14 million acres of land patented under the Act ended up in the hands of timber companies.

Toward the end of the nineteenth century, calls to conserve public forest lands became more prominent. In 1877, Secretary of the Interior Carl Schurz recommended that Congress enact a law "providing for the care and custody of such timber lands as are unfit for agriculture and for the gradual sale of the timber thereon and for the perpetuation of the growth of timber on such lands by such needful rules and regulations as may be required. . . ." REPORT OF THE LAND COMMISSIONER, 1877, *as quoted in* James L. Huffman, *A History of Forest Policy in the United States*, 8 ENVTL. L. 239, 258 (1978). Congress eventually responded with the General Revision Act of 1891, which provided that

> [T]he President of the United States may . . . set apart and reserve, in any State or Territory having public land bearing forests, in any part of the public lands wholly or in part covered with timber or undergrowth, whether of commercial value or not, as public reservations. . . .

Act of Mar. 3, 1891, ch. 561, 26 Stat. 1103. President Harrison took up his new authority with vigor. By the end of his term two years later he had set aside 15 reserves encompassing more than 13 million acres. Grover Cleveland followed Harrison with new reserves covering more than 25 million acres. President Cleveland's actions received strong support from the Eastern and Midwestern states, but were opposed by the Western states where the new reserves were located.

In the meantime, Cleveland's Interior Secretary, Hoke Smith, arranged for the appointment of a National Forest Commission to chart a plan for forest management and use. Gifford Pinchot, the renowned conservationist, was one of six members of the Commission.

The recommendations of the Commission along with the controversy surrounding Cleveland's forest reserves ultimately led Congress to adopt new legislation on June 4, 1897. The Organic Administration Act of 1897 authorized the President to continue to establish new reserves but subject to new conditions:

> No public forest reservation shall be established except to improve and protect the forest within the reservation, or for the purpose of securing favorable conditions of water flows, and to furnish a continuous supply of timber for the use and necessities of citizens of the United States; but it is not the purpose or intent of these provisions ... to authorize the inclusion ... of lands more valuable for the mineral therein or for agricultural purposes, than for forest purposes.

Act of June 4, 1897, ch. 2, 30 Stat. 34. The new law responded to the concerns of Western interests that forest lands should not be "locked up" or set aside for preservation. Rather, forests would be used to protect watersheds and provide "a continuous supply of timber." This approach fit well with Gifford Pinchot's "wise use" philosophy, and Pinchot was soon named the first chief of the nation's forests.

Pinchot's tenure began within the General Land Office at Interior, but Pinchot viewed Interior as too political and in 1905, with the help of his close ally, President Theodore Roosevelt, Congress transferred the forest reserves to the newly established U.S. Forest Service in the Department of Agriculture. On the day the forests were transferred, Pinchot set out his philosophy toward forest management in a famous letter that he wrote and arranged to have sent to him by Secretary of Agriculture James Wilson.

> All the resources of forest reserves are for *use*, and this use must be brought about in a thoroughly prompt and business-like manner, under such restrictions only as will insure the permanence of these resources ... You will see to it that the water, wood, and forage of the reserves are conserved and wisely used for the benefit of the homebuilder first of all, upon whom depends the best permanent use of lands and resources alike.

Quoted in CHARLES F. WILKINSON, CROSSING THE NEXT MERIDIAN 128 (1992) (emphasis in original). Pinchot's insistence on the *use* of forest resources, with timber as the dominant use, remains deeply ingrained in the agency's culture.

Despite the compromise that led to enactment of the 1897 Organic Act, controversy over forest reserves continued, due in large part to westerners' unease with Theodore Roosevelt's aggressive use of executive action to create federal forest reserves throughout the western states. In 1907, Congress enacted legislation that included an amendment that effectively revoked this presidential power by giving Congress the sole authority to create or enlarge forest reserves. HAROLD K. STEEN, THE U.S. FOREST SERVICE: A HISTORY 98–100 (1976). Bowing to political pressure, Theodore Roosevelt signed the legislation, but not until he designated 32 new forest reserves (renamed "national forests" by Pinchot) covering millions of acres. By the end of Roosevelt's tenure, there were 159 national forests covering 150 million acres of land.

Because the national forests were carved from the large tracts of public lands that remained at the end of the nineteenth and early part of the twentieth centuries, virtually all of them were in the Western states. The opportunity to establish eastern forests came about as a result of legislation sponsored by Republican Congressman John Weeks of Massachusetts. The Weeks Act of 1911 authorized the federal government to purchase forest lands to protect watersheds in navigable streams. Act of Mar. 1, 1911, ch. 186, 36 Stat. 961. Most of the 28 million acres of eastern forest lands—an area the size of Ohio—were acquired under this law. The following excerpt describes the Forest Service (FS) and the National Forest System (NFS) as it looks today.

Carol Hardy Vincent, *Federal Land Management Agencies: Background on Land and Resources Management*, Cong. Research Service., RL32393 (August 2, 2004)

The NFS includes 155 national forests with 188 million acres (97.6% of the system); 20 national grasslands with 4 million acres (2.0%); and 121 other areas, such as land utilization projects, purchase units, and research and experimental areas, with 0.8 million acres (0.4%). The NFS units are arranged into nine administrative regions, each headed by a regional forester. The nine regional foresters report to the NFS Deputy Chief, who reports to the Chief of the Forest Service. In contrast to the heads of other federal land management agencies, the Chief traditionally has been a career employee of the agency. The Chief reports to the Secretary through the Undersecretary for Natural Resources and Environment.

Table 4. The National Forest System

Forest Service Region		States containing NFS lands[a]	National Forest System Acreage[b]	
Region Name	No.	States	Federal	Inholdings
Northern	1	ID, MT, ND	25,411,585	2,727,271
Rocky Mountain	2	CO, NE, SD, WY	22,069,840	2,380,838
Southwestern	3	AZ, NM	20,805,767	1,668,087
Intermountain	4	ID, NV, UT, WY	32,003,788	2,250,034
Pacific Southwest	5	CA	20,137,345	3,629,680
Pacific Northwest	6	OR, WA	24,737,016	2,660,525
Southern	8	AL, AR, FL, GA, KY, LA, MS, NC, OK, PR, SC, TN, TX, VA	13,273,000	12,324,182
Eastern	9	IL, IN, ME, MI, MN, MO, NH, NY, OH, PA, VI, WI, WV	12,061,766	9,895,489
Alaska	10	AK	21,980,905	2,375,273
National Forest System Total			192,511,012	39,911,379

The NFS regions often are referred to by number, rather than by name. Table 4 identifies the number, states encompassed, and acreage for each region. Although the NFS lands are concentrated in the seven western FS regions, including Alaska (87%), the FS manages more than half of all federal land in the East. *Inholdings*, shown in Table 4, is land (primarily private) within the designated boundaries of the national forests (and other NFS units) that is not administered by the FS. Inholdings sometimes pose difficulties for FS land management, because the agency generally does not regulate the development and use of the inholdings. The uses of private inholdings may be incompatible with desired uses of the federal lands, and constraints on crossing inholdings may limit access to some federal lands. Many private landowners, however, object to federal restrictions on the use of their lands and to unfettered public access across their lands. This is particularly true in the Southern and Eastern Regions, where nearly half of the land within the NFS boundaries is inholdings.
* * *

Congress has provided further management direction within the NFS by creating special designations for certain areas. Some of these designations—wilderness areas, wild and scenic rivers, and national trails—are part of larger management systems affecting several federal land management agencies; these special systems are described in later chapters of this report.

In addition to these special systems, the NFS includes several other types of land designations. The NFS contains 21 national game refuges and wildlife preserves (1.2 million acres), 20 national recreation areas (2.9 million acres), 4 national monuments (3.7 million acres), 2 national volcanic monuments (167,-427 acres), 6 scenic areas (130,435 acres), a scenic-research area (6,637 acres), a scenic recreation area (12,645 acres), a recreation management area (43,900 acres), 3 special management areas (91,265 acres), 2 national protection areas (27,600 acres), 2 national botanical areas (8,256 acres), a primitive area (173,762 acres) and a national historic area (6,540 acres). Resource development and use is generally more restricted in these specially designated areas than on general NFS lands, and specific guidance typically is provided with each designation.

———

Gifford Pinchot's vision of using national forests and their resources to serve the needs of the American people was focused essentially on consumptive uses. Perhaps this narrow view was a product of the time in which he lived, but he did not see the forests as playgrounds or as biological reserves. He opposed the creation of national parks and he famously locked horns with John Muir over his support of the Hetch Hetchy dam in Yosemite National Park.

> Gifford Pinchot, who became head of the Forestry Service in 1898, envisioned the national forests as primarily a timber supply resource, and for nearly seventy years the Forest Service interpreted the Organic Act as allowing widespread extraction of timber. Indeed, after World War II, housing construction demands placed tremendous new pressure on the nation's timber supply, and on the Forest Service. Clearcutting became a common practice on private forest lands, thus depleting private timber supplies and causing the timber industry to pressure the Forest Service to increase the yield from national forests. The agency met this demand, but by doing so fueled a conflict between timber harvesting and another demand that boomed after the war—recreation. As clearcutting became common in the national forests, so too did the previously uncommon instance of public criticism of Forest Service decisions.

> Congress nevertheless gave the Forest Service basically a free hand in all such matters of national forest policy, intervening only once to enact the Multiple Use and Sustained Yield Act of 1960 (MUSYA). MUSYA expanded the purposes of national forest management from water flows and timber supply to include "outdoor recreation, range, timber, watershed, and wildlife and fish purposes." 16 U.S.C. § 528. Recognizing that "some land will be used for less than all the resources," MUSYA required that the five multiple uses, which Congress deliberately named in alphabetical order, be treated as co-equal and managed "with consideration being given to the relative values of the various resources." *Id.* The statute described the core mandate of multiple use as meaning

>> The management of all the various renewable surface resources of the national forests so that they are utilized in the combination that will best meet the needs of the American people; making the most judicious use of the land for some or all these resources or related services over areas large enough to provide sufficient latitude for periodic adjustments in use to conform to changing needs and conditions....

> *Id.* § 531.

> Conservation and recreation interests opposed the legislation while the agency and timber industry actively supported it. Critics of the Forest Service charged that the agency had elevated timber extraction above the other uses and exercised widespread clearcutting without due regard to the Organic Act, and would continue to do both under MUSYA. Indeed, for all practical purposes MUSYA codified precisely the policy discretion the agency sought (and argued it had even without MUSYA). After MUSYA, the law of national forests explicitly

recognized the breadth of the agency's discretion. While courts demanded that the agency give "due consideration" to each of the multiple use components, ... in the final analysis most courts agreed that "the decision as to the proper mix of uses within any particular area is left to the sound discretion and expertise of the Forest Service." *Sierra Club v. Hardin*, 325 F. Supp. 99, 123 (D. Alas. 1971). MUSY's multiple use mandate was essentially rendered directionless, leaving it to the agency to decide where to go and providing no meaningful legislative or judicial check on the path chosen.

JOHN NAGLE & J.B. RUHL, THE LAW OF BIODIVERSITY AND ECOSYSTEM MANAGEMENT 403–404 (2002).

The flexibility accorded the Forest Service under MUSYA might have been used to forge a new direction in forest management, but the Forest Service continued to manage the forests as it had always done, emphasizing consumptive use of forest resources and especially timber production. But even as timber production on national forests began rising, the times were beginning to change. In 1969, concerned about indiscriminate clearcutting in the Bitteroot National Forest near Missoula, Montana, Senator Lee Metcalf asked Arnold Bolle, head of the Department of Forestry at the University of Montana, to head a commission to study logging in the Bitteroot. The Bolle Report was released in November, 1970, and strongly criticized the Forest Service for its failure to promote true multiple use management and for its continuing "overriding concern for sawtimber production." A UNIVERSITY VIEW OF THE FOREST SERVICE, S. DOC. No. 92–115.

The Bolle Report was followed by the Church Report, which was also highly critical of clearcutting and the Forest Service's timber management program. The Church Report, named for Senator Frank Church, chair of the Public Lands Subcommittee of the Senate Interior Committee, focused on clearcutting in the Monongahela National Forest in West Virginia and four national forests in Wyoming and argued for limiting clearcutting and for prohibiting all timber production on public lands where logging would be uneconomical or incompatible with other important values. In 1974, Congress passed the Forest and Rangelands Renewable Resources Planning Act, Pub. L. No. 93–378, 88 Stat. 476, which required the Forest Service to prepare "land and resource management plans" for each forest unit. But the law did little to rein in the Agency. It took a lawsuit to force the Forest Service to confront the political problems posed by clearcutting. That case, which is excerpted below, involved the Monongahela National Forest in West Virginia. It effectively stopped clearcutting in the national forests, and ultimately led Congress to pass the National Forest Management Act (NFMA), which once again authorized clearcutting, albeit subject to some constraints. NFMA is discussed in the section following the decision.

WEST VIRGINIA DIV. OF IZAAK WALTON LEAGUE OF AMERICA, INC. v. BUTZ,
522 F.2d 945 (4th Cir. 1975)

FIELD, CIRCUIT JUDGE

Alleging that the Forest Service was entering into contracts for the sale of timber in the Monongahela National Forest of West Virginia the terms of which violated the Organic Act of 1897 (hereinafter "Organic Act"), the plaintiffs instituted this action seeking both declaratory and injunctive relief. Specifically, the plaintiffs challenged three proposed timber sales which in the aggregate covered the harvesting of 1077 acres. Under the sales contracts 649 acres were designated for selective cutting while the remaining 428 acres were to be harvested by clearcutting in units ranging in size from five to twenty-five acres. While the trees to be harvested by the selective method would be individually marked, the contracts provided that in the clearcut area all merchantable timber would be cut and none of the trees would be individually marked. The plaintiffs charged that the contracts with respect to the 428 acres violated the sales provision of the Act, 16 U.S.C. § 476, which reads in pertinent part as follows:

> "For the purpose of preserving the living and growing timber and promoting the younger growth on national forests, the Secretary of Agriculture, . . . may cause to be designated and appraised so much of the dead, matured or large growth of trees found upon such national forests as may be compatible with the utilization of the forests thereon, and may sell the same. . . . Such timber, before being sold, shall be marked and designated, and shall be cut and removed under the supervision of some person appointed for that purpose by the Secretary of Agriculture. . . ."

Both parties moved for summary judgment and filed supporting affidavits and exhibits as well as an agreed statement of facts. The statement of facts conceded that the three contracts in question were representative of other contracts for the sale of timber in the Monongahela National Forest and that they involved the sale and cutting of trees, some of which were neither dead, physiologically matured nor large. It was further stated that the Forest Service was selling timber pursuant to procedures under which each tree was not individually marked prior to cutting, although the boundaries of cutting areas were marked. Upon these admitted facts the district court granted the plaintiffs' motion for summary judgment. In doing so, the court declared that the practice, regulations and contracts of the Forest Service which (1) permit the cutting of trees which are not dead, mature or large growth, (2) permit the cutting of trees which have not been individually marked and (3) allow timber which has been cut to remain at the site violate the provisions of the Organic Act. The court enjoined the Forest Service from contracting for or otherwise allowing the cutting of timber in the Monongahela National Forest in violation of the Organic Act. The order further requires the Forest Service to revise its regulations, recognizing, however, certain specific statutory exceptions.

The district court concluded that the language of the Organic Act constituted a clear directive from Congress "that trees can be sold and cut only if they are 'dead, matured or large growth' and then may be sold only when the sale serves the purpose of preserving and promoting the younger growth of timber on the national forests." In reaching this conclusion the court applied the dictionary definitions to the statutory terms and held that "dead" means "deprived of life"; "mature" means "brought by natural process to completeness of growth and development"; and "large" means "exceeding most other things of like kind in bulk . . .; of considerable magnitude; big; great. . . ." The Forest Service does not, of course, take issue with the district court's definition of the word "dead" as used in the statute, but it does contend that the court erred in its interpretation of the statutory phrase "large growth of trees" and placed an unduly restrictive definition on the word "matured." * * *

The Service takes the position that "large growth of trees" signifies a sizeable stand or grouping of trees, and that the district court erroneously converted this phrase into "large growth trees" which in effect requires that each individual tree be identified as "large." We think the district court correctly construed this statutory phrase. The stated purpose of "promoting the younger growth" clearly refers to the characteristics of the individual trees, and in our opinion the use of the phrase "large growth of trees" in the latter part of the same sentence likewise refers to the individual trees, the words "large growth" being used in contradistinction to the prior reference to "younger growth." To accept this contention that "large growth of trees" means a sizeable stand or group of trees would treat the words "dead and mature" as surplusage, and violate the "well known maxim of statutory construction that all words and provisions of statutes are intended to have meaning and are to be given effect, and words of a statute are not to be construed as surplusage." *Wilderness Society v. Morton*, 479 F.2d 842, 856 (1973), *cert. denied*, 411 U.S. 917 (1973).

The interpretation urged by the defendants would lead to the absurd result that while in small areas of the forest the authority of the Secretary would be restricted, he would nevertheless be free to cut any trees he might desire from a sizeable stand or group of trees (defined by the Government as ten acres or more), regardless of whether the individual trees in such group or stand were small or large, young or old, immature or mature. In our opinion such a paradoxical result would be at odds with the purpose of the Organic Act as well as the plain language of the statute.

The Service further contends that in treating "mature" trees as only those which are physiologically mature, the court ignored other accepted silvicultural tests of maturity. Here again we agree with the district court that the language of the statute means physiological maturity rather than economic or management maturity. A tree is physiologically mature when because of age and condition its growth begins to taper off or it loses its health and vigor, and while age and size are indicators of physiological maturity, they are not exclusively so. From the economic viewpoint a tree is considered mature when it has the highest marketable value, and management maturity is defined as the state at which a tree or stand best fulfills the purpose for which it was maintained, e. g., produces the best supply of specified products. We think unquestionably that in using the word "mature" Congress was referring to physiological maturity. This appears to be the meaning of "mature" in forestry terminology today, and was the accepted meaning of the word at the time the Organic Act was passed by the Congress. * * *

Turning to that part of Section 476 which requires that the timber "before being sold, shall be marked and designated," we find the statutory language to be simple and unambiguous. The term "marked" in the context of forestry is well defined and means "selection and indication by a blaze, paint * * * or marking hammer on the stem of trees to be felled or retained." "Designate," on the other hand, is a much broader term and merely means to "indicate." The two words are not synonymous or interchangeable and in using them conjunctively it is evident that Congress intended that the Forest Service designate the area from which the timber was to be sold and, additionally, placed upon the Service the obligation to mark each individual tree which was authorized to be cut. This plain reading of the statutory language is buttressed by reference to the statement of Gifford Pinchot, the first Chief of the Forest Service, in his 1898 Surveys of Forest Reserves:

> "In reserves where timber is sold it will be necessary to indicate unmistakably before the cutting what trees are to be cut and afterwards to ascertain that these trees, and these only, have been taken."

Typical of the instructions with respect to sales of timber in Forest Reserves shortly after passage of the Act were those issued by the Secretary of the Interior on February 27, 1902:

> "If the application (to cut timber) is approved, the head ranger or supervisor (with assistance, if necessary) will mark at once all trees to be cut. This is imperative in all cases involving living timber.
>
> The marking of standing timber must be done with the 'U.S.' stamping hammer, and all trees must be marked near the ground in order that the stumps may afford positive evidence of the marking."

This emphasis placed on such selective marking by those who urged the passage of the Organic Act and were charged with the responsibility of its implementation is entitled to particular weight. *See Zuber v. Allen*, 396 U.S. 168, 192 (1969). * * *

While we base our decision primarily upon a literal reading of the statute we find convincing support for our conclusion in the background and legislative history of the Organic Act. From its initial settlement and continuing throughout the greater part of the nineteenth century, the nation's forest lands were wastefully exploited. Originally, some seventy per cent of the country's total land surface, or approximately 1¼ billion acres, was covered by forests, but by 1893 it was estimated that only 500 million acres of productive forests remained. Over 600 million acres of former forests had become waste and brush land, the greater portion of which had resulted from a combination of wasteful cutting and the careless use of fire. By the late nineteenth century responsible leaders, both in and out of Government, had become so alarmed that they warned the Congress and the country against the immediate and long range effects on both water flow and timber supply which would inevitably result if the irresponsible and profligate timber practices were permitted to continue.

The initial reported version [of the bill that would eventually become the Organic Act] in 1893 provided that "timber of commercial nature" could be cut when the cutting was consistent with the requirement that the Secretary of the Interior "preserve the forest." In 1894 this wording was deleted by House amendment and replaced by the more restrictive provision that "dead or matured trees" could be removed when necessary to preserve the remaining timber. To quiet the concern of those who were distrustful of the executive's ability to protect the forests, Congressman Coffeen, one of the authors of the amendment, stated:

> "As the bill now stands I think no one can reasonably object to its provisions. It provides, indeed, for sale of dead and nongrowing or matured timber where the elimination of that kind of timber is necessary for the better preservation of the living and growing trees; this all under strict supervision. Having myself prepared this section of the amended bill, I feel that the living timber can not in any manner be endangered under its careful wording and provisions. * * *

Despite assurances by the sponsors of the bill that it fully protected those interests about which Mr. Wells expressed concern, the bill did not pass at that session, and although introduced each year thereafter, passage was not effected until 1897. The phrase 'large growth of trees' appeared for the first time in the final version of the bill as passed, and while we find no recorded debate on the addition of this language, Senator Pettigrew, in offering the amendment stated:

> "We propose by this amendment, after this country has been surveyed, that the living trees shall be preserved that is, under the direction of the Secretary of the Interior so that the large trees, the dying trees, the trees

that will grow no better in time, may be sold and removed by the purchaser. . . ." (emphasis added)

It is significant that Congressman McRae supported the Pettigrew amendment in the House, stating that in his opinion it would accomplish the primary objectives of his bill.

This legislative history demonstrates that the primary concern of Congress in passing the Organic Act was the preservation of the national forests. While the Act as finally passed rejected the position of the extremists who wished to forbid all cutting in the forests, it specifically limited the authority of the Secretary in his selection of timber which could be sold. He could select the timber to be cut only from those trees which were dead, physiologically mature or large, and then only when such cutting would preserve the young and growing timber which remained. Following the addition of "large growth of trees" to the bill, the sponsors repeatedly made it clear that the Act would permit the sale only of the individual trees which met its specific requirements which, in the words of Senator Pettigrew, were "the large trees, the dying trees and trees that will grow no better in time. . . ."

Since the proposed legislation limited the types of trees which could be sold, it logically followed that Congress wanted to insure that only the selected trees would be cut. The original version of the McRae bill had no provision requiring that such trees be either marked or designated. In the face of sharp criticism on this point the Hermann amendment added the requirement that the Secretary of the Interior "shall carefully designate . . . said dead or mature trees." This change was insufficient to quiet the critics who were concerned that the loggers would cut whatever timber they wanted and continue to denude the forests. Finally, the Senate Committee on Public Lands amended the bill to include the requirement of marking as well as designating. This requirement remained in the McRae bill and was included in the Pettigrew amendment which became the present statute. It is clear from the legislative history that Congress considered marking to be a necessary adjunct to the pattern of the selective selling and cutting of individual trees under the Organic Act. * * *

We are not insensitive to the fact that our reading of the Organic Act will have serious and far-reaching consequences, and it may well be that this legislation enacted over seventy-five years ago is an anachronism which no longer serves the public interest. However, the appropriate forum to resolve this complex and controversial issue is not the courts but the Congress. * * *

The judgment of the district court is affirmed.

QUESTIONS AND DISCUSSION

1. In a portion of the opinion not included in the text, the court addressed the government's claim that the MUSYA, which, as explained above, directs the Forest Service to manage "renewable surface resources of the national forests for multiple use and sustained yield," allowed the agency to employ modern forestry practices in managing the forests. The court disagreed, noting in particular that Congress had stated that the purposes of MUSYA were supplemental to and not in derogation of the Organic Act.

2. If the practice of marking each tree has fallen out of use in modern forestry practices, should the Forest Service be obligated to continue to adhere to the anachronistic practice? In order to separate out this question of statutory interpretation from your substantive views about clearcutting, ask yourself whether you see the constitutional interpretation as similarly limited? Is it ever appropriate for statutory interpretation to be updated to reflect modern practice? What criteria would you apply to answer the question?

3. Although the costs of the timber program are substantial and often exceed revenues for individual sales, those revenues are nonetheless substantial. During the period between 1995 and 1997, for example, timber receipts generated $1.85 billion. Ninety-two percent of these revenues or about $1.7 billion was distributed to specific funds maintained by the Forest Service for various purposes. Only about $154 million went into the General Fund of the U.S. Treasury. *See* U.S. General Accounting Office, *Distribution of Timber Sales and Receipts, Fiscal Years 1995–1998*, GAO/ RCED 99–24 at 1–2 (1998). One of the biggest outlays—25% of timber receipts—goes to the States for the benefit of roads and schools in the counties where the forests are located. 16 U.S.C. § 500 (2000). An additional 10% of timber receipts goes into a fund for roads and trails on national forest lands. 16 U.S.C. § 501 (2000).

4. The Knutsen–Vandenberg Act was enacted in 1930 to provide a mechanism for funding the reforestation of logged lands. The statute authorizes the Forest Service to—

> require any purchaser of national-forest timber to make deposits of money in addition to the payments for the timber, to cover the cost to the United States of (1) planting . . ., (2) sowing with tree seeds . . ., (3) cutting, destroying, or otherwise removing undesirable trees or other growth . . . to improve the future stand of timber, or (4) protecting and improving the future productivity of the renewable resources of the forest land on such sale area. . . .

16 U.S.C. § 576b (2000). "K–V funds" are made directly available to the Forest Service to cover reforestation costs, and any excess K–V money that is not needed for reforestation is placed in a forest reserve account. Originally, the money paid under the K–V Act was a distinct premium over the purchase price of the timber. Beginning in 1957, however, the Forest Service simply included the K–V money in the overall purchase price, making it impossible to know how much of the purchase price was added for reforestation costs. Moreover, in order to recapture as much of this money as possible, the Forest Service treats all but $0.50/thousand board feet as available for K–V expenditure. Not surprisingly, the Forest Service has come to depend on this money to fund not only reforestation but also general overhead costs. The problem, of course, is that this gives the Forest Service a powerful incentive to sell more timber since the more timber it sells, the more K–V money becomes available. *See Who Says Money Doesn't Grow on Trees*, Forest Service Employees for Environmental Ethics, *available at* http://fseee.org/index.html?page=http%3A/fseee.org/projects/on-kv. shtml. In recent years, the KV Trust Fund has received about 24% of the total timber revenues. Between 1992 and 1997 this amounted to $1.274 billion. U.S. General Accounting Office, *Distribution of Timber Sales and Receipts, Fiscal Years 1995–1998*, GAO/RCED 99–24 at 19 (1998).

Should Congress repeal the K–V Act? Is there any way to retain those parts of the law that support important reforestation activities without promoting ill-advised timber sales?

5.   Most of the land managed by the Bureau of Land Management is not suitable for logging. The chief exception is the 2.2 million acres of timber-rich land in Oregon that was originally transferred to the Oregon and California Railroad Company (O & C) as part of a railroad land grant. The railroad defaulted on the agreement and the lands were restored to federal ownership. The history of the O & C lands was previously described in Chapter 2, *supra* at 126. Under the O & C Lands Act of 1937, the BLM is supposed to manage these lands "for permanent forest production" on a sustained yield basis. 43 U.S.C. §§ 1181a–1181j. In *Headwaters, Inc. v. BLM Medford District,* 914 F.2d 1174, 1183 (9th Cir. 1990), the court rejected a claim by an environmental group that the term "forest production" should be read broadly to encompass conservation values. According to the court, the O & C Act had two purposes: (1) to provide the counties where O & C lands are located with a permanent stream of revenue; and (2) to halt the historic practice of clearcutting O & C lands without reforestation. Does it strike you as odd that the federal government would be managing primarily to provide revenue to counties? Is the O & C Act an anachronism? Can it and should it be changed?

6.   The dispute in the *Monongahela* case was over clearcutting—a practice previously described in the section on silvicultural practices that involves removing all of the trees from a particular tract of land. Some foresters, especially on the industry side, believe that clearcutting mimics nature, and thus is the most appropriate logging method, at least in some circumstances. Others, however, disagree, noting for example that logging, unlike natural losses from windthrow, fire, and disease, removes most of the organic matter from the logged area. The controversy continues today. In 1993, the Sierra Club published a coffee table book of aerial photographs and text called, *Clearcut: The Tragedy of Industrial Forestry,* depicting numerous sites around the country that had suffered severe environmental damage from clearcutting. The American Forest and Paper Association responded the very next year with its own 28 page "book" called, *Closer Look: An On-the-Ground Investigation of the Sierra Club's Book, Clearcut.* Why do you suppose that the Sierra Club focused on aerial photos and the AFPA responded with on-the-ground pictures? Which one provides the more accurate ecological view?

———

2.   MODERN MANAGEMENT LAW, POLICIES, AND PRACTICES

The *Monongahela* decision, along with the Bolle and Church reports, paved the way for legislative reform. But the direction that reform would take was unclear. Many in Congress wanted to end the hold that timber production held on forest managers and limit their over-reliance on clearcutting. On the other hand, *Monongahela*'s flat ban on clearcutting was unlikely to survive. In 1976, Congress passed its reform legislation—the National Forest Management Act (NFMA). 16 U.S.C. §§ 1600–1614. National forest management today thus derives largely from three laws—NFMA and two to which you have already been introduced: The Multiple–Use, Sustained–Yield Act of 1960 (MUSYA), 16 U.S.C. § 528–531 (2000), and the Renewable Range and Resources Planning Act of 1974 (RPA), 16 U.S.C. §§ 1601–02.

NFMA, which is the most important of the three laws, establishes standards for individual forest "land and resource management plans" (LRMPs). Chapter 3 introduced you to LRMPs in the context of natural resource planning on the public lands (pages 298–307) and you may wish to review that section in conjunction with your study of NFMA below. Whereas Chapter 3 focused on the procedural benefits of planning for agency decision-making and accountability, the focus in this chapter is on the actual substantive requirements to which the Forest Service must adhere in its planning process. NFMA is, at its core, a planning statute and it gives the Forest Service significant management discretion, but the agency's discretion is not unbounded. The sections below introduce some of the limits on agency management of the national forests. We begin with a brief overview of how LRMPs and the planning process are supposed to work. The section then considers whether NFMA's planning process has substantive teeth. It looks first at the issue of whether NFMA imposes any real limits on the practice of clearcutting. Next, it briefly describes the process by which the Forest Service sells timber within the national forests. It then studies what obligations to conserve biodiversity are created by NFMA and the other forest management statutes. This section of the chapter concludes with a brief look at Forest Service management duties with respect to fire.

a. *National Forest Land and Resource Management Planning*

In developing LRMPs for national forests, NFMA requires the Forest Service, among other things, to

(b) use a systematic interdisciplinary approach to achieve integrated consideration of physical, biological, economic, and other sciences; * * *

(d) provide for public participation in the development, review, and revision of land management plans; * * *

(g)(1) specif[y] procedures to insure that land management plans are prepared in accordance with NEPA;* * *

(3) specif[y] guidelines for land management plans developed to achieve the goals of the [Resource Assessment] Program which—

(A) insure consideration of the economic and environmental aspects of various systems of renewable resource management ...;

(B) provide for diversity of plant and animal communities based upon the suitability and capability of the specific land area in order to meet overall multiple use objectives ...;

(C) insure research on and ... evaluation of the effects of each management system; * * *

(E) insure that timber will be harvested from National Forest System lands only where—

(i) soil, slope, or other watershed conditions will not be irreversibly damaged;

(ii) there is assurance that such lands can be adequately restocked within five years after harvest;

(iii) protection is provided for streams, streambanks, shorelines, lakes, wetlands, and other bodies of water from detrimental changes in water temperatures, blockages of water courses, and deposits of sediment, where harvests are likely to seriously and adversely affect water conditions or fish habitat; and

(iv) the harvesting system to be used is not selected primarily because it will give the greatest dollar return or the greatest unit output of timber; and

(F) insure that clearcutting, seed tree cutting, shelterwood cutting, and other cuts designed to regenerate an even-aged stand of timber will be used as a cutting method on National Forest System lands only where—

(i) for clearcutting, it is determined to be the optimum method, and for other such cuts it is determined to be appropriate, to meet the objectives and requirements of the relevant land management plan;

(ii) the interdisciplinary review as determined by the Secretary has been completed and the potential environmental, biological, esthetic, engineering, and economic impacts on each advertised sale area have been assessed, as well as the consistency of the sale with the multiple use of the general area;

(iii) cut blocks, patches, or strips are shaped and blended to the extent practicable with the natural terrain;

(iv) there are established according to geographic areas, forest types, or other suitable classifications the maximum size limits for areas to be cut in one harvest operation * * *; and

(v) such cuts are carried out in a manner consistent with the protection of soil, watershed, fish, wildlife, recreation, and esthetic resources, and the regeneration of the timber resource.

16 U.S.C. § 1604. LRMPs for national forests are required to be revised "when the Secretary finds conditions in a unit have significantly changed, but at least every fifteen years...." 16 U.S.C. § 1604(f)(5).

To assist the Forest Service in implementing the key provisions of 16 U.S.C. § 1604(g), which is excerpted above, Congress directed the agency to appoint "a committee of scientists who are not officers or employees of the Forest Service ... [to] provide scientific and technical advice and counsel on proposed guidelines and procedures to assure that an effective interdisciplinary approach is proposed and adopted." 16 U.S.C. § 1604(h). This "Committee of Scientists" was convened in 1977 and issued its report in 1979. *See* 44 Fed. Reg. 26,599, 53,967 (1979).

In 1982, the Forest Service largely adopted the committee's recommendations in its planning regulations at 36 C.F.R. part 219 (1998). Among other things, those rules required that—

> Fish and wildlife habitat shall be managed to maintain *viable populations* of existing native and desired non-native vertebrate species in the planning areas.
> * * *
>
> (a)(1) In order to estimate the effects of each alternative on fish and wildlife populations, certain vertebrate and/or invertebrate species present in the area shall be identified and selected as *management indicator species* and the reasons for their selection will be stated. These species shall be selected because their population changes are believed to indicate the effects of management activities.

36 C.F.R. § 219.18 (1999) (emphasis added). Endangered species are supposed to be represented as management indicator species (MIS) "where appropriate." *Id.* "Management prescriptions" for each land use area must "preserve and enhance the diversity of plant and animal communities, including endemic and desirable naturalized plant and animal species, so that it is at least as great as that which would be expected in a natural forest. . . ." *Id.* § 219.27 (1999).

While these 1982 rules, together with the language from NFMA, might have been construed to apply multiple use principles only after native biodiversity was protected, Pinchot's utilitarian legacy, as reflected by the Forest Service's longstanding affinity for timber sales, seems to have survived as the overriding influence on forest management. Further hampering the protection of native biodiversity is the agency's penchant for managing natural ecosystems to achieve "future desired conditions." In defining these desired conditions the agency can effectively manage the forest for whatever values it might choose. So, for example, if the Forest Service defines the future desired condition in a particular area as providing a mosaic of different land conditions—from old growth forests to open fields—activities that promote that condition, including timber sales, are presumably justified for that reason alone, even if those conditions were not the way that the natural landscape had evolved. Of course, as discussed in Chapter 1, there may be widely varying views as to what constitutes the "natural" landscape, but this fact only serves to underscore the breadth of discretion accorded the managing agency.

The Secretary of Agriculture appointed a second committee in 1997 in yet another effort to reorient the focus of the Forest Service. This Committee issued its report in 1999. *See* Sustaining the People's Lands: Recommendations for Stewardship for National Forests and Grasslands into the Next Century, *available at* http://www.fs.fed.us/news/news_archived/science/cosfrnt.pdf. As with the earlier Committee report, the Forest Service largely accepted the recommendations of the Second Committee of Scientists and adopted final rules implementing the recommendations in 2000. 65 Fed. Reg. 67,568 (2000). These rules established that "[t]he first priority for stewardship of the national forests and grasslands is to maintain or restore ecological sustainability to provide a sustainable flow of uses, values, products, and services from these lands." 36 C.F.R. § 219.19 (2001). They further make "[e]cosystem diversity and species diversity" components of ecological sustainability. 36 C.F.R. § 219.20 (2001). According to the rules:

> The planning process must include the development and analysis of information regarding these components at a variety of spatial and temporal scales. These scales include geographic areas such as bioregions and watersheds, scales of biological organization such as communities and species, and scales of time ranging from months to centuries.

Id. See also Charles F. Wilkinson, *A Case Study in the Intersection of Law and Science: The 1999 Report of the Committee of Scientists*, 42 ARIZ. L. REV. 307 (2000). The new rules provided a transition period until May 9, 2002, during which time individual forest supervisors could choose to follow the 1982 rules or the newly promulgated 2000 rules. 36 C.F.R. § 219.35 (2001)

On May 20, 2002, before the Clinton rules had a chance to influence planning documents, the Bush Administration issued an interim final rule suspending the Clinton rules. 67 Fed. Reg. 35,431 (2002). Public comment on the interim rules was accepted until April 7, 2003. Permanent new planning rules were proposed in December 2002, in part at least, because of the agency's skepticism about the ecological sustainability requirement:

> The planners particularly questioned whether or not the agency could achieve the ecological, social, and economic sustainability standards established in Sec. 219.19 of the 2000 rule.... The reviewers found that the ecological sustainability requirements in the rule are not only complex, but needlessly so. Although the 2000 rule was intended to increase the focus on ecosystem-level analyses for addressing the diversity of plant and animal communities and, thereby, reducing the far more costly species-by-species approach, the means to accomplish the intent of the rule are not clear.

67 Fed. Reg. 72,770, 72,772 (2002). In the meantime, the transition period authorized under the 2000 rules was extended until final new planning rules were promulgated. 67 Fed. Reg. 35,431, 35,432 (2002). On September 29, 2004, amid continued uncertainty due to its failure to promulgate permanent planning rules, the USDA issued an "interpretive rule" stating that the 1982 planning rules were no longer in effect, but could nonetheless continue to be used for plan amendments and revisions.

Finally, on January 5, 2005, the Forest Service promulgated comprehensive new planning rules, which it claimed were an outgrowth of the 2002 interim rules and comment period but which signaled a dramatic shift from any previous proposals. 70 Fed. Reg. 1023 (2005). Moreover, unlike previous planning rules, the Forest Service did not convene a new committee of scientists, and did not prepare an environmental impact statement or engage in consultation under the Endangered Species Act for the new rules, claiming that they were "strategic rather than prescriptive in nature" and thus would "not have environmental effects." *Id.* at 1031. At the same time that it published the 2005 rule, the Forest Service proposed to "categorically exclude[] from NEPA's procedural requirements all proposals to develop, amend, or revise land use plans which did not approve particular projects." 70 Fed. Reg. 1062. A final categorical exclusion for NFMA plans was published on December 15, 2006. 71 Fed. Reg. 75481 (2006).

The 2005 rules did not survive for long. In *Citizens for Better Forestry v. U.S. Department of Agriculture*, 481 F. Supp. 2d 1059 (N.D. Cal. 2007) the court enjoined the rules as contrary to NEPA, the ESA, and the public comment requirements of the APA. The court did not, however, reinstate the 1982 rules as the plaintiffs had requested, thus leaving the forest planning process in limbo. Although the Forest Service appealed the court's decision, it decided to move forward with new rules that complied with the court's order. A draft and final EIS were prepared along with proposed rules. Public comments were also accepted. Finally, on April 21, 2008, the Forest Service promulgated new planning rules that look very much like the 2005 rules.

Like the 2005 rules, the 2008 rules describe the planning process in broad terms. "Land management planning is an adaptive management process that includes social, economic, and ecological evaluation." 36 C.F.R. § 219.3 (2008). A plan "may include standards as a plan component" but apparently it does not have to include such standards. 36 C.F.R. § 219.7(a)(3) (2008).

The new rules somewhat cryptically state that "[a]pproval of a plan . . . will be done in accord with the Forest Service NEPA procedures," 36 C.F.R. § 219.4(b) (2008), but the preamble makes clear that the agency's procedures do not currently require NEPA compliance for forest planning because those decisions were categorically excluded by the agency. 71 Fed. Reg. 75481 (2006); Forest Service Handbook, 1909.15, § 31.2(16), *available at*, http://www.fs.fed.us/im/directives/. The decision to categorically exclude NFMA plans is the subject of ongoing litigation, *Defenders of Wildlife v. Kimbell*, 07–CV–194–RLJ (D.D.C), and the language of NFMA itself suggests that the agency may have an uphill fight. NFMA states that "land management plans [must be] prepared in accordance with [NEPA]," 16 U.S.C. § 1604(g)(1), and the Forest Service claims that its decision to categorically exclude such plans from NEPA satisfies this standard. Problematically, however, NFMA was enacted two years before the CEQ first established its rules authorizing categorical exclusions so it is hard to see how when Congress mandated compliance with NEPA for forest plans in 1976, it could have meant categorically excluding those plans from NEPA compliance. *See* 40 C.F.R. § 1508.4 (2008).

Notwithstanding the decision to avoid preparation of NEPA documents, the 2008 rules do promote a "collaborative and participatory approach to land management planning." 36 C.F.R. § 219.9 (2008). While collaborative processes risks giving undue weight to those with the time and resources to participate fully in the process, the Forest Service seems committed to a robust process that engages all interested parties.

The 2008 rules also require each forest to establish an "environmental management system" (EMS) that conforms to the consensus EMS standard developed by the International Organization for Standardization (ISO), known as ISO 14001. 36 C.F.R. § 219.5 (2008). While the ISO advertises its standards for government as well as business, its particular niche has been in the business world where companies are seeking to adhere to accepted conventions for responsible development. It is an odd fit for a government agency, particularly because the standards are proprietary. A member of the public cannot even view ISO 14001 without first purchasing it. *See* http://www.iso.org/iso/home.htm.

The new rules are quite vague about the issues that proved problematic for the 1982 and 2000 rules. The rules generally promote social, economic, and ecological sustainability but contain little in the way of specific standards or requirements to achieve those goals. 36 C.F.R. § 219.10 (2008). The rules also require the agency to "take into account the best available science," and to document how it did so, 36 C.F.R. § 219.11 (2008), but it is apparently free to ignore that science based upon "public input, competing use demands, budget projects, and many other factors...." 73 Fed. Reg. 21473–74.

Soon after the election of President Obama in November 2008, various citizen and environmental groups, as well as the Society for Conservation Biology, urged the Obama Administration to rescind the 2008 rules and reinstate the 1982 NFMA regulations. *See* http://www.americanlands.org/assets/docs/Forest_100_Day_Ltr_Priorities_FINAL_99.pdf; *see also* http://www.nccsp.org/files/100day_Draft_12_04_08_Booklet.pdf. At the time of this writing, the Obama Administration had taken no position on the 2008 planning rules.

b. *NFMA and Clearcutting*

As noted above, NFMA was enacted, in part at least, in response to the *Monongahela* decision's ban on clearcutting. NFMA, of course, allows clearcutting, but only where it is determined to be the "optimum" cutting method "to meet the objectives and requirements of the relevant land use plan." NFMA also requires the Forest Service to ensure that "the harvesting system to be used is not selected primarily because it will give the greatest dollar return or the greatest unit output of timber." 16 U.S.C. § 1604(g)(3)(E)(iv) (2000). Many people thought that these provisions would make clearcutting the exception rather than the rule. But the perceived economic advantages of clearcutting are so enticing that they tend to overwhelm other factors, especially for sales that are "below cost," since clearcutting brings in more revenue and thus helps to improve the revenue-cost ratio on such sales. "Below cost" timber sales are described in greater detail at Section IV.A.3. The term generally describes sales where the costs of carrying out the sale exceed the revenues from the sale of timber. Even where the ecological benefits of using other methods might be high, clearcutting often looks like a better choice because ecological and other intangible benefits are difficult to measure. Indeed, the Forest Service does not even attempt to quantify certain intangible benefits when it prepares a cost-benefit analysis for timber sale proposals, thus effectively ensuring that such benefits are ignored in the economic analysis of the sale.* Despite Congress' apparent desire to limit clearcutting, the vague language of NFMA has not made this easy, as the following case illustrates.

---

* The Forest Service Handbook describes the process for preparing a financial analysis as follows:

Express direct benefits in terms of dollars, based on such values as expected stumpage prices and payments-in-kind, for example, purchaser credit roads,

SIERRA CLUB V. ESPY,
38 F.3d 792 (5th Cir. 1994)

PATRICK E. HIGGINBOTHAM, CIRCUIT JUDGE:

The district court issued a preliminary injunction barring the Forest Service from conducting even-aged management in any of the four Texas national forests. The injunction was based on the district court's finding of probable success on plaintiffs' claims under two statutes: the National Forest Management Act, 16 U.S.C. §§ 1600–1614, and the National Environmental Policy Act, 42 U.S.C. §§ 4321–4347. The government and the timber industry intervenors bring this interlocutory appeal challenging the district court's order.

We disagree with the district court's insistence that NFMA restricts even-aged management to exceptional circumstances. We are persuaded that the district court erected too high a barrier to even-aged management. The standard that even-aged management may be used only in exceptional circumstances goes to the heart of the finding by the district court of a likelihood of success on the merits and upsets the delicate balance struck by Congress between friends and foes of this harvesting method. We must vacate the preliminary injunction and remand.

I.

A.

The Forest Service of the Department of Agriculture is charged with administering the resources of this country's national forests "for outdoor recreation, range, timber, watershed, and wildlife and fish purposes." Multiple–Use Sustained–Yield Act of 1960, 16 U.S.C. § 528. The principles of MUSYA were expressly incorporated into the statutory and regulatory scheme of NFMA. The pressures to enact NFMA came from many sources. On the one hand, there was increasing national concern over the Forest Service's use of clearcutting. On the other hand, Congress felt it necessary to counteract a Fourth Circuit decision which strictly construed the Organic Act of 1897 to effectively prohibit the practice of clearcutting in the national forests. *See West Va. Div. of the Izaak Walton League of Am., Inc. v. Butz*, 522 F.2d 945 (4th Cir. 1975) (the *Monongahela* decision). The result was a compromise expressed in a statute repealing the portion of the Organic Act interpreted in the *Monongahela* decision, Pub.L. No. 94–588, § 13, 1976 U.S.C.C.A.N. (90 Stat.) 2949, 2958, yet imposing new procedural and substantive restraints on the Forest Service.

Specifically, NFMA sets forth requirements for Land and Resource Management Plans under which the national forests are managed. The national forests are divided into management units, *see* 36 C.F.R. § 200.2, and the Forest Service must prepare an LRMP for each unit. An LRMP must "provide for multiple use and sustained yield of the products and services obtained [from units of the National Forest System], and, in particular, include coordination of

when appropriate. Where appropriate, projected stumpage prices shall reflect expectations of price trends and variations in values associated with differences in product size and quality resulting from different management prescriptions. *Do not assign benefit values to timber outputs for which there is no market or projected demand.*

FSH § 2409.13, 20(22.3) (1992) (emphasis added).

outdoor recreation, range, timber, watershed, wildlife and fish, and wilderness. . . ." 16 U.S.C. § 1604(e)(1). Once an LRMP is in place, the Forest Service can decide to sell timber only after analyzing timber management alternatives and the sale's particular environmental consequences. Site-specific analysis, sometimes referred to as compartment-level analysis, must be consistent with the LRMP. *Id.* § 1604(i).

Broadly stated, there are two ways to manage a forest's timber resources. The first method is even-aged management. *See* 36 C.F.R. § 219.3. Even-aged management includes clearcutting, where all the trees are cut down; seed tree cutting, where most of the trees are cut down, leaving only a few to naturally seed the cut area; and shelterwood cutting, where about double the number of trees are left standing as would be under the seed tree method. Even under the least intrusive even-aged management technique, shelterwood cutting, only about sixteen trees per acre remain after a cut. Moreover, under seed tree cutting, the older trees left to naturally seed the cut area are later removed. Even-aged management results in stands of trees that are essentially the same age. Before choosing to clearcut a portion of the forest, the Forest Service must find that clearcutting is the "optimum method" for achieving the objectives and requirements of the LRMP. 16 U.S.C. § 1604(g)(3)(F)(i). Similarly, before choosing to seed tree cut or shelterwood cut, the Forest Service must find that those methods are "appropriate" for achieving the objectives and requirements of the LRMP. *Id.*

The second method of timber resource management is uneven-aged management, also known as selection management. *See* 36 C.F.R. § 219.3. Uneven-aged management encompasses both single tree selection and group selection. Group selection involves cutting small patches of trees, while single tree selection involves selecting particular trees for cutting. Uneven-aged management maintains a continuous high-forest cover, and the stands are characterized by a number of differently aged trees. * * *

B.

On May 20, 1987, the Forest Service's Regional Forester signed the Record of Decision approving the LRMP and the Final EIS for the Texas national forests. The FEIS examined thirteen alternatives for managing the forests. Two of the alternatives provided for uneven-aged management of the forests' timber resources and the remainder for even-aged management. The Forest Service selected an alternative that provided for even-aged management. On June 8, 1987, the Texas Committee on Natural Resources, TCONR, filed an administrative appeal with the Forest Service challenging both the FEIS and the LRMP. TCONR also requested a stay of all timber operations under the even-aged management system. * * *

On April 1, 1989, the reviewing officer hearing TCONR's administrative appeal of the FEIS and the LRMP decided not to rule on the merits of TCONR's challenge, but instead remanded the LRMP for reanalysis. The reviewing officer reasoned that a change affecting one-third of Texas forests affects the level of goods and services that the forests can supply under the current LRMP. Forest Service Decision at 4. The reviewing officer promulgated interim guidelines to govern management of the forests until the Forest Service issued a new LRMP. *Id.* at 5. These guidelines provide that the appropriate timber management system is to be determined on a site-specific basis. *Id.* Specifically, even-aged management can be used if the Forest Service determines it to be appropriate to meet the "objectives and requirements" of the existing LRMP. *Id.* The Forest Service, however, must consider uneven-aged management alternatives during site-specific analysis. *Id.* at 6. In sum, although the LRMP was remanded for reanalysis, during the interim its "objectives and requirements" remain controlling on compartment-level decisions.

Frustrated by the Forest Service's refusal to rule on the merits of its administrative claim, TCONR, now joined by the Sierra Club and the Wilderness Society (collectively TCONR), turned to federal court to present its challenge to the FEIS and the LRMP. TCONR sought a declaration that the Forest Service's even-aged management practices did not comply with NEPA or NFMA and an injunction against all even-aged management practices. The government moved for summary judgment on TCONR's even-aged claims. * * *

On January 6, 1993, TCONR filed an "Urgent Motion for Injunction," seeking to enjoin the Forest Service's even-aged management practices, including twelve imminent timber sales. TCONR later dropped the number of challenged sales to nine. The district court ... denied the government's motion for summary judgment and issued a preliminary injunction prohibiting even-aged management in any of the four Texas forests. *Sierra Club v. Espy,* 822 F. Supp. 356, 369–70 (E.D.Tex.1993). * * *

The court ... focused on whether the EAs [on the timber sales] complied with NEPA and NFMA. The court found they did not. The court reasoned that TCONR was likely to succeed on its NFMA claim because the Forest Service employed even-aged management as the "rule" when, in fact, NFMA "contemplates that even-aged management techniques will be used only in exceptional circumstances." *Id.* at 363–64. * * *

IV.

A.

The government challenges the district court's interpretation of NFMA. Specifically, the government argues that the district court erred when it held that even-aged logging practices could only be used in exceptional circumstances. To hold otherwise, the district court reasoned, would violate the statutory provision that requires the Forest Service to use even-aged management only where "such cuts are carried out in a manner consistent with the *protection* of soil, watershed, fish, wildlife, recreation, and esthetic resources, and the regeneration of the timber resource." 16 U.S.C. § 1604(g)(3)(F)(v) (emphasis added); *accord* 36 C.F.R. § 219.27(c)(6). This duty to protect, the court held, "reflects the truism that the monoculture created by clearcutting and resultant even-aged management techniques is contrary to NFMA-mandated bio-diversity." 822 F. Supp. at 364 (*citing* 16 U.S.C. § 1604(g)(3)(B)).

The district court's holding that NFMA requires even-aged management be used only in exceptional circumstances is in tension with *Texas Comm. on Natural Resources v. Bergland,* 573 F.2d 201 (5th Cir.), *cert. denied,* 439 U.S. 966 (1978) (*TCONR I*). There we found that Congress, after hearing testimony on both sides of the clearcutting issue, struck a delicate balance between the benefits of clearcutting and the benefits of preserving the ecosystems and scenic quality of natural forests. *Id.* at 210. Specifically, NFMA "was an effort to place the initial technical, management responsibility for the application of NFMA guidelines on the responsible government agency, in this case the Forest Service. The NFMA is a set of outer boundaries within which the Forest Service must work." *Id.* We then cautioned the Forest Service that clearcutting could not be justified merely on the basis that it provided the greatest dollar return per unit output; "[r]ather[,] clearcutting must be used only where it is essential to accomplish the relevant forest management objectives." *Id.* at 212. We concluded by noting that "[a] decision to pursue even-aged management as the over-all management plan under the NFMA is subject to the narrow arbitrary and capricious standard of review." *Id.*

TCONR I recognized that the Forest Service may use even-aged management as an overall management strategy. That even-aged management must be the optimum or appropriate method to accomplish the objectives and requirements set forth in an LRMP does not mean that even-aged management is the exception to a rule that purportedly favors selection management. Similarly, the requirement that even-aged logging protect forest resources does not in itself limit its use. Rather, these provisions mean that the Forest Service must proceed cautiously in implementing an even-aged management alternative and only after a close examination of the effects that such management will have on other forest resources.

The conclusion that even-aged management is not the "exception" to the "rule" of uneven-aged management is supported by NFMA's legislative history. On three separate occasions, Congress rejected amendments that would have made uneven-aged management the preferred forest management technique. The first occurred during the joint markup sessions of the Senate Committees on Agriculture and Forestry, and on Interior and Insular Affairs. The language rejected by the Committees appeared in a bill introduced by Senator Randolph. The proposed bill would have required that "uneven-aged forest management primarily implemented by selection cutting shall be used in the eastern mixed hardwood forests." S. 2926, 94th Cong., 2d Sess. § 7(a) (1976).... The Committees rejected that amendment largely based on the advice of Forest Service Chief McGuire and another professional forester that even-aged management was often environmentally preferable to uneven-aged management. Following his defeat at the committee level, Senator Randolph offered an amendment on the Senate floor to create the same preference for uneven-aged management. The amendment was tabled and thereby defeated. *See* 122 Cong.Rec. 27625–27 (Aug. 25, 1976). Finally, during the markup sessions before the House Committee on Agriculture, the Committee rejected an amendment offered by Representative Brown, which would have mandated that uneven-aged management dominate eastern national forests.

TCONR points out that since the Randolph amendments would have *required* the use of uneven-aged management, they are not relevant on the issue of whether uneven-aged management is *preferred*. While TCONR correctly distinguishes the district court's holding from Senator Randolph's attempts to bar even-aged management, TCONR fails to persuade on the issue of whether rejection of congressional efforts to restrict even-aged logging sends a legislative message. That no amendment was specifically offered and rejected that proposed a preference for uneven-aged logging does not change the fact that legislators were loath to deprive the Forest Service of the option to select even-aged management. The final outcome of NFMA reflects those concerns.
* * *

Thus, NFMA does not bar even-aged management or require that it be undertaken only in exceptional circumstances; it requires that the Forest Service meet certain substantive restrictions before it selects even-aged management. To be sure, these restrictions reflect a congressional wariness towards even-aged management, constraining resort to its use. The sluicing effect of the required inquiries might be described as making a decision to employ even-aged management more difficult. However, it is not a description or characterization of the effects of the required decisional process that we face. The district court used "exceptional" as a decisional standard—and hence it upset the balance struck. * * *

We conclude that the district court erred in granting the preliminary injunction. * * *

QUESTIONS AND DISCUSSION

1. After *Espy*, are there any real limits on the ability of the Forest Service to allow clearcutting? Recall from Chapter 3 that in *Ohio Forestry v. Sierra Club*, 523 U.S. 726 (1998), the Supreme Court held that the plaintiff could not challenge the timber program approved in an LRMP until the Forest Service decided whether it would actually approve individual timber sales. On what grounds might a plaintiff challenge a timber program from an LRMP that imposes no restrictions on clearcutting?

2. As noted previously, supporters of clearcutting argue that it mimics fire, and thus contributes to the natural evolution of the forest ecosystem. Opponents respond that unlike fire, clearcutting takes most of the biomass and nutrients out of the forest rather than recycling them into the soil. Moreover, the rotation period for clearcutting, and consequently the catastrophic ecological changes caused by clearcutting, occur much more frequently than a catastrophic fire. Is this a sufficient reason under NFMA for banning clearcutting? For imposing any limits on clearcutting?

3. While the *Espy* case nominally involves a dispute over clearcutting it suggests a much broader and more fundamental disagreement about forest management generally and ecosystem management in particular. For many, biodiversity conservation and the preservation of natural ecosystems are important goals for their own sake. The Forest Service, however, has traditionally taken a more utilitarian view of ecosystem management. In *Krichbaum v. Kelley,* 844 F. Supp. 1107, 1115 (W.D. Va. 1994), *aff'd,* 61 F.3d 900 (4th Cir. 1995), the Forest Service offered the following defense of its policies:

> Ecosystem management is the means to an end. It is not the end itself. The Forest Service does not manage ecosystems just for the sake of managing them or for some notion of intrinsic ecosystem values....

The "end" that the Forest Service is seeking is therefore not a natural forest but a "desired" forest. In the district court's decision in the *Ohio Forestry* case, ultimately dismissed by the Supreme Court on ripeness grounds, *supra* at 314–315 the agency explained why logging remains so popular with forest managers:

> Timber sales are the most economically viable means of achieving desired plant and animal diversity. Our publics put high values on wildlife-associated recreation and the visual amenities of the Forest. If these benefits were provided through a method other than commercial timber sales, costs would be significantly higher and would eliminate returns to the Treasury.

Sierra Club v. Robertson, 845 F. Supp. 485, 498 (S.D. Ohio 1994). Since clearcutting usually provides the highest timber revenues for the Treasury, it should come as no surprise that clearcutting is the most popular logging method. How do you think the general public views "ecosystem management"? Do you think they understand it to mean a "means to an end"—an ecosystem manufactured through management policies—or an end in it-self—a natural ecosystem allowed to evolve on its own? If the former, is it misleading for the Forest Service to profess to be following an ecosystem management approach? Is utilitarianism compatible with ecosystem management? Is a timber-dependent community on the edge of a national forest a part of the forest ecosystem?

4. Although the process of managing national forests for timber production is complex, the basic approach followed by the Forest Service can be simply described. NFMA establishes the upper limit for timber sales from each national forest as "a quantity equal to or less than a quantity which can be removed from such forest annually in perpetuity on a sustained-yield basis." 16 U.S.C. § 1611(a) (2000). To determine this quantity, the Forest Service first calculates the "suitable timber base." *See* Forest Service Handbook (FSH), § 2409.13, 20. Lands are deemed unsuitable for a host of reasons. The land might not have trees, or it might be withdrawn from timber production (e.g., wilderness), or logging on the land might cause irreversible environmental damage, or be incapable of restocking within five years as required by law. *See* 16 U.S.C. § 1604(g)(3)(E)(ii). Lands might also be deemed unsuitable because logging is not cost-efficient, or because other preferred uses of the land are not compatible with logging. *Id.*

Land use planning conflicts might arise, for example, where lands are designated primarily for primitive, non-motorized recreation or where lands are designated primarily for managing old-growth dependent species. Unacceptable environmental damage might occur, for example, if logging were allowed on "hydric" or wet soils. Logging on wet soils causes soil compaction, which increases runoff, decreases infiltration, and inhibits root growth and regeneration of the forest. Likewise, logging near streams may cause erosion and siltation of the stream.

Once the suitable timber base is determined, the Forest Service can estimate the amount of timber available from those lands by calculating the "long-term sustained yield capacity" (LTSYC) for those lands. *See* FSH § 2409.13, 30. This is done by determining the "rotation age" of the trees, which is essentially the time it takes for new trees to reach harvest age. The Forest Service generally requires the tree stand to meet the "culmination of mean annual increment"—the age at which the average annual growth of a tree stand is greatest—before it is deemed ready for harvest. *See* FSH § 2409.13, 0.

This information allows the Forest Service to determine an "allowable sale quantity" or "ASQ." The ASQ is expressed in terms of "million board feet" (mmbf) and is defined as the quantity of timber that may be sold from the suitable timber lands within a forest over the planning period—usually ten years. FSH § 2409.13, 0. The average *annual* ASQ can thus be determined simply by dividing by ten.

5. The ASQ depends upon a host of land management choices made by the Forest Service at the individual forest level. The Resources Planning Act may set objectives for individual forests, including a proposed ASQ, and these objectives must be reflected in the environmental analysis prepared for the forest plan, but they don't bind the agency in making its planning decision. In *Wind River Multiple–Use Advocates v. Espy*, 835 F. Supp. 1362 (D. Wyo. 1993), for example, the court rejected a claim that a Forest Service decision to set the ASQ for the Bridger–Teton National Forest at about 12 mmbf annually was unlawful because the RPA had set an "objective" for the Forest of 46 mmbf. The court found that the RPA objectives were "tentative," and were not intended to be "mandatory." *Id.* at 1371–72. The decision to limit timber sales on the Bridger–Teton National Forest to 12 mmbf was based upon a variety of considerations, including the popularity of the Forest with recreational users and the Forest's important wildlife resources, including prime grizzly bear habitat. Suppose, however, that notwithstanding these resources the Forest Service had decided to set the annual ASQ at 46 mmbf—the level suggested by the RPA. How difficult would it likely be to successfully challenge such a decision? What does this suggest to you about the scope of the agency's discretion in setting the ASQ?

6.   How much discretion does the system of establishing a "suitable timber base" afford the Forest Service in setting timber production goals? In *Friends of the Bow v. Thompson*, 124 F.3d 1210 (10th Cir. 1997), the court rejected with little discussion plaintiffs' challenge to an individual timber sale based in part on a claim that flaws in the calculation of the suitable timber base resulted in an ASQ for the Medicine Bow National Forest that was far too high. Plaintiffs argued that the agency's own data showed that the 28.4 mmbf annual ASQ should have been set at less than 7 mmbf. But the court noted that the particular timber sale that was being challenged involved only 3.1 mmbf, and that it did not therefore by itself implicate the lower ASQ supported by the plaintiffs. *Id.* at 1218. Moreover, since the annual ASQ is an average over ten years, sales in any particular year that exceed the annual ASQ do not technically cause a violation of the forest plan. Does the decision in *Friends of the Bow* suggest that plaintiffs must wait until the agency decides to sell timber in excess of the ten year ASQ before they can raise issues about the accuracy of the suitable timber base calculation? Can you think of any legal arguments that might be made to counter this claim?

7.   The Forest Service uses the LRMP, the ASQ, and all of the timber resource information gathered during the planning process to establish a schedule of possible timber sales. This schedule offers a rough agenda for sale proposals over the course of the planning period. Timber sales are proposed by the Forest Service following preparation of a draft and final EA or EIS. After NEPA compliance the Forest Service decides whether to sell timber and, if so, how much. If the decision is made to sell timber, the Forest Service solicits bids on the sale and generally accepts the highest bid. Before entering a contract with the high bidder, the Forest Service will "cruise" the sale to determine how much timber is actually available. Because the Forest Service generally does not specifically assess the amount of available timber until a bidder is identified, it is not unusual for the sale quantity to vary—sometimes significantly—from the amount proposed in the record of decision. This can be problematic because the cost-benefit analysis prepared by the Forest Service in conjunction with the NEPA document is based upon the estimated sale quantity. If the amount of timber is lower than was estimated in the EIS then the cost-benefit analysis will offer more support for logging than is justified by the facts. In *Friends of the Bow v. Thompson,* 124 F.3d 1210 (10th Cir. 1997), for example, the plaintiffs argued that the information gained from cruising the sale changed a sale with a positive revenue-to-cost ratio into a sale with a negative revenue-to-cost ratio. That is, it went from a sale that would make money to one that would lose money. The court nonetheless upheld the sale. This particular sale is the subject of a problem exercise at pages 289–290.

8. The goal of the federal timber program is to achieve "non-declining even flow" (NDEF). Under this policy the volume of timber removed from a National Forest in each decade is supposed to equal or exceed that volume planned for removal in the previous decade. This policy is designed to ensure that the objectives of long-term sustained yield will be met. In fact, however, timber sales on national forests have declined dramatically in recent years from a peak of 12.7 bbf in 1987 to less than 3 bbf in 1999. The decline can probably be attributed to a host of factors, but one of the most prominent reasons is the growing concern for biodiversity conservation. That subject is explored in the next section.

———

c.   Biodiversity Conservation and National Forests

As described at the beginning of this chapter, forests support a wide range of plant and animal life. But the extensive logging that occurred in our Eastern and Northern forests throughout the nineteenth and most of the twentieth century eliminated most of our native forests (recall that only 6% of our remaining forests are over 175 years old). Much of what remains is in our national forests, and most of that is in the Western United States. As the following two cases illustrate, biodiversity conservation has become a hotly debated issue, especially when additional logging is proposed in what remains of the old growth stands in our national forests.

IDAHO SPORTING CONGRESS V. RITTENHOUSE,
305 F.3d 957 (9th Cir. 2002)

D.W. NELSON, SENIOR CIRCUIT JUDGE.

Plaintiffs Idaho Sporting Congress, Inc. and Alliance for the Wild Rockies (collectively "Conservation Groups") brought suit against the United States Forest Service ("Forest Service") to enjoin two timber sales ("Lightning Ridge sale and Long Prong sale") in the Boise National Forest ("Forest") for violation of the National Environmental Policy Act ("NEPA"), 42 U.S.C. § 4321–4370f, and for violation of the National Forest Management Act ("Forest Act"), 16 U.S.C. §§ 1600–1687. The district court granted summary judgment in favor of the Forest Service on all claims.... We remand to the district court with instructions to enjoin the Long Prong and Lightning Ridge timber sales consistent with this opinion.

I.   BACKGROUND AND PROCEDURAL HISTORY

The Forest covers approximately 2,272,000 acres in west-central Idaho, north and east of the capital city of Boise. Many free-flowing streams with outstanding wild, scenic, and recreational values traverse the Forest, including the middle and south forks of the Payette River, the south fork of the Salmon River, and the south fork of the Boise River. The Frank Church–River Of No Return Wilderness, which is the largest wilderness area in the contiguous 48 states, is located partially within the Forest, and thirty-eight roadless areas located in the Forest encompass over one million acres.

Over three hundred species of wildlife depend on the Forest for habitat, including black bear, mountain lion, grey wolf, river otter, golden eagle, and osprey. Cutthroat, rainbow, brook, and bull trout live in the creeks and rivers of the Boise, Payette, and Salmon River drainages. Chinook salmon spawn and hatch in the streams of the Forest and then travel down the Columbia River system through Oregon and Washington, returning to the Pacific Ocean to live until they embark on the long journey upstream, returning again to lay their eggs in the cold-water washed gravel beds of South Fork Salmon River, Johnson Creek, Sulphur Creek, Elk Creek, and Bear Valley Creek.

The Forest supports myriad recreational activities, including fishing, hunting, camping, and white-water rafting. Commercial exploitation of Forest resources occurs mainly in the form of timber harvest. Logging and recreational uses of the Forest help support the economies of surrounding communities.

The Forest Service manages the Forest, and is required by statute and regulation to safeguard the continued viability of wildlife in the Forest. In carrying out its management responsibilities, the Forest Service must comply with the mandates of the Forest Act, 16 U.S.C. §§ 1600–1687. The Forest Act requires the Forest Service to develop a land and resource management plan ("forest plan") for each forest that it manages. 16 U.S.C. § 1604. The forest plan must provide for multiple uses of the forest, including recreation, range, timber, wildlife and fish, and wilderness. 16 U.S.C. § 1604(e)(1). In providing for multiple uses, the forest plan must comply with substantive requirements of the Forest Act designed to ensure continued diversity of plant and animal communities and the continued viability of wildlife in the forest, including the requirement that "wildlife habitat shall be managed to maintain viable populations of existing native and desired non-native vertebrate species in the planning area." 16 U.S.C. § 1604(g)(3)(B); 36 C.F.R. § 219.19 (1999). In order to maintain viable populations of wildlife, "habitat must be provided to support, at least, a minimum number of reproductive individuals and that habitat must be well distributed so that those individuals can interact with others in the planning area." 36 C.F.R. § 219.19.

In summary, all management activities undertaken by the Forest Service must comply with the forest plan, which in turn must comply with the Forest Act, which requires that wildlife habitat must be managed to maintain viable populations of native and desired non-native wildlife species. In order to ensure compliance with the forest plan and the Forest Act, the Forest Service must conduct an analysis of each "site specific" action, such as a timber sale, to ensure that the action is consistent with the forest plan. *Inland Empire Pub. Lands Council v. U.S. Forest Serv.*, 88 F.3d 754, 757 (9th Cir. 1996) (*citing* 16 U.S.C. § 1604(i)).

In 1990, the Forest Service adopted a Land and Resource Management Plan to govern its management of the Boise National Forest ("Forest Plan"). The Boise Forest Plan employs a "proxy-on-proxy" approach to meet the requirement of maintaining viable wildlife populations. First, seven "management indicator species" were selected to represent the needs of various types of wildlife throughout the Forest. For example, the pileated woodpecker was selected to represent a "wide range of large snag users." By monitoring the health of the pileated woodpecker population, the health of a wide range of other species which use similar habitat would be monitored as well. In this way, the pileated woodpecker acts as an indicator, or proxy, for many other species. This indicator species approach is the first level of proxy.

Next, rather than actually monitoring the population of each indicator species to determine if viable populations are being maintained, the Forest Service designates certain types and quantities of habitat as sufficient to maintain viable populations of the selected indicator species. Then "[h]abitats used by management indicator species will be monitored to determine what population changes, if any, are induced by management activities." For example, the Forest Service determined that each breeding pair of pileated woodpeckers would require a 300 acre block of "mature timber," which would in turn contain at least 100 acres of "old growth" forest.

The Forest Plan sets out detailed and exacting requirements for old growth forest. It defines old growth as a "stand of trees that is past full maturity and showing signs of decadence." The Forest Plan also requires that, to qualify as old growth, a stand of trees must be at least ten acres in size and contain at least twenty trees per acre greater than 20′ in diameter at breast height and thirty trees per acre 10′ to 20′ in diameter at breast height. There also must be at least fifteen tons per acre of downed or dead trees and two logs per acre greater than 12′ in diameter at breast height. Finally, there must be at least two standing dead trees (snags) per acre greater than 20′ in diameter at breast height and greater than twenty feet tall.

In order to support the minimum viable population of pileated woodpeckers, which the Forest Service determined to be ninety breeding pairs, ninety blocks of such forest would need to be maintained in a well distributed pattern throughout the Forest. These blocks of habitat are the second level of proxy, each block "counting" as the presence of a breeding pair of pileated woodpeckers, which in turn indicates (in theory) the presence of numerous other species which share similar habitat needs.

For management purposes, the Forest is divided into fifty-nine management areas. The larger management areas are in turn divided into compartments. Management areas vary in size from about 2,000 acres to over 135,000 acres. Compartments average about 5,000 to 7,000 acres. The Forest Plan calls for one pair of pileated woodpeckers to be located in each management area less than 50,000 acres and two pairs to be located in each management area over 50,000 acres. In other words, consistent with the proxy on proxy approach, one 300 acre block of mature forest containing 100 acres of old growth must be identified and preserved in each management area less than 50,000 acres and two such blocks must be identified and set aside in each area over 50,000 acres. Additionally, in order to comply with the Forest Act and its implementing regulations, these blocks "must be well distributed so that those individuals [pileated woodpeckers] can interact with others in the planning area." 36 C.F.R. § 219.19. At a minimum, this means that the offspring of breeding pairs must be able to find each other and find suitable breeding and foraging habitat so that the species can survive.

Consistent with the established needs of the pileated woodpecker, the Forest Plan calls for a minimum of 27,000 acres (90 breeding pairs multiplied by 300 acre blocks) to be set aside for pileated woodpecker habitat. To meet this requirement, the Forest Plan calls for "[d]edication of 55,000 acres of old-growth habitat, well-distributed throughout the forest, by the year 1991." The Forest Plan also requires that when "significant" areas of old growth are lost to fire, new acres must be rededicated. The parties disagree as to how much forest must be lost to fire before it is considered significant, and disagree as to how quickly the Forest Service must act to rededicate acres lost to fire. * * *

In 1999, the Forest Service approved the two timber sales at issue here, the Lightning Ridge sale involving timber harvest from approximately 860 acres in Management Area 35, and the Long Prong sale involving timber harvest from approximately 2,000 acres in Management Area 53. The Conservation Groups brought administrative appeals challenging the two sales, and ultimately brought suit in federal district court challenging the two sales for failure to comply with the Forest Act and NEPA. * * *

The district court ... granted summary judgment [on procedural grounds] on all claims in favor of the Forest Service. The Conservation Groups timely appealed. * * *

III.   DISCUSSION

* * *

While the Conservation Groups make numerous assaults on the Lightning Ridge and Long Prong sales, and the organization of their arguments is less than a model of clarity, their claims essentially are that the Forest Service's approval of the sales was not in accordance with law because the Forest Plan's old growth species viability standard is invalid, and, in any event, the standard is not being met. All site specific actions must be consistent with adopted forest plans. *Inland Empire*, 88 F.3d at 757. Here, the site specific analyses of timber sales depend on the Forest Plan old growth viability standard to insure that the Forest Act's requirement of maintaining viable populations of native species, including old growth dependent species, is met. If the Forest Plan's standard is invalid, or is not being met, then the timber sales that depend upon it to comply with the Forest Act are not in accordance with law and must be set aside. *See id.*

First, the Conservation Groups argue that the old growth viability standard is invalid because the Forest Service's 1996 Monitoring Report, issued to reassess the Forest Plan, shows that the old growth standard is no longer tenable because new scientific information invalidates the Forest Plan assumptions regarding the viability of old growth dependent species.

Next, they argue that the Forest Plan requirements are not being met because recent uncharacteristic forest fires have destroyed a significant amount of the 55,000 acres of old growth habitat set aside in the Forest Plan, and the Forest Service has failed to rededicate replacement acres as required by the Forest Plan.

Finally, the Conservation Groups argue that the entire proxy-on-proxy approach, upon which the Forest Plan depends, is invalid because it does not comply with the requirements of 36 C.F.R. § 219.19(a)(6) that "[p]opulation trends of the management indicator species will be monitored and relationships to habitat changes determined." The Conservation Groups argue that the Forest Service must monitor the actual animals included in the seven management indicator species and may not use the existence of a predetermined amount of designated habitat as a proxy for the existence of an individual animal.

In order to ensure that forest plans remain in compliance with the Forest Act, the Forest Service is required to assess each forest plan and issue a monitoring report every five years. 36 C.F.R. § 219.10(g). Among other things, these periodic monitoring reports assess the forest plan's compliance with the Forest Act requirement that "wildlife habitat shall be managed to maintain existing native and desired non-native species in the planning area." 36 C.F.R. § 219.19.

In 1996, the Forest Service issued a five year monitoring report for the Boise Forest Plan ("Monitoring Report"). The Monitoring Report reveals that changed conditions and new scientific understanding render the Forest Plan inadequate over a wide range of forest management issues. * * *

Relevant to the issue now before us, Forest Service documentation prepared in conjunction with the Monitoring Report and upon which that report was based indicates in no uncertain terms that the Forest Plan old growth dependent species viability standard is, as the Conservation Groups claim, invalid. As discussed above, the Forest Plan old growth dependent species viability standard sets aside blocks of old growth habitat for the pileated woodpecker, a management indicator species. By monitoring these blocks of habitat the Forest Service seeks to ensure the continued existence of healthy pileated woodpecker populations in the Forest, which in turn indicates the continued health of many other species that use similar habitat. The same strategy is used for the red-backed vole, another management indicator species that uses old growth habitat. Monitoring Element D—Adequacy of Forest Plan Direction for Management Indicator Species—reveals the following conclusions of Forest Service scientists with regard to the pileated woodpecker and red-backed vole:

> Assumptions regarding the sustainability of dedicated old growth appear invalid. New information regarding dispersal distances and disturbance effects suggest the amount of dedicated old growth in the Forest Plan may be inadequate. New information also suggests that old growth definitions in the Forest Plan do not reflect diversity of old growth on the ground. . . . Analysis shows that the current Forest Plan approach to sustaining old growth through the planning period is invalid.

In addition, Monitoring Report Question D shows that changed conditions, in the form of extensive forest fires occurring after the original 55,000 acres was dedicated, mean that even the invalid standard is not being met. * * *

The Forest Service further argues that its requirement to rededicate acres of old growth lost to fire has not been triggered. It points out that the Forest Plan requires rededication only when "significant" areas of old growth are lost to fire. . . . We consider the Monitoring Report's conclusion that "40 percent of the [dedicated] compartments currently do not meet Forest Plan expectations for old growth" to establish a significant loss.

Thus, the record strongly indicates that the Forest Plan standard itself is invalid and that changed conditions removed a significant number of compartments of dedicated old growth, resulting in non-compliance with the standard because the Forest Service has failed to rededicate old growth. * * *

While we give deference to an administrative agency's judgment on matters within its expertise, here the Forest Service's own scientists have concluded that the "Forest Plan approach to sustaining old growth through the planning period is invalid"; . . . and have concluded that a significant amount of the dedicated compartments have been damaged by fire. We hold therefore that the approval of the Long Prong and Lightning Ridge timber sales was not in accordance with law. . . . Specifically, we hold that the Forest Plan standard for maintaining the viability of old growth dependent species was invalid. Further, we hold that the Forest Service failed to comply with the Forest Plan standard for maintaining the viability of old growth dependent species because the Forest Service failed to rededicate acres of old growth lost to fire and failed to take adequate steps to insure that compartments identified as containing dedicated old growth do, in fact, contain it. Because site specific actions, including approval of the Long Prong and Lightning Ridge sales, depend on a valid and adequately implemented Forest Plan old growth species viability standard to ensure compliance with the Forest Act's requirement of maintaining viable populations of native species, and the viability standard here was both invalid and inadequately implemented, the sales must be set aside and logging thereunder enjoined.

The Conservation Groups argue that the following two sections of the Code of Federal Regulations require the Forest Service to monitor the population trends of management indicator species in addition to monitoring habitat:

> In order to estimate the effects of each alternative on fish and wildlife populations, certain vertebrate and/ or invertebrate species present in the area shall be identified and selected as management indicator species and the reasons for their selection will be stated. These species shall be selected because their population changes are believed to indicate the effects of management activities. 36 C.F.R. § 219.19(a)(1).

> Populations trends of the management indicator species will be monitored and relationships to habitat changes determined. 36 C.F.R. § 219.19(a)(6).

In addition to these two sections, the Conservation Groups point to § 219.19(a)(2), which requires that "[p]lanning alternatives shall be stated and evaluated in terms of *both* amount and quality of habitat *and* of animal population trends of the management indicator species." 36 C.F.R. § 219.19(a)(2) (emphasis added).

The Forest Service, on the other hand, points out that this Court has interpreted these regulations to allow the evaluation of habitat as a proxy for monitoring population trends. *Inland Empire,* 88 F.3d at 761. However, in *Inland Empire* this Court was satisfied that the Forest Service's methodology was sound, *id.,* and the opinion states that *"[i]n this case,* the Service's methodology reasonably ensures such [viable] populations." *Id.* (emphasis added). We cannot say the same thing here. In the case before us, the Monitoring Report shows that the Forest Service's methodology does not reasonably ensure viable populations of the species at issue. In addition to the conclusions of the Monitoring Report, the record demonstrates that the Forest Service's methodology for dedicating old growth is so inaccurate that it turns out there is no old growth at all in management area 35, where the Forest Service has purported to dedicate 1,280 acres of old growth.

We therefore remand to the district court with instructions to enjoin the Lightning Ridge and Long Prong timber sales until such time as the Forest Service complies with the Forest Act and NEPA.

QUESTIONS AND DISCUSSION

1. Do you think the outcome of this case would have been the same if it had gone to court after the Supreme Court's decision in *Norton v. Southern Utah Wilderness Alliance* 542 U.S. 55 (2004), discussed, *supra,* Chapter 3? Unlike *SUWA,* which involved an alleged failure on the part of the agency to act, *Rittenhouse* involved "discrete" actions—two timber sales. But the legal claims were largely based upon an allegation that the sales violated the applicable forest plan. In *SUWA,* the Court described a comparable BLM land use plan as "generally a statement of priorities; it guides and constrains actions, but does not (at least in the usual case) prescribe them." *Id.* at 71. Thus, according to the Court, "allowing general enforcement of plan terms would lead to pervasive interference with BLM's own ordering of priorities." *Id.* The Court conceded, however, that "an action called for in a plan may be compelled when the plan merely reiterates duties the agency is already obligated to perform, or perhaps when language in the plan itself creates a commitment binding on the agency." *Id.* To what extent can the Forest Service use the *SUWA* decision to avoid cases like *Rittenhouse* on the future? Thus far, at least, district courts in the 9th Circuit appear to construe the reach of SUWA narrowly. *See, e.g., Center for Biological Diversity v. BLM*, 422 F. Supp. 2d 1115 (N.D. Cal. 2006); *Soda Mountain Wilderness Council v. Norton*, 424 F. Supp. 2d 1241 (E.D. Cal. 2006); *Envtl. Prot. Info. Ctr. v. Blackwell*, 389 F. Supp. 2d 1174, 1215 (N.D. Cal. 2004).

2.   The 1982 Forest Service planning rules provide for the selection of management indicator species (MIS) as follows:

> In order to estimate the effects of each alternative on fish and wildlife populations, certain vertebrate and/or invertebrate species present in the area shall be identified and selected as management indicator species and the reasons for their selection will be stated. These species shall be selected because their population changes are believed to indicate the effects of management activities. In the selection of management indicator species, the following categories shall be represented where appropriate: Endangered and threatened plant and animal species identified on State and Federal lists for the planning area; species with special habitat needs that may be influenced significantly by planned management programs; species commonly hunted, fished, or trapped; non-game species of special interest; and additional plant or animal species selected because their population changes are believed to indicate the effects of management activities on other species of selected major biological communities or on water quality. * * *

36 C.F.R. § 219.19(a)(1) (2000). What advantages and disadvantages can you see in following the MIS approach to addressing biodiversity conservation?

3.   The court describes the approach taken by the Forest Service in the *Idaho Sporting Congress* case as a "proxy-on-proxy approach." The MIS serves as the proxy for assessing the health of other species with similar habitat needs, and MIS habitat serves as a proxy for the species itself. In *Inland Empire Public Lands Council v. U.S. Forest Service*, 88 F.3d 754, 763 (9th Cir. 1996), the same court held that "the Service [did not] act[] arbitrarily or capriciously when it estimated the effects of the alternatives on the population of the management indicator species by analyzing the amount of the species' habitat that would be reduced by each alternative." What facts in *Idaho Sporting Congress* led the court to limit the holding in *Inland Empire*? After *Idaho Sporting Congress* can the Forest Service ever rely on the proxy-on-proxy approach? In *Environmental Protection Information Center v. Blackwell*, 389 F. Supp. 2d 1174, 1215 (N.D. Cal. 2004), the court construed *Inland Empire* to allow the proxy-on-proxy approach "for the smaller, more reclusive species, such as the pileated woodpecker, [for which] there is no technically reliable and cost-effective method of counting individual members of the species." Nonetheless, in *Blackwell,* the court rejected the use of the proxy-on-proxy approach where it relied on habitat models that have not been proved reliable. *Id.* at 1217.

4. Professor Oliver Houck has described three cases that he claims show that the Forest Service continues to exalt timber production and management over biodiversity conservation, despite NFMA and its implementing rules. In *Sierra Club v. Robertson*, 810 F. Supp. 1021 (W.D. Ark. 1992), *aff'd*, 28 F.3d 753 (8th Cir. 1994), the court upheld a plan that was designed "to cut existing trees and grow pines of uniform height, which in turn will be harvested." *Id.* at 1024. In *Sierra Club v. United States Forest Service*, 878 F. Supp. 1295 (D. S.D. 1993), *aff'd*, 46 F.3d 835 (8th Cir. 1995) the court upheld clearcuts that were designed to provide habitat for the ubiquitous game animal, the white-tailed deer. And in *Krichbaum v. Kelley*, 844 F. Supp. 1107 (W.D. Va. 1994), *aff'd*, 61 F.3d 900 (4th Cir. 1995) the court approved a plan providing for a "mosaic of even aged tree stands." After discussing these cases, Professor Houck observed:

> One emerges from these cases with the conviction that, at some early point, they took a wrong fork in the road. On reflection, Congress took the first wrong turn in assuming, with unrealistic optimism, that the Service could offset decades of timber-first training and continuing pressures to keep the cut high with precatory language about diversity goals and multiple use. Despite the Committee of Scientists' efforts to pin diversity down, it too left enough flexibility and ambiguity in its recommendations to allow diversity planning to continue as an afterthought, and even a justification for the status quo. The courts for their part could have interpreted the diversity regulations both by their intent and their literal word, rather than give up at the first mention of multiple use; they could do so still. So could the Forest Service itself.

Oliver A. Houck, *On the Law of Biodiversity and Ecosystem Management*, 81 MINN. L. REV. 869, 921 (1997). Professor Houck offers three "self-evident truths" for securing real biodiversity:

> (a) *The natural forest baseline.* The Committee of Scientists clearly had the unmanaged forest in mind as the baseline for diversity planning. The Forest Service has managed to pervert that concept to "natural forest," and from there to "desired" natural forest, and from there sideways, to diversity "equal to" that of a natural forest.... Either the objective for diversity is the historic natural forest in its unmanaged condition, or it is whatever set of "outputs" the dominant political pressure wants it to be. There is no in between.

> (b) *Viable populations.* The viable population concept is demanding, time-consuming, expensive, never certain and often inconclusive—but it works. It produces defensible conclusions on what habitat is needed and how much and where. No other approach provides that level of objectivity and specificity. For decisions that are then going to run a gauntlet of fire from every side, an objective, scientific basis is indispensable.

> (c) *Management indicator species.* The MIS approach is as excellent or as abysmal as the species selected. The Endangered Species Act is effective because it flatly requires the selection of its listed species for MIS-like analyses. The diversity regulations fail when they allow the selection of common species or species of convenience, obviously selected to continue a high level of locally popular "outputs."

Id. at 922–23.

5. In light of these problems, Professor Blumm argues that the preference of the Forest Service toward timber production can be readily explained by public choice theory. Michael C. Blumm, *Public Choice Theory and the Public Lands: Why "Multiple Use" Failed*, 18 HARV. ENVTL. L. REV. 405 (1994). Do you agree? What, if anything, can be done to change this preference?

6. In 1991, Congress passed an "appropriations rider" providing that certain studies of timber sales in northern spotted owl habitat in the Pacific Northwest should be deemed adequate consideration for the purpose of meeting statutory requirements, including NEPA and NFMA, that were the basis for two pending lawsuits. Can Congress direct a court to find that an agency shall be deemed in compliance when it plainly is not? In *Roberston v. Seattle Audubon Society*, 503 U.S. 429 (1992), the Supreme Court upheld the rider against a separation of powers claim. The Court found that the rider "compelled changes in law, not findings or results under old law." *Id.* at 438. Thus, according to the Court, the provision did not raise separation of powers concerns. Do you agree?

Following the *Robertson* decision, Congress amended NFMA to establish procedures for expediting salvage timber sales. Pub. L. No. 104–19, 109 Stat. 240 (1995). Congress found expedited sales necessary to ensure that salvage timber (typically timber damaged by fire or windthrow) could be removed before it became unmarketable. The law also responded to several post-*Robertson* decisions that had continued to impose logging bans in northern spotted owl habitat. *See, e.g., National Audubon Soc. v. U.S. Forest Service,* 4 F.3d 832 (9th Cir. 1993); *Seattle Audubon Soc. v. Moseley,* 798 F. Supp. 1484 (W.D. Wash.1992). It specifically authorized the Forest Service to conduct timber sales in spotted owl habitat "notwithstanding any decision, restraining order, or injunction issued by a United States court before the date of enactment of this section," and it provided that the expedited sale procedures "shall be deemed to satisfy" a host of federal laws, including NFMA, NEPA, and the ESA. *Id.* at § 2001(d). The new language went well beyond the limited exemption contained in the earlier rider. Are there policy reasons for and against the adoption of such selective exemptions from the law? Should it matter whether the exemption is contained in an appropriations rider as in *Robertson* or in regular legislation, as in the salvage timber bill? Does selective exemption legislation raise public choice concerns?

SIERRA CLUB v. MARITA,
46 F.3d 606 (7th Cir. 1995)

FLAUM, CIRCUIT JUDGE

Plaintiffs Sierra Club, Wisconsin Forest Conservation Task Force, and Wisconsin Audubon Council, Inc. (collectively, "Sierra Club") brought suit against defendant United States Forest Service ("Service") seeking to enjoin timber harvesting, road construction or reconstruction, and the creation of wildlife openings at two national forests in northern Wisconsin. The Sierra

Club claimed that the Service violated a number of environmental statutes and regulations in developing forest management plans for the two national forests by failing to consider properly certain ecological principles of biological diversity. The district court ... granted the Service summary judgment on the merits of those claims. We affirm.

I.

The National Forest Management Act ("NFMA") requires the Secretary of Agriculture, who is responsible for the Forest Service, to develop "land and resource management plans" to guide the maintenance and use of resources within national forests. 16 U.S.C. §§ 1601–1604. * * *

The process for developing plans is quite elaborate. The Service must develop its management plans in conjunction with coordinated planning by a specially-designated interdisciplinary team, extensive public participation and comment, and related efforts of other federal agencies, state and local governments, and Indian tribes. 36 C.F.R. §§ 219.4–219.7. Directors at all levels of the Service participate in the planning process for a given national forest. The Forest Supervisor, who is responsible for one particular forest, initially appoints and then supervises the interdisciplinary team in order to help develop a plan and coordinate public participation. The Supervisor and team then develop a draft plan and draft environmental impact statement ("EIS"), which is presented to the public for comment. 36 C.F.R. §§ 219.10(a), 219.10(b). After a period of comment and revision, a final plan and final EIS are sent to the Regional Forester, who directs one of four national forest regions, for review. If the Regional Forester approves them, she issues both along with a Record of Decision ("ROD") explaining her reasoning. 36 C.F.R. § 219.10(c). An approved plan and final EIS may be appealed to the Forest Service Chief ("Chief") as a final administrative decision. 36 C.F.R. §§ 219.10(d), 211.18.

The final plan is a large document, complete with glossary and appendices, dividing a forest into "management areas" and stipulating how resources in each of these areas will be administered. The plans are ordinarily to be revised on a ten-year cycle, or at least once every fifteen years. 36 C.F.R. § 219.10(g).

The present case concerns management plans developed for two forests: Nicolet National Forest ("Nicolet") and Chequamegon (She-WA-me-gon) National Forest ("Chequamegon"). Nicolet spreads over 973,000 acres, of which 655,000 acres are National Forest Land, in northeastern Wisconsin, while Chequamegon encompasses 845,000 publicly-owned acres in northwestern and north-central Wisconsin. Collectively, the Nicolet and the Chequamegon contain hundreds of lakes and streams, thousands of miles of roads and trails, and serve a wide variety of uses, including hiking, skiing, snowmobiling, logging, fishing, hunting, sightseeing, and scientific research. The forests are important for both the tourism and the forest product industries in northern Wisconsin.

In the late 1970s and early 1980s, the Nicolet and Chequamegon Forest Supervisors and interdisciplinary teams each began drafting a forest management plan for their respective forests. These plans were expected to guide forest management for ten to fifteen years beginning in 1986. Drafts of the Nicolet plan and an EIS comparing the proposed plan to several alternatives were issued on November 9, 1984, while similar drafts of the Chequamegon plan were issued on March 29, 1985. Both plans were followed by a period of public comment, pursuant to 16 U.S.C. § 1604(d), which resulted in a number of changes to both plans.

The Regional Forester issued final drafts of both plans on August 11, 1986, as well as final environmental impact statements ("FEIS") and RODs explaining the final planning decisions. Various citizens' groups, including the Sierra Club, challenged the plans in administrative appeals. Chief F. Dale Robertson affirmed in part and remanded in part the Nicolet plan on February 22, 1988, and affirmed in part and remanded in part the Chequamegon plan on January 31, 1990.

The Sierra Club brought an action against the Service in the district court on April 2, 1990, over the Nicolet plan and on October 10, 1990, over the Chequamegon plan. Suing under the Administrative Procedure Act ("APA"), 5 U.S.C. § 701–06, the Sierra Club argued in both cases that the Service had acted arbitrarily or capriciously in developing these forest management plans and FEISs. The Sierra Club requested both declaratory and injunctive relief. The Service, in turn, replied that the Sierra Club lacked standing to challenge the forest plans or FEISs. Both sides moved for summary judgment.

The Sierra Club's primary contention concerned the Service's failure to employ the science of conservation biology, which failure led it to violate a number of statutes and regulations regarding diversity in national forests. Conservation biology, the Sierra Club asserted, predicts that biological diversity can only be maintained if a given habitat is sufficiently large so that populations within that habitat will remain viable in the event of disturbances. Accordingly, dividing up large tracts of forest into a patchwork of different habitats, as the Nicolet and Chequamegon plans did, would not sustain the diversity within these patches unless each patch were sufficiently large so as to extend across an entire landscape or regional ecosystem. *See generally* Reed F. Noss, *Some Principles of Conservation Biology, As They Apply to Environmental Law,* 69 Chi.–Kent L.Rev. 893 (1994). Hence, the Sierra Club reasoned, the Service did not fulfill its mandates under the NFMA, NEPA and MUYSA to consider and promote biological diversity within the Nicolet and the Chequamegon.

On February 9, 1994, the district court denied the Sierra Club's motion for summary judgment and granted the Service's with regard to the Nicolet. The court held that ... because of the uncertain nature of application of many theories of conservation biology, the Service had not erred in failing to apply it and so had not violated the NFMA, NEPA, or MUSYA. *Sierra Club v. Marita,* 843 F. Supp. 1526 (E.D.Wis.1994) ("*Nicolet*"). The court issued a similar opinion with regard to the Chequamegon plan on March 7, 1994. *Sierra Club v. Marita,* 845 F. Supp. 1317 (E.D.Wis.1994) ("*Chequamegon*"). This consolidated appeal of the two cases followed. * * *

[The court first finds that the plaintiffs have standing and that the case is ripe for judicial review.]

III.

The Sierra Club claims that the Service violated the NFMA and NEPA by using scientifically unsupported techniques to address diversity concerns in its management plans and by arbitrarily disregarding certain principles of conservation biology in developing those plans. The Sierra Club asserts that the Service abdicated its duty to take a "hard look" at the environmental impact of its decisions on biological diversity in the forests on the erroneous contentions that the Sierra Club's proposed theories and predictions were "uncertain" in application and that the Service's own methodology was more than adequate to meet all statutory requirements. According to the Sierra Club, the Service, rather than address the important ecological issues the plaintiffs raised, stuck its head in the sand. The result, the Sierra Club argues, was a plan with "predictions about diversity directly at odds with the prevailing scientific literature."

A.

Several statutes and regulations mandate consideration of diversity in preparing forest management plans. Section 6(g) of the NFMA, the primary statute at issue, directs the Secretary of Agriculture in preparing a forest management plan to, among other things,

> provide for diversity of plant and animal communities based on the suitability and capability of the specific land area in order to meet overall multiple-use objectives, and within the multiple-use objectives of a land management plan adopted pursuant to this section, provide, where appropriate, to the degree practicable, for steps to be taken to preserve the diversity of tree species similar to that existing in the region controlled by the plan[.]

16 U.S.C. § 1604(g)(3)(B).

A number of regulations guide the application of this statute. The most general one stipulates that:

> Forest planning shall provide for diversity of plant and animal communities and tree species consistent with the overall multiple-use objectives of the planning area. Such diversity shall be considered throughout the planning process. Inventories shall include quantitative data making possible the evaluation of diversity in terms of its prior and present condition. For each planning alternative, the interdisciplinary team shall consider how diversity will be affected by various mixes of resource outputs and uses, including proposed management practices.

36 C.F.R. § 219.26. * * *

Regulations implementing the NFMA with regard to the management of fish and wildlife resources are more specific still. First,

> [f]ish and wildlife habitat shall be managed to maintain viable populations of existing native and desired non-native vertebrate species in the planning area.... In order to ensure that viable populations will be maintained, habitat must be provided to support, at least, a minimum number of reproductive individuals and that habitat must be well distributed so that those individuals can interact with others in the planning area.

36 C.F.R. § 219.19. * * *

The NFMA diversity statute does not provide much guidance as to its execution.... However, "when the section is read in light of the historical context and overall purposes of the NFMA, as well as the legislative history of the section, it is evident that section 6(g)(3)(B) requires Forest Service planners to treat the wildlife resource as a controlling, co-equal factor in forest management and, in particular, as a substantive limitation on timber production." *Id.* * * *

B.

The Service addressed diversity concerns in the Nicolet and Chequamegon in largely similar ways, both of which are extensively detailed in the district court opinions issued below. *See Nicolet,* 843 F. Supp. at 1533–40; *Chequamegon,* 845 F. Supp. at 1322–28. The Service defined diversity as "[t]he distribution and abundance of different plant and animal communities and species within the area covered by the Land and Resource Management Plan." The

Service assumed that "an increase in the diversity of habitats increases the potential livelihood of diverse kinds of organisms."

The Service focused its attention first on vegetative diversity. Diversity of vegetation was measured within tree stands as well as throughout the forest, noting that such diversity is "desirable for diverse wildlife habitat, visual variety, and as an aid to protecting the area from wildfire, insects, and disease." The Service assessed vegetative diversity based on vegetative types, age class structure of timber types, within-stand diversity of tree species, and the spatial distribution pattern of all these elements across the particular forest. The Service also factored in other considerations, including the desirability of "large areas of low human disturbance" and amount of "old-growth" forest, into its evaluations. Using these guidelines, the Service gathered and analyzed data on the current and historical composition of the forests to project an optimal vegetative diversity.

The Service assessed animal diversity primarily on the basis of vegetative diversity. Pursuant to the regulations, the Service identified all rare and uncommon vertebrate wildlife species as well as those species identified with a particular habitat and subject to significant change through planning alternatives. The Service grouped these species with a particular habitat type, identifying 14 categories in the Nicolet and 25 (reduced to 10 similar types) in the Chequamegon. For each of these habitat types, the Service selected [management indicator species] MIS (33 in the Nicolet and 18 in the Chequamegon) to determine the impact of management practices on these species in particular and, by proxy, on other species in general. For each MIS, the Service calculated the minimum viable population necessary in order to ensure the continued reproductive vitality of the species. Factors involved in this calculation included a determination of population size, the spatial distribution across the forest needed to ensure fitness and resilience, and the kinds, amounts and pattern of habitats needed to support the population.

Taking its diversity analysis into consideration, along with its numerous other mandates, the Service developed a number of plan alternatives for each of the forests (eight in the Nicolet and nine in the Chequamegon). Each alternative emphasized a different aspect of forest management, including cost efficiency, wildlife habitat, recreation, and hunting, although all were considered to be "environmentally, technically, and legally feasible." In the Nicolet, the Service selected the alternative emphasizing resource outputs associated with large diameter hardwood and softwood vegetation; in the Chequamegon an alternative emphasizing recreational opportunities, quality saw-timber, and aspen management was chosen.

C.

The Sierra Club argues that the diversity statute and regulations, as well as NEPA, required the Service to consider and apply certain principles of conservation biology in developing the forest plan. These principles, the Sierra Club asserts, dictate that diversity is not comprehensible solely through analysis of the numbers of plants and animals and the variety of species in a given area. Rather, diversity also requires an understanding of the relationships between differing landscape patterns and among various habitats. That understanding, the Sierra Club says, has led to the prediction that the size of a habitat—the "patch size"—tends to affect directly the survival of the habitat and the diversity of plant and animal species within that habitat.

A basic generalization of conservation biology is that smaller patches of habitat will not support life as well as one larger patch of that habitat, even if the total area of the smaller patches equals the total area of the large patch. This generalization derives from a number of observations and predictions. First, whereas a large-scale disturbance will wipe out many populations in a smaller patch, those in a larger patch have a better chance of survival. Second, smaller patches are subject to destruction through "edge effects." Edge effects occur when one habitat's environment suffers because it is surrounded by different type of habitat. Given basic geometry, among other factors, the smaller the patch size of the surrounded habitat, the greater the chance that a surrounding habitat will invade and devastate the surrounded habitat. Third, the more isolated similar habitats are from one another, the less chance organisms can migrate from one habitat to another in the event of a local disturbance. Consequently, fewer organisms will survive such a disturbance and diversity will decline. This third factor is known as the theory of "island biogeography." Thus, the mere fact that a given area contains diverse habitats does not ensure diversity at all; a "fragmented forest" is a recipe for ecological trouble. * * *

As a way of putting conservation biology into practice, the Sierra Club suggested that large blocks of land (at least 30,000 to 50,000 acres per block), so-called "Diversity Maintenance Areas" ("DMAs"), be set aside in each of the forests. The Sierra Club proposed and mapped three DMAs for the Nicolet and two for the Chequamegon. In these areas, which would have included about 25% of each forest, habitats were to be undisturbed by new roads, timber sales, or wildlife openings. Neither forest plan, however, ultimately contained a DMA; the Chequamegon Forest Supervisor initially did include two DMAs, but the Regional Forester removed them from the final Chequamegon plan.

The Sierra Club contends that the Service ignored its submissions, noting that the FEISs and RODs for both the Nicolet and the Chequamegon are devoid of reference to population dynamics, species turnover, patch size, recolonization problems, fragmentation problems, edge effects, and island biogeography. According to the Sierra Club, the Service simply disregarded extensive documentary and expert testimony, including over 100 articles and 13 affidavits, supporting the Sierra Club's assertions and thereby shirked its legal duties.

The Service replies that it correctly considered the implications of conservation biology for both the Nicolet and Chequamegon and appropriately declined to apply the science. The Service asserts that it duly noted the "concern [of the Sierra Club and others] that fragmentation of the ... forest canopy through timber harvesting and road building is detrimental to certain plant and animal species." The Service decided that the theory had "not been applied to forest management in the Lake States" and that the subject was worthy of further study. However, the Service found in both cases that while the theories of conservation biology in general and of island biogeography in particular were "of interest, ... there is not sufficient justification at this time to make research of the theory a Forest Service priority." Given its otherwise extensive analysis of diversity, as well as the deference owed its interpretation of applicable statutory and regulatory requirements, the Service contends that it clearly met all the "diversity" obligations imposed on it.

IV.

The case now turns to whether the Service was required to apply conservation biology in its analysis and whether the Service otherwise complied with its statutory mandates and regulatory prescriptions regarding diversity in national forests. We hold that the Service met all legal requirements in addressing the concerns the Sierra Club raises.

A.

We note at the outset that the Sierra Club faces a high standard in challenging the Service's planning decisions. The APA, under which the Sierra Club has brought this suit, requires a court to set aside an agency action determined to be "arbitrary, capricious, an abuse of discretion, or otherwise not in accordance with law," or "without observance of procedure required by law." 5 U.S.C. §§ 706(2)(A), 706(2)(D). In so doing, "the court must consider whether the decision was based on a consideration of the relevant factors and whether there has been a clear error of judgment." *Citizens to Preserve Overton Park, Inc. v. Volpe,* 401 U.S. 402, 416 (1971). "Although this inquiry into the facts is to be searching and careful, the ultimate standard of review is a narrow one. The court is not empowered to substitute its judgment for that of the agency." *Id.* The party challenging the agency action also bears the burden of proof in these cases. * * *

B.

The Sierra Club's arguments regarding the inadequacy of the Service's plans and FEISs can be distilled into five basic allegations, each of which we address in turn. First, the Sierra Club asserts that the law "treats ecosystems and ecological relationships as a separately cognizable issue from the species by species concepts driving game and timber issues." The Sierra Club relies on the NFMA's diversity language to argue that the NFMA treats diversity in two distinct respects: diversity of plant and animal communities and diversity of tree species. *See* 16 U.S.C. § 1604(g)(3)(B). The Sierra Club also points to NEPA's stipulations that environmental policy should focus on the "interrelations of all components of the natural environment," 42 U.S.C. § 4331, and regulations which require an EIS to include an analysis of "ecological" effects. *See* 40 C.F.R. § 1508.8. The Sierra Club concludes from these statutes and regulations that the Service was obligated to apply an ecological approach to forest management and failed to do so. In the Sierra Club's view, MISs and population viability analyses present only half the picture, a picture that the addition of conservation biology would make complete.

The Sierra Club errs in these assertions because it sees requirements in the NFMA and NEPA that simply do not exist. The drafters of the NFMA diversity regulations themselves recognized that diversity was a complex term and declined to adopt any particular means or methodology of providing for diversity.... Thus, conservation biology is not a necessary element of diversity analysis insofar as the regulations do not dictate that the service analyze diversity in any specific way.

Furthermore, the Sierra Club has overstated its case by claiming that MIS and population viability analyses do not gauge the diversity of ecological communities as required by the regulations. Except for those species to be monitored because they themselves are in danger, species are chosen to be on an MIS list precisely because they will indicate the effects management practices are having on a broader ecological community. Indeed, even if all that the Sierra Club has asserted about forest fragmentation and patch size and edge effects is true, an MIS should to some degree indicate their impact on diversity. * * *

In a second and related argument, the Sierra Club submits that the substantive law of diversity necessitated the set-aside of large, unfragmented habitats to protect at least some old-growth forest communities. The Sierra Club points out that 36 C.F.R. § 219.27(g) requires that "where appropriate and to the extent practicable" the Service "shall preserve and enhance the diversity of plant and animal communities ... so that it is at least as great as that which would be expected in a natural forest...." * * *

[A]s the Service points out, the regulations do not actually require the promotion of "natural forest" diversity but rather the promotion of diversity at least as great as that found in a natural forest. The Service maintains that it did provide for such diversity in the ways discussed above. Additionally, the Service did consider the maintenance of some old-growth forest, even though the Sierra Club disputes that the Service's efforts will have any positive effects. And to the extent the Service's final choice did not promote "natural diversity" above all else, the Service acted well within its regulatory discretion. * * *

Third, the Sierra Club asserts that the Service failed in its responsibility under NEPA to utilize "high quality" science in preparing EISs and evaluating diversity in them. 40 C.F.R. § 1500.1. * * *

Again, we disagree. The Service is entitled to use its own methodology, unless it is irrational. * * *

In supporting the Sierra Club's allegation that the Service used "bad" science, amici Society for Conservation Biology and the American Institute of Biological Sciences have suggested that we borrow the Supreme Court's test for admissibility of scientific expert testimony as set forth in *Daubert v. Merrell Dow Pharmaceuticals, Inc.*, 509 U.S. 579 (1993), as a way of determining whether the Service's scientific assertions are owed any deference under NEPA. We decline the suggestion. While such a proposal might assure better documentation of an agency's scientific decisions, we think that forcing an agency to make such a showing as a general rule is intrusive, undeferential, and not required. * * *

Fourth, the Sierra Club contends that the rejection of its "high quality" science argument on the basis of "uncertainty" in the application of conservation biology was unscrupulous. The Sierra Club asserts that conservation biology represented well-accepted and well-respected science even at the time the Service developed its management plans in the mid–1980s and that this evidence was before the Service when it drafted the forest plans. Thus, if the Service's only argument against applying the "high quality" science of conservation biology was its uncertainty, the Service has utterly failed to respond to the challenge of conservation biology.

A brief look at available evidence suggests that the district court's understanding of uncertainty was correct and the Service's explanation principled. The Service, in looking at island biogeography, noted that it had been developed as a result of research on actual islands or in the predominantly old-growth forests of the Pacific Northwest and therefore did not necessarily lend itself to application in the forests of Wisconsin. Literature submitted by the Sierra Club to the Service was not unequivocal in stipulating how to apply conservation biology principles in the Nicolet and Chequamegon. * * *

V.

The creation of a forest plan requires the Forest Service to make trade-offs among competing interests. *See Sierra Club v. Espy*, 38 F.3d at 802. The NFMA's diversity provisions do substantively limit the Forest Service's ability to sacrifice diversity in those trades, and NEPA does require that decisions regarding diversity comply with certain procedural requirements. However, the Service neither ignored nor abused those limits in the present case. Thus, while the Sierra Club did have standing to challenge the choices made by the Service, the Service made those choices within the boundaries of the applicable statutes and regulations. * * *

QUESTIONS AND DISCUSSION

1. The Forest Service found that the theories of conservation biology and island biogeography were "of interest," but declined to apply them "at this time." The approved forest plans, however, appear to authorize actions that will result in fragmentation of forest resources. Doesn't this mean that the Forest Service has effectively precluded application of these principles in the future? Is there any legal argument that would limit or prevent the Forest Service from making this irretrievable commitment of resources?

2. The court suggests that the literature on conservation biology was developed in the Pacific Northwest and cannot be applied directly to Wisconsin. Does this imply that conservation biology should be used in the forests of the Pacific Northwest?

3. Why do you think the Forest Service has resisted the movement by many scientists to conservation biology? If the Forest Service chose to protect large, relatively intact areas of national forests, how would this likely impact other uses? How might it affect the agency's ability to achieve the "future desired condition" that it has identified for the forest?

4. The amici in *Marita* suggested that the court follow the approach taken by the Supreme Court in *Daubert v. Merrell Dow Pharmaceuticals, Inc.*, 509 U.S. 579 (1993). *Daubert* established the test for determining the admissibility of scientific evidence in a trial. The key question is whether the evidence is reliable and the Court suggested several specific factors for evaluating the reliability of the scientific evidence: (1) whether the theory or technique has been scientifically tested; (2) whether the theory has been subject to peer review or publication; (3) the error rate of the technique used; and (4) acceptance of the theory or technique in the relevant scientific community. The Court made clear that the test was intended to be flexible. No single factor is dispositive. Moreover, some of these factors might not be relevant in a particular case, and other factors might be considered in an appropriate case. How did the amici propose to use *Daubert* in the *Marita* case? The court found that application of *Daubert* in this case would be "intrusive, undeferential, and not required." How would a test that required the Forest Service to show that its science was "reliable" be intrusive and undeferential? How should the court assess the argument made by the amici that the Forest Service used "bad science" in approving the Nicolet and Chequamegon forest plans? Is it arbitrary and capricious for an agency to use "bad science" in reaching a decision on a forest plan? Recall that in *Motor Vehicle Manufacturers Ass'n v. State Farm Ins. Co.*, 463 U.S. 29, 43 (1983), discussed above in Chapter 3, the Supreme Court held that an agency decision was arbitrary and capricious "if the agency has relied on factors which Congress has not intended it to consider, entirely failed to consider an important aspect of the problem, offered an explanation for its decision that runs counter to the evidence before the agency, or is so implausible that it could not be ascribed to a difference in view or the product of agency expertise."

5. The deference accorded the Forest Service in *Marita* as to its responsibility to apply "high quality" science in management decisions has been criticized, and some courts have refused to apply a similar standard. *See Lands Council v. Powell*, 395 F.3d 1019 (9th Cir. 2005). In an article evaluating the role of scientific uncertainty in Forest Service policies, Courtney Schultz argues that the *Marita* decision failed to demand that the Forest Service engage in the level of scrutiny that NEPA requires:

> While it is true that it is not the court's role to decide nuanced methodological disputes, in this case the court failed in their obligation to hold the agency to a standard of "high quality" science, especially in light of the amount of scientific support for the methodologies of conservation biology. The court particularly failed to uphold disclosure requirements under NEPA, given that the agency not only did not utilize conservation biology methods in any of its alternatives, but also did not explain in its final EIS, an important piece of public documentation, why it had declined to apply concepts of conservation biology despite the fact that this issue had been raised repeatedly during the public comment process.

Courtney Schultz, *Responding to Scientific Uncertainty in U.S. Forest Policy*, 11 ENVTL. SCI. & POL'Y 253, 260 (2008).

6. The idea of using science, and even requiring "peer-review" by scientific experts of agency analyses, has begun to creep into federal law. *See, e.g.,* 16 U.S.C. § 6554(b)(3) (requiring peer review of silvicultural assessments prepared under the provisions of the Healthy Forests Protection Act). To what extent should we entrust the management of our public lands to scientists? What difficulties would such a policy present?

7. *Marita* was decided several years before the Committee of Scientists was reconvened. As noted previously, the 1999 Committee report recommended that the Forest Service redirect its focus to ecological sustainability. The rules promulgated in response to that report (and now superseded by the agency's 2008 planning rule) provided:

> The first priority for stewardship of the national forests and grasslands is to maintain or restore ecological sustainability to provide a sustainable flow of uses, values, products, and services from these lands.

> To achieve ecological sustainability, the responsible official must ensure that plans provide for maintenance or restoration of ecosystems at appropriate spatial and temporal scales.... These scales include geographic areas such as bioregions and watersheds, scales of biological organization such as communities and species, and scales of time ranging from months to centuries.

36 C.F.R. §§ 219.19–219.20 (2003). As the report itself explains—

> The decisions of resource managers must be based upon the best available scientific information and analysis to provide ecological conditions needed to protect and, as necessary, restore the viability of focal species and of threatened, endangered, and sensitive species. A viable species is defined as consisting of self-sustaining populations that are well distributed throughout the species' range. Self-sustaining populations are those that are sufficiently abundant and have sufficient diversity to display the array of life-history strategies and forms that will provide for their persistence and adaptability in the planning area over time.

Sustaining the People's Lands: Recommendations for Stewardship of the National Forests and Grasslands into the Next Century (1999), at 151–52, *available at* http://www.fs.fed.us/news/news_archived/science/cosfrnt.pdf. *See also* Charles F. Wilkinson, *A Case Study in the Intersection of Law and Science: The 1999 Report of the Committee of Scientists,* 42 ARIZ. L. REV. 307 (2000). Would the outcome in *Marita* have been the same if these rules had been in effect? Recall that the Bush Administration suspended these rules largely because of doubts that the goal of ecological sustainability could be achieved.

————

d.   *Roads and National Forests*

An issue of particular importance to biodiversity conservation in the national forests is roads. As described in Chapter 6, roads can have a tremendous impact on biodiversity. Roads are probably the greatest source of erosion and increased sedimentation. Roads create barriers to the movement of many species. Roads can facilitate the introduction of non-native species into new areas. In many ways, the construction of logging roads can be more harmful to biodiversity than the logging itself. Moreover, in addition to logging, roads bring people, whether to hike, camp, fish, mine, or use their off-road vehicles. In the absence of roads, people and companies will still come, but in smaller numbers and in much different use patterns.

Given these impacts, it is not surprising that roads have long received the special attention of the preservation community. Roads, or more precisely the absence of roads, were at the core of the wilderness idea. To qualify as wilderness under the Wilderness Act, an area usually must contain 5000 roadless acres. 16 U.S.C. § 1131(c). Recall that the Wilderness Act required the Forest Service to inventory primitive areas and contiguous lands within national forests to determine whether those lands had wilderness potential. 16 U.S.C. § 1132. As described in Chapter 6, the Forest Service ended up inventorying all of its lands for potential wilderness in two separate Roadless Area Review and Evaluations (RARE I and RARE II). Those reviews found 62 million acres of potential wilderness within the national forests, but the Forest Service recommended only 15 million of those acres for wilderness designation and only a portion of the recommended acres have been incorporated into the National Wilderness Preservation System. *See* pages 639–642.

The undesignated roadless acreage within national forests has remained a source of significant tension in Forest Service management of the national forests. The preservation community would prefer the areas be protected as wilderness. On the other side, loggers, miners, off-road vehicle users, and forest-resource dependent rural communities have pushed to have the roadless areas open to multiple use. As logging, mining, recreation, and other forms of development have continued in the national forests, and as the number and size of the remaining roadless areas has declined, this tension has only increased.

The recent Supreme Court case *Norton v. Southern Utah Wilderness Alliance* exemplifies the current friction over potential wilderness areas. 542 U.S. 55 (2004). The Bureau of Land Management supervised a tract of land in Utah that had all the prerequisites of a wilderness area but had not yet received federal approval. When the BLM allowed some off road vehicle usage, plaintiffs brought suit claiming such usage was outside the protective stewardship provisions of 43 U.S.C. § 1782(c). Indeed, the case epitomized the classic tension between two inconsistent uses on the public lands, with some seeking multiple use designation including roads, and others demanding preservation of the precious remaining wilderness. To the chagrin of environmentalists, the Court held, citing largely procedural and textual arguments, that the BLM could independently conclude that off road vehicles and roads in potential wilderness did not adversely affect the character of the land, meaning land can somehow remain "untrammeled by man" as per 16 U.S.C. 1131(c) despite man's vehicles driving over it. Can you think of any other approaches that the Court could have taken to assuage both sides of the roadless issue? Is there a difference between management of potential wilderness area merely awaiting presidential approval and those already certified?

Conversely, however, in the waning days of the Clinton administration, preservation interests and biodiversity conservation received a significant boost when the Forest Service published its so-called "Roadless Rule," which prohibited the construction of new roads and the reconstruction of existing roads on approximately 58.5 million acres of inventoried roadless areas, or nearly one-third of all national forest land, subject to certain limited exceptions. 36 C.F.R. § 294 (2003); 66 Fed. Reg. 3244 (2001). Logging was also prohibited in these areas except to improve habitat for sensitive species, or species listed or proposed for listing under the Endangered Species Act, or "maintain or restore ecosystem composition or structure," such as to reduce the risk of uncharacteristic wildfire effects. *Id*. § 294.13(b)(1), 66 Fed. Reg. 3273. A proposal that would have allowed logging for "stewardship" purposes was omitted from the final rule.

Not surprisingly, the Clinton administration's Roadless Rule was immediately challenged by various parties interested in development of forest resources. Set forth below is an excerpt from the Ninth Circuit's decision in the case.

KOOTENAI TRIBE OF IDAHO V. VENEMAN, 313 F.3D 1094 (9TH CIR. 2002)

GOULD, CIRCUIT JUDGE

This case involves procedural challenges to a United States Forest Service rule, known commonly as the "Roadless Rule," with a potential environmental impact restricting development in national forest lands representing about two percent of the United States land mass. These challenges in essence urge that the Roadless Rule was promulgated without proper process and that it is invalid. * * *

But we must start closer to the beginning: This appeal arises out of litigation that began on January 8, 2001 when Kootenai Tribe of Idaho and Boise Cascade Corporation, joined by motorized recreation groups, livestock companies, and two Idaho counties filed suit in the United States District Court for the District of Idaho, alleging that the United States Forest Service's

Roadless Area Conservation Rule ("Roadless Rule") violated, *inter alia,* the National Environmental Policy Act ("NEPA"), 42 U.S.C. §§ 4321 et seq., and the Administrative Procedure Act ("APA"), 5 U.S.C. § 533. One day later, the State of Idaho and some state office-holders (collectively "Idaho plaintiffs") filed a separate complaint in the District of Idaho and stated similar allegations. Environmental groups intervened. The district court granted plaintiffs' motions for preliminary injunction against the implementation of the Roadless Rule. Although the federal defendants did not appeal the invalidation of the Roadless Rule, an appeal was taken in both cases by intervenors. We consolidated the appeals and have jurisdiction under 28 U.S.C. § 1292(a)(1).

We hold that the district court ... abused its discretion in granting preliminary injunction against implementation of the Roadless Rule.

II

A.   *History of the Roadless Rule*

In the 1970s, the United States Forest Service ("Forest Service") began to study and evaluate roadless areas in national forests. The Forest Service developed an "inventory" of roadless areas, each larger than five thousand acres. There are now 58.5 million acres of inventoried roadless areas in the National Forest System.

The Forest Service, in an odd semantic twist, has included in "inventoried roadless areas" some areas with roads. Since 1982, the Forest Service has permitted road construction, industrial logging and other development in the inventoried roadless areas on a local, site-specific basis. *See California v. Block,* 690 F.2d 753 (9th Cir. 1982). In the past two decades, 2.8 million acres of roadless areas have been developed by the Forest Service.

On October 13, 1999, President William Jefferson Clinton ordered the United States Forest Service to initiate a nationwide plan to protect inventoried and uninventoried roadless areas within our treasured national forests. Within a week of President Clinton's directive, the Forest Service published a Notice of Intent ("NOI") to prepare an Environmental Impact Statement ("EIS") for a nationwide Roadless Rule. The NOI gave sixty days for scoping and public comment. 64 Fed.Reg. 56,306 (Oct. 19, 1999). The Forest Service denied requests to extend the sixty-day scoping period. * * *

On May 10, 2000, the Forest Service published a 700 page DEIS, along with a Proposed Rule. The Proposed Rule identified 54.3 million acres of "inventoried roadless areas." Of these, 51.5 million acres were "unroaded" and 2.8 million acres were classified as "roaded." The Proposed Rule would have banned road building on the 51.5 million unroaded acres but exempted the 2.8 million roaded acres from the Rule's proscription. After the DEIS's release, the Forest Service allowed sixty-nine days for public comment. Again, some sought extensions of time to file comments and, again, the Forest Service denied requests for extensions, maintaining its schedule.

On November 13, 2000, the Forest Service published a final EIS ("FEIS"). The FEIS identified 58.5 million acres of "inventoried roadless areas" subject to the Roadless Rule's prohibition on road construction. Included were 4.2 million acres of inventoried roadless areas not identified in the DEIS and Proposed Rule. Also, the Proposed Rule now applied to the 2.8 million acres of "roaded" inventoried roadless areas, while relaxing standards for timber harvest in "roaded" areas. No maps in the FEIS identified the 2.8 million acres of "roaded" land.

On January 5, 2001, the Forest Service issued the Final [Roadless] Rule, applicable to the 58.5 million acres identified in the FEIS. [66 Fed. Reg. 3243 (2001).] It was to be implemented on March 13, 2001. It generally banned road building subject to limited exceptions including: the preservation of "reserved or outstanding rights" or discretionary Forest Service construction necessary for public health and safety. 36 C.F.R. § 294.12(b)(1), (3). Henceforth, this vast national forest acreage, for better or worse, was more committed to pristine wilderness, and less amenable to road development for purposes permitted by the Forest Service.

B.   Procedural History

On January 8, 2001, three days after the Final Rule was issued, the Kootenai Tribe, and the private and county plaintiffs joined with it, filed suit alleging that the Roadless Rule was illegal. On January 9, 2001, the Idaho plaintiffs filed suit with similar claims. Both sets of plaintiffs alleged violations of the NEPA and the APA.

On January 20, 2001, newly-inaugurated President George Walker Bush issued an order postponing by sixty days the effective date of all the prior administration's regulations and rules not yet implemented. The effective date of the Roadless Rule was thus postponed until May 12, 2001. Before then, on February 20, 2001, the Kootenai Tribe and its co-plaintiffs moved for a preliminary injunction against implementation of the Roadless Rule. The Idaho plaintiffs did the same on March 7, 2001. Both sets of plaintiffs argued that the Roadless Rule would cause them irreparable harm by preventing their access to the national forests for proper purposes. Plaintiffs argued that such access was necessary to counter wildfires and threats from insects and disease. The plaintiffs based their motion for preliminary injunction upon alleged violations of NEPA, National Forest Management Act ("NFMA") and the APA.

Thereafter, on March 14, 2001, the district court granted the motion of the Idaho Conservation League, joined by other environmental organizations (collectively, "ICL") to intervene as defendants in both cases. The district court also granted the motion of the Forest Service Employees for Environmental Ethics ("FSEEE") to intervene as a defendant in the complaint brought by Kootenai Tribe and its co-plaintiffs.

On April 5, 2001, the district court issued an order in each case, holding that the plaintiffs had a likelihood of success on their motions for a preliminary injunction. However, the district court reserved ruling on plaintiffs' preliminary injunction motions until the administration of President Bush updated the court on its ongoing review of the Roadless Rule. On May 4, 2001, eight days before the Roadless Rule was to go into effect, the Forest Service told the district court that because of "concerns about the process through which the Rule was promulgated," the Forest Service planned to "initiate an additional public process that [would] . . . examine possible modifications to the Rule." Although the Forest Service would let the Roadless Rule go into effect, the Forest Service told the district court that it would also "develop[] proposed amendments to the Rule that will seek to maintain the protections embodied in the current rule." In particular, the Forest Service planned to amend the Rule to allow "limited activities to prevent the negative effects of unnaturally severe wildfires, insect infestation and disease."

Thereafter, on May 10, 2001, the district court found that the plaintiffs had shown that there was "a strong likelihood of success on the merits"; that there existed, absent amendments to the Roadless Rule proposed by the federal government under President Bush's administration, a "substantial possibility that the Roadless Rule will result in irreparable harm to the National Forests"; that there was no date certain for amendments nor guarantee that amendments would "cure the defects identified by the Court and acknowledged to exist by the Federal Government"; and finally and accordingly, that "the Court finds that Plaintiffs have made the minimal showing of irreparable harm and will order that the injunction issue."

ICL and FSEEE filed their Notices of Appeal on May 11 and May 15, 2001, respectively. The federal defendants did not appeal.

III

This appeal presents an unusual procedural setting: The federal defendants, enjoined from "implementing all aspects of the Roadless Area Conservation Rule," have not appealed the injunctions. The interlocutory appeals before us were brought by the environmental groups granted status as defendant-intervenors by the district court.

[The court finds the defendant-intervenors are entitled to appeal under permissive intervention rules, and that the plaintiffs had standing to bring the case.]

VI

We next address whether the district court erred in issuing a preliminary injunction against the implementation of the Roadless Rule. We review the district court's grant of a preliminary injunction to determine if the district court abused its discretion or based its decision on an erroneous legal standard or clearly erroneous findings of fact. *Desert Citizens Against Pollution v. Bisson,* 231 F.3d 1172, 1176 (9th Cir. 2000).

To be entitled to preliminary injunctive relief, the plaintiffs must demonstrate either: (1) a combination of probable success on the merits combined with a possibility of irreparable injury; or (2) that serious questions are raised and the balance of hardships tips in plaintiffs' favor. *Idaho Sporting Cong. Inc. v. Alexander,* 222 F.3d 562, 565 (9th Cir. 2000).

A.   Success on the Merits

The district court found that plaintiffs had shown probable success on the merits of their NEPA claim. We discuss the substantive grounds considered by the district court and reach a different conclusion.

1.   Compliance with NEPA's Notice and Comment Procedures

It is settled that "NEPA is a procedural statute intended to ensure environmentally informed decision-making by federal agencies." *Tillamook County v. U.S. Army Corps of Eng'rs,* 288 F.3d 1140, 1142 (9th Cir. 2002). For this reason, we have held that "NEPA 'does not mandate particular results,' but 'simply provides the necessary process' to ensure that federal agencies take a 'hard look' at the environmental consequences of their actions." *Muckleshoot Indian Tribe v. U.S. Forest Service,* 177 F.3d 800, 814 (9th Cir. 1999) (quoting *Robertson v. Methow Valley Citizens Council,* 490 U.S. 332, 350 (1989)).

To ensure that the Forest Service took a "hard look" at the consequences of the Roadless Rule initiative, the Forest Service was required to "involve the public in preparing and implementing their NEPA procedures." 40 C.F.R. § 1506.6(a); *see also* 5 U.S.C. § 553(c) (the Forest Service was under an obligation to afford "interested persons an opportunity to participate in the rule making."). NEPA regulations also required that the Forest Service invite the participation of affected state and local governments, as well as Indian Tribes. 40 C.F.R. § 1501.7(a)(1).

Upon our review of the record, we are persuaded that the Forest Service did provide the public with extensive, relevant information on the Roadless Rule. We also conclude that the Forest Service allowed adequate time for meaningful public debate and comment.

2. Consideration of a Reasonable Range of Alternatives

Plaintiffs allege that the alternatives to the Roadless Rule proposed by the Forest Service in the DEIS and FEIS were impermissibly narrow under NEPA. The district court held that the Forest Service failed to consider the full range of reasonable alternatives consonant with its policy objectives, stressing that the Forest Service considered only three viable alternatives, all of which included a total ban on road construction within roadless areas. We disagree with the district court's conclusion in this regard. We conclude that the DEIS and FEIS analyzed an adequate range of alternatives. The NEPA alternatives requirement must be interpreted less stringently when the proposed agency action has a primary and central purpose to conserve and protect the natural environment, rather than to harm it. Certainly, it was not the original purpose of Congress in NEPA that government agencies in advancing conservation of the environment must consider alternatives less restrictive of developmental interests. See 42 U.S.C. §§ 4231 et seq. The reason for a proper concern with alternatives here is that plaintiffs have urged that an excess of conservation will be harmful to the environment by precluding appropriate actions in developing roads useful for fighting fires, or insects, or other hazards. * * *

We think that defendant-intervenors are correct in arguing that any inclusion of alternatives that allowed road construction outside of the few exceptions allowed in the Roadless Rule would be inconsistent with the Forest Service's policy objective in promulgating the Rule. That objective, as described by the Forest Service itself in the FEIS was to "prohibit[] activities that have the greatest likelihood of degrading desirable characteristics of inventoried roadless areas and [to] ensur[e] that ecological and social characteristics of inventoried roadless areas are identified and evaluated through local land management planning efforts." The Forest Service defined these values as, among other things, undisturbed landscapes, sources of water, biological diversity, protection against invasive species, and educational opportunities.

The district court also paid no heed to other interests asserted by intervenors such as FSEEE which, through its declarants, pointed out that there were inadequate funds available to maintain with safety existing Forest Service roads. The Roadless Rule ban would help ensure that adequate resources were available to keep existing roads in roaded areas safe. Stated another way, budget and safety considerations were offered by Forest Service to justify the Roadless Rule, in addition to the compelling environmental, conservation and wilderness values asserted by declarants and by Forest Service. * * *

As the case law and the statute itself reflect, the policy of NEPA is first and foremost to protect the natural environment. NEPA may not be used to preclude lawful conservation measures by the Forest Service and to force federal agencies, in contravention of their own policy objectives, to develop and degrade scarce environmental resources. The Forest Service, as steward of our priceless national forests, is in the best position, after hearing from the public, to assess whether current roads adequately aid forest management practices and whether a general ban on new roads in roadless areas of national forest serves appropriate conservation and budgetary interests. * * *

If plaintiffs had demonstrated a strong likelihood of success on the merits, then plaintiffs would have needed only to make a minimal showing of harm to justify the preliminary injunction. *See Idaho Sporting Cong. Inc.*, 222 F.3d at 565 (the stronger the probability of success on the merits, the less burden is placed on the plaintiffs to demonstrate irreparable harm). That is how the district court analyzed the injunction standard after, in our view, giving too much credence to the substantiality of plaintiffs' claims. The converse side of the sliding scale is applicable. Where, as here, only a serious question of liability is presented, then for injunction, the plaintiffs must show that the balance of hardships tips decidedly in their favor. We turn to consider the assertions of irreparable injury by plaintiffs and the balance of hardships.

B. *Balance of Hardships*

The intervenors argue that even if plaintiffs have shown probable success on the merits of their NEPA claims, the district court erred in issuing a preliminary injunction because the plaintiffs have not made the requisite showings that they will suffer "irreparable injury" and that they are favored by the balance of hardships.

In their status report to the district court, the Forest Service, now governed by a new presidential administration which is perhaps less sympathetic to the Roadless Rule, expressed concern "about the potential for irreparable harm in the long-term" caused by the Roadless Rule. Also, the district court made its own findings of irreparable injury based on the record before it. The district court based its finding of irreparable harm on a General Accounting Office Report, which found that the Roadless Rule would prevent officials in (1) Payette National Forest in Idaho from implementing a forest-wide plan to restore pine forests; (2) Shasta Trinity National Forest in California from rebuilding old jeep trails to provide short-term access for fire prevention measures; and (3) Routt National Forest in Colorado from undertaking fire prevention measures. As noted above, there is an argument that the evidence suggested that implementation of the Roadless Rule would restrict active management activities that have already been planned and would thus preclude Forest Service officials from considering management techniques designed to prevent harms, such as wildfires, disease outbreaks and insect infestation. *See Forest Conservation Council v. U.S. Forest Serv.*, 66 F.3d 1489, 1496–98 (9th Cir. 1995) (ban of timber removal could cause state and county intervenors irreparable harm due to inability to undertake "their legal duties to protect the public safety by preventing and fighting wildfires"); *see also Northern Cheyenne Tribe v. Hodel*, 851 F.2d 1152, 1158 (9th Cir. 1988) (cultural, social and economic harms to a tribe can constitute irreparable harm for purposes of NEPA injunction analysis). But the argument is overstated. * * *

This is an unusual case where an action, cessation of road development and repair in certain areas of our national forests, is being undertaken for the primary purpose of conservation, and the resulting benefit of the environment. There can be no serious argument that restrictions on human intervention in these wilderness areas will not result in immeasurable benefits from a conservationist standpoint. The question is whether the incidental harms that may result from such restrictions outweigh those benefits. We have already decided that, in a case such as this one where the purpose of the challenged action is to benefit the environment, the public's interest in preserving precious, unreplenishable resources must be taken into account in balancing the hardships. * * *

Many sensitive wildlife species—whether mammals, birds, reptiles, fish, insects or other organisms—make their homes in wild and roadless areas of forest, and can know no other life. Appellants Intervenors point out that many wildlife species that are hard-pressed for survival have final refuge in roadless areas. We cannot properly be unmindful of the fact that mountain lion, elk, wolverine, grizzly bears, wolves, and other threatened species need roadless areas to survive.

As for the forests themselves, which mankind itself needs to survive, they have not fared well in aggregate in recent decades. In a recent report, with comment on deforestation, the United Nations said 2.4 percent of the world's forests were destroyed during the 1990s; it estimated a total of 220 million acres of forest, an area larger that Venezuela, were lost. In the United States, our National Forests already are both benefited and burdened by extensive road development, some 380,000 miles of roads. Certainly, it is a policy decision for Congress and the responsible federal agencies such as the Forest Service to decide the proper balance for U.S. National Forests between conservation of wilderness and managed use that results in forest loss. * * *

VII

Plaintiffs have demonstrated at best a serious question of liability on the merits of their NEPA claim, and plaintiffs cannot prevail at this stage when we assess prospects of irreparable harm to all parties and the balance of hardships that would flow from injunction. Because of its incorrect legal conclusion on prospects of success, the district court proceeded on an incorrect legal premise, applied the wrong standard for injunction, and abused its discretion in issuing a preliminary injunction.

QUESTIONS AND DISCUSSION

1. In July 2003, the United States District Court for Wyoming rejected the 9th Circuit's decision in *Kootenai,* and enjoined the rule nationwide, on the grounds that it violated NEPA and the Wilderness Act. *Wyoming v. U.S. Dep't of Agric.,* 277 F. Supp. 2d 1197 (D. Wyo. 2003). In particular, the court found that "the promulgation of the Roadless Rule designated 58.5 million acres of National Forest land as a *de facto* wilderness area in violation of the Wilderness Act." *Id.* at 1236. Recall the discussion of the Wilderness Act in Chapter 6. Under that law only Congress can designate wilderness. Do you agree that the Roadless Rule is a *de facto* designation of wilderness?

In May 2004, while an appeal to the Wyoming district court decision was pending in the Tenth Circuit, the Bush Administration replaced the 2001 Roadless Rule with the State Petitions for Inventoried Roadless Area Management Rule (State Petitions Rule). 70 Fed. Reg. 25,654 (2005). As a result, the Tenth Circuit vacated the district court judgment. *Wyoming v. U.S. Dep't of Agric.,* 414 F.3d 1207, 1214 (10th Cir. 2005). However, in *California ex. rel. Lockyer v. U.S. Department of Agriculture,* 459 F. Supp. 2d 874 (N.D. Cal. 2006), the State Petitions Rule was enjoined because the Forest Service had failed to comply with NEPA or the ESA. In issuing her order, Judge Laporte not only enjoined the Bush Administration's rule, but also ordered reinstatement of original Roadless Rule. Following the *Lockyer* decision, and a motion by the State of Wyoming, the Wyoming district court responded by reinstating its earlier injunction of the Roadless Rule. *Wyoming v. U.S. Dep't of Agric.,* 570 F. Supp. 2d 1309 (D. Wyo. 2008). At the time of this writing, appeals were pending regarding both the *Lockyer* and *Wyoming* decisions. One advocacy group has argued that the net effect of the conflicting district court decisions and resulting injunctions is that the Forest Service cannot undertake activities that violate the Roadless Rule, nor can it use the rule to legally justify any management decisions. *See* http://wilderness.org/files/TWS-legal-primer.pdf.

2.   Due to uncertainty surrounding the status of the Roadless Rule, the Forest Service established state-specific rules under the rulemaking petition provision of the Administrative Procedure Act. 5 U.S.C. § 553(e). The Roadless Area Conservation National Advisory Committee (RACNAC), formed in 2005 by Agriculture Secretary Mike Johanns to administer the State Petition Rule, was asked to review state requests for specific Roadless Rule application in their state. RACNAC, which consists of fourteen members representing such diverse interests as state governments, ski resorts, labor unions, fisherman, and east and west coast wilderness advocates, has since approved proposals from Virginia, North Carolina, South Carolina, New Mexico, and California to maintain undiminished Roadless Rule protection for all eligible national forest lands in those states. RACNAC also approved Colorado's request for Roadless Rule protection for most roadless areas in the state, subject to limited exemptions for ski area expansion and coal mining. *See* http://roadless.fs.fed.us/colorado.shtml. Idaho is the only state thus far to ask for a significant reduction in roadless acreage, a proposal which RACNAC endorsed but not without considerable public outcry. *See* http://roadless.fs.fed.us/idaho.shtml. RACNAC's charter expired in April 2009. The co-chairs of the committee urged then President-elect Obama to renew the charter in December 2008. *See* http://fs.usda.gov/Internet/FSE_DOCUMENTS/stelprdb5050457.pdf.

3.   Another interesting twist regarding the current state of the Roadless Rule involves the Tongass National Forest in Alaska. The 16.8–million–acre Tongass National Forest is approximately 90 percent roadless. Congress has designated much of this land as wilderness and the Tongass LRMP prohibits logging on much additional land. Logging on the Tongass has long been controversial because it intrudes on one of the great temperate rainforests of the world and costs taxpayers lots of money. Between fiscal years 1989 and 1993 the Forest Service's own figures show losses of over $12 million on the Tongass. *See* Ross W. Gorte, *Below–Cost Timber Sales: An Overview,* Cong. Research Service Report 95–15 (1994). Using Forest Service data suggesting average losses of $178 per thousand board feet, some have estimated that future logging on the Tongass will cost taxpayers an additional $96 million. *See* Final EIS, *Forest Service Roadless Areas Conservation,* (Nov. 2000) at 7–35; *see also* Draft EIS, *Forest Service Roadless Area Conservation,* 3–184, 5–226 (May, 2000).

In 2003, the Bush administration exempted the Tongass from the Roadless Rule by creating a separate amendment that was based on the validity of the Tongass Land Management Plan. 68 Fed. Reg. 75,136 (2003). The 2003 rule followed from what some have characterized as a friendly settlement between the Forest Service and the State of Alaska, which sued the agency over claims that the Roadless Rule violated the Alaska National Interests Lands Conservation Act. *Id.* How does the "friendly settlement" of this lawsuit impact the public's right to notice and comment on this change of the Roadless Rule? Does the settlement violate the APA?

Although the Roadless Rule may not apply to the Tongass, the Ninth Circuit nonetheless enjoined implementation of the Tongass land and resource management plan because it was issued in violation of NEPA. *Natural Res. Def. Council v. U.S. Forest Serv.*, 421 F.3d 797, 816 (9th Cir. 2005). A revised plan was promulgated in January, 2008.

4. Consider the political context of the Roadless Rule. Why do you think the Clinton Administration Forest Service was unwilling to grant additional time for notice and comment on the scoping process and on the draft EIS? Why were the requests for additional time made? Given that user groups and environmental groups are usually on the opposite side of these process arguments, might either group have been concerned about the precedent it could create in the excerpted case? Is it possible to evaluate the process by which the Roadless Rule was made separately from whether roadless areas are a good idea? One public lands commentator recently opined that "[o]nly losers care about process." John Margolis, *Bush is Audacious, But Should That Be Surprising?*, HIGH COUNTRY NEWS, Mar. 2 2004, at 23. Is this true? Are process arguments ever really principled?

———

e. *The Role of Fire in Forest Management*

Fire policy provides another critical component of national forest management. Most forest ecosystems cannot be understood without some understanding of fire.

> Fire ... changes the chemical composition of the soil, promoting more varied vegetation and supporting more diverse wildlife. It releases soluble mineral salts in plant tissue, and increases the nitrogen, calcium, potassium, and phosphorus in the soil that act as fertilizers. It decreases soil acidity, neutralizing the effects of acid rain, not only in the earth but in the streams and lakes as well.... Burning forests stimulates germination in some trees, such as lodgepole pine; it produces habitat for nesting birds, such as the mountain bluebird. But the most important result of burning is that it arrests or reverses the normally inexorable seral succession.

> Left undisturbed, areas such as Yellowstone would progress from grasslands, to shrub, to deciduous stands or aspen, then to lodgepole pine, and finally to spruce and fir, a succession that takes around three hundred years. As succession progresses, the variety of plant life diminishes and thus the capacity of the land to support wildlife declines as well. Fire is the only way to interrupt seral succession....

ALSTON CHASE, PLAYING GOD IN YELLOWSTONE: THE DESTRUCTION OF AMERICA'S FIRST NATIONAL PARK 92–93 (1987). As discussed in Chapter 1, fire has been used as a forest management tool for many years. Native Americans used fire to clear land and to enhance wildlife habitat long before white settlers moved onto their land.

The story of fire management for most of the twentieth century, however, was not one of *using* fire but of *suppressing* fire. One of the government's most enduring symbols, Smokey the Bear, repeatedly warned us of the need to prevent forest fires. Tasked by its Organic Act with "furnish[ing] a continuous supply of timber for the use and necessities of citizens of the United States," 16 U.S.C. § 475, the Forest Service's suppression policy is not particularly surprising. But it has had significant consequences for forest ecosystems. In that regard, consider the following excerpt, which takes a particularly harsh view of United States fire policy.

––––––––

George Wuerthner, *Smokey the Bear's Legacy on the West,* in WILDFIRE!: AN ENDANGERED ECOSYSTEM PROCESS Vol. 1, Cascadia Fire Ecology Education Project, 1994 *available at* http://www.fire-ecology.org/ research/smokey_bear_legacy.htm.

No single human modification of the environment has had more pervasive and widespread negative consequences for the ecological integrity of North America than the suppression of fire. Fire suppression has destroyed the natural balance of the land more than overgrazing, logging, or the elimination of predators. One could easily build a case that an Environmental Impact Statement should be prepared prior to any fire suppression activities by government agencies since control of wildfires greatly alters the natural environment. Yet, most people are oblivious to the many long-term consequences of fire suppression policies.

Those who study fire ecology are painfully aware of the wounded landscape resulting from fire suppression. Wandering through Cascadia's eastside ponderosa pine forests and westside fir forests I see dying ecosystems. Old photos of these places show sunny, open and park-like cathedral stands of widely spaced large trees. Today these stands are choking on their own prodigy. With water, nutrients, and space divided among many more individuals, the overall health of the forest has declined. These forests are now more susceptible to disease and insects, and in some cases, to more intense burns than in the past.

Catastrophic fires are not abnormal, but rather, are ecologically important parts of the landscape. Indeed, while hundreds of small fires reduce fuels over many parts of the landscape, most of the acreage burned in forest fires occurs in a few very large fires. These might only visit a particular site once every couple of hundred years, when conditions of prolonged drought, wind, fuel loading, and ignition all unite to set the stage for significant fires. Large fires are not disasters, nor do they "damage" the land. Rather, they are an essential part of the ecological setting that no amount of suppression can ultimately prevent—nor should we want to.

Frequent fires have many ecological benefits for soils and plant fertility. Over much of the Pacific Northwest, wet winters are followed by predictable summer drought. Thus, the time of year when it's warmest and most conducive to bacterial and fungal decomposition, moisture is limited, and rapid decomposition of litter is precluded. There is usually only a short period of the year during the spring months when soils are both moist enough and warm enough to provide decomposing organisms the proper environment for composting litter. Without fires, dead material accumulates, locking up essential nutrients necessary for plant growth. Fires release these nutrients, and enhance the production of nitrogen-fixing plants that often revegetate recently burned areas. Fires are thus analogous to river floods which each year provide a new layer of life-giving soil for plant growth.

Fires also cleanse forests. Many tree pathogens are killed just by the smoke. In addition, insects and diseases are directly reduced by fires. Once a fire has burned through a forest, especially if it is a cool, slow burning fire, the younger trees are thinned out while leaving behind the more mature individuals. Some species like the Ponderosa pine, Douglas fir, western larch, jeffery pine, and sequoia are specifically adapted to survive fires by having a thick bark and tall limbless trunks which protect them from small, quick burns. These survivors experience increased viability due to reduced competition for nutrients, light and water. Hence their ability to resist forest insects and disease is increased. The increased occurrence of pine beetle, spruce budworm, and other forest pathogens we see today are the direct result of fire suppression which has weakened the overall ability of trees to resist infestation.

The public pays three ways for this policy of fire suppression. First, we pay the high cost of fire fighting, which is frequently the highest budgetary expenditure of public land agencies. One big fire will often cost five to ten million dollars for suppression. Think of how much better it would be to spend the millions of dollars it costs to suppress fires each summer on endangered species research or the acquisition of private lands which hold important wildlife habitat. Fire research has shown that, in addition to being expensive, fire fighting frequently has nothing to do with putting out the fire. Fires usually don't stop until the weather changes or the fire encounters another recent burn and runs out of fuel. In essence, we often throw money away at fires just so we have the appearance of doing something. For example, the Forest Service spent over $10 million attempting to suppress the Warner Creek Fire, yet it burned uncontrolled until a snow shower fell on the blaze.

Second, we pay for the below-cost sales which result when the agencies attempt to correct the ecological imbalances they have created. For example, after factoring in the $11 million spent on suppression and an Environmental Impact Statement (ostensibly to "save" the trees for wildlife habitat recovery) the Warner salvage sales will result in an unprecedented $9 million deficit timber sale on the Willamette National Forest!

Third, because many of these proposed logging sales are in presently roadless, wild areas, we lose these precious wilderness resources. We do not need to cut down Habitat Conservation Areas and Late–Succession Reserves, such as Warner Creek's native forest, to "protect" it from future wildfires. All we need to do is let natural fires burn.

Although many agencies are now experimenting with prescribed burns, their practices have several shortcomings. In the past, before fire suppression, the total acreage burned each summer in the western U.S. was in the millions of acres. Today, most prescribed burns are too small. Furthermore, most prescribed burns are set when the forests are moist, usually in the spring. Under natural conditions fires burn in the drier months. Small mammals, birds, etc. have usually completed breeding by the time natural fire seasons begin. But human-induced prescribed burns occur at a time when wildlife is less able to cope with a fire, with an attendant cost in life not usually associated with wildfires. Smokey lied. Studies have shown that under natural fire conditions, few wildlife species or individuals are hurt. They simply fly, walk or burrow away from the flames.

The problem with our fire policy is that we are not emulating natural systems. An analogy would be cutting off a leg from a table and expecting it to still stand upright. In cutting out natural fires, we have cut off the leg of a table. We continue to expend energy in the form of fire fighting, below-cost timber sales, etc. to hold up this table or ecosystem which wants to fall over. As more litter accumulates, the heavier the load piled on the table becomes and the more energy we must expend to keep it from falling over.

The western U.S. is sitting on a powderkeg. One of these summers the West will burn down. Fuel loading is so high, a fire-storm of incredible proportions will overwhelm our suppression capabilities. We also face greater possibilities of loss of human life and property as people continue to build houses in forested areas. This is analogous to building on the flood plain of a river. Sooner or later you pay the consequences. Communities have not recognized this problem and thus have not faced it with zoning restrictions.

What needs to be done? To begin, we must realize that fires are a natural and a needed part of our environment. Instead of spending money to put out fires everywhere they occur, we need a massive public education program to promote the merits of fire. We should replace statements like "a forest fire DAMAGED 100 acres of land today" with statements like "a forest fire CREATED 100 acres of new wildlife habitat and fire break today." Fire fighters, instead of being viewed as heroes, should be called what they are: money grubbing mercenaries out to kill fires. Fires have as much right to exist as grizzlies and wolves. Just as predator control has upset natural balances, fire control has had the same consequences. We must come to the realization that fire suppression, except in specific locations needed to protect human habitation and life, is a direct affront to the ecological balance of this continent. Smokey the Bear policies have done more to destroy the wildlife habitat and forest health of the western U.S. than any other human intrusion.

Many foresters and politicians argue that the decline in the forest's ecological health should be dealt with by surgery—"salvage" logging they call it. But logging a burned area like Warner Creek would be a grievous ecological affront. Fires are, like disease and insects, natural processes in forest ecosystems. We should not think of a forest as "recovering" from a fire, and hence, we do not need to fix such landscapes. Forests do not need to recover from a burn—they can only recover from abnormal or unusual events like timber harvests. Do not confuse forestry—which is an economic activity—with forest ecology. Never forget that foresters are trained to manipulate forests, not understand them.

I hesitate to prescribe any management options other than allowing Nature to reach whatever equilibrium or disequilibrium it chooses. On the whole, the best policy we could follow is to let Nature take its course. Protect our dwellings and human life when necessary, but let the bulk of the forests live and die from insects, disease, and even catastrophic fire. We can never emulate natural forests, and it is pure arrogance to assume that we know enough about how a forest works to presume that we can "manage" it at all.

Timothy Ingalsbee, *Wildfire*, OREGON QUARTERLY, Winter 2002, at 18–23 *available at* http://www.fire-ecology.org/research/wildfire_paradox.pdf.

The 2002 fire season caught everyone off guard. Coinciding with a record-breaking drought that affected most of the continental United States, wildfires erupted much earlier in the season, spread faster, and burned hotter than anticipated. News stories highlighted the peril to rural homeowners and whole communities that had unknowingly settled in a "fire plain" and faced the equivalent of the 100–year flood of fire. Despite thousands of extra fire fighters hired under the National Fire Plan, the world's largest fire fighting force couldn't stop one of nature's most powerful forces from imposing its will upon the land. Oregon was an epicenter of wildfire activity, home to two of the largest wildfires in the country: the 491,500–acre Biscuit Fire and the approximately 300,000–acre Toolbox Fire, and several other large fires that cumulatively burned over one million acres. The 2002 fire season was full of superlatives, with several Western states experiencing the largest, costliest, most destructive fires in their histories. Experts predict that the long, hot summer was but a harbinger of more frequent severe fire seasons to come, with potentially dire effects on species, ecosystems, and communities unless fundamental changes are made in society's relationship with forests and fires. Those changes will be difficult to make until we understand and resolve some of the cultural and institutional paradoxes that characterize our relationship with forest fires.

Paradox #1: Fighting Fire

Perhaps the greatest paradox of all is that we exist in an endless and escalating state of war against wildland fire, one of nature's most primal, vital, evolutionary forces. From the first instance when the federal government put out wildfires with U.S. cavalrymen in Yellowstone National Park in the 1880s, federal fire management policy has been framed by the war metaphor: "fighting" fire. Smokey Bear, in fact, was created in 1944 by the Wartime Advertising Council working at the behest of the U.S. Forest Service, and promoted militaristic slogans on fire prevention posters. Following World War II and the Korean War, surplus military aircraft, vehicles, and equipment were used for wildland fire fighting. Beginning with the "siege of '87" in Oregon and California, and continuing with the Yellowstone Fires of 1988, the severe fire seasons of the 1990s, and the firestorms of 2000 and 2002, infantry soldiers were mobilized to help fight forest fires. Thanks to Smokey Bear's "pyroganda" and news coverage that demonizes wildfires, most people believe that all forest fires should be attacked by any means necessary.

As in every other form of military combat, the war on wildfire exacts a toll in human casualties. The 2002 season cost the lives of twenty-one fire fighters. Dozens more were injured this year, and many others will suffer from sickness in the future due to lingering effects of excessive smoke inhalation. Wildland fire fighting is inherently hazardous duty. We should not send out young people to fight fire unless it is absolutely necessary. Protecting the lives and homes of fellow citizens is a valid and noble reason for assuming these risks; suppressing fire from burning through fire-dependent ecosystems in remote roadless and wilderness areas is not.

Making war also exacts an economic toll, and the 2002 season was the most expensive season in history. Suppression costs have exceeded $1.6 billion, and the bills are still pouring in. Oregon's Biscuit Fire was the nation's most expensive fire, costing nearly $150 million for suppression efforts alone, excluding the expense of rehabilitating areas damaged by fire fighting. Unlike all other federal agencies except, significantly, the Department of Defense, federal land management agencies can engage in deficit spending to fight fires. When the agencies exhaust their suppression budgets, they take money from their budgets for recreation, reforestation, or ironically, fuels reduction to pay for fire fighting, and then ask Congress for reimbursements. Congress routinely writes these checks for hundreds of millions of tax dollars with no questions asked. In this period when budgets for education, health care, and environmental protection are being dramatically cut, how long can the nation sustain billion-dollar expenses for an endless war against wildfire?

Finally, aggressive fire fighting does significant "collateral damage" to the natural environment. On the Biscuit Fire, for example, more than 400 miles of perimeter fire line were carved into steep, forested mountainsides using every-thing from shovels and bulldozers to explosives; more than 50,000 acres were torched by high-intensity backfires; hundreds of thousands of gallons of toxic fire retardant chemicals were dumped on the ground; and many big, old wildlife habitat trees were leveled as "hazard trees." These are all routine impacts of fire fighting, but unique to the Biscuit Fire, bulldozers plowed through mead-ows covered with rare endemic plants like the Darlingtonia, and fire engines and helicopters dropped water contaminated with the dreaded Port Orford Cedar root rot disease into previously unaffected watersheds. In actuality, fire fighting is a misnomer: We don't really fight fires, we fight forests.

The paradox of our hostile relations towards wildland fire is that what had formerly been revered as humankind's friend, enabling homo sapiens to become human beings and dwell in formerly uninhabitable regions of the planet, is now feared as a threat to civilization. Fire has been used on the landscape for millennia by nearly every indigenous culture on Earth. Native Americans increased the bounty of their harvests and hunts by using fire to stimulate nature's regenerative powers. Over the span of 700 human generations, most of the native flora and fauna in Western forests and grasslands coevolved with frequent Native American burning that often occurred in the early spring and late fall, supplementing the inevitable summer lightning storms. Our best hope of resolving the paradox and making peace with wildland fire is to recover that forgotten past and restore indigenous practices of "light burning:" safely herding low-intensity prescribed fires across the forest floor during cool, moist conditions in order to replenish our fire-starved forest ecosystems.

Paradox #2: Fire Fighters as Fire Lighters

Despite more than fifty years of Smokey Bear's social conditioning trying to instill pyrophobia (the fear and hatred of fire), every campfire attests to our innate and inextinguishable pyrophilia (the fascination and love of fire). In truth, fire fighters would much prefer to be fire lighters. The old adage "fight fire with fire" is standard procedure; indeed, fire lines are where fires are paradoxically started in order to be stopped. One of the reasons that Oregon was home to two of the largest "superfires" in the country was that the Toolbox and Winter Fires in southeastern Oregon, and the Florence and Sour Biscuit Fires in southwestern Oregon, were separate fires deliberately brought together through backfire operations, then renamed as the Toolbox and Biscuit Fires, respectively.

Backfires are ignited to burn up the vegetation ahead of an advancing flame front, or to merge several small fires into a single large fire that is more efficient for encircling with a fire line. On the Biscuit Fire, a daring thirty-mile-long, 40,000–acre burnout operation successfully stopped the wildfire from spreading into the Illinois Valley, home to 17,000 residents. But in 2000, errant backfires created their own firestorm disasters, including the destruction of hundreds of homes in Los Alamos, New Mexico, and in the Bitterroot Valley, Montana. Even when backfires are successful in containing wildfire spread, they can do serious damage to the environment. By design, backfires are intended to inflict high tree mortality and to consume all small-diameter fuels "from ground to crown." In effect, backfires are set to create a solid swath of scorched earth that leaves nothing for the main fire to burn. Residents of the Illinois Valley learned to identify backfires because they spewed large roiling black smoke columns—a sure sign of high-intensity fire hurling up larger-sized particulates—which differed from the diffuse clouds of gray-brown smoke normally emitted from the wildfire alone. * * *

Paradox #3: Logging-for-Fire Fighting

In response to the 2002 wildfires, President Bush visited Oregon and used the Squire Fire as a backdrop to announce his "Healthy Forests Initiative." In brief, the president's policy would increase the logging of commercially valuable large trees in national forests to pay for removal of highly flammable but non-merchantable small trees and underbrush. Most controversial, this proposal would limit the ability of citizens to raise legal challenges to management projects that they believe fail to conform to the best available science or social values, or otherwise violate the law. Congress this fall debated several bills related to the president's proposals, but conservationist critics have dubbed the president's approach "logging without laws," and highlight the paradox of passing a law that suspends forest protection laws supposedly for the protection of forests from fire.

Historically, flames have followed the ax, as some of the most deadly and destructive fires in U.S. history raged through logged-over lands in the Midwest. The *Los Angeles Times* recently published an analysis of U.S. Forest Service logging and fire statistics that showed that the peak periods of logging in the 1960s through 1980s created the conditions for the severe fire seasons of the 1990s to the present. The reason is that commercial logging removes the largest, oldest, most fire-resistant trees while leaving behind the smallest, youngest, most fire-susceptible trees. Logging also removes the least flammable portion of a tree—its large-diameter "trunk"—while leaving the most flammable portions of a tree—its small-diameter limbs and needles. Timber companies and land management agencies are supposed to reduce this logging debris or "slash" by burning or physically removing it, but that may take years, and often the slash is never cleaned up at all. Logging slash can whip up blazes for thirty years after the trees are cut. Commercial logging also alters the "microclimate." Removing large shadebearing trees exposes the ground surface to more sun and wind, which makes fuels and vegetation drier and hotter and easier to burn. What's more, increased sunlight and soil disturbance caused by logging often results in rapid growth of flammable brush and invasive weeds that replace the tall trees. These are all ingredients for more rapid fire spread, higher fire-line intensity, and more erratic, extreme fire behavior.

The debate over forest health often reduces the issue to the problem of "excess trees," presented as an unforeseen consequence resulting from well-intentioned but mistaken past fire suppression. However, it was not an accident but the intention of the U.S. Forest Service to grow as many trees per acre as possible. Indeed, not so long ago, the agency and timber industry boasted that they "planted six trees for every one cut." But densely stocked, even-aged, slash-covered plantations of young conifers ignite like fire bombs, causing fires to blow up into roaring infernos. Fire fighters reported that this summer's Tiller Fire in the Umpqua National Forest raged hot through old clear-cuts and young plantations, hurling flames into the crowns of adjacent old-growth stands; but, when flames entered unfragmented blocks of mature and old-growth stands, the fire typically burned at the ground surface with lower intensity. Thus, the use of commercial logging for fire hazard reduction poses yet another paradox: Logging removes the trees that normally survive fires, leaves behind the trees that are most often killed by fire, increases flammable fuel loads, and worsens fire weather conditions.

There is a role for strategic thinning of small-diameter understory trees and brush, but thinning should focus on genuinely thin trees, not the thick, tall, mature, and old trees most valuable to wildlife and watersheds. Moreover, thinning proposals should not be falsely advertised as a means of preventing wildfires, but rather, as a means of preparing forests for prescribed and wildland fires. Given the widespread sense of a wildfire crisis, Congress should consider setting a new mission for the federal agencies to prioritize thinning and burning for tinder reduction over logging for timber production until the crisis has passed.

Paradox #4: Public Lands Logging for Private Home Protection

What made the 2002 fire season such a crisis was that nearly every wildfire threatened homes and communities. In some cases, like Oregon's Eyerly Fire, the fire spread so fast that residents barely had time to flee. In the Cache Mountain Fire near the exclusive Black Butte Ranch, a mass evacuation was ordered. On the Biscuit Fire, communities lived for weeks with the prospect of getting a thirty-minute evacuation notice. Logging proponents argue that thinning across the landscape would reduce the threat of wildfires to homes and communities, but research from the Forest Service's own fire sciences lab refutes this claim. Fire scientist Jack Cohen discovered that the most important factors affecting home losses to wildfire are the building materials and design of houses, especially roofing materials, and the vegetation immediately surrounding houses up to a maximum of 200 feet. Cohen concluded that vegetation removal beyond this 200–foot radius ''home ignition zone'' is both ineffective and inefficient for protecting houses from wildfire. The two homes destroyed by the Cache Mountain Fire still had old cedar shake roofs and burned even though their Black Butte Ranch subdivision was buffered by green fairways of a golf course and dozens of fire engines were staged in the neighborhood. Nearby homes with nonflammable roofs and well-maintained yards survived.

Defending homes from advancing wildfires is dangerous duty for wildland fire fighters. But on fire after fire this summer, the same scene was replayed: Fire fighters furiously cut brush, pruned low-hanging tree branches, relocated firewood piles and other flammables away from homes, but did not cut down large trees or deal with vegetation much beyond one hose-length (approximately 100 feet) from a house. The paradox of using landscape-scale logging on public lands as a means of protecting homes and communities is that the vast majority of acres within the home ignition zone are located on private lands, and are most often bordered by corporate, state, or tribal-owned lands, not federal lands. A one-time investment in retrofitting homes with nonflammable roofs would be less expensive and more effective than spending endless tax dollars forever doing emergency fire fighting and hazardous fuels reduction across the landscape. This is an entirely solvable situation and the solution resides almost exclusively on private lands. Indeed, in comparison to the immense challenge and complexity of restoring fire to fire-adapted ecosystems, fireproofing homes will be a relatively simple, straightforward technical task.

* * *

How Can These Paradoxes of Fire be Resolved?

Some of them will be relatively easy, a matter of employing reason and facts and promoting community interests against hysteria, fallacies, and corporate interests. The public's taxes and trees should not be sacrificed for management practices that increase the occurrence of severe wildfires, accelerate the decline of forest ecosystem health, and fail to protect homes and communities. There is a legitimate role for government to help people fireproof their own homes and protect their communities through education, technical assistance, low-interest loans, and need-based grants. This would make a wise social investment, for the sooner we protect our communities from fire, the sooner we can begin restoring our forests with fire. Thus, we begin to develop fire-adapted communities instead of further degrading fire-dependent forests.

Other paradoxes will not be so easy to resolve without a paradigm shift in our relationship with nature. The war on wildfire strikes a deep, resonant chord with Western civilization's historical quest to control nature, and powerful political and economic forces have stakes in perpetuation of the war, for it is a source of power and profits. But making wildland fire an adversary puts us in an untenable position: We may win all the battles against blazes, but it is an endless, escalating, and unwinnable war. For as sure as the sun shines, the rain falls, vegetation grows and dies, and lightning strikes, there will be fires burning our pyrogenic wildlands. The ultimate resolution of these paradoxes is to learn to make peace with wildland fire and rediscover our ecological role as torchbearers wisely applying prescribed fire to nurture the vitality and sustainability of forest ecosystems and their human communities.

———

QUESTIONS AND DISCUSSION

1. Wuerthner offers an alternative fire management strategy as simply "let[ting] Nature take its course." Ingalsbee suggests that we should learn to "make peace with wildland fire." How practical are these strategies? What might be done to move toward these strategies even while recognizing the need to "fight" some wild fires?

2. In 1988, wildfire scorched over one third of Yellowstone National Park's more than 2.2 million acres. The fires were initially perceived by many as a disaster. But time and research on the long-term impact of the fires suggests that they may have gone a long way to restoring the natural ecological balance in the Park. Park policy is now designed "to preserve the process of natural fire in the park while minimizing adverse effects on park visitors and neighbors, recognizing the inevitability of this force to continue shaping the landscape as it has for centuries." Recall the Cronon excerpt in Chapter 1. Does this new fire policy make the Park more "natural" than it was under the fire suppression policy? *See* http://www.nps.gov/yell/nature science/wildlandfire.htm.

3. Sometimes "prescribed burns" get out of control. On May 4, 2000, the National Park Service set a fire in the Bandelier National Monument in New Mexico in an effort to remove some underbrush and reduce the risk of future fires. But high winds and dry conditions caused the fire to quickly spread. The fire burned more than 44,000 acres of land, and 25,000 people were forced to evacuate from the neighboring community of Los Alamos. More than 400 families lost their homes to the fire and it destroyed 115 buildings at the Los Alamos National Laboratory, birthplace of the atomic bomb. The fire came very close to a building that contained radioactive tritium. An investigation of the fire by the Interior Department determined that the Park Service had not followed proper procedures and had inadequate fire crews on hand to keep the blaze under control.

While the Park Service bears some responsibility for the Bandelier fire, isn't it inevitable that some prescribed fires will get out of control? Given that the government often spends more than $1 billion each year to fight fires, doesn't it make sense to encourage federal agencies to prescribe fires where necessary to reduce the risk of more catastrophic fires, even though we know that the government may lose control of some of these fires?

4. In October, 1997, an unusual wind storm swept through the Routt National Forest in northern Colorado near the Wyoming border. The winds were so powerful that they knocked over 100–foot tall Engelmann spruce trees like they were toothpicks. The storm affected 13,000 acres of land, much of it unroaded. The classic response of the Forest Service to this event would have been to quickly schedule several salvage timber sales in order to avoid an epidemic of bugs and the risk of catastrophic fire. But much of the blowdown area was in wilderness and otherwise inaccessible. Up until now at least, the agency has chosen chose not to respond in the classic way. Meanwhile, the expected epidemic of spruce beetles has come, and has infested areas beyond the blowdown. Fire may soon follow. Should the Forest Service let nature take its course, or is intervention appropriate? *See* Allen Best, *Beetlemania,* FOREST MAGAZINE, Spring 2004.

5. Ingalsbee uses the environmental "collateral damage" from Oregon's Biscuit Fire to illustrate his criticism of an aggressive fire suppression management approach. However, even after the flames from the Biscuit Fire subsided, the controversy over appropriate land management continued to fume. Four years after the 2002 fire burned through Southern Oregon forests, the journal *Science* published an article from an Oregon State University (OSU) study that found that the post-fire ("salvage") logging activities that occurred after the Biscuit Fire were detrimental to natural forest regeneration and health, and also increased the area's future fire risk. Dan C. Donato et al., *Post–Wildfire Logging Hinders Regeneration and Increases Fire Risk*, 311 SCIENCE 352 (2006). The *Donato* study findings conflicted with an earlier study by a group of OSU professors, John Session et al., *Hastening the Return of Complex Forests Following Fires: The Consequences of Delay*, 102 J. FORESTRY 38 (2004), as well as testimony from the dean of the OSU College of Forestry in favor of a U.S. House Bill that proposed to ease restrictions on salvage logging activities. While some professors, foresters, and politicians criticized the academic integrity of the *Donato* study, others found the study consistent with scientific findings on the negative impacts of salvage logging in various parts of the world. *See* D.B. Lindenmayer et al., *Salvage Harvesting Policies After Natural Disturbance*, 303 SCIENCE 1303 (2004). Additionally, efforts by some to prevent *Science* from publishing the *Donato* study, as well as the BLM's temporary suspension of study funding after its publication, raised concerns about infringement on academic freedom and the influence of the timber industry on forestry studies and management decisions. *Science* provided a forum in a later issue for both sides to respond and comment on the findings from the *Donato* study. *See* 313 SCIENCE 615 (2006). The controversy highlights the heated interplay between science, academia, politics, and industry that permeates federal forestry policy. *See* Blaine Harden, *In Fire's Wake, Logging Study Inflames Debate*, WASH. POST, Feb. 27, 2006, at A03. *See also* http://original.rlch.org/news/06_15_06_suit.html; Michael Milstein, *Logging Study Set Off Own Firestorm*, THE OREGONIAN, Jan. 20, 2006, at A01.

6. The National Interagency Fire Center (NIFC), based in Boise, Idaho, is the national support center for wildland firefighting. It was founded in 1965 as the Boise Interagency Fire Center, but its name was changed in 1993 to reflect its national mission. All of the major federal public land management agencies participate in the Center, including the BLM, the

Forest Service, the National Park Service, the Fish and Wildlife Service, and the Bureau of Indian Affairs. NIFC maintains wildland fire statistics which show an average of nearly nine million acres of burned land in the United States for each year between 2004 and 2007. *See* http://www.nifc.gov/fire_info/fires_acres.htm. Over that same time period, prescribed burns averaged over 2.5 million acres. *See* http://www.nifc.gov/fire_info/prescribed_fires.htm.

7. In 2003, in the wake of several costly and severe fire seasons, Congress passed the Healthy Forests Restoration Act. 16 U.S.C. §§ 6501–6591. HFRA is controversial because of the perception by some that it promotes large-scale commercial logging near urban areas claimed to be at risk from fire without the full environmental review otherwise required by NEPA. HFRA also limits judicial review of logging decisions that fall within its purview. In particular, HFRA—

- Calls for fuel reduction projects on up to 20 million acres of public land. *Id.* at § 6512(c).

- Requires that at least 50% of appropriated funds be spent on projects in at risk areas in the urban-wildlands interface. *Id.* at § 6513(d)(1)(A).

- Focuses on urban watersheds as well as areas that provide important habitat for threatened and endangered species.

- Directs the agencies to avoid old-growth forests (subject to broad exceptions).

- Limits the number of alternatives required in NEPA documents for "hazardous fuel reduction projects."(For example, projects in the urban-wildland interface require the analysis of only the proposed action and one action alternative.) *Id.* at § 6514(d)(1).

- Establishes an entirely new "predecisional" administrative review process in which all requests for review have to be made to the agency after it completes the EA or EIS but before it issues its final decision approving the project. *Id.* at § 6515(a).

- Allows only those who have submitted specific written comments that relate to the proposed action during the NEPA scoping process or public comment period to object to the project.

- Precludes anyone from litigating over a fuels reduction project unless they participated in the administrative process. *Id.* at § 6515(c).

For additional information about HFRA and how it is working, see the Red Lodge Clearinghouse website at http://rlch.org/content/view/254/41/#titleone.

8. In 2003, the Forest Service promulgated regulations that categorically excluded from NEPA compliance certain hazardous fuels reduction activities using prescribed fire, not exceeding 4,500 acres and salvage timber sales of 250 acres or less. In addition, these rules exempted such actions from the notice, comment, and appeal requirements of the Appeals Reform Act (ARA). 36 C.F.R. § 215.4(a) (2008). The Earth Island Institute and others challenged the ARA rules in a federal district court in California in the context of a challenge to a particular timber sale, the Burnt Ridge Project. The district court entered a preliminary injunction against the timber sale, after which the parties settled their dispute over that project. The case nonetheless went forward as a facial challenge to the ARA rules and the court struck down the rules. *Earth Island Institute v. Pengilly*, 376 F. Supp. 2d 994 (E.D. Cal. 2005). The Court of Appeals for the Ninth Circuit affirmed, holding that the ARA requires notice, the opportunity for comment, and a right of appeal from all Forest Service decisions, even if they are categorically excluded under NEPA. *Earth Island Institute v. Ruthenbeck*, 490 F.3d 687 (9th Cir. 2007). In a 5–4 decision the Supreme Court reversed on the grounds that plaintiff lacked standing to challenge the ARA rules because they had failed to show a concrete injury. *Summers v. Earth Island Institute*, 129 S.Ct. 1142 (2009). The Court also denied the plaintiffs' claim of a procedural injury claim because they had not shown a concrete interest that might be affected by the denial of the procedural right.

PROBLEM EXERCISE: FORESTS AND FIRE

The Evergreen National Forest is located in the State of Anxiety. For many years the Forest Service had suppressed fires on the Evergreen and by February, 2012, after a prolonged period of drought conditions in the region, the forest was highly susceptible to a catastrophic fire.

In an effort to address the problem proactively, the Forest Supervisor assembled an interdisciplinary (ID) team of experts to prepare an environmental assessment of the options available for addressing the risk of a catastrophic fire. Shortly thereafter, the ID team issued an EA addressing the following four alternatives:

(1) Set four strategic fires in the early Spring (around March 15) in an effort to reduce brush and fuel that might promote a catastrophic fire. The committee noted that even if these fires were successful in reducing the fuel load, a significant risk of catastrophic fire would remain so long as drought conditions persisted. Moreover, the committee made clear that the Forest Service could easily lose control of one or more of these fires depending on weather conditions, in which case unintended damage to private property would be likely. The cost of setting and managing these fires would be about $500,000. If they were to get out of control, fire fighting costs would, of course, be much higher. Private property damage could raise the losses even further.

(2) Schedule three timber sales totaling approximately 10 million board feet in areas where the fire danger is especially high. The committee noted that such timber sales would be the most cost-effective way to reduce the risk of fire, but would require three miles of new roads into a previously unroaded area, and would disrupt the habitat of the pine marten, a management indicator species on the Evergreen National Forest that prefers old growth habitat. The committee also noted that large clearcuts would bring in the highest revenues and do the most to prevent fire, but they would also cause

significant damage to the biological values of the area. Even with clearcuts, the Forest Service would lose about $2 million on this timber sale. Shelterwood cuts would increase the agency's losses to $3 million.

(3) Monitor natural fires and suppress only those fires that threaten homes or other important structures. The committee noted that it might be very difficult to contain these natural fires unless the drought ends in the Spring and Summer of 2004. The committee estimated that the cost of fighting fires in this area could range from a low of $50,000 to a high of $3 million. Damage to private property could be as much as $5 million more.

(4) Mechanically remove underbrush and other fuel that might promote fire, but leave all significant trees standing. The committee noted that this option would be expensive, costing approximately $5 million but that it might be very effective in reducing the risk of catastrophic fire.

The following table was included in the EA in an effort to summarize the agency's choices.

Option	Alternative 1	Alternative 2	Alternative 3	Alternative 4
Cost (in millions)	$0.5	$2.0–$3.0	$0.05–$3.0	$5.0
Risk of Private Property Damage	Moderate to high	Low	Moderate to high	Low
Impacts to Biological Values	Low to Moderate	High	Low	Low
Ongoing risk of fire	Moderate	Low	High	Low

If you were the Forest Supervisor what alternative would you choose and why? Review 16 U.S.C. § 1604 and ask yourself whether the Forest Service can justify any of the four alternatives under that law. Does NEPA pose any additional obstacle to the Forest Service in making its choice?

———

3. THE ECONOMICS OF LOGGING ON NATIONAL FORESTS

As the foregoing materials suggest, timber production on national forests sometimes seems to drive forest management. One might think that this is because the Forest Service makes a lot of money selling timber. In fact, logging on national forests is generally a money-losing proposition. A report by the Congressional Research Service in 1994 indicated that 77 of 120 national forests lost money over a 5–year period between 1989 and 1993, and overall losses increased every year during that period, from $60.9 million in fiscal year 1989 to $137.6 million in fiscal year 1993. Ross W. Gorte, *Below–Cost Timber Sales: An Overview*, at 8, Cong. Research Service, Report 95–15 (1994), *available at* http://ncseonline.org/nle/crsreports/forests/for-1.cfm. Timber losses aside, University of Montana economist Tom Power argues in the excerpt below that our national forests often have far greater value when used for purposes other than logging.

THOMAS MICHAEL POWER, LOST LANDSCAPES AND FAILED ECONOMIES:
THE SEARCH FOR A VALUE OF PLACE 151–69 (1996)

The Mirage of Timber Productivity

If federal forestland were to be managed for something besides logging, the "opportunity cost" of pursuing the other objective would be equivalent to the land's commercial timber value. However, not all forestland has equal commercial timber value. In fact, many forested areas have no such value because the costs of gaining access to and harvesting the timber are too high. Obviously, if these costs exceed the value of the timber, there is no economic loss incurred by choosing not to harvest. Thus in evaluating the opportunity cost of putting certain lands off-limits to harvest, one has to analyze their timber potential. The total number of acres does not tell us anything about the opportunity cost of managing land for nontimber values.

This consideration is especially important for federal land because the more productive timberland passed into private ownership years ago. The national forest reserve system created at the end of the nineteenth century included only land that no one had yet claimed for private use, primarily the mountainous lands of the West. Early in this century, the federal government bought up much of the land that had been logged and abandoned in the East, and today this land makes up most of the eastern national forests' 24 million acres. Generally, timber productivity on federal forestland is significantly lower than on nonfederal forestland.

The Forest Service's own classification of forestland as part of a commercial timber base is not tied directly to an economic measure of commercial viability. To be included in the Forest Service's commercial timber base, the commercial value of the trees does not have to exceed the cost of managing the land for its timber value. If potential timber productivity exceeds certain minimal levels, the land is assumed suitable for timber management regardless of those costs. Land that no private owner would judge as having commercial value is added to the Forest Service's timber base, and as a result its commercial value is overestimated.

Still, a substantial amount of national forestland whose management is currently being debated has not been classified as having commercial timber potential. This is true, for instance, for over 80 percent of the remaining roadless National Forest land in the Northern Rockies. The decision to manage this land for its nontimber value costs the nation nothing. In fact, it saves the nation the losses the Forest Service would incur in trying to manage the land for timber. In the past, land set aside as wilderness or national parks tended to be steep, dramatic, and inaccessible and with little commercial timber value. In that setting, the current debate about "locking up" the timber resource involves gross exaggeration.

The timber-producing capability of land can be determined in purely biological terms. A site can be studied for such factors as temperature, moisture, sunlight, nutrients, and competition from various plants. Then calculations can be made about what species to plant, how frequently they should be thinned, what pesticides and herbicides should be applied to control biological pests, and so on. This will produce an estimate of the wood fiber the site is capable of producing—but it won't be a measure of the site's timber productivity in economic terms. Potential biological productivity is not economic productivity.

To realize economic productivity, expensive access roads have to be built and maintained for 50 to 150 years. The area has to be planted, thinned, and nurtured for decades before the harvest. The value of that distant harvest is what has to justify all the high up-front costs. As might be expected, those future timber harvest values may not always justify the costs of realizing it.

The Forest Service tends to base its estimates of a site's timber value on biological potential, not economic productivity, requesting congressional budget support for intensive timber management regardless of the economic losses. Sites with almost no commercial timber, even relatively bare sites, are considered highly productive forestlands. In the Forest Service's evaluation of resource tradeoffs associated with wilderness protection in roadless areas, such exaggerated site productivity has been used to boost the apparent timber opportunity cost of wilderness preservation, thereby protecting the agency's ability to harvest the trees.

It is not only the dollar cost of intensive management that constrains the timber productivity of federal land. National forests are not private tree farms that can be operated without regard for the environmental impacts. Legislation guiding the management of national forestland makes clear that timber is just one of many forest values that are to be protected and developed, and timber is not identified as the dominant value. In addition, the Forest Service must see that its management decisions are consistent with state and federal clean-water laws, the Endangered Species Act, and other environmental regulations. The point is that economic, legal, and environmental constraints limit theoretically calculated timber productivity. The relevant measure in evaluating nontimber management of landscape is realizable economic productivity. * * *

The Relative Importance of Federal Timber Supplies

Some discussions of federal forest management give the impression that federal timber supplies are the dominant source of wood fiber for U.S. mills. The implication is that it is federal forest managers who determine whether there is enough wood fiber available to assure adequate housing for Americans and jobs for forest industry workers. This is an exaggeration. The Forest Service is rarely the sole or even most important local source of wood fiber. The Forest Service controls about 18 percent of the nation's commercial timberland but only 14 percent of annual fiber growth. That is, only one seventh of America's timberland productivity is controlled by the Forest Service. In the eastern half of the nation, the federal government controls an even smaller part of the total wood fiber supply, about 8 percent. Even in the West, where the national forest system is concentrated, federal land represents a minority, about 40 percent, of total timberland, and as mentioned, it tends to be less productive than private timberland.

It would stand to reason, then, that manipulation of federal supplies cannot control the timber industry or the future of America's timber dependent communities. In some areas the Forest Service will have more influence than in others, but it is misleading to assume that federal land management decisions are the dominant determinants of economic activity in timber communities. The Forest Service is just one player, and a minority player at that. This fact is obscured in public debate over federal forest use. Private timberland use is not subject to similar public comment, though it can have a much greater effect on the local community. Private land-use decisions are accepted, fatalistically by many, as an aspect of a private enterprise society. That is not true of less consequential federal land-use decisions. They get vigorously and emotionally debated, which lends them an air of exaggerated importance. * * *

Federal and Private Timber Supplies: A Case of Dynamic Interaction

Because timber sales from federal land flow into a national and international market, their impact on the overall timber industry cannot be determined in isolation. A competitive market generates interaction between federal and private timber supplies. When one source of supply is reduced, prices tend to rise, stimulating production from other sources of supply while reducing exports and increasing imports. As timber prices rise, so does the profitability of harvesting trees. Logs that were previously exported unprocessed to more lucrative foreign markets may now find the domestic market more profitable. Canadian sources of supply will find the American market more attractive. As a result, the net impact of reduced supply is significantly smaller than the initial reduction in federal harvest. * * *

Choosers Aren't Beggars: Preservation and the Local Economy

During the 1980s many forest-dependent communities lost their lumber mills and were forced to make adjustments to the new economic reality. As painful as the losses were, these towns did not fade into the ghost towns that were predicted before the mills shut down. Their economic vitality and that of many other forest-dependent communities facing a similar change hold important lessons for local communities.

Dubois, Wyoming

Until 1987 Dubois, Wyoming, a town of about 1,000 hosted one of the largest stud mills in the nation. That mill provided a third of both the jobs and the tax base in Dubois. It consumed an enormous number of trees. Supplying them from the Shoshone and Bridger–Teton National Forests grew more and more controversial as roads were built through wildlife habitat and recreation land. Controversy over the appropriateness of sacrificing the forest to keep the mill alive caused tension between Dubois and the neighboring communities of Pinedale and Jackson, whose economies were more clearly recreation oriented, and it split the population of the county, Fremont. Some argued that the survival of Dubois and of the regional economy was at stake. Others insisted that the mill's voracious appetite could never be satisfied, and that seeking to satisfy it in the short run would destroy the recreational economy that was developing in the area.

The Forest Service, after years of feeding the mill and leaving the woods with huge, spreading scars, decided that it could not continue to provide the flow of logs the mill required. The mill shut down amid protests that Dubois would "up and blow away." By 1993 the mayor was bragging, "Now our economy is steadier and stronger than ever." Real estate agents "were delighted to get rid of that mill." As retired economics professor and long-time Dubois resident John Murdock pointed out during the timber harvest debates in the late 1980s, even before the mill shut down the area had begun to attract residents and businesses because of its outdoor amenities.

The Dubois area, less than 100 miles southeast of Grand Teton and Yellowstone National Parks along a major highway, is home to the largest bighorn sheep herd in the country. To the south rise the Wind River Range and to the north the Absaroka, the highest mountain ranges in Wyoming. The town sits on the Wind River. One would think that the economic potential of such a spectacular setting would have been obvious. But to the majority it did not become obvious until the lumber mill shut down.

The director for economic development in Fremont County claims that this area "may be one of the few places in the country basing our economic revitalization on wildlife and wild-land rehabilitation". Local officials are formally implementing this commitment, opposing extractive developments such as oil and gas development that may threaten wildlands and the economic vitality that relies on them. In 1993 a National Bighorn Sheep Interpretive Center opened in Dubois and is expected to draw 120,000 visitors annually. This is just one of the many signs of the town's "somersault from logging camp to nature camp," and it has taken place in a short five years. In the years following the mill closure, real income in Dubois grew by 8.5 percent per year while the Wyoming economy showed almost no real growth and the national economy grew at less than a third of this rate—hardly the doom that proponents of feeding the landscape to the mill had forecast. * * *

Twenty Million Acres of Additional Wilderness: Locking Up Resources, or Creating Jobs?

One of the most contentious issues of public land management is wilderness classification. Because federal land classified as wilderness under the 1964 Wilderness Act is off-limits to commercial extraction and motorized vehicles, many people argue that the classification "locks up" resources that would otherwise support the local economy. The above cases suggest otherwise.

Beginning in the late 1980s, a coalition of environmental groups in the northern Rocky Mountains of the United States and Canada began advocating legal protection for almost all of the remnant roadless areas on public land that did not already have wilderness or national park classification. In the United States, this took the form of proposed federal legislation, the Northern Rockies Ecosystem Protection Act (NREPA), that would prohibit almost all commercial extractive activity on Forest Service roadless areas in Montana, Idaho, eastern Washington and Oregon, and northern Wyoming.

The NREPA represents a growing awareness among environmentalists that natural landscapes cannot be protected in piecemeal fashion. "Island" areas cut off from biological exchange with larger ecosystems cease to be natural or healthy. The NREPA seeks to save roadless areas that serve as wildlife "corridors" between existing national parks and wilderness areas and that provide habitat critical to the survival of the region's wildlife—grizzly bears, timber wolves, salmon, bull trout, woodland caribou, and other species that represent almost the complete set of natural fauna present when European settlers first arrived. Many of these species are on the verge of extinction because of human encroachment on their habitat. Under the NREPA, nearly 20 million acres of roadless natural landscape would be given official protection from further encroachment.

Extractive interests were upset by the proposal. From their point of view, the NREPA would lock up tens of millions of additional acres in nondevelopment status. The act would take logs from mills, block metal mining, prevent oil and gas development, and limit grazing on public land, impoverishing local communities by cutting them off from the natural resource base on which they depended.

However, a detailed economic analysis of the impact this preservation proposal would have on the industry most affected, timber, indicated that the negative impact on extraction would be minor and that the overall impact on the economy was likely to be positive. All twenty-eight national forests involved were analyzed, going roadless area by roadless area using Forest Service data. The timber industry, it was estimated, would directly lose about 1,400 of the five-state region's 1.2 million jobs, or about one-tenth of 1 percent of total employment. On average, over the last decade this number of jobs has been created every three weeks by growth in the overall regional economy. That is, the employment cost of protecting 20 million acres of natural landscape would be a three-week pause in normal job creation. Even this relatively modest setback for timber employment was expected to be more than offset by jobs gained from granting permanent protection to the environment and from recreational activities that were already the driving force in the region's economic growth. * * *

Juggling Extraction and Amenities

The timber industry is unstable and in long-term decline as a source of jobs and income. Logging, especially the massive clear-cutting of recent years, seriously threatens other forest amenities that support local economies. Landscapes stripped bare, silted streams with dead fish, fragmented ecosystems devoid of wildlife—this isn't what draws people and business. Lessons abound from America's past: aggressive logging in northern New England, the Great Lakes region, and the South left desolate landscapes and poverty behind.

The economic health of a community in a forested landscape does not depend on as high a rate of extraction of wood fiber as possible. In fact, the long-run economic health of the community depends on something quite different: weaning from dependency through systematic diversification. The primary economic alternatives facing forestland communities are associated with their natural and social amenities. By no means does logging have to come to a halt, but it does have to be practiced in harmony with preservation. In situations where it unavoidably threatens other forest values, an economically rational choice requires that the positive economic values associated with preservation be weighed against the limited support expanded timber harvest offers the local economy.

The Forest Service's official definition of community stability, with its emphasis on helping places adapt to change, recognizes the amenity-driven diversification that is currently taking place in many forestland communities. Logging locations, methods, and volumes must be adjusted in ways that do not stop diversification. Modifying forest management policies to protect environmental services does not threaten the economies of forest-dependent communities, it protects and enhances them.

QUESTIONS AND DISCUSSION

1. Environmental groups have opposed logging on national forest lands, especially clearcutting, and especially in roadless areas, for many years. More recently, taxpayer groups have become more vocal in opposing such sales because of the millions of dollars that the federal timber program loses each year. In a report issued in 2002, Taxpayers for Common Sense decried the waste and mismanagement in the Forest Service's timber program. It noted that in the most recent period for which government figures were available—FY 1998—the Forest Service itself estimated that its timber sales lost $126 million. Taxpayers for Common Sense estimated that the actual losses were in excess of $407 million. *See Lost in the Forest: How the Forest Service's Misdirection, Mismanagement, and Mischief Squanders Your Tax Dollars* (2002), *available at* http://www.forestcouncil. org/pdf/lostintheforest.pdf. Moreover, according to the General Accounting Office, there is no more recent data on timber sales than the 1998 report because the Forest Service's accounting practices are too poor for accurate assessment, posing a serious threat to the democratic accountability of this public office. *See* http://www.gao.gov/new.items/d011101r.pdf. Should the Forest Service be required to produce specific financial data on timber sales, regardless of cost? Why do you think the Forest Service continues to promote a program that costs taxpayers so much money even as it causes significant ecological problems?

2. The Forest Service prepares an economic analysis that shows a ratio of benefits to costs and revenues to costs of timber sales for each proposed timber sale. "Benefits," unlike "revenues," may include items that have market value but that do not provide any revenue to the government. A "below-cost" sale is one where the costs exceed the revenues. One of the chief alleged benefits of many timber sales in the Western United States is in the form of increased water yields. When trees are cut they no longer transpire water into the atmosphere. Land cleared of trees may also lead to faster runoff from an earlier snowmelt. Whether this actually results in an increase in useable water supplies, and whether the true value of these supplies can be accurately measured, is subject to debate. Among the unresolved questions is how to value increased water supplies during the spring, when water supplies are relatively plentiful. Nonetheless, economic analyses for timber sales frequently show significant economic benefits from increased water yields. These are not, of course, benefits for which the Forest Service receives any compensation. Indeed, it is almost impossible to know who might actually benefit under the prior appropriation system that applies throughout the western United States. *See* Chapter 7, *supra*. On the other hand, the Forest Service analysis does not include in its calculations costs and benefits for which there is no market or projected demand. *See* FSH § 2409.13, 22.3. Thus, while water yields and recreational benefits with a market value are included in the analysis, ecological values are generally not included. Why do you think that the Forest Service has decided not to include these values in its calculations? How useful is an economic analysis that omits certain potentially significant values?

3. As the earlier excerpt by Douglas Krieger made clear (pages 1206–1209), the ecosystem services provided by forests have significant value, sometimes greater than the commercial value of their timber. Yet there is no market for many of these services such as climate regulation, nutrient cycling, erosion control, and ecological control (A voluntary trading market for carbon credits currently exists, *see* http://www.chicagoclimatex.com/, but realizing the true market value of forests for carbon capture ecosystem services will depend on potential future laws or policies that find a way to impose the full costs of emitting carbon on the responsible party). How should the Forest Service address services for which there is no market value in its analysis? Economists use various methods to place a value on non-market goods. These include—(1) the "travel-cost method" whereby the costs incurred in visiting a site are used to determine the site's value for visitation purposes; (2) the hedonic approach, whereby the value of goods with associated amenities (*e.g.*, land on a lake or adjacent to a forest), is compared with the value of similar land without the associated amenity, and (3) contingent valuation, where an economist surveys the amount one is willing to pay for an amenity. To what extent should the Forest Service rely on these methods to assess value? What if the different methods give significantly different values for the same forest?

4. As previously described, a great debate continues over whether to preserve the remaining roadless areas in our national forests. One part of this debate not yet addressed is the economics of roads. Currently, our National Forests are home to nearly 400,000 miles of roads. The Forest Service estimates that over 80% of these roads are not maintained to the public safety and environmental standards to which they were built and the agency faces an $8.4 billion backlog in road reconstruction and maintenance on these roads. Most of these roads were built by logging companies to support logging activities and, until 1999, these companies received a credit for the cost of constructing these roads against the purchase price of the timber. Thus, roads have become a significant economic burden to the Forest Service. By contrast, roadless areas offer significant economic benefits that are generally not available from logged lands. One economic study prepared for The Wilderness Society and the Heritage Forests Campaign estimates that the 42 million acres of roadless areas on national forests in the lower 48 states provide nearly $600 million in recreation benefits, more than $280 million in "passive use" values, which include, for example, the value that people place on the option of visiting a roadless area in the future, $490 million in waste treatment services, and somewhere between $490 million and $1 billion in carbon sequestration value. JOHN B. LOOMIS & RICHARD RICHARDSON, ECONOMIC VALUES OF PROTECTING ROADLESS AREAS IN THE UNITED STATES (2000).

————

B.   PRIVATE FORESTS

1.   ACQUISITION OF PRIVATE TIMBER RIGHTS

As the foregoing materials suggest, timber is unique among natural resources. Like water, timber is a renewable resource, but the similarity seems to end there. Unlike water, which exists in a continuous cycle, timber lands are frequently converted to other uses after logging. Even where timber is allowed to regenerate, the ecological conditions that brought about the original forests cannot likely be replicated. Moreover, new trees take years to mature. This "rotation age" for trees depends on a variety of factors such as tree type, climate, slope, and soil conditions. These factors are not easily controlled, especially if native trees and natural regeneration are planned. In the more arid and rugged parts of the Rocky Mountain West, for example, large conifers take 100 years or more to regenerate and mature after they have been logged. By contrast, in the warmer and more humid climate in the southeastern United States, trees grow much more quickly and may grow to commercial size in as little as twenty years.

From the perspective of private property rights, timber probably has more in common with non-renewable resources like minerals, than it does with renewable resources like water. Those who want to log timber on forested lands are often interested only in the product presently on the land. They have no interest in the land itself or in successive timber harvests. As a result, timber rights can be bought and sold much like mineral rights, through leases, licenses, and *profits a prendre. See* Chapter 9, at 1043. But unlike minerals, timber production is not limited to particular tracts of land. With the right soil and climate, and sufficient water, a wide variety of timber species can be grown on many different soils and in many locations. Moreover, forests have commercial value that extends beyond timber. As previously described, forested lands provide a variety of ecosystem services, as well as opportunities for recreation and hunting, and private forest lands are often leased for these purposes.

Timber is, of course, an agricultural product, and while large quantities of timber are harvested from lands where regeneration occurs naturally, many timber companies own vast tracts of forest lands that are cultivated for timber production. Like other agricultural products, timber is susceptible to damage and destruction. Fire and disease can destroy a once healthy forest with little advance warning. As described previously, however, fire and disease also play an important role in the natural ecological cycle. Whatever limited inclination the Forest Service might have to allow fire and disease in national forests to take their natural course, such proclivities are generally not honored on private forests. Unlike national forests, private forests are usually held to maximize economic returns.

The materials that follow focus on some of the issues that arise in transactions to buy and sell timber rights. Keep in mind the unique aspects of timber resources as you consider these issues.

ARBOGAST V. PILOT ROCK LUMBER COMPANY,
215 Or. 579, 336 P.2d 329 (1959)

WARNER, J.

This suit is brought by the plaintiffs, Arbogast, against the defendants, Pilot Rock Lumber Co. (hereinafter called the Lumber Co.), and Travelers Insurance Company (hereinafter called the Insurance Co.), for a declaratory judgment that plaintiffs, as the owners of the fee to 240 acres of land in Grant County, Oregon, were entitled to have left all timber of every size on said lands which was not then deemed acceptable for cutting into saw logs and manufactured into lumber in October, 1924, a date when plaintiffs' predecessors in interest executed two similar timber deeds to the predecessor in interest of the defendant Lumber Co. * * *

The defendants appeal only from that part of the decree which declares the kind and size of the timber which they presently own and are entitled to cut. The plaintiffs by cross-appeal assail the same provision of the decree. * * *

Amelia Hector, on October 6, 1924, conveyed to the Hewitt Land Company timber situated on an 80–acre tract of land in Grant County, Oregon (hereinafter called the Hector tract). On October 23, 1924, Herman H. Rosenboom and Andrew Edling and his wife deeded to the same grantee timber on their nearby 160 acres in the same county (hereinafter called the Rosenboom–Edling tract).

Both deeds are identical in form. Both conveyed to the Land Company, "all of the Timber and Logs now standing, laying and being upon the following described tract of land...." Both deeds gave grantee "the exclusive right to enter upon the said lands and to cut and remove said timber and logs therefrom for and at any time during the period of twenty-five years from and after the date hereof...." The only other provision of interest in this matter was the right given to grantee to extend the time period from year to year upon payment of $6 per year upon each 40–acre tract for which an extension was requested.

Prior to 1951, the plaintiff Elmer L. Arbogast, and his wife (now deceased), acquired (as tenants by the entirety) from the grantor Rosenboom and the successors of the grantors Edling, grantors' respective interests in the Rosen-boom–Edling tract. In 1952, the plaintiffs, as tenants in common, took title from Amelia Hector for her interest in the Hector tract.

The defendant Lumber Company is successor in interest to all the timber originally conveyed to the Hewitt Land Company in 1924 by the Hector and Rosenboom–Edling deeds. The defendant Insurance Co. has an unchallenged first lien on the Lumber Co.'s interest in the timber. From this point, when we refer to the "defendant," we will mean the defendant Lumber Co.

Prior to June 30, 1954, the removal period had been extended as to both tracts by the annual payments stipulated in the deeds. . . . As of the time of trial, no timber had been cut or removed.

The prime question for solution is the meaning to be assigned to the phrase appearing in the granting clause of both 1924 deeds: "all of the Timber and Logs now standing, laying and being. . . ." Simplified, the issue is: How much timber may be cut and how much must be left.

That part of the decree over which both parties express dissatisfaction declares: that the defendant Lumber Co. is the owner of all Ponderosa Pine now 16 inches or more in diameter, all Douglas Fir 16.5 inches or more in diameter and all White Fir 17.75 inches or more in diameter. All of the foregoing diameter dimensions include the normal average increase in growth for each species since October, 1924, and all are measured at a height of from 24 to 30 inches.

Plaintiffs argue that "all timber" means trees of a *size* and quality suitable for the cutting into saw logs and manufacture of lumber at the time of the execution of the deeds; that "timber" does not include other trees not then suitable for lumber purposes but which have since attained that stature; in short, they claim the deeds conveyed only what was the near equivalent of "merchantable timber" in October, 1924.

Defendants urge that the words "all timber and logs" embraced all trees on the land in 1924 without limitation as to size, type or merchantability.

The defendants represent by their three assignments that the trial court erred in the construction of the granting clauses by refusing to consider and give proper weight to: (1) the evidence of the surrounding circumstances and intention of the parties, (2) the evidence of the usage peculiar to the timber industry in 1924 among buyers and sellers and dealers, and (3) the evidence of the alleged practical construction placed on the instruments by the parties involved. * * *

Ordinarily, timber deeds have more specific descriptions of the timber conveyed than we find in the instant deeds as, for example, the descriptions are qualified by more definite terms, such as "timber suitable for sawmills" or limited to timber of certain species, size and dimensions. But there is little in the instruments under review which is helpful in defining the language "all of the timber and logs now standing, laying and being . . . ," and particularly the meaning of "all timber." These terms are, in our opinion, not clear and are ambiguous in so far as the size and quality of the timber is concerned. They are wanting in the precise signification necessary to determine the issue here raised.

Under the circumstances, we turn to discover what is commonly under-stood in case law by the word "timber," particularly when it is employed alone in deeds and contracts for sale by the sellers of timber and buyers connected with the timber and lumbering industry.

In an early decision, *Roots v. Boring Junction Lumber Co.*, 50 Ore. 298, 300, 317, 92 P. 811, 94 P. 182 (1907), we held that "all the 'saw timber' over nine inches in diameter" was intended to embrace only timber fit for the manufacture of lumber; it did not comprehend smaller trees, or tops, useful only for cordwood.

In absence of modifying terms or expressions in the instrument or a construction peculiar to the locality, the general rule within the lumber industry is that the word "timber" denotes trees of a size suitable for manufacture into lumber for use in building and allied purposes. It does not, however, include saplings, brush, fruit trees or trees suitable only for firewood or decoration. * * *

Plaintiffs would, however, give the word a more restricted meaning. If followed, it would have a more limited effect upon the size of the trees and their availability for certain utilizations.

The definition of "timber" which we employ and which was the apparent definition utilized by the trial court leaves two questions unanswered: When does one determine the size of "timber" suitable for manufacture into lumber for use in buildings and allied purposes? And what measure of size is to be employed at that moment?

We find no evidence of any understanding between the parties in 1924 as to any growth of a particular size being conveyed or when the size of the "timber" was to be determined, except as may be hereinafter noticed. Whether or not such growth of timber occurring after 1924 was conveyed becomes a question of prime importance in this appeal, especially when the parties have not specifically provided for the inclusion of "growth." *Doherty v. Harris Pine Mills, Inc., supra* (211 Ore. at 419).

The question of time of determination is not a novel one in this court. . . . [O]n the question of *when* size is to be determined, the factor of time is as common to instruments conveying only "timber" as it is to those conveying "merchantable timber"; that is, when the point of such proper time is as vague or ambiguous as it is in the instant matter. . . . [T]he true rule is as was stated in *Hughes v. Heppner Lbr. Co.*, 205 Ore. 11, 37, 283 P.2d 142, and *Rayburn v. Crawford*, 187 Ore. 386, 398, 211 P.2d 483, the gist of which is: that where there is no specific provision in the instrument establishing the time for determining the size of the timber conveyed, it is to be determined as of the date of execution of the contract. * * *

Any doubt that the parties intended to include only those trees classifiable as "timber" at the time of execution in 1924 is dispelled by a further examination of the granting clause. It reads, in part: " . . . hereby grant, bargain, sell and convey . . . *all* of the Timber and Logs *now* standing, laying and being. . . ." (Emphasis ours.) The adverb "now" is pivotal in that phrase, for it identifies time. "Now" denotes the present time or instant; here, it is October 6, 1924, for the Hector deed and October 23, 1924, for the Rosenboom–Edling deed. * * *

The use of the word "now" in the deeds indicates to us that it was the intention of these parties that only those trees constituting "timber and logs" at the time of execution in 1924 were conveyed to defendants. To include by parol or judicial construction the "growth," or trees not of suitable size as "timber" in 1924, but which have since attained that stature, would be repugnant to the express terms of the instrument. . . .

We hold that the trial court was correct in determining, as it did, that the "timber" conveyed in 1924 was that which satisfied the definition of that word as of that time. This necessarily repudiates the all-inclusive theory of ownership urged by the defendants. * * *

Affirmed.

QUESTIONS AND DISCUSSION

1. What is the nature of the conveyances at issue in *Arbogast*? The court describes them as "timber deeds." Are they fee estates in the timber? Are they leases, *profits a prendre*, or licenses? Recall the discussion of the differences between these types of interests in Chapter 9, *supra* at 1043. The key to distinguishing these instruments is first deciding whether the grantor has conveyed a permanent estate. If so, then the grantor has likely conveyed a fee interest. If not, then the issue is whether the grantee has any right of possession to the land itself. Recall that leases are possessory estates while profits are not.

2. In *Hoglund v. Omak Wood Products, Inc.*, 81 Wash. App. 501, 914 P.2d 1197 (1996), a deed reserved to the grantors "all of the timber of all species upon the following described land ... together with the perpetual right to remove and use the same...." The Hoglunds, successors in interest to the grantee of the remaining estate, argued that the deed had reserved to the grantor a *profit a prendre* in the timber, rather than a fee estate as the defendant claimed. How should the court rule? Does the deed convey the right to trees that may grow on the land in the future?

3. In *M. & I. Timber Co. v. Hope Silver–Lead Mines, Inc.*, 91 Idaho 638, 428 P.2d 955 (1967), a deed reserved to the grantors and their heirs and assigns "the right and privilege to remove any and all timber from any and all of the above described tracts of land...." The parties agreed that this interest was assignable, but they could not agree whether the deed reserved a permanent right to remove trees from the land. Despite the lack of any time limit in the reservation clause, the court held that deed reserved a *profit a prendre* that gave the grantors and their successors the right to remove only those trees suitable for use when the deed was executed. The court noted in particular that the deed had not reserved the timber itself but only "cutting rights," *i.e.*, the right to *remove* the timber.

4. Compare the result in *M & I Timber* with *Baca Land & Cattle Co. v. Savage*, 440 F.2d 867 (10th Cir. 1971). The latter case involved a deed that reserved to the original owner

> all the timber, trees and wood and increment thereof, standing, growing, lying and being in and upon the above described premises, with the right of entry and re-entry at all times, for and during the term or period of ninety-nine (99) years from the date hereof [December 14, 1918] for the purpose of cutting, manufacturing, piling, storing, and removing of said timber, trees and wood and the increment thereof, with the right to ... generally occupy so much of the surface of said premises and in such manner and with such means, as may be necessary or convenient for the full enjoyment of the rights hereby reserved.

The court thought that this language made it obvious that "the parties to the 1918 agreement were looking forward to a century of substantial timber operations, during which many new trees would grow, new timbering methods would develop, and new uses for wood products would emerge." Accordingly, the court found that the reservation included new forest growth. How is the reservation in the *Baca Land* deed different from the reservation in *M & I Timber*? Do you agree with the *Baca Land* court's finding?

At the time the *Baca Land* deed was executed, timber practices were limited to the selective cutting method. Selective cutting had the effect of enhancing the use of the land by the fee owner for cattle ranching and other purposes. The reservation owner, however, had begun to employ clearcutting methods that resulted in cutting virtually all of the trees and leaving large piles of slash and debris. The few "snags" or lone trees (often dead) left standing attracted lightning and often blew down. The fee owner claimed that the deed did not authorize the use of clearcutting methods because such methods were not generally used in 1926 when the deed was executed. How should the court rule? Recall that in the context of strip mining for coal, the courts were split on whether coal owners were limited to the methods employed when the deeds were executed. *See, e.g., Martin v. Kentucky Oak Mining Co.,* 429 S.W.2d 395 (Ky.1968), *supra,* Chapter 9, where the court sustained the right of the coal owner to remove coal by strip mining, even though this method was not commonly practiced at the time of the deed. Should clearcutting be similarly allowed? Are the landowner's expectations regarding use of the land relevant to this inquiry? Suppose, for example, that the landowner had purchased the land for use as a game preserve and that large-scale clearcutting would interfere with that use.

5. The *Baca Land* court sustained the right of the timber owner to use clearcutting methods, but prohibited practices that "unreasonably impair the rights of the landowner." In *The Problem of Social Cost,* Professor Ronald Coase argued cases like *Baca Land* should not be analyzed simply from the perspective of the logger harming the landowner. Rather the problem is one of reciprocal harms, in which one must also consider the foregone income if logging is prohibited. The goal should be to choose the mix of uses that causes the least amount of harm and realizes the maximum benefit. For example, the landowner should consider foregone payments, which the logger might choose to pay to the owner in order to more efficiently harvest timber. Overall, it is important that the two sides be able to freely bargain and internalize the externality resulting from clearcutting, so as to reach the most efficient outcome for society. Ronald H. Coase, *The Problem of Social Cost,* 3 J. L. & ECON. 1 (1960). Should the court employ a Coasean analysis in deciding what practices are unreasonable? What would it look like?

6. In 2000, the United States purchased 89,000 acres of the former Baca Ranch and established the Valles Calderas National Preserve as a unit of the National Forest System with a unique management structure. Valles Caldera National Preserve Act, Pub. L. No. 106–248 (2000), 16 U.S.C. §§ 698v to 698v-10. The Preserve is managed by a Board of Trustees that includes the Forest Supervisor of the Santa Fe National Forest, the Superintendent of Bandelier National Monument, and seven individuals with a variety of backgrounds and skills. The President of the United States, in consultation with the New Mexico congressional delegation, appoints the seven individuals to represent expertise in livestock management, game and non-game wildlife and fish populations, sustainable forestry, nonprofit conservation organizations, financial management, cultural, and natural history of the region, and state or local government in New Mexico. *See* http://www.vallescaldera.gov.

7. In *Holmes v. Westvaco Corp.*, 289 S.C. 591, 592, 347 S.E.2d 887, 888 (1986), the landowner granted timber rights to a thirty-five acre tract for one year. The logging company marked the timber to be cut and removed, but, after the year expired, some marked trees remained on the land. The question was who owned the trees that had been marked but not removed. How should the Court rule?

8. *McKillop v. Crown Zellerbach, Inc.*, 46 Wash. App. 870, 872, 733 P.2d 559, 560 (1987), involved a dispute over a reservation of timber rights of "all of the timber of all species upon all of the land," subject to a right in the grantee *to use any fir or tamarack on said land* for posts for the fencing and maintenance of fences or poles for corrals upon said land, all such posts or poles "to be cut from timber having a stump diameter of 12 inches or less." *Id. (Emphasis in original.).* The trial court ruled that the reference to "timber" was ambiguous and should be construed to include only "merchantable timber-trees with a diameter greater than 12 inches." *Id.* at 561. How should the Court rule on appeal?

9. An interesting case involving the scope of timber rights is *Cushing v. Maine*, 434 A.2d 486 (Me. 1981), which addressed the ownership of timber on so-called public reserved lots in Maine. Under the Maine constitution, 1000 acre plots of land were reserved for the benefit of each unincorporated township in Maine. Pending incorporation, however, these public reserved lots were to be managed by the state. In 1850, the legislature authorized a state land agent to sell cutting rights to the lots within unincorporated townships. The cutting rights were to "continue" until the township was incorporated. Because many townships within Maine still have not been incorporated, the question in the case was whether the state's sale of continuing cutting rights included standing timber and future growth until the time of incorporation or only the timber standing on the lot at the time of the initial conveyance. The court concluded that the legislature had conveyed only the right to cut timber standing on the land at the time of the sale. In reaching this conclusion, the court emphasized that the state had a trust responsibility to all of its citizens with respect to the forest plots at issue:

> If this were an ordinary transaction between private parties, we would not be willing to infer an intent to convey future growth, where such intent is not manifested by the language of the deed. We are all the more reluctant to allow that inference to be drawn here where the grantor was the sovereign acting in a special capacity as trustee of the public reserved lots. * * *

> The State holds title to the public reserved lots as trustee and is constrained to hold and preserve these lots for the "public uses" contemplated by the Articles of Separation. In light of this constitutional restriction, we should not assume that the State intended to convey such an interest in the land as would impair for the indefinite future its ability to provide for the management of the public reserved lots. While we do not express any opinion on the ultimate limits of the

> State's power to convey interests in the public reserved lots to private parties,
> we note that the Referee's report fails to recognize the possibility of such limits.

Id. at 500. Does the Supreme Judicial Court's reasoning amount to a public trust doctrine for forests? Does its reference to the state's trust obligation differ from the public trust doctrine applied in *Illinois Central* (page 105) where the Court affirmed the Illinois legislature's voiding of a previous grant of submerged lands to the Illinois Central Railroad, and *National Audubon* (page 799), where the court restricted the water rights of the City of Los Angeles because of the harm caused to Mono Lake by the diversions? In comparing the three courts' approaches to the state's trust obligation, do you favor any particular approach? Is the public trust doctrine better understood as a rule of construction or a substantive limit on state power to alienate natural resources? Should it matter whether the resource involved is submerged lands, appropriative water rights, or forests?

The *Cushing* court declined to "express any opinion on the ultimate limits of the State's power to convey interests in the public reserved lots to private parties." *Id.* If the court had addressed this question, what decision should it have reached? Suppose, for example, that the 1850 legislation had been interpreted to grant a timber harvesting right in perpetuity. Could the court have used the public trust doctrine to invalidate the grant without obligating Maine to pay just compensation? What are the broader implications of extending the public trust to forests? How might this affect state and federal regulation of logging on lands acquired under railroad land grants or the 1878 Timber and Stone Act?

10. Timber rights, like other property rights, can be acquired through adverse possession. In *Stephenson Lumber Co. v. Hurst*, 259 Ky. 747, 83 S.W.2d 48 (1934) the lumber company assumed possession of the land even though tenants of the record owners were also in possession. The court held that the actual possession by the record owners of any part of the land was assumed to extend to all of the land within the boundaries set forth in the deed. Thus, the simultaneous possession by the lumber company of some part of the land was not sufficient to defeat the owner's title by adverse possession.

11. The sale of timber is considered the "sale of goods" and is thus covered by Article 2 of the Uniform Commercial Code. U.C.C. § 2–107[2]. But the timber must be existing and identified before any interest passes, and when these standards are not satisfied, the contract operates as the sale of future goods. *See* U.C.C. §§ 2–105[2], 2–401[1]. Once identified, the buyer obtains an insurable interest in the goods, but absent a specific agreement to the contrary, the seller likewise retains an insurable interest and may substitute like goods for the goods identified until the seller notifies the buyer that the identification is final. *See* U.C.C. §§ 2–501[1], [2]. In *Conservancy Holdings, Ltd. v. Perma–Treat Corp.*, 126 A.D.2d 114, 513 N.Y.S.2d 266 (1987), the court found that timber that was not identified at the time of the contract but that was to be marked at a later date by the seller was a contract to sell future goods, and that the seller was properly found to have breached that contract when it failed to timely mark the timber. In accordance with U.C.C. § 2–715, Perma–Treat, the buyer, was entitled to recover both incidental and consequential damages as a result of a breach. In light of the U.C.C., how should a timber contract be drafted to avoid any misunderstanding about the time for marking and removing timber or about the time when title to the timber passes to the buyer?

12.   Once loggers cut and clear the timber, they must transport the timber to a mill. The mill owner and the logger contract for delivery of timber of a particular type and quality for an established price. Historically, mill owners held significant control over these transactions with the result that loggers often believed that they were not fully compensated for their timber. One way that mill owners unfairly took advantage of loggers was by the method of "scaling" or measuring the timber. In order to ensure that loggers were fairly compensated for the logs hauled and delivered to the mills, Idaho adopted legislation that changed the way mill owners scale logs. Under the Idaho law, mill owners are required to pay for the gross weight of logs delivered to the mill. IDAHO CODE § 38–1202(c). In *Toivo Pottala Logging, Inc. v. Boise Cascade Corp.*, 112 Idaho 489, 733 P.2d 710 (1987), however, the Idaho Supreme Court held that this legislation does not restrict the mill owners and loggers from negotiating merchantability. Thus, a mill owner may still demand timber that meets its standards for type and quality, and pay only for timber that meets those standards. As a result, loggers must ensure that each load is up to the mill owners' expectations. Otherwise the logger may face a total loss.

---

2.   FEDERAL AND STATE REGULATION OF PRIVATE LOGGING ACTIVITIES

The federal government does not have a comprehensive program for regulating the environmental impacts associated with logging on private land as it does, for example, with coal mining, but several federal environmental requirements frequently apply to private logging activities. Most important, perhaps, is the Endangered Species Act, which prohibits the "taking" of any wildlife species listed under the law unless a habitat conservation plan is approved by the Secretary of the Interior in advance of any such taking. 16 U.S.C § 1539. While not all logging operations threaten endangered species, the strict interpretation of the law by the U.S. Supreme Court and the possibility of enforcement by interested environmental groups helps to ensure that logging companies carefully assess the impacts of their activities on wildlife.

In addition to the ESA, logging activities may be subject to various requirements under the Clean Water Act as nonpoint sources of pollution. Under Section 319, states are required to adopt management programs that establish "best management practices" (BMPs) for categories of nonpoint source pollution such as silviculture. Silvicultural activities may also have to meet state water quality standards (WQS), which are essentially ambient water standards for individual water bodies, established under Section 303 of the Clean Water Act. 33 U.S.C. § 1313 (2000). Under this program, states are required to attain and maintain WQS. For waters that fail to meet WQS, states must establish "total maximum daily loads" (TMDLs) for those waters. In order to meet these requirements, regulation of silvicultural activities may be necessary.

In 1999, EPA proposed to regulate silvicultural operations under the National Pollutant Discharge Elimination System (NPDES) permit program set out at Section 402 of the Clean Water Act. *See* 64 Fed. Reg. 46,058 (1999). EPA eventually backed-off that proposal when it adopted its final TMDL rules in 2000. *See* 65 Fed. Reg. 43,585 (2000), *codified at,* 40 C.F.R. § 130 (2003). Silvicultural activities are not generally subject to the dredge and fill requirements of Section 404 of the Clean Water Act. Section 404(f)(1)(A) expressly exempts "normal silvicultural activities" and "harvesting for the production of food, fiber, and forest products." 33 U.S.C. § 1344(f)(1)(A).

The Clean water Act's current impact on forestry practices, will depend in substantial part on how the scope of federal jurisdiction under the Act is ultimately resolved. In *Rapanos v. United States*, 547 U.S. 715 (2006), the Supreme Court split badly over how to construe the scope of the term "navigable waters of the United States" in the Clean Water Act. Justice Kennedy's concurring opinion, which is the basis for current law, requires a "significant nexus" between affected wetlands and traditional navigable waters. *Id.* at 780; *see also* Mark Squillace, *From "Navigable Waters" to "Constitutional Waters": The Future of Federal Wetlands Regulation*, 40 U. MICH. J.L. REFORM 799 (2007). Efforts to amend the Clean Water Act to address the problem posed by *Rapanos* and the Court's earlier decision in *Solid Waste Agency of Northern Cook County (SWANCC) v. U.S. Army Corps of Engineers*, 531 U.S. 159 (2001), have been ongoing for several years. Most recently, Senator Feingold (D–WI) introduced legislation (known as the "Clean Water Restoration Act") during the 111th Congress that would, if passed, essentially overturn *Rapanos* and *SWANCC*, by removing the term "navigable waters of the United States" from the statute and by defining "waters of the United States" as:

> "[A]ll waters subject to the ebb and flow of the tide, the territorial seas, and all interstate and intrastate waters and their tributaries, including lakes, rivers, streams (including intermittent streams), mudflats, sandflats, wetlands, sloughs, prairie potholes, wet meadows, playa lakes, natural ponds, and all impoundments of the foregoing, to the fullest extent that these waters, or activities affecting these waters, are subject to the legislative power of Congress under the Constitution." S. 787, 111th Cong. §§ 4–5 (2009).

If the Feingold amendment passes, federal Clean Water Act jurisdiction over forestry practices that impact wetlands or other waters would extend to any such waters that could satisfy the broadest interpretation of the commerce clause, the treaty clause (which would encompass waters used by migratory birds), and perhaps other sources of federal constitutional power.

On the funding side, the Cooperative Forestry Assistance Act, 16 U.S.C. § 2101, authorizes federal funds for federal-state cooperative forestry activities that promote environmental quality. In particular, the Secretary of Agriculture may establish stewardship programs that help promote recycling of wood fibers, improvement and maintenance of fish and wildlife habitat, the prevention and control of fires, insects and disease, and the planning and conduct of urban forestry programs. *Id.* § 2101(b).

Comprehensive state regulation of logging activities usually takes the form of a "forest practices act." Oregon was the first state to adopt such a law in 1971, OR. REV. CODE, Chap. 527, and a number of other states have followed Oregon's lead. *See, e.g.,* California Forest Practices Act of 1973, CAL. PUB. RES. CODE, §§ 4511 *et seq.*; Idaho Forest Practices Act, IDAHO CODE 38–1301; Washington Forest Practices Act, WASH. REV. CODE, Ch. 76.09. Some states like Virginia have comprehensive management of forestry and logging practices but their authority is not set out in a single law. *See* Michael J. Mortimer & James W. Garner, *Yes Virginia, There is a Forest Practices Act,* 17 VIRGINIA FOREST LANDOWNER UPDATE, No. 1 (Winter 2002– 03). The following case arises under California's forest practices law.

SIERRA CLUB V. STATE BOARD OF FORESTRY,
7 Cal. 4th 1215, 876 P.2d 505, 32 Cal. Rptr. 2d 19 (1994)

BAXTER, J.

Pacific Lumber Company submitted two timber harvesting plans covering old-growth forest in Humboldt County to the Department of Forestry (department). In response to a request by the Department of Fish and Game (Fish and Game), the department asked Pacific Lumber Company to provide information on old-growth-dependent wildlife species within the plan areas. Pacific Lumber Company refused to provide the requested information on the ground that it was not specified in the rules promulgated by the Board of Forestry (board). (Cal. Code Regs., tit. 14, § 895 *et seq.* [hereafter, sometimes, rules or forest practice rules].) The department then denied the plans on the ground that they were incomplete. Pacific Lumber Company appealed the department's denial to the board. The board approved the plans, ultimately finding that "there will not be any significant adverse effect on old-growth-dependent wildlife species or habitat from the harvesting that will occur under these two plans."

The legal issue before us, in its simplest form, is whether the board abused its discretion in approving the timber harvest plans. We conclude that the board did abuse its discretion when it evaluated and approved the plans on the basis of a record which lacked information regarding the presence in the subject areas of some old-growth-dependent species, information which both the department and Fish and Game had determined was necessary. By approving the plans without the necessary information regarding those species the board failed to comply with the obligation imposed on it by the California Environmental Quality Act (CEQA) (Pub. Resources Code, § 21000 *et seq.*) and the Z'Berg–Nejedly Forest Practice Act of 1973 (the Act or Forest Practice Act) (Pub. Resources Code, § 4511 *et seq.*). * * *

I. FACTS

On February 16, 1988, the Pacific Lumber Company submitted two timber harvesting plans to the department for the logging of two separate stands of what Pacific Lumber Company's registered professional forester described as "virgin old-growth redwood-type forest." Timber harvesting plan 1–88–65 HUM covers 82 acres in the Yager Creek drainage basin in Humboldt County; timber harvesting plan 1–88–74 HUM covers 237 acres in the basin approximately 1 mile from the area covered by 1–88–65 HUM. On February 18, 1988, the department returned timber harvesting plan 1–88–74 HUM to Pacific Lumber Company with the request that it provide additional information on certain aspects of the stand. This information was needed, according to the department, because the harvest area "appears to constitute habitat for old-growth-dependent species" and, if true, "the harvest could result in a significant adverse effect on these species." [The affected species included the goshawk, Olympic salamander, tailed frog, red tree vole, Pacific fisher, spotted owl, and marbled murrelet.] * * *

On April 19, 1988, the department denied both timber harvesting plans on the ground that "information contained in the plans you have submitted is incomplete in a material way. This conclusion is based on the request from the Department of Fish and Game, John Hummel, for wildlife surveys and the need to know of the presence or absence of old-growth dependent species in order to make adequate mitigation if those species exist in the [timber harvesting plan] areas." Pacific Lumber Company appealed the department's denial of the plans to the board.

In a hearing before the board on May 20, 1988, the department dropped its request for information in the "general vicinity" of the timber harvesting plan area, and confined its request to surveys of the old-growth-dependent wildlife on the plan property. On June 8, 1988, the board overturned the director's denial of the plans, finding that both plans were "in conformance with the rules and regulations of the Board of Forestry." The board, accordingly, "approve[d] the plans based on the record before the Director of the California Department of Forestry and Fire Protection." In its statement of reasons, the board concluded that it "is unable to determinatively say whether there will or there will not be significant adverse effects on old-growth-dependent wildlife species or habitat from harvesting that will occur under these two plans. The best that we can say is that the [Department of Fish and Game], the state agency responsible for protection of wildlife, believes that there may be possible significant effects, whereas other reputable experts for [Pacific Lumber Company] believe that there will not be. At best, the information is uncertain and speculative (based on available information). Given [Pacific Lumber Company's] efforts to date, and the fact that the issue of the effects on old-growth-dependent species will still remain debatable, even with the additional surveys, it is unreasonable to request further information." * * *

On June 16, 1988, the Sierra Club and the Environmental Protection Information Center, Inc., filed a petition for writ of mandate seeking an order compelling the board to withdraw its approval of these two timber harvesting plans. The petition alleged . . . that by either failing to perform an evaluation of the adverse effects of the plan itself or failing to require that Pacific Lumber Company perform such an evaluation, the board violated both its own rules and the requirements of the CEQA. The trial court concluded that the board had failed actually to determine whether harvesting under these two plans would have significant adverse effects on "old-growth-dependent species habitat." On February 9, 1989, the trial court returned the plans to the board. . . .

On March 20, 1989, the board filed its supplemental findings. It concluded that approval of both plans will not produce a significant effect on the environment, and further found "that there will not be any significant adverse effect on old-growth-dependent wildlife species or habitat from the harvesting that will occur under these two plans." A later statement in the supplemental findings provided: "The Board has evaluated the information provided in the THP record and the May 20, 1988 and June 8, 1988 hearing and found that there was no determinative evidence presented for reaching the conclusion that significant adverse effects will result to wildlife." The board's conclusion that these plans had no adverse impact on old-growth-dependent wildlife obviated its need to specify additional mitigation measures. The board noted, however,

the existing mitigation measures that would lessen the plans' impact on wildlife: the modified selection silvicultural system would lessen the impact on 200 acres of the plan area, leaving approximately half the trees in that area that could be used for habitat; watercourse protection zones would protect the integrity of the streams, keeping them as habitat for aquatic species; the decision not to use fire for site preparation would retain vegetative cover necessary for some of the species; and the retention of some downed trees would provide habitat for cavity dwellers. The board specifically found that it "was not appropriate to require extensive or costly species-wide surveys by forest landowners in an effort to address wildlife effects which are speculative."
* * *

The trial court, after receiving the board's supplemental findings, denied the petition for writ of mandate on October 23, 1989. The Court of Appeal stayed timber operations pending its review of the case, and addressed the issue as only whether the department could require the additional survey. Concluding that the department had the power to do so, the Court of Appeal reversed the judgment of the trial court and remanded the matter . . . with instructions to issue a peremptory writ of mandate directing the board to rescind its approval of both timber harvesting plans. We granted Pacific Lumber Company's petition for review.

II. STATUTORY BACKGROUND

Timber harvesting operations in this state must be conducted in accordance with the provisions of the Forest Practice Act. The Act was intended to create and maintain a comprehensive system for regulating timber harvesting in order to achieve two goals: (1) to ensure that "[w]here feasible, the productivity of timberlands is restored, enhanced, and maintained"; and (2) to ensure that "[t]he goal of maximum sustained production of high-quality timber products is achieved while giving consideration to values relating to recreation, watershed, wildlife, range and forage, fisheries, . . . and aesthetic enjoyment." (§ 4513.) The Act vests in the board the obligation to adopt forest practice rules and regulations specific to the various forest districts of the state in order "to assure the continuous growing and harvesting of commercial forest tree species and to protect the soil, air, fish, and wildlife, and water resources, including, but not limited to, streams, lakes, and estuaries." (§ 4551.)

Actual timber operations are controlled by means of a site-specific timber harvesting plan that must be submitted to the department before timber operations may commence. (§§ 4581 and 4582.5.) The Legislature has specified that the plan include the name and address of the timber owner and the timber operator, a description of the land upon which the work is proposed to be done, a description of the silviculture methods to be applied, an outline of the methods to mitigate erosion caused by operations performed in the vicinity of a stream, the provisions, if any, to protect any "unique area" within the area of operations, and the anticipated dates for commencement and completion of operations. (§ 4582, subds. (a)–(g).) In addition, the plan must include "[a]ny other information the board provides by regulation to meet its rules and the standards of this chapter." (§ 4582, subd. (j).)

The director of the department reviews the plan "to determine if [it] is in conformance with the rules and regulations of the board and with [the provisions of] this chapter." (§ 4582.7.) If the director determines that the plan does not conform to the rules and regulations of the board and with the other provisions of the Act, he or she must return the plan, indicating the reasons for the return and advising the plan submitter of his or her right to a public hearing before the board. Any appeal to the board must be filed within 10 days from the receipt of the returned plan, and the board must rule on the appeal within 30 days from the date it was filed, unless the parties agree to a later date. The board reviews the plan to determine whether it conforms to the rules and regulations of the board and the provisions of the Act itself. * * *

III. THE DEPARTMENT'S AUTHORITY TO REQUEST INFORMATION NOT SPECIFIED IN THE RULES

The uncertainty reflected in the record as to the presence or absence of old-growth-dependent species stemmed in part from a disagreement between the department and the board as to the department's authority to request, and the board's power to demand as a condition of approval of a timber harvest plan, information not specified in the forest practice rules. Although the rules have been amended to provide for the submission of information on the presence of old-growth-dependent species in appropriate cases (Cal. Code Regs., tit. 14, § 1034, subd. (w)), eliminating this particular controversy, the department's authority to request other types of information not specified in the rules remains a relevant concern for future cases. The Forest Practice Act does not expressly grant the department the authority to request information not expressly specified by the rules, nor do the rules themselves. We note, however, that even in its 1988 rules, the board had imposed upon the department (acting through its director) the obligation to disapprove those plans that did not incorporate "silvicultural systems, operating methods and procedures" that would substantially lessen significant adverse impacts on the environment. (Cal. Code Regs., tit. 14, § 898.1, subd. (c)(1).) The department cannot discharge its obligation to disapprove plans that do not incorporate feasible measures to reduce the significant adverse effects of the plan on the environment if it is unable to identify those significant adverse impacts due to a lack of information. Therefore, by vesting the department with the authority to determine whether timber harvesting plans incorporate the measures specified by the board to reduce significant impacts, the board impliedly vests the department with the authority to secure the information that it needs to make that determination.

Because we conclude that section 21160, a CEQA provision, gives the department express authority to request information that it needs to identify the significant adverse impacts of a timber harvesting plan, we need not rely on the department's implied authority alone. Section 21160 provides, in its relevant part, that "[w]henever any person applies to any public agency for a lease, permit, license, certificate, or other entitlement for use, the public agency may require that person to submit data and information which may be necessary to enable the public agency to determine whether the proposed project may have a significant effect on the environment or to prepare an environmental impact report." The department is the public agency initially charged with the duty of determining whether or not a proposed timber harvesting plan incorporates feasible silvicultural systems, operating methods, and procedures to substantially lessen significant adverse impacts on the environment. (Cal. Code Regs., tit. 14, § 898.1, subd. (c)(1).) Section 21160, by its express terms, therefore authorizes the public agency—here, the department—to request from the plan submitter the information that it needs to satisfy its obligations under the rule. * * *

In section 21000 of CEQA, the Legislature expressly declared its intent "that *all* agencies of the state government which regulate activities of private individuals, corporations, and public agencies which are found to affect the quality of the environment, shall regulate such activities so that major consideration is given to preventing environmental damage, while providing a decent home and satisfying living environment for every Californian." (§ 21000, subd.

(g), italics added.) In 1976, the Legislature clarified how public agencies were to discharge their obligations under CEQA: "The Legislature finds and declares that it is the policy of the state that public agencies should not approve projects as proposed if there are feasible alternatives or feasible mitigation measures available which would substantially lessen the significant environmental effects of such projects, and the procedures required by this division are intended to assist public agencies in systematically identifying both the significant effects of proposed projects and the feasible alternatives or feasible mitigation measures which will avoid or substantially lessen such significant effects. The Legislature further finds and declares that in the event specific economic, social, or other conditions make infeasible such project alternatives or such mitigation measures, individual projects may be approved in spite of one or more significant effects thereof." (§ 21002.)

We have stated that the environmental impact report (EIR) is "the primary means of achieving the Legislature's considered declaration that it is the policy of this state to 'take all action necessary to protect, rehabilitate, and enhance the environmental quality of the state.' (§ 21000, subd. (a).)" *Laurel Heights Improvement Assn. v. Regents of the University of California* (1988) 47 Cal.3d 376, 392. The environmental impact report is " 'the heart of CEQA' " and the "environmental 'alarm bell' whose purpose it is to alert the public and its responsible officials to environmental changes before they have reached ecological points of no return." * * *

Pacific Lumber Company, joined by various amici curiae, argues that section 4582.75 precludes the department from requesting information not expressly specified in the forest practice rules. Section 4582.75 provides: "The rules adopted by the board shall be the only criteria employed by the director when reviewing timber harvesting plans pursuant to Section 4582.7." A request for information, however, is not a criterion by which a plan is reviewed. Section 4582.75, as demonstrated below, was enacted to curtail the department's ability to make forest policy decisions outside the scope established by the board. Vesting the department with the ability to request information does not permit the department to make decisions outside the scope of the board's rules. * * *

Section 4582.75, providing that the rules would be the sole criteria employed by the director in reviewing timber harvesting plans, was added to limit the department director's discretion in reviewing timber harvesting plans. Its purpose is to assure that the director operates within the forest policies established by the board and articulated in the forest practice rules. *Environmental Protection Information Center, Inc. v. Johnson* (1985) 170 Cal.App.3d 604, 619. In other words, the director of the department is not to approve or disapprove timber harvesting plans based on his or her own conception of what is good forest policy, but rather, based on the board's conclusions. Hence, the board's rules provide that the director of the department "may only require incorporation into the plan of mitigation measures that are based on rules of the Board." (Cal. Code Regs., tit. 14, § 1037.5, subd. (f).)

As we stated above, however, a request for information is not a criterion for reviewing a timber harvesting plan, but is instead a prerequisite to application of the criteria established by the board, in particular, that rule requiring the director to disapprove those plans which do not incorporate procedures to substantially lessen significant adverse impacts on the environment. (Cal. Code Regs., tit. 14, § 898.1, subd. (c)(1).) The director of the department cannot discharge that obligation until the significant adverse impacts of the timber harvesting operation have been identified.

A construction of section 4582.75 that permits the director of the department to require the submission of information not otherwise specified in the rules does not upset the respective functions of the department and the board, since the information requested must be relevant to the manner in which the criteria expressed in the rules are applied, and the board retains the power to approve a plan that has significant adverse effects upon the environment, so long as it justifies its action in light of "specific economic, social, or other conditions." (§ 21002.) CEQA requires that the board identify the adverse effects of the proposed project before it exercises that power, however.

CEQA compels government first to identify the environmental effects of projects, and then to mitigate those adverse effects through the imposition of feasible mitigation measures or through the selection of feasible alternatives. It permits government agencies to approve projects that have an environmentally deleterious effect, but also requires them to justify those choices in light of specific social or economic conditions. (§ 21002.) The board cannot, as a practical matter, anticipate each and every significant adverse effect of timber harvesting, and therefore cannot promulgate rules that require the submission of all relevant information from timber harvest plan submitters. It is through the agency of the department that the board acquires the information on the impacts of timber harvesting that forms the basis for new rules.

The Legislature appears to have expressly contemplated the information-gathering role of the department in section 4582.6: "Upon receipt of the timber harvesting plan, the department shall place it ... in a file available for public inspection ... and, for the purpose of interdisciplinary review, shall transmit a copy to the Department of Fish and Game, [and] the appropriate California regional water quality control board, county planning agency.... The department shall invite, consider, and respond in writing to comments received from public agencies to which the plan has been transmitted and shall consult with those agencies at their request." (§ 4582.6, subd.(a).) For that consultation to be meaningful, the department must have the power to compel the applicant to obtain and produce relevant information requested by the participating agencies.

In summary, we find that a reading of section 4582.75 that authorizes the department to require the production of relevant information not specified in the rules furthers the ultimate purpose of both CEQA and the Act, and permits the director of the department to meaningfully discharge his or her obligations under the rules of the board itself.

We recognize that the Legislature cannot have intended the department to have unfettered discretion in the type of information that it may require. Section 21160 limits the agency's power to compel information to that "data and information which may be necessary to enable the public agency to determine whether the proposed project may have a significant effect on the environment...." To comply with the requirements of this section, the information sought by the department must be information that will reveal effects of timber harvesting that can be fairly described as "significant." Section 21068 defines "significant effect on the environment" as "a substantial, or potentially substantial, adverse change in the environment." * * *

IV. DID THE BOARD ABUSE ITS DISCRETION
BY APPROVING THESE PLANS?

* * *

The board performs an adjudicatory function in approving or rejecting a timber harvest plan following an appeal from the director's return of the plan to the submitter.... Its order is therefore subject to judicial review under the mandate procedure established by Code of Civil Procedure section 1094.5. The inquiry, in such review here, is whether the board abused its discretion in approving these plans. "Abuse of discretion is established if the respondent [agency] has not proceeded in the manner required by law, the order or decision is not supported by the findings, or the findings are not supported by the evidence." (*Ibid.*; *See also* § 21168.5.)....

Because the board believed that gathering the additional information sought by the department could not be required of Pacific Lumber Company, it evaluated the timber harvest plans based solely on the information already in the record. The mandate proceeding and, ultimately, this appeal, therefore require that the court first determine whether the board or department failed to comply with mandatory procedures of CEQA and the Forest Practice Act. As noted earlier, that record contained no site-specific data regarding the presence of four old-growth-dependent species, the red tree vole, the marbled murrelet, the goshawk, and the spotted owl, and indicated that neither the department nor Fish and Game had made site-specific recommendations regarding mitigation measures.

In evaluating and approving the timber harvest plan in the absence of such data and recommendations the board failed to proceed in the manner prescribed by CEQA. The record confirms that Fish and Game had reasonably determined that the proposed timber harvest could have a significant adverse effect on the old-growth-dependent wildlife habitat. Therefore, the board, through the department, had an obligation imposed by CEQA to collect information regarding the presence of old-growth-dependent species on the site of the proposed timber harvest. Without that information the board could not identify the environmental impacts of the project or carry out its obligation to protect wildlife as required by the Forest Practice Act (§ 4551), and to prevent environmental damage by refusing to approve projects if feasible mitigation measures are available which will avoid or substantially lessen significant environmental effects as required by CEQA. (§ 21000, 21002.) When it nonetheless approved the plan, the board failed to proceed in the manner prescribed by the Forest Practice Act and CEQA. * * *

The judgment of the Court of Appeal directing the superior court to issue a peremptory writ of mandate compelling the board to rescind its approval of timber harvesting plans 1–88–65 HUM and 1–88–74 HUM is affirmed.

QUESTIONS AND DISCUSSION

1. Review the opinion's description of California's Forest Practices Act and the California Environmental Quality Act (CEQA). What are the implications of the two statutes for questions of management scale? Is this an instance where state regulation may offer more protection of the forest resource than federal regulation? In light of the Supreme Court's decision in the *Granite Rock* case, discussed in Chapter 9 (page 1175), does California's Forest Practices Act apply to a timber sale in a national forest located in California?

2. Review the court's description of the California Environmental Quality Act (CEQA). How does CEQA differ from NEPA? Does it have more substantive content? What is your reaction to CEQA's provision that allows a project proponent to avoid mitigation of significant environmental effects where economic, social, or other conditions make project alternatives "infeasible"?

3. What are the implications of the court's decision? Why did Pacific Lumber oppose collecting more data? What were the Sierra Club's reasons for pursuing the writ of mandate?

4. The impetus for the adoption of forest practice acts was the desire to protect water resources, but over the years the laws have evolved to encompass harvesting practices, road construction and maintenance, reforestation, fish and wildlife protection, and pesticide use. Obviously, these concerns must be balanced with economic considerations, private property rights, and the societal need for wood products. Although there are many similarities among state forest practices law, there are also some differences. Some states such as California focus more on procedural tools like permits and planning requirements; while others like Oregon rely more on substantive performance standards. What are the advantages and disadvantages of focusing on planning? Of relying on performance standards? Which system is likely to afford the state more discretion? Which lends itself to more meaningful public participation?

COMMON ACRONYMS

The field of natural resources law is burdened with a multitude of acronyms. We have attempted throughout the casebook to define acronyms in relative proximity to their use but provide the following list as an additional reference.

ACEC	Area of Critical Environmental Concern
ALJ	Administrative Law Judge
ANILCA	Alaska National Interest Lands Conservation Act
ANSCA	Alaska Native Claims Settlement Act
APA	Administrative Procedure Act
APD	Application for Permit to Drill
ARPA	Archaeological Resources Protection Act
ASQ	Allowable Sale Quantity
AUM	Animal Unit Month
BA	Biological Assessment
BBF	Billion board feet
BIA	Bureau of Indian Affairs
BLM	Bureau of Land Management
BO	Biological Opinion
BoR	Bureau of Reclamation
CAFO	Concentrated Animal Feeding Operation
CAP	Central Arizona Project
CDM	Clean Development Mechanism
CDQ	Community Development Quota
CEQ	Council on Environmental Quality
CFR	Code of Federal Regulations
CITES	Convention on International Trade in Endangered Species
CMA	Cooperative Management Agreement
CMUA	Classification and Multiple Use Act
CWA	Clean Water Act
DLA	Desert Lands Act
DOI	Department of the Interior
DPCIA	Dolphin Protection Consumer Information Act of 1990
EA	Environmental Assessment
EEZ	Exclusive Economic Zone
EIS	Environmental Impact Statement
EPA	Environmental Protection Agency
ESA	Endangered Species Act
FAO	United Nations Food and Agriculture Organization
FCMA	Magnuson–Stevens Fishery Conservation and Management Act
FLPMA	Federal Land Policy and Management Act
FMC	Fishery Management Council
FMP	Fishery Management Plan
FONSI	Finding of No Significant Impact
FS	Forest Service
FTCA	Federal Tort Claims Act
FWS	Fish and Wildlife Service

GATT	General Agreement on Tariffs and Trade
GLO	General Land Office
GML	General Mining Law
HCP	Habitat Conservation Plan
IATTC	Inter–American Tropical Tuna Commission
IBLA	Interior Board of Land Appeals
ICRW	International Convention for the Regulation of Whaling
ITQ	Individual Transferable Quota
ITS	Incidental Take Statement
IWC	International Whaling Commission
LBMP	Land-based marine pollution
LRMP	Land and Resource Management Plan
LWCF	Land and Water Conservation Fund
MBF	Thousand board feet
MBTA	Migratory Bird Treaty Act
MFP	Management Framework Plan
MIS	Management Indicator Species
MLA	Mineral Leasing Act
MMBF	Million board feet
MMPA	Marine Mammal Protection Act
MMS	Minerals Management Service
MPA	Marine Protected Area
MSY	Maximum Sustainable Yield
MUSYA	Multiple–Use, Sustained–Yield Act
MWD	Metropolitan Water District
NAGPRA	Native American Graves Protection and Repatriation Act
NAMMCO	North Atlantic Marine Mammal Commission
NEPA	National Environmental Policy Act
NFMA	National Forest Management Act
NGO	Nongovernmental Organization
NHPA	National Historic Preservation Act
NMFS	National Marine Fisheries Service
NOAA	National Oceanic and Atmospheric Administration
NPS	National Park Service
NRA	National Recreation Area
NRCS	Natural Resources Conservation Service
NSO	No Surface Occupancy
NWPS	National Wilderness Preservation System
NWR	National Wildlife Refuge
O & C	Oregon and California
ORV	Off–Road Vehicle
OSM	Office of Surface Mining Reclamation and Enforcement
OY	Optimum Yield
PRIA	Public Rangeland Improvement Act
RAC	Range Advisory Council
RARE	Roadless Area Review and Evaluation
RMP	Resource Management Plan
ROD	Record of Decision
ROW	Right of Way
RPA	Forest and Rangelands Renewable Resources Planning Act or Reasonable and Prudent Alternatives
SFA	Sustainable Fisheries Act
SMCRA	Surface Mining Control and Reclamation Act
SRA	Surface Resources Act

SRHA	Stock–Raising Homestead Act
TAC	Total Allowable Catch
TGA	Taylor Grazing Act
TMDL	Total Maximum Daily Load
TVA	Tennessee Valley Authority
UNCLOS	United Nations Convention on the Law of the Sea
UNEP	United Nations Environment Programme
USGS	United States Geological Survey
WFRHBA	Wild Free–Roaming Horses and Burros Act
WSA	Wilderness Study Area
WSRA	Wild and Scenic Rivers Act
WTO	World Trade Organization

*

INDEX

References are to pages

ABORIGINAL SUBSISTENCE WHALING
Generally, 543–549

ACQUISITION OF PUBLIC LANDS
History of Natural Resources Law, this index

ADMINISTRATIVE AGENCIES
Generally, 208–319
Administrative Procedure Act, this index
Advocacy by nongovernmental organizations (NGOs), 238
Bureau of Indian Affairs, mission and organization, 218
Bureau of Land Management, mission and organization, 215–216
Bureau of Reclamation
    Generally, 212
  Mission and organization, 218
Citizen suits and litigation, 239–241
Constitutional challenges, 212–214
Council on Environmental Quality, mission and organization, 218
Department of the Interior, 210
Earth Day, 237
Environmental Protection Agency, mission and organization, 217–218
Exhaustion of remedies, nongovernmental organizations (NGOs), 257
Federal Land Policy Management Act, resource planning on public lands, 293, 297–319
Final agency actions, nongovernmental organizations (NGOs), 256–257
General Land Office, 210, 212, 213
Grazing Service, 212
Improvement of agency decision-making, generally, 223–319
Interagency disputes, 220–221
Litigation and citizen suits, 239–241
Lobbying for legislative and administrative action by nongovernmental organizations (NGOs), 237–239
Minerals Management Service, mission and organization, 218
Missions of agencies, 214–219
National Audobon Society, 236, 238
National Environmental Policy Act, this index
National Forest Management Act, resource planning on public lands, 293, 297–319

ADMINISTRATIVE AGENCIES—Cont'd
National Marine Fisheries Service, mission and organization, 217
National Park Service
    Generally, 212
  Mission and organization, 216
National Wildlife Federation, 236
Natural Resources Conservation Service, mission and organization, 218–219
Nongovernmental organizations (NGOs)
    Generally, 236–258
  Advocacy, 238
  Citizen suits and litigation, 239–241
  Earth Day, 237
  Exhaustion of remedies, 257
  Final agency actions, 256–257
  Injury in fact, standing to sue, 242–243
  Lobbying for legislative and administrative action, 237–239
  Market actors, 238
  National Audobon Society, 236, 238
  National Wildlife Federation, 236
  Ripeness, 257
  Sierra Club, 236, 238
  Standing to sue, 241–256, 257–258
  Think tanks and expert analysis, 238
  Timing of judicial review, 256–257
  Traceability and redressability, standing to sue, 243
  Wilderness Society, 236, 238
  Zone of interests, standing to sue, 243–244
Office of Surface Mining Regulation and Enforcement Service, mission and organization, 218
Organization of agencies, 214–219
Progressive Conservation Movement, 211–212
Public choice challenges for agency management of natural resources, 219–223
Rangelands, 983–1005
Redressability, standing to sue of nongovernmental organizations (NGOs), 243
Resource planning on public lands
    Generally, 292–319
  Federal Land Policy Management Act, 293, 297–319
  History, 294–297
  National Forest Management Act, 293, 297–319
  Scientific uncertainty, 293

1323

ADMINISTRATIVE AGENCIES—Cont'd

Ripeness, nongovernmental organizations (NGOs), 257

Rise in federal natural resource agencies, 210–212

Scientific uncertainty, resource planning on public lands, 293

Sierra Club, 236, 238

Standing to sue of nongovernmental organizations (NGOs), 241–256, 257–258

Think tanks and expert analysis, 238

Timing of judicial review, nongovernmental organizations (NGOs), 256–257

Traceability, standing to sue of nongovernmental organizations (NGOs), 243

U.S. Army Corps of Engineers, mission and organization, 217

U.S. Fish and Wildlife Service, mission and organization, 216–217

U.S. Forest Service
>Generally, 212, 213–214
>Mission and organization, 214–215

U.S. Geological Service, mission and organization, 218

Wilderness Society, 236, 238

Zone of interests, standing to sue of nongovernmental organizations (NGOs), 243–244

ADMINISTRATIVE PROCEDURE ACT

Generally, 223–236

Adjudication, 225–226

Deference to agency, 227–230

Enforcement actions, 225–226

Formal adjudications, 226

Formal rulemaking, 224

Informal adjudications, 226

Informal rulemaking, 224

Information bulletins, 225

Instruction memoranda, 225

Interpretative rules, 225

Judicial review
>Generally, 226–236
>Deference to agency, 227–230
>Standard of review, 226–228

Notice of proposed and final rules, 224–225

Permit issuance, 225–226

Policy statements, 225

Rulemaking, 224–225

Standard of review, 226–228

AESTHETIC RESOURCES AND VALUES

Biodiversity, 332, 333

Management of natural resources, 37–38

AGRICULTURAL SECURITY

Biodiversity, 331

AIR QUALITY

Forests, 1207–1208

ALASKA NATIONAL INTEREST LANDS CONSERVATION ACT

Generally, 145

ALASKA NATIVE CLAIM SETTLEMENT ACT

Generally, 145

ALIEN TORT CLAIMS ACT

Foreign countries, mineral development in, 1042

ALLOCATION

History of Natural Resources Law, this index

Water, this index

ALLUVIAL VALLEY FLOORS

Surface Mining Control And Reclamation Act, 1188–1189

AMENDMENTS

Minerals, staking claims, 1102–1103

AMERICAN REVOLUTION

History of natural resources law, 80

ANTHROPOCENTRISM

Magnuson–Stevens Fishery Conservation and Management Act, 21

Protection vs. use of natural resources, 16–20

ANTIQUITIES ACT

National monuments, 620–625

APPEALS

Judicial Review, this index

AQUACULTURE

Generally, 476–478

ARCHEOLOGICAL RESOURCES PROTECTION ACT

Federal power to manage natural resources, 202

ARCTIC NATIONAL WILDLIFE REFUGE

Generally, 8–9

Management of natural resources, 67–69

ASSESSMENT WORK

Minerals, staking claims, 1103–1111

BALD EAGLE PROTECTION ACT

Generally, 347–348

BEACHFRONT MANAGEMENT

Takings clause, 185–200

BEST SCIENTIFIC INFORMATION

Magnuson–Stevens Fishery Conservation and Management Act, national standards, 495–498

BIOCENTRISM

Endangered Species Act, 21

Marine mammals, 21–22

Protection vs. use of natural resources, 12–16

BIODIVERSITY

Generally, 320–440

Aesthetic values, 332, 333

Agriculture and food security, 331

Captive breeding, 344

Convention on Biological Diversity, 341

Defined, 321–323

BIODIVERSITY—Cont'd
Drugs and medicine, 331
Ecosystem diversity, 322
Ecosystem services, 18, 331–332
Endangered Species Act, this index
English game laws, 342–343
Existence values, 332
Extinction and extinction rate, 323–330
Forests, 1254–1272
Genetic diversity, 322
Intrinsic values, 332
Landscape management, 344
Market instruments, 344
Market values, 331
Non-market values, 331–332
Option values, 332
Ownership of wildlife, 338–342
Policy instruments
    Generally, 342–348
    English game laws, 342–343
    Landscape management and captive breeding, 344
    Market instruments, 344
    Restriction of access and take, 343–344
    Restriction of market for sale, 344–345
Population diversity, 322
Reasons to preserve biodiversity, 330–338
Restriction of access and take, 343–344
Restriction of market for sale, 344–345
Species diversity, 322
Spiritual values, 332
Traditional uses of wildlife, 331
Utilitarianism, 333

BIOPROSPECTING
National parks, 614–615

BONDS
Surface Mining Control And Reclamation Act, 1186

BOUNDARY WATERS CANOE AREA WILDERNESS ACT
Federal power to manage natural resources, 158–162

BUREAU OF INDIAN AFFAIRS
Mission and organization, 218

BUREAU OF LAND MANAGEMENT
Access across federal lands, impact of, 709–727
Creation, 140–141, 212
Exchange of federal lands for private lands, 144–145
Federal Land Policy Management Act, this index
History, 294–297
Mining, 1084–1087, 1097–1099
Mission and organization, 215–216
Multiple use lands, 673–687
National monuments, 634–635
Public land planning, 294–297, 298–317
Public Rangelands Improvement Act, 954–974
Rangeland planning, 950–972
Rulemaking, 225
Wilderness, 642–644
Withdrawal authority under Federal Land Policy Management Act, 687–692

BUREAU OF RECLAMATION
Generally, 212
Mission and organization, 218

BYCATCH
Fisheries, 451–452
Magnuson–Stevens Fishery Conservation and Management Act, national standards, 501–504

CALIFORNIA GOLD RUSH
Generally, 1024–1025

CAPTIVE BREEDING
Biodiversity, 344

CAPTURE RULE
Groundwater, 815–816

CAREY ACT
Federal disposition of land, 123

CATEGORICAL EXCLUSIONS
Environmental impact statements, 263, 274–275

CATEGORIES OF NATURE
Generally, 5–9

CITIZEN SUITS
Administrative agencies, 239–241
Endangered Species Act, 240
Federal Land Policy Management Act, 240
National Environmental Policy Act, 240
Surface Mining Control And Reclamation Act, 1188

CLASSIFICATION AND MULTIPLE USE ACT
Rangelands, 950–951

CLEAN WATER ACT
Generally, 851–868
Logging in private forests, 1308–1309
Rangelands, 1011–1012

CLEARCUTTING
Forests, 1212–1213, 1246–1252

CLIMATE CHANGE
Endangered Species Act, 381–384
Fisheries, collapse of, 454–455
Forests, 1208
Minerals, 1027–1030
Scientific uncertainty, 43–45

CLINTON, WILLIAM
National monuments, 625–636

COAL BED METHANE
Generally, 1067–1076

COASTAL ZONE MANAGEMENT ACT
Resource planning on public lands, 293

COLLABORATION
Rangelands, 978–980

COLORADO RIVER
Water allocation, 890–900

COMMAND–AND–CONTROL REGULA-TION
Management of natural resources, 71–72

COMMERCE CLAUSE
Management of natural resources, 163–168, 173–184

COMMON VARIETIES ACT
Minerals, 1147–1150

COMMONS, PROBLEMS OF THE
Generally, 39–41, 45–47

COMMUNITIES OF INTEREST
Water, 749–751

COMPACTION
Forests, impacts of logging, 1214–1215

COMPACTS AMONG STATES
Water, 884–887

CONCESSIONS
National parks, 615–617

CONSENSUS
Rangelands, 978–980

CONSERVATION EASEMENTS
Generally, 729–730, 734–736

CONSERVATION INTERNATIONAL
Market actors, 238

CONSTITUTIONAL LAW
Administrative agencies, 212–214
Management of natural resources, 146–184
Property Clause of U.S. Constitution, this index

CONTEST PROCEEDINGS
Minerals, 1135–1139

CONVENTION ON BIOLOGICAL DI-VERSITY
Generally, 341

COOPERATIVE ENDANGERED SPE-CIES CONSERVATION FUND
Land protected, 669

COOPERATIVE FORESTRY ASSIS-TANCE ACT
Logging in private forests, 1309

COOPERATIVE MANAGEMENT AGREEMENT PROGRAM
Rangelands, 984–988

CORAL REEFS
Sri Lanka, mining in, 11–12

CORRELATIVE RIGHTS
Groundwater, 816–817

COST–BENEFIT ANALYSIS
Ecosystem services, use and non-use values, 19–20, 24–26

COUNCIL ON ENVIRONMENTAL QUALITY
Mission and organization, 218

CULTURAL VALUES
Forests, 1209, 1216–1227
Land protected, 586

CUMULATIVE IMPACT
National Environmental Policy Act, environmental impact statements (EIS), 267–273

CUSTOMS
Logging, 1216–1227

CYANIDE HEAP–LEACH MINING
Generally, 1040–1041, 1183–1184

DAMS
Generally, 755–758

DDT
Natural, defined, 3
Utilitarianism, 17–18

DEBT–FOR–NATURE SWAPS
Land protected, 736–737

DECLARATION OF INDEPENDENCE
History of natural resources law, 80

DEEP ECOLOGY
Protection vs. use of natural resources, 12–13, 22–23, 26

DEFERENCE
Administrative Procedure Act, 227–230

DEFORESTATION
Generally, 1196–1203

DELHI SANDS FLOWER–LOVING FLY
Endangered Species Act, 426–440

DEPARTMENT OF THE INTERIOR
Generally, 210

DERBY FISHING
Generally, 466–467

DESERT LAND ACT
Generally, 829
Federal disposition of land, 123

DEVILS' TOWER
Federal power to manage natural resources, 203–207

DIAMOND CARTEL
Generally, 1035

DOLPHINS
Tuna fishery, 565–576

DRUGS
Biodiversity, 331

EARTH DAY
Generally, 237

ECOSYSTEM SERVICES
Biodiversity, 18, 331–332
Forests, 1206–1211
Management of natural resources, 37, 65–66
Protection vs. use of natural resources, 18–20
Water, use and non-use values, 18

ECOTOURISM
Generally, 595–596

ELITISM
Wilderness, 645–646

ELK
Yellowstone National Park, 3, 9

EMERGENCIES
National Environmental Policy Act, environmental impact statements (EIS), 286–288

EMERSON, RALPH WALDO
Wilderness, 30, 579

ENCLAVE CLAUSE OF U.S. CONSTITUTION
History of natural resources law, equal footing doctrine, 98–99, 102

ENDANGERED SPECIES ACT
Generally, 348–440
Adverse modification of critical habitat, 369–384
Biocentrism, 21
Citizen suits, 240
Conservation, 366–369
Consultation, 369–384
Designation of critical habitat, 362–366
Direct vs. indirect takes, 386–404
Federal power to manage natural resources, 174–183, 194
Habitat conservation plans, 418–424
Incentives for protection, 417–424
Incidental take permits, 418–424
Jeopardy, 369–384
Listing, 349–362
Logging in private forests, 1308
No Surprises policy, 418–424
Northern Spotted Owl, this index
Petition for listing, 350
Prairie dogs, 353–354
Prohibition against takes, 384–409
Rangelands, 1013–1014
Resource planning on public lands, 293
Safe Harbors policy, 418–424
Salmon, 354–362
Standing to sue, 244–254
Vicarious takes, 409–417
Water, 870–881

ENVIRONMENTAL AUDITS
Mining on public lands, mechanics of claim transactions, 1146

ENVIRONMENTAL IMPACT STATEMENTS
National Environmental Policy Act, this index

ENVIRONMENTAL LAW ALLIANCE WORLDWIDE
Nongovernmental organizations, 239

ENVIRONMENTAL LAW INSTITUTE
Think tanks and expert analysis, 238

ENVIRONMENTAL PROTECTION AGENCY
Mission and organization, 217–218

EQUAL FOOTING DOCTRINE
History of natural resources law, 96–104

EQUITABLE ALLOCATION
Water, 882–884

EXHAUSTION OF REMEDIES
Administrative agencies, nongovernmental organizations (NGOs), 257

EXPERT ANALYSIS
Administrative agencies, 238

EXTINCTION AND EXTINCTION RATE
Biodiversity, 323–330

FARM AND RANCH LANDS PROTECTION PROGRAM
Generally, 669

FARMABLE WETLANDS PROGRAM
Generally, 669

FEDERAL INSECTICIDE, FUNGICIDE, AND RODENTICIDE ACT
Citizen suits, 240

FEDERAL LAND POLICY MANAGEMENT ACT
Generally, 139, 141
Citizen suits, 240
Exchange of federal lands for private lands, 144
National parks, 604
Rangelands, 952–954, 959–962, 972–974
Resource planning on public lands, 293, 297–319
Withdrawal authority, multiple use lands, 687–696

FEDERAL LANDS RECREATION ENHANCEMENT ACT
Generally, 597

FEDERAL MINE SAFETY AND HEALTH ACT
Generally, 1031–1032

FEES
Rangelands, 975–977

FENCES
Rangelands, history of efforts to control western rangelands, 937–939

FIRES AND FIRE SUPPRESSION
Forest Service, 3
Forests, 1281–1293
Yellowstone national park, 3–4

FISHERIES
Generally, 441–528
Aquaculture, 476–478
Area restrictions, 467
Bycatch, 451–452
Capacity reduction, 468–469
Catch restrictions, 466
Climate change, collapse of fisheries, 454–455
Collapse of fisheries
Generally, 442–457
Bycatch, 451–452
Causes, 449–457
Climate change, 454–455
Habitat loss and degradation, 452–453
Invasive species, 453–454
Land-based marine pollution, 452–453, 455–456
Overfishing and overcapitalization, 450
Subsidies, 450–451
Community development quotas, 471–473
Derby fishing, 466–467
Entry restrictions, 466
Equipment restrictions, 468
Exclusive economic zones, 478–482
Fishing license retirement, 468
Gear retirement, 468
Habitat loss and degradation, collapse of fisheries, 452–453
Individual fishing quotas, 469
Individual transferable quotas, 469–473
Invasive species, 453–454
Land-based marine pollution, 452–453, 455–456
Limited access privilege programs, 469–476
Magnuson–Stevens Fishery Conservation and Management Act, this index
Management tools
Generally, 466–478
Aquaculture, 476–478
Area restrictions, 467
Capacity reduction, 468–469
Catch restrictions, 466
Community development quotas, 471–473
Derby fishing, 466–467
Entry restrictions, 466
Equipment restrictions, 468
Fishing license retirement, 468
Gear retirement, 468
Individual fishing quotas, 469
Individual transferable quotas, 469–473
Limited access privilege programs, 469–476
Restrictions, 466–468
Seasonal restrictions, 466
Vessel buyback schemes, 468
Overfishing and overcapitalization, 450
Restrictions, management tools, 466–468
Science of fisheries, 457–466
Seasonal restrictions, 466
Subsidies, collapse of fisheries, 450–451
United Nations Convention on the Law of the Sea, 478–482
Vessel buyback schemes, 468

FOOD SECURITY
Biodiversity, 331

FOREIGN COUNTRIES
Mineral development, 1041–1043

FOREST LEGACY PROGRAM
Generally, 668–669

FOREST STEWARDSHIP PROGRAM
Generally, 669

FORESTS
Generally, 1194–1309
Air quality, 1207–1208
Biodiversity conservation, 1254–1272
Biological diversity, 1208
Clearcutting, 1212–1213, 1246–1252
Climate regulation and carbon sequestration, 1208
Compaction, impacts of logging, 1214–1215
Cultural values, 1209, 1216–1227
Customs, logging, 1216–1227
Deforestation, 1196–1203
Economics of logging in national forests, 1293–1300
Ecosystem services, 1206–1211
Environmental impacts of logging, 1214–1216
Fire, 1281–1293
History of federal forestry law, 1228–1240
Local timber economies, logging, 1216–1227
Logging
Generally, 1211–1227
Clearcutting, 1212–1213
Customs, cultures and local timber economies, 1216–1227
Environmental impacts, 1214–1216
Methods, 1211–1213
National parks, 615
Seed tree harvesting, 1212
Selection harvesting, 1213–1214
Shelterwood harvesting, 1212
Soil erosion and compaction, 1214–1215
Water, impact on, 1215
Wildlife habitat, impact on, 1215–1216
Multiple Use and Sustained Yield Act, 1233–1234, 1238, 1241
National Forest Management Act. National forests, below, 1241 et seq.
National forests
Generally, 1227–1300
Biodiversity conservation, 1254–1272
Citizen suits, 240
Clearcutting, 1246–1252
Economics of logging in national forests, 1293–1300
Fire, 1281–1293
History of federal forestry law, 1228–1240
History of natural resources law, 131–133
Land and resource management plans, National Forest Management Act, 1241–1246
Minerals, 1085
Modern management law, policies and practices, 1240–1293
Multiple Use and Sustained Yield Act, 1233–1234, 1238, 1241

FORESTS—Cont'd
National Forest Management Act, 1241 et seq.
Prescribed burns, 1283, 1289
Resource planning on public lands, 293, 297–319
Roads, construction of, 1272–1281
Wilderness, 640–642
Non-timber commercial forest products, 1209
Old growth timber, 1200, 1202
Prescribed burns, 1283, 1289
Private forests
Generally, 1300–1309
Acquisition of timber rights, 1300–1308
Regulation of logging, 1308–1317
Rainforests, 1196–1197, 1205
Recreation and tourism, 1208–1209
Roads, construction in national forests, 1272–1281
Seed tree harvesting, 1212
Selection harvesting, 1213–1214
Shelterwood harvesting, 1212
Soil erosion and stabilization, 1207, 1214–1215
Spiking of trees, 1201–1202, 1206
U.S. forest resources, 1198–1206
Water, impact of logging on, 1215
Watershed services, 1207
Wildlife habitat, impact of logging on, 1215–1216
Worldwide forest resources, 1196–1197

FOUR–WHEEL DRIVE VEHICLES
National parks, 604–612

FREE EXERCISE AND ESTABLISH-MENT CLAUSE
Management of natural resources, 201–207

FRIENDS OF THE EARTH–INTERNATIONAL
Nongovernmental organizations, 239

GENERAL LAND OFFICE
Generally, 210, 212, 213

GENERAL MINING LAW
Minerals, this index

GENETIC DIVERSITY
Biodiversity, 322

GIANT SEQUOIA NATIONAL MONUMENT
Generally, 629–631

GRAND CANYON
Antiquities Act, 621–623

GRAND CANYON TRUST
Retirement of grazing permits, 1005–1011

GRAND STAIRCASE–ESCALANTE NATIONAL MONUMENT
Generally, 625–627

GRAZING SERVICE
Generally, 212

GREENPEACE
Nongovernmental organizations, 239

GRIZZLY BEARS
Endangered Species Act, 380–381, 404

GROUNDWATER
Water, this index

HARMON DOCTRINE
Water, 901–902

HETCH HETCHY DAM
Yosemite National Park, 32

HISTORY OF NATURAL RESOURCES LAW
Generally, 80–207
Acquisition of public lands
Generally, 82–94
European powers, 84–87
Indian tribes, 87–94
Western land claims, states with, 83–84
Allocation of public lands and natural resources
Generally, 94–115
Equal footing doctrine, 96–104
Public trust doctrine, 104–115
American Revolution, 80
Declaration of Independence, 80
Enclave Clause of U.S. Constitution, equal footing doctrine, 98–99, 102
Equal footing doctrine, 96–104
European powers, acquisition of public lands from, 84–87
Federal disposition of resources
Generally, 115–129
Homesteads, 121–123
Jeffersonian survey system, 116–118
Railroads, land grants to, 125–126
Settlors, land grants to, 119–125
Squatters, 120–121
States, land grants to, 118–119
Federal retention of resources
Generally, 129–146
Decision to retain public domain lands, 139–141
Early federal retention and national parks, 129–130
Geographic legacy of federal policy, 141
National forests, 131–133
National wildlife refuges and executive withdrawals, 133–139
Geographic legacy of federal policy, 141
Homesteads, 121–123
Indian tribes, acquisition of public lands from, 87–94
Jeffersonian survey system, 116–118
Management of Natural Resources, this index
Morrill Act, equal footing doctrine, 97
National forests, 131–133
National wildlife refuges and executive withdrawals, 133–139
Navigable waters, ownership of land under, 97–103, 104–115
Property Clause of U.S. Constitution, equal footing doctrine, 98
Public trust doctrine, 104–115
Railroads, land grants to, 125–126
Settlors, land grants to, 119–125
Squatters, 120–121

HISTORY OF NATURAL RESOURCES LAW—Cont'd
States, land grants to, 118–119
Washington tidelands, Indian treaty rights, 111–115
Western land claims, states with, 83–84

HOMESTEADS
History of natural resources law, 121–123

HYDROLOGIC CYCLE
Generally, 741–742

INCIDENTAL TAKE PERMITS
Endangered Species Act, 418–424

INDIAN TRIBES
Acquisition of public lands from tribes, 87–94
Water, 830–851

INDIVIDUAL FISHING QUOTAS
Generally, 469

INDIVIDUAL TRANSFERABLE QUOTAS
Generally, 469–473

INFORMATION BULLETINS
Administrative Procedure Act, 225

INSPECTIONS
Surface Mining Control And Reclamation Act, 1187

INSTRUCTION MEMORANDA
Administrative Procedure Act, 225

INTERGOVERNMENTAL PANEL ON CLIMATE CHANGE
Generally, 1028

INTERNATIONAL CONVENTION ON THE REGULATION OF WHALING
Generally, 531–543

INTERNATIONAL LAW
Water, this index

INTERNATIONAL UNION FOR THE CONSERVATION OF NATURE
Nongovernmental organizations, 238–239

INTERPRETATIVE RULES
Administrative Procedure Act, 225

INVASIVE SPECIES
Fisheries, 453–454

IZEMBEK NATIONAL WILDLIFE REFUGE
Generally, 661–662

JEFFERSONIAN SURVEY SYSTEM
Generally, 116–118

JEOPARDY
Endangered Species Act, 369–384

JUDICIAL REVIEW
Administrative Procedure Act, this index
Surface Mining Control And Reclamation Act, 1189

JURISDICTION
Management of natural resources, 56–57

KNUTSEN–VANDENBERG ACT
Reforestation of logged lands, 1239–1240

LACEY ACT
Generally, 347

LAKE TAHOE
Moratorium on development, 195–197

LAND AND WATER CONSERVATION ACT
Generally, 33

LAND AND WATER CONSERVATION FUND
Generally, 667–673

LAND PROTECTED
Generally, 577–738
Alternatives to preservation, 727–738
Bureau of Land Management, this index
Conservation easements, 729–730, 734–736
Cooperative Endangered Species Conservation Fund, 669
Cultural documentation, preservation as, 586
Darker side of preservation, 591–595
Debt-for-nature swaps, 736–737
Ecological case for preservation, 586–588
Economic case for preservation, 582–586
Ecotourism, 595–596
Farm and Ranch Lands Protection Program, 669
Farmable Wetlands Program, 669
Federal Land Policy Management Act withdrawal authority, multiple use lands, 687–696
Federal reacquisition of land and resources, 667–673
Forest Legacy Program, 668–669
Forest Stewardship Program, 669
Historical documentation, preservation as, 586
Impact of access on preservation
    Generally, 696–727
    Federal lands, access to private and state property across, 699–707
    Obtaining access to inholdings, 724–727
    Road construction, 707–724
Land and Water Conservation Fund, 667–673
Land trusts, 729–732, 733–734
Migratory Bird Conservation Fund, 668
Moral case for preservation, 588–591
Multiple use lands
    Generally, 673–696
    Defined, 673–674
    Federal Land Policy Management Act withdrawal authority, 687–696
    Utah Settlement Agreement, 684–687
National Monuments, this index
National Parks, this index
National Wildlife Refuge System, 662–665
North American Wetland Conservation Act, 668
Partners for Fish and Wildlife Program, 669–670

LAND PROTECTED—Cont'd
Preservation, case for, 582–599
Private Stewardship Grants Program, 669
Rangelands, this index
Road construction, 707–724
State parks, 727–728
Urban and suburban parks, 728–729, 737
Utah Settlement Agreement, multiple use lands, 684–687
Wetlands Reserve Program, 669
Wild and Scenic Rivers Act, 665–667
Wilderness, this index
Wildlands Project, 587–588

LAND TRUSTS
Generally, 729–732, 733–734

LANDSCAPE MANAGEMENT
Biodiversity, 344

LEASES
Minerals, this index

LISTING
Endangered Species Act, 349–362

LOBBYING
Legislative and administrative action, nongovernmental organizations (NGOs), 237–239

LODE AND PLACER CLAIMS
Minerals, 1087–1094

LOGGING
Forests, this index

LOS ANGELES
Water and public trust doctrine, 797–810

MAGNUSON–STEVENS FISHERY CONSERVATION AND MANAGEMENT ACT
Generally, 482–528
Anthropocentrism, 21
Best scientific information, conservation measures based on (National Standard Two), 495–498
Bycatch and bycatch mortality, minimization of (National Standard Nine), 501–504
Ecosystem management, 513–517
Essential fish habitats, 515–517
Fishery Management Plans, 488–493
Fishing communities, consideration of impact on (National Standard Eight), 499–501
National standards
　　Generally, 494–511
　　Best scientific information, conservation measures based on (National Standard Two), 495–498
　　Bycatch and bycatch mortality, minimization of (National Standard Nine), 501–504
　　Conflicts between standards, 504–511
　　Fishing communities, consideration of impact on (National Standard Eight), 499–501

MAGNUSON–STEVENS FISHERY CONSERVATION AND MANAGEMENT ACT—Cont'd
National standards—Cont'd
　　Prevention of overfishing and achievement of optimum yield (National Standard One), 495, 498
Optimum yield, achievement of (National Standard One), 495, 498
Overfishing, prevention of (National Standard One), 495, 498
Rebuilding of stocks, 511–513
Red snapper fishery, 518–528
Regional Fishery Management Councils, 486–488
Resource planning on public lands, 292

MANAGEMENT OF NATURAL RESOURCES
Generally, 36–79
Arctic National Wildlife Refuge, case study, 67–69
Beachfront management, takings clause, 185–200
Biophysical scale, 51–52
Clash of values among competing interests, 38–39
Coastal management, takings clause, 185–200
Command-and-control regulation, 71–72
Commerce Clause, 163–168, 173–184
Commons, problems of the, 39–41, 45–47
Constitutional power, 146–184
Ecosystem services, 37, 65–66
Extractive resources, scarcity, 36–37
Federal power
　　Generally, 146–207
　　Coastal and beachfront management, takings clause, 185–200
　　Commerce Clause, 163–168, 173–184
　　Constitutional power, 146–184
　　Free Exercise and Establishment Clause, limitation of, 201–207
　　Property Clause of U.S. Constitution, 148–162
　　Sagebrush Rebellion, 156–162
　　Takings Clause, limitation of, 184–201
　　Treaty power, 168–172
Financial penalties, 73
Free Exercise and Establishment Clause, limitation of, 201–207
Institutional inadequacy, 60–67
Jurisdiction and ownership, relationship between, 56–57
Market forces and market failures, 41–43, 47–49
Nonrenewable resources, scarcity, 36–37
Ownership and jurisdiction, relationship between, 56–57
Political scale, 52–57
Prescriptive regulation, 71–73
Privatization of parks, case study, 77–79
Property Clause of U.S. Constitution, 148–162
Property rights, 70–71
Public choice theory, 61–67
Public disclosure and persuasion, 74
Quincy Library Group, 58–60

**MANAGEMENT OF NATURAL RE-
SOURCES**—Cont'd
Renewable resources, scarcity, 37
Sagebrush Rebellion, 156–162
Scales
    Generally, 51–60
    Biophysical scale, 51–52
    Ownership and jurisdiction, relationship
        between, 56–57
    Political scale, 52–57
    Quincy Library Group, 58–60
    Temporal scale, 57–58
Scarcity, 36–38
Scientific uncertainty, 43–45, 49–51
Spiritual or aesthetic resources, 37–38
Subsidies, 41–42, 49, 73–74, 75
Sustainable development, 66–67
Takings Clause, limitation of, 184–201
Temporal scale, 57–58
Tools of management, 69–77
Tradable permits, 72–73
Treaty power, 168–172

MARINE MAMMALS
    Generally, 528–576
Biocentrism, 21–22
Conflicts with fisheries, 549–576
Dolphin mortality in tuna fishery, 565–576
Marine Mammal Protection Act
    Generally, 348, 549–576
    Biocentrism, 21–22
Pinnipeds and salmon fishery, 557–565
Porpoises, 550–551
Territorial reach of Marine Mammal Protec-
    tion Act, 556
Whales, this index

MARINE RESOURCES
    Generally, 441–576
Fisheries, this index
Marine Mammals, this index

MARKET ANALYSIS
Mining on public lands, mechanics of claim
    transactions, 1145

MARKET INSTRUMENTS
Biodiversity, 344

MARKET VALUES
Biodiversity, 331

MARKETABILITY TEST
Minerals, discovery of valuable minerals,
    1123–1126

MASTER TITLE AND USE PLATS
Minerals, 1086

MEDICINE
Biodiversity, 331

**MIGRATORY BIRD CONSERVATION
FUND**
Generally, 668

MIGRATORY BIRD TREATY ACT
    Generally, 347
Federal power to manage natural resources,
    168–172

MILL SITES
Minerals, 1094–1095

MINERALS
    Generally, 1021–1193
Alluvial valley floors, Surface Mining Control
    And Reclamation Act, 1188–1189
Amendment, staking claims, 1102–1103
Assessment work, staking claims, 1103–1111
Bonds, Surface Mining Control And Reclama-
    tion Act, 1186
Broad form deeds, 1046–1055
Bureau of Land Management, 1084–1087,
    1097–1099
California gold rush, 1024–1025
Challenges to mining claims, 1135–1139
Citizen complaints, Surface Mining Control
    And Reclamation Act, 1188
Citizen suits, Surface Mining Control And
    Reclamation Act, 1188
Climate change, 1027–1030
Coal bed methane, 1067–1076
Coal leasing, Mineral Leasing Act, 1160–1167
Common Varieties Act, 1147–1150
Concentration of ore, 1038
Contest proceedings, 1135–1139
Cyanide heap–leach mining, 1040–1041,
    1183–1184
Defining mineral resources
    Generally, 1059–1077
    Coal bed methane, 1067–1076
    Drafting of mineral lease, 1076–1077
Development methods, 1036–1041
Discovery of valuable minerals
    Generally, 1122–1135
    Marketability test, 1123–1126
    Present vs. prospective value, 1126–1130
    Prudent person test, 1122–1123
Drafting of mineral lease, 1076–1077
Economics, 1033–1036
Enforcement, Surface Mining Control And
    Reclamation Act, 1187
Environmental cost, 1030–1031
Environmental regulation
    Generally, 1170–1193
    Coal mining. Surface Mining Control And
        Reclamation Act, below
    Federal regulation of hard rock mining,
        1170–1174
    Hard rock mining, 1170–1185
    State regulation of hard rock mining,
        1174–1183
Federal disposition of land, 124–125
Fish and wildlife refuges, 1086
Foreign countries, mineral development in,
    1041–1043
General Mining Law. Public lands, below
History of mining, 1024–1030
Inspections, Surface Mining Control And
    Reclamation Act, 1187
Judicial review, Surface Mining Control And
    Reclamation Act, 1189
Leases or minerals. Sales and leases of miner-
    als, below
Location requirements, staking claims,
    1100–1101
Lode and placer claims, 1087–1094

MINERALS—Cont'd

Marketability test, discovery of valuable minerals, 1123–1126

Master title and use plats, 1086

Mill sites, 1094–1095

Mineral Leasing Act

Generally, 1153–1168

Coal leasing, 1160–1167

Federal retention of resources, 143

Onshore oil and gas leasing, 1154–1160

Phosphates, oil shale, sodium, sulfur and potash, 1167–1168

Mountaintop removal, Surface Mining Control And Reclamation Act, 1190–1192

Multiple mineral development, 1168–1169

National forests, 1085

National parks and monuments, 1084–1085

Notation rule, 1086–1087

Oil shale, Mineral Leasing Act, 1167–1168

Onshore oil and gas leasing, Mineral Leasing Act, 1154–1160

Open pit mines, 1021–1022

Ownership of minerals

Generally, 1043–1059

Broad form deeds, 1046–1055

Estates in land, generally, 1043–1046

Split estates, 1055–1059

Patents, 1139–1144

Pedis possessio, 1119–1122

Penalties, Surface Mining Control And Reclamation Act, 1187–1188

Performance standards, Surface Mining Control And Reclamation Act, 1187

Permits, Surface Mining Control And Reclamation Act, 1186

Phosphates, Mineral Leasing Act, 1167–1168

Placer and lode claims, 1087–1094

Pooling agreements, 1036–1037

Potash, Mineral Leasing Act, 1167–1168

Present vs. prospective value, discovery of valuable minerals, 1126–1130

Prime farmlands, Surface Mining Control And Reclamation Act, 1188–1189

Protest proceedings, 1135–1139

Prudent person test, discovery of valuable minerals, 1122–1123

Public lands

Generally, 1077–1146

Challenges to mining claims, 1135–1139

Contest proceedings, 1135–1139

Discovery of valuable minerals, above

Fish and wildlife refuges, 1086

General Mining Law, 1077 et seq.

Location, lands open to, 1084–1087

Lode and placer claims, 1087–1094

Master title and use plats, 1086

Mechanics of claim transactions, 1145–1146

Mill sites, 1094–1095

National forests, 1085

National parks and monuments, 1084–1085

Notation rule, 1086–1087

Patents, 1139–1144

Pedis possessio, 1119–1122

Protest proceedings, 1135–1139

MINERALS—Cont'd

Public lands—Cont'd

Sales and leases of minerals, below

Staking claims, below

Tunnel sites, 1094

Types of mining claims, 1087–1097

Wild and scenic rivers, 1085

Wilderness areas, 1085

Public participation, Surface Mining Control And Reclamation Act, 1188

Recording requirements, staking claims, 1100–1101, 1111–1119

Relocation, staking claims, 1102–1103

Sales and leases of minerals

Generally, 1146–1169

Common Varieties Act, 1147–1150

Mineral Leasing Act, above

Multiple mineral development, 1168–1169

Surface Resources Act, 1150–1153

Separation of metals, 1038–1039

Sodium, Mineral Leasing Act, 1167–1168

Split estates, 1055–1059

Sri Lanka, coral reefs, 11–12

Staking claims

Generally, 1097–1119

Amendment and relocation, 1102–1103

Assessment work, 1103–1111

Federal and state standards, 1097–1102

Location requirements, 1100–1101

Recording requirements, 1100–1101, 1111–1119

State regulation of hard rock mining, 1174–1183

Steep slopes, Surface Mining Control And Reclamation Act, 1188–1189

Sulfur, Mineral Leasing Act, 1167–1168

Surface mining, generally, 1037, 1039–1040

Surface Mining Control and Reclamation Act

Generally, 1053–1054, 1186–1193

Bonds, 1186

Citizen suits, 1188

Enforcement, 1187

Inspections, 1187

Judicial review, 1189

Mountaintop removal, 1190–1192

Penalties, 1187–1188

Performance standards, 1187

Permits, 1186

Public participation/citizen complaints, 1188

Steep slopes, prime farmlands and alluvial valley floors, 1188–1189

Unsuitability designations, 1188

Whistleblower protection, 1189

Surface Resources Act, 1150–1153

Tunnel sites, 1094

Underground mining, 1037–1038

Unitization agreements, 1037

Unsuitability designations, Surface Mining Control And Reclamation Act, 1188

Water, 777–779, 1145

Whistleblower protection, Surface Mining Control And Reclamation Act, 1189

Wild and scenic rivers, 1085

Wilderness areas, 660–661, 1085

Worker safety, 1031–1033

MINERALS MANAGEMENT SERVICE
Mission and organization, 218

MONO LAKE
Los Angeles, water and public trust doctrine, 799–809

MORRILL ACT
Equal footing doctrine, 97

MOUNTAINTOP REMOVAL
Surface Mining Control And Reclamation Act, 1190–1192

MUIR, JOHN
Wilderness, 31–32, 34–35, 580–581

MULTIPLE USE AND SUSTAINED YIELD ACT
Forests, 1233–1234, 1238, 1241

MULTIPLE USE LANDS
Land Protected, this index

NATIONAL AUDOBON SOCIETY
Generally, 236, 238

NATIONAL ENVIRONMENTAL POLICY ACT
Generally, 258–292
Alternatives analysis, environmental impact statements (EIS), 278–285
Citizen suits, 240
Council on Environmental Quality, 259–260
Cumulative impact, environmental impact statements (EIS), 267–273
Emergencies, environmental impact statements (EIS), 286–288
Environmental impact statements (EIS)
Generally, 258–292
Adequacy of analysis, 285–288
Alternatives analysis, 278–285
Cumulative impact, 267–273
Elements of EIS, 277–288
Emergencies, 286–288
Environmental assessments, 263
Finding of no significant impact, 263
Major actions, 266–277
Natural disasters and scientific uncertainty, 286–288
Record of decision, 263–264
Requirement for preparation of EIS, 262–277
Scale of proposed action and tiering, 265–266
Scope of agency action, 266–277
Supplemental EISs, 288–290
Timing, 264–265
Evolution of act, 261–262
Natural disasters, environmental impact statements (EIS), 286–288
Oil and gas leases, 1158–1159
Rangelands, 951–952, 962–968, 972–974
Record of decision, environmental impact statements (EIS), 263–264
Scientific uncertainty, environmental impact statements (EIS), 286–288
Supplemental environmental impact statements, 288–290
Timing of environmental impact statements, 264–265

NATIONAL FORESTS
Forests, this index

NATIONAL HISTORIC PRESERVATION ACT
Generally, 33
Federal power to manage natural resources, 202–203

NATIONAL MARINE FISHERIES SERVICE
Mission and organization, 217

NATIONAL MONUMENTS
Generally, 619–636
Antiquities Act, 620–625
Bureau of Land Management, 634–635
Minerals, 1084–1085
President Clinton, 625–636

NATIONAL PARKS
Generally, 599–619
Bioprospecting, 614–615
Concessions within parks, 615–617
Federal Land Policy Management Act, 604
Four-wheel drive vehicle usage, 604–612
Logging, 615
Minerals, 1084–1085
National Park Service, 212, 216
Park Service Organic Act, 601–603
Snowmobiles, 617–619
Yellowstone National Park. this index

NATIONAL WILD AND SCENIC RIVERS SYSTEM
Generally, 33

NATIONAL WILDERNESS PRESERVATION SYSTEM
Generally, 637–638

NATIONAL WILDLIFE FEDERATION
Generally, 236

NATIONAL WILDLIFE REFUGES
History of natural resources law, 133–139
Minerals, 1086
National Wildlife Refuge Improvement Act, resource planning on public lands, 293
National Wildlife Refuge System, 662–665

NATIVE AMERICAN GRAVES PROTECTION AND REPATRIATION ACT
Federal power to manage natural resources, 202

NATURAL
Defined, 2–11

NATURAL DISASTERS
National Environmental Policy Act, environmental impact statements (EIS), 286–288

NATURAL RESOURCES CONSERVATION SERVICE
Mission and organization, 218–219

NATURE COMPANY
Advertisements, 10–11

NATURE CONSERVANCY
Market actors, 238

NAVIGABLE WATERS
History of natural resources law, 97–103, 104–115

NAVY SONAR
Marine Mammal Protection Act, 552–555

NILE RIVER BASIN
Generally, 908–912

NO SURPRISES POLICY
Endangered Species Act, 418–424

NONGOVERNMENTAL ORGANIZATIONS (NGOS)
Administrative Agencies, this index

NORTH AMERICAN WETLAND CONSERVATION ACT
Generally, 668

NORTH ATLANTIC MARINE MAMMAL COMMISSION
Whales, 534–526, 542–543

NORTHERN SPOTTED OWL
Generally, 230–234
Listing under Endangered Species Act, 350, 388
Logging ban, 1224, 1262
Political scale, 53, 62

NOTATION RULE
Minerals, 1086–1087

NOTICE
Administrative Procedure Act, 224–225

OFFICE OF SURFACE MINING REGULATION AND ENFORCEMENT SERVICE
Mission and organization, 218

OIL AND GAS LEASES
National Environmental Policy Act, 1158–1159

OIL SHALE
Mineral Leasing Act, 1167–1168

OLD GROWTH TIMBER
Generally, 1200, 1202

OPEN PIT MINES
Generally, 1021–1022

OPTIMUM YIELD
Magnuson–Stevens Fishery Conservation and Management Act, national standards, 495, 498

OPTION VALUES
Biodiversity, 332

ORGANIZATION OF PETROLEUM EXPORTING COUNTRIES
Generally, 1033–1034

OUTER CONTINENTAL SHELF LANDS ACT
Offshore gas and oil leasing, 1158

OVERFISHING AND OVERCAPITALIZATION
Generally, 450

OWLS
Northern Spotted Owl, this index
Pygmy owls, Endangered Species Act, 404–405

OWNERSHIP
Biodiversity, 338–342
Management of natural resources, 56–57
Minerals, this index

PAPAHNAUMOKUKEA MARINE NATIONAL MONUMENT
Generally, 635

PARTNERS FOR FISH AND WILDLIFE PROGRAM
Generally, 669–670

PATENTS
Minerals, 1139–1144

PAYMENT–IN–LIEU–OF–TAXES ACT
Federal retention of resources, 143

PCB
Inuit people, 3

PEDIS POSSESSIO
Minerals, 1119–1122

PENALTIES
Management of natural resources, 73
Surface Mining Control And Reclamation Act, 1187–1188

PERFORMANCE STANDARDS
Surface Mining Control And Reclamation Act, 1187

PERMITS
Surface Mining Control And Reclamation Act, 1186
Water, prior appropriation, 790–793

PERSONNEL
Mining on public lands, mechanics of claim transactions, 1146

PHOSPHATES
Mineral Leasing Act, 1167–1168

PIKAS
Endangered Species Act, 381–384

PINELAND NATIONAL RESERVE
Generally, 738

PINNIPEDS
Salmon fishery, 557–565

PLACER AND LODE CLAIMS
Minerals, 1087–1094

POLLINATION
Ecosystem services, use and non-use values, 18

POOLING AGREEMENTS
Minerals, 1036–1037

POPULATION DIVERSITY
Biodiversity, 322

PORPOISES
Generally, 550–551

POTASH
Mineral Leasing Act, 1167–1168

PRAIRIE DOGS
Endangered Species Act, 353–354

PRESCRIBED BURNS
Forests, 1283, 1289

PRIOR APPROPRIATION
Water, this index

PRIVATE ACTIONS
Citizen Suits, this index

PRIVATE STEWARDSHIP GRANTS PROGRAM
Generally, 669

PRIVATIZATION OF PARKS
Management of natural resources, 77–79

PROGRESSIVE CONSERVATION MOVEMENT
Generally, 211–212

PROPERTY CLAUSE OF U.S. CONSTITUTION
Equal footing doctrine, 98
Management of natural resources, 148–162

PROTECTION VS. USE OF NATURAL RESOURCES
Generally, 11–36
Anthropocentrism, 16–20
Biocentrism, 12–16
Deep ecology, 12–13, 22–23, 26
Ecosystem services, use and non-use values, 18–20
Intergenerational equity, 20–21
Land ethic, 13–16, 22–23
Sri Lanka, mining of coral reefs, 11–12
Utilitarianism, 16–19
Values, 21–22

PROTEST PROCEEDINGS
Minerals, 1135–1139

PRUDENT PERSON TEST
Minerals, discovery of valuable minerals, 1122–1123

PUBLIC CHOICE THEORY
Management of natural resources, 61–67

PUBLIC RANGELANDS IMPROVEMENT ACT
Generally, 954–974

PUBLIC TRUST DOCTRINE
History of natural resources law, 104–115

PYGMY OWLS
Endangered Species Act, 404–405

QUINCY LIBRARY GROUP
Management of natural resources, 58–60

RAILROADS
History of natural resources law, 125–126

RAINFORESTS
Generally, 1196–1197, 1205

RANGELANDS
Generally, 913–1020
Administrative regulations, 983–1005
Bureau of Land Management, 950–972
Clean Water Act, 1011–1012
Collaboration, 978–980
Consensus, 978–980
Cooperative Management Agreement Program, 984–988
Defined, 914–915
Early range planning efforts, 950–952
Endangered Species Act, 1013–1014
Federal Land Policy Management Act, 952–954, 959–962, 972–974
Fees and subsidies, 975–977
Fences, history of efforts to control western rangelands, 937–939
Goods and services, 915–917
Grand Canyon Trust and retirement of grazing permits, 1005–1011
History of efforts to control western rangelands
Generally, 934–949
Ending open access to public rangelands, 941–949
Fences, 937–939
Initial federal limitations on open access grazing, 939–941
Rise of ranching, 934–937
Taylor Grazing Act, 941–949
Impact of grazing, 917–925
Intersecting laws, 1011–1014
Local control, 978–980
National Environmental Policy Act, 951–952, 962–968, 972–974
Passions stirred by grazing on public lands, 925–934
Privatization of grazing permits, 977–978
Public Rangelands Improvement Act, 954–974
Reforms
Generally, 975–1011
Administrative regulations, 983–1005
Collaboration, consensus and local control, 978–980
Cooperative Management Agreement program, 984–988
Fees and subsidies, 975–977
Privatization of grazing permits, 977–978
Repurchase of range, 978

RANGELANDS—Cont'd
Repurchase of range, 978
State lands, 1015–1020
Subsidies and fees, 975–977
Sufficiency of statutes to protect rangelands, 972–974
Taylor Grazing Act, 941–950, 972–974, 989–999
Value of public lands for grazing, 974–975
Wild and Scenic Rivers Act, 1012–1013

REASONABLE USE
Water, 760–765, 816, 817

RECORDING REQUIREMENTS
Minerals, staking claims, 1100–1101, 1111–1119

RED SNAPPER
Magnuson–Stevens Fishery Conservation and Management Act, 518–528

REDRESSABILITY
Administrative agencies, standing to sue of nongovernmental organizations (NGOs), 243

REGIONAL FISHERY MANAGEMENT COUNCILS
Magnuson–Stevens Fishery Conservation and Management Act, 486–488

REGIONAL GREENHOUSE GAS INITIATIVE
Generally, 1029

RELIGIOUS FREEDOM RESTORATION ACT
Federal power to manage natural resources, 201–202
Mining on public lands, 1185

RESOURCES FOR THE FUTURE
Think tanks and expert analysis, 238

REVISED MANAGEMENT PROCEDURE
Whales, 534

RIO GRANDE RIVER
Transboundary watercourses, international law, 901–902

RIPARIAN RIGHTS
Generally, 758–767

RIPENESS
Administrative agencies, nongovernmental organizations (NGOs), 257

RIVERS AND HARBORS APPROPRIATION ACT OF 1890
Generally, 827

ROADLESS RULE
National forests, 1272–1281

ROADS
Construction of roads, 707–724
Forests, construction in national, 1272–1281

ROCKY MOUNTAIN ARSENAL
Generally, 4–5, 9

SACRED SITES, EXECUTIVE ORDER ON
Federal power to manage natural resources, 203

SAFE HARBORS POLICY
Endangered Species Act, 418–424

SAGEBRUSH REBELLION
Management of natural resources, 156–162

SALES
Minerals, this index

SALMON
Endangered Species Act, 354–362

SALTON SEA
Generally, 788–790

SCALES
Management of Natural Resources, this index

SCARCITY
Management of natural resources, 36–38

SCIENTIFIC UNCERTAINTY
Administrative agencies, resource planning on public lands, 293
Management of natural resources, 43–45, 49–51
National Environmental Policy Act, environmental impact statements (EIS), 286–288

SEED TREE HARVESTING
Forests, 1212

SELECTION HARVESTING
Forests, 1213–1214

SHELTERWOOD HARVESTING
Forests, 1212

SIERRA CLUB
Administrative agencies, 236, 238

SNAIL DARTER
Endangered Species Act, 369–370

SNAKE RIVER BASIN ADJUDICATION
Generally, 848–851

SNOWMOBILES
National parks, 617–619
Wilderness, 659

SODIUM
Mineral Leasing Act, 1167–1168

SOIL EROSION AND STABILIZATION
Forests, 1207, 1214–1215

SONORAN DESERT NATIONAL MONUMENT
Generally, 632

SPIKING OF TREES
Forests, 1201–1202, 1206

SPIRITUAL RESOURCES AND VALUES
Biodiversity, 332
Management of natural resources, 37–38

SPLIT ESTATES
Minerals, 1055–1059

SPORT UTILITY VEHICLES
Advertisements, 10

SQUATTERS
History of natural resources law, 120–121

SRI LANKA
Mining of coral reefs, 11–12

STAKING OF CLAIMS
Minerals, this index

STANDARD OF REVIEW
Administrative Procedure Act, 226–228

STANDING TO SUE
Administrative agencies, nongovernmental
   organizations (NGOs), 241–256,
   257–258
Endangered Species Act, 244–254

STATE PARKS
Generally, 727–728

STEEP SLOPES
Surface Mining Control And Reclamation
   Act, 1188–1189

SUBSIDIES
Fisheries, collapse of, 450–451
Management of natural resources, 41–42, 49,
   73–74, 75
Rangelands, 975–977

SUBURBAN AND URBAN PARKS
Generally, 728–729, 737

SULFUR
Mineral Leasing Act, 1167–1168

**SUPPLEMENTAL ENVIRONMENTAL
   IMPACT STATEMENTS**
Generally, 288–290

**SURFACE MINING CONTROL AND
   RECLAMATION ACT**
Minerals, this index

TAKINGS CLAUSE
Management of natural resources, 184–201

TAYLOR GRAZING ACT
Rangelands, 941–950, 972–974, 989–999

THINK TANKS
Administrative agencies, 238

THOREAU, HENRY DAVID
Wilderness, 30, 579

TIMBER AND STONE ACT
Federal disposition of land, 124

TIMBER CULTURE ACT
Federal disposition of land, 123

TITLE SEARCHES
Mining on public lands, mechanics of claim
   transactions, 1145

TRACEABILITY
Administrative agencies, standing to sue of
   nongovernmental   organizations
   (NGOs), 243

TRADABLE PERMITS
Management of natural resources, 72–73

TREATY POWER
Management of natural resources, 168–172

**TROPICAL FOREST CONSERVATION
   ACT**
Generally, 736–737

TRUSTS
Land trusts, 729–732, 733–734
Water trust, formation of, 797

TUNNEL SITES
Minerals, 1094

UNDERGROUND MINING
Generally, 1037–1038

**UNITED NATIONS CONVENTION ON
   THE LAW OF THE NON–NAVIGA-
   TIONAL USES OF INTERNATIONAL
   WATERCOURSES**
Generally, 904–908

**UNITED NATIONS CONVENTION ON
   THE LAW OF THE SEA**
Fisheries, 478–482

**UNITED NATIONS FRAMEWORK CON-
   VENTION ON CLIMATE CHANGE**
Generally, 1028–1029

UNITIZATION AGREEMENTS
Minerals, 1037

UNSUITABILITY DESIGNATIONS
Surface Mining Control And Reclamation
   Act, 1188

URBAN AND SUBURBAN PARKS
Generally, 728–729, 737

U–REGULATIONS
Wilderness, 637

U.S. ARMY CORPS OF ENGINEERS
Mission and organization, 217

U.S. FISH AND WILDLIFE SERVICE
Mission and organization, 216–217

U.S. FOREST SERVICE
Generally, 212, 213–214
Mission and organization, 214–215

U.S. GEOLOGICAL SERVICE
Mission and organization, 218

UTAH SETTLEMENT AGREEMENT
Multiple use lands, 684–687

UTILITARIANISM
Biodiversity, 333
Protection vs. use of natural resources, 16–19

VALLES CALDERA NATIONAL PRE-SERVE
Generally, 737–738

VESSEL BUYBACK SCHEMES
Fisheries, 468

VICARIOUS TAKES
Endangered Species Act, 409–417

WALDEN
Wilderness, case study, 30

WASHINGTON TIDELANDS
Indian treaty rights, 111–115

WATER
Generally, 739–912
Allocation of water
    Generally, 758–825
    Eastern permit systems, 758–760, 767–777
    Groundwater, below
    Prior appropriation, below
    Reasonable use theory, 760–765
    Riparian rights, 758–767
    States, allocation of water among, below
Capture rule, groundwater, 815–816
Clean Water Act, this index
Communities of interest, 749–751
Compacts among states, 884–887
Congressional allocation among states, 887–888
Consumptive and nonconsumptive uses, 748
Correlative rights, groundwater, 816–817
Dams, 755–758
Eastern permit systems, 758–760, 767–777
Ecosystem services, use and non-use values, 18
Endangered Species Act, 870–881
Equitable allocation among states, 882–884
Federalism
    Generally, 825–900
    Clean Water Act and wetlands, 851–868
    Endangered Species Act, 870–881
    Indian and federal reserved water rights, 830–851
    Intersecting federal statutes, 851–881
    Navigation servitude, 868–869
    States, allocation of water among, below
Fisheries, this index
Forests, impact of logging in, 1215
Groundwater
    Generally, 810–825
    Allocation of groundwater, 815–825
    Capture rule, 815–816
    Correlative rights, 816–817
    Prior appropriation, 817–821
    Reasonable use, 816, 817
Harmon Doctrine, 901–902
Hydrologic cycle, 741–742

WATER—Cont'd
Indian and federal reserved water rights, 830–851
Instream and out-of-stream uses, 748
International law
    Generally, 900–912
    Harmon Doctrine, 901–902
    Nile River basin, 908–912
    Transboundary watercourses, 901–904
    UN Convention on the Law of the Non-Navigational Uses of International Watercourses, 904–908
Judicial allocation among states, 882–884
Los Angeles, water and public trust doctrine, 797–810
Marine Mammals, this index
Marine Resources, this index
Mining, 777–779, 1145
Navigation servitude, 868–869
Nile River basin, 908–912
Out-of-stream and instream uses, 748
Permit systems and public interest requirement, prior appropriation, 790–793
Prior appropriation
    Generally, 758–760, 777–810
    Beneficial use and waste, 784–790
    Groundwater, 817–821
    Instream flow appropriations, 793–797
    Los Angeles, water and public trust doctrine, 797–810
    Mining law, 777–779
    Permit systems and public interest requirement, 790–793
    Water trust, formation of, 797
Quality of water, 744
Reasonable use, 760–765, 816, 817
Riparian rights, 758–767
States, allocation of water among
    Generally, 881–900
    Compacts among states, 884–887
    Congressional allocation, 887–888
    Equitable allocation, 882–884
    Judicial allocation, 882–884
Transboundary watercourses, 901–904
UN Convention on the Law of the Non-Navigational Uses of International Watercourses, 904–908
Understanding the water resource
    Generally, 741–758
    Communities of interest, 749–751
    Consumptive and nonconsumptive uses, 748
    Dams, 755–758
    Hydrologic cycle, 741–742
    Instream and out-of-stream uses, 748
    Quality of water, 744
    United State's water, 744–748
    Uses and users, 748–751
    Valuation of water, 751–755
    World's water, 741–744
United State's water, 744–748
Uses and users, 748–751
Valuation of water, 751–755
Water trust, formation of, 797
World's water, 741–744

WESTERN REGIONAL CLIMATE AC-TION INITIATIVE
Generally, 1029

WETLANDS RESERVE PROGRAM
Generally, 669

WHALES
Generally, 529–549
Aboriginal subsistence whaling, 543–549
History of whaling, 529–531
International Convention on the Regulation of Whaling, 531–543
Moratorium on whaling, 533–538
North Atlantic Marine Mammal Commission, 534–526, 542–543
Revised Management Procedure, 534

WHISTLEBLOWER PROTECTION
Surface Mining Control And Reclamation Act, 1189

WILD AND SCENIC RIVERS ACT
Generally, 665–667
Rangelands, 1012–1013

WILD FREE–ROAMING HORSES AND BURROS ACT
Federal power to manage natural resources, 148–156

WILDERNESS
Generally, 636–662
Bureau of Land Management lands, 642–644
Case study, 28–36
Commercial services, 649–658
Designation of wilderness areas, 639–649
Elitism, 645–646
Evolution of wilderness idea, 636–637
Grazing of livestock, 659–660
Management of wilderness areas, 649–662
Minerals, 660–661, 1085
National forests, 640–642

WILDERNESS—Cont'd
National Wilderness Preservation System, 637–638
Snowmobiles, 659
U–Regulations, 637
Use of wilderness areas, 638
Wilderness Act, 22, 23, 637 et seq.

WILDERNESS SOCIETY
Generally, 236, 238

WILDLANDS PROJECT
Generally, 587–588

WILDLIFE HABITAT
Forests, impact of logging in, 1215–1216

WOLVES
Endangered Species Act, 405–409
Yellowstone National Park, 406–407

WORKER SAFETY
Minerals, 1031–1033

WORLD RESOURCES INSTITUTE
Think tanks and expert analysis, 238

WORLD WIDE FUND FOR NATURE
Nongovernmental organizations, 239

YELLOWSTONE NATIONAL PARK
Creation, 579
Elk population, 3, 9
Fires and fire suppression, 3–4
Snowmobiles, 617–619
Wolf reintroduction, Endangered Species Act, 406–407

YOSEMITE NATIONAL PARK
Hetch Hetchy Dam, 32

ZONE OF INTERESTS
Administrative agencies, standing to sue of nongovernmental organizations (NGOs), 243–244

†